APA Dictionary *of* Psychology

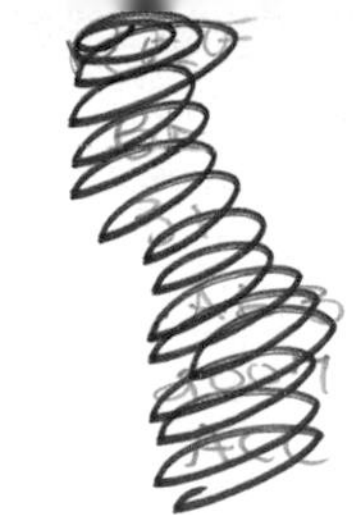

Ψ

APA Dictionary of Psychology

Gary R. VandenBos, PhD
Editor in Chief

American Psychological Association
Washington, DC

Published by
American Psychological Association
750 First Street, NE
Washington, DC 20002
www.apa.org

To order
APA Order Department
P.O. Box 92984
Washington, DC 20090-2984
Tel: (800) 374-2721; Direct: (202) 336-5510
Fax: (202) 336-5502; TDD/TTY: (202) 336-6123
Online: www.apa.org/books/
E-mail: order@apa.org

In the U.K., Europe, Africa, and the Middle East, copies may be ordered from
American Psychological Association
3 Henrietta Street
Covent Garden, London
WC2E 8LU England

Typeset in Aylesbury, England, by Market House Books, Ltd.
Printer: Sheridan Books, Ann Arbor, Michigan
Cover Designer: Naylor Design, Washington, DC

Library of Congress Cataloging-in-Publication Data

VandenBos, Gary R.
APA dictionary of psychology / edited by Gary R. VandenBos. — 1st ed.
p. cm.
ISBN-13: 978-1-59147-380-0
ISBN-10: 1-59147-380-2
1. Psychology—Dictionaries. I. American Psychological Association. II. Title.
III. Title: A.P.A. dictionary of psychology. IV. Title: Dictionary of psychology.

BF31.V295 2006
150.3—dc22

2006010293

British Library Cataloguing-in-Publication Data
A CIP record is available from the British Library.

Printed in the United States of America
First Edition

Contents

Preface

What does it mean when the largest scientific and professional organization representing psychology in the United States and the largest association of psychologists in the world—the American Psychological Association—compiles its first dictionary of psychology? Any response must be given both with pride and humility.

The expansion and permeation of a discipline known as *psychology* into the collective human experience—beginning from the mid-19th century and continuing with unabated vitality into the 21st—could hardly be either an unobserved or a disregarded phenomenon. As an ever-evolving science, psychology has creatively and productively examined the human condition and developed innovative diagnoses and often effective interventions for a broad array of mental and physical health issues as well as social and educational problems. Psychology has made significant leaps in our understanding of human behavior, perception, emotion, cognition, and the like. So too, has it become more closely associated with the physical sciences—for example, by being at the forefront of neuroscience research; by adapting the strict methodology and evaluation criteria long associated with scientific testing in the pursuit of evidence-based practices in mental health; and by its development of health psychology in close alliance with both general and specialized medicine. In such a restless environment of scholarly inquiry, the language of psychology has naturally grown, shedding old meanings, acquiring new ones, and adding its own distinctive color to vocabulary that it has subsumed from other disciplines.

For the American Psychological Association, the publication of its first dictionary is a signal—one among many—that a certain organizational maturity has been attained. Over the years, as the Association moved toward achievement of that developmental level, it increasingly felt a duty to collect and define the vocabulary of the field, recognizing that the responsibility was owed not just to its membership, but also to the field as a whole and, indeed, to the general public.

The work in your hands represents a snapshot of the lexicon of psychology as it exists at the beginning of the 21st century. It purports to be an exercise in description, not prescription. Although selective in scope, it seeks not to limit the vocabulary but, rather, to delineate the current and evolving understanding of the language used within the field.

APA and Information Dissemination

From a broad purview, scientific and professional societies essentially exist in order to define their fields and to facilitate communication within them. Over the 114 years of its existence (as of the 2006 release of this first edition), one of the chief means by which the Association has sought to fulfill these goals has been through its long history of information dissemination. In the very activity of sharing information, APA has inevitably played a major role in both the creation and the collection of the psychological lexicon.

In the domain of traditional print products, the Association's first two scholarly journals, *Psychological Review* and *Psychological Bulletin*, were first published in 1894 and 1904, respectively. As the field diversified into more focused subdisciplines, so did the need for parallel coverage of developing research, and APA gradually conceptualized and produced more and more serials, currently offering subscriptions for some 50 periodicals. A program for book publishing was not truly established until the early 1950s and it released only a small number of publications annually. A true book publishing entity, APA Books, came into its own in the early 1990s and has since become a leading scholarly publisher in psychology, releasing approximately 65 titles annually for researchers and practitioners, as well as producing several popular videotape series focused on the practice of different psychotherapy modalities and the treatment of specific behavioral problems and conditions.

In addition to scholarly journals and books and clinician-oriented videos, APA's Office of Publications and Databases (APA Books' parent division) compiles and offers for subscription the premier electronic database resource in psychology, with a suite of useful research tools: PsycINFO (a bibliographic database of citations with abstracts to the scholarly literature); PsycARTICLES (a database of full-text journal articles from APA and several other publishers); PsycBOOKS (a searchable, full-text database of scholarly books from APA and other publishers); PsycEXTRA (a database of gray literature—credible research published outside the traditional peer-reviewed journal and scholarly book context—covering psychology, behavioral science, and health); and PsycCRITIQUES (an electronic serial offering timely reviews of current psychology books).

Evolution of the APA Dictionary

As early as 1898, at its seventh annual meeting, the executive committee of the American Psychological Association established a "Standing Committee on Psychological and Philosophical Terminology," among whose members were some of psychology's earliest luminaries: Hugo Münsterberg, James McKeen Cattell, and James Mark Baldwin. According to the published proceedings, their duties were as follows:

> *(1) To recommend, from time to time, new terms in Psychology and Philosophy. (2) To recommend choice of alternative terms in those fields. (3) To recommend foreign equivalents for translating work both into English and into foreign languages. [and] (4) To keep the Association informed as to the growth of terminology in other departments, especially Neurology.*

More proximately, although the APA Office of Publications and Databases has considered publishing a dictionary for almost 20 years, the actual origins of the book you hold in your hands can be set at 1997, when APA Books acquired the rights to the *Longman Dictionary of Psychology and Psychiatry*, originally published in 1984. The *Longman* became one of the fundamental sources used in the development of the *APA Dictionary*, serving as the starting point for the identification of terms to include and the development of their definitions.

Perhaps the broadest source of terms (or headwords) came from a scan of APA's immense PsycINFO database, with its more than 2 million records. The 9th and 10th editions of the *Thesaurus of Psychological Index Terms* were enormously useful in helping editorial staff focus down to a workable pool of approximately 34,000 potential headwords.

Additionally, APA reference staff surveyed numerous other psychological dictionaries and glossaries for coverage, some historical in nature and out-of-print (the earliest examined was the four-volume *Dictionary of Philosophy and Psychology*, edited by James Mark Baldwin in 1901–1902) and some currently found on library and bookstore shelves. Many specialty area dictionaries were also reviewed.

A six-part editorial review process, involving several layers of participants, was designed and set in motion in 1999:

1. From the onset, APA recognized the benefits of finding a partner with strong lexicographic and general reference expertise for a publication so unlike any in the APA Books standard list. We were fortunate, indeed, to find those consummate reference professionals at Market House Books, Ltd. (MHB), a firm with over 30 years experience in compiling dictionaries for both British and American audiences. Market House editorial staff first dissected and categorized the pool of 34,000 potential headwords into over 90 separate lists by specific content area. Concurrently, APA Books recruited a pool of contributors (see p. xi) whose particular areas of content expertise more or less paralleled the MHB categorization. MHB set up the project's electronic database so that each list had a standard format that would readily guide contributors through a variety of editorial judgments and tasks. Each list contained (a) headwords derived from *Longman*, with their original definitions, and (b) undefined headwords from all other sources (most particularly, from PsycINFO).
2. Contributors then edited or entirely rewrote the *Longman* entries, which were often dated and heavily slanted toward the psychiatric and psychoanalytical contexts, and they wrote definitions for undefined headwords. Additionally, they identified new terms that they felt should be considered for inclusion and composed definitions for them—in so doing, increasing the list of potential headwords to somewhere over 37,000. Finally, they graded all entries using a tripartite ranking system, with only ranks 1 (*essential to include*) and 2 (*useful to include*) being slated for publication in the first edition. In assigning ranks, contributors needed to keep an eye simultaneously to currency and historical significance as well as to achieving adequate representation for their subareas.
3. MHB editorial staff then reviewed and edited each of the contributors' lists in order to check for clarity and proper lexicographic form. Crucially at this stage, they also provided an eagle-eyed perspective of each list's relationship to other subarea lists and to the dictionary as a whole. They returned each edited list to APA Books as it was received and processed.
4. APA reference staff now sent each list to a member of the project's board of editors (see p. xi), who had broader oversight for the project than did the more narrowly focused contributors. These editors reviewed the content-area lists, suggesting further edits and offering recommendations with regard to rankings and balance of coverage.
5. The editorial board returned lists to APA reference staff who conducted a final review and editing stage before submitting all lists to MHB for entry of APA edits and collapsing of the entire database into a preliminary A-to-Z file of entries.
6. The culminating editorial phase now occurred, in which Market House and APA staff jointly reviewed the master A-to-Z file to merge and order senses from different content areas. Because APA decided that the first edition would contain only approximately 25,000 of the potential 37,000 entries, APA reference staff made the extensive cuts, primarily through exclusion of all rank 3 headwords and secondarily through a final editorial balancing of content-area coverage. These tasks yielded a first set of galleys for a final round of substantive copyediting, and, from this point, the book followed a more-or-less routine path toward its publication.

The User

The core topics in psychology are remarkably diverse in their focus, content, and methods, encompassing such areas of research and application as personality, development, interpersonal relations, memory, motivation, cognition, language, communication, and aging, among others. The discipline is multi- and interdisciplinary, moreover, extending into and overlapping with fields such as artificial intelligence, biology, ergonomics, law, linguistics, education, political science, philosophy, computer science, management, engineering, and others.

Mirroring this breadth of underlying content is a diverse audience for the *APA Dictionary*. Although we naturally anticipate the primary users to be psychologists, graduate and undergraduate psychology students, and practitioners and researchers in allied mental health professions (e.g., psychiatrists and social workers), we also predict the work's value for other professionals (e.g., in education, medicine, human resources, and law) who draw upon psychological information in the course of their work. Because the language and influence of psychology have become so much a part of contemporary life and expression, moreover, we expect the dictionary to prove valuable to the general public.

To reach out successfully to such a broad universe of users is a daunting task, requiring a balance between comprehensibility at different levels of understanding and experience. We hope that we have made a reasonable start in reaching out to these individual perspectives in this first edition.

Features of the APA Dictionary

The approximately 25,000 entries in this dictionary cover psychological concepts, processes, and therapies, and offer basic coverage of important individuals, organizations and institutions, and psychological tests and assessment instruments. Self-imposed limitations for biographical, institutional, and psychological test and assessment entries in the first edition were strict, primarily due to space limitations and the availability of such information in other reference resources. Our choices about inclusion of these (indeed, about all) entries may be debated—editorial staff certainly debated a variety of options throughout development of the project—and we look forward to feedback from interested users with regard to all of our choices (see *Future Perspectives* below).

Most of these entries offer relatively brief definitions (averaging 40 words), but a small proportion can be characterized as verging on the "encyclopedic," providing greater than average scope that delves more deeply and suggestively into their subjects. Where "coinage" or initial use of terms could be determined, credit has been given.

Entries composed of multiple senses are ordered according to various demands and criteria in different dictionaries. In this dictionary, reference staff evolved a kind of general hierarchy by content area, so that clinical psychology senses typically precede experimental senses, and experimental precede social and personality senses, which precede developmental and educational senses, and so forth. Not unusually, if a term has a general, commonly understood sense in everyday usage that naturally informs any specific meaning in psychology or a shared meaning among subfields, the common or shared sense will appear first. That stated, the user should note that editorial staff approached the organizing hierarchy as a set of guidelines and not a rigid set of rules.

The user will also note that entries frequently contain cross-references to other pertinent entries, a procedure that allows the interested reader to develop fuller understanding because of such qualities as similarity or contrast with or amplification of the original entry. Many entries covering synonymous or variant headwords direct the reader to the central, more commonly used term or concept. The user will also find many acronym or initialism headwords that lead to entries under the fully spelled headword; this can be particularly helpful, for example, in cases where the general user only recognizes an organization, say, by its acronym or abbreviation. Occasionally, as sometimes occurs in psychopharmacology, the reverse is true: that is, the term may be defined under its abbreviation.

In the front matter of this book, the reader will find a *Guide to the Dictionary* that lays out the formal elements and editorial practices (style, format) of the work and enables the user to make the fullest use of the information contained herein. In the back matter, after the alphabetical listing of entries proper, are four appendixes, each gathering headwords from a particular context into one synoptic listing: biographical entries, institutional and organizational entries, psychological test and assessment instrument entries, and psychotherapy and psychotherapeutic approach entries.

Future Perspectives

All dictionaries are in some sense "attempts," an observation that harks back to the use of the word *humility* at the beginning of this preface. There are always problems and disagreements attached to editorial work that passes through as many hands and such a protracted process as that described above. It is an awesome task to incorporate as many perspectives in as consistent a form and style as possible. We hope that we have met this challenge with reasonable, if not total, success in this first edition.

Temporal imperatives—that is, *when* to release—are, moreover, at issue in reference publishing, indeed in much scholarly publishing. As any lexicographer will tell you, endless time could be spent on selection and delimitation of headwords, collection and review of citations, and refinement of definitions. Nevertheless, a time arises to put the product out for use and comment. The "answer" to any criticism associated with these restrictions and disadvantages must lie in our commitment to the product.

Given the history, effort, and participation leading to its publication, the Association anticipates a continuing life and healthy future for the *APA Dictionary of Psychology*. Certainly, we envision a number of evolutionary landmarks before the first decade of the 21st century runs its course: an abridgement, several specialty dictionaries, a second edition, and an electronic dictionary, the last of which will eventually be fully integrated into the suite of electronic databases offered by the Association.

In seeking to effect the expansion of its reference resources, APA Books will continually devote staff time to the refinement of this core source, the *APA Dictionary of Psychology*. There are weaknesses in any reference work—especially in a first edition—that demand amelioration. APA reference staff is aware of some of them and has already begun to monitor, correct, rewrite, and polish. Moreover, it will continue to scan the scholarly literature to identify new terms as well as newer senses and understandings of established vocabulary.

To assist APA reference staff in this task, we invite users to contact us, noting errors of omission and inclusion, inaccuracies, infelicities of phrasing, new vocabulary, historical terms and senses that deserve to remain for the record, printing errors, and the like. Please contact us by post in care of APA Books, 750 First Street, NE, Washington, DC 20002, Attention: Reference; or by e-mail at *apadictionary@apa.org* and we will consider all thoughtful criticism and suggestions.

There are two phrases that have been much associated with the American Psychological Association in the past few decades: "Giving psychology away" and "Making psychology a household word." Each phrase has become something of a mantra, as well as a kind of unofficial mission statement. Within the larger context of the APA Office of Publications and Databases, APA Books plays a central role in fulfilling these two ideals, and we like to think that the *APA Dictionary of Psychology* has a fundamental role to play in giving psychology away and making psychology a household word—in fact, a whole book of words.

Gary R. VandenBos, PhD
Editor in Chief
APA Publisher

Editorial Staff

Editorial Contributors (continued)

Editorial Consultants

Guide to the Dictionary

Headwords

All terms defined in the dictionary are described as headwords and are indicated in large boldface type:

aberrant response an abnormal or atypical behavior, commonly targeted during a behavioral intervention.

In this case the headword is **aberrant response**.

Alphabetical Order

The arrangement of headwords is on a strict letter-by-letter basis rather than by word. For example, the following sequence of headwords is used:

game
game reasoning
gamete
gamete intrafallopian transfer
game theory

Note that the headword **game theory** does not directly follow **game reasoning** (as it would in most telephone directories). In dictionaries, spaces, hyphens, or dashes between words are ignored in determining alphabetical order.

If two headwords differ only in whether the letters are upper- or lowercase, then the lowercase version comes first. For example, **ecstasy** (the emotional state) preceeds **Ecstasy** (the drug).

In the vast majority of cases, numbers in headwords are ignored for the purposes of alphabetization. For example, **6-hydroxydopamine** is alphabetized as if it were simply **hydroxydopamine**. The rare exceptions to this rule are terms in which the number is an essential element of the headword. For example, **80:20 rule** follows **eighth cranial nerve**.

Superscript and subscript numbers, letters, and words in headwords are also ignored for alphabetization purposes. Thus, for example, $\mathbf{H_1}$, $\mathbf{r_{alerting}}$, and $\mathbf{S_D}$ are positioned at the beginning of H, R, and S, respectively.

Abbreviations and Variants

Common abbreviations of headwords, as well as alternative spellings and other variant forms, are given in parentheses immediately after the headword:

American Association of Clinical Psychologists (**AACP**) a professional organization founded in 1917 . . . .

bulimia (**boulimia**) *n.* insatiable hunger for food . . . .

However, when a term is more commonly known in the abbreviated form than in the full form, the entry is given at the abbreviation. A typical example is:

DNA *d*eoxyribo*n*ucleic *a*cid: one of the two types of NUCLEIC ACID found in living organisms . . . .

Parts of Speech

Part-of-speech labels are given for single words (but not for multiple-word headwords). The labels immediately follow the headword (and any variant) and are in italic type:

hue *n.* the subjective quality of color, which is determined primarily by wavelength and secondarily by amplitude.

In this example, the headword is a noun. The labels used in this dictionary are:

adj. adjective
adv. adverb
n. noun
pl. n. plural noun
pron. pronoun
vb. verb

In addition, labels are used for:

combining form
prefix
suffix

Irregular Forms

Irregular plurals of words are placed after the part-of-speech label in parentheses:

ampulla *n.* (*pl.* **ampullae**) any saclike enlargement of a duct or passageway . . . .

microvillus *n.* (*pl.* **microvilli**) in taste perception, the hairlike extension of each TASTE CELL that projects through the pore of a TASTE BUD to sample the environment . . . .

A small number of noun headwords are most commonly used in their plural form, in which case the singular inflection is given:

data *pl. n.* (*sing.* **datum**) observations or measurements, usually quantified and obtained in the course of research.

labia *pl. n.* (*sing.* **labium**) four folds of tissue forming part of the female external genitalia (see VULVA) . . . .

Sense Numbers

Many entries have two or more distinct meanings (senses). These are indicated by boldface numbers. For example, the headword **reason** has four distinct senses:

reason *n.* **1.** consecutive thought, as in deduction or induction. Although at one time reason was considered a mental faculty, this is typically not intended in current usage. See DEDUCTIVE REASONING; INDUCTIVE REASONING. **2.** in philosophy, the intellect (or NOUS) regarded as the source of true knowledge. See RATIONALISM. **3.** soundness of mind. **4.** a statement offered to justify an action or decision or to explain the occurrence of an event.

Cross-references

The dictionary contains a large number of cross-references, which are indicated by using a small capitals typeface. Cross-references can occur in normal running text:

barricade incidents hostage and high-risk incidents, which require CRISIS MANAGEMENT and negotiation capabilities.

In this example, the cross-reference is to the headword **crisis management**.

Cross-references may also be introduced by "See," "See also," or "Compare":

saccade *n.* a ballistic movement of the eyes that allows visual fixation to jump from one location to another in the visual field. Once initiated, a saccade cannot change course. See also MICROSACCADES. Compare SMOOTH-PURSUIT MOVEMENT.

In this example, the cross-references are to the headwords **microsaccades** and **smooth-pursuit movement**.

Note that not all headwords in the book are cross-referenced when they are used in definitions. The intention is to direct the user of the dictionary to entries that will give additional information connected with the term of interest.

Some entries consist simply of a cross-reference. Entries for most abbreviations and for variants are treated in this way:

AACP abbreviation for AMERICAN ASSOCIATION OF CLINICAL PSYCHOLOGISTS.

boulimia *n.* see BULIMIA.

Such cross-reference entries are also provided for terms that are hidden entries or synonyms (see below).

Hidden Entries

Sometimes it is helpful to the user to define a term under the entry for a more general or a related term, rather than under its own headword. For example, the term **abductor pollicis** is treated as a hidden entry under the headword **abductor**:

abductor *n.* any muscle that moves a body part away from the midline of the body or of a limb or other part. Thus the **abductor pollicis** muscles move the thumb away from the palm. Compare ADDUCTOR.

Note that the hidden entry is indicated using a sans serif semibold typeface.

Another example is the hidden entry for **brain ablation** at the headword **ablation**:

ablation *n.* the removal or destruction of a biological tissue or structure by a surgical procedure or a toxic substance, usually for treatment or to study its function. For example, **brain ablation** entails the removal or destruction of function of a part of the brain . . . .

In such cases, there is a simple cross-reference from the headword for the hidden entry:

brain ablation see ABLATION.

Synonyms

Many of the terms defined in the dictionary have synonyms, which are displayed at the end of the definition, preceded by "Also called." If a headword has more than one synonym, these are presented in alphabetical order. Our general policy is to put the main definition under the most commonly used name; alternative names are treated as cross-reference entries. Examples are:

acetone *n.* a colorless volatile liquid with a sweet, fruity odor that occurs in excessive amounts in the blood and urine of people with diabetes or other metabolic disorders. Acetone also is a normal metabolite of ethyl alcohol and a sign of alcoholism. Also called **dimethyl ketone**.

dimethyl ketone see ACETONE.

latency of response the time that elapses between the onset of a stimulus and the onset of a response, which may be used as an indicator of the strength of CONDITIONING. Also called **latency of reply**; **response latency**. See REACTION TIME.

response latency see LATENCY OF RESPONSE.

Etymologies

Many entries provide information about the origin of the term defined. In most cases, this information will take the form of brief biographical notes on figures who are identified either in the headwords (eponymous entries) or within the definition. These figures may have originated a term or significantly developed its meaning. In most cases, etymologies are presented in brackets at the end of the definition, following any synonyms and terminal cross-references, but may alternatively be embedded within the definition. Some examples:

Addison's disease a disorder caused by a malfunction of the adrenal glands resulting in a deficiency of adrenal hormones. . . . Mental effects include depression, anxiety, and mood changes. [Thomas **Addison** (1793–1860), British physician]

accentuation theory the proposition that classification of items produces encoding biases, that is, that individuals tend to exaggerate (accentuate) the similarities among items placed in the same category and the differences among items placed in different categories. This accentuation effect is an important component of SOCIAL IDENTITY THEORY. [proposed in 1959 by Polish-born British social psychologist Henri Tajfel (1919–1982)]

Note that figures who are identified in eponymous headwords are treated as hidden entries—that is, their names are printed in sans serif semibold type.

In addition to the above, some foreign-language terms have etymologies in the form of translations or explanations:

ad baculum denoting a type of informal FALLACY or a persuasive technique in which claims to validity are based on an appeal to force or threat, either direct or implied. For example: Theory X should be accepted as true because failure to endorse it will result in loss of scientific status. [from Latin *baculus,* "walking stick," "staff," or "rod," implying the threat of force or punishment]

Derived Words

Derived words are words that can be formed formulaically from the headword using certain rules. They are shown at the end of the entry in boldface type, preceded by an em dash and followed by a part-of-speech label:

abiotrophy *n.* the loss of resistance to a disease through degeneration or failure of a body system . . . . Abiotrophy also may be accelerated by a genetic defect, as in Huntington's disease, which usually does not produce symptoms until middle age. **—abiotrophic** *adj.*

accessible *adj.* **1.** in social psychology and psychotherapy, receptive or responsive to personal interaction and other external stimuli. . . . **4.** of a tissue or organ, reachable by means of standard surgical or diagnostic procedures. **—accessibility** *n.*

Here, **abiotrophic** is an adjective derived from the noun **abiotrophy**, and **accessibility** is a noun derived from the adjective **accessible**.

Quick Guide to Format

Headword | Plural form

microvillus *n.* (*pl.* **microvilli**) in taste perception, the hairlike extension of each taste cell that projects through the pore of a taste bud to sample the environment. Although a microvillus accounts for only 3% of the surface area of a taste cell, it is studded with receptor proteins that recognize specific molecules and is the site of taste transduction.

Part-of-speech label | Alternative name

midbrain *n.* a relatively small region of neural tissue lying between the FOREBRAIN and HINDBRAIN. It contains the inferior and superior COLLICULI, a portion of the RETICULAR FORMATION, sensory and motor tracts, and reflex centers. Also called **mesencephalon.**

Cross-reference

middle-child syndrome a hypothetical condition purported to be shared by all middle-born children, based on the assumption that middle children in a family develop personality characteristics that are different from first-born and later born children. Current research indicates that a child's birth order in a particular family may have small, subtle influences on personality and intelligence but not strong and consistent effects on psychological outcomes. See also BIRTH ORDER.

Etymology

midlife crisis a period of psychological distress occurring in some individuals during the middle years of adulthood, roughly from ages 45 to 60. Causes may include significant life events and health or occupational problems and concerns. See also AGE CRISIS. [term coined in 1965 by Canadian consulting organizational psychologist Elliot Jaques (1917–2003)]

Abbreviation | Cross-reference

mild cognitive impairment (MCI) a transitional condition between normal healthy aging and early DEMENTIA, characterized by a memory impairment greater than would be expected for age and education. Other cognitive functions are intact, and activities of daily living are normal. Individuals with MCI are at increased risk for developing ALZHEIMER'S DISEASE.

Sense number | Sense number | Derived word

millenarianism *n.* **1.** belief in the imminent end of human history, to be followed by a thousand-year period of peace and blessedness (often associated with the Second Coming of Christ). Such beliefs were current in the early Christian church and appeared sporadically, primarily from the 11th through the 17th centuries, in periods of political or intellectual crisis and among marginalized groups. Some New Age groups proclaim similar beliefs but without the language and imagery of Christianity. **2.** by extension, any belief that rapid and violent change can lead to a golden age of justice and peace. **—millenarian** *adj.*

Hidden entry | Derived word

mimetic *adj.* relating to imitation, for example, a young chimpanzee's imitation of its parent's actions or a parrot imitating the words of its owner. A **mimetic response** is a copying or imitative response. Mimetic can also refer to physical features, such as the pseudopenis of female spotted hyenas, which is an enlargement of the clitoris and va gina through which mating and birth are accomplished. **—mimesis** *n.*

APA Dictionary *of* Psychology

Aa

a- (**an-**) *prefix* not or without.

AA 1. abbreviation for ACHIEVEMENT AGE. **2.** abbreviation for ALCOHOLICS ANONYMOUS.

AAAP abbreviation for AMERICAN ASSOCIATION OF APPLIED PSYCHOLOGY.

AAAPP abbreviation for AMERICAN ASSOCIATION OF APPLIED AND PREVENTIVE PSYCHOLOGY.

AAAS abbreviation for AMERICAN ASSOCIATION FOR THE ADVANCEMENT OF SCIENCE.

AAASP abbreviation for ASSOCIATION FOR THE ADVANCEMENT OF APPLIED SPORT PSYCHOLOGY.

AACD abbreviation for (the former) American Association for Counseling and Development. See AMERICAN COUNSELING ASSOCIATION.

AACP abbreviation for AMERICAN ASSOCIATION OF CLINICAL PSYCHOLOGISTS.

AACS abbreviation for AMERICAN ACADEMY OF CLINICAL SEXOLOGISTS.

AAHPERD abbreviation for AMERICAN ALLIANCE FOR HEALTH, PHYSICAL EDUCATION, RECREATION AND DANCE.

A-alpha fiber a myelinated (and therefore rapidly conducting) AXON, of large diameter (13–20 μm), that transmits information from proprioceptors of skeletal muscles to the central nervous system. See A FIBER.

AAMI abbreviation for AGE-ASSOCIATED MEMORY IMPAIRMENT.

AAMR abbreviation for AMERICAN ASSOCIATION OF MENTAL RETARDATION.

AAP abbreviation for ASSOCIATION FOR THE ADVANCEMENT OF PSYCHOLOGY.

AASECT abbreviation for AMERICAN ASSOCIATION OF SEX EDUCATORS, COUNSELORS AND THERAPISTS.

AAVE abbreviation for African American Vernacular English. See BLACK ENGLISH.

ab- *prefix* away from or opposite to.

ABA abbreviation for APPLIED BEHAVIOR ANALYSIS.

A-B-A-B-A design a SINGLE-CASE EXPERIMENTAL DESIGN in which participants are measured before, during, and after treatment (the A phase) and in which the treatment (the B phase) is administered twice.

A-B-A-B design a SINGLE-CASE EXPERIMENTAL DESIGN in which a baseline or other initial condition (A) is followed by a different condition (B), which is followed by a return to the initial condition (A), which is then followed by a return to the second condition (B).

A-B-A design a SINGLE-CASE EXPERIMENTAL DESIGN in which a baseline or other initial condition (A) is followed by a different condition (B) and then by a return to the initial condition (A).

abaissement n. a mental state in which the threshold of consciousness lowers and unconscious thoughts become conscious, as when slipping into sleep and becoming aware of dream content. [from French, in full: *abaissement du niveau mental*, first recognized and defined by French physician and psychologist Pierre Janet (1859–1947)]

abandonment *n.* desertion or neglect of a dependent by a parent or primary caregiver. Those abandoned are usually children but may be ill individuals or entire families. **—abandon** *vb.*

abandonment reaction a feeling of emotional deprivation, loss of support, and loneliness experienced by children who have been deserted or neglected by one or both parents. Abandonment reaction is also experienced by adults who have lost a loved one on whom they have depended.

abasement need a need to surrender oneself to another person, accept blame or punishment, or confess and atone. See also MASOCHISM. [defined by U.S. psychologist Henry A. Murray (1893–1988)]

abasia *n.* severe impairment or complete loss of the ability to walk. See also ASTASIA–ABASIA.

abatement *n.* a reduction or lessening in the severity of pain or other symptoms of illness or disorder.

A-B-B-A design a SINGLE-CASE EXPERIMENTAL DESIGN in which a baseline or other initial condition (A) is followed by a different condition (B), which is followed by an additional application of the second condition (B), which is followed by a return to the initial condition (A).

A-B-BC-B design a SINGLE-CASE EXPERIMENTAL DESIGN in which participants are measured before the introduction of the treatments (the A phase), then during Treatment B, during the combination of Treatments B and C, and finally during Treatment B alone again. The purpose of the design is to assess the effect of B both in combination with C and apart from C.

ABCDE technique a procedure used in RATIONAL EMOTIVE BEHAVIOR THERAPY, on the basis of ABC THEORY, which suggests that *A*ctivating experiences (i.e., adversities) are mediated by irrational *B*eliefs in bringing about inappropriate *C*onsequences. ABCDE technique involves *D*isputing these beliefs (i.e., in therapy under the guidance of the therapist), which results in several types of *E*ffects (e.g., cognitive or rational beliefs, appropriate feelings, desirable behaviors). [devised by U.S. psychologist Albert Ellis (1913–)]

ABCL abbreviation for AMERICAN BIRTH CONTROL LEAGUE.

ABC theory the theory underlying RATIONAL EMOTIVE BEHAVIOR THERAPY, which suggests that *A*ctivating events (i.e., adversities) are mediated by irrational *B*eliefs in determining inappropriate behavioral *C*onsequences. See also ABCDE TECHNIQUE. [devised by U.S. psychologist Albert Ellis (1913–)]

A-B design the simplest SINGLE-CASE EXPERIMENTAL DESIGN, in which the DEPENDENT VARIABLE is measured throughout the pretreatment or baseline period (the A phase) and then again following the treatment period (the B phase).

abdominal bloating see BLOATING.

abdominal migraine recurrent, severe episodes of abdominal pain that may be accompanied by nausea and vomiting. The episodes may last for hours or days but are separated by intervals of completely normal health. Abdominal migraine occurs most frequently in children.

abducens nerve the sixth CRANIAL NERVE, carrying motor fibers for control of the lateral rectus muscle of the eye. Also called **cranial nerve VI**.

abducens nucleus a collection of nerve cells in the floor of the fourth VENTRICLE of the brain, from which the ABDUCENS NERVE originates.

abduction *n.* **1.** movement of a body part away from the midline of the body or of a limb or other part. See also ABDUCTOR. Compare ADDUCTION. **2.** the act of taking a person away by force or deception. **—abduct** *vb.*

abductive inference a form of diagnostic reasoning in which conditions are considered in an attempt to determine their causes. This form of reasoning (unsound, in the mathematical sense) is often described as "reasoning to the best explanation."

abductor *n.* any muscle that moves a body part away from the midline of the body or of a limb or other part. Thus the **abductor pollicis** muscles move the thumb away from the palm. Compare ADDUCTOR.

Abecedarian Project a project that began in the 1970s at the University of North Carolina at Chapel Hill, the goal of which was to enrich the lives of preschool children from deprived rural areas. Children were enrolled in a full-time child-care center shortly after birth and attended until entering first grade. The Abecedarian Project is one of the few preschool ENRICHMENT programs to report intellectual gains in participants into young adulthood relative to participants in a control condition.

aberrant response an abnormal or atypical behavior, commonly targeted during a behavioral intervention.

aberration *n.* **1.** any deviation, but usually a significant one, from the normal or typical. See also MENTAL ABERRATION. **2.** in vision, the failure of light rays to converge at the same point, due either to distortion by a lens (**spherical aberration**) or to the formation of colored fringes by a lens (CHROMATIC ABERRATION).

A-beta fiber a myelinated (and therefore rapidly conducting) AXON, of large diameter (6–12 μm), that transmits information from mechanoreceptors of the skin to the central nervous system. See A FIBER.

abience *n.* a response or behavior that results in a movement away from a stimulus, either by physical withdrawal from the stimulus or by an action designed to avoid the stimulus entirely. **Abient behavior** is an AVOIDANCE RESPONSE or withdrawal behavior designed to prevent or minimize contact with a given stimulus. Compare ADIENCE. **—abient** *adj.*

Abilify *n.* a trade name for ARIPIPRAZOLE.

ability *n.* competence or capacity to perform a physical or mental act. Ability may be either innate or acquired by education and practice.

ability–achievement discrepancy the difference between an individual's known aptitude for a subject area or concept and his or her performance in that area or concept.

ability grouping **1.** the assignment of pupils to school classes on the basis of their learning ability. **2.** the process of dividing a class into sections based on student ability in one area, for example, the practice of assigning elementary-school children to reading groups for fast or slow readers.

ability level an index of achievement, performance, or potential that reports the absolute or relative ability of the organism being evaluated.

ability test **1.** a norm-referenced standardized test designed to measure competence or capacity to perform a physical or mental act. **2.** a test measuring achievement.

ability trait a personality trait that involves an individual's capacity to attain his or her goals. It is one of three classes of SOURCE TRAITS in CATTELL'S FACTORIAL THEORY OF PERSONALITY, the other two being DYNAMIC TRAITS and TEMPERAMENT TRAITS.

abiotic *adj.* nonliving.

abiotrophy *n.* the loss of resistance to a disease through degeneration or failure of a body system; for example, the decline of an individual's immune system with aging, resulting in an increased risk of cancer as the antibodies lose ability to reject the tumor cells. Abiotrophy also may be accelerated by a genetic defect, as in Huntington's disease, which usually does not produce symptoms until middle age. **—abiotrophic** *adj.*

ablation *n.* the removal or destruction of a biological tissue or structure by a surgical procedure or a toxic substance, usually for treatment or to study its function. For example, **brain ablation** entails the removal or destruction of function of a part of the brain. Also called **extirpation**. See also BIOPSY.

ableism *n.* discrimination against individuals with disabilities. See also DISABILITY; HANDICAP.

ablution *n.* **1.** a largely obsolete therapeutic technique utilizing water (such as wrapping wet towels around the body or immersing in water) to calm agitated patients. It was abandoned with the advent of psychotropic drugs. **2.** a symbolic cleansing of the body, or of possessions, with the intent of purification.

ABMS abbreviation for AMERICAN BOARD OF MEDICAL SPECIALTIES.

Abney's effect a perceptual phenomenon that occurs when a large area is suddenly illuminated or darkened. Light appears first in the center of an illuminated area and then spreads to the edges; when the light goes out, darkness appears first at the edges and last in the center. [Sir William **Abney** (1843–1920), British chemist and physicist]

abnormal *adj.* **1.** relating to any deviation from what is considered normal, typical, usual, or healthy, particularly if the deviation is considered harmful or maladjustive. **2.** in statistics, denoting scores that are outside the usual or expected range.

abnormal behavior behavior that is atypical or statistically uncommon within a particular culture or that is maladaptive or detrimental to an individual. Such behavior is often regarded as evidence of a mental or emotional disturbance, ranging from minor adjustment problems to severe mental disorder.

abnormal fixation in vision, the inability to focus on a given target of interest. Abnormal fixations may be the result of saccadic intrusions or oscillations (see SACCADE) or NYSTAGMUS.

abnormal grief see COMPLICATED GRIEF.

abnormality *n.* **1.** the state or condition of being ABNORMAL. **2.** a defect or malformation in structure or function.

abnormal psychology the branch of psychology devoted to the study, prevention, assessment, and treatment of ABNORMAL BEHAVIOR. See also PSYCHOPATHOLOGY.

aboiement *n.* the involuntary, uncontrollable production of animalistic sounds. Aboiement (French, "barking") is a symptom sometimes occurring in schizophrenia and Tourette's disorder.

abortifacient *n.* any agent that induces abortion. Also called **abortient**.

abortion *n.* the expulsion from the uterus of an embryo or fetus before it has reached full term or the stage of viability (the ability to live outside the uterus), that is, before about 20 weeks of gestation. An abortion may be either spontaneous or induced (see INDUCED ABORTION; SPONTANEOUS ABORTION). See also ELECTIVE ABORTION; THERAPEUTIC ABORTION.

abortion counseling counseling in which guidance, advice, information, and support are provided on issues concerning termination of pregnancy and the alternatives (e.g., adoption or raising the child). Abortion counseling is usually offered in special clinics in which abortions may be performed but may also be offered in general hospitals.

abortion laws laws concerning the rights of women to obtain an abortion, which in the United States are provisioned through the 1973 U.S. Supreme Court decision in *Roe v. Wade*.

aboulia *n.* see ABULIA.

above-down analysis see TOP-DOWN ANALYSIS.

ABPP abbreviation for AMERICAN BOARD OF PROFESSIONAL PSYCHOLOGY.

ABR abbreviation for auditory brainstem response. See ELECTROPHYSIOLOGIC AUDIOMETRY.

abreaction *n.* the therapeutic process of bringing forgotten or inhibited material (i.e., experiences, memories) from the unconscious into consciousness, with concurrent emotional release and discharge of tension and anxiety. See also CATHARSIS.

ABS abbreviation for the American Association on Mental Retardation's Adaptive Behavior Scale, in separate editions for school and adult service settings. See ADAPTIVE BEHAVIOR SCALE.

abscess *n.* a contained but often enlarging area of infection that includes pus and dead tissue. A BRAIN ABSCESS will often cause tissue damage and neurological symptoms, such as headaches and altered mental states. Treatment is usually with antibiotics, surgery, or both.

abscissa *n.* the horizontal coordinate in a graph or data plot; that is, the *x*-axis. See also ORDINATE.

absence *n.* a brief LOSS OF CONSCIOUSNESS or period of mental inattentiveness, particularly when associated with a seizure (see ABSENCE SEIZURE), with no memory for the event afterward.

absence culture an informal organizational NORM that leads employees and managers to believe that they are entitled to take more days off work than the number formally allowed. In some organizations, for example, employees may have come to regard a certain amount of sick leave as a benefit to be claimed rather than a provision to be utilized only when strictly necessary. See ABSENTEEISM.

absence seizure a type of GENERALIZED SEIZURE, formerly called **petit mal seizure**, in which the individual experiences an abrupt cessation of activity and cannot afterward remember the event. The absences usually last from 5 to 15 s, during which the individual is unresponsive and motionless, staring blankly. An absence seizure can easily be identified on an electroencephalogram (see ELECTROENCEPHALOGRAPHY) by characteristic spike-and-wave discharges at a rate of 3 Hz. Seizures of this type typically begin between ages 4 and 12 and rarely persist into adulthood.

absence without leave (**AWOL**) unauthorized or unreported absence, which may be grounds for disciplinary action.

absenteeism *n.* unjustified absence from work, school, or college, especially when regular or persistent. A record of the number, duration, and cause of absences is usually kept by supervisors and may be used as one JOB CRITERION. Although absenteeism has been shown to have a relation to JOB SATISFACTION other factors, such as ORGANIZATIONAL CULTURE, may be more relevant (see ABSENCE CULTURE). See also MALINGERING.

absent-mindedness *n.* a state of heedlessness or inattention marked by a tendency to be occupied by one's own thoughts and not to be fully aware of concurrent situations or the external reality of the moment.

absent state a vacant, dreamlike state of detachment that may occur in COMPLEX PARTIAL SEIZURES.

absolute *adj.* **1.** not limited or subject to restriction, as in **absolute power**. **2.** not conditional on or relative to anything else. In philosophy, the position that there are absolute ethical, aesthetic, or epistemological values is known as **absolutism**. Such a position involves a rejection (in whole or in part) of RELATIVISM. See also CULTURAL UNIVERSALISM. **3.** denoting an ultimate limit, as in **absolute zero**. **—absolutist** *adj.*

absolute error the degree to which an observation is inaccurate without specification of whether it errs by being too high or too low. Absolute error is computed as the average absolute difference (see ABSOLUTE VALUE) between the intended or expected value and the actual value. This measure may also describe the overall accuracy of a set of movements with a well-defined goal. Compare CONSTANT ERROR; RANDOM ERROR.

absolute idealism the philosophical position that both mental and material reality are manifestations of a universal and absolute mind or spirit. See IDEALISM; IDEALISTIC MONISM. [proposed by German philosopher Georg Wilhelm Friedrich Hegel (1770–1831)]

absolute impression a psychophysical judgment based on implied or vague standards, such as *It was a bright day*.

absolute judgment a psychophysical judgment in which a single stimulus is placed in a particular category (e.g., "bright," "loud"), as opposed to one in which several stimuli are compared to one another or to a given standard (e.g., "brighter," "louder"). Compare COMPARATIVE JUDGMENT.

absolute-judgment method a PSYCHOPHYSICAL METHOD in which participants are asked to make categorical judgments about individual stimuli rather than COMPARATIVE JUDGMENTS about a set of stimuli. The stimuli usually vary along one or two dimensions, such as brightness or loudness.

absolute limen see ABSOLUTE THRESHOLD.

absolute measurement a measurement made directly and independently of comparison with other measurements.

absolute pitch the ability to identify the pitch of a sound accurately without the use of a reference pitch. Also called **perfect pitch**. Compare RELATIVE PITCH.

absolute rating scale a type of rating instrument in which the targets (e.g., people, objects) are evaluated according to absolute values, that is, the targets to be rated are not compared with other targets but are judged according to independent criteria.

absolute reality in philosophy, the totality of what really exists, regarded as a unity transcending the world of PHENOMENA experienced and interpreted by humans.

The concept of an absolute reality is mainly of significance in the idealist tradition deriving from the work of German philosopher Immanuel Kant (1724–1804). See NOUMENON; TRANSCENDENTALISM.

absolute refractory period see REFRACTORY PERIOD.

absolute scotoma see SCOTOMA.

absolute threshold the minimum amount of stimulation required to trigger a reaction or produce a sensation. Absolute threshold is measured across several trials. It is the lowest or weakest level of stimulation (e.g., the slightest, most indistinct sound) that can be detected on 50% of trials. Although the name suggests a fixed level at which stimuli effectively elicit sensations, the absolute threshold fluctuates according to alterations in receptors and environmental conditions. Also called **absolute limen** (**AL**); **detection threshold**; **sensation threshold**.

absolute value the numerical value of a figure disregarding its algebraic sign.

absorption *n.* **1.** an extreme involvement or preoccupation with one object, idea, or pursuit, with inattention to other aspects of the environment. See also TELLEGEN ABSORPTION SCALE. **2.** the uptake of fluid and dissolved substances into a cell across the plasma membrane. An administered drug moves through various biological membranes from its site of administration to its target organ. Absorption into the target organ is dependent on a number of factors, including the method of ADMINISTRATION (e.g., oral, intravenous); the properties of the drug (e.g., molecular size, ability to cross lipid membranes); the amount of drug administered; and the characteristics or state of the individual (e.g., body mass, sex, age, presence of disease, presence of other drugs). **3.** in physics, the conversion of energy from one form to another on entering a medium, for example, the retention of light without transmission or reflection.

absorption curve a graph that plots the number of photons of light of different wavelengths absorbed by a PHOTOPIGMENT.

abstinence *n.* **1.** the act of refraining from the use of alcohol, drugs, or certain foods. In most instances, abstinence from drugs or alcohol is the primary goal of substance abuse treatment. See also SUBSTANCE WITHDRAWAL. **2.** the act of refraining from sexual activity. **—abstinent** *adj.*

abstinence delirium a form of DELIRIUM that occasionally accompanies withdrawal from alcohol or drugs of abuse. See ALCOHOL WITHDRAWAL DELIRIUM; DELIRIUM TREMENS.

abstinence rule see RULE OF ABSTINENCE.

abstinence syndrome the characteristic set of physiological and behavioral events that accompanies withdrawal from dependence-inducing substances.

abstract ability see ABSTRACT INTELLIGENCE.

abstract attitude a COGNITIVE STYLE that involves the ability to grasp essentials and common properties, to keep different aspects of a situation in mind and shift from one to another, to predict and plan ahead, and to think symbolically and draw conclusions. These capacities are often impaired in people with certain neurological or psychological disorders. Also called **categorical attitude**. Compare CONCRETE ATTITUDE. See also ABSTRACT THINKING. [defined by German-born U.S. neurologist Kurt Goldstein (1878–1965)]

abstract conceptualization the process of forming abstract concepts, which may be general and apply to numerous particular instances (e.g., "dog" or "fish") or wholly intangible and have no specific material referent (e.g., "liberty" or "youth"). See ABSTRACTION; CONCEPTUALIZATION.

abstract expressionism a nonrepresentational style of painting that flourished in the 1950s.

abstract idea an idea or concept that has no specific material referent, such as "justice," or one that applies to a great many particular instances, having a meaning apart from any particular, such as "dog." See also UNIVERSALS.

abstract intelligence the intellectual ability to think in terms of abstract concepts. Also called **abstract ability**. See ABSTRACT THINKING. Compare CONCRETE INTELLIGENCE.

abstraction *n.* **1.** the formation of general ideas or concepts, such as "fish" or "hypocrisy," from particular instances. The precise cognitive processes by which this occurs remain a subject of investigation. See also CONCEPT FORMATION; CONCEPTUALIZATION. **2.** such a concept, especially a wholly intangible one, such as "goodness" or "beauty." **3.** in conditioning, DISCRIMINATION based on a single property of multicomponent stimuli. **—abstract** *vb.*

abstraction experiment a study that investigates participants' ability to induce the general properties of a category or concept from specific instances that are presented to them as examples or nonexamples. See also CONCEPT-DISCOVERY TASK; CONCEPT-FORMATION TEST.

abstract learning acquiring knowledge of abstract (general or intangible) material, such as the meanings of CONCEPTS and PROPOSITIONS and the logical and systematic relations between them.

abstract representation in cognitive theory, a MENTAL REPRESENTATION of a stimulus in an abstract or essential form that is not tied to any one of its variable surface forms. For example, the letter *A* can be thought about at an abstract level with no reference to specific surface forms, such as *a*, *A*, or **a**. Compare CONCRETE PICTURE; ICONIC REPRESENTATION.

abstract thinking thinking characterized by the use of abstractions and generalizations. Compare CONCRETE THINKING. See also ABSTRACT ATTITUDE; CATEGORICAL THOUGHT.

abstract-versus-representational dimension the degree to which a work of art is nonrepresentational versus representational of reality. Representational art is characterized by a great amount of detail, whereas abstract art is highly selective in the inclusion of detail.

abstract word in linguistics, a word denoting a concept or idea not readily perceptible to the senses, such as *curiosity* or *metaphor*. Compare CONCRETE WORD.

absurdities test the type of test in which participants must identify absurdities, inconsistencies, or incongruities in a picture, story, or other written material. The STANFORD–BINET INTELLIGENCE SCALE incorporates absurdity tasks.

abulia (**aboulia**) *n.* extreme loss of initiative and drive, resulting in an inability to make decisions or initiate voluntary actions. It may be seen in individuals with brain damage or schizophrenia and sometimes accompanies severe depression. Also called **initiation deficit**. **—abulic** *adj.*

abundancy motive the tendency to seek a greater degree of satisfaction than that provided by meeting a particular need, for example, eating more food than the amount actually required to alleviate hunger. Compare DEFICIENCY MOTIVE.

abuse 1. *n.* interactions in which one person behaves in a violent, demeaning, or invasive manner toward another person (e.g., a child or a partner) or an animal. **2.** *vb.* to subject a person or animal to such treatment. **3.** *n.* misuse of a substance characterized by repeated occurrences of social, occupational, legal, or interpersonal consequences within a 12-month period (see SUBSTANCE ABUSE); *DSM–IV–TR* distinguishes between substance abuse and SUBSTANCE DEPENDENCE. **4.** *n.* colloquially, the misuse of a substance to an extent that it causes the individual difficulty, whether or not it meets the *DSM–IV–TR* definition of substance abuse. See also ALCOHOL ABUSE. **—abuser** *n.*

abuse excuse experience of prior abuse (e.g., physical, mental, or sexual) used as a defense for a person's violent acts.

abuse potential the ability of a drug to reinforce drug-taking behavior. Factors that determine abuse potential include route of drug administration (e.g., intravenous, inhalation, oral) and the speed of onset, duration, and nature of the drug effect. These factors are themselves determined by complex interactions between the individual, the substance, and the social environment. Substances with a high abuse potential include intravenous heroin, crack cocaine, morphine, and smoked opium. Substances with a low abuse potential include the hallucinogens and marijuana. Also called **abuse liability**.

ABX paradigm a psychophysical procedure in which a pair of auditory stimuli (A and B) are presented, followed by another stimulus (X). In one version of the task, participants are asked to judge whether or not X is identical to A or B; in another version, they have to judge whether or not X was included in the A–B pair.

ACA abbreviation for AMERICAN COUNSELING ASSOCIATION.

academic *adj.* relating to formal learning with conventional or theoretical study at a school or other educational institution.

academic achievement 1. any identifiable success in the areas of scholarship or disciplined study. **2.** in educational psychology, a specific level of proficiency in scholastic work in general or in a specific skill, such as arithmetic or reading. See also NEED FOR ACHIEVEMENT.

academic-achievement motivation an idea, need, desire, or impulse that causes a person to pursue success in the areas of scholarship or disciplined study. See also ACHIEVEMENT MOTIVATION.

academic-achievement prediction prediction of the amount of success a student can achieve in the areas of scholarship or disciplined study. Evidence of future academic achievement is usually based on the results of standardized ABILITY TESTS and assessment of performance by a teacher or other supervisor.

academic aptitude competence or capacity to perform a scholastic mental act, such as the ability to learn quickly in areas of scholarship or disciplined study. Academic aptitude may be either innate or acquired by education and practice. See also APTITUDE.

academic environment the sum of the physical surroundings, influences, and conditions in an educational setting, which can either detract from one's ability to learn or enhance it.

academic failure 1. any marked insufficiency or inadequacy in the area of scholarship or study, for example, when a learner does not achieve an expected competence. The usual reasons for academic failure are lack of academic ability or application in the learner, a substandard academic environment, or insufficient instruction. **2.** a weakening or decline in the ability to succeed in areas of scholarship.

academic freedom within an institution of learning, the liberty of a teacher to educate, of a student to study, and of both to hold and express opinions, particularly regarding controversial topics (e.g., morals, religion, and politics), without interference from or punishment by government, school officials, teachers, or community groups.

academic intelligence the intellectual skills that, according to some theories, are particularly important to success in school environments. These skills also predict success, to a lesser extent, in nonschool environments, such as the workplace.

academic intelligence tasks tasks that require the use of academic skills and knowledge, such as tasks that involve solving arithmetic problems or verbal analogies. Compare PRACTICAL INTELLIGENCE TASK.

academic intervention the active involvement of school officials and teachers in developing and implementing an effective plan for the prevention or remediation of inappropriate and disruptive student behavior. Successful programs of intervention are most often individualized, based on a cognitive-behavioral approach, child focused, and minimally restrictive. Academic intervention is the antithesis of reactive strategies, such as punishment, ridicule, loss of privileges, and time out.

academic overachievement 1. academic performance that exceeds the expected level for that person, or the usual predicted attainment level, especially as indicated by norm-referenced and standardized intelligence or aptitude tests. **2.** the act of driving oneself relentlessly in attempting to reach a difficult scholastic goal.

academic problem 1. a learning problem in a schoolchild who does not acquire the necessary grade-level knowledge or cannot successfully pursue the expected grade-level tasks and scholarly goals. It can be caused by the child's inability or unwillingness to learn. **2.** a behavioral problem caused by fear of school, frustration with schoolwork, or inability to relate appropriately with teachers or other children.

academic self-concept an individual's evaluation of his or her success in academic or educational studies. The two aspects of this evaluation are (a) a general academic self-concept in which students assess their overall learning skills and performance; and (b) a specific academic self-concept of their prowess in such specific subjects as mathematics, social science, or language studies. A major consideration for any individual is whether or not a positive self-concept is an aid to academic achievement. Another consideration is whether or not academic achievement, in itself, enhances a positive self-concept.

academic skills disorder in *DSM–III* and earlier editions, a disorder that in *DSM–IV–TR* is classified as a LEARNING DISORDER.

academic underachievement 1. performance below one's predicted capacity, especially as indicated by norm-referenced and standardized intelligence or aptitude tests. **2.** lack of drive in pursuit of scholastic goals. Causative factors can include unstimulating curriculum and instruction, negative attitudes of parents or teachers, changes in the student, and individual choices that militate against learning.

Academy of Certified Social Workers (**ACSW**) a professional organization founded in 1960 to provide certification of competence for social workers for independent, self-regulated practice and to ensure high standards of practice.

acalculia *n.* an inability to perform simple arithmetic operations. It is a form of APHASIA, usually resulting from damage to the PARIETAL LOBE. In some cases the individual may also be unable to read or write numbers. Also called **anarithmia**; **dyscalculia**.

acamprosate *n.* an analog of the inhibitory neurotransmitter GAMMA-AMINOBUTYRIC ACID (GABA) used in the management of alcohol dependence. Although exact mechanisms of action are unclear, acamprosate may act by directly binding to the GABA receptor complex (see $GABA_A$ RECEPTOR; $GABA_B$ RECEPTOR); it may also act by inhibiting the actions of the excitatory amino acid GLUTAMATE, for example by inhibiting NMDA RECEPTORS. When administered in combination with behavioral treatments, it has some efficacy in reducing alcohol intake or increasing alcohol-free periods in people recovering from alcohol dependence. U.S. trade name: **Campral**.

acarophobia *n.* a persistent and irrational fear of skin parasites (mites), ants, worms, and, by extension, small objects such as pins and needles. The condition is believed to be related to the sensation of insects crawling on or under the skin, which occurs in alcoholism, cocaine use, narcotic addiction, and delirium resulting from meningitis, encephalitis, rheumatic fever, or diphtheria. See also FORMICATION; LILLIPUTIAN HALLUCINATION. **—acarophobic** *adj.*

acatamathesia (**akatamathesia**) *n.* **1.** absence or loss of the ability to comprehend perceptions of objects or situations. **2.** inability to comprehend speech.

acataphasia (**akataphasia**) *n.* the use of inappropriate or grammatically incorrect words and expressions. It is a speech disturbance frequently found in individuals with schizophrenia or APHASIA. See also AGRAMMATISM; SYNTACTICAL APHASIA.

acathisia *n.* see AKATHISIA.

accelerated interaction the intensification of group processes and emotional interaction that occurs in experiential groups when the group sessions are continuous and secluded. See MARATHON GROUP; TIME-EXTENDED THERAPY.

acceleration *n.* **1.** an increase in speed of movement or rate of change. Compare DECELERATION. **2.** in mathematics and statistics, the rate of change in the SLOPE of a function; that is, the second derivative of $f(x)$ with respect to x.

acceleration–deceleration injury a form of HEAD INJURY caused by the head suddenly being placed into motion or abruptly stopped, as, for example, when the individual is in a car accident. The sudden motion or stop causes diffuse stretching and tearing of white matter tracts in addition to bleeding and other neurological effects. The injury may have a variety of consequences, including personality change, attention problems, memory disorders, and EXECUTIVE DYSFUNCTION.

acceleration effects physical, physiological, biochemical, or psychological changes in the body resulting from acceleration imposing g-forces greater than 1. Examples include displacement of body fluids, changes in pupil size, changes in or disturbances of heart rhythm, increases in blood pressure, deficiency of oxygen in the blood (see HYPOXEMIA), disorientation and confusion, amnesia, GRAY-OUT, BLACKOUT, and GRAVITY-INDUCED LOSS OF CONSCIOUSNESS.

acceleration forces forces exerted on an object by the rate of change of its velocity. In psychology, the focus is on the range of forces sustained by the human body when it is in a moving vehicle, such as an automobile or aircraft, and the resultant physical, physiological, and psychological consequences. See ACCELERATION EFFECTS.

accent *n.* **1.** in linguistics, phonetic features of an individual's speech that are associated with geographical region, social class, or native language. The standard version of a language (see STANDARD LANGUAGE) is usually considered by native speakers to be unaccented. Compare DIALECT. **2.** a STRESS placed on a syllable of a word, orthographically marked in some languages. **3.** a type of informal FALLACY or a persuasive technique in which a speaker or writer gives special emphasis to particular words in a proposition, thereby altering the nature of the argument. An example is emphasizing the word *patriotic* in the sentence *All patriotic Americans support the administration*, so that the statement becomes an example of CIRCULAR REASONING.

accentuation theory the proposition that classification of items produces encoding biases, that is, that individuals tend to exaggerate (accentuate) the similarities among items placed in the same category and the differences among items placed in different categories. This accentuation effect is an important component of SOCIAL IDENTITY THEORY. [proposed in 1959 by Polish-born British social psychologist Henri Tajfel (1919–1982)]

acceptance *n.* **1.** a favorable attitude toward an idea, situation, person, or group. In the context of psychotherapy and counseling, it is the receptive, nonjudgmental attitude of therapists or counselors, which conveys an implicit respect and regard for their clients as individuals. **2.** in recovery from substance abuse and other addictive behaviors, the first stage a person must reach (i.e., acceptance that he or she has a problem) before any interventions can be effective. Compare DENIAL.

acceptance and commitment therapy a form of COGNITIVE BEHAVIOR THERAPY that helps clients to abandon ineffective control strategies, to accept difficult thoughts and feelings without taking them to be literally true, and to take actions in accordance with their own values and goals. The therapy is based on the premise that ineffective strategies to control thoughts and feelings actually lead to problem behaviors. Also called **commitment therapy**.

acceptance region the set of values for a test statistic for which the NULL HYPOTHESIS is not rejected. Also called **region of acceptance**. Compare CRITICAL REGION.

acceptance sampling a statistical procedure by which a case is accepted into a sample on the grounds of whether it is within some prespecified TOLERANCE LIMIT.

acceptance stage the last of the five STAGES OF DYING described by Swiss-born U.S. psychiatrist Elisabeth Kübler-Ross (1926–2004). It is characterized by withdrawal from life and resignation to the reality of impending death.

acceptor *n.* see ALLOCATOR.

access *vb.* to retrieve or recall a memory.

accessibility *n.* see ACCESSIBLE; AVAILABILITY.

accessibility of an attitude the likelihood that an attitude will be automatically activated from memory on encountering the ATTITUDE OBJECT. Accessibility is assumed to depend on the strength of the associative link in memory between the representation of the object and the evaluation of the object: The stronger the memory link between the object and its evaluation, the more quickly will the attitude come to mind. Attitudes that come quickly to mind are believed to be better guides to behavior. Accessibility is a determinant of the STRENGTH OF AN ATTITUDE.

accessible *adj.* **1.** in social psychology and psychotherapy, receptive or responsive to personal interaction and other external stimuli. A client in psychotherapy is thought to be accessible if he or she responds to the therapist in a way that facilitates the development of rapport and, ultimately, fosters the examination of cognitive, emotional, and behavioral issues. **2.** retrievable through memory or other cognitive processes. **3.** of a building and its facilities and fixtures, a site, or the like, easy to approach, enter, or use, particularly by people with disabilities. **4.** of a tissue, reachable by means of standard surgical or diagnostic procedures. **—accessibility** *n.*

accessory 1. *adj.* ANCILLARY, supplemental, or contributory. **2.** *n.* a thing or person that is supplementary or subordinate.

accessory nerve the 11th CRANIAL NERVE, sometimes so named because one of its functions is that of serving as an accessory to the 10th cranial nerve (the VAGUS NERVE). It innervates the sternomastoid and trapezius muscles in the neck. Also called **cranial nerve XI**.

accessory structure in biology, a structure that assists or can take over the function of another (the primary) structure.

accessory symptoms see SECONDARY SYMPTOMS.

accident *n.* **1.** an unexpected or unintended event, especially one resulting in human injury or death, system damage, or system loss. **2.** chance or fortune. **3.** see ACCIDENTAL PROPERTY. **—accidental** *adj.*

accidental chaining learning, by REINFORCEMENT, a sequence of two or more actions that includes an act unnecessary to obtain reinforcement (see also CHAINING). This occurs as a result of accidental temporal conjunction between the unnecessary act and a stimulus circumstance that precedes a reinforced response.

accidental group any GROUP that comes into existence gradually as individuals find themselves repeatedly interacting with the same subset of individuals. Such a group will not normally have the defined goals, procedures, and structures of a FORMAL GROUP.

accidental hypothermia see HYPOTHERMIA.

accidental property a characteristic of an idea or entity that is not essential to its nature or existence. For example, being musical is an accidental property of human beings, whereas being mortal is an ESSENTIAL PROPERTY. Also called **accident**.

accidental reinforcement the accidental occurrence of a REINFORCER after an act, which may inadvertently strengthen the likelihood of occurrence of that act. Superstitious behavior is often a result of accidental reinforcement. For example, a golfer might lean as a putt nears the hole. Such leaning has been followed in the past by the ball going in the hole (the reinforcer), so even though leaning has no causal effect on whether the ball goes in or not, the accidental contingent relationship between leaning and the ball being holed leads to reinforcement of leaning. Also called **adventitious reinforcement**.

accidental stimulus any stimulus that intrudes into a dream, such as the sound of a telephone ringing or a muscle cramp. Such stimuli may be incorporated into dreams. Compare DREAM STIMULUS.

accident analysis a systematic process undertaken to determine the causes of an accident with the goal of reducing the likelihood that such an accident will occur again. See also ACCIDENT-PATH MODEL; FAILURE MODES AND EFFECTS ANALYSIS; FAULT-TREE ANALYSIS; JOB-SAFETY ANALYSIS.

accident behavior behavior that could result in injury to the individual or other people, or in physical damage to equipment or the environment. Such behavior may arise from purely personal factors, such as inattention or risk taking, but may also reflect situational factors, such as a fatiguing work schedule or poorly designed work systems. See ACCIDENT PREVENTION.

accident-path model a model used to illustrate the antecedents and causes of an accident using a chronological or otherwise ordered pattern. Accident-path models are used in ACCIDENT ANALYSIS to determine the types and extent of interventions necessary to prevent accidents. See also FAILURE MODES AND EFFECTS ANALYSIS; FAULT-TREE ANALYSIS; JOB-SAFETY ANALYSIS.

accident prevention the use of scientifically tested methods to reduce the number and severity of accidents. These include the systematic study of accidents and the circumstances in which they occur (see ACCIDENT ANALYSIS; JOB-SAFETY ANALYSIS); the psychological study of ACCIDENT PRONENESS; redesign of equipment such as vehicles and industrial machines (see EXCLUSION DESIGN); improved signs, warnings, and safety instructions; motivation of employees through GOAL SETTING, incentives, and intolerance of careless or negligent behavior; alcohol-detection tests; use of PERSONAL PROTECTIVE EQUIPMENT; reduction of personal stress and tension through counseling and psychotherapy; and such educational techniques as training programs, group discussion of safety problems, and role play. Also called **accident reduction**. See also ADMINISTRATIVE CONTROLS; HAZARD CONTROL; SAFETY ENGINEERING.

accident proneness a chronic susceptibility to accidents. This concept has been heavily debated since it was introduced around 1920, and many question the existence of a fixed accident-prone personality. However, a variety of individual variables and sociological and environmental (situational) factors have been identified as important predictors of accident involvement. These include aggressiveness, hostility, impulsiveness, thrill and adventure seeking, workload and cognitive demand, and stress. See also PURPOSIVE ACCIDENT.

accident reduction see ACCIDENT PREVENTION.

acclimatization *n.* **1.** adjustment or adaptation to new circumstances or environmental conditions. **2.** physiological changes that improve the ability of an individual to tolerate environmental alterations. Also called **acclimation**. **—acclimatize** *vb.*

accommodation *n.* **1.** adjustment or modification of the environment or a task in order to meet the needs of individuals with disabilities. This might include installing ramps for wheelchair accessibility, providing an interpreter for an individual with hearing loss, or altering the format of a test for an individual with learning disabilities. See also REASONABLE ACCOMMODATIONS. **2.** the process by which the focus of the eye is changed to allow near or distant objects to form sharp images on the retina. Accommodation is achieved mainly by contraction or relaxation of the CILIARY MUSCLES, which exert tension on the ZONULES attached to the lens, thereby flattening the lens (for distant objects) or allowing it to assume a more rounded shape (for near objects). Adjustments in the CONVERGENCE of the eyes and the size of the pupils also contribute to accommodation. **3.** the adjustment of mental SCHEMAS to match information acquired through experience, in contrast to ASSIMILATION, which involves alteration of the experience to fit existing schemas. See also ADAPTATION. [defined by Jean PIAGET]

4. in bargaining and interpersonal negotiations, modification or adjustment of the various parties' demands or actions, so that agreement or a mutually beneficial outcome can be achieved. **—accommodate** *vb.*

accommodation reflex the reflexive action involved in adjusting vision for various distances by the CONVERGENCE of the eyes, constriction of the pupils, and changing the shape of the lens through contraction or relaxation of the CILIARY MUSCLES.

accommodation time the time it takes for the eyes to focus on a visual stimulus following its presentation.

accommodative insufficiency a reduction in the efficiency of visual ACCOMMODATION, ranging from a slight to a very marked decrease. The primary symptom is blurring of near vision. Usually caused by dysfunction of the eye muscles involved in accommodation or by midbrain injury, accommodative insufficiency may also be observed after injury to oculomotor control centers in preoccipital regions of the brain. Approximately 20% of people with traumatic brain injury have an accommodative dysfunction.

accommodative spasm failure of the eye muscles involved in ACCOMMODATION to relax after focusing on near objects, resulting in transient myopia. Affecting one or both eyes, it is usually caused by an injury to the parasympathetic nervous system and can occur after head injury. The primary symptom is visual blurring at all distances, in many cases occurring over a period of months or even years.

accomplishment quotient a former name for ACHIEVEMENT QUOTIENT.

accountability *n.* **1.** the extent to which a person is answerable to another (e.g., a supervisor or official review body) for his or her behaviors, decisions, or judgments, especially in a professional capacity. **2.** in health care, the responsibility of individual providers, clinics, or hospitals to document their efforts, their resource utilization, and the outcome of their services and to report this information to insurance companies or state or federal agencies. **—accountable** *adj.*

accreditation *n.* the formal process in which an agency or institution evaluates and approves an institution or program of study as meeting predetermined standards. Accreditation applies to institutions as CERTIFICATION applies to individuals. **—accredited** *adj.*

accretion *n.* **1.** a form of learning resulting from the cumulative effect of repeated associations and reinforcements. **2.** the accumulation of objects or material in the environment, which may indicate the degree of individual responsibility of people who use a particular area. Littering is an example of accretion. Compare EROSION.

acculturation *n.* the process by which groups or individuals integrate the social and cultural values, ideas, beliefs, and behavioral patterns of their culture of origin with those of a different culture. **Psychological acculturation** is an individual's attitudinal and behavioral adjustment to another culture, which typically varies with regard to degree and type. Also called **cultural assimilation**; **cultural integration**. Compare DECULTURATION; ENCULTURATION. See also SOCIAL ASSIMILATION. **—acculturate** *vb.*

accumbens *n.* see NUCLEUS ACCUMBENS.

accuracy *n.* **1.** in a task or test, a measure of performance, usually based on the proportion of correct responses. **2.** more generally, the degree to which responses or statements are correct. **3.** exactness or freedom from error. See also PRECISION. **—accurate** *adj.*

accuracy standards criteria used to assess the scientific value of the information and conclusions presented in an evaluation report. Such standards include ensuring the completeness of data collection and the reliability and validity of procedures and measures, conducting appropriate qualitative and quantitative analyses, and impartially reporting results to arrive at justified conclusions. See also FEASIBILITY STANDARDS; PROPRIETY STANDARDS; UTILITY STANDARDS.

accuracy test a test scored for correctness only and not for other criteria, such as speed.

accusative *n.* in linguistics, the CASE of a noun, pronoun, or noun phrase that forms the direct OBJECT of a clause or sentence. In English, unlike more inflected languages, only certain personal and possessive pronouns change their form when they appear in accusative position (so that English speakers say, for example, *She hit me* and not *She hit I*). Also called **objective**. Compare DATIVE; GENITIVE; NOMINATIVE.

Accutane *n.* a trade name for ISOTRETINOIN.

acenesthesia *n.* **1.** loss of the sensation of physical existence. **2.** a lack of awareness of one's own body. See DEPERSONALIZATION.

ACEP abbreviation for American Coaching Effectiveness Program (see AMERICAN SPORT EDUCATION PROGRAM).

acetaminophen *n.* a common ANALGESIC and ANTIPYRETIC agent with an efficacy similar to aspirin, except that it does not possess antirheumatic or anti-inflammatory properties. It is rapidly distributed in the body and has a short HALF-LIFE (around 2 hours). Acetaminophen is a widely used alternative to aspirin, especially when usage of the latter is inadvisable (e.g., in patients with bleeding disorders). It is also sold in combination with other analgesics, antihistamines, decongestants, or cough suppressants. However, acute overdose or chronic daily dosing of acetaminophen may cause liver damage (hepatotoxicity), and consumption of alcohol increases the risk of liver damage. Rapid intervention, including the administration of *N*-acetylcysteine, is required to prevent fatal hepatotoxicity after acetaminophen poisoning. Also called **APAP**; **paracetamol**. U.S. trade name (among others): **Tylenol**.

acetanilide *n.* see ANILIDES.

acetazolamide *n.* see CARBONIC ANHYDRASE INHIBITORS.

acetone *n.* a colorless volatile liquid with a sweet, fruity odor that occurs in excessive amounts in the blood and urine of people with diabetes or other metabolic disorders. Acetone also is a normal metabolite of ethyl alcohol and a sign of alcoholism. Also called **dimethyl ketone**.

acetylcholine (**ACh**) *n.* a NEUROTRANSMITTER that causes excitation at synapses between motor neurons and skeletal muscles and inhibition between synapses of the VAGUS NERVE and heart muscle.

acetylcholine receptors RECEPTOR molecules that are stimulated by ACETYLCHOLINE or acetylcholine-like substances (i.e., acetylcholine agonists). Neurons that possess acetylcholine receptors include (a) effector cells of the postganglionic parasympathetic fibers, (b) preganglionic autonomic fibers connecting to sympathetic and parasympathetic ganglion cells and to the adrenal medulla, (c) motor nerve cells connecting to the skeletal muscles, and (d) some cells in the central nervous system. See also MUSCARINIC RECEPTOR; NICOTINIC RECEPTOR.

acetylcholinesterase (**AChE**) *n.* an enzyme that splits ACETYLCHOLINE into choline and acetic acid, thus inactivating the neurotransmitter after its release at a synaptic junction.

acetylcholinesterase inhibitors drugs that block the ability of the enzyme ACETYLCHOLINESTERASE to degrade the neurotransmitter acetylcholine in the SYNAPTIC CLEFT of cholinergic neurons. Some acetylcholinesterase inhibitors are used clinically as NOOTROPIC DRUGS to slow the progression of dementia in Alzheimer's disease. Also called **anticholinesterases**; **cholinesterase inhibitors**. See DONEPEZIL; GALANTAMINE; RIVASTIGMINE; TACRINE. See also CARBAMATES.

acetylsalicylic acid (**ASA**) the chemical name for ASPIRIN.

acetylureas *pl. n.* drugs that are analogs of HYDANTOINS used in the treatment of partial seizures.

ACh abbreviation for ACETYLCHOLINE.

AChE abbreviation for ACETYLCHOLINESTERASE.

acheiria (**achiria**) *n.* **1.** the condition of being born with only one or no hands. **2.** a disorder of sensation in which an individual cannot tell which side of the body is being externally stimulated.

achieved status social standing and prestige reflecting the ability of an individual to acquire an established position as a result of personal accomplishments.

achievement *n.* **1.** the attainment of some goal, or the goal attained. **2.** see ACADEMIC ACHIEVEMENT. See also NEED FOR ACHIEVEMENT.

achievement age (**AA**) the achievement rating of an individual as measured in terms of the norm or standard for a particular CHRONOLOGICAL AGE.

achievement battery any group of ACHIEVEMENT TESTS designed to provide an index of a person's knowledge or specific physical or mental skills across a range of related topics.

achievement drive a strong impulse to do one's best to achieve a goal and, often, to be recognized and approved for attaining it. Students with a strong achievement drive have been found to earn better grades than equally gifted students with a weaker achievement drive. Studies of the literature of different societies indicate that achievement themes predominate during periods of rapid economic growth. See also ACHIEVEMENT MOTIVATION.

achievement ethic a personal or cultural standard that requires a high level of accomplishment in both work and leisure activities. See also WORK ETHIC.

achievement goal theory any of various theories of motivation that identify two types of achievement goals, task-oriented (see TASK ORIENTATION) and ego-oriented (see EGO ORIENTATION), and that relate these to differences in individuals' perceived ability for the task and their achievement behavior.

achievement level **1.** the level of individual or group performance on a task as determined by objective or subjective criteria. **2.** the degree of proficiency attained in academic work in general. **3.** the degree of proficiency reached in a specific skill, such as reading, arithmetic, artistic performance, or athletic success.

achievement measures tasks, instruments, or systems designed to demonstrate a student's level of proficiency and to ascertain the value, strength, or quality of performance by comparison with a peer standard.

achievement motivation the desire to overcome obstacles and master difficult challenges. High scorers in achievement motivation are likely to set higher standards and work with greater perseverance than equally gifted low scorers. David MCCLELLAND found a significant relationship between high achievement motivation and early independence in childhood; in addition, there is a positive correlation between high achievement motivation and actual achievement in later life. See ACHIEVEMENT DRIVE; NEED FOR ACHIEVEMENT. [first described by U.S. psychologist Henry Alexander Murray (1893–1988)]

achievement-oriented leadership in the PATH–GOAL THEORY OF LEADERSHIP, a leadership style in which the leader encourages excellent performance and continuous improvement by showing a high degree of confidence in followers and setting challenging goals.

achievement potential **1.** the ability of a person to develop certain skills or traits in order to attain a certain projected level of proficiency. **2.** academic skills or abilities that may develop over time through education and practice.

achievement quotient (**AQ**) the ratio of actual performance, usually as measured on a norm-referenced standardized achievement test, to expected performance or age norm, usually as measured on a norm-referenced standardized intelligence test.

achievement test a norm-referenced and standardized test intended to measure an individual's current level of skill or knowledge in a given subject. Often the distinction is made that achievement tests emphasize ability acquired through formal learning or training, whereas APTITUDE TESTS (usually as measured by a norm-referenced and standardized intelligence test) emphasize innate potential. In addition to their use in academic areas, achievement tests are employed for a variety of vocational, professional, and diagnostic purposes. Also called **attainment test**.

achiever *n.* a person who is able to accomplish some action or desired result.

achiria *n.* see ACHEIRIA.

achondroplasia *n.* a form of autosomal dominant DWARFISM in which the bones derived from cartilage develop at a slower rate than the bones derived from connective tissue. This results in an enlarged cranial vault and abnormally high forehead. Motor development of infants with this disorder may be slow, but in most cases intelligence is normal. Also called **achondroplastic dwarfism**. —**achondroplastic** *adj.*

achromatic *adj.* **1.** without hue; colorless. **Achromatic stimuli** are black, white, or shades of gray. **2.** able to refract light without splitting it into its constituent wavelengths. **Achromatic lenses** do not distort the color of objects viewed through them.

achromatic–chromatic scale a scale of color values ranging through the CHROMATIC spectrum of hues and including the ACHROMATIC shades of black through gray to white.

achromatic colors colors without saturation and hue, that is, black, white, and gray. Compare CHROMATIC COLORS.

achromatic interval **1.** in vision, the interval of light intensity between the amount required for detection of a monochromatic stimulus and the amount required to perceive the color of the stimulus. **2.** in audition, a similar interval as applied to sound: the interval of sound intensity between the amount required for detection of a pure tone and the amount required to perceive the pitch of the tone.

achromatism *n.* a rare condition marked by the inability to perceive color: Everything is seen in different shades of gray. The major cause of achromatism is a congenital lack of RETINAL CONES, often associated with albinism, although it can also result from injury, OPTIC NEURITIS, lead poisoning, carbon disulfide poisoning, or occipital brain injury. Also called **achromatopsia**;

total color blindness. See also ACQUIRED COLOR BLINDNESS; CEREBRAL ACHROMATOPSIA.

acid 1. *adj.* denoting one of the four primary odor qualities in the CROCKER–HENDERSON ODOR SYSTEM. **2.** *n.* slang for LSD. See also HALLUCINOGEN.

acid flashback the experience reported by some users of LSD in which some part of the LSD experience recurs later when the individual has not been using the drug.

acid head slang for a user of LSD.

acidosis *n.* a disorder caused by a loss of the normal acid–base balance of body chemistry, resulting in an increase in the level of acidity in the blood and tissues or a depletion of alkaline reserves. The condition results in neurological abnormalities, such as muscle twitching, disorientation, and coma. It may also cause heart arrhythmias. Compare ALKALOSIS. **—acidotic** *adj.*

acid trip slang for an episode of LSD intoxication.

acme *n.* the highest point of sexual pleasure. Also called **summa libido**.

acmesthesia *n.* a form of PARESTHESIA in which a cutaneous stimulus normally sensed as pain is perceived instead as sharp touch or pressure.

ACOA abbreviation for ADULT CHILDREN OF ALCOHOLICS.

acoasm *n.* see ACOUSMA.

ACoA syndrome abbreviation for ANTERIOR COMMUNICATING ARTERY SYNDROME.

aconuresis *n.* involuntary passage of urine. See BEDWETTING; ENURESIS; URINARY INCONTINENCE.

acoria (**akoria**) *n.* a form of POLYPHAGIA marked by an excessive appetite and a loss of the sensation of satiety. See also BULIMIA NERVOSA.

Acosta's syndrome see ALTITUDE SICKNESS. [José de Acosta (1539–1600), Spanish geographer]

acousma *n.* a simple, nonverbal AUDITORY HALLUCINATION, such as a buzzing, ringing, or roaring sound. Also called **acoasm**; **akoasm**.

acoustic *adj.* associated with sound. The word is usually used to modify technical terms (e.g., acoustic wave, acoustic impedance, ACOUSTIC REFLEX). **Acoustical** is used as a modifier in all other contexts (e.g., acoustical engineer, ACOUSTICAL SOCIETY OF AMERICA).

Acoustical Society of America (**ASA**) the major professional organization in acoustics in the United States. The society consists of many technical areas, including psychological and physiological acoustics, speech communication, and musical acoustics. The ASA is part of the American Institute of Physics and publishes the *Journal of the Acoustical Society of America* (*JASA*).

acoustic cue in phonology, one of the physical properties of a speech sound (e.g., wave frequency, VOICE-ONSET TIME, or intensity) that mark its identity.

acoustic environments the acoustic or sound-propagating qualities of a physical environment. In addition to sound intensity (i.e., loudness), an important feature of acoustic environments is reverberation time: the time taken for a sound to decay 60 dB. Perception of sound inside differs from that outside because of reverberation.

acoustic filter a component of some versions of the WORKING MEMORY model that allows only speechlike stimuli to access the model's phonological store.

acoustic labyrinth see AUDITORY LABYRINTH.

acoustic-mnestic aphasia a form of APHASIA resulting from lesions in the central portions of the left temporal area of the brain or deep portions of the temporal cortex. It is marked by difficulty in comprehending words, recalling word lists, and comprehending and reproducing long sentences, as well as an inability to name objects. Also called **acousticoamnestic aphasia**.

acoustic nerve see AUDITORY NERVE.

acoustic neuroma a benign tumor arising from the AUDITORY NERVE, between the cochlea and the brainstem. Common symptoms include tinnitus, unilateral hearing loss, and vertigo.

acousticoamnestic aphasia see ACOUSTIC-MNESTIC APHASIA.

acoustic phonetics the branch of PHONETICS that studies the physical properties of human speech sounds and the physiological means by which they are perceived. Compare ARTICULATORY PHONETICS.

acoustic pressure see SOUND PRESSURE.

acoustic reflex 1. contraction of the middle ear muscles, elicited by intense sounds, vocalization, or bodily movement. This reflex reduces the low-frequency input to the inner ear and functions partly to protect the inner ear from the damaging effects of intense sounds. **2.** an automatic reaction to sound. Kinds of acoustic reflexes include the BLINK RESPONSE, condition-oriented reflex, MORO REFLEX, STRETCH REFLEX, and SUCKING REFLEX.

acoustic resonance a frequency-dependent change in the response of an acoustic system. The response of a system is a maximum at its **resonance frequency**.

acoustics *n.* the science of sound, including its production, transmission, and auditory effects.

acoustics as emotions acoustic patterns that are specific to particular emotions and therefore enable recognition of emotion in speech. These acoustic properties are measured by FORMANT analysis, spectral analysis, intonation scoring, and inverse filtering of the speech signal to arrive at an estimate of the glottal waveform.

acoustic spectrum see SOUND SPECTRUM.

acoustic store a component of short-term memory that retains auditory information based on how items sound. Forgetting occurs when words or letters in acoustic store sound alike. Compare ARTICULATORY STORE.

acoustic trauma a form of SENSORINEURAL HEARING LOSS resulting from exposure to intense noise. Even brief periods of exposure to jet-aircraft engine noise, gunfire, loud music, or heavy drills may cause permanent damage to the nerve fibers in the cochlea.

ACPT abbreviation for AUDITORY CONTINUOUS PERFORMANCE TEST.

acquaintance rape see DATE RAPE.

acquiescence *n.* agreement or acceptance, typically without protest or argument. **—acquiesce** *vb.* **—acquiescent** *adj.*

acquiescent response set the tendency of a participant presented with a series of statements in a test or questionnaire to agree with these statements, regardless of their content. Response acquiescence (or yea-saying) can distort the results of personality inventories and attitude scales.

acquired *adj.* denoting a response, behavior, idea, or information that has been learned or developed on the basis of experience rather than being innate or inborn.

acquired agraphia see AGRAPHIA.

acquired characteristic a structural or functional characteristic or a psychological feature (e.g., a trait or behavior) of a organism that arises from experience or through environmental factors rather than being the result of inheritance. Also called **acquired character**.

acquired color blindness defective color vision that

develops in a person with previously normal vision. Acquired forms of color blindness can be caused by retinal disease (e.g., GLAUCOMA, RETINITIS PIGMENTOSA), optic nerve disease (e.g., in multiple sclerosis), or injury to areas of the occipitotemporal cortex that are responsible for color processing (see CEREBRAL ACHROMATOPSIA; HEMIACHROMATOPSIA). Systemic disorders (e.g., diabetes mellitus and alcoholism), ANOXIA, and many toxins can also produce color deficiencies. Acquired color blindness often differs from genetic forms of the condition (see COLOR BLINDNESS). The discrimination of colors may be impaired in all parts of the spectrum, and the patient may have difficulty in identifying desaturated colors. Color blindness is typically present in the entire visual field, but that due to cerebral injury may be limited to the left or right half of the visual field.

acquired distinctiveness of cues prior learning about how to respond appropriately to certain stimuli in one situation that may facilitate learning to respond to stimuli in another situation. For example, rats may be trained to learn a maze by distinguishing between white and black arms of the maze. If these rats are later trained to distinguish between left and right arms of a different maze through reinforcement of the right arm when it is white and the left arm when it is black, they are likely to learn the maze faster than rats who were initially trained to distinguish between wide and narrow arms. Also called **acquired discrimination of cues**.

acquired drive see SECONDARY DRIVE.

acquired dyslexia see ALEXIA.

acquired dyspraxia DYSPRAXIA that is manifested as the loss of a previously acquired ability to perform coordinated movements. It usually follows or is associated with brain injury or stroke. Compare DEVELOPMENTAL DYSPRAXIA.

acquired immune deficiency syndrome see AIDS.

acquired response a response to a stimulus that has been learned, such as a classically conditioned response or a reinforced response. Also called **acquired reaction**.

acquired speech disorder a speech disorder that develops at some time after birth, which may be manifested as the loss of a previously acquired ability to produce articulate speech. Compare CONGENITAL SPEECH DISORDER.

acquired visual impairment see ADVENTITIOUS VISUAL IMPAIRMENT.

acquisition *n.* **1.** the addition of a new type of behavior, response, information, or idea to an individual's REPERTOIRE. **2.** the new behavior or information so added. See LEARNING. **—acquire** *vb.*

acquisition trial see LEARNING TRIAL.

acquisitiveness *n.* the tendency or desire to acquire and accumulate objects or possessions. Compare HOARDING. **—acquisitive** *adj.*

acro- *combining form* **1.** the extremities (e.g., ACROMEGALY). **2.** height (e.g., ACROPHOBIA).

acroagnosia *n.* lack of sensory recognition of a limb. Individuals with this disorder cannot feel the presence of a limb although they may be able to see it or acknowledge its existence. Also called **acroagnosis**.

acroanesthesia *n.* an absence of sensitivity in the extremities as a result of disease or as an aftereffect of anesthesia. See also ACROPARESTHESIA. Compare ACROESTHESIA.

acrocentric chromosome a chromosome in which the CENTROMERE is near one end, making one arm of the replicating chromosome shorter than the other. An acrocentric chromosome may be much smaller than others and may occur as additional genetic material in such disorders as CAT'S-EYE SYNDROME.

acrocephalopolysyndactyly *n.* see CARPENTER'S SYNDROME.

acrocephalosyndactyly *n.* any of several related inherited disorders (all dominant traits) that cause abnormalities of the skull, face, hands, and feet. APERT'S SYNDROME, Apert–Crouzon syndrome, and PFEIFFER'S SYNDROME (acrocephalosyndactyly Types I, II, and V) are due to different mutations in the *FGFR2* gene (encoding fibroblast growth factor receptor) on chromosome 10. CHOTZEN'S SYNDROME (Type III) is due to a mutation in the *TWIST* gene on chromosome 7 (locus 7p21.3–21.2), which affects the expression of *FGFR2*.

acrocephaly *n.* see OXYCEPHALY.

acrocinesis *n.* excessive motion or movement, as is sometimes observed, for example, in manic episodes. Also called **acrocinesia**; **acrokinesia**.

acroesthesia *n.* an abnormal sensitivity to stimuli applied to the extremities. Neurologists refer to this as DYSESTHESIA. Compare ACROANESTHESIA; ACROPARESTHESIA.

acromegaloid-hypertelorism-pectus carinatum syndrome a congenital condition, believed to be hereditary, marked by short stature, mental retardation, widely set eyes, and skeletal anomalies, including an enlarged head and a deformed sternum. Only males are known to be affected. All show slow psychomotor development and IQs estimated in the 20s.

acromegaloid personality a personality pattern observed in a large proportion of patients with ACROMEGALY. The chief features are frequent changes in mood, impulsiveness, temper outbursts, impatience, and, in advanced cases, loss of initiative, egocentricity, and somnolence.

acromegaly *n.* an abnormal enlargement of the skeletal extremities, such as the arms, legs, and parts of the skull. The condition is rare and usually occurs in adults whose normal bone growth has already stopped. The cause is a pituitary-gland abnormality that results in excessive secretion of growth hormone. In growing children, whose bones are still developing, the effect is known as GIGANTISM.

acromicria *n.* a type of underdevelopment marked by abnormally small fingers, toes, or facial features.

acronym *n.* an abbreviation formed from the initials or first few letters of the parts of a compound name and pronounced as a word, such as *AIDS* (for *a*cquired *i*mmune *d*eficiency *s*yndrome) or *sonar* (for *so*und *n*avigation *a*nd *r*anging). An abbreviation formed in the same way but pronounced letter by letter, such as *IRS* (for *I*nternal *R*evenue *S*ervice), is known as an **initialism**.

acroparesthesia *n.* a feeling of numbness, tingling, or other abnormal sensation in the extremities. Kinds of acroparesthesia include **Nothnagel's acroparesthesia**, which is accompanied by circulatory disorders, and **Schultze's acroparesthesia**, marked by peripheral-nerve irritability but without circulatory abnormalities. See also ACROANESTHESIA. Compare ACROESTHESIA.

acrophobia *n.* a SPECIFIC PHOBIA, natural environment type, characterized by an excessive fear of high places. The focus of apprehension may include anticipated harm (e.g., falling) or uncomfortable physical sensations (e.g., dizziness). Also called **height phobia**. **—acrophobic** *adj.*

acrotomophilia *n.* pathological interest in amputations. It may be expressed as a PARAPHILIA in which the person is sexually aroused by people whose body parts, typically arms or legs, have been amputated or by amputation sites in the body. Also called **acrotophilia**; **apotemnophilia**.

ACSI abbreviation for ATHLETIC COPING SKILLS INVENTORY.

ACSM abbreviation for AMERICAN COLLEGE OF SPORTS MEDICINE.

ACSW abbreviation for ACADEMY OF CERTIFIED SOCIAL WORKERS.

act *n.* a complex behavior, as distinct from a simple MOVEMENT.

ACT 1. abbreviation for ATROPINE-COMA THERAPY. **2.** abbreviation for ATTENTION-CONTROL TRAINING. **3.** abbreviation for AUDITORY CONSONANT TRIGRAM.

ACT* acronym (pronounced act-star) for *a*daptive *c*ontrol of *t*hought theory, in revised form. ACT* is a theory of the mental representation of knowledge and of skilled behaviors that implement knowledge. [formulated by U.S. cognitive psychologist John R. Anderson (1947–)]

ACT Assessment *A*merican *C*ollege *T*esting Assessment: a set of four multiple-choice academic college tests (English, mathematics, reading, science) administered nationwide five times yearly; an optional, supplemental essay writing test may also be given. The assessment consists of 215 total questions intended to evaluate the participant's overall academic achievement and mastery of the basic skills required for satisfactory performance in college, rather than the person's aptitude or intelligence. The ACT Assessment is one of four major components of the **American College Testing Program** (**ACTP**), a system for gathering data about students and providing it to designated educational institutions.

ACTH abbreviation for ADRENOCORTICOTROPIC HORMONE.

ACTH releasing factor see CORTICOTROPIN-RELEASING HORMONE.

actin *n.* a contractile protein that, together with MYOSIN, occurs in MUSCLE FIBERS and mediates MUSCLE CONTRACTION.

acting in 1. in psychoanalysis, a form of RESISTANCE in which the patient defends against repressed wishes, memories, or both by using actions (e.g., getting up and walking about) to impede the flow of FREE ASSOCIATION. **2.** the patient's reenactment of past relationships in the TRANSFERENCE relationship with the analyst.

acting out 1. the uncontrolled and inappropriate behavioral expression of denied emotions that serves to relieve tension associated with these emotions or to communicate them in a disguised, or indirect, way to others. Such behaviors may include (but are not limited to) arguing, fighting, stealing, threatening, or throwing tantrums. Acting out is often assumed to underlie antisocial or delinquent behavior in children and adolescents but is not limited to this age group. **2.** in psychoanalytic theory, the expression of unconscious emotional conflicts, feelings, or desires—often sexual or aggressive—through inappropriate action, with no attempt to understand the origin or meaning of these behaviors.

action *n.* **1.** a self-initiated sequence of movements, usually with respect to some goal. It may consist of an integrated set of component behaviors as opposed to a single response. **2.** the occurrence or performance of a process or function (e.g., the action of an enzyme). **3.** the state or process of being active.

actional verb in linguistics, a verb that denotes physical action, usually performed by an AGENT and resulting in an effect on a PATIENT, such as *kick* or *kiss*. A **nonactional verb** is one that denotes an occurrence, experience, state, or condition, such as *be, have, see, think,* or *explain*. Some psychologists believe that the distinction between actional and nonactional verbs is significant in explaining patterns of early language development. See also CAUSATIVE VERB.

action at a distance the interaction of bodies that are not in physical contact and have no intervening mechanical medium, as by a field of force, such as gravitation. See FIELD THEORY.

action current see ACTION POTENTIAL.

action disorganization syndrome (**ADS**) a disorder in which damage to the FRONTAL LOBES of the brain causes individuals to make many errors on multistepped tasks, even on tasks that are familiar. Individuals with ADS have impairments in their ability to control their behavior in both familiar and unfamiliar circumstances.

action group a TASK-ORIENTED GROUP that aims to have a direct impact on and achieve a modification of the environment. An action group may be contrasted to a therapy group, personal-growth group, or study group, in which the immediate aim is to improve the attitudes, behaviors, knowledge, or interpersonal relations of those within the group.

action identification the act of construing one's actions or those of another in a particular way, so that one says or thinks (for example) "I am running," "I am trying to catch the bus," or "I am getting to work." The same action may be construed at multiple levels of meaning, ranging from mere muscle movements (low level) to long-term goals (high level).

action interpretation the nonverbal reaction of a therapist to a patient's behavior or remarks.

action learning see ACTIVE LEARNING.

action orientation a style of responding to dilemmas or conflicts that is characterized by swift, decisive action rather than by prolonged analysis and planning. Compare STATE ORIENTATION.

action-oriented therapy any therapy that emphasizes doing and taking action rather than verbal communication or discussion.

action painting a form of painting, often used in ART THERAPY, in which individuals spontaneously create unplanned abstract works using unconventional techniques, for example, splashing, dribbling, trickling, or slapping the paint more or less randomly onto the canvas. When used therapeutically, these productions are reviewed and incorporated into treatment. Also called **tachisme**.

action pattern a predictable behavioral sequence that is elicited by certain requisite stimuli. For example, during the mating season, a male fish aggressively defends its territory against other males. See also FIXED-ACTION PATTERN.

action potential (**AP**) the change in electric potential that propagates along a cell during the transmission of a nerve impulse or the contraction of a muscle. It is marked by a rapid, transient DEPOLARIZATION of the cell's plasma membrane, from a RESTING POTENTIAL of about –70 mV (inside negative) to about +30 mV (inside positive), and back again, after a slight HYPERPOLARIZATION, to the resting potential. Each action potential takes just a few milliseconds. Also called **action current**; **spike potential**.

action readiness a state of preparedness for action that is elicited as part of an emotional response and associated with such physiological indicators as changes in heart rate, respiratory rate, and muscle tension. The term is often used synonymously with ACTION TENDENCY but also refers to a general readiness for action that does not involve a specific identifiable action tendency.

action research study or research that is directed toward a practical goal, usually an improvement in a particular process or system, in contrast to purely experimental research. In ORGANIZATIONAL DEVELOPMENT, action research involves not only systematically collecting data about an organization but also providing feedback to the organization, taking actions to improve the organization based on the feedback, and then evaluating the results of these actions.

action slip any error that involves some kind of cognitive lapse and results in an unintended action, as in putting one's spectacles in the refrigerator. Action slips are commonly referred to as "absent-minded" mistakes. See ABSENT-MINDEDNESS.

action-specific energy a hypothetical supply of motivational energy within an organism that is associated with specific unlearned behavioral responses known as FIXED-ACTION PATTERNS. Each response has its own energy supply, which builds up until the organism encounters the appropriate stimulus (see RELEASER) that triggers the response and thus depletes the energy supply. After the response and in the absence of the releaser, the action-specific energy begins to build up again. [proposed by Austrian ethologist Konrad Z. Lorenz (1903–1989)]

action stream see STREAM OF ACTION.

action tendency an urge to carry out certain expressive or instrumental behaviors that is linked to a specific emotion. For example, the action tendency of fear involves an urge to escape, and that of anger involves an urge to attack. Some theorists argue that the action tendency of an emotional reaction should be regarded as its essential defining characteristic. Compare ACTION READINESS.

action theory all those theories, collectively, that have as their model potentially reflexive human beings (i.e., able to think of themselves as being in a situation) who act intentionally with reference to the environment. Action theory was known originally as **will psychology**, founded in Germany by Wilhelm WUNDT, who emphasized and distinguished between motivation and volition of human behavior.

action tremor a tremor that arises when the individual is engaged in voluntary activity rather than at rest. Such tremors are common in Parkinson's disease. Also called **volitional tremor**. See INTENTION TREMOR.

action unit the simplest facial movement used as a code in the FACIAL ACTION CODING SYSTEM. Action units are the visible signs of the operation of single facial muscles.

Actiq *n.* a trade name for FENTANYL.

activated sleep see REM SLEEP.

activating event in RATIONAL EMOTIVE BEHAVIOR THERAPY, an event—current, past, or anticipated—that triggers irrational beliefs and disruptive emotions.

activation *n.* **1.** in many theories of memory, an attribute of the representational units (such as NODES or LOGOGENS) that varies from weaker to stronger, with more strongly activated representations competing to control processing. **2.** the process of alerting an organ or body system for action, particularly arousal of one organ or system by another. **—activate** *vb.* **—activational** *adj.*

activational effect a transient hormonal effect that typically causes a short-term change in behavior or physiological activity in adult animals. For example, increased testosterone in male songbirds in spring leads to increased aggression in territory defense and increased courtship behavior. Compare ORGANIZATIONAL EFFECT.

activation–arousal theory see ACTIVATION THEORY OF EMOTION.

activation–elaboration a dual-process theory of memory holding that concepts stored in memory vary in their levels both of ACTIVATION and ELABORATION.

activation hypothesis **1.** in cognitive theory, the principle that numerical weightings on the links or nodes of cognitive network models can represent their degree of activity or processing. Consciousness is sometimes attributed to the subset of most highly weighted elements in such models. **2.** in brain theory, the hypothesis that high metabolic activity reflects activation of brain areas subserving mental tasks.

activation pattern in electroencephalography, the suppression of ALPHA WAVES and a shift to low-voltage, rapid activity when the person undergoing the procedure opens his or her eyes to view an object or display. The alpha desynchronization may be localized or general, as measured in various cerebral areas, and transient or sustained.

activation–synthesis hypothesis a hypothesis that explains dreams as a product of cortical interpretation of random activation rising from the lower brain structures, including the PONS. See PGO SPIKES. [originated by U.S. psychiatrists J. Allan Hobson (1933–) and Robert W. McCarley]

activation theory of emotion the theory that emotion is measurable as change in the individual's level of energy expenditure (i.e., level of AROUSAL) and change in his or her degree of approach to or withdrawal from an object. Also called **activation–arousal theory**; **arousal theory**. [formulated in 1934 by U.S. psychologist Elizabeth Duffy (1904–1970)]

active *adj.* **1.** currently functioning or performing some action, either continuously or intermittently. **2.** exerting an effect or influence on a process or thing. **3.** in grammar, denoting the ACTIVE VOICE of a verb. **4.** vigorous, lively, or energetic.

active algolagnia arousal of sexual excitement by causing pain to another person. See SEXUAL SADISM.

active analytic psychotherapy the therapeutic approach of German psychoanalyst Wilhelm Stekel (1868–1940) in which the analyst takes a much more active role than prescribed in CLASSICAL PSYCHOANALYSIS and gives more attention to the intrapsychic conflicts in the patient's current life than to exploring early childhood experiences. The therapist intervenes in the process of free association to discuss important issues, confronts the patient's resistances directly, offers advice and exhortation, and helps the patient interpret his or her dreams intuitively in the light of current attitudes and problems. Through these methods, and by avoiding many of the Freudian steps such as ANALYSIS OF THE TRANSFERENCE, Stekel sought to shorten the therapeutic process considerably. Also called **active analysis**.

active avoidance a type of OPERANT CONDITIONING in which an explicit act prevents or postpones the delivery of an AVERSIVE STIMULUS, such as when pressing a lever blocks the delivery of an electric shock. That is, avoidance is achieved by an overt action. Compare PASSIVE AVOIDANCE.

active concretization in schizophrenia, the process of

transforming abstract concepts into concrete representations or forms. For example, an individual with paranoid schizophrenia who experiences feelings that the whole world is hostile may later become convinced that the neighbors are trying to harm him or her. If this individual should then begin to have specific perceptual experiences that support this conviction, such as auditory hallucinations of threatening remarks made by the neighbors, PERCEPTUALIZATION of the concept has occurred; this is the most advanced level of active concretization. [defined by Italian-born U.S. psychiatrist Silvano Arieti (1914–1982)]

active coping see PROBLEM-FOCUSED COPING.

active deception the process of intentionally misleading research participants, for example, by giving them false information about the purpose of the research or by having them unwittingly interact with CONFEDERATES. Also called **deception by commission**.

active euthanasia direct action intended to terminate the life of a person (or animal) who is suffering greatly and is considered to have no chance for recovery. Lethal injections and administration of carbon monoxide are the most common types of active euthanasia today. This practice is distinguished from PASSIVE EUTHANASIA, in which treatments are withheld but no direct action to terminate the life is taken. See also ASSISTED DEATH; EUTHANASIA.

active intermodal mapping the ability of young infants to integrate information from two or more senses. This cognitive ability is thought to underlie NEONATAL IMITATION. [postulated by U.S. psychologists Andrew N. Meltzoff (1950–) and M. Keith Moore]

active learning 1. learning that occurs through the ACTIVE PERFORMANCE of a task or cognitive operation. Also called **action learning**. **2.** the active seeking out of new information, rather than simply being a passive recipient of a learning experience. Active learners set goals, select strategies, recognize when they understand, and work with others to further learning. See METACOGNITION.

active listening a psychotherapeutic technique in which the therapist listens to a client closely and attentively, asking questions as needed, in an attempt to fully understand the content of the message and the depth of the client's emotion. The therapist typically restates what has been said to assure the client that he or she has been understood. Active listening is particularly associated with CLIENT-CENTERED THERAPY.

active memory a memory that is currently the focus of consciousness or was recently in awareness, as distinct from the vast body of stored memories that are currently inactive. Activation occurs through RETRIEVAL, cuing (see CUE), or prompting. According to one theory, an item in short-term memory is an item from long-term memory that has been activated.

active negativism see NEGATIVISM.

active noise cancellation a method of controlling noise levels that involves the production of sound signals to cancel other sounds. Compare ACTIVE NOISE REDUCTION.

active noise protection (**ANP**) any method of protecting people from unwanted or excessive noise based upon ACTIVE NOISE CANCELLATION or ACTIVE NOISE REDUCTION, as opposed to **passive noise protection**, which involves the use of simple barrier methods, such as earplugs.

active noise reduction (**ANR**) a method of noise reduction that makes use of sound absorbers or decouplers. Compare ACTIVE NOISE CANCELLATION.

active performance the actual performance of behavior or acting out an idea, in contrast to mentally rehearsing or imagining the action.

active placebo an agent used in DOUBLE-BLIND controlled trials of pharmacological products that has no therapeutic effect but—unlike a completely inert DUMMY placebo—may produce side effects characteristic of the drug under investigation. Active placebos are therefore considered by some to be more likely to reveal true differences in drug–placebo responding.

active recreation a form of RECREATIONAL THERAPY in which the individual is an active participant in an activity, such as dancing, that requires physical or mental exertion. Compare PASSIVE RECREATION.

active rehearsal see CUMULATIVE REHEARSAL.

active scopophilia pathological interest in viewing other people engaged in sexual activity or in viewing their genitals. It may be expressed as a PARAPHILIA in which the person is sexually aroused by these actions. See also SCOPOPHILIA.

active therapy 1. a form of psychotherapy in which the therapist assumes an active, directive role. An **active therapist** may express opinions, offer interpretations, make suggestions and recommendations, issue injunctions and prohibitions, or urge the client to take a particular action, such as facing an anxiety-provoking situation directly. [introduced by Hungarian psychoanalyst Sandor Ferenczi (1873–1933)] **2.** in psychoanalysis, a method of therapy in which the analyst departs from classic Freudian practice by (a) encouraging the patient to break the RULE OF ABSTINENCE and (b) ignoring the injunction against giving advice about the patient's actions and decisions.

active touch touch perception of the characteristics of an object through voluntary, intentional contact movement (especially by the hands) that is self-initiated. Compare PASSIVE TOUCH. See also HAPTIC.

active transport the movement of ions or molecules across a cell membrane by a mechanism that requires energy. The movement may depend on a special affinity between ions, a metabolic reaction, or some other energy-consuming process. Active transport is involved in the movement of sodium and potassium ions across the membrane of a nerve cell. Compare PASSIVE TRANSPORT.

active vocabulary see PRODUCTIVE VOCABULARY.

active voice in linguistics, the category of a verb in which the grammatical SUBJECT of the clause or sentence is the AGENT of the action and the grammatical OBJECT is its PATIENT. The great majority of English sentences are constructed using the active voice. Compare PASSIVE VOICE.

activism *n.* **1.** the policy or practice of taking committed action to achieve an end, in particular a political or social goal. See also COMMUNITY ACTION GROUP; SOCIAL ACTION PROGRAM. **2.** in philosophy, the doctrine that any relationship between thought and reality is characterized by continuous activity on the part of the mind, rather than passive receptivity. **—activist** *adj., n.*

activities, interests, opinions (**AIO**) see PSYCHOGRAPHICS.

activities of daily living (**ADLs**) activities essential to an individual's personal care, such as getting into and out of bed, dressing, eating, toileting and bathing, and grooming. Instruments measuring activities of daily living are often used to assess the functional capabilities of those with degenerative diseases (e.g., Alzheimer's disease). Individuals with disabilities or individuals who have experienced a sudden trauma (e.g., a stroke) may be required to relearn ADLs using new techniques or assistive devices (see ASSISTIVE TECHNOLOGY). See also INSTRUMENTAL ACTIVITIES OF DAILY LIVING.

activity analysis the objective evaluation of activity engaged in by an individual over a specified period, usually by breaking it down into smaller components, such as eating, working, social activities, resting, and so on.

activity cage an enclosed space in which animals move freely while their behavior is observed, recorded, or measured.

activity cycle any regularly recurring sequence of events characterized by fluctuating levels of activity. Unlike ACTIVITY RHYTHMS, activity cycles may be learned and thus are not always associated with BIOLOGICAL RHYTHMS.

activity deprivation lack of opportunity to engage in physical activity due to restrictive circumstances, for example, confinement in a small area, which may result in distress and physical discomfort. See also ACTIVITY DRIVE.

activity drive an organism's hypothetical innate desire or urge to be physically active, often expressed as a need to move about, even in the absence of any apparent stimuli motivating movement, such that ACTIVITY DEPRIVATION may cause distress.

activity-group therapy a form of GROUP PSYCHOTHERAPY for children and young adolescents that emphasizes active participation in games, crafts, and other age-appropriate activities and interplay. Activity-group therapy provides children with opportunities to express their feelings in a permissive, nonthreatening atmosphere. [introduced in the 1930s by 20th-century Russian-born U.S. psychotherapist Samuel Richard Slavson]

activity-interview group psychotherapy a form of ANALYTIC GROUP PSYCHOTHERAPY for children in the latency period (i.e., between infancy and adolescence). Hobbies and recreational activities are used to stimulate communication and the expression of conflicts and fantasies. During the process, the therapist asks questions that encourage the children to understand how their immediate problems (e.g., fears) are affecting their behavior and attitudes. [introduced by 20th-century Russian-born U.S. psychotherapist Samuel Richard Slavson]

activity log a diary kept by a research director or the research participant of hourly activities in various environmental settings. A typical activity log includes data regarding the location of the participant by time period (e.g., at home, at work, or traveling) and whether the time is spent alone or with family, friends, or work associates. An activity log as a method of obtaining a record of events is superior to interviews based on a participant's memory. See also ACTIVITY RECORD.

activity–passivity in psychoanalytic theory, polarities characterizing instinctual aims (see AIM OF THE INSTINCT). Sigmund FREUD asserted that instincts are always active but that their aims can be either active (e.g., SADISM and VOYEURISM) or passive (e.g., EXHIBITIONISM and MASOCHISM). Freud's equation of activity with masculinity and passivity with femininity was much criticized early on by women analysts, including Melanie KLEIN and German-born U.S. psychoanalyst Karen Horney (1885–1952), and has been rejected by many theorists, researchers, and therapists since.

activity-play therapy a controlled play technique in which a child is given a set of dolls and other play materials and encouraged to express and explore his or her feelings about them—such as sadness, guilt, and hostility—based on the theory that the child will then become less afraid of these emotions and will express them more freely.

activity pleasure the satisfaction derived from performing an activity. By extension, activity pleasure includes intellectual activities that satisfy an individual's curiosity. See also FUNCTION PLEASURE.

activity record the written or recorded data detailing a student's extracurricular involvement in school activities, clubs, or special projects. See also ACTIVITY LOG.

activity rhythm the pattern of animal behavior over the course of a day, month, or year that exhibits a clear cycle of activity more or less in synchrony with temporal cues. For example, rats are generally active for approximately 12 hours a day, during the hours of darkness, but this pattern persists even in the absence of regular changes in light and dark. See BIOLOGICAL RHYTHM.

activity system see BEHAVIOR SYSTEM.

activity theory 1. a school of thought, developed primarily by Soviet psychologists, that focuses on activity in general—rather than the distinct concepts of behavior or mental states—as the primary unit of analysis. In this context, an **activity** is a nonadditive unit that orients an organism in the world; it is essentially a system comprising an **operation** (a routine behavior requiring little thought, e.g., typing) that serves to accomplish an **action** (a behavior that involves planning, e.g., creating a bibliography) in the minimum meaningful context that provides understanding of the function of the individual in interacting with the environment (e.g., preparing a paper for a university course as part of a network of students). The theory emphasizes a hierarchical structure of activity, object-orientedness, internalization and externalization, mediation (by tools, language, and other cultural artifacts or instruments), and continuous development. Also called **activity psychology**. **2.** a social theory of aging that suggests that SUCCESSFUL AGING is characterized by maintaining social roles, activities, and relationships. Also called **activity theory of aging**. Compare DISENGAGEMENT THEORY.

activity therapy any type of therapy centered around various activities, such as arts and crafts, exercise, music, and dramatics groups.

activity wheel a revolving drum that turns by the weight of an animal running inside. The activity wheel records the number of revolutions and is often used for various research purposes. Also called **running wheel**.

actomyosin *n.* see MUSCLE FIBER.

actor–observer effect in ATTRIBUTION THEORY, the tendency for individuals acting in a situation to attribute the causes of their behavior to external or situational factors, such as social pressure, but for observers to attribute the same behavior to internal or dispositional factors, such as personality. See FUNDAMENTAL ATTRIBUTION ERROR. See also DISPOSITIONAL ATTRIBUTION; SITUATIONAL ATTRIBUTION.

ACTP abbreviation for American College Testing Program. See ACT ASSESSMENT.

act psychology a philosophical and psychological approach based on the proposition that the act and CONTENT of psychological processes are separate functions; for example, the act of seeing color leads to a perception of the visual content, or image. Proponents of act psychology hold that acts, rather than contents, are the proper subject of psychology, in contrast to Wilhelm WUNDT's emphasis on introspection and conscious contents. Compare CONTENT PSYCHOLOGY. See also INTENTIONALITY. [proposed by German psychologist and philosopher Franz Brentano (1838–1917)]

actual *adj.* in philosophy, existing as a real and present fact. The actual is often contrasted with the merely apparent. Something may appear to the senses to be real but may not actually exist. In the intellectual tradition founded by Greek philosopher Aristotle (384–322 BCE), the actual is contrasted to the **potential**, which is the capacity to change: An entity is actual when form and substance come together to produce it as an end. See also ENTELECHY.

actual incidence real or observed rates of a particular occurrence, as opposed to reported or assumed rates.

actualization *n.* the process of mobilizing one's potentialities and expressing or realizing them in concrete form. See also ACTUALIZING TENDENCY; SELF-ACTUALIZATION. **—actualize** *vb.*

actualizing tendency in the humanistic personality theory of Carl ROGERS, the innate tendency of humans to develop and actualize the self fully. See ACTUALIZATION; SELF-ACTUALIZATION.

actual neurosis in the classical psychoanalytic theory of Sigmund FREUD, a neurosis that stems from current sexual frustrations (e.g., coitus interruptus, otherwise incomplete sexual experience, or forced abstinence), as contrasted with one that stems from past experiences or psychological conflicts. The term, which was applied primarily to ANXIETY NEUROSIS and NEURASTHENIA, is now rarely used.

actual self in various psychodynamic writings, the REAL SELF or TRUE SELF as it exists at a particular point in time, as opposed to an idealized, grandiose, or otherwise distorted self.

actuarial *adj.* statistical, as opposed to clinical. The use of data about prior instances, in order to estimate the likelihood or risk of a particular outcome, is sometimes cited as an alternative to clinical diagnoses, which are open to human error.

actuarial prediction prediction based on quantified experience and data rather than on more subjective (e.g., clinical) experience. See also ACTUARIAL RISK ASSESSMENT.

actuarial risk assessment a statistically calculated prediction of the likelihood that an individual will pose a threat to others or engage in a certain behavior (e.g., violence) within a given period. Unlike CLINICAL RISK ASSESSMENT, it relies on data from specific, measurable variables (e.g., age, gender, prior criminal activity) that have been validated as predictors and uses mathematical analyses and formulas to calculate the probability of DANGEROUSNESS or violent behavior.

actus reus the illegal act (Latin, "guilty act") that, combined with a criminal intent in committing it (see MENS REA), constitutes a crime.

acuity *n.* sharpness of perception. SENSORY ACUITY is the precision with which any sensory stimulation is perceived; VISUAL ACUITY is sharpness of vision. See also VISUAL THRESHOLD; SNELLEN CHART.

acuity grating a device used to measure the VISUAL ACUITY of an individual. It consists of alternating black and white lines spaced closely together; the participant must determine whether the stimulus consists of lines or is homogeneous. The point at which the participant perceives the lines to be homogeneous gives an indication of visual acuity. When the contrast of the lines is varied, the acuity grating can be used to test CONTRAST SENSITIVITY.

aculalia *n.* nonsensical speech associated with lack of comprehension of written or spoken language. It is a form of APHASIA resulting from lesions in the left TEMPORAL LOBE of the brain. Aculalia is similar to WORD SALAD. See also WERNICKE'S APHASIA.

acupressure *n.* a form of COMPLEMENTARY AND ALTERNATIVE MEDICINE in which pressure is applied with the fingers or thumbs to points on the body to relieve pain, treat symptoms of disease or illness, or improve overall health. Compare ACUPUNCTURE.

acupuncture *n.* the technique of inserting fine needles into the body at specific points to relieve pain, to induce anesthesia for surgical procedures (see ACUPUNCTURE ANESTHESIA), or as a form of therapy. It is based on the concept in traditional Chinese medicine that "meridians," or pathways, conduct life-force energy known as CHI between places on the skin and the body's organ systems. Although scientists are unable to explain the processes by which acupuncture produces its effects (the needling sites may be related to trigger points in the GATE-CONTROL THEORY OF PAIN), the technique is highly popular in many Western societies and has been deemed appropriate by the World Health Organization for use in treating more than 40 medical conditions. Compare ACUPRESSURE. See also COMPLEMENTARY AND ALTERNATIVE MEDICINE; YIN AND YANG. **—acupuncturist** *n.*

acupuncture anesthesia the loss of sensation, often of pain, that results from the insertion of ACUPUNCTURE needles into the body at specific points. The technique may be used alone or in combination with other PAIN-MANAGEMENT techniques during surgery.

-acusia (**-acusis**; **-cusis**) *suffix* hearing (e.g., PARACUSIA).

acute *adj.* **1.** sharp, keen, or very sensitive (e.g., an acute sense of hearing). **2.** denoting an illness of sudden onset, intense symptoms, and short duration. Compare CHRONIC.

acute alcoholic hallucinosis the rapid or sudden onset of alcoholic hallucinosis (see ALCOHOL-INDUCED PSYCHOTIC DISORDER), usually either during a heavy drinking episode or during withdrawal. See also ALCOHOL WITHDRAWAL.

acute alcoholic myopathy a condition of severe pain, tenderness, and swelling of the muscles, accompanied by cramps and muscular weakness, that develops after a period of heavy drinking. The effects may be general or focused in one body area. In some cases, muscle fibers may undergo necrosis (death of constituent cells). Recovery may require several weeks to several months.

acute alcoholism the unusually rapid onset of the symptoms of ALCOHOL DEPENDENCE.

acute anxiety a sudden feeling of dread and apprehension accompanied by somatic symptoms of tension, usually precipitated by a threatening situation, such as an examination or court hearing. The feeling typically subsides as soon as the situation is over. See PERFORMANCE ANXIETY.

acute anxiety attack see PANIC ATTACK.

acute brain disorder any pattern of symptoms resulting from temporary, reversible impairment of brain functioning.

acute cerebellar ataxia a disorder that occurs suddenly, most often in children, following a viral infection. It is characterized by slurred speech, muscular incoordination (ATAXIA), rapid, involuntary eye movements (NYSTAGMUS), and INTENTION TREMOR. Also called **acute cerebral tremor**.

acute cerebrovascular accident see CEREBROVASCULAR ACCIDENT.

acute confusional state severe confusion that can include symptoms of agitation, memory disturbance, disorientation, and DELIRIUM. It often occurs as a result of severe mental or physical illness.

acute delirium a disorder of brain function, of sudden onset and brief duration, characterized by a disturbance in consciousness that ranges from extreme hyperactivity to near coma. Resulting from metabolic disturbance (e.g., high fever) or toxic agents (e.g., excessive amounts of alcohol), it is marked by illusions, hallucinations, delusions, excitement, restlessness, and incoherence.

acute delusional psychosis a diagnostic entity specific to French psychiatry, in which it is known as **bouffée délirante** (French, "delirious outburst"), involving the sudden onset of schizophrenic symptoms in response to a stressful life event. It is temporary (lasting no longer than 3 months), has no strong evidence of a genetic link, and has a favorable prognosis; spontaneous resolution of symptoms is not uncommon. Acute delusional psychosis is essentially equivalent to SCHIZOPHRENIFORM DISORDER. See also ACUTE SCHIZOPHRENIC EPISODE.

acute depression **1.** a recent, sudden onset of depression. **2.** a severe episode of depression, characterized by many more symptoms than are necessary to meet the criteria for a MAJOR DEPRESSIVE EPISODE.

acute dystonia a sudden loss of normal muscle tone. See DYSTONIA.

acute hallucinosis the sudden onset of hallucinations resulting from alcohol or drug intoxication or withdrawal. The condition usually remits within hours, though it may persist for a few days. See SUBSTANCE-INDUCED PSYCHOTIC DISORDER.

acute mania the manic phase of bipolar I disorder (see BIPOLAR DISORDERS), characterized by an extremely unstable euphoric or irritable mood with hyperactivity, excessively rapid thought and speech, uninhibited and reckless behavior, and FLIGHT OF IDEAS. See MANIC EPISODE.

acute mountain sickness an illness that can affect mountain climbers, hikers, or skiers who have ascended too rapidly above 2,400 m (8,000 ft), especially when coming from sea level. Caused by the effects of reduced atmospheric pressure and oxygen pressure at high altitudes, it affects the nervous system, lungs, muscles, and heart. The faster the ascent and the higher the altitude, the greater is the degree of illness. In 2 out of every 10,000 people, swelling occurs around the brain, causing confusion and leading to coma (**high-altitude cerebral edema**). See also ALTITUDE SICKNESS.

acute onset a sudden, rapid, or unanticipated development of a disease or symptoms of an illness or of a disorder.

acute otitis media see OTITIS MEDIA.

acute preparation an animal that has undergone an experimental procedure, often surgical in nature, and is then studied for a relatively short period, to observe the immediate or temporary effects of this procedure, before being euthanized. Compare CHRONIC PREPARATION.

acute psychotic episode an appearance of florid (blatant) psychotic symptoms, such as hallucinations, delusions, and disorganized speech, that is of sudden onset and usually short duration.

acute schizophrenic episode an appearance of florid (blatant) schizophrenic symptoms, such as disordered thinking and disturbances in emotional responsiveness and behavior, that is of sudden onset and usually short duration.

acute stress disorder (**ASD**) in *DSM–IV–TR*, a disorder representing the immediate psychological aftermath of exposure to a traumatic stressor. In addition to characteristics of posttraumatic stress, ASD may also include elements of DISSOCIATION and disorientation. ASD does not necessarily develop into POSTTRAUMATIC STRESS DISORDER.

acute tolerance a type of TOLERANCE that can develop rapidly and in response to a small dose of a particular drug. See also DEPENDENCE; TACHYPHYLAXIS.

ad- *prefix* **1.** to or toward. **2.** near or adjacent to.

ADA abbreviation for AMERICANS WITH DISABILITIES ACT.

Adam *n.* slang for MDMA, a hallucinogen.

ADAMHA abbreviation for ALCOHOL, DRUG ABUSE AND MENTAL HEALTH ADMINISTRATION.

adaptability *n.* **1.** the capacity to make appropriate responses to changed or changing situations. **2.** the ability to modify or adjust one's behavior in meeting different circumstances or different people. **—adaptable** *adj.*

adaptation *n.* **1.** adjustment of a sense organ to the intensity or quality of stimulation, resulting in a change in sensory or perceptual experience, as when the pupil of the eye adjusts to dim or bright light (see VISUAL ADAPTATION). See also SENSORY ADAPTATION. **2.** the diminished effect of a stimulus or circumstance as a result of prolonged or repeated exposure to it. **3.** in evolution, the modification of an organism in structure, function, or behavior that increases its ability to reproduce successfully and its offspring's ability to survive and reproduce successfully in a changing or different environment. **4.** see SOCIAL ADAPTATION. **5.** in Jean PIAGET's theory of cognitive development, the process of adjusting one's cognitive structures to meet environmental demands, which involves the complementary processes of ASSIMILATION and ACCOMMODATION. **—adapt** *vb.* **—adaptational** *adj.* **—adaptive** *adj.*

adaptational approach a form of psychoanalytic psychiatry that avoids the orthodox analytic emphasis on childhood experience and focuses instead on the nature and development of the patient's maladaptive behavior and the steps he or she should take to develop new, more effective patterns. Also called **adaptational psychodynamics**. [developed by Hungarian-born U.S. psychoanalyst Sandor Rado (1890–1972)]

adaptation level (**AL**) the level to which a person has adapted, which forms a standard against which new stimuli are evaluated. For example, the traffic in a small town may seem heavy to a farmer and light to a city dweller. Although it originated in studies of sensory perception, **adaptation-level theory** has since been applied in other fields, such as the study of attitude change. [originated by U.S. psychologist Harry Helson (1898–1977)]

adaptation mechanism a means of biological ADAPTATION through the interplay between the ASSIMILATION of data from experience and the modification of the organism to accommodate new data into its mental framework (see ACCOMMODATION). See also ADJUSTMENT PROCESS. [proposed by Jean PIAGET]

adaptation period a period of time during which a research participant becomes accustomed to instrumentation or experimental apparatus.

adaptation stage see GENERAL ADAPTATION SYNDROME.

adaptation syndrome see GENERAL ADAPTATION SYNDROME.

adaptation time the period of time from the start of a stimulus until the sense organ stimulated has adapted completely and no longer responds.

adapted child one of the child ego states in TRANSACTIONAL ANALYSIS, characterized as compliant, orderly, and manipulative. Compare NATURAL CHILD.

adaptive act the process whereby an organism learns to make the appropriate responses that are needed for an adjustment to the environment. For example, a caged pigeon learns to peck on a lighted key in order to receive food.

adaptive behavior **1.** the level of everyday performance of tasks that is required for a person to fulfill typical roles in society, including maintaining independence and meeting cultural expectations regarding personal and social responsibility. Specific categories in which adaptive behavior is usually assessed include self-help, mobility, health care, communication, domestic skills, consumer skills, community use, practical academic skills, and vocational skills. Limitations in adaptive behavior are one of the criteria for diagnosis or classification of MENTAL RETARDATION. See also ADAPTIVE BEHAVIOR SCALE. **2.** any behavior that enables an individual to adjust to the environment appropriately and effectively. It is often discussed in the context of evolution. See also ADAPTIVE ACT; ADJUSTMENT PROCESS.

adaptive behavior scale **1.** any standardized assessment protocol with established psychometric properties used to document and quantify everyday performance of skills necessary for personal independence and social responsibility, consistent with cultural expectations (see ADAPTIVE BEHAVIOR). Examples include the American Association on Mental Retardation's Adaptive Behavior Scale (ABS), Vineland Adaptive Behavior Scales (VABS), and Scales of Independent Behavior (SIB). **2.** any protocol assessing behavioral and social performance that is based on developmental norms, with domains structured in developmental sequence or degree of ascending task complexity or difficulty. **3.** a component of the BAYLEY SCALES OF INFANT AND TODDLER DEVELOPMENT.

adaptive control of thought theory see ACT*.

adaptive hypothesis the view that the function of the primary autonomous ego is to cope with an "average expectable environment" through perception, memory, affect regulation, and motility. This is the view taken by Austrian-born U.S. psychoanalyst Heinz Hartmann (1894–1970) in his version of EGO PSYCHOLOGY.

adaptive intelligence the ability to use knowledge for practical purposes, such as solving problems and interacting with others (i.e., understanding language), demonstrating an effective ability to interact with, and learn from, the environment.

adaptive nonresponding theory a theory that sleep evolved as a means of creating species-specific daily periods of inactivity concurrent with periods of greatest threat from predators.

adaptive process see ADJUSTMENT PROCESS.

adaptive production system a PRODUCTION SYSTEM able to change or adjust the rules in production memory as a result of interacting with an environment. Both SOAR and CLASSIFIER SYSTEMS fall into this category.

adaptive response see ADAPTIVE BEHAVIOR.

adaptive skills activities that require self-management, such as controlling impulses, being able to adjust to a new environment, and a willingness to learn new things.

adaptive strategy choice model (**ASCM**) a theoretical model that postulates the existence of multiple strategies of problem solving within a child's cognitive repertoire and describes how use of these strategies changes over time. According to this model, strategies compete with one another for use: With time and experience, more efficient strategies are used more frequently, whereas less efficient strategies are used less frequently but never totally disappear. This contrasts with **stage theory of strategy development**, which postulates that more efficient strategies replace less efficient ones. [proposed by U.S. developmental psychologist Robert S. Siegler (1949–) and Christopher Shipley]

adaptive system in ergonomics, a system with the capability to alter information presentation, interface design, or output according to the capabilities or characteristics of the user, system, or environmental state.

adaptive task allocation in ergonomics, a system design that supports allocation of tasks to the human operator or the machine according to the state of the system, the state of the operator (e.g., if fatigued), or other operational rules. Adaptive task allocation maintains a flexible FUNCTION ALLOCATION policy.

adaptive testing a testing technique (usually applied with the aid of a computer) designed to adjust to the response characteristics of individual examinees. For example, all examinations may start with an item of intermediate difficulty: If the examinee's response is correct, he or she will then be given a more difficult item; if the response is wrong, the examinee will then be given an easier item. The process continues until a stable estimate of the ABILITY LEVEL of the examinee can be determined.

adaptometer *n.* an instrument used to measure the time taken for VISUAL ADAPTATION, used in the diagnosis of night blindness and other visual disorders.

ad baculum denoting a type of informal FALLACY or a persuasive technique in which claims to validity are based on an appeal to force or threat, either direct or implied. For example: Theory X should be accepted as true because failure to endorse it will result in loss of scientific status. [from Latin *baculus*, "walking stick," "staff," or "rod," implying the threat of force or punishment]

ADC abbreviation for AIDS DEMENTIA COMPLEX.

ADD abbreviation for ATTENTION-DEFICIT DISORDER.

ADDH abbreviation for attention-deficit disorder with hyperactivity. See ATTENTION-DEFICIT/HYPERACTIVITY DISORDER.

addict *n.* a person who has developed a SUBSTANCE DEPENDENCE.

addicted athlete an individual habitually involved in an athletic activity who will experience withdrawal symptoms if deprived of participating in the activity. See also COMPULSIVE EXERCISER.

addiction *n.* a state of psychological or physical dependence (or both) on the use of alcohol or other drugs of abuse. The equivalent term SUBSTANCE DEPENDENCE is preferred to describe this state because it refers more explicitly to the criteria by which it is diagnosed. *DSM–IV–TR* criteria for substance dependence include TOLERANCE, withdrawal, loss of control, and compulsive use of the substance. See also PHYSICAL DEPENDENCE; PSYCHOLOGICAL DEPENDENCE. **—addictive** *adj.*

addictive alcoholism see GAMMA ALCOHOLISM.

addictive drugs drugs or other substances that cause SUBSTANCE DEPENDENCE. They include alcohol, AMPHETAMINES and amphetamine-like CNS STIMULANTS, caffeine, COCAINE and CRACK, HALLUCINOGENS, INHALANTS, NICOTINE, OPIOIDS, PCP (phencyclidine) and phencyclidine-like substances, and CNS DEPRESSANTS.

addictive personality a hypothetical personality pattern thought to increase the likelihood a person will become dependent on one or more substances. Research has not supported this view, although it has identified personality traits associated with substance abuse, such as impulsivity and neuroticism.

Addison's disease a disorder caused by a malfunction of the adrenal glands resulting in a deficiency of adrenal hormones. A major symptom is muscle fatigue with trembling, due in part to an inability to maintain a stable level of blood sugar for energy. Mental effects include depression, anxiety, and mood changes. [Thomas **Addison** (1793–1860), British physician]

addition test a task requiring the solution of arithmetic addition problems. Early tests of intelligence, such as those of Louis Leon THURSTONE, sometimes included such tasks, but with the advent of modern computational devices, such as calculators and computers, the tasks have seemed less relevant in contemporary times.

additive bilingualism the sociolinguistic situation in which a second language is adopted by a SPEECH COMMUNITY without threatening the status of the first language. For example, most English-speaking Canadians learn French in order to gain access to prestige jobs that require bilingualism but continue to use English as their main language. This contrasts with **subtractive bilingualism**, in which the second language comes to replace the functions of the first language. The bilingualism of most immigrant communities is considered subtractive, resulting in LANGUAGE SHIFT within one or two generations.

additive color mixture the process and effect of combining colored lights, as manifested in new, composite colors; for example, in stage lighting, red and green spotlights are blended to form yellow. The color in television is another example of additive COLOR MIXTURE.

additive effect in statistics, an effect in which the joint effect of two factors is the sum of their individual effects, unconditional upon the level of the other factor.

additive-factors method a procedure for analyzing reaction-time data to determine whether two variables affect the same or different processing stages. If two variables influence different stages, their effects should be additive. If two variables influence the same stage, their effects should be interactive.

additive scale a scale with all points distributed equally so that a meaningful result can be obtained by addition (e.g., a metric ruler).

additive task a task or project that a group can complete by aggregating individual members' efforts or contributions. Such tasks are in most cases divisible (they can be broken down into subcomponents that are assigned to each member), maximizing (they call for high quantities of product rather than high-quality solutions), and of such a nature that relatively little coordination of members' efforts and activities is required (as with people clapping after a performance or a five-person group pulling together on a rope). Groups usually outperform individuals on such tasks, but overall group productivity rarely reaches its maximum potential owing to SOCIAL LOAFING. Compare COMPENSATORY TASK; CONJUNCTIVE TASK; DISJUNCTIVE TASK.

adduction *n.* **1.** movement of a body part toward the midline of the body or of a limb or other part. See also ADDUCTOR. Compare ABDUCTION. **2.** in CONDITIONING, the production of new behavior by combining the DISCRIMINATIVE STIMULI of separate DISCRIMINATED OPERANTS.

adductor *n.* a muscle that moves a body part toward the midline of the body or of a limb or other part. Thus the **adductor pollicis** muscle moves the thumb toward the palm of the hand. Compare ABDUCTOR.

ADEA abbreviation for AGE DISCRIMINATION IN EMPLOYMENT ACT.

A-delta fiber a myelinated (and therefore rapidly conducting) AXON, of moderately large diameter (1–5 μm), transmitting pain or temperature information to the central nervous system. See A FIBER.

adendritic *adj.* describing neurons that lack DENDRITES.

adenine (symbol: A) *n.* a purine compound that is present in the nucleotides and nucleic acids of living organisms; it is found especially in nuclei. Adenine is one of the four bases in DNA and MESSENGER RNA that make up the elements of the GENETIC CODE.

adeno- (**aden-**) *combining form* gland or glandular.

adenohypophysis *n.* see PITUITARY GLAND.

adenoid type an individual whose pharyngeal tonsil is pathologically enlarged (a condition known as **adenoids**), which is associated with such constitutional anomalies as cretinism, deaf-mutism, or oxycephaly.

adenoma *n.* a usually benign tumor derived from epithelium that has glandular properties. The most common adenoma in the central nervous system is in the pituitary gland (**pituitary adenoma**). **—adenomatous** *adj.*

adenosine *n.* a compound, found in most living cells, consisting of an ADENINE molecule and a ribose sugar molecule. Adenosine functions as a neuromodulator: By binding to special receptors (**adenosine receptors**), it influences the release of several neurotransmitters in the central nervous system. Combined with three phosphate units, adenosine becomes ATP (adenosine triphosphate), which functions as an energy source in metabolic activities.

adenosine 3′,5′-monophosphate see CYCLIC AMP.

adenosine triphosphate see ATP.

adenylate cyclase an enzyme that catalyzes the conversion of ATP to CYCLIC AMP, which functions as a SECOND MESSENGER in signaling pathways within cells. Also called **adenyl cyclase**.

adequate sample a sample that adequately represents the population from which it was drawn in terms of size.

adequate stimulus the type of stimulus for which a given sensory organ is particularly adapted. Thus the adequate stimulus for the eye is photic (light) energy. Although mechanical pressure on the eye or an electrical shock can stimulate the retina and produce sensations of light, these are not adequate stimuli for the eye.

ADH abbreviation for antidiuretic hormone (see VASOPRESSIN).

ADHD abbreviation for ATTENTION-DEFICIT/HYPERACTIVITY DISORDER.

adherence *n.* **1.** the ability of an individual to conform to a treatment regimen, especially one involving drug treatment, as outlined by a health care provider. External factors affecting adherence may include appropriate education regarding a drug and its use, the individual's ability to pay for or otherwise obtain the treatment recommended, and familial or cultural value systems influencing the acceptability of the treatment to the individual. Internal factors include the individual's belief in the potency of the treatment, the presence or absence of unpleasant side effects, and the individual's capability to understand or conform to instructions given by the health care provider. See also NONADHERENCE. **2.** see EXERCISE ADHERENCE. Also called **compliance**.

adhesive otitis media see OTITIS MEDIA.

ad hoc for a particular purpose or in response to some particular event or occurrence. For example, an **ad hoc committee** is convened on a short-term basis to address a single problem, and an **ad hoc hypothesis** is an explanation of a particular phenomenon, rather than a general theory. [Latin, literally: "to this"]

ad hoc category a category formed to meet a special criterion or demand, usually in the moment it is needed. For example, one might form the category "things I would take from my house if it were on fire." Compare NATURAL CATEGORY.

ad hominem denoting a type of informal FALLACY or a persuasive technique in which an argument is held to be valid or invalid because of the (supposed) character defects of particular individuals who support or oppose it. For example: Theory X should be accepted as true because Professor Y, who opposes it, is an alcoholic. [Latin: "to (i.e., against) the man"]

adiadochokinesis (**adiadokokinesis**) *n.* see DYSDIADOCHOKINESIS.

adience *n.* a response or behavior that results in movement toward a stimulus, either by physical approach or by an action that increases contact with an already available stimulus. **Adient behavior** is an APPROACH RESPONSE or behavior designed to make or prolong contact with a given stimulus. Compare ABIENCE. **—adient** *adj.*

ad ignorantium (**ad ignorantiam**) denoting a type of informal FALLACY or a persuasive technique in which an argument is proposed to be true because it has not been proven false. It is thus an **appeal to ignorance**, specifically ignorance of evidence to the contrary. For example: UFOs exist because no evidence has been found that they do not. [Latin, literally: "to ignorance"]

adinazolam *n.* a BENZODIAZEPINE of the triazolobenzodiazepine class with antidepressant as well as anxiolytic properties. It currently is not available in the United States. Italian trade name: **Deracyn**.

Adipex *n.* a trade name for PHENTERMINE.

adipo- (**adip-**) *combining form* fat or fatty.

adipocyte *n.* a cell that forms ADIPOSE TISSUE and is specialized for the synthesis and storage of triglycerides (triacylglycerols), the form in which most fat is stored in the body. Adipocytes also contain enzymes that can mobilize the stored fat as fatty acids and glycerol (see FAT METABOLISM). Also called **fat cell**.

adipose tissue connective tissue consisting largely of fat cells (see ADIPOCYTE), which is found beneath the skin and around major organs. It provides protection and insulation and functions as an energy reserve. See also BROWN FAT; FAT METABOLISM.

adiposogenital dystrophy (**adiposogenitalism**) see FRÖHLICH'S SYNDROME.

adipsia *n.* an absence of thirst or an abnormal avoidance of beverages. Adipsia may be associated with lesions in the hypothalamus.

ADJ abbreviation for ADJUSTING SCHEDULE OF REINFORCEMENT.

adjective checklist 1. a self-inventory, used in personality assessment, consisting of a list of adjectives (e.g., intelligent, lazy, productive) that the respondent checks off as descriptive of or applicable to him- or herself. **2.** in CONSUMER PSYCHOLOGY, a list of adjectives used, for example, in the assessment of a product image and in advertising research.

adjudication *n.* **1.** any formal decision of a court. **2.** the act or process of settling a matter by judicial proceedings. **—adjudicate** *vb.*

adjudicative competence see COMPETENCY TO STAND TRIAL.

adjunct *n.* **1.** a drug that is used concurrently with another drug in treating a condition in order to provide additional therapeutic effects. It may have a mechanism of action that differs from that of the main drug used in treatment. **2.** a word or phrase in a sentence that is not a main structural element but that modifies, amplifies, or illustrates another element that is. **3.** more generally, a supplementary or nonessential part of something. **—adjunctive** *adj.*

adjunctive behavior relatively stereotyped behavior (i.e., behavior repeated with little variation) that follows the delivery of a stimulus. It differs from simple RESPONDENT BEHAVIOR in that the likelihood of its occurrence is influenced by the time between stimulus presentations. An example is **schedule-induced polydipsia**, in which excessive drinking of water occurs when small portions of food are delivered intermittently. Compare TERMINAL BEHAVIOR.

adjunctive therapist 1. in psychotherapy, a provider of any secondary ADJUNCTIVE THERAPY. **2.** in health care, a member of a multidisciplinary treatment team whose functions are ancillary to the main therapeutic program. Such therapists provide direct clinical services to patients in such areas as improvement of daily living skills, behavior management, coordination of educational activities, and management of leisure time.

adjunctive therapy one or more secondary interventions used concurrently with a primary intervention to enhance treatment effectiveness. For example, medication may be used concurrently with COGNITIVE BEHAVIOR THERAPY, with the latter as the primary form of intervention; GROUP PSYCHOTHERAPY may be used secondarily to individual PSYCHODYNAMIC PSYCHOTHERAPY, with each intervention bringing its own characteristic perspectives and methods to bear on the client's mental awareness and healing. Adjunctive therapy is typically conducted by a different practitioner than is the primary intervention. See also COLLABORATIVE CARE. Compare ADJUVANT THERAPY; COMBINATION THERAPY.

adjusted mean in the ANALYSIS OF COVARIANCE, the value that is obtained after the effects of a covariate are regressed out.

adjusted $\mathbf{R^2}$ the COEFFICIENT OF MULTIPLE CORRELATION (R^2) adjusted to take into account the number of individual variables and the sample size so as to provide a truer estimate of the extent to which the individual variables explain the dependent variable:

$$R^2_{adj} = 1 - [(n - 1)/(n - p)],$$

where n is the total number of observations and p is the number of predictor variables.

adjusting schedule of reinforcement (**ADJ**) any SCHEDULE OF REINFORCEMENT in which the requirements for reinforcement are changed, based on performance, either between reinforcements or from one reinforcement to another.

adjustive behavior any response of an organism that effectively incorporates environmental or situational demands.

adjustment *n.* **1.** a change in attitude, behavior, or both by an individual on the basis of some recognized need or desire to change. Adjustment may come about through forced external circumstances or through an understanding of the need for a different and improved way of functioning. Adjustment or modification of behavior is a goal of therapeutic intervention. **2.** modification to match a standard. See METHOD OF ADJUSTMENT. **3.** the degree of equilibrium or harmony between an individual and the environment. For example, a well-adjusted person is one who satisfies his or her needs in a healthy, beneficial manner and demonstrates appropriate social and psychological responses to situations and demands. **4.** the process of correcting or accounting for current, changing, atypical, or unexpected conditions. **—adjust** *vb.*

adjustment disorder in *DSM–IV–TR*, a maladaptive reaction occurring within three months after an individual is subjected to a specific identifiable stressful event, such as a divorce, business crisis, family discord, starting school, becoming a parent, or retirement. The event is not as stressful as a traumatic stressor, which can lead to POSTTRAUMATIC STRESS DISORDER. The individual's failure to adjust is not manifested by a single instance of overreaction but involves impairment in social or occupational functioning and unexpectedly severe symptoms, which generally subside when the stress ceases or when a new level of adaptation is reached. In **chronic adjustment disorder**, the symptoms last more than six months due to either the persistence or the severity of the stressor.

adjustment inventory a survey form used to assess a person's emotional and social adjustment as compared with a large and representative sample of individuals from the same population.

adjustment mechanism a habitual behavioral pattern that enables the individual to meet the demands of life.

adjustment method see METHOD OF ADJUSTMENT.

adjustment process any function or activity through which human beings attempt to adjust to environmental demands. Examples are language, which enables individuals to solve problems by gathering information and communicating with others; perception, which enables individuals to recognize and interpret experiences and events; memory, which stores knowledge to be called upon when needed; and imagination, which enables individuals to envisage new ideas and solutions. Also called **adaptive process**. See also ADAPTIVE BEHAVIOR.

adjustment reaction a temporary, maladjustive psychological response to a situation. Such reactions were subsumed under the category TRANSIENT SITUATIONAL PERSONALITY DISORDER in *DSM–I*, comprising adjustment reactions of infancy, childhood, adolescence, and later life, and under TRANSIENT SITUATIONAL DISTURBANCE in *DSM–II*; the corresponding category for these reactions in *DSM–III* and *DSM–IV–TR* is ADJUSTMENT DISORDER.

adjuvant therapy therapy provided after the initial (primary) form of treatment to enhance effectiveness or to increase the chances of a cure. Adjuvant therapy typically refers to medical rather than psychotherapeutic treatment, particularly any drug therapy used in support of nondrug interventions. For example, in the treatment of cancer, chemotherapy and radiation are often used as adjuvant therapies after the primary intervention of surgery. The term is sometimes used in psychotherapy as a synonym for the preferred ADJUNCTIVE THERAPY.

Adler, Alfred (1870–1937) Austrian psychiatrist. Trained in medicine at the University of Vienna, receiving his MD in 1895, Adler was the first disciple of Sigmund FREUD to break away and form his own school, known as INDIVIDUAL PSYCHOLOGY. This was based on the theory that human beings are governed by a conscious drive to express and fulfill themselves, as opposed to Freud's theory of dominance by early sexual trauma and blind unconscious instincts. The school revolved around such concepts as the STRIVING FOR SUPERIORITY, the INFERIORITY COMPLEX, COMPENSATION and overcompensation, social interests, and the creative development of an individual style of life that incorporates both personal and social goals. See also GUIDING FICTION; LIFE GOAL; LIFE PLAN; PERSUASION THERAPY; SOCIAL INSTINCT; SOCIAL INTEREST; WILL TO POWER. **—Adlerian** *adj.*

Adlerian psychology see INDIVIDUAL PSYCHOLOGY.

ad lib 1. in animal experiments, denoting or relating to a schedule of unlimited access to food and water. Also called **free feeding**. See also FREE-FEEDING WEIGHT. **2.** more generally, without restriction. [from Latin *ad libitum*, "as desired"]

ad litem for the purpose of the suit (in a court of law). See GUARDIAN AD LITEM. [Latin, literally: "for the lawsuit"]

ADLs abbreviation for ACTIVITIES OF DAILY LIVING.

administration *n.* **1.** the application of a drug or other agent in the diagnosis or treatment of a disorder. Routes of administration include TOPICAL APPLICATION (e.g., a TRANSDERMAL PATCH) and various **systemic routes**, including **oral** and **sublingual** (under the tongue) **administration**, **rectal administration** (by suppository or enema), **vaginal administration** (by suppository), and administration by injection. Injectable drugs may be administered directly into the venous system (see INTRAVENOUS INJECTION), into muscle (see INTRAMUSCULAR INJECTION), or under the skin (see SUBCUTANEOUS INJECTION). Drugs may also be inhaled through the mouth or nose (see INHALATION OF DRUGS). Drugs used for disorders of the nervous system are usually administered systemically. See also PARENTERAL DRUG ADMINISTRATION. **2.** see TEST ADMINISTRATION.

administrative controls in SAFETY ENGINEERING, administrative interventions, such as training, rotating work schedules to reduce exposure (e.g., to hazardous chemicals), and CLEARANCE REQUIREMENTS, that can help to maintain a safe environment in the workplace. Administrative controls, supplemented by the use of PERSONAL PROTECTIVE EQUIPMENT, are considered the second resort after ENGINEERING CONTROLS. See also HAZARD-CONTROL PROTOCOL.

ad misericordiam denoting a type of informal FALLACY or a persuasive technique in which support for the truth of an argument is based on an appeal to pity or sympathy. For example: Theory X should be accepted as true because if it is, this will encourage certain disadvantaged groups in society. [Latin, literally: "to pity"]

admission *n.* the act of registering an individual for treatment or observation in a health care facility. See FIRST ADMISSION; READMISSION; VOLUNTARY ADMISSION. **—admit** *vb.*

admission certification an aspect of UTILIZATION REVIEW in which the medical necessity of a patient's admission to a health care facility is determined.

admission criteria a set of standards or tests used to decide whether or not to allow a student entry to an educational program.

admission procedures the administrative and medical procedures of admitting a person as an inpatient to a health care facility.

adolescence *n.* the period of human development that starts with PUBERTY (10–12 years of age) and ends with physiological maturity (approximately 19 years of age), although the exact age span varies across individuals. During this period major changes occur at varying rates in sexual characteristics, body image, sexual interest, social roles, intellectual development, and self-concept. **—adolescent** *adj.*, *n.*

adolescent cognitive development the development of cognitive processing in adolescents as they mature physiologically, intellectually, and socially. Most young people develop enhanced abilities to think abstractly, plan cognitively, evaluate reality hypothetically, reconsider prior experiences from altered points of view, assess data from multiple dimensions, reflect inwardly, develop complex models of understanding, and project complicated future scenarios. In addition to standard rote learning, adolescents require multiple opportunities to use and practice their newly developed abstract skills in order to maximize their potential. Adults are important role models for young people as they develop the social applications of cognitive processing.

adolescent counseling the provision of professional guidance, advice, and information to adolescents through such means as personal interviews, analysis of case-history data, and the use of psychological tests.

adolescent crisis the emotional turmoil that may occur during adolescence as individuals seek to achieve independence (by casting off old emotional ties and developing new relationships) and adapt to a changed body.

adolescent egocentrism the feeling of personal uniqueness often experienced in adolescence; that is, the conviction that one is special and is or should be the constant focus of others' attention.

adolescent growth spurt see PUBESCENT GROWTH SPURT.

adolescent gynecomastia enlargement of the breasts in adolescent males, usually resulting from insufficiency of ANDROGENS. It is usually minor and transient. See GYNECOMASTIA.

adolescent homosexuality same-sex activity during the pubertal period. It has been estimated that at least 20% of boys and 3% of girls have engaged in such activity, resulting in orgasm, before the end of adolescence, and about twice that number have had casual or relatively uninvolved gay or lesbian experiences during adolescence. Many of these experiences, especially for boys, actually involve mutual masturbation to heterosexual stimuli and thus do not indicate same-sex eroticism or predict adult gay or lesbian sexual orientation.

adolescent pregnancy pregnancy that occurs during the period of adolescence. Adolescent pregnancy is a controversial social issue, particularly when it occurs during the early and middle years of adolescence, when teenagers are typically not emotionally or financially prepared to raise children. A number of possible causes contribute to variations in teenage pregnancy rates, including social and cultural customs, family background and education, and economic and social conditions. Also called **teenage** (or **teen**) **pregnancy**.

adolescent psychology the branch of psychology that describes and studies adolescents, their development, and their behavior.

adolescent psychotherapy psychotherapy for adolescents who are experiencing social, emotional, or behavioral problems.

adolescent rebellion the rejection by adolescents of family values and family control over their behavior, reflecting their desire for increased independence.

adolescent sex changes the physical and physiological changes that start at PUBERTY. They include accelerated development of sex organs, the appearance of secondary SEX CHARACTERISTICS, and the first occurrence of seminal ejaculation in boys and menstruation in girls. See ADOLESCENCE.

adopter categories categories into which consumers who buy a new product or service can be grouped on the basis of how soon they adopt the innovation after it first appears on the market. From this can be deduced their motive for the purchase. Typical categories include innovators (see CONSUMER INNOVATOR), early adopters, early majority, late majority, and laggards. Analysis of adopter categories is important in determining the likely success of a new product or service and in devising the most effective strategies for marketing it.

adoption *n.* the legal process by which an infant or child is permanently placed with a family other than his or her birth family. Types of adoption include **private adoption**, in which a birth parent voluntarily plans for the placement of the child with adoptive parents through agencies, attorneys, doctors, and other intermediaries; and **public adoption**, in which a child removed from his or her birth parent(s) because of neglect or abuse is placed with adoptive parents through public child welfare agencies. See also CLOSED ADOPTION; OPEN ADOPTION.

adoption study a research design that aims to estimate the degree of heritability of a given trait or disorder by such methods as comparing the incidence of that trait or disorder in adoptees and in their biological parents and adoptive families. For example, one might compare the incidence of schizophrenia in adoptive and biological parents when an adoptee has been diagnosed as having schizophrenia, or one might compare the incidence of schizophrenia among adoptees whose biological parents have schizophrenia with the incidence among adoptees whose parents do not have schizophrenia.

adoptive parents the adults who legally adopt a child (see ADOPTION) and raise him or her as their own. Compare BIRTH PARENT.

adoration *n.* **1.** great esteem or reverence held by one individual for another. **2.** worshipful devotion to a deity or divine being. **—adore** *vb.*

ad populum denoting a type of informal FALLACY or a persuasive technique in which claims for the truth of an argument are based on an appeal to popular opinion, belief, or feeling. For example: Theory X should be endorsed as true because most people believe that it is. See also BANDWAGON EFFECT. [Latin, literally: "to the people"]

adren- *combining form* see ADRENO-.

adrenal androgen any of the androgenic hormones (chiefly dehydroepiandrosterone and androstenedione) secreted by the ADRENAL CORTEX. See ADRENARCHE; ANDROGEN.

adrenal cortex the outer layer of the ADRENAL GLAND. It secretes a number of hormones, including ADRENAL ANDROGENS, GLUCOCORTICOIDS, and MINERALOCORTICOIDS. Adrenal cortical functions are controlled by ADRENOCORTICOTROPIC HORMONE, secreted by the anterior PITUITARY GLAND.

adrenal-cortical hyperfunction the excessive production of one or more of the hormones of the adrenal cortex. The manifestations vary with the hormone. For example, the presence of male characteristics in women (**adrenal virilism**) is a characteristic of androgen hypersecretion; excessive production of glucocorticoids results in CUSHING'S SYNDROME; and hypersecretion of aldosterone causes hypertension, sodium retention, and (in some cases) nerve damage (see ALDOSTERONISM). Because more than one hormone may be overproduced, the symptoms can overlap. Causes may include a benign or malignant tumor or ADRENAL HYPERPLASIA, which may be congenital or acquired.

adrenalectomy *n.* surgical removal of one or both of the ADRENAL GLANDS.

adrenal gland an ENDOCRINE GLAND adjacent to the kidney. Its outer layer, the ADRENAL CORTEX, secretes a number of hormones, including ADRENAL ANDROGENS, GLUCOCORTICOIDS, and MINERALOCORTICOIDS. Its inner core, the ADRENAL MEDULLA, secretes EPINEPHRINE and NOREPINEPHRINE. Also called **suprarenal gland**.

adrenal hormones hormones secreted from either the cortex or the medulla of the ADRENAL GLANDS. The cortex secretes mainly cortisol, aldosterone, and androgens; the medulla secretes mainly epinephrine.

adrenal hyperplasia a usually congenital disorder marked by increased adrenal production of cortisol precursors and androgens. Increased secretion of androgens during intrauterine life causes masculinization of female genitalia and an enlarged penis in boys. The children grow rapidly at first, but skeletal maturation is premature so that they are below average in height as adults.

adrenaline *n.* see EPINEPHRINE.

adrenal medulla the central portion of the ADRENAL GLAND. It secretes two hormones, EPINEPHRINE and NOREPINEPHRINE, both of which also serve as neurotransmitters.

adrenal virilism see ADRENAL-CORTICAL HYPERFUNCTION.

adrenarche *n.* the stage of prepubertal development marked by the start of androgen secretion by the adrenal cortex. Normally, it occurs between 6 to 8 years of age and does not result in ANDROGENIZATION. Premature adrenarche, characterized by pubertal levels of ADRENAL ANDROGENS, is manifested by the early appearance of pubic hair. It may be associated with psychological disturbances. By parent report on the DIAGNOSTIC INTERVIEW SCHEDULE for Children, 44% of the children with premature adrenarche met the diagnostic criteria for psychological disorders, primarily anxiety disorders. The condition is also associated with self-reported depression and parent-reported behavior problems and low scores on various intelligence tests.

adrenergic *adj.* relating to the activity or effects of EPINEPHRINE, NOREPINEPHRINE, or similar substances (see CATECHOLAMINE) released by the ADRENAL MEDULLA or nerve fibers or introduced into the body as a drug.

adrenergic drugs see SYMPATHOMIMETIC DRUGS.

adrenergic neuron a neuron that employs EPINEPHRINE or NOREPINEPHRINE as a NEUROTRANSMITTER.

adrenergic reaction the response of organs innervated by the SYMPATHETIC NERVOUS SYSTEM to stimulation by the adrenergic hormones NOREPINEPHRINE or EPINEPHRINE. Adrenergic reactions include increased heart rate, constriction of blood vessels, and dilation of the pupils.

adrenergic receptor see ADRENORECEPTOR.

adrenergic system the part of the AUTONOMIC NERVOUS SYSTEM, including receptor sites, that is influenced by ADRENERGIC neurotransmitters and drugs. The nerves included in the adrenergic system vary somewhat with species but generally include all postganglionic sympathetic fibers. Compare CHOLINERGIC SYSTEM.

adreno- (**adren-**) *combining form* the adrenal glands.

adrenoceptor *n.* see ADRENORECEPTOR.

adrenocortical insufficiency a condition caused by failure of the adrenal cortex to produce adequate levels of hormones required for normal metabolic functions. Symptoms may include muscle weakness and fatigue, dizziness, and depression. See ADDISON'S DISEASE.

adrenocorticoid *n.* see CORTICOSTEROID.

adrenocorticotropic hormone (**ACTH**) a hormone secreted by the anterior PITUITARY GLAND that controls the release of steroid hormones from the ADRENAL CORTEX. Also called **corticotropin**. See also CORTICOTROPIN-RELEASING HORMONE.

adrenogenital syndrome a group of symptoms associated with alterations of secondary sexual characteristics that is due to abnormally increased production of androgens by the adrenal glands. The term most commonly applies to the development of masculine traits in females or premature puberty in males.

adrenoleukodystrophy *n.* a genetic disease characterized by destruction of the MYELIN SHEATH surrounding the nerves of the brain (i.e., demyelination) and progressive dysfunction of the adrenal gland. Nerve function becomes erratic, resulting in a variety of physiological and behavioral symptoms involving changes in body tone, motor movements, gait, speech, ability to eat, vision, hearing, memory, attention, and cognitive processes. There are several types of adrenoleukodystrophy, of which the childhood X-chromosome-linked form is the most common and the most severe.

adrenoreceptor *n.* a receptor that binds and responds to norepinephrine and, to a lesser extent, epinephrine, which act as neurotransmitters in the sympathetic nervous system. There are two types: ALPHA ADRENORECEPTORS and BETA ADRENORECEPTORS. Also called **adrenergic receptor**; **adrenoceptor**.

adrenoreceptor blocking agents substances that either partially or completely inhibit the binding of the neurotransmitters norepinephrine or epinephrine to their appropriate receptor sites (adrenoreceptors) and thus block or disrupt the action of these neurotransmitters. Such blocking agents are classed according to whether they inhibit binding to ALPHA ADRENORECEPTORS (**alpha blockers**, or **alpha-adrenoreceptor blocking agents**, used clinically as VASODILATORS) or BETA ADRENORECEPTORS (see BETA BLOCKERS).

adrenosteroid *n.* see CORTICOSTEROID.

ADS abbreviation for ACTION DISORGANIZATION SYNDROME.

adult *n.* **1.** a person who has reached ADULTHOOD. **2.** a person who has reached the legal age of maturity. Although it may vary across jurisdictions, an individual 18 years of age is typically considered an adult.

adult attachment interview an hour-long PATTERNED INTERVIEW used for classifying a person's state of mind with respect to his or her own attachment experiences. It is based on reports by interviewees of experiences with their parents, especially centering on hurtful experiences, separations, and discipline. The categories of adult attachment that emerge from such interviews include (a) **dismissing** (of attachment-related experiences and relationships, corresponding to ANXIOUS–AVOIDANT ATTACHMENT of infancy); (b) **preoccupied** (by past attachment relationships and experiences, as well as angry, passive, or fearful in responses in the interview, corresponding to ANXIOUS–RESISTANT ATTACHMENT of infancy); (c) **unresolved** or **disorganized** (showing lapses in reasoning when discussing loss or abuse, corresponding to DISORGANIZED ATTACHMENT of infancy); and (d) **secure** or **autonomous** (giving coherent accounts that value attachment and appear objective regarding relationships, corresponding to SECURE ATTACHMENT of infancy).

Adult Children of Alcoholics (**ACOA**) a TWELVE-STEP PROGRAM for adults who were raised in a family environment where alcoholism or other family dysfunctions were present. See also SELF-HELP GROUP.

adult day care a group program for the nonresidential care and supervision of adults with functional impairments, designed to meet their health, social, and functional needs in a setting other than their homes. See DAY CARE CENTER.

adult development biological, psychological, and sociocultural developmental processes that begin in late adolescence and continue through old age.

adult education formal schooling, often offered at night, that is specifically appropriate for adults who wish either to improve their work or career performance or to learn about a particular subject area of interest. See also CONTINUING EDUCATION.

adultery *n.* voluntary sexual intercourse between a married person and an individual who is not his or her spouse. In most Western countries this is grounds for divorce; in some other cultures adulterers may face legal penalties or severe social sanctions. **—adulterer** *n.* **—adulterous** *adj.*

adult foster care the provision of community-based living arrangements to adults who require supervision, personal care, or other services in daily living because they are unable to live independently due to physical or mental impairments or disabilities. Adult foster care homes provide such services on a 24-hour basis and differ from other RESIDENTIAL CARE facilities both in terms of the size of the home and the family nature of the care setting. See FOSTER HOME.

adult home an assisted-living residence that provides room, board, personal care services, and protective oversight. See ASSISTED LIVING FACILITIES; REST HOME.

adulthood *n.* the period of human development in which full physical growth and maturity have been achieved and certain biological, cognitive, social, personality, and other changes associated with the aging process occur. Beginning after ADOLESCENCE, adulthood is sometimes divided into young adulthood (roughly 19 to 45 years of age); middle adulthood (about 45 to 60 years); and later adulthood (age 60 and beyond), which itself is sometimes subdivided into YOUNG-OLD, OLD-OLD, and OLDEST OLD.

adultomorphism *n.* **1.** the attribution of adult traits or motives to children. Also called **enelicomorphism**. Compare PEDOMORPHISM. **2.** more specifically, the tendency to reconstruct developmental phases by extrapolating from adult psychopathology. **—adultomorphic** *adj.*

adult sensorineural lesions organic damage to structures of the auditory system that develop from the inner ear to the areas of the brain in which sound is perceived. These lesions are generally located in the cochlea or the AUDITORY NERVE. A sensory lesion in the cochlea may be due to MÉNIÈRE'S DISEASE, prolonged exposure to loud noises, a viral infection, or drug effects. A lesion of the auditory nerve is frequently caused by a tumor. See also ACOUSTIC NEUROMA; SENSORINEURAL HEARING LOSS.

advance directive a legal mechanism for individuals to specify their wishes and instructions about prospective health care (e.g., future medical treatment) in the event they later become incompetent or otherwise unable to make such decisions. This can be achieved by means of a DURABLE POWER OF ATTORNEY or a LIVING WILL.

advanced organizers verbal or written information presented to students before a lecture or other teaching session to enhance their attentiveness and information acquisition in the subsequent lecture. The purposes are (a) to promote an initial understanding of the content, (b) to familiarize students with the way in which information is to be presented, and (c) to identify the purposes for learning the subsequent material. Schematic representations, templates, and prior knowledge information processing are ways of enhancing advanced organization.

advanced placement examinations achievement tests that (a) give high school students an opportunity to gain admission to college with advanced standing in one or more subjects (the **College Entrance Examination Board Advanced Placement Program**) or (b) evaluate college-level education acquired through independent study and other nontraditional procedures (see COLLEGE LEVEL EXAMINATION PROGRAM).

advantage by illness see SECONDARY GAINS.

advantage law see LAW OF ADVANTAGE.

adventitious *adj.* appearing or occurring unexpectedly or in an unusual place.

adventitious blindness see ADVENTITIOUS VISUAL IMPAIRMENT.

adventitious deafness a loss of hearing that results from injury or illness following a period of normal hearing ability. Compare CONGENITAL DEAFNESS.

adventitious reinforcement see ACCIDENTAL REINFORCEMENT.

adventitious visual impairment VISUAL IMPAIRMENT that results from injury or illness following a period of normal visual ability. Onset of the impairment can produce severe grief, mourning reactions, and dependency. As a consequence, any residual visual capacity may not be used effectively, exacerbating psychological and social-adjustment problems. Also called **acquired visual impairment**. Compare CONGENITAL VISUAL IMPAIRMENT.

adventure-recreation model a model for those who seek risk in outdoor recreational activities. It establishes the relationship among level of engagement, type and level of risk, social orientation, locus of decision making, frequency of participation, and preferred environment. Also called **risk-recreation model**.

ad verecundiam denoting a type of informal FALLACY or a persuasive technique in which claims for the truth of an argument are based on an appeal to some expert or other authority. For example: Theory X should be accepted as true because respected authorities in the field endorse it. See also FALSE AUTHORITY. [from Latin *verecundia*, "bashfulness" or "diffidence"; that is, "(due) to diffidence"]

adversarial system the type of legal system, as in the United States, that involves the dispute between opposing parties being heard before an independent TRIER OF FACT (i.e., a judge or jury). In many European countries, but not the United Kingdom, an **inquisitorial system** is used, in which the judge leads the investigation by interrogating the parties.

adverse drug reaction any unintended, harmful response (physical or mental) to a drug. Reactions may be highly individual and related to genetic susceptibility or they may arise through interactions with other prescribed or nonprescribed drugs (see DRUG INTERACTIONS) or with dietary items (as in the case of MONOAMINE OXIDASE INHIBITORS). Also called **adverse event**; **adverse reaction**. Compare SIDE EFFECTS.

adverse event **1.** in health care, an injury or harmful effect resulting from medical intervention or research. **2.** in pharmacology, see ADVERSE DRUG REACTION.

adverse impact the unfavorable or negative effect on certain groups (e.g., those defined by ethnicity, age, gender, disability, or sexual orientation) of employment or other practices deemed to be discriminatory. In PERSONNEL SELECTION, for example, testing for competence in written English might have an adverse impact on recent immigrants; such testing should therefore be avoided unless this competence is a BONA FIDE OCCUPATIONAL QUALIFICATION. Also called **disparate impact**. See also GRIGGS V. DUKE POWER CO.; UNIFORM GUIDELINES FOR EMPLOYEE SELECTION PROCEDURES.

adverse witness an individual who reveals bias against the party that called him or her to give evidence in a court of law. An adverse witness may be a HOSTILE WITNESS.

advertisement *n.* **1.** a public announcement appearing in print, broadcast, or electronic media that is designed to enhance individuals' knowledge about a particular item or service in order to encourage the purchase, consumption, or increased use of that item or service. See also ADVERTISING PSYCHOLOGY; ADVERTISING RESEARCH. **2.** in animal behavior, a type of signal or display that emphasizes or calls attention to the organism producing it. For example, a male bird defending a territory might use advertisement in the form of bright coloration and conspicuous song both to attract mates and to deter competing males. Compare CAMOUFLAGE.

advertising psychology the psychological study of the techniques and effectiveness of all types of advertising, including the motives that prompt consumers to buy, the use and value of slogans, and the physical characteristics of advertisements in terms of such factors as color, size, and position in print media and in terms of different elements of commercials, such as jingles, animated figures, and repetition. See ADVERTISING RESEARCH.

advertising research the study of (a) the selection of effective appeals for specific products or commodities; (b) the creation of product images, including trade names and package designs; and (c) the development of methods of measuring the effectiveness of advertising campaigns in different media. Advertising research is also used in generic advertising, for example, in the advertising of an industry or product category, such as cigars or coffee, rather than of specific brands. See also ADVERTISING PSYCHOLOGY.

advertising response modeling (**ARM**) statistical techniques used to assess the frequency and reach of advertising messages to particular audiences. In combination with sales data, these techniques are used to determine optimal levels of advertising.

advice giving a COUNSELING technique in which the therapist advises the client on alternatives or options for consideration.

advocacy *n.* speaking or acting on behalf of an individual or group to uphold their rights or explain their point of view. A therapist may, for example, be in a position to act as an ADVOCATE for a client in a court hearing, school situation, or other instance when a decision is to be made based on the client's mental health, intelligence, or the like.

advocate *n.* an individual who represents and defends the interests of another individual or of a group or cause. In health care, advocates represent consumers to protect their rights to effective treatment. There are two general types of such advocates: A **case advocate** represents a single individual, and a **class advocate** represents a whole group. See OMBUDSMAN. See also CHILD ADVOCACY.

AEP abbreviation for average evoked potential. See EVOKED POTENTIAL.

AEq abbreviation for AGE EQUIVALENT.

AERA abbreviation for AMERICAN EDUCATIONAL RESEARCH ASSOCIATION.

aerial perspective a MONOCULAR CUE to DEPTH PERCEPTION consisting of the relative clarity of objects under varying atmospheric conditions. Nearer objects are usually clearer in detail, whereas more distant objects are less distinct and appear bluer.

aero- (**aer-**) *combining form* air or gas.

aerobic activity see ENDURANCE ACTIVITY.

aerobic capacity see ENDURANCE ACTIVITY.

aerobic exercise the level of exercise that is maintained by an energy-producing system that involves the use of oxygen in the muscles; that is, exercise, typically prolonged and of moderate intensity, that increases the body's demand for, supply of, and use of oxygen and strengthens the cardiovascular and respiratory systems. Aerobic exercise, such as jogging or cycling, is associated with a variety of benefits to physical and mental health, including increased endurance, reduction of body fat, and alleviation of depressive symptoms. Also called **aerobics**. Compare ANAEROBIC EXERCISE.

AER technique abbreviation for AVERAGE-EVOKED-RESPONSE TECHNIQUE.

aesthesiometer *n.* see ESTHESIOMETER.

aesthesiometry *n.* see ESTHESIOMETRY.

aesthetic appreciation the extent to which a stimulus is enjoyed because of its aesthetic properties.

aesthetic emotion an emotion linked to the experience of natural beauty or art, including abstract visual displays, music, and dance.

aesthetic evolution the concept that the arts change in an orderly fashion because of intrinsic forces. By definition, art has to be novel; this leads to systematic changes in word usage and styles.

aesthetic overshadowing the fact that the most important determinant of preference in a stimulus generally accounts almost entirely for preference for the stimulus, with other determinants being largely ignored.

aesthetic preference the extent to which a particular stimulus is preferred to others for aesthetic reasons. See also AROUSAL POTENTIAL.

aesthetics *n.* the study of the psychological or philosophical aspects of beauty, or the lack of it, in nature and art. See PSYCHOLOGICAL AESTHETICS. See also ENVIRONMENTAL AESTHETICS; EXPERIMENTAL AESTHETICS. **—aesthetic** *adj.*

aesthetic taste judgment of works of art as being beautiful or appropriate according to generally accepted standards.

aesthetic threshold the threshold at which one can make a reliable aesthetic judgment. It appears to be very close to the sensory threshold.

aesthetic value the emotional or spiritual value imparted to a person by the beauty of a work of art or nature.

affair *n.* a sexual relationship between two individuals, especially one involving infidelity to a partner. See ADULTERY.

affect *n.* any experience of feeling or emotion, ranging from suffering to elation, from the simplest to the most complex sensations of feeling, and from the most normal to the most pathological emotional reactions. Affect is one of the three traditionally identified components of mind, the others being COGNITION and CONATION. An affect may be reflexive or irreflexive. **Irreflexive affect** is the direct experience in consciousness of the AFFECTIVE TONE of a particular emotional state. An example is a person's feeling of elation upon receiving good news. **Reflexive affect** occurs when a person makes his or her feelings objects of scrutiny. An example would be when a person wonders why he or she does not feel particularly elated upon receiving good news. See NEGATIVE AFFECT; POSITIVE AFFECT.

affectation *n.* an artificial manner that is assumed to impress others, which occasionally occurs during the manic phase of bipolar I disorder (see BIPOLAR DISORDERS).

affect-block *n.* a condition marked by an inability to adequately express or experience emotions, especially strong ones, because of a dissociation of these emotions from ideas or thoughts. It is characteristically seen in individuals with schizophrenia or obsessive-compulsive disorder.

affect display a facial, vocal, or gestural behavior that serves as an indicator of AFFECT. See EMOTIONAL EXPRESSION.

affect hunger a craving for affection and loving care.

affect intensity the tendency to experience emotional states very strongly, irrespective of the nature (e.g., positive versus negative) of those states.

affect inversion see REVERSAL OF AFFECT.

affection *n.* feelings of tenderness and attachment, especially when such feelings are nonsexual. **—affectionate** *adj.*

affectional bonds feelings of affection and emotional attachment between human beings, between animals, and between human beings and animals. Affectional bonds are manifested by such activities as clinging, cuddling, stroking, and embracing. The presence of affectional bonds is also evidenced by the sense of loss, grief, and anxiety experienced if separation occurs. See SEPARATION ANXIETY.

affective *adj.* **1.** pertaining to emotion or feelings. **2.** capable of producing or demonstrating AFFECT or emotion.

affective aggression see AGGRESSION.

affective amnesia see FUNCTIONAL AMNESIA.

affective assessment evaluation of an individual's emotional or psychological state and degree of emotional intensity.

affective–cognitive consistency the degree to which the affective and cognitive BASES OF AN ATTITUDE are evaluatively consistent with one another. For example, if the affective basis is extremely positive and the cognitive basis is extremely negative, affective–cognitive consistency is low. See also AFFECTIVE–EVALUATIVE CONSISTENCY; COGNITIVE–EVALUATIVE CONSISTENCY.

affective–cognitive structure the combination of an emotional experience with a thought or image, such as the linking of the emotions of relief and fear reduction to the idea of a parent as a haven of safety.

affective commitment that element of an employee's ORGANIZATIONAL COMMITMENT that can be attributed to a feeling of involvement with the organization and an identification with its goals and objectives. Compare CONTINUANCE COMMITMENT.

affective development see EMOTIONAL DEVELOPMENT.

affective discharge the expression of strong emotions (e.g., sorrow or anger) by clients undergoing therapy in which the therapist uses techniques aimed at facilitating deeper exploration of past experiences. Affective discharge is believed to be a release of psychic energy. Also called **cathectic discharge**.

affective disharmony a characteristic of schizophrenia in which there is an absence of conformity between emotional reaction and content of the idea or thought.

affective disorder in *DSM–III*, any of a group of disorders characterized by a prolonged, pervasive disturbance of mood not due to any other physical or mental disorder. This group included the **major affective disorders** (e.g., major depression [see MAJOR DEPRESSIVE DISORDER], BIPOLAR DISORDER), other specific affective disorders (CYCLOTHYMIC DISORDER, DYSTHYMIC DISORDER), atypical affective disorders (see ATYPICAL DEPRESSION), and sometimes MINOR DEPRESSIVE DISORDER. In *DSM–IV–TR*, affective disorders are classified as MOOD DISORDERS.

affective education any training that involves a learning process focused on or derived from emotion rather than reason, for example, a curriculum aimed at changing the emotional and social behavior of students and enhancing their understanding of such behavior. The concept is gaining popularity in reducing conflict and aggression in schools.

affective engineering see KANSEI ENGINEERING.

affective equilibrium the idea that a set of psychophysical judgments is formed around the median of the judgments made for individual stimuli in the set.

affective–evaluative consistency the degree to which the affective basis of an attitude (see BASES OF AN ATTITUDE) and the overall attitude are evaluatively consistent with one another. For example, if the affective basis is extremely positive and the overall attitude is extremely negative, affective–evaluative consistency is low. See also AFFECTIVE–COGNITIVE CONSISTENCY; COGNITIVE–EVALUATIVE CONSISTENCY.

affective experience any emotionally charged experience.

affective forecasting predicting one's own future emotional states, especially in connection with some event or outcome that one faces. People often "forecast" more extreme and lasting emotional reactions to events than they actually experience.

affective hallucination a hallucination that occurs in the context of AFFECTIVE PSYCHOSIS and has a manic or depressive content.

affective interaction highly emotional interpersonal interactions, as may occur in GROUP PSYCHOTHERAPY or in a family.

affective lability emotional instability; that is, sudden shifts in emotional expression. It is often seen in such disorders as schizophrenia, bipolar disorder, borderline personality disorder, senile dementia, and traumatic brain injury. Also called **labile affect**.

affective logic the hypothesis that emotions have their own independent set of mental operations, distinct from those governing other forms of mental life. [proposed by French psychologist Théodule A. Ribot (1839–1916)]

affectively based persuasion an active attempt to change an attitude primarily by altering the emotions, feelings, or mood states associated with the ATTITUDE OBJECT. Also called **emotionally based persuasion**. See also BASES OF AN ATTITUDE; FEAR APPEAL. Compare COGNITIVELY BASED PERSUASION.

affective meaning the attitude or emotion elicited by a stimulus, such as a musical piece, a drawing, or—especially—a word or phrase. The term is sometimes used interchangeably with **connotative meaning** (see DENOTATIVE MEANING).

affective psychosis a PSYCHOSIS that occurs in the context of severe MAJOR DEPRESSIVE EPISODES or MANIC EPISODES. The mood disruption precedes the psychotic symptoms, and the psychotic symptoms occur only during these episodes. See MOOD-CONGRUENT PSYCHOTIC FEATURES; MOOD-INCONGRUENT PSYCHOTIC FEATURES.

affective rigidity a condition in which emotions or feelings remain unchanged through varying situations in which such changes would normally occur. Affective rigidity is common in obsessive-compulsive disorder and schizophrenia.

affective state any type of emotional state. The term is often used in situations where emotions dominate the person's awareness.

affective theory a paradigm (framework) underlying approaches to psychotherapy that emphasizes the importance of feelings and emotions in therapeutic change.

affective tone the mood or feeling associated with a particular experience or stimulus. In psychotherapy, when a client fails to recognize his or her affective tone, the therapist may draw the client's attention to it as a primary element of the communication, thus focusing the client's attention on underlying or unconscious feelings. Also called **feeling tone**.

affectivity *n.* the degree of a person's response or susceptibility to pleasure, pain, and other emotional stimuli. Evaluation of affectivity is an important component of a psychological examination; the therapist or clinician may look for evidence of such reactions as BLUNTED AFFECT, INAPPROPRIATE AFFECT, LOSS OF AFFECT, AMBIVALENCE, DEPERSONALIZATION, ELATION, DEPRESSION, or ANXIETY.

affect regulation the attempt to alter or prolong one's mood or emotional state. Trying to get out of a bad mood is the most common example. Because people cannot usually change their emotions simply by deciding to feel differently, they use many indirect strategies for affect regulation.

affect scale any of several psychometric measures for quantifying the intensity of the subjective aspects of emotion. An example is the BECK DEPRESSION INVENTORY.

afferent *adj.* conducting or conveying from the periphery toward a central point. For example, AFFERENT NERVE FIBERS conduct impulses toward the brain or spinal cord. Compare EFFERENT.

afferent nerve fiber a nerve fiber, typically a sensory fiber, that conducts impulses toward the brain or spinal cord or from a lower to a higher center of the central nervous system. Compare EFFERENT NERVE FIBER.

afferent pathway a NEURAL PATHWAY that conducts impulses from a sense organ toward the brain or spinal cord or from one brain region to another. Compare EFFERENT PATHWAY.

afferent sensory neuron a neuron that conducts impulses from a sense organ to the brain or spinal cord.

afferent stimulation stimulation of a sensory system, leading to conduction of neural impulses to the brain or spinal cord.

affiliation *n.* in social psychology, a social relationship with one or more other individuals, usually based on liking or a personal attachment rather than on perceived material benefits. The sense of loneliness stemming from the absence of such relationships often leads to feelings of being worthless, hopeless, and powerless. See AFFILIATIVE BEHAVIOR; AFFILIATIVE DRIVE. **—affiliative** *adj.*

affiliation motivation see AFFILIATIVE DRIVE.

affiliative behavior any action that is carried out with the aim of maintaining or enhancing one's personal relationship with one or more other individuals or that is associated more generally with the urge to form, maintain, or enhance personal attachments. See AFFILIATION; AFFILIATIVE DRIVE.

affiliative drive in social psychology, the desire to have a personal relationship with one or more other individuals, usually a relationship that would not be based primarily on any material benefits that might be gained. This manifests itself in the urge to form friendships and attachments and to join organizations and enjoy social gatherings. AFFILIATION appears to be a basic source of emotional security; without it, most individuals feel lost, anxious, and frustrated. Although individuals differ in the strength of their desire to be with others, stressful situations typically intensify the need for affiliation; this is especially so when these others are undergoing the same stress, perhaps because being part of a group helps to reduce the unpleasantness of the situation. Also called **affiliation motivation**. See also AFFILIATIVE BEHAVIOR; GREGARIOUSNESS.

affiliative need the fundamental human need to seek cooperative, friendly association with others who resemble one or like one or whom one likes. [described by U.S. psychologist Henry Alexander Murray (1893–1988)]

affinity *n.* **1.** similarity in structure, form, or quality. **2.** relationship by marriage or adoption rather than blood. Compare CONSANGUINITY. **3.** in pharmacology, the tendency of a particular LIGAND (e.g., neurotransmitter, hormone, or drug) to bind to a particular RECEPTOR, measured by the percentage of receptors (binding sites) occupied by the ligand. **4.** an inherent attraction to or liking for a particular person, place, or thing, often based on some commonality. See ELECTIVE AFFINITY.

affirmation *n.* in many forms of psychotherapy, particularly COGNITIVE BEHAVIOR THERAPY, a short statement repeated frequently by the client to instill positive thoughts, beliefs, and behavior. For example, a client who feels unloved might repeat "I am a lovable person."

affirmative *n.* in linguistics, the form of a sentence used to make a positive assertion about something rather than a NEGATIVE statement or a question (see INTERROGATIVE).

affirmative action a U.S. government policy designed to promote equal opportunities by requiring firms with federal contracts or subcontracts to develop and submit plans for hiring, training, and promoting people from various disadvantaged groups, including ethnic minorities, women, and people with disabilities, and to keep extensive records of their progress toward these goals. The policy is controversial in some of its aspects and has been subject to legal challenges. See also ADVERSE IMPACT; BANDING; EQUAL OPPORTUNITY; FOUR-FIFTHS RULE; POSITIVE DISCRIMINATION; RACE NORMING.

affirmative defense a defense in which the defendant admits committing the act with which he or she is charged but provides evidence that undermines the prosecution's or plaintiff's claim of criminal intent. The INSANITY DEFENSE, DIMINISHED RESPONSIBILITY, contributory negligence (the defendant's claim that the plaintiff acted carelessly or with disregard and was partially at fault), and self-defense are examples of affirmative defenses.

affirmative postmodernism a perspective in POSTMODERNISM holding that social, cultural, and political progress is possible within a postmodern framework of assumptions. Compare SKEPTICAL POSTMODERNISM.

affirmative therapy a socioculturally informed intervention that empowers clients and their communities, particularly in situations in which ethnic, gender, or sexual orientation diversity has been resisted or in which normal conditions (e.g., gay identity) have been pathologized. Emphasizing self- and cultural awareness, this therapy may be practiced as a distinct intervention or within the context of other psychotherapies.

affirming the antecedent in logic, the principle that if a conditional statement of the type "if X, then Y" is accepted as true, then the affirmation of the CONSEQUENT (Y) can be validly inferred from the affirmation of the ANTECEDENT (X). For example: *If it is raining, then the grass will be wet: It is raining: Therefore the grass is wet.* Also called **modus ponens**. See also AFFIRMING THE CONSEQUENT; DENYING THE ANTECEDENT; DENYING THE CONSEQUENT.

affirming the consequent a formal FALLACY in which one affirms the CONSEQUENT of an "if...then" statement and concludes, on this basis, that the ANTECEDENT is also true. For example: *If it is raining, then the grass will be wet: The grass is wet: Therefore it is raining.* No valid conclusion can be drawn from the fact that the consequent is affirmed. See also AFFIRMING THE ANTECEDENT; DENYING THE ANTECEDENT; DENYING THE CONSEQUENT.

affixation *n.* the linguistic process in which **affixes** (PREFIXES, SUFFIXES, and INFIXES) are added to words to create inflected or derived forms (e.g., *un-glue*; *walk-ing*; *material-ize*). Languages vary in both extent of affixation and relative frequency of types of affixation. See also AGGLUTINATION; AGGLUTINATIVE LANGUAGE. **—affix** *vb.*

affordance *n.* the quality of a stimulus or an object that defines its usability to an organism, for example, an object that can be used as a seat affords support or sittability. The affordance of an object varies with the organism; thus a tree may serve as a landmark or supply food, shelter, fuel, lumber, or nest sites to different organisms. [defined in 1981 by James J. GIBSON]

affricate *n.* a speech sound consisting of a PLOSIVE (e.g., [t]) followed immediately by a FRICATIVE (e.g., [sh]), such as the [ch] sound in *chair.*

A fiber a large-diameter, myelinated fiber of the SOMATOSENSORY SYSTEM. A fibers range in diameter from 1 to about 20 μm and transmit impulses at a velocity of 5–120 m/s; the larger the diameter, the more rapid the velocity. The A-fiber group is subdivided by diameter, ranging from largest to smallest: A-ALPHA FIBERS, A-BETA FIBERS, and A-DELTA FIBERS.

AFMET acronym for Air Force Medical Evaluation Test, the former name for the BIOGRAPHICAL EVALUATION AND SCREENING OF TROOPS program.

a fortiori for a similar but stronger reason. In logical or philosophical argument the phrase is used to mean "even more certainly," as in *If I am too old to learn to fly, a fortiori my father is too.* [Latin, literally: "from stronger"]

AFP abbreviation for ALPHA-FETOPROTEIN.

AFQT abbreviation for ARMED FORCES QUALIFICATION TEST.

African American Vernacular English (AAVE) see BLACK ENGLISH.

African trypanosomiasis see SLEEPING SICKNESS.

afterbirth *n.* the third and final stage of birth, involving expulsion of the placenta and other membranes from the uterus. See also DELIVERY; LABOR.

aftercare *n.* **1.** a continuing program of outpatient treatment and rehabilitation services provided for patients who have been discharged from the hospital. The program is directed to maintenance of improvement, prevention of relapse, and adjustment of the individual to the community. Aftercare may also refer to inpatient services provided for convalescent patients, such as those who are recovering from surgery. **2.** a form of day care, as in programs designed to care for children after school. See CHILD CARE.

aftercurrent *n.* see AFTERPOTENTIAL.

afterdischarge *n.* continued production of nerve impulses after the stimulus that caused the activity has been removed.

aftereffect *n.* the altered perception of a sensory stimulus (usually visual) that results from prolonged exposure to another stimulus. Aftereffects are usually the inverted form of the original stimulus. For example, viewing a pattern of lines tilted to the left will make a pattern of vertical lines appear to be tilted to the right (see TILT AFTEREFFECT). Also called **aftersensation**; **perceptual aftereffect**. See also CONTINGENT AFTEREFFECT; MOTION AFTEREFFECT; ROTATIONAL AFTEREFFECT. Compare AFTERIMAGE.

afterexpulsion *n.* see REPRESSION PROPER.

afterimage *n.* the image that remains after a stimulus ends or is removed. A **positive afterimage** occurs rarely, lasts a few seconds, and is caused by a continuation of receptor and neural processes following cessation of the stimulus; it has approximately the color and brightness of the original stimulus. A **negative afterimage** is more common, often more intense, and lasts longer. It is usually complementary to the original stimulus in color and brightness; for example, if the stimulus was bright yellow, the negative afterimage will be dark blue. Compare AFTEREFFECT.

after-nystagmus *n.* the element of VESTIBULAR NYSTAGMUS that occurs after rotating the head, consisting of rapid, involuntary movement of the eyes in the direction opposite to that of the rotation.

afterplay *n.* affectionate and sensual activity (e.g., hugging, caressing, kissing) that continues after orgasm is achieved in sexual activity.

afterpotential *n.* the part of an ACTION POTENTIAL that remains after the electric potential has reached its peak, or spike. Also called **aftercurrent**. See also NEGATIVE AFTERPOTENTIAL; POSITIVE AFTERPOTENTIAL.

aftersensation *n.* see AFTEREFFECT.

agape *n.* a complex form of love involving feelings of tenderness, protectiveness, self-denial, and aesthetic preference for the features, gestures, speech, and other traits of a person; it may also involve erotic or sensual elements. The term, which derives from a Greek word meaning "brotherly love," is sometimes used to denote an unselfish love as taught by such religious figures as Jesus and the Buddha. Also called **agapism**.

AGCT abbreviation for Army General Classification Test. See ARMY TESTS.

age 1. *n.* the amount of time that has passed since an organism's birth; that is, an individual's CHRONOLOGICAL AGE. Compare GESTATIONAL AGE. **2.** *n.* a measure of physical or mental development (e.g., ANATOMICAL AGE, EDUCATIONAL AGE, or READING AGE). **3.** *n.* a specific period of human life (as in **middle age, old age**). See DEVELOPMENTAL LEVELS. **4.** *vb.* to grow older. See AGING; SECONDARY AGING.

age-appropriate maturity psychological maturity: the ability to deal effectively and resiliently with experience and to perform satisfactorily in developmental tasks (biological, social, cognitive) characteristic of one's age level.

age-associated memory impairment (**AAMI**) the minor memory deficits often associated with normal aging. These changes are not associated with dementias, such as Alzheimer's disease. Also called **benign senescence; benign senescent forgetfulness**.

age avoidance see AGEISM.

age calibration the standardization of a test in AGE EQUIVALENTS.

age crisis a theoretical, qualitative change in personality associated with inner conflicts occurring at a particular stage of life. Empirical research has failed to find indications of such radical changes in personality associated with a particular stage of life. See also MIDLIFE CRISIS.

âge critique the menopausal years. [French, literally: "critical age"]

âge de retour the years of SENILITY. [French, literally: "age of return," namely, to childhood]

age discrimination differential and typically unfavorable treatment of individuals because of their chronological age. In the United States, federal legislation has been enacted making age discrimination illegal in various contexts. An example is the AGE DISCRIMINATION IN EMPLOYMENT ACT. See AGEISM.

Age Discrimination in Employment Act (**ADEA**) a U.S. federal law, enacted in 1967, that prohibits employment practices that discriminate against those aged 40 or older, unless the employer can demonstrate that youth is a BONA FIDE OCCUPATIONAL QUALIFICATION for the job in question. See also FUNCTIONAL AGE.

age effect 1. any age-based change in psychological functioning and behavior, such as increased conformity during adolescence. See also COHORT EFFECT. **2.** in the psychology of groups, any of various cognitive and interpersonal consequences that result when group members respond to others on the basis of their age. See also AGEISM.

age equivalent (**AEq**) the average chronological age at which members of a defined population typically obtain a given test score.

age-equivalent scale a system of expressing test scores in terms of age norms or averages (see AGE EQUIVALENT).

age-grade scaling a method of standardizing a test by establishing norms based on a sample of children who are of the typical chronological age for their grade in school.

ageism *n.* **1.** discrimination against older adults because of their age, especially in employment and in health care. See AGE DISCRIMINATION. **2.** the tendency to be prejudiced against older adults and to negatively stereotype them as, for example, debilitated, inadequate, frail, or unable to care for themselves. **—ageist** *adj.*

agency *n.* the state of being active, usually in the service of a goal, or of exerting power or influence. See AGENT.

agency shop an arrangement between a labor union and an employer in which employees who are not union members pay a representational fee (usually equal to the dues paid by members) as a condition of employment. See also CLOSED SHOP; OPEN SHOP; UNION SHOP.

agency theory a theory that describes economic and organizational activity in terms of a series of agreements between principals, who require goods or services, and agents, who supply these goods or services. Central to this theory is the rational economic assumption that both agents and principals will attempt to maximize their respective UTILITIES. An **agency problem** may arise when the interests of principals (e.g., shareholders in a company) and agents (e.g., managers) are not congruent, or when principals have insufficient information about the activities of agents. Agency theory suggests ways in which these problems can be reduced, notably by redesigning contracts or compensation schemes so that agents have an incentive to act in the best interests of principals (e.g., by some form of GAINSHARING) and by improving monitoring procedures.

agenesis *n.* the failure of a body part to develop normally or to develop at all. An example is **callosal agenesis** (or **corpus callosum agenesis**), in which the nerve tract joining the two cerebral hemispheres (see CORPUS CALLOSUM) fails to develop. **—agenetic** *adj.*

agenitalism *n.* a condition due to lack of secretion by the testes or ovaries.

age norm the CHRONOLOGICAL AGE associated with an average or expected level of achievement.

agent *n.* **1.** a person or entity that acts or has the capacity to act. **2.** a person who acts on behalf of another or of a group. **3.** in PSYCHOTHERAPY, a therapist who helps a client gain self-understanding. **4.** in GROUP PSYCHOTHERAPY, the therapist or any individual client who helps another client. **5.** a means by which something is done or caused. For example, an infectious agent is a bacterium or other microorganism that causes a particular disease. **6.** in social psychology, the individual who initiates a dyadic or other social interaction. The object of the agent's action is the **patient**. **7.** in linguistics, the entity that performs the main action in a clause or sentence. It is prototypically an ANIMATE NOUN and usually, but not always, the grammatical SUBJECT of the clause. The agent is an important category in CASE GRAMMAR. Compare EXPERIENCER; INSTRUMENTAL; PATIENT. **8.** in parapsychology, the person who instigates an alleged occurrence of PSYCHOKINESIS or TELEPATHY. Compare PERCIPIENT. See also SENDER. **9.** in philosophy, an entity that possesses both the power to bring about an event and the power to refrain from bringing it about. In this sense, an agent possesses FREE WILL or some similar power to act or forbear. A person as agent is considered to be partly or wholly the originator of his or her own actions. **10.** a computer program that makes use of DISTRIBUTED COGNITION in problem solving. This type of program is designed for use in such areas as distributed sensing, telecommunications, and World Wide Web-based tasks. Besides being distributed, agents are designed for particular (and often limited) situations and are intended to work semiautonomously, to be flexible, and to be able to collaborate in problem-solving tasks. **—agentive** *adj.*

agentic orientation an emphasis on achieving, doing, succeeding, and making one's own mark in the world, which may be expressed through such traits as COMPETITIVENESS and SELF-FOCUS.

agentic state a psychological state that occurs when individuals, as subordinates to a higher authority in an organized status hierarchy, feel compelled to obey the orders issued by that authority. See BEHAVIORAL STUDY

OF OBEDIENCE; DESTRUCTIVE OBEDIENCE. [described by Stanley MILGRAM]

age of consent the age at which an individual is considered legally competent to assent to something, especially sexual intercourse or marriage.

age of onset the typical age at which a disease first occurs in predisposed individuals. One of the hallmarks of some genetic syndromes is that the age of onset is earlier in individuals with hereditary susceptibility than in sporadic cases.

agerasia *n.* youthful appearance in an old person. [from Greek, "eternal youth"]

age ratio one indicator of the predictive power of an APTITUDE TEST, obtained by dividing the student's chronological age at one administration of a test by his or her age at a later administration of the same test.

age regression a hypnotic technique in which the therapist helps the client recall a crucial experience by inducing amnesia for the present, then suggesting that he or she return, year by year, to the earlier date when a particular experience took place. This technique is also used in forensic contexts to help eyewitnesses and victims recall their experiences. The use of age regression in both psychotherapeutic and forensic settings is controversial.

age scale see AGE-EQUIVALENT SCALE.

age score a test score expressed in terms of the age at which most people reach a particular level of performance.

ageusia (**aguesia**) *n.* loss of the ability to taste. Causes may include a failure of taste receptors to form; a loss of taste receptors due to injury, disease, or advanced age; or damage to the sensory nerves that transport taste sensations to the central nervous system.

agglutination *n.* in linguistics, the creation of a word from the combination of several MORPHEMES that remain essentially unchanged in the process. For example, the word *unbeatable* is created by the agglutination of the morphemes *un-*, *beat*, and *-able*. See also AGGLUTINATIVE LANGUAGE. —**agglutinate** *vb.*

agglutinative language in LINGUISTIC TYPOLOGY, a language that expresses ideas in complex words formed by the AGGLUTINATION of numerous distinct MORPHEMES. Turkish is considered a typical agglutinative language. Compare FUSIONAL LANGUAGE; ISOLATING LANGUAGE.

aggravating factor a fact relating to a crime or to the defendant that makes the offense more serious or supports the argument for a harsher sentence. An example of an aggravating factor is the use of a deadly weapon in the commission of a crime. Also called **aggravating circumstance**. Compare MITIGATING FACTOR.

aggregate idea an idea that is formed by recombination of the elements of a complex stimulus (such as the set of tones of a clanging noise) into a new COMPOUND STIMULUS (such as a musical chord). The new, aggregate idea can be characterized by its elements but is not itself contained in those elements. [defined by Wilhelm WUNDT]

aggregate score a combination of two or more scores on variables that are related to one another conceptually or empirically.

aggregation *n.* **1.** a collection of organisms in one location with no obvious SOCIAL STRUCTURE or SOCIAL ORGANIZATION, possessing only a minimum of shared purpose or interdependence. Examples include people in a shopping mall, commuters on a subway platform, or a group of butterflies around a puddle of water. **2.** in statistics, a structured set of data elements. —**aggregate** *vb.* —**aggregative** *adj.*

aggregation problems the difficulty of separating individual effects from situational effects when established groups or institutions are used as the unit of analysis in an evaluation. For example, investigators are likely to attribute characteristics of the institution to the individual.

aggression *n.* behavior, motivated by competitiveness, anger, or hostility, that results in harm to or destruction or defeat of others or, in some cases, oneself. When the primary goal is intentional injury or destruction of the target, the behavior is called **hostile aggression**. It is distinguished from **instrumental** (or **operant**) **aggression**, in which the attack is carried out principally to achieve a goal other than the target's injury, such as acquiring a desired resource. Most instances of hostile aggression can also be regarded as **affective aggression** in that they are emotional reactions to an aversive state of affairs, which tend to be targeted toward the perceived source of the distress but may be displaced onto other people or objects if the disturbing agent cannot be attacked (see DISPLACED AGGRESSION). In the classical psychoanalytic theory of Sigmund FREUD, the aggressive impulse is innate and instinctual (see AGGRESSIVE INSTINCT), but most nonpsychoanalytically oriented psychologists view it as a socially learned reaction to frustration (see FRUSTRATION–AGGRESSION HYPOTHESIS). See also ANIMAL AGGRESSION. —**aggressive** *adj.*

aggression–frustration hypothesis see FRUSTRATION–AGGRESSION HYPOTHESIS.

aggressive character a personality characterized by a hostile or competitive attitude to others and the pursuit of power, prestige, and material possessions. German-born U.S. psychoanalyst Karen D. Horney (1885–1952) defined the development of such a character as one of three basic NEUROTIC TRENDS used as a defense against BASIC ANXIETY. Compare COMPLIANT CHARACTER; DETACHED CHARACTER.

aggressive cue a signal or stimulus in a person's environment that is interpreted as aggressive or that is typically associated with aggression.

aggressive erotic containing both violent and sexual elements. It may describe a type of pornography or behavior (e.g., rape).

aggressive instinct in psychoanalytic theory, a derivative of the DEATH INSTINCT that directs destructive impulses away from the self and toward the outside world. See AGGRESSION.

aggressive mimicry MIMICRY in which either the physical or behavioral traits (or both) of a predatory species closely resemble those of a nonpredatory species, with the result that potential prey are attracted to approach the predator more readily. For example, the females of a species of firefly can imitate the sexual flash patterns of a different species, luring males of that species close enough to be eaten.

aggressiveness *n.* a tendency toward assertiveness, social dominance, threatening behavior, and hostility. It may cause a transient change in behavior within an individual or be a characteristic trait of an individual. See also AGGRESSION. —**aggressive** *adj.*

aggressive script a SCRIPT based on anger, hostility, and overcompetitiveness that becomes stored in the memory of some individuals and guides their judgments and behavior. It is thought that such scripts are acquired from early family experiences, association with aggressive peers, and exposure to media violence.

aging *n.* the biological and psychological changes associated with chronological age. A distinction is often made between changes that are due to normal biological processes (i.e., SENESCENCE; see PRIMARY AGING) and changes that are caused by age-related pathologies (see SECONDARY AGING).

aging disorder the gradual structural and immune changes that occur with the passage of time, that are not due to disease or accident, and that eventually lead to increased probability of death as the individual ages.

agitated depression a MAJOR DEPRESSIVE EPISODE characterized by PSYCHOMOTOR AGITATION, restlessness, and irritability. It was formerly known as **agitated melancholia**.

agitation *n.* a state of increased activity, as in PSYCHOMOTOR AGITATION.

agitographia *n.* very rapid writing with unconscious omissions and distortions of letters, words, or parts of words.

agitophasia *n.* very rapid and cluttered speech in which sounds, words, or parts of words are omitted or distorted. Also called **agitolalia**.

aglossia *n.* partial or complete absence or loss of the tongue, resulting in difficulty in or failure to achieve articulation. Partial absence is sometimes referred to as **dysglossia**.

agnosia *n.* loss or impairment of the ability to recognize, interpret, or comprehend the meaning of sensory stimuli. The condition is associated with brain damage or neurological disorder and exists in a variety of forms (e.g., AUTOTOPAGNOSIA, FINGER AGNOSIA, PROSOPAGNOSIA, VISUAL AGNOSIA).

agnosic alexia see PURE ALEXIA.

agnosticism *n.* a skeptical position holding that the truth or falsity of certain metaphysical ideas or propositions cannot be known. The word is most often used in regard to theological doctrines, especially to belief in the existence of God. [coined in 1869 by British biologist Thomas Henry Huxley (1825–1895)] **—agnostic** *adj., n.*

agnus castus an herbal preparation derived from the flowers of the chasteberry tree and approved by Commission E of the German Federal Institute for Drugs and Medical Devices for use in the management of symptoms associated with the late luteal phase of the menstrual cycle (see PREMENSTRUAL DYSPHORIC DISORDER) and in the alleviation of menstrual cycle abnormalities or irregularities. Although its active components and mechanism of action are unknown, agnus castus has been shown to possess significant estrogenic activity and is thought to act upon the pituitary gland. Agnus castus may also possess dopaminergic activity and thus its concurrent use with either DOPAMINE-RECEPTOR AGONISTS or DOPAMINE-RECEPTOR ANTAGONISTS is not recommended, given the potential interactions that may occur. Side effects of agnus castus use are rare, but may include rashes and itching, nausea and vomiting, dizziness, headache, drowsiness, and confusion. Also called **vitex agnus castus**.

agonadal *adj.* **1.** having no sex glands. **2.** resulting from the absence of sex glands.

agonist *n.* **1.** a neurotransmitter, drug, hormone, or other agent that binds to a receptor site and initiates a response, thereby producing a physiological change. For example, the change could involve stimulation of a neuron, causing a nerve impulse to be fired, or it could inhibit nerve-cell discharge. A drug that acts as an agonist at a particular receptor normally produces a physiological effect similar to that of the body's own chemical messenger at that site. See INDIRECT AGONIST; INVERSE AGONIST; PARTIAL AGONIST. **2.** a contracting muscle whose action generates force in the intended direction. Compare ANTAGONIST. **—agonistic** *adj.*

agonist–antagonist *n.* a substance that simultaneously binds to multiple RECEPTORS, acting as an AGONIST or PARTIAL AGONIST at one particular type of receptor site and as an ANTAGONIST at another, different type of receptor site.

agonistic behavior competitive interactions involving components of both fear and aggression. In dominance or territorial encounters, behavioral interactions typically involve fluctuations in fearful and aggressive behavior within both parties, so that neither can be said to be purely aggressive or fearful.

agoraphobia *n.* literally, fear of the marketplace (from the Greek word *agora*), manifested as anxiety about being in places or situations for fear of having uncontrolled panic symptoms or a PANIC ATTACK. Apprehension is typically focused on fear of being unable to avoid a situation from which escape may be difficult or to control the panic symptoms that may result from exposure to the situation. The types of situations that are avoided (or endured with significant distress) include standing in line, being in a crowd, and traveling in a bus, train, or car. Agoraphobia may accompany PANIC DISORDER (**panic disorder with agoraphobia**), in which an individual experiences unexpected panic attacks, or it may occur in the absence of panic disorder (**agoraphobia without history of panic disorder**), when an individual fears paniclike symptoms or limited symptom attacks but has not experienced full-blown panic attacks. See also ANXIETY DISORDERS. **—agoraphobic** *adj.*

agrammatism *n.* a form of APHASIA characterized by speech that does not conform to grammatical rules, such as those governing word use, verb tense, and subject–verb agreement. Agrammatism occurs frequently in PICK'S DISEASE and Alzheimer's disease and occasionally in schizophrenia. Also called **agrammalogia**; **agrammaphasia**; **agrammata**; **agrammataphasia**; **agrammatologia**. See also DYSGRAMMATISM; SYNTACTICAL APHASIA.

agranular cortex the portion of the cerebral cortex that lacks GRANULE CELLS. It is found in layers I, III, and V of the cortex (see CORTICAL LAYERS) and refers particularly to the primary motor cortex (Brodmann's area 4), in which layer V (the major projection area) is very thick. Compare GRANULAR CORTEX.

agranulocytosis *n.* a decline in the number of certain white blood cells (neutrophils), typically as a result of an immune reaction to a drug or other chemical or the toxic effect of this substance on the bone marrow, causing production of white blood cells to fall. Agranulocytosis is diagnosed when the neutrophil count is below $200/mm^3$ or when the total white-blood-cell count is below $500/mm^3$. The condition results in suppression of the immune response, rendering individuals vulnerable to opportunistic infections. Psychotropic drugs, such as CLOZAPINE and PHENOTHIAZINE antipsychotics, can induce agranulocytosis.

agraphia *n.* loss or impairment of the ability to write. The disorder is most frequently a result of a stroke, head injury, ENCEPHALITIS, or other conditions resulting in brain damage, in which case it is known as **acquired agraphia**. However, agraphia is occasionally due to a localized congenital defect that may not result in other impairment. Also called **anorthography**; **written aphasia**. See also APHASIA.

agreeableness *n.* the tendency to act in a cooperative, unselfish manner, construed as one end of a dimension of individual differences (agreeableness versus disagreeableness) in the BIG FIVE PERSONALITY MODEL. It is also a dimension in the FIVE-FACTOR PERSONALITY MODEL. —**agreeable** *adj.*

agreement *n.* in linguistics, the correct relation between the different grammatical elements of a sentence, so that, for example, the NUMBER of the verb corresponds to that of its subject, and the number and gender of a pronoun correspond to those of its noun.

agreement coefficient see COEFFICIENT OF AGREEMENT.

agrypnia *n.* see INSOMNIA.

aguesia *n.* see AGEUSIA.

agyria *n.* see LISSENCEPHALY.

aha experience 1. the emotional reaction (**aha reaction**) that typically occurs at a moment of sudden insight into or understanding of a problem or other previously puzzling issue. It is the moment when the separate elements of the problem or issue come together and make sense or the moment when a solution is apparent. See also DISCONTINUITY HYPOTHESIS; EUREKA TASK; INSPIRATION. **2.** in psychotherapy, the client's sudden insight into his or her motives for cognitions, affects, or behaviors. See also EPIPHANY.

AHD abbreviation for ATTENTION-DEFICIT/HYPERACTIVITY DISORDER.

ahedonia *n.* see ANHEDONIA.

ahistorical *adj.* **1.** denoting a perspective that sees behavior in terms of contemporary causative factors, with emphasis on the here and now. Sometimes there is an implication that historical causes may be represented in current processes that produce their effects contemporaneously. See PRESENTIST. **2.** more generally, not concerned with or not taking into account history, historical factors, or historical perspective.

ahistoric therapy a therapeutic approach that focuses on here-and-now situations and behaviors. This approach is distinguished from approaches that place a strong emphasis on earlier events and circumstances.

AHP abbreviation for ALLIED HEALTH PROFESSIONAL.

ahypnia *n.* see INSOMNIA.

ahypnosia *n.* see INSOMNIA.

AI 1. abbreviation for ARTIFICIAL INSEMINATION. **2.** abbreviation for ARTIFICIAL INTELLIGENCE.

aided recall 1. the process of remembering something under circumstances where a prompt is given to assist recall. Measures of aided recall reflect the extent to which something is remembered when the prompt is provided. **2.** any of a number of methods used to assist a person, such as an eyewitness or victim of a crime, to retrieve memories relevant to an event. See also COGNITIVE INTERVIEW; CONTEXT REINSTATEMENT. **3.** the use of prompts to assist consumers in remembering information contained in a commercial message. It is used in testing the effectiveness of advertising and other messages and can include the use of **funnel interviews** (in which the research starts with general questions and then moves on to specific ones) as well as multiple-choice tests. For example, the interviewer might ask members of the public if they remember seeing a particular advertisement. If they do, the interviewer will ask about specific aspects of the advertisement.

aidoiomania *n.* see EROTOMANIA.

AIDS *a*cquired *i*mmune *d*eficiency *s*yndrome: a condition resulting from infection with human immunodeficiency virus (see HIV), which suppresses the body's immune response. The virus occurs in blood, semen, and vaginal fluid, and the initial transmission can occur from HIV-infected individuals through unprotected sex, intravenous drug use by contaminated needle sharing, and infusion of infected blood or blood products. HIV can also be transmitted from an infected mother to her child *in utero* or through breast feeding. AIDS is diagnosed in an HIV-infected person when the immune system is severely damaged, which results in certain serious opportunistic infections and diseases. Disclosing one's HIV-positive status can be difficult: The illness is stigmatizing, resulting in social rejection and leading to increased dependency on caregivers. To be supportive, family members and friends require detailed knowledge of the condition.

AIDS counseling counseling in which guidance, advice, and information are provided to individuals on issues related to HIV infection and AIDS. Such counseling typically covers ways to avoid exposure to HIV infection, provision of HIV antibody testing, and the importance of adhering to medication, as well as dealing with the myriad psychological and social issues associated with AIDS, including stigma, the anxiety in dealing with a life-threatening illness, and the nature of friendships and other support systems. Also called **HIV/AIDS counseling**.

AIDS dementia complex (**ADC**) neuropsychological dysfunction directly attributable to HIV infection, found most commonly in AIDS patients with advanced disease. It is marked by impairment in four areas: (a) cognition (e.g., memory loss, inability to concentrate); (b) behavior (e.g., inability to perform normal activities of daily living); (c) motor coordination (e.g., unsteady gait, loss of balance, incontinence); and (d) mood (e.g., severe depression, psychosis). Brain scans of affected individuals reveal cortical atrophy.

aim *n.* **1.** the symbolic or internal representation of a goal that may motivate and direct behavior toward achieving that goal: an intention or purpose. **2.** a goal toward which an organism voluntarily directs behavior, effort, or activity: an objective. **3.** in psychoanalytic theory, see AIM OF THE INSTINCT; OBJECT OF INSTINCT.

aiming test a test of VISUAL–MOTOR COORDINATION, precision, and speed. The participant either thrusts a stylus into a series of progressively smaller holes momentarily uncovered by a rotating shutter or places dots in small circles as rapidly as possible (see DOTTING TEST).

aim-inhibited *adj.* in psychoanalytic theory, describing a behavior—particularly an interpersonal behavior—in which the underlying drives are deflected from their original object and remain unconscious. According to the theory, aim inhibition characterizes those situations in which an INSTINCT fails to achieve direct satisfaction of its aim but obtains reduced gratification through activities or relationships similar to the original aim. Sigmund FREUD used this idea to explain affectional relationships within families and platonic friendships as deriving from an aim-inhibited sexual instinct.

aim of the instinct in psychoanalytic theory, the activity through which an INSTINCT is gratified, resulting in the release of internal tension. For example, kissing may satisfy the oral instinct. Also called **instinctual aim**. See also REVERSAL OF AFFECT.

AIO abbreviation for activities, interests, opinions. See PSYCHOGRAPHICS.

air–bone gap the difference between the air-conduction and bone-conduction hearing levels at specific frequencies, which indicates the amount of conductive impairment in the ear tested.

air conduction the process of conducting sound waves

through the ear canal to the eardrum, which vibrates in response to changes in adjacent air pressure.

air-conduction testing an audiological procedure that measures a person's threshold for PURE TONES in each ear at individual frequencies.

air-pollution adaptation habituation to local levels of air pollution through desensitization to their effects on health and aesthetic judgments. Signal detection analysis (see SIGNAL DETECTION THEORY) suggests a shift in RESPONSE BIAS rather than in actual threshold effects. See also AIR-POLLUTION BEHAVIORAL EFFECTS.

air-pollution behavioral effects the impact of air pollution on human behavior, over and above the behavioral effects of individual toxins (see BEHAVIORAL TOXICOLOGY). Exposure to air pollution has adverse effects on mood and emotions, increases feelings of annoyance, helplessness, and (under certain circumstances) aggression, and suppresses altruism. See also AIR-POLLUTION ADAPTATION.

air-pressure effects the adverse mental or physical effects of a significant variation from normal atmospheric pressure. Air-pressure effects experienced at high pressures, for example in diving more than 10 m (33 ft) beneath the surface of the sea, may include breathing difficulty, nitrogen poisoning marked by lightheadedness and mental instability, and oxygen poisoning caused by breathing oxygen under extreme pressure. Exposure to low pressures, as in mountain climbing or during airplane flights without oxygen or air-pressure modification, characteristically causes oxygen starvation, with impaired performance and eventual loss of consciousness and death. See also ACUTE MOUNTAIN SICKNESS; ALTITUDE SICKNESS; DECOMPRESSION SICKNESS; GRAY-OUT.

air sickness MOTION SICKNESS caused by air travel.

air traffic control personnel, equipment, and systems that support the safety and security of aircraft through information, communication, observation, and control of flight trajectories. See AVIATION PSYCHOLOGY.

AIS abbreviation for ANDROGEN-INSENSITIVITY SYNDROME.

Ajzen–Fishbein model the original framework for what is now known as the THEORY OF REASONED ACTION. [Icek **Ajzen** (1942–) and Martin **Fishbein** (1936–), U.S. social psychologists]

akatamathesia *n.* see ACATAMATHESIA.

akataphasia *n.* see ACATAPHASIA.

akathisia (**acathisia**) *n.* extreme restlessness characterized by an inability to sit or stand still for at least several minutes and by fidgety movements or jitteriness, as well as a subjective report of inner restlessness. It occurs as an EXTRAPYRAMIDAL EFFECT resulting from exposure to a neuroleptic (antipsychotic) medication (**neuroleptic-induced acute akathisia**) or in response to SSRI antidepressant medications (**medication-induced movement disorder not otherwise specified**). Akathisia is also a feature of some neurological and general medical conditions (e.g., Parkinson's disease and iron-deficiency anemia).

akinesia *n.* impaired or decreased ability to initiate voluntary movement in the absence of paralysis. This is most often observed in Parkinson's disease. Also called **akinesis**.

akinesia algera a condition in which pain is experienced with any body movement, a disorder often associated with psychogenic factors.

akinesis *n.* see AKINESIA.

akinesthesia *n.* the absence, loss, or impairment of the kinesthetic sense (see KINESTHESIS). —**akinesthesic** or **akinesthetic** *adj.*

akinetic *adj.* characterized by loss of voluntary movement not due to paralysis. See AKINESIA.

akinetic mutism an absence or gross reduction of voluntary movements and speech, although the individual does follow eye movements. The condition is associated with damage to the anterior CINGULATE GYRUS and supplementary motor area in the mesial part of the FRONTAL LOBES.

akinetic seizure see ATONIC SEIZURE.

Akineton *n.* a trade name for BIPERIDEN.

akinetopsia *n.* inability to see objects in motion, despite intact visual field, visual acuity, and eye movements, caused by bilateral injury to the occipitotemporal region of the brain. Patients with akinetopsia perceive moving stimuli as a series of stationary images, and stimuli moving at different speeds appear to be moving at the same speed.

akoasm *n.* see ACOUSMA.

akoria *n.* see ACORIA.

AL 1. abbreviation for absolute limen (see ABSOLUTE THRESHOLD). **2.** abbreviation for ADAPTATION LEVEL.

alalia *n.* partial or total inability to speak. Although mostly historical now, the term is occasionally used as a synonym for MUTISM.

Al-Anon *n.* an organization for people whose lives have been affected by the compulsive use of alcohol by a family member or friend. It uses the TWELVE-STEP PROGRAM adapted from ALCOHOLICS ANONYMOUS.

alarm call a vocalization produced by an animal, often in response to detecting a potential predator, that warns other individuals to either take cover or join in mutual attack of the predator. Alarm calls appear to be altruistic acts (placing the caller at increased risk), with the behavior often explained through KIN SELECTION or RECIPROCAL ALTRUISM.

alarm reaction see GENERAL ADAPTATION SYNDROME.

alaryngeal *adj.* without or not involving the LARYNX.

Alateen *n.* an organization composed of young people whose lives have been affected by someone else's drinking. An active adult member of AL-ANON serves as a sponsor for each group. It is based on the TWELVE-STEP PROGRAM adapted from ALCOHOLICS ANONYMOUS.

albinism *n.* any one of a group of genetic disorders in which the pigmentation of the eye, and frequently the skin, is defective. This is caused by the failure of the melanocytes (pigment-producing cells) to produce normal melanin pigment. The most common form of albinism results from a metabolic defect marked by a lack of the enzyme tyrosinase. **Tyrosinase-negative albinism** is the classic form of the disorder, affecting about 3 individuals per 100,000: It is characterized by unpigmented skin and hair. In **tyrosinase-positive albinism**, which affects Black individuals more frequently than White people, melanin is absent at birth, but pigmentation increases with age. Other forms include **cutaneous albinism**, a dominant genetic trait marked by a triangular white forelock and other effects limited to the skin and hair; and **ocular albinism**, in which only the eyes are affected, with incomplete development of the fovea (**foveal hypoplasia**) and a deficit of pigment in the iris and retina: Symptoms include STRABISMUS, NYSTAGMUS, PHOTOPHOBIA, severe ERRORS OF REFRACTION, and reduced visual acuity.

Albright's disease a disorder caused by dysfunction of

the pituitary gland and hypothalamus, characterized by pigment abnormalities, skeletal pseudocysts, and precocious puberty in females. [Fuller **Albright** (1900–1969), U.S. physician]

Albright's hereditary osteodystrophy a hereditary condition that clinically resembles hypoparathyroidism but is caused by failure of response to, rather than deficiency of, parathyroid hormone (see PSEUDOHYPOPARATHYROIDISM). It is commonly marked by short stature, obesity, short metacarpals, and ectopic calcification. [Fuller **Albright**]

alcohol *n.* **1.** ETHANOL (ethyl alcohol): the most frequently used and abused CNS DEPRESSANT in most cultures. When consumed, its primary effects are on the central nervous system, mood, and cognitive functions. **2.** any other member of the class of chemical compounds to which ethanol belongs.

Alcohol, Drug Abuse and Mental Health Administration (ADAMHA) an agency in the U.S. Department of Health and Human Services that was replaced in 1992 by the SUBSTANCE ABUSE AND MENTAL HEALTH SERVICES ADMINISTRATION (SAMHSA). In this reorganization, the three ADAMHA research institutes, the National Institute on Alcohol Abuse and Alcoholism (NIAAA), the National Institute on Drug Abuse (NIDA), and the NATIONAL INSTITUTE OF MENTAL HEALTH (NIMH), were moved to the National Institutes of Health. The substance abuse and mental health services programs provided by ADAMHA remain the responsibility of SAMHSA.

alcohol abuse in *DSM–IV–TR*, a pattern of alcohol use manifested by recurrent significant adverse consequences related to the repeated ingestion of alcohol. A diagnosis of alcohol abuse is preempted by the diagnosis of ALCOHOL DEPENDENCE: If the criteria for alcohol abuse and alcohol dependence are both met, only the latter diagnosis is given. See also SUBSTANCE ABUSE; SUBSTANCE DEPENDENCE.

alcohol addiction see ADDICTION; ALCOHOL DEPENDENCE.

alcohol-amnestic disorder the *DSM–III* designation for the condition classified in *DSM–IV–TR* as ALCOHOL-INDUCED PERSISTING AMNESTIC DISORDER.

alcohol dependence in *DSM–IV–TR*, a cluster of cognitive, behavioral, and physiological symptoms indicating continued use of alcohol despite significant alcohol-related problems. There is a pattern of repeated alcohol ingestion resulting in tolerance, characteristic symptoms if use is suspended (see ALCOHOL WITHDRAWAL), and an uncontrollable drive to continue use. Alcohol dependence is known popularly as **alcoholism**. See also ALCOHOL ABUSE; ALCOHOLISM TREATMENT.

alcohol derivatives drugs that utilize the sedative and hypnotic effects of alcohols for therapeutic purposes. In the 1890s, it was found that compounds derived from methyl alcohol had CNS DEPRESSANT effects. In the 1950s, a new generation of alcohol-based compounds with greater hypnotic activity was introduced. They included ETHCHLORVYNOL and **ethinamate**; the latter is a more potent sleep inducer than ethchlorvynol, but its abuse potential is similar to that of barbiturates. Due to their toxicity, alcohol derivatives are rarely used in modern clinical practice.

alcohol hallucinosis see ALCOHOL-INDUCED PSYCHOTIC DISORDER.

alcoholic *n.* a person who meets the *DSM–IV–TR* criteria for ALCOHOL DEPENDENCE.

alcoholic blackout see BLACKOUT.

alcoholic brain syndrome any of several syndromes associated with the acute or chronic effects of alcohol on brain function, including ALCOHOL INTOXICATION DELIRIUM, ALCOHOL WITHDRAWAL DELIRIUM, ALCOHOL-INDUCED PERSISTING DEMENTIA, ALCOHOL-INDUCED PERSISTING AMNESTIC DISORDER, and ALCOHOL-INDUCED PSYCHOTIC DISORDER.

alcoholic cerebellar degeneration degeneration of the CEREBELLUM caused by long-term alcohol abuse, commonly producing gait disturbances.

alcoholic dementia see ALCOHOL-INDUCED PERSISTING DEMENTIA.

alcoholic hallucinosis see ALCOHOL-INDUCED PSYCHOTIC DISORDER.

alcoholic Korsakoff's syndrome a form of KORSAKOFF'S SYNDROME caused by long-term alcohol abuse. See ALCOHOL-INDUCED PERSISTING AMNESTIC DISORDER.

alcoholic myopathy see ACUTE ALCOHOLIC MYOPATHY.

alcoholic neuropathy any of various neurological disturbances, including weakness and abnormal skin sensations, such as numbness, tingling, and burning (see PARESTHESIA), that are secondary to chronic alcoholism. The symptoms are similar to those of BERIBERI, suggesting that B-vitamin deficiency is a causative factor.

alcoholic psychosis in *DSM–II*, a category of mental disorders associated with the detrimental neurological effects of alcohol abuse. The equivalent *DSM–IV–TR* disorders include the following: ALCOHOL INTOXICATION DELIRIUM, ALCOHOL WITHDRAWAL DELIRIUM, ALCOHOL-INDUCED PSYCHOTIC DISORDER, ALCOHOL-INDUCED PERSISTING DEMENTIA, and ALCOHOL-INDUCED PERSISTING AMNESTIC DISORDER.

Alcoholics Anonymous (AA) a worldwide voluntary organization of men and women who, through a TWELVE-STEP PROGRAM, seek to help each other stay sober. The only requirement for membership is a desire to stop drinking. Supported by voluntary contributions of its members and groups, AA neither seeks nor accepts outside funding. Members observe personal anonymity at the public level, thus emphasizing AA principles rather than personalities. Founded in the United States in 1935, AA is the oldest, largest, and best-known self-help organization.

alcohol idiosyncratic intoxication in *DSM–III*, a condition characterized by marked behavioral change associated with consumption of an amount of alcohol usually insufficient to intoxicate most people. The idiosyncratic behavior is atypical of the individual when he or she is not drinking: For example, a quiet, shy person may become belligerent and assaultive. Although this diagnosis has been removed from *DSM–IV* because of its rarity, controversy over the decision to remove it remains.

alcohol-induced persisting amnestic disorder a disturbance in memory caused by the persisting effects of alcohol. The ability to learn new information or to recall previously learned information is impaired severely enough to interfere markedly with social or occupational functioning and to represent a significant decline from a previous level of functioning. See also KORSAKOFF'S SYNDROME; WERNICKE–KORSAKOFF SYNDROME.

alcohol-induced persisting dementia a deterioration of mental function resulting from the persisting effects of alcohol abuse. It is characterized by multiple COGNITIVE DEFICITS, especially of memory but also including impairment of speech (see APHASIA), movement (see APRAXIA), and sensory capabilities (see AGNOSIA), and EXECUTIVE DYSFUNCTION. Also called **alcoholic dementia**. See also SUBSTANCE-INDUCED PERSISTING DEMENTIA.

alcohol-induced psychotic disorder hallucinations or delusions due to the direct physiological effects of alcohol. Also called **alcoholic** (or **alcohol**) **hallucinosis**. See also SUBSTANCE-INDUCED PSYCHOTIC DISORDER.

alcohol intoxication a reversible condition that develops soon after the ingestion of alcohol. It comprises behavioral or psychological changes, such as inappropriate or aggressive behavior, impaired judgment, or impaired social functioning; and physiological changes, such as slurred speech, unsteady gait, and disruption of attention or memory. The effects typically become more marked with increased alcohol intake. See also SUBSTANCE INTOXICATION.

alcohol intoxication delirium a reversible syndrome that develops over a short period of time (usually hours to days) following heavy alcohol consumption. Disturbance of consciousness (e.g., reduced ability to focus, sustain, or shift attention) is accompanied by changes in cognition (e.g., memory deficit, disorientation, or language disturbance) in excess of those usually associated with ALCOHOL INTOXICATION. See also SUBSTANCE INTOXICATION DELIRIUM.

alcoholism *n.* see ALCOHOL DEPENDENCE.

alcoholism treatment interventions designed to enable the alcohol-dependent person either to achieve and maintain abstinence, which is the generally accepted goal of treatment for alcohol dependence, or to reach and maintain a stable pattern of nonproblem drinking, which is a controversial, less common goal of treatment. Also called **alcohol rehabilitation**.

alcohol withdrawal a withdrawal syndrome that develops after cessation of (or reduction in) prolonged, heavy alcohol consumption. Two or more of the following are required for a *DSM–IV–TR* diagnosis of alcohol withdrawal: (a) autonomic hyperactivity (sweating, pounding heart, dry mouth, etc.), (b) hand tremor, (c) insomnia, (d) nausea or vomiting, (e) hallucinations or illusions, (f) PSYCHOMOTOR AGITATION, (g) anxiety, and (h) tonic–clonic seizures. See also SUBSTANCE WITHDRAWAL.

alcohol withdrawal delirium a reversible syndrome that develops over a short period of time (usually hours to days) following cessation of prolonged, heavy alcohol consumption. The features are disturbed consciousness (e.g., reduced ability to focus, sustain, or shift attention) and changes in cognition (e.g., memory deficit, disorientation, or language disturbance) in excess of those usually associated with ALCOHOL WITHDRAWAL. See also DELIRIUM TREMENS.

aldolase (**ALS**) *n.* an enzyme found in muscle tissue, where it serves to split a complex sugar molecule. Excessive levels of aldolase in the blood may be an early indication of abnormal muscle function and a clue in the diagnosis of MUSCULAR DYSTROPHY.

Aldomet *n.* a trade name for METHYLDOPA.

aldosterone *n.* a MINERALOCORTICOID hormone secreted by the ADRENAL CORTEX. It helps to regulate mineral and water metabolism by promoting secretion of potassium and reabsorption of sodium in the kidneys. Production of aldosterone is regulated by the RENIN–ANGIOTENSIN SYSTEM.

aldosteronism *n.* a pathological condition caused by excess secretion of the CORTICOSTEROID hormone aldosterone. It is marked by headaches, urinary disturbances, fatigue, hypertension, and (in some cases) nerve damage, causing tingling sensations, muscle weakness, and transient paralysis. It may be primary (**Conn's syndrome**), due to an adrenocortical disorder, or secondary, as a result of a liver, heart, or kidney disease affecting the adrenal glands.

alert inactivity an INFANT STATE OF AROUSAL marked by facial relaxation, calm and even breathing, open, luminous eyes, and considerable visual exploration.

alerting correlation (symbol: r_{alerting}) the correlation between the MEANS and CONTRAST WEIGHTS of groups of experimental participants.

alerting device an ASSISTIVE TECHNOLOGY device that alerts individuals with hearing loss to the occurrence of an event that is typically signaled by auditory means, such as the ringing of a doorbell, the buzzing of an alarm clock, or the beeping of a smoke or fire alarm. It might employ extremely loud sounds, a flashing light, vibrations, or other nonauditory stimuli.

alerting mechanisms systems within the central nervous system that trigger a response or direct the attention of higher brain centers to possible threats. Most important is the arousal mechanism of the RETICULAR FORMATION in the brainstem.

alertness *n.* **1.** the state of being awake, aware, attentive, and prepared to act or react, as opposed to being inattentive or drowsy. **2.** in neurology, a high degree of cortical activity resulting from stimulation of the RETICULAR ACTIVATING SYSTEM. See also AROUSAL.

alexia *n.* a form of APHASIA that is manifested as the loss of a previously acquired ability to read written or printed words. It is associated with lesions, stroke, or other forms of brain injury or trauma. Also called **acquired dyslexia**; **visual aphasia**; **word blindness**. See also DYSLEXIA.

alexia with agraphia a form of acquired dyslexia (see ALEXIA) in which both reading and writing ability are impaired. Often, problems producing or comprehending speech are also present. The condition is thought to be associated with lesions of the ANGULAR GYRUS and may also be accompanied by lesions in the PARIETAL LOBE of the brain. See also PURE ALEXIA.

alexithymia *n.* an inability to express, describe, or distinguish between one's emotions. It may occur in a variety of disorders, especially psychosomatic and some substance use disorders, or following repeated exposure to a traumatic stressor.

Alfenta *n.* a trade name for alfentanil. See FENTANYL.

alfentanil *n.* see FENTANYL.

algebraic summation summation that takes into account the signs of the terms. Thus, when EXCITATORY POSTSYNAPTIC POTENTIALS and INHIBITORY POSTSYNAPTIC POTENTIALS are induced in a neuron, an ACTION POTENTIAL is evoked only if the excitatory potentials exceed the inhibitory potentials by at least a threshold amount.

algedonic *adj.* relating to pain associated with pleasure, or the pleasantness–unpleasantness dimension of experience. **Algedonics** is the study of the mixture of pleasure and pain.

algedonic aesthetics the concept that pleasure arises when sensory organs are in a hypernormal state of readiness to respond, and displeasure arises when they are in a hyponormal state of readiness. [formulated in the late 19th century by U.S. philosopher Henry R. Marshall (1852–1927)]

algesia *n.* the ability to experience the sensation of pain. Compare ANALGESIA.

algesimeter *n.* an instrument used to measure the sensitivity of an individual to pain. It contains a calibrated needle that is pressed against a body surface in order to determine the person's pain threshold. Also called **algesiometer**; **algometer**.

-algia *suffix* pain or a painful condition (e.g., NEURALGIA).

algo- (**alg-**) *combining form* pain.

algolagnia *n.* a sexual disorder in which sexual excitement is achieved by experiencing or inflicting pain. See ACTIVE ALGOLAGNIA; PASSIVE ALGOLAGNIA; SEXUAL MASOCHISM; SEXUAL SADISM.

algometer *n.* see ALGESIMETER.

algophilia *n.* liking for the experience or infliction of pain. See also ALGOLAGNIA; MASOCHISM; SADISM.

algopsychalia *n.* physical pain recognized by the patient as being of mental rather than physical origin, which sometimes accompanies mental difficulties (e.g., anxiety, schizophrenia, depression). See also PSYCHIC PAIN.

algorithm *n.* a precisely defined procedure or rule that is guaranteed to solve a particular problem or accomplish a particular task or that is used for conducting a series of computations. An example is trying all the possible combinations in sequence in order to open a combination lock. Algorithms, which may be represented visually as flow charts, are essential to computer programming and information processing. The word is derived from the name of the 9th-century Arab mathematician al-Khwarizmi. Compare HEURISTIC. See also BRITISH MUSEUM ALGORITHM; BRUTE FORCE; EXHAUSTIVE SEARCH. **—algorithmic** *adj.*

alias *n.* in statistics, a situation in which an effect is completely confounded with another effect in such a way that the two cannot be disentangled. For example, if one were examining weight gain in undernourished infants provided with high-protein food enriched with vitamins, it would not be possible to separate the effect of vitamin intake from the consumption of high-protein food. See CONFOUNDS.

Alice in Wonderland effect see METAMORPHOPSIA.

alien abduction a claim by individuals that they have been kidnapped by extraterrestrial beings. Although this phenomenon is commonly associated with delusional thinking, POSTTRAUMATIC STRESS DISORDER, and acute stress reactions, many of these individuals have no other clear symptoms of mental disorder. Historically, there is no conclusive physical evidence to support the validity of their claims. Also called **extraterrestrial kidnapping**.

alienatio mentis a legal term for INSANITY. [Latin, literally: "alienation of the mind"]

alienation *n.* **1.** estrangement from one's social group (e.g., family, workplace, community, school, or church). **2.** a deep-seated sense of dissatisfaction with one's personal experiences that can be a source of lack of trust in one's social or physical environment or in oneself. **3.** the experience of separation between thoughts and feelings, sometimes seen in OBSESSIVE-COMPULSIVE DISORDER and SCHIZOPHRENIA. **—alienated** *adj.*

alienation coefficient see COEFFICIENT OF ALIENATION.

alienation test an evaluation of an individual's feelings of estrangement or separation from his or her milieu, work, or self.

alien-hand syndrome a phenomenon in which an individual perceives his or her hand to be acting under its own control or to be "foreign." This is most often associated with lesions to the corpus callosum or frontal lobe.

alien limb syndrome a feature of UNILATERAL NEGLECT in which patients do not recognize, or may even disown, a limb as part of their body. Compare PHANTOM LIMB.

ALI Guidelines abbreviation for American Law Institute Guidelines (see AMERICAN LAW INSTITUTE MODEL PENAL CODE INSANITY TEST).

aliphatic phenothiazines PHENOTHIAZINE antipsychotic agents containing an aliphatic (fatty acid) side chain in their molecular structure. Including chlorpromazine, promazine, and triflupromazine, they are the least potent of the phenothiazines and are now rarely used.

alkalosis *n.* a pathological condition caused by an abnormally high level of alkalinity in the blood and tissues of the body. It also may result from a depletion of acids, thereby upsetting the body's acid-base balance. The condition is often marked by slow, shallow breathing but also may include such symptoms as muscle weakness, muscle twitching, confusion, irritability, and, in severe cases, convulsive seizures. Compare ACIDOSIS.

all- *combining form* see ALLO-.

allachesthesia *n.* the sensation of touch experienced in a place other than the point of stimulation. Also called **allesthesia**; **alloesthesia**. See also VISUAL ALLACHESTHESIA.

Allan Dent disease a form of moderate to severe mental retardation, often accompanied by tonic–clonic seizures in childhood. Clinical signs include sparse, dull, friable hair on the scalp and body. Large quantities of argininosuccinic acid are present in the urine. See also ARGININOSUCCINIC ACIDURIA.

allele *n.* one of the variant forms of a GENE at a particular locus (location) on each of the pairs of matching chromosomes inherited from the mother and father. Each person normally has two alleles for each gene, one inherited from each parent. Different alleles produce variation in inherited characteristics, such as hair color or blood type. See also DOMINANT ALLELE; RECESSIVE ALLELE.

allergen *n.* a normally harmless substance that is capable of producing an abnormal immune response in a sensitized individual (see ANTIGEN; ALLERGY). Allergens can be food items, house dust, animal dander (scales from hair or feathers), pollen, or tissues of another organism. **—allergenic** *adj.*

allergy *n.* a condition in which the body produces an abnormal or inappropriate IMMUNE RESPONSE to certain ANTIGENS (called ALLERGENS). In an allergic person the allergens stimulate the release of HISTAMINE, leading to inflammation and other symptoms. See also ANAPHYLAXIS. **—allergic** *adj.*

allesthesia *n.* see ALLACHESTHESIA.

alley maze an experimental device consisting of a series of enclosed and interconnected paths only one of which leads to a goal. It is used to study learning in rats or other nonhuman animals.

alley problem the conundrum posed by the apparent convergence of two parallel structures that extend from the viewer into the distance. Parallel rows of trees, railroad tracks, or walls of buildings forming an alley are all common stimuli that appear to meet in the distance. See also ILLUSION; LINEAR PERSPECTIVE.

alliaceous *adj.* in the ZWAARDEMAKER SMELL SYSTEM,

denoting an odor quality that is smelled in garlic and chlorine.

alliance *n.* in animal behavior, an association between two or more individuals that allows them collectively to control resources that one individual could not control alone. Two male primates of lower rank may act together to control resources that normally only the ALPHA MALE would control. A group of male lions (often related) will form an alliance to take over a pride of females from another male.

allied health professional (**AHP**) a licensed health care professional with specialized education and training who assists other professional staff in the prevention, treatment, and rehabilitation process.

allo- (**all-**) *combining form* difference or otherness.

allocation decision **1.** in DECISION THEORY, a choice in which an individual must decide how to distribute a limited resource across entities (e.g., hypothetical factories or hospitals). **2.** in group problem solving, the group's allocation of particular roles or jobs to individual members.

allocator *n.* in bargaining and GAME THEORY, the individual or group making the initial offer to the other party (the **acceptor** or **responder**).

allocentric **1.** *adj.* characterized by the focusing of interest or attention on other objects or people (i.e., not egocentric). **2.** *adj.* in anthropology, respecting the values and customs of other cultures (i.e., not ethnocentric). **3.** *n.* an individual who is dispositionally predisposed to put the goals and needs of the group above his or her own. Just as societies based on COLLECTIVISM stress connections among members and the welfare of the group, allocentrics emphasize their connections to others and are group-centered. They are more likely to join groups and to base their identities on their memberships. Also called **interdependent**. Compare IDIOCENTRIC. See also SOCIOCENTRISM. **—allocentrism** *n.*

allochiria (**allocheiria**) *n.* the transfer of pain or touch sensations to a point on the opposite side of the body corresponding to the place actually stimulated.

allochthonous *adj.* stemming from sources or forces external to a particular system: not indigenous or innate. Compare AUTOCHTHONOUS.

allocortex *n.* cerebral cortex that has fewer than the six CORTICAL LAYERS of NEOCORTEX. It includes the ARCHICORTEX and the PALEOCORTEX. Examples of allocortex are the three-layered DENTATE GYRUS and the CA1 region of the HIPPOCAMPUS.

alloeroticism *n.* the extension of erotic feelings toward and the derivation of sexual satisfaction from others, as opposed to AUTOEROTICISM. Also called **alloerotism**. **—alloerotic** *adj.*

alloesthesia *n.* see ALLACHESTHESIA.

allogrooming *n.* behavior that involves two or more individuals picking through each other's hair or feathers. Often thought to have a solely hygienic function (i.e., the removal of dirt and parasites), allogrooming has been shown to have positive social effects as well, through production of ENDOGENOUS OPIOIDS in recipients. It is thus a mechanism that reinforces social relationships.

allomone *n.* a chemical signal that is released outside the body by members of one species and affects the behavior of members of another species. Compare PHEROMONE.

allomorph *n.* in linguistics, any of several different speech sounds or written forms that are used to represent the same MORPHEME. For example, the [s] sound at the end of *cats* and the [z] sound at the end of *dogs* represent the same noun-plural morpheme and are therefore allomorphs. Similarly, in writing, the *-t* at the end of *burnt* and the *-ed* at the end of *turned* are allomorphs representing the same past-tense morpheme. **—allomorphic** *adj.*

alloparenting *n.* care of infants by individuals who are not their parents. It is seen especially among COOPERATIVE-BREEDING species where **alloparents** (also known as **helpers** or **helpers at the nest**) may provide essential services for infant survival.

allopathy *n.* a method of treating a disease or disorder by the use of agents, remedies, or situations that produce effects different from, or incompatible with, those caused by the disease or disorder. For example, in psychotherapy, it might include the use of relaxation in desensitizing a client to phobic situations (see DESENSITIZATION). Compare HOMEOPATHY. **—allopathic** *adj.*

allopatric *adj.* see SYMPATRIC SPECIES.

allophasis *n.* disorganized, incoherent speech.

allophone *n.* in linguistics, any of several slightly different speech sounds that are regarded as contextual variants of the same PHONEME. For example, in English the aspirated [p] sound at the beginning of *paid* and the unaspirated [p] sound in *spade* have no contrastive function in the phonological system of the language and are therefore regarded as allophones of the same phoneme, /p/. **—allophonic** *adj.*

alloplasty *n.* **1.** a process of adaptive response that aims to alter the environment, as opposed to altering the self. Also called **alloplastic adaptation**. **2.** surgical repair of diseased or damaged tissue through implantation using synthetic or organic material from outside the patient's body. Compare AUTOPLASTY. **—alloplastic** *adj.*

allopregnenolone *n.* a naturally occurring steroid that modulates $GABA_A$ RECEPTOR activity in a manner similar to that of BENZODIAZEPINE anxiolytics.

allopsychic delusion see AUTOPSYCHIC DELUSION.

all-or-none law the principle that the amplitude of the ACTION POTENTIAL in a given neuron is independent of the magnitude of the stimulus. Stimuli above a certain threshold trigger action potentials of identical magnitude (although they may vary in frequency); stimuli below this threshold may produce local GRADED POTENTIALS but no propagated impulses. Also called **all-or-none principle**. See also NONDECREMENTAL CONDUCTION.

all-or-none learning hypothesis the theory that, in any given learning trial, learning occurs either completely and fully or not at all. The all-or-none learning hypothesis contrasts with a trial-by-trial increment theory of learning (see CONTINUITY HYPOTHESIS).

allosteric modulation the binding of a substance (called an **allosteric modulator**) to a certain site on a RECEPTOR complex in a way that affects the binding of other agents (e.g., neurotransmitters, drugs) to their receptor sites on the same complex. Allosteric modulators alter the conformation of the target receptor site, thereby increasing or decreasing the affinity of the receptor for other molecules. For example, binding of benzodiazepines on one site of the GABA–benzodiazepine receptor complex increases the binding capability of GABA at other sites on the receptor complex (see GABA AGONISTS).

allotriogeusia (**allotriogeustia**) *n.* **1.** an abnormal sense of taste. **2.** an abnormal appetite. See ALLOTRIOPHAGY; DYSGEUSIA.

allotriophagy *n.* a desire to eat inappropriate foods or nonnutritive substances. Also called **allotriophagia**. See also PICA.

all-payer system a health care system in which prices for health care services and payment methods are the same regardless of who is paying (e.g., the patient or an insurance company). Also called **multipayer system**.

Allport, Gordon Willard (1897–1967) U.S. psychologist. Allport received his PhD from Harvard University in 1922. He is widely recognized as the originator of a theory of personality based on three categories of traits (see ALLPORT'S PERSONALITY TRAIT THEORY) and as coauthor of two personality inventories, the ALLPORT–VERNON–LINDZEY STUDY OF VALUES and the Allport AS Reaction Study. Allport was also a major contributor to the field of social psychology, emphasizing the role of attitudes in motivation and making major theoretical contributions to the study of prejudice. See also DIRECTEDNESS; FUNCTIONAL AUTONOMY; GROUP RELATIONS THEORY; HUMANISTIC PERSPECTIVE; PERSONALISTIC PSYCHOLOGY; PERSONALITY STRUCTURE; PROPRIATE STRIVING; PROPRIUM; SELF-EXTENSION; SELF-OBJECTIFICATION.

Allport's personality trait theory the theory that an individual's PERSONALITY TRAITS are the key to the uniqueness and consistency of his or her behavior. Traits are regarded as dynamic forces that interact with each other and the environment to determine the characteristic actions or reactions that define the self (see PROPRIUM). They develop largely from experience, learning, and imitation and fall into three main categories: (a) cardinal traits or master qualities (e.g., overweening ambition); (b) central traits, or clusters of distinctive attitudes and characteristics; and (c) secondary traits, which are more limited and not essential to personality description. [Gordon W. ALLPORT]

Allport–Vernon–Lindzey Study of Values (**SOV**) a two-part personality test designed to show the relative importance of six basic values in the participant's life: theoretical, economic, aesthetic, social, political, and religious. The categories are based on SPRANGER'S TYPOLOGY and presented in the form of 45 items to which participants respond. Part one consists of 30 statements, each describing a situation with two alternative choices; participants must choose which option they prefer and indicate the strength of that preference by distributing three points between the two alternatives. Part two consists of 15 questions, each with four alternative answers; participants must rank the answers in order of preference. The SOV was originally published in 1931 as the **Allport–Vernon Study of Values** but in 1951 was revised and renamed. The most recent version of the test was published in 1960. Also called **Study of Values**. [Gordon W. ALLPORT; Philip E. **Vernon** (1905–1987), British psychologist; Gardner **Lindzey** (1920–), U.S. psychologist]

allusive thinking a type of thinking marked by inference and suggestion rather than traditional logic and direct communication of ideas. The concepts employed may seem diffuse and indistinct. See also ANALOGICAL THINKING.

alogia *n.* inability to speak because of dysfunction in the central nervous system. In a less severe form, it is sometimes referred to as **dyslogia**.

alpha (symbol: α) *n.* the probability of a TYPE I ERROR.

L-alpha-acetyl-methadol *n.* see LAAM.

alpha adrenoreceptor a receptor that binds NOREPINEPHRINE and causes stimulation of smooth muscle in responses of the SYMPATHETIC NERVOUS SYSTEM, such as pupil dilation and increased vascular resistance (see VASOCONSTRICTION). There are two types, α_1-adrenoreceptors and α_2-adrenoreceptors, each of which is divided into subtypes designated by subscript capital letters (α_{1A}-adrenoreceptor, α_{2A}-adrenoreceptor, etc.). Also called **alpha adrenergic receptor**; **alpha adrenoceptor**; **alpha receptor**. Compare BETA ADRENORECEPTOR.

alpha-adrenoreceptor blocking agents see ADRENORECEPTOR BLOCKING AGENTS.

alpha alcoholism the first stage of alcoholism. It is characterized by undisciplined drinking and psychological dependence on the effects of alcohol for the relief of physical or psychological pain, but it does not involve losing control or inability to abstain. See also BETA ALCOHOLISM; GAMMA ALCOHOLISM; DELTA ALCOHOLISM; EPSILON ALCOHOLISM. [defined by U.S. physician Elvin M. Jellinek (1890–1963)]

alphabet *n.* a set of letters or signs, usually listed in a fixed order, that are used to represent the basic speech sounds of a language in writing. In linguistics, the term is restricted to those writing systems in which the symbols represent individual PHONEMES rather than syllables. Compare SYLLABARY. **—alphabetical** *adj.*

alpha biofeedback see ALPHA-WAVE TRAINING.

alpha-block conditioning the training of humans or other animals to block ALPHA WAVES by reinforcement or biofeedback. See ALPHA BLOCKING.

alpha blockers see ADRENORECEPTOR BLOCKING AGENTS.

alpha blocking the suppression of ALPHA WAVES by an unexpected stimulus or an active mental task, sometimes taken as an indicator of orienting or attention. Typically, blocked alpha waves are replaced by faster, irregular, low-voltage waves on the electroencephalogram. See DESYNCHRONIZATION.

alpha coefficient see CRONBACH'S ALPHA.

alpha-endorphin *n.* a polypeptide containing 16 amino acids whose behavioral significance is unknown. See ENDORPHINS.

alpha error see TYPE I ERROR.

Alpha examination see ARMY TESTS.

alpha female the top-ranked or dominant female within a group, with primary access to resources, including food and mates. In some species the alpha female inhibits reproduction among other females.

alpha-fetoprotein (**α-fetoprotein**; **AFP**) *n.* a protein found in the blood plasma of fetuses and produced by some tumors in adult humans. In rodents alpha-fetoprotein binds estrogens and prevents them from entering the brain, thus influencing sexual differentiation. In adult humans, measurement of alpha-fetoprotein is used to diagnose liver cancer. See also ALPHA-FETOPROTEIN TEST.

alpha-fetoprotein test a prenatal diagnostic test for risk of fetal abnormality in which a sample of blood is drawn from the pregnant woman and analyzed for the presence of ALPHA-FETOPROTEIN. Levels of this protein that are abnormally high or abnormally low suggest an abnormality in the fetus.

alpha fiber see ALPHA MOTOR NEURON.

alpha level see SIGNIFICANCE LEVEL.

alpha male the top-ranked or dominant male within a group, with primary access to resources, including food and mates. In many species the alpha male prevents other males from mating or from mating during the peak time of female fertility.

alpha-melanocyte stimulating hormone (**α-MSH**) a form of MELANOCYTE-STIMULATING HORMONE that binds the MELANOCORTIN-4 RECEPTOR and is involved in diverse functions, such as regulation of feeding and sexual function.

alpha-methylparatyrosine (**AMPT**) a drug that inhibits the synthesis, from the amino acid tyrosine, of the catecholamine neurotransmitters DOPAMINE, NOREPINEPHRINE, and EPINEPHRINE. It is sometimes used to treat catecholamine-secreting tumors of the adrenal gland (e.g., PHEOCHROMOCYTOMA). **Alpha-methyltyrosine** has a similar action.

alpha motor neuron a MOTOR NEURON that controls the main contractile fibers (EXTRAFUSAL FIBERS) of a muscle. Also called **alpha fiber**. Compare GAMMA EFFERENT NEURON.

alpha movement a form of APPARENT MOVEMENT in which an object appears to expand or contract when increasingly larger or smaller versions of it are presented in rapid succession. Also called **alpha motion**.

alpha-MSH (**α-MSH**) abbreviation for ALPHA-MELANOCYTE STIMULATING HORMONE.

alpha rhythm see ALPHA WAVE.

alpha state a state of relaxed wakefulness achieved by individuals who produce increased ALPHA WAVES. Alpha state may occur or be increased as a result of biofeedback training (see ALPHA-WAVE TRAINING), meditation, yoga, hypnosis, and other calmly focused activities.

Alpha test see ARMY TESTS.

alpha wave in electroencephalography, a type of low-amplitude BRAIN WAVE (frequency 8–12 Hz) often recorded from the scalp above the occipital cortex. Alpha waves typically occur when the eyes are unfocused and no active mental processes are taking place: They are often taken to indicate a wakeful but relaxed state. The occurrence of alpha waves may be increased through biofeedback training (see ALPHA-WAVE TRAINING) or meditation, for example. Also called **alpha rhythm**; **Berger rhythm**.

alpha-wave training a type of BIOFEEDBACK TRAINING in which clients learn to achieve a state of peaceful wakefulness and relaxation by increasing their ALPHA WAVES. The technique usually involves **alpha biofeedback**, the process of providing a feedback stimulus (typically an auditory tone) when alpha waves appear on the electroencephalogram (EEG). See also ALPHA STATE.

Alport's syndrome a familial condition characterized by hematuria (bloody urine), nephropathy (disease of the kidney), and deafness. Hematuria may first appear in infancy, while deafness is likely to develop around the age of puberty. The condition also may be accompanied by cataracts and mental retardation. It is caused by mutation of the genes *COL4A3*, *COL4A4*, *COL4A5*, or *COL4A6*, which specify chains of basement membrane (Type IV) collagen. [described in 1927 by Arthur Cecil **Alport** (1879–1959), British physician]

alprazolam *n.* a BENZODIAZEPINE anxiolytic drug characterized by rapid absorption and distribution and a relatively brief duration of action (an extended-release preparation is now available). It is used for the treatment of generalized anxiety. U.S. trade names (among others): **Xanax**; **Xanax SR**.

ALS 1. abbreviation for ALDOLASE. **2.** abbreviation for AMYOTROPHIC LATERAL SCLEROSIS.

als ob as if (German). The phrase is associated with the thought of German philosopher Hans Vaihinger (1852–1933), who proposed that certain "fictions," such as free will, immortality, and objective morality, should be supported and lived as if (*als ob*) they were true, because there is biological advantage in doing so. Vaihinger's work influenced that of Alfred ADLER. See also AS-IF PERSONALITY.

Alström–Hallgren syndrome a familial disorder characterized by obesity, deafness, visual disorders, and diabetes and occasionally associated with mental disorders. [Carl Henry **Alström** (1907–), Swedish physician; Bertil **Hallgren**, 20th-century Swedish geneticist]

ALT abbreviation for ALTERNATIVE SCHEDULE OF REINFORCEMENT.

alter *n.* **1.** any of the SECONDARY PERSONALITIES in a person with DISSOCIATIVE IDENTITY DISORDER. **2.** the other person in a social interaction.

alteration hypothesis the hypothesis that false or misleading information introduced after a witnessed event replaces, transforms, or impairs the original memory of the event, leading to erroneous reporting of that event. Also called **substitution hypothesis**; **overwritten hypothesis**. Compare COEXISTENCE HYPOTHESIS.

altercasting *n.* imposing identities and social roles on others, usually by treating them in ways that are consistent with the imposed identity or role. **—altercast** *vb.*

altered lovemap see LOVEMAP.

altered state of consciousness (**ASC**) a state of psychological functioning that is significantly different from ordinary states of CONSCIOUSNESS, being characterized by altered levels of self-awareness, affect, reality testing, orientation to time and place, wakefulness, responsiveness to external stimuli, or memorability or by a sense of ecstasy, boundlessness, or unity with the universe. Superficial ASCs—such as staring into space, being engrossed in reading a book or watching a movie, and lack of awareness due to repetitive, monotonous activity—are typically accompanied by disturbed temporal sense, constriction of perception, or a feeling of deep pleasurable involvement. Some individuals recounting the occurrence of more profound ASCs—as in meditation, hypnosis, sensory deprivation, or some drug-induced states—have noted the experience of mystical feelings, such as partaking in universal oneness, enhanced or complete understanding, or sensing the presence of the divine. Reporting of the experience of ASCs is highly subjective, but the phenomenon is susceptible to some degree of scientific study. Although, in some instances, ASCs are symptomatic of mental disorder (e.g., psychoanalysis has tended to regard them as regressive phenomena), in other contexts, such as in certain Eastern philosophies and TRANSPERSONAL PSYCHOLOGY, they are regarded as higher states of consciousness and, often, as indicative of a more profound level of personal and spiritual evolution.

alter ego 1. a second identity or aspect of a person that exists metaphorically as his or her substitute or representative, with different characteristics. **2.** an intimate, supportive friend with whom an individual can share all types of problems and experiences, as if he or she were "another self." **3.** in psychodrama, a group member, other than the therapist, who assumes the role of a significant figure in the PROTAGONIST's life (see AUXILIARY EGO) but who also speaks as part of the protagonist in order to give voice to and portray actions felt but not expressed by the protagonist.

alter-egoism *n.* an altruistic concern or a feeling of empathy for another person in the same situation as oneself.

alternate binaural loudness-balance test a test for abnormal sensitivity to loud sounds (see RECRUITMENT). The individual hears two tones of the same frequency played alternately into the two ears, but the intensity of the sound at one ear is set at a level 20 dB higher than the other. If the individual perceives the two sounds as having the same loudness, it indicates that one ear is more sensitive to loudness.

alternate form a scale of items so closely similar to another scale that each is considered a different version of the same test. Also called **alternate test form**; **parallel form**.

alternate-forms reliability the RELIABILITY of a measure as estimated from the correlation between parallel forms of the measure. Also called **comparable-forms reliability**.

alternate-response test a test requiring the participant to choose the correct response from two alternatives, such as true or false.

alternate-uses test a test of DIVERGENT THINKING that requires the participant to cite as many uses as possible for a specified object other than its common use. For example, a newspaper could be used for starting a fire or packing objects in a box.

alternating personality a personality with components that appear alternately. See DISSOCIATIVE IDENTITY DISORDER.

alternating perspective the abrupt transition from one perspective to another that occurs when an AMBIGUOUS FIGURE is viewed. Only one perspective can be perceived at a given time. See NECKER CUBE; REVERSIBLE FIGURE; RUBIN'S FIGURE.

alternating role shifting periodically from one pattern of behavior to another, for example, from an authoritarian to a democratic role and back to an authoritarian role.

alternation *n.* **1.** in experimental research, a pattern in which one event alternates with another. For example, in an OPERANT CONDITIONING experiment, a reinforced trial (R) may alternate with a nonreinforced trial (N), yielding the pattern RNRNRN.... **2.** the pattern of behavior produced by this schedule, which is stronger responding on R than on N trials. See also DOUBLE ALTERNATION.

alternation learning **1.** a learning task in which an individual must learn to alternate responses, never making the same response twice in a row. **2.** alternation of reward and nonreward for a single response. In this case, responding is faster for a reward than it is when no reward is available.

alternation method a technique used in studies of thinking, language, and problem solving among nonhuman animals and humans, in which the participant is required to follow an increasingly complex sequence of activities in order to reach a goal or receive a reward. An example is RRR LLL, or triple alternation: turning right three times, then left three times.

alternative behavior completion a technique in BEHAVIOR THERAPY for extinguishing unwanted habits by substituting an incompatible behavior for the nondesired behavior (e.g., substituting nail care for nail biting). This technique can be practiced in vivo (see IN VIVO DESENSITIZATION) or imaginally in the therapy session or assigned as homework. It is often used as an alternative to mild AVERSION THERAPY. See also COMPETING RESPONSE TRAINING.

alternative brain process theory the hypothesis that in some cases of brain damage another part of the brain assumes the functions of the damaged part. Also called **vicarious brain process hypothesis**. See also FUNCTIONAL PLASTICITY; VICARIOUS FUNCTION.

alternative dispute resolution the resolving of disputes between parties using neutral third parties, who act as arbitrators or mediators, rather than by engaging in a lawsuit.

alternative educational system any nontraditional or unconventional learning environment in which information, instruction, or education is given.

alternative hypothesis (symbol: H_1) a statement that experimental effects or relationships between variables exist. The alternative hypothesis is accepted when the NULL HYPOTHESIS is rejected at a predetermined SIGNIFICANCE LEVEL.

alternative medicine see COMPLEMENTARY AND ALTERNATIVE MEDICINE.

alternative psychology any approach to understanding psychological issues that ignores or rejects accepted academic, scientific, or mainstream views. These approaches may involve unorthodox metaphysical assumptions and focus on spiritualistic and mystical influences. Emphasis may be on aspects of human thought, feeling, and actions that are ignored by mainstream psychology.

alternative psychotherapy any treatment approach not considered to be within the mainstream of psychotherapy. For example, the use of LSD PSYCHOTHERAPY in the 1960s was considered alternative. PRIMAL THERAPY and REICHIAN ANALYSIS are also considered alternative approaches by most therapists.

alternative schedule of reinforcement (**ALT**) a technique in which reinforcement of a maintained response occurs according to either a FIXED-RATIO SCHEDULE or a FIXED-INTERVAL SCHEDULE, whichever is satisfied first.

alternative school any nontraditional or unconventional institution in which instruction is given to students.

alternative sentencing the imposition of sanctions other than traditional imprisonment on those convicted of crimes. Examples of alternative sentencing include shock incarceration programs (see SHOCK PROBATION), electronic monitoring, and group homes. Also called **community correction**.

altitude sickness illness resulting from oxygen deficiency at high altitudes (see HYPOXIA). Symptoms include nausea, breathlessness, nosebleed, and impaired mental processes. Also called **Acosta's syndrome**; **Acosta's disease**; **D'Acosta's syndrome**; **hypobaropathy**; **mountain-climber's syndrome**; **mountain sickness**. See also ACUTE MOUNTAIN SICKNESS.

altitude test a type of assessment or examination intended to calculate an individual's ability in a particular area as indicated by the level of performance that the individual can attain.

altricial *adj.* describing animals, such as primates (including humans), that are not fully developed at birth and hence require considerable and sustained PARENTAL BEHAVIOR or ALLOPARENTING beyond nursing or feeding in order to survive. Compare PRECOCIAL.

altruism *n.* an apparently unselfish concern for others or behavior that provides benefit to others at some cost to the individual. In contrast to selfishness, altruism represents a need to help or assist others, without regard to rewards or returned favors. In animal behavior it is difficult to understand how altruism could evolve since NATURAL SELECTION operates on individuals. However, organisms displaying altruism can benefit if they help their relatives (see KIN SELECTION) or if an altruistic act is subsequently reciprocated (see RECIPROCAL ALTRUISM). **—altruistic** *adj.* **—altruist** *n.*

altruistic aggression a form of ANIMAL AGGRESSION in which the aggressor defends not itself but other group or family members.

altruistic behavior behavior performed for the benefit of others. Altruistic behavior covers a wide range of actions, including expressions of interest, support, and sympathy; special favors performed for others; active defense of the rights of the oppressed or deprived; VOLUNTEERISM; and martyrdom (see ALTRUISTIC SUICIDE). The degree to which altruistic behavior is true—that is, without egoistic motivation—is subject to much debate. See also EGOISTIC HELPING; EMPATHY–ALTRUISM HELPING; HELPING BEHAVIOR; PROSOCIAL BEHAVIOR.

altruistic suicide suicide committed, or suicidal actions undertaken, in the belief that this will benefit the group or serve a greater good, as exemplified by terrorist suicide bombings, the Japanese KAMIKAZE attacks of World War II, or suicides by older adults who believe they are a burden to their families. Altruistic suicide is generally committed by members of highly integrated groups. See also MASS SUICIDE. [defined by French sociologist Emile Durkheim (1858–1917)]

alveolar 1. *adj.* denoting a speech sound made with the tongue touching or near the upper ALVEOLAR RIDGE, for example, [d], [t], [n], or [s]. See also DENTAL; INTERDENTAL. **2.** *n.* an alveolar speech sound.

alveolar ridge the bony ridge of either the upper or lower jawbones that contains the sockets of the teeth (i.e., the alveoli).

Alzheimer's disease a progressive neurological disease due to widespread degeneration of brain cells, with the formation of SENILE PLAQUES and NEUROFIBRILLARY TANGLES. The most common cause of DEMENTIA (called **dementia of the Alzheimer's type** in *DSM–IV–TR*), it is characterized by progressive memory and other cognitive impairments that cause a significant decline in social or occupational functioning. The age of onset is usually (but not always) after 65 years and prevalence doubles approximately every 5 years between the ages of 65 and 85. The presence of the ApoE4 allele (see APOLIPOPROTEIN E) on chromosome 19 is a major risk factor. [first described in 1907 by Alois **Alzheimer** (1864–1915), German neurologist]

Alzheimer's Disease and Related Disorders Association, Inc. an organization that provides support groups, assistance, and information for caregivers of patients with Alzheimer's disease.

Alzheimer's facilities facilities designed to augment the treatment of people who have Alzheimer's disease and assist their caregivers. Features may include, for example, small social areas (e.g., dining rooms, recreation areas) that are furnished in a style historically familiar to the residents; well-controlled walkways and spaces, with adequate markers for spatial orientation, that allow for safe wandering; and reduced levels of noise and other distraction.

amacrine cells a diverse class of neurons in the RETINA that make lateral connections between RETINAL BIPOLAR CELLS, RETINAL GANGLION CELLS, and other amacrine cells. Amacrine cells contribute to the CENTER–SURROUND ANTAGONISM of retinal ganglion cell receptive fields. However, they have no axons and do not contribute directly to the output of the retina.

amae *n.* a state of dependency in which people expect others to perform actions for them that they could actually perform for themselves. Amae differs from true dependency in that a person who is truly dependent may not be able to perform the relevant action. Amae is often said to constitute a fundamental component of the prototypical Japanese personality. [first described by Japanese psychologist Takeo Doi (1920–)]

Amalric's syndrome a condition in which deafness is associated with defects in central vision.

amantadine *n.* an ANTIVIRAL DRUG that is also a DOPAMINE-RECEPTOR AGONIST and is occasionally used to ameliorate the EXTRAPYRAMIDAL EFFECTS of antipsychotic drugs active at dopamine receptors. U.S. trade name: **Symmetrel**.

amative intercourse sexual intercourse that occurs as part of a loving, caring relationship. This is distinguished from sexual activity between people who neither know each other nor have an emotional relationship (e.g., a prostitute and a client).

amaurosis *n.* partial or complete loss of sight without evidence of organic abnormality of the affected eye or eyes. The cause is often damage to the optic nerve or the brain. The condition may be hereditary, as in LEBER'S DISEASE; transient (see AMAUROSIS FUGAX); part of a syndrome, such as TAY–SACHS DISEASE; or the result of complete destruction of the STRIATE CORTEX (**cortical amaurosis**). See also FUNCTIONAL BLINDNESS.

amaurosis fugax recurrent episodes of visual loss, which can be caused by, among other things, glaucoma, intoxication, optic neuritis, migraine, or retinal vascular disease. The visual loss is painless and usually lasts 2–3 min; recovery of vision is more gradual, marked by gray, blurred, or hazy vision. Also called **transient monocular blindness**.

amazon *n.* any strong, dominant, or aggressive woman. In Greek mythology, the Amazons are a race of female warriors. In ancient Greece, the name was understood to mean "breastless" (Greek *a* + *maza*, without breast), and the story was told that the Amazons removed the right breast so as not to impede their ability to throw the javelin.

ambenomium *n.* an anticholinesterase (see CHOLINERGIC DRUGS) that can be taken orally to relieve the symptoms of MYASTHENIA GRAVIS. U.S. trade name: **Mytelase**.

ambi- *prefix* both.

ambidextrous *adj.* able to use either hand with equal skill.

Ambien *n.* a trade name for ZOLPIDEM.

ambience (**ambiance**) *n.* an environment or milieu: the context and surroundings of an event or situation, particularly as they influence its emotional effect and the appreciation of it. **—ambient** *adj.*

ambient awareness awareness of unattended aspects of visual and auditory scenes. A unique stimulus element is processed at some level even when attention is engaged elsewhere.

ambient conditions the physical variables in a particular environment (e.g., temperature, humidity, air quality, noise level, and intensity of light) that, taken as a whole, create an atmosphere that may evoke a distinct feeling or mood. Ambient conditions can be distinguished from specific elements of the environment.

ambient light the naturally available light that illuminates or surrounds an object or other element within an environment or physical context.

ambiguity *n.* **1.** in linguistics, the property of a word, phrase, or sentence that has more than one possible meaning. Ambiguity in a phrase or sentence may be lexical, as in *The students are revolting,* or structural, as in *black cats and dogs*; often there is a combination of both factors. In PSYCHOLINGUISTICS, the main area of interest has been the process used to interpret sentences whose SURFACE STRUCTURE could reflect two quite different DEEP STRUCTURES, as in the instruction *Before opening tin, stand in boiling water for ten minutes*. In psychoanalytic theory, ambiguous words or phrases are usually interpreted as a symptom of the speaker's hidden feelings or unconscious wishes about the subject. See also HOMONYM; POLYSEMY; PUN. **2.** the property of a behavior, behavior pattern, or situation that might lead to interpretation in more than one way. **—ambiguous** *adj.*

ambiguity scale any questionnaire used in evaluating tolerance or intolerance for vagueness, ambiguity, and indefiniteness.

ambiguity tolerance see TOLERANCE OF AMBIGUITY.

ambiguous figure a figure that can be interpreted in different ways, or in which the perspective appears to change. See ALTERNATING PERSPECTIVE; NECKER CUBE; RABBIT–DUCK FIGURE; RUBIN'S FIGURE.

ambiguous genitalia sex organs that are not fully differentiated, as in girls born with a clitoris that could be mistaken for a penis. See also HERMAPHRODITE.

ambiguous stimulus a stimulus in any sensory modality that can be interpreted in more than one way. See BISTABLE PERCEPTUAL EVENTS.

ambisexual *adj.* **1.** denoting individuals or characteristics that manifest no sex or gender dominance. Compare ASEXUAL. **2.** an older term for bisexual (see BISEXUALITY), now rarely used. **—ambisexuality** *n.*

ambitendency *n.* **1.** the tendency to act in opposite ways, based on conflicting behavioral motivations. **2.** a pattern of incomplete motor responses in anticipation of a voluntary action. It occurs in catatonic states as a type of PSYCHOMOTOR RETARDATION in which the individual appears motorically stuck and exhibits hesitant, indecisive motions in the absence of voluntary movement. **3.** in Jungian psychology, the psychic ambivalence that is caused by the existence of opposing tendencies.

ambivalence *n.* **1.** the simultaneous existence of contradictory feelings and attitudes, such as pleasantness and unpleasantness or friendliness and hostility, toward the same person, object, event, or situation. Conflicting feelings are often strong toward parents, since they are agents of both discipline and affection. Swiss psychiatrist Eugen Bleuler (1857–1939), who first defined ambivalence in a psychological sense and referred to it as **affective ambivalence**, regarded extreme ambivalence, such as an individual expressing great love for his or her mother while also asking how to kill her, as a major symptom of schizophrenia. **2.** uncertainty or indecisiveness about a course of action. **—ambivalent** *adj.*

ambivalence of an attitude the extent to which the evaluative responses associated with an attitude are inconsistent with one another. If the evaluative responses are uniformly positive or uniformly negative, ambivalence is low. If both positive and negative responses are associated with the attitude, ambivalence is high. See also AFFECTIVE–COGNITIVE CONSISTENCY; AFFECTIVE–EVALUATIVE CONSISTENCY; COGNITIVE–EVALUATIVE CONSISTENCY; CROSS-DIMENSION ATTITUDE CONSISTENCY; WITHIN-DIMENSION ATTITUDE CONSISTENCY.

ambivalent attachment in the STRANGE SITUATION, a form of INSECURE ATTACHMENT in which infants show a combination of positive and negative responses toward a parent. After separation, for example, infants may simultaneously seek and resist close contact with the returning parent. Also called **resistant attachment**.

ambivalent sexism a type of SEXISM that is characterized by the coexistence of negative and positive attitudes toward one of the two sexes. For example, such attitudes toward women might involve fear and hostility on the one hand and an exaggerated chivalry and protectiveness on the other.

ambiversion *n.* the tendency to display characteristics of introversion and extraversion in approximately equal degrees. Such a person would be referred to as an **ambivert**.

ambly- *combining form* deficient or impaired.

amblyacousia *n.* dullness of hearing.

amblyopia *n.* poor vision in the absence of any organic defect of the eye. See CEREBRAL AMBLYOPIA; DEVELOPMENTAL AMBLYOPIA; FUNCTIONAL AMBLYOPIA; LAZY EYE; MERIDIONAL AMBLYOPIA.

amblyoscope *n.* an instrument used to determine the angle of deviation of the eyes (the degree of STRABISMUS), as well as the extent to which the eyes can be used together even though one or both are deviated. Also called **orthoptoscope**.

ambrosiac *adj.* in the ZWAARDEMAKER SMELL SYSTEM, denoting an odor quality that is smelled in musk and sandalwood. Also called **ambrosial**.

ambulation *n.* the act of walking from place to place. Ambulation training often is necessary in the rehabilitation of individuals who have had a spinal injury, stroke, or other trauma affecting the neuromuscular system and in the physical therapy of individuals with certain genetic or congenital disorders.

ambulatory care medical or psychological services provided to individuals on an outpatient, nonemergency basis. Such services may include observation, diagnosis, treatment (referred to as **ambulatory treatment**), and rehabilitation and are often provided at such places as a doctor's office, health center, or hospital outpatient department.

ambulatory psychotherapy psychological treatment on an outpatient basis.

ambulatory schizophrenia a condition in which a person who was previously hospitalized from extreme symptoms and then diagnosed as having schizophrenia no longer requires hospitalization but nonetheless behaves eccentrically and cannot function in a manner consistent with social expectations.

ambulatory services mental health, counseling, or medical services provided on an outpatient basis, that is, without the client needing to be in or remain in a hospital, clinic, or other provider facility. See also WALK-IN CLINIC.

ambulatory treatment see AMBULATORY CARE.

amelioration *n.* a change for the better in the severity of a disease or disorder, or a reduction of the intensity of its symptoms. **—ameliorative** *adj., n.*

amenity move a type of residence change, often occurring around the time of retirement, that is made to improve the quality of one's life.

amenorrhea *n.* the absence of menstruation during the period from puberty to menopause. When menstruation fails to begin after puberty, the condition is called **primary amenorrhea**. If menstrual periods stop, in the absence of pregnancy or menopause, after starting, the condition is known as **secondary amenorrhea**. Changes in physical or mental health can be a causal factor.

American Academy of Clinical Sexologists (**AACS**) an institution founded in 1986 as the educational arm of the American Board of Sexology. Since 1995 it has provided professional training for sex therapists at Maimonides University, Miami Beach, Florida.

American Alliance for Health, Physical Education, Recreation and Dance (**AAHPERD**) an alliance of six organizations (American Association for Active Lifestyles and Fitness, American Association for Health Education, American Association for Leisure and Recreation, National Association for Girls and Women in Sport, National Association for Sport and Physical Education, and National Dance Association) whose purpose is to promote healthy lifestyles through quality programs in physical and health education, recreation, dance, and sport. The primary focus of the alliance is the professionals in each field.

American Association for Counseling and Development (**AACD**) the former name for the AMERICAN COUNSELING ASSOCIATION.

American Association for the Advancement of Science (**AAAS**) a professional organization, founded in 1848 to represent all scientific disciplines, whose mission is to "advance science and innovation throughout the world for the benefit of all people." AAAS promotes education in, public understanding of, and responsible conduct and use of science and technology. The world's largest general scientific society, it publishes the journal *Science*.

American Association of Applied and Preventive Psychology (**AAAPP**) a professional organization whose purpose is to promote the interests of clinical and preventive psychology. It encourages a research orientation toward clinical and preventive work, emphasizing the consumer and public interest above guild or personal interests. Its main publication is the journal *Applied and Preventive Psychology: Current Scientific Perspectives*.

American Association of Applied Psychology (**AAAP**) a professional organization founded in 1937 by a group of consulting, clinical, educational, and industrial psychologists who broke from the AMERICAN PSYCHOLOGICAL ASSOCIATION in order to represent the applied interests of U.S. psychologists more effectively. Their main publication was the *Journal of Consulting Psychology*. In 1944 the group rejoined the American Psychological Association.

American Association of Clinical Psychologists (**AACP**) a professional organization founded in 1917 when clinical psychologists broke from the AMERICAN PSYCHOLOGICAL ASSOCIATION in order to promote training and certification standards for the practice of clinical psychology. The AACP returned to the American Psychological Association in 1919 as its first special-interest group, the Section of Clinical Psychology.

American Association of Mental Retardation (**AAMR**) a professional organization, founded in 1876, whose mission is to promote progressive policies, sound research, and effective practices in the field of mental retardation, together with universal human rights for people with intellectual disabilities. It is the oldest and largest interdisciplinary organization in this field.

American Association of Sex Educators, Counselors and Therapists (**AASECT**) a nonprofit, interdisciplinary, professional accrediting organization founded in 1967 whose mission is to provide professional education and certification of sex educators, counselors, and therapists and to promote understanding of human sexuality and healthy sexual behavior.

American Birth Control League (**ABCL**) a voluntary organization to promote birth control via public education, legislative reform, medical contraceptive research, and provision of services. In 1942 it was renamed the PLANNED PARENTHOOD FEDERATION OF AMERICA. [founded in 1921 by U.S. birth control pioneer Margaret Sanger (1883–1966)]

American Board of Medical Specialties (**ABMS**) the umbrella organization for 24 approved medical specialty boards in the United States. Established in 1933, its mission is to maintain and improve the quality of medical care in the United States by assisting the member boards in their efforts to develop and utilize professional and educational standards for the evaluation and certification of physician specialists.

American Board of Professional Psychology (**ABPP**) the umbrella organization for 13 psychological specialty boards in the United States. Established in 1947, its purpose is to establish, implement, and maintain standards and set examinations for specialty areas in the practice of psychology. A "specialty" is defined as a focused area in which special competency has been acquired through an organized sequence of education, training, and practical experience.

American Coaching Effectiveness Program (**ACEP**) see AMERICAN SPORT EDUCATION PROGRAM.

American College of Sports Medicine (**ACSM**) a multidisciplinary organization of exercise physiologists, sport medicine physicians, athletic trainers, and educators that strives to provide the most current information on health and fitness. The organization also provides certification in the areas of health and fitness.

American College Testing Program see ACT ASSESSMENT.

American Counseling Association (**ACA**) a professional and educational organization dedicated to promoting the development of the counseling profession. It is the world's largest association of professional counselors and has been instrumental in setting professional and ethical standards. Founded in 1952 as the American Personnel and Guidance Association (APGA), it changed its name to the American Association of Counseling and Development in 1983 and adopted its present name in 1992.

American Educational Research Association (**AERA**) a professional organization founded in 1916 to improve the educational process by encouraging scholarly inquiry related to education and by promoting the dissemination and practical application of research results.

American Indian see NATIVE AMERICAN.

American Law Institute Model Penal Code Insanity Test a legal standard for establishing CRIMINAL RESPONSIBILITY, adopted in 1962, that combines elements of the MCNAUGHTEN RULE and the IRRESISTIBLE IMPULSE RULE. According to this standard, individuals are not responsible for criminal conduct if at the time of such conduct, as a result of mental illness or defect, they lacked substantial capacity either to appreciate the criminality of their conduct or to conform their conduct to the requirements of the law. Also called **American Law Institute Guidelines** (**ALI Guidelines**); **Brawner decision**; **Brawner rule**.

American Manual Alphabet a means of communication for those with hearing loss in which the speaker uses specific finger and hand positions to represent the individual letters of the alphabet. It typically supplements SIGN LANGUAGE. See also INTERNATIONAL STANDARD MANUAL ALPHABET.

American Orthopsychiatric Association (**AOA**) an interdisciplinary professional organization engaged in preventive, treatment, and advocacy approaches to mental health. The prefix *ortho-* (from the Greek *orthos*, "straight") emphasizes the need for preventive approaches. The *American Journal of Orthopsychiatry* is its major publication. [founded in 1924 by U.S. physician Karl Menninger (1893–1990)]

American Pain Society (**APS**) a multidisciplinary professional organization whose mission is to advance pain-related research, education, treatment, and professional practice. It was founded in 1977 as the U.S. chapter of the International Association for the Study of Pain (IASP).

American Parkinson Disease Association, Inc. an organization that provides support groups, information, and referrals for individuals with Parkinson's disease and their families.

American Philosophical Society (**APS**) the oldest scholarly organization in the United States, founded in 1743 under the impetus of Benjamin Franklin in Philadelphia, Pennsylvania, where it is still headquartered. Members are elected on the basis of extraordinary accomplishments in the sciences and humanities. Publications include the society's *Transactions*, first published in 1771, *Memoirs*, *Proceedings*, and a *Year Book*. The society supports excellence in scholarly research through special prizes and grants.

American Psychiatric Association (**APA**) a national medical-specialty society whose physician members specialize in the diagnosis and treatment of mental and emotional illnesses and substance abuse disorders. It was founded in 1844 as the Association of Medical Superintendents of American Institutes for the Insane and renamed the American Medico-Psychological Association in 1892. The current name was adopted in 1922. Its objectives include the advancement and improvement of care for people with mental illnesses through nationwide public information, education, and awareness programs and materials. Among its extensive publications are eight scholarly journals and the *Diagnostic and Statistical Manual of Mental Disorders* (see DSM–IV–TR), the most widely used psychiatric reference in the world.

American Psychoanalytic Association (**APsaA**) a professional organization for psychoanalysts that focuses on education, research, and membership development. Founded in 1911, it is the oldest national psychoanalytic organization, with 29 accredited training institutes and 42 affiliate psychoanalytic societies. It is the U.S. chapter of the International Psychoanalytic Association. Its major publication is the *Journal of the American Psychoanalytic Association.*

American Psychological Association (**APA**) a scientific and professional organization founded in 1892 that represents psychology in the United States and is the largest association of psychologists worldwide. Its mission is to advance psychology as a science, as a profession, and as a means of promoting health and human welfare. Among its specific goals are the promotion of psychological research and improvement of research methods and conditions; the establishment and maintenance of high standards of professional ethics and conduct of its members; and the increase and diffusion of psychological knowledge through a variety of means, including 45 scholarly journals, the APA *Publication Manual,* 75 books and videotapes per year, and 5 electronic databases.

American Psychological Association code see CODE OF ETHICS.

American Psychological Association of Graduate Students (**APAGS**) the largest organized group of psychology graduate students worldwide, established in 1988 as a constituency group of the AMERICAN PSYCHOLOGICAL ASSOCIATION. It develops and disseminates information about relevant education and training issues and supports students through scholarships and awards, association advocacy work, and professional development opportunities.

American Psychological Foundation (**APF**) a nonprofit, philanthropic organization, founded in 1953, that provides scholarships, grants, and awards in order to advance the science and the practice of psychology for the understanding of behavior and the benefit of human welfare.

American Psychological Society (**APS**) a professional organization founded in 1988 to advance the needs and interests of scientific, applied, and academic psychologists as opposed to those engaged in clinical practice. Its mission is to promote, protect, and advance the interests of scientifically oriented psychology in research, application, and the improvement of human welfare. The APS publishes three journals: *Psychological Science, Current Directions in Psychological Science*, and *Psychological Science in the Public Interest.*

American Psychosomatic Society (**APS**) an interdisciplinary professional organization founded in 1942 whose mission is to promote a scientific understanding of the interrelationships among biological, psychological, social, and behavioral factors in human health and disease. Its main publication is *Psychosomatic Medicine.*

American Sign Language (**ASL**) a system, used for communication with or between people with hearing loss, in which hand signs and movements represent words. It is used primarily in the United States and Canada. See also SIGN LANGUAGE.

American Society for Psychical Research a scholarly society devoted to the scientific investigation of parapsychological and paranormal phenomena. Initially founded in 1885 by a group including William JAMES, it became a branch of the British SOCIETY FOR PSYCHICAL RESEARCH before becoming independent once more in 1906. It publishes the *Journal of the American Society for Psychical Research* (established 1907).

American Sport Education Program (**ASEP**) a series of educational courses for parents, coaches, officials, and administrators of volunteer youth sport that has an athlete-centered philosophy. It was formerly known as the **American Coaching Effectiveness Program** (**ACEP**).

Americans With Disabilities Act (**ADA**) a U.S. federal law that prohibits hiring and other employment practices that discriminate on the basis of physical or mental impairments, unless it can be shown that these would prevent the individual from performing the essential or primary functions of the job. Impairments are defined as real or perceived limitations that detract from one or more major life activities. The ADA also prohibits discrimination in other areas, such as access to programs, services and activities provided by a public agency (e.g., health care, social services, courts, community meetings); access to public accommodations (e.g., restaurants, hotels, schools and colleges, recreational facilities); and access to telecommunications (e.g., telephone, television). See also BONA FIDE OCCUPATIONAL QUALIFICATION.

Ames distortion room a room in which cues for

DEPTH PERCEPTION are used experimentally to distort the viewer's perception of the relative size of objects within the room. Also called **Ames room**. [Adelbert **Ames**, Jr. (1880–1955), U.S. psychologist, inventor, and artist]

Ameslan *n.* a contraction of AMERICAN SIGN LANGUAGE.

amethystic *n.* see ANTI-INTOXICANT.

ametropia *n.* any defect of the eye resulting in blurred vision due to ERRORS OF REFRACTION. Typical conditions of ametropia are MYOPIA, HYPEROPIA, ASTIGMATISM, PRESBYOPIA, and injury to the cornea.

AMH abbreviation for anti-Müllerian hormone (see MÜLLERIAN-INHIBITING HORMONE).

AMI 1. abbreviation for ATHLETIC MOTIVATION INVENTORY. **2.** abbreviation for AUTOBIOGRAPHICAL MEMORY INTERVIEW.

amicus curiae a third party (Latin, "friend of the court"), such as a psychologist, who is invited or volunteers to educate the court on a matter that has relevance to the dispute before it. See EXPERT WITNESS.

amiloride *n.* a heterocyclic carboxy-guanidinium compound used clinically as a DIURETIC to prevent sodium resorption in the kidneys and so lower blood pressure by blocking sodium channels. Amiloride is also used by taste researchers to block sodium channels on the tongue to study the perception of saltiness.

amimia *n.* **1.** a language or communication disorder characterized by an inability to convey meaning through appropriate gestures (**motor** or **expressive amimia**) or to interpret the gestures of others (**sensory** or **receptive amimia**). **2.** loss of memory.

amine *n.* a chemical compound that contains one or more amino groups ($-NH_2$). Several NEUROTRANSMITTERS are amines, including ACETYLCHOLINE, NOREPINEPHRINE, and SEROTONIN. See also AMINE HORMONE; AMINO ACID; BIOGENIC AMINE.

amine hormone any of a class of chemical compounds that contain a single AMINO ACID that has been modified into a hormone, such as MELATONIN or NOREPINEPHRINE. Also called **monoamine hormone**.

aminoacetic acid see GLYCINE.

amino acid an organic compound that contains an amino group ($-NH_2$) and a carboxyl group ($-COOH$). Amino acids occur naturally as the building blocks of PROTEIN molecules. Eight of the more than 20 amino acids in the human diet are **essential amino acids**, that is, they cannot be synthesized by the body and must be obtained from foods. Some amino acids on their derivatives are neurotransmitters, including GAMMA-AMINOBUTYRIC ACID, GLUTAMATE, GLYCINE, and HISTAMINE.

amino acid imbalance a disorder, genetic or acquired, characterized by a deficiency in the body's ability to transport or utilize certain amino acids. The cause is usually an absence or lack of an enzyme needed to carry an amino acid or its components through a step of a metabolic cycle. More than 80 kinds of amino acid imbalance have been identified, and many (e.g., PHENYLKETONURIA, HOMOCYSTINURIA) affect the central nervous system.

aminoketones *pl. n.* a class of antidepressant agents, represented clinically by BUPROPION, whose structure and mechanism of action differ from other marketed antidepressants.

aminopterin *n.* a drug similar to methotrexate (also called **amethopterin** and used in treating leukemia) that is sometimes used in nonclinical settings to induce abortions. Surviving infants show TERATOGENIC effects, such as HYDROCEPHALUS, craniosynostosis (premature skull ossification) with skull defects, and mild to moderate mental retardation. Aminopterin is in current use as a rodenticide and is under investigation as a treatment for certain forms of leukemia.

aminotransferase *n.* any of a class of TRANSFERASE enzymes that catalyze the transfer of an amino group ($-NH_2$) from a donor molecule to a recipient molecule. Two of the better known aminotransferases are ASPARTATE AMINOTRANSFERASE and alanine aminotransferase, which are normally found in the liver and heart, respectively, and are released into the bloodstream as a result of damage to those organs. Hence, they are used as indicators in liver and heart function tests.

amitriptyline *n.* a TRICYCLIC ANTIDEPRESSANT introduced into clinical use in 1961; with IMIPRAMINE, it was the first widely used antidepressant agent. Its tertiary amine structure makes it a more potent inhibitor of SEROTONIN reuptake than secondary amines (thereby increasing the availability of serotonin for neurotransmission), but also contributes to its significant antihistamine, anticholinergic, and adrenoreceptor-blocking activity (producing adverse side effects). It is an effective antidepressant, but its side effects and toxicity in overdose have led to a decline in its use in favor of the SSRIS and other agents. Although still used as an antidepressant, amitriptyline is no longer considered FIRST-LINE MEDICATION and is more likely to be employed in low doses for chronic pain management or the prevention of migraine. It is also sold in combination with a benzodiazepine ANXIOLYTIC (as **Limbitrol** in the United States) or an antipsychotic (as **Etrafon** or **Triavil** in the United States). U.S. trade name: **Elavil**.

amnesia *n.* a partial or complete loss of memory, either temporary or permanent, due to (a) organic factors (see AMNESTIC DISORDER) or (b) psychogenic factors, as in unconscious repression of painful or traumatic experiences (see FUNCTIONAL AMNESIA). See also ANTEROGRADE AMNESIA; RETROGRADE AMNESIA. **—amnesiac** *adj., n.* **—amnesic** or **amnestic** *adj.*

amnesic syndrome see AMNESTIC DISORDER.

amnestic aphasia an impaired ability to recognize the meanings of words and to recall the right names for objects. Mild forms may be due to anxiety, fatigue, intoxication, or senility; severe forms are indicative of a FOCAL LESION between the ANGULAR GYRUS and the first temporal gyrus on the left side of the brain. Also called **amnesic aphasia**; **anomic aphasia**; **nominal aphasia**.

amnestic apraxia an inability to remember and therefore carry out a command, although there is no loss of ability to perform the task. Also called **amnesic apraxia**.

amnestic disorder in *DSM–IV–TR*, a disturbance in memory marked by inability to learn new information (see ANTEROGRADE AMNESIA) or to recall previously learned information or past events (see RETROGRADE AMNESIA) that is severe enough to interfere markedly with social or occupational functioning or represents a significant decline from a previous level of functioning. A distinction is made between **amnestic disorder due to a general medical condition**, SUBSTANCE-INDUCED PERSISTING AMNESTIC DISORDER, and **amnestic disorder not otherwise specified**. The first of these can be caused by a variety of conditions, including head injury, ANOXIA, HERPES-SIMPLEX ENCEPHALITIS, and posterior cerebral artery stroke, resulting in lesions in specific brain regions, including the MEDIAL TEMPORAL LOBE and the DIENCEPHALON, and their connections with various cortical areas. It may be transient, lasting from several hours to no more than a month (see also TRANSIENT GLOBAL

AMNESIA), or chronic (lasting more than 1 month). In *DSM–III*, amnestic disorder was called **amnesic** (or **amnestic**) **syndrome**.

amniocentesis *n.* a method of examining fetal chromosomes for any abnormality or for determination of sex. A hollow needle is inserted through the mother's abdominal wall into the uterus, enabling the collection of amniotic fluid. Compare CHORIONIC VILLUS SAMPLING.

amniotic sac the fluid-filled membrane that encases and protects the embryo of a bird, reptile, or mammal.

amobarbital *n.* an intermediate-acting, rapidly excreted BARBITURATE that was formerly used as a sedative and hypnotic. Like other barbiturates, its toxicity has led to its clinical eclipse by safer agents, such as the BENZODIAZEPINES. Amobarbital abuse can result in addiction, stupor, and death. Amobarbital was occasionally used to conduct interviews (**Amytal interviews**) designed to elicit subconscious material from patients, as well as information that was consciously withheld. Such interviews were also used in attempting to distinguish between patients who were malingering and those who had a bona fide conversion disorder. Due to numerous legal and ethical issues surrounding amobarbital interviews, in addition to the medical risks associated with administration of barbiturates, such techniques are no longer acceptable in modern clinical practice. U.S. trade name: **Amytal**.

amok (**amuck**) *n.* a CULTURE-BOUND SYNDROME observed among males in Malaysia, the Philippines, and other parts of southeast Asia. The individual experiences a period of brooding and apathy, followed by a wild, unprovoked, homicidal attack on people or animals nearby. If he is not overpowered or killed by others in self-defense and does not commit suicide, the affected male eventually collapses from exhaustion and afterward has no memory of the event. Also called **mata elap**. See also FUROR; MAL DE PELEA.

amorphagnosia *n.* lack of awareness of shape. See also AGNOSIA.

amorphosynthesis *n.* an inability to perceive a specific form based on tactile sensations. The failure of the brain to synthesize an image from neural impressions received by touching an object is a type of AGNOSIA known as ASTEREOGNOSIS.

amotivational syndrome a behavior pattern associated with chronic use of cannabis, characterized by loss of drive and initiative. The concept is mainly conjectural and anecdotal, based on observations of the lifestyles of chronic cannabis users in various cultures around the world. See CANNABIS ABUSE; CANNABIS DEPENDENCE.

amoxapine *n.* an antidepressant, one of the secondary amine TRICYCLIC ANTIDEPRESSANTS (TCAs), that inhibits the reuptake of norepinephrine and serotonin. It may also have ANTIPSYCHOTIC activity due to the strong dopamine-receptor-blocking activity of one of its metabolites. Amoxapine may cause EXTRAPYRAMIDAL EFFECTS and TARDIVE DYSKINESIA but is less associated with anticholinergic side effects than other TCAs. U.S. trade name: **Asendin**.

AMPA abbreviation for alpha-amino-3-hydroxy-5-methyl-4-isoxazole-propionic acid: an AGONIST that binds to AMPA receptors.

AMPA receptor a type of GLUTAMATE RECEPTOR that binds AMPA as well as glutamate. AMPA receptors are coupled to LIGAND-GATED ION CHANNELS and are responsible for most of the activity at synapses where glutamate is the neurotransmitter. Compare NMDA RECEPTOR.

amphetamine *n.* a CNS STIMULANT, closely related in structure and activity to ephedrine (see EPHEDRA), that is the prototype of the group of drugs known as the AMPHETAMINES. U.S. trade name: **Benzedrine**.

amphetamine abuse in *DSM–IV–TR*, a pattern of use of AMPHETAMINES or amphetamine-like substances manifested by recurrent significant adverse consequences related to the repeated ingestion of these substances. This diagnosis is preempted by the diagnosis of AMPHETAMINE DEPENDENCE: If the criteria for amphetamine abuse and amphetamine dependence are both met, only the latter diagnosis is given. See also SUBSTANCE ABUSE; SUBSTANCE DEPENDENCE.

amphetamine dependence in *DSM–IV–TR*, a cluster of cognitive, behavioral, and physiological symptoms indicating continued use of an amphetamine or amphetamine-like substance despite significant substance-related problems. There is a pattern of repeated substance ingestion resulting in tolerance, characteristic symptoms if use is suspended (see AMPHETAMINE WITHDRAWAL), and an uncontrollable drive to continue use. See also AMPHETAMINE ABUSE.

amphetamine-induced psychotic disorder a condition marked by paranoid delusions due to the direct physiological effects of an amphetamine or amphetamine-like substance. The delusions can continue as long as the use of these substances continues and might persist for weeks or months after withdrawal from the substances has been completed. Also called **amphetamine psychosis**.

amphetamine intoxication a reversible syndrome caused by the recent ingestion of amphetamines or amphetamine-like substances. It is characterized by behavioral or psychological changes (e.g., inappropriate aggressive behavior, impaired judgment, suspiciousness, and paranoia), as well as one or more signs of physiological involvement (e.g., unsteady gait, impairment in attention or memory). See also SUBSTANCE INTOXICATION.

amphetamine intoxication delirium a reversible syndrome that develops over a short period of time (usually hours to days) following the heavy ingestion of amphetamines or amphetamine-like substances. The features include disturbed consciousness (e.g., reduced ability to focus, sustain, or shift attention) and changes in cognition (e.g., memory deficit, disorientation, or language disturbance) in excess of those usually associated with AMPHETAMINE INTOXICATION. See also SUBSTANCE INTOXICATION DELIRIUM.

amphetamine psychosis see AMPHETAMINE-INDUCED PSYCHOTIC DISORDER.

amphetamines *pl. n.* a group of drugs (substituted PHENYLETHYLAMINES) that stimulate the RETICULAR FORMATION in the brain and cause a release of stored norepinephrine. The effect is a prolonged state of arousal and relief from feelings of fatigue (see CNS STIMULANTS). Amphetamines were introduced in 1932 for a variety of clinical uses. During World War II, they were widely dispensed to combat soldiers to enable them to remain alert for periods of up to 60 hours. TOLERANCE develops progressively with continued use until the individual reaches a point of exhaustion and sleeps continuously for several days. AMPHETAMINE ABUSE can result in dependence and a well-defined state of psychosis (see AMPHETAMINE DEPENDENCE; AMPHETAMINE-INDUCED PSYCHOTIC DISORDER). Although widely used in the past for weight loss, relief of depression, and other indications, modern use of amphetamines is more circumscribed because of their adverse effects. They are now used mainly in short- and long-acting preparations to manage symptoms of attention deficit/hyperactivity disorder and to treat certain cases of severe depression or narcolepsy, and they still maintain a military use in the management of fatigue.

Amphetamines include AMPHETAMINE itself (the prototype), DEXTROAMPHETAMINE, and METHAMPHETAMINE. Related drugs, with a similar mode of action but different molecular structure, include METHYLPHENIDATE. In addition, some forms and derivatives (including DOM, MDA, and MDMA) have been manufactured as recreational hallucinogenic drugs.

amphetamine withdrawal a characteristic withdrawal syndrome that develops after cessation of (or reduction in) prolonged, heavy consumption of an amphetamine or amphetamine-like substance. The essential characteristic is depressed mood, sometimes severe, and there may also be fatigue, disturbed sleep, increased appetite, vivid and unpleasant dreams, or PSYCHOMOTOR RETARDATION or agitation, or all of these features. Marked withdrawal symptoms (see CRASH) often follow an episode of intense, high-dose use. See also SUBSTANCE WITHDRAWAL.

amphi- *prefix* **1.** uncertain or unclear (e.g., AMPHIBOLY). **2.** on both sides or of both kinds.

amphiboly *n.* a sentence that has an unclear or ambiguous meaning because of its construction. Such a sentence may be used in argument as a form of informal FALLACY, as in *Do not treat pathology, emphasize science.* Also called **amphibology**.

amplitude *n.* **1.** the magnitude of a stimulus or response. **2.** the peak value of a sinusoid wave.

amplitude distortion a hearing disorder in which loud sounds are distorted or misjudged.

amplitude modulation see MODULATION.

amplitude of light wave the maximum deviation of a wave of light from its median intensity. The greater the amplitude of a light wave, the brighter it appears.

amplitude of response see RESPONSE AMPLITUDE.

amplitude spectrum see SOUND SPECTRUM.

AMPT abbreviation for ALPHA-METHYLPARATYROSINE.

ampulla *n.* (*pl.* **ampullae**) any saclike enlargement of a duct or passageway. Ampullae located at each end of the SEMICIRCULAR CANALS of the inner ear contain HAIR CELLS that help maintain balance.

amputation *n.* the surgical or traumatic removal of a limb or other appendage from the body. Surgical amputation generally is performed as a life-saving measure following an injury, to prevent the spread of a malignant tumor or gangrene, or to remove a body part that no longer has an adequate blood circulation (e.g., as a result of diabetes or severe frostbite).

amputation fetish see ACROTOMOPHILIA.

Amsterdam criteria the classic criteria for identifying a family with hereditary nonpolyposis colorectal cancer (HNPCC). The criteria are characterized by a 3-2-1 paradigm: *3* patients with colon cancer, one of whom is a first-degree relative of the other, in at least *2* generations, with an age of onset before age 50 in at least *1* patient. See also MLH1; MSH2.

Amsterdam dwarf disease a congenital disorder characterized by delayed growth, small stature, MICROCEPHALY, and such features as cleft lip and palate, upturned nose, and hirsutism. Other manifestations can include malformed or missing limbs, fingers, or hands, seizure disorders, bowel abnormalities, and cardiac defects. Developmental delays are common, as is some degree of mental retardation (usually moderate to severe). Also called **Amsterdam type of retardation**; **Brachmann–de Lange syndrome**. See also DE LANGE'S SYNDROME.

amuck *n.* see AMOK.

amurakh *n.* a CULTURE-BOUND SYNDROME observed among Siberian women and characterized by compulsive mimicking of other people's words or behaviors. See also LATAH.

amusia *n.* a type of AUDITORY APHASIA in which individuals are unable to recognize melodies. The condition is usually associated with a lesion in the left PARIETAL LOBE of the brain. **Expressive amusia** is the inability to produce music. See also MOTOR AMUSIA; SENSORY AMUSIA.

amygdala *n.* an almond-shaped structure—a component of the LIMBIC SYSTEM—located in the medial part of the TEMPORAL LOBE of the brain. The main groups of nuclei in the amygdala are the CORTICOMEDIAL GROUP and the basolateral group. Through widespread connections with other brain areas, the amygdala has numerous viscerosensory and autonomic functions as well as an important role in memory, emotion, perception of threat, and fear learning. Also called **amygdaloid body**; **amygdaloid complex**; **amygdaloid nuclei**. —**amygdaloid** *adj.*

amygdaloid stimulation electrical activation of the AMYGDALA, which induces changes in the emotional, behavioral, and motivational responses of an animal.

amyl nitrite an organic nitrite, administered by nasal inhalation, that dilates (widens) arteries by relaxing smooth muscles in arterial walls. The main effects are to dilate the coronary arteries supplying the heart and to reduce blood pressure. Amyl nitrite has been used therapeutically in the treatment of angina pectoris and as an antidote in the treatment of cyanide poisoning. It is now best known as a recreational drug that is reputed to enhance orgasm and other aspects of the sexual experience; adverse effects can include anxiety, nausea, dizziness, faintness associated with a drop in blood pressure, and impaired oxygen-carrying capacity of the blood.

amyloidosis *n.* a disorder marked by the accumulation in the tissues of **amyloid**, a complex starchlike protein substance. The cause is believed to be an immune-deficiency disease. Amyloidosis is eventually destructive because it interferes with the normal function of tissues, forming tumors in the respiratory tract, liver, kidney, and other organs. **Primary amyloidosis** occurs in the absence of other diseases, while **secondary amyloidosis** is associated with a chronic disease.

amyloid precursor protein (**APP**) a protein that, when cleaved by several enzymes (including beta-secretase), produces BETA-AMYLOID. Buildup of beta-amyloid in the brain is thought to cause ALZHEIMER'S DISEASE.

amyotrophic lateral sclerosis (**ALS**) a MOTOR NEURON DISEASE in which both LOWER MOTOR NEURONS and UPPER MOTOR NEURONS are affected (sensory nerves are not affected). It is marked by progressive degeneration of the ANTERIOR HORN cells of the spinal cord, brainstem, and cerebral cortex. Symptoms usually appear after the age of 40 and include muscular atrophy and weakness, partial and complete paralysis, speech impairment, and difficulties swallowing or breathing. Spasticity and exaggerated TENDON REFLEXES may also be observed. Death typically occurs within 2 to 5 years of symptom onset. Amyotrophic lateral sclerosis is often used interchangeably with motor neuron disease, especially in the United States. Also called **Lou Gehrig's disease**.

Amytal *n.* a trade name for AMOBARBITAL.

Amytal interview see AMOBARBITAL.

an- *prefix* see A-.

ana- *prefix* **1.** up (e.g., ANABOLISM). **2.** back (e.g., ANACLISIS). **3.** again (e.g., ANALOGY).

anabolic-androgenic steroids steroids that are used to increase muscle bulk and also affect the secondary sex characteristics.

anabolic system a constitutional body type in which the abdomen is more prominent than the chest due to the presence of large visceral organs.

anabolism *n.* the constructive part of METABOLISM, in which complex molecules are formed from simpler ones. Compare CATABOLISM. **—anabolic** *adj.*

anaclisis *n.* **1.** an extreme dependence on another person for emotional and in some cases physical support, just as an infant is dependent on the parents for the satisfaction of his or her basic needs. See ANACLITIC OBJECT CHOICE. **2.** in the classical psychoanalytic theory of Sigmund FREUD, the attachment of the sex drive to the satisfaction of another instinct, such as hunger or defecation. **—anaclitic** *adj.*

anaclitic depression 1. a form of REACTIVE DEPRESSION seen in infants abruptly separated from their mothers or otherwise deprived of mothering care. It is characterized by such symptoms as social withdrawal, weight loss, and sleeplessness and often results in impairment of the infant's physical, social, and intellectual development. Although this term is primarily applied to humans, anaclitic depression has also been observed in monkeys and other primates. [described in 1946 by Austrian psychiatrist René Spitz (1887–1974)] **2.** depression that involves feelings of abandonment, helplessness, and fear. Compare INTROJECTIVE DEPRESSION.

anaclitic identification in psychoanalytic theory, the first phase of the IDENTIFICATION process, which is rooted in the child's initial total dependence on the mother (as well as others) for basic biological and emotional needs. The child acquires the mother's characteristics in the service of becoming his or her own source of reinforcement and comfort. The child incorporates the mother into his or her superego (see EGO-IDEAL). A weaker version of this is seen with other significant figures in the child's life (e.g., teachers).

anaclitic object choice in psychoanalytic theory, the selection of a mate or other LOVE OBJECT who will provide the same type of assistance, comfort, and support that the individual received from the parents during infancy and early childhood: A woman chooses a man resembling or modelled on her father and a man chooses a woman like his mother. Sigmund FREUD contrasted this with NARCISSISTIC OBJECT CHOICE, which involves selecting a mate who is similar to oneself. According to Freud, these are the only two possible types of object choice. Also called **anaclitic love**. See also ANACLISIS.

anaclitic personality according to some psychoanalytic theories, a line of personality development that is focused on feelings of loneliness or fear of abandonment with regard to interpersonal relationships and—if the personality fails to develop properly—may result in psychopathological dependency. Compare INTROJECTIVE PERSONALITY.

anacusis (**anakusis**) *n.* total deafness. Also called **anacousia**; **anacusia**.

anadanmide *n.* a neurotransmitter that binds to CANNABINOID receptors.

anaerobic exercise the level of exercise maintained by an energy-providing system that does not involve the use of oxygen in the muscles; that is, exercise, such as weight training and sprinting, that occurs in short, intense bursts of activity with limited oxygen intake. The **anaerobic threshold** is the point at which energy is expended too rapidly to be supplied by the oxygen-requiring system and the body must switch to the anaerobic system, producing energy in the absence of adequate oxygen. Compare AEROBIC EXERCISE.

anaesthesia *n.* see ANESTHESIA.

Anafranil *n.* a trade name for CLOMIPRAMINE.

anaglyph *n.* a single picture made from two copies of the same image that differ in color and are slightly displaced from one another in the horizontal plane. When viewed through colored glasses, only one image is visible through each eye, and the horizontal offset of the images is interpreted as stereoscopic depth. See STEREOPSIS; RANDOM-DOT STEREOGRAM.

anaglyptoscope *n.* a device that reverses the areas of light and shadow on an object, altering the perception of depth. Shadow is a powerful DEPTH CUE. Also called **anaglyphoscope**. See DEPTH PERCEPTION; DEPTH FROM SHADING.

anagogic interpretation the interpretation of dreams and other unconscious material as expressions of ideals or spiritual forces, in contrast to the instinct-based interpretations of psychoanalysis. [introduced by Carl JUNG and developed by Austrian psychoanalyst Herbert Silberer (1882–1923)]

anagram problem solving in studies of problem solving, a common task in which participants are asked to determine the word that corresponds to a series of scrambled letters (e.g., *rlmoebp–problem*).

anal-aggressive personality in psychoanalytic theory, a personality type characterized by obstinacy, obstructionism, defiance, and passive resistance. Such traits are held to stem from the ANAL STAGE, in which the child asserted himself or herself by withholding feces. Also called **anal-aggressive character**. See also ANAL PERSONALITY; ANAL SADISM; ANAL-SADISTIC PHASE.

anal character see ANAL PERSONALITY.

analeptics *pl. n.* stimulants other than amphetamines that produce subjective effects similar to those caused by amphetamine use. These effects may include alertness, elevated mood, increased feeling of energy, decreased appetite, irritability, and insomnia. The group includes DIETHYLPROPION, METHYLPHENIDATE, and PEMOLINE. See also APPETITE SUPPRESSANTS.

anal eroticism in psychoanalytic theory, pleasurable sensations associated with expulsion, retention, or observation of the feces or through stimulation of the anus. These sensations first arise in the ANAL STAGE of PSYCHOSEXUAL DEVELOPMENT, between the ages of 1 and 3. Also called **anal erotism**. See also ANAL PERSONALITY; COPROPHILIA.

anal-expulsive phase in psychoanalytic theory, a phase of the ANAL STAGE in which pleasure is obtained by expelling feces and the sadistic instinct is linked to destruction of the OBJECT. According to the theory, fixation at this phase results in an adult ANAL PERSONALITY. See also ANAL-SADISTIC PHASE. Compare ANAL-RETENTIVE PHASE.

analgesia *n.* the absence or loss of, or a reduction in, the sensation of pain. See also STRESS-INDUCED ANALGESIA. Compare ALGESIA. **—analgesic** *adj.*

analgesics *pl. n.* drugs or other agents that alleviate pain. Analgesic drugs usually are classed as opioid (narcotic) or nonopioid (nonnarcotic), depending on their chemical composition and potential for physical dependence. OPIOID ANALGESICS are generally the most effective in relieving pain. The most widely used of the less potent nonopioid analgesics are the NSAIDS (nonsteroidal anti-inflammatory drugs)—most notably ASPIRIN—and ACETAMINOPHEN.

anal intercourse a form of sexual activity in which pleasure is achieved through the insertion of the penis into the anus. Also called **coitus analis; coitus in ano**. See also SODOMY.

anal masturbation a form of anal eroticism in which sexual excitement is achieved through manual or mechanical self-stimulation of the anus.

analog *adj.* relating to the representation of information by means of a continuously varying physical quantity, such as voltage, rather than by means of discrete digits. Compare DIGITAL.

analog computer a computer that solves problems, usually mathematical, by using a physical analogue of the mathematical relationships expressed in the computer's program. These analogues of computational variables are usually an electrical voltage or the rotation of a shaft. See DIGITAL COMPUTER.

analogical thinking 1. a type of thinking marked by the use of ANALOGY rather than formal logic or consecutive reasoning. Also called **analogical reasoning**. See also ALLUSIVE THINKING. **2.** in problem solving, an approach in which an individual tries to solve a problem by thinking about the solutions to similar problems. See also PROBLEM ISOMORPHS.

analogies test a test of the participant's ability to comprehend the relationship between two items and then extend that relationship to a different situation: For example, paintbrush is to paint as pen is to __.

analogue *n.* **1.** something that is like, or similar in some respect to, something else. See ANALOGY. **2.** an organ of one species that has a similar function to an organ of another species, although they have different structures and PHYLOGENY. The wings of bats and flies are examples.

analogue experiment an experiment in which a phenomenon is produced in the laboratory in order to obtain greater experimental control over the phenomenon. Examples of an analogue experiment include the use of hypnosis, mind-altering drugs, and sensory deprivation to produce brief periods of abnormal behavior that simulate those of psychopathological conditions.

analogue study a research design or experiment in which the procedures or participants used are similar but not identical to the situation of interest. For example, if researchers are interested in the effects of therapist gender on client perceptions of therapist trustworthiness, they may use undergraduate students who are not clients and provide simulated counseling dialogues that are typed and identified as offered by a male or female therapist. The results of such studies are assumed to offer a high degree of experimental control and to generalize to actual clinical practice. Also called **analogue model**.

analogy *n.* **1.** a similarity between two entities in certain limited respects. In biology it refers to similarity of function in structures with different evolutionary origins. For example, the hand of a human and the trunk of an elephant are analogous in that both are used for manipulating objects. Compare HOMOLOGY; HOMOPLASY. **2.** a method of argument that relies on an inference that a similarity between two or more entities in some attributes justifies a probable assumption that they will be similar in other attributes (see FALSE ANALOGY). Analogy is often used in arguments about the existence of God and of other minds. **3.** in linguistics, the process by which the regular patterns of INFLECTION, word formation, and the like in a language are extended to novel or anomalous instances. This can be observed in historical language change as well as in LANGUAGE ACQUISITION. A notable form of analogy occurs when children regularize irregular grammatical forms, such as applying the *-ed* past-tense ending to irregular verbs, creating novel forms such as *go-ed*. **—analogical** *adj.* **—analogous** *adj.*

analogy of the cave a metaphor used by Greek philosopher Plato (c. 429–347 BCE) to illustrate his contention that humans are only dimly aware of the true nature of things. Plato likened human life to the state of being imprisoned in a cave, with the world outside casting shadows on the cave walls: He contended that these shadows are all one actually experiences of the real world, which is timeless and ideal. See PLATONIC IDEALISM; THEORY OF FORMS. See also TRANSCENDENTALISM.

anal personality in psychoanalytic theory, a pattern of personality traits believed to stem from the ANAL STAGE of PSYCHOSEXUAL DEVELOPMENT, when defecation is a primary source of pleasure. Special satisfaction from retention of the feces will result in an adult **anal-retentive personality**, marked by frugality, obstinacy, and orderliness, whereas fixation on expelling feces will produce an aggressive and disorderly **anal-expulsive personality**. Also called **anal character**. See also ANAL-AGGRESSIVE PERSONALITY; HOARDING ORIENTATION.

anal phase see ANAL STAGE.

anal-retentive phase in psychoanalytic theory, a phase of the ANAL STAGE marked by pleasure in retaining feces and thereby defying the parent, in which the sadistic instinct is linked to possession and control of the OBJECT. Fixation at this phase results in an adult ANAL PERSONALITY. See also ANAL-SADISTIC PHASE. Compare ANAL-EXPULSIVE PHASE.

anal sadism in psychoanalytic theory, the expression of aggressive impulses in the ANAL STAGE of psychosexual development, involving both the destruction of the OBJECT and its possession and control. It is manifested in the adult in the form of an ANAL-AGGRESSIVE PERSONALITY.

anal-sadistic phase in psychoanalytic theory, a phase of the ANAL STAGE in which the child manifests aggressive, destructive, and negative tendencies. One expression of these tendencies is withholding the feces in defiance of parental urging. See ANAL-AGGRESSIVE PERSONALITY. See also ANAL-EXPULSIVE PHASE; ANAL-RETENTIVE PHASE.

anal stage in psychoanalytic theory, the second stage of PSYCHOSEXUAL DEVELOPMENT, typically occurring during the 2nd year of life, in which the child's interest and sexual pleasure are focused on the expulsion and retention of feces and the sadistic instinct is linked to the desire to both possess and destroy the OBJECT. Fixation during this stage results in an ANAL PERSONALITY. Also called **anal phase**. See also ANAL-EXPULSIVE PHASE; ANAL-RETENTIVE PHASE; ANAL-SADISTIC PHASE.

analysand *n.* in psychoanalysis, a patient who is undergoing analysis.

analysis *n.* **1.** the division of any entity into its component parts, typically for the purpose of investigation or study. **2.** see PSYCHOANALYSIS. **—analytic** or **analytical** *adj.*

analysis by synthesis any theory of information processing stating that both DATA-DRIVEN PROCESSES and CONCEPTUALLY DRIVEN PROCESSES interact in the recognition and interpretation of sensory input. According to theories of this type, which are associated particularly with speech perception and language processing, the person initially assesses (analyzes) the physical attributes and constituent elements of a stimulus (data-driven processing) and then, guided by contextual information and knowledge acquired from previous experience or learning (conceptually driven processing), determines the significant information from this preliminary analysis of the stimulus and assembles (synthesizes) it into an internal representation or interpretation of what the stimulus might be. This internal representation is compared to the stimulus input: If the two match, then the stimulus is recognized; if not, alternative representations are assembled for comparison until a match is found. In other words, one analyzes the original stimulus input, hypothesizes what it is, determines what the input would be like if the hypothesis were correct, and then assesses whether the input is actually like that.

analysis of covariance (**ANCOVA**) an extension of the ANALYSIS OF VARIANCE that adjusts the dependent variable (or variables) for the influence of a correlated variable (COVARIATE). For example, in an experimental study of the effect of a particular form of training on a particular test of performance, one might make a statistical adjustment to the final performance values on the basis of the pretraining level of performance. An analysis of covariance is appropriate in two types of cases: (a) when experimental groups are suspected to differ on a background-correlated variable in addition to the differences attributed to the experimental treatment and (b) where adjustment on a covariate can increase the precision of the experiment.

analysis of the resistance a basic procedure in psychoanalysis, in which the patient's tendency to maintain the REPRESSION of unconscious impulses and experiences is subjected to analytic scrutiny. The process of explaining RESISTANCES is believed to be a major contribution to self-understanding and positive change.

analysis of the transference in psychoanalysis, the interpretation of a patient's early relationships and experiences as they are reflected and expressed in his or her present relationship to the analyst. Also called **transference analysis**. See TRANSFERENCE; TRANSFERENCE RESISTANCE.

analysis of variance (**ANOVA**) any of several statistical procedures that isolate the joint and separate effects of INDEPENDENT VARIABLES upon a DEPENDENT VARIABLE and test them for statistical significance. See also GENERAL LINEAR MODEL.

analysis unit see UNIT OF ANALYSIS.

analyst *n.* generally, one who practices psychoanalysis. This is usually a PSYCHOANALYST in the tradition of Sigmund FREUD; however, the term is also applied to therapists adhering to the methods of Carl JUNG (see ANALYTIC PSYCHOLOGY) or Alfred ADLER (see INDIVIDUAL PSYCHOLOGY).

analytical intelligence in the TRIARCHIC THEORY OF INTELLIGENCE, the skills measured by conventional tests of intelligence, such as analysis, comparison, evaluation, critique, and judgment. Compare CREATIVE INTELLIGENCE; PRACTICAL INTELLIGENCE.

analytical psychotherapy **1.** a short-term method of psychotherapy using psychoanalytic principles but with less depth of analysis, more active intervention on the part of the therapist, and less frequent sessions than are required for a true psychoanalysis. **2.** historically, an alternative method to psychoanalysis proposed by Viennese psychoanalyst Wilhelm Stekel (1868–1940).

analytic approach the breaking down of complex processes into their component parts in order to better understand these processes. Also called **analytic method**.

analytic couch see COUCH.

analytic group psychotherapy a form of group psychotherapy based on the application of psychoanalytic concepts and techniques to three principal age groups: (a) PLAY-GROUP PSYCHOTHERAPY for preschool children, (b) ACTIVITY-INTERVIEW GROUP PSYCHOTHERAPY for children before adolescence, and (c) INTERVIEW GROUP PSYCHOTHERAPY for adolescents and adults. [developed by 20th-century Russian-born U.S. psychotherapist Samuel Richard Slavson]

analytic philosophy an approach to philosophy developed by Austrian philosopher Ludwig Wittgenstein (1889–1951) and British philosopher Bertrand Russell (1872–1970) at the beginning of the 20th century. According to this view, the truth or falsity of complex statements could be determined by analyzing them into simple, elemental, logical propositions. The main task of philosophy is therefore the clarification of thought and language rather than the creation of speculative systems or theories. This approach influenced LOGICAL POSITIVISM and remained dominant in Britain and the United States during the 20th century. Compare CONTINENTAL PHILOSOPHY.

analytic psychology the system of psychoanalysis proposed by Carl JUNG, in which the psyche is interpreted primarily in terms of philosophical values, primordial images and symbols, and a drive for self-fulfillment. Jung's basic concepts are (a) the EGO, which maintains a balance between conscious and unconscious activities and gradually develops a unique self through INDIVIDUATION; (b) the PERSONAL UNCONSCIOUS, made up of memories, thoughts, and feelings based on personal experience; (c) the COLLECTIVE UNCONSCIOUS, made up of ancestral images, or ARCHETYPES, that constitute the inherited foundation of an individual's intellectual life and personality; and (d) dynamic polarities, or tension systems, which derive their psychic energy from the LIBIDO and influence the development and expression of the ego: conscious versus unconscious values, introversion versus extraversion, sublimation versus repression, rational versus irrational. The object of life, and of Jungian therapy, is to achieve a creative balance among all these forces. Also called **analytical psychology**.

analytic rules the three rules laid down by Sigmund FREUD for conducting psychoanalytic therapy: the BASIC RULE of free association, which gives free reign to the unconscious to bring repressed impulses and experiences to the surface; the RULE OF ABSTINENCE, which discourages gratifications that might drain off energy that could be utilized in the therapeutic process; and the rule against ACTING OUT feelings and events instead of talking them out.

analyzer *n.* a theoretical part or function of the central nervous system responsible for making evaluations of stimuli within particular senses. Each sense (e.g., vision) has a series of analyzers, and each analyzer is responsive to a particular stimulus dimension (e.g., color, length, orientation, or brightness). The concept was introduced by Ivan PAVLOV.

anamnesis *n.* in psychiatry, a patient's personal account of his or her developmental, family, and medical history prior to the onset of a psychological disorder or admission to a hospital. [first suggested by Swiss-born U.S. psychiatrist Adolf Meyer (1866–1950) as an aid to diagnosis and exploration of possible causes of a patient's disorder]

anamnestic analysis psychoanalysis that emphasizes the patient's historical account of his or her problem with added material from family and friends. [introduced by Carl JUNG]

anancastic personality (**anankastic personality**) an older name for OBSESSIVE-COMPULSIVE PERSONALITY DISORDER.

anandria *n.* the absence of masculinity in a male.

anaphia *n.* the absence or loss of ability to perceive tactile sensations or stimuli. Also called **anhaphia**.

anaphora *n.* in linguistics, the use of a word (often a PRONOUN) to refer back to a word used earlier, usually to avoid repetition. In *You take the high road, I'll take the low one,* the use of *one* to mean *road* is an example of anaphora. Ability to form and process such constructions has been a major preoccupation of GENERATIVE GRAMMAR and PSYCHOLINGUISTICS. See also ANTECEDENT. **—anaphoric** *adj.*

anaphrodisiac *n.* a drug or other agent that functions as a sexual sedative to reduce or repress sexual desire. Among substances claimed to have this effect are potassium bromide, heroin, and camphor. Anaphrodisiacs also may be a cause of SEXUAL ANESTHESIA. See also CHEMICAL CASTRATION.

anaphylaxis *n.* hypersensitivity to the introduction of an allergen into body tissues, resulting from previous exposure to it. The reaction may be localized or widespread and ranges from wheals on the face and elsewhere to **anaphylactic shock**—convulsions, coma, breathing difficulty, shock, and death—depending upon individual sensitivities. Anaphylactic reactions may occur in response to insect stings (e.g., by wasps or bees), certain foods (e.g., peanuts, fish), or drugs (e.g., penicillins), especially when injected. See also PSYCHOLOGICAL ANAPHYLAXIS. **—anaphylactic** *adj.*

anaplastic astrocytoma see GLIOBLASTOMA.

anarithmia *n.* see ACALCULIA.

anarthria *n.* inability to speak.

Anastasi, Anne (1908–2001) U.S. psychologist. A National Medal of Science winner, Anastasi made her greatest contributions in the area of psychological testing and the study of psychological traits. Anastasi earned her PhD in 1929 from Columbia University, where she studied under Harry L. HOLLINGWORTH. Her major works include *Differential Psychology* (1958), *Fields of Applied Psychology* (1979), and *Psychological Testing* (1997), as well as a 1958 *Psychological Review* article, now considered a classic, on the NATURE–NURTURE CONTROVERSY. Among her numerous professional appointments was her election to the presidency of the American Psychological Association in 1972: She was the first female to hold that office since Margaret Floy WASHBURN became president in 1921.

anastomosis *n.* (*pl.* **anastomoses**) **1.** a connection or opening between two normally separate structures, organs, or spaces. **2.** an alternate pathway formed by branching of a main circuit. Anastomoses are found in nerves, blood vessels, and lymphatic vessels. The brain is served by arterial anastomoses that help ensure a continuing blood flow in the event of one pathway being blocked by a blood clot or rupture of a blood vessel.

anatomical age a measure of the stage of physical development of an individual, based on the condition of certain skeletal features as compared with the normal state of the bones for a specified CHRONOLOGICAL AGE. Also called **physical age**. See also MENTAL AGE.

anatomically detailed doll a doll with anatomically correct genitalia that is used during an interview with a child to help a professional decide whether the child has been sexually abused. Also called **anatomically correct doll**; **physically correct doll**.

ancestor worship a practice found in various cultures, especially in Asia and Africa, that involves the veneration of departed kin and the summoning of **ancestral spirits** through rituals.

ancestral trait an evolutionary trait that is homologous within a group of organisms (see HOMOLOGY) but is not unique to members of that group, being shared by many other organisms that are descended from the common ancestor in which the trait first evolved. It therefore cannot be used as a defining characteristic of the group.

anchor *n.* a reference point used when making a series of subjective judgments. For example, in an experiment in which participants gauge distances between objects, the experimenter introduces an anchor by informing the participants that the distance between two of the stimulus objects is a given value. That value then functions as a reference for participants in their subsequent judgments. Also called **anchoring point**.

anchoring *n.* **1.** in ADAPTATION LEVEL theory, the assignment of set points (ANCHORS) for judgment scales. According to this theory, all judgments are relative to an implicit scale of comparison; for example, poverty is evaluated differently when people are given specific examples of either extreme or moderate poverty. **2.** the process in which one or more items in a list being learned serve as anchors with which the other items are associated. For instance, the first and last items in a list of words may serve as anchors, cuing the words in between.

anchoring bias the tendency, in forming perceptions or making quantitative judgments of some entity under conditions of uncertainty, to give excessive weight to the initial starting value (or ANCHOR), based on the first received information or one's initial judgment, and not to modify this anchor sufficiently in light of later information. For example, estimates of the product of $9 \times 8 \times 7 \times 6 \times 5 \times 4 \times 3 \times 2 \times 1$ tend to be higher than estimates of the product of $1 \times 2 \times 3 \times 4 \times 5 \times 6 \times 7 \times 8 \times 9$. Also called **anchoring effect**. See also ATMOSPHERE EFFECT.

anchoring point see ANCHOR.

anchor test a test used in establishing comparable norms for tests in the same field.

ancillary *adj.* supporting or supplemental but not necessarily critical to some function or event.

ANCOVA acronym for ANALYSIS OF COVARIANCE.

Andersen's disease a familial disorder marked by cirrhosis of the liver with involvement of the heart, kidneys, muscles, and nervous system. The disease is due to a deficit of an enzyme needed to convert glucose carried from the digestive tract into glycogen for storage by the liver. [Dorothy Hansine **Andersen** (1901–1963), U.S. pediatrician]

Andersen's syndrome a disorder consisting of three pathological conditions: cystic fibrosis of the pancreas, celiac disease, and vitamin A deficiency. The syndrome may be marked by symptoms of depression, muscle wasting, and hypotonia (weak, floppy muscles). Children may have difficulty in walking or standing. Also called **Andersen's triad**. [Dorothy Hansine **Andersen** (1901–1963), U.S. pediatrician]

Andrade's syndrome a form of AMYLOIDOSIS characterized by flaccid paralysis, sensory disorders, impotence, and premature menopause. Also called **Corino de Andrade's paramyloidosis**; **familial Portuguese polyneuritic amyloidosis**; **Wohlwill–Corino An-**

drade syndrome. [Corino de **Andrade**, Portuguese physician; Joachim Friedrich **Wohlwill** (1881–1958), German physician]

andro- (**andr-**) *combining form* male.

androcentric *adj.* denoting a male perspective, sometimes one that marginalizes or excludes women and their experience. See also PHALLOCENTRIC. **—androcentrism** *n.*

androgen *n.* any of a class of hormones that include TESTOSTERONE and other male hormones, manufactured mainly by the TESTES. Androgens are also secreted in small quantities by the adrenal cortex (see ADRENAL ANDROGEN) and can be produced synthetically. Also called **androgenic hormone**. See also ANDROSTENEDIONE; ANDROSTERONE.

androgen antagonist *n.* see ANTIANDROGEN.

androgen-insensitivity syndrome (**AIS**) an inherited X-linked (see SEX-LINKED) recessive condition affecting the development of reproductive and genital organs, caused by varying degrees of insensitivity to ANDROGENS. There are two forms: **complete AIS**, in which the insensitivity is total, resulting in external genitalia that are female; and **partial AIS**, in which some sensitivity to the hormones allows for external genitalia that may be structurally ambiguous, falling anywhere within the range of male to female. In both forms, however, the internal organs are male (i.e., testes). Also called **feminizing testes syndrome**; **male pseudohermaphroditism**; **testicular feminization syndrome**. See also INTERSEXUALITY; PSEUDOHERMAPHRODITISM.

androgenization *n.* the masculinizing effect of androgens, especially TESTOSTERONE, on body tissues and organs sensitive to them, as in the development of male sex characteristics.

androgyne *n.* see ANDROGYNY.

androgynophilia *n.* **1.** sexual attraction to both males and females. See BISEXUAL BEHAVIOR. **2.** sexual attraction to someone who is androgynous in appearance.

androgynous personality a personality style in which an individual displays both stereotypical masculine and stereotypical feminine psychological characteristics (e.g., both assertiveness and sensitivity).

androgynous sex role 1. a mixture of SEX ROLES in which there is confusion or uncertainty about gender identity and behavior that may be labeled both masculine and feminine. A male may play a feminine role and prefer a partner of his own sex, or a female may play a masculine role and prefer a partner of her own sex. **2.** a sex role that does not conform to either stereotypical male or female sex roles, but rather combines positive elements of both.

androgyny *n.* **1.** the presence of male and female characteristics in one individual. **2.** the state of being neither distinguishably masculine or feminine in appearance, as in dress. Also called **androgyneity**; **androgynism**. Compare GYNANDROMORPH; HERMAPHRODITE. **—androgyne** *n.* **—androgynous** *adj.*

android 1. *adj.* possessing human features. **2.** *n.* an automaton constructed entirely or mainly from biological materials and resembling a human being. The term was popularized by science fiction writers in the mid- and late 20th century. Also called **humanoid**.

andropause *n.* see MALE CLIMACTERIC.

androstenedione *n.* a steroid hormone secreted by the ADRENAL CORTEX and the gonads as a precursor of the male and female sex hormones, particularly testosterone and estrone.

androsterone *n.* a steroid hormone, secreted by the ADRENAL CORTEX and testis, with weak androgenic effects.

anecdotal evidence evidence based on informal, uncontrolled personal observations.

anecdotal method a technique of research based on personal observation rather than more systematic, controlled observation. The anecdotal method may not clearly reveal relationships but can offer clues as to areas of investigation that warrant more systematic research.

anecdotal record in education, a factual, written record containing spontaneous, succinct, cumulative descriptions of a student's behavior. Such observations are usually considered significant because they highlight a given aspect of the student's personality and may prove useful in future evaluations.

anechoic chamber an enclosure designed to eliminate sound reverberations and echoes. A **sound-attenuating chamber**, like an anechoic chamber, minimizes intrusion of externally generated sounds but does not minimize internally generated sounds.

Anectine *n.* a trade name for SUCCINYLCHOLINE.

anencephaly *n.* congenital absence of the cranial vault (the bones forming the rear of the skull), with cerebral hemispheres completely missing or reduced to small masses. Infants born with anencephaly are usually blind, deaf, unconscious, and unable to feel pain. Anencephaly is an example of a NEURAL TUBE DEFECT. **—anencephalic** *adj.*

anergia *n.* **1.** absence of energy. **2.** a state of passivity. Also called **anergy**. **—anergic** *adj.*

anesthesia (**anaesthesia**) *n.* the loss or impairment of sensitivity to stimuli due to nerve damage or destruction, the administration of drugs (see ANESTHETIC), therapeutic techniques (e.g., ACUPUNCTURE ANESTHESIA), hypnotic suggestion, or conversion disorder (see CONVERSION ANESTHESIA). **—anesthetic** *adj.*

anesthetic *n.* any agent that produces anesthesia, with or without unconsciousness. **General anesthetics** produce loss of consciousness and are administered by inhalation or intravenous injection; **local anesthetics** are administered by injection or topical application to produce loss of sensation in a circumscribed area or region of the body.

anethopath *n.* a person lacking ethical or moral inhibitions. See also ANTISOCIAL PERSONALITY DISORDER. **—anethopathy** *n.*

aneuploidy *n.* the condition in which a cell or organism has fewer or more than the normal number of chromosomes, for example (in humans), 45 or 49, instead of the normal 46. Aneuploidy is often associated with neurological or cognitive defects. See MONOSOMY; TRISOMY. **—aneuploid** *adj., n.*

aneurysm (**aneurism**) *n.* an enlargement (dilation) at some point in an artery caused by the pressure of blood on weakened tissues, often at junctions where arteries split off from one another. **—aneurysmal** *adj.*

angakok *n.* an Inuit name for a SHAMAN or spiritual guide. The angakok is a central figure of Inuit spiritual life; present at major ceremonies, he foretells weather and the movement of game animals, cures illness, retrieves lost or stolen souls, and converses with other spiritual beings.

angel dust a street name for crystals of PCP (phencyclidine). The crystals are sometimes sprinkled onto oregano, parsley, or alfalfa and sold as marijuana.

Angell, James Rowland (1869–1949) U.S. psychologist. After studying at the University of Michigan under

John DEWEY, Angell moved to Harvard University to study under William JAMES and Josiah Royce (1855–1916), before studying at various German universities, including the University of Halle. From 1894 through 1919 Angell taught at the University of Chicago, where he became professor of psychology, dean, and finally acting president of the university (1918–1919). He then became chair of the National Research Council, president of the Carnegie Corporation, and finally (in 1921) president of Yale University until his retirement in 1937. In all these positions, Angell used his considerable influence to promote the development of psychology as a science. He was a leading exponent of the school of FUNCTIONALISM, as outlined in his 1906 American Psychological Association presidential address. He argued that, rather than study the discrete elements of consciousness (e.g., memories, images, sensations) as Edward B. TITCHENER advocated, psychologists ought to study the evolutionary utility or functions of consciousness. Providing the foundation of the school of BEHAVIORISM, functionalism as Angell and others defined it has exerted widespread influence on psychology in the United States. Angell received many honors, including election to the National Academy of Sciences in 1920 and the American Academy of Arts and Sciences in 1932.

Angelman syndrome a congenital disorder, caused by a genetic abnormality on chromosome 15, characterized by abnormalities or impairments in neurological, motor, and cognitive functioning, including severe learning disabilities, absence of speech, and a stiff, jerky gait and movements (see ATAXIA). Individuals with Angelman syndrome have happy dispositions and a propensity for paroxysms of inappropriate laughter. Craniofacial abnormalities, including a small or unusually flattened head, a large mouth, and a protruding jaw, are also common. The condition was formerly called **happy-puppet syndrome**. [Harry **Angelman** (1915–1996), British pediatrician]

anger *n.* an EMOTION characterized by tension and hostility arising from such sources as frustration, real or imagined injury by another, or perceived injustice. It can manifest itself in behaviors designed to remove the object of the anger (e.g., determined action) or behaviors designed merely to express the emotion (e.g., swearing).

anger control therapy a treatment that makes use of therapist-guided progressive exposure to anger-provoking cues in conjunction with therapist modeling, client rehearsal, assertiveness training, and other forms of coping skills training. Practiced in both individual and group settings, the intervention is used with clients who have general difficulty with anger (e.g., intensity, frequency, or mode of expression) or with clients who have specific disorders. See also ANGER MANAGEMENT.

anger-in *n.* hostility turned inward, particularly as a source of depression. See also SELF-ACCUSATION.

anger management techniques used by individuals—sometimes in counseling or therapy—to control their inappropriate reactions to anger-provoking stimuli and to express their feelings of anger in appropriate ways that are respectful of others. Such techniques include using relaxation methods (breathing deeply, repeating a word or phrase, visualizing a relaxing experience) to reduce physiological responses to anger, replacing exaggerated or overly dramatic thoughts with more rational ones (see COGNITIVE RESTRUCTURING), communicating more calmly and thoughtfully about one's anger, and removing oneself from situations or circumstances that provoke anger or avoiding them altogether.

anger stage the second of the five STAGES OF DYING described by Swiss-born U.S. psychiatrist Elisabeth Kübler-Ross (1926–2004). It is characterized by rage, resentment, and the question "Why me?".

angio- (**angi-**) *combining form* blood vessels or lymph vessels.

angiography *n.* the visualization of blood vessels by radiological techniques, used as an aid in diagnosing abnormalities or discovering blockages in areas of the circulatory system. For example, it can identify blood clots, tumors, aneurysms, and the degree of narrowing of the coronary arteries, which supply the heart. A substance that is opaque to X-rays is injected into a blood vessel to follow the path of blood flow; any obstruction, aneurysm, or rupture in the blood vessels will be revealed as a contrasting pattern. When the imaging is of arteries it is also called **arteriography**. The image produced is called an **angiogram** (or **arteriogram**). See also CEREBRAL ANGIOGRAPHY; DIGITAL SUBTRACTION ANGIOGRAPHY.

angioma *n.* a swelling or tumor of the vascular system that is made up of blood vessels or lymph vessels.

angioneurotic edema a disorder marked by recurrent episodes of noninflammatory swelling of certain body tissues, particularly the skin, mucous membranes, viscera, and central nervous system. The disorder may begin suddenly and last for hours or days, sometimes causing death. Attacks may be triggered by food or drug allergies, insect stings or bites, or viral infection. A hereditary form may be associated with emotional stress. Also called **Quincke's disease**.

angioscotoma *n.* a type of VISUAL FIELD DEFECT caused by shadows of blood vessels on the retina.

angiotensin *n.* one of a family of peptides, including angiotensins I, II, and III, that are produced by the enzymatic action of RENIN on a precursor protein (**angiotensinogen**) in the bloodstream. Their effects include narrowing of blood vessels (VASOCONSTRICTION), increased blood pressure, thirst, and stimulation of ALDOSTERONE release from the adrenal glands. See also RENIN–ANGIOTENSIN SYSTEM.

angst *n.* **1.** fear or anxiety (German). **2.** in EXISTENTIALISM, a state of anguish or despair in which a person recognizes the fundamental uncertainty of existence and understands the significance of conscious choice and personal responsibility.

angular gyrus a gyrus (ridge) in the inferior PARIETAL LOBE of the brain, formed by a junction of the superior and middle temporal gyri. The angular gyrus arches over the end of the superior temporal SULCUS and becomes continuous with the middle temporal gyrus. A stroke in this region can cause word blindness (see ALEXIA), and deficient processing in this area has been linked to DYSLEXIA.

anhaphia *n.* see ANAPHIA.

anhedonia *n.* the inability to enjoy experiences or activities that would normally be pleasurable. It is one of two symptoms either of which must always be present to meet the diagnostic criteria for a MAJOR DEPRESSIVE EPISODE, the other being a persistent depressed mood. Anhedonia is also commonly seen in schizophrenia. Also called **ahedonia**. [first defined in 1897 by French psychologist Théodule Ribot (1839–1916)] **—anhedonic** *adj.*

anhypnia *n.* see INSOMNIA.

aniconia *n.* an absence of mental imagery.

aniliction *n.* see ANILINGUS.

anilides *pl. n.* a group of aniline derivatives developed as analgesics and antipyretics of which ACETAMINOPHEN is the only member in current use. The parent compound, **acetanilide**, was originally introduced in 1886 as an antipyretic, but its toxicity led to its disuse and the development of a number of derivatives, including **phenacetin** (**acetophenetidin**; no longer in clinical use) and acetaminophen.

anililagnia *n.* see ANILINGUS.

anilingus *n.* the practice of applying the mouth to the anus as a form of sexual activity. Also called **aniliction**; **anililagnia**.

anima *n.* **1.** in the earlier writings of Carl JUNG, a person's innermost being, which is in closest contact with the UNCONSCIOUS and is contrasted with the PERSONA, or the externally directed part of a person. **2.** in Jung's later writings, (a) an ARCHETYPE that represents universal feminine characteristics or (b) the unconscious feminine aspect of the male psyche. Compare ANIMUS.

animal 1. *n.* a living organism generally distinguished from plants by having motility and mechanisms for rapid response to outside events. **2.** *n.* any such organism other than humans. **3.** *adj.* beastlike, or characteristic of lower animals: lacking human faculties and sensitivities.

animal aggression behavior among animals that includes direct physical attack by one on another or the threat of such attack. Types of animal aggression include, among others, (a) MATERNAL AGGRESSION, when the female's young are threatened; (b) PREDATORY AGGRESSION, to obtain prey; (c) DOMINANCE AGGRESSION, to maintain status or rank; (d) SEXUAL AGGRESSION in the male, for purposes of securing mates; (e) ANTIPREDATORY AGGRESSION; (f) FEAR-INDUCED AGGRESSION; (g) INTERMALE AGGRESSION, elicited by a male competitor; and (h) **instrumental aggression**, where aggressive behavior has been rewarded in the past.

animal-assisted therapy the therapeutic use of pets to enhance individuals' physical, social, emotional, or cognitive functioning. Animal-assisted therapy may be used, for example, to help people receive and give affection, especially in developing communication and social skills. It may be most effective for people who have suffered losses or separation from loved ones. Also called **pet-assisted therapy**; **pet therapy**.

animal behavior the scientific study of the behavior of animals, typically nonhuman animals. It includes the fields of ETHOLOGY, COMPARATIVE PSYCHOLOGY, and BEHAVIORAL ECOLOGY. Areas of study include ANIMAL AGGRESSION, ANIMAL COGNITION, ANIMAL COMMUNICATION, ANIMAL COURTSHIP, ANIMAL DEFENSIVE BEHAVIOR, ANIMAL EMOTIONALITY, ANIMAL GROOMING BEHAVIOR, ANIMAL MATERNAL BEHAVIOR, animal MATE SELECTION, ANIMAL PATERNAL BEHAVIOR, ANIMAL PLAY, ANIMAL SOCIAL BEHAVIOR, FORAGING, and PARENTAL BEHAVIOR.

animal care and use the treatment of nonhuman animals used in research and experimentation. Various regulations, standards, and principles have been developed to protect the well-being of such animals and ensure that they are treated in a humane and ethical manner. In the United States, examples include the Animal Welfare Act, passed by the U.S. Congress in 1966 and amended in 1970, 1976, 1985, and 1990; and the American Psychological Association's "Guidelines for Ethical Conduct in the Care and Use of Animals," developed in 1968 by the Committee on Animal Research and Ethics (CARE) and revised in 1996. See INSTITUTIONAL ANIMAL CARE AND USE COMMITTEE.

animal circadian rhythm rhythmic fluctuations in behavior or physiology in animals with a period of approximately one day. See BIOLOGICAL RHYTHM; CIRCADIAN RHYTHM.

animal cognition the inferred processes that are used by animals in solving environmental and social problems but that cannot be observed directly. This includes PROBLEM-SOLVING abilities that appear not to depend on rote memory or trial-and-error learning, suggesting that animals may be able to reason about potential solutions and therefore to solve problems with apparent spontaneity. See ANIMAL INTELLIGENCE; SOCIAL COGNITION; THEORY OF MIND.

animal communication the study of how nonhuman animals communicate with each other either to provide HONEST SIGNALS or to manage or manipulate the behavior of others. See CHEMICAL COMMUNICATION; INFRASONIC COMMUNICATION; SEISMIC COMMUNICATION; TACTILE COMMUNICATION; ULTRASONIC COMMUNICATION; VISUAL COMMUNICATION; VOCAL COMMUNICATION.

animal cooperation behavior in which two or more animals act together in a way that leads to mutual benefit. Examples include the cooperative nest building, food finding, and care of young in SOCIAL INSECTS, the MOBBING BEHAVIOR of animals toward a predator, and the production of specific signals to indicate sources of food or shelter to others. It is not known whether cases of animal cooperation require that the animals understand the need to cooperate (see COOPERATION).

animal courtship the behavior of animals prior to or associated with SEXUAL BEHAVIOR that allows one or both sexes to identify each other, to advertise their qualities to one another for MATE SELECTION, to prepare each other physiologically for reproduction, or to form or strengthen PAIR BONDS between mates. See also COURTSHIP BEHAVIOR.

animal defensive behavior behavior used by an animal to avoid being harmed by another. This might involve **defensive aggression** against a potential predator or against a member of the same species, either from its own group or an outside group (see DEFENSIVE BEHAVIOR), or ANIMAL ESCAPE BEHAVIOR to avoid the source of harm. It might also involve strategies to become inconspicuous, through CAMOUFLAGE or inactivity, or highly conspicuous, as evidenced by the noise a rattlesnake makes to indicate potential danger if provoked or attacked.

animal dominance the relationship between animals that allows some individuals to have greater access to resources (e.g., food, shelter, mates) than others in the group. Dominance ranks are often thought to be linear, with a clear ordering from most to least dominant (see PECKING ORDER), but may also be dependent (i.e., based on kin or age relationships) or governed by COALITIONS in which some subordinate individuals can outrank more dominant ones by acting together. Although dominance is usually thought to be based on ANIMAL AGGRESSION, stable dominance relationships are in fact maintained through the use of ANIMAL VOCALIZATIONS or VISUAL COMMUNICATION, with minimal aggression.

animal emotionality emotional reactions in animals, often measured by EXPLORATORY BEHAVIOR in an open field or by physiological correlates, such as heart rate or defecation rate. Individuals showing less exploratory behavior or greater physiological arousal are assumed to exhibit higher emotional reactivity.

animal escape behavior the attempt of an animal to escape an AVERSIVE STIMULUS, such as pain, a distasteful food, a predator, or an attacking or threatening member of the same species. This is one form of ANIMAL DEFENSIVE BEHAVIOR. See also ESCAPE BEHAVIOR.

animal ethology see ETHOLOGY.

animal fear see ANIMAL PHOBIA.

animal grooming behavior behavior in which an animal picks through its own hair or feathers or the hair or feathers of another group member (see GROOMING; ALLOGROOMING). Whereas the main function of self-grooming is hygienic (i.e., to remove dirt and parasites), grooming of other individuals may have both hygienic and social functions.

animal homing the ability of an animal to return, through NAVIGATION, to its place of origin when displaced, either by MIGRATION BEHAVIOR or experimental dispersal. See HOMING.

animal–human comparison the use of results from studies of ANIMAL BEHAVIOR to make generalizations about human behavior. Often, studies of animals are specifically designed to provide explicit models for some aspect of human behavior, but studies of the diversity of behavior across different animal species can be used both to understand the origins of certain types of human behavior and to suggest alternative solutions to human problems based on solutions that animals have developed. See COMPARATIVE PSYCHOLOGY.

animal hypnosis a state of motor nonresponsiveness in animals, produced by stroking, salient stimuli, or physical restraint. It is called "hypnosis" because of a putative resemblance to human hypnosis and trance.

animal intelligence the various abilities of animals to solve problems in their environment through mechanisms of ANIMAL LEARNING and ANIMAL COGNITION. Psychologists formerly thought that animal intelligence was best measured relative to human skills, with a linear progression of intelligence from simple to complex organisms. Current thinking evaluates skills relative to the particular problems each species faces and argues against simple phylogenetic relationships.

animal learning a field of psychology that studies the learning ability of nonhuman animals. The forms of learning studied are often less complex than those studied in human beings, which enables a degree of precision and control in studies of animal learning that is not always possible with human participants.

animal magnetism a hypothetical physical force that allegedly can have a curative effect when focused on ailing parts of the body, often through the use of a magnetized wand, magnetized rods, or a magnetized bath (see BAQUET). See MESMERISM. [proposed by Austrian physician Franz Anton Mesmer (1734–1815), who claimed some success using this method]

animal maternal behavior aspects of animal PARENTAL BEHAVIOR that are specific to female parents. These can range from NURSING BEHAVIOR in mammals and feeding in other species to protection, thermoregulation, and teaching skills to the young. See MATERNAL BEHAVIOR.

animal maternal deprivation an experimental manipulation used to evaluate the importance of female parents in the early behavioral, physical, social, and emotional development of animals by rearing the young in isolation or in peer groups. In species in which group members other than the female parent are involved in care of the young, maternal deprivation can be used to evaluate the caregiving ability of these others. See also MATERNAL DEPRIVATION.

animal mate selection see MATE SELECTION.

animal mating behavior see MATE SELECTION; MATING BEHAVIOR.

animal mimicry see MIMICRY.

animal model characteristics or conditions of an animal that are similar to those of humans, thus making the animal suitable for studying human behavior, disorders, or diseases.

animal navigation see NAVIGATION.

animal open-field behavior the activity of an animal measured in the form of exploratory behavior, movement, and number of defecations when it is exposed to an enclosed but otherwise relatively unrestricted laboratory environment, such as the OPEN-FIELD CHAMBER.

animal parental behavior see ANIMAL MATERNAL BEHAVIOR; ANIMAL PATERNAL BEHAVIOR; PARENTAL BEHAVIOR.

animal paternal behavior behavior by the male parent or another male that contributes toward the survival of the young animal. Because many males, especially in birds and mammals, lack CERTAINTY OF PATERNITY, it is thought that direct paternal care (e.g., feeding and carrying the young) is rare; indeed most animal paternal behavior is seen in socially monogamous species. See PARENTAL BEHAVIOR; PATERNAL BEHAVIOR.

animal phobia a persistent and irrational fear of a particular type of animal, such as snakes, cats, dogs, insects, mice, birds, or spiders. The focus of fear is often anticipated harm or danger. The emotion of disgust may also play a role in the maintenance of certain animal phobias (e.g., insects, mice, spiders). Situations in which the phobic animal or insect may be encountered are often avoided or else endured with intense anxiety or distress. Animal phobias typically start in childhood. The *DSM–IV–TR* designation is SPECIFIC PHOBIA, animal type.

animal play interaction occurring between animals, typically young animals, that appears to have no apparent function or purpose. Animal play often includes components of ANIMAL COURTSHIP, ANIMAL AGGRESSION, PREDATORY BEHAVIOR, and ANIMAL SEXUAL BEHAVIOR in contexts where mating or aggression do not seem appropriate. However, play might well have important functions in developing future SOCIAL RELATIONSHIPS and social skills, developing confidence, or strengthening sensorimotor systems. See also PLAY.

animal predatory behavior see PREDATORY BEHAVIOR.

animal psychology see COMPARATIVE PSYCHOLOGY.

animal rights the rights of animals to be treated with respect and to be free from exploitation and abuse by humans. Proponents of animal rights believe that it is morally wrong to harm, kill, or exploit animals for any human uses, including any type of research, and many advocate that all sentient creatures are in some ways the moral equals of humans. Proponents of **animal welfare**, however, typically make a moral distinction between humans and animals and believe that, while individuals have an obligation to treat animals humanely, certain research involving animals is medically and scientifically necessary. See also ANIMAL CARE AND USE.

animal sexual behavior all reproductive behavior between animals, beginning with ANIMAL COURTSHIP, leading to MATE SELECTION, and culminating in COPULATORY BEHAVIOR.

animal social behavior the aggregate of interactions between members of an animal group or family, including ANIMAL AGGRESSION, ANIMAL COMMUNICATION,

ANIMAL COOPERATION, ANIMAL COURTSHIP, ANIMAL DOMINANCE, ANIMAL PLAY, and PARENTAL BEHAVIOR. SOCIAL ORGANIZATION and SOCIAL STRUCTURE can be inferred from a detailed knowledge of animal social behavior.

animal spirits in the system of Roman physician Galen (129–215), a vaguely defined force or substance that is pictured as flowing through hollow tubes from the brain to all parts of the body; as such, it is a precursor of the modern concept of the nerve impulse. Like other aspects of Galen's system, the concept of animal spirits remained current well into the 17th century. In the mechanistic physiology of French philosopher René Descartes (1596–1650), for example, the animal spirits are retained to provide a link between body and mind. Descartes, however, anticipated the modern concept of the peripheral nervous system by maintaining that nerves conduct in either direction between the muscles and sense organs. Also called **vital spirits**. See also HYDRAULIC MODEL.

animal tool use the use of materials extraneous to the body for various purposes, such as the location or extraction of food or water. TOOL-USING BEHAVIOR is seen in a wide variety of species, but until recently **tool making** was thought to be restricted to human beings. However, studies of apes and birds indicate that this is not the case.

animal vocalization any call or sound produced by an animal that can provide information about internal state or likelihood of subsequent action or can be used to assess or manage the behavior of others. Vocalizations are typically produced through vibration of an organ, such as the larynx in some mammals, the two syringes in birds, or the blowholes in whales. Frequently sounds are amplified through special organs, such as throat sacs in amphibians. See also VOCAL COMMUNICATION.

animal welfare see ANIMAL RIGHTS.

animate noun a noun denoting a living entity capable of being the AGENT of an action; an **inanimate noun** is one denoting any other entity. The distinction affects the form of the noun in some languages and can be significant in CASE GRAMMAR.

animatism *n.* the belief that within all entities, living and nonliving, there exist supernatural forces or powers.

animism *n.* **1.** the belief that natural phenomena, such as forests, rivers, and clouds, possess souls or spirits. **2.** belief in the existence of spiritual beings that are wholly supernatural and have no physical form. **3.** see ANIMISTIC THINKING. **—animistic** *adj.*

animistic thinking in Jean PIAGET's theory of cognitive development, a characteristic of the thinking of children in the PREOPERATIONAL STAGE in which inanimate objects are believed to be alive or to possess lifelike characteristics, such as intentions, desires, feelings, and beliefs. Compare PRECAUSAL THINKING.

animus *n.* in ANALYTIC PSYCHOLOGY, (a) an ARCHETYPE that represents universal masculine characteristics or (b) the unconscious masculine component of the female psyche. Compare ANIMA. [sense originated by Carl JUNG]

anion *n.* a negatively charged ION, such as a chloride ion. Compare CATION. **—anionic** *adj.*

aniridia *n.* a rare congenital disorder characterized by partial or almost complete absence of the iris, with abnormal development of the MACULA LUTEA and optic nerve. Glaucoma and cataract almost inevitably develop as a consequence of aniridia.

aniridia-oligophrenia-cerebellar ataxia syndrome a rare form of mental retardation in which the patient also suffers from lack of normal muscle control and has speech difficulty. Lenses and corneas may be normal, but the eyes lack irises and visual acuity is in a range between 20/100 and 20/200. Also called **Gillespie syndrome**.

aniseikonia *n.* a condition in which the two eyes perceive images of unequal size or shape when these are viewed through each eye separately. It may be an unintended consequence of clinical alterations made to the cornea or lens.

aniso- (**anis-**) *combining form* unequal or dissimilar.

anisocoria *n.* inequality in the size of the pupils. Roughly one quarter of the population has a clinically visible amount of pupillary inequality; this figure increases with age: One third of people over age 60 exhibit anisocoria.

anisometropia *n.* a condition in which the eyes have differing powers of REFRACTION.

anisometropic amblyopia see DEVELOPMENTAL AMBLYOPIA.

anisotropy *n.* the state of being different, especially with respect to direction or orientation, lack of symmetry of form, or lack of symmetry of responses in different parts of something. Anisotropy in vision can refer to differences between the right and left eyes (e.g., ANISOMETROPIA). Also called **anisotropia**. **—anisotropic** *adj.*

ankylo- (**ankyl-**) *combining form* bent or crooked.

ankyloglossia *n.* restricted movement of the tongue due to abnormal shortness of the lingual frenum. Normal speech production may be affected. Also called **tongue tie**.

ankylosis *n.* an immobility and consolidation of a joint, usually due to the destruction of membranes lining the joint or to a defect in bone structure. It may occur naturally, as in rheumatoid arthritis, or by surgical fusion (arthrodesis).

Anna O. the pseudonym of Austrian social worker and feminist Bertha Pappenheim (1859–1936), who was a patient of Austrian physician Josef Breuer (1842–1925), a colleague of Sigmund FREUD. Breuer's treatment of her hysteria was written up in an early case study that was an important precursor to PSYCHOANALYSIS. See also TALKING CURE.

annihilation *n.* complete destruction. In psychoanalytic theory, annihilation is destruction of the self. In OBJECT RELATIONS THEORY, fear of annihilation (**annihilation anxiety**) is viewed as the earliest form of anxiety. Melanie KLEIN attributed it to the experience of the DEATH INSTINCT; British psychoanalyst Donald Winnicott (1896–1971) saw it as the anxiety that accompanies IMPINGEMENTS from the environment. **—annihilate** *vb.*

anniversary event the annual occurrence of a date marking a significant event or experience that may be positive or negative.

anniversary reaction a strong emotional response on the anniversary of a significant event. It most commonly involves depressive symptoms around the same time of the year that the death of a loved one or a severe disappointment occurred.

annual cycle a pattern of behavior that recurs over the course of a year. Hibernating animals eat more food and gain weight in the months before winter, migratory animals experience periods of activity twice a year coincident with migration, and seasonally breeding animals undergo annual changes in reproductive physiology and related behavior (such as territory defense and SONG).

Some annual cycles will continue to be manifested even in the absence of external seasonal cues.

annulment *n.* **1.** a formal pronouncement that a marriage or judicial proceeding is terminated. **2.** in psychoanalytic theory, a process in which disagreeable ideas or events are neutralized or made ineffective by converting them into daydreams and fantasies. Compare REPRESSION.

annulospiral ending a type of nerve fiber ending in MUSCLE SPINDLES in which the nerve fiber is wrapped around the muscle fiber near the center of the spindle. Annulospiral endings show a maximal discharge early in the stretch of a muscle and then adapt to a lower discharge rate. Also called **primary sensory ending**. Compare FLOWER-SPRAY ENDING.

annunciator *n.* in ergonomics, an early-warning system that uses sensors to monitor specific system attributes and some form of alert to warn the operator when deviation from the normal limits occurs. Action can then be taken to return the system attribute to its normal state. Compare CHECK READING. **—annunciate** *vb.*

anodal polarization a condition in which the flow of electrical current is toward the positive pole. In a typical nerve cell, the positive pole would be in extracellular fluid, and the current flow would be from the inside toward the outside of the cell membrane.

anodmia *n.* see ANOSMIA.

anodyne *n.* any agent or procedure that relieves pain, including analgesics (e.g., aspirin), anesthetics, or acupuncture.

anoetic *adj.* **1.** not involving or subject to intellectual or cognitive processes. Emotions are sometimes considered anoetic. **2.** describing a level of knowledge or memory in which there is no consciousness of knowing or remembering (see ANOETIC MEMORY). **Anoetic consciousness** is a corresponding state of "unknowing knowing" in which one is aware of external stimuli but not of interpreting them. [defined by Estonian-born Canadian psychologist Endel Tulving (1927–)] **3.** lacking the capacity for understanding or concentrated thought. This meaning, originally applied to denote mental retardation, is no longer common. Compare AUTONOETIC; NOETIC. **—anoesis** *n.*

anoetic memory learning or knowledge that is recalled without conscious awareness and demonstrated by enhancement of speed or efficiency of performance. It is the most basic level of memory in the monohierarchic theory of memory proposed by Estonian-born Canadian psychologist Endel Tulving (1927–), being subordinate to NOETIC MEMORY and AUTONOETIC MEMORY.

anogenital *adj.* relating to the anatomical region in which the anus and genitalia are located.

anomalopia *n.* see ANOMALOUS TRICHROMATISM.

anomalous color vision see ACHROMATISM; COLOR BLINDNESS.

anomalous dichromatism partial color blindness in which only two colors (usually blue and yellow) can be seen. Also called **anomalous dichromasy**. See DICHROMATISM.

anomalous differences differences between expected and obtained data that require further investigation in order to be reconciled.

anomalous experience any of a set of conscious states, often categorized as ALTERED STATES OF CONSCIOUSNESS, that are felt to be unusual and inexplicable. Examples are OUT-OF-BODY EXPERIENCES, mystical experiences (see MYSTICISM), a SENSE OF PRESENCE, and epileptic AURAS.

anomalous stimulus a stimulus that is unexpected in relation to an organism's recent experience, which gives rise to unique neural events different from those caused by expected stimuli.

anomalous trichromatism a form of COLOR BLINDNESS or COLOR WEAKNESS in which affected individuals have three types of retinal cone but one of these has a color sensitivity that is different from that of the corresponding normal cone. It is usually marked by a diminished capacity to respond to the red–green color system. The ability to distinguish these colors increases in proportion to their intensity, that is, less brilliant shades are less easily identified. Also called **anomalopia**; **anomalous trichromasy**.

anomaly *n.* **1.** anything that is irregular or deviates from the norm. **2.** in the analysis of SCIENTIFIC REVOLUTIONS by U.S. philosopher of science Thomas Kuhn (1922–1996), an empirical fact that should be but cannot be explained or predicted by a particular theoretical system. **—anomalous** *adj.*

anomia *n.* **1.** an impaired ability to recall the names of objects. See AMNESTIC APHASIA. See also COLOR ANOMIA. **2.** a defective moral sense. [defined by U.S. physician Benjamin Rush (1745–1813)] **—anomic** *adj.*

anomic aphasia see AMNESTIC APHASIA.

anomic suicide a former name for a suicide in response to an unfavorable change in the person's financial or social situation. [first defined by French sociologist Émile Durkheim (1858–1917)]

anomie *n.* a sense of alienation and hopelessness in a society or group that is often a response to social upheaval. It may also be accompanied by changes in personal and social values. **—anomic** *adj.*

anopia *n.* blindness in one or both halves of the visual field as a result of a defect in the peripheral or central visual system. Also called **anopsia**. See HEMIANOPIA; QUADRANOPIA.

anopsia *n.* see ANOPIA.

anorchism *n.* congenital absence of one or both testes.

anorectants *pl. n.* see APPETITE SUPPRESSANTS.

anorexia *n.* **1.** the absence or loss of appetite for food, usually as a chronic or continuing condition as opposed to a temporary lack of appetite. Anorexia may be primarily psychological in origin (see ANOREXIA NERVOSA) or it may be associated with a physiological disorder, such as hypopituitarism. **2.** loss of appetite for other desires (e.g., sex). **—anorectic** or **anorexic** *adj., n.*

anorexia mirabilis a CULTURE-BOUND SYNDROME found in medieval Europe, characterized by severe restriction of food intake associated with religious devotion and piety. Also called **holy anorexia**.

anorexia nervosa an EATING DISORDER, occurring most frequently in adolescent girls, that involves persistent refusal of food, excessive fear of weight gain, refusal to maintain minimally normal body weight, disturbed perception of body image, and amenorrhea (absence of at least three menstrual periods). Compare BULIMIA NERVOSA; REVERSE ANOREXIA.

anorgasmia *n.* the inability to achieve orgasm. Also called **anorgasmy**. See also FEMALE ORGASMIC DISORDER; MALE ORGASMIC DISORDER. **—anorgasmic** *adj.*

anorthography *n.* see AGRAPHIA.

anorthopia *n.* asymmetrical or distorted vision, sometimes associated with STRABISMUS.

anorthoscope *n.* a device consisting of two disks, one in front of the other, that rotate in opposite directions. The front disk is opaque with four slits through which a highly distorted image on the back disk is viewed. Although the image on the rear disk is both rotating and distorted, it will appear normal and stationary when viewed through the front disk if both disks are rotated at the appropriate speed. [first constructed by Joseph Antoine Ferdinand Plateau (1801–1888), Belgian inventor and physician]

anorthoscopic perception distortions in the appearance of a moving stimulus that occur when the view of the stimulus is periodically interrupted. For example, the rotating spokes of a wagon wheel appear curved when viewed through the pickets of a fence. See ANORTHOSCOPE.

anosmia *n.* absence of the sense of smell, which may be general or limited to certain odors. Anosmia is associated with many disorders, including brain injuries and frontal lobe tumors. Also called **anodmia**; **anosphresia**. **—anosmic** *adj.*

anosognosia *n.* failure or refusal to recognize or deal with the existence of a defect or disorder, such as hearing loss, poor vision, speech defects, or paralysis. This may reflect psychological denial or it may arise from certain brain injuries, especially in the right cerebral hemisphere.

anosognosia for blindness see ANTON'S SYNDROME.

anosphresia *n.* see ANOSMIA.

A-not-B task see OBJECT PERMANENCE.

ANOVA acronym for ANALYSIS OF VARIANCE.

anovulatory menstrual cycle a menstrual cycle that occurs without ovulation. It results from an imbalance between hormone production of the pituitary gland and the ovaries and is marked by irregular menstruation. An anovulatory menstrual cycle is most likely to be associated with menarche or menopause.

anoxemia *n.* the absence of oxygen in the blood, a condition that frequently results in loss of consciousness and brain damage. Compare HYPOXEMIA.

anoxia *n.* reduced oxygen to the brain, due to decreased vascular perfusion or reduced oxygen content in the blood. This may be caused by cardiac arrest, CARBON MONOXIDE POISONING, or respiratory distress, which in turn may be a result of severe allergic reactions, strangulation, or near-drowning episodes. Consequences depend on the severity of the anoxia and the specific areas of the brain that are affected, but can include generalized cognitive deficits or more focal deficits in memory (see AMNESTIC DISORDER), perception, or EXECUTIVE FUNCTION. Compare HYPOXIA. **—anoxic** *adj.*

ANP abbreviation for ACTIVE NOISE PROTECTION.

ANR abbreviation for ACTIVE NOISE REDUCTION.

ANS abbreviation for AUTONOMIC NERVOUS SYSTEM.

Anschauung *n.* intuition (German, in which it can also mean "view" or "perception"). In the thought of German philosopher Immanuel Kant (1724–1804), *Anschauung* is that means of knowing in which knowledge is immediate and not based on concepts. According to Kant, one's knowledge of sensible objects is of this kind.

ant- *prefix* see ANTE-; ANTI-.

Antabuse *n.* a trade name for DISULFIRAM.

antagonist *n.* **1.** an agent (e.g., a drug) that inhibits or reduces the action of another substance (the AGONIST). For example, it may combine with the agonist, thus preventing it from binding to its receptor (**chemical antagonism**); it may oppose or reverse the effects of the agonist by competitively binding to the same receptor (see PHARMACOLOGICAL ANTAGONISM); or it may produce an opposite effect by binding to a different receptor (see PHYSIOLOGICAL ANTAGONISM). **2.** a contracting muscle whose action generates force opposing the intended direction of movement. This force may serve to slow the movement rapidly as it approaches the target (see TRIPHASIC PATTERN) or it may help to define the force equilibrium at the movement end point (see EQUILIBRIUM-POINT MODEL). **3.** an adversary: one who opposes or thwarts another. **—antagonism** *n.* **—antagonistic** *adj.*

antagonistic colors colors at opposite sides of the COLOR CIRCLE, such as red and green or blue and yellow. Also called **complementary colors**.

antagonistic muscles pairs of muscles (or muscle groups) that oppose each other in function. For example, the biceps flexes the arm at the elbow, whereas the opposing triceps straightens the arm.

ante- (**ant-**) *prefix* before or in front of.

antecedent *n.* **1.** an event, circumstance, or stimulus that precedes some other event and often elicits, signals, or sets the occasion for a particular behavior or response. See also CONTINGENCY. **2.** in linguistics, the noun or noun phrase to which a PRONOUN (especially a relative pronoun, such as *who, that,* or *which*) refers back. For example, in *the train that I caught yesterday*, the antecedent of *that* is *train*. See ANAPHORA. **3.** in a conditional proposition of the *if...then* form, the statement that follows *if*. The antecedent is what is posited to be the case as the condition for the CONSEQUENT (the statement following *then*) to be true. For example, in the conditional proposition *If Socrates is a man, then he is mortal*, the statement *Socrates is a man* is the antecedent. Also called **protasis**. See also AFFIRMING THE ANTECEDENT; DENYING THE ANTECEDENT.

antecedent variable a variable (*a*) that precedes another variable (*b*) but that may or may not be causally related to variable *b*.

antergic *adj.* exerting force in opposition. For example, antergic pairs of muscles or muscle groups oppose each other in flexing or extending a joint. Compare SYNERGY.

anterior *adj.* toward the front or head of an animal. Compare POSTERIOR; ROSTRAL. **—anteriorly** *adv.*

anterior cerebral artery a branch of the INTERNAL CAROTID ARTERY that begins near the lateral cerebral sulcus and passes above the optic nerve to the beginning of the longitudinal fissure. The left and right anterior cerebral arteries run parallel in the longitudinal fissure, then curve back along the upper surface of the CORPUS CALLOSUM. They supply blood to the frontal cortex and to much of the medial and superior surfaces of the cortex.

anterior chamber see EYE.

anterior choroidal artery a relatively narrow artery that is a posterior branch of the MIDDLE CEREBRAL ARTERY. It passes across the optic tract toward the temporal horn of the lateral ventricle and into the choroid plexus, hippocampus, thalamus, amygdala, and related deep structures.

anterior commissure a bundle of myelinated fibers connecting parts of the cerebral hemispheres in the brain. It also contains fibers of the OLFACTORY TRACT and is involved in certain disorders involving loss of the sense of smell. See also COMMISSURE.

anterior communicating artery syndrome (**ACoA syndrome**) a syndrome resulting from rupture of an aneurysm in the anterior communicating artery, a small blood vessel in the brain that links the right and left cerebral arteries. The acute phase is marked by severe confusion and gross attentional disturbances. When the confusional state clears, both ANTEROGRADE AMNESIA and RETROGRADE AMNESIA are seen, and disorientation and EXECUTIVE DYSFUNCTION are apparent. CONFABULATION and lack of insight may also occur. See also FRONTAL LOBE SYNDROME.

anterior corticospinal tract see CORTICOSPINAL TRACT.

anterior fossa see FOSSA.

anterior horn **1.** either of the regions of gray matter in the ventral SPINAL CORD that contain large motor neurons whose axons form the VENTRAL ROOTS. Also called **ventral horn**. See also CENTRAL GRAY. Compare DORSAL HORN. **2.** the anterior subdivision of each LATERAL VENTRICLE in the brain.

anterior pituitary the anterior lobe of the PITUITARY GLAND. Also called **adenohypophysis**.

anterior pituitary hormone any of the hormones secreted by the anterior PITUITARY GLAND. They include GROWTH HORMONE, PROLACTIN, and the TROPIC HORMONES.

anterior–posterior axis a line or plane running from the front to the back of the body.

anterior–posterior development gradient the more rapid growth of the head region compared with posterior areas of the body during fetal development. In the early embryonic stages, the head and brain make up half of the body mass, and at birth the head represents one quarter of the infant's total height. See CEPHALOCAUDAL DEVELOPMENT.

anterior rhizotomy see RHIZOTOMY.

anterior root see VENTRAL ROOT.

anterior spinothalamic tract see SPINOTHALAMIC TRACTS.

anterograde *adj.* moving or extending forward in time or in space.

anterograde amnesia loss of memory for events that occurred subsequent to the onset of the AMNESIA. For example, a boxer who receives a heavy blow to the head may not remember finishing the fight. Because anterograde amnesia is defined in relation to the onset of the precipitating event, it is synonymous with an **impairment in new learning**. Compare RETROGRADE AMNESIA.

anterograde degeneration the degeneration of a neuron after injury that spreads from the point of injury distally, away from the nerve cell body. Also called **Wallerian degeneration**. Compare RETROGRADE DEGENERATION.

anterolateral system a major SOMATOSENSORY SYSTEM consisting of ascending tracts in the anterior lateral white matter of the spinal cord. Its fibers originate mostly from DORSAL HORN cells and convey information about pain, temperature, and touch to higher centers. See also SPINOTHALAMIC TRACTS.

anthropo- *combining form* human.

anthropocentrism *n.* the explicit or implicit assumption that human experience is the central reality and, by extension, the idea that all phenomena can be evaluated in the light of their relationship to humans. **—anthropocentric** *adj.*

anthropogenesis *n.* the scientific study of the origins and development of humans. Also called **anthropogeny**. **—anthropogenetic** or **anthropogenic** *adj.*

anthropoid *adj.* resembling a human being. The term is usually applied to the tailless apes: specifically, gorillas, orangutans, chimpanzees, bonobos, and gibbons.

anthropological linguistics the branch of linguistics that draws connections between the characteristics of a particular language and the cultural practices, social structures, and worldview of the society in which it is spoken (see LINGUISTIC DETERMINISM; LINGUISTIC RELATIVITY). The field developed primarily from an interest in describing languages indigenous to North America, such as Navaho and Hopi.

anthropology *n.* the study of human beings. This typically involves the description and explanation of similarities and differences among human groups in their languages, aesthetic expressions, belief systems, and social structures over the range of human geography and chronology. **Physical anthropology** focuses on the origin, evolution, and environmental adaptation of human groups, while **cultural anthropology** and **social anthropology** are primarily concerned with the development and functioning of customs, beliefs, and institutions. Outside the United States, this latter subdivision is often called ETHNOLOGY. Although historically concentrating on preliterate peoples, anthropological interests have extended more recently to nontribal societies and urban groups. **—anthropological** *adj.* **—anthropologist** *n.*

anthropometry *n.* **1.** the scientific study of how the size and proportions of the human body are affected by such variables as age, sex, and ethnic and cultural groups. **2.** the taking of measurements of the human body for purposes of comparison and study. **—anthropometric** *adj.* **—anthropometrist** *n.*

anthropomorphism *n.* **1.** the attribution of human characteristics to nonhuman entities such as deities, spirits, animals, plants, or inanimate objects. From the scientific point of view, this must be considered a primitive and erroneous mode of thinking; nevertheless, it remains a fundamental tendency of the human imagination as reflected in language, religion, and art. **2.** in COMPARATIVE PSYCHOLOGY, the tendency to interpret the behavior and mental processes of nonhuman animals in terms of human abilities. A variation is ANTHROPOCENTRISM, which uses human behavior as the standard by which the behavior of nonhuman animals, for example, ANIMAL INTELLIGENCE, is evaluated. See also LLOYD MORGAN'S CANON. Compare ZOOMORPHISM. **—anthropomorphic** *adj.*

anthroponomy *n.* the science of human development as it relates to the development of other species and to the environment. **—anthroponomical** *adj.*

anthroposcopy *n.* the practice of judging the body build of an individual by inspection, rather than by the use of anthropometric techniques of body measurement. **—anthroposcopic** *adj.*

anti- (**ant-**) *prefix* **1.** opposing or against (e.g., ANTICONFORMITY). **2.** opposite to (e.g., ANTIMETROPIA). **3.** counteracting or inhibiting (e.g., ANTIDEPRESSANT).

antiaging remedy any intervention that is hypothesized to slow down or reverse the effects of aging. Typically these interventions are pharmacological (e.g., antioxidants, vitamin C, growth hormones), but they also can be lifestyle changes (e.g., exercise).

antiandrogen *n.* a substance that reduces or blocks the physiological effects of androgenic hormones on tissues normally responsive to these hormones. Antiandrogens may function by PHARMACOLOGICAL ANTAGONISM, by interfering with the metabolism of androgens, or by inhibiting the normal response to androgens. They include

bicalutamide, **finasteride**, **flutamide**, and **nilutamide**. Also called **androgen antagonist**.

antiandrogen therapy medical treatment using ANTIANDROGENS to correct the effects of excessive levels of male sex hormones. It may be used to control hair loss and cancer of the prostate in males and to reverse masculine traits (e.g., excessive facial hair) in females. More controversially, antiandrogens have been used in the treatment of repeat sex offenders (see CHEMICAL CASTRATION).

antianxiety medications see ANXIOLYTICS.

antibiotics *pl. n.* drugs that are used to destroy pathogenic or otherwise harmful microorganisms, especially bacteria. Antibiotics can be produced by or obtained from living cells (e.g., molds, yeasts, or bacteria) or manufactured as synthetic chemicals with effects similar to natural antibiotics. Some work by interfering with bacterial reproduction, while others may disrupt the normal life functions of the pathogen. Antibiotics are ineffective against viruses. Overuse and inappropriate use of antibiotics are contributing to the development of bacterial resistance to many commonly used antibiotics.

antibody *n.* a modified protein molecule, produced by B LYMPHOCYTES, that interacts with an ANTIGEN and renders it harmless (see IMMUNE RESPONSE). Each type of antibody is designed to interact with a specific antigen and can be mass-produced following previous exposure to an identical antigen. See ANTIGEN–ANTIBODY REACTION; IMMUNITY.

anticathexis *n.* in psychoanalytic theory, a process in which the EGO withdraws PSYCHIC ENERGY from certain unconscious wishes and ideas and uses it to strengthen other ideas and wishes capable of blocking their entrance into consciousness. The **anticathected** idea may be similar to the original idea or opposite but related to it: for example, philanthropy may neutralize an unconscious wish to hoard. Also called **countercathexis**. See also CATHEXIS.

anticholinergic drugs drugs that block or otherwise interfere with the release of the neurotransmitter acetylcholine by nerve endings and thus disrupt the transmission of impulses along parasympathetic routes. Because they act at MUSCARINIC RECEPTORS (a category of acetylcholine receptors), these agents are also known as **antimuscarinic drugs**. In large doses, they may also interfere with actions of histamine, serotonin, and norepinephrine. Natural anticholinergic drugs include ATROPINE and SCOPOLAMINE. A variety of synthetic anticholinergic drugs are used to treat neurological disorders, many as ANTIPARKINSONIAN AGENTS. They include BENZTROPINE, BIPERIDEN, PROCYCLIDINE, and TRIHEXYPHENIDYL, which are administered primarily to relieve the symptoms of muscular rigidity. Anticholinergic drugs are often used in combinations to control specific symptoms. TRICYCLIC ANTIDEPRESSANTS and some conventional ANTIPSYCHOTICS also have anticholinergic activity. Also called **parasympatholytic drugs**.

anticholinergic effects side effects that are characteristic of ANTICHOLINERGIC DRUGS and are also associated with other agents (e.g., TRICYCLIC ANTIDEPRESSANTS, MONOAMINE OXIDASE INHIBITORS) that exert antagonist effects at MUSCARINIC RECEPTORS. They include dry mouth, blurred vision, urinary hesitancy or retention, and constipation. Also called **antimuscarinic effects**. See also ANTICHOLINERGIC SYNDROME.

anticholinergic ileus obstruction of the small bowel (ileum) due to paralysis of its muscle, resulting from administration of agents that block MUSCARINIC RECEPTORS in the bowel. Though rare, it may be caused by strongly ANTICHOLINERGIC DRUGS, such as tricyclic antidepressants and some older antipsychotics. Ileus may be fatal and requires medical intervention.

anticholinergic syndrome a disorder produced by anticholinergic drugs and due to their ANTICHOLINERGIC EFFECTS, marked by symptoms involving both the peripheral and central nervous systems. The former include dry mucous membranes, dry mouth, and flushed skin and face, while the latter include ataxia (unsteady gait), drowsiness, slurred speech, confusion and disorientation, hallucinations, and memory deficits, particularly of short-term memory. Tricyclic antidepressants, aliphatic phenothiazines, antiparkinsonian agents, and scopolamine are examples of drugs that can cause anticholinergic syndrome. This syndrome is often observed in patients receiving combinations of such drugs. See CENTRAL ANTICHOLINERGIC SYNDROME; PERIPHERAL ANTICHOLINERGIC SYNDROME.

anticholinesterase *n.* see ACETYLCHOLINESTERASE INHIBITORS; CHOLINERGIC DRUGS.

anticipation *n.* **1.** looking forward to a future event or state, sometimes with an affective component (e.g., pleasure, anxiety). **2.** the onset of a hereditary disease at earlier and earlier ages in successive generations.

anticipation learning method a technique that involves learning to associate a stimulus (e.g., an item in a list or series) with a response that follows (e.g., the next item in the list or series), so that when subsequently given the stimulus, one can produce the response. The anticipation learning method is frequently used in PAIRED-ASSOCIATES LEARNING and SERIAL RECALL. Also called **anticipation method**; **serial anticipation method**.

anticipatory anxiety worry or apprehension about an upcoming event or situation because of the possibility of a negative outcome, such as danger, misfortune, or adverse judgment by others. The worry or apprehension is often accompanied by somatic symptoms of tension. Anticipatory anxiety is a common feature of PANIC DISORDER, in which the concern is over the possibility of experiencing future panic attacks.

anticipatory attitude change ATTITUDE CHANGE that depends on the expectation of receiving a persuasive message. When the topic of the anticipated message is very important, attitudes polarize in the direction of the initial attitude. When the topic is of little importance, attitudes become more moderate.

anticipatory coping a stress-management strategy used by an individual who faces a stressful upcoming event, situation, or task that involves avoiding or minimizing the occurrence of problems associated with the stress. Anticipatory coping is assumed to increase with middle and old age.

anticipatory error **1.** the error of making a response before it should be made. **2.** an error made when recalling items from a list in which an item is recalled as having been earlier in the list than it actually was.

anticipatory grief sorrow and anxiety experienced by someone who expects a loved one to die within a short period. The period of anticipatory grief can be regarded as having both stressful and constructive possibilities: It might cushion the emotional impact when the death actually occurs, but it could have the unfortunate consequence of leading a person to withdraw from the relationship, treating the other person as though he or she were already dead. See also COMPLICATED GRIEF; TRAUMATIC GRIEF. [introduced as a concept in 1944 by U.S. psychologist Erich Lindemann (1900–1974)]

anticipatory guidance counseling and educational services provided to individuals or families before they reach a turning point or significant developmental change in their lives. Examples include parental guidance before a child enters school and counseling of employees soon to reach retirement age.

anticipatory image a mental image that allows one to envision transformations of that image, even if one has never experienced such transformations in the past. According to Jean PIAGET's theory of cognitive development, anticipatory images are not produced until the CONCRETE OPERATIONAL STAGE. Compare REPRODUCTIVE IMAGE.

anticipatory movement a movement that is based on (a) expected changes in the environment (e.g., predictive smooth eye or hand movements to track a moving stimulus); (b) expected postural necessity (e.g., to maintain balance when shifting a limb); or (c) preparation for an upcoming action (e.g., prepositioning movements, such as lip rounding in speech).

anticipatory nausea nausea that occurs prior to chemotherapy (typically during the day before administration). Nausea and vomiting can also occur after an individual has received a few treatments, usually in response to triggers in the environment (e.g., odors and sights of the hospital room) that have been associated with the physical side effects of chemotherapy.

anticipatory regret a sense of the potential negative consequences of a decision that influences the choice made: For example, an individual may decide not to make an investment because of the feelings associated with an imagined loss. See PROSPECT THEORY.

anticipatory response a response that occurs before the evoking stimulus is presented.

anticipatory schema in the PERCEPTUAL CYCLE HYPOTHESIS, a structured pattern of knowledge (a "preunderstanding") that influences an organism's expectations in a given situation, thus guiding the organism's perception of that situation (i.e., by preparing it to receive certain kinds of information or to perceive particular aspects of the situation) and ultimately directing its exploration and action. For example, a student entering an unfamiliar classroom for the first time may invoke a general classroom schema, which likely contains information about the general characteristics of such a room (the presence of a floor, a ceiling, four walls, a blackboard, desks, etc.) and leads the person to expect to encounter these things within this novel classroom. Since the general classroom schema does not contain information suggesting the presence of, say, a clothes washing machine, the student would not spend time looking for this unanticipated item. Anticipatory schemas are dynamic rather than static; although based on previous experience, they are continuously being revised as a result of new experiences. [defined in 1976 by U.S. cognitive psychologist Ulric Neisser (1928–)]

anticonfirmationism *n.* the position that it is not possible to confirm the truth of general propositions, including scientific hypotheses, either by accruing positive instances or by probability estimates. See FALSIFICATIONISM.

anticonformity *n.* a deliberate, self-conscious refusal to comply with accepted social standards, often accompanied by the expression of ideas, beliefs, or judgments that challenge those standards. Anticonformity is motivated by rebelliousness or obstinacy rather than the need to express oneself sincerely. Also called **counterconformity**. Compare CONFORMITY; NONCONFORMITY.

anticonvulsants *pl. n.* drugs used to reduce the frequency or severity of epileptic seizures or to terminate a seizure already underway. Until the advent of the HYDANTOINS in the 1930s, anticonvulsants consisted mainly of BROMIDES and BARBITURATES: PHENOBARBITAL was first used in the treatment of epilepsy in 1912 and remained the mainstay of treatment until the introduction of the hydantoin PHENYTOIN. Drugs now used to treat partial or tonic–clonic seizures include phenytoin, CARBAMAZEPINE, VALPROIC ACID, phenobarbital, and newer anticonvulsants, such as LAMOTRIGINE, GABAPENTIN, tiagabine, TOPIRAMATE, vigabatrin, and zonisamide. Ethosuximide and other SUCCINIMIDES may be used in managing absence seizures. The BENZODIAZEPINES are also effective antiseizure medications. Also called **antiepileptics**.

antidepressants *pl. n.* a class of psychotropic drugs administered in the treatment of depression. Although exact mechanisms of action remain unclear, antidepressants apparently work by altering levels of various neurotransmitters available at receptor sites in the brain. At least four classes of antidepressants are in current clinical use: SSRIS (selective serotonin-reuptake inhibitors), MIXED-FUNCTION ANTIDEPRESSANTS (or dual-action agents), TRICYCLIC ANTIDEPRESSANTS (TCAs), and MONOAMINE OXIDASE INHIBITORS (MAOIs). Some stimulants may also function as antidepressants.

antidiuretic hormone (**ADH**) see VASOPRESSIN.

antidromic conduction the conduction of a nerve impulse in a reversed direction (i.e., from axon to cell body), produced for experimental purposes. Also called **antidromic activation**; **antidromic phenomenon**.

antiepileptics *pl. n.* see ANTICONVULSANTS.

antiestrogen *n.* a substance (e.g., tamoxifen) that reduces or blocks the physiological effects of estrogenic hormones on tissues normally responsive to these hormones. Antiestrogens may function by exerting a primarily antagonistic effect on estrogen receptors or by blocking estrogen receptor sites. Substances (e.g., raloxifene) that exhibit some degree of mixed agonist and antagonist effect at estrogen receptors are called **selective estrogen receptor modulators** (SERMs). These agents are variously used in the treatment or prevention of breast cancer and some estrogenically mediated effects of menopause and also in the treatment of some types of female infertility. Also called **estrogen antagonist**.

antigen *n.* any substance that is treated by the immune system as foreign and is therefore capable of inducing an IMMUNE RESPONSE, particularly the production of ANTIBODIES that render it harmless. The antigen may be a virus, a bacterium, a toxin (e.g., bee venom), or tissue (e.g., blood) of another individual with different genetic characteristics. See also ALLERGEN. **—antigenic** *adj.*

antigen–antibody reaction the binding of an ANTIBODY to its particular ANTIGEN as part of the body's natural defense against the introduction of a foreign substance. The bound antibody renders the foreign substance more susceptible to degradation by immune cells, for example, engulfment by phagocytic cells. Once the individual's IMMUNE SYSTEM has developed antibodies to fight a certain type of antigen, the antibodies can be mobilized quickly to destroy any repeated invasion by the antigen; thus the first antigen attack induces IMMUNITY to future attacks. See also IMMUNE RESPONSE.

antigonadal action the blocking of gonadal function by an agent or process, such as a lesion in the pituitary gland or amygdala.

antiharassment policies policies and procedures adopted by an organization or institution to prevent and counter harassment due to gender, race, or sexual orientation. They typically include conducting awareness training designed to educate people about harassment, implementing disciplinary measures when necessary, and having formal grievance procedures.

antihistamines *pl. n.* see HISTAMINE ANTAGONISTS.

anti-intoxicant *n.* a theoretical drug that would have the effect of countering the intoxicating effects of alcohol. Also called **amethystic**.

antilibidinal ego in the OBJECT RELATIONS THEORY of British psychoanalyst W. Ronald D. Fairbairn (1889–1964), the portion of the EGO STRUCTURE that is similar to Sigmund FREUD'S SUPEREGO The antilibidinal ego constitutes a nonpleasure-gratifying, self-deprecatory, or even hostile self-image; it is posited to develop out of the unitary ego present at birth when the infantile libidinal ego (similar to the ID) experiences deprivation at the hands of the parent and the infant suppresses his or her frustrated needs. Also called **internal saboteur**. See FAIRBAIRNIAN THEORY.

Antilirium *n.* a trade name for PHYSOSTIGMINE.

antimanic drugs see MOOD STABILIZERS.

antimetabolite *n.* a substance that has a molecular structure so similar to that of another substance required for a normal physiological function that it may be accepted as the required molecule, thereby disrupting a normal metabolic process. For example, the anticoagulant bishydroxycoumarin functions as an antimetabolite by interfering with vitamin K in producing the blood-clotting agent prothrombin.

antimetropia *n.* a condition in which one eye is myopic (nearsighted) and the other is hyperopic (farsighted).

anti-Müllerian hormone (**AMH**) see MÜLLERIAN-INHIBITING HORMONE.

antimuscarinic drugs see ANTICHOLINERGIC DRUGS.

antinociceptive *adj.* describing or relating to any factor that increases tolerance for, or reduces sensitivity to, harmful stimuli, usually stimuli that cause pain. See also PAIN PERCEPTION.

antinodal behavior see NODAL BEHAVIOR.

antinomy *n.* **1.** in common usage, a state of opposition or contradiction between two things. **2.** in the thought of German philosopher Immanuel Kant (1724–1804), a contradiction between two A PRIORI propositions in metaphysics, each of which can be supported by equally valid proofs. Kant cited a series of such antinomies as part of his argument against speculative metaphysics and in favor of his own position that the only world one can have knowledge of is the world of PHENOMENA.

antiparkinsonian agents drugs that reduce the severity of signs and symptoms of Parkinson's disease or drug-induced parkinsonism, including tremors, movement and gait abnormalities, and muscle rigidity. Antiparkinsonian agents are generally used in mental health to counter drug-induced parkinsonian symptoms, common with the use of conventional ANTIPSYCHOTICS. They include histamine antagonists (e.g., DIPHENHYDRAMINE), anticholinergic drugs (e.g., BENZTROPINE, TRIHEXYPHENIDYL), DOPAMINE-RECEPTOR AGONISTS (e.g., carbidopa, levodopa), and specific enzyme inhibitors.

antipathy *n.* strong aversion or deep-seated dislike. See also PREJUDICE. **—antipathetic** *adj.*

antipredator behavior all forms of action by an organism that function to avoid predation, including ANTIPREDATORY AGGRESSION, DEFENSIVE BEHAVIOR, CAMOUFLAGE, and MOBBING BEHAVIOR as well as IMMOBILITY, rapidly changing, unpredictable confusion behavior (see CONFUSION EFFECT), mass movement or activity (see DILUTION EFFECT), flight, or **evasive action** (turning away from the direction of the predator's approach).

antipredator defense any means by which animals avoid predation. It can take the form of CAMOUFLAGE, BATESIAN MIMICRY, MÜLLERIAN MIMICRY, WARNING COLORATION, or any of various forms of ANTIPREDATOR BEHAVIOR.

antipredatory aggression attack behavior directed toward a potential predator as a form of defense. See ANIMAL AGGRESSION; DEFENSIVE BEHAVIOR.

antipsychiatry *n.* an international movement that emerged in the 1960s under the leadership of British psychiatrist Ronnie D. Laing (1927–1989), South African psychiatrist David Cooper (1931–), Italian psychiatrist Franco Basaglia, and U.S. psychoanalyst Thomas Szasz (1920–). Antipsychiatrists contested the scientific and practical validity of psychiatry and radically opposed what they understood as a hospital-centered medical specialty legally empowered to treat and institutionalize individuals with mental disorders. Indeed, many antipsychiatrists argued against the very existence of mental disorders themselves, advancing the notion that mental illnesses are not illnesses at all but rather alternative ways of behaving that alarm people. They viewed psychiatry as a form of social repression and a means to control deviance, and treatment as a disguised form of punishment. **—antipsychiatrist** *n.*

antipsychotics *pl. n.* agents used in the treatment of schizophrenia, acute mania, delirium, and other forms of thought disorder and severe behavioral agitation. Formerly called **major tranquilizers**, antipsychotics are commonly divided into two major classes: **conventional** (**typical** or **first-generation**) **antipsychotics**, including the PHENOTHIAZINES, BUTYROPHENONES, and THIOXANTHENES; and the newer ATYPICAL ANTIPSYCHOTICS, of which CLOZAPINE is the prototype. The latter class has fewer adverse side effects than the former. Antipsychotics exert their effects by various mechanisms, including antagonism of dopamine D2 receptors (see DOPAMINE-RECEPTOR ANTAGONISTS). Those with EXTRAPYRAMIDAL EFFECTS are also called **neuroleptics**. See also HIGH-POTENCY ANTIPSYCHOTICS.

antipyretics *pl. n.* drugs that help control fever or other forms of hyperthermia (raised body temperature) by acting on the thermoregulatory center in the hypothalamus. They may also help the body to dissipate heat faster by dilating peripheral arteries. Aspirin and other nonopioid analgesics function as antipyretics.

antisocial *adj.* denoting or exhibiting behavior that not only sharply deviates from customary social norms but also violates other people's rights. See ANTISOCIAL BEHAVIOR. Compare PROSOCIAL.

antisocial aggression any act of AGGRESSION that has socially destructive and undesirable consequences. Compare PROSOCIAL AGGRESSION.

antisocial behavior aggressive, impulsive, and sometimes violent actions that violate the established rules, conventions, and codes of a society, such as the laws upholding personal and property rights. Compare PROSOCIAL BEHAVIOR.

antisocial personality disorder a personality disorder characterized by chronic antisocial behavior that is not due to severe mental retardation, schizophrenia, or manic episodes. This behavior pattern, which is more common in males than females, starts before age 15 with such infractions as lying, stealing, fighting, truancy, vandalism, theft, drunkenness, or substance abuse. It then continues after age 18 with at least four of the following manifestations: (a) inability to work consistently, (b) inability to function as a responsible parent, (c) repeated violations of the law, (d) inability to maintain an enduring sexual relationship, (e) frequent fights and beatings inside and outside the home, (f) failure to repay debts and provide child support, (g) travel from place to place without planning, (h) repeated lying and conning, and (i) extreme recklessness in driving and other activities.

Individuals with antisocial personality disorder were originally called constitutional psychopaths and CONSTITUTIONAL PSYCHOPATHIC INFERIORS. The disorder was subsequently known by various names, including **dyssocial personality**, **psychopathic personality**, **psychopathy**, **sociopathic personality**, **sociopathy**, and **antisocial reaction**; it was renamed antisocial personality disorder in *DSM–III*, and this continues to be the official nomenclature in *DSM–IV–TR*.

antispasmodic drugs drugs used in the management of muscle spasms, usually by relaxation of smooth muscle. Anticholinergic drugs are commonly used as antispasmodic drugs. See also MUSCLE RELAXANTS.

antiterrorist activities security programs to detect and counter terrorist activities, including those involving potential chemical and biological attacks.

antithesis *n.* **1.** a THESIS, idea, or proposition that is opposite to or contradicts another. **2.** in philosophy, the second stage of a dialectical process based on proposition, contradiction, and the reconciliation of these (thesis, antithesis, and SYNTHESIS). The term is often associated with German philosopher Georg Wilhelm Friedrich Hegel (1770–1831) and his theory of the dialectical development of ideas, although it was not a term he employed in his analysis. See also DIALECTICAL MATERIALISM. **—antithetical** *adj.*

antitussives *pl. n.* drugs that suppress coughing by affecting the cough-control center in the medulla oblongata of the brain. Because the cough center is sensitive to OPIOIDS, these drugs are effective in suppressing cough. Opioids used as antitussives include codeine and DEXTROMETHORPHAN. Also called **cough suppressants**.

antiviral drugs substances that interfere with the normal functioning of viruses. They may act by blocking host-cell enzyme systems required for viral reproduction, by blocking signals carried in messenger RNA, or by uncoating the nucleic acid molecule of the virus. Antiviral drugs are difficult to manage in clinical practice because chemicals that block viral processes may also interfere with the patient's normal cell functions. Antivirals occasionally interact with substances in human tissues to yield unexpected benefits, as with AMANTADINE, which can be used as an antiparkinsonian agent.

antivitamin *n.* a substance that interferes with the functions of vitamins. Most antivitamins are chemicals that are similar in structure to the vitamins they render ineffective. They are used mainly in studies and tests of vitamin deficiencies.

Anton's syndrome a rare disorder marked by the patient's lack of awareness and denial of blindness, despite clinical evidence of loss of vision. Such patients attempt to behave as if sighted, making elaborate explanations and rationalizations for their difficulties in getting around, handling objects, and so forth. The condition typically occurs after bilateral injury to the occipital lobe but may also be present after unilateral injury. Also called **anosognosia for blindness**; **denial of blindness**; **visual anosognosia**. [first described in 1899 by Gabriel **Anton** (1858–1933), Austrian physician]

antonym *n.* a word that has the directly opposite meaning to another word in the same language. *After*, for example, is the antonym of *before*. Compare SYNONYM. **—antonymous** *adj.*

antonym test an examination in which the respondent is presented with a word and asked to supply a word with the opposite meaning to it (e.g., being given "true" and replying "false"). Also called **opposites test**.

anvil *n.* see OSSICLES.

anxiety *n.* a mood state characterized by apprehension and somatic symptoms of tension in which an individual anticipates impending danger, catastrophe, or misfortune. The future threat may be real or imagined, internal or external. It may be an identifiable situation or a more vague fear of the unknown (e.g., a general sense of impending doom). The body often mobilizes itself to meet the threat: Muscles become tense, breathing is faster, and the heart beats more rapidly. Anxiety may be distinguished from FEAR both conceptually and physiologically, although the two terms are often mistakenly used interchangeably. See also ACUTE ANXIETY; ANTICIPATORY ANXIETY; ANXIETY DISORDERS; GENERALIZED ANXIETY DISORDER; SEPARATION ANXIETY; SOCIAL ANXIETY. **—anxious** *adj.*

anxiety attack see PANIC ATTACK.

anxiety discharge any anxiety-reducing action or repetitive activity (e.g., exercise, knitting, weeding a garden) associated with normal daily living, viewed as an alternative to suppression of anxiety.

anxiety disorder due to a general medical condition significant anxiety (e.g., generalized anxiety, panic attacks, obsessions, and compulsions) deemed to be caused directly by the physiological effects of a general medical condition. Anxiety may be caused by a number of such conditions, including endocrine disorders (e.g., hyperthyroidism), respiratory disorders (e.g., chronic obstructive pulmonary disease), cardiovascular disorders (e.g., arrhythmia), metabolic disorders (e.g., vitamin B_{12} deficiency), and neurological disorders (e.g., vestibular dysfunction).

anxiety disorder not otherwise specified clinically significant anxiety or phobic avoidance that does not meet the criteria for a specific anxiety disorder in *DSM–IV–TR*.

anxiety disorders a group of disorders in which anxiety is either the predominant disturbance or is experienced in confronting a dreaded object or situation or in resisting obsessions or compulsions. In *DSM–IV–TR* the disorders include PANIC DISORDER without agoraphobia, panic disorder with agoraphobia, AGORAPHOBIA without history of panic disorder, SPECIFIC PHOBIA, SOCIAL PHOBIA, OBSESSIVE-COMPULSIVE DISORDER, POSTTRAUMATIC STRESS DISORDER, ACUTE STRESS DISORDER, GENERALIZED ANXIETY DISORDER, ANXIETY DISORDER DUE TO A GENERAL MEDICAL CONDITION, SUBSTANCE-INDUCED ANXIETY DISORDER, and ANXIETY DISORDER NOT OTHERWISE SPECIFIED. Not included are conditions in which the anxiety is due to another mental disorder, such as schizophrenic or affective syndromes.

anxiety disturbance a condition characterized by a marked, persistent, and excessive anxiety that causes a significant degree of emotional distress, impairment in functioning (e.g., social, academic, occupational), or both. See ANXIETY DISORDERS.

anxiety equivalent in psychoanalysis, a conscious, observable symptom of ANXIETY, such as trembling or nausea.

anxiety fixation in psychoanalysis, the maintenance or continuation of an anxiety reaction from an earlier developmental stage into a later one.

anxiety hierarchy a series of graduated anxiety-arousing stimuli centering on a specific source of anxiety in a specific individual. It is used in the treatment of phobias by SYSTEMATIC DESENSITIZATION: Patients proceed along the hierarchy from the least threatening situation toward the most threatening situation.

anxiety hysteria in psychoanalysis, a neurosis in which the anxiety generated by unconscious sexual conflicts is expressed in phobic symptoms, such as an irrational fear of dirt or open spaces, and in physical disturbances that are conversion symptoms. The term is now seldom used because it combines disorders that are now classified separately. See ANXIETY DISORDERS; CONVERSION DISORDER. [defined by Sigmund FREUD]

anxiety management cognitive-behavioral, behavioral, or other techniques that aid in the reduction of anxiety, such as BIOFEEDBACK TRAINING, RELAXATION TECHNIQUES, or medication.

anxiety neurosis in psychoanalysis, a disturbance or neurosis in which the most prominent symptoms are persistent anxiety, feelings of impending disaster, and FREE-FLOATING FEAR accompanied by such symptoms as difficulty in making decisions, insomnia, loss of appetite, and heart palpitations. This term is now seldom used: The current classification of chronic anxiety of this nature is GENERALIZED ANXIETY DISORDER. Also called **anxiety state**. See also ANXIETY DISORDERS.

anxiety nightmare a frightening dream that is sometimes taken to represent the fears of the dreamer.

anxiety object in psychoanalysis, an object upon which anxiety originally caused by another source is displaced. For example, a nonhuman object may be feared because it represents the father who caused the original anxiety. See LITTLE HANS.

anxiety–performance relationship see AROUSAL–PERFORMANCE RELATIONSHIP.

anxiety reaction an emotional response characterized by marked apprehension and accompanied by somatic symptoms of tension.

anxiety-relief response in BEHAVIOR THERAPY, the repetition of reassuring or tranquilizing words (e.g., "calm") in anxiety-provoking situations.

anxiety scale any of numerous tests designed to measure manifest anxiety as opposed to assessing hidden or unconscious anxiety. An important example is the TAYLOR MANIFEST ANXIETY SCALE. Such scales usually take the form of self-report tests but can also be based on clinician ratings or actual performance.

anxiety sensitivity fear that sensations associated with anxiety will have harmful consequences. An individual with high anxiety sensitivity is more likely to respond fearfully to anxiety sensations than an individual with low anxiety sensitivity. For example, an individual with high anxiety sensitivity is likely to regard feeling lightheaded as a sign of impending illness or fainting, whereas an individual with low anxiety sensitivity would tend to regard this sensation as simply unpleasant. Research indicates that high anxiety sensitivity is a personality risk factor for the development of PANIC ATTACKS and PANIC DISORDER.

anxiety state **1.** see ANXIETY NEUROSIS. **2.** formerly, a traumatic neurosis precipitated by a wartime experience in which the ego-ideals of war conflict with customary ideals. [defined by Sigmund FREUD]

anxiolytics *pl. n.* a class of drugs used in the control of anxiety, mild behavioral agitation, and insomnia. Formerly called **minor tranquilizers**, they can also be used as adjunctive agents in the treatment of depression and panic disorder. The most widely used anxiolytics are the BENZODIAZEPINES. See also AZASPIRONES; SEDATIVE, HYPNOTIC, AND ANXIOLYTIC DRUGS.

anxious–ambivalent attachment style an interpersonal style characterized by worry that a partner will break off a relationship or by hesitancy in forming deeply committed relationships despite a desire to do so. See also ATTACHMENT THEORY.

anxious–avoidant attachment in the STRANGE SITUATION, a form of INSECURE ATTACHMENT in which an infant explores only minimally and tends to avoid or be indifferent to the parent.

anxious–avoidant attachment style see AVOIDANT ATTACHMENT STYLE.

anxious depression a MAJOR DEPRESSIVE EPISODE accompanied by high levels of anxiety.

anxious–resistant attachment in the STRANGE SITUATION, a form of INSECURE ATTACHMENT in which an infant appears anxious in the parent's presence, distressed in the parent's absence, and angry upon the parent's return, often resisting contact with him or her.

aortic arch syndrome a disorder caused by progressive obliteration of the main branches of the aortic arch because of arteriosclerosis, aneurysm, or a related problem. Usually only one or two of the branches are involved, affecting blood flow to a local area. If the carotid or vertebral arteries are involved, the brain will be affected. The patient may experience fainting spells, epilepsy-like seizures, temporary blindness, paralysis on one side of the body, aphasia, memory disturbances, or a combination of symptoms. A typical effect is the **carotid-sinus syndrome**, in which the patient faints after turning the head. Collateral circulation may develop to compensate for some degree of interrupted blood flow, but progressive loss of vision may occur in the meantime.

aortic stenosis see STENOSIS.

AP **1.** abbreviation for ACTION POTENTIAL. **2.** abbreviation for advanced placement. See ADVANCED PLACEMENT EXAMINATIONS.

APA **1.** abbreviation for AMERICAN PSYCHIATRIC ASSOCIATION. **2.** abbreviation for AMERICAN PSYCHOLOGICAL ASSOCIATION.

APAGS abbreviation for AMERICAN PSYCHOLOGICAL ASSOCIATION OF GRADUATE STUDENTS.

APAP *n.* see ACETAMINOPHEN.

apareunia *n.* **1.** the inability to perform sexual intercourse. **2.** abstinence from coitus.

apastia *n.* fasting or abstinence from food. Compare APHAGIA.

APA style guidelines and standards for writing (e.g., grammar) and formatting (e.g., data display, headings) for students, instructors, researchers, and clinicians in the social and behavioral sciences, as collected in the *Publication Manual of the American Psychological Association*.

apathetic hyperthyroidism a condition associated with THYROTOXICOSIS. In contrast to other hyperthyroid conditions, apathetic hyperthyroidism is usually characterized by lethargy or otherwise unexplained congestive heart failure.

apathy *n.* indifference and lack of response to one's surroundings. Apathy is commonly associated with severe depression or schizophrenia. **—apathetic** *adj.*

apathy syndrome the pattern of emotional insulation (indifference, detachment) adopted by many prisoners-of-war and other victims of catastrophes in an effort to maintain their stability.

aperiodic reinforcement schedule a former name for VARIABLE-INTERVAL REINFORCEMENT SCHEDULE.

Apert's syndrome an inherited condition in which an abnormally shaped head due to premature closure of some of the cranial sutures (see CRANIOSYNOSTOSIS SYNDROME) is accompanied by mental retardation and syndactyly (partial or complete fusion of the digits). The syndactyly usually involves both hands and feet and typically results in fusion of the skin and bones, marked by "mitten hands" and "sock feet." Apert's syndrome may be complicated by CROUZON'S SYNDROME (and called **Apert–Crouzon syndrome**), in which case fusion of the digits is partial. Both syndromes are dominant traits (see ACROCEPHALOSYNDACTYLY). [Eugène **Apert** (1868–1940), French pediatrician]

APF abbreviation for AMERICAN PSYCHOLOGICAL FOUNDATION.

Apgar score an evaluation of newborn infants on five factors: skin color, heart rate, respiratory effort, reflexes, and muscle tone. The evaluation is typically performed at 1 min and again at 5 min after birth to assess the physical condition of the infant and to determine quickly if he or she needs immediate medical care. Each factor is scored 0, 1, or 2, with a maximum total of 10 points. A score below 3 indicates that the infant is in severe distress; a score of 4–7 indicates moderate distress; and a score of 7–10 indicates that the infant's condition is normal. [developed in 1952 by Virginia **Apgar** (1909–1974), U.S. anesthesiologist]

aphagia *n.* inability to swallow or eat. Compare APASTIA. **—aphagic** *adj.*

aphakia *n.* the absence of the lens from the eye, a condition that may be congenital or the result of disease, injury, or surgery. **—aphakic** *adj.*

aphanisis *n.* an obsolete term indicating total extinction of sexual desire. [from Greek *aphanes*, "invisible": defined by British physician Ernest Jones (1879–1958)]

aphasia *n.* loss or impairment of the ability to understand language or express oneself through language due to brain injury or disease. RECEPTIVE APHASIA is an impaired ability to understand words, signs, or gestures. EXPRESSIVE APHASIA is an impaired ability to speak, write, or make meaningful gestures. Major causes of the cerebral damage are stroke, brain tumor, encephalitis, and head injury. There are numerous types and forms of aphasia, some of the most important or common of which are ALEXIA, AMNESTIC APHASIA, AUDITORY APHASIA, BROCA'S APHASIA, MOTOR APHASIA, and WERNICKE'S APHASIA. See also DYSPHASIA. **—aphasic** *adj.*

aphemia *n.* as originally defined by French physician Pierre Paul Broca (1824–1880), a MOTOR APHASIA with nonfluency (i.e., lack of speech) but intact language functions, as evidenced by intact writing. This condition was later renamed BROCA'S APHASIA.

aphonia *n.* loss of the voice resulting from disease, damage to the larynx, or psychological disturbance (see MOTOR CONVERSION SYMPTOMS). See also MUTISM.

aphrasia *n.* the inability to utter or understand words arranged in phrases, even though individual words may be used or understood.

aphrodisiac *n.* an agent or substance that is thought to stimulate sexual activity in humans or animals. Agents that folklore considers to be aphrodisiacs include odors (e.g., perfumes), foods (e.g., raw oysters and chestnuts), and drugs. Alcohol, various alkaloids (e.g., yohimbine), cantharidin from the Spanish fly, vitamin E, and amyl nitrite have been listed as aphrodisiacs, although evidence of any real efficacy is lacking, and some research shows such agents not to have any sexual effects.

apical dendrite the DENDRITE that extends from a PYRAMIDAL CELL to the outermost surface of the cerebral cortex. Compare BASAL DENDRITE.

aplasia *n.* the arrested development of a body tissue or organ or failure of body tissue to grow. See AGENESIS.

aplestia *n.* extreme greediness.

Aplysia *n.* a genus of molluscs that have a very simple nervous system and are often used to study neurophysiology, especially the neurophysiology of learning and memory.

apnea (**apnoea**) *n.* temporary suspension of respiration. If the **apneic period** is a long one, the heart may be slowed and EEG (electroencephalogram) changes may occur. Apnea can occur during sleep (see SLEEP APNEA) and is also found in many disorders, such as major epilepsy and concussion. **—apneic** *adj.*

apo- *prefix* away from.

apoclesis *n.* absence of a desire for, or an aversion to, food.

ApoE abbreviation for APOLIPOPROTEIN E.

apoenzyme *n.* the protein component of an ENZYME. It must combine with a second component, a COENZYME, to make the enzyme functional.

apolipoprotein E (**ApoE**) a protein that may help break down BETA-AMYLOID. Individuals carrying a particular allele of the ApoE gene, the ApoE4 allele, are more likely to develop ALZHEIMER'S DISEASE and other conditions that damage the nervous system.

Apollonian *adj.* describing a state of mind that is well ordered, rational, and harmonious (from Apollo, the god of prophecy, music, and healing in Greek mythology). This modern use of the term was originated by German philosopher Friedrich Nietzsche (1844–1900), who drew a contrast between the Apollonian and the DIONYSIAN sides of human nature.

apomorphine *n.* a morphine derivative used as an expectorant and to induce vomiting.

apopathetic behavior behavior influenced by the presence of others although not directed toward them, as in boasting about one's exploits.

apoplectic type a body type characterized by a heavy-set, rotund physique, which roughly corresponds to the PYKNIC TYPE in KRETSCHMER TYPOLOGY and the endomorphic type (see ENDOMORPH) in SHELDON'S CONSTITUTIONAL THEORY OF PERSONALITY. Also called **habitus apoplecticus**. [defined by Greek physician Hippocrates (c. 460–c. 377 BCE)]

apoplexy *n.* **1.** an obsolete term for a HEMORRHAGIC STROKE. **2.** hemorrhage into an organ, for example, a **pituitary apoplexy**.

apoptosis *n.* see PROGRAMMED CELL DEATH. **—apoptotic** *adj.*

aposematic *adj.* having or denoting bright colors or patterns or other distinctive morphology indicating that an organism is dangerous or unpalatable. See WARNING COLORATION.

a posteriori inferring causes or antecedents from observations. Compare A PRIORI.

a posteriori test a statistical test of a hypothesis formulated after a study is completed and the data have been examined.

apostilb *n.* a unit of LUMINANCE equal to the luminance of a uniform diffuser emitting $1/\pi$ cd/m^2.

apotemnophilia *n.* see ACROTOMOPHILIA.

APP abbreviation for AMYLOID PRECURSOR PROTEIN.

apparatus *n.* **1.** one or more instruments, pieces of equipment, or the like used for a particular purpose, such as providing stimuli or measuring responses during an experiment. **2.** in biology, a group or system of structures that perform a particular function. It may be microscopic, as in the intracellular GOLGI APPARATUS, or macroscopic, as in the VESTIBULAR APPARATUS.

apparent *adj.* **1.** seeming or illusory, as in **apparent modesty**. **2.** in physics, denoting an observed state that is not in accordance with actual physical conditions. For example, **apparent motion** is a perception of motion induced by the motion of the observer rather than that of the observed entity. **3.** obvious or manifest.

apparent distance the perceived distance of an object from an observer. The VISUAL ANGLE subtended by the image of the object is a powerful but imperfect cue for the apparent distance of the object.

apparent magnitude the BRIGHTNESS of an object, which depends on its LUMINOSITY and its distance from the observer.

apparent movement an illusion of motion or change of size, as in television animation. Also called **illusory movement**. See ALPHA MOVEMENT; BETA MOVEMENT; DELTA MOVEMENT; EPSILON MOVEMENT; GAMMA MOVEMENT.

apparent size the perceived size of a stimulus. This depends on many factors in addition to the size of the stimulus on the retina, most importantly the perceived distance from the observer to the object. See also SIZE CONSTANCY; SIZE CUE.

apparition *n.* **1.** a visual illusion that results from distortion of a perceived object. Often interpreted as threatening, apparitions may be associated with a neurological or toxic disorder, such as ALCOHOL-INDUCED PSYCHOTIC DISORDER. **2.** the perceived manifestation of a ghost or spirit. See also GHOST IMAGE; MATERIALIZATION; PHANTASM. **3.** the act of becoming visible.

appeal 1. *n.* an effort to arouse a sympathetic response from an individual or group, particularly from consumers who are the targets of advertising. Appeals may be based on psychological studies of consumer desires or needs and may be as obvious as a practical package design or as subtle as an implied suggestion that the product might enhance the purchaser's sexual attractiveness. Advertising appeals also may be directed toward the purchaser's competitive drives. See also PRODUCT APPEALS. **2.** *vb.* to make an appeal.

appeal to ignorance see AD IGNORANTIUM.

appearance–reality distinction the knowledge that the appearance of an object does not necessarily correspond to its reality, for example, a sponge shaped like a rock may look like a rock but it is really a sponge. Children younger than 3 may have difficulty making appearance–reality distinctions.

appeasement behavior actions by one organism that reduce the likelihood of attack or threatening behavior from another organism. This often involves reducing apparent body size (e.g., by crouching or sleeking fur or hair) or using vocal signals typical of young animals.

Appelt–Gerken–Lenz syndrome see ROBERTS SYNDROME.

apperception *n.* **1.** the act or process of perceiving something consciously. **2.** the mental process by which a perception or an idea is assimilated into an individual's existing knowledge, thoughts, and emotions (his or her APPERCEPTIVE MASS). See also TENDENTIOUS APPERCEPTION. **—apperceive** *vb.* **—apperceptive** *adj.*

apperceptive mass the previously acquired knowledge with which a new perception or idea must be assimilated if it is to be understood by the perceiver. [defined by German philosopher Johann Friedrich Herbart (1776–1841)]

apperceptive visual agnosia see VISUAL AGNOSIA.

appersonation *n.* a delusion in which the individual believes him- or herself to be another person and assumes the characteristics of that other person. Also called **appersonification**.

appestat *n.* a hypothetical area in the brain believed to regulate appetite and food intake. Although parts of the hypothalamus (see LATERAL HYPOTHALAMUS; VENTROMEDIAL NUCLEUS) and brainstem (see SOLITARY NUCLEUS) have been shown definitively to be involved in appetite and food intake, the idea of a single appestat is probably overly simplistic.

appetite *n.* **1.** a desire to satisfy the need for food or (more broadly) any other physiological need. Appetite may be innate or learned and therefore subject to modification by experience. **2.** a state of wanting or longing, which may elicit active searching behavior leading ultimately to a CONSUMMATORY RESPONSE. **—appetitive** *adj.*

appetite suppressants agents that reduce appetite and thus control body weight. They include the amphetamines and other stimulants (e.g., PHENTERMINE, DIETHYLPROPION), SIBUTRAMINE, and serotonin agonists (fenfluramine, dexfenfluramine). Use of the latter compounds, particularly in combination with phentermine (so-called "phen-fen"), resulted in heart-valve defects, and this combination was removed from the market. Although appetite suppressants may result in short-term weight loss, there is no evidence that they achieve long-term weight reduction unless used in conjunction with a behavioral management program. Also called **anorectants**.

appetition system EXTRAVERSION as represented by an individual's relative sensitivity to appetitive (positive, rewarding) cues and stimuli and his or her processes for approaching them. Compare AVERSION SYSTEM. [proposed by Hans EYSENCK]

appetitive behavior 1. an active searching process that precedes consummatory behavior (see CONSUMMATORY RESPONSE) and is indicative of desire. Influenced by learning and prior experience, it is highly flexible and—in MATING BEHAVIOR—helps to establish or maintain sexual interaction prior to copulation. **2.** feeding activity, which is influenced in part by the central nervous system, including areas of the brainstem and nuclei of the hypothalamus in the brain. For example, lesions of the VENTROMEDIAL NUCLEUS may result in excessive eating, whereas lesions of nuclei in the LATERAL HYPOTHALAMUS may cause deficient eating.

appetitive conditioning a type of PAVLOVIAN CONDITIONING in which the UNCONDITIONED STIMULUS is a positive reinforcer, such as food.

appetitive stimulus a positive reinforcer (see POSITIVE REINFORCEMENT) or an UNCONDITIONED STIMULUS that an organism will approach, the effectiveness of which can be modified by deprivation. For example, hunger can increase the effectiveness of food as an appetitive stimulus.

applied behavior analysis (**ABA**) the extension of SKINNER's behavioral principles (i.e., operant conditioning) to practical settings. Variations of applied behavior analysis may be used clinically (in the form of BEHAVIOR MODIFICATION or BEHAVIOR THERAPY) as treatment for abnormal or problematic behaviors.

applied linguistics the field in which linguistic theories and methods are put to practical use. Contexts in which this occurs include language teaching, the treatment of language disorders, and various aspects of artificial intelligence.

applied psychology the application of the theories, principles, and techniques of psychology to practical concerns, such as political campaigns, consumer affairs, industry, ergonomics, education, advertising, vocational guidance, problems of living or coping, and environmental issues. It may be contrasted with theoretical psychology or academic psychology, in which the emphasis is on understanding for its own sake rather than the utility of the knowledge.

applied relaxation a technique in which clients are taught, in a step-wise fashion, to relax more and more rapidly over a series of sessions in order to master panic, anxiety, phobias, pain, and other symptoms. The goal is for the client to be able to relax in 20–30 seconds in situations in which their symptoms typically occur. See also PROGRESSIVE RELAXATION.

applied research research aimed at answering a practical question rather than developing a theory or obtaining knowledge for its own sake. Compare BASIC RESEARCH; PURE RESEARCH.

applied science an approach to science in which scientific principles and theories are applied in practical ways.

applied sport psychology the use or study of the use of SPORT PSYCHOLOGY to enhance or make consistent the performance of athletes.

applied tension a technique in BEHAVIOR THERAPY and EXPOSURE THERAPY that focuses on changing physiological responses (e.g., low blood pressure leading to fainting) by teaching and having the client practice muscle tensing and releasing. The technique was developed and is still primarily used for blood, injury, and injection phobias.

apport *n.* **1.** in SPIRITUALISM, the manifestation, allegedly by supernatural means, of physical objects during a seance. Such objects are regarded as signs or gifts from the spirits. See also MATERIALIZATION. **2.** an object produced in this way.

appraisal *n.* the cognitive evaluation of a phenomenon or event. In theories of emotion, cognitive appraisals are seen as determinants of emotional experience. See COGNITIVE APPRAISAL THEORY. **—appraise** *vb.*

appraisal dimension any of the criteria that account for a person's evaluation of an interaction with the environment and the generation of an appropriate emotional response. Examples of appraisal dimensions include the goal relevance of an event, its stimulus novelty, its judged pleasantness or unpleasantness, and a judgment of one's COPING POTENTIAL in relation to this event. Different theories of APPRAISAL emphasize different appraisal dimensions. See also STIMULUS EVALUATION CHECKS.

appraisal motive the desire to gain accurate information about the self. It leads people to seek highly diagnosic feedback (see DIAGNOSTICITY) and to reject flattery or other bias. Compare CONSISTENCY MOTIVE; SELF-ENHANCEMENT MOTIVE.

appraisal theory a group of theories stating that people's cognitive appraisals or evaluations of a situation determine the emotions they feel in response to the situation. See also COGNITIVE APPRAISAL THEORY.

apprehension *n.* **1.** anxious expectation, uneasiness, or dread about a situation, event, or the future generally. Also called **apprehensiveness**. **2.** the act or capability of grasping something mentally, such as the nature of an object, event, or situation. Compare COMPREHENSION. **—apprehend** *vb.* **—apprehensible** *adj.* **—apprehensive** *adj.*

apprehension span the number of items an individual can report from a single glance at an array of items. Typically the number reported is four or five. Also called **span of apprehension**.

apprehension-span test a test in which participants report some aspect of a briefly presented array of items (e.g., letters). The WHOLE REPORT task requires participants to report as many letters as they can. Recent studies have used a PARTIAL REPORT task, in which individuals must report the presence of a particular letter among a group of distractor letters in the briefly flashed display. Also called **attention-span test**.

apprehensive expectation see GENERALIZED ANXIETY DISORDER.

apprehensiveness *n.* see APPREHENSION.

approach *n.* a particular method or strategy used to achieve a goal or purpose, for example, a psychodynamic approach in psychological research and practice.

approach–approach conflict a conflict situation involving a choice between two equally desirable but incompatible goals, for example, when an individual must choose between two attractive job opportunities. Also called **double-approach conflict**. See also APPROACH–AVOIDANCE CONFLICT; AVOIDANCE–AVOIDANCE CONFLICT.

approach–avoidance conflict ambivalence that arises when a goal has both desirable and undesirable aspects or consequences, for example, when a highly desired but lower paid job opportunity becomes available. The closer an individual comes to the goal, the greater the anxiety and fear in being close to that goal. Withdrawal from the goal then increases the desire, and a cycle of anxiety develops. See also APPROACH–APPROACH CONFLICT; AVOIDANCE–AVOIDANCE CONFLICT; DOUBLE APPROACH–AVOIDANCE CONFLICT.

Approach Control Test a test for simulation and assessment of air traffic control for management of aircraft approaching airports. It assesses the influence of stress factors, such as time pressures.

approach gradient the variation in the strength of a drive as a function of the organism's proximity to its goal. For example, a rat's goal-directed behavior increases in intensity as it nears its goal of food. The approach gradient appears less steep than the AVOIDANCE GRADIENT. See also APPROACH–APPROACH CONFLICT; APPROACH–AVOIDANCE CONFLICT.

approach motivation expectation of reward (e.g., a positive emotional experience), which is a condition for goal-directed behavior.

approach response any behavior that brings an organism closer to a stimulus. See ADIENCE.

appropriate affect an expression of mood or feeling that is in harmony with, or naturally indicative of, the accompanying thought, action, reaction, or verbal expression.

appropriate death the death a person would choose if given the opportunity. The concept of appropriate death has been influential in drawing attention to the needs and values of individuals in the terminal phase of life. It challenges the tendency to treat the disease rather than the patient and the assumption that a "good death" has the same meaning for all people. PALLIATIVE CARE, especially as given in HOSPICES, attempts to protect individuality and offers a communication process and caring environment providing the maximum possible opportunity for the dying person to make personally meaningful decisions.

approximation conditioning see BEHAVIOR SHAPING.

appurtenance *n.* in GESTALT PSYCHOLOGY, interaction or mutual influence between parts of a perceptual field so that the parts appear to belong together. [defined in 1935 by Kurt KOFFKA]

apractagnosia *n.* an impaired ability to organize, remember, and perform a sequence of movements or skilled motor activities or to analyze spatial relationships. The condition is due to lesions in the lower part of the occipital and parietal lobes of the brain. Also called **spatial apractagnosia**.

apraxia *n.* loss or absence of the ability to perform learned purposeful movements, such as dressing oneself or driving a car, despite intact motor function, sensation, attention, coordination, motivation, and comprehension. The condition is believed to represent an impairment of the ability to plan, select, and sequence the motor execution of movements. It may develop as a result of brain injury, tumor, or stroke (**acquired apraxia**) or it may be present at birth (**developmental apraxia**). There are several categories and types of apraxia, including DRESSING APRAXIA, IDEATIONAL APRAXIA, IDEOMOTOR APRAXIA, CONSTRUCTIONAL APRAXIA, and ORAL APRAXIA. —**apraxic** *adj.*

apraxia of gait impairment or loss of the ability to walk that does not involve sensory impairment or paralysis.

apraxia of speech a speech-articulation disorder due to lack of coordination of the muscles used in speaking, in the absence of sensory loss or paralysis. Also called **apraxic dysarthria**.

apraxic agraphia see GRAPHOMOTOR APRAXIA.

A prime (symbol: A′) a measure of the sensitivity for correctly detecting or remembering a stimulus in a task or test. This measure is based on the nonparametric theory of signal detection, which does not make stringent assumptions about the distribution of responses. See SIGNAL DETECTION THEORY.

a priori inferring effects from known or assumed causes. Compare A POSTERIORI. [Latin, "prior to"]

apriorism *n.* in philosophy, the position that asserts the reality of INNATE IDEAS and the validity of knowledge that is not created by or dependent upon experience. It is thus the opposite of EMPIRICISM.

a priori test a statistical test of a hypothesis formulated before a study is completed and the data have been examined.

aprosexia *n.* loss of the ability to focus attention, due to a brain lesion or psychiatric disorder.

aprosodia *n.* absence of the normal variations in the rhythm, stress, and pitch of speech, resulting in monotone speech. It may be due to a brain injury or have emotional origins. Also called **aprosody**. See MOTOR APROSODIA; SENSORY APROSODIA.

APS 1. abbreviation for AMERICAN PAIN SOCIETY. **2.** abbreviation for AMERICAN PSYCHOLOGICAL SOCIETY. **3.** abbreviation for AMERICAN PSYCHOSOMATIC SOCIETY.

APsaA abbreviation for AMERICAN PSYCHOANALYTIC ASSOCIATION.

aptitude *n.* the capacity to acquire competence or skill through training. Individuals who can learn to play the piano or perform arithmetical calculations with relative ease are frequently said to have a **natural aptitude** for these activities. **Specific aptitude** is potential in a particular area (e.g., artistic or mathematical aptitude); **general aptitude** is potential in several fields. See also ACADEMIC APTITUDE.

aptitude measure a unit, instrument, or system for calculating one's capacity to acquire competence or skill through training, by comparison with a peer standard.

Aptitude Research Project tests see ARP TESTS.

aptitude test an assessment instrument designed to measure (a) individual concrete abilities such as dexterity, visual acuity, and clerical performance; (b) abilities of candidates for professional training, such as in medicine, law, or nursing; or (c) a wide range of basic abilities required for academic or vocational success, such as verbal comprehension, numerical ability, mechanical knowledge, and reasoning.

aptitude–treatment interaction an interaction in which people with certain patterns of aptitudes respond better to one set of treatments, whereas people with a different pattern of aptitudes respond better to a different set of treatments. For example, people with high spatial aptitudes might learn better when material is presented to them visually with charts and diagrams, whereas people with high verbal aptitudes might learn better when the same material is presented in words.

AQ abbreviation for ACHIEVEMENT QUOTIENT.

Aquachloral *n.* a trade name for CHLORAL HYDRATE.

aqueduct of Sylvius see CEREBRAL AQUEDUCT. [Franciscus **Sylvius** (1614–1672), Dutch anatomist]

aqueous humor the clear fluid that occupies the anterior and posterior chambers of the EYE. It is produced by the epithelium of the CILIARY PROCESSES, which are part of the CILIARY BODY.

arachidonic acid a long-chain, polyunsaturated fatty acid that is a component of cell membranes. When liberated from the membrane by the enzyme phospholipase A2, it is transformed into a series of compounds known as eicosanoids, which serve as precursors for prostaglandins, thromboxanes, and leukotrienes.

arachneophobia *n.* see SPIDER PHOBIA.

arachnoid *n.* see ARACHNOID MATER.

arachnoid granulations a series of extensions of the middle layer of the meninges (ARACHNOID MATER) through the outer layer (DURA MATER) that permits CEREBROSPINAL FLUID to drain into the bloodstream.

arachnoid mater the middle one of the three membranous layers (MENINGES) covering the surface of the brain and spinal cord, so called because its strands of tissue resemble spiders' webs. Also called **arachnoid**; **arachnoid membrane**.

arachnophobia *n.* see SPIDER PHOBIA.

Arago phenomenon the impaired sensitivity to light that exists in the center of the visual field under poor light conditions. It is presumably caused by the absence of RETINAL RODS in the FOVEA CENTRALIS. See SCOTOPIC

VISION. [Dominique **Arago** (1786–1853), French physicist]

Aran–Duchenne disease see SPINAL MUSCULAR ATROPHY. [François **Aran** (1817–1861), French physician; Guillaume **Duchenne** (1806–1875), French neurologist]

ARAS abbreviation for ASCENDING RETICULAR ACTIVATING SYSTEM.

arbitrary inference a COGNITIVE DISTORTION in which a person draws a conclusion that is unrelated to or contradicted by the evidence.

arbitrary matching to sample a variation of MATCHING TO SAMPLE in which the correct alternative during the choice phase bears an arbitrary relationship to the stimulus presented as the sample. For example, after presentation of a blue stimulus as a sample, the correct choice may be to select a triangle. Also called **symbolic matching to sample**.

arbitrary symbol a linguistic SIGN (a written or spoken word) that bears no obvious resemblance to the thing or concept signified (see REFERENT). Because the vast majority of words in all languages are considered to fall into this category, arbitrariness is often cited as an important characteristic of human languages; this idea is of central significance in the structuralist approach to linguistics (see STRUCTURALISM). Compare ICONIC SYMBOL. See also PHONETIC SYMBOLISM.

arbitration *n.* a method of settling controversies in which the parties involved present their arguments and supporting information to an impartial agent, such as a judge or, in a labor dispute, an arbitrator or arbitration board. By mutual agreement the arbiter's decision is final. This process is distinguished from MEDIATION, in which the outside agent (the mediator or conciliator) seeks to help the parties reach a mutually acceptable agreement. **—arbitrate** *vb.*

arborization *n.* a branching, treelike structure, as of the DENDRITES of a neuron.

archaic inheritance presumed phylogenetic influences in the development of the individual's mental processes, such as the RACIAL MEMORY and ARCHETYPES of Carl Jung's ANALYTIC PSYCHOLOGY. See PHYLOGENY.

archaic thought a type of CONCRETE THINKING in which abstract concepts are characterized by the types of actions they inspire.

archetype *n.* **1.** a perfect or typical example of something or the original model from which something is held to derive. See also PROTOTYPE. **2.** in ANALYTIC PSYCHOLOGY, a structural component of the mind that derives from the accumulated experience of humankind. These inherited components are stored in the COLLECTIVE UNCONSCIOUS and serve as a frame of reference with which individuals view the world and as one of the major foundations on which the structure of the personality is built. Examples are ANIMA, ANIMUS, PERSONA, SHADOW, supreme being, MAGNA MATER, and hero. Also called **archetypal image**; **primordial image**. **—archetypal** *adj.*

archicerebellum *n.* the phylogenetically oldest part of the CEREBELLUM.

archicortex *n.* CEREBRAL CORTEX that has three CORTICAL LAYERS. See also ALLOCORTEX.

Archimedes spiral a simple spiral, formed by a curve whose tangent is maintained at a constant angle. A simple line drawing of an Archimedes spiral is often rotated to induce a MOTION AFTEREFFECT. [**Archimedes** of Syracuse (287–212 BCE), Greek philosopher and mathematician]

architectonic structure see CYTOARCHITECTURE.

architectural constraints ways in which the architecture of the brain dictates the type of information that can be processed by the brain and the manner in which it is processed. Also called **architectural innateness**. Compare CHRONOTOPIC CONSTRAINTS; REPRESENTATIONAL CONSTRAINTS.

architectural determinism the mistaken belief that the designed environment dictates behavior or directly causes certain behaviors to occur or not to occur. Design more typically facilitates or inhibits behavior, providing opportunities that influence the probability that certain behaviors will or will not occur. See also PERSON–ENVIRONMENT INTERACTION.

architectural programming determination of the performance requirements of buildings and other physical facilities prior to construction. Key considerations include the behavior and activity expected to occur or not to occur in the space, user groups with special needs, and any trade-offs in the behavioral consequences of various design decisions. See also BEHAVIOR MAPPING; POST-OCCUPANCY EVALUATION.

architectural psychology the study of the role of the built environment in human behavior, a major subtopic in ENVIRONMENTAL PSYCHOLOGY. Also called **design and behavior**.

archival records data available in storage. Examples include library records, telephone bills, computer time used, etc. Analysis of these records is used in unobtrusive studies of behavior and to validate self-reported behavior.

archival research the use of books, journals, documents, data sets, manuscripts, and other records or cultural artifacts in scientific research. As in other research methods, control of experimenter biases, appropriate sampling, and data analytic procedures must be evaluated.

archive *n.* a relatively permanent repository of data or material. **—archival** *adj.*

arch of Corti see RODS OF CORTI.

arc sine transformation (**arcsin transformation**) a mathematical TRANSFORMATION used to make sample variances across comparison groups more similar in order to satisfy the equality of variances assumption critical to certain statistical tests (e.g., ANALYSIS OF VARIANCE). Arc sine transformation is often performed on data in the form of frequencies and proportions: $p' = 2\arcsin\sqrt{p}$, where p is the percentage or proportion and p' the transformed value.

arctic hysteria see PIBLOKTO.

arcuate fasciculus a tract that runs from WERNICKE'S AREA to BROCA'S AREA. Individuals with lesions of this tract manifest fluent speech and relatively normal comprehension but poor ability to repeat words or sentences (see CONDUCTION APHASIA).

arcuate nucleus **1.** an arc-shaped nucleus in the HYPOTHALAMUS. **2.** any of various small groups of gray matter on the anterior surface of the PYRAMIDS of the medulla oblongata that are extensions of PONTINE NUCLEI. They are associated with the SOMATOSENSES of the face.

arcuate zone of the brain the bow-shaped portion of the RETICULAR FORMATION that extends from the spinal cord to the pons and includes the internal and external arcuate fibers and ARCUATE NUCLEI. The arcuate fibers are concentrated in the OLIVARY NUCLEUS of the medulla oblongata.

areal linguistics the study of languages and dialects

within a defined geographical area and with an emphasis on regional influences. This approach differs from both LINGUISTIC TYPOLOGY and GENETIC LINGUISTICS.

area postrema a highly vascularized region of the brain located in the basal wall of the lateral VENTRICLE. Brain capillaries in this area form a relatively permeable region of the BLOOD–BRAIN BARRIER, enabling the passage of toxic substances to the underlying CHEMORECEPTOR TRIGGER ZONE, which elicits a vomiting response.

area sampling a method of selecting individuals for research in which specific neighborhoods, streets, homes, or other geographic areas are designated in advance as the source of participants.

arecoline *n.* a drug, related to MUSCARINE, that stimulates smooth muscles and glands that respond to postganglionic cholinergic agents. It is used in veterinary medicine to eliminate internal parasites and was formerly used in the management of schizophrenia.

areflexia *n.* an absence of motor reflexes.

argininosuccinic aciduria a disorder characterized by the presence in the urine and cerebrospinal fluid of argininosuccinic acid, resulting from an inborn error of metabolism and accompanied by epilepsy and mental retardation. Treatment is based on control of protein intake to prevent hyperammonemia. The trait is transmitted by an autosomal recessive gene on chromosome 7. See also ALLAN DENT DISEASE.

argot *n.* unconventional jargon words or phrases (French, "slang"), generally of a particular group.

argument *n.* **1.** a sequence of propositions that provides logical reasons for accepting a CONCLUSION as valid or true. A single one of these statements is referred to as a PREMISE. **Argumentation** is the process of making an argument from premise to conclusion. **2.** a parameter on which the value of a mathematical FUNCTION depends. **3.** a disagreement involving varied, often opposite, positions.

argumentativeness *n.* a persistent tendency to dispute and argue. **—argumentative** *adj.*

argument framing the extent to which a persuasive message presents information in a manner that stresses the positive consequences of adopting the advocated position versus the negative consequences of failing to adopt the advocated position.

argument quality the extent to which an argument elicits primarily positive evaluative responses toward the ATTITUDE OBJECT versus primarily negative ones. The greater the number of positive responses relative to negative responses, the higher the quality of the argument. See also COGNITIVE RESPONSE.

argument quantity the number of arguments included in a persuasive message.

Argyll Robertson pupil a pupil that does not respond to light (see PUPILLARY REFLEX), reacts slowly to drugs that induce pupil contraction, but responds to ACCOMMODATION. It is a sign of several disorders of the central nervous system, such as a BRAIN TUMOR, MULTIPLE SCLEROSIS, and neurosyphilis. [Douglas **Argyll Robertson** (1837–1909), British ophthalmologist]

arhinencephaly *n.* see ARRHINENCEPHALY.

ARI abbreviation for ARMY RESEARCH INSTITUTE.

Aricept *n.* a trade name for DONEPEZIL.

aripiprazole *n.* an ATYPICAL ANTIPSYCHOTIC agent that is thought to exert its effects by binding to the presynaptic D2 dopamine AUTORECEPTOR, thereby inhibiting the release of dopamine from the presynaptic terminal. It is used in the treatment of schizophrenia. U.S. trade name: **Abilify**.

Aristotelian *adj.* **1.** of or relating to the tradition of formal logic founded by Greek philosopher Aristotle (384–322 BCE) and developed especially by the Scholastic philosophers of the Middle Ages (see SCHOLASTICISM). The term "Aristotelian" is often used to distinguish this tradition of logic from that of modern SYMBOLIC LOGIC. **2.** of or relating to Aristotle, his works, or his thought. In this more general sense, an Aristotelian approach, which gives primacy to particulars over UNIVERSALS and grants a higher value to empirical knowledge, is often contrasted with the approach of PLATONIC IDEALISM or NEOPLATONISM. **—Aristotelianism** *n.*

Aristotelian method an approach to knowledge emphasizing deductive (i.e., not primarily empirical) procedures. Compare GALILEAN METHOD.

Aristotle's illusion the tactile perception that a single object is two objects when held in the crossed index and middle fingers. [**Aristotle** (384–322 BCE), Greek philosopher]

arithmetic disability a disturbance in the ability to calculate and reason that is associated with neurological impairment. See ACALCULIA.

arithmetic mean see MEAN.

Arizona v. Fulminante a case resulting in an influential 1991 U.S. Supreme Court ruling that admitting a confession not voluntarily given into evidence can be considered a harmless error and does not violate DUE PROCESS rights if the remaining evidence is considered to be sufficient to convict the defendant.

ARM abbreviation for ADVERTISING RESPONSE MODELING.

armamentarium *n.* **1.** the complete equipment of an institution, often a medical institution, necessary or sufficient for instruction, research, or practice. Such equipment includes books, supplies, and instruments. **2.** the complete materials necessary to undertake any field of activity.

armchair psychology a form of psychological inquiry based on introspection and rational processes without recourse necessarily to empirical observation. It may be contrasted with EMPIRICAL PSYCHOLOGY, in which the data come from laboratory procedures or controlled forms of observation and measurement. See RATIONAL PSYCHOLOGY; SPECULATIVE PSYCHOLOGY.

Armed Forces Qualification Test (AFQT) a screening test developed in 1950 by the Department of Defense to determine a person's eligibility for acceptance into U.S. military service by assessing his or her mental ability qualification. Originally consisting of 100 multiple-choice items measuring vocabulary, arithmetic, spatial relations, and mechanical ability, the AFQT was used as a stand-alone test until 1976, when the ARMED SERVICES VOCATIONAL APTITUDE BATTERY (ASVAB) became the official screening instrument of all U.S. military branches.

Armed Services Vocational Aptitude Battery (ASVAB) a TEST BATTERY developed in 1966 by the Department of Defense for use by the U.S. military as a standardized instrument for personnel selection and classification (specific job assignment); in 1976 it became the official testing instrument of all U.S. military branches. It currently consists of nine timed multiple-choice tests in the areas of word knowledge, paragraph comprehension, arithmetic reasoning, mathematics knowledge, general science, auto and shop information, mechanical comprehension, electronics information, and assembling objects. The first four tests are used to determine eligibility for service (see ARMED FORCES QUALI-

FICATION TEST); the remainder are used to determine interests and aptitudes. Although sometimes administered to high school students to assist in career planning, the ASVAB is a required part of the application process for all potential military recruits.

armoring *n.* a defense mechanism used to distance oneself by withholding the expression of emotion through BLOCKING of one's experience and expression of life-affirming emotions (sadness, joy, anger, grief, and fear).

Armor's theta an index of the overall RELIABILITY of a measure. It comprises a set of items or other variables and is based on the EIGENVALUE of the first (unrotated) principal component.

Army Alpha Test see ARMY TESTS.

Army Beta Test see ARMY TESTS.

Army General Classification Test (**AGCT**) see ARMY TESTS.

Army Research Institute (**ARI**) the U.S. Army Research Institute for the Behavioral and Social Sciences, which has its headquarters in Alexandria, Virginia, and opened in 1939. Its function is to maximize combat effectiveness by means of research in the acquisition, development, training, and utilization of soldiers in military forces. It conducts basic, exploratory, and advanced research and development.

Army tests group intelligence tests for military personnel, developed by Lewis M. TERMAN, Robert M. YERKES, and others and used by the U.S. Army beginning in World War I. The **Army Alpha Test** (**Alpha test** or **examination**) was a verbal test, measuring such skills as ability to follow directions. The **Army Beta Test** (**Beta test** or **examination**) presented nonverbal problems to illiterate subjects and recent immigrants who were not proficient in English. Both the Alpha and Beta tests were replaced at the outbreak of World War II by the 150-item **Army General Classification Test** (**AGCT**), designed to measure verbal comprehension, quantitative reasoning, and spatial perception and used to classify inductees according to their ability to learn military duties. The AGCT was itself replaced in 1950 by the ARMED FORCES QUALIFICATION TEST.

Army Training and Evaluation Program see ARTEPS EXERCISE.

Arnold–Chiari malformation a congenital deformity in which the MEDULLA OBLONGATA and CEREBELLUM protrude through the FORAMEN MAGNUM, so that the cerebellum overlaps the top of the spinal cord. HYDROCEPHALUS and MENINGOMYELOCELE are commonly associated with the different types of the deformity. [Julius **Arnold** (1835–1915), German pathologist; Hans **Chiari** (1851–1916), Austrian pathologist]

ARO abbreviation for ASSOCIATION FOR RESEARCH IN OTOLARYNGOLOGY.

aromachology *n.* the field of scientific study that attempts to specify the relationships between psychology and fragrance technology. The focus is on temporary effects of stimuli mediated by the olfactory pathways and moderated by cognition.

Aromascan *n.* a company that makes ELECTRONIC NOSES.

aromatase *n.* an enzyme that converts many male sex hormones (ANDROGENS) into female sex hormones (ESTROGENS). See also AROMATIZATION HYPOTHESIS.

aromatherapy *n.* a type of therapy purported to improve psychological and physical health through the use of selected aromatic oils extracted from herbs, flowers, fruits, and trees. The fragrances of these oils are inhaled or the oils themselves massaged into the skin in an effort to induce relaxation, reduce stress and emotional distress, and enhance well-being. See also COMPLEMENTARY AND ALTERNATIVE MEDICINE.

aromatic *adj.* in the ZWAARDEMAKER SMELL SYSTEM, denoting an odor quality that is smelled in spices and camphor.

aromatization hypothesis the hypothesis that, in some rodents, testicular ANDROGENS enter the brain and are converted there into ESTROGENS by the action of the aromatase enzyme in order to masculinize the developing nervous system.

arousal *n.* **1.** a state of ALERTNESS and readiness for action. **2.** a pervasive state of cortical responsiveness believed to be associated with sensory stimulation and activation of fibers from the RETICULAR ACTIVATING SYSTEM. Also called **arousal state**. See PHYSIOLOGICAL AROUSAL; SEXUAL AROUSAL. **3.** a state of excitement or energy expenditure linked to an EMOTION. Usually, arousal is closely related to a person's appraisal of the significance of an event or to the physical intensity of a stimulus. Arousal can either facilitate or debilitate performance. See also CATASTROPHE CUSP THEORY. **—arouse** *vb.*

arousal-boost mechanism any stimulus pattern produced by contact with a work of art that gives rise to a measurable hedonic (pleasure) effect. The arousal is measured by various psychological tests as the participant views a selection of paintings by various masters. Compare AROUSAL-REDUCTION MECHANISM. [proposed in 1967 by British-born Canadian psychologist Daniel E. Berlyne (1924–1976) as part of his theory of positive hedonic value as a psychological effect of art]

arousal jag an increase of ACTIVATION followed by a more or less sudden decrease, often accompanied by LAUGHTER as a release of tension. The abrupt fall from elevated levels of AROUSAL to a lower, more appropriate level of arousal is thought to produce a pleasurable response. Common experiences that can produce an arousal jag include a roller-coaster ride or watching a scary movie. [introduced in 1970 by British-born Canadian psychologist Daniel E. Berlyne (1924–1976)]

arousal level the extent to which an organism is alert to stimuli.

arousal–performance relationship the pattern of association between cognitive or physiological AROUSAL (or both) and achievement at physical or cognitive tasks. Also called **anxiety–performance relationship**. See CATASTROPHE CUSP THEORY; INVERTED-U HYPOTHESIS; REVERSAL THEORY.

arousal phase see SEXUAL-RESPONSE CYCLE.

arousal potential the capability of a stimulus to induce arousal. According to British-born Canadian psychologist Daniel E. Berlyne (1924–1976), preference for a work of art is due to the amount of general arousal it produces, which derives from its PSYCHOPHYSICAL PROPERTIES (e.g., intensity), COLLATIVE PROPERTIES (e.g., novelty), and ecological properties (meaningfulness, or signal value). See also ISOHEDONIC TRAP.

arousal-reduction mechanism any stimulus or inhibitory reaction that decreases the degree of arousal of an individual after this has reached an uncomfortably high level. According to British-born Canadian psychologist Daniel E. Berlyne (1924–1976), a sharp increase in arousal can have unpleasant or aversive effects, but an arousal-reduction mechanism can produce positive hedonic value by lowering the arousal curve. An arousal-reduction mechanism may have a natural inhibitory effect on CNS circuits to strong stimulation or it may result from a stimulus that conveys a sense of harmony or CONCINNITY. Compare AROUSAL-BOOST MECHANISM.

arousal regulation the controlling of cognitive and physiological activation using cognitive-behavioral methods. See AUTOGENIC TRAINING; ENERGIZING; IMAGERY CUE; PROGRESSIVE RELAXATION.

arousal state see AROUSAL.

arousal system a diffuse system of nerve cells that controls AROUSAL by activating both the central nervous system and the autonomic nervous system. A principal component is the RETICULAR FORMATION.

arousal theory **1.** the theory that the physical environment can affect arousal levels by stimulation and by stress created when psychological or physical needs are not met. Arousal increases when personal space is diminished (see CROWDING) or when people are subjected to noise or traffic congestion. **2.** see ACTIVATION THEORY OF EMOTION.

arousal training a technique in BEHAVIOR THERAPY that teaches clients to detect levels of physiological arousal and then to enhance or reduce these levels depending on therapeutic goals. This technique is often used in ANGER CONTROL THERAPY and BEHAVIORAL SEX THERAPY.

arousal transfer an increase in the intensity of one emotion that follows the experience of another emotion. For instance, the intensity of love may increase following an intense experience of fear or anger.

arpeggio paradox the contradiction of the stimulus–response view of a CHAIN OF BEHAVIOR, evidenced by the speed at which accomplished pianists play arpeggios. Key strikes are too fast for nerve conduction to the brain to occur between them, so that one strike cannot serve as a stimulus for the next.

ARP tests *A*ptitude *R*esearch *P*roject tests: tests of divergent thinking produced by the Southern California Aptitude Research Project. Test items include writing a series of words containing a specified letter (word fluency), writing titles for short-story plots (ideational fluency, originality), writing words similar in meaning to a given word (associational fluency), writing sentences containing words beginning with given letters (expressional fluency), and listing different consequences of a hypothetical situation, such as people no longer needing sleep (see CREATIVITY TEST; DIVERGENT THINKING; TORRANCE TESTS OF CREATIVE THINKING). These tests received considerable attention from intelligence researchers in the 1960s and 1970s but less since then, largely because the STRUCTURE OF INTELLECT MODEL, which they were designed to operationalize and test, has become much less popular. [devised by Joy Paul GUILFORD and associates in the 1950s to 1980s]

arranged marriage a marriage planned and contracted by the parents or other relatives of the partners or by significant figures (e.g., elders) in the partners' culture or social group. In cultures in which arranged marriages are the norm and in contrast to the concept of the "love match," marriage is typically seen as the union of two kinship groups and not merely of two individuals.

array *n.* a two-dimensional, tabular grouping of data where the rows represent participants or cases and the columns represent measurements or variables. The concept may be extended to more than two dimensions. See MATRIX.

arrested testis a testis that lies within the inguinal canal but is unable to descend into the scrotum because the normal passage is obstructed. Also called **undescended testicle**. See CRYPTORCHIDISM.

arrest reaction a behavioral response, usually studied in cats, characterized by sudden immobility, or "freezing." The arrest reaction can be produced by electrically stimulating various areas of the brain. See also STARTLE RESPONSE.

arrhinencephaly (**arhinencephaly**) *n.* a congenital defect attributable to improper development of the RHINENCEPHALON, the part of the brain associated with the sense of smell. In various forms of the condition, the olfactory lobe of the brain and the external olfactory organ may be absent or imperfectly developed on one or both sides of the body. Also called **arrhinencephalia**; **arhinencephalia**.

arrhythmia *n.* any variation from the normal rhythm of the heartbeat. Changes in the heart rhythm are relatively important in terms of diagnosis and therapy. Normal rhythm for an infant may be as high as 150 beats per minute, which would be considered TACHYCARDIA (any rate above 100 per minute) and a sign of a cardiac emergency for an adult. A rate of less than 60 beats per minute (BRADYCARDIA) may also be a sign of heart disease. Other kinds of arrhythmias include premature beats; **atrial flutter**, in which one of the upper chambers contracts at a rate of as much as 400 times per minute; and **heart block**, marked by failure of the heart to contract because of the interruption or delay of an electrical stimulus needed to trigger the contraction.

arrowhead illusion see MÜLLER-LYER ILLUSION.

Artane *n.* a trade name for TRIHEXYPHENIDYL.

ARTEPS exercise Army Training and Evaluation Program exercise: a field exercise designed to assess the ability of units to perform assigned missions and functions under noncombat stressors.

arterial circle a ring of blood vessels at the base of the brain, formed by links between branches of the major arteries supplying the brain—the internal carotid and the basilar arteries (see POSTERIOR COMMUNICATING ARTERY). This arrangement provides alternate pathways of blood flow in the event of a cerebral hemorrhage or other disorder that could interrupt circulation in one part of the brain. Also called **circle of Willis**.

arterio- *combining form* arteries.

arteriogram *n.* see ANGIOGRAPHY.

arteriography *n.* see ANGIOGRAPHY.

arteriole reaction a response controlled by the AUTONOMIC NERVOUS SYSTEM and marked by a change in the diameter of the arterioles, which control the flow of blood from the arteries to the capillaries. Smooth muscle in the walls of the arterioles is particularly sensitive to sympathetic nerve impulses and may react to anger, fear, or other emotions by producing dramatic changes of blood pressure.

arteriopathia hypertonica a form of arterial degeneration associated with hypertension. The muscle and elastic tissue of the walls of the arterial system increases and forms layers that are eventually replaced by connective-tissue fibers. The condition can be both a cause and an effect of hypertension, leading to cerebrovascular accidents if not controlled by medication.

arteriosclerosis *n.* literally, hardening of the arteries, often resulting from deposition of plaques in the artery walls (see ATHEROSCLEROSIS) and consequent narrowing and loss of flexibility. This may lead to OCCLUSION of one or more arteries and, when involving cerebral vessels, stroke. **—arteriosclerotic** *adj.*

arteriovenous malformation (**AVM**) an abnormal, congenital tangle of arteries and veins that are directly connected and lack intervening capillaries. Such malformations may have no symptoms, but in the brain they can hemorrhage, causing mild to severe brain damage with symptoms ranging from headaches to paralysis and APHASIA.

arteritis *n.* inflammation of an artery or more than one artery. A common form is **temporal** (or **giant cell**) **arteritis**, a chronic disease of older people that largely involves the carotid arterial system, especially the arteries of the temple and scalp. It is marked by the appearance of giant, multinucleate cells and granulomas in the affected arteries; symptoms include severe temporal-area headaches on both sides and visual disturbances, which may result in loss of sight in one eye. See also PANARTERITIS.

arthritis *n.* any inflammation of a joint, often accompanied by muscle and bone stiffness around the affected joint. There are several types of arthritis, including **rheumatoid arthritis**, a chronic systemic form of the disease that is associated with inflammatory changes throughout the body's connective tissues and that is an autoimmune disorder (see AUTOIMMUNITY), and **osteoarthritis**, a degenerative disease affecting mainly weight-bearing joints and caused by wear and tear on the joint tissues. The psychosocial effects of arthritis, which can be chronic, painful, recurrent, and debilitating, can include lifestyle changes, stress on personal relationships, and depression. **—arthritic** *adj.*

arthro- (**arthr-**) *combining form* joints.

arthrogryposis multiplex congenita a congenital disorder, with evidence of hereditary factors in 30% of cases, marked by distorted joints in different body areas, clubfoot, and a greater than average incidence of mental retardation. In some cases arms are rotated inward, the hips are dislocated, and the muscles are small, weak, and hypotonic. The term itself means "crooked-joint disorder." Four separate types of the disease are known. Also called **arthrogryposis**.

arthropathy *n.* any inflammatory, neuropathic, or other disease involving a joint.

article *n.* in linguistics, a DETERMINER that limits a noun with respect to its definiteness and number (e.g., *a, the* in English) and with respect to its gender in many Romance languages (e.g., *el, la* in Spanish). See DEFINITE ARTICLE; INDEFINITE ARTICLE.

articular sensation a sensation derived from the position of the joints.

articulate speech oral language that is meaningful and intelligible.

articulation *n.* **1.** the act or process of producing and using the speech sounds required for intelligible speech. Articulation is a complex process that involves accuracy in the placement of the apparatus of the VOCAL TRACT, timing, direction of movements, force expended, speed of response, and neural integration of all actions. Compare MISARTICULATION. **2.** a clearly articulated sound or utterance. **3.** a joint between bones, which may be fixed or movable. **4.** in Gestalt psychology, the level of complexity within a structure. **—articulate** *vb.*

articulation disorder any disorder of speech involving the substitution, omission, distortion, or addition of speech sounds (PHONEMES). See also DYSARTHRIA; PHONOLOGICAL DISORDER; SPEECH DISORDER.

articulation index an index used to measure SPEECH INTELLIGIBILITY within an operational environment. It reflects the degree of separation between speech and background or other system noise.

articulation test **1.** the phonetic analysis and recording of the speech of an individual with faulty sound production according to such criteria as developmental sequence, correct placement of the ARTICULATORS, and intelligibility. **2.** in audition, a hearing test designed to measure the intelligibility of speech.

articulator *n.* any of the elements of the vocal tract (e.g., lips, tongue, soft palate) that are involved in articulation, that is, in the shaping and production of speech sounds. Some, but not all, authorities include the cheeks, larynx, uvula, alveolar ridge, nose, and teeth as articulators.

articulatory loop in models of WORKING MEMORY, a dedicated memory store for holding spoken, auditory information. If, for example, one tried to memorize a telephone number by repeating it mentally over and over (see ROTE REHEARSAL), this would take place in the articulatory loop.

articulatory phonetics the branch of PHONETICS concerned with the relationship between the physiology of the articulatory mechanisms in human beings and the physical properties of human speech sounds. Compare ACOUSTIC PHONETICS.

articulatory store a component of short-term memory that retains auditory information based on the motor systems involved in pronouncing items, rather than how they sound. Compare ACOUSTIC STORE.

articulatory suppression a method used to inhibit subvocal rehearsal of items in a memory test or experiment by requiring the participant to perform a distracting verbal task, such as counting or naming, during the RETENTION period.

artifact *n.* **1.** an error caused by improper statistical manipulation of experimental data or a logical flaw in experimental design that causes the experiment to be invalid. The experimental finding is the consequent of the flawed design or the analytic error rather than a reflection of the true state of nature. **2.** any manufactured object, particularly a product of historical significance.

artifact in assessment an extraneous factor affecting the results of assessment (evaluation), particularly one associated with the examiner and examinee. See ARTIFACT.

artifact in research an extraneous factor affecting the results of research, especially one associated with the researcher (e.g., expectations, personality) or with the participant (e.g., awareness of the researcher's intent, concern over being evaluated). See ARTIFACT.

artificial category see NATURAL CATEGORY.

artificial insemination (**AI**) the use of medical or surgical techniques to achieve conception by introducing sperm into the female reproductive system. In humans, this is done by introducing sperm from the donor (who masturbates to provide the semen) into the vagina or through the cervical opening, directly into the uterus. As with intercourse, artificial insemination may need to be done more than once for pregnancy to occur, but it is usually scheduled to coincide with the days of ovulation, to maximize success. Success rates of 75% are usual.

artificial intelligence (**AI**) a subdiscipline of computer science that aims to produce programs that simulate human intelligence. AI researchers often develop very high-level computer languages for this purpose, such as LISP, PROLOG, and SMALLTALK. There are many branches of AI, including ROBOTICS, computer vision, machine learning, game playing, and EXPERT SYSTEMS. AI has also supported research in other related areas, including COGNITIVE SCIENCE and computational linguistics. See also TURING TEST.

artificialism *n.* the assumption that any thing that exists must have been made by a conscious entity, such as God or a human being, who is directly responsible for its qualities and movements. Jean PIAGET, who introduced the term, drew a contrast between artificialism and ANIMISM, which assumes that entities have an innate power or energy to direct their movements and determine their ultimate nature. Both assumptions are characteristic of children in the PREOPERATIONAL STAGE of development. **—artificialist** *adj.*

artificial language any language or languagelike system that is not a NATURAL LANGUAGE. The category includes invented languages, such as Esperanto, and the various languages used in computer programming; the **formal languages** of logic and mathematics are also sometimes included. In linguistics and psycholinguistics, artificial languages are sometimes invented to simulate or to violate certain aspects of natural-language rules.

artificial life a research area of ARTIFICIAL INTELLIGENCE in which computer-based life forms are generated. Such forms, first proposed by Austrian-born U.S. mathematician John von Neumann (1903–1957), are often constructed from CELLULAR AUTOMATA. The state of each cell, together with the state of its immediate neighbors, determines its survival. This research area often attempts to simulate the results of communication and other society-based skills on survival.

artificial neurosis see EXPERIMENTAL NEUROSIS.

artificial pupil an artificial aperture that limits the amount of light entering the eye.

artificial selection human intervention in animal or plant reproduction to improve the value or utility of succeeding generations. Compare NATURAL SELECTION.

arts and crafts creative activities that involve skilled hand fabrication, such as painting, weaving, woodworking, or leatherworking. Arts and crafts are often used in rehabilitation programs as directed by recreational or occupational therapists. See also ART THERAPY.

art test a test designed to identify special abilities in the fine arts (e.g., painting, architecture), to assess creativity in the arts, or to evaluate art productions. A variety of techniques are utilized for these different purposes, which include comparing the individual's judgment of pictures with that of experts, reproducing an object from memory, and identifying mechanical or judgment errors in a standard drawing.

art therapy the use of artistic activities, such as painting and clay modeling, in psychotherapy and rehabilitation. The process of making art is seen as healing, an experience that provides the opportunity to express oneself imaginatively, authentically, and spontaneously; over time, this process can lead to personal fulfillment, emotional reparation, and transformation. The products made in art therapy are seen as a means of symbolic communication and a vehicle for developing new insights and understandings, resolving conflicts, solving problems, and formulating new perceptions to achieve positive changes, growth, and rehabilitation.

arugamama *n.* a Japanese concept that emphasizes the naturalness of feelings and the acceptance of one's feelings as they are. See MORITA THERAPY.

ASA 1. abbreviation for acetylsalicylic acid. See ASPIRIN. **2.** abbreviation for ACOUSTICAL SOCIETY OF AMERICA.

ASA model abbreviation for ATTRACTION–SELECTION–ATTRITION MODEL.

asana *n.* a yoga posture or position. Each asana is said to have both physical and psychological effects that may be therapeutic or cathartic.

asapholalia *n.* mumbled or indistinct speech.

ASC abbreviation for ALTERED STATE OF CONSCIOUSNESS.

ascendance *n.* a personality trait involving a desire to be prominent in group situations, to assert oneself, and to acquire positions of authority over others. Traditional paper-and-pencil measures of ascendance can predict an individual's emergence as the leader in small groups. Also called **ascendancy**. See also DOMINANCE. **—ascendant** *adj.*

ascendance–submission see DOMINANCE–SUBMISSION.

ascending–descending series in psychophysics, the two sets of stimuli—one of increasing magnitude, one of decreasing magnitude—used in the METHOD OF LIMITS. In the ascending series the stimulus, initially below threshold, is increased incrementally until it exceeds threshold; in the descending series the initial stimulus exceeds threshold and is decreased incrementally until it is below threshold. This procedure controls for HABITUATION and PERSEVERATION errors.

ascending pathway 1. a route formed by nerve fibers that carry nerve impulses toward the brain from lower levels of the nervous system. **2.** see ASCENDING TRACT.

ascending reticular activating system (**ARAS**) the pathways that transmit nervous impulses from the RETICULAR FORMATION of the midbrain upward through the thalamus to all parts of the cerebral cortex.

ascending tract a bundle of nerve fibers (see TRACT) within the central nervous system that carries nerve impulses toward the brain. Also called **ascending nerve tract**; **ascending pathway**. Compare DESCENDING TRACT.

asceticism *n.* a character trait or lifestyle characterized by simplicity, renunciation of physical pleasures and worldly goods, social withdrawal, and extreme self-discipline. **—ascetic** *adj.*

Asch, Solomon E. (1907–1996) Polish-born U.S. psychologist. Asch emigrated with his family to the United States in 1920 and earned his doctorate from Columbia University in 1932; his dominant influences were the Gestalt psychologists, especially Max WERTHEIMER. Asch taught at a number of universities, including Swarthmore College, where for some 19 years he was part of a group of Gestalt psychologists that also included Wolfgang KÖHLER, and the University of Pennsylvania, where he remained from 1972 until his retirement. Asch is best known for his contributions to social psychology, especially for his classic 1952 text on that field. He was particularly successful in designing laboratory experiments that reflected the complexity of human social life. His experiments were among the first to show how social context could influence even such fundamental processes as perception. For example, in his famous studies of CONFORMITY, he showed that people's perception of a line's length could be influenced by the false reports of others around them. His work was widely influential; the famous conformity experiments of Stanley MILGRAM grew directly out of Asch's work. Asch held many honors, including the Nicholas Murray Butler Medal from Columbia University and a Distinguished Scientific Contribution Award from the American Psychological Association. He was elected to the American Academy of Arts and Sciences in 1965.

Asch conformity effect the tendency for individuals to conform when in groups, particularly in situations such as those studied by Solomon ASCH (see ASCH SITUATION), in which the group's position is obviously incorrect or unfounded. See CONFORMITY.

Asch situation an experimental paradigm used to study CONFORMITY to group opinion. Participants are led to believe that they are making perceptual judgments as part of a group, but in reality the other members are confederates who make errors deliberately on certain trials. This paradigm measures the extent to which participants publicly conform to the erroneous group judgment or resist the pressure to do so and remain independent. [Solomon ASCH]

ASCM abbreviation for ADAPTIVE STRATEGY CHOICE MODEL.

ascorbic acid the chemical name for vitamin C, a nutrient found in many fruits and vegetables, particularly citrus fruits (see VITAMIN). Unlike most mammals, primates cannot make ascorbic acid, so they must obtain it from foods. Ascorbic acid aids formation of connective tissue and prevents oxidation of cellular components. Deficiency can result in scurvy (marked by bleeding gums and delayed wound healing) and neurological disorders.

ascriptive responsibility the judgment that an individual who has committed an illegal act can be ascribed CRIMINAL RESPONSIBILITY and should therefore be punished. Compare DESCRIPTIVE RESPONSIBILITY.

ASD abbreviation for ACUTE STRESS DISORDER.

-ase *suffix* an enzyme (e.g., TRANSFERASE).

A* search (pronounced "A star") a type of BEST-FIRST SEARCH in which "best" for any state is measured by the distance that state is from the start state plus the heuristic estimate of the quality of that state. The heuristic estimate must be less than or equal to the actual cost of going from that state to a goal state.

asemasia *n.* see ASYMBOLIA.

asemia *n.* see ASYMBOLIA.

Asendin *n.* a trade name for AMOXAPINE.

ASEP abbreviation for AMERICAN SPORT EDUCATION PROGRAM.

aseptic meningitis see MENINGITIS.

asexual *adj.* **1.** lacking sexual characteristics or drive. **2.** capable of reproduction without fertilization. **Asexual reproduction** occurs in many plants and in animal species that reproduce by budding or are capable of regenerating an entire individual from separate parts when cut into pieces. **—asexuality** *n.*

Asian influenza a type of influenza caused by the H2N2 strain of influenza virus, which first appeared in north China in 1957. The mortality rate was not high, but the infection was complicated by severe staphylococcal pneumonia in many cases. Some patients also developed postinfluenzal asthenia with psychogenic factors.

as-if hypothesis **1.** an unproven and perhaps unprovable hypothesis that is treated "as if" it were correct, usually because of its value as an explanatory model or its utility as a basis for experiment and research. Many of the hypothetical entities postulated by psychology and psychoanalysis are of this nature. See also CONSTRUCT; HEURISTIC. **2.** any unproven assumption that an individual accepts "as if" it were true because of its value to him or her as a guide for thought or action. See ALS OB. See also GUIDING FICTION. [introduced by German philosopher Hans Vaihinger (1852–1933)]

as-if personality a type of personality style in which the individual behaves as if well adjusted, but in fact is doing only what is expected and is unable to behave in a genuine or spontaneous manner. This condition has reportedly been observed in individuals with schizophrenia before they exhibit psychotic symptoms, such as hallucinations or delusions. [first described in 1942 by U.S. psychologist Helene Deutsch (1884–1982)]

-asis *suffix* see -IASIS.

asitia *n.* repulsion at the thought or sight of food. See also ANOREXIA.

ASL abbreviation for AMERICAN SIGN LANGUAGE.

asocial *adj.* **1.** declining to engage, or incapable of engaging, in social interaction. See also SCHIZOID PERSONALITY DISORDER. **2.** lacking sensitivity or regard for social values or norms. See also ANTISOCIAL PERSONALITY DISORDER. **—asociality** *n.*

asomatognosia *n.* lack of sensory awareness of one's body. Individuals with this disorder may be unable to recognize parts of their body as their own. See NEGLECT.

asonia *n.* a form of SENSORY AMUSIA characterized by inability to distinguish differences of pitch. Also called **tone deafness**.

aspartate *n.* an amino acid NEUROTRANSMITTER that is excitatory at many synapses.

aspartate aminotransferase an enzyme that may be involved in the cause of muscular dystrophy. Increased levels in the blood are a clinical sign of this disease and also of damage to the heart and liver, for example, in cases of jaundice or myocardial infarction. The former name of this enzyme was **glutamic–oxaloacetic transaminase**. Also called **aspartate transaminase**.

aspect *n.* see TENSE.

Asperger's disorder a pervasive developmental disorder associated with varying degrees of deficits in social and conversational skills, difficulties with transitions from one task to another or with changes in situations or environments, and preference for sameness and predictability of events. Obsessive routines and preoccupation with particular subjects of interest may be present, as may difficulty reading body language and maintaining proper social distance. Some people with Asperger's disorder have reported oversensitivity to sounds, tastes, smells, and sights, but the nature of such sensitivities is not well researched. In contrast to AUTISTIC DISORDER, language skills develop, and there is no clinically significant delay in cognitive or adaptive functioning other than in social interactions. By definition, people with Asperger's disorder have an IQ in the normal to superior range, and some may exhibit exceptional specific skills or talents. See also AUTISTIC SPECTRUM DISORDER. Also called **Asperger's syndrome**. [described in 1944 by Hans **Asperger** (1906–1980), Austrian psychiatrist]

aspermia *n.* failure of the male reproductive organs to produce or emit semen. Also called **aspermatism**.

asphyxia *n.* a condition in which the level of oxygen in the blood falls below normal, while the proportion of carbon dioxide increases. It may be associated with labored or difficult breathing and marked by signs of pallor or cyanosis. Causes include choking, drowning, electric shock, inhaled smoke or toxic fumes, or disease or injury involving the respiratory system.

asphyxophilia *n.* arousal and enjoyment obtained from being unable to breathe during sexual activity. As a PARAPHILIA, this may involve being choked or strangled by a partner.

aspiration *n.* in phonetics, the articulation of a stop consonant with a sudden plosive burst of air. In English the consonants *p*, *t*, and *k* are aspirated at the beginning of a syllable but not at the end or in combination with certain other consonants (see ALLOPHONE). The difference can be easily experienced by placing a finger close to one's mouth and saying *pot* (aspirated) and then *top* and *spot* (unaspirated).

aspirational group any group that an individual wishes or aspires to join. An aspirational group may be an actual group characterized by interaction and interpersonal structures (e.g., a professional association,a sports team) or an aggregation of individuals who are thought to possess one or more shared similarities (e.g., the rich, intellectuals). Compare MEMBERSHIP GROUP; REFERENCE GROUP.

aspirin *n.* acetylsalicylic acid: the most commonly used nonopioid ANALGESIC, which also has ANTIPYRETIC and anti-inflammatory properties and the ability to prevent formation of blood clots. Aspirin alleviates pain mainly by peripheral mechanisms (see NSAIDS); in controlling fever, it acts on the body's thermoregulatory center in the hypothalamus. Adverse effects include gastric irritation or ulceration with bleeding and occasional allergic reactions. Overdosage affects the central nervous system and other body systems (see SALICYLISM).

aspirin combinations drug mixtures that include ASPIRIN as one of the components, the others commonly being other analgesics (e.g., ACETAMINOPHEN, CODEINE, PROPOXYPHENE), stimulants (usually caffeine), or both. Aspirin combinations may also include a barbiturate (e.g., **butalbital**), a skeletal muscle relaxant (e.g., CARISOPRODOL, ORPHENADRINE), or other drugs. Because many of these preparations can be obtained without a doctor's prescription, individuals with the habit of regular self-medication are at risk of developing gastrointestinal symptoms (e.g., peptic ulcer) and other toxic reactions (see SALICYLISM; CAFFEINE INTOXICATION).

aspirin poisoning see SALICYLISM.

ASR abbreviation for AUTOMATED SPEECH RECOGNITION.

assault *n.* **1.** a violent attack on an individual. **2.** illegal conduct occurring when an individual either attempts to injure another person or threatens to do so, and has the capacity to carry out the threat. **—assaultive** *adj.*

assembly test a test requiring participants to put together elements, such as pieces of a puzzle or of an object.

assertion *n.* **1.** the forceful, sometimes aggressive, statement of or insistence on one's beliefs, claims, rights, or the like. **2.** in sport, the use of force within the rules of the game to achieve a strategic advantage over an opponent. Also called **proactive aggression**. Compare REACTIVE AGGRESSION.

assertiveness *n.* a style of communication in which individuals express their feelings and needs directly, while maintaining respect for others.

assertiveness training **1.** a method of teaching individuals to change verbal and nonverbal signals and behavioral patterns and to enhance interpersonal communication generally through techniques designed to help them express emotions, opinions, and preferences—positive and negative—clearly, directly, and in an appropriate manner. ROLE PLAY or BEHAVIOR REHEARSAL is often used to prepare clients to be appropriately assertive in real-life situations. Also called **assertive training**. **2.** in sport, the use of specific drills that have the purpose of increasing the physicality of play within the rules.

assessment *n.* **1.** in general, a judgment of the quality, worth, importance, or value of something or someone. **2.** see PSYCHOLOGICAL ASSESSMENT. **3.** in animal behavior, an evaluation of an individual based on its behavior or communication signals. A potential rival might use the degree of vigor and complexity of a male's song or the intensity of its plumage color to make an assessment of the probability of displacing that male. Similarly, a female might evaluate the relative quality of different potential mates in MATE SELECTION. Assessment may be a major function of animal communication.

assessment center an office or department in which participants are observed and evaluated with regard to their future growth and development within an organization. A variety of assessment procedures may be used, including IN-BASKET TESTS, ROLE PLAY, and individual or group exercises constructed to simulate important activities at the organizational level to which the participants aspire. The assessment center may be used for currently employed personnel, job applicants, or both.

assessment instrument an instrument for the evaluation of ability, achievement, interests, personality, psychopathology, or the like.

assessment of intelligence the administration of standardized tests to an individual in order to determine his or her ability to learn, reason, understand concepts, and acquire knowledge. See also MEASURES OF INTELLIGENCE.

assignment therapy a technique used in group therapy to enhance cohesiveness and communication among the participants so as to obtain maximum therapeutic benefit. A SOCIOMETRIC TEST is administered to determine the patterns of intermember relations within the group as a whole, and these patterns are then used to assign individuals to smaller, more focused groups. [articulated by Austrian psychiatrist and philosopher Jacob L. Moreno (1889–1974)]

assimilation *n.* **1.** in Jean PIAGET's theory of cognitive development, the process of incorporating information into already existing cognitive structures without modifying those structures. See PIAGETIAN THEORY OF INTELLIGENCE. See also ACCOMMODATION; ADAPTATION. **2.** in making judgments, finding similarities between the target being judged and features of the context in which it is judged. For example, meeting a person in a pleasant social context (e.g., an enjoyable party) could lead to a more positive evaluation of that person than would have been the case in a more neutral context. In such a case, the evaluation of the person has been assimilated toward the positive social context. Compare CONTRAST. **3.** the process by which an immigrant to a new culture adopts the culture's beliefs and practices. **—assimilate** *vb.*

assimilation effect in psychology experiments, an effect in which participants' judgments shift toward an ANCHOR after it is introduced. For example, judgments of relative distance or weight will usually be evenly distributed along a scale before the experimenter provides an anchor. If, once the anchor is introduced, judgments cluster around the anchor, an assimilation effect is said to have occurred. Compare CONTRAST EFFECT.

assisted death an action taken by one person to end the life of another, at the request of the latter. This action can take the form of either PASSIVE EUTHANASIA or ACTIVE EUTHANASIA. Assisted death differs from MERCY KILLING in that it is generally performed by a physician and is not in response to an acute situation. It is sometimes called **physician-assisted suicide**, which assumes a firm determination of the cause of death. See also EUTHANASIA.

assisted living facilities residential facilities for older adults requiring long-term care services that include meals, personal care, and health-related services that are available for both scheduled and unscheduled needs 24 hours a day. Such facilities encourage a degree of autonomy and independence in residents that is not provided for in NURSING HOMES.

assisted suicide suicide in which the person ending his or her own life is helped to do so by another. See ASSISTED DEATH.

assistive device see ASSISTIVE TECHNOLOGY.

assistive listening device a device used by a person with hearing loss to emphasize a single specific sound. Unlike conventional hearing aids, which amplify all sounds in the environment, assistive listening devices focus on a single sound, such as the voice of a person with whom one is conversing in a noisy restaurant, and make it more prominent than the background noise. An assistive listening device typically consists of a transmitter and microphone that are placed near the source of the sound in which one is interested and a receiver and output device, such as headphones, that direct the sound to a particular individual.

assistive software computer programs designed to enable individuals with disabilities to use computer applications. For example, a SCREEN READER, a software program designed for users with visual impairment, can be used with a SPEECH SYNTHESIZER to convert information on a computer monitor into speech.

assistive technology (**AT**) **1.** the field concerned with development and service provision of tools that improve the functioning of individuals with limitations or disabilities. See also BIOENGINEERING. **2.** equipment that assists individuals with disabilities to function more independently in such areas as mobility and personal care. **Assistive devices** (or **assistive technology devices**) range from simple LOW-TECHNOLOGY ASSISTIVE DEVICES, such as canes, walkers, reachers, and eating utensils with built-up handles, to HIGH-TECHNOLOGY ASSISTIVE DEVICES, such as voice-controlled computers and computerized speech-output devices. These devices are also occasionally referred to as **daily-living aids** or **independent-living aids**. See also INDEPENDENT LIVING.

assistive technology service any organization, business, facility, or supplier that directly assists individuals with disabilities in the choice, purchase or leasing, or use of an ASSISTIVE TECHNOLOGY device, including customization, maintenance, and replacement.

associate 1. *n.* something that accompanies or is categorized with something else. **2.** *n.* a friend, partner, colleague, or accomplice. **3.** *n.* in learning studies, a word that is paired with another word to be learned with it (see PAIRED-ASSOCIATES LEARNING). **4.** *n.* a word that is suggested by another word by virtue of some implicit connection. **5.** *vb.* to use mental processes to form a connection between ideas, events, objects, and so forth.

associated movement involuntary, unnecessary contractions of uninvolved muscles during a movement.

association *n.* **1.** a connection or relationship between ideas (see ASSOCIATION OF IDEAS), behaviors, events, objects, or feelings on a conscious or unconscious level. Associations are established by learning or experience and may be expressed spontaneously, as in FREE ASSOCIATION, or deliberately elicited, as in WORD-ASSOCIATION TESTS. See also BACKWARD ASSOCIATION; CONTROLLED ASSOCIATION; FORWARD ASSOCIATION; REMOTE ASSOCIATION. **2.** the degree of statistical dependence between two or more phenomena. See also STRENGTH OF ASSOCIATION. **3.** a group of individuals who gather occasionally for some common purpose. **—associative** *adj.* **—associational** *adj.*

association area see ASSOCIATION CORTEX.

association by contiguity see CONTIGUITY OF ASSOCIATIONS.

association cortex any of various areas of the CEREBRAL CORTEX that are not involved principally in sensory or motor representations but may be involved in integrative functions. Also called **association area**.

association disturbance see DISTURBANCE OF ASSOCIATION.

association fiber a nerve fiber that transmits impulses between different parts of the same CEREBRAL HEMISPHERE. Compare COMMISSURAL FIBER.

Association for Research in Otolaryngology (**ARO**) an association of scientists and physicians who are engaged in basic and clinical research on hearing, balance, speech, taste, and smell. The ARO publishes the *Journal of the Association for Research in Otolaryngology* (*JARO*).

Association for the Advancement of Applied Sport Psychology (**AAASP**) a professional organization founded in 1986 whose mission is to promote the development of psychological theory and applications in sport, exercise, and health psychology. Its main publication is the *Journal of Applied Sport Psychology*. See SPORT AND EXERCISE PSYCHOLOGY.

Association for the Advancement of Psychology (**AAP**) an organization founded in 1974 for the purpose of promoting human welfare through the advancement of the profession and science of psychology. The AAP promotes the interests of psychologists through (a) representation before public and governmental bodies, (b) cooperation with other organizations and agencies in furtherance of the profession and science of psychology, and (c) the operation of a political committee known as Psychologists for Legislative Action Now (AAP/PLAN).

associationism *n.* the theory that complex mental processes, such as thinking, learning, and memory, can be wholly or mainly explained by the associative links formed between ideas according to specific laws and principles (see ASSOCIATION OF IDEAS). Although Greek philosopher Aristotle (384–322 BCE) cited some of these laws (similarity, difference, contiguity in time or space, etc.), the theory was first stated systematically by English philosopher Thomas Hobbes (1588–1679), who held that all knowledge is compounded from relatively simple sense impressions. The laws and applications of association were later developed by John Locke (1632–1704) and other members of the British empiricist school (see EMPIRICISM), notably George Berkeley (1685–1753), David Hume (1711–1776), David Hartley (1705–1757), James Mill (1773–1836), and John Stuart Mill (1806–1873). Although the approach taken by such thinkers was relatively static and nonexperimental, there are echoes of associationism in much historical and contemporary psychology. Most importantly, associationism has been invoked to explain the pairing of stimuli and responses. As such, it is a fundamental assumption of modern LEARNING THEORY and all behaviorist approaches (see BEHAVIORISM). Also called **British associationism**.

associationist *n.* a theorist who believes that the process of learning can be best described as the acquisition, modification, or elaboration of ASSOCIATIONS. See ASSOCIATIONISM.

associationistic theory of learning any of various theories that describe learning as a process of forming ASSOCIATIONS among items, these items being either stimuli and responses or, in contemporary theories, cognitive representations. Historically, the associationistic theories of HULL and SPENCE are contrasted with the nonassociative and cognitive theory of TOLMAN.

association nuclei nuclei of the THALAMUS that do not receive direct input from ascending sensory systems. They connect widely with other thalamic nuclei and send axons to ASSOCIATION CORTEX.

association of ideas the process by which simple perceptions and ideas are combined into totalities of varying degrees of complexity and abstractness, as, for example, connecting the relatively simple ideas of four legs, furry coat, a certain shape and size, and so on, into the compound concept "cat." The same process is held to explain one's understanding of entirely ABSTRACT IDEAS, such as "power" or "liberalism." The association of ideas was a key concept for the British empiricist school of philosophers (see EMPIRICISM) and remains fundamental in LEARNING THEORY and BEHAVIORISM. See also MENTAL CHEMISTRY; MENTAL MECHANICS.

association psychology psychology based on the premise that learning and knowledge are derived from the formation of ASSOCIATIONS between ideas. Perception, learning, remembering, and thinking all use these acquired associations. Association psychology developed from British empiricist and associationist philosophy (see ASSOCIATIONISM).

association-reaction time in a word-association test, the elapsed time between stimulus and response.

association value 1. the extent to which a stimulus is associated with other ideas, memories, or values. **2.** the extent to which people are able to ascribe meaning to an apparently meaningless stimulus, for example, an arbitrary consonant-vowel-consonant trigram (e.g., KEX or DAG) presented during an association test.

associative anamnesis a psychiatric interview technique in which the client gives an autobiographical account of his or her history and difficulties, while the therapist listens for key words and expressions that are then used to establish an **associative linkage** that will bring the client closer to the unconscious roots of his or her disturbance. See also SECTOR THERAPY. [developed by Felix Deutsch (1884–1964)]

associative-chain theory in LEARNING THEORY and behaviorist psychology (see BEHAVIORISM), a theory of how complex behaviors, including linguistic behaviors, are formed from combinations of simple stimulus–response associations.

associative clustering the tendency for items with preexisting associations to be recalled together during memory recall.

associative–dissociative strategy a plan of shifting one's ATTENTIONAL FOCUS between internal (associative) feedback (e.g., breathing rate, muscle soreness) and external (dissociative) stimuli (e.g., what others are doing, the scenery). Athletes in ENDURANCE ACTIVITIES use such strategies to check body functions at specific times and to pay attention to external stimuli at others.

associative fluency the ability to make a wide range of connections when presented with an object, event, word, or concept. High associative fluency has been identified as an aspect of CREATIVITY that in many individuals is not positively correlated with high intelligence. See also CREATIVE THINKING; DIVERGENT THINKING.

associative illusion a visual illusion produced by the interaction of parts of a design (e.g., the MÜLLER-LYER ILLUSION).

associative law any of the principles according to which ASSOCIATIONS are acquired and strengthened, originally derived from British empiricist philosophy (see ASSOCIATIONISM). These include the LAW OF CONTIGUITY, the LAW OF FREQUENCY, and the law of recency (see RECENCY EFFECT).

associative learning a type of learning in which bonds are formed between elements. In different types of learning theories, these associated elements may be stimulus and response, mental representations of events, or elements in neural networks.

associative linkage see ASSOCIATIVE ANAMNESIS.

associative memory 1. revival of the memory of a past event or place by recalling something associated with it. **2.** retrieval of the memory of a stimulus or behavior in reaction to the presentation of an associated stimulus or response.

associative play a type of SOCIAL PLAY characteristic of young preschool children, in which two or more children interact, possibly sharing toys and talking to one another, but with each engaged in a different activity. See COLLECTIVE MONOLOGUE. Compare COOPERATIVE PLAY; PARALLEL PLAY; SOLITARY PLAY.

associative strength the strength of the ASSOCIATION between two or more items (e.g., between stimulus and response or between items in memory). Associative strength is typically measured by the capacity of the stimulus to elicit the response (e.g., a conditioned response) or the capacity of the first item to produce recall of the second.

associative thinking a relatively uncontrolled cognitive activity in which the mind "wanders" without specific direction among elements based on their associations with one another, as occurs during REVERIE, DAYDREAM, and FREE ASSOCIATION.

associative visual agnosia see VISUAL AGNOSIA.

assonance *n.* a similarity in the vowel sounds of two or more words, for example, *through* and *flute* or *sane* and *stay*.

assortative mating MATING BEHAVIOR in which mates are chosen on the basis of a particular trait or group of traits (e.g., attractiveness, similarity of body size). Also called **assortive mating**. See also MATE SELECTION. Compare RANDOM MATING.

assumed role a behavior pattern adopted by a person who chooses or accepts a particular social position or status in the belief that such behavior is expected for that position or status. An example of an assumed role is the SICK ROLE. Also called **role enactment**.

assumption *n.* **1.** the premise or supposition that something is fact; that is, the act of taking something for granted. **2.** one or more conditions that need to be met in order for a statistical procedure to be fully justified from a theoretical perspective. For example, ANALYSIS OF VARIANCE assumes HOMOGENEITY OF VARIANCE and independence of observations, among other criteria. If the assumptions were to be violated to an extreme extent, the results would be invalid. See ROBUSTNESS.

assurance *n.* see REASSURANCE.

astasia *n.* severe impairment or complete loss of the ability to stand due to problems in motor coordination. **—astatic** *adj.*

astasia–abasia 1. severe impairment or complete loss of the ability to stand (see ASTASIA) or walk (see ABASIA). **2.** the ability to walk only with a wobbly, staggering gait, although control is normal while lying down. This is believed to be psychogenic in origin and may be manifested as a symptom of CONVERSION DISORDER. Also called **Blocq's disease**.

astereognosis *n.* a form of AGNOSIA characterized by loss or marked impairment of the ability to identify objects or geometric forms by touch. The condition is frequently associated with a lesion in the PARIETAL LOBE of the brain caused by disease or injury. Also called **astereognosia**; **tactile agnosia**; **tactile amnesia**. See also AMORPHOSYNTHESIS.

asterixis *n.* transient loss of a fixed position of the hands or arms followed by a jerking recovery movement, usually occurring in association with tremulousness caused by metabolic disorders. Also called **flapping tremor**.

asthenia *n.* severe weakness or loss of strength, often associated with general fatigue and muscular pain, breathlessness, PSYCHOMOTOR AGITATION, and heart palpitations. In some cases, it is caused by dysfunction of the pituitary gland. Asthenia was formerly thought to be a common symptom of a MAJOR DEPRESSIVE EPISODE but is no longer defined as such. **—asthenic** *adj.*

asthenic type a body type characterized by a frail, long-limbed, narrow-chested physique. According to KRETSCHMER TYPOLOGY, such individuals tend to be shy, sensitive, and introversive in temperament (and in extreme cases schizophrenic). Also called **leptosome type**. See also CONSTITUTIONAL TYPE.

asthenopia *n.* weakness or fatigue involving the eyes and eye muscles, usually due to strain.

asthma *n.* a disorder in which blocking of the bronchial passages by spasmodic contractions and mucus produces wheezing and gasping. Though the precipitating cause is usually an allergen (dust or pollen), such irritants as tobacco smoke or pesticides, hypersensitivity to bacteria, or psychological factors, such as anxiety and stress, may aggravate or even precipitate an attack. Also called **bronchial asthma**.

astigmatism *n.* a visual disorder in which the light rays of a visual stimulus do not all focus at a single point on the retina. Astigmatism is caused by uneven curvature of the cornea. As a result, light rays are refracted more in one meridian (that of the greatest curvature) than in the other at right angles to it (that of least curvature). The effect is an aberration or distortion of the visual image not unlike the reflection seen in an amusement park mirror. Astigmatism causes MERIDIONAL AMBLYOPIA and can occur with the presence of MYOPIA or HYPEROPIA. **—astigmatic** *adj.*

astigmatoscope *n.* an instrument used to diagnose and measure ASTIGMATISM in the eye.

astral projection the alleged ability of certain MEDIUMS or SENSITIVES to enter a trance-like state in which they leave the physical body and operate in its supposed supersensible counterpart, the **astral body**. See OUT-OF-BODY EXPERIENCE.

astroblastoma *n.* a type of slow-growing tumor of neuroglial cells (see ASTROCYTOMA) in which the cells have abundant cytoplasm and multiple nuclei. Also called **Grade II astrocytoma**.

astrocyte *n.* a star-shaped glial cell (see NEUROGLIA) with numerous processes (extensions) that run in all directions. The processes provide structural support for the brain, are responsible for many homeostatic controls, and may isolate receptive surfaces.

astrocytoma *n.* a tumor composed of neuroglial cells (see NEUROGLIA). It can be classified from Grade I to Grade IV by its severity and rate of growth. Grade II tumors are also called ASTROBLASTOMAS; Grade III and IV tumors are often identified as GLIOBLASTOMA multiforme. Grade I tumors may be associated with minimal behavioral or cognitive impact, whereas faster growing tumors may lead to severe impairment depending on their location within the brain.

astrocytosis *n.* a pathological condition marked by a proliferation of ASTROCYTES, neuroglial cells with fibrous processes (see NEUROGLIA). The astrocytes spread into tissues of the central nervous system in which normal neurons have died due to lack of oxygen or glucose, as during episodes of HYPOXIA or HYPOGLYCEMIA.

astroglia *n.* NEUROGLIA composed of ASTROCYTES.

astrology *n.* a PSEUDOSCIENCE based on the belief that the movements and positions of the planets in relation to the constellations of the zodiac influence the lives of individuals and the course of events. The systematic study of astrology originated in ancient Babylon and spread to Greece, China, India, and the Islamic world. Despite the disapproval of the Church, it remained widely influential during the medieval and Renaissance periods in Europe. Even in the modern scientific world, many people believe that their HOROSCOPE (a map of the heavens at the time of their birth) determines their personal characteristics, tendencies to particular diseases, and liability to good or bad fortune. There is no evidence for this belief, except perhaps as a SELF-FULFILLING PROPHECY. Astrology is mainly of interest to psychology because it involved an early theory of personality types, relating the physical and psychological characteristics of individuals to the supposed influence of the heavens. **—astrologer** *n.* **—astrological** *adj.*

ASVAB abbreviation for ARMED SERVICES VOCATIONAL APTITUDE BATTERY.

asyllabia *n.* a type of APHASIA in which a person can recognize individual letters of the alphabet but is unable to form or comprehend syllables or words.

asylum *n.* originally, a refuge for criminals (from Greek *asylon*, "sanctuary"). From the 19th century, the terms "asylum" or "insane asylum" were applied to MENTAL INSTITUTIONS. These names are now obsolete, discarded because of their emphasis on refuge rather than treatment.

asymbolia *n.* loss of the ability to understand or use symbols of any kind, including words, gestures, signals, musical notes, chemical formulas, or signs. Asymbolia is a form of APHASIA and includes such conditions as ALEXIA, AGRAPHIA, and AMIMIA. Also called **asemasia**; **asemia**.

asymmetrical distribution a DISTRIBUTION in which the frequency of scores above the mean does not equal that below the mean.

asymptomatic *adj.* not showing any symptoms. A disease or disorder may be present in an individual but show no outright physical or behavioral symptoms; for example, hypertension is considered to be asymptomatic because, unless severe or acute, it does not have any associated symptoms and can be detected only by measuring the blood pressure.

asymptomatic neurosyphilis a form of NEUROSYPHILIS in which laboratory findings show abnormalities in the cerebrospinal fluid but the patient does not show symptoms of the disease.

asymptote *n.* **1.** in statistics, a straight line that a regular curve approaches but never reaches. **2.** in psychology, the approach to a full level of response after many learning trials. **—asymptotic** *adj.*

asymptotic normality a property of a distribution whereby that distribution becomes indistinguishable from the normal distribution as one or more of its parameters (e.g., *n* in the BINOMIAL DISTRIBUTION or ν in the CHI-SQUARE DISTRIBUTION) becomes very large.

asynchronous brood offspring (usually birds) that are hatched successively (rather than simultaneously, as in a **synchronous brood**). In cattle egrets, for example, eggs hatch 1 or 2 days apart, giving a growth advantage to the first-hatched chick. Often, older chicks will attack young siblings to the point of killing them (see SIBLICIDE). However, in terms of parental efficiency in feeding chicks and mean chick survival, producing asynchronous broods is a better strategy than producing synchronous broods.

asynchrony *n.* lack of temporal correspondence in the occurrence of different events or processes, for example, the delay in time between a child's language comprehension and language production.

asyndesis *n.* disjointed speech in which disconnected ideas are put together without adequate grammatical linkages. Asyndesis is observed frequently in schizophrenia and occasionally in other disorders. **—asyndetic** *adj.*

asyndetic thinking thought processes in which ideas and images are fragmented or unconnected. It is prevalent in schizophrenia.

asynergia *n.* faulty coordination of muscle groups involved in the performance of complex motor movements, such as standing, walking, or kneeling. Also called **asynergy**. **—asynergic** *adj.*

asynergic speech see CEREBELLAR SPEECH.

AT abbreviation for ASSISTIVE TECHNOLOGY.

ataque de nervios a CULTURE-BOUND SYNDROME observed mainly among Latinos. Common symptoms include trembling, crying, uncontrollable shaking, verbal or physical aggression (or both), and in some cases seizurelike or fainting episodes. Some individuals have no memory for the episode afterward. Attacks often occur as a result of a stressful event related to the family, and most patients quickly return to their previous level of functioning.

ataractic *adj.* see ATARAXY.

ataractics *pl. n.* agents that have a calming or quieting effect, producing a state of ATARAXY. The name was introduced as an alternative to TRANQUILIZER. Also called **ataraxics**.

Atarax *n.* a trade name for HYDROXYZINE.

ataraxy *n.* a state of mind that is characterized by perfect peace or detached serenity without loss of mental abilities or clouding of consciousness. Also called **ataraxia**. **—ataraxic** or **ataractic** *adj.*

atavism *n.* **1.** the presence of a genetic trait inherited from a remote ancestor that did not appear in more recent ancestors, that is, a reversion to an earlier type. **2.** more generally, the reappearance of or reversion to an earlier or more primitive characteristic or form (e.g., behavioral atavism). **—atavistic** *adj.*

ataxia *n.* impaired ability or inability to perform coordinated movements, such as walking or reaching for an object. This may be due to failure of the central nervous system to coordinate muscle movements or to loss of feedback from the muscles and joints, called SENSORY ATAXIA. Causes may include injury, drugs, or disorders affecting muscular coordination, such as cerebral palsy or multiple sclerosis. Ataxia may be mimicked by certain psychological disorders, such as SOMATIZATION DISORDER. There are several types of ataxia, including CEREBELLAR ATAXIA, FRIEDREICH'S ATAXIA, LOCOMOTOR ATAXIA, and OPTIC ATAXIA. **—ataxic** *adj.*

ataxiagraph *n.* a device that measures ATAXIA by assessing the amount a person's body sways when he or she is standing upright with eyes closed. Also called **ataxiameter**.

ataxia telangiectasia an AUTOSOMAL RECESSIVE genetic disorder characterized primarily by an inability to coordinate voluntary muscle movements (see ATAXIA) and by the dilation of small blood vessels in the eyes and skin of the nose and ears. Initial symptoms include limb ataxia and truncal ataxia (swaying of the head and trunk while standing or sitting), which eventually become so severe that the individual must remain in a wheelchair. Other symptoms include increasingly slowed speech, the appearance of such involuntary movements as MYOCLONUS or INTENTION TREMORS, and a proneness to infection, particularly respiratory infection. Also called **Louis-Bar syndrome**.

ataxic dysarthria a speech disorder characterized by slurring, poorly controlled volume, and sudden spastic irregularities of vocal cord function. Also called **ataxic speech**.

ataxic feeling a sense that the ability to coordinate muscular movement has been lost. The feeling may be psychogenic or caused by such psychotropic drugs as antipsychotics, benzodiazepines, and lithium.

ataxic gait a wide-based, staggering gait seen in individuals with cerebellar damage.

ataxic speech see ATAXIC DYSARTHRIA.

ataxic writing uncoordinated or irregular writing caused by brain damage.

ataxiophemia *n.* incoordination of the muscles used in speaking. It is essentially equivalent to DYSARTHRIA.

atCODAP see COMPREHENSIVE OCCUPATIONAL DATA ANALYSIS PROGRAM.

ateliosis *n.* **1.** incomplete development of the body or of any of its parts, as in infantilism or dwarfism. **2.** formerly, the persistence of infantile or childlike cognitive or emotional developmental stages. Also called **atelia**.

atheroma *n.* see ATHEROSCLEROSIS.

atherosclerosis *n.* a common form of ARTERIOSCLEROSIS in which the primary sign is **atheroma**, the deposition of yellowish lipid **atherosclerotic** (or **atheromatous**) **plaques**, on the inner walls of large and medium-sized arteries. **—atherosclerotic** *adj.*

athetosis *n.* slow, involuntary, snakelike, recurrent movements, typically of the fingers, toes, arms, or legs, due to lesions in the EXTRAPYRAMIDAL TRACT. It is generally most evident in the upper extremities of the body. **—athetoid** *adj.* **—athetotic** *adj.*

athlete-based intervention **1.** an intervention that develops an athlete's perceptions, experiences, or both. **2.** an intervention that is initiated and conducted by the athlete.

athlete identity the degree to which an individual defines him- or herself as an athlete; it is a domain of SELF-CONCEPT. Individuals who rely too strongly on the athletic role to define themselves are vulnerable to mental health problems at the end of their involvement in sporting activity.

Athletic Coping Skills Inventory (**ACSI**) a self-report inventory used to assess an individual's psychological skills in seven sports-specific areas: (a) coping with adversity, (b) peaking under pressure, (c) GOAL SETTING and mental preparation, (d) CONCENTRATION, (e) freedom from worry, (f) CONFIDENCE and ACHIEVEMENT MOTIVATION, and (g) coachability. The most recent version of the inventory is the **ACSI-28**, published in 1995. It consists of 28 statements (e.g., "I feel confident that I will play well") to which participants respond using a 4-point LIKERT SCALE, ranging from "almost never" to "almost always." [developed by U.S. psychologist Ronald E. Smith (1940–), statistician Robert W. Schutz, U.S. psychologist Frank L. Smoll (1941–), and U.S. psychologist John T. Ptacek (1962–)]

Athletic Motivation Inventory (**AMI**) a self-report inventory used to assess 11 personality traits purportedly associated with successful athletic performance: aggressiveness, coachability, conscientiousness, determination, drive, emotional control, guilt proneness, leadership, mental toughness, self-confidence, and trust. Originally published in the 1960s, the AMI currently consists of 190 sports-specific statements (e.g., "I usually compete best without the advice of others") or questions (e.g., "Which would you say is the most true of coaching?") to which participants respond using a multiple-choice format. See also SPORT PERSONALITY DEBATE. [developed by U.S. psychologist Thomas A. Tutko (1931–), Leland P. Lyon, and U.S. psychologist Bruce C. Ogilvie (1920–2003)]

athletic triad the combination of AMENORRHEA, ANOREXIA NERVOSA, and osteoporosis (see CALCIUM-DEFICIENCY DISORDERS) observed in some female athletes. This is more likely to be found among female athletes in subjectively evaluated sports (e.g., gymnastics, diving) or endurance sports (e.g., marathon or cross-country running).

athletic type a body type characterized by a muscular, well-proportioned, broad-shouldered physique. According to KRETSCHMER TYPOLOGY, such individuals tend to be energetic and aggressive in temperament. See also CARUS TYPOLOGY; CONSTITUTIONAL TYPE.

athymia *n.* **1.** absence of feeling or emotion. **2.** congenital absence of the THYMUS.

athyreosis *n.* a form of HYPOTHYROIDISM found in children in whom the thyroid gland has failed to develop normally. Affected children either have no thyroid gland or a gland that is abnormally small and whose essential elements are replaced by fibrous tissue. Also called **athyreotic cretinism**. See also CRETINISM.

Ativan *n.* a trade name for LORAZEPAM.

atmosphere effect 1. the tendency for particular behaviors to be stimulated by a particular environment or situation, even when inappropriate, such as gesturing when using the telephone or applauding a poor speech. **2.** the tendency for an individual's thinking on a question to be affected illogically by an impression made by the terms in which the question is stated, as when positively worded premises in a syllogism increase the perceived validity of a false but positively worded conclusion. Also called **framing effect**. See also ANCHORING BIAS.

atmospheric conditions various aspects of the atmosphere (e.g., temperature, humidity, airflow, barometric pressure, composition, toxic conditions) as they affect the comfort and performance of people in their living or working environment.

atmospheric perspective a cue that aids the perception of depth and distance. Atmospheric perspective is the acquired ability to differentiate near and distant objects on the basis of their clear or indistinct appearance.

atomism *n.* **1.** the view that psychological phenomena can best be understood by analyzing them into elementary units, such as sensations or conditioned responses, and by showing how these units combine to form thoughts, images, perceptions, and behavior. Also called **atomistic psychology**; **molecularism**. See also ELEMENTARISM; REDUCTIONISM. **2.** in vision, the principle that visual perception of a complex stimulus results from an analysis of its elementary components. **—atomistic** *adj.*

atonia *n.* lack of normal muscle tone or strength. See also DYSTONIA. Also called **atony**; **atonicity**. **—atonic** *adj.*

atonic seizure a rare type of GENERALIZED SEIZURE in which there is a rapid loss of muscle tone and the individual suddenly falls on the ground. It was formerly called an **akinetic seizure**.

ATP *a*denosine *t*ri*p*hosphate: a nucleotide, present in all living cells, that is the source of chemical energy for muscle contractions and transmission of nerve impulses. Consisting of ADENOSINE combined with three phosphate groups, it contains a high-energy bond that is easily split when a cell requires energy quickly.

atrial flutter see ARRHYTHMIA.

at risk vulnerable to a disorder or disease. Risk status for an individual is defined by genetic, physical, and behavioral factors or conditions. For example, children of people with schizophrenia may be considered at risk for schizophrenia, and heavy cigarette smokers are at risk for emphysema and lung cancer.

at-risk mental states psychological symptoms or mental processes that render individuals vulnerable to mental illnesses or to adverse behaviors, such as violence.

atrium *n.* (*pl.* **atria**) in anatomy, a body cavity or chamber, such as either of the two upper chambers of the heart. **—atrial** *adj.*

atrophy 1. *n.* a wasting away of the body or a part it, as from lack of nourishment, inactivity, degenerative disease, or normal aging. See CEREBRAL ATROPHY. **2.** *n.* degeneration from disuse. **3.** *vb.* to waste away or degenerate. **—atrophic** *adj.*

atropine *n.* an ANTICHOLINERGIC DRUG derived from certain plants, particularly belladonna (see BELLADONNA ALKALOIDS), and also produced synthetically. Its effects include increases in heart rate and rate of breathing, relaxation of smooth muscles, and reduction of secretions (e.g., saliva). It may be used to treat organophosphate poisoning and bradycardia (slowing of the heart rate), or as an adjunct to anesthesia, but is most commonly employed in eye examinations to dilate the pupil. Atropine is closely related, chemically and pharmacologically, to SCOPOLAMINE.

atropine-coma therapy (**ACT**) a now-abandoned method of treating tense, agitated, and anxious people with psychoses by administering atropine sulfate to induce coma.

attachment *n.* the tendency of human infants and young nonhuman animals to become emotionally close to certain individuals and to be calm while in their presence. Human infants develop strong emotional bonds with a caregiver, particularly a parent, and seek attachment to their caregivers as a step in establishing a feeling of security; when fearful or anxious they are comforted by contact with their attachment object. For humans, attachment also involves the tendency in adulthood to seek emotionally supportive relationships. In animals, attachment can be formed with male or female parents or with other siblings based on the degree of contact in early life; contact with the attachment object rapidly reduces stress responses.

attachment behavior 1. behavior associated with the formation of and investment in significant relationships. **2.** infant behavior that results in the infant gaining proximity to or contact with his or her caregiver. Its manifestations include crying, smiling, calling, and clinging. See ATTACHMENT THEORY. [first described by John BOWLBY]

attachment bond the primary, enduring, special relationship that gradually develops between an infant and caregiver.

attachment disorder see REACTIVE ATTACHMENT DISORDER.

attachment theory a theory that (a) postulates an evolutionarily advantageous need, especially in primates, to form close emotional bonds with significant others: specifically, a need for the young to maintain close proximity to and form ATTACHMENTS with their caregivers; and (b) characterizes the different types of relationships between human infants and caregivers. Different patterns of attachment established in infancy and early childhood have been shown to affect the individual's later emotional development and emotional stability. See ATTACHMENT BEHAVIOR; INSECURE ATTACHMENT; SECURE ATTACHMENT; STRANGE SITUATION. [originally developed by John BOWLBY and later expanded by Canadian-born U.S. psychologist Mary D. Salter Ainsworth (1913–1999)]

attack behavior an aggressive use of force or violence against an adversary, usually with intent to harm. Attack behavior often occurs when signals of warning or threat have been ignored. Animals, and some human beings, may use attack as a form of defense (defensive aggression: see DEFENSIVE BEHAVIOR).

attainment *n.* a particular educational achievement or accomplishment.

attainment test see ACHIEVEMENT TEST.

attempted suicide a deliberate but, by implication, unsuccessful attempt to commit SUICIDE. Also called **suicide attempt**.

attendance *n.* **1.** the number of pupils present in a class, school, or educational function. **2.** a record of how consistently a pupil has been present on the days that a class or school is in session.

attendant care **1.** nonmedical, in-home personal care provided to individuals with a physical or developmental disability who are able to live independently except that help is required for part of the day in dressing, undressing, feeding, or other activities of daily living. **2.** one-on-one direct supervision by a trained attendant of a juvenile who has been taken into custody in a nonsecure setting.

attending *n.* the act of directing ATTENTION to a person, location, object, or event, which is presumed to increase processing of the attended information and make it more prominent in conscious awareness.

attending behavior any behavior engaged in by an individual while attentively listening to and observing a speaker, for example, exhibiting an open, interested posture and maintaining eye contact. Helpful attending behaviors, along with ACTIVE LISTENING, are considered cornerstones of a therapist's or counselor's general ability.

attensity *n.* the sensory clarity or attention-producing effect of a sensation. [defined around 1900 by E. B. TITCHENER]

attention *n.* a state of awareness in which the senses are focused selectively on aspects of the environment and the central nervous system is in a state of readiness to respond to stimuli. Because human beings do not have an infinite capacity to attend to everything—focusing on certain items at the expense of others—much of the research in this field is devoted to discerning which factors influence attention and to understanding the neural mechanisms that are involved in the selective processing of information. For example, past experience affects perceptual experience (we notice things that have meaning for us), and some activities (e.g., reading) require conscious participation (i.e., intentional attention). However, attention can also be captured (i.e., directed unintentionally) by qualities of stimuli in the environment, such as intensity, movement, repetition, contrast, and novelty. See also ATTENUATION THEORY; DIVIDED ATTENTION; FILTER THEORY; FOCAL ATTENTION; SELECTIVE ATTENTION; VISUAL ATTENTION.

attentional blink impairment in the ability to detect a PROBE event (e.g., the letter X) in a rapidly presented stream of letters when it follows a target letter (e.g., a white letter) that must be identified. Because the impairment is usually largest at a lag of a few letters, it is attributed to attentional requirements for processing the target letter and not to perceptual impairment.

attentional capture the unintentional focusing of attention, for example by a change in a stimulus, which interrupts other processing.

attentional control of consciousness the concept that SELECTIVE ATTENTION to an event can increase the likelihood of the event becoming conscious.

attentional dyslexia a form of acquired dyslexia (see ALEXIA) in which a person is able to read words but has difficulty identifying their constituent letters. This is thought to be caused by a failure of the letter-to-word binding system, resulting in the "migration" of letters between words. People with attentional dyslexia are able to read letters or words significantly better when they are presented in isolation than when presented together with others as part of a text.

attentional focus the focus of an individual's attention at a particular moment. This focus may be internal (i.e., attending to cognitive, emotional, or pain cues) or it may be external (i.e., attending to environmental cues). See ASSOCIATIVE–DISSOCIATIVE STRATEGIES; TEST OF ATTENTIONAL AND INTERPERSONAL STYLE.

attentional narrowing the restricting of attention in high-stress situations to a small set of displays or information sources. If critical information occurs outside this set, performance will suffer; that is, in response to the anxiety of a situation, an individual will often attend to some but not all task-relevant cues and will therefore make errors by omission of task-relevant information. For example, when driving to the hospital for a medical emergency, the driver may focus attention only on the road ahead and not notice events at the side of the road, such as a pedestrian entering a crosswalk.

attentional strategy a pattern of ATTENTIONAL FOCUS for the purpose of efficient execution of a task. The pattern may be specifically learned or habitually developed. For example, a quarterback in football starts with a broad external focus (determining the opposition's defense pattern) and moves to an internal focus (selecting the appropriate play), then back to a broad external focus after snap (determining pass patterns), and finally to a narrow external focus (selecting the receiver and executing the throw). See also ASSOCIATIVE–DISSOCIATIVE STRATEGY.

attention-control training (**ACT**) a program that assists an individual to be more effective at maintaining appropriate ATTENTIONAL FOCUS. It is achieved by assessment of the individual's attentional strengths and weaknesses, the attentional demands of the environment in which the individual's performance occurs, environmental and personal characteristics likely to induce stress and dictate behavior under pressure, and typical error patterns and situations in which they occur. This assessment leads to the planning of an intervention protocol, the purpose of which is to teach the individual to concentrate on all the task-relevant cues and ignore all the task-irrelevant cues in a given situation.

attention decrement the tendency for items or events that receive less attention to be remembered less well than those that receive more attention.

attention-deficit disorder (**ADD**) a former and still commonly used name for ATTENTION-DEFICIT/HYPERACTIVITY DISORDER.

attention-deficit/hyperactivity disorder (**ADHD**; **AHD**) in *DSM–IV–TR,* a behavioral syndrome characterized by the persistent presence (i.e., for 6 months or more) of six or more symptoms involving (a) inattention (e.g., failure to complete tasks or listen carefully, difficulty in concentrating, distractibility) or (b) impulsivity or hyperactivity (e.g., blurting out answers; impatience; restlessness; fidgeting; difficulty in organizing work, taking turns, or staying seated; excessive talking; running about; climbing on things). The symptoms, which impair social, academic, or occupational functioning, start to appear before the age of 7 and are observed in more than one setting. ADHD is estimated to be present in 3–7% of schoolchildren. In *DSM–III,* ADHD was designated **attention-deficit disorder with hyperactivity**. There was a separate diagnostic category, **attention-deficit disorder without hyperactivity**, which in *DSM–IV–TR* is represented by the subtype **predominantly inattentive**.

attention-deficit/hyperactivity disorder not otherwise specified in *DSM–IV–TR,* a disorder characterized by inattention, hyperactivity, or impulsivity that impair performance in educational or social situations but do not meet the diagnostic criteria for ATTENTION-DEFICIT/HYPERACTIVITY DISORDER (ADHD). It may, for example, be marked by significant problems in attention that start after the age of 7 or that are not among the criteria listed for a diagnosis of ADHD (e.g., daydreaming).

attention disorder a disturbance characterized by an inability to maintain focus on an activity or by difficulties in taking notice of, responding to, or being aware of the behavior, demands, or requests of other people. Previously, this term was frequently used interchangeably with MINIMAL BRAIN DYSFUNCTION, as impairments of attention are among the most common manifestations of brain damage. See also LEARNING DISABILITY.

attention fluctuation see FLUCTUATION OF ATTENTION.

attention-getting *adj.* describing a type of behavior, often inappropriate, that is used to gain attention. Childhood TEMPER TANTRUMS are an example of such behavior.

attention level the degree to which a task or event is likely to be reportable or conscious. Tasks with high attention-level demands are likely to interfere with each other when they must be done at the same time. See also DUAL-TASK COMPETITION.

attention load measure a method that uses competing cognitive tasks to assess the processing demands made by each task. The degradation in performance of one task is taken to be a measure of the attentional demands made by the other task.

attention overload a psychological condition that results from excessive demands on attention. The effect is temporary depletion of available attention and an inability to cope with tasks that demand attention. Attention overload can occur in work tasks, such as supervising activity of commercial aircraft in an airport control tower. In resource models of attention, such as the UNITARY-RESOURCE MODEL, overload refers specifically to situations in which the demand for attentional resources exceeds the supply. See also INFORMATION OVERLOAD.

attention shifting moving the focus of attention from one location to another. Shifts can be made intentionally or caused automatically by the abrupt onset of a stimulus. For intentional shifts, a spatial cue must be presented a few hundred milliseconds before the displayed information to allow attention to be shifted to the cued location.

attention span **1.** the length of time an individual can concentrate on one subject. **2.** the amount of material grasped during exposure to stimuli or information.

attention-span test see APPREHENSION-SPAN TEST.

attentiveness *n.* **1.** the state of being alert and actively paying attention. **2.** the quality of actively attending to the needs of others.

attenuated positive symptoms in schizophrenia, a reduction in hallucinations, delusions, bizarre behavior, or conceptual thought problems. See also POSITIVE SYMPTOM.

attenuated psychotic symptoms in schizophrenia and other PSYCHOTIC DISORDERS, an increase in reality-based perceptions and a reduction in symptoms, such as delusions, hallucinations, markedly incoherent speech, and disorientation.

attenuation *n.* **1.** the lessening or weakening in strength, value, or quality of a stimulus. **2.** in statistics, a reduction in the estimated size of an effect because of errors of measurement.

attenuation theory a version of the FILTER THEORY of attention proposing that unattended messages are attenuated (i.e., processed weakly) but not entirely blocked from further processing. According to the theory, items in unattended channels of information have different thresholds of recognition depending on their significance to the individual. Thus a significant word (e.g., the person's name) would have a low threshold and, when mentioned, would be recognized even if that person's attention is concentrated elsewhere (e.g., in conversation with someone else). See also COCKTAIL-PARTY EFFECT. [proposed in 1960 by British psychologist Anne Marie Treisman (1935–)]

attenuator *n.* a calibrated device that accurately controls the decrease in the intensity of tones or light on electronic instruments, such as AUDIOMETERS, stereophonic sound systems, or video equipment.

attitude *n.* **1.** in social psychology, a relatively enduring and general evaluation of an object, person, group, issue, or concept on a scale ranging from negative to positive. **2.** any subjective belief or evaluation associated with an object. **—attitudinal** *adj.*

attitude–behavior consistency the extent to which behavior toward an ATTITUDE OBJECT is consistent with the attitude associated with that object. Positive attitudes are associated with approach behaviors; negative attitudes are associated with withdrawal behaviors.

attitude change any alteration in an attitude, which may result from active attempts by others to change the attitude or from processes initiated by the person holding the attitude.

attitude-congeniality memory effect the tendency to remember information that is evaluatively consistent with an attitude better than information that is evaluatively inconsistent with an attitude.

attitude measure a procedure in which individuals are assigned quantitative values that reflect systematic variation on some underlying attitude. Several broad categories have been developed, including DIRECT ATTITUDE MEASURES, INDIRECT ATTITUDE MEASURES, EXPLICIT ATTITUDE MEASURES, and IMPLICIT ATTITUDE MEASURES.

attitude object any target of judgment that has an attitude associated with it. Attitude objects may be people, social groups, policy positions, abstract concepts, or physical objects.

attitude-relevant knowledge information directly associated with an ATTITUDE OBJECT that is activated in memory when encountering the object. Attitude-relevant knowledge is usually measured in terms of the amount of information associated with the object. Also called **issue-relevant knowledge**; **working knowledge**.

attitude scale a measure used to assess an attitude. See LIKERT SCALE; SEMANTIC DIFFERENTIAL; THURSTONE ATTITUDE SCALES.

attitude-strength-related belief a subjective belief about an attitude or ATTITUDE OBJECT that is associated with the underlying STRENGTH OF AN ATTITUDE.

attitude survey a set of ATTITUDE MEASURES usually designed to assess attitudes toward more than one ATTITUDE OBJECT.

attitude system a set of two or more attitudes that are associated with one another in memory. Attitude systems can be characterized in terms of the number of attitudes in the system, the strength, number, and pattern of associations among the attitudes, and the evaluative consistency of the attitudes in the system. See also INTERATTITUDINAL CONSISTENCY.

attitude therapy a form of reeducative treatment that emphasizes current attitudes of the client in terms of the origins of these attitudes, the purpose such attitudes serve, and their distortions.

attitudinal group **1.** an aggregation, or set, of individuals who are highly similar in their attitudes toward a given subject. **2.** any personal growth or therapy group in which the members are given the chance to express and exchange feelings and thoughts in an accepting environment.

attitudinal involvement see EGO INVOLVEMENT.

attitudinal reflex a reflex that helps put an animal in a position or condition to make a complex response, as in preparing to attack an adversary.

attitudinal types in Carl Jung's ANALYTIC PSYCHOLOGY, two personality types defined by habitual EXTRAVERSION on the one hand and habitual INTROVERSION on the other. See INTROVERSION–EXTRAVERSION. See also FUNCTIONAL TYPES.

attraction *n.* **1.** in social psychology, the feeling of being drawn to one or more other individuals and desiring their company, usually but not necessarily always because of a personal liking for them. **2.** in environmental psychology, a quality affecting proximity relationships between individuals, usually reflecting such factors as their liking for each other. For example, male–female and female–female pairs who like each other position themselves closer to each other than do pairs who feel no personal attraction toward each other. Environmental influences, such as noise, heat, and humidity, decrease attraction between pairs of individuals. See PROXEMICS. **3.** power of attraction: the extent to which any one individual is attractive to or liked by others. See also INTERPERSONAL ATTRACTION. **—attractive** *adj.*

attraction relations patterns of liking–disliking, acceptance–rejection, and inclusion–exclusion among members of a group. Such patterns are also known as **sociometric structure**, particularly when assessed through the use of SOCIOMETRY.

attraction–selection–attrition model (**ASA model**) in industrial and organizational psychology, a model proposing that (a) people are attracted to organizations that are congruent with their values, personalities, and needs; (b) the organization, in turn, employs people with attributes that fit the ORGANIZATIONAL CULTURE; and (c) those employees who do not fit the organizational culture leave. Over time the characteristics of the people who constitute the organization become increasingly homogeneous as the result of this process. [proposed by U.S. organizational psychologist Benjamin Schneider (1938–) in 1987]

attractor dynamics an approach to analyzing and understanding the interactions of goals, FEEDBACK, and the environment in the evolution of a movement TRAJECTORY, especially for repetitive movements.

attributable risk in EPIDEMIOLOGY, the incidence rate of a disease or disorder that can be considered to have been caused by exposure to a RISK FACTOR. A large portion of lung cancers can be attributed to tobacco use, constituting a substantial attributable risk for this disease.

attribute **1.** *n.* a quality or property of a person, sensation, or object, for example, the TONAL ATTRIBUTE of a note. **2.** *vb.* to assign an effect to a particular causal factor or agent. See ATTRIBUTION THEORY.

attribute model of memory a model in which different brain regions process different dimensions or attributes of a learning or memory situation—space, time, sensory dimensions, response, and emotional aspects.

attribution *n.* **1.** an inference regarding the cause of a person's behavior or an interpersonal event. The cause may be stable or unstable, internal or external, and controllable or uncontrollable, and the character of the reason affects motivation. See ATTRIBUTION THEORY; LEARNED HELPLESSNESS. **2.** in the TWO-WORD STAGE of language development, a noun qualified by an attribute, for example, *blue car*.

attributional analysis of persuasion an approach to understanding PERSUASION in terms of the reasons given by people for why communicators of persuasive messages adopt particular attitudes.

attributional style a person's characteristic tendencies when inferring the cause of behavior or events. Three dimensions are often used to evaluate people's attributional styles: the internal–external dimension (whether they tend to attribute events to the self or to other factors), the stable–unstable dimension (whether they tend to attribute events to enduring or transient causes), and the global–specific dimension (whether they tend to attribute events to causes that affect many events or just a single event).

attribution error an error or bias in ascribing motives to behaviors or causes to outcomes. See FUNDAMENTAL ATTRIBUTION ERROR; GROUP ATTRIBUTION ERROR; GROUP-SERVING BIAS; SELF-SERVING BIAS.

attribution of emotion see SCHACHTER–SINGER THEORY.

attribution theory the study of the processes by which people ascribe motives to their own and others' behavior. The motives ascribed may be either internal and personal (DISPOSITIONAL ATTRIBUTION) or external and circumstantial (SITUATIONAL ATTRIBUTION). According to U.S. social psychologist Harold H. Kelley (1921–2003), observers choose between the two types of ATTRIBUTION on the basis of three factors: consistency (how has the same individual (actor) behaved in the same situation in the past?); distinctiveness (how has the actor behaved in different situations?); and consensus (how do other people behave in the same situation?). Kelley also stated three general principles of attribution: the COVARIATION PRINCIPLE, the DISCOUNTING PRINCIPLE, and the AUGMENTATION PRINCIPLE. Kelley's work and other prominent attribution theories (e.g., CORRESPONDENT INFERENCE THEORY) emerged from the "naive" or "lay" psychology developed in 1958 by Austrian-born U.S. psychologist Fritz Heider (1896–1988). See NAIVE ANALYSIS OF ACTION.

attribution theory of leadership a model of LEADERSHIP EMERGENCE and evaluation that assumes that individuals make inferences about leadership ability by observing and interpreting certain environmental and behavioral cues. Like LEADER-CATEGORIZATION THEORY, attribution theory assumes that followers respond more positively to a leader who displays the qualities and behaviors that match their IMPLICIT LEADERSHIP THEORIES. See also LEADER PROTOTYPE.

attribution therapy a form of therapy in which the therapist tries to change a client's views concerning the causes of events and behavior.

attrition *n.* dropout or loss of participants during an experiment or withdrawal of patients during a clinical trial. Also called **experimental attrition**; **mortality**.

A-type personality see TYPE A PERSONALITY.

atypical *adj.* differing from the norm in being unusual, unrepresentative, or uncharacteristic.

atypical, mixed, or other personality disorder in *DSM–IV–TR*, a category of personality disorders for which there is insufficient evidence for a more specific designation. Cases that involve features of several personality disorders without meeting the criteria for any one type are described as **mixed personality disorders**; **other personality disorders** are unclassified cases, such as masochistic, impulsive, or immature personality disorder.

atypical antipsychotics a class of ANTIPSYCHOTIC drugs that, compared to conventional (typical or first-generation) antipsychotics, produce fewer EXTRAPYRAMIDAL EFFECTS, are less likely to alter serum levels of PROLACTIN, and appear to be less likely to cause TARDIVE DYSKINESIA, all of which are significant adverse effects of the conventional drugs. They show some degree of activity as DOPAMINE-RECEPTOR ANTAGONISTS but also block the effects of serotonin or other neurotransmitters. Atypical antipsychotics are used in the treatment of schizophrenias, delusional disorders, dementias, and other disorders characterized by psychotic symptoms. They are also used as adjunctive agents in the treatment of some nonpsychotic conditions, such as obsessive-compulsive disorder, explosive disorder, or severe depression. The prototype of the group is CLOZAPINE; others in current clinical use include OLANZAPINE, RISPERIDONE, ILOPERIDONE, QUETIAPINE, ARIPIPRAZOLE, and ZIPRASIDONE. Also called **novel antipsychotics**; **second-generation antipsychotics**.

atypical autism see PERVASIVE DEVELOPMENTAL DISORDER NOT OTHERWISE SPECIFIED.

atypical conduct disorder in *DSM–III*, a diagnostic category for disorders that in *DSM–IV–TR* are classified as DISRUPTIVE BEHAVIOR DISORDER NOT OTHERWISE SPECIFIED.

atypical depression a MAJOR DEPRESSIVE EPISODE or, less commonly, DYSTHYMIC DISORDER characterized by ATYPICAL FEATURES.

atypical disorder in *DSM–III* and earlier editions, a residual category that included unusual or uncharacteristic variations of standard mental disorders. The equivalent *DSM–IV–TR* category is not otherwise specified.

atypical dissociative disorder in *DSM–III*, a residual category of dissociative disorders that in *DSM–IV–TR* is labeled DISSOCIATIVE DISORDER NOT OTHERWISE SPECIFIED.

atypical eating disorder in *DSM–III* and earlier editions, a residual category of disorders that in *DSM–IV–TR* is labeled EATING DISORDER not otherwise specified.

atypical features symptoms of a MAJOR DEPRESSIVE EPISODE or of DYSTHYMIC DISORDER other than the standard diagnostic criteria. They comprise improvement of mood in response to positive events, weight gain, HYPERSOMNIA, heavy feelings in the limbs, and sensitivity to interpersonal rejection.

atypical gender identity disorder in *DSM–III*, a residual category for disorders of gender identity that were not classifiable as any specific gender identity disorder. In *DSM–IV–TR* such disorders are designated GENDER IDENTITY DISORDER not otherwise specified.

atypical impulse-control disorder in *DSM–III* and earlier editions, a residual category of impulse-control disorders that in *DSM–IV–TR* is labeled impulse-control disorder not otherwise specified (see IMPULSE-CONTROL DISORDERS NOT ELSEWHERE CLASSIFIED).

atypical mental disorder see ATYPICAL DISORDER.

atypical paraphilia in *DSM–III*, a residual category of paraphilias that in *DSM–IV–TR* is labeled PARAPHILIA NOT OTHERWISE SPECIFIED.

atypical pervasive developmental disorder in *DSM–III*, a diagnostic category for disorders that in *DSM–IV–TR* are classified as PERVASIVE DEVELOPMENTAL DISORDER NOT OTHERWISE SPECIFIED.

atypical psychosexual disorder a sexual problem that does not meet diagnostic criteria for sexual dysfunction or sexual deviancy. In *DSM–IV–TR* such disorders are categorized as SEXUAL DISORDER NOT OTHERWISE SPECIFIED.

atypical psychosexual dysfunction in *DSM–III*, a category that included psychosexual dysfunctions outside the standard specific categories. In *DSM–IV–TR* this is labeled SEXUAL DYSFUNCTION NOT OTHERWISE SPECIFIED.

atypical psychosis in *DSM–III*, any of various conditions involving psychotic symptoms that do not meet the criteria for any specific disorder. The equivalent *DSM–IV–TR* classification is PSYCHOTIC DISORDER NOT OTHERWISE SPECIFIED.

atypical specific developmental disorder in *DSM–III*, a residual category for disorders that in *DSM–IV–TR* are categorized as LEARNING DISORDER NOT OTHERWISE SPECIFIED or COMMUNICATION DISORDER NOT OTHERWISE SPECIFIED.

atypical stereotyped-movement disorder in *DSM–III* and earlier editions, a diagnostic category for disorders that in *DSM–IV–TR* are classified as TIC DISORDER NOT OTHERWISE SPECIFIED or STEREOTYPIC MOVEMENT DISORDER.

atypical tic disorder in *DSM–III*, a diagnostic category for tic disorders that in *DSM–IV–TR* are labeled TIC DISORDER NOT OTHERWISE SPECIFIED.

Aubert phenomenon the illusion that a vertical line tilts in the opposite direction from the direction the head is tilted when viewing it. Also called **Aubert illusion**. [Hermann **Aubert** (1826–1892), German physician]

audibility curve the relationship between the threshold of hearing for a PURE TONE, expressed in DECIBELS sound-pressure level (dB SPL), and the frequency of the tone. Compare AUDIOGRAM.

audibility range see RANGE OF AUDIBILITY.

audible thought a type of hallucination in which one hears one's own thoughts as if they were projected by an inner voice.

audience *n.* **1.** a body of onlookers that observes some performance, event, or activity. Unlike street crowds or MOBS, audiences are usually restrained and conventional in manner; individuals usually join them deliberately and withdraw when the observed performance or activity is completed. Audiences are, in some cases, widely scattered, as in the audience for a television broadcast. **2.** the people reached by a communication, particularly when selected as the target of a persuasive message.

audience effect the influence on a person's behavior of the presence of other people or of the belief that other people may subsequently learn of the behavior. Performance is often improved when the action is simple and well learned (see SOCIAL FACILITATION) but may be inhibited when it is complicated, difficult to perform, or when the person believes the behavior might incur the audience's disapproval (see SOCIAL INHIBITION).

audience measurement techniques used to assess the number of individuals who are likely to be exposed to a particular media presentation.

audience task any performance, competition, work assignment, or goal-oriented activity that is executed in the presence of one or more individuals who watch the activity. Compare COACTION TASK.

auding *n.* a level of auditory reception that involves hearing, listening, and comprehension of information.

audio- *combining form* sound or hearing.

audiogenic seizure a seizure induced by loud noises. See REFLEX EPILEPSY.

audiogram *n.* a graph relating an individual's PURE-TONE thresholds at selected frequencies to those of people with normal hearing. The *x*-axis is the frequency of the tone; the *y*-axis is **hearing level** (HL), expressed in decibels (dB). For example, a person whose threshold is 30 dB above normal for a 4-kHz tone would have an audiogram that shows a point at 4 kHz and 30 dB HL. The audiogram is a basic clinical measurement for assessing and diagnosing hearing disorders. See AUDIOMETER; AUDIOMETRIC ZERO. Compare AUDIBILITY CURVE.

audiogravic illusion mislocalization of sounds that occurs when the body is tilted or the apparent direction of gravity is altered.

audiogyral illusion the apparent movement of a stationary source of sound when the listener is rotated.

audiology *n.* the study of hearing, with an emphasis on the evaluation and treatment of hearing disorders and the rehabilitation of individuals with hearing loss or related disorders (e.g., balance disorders). **—audiological** *adj.* **—audiologist** *n.*

audiometer *n.* an electronic device used to measure auditory sensitivity, usually in clinical settings. Its primary use is to produce an AUDIOGRAM. **—audiometric** *adj.*

audiometric zero the level of a PURE TONE of a given frequency that is just detectable by a person with normal hearing. For example, the audiometric zero for a 1-kHz pure tone is 7.5 dB SPL (sound-pressure level) for TDH49 headphones, according to U.S. standards (ANSI S3.6-1996 Specification for Audiometers). Audiometric zero is used to calibrate audiometers and, by definition, is 0 dB HL (hearing level). See AUDIOGRAM.

audiometry *n.* the measurement of an individual's hearing ability with electronic AUDIOMETERS to diagnose hearing loss and determine the nature and extent of such loss. Audiometry provides a guide to the use of hearing aids, aural habilitation (training to help the individual make use of any residual hearing), and possible surgical intervention. Also called **diagnostic audiometry**. See also ELECTROENCEPHALOGRAPHIC AUDIOMETRY; ELECTROPHYSIOLOGIC AUDIOMETRY; SCREENING AUDIOMETRY; SPEECH AUDIOMETRY. **—audiometrician** *n.*

audiotactile device an ASSISTIVE TECHNOLOGY device consisting of a touch-sensitive pad and a SPEECH SYNTHESIZER, which generates a voice output in response to input from the pad.

audioverbal amnesia a type of AUDITORY APHASIA in which the individual may be able to retain and repeat certain single words presented acoustically but is unable to retain and repeat series of words. The condition is often associated with a lesion in the middle temporal GYRUS of the brain.

audiovisual training instruction using audio aids, visual aids, or both, such as films, slides, filmstrips, videotapes, audiotapes, television, and computers, in academic education, technical training, and personnel training. Also called **audiovisual method**.

audit *n.* in health administration, an evaluation or review of the health care services proposed or rendered by a provider. See MEDICAL AUDIT; TREATMENT AUDIT.

audition *n.* see HEARING.

auditory abilities abilities to encode and discriminate different sounds or tones, which, according to some theories of intelligence (such as the THREE-STRATUM MODEL OF INTELLIGENCE and the CATTELL–HORN THEORY OF INTELLIGENCE), are distinguished from visual abilities of the kind used in discriminating visual stimuli.

auditory acuity the ability to detect and discriminate between sounds. For example, **auditory frequency acuity** is the ability to distinguish between sounds that differ in their frequency composition: A 1-kHz tone can be distinguished from a 1005-Hz tone (a 0.5% change), indicating a high degree of auditory frequency acuity.

auditory agnosia see AUDITORY APHASIA.

auditory amnesia loss of the ability to comprehend sounds or speech. See WERNICKE'S APHASIA.

auditory aphasia an impairment in or loss of the ability to comprehend spoken language due to disease, injury, or maldevelopment in the left hemisphere of the brain. It is a form of RECEPTIVE APHASIA. Also called **auditory agnosia**; **word deafness**.

auditory attributes perceptual qualities of sound, including LOUDNESS, PITCH, and TIMBRE.

auditory blending the ability to synthesize the individual sounds (PHONEMES) of a word so that the whole word can be recognized.

auditory brainstem response (**ABR**) see ELECTROPHYSIOLOGIC AUDIOMETRY.

auditory canal see EXTERNAL AUDITORY MEATUS.

auditory closure the ability to fill in parts of words that were omitted in auditory presentation. It is typically an automatic process. See CLOSURE; PHONEMIC RESTORATION EFFECT; RESTORATION EFFECT.

Auditory Consonant Trigram (**ACT**) a memory test in which a three-letter NONSENSE SYLLABLE consisting only of consonants, such as *DCJ*, is presented verbally and the participant is asked to recall the sequence following delays of varying lengths (e.g., 9, 18, and 36 s). During the delay intervals, the participant performs a distractor task (e.g., counting backwards from a specified number by threes). See BROWN–PETERSON DISTRACTOR TECHNIQUE.

Auditory Continuous Performance Test (**ACPT**) a test that measures a child's ability to attend to auditory stimuli for an extended period. The test comprises six trial lists of one-syllable words. The words are presented at a rapid rate, and the child is instructed to indicate each time a target word occurs. The number of incorrect responses for the entire test provides a measure of overall attention ability; the number of incorrect responses for each of the six trial lists provides an indication of changes in attention during the task. [developed in 1994 by audiologist Robert W. Keith]

auditory cortex the sensory area for hearing, located in the TEMPORAL LOBE of the cerebral cortex. Also called **auditory projection area**.

auditory discrimination the ability to distinguish between sounds. Intensity discrimination, for example, is the ability to detect differences between sounds that differ only in their intensity.

auditory display 1. acoustic information presented via headphones, which often includes simulations of realistic listening situations. See VIRTUAL REALITY. **2.** any presentation of acoustic information.

auditory distance cue see DISTANCE CUE.

auditory distance perception the ability to assess the distance of a sound source based only on acoustic information. Humans are relatively poor at auditory distance perception. The primary cue in realistic listening environments appears to be the ratio of direct to reverberant sound energy.

auditory evoked potential a biologically produced electrical response to sound. There are many types of auditory evoked potentials, which differ in their methods of recording and processing sounds.

auditory fatigue a transient form of hearing loss marked by reduced AUDITORY-THRESHOLD sensitivity due to exposure to loud noises. See also EXPOSURE DEAFNESS.

auditory feedback the sound of one's own voice heard while one is speaking, which enables adjustments in intensity, pacing, or clarity of speech to be made. In addition to naturally occurring feedback, there are several types of speaking control systems that provide auditory feedback in voice, speech, and language therapy, including REAL-TIME AMPLIFICATION, DELAYED AUDITORY FEEDBACK, and METRONOMIC PACING.

auditory filter the process responsible for the FREQUENCY SELECTIVITY of the auditory system. The initial stages of auditory processing are often described as consisting of a bank of auditory filters with different center frequencies. The term is closely related to the concept of a CRITICAL BAND but with more emphasis on the "shape" or characteristics of the filter rather than simply its critical bandwidth. See TONOTOPIC ORGANIZATION; TUNING CURVE.

auditory flicker sound presented as discrete units (with gaps) rather than as continuous. **Auditory fusion** occurs when, despite the gaps, the listener hears the sound as continuous. Also called **auditory flutter**. See also CRITICAL FLICKER FREQUENCY.

auditory fusion see AUDITORY FLICKER; FISSION.

auditory hallucination the perception of sound in the absence of an auditory stimulus. Hallucinations may, for example, be of accusatory or laudatory voices, strange noises, or muffled or disconnected words or commands. Auditory hallucinations occur frequently in schizophrenia and other psychotic disorders but may be associated with other conditions as well (e.g., DELIRIUM, DEMENTIA, or ALCOHOL-INDUCED PSYCHOTIC DISORDER).

auditory labyrinth the series of canals, ducts, and cavities within the temporal bone of the skull that contains the sensory receptors for hearing. The COCHLEA forms part of the bony LABYRINTH. The HAIR CELLS—the auditory receptors—are located within the SCALA MEDIA (cochlear duct), one of the membrane-lined ducts that form part of the membranous labyrinth. Also called **acoustic labyrinth**.

auditory localization the ability to identify the position and changes in position of sound sources based on acoustic information. When sounds are presented through headphones, the acoustic image usually appears to originate within the head and lacks the three-dimensional quality of real sound sources. The image can be lateralized on a left–right dimension (**auditory lateralization**)—that is, toward the left or right ear—but not localized in external space. Also called **sound localization**.

auditory masking a reduction in the ability to detect, discriminate, or recognize one sound (the signal or target) due to the presence of another sound (the masker), measured as an increase in the detection threshold caused by the masker. The **amount of masking** is the increase in threshold measured in decibels (dB). For example, if the detection threshold with no masker is 10 dB SPL (sound-pressure level) and the masker raises the threshold to 60 dB SPL, the amount of masking is 50 dB or, equivalently, the masker produces 50 dB of masking. The ability of one sound to mask another has been used extensively to assess the FREQUENCY SELECTIVITY of the auditory system. See also CRITICAL BAND; MASKING.

auditory memory the type of memory that retains information obtained by hearing. Auditory memory may be either SHORT-TERM MEMORY or LONG-TERM MEMORY, and the material retained may be linguistic (e.g., words) or nonlinguistic (e.g., music).

auditory memory span the number of simple items, such as words or numbers, that can be repeated in the same order by a person after hearing the series once. The auditory memory span indicates the capacity of a person's WORKING MEMORY. Also called **auditory span**. See also MEMORY SPAN.

auditory nerve the portion of the eighth cranial nerve (see VESTIBULOCOCHLEAR NERVE) concerned with the sense of hearing. It originates in the cochlea, from which nerve fibers pass through several layers of nuclei in the brainstem to terminate predominantly in the AUDITORY CORTEX. Also called **acoustic nerve**; **cochlear nerve**.

auditory object see FISSION.

auditory ossicles see OSSICLES.

auditory pathways the neural structures that convey auditory information from the cochlear HAIR CELLS to the AUDITORY CORTEX (the ascending pathway) and from the cortex to the cochlea (the descending, or centrifugal, pathway). The major structures in the auditory pathways are the AUDITORY NERVE, COCHLEAR NUCLEUS, SUPERIOR OLIVARY COMPLEX, LATERAL LEMNISCUS, INFE-

RIOR COLLICULUS, MEDIAL GENICULATE NUCLEUS, and the auditory cortex.

auditory perception the ability to interpret and organize sensory information received through the ear.

auditory perceptual disorders a series of language-cognition disorders associated with lesions in various areas of the brain. A lesion in the left hemisphere may result in AUDITORY APHASIA; a lesion in the superior temporal gyrus may cause difficulty in PHONEME discrimination, so that terms like *bitch* and *pitch* sound the same.

auditory processes see AUDITORY SKILLS.

auditory processing the processes or mechanisms that underlie HEARING.

auditory processing disorder see CENTRAL AUDITORY PROCESSING DISORDER.

auditory projection area see AUDITORY CORTEX.

auditory sensation the sensation produced by a sound or other AUDITORY STIMULUS.

auditory sensation level see SENSATION LEVEL.

auditory sensation unit the just noticeable difference in sound intensity. See DIFFERENCE THRESHOLD.

auditory sensory memory see ECHOIC MEMORY.

auditory skills the skills related to hearing, including AUDITORY DISCRIMINATION, auditory ATTENTION, and AUDITORY MEMORY. Also called **auditory processes**; **central auditory abilities**.

auditory space perception perception of the direction and distance of a sound source. See AUDITORY LOCALIZATION.

auditory span see AUDITORY MEMORY SPAN.

auditory spectrum see SOUND SPECTRUM.

auditory stimulus a stimulus capable of eliciting auditory sensation. It usually refers to airborne sound but can include vibration produced by BONE CONDUCTION or by internally generated events.

auditory system the biological structures and processes responsible for hearing. The **peripheral auditory system**, or **auditory periphery**, includes the external, middle, and inner ears and the AUDITORY NERVE. Auditory structures of the brain, including the AUDITORY CORTEX, constitute the **central auditory system**.

auditory threshold 1. the minimum level of sound that can be detected by an organism. See ABSOLUTE THRESHOLD; AUDIBILITY CURVE; AUDIOGRAM. **2.** any threshold pertaining to hearing, including DIFFERENCE THRESHOLDS, pain thresholds, acoustic reflex thresholds, and bone-conduction thresholds.

auditory thrombosis a blood clot in the internal auditory artery, resulting in sudden deafness.

auditory training helping people with hearing loss to better distinguish sounds and understand spoken language by teaching them how to make the most effective use of their residual hearing and to discern contextual clues related to situations and environments.

auditory verbal learning test a memory test that generally involves learning verbal material, usually single words, that is auditorily presented over repeated trials. Recall or recognition may be employed as a measure of learning over various delay periods.

Aufgabe *n.* assignment, task (German): a mental preparation or predisposition that unconsciously determines the way a person handles a situation or task. For example, if the problem involves the numbers 6 and 4 and the *Aufgabe* is "adding," the answer is 10, but if the *Aufgabe* is "subtracting," the answer is 2. The term was introduced by the WÜRZBURG SCHOOL in their introspective experiments on mental processes. See also DETERMINING TENDENCY; EINSTELLUNG; MENTAL SET; SET.

augmentation *n.* **1.** an increase in the amplitude of average evoked responses, either above background noise in the AVERAGE-EVOKED-RESPONSE TECHNIQUE or by more than would be expected from the increase in the stimulus. **2.** more generally, any increase, enlargement, growth, or intensification.

augmentation principle in ATTRIBUTION THEORY, the principle that if someone performs an action when there are known constraints, costs, or risks involved in doing so, then his or her motive for acting must be stronger than any of the inhibitory motives. Compare DISCOUNTING PRINCIPLE. [introduced by U.S. social psychologist Harold H. Kelley (1921–2003)]

augmentation strategies mechanisms to increase the effectiveness of psychotropic drugs by the addition of other agents. Augmentation strategies are most commonly used in the treatment of depression; they include addition of other antidepressants, lithium, thyroid hormones, or stimulants.

augmentative communication communication aided, facilitated, or expanded by a resource other than the communicator. An example is provision of an easy-to-access online dictionary or thesaurus to E-MAIL recipients, or of pointers to WEBSITES for additional information regarding news items. See also FACILITATED COMMUNICATION.

augury *n.* the DIVINATION of future events on the basis of OMENS, portents, or other signs. In ancient Rome, an **augur** was a priest whose interpretations of natural phenomena (e.g., meteorological events, the flights of birds) were used to guide public decisions.

aura *n.* **1.** a subjective sensation that precedes or warns the individual of an impending epileptic seizure or migraine headache. It may include such phenomena as strange tastes or odors, flashes of light (a **visual aura**), numbness, feelings of unreality, anxiety, stomach distress, or DÉJÀ VU. **2.** in PARAPSYCHOLOGY, a subtle halo or emanation that purportedly surrounds every person, animal, plant, or object. Some SENSITIVES claim to be able to discern such auras, which can allegedly reveal an individual's personal qualities as well as his or her state of physical health. It is also claimed that auras may be rendered visible by such means as KIRLIAN PHOTOGRAPHY and the use of KILNER SCREENS. In SPIRITUALISM and theosophy, a person's aura is sometimes identified with his or her astral body (see ASTRAL PROJECTION); in other traditions it may be seen as the manifestation of a life force or energy field. See also EFFLUVIUM; REICHENBACH PHENOMENON.

aural *adj.* pertaining to hearing or to the auditory system.

aural harmonic a distortion product generated within the ear. See HARMONIC.

auricle *n.* **1.** see PINNA. **2.** a small ear-shaped pouch that extends from the upper anterior portion of each ATRIUM of the heart.

auscultation *n.* a diagnostic method in which the examiner listens for sounds within the body either with the aid of a stethoscope (**mediate auscultation**) or directly by laying the ear on the surface of the body (**immediate auscultation**).

Austrian school the theoretical developments in psychology associated principally with the universities of Vienna and Graz in Austria at the end of the 19th century. Influenced by German psychologist and philosopher Franz Brentano (1838–1917) and Austrian philosopher Ernst Mach (1838–1916), the emphasis was on the mental processes that produced whole, organized perceptions, a focus that was a precursor to GESTALT PSYCHOLOGY. See ACT PSYCHOLOGY.

aut- *combining form* see AUTO-.

autarchy *n.* **1.** in psychiatry, the period of infancy in which the child exerts autocratic power over others, including the parents who satisfy all his or her instinctual demands. **2.** more generally, supreme and absolute power. See also OMNIPOTENCE. **—autarchic** *adj.*

autassassinophilia *n.* a PARAPHILIA in which sexual arousal and the achievement of orgasm are facilitated by the belief that one is in danger of being killed. This often includes the individual staging a sexual encounter characterized by extreme MASOCHISM with the real potential for his or her own murder. Also called **autassassinatophilia**. Compare HOMICIDOPHILIA.

autemesia *n.* vomiting for which no organic cause can be identified.

authenticity *n.* **1.** the quality of being genuine or of undisputed origin. **2.** in psychotherapy and counseling, a characteristic of the therapist or counselor who is considered to be genuine and caring. Authenticity is often demonstrated by a professional but down-to-earth attitude that the client senses to be a reflection of the true person and not simply of the therapist acting in his or her professional role. **3.** in EXISTENTIALISM, a mode of being that humans can achieve by accepting the burden of freedom, choice, and responsibility and the need to construct their own values and meanings in a meaningless universe. **—authentic** *adj.*

authentic schizophrenia see NUCLEAR SCHIZOPHRENIA.

authoritarian *adj.* **1.** describing or relating to a political system or social climate that involves the restriction of individual freedoms and the subjugation of individuals to a centralized, hierarchical authority. For example, an authoritarian group is one in which decisions rest solely with the leader. **2.** describing an individual, especially but not limited to one in a position of authority, who uses or favors restrictive, autocratic methods when interacting with others. See AUTHORITARIAN PERSONALITY. **—authoritarianism** *n.*

authoritarian conscience the type of conscience that is guided by (a) fear of an external authority or (b) the voice of an internalized external authority, such as the SUPEREGO. Compare HUMANISTIC CONSCIENCE. [defined by Erich FROMM]

authoritarian leader the type of LEADER who determines policy and makes decisions without seeking input from followers, rejects any suggestions from others, assigns tasks to group members without considering their preferences, and dominates interactions through frequent criticism. Studies have found that groups with authoritarian leaders work less when the leader is absent, display greater reliance on the leader, express more critical discontent, and make more aggressive demands for attention than do groups with DEMOCRATIC LEADERS or with LAISSEZ-FAIRE LEADERS. [defined by Kurt LEWIN and his colleagues in experimental studies of leadership styles]

authoritarian parenting a restrictive PARENTING style in which the parent or caregiver stresses obedience, deemphasizes collaboration and dialogue, and employs strong forms of punishment to deter unwanted behavior. Compare AUTHORITATIVE PARENTING; PERMISSIVE PARENTING; REJECTING–NEGLECTING PARENTING. [first described by U.S. developmental psychologist Diana Baumrind (1927–)]

authoritarian personality a personality pattern characterized by (a) preoccupation with power and status, (b) strict adherence to highly simplified conventional values, (c) an attitude of great deference to authority figures while demanding subservience from those regarded as lower in status, and (d) hostility toward minorities or other OUTGROUPS and to people who deviate from conventional moral prescriptions.

authoritative parenting a collaborative PARENTING style in which the parent or caregiver encourages a child's AUTONOMY and independence yet still places certain limitations or restrictions on the child's behavior. The parent typically explains and promotes discussion of the reasons for such limitations or restrictions. Compare AUTHORITARIAN PARENTING; PERMISSIVE PARENTING; REJECTING–NEGLECTING PARENTING. [first described by U.S. developmental psychologist Diana Baumrind (1927–)]

authority *n.* the capacity to influence others. Formal authority enables an individual to exert influence as a result of either high, legally recognized office (**legitimate authority**) or high rank in a long-established but not legally codified hierarchy (**traditional authority**). Informal authority is based on the individual having either attributes that facilitate the achievement of a group's goals (**rational** or **expert authority**) or an attractive and authoritative personality serving to enhance his or her credibility (**charismatic authority**). Whatever the specific basis of the authority, the individual exercising it is given, either explicitly or implicitly, the right to influence the others.

authority complex a pattern of emotionally charged concepts of authority that are partially or completely repressed. To satisfy an unconscious need for authority, a person projects power onto certain other people (see PROJECTION) and experiences inferiority in the presence of these others. Therefore, reactions to authority often take the form of oversubmission.

authority principle the concept that each member of a social hierarchy is expected to comply with the wishes of those above him or her.

authority relations see STATUS RELATIONS.

autism *n.* **1.** a behavioral syndrome of neurological dysfunction characterized by impaired reciprocal social interactions, impaired verbal and nonverbal communication, impoverished or diminished imaginative activity, and a markedly restricted repertoire of activities and interests relative to age. In *DSM–IV–TR*, autism that becomes evident by the age of 3 is designated AUTISTIC DISORDER and categorized as a PERVASIVE DEVELOPMENTAL DISORDER. **2.** abnormal introversion and egocentricity. It is one of the primary signs of schizophrenia described by Swiss psychiatrist Eugen Bleuler (1857–1939). See also FUNDAMENTAL SYMPTOMS. **—autistic** *adj.*

autistic disorder in *DSM–IV–TR*, a PERVASIVE DEVELOPMENTAL DISORDER characterized by an onset before the age of 3 and markedly abnormal or impaired development in social interactions and communication and markedly restricted behavior, activities, and interests, often with repetitive, stereotyped, inflexible adherence to routines and rituals. Manifestations and features of the disorder vary greatly across children according to developmental level, language skills, and chronological age. Autistic disorder is commonly associated with a degree of mental retardation. Its prevalence varies from 2 to 20 cases per 10,000 individuals. Also called **childhood autism**; **early infantile autism**; **infantile autism**; **Kanner's syndrome** (or **autism**). See also AUTISM.

autistic fantasy a DEFENSE MECHANISM in which a person deals with emotional conflict and stressors by indulging in excessive daydreaming as a substitute for human relationships or more active and direct problem solving.

autistic spectrum disorder any one of a group of pervasive developmental disorders with an onset typically occurring during the preschool years and characterized by varying but often marked difficulties in communication and social interaction. The group includes AUTISM, PERVASIVE DEVELOPMENTAL DISORDER NOT OTHERWISE SPECIFIED, RETT SYNDROME, ASPERGER'S DISORDER, and CHILDHOOD DISINTEGRATIVE DISORDER. Substantial proportions of children with autistic spectrum disorders, excluding Asperger's syndrome, are reported to also have varying degrees of mental retardation. Also called **autism spectrum disorder**.

autistic thinking narcissistic, egocentric thought processes, such as fantasizing and daydreaming, that have little or no relation to reality. It is similar to dereistic thinking (see DEREISM), but the emphasis is on self-absorption rather than disconnection from reality. See AUTISM.

auto- (**aut-**) *combining form* **1.** self (e.g., AUTOBIOGRAPHY). **2.** self-caused (e.g., AUTOHYPNOSIS).

autoagonistophilia *n.* sexual arousal from being observed or filmed while engaging in sexual activity.

autoallergy *n.* see AUTOIMMUNITY.

autoassassinatophilia *n.* see AUTASSASSINOPHILIA.

autobiographical memory **1.** a type of EPISODIC MEMORY comprising vivid personal memories recalling the time and place of events. **2.** narrative, factual knowledge about oneself.

Autobiographical Memory Interview (**AMI**) a semistructured interview designed to assess memory for autobiographical information, impairment of which is often indicative of retrograde amnesia and potentially associated with a variety of neurological and psychiatric disorders. The AMI contains an Autobiographical Incidents Schedule, which queries specific, personally experienced events from childhood, early adult life, and the recent past; and a Personal Semantic Memory Schedule, which queries generic or semantic facts about the self, divided into childhood, early adult life, and recent information. [developed in 1989 by British neuropsychiatrist Michael D. Kopelman, British clinical psychologist Barbara A. Wilson, and British cognitive psychologist Alan D. Baddeley (1934–)]

autobiography *n.* in therapy or counseling, a technique in which a LIFE HISTORY, written by the client from his or her own point of view, is used to obtain information regarding the client's behavioral patterns and feelings. A **structured autobiography** is based on explicit questions or topic guidelines supplied by the therapist or counselor. An **unstructured autobiography** contains no guidelines. See also LIFE REVIEW.

autocentric *adj.* centered on or within the self. Compare ALLOCENTRIC.

autochthonous *adj.* **1.** native, indigenous, or original. **2.** denoting ENDOGENOUS processes and events that originate within the individual, independently of external influences. Compare ALLOCHTHONOUS.

autochthonous gestalt a perceptual pattern induced by internal factors (autochthonous forces) rather than factors of the external stimulus.

autoclitic *n.* a unit of VERBAL BEHAVIOR (a verbal OPERANT) that depends on other verbal behavior and that alters the effect of that other verbal behavior on a listener. For example, in saying "I think that is a cat" the words *I think* serve as an autoclitic to indicate to the listener that the speaker is less than certain about the remaining verbal operants in the sentence. The *is* is also an autoclitic, indicating that the same stimulus is occasioning the words *that* and *cat*.

autocorrelation *n.* in statistics and experimental design, the correlation of observations with themselves over time, usually experienced in TIME SERIES or REPEATED MEASURES DESIGNS.

autocratic *adj.* **1.** dictatorial, high-handed, and undemocratic. **2.** wielding unlimited power and not permitting opposition. **—autocrat** *n.*

autocratic leader a LEADER who exercises unrestricted authority, reserving all decision making, problem solving, and goal setting for himself or herself rather than consulting with other group members. Autocratic leaders may, in some cases, seek information from members, but they do not seek their opinions on options or possible solutions. [defined by U.S. psychologist Victor Vroom (1932–) in his psychological analysis of leadership and decision making in organizations]

autocrine *adj.* describing or relating to a type of cellular signaling in which a chemical messenger is secreted by a cell into its environment and feeds back to elicit a response in the same cell. For example, some nerve cells have AUTORECEPTORS that are affected by neurotransmitter molecules released by the same cell. Compare ENDOCRINE; PARACRINE.

autoenucleation *n.* an act of self-mutilation in which an individual excises an organ or tumor from his or her own body, as, for example, when a person with a psychotic disorder removes an eyeball (see ENUCLEATION). Also called **self-enucleation**.

autoerotic asphyxiation sexual pleasure obtained from being unable to breathe during masturbation. It may involve the person hanging him- or herself, a practice that has been found to result in a number of accidental deaths each year when the person is unable to get free of the rope.

autoeroticism *n.* **1.** the creation of sexual excitement and gratification by the self, whether it be through masturbation, other sexual behaviors (e.g., stimulating nongenital portions of the body), or thoughts (e.g., daydreams, fantasies). See also SECONDARY AUTOEROTICISM. [defined by British sexologist Havelock Ellis (1859–1939)] **2.** formerly, GENITAL AROUSAL IN SLEEP, which is now understood to be a normal component of one stage of sleep and is not associated with erotic dreams. Also called **autoerotism**. Compare ALLOEROTICISM. **—autoerotic** *adj.*

autoerythrocyte sensitization syndrome see GARDNER–DIAMOND SYNDROME.

autoflagellation *n.* sexual pleasure derived from striking, whipping, or beating oneself.

autogenic training a relaxation technique in which a quasi-hypnotic state is self-induced and deep relaxation is achieved through mental imagery, breath control, and exercises that focus attention on physical sensations, including warmth and heaviness of the limbs, a regular heartbeat, abdominal warmth, and cooling of the forehead. The aim is to reduce stress by gaining control of autonomic arousal associated with anxiety and to obtain an IDEAL PERFORMANCE STATE. [developed in the early 20th century by German neurologist Johannes Heinrich Schultz (1884–1970)]

autogenital stimulation any form of stimulation by a human or an animal of its own genitalia. It may take the form of pelvic thrusts, MASTURBATION, or self-stimulation preceding sexual intercourse. Autogenital stimulation may occur in the presence of members of the same or opposite sex or in the absence of other individuals.

autognosis *n.* knowledge of self.

autographism *n.* see DERMATOGRAPHISM.

autohypnosis *n.* self-induced hypnosis. It may occur spontaneously or be achieved through training in AUTOSUGGESTION. See also SELF-HYPNOSIS. **—autohypnotic** *adj.*

autohypnotic amnesia a Jungian term for repression, based on the observation that HYPNOTIC AMNESIA may be induced by a person under hypnosis.

autoimmunity *n.* a condition in which the body's immune system fails to recognize its own tissues as "self" and attempts to reject its own cells. Autoimmunity increases with age, when the immune system deteriorates, and is a primary factor in the development of such diseases as rheumatoid arthritis and systemic lupus erythematosus (called **autoimmune disorders**). Also called **autoallergy**. **—autoimmune** *adj.*

autoinstructional device any equipment enabling self-teaching, as in programmed learning, including workbooks, CD-ROMs, cassettes, and so forth. It is used to further one's education without the direct, immediate aid of a teacher either physically present or at a remote site.

autokinesis *n.* **1.** any movement that is voluntary. **2.** an illusory perception of movement—often experienced by pilots flying at night—that occurs when fixating on a dim, stationary light source in the dark.

autokinetic effect the illusion of seeing a static spot of light moving in a dark room. The autokinetic effect has been utilized in certain psychological experiments, for example, investigating suggestibility or the establishment of group norms. Also called **autokinetic illusion**; **Charpentier's illusion**.

automaintenance *n.* maintenance of behavior established by behavior-independent stimulus–reinforcer pairings. It commonly refers to the maintenance of keypecking behavior in pigeons that is established through AUTOSHAPING.

automasochism *n.* sexual pleasure derived from inflicting pain on oneself during masturbation or during sexual activity with a partner.

automated assessment see COMPUTERIZED ASSESSMENT.

automated clinical records a computerized database used for such purposes as monitoring patient care, providing data for administrative decisions, and assisting the clinician in understanding and treating patients.

automated desensitization the use of such devices as audiotapes, video tapes, and digitized media to facilitate the presentation of anxiety-provoking and relaxing stimuli during SYSTEMATIC DESENSITIZATION. It is especially helpful in situations where a client is reluctant to undergo desensitization in the presence of the therapist. See DEVICE FOR AUTOMATED DESENSITIZATION.

automated learning a method of acquiring knowledge using electronic or mechanical devices. This is sometimes outside the scope of traditional institutions and includes individualized instructional modules, exercises, reading materials, interactive computers, online programs, and CD-ROMs.

automated natural language understanding understanding speech or writing through computer-based processes. Understanding, in this context, means determining the meaning of what is spoken or written, enabling an appropriate response to questions or commands. Compare AUTOMATED SPEECH RECOGNITION.

automated reasoning computer-based mathematical reasoning covering areas including geometric theorem proving, algebraic equation solving, and mathematical theorem proving. It is a subdiscipline of ARTIFICIAL INTELLIGENCE.

automated speech recognition (**ASR**) recognition of speech by means of a computer-based process. Recognition in this context usually means the production of a written representation of the words spoken. Unlike AUTOMATED NATURAL LANGUAGE UNDERSTANDING, ASR does not require an understanding of the meanings of the words recognized.

automatic action an act that is performed without requiring attention or conscious awareness.

automatic activation involuntary processing of stimuli and preparation for associated responses. This activation tends to occur more rapidly than that resulting from ATTENTION or INTENTION.

automatic activation of attitudes the spontaneous activation of an attitude from memory on encountering the ATTITUDE OBJECT. The likelihood of automatic activation depends on the ACCESSIBILITY OF AN ATTITUDE.

automatic anxiety see PRIMARY ANXIETY.

automatic decisions decisions made quickly or with little thought, based on habit or the use of mental shortcuts. For example, consumers may make automatic decisions when selecting one of a number of product brands.

automatic drawing the act of drawing images or objects while in a hypnotic trance or in a situation in which attention is distracted. It may be used in HYPNOTHERAPY to provide a therapist with access to unconscious material from the client. See also AUTOMATIC WRITING.

automaticity *n.* the quality of a mental process that can be carried out rapidly and without effort or intention (an **automatic process**). See also CONSCIOUS PROCESS; DEAUTOMATIZATION HYPOTHESIS; UNCONSCIOUS PROCESS.

automatic obedience excessive, uncritical, or mechanical compliance with the requests, suggestions, or commands of others. See also COMMAND AUTOMATISM.

automatic performance see ROUTINIZED BEHAVIOR.

automatic process see AUTOMATICITY.

automatic promotion **1.** advancing a student who has not sufficiently mastered the academic skills and knowledge of one grade level to a higher instruction or grade level. **2.** active support or encouragement given to a student whether or not that student has met the course requirements.

automatic reinforcer a physical or sensory consequence of a response that serves to reinforce the response.

automatic speaker recognition identification of a speaker by means of an analysis, usually computer-based, of the characteristics of his or her speech. Also called **automatic speaker identification**.

automatic speech **1.** speech that erupts involuntarily, or without conscious control. It sometimes occurs as a consequence of senility, Tourette's syndrome, or highly emotional states. Automatic speech is not to be confused with synthesized or SYNTHETIC SPEECH. **2.** speech that is uttered with little or no conscious consideration of the spoken material, such as the days of the week, numbers, the alphabet, and other well-learned material.

automatic thoughts 1. instantaneous, habitual, but unconscious thoughts that affect a person's mood and actions. Helping clients become aware of the presence and impact of automatic thoughts is a central task of cognitive therapy. Once clients become aware of these thoughts, they are encouraged to test their validity and, if indicated, generate other thoughts that are more reasonable and less incapacitating. **2.** thoughts that have been so well learned and habitually repeated that they occur without cognitive effort. For example, a seasoned athlete observing a particular alignment of the opposing team will consciously choose the correct personal behavior pattern without analysis. Also called **routinized thoughts**.

automatic writing the act of writing while one's attention is not focused on the task or of writing without conscious awareness, as during a hypnotic trance. It may be used in HYPNOTHERAPY to provide a therapist with access to unconscious material from the client. See also AUTOMATIC DRAWING.

automation *n.* the state or condition in which activities are carried out automatically, without ongoing outside direction, especially by electronically controlled systems.

automatism *n.* behavior performed mechanically, without intention, and without conscious awareness. It may be motor or verbal and ranges from simple repetitive acts, such as lipsmacking or repeatedly using the same phrase (e.g., *as it were*), to complex activities, such as sleepwalking and automatic writing. Automatism is seen in several disorders, including CATATONIC SCHIZOPHRENIA and COMPLEX PARTIAL SEIZURES.

automatism defense a legal defense consisting of the claim that criminal intent (see MENS REA) is lacking as a result of the defendant's dissociated or unconscious state at the time the criminal act was committed. The defense is more common in the United Kingdom and Canada than in the United States.

automatization *n.* **1.** the development of a skill or habit to a point at which it becomes routine and requires little if any conscious effort or direction. **2.** the state of individuals who obey compulsive impulses so automatically that they may be described as automata (see AUTOMATON).

automatograph *n.* a classic device used to measure movement. It consists of a plate that lies on metal balls and thus follows every impulse of the hand that lies flat on it: The plate has an attachment by which the slightest involuntary movements are registered.

automaton *n.* **1.** a machine that simulates human functions, such as a robot spot welder, or the "machina docilis," which was capable of conditioning, motility, problem solving, avoiding obstacles, and obeying a whistle. Some automatic machines are able to run mazes, take shortcuts, and even "choose" between goals. See also CYBERNETICS; FEEDBACK. **2.** a human acting in an autonomous and routine manner without an external driving force. See also AUTOMATIZATION.

automaton conformity beliefs or behaviors displayed by individuals who unthinkingly conform to the demands of the roles they occupy or imitate the actions and opinions displayed by others. See CONFORMITY.

automotive telematics technology for delivering information to moving automobiles and other road vehicles. The information can include traffic conditions on routes of interest, alternative routing, hotel accommodation, safety news, and entertainment for passengers.

automutilation *n.* sexual pleasure derived from mutilating parts of one's body or from fantasy about mutilated parts of one's body. It usually involves cutting some part of the body during masturbation.

autonecrophilia *n.* sexual pleasure derived from the fantasy that one is dead and that another person is having sexual relations with one's dead body.

autoneprophilia *n.* sexual pleasure derived from dressing as a baby, pretending to be a baby, or having a fantasy about being a baby.

autonoetic *adj.* describing a level of knowledge or memory in which one is aware not only of the known or remembered thing but also of one's personal experience in relation to that thing (see AUTONOETIC MEMORY). **Autonoetic consciousness** is a corresponding level of consciousness in which one's knowledge of facts, concepts, and meanings is mediated through an awareness of one's own existence in time. Compare ANOETIC; NOETIC. [defined by Estonian-born Canadian psychologist Endel Tulving (1927–)]

autonoetic memory the recall of a personal memory and the conscious awareness that one is reliving a moment from the past. Synonymous with EPISODIC MEMORY, it is the final level in the monohierarchic theory of memory proposed by Estonian-born Canadian psychologist Endel Tulving (1927–). Compare ANOETIC MEMORY; NOETIC MEMORY.

autonomasia *n.* a type of AMNESTIC APHASIA in which the person is unable to recall nouns or names.

autonomic *adj.* pertaining to the AUTONOMIC NERVOUS SYSTEM or the processes controlled by it. **—autonomically** *adv.*

autonomic apparatus all the body organs, including the endocrine glands and viscera, that are controlled by the AUTONOMIC NERVOUS SYSTEM.

autonomic balance the complementary and reciprocal interactions of the sympathetic and parasympathetic branches of the AUTONOMIC NERVOUS SYSTEM.

autonomic conditioning the process of achieving conscious or voluntary control over autonomic processes (e.g., heart rate) through such means as BIOFEEDBACK TRAINING, meditation, yoga, or CONDITIONING.

autonomic dysfunction see DYSAUTONOMIA.

autonomic dysreflexia exaggerated activity of the autonomic nervous system in an individual with a spinal-cord injury at or above the level of the sixth thoracic vertebra. It is caused by irritation, pain, or similar stimulation of the nervous system below the area of the injury and may be fatal. Symptoms include the sudden onset of headache and hypertension; there may also be BRADYCARDIA, sweating, dilated pupils, blurred vision, nasal stuffiness, flushing, and gooseflesh. Also called **autonomic hyperreflexia**.

autonomic ganglia the ganglia of the AUTONOMIC NERVOUS SYSTEM. They include the two chains of sympathetic ganglia (see SYMPATHETIC CHAIN) and the more peripheral parasympathetic ganglia (see PARASYMPATHETIC NERVOUS SYSTEM).

autonomic hyperactivity arousal of the AUTONOMIC NERVOUS SYSTEM (ANS) resulting in the physiological symptoms associated with anxiety and fear (e.g., sweating, palpitations, dry mouth, lightheadedness, upset stomach). The ANS consists of the SYMPATHETIC NERVOUS SYSTEM and PARASYMPATHETIC NERVOUS SYSTEM. The sympathetic system is involved in the preparation of the body for an emergency and acts to cause widespread changes in the body (e.g., accelerated heart rate, release of adrenaline into the blood, inhibition of digestion, elevated blood pressure).

autonomic hyperreflexia see AUTONOMIC DYSREFLEXIA.

autonomic learning a type of learning in which the responses learned consist of changes in functions involving the AUTONOMIC NERVOUS SYSTEM, such as heart rate or blood pressure. See also CONDITIONED RESPONSE.

autonomic motor pool MOTOR NEURONS in the brainstem and spinal cord that give rise to nerves that supply AUTONOMIC GANGLIA.

autonomic nervous system (**ANS**) the portion of the CENTRAL NERVOUS SYSTEM and PERIPHERAL NERVOUS SYSTEM involved primarily in involuntary bodily functions, such as those of the circulatory, digestive, and respiratory organs. It is divided into the SYMPATHETIC NERVOUS SYSTEM and PARASYMPATHETIC NERVOUS SYSTEM and includes both autonomic nerves and AUTONOMIC GANGLIA. **Autonomic responses** typically involve changes in smooth-muscle or glandular activity. They include changes in heart rate, salivation, digestion, perspiration, secretion of hormones from the ADRENAL MEDULLA, bladder contraction, and engorgement of the penis and clitoris. The system is called autonomic because it was once thought to function independently of the central nervous system.

autonomic neuropathy see DYSAUTONOMIA.

autonomic reactivity 1. the extent to which an organism responds physiologically to a stimulus, such as a stressor. **2.** a pattern of responses of the AUTONOMIC NERVOUS SYSTEM that is characteristic of an individual throughout life. Also called **autonomic response specificity**; **individual response stereotypy**.

autonomic response see AUTONOMIC NERVOUS SYSTEM.

autonomic restrictors people with GENERALIZED ANXIETY DISORDER (GAD), who have lower heart rate, blood pressure, skin conductance, and respiration rate than do people with other anxiety disorders.

autonomous *adj.* **1.** having an independent existence. **2.** having self-government. **3.** acting or operating under one's own direction. Compare HETERONOMOUS.

autonomous activity in GENERAL SYSTEMS THEORY, processes or behaviors that occur spontaneously, in the absence of external eliciting stimuli.

autonomous depression 1. a MAJOR DEPRESSIVE EPISODE that does not occur in response to any obvious psychosocial stressor. See also ENDOGENOUS DEPRESSION. **2.** an obsolete name for depression characterized by agitation and self-criticism.

autonomous stage in Jean PIAGET's theory of moral development, the stage during which the child, typically 10 years of age or older, eventually understands that rules and laws are not permanent, fixed properties of the world but rather are flexible, modifiable entities created by people. The child gradually relies less on parental authority and more on individual and independent morality and learns that intentions, not consequences or the likelihood of punishment, are important in determining the morality of an act. Also called **autonomous morality**. See MORAL INDEPENDENCE; MORAL RELATIVISM. Compare HETERONOMOUS STAGE; PREMORAL STAGE.

autonomous syntax the theory that SYNTAX is an autonomous component of language that operates independently of meaning (semantics) and function (pragmatics). Such a view explains how a sentence with no meaningful content or communicative function can nevertheless be recognized as grammatical by native speakers (see GRAMMATICALITY). It also explains why syntactic rules, such as number agreement between subject and verb, operate regardless of the semantic relationship between the sentence elements. For example, in the two sentences *The boy is slamming the doors* and *The doors are being slammed by the boy* the verb takes different forms to agree with the grammatical subject in each case (*boy is; doors are*), regardless of the fact that in both cases the boy is the AGENT of the action, and the doors are its PATIENT. See CASE GRAMMAR. [introduced by Noam CHOMSKY]

autonomous word see CONTENT WORD.

autonomous work groups small, self-regulated, worker-centered units within an organization that are given responsibility for developing procedures, organizing the production process, generating the required product, and maintaining quality without guidance by an external authority or manager.

autonomy *n.* a state of independence and self-determination in an individual, a group, or a society. According to some theories, an inordinate focus on self-determination and achievement represents a risk factor for the development of MAJOR DEPRESSIVE DISORDER. See also FUNCTIONAL AUTONOMY. Compare HETERONOMY.

autonomy of motives see FUNCTIONAL AUTONOMY.

autonomy versus shame and doubt the second of ERIKSON'S EIGHT STAGES OF DEVELOPMENT, between the ages of 1½ and 3 years. During this stage, children acquire a degree of self-reliance and self-confidence if allowed to develop at their own pace but may begin to doubt their ability to control themselves and their world if parents are overcritical, overprotective, or inconsistent.

autopagnosia *n.* see AUTOTOPAGNOSIA.

autopedophilia *n.* sexual pleasure derived from dressing as a child, pretending to be a child, or having a fantasy about being a child.

autophagy *n.* **1.** the chewing or eating of one's own flesh. **2.** the body's maintenance of nutrition by consumption of its own tissues, as in times of excessive fasting. Also called **autophagia**.

autophonic response the echolike reproduction and vibration of one's own voice, commonly referred to as "hearing one own voice." An autophonic response is usually due to disease of the middle ear or auditory canal in which the eustachian tube remains open. Also called **autophonia**; **autophony**.

autoplasty *n.* **1.** adaptation to reality by modifying one's own behavioral patterns, rather than by altering one's environment. Autoplastic behavior can be negative and psychologically harmful, as in the development of neurotic behavior, or positive and psychologically healthy, as in the tendency toward more adaptive thinking and action following psychotherapeutic intervention. Also called **autoplastic development**. **2.** surgical repair using tissue from another part of the patient's body. Compare ALLOPLASTY. **—autoplastic** *adj.*

autopoesis *n.* a system, often a COGNITIVE ARCHITECTURE, in which the constituent modular components support, nurture, and maintain each other.

autopsy *n.* a procedure in which the body of a person is examined after death in an effort to determine the exact cause and time of death. For legal, religious, and cultural reasons, an autopsy generally cannot be performed without permission of the next of kin or an order of the public authorities. The procedure usually requires a detailed dissection of body tissues, laboratory tests, and other techniques when the death occurs under suspicious circumstances. Also called **postmortem examination**. See also PSYCHOLOGICAL AUTOPSY.

autopsychic delusion a delusion about one's personality. It is distinguished from **allopsychic delusions**, which refer to the outside world, and SOMATIC DELUSIONS, which refer to one's own body. [defined by German neurologist Carl Wernicke (1848–1905)]

autopsychosis *n.* a delusional condition in which the individual maintains distorted ideas about him- or herself, such as being the world's savior, the devil incarnate, or an unrecognized genius. **—autopsychotic** *adj.*

autoradiography *n.* a histological technique that reveals the distribution of radioactive chemicals in tissues or in analytical media, such as electrophoretic plates. **—autoradiographic** *adj.*

autoreceptor *n.* a RECEPTOR molecule for a neurotransmitter that is located in the presynaptic membrane of a SYNAPSE. Autoreceptors "tell" the AXON TERMINAL how much transmitter has been released.

autoregressive model a model used primarily in the analysis of TIME SERIES, where each successive observation depends, at least in part, on one or more preceding observations. An example is a systematic structure of error in REGRESSION ANALYSIS in which the ERROR TERM at time *t* is a constant fraction of the error at the previous time point plus a new error term.

autoscope *n.* a device or instrument that records or magnifies small muscular movements.

autoscopophilia *n.* sexual pleasure derived from observing oneself disrobing, being nude, or watching oneself during sexual activity. It may involve viewing videos or pictures of these situations.

autoscopy *n.* seeing a double of oneself in external space. The image is generally short-lived and hazy, filmy, and colorless. Also called **autoscopic phenomenon**. See also DOPPELGANGER PHENOMENON; OUT-OF-BODY EXPERIENCE.

autosexuality *n.* any form of sexual arousal or stimulation that occurs without the participation of another person or animal, for example, masturbation, sexual dreams, or sexual fantasies.

autoshaping *n.* a method of establishing OPERANT performance that rewards only elicited responses. It is most commonly used with pigeons. Signals are presented, independently of behavior, on a response device (in the case of pigeons, a pecking disk), which records the response and then immediately presents reinforcement.

autosomal *adj.* denoting a genetic characteristic located on or transmitted by an AUTOSOME.

autosomal aberration any disorder of structure, function, or both that is associated with an alteration in the structure or number of any of the pairs of chromosomes that are not sex chromosomes (see AUTOSOME). An example of such a disorder is DOWN SYNDROME. Also called **autosomal abnormality**; **autosomal anomaly**.

autosomal dominant denoting or relating to a pattern of MENDELIAN INHERITANCE in which a physical or other feature of an offspring requires the presence of only one mutant ALLELE, carried on an AUTOSOME, to produce its effect (see DOMINANT ALLELE). Even when the other allele is normal, the individual has the characteristic or susceptibility that is conveyed by the mutant allele. Individuals with autosomal dominant diseases have a 50:50 chance of passing on the mutant allele (and hence the characteristic, disease, or susceptibility) to their children. An example of an autosomal dominant disorder is HUNTINGTON'S DISEASE.

autosomal recessive denoting or relating to a pattern of MENDELIAN INHERITANCE in which a mutant allele produces its effect in an offspring only if it is present on both members of a pair of HOMOLOGOUS chromosomes (see AUTOSOME; RECESSIVE ALLELE). An example of an autosomal recessive disorder is TAY–SACHS DISEASE.

autosomal trisomy of group G the condition in which either of the chromosome pairs 21 or 22 (known as group G) includes an additional autosome. The most common of these two autosome abnormalities is TRISOMY 21. See also DOWN SYNDROME.

autosome *n.* any chromosome that is not a SEX CHROMOSOME. A human normally has a total of 44 autosomes (arranged in 22 HOMOLOGOUS pairs) in the nucleus of each body cell, although irregular numbers may occur through the loss or addition of one or more autosomes. If a homologous pair of autosomes has an extra chromosome, the condition is called TRISOMY. If one member of a homologous pair is absent, the condition is called MONOSOMY.

autostereogram *n.* a two-dimensional arrangement of repeated elements that produces a perception of three-dimensional depth when viewed correctly. See RANDOM-DOT STEREOGRAM; STEREOGRAM.

autostereotyping *n.* incorporating STEREOTYPES about the groups to which one belongs into one's own SELF-CONCEPT. Also called **self-stereotyping**. See GROUP IDENTIFICATION. **—autostereotype** *vb.*

autosuggestibility *n.* susceptibility to being influenced by one's own suggestions, as in AUTOHYPNOSIS.

autosuggestion *n.* the process of making positive suggestions to oneself for such purposes as improving morale, inducing relaxation, or promoting recovery from illness. Also called **self-suggestion**. See also AFFIRMATION; AUTOGENIC TRAINING; SUGGESTION.

autotomy *n.* **1.** in animal behavior, the casting off of a body part, as, for example, when a lizard sheds its tail to escape from a predator. **2.** SELF-MUTILATION or the cutting off by an individual of his or her body parts.

autotopagnosia *n.* an inability to recognize, name, or point to parts of one's own or another person's body. It is a type of AGNOSIA resulting from lesions in the neural pathway between the PARIETAL LOBE and thalamus of the brain. Also called **autopagnosia**; **somatotopagnosia**.

auxiliary 1. *adj.* subsidiary or supporting. **2.** *n.* a person or thing that provides support, usually in a subsidiary capacity. **3.** *n.* see AUXILIARY VERB.

auxiliary ego in PSYCHODRAMA, a group member, other than the therapist, who assumes the role of a significant figure in the PROTAGONIST's life.

auxiliary inversion in grammar, the reversal of the usual order of SUBJECT and AUXILIARY VERB in a declarative sentence to create a question so that, for example, *The poodle is barking* becomes *Is the poodle barking?* Such constructions are of major interest in GENERATIVE GRAMMAR and PSYCHOLINGUISTICS. See INTERROGATIVE.

auxiliary organ see EXECUTIVE ORGAN.

auxiliary therapist a therapist who takes part in COTHERAPY.

auxiliary verb a verb that is used to indicate the TENSE, MOOD, or VOICE of another verb, such as *have* in *The ship had sunk*, *do* in *Do you pray?*, and *be* in *I was met by a friend*. Other common auxiliary verbs in English are *can*, *could*, *shall*, *should*, *will*, *would*, *may*, *might*, and *must*. Also called **auxiliary**.

ava *n.* see KAVA.

availability *n.* the presence of information in memory storage. Availability should be distinguished from **acces-**

sibility, which refers to the ability of a portion of information to be retrieved.

availability error in problem solving, an error that can arise when possible solutions that most easily come to mind are mistaken for the correct or best answer.

availability heuristic *n.* a common strategy for making judgments about likelihood of occurrence in which the individual bases such judgments on the amount of information held in his or her memory about the particular type of event: The more information there is, the more likely the event is judged to be. Use of this strategy may lead to errors of judgment when information that is highly available in memory (e.g., about well-publicized events, such as plane crashes) leads people to believe that those kinds of events are more probable than they actually are, or when the relative unavailability of information (e.g., about less well-publicized causes of death, as from diabetes) leads people to believe that those kinds of events are less probable than they are. Compare REPRESENTATIVENESS HEURISTIC. See HEURISTIC.

avalanche conduction the spreading of nerve impulses from a receptor to a number of other neurons, resulting in an effect that is disproportionate to the initial stimulus, as in a seizure.

Aventyl *n.* a trade name for NORTRIPTYLINE.

average *n.* see MEAN.

average absolute deviation a measure of the DISPERSION of scores obtained by finding the average absolute difference (see ABSOLUTE VALUE) between each score and the MEAN.

averaged electroencephalic audiometry see ELECTROENCEPHALOGRAPHIC AUDIOMETRY; ELECTROPHYSIOLOGIC AUDIOMETRY.

average error the typical degree to which a series of observations are inaccurate with respect to an absolute criterion (e.g., a standard weight or length) or a relative criterion (e.g., the mean of the observations within a given condition).

average-evoked-response technique (**AER technique**) a method of finding electrical responses of the brain, despite background "noise," by determining the average evoked response (see EVOKED POTENTIAL), usually with the aid of a computer. If the same stimulus is repeated, and the responses are summated, the evoked response will appear above random noise. See also AUGMENTATION; EVENT-RELATED POTENTIAL.

averse conditioning see AVERSIVE CONDITIONING.

aversion *n.* a physiological or emotional response indicating that a stimulus, such as another organism, an object, or a situation, should be avoided. It is usually accompanied by a desire to withdraw from or avoid the aversive stimulus. —**aversive** *n.*

aversion conditioning see AVERSIVE CONDITIONING.

aversion reaction a response expressed by avoiding a distasteful, threatening, or otherwise objectionable stimulus.

aversion system NEUROTICISM as represented by an individual's relative sensitivity to aversive (negative, punishing) cues and stimuli and his or her processes for avoiding them. Compare APPETITION SYSTEM. [proposed by Hans EYSENCK]

aversion therapy a form of BEHAVIOR THERAPY in which the client is conditioned to change or eliminate undesirable behavior or symptoms by associating them with noxious or unpleasant experiences, such as a bitter taste (for nail biting) or nausea (for alcoholism). Also called **aversive therapy**; **deterrent therapy**.

aversive conditioning the process by which a noxious or unpleasant stimulus is paired with an undesired behavior. This technique may be used therapeutically, for example, in the treatment of substance abuse. Also called **averse conditioning**; **aversion conditioning**. See also AVERSION THERAPY.

aversive control the use of an aversive outcome, such as punishment or negative reinforcement, to control behavior.

aversive event see AVERSIVE STIMULUS.

aversive racism a form of racial PREJUDICE felt by individuals who outwardly endorse egalitarian attitudes and values but nonetheless experience negative emotions in the presence of members of certain racial groups. See also MODERN RACISM; RACISM.

aversive stimulus any stimulus or occurrence that evokes AVOIDANCE BEHAVIOR or ESCAPE BEHAVIOR. Also called **aversive event**. See also AVOIDANCE CONDITIONING.

aversive therapy see AVERSION THERAPY.

Aveyron boy see WILD BOY OF AVEYRON.

aviation clinical psychology program a program developed at the Aeromedical Research Laboratory at Fort Rucker, Alabama (established in 1962). The Laboratory directs medical research, provides training support to Army aviation and airborne activities, and trains aviation psychologists.

aviation psychology a specialty in APPLIED PSYCHOLOGY that focuses on understanding human psychology as it relates to the operation and control of aviation systems and influences the safety and efficiency of flight.

aviator's neurasthenia a syndrome of gastrointestinal disorders, irritability, insomnia, emotional stress, and mental fatigue associated with pilots of military aircraft in the early 20th century.

aviophobia *n.* see FEAR OF FLYING.

AVM abbreviation for ARTERIOVENOUS MALFORMATION.

avoidance *n.* the practice or an instance of keeping away from particular situations, activities, environments, individuals, things, or subjects of thought or conversation because of either (a) the anticipated negative consequences of such an encounter or (b) anxious or painful feelings associated with those things or events. Psychology brings several theoretical perspectives to the study of avoidance: its use as a means of coping; its use as a response to fear or shame; and its existence as a component in ANXIETY DISORDERS. See also APPROACH–AVOIDANCE CONFLICT; AVOIDANCE BEHAVIOR; AVOIDANCE CONDITIONING.

avoidance–avoidance conflict a conflict situation involving a choice between two equally objectionable alternatives, for example, when an individual must choose between unemployment or a salary cut. Also called **double-avoidance conflict**. Compare APPROACH–APPROACH CONFLICT; APPROACH–AVOIDANCE CONFLICT.

avoidance behavior any act that enables an individual to avoid or anticipate unpleasant or painful situations, stimuli, or events, including conditioned aversive stimuli. See AVOIDANCE CONDITIONING. Compare ESCAPE BEHAVIOR.

avoidance conditioning the establishment of behavior that prevents, postpones, or reduces the frequency of aversive stimulation. In a typical conditioning experiment a buzzer is sounded, then a shock is applied to the subject (e.g., a dog) until it performs a particular act (e.g., jumping over a fence). After several trials, the dog jumps as soon as the buzzer sounds, avoiding the shock. Also called **avoidance learning**; **avoidance training**. See also ESCAPE LEARNING; SIDMAN AVOIDANCE SCHEDULE.

avoidance gradient the variation in the strength of a drive as a function of the organism's proximity to an AVERSIVE STIMULUS. For example, a rat's withdrawal behavior increases in intensity as it nears a feared stimulus (e.g., an electric shock). The avoidance gradient appears steeper than the APPROACH GRADIENT. See also APPROACH–APPROACH CONFLICT; APPROACH–AVOIDANCE CONFLICT.

avoidance learning see AVOIDANCE CONDITIONING.

avoidance response a response in which an organism anticipates an aversive stimulus and consequently attempts to prevent contact with this stimulus. The avoidance response is a form of abient behavior (see ABIENCE). Also called **avoidance reaction**.

avoidance training see AVOIDANCE CONDITIONING.

avoidance without warning signal see SIDMAN AVOIDANCE SCHEDULE.

avoidant attachment in the STRANGE SITUATION, a form of INSECURE ATTACHMENT in which infants do not seek proximity to their parent after separation. Instead, the infant does not appear distressed by the separation and avoids the returning parent.

avoidant attachment style an interpersonal style characterized by a discomfort in being close to others. Also called **anxious–avoidant attachment style**. See also ANXIOUS–AVOIDANT ATTACHMENT; ATTACHMENT THEORY.

avoidant disorder of childhood or adolescence in *DSM–III*, a disorder lasting at least 6 months between the ages of 2½ and 18 and characterized by persistent, excessive retreating from strangers. It interferes with peer relationships, but satisfying relationships with family members may be intact. In *DSM–IV–TR*, this diagnostic category has been subsumed under SOCIAL PHOBIA. Also called **shyness disorder**. See also AVOIDANT PERSONALITY DISORDER.

avoidant marriage a long-lasting marriage in which the partners seldom argue because they have "agreed to disagree" and accept their differences of opinions with no apparent rancor.

avoidant paruresis inability to urinate in the presence of other people. Also called **bashful bladder syndrome**.

avoidant personality a personality trait characterized by feeling uncomfortable when psychologically close to others, resulting in a tendency not to form intimate relations.

avoidant personality disorder in *DSM–IV–TR*, a personality disorder characterized by (a) hypersensitivity to rejection and criticism, (b) a desire for uncritical acceptance, (c) social withdrawal in spite of a desire for affection and acceptance, and (d) low self-esteem. This pattern is long-standing and severe enough to cause objective distress and seriously impair the ability to work and maintain relationships. [first defined in 1969 by U.S. psychologist Theodore Millon (1929–)]

avolition *n.* failure to engage in goal-directed behavior, occasionally occurring in severe MAJOR DEPRESSIVE EPISODES.

awareness *n.* a consciousness of internal or external events or experiences. There has been a continuing controversy over whether nonhuman animals have **self-awareness**. Evidence of self-awareness in animals is most often determined by whether or not an animal can use a mirror to groom an otherwise unseen mark or spot on its own forehead: A few chimpanzees, gorillas, and orangutans have passed this test. See also CONSCIOUSNESS.

awareness-training model an approach in psychology and education that stresses self-awareness, self-realization, exploration, and interpersonal sensitivity. The awareness-training model is associated with such writers as German-born U.S. psychologist Frederick (Fritz) S. Perls (1893–1970) and U.S. psychologist William C. Schutz (1925–2002).

awe *n.* the experience of admiration and elevation in response to physical beauty, displays of exceptional ability, or moral goodness. The awe-inspiring stimulus is experienced as "vast" and difficult to comprehend.

awfulizing *n.* an irrational thought pattern characterized by the tendency to overestimate the potential seriousness or negative consequences of events, situations, or perceived threats.

AWOL acronym for ABSENCE WITHOUT LEAVE.

axial *adj.* **1.** referring to the longitudinal AXIS of the body. **2.** referring to the central part of the body and not the limbs.

axial gradient the difference in development or metabolic rate of tissues along a body axis. See also ANTERIOR–POSTERIOR DEVELOPMENT GRADIENT; CEPHALOCAUDAL DEVELOPMENT.

axiodrama *n.* see PSYCHODRAMA.

axiom *n.* in logic and philosophy, a universally accepted proposition that is not capable of proof or disproof. An axiom can be used as the starting point for a chain of DEDUCTIVE REASONING. Also called **postulate**. [from Greek *axioma*, "worthy thing"] **—axiomatic** *adj.*

axis *n.* (*pl.* **axes**) **1.** in *DSM–IV–TR*, any of the dimensions that are helpful for describing individual behavior and thus facilitate CLINICAL ASSESSMENT. *DSM–IV–TR* uses a MULTIAXIAL CLASSIFICATION based on five axes: clinical disorders (Axis I), personality disorders and mental retardation (Axis II), GENERAL MEDICAL CONDITIONS (Axis III), psychosocial and environmental problems (Axis IV), and global assessment of functioning (Axis V). **2.** an imaginary line that bisects the body or an organ in a particular plane. For example, the **long** or (**cephalocaudal**) **axis** runs in the median plane, dividing the body into right and left halves. **3.** the second cervical vertebra, on which the skull rotates. **4.** see NEURAL AXIS. **5.** a system made up of interrelated parts, as in the HYPOTHALAMIC–PITUITARY–ADRENOCORTICAL SYSTEM (or axis). **6.** a fixed reference line in a coordinate system. See also ABSCISSA; ORDINATE.

axis cylinder the central core of an AXON, consisting of cytoplasm (or **axoplasm**) surrounded by the plasma membrane (or **axolemma**).

axo-axonal synapse a SYNAPSE between two nerve cells in which the nerve impulse travels from one axon to the other axon, rather than between axon and dendrite (**axodendritic synapse**) or axon and cell body (**axosomatic synapse**).

axolemma *n.* see AXIS CYLINDER.

axon *n.* the long, thin, cylindrical extension of a NEURON that normally carries a nerve impulse away from the CELL BODY. An axon may range in diameter from 0.25 to over 10 μm. In humans, axons extending from the spinal cord to the foot may be nearly a meter in length. Also called **nerve fiber**. **—axonal** *adj.*

axonal bundle a group of parallel axons. Also called **fasciculus**.

axonal myelination see MYELINATION.

axonal transport the transportation of materials along the AXON of a neuron. It may be directed from the CELL BODY to distant regions in the DENDRITES or from the axon terminals back to the cell body. Also called **axoplasmic flow**; **axoplasmic transport**.

axonal varicosities enlarged areas of an axon that contain SYNAPTIC VESICLES and release neurotransmitter molecules.

axon collateral a branch of a neuron's AXON.

axon hillock a cone-shaped part of the CELL BODY of a neuron from which the AXON originates. Depolarization must reach a critical threshold at the axon hillock for the axon to propagate a nerve impulse.

axon reflex a peripheral nerve reflex, often associated with pain, in which stimulation of nerve fibers causes impulses to pass up these fibers to their endings, where substances are released.

axon terminal the end of an axon or a branch of an axon, which forms a SYNAPSE on a neuron or other target. See TERMINAL BUTTON.

axoplasm *n.* see AXIS CYLINDER. **—axoplasmic** *adj.*

axoplasmic flow (**axoplasmic transport**) see AXONAL TRANSPORT.

axosomatic synapse see AXO-AXONAL SYNAPSE.

axotomy *n.* the severing of an AXON. This type of denervation is often used in experimental studies of neurophysiology or as a model of certain diseases of the nervous system.

ayahuasca *n.* a powerful hallucinogenic beverage made from the stems of a tropical South American woody vine, *Banisteriopsis caapi*, and used for centuries by indigenous peoples of the Amazon for religious, spiritual, and medicinal purposes and more recently in the United States to evoke ANOMALOUS EXPERIENCES. The pharmacologically active ingredients are HARMINE and **harmaline**. In smaller doses, these ingredients have hallucinogenic and euphoric effects but in larger doses cause nausea and vomiting, TINNITUS, and collapse, followed by sedation. Also called **caapi**; **yagé**.

Ayurveda *n.* a holistic system of healing, originating and practiced primarily in the Indian subcontinent, that has spread to some extent in Western cultures. It includes diet and herbal remedies and emphasizes the use of body, mind, and spirit in disease prevention and treatment.

azaspirones *pl. n.* a class of nonbenzodiazepine ANXIOLYTICS of which the prototype is BUSPIRONE. They relieve anxiety by acting as PARTIAL AGONISTS at the 5-HT_{1A} serotonin receptor (see SEROTONIN-RECEPTOR AGONISTS). Other drugs in this class include gepirone, tandospirone, and ipsapirone. Azaspirones produce less sedation than the BENZODIAZEPINES and they lack the abuse potential of these drugs. However, their onset of action is 2–3 weeks, and they cannot therefore be used to manage acute or paroxysmal anxiety. Also called **azaspirodecanediones**.

azathioprine *n.* a drug used to suppress the immune response. It is the most widely used drug in support of organ transplantation and other potentially severe cases of immune reactions. U.S. trade name (among others): **Imuran**.

azoospermia *n.* an absence of viable sperm in the semen, usually as a failure of spermatogenesis.

Bb

baah-ji *n.* see BAH-TSCHI.

babbling *n.* prespeech sounds, such as *dadada,* made by infants from around 6 months of age. Babbling is usually regarded as practice in vocalization, which facilitates later speech development. Also called **babble**. See BABY TALK; PRESPEECH DEVELOPMENT.

Babinski reflex the reflex occurring in a healthy infant in which the toes are extended upward when the sole of the foot is gently stimulated. This response disappears by the time the baby walks, but it may reappear in adults if there is a loss of function of the UPPER MOTOR NEURONS. Also called **Babinski's sign**. [Joseph F. **Babinski** (1857–1932), French neurologist]

Babkin reflex a neonatal reflex in which infants open their mouths and twist their heads in response to pressure on their palms. [Boris Petrovich **Babkin** (1877–1950), Russian-born Canadian neurologist]

baby blues a colloquial name for the transient depressive symptoms experienced by about 70% of women during the first 10 days after giving birth. It should be distinguished from POSTPARTUM DEPRESSION. Also called **maternity blues**; **postpartum blues**.

baby talk 1. sounds used by a child in the early stages of speech development. See BABBLING; PRESPEECH DEVELOPMENT. **2.** the type of speech used by adults and older children when talking to infants or very young children. See INFANT-DIRECTED SPEECH.

backbone *n.* see SPINAL COLUMN.

back-clipping *n.* see CLIPPING.

backcrossing *n.* the process of crossbreeding a HYBRID animal or plant with a member of the genetic line from which the hybrid was originally derived. The offspring of the mating is known as a **backcross**.

back-formation *n.* the creation of a new word on the mistaken assumption that an existing word must be derived from it. This usually involves the elimination of an apparent affix or inflection, as in the creation of the verb *enthuse* from *enthusiasm.* The term is also applied to a word formed in this way. Also called **inverse derivation**; **retrogressive formation**. See also CLIPPING.

background *n.* **1.** in perception, any aspect of the environment that forms a setting for the primary stimulus or stimuli. See also FIGURE-GROUND. **2.** in general, the sum total of a person's upbringing, education, training, and experience.

background noise see NOISE.

back-propagation algorithms (**backprop algorithms**) see PERCEPTRON.

backtrack search a GRAPH search strategy that considers states in a graph recursively: If the present state is not the goal state, then its first child (node) is examined. If this child is not the goal state, then its first child is taken. If there are no children of a state, then the next sibling of the present state is considered. If there are no further siblings of a state, then the sibling of the state's parent has to be considered. This process continues until either a goal state is found or there are no further states to examine. States, their siblings, and their children are usually (but not necessarily) considered in a left-to-right format.

back-translation *n.* see TRANSLATION AND BACK-TRANSLATION.

backup reinforcer in BEHAVIOR MODIFICATION, a reward given to a client or patient in return for tokens he or she has earned. See also TOKEN ECONOMY.

backward association the formation of an associative link between one item and an item that precedes it in a series or sequence. Compare FORWARD ASSOCIATION.

backward conditioning a procedure in which an UNCONDITIONED STIMULUS is consistently presented before a NEUTRAL STIMULUS. Generally, this arrangement is not thought to produce a change in the effect of a neutral stimulus. Occasionally, however, the neutral stimulus may take on inhibitory functions, presumably because it consistently predicts the absence of the unconditioned stimulus. It may also take on excitatory functions as a result of PSEUDOCONDITIONING. Also called **backward pairing**. Compare FORWARD CONDITIONING.

backward displacement in parapsychology experiments using ZENER CARDS or similar targets, a result in which the participant's "call" or guess matches the outcome of the previous trial in the series, rather than the current one. If this effect occurs consistently, it may be taken as evidence of POSTCOGNITION. Compare FORWARD DISPLACEMENT.

backward elimination a form of STEPWISE REGRESSION in which the least important variables are systematically removed from the prediction equation until a preset criterion is reached.

backward masking see MASKING.

backward pairing see BACKWARD CONDITIONING.

backward reading see PALINLEXIA.

backward search a problem-solving strategy in which the solver works backward from the end goal of the problem to the beginning state. An example would be finding the path through a maze by working from the end of the maze back to the beginning. See also WORKING BACKWARD.

baclofen *n.* a skeletal MUSCLE RELAXANT that inhibits transmission of synaptic reflexes at the spinal cord level. It is often used in the treatment of reversible spasticity associated with multiple sclerosis or spinal cord injury. U.S. trade name: **Lioresal**.

Baconian method the inductive method of scientific investigation first set out by English philosopher Francis Bacon (1561–1626). The method involves the inference of general laws or principles from particular instances observed under controlled conditions (i.e., in experiments). To make sure that any such generalization is valid, the observer must seek not only positive instances of an association between things in which one event or state brings about another, but also negative instances in which the event or state fails to occur in the absence of the other (see METHOD OF EXCLUSION; MILL'S CANONS). Finally, the observer tries to formulate an explanation for the causal connection so established. See INDUCTIVE REASONING.

bacteremia *n.* see BLOOD POISONING.

bacterial cerebral infection see CEREBRAL INFECTION.

bacterial endocarditis inflammation of the heart lining (endocardium) due to bacterial infection and causing damage to the heart valves and impaired pumping action of the heart. Fever and other systemic symptoms ensue, including embolism and heart failure. The infection can be acquired by unhygienic intravenous drug administration or abuse.

bacterial meningitis inflammation of the MENINGES, which form a protective covering for the brain and spinal cord, caused by bacterial infection, most commonly *Neisseria meningitidis* (the meningococcus), *Haemophilus influenzae*, or *Streptococcus pneumoniae* (the pneumococcus). **Meningococcal meningitis** is highly contagious because the bacteria are present in the throat as well as the cerebrospinal fluid. Common symptoms of bacterial meningitis, which can result in severe morbidity or mortality, include fever, headache, nausea, weakness, and confusion. See also MENINGITIS; TUBERCULOUS MENINGITIS.

bacterium *n.* (*pl.* **bacteria**) a unicellular, prokaryotic microorganism, that is, an organism whose chromosome is not contained in a nuclear envelope. Bacteria are considered to represent an earlier stage in the evolution of life than eukaryotes (organisms whose chromosomes are contained in nuclear envelopes, i.e., all organisms except bacteria). In humans, many bacteria cause disease (e.g., tetanus, syphilis, tuberculosis), while others are beneficial (e.g., preventing the growth of harmful microbes in the large intestine and enhancing the IMMUNE RESPONSE). **—bacterial** *adj.*

bad breast in the psychoanalytic theory of Melanie KLEIN, the internalized representation (see INTROJECTION) of the mother's breast as unsatisfying. According to Klein, the infant first experiences the mother and the nourishing breast as PART-OBJECTS with positive qualities—the GOOD BREAST—and negative qualities—the bad breast.

bad faith an individual's denial of his or her freedom as a human being or unwillingness to accept the undetermined and unforced nature of his or her actions. This often entails a denial of responsibility for the consequences of one's actions and choices or hiding the truth from oneself intentionally. See also EXISTENTIAL PSYCHOTHERAPY. [proposed by French existentialist philosopher Jean-Paul Sartre (1905–1980)]

bad is stronger than good the tendency for negative events, information, or feedback to have significantly more impact or influence on emotions, thoughts, or behavior than an equivalent positive event, information, or feedback. See TRAIT-NEGATIVITY BIAS.

bad me in the SELF-SYSTEM theory of U.S. psychoanalyst Harry Stack Sullivan (1892–1949), the internalized personification of impulses and behaviors that are considered to be negative by the self and, therefore, need to be hidden or disguised from others or from the self. In a child, for instance, the bad me may arise out of a sense of parental disapproval that in turn gives rise to anxiety and self-doubt. Compare GOOD ME. See also NOT ME.

bad object in the psychoanalytic theory of Melanie KLEIN, an introjected PART-OBJECT perceived as having negative qualities (see INTROJECTION). It is an early object representation that derives from SPLITTING of the object into parts containing negative qualities (i.e., the bad object) and positive qualities (i.e., the GOOD OBJECT).

bad trip an acute psychotic episode that is caused by ingestion of HALLUCINOGENS. The episode may also be marked by FLASHBACKS at a later date. See also HALLUCINOGEN INTOXICATION; HALLUCINOGEN-INDUCED MOOD DISORDER.

bah-tschi (**bah-tsi**; **baah-ji**) *n.* a CULTURE-BOUND SYNDROME found in Thailand, with symptoms similar to those of LATAH.

BAI abbreviation for BECK ANXIETY INVENTORY.

bait shyness the avoidance by animals of food that previously has been associated with gastric distress or other adverse effects. This learned avoidance is rapid (often occurring after a single trial) and long-lasting, even though the aversive effects may not be experienced for several minutes or even hours after ingestion. See also CONDITIONED TASTE AVERSION.

balance 1. *n.* a harmonious relationship or equilibrium of opposing forces or contrasting elements. See AUTONOMIC BALANCE; BALANCE THEORY; HOMEOSTASIS. **2.** *n.* the SENSE OF EQUILIBRIUM mediated by the VESTIBULAR SYSTEM of the inner ear. **3.** *vb.* to adjust forces to maintain something at a level from which it would ordinarily deviate.

balance control see BALANCE TRAINING.

balanced bilingual a person who has proficiency in two languages such that his or her skills in each language match those of a native speaker of the same age. Compare UNBALANCED BILINGUAL. See BILINGUALISM.

balanced design an experimental design in which the number of observations or measurements obtained in each experimental condition is equal. In the simplest case, a balanced design employs samples of equal size.

balanced Latin square a single LATIN SQUARE with an even number of treatments, or a pair of Latin squares with an odd number of treatments, in which each treatment occurs equally often in each position of the sequence (e.g., first, second, third, etc.) and each sequence of treatments (reading both forward and backward) also occurs equally often.

balanced replication a pair of studies that, taken together, show greater COUNTERBALANCING than does either study alone. See also REPLICATION.

balanced scale a scale in which, for each alternative, there is another alternative that means the opposite. An example is a rating scale with the four alternatives very poor, poor, good, and very good.

balance theory the theory that people tend to prefer elements within a cognitive system to be internally consistent with one another (i.e., balanced). Balanced systems are assumed to be more stable and psychologically pleasant than imbalanced systems. The theory has been primarily specified and tested within the context of systems involving three elements. These systems are sometimes referred to as **P-O-X triads**, in which P = person (i.e., self), O = other person, and X = some stimulus or event. See also COGNITIVE CONSISTENCY THEORY. [first proposed in 1946 by Austrian-born U.S. psychologist Fritz Heider (1896–1988)]

balance theory of wisdom see WISDOM.

balance training a form of physical or occupational therapy for individuals who experience difficulty with **balance control** (maintaining balance when standing, walking, or performing other activities). It involves a series of exercises designed to enhance muscular control and improve interpretation of information from the senses and may make use of trainer bicycles, tricycles with body supports and foot attachments, stilts, pogo sticks, rocker boards, and a rubber bouncing tube used like a trampoline. Balance training is also used by many athletes to enhance fitness, coordination, and performance.

balancing *n.* a statistical procedure for adjusting estimates of effects that takes into account the nonorthogonal structure of an experimental design (see NONORTHOGONAL DESIGN).

Baldwin, James Mark (1861–1934) U.S. psychologist. Baldwin earned his doctorate at Princeton University in 1887, studying under the philosopher James McCosh (1811–1895). He had earlier spent a year traveling in Germany, where he studied with Wilhelm WUNDT, among others. He taught at a number of universities, founding laboratories at the University of Toronto (1889) and Princeton University (1893) and reestablishing the laboratory originally founded by G. Stanley HALL at Johns Hopkins University (1903). Dismissed from Johns Hopkins in 1908 following a scandal, he taught in Mexico City for several years before settling at L'École des Hautes Études Sociales in Paris, where he remained from 1913 until 1934. A member of the founding generation of experimental psychologists in the United States, Baldwin founded and coedited (with James McKeen CATTELL) the *Psychological Review*, *Psychological Index*, and *Psychological Monographs*. He was president of the American Psychological Association in 1897. Baldwin is best known for his contributions to DEVELOPMENTAL PSYCHOLOGY. A proponent of FUNCTIONALISM in psychology, he applied evolutionary thinking to the study of human development, arguing that the child's mental development parallels the evolution of humankind, passing through stages from prelogical, through logical, to hyperlogical, involving flexible problem-solving abilities. Jean PIAGET's theory of COGNITIVE DEVELOPMENT was strongly influenced by Baldwin. His best known works include *Mental Development in the Child and in the Race* (1895) and the *Dictionary of Philosophy and Psychology* (1901–1902), which he edited.

Baldwin effect the influence on intraspecies evolution of phenotypic plasticity, that is, the capability of an organism to be flexible and creative in adapting its behavior to a changing environment. An individual member of the species acquires a new ability and behavior that enables that species member to adapt to the environment better and hence increase its probability of survival; the propensity for acquiring this characteristic is conferred in turn on descendants of that species member until a genetic variation occurs and the characteristic itself becomes hereditary. The Baldwin effect was originally called **organic selection**. [described in 1896 by James Mark BALDWIN]

Baldwin's figure a horizontal line with a square at each end. Small squares at the ends of the line make the line look longer than when large squares are at the ends of the line. Also called **Baldwin's illusion**. [James Mark BALDWIN]

Bálint's syndrome a disorder, resulting from lesions in the parieto-occipital portion of the brain, causing OPTIC ATAXIA, visual attention disorders, and psychogenic paralysis of visual fixation (inability to change visual gaze). Individuals with Bálint's syndrome have difficulty attending to more than one object at a time, although they can correctly identify each object in a display. For example, when shown a scene, the individual may focus on one object at a time within the scene and not be able to process the entire scene or its meaning. See also PSYCHIC PARALYSIS OF VISUAL IDEATION. [first described in 1909 by Rudolf **Bálint** (1874–1929), Hungarian physician]

Ballet's disease a disorder marked by the loss of movements of the eye and pupil while autonomic responses remain normal. The condition is associated with hyperthyroid disorders, such as exophthalmic goiter (see EXOPHTHALMOS). Also called **Ballet's sign**; **ophthalmoplegia externa**. [Gilbert **Ballet** (1853–1916), French neurologist]

ballet technique a structured form of DANCE THERAPY.

ballism *n.* a condition characterized by involuntary throwing or flinging movements, called **ballistic movements**, caused by severe muscle contractions in the limbs due to neurological damage. It may involve both sides of the body or, in the case of HEMIBALLISMUS, one side only. Also called **ballismus**.

ballistic *adj.* describing a movement (or part of a movement) in which the motion, once initiated, is not altered by feedback-based corrections. Ballistic is sometimes also used, incorrectly, to describe any rapid movement. See also BALLISM.

Baltimore Longitudinal Study of Aging (BLSA) the intramural scientific study of aging of the National Institute on Aging. Over 1,200 individuals are tested at regular intervals through their life spans. The study, which has been ongoing since 1958, examines changes due to age and changes due to disease within individuals.

B and D abbreviation for BONDAGE AND DISCIPLINE.

banding *n.* an approach to setting cutoff scores in PERSONNEL SELECTION. Several ranges of scores known as **score bands** are identified, usually on the basis of the STANDARD ERROR OF MEASUREMENT for the test or PREDICTOR. Rather than being considered individually, all scores falling within the same band are regarded as equivalent. If, as is usually the case, it becomes necessary to discriminate between applicants in the same band, then further tests or criteria must be used.

bandpass filter see FILTER.

band symmetry see SYMMETRY.

Bandura, Albert (1925–) Canadian-born U.S. psychologist. Born and raised in Alberta, Canada, Bandura received his PhD from the University of Iowa in 1952 under the direction of Arthur L. Benton (1909–). He then joined the faculty of Stanford University, where he remained throughout his career. Bandura is best known for his work on SOCIAL LEARNING THEORY. Early in his career, he studied the familial origins of antisocial aggression in adolescent boys, culminating in his first book, *Adolescent Aggression* (1959), and the later *Aggression: A Social Learning Analysis* (1973). These books showed that adolescents whose parents' behavior included hostile attitudes were more likely to display aggression, even when aggressive behavior was openly discouraged at home. Bandura and his colleagues went on to explore the role of OBSERVATIONAL LEARNING. In famous studies using a BOBO DOLL, Bandura showed that, contrary to the predictions of then-dominant behaviorist theory, humans could learn through social MODELING in the absence of positive reinforcement. Bandura's subsequent work centered on various topics in the field of SOCIAL-COGNITIVE THEORY, especially self-regulatory processes and their role in motivation and behavior. Among his other important works are *Social Learning Theory* (1977), *Social Foundations of Thought and Action: A Social Cognitive Theory* (1986), and *Self-Efficacy: The Exercise of Control* (1997). Bandura served as president of the American Psychological Association and was elected to the American

Academy of Arts and Sciences and the Institute of Medicine of the National Academy of Sciences.

bandwagon effect the tendency for large numbers of individuals, in social and sometimes political situations, to align themselves or their stated opinions with the majority opinion as they perceive it. See AD POPULUM.

bandwidth *n.* **1.** the range of information available from measuring instruments. Greater bandwidth is generally associated with lower FIDELITY. **2.** the width of a band of frequencies, usually expressed in hertz (cycles per second). It is a measure of the capacity of a communication channel, that is, of the amount of information that it can transmit per unit of time.

bangungut *n.* a CULTURE-BOUND SYNDROME observed mainly among young, healthy, Filipino males. The individual is often overheard screaming or moaning during sleep, apparently experiencing a terrifying nightmare; this is followed by unexpected death. Also called **oriental nightmare-death syndrome**.

banner advertisement a relatively small advertisement appearing on a web page, often inducing consumers to click on the advertisement (a small banner) to go to a website to learn more about a product. Banner advertisements are often related to the content of the website being viewed.

baquet *n.* a large, shallow, covered tub containing water, iron filings, ground glass, and bottles arranged in patterns from which metal rods protruded, used by Austrian physician Anton Mesmer (1734–1815) in his attempts to cure patients with a variety of hysterical symptoms. Mesmer had his patients place the rods on ailing parts of their bodies so that they would experience the supposed healing power of magnetism. See ANIMAL MAGNETISM; MESMERISM.

bar- *combining form* see BARO-.

baragnosis *n.* an inability to judge the weights of, or to detect weight differences between, objects held in the hand. It is typically attributable to a lesion in the PARIETAL LOBE of the brain. Compare BAROGNOSIS.

Bárány test a test designed to reveal whether the SEMICIRCULAR CANALS of the inner ear are functioning properly. The patient is rotated in a special chair—the **Bárány chair**—with his or her head in each of the planes that bring the three canals vertical to the direction of rotation. The resulting NYSTAGMUS (involuntary movements of the eyes) indicates whether the canals are functioning properly. Also called **Bárány method**. [Robert **Bárány** (1876–1936), Austrian physician]

barber's-pole effect the perception that a rotating vertical cylinder with spiral markings (a barber's pole) appears to be moving up, rather than simply rotating.

barbiturate abuse see SEDATIVE, HYPNOTIC, OR ANXIOLYTIC ABUSE.

barbiturate addiction see SEDATIVE, HYPNOTIC, OR ANXIOLYTIC DEPENDENCE.

barbiturate dependence see SEDATIVE, HYPNOTIC, OR ANXIOLYTIC DEPENDENCE.

barbiturate intoxication see SEDATIVE, HYPNOTIC, OR ANXIOLYTIC INTOXICATION.

barbiturates *pl. n.* a family of drugs, derived from barbituric acid, that depress activity of the central nervous system (see CNS DEPRESSANTS) and were previously widely used as anxiolytics, sedatives, and hypnotics. They typically induce profound TOLERANCE and withdrawal symptoms and depress respiration: They can depress breathing completely—hence their use by individuals wishing to commit suicide. Barbiturates are commonly categorized according to their rates of action (including onset of effect, absorption, and excretion) as long acting, intermediate acting, short acting, or ultrashort acting. Their use became common in the 1930s, but they were rapidly supplanted in the 1970s by the BENZODIAZEPINES, which lack the lethality associated with overdose of the barbiturates. The group includes AMOBARBITAL, BUTABARBITAL, PENTOBARBITAL, PHENOBARBITAL, PRIMIDONE, and THIOPENTAL, among others. See SEDATIVE, HYPNOTIC, AND ANXIOLYTIC DRUGS.

barbiturate withdrawal see SEDATIVE, HYPNOTIC, OR ANXIOLYTIC WITHDRAWAL.

barbiturate withdrawal delirium see SEDATIVE, HYPNOTIC, OR ANXIOLYTIC WITHDRAWAL DELIRIUM.

bar chart see BAR GRAPH.

Bard–Cannon theory see CANNON–BARD THEORY.

bar display in ergonomics, a machine display in which fluctuating values of a system attribute are indicated by the length of rectangular bars of equal width. See also OBJECT DISPLAY.

Barefoot v. Estelle a 1983 case resulting in a decision in which the U.S. Supreme Court upheld a death sentence after a psychiatrist testified at trial that the likelihood the defendant would reoffend was 100% and absolute, although the psychiatrist had never examined the defendant.

baresthesia *n.* the sensation of weight or pressure.

bargaining *n.* the process in which two parties attempt to resolve their conflicting interests by trading scarce resources in return for some benefits. **—bargain** *vb.*

bargaining stage the third of the five STAGES OF DYING described by Swiss-born U.S. psychiatrist Elisabeth Kübler-Ross (1926–2004). In this stage, the dying person is thought to be engaged in trying to negotiate a deal with God or fate that would delay the end of life.

bar graph a way of graphically displaying data using bars of varying length or height with spaces between them. A bar graph is appropriate when one of the two variables is discrete or is nonnumerical, such as males versus females, or political party affiliation. This variable would generally be represented along the *x*-axis, while the height of the bar would be proportional to the *y* variable, and the bars would be separated by space to denote their discrete nature. Compare HISTOGRAM. Also called **bar chart**.

bar hustlers see MALE HOMOSEXUAL PROSTITUTION.

bariatrics *n.* a field of medicine that focuses on the study of overweight: its causes, prevention, and treatment.

barK abbreviation for BETA-ADRENERGIC RECEPTOR KINASE.

Barnum effect the tendency of individuals to accept vague and generalized personal feedback—that is, to believe that vague predictions or general personality descriptions, such as those offered by astrology, have specific applications to themselves. Coinage of the term, which alludes to a remark allegedly made by U.S. showman Phineas T. Barnum (1810–1891), has been attributed to Paul E. MEEHL. The effect was termed the **fallacy of personal validation** by U.S. psychologist Bertram Robin Forer (1914–2000), who first studied it in 1949.

baro- (**bar-**) *combining form* pressure or weight.

barognosis *n.* the ability to detect weight differences of objects held in the hand. Compare BARAGNOSIS.

Barona equation an equation that uses demographic variables (such as age and education) to predict IQ. It is used primarily to estimate IQ prior to brain injury or disease. [Andres **Barona** (1945–), U.S. psychologist]

baroreceptor *n.* a pressure receptor in the heart or a major artery that detects changes in blood pressure and communicates that information to the brain via the autonomic nervous system. Also called **baroceptor**.

barotitis *n.* a disorder of the ear due to exposure to differing atmospheric pressures.

Barr body see SEX CHROMATIN. [Murray L. **Barr** (1908–1995), Canadian anatomist]

bar reflex a pathological phenomenon in which the lateral or vertical movement of one leg of a recumbent individual is followed by a similar movement of the other leg. This is usually a diagnostic sign of damage to the anterior region of the FRONTAL LOBE.

barricade incidents hostage and high-risk incidents, which require crisis management and negotiation capabilities.

barrier *n.* something that restricts, impedes, or blocks progress or the achievement of an ultimate objective or end. In psychological contexts barriers are mental, emotional, or behavioral limitations in individuals and groups.

barrier-free environment an environment that is free of obstacles to individuals with physical and cognitive disabilities whose normal movements are uncontrolled or unsteady or require the use of prosthetic devices (e.g., artificial limbs or wheelchairs). Environmental barriers can include street curbs, revolving doors or doors too narrow to admit wheelchairs, inaccessible toilets and washbowls, coin-operated telephones beyond the reach of users, and elevator buttons that cannot be read by people with visual impairment. See also UNIVERSAL DESIGN.

Barron–Welsh Art Scale (**BWAS**) an assessment of aesthetic preference in which participants indicate "like" or "dislike" for each of 86 black and white figures selected to differentiate between the judgment of CRITERION GROUPS of artists and nonartists. The figures vary in complexity from simple line drawings of geometric figures to detailed, multiline abstractions. Although available as a separate instrument, the Barron–Welsh scale is part of the larger WELSH FIGURE PREFERENCE TEST of personality characteristics; indeed, performance on the BWAS has been interpreted variously as an index of creativity and a reflection of underlying personality variables. [originally developed in 1952 by Frank X. **Barron** (1922–2002) and George S. **Welsh** (1918–1990), U.S. psychologists]

BARS abbreviation for BEHAVIORALLY ANCHORED RATING SCALE.

Barthel Index a form of FUNCTIONAL STATUS measurement that includes 10 items assessing an individual's ability to perform the ACTIVITIES OF DAILY LIVING independently. An individual is rated on a point scale regarding the degree of assistance required to perform each item, and the ratings are then combined to yield a total score. [Dorothea W. **Barthel**, 20th-century U.S. psychologist]

Bartholin's glands see VESTIBULAR GLANDS. [Caspar **Bartholin** (1655–1738), Danish anatomist]

Bartlett's test a statistical procedure designed to test the NULL HYPOTHESIS of HOMOGENEITY OF VARIANCE (i.e., equality of variance) in several populations, which is something that many parametric tests rely on. This procedure is highly dependent upon normality assumptions. See also LEVENE TEST. [Sir Frederic Charles **Bartlett** (1886–1969), British psychologist]

Bartlett technique a study of memory based on the theory that memory should be viewed as constructive and reconstructive (see CONSTRUCTIVE MEMORY; RECONSTRUCTIVE MEMORY), rather than being simply reproductive. In the original 1932 study, British college students attempted to recall a particular Native American folk tale. Successive reproductions of the tale demonstrated that the students' own cultural knowledge and expectations intruded into the recall, rationalizing and eliminating unusual elements and structuring unrelated items of the tale into a more coherent and familiar framework. Also called **Bartlett tradition**. See also EFFORT AFTER MEANING. [Sir Frederic **Bartlett**]

Bartley v. Kremens a lawsuit resulting in a Pennsylvania court decision (1976) that extended DUE PROCESS protection and provision of legal counsel to children committed to mental facilities by their parents.

baryphony *n.* speech characterized by a thick, heavy voice quality. Also called **baryphonia**.

BAS abbreviation for BEHAVIORAL APPROACH SYSTEM.

basal age see BASAL MENTAL AGE.

basal cell see TYPE IV CELL.

basal dendrite any of several DENDRITES on a PYRAMIDAL CELL that extend horizontally from the CELL BODY. Compare APICAL DENDRITE.

basal forebrain a region of the ventral FOREBRAIN near the corpus callosum containing cholinergic neurons that project widely to the cerebral cortex and HIPPOCAMPUS and are thought to be important in aspects of memory, learning, and attention. Subtle damage to this area may be observed in Alzheimer's disease; more extensive damage can result in amnesia and confabulation.

basal ganglia a group of nuclei (see NUCLEUS) deep within the cerebral hemispheres of the brain that includes the CAUDATE NUCLEUS, PUTAMEN, and GLOBUS PALLIDUS; the putamen and globus pallidus are together known as the lenticular (or lentiform) nucleus. The basal ganglia are involved in the generation of goal-directed voluntary movement. Also called **basal nuclei**.

basal mental age the mental age at which all items on a standardized test, such as the Stanford–Binet, are passed. This concept is less widely used than in the past because of the declining popularity of the mental-age construct (see MENTAL AGE). Also called **basal age**.

basal metabolism the minimum energy expenditure required to maintain the vital functions of the body while awake but at rest and not expending energy for thermoregulation. **Basal metabolic rate** is measured in kilojoules (or Calories) expended per kilogram of body weight or per square meter of body surface per hour.

basal nuclei see BASAL GANGLIA.

basal nucleus of Meynert see MAGNOCELLULAR NUCLEUS OF THE BASAL FOREBRAIN. [Theodor H. **Meynert** (1833–1892), Austrian neurologist]

basal reader approach a method of reading instruction through the use of a series of books. The vocabulary, content, and sequence of skills to be taught are thus determined by the authors. A teacher's manual and children's workbooks accompany the series.

basal skin resistance the level of electrical resistance of the skin, as measured by the GALVANIC SKIN RESPONSE and other criteria, in an individual during a resting state. Also called **basal-resistance level**. See SKIN CONDUCTANCE. See also POLYGRAPH.

base 1. *n.* the lowest or most fundamental part of something. **2.** *n.* a foundation or starting point for research or inquiry. **3.** *adj.* elemental, or having a primitive or basic nature.

baseline *n.* a stable behavioral performance that can be used as a yardstick, particularly to assess the effects of particular manipulations or interventions. For example, experimental treatments are expected to modify behavior relative to BASELINE MEASURES. See also BEHAVIORAL BASELINE.

baseline assessment **1.** the measurement of characteristics of an individual or population prior to planned interventions in order to evaluate the intervention effects. **2.** the measurement of characteristics of humans and other animals at a particular point in development in order to evaluate natural changes in these characteristics over time.

baseline measures observations of participants' responses before the administration of any experimental intervention.

baseline performance the measured rate of a behavior before introduction of an intervention, which allows comparison and assessment of the effects of the intervention. For example, a baseline for being off task is established before an intervention aimed at increasing on-task classroom behavior is delivered.

base pair see DNA.

base rate the unconditional, naturally occurring rate of a phenomenon in a population. This rate is often contrasted with the rate of the phenomenon under the influence of some changed condition in order to determine the degree to which the change influences the phenomenon.

base-rate fallacy a decision-making error in which information about rate of occurrence of some trait in a population (the base-rate information) is ignored or not given appropriate weight. For example, people might categorize a man as an engineer, rather than a lawyer, if they heard that he enjoyed physics at school, even if they knew that he was drawn from a population consisting of 90% lawyers and 10% engineers (i.e., the base-rate information). See REPRESENTATIVENESS HEURISTIC.

bases of an attitude the types of information from which an attitude is derived. Traditionally, researchers have distinguished between three categories of bases: The **affective basis** refers to the emotions, feelings, and moods associated with the ATTITUDE OBJECT; the **cognitive basis** refers to beliefs about attributes associated with the attitude object; and the **behavioral basis** refers to responses, such as past behaviors and future INTENTIONS, associated with the attitude object. Also called **components of an attitude**. See also TRIPARTITE THEORY OF ATTITUDES.

base structure see DEEP STRUCTURE.

bashful bladder syndrome see AVOIDANT PARURESIS.

Basic Achievement Skills Individual Screener (BASIS) an academic achievement test designed to provide both norm-referenced and criterion-referenced results for reading, mathematics, spelling, and writing for children in grades 1–12. The tests of reading, mathematics, and spelling are divided into grade-referenced clusters, each consisting of 6–10 items reflecting the curriculum of that grade. Testing begins with an easy cluster and progresses upward until the student fails to perform satisfactorily on a particular cluster. The 10-minute writing exercise is optional and designed to elicit a descriptive passage, which is then evaluated according to grade-level-specific comparison samples. Developed in 1983, the BASIS has been used as a general achievement measure or a quick initial screening device for grade-level placement.

basic anxiety in EGO PSYCHOLOGY, a feeling of being helpless, abandoned, and endangered in a hostile world. According to German-born U.S. psychoanalyst Karen D. Horney (1885–1952), it arises from the infant's helplessness and dependence on his or her parents or from parental indifference. Defenses against basic anxiety and hostility may produce NEUROTIC NEEDS and NEUROTIC TRENDS, such as a submissive attitude, the need to exert power over others, or withdrawal from relationships. See also BASIC HOSTILITY.

basic category see BASIC-LEVEL CATEGORY.

basic conflict in EGO PSYCHOLOGY, the conflict between a person's dominant NEUROTIC TREND and his or her incompatible nondominant NEUROTIC NEEDS, which must be kept repressed. [first described by German-born U.S. psychoanalyst Karen D. Horney (1885–1952)]

basic emotion see PRIMARY EMOTION.

basic encounter a meaningful experience in one person's relating to another that is characterized by mutual trust and empathy. The development and occurrence of such encounters in therapy and counseling contexts is considered to be beneficial to the therapeutic process and outcome for the client. See also CLIENT-CENTERED THERAPY.

basic hostility in EGO PSYCHOLOGY, a feeling of hostility and resentment toward the parents that develops as a result of the BASIC ANXIETY that the infant feels at being dependent on them. To the extent that the infant fears the parents, basic hostility and anxiety are repressed and give rise to NEUROTIC NEEDS and NEUROTIC TRENDS. [defined by German-born U.S. psychoanalyst Karen D. Horney (1885–1952)]

BASIC ID see MULTIMODAL THERAPY.

basic-level category a category formed at the level that people find most natural and appropriate in their normal, everyday experience of the things so categorized. A basic-level category (e.g., "bird," "table") will be broader than the more specific SUBORDINATE CATEGORIES into which it can be divided (e.g., "hawk," "dining table") but less abstract than the SUPERORDINATE CATEGORY into which it can be subsumed (e.g., "animals," "furniture"). A basic-level category will usually meet the following criteria: (a) It represents a level of CATEGORIZATION at which high resemblance among members of the category co-occurs with low resemblance with members of different categories; (b) it represents the highest level at which members have a similar general shape and is therefore the highest level at which a single mental image can stand for the entire category; (c) it represents the highest level at which numerous attributes can be listed, most of which will apply to most members of the category (see FAMILY RESEMBLANCE). The name of the basic-level category will generally be the term most frequently applied to the things in question in natural language, the term earliest learned, and the term that is most readily remembered. Also called **basic category**; **natural category**.

basic mistake in the psychology of Alfred ADLER, a factor arising in early childhood that affects a person's lifestyle in later life and that may need to be corrected in order to resolve conflicts.

basic mistrust the unsuccessful resolution of the first stage in ERIKSON'S EIGHT STAGES OF DEVELOPMENT, in which the child in the first 18 months of life comes to experience a fundamental distrust of his or her environment, often due to neglect, lack of love, or inconsistent treatment. The acquisition of BASIC TRUST or hope is considered essential for the development of self-esteem and normal relatedness.

basic need see BASIC PHYSIOLOGICAL NEED.

Basic Nordic Sleep Questionnaire (BNSQ) a standardized questionnaire that uses a five-point quantitative scale, ranging from never (1) to every night (5), for measuring the frequency of occurrence during the previous 3 months of various sleep disturbances and complaints. The questionnaire was initially developed in 1988 by the Scandinavian Sleep Research Society for use in Denmark, Norway, Sweden, Finland, and Iceland (i.e., the Nordic countries).

basic personality a distinctive pattern of thought, feeling, and behavior supposedly found in people raised in the same culture, largely as a result of their subjection to the same child-rearing practices. The basic personality is in turn held to be responsible for many of a culture's distinctive institutions, such as its religion and folklore. Also called **basic personality structure**; **basic personality type**. See also CULTURAL DETERMINISM; NATIONAL CHARACTER. [proposed by U.S. psychoanalyst Abram Kardiner (1891–1981)]

basic physiological need 1. any of the requirements to maintain life, namely, food, water, oxygen, shelter, security, and an environmental temperature within the range that allows life processes to continue. Also called **basic need**; **fundamental need**. **2.** the lowest level of MASLOW'S MOTIVATIONAL HIERARCHY of needs, comprising food, water, air, sleep, and other survival needs. See also PRIMARY NEED; VISCEROGENIC NEED.

basic reflexes the reflexes of sucking, eye movement, grasping, and sound orientation. According to Jean PIAGET's theory of cognitive development, basic reflexes are a feature of the first substage of the SENSORIMOTOR STAGE, in which infants know the world only in terms of their inherited action patterns.

basic research research conducted to obtain knowledge for its own sake rather than having a more direct practical goal. Compare APPLIED RESEARCH. See also PURE RESEARCH.

basic rest–activity cycle (BRAC) cyclic alternations between activity and nonactivity during waking and sleep, thought typically to involve a 90-min cycle.

basic rule the fundamental rule of psychoanalysis that the patient must attempt to put all spontaneous thoughts, feelings, and memories into words without censorship, so that they can be analyzed to reveal unconscious wishes and emotions. Also called **fundamental rule**.

basic skills in education, reading, writing, and arithmetic. Proficiency in the basic skills has traditionally been viewed as essential for scholastic achievement.

basic-skills testing 1. a standardized, often state-regulated assessment of BASIC SKILLS. **2.** an examination of an individual's ability to perform and understand fundamental tasks.

basic technique (BT) in parapsychology experiments using ZENER CARDS, the basic procedure in which each card is removed from the deck and laid aside after being "called" or guessed by the participant. The cards are not checked until the entire pack has been guessed in this way. See SCREENED TOUCH MATCHING. See also DOWN THROUGH; UP THROUGH.

basic trust the successful resolution of the first of ERIKSON'S EIGHT STAGES OF DEVELOPMENT, in which the child in the first 18 months of life comes to feel that his or her world is trustworthy. This lays the foundation for self-esteem and positive interpersonal relationships. The growth of basic trust is attributed to a primary caregiver who is responsively attuned to the baby's individual needs while conveying the quality of trustworthiness. Compare BASIC MISTRUST.

basilar artery an artery formed by the union of the two vertebral arteries. Its branches supply blood to the brainstem and to posterior portions of the cerebral hemispheres.

basilar membrane a fibrous membrane within the COCHLEA that supports the ORGAN OF CORTI. In response to sound the basilar membrane vibrates; this leads to stimulation of the HAIR CELLS—the auditory receptors within the organ of Corti. The mechanical properties of the basilar membrane vary over its length (34 mm in humans), giving rise to a pattern of movement known as a TRAVELING WAVE, or **Békésy traveling wave**. The location of the maximum movement depends on the frequency of the sound. This fundamental aspect of mammalian hearing was discovered by Hungarian-born U.S. physicist Georg von Békésy (1899–1972).

BASIS acronym for BASIC ACHIEVEMENT SKILLS INDIVIDUAL SCREENER.

basket cell a type of neuron found in the cerebellum.

basket endings nerve endings that are found around hair follicles and are responsible for sensations of contact and pressure.

basking in reflected glory (BIRG-ing) the tendency to enhance one's self-esteem by heightening one's association with a successful or prestigious group.

Bastian's aphasia see WERNICKE'S APHASIA. [Henry Charlton **Bastian** (1837–1915), British neurologist]

BAT abbreviation for BEHAVIORAL APPROACH TASK.

batch *n.* in EXPLORATORY DATA ANALYSIS, the set of data being considered.

Batesian mimicry a form of mimicry in which a species that is nontoxic or palatable to predators mimics the physical shape or coloration of a toxic species. For example, some species of flies have black and yellow coloration similar to bees and wasps with stingers. If predators can learn to avoid noxious prey quickly and form generalizations about similar-looking animals, then the nontoxic animals will be more likely to survive by mimicking a toxic species than if they did not. [Henry Walter **Bates** (1825–1892), British naturalist]

bath therapy the use of water immersion in therapy. See also HYDROTHERAPY.

bathy- *combining form* deep.

bathyesthesia *n.* sensitivity of the deep (subcutaneous) tissues of the body to pressure, pain, or muscle and joint sensations. Also called **deep-pressure sensitivity**; **deep sensibility**.

Batson v. Kentucky a legal case resulting in a U.S. Supreme Court ruling that it is unconstitutional to exercise PEREMPTORY CHALLENGES during VOIR DIRE for the purpose of removing jurors on account of their race.

battered-child syndrome the effects on a child of intentional and repeated physical abuse by parents or other caregivers. More broadly, it can include the effects on the child of the combination of physical abuse with severe physical, emotional, or nutritional neglect. In addition to physical injuries, the child may show signs of intellectual problems, childhood POSTTRAUMATIC STRESS DISORDER, conduct problems, and difficulties with ATTACHMENT. See also CHILD ABUSE.

battered-woman syndrome (BWS) the psychological effects of being battered by a spouse or domestic partner. The syndrome includes LEARNED HELPLESSNESS in relation to the abusive spouse, as well as symptoms of posttraumatic stress. Not all women who are battered will develop BWS: The severity and frequency of the abuse are factors in its development. See also CYCLE OF VIOLENCE.

battered women women who are physically abused by their spouses or domestic partners. Woman beating is considered to surpass rape as the most underreported act of violent assault in the United States. Current data suggest that violence against women is common and occurs in all social classes and ethnic and religious groups, as well as between same-sex partners.

battering men's excuses rationalizations given by men who beat their spouses or domestic partners. These may include claims of provocation, or that beating a spouse or partner is acceptable in the batterer's culture, or that the batterer was angry.

battery of tests see TEST BATTERY.

battlefield recovery tasks stressful tasks associated with the aftermath of an armed conflict, such as recovering casualties and bodies and identifying and burying the dead.

battle/garrison dimensions the dimensions of the risk (low to high) and types of mission (routine to unique) for a variety of operational settings, ranging from garrison (peacetime) to battlefield (combat) settings. The dimensions are influenced by training, previous exposure, and the cohesiveness of units.

battle inoculation training in simulated operational conditions (such as fire from real weapons) to prepare soldiers for deployment in combat. The battlefield performance of a soldier is directly related to the quality and amount of realistic unit and individual training that the soldier has received. Training must be related to the wartime mission of a unit and to the climatic conditions it can expect to face. Live-fire training prepares soldiers for the shock and noise of combat. Realistic training not only helps to inoculate soldiers to the stresses of operations (including combat) but also enables them to learn methods for coping with their reactions to these stresses. Previous operational experience (especially in combat) helps to prepare soldiers for future situations. See also STRESS TRAINING.

battle of the experts a scenario in which EXPERT WITNESSES from opposing sides of a legal dispute disagree over an issue that has to be decided to resolve the dispute. Such contradictory testimony is often of little help to the judge or jury in reaching a decision in the case.

battle shock psychological impairment resulting from COMBAT STRESS REACTIONS. The expression was used in the Israeli Yom Kippur war to describe the condition of a combat STRESS CASUALTY who was unable to tolerate further military combat.

Bayesian approach in evaluation research, the use of conditional probabilities as an aid in selecting between various PROGRAM OUTCOMES. [Thomas **Bayes** (1702–1761), British mathematician and theologian]

Bayesian belief network in artificial intelligence, a modeling and reasoning tool based on BAYES' THEOREM. Assumptions are made in the representation of the combinatorial problems of a full Bayesian analysis. These include an assumption of causality, in which causal situations (states of the world) are uniquely responsible for resulting states, that is, results cannot cause causes. Furthermore, the causing state is responsible for the result, with other events either conditionally independent or with co-relations so small that they may be ignored. [Thomas **Bayes**]

Bayes' theorem a formula derived from probability theory that relates two conditional probabilities: the probability of event A, given that event B has occurred, $p(A|B)$, and the probability of event B, given that event A has occurred, $p(B|A)$.

$p(A|B)p(B) = p(B|A)p(A)$

The formula may be used, for example, to calculate the probability that a certain antecedent, A_i, was associated with an observed event, B:

$p(A_i/B) = [p(B|A_i)p(A_i)]/ \Sigma\, p(B|A_i)\ i = 1$

It serves as the basis for linking prior and antecedent probabilities. [Thomas **Bayes**]

Bayley, Nancy (1899–1994) U.S. psychologist. Bayley received her PhD from the University of Iowa in 1926. Her publications covered a broad range of topics in human development, including influential studies on physical growth and sex differences in physical and psychological characteristics. She is best known for the BAYLEY SCALES OF INFANT AND TODDLER DEVELOPMENT. Most of her career was spent at the University of California at Berkeley; however, from 1954 to 1964 she was Chief of the Section on Child Development at the National Institute of Mental Health. She was the first woman to receive the American Psychological Association's Distinguished Scientific Contribution Award (1966).

Bayley Scales of Infant and Toddler Development scales for assessing the developmental status of infants and young children aged 1 month to 42 months. Test stimuli, such as form boards, blocks, shapes, household objects (e.g., utensils), and other common items, are used to engage the child in specific tasks of increasing difficulty and elicit particular responses. The Bayley scales currently have five components. Tasks from the **Mental scale** are designed to evaluate such functions as perception, memory, and learning; those from the **Motor scale** measure gross and fine motor abilities, such as crawling, sitting, grasping, and object manipulation. The **Behavior Rating scale** (formerly called the **Infant Behavior Record**) contains detailed descriptions of specific categories of behavior that are graded on a 5-point scale. It supplements the Mental and Motor scales and provides an assessment of overall attention and arousal, orientation and engagement, emotional regulation, and motor quality. The final two components, the **Social–Emotional scale** and the **Adaptive Behavior scale**, use questionnaires to obtain parent or caregiver perceptions of their child's development. The Bayley scales were originally published in 1969 and subsequently revised in 1993; the most recent version is the **Bayley–III**, published in 2005. [developed by Nancy BAYLEY]

BB a form of the enzyme CREATINE KINASE consisting of two identical B subunits, associated especially with brain tissue.

BBBG syndrome see TELECANTHUS-HYPOSPADIAS SYNDROME.

B cell see LYMPHOCYTE.

Bcl-2 *n.* a family of genes whose protein products regulate PROGRAMMED CELL DEATH.

B-cognition *n.* see BEING COGNITION.

BDD abbreviation for BODY DYSMORPHIC DISORDER.

BDI abbreviation for BECK DEPRESSION INVENTORY.

BDNF abbreviation for BRAIN-DERIVED NEUROTROPHIC FACTOR.

BDS abbreviation for BLESSED DEMENTIA SCALE.

BEAM abbreviation for BRAIN ELECTRICAL ACTIVITY MAPPING.

beast fetishism a PARAPHILIA involving contact with animal furs or hides, which serve as an APHRODISIAC.

beat *n.* **1.** a periodic change in loudness produced by superimposing two tones with similar frequencies. For example, the loudness of a 500-Hz tone and a 503-Hz tone when sounded together will fluctuate three times per second—the **beat rate**. **2.** the periodic change in AMPLITUDE produced by superimposing two sinusoidal signals that are relatively close in frequency. See also ROUGHNESS.

beat generation a group of writers who came of age in the United States in the 1950s, including the novelist Jack Kerouac (1922–1969) and the poets Lawrence Ferlinghetti (1919–), Allen Ginsberg (1926–1997), and Gregory Corso (1930–2001). The word "beat" expressed both exhaustion and beatification, in that the writers abjured traditional Western society, which they viewed as crass and commercial, and sought blissful illumination through Buddhism, literature, drink, sex, and drugs. A **beatnik** was a member of the subculture that adopted this alternative lifestyle. Older writers who related to the beat generation included Henry Miller (1891–1980), Kenneth Rexroth (1905–1982), and William S. Burroughs (1914–1997).

beating fantasy in the CLASSICAL PSYCHOANALYSIS of Sigmund FREUD, a male or female child's fantasy of being beaten by his or her father or mother. For both sexes, the fantasy is interpreted as an expression of the child's oedipal desires toward the father and is said to be based on the child's belief that the father beats the mother in the PRIMAL SCENE.

beauty *n.* the quality of a stimulus that elicits, usually immediately, admiration and pleasure.

Beck Anxiety Inventory (**BAI**) a self-report, 21-item measure used to assess the severity of anxiety experienced by patients. It is specifically designed to discriminate anxiety from depression and is appropriate for adult mental health populations. [Aaron T. **Beck** (1921–), U.S. psychiatrist]

Beck Depression Inventory (**BDI**) a self-report questionnaire designed to assess the severity of depressive symptoms in individuals aged 13 years to 80 years. Extensively used in both clinical and research settings, it consists of 21 item groups, each of which includes four statements of increasing severity. Each group reflects a symptom or attitude associated with depression (e.g., loss of energy, self-dislike), and each statement has a numerical value from 0 to 3. Participants choose the statement within each group that most accurately reflects how they have felt within the past two weeks. The BDI was originally published in 1961; the most recent version is the **BDI–II**, published in 1996. [Aaron T. **Beck** and colleagues]

Beck Hopelessness Scale (**BHS**) a scale of 20 true–false statements used to measure an individual's attitudes about the future, loss of motivation, and expectations. The scale is often used to predict suicide risk. [Aaron T. **Beck**]

Beck Scale for Suicide Ideation (**BSS**) a measure of the necessity for detailed questioning about a patient's intentions, administered to patients who are considered to be at risk of suicide. [Aaron T. **Beck**]

Beck therapy a COGNITIVE BEHAVIOR THERAPY, with individuals or groups, in which the therapist collaborates with the client to design in-session and homework tasks to test the validity of maladaptive thoughts and perceptions. Clients identify the negative thought or perception, label it (e.g., overgeneralization, polarized thinking), test its validity, devise alternative explanations, discuss the implications of these alternatives, and complete homework to practice the alternatives. [Aaron T. **Beck**]

Beckwith–Wiedemann syndrome a condition marked by neonatal hypoglycemia (low blood sugar), enlarged tongue, large abdominal hernia, and enlarged viscera. MICROCEPHALY and mental retardation are associated with the syndrome in some cases, possibly due to severe prolonged neonatal hypoglycemia. The majority of cases of this syndrome are thought to stem from loss of IMPRINTING of the gene encoding insulin growth factor 2. The relevant inhibitor is encoded by a paternally imprinted and maternally expressed gene located on the short arm of chromosome 11 (locus 11p15). [described in the 1960s by John Bruce **Beckwith** (1933–), U.S. physician, and Hans Rudolf **Wiedemann** (1915–), German pediatrician]

Bedlam *n.* the popular name for the Hospital of Saint Mary of Bethlehem in Bishopsgate, London, founded as a monastery in 1247 and converted into an asylum for the insane by Henry VIII in 1547. Many of the inmates were in a state of frenzy, and as they were shackled, starved, beaten, and exhibited to the public for a penny a look, general turmoil prevailed. The word "bedlam" thus became synonymous with wild confusion or frenzy. Sometimes **bedlamism** was used for psychotic behavior, and **bedlamite** for a psychotic individual.

bedsore *n.* see PRESSURE ULCER.

bed-wetting *n.* the involuntary discharge of urine during sleep. Bed-wetting is considered problematic if it occurs in children older than 4 or 5 years of age; it is twice as common in boys. Also called **sleep enuresis**. See also ELIMINATION DISORDER; ENURESIS.

bee communication the use of a set pattern of movements by a bee to communicate to other bees the direction and approximate distance to a source of food or a nest site. It comprises both a **round dance** and a **waggle dance** in the form of a figure 8; the intensity of these dances communicates the relative quality of the resource. The direction of the straight portion of the waggle dance with respect to gravity in the hive indicates the direction of the resource with respect to the sun. This **dancing language** is often cited as an example of bees' ability to communicate about objects distant in time and space, but alternative explanations suggest that other signals (e.g., odors) are equally important in locating food sources.

Beers, Clifford (1876–1943) U.S. philanthropist and founder of the MENTAL HYGIENE movement. In 1897 he earned his BA from Yale University's Sheffield Scientific School. Beers was secretary of the International Committee for Mental Hygiene, founded in 1909 to disseminate information on the nature and prevention of mental illness. Beers's interest in this field originated when, after attempting suicide, he was hospitalized with manic-depressive disorder. During the manic phase of the illness, he directed his considerable energy to public officials, demanding reform and improvement of conditions in mental institutions. He wrote *A Mind That Found Itself* (1908), which vividly described the phases of his illness and recovery, and advocated an enlightened approach to prevention and treatment.

before–after design an experimental design characterized by the administration of a PRETEST and a POSTTEST to one or more groups of participants. A before–after design may be an uncontrolled design, a quasi-experimental design, or a fully randomized design. Also called **pre–post design**.

begging *n.* in animal behavior, a series of vocalizations, often accompanied by mouth or bill opening, that guides parents toward feeding their young. In some species, each offspring has a distinct, individual form of begging that is used by parents for offspring recognition. Parents often give more food to the offspring with the most intense form of begging. In ANIMAL COURTSHIP some adult females engage in begging, receiving food from a potential mate. Begging also can reduce the aggression displayed by an animal toward a potential mate.

begging the question a type of CIRCULAR REASONING in which the proposition that is to be proved is assumed in the statement of the argument. An example would be to argue that all behaviors are produced or controlled by reinforcers, and then to define a reinforcer as anything that produces or controls behavior. Also called **petitio principii**; **question begging**. See also THEORY BEGGING.

behavior *n.* **1.** an organism's activities in response to external or internal stimuli, including objectively observable activities, introspectively observable activities (see COVERT BEHAVIOR), and unconscious processes. **2.** more restrictively, any action or function that can be objectively observed or measured in response to controlled stimuli. Historically, objective behavior was contrasted by behaviorists with mental activities, which were considered subjective and thus unsuitable for scientific study. See BEHAVIORISM. **—behavioral** *adj.*

behavioral approach system (**BAS**) a brain system theorized to underlie incentive motivation by activating approach behaviors in response to stimuli related to positive reinforcement. It has been suggested that the BAS is associated as well with the generation of positive affective responses, and that a strong or chronically active BAS tends to result in extraversion. Also called **behavioral activation system**. Compare BEHAVIORAL INHIBITION SYSTEM. [described by British psychologist Jeffrey Alan Gray (1934–2004)]

behavioral approach task (**BAT**) an observational assessment technique in which an individual approaches a feared situation until he or she is unable to go further. The BAT is used to assess levels of avoidance and fear of specific situations associated with SPECIFIC PHOBIA or panic disorder with AGORAPHOBIA. It may also be used to corroborate information obtained in the CLINICAL INTERVIEW and to measure treatment progress and outcome. Variables that can be measured using the BAT include physical symptoms (e.g., increased heart rate), escape or avoidance strategies, and subjective ratings of fear. Also called **behavioral approach test**; **behavioral avoidance test**.

behavioral assessment a wide variety of techniques for studying and evaluating behavior, including direct observation, interviews, psychological tests, and other methods of sampling attitudes and feelings in a situational context. The assessment procedure typically leads to the specific use of behavioral or cognitive-behavioral interventions. Also called **behavioral diagnosis**.

behavioral avoidance test see BEHAVIORAL APPROACH TASK.

behavioral baseline a STEADY STATE of behavior against which the effects of introducing an INDEPENDENT VARIABLE may be compared. For example, a child may throw between six and eight tantrums per week over the course of several weeks. This level of tantrums could then serve as a behavioral baseline to assess the effectiveness of a treatment regime. Also called **behavior baseline**.

behavioral chain see CHAIN OF BEHAVIOR.

behavioral clinic see MENTAL HEALTH CLINIC.

behavioral coaching the act of assisting an individual to change cognitive or physical behavior, or both, through demonstration, observation, and feedback.

behavioral congruence 1. consistency between the aims, attitudes, and values professed by an individual or group and observable behaviors. In personality research, behavioral congruence occurs when individuals' SELF-RATINGS are consistent with their actions. **2.** in organizational contexts, the situation in which employees' personal goals and work-related behaviors are consistent with the organizational goals.

behavioral consistency the principle that future JOB PERFORMANCE can usually be predicted on the basis of current and past job behavior. Also called **behavior consistency**.

behavioral contagion the rapid copying of the behavior of one or a few people by others in the vicinity, often in response to a salient rewarding or threatening stimulus. After the initiators first perform the behavior, the action is quickly adopted and copied by the others in an almost compulsive manner, with little analysis of the situation. Also called **behavior contagion**. See also CONTAGION; EMOTIONAL CONTAGION; MASS CONTAGION.

behavioral contingency the relationship between a specific response and the frequency, regularity, and level of REINFORCEMENT for that response.

behavioral contract an agreement between therapist and client in which the client agrees to carry out certain behaviors, usually between sessions but sometimes during the session as well. Also called **behavior contract**. See also CONTRACT; CONTINGENCY CONTRACT.

behavioral contrast 1. in clinical practice, an increase in the occurrence of a behavior in a nontreatment setting when a decrease in that behavior has been achieved in a treatment setting. For example, an intervention decreases tantrums in school, but the rate of tantrums increases at home, where the intervention is not in use. **2.** in research, an increased response for a more favorable reward following exposure to a less favorable reinforcer (**positive contrast**), or a decreased response for a less favorable reward following exposure to a more favorable reinforcer (**negative contrast**). The phenomenon illustrates that the effects of reinforcement depend on context.

behavioral counseling a system of counseling in which the primary focus is on changing client behavior through SELF-MANAGEMENT, OPERANT CONDITIONING, and related techniques. Specific behaviors are targeted for modification, and intervention strategies and environmental changes are then established in order to bring about the desired modification.

behavioral couples therapy a COUPLES THERAPY that focuses on interrupting negative interaction patterns through instruction, modeling, rehearsal, feedback, positive behavior exchange, and structured problem solving. This therapy can be conducted with individual couples or in a couples group format. When practiced with legally married partners, it is called **behavioral marital therapy**, though some practitioners use this term interchangeably with behavioral couples therapy. See also COMMUNICATION SKILLS TRAINING; INTEGRATIVE BEHAVIORAL COUPLES THERAPY.

behavioral criterion an aspect of actual (rather than self-reported) behavior that must exist in a person for an accurate diagnosis to be made. Also called **behavior criterion**.

behavioral deficit the lack of certain age-specific aspects of behavior in an individual, who is therefore not developmentally on target. Also called **behavior deficit**.

behavioral diagnosis see BEHAVIORAL ASSESSMENT.

behavioral diary a tool used to collect data in which the research participant keeps a record of events at the time they occur.

behavioral disorder see BEHAVIOR DISORDER.

behavioral dynamics the internal motivational patterns or causes underlying overt behavior.

behavioral ecology the study of the interaction between the environment and the behavior of organisms within that environment. Behavioral ecology is primarily concerned with adaptive aspects of ANIMAL BEHAVIOR, especially within a natural environment. Initially, many studies focused on the acquisition and use of resources, but more recent studies have focused on the adaptive significance of SOCIAL INTERACTIONS, blending behavioral ecology with SOCIOBIOLOGY.

behavioral economics the application of economic principles (e.g., the law of supply and demand) to the prediction, analysis, and potential modification of behavior. For example, substance abuse may be discussed in terms of the price of and demand for the substance in question.

behavioral embryology the study of the behavior of embryos. Embryonic chickens and ducks display sensitivity to different types of sensory stimuli before hatching, and motor movements similar to those needed for feeding can be seen. Embryonic rats also display many sensory and motor capacities, as well as learning, prior to birth.

behavioral endocrinology the study of the relationships between behavior and the functioning of the endocrine glands and neuroendocrine cells (see NEUROENDOCRINOLOGY). A variety of endocrine glands, including the hypothalamus, the pituitary gland, and the adrenal glands, have been shown to affect behavior. For example, gonadal secretion of sex hormones affects sexual behavior, and secretion of corticosteroids by the adrenal glands affects physiological and behavioral responses to stress.

behavioral family therapy a family treatment that is characterized by behavioral analysis of presenting problems and a focus on overt behavior change through application of learning-based behavioral principles and techniques of BEHAVIOR THERAPY. Techniques used to modify targeted behavior patterns include behavioral contracts, instruction, modeling, and rehearsal.

behavioral genetics see BEHAVIOR GENETICS.

behavioral group therapy a form of GROUP PSYCHOTHERAPY that applies learning-based behavioral principles and techniques, including modeling, rehearsal, social reinforcement, SYSTEMATIC DESENSITIZATION, and other methods of BEHAVIOR THERAPY, in the context of a group. See also COGNITIVE BEHAVIORAL GROUP THERAPY.

behavioral health an interdisciplinary subspecialty of BEHAVIORAL MEDICINE that promotes a philosophy of health emphasizing individual responsibility in the maintenance of one's own health and in the prevention of illness and dysfunction by means of self-initiated activities (jogging, exercising, healthy eating, no smoking, etc.). [proposed by U.S. psychologist Joseph D. Matarazzo (1925–)]

behavioral hierarchy see BEHAVIOR HIERARCHY.

behavioral homeostasis an organism's tendency to maintain stability or equilibrium through various behavioral processes. For example, temperature regulation is achieved via shivering, sweating, or panting, and satiety is achieved by the initiation and then cessation of feeding behavior. Also called **behavior homeostasis**. See also HOMEOSTASIS.

behavioral homology functional similarity (i.e., common behavior) across species, suggestive of a shared ancestral origin. Also called **behavior homology**.

behavioral immunogen a behavior or lifestyle associated with a decreased risk of illness and with longer life. Examples of behavioral immunogens are moderate consumption of alcohol, regular exercise, adequate sleep, and a healthy diet. Compare BEHAVIORAL PATHOGEN.

behavioral incident a single, separate behavioral event with a clearly defined start and finish (e.g., brushing one's teeth), which may be combined with other events to form a BEHAVIORAL SEQUENCE.

behavioral inhibition restraint in engaging with the world combined with a tendency to scrutinize the environment for potential threats and to avoid or withdraw from unfamiliar situations or people. This temperamental predisposition is characterized by shyness, timidity, negative emotionality, and fearfulness. [first described by U.S. psychologists Jerome Kagan (1929–) and J. Steven Reznick (1951–)]

behavioral inhibition system (**BIS**) a brain system theorized to underlie behavioral inhibition by activating avoidance behaviors in response to perceived threats. It has been suggested that the BIS is associated as well with the generation of negative affective responses, and that a strong or chronically active BIS tends to result in introversion. Compare BEHAVIORAL APPROACH SYSTEM. [described by British psychologist Jeffrey Alan Gray (1934–2004)]

behavioral integration 1. the combination of separate individual behaviors into a synchronized or coordinated behavioral unit. **2.** a model for environmentally sound behavior that specifies the relevant cognitions and affects and their interactions. Also called **behavior integration**.

behavioral interview an approach to clinical interviewing that focuses on relating a problem behavior to antecedent stimuli and the consequences of reinforcement.

behaviorally anchored rating scale (**BARS**) a behavior-based measure used in evaluating job performance. Employees are evaluated on each performance dimension by comparing their job behaviors with specific behavior examples that anchor each level of performance. The task of the rater is to find that point on the scale that is most typical of the employee's performance on the dimension. BARS can also be used to evaluate the performance of job applicants in a SITUATIONAL INTERVIEW. Compare BEHAVIORAL OBSERVATION SCALE; MIXED-STANDARD SCALE. See also CRITICAL-INCIDENT TECHNIQUE.

behavioral marital therapy see BEHAVIORAL COUPLES THERAPY.

behavioral medicine a discipline that draws on behavioral research for the clinical application of behavioral theories and methods to the prevention and treatment of medical and psychological disorders. Areas of application include chronic illness, lifestyle issues (e.g., tobacco, drugs, alcohol, obesity), SOMATOFORM DISORDERS, and the like. Behavioral medicine is a multidisciplinary field in which physicians, psychologists, psychiatrists, social workers, and others work together; it includes strong integration of biological, psychosocial, behavioral, and interpersonal perspectives in developing biopsychosocial models of illness and disease and interventions to treat and manage diseases, promote good health, and maintain healthy behaviors. See also BEHAVIORAL HEALTH.

behavioral model a systematic description or conceptualization of psychological disorders in terms of overt behavior patterns. Compare MEDICAL MODEL.

behavioral modeling 1. a type of personnel training in which supervisory and management-level workers are shown and instructed in appropriate methods of dealing with subordinates in such matters as poor work quality, absenteeism, or problems associated with racial or sexual discrimination. **2.** MODELING one's behavior consciously or unconsciously on that of another person.

behavioral momentum a hypothetical characteristic of behavior through time. It is indexed by the RESISTANCE TO CHANGE through time of some activity in the face of manipulations intended to disrupt the ongoing activity. The more difficult it is to disrupt an activity, the greater its behavioral momentum.

behavioral neurochemistry the study of the relationships between behavior and biochemical influences, including the effects of drugs on metabolic processes within the brain and the roles of different NEUROTRANSMITTERS and neuroregulatory substances.

behavioral neuroscience a branch of pyschology concerned with the simultaneous assessment or manipulation of both behavioral and neuroscience variables in an effort to understand and characterize the specific neural circuitry and mechanisms underlying behavioral propensities or capacities.

behavioral observation scale (**BOS**) a behavior-based measure used in evaluating job performance. The person carrying out the rating uses one or more scales to gauge the frequency with which the employee has demonstrated effective behaviors in the job. Compare BEHAVIORALLY ANCHORED RATING SCALE; MIXED-STANDARD SCALE. See also CRITICAL-INCIDENT TECHNIQUE.

behavioral pathogen a behavior or lifestyle that may increase the risk of developing illness or disability and may reduce life expectancy. Examples of behavioral pathogens are smoking, drug abuse, poor diet, unprotected sexual activity, and a sedentary lifestyle. Compare BEHAVIORAL IMMUNOGEN.

behavioral pattern see BEHAVIOR PATTERN.

behavioral pediatrics a multidisciplinary specialty in psychology that is often part of PEDIATRIC PSYCHOLOGY, clinical child psychology, and HEALTH PSYCHOLOGY. In prevention and intervention, practitioners address such problems as habit disorders, oppositional behavior, sleep and eating disorders, and physical health problems (e.g., traumatic brain injury). In the medical literature, it is also called **developmental-behavioral pediatrics**.

behavioral pharmacology a branch of psychology concerned with the physiological and behavioral mechanisms by which drugs operate, encompassing not only the effects of drugs on behavior but also how behavioral factors contribute to the actions of drugs and the ways in which they are used.

behavioral phenotype a pattern of motor, cognitive, linguistic, and social abnormalities that is consistently associated with a biological disorder. In some cases, the behavioral phenotype may constitute a discrete psychiatric disorder; in others, the abnormalities are usually not regarded as symptoms of a psychiatric disorder.

behavioral plasticity the degree to which a person's behavior can be influenced and modified by social experience and learning. High plasticity leaves ample room for change, whereas low plasticity involves inflexible behavior patterns.

behavioral procedure any psychological procedure based on the principles and techniques of BEHAVIOR THEORY. It may be used in basic research or in applied settings. See APPLIED BEHAVIOR ANALYSIS.

behavioral profile an overall representation of the behavioral characteristics of a participant in a test or experiment, obtained not only from the scores on each individual characteristic but also from the general pattern of these scores. The scores on each characteristic are often made more directly comparable by using percentiles or standard scores of one type or another.

behavioral psychology an approach to understanding psychological phenomena that focuses on observable aspects of behavior and makes use of BEHAVIOR THEORY for explanation. See also BEHAVIORISM.

behavioral psychotherapy see BEHAVIOR THERAPY.

behavioral rehearsal see BEHAVIOR REHEARSAL.

behavioral relaxation training a form of relaxation training and BEHAVIOR THERAPY that emphasizes labeling of sensations, modeling, reinforcement, and therapist feedback. See also PROGRESSIVE RELAXATION.

behavioral repertoire see REPERTOIRE.

behavioral risk factor any specific behavior or pattern of behaviors that increases an individual's likelihood of developing a disorder, disease, or syndrome (e.g., overeating or smoking).

behavioral science the study of the actions and reactions of human beings and animals using observational and experimental methods. Behavioral sciences comprise psychology, psychiatry, sociology, psychopharmacology, anthropology, and other disciplines.

behavioral segment see BEHAVIOR SEGMENT.

behavioral self-control training a technique in BEHAVIOR THERAPY that uses self-monitoring, self-evaluation, self-reinforcement, coaching, behavioral contracts, and relapse prevention techniques to help clients achieve active coping strategies, to increase their sense of mastery, and to decrease undesired habits (e.g., nail biting). See also BEHAVIORAL WEIGHT CONTROL THERAPIES.

behavioral sequence a combination of BEHAVIORAL INCIDENTS directed toward a particular goal or outcome (e.g., getting ready for work in the morning).

behavioral sex therapy a form of SEX THERAPY that focuses on behavioral analysis of presenting problems and on changes to behavioral sequences that hinder healthy sexual functioning through BEHAVIOR THERAPY methods. Behavioral sequences can include those that are relationship-based (e.g., communication behaviors) or specifically sexually based (e.g., avoidance of sexual stimuli).

behavioral sink the mutual attraction of animals into dense groupings with apparent detriment to individual animals. This was an unexpected result of studies in 1962 by U.S. experimental psychologist John B. Calhoun (1917–1995) in which animals were given unlimited food and water and allowed to reproduce without intervention. Population density increased rapidly, and the animals displayed increasing pathological behavior, typically close to the location of food and water.

behavioral specialization in animal behavior, adaptation to the conditions and challenges of a specific environment as applied to the selection of habitats, food, and mates. For example, when foraging for foods in competition with other species, those individuals that specialize on a few types of foods, known as **specialists**, should be more efficient in finding and processing food than generalists. Finches in the Galápagos Islands have diverged, some specializing on insects, others on seeds, and—within each of these broad groupings—some specialize on larger and others on smaller food items. Although behavioral specialization provides a competitive advantage in stable environments, generalists can respond more quickly to changing environments. Highly endangered species tend to show specialization.

behavioral study of obedience the experimental analysis, especially as carried out by Stanley MILGRAM in the 1960s, of individuals' willingness to obey the orders of an authority. In Milgram's experiment, each participant played the role of a teacher who was instructed to deliver painful electric shocks to another "participant" for each failure to answer a question correctly. The latter were in fact CONFEDERATES who did not actually receive shocks for their many deliberate errors. Milgram found that a substantial number of participants (65%) were completely obedient, delivering what they believed were shocks of increasing intensity despite the protestations and apparent suffering of the victim. See also AGENTIC STATE; DESTRUCTIVE OBEDIENCE.

behavioral technology experimentally established procedures (influenced by scientific behavior analysis) that are designed to produce behavioral change.

behavioral teratology the study of impairments in behavior that are produced by embryonic or fetal exposure to teratogens, that is, toxic substances that affect the developing organism (see TERATOGENIC).

behavioral theories of leadership see LEADERSHIP THEORIES.

behavioral toxicity an adverse behavioral change produced by psychotropic drugs, for example, insomnia, sedation, impaired psychomotor activity, or changes in mental status.

behavioral toxicology the study of the behavioral impact of toxic exposure. There is increasing evidence that many toxins have subclinical effects. At levels far below thresholds for detectable organic damage, subtle behavioral changes, often in neurosensory functioning, can occur. Perhaps the best known example is lead, which is now banned from gasoline and interior paint in many countries because of its low-level, behavioral-toxicological effects on developing children.

behavioral weight control therapies interventions that use the principles and techniques of BEHAVIOR THERAPY to help clients change eating and exercise habits to achieve and maintain a healthy weight. Practiced in group or individual sessions, these techniques include self-monitoring, behavioral contracts, environmental change (e.g., eating seated and only in a specific room), and reinforcement (e.g., social or monetary). See also BEHAVIORAL SELF-CONTROL TRAINING.

behavior analysis an approach to psychology, based on the experimental analysis of behavior, in which behavior is the subject matter for research rather than an indicator of underlying psychological entities or processes. Emphasis is placed on interactions between behavior and the environment. See APPLIED BEHAVIOR ANALYSIS; EXPERIMENTAL ANALYSIS OF BEHAVIOR. [originally developed by B. F. SKINNER]

behavior-based safety an approach in SAFETY ENGINEERING based on the premise that human behavior is learned and habitual and can thus be modified to avoid human error and accidents. Its main application is in the field of TRAINING SYSTEMS DESIGN, where the aim is to devise training programs that ingrain good safety habits. Additional applications include the design of organizational mechanisms to enhance workers' involvement in safety programs and the design of machines or equipment to accord with the behaviors and habits of workers or consumers.

behavior baseline see BEHAVIORAL BASELINE.

behavior chain see CHAIN OF BEHAVIOR.

behavior chaining see CHAINING.

behavior change 1. a systematic approach to changing behavior through the use of OPERANT CONDITIONING. **2.** any alteration or adjustment of behavior that affects a patient's functioning, brought about by psychotherapeutic or other interventions or occurring spontaneously.

behavior checklist a list of behaviors that are to be recorded each time they are observed by an experimental investigator or participant or by a clinician.

behavior clinic see MENTAL HEALTH CLINIC.

behavior consistency see BEHAVIORAL CONSISTENCY.

behavior-constraint theory the concept that an individual may acquire LEARNED HELPLESSNESS when repeated efforts fail to gain control over excessive or undesirable environmental stimuli.

behavior contagion see BEHAVIORAL CONTAGION.

behavior contract see BEHAVIORAL CONTRACT.

behavior control 1. the use of any type of psychological manipulation, such as threats or promises, to steer individual or group behavior in a desired direction. **2.** the misuse of invasive or intrusive treatments (e.g., drugs or aversive conditioning) to achieve control over the lives of individuals, including patients.

behavior criterion see BEHAVIORAL CRITERION.

behavior deficit see BEHAVIORAL DEFICIT.

behavior determinant any factor that produces a behavioral effect.

behavior disorder any persistent and repetitive pattern of behavior that violates societal norms or rules or that seriously impairs a person's functioning. The term is used in a very general sense to cover a wide range of disorders or other syndromes. Also called **behavioral disorder**. See also ATTENTION-DEFICIT/HYPERACTIVITY DISORDER; DISRUPTIVE BEHAVIOR DISORDER; PRIMARY BEHAVIOR DISORDER.

behavior disorders of childhood and adolescence observable behaviors in young people that deviate from the norm. The term is often used in SPECIAL EDUCATION and school placement.

behavior dysfunctions classification the classification of personal problems on the basis of behaviors rather than symptoms or hypothetical constructs. Such a classification leads the clinician to work on helping the patient change behaviors rather than treating syndromes or diseases.

behavior episode a unit or sequence of activity with a relatively well-defined start and end. Also called **behavior unit**.

behavior field any set of stimuli or conditions, or accumulation of factors, that produces a behavioral effect.

behavior genetics the study of familial or hereditary

behavior patterns and of the genetic mechanisms of behavior traits. Also called **behavioral genetics**.

behavior hierarchy a ranking of possible responses based on the relative probabilities of their being elicited, with more probable behaviors ranked higher than less probable behaviors. Also called **behavioral hierarchy**.

behavior homeostasis see BEHAVIORAL HOMEOSTASIS.

behavior homology see BEHAVIORAL HOMOLOGY.

behavior integration see BEHAVIORAL INTEGRATION.

behaviorism *n.* an approach to psychology, formulated in 1913 by John B. WATSON, based on the study of objective, observable facts rather than subjective, qualitative processes, such as feelings, motives, and consciousness. To make psychology a naturalistic science, Watson proposed to limit it to quantitative events, such as stimulus–response relationships, effects of conditioning, physiological processes, and a study of human and animal behavior, all of which can best be investigated through laboratory experiments that yield objective measures under controlled conditions. Historically, behaviorists held that mind was not a proper topic for scientific study since mental events are subjective and not independently verifiable. With its emphasis on activity as an adaptive function, behaviorism is seen as an outgrowth of FUNCTIONALISM. See DESCRIPTIVE BEHAVIORISM; METHODOLOGICAL BEHAVIORISM; NEOBEHAVIORISM; RADICAL BEHAVIORISM.

behaviorist *n.* a person who espouses the principles of BEHAVIORISM and whose activities are consciously guided by those principles. See also BEHAVIOR ANALYSIS; BEHAVIOR MODIFICATION.

behavior mapping a technique of studying the activities of individuals within a space by noting what happens where. The degree of variability of behavior, as well as its association with certain types of environmental features, is a useful starting point to build or test hypotheses about, for example, architectural design. See also ARCHITECTURAL PROGRAMMING.

behavior modification the use of OPERANT CONDITIONING, BIOFEEDBACK, MODELING, AVERSIVE CONDITIONING, RECIPROCAL INHIBITION, or other learning techniques as a means of changing human behavior. For example, behavioral modification is used in clinical contexts to improve adaptation and alleviate symptoms and in industrial and organizational contexts to encourage employees to adopt safe work practices. The term is often used synonymously with BEHAVIOR THERAPY.

behavior observation a recording or evaluation (or both) of the ongoing behavior of one or more research participants by one or more observers. Observations may be made—using charts, checklists, rating scales, etc.—either directly as the behavior occurs or from such media as film, videotape, or audiotape.

behavior pattern a complex arrangement of two or more responses that occur in a prescribed order. Behavior patterns are also referred to as CHAINS OF BEHAVIOR, highlighting their nature as a complex linking of simpler segments of behavior. They may be formed via the OPERANT CONDITIONING of various segments presented in the appropriate order. Also called **behavioral pattern**.

behavior problem a pattern of disruptive behavior that generally falls within social norms and does not seriously impair a person's functioning.

behavior rating a rating of the degree to which a participant shows each of several behaviors in a given situation.

Behavior Rating scale see BAYLEY SCALES OF INFANT AND TODDLER DEVELOPMENT.

behavior record a record of observations that provides a complete and accurate account of an organism's behavior within a specified time frame. In animal studies this involves documenting all observable actions of an individual within a time sample of behavior. In educational psychology, a behavioral record is a teacher's written observations regarding a student's behavior and personality (see ANECDOTAL RECORD).

behavior rehearsal 1. a technique used in BEHAVIOR THERAPY or COGNITIVE BEHAVIOR THERAPY for modifying or enhancing social or interpersonal skills. The therapist introduces effective interpersonal strategies or behavior patterns to be practiced and rehearsed by the client until these are ready to be used in a real-life situation. The technique is also commonly used in ASSERTIVENESS TRAINING. Also called **behavioral rehearsal**. **2.** more generally, the practice of an overt action.

behavior reversal a method of BEHAVIOR MODIFICATION in which the client, supervised by the therapist, practices desirable responses to interpersonal conflicts, which are often opposite to his or her usual behavior.

behavior sampling the process of recording a set of observations of a participant's behavior during a designated time frame. Behavior sampling may be conducted over multiple periods of observation in either natural or laboratory settings, with or without the awareness of the participant.

behavior segment a distinct response or BEHAVIOR EPISODE that, when linked with other responses, forms a BEHAVIOR PATTERN or chain. Also called **behavioral segment**.

behavior setting the geographical, physical, and social situation as it affects relationships and behavior. See also ECOLOGICAL PSYCHOLOGY. [identified by U.S. developmental psychologist Roger C. Barker (1903–1990)]

behavior shaping see SHAPING.

behavior system 1. the different activities that can be undertaken to reach the same goal or carry out the same function, for example, communication is achieved through writing, speaking, or gestures. **2.** the expression of important motives (e.g., hunger, sex, aggression), which varies between cultures and among individuals within the same culture who have had different training and experiences. Also called **activity system**.

behavior theory the assumption that behavior, including its acquisition, development, and maintenance, can be adequately explained by principles of learning. Behavior theory attempts to describe the general principles of behavior, often deriving these laws from controlled studies of animals. Behavior theory encompasses historical approaches to formal theorizing, such as those of C. L. HULL and K. W. SPENCE, and the operant theory of B. F. SKINNER, as well as contemporary approaches to behavior. Also called **general behavior theory**.

behavior therapy a form of psychotherapy that applies the principles of learning, OPERANT CONDITIONING, and PAVLOVIAN CONDITIONING to eliminate symptoms and modify ineffective or maladaptive patterns of behavior. The focus of this therapy is upon the behavior itself and the CONTINGENCIES and environmental factors that reinforce it, rather than exploration of the underlying psychological causes of the behavior. A wide variety of techniques are used in behavior therapy, such as BEHAVIOR REHEARSAL, BIOFEEDBACK, MODELING, and SYSTEMATIC DESENSITIZATION. Also called **behavioral psychotherapy**; **conditioning therapy**.

behavior unit see BEHAVIOR EPISODE.

Behrens–Fisher problem the classical and as yet unsolved statistical problem of testing for the equality of the means of two normally distributed populations without making any assumptions about the variances of the populations. [W. U. **Behrens**; Sir Ronald Aylmer **Fisher** (1890–1962), British statistician]

being-beyond-the-world *n.* in existential psychology, the potential for human beings to transcend the limitations of BEING-IN-THE-WORLD, usually through selfless love. See also DASEIN. [introduced by Swiss psychologist Ludwig Binswanger (1881–1966)]

being cognition 1. (**B-cognition**) in the humanistic psychology of Abraham MASLOW, an exceptional type of cognition that can be distinguished from one's everyday perception of reality (**deficiency cognition** or **D-cognition**). Being cognition takes one of two forms: In the first, a person is aware of the whole universe and the interrelatedness of everything within it, including the perceiver; in the second, a person becomes entirely focused on a single object (e.g., a natural phenomenon, a work of art, or a loved person) to the extent that the rest of the universe, including the perceiver, seems to disappear. According to Maslow, self-actualizers (see SELF-ACTUALIZATION) frequently experience being cognitions. See also PEAK EXPERIENCE; TIMELESS MOMENT. **2.** awareness of the inner core of one's existence, that is, one's self or identity.

being-in-the-world *n.* in theories and clinical approaches derived from EXISTENTIALISM, the particular type of being characteristic of humans, in contrast to the type of being of animals, inanimate objects, or abstractions. The term is roughly synonymous with DASEIN, the term used by German philosopher Martin Heidegger (1889–1976). The word "being" is meant to emphasize that human existence is an activity more than a state or condition. Similarly, "world" is meant to convey a much richer and more meaningful ground for human life than would be conveyed by a more sterile term, such as "environment." Being-in-the-world is by its very nature oriented toward meaning and growth; while it characterizes the type of being of all humans, it is also unique for every person, and can be seen to be offering an explanation of what in other psychological traditions might be called IDENTITY or SELF. Compare BEING-BEYOND-THE-WORLD. See also WORLD DESIGN.

being love (**B-love**) in Abraham MASLOW'S HUMANISTIC PSYCHOLOGY, a form of love characterized by mutuality, genuine concern for another's welfare and pleasure, and reduced dependency, selfishness, and jealousy. B-love is one of the qualities Maslow ascribes to self-actualizers (see SELF-ACTUALIZATION). Compare DEFICIENCY LOVE.

being motivation see METAMOTIVATION.

being–not being a paraphrase of the fundamental question that, according to German philosopher Martin Heidegger (1889–1976), motivates human beings, namely, the worry or concern about dying and not being here any longer. See also DASEIN.

being psychology a psychological perspective that deals with "persons insofar as they are ends-in-themselves." It is concerned with the sacred, the unique, and the incomparable in people and things. [developed by Abraham MASLOW]

being values see METANEEDS.

Békésy audiometer the first automatic AUDIOMETER with patient-controlled push-button responses and an ink recorder to graph the audiogram throughout the testing process. It yields tracings for continuous and interrupted tones at controlled frequencies. [Georg von **Békésy** (1899–1972), Hungarian-born U.S. physicist]

Békésy traveling wave see BASILAR MEMBRANE. [Georg von **Békésy**]

Bekhterev's nystagmus a form of NYSTAGMUS that develops after the loss of a second LABYRINTH. Nystagmus occurs after the destruction of the first of the two labyrinths but eventually subsides, only to recur as a compensatory effect after loss of the second labyrinth. Also called **compensatory nystagmus**. [Vladimir Mikhailovich **Bekhterev** (1857–1927), Russian neuropathologist]

bel (symbol: B) *n.* see DECIBEL.

belief *n.* **1.** in the psychology of attitudes, an association of some characteristic or attribute, usually evaluative in nature, with an ATTITUDE OBJECT (e.g., this car is reliable). See also BASES OF AN ATTITUDE. **2.** more generally, acceptance of the truth, reality, or validity of something (e.g., a phenomenon, a person's veracity, a theory). See also RELIGIOUS FAITH.

belief–desire reasoning the process by which one explains and predicts another's behavior on the basis of one's understanding of the other's desires and beliefs. Belief–desire reasoning is the basis for THEORY OF MIND. See also MINDBLINDNESS.

belief perseverance the tendency to maintain a belief even after the information that originally gave rise to it has been refuted or otherwise shown to be inaccurate.

belief system a set of beliefs, attitudes, or both that are associated with one another in memory. See also ATTITUDE SYSTEM.

belittling *n.* acting, speaking, or thinking in a way intended to lessen the perceived value or status of the target. **—belittle** *vb.*

belladonna alkaloids substances obtained from the shrub *Atropa belladonna* (commonly known as belladonna or deadly nightshade). They were known to the ancient Hindus and were used in the Middle Ages as poisons (the genus is named for Atropos, eldest of the mythological Fates, who cuts the thread of life). Their pharmacology was unknown until the 1860s, when they were found to affect heart rate, salivary secretion, and other body functions. ATROPINE and SCOPOLAMINE are the best known examples.

belladonna delirium delirium due to the effects on the central nervous system of large doses of belladonna alkaloids, such as atropine and scopolamine. Symptoms, in addition to delirium, include hallucinations and overactive coordinated limb movements.

belladonna poisoning poisoning due to ingestion of berries of the belladonna plant, *Atropa belladonna* (also called deadly nightshade). These contain atropine, which paralyzes the parasympathetic nervous system. The symptoms include visual hallucinations, mutism, dilated pupils, unresponsiveness, and disorientation.

bell and pad a device used in treatments aimed at controlling nocturnal enuresis (bed-wetting) in children. If the child urinates, an electric circuit is closed via the wetted pad and a bell rings, awakening the child.

bell curve the characteristic curve obtained by plotting a graph of a NORMAL DISTRIBUTION. With a large rounded peak tapering off on either side, it resembles a cross-sectional representation of a bell. Also called **bell-shaped curve**.

belle indifférence see LA BELLE INDIFFÉRENCE.

Bellevue scale see WECHSLER–BELLEVUE INTELLIGENCE SCALE.

Bell–Magendie law the principle that the VENTRAL ROOTS of the spinal cord are motor in function and DORSAL ROOTS are sensory. [Charles **Bell** (1774–1842), British surgeon and anatomist; François **Magendie** (1783–1855), French physiologist]

Bell's mania see LETHAL CATATONIA. [Charles **Bell**]

Bell's palsy paralysis of the seventh cranial nerve (see FACIAL NERVE) involving one side of the face, characterized by weakness of the muscles on the affected side evidenced by a distorted expression, inability to close the eye, and changes in taste. The onset is usually sudden, often beginning as a pain behind the ear and progressing to paralysis within a few hours. The condition most commonly results from a viral infection, leading to a swollen nerve that becomes compressed in its passage through the temporal bone, and usually resolves spontaneously. [Charles **Bell**]

Bell's phenomenon the upward and outward movement of the eye that normally occurs when attempting to close the eye. It is seen most prominently in individuals with Bell's palsy when they attempt to close the eye on the affected side. [Charles **Bell**]

belonging *n.* the feeling of being accepted and approved by a group or by society as a whole. Also called **belongingness**. Compare ALIENATION; ESTRANGEMENT.

belongingness principle see PRINCIPLE OF BELONGINGNESS.

below average denoting a range of intellectual functioning that is just below the average range, roughly between 80 and 90 on most IQ scales, and is inconsistent with the presence of mental retardation. Such a range may also be described as **low normal** or **dull normal**, but below average is now the preferred term.

Bem Sex Role Inventory (**BSRI**) a MASCULINITY–FEMININITY TEST in which participants rate themselves on 60 traits regarded as characteristically masculine or feminine. Masculinity and femininity are treated as independent variables; people with high scores for both types of traits (e.g., assertiveness plus warmth) are classified as androgynous (see ANDROGYNY), and people with low scores for both feminine and masculine traits are classified as undifferentiated. [Sandra **Bem** (1944–), U.S. psychologist]

Benadryl *n.* a trade name for DIPHENHYDRAMINE.

benchmark *n.* a measure of best performance for a particular process or outcome, which can be used as a reference to improve performance in other settings.

benchmark job a specific job that is used as a reference point in evaluating other jobs for the purpose of setting pay levels. Jobs chosen as benchmarks tend to be well known, to change very little over time, to have pay rates that are generally accepted as fair, and to represent significant points on the job evaluation scale that is being used. See CLASSIFICATION METHOD; FACTOR-COMPARISON METHOD.

bench trial a trial in which the judge, not the jury, decides the defendant's guilt or innocence.

Bender Visual–Motor Gestalt Test a visuoconstructive test in which the participant first copies line drawings of 16 geometric figures onto blank pieces of paper (Copy Phase) and then redraws them from memory (Recall Phase). All reproductions are scored on a 5-point scale, ranging from 0 (no resemblance) to 4 (nearly perfect). The test is appropriate for individuals aged 4 years and older and is used to assess visual–motor functioning and perceptual ability as well as to diagnose neuropsychological impairment. It is sometimes also used, albeit controversially, in conjunction with other personality tests to determine the presence of emotional and psychological disturbances, such as schizophrenia. Originally developed in 1938, the test (often shortened to **Bender-Gestalt**) is now in its second edition (published in 2003). [Lauretta **Bender** (1897–1987), U.S. psychiatrist]

bends *n.* see DECOMPRESSION SICKNESS.

beneffectance *n.* a combination of benevolence and effectiveness. According to U.S. social psychologist Anthony G. Greenwald (1939–), people routinely distort memories of their own prior actions so as to enhance their own sense of beneffectance. That is, they engage in self-deception so as to appear to themselves and others as morally good, well-intentioned, competent, and successful. See POSITIVE ILLUSION.

benevolent eclecticism the use of diverse models, methods, and perspectives to achieve valued scientific, therapeutic, or managerial goals. Hans EYSENCK, for example, argued for such an approach in the study of personality and individual differences. See ECLECTICISM.

Benham's top a disk with a black and white design that appears to consist of colored rings when rotated. [Charles E. **Benham** (1860–1929), British scientist]

benign *adj.* **1.** in mental health, denoting a disorder or illness that is not serious and has a favorable prognosis. **2.** denoting a disease condition that is relatively mild, transient, or not associated with serious pathology. See also NEOPLASM. Compare MALIGNANT.

benign hereditary tremor see ESSENTIAL TREMOR.

benign senescence (**benign senescent forgetfulness**) see AGE-ASSOCIATED MEMORY IMPAIRMENT.

benign stupor 1. a state of unresponsiveness, immobility, and indifference to one's surroundings that is unlikely to be permanent. **2.** PSYCHOMOTOR RETARDATION and apathy that often occur in severe MAJOR DEPRESSIVE EPISODES.

Bennett Differential Aptitude Tests see DIFFERENTIAL APTITUDE TESTS. [George Kettner **Bennett** (1904–1975), U.S. psychologist]

benny *n.* (*pl.* **bennies**) slang for an amphetamine tablet. See AMPHETAMINES.

Benton Visual Retention Test (**BVRT**) a drawing and recall task in which the participant is briefly shown cards containing two or three geometric designs and then asked to reproduce them from memory. The test assesses visual perception, short-term visual memory, and visuoconstructional ability; it is scored for the number of correct reproductions and for the number and types of errors. [developed in 1946 by Arthur Lester **Benton** (1909–), U.S. psychologist]

Benzedrine *n.* a trade name for AMPHETAMINE.

Benzedrine dependence see AMPHETAMINE DEPENDENCE.

benzene a volatile solvent that, when chronically inhaled, can cause kidney failure and death. See INHALANT. See also INHALANT ABUSE; INHALANT DEPENDENCE.

benzisoxazoles *pl. n.* a class of ATYPICAL ANTIPSYCHOTICS that include RISPERIDONE and ILOPERIDONE.

benzodiazepine agonists drugs that facilitate the binding of benzodiazepines to subunits of the benzodiazepine receptor complex (see $GABA_A$ RECEPTOR).

benzodiazepine antagonists agents that prevent the binding of benzodiazepines and related chemicals to the benzodiazepine receptor site on the $GABA_A$ RECEPTOR complex. Benzodiazepine antagonists in clinical use include FLUMAZENIL.

benzodiazepines *pl. n.* a family of drugs (CNS DEPRES-

SANTS) with hypnotic and anxiolytic properties that also produce sedation and relaxation of skeletal muscles. Benzodiazepines act as GABA AGONISTS. They are commonly used in the treatment of generalized anxiety and insomnia and are useful in the management of acute withdrawal from alcohol and in seizure disorders. Clinically introduced in the 1960s, they rapidly supplanted the barbiturates, largely due to their significantly lower toxicity in overdose. It is now known that members of the group show considerable variation in ABUSE POTENTIAL: Prolonged use can lead to tolerance and psychological and physical dependence (see SEDATIVE, HYPNOTIC, OR ANXIOLYTIC DEPENDENCE). The prototype drug of the group is CHLORDIAZEPOXIDE. See also ALPRAZOLAM; BROMAZEPAM; CLONAZEPAM; CLORAZEPATE; DIAZEPAM; ESTAZOLAM; FLURAZEPAM; LORAZEPAM; MIDAZOLAM; OXAZEPAM; QUAZEPAM; TEMAZEPAM; TRIAZOLAM.

benzothiadiazides *pl. n.* see THIAZIDE DIURETICS.

benztropine *n.* an ANTICHOLINERGIC DRUG used in the management of adverse side effects of conventional or first-generation antipsychotic drugs and as an adjunct in the treatment of Parkinson's disease. U.S. trade name: **Cogentin**.

berdache *n.* see TWO-SPIRIT.

bereavement *n.* a feeling of loss, especially over the death of a friend or loved one. The bereaved person may experience emotional pain and distress (see GRIEF; TRAUMATIC GRIEF) and may or may not express this distress to others (see MOURNING; DISENFRANCHISED GRIEF); individual grief and mourning responses vary. Bereavement may also signify a change in social status (e.g., from wife to widow). **—bereaved** *adj.*

bereavement program any of a variety of treatment services (e.g., support groups, GRIEF COUNSELING) offered to individuals coping with the death of a loved one.

bereavement therapy therapy or counseling provided to individuals who are experiencing loss and grief following the death of a loved one. The therapy may include issues of separation, grieving, and carrying on with life. See also GRIEF COUNSELING.

Berger rhythm see ALPHA WAVE. [Hans **Berger** (1873–1944), German neuropsychiatrist]

beriberi *n.* a nutritional disease caused by thiamine (vitamin B_1) deficiency and characterized by neurological symptoms and cardiovascular abnormalities. See also WERNICKE'S ENCEPHALOPATHY.

Berkeley Growth Study a study seeking to understand the mental abilities relevant at different ages of life, as well as their importance. A group of participants was followed over a period of over 50 years (from the late 1920s to the 1980s). [conducted by Nancy BAYLEY]

Bernoulli distribution see BINOMIAL DISTRIBUTION. [Jacques **Bernoulli** (1654–1705), Swiss mathematician and scientist]

Bernoulli trial a sequence of outcomes of an experiment of chance in which only one of two outcomes is possible on each trial (0 or 1; success or failure), the probability of each outcome is constant from trial to trial, and the trials are independent. [Jacques **Bernoulli**]

Berry syndrome see TREACHER COLLINS SYNDROME. [reported in 1889 by George Andreas **Berry** (1853–1929), British physician]

berserk 1. *adj.* destructive or violent. **2.** *n.* one who is destructive or violent. The term is derived from an Old Norse word literally meaning "bearshirt," used to describe ancient Norse warriors who wore bearskins during battle and fought with great strength and fury.

best-answer test a test in which participants examine several possible solutions to a problem, or reasons for a situation, and choose the one they consider most appropriate. Also called **best-reason test**.

best-first search a problem-solving strategy in which various possible paths to a solution are evaluated in terms of the likelihood that they will prove successful and the path judged most promising is attempted first. See HEURISTIC SEARCH.

best frequency (**BF**) see TONOTOPIC ORGANIZATION; TUNING CURVE.

bestiality *n.* see ZOOERASTY.

best interests of the child a standard used by courts to make child custody decisions in divorce proceedings, namely that the potential for the child to lead a happy and successful life should be given greater weight than the rights of either parent.

best-reason test see BEST-ANSWER TEST.

beta (symbol: β) *n.* **1.** the probability of a TYPE II ERROR. **2.** see BETA WEIGHT.

beta-adrenergic blocking agents see BETA BLOCKERS.

beta-adrenergic receptor kinase (**barK**) a CYCLIC AMP-dependent enzyme that is responsible for inactivating BETA ADRENORECEPTORS, thereby inhibiting the ability of these receptors to activate SECOND MESSENGERS within the cell. barK is a member of a family of G PROTEIN-coupled receptor kinases that work only when receptors are occupied by an agonist.

beta adrenoreceptor one of the two types of receptor that bind NOREPINEPHRINE, the other being the ALPHA ADRENORECEPTOR. There are two main subtypes, designated β_1 and β_2. β_1-Adrenoreceptors mediate stimulation of heart muscle, causing a faster and stronger heartbeat. β_2-Adrenoceptors are associated with relaxation of smooth muscle, causing (for example) dilation of blood vessels, widening of airways, and relaxation of the uterus. Also called **beta-adrenergic receptor**; **beta adrenoceptor**; **beta receptor**.

beta-adrenoreceptor blocking agents see BETA BLOCKERS.

beta alcoholism the second stage of alcoholism. It is characterized by undisciplined drinking that may affect the stomach, liver, pancreas, or kidneys and may cause POLYNEUROPATHY but does not yet involve physical or psychological dependence. The patient may also exhibit nutritional-deficiency symptoms, diminished job efficiency, or both. See also ALPHA ALCOHOLISM; GAMMA ALCOHOLISM; DELTA ALCOHOLISM; EPSILON ALCOHOLISM. [defined by U.S. physician Elvin M. Jellinek (1890–1963)]

beta-amyloid (**β-amyloid**) *n.* a protein that accumulates in SENILE PLAQUES in the brains of patients with ALZHEIMER'S DISEASE.

beta blockers drugs that act as competitive antagonists at BETA ADRENORECEPTORS, thereby reducing catecholamine-mediated neurotransmission. Beta blockers have a complex pharmacology, but their main effects are (a) to reduce activity of heart muscle and slow heart rate and (b) to constrict smooth muscle in the bronchial tree and vasculature. Beta blockers are used primarily in managing hypertension but also in the treatment of ESSENTIAL TREMOR. They have some application in mental health, occasionally to relieve symptoms of peripheral anxiety (tremor, quavering voice) accompanying certain types of social phobia or to reduce tremor induced by lithium or antipsychotic drugs. Also called **beta-adrenergic blocking agents**; **beta-adrenoreceptor blocking agents**.

beta coefficient see BETA WEIGHT.

beta-endorphin *n.* a neuropeptide involved in pain and hunger that produces its analgesic effects by binding to OPIOID RECEPTORS and disinhibiting dopamine pathways. See ENDOGENOUS OPIOID; ENDORPHINS.

beta error see TYPE II ERROR.

Beta examination see ARMY TESTS.

beta-glucuronidase deficiency deficiency of the enzyme β-glucuronidase, which is involved in the breakdown of complex carbohydrates (see MUCOPOLYSACCHARIDOSIS). This deficiency is characterized by enlarged liver or spleen, dermatan sulphate in the urine, bone malformations, white-cell inclusions, and mental retardation. The condition occurs in conjunction with abnormalities in the short arm of chromosome 7. Also called **mucopolysaccharidosis Type VII**; **Sly syndrome**.

beta level the probability of failing to reject the NULL HYPOTHESIS when it is in fact false, that is, making a TYPE II ERROR.

beta movement a form of APPARENT MOVEMENT in which successive presentations of stationary stimuli across the visual field produce the perception of a single, smoothly moving stimulus. Also called **beta motion**.

beta receptor see BETA ADRENORECEPTOR.

beta rhythm see BETA WAVE.

beta-secretase (**β-secretase**) *n.* an enzyme that cleaves AMYLOID PRECURSOR PROTEIN forming BETA-AMYLOID, accumulation of which in brain tissue can lead to ALZHEIMER'S DISEASE.

Beta test see ARMY TESTS.

beta wave in electroencephalography, the type of BRAIN WAVE associated with an alert and activated cerebral cortex. The frequency generally is above 12 Hz and may range upward of 40 Hz. Beta activity is recorded during intense mental activity, but it also occurs as a sign of anxiety or apprehension. Also called **beta rhythm**.

beta weight (symbol: β) in REGRESSION ANALYSIS, the multiplicative constant that reflects a variable's contribution to the prediction of a criterion, given the other variables in the prediction equation (e.g., b in $y = a + bx$). Also called **beta coefficient**.

betel nut the seed of the areca palm (*Areca catechu*), which is chewed as a stimulant by local populations of India and the islands of the Indian and Pacific Oceans. It contains the drug ARECOLINE.

bethanechol *n.* a CHOLINERGIC DRUG used to stimulate movement in the bladder in the management of such conditions as LOWER MOTOR NEURON disease and postoperative or postpartum urinary retention. U.S. trade name: **Urecholine**.

betrayal trauma a CONCEPTUAL MODEL for explaining why some children are unable to access memories of prior sexual abuse. According to the theory, this sort of REPRESSION occurs when the perpetrator of the abuse is an adult on whom the child is emotionally dependent and it develops out of the child's need to preserve the ATTACHMENT BOND; hence the child is unable to access the stored memories of the abuse while the need for attachment is still strong. [first proposed in 1991 by U.S. cognitive psychologist Jennifer J. Freyd]

between-groups design an experimental design in which the effect of one or more treatments is assessed by comparing the data generated by groups of participants that have each been exposed to only one of the treatments. Usually the participants have been randomly assigned to the single treatment to which they are exposed.

between-groups variance a statistic used in the ANALYSIS OF VARIANCE that reflects the degree to which the several group means differ from one another. An example is the variation in experimental scores that is attributable only to membership in different groups or exposure to different experimental conditions, which therefore reflects the effect of such differences. Compare WITHIN-GROUP VARIANCE.

between-subjects design any of a large number of experimental designs in which each person, or other sampling unit, experiences only one experimental condition (treatment) and therefore contributes only a single final score to enter into the analysis. Compare WITHIN-SUBJECTS DESIGN.

Betz cell a type of large PYRAMIDAL CELL found in the fifth layer of the cerebral cortex (see CORTICAL LAYERS), mainly in MOTOR CORTEX. Betz cells are associated with muscle movement and have a low threshold of stimulation. [Vladimir A. **Betz** (1834–1894), Russian anatomist]

BEV abbreviation for BLACK ENGLISH Vernacular.

bewildered *adj.* confused or puzzled, especially when presented with conflicting situations or statements. See also DISORIENTATION. **—bewilderment** *n.*

Bewusstseinslage *n.* state of consciousness (German): a term used by followers of the WÜRZBERG SCHOOL to denote mental experiences or activities that cannot readily be analyzed into a chain of associations based on images or sensations. See IMAGELESS THOUGHT.

beyondism *n.* a secular "religion" devised by British-born U.S. psychologist Raymond B. Cattell (1905–1998) on the basis of evolutionary theory. Beyondism holds that evolution will lead to the advancement of humanity; therefore, anything that furthers evolution is good, and anything that hinders it is not good. If allowed to operate freely, evolutionary processes will solve many of the world's problems through evolutionary competition, leading to the survival of some civilizations and the extinction of others. Because of this belief, and its support for voluntary EUGENICS, beyondism has received much criticism as racist. See POLITICAL GENETICS.

beyond reasonable doubt the standard of PROOF required in a criminal trial. In order to convict a defendant, a jury must be convinced of the defendant's guilt "beyond any reasonable doubt," meaning there is no justifiable, rational cause for jury members to doubt the defendant's guilt. This standard is considered to be equivalent to a moral certainty but is less than an absolute certainty.

Bezold–Brücke phenomenon the perception that bright illumination makes yellowish stimuli appear closer to yellow and bluish stimuli closer to blue. [Johann Friedrich W. von **Bezold** (1837–1907), German physicist; Ernst Wilhelm von **Brücker** (1819–1892), German physiologist]

BF abbreviation for best frequency. See TUNING CURVE.

B fiber a myelinated nerve fiber of the autonomic nervous system that transmits nerve impulses to the SYMPATHETIC CHAIN. B fibers are approximately 2 μm or less in diameter and carry impulses at speeds of 3–15 m/s. Compare A FIBER; C FIBER.

BFOQ abbreviation for BONA FIDE OCCUPATIONAL QUALIFICATION.

bhang *n.* the mildest preparation of CANNABIS, consisting of the whole *Cannabis sativa* plant, dried and powdered.

BHS abbreviation for BECK HOPELESSNESS SCALE.

bi- (**bin-**) *prefix* two, twice, or double.

BIA abbreviation for BODY IMAGE ASSESSMENT.

bias *n.* **1.** an inclination, tendency, or preference. See also PREJUDICE. **2.** in research, systematic and directional error arising during SAMPLING, data collection, data analysis, or data interpretation. **3.** see RESPONSE BIAS. **4.** any aspect of a test that is unrelated to the construct assessed by the test but that yields systematic, differential predictions or outcomes for individuals who are members of different groups. An example is CULTURAL TEST BIAS. See TEST BIAS. **5.** in statistics, the difference between the expected value of a statistic and the actual value that is obtained. **—biased** *adj.*

biased elaboration the tendency to generate particular evaluative responses preferentially when elaborating attitude-relevant information. See also BIASING FACTOR; ELABORATION; OBJECTIVE ELABORATION.

biased estimator an ESTIMATOR whose value differs from that of the population parameter it purports to estimate.

biased sampling drawing an unrepresentative sample of a population.

biased scanning a hypothetical process in which people alter or maintain a particular SELF-CONCEPT by searching the contents of their memory in a selective manner, focusing especially on memories that fit a predetermined impression. The theory assumes that people have a wide range of implicit memories, enabling them to support different views of the self by selectively remembering certain events.

biasing factor a variable that serves to bias the ELABORATION of attitude-relevant information. See also BIASED ELABORATION; MULTIPLE ROLES IN PERSUASION.

biastophilia *n.* a PARAPHILIA involving sexual arousal and excitement based on surprising or attacking a stranger sexually.

bibliotherapy *n.* a form of therapy that uses structured reading material. Bibliotherapy is often used as an adjunct to psychotherapy for such purposes as reinforcing specific in-session concepts or strategies or enhancing lifestyle changes. Carefully chosen readings are also used by some individuals as SELF-HELP tools to foster personal growth and development, for example, by facilitating communication and open discussion of problems, enhancing self-concept, and encouraging release of stress and emotional tension.

bicalutamide *n.* see ANTIANDROGEN.

bicameralism *n.* a highly controversial theory of primitive human mentality (posited to predate the development of consciousness) in which cognitive functions are separated into one section of the brain that "speaks" or "orders," specifically through auditory hallucination, and another section that "listens" or "obeys." The concept, proposed by U.S. psychologist John Jaynes in his 1976 publication *The Origins of Consciousness in the Breakdown of the Bicameral Mind,* has not received significant attention in neuropsychological research, although analogies have been drawn to neurological models describing the differing functions of the right and left hemispheres of the brain.

bicuculline *n.* an alkaloid derived from the plant *Dicentra cucullaria* that acts as a competitive GABA ANTAGONIST at $GABA_A$ RECEPTORS and has strong convulsant effects. It has no modern clinical applications but may be used experimentally in laboratory animals for various research purposes.

bidialectism *n.* the regular use of two or more DIALECTS of a language by a person or within a SPEECH COMMUNITY. Also called **bidialectalism**. See also CODE SWITCHING; DIGLOSSIA. **—bidialectal** *adj.*

bidirectionality of structure and function the reciprocal interaction of structure and function to produce a pattern of development, structure being some physical characteristic of an organism (e.g., brain cells) and function being activity emanating from that structure (e.g., the electrical firing of those cells). Such bidirectionality implies that development is not governed simply by a reading-out of the genetic code but is a dynamic process involving interaction at all levels of organization, from the genetic through the cultural.

Bidwell's ghost a second visual AFTERIMAGE that appears in a hue complementary to the stimulus. Also called **Purkinje afterimage**. [Shelford **Bidwell** (1848–1909), British physicist]

Bielschowsky's disease a condition marked by temporary loss of the ability to move the eyes in a vertical direction, up or down, in a synchronized manner. [Alfred **Bielschowsky** (1871–1940), German ophthalmologist]

Biemond's syndrome a disorder that combines mental retardation, growth impairment, abnormalities in the iris (a hole, split, or cleft), and excess fingers or toes. [A. **Biemond** (1902–), French physician]

bigamy *n.* the crime of marrying someone when already married to someone else. In cultures that permit individuals to have more than one spouse this practice should be referred to as POLYGAMY and not bigamy. Compare MONOGAMY. **—bigamist** *n.* **—bigamous** *adj.*

Big Brothers Big Sisters of America a volunteer association in which individuals act as mentors and positive role models to children typically from single-parent families. The Big Brother and Big Sister programs were created separately, and the two organizations merged in 1977.

Big Five personality model a model of the primary dimensions of individual differences in personality. The dimensions are usually labeled EXTRAVERSION, NEUROTICISM, AGREEABLENESS, CONSCIENTIOUSNESS, and OPENNESS TO EXPERIENCE, though the labels vary somewhat among researchers. See also FIVE-FACTOR PERSONALITY MODEL. [described by (among others) U.S. psychologists Lewis R. Goldberg (1932–) and Gerard T. Saucier]

big lie a PROPAGANDA device in which a false statement of extreme magnitude is constantly repeated in order to persuade the public. The assumption is that a big lie is less likely to be challenged than a lesser one because people will assume that evidence existed to support a statement of such magnitude. Josef Goebbels, the propaganda minister in Nazi Germany, repeatedly employed this technique when he charged the Nazis' enemies with heinous crimes.

bigorexia *n.* see MUSCLE DYSMORPHIA.

Big Sister program see BIG BROTHERS BIG SISTERS OF AMERICA.

bilabial 1. *adj.* pertaining to the two lips. **2.** *adj.* denoting a speech sound made with both lips, which stop or modify the airstream, for example, [b], [p], [m], or [w]. **3.** *n.* a bilabial speech sound. See LABIAL.

bilateral *adj.* **1.** having or formed of two sides. **2.** relating to or occurring on both sides of the body. **3.** having or marked by BILATERAL SYMMETRY. **—bilaterally** *adv.*

bilateral descent in anthropology, a system of descent or inheritance in which both the male and the female lines of descent are recognized. Also called **bilineal descent**. Compare UNILATERAL DESCENT. See also DESCENT GROUP; MATRIARCHY; PATRIARCHY.

bilateral lesion a lesion that involves both sides of an organ, especially both cerebral hemispheres, which can arise directly through injury or disease or secondarily through such mechanisms as EDEMA.

bilateral symmetry symmetrical arrangement around a central axis such that the right and left halves of an organism's body are approximately mirror images of each other. The human body shows bilateral symmetry.

bilateral transfer TRANSFER OF TRAINING or patterns of performance for a skill from one side of the body, where the skill was originally learned and primarily used, to the other side of the body. Observations of bilateral transfer in such skills as handwriting have been taken as evidence for the existence of a GENERALIZED MOTOR PROGRAM.

Bildungsroman *n.* a type of novel that describes the formation of the leading character's self in the course of his or her development (usually through a series of stages) from childhood to adulthood. The genre was established in Germany by Johann Wolfgang von Goethe's *Wilhelm Meister's Apprenticeship* (1795–1796) and has remained central to the German literary tradition. It was, therefore, an essential part of the intellectual climate in which the early psychoanalysts were educated and did their work. It might be argued that the classic "stage theories," such as Sigmund FREUD's psychosexual stages, Erik ERIKSON's psychosocial stages, Carl JUNG's process of individuation, and Jean PIAGET's stages of cognitive development, grew out of this tradition. [German, literally: "education novel"; coined by German philosopher Wilhelm Dilthey (1833–1911) in a biography of German philosopher Friederich Schleiermacher (1768–1834)]

bilineal descent see BILATERAL DESCENT.

bilingual education instruction in two languages, typically in one's native language and in the dominant language of the country in which one is educated. In the 1970s, the United States adopted a bilingual education program to help immigrant children learn English. By providing a bilingual facility, that is, the ability to perform equivalent academic work in two languages, this kind of education enables children to do regular schoolwork with their English-speaking classmates, thus receiving an equal educational opportunity. However, some programs now simply educate in the child's native language, failing to provide the bilingual facility.

bilingualism *n.* the regular use of two or more languages by a person or within a SPEECH COMMUNITY. See ADDITIVE BILINGUALISM; BILITERACY; EARLY BILINGUALISM; ELITE BILINGUALISM; FOLK BILINGUALISM. **—bilingual** *adj.*

bilirubin *n.* an orange bile pigment produced from breakdown products of the hemoglobin of red blood cells. Normally, the human body produces 0.25 g bilirubin per day, all of which is excreted in feces and urine. An excess of bilirubin is a sign of a disorder (such as abnormal destruction of red blood cells) and may be marked by deposits of yellowish pigments in the skin and other tissues, a condition known as JAUNDICE. See also HEPATITIS.

bilirubin encephalopathy a degenerative disease of the brain caused by deposition of the bile pigment BILIRUBIN in the basal ganglia and brainstem nuclei. The condition results from disorders in producing or breaking down bilirubin in the liver. This may be seen in newborns who are unable to metabolize bilirubin adequately.

bilis *n.* a CULTURE-BOUND SYNDROME found among Latino groups, who attribute it to extremely strong anger or rage. Symptoms include abrupt nervous tension, headache, screaming, stomach disturbances, vomiting, loss of weight, tremors, chronic tiredness, and—in extreme cases—loss of consciousness or death. The extreme anger is said to disturb the center of balance of hot and cold in the body, which upsets the material and spiritual aspects of the person. Also called **colera**; **muina**.

biliteracy *n.* the ability to read and write in two or more languages. See BILINGUALISM. **—biliterate** *adj.*

bill of rights in health care, a document stating the entitlements a patient has with respect to providers, institutions, and THIRD-PARTY PAYERS. See RIGHTS OF PATIENTS.

bimanual coordination coordination of the movements of the two hands.

bimanual interference problems encountered when the two hands must each perform different movements or the same movement with different timing (e.g., in piano playing).

bimodal distribution a set of scores that has two modes (represented by two peaks in their graphical distribution), reflecting a tendency for scores to cluster around two separate values.

bin- *prefix* see BI-.

binary choice in decision making, a choice between two alternatives.

binary feature in linguistics, a feature of the phonemic system of a language that has two mutually exclusive aspects, such as voiced–unvoiced (in English) or aspirated–unaspirated (in Hindi). Such features have a critical contrastive function, working rather like an on–off switch to distinguish one PHONEME from another; in English, for instance, the otherwise very similar sounds [b] and [p] are recognized as distinct phonemes because the former is VOICED and the latter UNVOICED. Binary opposition of this kind is a key concept in the structuralist interpretation of language and in the wider structuralist movement generally (see STRUCTURALISM). See also MINIMAL PAIR. [first described by Russian linguist Roman Jakobson (1896–1982)]

binary hue a hue that appears to be a mixture of two **unique hues**. Orange is a binary hue composed of red and yellow, which are considered unique because they are not produced by color mixing.

binary system a structure or organization composed of two elements or two kinds of elements. In computer science, it is a logical structure composed of two values, commonly called 0 and 1, based on the "off" and "on" modes of electrical circuits and devices. The principle of binary contrast is also of great importance in STRUCTURALISM, particularly structural linguistics. See BINARY FEATURE; MINIMAL PAIR.

binary variable a variable that may take on only two values, for example, male versus female, or 0 versus 1 in computer code.

binasal hemianopia the loss of vision in both the right half of the left visual field and the left half of the right visual field. It is caused by injury (compression) of the OPTIC CHIASM. See HEMIANOPIA.

binaural *adj.* pertaining to both ears or, more specifically, to hearing based on information from both ears. Compare DICHOTIC; MONAURAL.

binaural beat a periodic fluctuation in apparent position or in loudness when two tones differing slightly in frequency are presented to each ear separately but simultaneously. Unlike MONAURAL beats, binaural beats are not present in the stimulus; the binaural interaction between the tones occurs within the auditory system. See BEAT.

binaural cues differences in the sound arriving at the two ears from a given sound source. These **interaural differences** act as cues to permit localization or lateralization of the source using the binaural system. The common cues are **interaural level differences** (ILD), **interaural time differences** (ITD), and (closely related to ITD) **interaural phase differences** (IPD). Also called **binaural differences**. See also AUDITORY LOCALIZATION.

binaural fusion see FUSION.

binaural hearing see BINAURAL.

binaural interaction the interaction in the nervous system of signals from the two ears. It is especially important for localizing auditory stimuli.

binaural masking level difference see MASKING LEVEL DIFFERENCE.

binaural summation effect see SUMMATION EFFECT.

binding affinity 1. theoretically, the length of time a neurotransmitter or drug molecule binds to a RECEPTOR. **2.** in practice, the concentration of neurotransmitter or drug molecule that is required to bind half of the receptors at equilibrium.

binding hypothesis the theory that unified conscious percepts are produced by a complex process that draws together disparate sensory features. Feature binding is an element of both brain and psychological theories of consciousness. See FEATURE-INTEGRATION THEORY.

binding problem the difficulty of perceiving and representing different features, or conjunctions of properties, as one object or event. For example, to detect a green circle among blue circles and green squares one must correctly "bind" each shape to its color. This problem arises because different attributes of a stimulus (e.g., hue, form, spatial location, motion) are analyzed by different areas of the cerebral cortex; it is relevant in all areas of knowledge representation, including such complex cognitive representations as THEORY OF MIND.

Binet, Alfred (1857–1911) French psychologist. Although he had no formal training in psychology, Binet became a pioneer investigator of SUGGESTION and the thought processes of mentally gifted individuals and those with mental retardation. Opposing J. M. CATTELL's reduction of mental abilities to sensory and motor capacities, as measured by "brass instruments," Binet developed a variety of verbal and numerical test items in 1905, with the assistance of French psychologist Théodore Simon (1873–1961). These were used to determine a child's mental age and to identify pupils with mental retardation who might not be able to succeed in an ordinary academic curriculum. Later revisions of the Binet–Simon Scale led ultimately to the development of the STANFORD–BINET INTELLIGENCE SCALE, which is in wide use today. See also IQ.

Binet–Simon Scale see STANFORD–BINET INTELLIGENCE SCALE.

binge drinking a pattern of alcohol consumption characterized by alternation of periods of sobriety and shorter periods of intense, extremely heavy drinking. See also EPSILON ALCOHOLISM.

binge-eating disorder a disorder marked by recurring episodes of binge eating (i.e., discrete periods of uncontrolled consumption of abnormally large quantities of food) and distress associated with this behavior. There is an absence of inappropriate compensatory behaviors (e.g., vomiting, laxative misuse, excessive exercise, fasting). In *DSM–IV–TR* it is classified as EATING DISORDER not otherwise specified. Compare BULIMIA NERVOSA.

Bingham, Walter Van Dyke (1880–1952) U.S. psychologist. Bingham is best known as a founder of INDUSTRIAL AND ORGANIZATIONAL PSYCHOLOGY. Trained as an experimentalist at the University of Chicago (where he received his PhD in 1908) and strongly influenced by the Wundtian tradition (see WUNDT, WILHELM MAX), he became involved in the development of mental tests under Edward L. THORNDIKE's direction. He subsequently established the first American department of APPLIED PSYCHOLOGY at Carnegie Institute of Technology. Bingham was one of the key figures in the U.S. Army's World War I mental testing program, together with Robert M. YERKES and Walter Dill SCOTT. He became the Army's chief psychologist in World War II, putting to use the knowledge of aptitude and achievement testing that he had honed in both military and industrial settings. See also AMERICAN ASSOCIATION OF APPLIED PSYCHOLOGY.

binocular *adj.* relating to the two eyes.

binocular cells cortical cells that respond to a stimulus presented to either the left or the right eye. **Monocular cells**, in contrast, require stimulation through a specific eye to generate a response.

binocular cue any visual cue that requires the use of both eyes. RETINAL DISPARITY and CONVERGENCE are examples of binocular cues to DEPTH PERCEPTION. Compare MONOCULAR CUE.

binocular deprivation the deprivation of light to both eyes, as by sealing the eyelids. Compare MONOCULAR DEPRIVATION.

binocular disparity see RETINAL DISPARITY.

binocular flicker an experimental paradigm in which each eye is stimulated separately with an intermittent light. The phase relationships of the illumination of each eye can be varied to investigate binocular interactions. [devised by British physician and physiologist Sir Charles Scott Sherrington (1857–1952)]

binocular fusion the combination of stimuli viewed through each eye to give a single percept. See BINOCULAR VISION; FUSION.

binocular parallax the differences in the two retinal images due to separation of the eyes.

binocular perception any visual experience enabled by stimulation through both eyes.

binocular rivalry the failure of the eyes to fuse stimuli (see FUSION). For example, if horizontal bars are viewed through the left eye and vertical bars through the right eye, the perception is a patchy and fluctuating alternation of the two patterns, rather than a superimposition of the patterns to form a stable checkerboard. Also called **retinal rivalry**. Compare BINOCULAR FUSION.

binocular summation the phenomenon of increased sensation or increased magnitude of perceptual response that results from stimulation through both eyes, as compared to stimulation through one eye.

binocular suppression the ability of stimulation through one eye to inhibit the response or sensitivity to stimulation through the other eye.

binocular vision the normal coordinated function of the eyes that permits viewing of the surroundings in three dimensions. See STEREOPSIS. Compare BINOCULAR FUSION.

binomial distribution the distribution of the number of successes in a sequence of *n* independent trials, each of which has only two possible outcomes (success or failure), with a fixed probability of success θ on each trial. This distribution is often denoted by b(*n*,θ). Also called **Bernoulli distribution**.

binomial effect size display a method of arraying experimental results that emphasizes the effect of two or more treatments based on the success rates (e.g., survival rates, improvement rates, etc.) under each of the treatments.

binomial nomenclature see BIOLOGICAL TAXONOMY.

binomial test a statistical procedure to test a hypothesis concerning the value of the parameter θ in a BINOMIAL DISTRIBUTION.

Binswanger's disease a progressive VASCULAR DEMENTIA characterized by loss of cognitive functioning, memory impairment, and mood changes. The symptoms are associated with DEMYELINATION of subcortical white matter due to hypertension and arteriosclerosis affecting the arteries supplying the brain. The cerebral cortex is not affected. Also called **Binswanger's dementia**; **subcortical arteriosclerotic encephalopathy**. [Otto Ludvig **Binswanger** (1852–1929), German neurologist]

bio- *combining form* life or living.

bioacoustics *n.* the study of acoustic communication and related behavior of animals. This can involve study of the mechanisms of sound production and perception, the physical structure of animal signals, the alteration of animal sounds as they pass through different environments, and the influence of animal sounds on the behavior of other animals.

bioavailability *n.* the quantity of an administered agent (e.g., a drug) that is available for distribution within the body to the target organ or site.

biochemical approach 1. the study of behavioral patterns, including mental disorders, from the standpoint of chemical changes. An example of this approach is the view that a mental disorder can be explained in terms of an excess or deficiency of certain substances in the nervous system, such as serotonin. **2.** the use of psychotropic drugs in the treatment of mental disorders. See PSYCHOPHARMACOTHERAPY.

biochemical defect any of numerous chemical imbalances or aberrations in the brain that may be associated with neurological or psychiatric disorder. Such disorders may be related to the production of specific NEUROTRANSMITTERS or the availability of other biochemical substances necessary for brain function.

biochemical marker a biochemical variable that accompanies a disorder, irrespective of whether it directly causes the disorder; an example is demonstrated in the DEXAMETHASONE SUPPRESSION TEST. See also BIOLOGICAL MARKER; CLINICAL MARKER.

biochemistry *n.* the study of the chemical substances and processes occurring in living organisms. Also called **biological chemistry**. **—biochemical** *adj.*

biocybernetics *n.* the study of communication and self-regulatory activities within the body. **—biocybernetic** or **biocybernetical** *adj.*

biodata *pl. n.* see BIOGRAPHICAL DATA.

biodynamics *n.* the study of dynamic processes within living organisms. See DYNAMIC.

bioecological model a paradigm that treats human development as a process that continues both through the life span and across successive generations, thus according importance to historical continuity and change as forces indirectly affecting human development through their impact on proximal processes.

bioecological theory of intelligence a theory of intelligence postulating that intelligence develops as an interaction between biological dispositions and the environment in which these biological dispositions develop. [proposed by U.S. psychologist Stephen J. Ceci (1950–)]

bioelectric potential the electric potential of nerve, muscle, and other living tissue.

bioenergetics *n.* a form of alternative psychotherapy that combines work with the body and the mind in treating emotional problems. Bioenergetics proposes that body and mind are functionally identical: What happens in the mind reflects what is happening in the body, and vice versa. It uses exercises and postural changes in an attempt to relieve chronic muscular tensions and rigidity attributed to emotional stress and unresolved emotional conflicts. The approach was developed by U.S. physician Alexander Lowen (1910–) and is based on the work of Austrian psychoanalyst Wilhelm Reich (1897–1957).

bioengineering *n.* the application of engineering principles and knowledge to living organisms and biological processes, particularly in the design, testing, and manufacture of devices that can substitute for impaired body parts or functions. Examples include hip replacements, artificial organs, and NEUROCONTROL devices that enable an individual with quadriplegia to feed, dress, and wash himself or herself. See also REHABILITATION ENGINEERING. **—bioengineer** *n.*

bioequivalence *n.* a measure comparing the relative BIOAVAILABILITY of two forms or preparations of a drug. In bioequivalent drug preparations, the same proportion of unchanged, active drug reaches the systemic circulation. Bioequivalence may be a clinical issue when comparing two preparations of a drug (i.e., immediate-release versus delayed-release) or when comparing trademarked drugs and their generic counterparts. **—bioequivalent** *adj.*

bioethics *n.* the study of ETHICS and values relevant to the conduct of clinical practice and research in medicine and the life sciences. **—bioethical** *adj.*

biofeedback *n.* **1.** the impulses received from muscles, visceral organs, and the nervous system that provide information for an organism's internal regulatory systems in order to control and maintain organs at a physiologically desirable level. See FEEDBACK. **2.** the use of an external monitoring device to provide an individual with information regarding his or her physiological state, which may enable voluntary control over autonomic body functions, such as heart rate (see BIOFEEDBACK TRAINING). Also called **sensory feedback**.

biofeedback training a technique by which a person learns to control a normally involuntary autonomic response (e.g., blood pressure, heart rate, or alpha rhythm in the brain) by watching the output of a device that monitors the response continuously (e.g., a blood pressure monitor, an electrocardiograph, or an electroencephalograph). Biofeedback training is sometimes used to treat stress disorders, such as migraine headaches and hypertension. It is also used as an adjunctive treatment for other disorders, such as insomnia, substance abuse, attention-deficit/hyperactivity disorder, and epilepsy. See also ALPHA-WAVE TRAINING.

biogenesis *n.* the origin of living things from other living things. **Biogenetics** is the scientific study of the principles and processes governing the production of living organisms from other living organisms, including the mechanisms of heredity. **—biogenetic** *adj.*

biogenic *adj.* **1.** produced by living organisms or biological processes. **2.** necessary for the maintenance of life.

biogenic amine any of a group of psychoactive AMINES, including the CATECHOLAMINE neurotransmitters dopamine, epinephrine, and norepinephrine and the indoleamine neurotransmitter serotonin. These biogenic amines are sometimes identified as NEUROHORMONES.

biogenic amine hypothesis the concept that abnormalities in the physiology and metabolism of biogenic amines, particularly norepinephrine, dopamine, and serotonin, are involved in the causes and courses of certain mental disorders. See CATECHOLAMINE HYPOTHESIS; DOPAMINE HYPOTHESIS.

biogram *n.* a pattern of possible events involved in learning a BIOFEEDBACK experience. The biogram may begin as a conscious memory device but through repeated trials eventually becomes subconscious in a manner similar to other learning experiences acquired through repeated trials.

biographical data 1. information gathered by a therapist or medical professional about a client's history and behavioral patterns, primarily from the client but sometimes—when permitted by the client or deemed necessary—from individuals who know or are related to the client. **2.** information on job candidates for use in personnel selection. The data are usually obtained from application forms or special questionnaires (**biographical inventories**) and include such items as age, sex, education, work experience, and interests. Also called **biodata**.

Biographical Evaluation and Screening of Troops a program used for the selection and classification of military personnel. Formerly called the **Air Force Medical Evaluation Test** (**AFMET**), it is used to identify individuals who are unlikely to complete the Air Force basic training or who might find it difficult to function in a military system.

biographical inventory see BIOGRAPHICAL DATA.

biographical method the systematic use of personal data in studying the relationships between the factors, events, and outcomes of a person's life.

bioinformational theory a theory that attempts to explain how and why IMAGERY works in PERFORMANCE ENHANCEMENT. Mental images are stored in long-term memory as STIMULUS PROPOSITIONS and RESPONSE PROPOSITIONS. Both must be activated so that each can be modified.

biological aging see AGING; PRIMARY AGING. Compare SECONDARY AGING.

biological clock the mechanism within an organism that controls the periodicity of BIOLOGICAL RHYTHMS, including ACTIVITY RHYTHMS, even in the absence of any external cues. For example, a bird housed in constant light will continue to show patterns of activity and rest with approximately 24-hour rhythms due to the action of the biological clock. A biological clock in mammals is located in the SUPRACHIASMATIC NUCLEUS of the hypothalamus. Molecular mechanisms of the CIRCADIAN RHYTHM are the same in insects and mammals. Also called **internal clock**.

biological determinism the concept that psychological and behavioral characteristics are entirely the result of constitutional and biological factors. Environmental conditions serve only as occasions for the manifestation of such characteristics. Compare ENVIRONMENTAL DETERMINISM. See DETERMINISM; GENETIC DETERMINISM; NATURE–NURTURE CONTROVERSY.

biological drive an innate motivational state produced by depletion or deprivation of a needed substance (e.g., water, oxygen) in order to impel behavior that will restore physiological equilibrium. See also DRIVE.

biological factor any physical, chemical, genetic, or neurological condition associated with psychological disturbances.

biological fallacy 1. the questionable assumption that all human phenomena, including rationality, culture, and ethics, can be explained with reference to strictly biological processes. In this sense, the biological fallacy is one of naturalistic REDUCTIONISM. **2.** in the controversial view of some ecological theorists, the "fallacy" of equating life with the life of individual organisms. The term implies that the vital force referred to as "life" is better understood as inherent in, or as a quality of, the totality of the ecosystem.

biological family a person's blood relations as opposed to relations acquired through marriage, adoption, or fostering. See AFFINITY; CONSANGUINITY.

biological intelligence a level of mental ability of presumed biological origins required primarily for cognitive activity. The term was introduced to differentiate forebrain-functioning ability from traditional concepts of intelligence. Biological intelligence is measured with a battery of tests that also indicate evidence of brain injury. Although biological in nature, this kind of intelligence is affected by the environment, as illustrated by the fact that some kinds of brain damage result from head injuries that are environmentally caused. [defined by U.S. psychologist Ward C. Halstead (1908–1969)]

biological life events age-determined biological changes, such as PUBERTY or menopause (see CLIMACTERIC).

biologically primary ability an ability, such as language acquisition, that has been selected for in evolution and is acquired universally. Children typically are highly motivated to perform tasks involving these abilities. Compare BIOLOGICALLY SECONDARY ABILITY. [postulated by U.S. psychologist David Geary (1957–)]

biologically secondary ability an ability, such as reading, that builds upon a BIOLOGICALLY PRIMARY ABILITY but is principally a cultural invention and often requires extensive repetition and external motivation for its mastery. [postulated by David Geary]

biological marker a biological variable that accompanies a disorder, irrespective of whether it directly causes the disorder. See also BIOCHEMICAL MARKER; CLINICAL MARKER.

biological measures assessments or other markers of processes or outcomes that are drawn from bodily activity or other natural biological systems or events. Such measures include assessments of cardiopulmonary, endocrine, nervous-system, and immune-system activity.

biological motion 1. the kinds of motion performed by living organisms. See LOCOMOTION; TAXIS. **2.** a display, consisting of about 12 point lights, that is attached to the head and main joints. When the lights move appropriately in relation to each other, they induce a compelling impression of an organism in motion. [devised in the 1970s by Swedish psychologist Gunnar Johansson (1911–1998)]

biological psychology the science that deals with the area of overlap between psychology and biology and with the reciprocal relations between biological and psychological processes. It includes such fields as BEHAV-

IORAL NEUROSCIENCE, clinical NEUROSCIENCE, COGNITIVE NEUROSCIENCE, BEHAVIORAL ENDOCRINOLOGY, and PSYCHONEUROIMMUNOLOGY, and involves reciprocal interactions between the neural, endocrine, and immune systems as they affect and are affected by behavior. It was formerly known as **physiological psychology**. Also called **biopsychology**.

biological rhythm any periodic variation in a living organism's physiological or psychological function, such as energy level, sexual desire, or menstruation. Such rhythms are usually linked to cyclical changes in environmental cues, such as daylength or passing of the seasons, and tend to be daily (see CIRCADIAN RHYTHM) or annual (see CIRCANNUAL RHYTHM). They also can vary with individuals and with the period of the individual's life. Also called **biorhythm; endogenous rhythm; internal rhythm; life rhythm**. See also INFRADIAN RHYTHM; ULTRADIAN RHYTHM.

biological stress a condition that imposes severe demands on the physical and psychological defenses of the organism. Examples include acute or chronic disease, a congenital or acquired disability or defect, exposure to extreme heat or cold, malnutrition or starvation, hallucinogens or other drugs, and the ingestion of toxic substances. See also STRESS.

biological symbiosis see SYMBIOSIS.

biological taxonomy the science of the classification of organisms. Traditional classifications group organisms into a hierarchical system of ranks, in ascending order: species, genus, family, order, class, phylum, and kingdom (see also DOMAIN). Species are named using **binomial nomenclature**, devised by Swedish biologist Carolus Linnaeus (1707–1778) in 1758: Each species is given two names, the first for the genus to which it belongs and the second identifying the species itself; thus human beings are classified as *Homo sapiens*. Also called **systematics**. See also CLADISTICS.

biological theory of aging any of various explanations of aging based on either programmed biological changes (genetic SENESCENCE) or unpredicted, stochastic changes (DNA damage).

biological therapy any form of treatment for mental disorders that attempts to alter physiological functioning, including various drug therapies, ELECTROCONVULSIVE THERAPY, and PSYCHOSURGERY. Also called **biomedical therapy**. See also CLINICAL PSYCHOPHARMACOLOGY.

biological transducing system a biological system that converts energy or information from one form to another. See TRANSDUCTION.

biological viewpoint an approach to abnormal psychology based on causative factors that are organic, such as the SENILE PLAQUES that are assumed to be a causative factor in Alzheimer's disease.

biological warfare the use of disease-producing agents (such as bacteria and viruses) to incapacitate or kill opponents.

biologism *n.* a predilection to make use of BIOLOGICAL DETERMINISM and concepts from biology to explain behavior and psychological phenomena and to avoid psychological concepts and principles for such explanation. See also REDUCTIONISM.

biology *n.* the science that deals with living organisms and life processes. **—biological** *adj.* **—biologist** *n.*

biomechanics *n.* the application of the principles of mechanics to the study of the structure and function of biological systems, which includes the study of the physical stresses and strains on organisms while at rest and in motion. The discipline includes **occupational biomechanics**, which examines the physical interaction of workers with their tools, machines, and materials so as to maximize performance while minimizing the risk of musculoskeletal disorders. **—biomechanical** *adj.*

biomedical engineering the branch of engineering that specializes in research and development of equipment for medical treatment, rehabilitation, and special needs. Examples of applications include devices to monitor the physiological condition of astronauts in space, the design and creation of artificial limbs and organs, and the development of ULTRASOUND devices. See also BIOENGINEERING.

biomedical therapy see BIOLOGICAL THERAPY.

biometrics *n.* see BIOSTATISTICS.

bion *n.* a hypothetical microscopic vesicle charged with sexual energy, postulated by Austrian psychoanalyst Wilhelm Reich (1897–1957) as the ultimate source of the orgasm. See also ORGONE; ORGONE THERAPY.

bionics *n.* the study of biological systems to learn how aspects of their perceptual and problem-solving behavior might be built into an electronic system, such as a computer. [bi(ology) + (electr)onics]

bionomic factor any factor in the environment that controls or limits the development or evolution of organisms.

biophysical system 1. any biological system that is described or studied in terms of its physical aspects, including the application of physical laws and the techniques of physics. **2.** the hormonal and genital components of the human sexual response. [defined by U.S. sex therapists William H. Masters (1915–2001) and Virginia E. Johnson (1925–)]

biophysics *n.* the interface of biology and physics, involving the study of biological structures and processes by means of the methods of physics, for example, the application of the principles of physics in the study of vision or hearing.

biopsy *n.* the surgical removal and microscopic study of a small amount of tissue from an organ or body part believed to be diseased or otherwise abnormal. The biopsy specimen is examined for signs of malignancy or other abnormalities that would help determine the proper diagnosis and course of therapy. Compare AUTOPSY.

biopsychology *n.* see BIOLOGICAL PSYCHOLOGY.

biopsychosocial system a systematic integration of biological, psychological, and social approaches to the study of mental health and specific mental disorders. See GENERAL SYSTEMS THEORY.

biorhythms *pl. n.* **1.** according to pseudoscientific belief, three basic cycles (physical, emotional, and intellectual), with which every individual is programmed at birth. It is maintained that these rhythms continue unaltered until death and that good and bad days for various activities can be calculated accordingly. As with astrology, predictions made on this basis do not have a significantly different success rate from those made on a basis of pure chance. **2.** see BIOLOGICAL RHYTHM.

biosocial *adj.* pertaining to the interplay or mingling of biological and social forces, as with human behavior that is influenced simultaneously by complex neurophysiological processes and learned social meanings.

biosocial experimenter effect the unintended effect of the biological or social characteristics of data collectors on the results of their research.

biosocial theory any approach that explains personality or human behavior in terms of biological predispositions that are influenced by social or environmental factors.

biosphere *n.* collectively, all parts of the earth and its atmosphere in which living organisms subsist.

biostatistics *n.* **1.** data compiled about a population, including rates of birth, disease, and death (see VITAL STATISTICS). See also DEMOGRAPHY. **2.** a branch of statistics concerned with the application of statistical methods to biological processes, especially in medicine and epidemiology. Also called **biometrics**. **—biostatistical** *adj.* **—biostatistician** *n.*

biosynthesis *n.* **1.** the production of chemical compounds by living organisms from nutrients by means of enzyme-catalyzed reactions. **2.** the production of molecules of biological or medical interest, either in the laboratory or commercially, for example, by recombinant DNA technology. **—biosynthetic** *adj.*

biotaxis *n.* **1.** the classification of living organisms by their anatomical features and traits. **2.** the ability of living cells to orient themselves with respect to their environment. See NEUROBIOTAXIS. **—biotactic** *adj.*

biotechnology any technique that uses biological organisms, cells, or processes to produce products and services to meet human needs.

biotope *n.* in ecology, a physical region that can be defined by particular environmental characteristics.

biotransformation *n.* the metabolic process by which a substance (e.g., a drug) is changed from one chemical to another by means of a chemical reaction within a living system. The metabolites, or products, of this change may be active or inactive within the system.

biotransport *n.* the transportation of substances within cells or into and out of cells across biological membranes. See ACTIVE TRANSPORT; ION PUMP; PASSIVE TRANSPORT.

biotype *n.* **1.** a group of individuals who are very similar or identical in their GENOTYPE (genetic makeup), although they may vary in PHENOTYPE (visible features). **2.** a physical characteristic that distinguishes a population of organisms adapted to a particular environment and that does not occur in populations of the same species in other environments. **—biotypic** *adj.*

biotypology *n.* the classification of human beings according to their constitutional, anatomical, physiological, and psychological characteristics. See also CONSTITUTIONAL TYPE.

biparental care the bringing up of the young by both parents.

bipedal locomotion the ability to walk or run on two feet and in an upright position, as in human beings and birds. Great apes and bears also engage in short periods of bipedal locomotion, especially when the animal is carrying food, traveling over wet ground, or looking for something to eat.

biperiden *n.* a synthetic ANTICHOLINERGIC DRUG closely related to TRIHEXYPHENIDYL but having greater affinity for NICOTINIC RECEPTORS than for MUSCARINIC RECEPTORS, compared with trihexyphenidyl. It is used to manage symptoms of Parkinson's disease and parkinsonian symptoms induced by antipsychotic drugs. U.S. trade name: **Akineton**.

biphasic sleep see POLYPHASIC SLEEP.

biplot *n.* a graphical representation of data that allows the simultaneous display of both the rows and columns of a data ARRAY.

bipolar *adj.* **1.** denoting a structure with two ends, such as a BIPOLAR NEURON. **2.** referring to a mood disorder in which a person's state ranges from mania to depression. See BIPOLAR DISORDERS. **—bipolarity** *n.*

bipolar cell see BIPOLAR NEURON.

bipolar concept the notion, often applied to MOOD and AFFECT, that a particular phenomenon can accurately be described by reference to a dimension characterized by opposing attributes, such as happiness versus sadness. It is contrasted with a **unidimensional concept**, which is characterized by the extent of one particular attribute, such as a greater or lesser degree of sadness.

bipolar disorders a group of MOOD DISORDERS in which both manic (or hypomanic) and depressive symptoms occur. *DSM–IV–TR* distinguishes between **bipolar I disorder**, in which the individual has experienced one or more MANIC EPISODES or MIXED EPISODES and usually (but not necessarily) one or more MAJOR DEPRESSIVE EPISODES, and **bipolar II disorder**, characterized by one or more major depressive episodes and at least one HYPOMANIC EPISODE. Also categorized as bipolar disorders in *DSM–IV–TR* are CYCLOTHYMIC DISORDER and **bipolar disorder not otherwise specified**, which does not meet the criteria for more specific bipolar disorders. In *DSM–III* the bipolar disorders were grouped into the types **depressive**, **manic**, and **mixed**, according to the nature of the current or most recent episode. The former official name for bipolar disorders, **manic-depressive illness**, is still in frequent use.

bipolar electrode see ELECTRODE.

bipolar factor in FACTOR ANALYSIS, a factor (variable) characterized as having a neutral aspect at a relatively central position on a spectrum ranging from positive to negative extremes at either end, for example, attitudes toward work ranging from strong engagement to neutrality to sheer boredom.

bipolar neuron a neuron with only two processes—an AXON and a DENDRITE—that extend from opposite sides of the CELL BODY. Cells of this type are found in the retina (see RETINAL BIPOLAR CELLS) and also elsewhere in the nervous system. Also called **bipolar cell**. Compare MULTIPOLAR NEURON; UNIPOLAR NEURON.

bipolar rating scale a rating scale anchored at each end by opposite terms (e.g., very fast to very slow). It is distinguished from a **unipolar rating scale** (e.g., very fast to not at all fast, or very slow to not at all slow).

bipolar stimulation the activation of a particular NEURON or part of the brain through the use of an electrical current generated by a cathode and anode (see ELECTRODE) placed relatively close to each other.

birds-of-a-feather phenomenon the tendency to affiliate with or be attracted to others similar to oneself. As a result, groups and other interpersonal aggregates (e.g., romantic couples, friendship networks) tend to be composed of individuals who are similar to one another rather than dissimilar. See also HOMOPHILY.

BIRG-ing acronym for BASKING IN REFLECTED GLORY.

birth cohort a group of individuals born at approximately the same time who share the same pattern of historical experiences in childhood and adulthood.

birth control voluntary regulation of the number and spacing of offspring, including the prevention of conception using INTRAUTERINE DEVICES, ORAL CONTRACEPTIVES, spermicides, the RHYTHM METHOD, male contraceptive devices, surgical methods of STERILIZATION (e.g., salpingectomy, VASECTOMY), and the termination of pregnancy by induced ABORTION.

birth cry the initial reflexive sound produced by a newborn infant when respiration begins.

birth defect see CONGENITAL DEFECT.

birth injury physical damage incurred during birth, especially malformation or brain injury. Damage is most likely to occur in transverse or breech births, in instrumental deliveries, in premature infants and multiple births, in episodes of ANOXIA or HYPOXIA, or in prolonged labor.

birth mother see BIRTH PARENT.

birth order the ordinal position of a child in the family (firstborn, second-born, youngest, etc.). There has been much psychological research into how birth order affects personal adjustment and family status. Early interest in birth order appears in the work of British scientist Francis Galton (1822–1911) and Sigmund FREUD, but it was Alfred ADLER who first proposed that birth order is an important factor in personality development. Current family-structure research sees birth order not so much as a causal factor but rather as an indirect variable that follows more process-oriented variables (e.g., parental discipline, sibling interaction, and genetic and hormonal makeup) in importance. Birth order appears to have small and subtle influences (somewhat stronger for personality than for intelligence) that need further study, but the notion that it has strong and consistent effects on psychological outcomes is not supported.

birth parent the biological parent of a child, particularly the mother (**birth mother**), contrasted with the parent who may rear the child (see ADOPTIVE PARENTS).

birth rate the ratio of total live births to total population in a given community or geographical area within a specified period, often expressed as the number of live births per 1,000 population per year. Also called **natality**. See also FECUNDITY; FERTILITY.

birth ratio the ratio of one kind of birth to another, such as the ratio of male to female births, multiple to total births, or teen births (births to teenage mothers) to total births. See also SEX RATIO.

birth rite a culture-bound ceremony, religious ritual, or other customary practice associated with the prenatal period, birth, or infancy. In Western societies such rites may include baptism, CIRCUMCISION, or a secular naming ceremony. See RITE OF PASSAGE.

birth trauma the psychological shock of being born, due to the sudden change from the security of the womb to being bombarded with stimuli from the external world. Sigmund FREUD viewed birth as the child's first anxiety experience and the prototype of separation anxiety. To Austrian psychoanalyst Otto Rank (1884–1939), who first proposed the idea of birth trauma, it was the crucial factor in causing neuroses. See also PRIMAL ANXIETY; PRIMAL TRAUMA.

BIS abbreviation for BEHAVIORAL INHIBITION SYSTEM.

bisection *n.* the act of splitting something into two equal parts. In psychophysics it refers to a scaling method in which a participant adjusts a stimulus until it is perceived as halfway between two other stimuli with respect to a particular dimension.

biserial correlation a measure of the association between continuous and DICHOTOMOUS VARIABLES.

bisexual behavior behavior of a person who is attracted sexually to both sexes and is usually able to achieve orgasm in contact with members of either sex.

bisexuality *n.* **1.** sexual attraction to or sexual behavior with both men and women. Although much psychological research demonstrates the existence of a continuum of sexual attraction within most individuals, equal responsiveness to both sexes over the life span is rare, appearing to be more common in women than in men. Same-sex attractions and behaviors generally occur after those to the opposite sex for bisexual women, whereas bisexual men typically experience their first homosexual attractions and behavior before or at the same age as their first heterosexual experiences. Anthropological studies note that bisexuality is present in many cultures. **2.** the existence of both male and female genitals in the same organism. See HERMAPHRODITE; INTERSEXUALITY. **—bisexual** *adj., n.*

bistable perceptual events perceptions in which sensory stimuli, most often visual, are experienced as alternating, or "flipping," between two mutually exclusive perspectives or meanings (see ALTERNATING PERSPECTIVE). For example, the NECKER CUBE is usually seen in one of two alternating perspectives; the "young–old woman" visual illusion consists of alternating images of a young woman and then an old woman. See also AMBIGUOUS FIGURE.

bit *n.* **1.** in computing, a variable that can only take the values of zero or one. [bi(nary) + (digi)t] **2.** in information theory, the quantity of information that decreases uncertainty or the germane alternatives of a problem by one half. For example, if a dollar bill has been placed in one of 16 identical books standing side by side on a shelf, and one has to identify this book by asking a minimum number of questions that can be answered only by "yes" or "no," the best way to begin would be to ask if the book is to the right (or to the left) of center. The answer to this question would provide one bit of information.

bite bar 1. a device used to immobilize a participant's head during studies of visual perception. A bite bar contains an impression of the participant's teeth, so that when the bar is held between the jaws the head cannot move. **2.** in animal research, a bar placed in the mouth to restrain animals during surgery or to immobilize animals that are being tested.

bitemporal hemianopia a loss of vision in both the left half of the left visual field and the right half of the right visual field. It is caused by injury (compression) of the OPTIC CHIASM. See HEMIANOPIA.

biting mania a 15th-century epidemic of COLLECTIVE HYSTERIA that began when a German nun developed a compulsive urge to bite her associates, who in turn bit others. The mania eventually spread to convents throughout Germany, Holland, and Italy.

biting stage see ORAL-BITING PHASE.

bitter *adj.* denoting the unpleasant TASTE evoked by most alkaloids, glycosides, vitamins, and some salts. Each bitter chemical is recognized by one or more of a family of about 60 receptor proteins; some 15% of the human TASTE CELLS possess these proteins and therefore the capacity to signal bitterness. Bitter tastes are also associated with toxic chemicals. **—bitterness** *n.*

bivalence *n.* in logic, the principle that there are two and only two TRUTH VALUES, so that every proposition is necessarily either true or false. This is related to, but not identical with, the EXCLUDED MIDDLE PRINCIPLE. Compare INFINITE-VALUED LOGIC.

bivariate *adj.* characterized by two variables or attributes.

bivariate frequency distribution a simultaneous display (e.g., a graph or table) or mathematical representation of two RANDOM VARIABLES.

bizarre behavior behavior that is odd, strange, or unexpected, particularly if it is out of the ordinary for a given person. It may be a symptom of brain damage or a mental disorder, especially a psychotic disorder, such as schizophrenia.

bizarre delusion a belief that is clearly fantastic and implausible but is nonetheless maintained with conviction. For example, an individual with schizophrenia may believe that external forces are removing the thoughts from his or her mind (see THOUGHT WITHDRAWAL).

blackboard *n.* a software architecture consisting of a generally accessible global database (the blackboard) accessed by a number of "knowledge sources." The modular knowledge sources interact independently, posting and consuming information to and from the blackboard. An early use of the blackboard approach was in the development of Hearsay, a program that recognized and interpreted voiced speech.

black box a model for a device, system, or other complex entity or construct whose internal properties and processes are either unknown or unspecified and must be hypothesized on the basis of observed empirical relationships between external factors (input) and the resulting effects (output).

Black English a VERNACULAR of English used by the African American SPEECH COMMUNITY. Its formal and sociolinguistic properties have been the subject of intensive linguistic scholarship, notably by U.S. linguist William Labov (1927–). Also called **African American Vernacular English (AAVE)**; **Black English Vernacular (BEV)**; **Ebonics**.

blacking out see FALLING OUT.

blackout *n.* **1.** total loss of consciousness produced, for example, by sudden lowering of the blood supply to the brain or by decreased oxygen supply. **2.** amnesia produced by alcoholic intoxication. Also called **alcoholic blackout**.

blackout level the point at which an individual loses consciousness as a result of physiological changes. A blackout may be caused by excessive intake of such substances as alcohol or by scuba diving at extreme depths. The condition is of particular concern when the individual is operating equipment. Also called **blackout threshold**.

bladder control the ability to regulate urination so that voiding occurs in the proper place and at the proper time. See TOILET TRAINING. Compare ENURESIS.

bladder reflex see MICTURITION REFLEX.

Blake–Mouton managerial grid a model of leadership in which the behavior of the leader is assessed on two dimensions: concern for people and concern for production. The LEADERSHIP STYLE of a manager is described on nine-point scales on each dimension, giving a total of 81 possible styles. The five most often discussed styles are 9,1 (high concern for production, low concern for people: authoritarian); 1,9 (low production, high people: country club); 5,5 (medium production, medium people: compromiser); 1,1 (low production, low people: laissez faire); and 9,9 (high production, high people: team leadership). Also called **two-dimensional leader behavior space**. See also GRID ORGANIZATIONAL DEVELOPMENT. [developed in 1964 by Robert R. **Blake** (1918–) and Jane S. **Mouton** (1930–), U.S. psychologists]

blaming the victim a social psychological phenomenon in which individuals or groups attempt to cope with the bad things that have happened to others by assigning blame to the victim of the trauma or tragedy. Victim blaming serves to create psychological distance between the blamer and the victim, may rationalize a failure to intervene if the blamer was a bystander, and creates a psychological defense for the blamer against feelings of vulnerability.

blanket group a category comprising a large class of people, things, or situations that are in many respects quite diverse, so that any generalization made about such a group (e.g., women, Hispanics) is likely to be of little value.

blank hallucination a HALLUCINATION involving a sense of floating in space, changes in equilibrium or body size, or other hazy sensations, occurring mostly in response to stress or when falling asleep. In psychoanalytic theory, a blank hallucination is thought to repeat an early defensive mechanism by reproducing the soothing experience of suckling at the breast.

blank screen in psychoanalysis, the metaphorical backdrop onto which the patient projects his or her feelings and fantasies during the TRANSFERENCE process. The screen is the psychoanalyst, who is described as blank because he or she must remain passive and neutral to enable the patient to feel free to give voice to his or her innermost thoughts.

blank trial a trial within an experiment that uses irregular or meaningless stimulus conditions to prevent the participant from guessing or giving automatic responses. See also CATCH TRIAL.

blast noise excessive acoustic exposure (noise), which may rupture the tympanic membrane (eardrum) or cause damage to the inner ear.

blastocyst *n.* the mammalian EMBRYO at a very early stage of development. It consists of a tiny hollow sphere containing an inner cell mass and yolk sac, enclosed in a thin layer of cells that help implant the blastocyst in the uterine lining. Blastocyst formation in humans generally occurs on the 5th or 6th day following fertilization.

blast olfactometer an OLFACTOMETER that pulses an ODORANT into the nasal cavities via a blast of air. Because the blast has tactile as well as odor effects, most olfactometers now have a constant airstream into which odorants are introduced. See also STREAM OLFACTOMETER; ZWAARDEMAKER OLFACTOMETER.

blastula *n.* a roughly spherical group of cells formed by division of the fertilized egg (zygote) during the early stages of embryonic development. It consists of a single layer of cells (the **blastoderm**) surrounding a fluid-filled cavity (the **blastocele**). In mammals the blastula is called a BLASTOCYST.

blended family a family unit resulting from the union of partners both of whom have dependent offspring from prior relationships. Also called **reconstituted family**. Compare SIMPLE STEPFAMILY. See also PERMEABLE FAMILY; STEPFAMILY.

blending *n.* in linguistics, the process of combining the beginning of one word with the end of another to create a wholly new term; for example, *Reaganomics* is a blend of (Ronald) *Reagan* and *economics*. See PORTMANTEAU NEOLOGISM.

blepharospasm *n.* a tonic SPASM of the eyelid muscle that is manifested by an involuntary blinking or eye closure.

Blessed Dementia Scale (**BDS**) a behavioral rating scale used in the assessment of DEMENTIA severity. It is administered to a caregiver and has subscales measuring changes in the performance of everyday tasks, changes in daily activities and habits, and changes in personality and motivation. [developed in 1968 by Gary **Blessed**, British psychogeriatrician; Bernard E. Tomlinson, British neuropathologist; and Martin Roth, British psychiatrist]

Bleuler's theory a theory proposing a basic underlying symptomatology for SCHIZOPHRENIA. It defined four FUNDAMENTAL SYMPTOMS required for a diagnosis of the condition; the more obvious manifestations of schizophrenia (e.g., delusions, hallucinations) were regarded as accessory symptoms (see SECONDARY SYMPTOMS) because they are shared with other disorders. [Eugen **Bleuler** (1857–1939), Swiss psychiatrist]

blind *adj.* **1.** see BLINDNESS. **2.** denoting the condition in which a data collector, research participant, or both are kept unaware of the experimental conditions under which they are operating. See also SINGLE BLIND; DOUBLE BLIND; TRIPLE BLIND.

blind alley a type of MAZE pathway or passage whose only exit is its entrance. Also called **cul-de-sac**; **dead end**.

blind analysis a study or interpretation of data or conditions without specific knowledge or previous information about the topic being examined. For example, a clinical psychologist might diagnose a patient without having information concerning any previous psychological diagnoses.

blinding headache a migrainelike headache marked by intense pain over the eye and forehead with flushing and watering of the eyes and nose. Attacks last about an hour and occur in clusters. Also called **blind headache**.

blind judgment an evaluation made without knowledge of information that might influence one's assessment of the situation. Such an approach is used to eliminate conscious or unconscious bias. Blind judgments are often used in clinical experiments, for example, judging patients' current level of depression in the absence of information about which, if any, treatment they have received; and in scholarly peer review of manuscripts, in which the author's institutional affiliation is not disclosed to the reviewer.

blind-matching technique a procedure in which participants match different protocols or sets of diagnostic data based on incomplete or inadequate knowledge. For example, a person might be asked to associate each test score in a set of scores with the actual individual who obtained the score.

blindness *n.* **1.** profound, near-total, or total impairment of the ability to perceive visual stimuli. According to the World Health Organization's international classification (1977), blindness is defined as VISUAL ACUITY worse than 20/400 in the better eye with best correction or a VISUAL FIELD less than 10° in the widest meridian in the better eye. In the United States, the criterion for **legal blindness** is visual acuity of 20/200 or worse in the better eye with best correction or a visual field of 20° or less in the widest meridian of the better eye. **2.** absence of usable vision with the exception of light perception. Major causes of organic blindness include inoperable CATARACT, uncontrolled GLAUCOMA, RETINITIS PIGMENTOSA, DIABETIC RETINOPATHY, age-related MACULAR DEGENERATION, rubella, and brain injury. See also CORTICAL BLINDNESS; FUNCTIONAL BLINDNESS; LOW VISION; VISUAL IMPAIRMENT. **—blind** *adj.*

blind review a review of a manuscript or grant proposal to evaluate its quality and suitability for publication or funding by a person who does not know the identity of the author.

blindsight *n.* the capacity of some individuals with blindness in parts or all of the visual field to detect and localize visual stimuli presented within the blind field region. Discrimination of movement, flicker, wavelength, and orientation may also be present. However, these visual capacities are not accompanied by awareness: They have been demonstrated only in experimental conditions, when participants are forced to guess. Blindsight therefore does not help individuals to compensate for their loss of vision. The causes of blindsight are the subject of some debate: Since the neural pathway from the LATERAL GENICULATE NUCLEUS to the STRIATE CORTEX is nonfunctional in blind-sighted people, it is thought that their capacities are either based on other visual pathways, that is, via the midbrain to extrastriate areas, or represent RESIDUAL VISION of surviving striate cortex.

blind spot 1. a lack of insight or awareness—often persistent—into a specific area of one's behavior or personality, typically because recognition of one's true feelings and motives would be painful. In classical psychoanalysis, it is regarded as a defense against recognition of repressed impulses or memories that would threaten the patient's EGO. See SCOTOMIZATION. **2.** in vision, the area of the monocular visual field in which stimulation cannot be perceived because the image falls on the site of the OPTIC DISK in the eye. See also SCOTOMA.

blind testing a method used to test products in which consumers are asked to indicate their preference from among a number of unidentified products, which may be different brands of a product (see BRAND PREFERENCE) or new and established versions of a product. In some cases, the tests are designed so that the tester is also unaware of the identity of the product being tested (this is called **double-blind testing**).

blind walk a TRUST EXERCISE used in a group setting (e.g., an ENCOUNTER GROUP) to help members develop mutual trust. Half of the group close their eyes; the other half become their partners and lead the "blind" people through various events and experiences. Roles are then reversed, and finally all members discuss their reactions to the experience.

blink response abrupt closure of the eyelids in response to bright light, shifting attention, or irritation of the eye. Also called **blink reflex**.

Blix's temperature experiment an experiment to locate areas on the skin that are sensitive to thermal sensations. Spots on the skin were found to be sensitive to warmth or coldness, but not both, when stimulated with hot or cold contacts. [Magnus **Blix**, 20th-century Swedish physiologist]

BLM (**BLMS**) abbreviation for BUCCOLINGUAL MASTICATORY SYNDROME.

bloating *n.* a feeling of distension in the abdomen, which may be a feature of IRRITABLE BOWEL SYNDROME and is also frequently encountered as a symptom of SOMATIZATION DISORDER. Also called **abdominal bloating**.

blob *n.* see CYTOCHROME OXIDASE BLOB.

Bloch's law a rule of TEMPORAL SUMMATION stating that visual threshold is reached when luminance × duration reaches a constant. If the brightness of a stimulus is halved, the stimulus can still be detected if its duration is doubled. Bloch's law only holds for relatively brief (≤100 ms), dim stimuli. Also called **Bunsen–Roscoe law**.

block 1. *n.* an abrupt, involuntary interruption in the flow of thought or speech in which the individual is suddenly aware of not being able to perform a particular mental act, such as finding the words to express something he or she wishes to say. Also called **mental block**. See RETRIEVAL BLOCK; TIP-OF-THE-TONGUE PHENOMENON. **2.** *n.* in psychotherapy, an obstacle to progress that is perceived as a barrier that cannot be crossed. **3.** *n.* any physical, biochemical, or psychological barrier or obstacle that obstructs or impedes a process, function, or activity. **4.** *n.* in an experimental BLOCK DESIGN, any of the relatively homogeneous subsets or levels into which the entire sample of participants is subdivided. **5.** *vb.* to subdivide the participants into such subsets. **6.** *vb.* to obstruct or impede.

block design an experimental design that divides participants into BLOCKS of relatively homogeneous participants. Each block is exposed to some or all of the experimental conditions. The greater the homogeneity of each of the blocks, the greater the statistical power of the analysis. See INCOMPLETE BLOCK DESIGN; RANDOMIZED BLOCK DESIGN.

block-design test an intelligence subtest, found most notably on the Wechsler Intelligence Scales, in which the respondent is asked to use colored blocks to match a specified design. The block-design test also is utilized in the diagnosis of mental disorder and mental deterioration. See also KOHS BLOCK DESIGN TEST.

blocking *n.* **1.** a process in which one's flow of thought or speech is suddenly interrupted (see BLOCK). Also called **thought deprivation**; **thought obstruction**. **2.** a phenomenon of STIMULUS CONTROL in which previous learning restricts or prevents conditioning of a response to a new stimulus. For example, a light paired with an unconditioned stimulus for several trials results in some conditioning for the light. Adding a tone at this point, to form a COMPOUND STIMULUS, would result in the tone being less effective as an elicitor than it would if it had been present from the beginning. Also called **blocking effect**; **Kamin effect**.

blocking factor any variable used as a basis for subdividing participants or other sampling units into different groups for the purpose of increasing the precision of an experiment.

block sampling a technique, usually part of a multistage procedure, in which samples are taken first from a defined population and subsequently from a list of BLOCKS within each sample.

Blocq's disease see ASTASIA–ABASIA. [Paul O. **Blocq** (1860–1896), French physician]

blood–brain barrier a semipermeable barrier formed by cells lining the blood capillaries that supply the brain and other parts of the central nervous system. It prevents large molecules, including many drugs, passing from the blood to the fluid surrounding brain cells and to the cerebrospinal fluid, and thus protects the brain from potentially harmful substances. Ions and small molecules, such as water, oxygen, carbon dioxide, and alcohol, can cross relatively freely. Entry is also possible for lipid-soluble compounds, such as anesthetics, which diffuse through plasma membranes. Several anatomical features contribute to the barrier. Cells lining the capillary walls are joined together by tight junctions, which block the passage of molecules through the intercellular spaces found in capillaries elsewhere. Also, the brain capillaries lack pores, called fenestrations, which normally promote the passage of fluid and solutes. Furthermore, the brain capillaries are tightly enveloped in a sheath formed by star-shaped glial cells, called ASTROCYTES. The barrier formed by these features helps maintain a constant environment in which the brain can function, but it also means that many potentially useful drugs cannot enter the brain from the bloodstream. See also AREA POSTREMA.

blood glucose see BLOOD SUGAR.

blood group a category of immunologically distinct, genetically determined traits based on the presence or absence of certain ANTIGENS on the surface of red blood cells. The most commonly used is the ABO system, in which the basic categories are A, B, AB, and O. There are more than 20 other blood group systems, including the rhesus system (see RH FACTOR). The major initial work on blood groups and on the nature of blood transfusion was done at the beginning of the 20th century by Austrian physician Karl Landsteiner (1868–1943), who received a Nobel Prize for this research in 1930. Also called **blood type**.

bloodletting *n.* see PHLEBOTOMY.

blood levels the relative amounts of various substances in a measured amount of blood. Blood levels involve comparison of observed levels with an amount or range taken to be normal or toxic. The amount may be expressed as a percentage, in milligrams or micrograms per 100 milliliters, millimoles or micromoles per liter, or a similar measure. Also called **circulating levels**.

blood phobia a persistent and irrational fear of blood, specifically of seeing blood, also called **hematophobia** (although this name is now seldom used). In *DSM–IV–TR* blood phobia is classified as a SPECIFIC PHOBIA, blood-injection-injury type.

blood poisoning a severe or significant bacterial infection of the bloodstream, usually by microorganisms invading from an infection site elsewhere in the body. Blood poisoning may be characterized by fever, chills, and skin eruptions. A particularly hazardous complication is spread of the infection to tissues of the nervous system. Also called **bacteremia**; **septicemia**. See also SEPSIS.

blood pressure the pressure exerted by the blood against the walls of the blood vessels, especially the arteries. It varies with the strength of the heartbeat, the elasticity of the artery walls and resistance of the arterioles, and the person's health, age, and state of activity. Blood pressure is measured using an instrument called a sphygmomanometer. The pressure measured during heart contraction (see SYSTOLIC BLOOD PRESSURE) is higher than that measured when the heart is relaxed (see DIASTOLIC BLOOD PRESSURE). The readings are recorded (in millimeters of mercury) as systolic/diastolic; the normal resting blood pressure for an adult is approximately 120/80. See also HYPERTENSION.

blood sugar the concentration of GLUCOSE in the blood, which is regulated by the pancreatic hormones INSULIN and GLUCAGON. Glucose is an important source of energy for the body, particularly the brain. The normal level of blood sugar for humans, measured 12 hours after the last meal, generally ranges between 70 and 110 mg glucose per deciliter of blood. Abnormally high or low levels (see HYPERGLYCEMIA; HYPOGLYCEMIA) may indicate any of several disease states.

blood type see BLOOD GROUP.

B-love *n.* see BEING LOVE.

blow 1. *n.* slang for COCAINE. **2.** *vb.* to inhale cocaine or to smoke marijuana. See also COCAINE INTOXICATION; CANNABIS INTOXICATION.

blow job slang for oral stimulation of the penis by a partner, which may occur as a part of FOREPLAY or may be continued to the point of orgasm.

BLSA abbreviation for BALTIMORE LONGITUDINAL STUDY OF AGING.

blue *n.* the color experienced when the eye is stimulated by energy in the short-wavelength portion (c. 500–445 nm) of the visible SPECTRUM.

blue-collar worker an employee, such as a factory worker, who performs manual or technical physical labor. The term derives from the blue shirts traditionally (in some cases still) worn by many industrial workers. Compare WHITE-COLLAR WORKER.

blue color blindness see TRITANOPIA.

blues *pl. n.* a colloquial name for depressive symptoms, especially sadness or ANHEDONIA. See also BABY BLUES.

blue-sighted *adj.* having unusual sensitivity to blue stimuli. When a yellowed lens is removed to alleviate a cataract, many patients report heightened sensitivity to blue stimuli.

blue–yellow blindness a rare type of partial color blindness marked by blue and yellow confusion.

blunted affect a disturbance in which AFFECTIVE TONE is dulled. It was cited by Swiss psychiatrist Eugen Bleuler (1857–1939) as one of the basic symptoms of schizophrenia.

blur *n.* the quality of an image that causes it to be indistinct, with smeared or vague borders.

blur point the minimum distance from the eye that a stimulus must be placed to appear blurred. See BLUR.

blurred vision see VISUAL BLURRING.

blushing *n.* an involuntary reddening of the face, sometimes associated with feelings of embarrassment, self-consciousness, modesty, or shame.

B lymphocyte see LYMPHOCYTE.

BMI abbreviation for BODY MASS INDEX.

BMLD abbreviation for binaural MASKING LEVEL DIFFERENCE.

B-motivation *n.* see METAMOTIVATION.

BMR abbreviation for basal metabolic rate. See BASAL METABOLISM.

BNSQ abbreviation for BASIC NORDIC SLEEP QUESTIONNAIRE.

BNT abbreviation for BOSTON NAMING TEST.

board certified denoting a physician or other health care professional who has passed an examination set by a specialty board and has been certified as a specialist in that area. A board-certified (or **boarded**) individual is known as a **diplomate**.

boarding home see ADULT HOME; GROUP HOME; HALFWAY HOUSE.

boarding-out system a system in which patients with psychoses are cared for in private homes. See also GHEEL COLONY.

Bobo doll an inflatable plastic clown. In his studies of observational learning, Albert BANDURA demonstrated that children who had watched a videotape of an adult being violent with a Bobo doll were more likely to behave aggressively toward the doll than children who had watched an adult being nonviolent toward it.

bodily-kinesthetic intelligence in the MULTIPLE-INTELLIGENCES THEORY, the intelligence involved in forming and coordinating bodily movements, such as those used in dancing, playing a violin, or playing basketball.

body *n.* **1.** the entire physical structure of an organism, such as the human body. **2.** the physical body as opposed to the mental processes of a human being. See MIND–BODY PROBLEM. **3.** the trunk or torso of a human being or an animal. **4.** the main part of a structure or organ, such as the body of the penis. **5.** a discrete anatomical or cytological structure, such as the Barr body (see SEX CHROMATIN).

body awareness the perception of one's body structure as a component of the image of self, which is derived from internal sensations, movement, and contact with the external world.

body boundaries a component of the body image consisting of the definiteness or indefiniteness of the boundary of the body. Barrier responses in RORSCHACH INKBLOT TESTS, such as "turtle with shell" and "man in armor," indicate a definite body boundary, while PENETRATION RESPONSES, such as "person bleeding" and "torn coat," indicate indefinite boundaries.

body buffer zone the physical distance a person prefers to maintain between him- or herself and one or more other individuals to avoid feeling uncomfortable. This zone varies depending on the relationship with the others; it is smaller, for example, when there is a close relationship. It also varies according to culture.

body build a general measure of the body in terms of trunk, limb length, and girth.

body-build index an index of constitutional types. Individuals are grouped according to the formula: (height × 100)/(transverse chest diameter × 6). **Mesomorphs**, who are muscular, fall within one standard deviation of the mean; **leptomorphs** one standard deviation or more above the mean; and broadly built **eurymorphs** one standard deviation or more below the mean. [proposed by Hans Jürgen EYSENCK]

bodybuilding *n.* the use of a weight-lifting program to build muscle bulk and to acquire muscle definition.

body cell any tissue cell that is not a GERM CELL. It normally has the DIPLOID number of chromosomes. Also called **somatic cell**.

body cognitions beliefs or attitudes about the features of one's appearance. Characteristically negative and self-defeating thoughts are related to subjective dissatisfaction.

body concept the thoughts, feelings, and perceptions that constitute the way an individual views his or her body: that is, the conceptual image of one's body. Compare BODY PERCEPT. See BODY IMAGE.

body disfigurement an objective defect of appearance related to a congenital malformation, physical injury, or any disease process that modifies the physical integrity of the individual.

body distortion a tendency to overestimate one's body size or to have bizarre perceptual experiences. See also BODY-SIZE OVERESTIMATION; BODY-IMAGE DISTORTION.

body dysmorphia an extreme disparagement of some aspect of appearance that is not supported by the objective evidence. There may be a mild defect in the body feature or, in extreme cases, there may be no objective evidence of any malformation or oddity of appearance. See also BODY DYSMORPHIC DISORDER; MUSCLE DYSMORPHIA.

body dysmorphic disorder (**BDD**) in *DSM–IV–TR*, a SOMATOFORM DISORDER characterized by excessive preoccupation with an imagined defect in physical appearance or markedly excessive concern with a slight physical anomaly, formerly called **dysmorphophobia**. The preoccupation is typically accompanied by frequent checking of the defect. BDD shares features of OBSESSIVE-COMPULSIVE DISORDER, such as obsessions with appearance and associated compulsions (e.g., mirror-checking), and causes significant distress or impairment in social, occupational, or other important areas of functioning.

body ego in psychoanalytic theory, the part of the EGO that develops out of self-perceptions of the body. It is the core of the ego around which all perceptions of the self are grouped, including individual memories, sensations, ideas, wishes, strivings, and fantasies. See also PERSONALIZATION.

body electrode placement the pattern or location of individual electrodes used to measure electrical properties of the heart, brain, skin, or other organ or system.

body esteem the degree of positiveness with which individuals regard the various parts of their body and the appearance of those parts.

body ideal the BODY TYPE considered most attractive or most appropriate to one's age and sex by a particular individual, culture, or generation. See BODY IMAGE.

body image the mental picture one forms of one's body as a whole, including both its physical and functional characteristics (BODY PERCEPT) and one's attitudes toward these characteristics (BODY CONCEPT). Also called **body identity**. See also BODY SCHEMA.

Body Image Assessment (**BIA**) a measure of body image in which a participant is shown silhouettes of figures that increase incrementally in size from very thin to very overweight and is asked to choose the one that represents his or her actual figure and the one that represents his or her ideal figure. In addition to the BIA for adults, there are three other forms of the instrument: BIA-O for obese adults, BIA-C for younger children, and BIA-P for preadolescents. [originally developed in 1985 by U.S. psychologist Donald A. Williamson (1950–) and colleagues]

body-image avoidance behavioral manifestations of excessive concern with one's appearance, evidenced by such behaviors as avoiding social functions and engaging in cover-up activities (e.g., wearing bulky and loose-fitting clothing) to obscure and hide aspects of the body with which one is dissatisfied.

body-image distortion distortion in the subjective image or mental representation of one's own body appearance, size, or movement. The term is usually applied to overestimation of body size or used to define the perceptual experiences of individuals with psychoses. Also called **body-image disturbance**. See also ANOREXIA NERVOSA; BODY DISTORTION. Compare BODY DYSMORPHIC DISORDER.

body-image ideals personal standards of optimal appearance for various body features: idealized features as opposed to actual attributes of appearance.

body language the expression of feelings and thoughts, which may or may not be verbalized, through posture, gesture, facial expression, or other movements. For example, anger is usually indicated by a facial expression in which there are downward lines in the forehead, cheeks, and mouth, and the fist may be clenched. Although body language is often called NONVERBAL COMMUNICATION, such movements may be unintentional, and many investigators therefore believe the term "communication" is often inappropriate in this context.

body mass index (**BMI**) a widely used index of adiposity or OBESITY based on the following formula: weight (kg) divided by height squared (m^2).

body memory a sensory recollection of trauma in the form of pain, arousal, tension, or discomfort, usually unaccompanied by words or images. Body memory is frequently the result of trauma occurring during the period of INFANTILE AMNESIA, leading to a sensorimotor, rather than cognitive, encoding of the traumatic event. See also SENSORIMOTOR MEMORY.

body–mind problem see MIND–BODY PROBLEM.

body narcissism 1. an exaggerated preoccupation or fascination with one's own body and its erogenous zones. See also NARCISSISM. **2.** in psychoanalytic theory, the PRIMARY NARCISSISM of the young infant.

body odor the odor produced by the action of bacteria on skin secretions, such as perspiration (which itself is nearly odorless). Attitudes toward body odor vary in different cultures.

body percept the mental image one forms of the physical characteristics of one's own body, that is, whether one is slim or stocky, strong or weak, attractive or unattractive, tall or short. Compare BODY CONCEPT. See BODY IMAGE.

body positioning the notion that body posture can affect memory. Specific kinesthetic and proprioceptive feedback may provide a context for enhancing learning and recall.

body rocking see ROCKING.

body schema the cognitive organization of one's appearance, including internal image, thoughts, and feelings. See BODY PERCEPT.

body-size overestimation the specific tendency to overestimate the size of body features (e.g., width of waist, hips, or thighs) in relation to objective size measurements. It was once thought to be an essential feature of ANOREXIA NERVOSA. See BODY DISTORTION; BODY-IMAGE DISTORTION.

body temperature the temperature of the body, which is normally about 98.6 °F (37 °C) in humans. Body temperature affects all metabolic processes, and most cells must remain within the range of 32–113 °F (0–45 °C). Animals are characterized as ENDOTHERMS or ECTOTHERMS according to their ability to regulate body temperature. See also HEAT EFFECTS; HYPOTHERMIA.

body therapies a group of therapies that seek the relief of psychological tensions and other symptoms through body manipulation, relaxation, massage, breathing exercises, and changes in posture and position of body parts. The therapies are based on the theory that the body and its functioning embody an individual's basic personality and way of life. See also BODYWORK.

body type a classification of individuals according to body build or physique. See CONSTITUTIONAL TYPE; ECTOMORPH; ENDOMORPH; MESOMORPH; ASTHENIC TYPE; ATHLETIC TYPE; DYSPLASTIC TYPE; PYKNIC TYPE.

body-type theories a set of theories holding that aspects of physique and size determine such associated characteristics as psychological traits.

bodywork *n.* an adjunctive treatment (see ADJUNCTIVE THERAPY) that may be recommended in addition to psychotherapy. It typically includes massage, movement, and exercises involving touch.

Bogardus Social Distance Scale a SOCIAL DISTANCE SCALE used to measure individuals' attitudes toward particular ethnic groups. It is assumed that individuals who would prefer to keep a greater social distance between themselves and members of a specific group are prejudiced against that group. [Emory **Bogardus** (1882–1973), U.S. sociologist]

bogus pipeline fake apparatus used in attitude research to ascertain attitudes toward controversial or sensitive issues. The apparatus is attached to the participant, who is then informed, incorrectly, that it can detect whether or not the attitude he or she reports is a true one. In one study, it was found that use of the bogus pipeline resulted in a greater likelihood of admitting cocaine abuse, excessive drinking, and oral sex.

boilermaker's deafness a high-frequency hearing loss resulting from exposure to high-intensity noise. The condition has been known for many years but is increasingly prevalent due to the increased noise of highly industrialized society. See ACOUSTIC TRAUMA.

bolstering of an attitude a method of reducing COGNITIVE DISSONANCE by generating new cognitive elements that are consistent with an attitude. This is presumed to offset the dissonance resulting from an inconsistent element.

bona fide occupational qualification (**BFOQ**) a qualification or personal characteristic (e.g., age, sex, physical abilities) that is genuinely necessary to perform a particular job successfully, as opposed to one that is often associated with the job but not in fact necessary for effective performance. See also ADVERSE IMPACT; AGE DISCRIMINATION IN EMPLOYMENT ACT; AMERICANS WITH DISABILITIES ACT.

bona fide pipeline measure of attitudes see EVALUATIVE SEMANTIC PRIMING MEASURE OF ATTITUDES.

bond 1. *n.* a relationship between two or more individuals that signifies trust and alliance. In a social context, the existence of such an ATTACHMENT enables individuals to provide emotional support for each other (see also PAIR BOND). In psychotherapy, the bond of a THERAPEUTIC ALLIANCE between therapist and client is considered beneficial to the treatment. **2.** *n.* a chemical bond, such as an ionic or covalent bond, by which atoms are bound into a molecule. **3.** *vb.* to form a bond of either of these types. **4.** *n.* see BOND-SAMPLING THEORY OF HUMAN INTELLIGENCE.

bondage *n.* a form of mock enslavement of one person by another to arouse sexual pleasure in one or both partners. The bondage scenario, which is usually accompanied by threats or acts of danger and humiliation, may involve heterosexual, gay, lesbian, or bisexual participants. The enslaved person may be immobilized with ropes, straps, chains, or other restraining devices.

bondage and discipline (**B and D**) a phase of sexual BONDAGE that is accompanied by such acts as whipping or spanking. Because of the potential physical danger, the partners usually agree on a signal, called a safe word, to be used when the erotic activity exceeds the pleasurable limits.

bonding *n.* the process in which ATTACHMENTS or other close relationships are formed between individuals, especially between mother and infant. An early, positive relationship between a mother and a newborn child is considered to be essential in establishing unconditional love on the part of the parent, as well as security and trust on the part of the child. In subsequent development, bonding establishes friendship and trust (see BOND).

bond-sampling theory of human intelligence a theory postulating that the GENERAL FACTOR of intelligence is due not to a single psychological entity (general ability, or *g*) but rather to sampling of a wide variety of elements (called **bonds**), which might include such skills as understanding directions, responding to questions, and inferring relations. According to the theory, these multiple bonds mingle to form a general factor because all of them are required for all the subtests on a battery that measures intelligence. [proposed by Sir Godfrey Thomson (1881–1955), British psychologist]

bone age a measure of the skeletal maturity of an individual based on the stage of ossification of bone, usually determined from X-rays of the hand and wrist.

bone conduction the transmission of sound waves to the inner ear through vibrations of bones in the skull.

bone-conduction testing an audiological procedure to determine if the hearing loss detected in AIR-CONDUCTION TESTING is a result of conductive or sensorineural factors. It is performed at controlled frequencies with a small bone-conduction vibrator, attached to a headband, placed on the temporal bone behind the ear. See AIR–BONE GAP.

bone pointing see VOODOO DEATH.

Bonferroni t test a procedure for adjusting the *p*-value (see SIGNIFICANCE LEVEL) of individual related T TESTS in such a way that, for a collection of *c* related tests, the joint probability of rejecting any of the *c* NULL HYPOTHESES, when the combined null is true, is held at α. The procedure involves dividing the usual significance level value by the number of comparisons being made, so as to avoid the increased risk of TYPE I ERROR that comes with multiple comparisons. Also called **Bonferroni adjustment**; **Dunn's multiple comparison test**. [developed by O. J. Dunn]

Bonnet syndrome see CHARLES BONNET SYNDROME.

Boolean algebra a logical system that translates statements from various domains into symbolic equations that can be manipulated according to axiomatic rules to yield logical conclusions. In computer science, Boolean algebra underlies and models the complex chains of circuit logic of the digital computer. [George **Boole** (1815–1864), British mathematician and logician]

boomerang effect a situation in which a persuasive message produces ATTITUDE CHANGE in the direction opposite to that intended. Boomerang effects occur when recipients generate COUNTERARGUMENTS substantially stronger than the ARGUMENTS contained in the original message.

booster sessions in therapy, particularly COGNITIVE BEHAVIOR THERAPY, occasional periodic sessions, after the main sessions are officially ended, in order to reinforce progress or troubleshoot obstacles to continuance of positive changes made during the therapy.

bootstrapping *n.* **1.** in information processing, any process or operation in which a system uses its initial resources to develop more powerful and complex processing routines, which are then used in the same fashion, and so on cumulatively. In LANGUAGE ACQUISITION, the term is used of children's ability to learn complex linguistic rules, which can be endlessly reapplied, from extremely limited data (see COMPETENCE; LANGUAGE ACQUISITION DEVICE). The term derives from the idiom "to pull oneself up by one's bootstraps." **2.** a computational method for estimating the precision of an estimate of a parameter. A random sample of *n* observations is taken, and from this a number of other samples of equal size are obtained by sampling with replacement. **—bootstrap** *vb.*

borderline 1. *adj.* pertaining to any phenomenon difficult to categorize because it straddles two distinct classes, showing characteristics of both. Thus, BORDERLINE INTELLIGENCE is supposed to show characteristics of both the average and subaverage categories. See also BORDERLINE DISORDER; BORDERLINE STATE. **2.** *n.* an inappropriate designation for someone with BORDERLINE PERSONALITY DISORDER or its symptoms.

borderline case see CASE.

borderline disorder 1. BORDERLINE PERSONALITY DISORDER or, more broadly, any personality disorder. **2.** historically, any psychological condition that lies between normality and neurosis, between normality and psychosis, or between normal intelligence and mental retardation. See also BORDERLINE INTELLIGENCE.

borderline intelligence a level of measured intellectual performance between average and significantly subaverage intelligence. Some researchers define it as an IQ between 68 and 83, others as any IQ in the 70s, but it is most often associated with IQs in the range 70–75. IQs in the borderline range, especially above 75, do not justify a basis for diagnosis of mental retardation. Also called **borderline intellectual functioning**; **borderline mental retardation**.

borderline personality disorder in *DSM–IV–TR*, a personality disorder characterized by a long-standing pattern of instability in mood, interpersonal relationships, and self-image that is severe enough to cause extreme distress or interfere with social and occupational functioning. Among the manifestations of this disorder are (a) self-damaging behavior in such areas as gambling, sex, spending, overeating, and substance use; (b) intense but unstable relationships; (c) uncontrollable temper outbursts; (d) uncertainty about self-image, gender, goals, and loyalties; (e) shifting moods; (f) self-defeating behavior, such as fights, suicidal gestures, or self-mutilation; and (g) chronic feelings of emptiness and boredom. An alternative name for this disorder, **unstable personality disorder**, was proposed in the *DSM–III* task force.

borderline psychosis see BORDERLINE STATE.

borderline schizophrenia historically, a condition in which an individual inconsistently displays symptoms of schizophrenia (e.g., only under circumstances of high stress) but is in touch with reality most of the time. In *DSM–II*, this condition was included within the diagnostic category of latent schizophrenia.

borderline state any condition in which an individual's presenting symptoms are difficult to classify. Historically, borderline state (or **borderline psychosis**) more specifically referred to a condition in which an individual may become psychotic if exposed to unfavorable circumstances but has not currently lost touch with reality.

boredom *n.* a state of weariness or ennui resulting from a lack of engagement with stimuli in the environment. **—bored** *adj.*

Borg scale either of two scales for measuring intensity of sensation and experience, enabling comparisons across people and across tasks. The **RPE scale** (rating of perceived exertion) is used specifically for measuring perceived exertion and effort in physical work. The **CR10 scale** (categorical rating with a scale from 1 to 10) is a general method that measures the magnitude of different sensations, including pain, loudness and noise, and brightness. These scales are used in psychophysics as well as in fitness training, ergonomics, and REHABILITATION. [Gunnar **Borg**, 20th-century Swedish psychologist]

Boring, Edwin Garrigues (1886–1968) U.S. psychologist, who was an influential leader of EXPERIMENTAL PSYCHOLOGY and an American Psychological Foundation gold medalist. Boring was trained as a psychophysicist by Edward B. TITCHENER at Cornell University, receiving his PhD in 1914. He was recruited by Robert M. YERKES during World War I to work in the U.S. Army's mental testing program and was instrumental in creating the infamous report summarizing its results. Boring's most famous empirical work involved experiments on the MOON ILLUSION. However, he is perhaps best known for his *History of Experimental Psychology* (1929; revised 1950). This work was a required text for many psychology graduate students from its publication through the 1960s and beyond, and it helped to define the scope and methods of experimental psychology through its treatment of the subject's history. Boring served as director of the Psychology Laboratory at Harvard University for 25 years and remained there until his retirement in 1957. A number of contemporary historians have criticized Boring's work for selectively highlighting the pure versus the applied aspects of psychology's history and for relying heavily on the notion of a ZEITGEIST, or prevailing temper of a period, rather than on more complex historical explanations for psychology's evolution.

Börjeson–Forssman–Lehmann syndrome a disorder characterized by MICROCEPHALY, severe mental retardation, short stature, and hypogonadism. Affected individuals have severe to profound mental retardation and little or no pubic hair, even as adults. The syndrome is related to an X-linked recessive mutant gene (locus Xq26–27). [Mats Gunnar **Börjeson** (1922–), Hans Axel **Forssman** (1912–), and J. O. Orla **Lehmann** (1927–), Swedish physicians]

borna disease a disease of mammals (especially horses) that is caused by a virus and can be transmitted to humans, typically via intranasal infection. It usually results in ENCEPHALOPATHY, which leads to ATAXIA, blindness, and other neurological disorders.

borstal system a treatment approach for juvenile offenders that emphasizes rehabilitation through hard work and recreation, along with a period of supervision during reentry to society. The approach is named after the prison at Borstal in Kent, England, where it was first introduced in 1908.

BOS abbreviation for BEHAVIORAL OBSERVATION SCALE.

Boston Naming Test (**BNT**) a 60-item fluency test of word retrieval used to evaluate DYSPHASIA. Line drawings of objects—ranging in difficulty from the commonly encountered (e.g., tree, bed) to the rarely encountered (e.g., sphinx, abacus)—are presented, and the participant provides the name of each object. [originally developed in 1978 by U.S. neuropsychologist Edith F. Kaplan (1924–), U.S. clinical psychologist Harold Goodglass (1920–), and U.S. neuropsychologist Sandra Weintraub (1946–)]

BOT abbreviation for BRUININKS–OSERETSKY TEST OF MOTOR PROFICIENCY.

botany *n.* the scientific study of plants. **—botanical** *adj.* **—botanist** *n.*

bottle baby slang for an infant born addicted to CRACK.

bottle feeding see FEEDING TECHNIQUE.

bottleneck model any model of attention that assumes the existence of a limited-capacity channel (typically with a capacity of one item) at some specific stage of human information processing. In LATE-SELECTION THEORIES this channel (the "bottleneck") occurs after stimulus identification.

bottoming out a state of despair characterized by financial ruin, suicide attempts, or shattered family and other intimate interpersonal relationships that is frequently experienced by people with severe depression or addiction disorders (e.g., substance abusers and pathological gamblers).

bottom-up analysis **1.** an inductive approach to problem solving that begins with specific instances or empirical data and works up to a more abstract level of analysis, such as a general principle or hypothesis. See INDUCTIVE REASONING. Compare TOP-DOWN ANALYSIS. **2.** in information processing, see BOTTOM-UP PROCESSING.

bottom-up design an inductive approach to the design of a system or product. Such an approach involves identifying basic user requirements and allowing these to drive the design, as opposed to basing it on existing product designs or abstract models. Compare TOP-DOWN DESIGN.

bottom-up processing INFORMATION PROCESSING that proceeds from the data in the stimulus input to higher level processes, such as recognition, interpretation, and categorization. For example, in vision, features would be combined into objects, and objects into scenes, recognition of which would be based only on the information in the stimulus input. Typically, perceptual or cognitive mechanisms use bottom-up processing when information is unfamiliar or highly complex. Also called **bottom-up analysis**. Compare TOP-DOWN PROCESSING. See also DATA-DRIVEN PROCESS; SHALLOW PROCESSING.

bouffée délirante see ACUTE DELUSIONAL PSYCHOSIS.

Boulder model see SCIENTIST-PRACTITIONER MODEL.

boulimia *n.* see BULIMIA.

boundary *n.* **1.** a psychological demarcation that protects the integrity of an individual or group or that helps the person or group set realistic limits on participation in a relationship or activity. **2.** in psychotherapy, an important limit that is usually set by the therapist as part of the GROUND RULES in treatment. Boundaries may involve areas of discussion (e.g., the therapist's personal life is off limits) or physical limits (e.g., rules about touching), which are guided by ethical codes and standards. Respect for boundaries by both the therapist and client is an important concept in the therapeutic relationship.

boundary ambiguity uncertainty that arises in a family system when an individual's status, role, or family membership is brought into question, most often as a result of separation, divorce, and remarriage. See PERMEABLE FAMILY.

boundary detector **1.** any of the RETINAL GANGLION CELLS that respond to a sharp edge in a receptive field, regardless of brightness or contrast on either side of the edge. These cells are most common in the retinas of frogs. See also FEATURE DETECTOR. **2.** any of a class of computational algorithms designed to detect edges in artificial vision or word segmentation in speech processing.

boundary issues **1.** ethical issues relating to the proper limits of a professional relationship between a provider of services (e.g., a physician or a psychotherapist) and his or her patient or client, such that the trust and vulnerability of the latter are not abused (see BOUNDARY). A particular area of concern is PROFESSIONAL–CLIENT SEXUAL RELATIONS. **2.** in health care, issues relating to the demarcations between different areas and levels of expertise and questions of who is best qualified to give certain types of treatment or advice.

boundary system in GENERAL SYSTEMS THEORY, the semipermeable boundaries between living systems, permitting information to flow in either direction but posing the question of how much interpenetration and interdependence is feasible in a given social system. See also EGO BOUNDARY.

bounded rationality decision making in which the processes used are rational within the constraints imposed by (a) limitations in the individual's knowledge; (b) human cognitive limitations generally; and (c) empirical factors arising from the complex, real-life situations in which decisions have to be made. The concept was introduced by Herbert SIMON as a corrective to the assumption of classical economic theory that individuals can and will make ideally informed and rational decisions in pursuit of their own self-interest (see RATIONAL-ECONOMIC MAN). See PROCEDURAL RATIONALITY; SUBSTANTIVE RATIONALITY. See also SATISFICE.

bound energy in psychoanalytic theory, PSYCHIC ENERGY that is located within the ego and focused on the individual's external reality. Bound energy is associated with the SECONDARY PROCESSES and is contrasted with the FREE ENERGY of the id.

bound morpheme in linguistics, a MORPHEME that can occur only in combination with other morphemes. For example, the morpheme for the past tense *-ed* can only occur with a verb stem, as in *kissed*. Compare FREE MORPHEME.

bourgeoisie see MIDDLE CLASS.

bouton terminal see TERMINAL BUTTON.

bowel control the ability to regulate defecation so that elimination occurs in the proper place at the proper time. See TOILET TRAINING. Compare ENCOPRESIS.

bowel disorders disorders of the bowels, which frequently occur as responses to stress and anxiety. In some cases, transient disturbances, such as constipation and diarrhea, may occur as side effects of psychotropic drugs. Major bowel disorders that may be psychologically caused or aggravated include chronic CONSTIPATION, IRRITABLE BOWEL SYNDROME, and ulcerative COLITIS.

bowel incontinence see FECAL INCONTINENCE.

Bowen family systems theory see FAMILY SYSTEMS THEORY.

Bowlby, Edward John Mostyn (1907–1990) British psychiatrist. Bowlby received his MD in 1933 from University College in London and trained as a psychoanalyst. Influenced by the studies of IMPRINTING in animals that Austrian ethologist Konrad Lorenz (1903–1989) conducted, Bowlby integrated psychoanalytic ideas with evolutionary biology and cognitive psychology to create his ATTACHMENT THEORY. He argued that the attachment of human infants to their caregivers and their distress at being separated from them have an evolutionary advantage: They increase the infants' likelihood of survival by keeping them close to their caregivers. Patterns of attachment (secure and insecure) established in early childhood affect later emotional development and emotional stability in the child and adult. Bowlby's work has been very influential in developmental psychology since the 1970s, initiating a rich body of research on the importance of early attachment patterns to psychological well-being.

Box–Cox transformation a procedure for finding a data TRANSFORMATION that brings the transformed data into greater compliance with the assumptions of the GENERAL LINEAR MODEL. The transformations possible under Box–Cox are of the form $Y' = Y^{\lambda}$ and include the square root, log, exponential, and power transformations. [George E. P. **Box** (1919–) and David Roxbee **Cox** (1924–), British statisticians]

boxer's dementia a chronic, slowly progressive DEMENTIA resulting from scattered PETECHIAL HEMORRHAGES in the brain produced by repeated blows to the head. Affected individuals are often described as "punch-drunk." Common symptoms include poorly articulated speech (see DYSARTHRIA), poor balance, impaired memory and concentration, and involuntary movements. The term is often applied to the more advanced cases, while **boxer's traumatic encephalopathy** refers to all types of cases. Also called **dementia pugilistica**.

box plot in EXPLORATORY DATA ANALYSIS, a graphical display of a batch of data created exclusively from the extreme scores, the HINGES, and the MEDIAN of the batch.

BPRS abbreviation for BRIEF PSYCHIATRIC RATING SCALE.

BPS abbreviation for BRITISH PSYCHOLOGICAL SOCIETY.

BRAC abbreviation for BASIC REST–ACTIVITY CYCLE.

brace *n.* a device that supports or maintains the correct positioning of a part of the body, such as a limb, a joint, or the spine. Braces may be designed to permit flexion and motion and are typically intended for permanent or long-term use. They are distinct from splints, which are used to temporarily immobilize or protect a part of the body.

brachial plexus a network of nerves that carries signals from the spinal cord to the shoulder, arm, and hand. Injury to the brachial plexus can impair control of these parts.

brachium *n.* (*pl.* **brachia**) **1.** the upper arm, extending from the shoulder to the elbow. **2.** in anatomy, a structure that resembles an arm, such as the BRACHIUM CONJUNCTIVUM. **—brachial** *adj.*

brachium conjunctivum the superior CEREBELLAR PEDUNCLE, a band of fibrous tissue extending from each hemisphere of the cerebellum to the pons.

Brachmann–de Lange syndrome see AMSTERDAM DWARF DISEASE; DE LANGE'S SYNDROME. [described in 1916 by Winfried **Brachmann** (1888–c. 1915), German physician, and in 1933 by Cornelia **de Lange** (1871–1950), Dutch pediatrician]

brachy- *combining form* short.

brachycephalic *adj.* denoting a head that is abnormally short and wide. See CEPHALIC INDEX. **—brachycephaly** *n.*

brachymorph *n.* a body type characterized by an abnormally short, broad physique. Also called **brachytype**. **—brachymorphic** *adj.*

brachyskeletal *adj.* having abnormally short bones, particularly short leg bones. Also called **brachyskelic**.

brachytype *n.* see BRACHYMORPH.

bracketed morality a temporary suspension of the level of moral reasoning used in daily life due to contextual factors in a particular situation. See GAME REASONING.

brady- *combining form* slow.

bradyarthria *n.* see BRADYLALIA.

bradycardia *n.* a slow heartbeat due to an organic or psychogenic condition. See ARRHYTHMIA.

bradyesthesia *n.* slowed or dulled sensation.

bradykinesia *n.* abnormal slowness of movements with a decrease in spontaneous motor activity. Also called **bradykinesis**.

bradylalia *n.* abnormal slowness or hesitation in speech. Also called **bradyarthria**; **bradylogia**.

bradylexia *n.* extreme slowness in reading that is not attributable to intellectual impairment. **—bradylexic** *adj.*

bradylogia *n.* see BRADYLALIA.

bradyrhythmia *n.* slowness of the rhythms of the heart.

brahmacharya *n.* **1.** continence or chastity (Sanskrit). In the Hindu tradition (see HINDUISM), the term signifies continence in thought, word, and deed, which is one of the five virtues of the first stage of Raja-Yoga. It is also used to denote an ordination ceremony for novice monks as well as the first of the four stages into which human life is divided according to Vedic tradition. **2.** in BUDDHISM, holy conduct of life. The term signifies a life lived in harmony with Buddhist rules of discipline and is used to describe the chaste lifestyle of a Buddhist monk.

braid cutting a hair fetish in which a person's hair is cut as part of sexual activity.

Braid's strabismus a form of STRABISMUS in which hypnosis can be induced by causing the eyes to converge and turn upward. [James **Braid** (1795–1860), British surgeon and hypnosis researcher]

braille *n.* a system of letters, numbers, punctuation marks, and scientific and musical symbols adapted as a written language for people with severe visual impairment, using combinations of raised dots that can be touched. Each character comprises a specific pattern of six dots organized in two parallel vertical columns. Prefix symbols are used to indicate capitalization and numbers, and various other conventions are used to represent more than 200 common words or recurring letter combinations. [introduced in 1829 by Louis **Braille** (1809–1852), French teacher and inventor]

brain *n.* the enlarged, anterior part of the CENTRAL NERVOUS SYSTEM within the skull. The young adult human brain weighs about 1,450 g, and its outer layer (the CEREBRAL CORTEX) contains over 10 billion nerve cells. The brain develops by differentiation of the embryonic NEURAL TUBE along an anterior–posterior axis to form three main regions—the FOREBRAIN, MIDBRAIN, and HINDBRAIN—that can be further subdivided on the basis of anatomical and functional criteria. The cortical tissue is concentrated in the forebrain, and the midbrain and hindbrain structures are often considered together as the BRAINSTEM. The functions of the brain are discussed in entries for the different parts of the brain. Also called **encephalon**. See also BRAIN LOCALIZATION THEORY; EVOLUTION OF THE BRAIN; SPLIT BRAIN.

brain ablation see ABLATION.

brain abscess a circumscribed collection of pus that may occur in any part of the brain and, depending on its location, may produce deficits in any neurological function. Brain abscesses are often secondary to infections.

brain atlas a collection of illustrations of details of brain structure.

brain atrophy see CEREBRAL ATROPHY.

brain bank a program in which brains of people with specific neurological disorders are gathered to enable scientists to conduct intensive pathological studies.

brain biorhythm a BIOLOGICAL RHYTHM involving recurring periods of altered excitability or activity of the brain. Some practitioners claim to be able to predict an individual's brain biorhythms from his or her birthdate, and to use this information to improve performance.

brain center any of various regions of the brain that have specific functions, such as the visual centers and the (alleged) hunger center.

brain comparator a theoretical structure in the brain that compares an intended movement with sensory feedback that results from the movement (see COMPARATOR). The cerebellum is believed to act as a brain comparator to coordinate and calibrate movements in response to visual and somatosensory feedback. See also COROLLARY DISCHARGE.

brain concussion mild injury to the brain, due to trauma or jarring, that disrupts brain function but is typically followed by spontaneous recovery. Concussion usually involves at least brief unconsciousness, although it may be diagnosed in the absence of unconsciousness. The symptoms may include memory loss, headache, irritability, inappropriate emotional reactions, and changes in behavior. Concussions may be classified by severity based on the period of unconsciousness or the extent of memory loss for events before and after the trauma. See HEAD INJURY.

brain contusion see CEREBRAL CONTUSION.

brain damage injury to the brain. It can have various causes, including prenatal infection, birth injury, head injury, toxic agents, BRAIN TUMOR, brain inflammation, severe seizures, certain metabolic disorders, vitamin deficiency, intracranial hemorrhage, stroke, and surgical procedures. Brain damage is manifested by impairment of cognitive, motor, or sensory skills mediated by the brain.

brain-damage language disorder any loss of the ability to communicate effectively by means of symbolic stimuli, arising as a result of an acquired BRAIN DISORDER. See APHASIA; ALEXIA.

brain death the cessation of neurological signs of life. Medical criteria for brain death include absence of reflex response or response to noxious stimuli, fixed pupils, and absence of electroencephalogram (EEG) activity. The absence of EEG activity alone is not a final diagnostic sign, but brain death cannot be diagnosed if there is any sign of EEG activity.

brain-derived neurotrophic factor (**BDNF**) a NEUROTROPHIC FACTOR thought to be important in regulating synaptic plasticity, neurogenesis, and neuronal survival. It has been linked to some psychiatric disorders.

brain disease any disease that leads to BRAIN DAMAGE. Such diseases can include degenerative, metabolic, and infectious disorders.

brain disorder 1. any condition marked by disruption of the normal functioning of the brain. **2.** an older (*DSM–I*) term for an acute or chronic mental disorder caused by or associated with impairment of brain function and characterized by mild to severe impairment of cognition and mood. Also called **brain syndrome**.

brain electrical activity mapping (**BEAM**) a system of computerized ELECTROENCEPHALOGRAPHY used to analyze and display electrical activity of the brain.

brain explant a small piece of brain tissue that is isolated from the body and used for experimental purposes.

brain fag a CULTURE-BOUND SYNDROME originating in west Africa and most often experienced by high school or college students. Symptoms typically include difficulties with concentration, memory, and understanding information; feelings of pain, tightness, and burning around the head and neck; blurred vision; and tiredness associated with excessive thinking.

brain graft the surgical transplantation or implantation of brain tissue to replace a damaged part or compensate for a defect.

brain growth the increase in size, mass, and complexity of the brain. In humans, the brain grows very rapidly in the fetus and during the early postnatal years, reaching its maximum mass at about 20 years, after which there is a slow decline. Some regions of the brain grow more rapidly than others, well into the teenage years.

brain imaging 1. study of the anatomy of the brain through the intact skull by noninvasive computerized techniques, such as MAGNETIC RESONANCE IMAGING and COMPUTED TOMOGRAPHY. **2.** study of the relative activity of different parts of the brain by noninvasive computerized techniques, such as POSITRON EMISSION TOMOGRAPHY or FUNCTIONAL MAGNETIC RESONANCE IMAGING, in order to find how the different parts are involved in various cognitive functions. See also FUNCTIONAL BRAIN IMAGING; NUCLEAR IMAGING.

brain injury see BRAIN DAMAGE; BRAIN TRAUMA.

brain lesion any damage to an area of brain tissue caused by injury, disease, surgery, tumor, stroke, or infection. Also called **cerebral lesion**.

brain localization theory any of various theories that different areas of the brain serve different functions. Since the early 19th century, opinion has varied between notions of highly precise localization and a belief that the brain, or large portions of it, function as a whole. In 1861 French physician Paul Broca (1824–1880) deduced from localized brain lesions that the speech center of the brain is in the left frontal lobe (see BROCA'S AREA). Since then, many techniques, including localized electrical stimulation of the brain, electrical recording from the brain, and BRAIN IMAGING, have added information about localization of function in the brain. For many investigators, however, the concept of extreme parcellation of functions has given way to concepts of distributed control by collective activity of different regions. See also MASS ACTION.

brain mapping the creation of a visual representation of the brain in which different functions are assigned to different brain regions. Mapping may be based on a variety of sources of information, including effects of localized brain lesions, recording electrical activity of the brain, and BRAIN IMAGING during various behavioral states. See also BRAIN LOCALIZATION THEORY.

brain neoplasm see BRAIN TUMOR.

brain nucleus a cluster of cells within the cerebrum or cerebellum. See NUCLEUS.

brain pathology the study of any disorder or disease of the brain.

brain plasticity 1. the capacity of the brain to compensate for losses in brain tissue caused by injury or disease. **2.** the capacity of the brain to change as a function of experience. The term plasticity in this sense was first used by William JAMES in 1890. See also RECOVERY OF FUNCTION.

brain potential the electric potential of brain cells. See ELECTROENCEPHALOGRAPHY.

brain research investigation of the structure and functions of the brain, using such techniques as (a) the administration of psychological and neurological tests after lesions have occurred in various areas; (b) the observation or measurement of the effects of stimulation or ablation of parts of the brain; (c) the study of the electrical properties of the cortex; (d) the study of the nature and functions of chemicals involved in neurotransmission; and (e) the use of ELECTROENCEPHALOGRAPHY and BRAIN IMAGING techniques.

brain reserve capacity 1. the ability of remaining brain tissue to take over the function of damaged or destroyed tissue. See RECOVERY OF FUNCTION. **2.** a capacity outside of behaviors usually acknowledged, for example, the capacity for TELEPATHY or CLAIRVOYANCE.

brain scan any of a variety of techniques designed either to reveal structural or functional abnormalities of the diseased brain or to measure activity of the healthy brain. See BRAIN IMAGING.

brain self-stimulation see INTRACRANIAL SELF-STIMULATION.

brain splitting surgical separation of the cerebral hemispheres of the brain. See COMMISSUROTOMY; SPLIT BRAIN.

brainstem *n.* the part of the BRAIN that connects the cerebrum with the spinal cord. It includes the MIDBRAIN, PONS, CEREBELLUM, and MEDULLA OBLONGATA (the last three comprising the HINDBRAIN).

brainstem auditory evoked response an EVENT-RELATED POTENTIAL recorded from the BRAINSTEM in response to an auditory stimulus (see AUDITORY EVOKED POTENTIAL). Such recordings are used to diagnose abnormalities of the nervous system, hearing deficits in infants and young children, and neurological malfunctioning.

brainstem evoked response (**BSER**) see ELECTROPHYSIOLOGIC AUDIOMETRY.

brainstem reticular formation see RETICULAR FORMATION.

brain stimulation stimulation of specific areas of the brain, such as the motor cortex or the visual cortex, as a means of determining their functions and their effects on behavior. Kinds of brain stimulation include ELECTRICAL STIMULATION, TRANSCRANIAL MAGNETIC STIMULATION, and stimulation through a sense organ. Also called **cerebral stimulation**.

brainstorming *n.* a problem-solving strategy in which ideas are generated spontaneously and uninhibitedly, usually in a group setting, without any immediate critical judgment about their potential value. See also CREATIVE THINKING; DIVERGENT THINKING. —**brainstorm** *vb.*

brain syndrome see BRAIN DISORDER.

brain trauma physical injury to the brain. It can be produced by, for example, a blow to the head, a gunshot wound, or a cerebrovascular accident. See BRAIN CONCUSSION; HEAD INJURY.

brain tumor any abnormal tissue growth (see NEOPLASM) within the confines of the skull. Damage may occur by the destruction of healthy tissue or through increased INTRACRANIAL PRESSURE as there is little room for the tumor to grow within the skull without compressing healthy tissue and interfering with the flow of blood and nutrients into the brain. Brain tumors can occur at any age, producing initial symptoms of headache, nausea, or sudden vomiting without apparent cause. As the tumor progresses, the patient may experience disturbances of vision, hearing, and smell, loss of coordination, changes in mental status, weakness, and paralysis. Seizures sometimes are caused by a tumor. See also ASTROCYTOMA; GLIOMA; GLIOBLASTOMA; MENINGIOMA.

brain ventricle see VENTRICLE.

brainwashing *n.* a broad class of intense and often coercive tactics intended to produce profound changes in attitudes, beliefs, and emotions. Targets of such tactics have typically been prisoners of war and members of religious cults. See also PSYCHOLOGICAL KIDNAPPING.

brain waves spontaneous, rhythmic electrical impulses emanating from different areas of the brain. Electroencephalographic brain-wave recordings are used to study SLEEP STAGES and cognitive processes. According to their frequencies, brain waves are classified as ALPHA WAVES (8–12 Hz), BETA WAVES (12–40 Hz), DELTA WAVES (1–3 Hz), GAMMA WAVES (40–50 Hz), or THETA WAVES (4–7 Hz). The first substantial account of brain waves was given in 1929 by German neuropsychiatrist Hans Berger (1873–1944).

brain-wave therapy an alternative or adjunctive therapy in which ALPHA WAVES and THETA WAVES are stimulated because they are posited to have a vital role in learning and memory and, hence, in therapeutic INSIGHT.

brain weight the weight of a brain, which is about 1,450 g for a young adult human. Brain weights for elephants and whales may exceed 7,000 g and 9,000 g, respectively. Human brain sizes usually increase until around the age of 20, then gradually diminish. Brain weight correlates significantly ($r = .4$) with intelligence. See also BRAIN GROWTH.

branching *n.* **1.** a form of PROGRAMMED INSTRUCTION that provides additional steps, or branches, to be followed if the standard teaching material has not been adequately mastered to a given level of proficiency. Correct and incorrect answers lead to different branches of new questions so that students complete different sequences depending on how well they perform. Also called **branching program**. **2.** in linguistics, a method of analyzing the formal structure of a sentence in which this is represented diagrammatically as a treelike structure with an organized hierarchy of branches and subbranches. In PHRASE-STRUCTURE GRAMMAR, a **tree diagram** of this kind (also known as a **phrase marker**) is often used to illustrate the set of phrase-structure rules that generates a particular grammatical sentence: The diagram so produced will also be a CONSTITUENT analysis of the sentence in question. Theories of branching have been used in predicting psycholinguistic phenomena and in creating LINGUISTIC TYPOLOGIES.

Brandeis brief a summary presented to the court in the case of *Muller v. Oregon* in 1908 that outlined the damaging effects on women of long working hours. It is considered to be one of the first examples of a legal brief that relies on extensive documentation of social science research in its argument. [Louis Dembitz **Brandeis** (1856–1941), U.S. Supreme Court justice]

brand loyalty the tendency of consumers to purchase a particular brand consistently. Strong brand loyalty may be revealed by the willingness of consumers to pay higher prices or to exert more effort to obtain a favorite brand.

brand name the unique identifier that characterizes a product as belonging to a particular class or family. Examples are Pepsi-Cola and Nike athletic shoes. Brand names enable consumers to differentiate between many products that serve the same function. A particular brand name carries expectations of value, reliability, service, and perhaps status for the user.

brand preference preference for a particular brand of beer, margarine, or other product (see also BRAND LOYALTY). Two types of tests are frequently used to determine if consumers can recognize their own preferred brands: blindfold testing, and submission of unlabeled packages or bottles to a consumer panel (see BLIND TESTING).

brand-use survey a test of advertising psychology in which consumers are interviewed to determine whether or not they purchased a particular brand of product that was featured in a specific advertising appeal. The brand-use survey may be accompanied by use of the PANTRY-CHECK TECHNIQUE to validate results of the survey.

Brattleboro rat a rat that has a mutation in the gene for VASOPRESSIN that prevents the animal from producing functional hormone. Brattleboro rats show symptoms of DIABETES INSIPIDUS.

bravery *n.* see COURAGE.

Brawner rule see AMERICAN LAW INSTITUTE MODEL PENAL CODE INSANITY TEST.

Brazelton Neonatal Behavioral Assessment Scale an instrument used in both research and clinical settings to assess the neurological and behavioral status of newborns and infants up to 2 months old, as indicated by their responses to various stimuli (a light directed to the eye, a moving ball, a rattle, etc.). The Brazelton scale currently contains 14 neurologically and 26 behaviorally oriented items; the former are graded on a 4-point scale of intensity of response, and the latter on a 9-point scale. Originally developed in 1973, the Brazelton Neonatal Behavioral Assessment Scale was revised in 2000. Also called **Neonatal Behavioral Assessment Scale** (**NBAS**). [Thomas Berry **Brazelton** (1918–), U.S. pediatrician]

BRCA1 and BRCA2 the first two major genes found to be associated with susceptibility to breast and ovarian cancer. Cloned respectively in 1994 and 1995, *BRCA1* and *BRCA2* were the first major cancer genes for which widespread genetic testing was made available; within several years, direct screening became available. The risk of breast cancer in women with mutations in one of these genes ranges from 56% to 85%, and this type of breast cancer tends to occur at younger ages than do most other types. Risk of ovarian cancer is also greatly increased. *BRCA2* mutations are also associated with increased rates of male breast cancer, although these rates remain low (around 5%). Because of incomplete PENETRANCE of these genes, a small percentage of mutation CARRIERS never develop breast, ovarian, or associated cancers. See also RISK PERCEPTION.

breadth-first search a GRAPH search strategy that considers states in a graph recursively: If the present state is not the goal state, then its sibling state is considered. If this sibling is not the goal state, then its sibling is considered. If there are no more siblings, then the first child of the first state is considered. This process continues until either a goal state is found or there are no further states to examine. States, their siblings, and their children are usually (but not necessarily) considered in a left-to-right format. Breadth-first search is often organized by a "queue" or "first-in is first-out" data structure.

breakdown *n.* see NERVOUS BREAKDOWN.

breakthrough *n.* **1.** a significant, sometimes sudden, forward step in therapy, especially after an unproductive plateau. **2.** a major or significant advance in knowledge, research, or treatment.

breast *n.* the human mammary (milk-producing) gland, consisting of milk-secreting cells and their ducts, fat cells, and connective tissue. Enlarged breasts in adult females are a characteristic of the human species that is not shared by other mammals; it may result from SEXUAL SELECTION. Enlarged breasts may occur abnormally in males (see GYNECOMASTIA).

breast envy in the psychoanalytic theory of Melanie KLEIN, the idea that infants envy the nourishing capacity and creative power of the mother's breast. Such envy may later be transformed into PENIS ENVY.

breast feeding see FEEDING TECHNIQUE.

breast-phantom phenomenon the illusion that an amputated breast is still present, often manifested as a tingling or, occasionally, painful sensation in the area of the missing organ; in some cases the individual may even deny that the breast has been removed. It is thought that the brain's representation of the breast remains intact and, in the absence of normal SOMESTHETIC STIMULATION, becomes active either spontaneously or as a result of stimulation from other brain tissue. See also PHANTOM LIMB.

breathing *n.* the mechanism for ventilating the lungs, consisting of cycles of alternate inhalation and exhalation. See also HYPERVENTILATION; INSPIRATION–EXPIRATION RATIO; RESPIRATION.

breathing-related sleep disorder in *DSM–IV–TR*, a primary SLEEP DISORDER marked by excessive sleepiness or insomnia arising from sleep disruption due to breathing difficulties during sleep, for example, SLEEP APNEA. See DYSSOMNIA.

breathing retraining a technique used in BEHAVIOR THERAPY and COGNITIVE BEHAVIOR THERAPY, particularly in the treatment of hyperventilation in anxiety and panic disorders. The technique teaches clients slow diaphragmatic breathing through various methods, including therapist modeling and corrective feedback. See also PROGRESSIVE RELAXATION; STRESS MANAGEMENT.

breathwork *n.* see REBIRTHING.

breathy voice a type of PHONATION in which the vocal cords vibrate as in normal voicing, but the glottal closure is incomplete, allowing air to leak between the cords throughout the vibration cycle. Examples are heard in normal articulation in the [h] sound in such words as *behind* and *hippopotamus*. When the voice is both weak and breathy, the condition is sometimes described as **phonasthenia**.

breech birth delivery of a baby buttocks first (rather than the normal head-first position), which increases the risk of BIRTH INJURY.

breed *n.* a subtype within a SPECIES sharing certain characteristics that are distinct from other members of the species. German shepherds and chihuahuas, for example, are different breeds of dogs. The term is typically used for variations that have been induced through selective breeding, as distinguished from **subspecies**, which are naturally occurring variations within a species.

breeding behavior see ANIMAL SEXUAL BEHAVIOR; MATING BEHAVIOR.

bregma *n.* the location on the top of the skull that marks the junction of the sutures (immovable joints) between the FRONTAL bone and the two parietal bones (forming the sides of the skull). It is used as a landmark for stereotactic and other procedures (see STEREOTAXY).

bride price in some cultures, a payment to the bride's family made by the future husband or his family. Also called **bridewealth**. Compare DOWRY.

bridge to reality see REMOTIVATION.

bridging *n.* a method used in MULTIMODAL THERAPY in which the therapist first focuses on the client's preferred aspect of treatment (e.g., cognitions) before moving to another aspect (e.g., sensations) that the therapist believes may be more effective.

brief group therapy group psychotherapy conducted on a short-term (time- or session-limited) or CRISIS-INTERVENTION basis and focused clearly upon a specific treatment goal.

brief intensive group cognitive behavior therapy a form of COGNITIVE BEHAVIOR THERAPY conducted in a group setting over a relatively brief period of time but in lengthy sessions (e.g., all day) and often on consecutive days (e.g., weekends). The therapy is typically used to treat anxiety disorders, particularly panic disorder.

Brief Psychiatric Rating Scale (**BPRS**) a system of evaluating the presence and severity of clinical psychiatric signs on the basis of 24 factors, such as bizarre behavior, hostility, emotional withdrawal, and disorientation. Each factor is rated on a 7-point scale ranging from "not present" to "extremely severe," based on the judgments of trained observers. [introduced in its original version in 1962 by U.S. psychiatrist John E. Overall and U.S. clinical psychologist Donald R. Gorman]

brief psychodynamic psychotherapy a collection of time-limited PSYCHODYNAMIC PSYCHOTHERAPY approaches that actively address the issue of time to encourage therapeutic change. Therapists are typically active and confronting, focused on present-day client problems particularly as they manifest in the session, and limit the number of sessions in a fixed or flexible way. Also called **short-term dynamic psychotherapy**. [originally developed by Hungarian psychoanalyst Franz Alexander (1891–1964) and his colleague Thomas French]

brief psychotherapy see SHORT-TERM THERAPY.

brief psychotic disorder in *DSM–IV–TR*, a disturbance involving the sudden onset of at least one psychotic symptom (e.g., incoherence or loosening of associations, delusions, hallucinations, or grossly disorganized or catatonic behavior). The condition is often accompanied by emotional turmoil and lasts from 1 day to 1 month, with complete remission of all symptoms and a full return to previous levels of functioning. It may develop following a period of extreme stress, such as the loss of a loved one; in *DSM–III*, brief psychotic disorder involving a precipitating stressor was termed **brief reactive psychosis**.

brief stimulus therapy (**BST**) ELECTROCONVULSIVE THERAPY (ECT) in which the electric current is modified significantly to decrease the duration of stimulus needed to produce a seizure. Some researchers and clinicians claim that this technique not only achieves satisfactory clinical results comparable to those of standard ECT but also diminishes the duration of confusion or memory impairment. Also called **brief stimuli therapy**; **brief stimulus technique**.

bright light therapy see PHOTOTHERAPY.

brightness *n.* the perceptual correlate of light intensity. The brightness of a stimulus depends on its amplitude (energy), wavelength, the ADAPTATION state of the observer, and the nature of any surrounding or intervening stimuli. See LUMINANCE; BRIGHTNESS CONTRAST.

brightness adaptation an apparent decrease in the intensity of a stimulus after exposure to a high level of incident illumination. For example, the inside of a house appears very dim to someone coming in from a snow-covered garden.

brightness constancy the tendency to perceive a familiar object as having the same brightness under different conditions of illumination. For example, a piece of white paper has a similar brightness in daylight as it does at dusk, even though the energy it reflects may be quite different. Brightness constancy is one of the PERCEPTUAL CONSTANCIES. Also called **lightness constancy**. See also COLOR CONSTANCY; OBJECT CONSTANCY.

brightness contrast the apparent enhanced difference in brightness resulting from simultaneous stimulation by two stimuli of differing brightness. For example, a gray disk looks darker on a white background than on a black background. Also called **simultaneous lightness contrast**.

brightness discrimination the ability to distinguish differences in brightness. This appears to vary according to the wavelength of light.

brightness perception the ability to form impressions about the light intensity of a stimulus. See BRIGHTNESS; BRIGHTNESS ADAPTATION; BRIGHTNESS CONTRAST.

brightness threshold the minimum light intensity of a designated wavelength that can be detected against a surrounding field.

bril *n.* see BRIL SCALE.

brilliance *n.* a visual quality related to BRIGHTNESS but with an added dimension of SALIENCE. Brilliant stimuli are not just bright, they seem to radiate brightness. —**brilliant** *adj.*

bril scale a decibel (db) scale used to measure the perceived brightness of stimuli, developed from DIRECT SCALING methods, in which 0 db approximates the ABSOLUTE THRESHOLD. A **bril** is a unit of LUMINANCE representing the brightness perceived by a typical observer when the brightness is 40 db above the 0 db reference level; it is equivalent to one hundredth of a millilambert.

Briquet's syndrome a former name for SOMATIZATION DISORDER. [Paul **Briquet** (1796–1881), French physician, who provided the first systematic description of its characteristics in 1859]

Brissaud's infantilism a developmental anomaly in which infantile mental and physical characteristics continue past puberty. The condition is the result of faulty functioning of the thyroid gland. Also called **infantile myxedema**; **Brissaud–Meige syndrome**. [Edouard **Brissaud** (1852–1909) and Henry **Meige** (1866–1940), French physicians]

British associationism see ASSOCIATIONISM.

British Museum algorithm a problem-solving strategy in which all possible solutions are tried one by one, beginning with those involving the fewest steps. It is so named from the facetious idea that, given enough time, an army of monkeys banging on typewriters would eventually write all the books in the British Museum. See ALGORITHM. See also BRUTE FORCE; EXHAUSTIVE SEARCH.

British Psychological Society (**BPS**) a professional organization, founded in 1901, that is the representative body for psychologists and psychology in the United Kingdom. By royal charter, it is charged with national responsibility for the development, promotion, and application of psychology for the public good.

broadband *n.* a communication channel with very high bit-rate capacity. It is increasingly becoming the technology of choice for very short-range (tens of meters) data transfer from computer to computer at rates of tens of millions of bits per second.

broadband noise see NOISE.

Broadbent, Donald E. (1926–1993) British psychologist. Broadbent received his PhD from Cambridge University in 1949 under Sir Frederick Bartlett (1886–1969). Having earlier served in the Royal Air Force during World War II, he had become interested in how problems in attention, perception, and memory affected military communications. He is best known for applying ideas from communications engineering and mathematical decision theory to psychology; he compared the human mind to an information processor with input channels and filters that could be tuned to one or another competing channels (see FILTER THEORY). His theoretical and experimental work on the attentional processes broke new ground. His most important works include *Perception and Communication* (1958), *Behaviour* (1961), and *Decision and Stress* (1971). Broadbent received many honors: He was elected a Fellow of the Royal Society (1968) and a Foreign Associate of the U.S. National Academy of Sciences (1971), and he received the Distinguished Scientific Contribution Award of the American Psychological Association in 1975.

Broca's aphasia an EXPRESSIVE APHASIA in which the individual has difficulty speaking or writing words but may still be able to use gestures. It is associated with a lesion in the posterior part of the inferior frontal gyrus, a region of the brain sometimes identified as area 44 (see also BROCA'S AREA). [Pierre Paul **Broca** (1824–1880), French physician]

Broca's area a region of the posterior portion of the inferior frontal convolution of a CEREBRAL HEMISPHERE that is associated with the control of speech. It is located on the left hemisphere of right-handed people and of some left-handed individuals. [discovered in 1861 by Pierre Paul **Broca**]

Brodmann's area an area of cerebral cortex characterized by variation in the occurrence and arrangement of cells (see CYTOARCHITECTURE) from that of neighboring areas. These areas are identified by numbers and in many cases have been associated with specific brain functions, such as area 17 (STRIATE CORTEX, or primary visual cortex), areas 18 and 19 (PRESTRIATE CORTEX), area 4 (MOTOR AREA), and area 6 (PREMOTOR AREA). Brodmann's original map of 1909 identified 47 different cortical areas, but investigators have refined the mapping to identify more than 200 distinctive cortical areas. Also called **Brodmann's cytoarchitectonic area**. [Korbinian **Brodmann** (1868–1918), German neurologist]

brofaromine *n.* an antidepressant drug that is a reversible MONOAMINE OXIDASE INHIBITOR (RIMA) and relatively selective for MONOAMINE OXIDASE A. It therefore lacks many of the food interactions that limit the use of irreversible nonselective MAO inhibitors. Brofaromine is not currently available in the United States. European trade name: **Consonar**.

broken home a single-parent household resulting from the divorce or separation of the parents. The term is now generally avoided by social scientists as it seems to imply that all such families will be dysfunctional.

bromazepam *n.* a BENZODIAZEPINE used for the treatment of anxiety. It has a short to intermediate duration of action (serum HALF-LIFE up to 30 hours) and a slow onset of action due to its low lipid solubility (see BLOOD–BRAIN BARRIER). Bromazepam is not currently available in the United States. Canadian trade name: **Lectopam**.

bromide hallucinosis an extended hallucinatory state accompanied by marked fear reactions occurring as a result of bromide intoxication.

bromides *pl. n.* a class of drugs formerly used as anticonvulsants and as sedatives in the treatment of anxiety. Because of their toxicity and the frequency of adverse side effects, bromides were largely supplanted by phenobarbital in the early 20th century. Bromide intoxication (**bromism**) was a recognized complication, manifested in early stages by cognitive impairment and emotional disturbances and in later stages by psychosis, coma, and death.

bromocriptine *n.* a DOPAMINE-RECEPTOR AGONIST used to relieve the symptoms of PARKINSON'S DISEASE and, due to its ability to inhibit release of the pituitary hormone PROLACTIN, to treat GALACTORRHEA. It is also used to treat amenorrhea, infertility, prolactin-secreting adenomas, and parkinsonism, including drug-induced EXTRAPYRAMIDAL EFFECTS of conventional (typical or first-generation) antipsychotic agents. U.S. trade name: **Parlodel**.

bronchodilator medications drugs administered to widen the airways in the treatment of asthma, bronchitis, and related respiratory disorders. They include METHYLXANTHINES and SYMPATHOMIMETIC DRUGS.

bronchus *n.* (*pl.* **bronchi**) either of the two main branches of the windpipe (trachea). **—bronchial** *adj.*

brooding compulsion an irresistible drive to mentally review trivial details or ponder abstract concepts as a means of reducing distress or preventing some dreaded event or situation. This is a common symptom of OBSESSIVE-COMPULSIVE DISORDER.

brood parasitism a practice in which female birds of some species lay their eggs in the nest of another species, leaving the other parents to rear the chicks. Both cowbirds and cuckoos display brood parasitism. The parasitic species may eject some of the eggs of the host species already in the nest, and the young of the parasitic species often hatch earlier and beg more intensively, successfully competing for food against the foster parents' own offspring.

Brooklands experiment an experiment that studied the benefits of homelike and family living environments for children with severe mental retardation, at a time when many such children lived in residential facilities. Sixteen children (average age 7 years; average IQ 25) moved from a residential institution to a large house, together with a staff of nurses, a supervisor, and an educator. A similar group of children stayed at the institution. At follow-up, the children who had moved showed improvement in their ability to use and understand language and in other skills, but the institutional group did not. [reported in 1964 by New Zealand psychologist Jack Tizard (1919–1989), working in England]

brotherliness *n.* the feeling of human unity or solidarity, as expressed in productive involvement with others, care for their well-being, and concern for society as a whole. According to Erich FROMM, brotherliness represents the positive or ideal resolution of the search for ROOTEDNESS.

Brown, Roger (1925–1997) U.S. psychologist. Brown earned his doctorate at the University of Michigan in 1952 with a study of the social psychology of the AUTHORITARIAN PERSONALITY. He then joined the faculty of Harvard University, where he remained throughout his career except for a relatively brief interlude (1957–1962) at the Massachusetts Institute of Technology. His most important contributions to psychology were in the fields of social psychology and psycholinguistics. At Harvard, Brown became involved with the research group of U.S. development psychologist Jerome Bruner (1915–) studying cognitive processes and he became interested in the relationship between language and mind. His *Words and Things* (1957) is considered a classic in the field of psycholinguistics. Arguably his most important contribution to that field was his intensive study of language development in three children, published as *A First Language: The Early Stages* (1973). Brown is also noted for devising successful scientific experiments to study cognitive problems not previously thought amenable to scientific inquiry, such as the TIP-OF-THE-TONGUE PHENOMENON, and he coined the term FLASHBULB MEMORY. Among Brown's other important writings are the two editions of his widely used textbook *Social Psychology* (1965; 1986). He was elected to the American Academy of Arts and Sciences and the National Academy of Sciences and received the Distinguished Scientific Contribution Award from the American Psychological Association.

brown fat tissue made up of fat cells (see ADIPOCYTE) that is found especially around vital organs in the trunk and around the spinal column in the neck and chest. It is capable of intense metabolic activity to generate heat. See also ADIPOSE TISSUE.

Brown–Peterson distractor technique a technique used in memory studies in which participants are allowed a brief period for remembering during which REHEARSAL is minimized. Typically, three items (e.g., words) are presented, after which the participant is asked to count backward for a certain time (as a DISTRACTOR) before attempting to recall the presented items. [John A. **Brown**; Lloyd R. **Peterson** (1922–) and Margaret Jean **Peterson** (1930–), U.S. psychologists]

Brown-Séquard's syndrome a condition resulting from damage along one side of the spinal cord. It is characterized by a set of symptoms that include loss of the sense of pain and temperature along the opposite side of the body and spastic paralysis and loss of vibratory, joint, and tendon sensations on the same side as the lesion. [Charles **Brown-Séquard** (1817–1894), French neurophysiologist]

Brown–Spearman formula see SPEARMAN–BROWN PROPHECY FORMULA.

Bruce effect the effect of CHEMICAL COMMUNICATION in inducing miscarriage in pregnant females. Exposure to odors from an unfamiliar male within a few days of initial mating can disrupt pregnancy in female rodents. See also WHITTEN EFFECT. [described in 1959 by Hilda M. **Bruce**, 20th-century British endocrinologist]

brucine *n.* an alkaloid obtained from the *Brucea* genus of shrubs that is an antagonist at receptor sites for the inhibitory neurotransmitter GLYCINE. Brucine is also found (with strychnine) in NUX VOMICA; it resembles strychnine but is less potent.

Bruck–de Lange type see DE LANGE'S SYNDROME. [described in 1889 by F. **Bruck**, German physician, and in 1934 by Cornelia **de Lange** (1871–1950), Dutch pediatrician]

Brugsch's index a system of measuring the chest circumference in anthropometric studies. The procedure involves multiplying the chest circumference by 100 and dividing the result by the height of the individual. [Theodor **Brugsch** (1827–1894), German physician]

Bruininks–Oseretsky Test of Motor Proficiency (**BOT**) a set of standardized tests to assess FINE MOTOR and GROSS MOTOR skills in children aged 4 to 21 years. Its 53 items are grouped into eight subtests: fine motor precision, fine motor integration, manual dexterity, bilateral coordination, balance, running speed and agility, upper-limb coordination, and strength. The BOT, originally published in 1978 as a revision of the 1923 **Oseretsky Tests of Motor Proficiency**, is now in its second edition (published in 2005). [Robert H. **Bruininks** (1942–), U.S. psychologist; N. I. **Oseretsky**, 20th-century Russian psychologist]

brujeria *n.* see ROOTWORK.

Brunswik faces simple line drawings of faces in which such parameters as eye separation and height, nose length, and mouth height can be varied. The drawings are used in perceptual research for studies of discrimination and categorization. [Egon **Brunswik** (1903–1955), Austrian-born U.S. psychologist]

Brunswik ratio a mathematical expression of PERCEPTUAL CONSTANCY as environmental factors vary: $(P - R)/(O - R)$, where (in the case of size constancy, for example) P = perceived size, R = image size on retina, and O = objective (i.e., actual) size. [Egon **Brunswik**]

Brushfield–Wyatt syndrome a form of mental retardation associated with several other anomalies, including an extensive port-wine birthmark, paralysis on the side opposite to the causal lesion, and cerebral tumor. [Thomas **Brushfield** (1858–1937), British physician]

brute force a problem-solving strategy in which every possible solution to a problem is generated and tested (often by a computer). See ALGORITHM; EXHAUSTIVE SEARCH.

bruxism *n.* persistent grinding, clenching, or gnashing of teeth, usually during sleep. It can be associated with feelings of tension, anger, frustration, or fear. Also called **bruxomania**; **stridor dentium**.

BSER abbreviation for brainstem evoked response. See ELECTROPHYSIOLOGIC AUDIOMETRY.

BSRI abbreviation for BEM SEX ROLE INVENTORY.

BSS abbreviation for BECK SCALE FOR SUICIDE IDEATION.

BST abbreviation for BRIEF STIMULUS THERAPY.

BT abbreviation for BASIC TECHNIQUE.

B-type personality see TYPE B PERSONALITY.

bubble concept of personal space the theory that an imaginary, private region surrounds a person, serving as a buffer against potential emotional or physical threats and determining the distance to be maintained in communicating with others. The size of the "bubble" varies with different individuals and situations, being smaller, for example, for lovemaking than when conducting business. For most people, it extends from about 0.5 to 1.2 m (18 in to 4 ft) for contact with close friends, from 1.2 to 3.6 m (4 to 12 ft) for business acquaintances, and beyond 3.6 m (12 ft) for strangers. The distance also may vary in different cultures: Americans may back away from Europeans who are perceived as standing too close during conversations. See also PROXEMICS; TERRITORIALITY.

buccal *adj.* relating to the cheeks or the mouth cavity.

buccal intercourse see OROGENITAL ACTIVITY.

buccal speech a type of PHONATION that does not depend on laryngeal voice generation but, rather, is produced by shaping an air pocket in the buccal (i.e., oral) cavity. While the cheeks and upper jaw form a neoglottis (substitute vibrating agent), the tongue remains free to serve as an ARTICULATOR to shape the sound. Compare ESOPHAGEAL SPEECH.

buccinator *n.* a muscle that compresses the cheek and retracts the angle of the mouth for eating, speaking, and smiling. During mastication, the buccinator helps hold the food between the teeth. In speech, the buccinator compresses air in the mouth and forces it out between the lips.

buccofacial apraxia see ORAL APRAXIA.

buccolingual masticatory syndrome (**BLM**; **BLMS**) a movement disorder associated with the use of conventional ANTIPSYCHOTIC agents and characterized by involuntary movements of the tongue and musculature of the mouth and face. Patients may involuntarily chew, protrude the tongue, or make grimacing or pursing movements of the lips and cheeks. Also called **buccal–lingual masticatory syndrome**; **oral–lingual dyskinesia**. See also TARDIVE DYSKINESIA.

Buddhism *n.* the nontheistic religion and philosophy founded in India by Siddhartha Gautama (c. 563–c. 483 BCE), known as the Buddha (Sanskrit, Pali, literally: "awakened one"). Buddhism holds that the end toward which one ought to strive is enlightenment, a transformation of consciousness that offers the only escape from the cycle of rebirth. Enlightenment involves the overcoming of desire or craving and is achieved by following the eightfold path (right speech, right action, right livelihood, right effort, right mindfulness, right concentration, right views, and right intentions). The escape from the cycle of rebirth involves the dissolution of individual consciousness into a larger whole, a state referred to as NIRVANA, which represents an end of striving. Sigmund FREUD attempted to capture this sense of quiescence in his NIRVANA PRINCIPLE. See also ZEN BUDDHISM. —**Buddhist** *adj., n.*

buffer 1. *n.* see BUFFER ITEM. **2.** *n.* a temporary store in memory. For example, SHORT-TERM MEMORY is a buffer. **3.** *vb.* see BUFFERING.

buffering *n.* **1.** the protection against stressful experiences that is afforded by an individual's social support. **2.** in industrial and organizational theory, any practice by which an organization protects its operations from environmental uncertainty, for example, by accruing excess inventory to provide a safety margin. Such practices are generally deprecated by modern management theory. —**buffer** *vb.*

buffer item an irrelevant item interspersed between others in a test or experiment. For example, a buffer item may be a question that is not scored and is introduced only to separate or disguise other items.

bufotenin a naturally occurring, mildly hallucinogenic substance found on the skin of a species of toad (genus *Bufo*) and in plants of the genus *Anadenanthera*; it is also reported to be a component of the urine of certain patients with schizophrenia. Bufotenin is related chemically to LSD, PSILOCIN, and DMT. See also HALLUCINOGEN.

buggery *n.* SODOMY or ANAL INTERCOURSE.

bulb *n.* **1.** a globe-shaped structure. **2.** an obsolete name for the MEDULLA OBLONGATA. See BULBAR.

bulbar *adj.* pertaining to a bulb or bulblike structure, such as the eyeball (as in BULBAR RETRACTION REFLEX), but especially the MEDULLA OBLONGATA, as in BULBAR PARALYSIS.

bulbar paralysis a condition involving paralysis of the muscles of the lips, tongue, mouth, pharynx, and larynx, resulting in difficulties in chewing, swallowing, and talking. Causes may include myasthenia gravis, motor neuron disease, or tumor. Also called **bulbar palsy**; **progressive bulbar palsy**.

bulbar retraction reflex the reflex retraction of the eyeball and closing of the NICTITATING MEMBRANE in animals when the conjunctiva or cornea is touched.

bulbi xanthomatosis see XANTHOMATOSIS.

bulbocavernosus muscle a muscle of the perineum in men and women, which constricts the urethra. It therefore accelereates the passage of urine in both sexes and aids ejaculation in men; in women it also serves as a weak vaginal sphincter. Also called **bulbospongiosus muscle**.

bulbocavernous reflex contraction of the BULBOCAVERNOSUS MUSCLE of the penis in response to stimulation of the head of the penis. Absence of this reflex can indicate SPINAL SHOCK or impairment of the nerves connecting the penis to the spinal cord.

bulbopontine region the part of the brain consisting of the PONS and the portion of the MEDULLA OBLONGATA adjacent to the pons.

bulbospongiosus muscle see BULBOCAVERNOSUS MUSCLE.

bulbotegmental reticular formation the portion of the RETICULAR FORMATION that passes through the MEDULLA OBLONGATA.

bulbourethral glands a pair of glands in males whose ducts open into the urethra, near the base of the penis. Their secretion contributes to semen. Also called **Cowper's glands**.

bulimia (**boulimia**) *n.* insatiable hunger for food. It may have physiological causes, such as a brain lesion or endocrine disturbance, or be primarily a psychological disorder (see BINGE-EATING DISORDER; BULIMIA NERVOSA). See also HYPERBULIMIA; HYPERPHAGIA. —**bulimic** *adj., n.*

bulimia nervosa an EATING DISORDER involving recurrent episodes of binge eating (i.e., discrete periods of uncontrolled consumption of abnormally large quantities of food) followed by inappropriate compensatory behaviors (e.g., self-induced vomiting, misuse of laxatives, fasting, excessive exercise). Compare BINGE-EATING DISORDER.

bulky color the attribute of color when color is a property throughout the volume of the stimulus, as in a colored liquid. Also called **volume color**. Compare FILM COLOR; SURFACE COLOR.

bullying *n.* persistent threatening and aggressive behavior directed toward other people, especially those who are smaller or weaker.

bundle hypothesis the notion that sensory features are "bundled," or bound together, in conscious experience. See BINDING HYPOTHESIS. [proposed by Max WERTHEIMER]

bundling *n.* a former custom, found in various parts of Europe and North America, in which courting couples were permitted to sleep together fully clothed as long as various physical impediments to sexual intercourse were in place.

Bunsen–Roscoe law see BLOCH'S LAW. [Robert Wilhelm Eberhard **Bunsen** (1811–1899), German chemist; Henry Enfield **Roscoe** (1833–1915), British chemist]

buphthalmos *n.* the enlargement of the eye that is characteristic of CONGENITAL GLAUCOMA.

buprenorphine *n.* an OPIOID ANALGESIC with both agonist and antagonist activity at opioid receptors, used for the treatment of moderate to severe pain and also for the management of opioid dependence. Because of its ability to partially block the mu OPIOID RECEPTOR, it can attenuate the euphoria and other subjective and physiological effects associated with opioids, and therefore may be useful in both opioid withdrawal and as a substitute for illicit opioids in long-term maintenance treatment of opioid dependence. U.S. trade name: **Buprenex**.

bupropion *n.* an aminoketone stimulant agent commonly used in the treatment of depression. It is also appropriate as an adjuvant to behavioral treatment for smoking cessation. It is occasionally used in combination with other antidepressants to augment antidepressant response (see AUGMENTATION STRATEGIES), and has also been used in the treatment of attention-deficit/hyperactivity disorder. Bupropion is available in both immediate-release and extended-release preparations. U.S. trade names: **Wellbutrin**; **Zyban**.

bureaucracy *n.* **1.** a system of administration or organizational structure, often in a government body, that is characterized by standardized rule-bound procedures, specialization of skills, and an elaborate hierarchy. **2.** unnecessarily lengthy or complex official procedures resulting in delay, inaction, or inflexibility. —**bureaucrat** *n.* —**bureaucratic** *adj.*

bureaucratic leader 1. the type of LEADER whose responsibilities and leadership style are largely determined by his or her position in a hierarchical organization, such as a government department or military unit. **2.** a leader who rigidly adheres to prescribed routine and makes no allowance for extenuating circumstances.

Buridan's ass an example used to illustrate the difficulty of making decisions based solely on the relative desirability of alternatives. The unfortunate ass in the example starves to death while standing equidistant between two equally appealing haystacks. This image is named for French philosopher Jean Buridan (c. 1300–c. 1358), although he was not the originator of the example. The term may have reference to Buridan's attempt to find a philosophical middle ground in ACTION THEORY between strict voluntarism and strict rationalism.

burned out 1. describing an individual who is mentally or physically exhausted or overwhelmed. See BURNOUT. **2.** historically, describing individuals with chronic schizophrenia who are apathetic, withdrawn, and show progressive deterioration, with little hope of significant improvement, personal growth, or adaptive functioning.

burn injuries tissue damage caused by exposure to flame, intense heat without flame (e.g., contact with high-voltage electricity, red-hot metal, or scalding liquids), or ultraviolet radiation. **Superficial** (or **first-degree**) **burns** are characterized by redness, swelling, and peeling of the skin; **partial-thickness** (or **second-degree**) **burns** are marked by penetration of damage beyond the skin layer, which can be blistered and dull white to cherry red and streaked with coagulated capillaries; **full-thickness** (or **third-degree**) **burns** damage tissues that are subcutaneous or deeper, including epithelial tissue, nerve endings, and blood vessels; and **fourth-degree burns** are usually identified by a distinct odor and the appearance of charred flesh. Because of sometimes excruciating pain and cosmetic damage, burn injuries are often mentally traumatic, and psychological or psychiatric help is recommended.

burnout *n.* physical, emotional, or mental exhaustion, especially in one's job or career, accompanied by decreased motivation, lowered performance, and negative attitudes towards oneself and others. It results from performing at a high level until stress and tension, especially from extreme and prolonged physical or mental exertion or an overburdening workload, take their toll. The word was first used in this sense in 1975 by U.S. psychologist Herbert J. Freudenberger (1926–1999) in referring to workers in clinics with heavy caseloads. Burnout is most often observed in professionals who work closely with people (e.g., social workers, teachers, correctional officers) in service-oriented vocations and experience chronic high levels of STRESS. It can be particularly acute in therapists or counselors doing TRAUMA WORK, who feel overwhelmed by the cumulative secondary trauma of witnessing the effects. Burnout is also experienced by athletes when continually exposed to stress associated with performance without commensurate rewards or rest. See also OVERTRAINING SYNDROME.

burnt *adj.* denoting one of the primary odor qualities in HENNING'S ODOR PRISM and in the CROCKER–HENDERSON ODOR SYSTEM.

burst *n.* a series of responses elicited at a relatively high rate, often occurring at the onset of EXTINCTION, when conditioned responses are no longer rewarded.

burst–pause firing the simultaneous firing and pausing of neurons in the THALAMUS during deep sleep that produces large-amplitude electroencephalogram waves characteristic of SLOW-WAVE SLEEP.

business game a method of personnel training in which teams of employees compete against one another in solving typical but simulated management problems. Success will require an organized approach, interaction among the team members, and the analysis and application of information appropriate to the problem. See also CASE METHOD; CONFERENCE METHOD; MULTIPLE-ROLE PLAYING; SCENARIO ANALYSIS.

business psychology see INDUSTRIAL AND ORGANIZATIONAL PSYCHOLOGY.

buspirone *n.* a nonbenzodiazepine anxiolytic of the AZASPIRONE class. Both it and its primary metabolic product, 6-hydroxybuspirone, produce relief of subjective symptoms of anxiety without the sedation, behavioral disinhibition, and risk of dependence associated with the benzodiazepines. Its use has been limited due to its relative lack of efficacy compared with benzodiazepines. U.S. trade name: **BuSpar**.

bust-to-waist ratio a ratio of curvaceousness determined by dividing bust circumference by waist circumference.

butabarbital *n.* an intermediate-acting BARBITURATE used in the treatment of insomnia and for daytime and preoperative sedation. Like other barbiturates, it is a nonselective CNS DEPRESSANT and therefore quite toxic in overdose. Because tolerance to its sedative and hypnotic effects accrues much more rapidly than tolerance to its CNS depressant effects, its THERAPEUTIC INDEX drops and its potential lethality increases as the dose is increased. These factors, plus its potential for abuse, have caused a decline in its clinical use. U.S. trade name: **Butisol Sodium**.

butorphanol *n.* a synthetic OPIOID that acts as a mixed agonist–antagonist: It is an agonist at kappa OPIOID RECEPTORS but an antagonist at mu opioid receptors. It is used clinically for the management of moderate to severe pain, including migraine headaches, and as a preoperative medication. It is available in an injectable preparation and an intranasal spray, but the ease of use of the latter has made it a common drug of abuse. As with other opioid agents, butorphanol may cause respiratory depression, nausea, and dependence. U.S. trade name: **Stadol**.

butterfly effect the tendency of a complex, dynamic system to be sensitive to initial conditions, so that over time a small cause may have large, unpredictable effects (see SENSITIVE DEPENDENCE). The term refers to an example in which the fluttering of the wings of a butterfly in one part of the world is seen to contribute to the causation of a tornado in another. The term is used in CHAOS THEORY and more generally to describe nonlinear causal connections.

butyrophenones *pl. n.* a class of conventional ANTIPSYCHOTICS used primarily in the treatment of schizophrenia, mania, and severe agitation. The prototypical butyrophenone is HALOPERIDOL. Butyrophenones are classified as HIGH-POTENCY ANTIPSYCHOTICS, and their use is associated with numerous EXTRAPYRAMIDAL EFFECTS, as well as NEUROLEPTIC MALIGNANT SYNDROME and TARDIVE DYSKINESIA.

butyrylcholinesterase *n.* an enzyme, found in the brain and other tissues, that is involved in the breakdown of acetylcholine. Some drugs used in the management of Alzheimer's disease (e.g., TACRINE) inhibit both ACETYLCHOLINESTERASE (the principal enzyme responsible for acetylcholine degradation) and butyrylcholinesterase, and there is speculation that agents acting on both enzymes may be beneficial in reducing the formation of the plaques and NEUROFIBRILLARY TANGLES associated with the disease. Also called **pseudocholinesterase**.

buying behavior the sum total of the mental processes and physical activities associated with the purchase of products or services. The decision to buy a particular product can occur in a number of stages. Recognition of a need for the product is followed by searching for information about it, evaluating alternative products, and finally making a choice. Experience of using the product after purchase will become a factor in deciding whether or not to purchase it (or a similar product) in the future.

buzz group a subdivision of a group that has been broken up so that each member may be involved in more direct and active discussion to ascertain his or her feelings or opinions. The results are then typically conveyed to the primary (i.e., entire) group by a spokesperson. Also called **buzz session**.

B-values *pl. n.* see METANEEDS.

BVRT abbreviation for BENTON VISUAL RETENTION TEST.

BWAS abbreviation for BARRON–WELSH ART SCALE.

B wave of electroretinogram a large, positive electrical wave pattern that is recorded from the eye when the retina is stimulated by light. The electrical response is detected by an electrode placed on the anesthetized surface of the eye. See ELECTRORETINOGRAM.

BWS abbreviation for BATTERED-WOMAN SYNDROME.

bystander effect the tendency for people not to offer help when they know that others are present and capable of helping. This was initially thought to be the result of apathy and a selfish unwillingness to get involved, but more recent research suggests that a number of cognitive and social processes contribute to the effect, including misinterpreting other people's lack of response as an indication that help is not needed, CONFUSION OF RESPONSIBILITY, and DIFFUSION OF RESPONSIBILITY.

Cc

CA abbreviation for CHRONOLOGICAL AGE.

CA1, CA2, CA3, and CA4 see HIPPOCAMPUS.

caapi *n.* see AYAHUASCA.

CAB abbreviation for COOLIDGE ASSESSMENT BATTERY.

cable properties the physical properties of an axon such that a small, nonpropagated electrical disturbance spreads and decrements exponentially with distance, as along a nonorganic cable. See also CONDUCTION WITH DECREMENT.

cable tensiometry a method of measuring muscular strength in which the participant pulls on a cable and the change in the tension of the cable is measured with a tensiometer. See also ERGOGRAPH.

cachexia *n.* an extreme state of poor health, physical wasting away, and malnutrition, usually associated with chronic illness.

cachinnation *n.* an unrestrained and inappropriate type of laughter, which is often observed in DISORGANIZED SCHIZOPHRENIA.

caco- (**cac-**) *combining form* bad or unpleasant.

cacoethes *n.* an irresistible, and sometimes irrational, desire or compulsion.

caduceus *n.* a symbol of the healing professions, consisting of a short rod with two serpents coiled about it and topped by a pair of wings. In Greek mythology, the caduceus, a magical wand, is the property of Hermes, messenger of the gods. In the 7th century he became associated with alchemy, which may explain the tenuous link between the caduceus and medicine. Some medical organizations use as their emblem a representation of the **staff of Asclepius** (the Greek and Roman god of healing), which shows a single serpent coiled about a staff made from a rough-hewn tree limb.

caesarian section see CESAREAN SECTION.

cafard *n.* a CULTURE-BOUND SYNDROME found in Polynesia, with symptoms similar to those of AMOK. Also called **cathard**.

Cafergot *n.* a trade name for ERGOTAMINE.

cafeteria feeding a technique for studying the HUNGER DRIVE in children and nonhuman animals by offering a variety of foods and observing the extent to which the participants choose those providing balanced, life-sustaining nutrition. See SELF-SELECTION OF DIET.

cafeteria-style benefit plan a form of compensation in which employees are allowed to choose among a mix of benefit options. In cafeteria-style benefit plans, employees are provided with minimum coverage in medical insurance and retirement benefits but are given credits with which they can buy additional benefits of their choice, such as more life insurance, dental insurance, and so forth.

caffeine *n.* a CNS STIMULANT found in coffee, tea, cola, cocoa, chocolate, and certain prescribed and over-the-counter medications. It is an antagonist of the neuromodulator ADENOSINE. Caffeine belongs to the METHYLXANTHINE group of alkaloids, and its effects include rapid breathing, increased pulse rate and blood pressure, and diminished fatigue. Precise effects vary with the amount ingested and the tolerance of the individual. Moderate doses produce an improved flow of thought and clearness of ideas, together with increased respiratory and vasomotor activity; large doses may make concentration or continued attention difficult and cause insomnia, headaches, and confusion in some individuals (see CAFFEINE INTOXICATION; SUBSTANCE-INDUCED ANXIETY DISORDER). Because of its stimulant effects, caffeine is used in KEEP-AWAKE PILLS and in certain analgesics and cold remedies containing ingredients that usually cause drowsiness. See also ASPIRIN COMBINATIONS.

caffeine intoxication intoxication due to recent consumption of large amounts of caffeine (typically over 250 mg), in the form of coffee, tea, cola, or medications, and involving at least five of the following symptoms: restlessness, nervousness, excitement, insomnia, flushed face, diuresis (increased urination), gastrointestinal complaints, muscle twitching, rambling thought and speech, rapid or irregular heart rhythm, periods of inexhaustibility, or psychomotor agitation. Brewed coffee contains 100–150 mg caffeine per cup; tea contains about 50 mg, and cola about 35 mg. Also called **caffeinism**.

CAGE *n.* a screening instrument to detect alcohol dependence. It consists of the following four questions: (a) Have you ever felt you should *C*ut down on your drinking? (b) Have people *A*nnoyed you by criticizing your drinking? (c) Have you ever felt bad or *G*uilty about your drinking? (d) Have you ever used a drink as an *E*ye-opener?

cage apparatus see CONDITIONING APPARATUS.

CAI abbreviation for COMPUTER-ASSISTED INSTRUCTION.

CAL abbreviation for computer-assisted learning (see COMPUTER-ASSISTED INSTRUCTION).

calamus scriptorius the caudal end of the floor of the fourth VENTRICLE on the dorsal surface of the MEDULLA OBLONGATA.

calcarine area the region on the medial surface of the occipital lobe of the brain that surrounds the CALCARINE FISSURE. It includes parts of the STRIATE CORTEX and the PRESTRIATE CORTEX.

calcarine fissure a fissure on the medial surface of each cerebral hemisphere, extending from the most posterior prominence of the OCCIPITAL LOBE to the PARIETO-OCCIPITAL SULCUS. Also called **calcarine sulcus**. See also CALCARINE AREA.

calcitonin *n.* a hormone produced by the parafollicular (or C) cells of the THYROID GLAND. It controls calcium and phosphate levels in the blood by promoting the resorption of calcium and phosphate by bone tissue, thus lowering their concentrations in the blood. See CALCIUM REGULATION.

calcium channel a VOLTAGE-GATED ION CHANNEL in the presynaptic membrane of a neuron that is involved in the release of neurotransmitter (and therefore passage of a neural signal) at a SYNAPSE. The arrival of an ACTION POTENTIAL at the TERMINAL BUTTONS of the neuron is accompanied by DEPOLARIZATION of the presynaptic membrane, which results in opening of the calcium channels and influx of calcium ions into the terminal buttons. This triggers fusion of the SYNAPTIC VESICLES (which contain neurotransmitter) with the presynaptic membrane and the release of neurotransmitter into the SYNAPTIC CLEFT.

calcium-channel blockers a class of drugs, the prototype of which is **verapamil**, used in the treatment of hypertension and abnormal heart rhythms (arrhythmias). Calcium-channel blockers inhibit the flow of calcium ions into the smooth-muscle cells of blood vessels and the cells of heart muscle, which need calcium to contract. They act by binding to CALCIUM CHANNELS on the surface of depolarized muscle-cell membranes, causing a decrease in transmembrane calcium transmission and prolonged relaxation of the muscles. Verapamil has been studied as a potential MOOD STABILIZER, with equivocal results in the treatment of mania.

calcium-deficiency disorders diseases caused by a deficiency of calcium in the tissues. Absorption of calcium from food and its deposition in bone is facilitated by vitamin D, and deficiency of this vitamin is the usual cause of **rickets**, a disease of childhood marked by deformed bones and teeth and lax muscles, and **osteomalacia**, the adult form of rickets. **Osteoporosis**, in which the bones become brittle and break easily, is caused by resorption (loss) of calcified bone, due to disease or aging (it is common in postmenopausal women). **Tetany** (muscle spasms) is due to a deficiency of calcium in the blood.

calcium regulation the maintenance of calcium levels in the blood and other extracellular fluids. Secretion of PARATHYROID HORMONE by the parathyroid glands causes release of ionic calcium from the bones, whereas CALCITONIN, produced by the thyroid gland, inhibits calcium release.

calendar age see CHRONOLOGICAL AGE.

calendar calculation the rare ability to identify the day of the week for any given date, such as February 19, 1878, in a matter of seconds. **Calendar calculators** are frequently savants who usually have no evident mathematical ability but may be able to perform other feats with the calendar, such as correctly answering the question "In what years did April 16 fall on a Sunday?" No satisfactory explanation has been found for this skill. See also IDIOT SAVANT.

calendar method of birth control attempting to avoid pregnancy by not having intercourse during the middle days of the woman's menstrual cycle, when ovulation occurs. However, because ovulation is not completely regular, and sperm have been found to stay active for up to 3 days in the uterus, this method is not very successful. See also RHYTHM METHOD.

calibration *n.* the process of assigning values to a measuring device (instrument, test, or scale) relative to a reference standard.

California Achievement Tests (CAT) an achievement test battery developed by the California Test Bureau to assess the basic skills of students in kindergarten through 12th grade. Now in its fifth edition (published in 1992), the CAT consists of various multiple-choice subtests across 13 levels (K, 10–21/22) and six thinking process categories (gathering information, organizing information, analyzing information, generating ideas, synthesizing elements, evaluating outcomes). Among the academic areas covered (at appropriate levels) are reading, language, spelling, mathematics, study skills, science, and social studies. The CAT currently is available in five formats: Basic Battery, Complete Battery, Survey Battery, Math Separates, and Short Form. It was originally published in 1943 as a revision of the now obsolete 1933 **Progressive Achievement Tests**, which were also developed by the California Test Bureau and consisted of four batteries of tests (primary, elementary, intermediate, advanced), each measuring progress in the same general areas of school education: reading vocabulary, arithmetic reasoning, reading comprehension, arithmetic fundamentals, spelling, and the mechanics of English and grammar.

California Psychological Inventory (CPI) a self-report inventory designed to evaluate adult and adolescent personality characteristics, interpersonal behavior, and social interaction. It currently consists of 434 true–false statements (a 260-statement short form is also available) that produces scores on 20 scales divided into four measurement classes: (a) poise, ascendancy, self-assurance, and interpersonal adequacy; (b) socialization, responsibility, intrapersonal values, and character; (c) achievement potential and intellectual efficacy; and (d) intellectual and interest modes. Originally published in 1957, the CPI is now in its third edition (published 1996). Also called **California Psychological Inventory Test**. [devised by U.S. psychologist Harrison G. Gough (1921–) at the University of California, Berkeley]

California Verbal Learning Test (CVLT) a word-list learning test consisting of 16 items belonging to one of four categories. Currently in its second edition (**CVLT–II**), the test assesses immediate FREE RECALL following each of five learning trials as well as an interference trial. Free recall and CUED RECALL are also assessed following a short-term delay (immediately after the interference trial) and a long-term (20-min) delay. Finally, long-term recognition is assessed using distractors that vary in their likelihood of eliciting false positive errors. In addition to the adult version, a 9-item version has been developed for use with individuals with memory impairment (**CVLT–II short form**). There is also a 15-item version for children aged 5–16, **California Verbal Learning Test for Children** (**CVLT–C**). See also RECALL SCORE METHOD.

Calkins, Mary Whiton (1863–1930) U.S. psychologist. Calkins was an important member of the first generation of U.S. psychologists. Although she completed all requirements for the PhD at Harvard University (1895), she was never awarded the degree because she was a woman. Her best known empirical contribution was her development of the technique of PAIRED-ASSOCIATES LEARNING for studying memory, a technique that is still in use today. Calkins's major theoretical contribution was her development of SELF PSYCHOLOGY. During the 1910s and 1920s BEHAVIORISM was rising in importance within psychology and was abandoning the notions of self and consciousness, due to their uncertain metaphysical status, as well as rejecting the method of introspection. Calkins countered that psychology must be true to its philosophical origins and remain a science of the SELF and should make use of introspection to study the experiencing self in its relation to the physical and social world. Her self psychology is also called a PERSONALISTIC PSYCHOLOGY because she held that selves were inherently personal, a fact that had to be accommodated by an adequate science of psychology. Although she swam against the intellectual current, Calkins remained a well-respected psychologist. She had a life-long career on the faculty of Wellesley College and was the first woman president of both the American Psychological Association (1905) and the American Philosophical Association (1918).

callback *n.* in consumer psychology, a follow-up interview usually undertaken with a consumer after an initial interview about a product or service. Callbacks are carried out to assess continued satisfaction or possible changes in opinion.

call boy see MALE HOMOSEXUAL PROSTITUTION.

call girl *n.* a female prostitute who does not work out of a brothel or by soliciting in the street. Instead, her services are ordered by telephone, and she may then be collected by the client or come to the client's home or hotel. Call girls typically charge higher prices than other types of prostitutes.

calling card see SIGNATURE.

callosal *adj.* referring to the CORPUS CALLOSUM.

callosal apraxia an inability to perform learned, purposeful movements (see APRAXIA) due to lesions of the CORPUS CALLOSUM.

callosal gyrus see CINGULATE GYRUS.

callosal sulcus a fissure or groove that separates the CORPUS CALLOSUM from the CINGULATE GYRUS along the medial side of each cerebral hemisphere.

callosectomy *n.* see COMMISSUROTOMY.

callosotomy *n.* see COMMISSUROTOMY.

callosum *n.* see CORPUS CALLOSUM.

calmodulin *n.* a protein that binds calcium ions in many calcium-regulated processes in living cells. For example, calmodulin is involved in muscle contraction and in the cascade of neurochemical events that underlies memory formation.

caloric intake the consumption of food as measured in CALORIES.

caloric nystagmus a test that involves pouring water, either above or below body temperature, into the ear and measuring NYSTAGMUS.

calorie (symbol: cal) *n.* the amount of energy required to raise the temperature of 1 g of water by 1 °C. For most purposes the calorie (a c.g.s. unit) has been replaced by the SI unit of work and energy, the joule: 1 cal = 4.1868 J. However, the energy values of foods are sometimes still expressed in **kilocalories** (or Calories [Cal]: 1 Cal = 1000 cal).

Calvinism *n.* a form of Protestant Christianity based on the teachings of French-born reformer John Calvin (1509–1564), who is also known as Jean Cauvin. He taught that God will grant salvation only to those who are predestined to receive it as an unmerited gift, the rest of humanity being predestined to damnation. Humans therefore can do nothing to save themselves and have no free will. See PREDESTINATION.

CAM **1.** abbreviation for CELL ADHESION MOLECULE. **2.** abbreviation for COMPLEMENTARY AND ALTERNATIVE MEDICINE.

camaraderie *n.* goodwill and light-hearted rapport between friends or members of a social group, especially of a military unit; comradeship. Camaraderie is an important component of the morale, unit cohesion, and esprit de corps required in forming and sustaining unit dynamics. It can also serve as a buffer in protecting members of a unit.

camisole *n.* see STRAITJACKET.

camouflage *n.* the use of cryptic coloration and vocal signals that are difficult to localize in order to conceal one's location (see CRYPSIS). Many animal species use camouflage, either to escape the notice of predators or to avoid detection by prey. For example, a bird might have plumage that blends in with other features of the environment, making it difficult to detect. ALARM CALLS have acoustic features that make specific localization of the caller difficult. See also COUNTERSHADING. Compare ADVERTISEMENT.

cAMP abbreviation for CYCLIC AMP.

Campbell, Donald Thomas (1916–1996) U.S. psychologist. Trained as a social psychologist, Campbell received his PhD in 1947 from the University of California at Berkeley, where he studied under Edward C. TOLMAN. Among his most significant contributions were those he made to the methodologies of psychology: He developed methods for determining the CONSTRUCT VALIDITY of psychological measures and introduced the now-standard notions of INTERNAL VALIDITY and EXTERNAL VALIDITY in experimental design. His contributions to experimental design and his introduction, with Julian Stanley (1918–), of QUASI-EXPERIMENTAL DESIGN are considered landmarks in the field of social science methodology. Campbell's later work included contributions to the sociology and philosophy of science, in which he developed a theory of EVOLUTIONARY EPISTEMOLOGY. The bulk of his career was spent at Northwestern University. He was elected president of the American Psychological Association in 1973 and received distinguished scientist awards from the APA and several other scholarly societies in recognition of his significance to psychology, education, and the social sciences in general.

camphoraceous *adj.* denoting one of the seven classes of odorants in the STEREOCHEMICAL SMELL THEORY.

camphorated tincture of opium see PAREGORIC.

Campral *n.* a trade name for ACAMPROSATE.

camptocormia *n.* a condition in which the back is bent forward at a sharp angle (30–90°). In some cases it may be a rare manifestation of CONVERSION DISORDER and may be accompanied by back pain, tremors, or both.

campus crisis center a campus organization created to provide support and advice for students experiencing personal difficulty or trauma in their school, college, or university. Substance abuse, rape, depression, academic failure, and suicidal tendencies are typical of the problems or traumas encountered by students. A campus crisis center may offer such services as counseling, a hotline, or an escort service for students returning to housing late at night.

Canadian Mental Training Registry a registry system in Canada for certifying individuals in the use of mental skills to increase or make more consistent performance in various domains, including sport.

Canadian Psychological Association (**CPA**) a professional organization representing psychologists in Canada, organized in 1939 and incorporated in 1950. Its objectives are to lead, advance, and promote psychology as a science and profession for the benefit of humanity; to provide leadership in psychology in Canada; to promote the advancement, dissemination, and application of psychological knowledge; and to develop standards and ethical principles for education, training, science, and practice in psychology.

canalization *n.* **1.** in evolutionary genetics, the containment of variation of certain characters within narrow bounds so that expression of underlying genetic variation is repressed. It is a developmental mechanism that maintains a constant PHENOTYPE over a range of different environments in which the organism might normally occur. **2.** in neurology, the hypothetical process by which repeated use of a neural pathway leads to greater ease of transmission of impulses and hence its establishment as permanent. **3.** in psychology, the channeling by an organism of its needs into fixed patterns of gratification, for example, food preferences and recreational preferences.

cancellation test a test of perceptual and motor speed requiring the participant to cancel out randomly scattered symbols on a page or screen.

cancer *n.* any one of a group of diseases characterized by the unregulated, abnormal growth of cells to form malignant tumors (see NEOPLASM), which invade neighboring tissues; the abnormal cells are generally capable of spreading via the bloodstream or lymphatic system to other body areas or organs by the process of **metastasis**. Causes of cancer include viruses, hormones, environmental carcinogenic chemicals, radiation from sunlight, X-rays, or radioactive substances; hereditary factors are important in the etiology of many cancers. Cancers are generally classified as **carcinomas** if they involve cells of epithelial origin (e.g., cancers of the uterus, breast, stomach, or skin) and **sarcomas** if the affected tissues are derived from MESODERM (e.g., bone, muscle, blood). More than 150 different kinds of cancer have been identified in humans, based on cell types, rate of growth, and other factors. Because cancers can be disfiguring and life-threatening, psychological counseling is often helpful for patients. **—cancerous** *adj.*

cancer phobia a persistent and irrational fear of cancer. Fear of developing cancer may be a symptom of OBSESSIVE-COMPULSIVE DISORDER; it may also be classified as a SPECIFIC PHOBIA, other type. The belief that one has cancer based on the misinterpretation of bodily symptoms is classified as HYPOCHONDRIASIS.

candidiasis *n.* infection caused by yeastlike fungi of the genus *Candida*, especially the species *Candida albicans*. These fungi are part of the normal flora of the mouth, skin, intestinal tract, and vagina but under certain circumstances can cause a variety of infections. Candidiasis commonly affects the mouth, skin folds, and vagina. Less commonly, but more seriously, *Candida* can cause systemic infection leading to septicemia, endocarditis, meningitis, or osteomyelitis. Such serious infections are more common in debilitated or immunocompromised patients, such as those with AIDS. Candidiasis was formerly called **moniliasis**.

Candlelighters Childhood Cancer Foundation an organization that links children with cancer and their families to SUPPORT GROUPS in which they can share feelings and exchange information.

cane *n.* an aid for sitting, standing, or MOBILITY for people with visual impairment or other disabilities. Canes for individuals with neuromuscular disabilities, often called **orthopedic canes**, are usually sturdy shafts of solid wood or metal designed for weight bearing, with a curved or horizontal handle at the top, a rubber tip at the bottom, and sometimes three or four feet. Canes for individuals with visual impairment generally are slimmer, lighter, longer, made of metal, and used for orientation. See ORIENTATION AND MOBILITY TRAINING.

cannabinoid *n.* any of a class of about 60 substances in the CANNABIS plant that includes those responsible for the psychoactive properties of the plant. The most important cannabinoid is TETRAHYDROCANNABINOL.

cannabis *n.* any of three related plant species (*Cannabis sativa*, *C. indica*, or *C. ruderalis*) whose dried flowering or fruiting tops or leaves are widely used as a recreational drug, known as **marijuana**. The principal psychoactive agent in these plants, delta-9-TETRAHYDROCANNABINOL (THC), is concentrated in the resin, most of which is in the plants' flowering tops. When smoked, THC is rapidly absorbed into the blood and almost immediately distributed to the brain, causing the rapid onset of subjective effects that last 2–3 hours. These effects include a sense of euphoria or well-being, easy laughter, perceptual distortions, impairment of concentration and short-term memory, and craving for food. Adverse effects of anxiety or panic are not uncommon, and hallucinations may occur with high doses (see also CANNABIS-INDUCED PSYCHOTIC DISORDER; CANNABIS INTOXICATION). Tolerance to the effects of THC develops with repeated use, but reports of CANNABIS DEPENDENCE are rare. The most potent marijuana preparation is HASHISH, which consists of pure resin. A less potent preparation is sinsemilla, also called GANJA; it is made from the plants' flowering tops. The weakest preparation is BHANG. Also called **hemp**.

cannabis abuse in *DSM–IV–TR*, a pattern of CANNABIS use manifested by recurrent significant adverse consequences related to its repeated ingestion. This diagnosis is preempted by the diagnosis of CANNABIS DEPENDENCE: If the criteria for cannabis abuse and cannabis dependence are both met, only the latter diagnosis is given.

cannabis dependence in *DSM–IV–TR*, a cluster of cognitive, behavioral, and physiological symptoms indicating continued use of cannabis despite significant cannabis-related problems. There is a pattern of repeated cannabis ingestion resulting in tolerance, withdrawal symptoms (chiefly motor agitation) if use is suspended, and an uncontrollable drive to continue use. See CANNABIS ABUSE. See also SUBSTANCE DEPENDENCE.

cannabis-induced psychotic disorder a rare disorder marked by persecutory delusions associated with CANNABIS INTOXICATION, sometimes accompanied by marked anxiety, emotional lability, depersonalization, and subsequent amnesia for the episode. The disorder usually remits within a day, although it may persist for a few days. Hallucinations occur rarely. Also called **cannabis psychosis**.

cannabis intoxication a reversible syndrome that occurs during or shortly after the ingestion or smoking of CANNABIS. It consists of clinically significant behavioral or psychological changes (e.g., enhanced sense of well-being, intensification of perceptions, a sense of slowed time), as well as one or more signs of physiological involvement (e.g., increased pulse rate, conjunctivitis, dry mouth and throat). See also SUBSTANCE INTOXICATION.

cannabis psychosis see CANNABIS-INDUCED PSYCHOTIC DISORDER.

cannibalism *n.* **1.** the consumption of human flesh. See also KURU. **2.** a pathological urge to devour human flesh, occasionally observed in schizophrenia and similar mental disturbances, such as WINDIGO. In classical psychoanalytic theory, cannibalistic impulses are associated with fixation at the ORAL-BITING PHASE of PSYCHOSEXUAL DEVELOPMENT. **3.** the ingestion by a nonhuman animal of a member of its own species. Some female insects kill their mate at the time of copulation and eat it as a source of protein for developing eggs. In some animal species offspring are eaten, often in times of nutritional stress or when infants are malformed and unlikely to survive. **—cannibalistic** *adj.*

Cannon–Bard theory the theory that emotional states result from the influence of lower brain centers (the hypothalamus and thalamus) on higher ones (the cortex), rather than from sensory feedback to the brain produced by peripheral internal organs and voluntary musculature. According to this theory, the thalamus controls the experience of emotion, and the hypothalamus controls the expression of emotion. Also called **Bard–Cannon theory**; **Cannon's theory**; **hypothalamic theory of Cannon**; **thalamic theory of Cannon**. See also

EMERGENCY THEORY OF EMOTIONS; FIGHT–FLIGHT REACTION. [proposed in the 1920s and early 1930s by Walter B. **Cannon** (1871–1945) and Philip **Bard** (1898–1977), U.S. psychologists]

cannula *n.* a tube that can be inserted into a body cavity to provide a channel for the escape of fluid from the cavity. It can also be inserted into a blood vessel to introduce substances into the body to avoid repeated injections by a hypodermic needle or to take blood samples.

canon *n.* a fundamental working principle or rule believed to increase the likelihood of making accurate inferences and meaningful discoveries. **—canonical** *adj.*

canonical analysis a class of statistical analyses that assess the degree of relationship between two or more sets of measurements. Examples are DISCRIMINANT ANALYSIS and MULTIPLE REGRESSION analysis, among others.

canonical correlation a CORRELATION COEFFICIENT that quantifies the magnitude of linear relationship between a linear combination of one set of variables and a linear combination of a different set of variables. Canonical correlation might be used, for example, in an experimental design studying the relationship between intelligence and productivity, where there are three different measures of intelligence and five different measures of productivity. This statistical procedure, however, is now used less frequently because it has largely been replaced by STRUCTURAL EQUATION MODELING.

capability *n.* **1.** the possession of able qualities. **2.** an ability, talent, or facility that a person can put to constructive use. For example, a child may have great musical capability. **3.** a characteristic that can be developed for functional use.

capacity *n.* **1.** the maximum ability of an individual to receive or retain information and knowledge or to function in mental or physical tasks. **2.** the potential of an individual for intellectual or creative development or accomplishment. **3.** inborn potential, as contrasted with developed potential (see ABILITY).

capacity model one of a number of models of attention that characterize attention as a limited-capacity resource. Attentional deficits occur when the demands on this resource exceed the supply.

capacity sharing in DUAL-TASK PERFORMANCE, the dividing of attentional resources between the tasks, that is, the tasks are processed in parallel (see PARALLEL PROCESSING), but the processing efficiency varies with the available capacity of attention.

CAPD abbreviation for CENTRAL AUDITORY PROCESSING DISORDER.

Capgras syndrome a condition characterized by a delusional belief that the self or known individuals have been replaced by doubles or impostors. This type of MISIDENTIFICATION SYNDROME may be associated with paranoid schizophrenia, a neurological disorder, or a mood disorder. Also called **illusion of doubles**. [Jean Marie Joseph **Capgras** (1873–1950), French psychiatrist]

capitalism *n.* an economic system emphasizing individual enterprise, free-market principles, profit-taking, and private or corporate ownership of capital, rather than state control of the economy as in socialism or communism. **—capitalist** *n., adj.*

capitalization on chance the process of inferring causality from a phenomenon that is in truth a result of chance alone (i.e., a random phenomenon). Capitalization on chance often occurs when one selects an extreme case from among several cases available.

capitation *n.* a method of payment for health care services in which a provider or health care facility is paid a fixed amount for each person served under a risk contract. Capitation is the characteristic payment method of HMOS. **—capitated** *adj.*

caprylic *adj.* denoting one of the four primary odor qualities in the CROCKER–HENDERSON ODOR SYSTEM. This quality is called HIRCINE in the ZWAARDEMAKER SMELL SYSTEM.

capsaicin *n.* a compound, synthesized by various plants to deter predators, that elicits the sensation of burning. Capsaicin is responsible for the "hot" taste of chili peppers. It is used medicinally in topical ointments to relieve peripheral neuropathy.

capsula externa see EXTERNAL CAPSULE.

captioning *n.* the display of the text of spoken words, typically used in theaters, on television (see CLOSE-CAPTIONED TELEVISION), and in films, to allow those with hearing loss to follow verbal presentations or dramatic dialogue and action.

captivity *n.* **1.** the state or period of being confined, detained, incarcerated, imprisoned, or enslaved. See also POSTCAPTIVITY HEALTH PROBLEMS; PRISONER OF WAR. **2.** the state of an animal that is housed in an environment different from its natural environment and is prevented from returning to its natural environment. Much research is done on animals in captivity in order to have careful experimental control over environmental and social variables. Compare FIELD RESEARCH.

capture–tag–recapture sampling a type of SAMPLING used to estimate population size. For example, in order to estimate the number of fish in a lake, a random sample of fish (e.g., 100) would be drawn and tagged, then returned to the lake. The lake would be resampled, and the results (i.e., the fraction of tagged fish in the new sample) would be used to estimate the total number of fish in the lake.

CAR abbreviation for CONDITIONED AVOIDANCE RESPONSE.

carbamates *pl. n.* a class of ACETYLCHOLINESTERASE INHIBITORS (e.g., RIVASTIGMINE) used in the treatment of dementia. Carbamates can delay the progression of certain dementias, slowing declines in cognitive function and in activities of daily living. They are preferred to earlier generations of acetylcholinesterase inhibitors because of their relatively benign side effects, relative lack of liver toxicity, and improved dosing schedule (they need to be administered only once or twice a day).

carbamazepine (**CBZ**) *n.* a drug that is related to the TRICYCLIC ANTIDEPRESSANTS, used mainly as an ANTICONVULSANT but also for the relief of symptoms of TRIGEMINAL NEURALGIA and as a MOOD STABILIZER in mania. U.S. trade name (among others): **Tegretol**.

carbidopa *n.* see SINEMET.

carbohydrate *n.* any of a group of organic compounds that have the general formula $C_x(H_2O)_y$. They range from relatively small molecules, such as simple sugars (e.g., GLUCOSE), to macromolecular substances, such as starch, glycogen, and cellulose. Carbohydrates of plant origin form a major source of energy in the diet of animals.

carbohydrate metabolism the utilization by the body of starches, sugars, and other CARBOHYDRATES, which are broken down by various enzymes to GLUCOSE molecules. Glucose is the ultimate source of cellular energy for the brain and other organs.

carbon dioxide (formula: CO_2) a colorless, odorless, incombustible gas formed during respiration, combustion, and decomposition of organic substances. Plants obtain carbon for organic molecules from CO_2 by photosynthesis. The increasing CO_2 concentration in the atmosphere is considered to be a main cause of global warming.

carbon dioxide therapy a form of inhalation therapy, now no longer in use, that was occasionally applied (in conjunction with psychotherapy) to patients with anxiety, conversion, or psychophysiological symptoms. [first used in the 1920s by Hungarian-born U.S. psychiatrist Ladislaus Joseph Meduna (1896–1964) to induce unconsciousness as a means of interrupting pathological brain circuits]

carbonic anhydrase inhibitors a group of drugs that interfere with the action of the enzyme carbonic anhydrase in the body. Although their primary role was originally as diuretics, via their ability to block reabsorption of sodium bicarbonate from the proximal renal tubule, thus improving urine excretion and electrolyte balance, their use has been supplanted by less toxic diuretics. At present, **acetazolamide** (the prototype; U.S. trade name: **Diamox**) and other carbonic anhydrase inhibitors are used primarily for the management of GLAUCOMA and ACUTE MOUNTAIN SICKNESS. The drugs are also used as adjunctive agents in the management of epilepsy. Acetazolamide inhibits epileptic seizures and decreases the rate of cerebrospinal fluid formation.

carbon monoxide poisoning a toxic disorder resulting from inhalation of carbon monoxide, a colorless, odorless gas. Symptoms are produced by lack of oxygen in the tissues (anoxia); they range from headache and light-headedness due to mild exposure to an acute, transient state of confusion and delirium and, in cases of a severe exposure, deep coma followed by permanent brain damage and death by asphyxiation. Also called **carbon monoxide intoxication**.

carbon tetrachloride a volatile solvent that, when inhaled, can produce euphoria, disorientation and depersonalization, and other behavioral effects similar to those produced by the major sedatives. Continued use can lead to the rapid development of persisting dementia, as well as a variety of physical problems. See also INHALANT; INHALANT ABUSE; INHALANT DEPENDENCE; INHALANT INTOXICATION.

carcinogen *n.* any substance that initiates the development of CANCER (**carcinogenesis**). Tobacco smoke, which induces lung cancer, is an example. **—carcinogenic** *adj.*

carcinoma *n.* see CANCER.

cardi- *combining form* see CARDIO-.

cardiac index a measure of the cardiac output (i.e., the volume of blood pumped by the heart per minute) per square meter of body surface.

cardiac muscle the specialized muscle tissue of the heart. It consists of striated fibers that branch and interlock and are in electrical continuity with each other. This arrangement permits ACTION POTENTIALS to spread rapidly from cell to cell, allowing large groups of cells to contract in unison.

cardiac neurosis an anxiety reaction precipitated by a heart condition, the suspicion of having a heart condition, or the fear of developing coronary disease. In some cases a cardiac neurosis develops when the patient detects a harmless heart murmur, palpitations, or a chest pain due to emotional stress. In other cases it may be caused or aggravated by a physician's examination (see IATROGENIC ILLNESS). Cardiac anxiety is a common symptom of PANIC DISORDER; it may also be a focus in HYPOCHONDRIASIS.

cardiac pacemaker an electrical device that is surgically implanted into the chest to regulate an abnormal heart rhythm. Electrical leads from the device are placed in specific areas of the heart, and transducers can monitor the heart's rate of contraction and deliver an electric charge only when the organ is not functioning as desired.

cardiac psychology a specialization within HEALTH PSYCHOLOGY that focuses solely on health and disease related to the cardiovascular system.

cardiac psychosis a disorganization of thought processes that is associated with an acute state of fear and anxiety following a heart attack.

cardinal humors see HUMORAL THEORY.

cardinal trait a basic and pervasive characteristic or PERSONALITY TRAIT that dominates an individual's total behavior. [defined by Gordon Willard ALLPORT]

cardinal virtues in medieval philosophy, the four virtues on which all other virtues were thought to hinge, namely, prudence, courage, temperance, and justice. The cardinal or "natural" virtues were seen as available to all humans without the aid of divine grace; as such they were often contrasted with the "theological" virtues of faith, hope, and charity.

cardio- (**cardi-**) *combining form* heart.

cardiogram *n.* a graphic tracing of some aspect of heart activity, usually electrical activity of the heart (see ELECTROCARDIOGRAM). The tracing is produced by the stylet of a recording instrument called a **cardiograph**, and the procedure itself is called **cardiography**.

cardiomyopathy *n.* any disease involving the heart muscle, particularly when the specific cause is uncertain.

cardiophobia *n.* an excessive fear of the heart or, more specifically, of having or developing a heart condition. See CARDIAC NEUROSIS.

cardiopulmonary bypass machine a mechanical device that carries out the functions of the heart and lungs for short periods during surgery involving these organs. The machine collects blood from the veins before it reaches the heart and circulates it through a plastic chamber in which it is freshly oxygenated before being pumped back into the patient's arteries.

cardiovascular (**CV**) *adj.* relating to the heart and blood vessels or to blood circulation.

cardiovascular disease any disease, congenital or acquired, that affects the heart and blood vessels. Cardiovascular diseases include high blood pressure (see HYPERTENSION), congestive heart failure, myocardial INFARCTION, ARTERIOSCLEROSIS, CORONARY HEART DISEASE, and rheumatic heart disease.

cardiovascular reactivity the degree of change of cardiovascular responses (e.g., blood pressure, heart rate) to a psychological or physiological challenge or stressor. Exaggerated cardiovascular reactivity may indicate risk for development of cardiovascular symptoms, such as HYPERTENSION or CORONARY HEART DISEASE.

cardiovascular system the heart and blood vessels, which are responsible for the circulation of blood around the body. Also called **circulatory system**.

card-sorting test a test in which the participant is asked to sort randomly mixed cards into specific categories. Such tests may be used to determine frontal lobe functioning, learning ability, discriminatory powers, or clerical aptitude.

card-stacking *n.* a technique of persuasion that attempts to influence opinion through deliberate distortions, as in suppressing information, overemphasizing selected facts, manipulating statistics, and quoting rigged or questionable research.

CARE acronym for COMMUNICATED AUTHENTICITY, REGARD, EMPATHY.

care-and-protection proceedings court intervention on behalf of a child when the parents or caregivers do not adequately provide for the child's welfare.

carebaria *n.* a form of headache characterized by distressing sensations of pressure or heaviness.

career anchor a pattern of self-perceived work skills, interests, abilities, and values that are developed in the early stages of a person's career and that guide subsequent career decisions. Among the career anchors proposed in this theory are technical or functional competence, managerial competence, creativity, security, and autonomy. See CAREER PATTERN THEORY. [proposed by U.S. psychologist Edgar H. Schein (1928–)]

career aspirations longer-term goals that individuals set for their working lives, typically including pay, status, and accomplishments.

career choice the selection of a vocation, usually on the basis of such factors as parental guidance, vocational counseling, identification with admired figures, trial or part-time jobs, training opportunities, personal interests, and ability tests.

career conference a vocational meeting provided by many schools in which representatives of a given occupational field meet interested students to provide information and answer questions related to the requirements for, and opportunities available in, that field.

career counseling consultation, advice, or guidance specifically focused on a person's career opportunities, most often in educational, work, and some community settings. It also may provide consultation with the specific goal of enabling a person to change the direction of his or her career. The counseling will take account of an individual's preferences, intelligence, skill sets, work values, and experience. Such counseling is offered to groups as well as individuals. Also called **career guidance**.

career development 1. the manner in which a person manages the progress of his or her career, both within and between organizations. The issues that individuals must confront in their career development differ as a function of whether they are in the early, middle, or late stage of their careers. See also PROFESSIONAL DEVELOPMENT. **2.** the ways in which an organization structures the career progress of its employees, typically so that they are rewarded with higher levels of pay, status, responsibility, and satisfaction as they gain skills and experience.

career education a program of instruction designed to prepare one for employment or employment possibilities.

career guidance see CAREER COUNSELING.

career pattern theory any theory that attempts to describe the stages through which people pass during the course of their working lives. Careers are often depicted as passing through repeated cycles in which individuals grow by acquiring new skills and experience, stabilize their career gains, and then move into a period of transition as they prepare themselves for the next move.

career planning a VOCATIONAL GUIDANCE program designed to assist a client in choosing an occupation. A realistic appraisal of the individual's desires and abilities is formulated in relation to existing occupational opportunities. Various tests may be administered to aid a counselor in assessing a client's skills and aptitudes.

career workshop a VOCATIONAL GUIDANCE intervention consisting of a study group in which occupational opportunities and requirements are discussed and explored.

caregiver *n.* **1.** a person who attends to the needs of and provides assistance to someone else, such as an infant or an older adult. **2.** in health care, any individual involved in the process of identifying, preventing, or treating an illness or disability. —**caregiving** *adj.*

caregiver burden the stress and other psychological symptoms experienced by family members and other nonprofessional caregivers in response to looking after individuals with mental or physical disabilities. See also BURNOUT; COMPASSION FATIGUE.

care of young a manifestation of PARENTAL BEHAVIOR or ALLOPARENTING in animals, usually stimulated by certain hormonal and other physiological changes when in the presence of offspring. These include the secretion of PROLACTIN, which induces broodiness and parental feeding of young in birds and milk production in mammals.

caretaking behavior the behavior of parents or alloparents (**caretakers**) in attending to the needs of infants, responding to them when they approach, and protecting them from the aggression of others. See ALLOPARENTING; CARE OF YOUNG; PARENTAL BEHAVIOR.

carezza (**karezza**) *n.* a form of coitus in which the man does not reach orgasm. It is sometimes used as a means of birth control, but if combined with meditation it is similar to the COITUS RESERVATUS technique. Carezza techniques are derived from principles of Hindu Tantrism, and in this sense were first described by U.S. gynecologist Alice B. Stockham in 1896. Also called **coitus prolongatus**.

cargo cult 1. a system of beliefs found in the South Pacific islands, based on the notion that ritual worship will result in the attainment of modern material goods through supernatural means. It originated in indigenous religious practices in the 19th century and was altered, stimulated, and broadened from contact with Western cultures during World War II, when military forces stationed in the islands received regular deliveries of goods by air. **2.** the naive assumption that a superficial imitation of the manners, behavior, or style of influential or prosperous groups in society will bring one comparable wealth or status.

carisoprodol *n.* a drug belonging to the PROPANEDIOLS, a group originally developed as anxiolytics. Carisoprodol is now used as a MUSCLE RELAXANT and is increasingly seen as an intoxicant drug of abuse. U.S. trade name: **Soma**.

carnal *adj.* relating to the physical desires and appetites of the body, particularly sexual ones. **Carnal knowledge** is a mainly legal term for sexual intercourse.

carotid artery either of the two major arteries that ascend the right and left sides of the neck to the head and brain. The branch that enters the brain is the INTERNAL CAROTID ARTERY, whereas the **external carotid artery** supplies the face and scalp. Both branches arise from the **common carotid artery** on each side of the lower neck.

carotid sinus a small dilation in the common CAROTID ARTERY, at its bifurcation into the external and internal carotids. It contains BARORECEPTORS that, when stimulated, cause slowing of the heart rate, vasodilation, and a fall in blood pressure. It is innervated primarily by the GLOSSOPHARYNGEAL NERVE.

carotid-sinus syndrome see AORTIC ARCH SYNDROME.

carotid stenosis see STENOSIS.

carotodynia *n.* pain in the cheek, neck, and region of the eyes resulting from pressure on the common carotid artery.

carpal age an individual's ANATOMICAL AGE as estimated from the degree of ossification of the carpal (wrist) bones.

carpal tunnel syndrome (**CTS**) an inflammatory disorder of the hand caused by repetitive stress, physical injury, or other conditions that cause the tissues around the median nerve to become swollen. It occurs either when the protective lining of the tendons within the **carpal tunnel** become inflamed and swell or when the ligament that forms the roof of the tunnel becomes thicker and broader. See REPETITIVE STRAIN INJURY.

carpentered environment an environment consisting of built structures in which rectangles are predominant. Some hypotheses about DEPTH PERCEPTION and OPTICAL ILLUSIONS have suggested that people in carpentered environments interpret parallelograms (or parts of parallelograms) in two-dimensional drawings in ways that are consistent with perception of three-dimensional objects, such as doors, windows, and corners.

Carpenter's syndrome an autosomal recessive hereditary disorder marked by a pointed skull, webbing of the fingers and toes, subaverage intelligence, and usually obesity. Also called **acrocephalopolysyndactyly**. [George Alfred **Carpenter** (1859–1910), British physician]

carphology *n.* see FLOCCILLATION.

carrier *n.* an individual who has a mutation in a gene that conveys either increased susceptibility to a disease or other condition or the certainty that the condition will develop. A *BRCA1* mutation carrier, for example, is a person who carries an altered *BRCA1* gene (see BRCA1 AND BRCA2). This alteration is responsible for significantly raising the likelihood that the person, if female, will develop breast or ovarian cancer. See also OBLIGATE CARRIER.

carryover effect the effect on the current performance of a research participant of the experimental conditions that preceded the current conditions.

Cartesian coordinate system a system for locating a point in an *n*-dimensional space by indicating the distance of the point from a common origin along each of the *n* mutually orthogonal axes of the space. [René **Descartes** (1596–1650), French philosopher, mathematician, and scientist]

Cartesian dualism the position taken by French philosopher, mathematician, and scientist René Descartes (1596–1650) that the world comprises two distinct and incompatible classes of substance: RES EXTENSA, or extended substance, which extends through space; and RES COGITANS, or thinking substance, which has no extension in space. The body (including the brain) is composed of extended and divisible substance, whereas the mind is not. For Descartes, this means that the mind would continue to exist even if the material body did not. He accepted that there is interaction between mind and body, holding that in some activities the mind operates independently of bodily influences, whereas in others the body exerts an influence. Similarly, in some bodily activities there is influence from the mind, while in others there is not. Descartes proposed that the locus for the interaction of the mind and body is the point in the pineal gland in the brain termed the CONARIUM. However, to the question of how such incompatible substances can interact at all, Descartes had no answer. See DUALISM; GHOST IN THE MACHINE; MIND–BODY PROBLEM.

Cartesianism *n.* the system of philosophy developed by French philosopher, mathematician, and scientist René Descartes (1596–1650). The three fundamental tenets of the system are (a) that all knowledge forms a unity; (b) that the purpose of knowledge is to provide humankind with the means of mastery over the natural world; and (c) that all knowledge must be built up from a foundation of indubitable first principles, the truth of which can be known intuitively (see INNATE IDEAS). Many ideas and assumptions influential in psychology can be traced back to Descartes, including the notion of a rational self capable of knowing truth, the contention that the most trustworthy knowledge is of the contents of one's own mind, and the idea that the deductive methods that have been successful in producing certainty in mathematics can be applied to produce equally valid knowledge in other fields of human endeavor. Of particular importance to the development of psychology are Descartes' understanding of the ego (see CARTESIAN SELF) and his attempt to explain the relation of the mind to the body (see CARTESIAN DUALISM). See also MODERNISM; RATIONALISM. **—Cartesian** *adj.*

Cartesian self in the system of French philosopher, mathematician, and scientist René Descartes (1596–1650), the knowing subject or ego. The Cartesian self is capable of one fundamental certainty since, even if all else is subject to doubt, one cannot seriously doubt that one is thinking, as to doubt is to think. Thus, Descartes concludes, COGITO ERGO SUM ("I am thinking, therefore I exist"). From this position Descartes argues that all ideas intuited by the self with the same clarity and distinctness as the *cogito* must be equally true; this enables the intuition of further indubitable truths, such as the existence of God and the external world. However, since the ideas clearest to the self are the contents of the mind, the notion of the Cartesian self has led to a radical DUALISM between the inner life of the mind (subjectivity) and the outer world of things (objectivity). It has also led to the idea that knowledge is necessarily subjective and has opened the question as to how the outer world, including other human beings, can be known except as an idea. See CARTESIAN DUALISM; EGOCENTRIC PREDICAMENT; SOLIPSISM.

Cartesian theater a metaphorical conception of CONSCIOUSNESS identified as the traditional view by U.S. philosopher Daniel Dennett (1942–), who has challenged its adequacy. Based on the idea of the knowing subject or ego defined by French philosopher, mathematician, and scientist René Descartes (1596–1650), the Cartesian theater is envisioned as a place where all aspects of experience come together to provide a unified phenomenal world. See CARTESIAN DUALISM; CARTESIAN SELF.

Carus typology a classification of individuals into five body types: ATHLETIC TYPE, PHLEGMATIC TYPE, PHTHISIC TYPE, CEREBRAL TYPE, and sterile type. [Carl Gustav **Carus** (1789–1868), German physiologist and psychologist]

carve out to eliminate coverage for specific health care services (e.g., mental health or substance abuse) from a health care plan and contract for those services from a separate provider. **—carve-out** *n.*

CAS abbreviation for COGNITIVE ASSESSMENT SYSTEM.

Casanova complex a man's desire to have a large number of lovers, leading to very active pursuit of women and attempts to seduce or entice women into having sexual intercourse without any emotional relationship or commitment. The complex is named for Giovanni Jacopo

Casanova (1725–1798), an Italian adventurer noted for his sexual conquests.

case *n.* **1.** an instance of a disease or disorder, usually at the level of the individual patient. In a **borderline case**, the symptoms resemble those of a disease or disorder but do not fully meet the criteria. See also PROBAND. **2.** a person about whom data are collected or who is the recipient of assistance (e.g., from a health care professional or lawyer). **3.** a specific instance, occurrence, or example or a type thereof. **4.** a feature of certain languages in which the forms of nouns, pronouns, and (sometimes) adjectives are altered to indicate their syntactic relations with other words in a sentence. The role of case is most significant in highly inflected languages, such as German or Latin. In English, case endings are now restricted to the personal and possessive pronouns (*I, me, mine,* etc.) and to plural and possessive nouns (e.g., *dogs, children, girl's, girls'*). See ACCUSATIVE; DATIVE; GENITIVE; NOMINATIVE. **5.** one of various categories used in CASE GRAMMAR to classify the elements of a sentence in terms of their semantic relations with the main verb. See AGENT; EXPERIENCER; INSTRUMENTAL; PATIENT.

case advocate see ADVOCATE.

case alternation in reading research, a procedure for stimulus presentation in which the characters of stimulus words switch between upper and lower case. The change is usually made in one of six ways: (a) to the complete word (*APPLE/apple*), (b) to alternate letters (*ApPlE*), (c) after the second letter (*APple*), (d) after the third letter (*APPle*), (e) after the fourth letter (*APPLe*), or (f) after each pair (*APplE*).

case-based reasoning 1. an approach in which information about or obtained from previous similar situations (cases) is applied to the current situation, typically to make a decision or prediction or to solve a problem. See also ANALOGICAL THINKING. **2.** in ergonomics, the use of detailed scenarios or cases to elicit users' knowledge, reasoning patterns, motivations, or assumptions regarding a product or system. See KNOWLEDGE ELICITATION.

case-finding *n.* the process of identifying individuals who need treatment for mental disorders by administering screening tests, locating individuals who have contacted social agencies or mental health facilities, obtaining referrals from general practitioners, or via triage after a disaster.

case grammar in linguistics, an analysis of sentences that gives primacy to the semantic relations between words (e.g., whether they are the AGENT or the PATIENT of the action described) rather than to their syntactic relations (e.g., whether they are the SUBJECT or the OBJECT of the sentence). In the two sentences *The boy hit the ball* and *The ball was hit by the boy*, a case-grammar analysis would focus on the fact that *boy* is the agent of the action in both sentences, rather than the fact that it is the subject of the first sentence and the object in the second. Psychologists have shown a strong interest in case grammar because of its affinity to psychological categories of meaning. See also EXPERIENCER; INSTRUMENTAL.

case history a record of information relating to a person's psychological or medical condition used as an aid to diagnosis and treatment. It usually contains test results, interviews, professional evaluations, and sociological, occupational, and educational data.

case law a body of law established by a series of court decisions. Case law is distinguished from laws that arise from legislation. See also COMMON LAW.

case load the amount of work required of a psychotherapist, psychiatrist, doctor, social worker, or counselor during a particular period, as computed by the number of clients assigned to him or her and the comparative difficulty of their cases.

case management a system of managing and coordinating the delivery of health care in order to improve the continuity and quality of care as well as reducing costs. Case management is usually a function of a hospital's UTILIZATION REVIEW department.

case manager a health care professional, usually a nurse or social worker, who works with patients, providers, and health insurance plans to coordinate the continuity and cost-effectiveness of services.

case method in industrial and organizational psychology, a PERSONNEL TRAINING technique in which a group of managers or supervisors are presented with an actual or hypothetical business problem through written materials, audiovisual media, or live role play, and required to generate solutions. See also BUSINESS GAME; CONFERENCE METHOD; MULTIPLE-ROLE PLAYING; SCENARIO ANALYSIS.

case report a collection of data relating to a person's psychological or medical condition.

case study an in-depth investigation of an individual, a family, or other social unit. Multiple types of data (psychological, physiological, biographical, environmental) are assembled in order to understand the subject's background, relationships, and behavior.

casework *n.* the tasks carried out by a professional, usually a social worker known as a **caseworker**, who provides or oversees services being delivered, including counseling or therapy. Casework includes identifying and assessing the needs of the individual and his or her family and providing or coordinating and monitoring the provision of support and services. These services may include private counseling, treatment in a hospital or other institution, or such concrete services as arranging for public assistance, housing, and other aid. Also called **social casework**.

Caspar Hauser experiment any procedure in which an animal is deprived of its natural environment or sensory stimulation from birth onward. The experiment is named for a 19th-century German child who was allegedly raised in this manner.

cassina *n.* a perennial evergreen shrub, *Ilex vomitoria*, that grows wild in eastern North America, particularly Virginia and the Carolinas. The leaves contain caffeine and have been used by Native Americans to prepare a tealike beverage known as the "black drink" for medicinal, ceremonial, and social purposes. Also called **yaupon**; **youpon**.

CAST abbreviation for COMPUTERIZED ADAPTIVE SCREENING TEST.

caste *n.* **1.** any of the fixed hereditary classes of the **Hindu caste system**, which are held to be distinguished by different levels of ritual purity. The main classes are (in order of status): brahmins or priests, warriors, merchants, laborers, and outcastes or untouchables. Until recently, mobility or intermarriage between castes was exceptional. See also FIXED CLASS SOCIETY; HINDUISM; SOCIAL IMMOBILITY. **2.** any system of social stratification regarded as being comparably rigid. **3.** any class of society distinguished by inherited privilege and exclusivity.

castration *n.* surgical removal of the testes (see ORCHIDECTOMY); less commonly it can indicate removal of the ovaries (see OVARIECTOMY). In either men or women, inactivation of these glands can also be accomplished with radiation, by illness, or with drugs (see

CHEMICAL CASTRATION). Castration eliminates sex hormone production and, in men, may lower sexual drive and function. However, as hormones are also produced by the adrenal glands, this latter effect is not always obtained. In women, removal of the ovaries may reduce vaginal lubrication, and hormone replacement therapy has become usual for women who have had their ovaries removed for medical reasons.

castration anxiety fear of injury to or loss of the genitals. In the PREGENITAL PHASE posited by psychoanalytic theory, the various losses and deprivations experienced by the infant boy may give rise to the fear that he will also lose his penis. See also CASTRATION COMPLEX.

castration complex in psychoanalytic theory, the whole combination of the child's unconscious feelings and fantasies associated with being deprived of the PHALLUS, which in boys means the loss of the penis and in girls the belief that it has already been removed. It derives from the discovery that girls have no penis and is closely tied to the OEDIPUS COMPLEX.

casual crowd a crowd that forms by chance, usually in a public place, to share a temporary focus. Examples include passersby pausing to watch two people arguing loudly and people gathered behind police barricades around a burning building. Members of a casual crowd usually lack any definite intentions and often seem indifferent to or unconcerned with what they are witnessing.

casualty *n.* **1.** a person or group harmed, psychologically or physically, by such negative life experiences as accidents, abuse, warfare, and disasters. **2.** an individual whose psychological well-being declines, rather than improves, as a result of his or her experiences in a change-promoting group.

CAT **1.** abbreviation for CALIFORNIA ACHIEVEMENT TESTS. **2.** abbreviation for the British version of the COGNITIVE ABILITIES TEST. **3.** abbreviation for COMPUTER ADAPTIVE TESTING. **4.** acronym for computerized axial tomography (see COMPUTED TOMOGRAPHY).

cata- (**cat-**; **kata-**; **kat-**) *combining form* **1.** down or beneath (e.g., CATABOLISM). **2.** reversal or degeneration (e.g., CATATONIA).

catabolism *n.* the part of METABOLISM concerned with the breakdown of complex molecules from food or tissues, often with the release of energy. Compare ANABOLISM. **—catabolic** *adj.*

catabolite *n.* a product of CATABOLISM.

catalepsy *n.* a state of sustained unresponsiveness in which a fixed body posture or physical attitude is maintained over a long period of time. It is seen in cases of CATATONIC SCHIZOPHRENIA, EPILEPSY, and other disorders. Also called **catatonic rigidity**; **cerea flexibilitas**; **flexibilitas cerea**; **waxy flexibility**. See also EPIDEMIC CATALEPSY. **—cataleptic** *adj.*

catalogia *n.* see VERBIGERATION.

catalysis *n.* the speeding of a chemical reaction by a CATALYST.

catalyst *n.* a substance that increases the rate of a chemical reaction without itself being used up. An ENZYME is an organic catalyst.

catalytic agent in group psychotherapy, a member who stimulates emotional reactions in other members.

catalytic variable a variable whose presence facilitates a biological or social process.

catamite *n.* a boy who participates in PEDERASTY.

catamnesis *n.* the medical history of a patient following the onset of a mental or physical disorder, either after the initial examination or after discharge from treatment (in the latter case it is also known as **follow-up history**).

cataphasia *n.* **1.** a language disorder characterized by repetition of a single word. **2.** see SYNTACTICAL APHASIA. **3.** see VERBIGERATION.

cataphora *n.* a type of coma that may be interrupted by intervals of partial consciousness.

cataplexy *n.* a sudden loss of muscle tone that may be localized, causing (for example) loss of grasp or head nodding, or generalized, resulting in collapse of the entire body. It is a temporary condition usually precipitated by an extreme emotional stimulus (e.g., an uncontrollable fit of laughter, overwhelming anxiety, excitement, or anger). See NARCOLEPSY; NARCOLEPSY–CATAPLEXY SYNDROME. **—cataplectic** *adj.*

Catapres *n.* a trade name for CLONIDINE.

cataract *n.* a progressive clouding (opacification) of the lens of the eye that eventually results in severe visual impairment if untreated. Central vision in particular is impaired, but peripheral vision can also be affected. The typical (and often only) symptom is a gradual dimming of vision marked by the need for brighter illumination, larger print, or a particular way of holding reading material. Cataract is frequently associated with the degenerative processes of aging, but it may also be congenital (see CONGENITAL CATARACT) or due to disease, injury, exposure to radiation, dietary deficiencies, or uncontrolled diabetes.

catarrhal ophthalmia see OPHTHALMIA.

catastrophe cusp theory a theory concerning the interaction of COGNITIVE ANXIETY and physiological arousal. Under conditions of high cognitive anxiety, as physiological arousal increases, performance will increase to a certain point, but past this point a catastrophic drop in performance will occur. To regain an optimal level of performance, a substantial lowering of physiological arousal is necessary.

catastrophe theory a mathematical theory regarding discontinuous changes in one variable as a function of continuous change in some other variable or variables. It proposes that a small change in one factor may cause an abrupt and large change in another, for example, the dramatic change in the physical properties of water as the temperature reaches 0 °C or 100 °C (32 or 212 °F). Catastrophe theory models are classified according to the number of control parameters, the most common being the **cusp catastrophe model**, in which two control parameters are varied simultaneously.

catastrophic behavior see CATASTROPHIC REACTION.

catastrophic illness a severe illness, acute or chronic, that is likely to result in serious disability or death. Treatment is typically prolonged, intense, and costly.

catastrophic reaction **1.** a breakdown in the ability to cope with a threatening or traumatic situation. The individual experiences acute feelings of inadequacy, anxiety, frustration, and helplessness. **2.** highly emotional behavior (extreme anxiety, sudden crying, aggressive or hostile behavior, etc.) sometimes observed in individuals who have suffered brain damage, including those with APHASIA. The origin of this behavior remains unclear, although U.S. neurologist D. Frank Benson (1928–1996) ascribed such reactions to individuals' frustration, embarrassment, or agitation at their struggle to communicate or perform tasks they had previously performed with ease. Also called **catastrophic behavior**. [first described by German-born U.S. psychologist Kurt Goldstein (1878–1965)]

catastrophic stress an overwhelming reaction to a

traumatic event that is beyond the limits of normal life. Traumatic events, such as rape, torture, genocide, or severe war-zone experiences, are filtered through cognitive and emotional processes before being appraised as extreme threats.

catastrophize *vb.* to exaggerate the negative consequences of events or decisions. People are said to be catastrophizing when they think that the worst possible outcome will occur from a particular action or in a particular situation or when they feel as if they are in the midst of a catastrophe in situations that may be serious and upsetting but are not necessarily disastrous. The tendency to catastrophize can unnecessarily increase levels of anxiety and lead to maladaptive behavior.

catathymic crisis see ISOLATED EXPLOSIVE DISORDER.

catatonia *n.* a state of muscular rigidity or other disturbance of motor behavior, such as CATALEPSY, extreme overactivity, or adoption of bizarre postures. It is most frequently observed in CATATONIC SCHIZOPHRENIA. Also called **catatonic state**. **—catatonic** *adj.*

catatonic excitement periods of extreme restlessness and excessive and apparently purposeless motor activity, often as a symptom of CATATONIC SCHIZOPHRENIA.

catatonic rigidity see CATALEPSY.

catatonic schizophrenia in *DSM–IV–TR*, a relatively rare subtype of schizophrenia characterized by abnormal motor activity, specifically motor immobility (see CATALEPSY; CATATONIC STUPOR) or excessive motor activity (see CATATONIC EXCITEMENT). Other common features include extreme NEGATIVISM (apparently motiveless resistance to all instructions or maintenance of a rigid posture against attempts to be moved) or MUTISM; peculiarities of voluntary movement, such as POSTURING or stereotyped movements; and ECHOLALIA or ECHOPRAXIA. The *DSM–III* designation was **catatonic type schizophrenic disorder**.

catatonic state see CATATONIA.

catatonic stupor a state of significantly decreased reactivity to environmental stimuli and events and reduced spontaneous movement, often as a symptom of CATATONIC SCHIZOPHRENIA.

catchment area the geographic area served by a health care program (e.g., a community mental health center).

catch trial a trial within an experiment in which the INDEPENDENT VARIABLE is not present but the participants' responses are recorded as usual. For example, in an experiment in which participants identify auditory signals, catch trials are those in which no signal is given. See also BLANK TRIAL.

catch-up growth a period of relatively rapid growth that follows a period of retarded growth, for example, during prolonged illness. Catch-up growth allows the child to return to a normal level of development.

cat-cry syndrome see CRI DU CHAT SYNDROME.

catechetical method a form of instruction or means of persuasion that uses a skillfully devised series of questions, the answers to which gradually lead the person being questioned to accept the conclusions desired by the questioner. Also called **catechetical procedure**. See SOCRATIC DIALOGUE.

catecholamine *n.* any of a class of BIOGENIC AMINES that are the predominant neurotransmitters in the SYMPATHETIC NERVOUS SYSTEM. Naturally occurring catecholamine neurotransmitters are DOPAMINE and its metabolites EPINEPHRINE and NOREPINEPHRINE.

catecholamine hypothesis the hypothesis that deficiencies in the catecholamine neurotransmitters norepinephrine, epinephrine, and dopamine at receptor sites in the brain lead to a state of physiological and psychological depression, and that an excess of such neurotransmitters at these sites is responsible for the production of mania. The catecholamine hypothesis underlay the development of the early tricyclic antidepressants in the late 1950s, as it had been known that these compounds inhibited the reuptake of norepinephrine into presynaptic neurons. Despite numerous shortcomings, the catecholamine hypothesis, and the related MONOAMINE HYPOTHESIS, became the dominant hypotheses in the biological treatment of depression in the last half of the 20th century.

catecholaminergic neuron a nerve cell that releases a CATECHOLAMINE, such as norepinephrine, as a neurotransmitter. See also ADRENERGIC NEURON.

catechol-O-methyltransferase *n.* an enzyme, found at synapses of neurons, that deactivates CATECHOLAMINES.

categorical attitude see ABSTRACT ATTITUDE.

categorical classification see CONCEPTUAL CLASSIFICATION.

categorical data data that consist of counts as opposed to measurements. Religion or political party affiliation are examples of categorical data. Also called **nominal data**.

categorical data analysis any of several statistical procedures used to model the number of cases that fall into any category of a classification system as a function of one or more predictor variables.

categorical imperative the moral directive articulated by German philosopher Immanuel Kant (1724–1804) that one's behavior should be guided by maxims that one would be comfortable to hold as universal laws governing the actions of all people in the same circumstances. Because it is absolute and unconditional, the categorical imperative contrasts with a HYPOTHETICAL IMPERATIVE of the type "If you would achieve end Y, take action Z." The categorical imperative has been extremely influential in moral philosophy and in theories of moral behavior in psychology. See also UNIVERSALIZABILITY.

categorical intrusion in a memory recall test, the recall by the participant of one or more items that were not presented for memorization but are from the same semantic category (e.g., names, animals, foods) as the presented items. See CATEGORIZED LIST; DEESE PARADIGM.

categorical perception in speech perception, the phenomenon in which a continuous acoustic dimension, such as VOICE-ONSET TIME, is perceived as having distinct categories with sharp discontinuities at certain points. Moreover, individuals tested are often unable to discriminate between acoustically different stimuli that fall within the same categorical boundaries. Categorical perception is crucial in the identification of PHONEMES.

categorical scale see NOMINAL SCALE.

categorical thought in Jean PIAGET's theory of cognitive development, ABSTRACT THINKING that involves the use of general concepts and classifications. It is particularly lacking in young children, who tend to think concretely (see CONCRETE THINKING). See also ABSTRACT ATTITUDE.

categorical variable a variable defined by membership in a group, class, or category, rather than by rank or by scores on more continuous scales of measurement.

categories of thought in the thought of German philosopher Immanuel Kant (1724–1804), 12 basic concepts of human understanding that are essential to the interpretation of empirical experience. These include such fundamental ideas as unity, plurality, reality, negation, causality, and so on. Although they are necessary to the understanding of sense experience, the categories are themselves A PRIORI rather than empirically given. Time and space play a similar role in ordering one's sense impressions but are classed by Kant as immediate intuitions rather than categories of thought. The categories are applicable only to the world of appearances or PHENOMENA; there is no reason to suppose that they apply to things-in-themselves (see NOUMENON).

categorization *n.* the process by which objects, events, people, or experiences are grouped into classes on the basis of (a) characteristics shared by members of the same class and (b) features distinguishing the members of one class from those of another. Theories of categorization include the PROTOTYPE MODEL, INSTANCE THEORY, and the FAMILY RESEMBLANCE hypothesis. Also called **classification**. See also ABSTRACTION; CONCEPTUALIZATION. **—categorize** *vb.*

categorized list a list used in memory experiments in which the items come from one or more semantic categories (e.g., names, animals, foods). Categorized lists are often used to test FREE RECALL; the category labels (animals, foods, etc.) may be used to prompt recall.

category fluency see SEMANTIC FLUENCY.

category midpoint the halfway point between the upper and lower limits of a class or category.

category-system method any method of measurement or classification assessment that involves the use of STRUCTURED OBSERVATIONAL MEASURES to sort data elements into categories according to a set of rules. See also INTERACTION-PROCESS ANALYSIS; SYMLOG.

Category Test a nonverbal problem-solving task that requires abstract reasoning, concept formation, and mental flexibility. The participant is presented with six subtests each comprising a different set of stimuli organized according to a specific principle and each stimulus within each set associated with a particular number. The participant must respond by choosing a number and, using feedback about response accuracy, determine the principle of organization underlying the set of stimuli within a particular subtest. Once the principle is correctly identified, the participant can solve each item correctly within the subtest. A final subtest contains items from the previous six. The Category Test is part of the HALSTEAD–REITAN NEUROPSYCHOLOGICAL BATTERY. Also called **Halstead Category Test**. [designed in 1947 by U.S. psychologist Ward Halstead (1908–1969)]

catelectrotonus *n.* increased excitability of the tissue of a nerve or a muscle near the cathode (see ELECTRODE) as an electric current passes through it. **—catelectrotonic** *adj.*

cathard *n.* see CAFARD.

catharsis *n.* **1.** in psychoanalytic theory, the discharge of affects connected to traumatic events that had previously been repressed by bringing these events back into consciousness and reexperiencing them. See also ABREACTION. **2.** more generally, the release of strong, pent-up emotions. [from Greek, literally: "purgation, purification"] **—cathartic** *adj.*

cathected *adj.* see CATHEXIS.

cathectic discharge see AFFECTIVE DISCHARGE.

catheter *n.* any flexible tubular instrument inserted into a body cavity to introduce or remove fluids or to keep a body passage open. A catheter may be indwelling, if required for a long period of time, or temporary.

cathexis *n.* in psychoanalytic theory, the investment of PSYCHIC ENERGY in an OBJECT of any kind, such as a wish, fantasy, person, goal, idea, social group, or the self. Such objects are said to be **cathected** when an individual attaches emotional significance (positive or negative AFFECT) to them. See also ANTICATHEXIS; DECATHEXIS; EGO CATHEXIS; HYPERCATHEXIS; OBJECT CATHEXIS.

cathinone *n.* see KHAT.

cation *n.* a positively charged ION, such as a potassium ion (K^+) or sodium ion (Na^+). Compare ANION. **—cationic** *adj.*

catoptrics *n.* the field of optics concerned with the reflection of light. Compare DIOPTRICS.

cat's-eye syndrome a rare chromosomal disorder caused by the presence of a small additional section of chromosome material (see ACROCENTRIC CHROMOSOME), possibly from chromosome 14, resulting in a set of birth defects that include an imperforate anus and a cleft iris that produces a cat's-eye appearance. Affected individuals show normal or near normal mental development (some may have mild mental retardation). Also called **extra-small acrocentric chromosome syndrome**; **partial trisomy 6 syndrome**; **Schachenmann's syndrome**; **Schmid–Fraccaro syndrome**.

Cattell, James McKeen (1860–1944) U.S. psychologist. In 1886 Cattell became the first American to earn a German doctorate, studying under Wilhelm WUNDT in Leipzig and subsequently with Frances Galton (1822–1911) in England. At 28 he was appointed professor of psychology at the University of Pennsylvania. Shortly thereafter he transferred to Columbia University, where he exerted a broad influence as mentor to such distinguished psychologists as Robert S. WOODWORTH and Edward L. THORNDIKE. He was also influential as editor of many important scientific publications, such as *Science*, which became the main organ of the American Association for the Advancement of Science under his leadership, *Popular Science Monthly*, *The American Naturalist*, and *School and Society*. He also created and edited the influential *American Men of Science*, a directory of U.S. scientists with starred entries for the most eminent thousand (which Cattell determined by using his own statistical techniques). He was one of the founders of the Psychological Corporation. His empirical work included experiments on reaction time, perception, and word association and devising the first battery of psychological tests of special ability.

Cattell–Horn theory of intelligence a theory proposing that there are two main kinds of intellectual abilities nested under general intelligence: *g-c*, or crystallized ability, which is the sum of one's knowledge and is measured by tests of vocabulary, general information, etc.; and *g-f*, or fluid ability, which is the set of mental processes that is used in dealing with relatively novel tasks and is used in the acquisition of *g-c*. In later versions of the theory, other abilities have been added, such as *g-v*, or visual ability, which is the set of mental processes used in handling visual-spatial tasks, such as mentally rotating a geometric figure or visualizing what pieces of paper would look like were they folded. [Raymond Bernard **Cattell** (1905–1998), British-born U.S. personality psychologist; John L. **Horn** (1928–), U.S. psychologist]

Cattell inventory any of several self-report inventories based on a study of personality traits by FACTOR ANALYSIS. The best known of these inventories is the **Sixteen Personality Factor Questionnaire**, which yields 16 scores on such traits as trusting versus suspicious, humble versus assertive, and reserved versus outgoing. [Raymond **Cattell**]

Cattell's factorial theory of personality an approach to personality description based on the identification of traits, their measurement through FACTOR ANALYSIS, and their classification into 35 SURFACE TRAITS and the 12 SOURCE TRAITS that underlie them. [Raymond **Cattell**]

cauda equina the bundle of nerve roots at the base of the spinal cord, so called because of its resemblance to a horse's tail.

caudal *adj.* **1.** pertaining to a tail. **2.** situated at or toward the tail end of an organism. Compare ROSTRAL.

caudate nucleus one of the BASAL GANGLIA, so named because it has a long extension, or tail.

causal ambiguity a situation in which it is not known which one (or which set) of several phenomena is the cause of a particular effect. Sometimes the ambiguity attaches to the more complex question of which phenomena are causes and which are effects (see REVERSE CAUSALITY). Controlled empirical research is often used to resolve issues of causal ambiguity.

causal analysis an attempt to draw dependable causal inferences from data not obtained from true (randomized) experiments. Such analyses differ in the degree to which they are statistically complex and the degree to which causal inferences are, in fact, justified.

causal attribution see ATTRIBUTION.

causal chain a sequence of conditions or events, either hypothetical or empirically derived, that results in a particular effect. Explanation in terms of causal chains presumes that causation is transitive (see TRANSITIVITY). Also called **causal path**.

causalgia *n.* a sensation of intense, burning pain resulting from injury to the peripheral nerves. The condition is most often due to a penetrating wound inflicted by a bullet or knife and involves swelling, redness, and sweating in addition to almost unbearable pain.

causal inference the reasoned process of concluding that one variable is the cause of another.

causality *n.* in philosophy, the position that all events have causes, that is, that they are consequences of antecedent events. Traditionally, causality has been seen as an essential assumption of NATURALISM and all scientific explanation, although some have questioned whether causality is a necessary assumption of science. Others have suggested that, while causality must be assumed, there are different types of causality, each of which makes different metaphysical assumptions about the nature of the world and adopts different criteria about what types of relationships between phenomena can be considered as legitimately causal. See also CAUSATION; DETERMINISM. **—causal** *adj.*

causal latency 1. the temporal separation of a cause from its effect. Not all causes need have immediate effects; indeed, there may be a lengthy interval between a cause and the effect it produces. Causal latency may be expected to increase when there are other factors in a situation that may influence the cause-and-effect relationship. Some causes studied in psychology and the other social sciences are REMOTE CAUSES, in that they require the presence or activity of other factors or conditions before their effects become manifest. Remote causes may be expected to have large causal latencies. See DELAYED EFFECT. **2.** in the statistical procedure known as PATH ANALYSIS, the quality of a variable that has a measurable statistical effect on prediction only when other predictor variables are also included in the prediction model. Although the statistical relationships identified in such analyses are not, strictly speaking, causal, the language of causality is commonly employed. See CAUSAL PATH.

causal law a statement of a consistent or invariant relationship between phenomena in which the relationship is one of causation. A causal LAW is thus distinguished from other statements of invariant regularity, such as "In temperate climates, when the seasons change, the leaves turn color." Causal laws may reflect different types of CAUSALITY, ranging from strict DETERMINISM, through PROBABILISM, to TELEOLOGY. Sometimes, in superficial usage, causal laws are understood not as mere statements of consistent relationships, but as metaphysical entities or forces that produce the effects that consistently accrue. In such usage, a causal law becomes indistinguishable from a CAUSE.

causal mechanism the most immediate and physical means by which something is accomplished. For example, the causal mechanism for opening a door is the turning of the knob and the exertion of pressure on the door. The discovery of a causal mechanism does not resolve questions of causation, as there may well be other latent or REMOTE CAUSES. Nor does the recognition of a causal mechanism imply that the world is inherently mechanical. For example, although a mechanism is required for opening a door, the ultimate cause may be a nonmechanical intention to leave the room. See also MECHANICAL CAUSALITY; PROXIMATE CAUSE.

causal nexus a NEXUS or connection between phenomena that is one of CAUSATION. See CAUSAL CHAIN.

causal ordering 1. the principle that causes must temporally precede their effects, and never vice versa. See also FALSE CAUSE; REVERSE CAUSALITY. **2.** in PATH ANALYSIS and similar statistical procedures, the categorizing of causal variables as either more or less direct. See CAUSAL LATENCY; CAUSAL PATH.

causal path 1. see CAUSAL CHAIN. **2.** in PATH ANALYSIS and similar statistical procedures, a relatively probable causal sequence among a complex set of potential causes and effects. The analysis is based on first-order and partial correlations among variables indicating possible relations of cause and effect. From the pattern of correlations, conclusions are drawn regarding which set of variables, in which order, represents the most likely path from some presumed cause of interest to some presumed effect of interest.

causal texture the very large number of mutually dependent events that make up the fabric of reality. Those philosophers and psychologists who use this term conceive of the interdependencies among events in terms of probability rather than certainty, in part because such interdependencies change and develop over time. [introduced into psychology by Edward Chase TOLMAN and Austrian psychologist Egon Brunswick (1903–1955)]

causation *n.* **1.** the empirical relation between two events or states such that one (the cause) is held to bring about the other (the effect). See also CAUSALITY. **2.** in statistical analysis, the relation between two variables *X* and *Y* such that *X* is known to bring about *Y*. **3.** in Aristotelian and rationalist philosophy, the hypothetical relation between two phenomena (entities or events), such that one (the cause) either constitutes the necessary and sufficient grounds for the existence of the other (the effect), or the one possesses the capacity to bring about the other. **—causal** *adj.*

causative verb a verb that expresses the notion of something being caused, for example *convince, harmonize, enliven.* Children's acquisition of causative concepts is a lively area of developmental research at the intersection of linguistic, cognitive, and social development. See also ACTIONAL VERB.

cause *n.* **1.** an event or state that brings about another (its effect). **2.** in Aristotelian and rationalist philosophy, an entity or event that is a requirement for another entity or event's coming to be. Greek philosopher Aristotle (384–322 BCE) proposed that there were four types of cause—material, formal, efficient, and final. In the case of a sculpture, for example, the **material cause** is the stone or metal from which it is made, the **formal cause** is the form or structure that it takes, the EFFICIENT CAUSE is the sculptor, and the **final cause** is the sculptor's aim or purpose in making it. **—causal** *adj.*

cause-and-effect diagram a graphical analytical tool for discovering a set of causes for a particular effect. It was developed by Japanese management expert Kaoru Ishikawa (1915–1989) and first used in 1943. It is also referred to as an **Ishikawa diagram** or as a **fishbone diagram** because of its characteristic shape.

cause-and-effect test an intelligence test that offers alternative causes for different effects and alternative effects for different causes, requiring the examinee to choose the most logical explanations. It measures causal reasoning.

causism *n.* the practice of ascribing causal relations between two variables when evidence is inadequate to support a relationship as strong as causation. **—causist** *adj., n.*

cautious shift a CHOICE SHIFT in which an individual making a decision as part of a group adopts a more cautious approach than the same individual would have adopted had he or she made the decision alone. Studies suggest that such shifts are (a) rarer than the opposite RISKY SHIFT and (b) most likely to occur when the majority of the members of the group, prior to discussion, favor a cautious rather than a risky choice. See also GROUP POLARIZATION.

CBAS abbreviation for COACHING BEHAVIOR ASSESSMENT SYSTEM.

CBCA abbreviation for CRITERION-BASED CONTENT ANALYSIS.

CBCL abbreviation for CHILD BEHAVIOR CHECKLIST.

CBGD abbreviation for CORTICOBASAL GANGLIONIC DEGENERATION.

CBT abbreviation for COGNITIVE BEHAVIOR THERAPY.

CBZ abbreviation for CARBAMAZEPINE.

CCC theory abbreviation for COGNITIVE COMPLEXITY AND CONTROL THEORY.

CCK abbreviation for CHOLECYSTOKININ.

CCTV system abbreviation for CLOSED-CIRCUIT TELEVISION SYSTEM.

CCU 1. abbreviation for CONTINUING CARE UNIT. **2.** abbreviation for critical care unit (see INTENSIVE CARE UNIT).

CD abbreviation for COMMUNICATION DEVIANCE.

CDC abbreviation for CENTERS FOR DISEASE CONTROL AND PREVENTION.

CDI abbreviation for CHILDREN'S DEPRESSION INVENTORY.

CDQ abbreviation for CHOICE DILEMMA QUESTIONNAIRE.

cebocephaly *n.* a type of congenital defect in which the eyes are abnormally close to each other, the nose may be missing or not fully formed, and the facial features resemble those of a monkey. In some cases, the defect pattern may include CYCLOPIA. Cebocephaly is associated with chromosomal abnormalities, such as CHROMOSOME-13 TRISOMY.

CEFT abbreviation for CHILDREN'S EMBEDDED FIGURES TEST.

ceiling age the maximum level reached on a scaled test, such as the Stanford–Binet, that is, the level at which all tests are failed and the test is discontinued. This concept assumes the use of MENTAL AGES, which, in current testing, are used only relatively rarely.

ceiling effect the inability of a test to measure or discriminate above a certain point, usually because its items are too easy. Compare FLOOR EFFECT.

Celexa *n.* a trade name for CITALOPRAM.

celiac plexus 1. in the nervous system, a network of fibers lying anterior to the aorta at the level of the 12th thoracic vertebra. Most autonomic and visceral afferent nerves pass through this plexus. Also called **celiac nervous plexus**. **2.** in the lymphatic system, a network of afferent and efferent lymphatic vessels in the abdomen. Also called **celiac lymphatic plexus**.

celibacy *n.* **1.** the state of being unmarried, especially as the result of a religious vow. **2.** abstinence from sexual activity. See also CHASTITY. **—celibate** *adj., n.*

cell *n.* **1.** in biology, the basic unit of organized tissue, consisting of an outer plasma membrane, the NUCLEUS, and various ORGANELLES in a watery fluid together comprising the CYTOPLASM. Bacteria lack a nucleus and most organelles. The term was first applied to biological structure by English physicist Robert Hooke (1635–1703) when describing the microscopic appearance of cork. See also CELL THEORY. **2.** in statistics, the space formed at the intersection of a row and a column in a statistical table. For example, a tabular display of a study of handedness in men and women would consist of four cells: left-handed females, left-handed males, right-handed females, and right-handed males.

cell adhesion molecule (**CAM**) any of various proteins on cell surfaces that bind cells to each other and to the extracellular matrix. Certain CAMs play roles in cell migration or extension during development, including axonal pathfinding.

cell assembly a group of neurons that are repeatedly active at the same time and develop as a single functional unit, which may become active when any of its constituent neurons is stimulated. This enables, for example, a person to form a complete mental image of an object when only a portion is visible or to recall a memory from a partial cue. Cell assembly is influential in biological theories of memory. [proposed in 1949 by Donald O. HEBB]

cell body the part of a NEURON (nerve cell) that contains the nucleus and most organelles. Also called **perikaryon**; **soma**. See also AXON.

cell–cell interactions the general processes during embryological development in which one cell affects the differentiation of other, usually neighboring, cells. Also called **cell interactions**.

cell death see PROGRAMMED CELL DEATH.

cell differentiation see DIFFERENTIATION.

cell division the division of a cell to form daughter cells. It usually involves division of the nucleus (see MITOSIS; MEIOSIS) followed by partitioning of the cytoplasm.

cell interactions see CELL–CELL INTERACTIONS.

cell-means model any of a class of linear ANOVA (ANALYSIS OF VARIANCE) models in which the observed score is modeled as a function of the population mean of the CELL in which the score occurs plus a random error. The population cell means are the parameters of the model.

cell-mediated immunity see IMMUNE RESPONSE.

cell migration the movement of cells during development from their site of origin to their final location.

cell nucleus see NUCLEUS.

cell proliferation the multiplication of cells by MITOSIS.

cell theory the principle that all organisms are composed of one or more CELLS. [proposed in 1839 for animals by German physiologist Theodor Schwann (1810–1882) and for plants by German botanist Matthias Jakob Schleiden (1804–1881)]

cellular automata computer programs used in the study of ARTIFICIAL LIFE. Typically, a display is used on a computer screen, split into an array of cells, with an initial pattern of occupied cells. The pattern evolves through a sequence of steps according to certain rules (for example, whether or not certain numbers of neighboring cells are occupied). Programs of this type have been used in investigations of such phenomena as social behavior and evolutionary development.

CEM abbreviation for COLLECTIVE EFFORT MODEL.

cenesthesia (**coenesthesia**) *n.* awareness of bodily sensations, in a state ranging from health and vitality to illness and lethargy. **—cenesthetic** *adj.*

cenesthopathy *n.* a general feeling of illness or lack of well-being that is not identified with any particular part of the body.

ceno- *combining form* see COENO-.

censor *n.* in psychoanalytic theory, the mental agency, located in the PRECONSCIOUS, that is responsible for REPRESSION. The censor is posited to determine which of one's wishes, thoughts, and ideas may enter consciousness and which must be kept unconscious because they violate one's conscience or society's standards. The censor is also posited to be responsible for the distortion of wishes that occurs in dreams (see DREAM CENSORSHIP). The idea was introduced in the early writings of Sigmund FREUD, who later developed it into the concept of the SUPEREGO. **—censorship** *n.*

censored data a set of data in which some values are unobserved, often because the event of interest has not occurred by the end of the study or because the response falls into an unmeasurable portion of the scale. For example, a study done in 2006 of the marriage rate of individuals born in 1970 could be characterized as a censored data set, because some of those individuals might marry for the first time in 2007 or some year thereafter.

census *n.* the complete count of an entire population. A census differs from most experimental studies, which use a SAMPLE from a population in hopes of generalizing from the observed sample to the entire population.

census tract a small, generally homogeneous geographic area with boundaries established to facilitate the collection and reporting of census data. Community demographic data are frequently used in the assessment of the area's characteristics and needs, including mental health needs. See also CATCHMENT AREA.

cent *n.* in acoustics, a logarithmic unit used to express frequency ratios. There are 1200 cents in an OCTAVE, and successive notes or intervals on the equally tempered musical scale are separated by 100 cents, or one SEMITONE.

center *n.* in neurophysiology, a structure or region that controls a particular function, for example, the respiratory center of the brain.

centered *adj.* **1.** describing the state of an organism that is perfectly integrated with its environment. [defined by German-born U.S. neurologist Kurt Goldstein (1878–1965)] **2.** denoting a state of mind characterized by having a firm grip on reality, knowing who one is and what one wants out of life, and being prepared to meet most eventualities in an efficient manner. **3.** in a posture for defense or attack, with body balanced and crouching forward.

Center for Epidemiologic Studies Depression Scale (**CES-D**) a 20-item self-administered rating scale used to determine an individual's depression quotient. The test provides a quantitative measure of different depressive feelings and behaviors during the previous week. [developed in 1971 by Lenore Sawyer Radloff (1935–) while a researcher at the National Institute of Mental Health]

Center for Independent Living (**CIL**) see INDEPENDENT LIVING.

centering *n.* in sport psychology, a technique used by athletes to assist them in achieving an IDEAL PERFORMANCE STATE that involves focusing on a spot in the center of the body and imagining being in that state. The technique is most useful in "closed skill" sports, such as diving, hitting in baseball, sprinting, and foul shooting in basketball.

center median the largest of the INTRALAMINAL NUCLEI of the THALAMUS in the brain. Unlike other thalamic nuclei, it has no connections with the cerebral cortex and communicates only with the BASAL GANGLIA. Also called **centromedian nucleus**.

center of gravity a balance point, that is, the location about which the mass of an object is evenly distributed. The position of the center of gravity of the body relative to the legs determines whether, for example, a standing posture is stable.

Centers for Disease Control and Prevention (**CDC**) an agency founded in 1946 (now one of the 13 major operating components of the U.S. Department of Health and Human Services) that stands at the forefront of public health efforts to prevent and control infectious and chronic diseases, injuries, workplace hazards, disabilities, and environmental health threats. The CDC works with public health partners, both nationally and internationally, to monitor health, detect and investigate health problems, conduct research to enhance and implement prevention, promote healthy behaviors and safe and healthful environments, and develop and advocate sound public health policies.

Centers for Medicare and Medicaid Services (**CMS**) a federal government agency within the Department of Health and Human Services that is responsible for the administration of the MEDICARE and MEDICAID programs, as well as the State Children's Health Insurance Program. Formerly known as the **Health Care Financing Administration** (HCFA), the CMS consists of three business offices: the Center for Beneficiary Choices, the Center for Medicare Management, and the Center for Medicaid and State Operations.

center–surround antagonism a characteristic of the receptive fields of many visual and somatosensory neurons in which stimulation in the center of the receptive field evokes opposite responses to stimulation in the periphery. Thus some neurons depolarize with center stimulation and hyperpolarize when the same stimulus appears in the surrounding region of the receptive field, whereas other neurons have the opposite pattern of responses. Center–surround antagonism greatly increases the sensitivity of the nervous system to CONTRAST. See also OFF RESPONSE; ON RESPONSE; SIMPLE CELL.

center–surround receptive field a type of receptive field, common in the visual and somatosensory systems, that exhibits CENTER–SURROUND ANTAGONISM. Most center–surround receptive fields consist of a circular center area and an annular surrounding area.

central *adj.* of or relating to the CENTRAL NERVOUS SYSTEM (CNS), especially to disorders that occur as a result of injury to or dysfunction of the CNS.

central anticholinergic syndrome a syndrome observed in patients receiving combinations of agents with psychopharmacological effects and due to the additive ANTICHOLINERGIC EFFECTS on the central nervous system of, among others, tricyclic antidepressants, the weaker phenothiazines, and antiparkinsonian agents. The symptoms include anxiety, disorientation, short-term memory loss, visual distortions or hallucinations, and agitation. See also ANTICHOLINERGIC SYNDROME; PERIPHERAL ANTICHOLINERGIC SYNDROME.

central aphasia loss of the ability to understand or express language resulting from brain lesions; that is, APHASIA. [first defined in 1948 by German-born U.S. psychologist Kurt Goldstein (1878–1965)]

central auditory abilities see AUDITORY SKILLS.

central auditory processing disorder (**CAPD**) an impaired ability to decode acoustic messages into meaningful information and to discriminate speech, despite only minor changes in auditory sensitivity to sound. In adults, CAPD is typically associated with brain damage caused by stroke, lesions, and neurodegenerative diseases, such as multiple sclerosis; in children, it is most often associated with microscopic pathology in the brain and maturational delays in language acquisition. Also called **auditory processing disorder**.

central auditory system see AUDITORY SYSTEM.

central canal the channel in the center of the SPINAL CORD, which contains CEREBROSPINAL FLUID.

central conceptual structure an integrated network of concepts and cognitive processes that plays a central role in mediating children's performances across a broad range of tasks during cognitive development. [proposed by Canadian developmental psychologist Robbie Case (1944–2000)]

central conflict the intrapsychic struggle between the healthy constructive forces of the real self and the obstructive, neurotic forces of the idealized self-image. [first described by German-born U.S. psychiatrist Karen Horney (1885–1952)]

central deafness loss or absence of hearing caused by damage to the central AUDITORY SYSTEM, rather than by sensorineural or conductive impairment. Pure-tone acuity may be normal in people with central deafness. Compare CONDUCTION DEAFNESS; SENSORINEURAL HEARING LOSS.

central dyslexia a form of acquired dyslexia (see ALEXIA) characterized by difficulties with the pronunciation and comprehension of written words. Unlike PERIPHERAL DYSLEXIA, the visual analysis system is intact, and the damage is to other pathways and systems involved in reading (e.g., the semantic system).

central executive a component of WORKING MEMORY that distributes and directs attention to various tasks in which SHORT-TERM MEMORY might be engaged. In the multicomponent model of working memory, the two processing systems, one verbal and one spatial, are under the control of the central executive. See also PHONOLOGICAL LOOP; VISUOSPATIAL SCRATCHPAD. [proposed by British cognitive psychologist Alan D. Baddeley (1934–)]

central fissure see CENTRAL SULCUS.

central gray the UNMYELINATED (and therefore gray-colored) neurons and nerve fibers that form a generally H-shaped pattern in the central portion of the spinal cord. It consists of bilateral ANTERIOR and DORSAL HORNS connected by the GRAY COMMISSURE.

central inhibition a process within the central nervous system that prevents or interrupts the flow of neural impulses that control behavior.

centralism *n.* the concept that behavior is a function of the central nervous system mediated by the brain. See CENTRALIST PSYCHOLOGY. Compare PERIPHERALISM.

centralist psychology **1.** a psychological approach that focuses on behavior as a function of the higher brain centers, as opposed to peripheralist psychology (see PERIPHERALISM), which focuses on the effects of the receptors, glands, and muscles on behavior. Centralist psychology is essentially equivalent to CENTRALISM. **2.** more generally, the idea that mental activity or mind occurs in or is a function of the brain alone.

centrality of an attitude **1.** the extent to which an ATTITUDE OBJECT is thought about, reflected in the amount of time devoted to this thinking over an extended period. **2.** the extent to which an attitude is linked to other attitudes in memory. Increased centrality is associated with enhanced STRENGTH OF AN ATTITUDE.

centralized organization an ORGANIZATIONAL STRUCTURE in which those holding positions of authority at the upper levels of the hierarchy retain control over decision making. Compare DECENTRALIZED ORGANIZATION.

central limited capacity the observed constraint on processing capacity of the cognitive system associated with consciousness, such that only one conscious or effortful task can be accomplished at any given moment. Simultaneous conscious or effortful tasks will result in degraded performance. See DUAL-TASK COMPETITION.

central limit theorem the statistical principle that a linear combination of values (including the mean of those values) tends to be normally distributed over repeated samples as the sample sizes increase, whether or not the population from which the observations are drawn is normal in distribution.

central lobe see INSULA.

central moment a moment of a probability distribution taken about the mean. The *k*th central moment of the random variable X is $E[X - E(X)^k]$, where E indicates expectation. Also called **moment about the mean**.

central motive state a theoretical function of the nervous system that accounts for a persistent level of activity in the absence of external stimuli or a continuation of nervous activity when the original motive no longer exists.

central nervous system (**CNS**) the entire complex of NEURONS, AXONS, and supporting tissue that constitute the brain and spinal cord. The CNS is primarily involved in mental activities and in coordinating and integrating incoming sensory messages and outgoing motor messages. Compare PERIPHERAL NERVOUS SYSTEM.

central nervous system disorder any neurological disorder of the central nervous system (i.e., brain and spinal cord).

central neuron a neuron contained entirely within the central nervous system.

central nucleus a nucleus forming part of the CORTICOMEDIAL GROUP in the AMYGDALA within the brain. It receives input from other amygdaloid nuclei and projects to the hypothalamus and many brainstem structures, including the PERIAQUEDUCTAL GRAY. It is involved (among other things) in fear behavior.

central organizing trait see CENTRAL TRAIT.

central pain pain that is caused by a disorder of the central nervous system, such as a brain tumor or infection or injury of the spinal cord.

central pattern generator any of the sets of neurons in the spinal cord capable of producing oscillatory behavior and thought to be involved in the control of locomotion and other tasks. A central pattern generator is the neural substrate responsible for repetitive coordinated movements that can be modeled using COUPLED OSCILLATORS.

central processing dysfunction impairment in the analysis, storage, synthesis, and symbolic use of information. Because these processes involve memory tasks, the dysfunction is believed to be related to difficulties in learning.

central processor **1.** the part of a computer that controls and executes operations on data. **2.** in models of cognition based on analogies to INFORMATION PROCESSING in a computer, that part of the system that carries out operations on stored representations. The idea of a single central processor in the human cognitive system has been challenged by models based on DISTRIBUTED PROCESSING, PARALLEL DISTRIBUTED PROCESSING, and PARALLEL PROCESSING.

central reflex time the portion of REFLEX LATENCY that is occupied by activity within the central nervous system; it excludes the latency of muscular or endocrine response.

central route to persuasion the process by which attitudes are formed or changed as a result of carefully scrutinizing and thinking about the central merits of attitude-relevant information. See also ELABORATION; ELABORATION-LIKELIHOOD MODEL. Compare PERIPHERAL ROUTE TO PERSUASION.

central scotoma depressed vision in the central part of the visual field, which may be either absolute (total loss of vision) or relative (partial loss of vision). When caused by unilateral injury to or disease of the peripheral visual system (e.g., the retina or optic nerve), the central visual field of only one eye is affected. When associated with injury to the central visual system (i.e., beyond the optic nerve, in the brain), the central visual fields of both eyes are affected, and patients have great difficulty in guiding their fixation, localizing objects, reading, and recognizing faces. See SCOTOMA.

central state theory see IDENTITY THEORY.

central stimulation electrical or chemical stimulation of the brain. See INTRACRANIAL STIMULATION; INTRACRANIAL SELF-STIMULATION.

central sulcus a major cleft (see SULCUS) that passes roughly vertically along the lateral surface of each CEREBRAL HEMISPHERE from a point beginning near the top of the cerebrum. It marks the border between the FRONTAL LOBE and the PARIETAL LOBE. Also called **central fissure**; **fissure of Rolando**; **Rolandic fissure**; **Rolandic sulcus**; **sulcus centralis**.

central tendency the middle or center point of a DISTRIBUTION, estimated by a number of different statistics (e.g., MEAN and MEDIAN).

central-tendency error the error of making assessments (e.g., judgments or ratings) that do not accurately reflect the entire range of possible assessments that could be made because they cluster closely around an average or midpoint (see CENTRAL TENDENCY) rather than vary widely.

central trait any of a cluster of traits (e.g., compassion, ambition, sociability, helpfulness) that comprise the basic pattern of an individual's personality. [defined by Gordon W. ALLPORT]

central vision the ability to see stimuli in the middle of the visual field, surrounding and including the point of fixation. Central vision is provided by the FOVEA CENTRALIS. Also called **foveal vision**. Compare PARACENTRAL VISION; PERIPHERAL VISION.

centration *n.* in Jean PIAGET's theory of cognitive development, the tendency of children in the PREOPERATIONAL STAGE to attend to one aspect of a problem, object, or situation at a time, to the exclusion of others. Compare DECENTRATION.

centrencephalic *adj.* located in or near the center of the brain.

centrencephalic epilepsy a form of epilepsy marked by GENERALIZED SEIZURES (absence seizures and some tonic–clonic seizures) that appear to originate near the center of the brain. It is not associated with any particular local anatomical or functional system but instead radiates outward through both cerebral hemispheres. The term was coined in the 1940s by U.S.-born Canadian neurosurgeon Wilder Penfield (1891–1976) and U.S.-born Canadian neuroscientist Herbert Jasper (1906–1999), and its use is restricted primarily to historic contexts.

centrencephalic system the concept of a central anatomical brain region (the **centrencephalon**) whose activities provide a coherent unity for mental processes and the seat of free will. [proposed by U.S.-born Canadian neurosurgeon Wilder Penfield (1891–1976)]

centrifugal *adj.* directed away from the center. For example, a **centrifugal nerve** carries impulses from the central nervous system to a peripheral region of the body. Compare CENTRIPETAL.

centripetal *adj.* **1.** directed toward the center. For example, a **centripetal nerve** carries nerve impulses from the periphery to the central nervous system. Compare CENTRIFUGAL. **2.** in psychiatry, characterizing treatment or approaches that focus inward on minute changes in feelings and impulses, as in psychoanalysis.

centripetal impulse a nerve impulse that travels from the periphery toward the central nervous system, that is, a sensory impulse.

centroid *n.* the mean VECTOR of a p-dimensional distribution. The ith element of the vector is the mean of the marginal distribution of the ith component of the multivariate distribution.

centromedian nucleus see CENTER MEDIAN.

centromere *n.* the part of a chromosome at which the CHROMATIDs are joined and that is attached to the equatorial plane of the spindle during cell division. The centromere occasionally becomes a separate body of genetic material, accounting for certain types of anomalies. See CAT'S-EYE SYNDROME.

cephalalgia *n.* pain in the head (see HEADACHE).

cephalic *adj.* pertaining to or located in the head.

cephalic index the ratio of the maximum breadth of the head to its maximum length, multiplied by 100. The average, or medium, cephalic index for humans is between 75 and 81 (**mesocephalic**). A measure below 75 indicates a narrow head that is long in proportion to its width (**dolichocephalic**); a measure above 81 indicates a head that is wide in proportion to its length (**brachycephalic**). Compare CRANIAL INDEX. [defined by Swedish anatomist Anders Retzius (1796–1860)]

cephalization *n.* **1.** the evolutionary tendency for important structures (brain, major sense organs, etc.) to develop at the anterior (front) end of organisms. **2.** the evolutionary tendency for the brain to increase in size. See ENCEPHALIZATION; EVOLUTION OF THE BRAIN.

cephalo- (**cephal-**) *combining form* head.

cephalocaudal axis see AXIS.

cephalocaudal development the head-to-tail progression of anatomical and motor development, as determined by the ANTERIOR–POSTERIOR DEVELOPMENT GRADIENT. The head and its movements develop first, then the upper trunk, arms, and hands, followed by the lower trunk and legs, feet, and toes.

cephalogenesis *n.* formation of the head in embryonic development.

cephalometry *n.* the scientific measurement of the dimensions of the head. Cephalometry is used in orthodontics to predict and evaluate craniofacial development. **Fetal cephalometry** is the measurement of the skull of the fetus while in the uterus, using ultrasound or X-ray techniques.

CER abbreviation for CONDITIONED EMOTIONAL RESPONSE.

cerea flexibilitas see CATALEPSY.

cereb- *combining form* see CEREBRO-.

cerebellar *adj.* of or relating to the CEREBELLUM.

cerebellar ataxia poor muscular coordination (see ATAXIA) due to damage in the CEREBELLUM. Individuals cannot integrate voluntary movements and therefore find it difficult to stand or walk, feed themselves, and perform complex activities (e.g., playing the piano).

cerebellar cortex the GRAY MATTER, or unmyelinated nerve cells, covering the surface of the CEREBELLUM.

cerebellar folia the pattern of thin folds that subdivide the CEREBELLAR CORTEX.

cerebellar gait an unsteady, wobbly, wide-based gait, resembling that of an intoxicated individual and associated with cerebellar lesions or dysfunction.

cerebellar hemisphere either of the two main lobes of the CEREBELLUM.

cerebellar nucleus any of the small masses of neurons that lie within the white matter of the CEREBELLUM.

cerebellar peduncle any of the three bundles of nerve fibers that connect each main lobe (hemisphere) of the CEREBELLUM with other parts of the brain. The superior cerebellar peduncle, or BRACHIUM CONJUNCTIVUM, connects the cerebellum with the MIDBRAIN; the middle peduncle connects the cerebellum with the PONS; and the inferior peduncle connects the cerebellum with the MEDULLA OBLONGATA.

cerebellar rigidity see EXTENSOR RIGIDITY.

cerebellar speech a type of speech that is jerky, irregular, and poorly coordinated due to a lesion of the cerebellum. Also called **asynergic speech**.

cerebellopontine angle a region of the human brain where the CEREBELLUM touches the PONS. The FACIAL NERVE and the VESTIBULOCOCHLEAR NERVE enter the brainstem in this region, and tumors frequently occur in either of these nerves in this region.

cerebellum *n.* (*pl.* **cerebella**) a portion of the HINDBRAIN dorsal to the rest of the BRAINSTEM, to which it is connected by the CEREBELLAR PEDUNCLES. The cerebellum modulates muscular contractions to produce smooth, accurately timed movements; it helps maintain equilibrium by predicting body positions ahead of actual body movements, and it is required for some kinds of motor conditioning.

cerebral *adj.* referring to the CEREBRUM of the brain.

cerebral achromatopsia a condition in which brain injury results in a severe loss of color vision. In its extreme form the visual world becomes pale, washed out, and devoid of color, appearing only in shades of gray. The typical site of injury is the ventromedial occipital cortex of the brain (see V4). See also HEMIACHROMATOPSIA.

cerebral amblyopia a depression of light vision and complete loss of form and color vision in either the left or right half of the visual field (**unilateral hemiamblyopia**) or in both the left and right halves (**bilateral hemiamblyopia**). Movement vision is typically not affected. See also RIDDOCH'S PHENOMENON.

cerebral anemia a condition of abnormally low levels of hemoglobin or red blood cells in the blood reaching brain tissues, which may cause CEREBRAL INFARCTION.

cerebral angiography a noninvasive technique for examining brain structure by taking X-rays after special dyes have been injected into cerebral blood vessels. Inferences about adjacent tissue can be made from examination of the principal blood vessels. It has been largely superseded by such techniques as MAGNETIC RESONANCE IMAGING. Also called **cerebral arteriography**.

cerebral angiomatosis a disease characterized by the formation of multiple tumors in the blood vessels that supply brain tissue. A congenital form of the disorder is marked by frequent seizures and muscular weakness on one side of the body as a result of impaired blood flow to the brain.

cerebral aqueduct a passage that extends through the MIDBRAIN to link the third and fourth cerebral VENTRICLES of the brain. It contains CEREBROSPINAL FLUID. Also called **aqueduct of Sylvius**.

cerebral arteriography see CEREBRAL ANGIOGRAPHY.

cerebral arteriosclerosis a hardening of the arteries that supply the brain. See ARTERIOSCLEROSIS.

cerebral atrophy degeneration and shrinkage of the brain, usually due to aging, disease, or injury. It is marked by enlargement of the surface clefts (SULCI) and inner cavities (VENTRICLES) of the brain. In normal aging there may be few or no cognitive effects, but cerebral atrophy may be secondary to more serious disorders, such as cerebrovascular disease, encephalitis, Alzheimer's disease, or head injury. Also called **brain atrophy**.

cerebral beriberi see WERNICKE'S ENCEPHALOPATHY.

cerebral blindness see CORTICAL BLINDNESS.

cerebral contusion bruising of the brain, in which blood vessels are damaged but not ruptured, resulting from head injury. The effects vary with the severity of the injury, ranging from temporary neurological symptoms to permanent disability. Also called **brain contusion**.

cerebral cortex the layer of GRAY MATTER that covers the outside of the CEREBRAL HEMISPHERES in the brain. It consists mostly of NEOCORTEX, which has six main layers of cells (see CORTICAL LAYERS). Regional differences in the CYTOARCHITECTURE of the layers led to the recognition of distinct areas, called BRODMANN'S AREAS, many of which are known to serve different functions. Regions of cerebral cortex that do not have six layers are known as ALLOCORTEX. The cerebral cortex is associated with higher cognitive functions, such as language, learning, memory, perception, and planning.

cerebral diplopia see DIPLOPIA.

cerebral dominance 1. the control of lower brain centers by the cerebrum or cerebral cortex. **2.** the controlling or disproportionate influence on certain aspects of behavior by one CEREBRAL HEMISPHERE (e.g., language is typically left-lateralized in right-handed people). See DOMINANCE; HEMISPHERIC LATERALIZATION.

cerebral dyschromatopsia 1. incomplete CEREBRAL ACHROMATOPSIA. **2.** a distortion of color vision, as if the individual is seeing through a color filter. See also VISUAL ILLUSION.

cerebral dysfunction any impairment in cerebral processes, including disturbances of memory, language, attention, or executive functioning.

cerebral dysplasia any abnormality in the development of the brain. There are various types of cerebral dysplasia, including ANENCEPHALY, marked by failure of the cerebral hemispheres to develop; **porencephaly**, characterized by development of a hemisphere containing abnormal cavities; and callosal AGENESIS.

cerebral dysrhythmia a condition of abnormal brainwave rhythms associated with neurological disease or other pathological conditions, such as a drug overdose.

cerebral edema an abnormal accumulation of fluid in the intercellular spaces of brain tissues, which may be caused by injury, disease, cerebrovascular accident, or tumor (see also ACUTE MOUNTAIN SICKNESS). The condition results in swelling and a rise in INTRACRANIAL PRESSURE; if uncorrected, this may be followed by herniation of cerebral tissue through weakened areas. It may be reversible unless the damage extends to the brainstem, where the effects can be fatal. The increase in intracranial pressure may result in headaches and visual disorders. Cerebral edema can also cause dementia that recedes when the defect is corrected.

cerebral electrotherapy (**CET**) the application of low-voltage pulses of direct electrical current to the brain, occasionally used in the treatment of depression, anxiety, and insomnia. See ELECTRONARCOSIS.

cerebral embolism the presence of a small mass of material in the blood vessels of the brain (see EMBOLISM), which blocks or impedes the flow of blood to a part of the brain, resulting in an acute or chronic neurological deficit. See EMBOLIC STROKE; STROKE.

cerebral gigantism see SOTOS SYNDROME.

cerebral hemisphere either half (left or right) of the cerebrum. The hemispheres are separated by a deep LONGITUDINAL FISSURE but they are connected by commissural, projection, and association fibers so that each side of the brain normally is linked to functions of tissues on either side of the body. See also HEMISPHERIC LATERALIZATION.

cerebral hemorrhage any bleeding into the brain tissue due to a damaged blood vessel. The cause may be cerebrovascular disease, a ruptured aneurysm, a penetrating injury or blow to the head, or other factors. The neurological effects vary with the extent of the hemorrhage. Also called **intracerebral hemorrhage**. See HEMORRHAGIC STROKE; STROKE.

cerebral hyperplasia an abnormal increase in the volume of brain tissue, usually due to a proliferation of new, normal cells. Although neurons do not proliferate after the central nervous system has reached maturity, cells of the NEUROGLIA do continue to multiply into adulthood; in some cases neuroglial cell growth is associated with HYDROCEPHALUS.

cerebral hypoplasia the incomplete development of the cerebral hemispheres. It may be due to a congenital defect or malnutrition during early childhood.

cerebral infarction the death of brain tissue due to an interruption of blood flow caused by rupture of a blood vessel, blockage of a blood vessel by a clot, or a narrowing (stenosis) of a blood vessel.

cerebral infection the invasion of brain tissues by a pathogenic organism, such as a virus or bacterium. Most cases occur as a complication of a viral infection (see ENCEPHALITIS); the most common bacterial infection is MENINGITIS.

cerebral ischemia a condition in which brain tissue is deprived of an adequate blood supply and thus lacks oxygen and nutrients. It is usually marked by loss of normal function of the affected area and may be accompanied by CEREBRAL EDEMA. A brief interruption in blood supply—a TRANSIENT ISCHEMIC ATTACK (TIA)—usually causes no serious damage. An interruption lasting more than several minutes may result in CEREBRAL INFARCTION. See CEREBROVASCULAR ACCIDENT; STROKE.

cerebral laceration the tearing or cutting of brain tissue due to a severe head injury or penetration of the skull by a foreign object (e.g., a bullet).

cerebral lesion see BRAIN LESION.

cerebral pacemaker a hypothetical group of nerve cells in the brain that are believed to regulate the rhythms of BRAIN WAVES in the cerebral hemispheres. The cerebral pacemaker is believed to be located at the base of the brain, in the region of the HYPOTHALAMUS or in the RETICULAR FORMATION.

cerebral palsy (**CP**) a set of nonprogressive movement and posture disorders that results from trauma to the brain occurring prenatally, during the birth process, or before the age of 5. Symptoms include spasticity, uncontrolled movements (see ATHETOSIS), paralysis, unsteady gait, and speech abnormalities (see DYSARTHRIA) but may be accompanied by disorders of any other brain function, resulting in cognitive changes, seizures, visual defects, tactile impairment, hearing loss, and mental retardation. CP is commonly classified into the following types: **spastic**, the most common, resulting from damage to the motor cortex, corticospinal tract, or pyramidal tract; **dyskinetic**, resulting from damage to the basal ganglia; **ataxic**, resulting from damage to the cerebellum; and **mixed**, in which more than one type is evident.

cerebral peduncle either of two cylindrical bundles of nerve fibers that pass through the PONS to form the main connection between the CEREBRAL HEMISPHERES and the spinal cord. Also called **crus cerebri**.

cerebral specialization the differential contribution of the two cerebral hemispheres to many functions. Also called **hemispheric specialization**. See HEMISPHERIC LATERALIZATION.

cerebral stimulation see BRAIN STIMULATION.

cerebral syphilis a condition that results when untreated syphilis involves the cerebral cortex and surrounding meningeal membranes, causing GENERAL PARESIS. The condition, which usually develops about 10 years after the initial infection, is marked by irritability, memory impairment, inability to concentrate, headaches, insomnia, and behavioral deterioration.

cerebral thrombosis see THROMBOSIS.

cerebral trauma any damage to the brain, which may be temporary or permanent, following a blow to the head of sufficient severity to produce a concussion, contusion, or laceration.

cerebral type a body type in which the central nervous system is thought to have a dominant role, resulting in pronounced intellectual and cognitive abilities. See CARUS TYPOLOGY; ROSTAN TYPES.

cerebral vascular accident see CEREBROVASCULAR ACCIDENT.

cerebral vascular disease see CEREBROVASCULAR DISEASE.

cerebral vascular insufficiency see CEREBROVASCULAR INSUFFICIENCY.

cerebral ventricle see VENTRICLE.

cerebral vesicle an outgrowth of the embryonic NEURAL TUBE that develops into one of the three main regions of the brain: namely, the FOREBRAIN, MIDBRAIN, or HINDBRAIN.

cerebration *n.* any kind of conscious thinking, such as pondering or problem solving. **—cerebrate** *vb.*

cerebritis *n.* an infection of the brain. See CEREBRAL INFECTION.

cerebro- (**cereb-**) *combining form* brain.

cerebrocranial defect a deformity or dysfunction involving the cerebrum and the eight bones of the skull that form a protective layer around it. An example is the premature closing of the sutures of the skull, resulting in a displacement of cerebral tissues.

cerebromacular *adj.* referring to diseases, such as TAY–SACHS DISEASE, that are characterized by impairment of the brain and sometimes also by degeneration of the retina.

cerebroside *n.* a type of lipid present in the MYELIN SHEATH of nerve fibers.

cerebrospinal fluid (**CSF**) the fluid within the CENTRAL CANAL of the spinal cord, the four VENTRICLES of the brain, and the SUBARACHNOID SPACE of the brain. It serves as a watery cushion to protect vital tissues of the central nervous system from damage by shock pressure, and it mediates between blood vessels and brain tissue in exchange of materials, including nutrients.

cerebrotonia *n.* the personality type that, according to SHELDON'S CONSTITUTIONAL THEORY OF PERSONALITY, is associated with an ectomorphic (linear, fragile) physique (see ECTOMORPH). Cerebrotonia is characterized by a tendency toward introversion, restraint, inhibition, love of privacy and solitude, and sensitivity. **—cerebrotonic** *adj.*

cerebrovascular accident (**CVA**) a disorder of the brain arising from CEREBROVASCULAR DISEASE, such as CEREBRAL HEMORRHAGE, CEREBRAL EMBOLISM, or cerebral THROMBOSIS, resulting in temporary or permanent alterations in cognition, motor and sensory skills, or levels of consciousness. This term is often used interchangeably with STROKE. Also called **cerebral vascular accident**.

cerebrovascular disease a pathological condition of the blood vessels of the brain. It may manifest itself as symptoms of STROKE or a TRANSIENT ISCHEMIC ATTACK. Also called **cerebral vascular disease**. See also CEREBROVASCULAR ACCIDENT.

cerebrovascular insufficiency failure of the cardiovascular system to supply adequate levels of oxygenated blood to the brain tissues. The condition usually arises when one of the four main arteries supplying the brain, namely the two carotid and two vertebral arteries, is interrupted. It may also result from generalized ARTERIOSCLEROSIS or the inability of the heart to maintain adequate blood flow to the brain. Also called **cerebral vascular insufficiency**.

cerebrum *n.* the largest part of the brain, forming most of the FOREBRAIN and lying in front of and above the cerebellum. It consists of two CEREBRAL HEMISPHERES bridged by the CORPUS CALLOSUM. Each hemisphere is divided into four main lobes: the FRONTAL LOBE, OCCIPITAL LOBE, PARIETAL LOBE, and TEMPORAL LOBE. The outer layer of the cerebrum—the CEREBRAL CORTEX—is intricately folded and composed of GRAY MATTER. Also called **telencephalon**.

certainty of an attitude the level of subjective confidence that a person has regarding the validity of his or her attitude. It is related to the STRENGTH OF AN ATTITUDE.

certainty of paternity the degree to which a putative parent can be certain that it is the parent of an offspring. Because of internal fertilization and gestation, all female mammals are certain of maternity, but no male mammal can be 100% certain of paternity. In birds, BROOD PARASITISM can trick parents of both sexes into caring for chicks unrelated to either parent.

certifiable *adj.* **1.** describing people who, because of mental illness, may be a danger to themselves or others and are therefore eligible to be institutionalized. See CERTIFICATION LAWS; COMMITMENT LAWS. **2.** having met the requirements to be formally recognized by the relevant licensing or sanctioning body.

certificate of need (**CON**) written permission that a health care organization must obtain from a government body before making changes that involve expansion or reconstruction. The purpose of this requirement is to certify that the new services so provided will meet the needs of those for whom they are intended and to prevent excessive or duplicative development.

certification *n.* the process by which an external agency evaluates a person according to predetermined standards. Certification applies to individuals and ACCREDITATION applies to institutions. See also CREDENTIALING; PROFESSIONAL LICENSING. **—certificated** *adj.*

certification laws **1.** legislation governing the admission of individuals to mental institutions, including commitment proceedings as well as a review of case records to determine whether health care is necessary and whether the institution and type of care are appropriate. **2.** state laws governing the right of an individual to describe himself or herself as a psychologist.

certiorari *n.* a writ issued by a superior court demanding review of the action of a lower court. For example, if the U.S. Supreme Court issues a writ of certiorari (Latin, literally: "to be informed"), it has agreed to review a case that was decided by a lower court and subsequently appealed.

cerumen *n.* the waxlike secretion normally present in the EXTERNAL AUDITORY MEATUS of the ear. Also called **earwax**.

cerveau isolé an animal whose MIDBRAIN has been transected between the inferior and superior colliculi (see COLLICULUS) for experimental purposes. See also ENCÉPHALE ISOLÉ. [French, "isolated brain"]

cervical *adj.* **1.** relating to, occurring in, or affecting the neck, for example, the CERVICAL NERVES. **2.** pertaining to a necklike structure, especially the CERVIX of the uterus.

cervical angina see PSEUDOANGINA.

cervical ganglion any of the ganglia of the SYMPATHETIC NERVOUS SYSTEM that occur in the neck region. They innervate the pupils, sweat glands of the head, the salivary glands, and the heart.

cervical nerve any of the eight SPINAL NERVES in the neck area. Each has a DORSAL ROOT that is sensory in function and a VENTRAL ROOT that has motor function. See also CERVICAL GANGLION.

cervical plexus a nerve network formed from the VENTRAL ROOTS of the upper four CERVICAL NERVES. This plexus is anesthetized for surgical operations in the region between the jaw and the collarbone.

cervical sprain syndrome see WHIPLASH EFFECT.

cervix *n.* in anatomy, any necklike part, especially the neck of the UTERUS, which is the portion of the uterus that projects into the vagina. The cervix of a tooth is the slightly constricted part between the crown and the root.

CES abbreviation for cranial electrical stimulation. See ELECTROSLEEP THERAPY.

Cesamet *n.* a trade name for NABILONE.

cesarean section (**caesarean section**; **C-section**) a surgical procedure in which incisions are made through a woman's abdominal and uterine walls to deliver a baby under circumstances in which vaginal delivery is inadvisable. The name derives from the erroneous belief that Gaius Julius Caesar (100–44 BCE) was delivered in this manner.

CES-D abbreviation for CENTER FOR EPIDEMIOLOGIC STUDIES DEPRESSION SCALE.

CET abbreviation for CEREBRAL ELECTROTHERAPY.

CF abbreviation for characteristic frequency. See TUNING CURVE.

CFF abbreviation for CRITICAL FLICKER FREQUENCY.

C fiber a small-diameter UNMYELINATED nerve fiber that conducts pain information slowly and adapts slowly.

CFS abbreviation for CHRONIC FATIGUE SYNDROME.

cGMP abbreviation for CYCLIC GMP.

chained schedule a SCHEDULE OF REINFORCEMENT for a single response in which a sequence of at least two schedules, each accompanied by a distinctive stimulus, must be completed before primary reinforcement occurs. For example, in a chained fixed-ratio 10, fixed-ratio 50 schedule, 10 responses change the stimulus situation and then 50 more result in primary reinforcement. Chained schedules are often used to study conditioned reinforcement. Also called **chained reinforcement**. Compare TANDEM REINFORCEMENT.

chaining *n.* an OPERANT CONDITIONING technique in which a complex CHAIN OF BEHAVIOR is learned. Animals, both human and nonhuman, can be taught to perform relatively elaborate sequences of activities by this method, which makes PRIMARY REINFORCEMENT contingent on the final response in the series. In **backward chaining**, the final response is taught first. Once established, the stimulus for that response becomes a CONDITIONED REINFORCER that is used to reinforce the next-to-last response in the chain; this stimulus is then used to reinforce another response. The chain is thus taught backward, one response at a time. In **forward chaining**, the chain is taught by reinforcing the first step in the sequence, then the second, and so on until the entire sequence is learned. Also called **behavior chaining**.

chain of behavior a sequence of actions in which one action produces the stimulus or circumstance that sets the occasion for the next action. For example, when opening a locked door, turning the key produces a click that sets the occasion for turning the doorknob, which, when turned, allows the door to be pushed (or pulled) open. Also called **behavioral chain**; **behavior chain**.

chain reproduction in social and cultural psychology, the process by which material (e.g., ideas or stories) is relayed from person to person or group to group and altered slightly at each stage of transmission. In group exercises based on this process the ultimate product can be compared with the original in order to show, for example, that a picture of a cat has gradually become that of an owl. The same type of distortion occurs in the passing on of rumors and gossip through the processes of leveling (simplification), sharpening (emphasis on selected details), and assimilation (altering the accounts to suit attitudes, expectations, and prejudices).

chakra *n.* in oriental philosophy, one of the seven energy centers in the body. The chakras roughly correspond with the endocrine system. Each chakra symbolizes different, ascending human needs and has a sound (MANTRA) and color associated with it. Focused awareness and contemplation of the chakras may be practiced in YOGA and in other therapeutic approaches and traditions.

challenge 1. *n.* an obstacle appraised as an opportunity rather than a threat. A threat becomes a challenge when the individual judges that his or her coping resources are adequate not only to overcome the stress associated with the obstacle but also to improve the situation in a measurable way. **2.** *vb.* to pose or face with an obstacle or threat.

challenged *adj.* describing an individual with a DISABILITY or HANDICAP. The word is often considered to be euphemistic.

challenge for cause a request made to the judge during VOIR DIRE that a prospective juror be removed for some specific reason. For example, a juror with some relationship to either the prosecution or the defense may be removed as a result of a challenge for cause. Compare PEREMPTORY CHALLENGE.

challenging behavior behavior that is dangerous, or that interferes in participation in preschool, educational, or adult services, and often necessitates the design and use of special interventions. The term is used principally in human services in the United Kingdom and within educational services in the United States and most typically refers to behaviors of people with mental retardation or related conditions.

CHAMPUS acronym for CIVILIAN HEALTH AND MEDICAL PROGRAM OF THE UNIFORMED SERVICES.

chance occurrence 1. the occurrence of a phenomenon not resulting from CAUSATION. It is a matter of debate whether there are genuinely chance occurrences. Because CAUSALITY is a dominant assumption in much of philosophy and nearly all science, many would argue that what appear to be chance occurrences are merely occurrences the causes of which are not yet known, or not knowable. **2.** in statistical analysis, the occurrence of a predicted phenomenon under conditions of the NULL HYPOTHESIS. One purpose of statistical hypothesis testing is to assess the probability of chance occurrences.

chance variations changes in hereditary traits due to unknown factors.

change agent 1. a specific causative factor or element or an entire process that results in change, particularly in the sense of improvement. In psychotherapy research, a change agent may be a component or process in therapy that results in improvement in the behavior or psychological adaptation of a patient or client. **2.** an individual who instigates or implements change within an organization or group, such as a mental health professional who takes an active role in social policy planning, social action, and social engineering directed to improving community mental health.

change blindness an inability to notice changes in the visual array between one scene and another. For example, when a picture of an airplane is shown, followed by a blank screen, participants have surprising difficulty detecting a missing engine in a second picture of the airplane. See also INATTENTIONAL BLINDNESS; MINDSIGHT.

change effect in parapsychology, a phenomenon in which the physical structure of an object appears to have been altered by paranormal means, as in the alleged structural changes to metal in "spoon-bending" demonstrations. See PSYCHOKINESIS.

change management the process of planning, implementing, and evaluating change within organizations or communities with the goal of realizing the benefits of change while implementing it as efficiently, smoothly, and cost-effectively as possible. Change management practices include effective communication regarding the change, such as the identification of intended consequences, and the prediction of and preparation for unintended consequences.

change of life see CLIMACTERIC.

change of venue the transfer of a trial to another location if there is evidence that obtaining a fair and unbiased jury may be difficult in the original location owing to extensive PRETRIAL PUBLICITY.

change-over delay (**COD**) in CONCURRENT SCHEDULES OF REINFORCEMENT, a delay imposed between an organism's switch between alternative responses and the presentation of REINFORCEMENT.

change score a score based on two or more measurements made on the same person over time. The simplest change score is postscore minus prescore. More complex change scores can also be used to index, for example, the linearity of change over three, four, five, or more occasions of measurement.

channel *n.* an information transmission system. For example, the nervous system transmits coded messages from sense receptors (input) to effectors (output).

channel capacity in information theory, the maximum capacity of information or messages that a given channel can accommodate.

channel factors characteristics of the mode by which a persuasive message is communicated. For example, presentation of a message via written text (versus an audio recording) is a channel factor. See also MESSAGE-LEARNING APPROACH.

channels of communication 1. in the social psychology of groups, the paths that are usually available for the transmission of information from one person to one or more other people in the group or organization. For example, in a highly centralized communication structure (sometimes termed a **star**) all the channels of communication pass through the individual at the center of the structure, so that all information must go through this individual in order to reach any other member of the organization. **2.** the channels by which information is conveyed in face-to-face communication between people, comprising speech (source: vocal track; destination: ear), kinesics (body movement; eye), odor (chemical processes; nose), touch (body surface; skin), observation (body surface; eye), and proxemics (body placement; eye).

chaos theory an area of mathematics dealing with systems that are profoundly affected by their initial conditions, tiny variations in which can produce complex, unpredictable, and erratic effects. It has been applied by some psychological researchers to the study of human behavior. See BUTTERFLY EFFECT; NONLINEAR DYNAMICS THEORIES; SENSITIVE DEPENDENCE.

chaotic system a system that is too complex to be analyzed by traditional approaches, although it can still obey simple laws.

character *n.* **1.** the totality of an individual's attributes and PERSONALITY TRAITS, particularly his or her characteristic moral, social, and religious attitudes. Character is often used synonymously with PERSONALITY. **2.** see CHARACTER TYPE.

character analysis 1. in psychoanalysis, the treatment of a CHARACTER DISORDER. **2.** see CHARACTEROLOGY.

character development the gradual development of moral concepts, conscience, religious values or views, and social attitudes as an essential aspect of personality development.

character disorder formerly, in psychoanalysis, an alternative name for PERSONALITY DISORDER.

character displacement a change in a physical, physiological, or behavioral trait within two or more populations of a species that reduces competition between those populations and, over time, leads to the development of separate species. British naturalist Charles Darwin (1809–1882) found several types of finches in the Galápagos Islands with different forms of bills for eating seeds of different sizes or capturing insects of different sizes. This differentiation of bill size and shape from a founder species is a classic example of character displacement.

characteristic *n.* **1.** a quality of a person, especially any of the enduring qualities that define an individual's nature or personality in relation to others. **2.** any distinguishing feature of an organism, object, place, process, condition, or event.

characteristic frequency (**CF**) see TUNING CURVE.

characteristic value see EIGENVALUE.

characteristic vector see EIGENVECTOR.

characterization *n.* a description of psychological aspects of an individual, including ascriptions of personality traits, characteristics, or motives. **—characterize** *vb.*

character neurosis in psychoanalysis, a former name, used interchangeably with **neurotic character**, for PERSONALITY DISORDER.

characterology *n.* **1.** formerly, the branch of psychology concerned with character and personality. Also called **character analysis**. **2.** a pseudoscience in which character is "read" by external signs, such as hair color or facial type.

character strength a positive trait, such as kindness, teamwork, or hope, that is morally valued in its own right and contributes to the fulfillment of the self and others. Also called **human strength**. See POSITIVE PSYCHOLOGY.

character structure the organization of the traits and attributes that make up a person's CHARACTER.

character traits in trait conceptions of personality functioning, dispositional tendencies having to do with values, motives, and the regulation of behavior in accord with moral and ethical standards.

character type 1. see PERSONALITY TYPE. **2.** in psychoanalytic theory, a personality type defined by the kinds of DEFENSE MECHANISM used (e.g., a PHOBIC CHARACTER) or FIXATION at a particular stage in PSYCHOSEXUAL DEVELOPMENT (e.g., an ORAL PERSONALITY).

Charcot–Marie–Tooth disease a slowly progressive neuromuscular disorder characterized by muscle wasting (atrophy) and weakness in the arms (from the elbows down) and legs (from the knees down); feeling and movement in these areas may be lost. The disease, which results from degeneration of peripheral motor and sensory nerves, typically does not affect life expectancy. Usually AUTOSOMAL DOMINANT, it occasionally has recessive forms resulting in more severe symptoms. Also called **peroneal muscular atrophy**. [Jean **Charcot** (1825–1893) and Pierre **Marie** (1853–1940), French neurologists; Howard **Tooth** (1856–1925), British physician]

charisma *n.* the special quality of personality that enables an individual to gain the confidence of large numbers of people. It is exemplified in outstanding political, social, and religious leaders. **—charismatic** *adj.*

charismatic authority see AUTHORITY.

charismatic leader the type of political or social leader who commands high levels of devotion, enthusiasm, and commitment from his or her followers. German sociologist Max Weber (1864–1920) defined charismatic leaders as those who are widely admired and respected by their followers (e.g., Napoleon, Churchill), but the term is more popularly used to mean leaders who owe their success to personal charm or magnetism.

charitable behavior any act that benefits other people who are in need of assistance, usually because they lack resources necessary to thrive in society. Unlike ALTRUISM, charitable behavior may be carried out with the expectation of benefits in return. See also PROSOCIAL BEHAVIOR.

charlatan *n.* **1.** a person who makes pretense of having knowledge or skills that he or she does not in fact possess, especially in the field of medicine. See also QUACK. **2.** in parapsychology, a person who uses conjuring tricks or other forms of deliberate deception in order to claim paranormal powers.

Charles Bonnet syndrome complex visual hallucinations without delusions or the loss of insightful cognition, typically seen in older adults who have severe visual impairment. Such hallucinations are usually nonthreatening and often pleasant and are not indicative of mental illness or psychological disorder. Also called **Bonnet syndrome**. [Charles **Bonnet** (1720–1793), Swiss naturalist and philosopher]

charm *n.* **1.** the power of pleasing, attracting, or arousing interest in other people through one's manner or other personal qualities. **2.** an amulet often worn for its associative value to bring good luck or to protect from evil. **3.** a magic spell, usually consisting of an INCANTATION with associated ritual actions.

Charpentier's bands illusory light and dark bands that appear to follow a moving slit of light in the dark. [Pierre Marie Augustin **Charpentier** (1852–1916), French experimentalist]

Charpentier's illusion 1. see AUTOKINETIC EFFECT. **2.** see SIZE–WEIGHT ILLUSION. [Pierre **Charpentier**]

chart 1. *n.* a graphic representation of data. **2.** *vb.* to create such a representation. **3.** *vb.* to set out a plan for something, such as a course of psychotherapy.

chastity *n.* the state of abstaining from illicit sexual intercourse or—by extension—from all sexual activity. In religious usage it also includes the concept of not having sexual urges or impure thoughts. See also CELIBACY. **—chaste** *adj.*

chastity belt a device used to ensure that a woman remains incapable of having intercourse. It usually consists of a metal part that covers the pelvic area, between the legs, with straps holding it to the hips and small holes to allow urination and defecation. Chastity belts were first mentioned in medieval documents, but it is not clear how commonly they were used at any time in history.

chat *n.* see KHAT.

chatterbox effect the conversational behavior of many people with hydrocephalus and mental retardation or with spina bifida. The person may appear quite fluent and sociable in conversations but does not communicate in a meaningful manner, may tend to fabricate information as long as it seems interesting to the listener, and may be unable later to recall what was discussed. Also called **cocktail-party syndrome**.

chauvinism *n.* excessive favoritism toward a social, political, or ethnic group. Initially the word referred to extreme patriotism, as it derives from the name of a French soldier (Nicolas Chauvin) who displayed excessive devotion to Napoleon; now, however, it is often used to mean the mistaken belief that men are superior to women (MALE CHAUVINISM). **—chauvinistic** *adj.* **—chauvinist** *n.*

CHD abbreviation for CORONARY HEART DISEASE.

cheating *n.* **1.** influencing one's own or others' outcomes by deceit, trickery, or other unfair maneuvers. Because cheating is disruptive to maintaining a variety of social relationships, human beings and other animals have developed strategies to detect and punish it. **2.** in evolutionary psychology, using asocial strategies to gain an evolutionary advantage. For example, males of some species who have formed an exclusive PAIR BOND with a female may nonetheless seek to mate with other females so as to increase their chances of producing offspring. **3.** in RECIPROCAL ALTRUISM, the failure of an individual to aid another individual who has provided assistance in the past. **—cheat** *vb., n.*

check 1. *n.* the verification of the accuracy of an observation or calculation. **2.** *vb.* to verify the accuracy of an observation or calculation.

checkerboard pattern a pattern of alternating light and dark squares used in visual psychophysical tests and to stimulate visually responsive cells in the brain.

checklist *n.* a list of items that are to be observed, recorded, or corrected. See also BEHAVIOR CHECKLIST.

check reading in ergonomics, a machine display that provides information about the particular state of a system and is used by an operator to assess whether that system is operating within normal limits. Compare ANNUNCIATOR.

cheilophagia (**chilophagia**) *n.* the repeated biting of one's own lips.

cheiromancy *n.* see PALMISTRY. **—cheiromancer** *n.*

chelation *n.* the formation of chemical bonds between a metal ion and two or more nonmetallic ions. It can be used to remove certain types of ions from biological reactions or from the body, as in the removal of lead or mercury from the body by use of chelating agents.

chemesthesis *n.* the sense receptive to chemical stimuli through activation of receptors in the eye, nose, mouth, and throat other than those associated with the CHEMICAL SENSES, typically those involved in pain, touch, and thermal awareness. An example is the activation of pain receptors deriving from the burn in the taste of a chili pepper. Also called **common chemical sense**.

chemical antagonism see ANTAGONIST.

chemical brain stimulation the placing of various NEUROTRANSMITTERS or other brain-active chemicals in specific brain locations for therapeutic or experimental purposes.

chemical castration the administration of ANTIANDROGENS for the purposes of managing advanced prostate cancer or, more controversially, to reduce sexual drive in repeat sex offenders. Research has shown that a minority of sex offenders will offend again after chemical castration, indicating that sex drive is not the only cause of sexual offenses.

chemical communication the use of ODORANTS and other substances (see EXTERNAL CHEMICAL MESSENGER) to communicate between individuals. Many animals have specialized scent glands for scent production and specialized behavior for depositing scents. Chemical signals communicate the identity of species, subspecies, and individuals, reproductive status, dominance status, fear, and territorial boundaries. An advantage of chemical communication is that signals can remain long after the communicator has left.

chemical dependence see SUBSTANCE DEPENDENCE.

chemical methods of brain study methods of studying brain anatomy and neurophysiology that use chemicals or analyze the brain's chemical constituents. In in vivo preparations, chemical processes can be studied in the intact brain, using such methods as chemical sampling, CHEMICAL BRAIN STIMULATION, or POSITRON EMISSION TOMOGRAPHY. In in vitro preparations, tissue slices or cells can be maintained in nutrient solutions and studied by such techniques as the PATCH-CLAMP TECHNIQUE. In processed tissues, neurons can be stained chemically for anatomical analyses, treated for chemical analyses, or studied by AUTORADIOGRAPHY or IMMUNOCYTOCHEMISTRY.

chemical senses the senses receptive to chemical stimulation (i.e., through contact with chemical molecules or electrolytes), particularly the senses of SMELL and TASTE. Airborne molecules are inhaled and dissolved in the mucous membrane of the OLFACTORY EPITHELIUM to confer odors. Molecules dissolved in liquids are delivered to the TASTE CELLS on the tongue, soft palate, larynx, and pharynx to confer tastes.

chemical stimulation activity or a change of activity generated in olfactory (smell) or gustatory (taste) receptor cells by contact with specific electrolytes or molecules. Both CHEMICAL SENSES have specialized receptor proteins to which stimulating molecules bind to create electrical potentials. These potentials are passed on to peripheral nerves that transmit the message to the central nervous system for interpretation. See CHEMORECEPTOR.

chemical trail a track of chemical signals along the ground or another surface that allows group members to follow in the same direction as the trail maker but at a different time. Ants, for example, often leave chemical trails that provide direction toward foraging sites or the home nest.

chemical transmission the transmission of nerve impulses between nerve cells by NEUROTRANSMITTER molecules. See also SYNAPSE.

chemical transmitter see NEUROTRANSMITTER.

chemical warfare combat and associated military operations involving the use of incapacitating agents (e.g., poisons, contaminants, irritants), some of which may be lethal. Chemical weapons conventions prohibit the development, production, stockpiling, and use of such agents.

chemoaffinity hypothesis the notion that each neuron has a chemical identity that directs it to synapse on the proper target cell during development. [developed in the 1940s by U.S. psychologist Roger SPERRY]

chemoattractant *n.* a chemical compound that attracts particular classes of GROWTH CONES of neurons and so directs the growth of their axons. Compare CHEMOREPELLANT.

chemoreceptor *n.* a sensory nerve ending, such as any of those in the TASTE BUDS or OLFACTORY EPITHELIUM, that is capable of reacting to certain chemical stimuli. The chemical molecule or electrolyte generally must be in solution to be detected by the chemoreceptors for taste; it must be volatile to be detected by those involved in smell. In humans, there are hundreds of different taste receptor proteins and a total of about 300,000 TASTE CELLS, with some taste receptors reacting only to certain stimuli, such as those producing a bitter taste. Humans also have about 1,000 types of OLFACTORY RECEPTORS and about 1,000 receptors of each type, giving a total of one million olfactory receptors; other mammals (e.g., dogs) may have ten times that number. The relation between specific olfactory stimuli and particular olfactory receptors is still being debated.

chemoreceptor trigger zone (**CTZ**) a cluster of cells in the MEDULLA OBLONGATA that is sensitive to certain toxic chemicals and reacts by causing vomiting. The trigger zone is particularly sensitive to narcotics and responds by producing dizziness, nausea, and vomiting, the precise effects depending on the agent and the dosage. See also AREA POSTREMA.

chemorepellant *n.* a chemical compound that repels particular classes of GROWTH CONES of neurons and so directs the growth of their axons. Compare CHEMOATTRACTANT.

chemosensory event-related potential (**CSERP**) an electrical BRAIN POTENTIAL produced by a chemosensory event. This is a more general term than **olfactory-evoked potential** (**OEP**), which refers specifically to electrical potentials produced by olfactory events rather than trigeminal events (see TRIGEMINAL CHEMORECEPTION) or gustatory events.

chemotaxis *n.* see TAXIS.

chemotherapy *n.* the use of chemical agents (as opposed to RADIATION THERAPY) to treat cancer. **—chemotherapeutic** *adj.* **—chemotherapist** *n.*

Chernoff faces a representation of data in the form of stylized faces, designed to take advantage of the ability of observers to discern subtle changes in facial expressions. [Herman **Chernoff**, 20th-century U.S. statistician]

chessboard illusion an illusion of depth that occurs if a systematically distorted checkerboard pattern (known as the **Helmholtz chessboard**) is viewed close to the retina. The pattern contains small squares in the center, which become progressively larger toward the periphery. The progressive enlargement of the squares compensates for the progressive distortion of the image in the peripheral retina, caused by the optics of the eye. [described by Hermann Ludwig Ferdinand von Helmholtz (1821–1894), German physiologist and physicist]

chest voice the lower reaches, or range, of the speaking or singing voice, in which tone is created by pectoral breathing and chest resonance with little or no nasal resonance. A calm and relaxed normal speaking tone is generally delivered in a chest voice. Compare HEAD VOICE.

Cheyne–Stokes breathing labored breathing that alternates between increasing and decreasing rates, as in premature infants and individuals in a coma. [John **Cheyne** (1777–1836), Scottish medical writer; William **Stokes** (1804–1878), Irish physician]

chi (**qi**) *n.* in oriental philosophy, life-force energy (from Chinese, "energy"). Blockages in chi are believed to create illness. The equivalent Hindu concept is **prana** (Sanskrit, literally: "breath of life"). See also ACUPUNCTURE.

chiaroscuro *n.* the illusion of depth or distance in a picture produced by the use of light and shade.

chiasmal syndrome loss of visual acuity and abnormalities of the visual field associated with damage to the

OPTIC CHIASM and the adjacent optic nerve or OPTIC TRACT. Typical features are BITEMPORAL HEMIANOPIA and OPTIC ATROPHY. The great majority of cases are caused by brain tumors.

chibih *n.* see SUSTO.

Chicago school a school of psychology that emerged at the University of Chicago in the early 20th century, associated with psychologists John DEWEY, James R. ANGELL, and Harvey Carr (1873–1954). Their approach, called FUNCTIONALISM, was related to the ACT PSYCHOLOGY of Franz Brentano (1838–1917); it was an attempt to modify the subject matter of psychology by introducing the Darwinian idea that mental activities subserve an adaptive biological action function that should be the focus of psychology.

chicken game a type of laboratory game used in experimental investigations of bargaining and competition, in which each party in the interaction can win by selecting the noncooperative rather than the cooperative alternative. For example, if two cars traveling in opposite directions are stopped at a narrow intersection without traffic lights and both drivers are in a hurry (i.e., are motivated to attain their own individual goals), each motorist may want to start first across the intersection, pursuing his or her own interest (i.e., choosing the noncooperative alternative) and hoping that the other will give way (i.e., will adopt the more cooperative strategy). The danger is that both parties may become committed to the noncooperative strategy. This game differs from the PRISONER'S DILEMMA, in which both parties have incentives to both cooperate and compete with their partner. See also GAME THEORY.

chicken pox a highly contagious viral infection characterized by skin eruptions with fever, headache, anorexia, and other mild constitutional symptoms. The **varicella-zoster** virus, which causes chicken pox in children, also causes shingles in adults, although children or adults may experience both forms (see HERPES INFECTION). A common neurological complication is acute CEREBELLAR ATAXIA. Cranial nerve paralysis also may follow a chicken pox infection. Also called **varicella**.

child *n.* a young boy or girl between infancy and adolescence. See CHILDHOOD.

child abuse abuse of a child by a parent or other caregiver. It commonly implies physical abuse but can also encompass sexual and emotional abuse or neglect. See also BATTERED-CHILD SYNDROME; CHILD NEGLECT; EMOTIONAL INCEST; RITUAL ABUSE; SEXUAL ABUSE.

child advocacy any organized and structured interventions on behalf of children by professionals or institutions, often in relation to such issues as special parenting needs, child abuse, and adoption or foster care.

child analysis the application of psychoanalytic principles (considerably modified from those of CLASSICAL PSYCHOANALYSIS) to the treatment of children. In his first and most famous case, Sigmund FREUD analyzed 5-year-old LITTLE HANS by having the child answer questions through his father, but Freud never directly analyzed a child patient. Pioneers in the field are Melanie KLEIN, who developed the PSYCHOANALYTIC PLAY TECHNIQUE to achieve a deep analysis of the child's unconscious, and Anna FREUD, whose method was more pedagogical and encouraged EGO DEVELOPMENT. See also PLAY THERAPY.

Child Behavior Checklist (**CBCL**) a standardized instrument used to assess the behavioral problems and competencies of children between the ages of 4 and 18 years (a separate version is available for assessing the behavior of children ages 2 to 3). The CBCL is administered to parents, who describe their children's behavior by assigning a rating to each of the more than 100 items on the checklist. The items assessed range from "internalizing behaviors" (e.g., fearful, shy, anxious, inhibited) to "externalizing behaviors" (e.g., aggressive, antisocial, undercontrolled). [developed in 1983 by U.S. psychologists Thomas M. Achenbach (1940–) and Craig S. Edelbrock (1951–)]

child care 1. the care of children of any age in any setting. **2.** the daytime care of children by a nursery or childminder while parents are at work. **3.** the full-time residential care of children who have no other home or whose home life is seriously troubled.

child care facilities facilities licensed to provide regular out-of-home care to children during the working day. Child care facilities may be privately run but may also be associated with firms, churches, or social agencies. Such a facility is often referred to as a **day care center**.

child care worker an individual trained to attend to children on a day-to-day basis in a variety of group settings, including child care centers, schools, businesses, private households, and health care institutions. Child care workers perform such tasks as dressing, feeding, bathing, and overseeing play.

child-centered *adj.* focused on the needs, interests, safety, and well-being of children, as in **child-centered home** or **child-centered education**. See also CHILD-FOCUSED FAMILY.

child custody the care, protection, and supervision of a child. In certain legal proceedings, such as divorce or separation, the court may grant custody to one or both parents following a CHILD CUSTODY EVALUATION.

child custody evaluation a procedure, often conducted by clinical psychologists, that involves evaluating parenting behavior, analyzing parents' capacity to address children's needs, and providing the court with a recommendation regarding CHILD CUSTODY arrangements. See PRIMARY CARETAKER STANDARD.

child day care see CHILD CARE.

child development the sequential changes in the behavior, cognition, and physiology of children as they grow and mature from infancy through adolescence. See DEVELOPMENTAL TASK.

child-directed speech the specialized REGISTER of speech that adults and older children use when talking to young children. It is simplified and often more grammatically correct than adult-directed speech. See also INFANT-DIRECTED SPEECH.

child find in the U.S. educational system, an organized screening and identification program, directed by each state's Department of Education, that identifies preschool children in need of particular services and evaluates their readiness for school entry as well as their risk for developmental disabilities.

child-focused family a family in which the children's needs are paramount, sometimes to a point where they dominate the FAMILY CONSTELLATION and the parents' needs become secondary. Also called **child-centered family**.

child guidance a mental health approach for children that focuses not only on treatment but also on the prevention of possible future disorders by offering instruction, information, and therapeutic aid to the child and his or her family. Child guidance services and treatment are typically provided by specialized **child-guidance clinics**. The child-guidance movement emerged in the early

20th century and was at its strongest from the 1940s to 1970s.

childhood *n.* **1.** the period between the end of infancy (about 2 years of age) and the onset of puberty marking the beginning of ADOLESCENCE (10–12 years of age). This period is sometimes divided into (a) early childhood, from 2 years through the preschool age of 5 or 6 years; (b) middle childhood, from 6 to 8–10 years of age; and (c) late childhood or PREADOLESCENCE, which is identified as the 2-year period before the onset of puberty. **2.** the period between 3 or 4 years of age and about 7 years of age. In this context, childhood represents the period after weaning and before children can fend for themselves. Childhood in this more technical sense is unique to humans; other mammals advance directly from infancy to juvenility. See JUVENILE PERIOD. [defined by U.S. anthropologist Barry Bogin (1950–)]

childhood absence epilepsy a form of epilepsy in which children below the age of 7 experience frequent ABSENCE SEIZURES. It was formerly called **pyknolepsy**.

childhood amnesia the inability to recall events from early childhood (see EARLY MEMORY). Childhood amnesia has been attributed to the facts that (a) cognitive abilities necessary for encoding events for the long term have not yet been fully developed and (b) parts of the brain responsible for remembering personal events have not yet matured. Also called **infantile amnesia**.

childhood autism see AUTISTIC DISORDER.

childhood depression a MAJOR DEPRESSIVE EPISODE that occurs in childhood. Defining symptoms may differ from those of major depressive episodes in adults in that irritable mood is more characteristic than depressed mood, and failure to make expected weight gains often replaces an actual weight loss.

childhood disintegrative disorder in *DSM–IV–TR*, a PERVASIVE DEVELOPMENTAL DISORDER characterized by a significant loss of two or more of the following: previously acquired language skills, social skills or adaptive behavior, bowel or bladder control, play, or motor skills. This regression in functioning follows a period of normal development and occurs between the ages of 2 and 10. Impairments in social interaction and communication are also evident.

childhood disorder any social, emotional, behavioral, or educational disorder of childhood.

childhood fears fears occurring at different stages of childhood, such as fear of strangers, which usually develops around 8 months of age, and fear of heights, which emerges after the child learns to crawl. The content of fear changes for children from 2 to 6 years of age, with fears of darkness, animals, doctors, ghosts, monsters, and storms being common occurrences that usually pass in a few months or years without treatment.

childhood neurosis in Freudian theory, the development of psychological symptoms in childhood in response to efforts of defense against conflict.

childhood psychosis a PSYCHOTIC DISORDER with onset in childhood: In *DSM–IV–TR*, the defining features of psychotic disorders are essentially equivalent across all age groups. Historically, the term has been used much more widely to denote any of a variety of disorders or mental conditions of children that result in severe functional impairment, encompassing, for example, mental retardation and PERVASIVE DEVELOPMENTAL DISORDERS.

childhood schizophrenia SCHIZOPHRENIA with onset prior to age 12: In *DSM–IV–TR*, the defining features of schizophrenia are essentially equivalent across all age groups. Historically, the term has been used more widely to denote schizophrenic behavior that appears early in life, encompassing PERVASIVE DEVELOPMENTAL DISORDERS and AUTISTIC DISORDER in particular.

childhood sensorineural lesions organic disorders of the auditory system that may be a cause of hearing loss in children. The condition may be congenital and due to a failure of the inner ear to develop normally in the fetal stage or the result of an infection. Measles, mumps, and scarlet fever are among infectious causes. Childhood sensorineural lesions can also result from a GERMAN MEASLES infection of the mother during pregnancy.

child molestation child SEXUAL ABUSE: any sexual behavior toward a child by an adult. See also EMOTIONAL INCEST; RITUAL ABUSE.

child neglect the denial of attention, care, or affection considered essential for the normal development of a child's physical, emotional, and intellectual qualities, usually due to indifference, disregard, or impairment of the child's caregivers. See also PARENTAL REJECTION.

child pornography pornographic material featuring children. This may include written stories, pictures, or videos of naked children or of children engaging in sexual activity. Child pornography is illegal in the United States, and production or circulation of such materials is usually vigorously prosecuted.

child psychology the branch of psychology concerned with the systematic study of the behavior, adjustment, and growth of individuals from birth to adolescence, as well as with the treatment of their behavioral, mental, and emotional disorders. See also DEVELOPMENTAL PSYCHOLOGY.

child psychotherapy psychotherapy for children up to the age at which they reach puberty. The focus may be on emotions, cognitions, or behavior. The level of parental involvement is typically dependent upon the age of the child, type of problem, or approach used. The child may be treated concurrently in group or family therapy.

child-rearing practice a pattern of raising children that is specific to a particular society, subculture, family, or period in cultural history. Child-rearing practices vary in such areas as methods of discipline, expression of affection, and toilet-training and feeding techniques.

children in need of supervision (**CHINS**) children who commit offenses that may lead the court to act in service to them when they cannot be adequately controlled by parents or guardians. The child will typically appear before the court and receive some form of sanction. The crimes that lead to a CHINS classification are STATUS OFFENSES, such as truancy, running away from home, and misbehavior at school.

Children's Depression Inventory (**CDI**) a self-report questionnaire, based on the BECK DEPRESSION INVENTORY, designed to assess the severity of depression in children aged between 7 and 17 years. Intended primarily as a research tool, the CDI comprises 27 items that each consist of three statements reflecting different levels of severity of a particular symptom. For each item, the participant chooses the statement that best describes him or her during the previous two weeks. [originally published in 1977 by U.S. clinical psychologist Maria Kovacs (1944–)]

Children's Embedded Figures Test (**CEFT**) a version of the EMBEDDED FIGURES TEST of cognitive style that is designed for children aged 5 to 12 years. Participants are required to detect a simple shape within 25 increasingly complex figures or colored backgrounds. [developed in 1971 by U.S. clinical psychologist Stephen A. Karp (1928–) and Norma Konstadt]

Children's Manifest Anxiety Scale (**CMAS**) a 53-item modification of the TAYLOR MANIFEST ANXIETY SCALE that is appropriate for children. Originally developed in 1956 by U.S. psychologists Alfred Castaneda (1923–), Boyd R. McCandless (1915–), and David S. Palermo (1929–), the CMAS was subsequently revised in 1978 by U.S. educational psychologists Cecil R. Reynolds (1952–) and Bert O. Richmond (1929–). This **Revised Children's Manifest Anxiety Scale** (**RCMAS**) comprises 37 yes–no items measuring the nature and level of anxiety symptoms in children and adolescents aged between 6 and 19 years.

Children's Personality Questionnaire (**CPQ**) a 140-item self-report inventory for children aged 8 to 12 years that is based on CATTELL'S FACTORIAL THEORY OF PERSONALITY. It assesses 14 dimensions of personality (e.g., shy versus bold, self-assured versus apprehensive, sober versus enthusiastic) conceptualized as useful in evaluating, understanding, and predicting personal adjustment, social development, and academic performance. [originally developed in 1959 by U.S. educator Rutherford Burchard Porter (1909–2002) and British-born U.S. personality psychologist Raymond Bernard Cattell (1905–1998)]

child study movement the first organized effort, launched in the late 19th century by G. Stanley HALL, to apply scientific methods to the study of children. The movement focused on child welfare and, among other things, helped to bring about the passage of laws governing child labor and compulsory education.

child support a legally enforceable requirement that parents meet the economic and educational needs of their children. This includes providing the financial means to meet these needs.

child visitation in the context of divorce or situations in which children have been legally placed in the care of another (e.g., foster care), the permission granted by the court allowing a noncustodial parent some time to visit the child, provided this contact remains in the best interests of the child. Also called **visitation rights**.

child welfare the emotional or physical well-being of children, particularly in the context of legal issues or of social programs designed to enrich or intervene in their lives.

chilophagia see CHEILOPHAGIA.

chimera *n.* **1.** an organism composed of two or more kinds of genetically dissimilar cells. For example, a chimera may have received a transplant of genetically different tissue, such as bone marrow, or may have been produced by grafting an embryonic part of one animal onto the embryo of a genetically different animal; the graft may be either from a different species (a xenograft) or from the same species. **2.** an illusion of the imagination, sometimes something desired but impossible to realize. —**chimeric** *adj.*

chimeric stimulation a procedure, used by Roger SPERRY in the split-brain technique (see COMMISSUROTOMY), for studying the functions of the two cerebral hemispheres of the brain. In a typical experiment participants are shown an image of a **chimeric face**, consisting of the left half of one person's face joined to the right half of another person's face. In participants with a severed corpus callosum (i.e., a SPLIT BRAIN), one hemisphere perceives only one face, while the other hemisphere perceives the other, suggesting that there are two separate spheres of conscious awareness located in the two hemispheres. See also RIGHT-HEMISPHERE CONSCIOUSNESS.

chimerism *n.* the presence in an individual of cells with different genotypes, derived from different zygotes. Compare MOSAICISM.

Chinese Room argument a philosophical argument that computers or symbol-processing systems can receive only syntactical streams of ordered signs, and not semantic information. The name derives from a thought experiment in which a monolingual English speaker imagines him- or herself in a sealed room attempting to match streams of Chinese characters with Chinese script based only on a set of correspondence rules. [proposed by U.S. philosopher John R. Searle (1932–)]

chin reflex see JAW JERK.

CHINS acronym for CHILDREN IN NEED OF SUPERVISION.

chiromancy (**cheiromancy**) *n.* see PALMISTRY. —**chiromancer** *n.*

chiropractic *n.* an alternative health care system concerned with the relationship between the structure of the body (particularly the spine) and disease processes. Treatment comprises noninvasive drug-free methods, primarily manipulations and adjustments to the body, designed to restore proper nerve functioning and to promote health. See also COMPLEMENTARY AND ALTERNATIVE MEDICINE. —**chiropractor** *n.*

chirosophy *n.* see PALMISTRY. —**chirosopher** *n.*

chi-square distribution (**χ^2 distribution**) the distribution of the sum of a set of independent squared normal random deviates. If p independent variables are involved, the distribution is said to have p DEGREES OF FREEDOM. The CHI-SQUARE TEST is based upon it.

chi-square test a measure of how well a theoretical probability distribution fits a set of data. If values x_1, x_2, ... x_p are observed o_1, o_2, ... o_p times and are expected by theory to occur e_1, e_2, ... e_p times, then chi-square is calculated as

$$(o_1 - e_1)^2/e_1 + (o_2 - e_2)^2/e_2 + \ldots$$

Tables of chi-square for different degrees of freedom can be used to indicate the probability that the theory is correct. Also called **chi-square procedure**.

chloral hydrate a short-acting depressant of the central nervous system, first synthesized in 1832 and formerly widely used clinically, chiefly as a hypnotic. It is occasionally still used to induce sleep, but its use is limited by its potential toxicity. U.S. trade name: **Aquachloral**. See also KNOCKOUT DROPS.

chlordiazepoxide *n.* the first commercially available BENZODIAZEPINE anxiolytic. Developed in 1957 and in clinical use in the early 1960s, it became one of the most heavily prescribed medications ever developed. It is characterized by extensive metabolism in the liver and possesses a number of metabolic products, giving it a lengthy HALF-LIFE and a consequent long-acting anxiolytic effect. Its use in the management of anxiety and insomnia has been largely supplanted by benzodiazepines with less complicated metabolism and more predictable half-lives, but it remains in common use to protect against the effects of alcohol withdrawal. It is available in oral and injectable form. Because of erratic absorption, intramuscular administration is not advised. U.S. trade name: **Librium**.

chloride channel see ION CHANNEL.

chloropsia *n.* see CHROMATOPSIA.

chlorpromazine (**CPZ**) *n.* the first synthesized ANTIPSYCHOTIC agent, introduced into clinical use in Europe in 1952 and in Canada and the United States in 1954. It was initially used to reduce presurgical anxiety and deepen conscious sedation during surgical procedures;

its antipsychotic effects were discovered serendipitously. This low-potency PHENOTHIAZINE provided a degree of behavioral control and management of positive psychotic symptoms previously unavailable and ushered in the modern era of psychopharmacological treatment. However, although effective in managing the acute symptoms of schizophrenia, acute mania, and other psychoses, chlorpromazine caused a number of unwanted adverse effects, including neuromuscular rigidity and other EXTRAPYRAMIDAL EFFECTS, sedation, ORTHOSTATIC HYPOTENSION, cognitive slowing, and long-term association with TARDIVE DYSKINESIA. Although chlorpromazine has been largely supplanted by newer antipsychotic agents, it is still used as a referent for dose equivalency of other antipsychotics. It has also been used in lower doses to treat nausea, vomiting, and intractable hiccups. U.S. trade name: **Thorazine**.

chlorprothixene *n.* a low-potency antipsychotic of the THIOXANTHENE class, similar in its effects to other thioxanthenes. U.S. trade names: **Taractan**; **Taractin**.

choice *n.* a decision-making problem in which a person has to indicate a preference for one of a set of alternatives. See also BINARY CHOICE. **—choose** *vb.*

choice axiom a mathematical model of decision making that assumes, given several alternatives from which to choose, the probability that a particular alternative will be picked is independent of the sequence of decisions. [developed in 1959 by U.S. mathematician and psychologist R. Duncan Luce (1925–)]

choice behavior the selection of one of many available options or behavioral alternatives.

Choice Dilemma Questionnaire (**CDQ**) a research instrument used in early studies of the RISKY SHIFT to measure an individual's willingness to make risky or cautious decisions. Respondents were presented with a series of scenarios involving a course of action that might or might not yield financial, interpersonal, or educational benefits; they then indicated what the odds of success would have to be before they would recommend the course of action. See also CHOICE-SHIFT EFFECT.

choice point a position in a sequence of events at which a choice or decision must be made.

choice reaction time the REACTION TIME of a participant in a task that requires him or her to make a simple response (e.g., pressing a key) whenever one stimulus from a predefined set of stimuli is presented. Compare COMPLEX REACTION TIME; SIMPLE REACTION TIME. See also COMPOUND REACTION TIME; DISCRIMINATION REACTION TIME.

choice shift any shift in an individual's choices or decisions that occurs as a result of group discussion, as measured by comparing his or her prediscussion and postdiscussion responses. In many cases the result of such shifts is a CHOICE-SHIFT EFFECT within the group as a whole. See also CAUTIOUS SHIFT; RISKY SHIFT.

choice-shift effect the tendency for groups making a choice or decision to opt for a more extreme or risky alternative than most of their members would have done had they made the decision alone. See GROUP POLARIZATION; GROUP RISK TAKING; RISKY SHIFT. See also CAUTIOUS SHIFT.

choice stimuli in REACTION-TIME tasks, the array of possible stimuli that may occur in a particular trial. Each stimulus or item in the array is mapped to a different response (e.g., a different key to be pressed). Participants must decide which response to make to a particular stimulus.

choked disk see PAPILLEDEMA.

chokes *n.* see DECOMPRESSION SICKNESS.

choking *n.* in sport psychology, the deterioration in performance that occurs when an athlete is unable to gain control over the performance without outside assistance. This occurs most frequently in situations where the athlete encounters high levels of stress that cause physical and mental impediments to performance.

choking under pressure a paradoxical effect in which the demands of a situation that calls for good performance, such as a school test or job interview, cause an individual to perform poorly relative to his or her capabilities. "Pressure" denotes the individual's awareness of the need to perform well; "choking" refers to the actual decrement in performance that results.

cholecystokinin (**CCK**) *n.* a PEPTIDE HORMONE that is released from the duodenum and may be involved in the satiation of hunger. It also serves as a NEUROTRANSMITTER at some locations in the nervous system.

choleric type a type of temperament characterized by irritability and quick temper, as described by Roman physician Galen (129–199 CE). See HUMORAL THEORY.

Cholesky factorization a matrix algebra procedure that begins with a real, symmetric, POSITIVE-DEFINITE matrix A and allows one to obtain a matrix F such that $A = FF'$. The resulting matrix F plays a central role in multivariate statistics and factor analysis. [André-Louis **Cholesky** (1875–1918), French mathematician]

cholesterol *n.* a steroid derivative abundant in animal tissues, found especially in foods rich in animal fats. Cholesterol is a constituent of plasma membranes, the precursor of other steroids (e.g., the sex hormones), and a component of plasma lipoproteins, especially low-density lipoproteins (LDLs), which are believed to play an important role in forming atherosclerotic plaques (see ATHEROSCLEROSIS).

choline *n.* a BIOGENIC AMINE, often classed as a B vitamin, that is a constituent of many important compounds, such as ACETYLCHOLINE and lecithin (a component of plasma membranes). See also CHOLINE ACETYLASE.

choline acetylase an enzyme that is involved in the production of the neurotransmitter ACETYLCHOLINE from CHOLINE and acetyl coenzyme A. Also called **choline acetyltransferase**.

cholinergic *adj.* pertaining to nerve cells and organs that respond to the neurotransmitter ACETYLCHOLINE.

cholinergic drugs agents that potentiate the activity of the neurotransmitter ACETYLCHOLINE or have effects similar to acetylcholine, and therefore have the effect of stimulating the PARASYMPATHETIC NERVOUS SYSTEM. Cholinergic drugs include such alkaloids as PHYSOSTIGMINE and PILOCARPINE; BETHANECHOL; and anticholinesterases (CHOLINESTERASE inhibitors; e.g., EDROPHONIUM, NEOSTIGMINE, and PYRIDOSTIGMINE), used in the treatment and diagnosis of myasthenia gravis because they potentiate the action of acetylcholine at neuromuscular junctions. Other uses for cholinergic drugs include management of glaucoma and urinary retention, and as antidotes for toxic effects of ANTICHOLINERGIC DRUGS. Also called **parasympathetic drugs**; **parasympathomimetic drugs**.

cholinergic synapse a SYNAPSE that uses ACETYLCHOLINE as a neurotransmitter. Cholinergic synapses are found in postganglionic parasympathetic fibers, autonomic preganglionic fibers, preganglionic fibers to the adrenal medulla, somatic motor nerves to the skeletal muscles, and fibers to the sweat glands.

cholinergic system the part of the AUTONOMIC NER-

VOUS SYSTEM that reacts to the neurotransmitter ACETYLCHOLINE and to cholinergic drugs. Activities of this system are inhibited by ANTICHOLINERGIC DRUGS, such as atropine. Compare ADRENERGIC SYSTEM.

cholinesterase *n.* an enzyme that splits and inactivates ACETYLCHOLINE after it has been released into the SYNAPTIC CLEFT. Cholinesterase occurs in two forms: ACETYLCHOLINESTERASE, found in nerve tissue and red blood cells; and pseudocholinesterase, found in blood plasma and tissues other than neurons.

cholinesterase inhibitors see ACETYLCHOLINESTERASE INHIBITORS; CHOLINERGIC DRUGS.

Chomsky, Noam (1928–) U.S. linguist. Chomsky was awarded his doctorate in linguistics at the University of Pennsylvania in 1955. From 1951 to 1955 he was a junior fellow in Harvard University's elite Society of Fellows. In 1955 he joined the faculty of the Massachusetts Institute of Technology, where he remained throughout his career. His first book, *Syntactic Structure* (1957), was based on his doctoral dissertation. Chomsky is best known for his theory of TRANSFORMATIONAL GENERATIVE GRAMMAR, which revolutionized linguistic analysis and theory in the 20th century. He argued that the fundamental capacity for learning the structure of grammar is innate in humans, in the form of "DEEP STRUCTURES that correspond to a small number of abstract transformational rules of grammar common to all languages and cultures" (see COMPETENCE; LANGUAGE UNIVERSAL). This view brought him into direct conflict with both the dominant linguistic theorists of his day and psychologist B. F. SKINNER, who argued in his book *Verbal Behavior* (1957) that the fundamentals of grammatical structure and linguistic meaning were learned through experience. In 1959 Chomsky publicly attacked Skinner's view in the journal *Language*, in a widely reprinted review of "Verbal Behavior." Chomsky elaborated his theory in many subsequent works, including his book *The Logical Structure of Linguistic Theory* (1975). Chomsky is also widely known as a vocal critic of U.S. foreign policy and social policy. His honors include fellowships of the American Academy of Arts and Sciences and the National Academy of Science and the American Psychological Association's Distinguished Scientific Contribution Award.

chondroectodermal dysplasia see ELLIS–VAN CREVELD SYNDROME.

chorda tympani see GREATER SUPERFICIAL PETROSAL NERVE.

chord keyboard a keyboard with a limited number of keys that can be used to enter a wide range of alphanumeric information by pressing various keys in combination. Some can support one-handed entry. See also DVORAK KEYBOARD.

chorea *n.* irregular and involuntary jerky movements of the limbs and facial muscles. Chorea is associated with various disorders, including HUNTINGTON'S DISEASE and **Sydenham's chorea** (formerly known as **Saint Vitus's dance**), which occurs as a complication of a streptococcal infection (e.g., rheumatic fever). **—choreal** *adj.* **—choreic** *adj.*

choreiform *adj.* involving involuntary movement that resembles CHOREA. Also called **choreoid**.

choreoathetosis *n.* CHOREA accompanied by ATHETOSIS (involuntary writhing) of the face, tongue, hands, and feet. The condition is characteristic of HUNTINGTON'S DISEASE.

choreoid *adj.* see CHOREIFORM.

choreomania *n.* an uncontrollable urge to dance, especially in a frenzied, convulsive manner. Major outbreaks of choreomania occurred in the European DANCE EPIDEMICS of the Middle Ages. Also called **dancing madness**; **dancing mania**.

chorion *n.* the outermost of the membranes that surround and protect the developing embryo. In most mammals (including humans) a section of it forms the embryonic part of the PLACENTA. **—chorionic** *adj.*

chorionic sac the outermost membrane that protects the embryo and fetus.

chorionic villus sampling (**CVS**) a method of diagnosing diseases and genetic and chromosomal abnormalities in a fetus. Samples of cells of the chorionic villi, the microscopic projections in the protective membrane surrounding the fetus, are obtained for analysis of bacteria, metabolites, or DNA. Unlike AMNIOCENTESIS, this procedure can be carried out in the first trimester of pregnancy.

choroid layer the vascular pigmented layer of tissue that covers the back of the eye and is located between the retina and the sclera. In the anterior portion of the eye it is continuous with the pigmented portion of the CILIARY BODY. The pigment in the choroid layer absorbs stray light; the blood vessels include the **choriocapillaris**, a plexus of capillaries that provides oxygen and sustenance to the photoreceptors of the retina. Also called **choroid**; **choroid coat**.

choroid plexus a highly vascularized portion of the lining of the cerebral VENTRICLES that is responsible for the production of CEREBROSPINAL FLUID.

Chotzen's syndrome an inherited condition in which an abnormally shaped head due to premature closing of one or more of the cranial sutures, usually involving the coronal suture (see CRANIOSYNOSTOSIS SYNDROME), is accompanied by webbing of the fingers and toes. Mental retardation may be associated with the disorder, but affected children often have average intelligence. The trait is transmitted by an autosomal dominant gene (see ACROCEPHALOSYNDACTYLY). Also called **acrocephalosyndactyly Type III**; **Saethre–Chotzen syndrome**. [F. **Chotzen**, German physician]

chrematisophilia *n.* sexual arousal obtained by paying for sex, as opposed to having sexual relations with a willing partner who is not a prostitute.

Christian Science a Protestant Christian religious denomination founded in 1879 by U.S. spiritual leader Mary Baker Eddy (1821–1910). It is based on the idea that mind has power over matter, enabling MENTAL HEALING, particularly through prayer, of both spiritual ill health (i.e., sin) and physical illness and disease. The reliance of adherents on their beliefs has sparked many controversies regarding refusal of medical and mental health care.

chrom- *combining form* see CHROMO-.

chroma–brightness coefficient the relationship between saturation and intensity in the MUNSELL COLOR SYSTEM.

chromatic 1. *adj.* in vision, relating to the attribute of color. **2.** *n.* in music, an octave in which each tone differs from the preceding tone by one semitone.

chromatic aberration a defect in the image formed by a simple glass lens resulting from the fact that light of short wavelength is refracted to a greater extent than light of long wavelength. It causes different colors to be focused at different distances, so that the image has colored fringes. Chromatic aberration can be corrected by the use of an ACHROMATIC lens. Also called **chromatic error**.

chromatic adaptation decreased sensitivity to a particular color as a result of prolonged exposure to a colored stimulus. Also called **color adaptation**.

chromatic audition a type of SYNESTHESIA in which color sensations are experienced when sounds are heard. Also called **phonopsia**. See CHROMESTHESIA.

chromatic colors all colors other than black, white, and gray, that is, those colors that possess saturation and hue. Compare ACHROMATIC COLORS.

chromaticity *n.* a color-stimulus quality determined by the purity and wavelength of the stimulus, independent of its LUMINANCE. Chromaticity and luminance together provide a description of a colored stimulus that is independent of an observer's perceptions. Also called **chromaticness**.

chromatics *n.* in optics, the study of color and the sensation of color.

chromatic scale a musical scale with 12 SEMITONE steps to an OCTAVE.

chromatid *n.* in cell division, one of the two duplicate, filamentlike subunits, joined at the CENTROMERE, that make up a chromosome and then separate, each going to a different pole of the dividing cell to become a new chromosome in one of the daughter cells.

chromatin *n.* a substance present in chromosomes and cell nuclei that readily stains with certain identifying dyes. It consists of nucleic acids (mainly DNA) combined with protein (i.e., nucleoprotein).

chromatin negative denoting the absence of SEX CHROMATIN in the nucleus of a human somatic cell, which identifies the cell as being from a male.

chromatin positive denoting the presence in a human somatic cell of SEX CHROMATIN, which identifies the cell as being from a female.

chromatopsia *n.* an aberration in color vision in which there is excessive visual sensitivity to one color. Chromatopsia is caused by drugs, intense stimulation, or SNOW BLINDNESS and it can occur after eye hemorrhages, cataract extraction, electric shock, or optic atrophy. There are several forms: **erythropsia** (red vision), **chloropsia** (green vision), **xanthopsia** (yellow vision), and **cyanopsia** (blue vision). Also called **chromopsia**; **dyschromatopsia**.

chromesthesia *n.* a type of SYNESTHESIA in which perception of nonvisual stimuli (e.g., sounds, tastes, odors) is accompanied by color sensations. Strictly, chromesthesia is not a conscious juxtaposition of two different sense perceptions: The two perceptions coincide as responses to the same stimulus (e.g., the musical note G may be consistently experienced as blue). Also called **pseudochromesthesia**.

chromic myopia see MYOPIA.

chromo- (**chrom-**; **chromato-**) *combining form* color.

chromopsia *n.* see CHROMATOPSIA.

chromosomal aberration 1. an abnormal change in the structure of a chromosome. **2.** a congenital defect that can be attributed to an abnormal chromosome. See AUTOSOMAL ABERRATION; SEX-CHROMOSOMAL ABERRATION.

chromosomal map the appearance of a stained chromosome when observed under a microscope. Visually distinct light and dark bands give each chromosome a unique pattern, which enables KARYOTYPE testing to be carried out.

chromosomal mosaicism see CHROMOSOME MOSAICISM.

chromosome *n.* a usually invisible strand or filament composed of nucleic acid (mainly DNA in humans) and proteins (see CHROMATIN) that carries the genetic, or hereditary, traits of an individual. Located in the cell nucleus, chromosomes are visible, through a microscope, only during cell division. The normal human complement of chromosomes totals 46, or 23 pairs (44 AUTOSOMES and 2 SEX CHROMOSOMES), which contain more than 30,000 genes (see GENOME). Each parent contributes one chromosome to each pair, so a child receives half its chromosomes from its mother and half from its father. **—chromosomal** *adj.*

chromosome 4, deletion of short arm a chromosomal disorder involving absence of a portion of chromosome 4, resulting in microcephaly (small head), visual defects, severe mental retardation, and indifference to painful stimuli. Until 1965 the condition was considered a variation of CRI DU CHAT SYNDROME, involving chromosome 5, although the cat-cry effect was rarely noted.

chromosome 5, deletion of short arm see CRI DU CHAT SYNDROME.

chromosome 18, deletion of long arm a chromosomal disorder characterized by microcephaly (small head), deafness, and mental retardation associated with the absence of part of the long arm of chromosome 18. Reduced muscle tone and nystagmus (involuntary eye movements) are other neurological effects observed in affected individuals.

chromosome abnormality an abnormality that is evidenced by either an abnormal number of chromosomes or some alteration in the structure of one or more chromosomes.

chromosome disorder any disorder caused by a defect in the structure or number of one or more chromosomes. Such disorders can result from AUTOSOMAL ABERRATIONS or SEX-CHROMOSOMAL ABERRATIONS.

chromosome mosaicism a condition resulting from an error in the distribution of chromosomes between daughter cells during an early embryonic cell division, producing two and sometimes three populations of cells with different chromosome numbers in the same individual. Mosaicism involving the sex chromosomes is not uncommon (see HERMAPHRODITE).

chromosome number the number of chromosomes present in the tissue cells of an individual. All members of a species normally have the same number of chromosomes. The normal number for humans is 46. The chromosome number of a gamete, or reproductive cell, of a human is half the somatic chromosome number, or 23. See DELETION.

chromosome-13 trisomy a chromosomal syndrome involving an extra chromosome 13, resulting in the birth of an infant with a variety of defects, including mental retardation, cleft lip and palate, polydactyly (extra fingers or toes), cerebral anomalies, and ocular abnormalities, such as missing or very small eyes, cataracts, and defects in the iris. Also called **D trisomy**; **Patau's syndrome**; **trisomy 13**; **trisomy 13–15**.

chromotherapy *n.* see PHOTOBIOLOGY.

chron- *combining form* see CHRONO-.

chronaxie (**chronaxy**) *n.* an index of excitability of a nerve or muscle, measured as the duration of an electrical current of twice the THRESHOLD intensity required to elicit a nerve impulse or a muscular contraction. Also called **chronaxia**.

chronesthesia *n.* a hypothetical ability or capacity of the human brain or mind, acquired through evolution, that allows humans to be constantly aware of the past and the future. The key feature of this "mental time travel" is to enable people to anticipate the future—that is, to learn what to avoid and how to behave in the future—by recalling past events. For example, chronesthesia enables people over time to "distinguish friends from foes" in social relationships and to develop tools that work well (and discard those that do not) in occupational activities. [introduced by Estonian-born Canadian psychologist Endel Tulving (1927–)]

chronic *adj.* denoting conditions or symptoms that persist or progress over a long period of time and are resistant to cure. Compare ACUTE.

chronic adjustment disorder see ADJUSTMENT DISORDER.

chronic alcoholism habitual, long-term dependence on alcohol (see ALCOHOL DEPENDENCE). See also GAMMA ALCOHOLISM.

chronically accessible constructs mental contents (e.g., ideas or categories) that are frequently used and therefore come to mind particularly readily.

chronically suicidal describing an individual with a history of multiple suicide attempts or episodes that include serious thoughts about or plans for committing suicide. Such a history often occurs in individuals with BORDERLINE PERSONALITY DISORDER.

chronic anxiety a persistent, pervasive state of apprehension that may be associated with aspects of a number of anxiety disorders. These include uncontrollable worries in GENERALIZED ANXIETY DISORDER, fear of a panic attack in PANIC DISORDER, and obsessions in OBSESSIVE-COMPULSIVE DISORDER.

chronic brain disorder any disorder caused by or associated with brain damage and producing permanent impairment in one or more areas of brain function (cognitive, motor, sensory, and emotional). Such disorders may arise from trauma, stroke, infection, degenerative diseases, or many other conditions. In older literature, these disorders are also referred to as **chronic brain syndrome**.

chronic care long-term care and treatment of patients with long-standing health care problems.

chronic fatigue syndrome (**CFS**) an illness characterized by fatigue, decrease in physical activity, and flulike symptoms, such as muscle weakness, swelling of the lymph nodes, headache, sore throat, and sometimes depression. The condition can last for years; the cause is unknown.

chronic illness illness that persists for a long period. Chronic illnesses include many major diseases and conditions, such as heart disease, cancer, diabetes, and arthritis. Disease management is important when dealing with chronic illness; this includes ensuring adherence to treatment and maintaining quality of life.

chronicity *n.* **1.** the state of being CHRONIC. **2.** see SOCIAL BREAKDOWN SYNDROME.

chronic mania a manic state that persists indefinitely.

chronic mental illness a mental illness that continues for a prolonged period of time.

chronic mood disorder a mood disorder, such as DYSTHYMIC DISORDER or CYCLOTHYMIC DISORDER, in which symptoms rarely remit.

chronic motor or vocal tic disorder in *DSM–IV–TR*, a TIC DISORDER characterized by motor or vocal tics (but not both) for a period of more than 1 year, during which any period without tics lasts for no more than 3 months. The disorder has an onset before the age of 18. Compare TOURETTE'S DISORDER.

chronic myofascial pain (**CMP**) a MUSCULOSKELETAL DISORDER characterized by pain and stiffness that is restricted to certain locations on the body, called "trigger points." It is nonprogressive, nondegenerative, and noninflammatory. Chronic myofascial pain is sometimes referred to as **myofascial pain syndrome** (**MPS**), especially in older literature.

chronic obstructive pulmonary disease (**COPD**) a group of lung diseases, most commonly chronic bronchitis and emphysema, that are characterized by limited airflow with varying degrees of lung-tissue damage and alveolar (air-sack) enlargement. Marked by coughing, wheezing, and shortness of breath, COPD is caused by cigarette smoking, exposure to other irritants and pollutants, lung infections, or genetic factors. Individuals with COPD frequently experience depression, anxiety, and problems with sexual function; they also sometimes have cognitive and neuropsychological difficulties that may be associated with chronic deficiencies of oxygen to the brain. In addition to medical treatments, behavioral interventions (e.g., those that promote smoking cessation and exercise), psychotherapy, and treatment with psychoactive drugs can benefit patients with this condition. Also called **chronic obstructive lung disease**.

chronic pain pain that may have been caused by actual tissue damage, disease, or emotional trauma but continues to occur despite all medical and pharmacological efforts at treatment. Cognitive factors and beliefs influence the course of rehabilitation and the subjective experience of pain and may lead to maladaptive avoidance behaviors and family problems if left unattended.

chronic posttraumatic stress disorder a form of POSTTRAUMATIC STRESS DISORDER that is diagnosed when the symptoms persist over a period of more than 2 years, regardless of when they first appeared.

chronic preparation an animal that has undergone an experimental procedure, often surgical and permanent in nature, and is then observed over an extended period of time. Compare ACUTE PREPARATION.

chronic psychosis **1.** a delusional or hallucinatory state that persists indefinitely. **2.** a former name for CHRONIC SCHIZOPHRENIA. **3.** historically, any irreversible disorder of cognition, mood or affect, and behavior.

chronic schizophrenia schizophrenia of any type—paranoid, disorganized, catatonic, or undifferentiated—in which the symptoms persist for an extended period and are generally resistant to treatment. It is contrasted with ACUTE SCHIZOPHRENIC EPISODES, in which the symptoms are florid (blatant) but transient.

chronic tic disorder any TIC DISORDER that lasts for more than a year. See CHRONIC MOTOR OR VOCAL TIC DISORDER; TOURETTE'S DISORDER.

chrono- (**chron-**) *combining form* time.

chronobiology *n.* the branch of biology concerned with BIOLOGICAL RHYTHMS, such as the sleep–wake cycle.

chronograph *n.* an instrument that records time sequences graphically. **—chronographic** *adj.*

chronological age (**CA**) the amount of time elapsed since an individual's birth, typically expressed in terms of months and years. Also called **calendar age**; **life age**.

chronometer *n.* a precise clock that runs continuously and is designed to maintain its accuracy under all conditions of temperature, pressure, and the like.

chronometric analysis a method for studying a mental process that involves varying stimulus input conditions and measuring participants' REACTION TIMES to those stimuli. The relations between the stimulus variables and reaction times are then used to make inferences about the underlying mental processes. Also called **mental chronometry**. See DONDERS'S METHOD.

chronometry *n.* the measurement of time. **—chronometric** *adj.*

chronopsychology *n.* the scientific study of the way in which changes to daily SLEEP–WAKE CYCLES can affect the ability to work and function.

chronoscope *n.* an instrument for the accurate measurement, either mechanically or electronically, of small time intervals.

chronotaraxis *n.* a condition of time confusion in which the individual tends to underestimate or overestimate the passage of time or is confused about the time of day or day of the week.

chronotaxis *n.* see DISCHRONATION.

chronotherapy *n.* a treatment for CIRCADIAN RHYTHM SLEEP DISORDERS that systematically moves bedtime progressively later by intervals (phase delays) until it approaches the desired bedtime.

chronotopic constraints neural limitations on the timing of developmental events (e.g., language-processing ability). Also called **chronotopic innateness**. Compare ARCHITECTURAL CONSTRAINTS; REPRESENTATIONAL CONSTRAINTS.

chunking *n.* **1.** the process by which the mind sorts information into small, easily digestible units (**chunks**) that can be retained in SHORT-TERM MEMORY. As a result of this RECODING, one item in memory (e.g., a keyword or key idea) can stand for multiple other items (e.g., a short list of associated points). The capacity of short-term memory is believed to be constant for the number of individual units it can store (see SEVEN PLUS OR MINUS TWO), but the units themselves can range from simple chunks (e.g., individual letters or numbers) to complex chunks (e.g., words or phrases). The exact number of chunks remembered can depend on the size of each chunk or the subunits contained within each chunk. **2.** the associated principle that effective communication between humans depends on sorting information into units that do not exceed the mind's capacity to chunk them (the **chunking limit**). This has implications for the content and layout of written documents, diagrams and visual aids, websites, and so on. For example, any list of more than nine bullet points should normally be subdivided into two or more shorter lists. [coined by U.S. cognitive psychologist George Armitage Miller (1920–) in 1956]

cicatrization *n.* **1.** the formation of a scar, or **cicatrix**, after a wound has healed. **2.** the deliberate scarring of some part of the body for cosmetic or religious purposes. **—cicatrize** *vb.*

cichlid *n.* a tropical spiny-finned freshwater fish that is commonly the subject of behavioral studies.

-cide *suffix* killer or killing (e.g., INFANTICIDE).

cigarette smoking a common form of substance abuse. See NICOTINE; NICOTINE DEPENDENCE; TOBACCO.

CIL abbreviation for Center for Independent Living. See INDEPENDENT LIVING.

cilia *pl. n.* see CILIUM.

ciliary body a part of the eye located behind the iris and consisting of the CILIARY PROCESSES and the CILIARY MUSCLES.

ciliary muscle smooth muscle in the CILIARY BODY of the eye that changes the shape of the lens to bring objects into focus on the retina. The ciliary muscle regulates the tension of the ZONULES, causing the lens to flatten (which lessens the power of the lens and allows focus of distant objects) or become more curved (which increases the power of the lens and allows focus of near objects). The action of the ciliary muscle is a large component of ACCOMMODATION.

ciliary processes the extensions of the CILIARY BODY that project into the posterior chamber of the eye. The ciliary processes are covered by epithelial cells that produce the AQUEOUS HUMOR and are connected by the ZONULES to the capsule of the lens.

cilium *n.* (*pl.* **cilia**) **1.** an eyelash. **2.** a hairlike extension of a cell, usually occurring in tufts or tracts, as in the stereocilia of HAIR CELLS in the cochlea of the inner ear. **—ciliary** *adj.*

Cinderella syndrome behavior in childhood based on the child's belief of being a "Cinderella," or a victim of parental rejection, neglect, or abuse.

cingulate gyrus a long strip of CEREBRAL CORTEX on the medial surface of each cerebral hemisphere. The cingulate gyrus arches over and generally outlines the location of the CORPUS CALLOSUM, from which it is separated by the CALLOSAL SULCUS. It is a component of the LIMBIC SYSTEM. Also called **callosal gyrus**; **cingulate cortex**; **gyrus cinguli**.

cingulate sulcus the fissure that separates the CINGULATE GYRUS from the superior frontal gyrus on the medial surface of each cerebral hemisphere.

cingulotomy *n.* a procedure used in the treatment of chronic pain in which electrodes are used to destroy portions of the CINGULUM BUNDLE. It is also, albeit rarely, used in the treatment of some chronic mental disorders (e.g., OBSESSIVE-COMPULSIVE DISORDER) that have not responded to other, nonsurgical forms of treatment. Also called **cingulumotomy**.

cingulum bundle a longitudinal tract of nerve fibers, lying beneath the CINGULATE GYRUS, that connects the FRONTAL LOBE with the PARAHIPPOCAMPAL GYRUS and adjacent regions in the TEMPORAL LOBE.

circadian dysrhythmia a disruption of the normal cycles of wakefulness and sleep. See CIRCADIAN RHYTHM SLEEP DISORDER.

circadian oscillator a neural circuit with an output that repeats about once per day. A circadian oscillator is located in the SUPRACHIASMATIC NUCLEUS of the hypothalamus and is thought to be important in sleep–wake cycles.

circadian rhythm any variation in physiological or behavioral activity that repeats at approximately 24-hour intervals, such as the SLEEP–WAKE CYCLE. Also called **diurnal rhythm**. See also BIOLOGICAL RHYTHM.

circadian rhythm sleep disorder in *DSM–IV–TR*, a sleep disorder that is due to a mismatch between the sleep–wake schedule required by a person's environment and his or her circadian sleep–wake pattern, resulting in excessive sleepiness or insomnia. In the **delayed sleep-phase type**, sleep onset and awakening times are later than is socially typical or appropriate and the person is unable to fall asleep and wake up at a desired earlier time. In the **jet-lag type**, which affects people who repeatedly travel across two or more time zones, sleepiness and alertness occur at times inappropriate to the local time (see JET LAG). In the **shift-work type**, sleep disruption is produced by recurrent changes in work shifts; it is characterized by insomnia during the major sleep period or excessive sleepiness during the major wake period. This disorder was formerly called **sleep–wake schedule disor-**

der. See DYSSOMNIA. See also DISORDERS OF THE SLEEP–WAKE CYCLE SCHEDULE.

circannual rhythm a BIOLOGICAL RHYTHM of behavior, growth, or some other physiological variable that recurs on a yearly basis.

circle of support a group of people who provide support for an individual. For a person with a developmental disability, the circle often includes family members, friends, acquaintances, coworkers, and sometimes service providers or coordinators, who meet on a regular basis and help the individual accomplish personal goals. These goals are selected based on extensive and recurrent review of the person's past and current preferences and interests; they are addressed one stage at a time.

circle of Willis see ARTERIAL CIRCLE.

circles of learning see SYNERGOGY.

circuit *n.* see NEURAL CIRCUIT.

circuit resistance training a series of different exercises set out in a specific order, with a specific time or number of repetitions for each exercise. The type and order of exercises will be set according to their use as rehabilitation—health-related exercise for individuals with spinal cord injuries, diabetes, obesity, and other conditions—or as fitness training for athletes.

circular argument see CIRCULAR REASONING.

circular behavior any action that stimulates a similar action in others, such as yawning or laughing. Also called **circular response**.

circular causality 1. a sequence of causes and effects that leads back to the original cause and either alters or confirms it, thus producing a new sequence, as in a FEEDBACK loop. **2.** a form of CIRCULAR REASONING in which the cause of some event is held to exist in or be implied by the event itself.

circular questioning a technique used in some methods of family therapy to yield information about the dynamics and relationships in a family. For example, one family member may be asked to answer a question about who in the family is most depressed; subsequent family members each respond to the same question. This method of questioning everyone in the "circle" is intended to elicit the various perspectives within the group.

circular reaction 1. any action that generates a response that provides the stimulation for repetition of the action, often such that responses increase in intensity and duration. An example is the contraction of a muscle that sends a nerve impulse toward the brain or spinal cord, which in turn sends a nerve impulse back to the muscle to maintain the contraction. Also called **circular reflex**. **2.** in Jean PIAGET's theory of cognitive development, repetitive behavior observed in children during the SENSORIMOTOR STAGE, characterized as primary, secondary, or tertiary circular reactions. The primary phase involves ineffective repetitive behaviors; the secondary phase involves repetition of actions that are followed by reinforcement, typically without understanding causation; and the tertiary phase involves repetitive object manipulation, typically with slight variations among subsequent behaviors.

circular reasoning a type of informal FALLACY in which a conclusion is reached that is not materially different from something that was assumed as a premise of the argument. In other words, the argument assumes what it is supposed to prove. Circular reasoning is sometimes difficult to detect because the premise and conclusion are not articulated in precisely the same terms, obscuring the fact that they are really the same proposition. See also BEGGING THE QUESTION; THEORY BEGGING.

circulating levels see BLOOD LEVELS.

circulatory system see CARDIOVASCULAR SYSTEM.

circumcision *n.* the surgical removal of the FORESKIN of the penis, typically for religious, cultural, or medical reasons. Circumcision is often performed in infancy but may be performed at any age. Compare CLITORIDECTOMY.

circumlocution *n.* **1.** a mode of speaking characterized by difficulty or inability in finding the right words to identify or explain an object that has been perceived and recognized. It involves the use of a variety of words or phrases that indirectly communicate the individual's meaning. Circumlocution can be a manifestation of AMNESTIC APHASIA caused by damage to the left posterior temporal lobe of the brain, but in some cases it is an indication of disorganized thought processes, as in schizophrenia. See CIRCUMSTANTIALITY. **2.** a style of speaking used consciously by healthy individuals to convey meaning indirectly, so that the meaning is inferred by the listener.

circumplex model of personality and emotion a type of model for determining the degree of similarity between personality traits and emotions by depicting in a circular form the relations and interactions between those traits and emotions. Elements adjacent to one another on the circle are highly similar (positively correlated); the similarity (and correlation) between elements declines as the distance between them on the circle increases. Certain elements may be completely unrelated to each other (a correlation of 0). Elements opposite each other on the circle are highly dissimilar (negatively correlated) and represent dimensional extremes (e.g., agreeableness versus contrariness, joy versus sorrow, pessimism versus optimism).

circumscribed amnesia see LOCALIZED AMNESIA.

circumscribed belief a narrowly defined delusional belief held by some people with paranoia or brain damage who otherwise seem to function entirely normally. For example, such people may believe they are being persecuted by the CIA, or be convinced that they are Jesus, or suspect that the interviewer has hidden hostility toward them. The delusional belief system is generally highly consistent and resistant to disproof and appears to function separately from other beliefs held by the same person.

circumstantial bilingualism see FOLK BILINGUALISM.

circumstantial evidence evidence from which the existence of a fact may be inferred but which does not constitute direct proof of that fact.

circumstantiality *n.* circuitous, indirect speech in which the individual digresses to give unnecessary and often irrelevant details before arriving at the main point. An extreme form, arising from disorganized associative processes, may occur in schizophrenia, obsessional disorders, and certain types of dementia. Circumstantiality differs from TANGENTIALITY in that the main point is never lost but rather accompanied by a large amount of nonessential information.

circumstriate cortex see PRESTRIATE CORTEX.

circumthanatology *n.* the study of NEAR-DEATH EXPERIENCES.

circumvallate papillae swellings on the posterior portion (back) of the tongue, each surrounded by a trench. In humans, there are 7–11 circumvallate papillae, arranged in a chevron; each papilla contains about 250 TASTE BUDS, lining the trench and oriented horizontally. Receptors in circumvallate papillae are particularly sensitive to bitter chemicals. See also PAPILLA.

circumventricular organs four small structures located along the third and fourth ventricles at the base of the brain, outside the BLOOD–BRAIN BARRIER, that are believed to influence body fluid HOMEOSTASIS, thirst, vomiting, and other physiological functions. Also called **circumventricular system**. See also AREA POSTREMA; ORGANUM VASCULOSUM OF THE LAMINA TERMINALIS; SUBCOMMISSURAL ORGAN; SUBFORNICAL ORGAN.

CIRCUS *n.* an achievement test battery with a circus theme developed by the EDUCATIONAL TESTING SERVICE to assess the knowledge and skills of students in preschool through third grade. It consists of 15 subtests across four grade levels (A–D) and three categories (basic measures, other measures, and measures for special purposes). Among the areas covered (at appropriate levels) are listening comprehension, reading comprehension, reading vocabulary, writing skills, mathematics concepts and computation, problem solving, perceptual-motor coordination, visual memory, and visual discrimination. In addition, two questionnaires are included to enable teachers to report on the children's classroom behavior and the educational background of their families. Originally developed in the 1970s, the CIRCUS is no longer available.

cirrhosis *n.* a liver disease marked by widespread formation of fibrous tissue and loss of normal liver function. In most cases, it is a consequence of chronic alcohol abuse, although it may also be due to congenital defects involving metabolic deficiencies, exposure to toxic chemicals, or infections (e.g., hepatitis). **—cirrhotic** *adj.*

CISD abbreviation for CRITICAL-INCIDENT STRESS DEBRIEFING.

cissa *n.* a craving for unusual foods or nonnutritive substances while pregnant. See also PICA.

cisterna *n.* (*pl.* **cisternae**) **1.** in anatomy, an enlarged space, such as the CISTERNA MAGNA in the brain. **2.** in cell biology, a flattened membranous sac within the GOLGI APPARATUS of a cell. **—cisternal** *adj.*

cisterna magna an enlarged space between the lower surface of the CEREBELLUM and the dorsal surface of the MEDULLA OBLONGATA, which serves as a reservoir of CEREBROSPINAL FLUID. Also called **cisterna cerebellomedullaris; posterior subarachnoidean space**.

cistern puncture see SUBOCCIPITAL PUNCTURE.

CIT abbreviation for CRITICAL-INCIDENT TECHNIQUE.

citalopram *n.* an antidepressant of the SSRI class. It exerts its action by blocking the presynaptic serotonin TRANSPORTER, preventing reabsorption of serotonin into the presynaptic neuron and thereby increasing levels of available serotonin in the SYNAPTIC CLEFT without increasing overall levels of serotonin in the brain. U.S. trade name: **Celexa**.

citation analysis a form of research that traces the history of citations of particular researchers in particular books, articles, or other sources.

citizen *n.* one who is a formal member of a particular political community, such as a country or state, and is therefore entitled to full CIVIL RIGHTS as defined, guaranteed, and protected by that political entity. **—citizenship** *n.*

cittosis *n.* an abnormal desire for unusual foods or nonnutritive substances. See CISSA; PICA.

civil commitment a legal procedure that permits a person who is not charged with criminal conduct to be certified as mentally ill and to be institutionalized involuntarily.

civil disobedience nonviolent opposition or protest, usually on the grounds of conscience, to a government or its policies that takes the form of refusing to obey certain laws or to pay taxes. See also PASSIVE RESISTANCE.

civil emergency a disastrous event, either natural or caused by human activities, that threatens civilian populations. Such emergencies often require the cooperative effort of both civilian and military authorities to provide civil defense and crisis and disaster management.

Civilian Health and Medical Program of the Uniformed Services (**CHAMPUS**) the medical insurer that since 1967 has provided and paid for health care to U.S. military retirees and families and surviving family members of deceased military sponsors. Many new benefits have been added since the program was first established. The current program is called TRICARE.

civilization *n.* **1.** a highly developed society, advanced in such areas as arts, sciences, technology, law, religion, and moral and social values. **2.** human society as a whole in its present highly advanced state of cultural, intellectual, and technical development. **3.** the process of attaining this level of development. **—civilized** *adj.*

civil rights the rights of personal liberty and equality guaranteed to citizens by law. Also called **civil liberties**.

civil rights movement any collective effort to gain political or social rights denied by government, usually by nonviolent means such as demonstrations, lobbying, and CIVIL DISOBEDIENCE. When capitalized the term usually refers to the struggle for full constitutional rights by African Americans as it originated and developed in the United States in the 1950s and 1960s.

CJD abbreviation for CREUTZFELDT–JAKOB DISEASE.

CK abbreviation for CREATINE KINASE.

CL abbreviation for COMPARISON LEVEL.

cladistics *n.* a method for classifying organisms on the basis of their evolutionary relationships, which are expressed in treelike diagrams called **cladograms**. **—cladism** *n.* **—cladist** *n.*

claims review an evaluation of the appropriateness of a claim for payment for a medical or mental health service rendered. It will consider whether the claimant is eligible for reimbursement, whether the charges are consistent with customary fees or published institutional rates, and whether the service was necessary.

clairaudience *n.* in parapsychology, the alleged ability to "hear" voices or sounds beyond the normal range of hearing, including supposed messages from spirit guides or the dead. It is the auditory equivalent of CLAIRVOYANCE. See also EXTRASENSORY PERCEPTION. **—clairaudient** *n., adj.*

clairvoyance *n.* in parapsychology, the alleged ability to "see" things beyond the normal range of sight, such as distant or hidden objects or events in the past or future. Compare CLAIRAUDIENCE. Also called **remote viewing**. See also EXTRASENSORY PERCEPTION; SECOND SIGHT. **—clairvoyant** *n., adj.*

clairvoyant dream in parapsychology, a dream that appears to be confirmed by later events or knowledge. See CLAIRVOYANCE; PREMONITORY DREAM.

CLAlt abbreviation for COMPARISON LEVEL FOR ALTERNATIVES.

clamminess *n.* a sensory blend that consists of coldness, moistness, and stickiness. **—clammy** *adj.*

clan *n.* **1.** in anthropology, a major social division of many traditional societies consisting of a group of families that claim common ancestry. Clans often prohibit marriage between members and are often associated with reverence for a particular TOTEM. See also DESCENT GROUP; PHRATRY; SEPT. **2.** in Scotland and Ireland, a former social unit based on traditional patterns of land tenure and the concept of loyalty to a clan chief. Clan members often took the name of the supposed clan founder prefaced by *Mac* (Scotland) or *O'* (Ireland) but were not necessarily linked by common ancestry.

clang association an association of words by similarity of sound rather than meaning. Clang association occurs as a pathological disturbance in manic states and schizophrenia. Also called **clanging**.

clarification *n.* a counselor's formulation, in clearer terms and without indicating approval or disapproval, of a client's statement or expression of feelings. Clarification goes further than restatement and REFLECTION OF FEELING but stops short of interpretation.

Clark, Kenneth Bancroft (1914–2005) U.S. psychologist. Clark received his PhD from Columbia University in 1940 and spent his career at City College in the City University of New York from 1946 through his retirement in 1975. He is best known for studies, jointly conducted with his wife Mamie Phipps Clark (1917–1983), on the relationship between self-esteem and skin color in children. This work was influential in the U.S. Supreme Court's 1954 ruling on *Brown v. the Board of Education*, in which the court banned racial segregation in public schools. Among Clark's most important published works are *Prejudice and Your Child* (1955) and *Dark Ghetto: Dilemmas of Social Power* (1965). Clark was the first African American to become president of the American Psychological Association (1971) and was the first recipient of APA's award for Distinguished Contributions to Psychology in the Public Interest (1959). See also CROSS-CULTURAL PSYCHOLOGY; RACE PSYCHOLOGY; SELF-ESTEEM.

class *n.* **1.** a group, category, or division. See CATEGORIZATION. **2.** in sociology and political theory, see SOCIAL CLASS. **3.** in BIOLOGICAL TAXONOMY, a main subdivision of a PHYLUM, consisting of a group of similar, related ORDERS. **4.** in logic and philosophy, a collection of entities that have a specified property or properties in common: that is, a SET defined by a condition.

class advocate see ADVOCATE.

class consciousness awareness of belonging to a particular economic or social group. Originally relating to the struggle of the oppressed and exploited working class, as enunciated most famously by German social theorist Karl Marx (1818–1883), the concept was extended in the late 20th century to include gender, race, and ethnic consciousness, with similar implications. Here the sense of "consciousness" derives from German philosophy and implies a social worldview (see WELTANSCHAUUNG) rather than an individual state.

classical *adj.* denoting a style, mode of operation, or function that was typical or standard at some time in the past. In psychology, it was applied to PAVLOVIAN CONDITIONING to contrast it with newly recognized OPERANT CONDITIONING when the distinction between the two forms of learning was pointed out by B. F. SKINNER in 1938.

classical conditioning see PAVLOVIAN CONDITIONING.

classical depression a MAJOR DEPRESSIVE EPISODE characterized by intense sadness, difficulty in concentrating, PSYCHOMOTOR RETARDATION, decreased appetite, insomnia, and weight loss, as well as psychotic features (i.e., delusions or hallucinations). It is often thought to be prototypical of DEPRESSIVE DISORDERS.

classical humors see HUMORAL THEORY.

classical paranoia as conceptualized in the 19th century by German physician Karl Ludwig Kahlbaum (1828–1899) and later refined by German psychiatrist Emil Kraepelin (1856–1926), a rare disorder characterized by elaborate, fixed, and systematic DELUSIONS, usually of a persecutory, grandiose, or jealous character, that develop insidiously, cannot be accounted for by any psychiatric disorder, and exist in the context of preserved logical and orderly thinking. The basic definition of DELUSIONAL DISORDER in *DSM–IV–TR* retains much of the original concept of Kahlbaum and Kraepelin.

classical psychoanalysis 1. psychoanalytic theory in which major emphasis is placed on the LIBIDO, the stages of PSYCHOSEXUAL DEVELOPMENT, and the ID instincts or drives. The prototypical theory of this kind is that of Sigmund FREUD. Also called **classical theory**; **drive theory**. **2.** psychoanalytic treatment that adheres to Sigmund Freud's basic procedures, using dream interpretation, free association, and analysis of RESISTANCE, and to his basic aim of developing insight into the patient's unconscious life as a way to restructure personality. Also called **orthodox psychoanalysis**.

classical test theory (**CTT**) a body of psychometric theory of measurement that partitions observed scores into two components—TRUE SCORES and ERROR SCORES—and estimates error variance by calculating INTERNAL CONSISTENCY reliability, RETEST RELIABILITY, and ALTERNATE-FORMS RELIABILITY. Among the key benefits of CTT—the principal framework for test development prior to the 1970s—are that it is relatively simple to execute and that it can be applied to a broad range of measurement situations. Among its major limitations are that examinee characteristics cannot be separated from test characteristics and that the measurement statistics derived from it are fundamentally concerned with how people perform on a given test as opposed to any single item on that test. These inherent limitations of CTT prompted the development of ITEM RESPONSE THEORY and other models that are not subject to these limitations, that more accurately detect BIAS, and that offer enhanced reliability assessment and increased precision in ability measurement.

classical theory see CLASSICAL PSYCHOANALYSIS.

classic categorical approach a method for classifying disorders founded on the assumption that there are clear-cut differences between disorders.

classicism factor the role of traditional values of artistic style, particularly those associated with the art and architecture of ancient Greece and Rome, in evaluation of any artistic endeavor. The classicism factor is also used to distinguish formal art forms from art forms that are influenced by imagination (the **romanticism factor**).

classification *n.* **1.** in cognitive psychology, see CATEGORIZATION. **2.** in clinical psychology and psychiatry, the grouping of mental disorders on the basis of their characteristics or symptoms. See also DSM–IV–TR; INTERNATIONAL CLASSIFICATION OF DISEASES; NOSOLOGY. **3.** in biology, see BIOLOGICAL TAXONOMY. **—classify** *vb.*

classification method in industrial and organizational psychology, a method of evaluating jobs for the purpose of setting wages or salaries in which jobs are assigned to predefined classes or categories, usually on the basis of job title and job description. This usually involves comparison with one or more BENCHMARK JOBS. An example of such a method is the **General Schedule** system of the United States Civil Service System. Compare FACTOR-COMPARISON METHOD; JOB-COMPONENT METHOD; POINT METHOD; RANKING METHOD. See JOB EVALUATION.

classification table a table (usually two-dimensional) in which the number of cases in a sample are arranged on the basis of their joint membership in the row and column classes of the table.

classification test 1. a test in which participants are required to sort objects, people, events, or stimuli into specific categories. See CATEGORIZATION. **2.** a test in which participants are themselves sorted into categories (e.g., of ability or psychological type) according to the responses given.

classifier system a COGNITIVE ARCHITECTURE consisting of a computational system in which knowledge, in the form of "if → then" classifier rules, is exposed to a reacting environment and as a result undergoes modification over time (learning). The entire system is evaluated over time, with the importance of the individual classifier seen as minimal. See ADAPTIVE PRODUCTION SYSTEM. [created in 1986 by computer scientist John Henry Holland (1929–)]

class inclusion the concept that a subordinate class (e.g., dogs) must always be smaller than the superordinate class in which it is contained (e.g., animals). Jean PIAGET believed that understanding the concept of class inclusion represented an important developmental step. Children progress from classifications based on personal factors, perceptual features, and common function to classifications based on hierarchical relationships; for example, a monkey is a primate, a mammal, and a vertebrate animal. See CONCRETE OPERATION.

class interval the range of scores or numerical values that constitute one segment or class in a frequency distribution; for example, weights might be grouped in class intervals of 5 kg each. Also called **class size**.

class limits the limits of a CLASS INTERVAL; that is, the lowest and uppermost values that define the boundaries of a particular interval or range. Also called **class range**.

classroom-behavior modification an instructor's use of basic learning techniques, such as conditioning, to alter the behavior of the students within a learning environment. Specifically, classroom behavior modification may utilize such methods as adjusting classroom seating, providing a flexible time deadline for assignments, or altering the lesson requirements. Direct intervention, however, is the most effective modification procedure, using cognitive-behavioral techniques to address inappropriate classroom behavior. Such procedures are most useful for students with learning disabilities, attention-deficit/hyperactivity disorder, and other special needs.

classroom discipline 1. traditionally, any form of compliance with discipline imposed on school pupils in class. **2.** the methods of correction used by teachers or schools for student behavior that does not comply with the rules and regulations that have been established for an optimal learning environment. **3.** any type of training expected to produce a specific pattern of behavior within a classroom. In some countries, classroom discipline now excludes physical punishment.

classroom environment the physical, social, psychological, and intellectual conditions that characterize an instructional setting. Although the physical environment usually includes typical classrooms, laboratories, and lecture halls, it may also include alternative locations, such as a museum, home, gymnasium, or even the outdoors. Regardless of the setting, the degree of enclosure or openness, noise, seating arrangements, DENSITY, and size have all been shown to have an effect on student behavior and learning. See also OPEN-CLASSROOM DESIGN.

classroom test a test devised by a teacher for use in class, as contrasted with a STANDARDIZED TEST.

class size see CLASS INTERVAL.

class structure the composition, organization, and interrelationship of SOCIAL CLASSES within a society. The term encompasses the makeup of individual classes as well as their economic, political, and other roles within the larger SOCIAL ORDER.

class theory 1. the notion that conflict between social and economic classes is a fundamental determining force in human affairs, affecting not only systems of government and social organization but also individual psychology. It is held that one's perceptions, goals, and expectations, and even one's conceptions of psychological health and illness, are heavily influenced by the class of which one is a member. Most modern manifestations of class theory trace their origins to German social theorist Karl Marx (1818–1883), although the work of the critical theorists of the Frankfurt school (1930s onward) has also been influential. See MARXISM. **2.** the branch of SET THEORY that is concerned with the properties of CLASSES. It is particularly interested in defining the distinction between classes and sets that are not classes.

claudication *n.* **1.** limping. **2.** a cramping pain in the muscles (intermittent claudication), occurring especially in the calf muscles. See also MENTAL CLAUDICATION.

clause *n.* a linguistic unit smaller than a sentence but larger than a PHRASE; in traditional grammar, a clause is defined as having both a subject and a finite verb (i.e., one that agrees with the subject in number and person). Clauses are usually divided into two principal types: **main clauses**, which make sense by themselves and can constitute a sentence in their own right, and **subordinate clauses**, which are dependent on a main clause in both these respects. In *I smiled at Jane, who waved back,* for example, the words before the comma constitute a main clause and those after the comma are a subordinate clause. In psycholinguistics, clauses are considered to be an important unit of sentence processing. Sentences that are complex from a syntactic point of view, in that they contain one or more subordinate clauses, are also considered psychologically more complex. See COMPLEX SENTENCE; COORDINATION. **—clausal** *adj.*

claustrophobia *n.* a persistent and irrational fear of enclosed places (e.g., elevators, small rooms, tunnels, the backseat of a small car) or of being confined or unable to escape (e.g., in a dentist's chair, a crowd, or the middle of an aisle). The focus of fear is typically on panic symptoms triggered in these situations (e.g., feelings of being unable to breathe, choking, palpitations, sweating, depersonalization, fears of losing control or going crazy). In *DSM–IV–TR,* claustrophobia is classified as a SPECIFIC PHOBIA, situational type. When a wide range of situations is feared, a diagnosis of AGORAPHOBIA may be more appropriate. **—claustrophobic** *adj.*

claustrum *n.* (*pl.* **claustra**) a thin layer of gray matter in the brain that separates the white matter of the LENTICULAR NUCLEUS from the INSULA. It forms part of the BASAL GANGLIA and its function is unknown. (Latin, "barrier") **—claustral** *adj.*

clavus *n.* a sharp sensation as if a nail were being driven into the head.

clay therapy a form of therapy in which children manipulate clay, often used in physical rehabilitation, in stimulating individuals with mental retardation, and in the assessment and treatment of various disorders. The clay can be a metaphor for feelings, yet at the same time it serves as a tangible item that is visible, changeable, and under the child's control. A child can look at the clay, focus on it, manipulate it, squeeze it, and pound it, which can help reduce anxiety, enable the acting out of hostile emotions, and provide opportunities for gratification, achievement, and acceptance.

clean *adj.* denoting data from which errors of observation, recording, and computation have been eliminated or reduced.

clearance (**CL**) *n.* the rate of elimination of a drug from the body in relation to its concentration in a body fluid, as expressed by the equation CL = rate of elimination/C, where C is the concentration of the drug in the body fluid. Clearance is additive, that is, drugs are eliminated by various mechanisms (renal, hepatic, etc.) at differing rates; thus, total clearance is the sum of clearance from each individual organ system.

clearance requirement 1. in the design of security systems, the requirement that only specifically authorized personnel should have access to certain physical areas or types of information. **2.** in SAFETY ENGINEERING, a mandate or guideline specifying the minimal distance or elevation of objects from a potentially hazardous source.

clear sensorium see SENSORIUM.

cleavage *n.* the first stage of embryonic development, in which a fertilized ovum divides repeatedly to form a mass of smaller and smaller cells (see BLASTULA). Also called **segmentation**.

cleft palate a congenital disorder characterized by a fissure in the roof of the mouth caused by failure of bones of the palate to fuse properly during prenatal development. The extent of a cleft palate may vary in different individuals, affecting only the hard palate, both hard and soft palates, or extending completely through to the uvula; a **cleft lip** may or may not co-occur. The condition is typically corrected through surgery between 9 and 18 months of age, and repeated surgeries during childhood may be necessary to complete correction. Also called **uranoschisis**.

CLEP acronym for COLLEGE LEVEL EXAMINATION PROGRAM.

Clérambault's syndrome a form of EROTIC PARANOIA in which a person has EROTIC DELUSIONS that someone else, who is typically older and of higher social status, is in love with him or her. The person continues to hold this belief despite having little contact with the other person and no reciprocation of feelings. The condition is more common in females than in males. Also called **de Clérambault's syndrome**. [first described in 1922 by Gaëtan Gatian de **Clérambault** (1872–1934), French physician]

clerical aptitude 1. the ability to learn specific skills required for office work, such as perceptual speed (e.g., comparing names or numbers), speed in typing, learning shorthand, alphabetizing, error location, and vocabulary. **2.** the measure of individual abilities in the following areas: vocabulary (understanding words and ideas), arithmetic (handling figures easily and accurately), and checking (recognizing similarities and differences rapidly).

clerical test an examination to assess a person's knowledge or skills needed for office, clerical, or administrative support positions. Also called **clerical-aptitude test**.

CLES abbreviation for CONSTRUCTIVIST LEARNING ENVIRONMENT SURVEY.

Clever Hans the "thinking horse," reputed to be able to solve mathematical problems, spell words, distinguish colors, and identify coins, that became famous in Berlin around 1900. It signaled its answers by tapping its foot. However, German psychologist Oskar Pfungst (1874–1932), using experimental methods, demonstrated that the horse was responding to minimal cues in the form of involuntary movements on the part of its owner.

click thru rate the extent to which consumers actually click on BANNER ADVERTISEMENTS and go to a different website. This is viewed as one measure of banner advertising success.

client *n.* a person receiving treatment or services, especially in the context of counseling or social work. See PATIENT–CLIENT ISSUE.

client abuse harm to clients caused by therapists and counselors who exploit their clients' vulnerability and their own position of influence and trust to engage in inappropriate, unprofessional behavior. Client abuse, which sometimes takes the form of sexual involvement with a client, is usually grounds for legal and professional action against the practitioner. See also PROFESSIONAL ETHICS; PROFESSIONAL STANDARDS.

client-centered therapy a nondirective form of psychotherapy developed by Carl ROGERS in the early 1940s. According to Rogers, an orderly process of client self-discovery and actualization occurs in response to the therapist's consistent empathic understanding of, acceptance of, and respect for the client's FRAME OF REFERENCE. The therapist sets the stage for personality growth by reflecting and clarifying the ideas of the client, who is able to see himself or herself more clearly and come into closer touch with his or her real self. As therapy progresses, the client resolves conflicts, reorganizes values and approaches to life, and learns how to interpret his or her thoughts and feelings, consequently changing behavior that he or she considers problematic. It was originally known as **nondirective counseling** or **nondirective therapy**. Also called **client-centered psychotherapy**; **person-centered psychotherapy**; **Rogerian therapy**.

client characteristics aspects of a client that define his or her physical and personality attributes as well as the problems and symptoms that the client brings into therapy for resolution and healing.

client education interventions aimed at giving clients information intended to change their cognitions, beliefs, affect, and behaviors. This educational process can take place in formal groups (psychoeducational groups) or as a routine part of initiating psychotherapy.

client obligations see CONTRACT.

client–patient issue see PATIENT–CLIENT ISSUE.

client rights the rights of patients or clients to be fully informed of the benefits or risks of treatment procedures and to make informed decisions to accept or reject treatment.

client satisfaction the extent to which a person seeking mental health services is content with the results.

client self-monitoring see SELF-MONITORING.

client–treatment matching the selection of therapies and psychotherapists most appropriate for the clients' needs and characteristics (e.g., ethnicity, gender, personality traits). Client–treatment matching is assumed to enhance therapeutic outcomes.

climacteric *n.* the biological stage of life in which reproductive capacity declines and finally ceases. In women this period, which results from changes in the levels of estrogens and progesterone and is known as **menopause** (popularly, **change of life**), occurs between 40 and 55 years of age and lasts 2–3 years. During this time, menstrual flow gradually decreases and finally ceases altogether, and such symptoms as hot flashes, chills, mood swings, body aches and throbbing, fatigue, joint pains, and depression may occur in varying combinations and degrees. Some men undergo a similar period about 10 years later than is typical for women (see MALE CLIMACTERIC). See also GONADOPAUSE.

climate *n.* environmental conditions such as temperature, humidity, hours of daylight, and sunshine, all of which can influence mood and feelings. Temperature has a complex relationship with performance and can also influence social behaviors, such as aggression (see COLD EFFECTS; HEAT EFFECTS). **—climatic** *adj.*

climax *n.* see ORGASM.

clinging behavior a form of ATTACHMENT BEHAVIOR in which a child of 6 months or older clings to the primary caregiver and becomes acutely distressed when left alone. Clinging behavior reaches a maximum in the 2nd and 3rd years and then slowly subsides. The behavior is also observed in the young of other primates and of some rodents.

clinic *n.* **1.** a health care facility for the diagnosis and treatment of emergency and ambulatory patients. **2.** a brief instructional program or session with diagnostic, therapeutic, or remedial purpose in the areas of mental or physical health or education.

clinical *adj.* **1.** of or relating to the diagnosis and treatment of psychological, medical, or other disorders. Originally involving only direct observation of patients, clinical methods have now broadened to take into account biological and statistical factors in treating patients and diagnosing disorders. **2.** relating to or occurring in a clinic.

clinical assessment the systematic evaluation and measurement of psychological, biological, and social factors in a person presenting with a possible psychological disorder. See also DYNAMIC ASSESSMENT.

clinical counseling counseling that addresses a client's personal or emotional difficulties. The counseling encompasses general goals for the client, for example, greater self-acceptance, better reality orientation, improved decision-making ability, and greater effectiveness in interpersonal relationships. The counselor's responsibilities include gathering and interpretating data, identifying the client's major problems, and formulating and (sometimes) implementing a treatment plan.

clinical diagnosis the diagnosis of possible mental disorder through the study of the symptom pattern, investigation of background factors, analysis of significant relationships, and, where indicated, administration of psychological tests.

clinical efficacy the effectiveness of clinical interventions based on the evidence of controlled studies. Such studies typically include random assignment to control groups and treatment manuals that guide therapist actions.

clinical evidence information about clients or patients that is relevant to clinical diagnosis and therapy, obtained either directly, through questioning (see CLINICAL INTERVIEW), or indirectly, through observation of their behavior in a clinical setting, their CASE HISTORIES, and the like.

clinical grouping the classification of patients into groups according to their behavioral symptoms.

clinical health psychology a specialty field in HEALTH PSYCHOLOGY that applies biopsychosocial theory, research, and practice principles to promote physical health and to help resolve the immediate problems of patients with medical conditions and related family difficulties. Biofeedback, relaxation training, hypnotherapy, and coping skills are among the many methods used by **clinical health psychologists**, who are also active in health policy and in developing and implementing models of preventive intervention.

clinical interview a meeting between a patient or client and an interviewer, such as a clinical psychologist or a psychiatrist, for the purpose of obtaining relevant information. See CLINICAL EVIDENCE.

clinical investigation 1. examination of an individual by means of interviews, testing, behavioral observation, or document analysis. **2.** an in-depth analysis of an individual's life experiences and personal history.

clinical judgment analysis, evaluation, or prediction of disordered behavior, symptoms, or other aspects of psychological functioning. It includes assessing the appropriateness of particular treatments and the degree or likelihood of clinical improvement. These conclusions are derived from the expert knowledge of mental health professionals, as opposed to conclusions drawn from actuarial tables or statistical methods.

clinical judgment research empirical studies of the factors influencing the judgments mental health practitioners make with regard to assessment, treatment, predictions (e.g., dangerousness, suicidality), and prognosis in therapeutic and legal settings. Factors researched include individual differences of the practitioner (e.g., values, gender, sexual orientation), social contexts, and complex cognitive thought processes involved in judgment.

clinical marker an observable sign that is noteworthy as an indicator of a psychological disorder or as a predictor of an upcoming event of special interest. For example, sighing could be a clinical marker for the presence of anxiety.

clinical method 1. the process by which a clinical psychologist, psychiatrist, or other mental health or medical professional arrives at a conclusion, judgment, or diagnosis about a client or patient in a clinical situation. **2.** the process of collecting data in a natural situation (e.g., home, office, school) rather than in the formal setting of a laboratory.

clinical neurology see NEUROLOGY.

clinical neuropsychology an applied specialty in NEUROPSYCHOLOGY that comprises neuropsychological assessment and rehabilitation, which are critical in cases of neuropsychological injury that results in a range of impairments that disrupt an individual's abilities to function.

clinical practice guidelines systematically developed statements to assist providers, as well as clients or patients, in making decisions about appropriate medical or mental health care for specific clinical conditions.

clinical prediction the process of matching such factors as signs and symptoms with personality profiles and case history to determine the CLINICAL DIAGNOSIS and likely progress of patients. Clinical prediction can be contrasted with statistical prediction, in which formal statistical methods combine numerical information for the same purposes. See CLINICAL JUDGMENT.

clinical psychology the branch of psychology that specializes in the research, assessment, diagnosis, evaluation, prevention, and treatment of emotional and behavioral disorders. The **clinical psychologist** is a doctorate-level professional who has received training in research methods and techniques for the diagnosis and treatment of various psychological disorders (see also PSYCHOLOGIST). Clinical psychologists work primarily in health and mental health clinics, in research, or in group and independent practices. They also serve as consultants to other professionals in the medical, legal, social-work, and community-relations fields. Clinical psychologists comprise approximately one third of the psychologists working in the United States and are governed by the code of practice of the American Psychological Association.

clinical psychopharmacology a branch of pharmacology concerned with how drugs affect the brain and behavior and specifically with the clinical evaluation and management of drugs developed for the treatment of mental disorders. See also PSYCHOPHARMACOTHERAPY.

clinical risk assessment a clinician-based prediction of the likelihood that an individual will pose a threat to others or engage in a certain behavior (e.g., violence) within a given period. Unlike ACTUARIAL RISK ASSESSMENT, a specific formula or weighting system using empirically derived predictors is not applied. Instead, clinicians make predictions of dangerousness or violent behavior based primarily on their own experience, reasoning, and judgment; their observations, examination, and psychological testing of the client; and information obtained from client life histories.

clinical social worker a person who has been educated and trained to provide individual, family, and group treatment from a psychosocial perspective in such areas as health, mental health, family and child welfare, and correction. Clinical social workers have a graduate degree in social work and two years of postgraduate supervised clinical experience in an agency or other organized setting. They are trained additionally in client-centered advocacy that assists clients with information, referral, and in dealing with local, state, and federal agencies. Credentials of clinical social workers include Qualified Clinical Social Worker (QCSW), Board Certified Diplomat in Clinical Social Work (BCD), and Licensed Clinical Social Worker (LCSW).

clinical sociology a multidisciplinary, practice-oriented specialization in the field of sociology that seeks to effect social change through analysis, applied sociological theory, and problem-focused intervention.

clinical sport psychologist a person educated and trained in clinical psychology who works with individuals involved in sport. Clinical sport psychologists perform much the same services for athletes as do EDUCATIONAL SPORT PSYCHOLOGISTS (i.e., helping with performance enhancement and consistency), but they also assist athletes with clinical issues that are beyond the training of educational sport psychologists (e.g., depression, eating disorders).

clinical study an in-depth psychological, medical, or psychiatric study of an individual or group, using such techniques as diagnostic observation, psychiatric examination, psychological testing, depth interviewing, questionnaires, and the taking of a detailed case history.

clinical teaching a method of instruction designed to meet the needs of a particular, and usually atypical, child.

clinical test a test or measurement made in a clinical or research context for the purpose of diagnosis or treatment of a disorder.

clinical trial a research study designed to compare a new treatment or drug with an existing standard of care or other control condition (see CONTROL GROUP). Trials are generally designed to answer scientific questions and to find better ways to treat individuals who have a specific disease or disorder.

clinical type an individual whose pattern of symptoms or behaviors is consistent with a recognizable disorder of clinical psychology and psychiatry.

clinical utility the extent to which clinical interventions can be applied successfully and cost-effectively in real clinical settings. It is one of a proposed set of guidelines for evaluating clinical interventions.

clinical validation the act of acquiring evidence to support the accuracy of a theory by studying multiple cases with specific procedures for diagnosis or treatment.

clinician *n.* a medical or mental health care professional who is directly involved in the care and treatment of patients, as distinguished from one working in other areas, such as research or administration.

clinodactyly *n.* a permanent deflection of one or more of the fingers. This is a rather common physical trait associated with genetic or chromosomal disorders that also may be related to mental retardation.

clipping *n.* the shortening of a word in such a way that the new word is used with exactly the same meaning, for example, *exam* from *examination*. In general, adults prefer **back-clipping**, for example, *prof* for *professor*, while children prefer **front-clipping**, for example, *fessor* for *professor*. Unlike a BACK-FORMATION, the clipped word has the same part of speech as the full form.

clique *n.* a status- or friendship-based subgroup within a larger group or organization. Cliques are particularly common during adolescence, when they are often used to raise social standing, strengthen friendship ties, and reduce feelings of isolation and exclusion.

clitoral hood a fold of skin that covers the clitoris when it is flaccid. It is homologous to the FORESKIN of the penis. See also PREPUCE.

clitoridectomy *n.* the surgical removal of all or part of the clitoris. This highly controversial practice is performed predominantly in Africa, Asia, and the Middle East, typically for cultural or religious reasons, such as for purported curbing of sexual desire, preventing premarital sex, enhancing aesthetic appeal, or as part of an initiation. It is the most widely practiced of the procedures known as **female circumcision**, or FEMALE GENITAL MUTILATION. Compare CIRCUMCISION.

clitoris *n.* a small body of erectile tissue situated anterior to the vaginal opening. It is homologous to the penis but usually much smaller. —**clitoral** *adj.*

cloaca *n.* **1.** the common cavity, occurring in early mammalian embryos, into which the intestinal, urinary, and reproductive canals open. The proximity of these functions and the pleasure involved in them are a major factor in Sigmund FREUD's psychosexual theory. **2.** in nonmammalian vertebrates, the cavity through which sperm are discharged in the male, and eggs are laid in the female, and through which wastes are eliminated. [Latin, literally: "sewer, drain"] —**cloacal** *adj.*

cloacal theory a theory, sometimes held by young children, that combines the vagina and the anus into a single orifice and includes the belief that birth takes place through the anus and is a form of defecation. See PRIMAL FANTASY.

clomipramine *n.* a TRICYCLIC ANTIDEPRESSANT drug used for the treatment of obsessive-compulsive disorder (OCD) as well as depression and panic disorder. Clomipramine is a more potent inhibitor of serotonin reuptake than other tricyclic antidepressants, and its active metabolite inhibits norepinephrine reuptake; it thus is classified as a mixed serotonin–norepinephrine reuptake inhibitor. Because of its tricyclic structure, it has the same adverse side effects and toxicity as other tricyclic antidepressants, and it has been largely supplanted by the SSRIS, one of which—FLUVOXAMINE—is also used for the treatment of OCD. U.S. trade name: **Anafranil**.

clonazepam *n.* a highly potent BENZODIAZEPINE originally developed to treat absence seizures but now used for the treatment of panic disorder and other anxiety disorders and as a MOOD STABILIZER. Because it has a slow onset of action, long HALF-LIFE, and slow rate of CLEARANCE, it needs to be taken less frequently (twice a day) than some other benzodiazepines. U.S. trade name: **Klonopin**.

clone 1. *n.* an organism that is genetically identical to another. This may be because both organisms originate naturally from a single common parent as a result of ASEXUAL reproduction or because one is derived from genetic material taken from the other, by reproductive CLONING. Any observable differences in characters between cloned individuals are assumed to be the result of environmental factors. **2.** *n.* a group of genetically identical organisms. **3.** *n.* a group of cells derived from a single parent cell. **4.** *vb.* to produce genetically identical copies of a particular organism or cell. See CLONING. **—clonal** *adj.*

clonic *adj.* of, relating to, or characterized by CLONUS.

clonic phase see TONIC–CLONIC SEIZURE.

clonic spasm see SPASM.

clonidine *n.* a drug used for the treatment of hypertension. It functions by direct stimulation of ALPHA ADRENORECEPTORS in the brainstem to restrict the flow of impulses in peripheral sympathetic nerves supplying the arteries, thus causing them to relax (widen); most of the other commonly prescribed antihypertensive drugs act as beta blockers or as diuretics. Clonidine has been used as an adjunctive agent in the management of alcohol and opioid withdrawal, as a nonstimulant treatment for attention-deficit/hyperactivity disorder, and in the management of clozapine-induced sialorrhea (i.e., drooling). It has also been tried in patients with bipolar disorder resistant to other drug treatments, but with limited effectiveness. U.S. trade name (among others): **Catapres**.

cloning *n.* **1.** the process of making copies of a specific piece of DNA, usually a gene. This uses the techniques of GENETIC ENGINEERING to isolate the desired gene and transfer it to a suitable host cell, such as a bacterium, inside which it will undergo replication. Cloning facilitates investigation of gene structure and function and enables identification and analysis of particular gene products. Also called **gene cloning**. **2.** the process of making genetically identical copies of an entire organism. The potential cloning of human beings raises major ethical and social questions.

clonus *n.* a type of involuntary movement caused by a rapid succession of alternate muscular contractions and relaxations. Although some forms of clonus, such as hiccups, are considered normal, most such movements are abnormal; for example, clonus occurs as part of a TONIC–CLONIC SEIZURE. More severe forms are associated with spinal cord damage, poisoning (e.g., from strychnine), or an infection (e.g., syphilis).

Clopixol *n.* a trade name for ZUCLOPENTHIXOL.

clorazepate *n.* a long-acting BENZODIAZEPINE used in the treatment of anxiety, alcohol withdrawal, and PARTIAL SEIZURES. U.S. trade name (among others): **Tranxene**.

close-captioned television television programs supplemented with printed captions, usually placed at the bottom of the screen, that provide a visual representation of the speech on the audio channel. Close captioning is used for the benefit of viewers with hearing loss.

closed adoption a form of adoption that does not allow either pre- or postplacement contact between a child's birth family and adoptive family. Compare OPEN ADOPTION.

closed call system a system of vocal communication in which there is a limited number of vocalizations that can be used by an organism or where the vocalizations are not modifiable after a certain age. For example, in some bird species there is little evidence of environmentally induced change in calls after hatching, and in others there is little or no change in vocalizations after a CRITICAL PERIOD for learning has ended. Compare OPEN CALL SYSTEM.

closed-circuit television system (**CCTV system**) a type of PRINT ENLARGEMENT SYSTEM for individuals with LOW VISION that uses a video camera to magnify and project printed or handwritten text onto a video monitor or television screen.

closed-class words in a language, a category of words that does not readily admit new members, consisting mainly of words that serve key grammatical functions, such as pronouns, prepositions, and determiners (see FUNCTION WORD). Compare OPEN-CLASS WORDS.

closed economy an experimental design used in instrumental- or operant-conditioning procedures in which all arranged reinforcement (e.g., food) is obtained within experimental tests, with no supplements occurring outside the experimental context. Compare OPEN ECONOMY.

closed-ended question a question that provides respondents with alternative answers from which to select their response. Also called **fixed-alternative question**; **multiple-choice question**. Compare OPEN-ENDED QUESTION.

closed group a counseling or therapy group consisting of only those members who constituted the original group. New members may not join during the course of therapy. Compare OPEN GROUP.

closed head injury a head injury, such as a concussion, in which the head strikes against an object but the skull is not broken open or pierced. Compare OPEN HEAD INJURY.

closed-loop system 1. a system that recirculates materials, information, or energy without external input. **2.** a self-regulating system in which FEEDBACK from sensors enables a control mechanism to maintain a set of operating conditions. An example would be a central heating or air-conditioning system that is set to maintain an environment at a particular temperature. Compare OPEN-LOOP SYSTEM.

closed marriage a marriage that changes little over the years and that involves relatively little change in the individual partners. A closed marriage relies on the legal bond between the parties to enforce permanence and sexual exclusivity. Also called **static marriage**. Compare OPEN MARRIAGE.

closedmindedness *n.* see DOGMATISM.

closed scenario an experiment in which the participant is required to choose between a limited number of options for solving an assigned problem.

closed shop a work arrangement in which union membership is a precondition for hiring. The LABOR MANAGEMENT RELATIONS ACT prohibits such a precondition but does allow UNION SHOPS and AGENCY SHOPS. Compare OPEN SHOP.

closed skills motor skills that are performed under the same conditions on every occasion, as in making a free-throw shot in a game of basketball. Compare OPEN SKILLS.

closed society see OPEN SOCIETY.

closed system **1.** an isolated system having no contact with the environment. **2.** a self-contained system, such as the blood vascular system or a space module. **3.** by analogy, a social system that is resistant to new information or change. Compare OPEN SYSTEM.

closesightedness *n.* see MYOPIA.

closet homosexual a gay man or lesbian who does not reveal his or her sexual orientation to others, particularly to family members, parents, or employers. Compare COMING OUT.

closing *n.* ending a session in psychotherapy or counseling. Approaches to closing vary among therapists: Some allow the client to initiate the end of the session; others initiate it themselves.

closure *n.* **1.** the act, achievement, or sense of completing or resolving something. In psychotherapy, for example, a client achieves closure with the recognition that he or she has reached a resolution to a particular psychological issue or relationship problem. **2.** in GESTALT PSYCHOLOGY, the principle that people tend to perceive incomplete forms (e.g., images, sounds) as complete, synthesizing the missing units so as to perceive the image or sound as a whole—in effect closing the gap between the incomplete and complete forms. Also called **law of closure**; **principle of closure**. See also AUDITORY CLOSURE; GOODNESS OF CONFIGURATION; PRINCIPLE OF PRÄGNANZ; VISUAL CLOSURE. **3.** more generally, the act of closing or the state of being closed.

clouded sensorium see SENSORIUM.

clouding of consciousness a mental state involving a reduced awareness of the environment, inability to concentrate, and confusion. Also called **mental fog**.

cloverleaf skull see KLEEBLATTSCHÄDEL SYNDROME.

clozapine *n.* an ATYPICAL ANTIPSYCHOTIC agent of the DIBENZODIAZEPINE class: the first of the atypical antipsychotics to be used clinically and released into the U.S. market in 1990. Although regarded by some as the most effective of all antipsychotic drugs, clozapine has problematic side effects that have limited its use. Among others, these adverse effects may include weight gain, sedation, and—importantly—AGRANULOCYTOSIS, which may occur in 1–2% of patients treated with the drug. Use of clozapine therefore requires frequent monitoring of white blood cell counts in patients and is generally reserved for patients who have responded suboptimally to other antipsychotic agents. U.S. trade name: **Clorazil**.

cloze procedure a technique used in both testing and teaching reading and comprehension, in which words are deleted from a text, leaving blank spaces. The number of blanks that students fill in correctly is used as a measure of progress in these subjects. The cloze procedure is based on the Gestalt principle of CLOSURE.

club drugs substances used by teenagers and young adults at bars, dance clubs, or all-night parties known as "raves." Such substances include MDMA (Ecstasy); GHB and FLUNITRAZEPAM (see also DATE-RAPE DRUG); KETAMINE; METHAMPHETAMINE; and LSD. Chronic abuse can have severe physiological or psychological repercussions (or both) and, when combined with the intake of alcohol, might also prove fatal.

clubfoot *n.* a type of deformity in which the foot is twisted out of normal position, resulting—in most cases—in more than one positional distortion (e.g., the foot may be turned inward and downward, outward and upward, or in some other variation). The cause may be congenital, or the condition may be due to injury or a disease, such as poliomyelitis. Clubfoot often is associated with another anomaly, such as MENINGOMYELOCELE. Also called **talipes**.

clumsy automation in ergonomics, any reallocation of system functions from humans to machines that does not lead to the expected gains in safety and efficiency. This is usually because automation alters the human operator's task, resulting in increased workload or UNDERLOAD. Similarly, machine functions may be misallocated to humans. See also ADAPTIVE TASK ALLOCATION; FUNCTION ALLOCATION. [defined in 1989 by U.S. management scientist Earl Wiener (1949–)]

clumsy child syndrome an outdated and pejorative name for DEVELOPMENTAL DYSPRAXIA or DEVELOPMENTAL COORDINATION DISORDER.

cluster analysis a method of data analysis in which individuals (cases) are grouped together into clusters based on a criterion of being close to each other and distant from other cases in the multidimensional space defined by the variables entered into the analysis.

clustered random sample a random sample of groups of individuals, rather than of single individuals. See CLUSTER SAMPLING.

cluster evaluation **1.** a type of PROGRAM EVALUATION, either a FORMATIVE EVALUATION or a SUMMATIVE EVALUATION, carried out at several sites. Each site has the same EVALUATION OBJECTIVES, which are assessed in a coordinated effort by different evaluators in a continuous process. Information so obtained is then shared to enable common PROGRAM OUTCOMES to be assessed and to identify elements that contributed to the failures or successes of the program. **2.** a strategy for accumulating information in evaluation research that involves combining and reconciling studies with somewhat different conclusions. This approach suggests criteria for determining when data from dissimilar studies can be pooled. **3.** an approach in which individual evaluators in separate projects collaborate with an overarching evaluator. See also METAEVALUATION.

cluster headache a headache, typically limited to the area around one eye, that lasts between 15 min and 3 hr and occurs in bouts, or "clusters," every day (sometimes twice or more a day or every other day) for a period of up to 3 months, followed by a headache-free period of months or years.

clustering *n.* **1.** the tendency for items to be consistently grouped together in the course of recall. This grouping typically occurs for related items. It is readily apparent in memory tasks in which items from the same category, such as animals, are recalled together. **2.** in statistics, the process by which a CLUSTER ANALYSIS is conducted. **3.** in ergonomics, a method of KNOWLEDGE

ELICITATION in which a researcher interviewing users of a product or system jots down key ideas or words as they occur and then groups together linked ideas and meanings. The clusters so formed are then used to create taxonomies, task hierarchies, or menu structures. **—cluster** *n., vb.*

cluster sampling a survey sampling method in which the complete population is first subdivided into groups, or clusters, and random samples are then drawn from certain clusters. A common example would be sampling voters in a large jurisdiction (e.g., a state) by identifying clusters on the basis of close geographical proximity (e.g., counties) and then drawing samples from the county clusters (e.g., towns and cities). Such procedures are more economical, enabling participants to be contacted at a lower cost per person than if dispersed individuals were sampled. See CLUSTERED RANDOM SAMPLE.

cluster suicides a statistically high occurrence of suicides within a circumscribed geographic area, social group, or time period. Such clusters typically occur among adolescents who imitate the suicide of a high-status peer or among dispersed individuals, all exposed to the same or similar media coverage, who imitate the suicide of a widely admired role model (see WERTHER SYNDROME). Compare MASS SUICIDE.

cluttering *n.* rapid speech that is confused, jumbled, and imprecise, often occurring during a MANIC EPISODE.

CM abbreviation for COCHLEAR MICROPHONIC.

CMAS abbreviation for CHILDREN'S MANIFEST ANXIETY SCALE.

CME abbreviation for CONTINUING MEDICAL EDUCATION.

CMHC abbreviation for COMMUNITY MENTAL HEALTH CENTER.

CMI abbreviation for CORNELL MEDICAL INDEX.

CMP abbreviation for CHRONIC MYOFASCIAL PAIN.

CMS abbreviation for CENTERS FOR MEDICARE AND MEDICAID SERVICES.

CNS abbreviation for CENTRAL NERVOUS SYSTEM.

CNS abnormality any defect in structure or function of the tissues of the brain and spinal cord, that is, the central nervous system (CNS).

CNS depressants a group of drugs that, at low doses, depress the inhibitory centers of the brain. At somewhat higher doses, they depress other neural functions, slow reaction times, and lower respiration and heart rate. At still higher doses, they can induce unconsciousness, coma, and death. Examples of CNS depressants are ALCOHOL, BARBITURATES, BENZODIAZEPINES, INHALANTS, and MEPROBAMATE. See also SEDATIVE, HYPNOTIC, AND ANXIOLYTIC DRUGS.

CNS stimulants a group of drugs that, at low to moderate doses, heighten wakefulness and alertness, diminish fatigue, and provoke feelings of energy and well-being. At higher doses, the more powerful stimulants can produce agitation, panic excitement, hallucinations, and paranoia. In general, stimulants exert their effects by enhancing CATECHOLAMINE neurotransmission and increasing activity in the SYMPATHETIC NERVOUS SYSTEM. COCAINE and the AMPHETAMINES are examples of stimulants thought to activate the reward system (nucleus accumbens, limbic, and frontal cortex) by potentiating dopaminergic neurotransmission. CAFFEINE and NICOTINE are CNS stimulants with different mechanisms of action at ADENOSINE receptors and NICOTINIC RECEPTORS, respectively. In non-Western cultures, BETEL NUT, COCA leaves, GUARANA, KHAT, and numerous other substances are used as stimulants. Some stimulants are used clinically in mental health, and in psychiatric contexts are often referred to as **psychostimulants**. These drugs include the amphetamines and related or similarly acting compounds (e.g., METHYLPHENIDATE, PEMOLINE, MODAFINIL), used for the treatment of attention-deficit/hyperactivity disorder, narcolepsy, depression, and organic brain syndromes and as appetite suppressants. Caffeine and ephedrine are ingredients of over-the-counter "alertness" medications.

CNS vasodilation dilation of cerebral blood vessels leading to increased cerebral blood flow. It can be caused by various agents, such as nitrous oxide.

CNV abbreviation for CONTINGENT NEGATIVE VARIATION.

Co abbreviation for COMPARISON STIMULUS.

coaching *n.* **1.** a form of teaching and encouragement (one-to-one or coach-to-group) based on counseling principles of sensitivity to needs and personality differences. Also called **life coaching**. **2.** specialized instruction, training, and practice in taking academic or other intellectual psychological tests. **3.** in business and industry, an intervention technique for managers, administrators, and leaders who need skills for problem solving, interpersonal relationships, and motivating colleagues and other personnel in an organizational or other group setting.

Coaching Behavior Assessment System (CBAS) an observation system for determining the frequency of 12 specific coaching behaviors and their effect on athletes. The behaviors may be exhibited by the coach in anticipation of or in reaction to an athlete's or a team's performance and include correcting, rewarding, giving negative feedback, instructing, and disciplining.

coacting group a group consisting of two or more individuals working in one another's presence on tasks and activities that require little or no interaction or communication (COACTION TASKS), such as clerical staff working at individual desks in an open-design office. Researchers often create coacting groups in laboratory studies to determine the impact of the mere presence of others on performance.

coaction task any performance, competition, work assignment, or other goal-oriented activity that individuals execute in the presence of one or more other individuals who are performing a similar type of task. Examples include an aerobics exercise session and students taking a written test in a classroom. Compare AUDIENCE TASK.

coactivation *n.* the activation of the same response at the same time by two different stimuli.

coactive–interactive sport a sport that requires participants to perform independently, the result being determined by the accumulation of individual performances. Rowing and baseball are examples of coactive–interactive sports. Compare COACTIVE SPORT; INTERACTIVE SPORT.

coactive sport a sport in which participants perform the same task without the need for interaction or for coordination of their actions. Bowling and golf are examples of coactive sports. Compare COACTIVE–INTERACTIVE SPORT; INTERACTIVE SPORT.

coadaptation *n.* the interdependence of behavioral adaptations between species. For example, a type of fruit tree that depends on a bird or mammal to disperse seeds away from the parent tree may have fruit coloration and taste that engages the sensory and perceptual systems of these primary dispersers. Many animals depend on parasitic bacteria in the gut to digest food: Both the bacteria and the host gain and show a mutual coadaptation. See also SYMBIOSIS.

coalition *n.* a temporary alliance formed by two or more individuals in order to gain a better outcome (e.g., power and influence) than can be achieved by each individual alone. Coalitions tend to be adversarial, in that they seek outcomes that will benefit the coalition members at the expense of nonmembers. They also tend to be unstable because (a) they include individuals who would not naturally form an alliance but are obliged or encouraged to do so by circumstances and (b) members frequently abandon one alliance to form a more profitable one. Such alliances are also formed among nonhuman animals. In chimpanzees, for example, two or more lower ranking males can form a coalition to overtake the dominant male in the group, and male dolphins may form a coalition in order to be able to mate with a female that can successfully evade sexual approaches by one male but not by two. See also MINIMUM POWER THEORY; MINIMUM RESOURCE THEORY.

coarse tremor see TREMOR.

coarticulation effect a phenomenon in which the performance of one or more actions in a sequence of actions varies according to the other actions in the sequence. The effect is particularly important in speech, where the formation of certain PHONEMES varies according to the speech sounds that immediately precede or follow: So, for example, the aspirated [p] sound in *pin* differs slightly from the unaspirated [p] in *spin* (see ASPIRATION). The effect also occurs in keyboarding, where the movements used to type a particular key are different when the preceding or following keys are different. See also ALLOMORPH; ALLOPHONE.

CO blob abbreviation for CYTOCHROME OXIDASE BLOB.

coca *n.* a shrub, *Erythroxylum coca*, that is indigenous to Peru, Bolivia, and other South American countries and cultivated in India, Sri Lanka, and Indonesia. The leaves have been used for centuries as the source of COCAINE.

cocaine *n.* a drug, obtained from leaves of the coca shrub (*Erythroxylum coca*), that stimulates the central nervous system (see CNS STIMULANTS), with the effects of reducing fatigue and increasing well-being. These are followed by a period of depression as the initial effects diminish. The drug acts by blocking the reuptake of the neurotransmitters DOPAMINE, SEROTONIN, and NOREPINEPHRINE. The psychoactive properties of the coca plant were recognized by the Peruvian Incas before 4000 BCE, and in the 1880s the possible therapeutic uses of cocaine were investigated. Sigmund FREUD observed that the drug functioned as a topical anesthetic. See also CRACK; FREEBASE.

cocaine abuse in *DSM–IV–TR*, a pattern of cocaine use manifested by recurrent significant adverse consequences related to the repeated ingestion of the substance. This diagnosis is preempted by the diagnosis of COCAINE DEPENDENCE: If the criteria for cocaine abuse and cocaine dependence are both met, only the latter diagnosis is given. See also SUBSTANCE ABUSE.

Cocaine Anonymous a voluntary organization of men and women who seek to recover from cocaine addiction by using a TWELVE-STEP PROGRAM. See also SELF-HELP GROUP.

cocaine dependence in *DSM–IV–TR*, a cluster of cognitive, behavioral, and physiological symptoms indicating continued use of cocaine despite significant cocaine-related problems. There is a pattern of repeated cocaine ingestion resulting in tolerance, withdrawal symptoms if use is suspended, and an uncontrollable drive to continue use. See also COCAINE ABUSE; SUBSTANCE DEPENDENCE.

cocaine intoxication a reversible syndrome due to the recent ingestion of cocaine. It includes clinically significant behavioral or psychological changes (e.g., agitation, aggressive behavior, elation, grandiosity, impaired judgment, talkativeness, hypervigilance), as well as one or more physiological signs (e.g., rapid heartbeat, elevated blood pressure, perspiration or chills, nausea and vomiting). Large doses, especially when taken intravenously, may produce confusion, incoherence, apprehension, transient paranoid ideas, increased sexual interest, and perceptual disturbances (e.g., a sensation of insects crawling on the skin). An hour or so after these effects subside, the user may experience tremulousness, anxiety, irritability, fatigue, and depression. See also SUBSTANCE INTOXICATION.

cocaine intoxication delirium a reversible syndrome that develops over a short period of time (usually hours to days) following the heavy ingestion of cocaine. It includes disturbance of consciousness (e.g., reduced ability to focus, sustain, or shift attention), accompanied by changes in cognition (e.g., memory deficit, disorientation, or language disturbance) in excess of those usually associated with COCAINE INTOXICATION. See also SUBSTANCE INTOXICATION DELIRIUM.

cocaine withdrawal a characteristic withdrawal syndrome that develops after cessation of (or reduction in) prolonged, heavy consumption of cocaine. The essential characteristic is depressed mood, sometimes severe, and there may also be fatigue, disturbed sleep, increased appetite, vivid and unpleasant dreams, or PSYCHOMOTOR RETARDATION or agitation, or all of these features. Marked withdrawal symptoms (see CRASH) often follow an episode of intense, high-dose use. See also SUBSTANCE WITHDRAWAL.

coccygeal nerve see SPINAL NERVE.

coccyx *n.* (*pl.* **coccyges**) the last bone of the SPINAL COLUMN in apes and humans, formed by fusion of the caudal vertebrae. **—coccygeal** *adj.*

cochlea *n.* the bony fluid-filled part of the inner ear that is concerned with hearing. Shaped like a snail shell, it forms part of the bony labyrinth (see AUDITORY LABYRINTH). Along its length run three canals: the SCALA VESTIBULI, SCALA TYMPANI, and SCALA MEDIA, or cochlear duct. The floor of the scala media is formed by the BASILAR MEMBRANE; the ORGAN OF CORTI, which rests on the basilar membrane, contains the HAIR CELLS that act as auditory receptor organs. **—cochlear** *adj.*

cochlear aplasia the clinical absence or defective development of the cochlea in the inner ear.

cochlear duct see SCALA MEDIA.

cochlear echo see OTOACOUSTIC EMISSIONS.

cochlear emissions see OTOACOUSTIC EMISSIONS.

cochlear implant an electronic device designed to enable individuals with profound SENSORINEURAL HEARING LOSS to hear and interpret some sounds, particularly those associated with speech. It consists of a microphone to detect sound, a headpiece to transmit sound, a processor to digitize sound, and a receiver to signal electrodes that are surgically implanted in the cochlea to stimulate the auditory nerve.

cochlear microphonic (**CM**) an alternating-current electric potential generated by HAIR CELLS in the inner ear that has a waveform similar to that of the acoustic input. Also called **Wever–Bray effect**.

cochlear nerve see AUDITORY NERVE.

cochlear nuclei the cell bodies of second-order auditory neurons in the brainstem. The principal subdivisions are the ventral, dorsal, and anterior cochlear nuclei.

cochlear recruitment the RECRUITMENT of previously unstimulated neurons in the cochlea with an increase in stimulus intensity.

Cochran Q test a nonparametric statistical test used when each experimental unit is observed under multiple experimental conditions and one wishes to test the hypothesis of equality of the conditions when the case outcomes are binary. [William Gemmell **Cochran** (1909–1980), Scottish-born U.S. statistician]

Cockayne's syndrome a hereditary disorder involving dwarfism, microcephaly (small head), mental retardation, visual disorders, hypersensitivity to sunlight, and progressive neurological deterioration. Early psychomotor development is slow, and most affected individuals show an IQ of less than 50. Affected individuals eventually become blind and deaf and typically do not live past the age of 20. Also called **Cockayne–Neill dwarfism**. [reported in 1936 by Edward Alfred **Cockayne** (1880–1956), British physician, and in about 1950 by Catherine A. **Neill** (1922–2006), British-born U.S. pediatrician]

cocktail-party effect the ability to attend to one of several speech streams while ignoring others, just as one is able to attend to one conversation among others at a cocktail party. Research in this area in the early 1950s suggested that the unattended messages are not processed, but later findings indicated that meaning is identified in at least some cases. For example, the mention of one's name is processed even if it occurs in an unattended speech stream. See also ATTENUATION THEORY.

cocktail-party syndrome see CHATTERBOX EFFECT.

cocktail-party universal see PSYCHOLOGICAL UNIVERSAL.

cocoa *n.* a product derived from the cacao plant (*Theobroma cacao*) by roasting and grinding the beans (seeds) and removing the oils. The pharmacologically active ingredients are THEOBROMINE (typically about 1–3% of dry weight) and CAFFEINE.

coconsciousness *n.* **1.** in psychology, the relationship among multiple selves, or mental processes, that are simultaneously available but separated by a "diaphanous veil" from everyday awareness. [defined by William JAMES] **2.** in contemporary philosophy, the unity of consciousness. **—coconscious** *adj.*

coconscious personality a personality that is "split-off and independently acting," as in cases of DISSOCIATIVE IDENTITY DISORDER. [defined by U.S. psychologist Morton Prince (1854–1929)]

cocontraction *n.* concurrent activity in the AGONIST and ANTAGONIST muscles controlling a joint.

cocounseling *n.* the counseling of peers by each other, as opposed to one-way professionally led counseling.

COD abbreviation for CHANGE-OVER DELAY.

codability *n.* the extent to which speakers of a language agree on a name for something. For example, the codability of a color is defined by how much agreement there is about a name for that color. **—codable** *adj.*

CODAP abbreviation for COMPREHENSIVE OCCUPATIONAL DATA ANALYSIS PROGRAM.

codeine *n.* an OPIATE derived from morphine, with which it shares many properties—it is a potent analgesic (used alone or in combination with other analgesics, e.g., aspirin) and it induces euphoria. However, its addiction potential is substantially less than that of heroin. See OPIOID ANALGESIC.

code of ethics a set of standards and principles of professional conduct, such as the *Ethical Principles of Psychologists and Code of Conduct* of the American Psychological Association. See ETHICS; PROFESSIONAL ETHICS; STANDARDS OF PRACTICE.

codependency *n.* **1.** the state of being mutually dependent, for example, a relationship between two individuals who are emotionally dependent on one another. **2.** a dysfunctional relationship pattern in which an individual is psychologically dependent on (or controlled by) a person who has a pathological addiction (e.g., alcohol, gambling). **—codependent** *adj.*

Co-Dependents Anonymous a SELF-HELP GROUP for individuals who seek to improve problematic codependent relationships with others by using a TWELVE-STEP PROGRAM.

code switching in sociolinguistics, the practice typical of individuals proficient in two or more REGISTERS, dialects, or languages who will switch from one to the other depending on the conversational context or in order to enhance linguistic or social meaning. See also DIGLOSSIA.

code test a test that requires participants to translate one set of symbols into another, for example, by writing *California* in numbers that stand for letters according to the code A = 3, B = 4, C = 5, and so on. Also called **coding test**; **symbol-substitution test**. See CRYPTARITHMETIC; CRYPTOGRAM. See also SYMBOL–DIGIT TEST.

codification *n.* **1.** the systematic arrangement of items in an organized fashion or the classification of items into identifiable categories. **2.** the conversion of data or other information into a code that can be translated by others. Also called **coding**.

codification-of-rules stage in Jean PIAGET's theory of moral development, the stage at which children of 11 and 12 years of age and older view rules as binding once they are agreed to, and games are seen as a system of interconnecting laws. Although the awareness of rules emerges at an earlier age, systematic adherence is not manifested until the codification-of-rules stage.

coding *n.* see CODIFICATION.

coding test see CODE TEST.

codominance *n.* a sharing of high rank in certain animal populations. Wild macaques, baboons, and chimpanzees may control their groups through a few small males exhibiting codominance, rather than through a linear hierarchy of animal dominance. Coalitions may be formed by lower ranking individuals either to counter the influence of more dominant individuals or to overthrow them. Often coalitions are short-lived as one coalition member assumes dominance over the others.

codon *n.* a unit of the GENETIC CODE consisting of three consecutive bases in a DNA or MESSENGER RNA sequence. Most codons specify a particular amino acid in protein synthesis, although some act as "start" or "stop" signals. Codons on a gene are numbered, and genetic mutations are described as occurring at particular codons or locations on the gene. Thus a family might be described as having a mutation at codon 630 on EXON 11 of chromosome 10.

coefficient *n.* **1.** a number that functions as a measure of some property. For example, the CORRELATION COEFFICIENT is a measure of the degree of linear relatedness. **2.** in algebra, a scalar that multiplies a variable in an equation. For example, in the equation $y = \boldsymbol{b}x$, the scalar quantity $\boldsymbol{b}$ is said to be a coefficient.

coefficient alpha an index of reliability based on the internal consistency or average interitem correlation of a set of items that comprise a measuring instrument. See also CRONBACH'S ALPHA.

coefficient of agreement a numerical index that reflects the degree of agreement among a set of raters, judges, or instruments on which of several categories a case belongs to. Coefficients of agreement, such as KAPPA, are often corrected for chance agreement. Also called **agreement coefficient**. See also INTERRATER AGREEMENT.

coefficient of alienation (symbol: *k*) a numerical index that reflects the amount of unexplained variance between two variables. It is a measure of the lack of relationship between the two variables. Also called **alienation coefficient**.

coefficient of concordance (symbol: *W*) a numerical index that reflects the degree to which the rankings of *k* conditions or objects by *m* raters are in agreement. Also called **Kendall's coefficient of concordance**.

coefficient of determination (symbol: r^2) a numerical index that reflects the degree to which variation in the DEPENDENT VARIABLE is accounted for by one INDEPENDENT VARIABLE. Also called **determination coefficient**. See also COEFFICIENT OF MULTIPLE CORRELATION.

coefficient of multiple correlation (symbol: R^2) a numerical index that reflects the degree to which variation in the DEPENDENT VARIABLE is accounted for by two or more INDEPENDENT VARIABLES. For example, government policy analysts might use multiple correlations to measure the combined effect of age, gender, and years of education on workers' incomes. Also called **coefficient of multiple determination**; **multiple correlation squared**; **squared multiple correlation**. See also COEFFICIENT OF DETERMINATION.

coefficient of relatedness the mean number of genes shared between two related individuals. Identical twins share 100% of their genes and have a coefficient of relatedness of 1.0. Between siblings and between parents and offspring the coefficient of relatedness is 0.50, between uncles or aunts and nieces or nephews and between grandparents and grand-offspring it is 0.25, and between first cousins it is 0.125. Most studies of KIN RECOGNITION and kin-directed behavior show effects only with coefficients of relatedness of 0.25 and greater. See also INCLUSIVE FITNESS.

coefficient of variation a measure of the spread (see DISPERSION) of a set of data. It is determined by dividing the distribution's STANDARD DEVIATION by its MEAN.

coefficient of visibility a measure of the visibility of light of a particular wavelength. The coefficient of visibility for PHOTOPIC VISION is 1 at 555 nm, the wavelength at which humans have peak photopic sensitivity. Also called **luminosity coefficient**.

coenesthesia *n.* see CENESTHESIA.

coeno- (**coen-**; **cene-**; **ceno-**) *combining form* common or general.

coenzyme *n.* a nonprotein, organic compound that functions with the protein portion of an enzyme (an APOENZYME). Most enzymes fail to function without a specific coenzyme, which is often a vitamin.

coerced confession an accused person's admission of guilt elicited by the use of threats, torture, or promises made by authorities. Also called **involuntary confession**.

coercion *n.* the process of attempting to influence another person through the exercise of physical, psychological, or social power. **—coerce** *vb.* **—coercive** *adj.*

coercive behavior behavior designed to force others to do one's bidding, often masked as filial devotion or as marital or parental concern and sometimes expressed in undisguised form (e.g., "If you don't do what I say, I'll kill myself").

coercive persuasion 1. systematic, intensive indoctrination of political or military prisoners, using such methods as threats, punishments, bribes, isolation, continuous interrogation, and repetitious "instruction." Also called **thought reform**. See BRAINWASHING. **2.** broadly, a controlled program of social influence to bring about substantial changes in behavior and attitude. An example is U.S. Marine Corps basic training, which relies on changing attitudes from civilian perspectives to those of marines. As a countermeasure, military personnel are also trained in methods of **coercive persuasion resistance**, which are designed to enable them to function and survive to the best of their ability under circumstances in which they are subjected to techniques that may produce behavior and attitude changes.

coercive power the capacity to influence others through punishment or the threat of punishment. See POWER.

coercive strategy a goal-directed plan that uses threats, punishment, force, direct pressure, and other negative forms of influence to achieve its aims.

coercive treatment see FORCED TREATMENT.

coevolution *n.* the concurrent evolution of two or more species that mutually affect each other's evolution.

coexistence hypothesis the hypothesis that when misleading information is introduced after a witnessed event, it exists in competition with the original memory of the event. The FALSE MEMORY based on post-event information is more accessible due to RECENCY EFFECT and is more likely to be retrieved upon questioning, leading to erroneous reporting of the event. Compare ALTERATION HYPOTHESIS.

coexistent cultures two or more cultures with distinctive characteristics that exist in close proximity with one another in a conflict-free, if not symbiotic, relationship. Compare CULTURE CONFLICT.

coexperimenter *n.* an experimenter who assists the primary experimenter, especially by maintaining DOUBLE-BLIND conditions or otherwise helping to reduce potential sources of experimental BIAS.

cofacilitator *n.* a therapist or student in training who assists in leading a therapy group. The cofacilitator may act as an observer or as one who balances the approach of the other group leader.

coffee *n.* a product derived from evergreen trees of the genus *Coffea*, which grow wild or are cultivated in tropical regions worldwide, including Brazil, Columbia, and Ethiopia. Of more than 100 species of *Coffea*, two are commercially important sources of coffee beans (seeds), used in beverages. They are *C. arabica* and *C. robusta*, whose beans contain significant concentrations (about 1% and 2%, respectively) of the stimulant CAFFEINE.

cofigurative culture a society or culture in which people learn chiefly from other people in the same age group, so that, for example, children learn mostly from children and young adults from young adults. Also called **configurative culture**. Compare POSTFIGURATIVE CULTURE; PREFIGURATIVE CULTURE. [coined by U.S. anthropologist Margaret Mead (1901–1978)]

Cogan's syndrome a condition in which KERATITIS is

associated with attacks of vertigo, tinnitus, and deafness. Pain in the eyes and reduced vision are experienced; as the vertigo subsides, the patient becomes deaf. Also called **nonsyphilitic interstitial keratitis**. [described in 1945 by David Glendenning **Cogan** (1908–1993), U.S. physician]

CogAT acronym for COGNITIVE ABILITIES TEST.

Cogentin *n.* a trade name for BENZTROPINE.

cogito ergo sum I am thinking, therefore I exist. This Latin statement, made by French philosopher, mathematician, and scientist René Descartes (1596–1650), forms the basis for his rejection of metaphysical SKEPTICISM, the doctrine that nothing can be proven to have a real existence: If he (i.e., Descartes) thinks, then he must exist, and if he exists, the doctrine is wrong, leaving open the possibility of the existence of other beings and things. See CARTESIAN SELF.

cognate *adj.* denoting a word that is derived from the same historical root as another word, especially one in another language with a similar form and meaning. For example, the words *picture* (English), *pictura* (Spanish), and *pictora* (Italian) are said to be cognate.

Cognex *n.* a trade name for TACRINE.

cognition *n.* **1.** all forms of knowing and awareness, such as perceiving, conceiving, remembering, reasoning, judging, imagining, and problem solving. See also SYMBOLIC PROCESS; THINKING. **2.** an individual percept, idea, memory, or the like. **—cognitional** *adj.* **—cognitive** *adj.*

Cognitive Abilities Test (**CogAT**) a group of multiple-choice tests measuring students' abstract reasoning and problem-solving abilities. It is divided into a primary edition (for kindergarten–grade 2) and a multilevel edition (for grades 3–12), which are further divided into three levels (K, 1, and 2) and eight levels (A–H), respectively. Each edition contains various subtests (e.g., sentence completion, equation building, and figure synthesis) in three groups: verbal, quantitative, and nonverbal. The CogAT, a revision of the now obsolete 1954 **Lorge–Thorndike Intelligence Tests**, was originally published in 1968; the most recent version is the CogAT Form 6, published in 2001. A British version of the Cognitive Abilities Test is also available. Designed for use with students aged 7½ to 17 years and over, it is known as the **CAT** and is now in its third edition (published in 2003). [developed by U.S. psychologists Robert L. THORNDIKE, Irving D. Lorge (1905–1961), Elizabeth P. Hagen (1915–), and David F. Lohman (1949–)]

cognitive ability the skill of, or aptitude for, perception, learning, memory, understanding, awareness, reasoning, judgment, intuition, and language.

cognitive–affective crossfire a state of conflict between a person's cognitive responses to feedback about the self and his or her affective responses. In particular, an individual's thoughts (cognitions) may favor information that confirms his or her existing SELF-CONCEPT (see CONSISTENCY MOTIVE), whereas the same individual's emotional reactions (affects) may favor pleasant or positive views of the self (see SELF-ENHANCEMENT MOTIVE).

cognitive–affective personality system a theoretical conception of personality structure in which personality is viewed as a complex system that features a large number of highly interconnected cognitions and emotional tendencies. [developed by U.S. personality psychologists Walter Mischel (1930–) and Yuichi Shoda]

cognitive aging nonpathological age-related changes in mental functioning (e.g., attention, memory, decision making) that occur naturally across the adult age span.

cognitive aids external representations that support various mental processes. Examples are reminders, checklists, and other prompts provided to prevent forgetting of critical tasks.

cognitive-analytic therapy a time-limited integrative, collaborative psychotherapy that emphasizes SCHEMAS and integrates principles and techniques from PSYCHODYNAMIC PSYCHOTHERAPY and COGNITIVE BEHAVIOR THERAPY.

cognitive anxiety the level of worry and apprehension an individual experiences in a particular situation.

cognitive appraisal theory the theory that cognitive evaluation is involved in the generation of each and every emotion (see APPRAISAL). This concept is more appropriately expressed in the COGNITIVE–MOTIVATIONAL–RELATIONAL THEORY, as the latter recognizes that cognition is only one of three simultaneously operating processes that contribute to the generation of any emotion. See also CORE RELATIONAL THEMES. [proposed by U.S. psychologist Richard S. Lazarus (1922–2002)]

cognitive architecture a hypothesized architecture for human problem solving, usually represented as a component of a computer program. Examples include the PRODUCTION SYSTEM and SOAR. Empirical testing of cognitive phenomena is often used to establish the validity of aspects of this model.

cognitive arousal theory of emotion see SCHACHTER–SINGER THEORY.

cognitive assessment assessment of such skills as learning, memory, judgment, and reasoning.

Cognitive Assessment System (**CAS**) an individual test of intelligence based upon the neuropsychological theory of intelligence of Alexander LURIA. Applicable to both children and adolescents, the test yields separate scores for planning, attentional, simultaneous-processing, and successive-processing abilities, as well as an overall score. Scores on the test are correlated with scores on more conventional tests of intelligence (such as the WECHSLER ADULT INTELLIGENCE SCALE and the STANFORD–BINET INTELLIGENCE SCALE, but are not as highly correlated with such scores as they are with each other, because the test is based upon a different theory. See also PASS MODEL. [devised in the late 1980s by U.S. psychologists J. P. Das (1931–) and Jack A. Naglieri (1950–)]

cognitive balance theory the theory that people seek an equilibrium of positive and negative attitudes in their cognitive processes and that an unbalanced state creates stress and prompts change. [derived from the work of Austrian-born U.S. psychologist Fritz Heider (1896–1988)]

cognitive behavioral couples therapy couples therapy that uses BEHAVIORAL COUPLES THERAPY techniques yet also focuses on the reciprocal influence of the partners' idiosyncratic patterns of ideas about each other and about couples in general. Interfering ideas are made conscious and explicit, and then modified to improve the couple's relationship using techniques modified from COGNITIVE BEHAVIOR THERAPY. Compare INTEGRATIVE BEHAVIORAL COUPLES THERAPY.

cognitive behavioral group therapy a type of group psychotherapy that uses techniques and methods of COGNITIVE BEHAVIOR THERAPY, such as modeling, restructuring thoughts, relaxation training, and communication skills training, to achieve behaviorally defined goals. Groups can include clients with diverse issues or can be limited to clients with specific problems (e.g., agoraphobia, anger). See also BECK THERAPY.

cognitive–behavioral strategy any strategy to alter behavior by altering cognitions about a task or situation. For example, perceiving a situation as a challenge rather than a crisis will lead to a change in how one approaches the situation.

cognitive behaviorism see PURPOSIVE BEHAVIORISM.

cognitive behavior modification see COGNITIVE BEHAVIOR THERAPY.

cognitive behavior theory any theory deriving from general behavioral theory that considers cognitive or thought processes as significant mediators of behavioral change. A central feature in the theoretical formulations of the process is that the human organism responds primarily to cognitive representations of its environments rather than to the environments themselves. The theory has led to popular therapeutic procedures that incorporate cognitive behavior techniques to effect changes in self-image as well as behaviors.

cognitive behavior therapy (**CBT**) a form of psychotherapy that integrates theories of cognition and learning with treatment techniques derived from COGNITIVE THERAPY and BEHAVIOR THERAPY. CBT assumes that cognitive, emotional, and behavioral variables are functionally interrelated. Treatment is aimed at identifying and modifying the client's maladaptive thought processes and problematic behaviors through COGNITIVE RESTRUCTURING and behavioral techniques to achieve change. Also called **cognitive behavior modification**; **cognitive behavioral therapy**.

cognitive capacity one's inborn cognitive potential, which is not fully knowable through any existing means.

cognitive click a moment in psychotherapy in which it becomes suddenly clear to the client that his or her thinking is incorrect and therefore that he or she must change his or her attitudes and beliefs.

cognitive closure 1. the state in which an individual recognizes that he or she has achieved understanding of something. **2.** the final stage in figuratively seeing the total picture and how all pieces of it fit together.

cognitive complexity the state or quality of a thought process that involves numerous constructs, with many interrelationships among them. Such processing is often experienced as difficult or effortful. See also CONCEPTUAL COMPLEXITY.

cognitive complexity and control theory (**CCC theory**) the proposal that the ability to follow rules depends on the development of conscious awareness and self-control and is therefore age related. In general, a 4-year-old child can solve problems requiring the application of more complex rules than he or she could when aged 3. [proposed by Canadian psychologist Philip R. Zelazo (1940–) and U.S. psychologist Douglas Frye (1952–)]

cognitive conditioning a process in which a stimulus is repeatedly paired with an imagined or anticipated response or behavior. Cognitive conditioning has been used as a therapeutic technique, in which case the stimulus is typically aversive. For example, the client imagines that he or she is smoking a cigarette and gives himself or herself a pinch; the procedure is repeated until the thought produces the effect of discouraging the behavior. See also COGNITIVE REHEARSAL.

cognitive consistency the extent to which one cognitive element follows from or is implied by another cognitive element. See also COGNITIVE CONSONANCE; COGNITIVE DISSONANCE.

cognitive consistency theory any of a broad class of theories postulating that attitude change is a result of the desire to maintain consistency among elements of a cognitive system. See also BALANCE THEORY; COGNITIVE DISSONANCE THEORY; CONGRUITY THEORY.

cognitive consonance in COGNITIVE DISSONANCE THEORY, a situation in which two cognitive elements are consistent with one another, that is, one cognitive element follows from or is implied by the other.

cognitive construct see CONSTRUCT.

cognitive control the set of processes that organize, plan, and schedule mental operations. See also CONTROL PROCESSES; EXECUTIVE.

cognitive coping strategy any COPING STRATEGY in which mental activity is used to counter the problem or situation. Examples include thinking out the cause of the problem, working out how others might handle it, diverting one's attention to something less stressful or anxiety-provoking (e.g., remembering happy times, solving mathematical problems), and meditation or prayer.

cognitive decline reduction in one or more cognitive abilities, such as memory, awareness, judgment, and mental acuity, across the adult life span. The presence and degree of decline varies with the cognitive ability being measured: FLUID ABILITIES often show greater declines than CRYSTALLIZED ABILITIES. Cognitive decline is a part of normal healthy aging, but a severe decline could be symptomatic of disease: It is the primary symptom of disease-induced dementia (e.g., ALZHEIMER'S DISEASE).

cognitive deconstruction a mental state characterized by lack of emotion, the absence of any sense of future, a concentration on the here-and-now, and focus on concrete sensation rather than abstract thought. People may cultivate this state to escape from emotional distress or troublesome thoughts.

cognitive defect any impairment in knowing, understanding, and interpreting reality, for example, (a) in recognizing and identifying objects or individuals, (b) in reasoning and judging, (c) in thinking abstractly, (d) in remembering, (e) in comprehending or using language, or (f) in performing numerical calculations. Multiple cognitive defects, including memory impairment, are characteristic of DEMENTIA.

cognitive deficit cognitive performance (e.g., in memory tasks), as measured by individually administered standardized assessments (verbal and nonverbal cognitive measures), that is substantially below that expected given the individual's chronological age and formal educational experience.

cognitive derailment the often abrupt shifting of thoughts or associations so that they do not follow one another in a logical sequence. Cognitive derailment is a symptom of schizophrenia; the term is essentially equivalent to THOUGHT DERAILMENT. See DERAILMENT. See also COGNITIVE SLIPPAGE.

cognitive development the growth and maturation of thinking processes of all kinds, including perceiving, remembering, concept formation, problem solving, imagining, and reasoning.

cognitive developmental theory any theory that attempts to explain the mechanisms underlying the growth and maturation of thinking processes. Explanations may be in terms of stages of development in which the changes in thinking are relatively abrupt and discontinuous, or the changes may be viewed as occurring gradually and continuously over time.

cognitive discrimination the ability to make distinctions between concepts and to distinguish between examples and nonexamples of a particular concept.

cognitive disorder disordered thinking that involves impairment of the EXECUTIVE FUNCTIONS, such as organization, regulation, and perception. These fundamental abilities can affect performance in many cognitive areas, including speed, reasoning, planning, judgment, decision making, emotional engagement, perseveration, impulse control, temper control, awareness, attention, language, learning, memory, and timing.

cognitive dissonance an unpleasant psychological state resulting from inconsistency between two or more elements in a cognitive system. It is presumed to involve a state of heightened arousal and to have characteristics similar to physiological drives (e.g., hunger). Thus, cognitive dissonance creates a motivational drive in an individual to reduce the dissonance (see DISSONANCE REDUCTION). See also COGNITIVE CONSONANCE. [first described by Leon FESTINGER]

cognitive dissonance theory a theory proposing that people have a fundamental motivation to maintain consistency among elements in their cognitive systems. When inconsistency occurs, people experience an unpleasant psychological state that motivates them to reduce the dissonance in a variety of ways (see DISSONANCE REDUCTION). See also COGNITIVE CONSONANCE; NEW-LOOK THEORY OF COGNITIVE DISSONANCE; SELF-CONSISTENCY PERSPECTIVE OF COGNITIVE DISSONANCE THEORY. [first proposed by Leon FESTINGER]

cognitive distortion faulty or inaccurate thinking, perception, or belief. Cognitive distortion is a normal psychological process that can occur in all people to a greater or lesser extent.

cognitive dysfunction any disruption in mental activities associated with thinking, knowing, and remembering.

cognitive electrophysiology see ELECTROENCEPHALOGRAPHY.

cognitive enhancers see NOOTROPIC DRUGS.

cognitive ergonomics a specialty area of ERGONOMICS that seeks to understand the cognitive processes and representations involved in human performance. Cognitive ergonomics studies the combined effect of information-processing characteristics, task constraints, and task environment on human performance and applies the results of such studies to the design and evaluation of work systems.

cognitive ethology the study of the cognitive ability of an animal with respect to the problems it faces in its natural environment. A species that might perform poorly on a traditional laboratory task may display apparently complex cognitive skills in the wild. For example, some birds that store seeds over the winter display a high level of SPATIAL MEMORY for large numbers of objects. Homing salmon remember the odors of the stream in which they were hatched during the years they live in the ocean before returning to that stream to spawn.

cognitive evaluation theory a theory postulating that an individual's performance will improve or decline depending on his or her attitude about the reward for good performance, that is, about whether it is conferred as a true reward for effective performance or as a means by which the grantor of the reward asserts control over the performer. [posited by Leon FESTINGER]

cognitive–evaluative consistency the degree to which the cognitive basis of an attitude (see BASES OF AN ATTITUDE) and the overall attitude are evaluatively consistent with one another. For example, if the cognitive basis is extremely positive and the overall attitude is extremely negative, cognitive–evaluative consistency is low. See also AFFECTIVE–COGNITIVE CONSISTENCY; AFFECTIVE–EVALUATIVE CONSISTENCY.

cognitive faculty a specific aspect or domain of mental function, such as language, object recognition, or face perception. See FACULTY PSYCHOLOGY.

cognitive flexibility the capacity for objective appraisal and appropriately flexible action, most often in reference to teachers. Cognitive flexibility also implies adaptability, objectivity, and fair-mindedness.

cognitive flooding a method used in psychotherapy, mainly to treat phobias, in which the client is encouraged to focus on negative or aversive mental images to generate emotional states similar to those experienced when faced with a feared object or situation. The simulated fear is then seen to be manageable and associated with images that will reduce the original fear. See also IMPLOSIVE THERAPY.

cognitive generalization **1.** the ability to apply knowledge, concepts, or cognitive skills acquired in one context or domain to problems in another. See GENERALIZATION; GENERAL TRANSFER. **2.** a general principle of human cognition, such as association or categorization, that applies across cognitive faculties or domains. In the theory of COGNITIVE GRAMMAR such generalities are held to underlie the construction of meaning in language.

cognitive grammar in linguistics and psycholinguistics, a theory of grammar in which the constituent units are derived from general cognitive principles, such as associative memory, categorization, and so on, rather than from autonomous linguistic principles. This assumption that language is an integral part of cognition runs counter to the theory of the TASK SPECIFICITY OF LANGUAGE. [introduced in 1987 by U.S. linguist Ronald W. Langacker (1942–)]

cognitive growth see COGNITIVE DEVELOPMENT.

cognitive heuristic see HEURISTIC.

cognitive hypothesis testing problem-solving behavior in which the individual derives a set of rules (hypotheses) that are then sampled and tested until the one rule is discovered that consistently results in correct solutions to the problem.

cognitive intelligence one's abilities to learn, remember, reason, solve problems, and make sound judgments.

cognitive interview a structured technique developed for enhancing eyewitness recollection in criminal investigation. It relies on principles of cognition and memory retrieval, such as CONTEXT REINSTATEMENT, reporting everything (however seemingly irrelevant), recalling events in different order, and changing perspectives. See also AIDED RECALL.

cognitive learning the acquisition and retention of a mental representation of information and the use of this representation as the basis for behavior.

cognitive load the relative demand imposed by a particular task, in terms of mental resources required. Also called **mental load**; **mental workload**. See also COGNITIVE OVERLOAD; MENTAL EFFORT.

cognitively based persuasion an active attempt to change an attitude, primarily by altering beliefs regarding attributes associated with the ATTITUDE OBJECT. Also called **rationally based persuasion**. See also BASES OF AN ATTITUDE. Compare AFFECTIVELY BASED PERSUASION.

cognitively guided instruction an educational approach in which teachers make decisions about their instruction based on the knowledge and performance level of their students. Students are encouraged to create their own solutions to problems, rather than rely on a set of preconceived, teacher-directed procedures.

cognitive map a mental understanding of an environment, formed through trial and error as well as observation. The concept is based on the assumption that an individual seeks and collects contextual clues, such as environmental relationships, rather than acting as a passive receptor of information needed to achieve a goal. Human beings and other animals have well-developed cognitive maps that contain spatial information enabling them to orient themselves and find their way in the real world; symbolism and meaning are also contained in such maps. See also ENVIRONMENTAL COGNITION; LANDMARK; MENTAL MAP. [introduced by Edward Chace TOLMAN]

cognitive mediation the processing that is presumed to occur in the mind between arrival of a stimulus and initiation of the response. See also MEDIATION PROCESS.

cognitive miser a person who characteristically seeks quick, adequate solutions to problems rather than slow, careful ones. Such people will tend to employ mental shortcuts in making judgments and drawing inferences. See COGNITIVE STYLE; CONCEPTUAL TEMPO; REFLECTIVITY–IMPULSIVITY.

cognitive–motivational–relational theory an extension of the COGNITIVE APPRAISAL THEORY that puts equal emphasis on three processes involved in the generation of an emotion: (a) appraisal (the cognitive process), (b) the central role of the individual's strivings, intentions, and goals (the motivational process), and (c) the relevance of external events to these strivings (the relational process). [proposed by U.S. psychologist Richard S. Lazarus (1922–2002)]

cognitive narrowing focusing on a single aspect or individual grouping of aspects of a situation or object rather than on the whole. Examples include concentrating on the essay portion of a test or questionnaire in multiple formats, centering on negative factors in an overall assessment of deficits and benefits associated with accepting a new job, and focusing on a single figure or object in a large painting.

cognitive need see NEED FOR COGNITION.

cognitive neuroscience a branch of NEUROSCIENCE and BIOLOGICAL PSYCHOLOGY that focuses on the neural mechanisms of cognition. Although overlapping with the study of the mind in COGNITIVE PSYCHOLOGY, cognitive neuroscience, with its grounding in such areas as experimental psychology, neurobiology, physics, and mathematics, specifically examines how mental processes occur in the brain, but the two perspectives continually exert significant influence on each other.

cognitive operations the mental manipulation of MENTAL REPRESENTATIONS. See also OPERATION; SYMBOLIC PROCESS; THINKING.

cognitive overload the situation in which the demands placed on a person by mental work (the COGNITIVE LOAD) are greater than the person's mental abilities can cope with. See also COMMUNICATION OVERLOAD; SENSORY OVERLOAD; STIMULUS OVERLOAD.

cognitive penetrability the capacity of a mental process to be influenced by an individual's knowledge, beliefs, or goals. Reflex behavior is said to be **cognitively impenetrable**.

cognitive plan in problem solving, a mental outline of the steps to be undertaken to solve a problem or complete a task. See also PLAN.

cognitive play play behavior, such as CONSTRUCTIVE PLAY, that involves thinking and reasoning.

cognitive process 1. any of the mental functions assumed to be involved in cognitive activities, such as attention, perception, language, learning, memory, problem solving, and thinking. This term is often used synonymously with MENTAL PROCESS. See COGNITION; MEDIATION PROCESS; SYMBOLIC PROCESS. See also CONCEPTUALLY DRIVEN PROCESS; DATA-DRIVEN PROCESS. **2.** the acquisition, storage, interpretation, manipulation, transformation, and use of knowledge. These processes are commonly understood through several basic theories, including the SERIAL PROCESSING approach, which suggests that information is processed by the brain in discrete stages; the PARALLEL DISTRIBUTED PROCESSING approach, which assumes no discrete stages of processing and postulates many interactive operations that act simultaneously; and a combination theory, which assumes that cognitive processes are both serial and parallel, depending on the demands of the task.

cognitive processing the operation of COGNITIVE PROCESSES on information supplied by the senses or stored in memory. See INFORMATION PROCESSING. See also BOTTOM-UP PROCESSING; TOP-DOWN PROCESSING.

cognitive processing therapy (**CPT**) a treatment approach, based on INFORMATION PROCESSING theory, that deals with the client's conceptualizations of the self, others, and events. It is often used in the treatment of posttraumatic stress disorder resulting from sexual assault to facilitate the expression of affect and the appropriate accommodation of the traumatic event with more general cognitive schemas regarding one's self and the world.

cognitive prototype see PROTOTYPE.

cognitive psychology the branch of psychology that explores the operation of mental processes related to perceiving, attending, thinking, language, and memory, mainly through inferences from behavior. The cognitive approach, which developed in the 1940s and 1950s, diverged sharply from contemporary BEHAVIORISM in (a) emphasizing unseen knowledge processes instead of directly observable behaviors and (b) arguing that the relationship between stimulus and response was complex and mediated rather than simple and direct. Its concentration on the higher mental processes also contrasted with the focus on the instincts and other unconscious forces typical of psychoanalysis. More recently, cognitive psychology has been influenced by approaches to INFORMATION PROCESSING and INFORMATION THEORY developed in computer science and ARTIFICIAL INTELLIGENCE. See also COGNITIVE SCIENCE.

cognitive reaction time see REACTION TIME.

cognitive rehabilitation specific REHABILITATION interventions designed to address problems in mental processing that are associated with chronic illness, brain injury, or trauma, such as stroke. Rehabilitation may include relearning specific mental abilities, strengthening unaffected abilities, or substituting new abilities to compensate for lost ones.

cognitive rehearsal a therapeutic technique in which a client imagines those situations that tend to produce anxiety or self-defeating behavior and then repeats positive coping statements or mentally rehearses more appropriate behavior.

cognitive resource theory 1. in cognitive psychology, a general theoretical framework that assumes that individuals respond to problems, challenges, and choices by actively encoding, processing, and recalling needed information, but that these mental activities place demands on cognitive capacity such that heavy loads in one cognitive domain will lead to reductions in activity in another. **2.** a conceptual analysis of leadership effectiveness that assumes that team performance depends on a combination of the leader's cognitive resources (e.g., intelligence, personality traits, skills, and experience) and the particular group setting, especially with regard to the level of interpersonal conflict and stress in the group. This model was developed from the CONTINGENCY THEORY OF LEADERSHIP to give greater weight to the traits of individual leaders. See LEADERSHIP THEORIES. [developed in 1987 by Austrian-born U.S. psychologist Fred Fiedler (1922–) and his colleagues]

cognitive response an evaluative response to attitude-relevant information. Cognitive responses include inferences generated about the information, assessments of its validity, and other evaluative reactions that may or may not be cognitive in nature (e.g., emotional responses). Positive cognitive responses are associated with the formation or bolstering of positive attitudes; negative cognitive responses are associated with the formation or bolstering of negative attitudes. See also COGNITIVE RESPONSE THEORY; ELABORATION.

cognitive response theory a theory postulating that attitude change occurs primarily as a function of people's COGNITIVE RESPONSES to attitude-relevant information. This theory holds that it is primarily the number and VALENCE of these responses, rather than memory for the information itself, that determines the magnitude and duration of attitude change. See also MESSAGE-LEARNING APPROACH.

cognitive restructuring a technique used in COGNITIVE THERAPY and COGNITIVE BEHAVIOR THERAPY to help the client identify his or her self-defeating beliefs or cognitive distortions, refute them, and then modify them so that they are adaptive and reasonable.

cognitive schema see SCHEMA.

cognitive science an interdisciplinary approach to understanding the mind and mental processes that combines aspects of cognitive psychology, the philosophy of mind, epistemology, neuroscience, anthropology, psycholinguistics, and computer science.

cognitive self-guidance system the use of private, self-directed speech to guide problem-solving behavior. [proposed by Lev VYGOTSKY]

cognitive self-management the use of self-talk, imagery, or both to direct one's behavior in demanding or stressful situations.

cognitive set the predetermined way an individual construes a situation, which is based on a group of concepts, related to the self and other things, that determines a person's view of the world and influences his or her ability to negotiate living.

cognitive sign principle the belief that, through learning, stimuli come to signal outcomes or events in the environment (see S–S LEARNING MODEL). Edward C. TOLMAN offered cognitive sign learning as an alternative to the ideas of other behavioral theorists, such as Clark L. HULL, who postulated that stimuli become directly associated with responses (see S–R LEARNING MODEL).

cognitive slippage a mild form of disconnected thought processes or LOOSENING OF ASSOCIATIONS. Cognitive slippage may be seen in patients with a range of physical and mental disorders; it is a common characteristic of individuals with schizophrenia. [coined by Paul Everett MEEHL]

cognitive specificity hypothesis the belief that specific feeling states, such as depression and anxiety, are linked to particular kinds of automatic thoughts. [proposed by U.S. psychiatrist Aaron T. Beck (1921–)]

cognitive sports strategy a predetermined method used in sport to control cognition in order to facilitate high levels of performance. See COGNITIVE STRATEGY.

cognitive stage in some theories of cognitive development, especially that of Jean PIAGET, a plane of cognition that is characterized by a particular, qualitatively different level of thinking than preceding or later stages.

cognitive strategy any predetermined plan to control the process and content of thought. In sport psychology, for example, such strategies involve use of the SELF-TALK dialogue to assist athletes to keep focused, energized, confident, and "in the zone."

cognitive structure 1. a mental framework, pattern, or SCHEMA that maintains and organizes a body of information relating to a particular topic. When a need arises for the cognitive structure, as in a college test, the individual is thought to engage in a memory search in which the stored cognitive structure is retrieved and applied to the present requirements. **2.** a unified structure of facts, beliefs, and attitudes about the world or society. See COGNITIVE MAP; CONCEPTUAL SYSTEM; FRAME OF REFERENCE.

cognitive style a person's characteristic mode of perceiving, thinking, remembering, and problem solving. Cognitive styles might differ in preferred elements or activities, such as group work versus working individually, more structured versus less defined activities, or visual versus verbal ENCODING. Other dimensions along which cognitive styles vary include REFLECTIVITY–IMPULSIVITY and ABSTRACT ATTITUDE versus CONCRETE ATTITUDE. Also called **learning style**; **thinking style**. See also LEARNING TYPES; THEORY OF MENTAL SELF-GOVERNMENT.

cognitive system a set of cognitions that are organized into a meaningful complex with implied or stated relationships between them. See also COMPLEX OF IDEAS.

cognitive task a task requiring mental processes related to such activities as perceiving, attending, problem solving, thinking, or remembering.

cognitive task analysis a form of TASK ANALYSIS used to identify the different cognitive processes necessary to perform a task.

cognitive theories of leadership see LEADERSHIP THEORIES.

cognitive theory any theory of mind that focuses on mental activities, such as perceiving, attending, thinking, remembering, evaluating, planning, language, and creativity, especially one that suggests a model for the various processes involved.

cognitive theory of learning any theory postulating that learning requires central constructs and new ways of perceiving events (see S–S LEARNING MODEL). An example is the PURPOSIVE BEHAVIORISM of Edward C. TOLMAN. Cognitive theory is usually contrasted with behavioral learning theories, which suggest that behaviors or responses are acquired through experience (see S–R PSYCHOLOGY).

cognitive therapy (**CT**) a form of psychotherapy based on the concept that emotional and behavioral problems in an individual are, at least in part, the result of maladaptive or faulty ways of thinking and distorted attitudes toward oneself and others. The objective of the therapy is to identify these faulty cognitions and replace them with more adaptive ones, a process known as COGNITIVE RESTRUCTURING. The therapist takes the role of an active guide who attempts to make the client aware of these distorted thinking patterns and who helps the client correct and revise his or her perceptions and attitudes by citing evidence to the contrary or by eliciting it from the client. See also COGNITIVE BEHAVIOR THERAPY. [developed by U.S. psychiatrist Aaron T. Beck (1921–)]

cognitive triad a set of three beliefs thought to characterize MAJOR DEPRESSIVE EPISODES. These are negative beliefs about the self, the world, and the future. Also called **negative triad**.

cognitive tunneling a psychological state, typical of people concentrating on a demanding task or operating under conditions of stress, in which a single, narrowly defined category of information is attended to and processed. Cognitive tunneling involves the processing of highly critical task-relevant information, with limited or no processing of secondary information that may also be important to the task. Compare SOCIAL TUNNELING.

cognitive unconscious unreportable mental processes, collectively. There are many sources of evidence for a cognitive unconscious, including regularities of behavior due to habit or AUTOMATICITY, inferred grammatical rules, the details of sensorimotor control, and implicit knowledge after brain damage (see TACIT KNOWLEDGE). It is often contrasted with the psychoanalytically derived notion of the dynamic UNCONSCIOUS, which involves material that is kept out of consciousness to avoid anxiety, shame, or guilt.

cognitive vulnerability a set of beliefs or attitudes thought to make a person vulnerable to depression. Examples include PERFECTIONISM, DEPENDENCE, and SOCIOTROPY.

cognitive walkthrough method in ergonomics, a method of assessing the usability of a product or design in which several evaluators, representing the targeted user group, perform its various functions while discussing and identifying or anticipating problems arising from flawed design.

cognitivism *n.* adherence to the principles of COGNITIVE PSYCHOLOGY, especially as opposed to those of BEHAVIORISM.

cognitivist 1. *n.* a theorist concerned primarily with describing either intellectual development (e.g., Jean PIAGET, U.S. developmental psychologist Jerome Bruner [1915–]) or early language behavior (e.g., Roger BROWN). **2.** *adj.* describing a perspective or approach that is based on COGNITIVISM.

cognizance need the drive to acquire knowledge through questions, exploration, and study. [proposed by U.S. psychologist Henry Alexander Murray (1893–1988)]

cognize *vb.* to know or become aware of. **—cognizance** *n.* **—cognizant** *adj.*

cogwheel rigidity MUSCULAR RIGIDITY that produces a ratcheted resistance to passive movement of the limbs of people who have PARKINSON'S DISEASE. It may also be seen as the side effect of medication, especially antipsychotic drugs such as the PHENOTHIAZINES. Also called **cogwheeling**. Compare LEAD-PIPE RIGIDITY.

cohabitation *n.* the state or condition of living together as sexual and domestic partners without being married. See COMMON-LAW MARRIAGE; DOMESTIC PARTNERSHIP; SAME-SEX MARRIAGE. **—cohabit** *vb.* **—cohabitee** *n.*

Cohen's kappa (symbol: κ) a numerical index that reflects the degree of agreement between two raters or rating systems corrected for the level of agreement expected by chance alone. [Jacob **Cohen** (1923–1998), U.S. psychologist and statistician]

coherence *n.* **1.** meaningful interconnections between distinct psychological entities. For example, a system of independent beliefs that is logically consistent from one belief to another would be described as **coherent**. **2.** a measure of the extent to which energy waves (such as light waves) are correlated between two times (**temporal coherence**) or two points (**spatial coherence**). Beams of such waves that are in phase, or have a constant phase relationship, are said to be coherent. **3.** in imagery, the tendency for an image to be influenced by its background.

cohesion *n.* **1.** the unity or solidarity of a group, as indicated by the strength of the bonds that link group members to the group as a whole, the sense of belongingness and community within the group, the feelings of attraction for specific group members and the group itself experienced by individuals, and the degree to which members coordinate their efforts to achieve goals. According to Leon FESTINGER, cohesion reflects the degree to which group members are attracted to the group, which in turn depends on their liking for each other or the group's prestige or activities. The higher the cohesion, the stronger the members' motivation to adhere to the group's standards. Group cohesion is frequently considered essential to effective GROUP PSYCHOTHERAPY. **2.** in sport, the attraction to and integration of a team for both social reasons (i.e., relations with others on the team) and task-related reasons (i.e., the goals and purposes of the team). Also called **cohesiveness; group cohesion**. See also ESPRIT DE CORPS; GROUP SOLIDARITY. **—cohesive** *adj.*

cohesiveness *n.* **1.** see COHESION. **2.** a tendency of acts, either successive or simultaneous, to become connected or affiliated so as to form a unified whole.

cohort *n.* a group of people who share some characteristic, especially a group of individuals born during the same period (often the same year). See BIRTH COHORT.

cohort analysis an analysis of the effects attributed to members of a group sharing a particular characteristic, experience, or event.

cohort effect any adventitious effect associated with being a member of a group born at a particular time (see COHORT) and therefore influenced by pressures and challenges typical of the era of development. See also AGE EFFECT.

cohort sampling a SAMPLING method in which one or more COHORTS are selected for observation.

cohort-sequential design an experimental design in which multiple measures are taken over a period of time from two or more groups of participants of different ages (see COHORT). Such longitudinal studies avoid some of the problems of CROSS-SECTIONAL DESIGNS.

coil *n.* see INTRAUTERINE DEVICE.

coincidence *n.* a noncausal or noncontingent relationship between or among phenomena. **—coincidental** *adj.*

coital anorgasmia failure of a woman to reach orgasm during penile–vaginal intercourse. Studies show that roughly half of women do not have coital orgasms in the absence of concurrent clitoral stimulation. Sex therapists do not consider this a dysfunction; if the woman can have orgasm with her partner in other ways, and enjoys intercourse, there is no requirement that both happen simultaneously.

coital position any of various postures that may be assumed by sexual partners during intercourse.

coitus *n.* an act of sexual union, usually the insertion of the penis into the vagina followed by ejaculation. Variations include **coitus a tergo**, in which the penis is inserted from the rear; and **coitus inter femora** (**interfemoral sex**), in which the penis is inserted between the pressed thighs of the female. Also called **coition**; **intercourse**; **sexual intercourse**. See also ANAL INTERCOURSE; CAREZZA; PAINFUL SEXUAL INTERCOURSE. —**coital** *adj.*

coitus analis see ANAL INTERCOURSE.

coitus a tergo see COITUS.

coitus in ano see ANAL INTERCOURSE.

coitus inter femora see COITUS.

coitus interruptus the withdrawal of the penis during intercourse, prior to orgasm, with orgasm occurring external to the vagina. This is done mainly to reduce the likelihood of conception but is not very effective, as some semen is often released prior to orgasm.

coitus intra mammas coitus in which the penis is inserted between the breasts of the female.

coitus prolongatus see CAREZZA.

coitus reservatus sexual intercourse in which the man suppresses the ejaculation of semen. Coitus reservatus has been practiced for generations in eastern Asia, by the application of opium paste to the glans penis to reduce its sensitivity. In the Oneida community (a 19th-century Methodist commune in the northeastern United States), young men were encouraged to practice coitus reservatus with menopausal women until they were able to achieve a state of male continence. See also CAREZZA.

coke *n.* slang for COCAINE.

cola nut see KOLA NUT.

cold-blooded animal see ECTOTHERM.

cold cognition a mental process or activity that does not involve feelings or emotions. For instance, reading a list of nonsense syllables or factoids (brief pieces of invented or inaccurate information) typically involves cold cognition.

cold effects the effects of low temperatures on physical and mental health. Research indicates that reaction time, tracking proficiency, tactile discrimination, and other types of performance begin to deteriorate at temperatures of 13 °C (55 °F) or below. Studies of cold effects on social behavior have produced conflicting evidence of both increased and decreased aggression.

cold emotion a reaction to some stimulants (e.g., epinephrine) that entails the physiological responses of emotional arousal without an identifiable affective root.

coldness *n.* **1.** a thermal sensation produced by a stimulus that is below skin temperature. **2.** a psychological characteristic featuring a relative absence of empathy toward and emotional support of others.

cold pressor pain test a test of pain produced by immersing a limb in iced water. Also called **cold pressor test**.

cold sense the ability to experience COLDNESS. See TEMPERATURE SENSE.

cold spot any point on the surface of the skin containing nerve receptors sensitive to low-temperature stimuli.

cold stimulus a stimulus that is below skin temperature.

cold turkey the abrupt cessation of the use of drugs, particularly opiates, without cushioning the impact by the use of methadone or tranquilizers. The name refers specifically to the chills and gooseflesh experienced during OPIOID WITHDRAWAL.

coleadership *n.* **1.** the state of affairs in which the organizational, directive, and motivational duties of LEADERSHIP are shared between two or more individuals. The leadership role may be deliberately divided, or this may occur spontaneously as the various leadership duties become associated with several individuals (see ROLE DIFFERENTIATION). In some cases the leaders are equal in status and responsibilities, but in other cases one leader may have more status than another. In some groups one leader may focus on relationship matters (CONSIDERATION) and another on INITIATING STRUCTURE. **2.** leadership by two equal therapists or counselors, often used in GROUP PSYCHOTHERAPY.

colera *n.* see BILIS.

colic *n.* acute, paroxysmal, abdominal pain.

colitis *n.* inflammation of the colon, the main part of the large intestine. Colitis may be caused or aggravated by emotional disturbances, such as depression or anxiety.

collaboration *n.* **1.** the act or process of two or more people working together in order to obtain an outcome desired by all. **2.** an interpersonal relationship in which the parties show cooperation and sensitivity to the others' needs. [first described by U.S. psychiatrist Henry Stack Sullivan (1892–1949)] —**collaborative** *adj.*

collaborative care 1. collaboration between two or more disciplines or practitioners to assess a client's problem or problems, develop a treatment plan, and monitor progress. **2.** collaboration across agencies to coordinate services to a particular client or client group.

collaborative empiricism an approach to psychotherapy in which the therapist and client work together as equal partners in addressing issues and fostering change through mutual understanding, communication, and respect. The therapist views the client as a peer who is capable of objective analyses and conclusions.

collaborative evaluation see PARTICIPATORY EVALUATION.

collaborative family health care a form of interdisciplinary practice asserting that health events occur simultaneously on biological, psychological, and social levels and that offers treatment incorporating individual, family, community, and cultural influences. Collaborative clinicians share decision making and responsibility with patients and their families and integrate clinical expertise from relevant disciplines to provide patients with comprehensive and coordinated care.

collaborative filtering 1. in therapeutic and social interactions, the cooperative screening out of unproductive information and ideas during a discussion. **2.** any process of acquiring from other people the information needed to make a choice or decision, whether by asking them individually (word of mouth) or by polling them in large numbers. **3.** a partially automated decision-making procedure in which a computer recommends certain choices on the basis of choices made by others who are similar to the present chooser.

collaborative learning 1. the interaction between two or more people working on a task that allows greater learning to be achieved, particularly by those who are less skilled, than would occur if the participants worked alone. **2.** learning that occurs when two or more individuals who are equal in expertise or authority work together to solve a common problem. According to CULTURAL LEARNING theorists, collaborative learning is the third stage of cultural learning. See also IMITATIVE LEARNING; INSTRUCTED LEARNING. [proposed by U.S. psychologist Michael Tomasello (1950–) and colleagues]

collaborative therapy 1. any form of therapy employing COLLABORATIVE EMPIRICISM. **2.** MARITAL THERAPY conducted by two therapists, each seeing one spouse but conferring from time to time. Also called **collabora-**

tive marriage therapy; **collaborative marital therapy**.

collagen *n.* the major protein of the white fibers of the body's connective tissue (e.g., in skin, cartilage, bone, and tendons).

collapse *n.* a state of extreme prostration and depression with failure of circulation but without congestive heart failure.

collateral *adj.* secondary to something else. For example, a **collateral fiber** is a nerve fiber that branches off the main axon of a neuron, and **collateral circulation** is an alternative route for blood when the primary vessel is obstructed (see ANASTOMOSIS). **—collaterally** *adv.*

collateral behavior behavior that is not required by a REINFORCEMENT CONTINGENCY but occurs in a regular, temporal relation to behavior directly reinforced by the contingency. Compare ADJUNCTIVE BEHAVIOR; INTERIM BEHAVIOR; MEDIATING BEHAVIOR.

collateral heredity descent along different lines, but from a common ancestry.

collateral sulcus a fissure that runs along the inferior surface of each cerebral hemisphere from approximately the posterior end of the OCCIPITAL LOBE to the anterior end of the TEMPORAL LOBE.

collative properties the structural properties of such stimulus patterns in art forms as complexity and novelty. Studies indicate that people tend to prefer stimuli with moderate levels of collative properties. See also AROUSAL POTENTIAL.

collecting mania an obsessive preoccupation with indiscriminate collecting, often of useless articles or trash. The condition is most frequently found in chronic schizophrenia, dementia, and severe obsessive-compulsive disorder (see HOARDING).

collective *n.* any aggregate of two or more individuals, but especially a larger, spontaneous, and relatively ephemeral social grouping, such as a crowd or mob. A collective often includes individuals who are dispersed over a wide area and have no direct contact with one another, but who nonetheless display common shifts in opinion or action.

collective bargaining the process in which unionized employers negotiate with employee representatives on wages, benefits, hours, and other conditions of work, such as seniority, discipline, and discharge procedures. See also GOOD-FAITH BARGAINING.

collective behavior joint or similar actions performed by members of a COLLECTIVE, especially when these actions would be atypical of the same individuals outside the collective. Examples of collective behavior by groups or aggregations concentrated in a specific location include lynchings, rioting, and panics. Others, such as fads, rumors, COLLECTIVE HYSTERIA, and SOCIAL MOVEMENTS, involve widely dispersed individuals who nonetheless engage in similar actions (see COLLECTIVE MOVEMENTS).

collective conscience the shared values, norms, sentiments, and beliefs that form the basis of moral thinking and action in a cohesive society. Also called **common conscience**. [introduced by French sociologist and philosopher Émile Durkheim (1858–1917)]

collective consciousness see GROUP MIND.

collective efficacy the belief that a team or group is capable of integrating skills, efforts, and the persistence of its members to successfully complete the demands of a task. Compare COMMUNITY COMPETENCE.

collective effort model (**CEM**) an EXPECTANCY-VALUE MODEL of productivity losses in groups (SOCIAL LOAFING) that posits that working on a task collectively reduces members' motivation by lowering their expectations of successful goal attainment and diminishing the value of group goals. See also SUCKER EFFECT. [developed in 1993 by U.S. social psychologist Steven J. Karau (1965–) and U.S.-born Australian social psychologist Kipling D. Williams (1953–)]

collective experience in group psychotherapy, the common body of emotional experience that develops out of the individual members' identification with each other's problems and mutual support and empathy. [first described by 20th-century Russian-born U.S. psychotherapist Samuel Richard Slavson]

collective formation 1. generally, the initial constitution of a social aggregate or group, particularly when a group forms naturally as individuals interact with one another frequently (see ACCIDENTAL GROUP). **2.** in the psychoanalytic theory of Sigmund FREUD, the human tendency to form and interact in groups, as when a multiplicity of individuals take the same object as the EGO-IDEAL.

collective guilt 1. an unpleasant emotional state involving a shared realization that one's group or social unit has violated ethical or social principles, together with associated feelings of regret. See GUILT. **2.** the idea, usually seen as false and harmful, that members of a group may be held responsible for violations of norms or laws committed by other members of the same group. See GROUP FALLACY; GUILT BY ASSOCIATION.

collective hypnotization the act of hypnotizing a group of people at the same time. Also called **group hypnosis**.

collective hysteria the spontaneous outbreak of atypical thoughts, feelings, or actions in a group or social aggregate. Manifestations may include psychogenic illness, collective hallucinations, and bizarre actions. Instances of epidemic manias and panics, such as the DANCE EPIDEMICS of the Middle Ages, TULIPMANIA in 17th-century Holland, and listeners' reactions to the Orson Welles broadcast based on H. G. Wells's *War of the Worlds* in 1938, have been attributed to contagious hysteria (see CONTAGION) rather than conventional, individualistic disorders. Also called **group hysteria**; **mass hysteria**.

collective induction group discussion or problem solving, especially when this involves identifying general conclusions and rules from a set of specific facts and instances. See INDUCTION.

collective information-processing model a general theoretical explanation of group decision making that assumes that group members combine information through group discussion and process that information to formulate decisions, choices, and judgments.

collective memory theory a theory based on Carl JUNG's concept of the COLLECTIVE UNCONSCIOUS and related to human learning. The theory, postulated by British biologist Rupert Sheldrake (1942–) in 1981, was investigated in 1987 by U.S. psychologist Arlen Mahlberg (1948–) in a test involving the learning of two equally difficult sets of codes. Test results indicated that learning the codes became easier with exposure to them. Mahlberg subsequently applied the theory to explain, in 1997, a rise in IQ test scores over time.

collective method 1. any method that relies on groups rather than single individuals to solve problems, perform tasks, make decisions, and so on. **2.** the use of group methods in psychological treatment, as in GROUP PSYCHOTHERAPY, ENCOUNTER GROUPS, and the like.

collective mind see GROUP MIND.

collective monologue a form of egocentric, unsocialized speech in which 2- or 3-year-old children talk among themselves without apparently communicating with each other in a meaningful way, that is, the statements of one child seem unrelated to the statements of the others. Also called **pseudoconversation**. [first described by Jean PIAGET]

collective movements instances of COLLECTIVE BEHAVIOR in which the number of individuals responding similarly to some event or experience increases over time until numerous people are affected across physically distant locations. Some movements, which include SOCIAL MOVEMENTS, are organized, deliberate attempts to involve and influence individuals, whereas others (fads, crazes, or instances of COLLECTIVE HYSTERIA) occur spontaneously.

collective neurosis an archaic name for any fairly mild and transient disorder (e.g., hysteria, an obsession or phobia, anxiety) exhibited by an entire group of people rather than by a single individual. Compare COLLECTIVE PSYCHOSIS. See COLLECTIVE HYSTERIA.

collective psychology **1.** the mental and emotional states and processes unique to individuals when aggregated in such groups as audiences, crowds, or SOCIAL MOVEMENTS. **2.** the scientific study of these phenomena.

collective psychosis an archaic name for any grossly distorted reaction (e.g., hallucination, depression, delusion) exhibited by an entire group of people rather than by a single individual. Compare COLLECTIVE NEUROSIS. See COLLECTIVE HYSTERIA.

collective representations the institutions, laws, symbols, rituals, and stories that embody a society's key concepts and values and its sense of itself as a distinct community with its own identity and way of life. [introduced by French sociologist and philosopher Émile Durkheim (1858–1917)]

collective self the part of the self (or self-concept) that derives from one's relationships with other people and memberships in groups or categories, ranging from family to nationality or race. The collective self is distinguished from the PUBLIC SELF and the PRIVATE SELF. Also called **social identity**. See also SOCIAL SELF.

collective self-esteem individuals' subjective assessment of that portion of their self-concept that is based on their membership in social groups, including families, cliques, neighborhoods, tribes, cities, countries, and regions. Collective self-esteem is often measured using the **Collective Self-Esteem Scale** (**CSES**), developed in 1992 by U.S. social psychologists Riia K. Luhtanen and Jennifer Crocker (1952–). Respondents evaluate their general group memberships across four subscales pertaining to membership esteem (evaluation of their worthiness as members of a group), private collective self-esteem (evaluation of the worthiness of the group), public collective self-esteem (evaluation of others' perceptions of the group), and the importance of the group to their identity.

collective suicide see MASS SUICIDE.

collective unconscious the part of the UNCONSCIOUS that, according to Carl JUNG, is common to all humankind and contains the inherited accumulation of primitive human experiences in the form of ideas and images called ARCHETYPES. It is the deepest and least accessible part of the unconscious mind. See also PERSONAL UNCONSCIOUS; RACIAL MEMORY.

collectivism *n.* **1.** the tendency to view oneself as a member of a larger (family or social) group, rather than as an isolated, independent being. **2.** a social or cultural tradition, ideology, or personal outlook that emphasizes the unity of the group or community rather than each person's individuality. Asian, African, and South American societies tend to put more value on collectivism than do Western societies, in so far as they stress cooperation, communalism, constructive interdependence, and conformity to cultural roles and mores. Compare INDIVIDUALISM. **—collectivist** *adj.*

college admission tests tests for college applicants, which help colleges decide whether or not to accept them. These tests often include the SCHOLASTIC ASSESSMENT TEST (SAT) and the American College tests (ACT; see ACT ASSESSMENT). Also called **college boards**.

College Entrance Examination Board Advanced Placement Program see ADVANCED PLACEMENT EXAMINATIONS.

college environment the total physical and social environment, including buildings, classes, people, influences, conditions, and stimuli, that surround students enrolled in a college or university setting.

College Level Examination Program (**CLEP**) the most widely accepted credit-by-examination program in the United States, helping students of any age earn college credits by obtaining certified evidence of what they already know. A student can earn from 3 to 12 college units of credit toward a college degree for each CLEP examination that is successfully completed.

collegiality *n.* an arrangement or situation in which coworkers share authority and responsibility and are encouraged to treat one another as equals. **—collegial** *adj.*

collegial model any collaborative approach that encourages equal participation by all interactants while minimizing status differences. In research, for example, this approach enjoins researchers to involve participants fully in the research process; in therapeutic settings the model requires therapists to treat clients as equals.

colliculus *n.* (*pl.* **colliculi**) a small elevation. Two pairs of colliculi are found on the dorsal surface of the MIDBRAIN. The rostral pair, the SUPERIOR COLLICULI, receive and process visual information and help control eye movements. The caudal pair, the INFERIOR COLLICULI, receive and process auditory information.

collinearity *n.* the degree to which a set of variables are so highly interrelated that one of more of the variables in the set can be completely predicted from the remaining variables in the set. **—collinear** *adj.*

colloid *n.* **1.** a large, gluelike molecule that cannot pass through the plasma membrane of a cell. When injected into the peritoneum, colloids attract and retain water by OSMOSIS. **2.** a system consisting of two or more phases in which one phase (the **dispersed phase**) is distributed throughout the other phase (the **continuous phase**). A sol, for example, consists of large molecules or small solid particles distributed in a liquid, as when starch is mixed with water. **—colloidal** *adj.*

collusion *n.* in psychotherapy, the process in which a therapist consciously or unconsciously participates with a client or third party to avoid an issue that needs to be addressed. **—collusional** *adj.*

collusional marriage a marriage in which one partner instigates or engages in inordinate, deficient, irregular, or illegal conduct, and the other covertly endorses it or covers it up, while ostensibly being in the role of passive victim or martyr. See also MARITAL SKEW.

coloboma *n.* an apparent absence or defect of some ocular tissue, usually due to failure of a part of the fetal fissure to close. See IRIS COLOBOMA.

colocalization *n.* spatial overlap, in particular the presence of more than one neurotransmitter in the same PRESYNAPTIC terminal or of more than one brain activation in neuroimaging.

colonial nesting the gathering of several breeding pairs of birds of a COLONIAL SPECIES in one place to build nests, breed, and rear offspring. Colonial nesting provides the advantage of having many individuals to detect and attack potential predators and it is an important adaptation when suitable nesting sites are rare and clustered. The costs of colonial nesting are increased potential for disease transmission between groups and the need for large amounts of available food.

colonial species a species in which several breeding groups live in close spatial proximity. Cliff swallows and herring gulls, for example, build nests in close proximity to many others of their species (see COLONIAL NESTING). Colonial species can benefit from their close proximity in collective defense against predators. However, there may be extreme competition or INFANTICIDE between neighbors and increased risk of disease transmission.

colony *n.* **1.** a gathering of animals of the same species into a relatively large group that may or may not display SOCIAL ORGANIZATION. A colony may provide the advantage of having many individuals available for locating food and defending against predators, but it has potential costs in terms of increased competition for food or breeding opportunities and increased potential for disease transmission. **2.** a group of people who settle in a new territory but continue to have some relationship with their homeland. **3.** a territory that has become subject to the political and economic control of another country, usually a distant one, as a result of settlement from that country. The settlers or their descendants usually form the ruling class, despite being a minority. **4.** a group of individuals who share a common interest and live in close proximity, such as an artists' colony or nudist colony, or the place inhabited by such a group. **—colonial** *adj.* **—colonialism** *n.* **—colonist** *n.* **—colonize** *vb.*

color *n.* the quality of light that corresponds to wavelength as perceived by retinal receptors. Color can be characterized by its HUE, SATURATION, and LUMINOUS INTENSITY. See also ACHROMATIC COLORS; CHROMATIC COLORS.

color adaptation see CHROMATIC ADAPTATION.

color agnosia a condition in which an individual with intact color vision can neither name a color on presentation nor point to a given color when the name is offered. In addition, object–color relations are impaired, that is, individuals are unable to match the appropriate color with a given object or to state the correct color of a given object (e.g., "yellow" for "banana"). Color agnosia can occur after bilateral injury to the occipitotemporal region of the brain. The condition should not be confused with COLOR BLINDNESS.

color amnesia an inability to recall the characteristic colors of objects (e.g., a fire truck is red), despite intact color vision and perception.

color anomia the inability to name a presented color while being able to point to it when the name is given and to match colors correctly. Color anomia is explained as a disconnection of the cortical color centers from the language areas in the left hemisphere of the brain.

color attribute any of the basic characteristics of color: HUE, SATURATION, or LUMINOUS INTENSITY.

color balance the amounts of different colors that are most pleasing with each other. German poet and scholar Johann von Goethe (1749–1832) was the first to formulate a mathematical description of color balance; his work was amplified by U.S. painter Albert H. Munsell (1858–1918). See also MUNSELL COLOR SYSTEM.

color blindness the inability to discriminate between colors and to perceive color hues. Color blindness may be caused by disease, drugs, or brain injury (see ACQUIRED COLOR BLINDNESS), but most often is an inherited trait (**congenital color blindness**) that affects about 10% of men (it is rare in women). The most widely used classification of the different types of color blindness is based on the trichromatic nature of normal color perception, using prefixes to indicate the three primary colors: **proto-** (red), **deutero-** (green), and **trit-** (blue). The type of deficiency is indicated by suffixes: **-anomaly** for partial inability to perceive one or more of the primary colors and **-anopia** for complete inability to do this. The most common form of the disorder involves the green or red receptors of the cone cells in the retina, causing a red–green confusion (see DEUTERANOPIA; PROTANOPIA). Total color blindness is rare, affecting about 3 individuals out of 1 million (see ACHROMATISM). See also DICHROMATISM; TRITANOPIA.

color-blindness test any task or device that tests the ability to distinguish different colored stimuli, specifically to discover abnormalities in the perception of color. The most common tests involve the detection of colored figures against a colored background under conditions that require the use of hue information, rather than luminous intensity or saturation. See also ISHIHARA TEST FOR COLOR BLINDNESS.

color cells the three types of RETINAL CONES, each of which is sensitive to one of the visual primary colors: red, green, and blue. See PHOTOPIGMENT; TRICHROMATIC THEORY. See also COLOR BLINDNESS.

color circle 1. an array of CHROMATIC COLORS around the circumference of a circle. The colors are arranged in the order in which they are seen in the spectrum, but nonspectral purples and reds are also included. Complementary colors are opposite each other. **2.** the arrangement of color sectors on a disk such that the disk appears gray when the colors are "mixed" by rotation of the disk. [first devised by Sir Isaac Newton (1642–1727), British mathematician and physicist]

color cone a three-dimensional representation of all visible colors that takes into account HUE, SATURATION, and LUMINOUS INTENSITY. Luminous intensity is represented on the vertical axis, hue is represented in polar coordinates around the vertical axis, and saturation is represented radially around the vertical axis. See COLOR SOLID.

color constancy the tendency to perceive a familiar object as having the same color under different conditions of illumination. For example, a red apple will be perceived as red in well or poorly illuminated surroundings. Color constancy is an example of PERCEPTUAL CONSTANCY. Compare BRIGHTNESS CONSTANCY; OBJECT CONSTANCY; SHAPE CONSTANCY; SIZE CONSTANCY.

color contrast the effect of one color upon another when they are perceived in close proximity. In **simultaneous contrast**, complementary colors, such as yellow and blue, are enhanced by each other: The yellow appears yellower, and the blue appears bluer. In **successive contrast**, the complement of a fixated color is perceived when the FIXATION is shifted to a neutral surface. Also called **chromatic contrast**.

color deficiency a departure from normal trichromatic color vision. See also ACHROMATISM.

Colored Progressive Matrices a version of RAVEN'S PROGRESSIVE MATRICES designed especially for children and older adults. The test comprises 36 designs printed on colored backgrounds and arranged in three groups of 12. The items within each group become progressively more difficult, but overall are simpler and easier to solve than those on the standard matrices. Also called **Raven's Colored Progressive Matrices**.

color fusion see COLOR MIXTURE.

color harmony the extent to which colors are pleasing in combination with one another. At least in isolation, complementary colors and colors of the same hue but differing considerably in saturation or lightness are judged to be most harmonious.

color hearing see CHROMATIC AUDITION.

colorimeter *n.* an instrument used to compare, identify, or reproduce colors by comparison with a known mixture of monochromatic and white lights or a mixture of the three primary colors.

color induction see INDUCED COLOR.

color mixer a device that enables light of two different wavelengths to be presented simultaneously or in rapid sequence to the same region of the retina.

color mixture a fusion effect produced by combining pigments (SUBTRACTIVE MIXTURE), projecting lights simultaneously (ADDITIVE COLOR MIXTURE), or rapid rotation in a COLOR MIXER (retinal mixture).

color-mixture laws principles describing the perception that results when stimuli of different hue are presented simultaneously. An example is **Newton's law of color mixture**, which states that if two color mixtures evoke the same perception of color, then mixing them together will evoke the same perception of color.

color-mixture primaries the PRIMARY COLORS, usually red, green, and blue, which produce a total range of hues when mixed.

color perception the awareness of the stimulus attribute of HUE.

color purity a measure of the extent to which a color is free of white, gray, or black. A color that is predominantly free of such admixtures is said to have **high chromaticity**.

color pyramid see COLOR SOLID.

color saturation the degree of purity or richness of a color: that is, the attribute of a chromatic stimulus that describes the extent to which it differs from an achromatic stimulus of the same luminous intensity. See SATURATION.

color scotoma an area of depressed or lost color vision in one or both eyes. Color scotomas may be present in cases of OPTIC NEURITIS and are found in the contralateral half of the visual field of each eye after unilateral brain injury (see HEMIACHROMATOPSIA).

color sensation the experience evoked by exposure of the visual system to chromatic stimuli. Mental awareness and the integration of color sensations lead to COLOR PERCEPTION.

color solid a three-dimensional representation of all aspects of color, including the various degrees and combinations of hue, luminous intensity, and saturation. Various solid shapes can be used to form such a representation; these give rise to different types of color solids, such as the COLOR CONE, **color pyramid**, and **color spindle**.

color subtraction a process in which some wavelengths of an illuminating light source are absorbed by pigments in an object, while the remaining wavelengths are reflected. The reflected wavelengths are therefore the only ones that can be perceived, regardless of the wavelength composition of the original illumination. See also COLOR MIXTURE; SUBTRACTIVE MIXTURE. Compare ADDITIVE COLOR MIXTURE.

color surface a plane made by cutting through a COLOR SOLID to show all possible hues and saturations at a specific level of luminous intensity.

color system any system devised to organize colored stimuli that takes into account the attributes of hue, saturation, and luminous intensity. Examples include the DIN COLOR SYSTEM, MUNSELL COLOR SYSTEM, Ostwald color system, and Ridgway color system.

color temperature the temperature in kelvins (K) of a nonblack body indicated by the temperature to which a black body would need to be heated to give the same spectral distribution as that of the nonblack body. For example, candlelight has a color temperature of 1500 K, whereas blue sky is over 9000 K.

color theories theories formulated to explain color phenomena. See GRANIT THEORY OF COLOR VISION; HERING THEORY OF COLOR VISION; LADD-FRANKLIN THEORY; LAND THEORY OF COLOR VISION; OPPONENTS THEORY OF COLOR VISION; TRICHROMATIC THEORY; YOUNG–HELMHOLTZ THEORY OF COLOR VISION.

color tint a variant of any color that is lighter than a medium gray.

color tone the HUE of a color.

color triangle a triangular two-dimensional representation of the relationship between hue, luminous intensity, and saturation. Compare COLOR SOLID.

color value **1.** an attribute of a colored stimulus related to its LUMINANCE or perceived amount of gray. **2.** a dimension in the MUNSELL COLOR SYSTEM that specifies the lightness of a stimulus.

color vision the ability to distinguish visual stimuli on the basis of the wavelengths of light they emit or reflect. See COLOR THEORIES.

color weakness an impaired ability to perceive hues accurately. The term is often (inaccurately) used interchangeably with COLOR BLINDNESS. See also ACHROMATISM; DYSCHROMATOPSIA.

color wheel a disk divided into sectors of different colors. The wheel is rotated to investigate COLOR MIXTURE.

color zones **1.** areas of the retina that are differentially sensitive to different colors. All colors are perceived in the FOVEA CENTRALIS; blues, yellows, and grays in the middle zone; and (with some overlap) only ACHROMATIC COLORS in the periphery. **2.** in PERIMETRY, regions in the visual field with different color sensitivity, corresponding to the regions of retinal color sensitivity.

colostrum *n.* the first milk secreted by a woman immediately following the end of pregnancy. The milk is thin and opalescent and differs in nutrient composition compared with milk secreted during the remaining lactation period, having high levels of antibodies, which confer passive IMMUNITY on the infant.

column *n.* in anatomy, a structure that resembles an architectural pillar. Columns range from macroscopic, such as the SPINAL COLUMN, to microscopic, such as CORTICAL COLUMNS and DORSAL COLUMNS. —**columnar** *adj.*

columnar organization of the cortex see CORTICAL COLUMN.

coma *n.* a profound state of unconsciousness characterized by little or no response to stimuli, absence of reflexes, and suspension of voluntary activity. Common causes include severe brain injury, intracranial tumor, encephalitis, cerebral hemorrhage or embolism, diabetes, and drug or alcohol intoxication. Also called **comatose state**. See also GLASGOW COMA SCALE.

coma stimulation the use of multimodal sensory stimulation in an attempt to speed up the process of recovery from coma or improve arousal level. The efficacy of such approaches remains unknown.

coma therapy a treatment for schizophrenia, developed in the 1930s but rarely used after 1960, in which hypoglycemia was induced by intramuscular injection of insulin to produce a temporary coma. Inductions might last for 15 to 60 min, and a full course of coma treatment typically involved numerous coma inductions over a given period. Also called **insulin-coma therapy**; **insulin-shock therapy**.

comatose state see COMA.

coma vigil a coma with the eyes open, occurring in patients with acute impairment of brain function resulting from systemic infection, ingestion of drugs, or brain trauma. See LOCKED-IN SYNDROME.

combat stress reactions (**CSR**) psychological reactions to traumatic events in military operations, which can range from mild to severe and are normal reactions to the abnormal events. In World War I such reactions were known as SHELL SHOCK, whereas in World War II the terms **battle fatigue**, **combat fatigue**, **combat hysteria**, and **combat neurosis** were widely used. In *DSM–IV–TR* they are categorized as POSTTRAUMATIC STRESS DISORDERS. See also STRESS CASUALTY.

combat stress reduction measures designed to develop skills to reduce COMBAT STRESS REACTIONS. Stress reduction entails remediation procedures, regulatory techniques, and preventive strategies (psychological coping techniques).

combination *n.* in statistics, the selection of *r* objects from among *n* objects without regard to the order in which the objects are selected. The number of combinations of *n* objects taken *r* at a time is often denoted as ${}_nC_r$.

combination law see LAW OF COMBINATION.

combination test a type of test in which the main task is to assemble or combine words or objects into a more complex whole.

combination therapy the application of two or more distinct therapeutic approaches by the same therapist to a client's presenting problem. Compare ADJUNCTIVE THERAPY; COLLABORATIVE CARE.

combination tone a tone generated in the ear that is produced when two **primary tones** (i.e., two tones differing in frequency) are presented simultaneously. For example, under certain conditions a 1-kHz tone and a 1.2-kHz tone will produce audible combination tones whose frequencies are 200 Hz (a **difference tone**) and 800 Hz (a **cubic difference tone**). Most combination tones are produced by nonlinear distortion that occurs within the cochlea.

combinatorial operations mental processes that generate new representations by merging constituents according to a set of rules. For example, sentences are constructed by combinatorial operations on words and phrases according to the rules of syntax.

combined motor method a technique for measuring and assessing emotional responses to stimuli, in which participants perform a simple movement (e.g., pressing a key) when exposed to a stimulus. The reaction time and dynamics of the movement (e.g., strength with which the key is pressed and the duration of the key press) are recorded and are assumed to indicate the intensity of different emotions. Devised by Alexander LURIA, it is known informally as the **Luria technique**.

combined therapy 1. psychotherapy in which the client is engaged in two or more treatments with the same or different therapists. For example, MARITAL THERAPY may include group therapy with several other couples in addition to individual therapy or CONJOINT THERAPY for each couple. **2.** treatment using a combination of psychotherapy and medication. See also ADJUNCTIVE THERAPY; ADJUVANT THERAPY.

combined transcortical aphasia (**CTA**) a form of APHASIA resulting from lesions in both the anterior speech areas (**transcortical motor aphasia**; **TMA**) and the posterior speech areas (**transcortical sensory aphasia**; **TSA**) of the brain. Individuals can neither produce nor comprehend speech, resulting in the so-called "isolation syndrome" characterized by ECHOLALIA.

combined treatment see COMBINED THERAPY.

combining effect sizes a process for bringing together estimates of EFFECT SIZES from different studies in order to obtain a single estimate of the magnitude of an effect.

combining significance levels calculating the overall SIGNIFICANCE LEVELS resulting from multiple tests of the same hypothesis.

comedian *n.* in the psychology of groups, see RELATIONSHIP ROLE.

coming out revealing that one is gay, lesbian, bisexual, or transgender. Such a declaration can sometimes lead to problems with the individual's family, employers, or friends and can therefore be a difficult step, even for those who accept and are comfortable with their sexual orientation. Also called **coming out of the closet**.

command automatism actions performed by command or self-initiation, without critical judgment or conscious control. Such behavior may be observed in individuals with schizophrenia or those who are in a hypnotized state.

command style in education, a highly structured, authoritarian instruction method dominated by the teacher and excluding or greatly limiting student participation. Compare INDIVIDUAL PROGRAM.

commensalism *n.* an INTERSPECIES INTERACTION in which two species live closely together with neither species gaining or losing any benefits from the association. Compare MUTUALISM; PARASITISM. —**commensal** *adj.*, *n.*

commercial *n.* an advertisement on radio or television to promote a product or service. Commercials typically last 15–60 seconds. **Infomercials** are longer commercials (usually 30 minutes) in which a product or service is demonstrated and discussed in detail.

commissural fiber a MYELINATED FIBER of a nerve cell that connects the same or equivalent structures in the left and right cerebral hemispheres. Also called **intercerebral fiber**. Compare ASSOCIATION FIBER.

commissure *n.* a structure that forms a bridge or junction between two anatomical areas. Examples of commissures include the ANTERIOR COMMISSURE, which joins parts of the two cerebral hemispheres; and the **hippocampal commissure**, which joins the posterior columns of the FORNIX. The CORPUS CALLOSUM, connecting the two cerebral hemispheres, is the largest of the interhemispheric commissures; it is known as the **great commissure**. The anterior commissure and POSTERIOR COMMISSURE are key landmarks in BRAIN MAPPING. See also GRAY COMMISSURE; WHITE COMMISSURE. **—commissural** *adj.*

commissurotomy *n.* surgical transection or severing of a COMMISSURE, especially surgical separation of the cerebral hemispheres of the brain by severing the CORPUS CALLOSUM (called **callosectomy**, **callosotomy**, or **corpuscallosotomy**) and often the ANTERIOR COMMISSURE. This procedure is used clinically to treat severe epilepsy and has been used experimentally in animals to study the functions of each hemisphere. Because commissurotomy allows each hemisphere to function relatively independently, considerable information has been obtained about HEMISPHERIC LATERALIZATION in humans and animals. Research in this area was pioneered by Roger SPERRY, who—by directing stimuli to one or the other hemisphere—provided compelling evidence that the two hemispheres have different roles (see also CHIMERIC STIMULATION). Also called **split-brain procedure**; **split-brain technique**.

commitment *n.* confinement to a mental institution by court order following certification by appropriate psychiatric or other mental health authorities. The process may be voluntary but is generally involuntary. See CERTIFICATION LAWS. See also CIVIL COMMITMENT; CRIMINAL COMMITMENT; OBSERVATION COMMITMENT; TEMPORARY COMMITMENT; VOLUNTARY ADMISSION.

commitment laws legislation governing the holding of a patient in a mental hospital involuntarily upon certification. See CERTIFICATION LAWS.

commitment therapy see ACCEPTANCE AND COMMITMENT THERAPY.

commodity theory a theory proposing that the value of a product or service is related to its availability. In general, a product that is in short supply is perceived as having greater value than one that is readily available. However, a product's value is also related to the demand for it. It may be scarce, but if no one wants it, it will not have a high value. Commodity theory is used to explain consumer behavior in times of product or service restriction.

common cause hypothesis the hypothesis that all changes in sensory ability and intellectual functioning (COGNITIVE AGING) in old age are due to a common factor, the deterioration of brain function.

common chemical sense see CHEMESTHESIS.

common conscience see COLLECTIVE CONSCIENCE.

common factors in psychotherapy, variables that are common to various therapies with individuals, such as THERAPEUTIC ALLIANCE and length of treatment, as opposed to factors that are unique to a particular therapy, such as the use of interpretation. THERAPEUTIC FACTORS are similar, but typically apply to therapies with groups.

common fate in GESTALT PSYCHOLOGY, a principle of perception that objects functioning or moving in the same direction appear to belong together, that is, they are perceived as a single unit (e.g., a flock of birds). WERTHEIMER called this principle the **factor of uniform density**. Also called **law of common fate**; **principle of common fate**. See GESTALT PRINCIPLES OF ORGANIZATION.

common law 1. the legal principles deriving from previous decisions of the courts, as opposed to those established by statute. Also called **judge-made law**. See CASE LAW. **2.** the legal system originating in England and used in the United States and some other English-speaking countries, especially as opposed to those systems deriving from Roman law used in Continental Europe.

common-law marriage a relationship between an unmarried but long-term cohabiting couple that is considered legally equivalent to marriage. Most states in the United States do not recognize common-law marriages, although cohabitees may be regarded as equivalent to married partners for some purposes.

common sense 1. beliefs or propositions that are generally agreed upon to reflect sound judgment and nonesoteric reasoning. **2.** see SENSUS COMMUNIS. **—commonsense** *adj.*

commonsense justice practices and procedures that ordinary people consider to be fair and just, which may differ from legal conceptions of justice and fairness.

commonsense psychology ideas about psychological issues derived from common experience and not necessarily from empirical laboratory or clinical studies. See FOLK PSYCHOLOGY; POPULAR PSYCHOLOGY.

common social motive an interpersonal want or need that is shared by a significant proportion of a social, ethnic, regional, or cultural group. Unlike a biological motive, such as hunger or thirst, a common social motive prompts individuals to pursue in unison the same interpersonal goals, such as social contact, safety, achievement, or power.

common traits in personality theory, those traits that are shared in varying degrees by all individuals in a specific group or culture. The BIG FIVE PERSONALITY MODEL maintains that the personalities of virtually all individuals may be classified according to their degree of introversion–extraversion, warmth, achievement orientation, stability, and openness to experiences.

communal feeling a general sense of belonging to a unified, socially integrated group that can prompt members to act in ways that enhance the group's interests rather than their individualistic, personal interests. Also called **community feeling**. See also COHESION; COMMUNAL SPIRIT; ESPRIT DE CORPS; GROUP SOLIDARITY.

communality *n.* the proportion of the VARIANCE in a variable accounted for by the common factors that make up the variable in FACTOR ANALYSIS. The communality is scaled so that, if the factors completely account for all the variability in the variable, the communality is 1.0. The communality is the sum of squared FACTOR LOADINGS of that variable over all of the common factors in the factor analysis. See UNIQUENESS.

communal relationship a relationship in which interaction is governed primarily by consideration of the other's needs and wishes. This contrasts with an **exchange relationship**, in which the people involved are concerned mainly with receiving as much as they give. See also EQUITY THEORY. [discussed by U.S. social psychologists Margaret Clark and Judson Mills]

communal spirit a sense of unity and shared purpose felt by a group or community. Also called **community spirit**. See also COHESION; COMMUNAL FEELING; ESPRIT DE CORPS; GROUP SOLIDARITY.

commune *n.* a collective living arrangement among individuals or families, typically involving shared chores, resources, and child-rearing, as an alternative to marriage and the NUCLEAR FAMILY. Such arrangements were fashionable in the COUNTERCULTURE of the 1960s and 1970s.

communicated authenticity, regard, empathy (**CARE**) qualities of a psychotherapist regarded by some theorists as necessary for therapy to be effective and, ultimately, successful. CARE is considered essential to CLIENT-CENTERED THERAPY.

communicating hydrocephalus HYDROCEPHALUS in the absence of any blockage in the flow of cerebrospinal fluid in the ventricular system. Cerebrospinal fluid passes freely from the brain into the spinal canal but is overproduced or abnormally or inadequately reabsorbed. Compare NONCOMMUNICATING HYDROCEPHALUS.

communication *n.* the transmission of information, which may be by verbal (oral or written) or nonverbal means (see NONVERBAL COMMUNICATION). Humans communicate to relate and exchange ideas, knowledge, feelings, experiences and for many other interpersonal and social purposes. Nonhuman animals likewise communicate vocally or nonvocally for a variety of purposes (see ANIMAL COMMUNICATION). Communication is studied by cognitive and experimental psychologists, and COMMUNICATION DISORDERS are treated by mental and behavioral health therapists and by speech and language therapists. **Communications** is the discipline that studies the processes and systems involved in communication, especially the publishing media and telecommunication systems (telephones, radio, television, etc.).

communication analysis the study of the oral and written communications among people, particularly employees in an organization, with the objective of understanding and improving the process. It can include a determination of the patterns and types of these communications as well as an analysis of breakdowns in the communication process. See COMMUNICATION ERGONOMICS.

communication apprehension anxiety related to initiating or maintaining conversation with others. This is a common feature of SOCIAL PHOBIA. See also PUBLIC-SPEAKING ANXIETY.

communication channels see CHANNELS OF COMMUNICATION.

communication deviance (**CD**) lack of clarity in communication, making it hard to follow and difficult for the listener to share a common focus of attention and meaning with the speaker. Communication deviance is thought to be a long-term trait within families that may engender inefficient patterns of thinking and information processing. It is also thought to be associated with schizophrenia and other psychological disorders.

communication disorder any of a group of disorders characterized by difficulties with speech and language. In *DSM–IV–TR* communication disorders include EXPRESSIVE LANGUAGE DISORDER, MIXED RECEPTIVE-EXPRESSIVE LANGUAGE DISORDER, PHONOLOGICAL DISORDER, STUTTERING, and COMMUNICATION DISORDER NOT OTHERWISE SPECIFIED.

communication disorder not otherwise specified in *DSM–IV–TR,* a communication disorder that does not meet the diagnostic criteria for any of the specific disorders of this category. An example is a VOICE DISORDER.

communication engineering the application of scientific principles to the development of technical systems for communication, such as telephone, radio, television, and computer networks. The development and proliferation of computer networks have made knowledge of computer technology essential to communication engineering.

communication ergonomics a specialty area of ERGONOMICS that identifies those factors that support or undermine communication in shared tasks. Such factors, including information systems, technical systems, and COMMUNICATION NETWORKS and protocols, may be especially important when participants in a task are widely distributed and safety depends on clear, unambiguous communication (as, for example, in air traffic control).

communication network the patterns of information transmission and exchange that occur in a group or organization, showing who communicates most frequently (and to what extent) with whom. Such nets may be either centralized or decentralized and characterized mainly by DOWNWARD COMMUNICATION or UPWARD COMMUNICATION. Also called **communication net**. See also CHANNELS OF COMMUNICATION.

communication overload a condition in which more information is presented to a computer system or a person than can be processed or otherwise effectively utilized by the system or person. See also COGNITIVE OVERLOAD; INFORMATION OVERLOAD; SENSORY OVERLOAD; STIMULUS OVERLOAD.

communication skills the skills required to achieve effective communication. In addition to general language proficiency (adequate vocabulary and knowledge of syntax), effective communication involves the ability to listen and read with comprehension, to present one's thoughts clearly both in speech and in writing, to accept that the perspectives of others may differ from one's own, and to anticipate the effect of what one says or writes on listeners or readers.

communication skills training an intervention that teaches individuals to express themselves clearly and directly and to listen in an active and empathic way, using such techniques as feedback and modeling, in group, family, or work contexts. Training sessions typically focus on a specific theme (e.g., active listening, problem solving, or conflict resolution) after which homework is assigned. Initially developed for couples and families, the training is now used with such populations as people with developmental impairment and with teams in industry settings.

communication system an organized scheme or mechanism for transmitting and receiving information for the purposes of communication. The communication may be between people, between machines (usually computers), or between people and machines. Traditional systems include one-way communication (e.g., broadcast radio, television) and two-way communication (e.g., telephone, citizens-band radio). Computers and computer networks provide both one-way communication (e.g., WEBSITES, ELECTRONIC BULLETIN BOARDS) and two-way communication (e.g., E-MAIL, chat rooms).

communication theory 1. the theoretical treatment of the interchange of signs and signals that constitutes communication. **2.** the branch of science concerned with all aspects (technical, physiological, psychological, and social) of the storage and transmission of information. See INFORMATION THEORY.

communicative acts verbal or nonverbal behaviors through which one party deliberately or unintentionally transmits information to others.

communicative competence a speaker's knowledge of language and ability to use it appropriately in various communicative settings and with a range of different interlocutors. In contrast to Noam CHOMSKY's notion of COMPETENCE, which explicitly excludes nonlinguistic factors, the idea of communicative competence stresses the social uses of language and the importance of context. See also COMMUNICATION SKILLS. [first described by U.S. sociolinguist Dell H. Hymes (1927–)]

communicology *n.* an area covering the theory and practice of AUDIOLOGY, speech and language pathology, and improvement in communication by means of exchanging ideas, relating experiences, and giving voice to feelings.

communion principle a theory that the first requisite

of individual and group psychotherapy is a sense of unity and mutuality between client and therapist, thus enabling both parties to feel that they are engaged in a common enterprise to bring about improvement for the client.

communitas *n.* a society or social group with a strong sense of COMMUNAL SPIRIT and COMMUNAL FEELING, especially one bound together by shared rituals and traditions. *Communitas* (Latin for COMMUNITY) was also the title of the classic 1947 text on city planning by U.S. psychologist Paul Goodman (1911–1972) and his architect brother Percival Goodman, which stressed the relationship between city design and human potential.

communities for people with mental retardation service settings that consist of clusters of houses in which adults with mental retardation who can function somewhat independently participate in work and daily routines with people without disabilities. With the help of staff members, these adults manage the houses independently—planning meals, purchasing and preparing food, and participating in household maintenance chores—and enjoy leisure activities with their peers. In many instances staff live in the community as well.

community *n.* **1.** a socially organized set of species members living in a physically defined locality. Human communities are often characterized by (a) commonality of interests, attitudes, and values; (b) COMMUNAL FEELING; (c) members' self-identification as community members; and (d) some system of communication, governance, education, and commerce. In general parlance "the community" often means society or the general public. **2.** a collection of individuals who are not socially connected but do share common interests or qualities and are therefore perceived by others or by themselves as distinctive in some way (e.g., the scientific community). **3.** in BEHAVIORAL ECOLOGY, a unit comprising all the animal and plant species that coexist and are necessary for each other's survival. Thus a community includes predator and prey species as well as the various plants that animals need for food, shelter, and so forth; the plants may benefit from the presence of the animals in the community through seed dispersal or INTERSPECIES INTERACTIONS.

community action group a group of citizens organized to campaign against specific problems within the local community, such as inadequate delivery of health services, homelessness, or crime.

community attitude a feeling of approval or disapproval that is shared by most or all of the members of a community for particular behaviors, traits, and so on.

community care in psychiatry, psychology, and rehabilitation, comprehensive community-based services and supports for people with developmental or physical disabilities. These facilities or services include halfway houses, group homes, sheltered workshops and supported work arrangements, supervised and supportive residences for people with multiple disabilities or mental retardation, special education or integrated education programs for children and young people, in-home treatment and family support, personal-care or home-care assistance, case management or service coordination, cooperative living, and hospital-based or free-standing clinics.

community-centered approach a concerted, coordinated approach to such problems as mental disorder, delinquency, and substance abuse on the part of agencies and facilities in the local community or catchment area. The community-centered approach holds that since these problems developed in the community, efforts at prevention and treatment should be community-based rather than being the province primarily of state institutions or federal agencies. See COMMUNITY MENTAL HEALTH CENTER; COMMUNITY MENTAL HEALTH PROGRAM; COMMUNITY SERVICES.

community competence a COMMUNITY's efficacy in producing and regulating its outcomes, or its members' perceptions of this efficacy. Compare COLLECTIVE EFFICACY.

community correction see ALTERNATIVE SENTENCING.

community ergonomics the application of ergonomic principles and practices to address cumulative social trauma in complex societal systems. Community ergonomics focuses on distressed community settings characterized by poverty, social isolation, dependency, and low levels of self-regulation and control. In practice, community ergonomics seeks to identify and implement a community–environment interface to bridge the gap between the disadvantaged residents of a community and the resources defining the social environment within which they function.

community feeling see COMMUNAL FEELING.

community inclusion the practice of accepting and encouraging the presence and participation of people with disabilities, in particular developmental disabilities, in the full range of social, educational, work, and community activities. See also FULL INCLUSION.

community integration the practice of assisting people with disabilities, especially developmental disabilities, to participate in community activities. Those with such disabilities are encouraged to attend community functions, engage in social interactions with peers and community members without disabilities, and join formal and informal community groups.

community mental health activities undertaken in the community, rather than in institutional settings, to promote mental health. The community approach focuses primarily on the total population of a single catchment area and involves overall planning and demographic analyses. It emphasizes preventive services as distinguished from therapeutic services (e.g., by identifying sources of stress within the community) and seeks to provide a continuous, comprehensive system of services designed to meet all mental health-related needs in the community. Mental health is approached indirectly through consultation and education, with emphasis on such strategies as SHORT-TERM THERAPY and CRISIS INTERVENTION and using new types of workers, such as paraprofessionals and indigenous mental health workers.

community mental health center **(CMHC)** a community-based facility or group of facilities providing a full range of prevention, treatment, and rehabilitation services, sometimes organized as a practical alternative to the largely custodial care given in mental hospitals. Typical services are full diagnostic evaluation; outpatient individual and group psychotherapy; emergency inpatient treatment; specialized clinics for people with substance abuse and for disturbed children and families; aftercare (foster homes, halfway houses, home visiting); vocational, educational, and social rehabilitation programs for current and former patients; consultation to physicians, members of the clergy, courts, schools, health departments, and welfare agencies; and training for all types of mental health personnel. Also called **comprehensive mental health center**.

community mental health program an integrated program designed to meet the overall mental health needs of a particular community, including inpatient, outpatient, and emergency treatment; special facilities for treating children and patients with alcohol and drug dependence; and educational, counseling, rehabilitation, research, and training programs. See COMMUNITY-CENTERED APPROACH; COMMUNITY MENTAL HEALTH CENTER.

community mental health services see COMMUNITY SERVICES.

community mental health training training for mental health professionals in order to facilitate programs and services offered to the community.

community needs assessment see NEEDS ASSESSMENT.

Community Notification Act see MEGAN'S LAW.

community prevention and intervention organized efforts by professionals, indigenous non-professionals, and others with special competence to deal actively and constructively with community problems and to implement preventive programs as well as systems for intervention. Issues addressed in this way include substance abuse, homelessness, child abuse, juvenile delinquency, cigarette smoking, and a high suicide rate. Such broad-based efforts are typically most effective where the residents are themselves involved in dealing with such problems through existing community groups, such as neighborhood councils, block committees, service groups, social and fraternal organizations, and community educational and self-help programs.

community psychology the branch of psychology concerned with person–environment interactions and the way society affects individual and community functioning. Community psychology focuses on social issues, social institutions, and other settings that influence individuals, groups, and organizations. Community researchers examine the ways that individuals interact with each other, social groups (e.g., clubs, churches, schools, families), and the larger culture and environment. Research findings and methods are applied with regard to poverty, substance abuse, violence, school failure, and many other social issues. See COMMUNITY-CENTERED APPROACH; COMMUNITY SERVICES.

community residence a residential setting, usually serving 3 to 15 people and located in a regular house, with live-in or shift staffing. Community residences, some of which provide clinical services in addition to supervision, personal assistance, and training in everyday living skills, represent the most common out-of-home residential setting for people with mental retardation or developmental disabilities. Their use as a residential alternative for people with severe and persistent mental disorders is growing.

community services the complex of community-based services and facilities designed to maintain health and welfare, including mental health clinics, public health and adoption services, family services, vocational training facilities, rehabilitation centers, and living facilities (e.g., halfway houses, home care, and foster-family care). Also called **community mental health services**. See COMMUNITY CARE; COMMUNITY-CENTERED APPROACH.

community social worker a SOCIAL WORKER who maintains liaison between local, state, and federal government officials and the public on matters affecting the physical and psychological health of the community. For example, community social workers may try to raise the social consciousness of the community regarding recreational facilities, adequate housing, local employment problems, and environmental obstacles to the mobility of people with physical impairment.

community speech and hearing center see SPEECH, LANGUAGE, AND HEARING CENTER.

community spirit see COMMUNAL SPIRIT.

comorbidity *n.* the simultaneous presence in an individual of two or more mental or physical illnesses, diseases, or disorders. **—comorbid** *adj.*

companionate grandparent the type of grandparent who has a warm, loving relationship with his or her grandchildren but does not take on day-to-day responsibility for them. See also INVOLVED GRANDPARENT. Compare REMOTE GRANDPARENT.

companionate love a type of LOVE characterized by strong feelings of intimacy and affection for another person but not accompanied by strong passion or emotional arousal in the other's presence. In these respects, companionate love is distinguished from PASSIONATE LOVE. From the perspective of Robert J. Sternberg's TRIANGULAR THEORY OF LOVE, the relationship is high in intimacy and commitment.

companionate marriage a MARRIAGE without passion, usually one in which there is little if any sex.

comparable-forms reliability see ALTERNATE-FORMS RELIABILITY.

comparable groups two or more representative samples drawn from the same population for the purpose of observation or experiment.

comparable worth the principle that people should be paid the same if they perform similar work, as determined by evaluating jobs using procedures that provide objective comparisons on broad dimensions. According to the principle of comparable worth, if two jobs make similar behavioral demands, then the people thus employed should be paid the same despite differences in job titles, actual tasks performed, traditional compensation levels, or current market rates. The principle has been invoked chiefly by feminist campaigners, who argue that traditionally "female" occupations are paid less well than "male" occupations, despite the similarity of the behaviors and demands involved. Also called **pay equity**. See EQUITY THEORY.

comparative analysis see COMPARATIVE METHOD.

comparative judgment a psychophysical judgment in which two or more stimuli are compared with one another or with a given standard. Also called **relative judgment**. Compare ABSOLUTE JUDGMENT.

comparative linguistics the branch of linguistics that studies similarities and differences between languages with the general purpose of understanding the historical relationships between them. See DIACHRONIC LINGUISTICS; GENETIC LINGUISTICS; PHILOLOGY.

comparative method an experimental research method of analyzing and comparing the behavior of different species of animals, different cultures of humans, and different age groups of humans and other animals. For example, macaques are often used as a model for understanding human mother–infant relationships. However, male macaques rarely become interested in or involved with care of the young, and so comparative study of other species is needed to understand when and how male care of young develops.

comparative neuropsychology the study of the relationships between behavior and neural mechanisms in different animal species and human populations in order to understand the neural mechanisms that underlie behavior and the evolution of brain and behavior.

comparative psychology the study of animal behavior with the dual objective of understanding the behavior of nonhuman animals for its own sake as well as furthering the understanding of human behavior. Comparative psychology usually involves laboratory studies (compare ETHOLOGY) and typically refers to any study involving nonhuman species, whether or not the COMPARATIVE METHOD is used. Some **comparative psychologists** engage in both field and laboratory studies. See YERKES, ROBERT MEARNS. See also ANIMAL–HUMAN COMPARISON.

comparator *n.* an information-processing unit that compares one variable against a similar variable or standard measure and—based on the difference—may act to bring the variable within desired limits. For example, a thermostat may compare the ambient temperature against a preset temperature, turning the heating system on or off to minimize or eliminate any difference. See also BRAIN COMPARATOR; SERVOMECHANISM.

comparator hypothesis a theory of PAVLOVIAN CONDITIONING proposing that the strength of conditioning is based on comparing the likelihood that an unconditioned stimulus will occur following a conditioned stimulus with the likelihood that it will occur in the absence of a conditioned stimulus. It predicts that a response will be observed only if the former probability is higher.

comparison group see SOCIAL COMPARISON THEORY.

comparison level (**CL**) in SOCIAL EXCHANGE THEORY, the standard by which an individual evaluates the quality of any social relationship in which he or she is currently engaged. The CL derives from the average of all outcomes experienced by the individual in previous similar relationships or observed by the individual in similar relationships of others. In most cases, individuals whose prior relationships yielded positive rewards with few costs will have higher CLs than those who experienced fewer rewards and more costs in prior relationships. If the reward-to-cost ratio of the current relationship falls below the CL, the individual will experience dissatisfaction. [proposed in 1959 by U.S. social psychologists Harold H. Kelley (1921–) and John W. Thibaut (1917–1986)]

comparison level for alternatives (**CLAlt**) in social exchange theory, a standard used by individuals making decisions about whether to remain in a relationship. According to this theory, such decisions are based on a comparison of the outcomes (reward-to-cost ratios) of the current relationship with the possible outcomes of available alternative relationships. If the latter is higher, the relationship will become unstable and may not last. [proposed in 1959 by U.S. social psychologists John Thibaut (1917–1986) and Harold H. Kelley (1921–)]

comparison process in self psychology, any process in which an individual comes to understand and appraise the SELF by comparing its traits and performances with those of selected other people.

comparison stimulus (**Co**) one of a number of stimuli to be compared with a standard stimulus.

compartmentalization *n.* a DEFENSE MECHANISM in which thoughts and feelings that seem to conflict or to be incompatible are isolated from each other in separate and apparently impermeable psychic compartments. In the classical psychoanalytic tradition, compartmentalization produces fragmentation of the EGO, which ideally should be able to tolerate ambiguity and ambivalence. See also ISOLATION. **—compartmentalize** *vb.*

compassion *n.* a strong feeling of SYMPATHY with another person's feelings of sorrow or distress, usually involving a desire to help or comfort that person. Compare EMPATHY. **—compassionate** *adj.*

Compassionate Friends a voluntary organization that offers support, friendship, and understanding to parents and siblings grieving the death of a child. See SELF-HELP GROUP.

compassion fatigue the BURNOUT and stress-related symptoms experienced by caregivers and other helping professionals in reaction to working with traumatized people over an extended period of time. See also POST-TRAUMATIC STRESS DISORDER. [defined by U.S. psychologist Charles R. Figley (1944–)]

compatibility *n.* **1.** the state in which two or more people relate to each other harmoniously because their attitudes and desires do not conflict. Compare incompatibility. **2.** in philosophy, the position that FREE WILL and DETERMINISM are compatible and can, in some sense, coexist. See also HARD DETERMINISM; SOFT DETERMINISM. Compare INCOMPATIBILISM. **—compatible** *adj.*

Compazine *n.* a trade name for PROCHLORPERAZINE.

compensable job factor any of the factors that determine the worth of a particular job to the organization and hence the rate of compensation offered to those who perform it. The most commonly cited compensable job factors include skills, effort, or education required, amount of responsibilty entailed, and working conditions. The identification of such factors is the basis of the FACTOR-COMPARISON METHOD and the POINT METHOD of JOB EVALUATION.

compensating error an individual error that cancels the effects of another individual error, or, more generally, a set of errors that offset one another, leaving no net error or BIAS.

compensation *n.* **1.** substitution or development of strength or capability in one area to offset real or imagined lack or deficiency in another. This may be referred to as **overcompensation** when the substitute behavior exceeds what might actually be necessary in terms of level of compensation for the lack or deficiency. Compensation may be a conscious or unconscious process. In his classical psychoanalytic theory, Sigmund FREUD described compensation as a DEFENSE MECHANISM that protects the individual against the conscious realization of such lacks or deficiencies. The idea of compensation is central to Alfred ADLER's theory of personality, which sees all human striving as a response to feelings of inferiority (see also INFERIORITY COMPLEX). However, many psychologists emphasize the positive aspects of compensation in mitigating the effects of a weakness or deficiency (see COMPENSATORY MECHANISM). For example, it can be regarded as an important component of successful aging because it reduces the negative effects of cognitive and physical decline associated with the aging process. **2.** in Jean PIAGET's theory of cognitive development, a mental process—a form of REVERSIBILITY—in which one realizes that for any operation there exists another operation that compensates for the effects of the first, that is, a change in one dimension can compensate for changes in another. Also called **reciprocity**. **—compensate** *vb.* **—compensatory** *adj.*

compensation effect an increase in group performance that occurs when one or more members work harder to compensate for the real or imagined shortcomings of their fellow members. Compare KÖHLER EFFECT; SUCKER EFFECT.

compensatory damages a sum of money awarded in

a civil action ideally to restore the injured party to his or her state prior to the injury. Typical losses recoverable in compensatory damages are medical expenses, lost wages, and compensation for pain and suffering. Compare PUNITIVE DAMAGES.

compensatory education educational programs that are specially designed to enhance the intellectual and social skills of disadvantaged children. An example of such a program is PROJECT HEAD START.

compensatory eye movements movements of the eyes that counteract movement of the head. An example is the VESTIBULOOCULAR REFLEX.

compensatory mechanism a cognitive process that is used to offset a cognitive weakness. For example, someone who is weaker in spatial abilities than in verbal abilities might use compensatory mechanisms to attempt to solve spatial problems, such as mentally rotating a geometric figure by using verbal processes. The underlying theory is that intelligence partly consists of finding ways to compensate for the skills that one has lost over time or in which one was not adept in the first place. See also COMPENSATION.

compensatory nystagmus see BEKHTEREV'S NYSTAGMUS.

compensatory reflex a response that is opposite to, and therefore compensates for, another response. For example, a compensatory response to the suppression of pain by opioid drugs would be an increase in pain sensitivity, that is, with extended use, more of the drug is needed to achieve the same effect.

compensatory self-enhancement a strategy for self-presentation or boosting self-esteem in which people respond to bad feedback in one sphere by focusing on or emphasizing their positive traits in an unrelated sphere. The positive traits seem to offset the unwelcome implications of the bad feedback. Also called **self-affirmation**. See SELF-ENHANCEMENT.

compensatory task a task or project that a group can complete by averaging together individual members' solutions or recommendations. Such tasks are in most cases nondivisible (they cannot be broken down into subcomponents), optimizing (they call for high-quality solutions rather than high quantities of product), and of such a nature that relatively little coordination of members' efforts and activities is required. Groups outperform individuals on such tasks when (a) the members are equally proficient at the task and (b) the members do not share common biases that produce systematic tendencies toward overestimation or underestimation. Compare ADDITIVE TASK; CONJUNCTIVE TASK; DISJUNCTIVE TASK.

compensatory tracking in ergonomics, a TRACKING task requiring the operator to use a control (e.g., a joystick) to compensate for the movement of a cursor or other indicator on a display so that it remains within a defined target area. A driver, for example, must control his or her speed so that the needle on the speedometer remains below the mark showing the legal speed limit.

competence *n.* **1.** the ability to exert control over one's life, to cope with specific problems effectively, and to make changes to one's behavior and one's environment, as opposed to the mere ability to adjust or adapt to circumstances as they are. Affirming, strengthening, or achieving a client's competence is often a basic goal in psychotherapy. **2.** one's developed repertoire of skills, especially as it is applied to a task or set of tasks. A distinction is sometimes made between competence and performance, which is the extent to which competence is realized in one's actual work on a problem or set of problems. **3.** in linguistics and psycholinguistics, the unconscious knowledge of the underlying rules of a language that enables individuals to speak and understand it. In this sense, competence is a rationalist concept that must be kept distinct from the actual linguistic **performance** of any particular speaker, which may be constrained by such nonlinguistic factors as memory, attention, or fatigue. Both terms were introduced by Noam CHOMSKY, who proposed the study of linguistic competence as the true task of linguistics; in doing so, he effectively declared linguistics to be a branch of cognitive psychology. See GENERATIVE GRAMMAR; GRAMMATICALITY; LANGUAGE ACQUISITION DEVICE. **4.** in law, the capacity to comprehend the nature of a transaction and to assume legal responsibility for one's actions. See COMPETENCY TO STAND TRIAL; INCOMPETENCE. **—competent** *adj.*

competence knowledge in social psychology, SELF-ESTEEM and SELF-WORTH based on appraisals of one's competence made by others. Competence knowledge is the component of SELF-IMAGE that derives from an individual's unique talents and accomplishments; as such it is often contrasted with LEGITIMACY KNOWLEDGE, which derives from group identifications.

competence motivation the drive to interact effectively with the environment and develop personal skill and capability in solving problems and performing tasks, such mastery being reinforced by a sense of control and positive self-esteem.

competency-based instruction a teaching method in which students work at their own pace toward individual goals in a noncompetitive setting. The teacher works with students in identifying appropriate goals and monitoring their progress toward those goals.

competency evaluation evaluation of the defendant by a psychologist to determine his or her competency to stand trial.

competency to stand trial the capacity to be tried in court as determined by a person's ability, at the time of trial, to understand the nature of the charge and the potential consequences of conviction and to assist the attorney in his or her defense. Also called **adjudicative competence**; **fitness for trial**. See DUSKY STANDARD. See also INCOMPETENCY PLEA.

competing response training a technique in BEHAVIOR THERAPY that involves two sequential stages: (a) identification of habit occurrence, including antecedents and warning signs; and (b) creation and practice, in session and through homework, of a competing (i.e., alternative) response to the problem behavior. The competing response should be physically incompatible with the behavioral habit, inconspicuous, and easy to practice. This technique is typically used with habit disorders and is also used in ANGER MANAGEMENT training. See also ALTERNATIVE BEHAVIOR COMPLETION.

competition *n.* **1.** any performance situation structured in such a way that success depends on performing better than others. **Interpersonal competition** involves individuals striving to outperform each other; **intergroup competition** involves groups competing against other groups; **intragroup competition** involves individuals within a group trying to best each other. Because competing individuals sometimes increase their chances of success by actively undermining others' performances, such goal structures can create intense rivalries. Compare COOPERATION. **2.** in sport psychology, an OBJECTIVE COMPETITIVE SITUATION in which participants also experience a SUBJECTIVE COMPETITIVE SITUATION. **—compete** *vb.* **—competitive** *adj.*

competition by resource defense the use of territory or other defended space to exclude others from access to resources (see TERRITORIALITY). The resources are defended indirectly rather than by direct aggression or competition. A special case is RESOURCE DEFENSE POLYGYNY, in which a male can acquire additional mates if it is able to defend a larger than average set of resources.

competition for resources in ECOLOGY, the use of the same resource by individuals of the same species (**intraspecific competition**) or of different species (**interspecific competition**) when the supply of the resource is insufficient for the combined needs of all individuals. It is a major factor in NATURAL SELECTION. Also called **struggle for existence**. See also DARWINISM; SURVIVAL OF THE FITTEST.

competition goals see COMPETITIVE GOALS.

competition routine a predetermined pattern of behavior, SELF-TALK, and IMAGERY used during competition to enhance performance.

competition tolerance 1. acceptance of goal structures that require interactants to compete with one another. **2.** a positive, healthy reaction when one must perform competitively.

competitive bargaining see DISTRIBUTIVE BARGAINING.

competitive goals 1. standards of excellence to be achieved during a COMPETITION. Also called **competition goals**. **2.** established goals that cannot be achieved simultaneously—that in effect compete or conflict with one another. By spending time and effort to achieve one goal, an individual cannot achieve another goal.

competitive goal structure a performance situation structured in such a way that an interactant can reach his or her goals only by outperforming others or preventing others from reaching their goals. When goal structures are purely competitive, individual success requires that all others fail. Because competition creates incompatibility between people, such goal structures can generate interpersonal conflict. Compare COOPERATIVE GOAL STRUCTURE.

competitive motive the drive or dispositional tendency to respond competitively in interpersonal and performance settings by maximizing one's own outcomes and frustrating the progress of others. Compare COOPERATIVE MOTIVE.

competitiveness *n.* a disposition to seek out OBJECTIVE COMPETITIVE SITUATIONS and to compare one's performance against a standard or another person of comparable ability. **—competitive** *adj.*

competitive reward structure a performance setting in which rewards are assigned on the basis of individual rather than group achievement and which is structured in such a way that the success of any one individual decreases the rewards received by the other group members. Compare COOPERATIVE REWARD STRUCTURE; INDIVIDUALISTIC REWARD STRUCTURE.

competitive setting the environment in which an OBJECTIVE COMPETITIVE SITUATION occurs.

Competitive State Anxiety Inventory (**CSAI**) an instrument that assesses self-confidence and physical and cognitive elements of anxiety that are associated with an immediately upcoming competition (see STATE ANXIETY). It currently consists of 27 statements (e.g., "I am concerned about performing poorly") to which participants respond using a 4-point LIKERT SCALE, ranging from "not at all" to "very much so." [originally developed by sport psychologist Rainer Martens (1942–) and colleagues]

complement *n.* in linguistics, a word, phrase, or clause added to a verb to complete the sense of the PREDICATE. The term is most closely associated with the type of phrase that follows a COPULA (linking verb), such as *my father* in *He is my father* or *very unhappy* in *She looked very unhappy*.

complementarity *n.* in any DYADIC RELATIONSHIP, the existence of different personal qualities in each of the partners that contribute a sense of completeness to the other person and provide balance in the relationship. **—complementary** *adj.*

complementarity of interaction the concept that each individual in a DYNAMIC situation plays both a provocation role and a response role. It places emphasis on interaction as opposed to REACTION.

complementary and alternative medicine (**CAM**) a group of therapies and health care systems that fall outside the realm of conventional Western medical practice. These include but are not limited to ACUPUNCTURE, CHIROPRACTIC, MEDITATION, AROMATHERAPY, HOMEOPATHY, NATUROPATHY, OSTEOPATHY, TOUCH THERAPY, REFLEXOLOGY, REIKI, and the use of certain dietary supplements. Complementary medicine is used as an adjunct to conventional treatment; alternative medicine stands alone and replaces conventional treatment.

complementary class in SET THEORY, the totality of elements that do not belong to a particular CLASS. For example, if A is the class of all psychologists, then its complementary class is the class of all people who are not psychologists.

complementary classification in classification tasks, the grouping together of items from conceptually different categories into a superordinate class based on an individual's mental associations from past experience. For example, cow, tractor, and farmer may be grouped together because they are all found on a farm. Also called **functional classification**; **schematic classification**; **thematic classification**. Compare CONCEPTUAL CLASSIFICATION; IDIOSYNCRATIC CLASSIFICATION; PERCEPTUAL CLASSIFICATION.

complementary colors see ANTAGONISTIC COLORS.

complementary distribution the situation in which two or more ALLOPHONES of a PHONEME occur in mutually exclusive phonetic environments. Compare FREE VARIATION.

complete mother according to Austrian psychoanalyst Paul Federn (1871–1950), the ideal mother sought, both in fantasy and real life, by a person with schizophrenia: a mother who loves the child for him- or herself alone and not as a means of gratifying her own needs.

completion test a type of test in which the participant is usually required to supply a missing phrase, word, or letter in a written text. In nonverbal completion tests, a missing number, symbol, or representation must be supplied. See also STEM-COMPLETION TASK.

complex *n.* a group or system of related ideas or impulses that have a common emotional tone and exert a strong but usually unconscious influence on the individual's attitudes and behavior. The term, introduced by Carl JUNG to denote the contents of the PERSONAL UNCONSCIOUS, has taken on an almost purely pathological connotation in popular usage, which does not necessarily reflect usage in psychology. Primary examples from CLASSICAL PSYCHOANALYSIS and its offshoots are Jung's power complex, Sigmund FREUD'S CASTRATION COMPLEX and OEDIPUS COMPLEX, and Alfred ADLER'S INFERIORITY COMPLEX.

complex behavior an activity that requires many decisions and actions in rapid order or simultaneously. Dancing in a ballet is an example of a complex behavior.

complex cell a neuron in the cerebral cortex that responds to visual stimulation of appropriate contrast, orientation, and direction anywhere in the receptive field. Compare SIMPLE CELL.

Complex Figure Test a nonverbal memory test for a complex design. The individual is first asked to copy a complex design without being forewarned about a later memory test. This is followed by immediate and delayed recall trials in which the individual is asked to reproduce the complex figure from memory. A comparison of performance on the copy and recall trials allows the examiner to estimate the contribution of visuospatial and visuomotor processes, task strategy, and memory abilities to the individual's performance. The **Children's Complex Figure Test** is a version of this test for children. Also called **Rey Complex Figure Test (RCFT)**; **Rey–Osterrieth Complex Figure Test**.

complex ideas in ASSOCIATIONISM, those conceptions that are more abstract and involved than SIMPLE IDEAS. Associationists held that complex ideas, such as beauty, were derived from simple sensations by means of mental processes, such as comparing and generalizing. See ASSOCIATION OF IDEAS; REFLECTION. [defined by English philosopher John Locke (1632–1704)]

complexity–curvilinearity factor a factor in the judgment of art that combines simple–complex and curved–angular factors. The complexity–curvilinearity factor is a property of paintings that receive high positive ratings for simple–complex, emotions, and surface judgments and high negative ratings for curved–angular, disorderly–orderly, and line judgments from participants asked to evaluate the artistic work.

complexity factor in psychological aesthetics, a property of a work of art in which complexity is the main component of its stylistic ratings. The complexity factor may represent an information overload in a painting, such as Picasso's *Guernica*, and a reflection of the artist's feelings of tension. By contrast, a simple work of art may convey a feeling of tranquillity.

complexity hypothesis a hypothesis that conscious events result from neural systems in the DYNAMIC CORE that have high levels of complexity, a mathematical quantity defined as a joint function of neuronal integration and differentiation. [proposed by Italian–U.S. psychologist Giulio Tononi (1960–) and U.S. neuroscientist Gerald M. Edelman (1929–)]

complexity of an attitude the number of distinct dimensions underlying ATTITUDE-RELEVANT KNOWLEDGE. The greater the number of dimensions (i.e., distinct categories of attitude-relevant information), the greater the complexity of an attitude. Researchers have distinguished between two types of complex attitudes: those in which the underlying dimensions are seen as unrelated to one another (referred to as **differentiation**) and those in which the underlying dimensions are seen as related to one another (referred to as **integration**).

complex motives simultaneous, multiple desires to achieve one or more goals. For example, desires may be compatible and oriented toward the same goal (e.g., working hard due to a desire for success as well as a desire for money) or incompatible and oriented toward opposing goals (e.g., desiring to achieve success through work while simultaneously desiring to relax by not working).

complex of ideas a set of related ideas closely associated with emotions, memories, and other psychic factors so that when one of the ideas is recalled, other aspects of the complex are recalled with it. See also COGNITIVE SYSTEM.

complex partial seizure a PARTIAL SEIZURE that is characterized by complex psychological symptoms, repetitive motor activities, and specific sensory experiences. During the seizure the individual is in an impaired or altered, often trancelike, state of consciousness, typically accompanied by PARAMNESIAS (e.g. déjà vu), and may experience such emotions as fear, anxiety, or (less commonly) sadness or pleasure. Stereotyped motor behavior includes grimacing, sucking, chewing, and swallowing, and there may also be visual or olfactory hallucinations. Complex partial seizures are most commonly associated with abnormal discharges from neurons in the temporal lobe and were formerly called **temporal lobe seizures**. Also called **psychomotor seizure**.

complex reaction in reaction-time experiments, a situation in which the participant must make a decision before responding.

complex reaction time the REACTION TIME of a participant in a task that requires him or her to make one of several different responses depending on which one of several different stimuli is presented. Also called **disjunctive reaction time**. Compare CHOICE REACTION TIME; SIMPLE REACTION TIME. See also COMPOUND REACTION TIME; DISCRIMINATION REACTION TIME.

complex schedule of reinforcement a SCHEDULE OF REINFORCEMENT in which simple schedules are presented in combination. Examples include the CONJOINT SCHEDULE, CONJUNCTIVE REINFORCEMENT, and INTERLOCKING REINFORCEMENT SCHEDULE.

complex sentence in linguistics, a sentence consisting of a main CLAUSE and one or more subordinate clauses, as contrasted with a **simple sentence** consisting of a single main clause or a **compound sentence** consisting of several main clauses linked by coordinating conjunctions (see COORDINATION). See also EMBEDDED SENTENCE.

complex tone a sound that consists of two or more components of different frequencies. See SOUND SPECTRUM. Compare PURE TONE.

compliance *n.* **1.** submission to the demands, wishes, or suggestions of others. See also CONFORMITY. **2.** a change in a person's behavior in response to a direct request. A variety of techniques have been developed to enhance compliance with requests. Although some techniques may enhance compliance by producing ATTITUDE CHANGE, behavioral change is the primary goal of these techniques. See DOOR-IN-THE-FACE TECHNIQUE; FOOT-IN-THE-DOOR TECHNIQUE; LOW-BALL TECHNIQUE; THAT'S-NOT-ALL TECHNIQUE. **3.** in pharmacotherapy, see ADHERENCE. **4.** in SAFETY ENGINEERING, adherence to workplace codes or guidelines designed to enforce safe behaviors and exclude behaviors that increase the risk of injury or illness. Compliance is the end goal of workplace attempts to train or warn employees exposed to hazards. **—compliant** *adj.* **—comply** *vb.*

compliant character a submissive personality whose prime motive is to seek affection from others. German-born U.S. psychoanalyst Karen D. Horney (1885–1952) defined the development of such a character as one of three basic NEUROTIC TRENDS used as a defense against

BASIC ANXIETY. Compare AGGRESSIVE CHARACTER; DETACHED CHARACTER.

complicated grief a response to a death that deviates significantly from normal expectations. There are at least three different types of complicated grief: chronic grief, which is more intense, prolonged, or both; delayed grief; and absent grief. Most often observed is the pattern in which the immediate response to the loss is exceptionally devastating and in which the passage of time does not moderate the emotional pain or restore competent functioning. The concept of complicated grief was intended to replace the earlier terms abnormal grief and pathological grief.

complication *n.* **1.** an additional disease, disorder, or condition that occurs or develops during the course of another disease or disorder or during a medical procedure. See also COMORBIDITY. **2.** in perception, the perceived temporal position of stimuli from different senses.

complication experiment an experiment in which two or more events occur simultaneously, but only one is in the focus of attention. Such experiments indicate that the events occurring outside the focus of attention are perceived as being displaced in time. See LAW OF PRIOR ENTRY.

component evaluation an approach in PROGRAM EVALUATION that examines the separate elements comprising a HUMAN SERVICE DELIVERY SYSTEM or intervention program. The unit of analysis in the evaluation shifts from the program level to components or links between components and subsequent PROGRAM OUTCOMES.

componential analysis **1.** any analysis in which a process or system is separated into a series of subprocesses or components. **2.** a set of information-processing and mathematical techniques that enables an investigator to decompose an individual's performance on a cognitive task into the underlying elementary COGNITIVE PROCESSES. For example, solving an analogy requires encoding of stimuli, inference of the relation between the first two terms of the analogy, and so forth. Componential analysis enables the investigator to ascertain, for each individual, (a) the identities of the components used, (b) the strategy into which the components are combined, (c) the amount of time spent on each component, (d) the susceptibility of the component to erroneous execution, and (e) information regarding the mental representation upon which the component acts. [devised by U.S. psychologist Robert J. Sternberg (1949–)] **3.** a formal semantic analysis in which words are broken down into their separate elements, for example, man = human + male. Componential analysis is often employed to aid understanding of the meaning of words used by members of a particular culture.

componential subtheory a subtheory in the TRIARCHIC THEORY OF INTELLIGENCE that specifies three kinds of information-processing components in human intelligence. The three components are (a) metacomponents, which are used to plan, monitor, and evaluate problem solving and decision making; (b) performance components, which are used actually to solve the problems or make the decisions; and (c) knowledge-acquisition components, which are used to learn how to solve the problems or make the decisions in the first place.

component instinct in psychoanalytic theory, a fundamental element of the SEXUAL INSTINCT that has a specific source in one part of the body (e.g., the oral instinct) and a particular aim (e.g., instinct to master). The component instincts are posited to function independently during the early stages of PSYCHOSEXUAL DEVELOPMENT and later to fuse together during the GENITAL STAGE, which begins at puberty. Also called **partial instinct**; **part instinct**.

components of an attitude see BASES OF AN ATTITUDE.

components-of-variance model an ANOVA (ANALYSIS OF VARIANCE) model in which the parameters of the model are conceived of as RANDOM VARIABLES rather than fixed constants. Also called **random model**.

composite figure in psychoanalytic theory, a person or object in a dream whose image is created from the features or qualities of two or more individuals or objects (actual or existing in fantasy or imagination) by the process of CONDENSATION.

composite reliability the aggregate reliability of two or more items or judges' ratings. ARMOR'S THETA and CRONBACH'S ALPHA serve as two examples.

composition of movement the sequence and pattern of neuromuscular activity involved in movement (e.g., walking), including the integration of signals in the premotor and cerebellar areas of the brain.

compos mentis in law, mentally competent, that is, neither mentally deficient nor legally insane. See COMPETENCE. Compare NON COMPOS MENTIS.

compound *n.* in linguistics, two or more words or other linguistic units combined into a single unit, as in a compound noun (e.g., *bypass*), a compound verb (e.g., *shall go*), or a compound sentence (e.g., *John ate a sandwich, and Mary did too*).

compound action potential a recording of the ACTION POTENTIALS from several axons of a nerve when different axons are stimulated together. The different amplitudes and conduction velocities of the fibers account for the compound nature of the response. See also EVOKED POTENTIAL.

compound bilingual see COORDINATE BILINGUAL.

compound event an event that is the intersection of two or more simpler events. For example, being a male with schizophrenia is the intersection of the event classes being male and having schizophrenia.

compound eye the type of eye found in certain lower forms of animals (e.g., insects), which is composed of a number of separate visual units (**ommatidia**). Compare SIMPLE EYE.

compound reaction time the total time that elapses between the presentation of a stimulus and the occurrence of a response in a task that requires the participant to make a conscious decision before responding. The time actually required to decide on a response can be calculated using DONDERS'S METHOD. See DISCRIMINATION REACTION TIME. See also CHOICE REACTION TIME; COMPLEX REACTION TIME; SIMPLE REACTION TIME.

compound reflex a set of reflexes that are evoked together.

compound schedule of reinforcement a procedure for studying a single response in which two or more schedules of reinforcement are arranged to alternate, to appear in succession, or to be in effect simultaneously (i.e., concurrently). See CONJOINT SCHEDULE; MIXED REINFORCEMENT SCHEDULE; MULTIPLE REINFORCEMENT SCHEDULE; TANDEM REINFORCEMENT.

compound sentence see COMPLEX SENTENCE.

compound stimulus a stimulus comprising two or more simple stimuli that occur at the same time.

comprehension *n.* the act or capability of understanding something, especially the meaning of a communication. Compare APPREHENSION. See also VERBAL COMPREHENSION. **—comprehend** *vb.*

comprehension test 1. a reading-ability test in which understanding is assessed by asking questions about the passages read. **2.** a test requiring individuals to state how they would deal with a given practical situation. For example, a testee might be asked what he or she would do upon finding a letter on the street that has an address written on it and that is stamped with the proper postage.

comprehensive assessment service a team of professionals, often affiliated with a health care system or hospital, who perform multiple assessments of patients. The team's purposes are to identify specific health conditions and behavioral factors affecting an individual's growth and development and to enhance the value of the individual's referral to subsequent specialized educational or developmental services.

comprehensive functional assessment an assessment that is broad in scope, often implemented by an interdisciplinary team, and most frequently focuses on a person with mental retardation or a related condition. It typically incorporates findings regarding specific developmental strengths and individual preferences, specific functional and adaptive social skills that the individual needs to learn, the nature of any presenting disabilities and their causes, and the need for a wide range of services.

comprehensive mental health center see COMMUNITY MENTAL HEALTH CENTER.

Comprehensive Occupational Data Analysis Program (CODAP) an early attempt of the U.S. Air Force to develop a large computerized task database identifying the specific tasks performed as part of each job. A redesigned version (**atCODAP**) with a broader JOB ANALYSIS mission was launched in 1987.

compressed speech recorded speech that has been transformed so that it can be replayed without unacceptable distortion at a higher rate (in words per minute) than that at which it was originally produced. Speech compression is usually accomplished by DIGITAL coding and modifying the coded representation to preserve the characteristics of speech that are essential to its intelligibility while speeding its flow.

compression *n.* in neurology, pressure on the brain, spinal cord, or a nerve. Compression inside the skull raises INTRACRANIAL PRESSURE and may be caused by, for example, edema, hydrocephalus, or a tumor. Symptoms include motor disorders and disturbances of sensation, memory, or consciousness.

compromise formation in psychoanalytic theory, the conscious form of a repressed wish or idea that has been modified or disguised, as in a dream or symptom, so as to be unrecognizable. Thus it represents a compromise between the demands of the ego's DEFENSES and the unconscious wish.

compromiser *n.* in the social psychology of groups, the RELATIONSHIP ROLE adopted by a group member who, having previously advocated a specific policy, accedes partly or wholly to the opposing viewpoint to facilitate group progress.

compulsion *n.* a type of behavior (e.g., hand washing, checking) or a mental act (e.g., counting, praying) engaged in to reduce anxiety or distress. Typically the individual feels driven or compelled to perform the compulsion to reduce the distress associated with an OBSESSION or to prevent a dreaded event or situation. For example, individuals with an obsession about contamination may wash their hands until their skin is cracked and bleeding. Compulsions may also take the form of rigid or stereotyped acts based on idiosyncratic rules that do not have a rational basis (e.g., having to perform a task in a certain ritualized way). Compulsions do not provide pleasure or gratification and are disproportionate or irrelevant to the feared situation they are used to neutralize. See COUNTERCOMPULSION; OBSESSIVE-COMPULSIVE DISORDER. **—compulsive** *adj.*

compulsion to repeat see REPETITION COMPULSION.

compulsive character a personality pattern characterized by rigid, perfectionistic standards, an exaggerated sense of duty, and meticulous, obsessive attention to order and detail. Individuals of this type are usually humorless, parsimonious, stubborn, inhibited, rigid, and unable to relax. Also called **compulsive personality**.

compulsive disorders disorders of impulse control in which the individual feels forced to perform acts that are against his or her wishes or better judgment. The act may be associated with an experience of pleasure or gratification (e.g., compulsive gambling, drinking, or drug taking) or with the reduction of anxiety or distress (e.g., rituals in OBSESSIVE-COMPULSIVE DISORDER). See INTERMITTENT EXPLOSIVE DISORDER; KLEPTOMANIA; PARAPHILIA; PATHOLOGICAL GAMBLING; PYROMANIA; SUBSTANCE ABUSE; TRICHOTILLOMANIA. See also IMPULSE-CONTROL DISORDER.

compulsive drinker an individual who has an uncontrollable urge to drink excessively: an ALCOHOLIC. See ALCOHOL DEPENDENCE.

compulsive eating an irresistible drive to overeat, in some cases as a reaction to frustration or disappointment. See also BINGE-EATING DISORDER; BULIMIA NERVOSA; FOOD ADDICTION.

compulsive exerciser an individual who feels it is necessary to participate in moderate to high-level physical activity on a regular basis.

compulsive gambling see PATHOLOGICAL GAMBLING.

compulsive laughter persistent, inappropriate, and apparently uncontrollable laughter of which the individual may be unaware. See also INAPPROPRIATE AFFECT.

compulsiveness *n.* a behavior pattern associated with OBSESSIVE-COMPULSIVE DISORDER or OBSESSIVE-COMPULSIVE PERSONALITY DISORDER. See COMPULSION.

compulsive orderliness overconcern with everyday arrangements, such as a clean desk or dust-free house, with unbearable anxiety if there is any variation. See OBSESSIVE-COMPULSIVE DISORDER; OBSESSIVE-COMPULSIVE PERSONALITY DISORDER.

compulsive personality see COMPULSIVE CHARACTER.

compulsive personality disorder a personality disorder involving a long-standing disruptive pattern manifested in such behavior as difficulty in expressing warm emotions, stilted attitudes, stinginess, perfectionism, preoccupation with details and schedules, emphasis on work to the exclusion of pleasure, and avoidance or postponement of decisions for fear of making a mistake. See also OBSESSIVE-COMPULSIVE PERSONALITY DISORDER.

compulsive repetition the irresistible drive to perform needless acts, such as checking and rechecking a door to see whether it has been locked. See COMPULSION; OBSESSIVE-COMPULSIVE DISORDER.

compulsive stealing see KLEPTOMANIA.

compunction *n.* **1.** anxiety arising from an awareness of guilt. **2.** distress over an anticipated action or result.

computational epistemology see CYBERNETIC EPISTEMOLOGY.

computational linguistics an interdisciplinary field of study in which techniques from computer science and artificial intelligence are used to model theories based on linguistic analysis. Computers have been used experimentally to evaluate a range of hypotheses about phonetic perception and language processing. More practical applications have included the development of automatic translation systems and programs that can simulate or transcribe human speech.

computational metaphor a model of the mind as a device for performing operations on symbols that are analogous to those performed by a computer.

computational model any account of cognitive or psychobiological processes that assumes that the human mind functions like a digital computer, specifically in its ability to form representations of events and objects and to carry out complex sequences of operations on these representations.

computed tomography (**CT**) a radiographic technique for quickly producing detailed, three-dimensional images of the brain or other soft tissues. An X-ray beam is passed through the tissue from many different locations, and the different patterns of radiation absorption are analyzed and synthesized by a computer. Because a **CT scan** produces many slice-by-slice pictures of the head, chest, or abdomen, it is possible to locate abnormalities, such as lesions or tumors, without exploratory surgery. Also called **computer-assisted tomography**; **computerized axial tomography** (**CAT**); **computerized tomography**. See also MAGNETIC RESONANCE IMAGING.

computer *n.* **1.** an electronic device that can retrieve, process, store, and output information. It can follow encoded instructions (the program) to produce deterministic results. See ANALOG COMPUTER; DIGITAL COMPUTER. **2.** a person who does routine mathematical calculations, such as determining the ranges for military ballistic systems.

computer adaptive testing (**CAT**) a method of computer testing for particular skills or abilities in which the test items are automatically adjusted to match the level of proficiency demonstrated by the participant. The difficulty level of the items is reduced after an incorrect answer and increased after a correct answer. The testing stops once the participant's ability has been estimated to a predetermined level of accuracy.

computer address 1. a number that specifies the location of information stored in a computer's memory. **2.** a name or code that specifies a particular computer or site on the Internet or a particular e-mail destination.

computer-administered test an individually administered test in which items are presented by computer.

computer anxiety strong apprehension about computers and computer use that is disproportionate to the actual threat posed by these machines. The anxiety may be related to fear of the unknown or fear of the possible outcome of trying to use a computer (e.g., failure, frustration, embarrassment, or disappointment). If the anxiety is sufficient to cause significant distress and impairment, it may be classified as a SPECIFIC PHOBIA, situational type. Also called **computer phobia**.

computer-assisted diagnosis see COMPUTERIZED DIAGNOSIS.

computer-assisted instruction (**CAI**) a sophisticated offshoot of programmed learning, in which the memory-storage and retrieval capabilities of the computer are used to provide drill and practice, problem solving, simulation, and gaming forms of instruction. It is also useful for relatively individualized tutorial instruction. Also called **computer-assisted learning** (**CAL**). See also COMPUTER-MANAGED INSTRUCTION.

computer-assisted testing 1. assessment of skills that is given on, or with the support of, a computer. It can assess the ability of an individual (usually a student or an employee) to access specific material using a computer or to interact directly with a computer in order to complete an assessment. **2.** any testing that uses a computer. Such testing does not assess computer skills, and no previous computer experience or skills are required.

computer illiteracy the inability to understand computers or how to use them effectively. Compare COMPUTER LITERACY.

Computerized Adaptive Screening Test (**CAST**) a test developed by military research laboratories and implemented in 1984 to provide a quick estimate of the chance a military candidate has of passing the full ARMED SERVICES VOCATIONAL APTITUDE BATTERY.

computerized assessment evaluation of psychological information about an individual using a computer with access to databases that store previously acquired information from many other individuals in order to make comparisons, diagnoses, and prognoses. Also called **automated assessment**.

computerized diagnosis the use of computer programs for cataloging, storing, comparing, and evaluating psychological and medical data as an aid to CLINICAL DIAGNOSIS. In view of the many possible variables involved in a particular type of disorder, computerized diagnosis makes use of information based on thousands of similar or related sets of signs and symptoms of previous patients, as well as information on diagnoses and effective treatments stored in databases. Also called **computer-assisted diagnosis**. See PROBLEM-ORIENTED RECORD.

computerized therapy the use of a specially programmed computer to provide therapy, under the auspices of a trained therapist. Computers have been used for assessment, history taking, diagnosis, patient education, and intervention. Computer therapy software operates through a series of if–then statements, which determine how the computer responds to explicit input by the individual.

computer literacy the ability to understand what computers and computer networks do, how they function, and how to use them effectively for such purposes as composing and editing text, sending and receiving E-MAIL, and finding information through the Internet.

computer-managed instruction a method of instruction in which a computer is used to assist the teacher in carrying out a plan of individualized instruction. The computer processes daily data regarding the performance of each student; such data can then be used in prescribing the next instructional step for each student. The learner does not interact directly with the computer.

computer model a computer simulation of an external entity, such as a psychological function, for the purpose of helping to understand its components. Such models are often explicitly designed, for example, to enable a scientist to approximate, manipulate, and revise the decision-making processes of a human playing a game of chess.

computer network a group of computers interconnected by communication lines. Computer networks vary in size and complexity from local area networks (LANs) to the global Internet. Connections between network nodes (i.e., computers) can be WIRELESS (for short distances) or via copper wires (as in traditional telephone lines) or optical fibers.

computer of averaged transients an instrument that enables the computerized averaging of several successive responses to stimuli, as recorded by ELECTROENCEPHALOGRAPHY, in order to raise the ratio of signal to noise so that EVENT-RELATED POTENTIALS can be seen. This enables the responses to be distinguished above the noise of ongoing activity. See also AVERAGE-EVOKED-RESPONSE TECHNIQUE.

computer phobia see COMPUTER ANXIETY.

computer programming the process of giving coded instructions to a computer that direct it to perform a specific set of operations. The instructions are given in a computer programming language that the computer can read and understand.

computer programming language a formal language designed for encoding and submitting programs to a computer. There are hierarchies of programming languages from low-level machine code and assembly languages to high-level languages, such as LISP, LOGO, and PROLOG.

computer simulation 1. in cognitive psychology, a technique in which a model of cognitive processes is implemented as a computer program. This is generally to investigate specific theories of cognitive processing rather than to explore the more general issues that are the province of ARTIFICIAL INTELLIGENCE. **2.** in linguistics, see COMPUTATIONAL LINGUISTICS.

computer slanguage slang or jargon used in computer contexts. Examples include *flaming* to denote the sending of intemperate e-mail or messages to a computer addressee list and *snail mail* to refer to conventional mail.

Comrey Personality Scales (CPS) an inventory of individual differences in eight personality traits constructed primarily through FACTOR ANALYSIS and yielding scores on eight scales: trust versus defensiveness, orderliness versus lack of compulsion, social conformity versus rebelliousness, activity versus lack of energy, emotional stability versus neuroticism, extraversion versus introversion, masculinity versus femininity, and empathy versus egocentrism. Designed for individuals aged 16 years and over, it consists of 180 statements to which participants respond using a 7-point LIKERT SCALE format, ranging from "never" to "always" or from "definitely not" to "definitely." [developed in 1970 by Andrew Laurence **Comrey** (1923–), U.S. psychologist]

Comte's paradox an articulation, attributed by William JAMES to French positivist thinker Auguste Comte (1798–1857), of the difficulty associated with any science of human beings in which the mind becomes both the instrument of study and the object of study. Objective study of the rational mind by the rational mind seems paradoxical.

CON abbreviation for CERTIFICATE OF NEED.

conarium *n.* in the theory of French philosopher René Descartes (1596–1650), the point of contact between mind (RES COGITANS) and body (RES EXTENSA), which he located in the pineal gland of the brain. According to some interpreters, Freud's ID represents much the same concept. See CARTESIAN DUALISM.

conation *n.* the proactive (as opposed to habitual) part of motivation that connects knowledge, affect, drives, desires, and instincts to behavior. Along with COGNITION and affect, conation is one of the three traditionally identified components of mind. The behavioral basis of attitudes is sometimes referred to as the **conative component**. See also BASES OF AN ATTITUDE; TRIPARTITE THEORY OF ATTITUDES.

conative *adj.* characterized by volition or self-activation toward a goal.

concaveation *n.* in animal behavior, a form of SENSITIZATION whereby a virgin female, through repeated exposure to young animals, begins to display appropriate MATERNAL BEHAVIOR despite having no prior experience and undergoing none of the hormonal changes associated with pregnancy and nursing.

concealed-figures test a perceptual test in which the participant tries to find certain forms that are hidden or obscured by other contours. See also EMBEDDED FIGURES TEST.

concealed measurement a measurement made in such a way that the participant is unaware that an attribute is being measured.

concentration *n.* **1.** the act of bringing together or focusing, as, for example, bringing one's thought processes to bear on a central problem or subject (see ATTENTION). **2.** the proportion of a dissolved substance in a solution or mixture. **—concentrate** *vb.*

concentration-camp syndrome a variant form of POSTTRAUMATIC STRESS DISORDER suffered by survivors of concentration camps. Persistent stress symptoms in concentration-camp victims consist of severe anxiety, defenses against anxiety, an obsessive ruminative state, psychosomatic reactions, depression, and SURVIVOR GUILT produced by remaining alive while so many others died.

concentration difficulty a common symptom of a MAJOR DEPRESSIVE EPISODE in which the ability to concentrate and think clearly is diminished.

concentrative meditation a type of MEDITATION that focuses on a single stimulus (e.g., breathing); a specific image (e.g., a YANTRA); a specific sound, syllable, word, or phrase (see MANTRA); or a specific thought. It is the opposite of INSIGHT in that thoughts unrelated to the stimulus do not enter the consciousness. See also TRANSCENDENTAL MEDITATION. Compare MINDFULNESS MEDITATION.

concept *n.* **1.** an idea that represents a class of objects or events or their properties, such as "cats," "walking," "honesty," "blue," or "fast." See CONCEPTUALIZATION; CONJUNCTIVE CONCEPT; DISJUNCTIVE CONCEPT. See also ABSTRACT IDEA. **2.** in conditioning, a class of stimuli to which an organism responds in a similar or identical manner (see STIMULUS GENERALIZATION) and that an organism discriminates from other classes. **—conceptual** *adj.*

concept acquisition see CONCEPT FORMATION.

concept-discovery task a task in which the participant must try to discern the rule used to define members and nonmembers of a category. Also called **concept-identification task**. See also ABSTRACTION EXPERIMENT; CONCEPT-FORMATION TEST.

concept formation the process by which a person abstracts a common idea or CONCEPT from particular examples, such as learning what dogs are by experience of various different dogs. Also called **concept acquisition**. See also ABSTRACTION.

concept-formation test any test used in studying the process of concept formation and in assessing the level of concept acquisition achieved by a specific individual. See also ABSTRACTION EXPERIMENT; CONCEPT-DISCOVERY TASK.

concept-identification task see CONCEPT-DISCOVERY TASK.

conception ratio 1. in human demography, the proportion of males to females conceived, which is about 150:100. Male embryos are more vulnerable than female embryos, so the ratio of live births (the BIRTH RATIO) is about 110–105 boys to 100 girls. Also called **primary sex ratio**. See SEX RATIO. **2.** in animal husbandry, the ratio of the number of times a female becomes pregnant to the number of times she is serviced.

concept learning 1. learning the defining features that are characteristic or prototypical of a class (e.g., those describing a bird) or those features that are necessary and sufficient to identify members of a class of objects, relations, or actions (e.g., the concepts triangle, above, or move). **2.** the acquisition of new concepts or the modification of existing concepts. Also called **conceptual learning**.

conceptual apraxia a profound inability to use tools in an appropriate way. Conceptual apraxia is characterized by conceptual errors, in contrast to IDEOMOTOR APRAXIA, in which spatial errors are typically encountered.

conceptual classification in classification tasks, the grouping together of items on the basis of their shared function or membership in a similar category, for example, cow, dog, horse; tractor, bus, motorcycle. Also called **categorical classification**; **nominal classification**; **similarity classification**; **taxonomic classification**. Compare COMPLEMENTARY CLASSIFICATION; IDIOSYNCRATIC CLASSIFICATION; PERCEPTUAL CLASSIFICATION.

conceptual complexity the degree to which an idea or an argument is difficult to understand, owing to the number of abstract CONCEPTS involved and the intricate ways in which they connect. See also COGNITIVE COMPLEXITY.

conceptual dependency a formalized SEMANTIC NETWORK designed to capture semantic relationships in human language for use in computer programs related to understanding NATURAL LANGUAGE. There are four primitive (or atomic) components of this theory: actions, objects (picture producers), modifiers of actions, and modifiers of objects. Networks of these components are constructed to capture the semantic relationships of sentences in a natural language. See also COMPUTATIONAL LINGUISTICS.

conceptual disorder a disturbance in the thinking process or in the ability to formulate abstract ideas from generalized concepts.

conceptual disorganization irrelevant, rambling, or incoherent verbalizations, frequently including NEOLOGISMS and stereotyped expressions. It is one of the major signs of disorganized thought processes. See also SCHIZOPHRENIC THINKING.

conceptual imagery the MENTAL REPRESENTATION of concepts or conceptual relationships. See IMAGERY.

conceptualization *n.* the process of forming CONCEPTS, particularly concepts of an abstract nature, out of experience or learned material using thought processes and verbalization. See also ABSTRACT CONCEPTUALIZATION; ABSTRACTION; CONCEPT FORMATION. **—conceptualize** *vb.*

conceptual learning see CONCEPT LEARNING.

conceptually driven process a mental activity that focuses primarily on the meaningful aspects of a stimulus as opposed to its perceptual aspects. This is TOP-DOWN PROCESSING in which processing of the sensory input is guided by CONCEPTS acquired from experience or learning. Compare DATA-DRIVEN PROCESS. See also DEEP PROCESSING; SEMANTIC ENCODING.

conceptually guided control a stage or level of human INFORMATION PROCESSING that is controlled by HIGHER ORDER CONSTRUCTS, such as concepts or CONCEPTUAL SYSTEMS. Conceptually guided control functions primarily to direct thinking processes toward certain well-established goals.

conceptual model 1. a diagram, such as a VENN DIAGRAM or a tree diagram, used to represent in visual form the relations between concepts or between concepts and their attributes. **2.** in computing, an organizing principle that is used to structure the presentation of programs, files, and information to the end-user in ways that he or she will find conceptually familiar. Such a model is often based on a real-world analogy, as with the desktop and the spreadsheet.

conceptual nervous system a hypothetical model of the neurological and physiological functions of the nervous system that can be manipulated to provide analogies of behavioral activities. Critics claim that research should be concentrated on the actual nervous system rather than on this type of model. However, Donald O. HEBB pointed out that, over time, conceptual models of the nervous system have acquired more of the properties of the actual nervous system, and that modeling properties of the nervous system has been fruitful in encouraging research.

conceptual replication see REPLICATION.

conceptual system the organization of a person's cognitive abilities, emotional awareness, experience, and philosophical or religious orientation into a system for understanding events, data, or experience. See also COGNITIVE STRUCTURE; FRAME OF REFERENCE.

conceptual tempo the pace that is typical of a person's approach to cognitive tasks, for example, a hasty rather than a deliberate approach to observing, thinking, and responding. Conceptual tempo is an aspect of COGNITIVE STYLE. See also REFLECTIVITY–IMPULSIVITY.

Concerta *n.* a trade name for METHYLPHENIDATE.

conciliation *n.* the act or process of reconciling the positions of individuals or groups whose interests and goals are, at least initially, in opposition or incompatible. **—conciliate** *vb.*

concinnity *n.* the quality of an artistic design that features a harmonious arrangement of the various parts to each other as well as to the whole design.

conclusion *n.* **1.** in logic and philosophy, the proposition to which a line of argument or analysis leads. The conclusion is that which an argument is intended to establish as valid. See INFERENCE. **2.** in science, a general law or principle derived from experimental evidence by a process of INDUCTION.

conclusion drawing in a message explicitly stating the conclusions that are intended to be derived from a persuasive message.

concomitance *n.* **1.** the co-occurrence of two or more phenomena, especially such that the phenomena are essentially different manifestations of a single underlying reality. For example, a symbol and its meaning may be concomitant. According to Jungian psychology, synchronous events may be concomitant in this way (see SYNCHRONICITY). **2.** in statistics and experimental psychology, unwanted co-occurrence between the dependent variable (i.e., the one under investigation) and a variable other than the independent variable. Certain statistical procedures, such as ANALYSIS OF COVARIANCE, allow the effect to be controlled. **—concomitant** *adj.*

concomitant sensation see SYNESTHESIA.

concomitant variable see COVARIATE.

concomitant variation 1. the variation of two phenomena at the same time, in which the variables may be causally related or both may be influenced by a third variable. **2.** a correlation between variables.

concordance in twins in TWIN STUDIES, the probability that a given trait or disorder in one twin will be shown by the other. Evidence for genetic factors in the production of the trait or disorder comes from the comparison of concordance rates between identical and fraternal twins. Compare DISCORDANCE.

concordance rate the percentage of pairs of twins or other blood relatives who exhibit a particular trait or disorder. Also called **concordance ratio**. See also TWIN STUDIES.

concrete attitude a COGNITIVE STYLE that is directed to specific objects and immediate stimuli. A person who exhibits a concrete attitude tends not to make abstract comparisons and will not usually respond to abstract qualities, concepts, or categories. Compare ABSTRACT ATTITUDE. [defined by German-born U.S. neurologist Kurt Goldstein (1878–1965)]

concrete image an image that is recalled in terms of specific sense qualities, such as the taste of a particular kind of cheese or the sound of a ship's bell.

concrete intelligence the ability to handle concrete, practical relationships and situations. For example, a test of this ability might measure one's ability to solve a syllogism such as "All men are mortals. Socrates is a man. Can we be sure Socrates is mortal" Compare ABSTRACT INTELLIGENCE.

concrete operation the ability of a growing child to mentally represent items in the physical world and to understand the logical relations between them. Concrete operational children are, for example, able to understand the concept of CLASS INCLUSION and to represent part–whole relations in the physical world correctly (e.g., to grasp that dogs are a subset of animals or houses are a subset of buildings).

concrete operational stage in Jean PIAGET's theory, the third major stage of cognitive development, occurring approximately from 7 to 11 years of age, in which children can decenter their perception (see DECENTRATION), are less egocentric, and can think logically about concrete objects (see CONCRETE OPERATION) and about specific situations or experiences involving those objects.

concrete picture a MENTAL REPRESENTATION that is based on a specific object or event in the physical world with little or no abstraction. It was once widely assumed that humans in traditional societies thought in concrete pictures, but this is no longer held to be the case. Compare ABSTRACT REPRESENTATION. See also ICONIC REPRESENTATION; SYMBOLIC THINKING.

concrete thinking thinking focused on immediate experiences and specific objects or events. It is characteristic of young children and may also be seen in people with schizophrenia and people who have suffered a brain injury, especially frontal-lobe damage. Compare ABSTRACT THINKING.

concrete word in linguistics, a word denoting a physically real and perceptible entity, such as *tree, airplane, James*. Compare ABSTRACT WORD.

concretism *n.* **1.** in the ANALYTIC PSYCHOLOGY of Carl JUNG, a type of thought or feeling that is dependent on immediate physical sensation and displays little or no capacity for abstraction. In some traditional societies, such thinking may manifest itself in fetishism and belief in magic. In the modern world, it may display itself as an inability to think beyond the obvious material facts of a situation. **2.** in PIAGET's theory, see CONCRETE OPERATIONAL STAGE.

concretization *n.* **1.** inability to think abstractly in which there is an overemphasis on details and immediate experience. It occurs in such conditions as dementia and schizophrenia. **2.** in general usage, the process of being specific or of giving an example of a concept or relationship.

concretizing attitude converting an abstract idea into a concrete representation; for example, transforming a vague sense of someone's being angry with one into a DELUSION that the person is planning to murder one.

concurrence seeking striving to avoid disagreements and debates within a group, particularly during discussions or decision making. Concurrence seeking is a major cause of GROUPTHINK.

concurrent-chains procedure a procedure in which completion of either of two CONCURRENT SCHEDULES OF REINFORCEMENT, called the initial links, results in presentation of another schedule of reinforcement, called a terminal link, rather than primary reinforcement itself. Completion of the terminal-link schedule results in primary reinforcement. The initial links are concurrently available, in effect giving the organism an opportunity to choose between two terminal links. Once a terminal link is earned, however, it must be completed before the next period of choosing is made available.

concurrent medical audit see MEDICAL AUDIT.

concurrent operants a situation in which more than one OPERANT can be emitted and reinforced.

concurrent review an analysis of admissions to a psychiatric hospital or clinic carried out while care is being provided. It comprises certification of the necessity for admission (see ADMISSION CERTIFICATION) and assessment of the need for care to be continued (see CONTINUED-STAY REVIEW).

concurrent schedules of reinforcement a procedure in OPERANT CONDITIONING in which two or more separate reinforcement schedules, each associated with an independent OPERANT (response), are in effect simultaneously.

concurrent therapy 1. the use of two treatments at the same time. **2.** in MARITAL THERAPY and FAMILY THERAPY, the simultaneous treatment of spouses or other family members in individual or group therapy, either by the same therapist or different therapists. See also COMBINED THERAPY.

concurrent validity the extent of correspondence between two measurements at about the same point in time: specifically, the assessment of one test's validity by comparison of its results with a separate but related measurement, such as a standardized test, at the same point in time. See also CONTENT VALIDITY; CRITERION VALIDITY.

concussion *n.* see BRAIN CONCUSSION.

condensation *n.* the fusion of several meanings, concepts, or emotions into one image or symbol. Condensation is particularly common in dreams, in which (for example) one person may exhibit the characteristics of several or one behavior may represent several feelings or reactions.

condition 1. *n.* a logical antecedent on which a conclusion is dependent or an empirical antecedent on which an event or state is dependent. Conditions are often characterized as being either necessary or sufficient. A **necessary condition** is one without which the idea would not logically follow or the event would not occur. A **sufficient condition** is one that directly entails a particular conclusion or that has the power to produce a particular event regardless of other conditions. **2.** *vb.* to inculcate a response or a behavior in an organism by means of PAVLOVIAN CONDITIONING, OPERANT CONDITIONING, or other behaviorist paradigms (see BEHAVIORISM). The term implies that the learning is largely automatic, based on processes more like reflexes than conscious mental activity. **—conditional** *adj.*

conditional clause a subordinate CLAUSE that expresses a hypothesis or possibility, typically one introduced by *if* or *unless*. See also COUNTERFACTUAL.

conditional discharge the release of a patient from a psychiatric facility with imposition of certain conditions and limitations (such as periodically reporting to a supervisor or taking medications), during which time the patient is still under commitment.

conditional discrimination a DISCRIMINATION in which reinforcement of a response in the presence of a stimulus depends on the presence of other stimuli. For example, in a MATCHING-TO-SAMPLE procedure, responding to a comparison stimulus that matches the sample stimulus is reinforced; that is, determining the correctness of a response depends on the sample stimulus. See also SIMULTANEOUS DISCRIMINATION; SUCCESSIVE DISCRIMINATION.

conditionalism *n.* the view that one can predict an effect by knowing the CAUSE and that an effect can be explained in terms of its cause.

conditional positive regard an attitude of acceptance and esteem expressed by others on a conditional basis, that is, depending on the acceptability of the individual's behavior and the other's personal standards. In his theory of personality, Carl ROGERS proposed that while the need for positive regard is universal, conditional regard works against sound psychological development and adjustment in the recipient. Compare UNCONDITIONAL POSITIVE REGARD.

conditional probability the probability that an event will occur given that another event is known to have occurred.

conditional reasoning reasoning that takes the form "if X, then Y," as in *If Sam is male, then Sam is not a mother*. In formal logic, the statement that follows *if* is called the ANTECEDENT and that following *then* is called the CONSEQUENT.

conditional strategy the ability of organisms to develop different behavioral strategies appropriate for current contexts and conditions. An experienced adult male animal, for example, might actively defend a territory and guard females (see MATE GUARDING), while a young male stays as a SATELLITE MALE, not forming or defending the territory but attempting to copulate with available females (see SNEAK MATING). If the resident male dies or disappears, the young male can rapidly change strategies to become a territory-defending male.

conditioned *adj.* relating to or describing behavior whose occurrence, form of display, or both is a result of experience. The two main classes of experience resulting in conditioned behavior are OPERANT CONDITIONING and PAVLOVIAN CONDITIONING.

conditioned avoidance response (**CAR**) a conditioned response that prevents, postpones, or reduces the frequency or intensity of an aversive stimulus. A conditioned response that stops an aversive stimulus is known as a **conditioned escape response**. For example, if a monkey learns to press a lever that turns off a loud noise, the lever press is a conditioned escape response. See AVOIDANCE CONDITIONING.

conditioned discrimination a DISCRIMINATION based on experience.

conditioned emotional response (**CER**) any negative emotional response, typically fear or anxiety, that becomes associated with a neutral stimulus as a result of PAVLOVIAN CONDITIONING. It is the basis for CONDITIONED SUPPRESSION.

conditioned escape response see CONDITIONED AVOIDANCE RESPONSE.

conditioned inhibition the diminution of a CONDITIONED RESPONSE that occurs on presentation of a stimulus that has previously been experienced in different circumstances.

conditioned place preference (**CPP**) a technique for determining if experience with certain stimuli renders the place where that experience occurred reinforcing. For example, a rat might be injected with cocaine and then restricted to one side of a two-compartment chamber. After a number of trials, a test is conducted in which the rat can freely move between the two compartments. If the rat spends a majority of its time on the side in which it experienced cocaine, an inference is drawn that the dose of cocaine was reinforcing. Also called **place conditioning**.

conditioned reflex see CONDITIONED RESPONSE.

conditioned reinforcer a neutral stimulus that acquires the ability to act as a reinforcer, usually by being paired with a primary reinforcer (see PRIMARY REINFORCEMENT) or established as a DISCRIMINATIVE STIMULUS. For example, food may be paired with a token, which then becomes the conditioned reinforcer. Also called **secondary reinforcer**.

conditioned response (**CR**) in PAVLOVIAN CONDITIONING, the learned or acquired response to a conditioned stimulus. Also called **conditioned reflex**.

conditioned stimulus (**CS**) a neutral stimulus that is repeatedly associated (see PAIRING) with an UNCONDITIONED STIMULUS until it acquires the ability to elicit a response that it previously did not. In many (but not all) cases, the response elicited by the conditioned stimulus is similar to that elicited by the unconditioned stimulus. A light, for example, by being repeatedly paired with food (the unconditioned stimulus), eventually comes to elicit the same response as food (i.e., salivation) when presented alone. Also called **conditional stimulus**.

conditioned stimulus preexposure effect see LATENT INHIBITION.

conditioned suppression a phenomenon that occurs during an OPERANT performance test when a CONDITIONED RESPONSE to a positive stimulus is reduced by another stimulus that is associated with an aversive stimulus. For example, a rat may be trained to press a lever in order to receive food. During this procedure, the rat is occasionally exposed to a series of brief electric shocks that are preceded by a tone (the conditioned stimulus). As a result, when the rat subsequently hears the tone alone, its rate of lever pressing is reduced. Conditioned suppression is also used to study PAVLOVIAN CONDITIONING. See also ESTES–SKINNER PROCEDURE.

conditioned taste aversion the association of the taste of a food or fluid with an aversive stimulus (usually gastrointestinal discomfort or illness), leading to a very rapid and long-lasting aversion to, or at the least a decreased preference for, that particular taste. Conditioned taste aversion challenges traditional theories of associative learning, since very few PAIRINGS between the food and illness are needed to produce the effect (often one pairing will suffice), the delay between experiencing the taste and then feeling ill can be relatively long (i.e., a long DELAY OF REINFORCEMENT), and the aversion is highly resistant to EXTINCTION. Also called **learned taste aversion**; **taste-aversion learning**; **toxicosis**.

conditioning *n.* the process by which certain kinds of experience make particular actions more or less likely. See INSTRUMENTAL CONDITIONING; OPERANT CONDITIONING; PAVLOVIAN CONDITIONING.

conditioning apparatus in animal research, any apparatus used in conditioning procedures. The most common conditioning apparatus is the OPERANT CHAMBER. See also OPERANT CONDITIONING CHAMBER.

conditioning by successive approximations see SHAPING.

conditioning of attitudes the formation or change of an attitude as a result of the association of an ATTITUDE OBJECT with a pleasant or unpleasant stimulus in the environment. Attitudes may be conditioned via PAVLOVIAN CONDITIONING or OPERANT CONDITIONING processes.

conditioning therapy see BEHAVIOR THERAPY.

conditions not attributable to a mental disorder in *DSM–III* and earlier editions, a residual category of conditions that in *DSM–IV–TR* is labeled OTHER CONDITIONS THAT MAY BE A FOCUS OF CLINICAL ATTENTION.

conditions of worth the state in which an individual considers love and respect to be conditional on meeting the approval of others. This belief derives from the child's sense of being worthy of love on the basis of parental approval: As the individual matures, he or she may continue to feel worthy of affection and respect only when expressing desirable behaviors. [proposed by Carl ROGERS]

condom *n.* a sheath, usually made of latex rubber, placed over the erect penis to prevent pregnancy and to avoid sexually transmitted diseases.

conduct *n.* the behavior of an individual, either generally or on a specific occasion, usually as it conforms to or violates social norms.

conduct disorder in *DSM–IV–TR*, a persistent pattern of behavior that involves violating the basic rights of others and ignoring age-appropriate social standards. Specific behaviors include lying, theft, arson, running away from home, aggression, truancy, burglary, cruelty to animals, and fighting. This disorder is distinguished from OPPOSITIONAL DEFIANT DISORDER by the increased severity of the behaviors and their occurrence independently of an event occasioning opposition. ATTENTION-DEFICIT/HYPERACTIVITY DISORDER frequently coexists with or is misdiagnosed as conduct disorder.

conduction *n.* in physiology, the transmission of excitation along a nerve, muscle, or other tissue. In a neuron, subthreshold stimulation results in CONDUCTION WITH DECREMENT, whereas suprathreshold stimulation results in a propagated ACTION POTENTIAL, or nerve impulse.

conduction aphasia a form of APHASIA characterized by difficulty in differentiating speech sounds and repeating them accurately, even though spontaneous articulation may be intact. It is associated with lesions in the ARCUATE FASCICULUS, the tract linking the areas of the brain involved in the interpretation and control of speech.

conduction deafness loss of hearing due to a disorder in the structures that transmit sound to the cochlea. The cause may be an injury or disease that interferes with the normal functioning of the OSSICLES. Also called **conductive deafness**. See AIR–BONE GAP.

conduction time (**CT**) the time required for transmission of activity, such as an ACTION POTENTIAL, between two points.

conduction velocity see VELOCITY OF CONDUCTION.

conduction with decrement the exponential decay in the size of a membrane potential with distance from the site of stimulation when a subthreshold stimulus is applied to an axon. Compare NONDECREMENTAL CONDUCTION. See also CABLE PROPERTIES.

conductivity *n.* **1.** the ability of a substance to transmit energy, as in electrical conduction, thermal conduction, or skin conduction. **2.** the ability of a tissue to convey SIGNALS and respond to stimuli.

cone opsin see IODOPSIN.

cones *pl. n.* see RETINAL CONES.

confabulation *n.* the falsification of memory in which gaps in recall are filled by fabrications that the individual accepts as fact. It is not typically considered to be a conscious attempt to deceive others. Confabulation occurs most frequently in KORSAKOFF'S SYNDROME and to a lesser extent in other conditions associated with organically derived amnesia. In forensic contexts, eyewitnesses may resort to confabulation if they feel pressured to recall more information than they can remember. **—confabulate** *vb.*

confederate *n.* **1.** in an experimental situation, an aide of the experimenter who poses as a participant but whose behavior is rehearsed prior to the experiment. The real participants are sometimes referred to as NAIVE PARTICIPANTS. See also ACTIVE DECEPTION. **2.** in parapsychology, an individual who assists a supposed PSYCHIC by covertly providing him or her with information about a client's concerns, preferences, background, or situation, thus creating or strengthening the illusion of the psychic's paranormal abilities.

conference method a method of PERSONNEL TRAINING in which participants work together in an attempt to resolve typical work-related problems and issues. Participants develop their problem-solving and decision-making abilities, acquire new information, and modify their attitudes in the process of pooling ideas, testing assumptions, discussing new approaches, and drawing inferences and conclusions. See also BUSINESS GAME; CASE METHOD; MULTIPLE-ROLE PLAYING; SCENARIO ANALYSIS.

confidant *n.* an individual to whom another individual reveals private, often intimate, thoughts and feelings.

confidence interval a range of values (an interval), used for estimating the value of a population parameter from data obtained in a SAMPLE, with a preset, fixed probability that the interval will include the true value of the population parameter being estimated. Most research is done on samples, but it is done in order to draw inferences about the entire relevant population. Compare POINT ESTIMATE.

confidence limits the upper and lower end points of a CONFIDENCE INTERVAL; that is, the values between which the value of the parameter is anticipated with a known probability to be.

confidentiality *n.* a principle of PROFESSIONAL ETHICS requiring providers of mental health care or medical care to limit the disclosure of a patient's identity, his or her condition or treatment, and any data entrusted to professionals during assessment, diagnosis, and treatment. Similar protection is given to research participants and survey respondents against unauthorized access to information they reveal in confidence. See INFORMED CONSENT; TARASOFF DECISION. —**confidential** *adj.*

configural display see OBJECT DISPLAY.

configural learning learning to respond to a combination of two or more stimuli paired with an outcome when none of the stimuli presented alone is paired with that outcome. For example, if neither a tone nor a light presented separately is followed by food, but a tone–light combination is followed by food, configural learning has occurred when a conditioned response is elicited by the tone–light combination.

configural superiority effect in visual perception, a phenomenon in which a CONFIGURATION of elements or features is easier to identify than a single feature alone. Examples include the WORD-SUPERIORITY EFFECT and the OBJECT-SUPERIORITY EFFECT.

configuration *n.* **1.** an arrangement of elements or components in a particular pattern or figure. See GOODNESS OF CONFIGURATION. **2.** the usual English translation of GESTALT. —**configurational** *adj.*

configurational analysis an integrative psychodynamic model for case formulation, psychotherapy, and outcome evaluation. Maladaptive states of mind in the context of the client's problems, topics of concern, defenses, identity, and relationships are the focus of assessment and therapy. [developed by 21st-century U.S. psychiatrist Mardi Horowitz]

confinement study a study in a controlled environment to determine at what point physiological and psychological impairment occurs as a result of spatial restrictions. Such studies are important in space or undersea travel, during which individuals live and work in an artificial environment. The variables studied include length of time in confinement, area available, and crew size. These may have effects on sleep loss and ability to perform operational tasks.

confirmable proposition a statement or conclusion that is capable of being confirmed or falsified by experimental procedures. In LOGICAL POSITIVISM, all other propositions (except those of logic and mathematics) are considered essentially meaningless.

confirmation *n.* in PURPOSIVE BEHAVIORISM, the fulfillment of an expectancy that reinforces the behavior that led to the fulfillment.

confirmation bias the tendency to gather evidence that confirms preexisting expectations, typically by emphasizing or pursuing supporting evidence while dismissing or failing to seek contradictory evidence.

confirmatory data analysis statistical data analysis designed to address one or more specific research questions. Compare EXPLORATORY DATA ANALYSIS.

confirmatory factor analysis one of a set of procedures used in FACTOR ANALYSIS to demonstrate that a group of variables possess a theoretically expected factor structure.

confirmatory research research conducted with the goal of being able to test certain prespecified hypotheses.

conflict *n.* **1.** in psychology, the clash of opposing or incompatible emotional or motivational forces (e.g., attitudes, impulses, drives) in the same individual. **2.** in psychoanalysis, the struggle between conscious and unconscious forces, especially between the ID, EGO, and SUPEREGO, that is considered to be a major source of neuroses. **3.** in interpersonal relations, the disagreement, discord, and friction that occur when the actions or beliefs of one or more individuals are unacceptable to and resisted by others. See INTERGROUP CONFLICT; INTRAGROUP CONFLICT.

conflict behavior behavior that results from experiencing two incompatible motivational states at the same time. It commonly occurs as a result of an APPROACH–AVOIDANCE CONFLICT, for example when a hungry animal must leave shelter to feed in the presence of a predator (feeding versus fear) or when a territorial male is in the presence of a potential mate (aggression versus sex). Conflict behavior may be manifested in alternations of approach and retreat or in behavior unrelated to either of the behaviors relevant to the conflict (see DISPLACEMENT BEHAVIOR).

conflict-free sphere in EGO PSYCHOLOGY, an area of the ego that develops and functions without giving rise to internal conflict. Functions ordinarily controlled by the conflict-free sphere include speech, motility, and other autonomous ego functions. Also called **conflict-free area**.

conflict of interest a situation in which individuals or groups are drawn to the pursuit of goals or outcomes that are incompatible with the goals they are supposed to be pursuing. For example, psychologists who are employed by a health agency may find that their obligation to help their clients is incompatible with the agency's requirement to minimize treatment costs. See also DOUBLE-AGENTRY.

conflict resolution the reduction of discord and friction between individuals or groups, usually through the use of active strategies, such as CONCILIATION, NEGOTIATION, and BARGAINING. See also CONSTRUCTIVE CONFLICT RESOLUTION; DESTRUCTIVE CONFLICT RESOLUTION.

conflict spiral a pattern of escalating tension and discord between two or more parties. Parties in such conflicts counter one another's responses with more negative and more extreme responses.

conflict theory **1.** any conceptual analysis of the causes and consequences of interpersonal conflict. **2.** more specifically, a sociological approach that stresses the inevitability of conflict in any setting in which resources are unevenly distributed among interactants. See REALISTIC GROUP-CONFLICT THEORY.

confluence *n.* a fusion or merging of several elements, for example, motives or perceptual elements. —**confluent** *adj.*

confluence model a controversial and probably untenable theory that intelligence of siblings is correlated with family size. According to this model, average intelligence generally declines as the number of children in a family increases. Thus, in general, the greater the number of children, the less intelligent they would be expected to be. Intelligence is also held to decline with BIRTH ORDER. The one exception is an only child, whose intelligence suffers because he or she does not have an older sibling to serve as a teacher. However, many variables, e.g., spacing of children, could affect and reverse such generalizations.

conformity *n.* the adjustment of one's opinions, judgments, or actions so that they match either (a) the opinions, judgments, or actions of other people or (b) the normative standards of a social group or situation. Conformity includes the temporary COMPLIANCE of individuals, who agree publicly with the group but do not accept its position as their own, as well as the CONVER-

SION of individuals, who fully adopt the group position. Compare ANTICONFORMITY; NONCONFORMITY. See also MAJORITY INFLUENCE; PEER PRESSURE.

conformity curve see TELIC CONTINUUM.

confounds *pl. n.* variables that vary with the INDEPENDENT VARIABLE and whose influences on the DEPENDENT VARIABLE are therefore indistinguishable empirically from the effects of the independent variable. **Confounding** is usually inadvertent and damaging to the drawing of accurate inferences; however, sometimes it is employed intentionally. See ALIAS; FRACTIONAL FACTORIAL DESIGN; INCOMPLETE BLOCK DESIGN.

confrontation *n.* **1.** an argument or hostile disagreement. **2.** the act of directly facing, or being encouraged or required to face, a difficult situation, realization, discrepancy, or contradiction involving information, beliefs, attitudes, or behavior. Confrontational techniques may be used therapeutically, for example, to reveal and invite self-examination of inconsistencies in a client's reported and actual behavior, but they have a potential for disruptive as well as constructive effects. **3.** in INDIVIDUAL PSYCHOLOGY, a statement or question calculated to motivate the client to make a decision or face the reality of a situation. **—confrontational** *adj.*

confrontational meeting see CONSTRUCTIVE CONFRONTATION.

confrontational methods methods intended to change behavior in which individuals are aggressively forced to confront their failures and weaknesses. Such methods are used, for example, in residential drug programs staffed by ex-addicts. Similar but less aggressive methods are used in ENCOUNTER GROUPS as a means of increasing awareness and modifying behavior. Research has not supported the efficacy of confrontational approaches, and many patients respond negatively.

confrontation naming any procedure that requires the naming of an object presented visually or its pictorial representation.

confusability index in ergonomics, any quantity used to express the degree to which a symbol, graphic, display item, or other object is capable of being misunderstood by the user or assigned a meaning other than its intended meaning.

confusion *n.* a disturbance of consciousness characterized by bewilderment, inability to think clearly or act decisively, and DISORIENTATION for time, place, and person. Also called **mental confusion**.

confusional psychosis a form of CYCLOID PSYCHOSIS in which disturbances of cognitive processes are prominent and accompanied by a labile (highly changeable) emotional state characterized alternately by manifest anxiety, with the individual often misidentifying other people, and by mutism and greatly decreased movement. The latter differs from CATATONIC STUPOR in that self-care and spontaneity are preserved and negativism is absent. [defined by German psychiatrist Karl Leonhard (1904–1988)]

confusional state a state of impaired mental functioning in which awareness is retained but with loss of cognitive coherence and orientation to time, place, and sometimes identity. It may be accompanied by rambling or incoherent speech, visual hallucinations, and PSYCHOMOTOR disturbances. It can arise from a wide variety of causes, including brain lesions, trauma, toxicity, medications, neurotransmitter imbalances, sleep disturbances, Alzheimer's disease, sedation, or fever.

confusion effect an antipredator defense in which each of several animals may be moving or vocalizing in a highly random way, making it difficult for predators to locate and attack any one individual. See also ANTIPREDATOR BEHAVIOR; DILUTION EFFECT.

confusion of responsibility the tendency for bystanders to refrain from helping in both emergencies and nonemergencies in order to avoid being blamed by others for causing the problem. This is a contributing factor in the BYSTANDER EFFECT. See also DIFFUSION OF RESPONSIBILITY.

congenital *adj.* denoting a condition or disorder that is present at birth. Also called **connate**.

congenital acromicria see DOWN SYNDROME.

congenital adrenal hyperplasia see ADRENAL HYPERPLASIA.

congenital anomaly see CONGENITAL DEFECT.

congenital aphasia any disorder of written or spoken communication ability resulting from a defect present at birth.

congenital cataract opacity of the lens of the eye that is present at birth or occurs soon after birth. Its effect is to scatter light and blur the image on the retina, which prohibits the development of pattern vision because of visual deprivation. Central vision is always affected, and peripheral vision may also be reduced. Congenital cataract can occur in one or both eyes; it may be hereditary or caused by congenital infection or metabolic disorders.

congenital character a character or trait that is present at birth. It may be hereditary or result from the influence of factors experienced during fetal development or delivery.

congenital color blindness see COLOR BLINDNESS.

congenital deafness deafness that exists from birth, regardless of the cause. Compare ADVENTITIOUS DEAFNESS.

congenital defect any abnormality present at birth, regardless of the cause. It may be caused by faulty fetal development (e.g., spina bifida, cleft palate), hereditary factors (e.g., Huntington's disease), chromosomal aberration (e.g., Down syndrome), maternal conditions affecting the developing fetus (e.g., fetal alcohol syndrome), metabolic defects (e.g., phenylketonuria), or injury to the brain before or during birth (e.g., some cases of cerebral palsy). A congenital defect may not be apparent until several years after birth (for example, an allergy or a metabolic disorder) or even until after the individual has reached adulthood (e.g., Huntington's disease). Also called **birth defect**; **congenital anomaly**.

congenital glaucoma an eye disease, present at birth, in which a sustained, abnormally high fluid pressure within the eyeball damages the optic nerve (see GLAUCOMA). This causes enlargement of the eye (**buphthalmos**). In 70% of cases both eyes are affected; the condition is found more frequently in males than in females and carries a 5% increased risk of occurrence in siblings and offspring. Congenital glaucoma may occur in association with many developmental syndromes (e.g., ANIRIDIA, STURGE–WEBER SYNDROME). Decreased vision may result from optic atrophy, corneal clouding, astigmatism, visual deprivation, high myopia, and strabismus. In addition, children typically show PHOTOPHOBIA and BLEPHAROSPASM.

congenital hypothyroidism a condition of motor and mental retardation associated with a deficiency of thyroid hormone. More than a dozen causes, mostly hereditary metabolic defects, have been identified with the disorder. The prognosis varies with the degree of thyroid deficiency during fetal and early infant life, but early and adequate thyroid-hormone therapy generally reverses signs and symptoms. See CRETINISM.

congenital oculomotor apraxia a condition, present at birth, in which a child is unable to fixate objects normally. It is characterized by the absence of SACCADES and SMOOTH-PURSUIT MOVEMENTS in the horizontal plane, but vertical eye movements are preserved: Children with this condition are often mistakenly thought to be blind. Between the ages of 4 and 6 months, they develop thrusting, horizontal head movements, sometimes blinking prominently or rubbing their eyelids when they attempt to change fixation. The cause of congenital oculomotor apraxia is unknown, but there is usually an improvement with age.

congenital rubella syndrome a complex of congenital defects in infants whose mothers were infected by the rubella virus early in pregnancy. The defects may include deaf-mutism, cataracts, heart disease, cerebral palsy, microcephaly (small head), and mental retardation. Neurological abnormalities occur in about 80% of affected individuals, and brain weight is usually subnormal. Psychomotor retardation, marked by general lack of response to stimuli, and intellectual impairment are common. In developed nations rubella vaccination has resulted in a massive decline in the occurrence of this syndrome. See also GERMAN MEASLES.

congenital sensory neuropathy with anhidrosis a disorder marked by the absence of pain perception. Severe injuries, such as multiple fractures, may go untreated because they cause no pain. Affected individuals tend to show delayed intellectual development, with IQs below 80. Skin biopsies show normal but nonfunctional sweat glands.

congenital speech disorder a SPEECH DISORDER present at birth, usually due to genetic factors or events associated with the birth process. Compare ACQUIRED SPEECH DISORDER.

congenital visual agnosia a form of VISUAL AGNOSIA that is present at birth, due to abnormal development of those parts of the brain responsible for the visual identification of objects (congenital object agnosia), faces (congenital PROSOPAGNOSIA), or both. Congenital visual agnosia represents a specific visual cognitive disorder that cannot be explained by visual, cognitive, or language deficits. Also called **developmental visual agnosia**.

congenital visual impairment visual impairment already present at birth or occurring soon after birth. Major causes are infections, bilateral cataracts, and prematurity. Unless specially stimulated, children with this impairment are likely to show delay in sensory, motor, and social development. Compare ADVENTITIOUS VISUAL IMPAIRMENT.

congestive dysmenorrhea see DYSMENORRHEA.

congregate living facility a residential complex in which older adults live independently but take meals together as well as share some other social activities.

congruence *n.* **1.** in general, agreement, harmony, or conformity. **2.** in the phenomenological personality theory of Carl ROGERS, (a) the need for a therapist to act in accordance with his or her true feelings rather than with a stylized image of a therapist or (b) the conscious integration of an experience into the self. **3.** in environmental psychology, see PERSON–ENVIRONMENT INTERACTION. **—congruent** *adj.*

congruence conformity in congruity theory, a change in attitude in the target of a persuasive communication that brings the target's own attitude closer to the position taken in the communication.

congruity theory a COGNITIVE CONSISTENCY THEORY that focuses on the role of persuasive communications in attitude change. Congruity theory is similar to BALANCE THEORY in that it postulates that people tend to prefer elements within a cognitive system to be internally consistent with one another. Accordingly, if the person receiving a persuasive communication has a negative attitude to the content of the message but a positive attitude to the source of the message, or vice versa, then he or she will be motivated to revise both of these attitudes in some degree in order to restore congruity. Congruity theory differs from balance theory in that it takes into account gradations of evaluation of elements and therefore makes more precise predictions regarding the magnitude of change required to restore congruity among elements. [first proposed by U.S. psychologists Charles OSGOOD and Percy Tannenbaum (1927–)]

CONJ abbreviation for CONJUNCTIVE REINFORCEMENT.

conjoined twins MONOZYGOTIC TWINS whose bodies fail to separate completely during embryonic life. The result, at birth, is two conjoined bodies that may be separated by surgery, or variations of one body with two heads or four legs, or two individuals with shared vital organs, or some other combination. The popular name, **Siamese twins**, derives from the brothers Eng and Chang (1811–1874), who were born in Thailand (Siam) and exhibited in sideshows.

conjoint marital therapy see CONJOINT THERAPY.

conjoint schedule a type of COMPOUND SCHEDULE OF REINFORCEMENT under which two or more schedules of reinforcement operate simultaneously for a single response.

conjoint therapy therapy in which the partners in a relationship or members of a family are treated together in joint sessions by one or more therapists, instead of being treated separately. The technique is commonly applied in resolving marital disputes, when it is also known as **conjoint marital therapy**. Also called **conjoint counseling**. See also COUPLES THERAPY; FAMILY THERAPY; MARITAL THERAPY.

conjugate movements coordinated movements of the two eyes.

conjugate reinforcement a REINFORCEMENT CONTINGENCY in which some aspect of the reinforcer (e.g., its magnitude) varies systematically with some property of behavior (e.g., rate or force).

conjunction *n.* in linguistics, a FUNCTION WORD that serves to conjoin two or more sentence constituents or sentences, the most common being *and*, as in *John and Mary got married*. Other common conjunctions include *but*, *because*, *or*, and *if*. See COORDINATION.

conjunction search a search task in which the target has two or more relevant features. According to FEATURE-INTEGRATION THEORY, conjunction search proceeds in a serial manner.

conjunctival reflex the automatic closing of the eyelid when the cornea is stimulated.

conjunctive concept a concept that is defined by a set of attributes, every member of which must be present for the concept to apply. For example, the concept "brother" requires the joint presence of the attributes (a) male and (b) sibling, neither of which may be omitted. Compare DISJUNCTIVE CONCEPT.

conjunctive motivation the drive to achieve true and lasting (rather than temporary or substitute) satisfaction.

Compare DISJUNCTIVE MOTIVATION. [defined by U.S. psychiatrist Harry Stack Sullivan (1892–1949)]

conjunctive reinforcement (CONJ) a type of INTERMITTENT REINFORCEMENT in which two or more SCHEDULES OF REINFORCEMENT must be completed before reinforcement can be given. The order in which the schedules are completed is irrelevant. Also called **conjunctive reinforcement schedule**; **conjunctive schedule of reinforcement**.

conjunctive task a group task that cannot be completed successfully until all members of the group have completed their portion of the job. This means that the speed and quality of the work is determined by the least skilled member. Compare ADDITIVE TASK; COMPENSATORY TASK; DISJUNCTIVE TASK.

connate *adj.* see CONGENITAL.

connected discourse a relatively long and integrated unit of language, such as a written argument or spoken conversation. See DISCOURSE ANALYSIS.

connectionism *n.* the concept that learning involves the acquisition of neural links, or connections, between stimulus and response. [proposed by Edward L. THORNDIKE] **—connectionist** *adj.*

connectionist models of memory a class of theories hypothesizing that knowledge is encoded by the connections among representations stored in the brain rather than in the representations themselves. Connectionist models suggest that knowledge is distributed rather than being localized and that it is retrieved through SPREADING ACTIVATION among connections. The connectionist model concept has been extended to artificial intelligence, particularly to its NEURAL NETWORK models of problem solving.

connector neuron see INTERNEURON.

connotative meaning see DENOTATIVE MEANING.

Conn's syndrome see ALDOSTERONISM. [Jerome W. **Conn** (1907–1994), U.S. physician]

CONOPS acronym for CONTINUOUS OPERATIONS.

Conradi's disease a congenital disorder marked by short limbs, anomalies of the head and face, cataracts, dry skin, and, in some cases, degenerating cartilage at the ends of the long bones. In the RHIZOMELIC form of the disease mental retardation is common. However, it is rarely present in the **Conradi–Hunermann** form of the disease. [Erich **Conradi**, 20th-century German physician]

consanguinity *n.* **1.** a biological relationship between two or more individuals who are descended from a common ancestor. **2.** a close AFFINITY or connection.

conscience *n.* an individual's sense of right and wrong. In psychoanalysis, conscience is the SUPEREGO, or ethical component of personality, which acts as judge and critic of one's actions and attitudes. See also AUTHORITARIAN CONSCIENCE; HUMANISTIC CONSCIENCE.

conscientiousness *n.* the tendency to be organized, responsible, and hardworking, construed as one end of a dimension of individual differences (conscientiousness versus lack of direction) in the BIG FIVE PERSONALITY MODEL. It is also a dimension in the FIVE-FACTOR PERSONALITY MODEL. **—conscientious** *adj.*

conscientious objector an individual who is opposed to war and preparations for war and who refuses to serve in the armed forces for religious reasons or for other beliefs of conscience.

conscious 1. **(Cs)** *n.* in the classical psychoanalytic theory of Sigmund FREUD, the region of the psyche that contains thoughts, feelings, perceptions, and other aspects of mental life currently present in awareness. The content of the conscious is thus inherently transitory and continuously changing. Compare PRECONSCIOUS; UNCONSCIOUS. **2.** *adj.* relating to or marked by awareness or consciousness.

conscious access hypothesis the notion that the primary function of consciousness is to mobilize and integrate brain functions that are otherwise separate and independent.

conscious intentions goals that can be reported and carried out accurately. Compare UNCONSCIOUS INTENTIONS.

conscious memory see DECLARATIVE MEMORY; EXPLICIT MEMORY.

conscious mentalism any theory that posits the reality of purely mental phenomena, such as thinking, feeling, desiring, preferring, and (particularly) intention, holding that these mental phenomena are the chief causes of behavior and that they are available to the conscious mind. The rise of BEHAVIORISM was largely a reaction against MENTALISM as a causal explanation for behavior. While most forms of conscious mentalism hold that mental phenomena have a nonmaterial existence, some recent mentalistic positions have been materialistic, accepting that mental states and processes have their origin in physical states and processes. Compare ELIMINATIVISM; EPIPHENOMENALISM; REDUCTIONISM.

conscious moment the present moment, often thought to be about 3 s in duration. This theoretical measurement approximates to the decay time for conscious sensory images. See also FLEETING PRESENT.

consciousness *n.* **1.** the phenomena that humans report experiencing, including mental contents ranging from sensory and somatic perception to mental images, reportable ideas, inner speech, intentions to act, recalled memories, semantics, dreams, hallucinations, emotional feelings, "fringe" feelings (e.g., a sense of knowing), and aspects of cognitive and motor control. Operationally, these **contents of consciousness** are generally assessed by the ability to report an event accurately (see REPORTABILITY). **2.** any of various subjective states of awareness in which conscious contents can be reported. Consciousness most often refers to the ordinary waking state (see WAKEFULNESS), but it may also refer to the state of sleeping or to an ALTERED STATE OF CONSCIOUSNESS. In cognitive theory, consciousness appears to have a global-access function, presenting an endless variety of focal contents to executive control and decision making. In medicine and brain science, the distinctive electrical activity of the brain, as recorded on an electroencephalogram, is often used to identify conscious states (see BRAIN WAVES). **Sensory consciousness** of the perceptual world depends on the posterior SENSORY AREA of the brain. **Abstract consciousness** refers to abstract ideas, judgments, specific intentions, expectations, and events of FRINGE CONSCIOUSNESS; it may involve the FRONTAL CORTEX in addition to sensory cortex. The distinction between sensory and abstract experiences was originally made by Greek philosopher Plato (c. 427–c. 347 BCE). See also EVOLUTION OF CONSCIOUSNESS; HIGHER ORDER CONSCIOUSNESS.

consciousness-altering substances a large class of psychoactive compounds that affect conscious experience and perception. These substances are related to neurotransmitters (e.g., serotonin) and include LSD, CANNABIS, and alcoholic beverages. See also ALTERED STATE OF CONSCIOUSNESS.

consciousness of effort see EFFORTFULNESS.

consciousness of freedom the sense of choice people

tend to have in making decisions and controlling actions. It may be the intuitive basis for the widespread belief in free will. See also SENSE OF FREE WILL.

consciousness raising a process, often used in group discussion, directed toward greater awareness of (a) oneself, for example, one's condition, needs, values, and goals; or (b) a political or social issue, such as discrimination against a particular group of people.

conscious process a mental operation of which a person is aware and often in control. Compare UNCONSCIOUS PROCESS. See also AUTOMATICITY.

conscious resistance in psychoanalysis, the patient's deliberate withholding of unconscious material that has newly risen into consciousness because of shame, fear of rejection, or distrust of the analyst. See RESISTANCE. Compare ID RESISTANCE; REPRESSION-RESISTANCE.

conscious state see CONSCIOUSNESS.

consensual eye reflex a phenomenon in which the pupil of a shaded eye contracts when the other eye is stimulated by bright light. Also called **consensual light reflex**.

consensual validation the process by which a therapist helps a client check the accuracy of his or her perception or the results of his or her experience by comparing it with those of others, often in the context of GROUP PSYCHOTHERAPY.

consensus *n.* general agreement among the members of a group, especially when making an appraisal or decision. In tests of PERSON PERCEPTION, a consensus that a target person has a certain trait can act as a standard against which to compare the self-related biases of those who disagree with the group view. See also FALSE CONSENSUS.

consensus trance a continuous state of culture-induced trance in which individuals are hypothesized to exist. According to this idea, feelings, impressions, and images considered to be part of conscious reality are the result of powerful, repeated suggestions instilled in people since birth.

consent *n.* voluntary assent or approval given by an individual: specifically, permission granted by an individual for medical or psychological treatment, participation in research, or both. Individuals should be fully informed about the treatment or study and its risks and potential benefits (see INFORMED CONSENT).

consentience *n.* a lesser form of consciousness attributed to nonhuman animals.

consequate *vb.* to occur as a result of a response. If the response becomes more probable, consequation is said to have resulted in REINFORCEMENT. If the response becomes less probable, consequation has resulted in PUNISHMENT. **—consequation** *n.*

consequence *n.* an outcome of behavior in a given situation.

consequent *n.* in a conditional proposition of the *if…then* form, the statement that follows the connective *then.* The consequent is what is expected to be the case given that the ANTECEDENT (the statement following *if*) is true. For example, in the conditional proposition, *If Socrates is a man, then he is mortal*, the statement *he is mortal* is the consequent. See also AFFIRMING THE CONSEQUENT; DENYING THE CONSEQUENT.

conservation *n.* the awareness that physical quantities do not change in amount when they are altered in appearance. Conservation is a key element in the cognitive development theory of Swiss psychologist Jean PIAGET. In his famous conservation experiment, all the water from one beaker is poured into a taller, thinner beaker, whereupon the child is asked whether the amount of water has changed. By age 7 or 8 (i.e., at the CONCRETE OPERATIONAL STAGE), children will give the correct answer and understand the underlying principles. See also CONSTANCY; PERCEPTUAL CONSTANCY; REVERSIBILITY.

conservation of energy the physical law that energy can be neither created nor destroyed, only changed in form.

conservation withdrawal a response to emotional or physical stressors (or both) in which a person tends to withdraw from family and friends, become fatigued, and have less energy and strength for activities. A means of conserving energy and recouping psychological and physical strength, this response resembles symptoms experienced as part of a MAJOR DEPRESSIVE EPISODE.

conservatism *n.* **1.** an attitude characterized by a positive regard for the past or the status quo (e.g., established principles and procedures) and sometimes by dislike or distrust of change. **2.** a measurement scale used to assess the degree to which individuals display this attitude. **3.** a political stance reflecting this attitude. **—conservative** *adj.*

conservator *n.* an individual appointed by a court to protect the interests and property of a person who cannot be declared incompetent (see INCOMPETENCE) but is unable by reason of a physical or mental condition to take full responsibility for managing his or her own affairs. **—conservatorship** *n.*

conserve **1.** *vb.* to be aware that physical quantity does not change even though shape or appearance is altered. See CONSERVATION. **2.** *n.* the total knowledge, habits, and skills of a person. [derived from the work of Austrian-born U.S. psychiatrist Jacob Levi Moreno (1892–1974)]

consideration *n.* in leadership theory, a component of effective leadership that involves showing concern for the feelings of subordinates, thereby reducing conflict, maintaining positive relationships, and enhancing feelings of satisfaction and trust in the group. Compare INITIATING STRUCTURE.

consilience *n.* the view that the laws of physics and the rules of biological evolution underlie all aspects of human existence. All human endeavor should reflect these influences and exhibit a unity based on a few basic scientific principles arising from them. [proposed by U.S. biologist Edward O. Wilson (1929–) in his book *Consilience: The Unity of Knowledge* (1998)]

consistency motive the desire to get feedback that confirms what one already believes about one's self. This contributes to maintaining a stable, unchanging SELF-CONCEPT, whether positive or negative. Compare APPRAISAL MOTIVE; SELF-ENHANCEMENT MOTIVE. See also SELF-VERIFICATION HYPOTHESIS.

consistency principle the theory that healthy and well-adjusted people strive to be consistent in their behavior, opinions, and attitudes.

consistency theory a class of social psychological theory holding that people are chiefly motivated by a desire to maintain congruence or consistency among their cognitions. Originally introduced by Austrian-born U.S. psychologist Fritz Heider (1896–1988), Leon FESTINGER, and others, consistency theory was first applied specifically to work behavior by Abraham K. Korman (1933–) in 1970. Korman's theory is based on a two-point premise: a balance notion and a self-image standard. The theory states that workers will engage in, and find satisfying, behaviors that maximize their sense of cognitive balance and will be motivated to perform in a manner consistent with their self-image. Also called **self-consistency theory**. See CONSISTENCY MOTIVE; SELF-VERIFICATION HYPOTHESIS.

consistent mapping a condition of a SEARCH task in which a given stimulus is either (a) always a target or (b) always one of the DISTRACTOR stimuli among which the target is embedded: It is never a target at one time and a distractor at another. Consistent mapping usually produces a much more efficient search performance. Compare VARIED MAPPING.

consistent missing in parapsychology experiments using ZENER CARDS or similar targets, the phenomenon in which a participant's "calls" or guesses are consistently wrong or significantly below chance expectations.

consolidation *n.* **1.** the formation of a permanent memory during the time following a learning experience. **2.** the biological processes by which long-term memory is formed. See CONSOLIDATION PERIOD; PERSEVERATION–CONSOLIDATION HYPOTHESIS.

consolidation hypothesis see PERSEVERATION–CONSOLIDATION HYPOTHESIS.

consolidation period the time following a learning experience during which a permanent memory for the experience develops. According to different theories, the consolidation of long-term memory is said to take from seconds to days.

consonance *n.* **1.** the quality of harmony between elements, for example, in music. **2.** in communication, harmony between content (denotative meaning) and intent (connotative meaning); for example, if a talk on the subject of peace is uttered in peaceful tones, content and intent agree and the communication is said to possess consonance. **3.** in social psychology, the extent to which the components of an attitude are internally consistent or in agreement with each other. See COGNITIVE CONSONANCE.

consonant **1.** *n.* a VOICED or unvoiced speech sound that is produced when the vocal tract is partly or wholly constricted. **2.** *n.* one of the letters of the alphabet used to represent these sounds in writing. Compare VOWEL. **3.** *adj.* characterized by or exhibiting consonance.

consonant trigram three consonants, which normally do not spell a word, used in verbal learning experiments, e.g., JCL. See NONSENSE SYLLABLE. See also AUDITORY CONSONANT TRIGRAM.

Consonar *n.* a trade name for BROFAROMINE.

conspecific **1.** *adj.* belonging to the same species. **2.** *n.* a member of the same species.

conspicuity *n.* the ability of an object to attract attention. In attention studies, when a participant searches for a target among DISTRACTORS in a visual display, a target that has conspicuity (i.e., is conspicuous or salient) will tend to be detected rapidly. See POP-OUT.

constancy *n.* the tendency of perceptions to remain unchanged despite variations in the external conditions of observation. See BRIGHTNESS CONSTANCY; COLOR CONSTANCY; OBJECT CONSTANCY; PERCEPTUAL CONSTANCY; SHAPE CONSTANCY; SIZE CONSTANCY.

constancy law see PRINCIPLE OF CONSTANCY.

constancy of the IQ a tendency for IQ results to remain approximately the same when the same or a similar test is administered. IQ tends, on average, to remain remarkably constant throughout life, starting after infancy and lasting until old age, when there are often declines (starting roughly 10 years before death). New measures of intelligence in infancy, such as of preference for novelty and of recognition memory, suggest that even infant intelligence may predict intelligence in later childhood and adulthood. However, radical changes in environment can result in radical changes in IQ, as when children are adopted out of orphanages or families in which they have experienced severe privation. Usually, such adoptions produce larger changes in IQ if they occur earlier (e.g., by age 2) rather than later.

constancy principle the general principle that psychic forces and energies tend to remain in a steady or balanced state or tend to seek a return to a state of balance or of decreased energy. The idea is related to other general conceptions of constancy found in many scientific fields. In the psychology of Sigmund FREUD, constancy refers specifically to the tendency of psychic energy, or LIBIDO, to seek a homeostatic or balanced state. The same principle lies behind Freud's notion of CATHARSIS.

constancy scaling the mental readjustment of a stimulus attribute (most commonly size) so that the stimulus is perceived as unaffected by the viewing conditions. For example, the small retinal angle subtended by a person seen in the distance is mentally scaled to a larger size so that the person is perceived to be of normal size rather than tiny.

constant error a systematic BIAS or error in some particular direction. In psychophysics and motor control, constant error is evident in a deviation of the mean of the judgments from a standard. For example, if a weight of 1 kg is judged on average to be 1.5 kg, the constant error is 500 g. Compare ABSOLUTE ERROR; RANDOM ERROR.

constant stimulus method see METHOD OF CONSTANT STIMULI.

constellation *n.* in cognitive psychology, a group of ideas with a common theme or association. **—constellatory** *adj.*

constipation *n.* difficult or infrequent excretion of feces. The normal frequency of human bowel movements varies from three times a day to one every 3 days. In addition to diseases and mechanical obstructions, constipation may be caused by psychogenic factors. **Psychogenic constipation** is observed in individuals with obsessive-compulsive disorder who assign such importance to "regularity" that abnormal amounts of time and effort are devoted to daily bowel movements.

constituent *n.* a linguistic unit that is a component of a larger and more complex unit. Although the term is used in the more traditional forms of sentence parsing, it is now mainly associated with the type of **constituent analysis** practiced in PHRASE-STRUCTURE GRAMMAR and other forms of GENERATIVE GRAMMAR. In this form of analysis a canonical English sentence, such as *The man opened a window*, is usually said to have the immediate constituents "noun phrase" (NP) and "verb phrase" (VP); the verb phrase can be further subdivided into the constituents "verb" (V) and "noun phrase," and both noun phrases into "determiner" (det) and "noun" (N).

constitution *n.* **1.** the sum of an individual's innate characteristics. **2.** more broadly, the basic psychological and physical makeup of an individual, due partly to heredity and partly to life experience and environmental factors. **—constitutional** *adj.*

constitutional disorder a condition, disease, behavior, or constellation of behaviors arising from or inherent within some aspect of the individual's physical makeup or physiological characteristics.

constitutional factor a basic physiological tendency that is believed to contribute to personality, temperament, and the etiology of specific mental and physical disorders. These factors include hereditary predispositions and physiological characteristics (circulatory, musculoskeletal, glandular, etc.).

constitutional psychopathic inferior a former name for an individual with ANTISOCIAL PERSONALITY DISORDER. The term **psychopathic inferior** was introduced in 1888 by German physician Robert Koch (1843–1910) and included by German psychiatrist Emil Kraepelin (1856–1928) in his classification of mental disorders (1893). U.S. psychiatrist Adolf Meyer (1866–1950) added the word constitutional in the sense of deep-seated (but not congenital).

constitutional type a classification of individuals based on physique and other biological characteristics or on a hypothetical relationship between physical and psychological characteristics, such as temperament, personality, and a tendency to develop a specific type of mental disorder. See KRETSCHMER TYPOLOGY; SHELDON'S CONSTITUTIONAL THEORY OF PERSONALITY; CARUS TYPOLOGY.

constrained association see CONTROLLED ASSOCIATION.

constraint *n.* a limit on the operation of a linguistic rule such that it can apply only under certain conditions. For example, English has a complex noun-phrase constraint specifying that one cannot formulate a *wh-* question (*who?*, *where?*, *why?*, *when?*, *what?*, etc.) on a constituent of an EMBEDDED SENTENCE. This means, for example, that a *who*? question cannot be formed out of the COMPLEX SENTENCE *I know the boy that Mary likes* such that the answer would be *Mary*.

constraint of movement a belief, held without supporting evidence, that one's movements are controlled by others.

constraint of thought a belief that one's thoughts are controlled or influenced by others.

constraint question one of a series of questions that narrow the field of inquiry, particularly in psychotherapy.

construct *n.* **1.** a complex idea or concept formed from a synthesis of simpler ideas. See HIGHER ORDER CONSTRUCT. **2.** an explanatory model based on empirically verifiable and measurable events or processes—an **empirical construct**—or on processes inferred from data of this kind but not themselves directly observable—a **hypothetical construct**. Many models used in psychology are hypothetical constructs. See also AS-IF HYPOTHESIS; HEURISTIC. **3.** in the study of social cognition, an element of knowledge (a **cognitive construct**).

constructional apraxia an inability, because of brain damage, to copy an object or assemble it from its component parts. Tests for the condition include drawing from a model, reconstructions of puzzles, and building a particular structure using wooden sticks or blocks. See APRAXIA.

constructional dyspraxia an impaired ability to recreate visual images as drawings or other forms of construction (e.g., blocks or puzzle pieces). See DYSPRAXIA.

constructional praxis the ability to draw, copy, or manipulate spatial patterns or designs.

constructionism *n.* see CONSTRUCTIVISM.

constructive alternativism in the personality construct theory of U.S. psychologist George A. Kelly (1905–1967), the capacity to view the world from multiple perspectives, that is, to envision a variety of alternative constructs.

constructive conflict resolution the use of collaborative, salutary methods, such as BARGAINING, NEGOTIATION, ACCOMMODATION, and COOPERATION, to resolve interpersonal or intergroup disagreements. Parties are more likely to use these methods when they are prepared at the outset to cooperate, and the methods themselves often result in greater satisfaction with the solution as well as harmony in future interactions. Compare DESTRUCTIVE CONFLICT RESOLUTION.

constructive confrontation an ORGANIZATIONAL DEVELOPMENT initiative in which employees gather in a **confrontational meeting** to identify, analyze, and plan solutions to work-related problems. At the heart of the method is a free and open discussion in which individuals can be frank without fear of punishment or blame.

constructive criticism see CRITICISM.

constructive hypothesis of consciousness the hypothesis that the function of consciousness is to construct experience in a flexible way depending on the context and available mental contents. [originated by Austrian-born U.S. psychologist George A. Mandler (1924–)]

constructive memory a form of remembering marked by the use of general knowledge stored in one's memory to construct a more complete and detailed account of an event or experience. See BARTLETT TECHNIQUE; RECONSTRUCTIVE MEMORY.

constructive play a form of OBJECT-ORIENTED PLAY in which children manipulate materials in order to create or build objects, for example, making a sand castle or using blocks to build a house. Constructive play facilitates creativity, learning, and the development of skills.

constructive theory of perception any theory proposing that perceivers unconsciously combine information from a stimulus (such as a retinal image) with other information (such as apparent or expected distance and previous experience) to construct a perception.

constructive thinking the ability to solve problems in everyday life with minimal stress.

Constructive Thinking Inventory (**CTI**) a self-report measure of experiential intelligence, yielding scores on such dimensions as superstitious thinking, categorical thinking, naive optimism, and defensiveness. Designed for individuals aged 18 to 80 years, it consists of 108 self-statements about thoughts and behavior to which participants respond using a 5-point LIKERT SCALE format, ranging from "definitely false" to "definitely true." [originally developed in 1989 by U.S. psychologist Seymour Epstein (1924–)]

constructivism *n.* the theoretical perspective, central to the work of Jean PIAGET, that people actively build their perception of the world and interpret objects and events that surround them in terms of what they already know. Thus, their current state of knowledge guides processing, substantially influencing how (and what) new information is acquired. Also called **constructionism**. See also SOCIAL CONSTRUCTIVISM. Compare DIRECT PERCEPTION.

constructivist *adj.* relating to, based on, or derived from constructivism. In a constructivist approach, often represented in a COGNITIVE ARCHITECTURE, the discovery of invariants in a domain can enable developmental growth stages, while model building and refinement can assist learning.

Constructivist Learning Environment Survey (**CLES**) a questionnaire consisting of 30 statements (e.g., "I help the teacher to assess my learning") that students rate using a 5-point LIKERT SCALE format, ranging from "almost never" to "almost always." It assesses the degree to which a particular classroom's environment is consistent with a CONSTRUCTIVIST epistemology and assists teachers to reflect on their epistemological assumptions and reshape their teaching practice. [developed by Australian educators Peter Charles Taylor and Barry J. Fraser]

constructivist psychotherapy **1.** a form of individual psychotherapy, derived from CONSTRUCTIVISM, that focuses on meaning-making to help clients reconceptualize their problems in a more life-enhancing way using story, myth, poetry, and other linguistic and nonverbal forms. **2.** a group of psychotherapies all of which rely on a philosophy of interpersonal and social processes of meaning-making. Such therapies are typically derived from constructivism and encompass developments in existential, humanistic, and family therapy. See also NARRATIVE PSYCHOTHERAPY. [developed by U.S. clinical psychologist George Kelly (1905–1967)]

constructivist theory of emotion any theory holding that emotions are not INNATE but constructed through social and cultural experience. See SOCIAL CONSTRUCTIVISM.

construct validation the process of establishing the CONSTRUCT VALIDITY of an instrument. The process usually requires the simultaneous examination of CONVERGENT VALIDITY, DISCRIMINANT VALIDITY, and CONTENT VALIDITY.

construct validity the degree to which a test or instrument is capable of measuring a theoretical construct, trait, or ability (e.g., intelligence).

consultant *n.* **1.** a mental health care or medical specialist called upon to provide professional advice or services in terms of diagnosis, treatment, or rehabilitation. **2.** in the United Kingdom, a hospital doctor of the most senior rank in his or her field.

consulting *n.* the use of the particular skill, experience, and expertise of an individual or group to advise individuals, groups, or organizations.

consulting psychologist a psychologist who provides specialized, technical advisory assistance to individuals or organizations in regard to psychological aspects of their work. Consulting psychologists may have as clients individuals, institutions, corporations, or other kinds of organizations.

consulting psychology the branch of psychology that provides expert psychological guidance to business and industry, federal and state agencies, the armed forces, educational and scientific groups, religious groups, and volunteer and public service organizations. Consulting psychologists specialize in a variety of approaches—clinical, community, school, education, and industrial and organizational—and offer a wide variety of services, the most common of which are individual assessment, individual and group-process consultation, organizational development, education and training, employee selection and appraisal, research and evaluation test construction, management coaching, and change management.

consumer *n.* an individual who purchases (or otherwise acquires) and uses goods or services. In the context of medical and mental health care, consumers are those who purchase or receive health care services.

consumer behavior the acts of individuals or groups involved in obtaining, consuming, and disposing of economic goods and services, including the decision processes that precede and follow these acts.

consumer characteristics personality traits of consumers that can influence the planning of advertising campaigns. Most sophisticated studies of consumer characteristics go beyond area, sex, income, and neighborhood of residence and use established psychological techniques to analyze motives behind buying decisions. See also PSYCHOGRAPHICS.

consumer counseling counseling for individuals that focuses on good decision making in personal money management.

consumer education programs that educate consumers primarily in (a) the criteria by which to evaluate complex technical products and services; (b) decision-making skills; (c) the workings of business, government, and the marketplace; (d) techniques for judging advertising and selling claims; and (e) money-saving buying strategies.

consumer empowerment a practice in which the end-users of services increase their exercise of service choice and their influence over how, when, and by whom services are developed, delivered, and changed.

consumer innovator one of the first individuals to use a new product or service (see ADOPTER CATEGORIES). Innovators tend to be risk takers.

consumerism *n.* a movement to protect the rights of the consumer with regard to the quality and safety of available products and services (including psychotherapeutic and medical care). Consumerism has resulted in the legally enforceable rights of individuals to have access to treatment, to refuse treatment, and not to be given experimental, unusual, or hazardous treatment without INFORMED CONSENT. **—consumerist** *adj.*

consumer-jury technique a method of testing advertising appeals before an actual product promotion campaign is started in a test market. "Jury" members usually consist of typical consumers of the product category. They are shown a selection of different proposed advertisements and asked to evaluate them in terms of which advertisement would be most likely to induce them to purchase the product. The consumer-jury technique has been found to be an accurate predictor of advertising effectiveness. See also CONTINUOUS PANEL.

consumer psychology the branch of psychology that specializes in the behavior of individuals as consumers and in the techniques of communicating information to influence consumer decisions to purchase a manufacturer's product. **Consumer psychologists** investigate the reasons and psychological processes underlying behavior in for-profit as well as not-for-profit marketing.

consumer research the application of clinical, scientific, and statistical research techniques to the study of consumer behavior. Consumer research may include studies of consumer tastes and preferences, the influence of the package design, and the personality traits of a target audience. See also MARKET RESEARCH; MOTIVATION RESEARCH.

consumer survey a survey of consumer likes and dislikes in certain product categories (e.g., beverages) that may yield information about designing and packaging a product in ways the consumer will find attractive. Consumer surveys may be conducted by questionnaires, in-depth interviews, group interviews, visualization, and similar techniques.

consummatory communication a message that has the sole purpose of conveying the sender's ideas or feelings and does not require any response or action from the recipient.

consummatory response the final response in a chain of behavior directed toward the satisfaction of a need, resulting in a reduction in a particular DRIVE. Thus eating (to reduce hunger) is the final act of foraging behavior, and copulation (to reduce the sex drive) is the final act of sexual behavior. In 1918 U.S. ethologist

Wallace Craig distinguished between consummatory behavior as an innate stereotyped activity and APPETITIVE BEHAVIOR as the active searching process that precedes it. Also called **consummatory act; consummatory behavior**. See also GOAL-DIRECTED BEHAVIOR.

consummatory response theory of reinforcement see DRIVE-INDUCTION THEORY.

contact behavior actions and interactions occurring during an interpersonal relationship, which may be either an intimate, personal relationship (e.g., sexual contact) or a relatively impersonal relationship (e.g., buying and selling).

contact comfort the positive effects experienced by infants or young animals when in close contact with the mother or a MOTHER SURROGATE. The term originates from Harry HARLOW's classic experiments, in which young rhesus monkeys exposed both to an artificial cloth mother without a bottle for feeding and to an artificial wire mother with a bottle for feeding spent more time on the cloth mother and, when frightened, were more readily soothed by the presence of the cloth mother than the wire mother.

contact desensitization a variation of SYSTEMATIC DESENSITIZATION involving PARTICIPANT MODELING instead of relaxation training: used especially in the treatment of anxiety. The therapist demonstrates appropriate behaviors, beginning with those in the weakest anxiety-provoking situation for the client, and then assists the client in performing such behaviors. For example, in working with an client who is afraid of spiders, the therapist might first sit near a spider, then touch the spider, and then pick it up while the client observes. The client, with the guidance and assistance of the therapist, would then perform the same activities in the same order.

contact hypothesis the theory that people belonging to one group can become less prejudiced against (and perhaps more favorably disposed toward) members of other groups merely through increased contact with them. It is now thought that greater contact is unlikely to reduce intergroup prejudice unless the people from the different groups are of equal status, are not in competition with each other, and do not readily categorize the others as very different from themselves. Also called **intergroup-contact hypothesis**.

contact language an improvised system of communication, such as a PIDGIN, that emerges in situations of contact between speakers of different languages. Contact languages are usually characterized by a restricted lexicon, simplified sentence structures, and the absence of complex grammatical inflections.

contact lenses see CORRECTIVE LENS.

contact sense a sense in which sensory awareness arises from direct contact of the stimuli with the receptors. Contact senses include the CHEMICAL SENSES (i.e., taste and smell) and the TOUCH SENSE.

contagion *n.* in social theory, the spread of behaviors, attitudes, and affect through crowds and other types of social aggregation from one member to another. Early analyses of contagion suggested that it resulted from the heightened suggestibility of members and likened the process to the spread of contagious diseases. Subsequent studies have argued that contagion is sustained by relatively mundane interpersonal processes, such as social comparison (see SOCIAL COMPARISON THEORY), IMITATION, SOCIAL FACILITATION, CONFORMITY, UNIVERSALITY, and CIRCULAR REACTIONS. Also called **social contagion**. See also COLLECTIVE HYSTERIA; CROWD MIND; MASS CONTAGION.

containment *n.* in OBJECT RELATIONS THEORY, the notion that either the mother or the analyst aids growth and alleviates anxieties by acting as a "container," or "holding environment," for the projected aspects of the child's or patient's psyche (see PROJECTION). For instance, the infant, overwhelmed by distress and having no context to understand the experience, is held and soothed by the parent, who thus creates a safe context for the child and endows the experience with meaning.

contamination *n.* **1.** in testing and experimentation, the process of permitting knowledge, expectations, or other factors about the variable under study to influence the collection and interpretation of data about that variable. **2.** the mixing together of two or more discrete percepts, such as might occur on the RORSCHACH INKBLOT TEST or the MACHOVER DRAW-A-PERSON TEST. **3.** the creation of a NEOLOGISM by combining a part of one word with a part of another, usually resulting in a word that is unintelligible.

contamination obsession an intense preoccupation with disease, dirt, germs, mud, excrement, sputum, and so forth, based on a feeling that the world is disgusting, decaying, and dying. In extreme cases, it is regarded as a symptom of schizophrenia.

contemporaneity *n.* in psychotherapy, the principle of focusing on immediate experience. See also HERE AND NOW.

contempt *n.* an emotion characterized by negative regard for anything or anybody considered to be inferior, vile, or worthless. **—contemptuous** *adj.*

content *n.* **1.** in psychology, the thoughts, images, and sensations that occur in conscious experience: the objects of Wilhelm WUNDT's introspection and the subject matter of his psychological framework. Contents are contrasted with the mental processes or the neural structures that underlie them. **2.** more generally, that which is part of or contained within something (e.g., the content of a message, the contents of a book).

content-addressable store a model of memory, borrowed from computer science, in which a memory is stored and retrieved based on representation of its contents rather than by an arbitrary tag. Knowledge or memory is represented by values along certain dimensions, such as temporal (e.g., last summer) or semantic (a vacation); an effective retrieval cue using the same values along those dimensions will access the information stored.

content analysis 1. a systematic, quantitative procedure for coding the themes in qualitative material, such as projective-test responses, propaganda, or fiction. **2.** a systematic, quantitative study of verbally communicated material (e.g., articles, speeches, films) by determining the frequency of specific ideas, concepts, or terms. Also called **quantitative semantics**.

contentiousness *n.* a tendency toward disputes and strife: quarrelsomeness. Contentiousness may be observed in MANIA and in the early stages of predominantly persecutory DELUSIONAL DISORDERS when individuals perceive that they are being treated unfairly.

content psychology an approach to psychology that is concerned with the role of conscious experience and the CONTENT of that experience. The term is mainly applied to early STRUCTURALISM. Compare ACT PSYCHOLOGY.

contents of consciousness see CONSCIOUSNESS.

content-thought disorder a type of thought disturbance, typically found in schizophrenia and some other mental disorders (e.g., OBSESSIVE-COMPULSIVE DISOR-

DER, MANIA), characterized by multiple, fragmented, bizarre delusions.

contentual objectivism versus contentual subjectivism the question of whether the proper subject matter (CONTENT) of psychology is objective behavior or the subjective realm of the mind or consciousness. This question is often seen as the principal issue at stake in the conceptual confrontation between STRUCTURALISM and BEHAVIORISM in the early history of psychology. See also METHODOLOGICAL OBJECTIVISM VERSUS METHODOLOGICAL SUBJECTIVISM.

content validity the extent to which a test measures a representative sample of the subject matter or behavior under investigation. For example, if a test is designed to survey arithmetic skills at third-grade level, content validity will indicate how well it represents the range of arithmetic operations possible at that level.

content word in linguistics, a word with an independent lexical meaning, that is, one that can be defined with reference to the physical world or abstract concepts and without reference to any sentence in which the word may appear. In practice, the category of content words is virtually identical with that of OPEN-CLASS WORDS. Also called **autonomous word**; **lexical word**. Compare FUNCTION WORD.

context *n.* **1.** generally, the conditions or circumstances in which a particular phenomenon occurs. **2.** in linguistics, the parts of a speech or written passage that precede or follow a word, phrase, or other unit and clarify its meaning. **3.** in studies of cognition, the environment in which a stimulus event occurs, especially as this influences memory, learning, judgment, or other cognitive processes. **4.** in laboratory tasks involving the recognition of stimuli, the setting in which a target stimulus is presented, including any distractors or maskers (see MASKING). **—contextual** *adj.*

context clues clues provided by the immediate context (i.e., the sentence or paragraph) that enable a reader to recognize a word that is not a SIGHT WORD. See WORD-RECOGNITION SKILLS.

context-independent learning the learning of a skill or strategy independently of a specific situation in which the skill will be applied.

context reinstatement a method used to aid the retrieval of memories. In the case of eyewitness recall, the individual is asked to re-create the event to be remembered in its original context and is encouraged to think about a variety of stimuli surrounding the event (e.g., smells, sounds) in the hope of providing additional retrieval cues. See also COGNITIVE INTERVIEW.

context shifting in conversation or therapy, a tendency to change subjects abruptly, generally to avoid anxiety-laden issues.

context-specific learning learning that has occurred in a particular place, or context, and is displayed only in that context and not when testing occurs in another context. See also CONTEXTUAL ASSOCIATIONS.

context theory of meaning the theory that the meaning of a word or concept depends upon mental images associated with a specific body of sensations, as in the concept of fire. [formulated by Edward Bradford TITCHENER]

contextual associations ASSOCIATIONS learned between items or material an organism is exposed to and the context in which exposure occurs. For instance, a lecture may be associated with the classroom in which it occurs: The contextual associations facilitate retrieval, so recall of the lecture should be better in the classroom than outside it.

contextual interference effect an effect on learning that may occur when training occurs in different contexts or when trials on one task are alternated with those on a different task. Learning is slowed by changing contexts or by intervening tasks, but the knowledge is more enduring and more readily transferable to different tasks or domains.

contextualism *n.* **1.** the theory that the memory of experiences is not the result only of linkages between events, as in the associationist doctrine, but is due to the meaning given to events by the context surrounding the experiences. **2.** a worldview asserting that the environment in which an event occurs intrinsically informs the event and its interpretation.

contextualize *vb.* to interpret an event within a preexisting mental framework. See CONTEXT. **—contextualization** *n.*

contextual subtheory a part of the TRIARCHIC THEORY OF INTELLIGENCE according to which factors in the environment affect both an individual's intelligence and what constitutes an intelligent response to a given situation. The subtheory postulates that people are intelligent in context to the extent that they effectively adapt to, shape, and select environments.

contiguity *n.* the co-occurrence of stimuli in time or space. Learning an association between two stimuli is generally thought to depend at least partly on the contiguity of those stimuli. See CONTIGUITY OF ASSOCIATIONS; LAW OF CONTIGUITY. **—contiguous** *adj.*

contiguity learning theory a theory stating that if a pattern of stimulation and a response occur together in time and space, learning occurs by the formation of ASSOCIATIONS between them, so that the same stimulus pattern will elicit the same response on subsequent occasions. See also S–R PSYCHOLOGY. [proposed by Edwin R. GUTHRIE]

contiguity of associations the concept that a mental connection, or ASSOCIATION, is usually established between two objects, experiences, or behaviors that are close together in space or time. See also LAW OF CONTIGUITY.

contiguity principle see LAW OF CONTIGUITY.

continence *n.* the ability to control sexual urges or the urge to defecate or urinate. **—continent** *adj.*

continental philosophy philosophical developments originating in continental Europe from the middle of the 20th century, encompassing such movements as PHENOMENOLOGY, EXISTENTIALISM, STRUCTURALISM, and DECONSTRUCTION. Continental philosophy is often contrasted with the Anglo-American tradition of ANALYTIC PHILOSOPHY.

contingencies of self-worth particular areas of life in which people invest their SELF-ESTEEM, such that feedback regarding their standing or abilities in these domains has a crucial impact on their SELF-CONCEPT. Research indicates that people choose to stake their self-esteem in different domains, so that for some people material or professional success is vital to their sense of self-worth, whereas for others this is much less important than being well liked or sexually attractive.

contingency *n.* a conditional, probabilistic relation between two events. When the probability of Event B given Event A is 1.0, a perfect **positive contingency** is said to exist. When Event A predicts with certainty the absence of Event B, a perfect **negative contingency** is said to exist. Probabilities between –1.0 and 1.0 define a continuum from negative to positive contingencies, with a probability of zero indicating no contingency. Contingencies may be arranged via dependencies or they may emerge by accident (see ACCIDENTAL REINFORCEMENT). See also REINFORCEMENT CONTINGENCY.

contingency awareness **1.** awareness of a relationship or connection between two occurrences. See CO-OCCURRENCE. **2.** awareness of the dependence of one variable upon another. See COVARIATION.

contingency contract a mutually agreed-upon statement between a teacher and student, a parent and child, or a client and therapist regarding the change or changes desired, typically specifying behaviors and their positive and negative consequences.

contingency-governed behavior behavior that is directly and solely the result of REINFORCEMENT CONTINGENCIES. It occurs without deliberation. Compare RULE-GOVERNED BEHAVIOR.

contingency management the regulation of REINFORCEMENT management, with reference to such questions as: Who does the reinforcing? How much reinforcement for how much work? When is reinforcement to be delivered? What does it consist of?

contingency model any theory or model based on the generalization that there is no universal, ideal approach to structuring organizations and managing people. Rather, the most effective approach will depend on factors such as the nature of the task, the culture and environment of the organization, and the characteristics of the people involved. Also called **situational approach**. See also CONTINGENCY THEORIES OF LEADERSHIP.

contingency reinforcement in BEHAVIOR THERAPY, a technique in which a reinforcement, or reward, is given each time the desired behavior is performed; that is, the reward is contingent on the behavior.

contingency table a two-dimensional table in which the number of cases that are simultaneously in a given spot in a given row and column of the table are specified. For example, the ages and geographical locations of a sample of individuals applying for a particular job may be displayed in a contingency table, such that there are X number of individuals under 25 from New York City, Y number of individuals under 25 from Los Angeles, Z number of individuals between the ages of 25 and 35 from New York City, and so on. See CROSS-CLASSIFICATION.

contingency theories of leadership various models predicting that leadership performance depends on the interaction of the personal characteristics of the LEADER and the nature of the group situation. The prototypical contingency theory emerged from the conceptual analysis of leadership effectiveness developed by U.S. social psychologist Fred Fiedler (1922–) in the 1960s. Fiedler's model differentiates between TASK-MOTIVATED and RELATIONSHIP-MOTIVATED leaders, as indicated by scores on the LEAST PREFERRED COWORKER SCALE. The favorability of the leadership setting is determined by the quality of the leader's personal relationships with group members, the extent of the leader's actual authority or power, and the clarity of the tasks the group members must complete (see TASK STRUCTURE). The model predicts that task-motivated leaders will be most effective in extremely favorable or unfavorable group settings, whereas relationship-motivated leaders will be more effective in moderately favorable settings. Other models of this kind include the SITUATIONAL LEADERSHIP THEORY, the SUBSTITUTES FOR LEADERSHIP THEORY, and the VROOM–YETTON–JAGO MODEL OF LEADERSHIP. See also COGNITIVE RESOURCE THEORY; LEADERSHIP THEORIES.

contingent *adj.* **1.** dependent on circumstances, events, or conditions. See also CONTINGENCY. **2.** in philosophy, denoting a proposition that is true under certain conditions but not all, or a being that exists as a matter of fact but not as a matter of necessity.

contingent aftereffect a visual phenomenon in which the AFTEREFFECT in one stimulus dimension (e.g., color) is dependent on a separate stimulus dimension (e.g., orientation). The **McCullough effect** is an example in which repeated serial exposure to horizontal red bars followed by vertical green bars induces an aftereffect of horizontal white bars appearing green and vertical white bars appearing red. The color of the aftereffect is contingent on the orientation of the test stimulus.

contingent employee an employee hired on a temporary contract to work on specific projects or tasks. Also called **contingent worker**.

contingent negative variation (**CNV**) a slow EVENT-RELATED POTENTIAL that is recorded from the scalp. A CNV arises in the interval between a warning signal and a signal that directs action. Also called **expectancy wave**. See also EVOKED POTENTIAL.

contingent probability the probability, expressed as a number between 0 and 1, that one specific factor will occur if another one does, for example, the probability that the child of a drug user will become a drug user himself or herself. Unusually high or low contingent probabilities (compared to the general population) may, but do not necessarily, imply a causal relationship between the two factors.

contingent reinforcement in behaviorism, making the delivery of positive stimulus events (e.g., social or material rewards) and, more rarely, the elimination of negative stimulus events (e.g., penalties) dependent on the performance of desired behavior. In leadership and management, the term is applied to any approach in which a leader relies on rewards and penalties to motivate his or her followers. See REINFORCEMENT.

contingent reward in behaviorist theory, any social, symbolic, or material reward whose delivery to an individual depends on that individual performing a specific behavior.

continuance commitment that element of an employee's ORGANIZATIONAL COMMITMENT that can be attributed to the cost, inconvenience, or difficulty of changing employers. Compare AFFECTIVE COMMITMENT.

continued-stay review (**CSR**) a UTILIZATION REVIEW in which an internal or external auditor determines if continued inpatient care is medically necessary or if the current health care facility is still the most appropriate to provide the level of care required by the patient. See also CONCURRENT REVIEW; EXTENDED-STAY REVIEW.

continuing bond the emotional attachment that a bereaved person continues to maintain with the deceased long after the death. The increasingly influential continuing-bond approach focuses on ways in which the emotional and symbolic relationship with the deceased can be reconstructed and integrated into the individual's life. See also BEREAVEMENT; GRIEF; MOURNING; OBJECT LOSS.

continuing care unit (**CCU**) a hospital unit to which a patient with a catastrophic or chronic illness is transferred for additional care after the acute hospitalization period. Compare INTENSIVE CARE UNIT. See also CONVALESCENT CENTER; SKILLED NURSING FACILITY.

continuing education a subset of ADULT EDUCATION

in which an adult updates or augments a previously acquired skill set, knowledge base, or area of expertise.

continuing medical education (**CME**) postdoctoral educational activities that serve to develop or extend the knowledge, skills, and professional qualities that a physician uses to provide health care services.

continuity-care retirement community a facility that offers a range of services and living arrangements that older adult residents can use as the need arises. A full sprectrum of such services and arrangements might include independent living arrangements for the healthy and comparatively healthy; accessibility of on-site nursing care and other medical services for those temporarily ill, recovering from surgery, or returning from an extended stay in a hospital or rehabilitation facility; and terminal care for the dying.

continuity hypothesis 1. the assumption that successful DISCRIMINATION LEARNING or problem solving results from a progressive, incremental, continuous process of trial and error. Responses that prove unproductive are extinguished, whereas every reinforced response results in an increase in ASSOCIATIVE STRENGTH, thus producing the gradual rise of the LEARNING CURVE. Problem solving is conceived as a step-by-step learning process in which the correct response is discovered, practiced, and reinforced. Compare DISCONTINUITY HYPOTHESIS. **2.** the contention that psychological processes of various kinds (e.g., learning, childhood development) take place either in small steps or continuously, rather than in jumps from one identifiable stage to another. Also called **continuity theory**.

continuity of germ plasm see GERM PLASM.

continuity versus discontinuity of development the scientific debate over whether developmental change is gradual (continuous) or relatively abrupt (discontinuous).

continuous amnesia ongoing memory loss for all events after a particular period of time, up to and including the present.

continuous avoidance see SIDMAN AVOIDANCE SCHEDULE.

continuous bath treatment see HYDROTHERAPY.

continuous control in ergonomics, a control device operated by continuous movements, such as a joystick used to move a cursor on a screen, as opposed to a **discrete control** device, such as an on–off switch or the like. See also ISOMETRIC CONTROL; ISOTONIC CONTROL.

continuous distractor task a test of memory retention in which a continuous string of items to be remembered is presented: Every few items, the participant is presented with one of the items previously presented and must remember the item following it, while also retaining the other items in sequence. A continuous distractor task contrasts with a study-trial–test-trial procedure.

continuous group see OPEN GROUP.

continuous movement task a movement task that has no recognizable beginning or end—the behavior continues until it is arbitrarily stopped. Examples include running and steering a car. Compare DISCRETE MOVEMENT TASK.

continuous operations (**CONOPS**) operations conducted without interruption, which require strict discipline, planning, time management, and coordination. They may cause sleep loss and affect ability to perform operational tasks.

continuous panel a form of consumer jury in which members serve on a more or less permanent basis so that consumer psychologists can detect shifts in attitudes, values, or behavior (see CONSUMER-JURY TECHNIQUE). The panel members are carefully selected to represent the demographic or psychographic characteristics of a population, and they are tested periodically for signs of psychic mobility that may also represent attitude changes in the general population.

continuous performance test (**CPT**) any test that measures sustained attention and concentration, usually by requiring responses to an auditory or verbal target stimulus while ignoring nontarget stimuli.

continuous rating scale a scale on which ratings are assigned along a continuum (e.g., a line) rather than according to categories. Such ratings are made by making a mark on the scale to indicate the "placement" of the rating or by assigning a numerical value to indicate the magnitude of response. See CONTINUOUS SCALE.

continuous recognition task a memory task in which a series of items is presented, with some items presented on multiple occasions in the series. The participant responds to each item by indicating whether it is old (seen previously in the series) or new (not seen earlier in the series).

continuous reinforcement (**CRF**) in operant and instrumental conditioning, the REINFORCEMENT of every response. It is identical to a fixed-ratio 1 schedule of reinforcement (see FIXED-RATIO SCHEDULE). Also called **continuous reinforcement schedule**; **continuous schedule of reinforcement**.

continuous scale a scale in which additional values can always be inserted between any two adjacent scores.

continuous spectrum see SOUND SPECTRUM.

continuous variable a RANDOM VARIABLE that can take on an infinite number of values; that is, a variable measured on a continuous scale, as opposed to a CATEGORICAL VARIABLE. Also called **continuous random variable**.

continuum approach an approach based on the view that behavior ranges over a continuum from effective functioning to severe personality disorganization. It assumes that differences between people's behavior are a matter of degree rather than kind. A scale can be established to judge the severity of behavioral abnormality.

contra- *prefix* against or opposing.

contraception *n.* the prevention of conception, that is, the natural fertilization of the female ovum by the male spermatozoa. See BIRTH CONTROL. **—contraceptive** *n., adj.*

contract *n.* an explicit written agreement between parties or individuals. A contract between a client and therapist may detail (a) both the client's and the therapist's obligations, (b) the provisions for benefits or privileges to be gained through achievements, and (c) the specified consequences of failures (e.g., missing sessions). See also BEHAVIORAL CONTRACT; CONTINGENCY CONTRACT.

contractility *n.* the capacity of living tissue, particularly muscle, to contract in response to a stimulus. Also called **contractibility**.

contract plan a plan used in some schools in which a student signs a contract agreeing to change a certain behavior, such as raising a grade in a class. The contract enhances accountability for behavior; it often carries with it a reward for completion and sometimes a RESPONSE COST for failure to perform.

contracture *n.* an abnormal shortening or tightening of a muscle, which can result in permanent disability due to difficulty in stretching the muscle. A contracture often follows a disorder or injury that makes movement painful or is a consequence of prolonged, enforced inactivity (e.g., a coma).

contradiction principle in logic, the principle that a statement and its negation cannot simultaneously be true. As originally articulated by Greek philosopher Aristotle (384–322 BCE), the principle applies to more than propositions, stating that "Nothing can both be and not be at the same time." Also called **principle of contradiction; principle of noncontradiction**. See also EXCLUDED MIDDLE PRINCIPLE.

contradictory representation a condition in which one mental image prevents another from occurring owing to conflict between the two images. For example, it is impossible to hold an image of the same object as both round and square. The effect of contradictory representation is to inhibit further mental activity of which the image in question is an essential part. Contradictory representation is related to the more general CONTRADICTION PRINCIPLE.

contralateral *adj.* situated on or affecting the opposite side of the body. For example, motor paralysis occurs on the side of the body contralateral to the side on which a brain lesion is found. Compare IPSILATERAL. **—contralaterally** *adv.*

contralateral control the arrangement whereby the MOTOR CORTEX of each cerebral hemisphere is mainly responsible for control of movements of the contralateral (opposite) side of the body.

contralateral deficit see IPSILATERAL DEFICIT.

contralateral eye the eye located on the opposite side of the body to another structure or object. For example, layer 6 of the left LATERAL GENICULATE NUCLEUS receives input from the RETINAL GANGLION CELL axons that originate in the right (i.e., contralateral) eye. Compare IPSILATERAL EYE.

contralateral hemisphere the CEREBRAL HEMISPHERE on the opposite side of the body from any organ or part that is being considered as the reference point. See also CONTRALATERAL CONTROL.

contraprepared *adj.* denoting the state of an organism in relation to responses or associations that are difficult to learn, particularly in reaction to certain stimuli or in the presence of certain reinforcers. In conditioning experiments, for example, rats are contraprepared to associate a tone stimulus with gastric illness but readily learn to associate a distinctive taste with illness (see CONDITIONED TASTE AVERSION). One explanation for this is that the evolutionary history of the organism has not prepared it to learn some associations. Compare PREPARED LEARNING; PRINCIPLE OF BELONGINGNESS.

contraprepared behavior a behavior that is very difficult or even impossible for a certain species to learn.

contrarian *n.* a person who tends to disagree with someone or argue against something, regardless of the validity of the topic under discussion.

contrast *n.* **1.** that state in which the differences between one thing, event, or idea and another are emphasized by a comparison of their qualities. **2.** in cognitive psychology, see CONTRAST EFFECT. **3.** in the ANALYSIS OF VARIANCE, a comparison among group means using one DEGREE OF FREEDOM. **4.** in making judgments, the difference found between a target being judged and features of the context in which it is judged. For example, meeting a person in a social context that includes physically attractive people (e.g., a party of Hollywood stars) could lead to a more negative evaluation of the attractiveness of that person than would have been the case in a more neutral context. In such a case, the evaluation of the person's attractiveness has been contrasted away from the social context. Compare ASSIMILATION.

contrast analysis 1. comparisons between two or more groups that address specific questions about the patterning of the MEANS of these groups. **2.** a focused analysis of data that is designed to determine the specific degree to which obtained data agree with predicted data (i.e., to which they support a hypothesis or theory). Contrast analysis yields an estimate of EFFECT SIZE and an associated level of significance for each contrast computed.

contrast correlation (symbol: r_{contrast}) the correlation between scores on the DEPENDENT VARIABLE and the contrast weights (i.e., predicted values) after removing any other sources of variation in the data.

contrast detector 1. any of the RETINAL GANGLION CELLS that are sensitive to contrast (i.e., light–dark borders). See also FEATURE DETECTOR. **2.** any structure, neural or theoretical, that is sensitive to contrast.

contrast effect 1. the perception of an intensified or heightened difference between two stimuli or sensations when they are juxtaposed (simultaneous contrast) or when one immediately follows the other (successive contrast). Examples include the effect produced when a trombone follows a violin or when bright yellow and red are viewed simultaneously. **2.** in psychology experiments, an effect in which participants' judgments shift away from an ANCHOR after it is introduced. Compare ASSIMILATION EFFECT.

contrast error a type of RATING ERROR in which the evaluation of a target person in a group is affected by the level of performance of others in the group. When the others are high in performance, there may be a tendency to rate the target lower than is correct. When the others are low in performance, there may be a tendency to rate the target higher than is correct.

contrast illusion a class of visual illusions in which the degree of a stimulus attribute, such as perceived size, color, brightness, or angle, is affected by the presence of additional stimuli that differ in the same attribute. For example, a small circle at the center of many large circles will appear to be smaller than the same circle at the center of many smaller circles.

contrastive analysis in linguistics, a comparison of the structures of two languages, usually with the goal of providing insight into effective second- or foreign-language instruction. See also LANGUAGE TRANSFER.

contrastive rhetoric in linguistics, the theory that different languages have different rhetorical characteristics, as seen, for example, in the different ways they structure and present an argument. The idea of contrastive rhetoric has been much discussed in the field of second-language teaching, especially at the more advanced levels. It is said to explain, for example, why native speakers will often feel that there is something odd or "wrong" about essays, business letters, and so on produced by nonnative speakers, even when the grammar and vocabulary are flawless. Contrastive rhetoric has sometimes been linked to the wider hypothesis that languages embody culture-bound thought patterns (see LINGUISTIC DETERMINISM). [introduced in 1966 by U.S. applied linguist Robert B. Kaplan]

contrast polarity the degree of contrast between two visual elements, particularly figure and background. Contrast can be positive (light objects against dark backgrounds, e.g., a white letter printed upon black paper) or negative (dark objects against light backgrounds, e.g., a black letter printed upon white paper).

contrast sensitivity a measure of spatial RESOLUTION based on an individual's ability to detect subtle differences in light and dark coloring or shading in an object of a fixed size. Detection is affected by the size of contrasting elements and is usually tested using a grating of alternating light and dark bars, being defined by the minimum contrast required to distinguish that there is a bar pattern rather than a uniform screen. Contrast sensitivity is less for both coarse and fine gratings than it is for gratings of intermediate frequency. Humans have peak contrast sensitivity for gratings with 4–8 cpd (cycles per degree) and can detect contrast over a range from about 0.5 cpd to 50–60 cpd. Contrast sensitivity can be reduced after injury to the peripheral or central visual system: Patients complain of VISUAL BLURRING, although visual acuity may be only moderately affected. Also called **spatial contrast sensitivity**. See also SPATIAL FREQUENCY.

contrast-sensitivity function (**CSF**) a graphical representation of CONTRAST SENSITIVITY as a function of SPATIAL FREQUENCY. The CSF for normal humans peaks at about 4–8 cpd (cycles per degree).

contrast theory the view that aspects of an object can become known by comparing it with other similar objects that vary slightly in size, shape, color, texture, and so forth.

contrast weight the WEIGHT assigned to each set of observations or data obtained from a particular experimental condition in an experimental design in order to produce a one-DEGREE OF FREEDOM contrast.

contrasuggestibility *n.* a tendency to do or say the opposite of what has been suggested or requested.

contravolitional *adj.* against the wishes of an individual or beyond his or her control.

contrecoup *n.* brain injury on one side of the head resulting from a blow to the opposite side.

contributing cause a cause that is not sufficient to bring about an end or event but that helps in some way to bring about that end or event. A contributing cause may be a necessary CONDITION or it may influence events more indirectly by affecting other conditions that make the event more likely.

contrient interdependence a relationship between parties' outcomes such that one party's success increases the likelihood of the other party's failure. Such structures are associated with competition and conflict. Compare POSITIVE INTERDEPENDENCE. [described by U.S. psychologist Morton Deutsch (1920–)]

control *n.* **1.** authority, power, or influence over events, behaviors, situations, or people. **2.** the regulation of all extraneous conditions and variables in an experiment so that any change in the DEPENDENT VARIABLE can be attributed solely to manipulation of the INDEPENDENT VARIABLE. In other words, the results obtained will be due solely to the experimental condition or conditions and not to any other factors. **3.** any mechanism or instrument for operating or regulating a machine.

control adoptees see CROSS-FOSTERING.

control analysis psychoanalytic treatment conducted by a trainee under the guidance of a qualified PSYCHOANALYST, who helps the trainee to decide the direction of the treatment and to become aware of his or her COUNTERTRANSFERENCE. Also called **supervised analysis**; **supervisory analysis**.

control condition see CONTROL GROUP.

control device the mechanism that allows the operator of an ENVIRONMENTAL CONTROL DEVICE to transmit instructions to a TARGET DEVICE to perform a function. See also FEEDBACK DEVICE; SWITCH DEVICE.

control discriminability in ergonomics, the ease with which a control can be distinguished from other controls or objects on the interface and matched correctly to the impact that its activation or use will have on the system. The discriminability of a control will be a function of size, shape, color, and other design features.

control–display ratio in ergonomics, the ratio between the distance that a control or input device (e.g., a computer mouse) is moved by the operator and the consequent distance that the object it controls (e.g., the cursor) is moved on the display (e.g., the computer screen).

control experiment an experiment repeated for the purpose of increasing the validity of the original experiment. The experimental conditions may be duplicated exactly either to provide another measure of the DEPENDENT VARIABLE or to assess the impact of a variable that experimenters suspect was not previously controlled.

control function logic in ergonomics, a logical or typical and expected relationship between the operation of a control or input device and the resulting action or effect on a display. For example, if a person moves a computer mouse to the left, the on-screen cursor should also move to the left to preserve control function logic. See also DISPLAY–CONTROL COMPATIBILITY.

control group a group of participants in an experiment that are exposed to the **control conditions**, that is, the conditions of the experiment not involving a treatment or exposure to the INDEPENDENT VARIABLE. Compare EXPERIMENTAL GROUP.

controllability training exercises for teaching and improving an individual's ability to control IMAGERY.

controllable turnover see TURNOVER.

controlled association a technique in which a constraint is imposed on the participant's responses such that the given response relates to the stimulus in accordance with specific directions. For example, in an experiment involving presentation of stimulus words, the participant may be directed to give a synonym or antonym of each word. Also called **constrained association**. See FREE ASSOCIATION.

controlled attention see SELECTIVE ATTENTION.

controlled drinking a controversial approach to ALCOHOLISM TREATMENT formerly advocated by some behaviorists as a viable alternative to total abstinence. The development of treatment programs based on social learning approaches and training in self-regulation and coping skills did not consistently materialize, and, since the 1980s, research has not supported controlled drinking as an efficacious or ethical primary goal of intervention.

controlled-exposure technique a method of pretesting advertising effectiveness by presenting advertisements to a limited audience in the setting of a magazine display or radio or television broadcast. Several variations of the advertisement may be used and tested by TACHISTOSCOPES, hidden cameras, or GSR (GALVANIC SKIN RESPONSE) equipment to detect physiological reactions and by questionnaire surveys of the potential consumer responses.

controlled observation an observation made under standard and systematic conditions rather than casual or incidental conditions.

Controlled Oral Word Association (**COWA**) a test that requires participants to name all the words that they can beginning with specific letters (most commonly F, A, and S). The words cannot include proper names and cannot consist of previously used words with a suffix. The most widely utilized word fluency task, COWA is used to measure EXECUTIVE FUNCTIONS. Also called **FAS Test**. [originally developed in 1968 by U.S. neuropsychologist Arthur Lester Benton (1909–)]

controlled processing in cognitive psychology, attentive processing: that is, processing that requires control, effort, and intention. See ATTENTION.

controlling goal a goal, usually set by others, that must be achieved in order to receive an EXTRINSIC REWARD.

control-mastery theory 1. a perspective that underlies an integrative form of psychotherapy that focuses on changing a client's unconscious and maladaptive beliefs developed in childhood due to thwarted attempts to achieve attachment and safety in the client's family. The client is seen to have an inherent motivation toward health that results in testing these beliefs through TRANSFERENCE and through passive-into-active behaviors; when such testing is productive, the client is then free to pursue adaptive goals. [developed by U.S. psychiatrist Joseph Weiss] **2.** an integrative approach to child development that focuses on thoughts, feelings, and behaviors resulting from children's needs for attachment and safety in the family.

control order in ergonomics, the specific type of relationship between the operation of a control or input device and the resulting action or effect on a display. For example, a joystick may have either position or velocity control over cursor movements on a monitor.

control processes 1. in the theory of memory proposed by U.S. cognitive psychologists Richard C. Atkinson (1930–) and Richard M. Shiffrin (1942–), those processes that manipulate information in short-term memory, such as REHEARSAL or RECODING. **2.** those processes that organize the flow of information in an INFORMATION-PROCESSING system. See also COGNITIVE CONTROL; EXECUTIVE.

control question test (**CQT**) a technique used in POLYGRAPH testing, typically for criminal investigations. In addition to questions relevant to the crime and general questions to get a baseline pattern of physiological responses (i.e., irrelevant questions), the CQT also includes questions about past behavior (e.g., "Have you ever cheated on your taxes?") with the aim of eliciting strong physiological reactions on the part of examinees. See ZONE OF COMPARISON TEST. See also GUILTY KNOWLEDGE TEST; RELEVANT–IRRELEVANT TEST.

control series replications of experiments or experimental trials, often including checks on procedures, instruments, instructions, and the like.

contusion *n.* a bruise or bruising. Various kinds of HEAD INJURY can result in CEREBRAL CONTUSION.

convalescent center an EXTENDED CARE facility for patients whose recovery from disease or injury has reached a stage where full-time hospital inpatient services are no longer required. Convalescent centers generally provide professional personnel, including an available physician and 24-hour nursing service, rehabilitation services, and an authorized system of dispensing medications. See also CONTINUING CARE UNIT; SKILLED NURSING FACILITY.

convenience sampling the process of obtaining a sample because it is convenient for the purpose, regardless of whether it is representative of the population being investigated.

convenience shopper a shopper who pays attention less to the costs of products than to their ease of access. Convenience shoppers are primarily concerned with the efficient use of their time in product acquisition.

conventional antipsychotics see ANTIPSYCHOTICS.

conventionalism *n.* a personality trait marked by excessive concern with and inflexible adherence to social customs and traditional or accepted values and standards of behavior. The term is also used to refer specifically to one of the traits associated with the AUTHORITARIAN PERSONALITY.

conventional level in KOHLBERG'S THEORY OF MORAL DEVELOPMENT, the intermediate level of moral reasoning, characterized by an individual's identification with and conformity to the moral rules of family and society. The earlier stage of this level (Stage 3 of the model as a whole; see INTERPERSONAL CONCORDANCE) is marked by approval-seeking behavior and an individual's evaluation of his or her own underlying intentions. The later stage (Stage 4; see LAW-AND-ORDER ORIENTATION) is marked by an individual's emphasis on fixed rules, duty, obedience to authority, and defense of the existing social order. See also PRECONVENTIONAL LEVEL; POSTCONVENTIONAL LEVEL.

conventional morality see CONVENTIONAL LEVEL; KOHLBERG'S THEORY OF MORAL DEVELOPMENT.

convergence *n.* the rotation of the two eyes inward toward a light source so that the image falls on corresponding points on the foveas. Convergence enables the slightly different images of an object seen by each eye to come together and form a single image. The muscular tension exerted is also a cue to the distance of the object from the eyes.

convergence theory a conceptual analysis of COLLECTIVE BEHAVIOR that assumes that MOBS, SOCIAL MOVEMENTS, and other forms of mass action occur when individuals with similar needs, values, goals, or personalities join together to form a collective.

convergent evolution the tendency of unrelated organisms in a particular environment to evolve superficially similar body structures that enable them to adapt effectively to their habitat. Thus, many aquatic animals acquire a streamlined form and smooth surfaces for rapid movement through water. See also HOMOPLASY. Compare DIVERGENT EVOLUTION.

convergent production the capacity to produce the right answer to a question or to choose the best solution to a problem. It is one of the abilities recognized in Joy P. GUILFORD's theory of intelligence (see GUILFORD DIMENSIONS OF INTELLIGENCE). Compare DIVERGENT PRODUCTION.

convergent strabismus see CROSS-EYE; STRABISMUS.

convergent thinking the type of CRITICAL THINKING in which an individual analyzes a number of already formulated solutions to a problem to determine the one that is most likely to be successful. Compare DIVERGENT THINKING.

convergent validity a form of CONSTRUCT VALIDITY based on the degree to which the measurement instrument in question exhibits high correlation with conceptually similar instruments. Compare DISCRIMINANT VALIDITY.

conversation *n.* the use of speech to communicate ideas and information between or among people. Conversations are purposive but unplanned, arising flexibly from coordination in response to such elements as topic, private and public goals, rhetorical devices, temporal constraints, and individual speaking styles. Conversations proceed only through the mutual belief that the addressee has understood the speaker well enough for immediate purposes. Forms of this type of verbal exchange include small talk, gossip, repartee, debate, and negotiation, among others. **—conversational** *adj.*

conversational inference the process by which people engaged in a conversation can frequently infer the meanings intended by the other speakers, even when these are unstated or inexplicit. Such inferences will be based partly on a knowledge of the personal background and general context but more importantly on an awareness of conversational norms within a particular culture and the expectations that these create. Conversational inference does not depend on logical inference. For example, if a speaker says *My boss has been sober all week*, most listeners will understand that this person is frequently drunk, even though such an inference is not valid in logic. The listeners will assume, probably correctly, that such a statement would not be made in such a form unless it reflected an exceptional, rather than the usual, state of affairs. See also IMPLICATURE; INDIRECT SPEECH ACT.

conversational maxims the four basic rules governing interpersonal communications. The rules state that such communications should be (a) truthful; (b) as informative as is required; (c) relevant to the matter under discussion; and (d) clear, orderly, and brief. Violations of these maxims are usually presumed to be deliberate or indicative of a cognitive disturbance. [introduced by U.S. philosopher H. Paul Grice (1913–1988)]

conversational repair see REPAIR.

conversation analysis 1. in ergonomics, a method of evaluating a system or product that involves the examination of conversations occurring between two or more users interacting with it. Conversation analysis can be either qualitative or quantitative. It is a form of KNOWLEDGE ELICITATION. **2.** in linguistics, see DISCOURSE ANALYSIS.

converse accident a type of informal FALLACY or a persuasive technique that involves arguing from a qualified position or particular case to an unqualified and general rule. For example: Because patients with certain illnesses are permitted to use marijuana, marijuana use should be legal for everyone. In empirical research, the same fallacy can result from drawing conclusions from data based on small or nonrepresentative samples. Also called **hasty generalization**.

conversion *n.* **1.** an unconscious process in which anxiety generated by psychological conflicts is transformed into physical symptoms. Traditionally, this process was presumed to be involved in CONVERSION DISORDER, but current *DSM–IV–TR* diagnostic criteria for the disorder do not make such an implication. **2.** actual change in an individual's beliefs, attitudes, or behaviors that occurs as a result of SOCIAL INFLUENCE. Unlike COMPLIANCE, which is outward and temporary, conversion occurs when the targeted individual is personally convinced by a persuasive message or internalizes and accepts as his or her own the beliefs expressed by other group members. Also called **private acceptance**. See also CONFORMITY. **3.** the movement of all members of a group to a single, mutually shared position, as when individuals who initially offer diverse opinions on a subject eventually come to share the same position. See GROUP POLARIZATION. **4.** in a therapeutic context, the movement of clients away from their initial interpretations to one recommended by their therapists. **—convert** *vb.*

conversion anesthesia a SENSORY CONVERSION SYMPTOM marked by the absence of sensation in certain areas of the body that cannot be accounted for by any identifiable organic pathology or defect. See GLOVE ANESTHESIA; STOCKING ANESTHESIA.

conversion disorder in *DSM–IV–TR*, a SOMATOFORM DISORDER in which patients present with one or more symptoms or deficits affecting voluntary motor and sensory functioning that suggest a physical disorder but for which there is instead evidence of psychological involvement. These **conversion symptoms** are not intentionally produced or feigned and are not under voluntary control. They include paralysis, loss of voice, blindness, seizures, GLOBUS PHARYNGEUS, disturbance in coordination and balance, and loss of pain and touch sensations (see MOTOR CONVERSION SYMPTOMS; SENSORY CONVERSION SYMPTOMS).

conversion hysteria a former name for CONVERSION DISORDER.

conversion nonepileptic seizure a form of PSYCHOGENIC NONEPILEPTIC SEIZURE (PNES) that is a result of a diagnosed CONVERSION DISORDER. It is not associated with abnormal electrical activity on an electroencephalogram. Most PNESs are conversion nonepileptic seizures. Also called **conversion seizure**.

conversion paralysis a PSYCHOGENIC DISORDER in which there is an apparent loss of function of the muscles of a limb or a portion of the body for which no neurological cause can be identified. Unlike ORGANIC PARALYSIS, reflexes may be intact, muscle tone may be normal, and the paralyzed limb may be moved inadvertently when the patient's attention is elsewhere. This is one of the possible symptoms of CONVERSION DISORDER.

conversion seizure see CONVERSION NONEPILEPTIC SEIZURE.

conversion symptom see CONVERSION DISORDER.

conversion therapy a highly controversial and generally discredited therapy based on the belief that individuals of same-gender sexual orientation may become heterosexual.

conviction *n.* in social psychology, the subjective sense that an ATTITUDE is a valued possession or an important aspect of the SELF-CONCEPT. Conviction is related to the STRENGTH OF AN ATTITUDE.

convolution *n.* a folding or twisting, especially of the surface of the brain (see GYRUS; SULCUS).

convoy *n.* the set of people with whom an adult has close and intimate relationships and who remain present in that person's life over time. [first described in 1980 by U.S. developmental psychologist Toni Antonucci (1948–)]

convulsant *n.* any substance that causes or otherwise results in convulsions, usually by blocking inhibitory neurotransmission.

convulsion *n.* an involuntary, generalized, violent muscular contraction, in some cases tonic (contractions without relaxation), in others clonic (alternating contractions and relaxations of skeletal muscles).

convulsive disorder any form of EPILEPSY that involves recurrent GENERALIZED SEIZURES or PARTIAL SEIZURES with convulsions.

convulsive therapy any treatment that is based on the induction of a generalized seizure by electrical or chemical means. See ELECTROCONVULSIVE THERAPY.

co-occurrence *n.* a relation between two or more phenomena (objects or events) such that they tend to occur together. So, for example, thunder co-occurs with lightning and in English the letter *Q* typically co-occurs with the letter *U*. By itself, co-occurrence does not imply a causal link: For co-occurrence to become COVARIATION there must be a systematic correlation between both the occurrence of the phenomena and their nonoccurrence. —**co-occur** *vb.*

cooing *n.* vowellike sounds produced by young infants when they are seemingly happy and contented.

cookies *pl. n.* small files automatically saved on computers that provide records of websites an individual has viewed. They enable web servers to identify and track an individual user's online activities and preferences, thereby making it possible, for example, for web-based marketers to pitch a different product or service advertisement to the user each time he or she returns to a website. Cookies are considered by many users to be an invasion of privacy and may be disabled.

Cook's D an index used in REGRESSION ANALYSIS to show the influence of a particular case on the complete set of fitted values. [R. Denis **Cook** (1944–), U.S. statistician]

Coolidge Assessment Battery (**CAB**) a self-administered rating-scale instrument used to measure *DSM–IV–TR* personality (Axis II) disorders, as well as five major clinical (Axis I) disorders and EXECUTIVE FUNCTION. Developed in 1999, it comprises 225 items to which participants respond using a 4-point LIKERT SCALE ranging from strongly false (1) to strongly true (4). The CAB is a more comprehensive successor to the **Coolidge Axis II Inventory**. [Frederick L. **Coolidge** (1948–), U.S. neuropsychologist]

Coolidge effect increased sexual vigor when an animal or human being mates with multiple partners. The phenomenon is named for U.S. President Calvin Coolidge, alluding to a visit that he and his wife made to a farm where Mrs. Coolidge observed a rooster mating frequently. She allegedly asked the farmer to point this out to her husband, who is said to have replied "Same hen each time?"

cooperating teacher 1. the experienced master teacher in the teacher–apprentice relationship. **2.** an experienced teacher assigned to supervise student teacher trainees who are learning to teach in classrooms. Student teachers are thus provided with an opportunity to put into practice the principles of teaching that they have learned in their teacher education training programs. Cooperating teachers introduce the teacher trainees to the practical component of teaching in such a manner as to minimize the mistakes that they are likely to make.

cooperation *n.* the process of working together toward the attainment of a goal. This contrasts with COMPETITION, in which an individual's actions in working toward a goal lessen the likelihood of others achieving the same goal. In GAME THEORY, cooperation is regarded as the strategy that maximizes the rewards and minimizes the costs for all participants in the game; this is sometimes posited as an explanation for ALTRUISM. Studies of animals often suggest cooperation, but whether nonhuman animals understand that individuals must act together to reach a common solution or whether they act randomly and occasionally appear to cooperate by chance is still unclear. Often cooperation leads to outcomes, such as increased food, predator avoidance, or survival of kin, that make it adaptive (see ADAPTATION), but the benefit to each individual is not always obvious. See also ANIMAL COOPERATION. —**cooperate** *vb.* —**cooperative** *adj.*

cooperative breeding a type of MATING SYSTEM in which typically only one male and female breed while other group members help in taking care of the offspring (see ALLOPARENTING). Subordinate animals are reproductively inhibited, either physiologically or behaviorally; they have few other breeding options than to assist the breeding pair and wait for a breeding vacancy to occur.

cooperative education a school-administered program that combines study with employment. In higher education, the program especially seeks to enrich academic studies by supplementing them with practical field experience, ideally in responsible jobs in the student's field of interest. Periods of full- or part-time study alternate at intervals of 3 or 6 months.

cooperative goal structure a performance setting structured in such a way that individuals can reach their goals more easily if they work with others rather than against them. When goal structures are purely cooperative, individuals can succeed only when others succeed as well. Compare COMPETITIVE GOAL STRUCTURE.

cooperative learning 1. learning in small groups, to which each student in the group is expected to contribute using interpersonal skills and face-to-face interaction. Students also participate in regular assessment of the group process. **2.** a formal method of acquiring information that combines knowledge obtained in a classroom setting with that obtained in a work or applied setting. Typically, the formal classroom aspect of instruction is focused specifically on the actual work experience. See also COOPERATIVE TRAINING.

cooperative motive the drive or dispositional tendency to respond cooperatively in interpersonal and performance settings by helping others achieve their goals. Compare COMPETITIVE MOTIVE.

cooperative play SOCIAL PLAY in which children interact with one another on shared activities, for example, by taking turns, playing games together, and possibly competing with one another. Compare ASSOCIATIVE PLAY; PARALLEL PLAY; SOLITARY PLAY.

cooperative reward structure a performance setting in which rewards are assigned on the basis of group rather than individual achievement, and the success of each member promotes the success of the group as a whole. In most cases, such structures improve group trust and communication, and possibly foster greater achievement. Compare COMPETITIVE REWARD STRUCTURE; INDIVIDUALISTIC REWARD STRUCTURE.

cooperative training a vocational program for high school students who are placed in jobs related to the occupational fields of their choice. A program coordinator provides classroom instruction that supplements the job experience while monitoring the students' progress on the job by consulting with employers.

Cooper–Harper Handling Qualities Rating Scale a standardized measure of COGNITIVE LOAD devised for use by NASA. After a test flight, pilots were asked to evaluate the handling qualities of the aircraft and the demands placed on themselves as a result of any deficiencies using a simple decision tree. It has since been adapted to many other settings. Also called **Cooper–Harper rating scale**; **Cooper–Harper scale**. [introduced in 1969 by George E. **Cooper** and Robert P. **Harper**, Jr., U.S. pilots]

coordinate bilingual a person who regularly uses two languages, the second language having been learned independently from the first and within a different contextual environment. The mental representation of knowledge about the two languages is thought to be relatively independent. In contrast, a **compound bilingual** is a person who regularly uses two languages but who learned the languages as a result of equal and simultaneous exposure to them. See CODE SWITCHING; DUAL CODING THEORY. See also BILINGUALISM.

coordination *n.* **1.** the capacity of various parts to function together. This can be applied to body parts (e.g., the two legs while walking or the eyes and hands in visually guided reaching), to joints (e.g., the motion at the elbow and shoulder as the arm is swung back and forth), and to the muscles producing force at a joint (see ANTAGONISTIC MUSCLES). **2.** in linguistics, the linking of two or more CLAUSES of equal status by means of a coordinating CONJUNCTION (e.g., *and* or *but*), as in *The boy ate the cake, and the girl drank the milk*. This contrasts with **subordination**, in which one of the clauses is dependent on the other for its meaning, as in *The boy ate the cake that the girl liked*. See COMPLEX SENTENCE. **—coordinate** *vb.*

coordination loss in groups, a reduction in productivity caused by the imperfect integration of the efforts, activities, and contributions of each member of the group. See PROCESS LOSS.

coordination of secondary circular reactions in Jean PIAGET's theory, the fourth substage of sensorimotor development (see SENSORIMOTOR STAGE), in which infants are able to coordinate two or more behavior patterns to achieve a goal. Children become increasingly adept at the purposeful combination of repetitive, SECONDARY CIRCULAR REACTIONS to achieve a desired aim, such as picking up a pillow to get a toy placed underneath. This behavior usually emerges near the end of an infant's 1st year; it is distinguished from earlier behavior by the child's ability to choose and coordinate previously developed SCHEMES that are logically related to the requirements of new situations. Also called **coordination of secondary schemes**.

coordinative structure see SYNERGY.

COPD abbreviation for CHRONIC OBSTRUCTIVE PULMONARY DISEASE.

COPE model a model for dealing with unpleasant input from others. The name is an acronym of the methods outlined in the model: *C*ontrol emotions, *O*rganize input, *P*lan responses, *E*xecute.

Copernican theory see HELIOCENTRIC THEORY.

coping *n.* the use of cognitive and behavioral strategies to manage the demands of a situation when these are appraised as taxing or exceeding one's resources or to reduce the negative emotions and conflict caused by stress. See also COPING STRATEGY. **—cope** *vb.*

coping behavior a characteristic and often automatic action or set of actions taken in dealing with stressful or threatening situations. Coping behaviors can be both positive (i.e., adaptive), for example, taking time to meditate or exercise in the middle of a hectic day; or negative (i.e., maladaptive, avoidant), for example, not consulting a doctor when symptoms of serious illness appear or persist. See also COPING MECHANISM; COPING STRATEGY.

coping imagery a DESENSITIZATION technique in which relaxation is accompanied by images that have proved successful in controlling anxiety in situations that had previously aroused fear. See also COPING-SKILLS TRAINING. [developed by U.S. psychologist Joseph R. Cautela (1927–1999)]

coping mechanism any conscious or unconscious adjustment or adaptation that decreases tension and anxiety in a stressful experience or situation. Modifying maladaptive coping mechanisms is often the focus of psychological interventions. See also COPING BEHAVIOR; COPING STRATEGY.

coping potential an individual's evaluation of the prospects of successfully managing environmental demands or personal commitments. Coping potential differs from COPING in that it deals with prospects of successful management (rather than with actual deployment of resources).

coping-skills training therapy or educational interventions to increase an individual's ability to manage a variety of often uncomfortable or anxiety-provoking situations, ranging from relatively normal or situational problems (e.g., test taking, divorce) to diagnosed disorders (e.g., phobias). The types of skills taught are tailored to the situation and can involve increasing cognitive, behavioral, and affective proficiencies.

coping strategy an action, a series of actions, or a thought process used in meeting a stressful or unpleasant situation or in modifying one's reaction to such a situation. Coping strategies typically involve a conscious and direct approach to problems, in contrast to DEFENSE MECHANISMS. See also COPING BEHAVIOR; COPING MECHANISM; EMOTION-FOCUSED COPING; PROBLEM-FOCUSED COPING.

coping style the characteristic manner in which an individual confronts and deals with stress, anxiety-provoking situations, or emergencies.

copro- (**copr-**; **kopro-**; **kopr-**) *combining form* **1.** feces or filth (e.g., COPROPHILIA). **2.** obscenity (e.g., COPROPHEMIA).

coprolagnia (**koprolagnia**) *n.* a PARAPHILIA in which the sight, or even the thought, of excrement may result in sexual pleasure.

coprolalia *n.* spontaneous, unprovoked, and uncontrollable use of obscene or profane words and expressions, particularly those related to feces. It is a symptom that may be observed in individuals with a variety of neurological disorders, particularly TOURETTE'S DISORDER. See also LATAH. Also called **coprophrasia**.

coprophagia *n.* the eating of feces. Also called **coprophagy**.

coprophemia (**koprophemia**) *n.* the use of obscenities as a PARAPHILIA, for example to stimulate sexual excitement. See SCATOPHILIA.

coprophilia *n.* literally, the love of FECES, which is manifested in behavior as an excessive or pathological preoccupation with the bodily product itself or with objects and words that represent it. In classical psychoanalytic theory, these tendencies are held to represent a fixation during the ANAL STAGE of development. See also PARAPHILIA NOT OTHERWISE SPECIFIED.

coprophrasia *n.* see COPROLALIA.

copula *n.* in linguistics, a verb used so that it has little meaning other than to express equivalence between the SUBJECT and the COMPLEMENT in a sentence. In English the most important copula is the verb *be*, as in *He is my uncle* or *She is angry*. Other verbs that can function as copulas include *become, feel, get, seem,* and *look*. Also called **linking verb**.

copulatory behavior behavior patterns associated with sexual intercourse. Copulatory behavior is distinct from ANIMAL COURTSHIP, which refers to behavior preparatory to copulation. Copulatory behavior usually includes mounting, intromission (insertion of the penis into the vagina), and ejaculation. In some species (e.g., rats), several intromissions are necessary prior to ejaculation, and a female must receive several intromissions in order for ova to be implanted in the uterus. In other species, copulatory behavior is necessary to induce ovulation. In many socially monogamous species, such as human beings, copulatory behavior can occur irrespective of a female's stage in the ovulatory cycle.

copulatory lock see MATE GUARDING.

copy *n.* in consumer psychology, textual or verbal information concerning the attributes and use of a product or service as presented in an advertisement. Copy usually provides examples of the benefit of a product or service (e.g., a car engine will last longer if brand X motor oil is used) in order to persuade the user to purchase it.

copying mania an excessive preoccupation with imitating the speech or actions of other people, sometimes observed in catatonic schizophrenia (see ECHOLALIA; ECHOPRAXIA) and certain culture-bound syndromes, such as AMURAKH and MYRIACHIT.

core area the central part of a group's HOME RANGE that is used most extensively, often where the major locations of food or shelter are found. Home ranges of groups may overlap considerably, but it is rare to find overlap in core areas.

core conflictual relationship theme a method of research, case formulation, and PSYCHODYNAMIC PSYCHOTHERAPY that emphasizes central relationship patterns in clients' stories. Three components are analyzed: the wishes, needs, or intentions of the client with regard to the other person; the other person's expected or actual reaction to these; and the client's emotion, behavior, or symptoms as they relate to the other person's reaction. [developed by U.S. psychologist Lester Luborsky (1920–)]

core gender identity in psychoanalytic theory, an infant's sense of himself or herself as male or female, typically solidifying in the second year of life. Compare GENDER IDENTITY; SEX IDENTITY.

core hours see FLEXTIME.

coreometer *n.* see PUPILLOMETER.

core relational themes 1. in the COGNITIVE APPRAISAL THEORY of emotions, a person's judgments of the specific significance of particular events to himself or herself, resulting in the generation of specific emotional states (e.g., anger, joy, envy, or shame) in that person. Any core relational theme has three components: goal relevance, ego involvement, and COPING POTENTIAL. See APPRAISAL DIMENSION; PRIMARY APPRAISAL; SECONDARY APPRAISAL. **2.** repetitive patterns of relating to others that are presumed to be determined by relationships with parents and other influential individuals in early life. These relational themes can include dependent patterns and distrustful patterns, among others.

core temperature see DEEP BODY TEMPERATURE.

Coricidin *n.* a trade name for DEXTROMETHORPHAN.

Corino de Andrade's paramyloidosis see ANDRADE'S SYNDROME.

Coriolis effects the tendency for any moving body on or above the earth's surface (air, ocean current, artillery shells, etc.) to drift sideways from its course because of the earth's rotation. These effects are taken into account when considering projectile trajectories, terrestrial wind systems, and ocean currents. [Gaspard de **Coriolis** (1792–1843), French physicist]

cornea *n.* the transparent part of the outer covering of the eye, through which light first passes. It is continuous laterally with the SCLERA. The cornea provides the primary refractive power of the eye. **—corneal** *adj.*

corneal reflection technique a method of studying eye movements using light reflected from the cornea.

corneal reflex the reflexive closing of the eyelids when the cornea is touched.

Cornelia de Lange's syndrome see DE LANGE'S SYNDROME.

Cornell Medical Index (**CMI**) a psychological test originally designed for screening military personnel in World War II and later adapted for other purposes, such as diagnosing psychosomatic disorders on the basis of pathological mood and anxiety. The test is now rarely used. Also called **Cornell Selective Index**.

cornu ammonis see HIPPOCAMPUS.

corollary discharge a neuronal signal that encodes a copy of an intended motor command, which is sent to a structure in the brain (a BRAIN COMPARATOR) that can compare the intended movement with the sensory feedback (REAFFERENCE) that results from the actual movement. For example, when the eyes move, the world does not appear to move, even though the image of the world moves across the retina. The corollary discharge of the intended movement in effect cancels out the movement of the world over the retina. When the eye is moved passively by gently pushing on the eyelid, there is no corollary discharge, and the world appears to jump. Also called **efference copy**.

corona glandis the prominent posterior border of the head of the penis. See GLANS PENIS.

coronal plane the plane that divides the front (anterior) half of the body or brain from the back (posterior) half. Also called **frontal plane**.

coronal section the CROSS SECTION made by the CORONAL PLANE. Also called **frontal section**.

coronary heart disease (**CHD**) a cardiovascular disorder characterized by restricted flow of blood through the coronary arteries supplying the heart muscle. The cause is usually ATHEROSCLEROSIS of the coronary arteries and often leads to fatal myocardial INFARCTION. Behavioral and psychosocial factors are frequently involved in the development and prognosis of the disease. Also called **coronary artery disease**.

coronary-prone behavior actions or patterns of actions believed to be associated with an increased risk of coronary heart disease. The preferred term for such a behavior pattern is now TYPE A BEHAVIOR.

corp- *combining form* body or structure.

corpora *pl. n.* see CORPUS.

corporal *adj.* of or relating to the body.

corporal punishment physical punishment, that is, punishment that uses physical force that causes pain, but not injury, in order to correct or control an individual's behavior. Spanking a child is an example of corporal punishment.

corporeal *adj.* of a material, tangible nature, as opposed to spiritual.

corpse phobia see NECROPHOBIA.

corpus *n.* (*pl.* **corpora**) **1.** a body or distinct anatomical structure, such as the CORPUS CALLOSUM or CORPUS LUTEUM. **2.** a body of linguistic data, such as recorded conversation or written text, that is subjected to linguistic or psycholinguistic analysis.

corpuscallosotomy *n.* see COMMISSUROTOMY.

corpus callosum a large tract of nerve fibers running across the LONGITUDINAL FISSURE of the brain and connecting the CEREBRAL HEMISPHERES. It is the principal connection between the two sides of the brain. See also COMMISSURAL FIBER.

corpus callosum agenesis see AGENESIS.

corpus cavernosum (*pl.* **corpora cavernosa**) either of the columns of erectile tissue that form the superior (upper) portion of the body of the penis. A third column of tissue, the CORPUS SPONGIOSUM, lies inferior to corpora cavernosa.

corpus luteum a yellowish glandular mass in the ovary that remains after a GRAAFIAN FOLLICLE has ruptured and released an ovum. Its development is stimulated by LUTEINIZING HORMONE secreted by the anterior pituitary gland, and it functions as a transient endocrine gland, secreting PROGESTERONE.

corpus mammillare see MAMMILLARY BODY.

corpus planning see LANGUAGE PLANNING.

corpus spongiosum a column of tissue on the inferior (lower) side of the body of the penis that surrounds the urethra and extends into the GLANS PENIS. Above it lie the two columns of the corpora cavernosa (see CORPUS CAVERNOSUM), and the three columns comprise the erectile tissue of the penis, bound together by connective tissue. Also called **corpus cavernosum urethrae**.

corpus striatum a mass of nuclei and myelinated nerve fibers beneath the CEREBRAL CORTEX and in front of the THALAMUS in each cerebral hemisphere. It comprises the caudate nucleus and lenticular nucleus (see BASAL GANGLIA) and bands of PROJECTION FIBERS passing in both directions between them, through the INTERNAL CAPSULE, giving it a striped appearance in cross section.

correct detection in SIGNAL DETECTION TASKS, an accurate perception of a target stimulus (signal) by the participant in trials in which the signal is present, often expressed as a percentage accuracy rate (see HIT RATE). See also CORRECT REJECTION; FALSE DETECTION; FALSE REJECTION.

correction *n.* **1.** a quantity that is added, subtracted, or otherwise adjusted to increase the accuracy of a measure, such as a statistical calculation. Corrections are made, for example, to improve the correspondence between an ASSUMPTION of a technique and the nature of the data being analyzed. **2.** in optometry, the rectification of visual defects that are due to refractive errors through the use of lenses (see CORRECTIVE LENS).

correctional facility any facility that houses or detains individuals, who have been formally processed by the criminal or juvenile justice system, for the purpose of reform or rehabilitation. Examples include prisons, juvenile halls, and jails. Also called **correctional institution**.

correctional psychology a branch of FORENSIC PSYCHOLOGY concerned with the application of counseling and clinical techniques to criminal and juvenile offenders in penal and correctional institutions (e.g., reformatories, training schools, penitentiaries). **Correctional psychologists** also participate professionally in court activities, probation departments, parole boards, prison administration, supervision of inmate behavior, and programs for the rehabilitation of offenders.

correction for attenuation a method for estimating the correlations between the true scores of two measures by adjusting the observed correlation in accordance with the reliabilities of the two measures.

correction for continuity a set of statistical procedures that are applied to correct for the fact that a statistical procedure is based on an assumption that the data have a continuous distribution when, in fact, the distribution is discrete. It is used, for example, in the YATES CORRECTION.

correction for guessing a scoring rule for multiple choice items such that the expected value of getting an item correct under the assumption of no knowledge is 0 rather than $1/n$, where n is the number of alternatives.

correction procedure the repetition or continuation of particular stimulus conditions (usually in DISCRIMINATION training) after certain responses (usually errors) or in the absence of certain responses.

corrective advertising advertising required of companies found guilty of DECEPTIVE ADVERTISING by the Federal Trade Commission. Such advertising should successfully counter the incorrect inferences deduced from the deceptive advertisement.

corrective emotional experience a concept from psychoanalysis positing that clients achieve meaningful and lasting change through new interpersonal affective experiences with the therapist, particularly with regard to situations that clients were unable to master as children. This concept has been debated both within and outside psychoanalytic treatment circles. [advocated by Hungarian psychoanalyst Franz Alexander (1891–1964)]

corrective lens a lens worn on or in front of the eye to correct or improve vision. In **eyeglasses**, a pair of corrective lenses is mounted in a frame worn on the face; in **contact lenses**, the corrective lens is applied directly to the eye.

corrective therapy see KINESIOTHERAPY.

correct rejection in SIGNAL DETECTION TASKS, an accurate decision by the participant that a target stimulus (signal) is not present. See also CORRECT DETECTION; FALSE DETECTION; FALSE REJECTION.

correlate 1. *n.* a variable that is related to another variable. **2.** *vb.* to calculate a CORRELATION COEFFICIENT.

correlation *n.* the degree of a relationship (usually linear) between two attributes.

correlational redundancy see DISTRIBUTIONAL REDUNDANCY.

correlational study a study of the relationship between two or more variables.

correlation barrier the notion that there is a maximum correlation that can be obtained between tests of intelligence and the criteria that these tests are intended to predict, such as various measures of life success. Typically, such tests have only a moderate relationship (e.g., correlation coefficients between .3 and .5) with school performance and measures of success in later life.

correlation cluster a set of variables that are all substantially correlated with one another.

correlation coefficient a numerical index reflecting the degree of relationship (usually linear) between two attributes scaled so that the value of +1 indicates a perfect positive relationship, –1 a perfect negative relationship, and 0 no relationship.

correlation matrix a square symmetric MATRIX in which the correlation coefficient between the ith and jth variables in a set of variables is displayed in the intersection of the ith row and the jth column of the matrix. The diagonal elements of a correlation matrix are all equal to 1.

correlation ratio a statistical index, often referred to as **eta**, that reflects the magnitude of a nonlinear relationship between two variables.

correspondence *n.* in ATTRIBUTION THEORY, the extent to which an observed behavior, such as pushing past others to go to the front of a line, correlates to a general personality trait in the actor, such as rudeness or aggressiveness. Observers have a strong tendency to overestimate the correspondence of behaviors with traits (the FUNDAMENTAL ATTRIBUTION ERROR). See CORRESPONDENT INFERENCE THEORY. **—correspondent** *adj.*

correspondence bias see FUNDAMENTAL ATTRIBUTION ERROR.

correspondence problem the requirement that elements in one image must be matched by the visual system with the same elements in another image when the two images differ from one another in some respect. In STEREOPSIS the features seen through the left eye must be matched to the features seen through the right eye before depth information can be inferred. In APPARENT MOVEMENT the elements in one stationary image must be matched with the same elements in the next stationary image if the elements are to be perceived as moving. Theories of object recognition must take into account the ability to recognize objects as the same, even though they may appear from different perspectives in two different scenes. The correspondence problem is solved effortlessly by the visual system but has proven to be extremely difficult to solve in artificial vision.

correspondence training a BEHAVIOR THERAPY intervention for children and adolescents in which the clients are tangibly or socially reinforced either for verbally promising to do something and then following through or for doing a desired behavior and then verbally reporting on the activity. Promises and reports can be made to either an adult or a peer.

correspondent inference theory a model describing how people form inferences about other people's stable personality characteristics from observing their behaviors. CORRESPONDENCE between behaviors and traits is more likely to be inferred if the actor is judged to have acted (a) freely, (b) intentionally, (c) in a way that is unusual for someone in the situation, and (d) in a way that does not usually bring rewards or social approval. See also ATTRIBUTION THEORY. [proposed in 1965 by U.S. social psychologists Edward Jones (1926–) and Keith E. Davis (1936–)]

corresponding retinal points two sites, one on each retina, that receive stimulation from a single point in visual space. Also called **congruent retinal points**.

corridor illusion an illustration of SIZE CONSTANCY in which two identical figures appear to be radically different in size. If the figures are placed in a picture of a corridor, the one placed in the distance appears larger than the one placed in the foreground. This is because DEPTH CUES affect expectations about true size.

corroboration *n.* evidence to support a theory, fact, opinion, or the like. Austrian-born British philosopher Karl Popper (1902–1994) regarded mere corroboration as insufficient grounds for acceptance of a theory. He held instead that the proper test of a theory was one that had a high probability of refuting the theory if it was wrong, and that a theory lacking FALSIFIABILITY was not scientific. **—corroborate** *vb.*

cortex *n.* (*pl.* **cortices**) the outer or superficial layer or layers of a structure, as distinguished from the central core. In mammals, the cortex of a structure is identified with the name of the gland or organ, for example, the ADRENAL CORTEX, CEREBELLAR CORTEX, or CEREBRAL CORTEX. Compare MEDULLA. **—cortical** *adj.*

cortical activation activation of regions of the cerebral cortex or cerebellar cortex. It can be achieved by sensory stimulation or cognitive tasks or by such techniques as TRANSCRANIAL MAGNETIC STIMULATION. The activation can be recorded by noninvasive techniques, such as ELECTROENCEPHALOGRAPHY, FUNCTIONAL MAGNETIC RESONANCE IMAGING, or POSITRON EMISSION TOMOGRAPHY.

cortical amaurosis see AMAUROSIS.

cortical amnesia a form of amnesia due to organic causes, such as a stroke or brain injury.

cortical area see BRODMANN'S AREA; CEREBRAL CORTEX.

cortical-arousal factor the property of a work of art that is related to ratings that are high on the drowsy–alert and weak–powerful scales. [proposed by British-born Canadian psychologist Daniel E. Berlyne (1924–1976)]

cortical barrel in animals with facial whiskers, a column of neurons in the SOMATOSENSORY AREA that receives sensory information from the facial whiskers. The cortical barrels correspond to the facial whiskers in a somatotopic fashion (see SOMATOTOPIC ORGANIZATION).

cortical blindness blindness with normal pupillary responses due to complete destruction of the OPTIC RADIATIONS or the STRIATE CORTEX. Because the subcortical structures (white matter) of the visual system are involved, it is also called **cerebral blindness**. Typically caused by a stroke affecting the occipital lobe of the brain, cortical blindness can also result from traumatic injury or HYPOXIA. In children it is often a consequence of hydrocephalus, meningitis, toxic or hypertensive encephalopathy, trauma, or diffuse demyelinating degenerative disease. Complete loss of vision in a portion of the visual field is called **partial cortical blindness**.

cortical center 1. an area of the CEREBRAL CORTEX where sensory fibers terminate or motor fibers originate. **2.** an area of the cerebral cortex specialized for a certain function, such as the speech center or the vision center.

cortical column one of the vertical groups of interconnected neurons that span several CORTICAL LAYERS and constitute the basic functional organization of the NEOCORTEX. Columnar organization is most evident in visual cortex (see OCULAR DOMINANCE COLUMN; ORIENTATION COLUMN).

cortical control 1. the normal regulation of an activity, such as movement of a limb, by the CEREBRAL CORTEX. **2.** control of a PROSTHESIS by signals recorded from the cerebral cortex, which are computer-processed and amplified.

cortical deafness deafness that is caused by damage to auditory centers in the cerebral cortex of the brain. The peripheral auditory system (which includes the retrocochlear neural pathways terminating in the brainstem) can be intact in this condition.

cortical dementia DEMENTIA arising from degeneration of the cortical areas of the brain, rather than the subcortical (deeper) areas. The most common dementia of this type is ALZHEIMER'S DISEASE. Compare SUBCORTICAL DEMENTIA.

cortical dysplasia abnormality in the development (e.g., size, shape) of the cerebral cortex.

cortical-evoked potential an EVOKED POTENTIAL observed in the cerebral cortex. Also called **cortical-evoked response**.

cortical hearing loss hearing loss associated with auditory disorders due to damage to the higher neurological centers of the brain.

cortical inhibition inhibition of activity originating in the CEREBRAL CORTEX or CEREBELLAR CORTEX.

corticalization *n.* see ENCEPHALIZATION.

cortical lamina any of the layers of cells in the cerebral cortex. See BRODMANN'S AREA; CORTICAL LAYERS.

cortical layers the layers of neurons that constitute the structure of the cerebral cortex and cerebellar cortex. In the cerebral cortex the number of layers varies, reaching a maximum of six in the NEOCORTEX. These six layers, identified by Roman numerals and starting from the outer surface, are: I, the **plexiform molecular layer**, a narrow band of MYELINATED FIBERS; II, the **external granular**

layer, containing GRANULE CELLS and PYRAMIDAL CELLS; III, the **external pyramidal layer**, with medium-sized pyramidal cells in the outer zone and larger pyramidal cells in the inner zone; IV, the **internal granular layer**, which contains synapses of layer-III cells along with STELLATE CELLS categorized as granule cells; V, the **ganglionic** (or **internal pyramidal**) **layer**, which includes large pyramidal cells and the giant BETZ CELLS; and VI, the **polymorphic fusiform** (or **multiform**) **layer**, which contains cells of many shapes but mainly spindle-shaped and pyramidal cells.

cortical lesion a pathological change in the CEREBRAL CORTEX of the brain, which may be congenital or acquired and due to any cause.

cortical localization of function see LOCALIZATION OF FUNCTION.

cortical magnification factor an indication of the spatial extent of the VISUAL CORTEX that represents a given spatial extent in the visual field: used in scaling a RETINOTOPIC MAP. The cortical magnification factor can be expressed as the millimeters of visual cortex needed to represent each degree of visual angle. The center of gaze has a high cortical magnification factor, because a small part of the visual field is processed by neurons that occupy a large region of the cortex, whereas the opposite is true for the visual periphery. The cortical magnification factor therefore decreases steadily from the fovea to the periphery of the retina. Also called **magnification factor**.

cortical map a representation of a sensory modality or motor function in the cerebral cortex. Examples are the representations of the visual field in areas of visual cortex (see RETINOTOPIC MAP) and the tonotopic representations in regions of auditory cortex (see TONOTOPIC ORGANIZATION). The mapping is usually topographic rather than linear (see TOPOGRAPHIC ORGANIZATION). See also LOCALIZATION OF FUNCTION.

cortical motor aphasia see EXPRESSIVE APHASIA.

cortical neuron a nerve cell that has its cell body in the CEREBRAL CORTEX.

cortical potential an electric potential that originates in neurons of the cerebral cortex. See BRAIN WAVES; ELECTROENCEPHALOGRAPHY.

cortical process any of the mechanisms of the cerebral cortex that are involved in cognition. The early stages of a cognitive process are called **lower cortical processes** or **early cortical processes**; the later, more complex mechanisms are called **higher cortical processes**. See also EXECUTIVE FUNCTION.

cortical sensory aphasia see WERNICKE'S APHASIA.

cortical–subcortical motor loop a loop made up of projections between the MOTOR CORTEX and structures in the BASAL GANGLIA and the THALAMUS that monitors and sequences ongoing motor behaviors.

cortical undercutting a former psychosurgical procedure—a type of prefrontal lobotomy (see LEUKOTOMY)—used in controlling severe emotional and mental disturbance. In this procedure the skull was opened and long association fibers severed. The object was to prevent frontal lobe damage, which affects thinking processes.

cortico- *combining form* cortex.

corticobasal ganglionic degeneration (**CBGD**) a degenerative condition of the BASAL GANGLIA resulting in APRAXIA, rigidity, DYSTONIA, and cognitive deficits. Also called **corticostriatonigral degeneration**.

corticobulbar fiber see CORTICONUCLEAR FIBER.

corticofugal *adj.* describing nerve fibers or tracts that exit from the cerebral or cerebellar cortex. Corticofugal nerve fibers from the cerebral cortex include corticospinal, corticonuclear, and corticopontine fibers. Compare CORTICOPETAL.

corticomedial group one of the two main groups of nuclei in the AMYGDALA within the brain. It includes the CENTRAL NUCLEUS and receives mainly olfactory and pheromonal information; its output, via the STRIA TERMINALIS, is to the HYPOTHALAMUS and the basomedial FOREBRAIN.

corticonuclear fiber any of a group of fibers forming part of the PYRAMIDAL TRACT that extend from the cerebral cortex to nuclei in the midbrain, pons, and medulla oblongata. Also called **corticobulbar fiber**.

corticopetal *adj.* describing nerve fibers or tracts that are directed toward the cerebral or cerebellar cortex. Compare CORTICOFUGAL.

corticopontine *adj.* relating to or connecting the cerebral cortex and the pons in the brain.

corticospinal fiber a nerve fiber of the corticospinal tract.

corticospinal tract a major MOTOR PATHWAY that originates in the cerebral cortex (see MOTOR CORTEX), passes through the PYRAMID of the medulla oblongata, and descends to terminate in the spinal cord. At the pyramid most of its fibers cross over to form the LATERAL CORTICOSPINAL TRACT; the remaining fibers, forming the smaller **anterior corticospinal tract**, descend anteriorly in the white matter of the spinal cord to terminate in the ANTERIOR HORNS. See also PYRAMIDAL TRACT.

corticosteroid *n.* any of the steroid hormones produced by the ADRENAL CORTEX. They include the GLUCOCORTICOIDS (e.g., CORTISOL), which are involved in carbohydrate metabolism; and the MINERALOCORTICOIDS (e.g., ALDOSTERONE), which have a role in electrolyte balance and sodium retention. Also called **adrenocorticoid**; **adrenosteroid**.

corticosteroid therapy medical treatment that involves the use of CORTICOSTEROID drugs. Both MINERALOCORTICOIDS and GLUCOCORTICOIDS may be used as replacement therapy in patients whose secretion of the natural hormones is deficient, either through disease or surgical removal of one or both adrenal glands. However, glucocorticoids are most widely used as anti-inflammatory agents; they are also used in the treatment of asthma, dermatologic conditions, and seasonal rhinitis.

corticosterone *n.* a CORTICOSTEROID hormone with GLUCOCORTICOID functions that include regulating the metabolism of proteins, fats, and carbohydrates into energy sources for body cells. The concentration of corticosterone in the plasma is used as an index of stress.

corticostriatonigral degeneration see CORTICOBASAL GANGLIONIC DEGENERATION.

corticotropin *n.* see ADRENOCORTICOTROPIC HORMONE.

corticotropin-releasing hormone (**CRH**) a RELEASING HORMONE, produced by the hypothalamus, that controls the daily rhythm of ADRENOCORTICOTROPIC HORMONE release by the pituitary gland. Also called **ACTH-releasing factor**; **corticotropin-releasing factor** (**CRF**).

cortisol *n.* a CORTICOSTEROID hormone whose GLUCOCORTICOID activity increases BLOOD SUGAR levels. Blood levels of cortisol in humans vary according to sleep–wake cycles (being highest around 9:00 a.m. and lowest at midnight) and other factors; for example, they increase with stress and during pregnancy but decrease during diseases of the liver and kidneys. Since 1963, cortisol and its synthetic analogs have been administered in the treatment of chronic inflammatory and autoimmune disorders. Also called **hydrocortisone**.

cortisone *n.* a CORTICOSTEROID that is produced naturally by the adrenal cortex or synthetically. Cortisone is biologically inactive but is converted to the active hormone CORTISOL in the liver and other organs. It is used therapeutically in the management of disorders due to corticosteroid deficiency.

Corybantic rites in the classical world, orgiastic rites performed in honor of Cybele, the great mother-goddess of Anatolia (often identified with the Greek Demeter), and Dionysus, Greek god of wine, intoxication, and ritual madness or ecstasy. Corybantic rites were so called because they were thought to have been originated by Corybantes, half-divine, half-demonic beings. The rites, which included frenzied dancing to the sound of flutes, tambourines, cymbals, and castanets, wild cries, and self-infliction of wounds, produced an emotional release, followed by a state of euphoria and relaxation. Corybantic rites are referred to in the *Dialogues* of Greek philosopher Plato (c. 427–347 BCE), whose description of a kind of divine madness induced by the gods may also be an allusion to the state entered into by the participants. Later described in the writings of Greek historians Strabo (c. 64 BCE–c. 24 CE) and Diodorus Siculus (1st century BCE), Corybantic rites are of interest to psychology largely because they were believed to have a therapeutic effect on certain types of mental disorder; as such they provide a precedent for the more modern concept of CATHARSIS. They also suggest that some forms of what may be considered to be madness may have other meanings and origins. See also CHOREOMANIA.

coryza *n.* profuse discharge from the mucous membrane of the nose, especially when caused by a common cold.

cosmetic surgery a general category of multiple specific surgical procedures designed to improve or enhance some aspect of physical appearance. See PLASTIC SURGERY.

cosmic consciousness a purported sense of awareness of the universe as a whole. This is variously reported to be achieved through PEAK EXPERIENCES, religious ecstasy, the use of hallucinogenic drugs, or metaphysical disciplines, such as meditation, YOGA, and ZEN BUDDHISM. See also ALTERED STATE OF CONSCIOUSNESS; MYSTIC UNION.

cosmic identification a feeling of identification with the universe, which is most often seen in patients with SCHIZOID PERSONALITY DISORDER or BORDERLINE DISORDERS. The patient cannot distinguish between that which is himself or herself and the outside world. Also called **magic omnipotence**. See also MYSTIC UNION; OCEANIC FEELING.

costal stigma see STILLER'S SIGN.

cost analysis a systematic determination of the costs associated with the implementation of a program's services. These include direct personnel, material, and administrative costs, calculated from the perspective of a given purchaser (e.g., government agency, client), budgetary category, and time period. Once determined, these costs are utilized further in COST–BENEFIT ANALYSIS or COST-EFFECTIVENESS ANALYSIS.

cost–benefit analysis 1. an analytic procedure that attempts to determine and compare the economic efficiency of different programs. Costs and benefits are reduced to their monetary value and expressed in a **cost–benefit** (or **benefit–cost**) **ratio**. **2.** in BEHAVIORAL ECOLOGY, a method of predicting which behavioral strategies are likely to be adaptive by comparing the potential costs and potential benefits of each possible behavior. Those behaviors that will lead to greater benefits relative to costs will be those that survive through NATURAL SELECTION.

cost containment a program goal that seeks to control the costs involved in managing and delivering the PROGRAM OUTCOME. In health administration, a range of fiscal strategies is used to prevent health care costs from increasing. See also COST ANALYSIS.

cost-effectiveness analysis a measure of PROGRAM EFFICACY or economic efficiency expressed in terms of the cost of achieving a unit of PROGRAM OUTCOME. The analysis is most appropriate when programs have one main identifiable evaluation outcome, when future costs are not confounded with changes in outcome, or when outcomes are not directly reducible to monetary payoffs.

cost of concurrence the decrease that occurs in performance of a task that is placed in a dual-task context, even when the instructions are to emphasize that task. This cost is measured in terms of changes in reaction time or accuracy and is estimated from an analysis of a PERFORMANCE-OPERATING CHARACTERISTIC.

cost–reward analysis in social psychology, a model that attempts to explain HELPING BEHAVIOR in terms of the reinforcements and costs associated with specific helping actions. A helping act that possesses either high reinforcement value or very low cost value is more likely to be performed than a low-reinforcement, high-cost act.

Cotard's syndrome a psychotic condition characterized by severe depression and intense nihilistic delusions (see NIHILISM) in which individuals insist that their bodies or parts thereof, and in some cases the whole of reality, have disintegrated or ceased to exist. [first reported in 1880 by Jules **Cotard** (1840–1887), French neurologist, who called it **délire de négation** ("delirium of negation")]

cot death see SUDDEN INFANT DEATH SYNDROME.

cotherapy *n.* therapy by two therapists working with a client, pair of clients (e.g., a married couple), family, or group to enhance understanding and change behavior and relationships during treatment. Also called **dual-leadership therapy**.

cotwin control see TWIN CONTROL.

couch *n.* in psychoanalysis, the article of furniture on which the patient reclines. The use of the couch is based on the theory that this posture will facilitate FREE ASSOCIATION, encourage the patient to direct attention to his or her inward world of feeling and fantasy, and enable the patient to uncover his or her unconscious mind. The expression "on the couch" is sometimes used popularly to indicate psychoanalytic treatment. Also called **analytic couch**.

cough suppressants see ANTITUSSIVES.

counseling *n.* professional assistance in coping with personal problems, including emotional, behavioral, vocational, marital, educational, rehabilitation, and life-stage (e.g., retirement) problems. The COUNSELOR makes use of such techniques as ACTIVE LISTENING, guidance, advice, discussion, CLARIFICATION, and the administration of tests.

counseling process the interpersonal process engaged in by COUNSELOR and client as they attempt to define, address, and resolve specific problems of the client in face-to-face interviews. See also COUNSELING.

counseling psychology the branch of PSYCHOLOGY that specializes in facilitating personal and interpersonal functioning across the life span. Counseling psychology focuses on emotional, social, vocational, educational, health-related, developmental, and organizational concerns—such as improving well-being, alleviating distress and maladjustment, and resolving crises—and addresses issues from individual, family, group, systems, and organizational perspectives. The **counseling psychologist** has received professional education and training in one or more COUNSELING areas, such as educational, vocational, employee, aging, personal, marriage, or rehabilitation counseling. In contrast to a clinical psychologist (see CLINICAL PSYCHOLOGY), who usually emphasizes origins of maladaptations, a counseling psychologist emphasizes adaptation, adjustment, and more efficient use of the individual's available resources.

counseling relationship the interaction between counselor and client in which the relationship is professional yet also characterized by empathic warmth and AUTHENTICITY, with the counselor bringing professional training, experience, and personal insight to bear on the problems revealed by the client. The relationship is considered to be of central importance in bringing about desired change.

counseling services professional help provided by a government, social service, or mental health agency to individuals, families, and groups. Services are typically provided by licensed counselors, psychologists, social workers, and nurses. See also COUNSELING.

counselor *n.* an individual professionally trained in counseling, psychology, social work, or nursing who specializes in one or more counseling areas, such as vocational, rehabilitation, educational, substance abuse, marriage, relationship, or family counseling. A counselor provides professional evaluations, information, and suggestions designed to enhance the client's ability to solve problems, make decisions, and effect desired changes in attitude and behavior.

counteraction need the drive to overcome difficult challenges rather than accept defeat. It is motivated by the desire for power, knowledge, prestige, or creative achievement. [defined by U.S. psychologist Henry Alexander Murray (1893–1988)]

counterargument *n.* a COGNITIVE RESPONSE to a persuasive message that refutes attitude-relevant information presented in the message.

counterattitudinal advocacy a persuasive message that contradicts a person's current attitude.

counterattitudinal behavior behavior that is inconsistent with an attitude. Having a negative attitude toward a political candidate but agreeing to donate money to that candidate's political campaign is an example of counterattitudinal behavior. See also ATTITUDE–BEHAVIOR CONSISTENCY. Compare PROATTITUDINAL BEHAVIOR.

counterattitudinal role play a technique used in PSYCHODRAMA or ROLE PLAY in which the individuals taking part are directed to express opinions contrary to those in which they believe.

counterbalancing *n.* the process of arranging a series of experimental conditions or treatments in such a way as to minimize the influence of other factors, such as practice or fatigue, on experimental effects. A simple form of counterbalancing would be to administer experimental conditions in the order AB to half the participants and in the order BA to the other half.

countercathexis *n.* see ANTICATHEXIS.

countercompulsion *n.* a COMPULSION that is secondarily developed to resist the original compulsion when the latter cannot be continued. The new compulsion then replaces the original so that the compulsive behavior can continue. See OBSESSIVE-COMPULSIVE DISORDER.

counterconditioning *n.* an experimental procedure in which an animal, already conditioned to respond to a stimulus in a particular way, is trained to produce a different response to the same stimulus that is incompatible with the original response. This same principle underlies many of the techniques used in BEHAVIOR THERAPY to eliminate unwanted behavior.

counterconformity *n.* see ANTICONFORMITY.

counterculture *n.* a SOCIAL MOVEMENT that maintains its own alternative mores and values in opposition to prevailing cultural norms. The term is historically associated with the HIPPIE movement and attendant DRUG CULTURE of the late 1960s and early 1970s, which rejected such societal norms as the work ethic and the traditional family unit. See also SUBCULTURE; YOUTH CULTURE. **—countercultural** *adj.*

counterfactual *n.* in linguistics, a statement that is contrary to fact, particularly when used to form a CONDITIONAL CLAUSE, as in *If the Japanese had not bombed Pearl Harbor, the United States would not have become engaged in World War II.*

counterfactual thinking **1.** imagining ways in which events in one's life might have turned out differently. This often involves feelings of regret or disappointment (e.g., *If only I hadn't been so hasty*) but may also involve a sense of relief, as at a narrow escape (e.g., *If I had been standing three feet to the left . . .*). **2.** any process of reasoning based on a conditional statement of the type "If X, then Y" where X is known to be contrary to fact, impossible, or incapable of empirical verification. Counterfactual thinking of the first sort is common in such historical speculations as *If Hitler had been killed in July 1944, then . . . .* Counterfactual thinking of the second and third types can play a useful role in evaluating the implications of a theory or HEURISTIC and in THOUGHT EXPERIMENTS. See also AS-IF HYPOTHESIS; CONDITIONAL REASONING.

counterfeit role a false (i.e., inaccurate or deceptive) role. See also ROLE PLAY.

counteridentification *n.* in psychoanalysis, a form of COUNTERTRANSFERENCE in which the psychoanalyst identifies with the patient. **—counteridentify** *vb.*

countermeasure *n.* in POLYGRAPH testing, any effort on the part of an individual to avoid being classified as deceitful or dishonest. Typically, individuals may use either drugs to reduce their level of physiological arousal or physical means (e.g., biting their tongue) to increase arousal to questions unrelated to the issue of interest.

countermeasure-intervention program see SOCIAL REFORM PROGRAM.

counternull value the nonnull magnitude of EFFECT SIZE that is supported by exactly the same amount of evidence as is the null value of the effect size.

counterphobic character a personality that takes pleasure in pursuing risky or dangerous activities that other people would normally find anxiety-provoking. In psychoanalytic theory, this is explained as a manic DEFENSE that achieves satisfaction from the feeling of mastering anxiety.

countershading *n.* a form of CAMOUFLAGE that involves using differential light and dark areas on the body to minimize the ability of predators to detect the organism. For example, fish often have dark-colored backs and light-colored bellies. A predator from below has difficulty discriminating the fish from the sky above, and a predator from above has difficulty discriminating the fish from the dark substrate below.

countershock *n.* a mild electric shock administered to a patient undergoing ELECTROCONVULSIVE THERAPY (ECT) for 1 min after the convulsive shock. The countershock is intended to relieve some of the common aftereffects of ECT, such as postconvulsion confusion or amnesia.

countershock phase see GENERAL ADAPTATION SYNDROME.

countersuggestion *n.* in psychotherapy, a suggestion by the therapist that contradicts or opposes a previous suggestion or a particular fixed idea. This strategy is used to decrease the influence of the previous suggestion or idea, provide an alternative, or both.

countertransference *n.* the therapist's unconscious reactions to the patient and to the patient's TRANSFERENCE. These thoughts and feelings are based on the therapist's own psychological needs and conflicts and may be unexpressed or revealed through conscious responses to patient behavior. The term was originally used to describe this process in psychoanalysis but has since become part of the common lexicon in other forms of psychodynamic psychotherapy and in other therapies. In CLASSICAL PSYCHOANALYSIS, countertransference is viewed as a hindrance to the analyst's understanding of the patient, but to some modern analysts and therapists it may serve as a source of insight into the patient's impact on other people. In either case, the analyst or therapist must be aware of, and analyze, countertransference so that it does not interfere with the therapeutic process. See also CONTROL ANALYSIS.

counting *n.* see NUMERICAL COMPETENCE.

coupled oscillators a DYNAMIC SYSTEM model used to represent many aspects of rhythmical movements, such as those of the lower limbs during locomotion. See also CENTRAL PATTERN GENERATOR.

couples counseling COUNSELING in which guidance and advice focuses on issues confronting relationships between partners. Couples counseling is short-term and problem oriented; it may include a variety of approaches to such difficult areas as shared responsibilities, expectations for the future, and loyalties. Compare COUPLES THERAPY.

couples therapy therapy in which both partners in a committed relationship are treated at the same time by the same therapist or therapists. Couples therapy is concerned with problems within and between the individuals that affect the relationship. For example, one partner may have an undiagnosed, physiologically based depression that is affecting the relationship, and both partners may have trouble communicating effectively with one another. Individual sessions may be provided separately to each partner, particularly at the beginning of therapy; most of the course of therapy, however, is provided to both partners together. Couples therapy for married couples is known as **marital therapy**.

coupon-return technique a method of testing advertising effectiveness in a printed medium, such as a magazine or newspaper, by inducing the consumer to return a coupon by mail. The technique is sometimes used on a SPLIT-RUN basis in which the coupon is offered only to a part of the publication's audience, or several variations may be tested in different demographic areas in which the publication is sold. Some publications cooperate with advertisers using the coupon-return technique by charging for advertising space on a **per-inquiry (p.i.) basis**, each coupon returned counting as an inquiry.

courage *n.* the ability to meet a difficult challenge despite the physical, psychological, or moral risks involved in doing so. Examples of acts of courage include saving another's or one's own life against a meaningful threat; coping with a painful, debilitating, or terminal illness; overcoming a destructive habit; and voicing an unpopular opinion. Also called **bravery**; **valor**. **—courageous** *adj.*

course *n.* the length of time a disorder, illness, or treatment typically lasts, its natural progression, and (if applicable) its recurrence over time.

course modifier a pattern that develops in a disorder (e.g., recurrence, seasonal variation) that helps to predict its future course or may serve to alter its usual course.

courtesan fantasy see HETAERAL FANTASY.

court-ordered treatment any assessment, treatment, consultation, or other service for defendants, plaintiffs, or criminal offenders that is mandated by a judge or magistrate.

courtship behavior the behavior of different species of animals and of human beings in different societies or social strata during the period prior to reproduction or, in humans, marriage. In animals it involves evaluating a potential mate as well as locating and defending appropriate sites for nests or dens and synchronizing the hormones involved in reproduction (see ANIMAL COURTSHIP). In HUMAN COURTSHIP, such behavior may take widely different forms in different cultures.

couvade *n.* **1.** a custom in some cultures in which the father takes to bed before or after his child is born, as if he himself suffered the pain of childbirth. **2.** abdominal pain or other somatic symptoms appearing in male partners of pregnant women, usually presumed to be PSYCHOGENIC in origin. Also called **couvade syndrome**.

covariance *n.* a scale-dependent measure of the relationship between two variables.

covariate *n.* a correlated variable that is often controlled or held constant through the ANALYSIS OF COVARIANCE. Also called **concomitant variable**.

covariation *n.* a relationship between two phenomena (objects or events) such that there is a systematic correlation between variation of the one and variation of the other. So, for example, under stable conditions the volume of a substance will be found to covary with its weight: An increase or decrease to the volume will be found to entail a proportionate increase or decrease to the weight, and vice versa. Unlike mere CO-OCCURRENCE, covariation carries a strong presumption that there is a causal link between the covarying phenomena. See also ILLUSORY COVARIATION. **—covary** *vb.*

covariation principle in ATTRIBUTION THEORY, the principle that for a factor to be a cause of a behavior it must be present when the behavior occurs and not be present when it does not occur. [introduced by U.S. social psychologist Harold H. Kelley (1921–2003)]

coverage *n.* health care benefits and services provided within a given HEALTH PLAN.

covering-law model a model for SCIENTIFIC EXPLANATION positing that a phenomenon is explained only if it can be deduced from a set of statements among which is at least one general scientific law. Thus, a phenomenon can be explained only if it can be predicted. See also DEDUCTIVE-NOMOLOGICAL MODEL. [proposed by German philosopher of science Carl Gustav Hempel (1905–1997)]

cover memory see SCREEN MEMORY.

cover story a plausible but incorrect statement about the purpose of a research study given to research participants to avoid disclosing to them the research hypothesis being investigated. This deception is practiced when the participants' behavior in the study is apt to be affected by knowledge of the experiment's true purpose. For ethical reasons, the deception should not flagrantly violate the participants' right to know what they will be getting into by taking part in the investigation.

covert attention attention directed to a location that is different from that on which the eyes are fixated. See COVERT ORIENTING.

covert behavior behavior that is not directly observable and can only be inferred or self-reported. For example, imagining something is covert behavior. See also PRIVATE EVENT.

covert conditioning a technique of BEHAVIOR THERAPY that relies on the use of imagination and assumes that overt and covert behavior are associated, that each affects the other, and that both forms of behavior depend on the laws of learning. The individual imagines performing a desired behavior in a problematic real-life situation, rewards himself or herself for mentally engaging in the behavior, and finally achieves an actual change in behavior. Also called **covert behavioral reinforcement**. [developed in 1966 by U.S. psychologist Joseph R. Cautela (1927–1999)]

covert desensitization a form of DESENSITIZATION therapy in which an individual is helped to overcome a fear or anxiety by learning to relax while recollecting the anxiety-producing stimulus in his or her imagination. A hierarchy is devised with a sequence of items that range from the least to the most anxiety-producing aspects of the stimulus. The client then uses relaxation techniques while progressively imagining items on the hierarchy until able to imagine the stimulus without feeling anxious. Compare IN VIVO DESENSITIZATION. See also SYSTEMATIC DESENSITIZATION.

covert extinction a COVERT CONDITIONING procedure in which the client first imagines performing an unwanted behavior and then imagines failing to be rewarded or to receive REINFORCEMENT for the behavior. See also COVERT POSITIVE REINFORCEMENT.

covert modeling a COVERT CONDITIONING procedure in which the client pictures a role model, imagines behaving as this person might, and then visualizes specific favorable consequences of the behavior. See also COVERT POSITIVE REINFORCEMENT.

covert negative reinforcement in BEHAVIOR THERAPY, a technique in which the client first imagines an aversive event and then switches to imagining engaging in the target behavior. For example, a client might imagine that he or she is alone at a restaurant, feeling insecure and unhappy, and then switches the imaginary scene to one in which he or she is asking another person for a date and that person says yes. Compare COVERT POSITIVE REINFORCEMENT.

covert orienting the shifting of attentional focus independently of the direction of gaze. Covert orienting can be shown by improved detection or identification of target stimuli at a cued location in the absence of eye movements. See COVERT ATTENTION.

covert positive reinforcement in BEHAVIOR THERAPY, a technique in which a person imagines performing a desired behavior that is followed by a pleasant consequence and subsequently rehearsing the behavior in the hope that it will eventually be adopted. Also called **covert reinforcement**. Compare COVERT NEGATIVE REINFORCEMENT.

covert rehearsal a technique in which either rote or elaborate repetitive rehearsing in one's mind of words or behaviors is used to improve memory or to prepare for overt speech or behavior. See also BEHAVIOR REHEARSAL.

covert reinforcement see COVERT POSITIVE REINFORCEMENT.

covert response any generally unobservable response, such as a thought, image, emotion, or internal physiological reaction, the existence of which is typically inferred or measured indirectly. For example, covert preparation for physical responses can be observed in an electric brain potential called the LATERALIZED READINESS POTENTIAL and in electromyographic measures of muscle activity. Also called **implicit response**. Compare OVERT RESPONSE.

covert self an individual's perception of his or her true nature.

covert sensitization a BEHAVIOR THERAPY technique for reducing an undesired behavior in which the client imagines performing the undesired behavior (e.g., overeating) and then imagines an unpleasant consequence (e.g., vomiting).

covert speech talking to oneself. Covert speech is usually seen as the externalization of a person's inner voice: Some explanations have equated it with thought itself. See also SUBVOCAL SPEECH.

COWA abbreviation for CONTROLLED ORAL WORD ASSOCIATION.

Cowper's glands see BULBOURETHRAL GLANDS. [William **Cowper** (1660–1709), English surgeon]

CP abbreviation for CEREBRAL PALSY.

CPA 1. abbreviation for CANADIAN PSYCHOLOGICAL ASSOCIATION. **2.** abbreviation for critical path analysis (see CRITICAL PATH METHOD).

CPI abbreviation for CALIFORNIA PSYCHOLOGICAL INVENTORY.

CPM abbreviation for CRITICAL PATH METHOD.

CPP abbreviation for CONDITIONED PLACE PREFERENCE.

CPQ abbreviation for CHILDREN'S PERSONALITY QUESTIONNAIRE.

CPR fees abbreviation for CUSTOMARY, PREVAILING, AND REASONABLE FEES.

CPS abbreviation for COMREY PERSONALITY SCALES.

CPT 1. abbreviation for COGNITIVE PROCESSING THERAPY. **2.** abbreviation for CONTINUOUS PERFORMANCE TEST.

CPZ abbreviation for CHLORPROMAZINE.

CQT abbreviation for CONTROL QUESTION TEST.

CR abbreviation for CONDITIONED RESPONSE.

crack *n.* a dried mixture of COCAINE and baking soda that can be smoked. It contains a relatively small, inexpensive amount of cocaine, which produces a rapid and short-lived high, thus increasing the drug's accessibility.

cracking facades the process of encouraging people to reveal their true selves. It is associated with Carl ROGERS's encounter-group work.

Cramér's V coefficient (symbol: *V*) a correlation-like index that reflects the ASSOCIATION between two CATEGORICAL VARIABLES. [Carl Harald **Cramér** (1893–1985), Swedish statistician]

cramp *n.* a painful muscle spasm (contraction). See also DYSTONIA.

cranial *adj.* referring or relating to the CRANIUM.

cranial anomaly an abnormal head due to a congenital defect. The head may be abnormally large (as in HYDROCEPHALUS), abnormally small (as in MICROCEPHALY), or square-shaped (as in some cases of osteopetrosis) or it may have sutures that fail to close. The defect is often related to a chromosome abnormality. Chromosomes 17 and 18 are often involved through trisomy or other aberrations.

cranial bifida a congenital disorder manifested by a horseshoe-shaped depression of the medial (middle) plane of the forehead. A median-cleft palate, a cleft of the nose ranging from a notch to complete division, and widely spaced eyes are present. Because of a failure of the two sides of the head to fuse normally during prenatal development, the corpus callosum, the nerve tract connecting the two sides of the brain, may be defective. Mental retardation is common.

cranial capacity the volume of the skull.

cranial diameter the maximal width of the skull.

cranial division the part of the PARASYMPATHETIC NERVOUS SYSTEM whose fibers extend from CRANIAL NERVES. Compare SACRAL DIVISION.

cranial electrical stimulation see ELECTROSLEEP THERAPY.

cranial index the ratio of the maximum breadth of the skull to its maximum length, multiplied by 100. Compare CEPHALIC INDEX.

cranial nerve any of the 12 pairs of nerves that arise directly from the brain and are distributed mainly to structures in the head and neck. Some of the cranial nerves are sensory, some are motor, and some are mixed (i.e., both sensory and motor). Cranial nerves are designated by Roman numerals, as follows: I, OLFACTORY NERVE; II, OPTIC NERVE; III, OCULOMOTOR NERVE; IV, TROCHLEAR NERVE; V, TRIGEMINAL NERVE; VI, ABDUCENS NERVE; VII, FACIAL NERVE; VIII, VESTIBULOCOCHLEAR NERVE; IX, GLOSSOPHARYNGEAL NERVE; X, VAGUS NERVE; XI, ACCESSORY NERVE; XII, HYPOGLOSSAL NERVE.

cranial pia mater see PIA MATER.

cranial reflex a reflex mediated by one of the CRANIAL NERVES, such as the blink reflex in response to a bright light or to a touch to the cornea.

craniofacial anomaly a structural deformity, usually congenital, that involves the face and cranium. Disorders characterized by such anomalies include TREACHER COLLINS SYNDROME, CROUZON'S SYNDROME, and Hurler's syndrome (see GARGOYLISM).

craniofacial dysostosis see CROUZON'S SYNDROME.

craniograph *n.* **1.** a chart or photograph of the skull. **2.** an instrument for measuring the skull.

craniography *n.* the study of the skull using photographs and drawings made from measurements of the configuration of the skull and the relations of its angles and craniometric points. The technique is not widely used now.

craniology *n.* **1.** the scientific study of the size, shape, and other characteristics of the human skull. **2.** see PHRENOLOGY.

craniometry *n.* the scientific measurement of the skull. **—craniometric** *adj.*

craniosacral system a less common name for the PARASYMPATHETIC NERVOUS SYSTEM.

craniosinus fistula see FISTULA.

craniostenosis *n.* a skull deformity caused by premature closing of the cranial sutures. The condition restricts normal development of brain structures and usually results in mental retardation.

craniosynostosis syndrome a condition caused by premature fusion of cranial bones, resulting in a skull deformity. The sagittal suture along the top of the skull is most often involved. Premature closing of one suture is unlikely to affect brain growth or intelligence, but premature fusion of multiple sutures increases the risk of neurological disorders.

craniotelencephalic dysplasia premature closure of some of the cranial sutures (see CRANIOSYNOSTOSIS SYNDROME) accompanied by protrusion of the frontal skull bone and mental retardation, with or without encephalocele (brain herniation through the skull). Chromosomes of affected individuals do not show abnormalities, but it is possible that the disorder is associated with unspecified autosomal recessive inheritance.

craniotomy *n.* the surgical opening of the skull, a procedure that may be performed, for example, to administer surgical treatment or to release pressure when the brain is expanding due to HYDROCEPHALUS or CEREBRAL EDEMA. Craniotomy is one of the oldest types of surgery: Evidence of it has been found in prehistoric skulls in nearly every part of the world. See also TREPHINATION.

cranium *n.* **1.** the skull. **2.** the portion of the skull that encloses the brain.

crank *n.* a street name for smokable METHAMPHETAMINE.

crash *n.* **1.** the withdrawal symptoms, usually dominated by feelings of severe depression, that occur following a lengthy period of amphetamine intoxication. The user may sleep for several days more or less continuously, displaying signs of exhaustion and irritation during waking periods. See AMPHETAMINE WITHDRAWAL. **2.** the period following the "rush" or "high" produced by intravenous cocaine. As feelings of euphoria wear off, they are replaced by irritability, depression, and anxiety, as well as strong craving for another dose. See COCAINE WITHDRAWAL.

craze *n.* see FAD.

creatine kinase (**CK**) an enzyme present in heart muscle, skeletal muscle, and brain tissues. High levels in the blood may be a sign of disease or tissue damage, for example, muscular dystrophy or myocardial infarction. The enzyme consists of two subunits, of which there are two possible alternatives, M and B. The combination of subunits is characteristic of certain tissues and can be identified by electrophoresis techniques as myocardial (MB), skeletal muscle (MM), and brain (BB). The MB form is usually specific for myocardial infarction.

creationism *n.* **1.** in its most general sense, the view that the universe was created out of nothing by a higher intelligence, in contrast to the view that it came into being without any such intervention, or that it has existed forever. While most varieties of this view are religious, all need not be. **2.** in a more restricted sense, a family of views that reject evolutionary theories in favor of a literal acceptance of the biblical creation story, holding (among other things) that the world was created by God in six days (or fairly short time periods) and that each species of animal (including humans) was created by a separate act of God. See also INTELLIGENT DESIGN. **—creationist** *adj., n.*

creative arts therapy therapeutic interventions that use artistic endeavors or mediums, such as music, poetry, dance, and drama, to facilitate communication and emotional expression, enhance self-awareness, and foster health and change. See also ART THERAPY; DANCE THERAPY; DRAMA THERAPY; MUSIC THERAPY; POETRY THERAPY.

creative dramatics the use, especially with children,

of spontaneous drama-oriented play ("pretending") as a therapeutic technique designed to enhance creativity and imagination, improve communication and social skills, and foster health. The emphasis in creative dramatics is not on the end product (e.g., performance) but rather on the creative process itself.

creative genius see EXCEPTIONAL CREATIVITY.

creative imagination the faculty by which new, uncommon ideas are produced, especially when this does not seem explicable by the mere combination of existing ideas. The operations of the creative imagination are sometimes explained by the interaction of dormant or unconscious elements with active, conscious thoughts. See also CREATIVE THINKING; CREATIVITY; DIVERGENT THINKING; IMAGINATION.

creative intelligence in the TRIARCHIC THEORY OF INTELLIGENCE, the set of skills used to create, invent, discover, explore, imagine, and suppose. This set of skills is alleged to be relatively (although not wholly) distinctive with respect to analytical and practical skills. Compare ANALYTICAL INTELLIGENCE; PRACTICAL INTELLIGENCE.

creative synthesis the combination of several ideas, images, or associations into a new whole, especially when this differs fundamentally from any of its components. See also MENTAL SYNTHESIS. [coined by Wilhelm WUNDT]

creative thinking the mental processes leading to a new invention, solution, or synthesis in any area. A creative solution may use preexisting objects or ideas but creates a new relationship between the elements it utilizes. Examples include new machines, social ideas, scientific theories, and artistic creations. Compare CRITICAL THINKING. See also DIVERGENT THINKING.

creativity *n.* the ability to produce or develop original work, theories, techniques, or thoughts. A creative individual typically displays originality, imagination, and expressiveness. Analyses have failed to ascertain why one individual is more creative than another, but creativity does appear to be a very durable trait. See also CREATIVE IMAGINATION; CREATIVE THINKING; DIVERGENT THINKING. **—creative** *adj.*

creativity test any psychological test designed to identify CREATIVITY or DIVERGENT THINKING. Existing tests focus on a variety of factors, such as an individual's FLUENCY with words and ideas or ability to generate original associations; tasks may involve finding solutions to practical problems, suggesting different endings to stories, or listing unusual uses for objects (see ALTERNATE-USES TEST). See also ARP TESTS; TORRANCE TESTS OF CREATIVE THINKING.

credentialing *n.* the process of reviewing a health care provider's credentials, practice history, and medical CERTIFICATION or license to determine if criteria for clinical privileges are met. See also PROFESSIONAL LICENSING.

credibility of a source see SOURCE CREDIBILITY.

credulous argument the element of the SPORT PERSONALITY DEBATE supporting the concept that personality variables are related to athletic achievement. See also SKEPTICAL ARGUMENT.

creeping commitment see ESCALATION OF COMMITMENT.

cremasteric reflex the contraction of the **cremaster muscle**, which causes retraction of the TESTES toward the abdomen, caused by cold temperature or by stroking the skin on the inside of the thigh.

creole *n.* a language that has evolved from prolonged contact between two or more languages (often one of a European colonist and the other of the colonized people) and become the native language of a SPEECH COMMUNITY. Unlike a PIDGIN, a creole will usually have a fully developed grammatical system. See also DECREOLIZATION.

crepitation *n.* **1.** a soft, crackling sound heard on AUSCULTATION of the chest, which indicates disease of the lungs or airways. **2.** the sound of bones or damaged cartilage surfaces rubbing against each other, as occurs in ARTHRITIS and other degenerative skeletal conditions.

crepuscular animals animals that are most active in a dimly lighted environment, for example, at dawn or dusk.

Crespi effect in conditioning, an increase (or decrease) in a response that is disproportionate to the reinforcement. This occurs when there is a sudden shift in the amount of reinforcement; for example, if the amount of food given as reinforcement is suddenly increased from 1 g to 6 g, the level of performance is higher than if 6 g of food had been the only reinforcement given. Compare BEHAVIORAL CONTRAST. [Leo P. **Crespi** (1916–), U.S. psychologist]

cretinism *n.* a condition associated with thyroid deficiency. The term is derived from an Old French word, *chrétien*, "Christian," because many early victims were children of a European Christian sect that lived on iodine-deficient food in isolated valleys in the Alps. See ATHYREOSIS; CONGENITAL HYPOTHYROIDISM. [first described in 1657 by Austrian physician Wolfgang Hoefer]

Creutzfeldt–Jakob disease (**CJD**) a rapidly progressive neurological disease caused by abnormal PRION proteins and characterized by DEMENTIA, involuntary muscle movements (especially MYOCLONUS), ATAXIA, visual disturbances, and seizures. Vacuoles form in the gray matter of the brain and spinal cord, giving it a spongy appearance; the prion is thought to cause misfolding of other proteins, leading to the cellular pathology. **Classical CJD** occurs sporadically worldwide and typically affects individuals who are middle-aged or older. A small proportion (about 10%) of cases are inherited. Early symptoms are muscular incoordination (ataxia), with abnormalities of gait and speech, followed by worsening dementia and myoclonus. Death occurs usually within 1 year of the onset of symptoms. **Variant CJD** (**vCJD**) was first reported in Great Britain in the 1990s. It causes similar symptoms but typically affects younger people, who are believed to have acquired the disease by eating meat or meat products from cattle infected with bovine spongiform encephalopathy (BSE). Also called **Jakob–Creutzfeldt disease**; **subacute spongiform encephalopathy** (**SSE**). See also PRION DISEASE. [Hans Gerhard **Creutzfeldt** (1885–1964) and Alfons **Jakob** (1884–1931), German neuropathologists]

CRF **1.** abbreviation for CONTINUOUS REINFORCEMENT. **2.** abbreviation for corticotropin-releasing factor (see CORTICOTROPIN-RELEASING HORMONE).

CRH abbreviation for CORTICOTROPIN-RELEASING HORMONE.

crib death see SUDDEN INFANT DEATH SYNDROME.

cribriform plate a sievelike layer in the skull that supports the OLFACTORY BULB and permits olfactory receptor fibers to extend through its holes to the OLFACTORY EPITHELIUM.

cri du chat syndrome a chromosomal disorder involving deletion of the short arm of chromosome 5, which results in severe mental retardation, walking and talking difficulty or inability, and an anomaly of the epiglottis and larynx that causes a high-pitched wailing cry like that of a cat. Almost all affected individuals have very small heads (see MICROCEPHALY). The defect seems to be hereditary. Also called **cat-cry syndrome**; **chromosome 5, deletion of short arm**; **crying-cat syndrome**; **Lejeune syndrome**; **monosomy 5p**.

crime control model a view of legal process that places a premium on upholding law and order, the protection and safety of the public, and the apprehension and efficient processing of criminals. Compare DUE PROCESS MODEL.

criminal anthropology an early positivist approach to criminology (see POSITIVIST CRIMINOLOGY) associated with the theories of Italian criminologist Cesare Lombroso (1835–1909). It embraced the notion of the "born criminal" or criminal type, based on the belief that criminals had certain physical characteristics that distinguished them from noncriminals.

criminal commitment the confinement of people in mental institutions either because they have been found NOT GUILTY BY REASON OF INSANITY or in order to establish their COMPETENCY TO STAND TRIAL as responsible defendants.

criminal intent see MENS REA.

criminally insane describing defendants who are judged to be suffering from a mental illness or defect that absolves them of legal responsibility for the criminal acts they are alleged to have committed. The term is now seldom used.

criminal profiling methods used to identify characteristics of likely perpetrators of a crime based on a systematic evaluation of the crime scene together with other information, such as the background of the victim or victims (i.e., victimology).

criminal psychopath a person with ANTISOCIAL PERSONALITY DISORDER who repeatedly violates the law.

criminal responsibility a defendant's ability to formulate a criminal intent (see MENS REA) at the time of the crime with which he or she is charged, which must be proved in court before the person can be convicted. Criminal responsibility may be excluded for reason of INSANITY (see DURHAM RULE; IRRESISTIBLE IMPULSE RULE; MCNAUGHTEN RULE) or mitigated for a number of other reasons (see DIMINISHED CAPACITY; DIMINISHED RESPONSIBILITY).

criminal type a classification of individuals who repeatedly engage in criminal or illegal acts, supposedly because of a genetic predisposition to do so.

criminology *n.* the scientific study of crime and criminal behavior, including its causes, prevention, and punishment. See also POSITIVIST CRIMINOLOGY. **—criminologist** *n.*

crisis *n.* (*pl.* **crises**) **1.** a situation that produces significant stress in those involved in it. **2.** a traumatic change in an individual's life that often produces cognitive or emotional stress. **3.** a turning point for better or worse in the course of an illness. **4.** a state of affairs marked by instability and the possibility of impending change for the worse, for example, in a political or social situation. **5.** in the analysis of SCIENTIFIC REVOLUTIONS by U.S. philosopher of science Thomas Kuhn (1922–1996), the situation that occurs when a particular theoretical system is overcome by so many ANOMALIES that the system is perceived to be failing and a search for a better theoretical system is under way.

crisis center a facility established for emergency therapy or referral, sometimes staffed by medical and mental health professionals and paraprofessionals. See DROP-IN CENTER.

crisis counseling immediate drop-in, phone-in, or onsite professional counseling provided following a trauma or sudden stressful event, often for emergency situations or in the aftermath of a disaster. See DISASTER COUNSELING; HOTLINE.

crisis intervention 1. the brief ameliorative, rather than specifically curative, use of psychotherapy or counseling to aid individuals, families, and groups who have undergone a highly disruptive experience, such as an unexpected bereavement or a disaster. Crisis intervention may prevent more serious consequences of the experience, such as POSTTRAUMATIC STRESS DISORDER. **2.** psychological intervention provided on a short-term, emergency basis for individuals experiencing mental health crises, such as an ACUTE PSYCHOTIC EPISODE or ATTEMPTED SUICIDE.

crisis intervention service any of the services provided (usually by governmental or social agencies) during emergencies, disasters, and for personal crises. Such services include hot lines, drop-in services, and on-site intervention at the scene of a disaster.

crisis management the organization and mobilization of resources to overcome the difficulties presented by a sudden and unexpected threat. The psychological stress produced by a crisis can reduce the information-processing capacities of those affected, which should be taken into account by crisis managers when considering possible solutions.

crisis team a group of professionals and paraprofessionals trained and prepared to help individuals cope with psychological reactions during and following emergencies or mental health crises, for example, natural disasters or suicide threats or attempts.

crisis theory the body of concepts that deals with the nature of a crisis, crisis behavior, crisis precipitants, crisis prevention, crisis intervention, and crisis resolution.

crista (**crysta**) *n.* the structure within the ampulla at the end of each SEMICIRCULAR CANAL that contains hair cells sensitive to the direction and rate of movements of the head.

criteria of evaluation the criteria used to specify or measure PROGRAM IMPACT or, often, PROGRAM OUTCOME as stated in the EVALUATION OBJECTIVES of a study.

criteria of the psychic a proposed set of signs or indicators that would allow one to be confident in concluding that an organism possesses consciousness, or that a behavior arises from consciousness as opposed to purely physiological sources. The idea that such criteria could be formulated was proposed by Robert YERKES. Yerkes's structural criteria were general morphology, neural organization, and neural specialization; his proposed functional criteria were discrimination, modifiability of reaction, and variability of reaction.

criterion *n.* (*pl.* **criteria**) **1.** a standard against which a judgment, evaluation, or comparisons can be made. **2.** a test score or item against which other tests or items can be validated. For example, a well-validated test of creativity might be used as the criterion to select new tests of creativity.

criterion-based content analysis (**CBCA**) a form of STATEMENT VALIDITY ANALYSIS in which children's statements in instances of alleged abuse are analyzed in terms of key content criteria, in order to evaluate their truth.

criterion contamination an experimental situation in which the variable to be validated is allowed to influence the criterion (i.e., the variable used for VALIDATION).

criterion cutoff the score on an assessment instrument

that serves as a cutoff point separating participants into distinct categories. For example, in industrial and organizational psychology, the criterion cutoff on a particular measure of JOB PERFORMANCE separates what is considered a successful performance on this dimension from an unsuccessful performance. See JOB CRITERION.

criterion data information obtained from supervisors or other sources, such as absence records, that may be used in measuring the performance of employees in a job. See JOB CRITERION; JOB PERFORMANCE.

criterion dimensions in industrial and organizational psychology, multiple JOB CRITERIA used to evaluate the overall JOB PERFORMANCE of an employee. These may include such aspects of performance as productivity, effectiveness, absences, errors, and accidents. Multiple criteria are often preferred over the use of a single criterion because an individual may be outstanding in one aspect of job performance but below average in another.

criterion group a group tested for traits its members are already known to possess, usually for the purpose of validating a test. For example, a group of children with diagnosed visual disabilities may be given a visual test to assess its VALIDITY as a means of evaluating the presence of visual disabilities.

criterion problem see PARTICULARISM.

criterion-referenced testing an approach to testing based on the comparison of a person's performance with an established standard or criterion. The criterion is fixed, that is, each person's score is measured against the same criterion and is not influenced by the performance of others. See NORM-REFERENCED TESTING.

criterion score a predicted score on an attribute or variable that is derived from REGRESSION ANALYSIS.

criterion validity an index of how well a test correlates with a criterion, that is, an established standard of comparison. The criterion can be measured before, after, or at the same time as the test being validated.

criterion variable in statistical analysis, a variable to be predicted; that is, a DEPENDENT VARIABLE.

critical *adj.* **1.** essential or necessary for some process. A CRITICAL PERIOD, for example, is an essential stage in the developmental process. **2.** emphasizing real or imagined faults. **3.** characterized by or denoting thorough, impartial evaluation or review. **4.** crucial, decisive, or highly important.

critical band the band of frequencies in a masking noise that are effective in masking a tone of a given frequency (see AUDITORY MASKING). The width of this band, in hertz (Hz), is the **critical bandwidth**. For example, in detecting a 1-kHz tone in white NOISE, only frequency components in the noise between 920 Hz and 1080 Hz contribute significantly to the masking: The critical band is from 920 to 1080 Hz, and the critical bandwidth is 160 Hz. In psychoacoustics there are many manifestations of critical-band "filtering," including spectral effects in LOUDNESS SUMMATION and monaural phase effects. See also AUDITORY FILTER; FREQUENCY SELECTIVITY. [first described in 1940 by U.S. physicist Harvey Fletcher (1884–1981)]

critical care unit (**CCU**) see INTENSIVE CARE UNIT.

critical flicker frequency (**CFF**) the rate at which a periodic change, or flicker, in an intense visual stimulus fuses into a smooth, continuous stimulus. A similar phenomenon can occur with rapidly changing auditory stimuli. Also called **fusion frequency**.

critical-incident stress debriefing (**CISD**) a systematic and programmed process designed to help individuals who witness or work at the scene of a critical incident or disaster (e.g., firefighters). The process uses basic stress counseling techniques; formal training in CISD is provided in workshops for personnel in emergency services as well as for mental health professionals. [developed by U.S. psychologist Jeffrey T. Mitchell (1948–)]

critical-incident technique (**CIT**) a method designed to investigate factors associated with unusually good or unusually poor job performance. Observers record unusual outcomes and specific incidents, behaviors, or system features that may have triggered these outcomes. Data collected in this way are then classified and analyzed to identify key themes. The critical-incident technique is widely used in such areas as ACCIDENT PREVENTION and the creation of behaviorally based rating scales for use in EMPLOYEE EVALUATION (see BEHAVIORALLY ANCHORED RATING SCALE; BEHAVIORAL OBSERVATION SCALE; MIXED-STANDARD SCALE).

critical life event an event in life that requires major ADJUSTMENT and adaptive behavior. Such events may be regarded in retrospect as unusually formative or pivotal in shaping attitudes and beliefs. Common critical life events include bereavement, divorce, and unemployment. See also LIFE EVENTS.

critical path method (**CPM**) a project-management technique, developed in the early 1950s, that involves identifying, sequencing, and scheduling the essential subtasks in a complex, time-limited project. This analysis is usually represented as a diagram showing the "critical path" to successful completion. Also called **critical path analysis** (**CPA**).

critical period 1. an early stage in life when an organism is especially open to specific learning, emotional, or socializing experiences that occur as part of normal development and will not recur at a later stage. For example, the first 3 days of life are thought to constitute a critical period for IMPRINTING in ducks, and there may be a critical period for language acquisition in human infants. See also SENSITIVE PERIOD. **2.** in vision, the period of time after birth, varying from weeks (in cats) to months (in humans), in which full, binocular visual stimulation is necessary for the structural and functional maturation of the VISUAL SYSTEM. See also MONOCULAR REARING.

critical point a point in the course of psychotherapy at which the client sees his or her problem clearly and decides on an appropriate course of action to handle or resolve it.

critical range the range within which a particular biological measure must remain to ensure good health. See also SET ZONE.

critical region the set of values of a test statistic that will lead to the rejection of the null hypothesis. Also called **region of rejection**. Compare ACCEPTANCE REGION.

critical thinking a form of directed, problem-focused thinking in which the individual tests ideas or possible solutions for errors or drawbacks. It is essential to such activities as examining the validity of a hypothesis or interpreting the meaning of research results. Compare CREATIVE THINKING. See CONVERGENT THINKING.

critical value the value of either end point of the CRITICAL REGION; that is, either of the values of the test statistic above and below which the NULL HYPOTHESIS will be rejected.

critical variable a variable required to bring about a particular result or to make a particular prediction.

criticism *n.* **1.** a thoughtful evaluation or judgment of something, such as a person's performance or behavior, especially to help improve future performance or behavior or to offer different solutions. This is sometimes referred to as **constructive criticism**. **2.** expression of a negative evaluation in the form of disapproval that points out faults and shortcomings. Such criticism may be displayed by words or behavior and often has no constructive aim. **—criticize** *vb.*

critique *n.* a comprehensive analysis that identifies and explains both strengths and weaknesses.

Crocker–Henderson odor system a theory that posits four PRIMARY ODOR qualities: acid, burnt, caprylic, and fragrant. The presence of each primary in an odor is assessed via a 9-point scale (0–8) indicating the relative intensity of each quality. See also HENNING'S ODOR PRISM. [Ernest C. **Crocker** (1888–1964) and Lloyd F. **Henderson**, U.S. chemists]

Cro-Magnon *n.* an early form of modern human (*Homo sapiens*) inhabiting Europe in the late Paleolithic period. Its skeletal remains were first found in the Cro-Magnon cave in southern France.

Cronbach, Lee J. (1916–2001) U.S. psychologist. Cronbach received his doctorate in education from the University of Chicago in 1940. As a child, he was a participant in TERMAN'S GIFTEDNESS STUDY, graduating from high school at the age of 14. He held faculty positions at a number of universities, spending the longest periods at the University of Illinois (1948–1964) and Stanford University (from 1964 until his retirement). Cronbach is best known for his contributions to the fields of educational psychology and psychological testing. He developed a measure of test reliability that became known as CRONBACH'S ALPHA; he also contributed importantly to the topic of test VALIDITY. His widely cited paper "Construct Validity in Psychological Tests" (1955, coauthored by Paul MEEHL) helped to establish validity as a keystone of psychological testing. Cronbach was particularly influential in the field of education in California, where he headed a faculty consortium involved in evaluating education in the state. His book *Designing Educational Evaluations* (1982) summarized his ideas resulting from the work of the consortium. Cronbach also made important contributions to the field of instruction, with research focusing on the need to match student aptitude with the appropriate learning environment. This work is summarized in *Aptitudes and Instructional Methods* (1977, coauthored with R. E. Snow). Cronbach's honors included the Distinguished Scientific Contribution Award of the American Psychological Association and membership of the American Academy of Arts and Sciences, the National Academy of Education, and the National Academy of Sciences. He served as president of the American Psychological Association in 1956.

Cronbach's alpha an index of INTERNAL CONSISTENCY reliability, that is, the degree to which a set of items tap a single, unidimensional construct. Also called **alpha coefficient**. [Lee J. CRONBACH]

cross-adaptation *n.* the change in sensitivity to one stimulus caused by adaptation to another. See CROSS-NASAL ADAPTATION.

cross-addiction *n.* see CROSS-TOLERANCE.

crossbreeding *n.* see OUTBREEDING.

cross-classification *n.* classification of items according to more than one characteristic. More specifically, it is a two-way system of classification used in experimentation in which each person or other sampling unit is assigned to the intersection of a row category and a column category. For example, each person may be assigned to a treatment or control (no treatment) row condition and a pass or fail column condition.

cross-conditioning *n.* conditioning to a NEUTRAL STIMULUS when this stimulus by coincidence occurs simultaneously with an UNCONDITIONED STIMULUS.

cross-correlation mechanism the auditory mechanism thought to underlie sound localization based on interaural time differences (see BINAURAL CUES).

cross-correspondence *n.* in SPIRITUALISM and parapsychology, the situation in which two or more MEDIUMS, who claim to be in touch with the same spirit source but not with each other, produce similar or complementary messages. A famous and well-documented case of cross-correspondence occurred in 1901–1932, when three British mediums, working independently, produced strikingly similar messages (in AUTOMATIC WRITING) from the same deceased individuals.

To the believer, cross-correspondence provides firm evidence for the objective reality of spirit messages (or, at the very least, for some form of telepathy between the mediums). A more mundane explanation might stress (a) the mediums' access to the same biographical facts about the dead person and the same information regarding his or her interests, tastes, and opinions; and (b) the mediums' knowledge of the same spiritualist texts concerning the nature of the afterlife and the spirit world.

cross-cuing *n.* the use of one sense to identify an object when another, more appropriate sense is not available. For example, COMMISSUROTOMY (the split-brain technique) has revealed that auditory information is used to name an object when visual information is not available to the cerebral hemisphere mainly responsible for speech.

cross-cultural approach in the social sciences, a research method in which specific social practices, such as courtship behavior, child-rearing practices, or therapeutic attitudes and techniques, are studied and compared across a number of different cultures. Also called **cross-cultural method**. See also CROSS-CULTURAL PSYCHOLOGY.

cross-cultural counseling see MULTICULTURAL COUNSELING.

cross-cultural psychology a branch of psychology that studies similarities and variances in human behavior across different cultures and identifies the different psychological constructs and explanatory models used by these cultures. It may be contrasted with CULTURAL PSYCHOLOGY, which tends to adopt a systemic, within-culture approach. Also called **ethnopsychology**.

cross-cultural testing testing individuals with diverse cultural backgrounds and experiences using a method and materials that do not favor certain individuals over others. Typically, CULTURE-FAIR TESTS are administered with nonverbal instructions and content, avoid objects indigenous to a particular culture, and do not depend on speed.

cross-cultural treatment treatment in situations in which therapist and client differ in terms of race, ethnicity, gender, language, or lifestyle. Mental health providers should be attentive to cultural differences with clients for the following (among other) reasons: (a) Social and cultural beliefs influence diagnosis and treatment; (b) diagnosis differs across cultures; (c) symptoms are expressed differently across cultures; (d) diagnostic categories reflect majority cultural values; and (e) most providers are from the majority culture.

cross-dimension attitude consistency the extent to which the dimensions (i.e., distinct categories of information) underlying ATTITUDE-RELEVANT KNOWLEDGE are evaluatively consistent with one another. For example, if the information related to one dimension is extremely positive and the information related to a second dimension is extremely negative, cross-dimension attitude consistency is low. See also AMBIVALENCE OF AN ATTITUDE; COMPLEXITY OF AN ATTITUDE; WITHIN-DIMENSION ATTITUDE CONSISTENCY.

cross-dressing *n.* the process or habit of putting on the clothes of the opposite sex. It is done for a variety of reasons, for example, as part of a performance, as social commentary, or as a preliminary stage in sex-reversal procedures (see also TRANSSEXUALISM). Although synonymous with transvestism, cross-dressing is distinct from TRANSVESTIC FETISHISM.

crossed aphasia APHASIA resulting from damage to the right hemisphere of the brain rather than the left hemisphere, which is more common.

crossed disparity see UNCROSSED DISPARITY.

crossed dominance the tendency for some right-handed people to have a stronger or dominant left eye, and vice versa for the left-handed.

crossed-extension reflex a reflexive action by a contralateral limb to compensate for loss of support when the ipsilateral limb withdraws from a painful stimulus. The reflex, which helps shift the burden of body weight, is also associated with the coordination of legs in walking by flexing muscles on the left side when those on the right are extending, and vice versa.

crossed-factor design an experimental design in which each level of one factor occurs together with each level of another (crossed) factor. Thus, if there are four levels of reading ability in a study, and three levels of numbers of hours of tutoring, the factors of reading ability and of amount of tutoring are said to be crossed in a 4×3 crossed-factor design. Such a design yields 12 different cells, with each cell containing a set of observations or data obtained from a specific combination of the factor levels.

crossed reflex a reflex that occurs on the opposite side of the body from the part stimulated, such as the CROSSED-EXTENSION REFLEX.

cross-education *n.* see CROSS-TRAINING.

cross-eye *n.* a type of STRABISMUS (squint) in which there is a deviation of one or both eyes toward the other. The condition usually begins in infancy and is caused by deficient activity of one or more extrinsic EYE MUSCLES. Uncorrected cross-eye results in double visual images or FUNCTIONAL AMBLYOPIA. Cross-eye can be treated surgically in most cases. Also called **convergent strabismus**; **esotropia**.

cross-fostering *n.* **1.** in ANIMAL BEHAVIOR studies, the exchange of offspring between litters as a means of separating the effects of genetics from early experience. Wild rats reared by laboratory rats display less aggressive behavior, and mice from a polygynous species with low levels of territorial aggression that are cross-fostered to monogamous territorial mice display increased aggression and have patterns of brain neuropeptides more similar to their foster parents than to their natural parents. See also SEXUAL IMPRINTING. **2.** a similar technique used for investigating the effect of genetic factors in the development of a disorder. It involves either (a) having the offspring of biological parents who do not show the disorder being studied reared by adoptive parents who do or (b) having offspring of parents who show the disorder reared by parents who do not. Children cross-fostered in this manner are called **index adoptees**, whereas **control adoptees** are children of biological parents who do not show the disorder reared by adoptive parents who also do not show the disorder.

cross-gender behavior the process or habit of assuming the role of the opposite sex by adopting the clothes, hair style, and manner of speaking and gesturing that society considers characteristic of the opposite sex. See CROSS-DRESSING.

crossing over in genetics, see RECOMBINATION.

cross-lagged panel design a longitudinal experimental design used to increase the plausibility of causal inference in which two variables, *A* and *B*, are measured at time 1 (A_1, B_1) and at time 2 (A_2, B_2). Comparison of **cross-lagged panel correlations** between A_1 B_2 and B_1 A_2 may suggest a preponderance of causal influence of *A* over *B* or of *B* over *A*.

cross-linkage theory see EVERSION THEORY OF AGING.

cross-modal association 1. the coordination of sensory inputs involving different brain regions. It is usually required in tasks that involve matching auditory and visual inputs, tactile and visual inputs, or a similar combination of cognitive functions. Lesions in the temporal, parietal, or occipital lobes may be diagnosed by cross-modal association testing. See PERCEPTUAL SYNTHESIS; SENSORY INTERACTION. **2.** a phenomenon in which the input to one sense reliably generates an additional sensory output that is usually generated by the input to a separate sense.

cross-modality matching a DIRECT SCALING method of matching the magnitude of a stimulus (e.g., the brightness of a light) to the magnitude of another stimulus to which a different sense responds (e.g., the loudness of a sound).

cross-modal matching see INTERMODAL MATCHING.

cross-modal perception see INTERSENSORY PERCEPTION.

cross-modal transfer recognition of an object through a sense that differs from the sense through which it was originally encountered.

cross-nasal adaptation OLFACTORY ADAPTATION in one side of the nose after presenting a stimulus to the other side of the nose. Typically, cross-nasal adaptation is less pronounced than the adaptation in the side of the nose that receives the stimulus.

crossover design an experimental design in which different treatments are applied to the same sampling units (e.g., individuals) during different periods, as in LATIN SQUARES.

cross section a slice cut through any plane of an object or organ for examination. See CORONAL SECTION; HORIZONTAL SECTION. —**cross-sectional** *adj.*

cross-sectional design an experimental design in which individuals of different ages or developmental levels are directly compared, for example, in a **cross-sectional study** comparing 5-year-olds with 10-year-olds. Compare LONGITUDINAL DESIGN.

cross-sectional sampling selecting samples suitable for an experiment using a CROSS-SECTIONAL DESIGN.

cross-situational consistency the degree to which a psychological attribute, such as a personal disposition or a cognitive style, is displayed in the same, or a functionally equivalent, manner in different social environments.

cross-tabulation *n.* a method of arranging or presenting data (e.g., values, levels) in tabular form to show the mutual influence of one variable or variables on another variable or variables.

cross-talk *n.* a pattern of errors that occurs during the concurrent performance of tasks when the components of one task impinge on those of the other task, for example, when performing a different task with each hand.

cross-tolerance *n.* the potential for a drug, often a CNS DEPRESSANT, to produce the diminished effects of another drug of the same type when tissue tolerance for the effects of the latter substance has developed. Thus, a person with alcohol dependence can substitute a barbiturate or another sedative to prevent withdrawal symptoms, and vice versa. Similarly, cross-tolerance exists among most of the hallucinogens, except marijuana. Also called **cross-addiction**.

cross-training *n.* **1.** improvement in skill performance of one part of the body (e.g., the left hand) as a result of practice with another part of the body (e.g., the right hand). Also called **cross-education**. **2.** training employees in a variety of tasks or jobs that are outside their specialty areas so that they can substitute for one another when unforeseen absences occur. Cross-training is used to develop employee skills and to increase the flexibility with which a group or organization can deal with work demands. **3.** in sport, combining different sport or fitness activities to improve such areas as performance, endurance, flexibility, or weight loss. Combinations such as running (track), swimming, and weightlifting are typical. **—cross-train** *vb.*

cross-validation *n.* a model-evaluation approach in which the VALIDITY of a model is assessed by applying it to new data (i.e., data that were not used in developing the model). For example, a test's validity may be confirmed by administering the same test to a new sample in order to check the correctness of the initial validation. Cross-validation is necessary because chance and other factors may have inflated or biased the original validation.

Crouzon's syndrome a condition in which a wide skull with a protrusion near the anterior fontanel (on top of the head, at the front) is associated with a beaked nose and ocular abnormalities (see CRANIOSYNOSTOSIS SYNDROME). The latter may include atrophy, divergent strabismus, and blindness. Mild to moderate mental retardation is typical. Other neurological disorders may result from intracranial pressure. Also called **craniofacial dysostosis**. See also APERT'S SYNDROME. [described in 1912 by Octave **Crouzon** (1874–1938), French neurologist]

crowd *n.* a sizable gathering of people who temporarily share a common focus and a single location. Crowds vary in shape, size, and type; some common types include CASUAL CROWDS and MILLING CROWDS that form in the street, AUDIENCES, QUEUES, and MOBS.

crowd behavior the characteristic behavior of a group of people who congregate temporarily while their attention is focused on the same object or event. Typically, an AUDIENCE is relatively passive (smiling, laughing, applauding), a street crowd moves without apparent aim (see MILLING CROWD), and a MOB may stampede or act violently. See also COLLECTIVE BEHAVIOR.

crowd consciousness see CROWD MIND.

crowding *n.* **1.** psychological tension produced in environments of high population density, especially when individuals feel that the amount of space available to them is insufficient for their needs. Crowding may have a damaging effect on mental health and may result in poor performance of complex tasks, STRESSOR AFTEREFFECTS, and increased physiological stress. In animals, crowding can lead to impaired reproduction, decreased life expectancy, and a variety of pathological behaviors. However, crowding per se is often not the main source of pathology, since human beings and animals can live in high densities if appropriate resources are available. Two key mechanisms underlying crowding are lack of control over social interaction (i.e., privacy) and the deterioration of socially supportive relationships. See also BEHAVIORAL SINK; DENSITY; ENVIRONMENTAL STRESS. **2.** in learning, a situation in which there are too many items or tasks for the time allowed. Crowding would occur, for example, in an exam requiring the student to respond to 20 in-depth essay questions in 1 hour.

crowd mind a hypothetical explanation for the apparent uniformity of individuals' emotional, cognitive, and behavioral reactions when in large crowds; it supposes that a crowd of people can, in certain instances, become a unified entity that acts as if guided by a single collective mind. This hypothesis is not generally accepted now (see GROUP FALLACY). Also called **crowd consciousness**. Compare GROUP MIND. [introduced by French psychologist Gustave Le Bon (1841–1931)]

crowd psychology 1. the mental and emotional states and processes unique to individuals when they are members of street crowds, MOBS, and other such collectives. **2.** the scientific study of these phenomena.

CR10 scale see BORG SCALE.

crucial experiment an experiment so constructed that its result will determine which one of two opposing theories has made the correct prediction, thus refuting the other.

cruelty *n.* indifference to or deliberate infliction of injury, pain, grief, suffering, or other form of physical or psychological distress. **—cruel** *adj.*

crura *pl. n.* see CRUS.

crus *n.* (*pl.* **crura**) **1.** the portion of the leg between the knee and the ankle. **2.** a leglike part of the body, such as the ventral portion of a CEREBRAL PEDUNCLE. **—crural** *adj.*

crus cerebri see CEREBRAL PEDUNCLE.

crutch *n.* **1.** a device, usually made of metal or wood, designed to aid people with disabilities or other problems affecting the lower limbs by providing support in walking. The simplest type of crutch consists of two long parallel shafts that taper to a single point at the bottom and fit under the armpit at the top; a crosspiece in the middle functions as a handgrip. In contrast, arm crutches consist of a single shaft with a handgrip and a cuff that fits either the forearm or the upper arm. **2.** colloquially, a nonspecific coping or support mechanism, which may be of a psychological, medicinal, or other nature. **3.** a learning aid.

crying-cat syndrome see CRI DU CHAT SYNDROME.

cryo- *combining form* cold or freezing.

cryogenic method the use of extremely cold temperatures in diagnostic, therapeutic, or investigational procedures. For example, certain immunoglobulins associated with a variety of diseases are detected in the blood by reducing the temperature of a blood sample to the point at which the substances separate from the blood serum. Cryogenic methods are also used to freeze tissue samples to be sliced for microscopic examination. **Cryogenic surgery** is employed, for example, in the destruction of thalamic lesions responsible for symptoms of Parkinson's disease. **Cryogenics** is the branch of physics concerned with the scientific study and application of low temperatures and resulting phenomena.

cryonic suspension the attempt to preserve a corpse with the intention of subsequent revival and restoration to healthy life. A retired professor of psychology, Dr. James H. Bedford, is thought to have been the first person to be placed in cryonic suspension (in 1967, in a stainless steel chamber filled with liquid nitrogen).

cryotherapy *n.* the use of cold for therapeutic effect; for example, abnormal tissue is destroyed by freezing it. Cryotherapy is commonly used in sports medicine, though its effects on motor control remain unclear. It is possible that cryotherapy elevates the pain threshold.

crypsis *n.* the ability to remain inconspicuous through body coloration that blends in with the environment, through such behavior as freezing or IMMOBILITY, or through use of vocal signals that are difficult to localize. See also CAMOUFLAGE. —**cryptic** *adj.*

cryptarithmetic *n.* a type of problem sometimes used in studies of problem solving, in which the digits in an arithmetic problem are replaced with letters. The participant must determine which digit is represented by each letter. See also CODE TEST; CRYPTOGRAM.

cryptesthesia (**cryptaesthesia**) *n.* an experience of CLAIRVOYANCE, CLAIRAUDIENCE, TELEPATHY, or some other form of EXTRASENSORY PERCEPTION that cannot be explained with reference to any known sensory stimulus. Also called **telesthesia**. —**cryptesthetic** *adj.*

cryptic female choice a practice in which females mate with several males but "choose" which one's sperm will fertilize their eggs, concealing these decisions from the males. This practice allows females more choice in MATE SELECTION. In studies demonstrating cryptic female choice, it is the sperm that is genetically most compatible that fertilizes the female's eggs, rather than sperm from the most attractive males.

crypto- (**crypt-**) *combining form* concealed.

cryptogram *n.* a type of problem sometimes used in studies of problem solving, in which a short quip or quotation is ciphered so that letters of the alphabet are randomly assigned to replace one another (e.g., *s* stands for *a*, *a* stands for *n*, and so on). The participant must determine the letter correspondences used in the code, and thus decode the message. See also CODE TEST; CRYPTARITHMETIC.

cryptophasia *n.* secret or incomprehensible language, especially the peculiar communication patterns that are sometimes developed between twins and are understandable only to them.

cryptophoric symbolism a type of REPRESENTATION expressed indirectly in the form of a METAPHOR. For example, a person may describe a difficult relationship in terms of an illegible map or a stuck door. In METAPHOR THERAPY patients are encouraged to alter their attitudes or perceptions by finding new metaphors. Also called **metaphoric symbolism**. [described by U.S. psychotherapist Richard Royal Kopp (1942–)]

cryptophthalmos syndrome a familial or hereditary disorder in which a child is born with skin covering the eyes. The anomaly may occur on one side or both. The eyes are usually present under the facial skin, which lacks eyelids, eyelashes, and, usually, tear ducts, and the individual may be able to discern light and colors. Hearing loss is common, as are ear anomalies. This syndrome often occurs with mental retardation.

cryptorchidism *n.* the condition of a male whose testes have not descended into the scrotum. It is not unusual and does not interfere with male hormonal function, but spermatogenesis is unlikely if the individual is not treated in childhood. Untreated, the condition is also associated with an increased incidence of testicular cancer in later life. See also ARRESTED TESTIS; HYPERMOBILE TESTES. —**cryptorchid** *adj., n.*

crysta *n.* see CRISTA.

crystal gazing 1. in certain alternative therapies, a technique in which an individual is instructed to visualize significant experiences, or produce associations, while staring into a glass ball, light bulb, or mirror. **2.** the occult practice in which a fortune teller or clairvoyant looks into a crystal ball in order to "see" visions of future or hidden events, usually in the life of a particular client. Also called **scrying**.

crystal healing a pseudoscientific medical practice in which the alleged power of certain crystals to affect the human energy field is used to treat physical or mental ailments. See REICHENBACH PHENOMENON. See also FAITH HEALING; PSYCHIC HEALING.

crystallization *n.* in social psychology, the STRENGTH OF AN ATTITUDE or, more specifically, the level of PERSISTENCE OF AN ATTITUDE over time and the level of RESISTANCE OF THE ATTITUDE to active attempts to change it.

crystallized abilities those abilities, such as vocabulary and cultural knowledge, that are a function of learning and experience in a specific culture. Crystallized abilities are believed to depend on physiological condition somewhat less than do FLUID ABILITIES; thus they may be better sustained in old age. They are also believed by some to derive from fluid abilities. See FLUID–CRYSTALLIZED INTELLIGENCE THEORY.

crystallized intelligence the form of intelligence that comprises CRYSTALLIZED ABILITIES. See FLUID–CRYSTALLIZED INTELLIGENCE THEORY.

Cs abbreviation for CONSCIOUS.

CS abbreviation for CONDITIONED STIMULUS.

CSAI abbreviation for COMPETITIVE STATE ANXIETY INVENTORY.

C-section *n.* abbreviation for CESAREAN SECTION.

CSERP abbreviation for CHEMOSENSORY EVENT-RELATED POTENTIAL.

CSES abbreviation for Collective Self-Esteem Scale (see COLLECTIVE SELF-ESTEEM).

CSF 1. abbreviation for CEREBROSPINAL FLUID. **2.** abbreviation for CONTRAST-SENSITIVITY FUNCTION.

CSR 1. abbreviation for COMBAT STRESS REACTIONS. **2.** abbreviation for CONTINUED-STAY REVIEW.

CT 1. abbreviation for COGNITIVE THERAPY. **2.** abbreviation for COMPUTED TOMOGRAPHY. **3.** abbreviation for CONDUCTION TIME.

CTA abbreviation for COMBINED TRANSCORTICAL APHASIA.

CTD abbreviation for cumulative trauma disorder (see REPETITIVE STRAIN INJURY).

CTI abbreviation for CONSTRUCTIVE THINKING INVENTORY.

CTS abbreviation for CARPAL TUNNEL SYNDROME.

CT scan abbreviation for COMPUTED TOMOGRAPHY scan.

CTT abbreviation for CLASSICAL TEST THEORY.

CTZ abbreviation for CHEMORECEPTOR TRIGGER ZONE.

cube model a three-dimensional model of the information cues that determine causal attributions. The cues are consistency (the extent to which observed behavior agrees with previous behavior), distinctiveness (the contextual, or situational, variability surrounding the behavior), and consensus (the extent to which others act similarly in the same situations). See ATTRIBUTION THEORY.

cubic difference tone see COMBINATION TONE.

cuckoldry *n.* sexual behavior in which a pair-bonded female mates with a male other than her partner. Only about 10% of bird species that are socially monogamous are genetically monogamous as well (see MONOGAMY). Males whose mates engage in EXTRAPAIR MATING assist in the rearing of resultant unrelated offspring. Females practicing cuckoldry may benefit from having progeny from genetically higher quality males: Female blackbirds that do this have more surviving offspring than monogamous blackbirds.

cuddling behavior holding close, a form of ATTACHMENT BEHAVIOR between individuals that is intended to convey affection or give comfort. In developmental psychology, it typically refers to such behavior between a parent or caregiver and a child.

cue *n.* **1.** a stimulus that serves to guide behavior. **2.** see RETRIEVAL CUE.

cue-controlled relaxation a technique in which a client is taught to associate a cue word with the practice of relaxing. See also APPLIED RELAXATION.

cue-dependent forgetting forgetting caused by the absence at testing of a stimulus (or cue) that was present when the learning occurred. See also CONTEXT-SPECIFIC LEARNING; MOOD-DEPENDENT MEMORY; STATE-DEPENDENT LEARNING.

cued panic attack in *DSM–IV–TR*, a PANIC ATTACK that occurs almost invariably upon exposure to, or in anticipation of, a specific situational trigger. For example, an individual with social phobia may have a panic attack as a result of just thinking about an upcoming presentation. Also called **situationally bound panic attack**. See also SITUATIONALLY PREDISPOSED PANIC ATTACK. Compare UNCUED PANIC ATTACK.

cued recall a memory experiment in which an item to be remembered is presented for study along with a CUE and the participant subsequently attempts to recall the item when given the cue.

cued speech speech that is supplemented with manual gestures for the benefit of people with hearing impairment. Hand positions are used to indicate certain phonemic distinctions that are not visible. For example, the distinction between /p/ and /t/ when spoken is visible, whereas the distinction between /t/ and /d/ is not. Unlike SIGN LANGUAGE and FINGER SPELLING, the hand positions are not adequate to convey communication without the accompanying speech.

cue exposure a BEHAVIOR THERAPY technique in which a client is exposed to stimuli that induce cravings for substances (e.g., alcohol, tobacco), while the therapist uses other techniques to reduce or eliminate the craving. This technique is most frequently used in substance abuse and smoking cessation programs. See also EXPOSURE THERAPY.

cue-overload principle the principle that a RETRIEVAL CUE starts to lose its effectiveness in aiding recall as items associated with that particular cue increase in number.

cue reversal changing the outcome of a stimulus so that it signals the opposite of that with which it was first associated. For example, after learning that stimulus A signals food and stimulus B does not, during cue reversal the outcomes are exchanged, and the individual must learn that stimulus B signals food and stimulus A does not.

cues to localization see BINAURAL CUES.

cul-de-sac *n.* see BLIND ALLEY.

culpability *n.* **1.** responsibility for an adverse outcome. **2.** in law, the state of being found criminally responsible for one's actions and subject to legal sanctions. See CRIMINAL RESPONSIBILITY. **—culpable** *adj.*

cult *n.* **1.** a religious or quasi-religious group characterized by unusual or atypical beliefs, seclusion from the outside world, and an authoritarian structure. Cults tend to be highly cohesive, well-organized, secretive, and hostile to nonmembers. **2.** the system of beliefs and rituals specific to a particular religious group. Also called **cultus**.

cult of personality exaggerated devotion to a charismatic political, religious, or other leader, often fomented by authoritarian figures or regimes as a means of maintaining their power. Also called **personality cult**.

cultural absolutism see CULTURAL UNIVERSALISM.

cultural adaptability the ability of individuals or groups to adjust and become accustomed to a different culture, such as that of a new community to which they have migrated. See ACCULTURATION.

cultural anthropology see ANTHROPOLOGY.

cultural assimilation see ACCULTURATION.

cultural blindness the inability to understand how particular matters might be viewed by people of a different culture because of a rigid adherence to the views, attitudes, and values of one's own culture.

cultural change see CULTURE CHANGE.

cultural competency **1.** possession of the skills and knowledge that are appropriate for and specific to a given culture. **2.** the capacity to function effectively in cultural settings other than one's own. This will usually involve a recognition of the diversity both between and within cultures, a capacity for cultural self-assessment, and a willingness to adapt personal behaviors and practices. See also CULTURAL SENSITIVITY.

cultural conserve anything (e.g., a legend, tradition, or artifact) that has the effect of preserving valuable cultural memories, such as skills, discoveries, concepts, or moral values. See also CULTURAL HERITAGE; HERITAGE. [introduced by Austrian-born U.S. psychiatrist Jacob L. Moreno (1890–1974)]

cultural deprivation **1.** lack of opportunity to participate in the cultural offerings of the larger society due to such factors as economic deprivation, substandard living conditions, or discrimination. See PSEUDORETARDATION. **2.** loss of identification with one's cultural heritage as a result of assimilation into a larger or dominant culture. See DECULTURATION. **3.** lack of culturally stimulating phenomena in one's environment.

cultural determinism the theory or premise that individual and group character patterns are produced largely by a given society's economic, social, political, and religious organization. See NATIONAL CHARACTER. See also DETERMINISM; SOCIAL DETERMINISM.

cultural drift the gradual, uncontrolled changing of a culture, with its distinctive norms, values, and patterns of behavior, over time. Also called **culture drift**. See also CULTURE CHANGE; SOCIAL CHANGE; SOCIAL EVOLUTION.

cultural epoch theory the theory, formerly influential but now largely discredited, that all human cultures pass through the same stages of social and economic organization in the same order. In most versions of the theory this involves progress from a hunting-based society through pastoral, agricultural, and early industrial epochs to the modern developed world, with each stage being seen as more complex, organized, and secular than previous stages. See MODERNIZATION; PRIMITIVE; RECAPITULATION THEORY; SOCIAL DARWINISM.

cultural ergonomics a specialty area of ERGONOMICS that focuses on cultural factors relevant to human performance and the design and evaluation of work systems. Such factors as national culture, ethnicity, gender, and class are assessed as part of the task of creating systems that can be used efficiently and safely by a particular culture or subculture. See also INDIGENOUS RESEARCHER; POPULATION STEREOTYPE.

cultural-familial mental retardation mental retardation, usually mild, that occurs in the absence of any known organic cause and is therefore attributed to hereditary or early (preschool) environmental factors. Hereditary factors include natural variation, in the absence of genetic anomalies, in intellectual abilities among members of populations. Also called **familial retardation**; **sociocultural mental retardation**.

cultural genocide destruction of a culture's heritage, values, and practices, usually by another, dominant cultural group.

cultural heritage the customs, language, values, and skills that are handed down from each generation to the next in a particular cultural group and help to maintain its sense of identity. The cultural heritage also includes specific technological or artistic achievements. See HERITAGE; SOCIAL HERITAGE; SOCIAL TRANSMISSION.

cultural integration see ACCULTURATION.

cultural lag see CULTURE LAG.

cultural learning the transmission of acquired information and behavior both within and across generations with a high degree of fidelity. Cultural learning theory proposes three stagelike levels of cultural learning: IMITATIVE LEARNING, INSTRUCTED LEARNING, and COLLABORATIVE LEARNING. [proposed by U.S. psychologist Michael Tomasello (1950–) and colleagues]

culturally different describing individuals who are members of a subculture that differs substantially from the larger society.

culturally disadvantaged describing children whose environments hinder their social and intellectual development. See CULTURAL DEPRIVATION.

culturally loaded items test questions that cannot be correctly answered unless the participants are sufficiently familiar with their cultural or subcultural meanings. Culturally loaded items tend to bias a test in favor of the group or social class from whose experience they are drawn. It often is difficult to discern cultural loadings just from looking at test items, as the effects of culture may be subtle. See CULTURE-FAIR TESTS.

cultural monism a view or perspective holding that MULTICULTURALISM operates against social cohesion and that ethnic and other minorities should therefore be encouraged to assimilate with the dominant culture.

cultural norm a societal rule, value, or standard that delineates an accepted and appropriate behavior within a culture. See also NORMATIVE INFLUENCE; SOCIAL NORMS.

cultural parallelism in anthropology, the development of analogous cultural patterns, such as sun worship, in geographically separate groups assumed to have had no communication with each other.

cultural pluralism see MULTICULTURALISM.

cultural process the process by which ethnic and social values are transmitted across generations and modified by the influences prevailing over each.

cultural psychology an interdisciplinary extension of general psychology concerned with those psychological processes that are inherently organized by culture. It is a heterogeneous class of perspectives that focus on explaining how human psychological functions are culturally constituted through various forms of relations between people and their social contexts. As a discipline, cultural psychology relates to cultural anthropology, sociology, semiotics, language philosophy, and culture studies. Within psychology, cultural psychology relates most closely to cross-cultural, social, developmental, and cognitive issues.

cultural relativism the view that attitudes, behaviors, values, concepts, and achievements must be understood in the light of their own cultural milieu and not judged according to the standards of a different culture. In psychology, the relativist position questions the universal application of psychological theory, research, therapeutic techniques, and clinical approaches, since those used or developed in one culture may not be appropriate or applicable to another. See also RELATIVISM. Compare CULTURAL UNIVERSALISM.

cultural residue see CULTURE LAG.

cultural sensitivity awareness and appreciation of the values, norms, and beliefs characteristic of a particular cultural, ethnic, or racial group, accompanied by a willingness to adapt one's behavior accordingly. See CULTURAL COMPETENCY.

cultural specificity of emotions the finding that the elicitors and the expressions of emotions differ dramatically in members of different cultures and societies. Compare UNIVERSALITY OF EMOTIONS.

cultural test bias bias of a test in favor of those individuals from certain cultures at the expense of those individuals from other cultures. The bias may be in the content of the items, in the format of the items, or in the very act of taking a test itself. See also CULTURALLY LOADED ITEMS.

cultural transmission the processes by which customs, beliefs, rites, and knowledge are imparted to successive generations within a society.

cultural universalism the view that the values, concepts, and behaviors characteristic of diverse cultures can be viewed, understood, and judged according to universal standards. Such a view involves the rejection, at least in part, of CULTURAL RELATIVISM. Also called **cultural absolutism**.

culture *n.* **1.** the distinctive customs, values, beliefs, knowledge, art, and language of a society or a community. **2.** the characteristic attitudes and behaviors of a particular group within society, such as a profession, social class, or age group. See also COUNTERCULTURE; SUBCULTURE; YOUTH CULTURE. **—cultural** *adj.*

culture-bias theory the theory that measurements of intelligence may be biased in favor of members of certain cultural groups and against members of other cultural groups.

culture bound describing attitudes, practices, or behaviors that are the products of a particular culture and that are not widely found in other cultures.

culture-bound syndrome a pattern of mental illness and abnormal behavior that is unique to a small ethnic or cultural population and does not conform to Western classifications of psychiatric disorders. Culture-bound syndromes include, among others, AMOK, AMURAKH, BANGUNGUT, HSIEH-PING, IMU, JUMPING FRENCHMEN OF MAINE SYNDROME, KORO, LATAH, MAL DE PELEA, MYRIACHIT, PIBLOKTO, SUSTO, VOODOO DEATH, and WINDIGO. Also called **culture-specific syndrome**.

culture change modification of a community's culture, whether gradually over time (see CULTURAL DRIFT) or more rapidly as the result of contact with other cultures (see ACCULTURATION; DECULTURATION). Also called **cultural change**. See also SOCIAL CHANGE.

culture clash a situation in which the diverging attitudes, morals, opinions, or customs of two dissimilar cultures or subcultures are revealed. This may occur, for example, when people in different professions, such as academics and business people, collaborate on a project. See also CULTURE CONFLICT; CULTURE SHOCK.

culture complex a distinctive pattern of activities, beliefs, rites, and traditions associated with one central feature of life in a particular culture. An example is the cluster of activities, ceremonies, folklore, songs, and stories associated with the hunting and use of the buffalo by Native American peoples. Compare CULTURE TRAIT. Also called **culture pattern**.

culture conflict 1. tension or competition between different cultures. It often results in the weakening of a minority group's adherence to cultural practices and beliefs as these are superseded by those of a dominant or adjoining culture. Also called **intergroup culture conflict**. **2.** the conflicting loyalties experienced by individuals who endorse the cultural beliefs of their subgroup but are also drawn to the practices and beliefs of the dominant culture. Also called **internal culture conflict**. See CULTURE SHOCK.

culture drift see CULTURAL DRIFT.

culture epochs see CULTURAL EPOCH THEORY.

culture-fair tests intelligence tests based on common human experience and alleged to be relatively fair with respect to special cultural influences. Unlike the standard intelligence tests, which reflect predominantly middle-class experience, these tests are designed to apply across social lines and to permit fair comparisons among people from different cultures. Nonverbal, nonacademic items are used, such as matching identical forms, selecting a design that completes a given series, or drawing human figures. Studies have shown, however, that any test reflects certain cultural norms in some degree, and hence may tend to favor members of certain cultures over members of others. For example, "a circle in one place may be associated with the sun, in another with a copper coin, and [in] still another with a wheel" (D. WECHSLER, 1966). See also CROSS-CULTURAL TESTING.

culture-free tests intelligence tests designed completely to eliminate cultural bias by constructing questions that contain either no environmental influences or no environmental influences that reflect any specific culture. However, the creation of such a test is probably impossible. See CULTURE-FAIR TESTS.

culture lag 1. the tendency for some aspects of a culture to change at a slower rate than others, resulting in the retention of beliefs, customs, and values that no longer seem appropriate to altered economic or technological conditions. **2.** a specific cultural survival of this kind. Compare CULTURE LEAD. Also called **cultural lag**; **cultural residue**.

culture lead a particular aspect of a culture that appears to be changing faster than the culture as a whole. Technological and economic changes are often of this kind. Compare CULTURE LAG.

culture of honor a CULTURAL NORM in a region, nation, or ethnic group prescribing violence as the preferred reaction to an insult or other threat to a person's honor. It has been held to account for regional and national differences in violent crime rates, for example, to explain the relatively high rates of homicide in the U.S. South, Sardinia, and Colombia. A related concept is **subculture of violence**, used by U.S. criminologist Marvin Wolfgang (1924–1998) and Italian criminologist Franco Ferracuti to explain the relatively high rates of violent crime in certain minority populations in poverty-stricken urban areas.

culture pattern see CULTURE COMPLEX.

culture-relevant tests tests that are designed specifically to be relevant to a given cultural context. These tests typically differ at least somewhat from one culture to another beyond mere differences in language, and they have been carefully screened for appropriateness.

culture shock feelings of inner tension or conflict experienced by an individual or group that has been suddenly thrust into an alien culture or that experiences loyalties to two different cultures.

culture-specific syndrome see CULTURE-BOUND SYNDROME.

culture trait any basic belief, practice, technique, or object that can be said to identify a given culture in some aspect of its economic, political, social, or religious organization, such as a specific agricultural practice, law, ritual, belief about child-rearing, or architectural design. Compare CULTURE COMPLEX.

cumulative continuity the process by which an individual's actions produce results that accumulate over time and move him or her along specific life trajectories.

cumulative curve a graph of the cumulative value of a dependent variable.

cumulative educational advantage an advantageous position that is achieved as the result of knowledge acquired over a period of time.

cumulative frequency distribution a graphical representation of a batch of data that displays as the *y*-axis the number of cases that fall at or below a particular value or interval (the *x*-axis).

cumulative probability distribution 1. a graphical representation of a batch of data that displays as the *y*-axis the probability that a case picked at random from that batch will have a value less than or equal to the corresponding value on the *x*-axis. **2.** a representation of a probability density function, f(*x*), given by

$$x\, y = \Pr(X \le x) = \int_{-\infty}^{x} f(x)dx.$$

cumulative record a continuous record to which new data are added. In CONDITIONING, for example, a cumulative record is a graph showing the cumulative number of responses over a continuous period of time. It is often used in such contexts to display performance of FREE-OPERANT behavior under SCHEDULES OF REINFORCEMENT and provides a direct and continuous indicator of the rate of response.

cumulative rehearsal a strategy for retaining information in short-term memory in which a person repeats the most recently presented item (e.g., a word) and then rehearses it (see REHEARSAL) with all the items that have been presented before it, thus reviewing earlier items upon each presentation of a new item. Cumulative rehearsal is associated with higher levels of free-recall performance than is PASSIVE REHEARSAL. Also called **active rehearsal**.

cumulative response curve a cumulative record, in the form of a graph, of the responses in a conditioning experiment. Lack of response is indicated by a flat horizontal line, whereas faster responses are indicated by steeper slopes away from the horizontal. Also called **cumulative response record**.

cumulative scale an ATTITUDE SCALE consisting of multiple verbal statements related to an ATTITUDE OB-

JECT that can be ordered to reflect increasing levels of positive evaluation. Endorsement of a particular statement implies endorsement of all statements less extreme than that statement. Although generally used to measure attitudes, this type of scale can also be used to assess other properties of a target of judgment. Also called **Guttman scale; scalogram**. [first described in 1944 by U.S. experimental psychologist Louis Guttman (1916–1987]

cumulative trauma disorder (CTD) see REPETITIVE STRAIN INJURY.

cuneate *adj.* wedge-shaped. See CUNEUS.

cuneate fasciculus the lateral portion of either of the DORSAL COLUMNS of the spinal cord, which is wedge-shaped in transverse section. It is composed of ascending fibers that terminate in the NUCLEUS CUNEATUS of the medulla oblongata. Also called **fasciculus cuneatus**. See also GRACILE FASCICULUS.

cuneate nucleus see NUCLEUS CUNEATUS.

cuneate tubercle a swelling at the upper end of the CUNEATE FASCICULUS that contains the NUCLEUS CUNEATUS, which receives fibers from sensory nerves of the upper part of the body. The cuneate tubercle is the largest of the three nuclear swellings on the dorsal surface of the MEDULLA OBLONGATA; together with the GRACILE TUBERCLE, it forms the origin of the MEDIAL LEMNISCUS.

cuneus *n.* (*pl.* **cunei**) the wedge-shaped portion of the OCCIPITAL LOBE on the medial surface of each cerebral hemisphere above the posterior CALCARINE FISSURE.

cunnilingus *n.* stimulation of the external female genital organs (i.e., the clitoris and vulva) with the mouth or tongue. Also called **cunnilinctio**; **cunnilinction**; **cunnilinctus**; **cunnilingam**. See also OROGENITAL ACTIVITY.

cupula *n.* a gelatinous cap that forms part of the crista within the ampulla at the end of a SEMICIRCULAR CANAL.

curare *n.* any of various toxic plant extracts, especially extracts from plants of the genus *Strychnos*. Curare and related compounds exert their effects by blocking the activity of ACETYLCHOLINE at neuromuscular junctions, resulting in paralysis. Curare has a long ethnopharmacological history among indigenous peoples of the Amazon and Orinoco river basins, where it was applied to the tips of arrows to paralyze prey. It was brought to Europe in the 16th century by explorers of South America, but was not introduced into clinical use until the 1930s, when it was used to treat patients with tetanus and other spastic disorders. It has also been used in experiments showing that stimulus–response associations can be formed in paralyzed animals. The development of neuromuscular blocking agents with more predictable pharmacological profiles led to the abandonment of curare as a clinical agent.

curative factors model a model that seeks to identify those elements present in therapeutic groups that aid and promote personal growth and adjustment. U.S. psychologist Irwin Yalom (1931–) identified 10–15 curative factors, including the installation of hope, UNIVERSALITY, the imparting of information, altruism, and interpersonal learning.

curiosity *n.* the impulse or desire to investigate, observe, or gather information, particularly when the material is novel or interesting. This drive appears spontaneously in animals and in young children, who use sensory exploration and motor manipulation to inspect, bite, handle, taste, or smell practically everything in the immediate environment. See EXPLORATORY DRIVE. **—curious** *adj.*

current material information about a client's present feelings, interpersonal relationships, and life events that is used in understanding that person's PSYCHODYNAMICS, especially by contrasting it with data from past experiences.

curricular field experience knowledge gained from on-the-job activity or observation in a specific area of professional interest or academic pursuit. It often fulfills partial requirements for a course of study or an academic course.

curriculum *n.* **1.** a set of required or prescribed courses of study, across many subjects or within a specific subject area, that a student must fulfill in order to meet the requirements of a particular degree or educational program. **2.** all of the coursework available at an educational institution or within a department of that institution. **3.** the total combined unit of coursework constituting a specialized major or minor area of emphasis, most often in a college setting.

curriculum-based assessment 1. a complete, broad evaluation profile that reveals the degree of student mastery of a given defined body of content. The evaluation includes teacher-based testing (see CURRICULUM-BASED MEASUREMENT), classroom observation and interactions, standardized tests when relevant, and any other method of evaluation that yields data that can contribute to the overall assessment profile. **2.** data that help determine specific standards, such as those involved in individualized educational planning, direct performance referrals, and other forms of systematic planning relative to student progress.

curriculum-based measurement a narrow evaluation of student performance based on the material that has actually been taught, as opposed to CURRICULUM-BASED ASSESSMENTS, which are much broader and compare students to state, national, or other standard norms.

curriculum development the process of designing materials for instruction that will be used within a particular school district, school, or classroom. This process takes account of several important factors: The curriculum must not conflict with the standard practice adopted by similar programs of study; it must identify and articulate core concepts; and it must include an empirical base as a foundation for the actual learning content, thus facilitating teaching strategies, assessment, and accountability.

curve fitting any of various statistical techniques for obtaining a curve that graphically represents a given set of data.

curvilinear correlation a functional relationship between variables that is not of a straight-line form when depicted graphically.

curvilinear regression model see NONLINEAR REGRESSION MODEL.

Cushing's syndrome a group of signs and symptoms related to a chronic overproduction of corticosteroid hormones, mainly CORTISOL, by the adrenal cortex. The condition occurs most commonly in women and is usually associated with a tumor of the adrenal or pituitary gland. Cushing's syndrome is characterized by a "moon face" due to fat deposits, "buffalo hump" fat pads on the trunk, hypertension, glucose intolerance, and psychiatric disturbances. [Harvey W. **Cushing** (1869–1939), U.S. surgeon]

-cusis *suffix* see -ACUSIA.

custodial care 1. care rendered to a patient with prolonged mental or physical disability that includes assisted daily living (e.g., the regular feeding and washing of bedridden patients) but typically not mental health services themselves. **2.** confinement in such institutions as prisons and military correctional facilities that place restrictions on individuals' liberty under the rules of law and that protect and monitor the individual or protect others from the individual's violent and harmful tendencies or potential.

custodial case a court case concerning who should maintain legal custody of a child. See CHILD CUSTODY.

custom *n.* a traditional behavior, ritual, or action that is transmitted through the generations and is defined by a culture as appropriate or desirable for a particular situation.

customary, prevailing, and reasonable fees (**CPR fees**) a criterion invoked in reimbursing health care providers. It is determined by profiling the prevailing fees in a geographic area. Also called **usual, customary, and reasonable** (**UCR**) **fees**.

customer-relationship management the practice by companies of anticipating the future needs of their customers based on knowledge of past purchasing behaviors. Databases of information about consumers are used for this purpose.

cutaneous experience a sensation resulting from the stimulation of receptors in the skin. Such sensations include warmth, coldness, tickle, itch, pinprick (see PRICK EXPERIENCE), sharp pain, and dull pain. Also called **cutaneous sensation**; **dermal sensation**.

cutaneous perception perception of stimuli via activation of receptors in the skin. See CUTANEOUS SENSE.

cutaneous perception of color see DERMO-OPTICAL PERCEPTION.

cutaneous-pupillary reflex dilation of the pupil caused by scratching the skin of the cheek or chin. Also called **pupillary-skin reflex**.

cutaneous receptive field the area of skin being supplied by specific peripheral nerves and localized synaptic distribution in the central nervous system. See also RECEPTIVE FIELD.

cutaneous receptor a receptor organ in the skin that is responsible for CUTANEOUS EXPERIENCE. Cutaneous receptors include PACINIAN CORPUSCLES, BASKET ENDINGS, MEISSNER'S CORPUSCLES, and MERKEL'S TACTILE DISKS.

cutaneous sense any of the senses that are dependent on receptors in the skin sensitive to contact, pressure, vibration, temperature, or pain. Also called **skin sense**. See PRESSURE SENSE; TEMPERATURE SENSE; TOUCH SENSE.

cutoff point a numerical value that divides a DISTRIBUTION into two distinct parts.

cutting *n.* the act of cutting one's wrists or the inside of one's forearms, often accompanied by a sense of heightened arousal and little sensation of pain. This occurs most frequently in the context of BORDERLINE PERSONALITY DISORDER and occasionally in MAJOR DEPRESSIVE EPISODES.

CV 1. abbreviation for CARDIOVASCULAR. **2.** abbreviation for curriculum vitae.

CVA abbreviation for CEREBROVASCULAR ACCIDENT.

CVLT abbreviation for CALIFORNIA VERBAL LEARNING TEST.

CVLT–C abbreviation for California Verbal Learning Test for Children. See CALIFORNIA VERBAL LEARNING TEST.

CVLT–II abbreviation for California Verbal Learning Test–II. See CALIFORNIA VERBAL LEARNING TEST.

CVS abbreviation for CHORIONIC VILLUS SAMPLING.

cyanopsia *n.* see CHROMATOPSIA.

cybernetic epistemology a study that addresses the philosophical issues of EPISTEMOLOGY in terms of computation, often by making use of computational KNOWLEDGE REPRESENTATION and other techniques of ARTIFICIAL INTELLIGENCE. Grounding (how a system incorporates meaning into its problem solving), SCAFFOLDING (how a system uses its world as an essential component of its problem solving), and embodiment (how a system is defined as part of, and integrated into, an environment) are essential components of this study. Also called **computational epistemology**.

cybernetics *n.* the scientific study of communication and control as applied to machines and living organisms. It includes the study of self-regulation mechanisms, as in thermostats or feedback circuits in the nervous system, as well as transmission and self-correction of information in both computers and human communications. Cybernetics was formerly used to describe research in ARTIFICIAL INTELLIGENCE. [first defined in 1948 by U.S. mathematician Norbert Wiener (1894–1964)] **—cybernetic** *adj.*

cybernetic theory the study of how machines or other artificial systems can be made to regulate and guide themselves in the manner of living organisms. Its main application is the design of computer-controlled automated systems in manufacturing, transport, telecommunications, and other fields. The most widely used aspect of cybernetic theory is the self-regulatory model known as the FEEDBACK LOOP. [developed by U.S. mathematician Norbert Wiener (1894–1964)]

cycle of violence a conceptual framework for understanding the persistence of battering relationships. The cycle has three phases: (a) a "honeymoon phase," in which the batterer treats the battered partner lovingly; (b) a "tension build-up phase," in which the batterer begins to display irritability and anger toward the battered partner; and (c) the violence phase, in which battering occurs. The phases are then proposed to recycle. As a battering relationship persists over time, the honeymoon phases shorten, and the tension-building and violence phases lengthen. Also called **cycle of abuse**. [proposed in 1979 by U.S. clinical and forensic psychologist Lenore Walker (1942–)]

cyclic *adj.* characterized by alternating phases. Also called **cyclical**.

cyclic adenosine monophosphate see CYCLIC AMP.

cyclical vomiting syndrome recurrent, severe episodes of vomiting that may last for hours or days but are separated by intervals of completely normal health. Stress may be an important precipitant of cyclical vomiting, which occurs frequently in children.

cyclic AMP (**cAMP**; **cyclic adenosine monophosphate**) a SECOND MESSENGER that is involved in the activities of DOPAMINE, NOREPINEPHRINE, and SEROTONIN in transmitting signals at nerve synapses. Also called **adenosine 3′,5′-monophosphate**.

cyclic GMP (**cGMP**; **cyclic guanosine monophosphate**) a SECOND MESSENGER that is common in POSTSYNAPTIC neurons.

cyclic illness 1. any disorder characterized by alternating phases. **2.** bipolar I disorder (see BIPOLAR DISORDERS) in which both MAJOR DEPRESSIVE EPISODES and MANIC EPISODES occur alternately.

cyclic nucleotide a substance, such as CYCLIC AMP or CYCLIC GMP, that functions as a SECOND MESSENGER in cells to transduce an incoming signal, such as a hormone or neurotransmitter, into specific activity within the cell.

cyclobenzaprine *n.* a drug used for the treatment of

acute skeletal muscle spasm (see MUSCLE RELAXANTS). Structurally related to the tricyclic antidepressants, it has many features in common with them, including sedation and significant ANTICHOLINERGIC EFFECTS. Low doses are moderately effective in treating FIBROMYALGIA SYNDROME. Because of its resemblance to the tricyclic drugs, cyclobenzaprine should not be taken concurrently with MONOAMINE OXIDASE INHIBITORS. U.S. trade name: **Flexeril**.

cycloid psychosis an atypical and controversial psychiatric disorder with three forms: **motility**, **confusional**, and **anxiety–happiness**. Symptoms, which resemble those of both a SCHIZOAFFECTIVE DISORDER and a PSYCHOTIC DISORDER NOT OTHERWISE SPECIFIED, follow a phasically recurring course and may change rapidly. [as modified in 1957 by German psychiatrist Karl Leonhard (1904–1988) from the original 1924 conceptualization of German neuropsychiatrist Karl Kleist (1879–1960)]

cyclopean eye a theoretical eye, located on the midline between the real eyes, that has access to the functions of both eyes and is used in descriptions of space perception and eye movements.

cyclophoria *n.* an imbalance of the extrinsic eye muscles in which one eye deviates when not focused on an object.

cyclopia *n.* a hereditary birth defect transmitted as an autosomal recessive trait and characterized by the merging of the two eye orbits into a single cavity that contains one eye. The pituitary gland is usually absent. Cyclopia is associated with CHROMOSOME-13 TRISOMY, GROUP G MONOSOMY, and 18p– syndromes. Also called **Fraser–François syndrome**; **Fraser syndrome**.

cyclosporine (**cyclosporin**) *n.* an immunosuppressive agent used primarily to prevent rejection of organ transplants but also used in the treatment of some autoimmune disorders, such as inflammatory bowel disease and severe atopic dermatitis. It is extensively metabolized by the CYTOCHROME P450 3A4 enzyme, and accordingly has numerous potential interactions with psychotropic drugs metabolized via the same enzyme (e.g., clonidine, nefazodone, St. John's wort). Depression, anxiety, and other psychological disturbances are rare side effects. U.S. trade name (among others): **Sandimmune**.

cyclothymic disorder in *DSM–IV–TR*, a MOOD DISORDER characterized by periods of hypomanic symptoms and periods of depressive symptoms that occur over the course of at least 2 years (1 year in children and adolescents), during which any symptom-free periods must last no longer than 2 months. The symptoms are those of a MAJOR DEPRESSIVE EPISODE or a HYPOMANIC EPISODE, but the number, duration, and severity of these symptoms do not meet the full criteria for a major depressive episode or a hypomanic episode. Also called **cyclothymia**.

cyclotropia *n.* see STRABISMUS.

Cylert *n.* a trade name for PEMOLINE.

cyproheptadine *n.* a drug that acts as a HISTAMINE ANTAGONIST and SEROTONIN ANTAGONIST and is used for the the treatment of allergic symptoms (e.g., runny nose and watery eyes), appetite stimulation, and relief of migraine headaches. U.S. trade name (among others): **Periactin**.

cystathionine synthetase deficiency see HOMOCYSTINURIA.

cystathioninuria *n.* an inherited disorder of amino acid metabolism marked by deficiency of the enzyme cystathionase. The effects include vascular, skeletal, and ocular abnormalities. Mental retardation occurs in less than 50% of cases, often accompanied by behavioral disorders. Also called **gamma-cystathionase deficiency**.

cyto- *combining form* cells.

cytoarchitecture *n.* the arrangement of cells in organs and tissues, particularly those in the NEOCORTEX. The different types of cortical cells are organized in CORTICAL LAYERS and zones. The number of layers varies in different brain areas, but a typical section of neocortex shows six distinct layers. Differences in cytoarchitecture have been used to divide the neocortex into 50 or more regions, many of which differ in function. The scientific study of the cytoarchitecture of an organ is called **cytoarchitectonics**. Also called **architectonic structure**. See also BRODMANN'S AREA. **—cytoarchitectural** *adj.*

cytochrome oxidase an enzyme that occurs in the inner membrane of MITOCHONDRIA and is important in aerobic respiration. "Blobs" of cytochrome oxidase activity have been demonstrated in visual cortex (see CYTOCHROME OXIDASE BLOB).

cytochrome oxidase blob (**CO blob**) a small patch of neurons in the STRIATE CORTEX with greater than background levels of CYTOCHROME OXIDASE activity. Neurons in the CO blobs are sensitive to the wavelength of a visual stimulus. Also called **blob**.

cytochrome P450 (**CYP**) a group of proteins located in the smooth ENDOPLASMIC RETICULUM of liver and other cells that, in combination with other oxidative enzymes, is responsible for the metabolism of various chemicals, including many psychotropic drugs. Approximately 50 cytochrome P450 enzymes (so named because their reduced forms show a spectroscopic absorption peak at 450 nm) are currently identified as being active in humans, of which cytochromes belonging to the CYP2D6 subclass, CYP2C variants, and CYP3A4/5 subclass predominate. Cytochromes are mainly active in Phase I DRUG METABOLISM; by donating an atom of oxygen, they tend to make parent drugs more water soluble and therefore more easily excreted. Because numerous drugs are metabolized via the same cytochrome, these enzymes are important in DRUG INTERACTIONS.

cytogenetic map a type of chromosome map that depicts and enumerates the pattern of differentially staining bands produced when the chromosomes are treated with certain cytological stains. These bands are correlated with the physical location of particular genes. See also MAPPING OF GENES.

cytokine *n.* any of a variety of small proteins or peptides that are released by cells as signals to those or other cells. Each type stimulates a target cell that has a specific receptor for that cytokine. Cytokines mediate many IMMUNE RESPONSES, including proliferation and differentiation of lymphocytes, inflammation, allergies, and fever.

cytology *n.* the branch of biology that deals with the development, structure, and function of cells. **—cytological** *adj.* **—cytologist** *n.*

cytomegalovirus *n.* a virus of the herpes group. Infection usually causes no symptoms and no long-term health implications, but if acquired during pregnancy it may have serious consequences for the fetus, such as MICROCEPHALY, jaundice, liver and spleen infection, pneumonia, deafness, PSYCHOMOTOR RETARDATION, and mental retardation.

Cytomel *n.* a trade name for LIOTHYRONINE.

cytoplasm *n.* the contents of a cell excluding the NUCLEUS. **—cytoplasmic** *adj.*

cytosine (symbol: C) *n.* a pyrimidine compound that is one of the four bases in DNA and RNA constituting the elements of the GENETIC CODE.

Dd

d′ symbol for D PRIME.

DA 1. abbreviation for DEVELOPMENTAL AGE. **2.** abbreviation for DOPAMINE.

dabbler *n.* in magic and the esoteric arts, a person who engages in occult practices for superficial or frivolous reasons. **—dabble** *vb.*

Da Costa's syndrome an anxiety state identified in soldiers during the American Civil War (1861–1865) in which heart palpitations were the most prominent symptom. It is now recognized as a form of PANIC DISORDER observed in soldiers during the stress of combat and marked by fatigue, heart palpitations, chest pain, and breathing difficulty. Also called **neurocirculatory asthenia; soldier's heart**. See also EFFORT SYNDROME. [Jacob Méndes **Da Costa** (1833–1900), U.S. surgeon]

D'Acosta's syndrome see ALTITUDE SICKNESS. [José de **Acosta** (1539–1600), Spanish geographer]

dactylology *n.* the communication of ideas by means of signs formed with the fingers. See FINGER SPELLING; SIGN LANGUAGE.

DAD abbreviation for DEVICE FOR AUTOMATED DESENSITIZATION.

DAF abbreviation for DELAYED AUDITORY FEEDBACK.

DAH test abbreviation for Machover Draw-a-House Test. See MACHOVER DRAW-A-PERSON TEST.

DAI abbreviation for DIFFUSE AXONAL INJURY.

daily biological rhythm see CIRCADIAN RHYTHM.

daily living see ACTIVITIES OF DAILY LIVING.

daily-living aid see ASSISTIVE TECHNOLOGY.

Dale's law the concept, now known to be incorrect for many neurons, that each TERMINAL BUTTON of a neuron contains only one kind of neurotransmitter. Also called **Dale's principle**. [Henry Hallet **Dale** (1875–1968), British neurophysiologist]

Dallenbach stimulator a device for providing controlled thermal stimulation to the skin. [Karl M. **Dallenbach** (1887–1941), U.S. psychologist]

Dalmane *n.* a trade name for FLURAZEPAM.

damage-risk criteria (**DRC**) the levels and durations of sound exposures that are likely to cause permanent hearing loss. For example, according to the Occupational Safety and Health Administration (OSHA) standards, a continuous 8-hour noise exposure of less than 85 dB is acceptable, as is a continuous half-hour exposure of less than 110 dB. See SOUND-LEVEL METER.

damping *n.* a diminution of the amplitude of vibrations, often as a result of absorption of energy (e.g., electricity, sound) by the surrounding medium. In speech and singing, it refers to the tension and elongation of the vocal cords beyond the normal maximal level in an attempt to reach still higher tones on the ascending scale.

dance epidemic a phenomenon in which apparently spontaneous and compulsive dancing spreads through CONTAGION to affect a large segment of a population across a wide geographic area. The term is particularly associated with several instances of odd, manic, and compulsive dancing reported in Italy in the 10th century and in portions of Europe during the period of the bubonic plague (14th and 15th centuries). See CHOREOMANIA.

dance therapy the use of various forms of rhythmic movement—classical, modern, folk, or ballroom dancing; exercises to music; and the like—as a therapeutic technique to help individuals achieve greater body awareness and social interaction and enhance their psychological and physical functioning. See also MOVEMENT THERAPY. [pioneered in 1942 by U.S. dance professional Marian Chace (1896–1970)]

dancing language see BEE COMMUNICATION.

dancing madness see CHOREOMANIA.

dancing mania see CHOREOMANIA.

dancing mouse a strain of mice displaying behavior that resembles dancing. Mice of this strain have a genetic defect that causes degeneration of the HAIR CELLS of the inner ear. This degeneration produces deafness and impaired functioning of the VESTIBULAR SYSTEM of the ear, which is thought to cause the dancelike behavior.

Dandy–Walker syndrome a congenital anomaly involving a large cyst formed in the posterior region of the fetal brain. The syndrome is characterized by (a) blockage of the fourth ventricle, resulting in increased volume of brain fluid (see HYDROCEPHALUS), and (b) complete or partial AGENESIS (failure to develop) of the middle portion of the cerebellum (the vermis) because of its displacement by the cyst. [Walter **Dandy** (1886–1946), U.S. neurosurgeon; Arthur Earl **Walker** (1907–1995), U.S. neurologist]

dangerousness *n.* the state in which individuals become likely to do harm either to themselves or to others, representing a threat to their own or other people's safety. **—dangerous** *adj.*

dantrolene *n.* a MUSCLE RELAXANT whose primary action is directly on skeletal muscles; it also indirectly affects the central nervous system as a secondary action. Dantrolene is used in the treatment of muscular spasm associated with spinal cord injury, stroke, cerebral palsy, and multiple sclerosis, as well as with NEUROLEPTIC MALIGNANT SYNDROME. U.S. trade name: **Dantrium**.

Daoism *n.* see TAOISM.

DAP test abbreviation for MACHOVER DRAW-A-PERSON TEST.

dark adaptation the ability of the eye to adjust to conditions of low illumination by means of an increased sensitivity to light. The bulk of the process takes 30 min and involves expansion of the pupils and retinal alterations, specifically the regeneration of RHODOPSIN and IODOPSIN. See also ROD–CONE BREAK. Compare LIGHT ADAPTATION.

dark-adaptation curve a graph of light sensitivity over time for an individual asked to detect dim flashes in total darkness. See also ROD–CONE BREAK.

dark cell see TYPE I CELL.

dark light the sensation of light evoked by the spontaneous activity of retinal photoreceptors, which occurs even in the absence of light.

darkness fear see FEAR OF DARKNESS.

Darvocet *n.* a trade name for the analgesic combination PROPOXYPHENE and ACETAMINOPHEN.

Darvon *n.* a trade name for PROPOXYPHENE.

Darwinian algorithm in EVOLUTIONARY DEVELOPMENTAL PSYCHOLOGY, an innate domain-specific cognitive program that evolved to accomplish specific adaptive functions. An example is the cognitive mechanism for face recognition. [Charles **Darwin** (1809–1892), British naturalist]

Darwinian fitness the relative success of a particular organism or genotype in producing viable offspring, which is determined by NATURAL SELECTION. [Charles **Darwin**]

Darwinian psychology see EVOLUTIONARY PSYCHOLOGY. [Charles **Darwin**]

Darwinian reflex a grasping response shown by newborn infants. See GRASP REFLEX. [Charles **Darwin**]

Darwinism *n.* the theory of evolution by NATURAL SELECTION, as originally proposed by British naturalists Charles Darwin (1809–1882) and Alfred Russel Wallace (1823–1913). In the 20th century it was modified, as **neo-Darwinism**, to account for genetic mechanisms of heredity, particularly the sources of genetic variation upon which natural selection works. See also SURVIVAL OF THE FITTEST.

DAS abbreviation for DIFFERENTIAL ABILITY SCALES.

Dasein *n.* in the thought of German philosopher Martin Heidegger (1889–1976), the particular kind of being manifest in humans. It is their being as *Dasein* that allows human beings access to the larger question of being in general, since our access to the world is always through what our own being makes possible. The term is commonly used in EXISTENTIAL PSYCHOLOGY and related therapeutic approaches. See BEING-IN-THE-WORLD. [German, literally: "being there"]

Dasein analysis a method of EXISTENTIAL PSYCHOTHERAPY emphasizing the need to recognize not only one's BEING-IN-THE-WORLD but also what one can become (see DASEIN). Through examination of such concepts as intentionality and intuition, Dasein analysis attempts to help clients not to adapt to others or eliminate anxiety (which tends to submerge individuality and encourage outer conformity), but rather to accept themselves and realize their potential. [developed by Swiss psychiatrist Medard Boss (1903–1990)]

DAT 1. abbreviation for dementia of the Alzheimer's type. See ALZHEIMER'S DISEASE; DEMENTIA. **2.** abbreviation for DIFFERENTIAL APTITUDE TESTS.

data *pl. n.* (*sing.* **datum**) observations or measurements, usually quantified and obtained in the course of research.

data analysis the process of applying graphical, statistical, or quantitative techniques to a set of data (observations or measurements) in order to summarize it or to find general patterns.

database *n.* **1.** a large, structured collection of information stored in retrievable form on a computer. **2.** in medical records, one of five parts of a PROBLEM-ORIENTED RECORD.

data collection a systematic gathering of information for research or practical purposes. Examples include mail surveys, interviews, laboratory experiments, and psychological testing.

data-driven process a mental activity that focuses primarily on the physical attributes of a stimulus as opposed to its meaning. This is BOTTOM-UP PROCESSING in which sensory input is processed with little or no guidance from acquired concepts. Compare CONCEPTUALLY DRIVEN PROCESS. See also SHALLOW PROCESSING.

data pooling combining the data of two or more studies or substudies. This procedure can sometimes lead to misleading conclusions. See SIMPSON'S PARADOX.

data reduction the process of reducing a set of measurements or variables into a smaller, more manageable, more reliable, or better theoretically justified set or form.

data snooping 1. looking for unpredicted, post hoc effects in a body of data. **2.** examining data before an experiment has been completed, which can sometimes result in erroneous or misleading conclusions.

date rape sexual assault by an acquaintance, date, or other person known to the victim, often involving alcohol or DATE-RAPE DRUGS that may hinder the victim's ability to withhold consent. Also called **acquaintance rape**.

date-rape drug a drug that is surreptitiously administered to impair consciousness or memory for the purpose of sexual exploitation of the victim. Such drugs are commonly introduced into alcoholic beverages in social settings. Common date-rape drugs include barbiturates, high-potency benzodiazepines (FLUNITRAZEPAM, TRIAZOLAM), and the illicit substance GHB (gamma-hydroxybutyrate). The U.S. Congress passed the Drug-Induced Rape Prevention and Punishment Act in 1996, making it a federal crime to give an unaware person a controlled substance with the intent of committing a violent crime.

dative *n.* a CASE of nouns, pronouns, and noun phrases that identifies the indirect OBJECT of a verb. In modern English, unlike more inflected languages, the dative case affects only a few personal pronouns, when it is indistinguishable from the ACCUSATIVE. Compare GENITIVE; NOMINATIVE.

Daubert hearing a formal presentation and assessment of facts that is conducted by U.S. federal courts to determine whether expert scientific testimony meets criteria established by Federal Rules of Evidence 702 for reliability and relevance. This hearing typically takes place before the trial begins and evaluates whether the research presented in the testimony is both relevant and reliable, considering such factors as testability, error rate, evidence of peer review, and general acceptance within the scientific community.

Daubert test a test used in U.S. federal courts, in place of the earlier FRYE TEST, to determine if expert scientific testimony is admissible under Federal Rules of Evidence 702. It generally takes place during a DAUBERT HEARING, at which judges evaluate whether the testimony is both relevant and reliable, considering such factors as testability, error rate, evidence of peer review, and general acceptance within the scientific community.

Daubert v. Merrell Dow Pharmaceuticals Inc. a case resulting in an influential 1993 U.S. Supreme Court ruling that Federal Rules of Evidence, rather than the restrictive FRYE TEST, should be the standard to determine whether expert scientific testimony is admissible. The court noted that judges should evaluate the validity of the scientific testimony according to whether the research reported (a) is peer-reviewed, (b) is testable (i.e., capable of being falsified), (c) has known error rates, and (d) is generally accepted within the scientific community.

Dauerschlaf *n.* a type of therapy in which prolonged sleep is induced with drugs (e.g., barbiturates). Dauerschlaf (German, "perpetual sleep") has been used in the treatment of substance dependence, status epilepticus, and acute psychotic episodes. Its efficacy and use have been the subject of extreme controversy, and it is now rarely encountered clinically.

day blindness abnormal sensitivity of the FOVEA CENTRALIS to bright light. See also HEMERALOPIA.

day camp a facility that provides educational and recreational services to children, as well as rehabilitation services for children with disabilities, on a short-term, day-by-day basis, as opposed to long-term camps that require overnight accommodation. Day camps are often organized by local social, civic, or church groups or health care agencies, using the facilities of schools, churches, parks, private estates, country clubs, or private or public recreation centers.

day care center 1. a nonresidential facility that provides health and social services in a community setting for adults who are unable to perform many ordinary tasks without supervision or assistance. See ADULT DAY CARE. **2.** see CHILD CARE FACILITIES.

daydream *n.* a waking FANTASY, or reverie, in which conscious or unconscious wishes, and sometimes fears, are played out in imagination. Part of the stream of thoughts and images that occupy most of a person's waking hours, daydreams may be unbidden and apparently purposeless or simply fanciful thoughts, whether spontaneous or intentional. Researchers have identified at least three ways in which individuals' daydreaming styles differ: positive-constructive daydreaming, guilty and fearful daydreaming, and poor attentional control. These styles are posited to reflect the daydreamer's overall tendencies toward positive emotion, negative emotion, and other personality traits. Among the important positive functions that daydreams may serve are the release of strong affect, the gaining of self-insight when reviewing past experiences or rehearsing for future situations, the generation of creative solutions, and the production of greater empathy for others. See also WISH-FULFILLMENT.

day habilitation a HOME AND COMMUNITY-BASED SERVICE provided for a person with mental retardation or a related condition. This service provides productive daily schedules of activity based on individualized service and support planning, including clinical services, companion services, socialization, recreation, vocational development, and lifestyle enrichment. In practice, these services may be delivered on a person-by-person basis or in small groups, in any location during daytime hours.

day hospital a hospital where patients receive a full range of treatment services during the day and return to their homes at night. Services include individual and group therapy, psychological evaluation, occupational and recreational therapy, and somatic therapy. The concept was introduced to North America in 1946 by Scottish-born psychiatrist Donald Ewen Cameron (1901–1967) as an alternative to inpatient treatment and, together with partial hospitalization, grew as a result of deinstitutionalization. It is now used in rehabilitation as well as mental health care. See also DAY TREATMENT; NIGHT HOSPITAL.

daylight vision see PHOTOPIC VISION.

daymare *n.* an attack of acute anxiety, distress, or terror, which is similar to a NIGHTMARE but occurs in a period of wakefulness and is precipitated by waking-state fantasies.

day treatment a program of coordinated interdisciplinary assessment, treatment, and rehabilitation services provided by professionals and paraprofessionals for people with disabilities, mental or physical disorders, or substance abuse problems, usually at a single location for 6 or more hours. Services also address skill and vocational development and may include adjustment programs or SHELTERED WORKSHOPS.

dB symbol for DECIBEL.

DBI abbreviation for DIAZEPAM-BINDING INHIBITOR.

dc (**d/c**) in pharmacology, abbreviation for discontinue.

DC amplifier a direct-current device used to amplify the POTENTIAL difference across a neural membrane so that the cortical current can be recorded and studied.

D-cognition *n.* see BEING COGNITION.

DDAVP *n.* a trade name for DESMOPRESSIN.

dead end see BLIND ALLEY.

deadly catatonia see LETHAL CATATONIA.

deadly nightshade see BELLADONNA ALKALOIDS.

deaf-blind *adj.* lacking or having severely compromised vision and hearing concomitantly. People with deaf-blind impairment encounter significant—sometimes lifelong—challenges in communication, development, and education. Solutions involving tactile devices are often appropriate (e.g., BRAILLE). There is a large number of known causes, including MENINGITIS, CONGENITAL RUBELLA SYNDROME, and USHER SYNDROME. **—deaf-blindness** *n.*

deafferentation *n.* the cutting or removal of NEURONS or AXONS that conduct impulses toward a particular nervous system structure (e.g., the olfactory bulb).

deaf-mute *n.* an obsolescent and pejorative name for an individual who cannot speak, or chooses not to speak, because of congenital or early-acquired profound deafness.

deafness *n.* the partial or complete absence or loss of the sense of hearing. The condition may be hereditary or acquired by injury or disease at any stage of life, including in utero. The major kinds are CONDUCTION DEAFNESS, due to a disruption in sound vibrations before they reach the nerve endings of the inner ear; and sensorineural, or nerve, deafness (see SENSORINEURAL HEARING LOSS), caused by a failure of the nerves or brain centers associated with the sense of hearing to transmit or interpret properly the impulses from the inner ear. Some individuals experience both conduction and sensorineural deafness, a form called **mixed deafness**. See also ADVENTITIOUS DEAFNESS; BOILERMAKER'S DEAFNESS; CENTRAL DEAFNESS; CONGENITAL DEAFNESS; CORTICAL DEAFNESS; EXPOSURE DEAFNESS; PERCEPTION DEAFNESS. **—deaf** *adj.*

deaggressivization *n.* in psychoanalytic theory, the NEUTRALIZATION of the aggressive drive so that its energy can be diverted to various tasks and wishes of the EGO. See also SUBLIMATION.

death *n.* **1.** the permanent cessation of physical and mental processes in an organism. In the United States in the early 1980s, the American Medical Association and the American Bar Association drafted and approved the Uniform Determination of Death Act, in which death is defined as either the irreversible cessation of core physiological functioning (i.e., spontaneous circulatory and respiratory functions) or the irreversible loss of cerebral functioning (i.e., BRAIN DEATH). Given the emergence of sophisticated technologies for cardiopulmonary support, brain death is more often considered the essential determining factor, particularly within the legal profession. See also ASSISTED DEATH; DYING PROCESS; THANATOLOGY. **2.** the degeneration or disintegration of a biological cell. See NECROSIS; NEURONAL CELL DEATH; PROGRAMMED CELL DEATH.

death anxiety emotional distress and insecurity

aroused by reminders of mortality, including one's own memories and thoughts (see also ONTOLOGICAL CONFRONTATION). Classical psychoanalytic theory asserted that the unconscious cannot believe in its own death, therefore THANATOPHOBIA was a disguise for some deeper fear. Existentialists later proposed that death anxiety is at the root of all fears, though often disguised. A mass of research using self-report scales (see DEATH-ANXIETY SCALES) suggests that most people have a low to moderate level of death anxiety. See also EDGE THEORY; TERROR MANAGEMENT THEORY.

death-anxiety scales questionnaires that yield scores for the level of self-reported concern about death. Some scales distinguish between several types of concern, such as fear of pain or fear of nonbeing. See also THANATOPHOBIA.

deathbed escorts and visions auditory or visual hallucinations (or both) experienced near the end of life in which the "visitors" make themselves known only to the dying person. Sometimes the person describes the interaction or can be heard speaking with the apparition; sometimes the event can only be inferred from observing the person's behavior. The visitors, when known, are usually deceased family members or spiritual beings in the ancient tradition of psychopomps (deathbed escorts to accompany the soul on its journey). See also NEAR-DEATH EXPERIENCE.

death concepts cognitive constructions of linear time, finality, certainty, irreversibility, universality, and personal vulnerability, which cohere with other elements to form a general understanding of mortality. The infant's fear of separation is seen as an early precursor of these abstract and differentiated ideas, which usually do not develop until early adolescence. Even then, fantasy often continues to contend with reality in the acceptance of the finality and inevitability of death.

death education learning activities or programs designed to educate people about death, dying, and related issues, such as the emotional effects of bereavement. Death education is provided through information, discussion, guided experiences, and exploration of attitudes and feelings.

death feigning the act of becoming immobile, or "playing dead," when threatened. Also called **tonic immobility**. See ANIMAL DEFENSIVE BEHAVIOR; IMMOBILITY.

death gene a gene that is expressed only when a cell becomes committed to PROGRAMMED CELL DEATH.

death instinct in psychoanalytic theory, a drive whose aim is the reduction of psychical tension to the lowest possible point, that is, death. It is first directed inward as a self-destructive tendency and is later turned outward in the form of the AGGRESSIVE INSTINCT. In the DUAL INSTINCT THEORY of Sigmund FREUD, the death instinct, or THANATOS, stands opposed to the LIFE INSTINCT, or EROS, and is believed to be the drive underlying such behaviors as aggressiveness, sadism, and masochism. Also called **destructive instinct**. See also DESTRUDO; MORTIDO; NIRVANA PRINCIPLE.

death phobia see THANATOPHOBIA.

death-qualified jury a jury whose members have been questioned under oath by either judges or attorneys and deemed to be capable of imposing the death penalty. See also WAINWRIGHT V. WITT; WITHERSPOON EXCLUDABLES.

death rite a culture-bound ceremony, ritual, or other religious or customary practice associated with dying and the dead, such as a funeral rite. See RITE OF PASSAGE.

death system the dynamic patterns through which a society mediates its relationship with mortality in order to remain viable as a culture and meet the needs of the individual. All cultures have a death system whose primary functions are warning and prediction, prevention, care for the dying, disposing of the dead, social consolidation after death, killing, and making sense of death. How these functions are performed is significantly influenced by a number of factors, including economic priorities, religious values, traditions of discrimination and enmity, and level of technological development. [first described in 1977 by U.S. psychologist Robert J. Kastenbaum (1932–)]

death taboo (**death tabu**) the belief that death is so dangerous and disturbing a subject that one should not only avoid contact with the dead, the dying, and the recently bereaved but also refrain from talking or even thinking about it. In 1959, U.S. psychologist Herman Feifel (1915–) proposed that the United States had such a denying and avoiding attitude toward death that it could be compared with the rigid and extreme patterns observed by anthropologists in many band-and-village societies.

death trance a state of apparent suspended animation of an individual, characterized by minimal physiological functioning.

death wish 1. in psychoanalytic theory, a conscious or unconscious wish that another person, particularly a parent, will die. According to Sigmund FREUD, such wishes are a major source of guilt, desire for self-punishment, and depression. **2.** an unconscious desire for one's own death, as manifested in self-destructive or dangerous behaviors. See also DEATH INSTINCT.

deautomatization hypothesis the idea that automatic processes can be brought under conscious, voluntary control. See AUTOMATICITY.

debilitative anxiety a level of anxiety that an individual (e.g., an athlete) perceives as interfering with performance, for example, being psyched out (see PSYCHING OUT) or "out of the zone."

Debré–Sémélaigne syndrome see KOCHER–DEBRÉ–SÉMÉLAIGNE SYNDROME.

debriefing *n.* the process of giving participants in a completed research project a fuller explanation of the study in which they participated than was possible before or during the research.

debt counseling counseling specifically aimed at helping individuals with financial problems. The help and advice given includes budgeting, credit-card usage, debt consolidation, and awareness of difficulties in managing money. Debt counseling may be part of the counseling or therapy for other problems or it may be carried out by financial planners and accountants.

decadence *n.* **1.** a presumed deterioration of a culture, society, or civilization because of a general collapse of moral character and traditional values. **2.** generally, a loss or diminution of excellence or some other quality. **3.** (typically capitalized) loosely, an artistic movement of the mid- and late 19th century, particularly in literature and the visual arts, that valued extreme aesthetic refinement, the superiority of artifice (i.e., human invention) over nature, and innovative and atypical experiential perspectives and modes of being. Also called **Decadent movement**.

Decadron *n.* a trade name for DEXAMETHASONE.

décalage *n.* in Jean PIAGET's theory of cognitive development, the invariant order in which cognitive accomplishments develop. See HORIZONTAL DÉCALAGE; VERTICAL DÉCALAGE. [French, "interval," "shift"]

decarboxylase *n.* an enzyme that catalyzes the removal of a carboxyl group (–COOH) from a compound.

decarceration *n.* **1.** the process of removing offenders from correctional facilities, often to community facilities. **2.** see DEINSTITUTIONALIZATION.

decatastrophizing *n.* a technique, used in treating people with irrational or exaggerated fears, that explores the reality of the situation rather than imagined or anticipated events.

decathexis *n.* in psychoanalytic theory, the withdrawal of LIBIDO from objects (i.e., other people) in the external world. Compare CATHEXIS.

decay theory the theory that learned material leaves in the brain a trace or impression that autonomously recedes and disappears unless the material is practiced and used. Decay theory is a theory of forgetting. Also called **trace-decay theory**.

deceleration *n.* a decrease in speed of movement or rate of change. Compare ACCELERATION.

decentering *n.* **1.** any of a variety of techniques aimed at changing centered thinking to open-minded thinking. A person with centered thinking is focused on only one salient feature at a time, to the total exclusion of other important characteristics. **2.** dissolution of unity between self and identity. **3.** see DECENTRATION. **—decenter** *vb.*

decentralization *n.* the trend to relocate patients with chronic mental illness from long-term institutionalization, usually at government hospitals, to outpatient care in community-based, residential facilities. **—decentralize** *vb.*

decentralized organization an ORGANIZATIONAL STRUCTURE in which decision-making authority is spread throughout the organization rather than being reserved for those at the top of the hierarchy. Compare CENTRALIZED ORGANIZATION.

decentration *n.* in Jean PIAGET's theory of cognitive development, the gradual progression of a child away from egocentrism toward a reality shared with others. Decentration includes understanding how others perceive the world, knowing in what ways one's own perceptions differ, and recognizing that people have motivations and feelings different from one's own. It can also be extended to the ability to consider many aspects of a situation, problem, or object, as reflected, for example, in the child's grasp of the concept of CONSERVATION. Also called **decentering**. Compare CENTRATION. **—decenter** *vb.*

deception *n.* **1.** any distortion of fact or withholding of fact with the purpose of misleading others. **2.** in animal behavior, the providing of false information that results in the individual obtaining increased resources at the expense of others. Some animals give false alarm calls that disperse competitors and thus gain more food (see DISHONEST SIGNAL). Animals may engage in aggressive displays that make themselves appear larger than they really are. **—deceive** *vb.* **—deceptive** *adj.*

deception by commission see ACTIVE DECEPTION.

deception by omission see PASSIVE DECEPTION.

deception clue a behavioral indication that an individual is not telling the truth. Deception clues include inconsistencies between voluntary and involuntary behavior and unusual or exaggerated physiological or expressive responses to knowledge that only a guilty person possesses. To date, behavioral scientists have discovered no behavioral or physiological response that, by itself, shows a 1:1 relation to deception.

deception research research in which participants are misled or not informed about the nature of the investigation. See ACTIVE DECEPTION; DOUBLE DECEPTION; PASSIVE DECEPTION.

deceptive advertising advertising that leads to incorrect inferences on the part of consumers, for example, that taking a particular food supplement will help individuals lose weight.

decerebrate rigidity rigidity of the body that occurs when the brainstem is functionally separated from the cerebral cortex, typically as a result of a brain lesion or vascular disorder. It is marked by bilateral rigid extension, adduction, and hyperpronation of the legs and arms. Also called **decerebrate posturing**; **extensor posturing**.

decerebration *n.* loss of the ability to discriminate, learn, and control movements as a result of transecting the brainstem, surgically removing the CEREBRUM, or cutting off the cerebral blood supply. A **decerebrate** is an animal that has undergone decerebration.

decibel (symbol: dB) *n.* a logarithmic unit used to express the ratio of acoustic or electric power (intensity). An increase of 1 bel is a 10-fold increase in intensity; a decibel is one tenth of a bel and is the more commonly used unit, partly because a 1-dB change in intensity is just detectable (approximately and under laboratory conditions). The SOUND INTENSITY (the numerator of the intensity ratio) or **sound level** is usually specified in **decibels sound-pressure level** (dB SPL). The reference intensity (the denominator of the intensity ratio) for dB SPL is $10^{-12}W/m^2$ and corresponds to a SOUND PRESSURE of 20 μPa (micropascal). A sound presented at the reference intensity has a level of 0 dB SPL and is close to the absolute threshold for a 1-kHz tone. Often SPL is omitted but is implied from the context: A "60-dB sound" usually means 60 dB SPL. The decibel, because it is a logarithmic measure, has caused much confusion. For example, decibels do not add: Two unrelated 60 dB SPL sounds when sounded simultaneously produce a 63-dB SPL sound, not a 120-dB SPL sound.

decile *n.* the tenth part of a statistical distribution. The first 10% of cases comprises the first decile, the second 10% is the second decile, and so on.

decisional balance a method of assessing the positive and negative consequences, for oneself and others, of selecting a new behavior. Decisional balance is frequently used in weighing the consequences of exercise behavior. For example, by beginning a regular early-morning exercise program, an individual would lose weight (a positive consequence), would not be available for early-morning meetings at work (a negative consequence), would gain greater respect from others (e.g., family, friends) for getting in shape (a positive consequence), and would incur costs in terms of gym fees and workout clothes (a negative consequence).

decisional competence the ability of a defendant to make the decisions normally faced by defendants in a criminal defense (e.g., deciding among various plea agreements). See also COMPETENCY EVALUATION; COMPETENCY TO STAND TRIAL; DUSKY STANDARD.

decision making the cognitive process of choosing between two or more alternatives, ranging from the relatively clear cut (e.g., ordering a meal at a restaurant) to the complex (e.g., selecting a mate). Psychologists have adopted two converging strategies to understand decision making: (a) statistical analysis of multiple decisions involving complex tasks and (b) experimental manipulation of simple decisions, looking at elements that recur within these decisions.

decision-making model of counseling an approach that envisions counseling as a process with three stages: the problem definition phase, the work phase, and the action phase. The problem definition phase includes considering alternative definitions of the problem and committing to one of these. During the work phase the problem is examined from different perspectives to identify facts as well as the thoughts and feelings of the client. The counselor helps the client to look at issues, answers, and solutions in new ways. The action phase deals with finding alternative solutions and choosing one to test in the home environment.

decision-plane model a two-dimensional schema of the risks and benefits of doing research. This permits an informed evaluation of the ethical implications of conducting a particular study.

decision–redecision method a technique used in TRANSACTIONAL ANALYSIS that allows clients to reexperience decision moments in their childhood and choose to redecide. These decision moments resulted from such self-injunctions as "Don't be you," "Don't feel," "Don't be a child," and so forth, and have associated habitual patterns of emotion.

decision rule in hypothesis testing, the formal statement of the set of values of the test statistic that will lead to rejection of the NULL HYPOTHESIS.

decision theory a broad class of theories in the quantitative, social, and behavioral sciences that aim to explain the decision-making process and identify optimal ways of arriving at decisions (e.g., under conditions of uncertainty) in such a way that prespecified criteria are met.

decisive moment in psychotherapy, that moment at which a client makes a momentous decision, such as revealing a secret or deciding to make a major change in his or her life.

deck *n.* on small computer-based devices, such as cell phones or personal digital assistants, a set of displays relating to a particular function, concept, or category that can be "stacked" on screen like the cards in a deck of cards.

declarative *adj.* denoting a sentence or clause that takes the form of a straightforward statement rather than a question, request, or command. See INDICATIVE.

declarative memory memory that can be consciously recalled in response to a request to remember. This form of memory is selectively impaired in AMNESIA. In some theories, declarative memory includes EPISODIC MEMORY and SEMANTIC MEMORY. Also called **declarative knowledge**. See also EXPLICIT MEMORY. Compare NONDECLARATIVE MEMORY; PROCEDURAL MEMORY.

de Clérambault's syndrome see CLÉRAMBAULT'S SYNDROME.

decline effect in parapsychology experiments using ZENER CARDS or similar targets, the situation in which the accuracy of the participant's "calls" or guesses begins at above-chance levels but progressively drops to chance levels as further trials are carried out. See REGRESSION TOWARD THE MEAN. See also DIFFERENTIAL EFFECT; FOCUSING EFFECT; PREFERENTIAL EFFECT; SHEEP–GOAT EFFECT.

decoding *n.* in information theory, the process in which a receiver (e.g., the brain or a device, such as a cell phone) translates signals (sounds, writing, gestures, electrical impulses) into meaningful messages. Compare ENCODING. **—decode** *vb.*

decompensation *n.* a breakdown in an individual's DEFENSE MECHANISMS, resulting in progressive loss of normal functioning or worsening of psychiatric symptoms.

decomposition *n.* a process in which a complex item is separated into its simpler constituent elements. For example, in problem solving it is a strategy in which a problem is transformed into two or more simpler problems.

decomposition of movement difficulty of movement in which gestures are broken up into individual segments instead of being executed smoothly. It is a symptom of cerebellar lesions.

decompression sickness an adverse effect of exposure of the body to extremely high air pressure, resulting in the formation of nitrogen bubbles in the body tissues. The circulatory system is particularly sensitive to the effect. Decompression sickness develops as a person rapidly moves from an environment of high pressure to one of lower air pressure, causing dissolved gases to form bubbles. Neurological effects may include loss of consciousness, convulsions, paresthesias, and damage to the brain and spinal cord. A form of decompression sickness that affects the cardiopulmonary system and may lead to circulatory collapse is called **chokes**; it is characterized by discomfort underneath the sternum and coughing on deep inspiration. When decompression sickness affects mainly the bones and joints, the disorder is called **bends**.

deconditioning *n.* a technique in BEHAVIOR THERAPY in which learned responses, such as phobias, are "unlearned" (deconditioned). For example, a person with a phobic reaction to flying might be deconditioned initially by practicing going to the airport when not actually taking a flight and using breathing techniques to control anxiety. See also DESENSITIZATION.

deconstruction *n.* a form of critical analysis of literary texts and philosophical positions based on the twin assumptions that there can be no firm REFERENTS for language and no adequate grounding for truth claims. Although deconstruction challenges the fundamental grounds of the Western philosophical tradition, it recognizes that both the tools and the motivation for doing so arise from that very tradition. A deconstructive reading of a text will generally use traditional analytical methods to expose the innumerable ways in which the text subverts its own claims to meaning and coherence. In much general usage, the term is now taken to be synonymous with the destruction of an idea or a truth claim. See also POSTSTRUCTURALISM. [introduced by French philosopher Jacques Derrida (1930–2004)] **—deconstruct** *vb.* **—deconstructive** *adj.*

decontextualization *n.* **1.** the process of examining, considering, or interpreting something separately from the context within which it is embedded. Decontextualization may occur consciously (e.g., with the aim of subjecting a constituent element of some phenomenon or process to closer, individual study) or unconsciously. Either mode may result on the one hand in greater clarity but on the other in oversimplification and inaccuracies in comprehension. **2.** in perception, the process of turning implicit or contextual events into objects of conscious perception or belief. **—decontextualize** *vb.*

decortication *n.* surgical removal of the outer layer (cortex) of the brain while allowing deeper tissues to remain functional.

decreolization *n.* a stage of linguistic evolution that sometimes follows the formation of a CREOLE, in which its structure is further elaborated through the influence of the standard language and other languages in contact. The complex linguistic situation that arises in such cases is often referred to as a **postcreolization continuum**.

Decroly method of schooling **1.** an educational method based on a program implemented at the Hermitage School, which opened in Brussels, Belgium, in 1907. This program presented the classroom as a workshop, with a curriculum based on four categories: food, defense, shelter, and work. These needs formed the focus of a year's study, and children were encouraged to develop their own interests within the framework of those needs. **2.** historically, a specific application in special education used in the Institute for Abnormal Children established in 1901 in Uccle, Belgium. The school had a homelike atmosphere, enabling the children to demonstrate higher learning achievement than children without disabilities demonstrated in standard schools of the day. This method has been utilized for broadly based education. [Ovide **Decroly** (1871–1932), Belgian educator]

decubitus ulcer see PRESSURE ULCER.

deculturation *n.* the processes, intentional or unintentional, by which traditional cultural beliefs or practices are suppressed or altered as a result of contact with a different, dominant culture. Compare ACCULTURATION. **—deculturate** *vb.*

decussation *n.* a crossing or intersection in the form of a letter X, as in the decussation of the PYRAMIDS of the medulla oblongata and of the fibers of the left and right optic nerves in the OPTIC CHIASM.

dedifferentiation *n.* loss of specialization or of advanced organizational and functional abilities. This may occur, for example, when mature cells within an organism regress to a more general, simplified state, as is sometimes seen in the progression of certain cancers, or as a form of thought disorganization seen in schizophrenia.

deduction *n.* **1.** a conclusion derived from formal premises by a valid process of DEDUCTIVE REASONING. **2.** the process of deductive reasoning itself. Compare INDUCTION. **—deductive** *adj.*

deductive-nomological model an influential model of SCIENTIFIC EXPLANATION in which laws describing regularities in nature (see NATURAL LAW) are used as initial premises or axioms to deduce working explanations of phenomena, which are then used to deduce specific testable predictions. See HYPOTHETICO-DEDUCTIVE METHOD; NOMOLOGY. See also COVERING-LAW MODEL. [identified by German philosopher of science Carl Gustav Hempel (1905–1997)]

deductive reasoning the form of logical reasoning in which a conclusion is shown to follow necessarily from a sequence of premises, the first of which stands for a self-evident truth (see AXIOM) or agreed-upon data. In the empirical sciences, deductive reasoning underlies the process of deriving predictions from general laws or theories. Compare INDUCTIVE REASONING. See also LOGIC; TOP-DOWN ANALYSIS.

deep body temperature the temperature of the body's internal organs. Also called **core temperature**. See BODY TEMPERATURE.

deep cerebellar nucleus any of the nuclei at the base of the CEREBELLUM, such as the interpositus nucleus.

deep depression a severe MAJOR DEPRESSIVE EPISODE characterized by PSYCHOMOTOR RETARDATION, guilt, SUICIDAL IDEATION, and psychotic features. RUMINATION is frequent, and risk of suicide is high.

deep dyslexia a form of acquired dyslexia (see ALEXIA) characterized by semantic errors (e.g., reading *parrot* as *canary*), difficulties in reading abstract words (e.g., *idea, usual*) and function words (e.g., *the, and*), and an inability to read pronounceable nonwords. See also PHONOLOGICAL DYSLEXIA; SURFACE DYSLEXIA. [first described in 1973 by British neuropsychologists John C. Marshall and Freda Newcombe (1925–2001)]

deep-pockets effect the theory that juries are influenced by the wealth of the defendant when assessing COMPENSATORY DAMAGES, so that they are more likely both to find in the favor of the plaintiff and to make larger awards when the defendant is wealthy.

deep-pressure sensitivity see BATHYESTHESIA.

deep processing cognitive processing of a stimulus that focuses on its meaningful properties rather than its perceptual characteristics. It is considered that processing at this semantic level, which usually involves a degree of ELABORATION, produces stronger, longer-lasting memories than SHALLOW PROCESSING. See LEVELS-OF-PROCESSING MODEL OF MEMORY. See also CONCEPTUALLY DRIVEN PROCESS; SEMANTIC ENCODING; TOP-DOWN PROCESSING. [proposed in 1972 by Canadian psychologists Fergus I. M. Craik (1935–) and Robert S. Lockhart]

deep reflex see TENDON REFLEX.

deep sensibility see BATHYESTHESIA.

deep sleep the stage of the sleep cycle in which arousal thresholds are highest and consciousness is taken to be least likely. In deep sleep, DELTA WAVES are prominent in the electroencephalogram. See SLOW-WAVE SLEEP.

deep structure 1. in anatomy, any organ or tissue that is located beneath the surface layers of the body, such as the heart, liver, or kidney. **2.** in the TRANSFORMATIONAL GENERATIVE GRAMMAR developed by Noam CHOMSKY, an abstract base form of a sentence in which the logical and grammatical relations between the constituents are made explicit. The deep structure generates the SURFACE STRUCTURE of a sentence through transformations, such as changes in word order or addition or deletion of elements. Also called **base structure**.

deep trance in hypnosis and shamanistic practices, a state in which participants are minimally responsive to environmental cues except for suggestions consistent with their beliefs. See TRANCE.

deep vein thrombosis (**DVT**) the presence of a thrombus (clot) in a vein, most often in the leg or thigh, which may result from prolonged immobility and can lead to a PULMONARY EMBOLISM. See also THROMBOSIS.

Deese paradigm a laboratory memory task used to study false recall. It is based on the report in 1959 that, after presentation of a list of related words (e.g., *snore, rest, dream, awake*), participants mistakenly recalled an unpresented but strongly associated item (e.g., *sleep*). Following renewed research into the technique, it is now generally referred to as the **Deese–Roediger–McDermott paradigm**. [James **Deese** (1921–1999), U.S. psychologist; Henry L. **Roediger** III (1947–) and Kathleen B. **McDermott** (1968–), U.S. cognitive psychologists]

defecation reflex emptying of the rectum and lower portion of the colon in response to movement or pressure of fecal material. As the rectum fills, receptors send impulses to the spinal cord. Motor nerve impulses are transmitted through sacral fibers of the PARASYMPATHETIC NERVOUS SYSTEM, causing relaxation of the inner anal sphincter and contraction of muscles of the abdominal wall. In order for the act to be completed, the external sphincter muscle, which is controlled by voluntary, skeletal muscle nerves, must also be relaxed. The voluntary nervous system can override the reflex and, under normal conditions, prevent automatic defecation. Also called **rectal reflex**. See also ANAL STAGE; TOILET TRAINING.

defect *n.* a fault, product of error, or lack of an essential element in something that prevents it from functioning correctly. See CONGENITAL DEFECT; GENETIC DEFECT. **—defective** *adj.*

defective delinquent an outdated legal name for an individual who engages in repeated criminal behavior and is considered to be below average in intelligence.

defectology *n.* in Russian psychology, the area of abnormal psychology and learning disabilities. More specifically, defectology is concerned with the education of children with sensory, physical, cognitive, or neurological impairment. Russian defectology offers services to roughly the same population as special education and school psychology in the United States. It is based on the view that the primary problem of a disability is not the organic impairment itself but its social implications. [originally defined by Lev VYGOTSKY]

defect orientation **1.** in interdisciplinary team or other individual service-planning processes, an emphasis that focuses on the impairments, limitations, deficits, or defects in functioning of individuals with disabilities, but that excludes corresponding assessment of and emphasis on their skills, abilities, and strengths. **2.** see DEFECT THEORY. Compare DEVELOPMENTAL ORIENTATION.

defect theory the proposition that the cognitive processes and behavioral development of people with mental retardation are qualitatively different from those of their peers without mental retardation. Also called **defect orientation**; **difference hypothesis**. Compare DEVELOPMENTAL THEORY.

defender strategy a business strategy in which an organization attempts to compete in the marketplace by focusing on a narrow range of products and services and then protecting this niche by offering higher quality, superior service, and lower prices. To implement this strategy, the organization must be structured to maintain efficiency of operation.

defense *n.* behavior or physical features that reduce the likelihood of an individual being harmed by another. In nonhuman animals, for example, defensive physical features include hard body parts and toxic or noxious substances (e.g., odor from a skunk, poison from snakes and spiders); DEFENSIVE BEHAVIOR includes SUBMISSIVE SIGNALS, defensive aggression, immobility, and flight. **—defensive** *adj.*

defense interpretation in psychoanalysis, an interpretation of the ways in which the patient protects himself or herself from anxiety. Such an interpretation aims to make the patient aware of his or her defenses and to uncover the source of the anxiety in intrapsychic conflict.

defense mechanism in classical psychoanalytic theory, an unconscious reaction pattern employed by the EGO to protect itself from the anxiety that arises from psychic conflict. Such mechanisms range from mature to immature, depending on how much they distort reality: DENIAL is very immature because it negates reality, whereas SUBLIMATION is one of the most mature forms of defense because it allows indirect satisfaction of a true wish. In more recent psychological theories, defense mechanisms are seen as normal means of coping with everyday problems, but excessive use of any one, or the use of immature defenses (e.g., DISPLACEMENT or REPRESSION), is still considered pathological. Also called **escape mechanism**. See also AVOIDANCE; PROJECTION; REGRESSION; SUBSTITUTION. [proposed in 1894 by Sigmund FREUD]

defense reflex a sudden response elicited by a painful or unexpected stimulus. The term is applied to a variety of responses, ranging from an acceleration in heart rate in reaction to a startling auditory stimulus, through flight, fight, or freezing elicited by perceived threat, to complex psychological responses. Also called **defense response**.

defensible space a set of principles and guidelines for the design and planning of settings to reduce crime. Among the critical elements of defensible space are the creation of shared territories in which people have collective control, good surveillance, and markers and other symbols of ownership and primary territory. See TERRITORIALITY.

defensive aggression see ANIMAL DEFENSIVE BEHAVIOR.

defensive attribution a bias or error in attributing cause for some event such that a perceived threat to oneself is minimized. For example, people might blame an automobile accident on the driver's mistake rather than on a chance occurrence because this attribution lessens their perception that they themselves could be victimized by chance.

defensive behavior **1.** aggressive or submissive behavior in response to real or imagined threats of bodily or psychic (particularly emotional) harm. A cat, for example, may exhibit defensive aggression by spitting and hissing, arching its back, and raising the hair along the back of the neck in anticipation of a physical threat (see ANIMAL DEFENSIVE BEHAVIOR). A human might unconsciously fend off criticism by putting forth self-justifying excuses or by expressing an emotional reaction (e.g., crying) to limit another's disapproval or anger. **2.** in psychoanalytic theory, behavior characterized by the use or overuse of DEFENSE MECHANISMS operating at an unconscious level.

defensive conditioning a form of PAVLOVIAN CONDITIONING in which the UNCONDITIONED STIMULUS is noxious.

defensive identification the process by which a victim of abuse psychologically identifies with the perpetrator of abuse, or with the group with which the perpetrator is identified, as a defensive strategy against continuing feelings of vulnerability to further victimization.

defensiveness *n.* a tendency to be sensitive to criticism or comment about one's deficiencies and to counter or deny such criticisms. **—defensive** *adj.*

defensive processing the seeking out, attending to, encoding, interpreting, or elaborating of attitude-relevant information to support or confirm one's initial attitude. For example, defensive processing can involve avoiding attitude-inconsistent information and seeking out attitude-consistent information. Similarly, it can involve elaborating attitude-inconsistent information in a highly critical fashion in order to refute it. See also BIASED ELABORATION; COUNTERARGUMENT; SELECTIVE INFORMATION PROCESSING.

deferred imitation imitation of an act minutes, hours, or days after viewing the behavior. Jean PIAGET proposed that deferred imitation is first seen at about 18 months of age and is a reflection of the SYMBOLIC FUNCTION. More recent research, however, indicates that deferred imitation of simple tasks can be observed in infants late in their 1st year.

deferred prosecution see DIVERSION PROGRAM.

deficiency *n.* a lack or shortage of something. A deficiency may, for example, be a relative or absolute lack of a skill, of a biological substrate or process, or of resources that enable specific functions or actions to be performed.

deficiency cognition see BEING COGNITION.

deficiency love (**D-love**) in Abraham MASLOW's humanistic psychology, a type of love that is fulfillment-oriented (e.g., based on a need for belonging, self-esteem, security, or power) and characterized by dependency, possessiveness, lack of mutuality, and little concern for the other's true welfare. Compare BEING LOVE.

deficiency motivation in Abraham MASLOW's humanistic psychology, the type of motivation operating on the lower four levels of his hierarchy of needs (see MASLOW'S MOTIVATIONAL HIERARCHY). Deficiency motivation is characterized by the striving to correct a deficit that may be physiological or psychological in nature. Compare METAMOTIVATION.

deficiency motive the tendency to satisfy a particular need simply in order to counter a deficiency, for example, eating only the amount of food required to alleviate hunger. Compare ABUNDANCY MOTIVE.

deficiency need any need created by lack of a substance required for survival (e.g., food, water) or of a state required for well-being (e.g., security, love).

definite article in linguistics, an ARTICLE (*the* in English) used with a noun phrase to indicate reference to a specific entity that has been or is about to be defined, as in *The patient died last night* or *the patient who died last night*. Compare INDEFINITE ARTICLE.

definition *n.* in optics, the clarity of an image reproduced by photography or an optical system. Compare RESOLUTION.

deformity *n.* distortion or malformation of any part of the body. See DISFIGUREMENT.

defusion *n.* in psychoanalytic theory, the separation of INSTINCTS that usually operate together. Defusion is posited to lead to various neuroses. Compare FUSION. **—defused** *adj.*

degeneracy *n.* **1.** a state in which a person has declined or reverted to a much earlier state of development in physical, mental, or moral qualities. **2.** the state of possessing few if any of the moral standards considered normal in one's society. Degeneracy is often popularly used with special reference to sexual offenses. **3.** in biology, reversion to a less highly organized and simpler stage of development. **—degenerate** *adj.*

degenerating axon the remnant of an injured or dead AXON. Degenerating axons leave a residue that absorbs particular dyes. Thus, a degenerating myelinated nerve fiber releases MYELIN, which absorbs osmium, producing a black trail where the healthy fiber had been.

degeneration *n.* **1.** deterioration or decline of organs or tissues, especially of neural tissue to a less functional form. **2.** deterioration or decline of moral values. **—degenerate** *vb.*

degenerative status a constitutional body type marked by an accumulation of deviations from that considered normal, although a single deviant feature would have no particular pathological significance.

deglutition *n.* see SWALLOWING.

degradation *n.* **1.** in neurophysiology, the process by which NEUROTRANSMITTER molecules are broken down into inactive metabolites. **2.** more generally, the process or result of declining or reducing in value, quality, level, or status.

degraded stimulus a stimulus to which NOISE (visual or auditory) has been added to make it more difficult to perceive.

degrees of freedom 1. (symbol: *df*; ν) the number of elements that are free to vary in a statistical calculation, or the number of scores minus the number of mathematical restrictions. If the mean of a set of scores is fixed, then the number of degrees of freedom is one less than the number of scores. For example, if four individuals have a mean IQ of 100, then there are three degrees of freedom, because knowing three of the IQs determines the fourth IQ. See also CHI-SQUARE DISTRIBUTION. **2.** in motor control, the various joints that can move or the various muscles that can contract to produce a movement.

degrees of freedom problem the fact that, in most movement situations, the brain has access to many more DEGREES OF FREEDOM than are necessary to accomplish the task and thus selects which posture or movement TRAJECTORY to use from the large set of those that are possible.

dehoaxing *n.* DEBRIEFING participants who have been involved in DECEPTION RESEARCH.

dehumanization *n.* any process or practice that is thought to reduce human beings to the level of nonhuman animals or mechanisms, especially by denying them autonomy, individuality, and a sense of dignity. **—dehumanize** *vb.*

dehydration *n.* lack of water in the body tissues. Dehydration may be absolute, as measured in terms of the difference from normal body-water content, or relative, as considered in terms of fluid needed to maintain effective osmotic pressure. The physiological lag between water loss through excretion and the development of thirst sensations that stimulate replacement of the water is called **voluntary dehydration**. Compare HYDRATION.

dehydration reactions metabolic and psychological disturbances occurring when the body's water supply falls far below its normal quota. Early symptoms are apathy, irritability, drowsiness, inability to concentrate, and anxiety. Dehydration reactions may progress to delirium, spasticity, blindness, deafness, stupor, and death if more than 10% of body weight is lost.

dehydrogenase *n.* an enzyme that catalyzes the removal of hydrogen atoms in biological reactions. See LACTATE DEHYDROGENASE.

dehypnosis *n.* in hypnosis, the process of eliminating the belief that hypnotic fantasies are actual.

deictic *adj.* see DEIXIS.

deification *n.* **1.** the elevation of a living or dead person to the position of a god, as in the case of certain Roman emperors and other rulers of the ancient world. **2.** extreme adulation, or the endowment of a person or thing with godlike status. **—deify** *vb.*

deindividuation *n.* an experiential state characterized by loss of self-awareness, altered perceptions, and a reduction of inner restraints that results in the performance of unusual, atypical behavior. It can be caused by a number of factors, such as a sense of anonymity or of submersion in a group (see GROUP IDENTIFICATION).

deinstitutionalization *n.* the joint process of moving people with developmental or psychiatric disabilities from structured institutional facilities to their home communities and developing comprehensive community-based residential, day, vocational, clinical, and supportive services to address their needs. See COMMUNITY CARE. **—deinstitutionalize** *vb.*

deism *n.* a type of natural religion associated chiefly with the 18th-century Enlightenment. It is based on the premise that a benevolent God will make sure that the knowledge necessary for human happiness is (a) universally available and (b) accessible to the intellectual powers natural to human beings. It follows that divine truth will conform to human reason and the evidence provided by the natural creation. Deism thus contrasts with revealed religion, which requires a divine revelation of truth beyond what is available by the light of nature. Most forms of deism hold that God created the universe and the natural laws that govern it but has since dispassionately and detachedly allowed it to run its course. Compare PANTHEISM; THEISM. **—deist** *adj., n.*

Deiters cells cells that support the outer hair cells in the ORGAN OF CORTI. [Otto **Deiters** (1834–1863), German anatomist]

deixis *n.* in linguistics, the use of a word or phrase whose meaning is dependent on the situation in which it is used. For example, the meaning of *The tree on my side of the fence* depends on who says it and where that person is standing. Some words, including the personal and demonstrative pronouns and such adverbs as *here, there,* and *now,* are always deictic. The psychological interest in deixis stems from the recognition of different possible perspectives that it entails. **—deictic** *adj.*

déjà entendu the feeling that what is now being heard has a familiar ring, even though it has not been heard before (French, "already heard"). Déjà entendu is a FALSE MEMORY.

déjà pensé the feeling that one has had the same thoughts before, even though this is not the case (French, "already thought"). Déjà pensé is a FALSE MEMORY.

déjà raconté the feeling that a long-forgotten event, now recalled, has been told before (French, "already told"). Some theorists believe that the illusion arises from the need for reassurance that a threatening experience was previously mastered and can therefore be mastered again. See also FALSE MEMORY.

déjà vécu the feeling that one has lived previously (French, "already lived"), an experience in which feelings of familiarity in novel situations are attributed to recollection of experiences from another life. See FALSE MEMORY.

déjà vu the feeling that a new event has already been experienced or that the same scene has been witnessed before (French, "already seen"). The feeling of familiarity may be due to a neurological anomaly, to resemblance between the present and the past scenes, or to the fact that a similar scene has been pictured in a daydream or night dream. See FALSE MEMORY.

de Lange's syndrome a congenital disorder that occurs in two forms, both of which include moderate to severe mental retardation and are associated with autosomal dominant inheritance or duplication of the long arm of chromosome 3. One form, the **Bruck–de Lange type**, features a short, broad neck, broad shoulders, short and thick extremities, and muscular hypertrophy, which gives the child the appearance of a small professional wrestler. The other, **Brachmann–de Lange type**, is also known as AMSTERDAM DWARF DISEASE or Amsterdam type of retardation, because the disorder was identified among patients in the Amsterdam area. Also called **Cornelia de Lange's syndrome**. [Cornelia **de Lange** (1871–1950), Dutch physician]

delay conditioning in PAVLOVIAN CONDITIONING, a procedure in which the CONDITIONED STIMULUS is presented, and remains present, for a fixed period (the delay) before the UNCONDITIONED STIMULUS is introduced. After repeated exposure to such pairings, a conditioned response develops. If the delay is long enough, INHIBITION OF DELAY may be observed. Also called **delayed conditioning**.

delayed alternation task a DELAYED RESPONSE task in which a nonhuman animal must alternate responses between trials. The most common version of this task is one in which a food reward is alternated from side to side with a delay between trials. The animal must learn that a well (cup) containing food is always on the opposite side from the previous trial. Also called **delayed response alternation**.

delayed auditory feedback (**DAF**) a technique of AUDITORY FEEDBACK in which speakers listen through headphones to their own speech, which is heard a short time after it is spoken. It is one of several techniques that may be used to induce greater fluency and clearer articulation in those with various speech and language disorders, particularly in those who stutter. Paradoxically, however, the delay in DAF has also been found to cause DYSFLUENCY in normally fluent speakers.

delayed conditioning see DELAY CONDITIONING.

delayed development slower than expected developmental increases in physical, emotional, social, or cognitive abilities or capacities. A child with delayed development may hold attitudes, exhibit habits, or engage in behaviors consistent with an earlier developmental level.

delayed effect an effect that is not observed for some period of time after the event or factor that is held to have caused it. Usually the precipitating event exerts an indirect influence by starting a process or chain of events that ultimately has a demonstrable effect. See CAUSAL LATENCY; REMOTE CAUSE.

delayed feedback the delay of feedback from the senses that is used to guide or monitor specific motor movements. Delayed feedback interferes with decision making and behavior; for example, DELAYED AUDITORY FEEDBACK when speaking can substantially interfere with the speed and processing of speech.

delayed matching to sample (**DMTS**) a procedure involving CONDITIONAL DISCRIMINATION in which the participant is shown initially one stimulus as a sample (the study phase) and subsequently, after a variable interval, a pair of stimuli (the test phase), the task being to choose the stimulus in the test phase that matches the sample presented in the study phase. Responding to the stimulus that matches the sample is reinforced. In **zero-delay matching to sample**, the sample stimulus is removed, once the participant has responded to it, at the same instant that the comparison stimuli are presented. The task is more difficult the longer the delay between the two presentations. In **delayed nonmatching to sample**, the participant must choose the stimulus that was not presented in the study phase. See also MATCHING TO SAMPLE.

delayed parenthood the state of people who have their first child relatively late in life, usually after their 30th birthday.

delayed posttraumatic stress disorder a form of POSTTRAUMATIC STRESS DISORDER that is diagnosed when the symptoms first appear more than 6 months after exposure to the traumatic stressor.

delayed recall the ability to recollect information acquired earlier. Frequently used in laboratory studies of memory, delayed recall is also used in neuropsychological examinations to determine the rate of loss of information presented earlier, in comparison to established norms.

delayed reflex a reflexive response that has an abnormally long latency after stimulation.

delayed reinforcement REINFORCEMENT that does not occur immediately after a response has been made. The delay may be signaled or unsignaled. If it is signaled, a stimulus change occurs immediately after the response, and this stimulus remains present until the reinforcer is delivered. If the delay is unsignaled, there is no change of stimulus.

delayed response a response that occurs some time after its DISCRIMINATIVE STIMULUS has been removed. The most common **delayed response task** for nonhuman animals is one in which the animal is required to recall the location of a reward after a delay period has elapsed.

delayed response alternation see DELAYED ALTERNATION TASK.

delayed speech the failure of speech to develop at the expected age. It may be due to DEVELOPMENTAL DELAY, hearing loss, brain injury, mental retardation or other psychological disorders, or emotional disturbance.

delay of gratification forgoing immediate reward in order to obtain a larger, more desired, or more pleasurable reward in the future. Compare IMMEDIATE GRATIFICATION.

delay of reinforcement the time between a response and its reinforcer.

delay-of-reward gradient the relation between DELAY OF REINFORCEMENT and the effectiveness of REINFORCEMENT. The effectiveness of reinforcement decreases as the delay between response and reinforcement increases. Also called **delay-of-reinforcement gradient**.

Delboeuf illusion a size CONTRAST ILLUSION in which a concentric ring of large circles makes a medium-sized circle in the center of the ring look small, whereas the same circle in the center of a ring of smaller circles looks large. [Joseph Remi Leopold **Delboeuf** (1831–1896), French psychophysicist]

deletion *n.* **1.** in genetics, a particular kind of MUTATION characterized by the loss of genetic material from a chromosome. Deletion of a gene or part of a gene may result in development of a disease or abnormality. The deletion may involve the loss of one or several base pairs (see POINT MUTATION) or a much larger segment of a chromosome (i.e., a type of chromosome mutation). **2.** in GENERATIVE GRAMMAR, the process in which a constituent of the DEEP STRUCTURE of a sentence is deleted from the SURFACE STRUCTURE (i.e., the sentence as used). For example, the sentence *I am happy, my mother is too* is derived from the deep structure *I am happy, my mother is happy too*, with the second *happy* deleted. The question of whether deletion can serve as a psychological model of sentence processing has been a subject of much psycholinguistic investigation. See also ELLIPSIS.

deliberate psychological education (**DPE**) a curriculum that is designed to affect personal, ethical, aesthetic, and philosophical development in adolescents and young adults, through a balance of real and role-taking experiences and reflective inquiry. Counselors act as psychological educators or developmental instructors.

delibidinization *n.* see DESEXUALIZATION.

delinquency *n.* behavior violating social rules or conventions. The term is often used to denote the misbehavior of children or adolescents. See JUVENILE DELINQUENCY. —**delinquent** *adj., n.*

délire de négation see COTARD'S SYNDROME.

délire du toucher the compulsion to touch objects, which may be associated with OBSESSIVE-COMPULSIVE DISORDER or may be a complex tic in TOURETTE'S DISORDER.

deliriant *n.* a substance capable of inducing a state of acute DELIRIUM, commonly associated with restlessness or agitation. An acute delirium may result from excess ingestion of anticholinergic drugs (see CENTRAL ANTICHOLINERGIC SYNDROME) or withdrawal from alcohol and certain other substances.

delirious state a clinical state exhibiting the essential features of DELIRIUM. Delirious states can develop during amphetamine, barbiturate, or phencyclidine intoxication; during alcohol withdrawal; or as a result of other toxic conditions, systemic infections, hypoxia, head trauma, thiamine deficiency, postoperative conditions, or seizures.

delirium *n.* a state of disturbed consciousness in which attention cannot be sustained, the environment is misperceived, and the stream of thought is disordered. The individual may experience changes in cognition (which can include disorientation, memory impairment, or disturbance in language), perceptual disturbances, hallucinations, illusions, and misinterpretation of sounds or sights. The episode develops quickly and can fluctuate over a short period. Delirium may be caused by a variety of conditions including, but not limited to, infections, cerebral tumors, substance intoxication and withdrawal, head trauma, and seizures. The various types of delirium are discussed in their own individual entries.

delirium of persecution DELIRIUM in which the predominant symptoms include intense mistrust and hallucinations that one is being threatened.

delirium tremens (**DTs**) a relatively uncommon alcohol withdrawal syndrome involving extreme agitation, fearfulness, paranoia, and visual and tactile hallucinations. It is life-threatening if untreated. See also ALCOHOL WITHDRAWAL DELIRIUM.

delivery *n.* the second stage of childbirth, during which the infant travels through the birth canal and into the external world. See also AFTERBIRTH; LABOR.

Delphi technique a method of developing and improving group consensus by eliminating the effects of personal relationships and dominating personalities. Conflict is managed by circulating a questionnaire, which is edited and summarized based on the last round of comments and then reissued for further response by those participating in the survey. The Delphi technique is used in many situations where convergence of opinion is desirable (e.g., for defining goals, setting standards, or identifying and ranking needs and priorities).

delta alcoholism the fourth stage of alcoholism. It is characterized by daily drinking, increased tolerance due to cellular adaptation, and withdrawal symptoms if the person stops drinking for even a day or two. However, these individuals do not experience compulsive craving, and their control over intake is not completely lost. See also ALPHA ALCOHOLISM; BETA ALCOHOLISM; GAMMA ALCOHOLISM; EPSILON ALCOHOLISM. [defined by U.S. physician Elvin M. Jellinek (1890–1963)]

delta movement a form of APPARENT MOVEMENT in which a brighter stimulus appears to move toward a darker stimulus, provided that certain conditions of stimulus size, distance, and time between stimuli are met. Also called **delta motion**.

delta receptor see OPIOID RECEPTOR.

delta rule the principle that the change in strength of an association during learning is a function of the difference between the maximal strength possible and the current strength of the association. The delta rule is used in ASSOCIATIONISTIC THEORIES OF LEARNING and conditioning.

delta-9-tetrahydrocannabinol *n.* see CANNABIS.

delta wave the lowest frequency BRAIN WAVE recorded in electroencephalography. Delta waves are large, regular-shaped waves that have a frequency of 1–3 Hz. They are associated with deep, often dreamless, sleep (**delta-wave sleep**) and indicate a synchronization of cells of the cerebral cortex. Also called **delta rhythm**; **slow wave**. See NREM SLEEP; STAGE 3 SLEEP; STAGE 4 SLEEP.

deltoid **1.** *n.* a muscle that covers the shoulder and is used to raise the arm to the side. **2.** *adj.* pertaining to the deltoid muscle.

delusion *n.* an improbable, often highly personal, idea or belief system, not endorsed by one's culture or subculture, that is maintained with conviction in spite of irrationality or evidence to the contrary. Delusions may be transient and fragmentary, as in DELIRIUM, or highly systematized and elaborate, as in DELUSIONAL DISORDERS, though most of them fall between these two extremes. Common types include DELUSIONAL JEALOUSY, DELUSIONS OF BEING CONTROLLED, DELUSIONS OF GRANDEUR, DELUSIONS OF PERSECUTION, DELUSIONS OF REFERENCE, nihilistic delusions (see NIHILISM), and SOMATIC DELUSIONS. Data suggest delusions are not primarily logical errors but are derived from emotional material. Delusions have come to represent one of the most important factors in systems for classifying diagnostic categories. Some researchers believe that delusions may be the most important symptom of schizophrenia. See also BIZARRE DELUSION; ENCAPSULATED DELUSION; FRAGMENTARY DELUSION; SYSTEMATIZED DELUSION.

delusional disorder in *DSM–IV–TR*, any one of a group of psychotic disorders with the essential feature of one or more nonbizarre DELUSIONS that persist for at least 1 month but are not due to schizophrenia. The delusions are nonbizarre in that they feature situations that could conceivably occur in real life (e.g., being followed, poisoned, infected, deceived by one's government, etc.). Seven types of delusional disorder are specified, according to the theme of the delusion: **erotomanic type**, **grandiose type**, **jealous type**, **persecutory type**, **somatic type**, **mixed type**, and **unspecified type**. In *DSM–III*, delusional disorder was called **paranoid disorder**.

delusional jealousy a fixed delusion that a spouse or partner is unfaithful. The individual is constantly on the watch for indications that this false belief is justified, manufactures evidence if it is not to be found, and completely disregards facts that contravene the conviction. This type of delusion was formerly called **amorous** (or **conjugal**) **paranoia**. Also called **morbid jealousy**; **Othello syndrome** or **delusion**; **pathological jealousy**.

delusional mania a MANIC EPISODE characterized by delusions. Delusional mania is now more often described as a **manic episode with psychotic features**.

delusional misidentification see MISIDENTIFICATION.

delusional misidentification syndrome see MISIDENTIFICATION SYNDROME.

delusional system a more or less logically interconnected group of DELUSIONS held by the same person. Delusions that are tightly logical, but based on a false premise, are characteristic of persecutory type DELUSIONAL DISORDER. Also called **delusion system**.

delusion of being controlled the false belief that external forces, such as machines or other people, are controlling one's thoughts, feelings, or actions.

delusion of grandeur false attribution to oneself of great ability, knowledge, importance or worth, identity, prestige, power, accomplishment, or the like. Also called **grandiose delusion**. See also MEGALOMANIA.

delusion of influence **1.** the false supposition that other people or external agents are covertly exerting powers over oneself. **Idea of influence** is used synonymously, but with the implication that the condition is less definite, of shorter duration, or less severe. **2.** the false belief that one's intentions or actions directly control external events or the thoughts and behavior of other people.

delusion of negation see NIHILISM.

delusion of observation the false belief that one is being watched by others. Also called **observation delusion**.

delusion of persecution the false conviction that others are threatening or conspiring against one. Also called **persecutory delusion**.

delusion of poverty a false belief in which the individual insists that he or she is, or will soon be, entirely destitute.

delusion of reference the false conviction that the actions of others and events occurring in the external world have some special meaning or significance (typically negative) in relation to oneself. See also IDEA OF REFERENCE.

delusion of sin a delusion in which the individual is convinced of having committed unpardonable sins, for example, being to blame for wars, droughts, and other catastrophes. Such a delusion is frequently accompanied by intense fear of punishment.

delusion system see DELUSIONAL SYSTEM.

demand *n.* **1.** any internal or external condition that arouses a DRIVE in an organism. **2.** generally, a requirement or urgent need.

demand characteristics in an experiment or research project, cues that may influence or bias participants' behavior, for example, by suggesting the outcome or response that the experimenter expects or desires. Such cues can distort the findings of a study. See also EXPERIMENTER EFFECT; SENSORY LEAKAGE.

demand feeding see SELF-DEMAND SCHEDULE.

demandingness *n.* insistence upon attention, help, or advice from others. It is commonly associated with depression. See also DEPENDENCE. **—demanding** *adj.*

demandments *pl. n.* self-constructed and often self-defeating and unconscious imperatives that convert important desires and goals into absolute demands: "Because I am not performing well, as I *absolutely must,* I am a terrible person." See RATIONAL EMOTIVE BEHAVIOR THERAPY. [defined by U.S. psychotherapist Albert Ellis (1913–)]

demasculinization *n.* inhibition of masculine development in the fetus by insufficiency of androgens.

démence précoce see DEMENTIA PRAECOX.

dementia *n.* a generalized, pervasive deterioration of cognitive functions, such as memory, language, and EXECUTIVE FUNCTIONS, due to any of various causes. The loss of intellectual abilities is severe enough to interfere with an individual's daily functioning and social and occupational activity. In *DSM–IV–TR* dementias are categorized according to the cause, which may be Alzheimer's disease, cerebrovascular disease (see VASCULAR DEMENTIA), Pick's disease (mainly affecting the frontal and temporal lobes), Parkinson's disease (see also LEWY BODY DEMENTIA), Huntington's disease, HIV infection (see AIDS DEMENTIA COMPLEX), Creutzfeldt–Jakob disease, head injury, alcoholism (see ALCOHOL-INDUCED PERSISTING DEMENTIA), or substance abuse (see SUBSTANCE-INDUCED PERSISTING DEMENTIA). Brain tumor, HYPOTHYROIDISM, HEMATOMA, or other conditions, which may be treatable, can also cause dementia. The age of onset varies with the cause but is usually late in life (after 65 years). However, dementia should not be confused with AGE-ASSOCIATED MEMORY IMPAIRMENT, which has a much less deleterious impact on day-to-day functioning.

dementia of the Alzheimer's type (**DAT**) see ALZHEIMER'S DISEASE.

dementia paralytica see GENERAL PARESIS.

dementia praecox the original, now obsolete, name for SCHIZOPHRENIA, first used in 1896 by German psychiatrist Emil Kraepelin (1856–1926). It is derived from **démence précoce** (French, "early deterioration of the mind"), coined in 1857 by Austrian-born French psychiatrist Bénédict A. Morel (1809–1873), this name reflecting the belief that the symptoms of the disorder arose in adolescence or before and involved incurable degeneration. Swiss psychiatrist Eugen Bleuler (1857–1939) questioned both of these views and in 1911 renamed the disorder schizophrenia.

dementia pugilistica see BOXER'S DEMENTIA.

Dementia Rating Scale (**DRS**) a neuropsychological assessment instrument used to measure cognitive status in adults with cognitive impairments due to brain pathologies. It comprises 36 tasks of varying difficulty (e.g., repeating a series of numbers, naming objects present in the immediate environment, copying designs from stimulus cards onto blank pieces of paper) that are presented to participants in a fixed order. The scale evaluates performance on five subscales: attention, initiation–perseveration, construction, conceptualization, and memory. Originally developed in 1973 by U.S. neuropsychologist Steven Marris (1938–) and published commercially in 1988, the DRS subsequently was revised in 2001 (**DRS–2**).

dementia syndrome of depression see PSEUDODEMENTIA.

Demerol *n.* a trade name for MEPERIDINE.

Deming management method an approach to management that emphasizes the strategic role of senior management in meeting customer needs by implementing continuous improvement in the quality of products and services. The method was important in the development of TOTAL QUALITY MANAGEMENT. See also JAPANESE MANAGEMENT; THEORY Z. [W. Edwards **Deming** (1900–1993), U.S. management expert]

demo- (**dem-**) *combining form* people or population.

democracy *n.* **1.** a form of government in which the people either participate in the political process themselves or elect others to do so on their behalf (**representative democracy**) and in which decisions are made by majority vote. **2.** more loosely, any society in which all citizens have equal rights and in which certain basic freedoms, such as freedom of speech, are upheld. See also OPEN SOCIETY. **—democrat** *n.* **—democratic** *adj.*

democratic atmosphere a climate of social and political equality in which group members resolve issues and make choices through the use of procedures that ensure that the final decision accurately reflects the predominant desires and intentions of the group.

democratic leader the type of leader who establishes and maintains an egalitarian group climate in which members themselves plan activities, resolve issues, and make choices. Studies have found that groups with democratic leaders show greater originality, higher morale, and less anxiety, aggression, and apathy than do groups with AUTHORITARIAN LEADERS or with LAISSEZ-FAIRE LEADERS. [defined by Kurt LEWIN and his colleagues in experimental studies of leadership styles]

democratic parenting a parenting style, derived from the ideas of Alfred ADLER, in which the parent guides the child's development in an accepting but steady manner and fosters a climate in which cooperation, fairness, equality, and mutual respect between parent and child are assumed.

demographic analysis see DEMOGRAPHY.

demographic pattern a significant pattern revealed by a statistical study of population variables, such as marriages, births, infant mortality, income, or geographical distribution of the use of medical or mental health services.

demographic research see POPULATION RESEARCH.

demography *n.* the statistical study of human populations in regard to various factors and characteristics, including geographical distribution, sex and age distribution, size, structure, and growth trends. Such analyses are used in many types of study, including epidemiological studies. See also BIOSTATISTICS; SOCIAL STATISTICS. **—demographer** *n.* **—demographic** *adj.*

demonic possession the supposed invasion of the body by an evil spirit or devil that gains control of the mind or soul, producing mental disorder, illness, or criminal behavior. Many forms of physical and psychological illness were formerly attributed to such possession, notably EPILEPSY, SCHIZOPHRENIA, and TOURETTE'S DISORDER. The traditional remedy for possession was ritual EXORCISM.

demonolatry *n.* the worship of devils or demons. See also SATANISM; WITCHCRAFT. **—demonolator** *n.*

demonology *n.* the systematic study of belief in demons and evil spirits, frequently depicted in folklore and mythology as invading the mind, gaining possession of the soul, and producing disordered behavior. See also EXORCISM; FAMILIAR; INCUBUS; SUCCUBUS; WITCHCRAFT. **—demonological** *adj.* **—demonologist** *n.*

demonomania *n.* a morbid preoccupation with demons and demonic possession, including the belief that one is possessed by or under the control of an evil spirit or demon.

demonstration experiment a demonstration, often by a teacher in a classroom, of a well-established fact. Demonstration experiments are usually not experiments in the technical sense of comparing experimental to control conditions after randomization.

demoralization *n.* a breakdown of values, standards, and mores in an individual or group, such as may occur in periods of rapid social change, extended crises (e.g., war, economic depression), or personal traumas. A demoralized person may be disorganized and feel lost, bewildered, and insecure. **—demoralize** *vb.*

demoralization hypothesis the idea that effective psychotherapy depends on the therapist overcoming the client's state of demoralization, which can be achieved by encouraging the client to confide, explaining his or her symptoms, and providing a therapeutic ritual through which these may be resolved. Such an approach is held to be a common factor underlying the success of various therapies. [proposed by U.S. psychologist Jerome D. Frank (1909–2005)]

demotivation *n.* NEGATIVE IMAGERY or NEGATIVE SELF-TALK that emphasizes why one cannot do well in a task and thus discourages any attempt to perform it.

demyelinating disease any of various pathological conditions, such as multiple sclerosis, resulting from destruction of the MYELIN SHEATH covering nerve fibers in the central and peripheral nervous systems.

demyelination *n.* the loss of the MYELIN SHEATH that covers nerve fibers.

demyelination plaque see PLAQUE.

denasality *n.* see HYPONASALITY.

dendrite *n.* a threadlike extension of the CELL BODY that increases the receptive surface of a NEURON. **—dendritic** *adj.*

dendritic branching the pattern and quality of branching of the DENDRITES of a neuron.

dendritic pathology abnormalities of DENDRITES associated with specific psychological disorders and neurological illnesses or injuries.

dendritic potential the electric potential across the membrane of a DENDRITE, usually its RESTING POTENTIAL.

dendritic spine an outgrowth along the DENDRITE of a neuron. Many synapses occur between axon terminals and dendritic spines. Also called **dendritic thorn**.

dendritic tree the full arrangement of the DENDRITES of a single neuron.

dendritic zone any part of the receptive surface of a neuron, including the membrane of the CELL BODY.

dendrodendritic synapse a SYNAPSE between DENDRITES of two neurons.

dendrophilia *n.* a PARAPHILIA characterized by sexual attraction to trees. The person may have actual sexual contact with trees, may venerate them as phallic symbols, or both. Also called **dendrophily**.

denervation *n.* removal or interruption of the nerves that supply a part of the body.

denervation sensitivity see DISUSE SUPERSENSITIVITY.

denial *n.* a DEFENSE MECHANISM in which unpleasant thoughts, feelings, wishes, or events are ignored or excluded from conscious awareness. It may take such forms as refusal to acknowledge the reality of a terminal illness, a financial problem, an addiction, or a partner's infidelity. Denial is an unconscious process that functions to resolve emotional conflict or reduce anxiety. Also called **disavowal**. **—deny** *vb.*

denial and shock stage the first of the five STAGES OF DYING described by Swiss-born U.S. psychiatrist Elisabeth Kübler-Ross (1926–2004). It consists of an intense but brief state in which an all-encompassing wave of anxiety interferes with a person's ability to acknowledge or accept that he or she has a fatal condition.

denial of blindness see ANTON'S SYNDROME.

denotative meaning the objective or literal meaning of a word or phrase as opposed to its **connotative meaning**, which includes the various ideas and emotions that it suggests within a particular culture. So, for example, the word *father* denotes "male parent" but may connote a range of ideas involving protection, authority, and love.

density *n.* **1.** the compactness of the constituent elements of something, reflecting its degree of impenetrability. **2.** a measure of the amount of physical space per individual. High density can produce crowding, a psychological state of needing more space. Interior indices of density (e.g., people per room) are consistently related to negative psychological consequences, whereas external indices (e.g., people per square mile) are not. See also POPULATION DENSITY; SOCIAL DENSITY; SPATIAL DENSITY. **3.** in auditory perception, the quality of a sound representing a TONAL ATTRIBUTE of solidity distinct from PITCH, volume, or TIMBRE. **4.** in physics, the mass per unit volume of a substance. **—dense** *adj.*

density function the mathematical function rule that defines a probability distribution.

density–intensity hypothesis an explanation of psychological reactions to overcrowding positing that high DENSITY makes unpleasant situations more unpleasant but pleasant situations more pleasant. [proposed by U.S. psychologist Jonathan M. Freedman (1952–)]

dent- *combining form* see DENTI-.

dental 1. *adj.* of or relating to the teeth. **2.** *adj.* denoting a speech sound produced with the tongue touching the upper front teeth, as in the French [t] sound. **3.** *adj.* more loosely, denoting any ALVEOLAR, dental, or INTERDENTAL speech sound. **4.** *n.* a dental speech sound.

dental age a measure of dental development based on the number of permanent teeth present. Dental age may be used to calculate CHRONOLOGICAL AGE.

dental lisp see LISP.

dental pattern the species-specific arrangement of teeth by type (i.e. incisors, canines, bicuspids, and molars) in each quadrant of the mouth, from front to back.

dental phobia a persistent and irrational fear of dentists or of dental treatment that may be related to a prior traumatic dental experience, a lower-than-normal pain threshold, or fear of having a PANIC ATTACK. In *DSM–IV–TR* dental phobia is classified as a SPECIFIC PHOBIA.

dentate gyrus a strip of gray matter that connects the HIPPOCAMPUS with the ENTORHINAL CORTEX. It is part of the HIPPOCAMPAL FORMATION.

dentate nucleus a cluster of cell bodies in the CEREBELLUM believed to be associated with skilled and rapid movement.

denti- (**dent-**) *combining form* teeth.

denying the antecedent a formal FALLACY in which one denies (or negates) the ANTECEDENT of an *if...then* statement and concludes, on this basis, that the CONSEQUENT is also false. For example: *If it is raining, then the ground will be wet: It is not raining: Therefore the ground is not wet.* No valid conclusion can be drawn from the fact that the antecedent is not validated. See also AFFIRMING THE ANTECEDENT; AFFIRMING THE CONSEQUENT.

denying the consequent in logic, the principle that if a conditional statement of the type "if X, then Y" is accepted as true, then the negation of the ANTECEDENT (X) can be validly inferred from the negation of the CONSEQUENT (Y). For example: *If it is raining, then the grass will be wet: The grass is not wet: Therefore it is not raining.* Also called **modus tollens**. See also AFFIRMING THE ANTECEDENT; AFFIRMING THE CONSEQUENT.

deoxycorticosterone *n.* a potent MINERALOCORTICOID hormone synthesized by the adrenal glands. It is a precursor of CORTICOSTERONE.

deoxyglucose *n.* a compound that is related to glucose but cannot be metabolized. It is therefore used, in various forms, to label cells for histological examination or imaging techniques; for example, radiolabeled 2-deoxyglucose is used in POSITRON EMISSION TOMOGRAPHY.

deoxyribonucleic acid see DNA.

Depacon *n.* a trade name for valproate sodium. See VALPROIC ACID.

Depakene *n.* a trade name for VALPROIC ACID.

Depakote *n.* a trade name for DIVALPROEX SODIUM.

dependence *n.* **1.** a state in which assistance from others is intuitively expected or actively sought for emotional or financial support, protection, security, or daily care. The dependent person leans on others for guidance, decision making, and nurturance. Whereas some degree of dependence is natural in interpersonal relations, excessive, inappropriate, or misdirected reliance on others is often a focus of psychological treatment. Personality, social, and behavioral psychology, as well as psychoanalytic theory, all contribute different perspectives to the study and treatment of pathological dependence. **2.** see SUBSTANCE DEPENDENCE. **3.** in OPERANT CONDITIONING, a causal relation between a response and a consequence, which results in a CONTINGENCY. Also called **dependency**. **—dependent** *adj.*

Dependency Court in the United States, a court dealing with all issues concerned with child abuse and neglect; such issues are brought to the attention of the court by a government agency (typically Child Protective Services), which intervenes on behalf of the child by filing a petition alleging abuse or neglect.

dependency needs personal needs that must be satisfied by others, including the need for affection, love, shelter, physical care, food, warmth, protection, and security. Such needs are considered universal and normal for both sexes and at all ages. It is also recognized that dependence can be maladaptive (e.g., excessive and over-encouraged) and generate a variety of issues surrounding attachment. See also CODEPENDENCY; MORBID DEPENDENCY.

dependency ratio the percentage of a population that is not working for pay: a measure of the portion of a population that is composed of people who are too young to work or who have retired. The dependency ratio is often defined as the number of individuals aged below 15 or above 64 divided by the number of individuals aged 15 to 64.

dependency-support script a strategy in which caregivers consistently and immediately meet all the needs of an older adult receiving care. The adoption of this SCRIPT often reduces the autonomy and independence of the person receiving care.

dependent model see INTEGRATED MODEL.

dependent-part quality in GESTALT PSYCHOLOGY, the quality that a part of a larger whole derives by virtue of the part–whole relationship.

dependent personality disorder in *DSM–IV–TR*, a personality disorder manifested in a long-term pattern of passively allowing others to take responsibility for major areas of life and of subordinating personal needs to the needs of others, due to lack of self-confidence and self-dependence. It was formerly known as **passive-dependent personality**.

dependent variable (**DV**) the "outcome" variable that is observed to occur or change after the occurrence or variation of the INDEPENDENT VARIABLE. Dependent variables may or may not be related causally to the independent variable.

depersonalization *n.* a state of mind in which the self appears unreal. Individuals feel estranged from themselves and usually from the external world, and thoughts and experiences have a distant, dreamlike character. In its persistent form, depersonalization is observed in such disorders as depression, hypochondriasis, dissociative states, temporal-lobe epilepsy, and early schizophrenia. The extreme form is called **depersonalization syndrome**.

depersonalization disorder a DISSOCIATIVE DISORDER characterized by one or more episodes of DEPERSONALIZATION severe enough to impair social and occupational functioning. Onset of depersonalization is rapid and usually manifested in a sensation of self-estrangement, a feeling that one's extremities are changed in size, a sense of being mechanical, perceiving oneself at a distance, and, in some cases, a feeling that the external world is unreal (DEREALIZATION).

depersonalization syndrome see DEPERSONALIZATION.

depersonification *n.* **1.** treatment of another person as something other than the unique individual that he or she really is. For example, parents may treat their child as an extension of themselves, which leads to the child having a distorted sense of self. **2.** in psychoanalytic theory, a stage in the maturation of the SUPEREGO that follows INTROJECTION of parental IMAGOES and leads to integration of parental values as abstract ideas. **—depersonify** *vb.*

depletive treatment a type of treatment that involves deliberately weakening the organism and thereby (it is supposed) depleting it of some substance believed to be harmful, as by bleeding, purging, blistering, or making the patient vomit. Depletive treatment originated in the time of Greek physician Hippocrates (c. 460–c. 377 BCE) and was practiced for many centuries. More recently, certain psychiatric disorders have been treated by depletive therapies, as in various shock therapies.

depolarization *n.* a reduction in the MEMBRANE POTENTIAL of a cell, especially a neuron. When a neuron is at rest, the inner surface of the membrane is negative in relation to the outer surface. Depolarization occurs when the membrane is stimulated or a nerve impulse is transmitted. See ACTION POTENTIAL. Compare HYPERPOLARIZATION.

Depo-Provera *n.* a trade name for medroxyprogesterone acetate, an ANTIANDROGEN used in the treatment of sex offenders. See CHEMICAL CASTRATION.

deprenyl *n.* see SELEGILINE.

depressant *n.* any agent that diminishes or retards any function or activity of a body system or organ. See CNS DEPRESSANTS.

depressed skull fracture a skull fracture in which part of the skull is pressed in toward the brain. In some cases, skull fragments may enter the brain tissue.

depression *n.* **1.** DYSPHORIA that can vary in severity from a fluctuation in normal mood to an extreme feeling of sadness, pessimism, and despondency. **2.** in psychiatry, any of the DEPRESSIVE DISORDERS. **—depressed** *adj.*

depression after delivery a less common name for POSTPARTUM DEPRESSION.

depression stage the fourth of the five STAGES OF DYING described by Swiss-born U.S. psychiatrist Elisabeth Kübler-Ross (1926–2004). It occurs as the person experiences increasing weakness and loss of function.

depressive anxiety in psychoanalytic theory, anxiety provoked by fear of one's own hostile feelings toward others. It is based on the theory that depression is hostility turned inward.

depressive disorder in *DSM–IV–TR*, any of the MOOD DISORDERS that typically have sadness as one of their symptoms. They include DYSTHYMIC DISORDER, MAJOR DEPRESSIVE DISORDER, and DEPRESSIVE DISORDER NOT OTHERWISE SPECIFIED. See UNIPOLAR DEPRESSION.

depressive disorder not otherwise specified in *DSM–IV–TR*, a mood disorder with depressive symptoms that does not meet the criteria for either of the specific DEPRESSIVE DISORDERS (i.e., major depressive disorder or dysthymic disorder). This category includes MINOR DE-

PRESSIVE DISORDER and PREMENSTRUAL DYSPHORIC DISORDER.

depressive episode see MAJOR DEPRESSIVE EPISODE.

depressive neurosis a former name for DYSTHYMIC DISORDER.

depressive personality disorder a recently classified personality disorder (in the appendix of *DSM–IV–TR*) characterized by glumness, pessimism, a lack of joy, the inability to experience pleasure, and motor retardation. Feelings of loss, a sense of giving up, and an orientation to pain are notable. There are vegetative signs, despair regarding the future, and a disheartened outlook.

depressive position in the OBJECT RELATIONS THEORY of Melanie KLEIN, the stage of infant development that reaches its peak at about 6 months of age. In the depressive position the infant begins to perceive the GOOD OBJECT and BAD OBJECT as a single whole and feels guilt for having attacked the good object during the preceding PARANOID-SCHIZOID POSITION. In this—Klein's most mature—phase of primary psychological organization, the infant fears that he or she will lose or destroy the good object and attempts to make REPARATION for earlier hostility.

depressive reaction see REACTIVE DEPRESSION.

depressive spectrum the range of severity and disparate symptoms that characterize DEPRESSIVE DISORDERS. The underlying concept is that depression is a range of related disorders, rather than a single diagnostic entity.

depressor nerve an afferent nerve that depresses motor or glandular activity when stimulated, for example, a nerve that causes a fall in blood pressure via a brainstem reflex.

deprivation *n.* **1.** the removal, denial, or unavailability of something needed or desired. See CULTURAL DEPRIVATION; MATERNAL DEPRIVATION. **2.** in CONDITIONING, reduction of access to or intake of a REINFORCER. **—deprive** *vb.*

deprivation dwarfism stunting of physical growth in infancy and early childhood due to such nonorganic factors as maternal separation or emotional neglect. See also FAILURE TO THRIVE.

deprivation index a measure of the degree of inadequacy in a child's intellectual environment with respect to such variables as achievement expectations, incentives to explore and understand the environment, provision for general learning, emphasis on language development, and communication and interaction with significant adult role models.

deprogramming *n.* the process by which people who have adopted profoundly new sets of attitudes, beliefs, and values have their original attitudes, beliefs, and values restored. Deprogramming techniques are typically used on people who have left or been removed from highly coercive social groups, such as religious cults. See also BRAINWASHING.

depth cue any of a variety of means used to inform the visual system about the depth of a target or its distance from the observer. **Monocular depth cues** require only one eye and include signals about the state of the CILIARY MUSCLES, ATMOSPHERIC PERSPECTIVE, and occlusion of distant objects by near objects. **Binocular depth cues** require integration of information from the two eyes and include signals about the CONVERGENCE of the eyes and RETINAL DISPARITY.

depth-first search a GRAPH search strategy, equivalent to BACKTRACK SEARCH, that considers states in a graph recursively. The search is often organized by a "stack" or "last-in is first-out" data structure.

depth from motion a DEPTH CUE obtained from the distance that an image moves across the retina. Motion cues are particularly effective when more than one object is moving. Depth from motion can be inferred when the observer is stationary and the objects move, as in the KINETIC DEPTH EFFECT, or when the objects are stationary but the observer's head moves, inducing MOTION PARALLAX.

depth from shading a DEPTH CUE obtained from the pattern of light and shadow on an illuminated solid object. The shading alone, without any outline of an object, can also convey a sense of three-dimensional depth.

depth interview an interview designed to reveal deep-seated feelings, attitudes, opinions, and motives by encouraging the individual to express himself or herself freely without fear of disapproval or concern about the interviewer's reactions. Such interviews may be conducted, for example, in counseling and as part of qualitative market research. They tend to be relatively lengthy, unstructured, one-on-one conversations.

depth-of-processing hypothesis the theory that the strength of memory is dependent on the degree of cognitive processing the material receives. Depth has been defined variously as ELABORATION, amount of cognitive effort expended, and the distinctiveness of the MEMORY TRACE formed. This theory is an expanded empirical investigation of the LEVELS-OF-PROCESSING MODEL OF MEMORY. [expounded in 1972 by Canadian psychologist Fergus I. M. Craik (1935–) and Robert S. Lockhart and in 1975 by Craik and Estonian-born Canadian psychologist Endel Tulving (1927–)]

depth-oriented brief therapy a form of brief psychotherapy that applies principles of CONSTRUCTIVIST PSYCHOTHERAPY in a time-limited fashion.

depth perception awareness of three-dimensionality, solidity, and the distance between the observer and the object. Depth perception is achieved through such cues as ATMOSPHERIC PERSPECTIVE, MOTION PARALLAX, visual ACCOMMODATION, RETINAL DISPARITY, and CONVERGENCE. See also VISUAL CLIFF.

depth psychology a general approach to psychology and psychotherapy that focuses on unconscious mental processes as the source of emotional disturbance and symptoms, as well as personality, attitudes, creativity, and lifestyle. A typical example is CLASSICAL PSYCHOANALYSIS, but others include Carl JUNG'S ANALYTIC PSYCHOLOGY and Alfred ADLER'S INDIVIDUAL PSYCHOLOGY.

depth therapy any form of psychotherapy, brief or extended, that involves identifying and working through unconscious conflicts and experiences that underlie and interfere with behavior and adjustment. Compare SURFACE THERAPY.

Deracyn *n.* a trade name for ADINAZOLAM.

derailment *n.* a symptom of thought disorder, often occurring in individuals with schizophrenia, marked by frequent interruptions in thought and jumping from one idea to another unrelated or indirectly related idea. It is usually manifested in speech (**speech derailment**) but can also be observed in writing. Derailment is essentially equivalent to LOOSENING OF ASSOCIATIONS. See COGNITIVE DERAILMENT; DERAILMENT OF VOLITION; THOUGHT DERAILMENT.

derailment of volition a type of indecisiveness in which consistency of goals and purposes is replaced by tangential and irrelevant impulses, contradictory wishes, and short-lived causes.

derangement *n.* **1.** disturbance in the regular order or normal functioning of something. **2.** loosely, mental illness or mental disturbance.

derealization *n.* a state characterized by a sense of unreality; that is, an alteration in the perception of external reality so that it seems strange or unreal ("This can't be happening"), often due to trauma or stress. It may also occur as a feature of SCHIZOPHRENIA or of certain DISSOCIATIVE DISORDERS. See also DEPERSONALIZATION.

dereflection *n.* a common technique used to allay anxiety or stop inappropriate behavior by diverting attention to a different topic and away from the self. It is used to reduce excessive self-concern, shyness, and worry about the self and is a central component in MORITA THERAPY.

dereism *n.* mental activity that is not in accord with reality, experience, or logic. It is similar to AUTISTIC THINKING. Also called **dereistic thinking**.

derivative insight an insight into a problem that is achieved by the client without interpretation by the therapist.

derived ideas ideas that have causes outside the mind and thus derive from external sources, such as particular sense impressions. French philosopher and mathematician René Descartes (1596–1650) distinguished between derived ideas and INNATE IDEAS, which arise from processes of thought that occur naturally in the mind. According to Descartes, derived ideas are less clear and distinct, and less obviously trustworthy, than innate ideas. See CARTESIANISM; CARTESIAN SELF.

derived need a need developed through association with or generalization from a PRIMARY NEED.

derived property in GESTALT PSYCHOLOGY, a property taken on by a part of a whole by virtue of its being in a particular configuration or context. For example, if three noncollinear dots are seen as forming a triangle, each dot then has the derived property of being a vertex of the triangle.

derma *n.* the skin, particularly the DERMIS.

dermal sensation see CUTANEOUS EXPERIENCE.

dermal sensitivity the cutaneous sensations detected by nerve receptors in the skin.

dermato- (dermo-) *combining form* skin.

dermatoglyphics *n.* the study of the patterns of lines on the skin of the fingers, palms, and soles. The technique is used in the diagnosis of certain kinds of chromosomal abnormalities based on observations that some patterns are associated with certain types of birth defects or disorders. For example, people with Down syndrome have a single crease across the palm and a single crease on the skin of the little (fifth) finger.

dermatographism *n.* a kind of HIVES (urticaria) due to physical allergy in which a pale raised welt or wheal with a red flare on each side appears when the skin is scratched with a dull instrument. Also called **autographism**; **dermographia**.

dermatological disorder any disorder or disease of the skin. See also PSYCHOCUTANEOUS DISORDER.

dermatome *n.* **1.** an area of skin that is innervated primarily by fibers from the dorsal root of a particular SPINAL NERVE. **2.** a surgical instrument for removing thin slices of skin to be used as skin grafts or for removing lesions.

dermis *n.* the layer of skin beneath the outermost layer (EPIDERMIS). The dermis contains blood and lymphatic vessels, nerves and nerve endings, and the hair follicles. **—dermal** *adj.*

dermographia *n.* see DERMATOGRAPHISM.

dermo-optical perception (DOP) an alleged ability to see or to identify the color of objects by touch alone. U.S. psychologist Richard P. Youtz (1910–1986) suggested that people with this ability detect colors by means of temperature differences due to reflection of hand heat or other heat from the object. Also called **cutaneous perception of color**.

DES 1. abbreviation for DIETHYLSTILBESTROL. **2.** abbreviation for DYSEXECUTIVE SYNDROME.

descending pathway 1. a NEURAL PATHWAY from a higher center that modulates sensory input, such as tracts from the cerebral cortex to the spinal cord that gate pain input (see SPINAL GATE). **2.** see DESCENDING TRACT.

descending reticular system part of the RETICULAR FORMATION that receives information from the hypothalamus and is involved in activity of the autonomic nervous system. It also plays a role in motor activity.

descending tract a bundle of nerve fibers (see TRACT) that carries impulses from the brain to the spinal cord. There are three major descending tracts: the CORTICOSPINAL TRACT, VESTIBULOSPINAL TRACT, and RETICULOSPINAL TRACT. Also called **descending nerve tract**; **descending pathway**. Compare ASCENDING TRACT.

descent group any social group, such as a CLAN, PHRATRY, or SEPT, membership in which depends on real or supposed descent from a common ancestor. The group may be defined by UNILATERAL DESCENT (as in PATRIARCHY or MATRIARCHY) or BILATERAL DESCENT. See also KINSHIP NETWORK.

deschooling *n.* an informal movement of the late 1960s and 1970s that criticized the formal educational system for emphasizing a narrow idea of academic knowledge and ignoring people's real-life experience and the wider social context in which all learning takes place. Such thinkers and polemicists as Austrian-born U.S. writer Ivan Illich (1926–2002) sought to separate education from its institutional context and to promote the idea of informal life-long learning. **—deschool** *vb.*

descriptive approach see TOPOGRAPHIC MODEL.

descriptive average an approximate estimate of the average calculated on the basis of imprecise or partial data.

descriptive behaviorism an approach to the study of behavior espoused by B. F. SKINNER, who felt that psychology should limit itself to a description of behaviors of organisms, the conditions under which they occur, and their effects on the environment. It requires that theoretical explanations in terms of underlying biological or hypothetical psychological processes be avoided. See BEHAVIORISM; RADICAL BEHAVIORISM.

descriptive grammar see PRESCRIPTIVE GRAMMAR.

descriptive norms socially determined consensual standards (SOCIAL NORMS) that describe how people typically act, feel, and think in a given situation. These tacit standards, by identifying what actions and reactions are expected, also delineate those actions and reactions that are so uncommon that they would be considered odd or unusual if they occurred in that setting. Compare INJUNCTIVE NORMS.

descriptive operant in experimental studies of behavior, the formal, physical requirements for reinforcement (see OPERANT). For example, the descriptive operant for pressing a lever might be as follows: Any action on the part of the subject that exerts a force on the lever of 0.2 N through a distance of 5 mm will be reinforced. Compare FUNCTIONAL OPERANT.

descriptive research an empirical investigation designed to test prespecified hypotheses or to provide an overview of existing conditions and, sometimes, relationships, without aspiring to draw causal inferences.

descriptive responsibility the judgment that a defendant has performed an illegal act, as opposed to the judgment that he or she can be ascribed CRIMINAL RESPONSIBILITY. Compare ASCRIPTIVE RESPONSIBILITY.

descriptive science see NORMATIVE SCIENCE.

descriptive statistic a numerical index used to describe a particular feature of the data.

desegregation *n.* see SOCIAL INTEGRATION.

desensitization *n.* a reduction in emotional or physical reactivity to stimuli that is achieved by such means as gaining insight into its nature or origin, CATHARSIS, or DECONDITIONING techniques. See also COVERT DESENSITIZATION; IN VIVO DESENSITIZATION; SYSTEMATIC DESENSITIZATION.

desertion *n.* see ABANDONMENT.

desexualization *n.* in psychoanalytic theory, the elimination or NEUTRALIZATION of a sexual aim. Also called **delibidinization**. See also SUBLIMATION. **—desexualize** *vb.*

design and behavior see ARCHITECTURAL PSYCHOLOGY.

designer drugs synthetic opioids, usually with heroin-like effects, designed with chemical structures that circumvent existing legal definitions of controlled substances and hence avoid restrictions on their use. These drugs tend to be abused by young middle-class people. See also CLUB DRUGS.

design fluency test any of a group of tests in which participants must generate (within a given time) a series of figures that have specific criteria. The tests were developed to provide clinical information regarding nonverbal capacity for flexibility and planning similar to VERBAL FLUENCY TESTS. For example, participants may be required to produce figures made from five lines and must devise new ways to put the lines together in an organized manner to make new figures or designs. Also called **figural fluency test**.

design for adjustable range the practice of designing equipment so that it can be adjusted to suit the physical characteristics of a large portion of the population. Compare DESIGN FOR THE AVERAGE; UNIVERSAL DESIGN.

design for the average the principle that equipment for human use should be designed for average human dimensions, thereby sacrificing the extreme dimensions (e.g., below the 5th and above the 95th percentiles). Although no truly "average" person exists, this principle is used when adjustable designs cannot be developed and it is impossible or impracticable to design for the extremes. Compare DESIGN FOR ADJUSTABLE RANGE; UNIVERSAL DESIGN.

design matrix a matrix whose elements denote the presence or absence of each participant (row) in a treatment (column) of an experimental design.

design trade-off the situation in which one attribute of a system or product is made less usable because another attribute has been given priority. An example is the press-and-hold requirement on cell phones, which is used to reduce the chance of accidental power-up: The press-and-hold is not intuitive and may be frustrating at times, but eliminating accidental activation is considered to be a greater benefit.

desipramine *n.* a TRICYCLIC ANTIDEPRESSANT and the principal metabolic product of IMIPRAMINE, produced in the body by the demethylation of imipramine in the liver. Desipramine is a stronger inhibitor of norepinephrine reuptake than of serotonin reuptake relative to imipramine. In general, it is less sedating and has fewer ANTICHOLINERGIC EFFECTS than imipramine and was previously frequently used to treat behavior disorders and insomnia in children. However, like all tricyclic antidepressants, it has fallen into relative disuse as safer medications have become available. U.S. trade name: **Norpramin**.

deskilling *n.* the redesign of tasks in an organization so that they require less knowledge, skill, and ability and take less time to learn. Deskilling is often a consequence of technological and organizational change; it usually results in a loss of motivation on the part of employees. **—deskill** *vb.*

desmopressin *n.* a synthetic analog of the pituitary hormone VASOPRESSIN that, among other functions, stimulates water retention and raises blood pressure. Desmopressin is used in the form of a nasal spray to treat nocturnal enuresis (bed-wetting) and DIABETES INSIPIDUS. It possesses more antidiuretic activity (i.e., prevents excessive water loss from the body) and less potential to raise blood pressure than vasopressin. U.S. trade name (among others): **DDAVP**.

desocialization *n.* gradual withdrawal from social contacts and interpersonal communication, with absorption in private thought processes and adoption of idiosyncratic and often bizarre behavior.

Desoxyn *n.* a trade name for METHAMPHETAMINE.

despair *n.* **1.** the emotion or feeling of hopelessness, that is, that things are profoundly wrong and will not change for the better. Despair is one of the most negative and destructive of human affects and behaviors, and as such is a primary area for psychotherapeutic intervention. **2.** in ERIKSON'S EIGHT STAGES OF DEVELOPMENT, see INTEGRITY VERSUS DESPAIR.

despondency *n.* a state characterized by both APATHY and depressed mood. **—despondent** *adj.*

destiny neurosis see FATE NEUROSIS.

destructive behavior the expression of anger, hostility, or aggression by damaging or destroying external objects or oneself (see SELF-DESTRUCTIVENESS).

destructive conflict resolution the use of negative methods, such as threats, arguments, and coercion, to resolve interpersonal disagreements. Parties are more likely to use these methods when they are not prepared at the outset to consider each other's perspective, and the methods themselves are often counterproductive, resulting in greater antagonism in future interactions. Compare CONSTRUCTIVE CONFLICT RESOLUTION.

destructive instinct see DEATH INSTINCT.

destructiveness *n.* a tendency toward the expression of aggressive behavior by destroying, damaging, or defacing objects. See also SELF-DESTRUCTIVENESS.

destructive obedience compliance with the direct or indirect orders of a social, military, or moral authority that results in negative outcomes, such as injury inflicted on innocent victims, harm to the community, or the loss of confidence in social institutions. Stanley MILGRAM studied destructive obedience by ordering participants to engage in behavior that apparently harmed another person (see BEHAVIORAL STUDY OF OBEDIENCE). Other examples of destructive obedience include soldiers obeying when ordered to attack innocent civilians or medical personnel following a doctor's orders even when they know the doctor is mistaken.

destrudo *n.* the energy associated with THANATOS, the

DEATH INSTINCT. Destrudo contrasts with LIBIDO, the energy of EROS, the LIFE INSTINCT. See also MORTIDO. [defined by Austrian-Italian psychoanalyst Edoardo Weiss (1889–1970)]

desurgency *n.* a personality trait characterized by anxiety, brooding, and seclusion. [defined by British-born U.S. personality psychologist Raymond Bernard Cattell (1905–1998)]

desymbolization *n.* the process of depriving symbols, especially words, of their accepted meanings and substituting distorted, neologistic, autistic, or concrete ideas for them.

desynchronization *n.* in electroencephalography, the replacement of ALPHA WAVES by fast, low-amplitude, irregular waveforms, often because of an external stimulus, usually one that alerts the individual. See ALPHA BLOCKING.

desynchronized sleep see REM SLEEP.

Desyrel *n.* a trade name for TRAZODONE.

DET *di*ethyl*t*ryptamine: a synthetic HALLUCINOGEN belonging to the indolealkylamine family, to which LSD, PSILOCIN, and DMT also belong.

detached character a personality characterized by extreme self-sufficiency and lack of feeling for others. German-born U.S. psychoanalyst Karen D. Horney (1885–1952) identified the development of such a character as one of three basic NEUROTIC TRENDS used as a defense against BASIC ANXIETY. Compare AGGRESSIVE CHARACTER; COMPLIANT CHARACTER.

detached retina the separation of the inner layer of the RETINA (the neural retina) from the outer PIGMENT EPITHELIUM layer. The onset of symptoms, depending upon the size and site of the detachment, may include flashes of light followed later by a clouding of vision, the appearance of spots or visual artifacts before the eye (known as "floaters"), or a sudden complete loss of vision. Detached retina is usually treated by surgery. Also called **retinal detachment**. See also DIABETIC RETINOPATHY.

detachment *n.* **1.** a feeling of emotional freedom resulting from a lack of involvement in a problem or with another situation or person. **2.** objectivity: that is, the ability to consider a problem on its merits alone. Also called **intellectual detachment**. **3.** in developmental psychology, the child's desire to have new experiences and develop new skills. This occurs at about 2 years of age, as the child begins to outgrow the period of total attachment to and dependence on the parent or caregiver.

detailed inquiry a phase of a CLINICAL INTERVIEW during which the therapist gains an understanding of the patient by asking direct questions on many diverse topics, ranging from mundane questions about everyday life to highly detailed questions, for example, about particular reactions to specific events.

detail perspective a DEPTH CUE related to texture. Features or details on a surface appear closer together on a distant object and farther apart on a near object.

detection task see SIGNAL DETECTION TASK.

detection theory see SIGNAL DETECTION THEORY.

detection threshold see ABSOLUTE THRESHOLD.

deterioration *n.* progressive impairment or loss of basic functions, such as emotional, judgmental, intellectual, muscular, and memory functions.

deterioration effect an adverse effect or negative outcome from participating in psychotherapy.

deterioration index a pattern of subtest scores on the WECHSLER ADULT INTELLIGENCE SCALE viewed as suggestive of neurological deficit and used in measuring the degree of reduced performance that can be attributed to aging. Also called **deterioration quotient**. See also DON'T-HOLD FUNCTIONS; HOLD FUNCTIONS.

deterioration of attention inconstant and shifting attention and impaired ability to concentrate on external reality.

deterioration quotient see DETERIORATION INDEX.

determinant *n.* any internal or external condition that is the cause of an event.

determinant of elaboration any factor that influences the amount of ELABORATION a person engages in when encountering attitude-relevant information. Such factors may regulate ability to elaborate (e.g., distractions in the social context) or motivation to elaborate (e.g., the personal relevance of the ATTITUDE OBJECT). See also ELABORATION-LIKELIHOOD MODEL.

determination *n.* **1.** a mental attitude characterized by a strong commitment to achieving a particular goal despite barriers and hardships. **2.** the act or process of making a decision, reaching a conclusion, or ascertaining the characteristics or exact nature of something, or the end result of such a process. **3.** the precise definition or qualification of the attributes of a concept or proposal (e.g., determination of the dependent variable in an experiment).

determination coefficient see COEFFICIENT OF DETERMINATION.

determiner *n.* in linguistics, a word that appears with a noun or pronoun and limits (determines) its reference in some way, such as *a, the, this, that, some, all, any, every,* and so on. Numbers (as in *three cats*) and personal pronouns (as in *her cats*) can also be determiners. See also ARTICLE; QUANTIFIER.

determining tendency a goal direction or SET that arouses and maintains a particular behavior sequence. The term, introduced by German psychologist Narziss Ach (1871–1946), has a broader implication than the nearly synonymous AUFGABE, EINSTELLUNG, or MENTAL SET. Also called **determining set**.

determinism *n.* **1.** in philosophy, the position that all events, physical or mental, including human behavior, are the necessary results of antecedent causes or other entities or forces. Determinism requires that both the past and the future are fixed. See also CAUSALITY. **2.** in psychology, the position that all human behaviors result from specific efficient causal antecedents, such as biological structures or processes, environmental conditions, or past experience. The relationships between these antecedents and the behaviors they produce can be described by generalizations much like the laws that describe regularities in nature. Determinism contrasts with belief in FREE WILL, which implies that individuals can choose to act in some ways independent of antecedent events and conditions. Those who advocate free-will positions often adopt a position of SOFT DETERMINISM, which holds that free will and responsibility are compatible with determinism. Others hold that free will is illusory, a position known as HARD DETERMINISM. Of contemporary psychological theories, BEHAVIORISM takes most clearly a hard determinist position. See also GENETIC DETERMINISM; PHYSICAL DETERMINISM; PSYCHIC DETERMINISM; PSYCHOLOGICAL DETERMINISM. Compare INDETERMINISM. —**determinist** *adj., n.* —**deterministic** *adj.*

deterministic psychology any psychology that assumes DETERMINISM, most notably BEHAVIORISM.

deterrence *n.* the notion that punishing an individual who has committed an undesirable act, particularly a criminal one, will deter that person, as well as others, from committing such acts in the future. **—deter** *vb.* **—deterrent** *n., adj.*

deterrent therapy see AVERSION THERAPY.

detour problem in studies of problem solving, any problem or task that must be solved or performed indirectly or circuitously, often because the most direct solution is ineffective or blocked. Also called **Umweg problem**.

detoxification *n.* a therapeutic procedure, popularly known as **detox**, that reduces or eliminates toxic substances in the body. These procedures may be metabolic (by converting the toxic substance to a less harmful agent that is more easily excreted) or they may require induced vomiting, gastric lavage (washing), or dialysis, depending upon the nature of the poison and other factors. Examples are the use of methadone in opioid intoxication, tranquilizers to ease alcohol withdrawal, and lavage and artificial respiration in barbiturate poisoning.

detoxification center a clinic, hospital unit, or other facility devoted to the alleviation of the toxic effects of drug or alcohol overdose and to the management of acute withdrawal symptoms. These centers may focus on either medical or nonmedical procedures, depending on the severity of the syndromes handled. See ALCOHOL WITHDRAWAL; SUBSTANCE WITHDRAWAL.

detoxification effects see SUBSTANCE WITHDRAWAL.

detumescence *n.* the reduction or subsidence of a swelling, especially in the genital organs of either sex following orgasm. Compare TUMESCENCE. **—detumescent** *adj.*

Detussin *n.* a trade name for a combination of HYDROCODONE and pseudoephedrine.

deutan color blindness a type of color blindness in which green hues are perceived imperfectly or green is confused with red. In some cases, the condition results from an ability to perceive only two distinct hues, blue and yellow.

deuteranomaly *n.* a form of color blindness in which the green part of the spectrum is perceived inadequately. In testing for deuteranomaly, an unusual amount of green would be required in a red–green mixture to match a given yellow.

deuteranopia *n.* red–green color blindness, in which the deficiency is due to absence of the cone PHOTOPIGMENT sensitive to green light, resulting in loss of green sensitivity and confusion between red and green (see DICHROMATISM). The condition may be unilateral (i.e., color vision may be normal in one eye). See also PROTANOPIA.

deutero- (**deuter-**; **deut-**) *combining form* second or secondary. See COLOR BLINDNESS.

deutoplasm *n.* a substance, rich in protein and fat, that is laid down within the yolk of an egg cell to serve as nourishment for the embryo. It is absent from the egg cells of mammals, whose embryos absorb nutrients from their mothers via the placenta.

devaluation *n.* a DEFENSE MECHANISM that involves denying the importance of something or someone, including the self. **—devalue** *vb.*

development *n.* the progressive series of changes in structure, function, and behavior patterns that occur over the life span of a human being or other organism. **—developmental** *adj.*

developmental acceleration an abnormal or precocious growth in one or more functions (e.g., language).

developmental age (**DA**) a measure of development expressed in an age unit or AGE EQUIVALENT. For example, a 4-year-old child may have a developmental age of 6 in verbal skills.

developmental amblyopia a condition affecting central vision in which the early development of neural circuits for fine-pattern discrimination is disrupted due to inadequate detail in foveal imagery. There are two forms of developmental amblyopia: **anisometropic amblyopia**, in which the two eyes have differing powers of refraction, and **strabismic amblyopia**, in which the image from one eye is favored because of imbalance in the extrinsic EYE MUSCLES.

developmental aphasia see DEVELOPMENTAL DYSPHASIA.

developmental arithmetic disorder the *DSM–III* designation for MATHEMATICS DISORDER.

developmental articulation disorder see PHONOLOGICAL DISORDER.

developmental assessment the evaluation of a child's level of physical, cognitive, emotional, and social development, as assessed by specific DEVELOPMENTAL SCALES.

developmental-behavioral pediatrics see BEHAVIORAL PEDIATRICS.

developmental cognitive neuroscience the area of study that seeks to understand how the mind and brain jointly develop. It uses data from a variety of sources, including molecular biology, cell biology, artificial intelligence, and evolutionary theory, as well as conventional studies of cognitive development. See also COGNITIVE NEUROSCIENCE.

developmental contextual model see DEVELOPMENTAL SYSTEMS APPROACH.

developmental coordination disorder in *DSM–IV–TR*, a motor skills disorder characterized by marked impairment in the development of motor coordination. Performance in activities that require motor coordination is substantially below that expected given the child's chronological age and measured intelligence. Significant impairment of academic performance or daily living activities is also observed. However, the difficulties are not due to mental retardation or PERVASIVE DEVELOPMENTAL DISORDERS. See also DEVELOPMENTAL DYSPRAXIA.

developmental crisis see MATURATIONAL CRISIS.

developmental delay delay in the age at which developmental milestones are achieved by a child or delay in the development of communication, social, and daily living skills. It most typically refers to delays in infants, toddlers, and preschool children that are meaningful but do not constitute substantial handicap. Children with developmental delays are often eligible for early intervention or preschool services to ameliorate these delays.

developmental disability a developmental level or status that is attributable to a cognitive or physical impairment, or both, originating before the age of 22. Such an impairment is likely to continue indefinitely and results in substantial functional or adaptive limitations. Examples of developmental disabilities include, but are not limited to, mental retardation, PERVASIVE DEVELOPMENTAL DISORDERS, learning disorders, DEVELOPMENTAL COORDINATION DISORDER, communication disorders, cerebral palsy, epilepsy, blindness, deafness, mutism, and muscular dystrophy. Also called **developmental disorder**.

developmental dyslexia a form of DYSLEXIA that is apparent during an early developmental age or phase and manifested as difficulty in learning to read and spell single words.

developmental dysphasia language difficulty or delayed language acquisition believed to be associated with brain damage or cerebral maturation lag. It is characterized by defects in expressive language and articulation (**expressive dysphasia**) and in more severe cases by defects in comprehension of language (**receptive dysphasia**). Also called **developmental aphasia**.

developmental dyspraxia DYSPRAXIA present since birth and manifested during an early developmental age or phase as difficulty in performing coordinated movements. In *DSM–IV–TR* this condition is equivalent to DEVELOPMENTAL COORDINATION DISORDER. Compare ACQUIRED DYSPRAXIA.

developmental expressive writing disorder see DISORDER OF WRITTEN EXPRESSION.

developmental factors the conditions and variables that influence emotional, intellectual, social, and physical development from conception to maturity. Examples include parental attitudes and stimulation, peer relationships, learning experiences, recreational activities, and hereditary predispositions.

developmental function 1. the form that development takes over time. Different aspects of development (e.g., physical versus cognitive) may show different patterns of change over time. **2.** the role played by an entity (e.g., a gene), activity (e.g., play), stage (e.g., adolescence), or other phenomenon in the development of an organism.

developmental hyperactivity a condition shown by children who are within or above the average range intellectually but display high activity levels as an integral part of their behavior.

developmental immaturity the status of a child who exhibits a delay (usually temporary) in reaching developmental landmarks without clinical or historical evidence of damage to the central nervous system. The child may appear younger than his or her chronological age in physical development, gross and fine motor abilities, language development, social awareness, or any combination of these. See also DEVELOPMENTAL DELAY; DEVELOPMENTAL RETARDATION.

developmental invariance a pattern of development in which a skill reaches adult competence early in life and remains stable thereafter. For example, certain sensory and perceptual skills (e.g., vision) function at a high level early in life.

developmental language disorder in *DSM–III*, a diagnostic category comprising two types of disorder in which the development of language skills is impaired: an expressive type and a receptive type. The equivalent *DSM–IV–TR* classifications for these types are EXPRESSIVE LANGUAGE DISORDER and MIXED RECEPTIVE-EXPRESSIVE LANGUAGE DISORDER, respectively.

developmental levels the stages into which the human life span is typically divided: (a) neonatal period; (b) infancy; (c) early, middle, and late childhood; (d) adolescence; and (e) adulthood.

developmental milestone any aspect of physical, cognitive, social, or emotional development that is significant and predictable, such that children throughout the world develop this ability, characteristic, or behavior at about the same time. Developmental milestones include presence of first teeth and language acquisition.

developmental norm the typical skills and expected level of achievement associated with a particular stage of development.

developmental orientation 1. in interdisciplinary team or other individual service-planning processes, an emphasis on the skills, abilities, and strengths of people with disabilities in relation to expected developmental attainments and performance of children or young people without disabilities. **2.** see DEVELOPMENTAL THEORY. Compare DEFECT ORIENTATION.

developmental pharmacokinetics the study of how pharmacological agents are processed (see PHARMACOKINETICS) in infants and children.

developmental psycholinguistics the branch of PSYCHOLINGUISTICS that investigates LANGUAGE ACQUISITION by children.

developmental psychology the branch of psychology that studies the changes—physical, mental, and behavioral—that occur from conception to old age. See also GENETIC PSYCHOLOGY; LIFE-SPAN DEVELOPMENTAL PSYCHOLOGY.

developmental quotient (**DQ**) the DEVELOPMENTAL AGE, or a substitute measure of development, divided by the CHRONOLOGICAL AGE.

developmental readiness a student's state of psychological and intellectual preparedness for a given task, subject, or grade level.

developmental reading disorder the *DSM–III* designation for READING DISORDER.

developmental retardation abnormally slow growth in any or all areas—intellectual, motor, perceptual, linguistic, or social. See also DEVELOPMENTAL DELAY; DEVELOPMENTAL IMMATURITY.

developmental scale a measurement instrument used to assess the degree to which an individual has progressed through the typical DEVELOPMENTAL MILESTONES.

developmental schedules normative timetables of when certain aspects of physical and behavioral development typically occur (see DEVELOPMENTAL MILESTONE). See BRAZELTON NEONATAL BEHAVIORAL ASSESSMENT SCALE.

developmental sequence the order in which changes in structure or function occur during the process of development of an organism.

developmental stage a period of development during which specific abilities, characteristics, or behavior patterns appear.

developmental systems approach the view that development is the result of bidirectional interaction between all levels of biological and experiential variables, from the genetic through the cultural. Also called **developmental contextual model**. See also BIDIRECTIONALITY OF STRUCTURE AND FUNCTION; TRANSACTIONAL MODEL OF DEVELOPMENT.

developmental task any of the fundamental physical, social, intellectual, and emotional achievements and abilities that must be acquired at each stage of life for normal and healthy development. Because development is largely cumulative, the inability to master developmental tasks at one stage is likely to inhibit development in later stages. See also DEVELOPMENTAL SEQUENCE.

developmental teaching model a general approach in education based on the work of Jean PIAGET and others. Cognitive, social, and moral development are considered to advance in discrete and distinctive stages. In cognitive development, the emphasis is on logical reasoning and the enhancement of intellectual development. There is an effort to orient school curricula toward operative knowledge.

Developmental Test of Visual–Motor Integration (VMI) a measure of visuomotor development that requires the participant to copy onto blank pieces of paper geometric designs increasing in difficulty from a straight line to complex figures. Now in its fifth edition, the VMI is used to identify problems with visual perception, motor coordination, and visual–motor integration. It is available in two versions: the Short Format, containing 15 designs and appropriate for children aged 2 to 8 years, and the Full Format, containing 24 designs and appropriate for children through age 18. [originally developed in 1967 by U.S. psychologists Keith E. Beery (1932–) and Norman A. Buktenica (1930–)]

developmental theory 1. any theory based on the continuity of human development and the importance of early experiences in shaping the personality. Examples are the psychoanalytic theory of PSYCHOSEXUAL DEVELOPMENT, ERIKSON'S EIGHT STAGES OF DEVELOPMENT, learning theories that stress early conditioning, and role theories that focus on the gradual acquisition of different roles in life. **2.** the proposition that mental retardation is due to slower than normal development of cognitive processes and is not qualitatively different from the cognitive processes of other people. Also called **developmental orientation**. Compare DEFECT THEORY.

developmental therapy a method of treatment for children and adolescents with emotional, social, or behavioral problems. A series of graded experiences is used to help clients to function better in various areas, such as interacting with others or managing anger.

developmental toxicology the study of the effects of toxic (poisonous) substances on the normal development of infants and children: specifically, the study of the adverse effects of certain drugs (e.g., aspirin, valproic acid, drugs of abuse) administered to them or to which they may have been exposed in the uterus.

developmental visual agnosia see CONGENITAL VISUAL AGNOSIA.

development cycle in ergonomics, the process of developing a product or system, beginning with a formative idea and continuing through research, design, testing, and improvement, to final release.

deviant behavior any behavior that deviates significantly from what is considered appropriate or typical for a social group. Also called **deviance**.

deviant sexuality see SEXUAL DEVIANCY.

deviant verbalization see SCHIZOPHRENIC THINKING.

deviation IQ the absolute measure of how far an individual differs from the mean on an individually administered IQ test. This is the approach now most commonly used in standard IQ tests. A reported deviation IQ is a standard score on an IQ test that has a mean of 100 and a standard deviation specific to that of the test administered, usually 15 or 16 for intelligence tests. The test scores represent a deviation from the mean score rather than a quotient, as was typical in the early days of IQ testing.

deviation score a RAW SCORE subtracted from the mean, indicating the value of the score relative to the mean.

device for automated desensitization (DAD) a computerized system for applying DESENSITIZATION therapy to the treatment of focused phobic behavior. The device administers visual or audio instructions for muscle relaxation and visualization of feared stimuli arranged in a hierarchical order. See also COVERT DESENSITIZATION; SYSTEMATIC DESENSITIZATION.

devil's trumpet see JIMSONWEED.

Dewey, John (1859–1952) U.S. philosopher, educator, and psychologist. After receiving his doctorate in 1884 under George S. Morris (1840–1889) at Johns Hopkins University, Dewey taught for a decade at each of the universities of Michigan and Chicago before moving to Columbia University, where he spent the rest of his career. Dewey wrote the first scientific text on psychology in the United States (*Psychology*, 1886) and went on to develop the functionalist, or instrumentalist, approach, in conjunction with William JAMES, James Rowland ANGELL, and others. Dewey's 1896 essay, "The Reflex Arc Concept in Psychology," is considered to be the debut of FUNCTIONALISM in psychology. Dewey's work also had a great impact in the fields of education and philosophy. In keeping with his functionalist views, he held that education must relate to the child's own experience, involve the child's participation, and develop a spirit of inquiry leading to the solution of real rather than merely academic problems. In philosophy, Dewey is famous as one of the founders of the American school of PRAGMATISM, together with William James, Charles S. Peirce (1839–1914), and George Herbert Mead (1863–1931). See also INSTRUMENTALISM; PROGRESSIVE EDUCATION.

DEX abbreviation for Dysexecutive Questionnaire. See DYSEXECUTIVE SYNDROME.

dexamethasone *n.* a synthetic analog of CORTISOL, with similar biological action. It is used to treat nausea and vomiting and as an anti-inflammatory agent. U.S. trade name (among others): **Decadron**.

dexamethasone suppression test (DST) a test of the ability of dexamethasone, a synthetic analogue of CORTISOL, to inhibit the secretion of ADRENOCORTICOTROPIC HORMONE and hence suppress levels of cortisol in the blood. In the test, dexamethasone is administered and, after a waiting period, cortisol levels are assessed. In normal individuals cortisol levels will be suppressed by dexamethasone. If cortisol is still elevated, the individual is categorized as a nonsuppressor. The test is used primarily to aid in the diagnosis of Cushing's syndrome. Dexamethasone nonsuppression was thought at one time to be good indication that the individual has, or is likely to develop, MAJOR DEPRESSIVE DISORDER, but it does not reliably predict this condition. Because of this, and the development of less invasive and less costly diagnostics, the DST has been generally abandoned as a clinical maneuver in depression.

dexamphetamine *n.* see DEXTROAMPHETAMINE.

Dexedrine *n.* a trade name for DEXTROAMPHETAMINE.

dexterity test a manual test of speed and accuracy.

dextrality *n.* a tendency or preference to be right-handed or to use the right side of the body in motor activities. See also RIGHT-HANDEDNESS. Compare SINISTRALITY.

dextro- (dextr-) *combining form* on or toward the right.

dextroamphetamine *n.* a sympathomimetic agent and CNS STIMULANT that is the dextrorotated form of the amphetamine molecule. It is used in the treatment of narcolepsy and attention-deficit/hyperactivity disorder. Like all AMPHETAMINES, it is prone to abuse and dependence. Also called **dexamphetamine**. U.S. trade names (among others): **Dexedrine**; **Adderall** (in combination with AMPHETAMINE).

dextromethorphan *n.* a synthetic OPIOID used clinically as a cough suppressant. Its mechanism of action is unknown, but it is known to bind to NMDA RECEPTORS. Dextromethorphan is a common ingredient in over-the-counter cough and cold preparations and is increasingly used as a drug of abuse, particularly among adolescents.

Because it is metabolized extensively by the CYTOCHROME P450 (CYP) 2D6 liver enzyme, it is used in pharmacology as a comparison when calculating the degree to which certain drugs inhibit CYP enzymes. It should not be taken by individuals who are taking MONOAMINE OXIDASE INHIBITORS, and it should be used with caution by those taking inhibitors of the CYP2D6 enzyme (i.e., fluoxetine, paroxetine) because unexpectedly high plasma concentrations of either drug may occur (see ENZYME INHIBITION). Examples of some common U.S. proprietary products that include dextromethorphan are **Coricidin**, **NyQuil**, **Robitussin**, **Tylenol PM**, and **Vicks 44**.

dextrosinistral *adj.* oriented or directed from the right side of the body to the left side.

df symbol for DEGREES OF FREEDOM.

DFBETAS in REGRESSION ANALYSIS, *d*ifferences in *beta* values: an index that describes the influence of the *i*th case upon the estimates of REGRESSION COEFFICIENTS. It is one of several indices that are useful in diagnosing problems in regression analysis.

DFFITS in REGRESSION ANALYSIS, *d*ifference in *fits*: an index of the influence that a particular case (i) has upon the fitted value $\hat{Y}_i$. It is one of several indices that are useful in diagnosing problems in regression analysis.

dharma *n.* **1.** in Hinduism, the principle of natural law that sustains and governs the cosmos. In a narrower sense, the term denotes the social laws and customs that must be followed to achieve the right path of spiritual advancement. **2.** in Buddhism, the cosmic law underlying the world of humans, above all, the law of karmic rebirth (see KARMA). The term has multiple other meanings, including the truth as set out in the teachings of the Buddha, norms of behavior and ethical rules, the manifestation of reality, and the content of human thought. [Sanskrit, literally: "carrying, holding"]

dhat *n.* in *DSM–IV–TR*, a CULTURE-BOUND SYNDROME specific to India. Dhat involves severe anxiety and hypochondriacal concerns about the discharge of semen, whitish discoloration of the urine, and feelings of weakness and exhaustion. It is similar to SHEN-K'UEI.

DHE 45 *n.* a trade name for DIHYDROERGOTAMINE.

di- *prefix* twice or double.

dia- *prefix* through, across, or apart.

diabetes insipidus a metabolic disorder marked by a deficiency of VASOPRESSIN (antidiuretic hormone), which promotes the reabsorption of water from the kidney tubules. The patient experiences excessive thirst and excretes large amounts of urine, but without the high level of sugar found in the urine of people with diabetes mellitus. See also NEPHROGENIC DIABETES INSIPIDUS.

diabetes mellitus a metabolic disorder caused by ineffective production or utilization of the hormone INSULIN. Because of the insulin disruption, the patient is unable to oxidize and utilize carbohydrates in food. Glucose accumulates in the blood, causing weakness, fatigue, and the appearance of sugar in the urine. Fat metabolism is also disrupted so that end products of fat metabolism (ketones) accumulate in the blood.

diabetic enteropathy a gastrointestinal complication of diabetes mellitus, marked by intermittent occurrence of nocturnal fecal incontinence. The condition is often associated with autonomic and peripheral neuropathy and is regarded as one of several manifestations of visceral neuropathy in people with diabetes. See also GASTRIC NEUROPATHY.

diabetic gastropathy any disorder of the stomach or related digestive organs that is due primarily to the effects of diabetes on the autonomic nervous system. See also GASTRIC NEUROPATHY.

diabetic retinopathy deterioration of the retina as a complication of DIABETES MELLITUS, marked by tiny ANEURYSMS of the retinal capillaries. These first appear as small venous dilations and red dots, observed during ophthalmological examination; they progress to retinal hemorrhages and exudates that impair vision. New, abnormal vessels may form in the vitreous cavity and these may also hemorrhage. DETACHED RETINA is a complication. Treatment includes control of diabetes and hypertension, laser photocoagulation, and vitreous surgery.

diabetogenic factor an agent that causes diabetes.

diacetylmorphine *n.* the chemical name for HEROIN. A synthetic analog of MORPHINE (produced by substituting acetyl groups for hydroxyl groups at two positions on the morphine molecule), it is, like morphine and CODEINE, a pure opioid agonist, activating receptors for endorphins and enkephalins (see ENDOGENOUS OPIOID). Diacetylmorphine is characterized by a rapid onset of action and a duration of action similar to that of morphine; however, it is three times more potent than morphine. In Great Britain and Canada it is used clinically in the management of severe pain, for example, in terminally ill patients, but it is not legally available in the United States due to concerns about its potential for abuse. Also called **diamorphine**. See OPIOID ANALGESIC.

diachronic linguistics the study of languages as they change over time, as practiced in PHILOLOGY or COMPARATIVE LINGUISTICS. This is often contrasted with **synchronic linguistics**, the study of languages or (more often) a particular language at a single point in time, with no reference to historical or developmental factors. The synchronic approach to language is the basis of linguistic STRUCTURALISM. [introduced by Swiss linguist Ferdinand de Saussure (1857–1913)]

diachronic universal see PSYCHOLOGICAL UNIVERSAL.

diacritical marking system (**DMS**) a unified arrangement or series of symbols used to denote phonetic sounds.

diadochokinesis *n.* the ability to rapidly perform repetitive muscular movements, such as finger tapping or pursing and retracting the lips. This ability is often examined during clinical assessments of motor behavior.

diagnosis (**Dx**) *n.* (*pl.* **diagnoses**) **1.** the process of identifying and determining the nature of a disease or disorder by its signs and symptoms, through the use of assessment techniques (e.g., tests and examinations) and other available evidence. **2.** the classification of individuals on the basis of a disease, disorder, abnormality, or set of characteristics. Psychological diagnoses have been codified for professional use, notably in the DSM–IV–TR. **—diagnostic** *adj.*

diagnosis-related groups (**DRGs**) an inpatient or hospital classification used as a financing tool to reimburse health care providers. Each of the DRGs (of which there are currently over 500) has a preset price based on diagnosis, age and sex of patient, therapeutic procedure, and length of stay.

Diagnostic and Statistical Manual of Mental Disorders see DSM–IV–TR.

diagnostic audiometry see AUDIOMETRY.

diagnostic baseline the entry or pretreatment levels of condition- or disease-related symptoms used in identifying or treating diseases or disorders. Such levels are often used to assign patients or participants in a study to correlational groups. See also BASELINE.

diagnostic center a facility equipped with skilled personnel and appropriate laboratory and other equipment for evaluating the condition of a patient and determining the cause of his or her physical or psychological disorder. The diagnostic center may be a part of a larger health care facility or a separate institution.

diagnostic educational tests tests designed to identify and measure academic deficiencies. Examples include the PEABODY PICTURE VOCABULARY TEST, the IOWA TESTS OF BASIC SKILLS, and the NELSON–DENNY READING TEST. Also called **educational tests**.

diagnostic formulation a comprehensive evaluation of a patient, including a summary of his or her behavioral, emotional, and psychophysiological disturbances. Diagnostic formulation includes the most significant features of the patient's total history; the results of psychological and medical examinations; a tentative explanation of the origin and development of his or her disorder; the diagnostic classification of the disorder; a therapeutic plan, including basic and adjunctive treatments; and a prognostic evaluation based on carrying out this plan.

diagnostic interview an interview in which a psychologist or other mental health professional explores a patient's presenting problem, current situation, and background, with the aim of formulating a diagnosis and prognosis as well as developing a treatment program.

Diagnostic Interview Schedule (**DIS**) a STRUCTURED INTERVIEW assessing an individual's current and past symptoms of a variety of psychiatric disorders, including depression, schizophrenia, and alcohol and substance dependence. Designed to be an objective diagnostic instrument requiring a minimum of clinical judgment, the DIS consists of a predetermined set of questions that are asked in a specific order. It was originally developed in the late 1970s by the NATIONAL INSTITUTE OF MENTAL HEALTH for use in the EPIDEMIOLOGIC CATCHMENT AREA SURVEY. The **Diagnostic Interview Schedule for Children** (**DISC**) is also available.

diagnosticity *n.* the informational value of an interaction, event, or feedback for someone seeking self-knowledge. Information with high diagnosticity has clear implications for the SELF-CONCEPT, whereas information with low diagnosticity may be unclear, ambiguous, or inaccurate. The impulse to seek highly diagnostic information about the self is called the APPRAISAL MOTIVE.

diagnostic overshadowing the failure, when assessing an individual with multiple disabilities, to discern the presence of one disability because its features are attributed to another, primary disability. In particular, it refers to the failure to recognize a psychiatric condition or mental disorder in a person with mental retardation, because characteristics of that condition are erroneously attributed to the mental retardation. See also DUAL DIAGNOSIS.

diagnostic prescriptive educational approach the concept that effectiveness of classroom teaching of children with disabilities depends in large part upon the teacher's understanding of the disability. For example, the more the teacher and educational administrators know about hydrocephalus, the more effectively they can design and individualize an appropriate educational program for students with this particular disability.

diagnostic test any examination or assessment measure that may help reveal the nature and source of an individual's physical, mental, or behavioral problem or anomalies.

dialect *n.* **1.** a variety of a language that is associated with a particular geographical region, social class, or ethnic group and has its own characteristic words, grammatical forms, and pronunciation. Dialects of a language are generally mutually intelligible. Compare ACCENT; REGISTER. **2.** in animal communication, a variant of the standard form of communication that is specific to a population or a geographical region. For example, cardinals in different parts of North America have regional differences in song. **—dialectal** *adj.*

dialectic *n.* **1.** in general language, any investigation of the truth of ideas through juxtaposition of opposing or contradictory opinions. **2.** the conversational mode of argument attributed to Greek philosopher Socrates (c. 470–399 BCE), in which knowledge is sought through a process of question and answer. **3.** in the work of German philosopher Georg Wilhelm Friedrich Hegel (1770–1831), the pattern of statement, contradiction, and reconciliation (THESIS, ANTITHESIS, and SYNTHESIS) that he held to govern both the progress of thought and the process of human history. See also DIALECTICAL MATERIALISM. **—dialectical** *adj.*

dialectical behavior therapy a flexible, stage-based therapy that combines principles of BEHAVIOR THERAPY, COGNITIVE BEHAVIOR THERAPY, and MINDFULNESS. Dialectical behavior therapy concurrently promotes acceptance and change, especially with difficult-to-treat patients. [developed by U.S. clinical psychologist Marsha Linehan (1943–)]

dialectical materialism in the philosophy of German social thinker Karl Marx (1818–1883), the principle that accounts for the progress of history and the succession of economic and government systems. The process is one in which the clash of the prevailing system (the THESIS) with an insurgent system (the ANTITHESIS) results in a new system (the SYNTHESIS). This movement is driven by purely material factors, most notably those attending the control of the means of production. Marx's dialectical account of history thus inverts what may be referred to as the dialectical idealism of German philosopher Georg Wilhelm Friedrich Hegel (1770–1831). See also CLASS THEORY; MARXISM.

dialectical method see DIALECTICAL TEACHING.

dialectical operations mechanisms by which development occurs as a result of interactions between the individual and the environment. Rather than emphasizing universal stages of development, theorists taking a dialectical perspective, such as Lev VYGOTSKY, argue that development takes place as individuals both react to and influence their social environment. Models of this sort are based on the theories of German philosopher Georg Wilhelm Friedrich Hegel (1770–1831).

dialectical teaching a method that engages students in a critical examination of their reasoning through repeated questioning of their answers, much as Socrates is portrayed as doing in the Platonic dialogues. Also called **dialectical method**.

dialectology *n.* the branch of linguistics concerned with the study of DIALECTS.

dialogue (**dialog**) *n.* **1.** in general, an exchange of ideas between two or more people. **2.** in GESTALT THERAPY, a technique in which the client engages in an imaginary conversation (a) with a body part from which he or she feels alienated; (b) with a person, such as his or her mother or father, who is pictured sitting in an empty chair (see EMPTY-CHAIR TECHNIQUE); or (c) with an object associated with a dream. The technique often elicits strong feelings. Also called **dialogue technique**.

dialysis dementia an aluminum-induced brain disease affecting patients undergoing long-term dialysis. Major symptoms are progressive mental deterioration, personality changes, and speech impairment, with such neurological signs as seizures, DYSARTHRIA, dysnomia (difficulty in naming objects), and DYSPRAXIA.

diamorphine *n.* see DIACETYLMORPHINE.

dianetics *n.* a controversial therapeutic technique claiming to treat, according to its founder, "all inorganic mental ills and all inorganic psychosomatic ills, with assurance of complete cure." Dianetics has been largely discredited within the fields of psychology and psychiatry. [introduced in 1950 by L(afayette) Ron(ald) Hubbard (1911–1986), U.S. writer and subsequent founder of SCIENTOLOGY]

dianoia *n.* in philosophy, reasoning based on sensory perception and experience, especially as contrasted with the purely intellectual operation of the NOUS. Compare NOESIS. See also UNDERSTANDING. **—dianoetic** *adj.*

diaphragm *n.* **1.** a muscular sheet that separates the thoracic and abdominal cavities. **2.** a cup-shaped contraceptive device made from a layer of thick latex rubber fitted over a round or spiral spring. The diaphragm is filled with a contraceptive jelly and inserted in the vagina so that it forms a barrier between the cervix and any spermatozoa that enter the vagina during coitus. The spring holds it in place. The diaphragm has been used by women since 1882. **—diaphragmatic** *adj.*

diary method a technique for compiling detailed data about an individual who is being observed or studied by having the individual record daily events in his or her life.

diaschisis *n.* a loss or deficiency of function in brain regions surrounding or connected to an area of localized damage.

diastolic blood pressure the pressure of blood flowing in a major artery while the heart rests briefly between contractions. On blood-pressure readings, it is the smaller number, usually noted after the SYSTOLIC BLOOD PRESSURE. See BLOOD PRESSURE.

diathesis *n.* an inherited susceptibility to certain diseases or disorders (e.g., arthritic diathesis). See also GENETIC PREDISPOSITION.

diathesis–stress model the theory that mental and physical disorders develop from a genetic or biological predisposition for that illness (diathesis) combined with stressful conditions that play a precipitating or facilitating role. Also called **diathesis–stress hypothesis**; **diathesis–stress paradigm**; **diathesis–stress theory**. See also STRESS–VULNERABILITY MODEL.

diazepam *n.* a long-acting BENZODIAZEPINE that is used for the management of alcohol withdrawal and as an ANTICONVULSANT, ANXIOLYTIC, and MUSCLE RELAXANT. It is broken down in the liver to produce a number of metabolites (metabolic products) of varying HALF-LIVES, including the active compounds desmethyldiazepam (nordiazepam) and OXAZEPAM. Its complex metabolism and lengthy half-life make diazepam unsuitable for use in older adults and those with liver disease. U.S. trade name (among others): **Valium**.

diazepam-binding inhibitor (**DBI**) an endogenous NEUROPEPTIDE that binds to molecular receptors for BENZODIAZEPINES. It counters the effectiveness of these drugs, thus increasing anxiety, and may be involved in the development of drug dependence.

dibenzodiazepine *n.* any member of a class of chemically related compounds that include CLOZAPINE, the first ATYPICAL ANTIPSYCHOTIC introduced into clinical medicine. This class is structurally similar to the DIBENZOXAZEPINES.

dibenzothiazepine *n.* any member of a class of chemically related compounds that include QUETIAPINE, an atypical antipsychotic. This class is structurally similar to the DIBENZODIAZEPINES and the DIBENZOXAZEPINES.

dibenzoxazepine *n.* any member of a class of chemically related compounds that include LOXAPINE, one of the older antipsychotics that does not belong to the phenothiazine class. This class is structurally similar to the DIBENZODIAZEPINES.

DICE model *d*issociable *i*nteractions and *c*onscious *e*xperience model: a cognitive model that relates consciousness to an executive awareness system. [devised by U.S. psychologist Daniel L. Schacter (1952–)]

dichoptic stimulation the simultaneous presentation of different stimuli to each of the eyes. Dichoptic stimulation usually causes BINOCULAR RIVALRY.

dichorhinic *adj.* relating to the presentation of different odorants in each nostril via an OLFACTOMETER.

dichorial twins a set of twins that had separate chorionic membranes as embryos. They include DIZYGOTIC TWINS as well as MONOZYGOTIC TWINS that are separated shortly after fertilization. Compare MONOCHORIAL TWINS.

dichotic *adj.* affecting or relating to the left and right ears differently, as with the presentation of different sounds to each ear. Compare DIOTIC.

dichotic listening the process of receiving different auditory messages presented simultaneously to each ear. Listeners experience two streams of sound, each localized at the ear to which it is presented, and are able to focus on the message from one ear while ignoring the message from the other ear.

dichotomous thinking the tendency to think in terms of bipolar opposites, that is, in terms of the best and worst, without accepting the possibilities that lie between these two extremes. This has been found to be especially common among individuals with MAJOR DEPRESSIVE EPISODES, and is sometimes thought to be a risk factor for MAJOR DEPRESSIVE DISORDER. Also called **polarized thinking**.

dichotomous variable a variable that can have only two values (e.g., 0 and 1) to designate membership in one of two possible categories, for example, female versus male, Republican versus Democrat, answering a question yes versus no.

dichotomy *n.* in statistics, the division of scores into two units (e.g., above versus below the median).

dichromatism *n.* partial color blindness in which the eye contains only two types of cone PHOTOPIGMENT. Consequently, the individual identifies colors on the basis of two wavelengths of light, rather than the three required for normal color perception. Red–green color blindness (see DEUTERANOPIA) is observed fairly frequently, whereas the blue–green variety (see TRITANOPIA) is relatively rare. Also called **dichromacy**; **dichromatic vision**; **dichromatopsia**. See also ANOMALOUS TRICHROMATISM; ACHROMATISM. **—dichromatic** *adj.*

dichromic *adj.* distinguishing only two colors.

didactic analysis see TRAINING ANALYSIS.

didactic group therapy an early form of group psychotherapy based on the theory that institutionalized individuals will respond most effectively to the active guidance of a professional leader. In one form of didactic group therapy the group members bring up their own problems and the therapist leads the discussion, often giving his or her own interpretations. In another form, the therapist presents a short lecture based on printed material designed to stimulate the members to break through their resistances and express themselves. The didactic approach is also used in self-help groups.

didactic teaching 1. a technique in which behavioral and therapeutic concepts and techniques are explained to clients, and instructions are given in both verbal and written form. Such instruction is common in many forms of therapy, with the exception of long-term PSYCHODYNAMIC PSYCHOTHERAPY and PSYCHOANALYSIS. **2.** a component of many courses in undergraduate and graduate psychology courses and multidisciplinary psychotherapy training.

diencephalic amnesia amnesia caused by lesions of the DIENCEPHALON. Causes include infarction of the paramedian artery, trauma, diencephalic tumors, and WERNICKE–KORSAKOFF SYNDROME.

diencephalon *n.* the posterior part of the FOREBRAIN that includes the THALAMUS, EPITHALAMUS, HYPOTHALAMUS, and PINEAL GLAND. **—diencephalic** *adj.*

diestrus *n.* in the polyestrous mammalian female, a period of sexual inactivity between two ESTROUS CYCLES, during which the reproductive system prepares for potential conception and gestation.

diet *n.* **1.** food substances and liquids habitually consumed by an organism. **2.** a prescribed course of eating and drinking for a particular reason (e.g., a low-cholesterol diet). **—dietary** *adj.*

dietary neophobia avoidance of new foods. A nonpathological form is commonly seen in children who display a reluctance to try unfamiliar food. Acceptance of novel diets may be facilitated through observation of others eating similar foods or, in some cases, by simply observing others eating familiar foods. Young rats can accept novel foods ingested by their dam through smelling odors on her breath. In some primates, parents or other caretakers appear more likely to offer or share with the young foods that are novel to the young than foods that are familiar to them.

dietary selection the ability of an organism to select various components of its diet that maintain a good nutritional balance, not only with respect to calories but also fats, protein, minerals, and vitamins. Many species appear to be able to self-select an appropriate diet, but this may be due to sampling of foods that reduce illness induced by lack of one item or another. Most species studied, however, demonstrate a specific appetite for sodium, a critical mineral for survival.

diethylpropion *n.* a CNS STIMULANT used as an appetite suppressant in the treatment of obesity. See also ANALEPTICS. U.S. trade name: **Tenuate**.

diethylstilbestrol (**DES**) *n.* a synthetic, nonsteroidal compound with the activity of estrogen. It was formerly widely prescribed to pregnant women to prevent miscarriages or premature deliveries, but such use was discontinued in the early 1970s due to the health risks associated with DES, including increased risk of reproductive abnormalities and cancer in female offspring. It is still used clinically to treat selected cases of breast cancer or prostate cancer, but this is very rare.

diethyltryptamine *n.* see DET.

dieting *n.* the deliberate restriction of the types or amounts of food one eats, usually in an effort to lose weight or to improve one's health. Dieting is viewed by some medical and mental health professionals as a solution to obesity and by others as a primary pathology associated with EATING DISORDERS.

difference canon see METHOD OF DIFFERENCE.

difference hypothesis see DEFECT THEORY.

difference judgment the ability to distinguish between two similar stimuli. The minimum difference between the stimuli necessary to do this is called the DIFFERENCE THRESHOLD (or just noticeable difference).

difference threshold the smallest perceptible difference between two stimuli that can be consistently and accurately detected on 75% of trials. Difference threshold is measured across several trials. Also called **difference limen** (**DL**); **differential limen; differential threshold; equally noticeable difference; just noticeable difference** (**JND**; **jnd**); **least noticeable difference**; **sensation unit**. See also ABSOLUTE THRESHOLD; WEBER'S LAW.

difference tone see COMBINATION TONE.

Differential Ability Scales (**DAS**) an individual test of intelligence that is not based on any particular theory but is designed to yield a broad index of intelligence. It comprises 17 cognitive and 3 achievement tests; the former are divided into core and diagnostic subtests. The core subtests are good measures of *g* (see GENERAL FACTOR), while the diagnostic subtests measure such abilities as short-term memory and processing speed. Six of the core subtests at the school-age level yield separate scores for verbal ability, nonverbal reasoning, and spatial ability. [developed in 1990 by British psychologist Colin D. Elliott (1937–)]

differential accuracy the ability to determine accurately in what way and to what extent a person's traits differ from a STEREOTYPE associated with his or her age group, ethnic group, professional group, or other relevant group. Compare STEREOTYPE ACCURACY.

differential amplifier an electrical device that amplifies the voltage difference between two input leads. In neural research, potential changes may be as small as 1 μV, and electrical resistances and sources of interference may be greater than the voltages being studied. Thus, complex electronic equipment, such as a differential amplifier, is required.

Differential Aptitude Tests (**DAT**) a battery of tests designed for use in the educational and vocational counseling of students in grades 7 to 12 as well as adults. The battery—which measures abstract reasoning, mechanical reasoning, verbal reasoning, language usage, numerical ability, spatial relations, and perceptual speed and accuracy—pinpoints mental strengths and weaknesses and predicts success both in school and in the workplace. The DAT is now in its fifth edition, published in 1990. [originally developed in 1947 by U.S. psychologists George Kettner Bennett (1904–1975), Harold G. Seashore (1906–1965), and Alexander G. Wesman (1914–1973)]

differential association the theory that an individual's behavior is influenced by the particular people with whom the individual associates, usually over a prolonged period. This concept was proposed to explain why people living in a neighborhood with a high crime rate were more likely to commit crimes themselves. Moreover, it was suggested that association with a particular type of criminal determined what kind of criminal one became. [proposed by U.S. criminologist Edwin H. Sutherland (1883–1950)]

differential conditioning a PAVLOVIAN CONDITIONING experiment in which two or more stimuli are used, only one of which produces a CONDITIONED RESPONSE. The stimuli are paired with different outcomes. Most commonly, one stimulus (the positive conditioned stimulus, e.g., a light) is paired with an unconditioned stimulus (e.g., food), and another (e.g., a tone) is not paired. The usual outcome is that a conditioned response is elicited by the positive conditioned stimulus but not by the other stimulus.

differential diagnosis 1. the process of determining which of two or more diseases or disorders with overlapping symptoms a particular patient has. **2.** the distinction between two or more similar conditions by identifying critical symptoms present in one but not the other.

differential effect in parapsychology experiments using ZENER CARDS or similar targets, the finding that a participant shows an above-chance difference in performance under two contrasting conditions of testing. See also DECLINE EFFECT; FOCUSING EFFECT; POSITION EFFECT; PREFERENTIAL EFFECT; SHEEP–GOAT EFFECT.

differential emotions theory a theory proposing the existence of a large but limited set of specific emotions that appear without social learning at the age when the emotions can first play an adaptive role in the behavior of the child. [associated with the work of U.S. psychologist Carroll E. Izard (1923–)]

differential extinction the EXTINCTION of one or more responses established through conditioning while other, related conditioned responses remain.

differential fertility the fertility rate of any group (e.g., an ethnic or socioeconomic group) in relation to that of another group.

differential growth the growth of an organ at a rate different from that of other organs in the body.

differential limen see DIFFERENCE THRESHOLD.

differential psychology the branch of psychology that studies the nature, magnitude, causes, and consequences of psychological differences between individuals and groups, as well as the methods for assessing these differences.

differential reinforcement in conditioning, the REINFORCEMENT of only selected behavior. For example, one might reinforce lever presses that are more than 1 s in duration, but not reinforce those that are less than 1 s in duration.

differential reinforcement of alternative behavior (DRA) the REINFORCEMENT of a particular behavior as a means of decreasing another, targeted behavior. It combines EXTINCTION of the targeted response with competition from the reinforced alternative.

differential reinforcement of high rate (DRH) a SCHEDULE OF REINFORCEMENT in which reinforcement depends on fast responses to stimuli. It is often dependent on the interval between responses being less than an allowed maximum.

differential reinforcement of low rate (DRL) a SCHEDULE OF REINFORCEMENT in which reinforcement is given only when the rate of response to stimuli is low. It is often dependent on the interval between responses being greater than an allowed minimum. Also called **differential reinforcement of long response times**.

differential reinforcement of other behavior (DRO) a procedure in which REINFORCEMENT occurs if a particular response does not occur for a fixed period of time. It is used to decrease the rate of the targeted response. Also called **omission training**.

differential relaxation a technique for exertion of only the amount of muscular tension or energy required to perform an activity successfully. For example, an individual driving an automobile can practice easing and releasing contracted muscles that are not primarily involved in the act of driving (e.g., the shoulders and upper back or the neck and facial muscles) and thus permit more appropriate focus and engagement of those muscles directly involved (e.g., in the hands, arms, legs, and back).

differential threshold see DIFFERENCE THRESHOLD.

differential validity the VALIDITY or accuracy of a battery of tests in differentiating a person's subsequent success in two or more different CRITERION tasks.

differentiation *n.* **1.** sensory discrimination of differences among stimuli. For example, wines that at first taste identical may, with experience, be readily distinguished. **2.** a conditioning process in which a limited range of behavior types is achieved through selective REINFORCEMENT of only some forms of behavior. Also called **response differentiation**. **3.** in embryology, the process whereby cells of a developing embryo undergo the changes necessary to become specialized in structure and function so that they or their successors can form tissues, such as muscle, neurons, or bone. **4.** in mathematics, the process used in calculus for obtaining the differential coefficient of a function or variable.

differentiation of self the ability to distinguish and maintain personal thoughts, feelings, goals, and identity in the presence of emotional and societal pressures to do otherwise, especially in family systems.

differentiation theory the theory that perception can be understood as an incremental filtering process enabling environmental noise (i.e., dispensable, incidental information) to be screened out while one learns to distinguish the essential characteristics of sensory patterns.

difficulty value the difficulty of a test item as measured by the percentage of participants or students in a designated class, age level, or experimental group who respond to the item correctly.

diffraction *n.* the bending or scattering of waves as they pass through an aperture or around the edge of a barrier. Diffraction most often refers to this phenomenon in light waves, but it may occur with waves of any type, including sound waves, radio waves, water waves, and so forth.

diffraction grating a piece of glass or metal containing closely spaced parallel slits or transparencies, used to separate light into its component wavelengths.

diffuse axonal injury (DAI) widespread stretching and tearing of the white-matter (axonal) tracts of the brain typically caused by ACCELERATION–DECELERATION INJURIES.

diffuse bipolar cell a RETINAL BIPOLAR CELL that receives input from several receptors. Compare MIDGET BIPOLAR CELL.

diffuse-status characteristics general personal qualities, such as age, sex, and ethnicity, that people intentionally and unintentionally consider when estimating the relative competency, ability, and social value of themselves and others. Unlike SPECIFIC-STATUS CHARACTERISTICS, diffuse-status characteristics will have no particular relevance in the given setting and are not indicators of competence, ability, and status. See EXPECTATION-STATES THEORY; STATUS GENERALIZATION.

diffuse thalamic projection system (DTPS) a set of thalamic nuclei that project numerous fibers to all parts of the cerebral cortex. It is the projection system for the RETICULAR FORMATION and sets the tone of the cerebral cortex. See THALAMUS.

diffusion *n.* **1.** the process in which knowledge, innovation, language, or cultural characteristics are spread within or between cultures or communities. **2.** in biology, see PASSIVE TRANSPORT. **3.** more generally, any process by which something becomes spread or distributed throughout something else. **—diffuse** *vb.*

diffusion model a model of reaction time and accuracy proposing that an individual accumulates evidence continuously, rather than in discrete steps, until a response criterion is reached. [proposed in 1978 by U.S. psychologist Roger Ratcliff (1947–)]

diffusion of responsibility the lessening of responsibility often experienced by individuals in groups and social collectives. This has been proposed as one reason for the BYSTANDER EFFECT, in which groups of bystanders are less likely to help someone in need than are isolated onlookers. In groups the obligation to intervene is shared by all onlookers rather than focused on any specific individual. This diffusion process has also been identified as a possible mediator of a number of other group-level phenomena, including CHOICE SHIFTS, DEINDIVIDUATION, SOCIAL LOAFING, and reactions to SOCIAL DILEMMAS. See also CONFUSION OF RESPONSIBILITY; CROWD BEHAVIOR. [first described in 1970 by U.S. social psychologists John M. Darley (1938–) and Bibb Latané (1937–)]

diffusion process in marketing and advertising, the technique employed in gaining the public's general acceptance of a new concept or product. The process is based on the analogy of a stone dropped into a pond so that it produces waves that spread outward to cover the entire pond. The diffusion process depends on acceptance by an initial core of people, whose influence then ripples outward through the surrounding population.

digestion *n.* the process by which food is broken down so that it may be absorbed and assimilated by the body, thus providing energy and nutrients.

digestive type a constitutional body type in which the alimentary system dominates other systems (see ROSTAN TYPES). It corresponds to the PYKNIC TYPE in KRETSCHMER TYPOLOGY.

digital *adj.* **1.** relating to the representation of information in discrete or numerical (typically binary) form. Compare ANALOG. **2.** of or relating to the fingers or toes.

digital computer an electronic device that processes information, including making numeric calculations. It is called "digital" because the machine's primary mechanisms include counting, comparing, and rearranging digits in its memory and processing modules. The (digital) unit for these computations is called a BIT. Compare ANALOG COMPUTER.

digital subtraction angiography angiography to visualize blood vessels that have been injected with contrast medium in which minimalization or elimination of the background and other soft tissues by computer results in a clear image.

digitized speech speech that has been coded in DIGITAL form, usually for storage in a computer or transmission over a COMPUTER NETWORK.

Digit Span an attentional subtest in the WECHSLER ADULT INTELLIGENCE SCALE that assesses the ability of an individual to repeat a series of digits of increasing length. **Digit Span Forward** assesses the number of digits an individual is able to repeat immediately following their presentation, in the exact order they were presented. **Digit Span Backward** assesses the number of digits an individual is able to repeat immediately following their presentation, but in reverse order. The former is regarded as a measure of IMMEDIATE MEMORY; the latter provides a measure of WORKING MEMORY.

Digit Symbol a performance subtest in the WECHSLER ADULT INTELLIGENCE SCALE that measures the time taken to indicate digits associated with abstract symbols using a substitution key. It is a measure of FLUID ABILITIES and performance and is negatively correlated with adult age.

diglossia *n.* the situation in which two varieties of a language coexist and have distinct social functions within a community; these are usually characterized by high (H) and low (L) uses, H being associated with formality and literacy, and L with everyday colloquial usage. See also CODE SWITCHING; MULTILINGUALISM; VERNACULAR. [first described in 1959 by U.S. linguist Charles Ferguson (1921–1998)]

digraph *n.* a combination of two letters or other symbols used to represent a single speech sound, for example, *ph* in *digraph* or *ou* in *house*. The corresponding term **trigraph** refers to three letters or symbols, for example, *tth* in *Matthew*. Compare DIPHTHONG.

dihydrocodeine *n.* see OPIOID ANALGESIC; OPIOIDS.

dihydroergotamine *n.* a semisynthetic derivative of the ergot alkaloid ERGOTAMINE, used in the treatment of acute migraine headache. It is a potent VASOCONSTRICTOR due to its ability to antagonize ALPHA ADRENORECEPTORS in blood-vessel walls as well as serotonin and dopamine receptors. U.S. trade names: **DHE 45**; **Migranal**.

dihydroindolone *n.* any member of a class of chemically related compounds whose molecular structure incorporates an indole nucleus similar to that of serotonin. The group includes MOLINDONE, a conventional ANTIPSYCHOTIC.

dihydromorphine *n.* a semisynthetic OPIOID ANALGESIC used primarily in research on OPIOID RECEPTORS. It is also a metabolite (metabolic product) of dihydrocodeine. See also OPIOIDS.

dihydrotestosterone *n.* a potent androgenic hormone produced by the metabolic breakdown of TESTOSTERONE, many of whose effects it mediates in target tissues. It is important in the development of reproductive organs in the male fetus and of male secondary SEX CHARACTERISTICS. A semisynthetic form is used therapeutically (see STANOLONE).

dihydroxyphenylacetic acid see DOPAC.

3,4-dihydroxyphenylalanine *n.* see DOPA.

Dilantin *n.* a trade name for PHENYTOIN.

dilation *n.* the process of enlargement, usually of an aperture, such as the pupil of the eye.

dilator *n.* **1.** a muscle or nerve that causes opening or enlargement of a bodily structure. **2.** an instrument for opening up an orifice or passage in the body. **3.** a drug or other agent that causes dilation or enlargement of an organ or opening. See VASODILATOR.

dildo *n.* an artificial penis, made usually of rubber or plastic but occasionally of wood or other materials. A dildo is used in autoerotic practices and other sexual activities. Also called **olisbos**; **lingam**; **godemiche**. See also VIBRATOR.

dilemma *n.* a situation necessitating a choice between two equally desirable or undesirable alternatives. Psychologists, economists, or sociologists may invent dilemmas and present them to individuals or groups in order to study decision making. See ETHICAL DILEMMA; PRISONER'S DILEMMA; SOCIAL DILEMMA.

dilution effect in animal behavior, the activity of many individuals at the same time, reducing the average probability that any one individual will be preyed on. For example, young birds may leave a nesting colony en masse, or insects may emerge synchronously; as a result, predators are able to take proportionally fewer prey. See also ANTIPREDATOR BEHAVIOR; CONFUSION EFFECT.

dimenhydrinate *n.* a nonprescription HISTAMINE ANTAGONIST at H_1 receptors that is commonly taken to suppress symptoms of motion sickness. U.S. trade name (among others): **Dramamine**.

dimensional theory of emotion any theory postulating that emotions have two or more fundamental dimensions. There is universal agreement among theories on two fundamental dimensions—pleasantness–unpleasantness (hedonic level) and arousal–relaxation (level of activation)—but considerable differences in labeling others. See also FEELING THEORY OF THREE DIMENSIONS.

dimensions of consciousness dimensions along which the overall quality of awareness can vary, including mood, involvement with inner or outer events, changes in immediate memory, sensation and perception, self-awareness, and identification with events outside of oneself.

dimer *n.* a complex in which two macromolecular subunits (e.g., of a protein) are bound together. **—dimeric** *adj.*

dimethoxymethylamphetamine *n.* see DOM.

dimethyl ketone see ACETONE.

dimethyltryptamine *n.* see DMT.

diminished capacity a legal defense in which a mental abnormality, due either to intoxication (see INTOXICATION DEFENSE) or mental defect, is claimed to have limited the defendant's ability to form the requisite criminal intent (see MENS REA) for the crime with which he or she is charged.

diminished responsibility a form of AFFIRMATIVE DEFENSE in which evidence of mental abnormality is presented to mitigate or reduce a defendant's accountability for an act. It is distinct from an INSANITY DEFENSE, which takes an all-or-none perspective with regard to CRIMINAL RESPONSIBILITY. Also called **limited responsibility**. See also PARTIAL INSANITY.

diminutive visual hallucination see LILLIPUTIAN HALLUCINATION.

dimming effect 1. the effect of a bright light in a scene with other, fainter elements. The faint elements appear dimmer in the presence of the light source than they do when the light source is absent. **2.** the increase in brightness of an afterimage that results from dimming its background.

dimorphism *n.* the existence among members of the same species of two distinct forms that differ in one or more characteristics, such as size, shape, or color. See also SEXUAL DIMORPHISM. **—dimorphic** *adj.*

DIMS abbreviation for DISORDERS OF INITIATING AND MAINTAINING SLEEP.

DIN color system a European system for representing colors by their attributes of hue, luminous intensity, and saturation (from German *D(eutsche) I(ndustrie-)N(orm)*, German Industry Standard). It is similar to the U.S. MUNSELL COLOR SYSTEM.

Dionysian *adj.* describing a state of mind that is irrational, sensuous, disordered, and even drunken or mad (from Dionysus, Greek god of wine, intoxication, and ritual madness or ecstasy). This modern use of the term was originated by German philosopher Friedrich Nietzsche (1844–1900), who drew a contrast between the Dionysian and the APOLLONIAN sides of human nature. He felt that a Dionysian attitude would counter the enervating effects of the Apollonian attitude then dominant in morality, religion, and philosophy.

diopter *n.* a unit of the power of a lens, equal to the reciprocal of its FOCAL LENGTH in meters. A lens of 1 diopter will focus parallel rays of light to a point 1 m behind the lens.

dioptrics *n.* the field of optics concerned with the refraction of light. Compare CATOPTRICS.

diotic *adj.* denoting, resulting from, or relating to the presentation of the same sound to both ears. Compare DICHOTIC; MONOTIC.

diphenhydramine *n.* a sedating HISTAMINE ANTAGONIST at H_1 receptors that also possesses activity at cholinergic and other receptor sites. It is used generally to suppress allergic responses and, in mental health, as a sedative and hypnotic or to suppress the parkinsonian symptoms induced by conventional antipsychotic drugs. U.S. trade name (among others): **Benadryl**.

diphenylbutylpiperidine *n.* any member of a class of chemically related compounds that include the conventional antipsychotic PIMOZIDE.

diphenylmethanes *pl. n.* a class of sedating HISTAMINE ANTAGONISTS at H_1 receptors that are used primarily as ANXIOLYTICS. They also prevent cardiac FIBRILLATION and have local anesthetic effects. The prototype is HYDROXYZINE.

diphthong *n.* a speech sound in which one vowel glides imperceptibly into another, as in English *boy* or *great*.

diplacusis *n.* a condition in which one tone is heard as two.

diplegia *n.* a paralysis that affects corresponding parts on both sides of the body (e.g., both arms). **—diplegic** *adj.*

diplo- (**dipl-**) *combining form* double or doubled.

diploid *adj.* denoting or possessing the normal number of chromosomes, which in humans is 46: 22 HOMOLOGOUS pairs of AUTOSOMES plus the male or female set of XY or XX SEX CHROMOSOMES. Compare HAPLOID.

diplomate *n.* see BOARD CERTIFIED.

diplopia *n.* a visual disorder in which images from the two eyes are seen separately and simultaneously. Diplopia is usually due to weak or paralyzed eye muscles, resulting in a failure of coordination and focus. Diplopia may also be a functional symptom or result from brain injury (**cerebral diplopia**). See also DOUBLE VISION.

dipsomania *n.* formerly, episodic binge drinking. See EPSILON ALCOHOLISM. **—dipsomaniac** *n.*

direct aggression aggressive behavior directed toward the source of the frustration or anger. Compare DISPLACED AGGRESSION.

direct attitude measure any procedure for assessing attitudes that requires a person to provide a report of his or her attitude. Traditional approaches to attitude measurement, such as LIKERT SCALES, SEMANTIC DIFFERENTIALS, and THURSTONE ATTITUDE SCALES, are examples of direct attitude measures. See also EXPLICIT ATTITUDE MEASURE; IMPLICIT ATTITUDE MEASURE. Compare INDIRECT ATTITUDE MEASURE.

direct-contact group see FACE-TO-FACE GROUP.

direct coping active, focused confrontation and management or resolution of stressful or otherwise problematic situations.

direct dyslexia a form of acquired dyslexia (see ALEXIA) characterized by an ability to read words aloud but an inability to understand what is being read. Some have suggested this is a parallel to developmental HYPERLEXIA.

directed analysis see FOCUSED ANALYSIS.

directed attention see SELECTIVE ATTENTION.

directed discussion method dialogue between two or more people about a specific topic in which one person's role is to keep the dialogue focused on a certain path or moving in a certain direction. That person may be a teacher, group leader, or mediator. In an educational setting, for example, a professor would provide curriculum-directed focus based on experience, while the students would contribute varied perspectives and broad-ranging information from their research.

directed facial action studies studies in which participants are instructed to contract specific facial muscles to produce prototypical emotional facial expressions without any verbal reference being made to the emotions themselves (e.g., "anger," "frown"). These studies have reported that facial configurations of negative emotions produce distinctive patterns of autonomic physiological activity.

directed movement movement targeted toward achieving a specific goal.

directedness *n.* the sense of unified purpose that provides the mature individual with enduring motivation, continuity, and orientation to the future. [first described by G. W. ALLPORT]

directed reverie in individual and group therapy, a technique in which the therapist directs the client to reexperience a dream or something that happened in early life by creating and then describing a mental image of that dream or event. See also GUIDED AFFECTIVE IMAGERY.

directed thinking controlled, purposeful thinking that is focused on a specific goal, such as the solution to a problem, and guided by the requirements of that goal. See also CRITICAL THINKING.

direct glare interference with vision caused by bright light from a source in the visual field, as opposed to **reflected glare**, which is interference caused by light reflected from a surface.

directional confusion difficulty in distinguishing left from right and, in some cases, other directions, such as uptown from downtown. Some directional confusion is common up to the age of 6 or 7, especially during the early stages of reading, writing, and spelling, and also in people with MIXED LATERALITY. Persistent directional confusion may indicate MINIMAL BRAIN DAMAGE or forced conversion from left-handedness to right-handedness.

directional hypothesis a prediction regarding the direction in which one experimental group's scores on a measure will differ from another group's scores or whether the sign of a COEFFICIENT will be positive rather than negative.

directionality problem in correlational studies, a problem in which it is known that two variables are related although it is not known which is the cause and which is the effect.

directional test see ONE-TAILED TEST.

direction perception the ability to determine the location in space of a moving visual target or of an auditory stimulus.

directions test a type of intelligence test that measures the participant's ability to follow instructions on a series of tasks. Although most directions tests do not explicitly measure following of directions, they implicitly measure it, because misunderstanding of directions typically results in a reduced score.

directive *n.* a command, suggestion, or order specifying the type of action that should be performed. In therapeutic contexts, a directive is a specific statement by the therapist that enjoins the client to act, feel, or think in a particular way when he or she confronts a particular problem or situation. The use of directives in therapy depends a great deal on the particular mode of therapy; in some modes (e.g., psychoanalysis) directives occur rarely if at all, whereas in others (e.g., behavior therapy) they occur more frequently.

directive counseling an approach to counseling and psychotherapy in which the therapeutic process is directed along lines considered relevant by the counselor or therapist. Directive counseling is based on the assumption that the professional training and experience of the counselor or therapist equip him or her to manage the therapeutic process and to guide the client's behavior. Therapy is considered to progress along primarily intellectual lines in contrast to the approaches of PSYCHODYNAMIC PSYCHOTHERAPY, which emphasizes unconscious motivation and affective dynamics. Also called **directive psychotherapy**.

directive discipline a field of study, particularly within the social sciences or humanities, that provides explicit or implicit answers to prescriptive questions regarding society and the conduct of individual lives. For example, philosophy is a directive discipline when it suggests that some ethical system is to be recommended over another. Psychology is a directive discipline to the extent that it describes a healthy or fully functioning life and may attempt to modify behaviors that fall short of this ideal.

directive group psychotherapy a type of group psychotherapy designed to help members adjust to their environment through educational tasks, group guidance, group counseling, and therapeutic recreation. [developed by 20th-century Russian-born U.S. psychotherapist Samuel Richard Slavson]

directive leader a group leader who actively guides the group's planning, activities, and decision making. In therapeutic groups, a directive leader is one who guides the course of the interaction, assigns various tasks to the group members, and offers verbal interpretations and recommendations. In contrast, nondirective GROUP-CENTERED LEADERS refrain from providing direction or interpretation.

directive play therapy a controlled approach to PLAY THERAPY in which the therapist is actively involved, structuring a child's activities by providing selected play materials and encouraging the child to use them in the enactment of "pretend" situations and the expression of feelings. Compare NONDIRECTIVE PLAY THERAPY.

directive therapy see DIRECTIVE COUNSELING.

direct marketing promoting a product by means of communication strategies addressed to individuals, rather than disseminated via the mass media, using knowledge of past purchases, demographics, and other factors. Examples are direct mail campaigns, telemarketing, and targeted e-mailing.

direct object see OBJECT.

direct odor effect a change in the nervous system caused by direct stimulation of the OLFACTORY TRACT and related brain structures. In contrast, an **indirect odor effect** is a change in the central nervous system arising from cognitions, such as expectations, associated with the odor.

director *n.* in a PSYCHODRAMA, the therapist who establishes the scenario or ROLE PLAY and manages the interactions therein.

Directory of Psychological Tests in the Sport and Exercise Sciences a collection of psychological scales, questionnaires, and inventories related to sport and exercise. It provides the source, purpose, description, construction, reliability, validity, norms, availability, and references for each instrument.

direct perception the theory that the information required for perception is external to the observer, that is, one can directly perceive an object based on the properties of the DISTAL STIMULUS alone, unaided by inference, memories, the construction of representations, or the influence of other cognitive processes. See ECOLOGICAL PERCEPTION. Compare CONSTRUCTIVISM. [proposed by James J. GIBSON]

direct realism 1. see NAIVE REALISM. **2.** an occasional synonym for DIRECT PERCEPTION.

direct reflex a reflex involving a receptor and effector on the same side of the body.

direct scaling a procedure for developing numerical scales of magnitude of psychophysical factors in which the observer makes judgments of the magnitude of stimuli. This is in contrast to **indirect scaling**, in which the magnitude scales are derived from PAIRED COMPARISON judgments.

direct selection a form of NATURAL SELECTION in which some behavioral, physical, or physiological trait in an individual improves the likelihood that its offspring will survive to reproduce. This contrasts with KIN SELECTION, in which the behavior of an organism may not help survival of its direct descendants but may benefit its relatives instead.

direct suggestion 1. a technique in SUPPORTIVE PSYCHOTHERAPY in which attempts are made to alleviate emotional distress and disturbance in an individual through reassurance, encouragement, and direct instructions. **2.** a technique in HYPNOTHERAPY in which a client under hypnosis is directed to follow instructions of the therapist either in the session or in his or her daily life.

dirhinic *adj.* relating to the presentation of the same ODORANT in each nostril via an OLFACTOMETER.

dirt phobia a persistent and irrational fear of dirt, often accompanied by a fear of contamination and a handwashing compulsion. Fear of dirt is a common OBSESSION associated with OBSESSIVE-COMPULSIVE DISORDER.

DIS abbreviation for DIAGNOSTIC INTERVIEW SCHEDULE.

disability *n.* a lasting physical or mental impairment that significantly interferes with an individual's ability to function in one or more central life activities, such as self-care, ambulation, communication, social interaction, sexual expression, or employment. For example, an individual who cannot see has visual disability. See also HANDICAP. **—disabled** *adj.*

disability evaluation an evaluation of the effect of an impairment (i.e., a loss of function) on an individual's capabilities, particularly in terms of his or her capacity for gainful employment.

disability laws legislation relating to the treatment of people with mental or physical disabilities. An example in the United States is the 1990 AMERICANS WITH DISABILITIES ACT (ADA).

Disability Rating Scale (**DRS**) a rating scale, used primarily in rehabilitation facilities to monitor the rehabilitative progress of individuals with moderate to severe brain damage, that measures arousal and awareness, cognitive ability, dependence on others, and psychosocial adaptability. Each of the 8 items on the scale (eye opening, communication ability, motor response, feeding, toileting, grooming, level of functioning in self-care, and employability) is assigned a value from 0 to either 3, 4, or 5. These values are then added together to obtain a total score, which may range from 0 (no disability) to 29 (extreme vegetative state). [originally developed in 1982 by psychiatrist Maurice Rappaport (1926–) and colleagues]

disadvantaged *adj.* denoting individuals, families, or communities deprived of equal access to society's resources, especially the necessities of life or the advantages of education and employment. See also CULTURALLY DISADVANTAGED.

disarranged-sentence test a test or test item whose objective is to put a scrambled sentence in proper order. For example, the individual being tested could be required to reorder "Boy town the to went bustling the" to read "The boy went to the bustling town."

disaster counseling counseling offered to victims and their families, emergency workers, and witnesses during or immediately following a traumatic event. Individual therapists and counselors and mental health teams are specially trained (e.g., by the American Red Cross) to respond in disaster situations. Disaster counseling may include defusing, debriefing (e.g., CRITICAL-INCIDENT STRESS DEBRIEFING), and other counseling techniques to help traumatized people cope with stress. One aim of the counseling might be to reduce the potential for POST-TRAUMATIC STRESS DISORDER, which may develop after the event.

disavowal *n.* see DENIAL.

discharge *n.* **1.** in clinical psychology, the abrupt reduction in psychic tension that occurs in symptomatic acts, dreams, or fantasies. **2.** in neurophysiology, the firing or activity of a neuron or group of neurons, resulting in an ACTION POTENTIAL. **3.** in hospitals and other mental and physical health facilities, the dismissal of a patient from treatment or other services. **4.** the dismissal of an employee.

discharge of affect the reduction of an emotion by giving it active expression, for example, by crying. [described by Sigmund FREUD]

discharge procedure the process of releasing a patient from a mental hospital or psychiatric unit. Common steps in the process include a final clinical interview and evaluation, instructions regarding prescribed medication (if relevant), and discussion of follow-up treatment and services.

discharge rate the ratio of the number of patients discharged from a hospital or other institution in a given period to the number admitted. Also called **improvement rate**; **recovery ratio**.

dischronation *n.* an aspect of DISORIENTATION in which there is confusion about time. Also called **chronotaxis**.

disciple *n.* **1.** a student under a teacher's direction, a supporter of a cause, or a follower. **2.** one who spreads the doctrine of another.

discipline *n.* **1.** training that is designed to establish desired habits of mind and behavior. **2.** control of conduct, usually a child's, by means of punishment or reward. **3.** a field of study.

discomfort anxiety tension and consequent low frustration tolerance that arise from irrational beliefs about perceived threats to well-being. For example, one may experience discomfort anxiety when one has the AW-

FULIZING belief "I can't stand it when things don't go my way." [proposed in 1979 by U.S. psychologist Albert Ellis (1913–)]

discomfort disturbance a low tolerance to either discomfort or frustration that may make people overreact to unpleasant life experiences, frustration, or their own negative feelings. [proposed by U.S. psychologist Albert Ellis (1913–)]

discomfort–relief quotient see DISTRESS–RELIEF QUOTIENT.

disconfirmability *n.* see FALSIFIABILITY.

disconnection syndrome any neurological disorder resulting from a separation or isolation of cortical areas that usually work together. Several neurobehavioral symptoms, including some apraxias and agnosias, are thought to be attributable to disconnection syndrome. [defined by U.S. neurologist Norman Geschwind (1926–1984)]

discontinuity effect the markedly greater competitiveness of intergroup interactions relative to the competitiveness of interactions involving individuals.

discontinuity hypothesis in GESTALT PSYCHOLOGY, the viewpoint that emphasizes the role of sudden insight and perceptual reorganization in successful DISCRIMINATION LEARNING and problem solving. According to this view, a correct answer is only recognized when its relation to the issue as a whole is discovered. Also called **discontinuity theory**. Compare CONTINUITY HYPOTHESIS. See also AHA EXPERIENCE; ALL-OR-NONE LEARNING HYPOTHESIS; EUREKA TASK.

discordance *n.* **1.** the state or condition of being at variance. **Affective discordance** may be observed during psychotherapy when a client relates a particularly disturbing experience without a trace of feeling. **2.** in TWIN STUDIES, dissimilarity between a pair of twins with respect to a particular trait or disease. Compare CONCORDANCE IN TWINS. **—discordant** *adj.*

discounting principle in ATTRIBUTION THEORY, the principle that the role of a particular cause in producing a particular effect should be given less weight if other plausible causes are also present. Compare AUGMENTATION PRINCIPLE. [introduced by U.S. social psychologist Harold H. Kelley (1921–2003)]

discourse analysis in linguistics, the study of structures that extend beyond the single sentence, such as conversations, narratives, or written arguments. Discourse analysis is particularly concerned with the ways in which a sequence of two or more sentences can produce meanings that are different from or additional to any found in the sentences considered separately. An important source of such meanings is the "frame" or format of the discourse (news item, fairytale, joke, etc.), and a recognition of the various norms that this implies. The norms and expectations that govern conversation are a major concern of discourse analysis, as is the structure of conversational language generally. Particular areas of interest here include the distinction between background and foreground information (see FOREGROUNDING; GIVEN–NEW DISTINCTION) and the relations between explicit and inferred meanings (see CONVERSATIONAL INFERENCE; IMPLICATURE; PRESUPPOSITION).

discourse routine a highly structured and ritualized conversational act in which the participants have set expectations about turn taking and participation. Discourse routine is important in institutional contexts, such as classroom instruction.

discovery *n.* in a legal dispute, a motion usually put forward by the defense that the prosecution make available for copy all documents relevant to its case. These include both paper documents and any information stored on computer or video.

discovery learning learning that occurs through solving problems, by formulating and testing hypotheses, and in actual experience and manipulation in attempting solutions.

discovery method a teaching method that seeks to provide students with experience of the processes of science or other disciplines through inductive reasoning and active experimentation, with minimal teacher supervision. Students are encouraged to organize data, develop and test hypotheses, and formulate conclusions or general principles. The discovery method is associated with the cognitivist school of Jean PIAGET, U.S. psychologist Jerome Bruner (1915–), and others.

discovery of new means through active experimentation see TERTIARY CIRCULAR REACTION.

discrepancy evaluation in evaluation research, the search for differences between two or more elements or variables of a program that should be in agreement. Reconciling these differences may then become a major objective in the program's development.

discrepancy principle the assumption that infants are most attentive to novel stimuli, which forms the basis for studies of infant perception.

discrepant stimulus a stimulus that varies moderately from a known stimulus or schematic image. For example, a stranger's face represents a discrepant stimulus for an infant.

discrete control see CONTINUOUS CONTROL.

discrete data data that are not on a continuous scale but are limited to specific categories or values, which may be ordered or not ordered. See CATEGORICAL DATA; DISCRETE VARIABLE.

discrete measure a measure of a discrete (i.e., discontinuous, distinct, and limited) value, for example, the grade level of a student.

discrete movement task a movement task that has a recognizable beginning and end. Examples include grasping an object, kicking a ball, and shifting the gears of a car. Compare CONTINUOUS MOVEMENT TASK.

discrete trial a defined, limited occasion to engage in some behavior. For example, each trip through a maze by a rat can be considered a discrete trial. Such trials may be contrasted with those in which the behavior in question can occur at any time (see FREE OPERANT).

discrete variable a RANDOM VARIABLE that is not continuous but takes on only a relatively small number of distinct values. Also called **discrete random variable**. Compare CONTINUOUS VARIABLE.

discretionary task a relatively unstructured task that can be solved at the discretion of the group or group leader using a variety of procedures. See ADDITIVE TASK; COMPENSATORY TASK; CONJUNCTIVE TASK; DISJUNCTIVE TASK.

discriminability *n.* the quality that enables an object or person to be readily distinguished from something or someone else.

discriminal dispersion the distribution of responses around a given MEAN in an experiment involving DISCRIMINATIONS.

discriminanda *pl. n.* (*sing.* **discriminandum**) stimuli that can be distinguished from one another.

discriminant analysis a MULTIVARIATE statistical method that combines information from a set of predictor variables in order to allow maximal discrimination among a set of predefined groups.

discriminant function any of a range of statistical techniques to situate an item that could belong to any of two or more variables in the correct set, with minimal probability of error.

discriminant validity a form of CONSTRUCT VALIDITY demonstrated by showing that measures of constructs that are conceptually unrelated do not correlate in the data. Compare CONVERGENT VALIDITY.

discriminated operant a conditioned OPERANT that is under stimulus control, that is, a response that is more likely to occur when its DISCRIMINATIVE STIMULUS is present than when it is not present.

discriminating power a measure of the ability of a test to distinguish between two groups being measured.

discrimination *n.* **1.** the ability to distinguish between stimuli or objects that differ quantitatively or qualitatively from one another. **2.** the ability to respond in different ways in the presence of different stimuli. In conditioning, this is usually established in experiments by DIFFERENTIAL REINFORCEMENT or DIFFERENTIAL CONDITIONING techniques. See DISCRIMINATION LEARNING; DISCRIMINATION TRAINING. **3.** differential treatment of the members of different ethnic, religious, national, or other groups. Discrimination is usually the behavioral manifestation of PREJUDICE and therefore involves negative, hostile, and injurious treatment of the members of rejected groups. By contrast, POSITIVE DISCRIMINATION is the favorable treatment of the oppressed group rather than the typically favored group. See also RACIAL DISCRIMINATION; SEX DISCRIMINATION; SOCIAL DISCRIMINATION. **—discriminate** *vb.*

discrimination index see INDEX OF DISCRIMINATION.

discrimination learning a conditioning or learning experience in which an individual must learn to make choices between seemingly identical or similar alternatives in order to reach a goal. For example, a cat may have to learn to find food under a white cup on the left side of an area in which there are white and black cups on both sides. Also called **discriminative learning**.

discrimination of cues the ability to distinguish between or two or more stimuli. Operant or Pavlovian DISCRIMINATION TRAINING procedures are often used to allow behavior to reflect this ability.

discrimination reaction time the REACTION TIME of a participant in a task that requires him or her to discriminate between different stimuli, as in a CHOICE REACTION TIME task or a COMPLEX REACTION TIME task. See also COMPOUND REACTION TIME; SIMPLE REACTION TIME.

discrimination training 1. a procedure in which an OPERANT RESPONSE is reinforced in the presence of a particular stimulus but not in the absence of that stimulus. For example, a rat's lever-press response might be reinforced when a stimulus light is on but not when the light is off. This rat will eventually learn to press the lever only when the light is on. See DISCRIMINATION OF CUES. **2.** in sport, the training of the ability to identify task-relevant cues and their meaning.

discriminative learning see DISCRIMINATION LEARNING.

discriminative response in conditioning, a response that is controlled by the stimulus.

discriminative stimulus (symbol: S^D) in OPERANT CONDITIONING, a stimulus that increases the probability of a response because of a previous history of DIFFERENTIAL REINFORCEMENT in the presence of that stimulus. For example, if a pigeon's key pecks are reinforced when the key is illuminated red, but not when the key is green, the red stimulus will come to serve as an S^D and the pigeon will learn to peck only when the key is red. Compare NEGATIVE DISCRIMINATIVE STIMULUS.

discussion group any group set up to explore problems and questions in a variety of vocational, educational, guidance, therapeutic, and community settings. In schools, a discussion group is usually an instructional technique; in psychiatric and other therapeutic settings, the focus is emotional and interpersonal; in vocational, guidance, and community settings, the objective may be to stimulate decision-making processes and to channel recommendations to a study or action group.

discussion leader the member of a DISCUSSION GROUP who is responsible for stimulating and guiding discussions.

discussion method a teaching method in which both teacher and students actively contribute to the instructional process through classroom dialogue.

disease *n.* a definite pathological process with organic origins, marked by a characteristic set of symptoms that may affect the entire body or a part of the body and that impairs functioning.

disease course the progress of a pathological condition or process from inception, manifestation, and DIAGNOSIS through treatment and resolution.

disease model 1. any of several theories concerning the causes and course of a pathological condition or process. **2.** see MEDICAL MODEL.

disease of adaptation any of a group of illnesses, including high blood pressure and heart attacks, that are associated with or partly caused by long-term defective physiological or psychological reactions to stress. [named and defined by Austrian physician Hans Selye (1907–1982)]

disease phobia a persistent and irrational fear of disease in general or of a particular disease, formerly called **nosophobia**. Fear of disease may be a SPECIFIC PHOBIA or a feature of HYPOCHONDRIASIS or OBSESSIVE-COMPULSIVE DISORDER. Also called **pathophobia**.

disenfranchised grief grief that society (or some element of it) does not expect or may not allow a person to express. Examples include the grief of parents for stillborn babies, of teachers for the death of students, and of nurses for the death of patients. People who have lost an animal companion are often expected to keep their sorrow to themselves. Disenfranchised grief tends to isolate the bereaved individual from others and thus impede recovery. Also called **hidden grief**. See also GRIEF COUNSELING; GRIEFWORK; MOURNING.

disengaged family a family whose members are mutually withdrawn from each other psychologically and emotionally.

disengagement *n.* the act of withdrawing from an attachment or relationship or, more generally, from an unpleasant situation. **—disengaged** *adj.*

disengagement theory a theory proposing that old age involves a sharp decline in social interaction, a reduced LIFE SPACE, and loss of social esteem and morale. According to this theory, there is a withdrawal of the individual from society and of society from the individual. Empirical research has shown, however, that this mutual withdrawal is not a necessary component of old age. Compare ACTIVITY THEORY. [developed by 20th-century U.S. psychologists Elaine Cumming and William E. Henry]

disequilibrium *n.* **1.** a loss of physical balance, as in PARKINSON'S DISEASE and ATAXIAS due to cerebellar disorder or injury. **2.** emotional imbalance, as in individuals with extreme mood swings or AFFECTIVE LABILITY. **3.** in developmental psychology, a state of tension between cognitive processes competing against each other. In contrast to Jean PIAGET, some theorists believe that disequilibrium is the optimal state for significant cognitive advances to occur. See also EQUILIBRATION.

disesthesia *n.* see DYSESTHESIA.

disfigurement *n.* a blemish or deformity that mars the appearance of the face or body. Disfigurement can result from severe burn scars; mutilations due to wounds, accidents, or radical surgery; and a wide variety of congenital anomalies, some of which are at least partially reparable. The psychological effects of disfigurement are often devastating, especially since they are due in part to the negative and often humiliating reactions of others in a society that places a high value on physical attractiveness. Among these effects are damage to the self-image, loss of self-esteem, feelings of inferiority, self-consciousness, shame, resentment, hypersensitivity, withdrawal, antisocial behavior, and paranoid reactions. See also FACIAL DISFIGUREMENT.

disgust *n.* **1.** a strong aversion, for example, to the taste, smell, or touch of something deemed revolting. **2.** strong distaste for a person or behavior deemed morally repugnant. **—disgusting** *adj.*

dishabituation *n.* the reappearance or enhancement of a habituated response (i.e., one that has been weakened following repeated exposure to the evoking stimulus) due to the presentation of a new stimulus. Dishabituation can be interpreted as a signal that a given stimulus can be discriminated from another habituated stimulus and is a useful method for investigating perception in nonverbal individuals or animals. Compare HABITUATION.

dishonest signal in animal communication, a signal that provides misleading information about the size, quality, or intention of an individual. Dishonest signals include ALARM CALLS that scare away other group members, with the result that the animal gains better access to food, and a misleading impression of great vigor that attracts mates. Some have argued that dishonest signals are more compatible with the competitive process of NATURAL SELECTION than are HONEST SIGNALS. See DECEPTION.

disincentive *n.* a deterrent. Specifically, in industrial and organizational psychology, it is any factor that tends to discourage effort or productivity and to lower MOTIVATION, such as unpleasant working conditions. In some situations factors outside the workplace, such as aspects of the tax or welfare system, may act as disincentives. See also HYGIENE FACTORS.

disinformation *n.* PROPAGANDA or false information publicly announced or planted in the news media for the purpose of deception.

disinhibition *n.* **1.** diminution or loss of the normal control exerted by the cerebral cortex, resulting in poorly controlled or poorly restrained emotions or actions. Disinhibition may be due to the effects of alcohol, drugs, or brain injury, particularly to the frontal lobes. **2.** in conditioning experiments, the reappearance of responding, which has stopped occurring as a result of exposure to EXTINCTION, when a new stimulus is presented.

disinhibitory effect activity within the brain that permits individuals to behave in a manner that they would not normally find acceptable. It can result from the consumption of alcohol, prescription medication, or other drugs.

disintegration *n.* a breakup or severe disorganization of some structure or system of functioning, for example, of psychic and behavioral functions.

disintegration of personality fragmentation of the personality to such an extent that the individual no longer presents a unified, predictable set of beliefs, attitudes, traits, and behavioral responses. The most extreme examples of disintegrated, disorganized personality are found in the schizophrenias.

disjoint sets in SET THEORY, two sets that have no elements in common. The intersection of the sets is empty, and they are mutually exclusive.

disjunctive concept a concept that is based on a set of attributes not all of which are required to be present in every instance. For example, the concept "car" could be defined by citing the attributes (a) has an internal combustion engine, (b) has four wheels, (c) has a steering wheel, (d) has headlights, and so on: However, it is quite possible to conceive of a car that lacks one or more of these attributes. Compare CONJUNCTIVE CONCEPT. See also FAMILY RESEMBLANCE.

disjunctive motivation striving for substitute or temporary (rather than true and lasting) satisfaction. Compare CONJUNCTIVE MOTIVATION. [defined by U.S. psychiatrist Harry Stack Sullivan (1892–1949)]

disjunctive reaction time see COMPLEX REACTION TIME.

disjunctive task a group task or project that is completed when a single solution, decision, or group member's recommendation is adopted by the group. Such tasks are in most cases nondivisible (they cannot be broken down into subcomponents), optimizing (they require a correct or best solution rather than a high quantity of production), and they require that groups develop some means of selecting an alternative from a pool of alternatives. Compare ADDITIVE TASK; COMPENSATORY TASK; CONJUNCTIVE TASK.

dismissive attachment an adult attachment style that combines a positive INTERNAL WORKING MODEL OF ATTACHMENT of oneself, characterized by a view of oneself as competent and worthy of love, and a negative internal working model of attachment of others, characterized by one's view that others are untrustworthy or undependable. Individuals with dismissive attachment are presumed to discount the importance of close relationships and to maintain rigid self-sufficiency. Compare FEARFUL ATTACHMENT; PREOCCUPIED ATTACHMENT; SECURE ATTACHMENT.

disorder *n.* a group of symptoms involving abnormal behaviors, persistent or intense distress, or a disruption of physiological functioning. See also MENTAL DISORDER.

disorder of written expression in *DSM–IV–TR*, a LEARNING DISORDER in which writing skills are substantially below those expected, given the person's chronological age, formal education experience, and measured intelligence. The writing difficulties, which may involve errors in grammar, punctuation, and paragraph organization, often combined with extremely poor handwriting and spelling errors, significantly interfere with academic achievement and activities of daily living that require writing skills. Also called **developmental expressive writing disorder**.

disorders of excessive somnolence (**DOES**) one of four basic types of SLEEP DISORDERS, differentiated from the other types by the presence of excessive sleepiness for at least 1 month. The equivalent classification in *DSM–*

IV–TR is PRIMARY HYPERSOMNIA. Diagnosis can involve observation in a SLEEP LABORATORY, in which such criteria as nocturnal awakenings, sleep time, sleep continuity, SLEEP LATENCY, percentage of time in STAGE 2 SLEEP, and percentage of time in STAGE 3 SLEEP and STAGE 4 SLEEP are measured.

disorders of infancy, childhood, or adolescence not otherwise specified in *DSM–IV–TR*, disorders with an onset during infancy, childhood, or adolescence that do not meet *DSM–IV–TR* criteria for any specific disorder.

disorders of initiating and maintaining sleep (**DIMS**) one of four basic types of SLEEP DISORDERS, differentiated from the other types by the presence of INSOMNIA, that is, persistent inability to fall asleep or stay asleep. The equivalent classification in *DSM–IV–TR* is PRIMARY INSOMNIA. Diagnosis can involve observation in a SLEEP LABORATORY, in which such criteria as nocturnal awakenings, sleep time, sleep efficiency, breathing patterns, percentage of time in STAGE 2 SLEEP, percentage of time in STAGE 3 SLEEP and STAGE 4 SLEEP, minutes of REM SLEEP, and REM SLEEP LATENCY are measured.

disorders of the self in SELF PSYCHOLOGY, narcissistic problems resulting from insufficient response by others (such as parents) to one's needs. According to this view, an individual's self-cohesion, self-esteem, and vitality derive from and are maintained by the empathic responsiveness of others; lack of this response can lead to deficiencies or inabilities in loving other people and a focus on oneself. [defined by Austrian psychoanalyst Heinz Kohut (1913–1981)]

disorders of the sleep–wake cycle schedule one of four basic types of SLEEP DISORDERS, differentiated from the other types in that it results from a mismatch between one's internal CIRCADIAN RHYTHM and one's actual sleep schedule. The equivalent classification in *DSM–IV–TR* is CIRCADIAN RHYTHM SLEEP DISORDER. Rotating work-shift schedules and JET LAG are two common causes of this disorder. Diagnosis can involve observation in a SLEEP LABORATORY, in which such criteria as nocturnal awakening, sleep time, sleep efficiency, breathing patterns, body temperature, minutes of REM SLEEP, and REM SLEEP LATENCY are measured.

disorganization *n.* loss or disruption of orderly or systematic structure or functioning. For example, thought disorganization is an inability to integrate thought processes; behavior disorganization is a disruption of behavior.

disorganized attachment in the STRANGE SITUATION, a form of INSECURE ATTACHMENT in which infants show no coherent or consistent behavior during separation from and reunion with their parent. Also called **disoriented attachment**.

disorganized behavior behavior that is self-contradictory or inconsistent. It may include childlike silliness, unpurposeful or aimless behavior, unpredictable agitation, or extreme emotional reaction (e.g., laughing after a catastrophe). A typical example is dressing in clothing inappropriate for the weather (e.g., wearing several layers on a warm summer day). Disorganized behavior is commonly seen in individuals with schizophrenia.

disorganized development disruption in the normal course of ATTACHMENT in children in which the child does not learn how to deal with separation from or reunion with a parent. As infants, these children react to their parents with fear or apprehension and do not know how to seek them out when stressed (see DISORGANIZED ATTACHMENT).

disorganized offender the type of offender who approaches his or her crimes in a frenzied and impulsive manner, is typically of low to moderate intelligence and socially withdrawn, and has a poor work history. Compare ORGANIZED OFFENDER.

disorganized schizophrenia in *DSM–IV–TR*, a subtype of schizophrenia characterized primarily by random and fragmented speech and behavior and by flat or inappropriate affect, frequently associated with grimaces, mannerisms, laughter, and extreme social withdrawal. It tends to be the most severe of the schizophrenia subtypes and is often associated with poor premorbid personality and early and insidious onset. In *DSM–III*, it was called **disorganized type schizophrenic disorder**; historically, and in other classifications, this subtype is known as **hebephrenia** or **hebephrenic schizophrenia**.

disorganized speech incoherent speech. This may be speech in which ideas shift from one subject to another, seemingly unrelated, subject, sometimes described as LOOSENING OF ASSOCIATIONS. Other types of disorganized speech include responding to questions in an irrelevant way, reaching illogical conclusions, and making up words. See METONYMIC DISTORTION; NEOLOGISM; PARALOGIA.

disorientation *n.* a state of impaired ability to identify oneself or to locate oneself in relation to time, place, or other aspects of one's surroundings. Long-term disorientation can be characteristic of organic neurological and psychological disorders; temporary disorientation can be caused by alcohol or drugs or can occur in situations of acute stress, such as fires or earthquakes. See also CONFUSION; TIME DISORIENTATION; TOPOGRAPHICAL DISORIENTATION. **—disoriented** *adj.*

disoriented attachment see DISORGANIZED ATTACHMENT.

disparate impact see ADVERSE IMPACT.

disparate sensations 1. different sensory or cognitive responses arising from a single object or idea. **2.** the bases for thought and perception, which are integrated by the brain into wholes.

dispersal *n.* the departure of animals from their natal group to join a different group or find mates elsewhere. Dispersal is thought to be important in reducing inbreeding and avoiding competition with older individuals of the same sex. Species vary in terms of whether dispersal is male-biased or female-biased or whether both sexes disperse. It is a costly behavior, because the dispersing individual is more subject to predation as well as to aggression from other members of the same species. See also PHILOPATRY.

dispersion *n.* the degree to which a batch of scores deviate from the mean. Also called **spread**.

displaced aggression the direction of hostility away from the source of frustration or anger and toward either the self or a different person or object. Displaced aggression may occur, for example, when circumstances preclude direct confrontation with the responsible person or institution because that person or institution is perceived as too powerful to attack without fear of reprisal. See DISPLACEMENT. Compare DIRECT AGGRESSION.

displacement *n.* the transfer of feelings or behavior from their original object to another person or thing. In psychoanalytic theory, displacement is considered to be a DEFENSE MECHANISM in which the individual discharges tensions associated with, for example, hostility and fear by taking them out on a neutral, nonthreatening or less threatening target. Thus, an angry child might hurt a sibling instead of attacking the father; a frustrated employee might criticize his or her spouse instead of the boss; or a person who fears his or her own hostile impulses might transfer that fear to knives, guns, or other objects that might be used as a weapon. See also DISPLACED AGGRESSION; DRIVE DISPLACEMENT; SCAPEGOATING. **—displace** *vb.*

displacement behavior a behavior in which an individual substitutes one type of action for another when the first action is unsuccessful or when two competing motivations are present that lead to incompatible actions. A gull at a territory boundary may direct attacklike actions toward the ground rather than its rival due to simultaneous aggressive and fearful responses to the opponent. A laboratory animal that is frustrated by servings of food that are small and delivered slowly may express displacement behavior by drinking instead of eating. Also called **displacement activity**.

displacement of affect see TRANSPOSITION OF AFFECT.

display *n.* **1.** the presentation of stimuli to any of the senses. **2.** a device used for such a purpose.

display behavior more or less stereotyped actions (i.e., actions repeated with little variation) that bring about a response in another individual: an integral part of ANIMAL COMMUNICATION. Display behavior may be verbal or nonverbal, usually involving stimulation of the visual or auditory senses. It may include body language that would convey a message of courtship to a member of the opposite sex (e.g., a show of plumage or color) or a suggestion that would be interpreted by an opponent as threatening (e.g., bared teeth or hissing noises). Because of their stereotyped nature, displays are thought to have evolved from physiological or behavioral responses to previously direct interactions that have now become symbolic. For example, a human being may be flushed when aggressive or pale when fearful due to vasodilation or vasoconstriction associated with attack or avoidance. These vascular changes have now become predictive of the behavior likely to follow and serve as communication signals. See also DISPLAY RULES.

display–control compatibility in ergonomics, a design principle stating that controls and their corresponding displays should be compatible on such dimensions as direction of movement, color, and location or alignment. See also CONTROL FUNCTION LOGIC; PROXIMITY COMPATIBILITY.

display design in ergonomics, the design of displays for effective transmission of information in different situations. Displays may be static devices (such as signs, labels, and diagrams) or dynamic devices (such as speedometers, clocks, and temperature gauges). Other dimensions on which display design may vary include: numerical scales with moving pointers versus moving scales with fixed pointers, circular versus linear displays, horizontal versus vertical scales, pictorial versus verbal signs, and simple versus detailed signs. The information conveyed may include directions and instructions, safety messages and alerts, and fluctuating information about the state of a particular system (e.g., speed, volume, or temperature). See BAR DISPLAY; OBJECT DISPLAY; INTEGRATED DISPLAY; SEPARATED DISPLAY. See also DISPLAY–CONTROL COMPATIBILITY.

display rules in human behavior, the socially learned standards that regulate the expression of emotion. Display rules vary from culture to culture; for example, the expression of anger may be considered appropriate in some cultures but not in others.

disposition *n.* a recurrent behavioral or affective tendency that distinguishes an individual from others. Also called **personal disposition** (**PD**).

dispositional attribution 1. in ATTRIBUTION THEORY, the ascription of one's own or another's actions to internal or psychological causes, such as personality, moods, or attitudes. **2.** the ascription of an event or outcome to internal or psychological causes specific to the person concerned, such as decisions and judgments, abilities, or effort. Also called **internal attribution**; **personal attribution**. Compare SITUATIONAL ATTRIBUTION.

dispositional hearing a proceeding held in juvenile court cases after the court finds that an offense has been committed. It is similar to the sentencing hearing or penalty phase in an adult criminal court.

disruptive behavior behavior that chronically threatens and intimidates others or violates social norms. The term is typically applied to the behavior of children, but it can also be used to describe adult behavior. According to *DSM–IV–TR* criteria, children exhibiting disruptive behavior are diagnosed with one of the DISRUPTIVE BEHAVIOR DISORDERS, whereas those older than 18 years of age are diagnosed with ANTISOCIAL PERSONALITY DISORDER.

disruptive behavior disorder a psychiatric disorder in which the primary symptom involves DISRUPTIVE BEHAVIOR (e.g., violation of social rules and rights of others, defiance, hostile behavior) that is severe enough to produce significant impairment in social or occupational functioning. In *DSM–IV–TR*, disruptive behavior disorders include CONDUCT DISORDER, OPPOSITIONAL DEFIANT DISORDER, and DISRUPTIVE BEHAVIOR DISORDER NOT OTHERWISE SPECIFIED.

disruptive behavior disorder not otherwise specified in *DSM–IV–TR*, a pattern of behavior involving violation of social rules or the basic rights of others, aggression, or defiance that results in clinically significant impairment but does not conform to the full *DSM–IV–TR* criteria of other, specific disruptive behavior disorders.

dissent *n.* **1.** disagreement with majority opinion or established social norms. **2.** disagreement with government policies, especially as expressed through organized protests or social ACTIVISM. See also CIVIL DISOBEDIENCE; PASSIVE RESISTANCE. **—dissenter** *n.*

dissociated learning see STATE-DEPENDENT LEARNING.

dissociated state a reaction to a traumatic event in which the individual splits the components of the event into those that can be faced in the present and those that are too harmful to process. The latter components are repressed and can be recalled later in life if triggered by a similarly traumatic event, introspection, or psychotherapy. In the normal psyche, the functioning of consciousness, memory, identity, and perception of the environment are integrated rather than split into separate components. See also DISSOCIATIVE DISORDERS.

dissociation *n.* **1.** an unconscious DEFENSE MECHANISM in which conflicting impulses are kept apart or threatening ideas and feelings are separated from the rest of the psyche. See COMPARTMENTALIZATION; DISSOCIATIVE DISORDERS. **2.** in research, a method used to differentiate processes, components, or variables. For instance, it might involve discovering a variable that influences short-term memory but not long-term memory. See DOUBLE DISSOCIATION.

dissociative amnesia in *DSM–IV–TR*, a DISSOCIATIVE DISORDER characterized by failure to recall important information about one's personal experiences, usually of a traumatic or stressful nature, that is too extensive to be explained by normal forgetfulness. Recovery of memory often occurs spontaneously within a few hours and is usually connected with removal from the traumatic circumstances with which the amnesia was associated. In *DSM–III* this disorder was called **psychogenic amnesia**.

dissociative anesthetic an anesthetic agent capable of producing amnesia, analgesia, and sedation without inducing loss of consciousness.

dissociative barriers in dissociative disorders, the barriers to full conscious access by individuals to their recollections of a traumatic event. The trauma is presumed to be implicated in the development of the disorder, and the dissociative barriers are theorized to serve a protective function, allowing the traumatized person to avoid knowledge of horrific life events.

dissociative disorder not otherwise specified in *DSM–IV–TR*, a residual category of disorders that do not meet the diagnostic criteria for any of the specific DISSOCIATIVE DISORDERS. It includes DISSOCIATIVE TRANCE DISORDER, DEREALIZATION without depersonalization, DISSOCIATED STATES resulting from brainwashing or other forms of coercion, and GANSER SYNDROME.

dissociative disorders in *DSM–IV–TR*, a group of disorders characterized by a sudden, gradual, transient, or chronic disruption in the normal integrative functions of consciousness, memory, or perception of the environment. Such disruption may last for minutes or years, depending on the type of disorder. Included in this category are DISSOCIATIVE AMNESIA, DISSOCIATIVE FUGUE, DISSOCIATIVE IDENTITY DISORDER, DEPERSONALIZATION DISORDER, and DISSOCIATIVE DISORDER NOT OTHERWISE SPECIFIED.

dissociative fugue in *DSM–IV–TR*, a DISSOCIATIVE DISORDER in which the individual suddenly and unexpectedly travels away from home or a customary place of daily activities and is unable to recall some or all of his or her past. Symptoms also include either confusion about personal identity or assumption of a new identity. No other signs of mental disorder are present, and the fugue state can last from hours to months. Travel can be brief or extended in duration, and there may be no memory of travel once the individual is brought back to the prefugue state. In *DSM–III* this disorder was called **psychogenic fugue**.

dissociative group a group with which one wishes not to be associated. Compare ASPIRATIONAL GROUP.

dissociative hysteria a former name for a DISSOCIATIVE DISORDER.

dissociative identity disorder in *DSM–IV–TR*, a DISSOCIATIVE DISORDER characterized by the presence in one individual of two or more distinct identities or personality states that each recurrently take control of the individual's behavior. It is typically associated with severe physical and sexual abuse, especially during childhood. An increase in reported cases has been seen in the United States in recent years, and research suggests that there may be a hereditary component. In *DSM–III* this disorder was called **multiple personality disorder**.

dissociative pattern a pattern of behavior consistent with DISSOCIATIVE DISORDERS, as evidenced by disruption in the normal integrative functions of consciousness, memory, or perception of the environment.

dissociative process a process of disruption of the normal integrative functions of consciousness, memory, or perception of the environment. It typically occurs as a result of a traumatic or profoundly disturbing event, such as physical or sexual abuse, wartime experience, or involvement in an accident in which someone else died. See also DISSOCIATIVE DISORDERS.

dissociative stupor a profound decrease in or absence of voluntary movement and responsiveness to external stimuli, apparently resulting from acute STRESS.

dissociative trance disorder a DISSOCIATIVE DISORDER characterized by involuntary alterations in consciousness, identity, awareness or memory, and motor functioning that result in significant distress or impairment. The two subtypes of the disorder are distinguished by the individual's identity state. In **possession trance**, the individual's usual identity is replaced by a new identity perceived to be an external force, such as a ghost, another person, or a divine being, and there is loss of memory for the episode of trance. In **trance disorder**, individuals retain their usual identity but have an altered perception of their milieu. These types of dissociative experiences are common in various cultures and may be part of customary religious practice; they should not be regarded as pathological unless considered abnormal within the context of that cultural or religious group. Also called **possession trance disorder**; **trance and possession disorder** (**TPD**). See DISSOCIATIVE DISORDER NOT OTHERWISE SPECIFIED. See also AMOK; ATAQUE DE NERVIOS; LATAH; PIBLOKTO.

dissonance *n.* see COGNITIVE DISSONANCE.

dissonance reduction the process by which a person reduces the uncomfortable psychological state that results from inconsistency among elements of a cognitive system (see COGNITIVE DISSONANCE). Dissonance can be reduced by making one or more inconsistent elements consistent with other elements in the system, by decreasing the perceived importance of an inconsistent element, or by adding new consistent elements to the system. Finally, SELF-AFFIRMATION THEORY postulates that merely affirming some valued aspect of the self, even if it is not directly relevant to the inconsistency, can reduce dissonance. See also BOLSTERING OF AN ATTITUDE; FORCED COMPLIANCE EFFECT.

distal *adj.* **1.** situated or directed toward the periphery of the body or toward the end of a limb. **2.** remote from or mostly distantly related to the point of reference or origin. Compare PROXIMAL.

distal effect any influence that particular responses of an organism may have on the environment.

distal response a response of an organism that produces an effect in the environment. Compare PROXIMAL RESPONSE.

distal stimulus in perception, the actual object in the environment that stimulates or acts on a sense organ. Also called **distal variable**. Compare PROXIMAL STIMULUS.

distance cue any of the auditory or visual cues that enable an individual to judge the distance of the source of a stimulus. Auditory distance cues include intensity of familiar sounds (e.g., voices), intensity differences between the ears, and changes in spectral content. In vision, distance cues include the size of familiar objects and ACCOMMODATION. See also DEPTH CUE.

distance learning the process of acquiring knowledge from a location remote from the teaching source. Typical methods include correspondence coursework, coursework presented over radio or television, computerized software programmed learning, coursework programmed and accessible on the Internet, live Internet hook-up to an instructor, direct live remote television, and live group video conferencing.

distance paradox see SIZE–DISTANCE PARADOX.

distance perception the ability of a viewer to judge the distance between him- or herself and a visual target. See also DEPTH CUE.

distance receptor see TELECEPTOR.

distance therapy any type of psychotherapy in which sessions are not conducted face-to-face because of problems of mobility, geographical isolation, or other limiting factors. Distance therapy includes interventions by telephone, audioconference, or videoconference (known collectively as **telepsychotherapy**) and the Internet (see E-THERAPY).

distance vision vision that permits discrimination of objects more than 6 m (20 ft) from the observer.

distance zone in social psychology, the area of physical distance commonly adopted between interacting individuals. Interpersonal distance tends to be relatively small the more familiar the people are to each other and usually increases in proportion to the formality of the relationship, the setting, and the interaction's function. See INTIMATE ZONE; PERSONAL DISTANCE ZONE; PUBLIC DISTANCE ZONE; SOCIAL ZONE. See also PROXEMICS.

distinctiveness effect see VON RESTORFF EFFECT.

distinctness *n.* **1.** the quality of an object on which attention is focused of being perceived clearly and as separate from other stimuli. **2.** in tasks requiring SELECTIVE ATTENTION, the extent to which the target is different from DISTRACTOR stimuli. Performance on selective attention tasks is better when the target is distinct from the distractors.

distorted room see AMES DISTORTION ROOM.

distorted speech test a test used to evaluate auditory and perceptual processing problems. In such tests certain elements of the acoustic signal are removed. Examples are FILTERED SPEECH and TIME-COMPRESSED SPEECH.

distorting-image procedure see DISTORTING-MIRROR PROCEDURE; DISTORTING-PHOTOGRAPH PROCEDURE; DISTORTING-VIDEO PROCEDURE.

distorting-mirror procedure a method of documenting accuracy of body-size perception by using a mirror distorted to represent an appearance that is either smaller or larger than one's actual dimensions. Accuracy of image perception is determined by comparison with objective size level.

distorting-photograph procedure a method of documenting accuracy of body-size perception by using a photograph distorted to provide an image of an individual that is smaller or larger than actual size. Discrepancy between the size of the selected image and that of an accurate image is used as an index of perceptual accuracy of body size.

distorting-video procedure a method of documenting accuracy of body-size perception by using a video image modified to be smaller or larger than one's actual size.

distortion *n.* **1.** either the unconscious process of altering emotions and thoughts that are unacceptable in the individual's psyche or the conscious misrepresentation of facts, which often serves the same underlying purpose of disguising that which is unacceptable to or in the self. **2.** in psychoanalytic theory, the outcome of the DREAM-WORK that modifies forbidden thoughts and wishes to make them more acceptable to the EGO. Such distortion of the dream WISH through the use of substitutes and symbols means that only an act of INTERPRETATION can uncover the true meaning of the dream.

distractibility *n.* difficulty in maintaining attention or a tendency to be easily diverted from the matter at hand. Excessive distractibility is frequently found in children with learning disorders or ATTENTION-DEFICIT/HYPERACTIVITY DISORDER and in people experiencing MANIC EPISODES or HYPOMANIC EPISODES.

distractible speech a speech pattern in which the individual shifts rapidly from topic to topic in response to external or internal stimuli. It is a common symptom in mania. See also FLIGHT OF IDEAS.

distraction *n.* **1.** the process of interrupting attention. **2.** a stimulus or task that draws attention away from the task of primary interest.

distractor *n.* a stimulus or an aspect of a stimulus that is irrelevant to the task or activity being performed. In memory studies, an item or task may be used as a distractor either to fill time before the participant attempts to recall or to minimize rehearsal of the material to be remembered. For instance, the participant might be given some arithmetic problems to solve as a distractor task between the study and recall phases of an experiment. See also VISUAL ATTENTION.

distractor task see BROWN–PETERSON DISTRACTOR TECHNIQUE; DISTRACTOR.

distress *n.* a negative emotional state in which the specific quality of the emotion is unspecified or unidentifiable. For example, STRANGER ANXIETY in infants is more properly designated **stranger distress** because the infant's negative behavior, typically crying, allows no more specific identification of the emotion. **—distressing** *adj.*

distress–relief quotient the ratio of verbal expressions of distress to those of relief, used as an index of improvement in counseling and psychotherapy. Also called **discomfort–relief quotient; relief–discomfort quotient; relief–distress quotient**.

distributed actions theory a model of leadership (see LEADERSHIP THEORIES) that assumes that group effectiveness and member satisfaction increase when certain key functions of a leader, such as decision making, task orientation, INITIATING STRUCTURE, and the improvement of intermember relations, are not the sole responsibility of the leader but are instead distributed throughout the group.

distributed cognition a model for intelligent problem solving in which either the input information comes from separated and independent sources or the processing of this input information takes place across autonomous computational devices. Agent-based problem solving is sometimes described as distributed cognition.

distributed knowledge see DISTRIBUTED REPRESENTATION.

distributed practice a learning procedure in which practice periods for a particular activity or to improve recall of specific material are separated by regular, lengthy rest periods or periods of practicing different activities or studying other material, rather than practice being consecutive. In many learning situations, distributed practice is found to be more effective than MASSED PRACTICE. Also called **distribution of practice**; **spaced learning**; **spaced practice**.

distributed processing information processing in which computations are made across a series of processors or units, rather than being handled in a single, dedicated CENTRAL PROCESSOR. See also PARALLEL DISTRIBUTED PROCESSING; PARALLEL PROCESSING.

distributed representation in information processing, a system of representation in which information pertaining to a given unit of knowledge is carried by many separate components of the processing system, rather than being stored together as a single entity.

distribution *n.* the relation between the values that a variable may take and the relative number of cases taking on each value. A distribution may be simply an empirical description of that relationship or a mathematical (probabilistic) specification of the relationship.

distributional redundancy in psychological aesthetics, the development of uncertainty in an artistic pattern by making some elements occur more frequently than others. Distributional redundancy is one of two kinds of internal restraint in pattern variation, the other being **correlational redundancy**, in which certain combinations of elements are made to occur more frequently than others.

distribution-free test a test of statistical significance that makes relatively few, if any, assumptions about the underlying distribution of scores. See NONPARAMETRIC STATISTICS.

distribution of practice see DISTRIBUTED PRACTICE.

distributive analysis and synthesis an approach to psychotherapy, developed within PSYCHOBIOLOGY. In the first stage, a systematic analysis is made from information gained from the client about past and present experience and distributed into such categories as symptoms and complaints, assets and liabilities, and pathological or immature reactions. In the second stage this study is used as a prelude to a constructive synthesis built on the client's own strengths, goals, and abilities. [developed by Swiss-born U.S. psychiatrist Adolf Meyer (1866–1950)]

distributive bargaining a type of bargaining procedure in competitive situations in which the parties involved make demands of each other by indicating their preferred outcomes, using such contentious tactics as threats and arguments, and insisting on their firm commitment to their positions. Also called **competitive bargaining**.

distributive justice **1.** the belief that rules can be changed and punishments and rewards distributed according to relative standards, specifically according to equality and equity. In the **equality stage** (ages 8 to 10), children demand that everyone be treated in the same way. In the **equity stage** (ages 11 and older), children make allowances for subjective considerations, personal circumstances, and motive. Compare IMMANENT JUSTICE. [postulated by Jean PIAGET] **2.** see ORGANIZATIONAL JUSTICE.

disturbance in executive functioning see EXECUTIVE DYSFUNCTION.

disturbance of association interruption of a logical chain of culturally accepted thought, leading to apparently confused and haphazard thinking that is difficult for others to comprehend. It is one of the FUNDAMENTAL SYMPTOMS of schizophrenia described by Swiss psychiatrist Eugen Bleuler (1857–1939). See also SCHIZOPHRENIC THINKING; THOUGHT DISORDER.

disturbance term see ERROR TERM.

disulfiram *n.* a drug used as an aversive agent in managing alcohol abuse or dependence. Disulfiram inhibits the activity of acetaldehyde dehydrogenase, an enzyme responsible for the metabolism of alcohol (ethanol) in the liver. Consumption of alcohol following administration of disulfiram results in accumulation of acetaldehyde, a toxic metabolic product of ethanol, with such unpleasant effects as nausea, vomiting, sweating, headache, a fast heart rate, and palpitations. Because of the serious nature of some of these effects (which can include damage to the liver and heart), careful INFORMED CONSENT is required before use of disulfiram. Disulfiram by itself is rarely effective in managing alcoholism and should be administered only in concert with a carefully designed behavioral regimen. U.S. trade name: **Antabuse**.

disuse supersensitivity a condition in which target cells, on losing neural input either through denervation or chronic application of an ANTAGONIST drug, produce more than the normal number of RECEPTOR molecules, resulting in an exaggerated response when a neurotransmitter is applied. When this condition results from denervation, it is also called **denervation sensitivity**.

disuse theory of aging the theory that some decline in psychological abilities with aging may be due to the lack of use of those abilities. According to this theory, as adults grow older, they engage their minds less and less with the types of tasks that are found on most psychological tests.

disynaptic arc a NEURAL ARC in which there is an INTERNEURON between a sensory neuron and a motor neuron, requiring a neural signal to cross two synapses to complete the arc. See also REFLEX ARC.

diuretic *n.* a substance that increases the flow of urine. Diuretics may be endogenous agents (e.g., dopamine) or prescription or nonprescription drugs (e.g., THIAZIDE DIURETICS). Many diuretics (including thiazides) work by inhibiting or blocking the reabsorption of sodium and potassium ions from the kidney filtrate, so that less water is reabsorbed across the kidney tubules. Others, called osmotic diuretics, increase the osmolality of the filtrate. Both mechanisms result in increased urine volume. Some diuretics may produce adverse effects with psychological implications, for example, lassitude, weakness, vertigo, sexual impotence, headaches, polydipsia (intense thirst), irritability, or excitability.

diurnal *adj.* **1.** daily; that is, recurring every 24 hours. See BIOLOGICAL CLOCK; CIRCADIAN RHYTHM. **2.** occurring or active during daylight hours. Compare NOCTURNAL. —**diurnality** *n.*

diurnal enuresis see ENURESIS.

diurnal mood variation a feature of some BIPOLAR DISORDERS and DEPRESSIVE DISORDERS in which daily, predictable fluctuations in mood occur. Typically, this pattern consists of an elevation of mood during the daytime and evening hours and a depression of mood during the overnight and morning hours. See also SEASONAL AFFECTIVE DISORDER.

diurnal rhythm see CIRCADIAN RHYTHM.

divagation *n.* rambling, digressive speech, writing, or thought. See also DISORGANIZED SPEECH.

divalproex sodium an ANTICONVULSANT drug, derived from VALPROIC ACID, originally used in the treatment of absence seizures and now used primarily for the stabilization of mania and for prophylaxis in individuals with bipolar disorder. It has also been used in the treatment of various other conditions, including autism, migrainous and other forms of head pain, other chronic pain syndromes, and mood symptoms associated with borderline personality disorder. Liver damage and reduction in blood platelets (thrombocytopenia) may occur with use of the drug, and monitoring of blood count and liver function should be carried out, particularly in the early course of treatment and particularly in children, as most fatalities due to liver failure have occurred in children. Because of its possible association with NEURAL TUBE DEFECTS, divalproex sodium should not be prescribed during pregnancy. The drug has significant interactions with antidepressants, antipsychotics, anxiolytics, and numerous other classes of medication. U.S. trade name: **Depakote**.

divergence *n.* the tendency for the eyes to turn outward when shifting from near to far fixation. A permanent divergence (**walleye**) of one eye is termed EXOTROPIA. See also VERGENCE. **—divergent** *adj.*

divergent evolution the process by which populations become increasingly different from each other through different SELECTION PRESSURES acting in different habitats. Divergent evolution is a major way in which new species are formed. It contrasts with CONVERGENT EVOLUTION, in which different species become more similar to each other through adaptation to similar habitats.

divergent production the capacity to produce novel solutions to a problem. It is one of the abilities recognized in Joy P. GUILFORD's theory of intelligence (see GUILFORD DIMENSIONS OF INTELLIGENCE). Compare CONVERGENT PRODUCTION.

divergent strabismus see EXOTROPIA; STRABISMUS.

divergent thinking the type of CREATIVE THINKING in which an individual formulates new solutions to problems. The aim of such thinking is often to generate a variety of possible answers, which can then be analyzed and evaluated (see BRAINSTORMING). Compare CONVERGENT THINKING.

diversion program a program that may be available in some circumstances for individuals who have been arrested but have not been tried and sentenced. After the defendant has been formally charged with a crime and has entered a plea, he or she may be sent to a diversion program (e.g., for drug treatment) instead of proceeding to trial; the charges are dropped if the individual successfully completes the program. Also called **deferred prosecution**.

diversity training personnel training programs that help employees to appreciate and deal effectively with cultural, ethnic, racial, gender, sexual orientation, and other differences among people.

diversive exploration EXPLORATORY BEHAVIOR used as a means of seeking novel or otherwise activating stimuli and thus increasing arousal. Compare INSPECTIVE EXPLORATION. [defined by British-born Canadian psychologist Daniel E. Berlyne (1924–1976)]

divided attention attention to two or more channels of information at the same time, so that two or more tasks may be performed concurrently. Divided attention can occur through just one sense (e.g., hearing), or two or more senses (e.g., hearing and vision) may be engaged in the process.

divided brain see SPLIT BRAIN.

divided consciousness a state in which two or more mental activities appear to be carried out at the same time, for example, listening, planning questions, and taking notes during an interview. To the extent that the activities require consciousness and attention, they will tend to degrade each other. See also DUAL-TASK COMPETITION.

divination *n.* the art or practice of discerning future events or hidden knowledge by supernatural means. The numerous forms of divination include ASTROLOGY, AUGURY, CRYSTAL GAZING, LECANOMANCY, NECROMANCY, NUMEROLOGY, ONEIROMANCY, PALMISTRY, and RHABDOMANCY. **—divinatory** *adj.* **—divine** *vb.*

divine right the theory or presumption that monarchs derive their authority to govern directly from God and not from the governed or any entity representative of them. The theory saw its heyday under the reigns of the English kings James I (1603–1625) and Charles I (1625–1649) and the French king Louis XIV (1643–1715). Also called **divine right of kings**. See also SOCIAL CONTRACT.

divorce *n.* the legal dissolution of marriage, leaving the partners free to remarry. See also EMOTIONAL DIVORCE. **—divorcee** *n.*

divorce counseling counseling provided to individuals and their family members to help them cope with the problems resulting from divorce. The counseling can be conducted with the entire family or with one parent and children to provide group support and encourage a sense of belonging and identity during the transitional period. In either a family or individual context, family members may be encouraged to let go of the past and learn to deal with their present emotions. Spouses seen either individually or together may explore what their own contributions to the breakup may have been so as to decrease blame and increase probability of future relationship success.

divorce mediation counseling aimed at resolving issues for couples facing separation or divorce. The mediator remains neutral and impartial while assisting in negotiations to come to an agreed settlement over such issues as financial arrangements, child custody and visitation, and child support. Divorce mediation attempts to avoid confrontation and undue litigation prior to final settlement.

dizygotic twins (**DZ twins**) twins, of the same or different sexes, that have developed from two separate ova fertilized by two separate sperm. DZ twins are genetically as much alike as ordinary full siblings born as SINGLETONS, with each individual inheriting a random half of each parent's genes. On average, DZ twins are approximately half as genetically similar to one another as MONOZYGOTIC TWINS. For every 1,000 pregnancies there are, on average, 7–12 DZ twins. Also called **fraternal twins**. See also TWIN STUDIES.

dizziness *n.* a sensation of light-headedness or unsteadiness, sometimes with nausea and a fear of fainting. See VERTIGO.

DL abbreviation for difference limen (see DIFFERENCE THRESHOLD).

D-love *n.* see DEFICIENCY LOVE.

DLPFC abbreviation for DORSOLATERAL PREFRONTAL CORTEX.

DMS abbreviation for DIACRITICAL MARKING SYSTEM.

DMT *di*methyl*t*ryptamine: a HALLUCINOGEN belonging to the indolealkylamine family, to which LSD, PSILOCIN, and DET also belong.

DMTS abbreviation for DELAYED MATCHING TO SAMPLE.

DNA *d*eoxyribo*n*ucleic *a*cid: one of the two types of NUCLEIC ACID found in living organisms, which is the principal carrier of genetic information in chromosomes and, to a much lesser extent, in MITOCHONDRIA. Certain segments of the DNA molecules constitute the organism's genes. Structurally, DNA consists of two intertwined, helically coiled strands of nucleotides—the **double helix**. The nucleotides each contain one of four bases: adenine, guanine, cytosine, or thymine. Each base forms hydrogen bonds with the adjacent base on the other, sister strand, producing consecutive **base pairs** arranged rather like the "rungs" on a helical ladder. Adenine (A) is always paired with thymine (T), and guanine (G) with cytosine (C). DNA can undergo self-replication in such a way that each strand serves as the template for the assembly of a complementary matching strand, resulting in two molecules exactly like the original helix in terms of base pairing. The sequence of bases in the DNA of genes contains information according to the GENETIC CODE. Each gene specifies the manufacture of a particular protein or ribosome. Because of DNA's ability to conserve its base sequence when replicating, the genetic instructions it carries are also conserved, both during cell division within a single organism and for that organism's offspring following reproduction. Compare RNA. See also RECOMBINANT DNA.

DNR abbreviation for do not resuscitate. See INFORMED CONSENT.

docility *n.* the state of being passive or calm, easy to handle, or unlikely to attack. Docility can be induced in a strain of animals through selective breeding but may occur as part of natural variation within a population. A continuum of TEMPERAMENT from shy to bold has been observed in species ranging from fish to human beings. **—docile** *adj.*

doctor *n.* an individual, usually an MD, PhD, or PsyD, trained and licensed to deliver medical or mental health care services.

doctrine *n.* a teaching, dogma, or tenet of a system of belief or a body of such teachings. **—doctrinal** *adj.*

doctrine of causes the belief of Greek philosopher Aristotle (384–322 BCE) that explanations of the causality of an object had four different modes or types—formal, final, material, and efficient—corresponding roughly to its plan, its goal, the substance of which it was made, and the work done to produce it. See CAUSE.

doctrine of formal discipline the idea, no longer widely believed, that the mind can be trained to learn by first studying certain fields, such as languages, mathematics, and philosophy. The mind would then be ready to learn other topics. See also TRANSFER OF TRAINING.

Doerfler–Stewart test a test originated during World War II for screening for functional hearing loss. It is used to examine a person's ability to respond to selected two-syllable words in quiet and in the presence of a MASKING noise. [Leo G. **Doerfler** (1919–), U.S. audiologist; J. P. **Stewart**]

DOES abbreviation for DISORDERS OF EXCESSIVE SOMNOLENCE.

dogmatism *n.* **1.** the tendency to act in a blindly certain, assertive, and authoritative manner in accord with a strongly held set of beliefs. **2.** a personality trait characterized by the development of BELIEF SYSTEMS containing elements that are isolated from one another and thus may contradict one another. These belief systems are presumed to be resistant to change. Dogmatic people tend to be intolerant of those who hold different beliefs and of members of socially deviant groups. See ROKEACH DOGMATISM SCALE. [first proposed by U.S. psychologist Milton Rokeach (1918–1988)] **—dogmatic** *adj.*

dol *n.* a unit of pain sensation. One dol equals twice the threshold value.

dolichocephalic *adj.* denoting a head that is long and narrow. See CEPHALIC INDEX. **—dolichocephaly** *n.*

dolichomorphic *adj.* denoting a body that is tall and thin. **—dolichomorphy** *n.*

doll play in PLAY THERAPY, the use of dolls and figurines, which may represent individuals familiar to the child, to facilitate the expression of feelings, to enact stories that express emotional needs, or to reveal significant family relationships. Also called **projective doll play**.

Dolophine *n.* a trade name for METHADONE.

dolorimeter *n.* a device for the measurement of pain. **—dolorimetry** *n.*

DOM *d*imethoxy*m*ethylamphetamine: a synthetic HALLUCINOGEN that is also called **STP**—*s*erenity, *t*ranquillity, and *p*eace, which the substance is said to induce. It is a member of the phenylisopropylamine family, to which MDA and MDMA also belong.

domain *n.* **1.** the class of entities or events that constitutes the subject matter of a science or other discipline. **2.** a field of mastery, dominance, or endeavor. **3.** in BIOLOGICAL TAXONOMY, the highest category used in some classification systems, comprising one or more kingdoms. Three domains are recognized: Archaea (archaebacteria), Bacteria, and Eukarya (including animals, plants, fungi, and protists). **4.** in SET THEORY, the set of elements over which a function is defined.

domain-free problem in the literature on problem solving, a problem that can be solved without knowledge of a particular content domain, such as mathematics or science.

domain-general ability a cognitive ability, such as general intelligence or speed of information processing, that influences performance over a wide range of situations and tasks. Compare DOMAIN-SPECIFIC ABILITY.

domain identification **1.** the process by which individuals tacitly form a relationship between themselves and some field or pursuit, such as the academic, occupational, or athletic domain. Identification with the academic domain, for example, occurs for adolescents who value the rewards offered by success in educational settings, who feel they have the skills and resources needed in school, and who feel that others value achievements in this domain. **2.** in organizational theory, the specification of the methods used, the goals sought, and the population served by an organization.

domain name a name reserved for use in finding a website. Ideally, domain names for consumer products or companies are the same as the names used in the physical world.

domain-specific ability a cognitive ability, such as face recognition, that is specific to a task and under control of a specific function of the mind, brain, or both. Compare DOMAIN-GENERAL ABILITY.

domain-specific knowledge specialized knowledge within a topic, such as knowledge of chess, baseball, or music.

domestication *n.* the selective breeding of animals so that they can live in close association with human beings. All domestic livestock, as well as pets and laboratory mice and rats, have been selectively bred to exhibit features that allow close association with human beings, typically by being more docile and less aggressive than wild animals. **—domesticate** *vb.*

domestic partnership two people who live together in a stable, intimate relationship and share the responsibilities of a household in the same way that a married couple would. Some states and companies in the United States and some other countries provide legal and economic rights to domestic partners (e.g., insurance and death benefits) that are similar to those granted to married couples. See COMMON-LAW MARRIAGE; SAME-SEX MARRIAGE.

domestic violence any action by a person that causes physical harm to one or more members of his or her family unit. For example, it can involve battering of one partner by another, violence against children by a parent, or violence against elders by younger family members. See also BATTERED WOMEN; CHILD ABUSE; ELDER ABUSE.

domiciliary care inpatient institutional care provided because care in the individual's home is not available or not suitable. See also RESIDENTIAL CARE.

dominance *n.* **1.** the exercise of major influence or control over others. See also ANIMAL DOMINANCE. **2.** the tendency for one hemisphere of the brain to exert greater influence than the other over certain functions, such as language or handedness. The two hemispheres contribute differently to many functions; researchers therefore use the terms **hemispheric specialization** or HEMISPHERIC LATERALIZATION in preference to dominance (or **hemispheric dominance**). **3.** in genetics, the ability of one allele to determine the PHENOTYPE of a HETEROZYGOUS individual. See DOMINANT ALLELE; DOMINANT TRAIT. **—dominant** *adj.*

dominance aggression a form of ANIMAL AGGRESSION that involves one individual maintaining a higher status over another through threats or actual attacks. See ANIMAL DOMINANCE.

dominance hierarchy **1.** in social psychology, a system of stable linear variations in prestige, status, and authority among group members. It is the PECKING ORDER of the group, which defines who gives orders and who carries them out. See also STATUS RELATIONS. **2.** any ordering of motives, needs, or other psychological or physical responses based on priority or importance. An example is MASLOW'S MOTIVATIONAL HIERARCHY.

dominance need the need to dominate, lead, or otherwise control others. It is motivated by the desire for power, knowledge, prestige, or creative achievement. [proposed by U.S. psychologist Henry Alexander Murray (1893–1988)]

dominance statistic an index that quantifies the number of cases in one group that outscore cases in another group.

dominance–submission a key dimension of interpersonal behavior, identified through FACTOR ANALYSIS, in which behavior is differentiated along a continuum ranging from extreme dominance (active, talkative, extraverted, assertive, controlling, powerful) to extreme subordination (passive, quiet, introverted, submissive, weak). Also called **ascendance–submission**.

dominance–subordination relationship a form of social relationship within groups with a leader or dominant member who has priority of access to resources over other, subordinate members of the community. Dominance–subordination relationships are highly organized in troops of baboons, in which dominant males have more access to food resources and mates than do subordinate males and all males often appear to have dominance over females. In hyena groups the relationship is reversed, with males subordinate to females.

dominant allele the version of a gene (see ALLELE) whose effects are manifest in preference to another version of the same gene (the RECESSIVE ALLELE) when both are present in the same cell. Hence, the trait determined by a dominant allele (the DOMINANT TRAIT) is apparent even when the allele is carried on only one of a pair of HOMOLOGOUS chromosomes; that is, when it occurs in the HETEROZYGOUS state (as well as the HOMOZYGOUS state). If one parent is heterozygous for a dominant allele, there is a 50:50 chance of each offspring inheriting the dominant allele and displaying the trait.

dominant complex an emotional disturbance that dominates or controls one's conduct.

dominant eye the eye that is used preferentially or through which stimulation is preferentially effective.

dominant hemisphere formerly, the hemisphere regarded as having primary control of speech or handedness. See DOMINANCE; HEMISPHERIC LATERALIZATION.

dominant ideology thesis in Marxist theory, the view that the ruling class consolidates its position in society by enforcing its ideology on subordinate classes, who come to accept it uncritically. See HEGEMONY.

dominant trait in genetics, a trait, such as a particular eye color, that is manifest in preference to an alternative version of the same trait (i.e., the RECESSIVE TRAIT) when the individual concerned carries both dominant and recessive versions of the gene determining the trait. See DOMINANT ALLELE.

dominant wavelength a single wavelength that when mixed with white will match a given hue.

dominatrix *n.* a woman who takes the dominant role in sexual activity, often associated with BONDAGE AND DISCIPLINE or SADOMASOCHISM.

Donders's law the principle that the position of the eyes in looking at an object is independent of their movement to that position. [Franciscus Cornelis **Donders** (1818–1889), Dutch physician and physiologist]

Donders's method a method of separating out hypothetical stages of mental processing by requiring participants to perform a set of REACTION TIME tasks in which each successive task differs from its predecessor by the addition of a single mental stage. The time required to complete a particular stage of processing can be inferred by subtracting from the reaction time in one task the reaction time in the preceding task. For example, task A, in which a person responds to one signal by pressing one key and to another by pressing another key, adds a response-decision stage to task B, in which a person responds to one signal by pressing a key and makes no response to the other signal. Also called **subtraction method**. See also CHRONOMETRIC ANALYSIS; COMPOUND REACTION TIME. [Franciscus **Donders**]

donepezil *n.* an ACETYLCHOLINESTERASE INHIBITOR used as a NOOTROPIC DRUG in the management of mild to moderate dementia. By inhibiting the degradation of acetylcholine in the SYNAPTIC CLEFT, donepezil increases available levels of acetylcholine in the MAGNOCELLULAR NUCLEUS OF THE BASAL FOREBRAIN, thought to be associated with improved memory and other aspects of cognitive functioning. U.S. trade name: **Aricept**.

dong quai an herbal agent derived from the plant *Angelica sinensis*, native to mountainous regions of China, Korea, and Japan, with extensive folk use in Asia, America, and western Europe for a variety of conditions but particularly as a remedy for AMENORRHEA, DYSMENORRHEA, and other menstrual irregularities. It also is reputed to ameliorate the physical and psychological symptoms associated with premenstrual syndrome and menopause. The limited research that has been done on dong quai is inconclusive, providing conflicting results on its effectiveness for any of these uses. Side effects include abdominal bloating, diarrhea and other gastrointestinal disturbances, fever, photosensitivity, and increased bleeding. Additionally, the plant contains numerous phytoestrogens (see ESTROGEN) and coumarinlike compounds and may therefore interact with pharmaceutical estrogenic compounds and prescribed blood thinners.

Don Juan a man who ruthlessly seduces women, concerned only with sexual conquest, after which he abruptly loses interest in them (**Don Juanism**). The original Don Juan was a legendary Spanish libertine, the subject of literature and Mozart's opera *Don Giovanni*. In contrast to men with a CASANOVA COMPLEX, who adore women, a Don Juan may think of women as prey. See also SATYRIASIS; EROTOMANIA.

Donohue's syndrome see LEPRECHAUNISM. [William Leslie **Donohue** (1906–1984), Canadian pediatric pathologist]

don't-hold functions cognitive abilities, such as those involved in digit–symbol association (see DIGIT SYMBOL), that often deteriorate with adult aging as observed on intellectual or cognitive tests (e.g., the WECHSLER ADULT INTELLIGENCE SCALE).

door-in-the-face technique a two-step procedure for enhancing COMPLIANCE in which an extreme initial request is presented immediately before the more moderate target request. Rejection of the initial request makes people more likely to accept the target request than would have been the case if the latter had been presented on its own. See also FOOT-IN-THE-DOOR TECHNIQUE; LOW-BALL TECHNIQUE; THAT'S-NOT-ALL TECHNIQUE.

DOP abbreviation for DERMO-OPTICAL PERCEPTION.

dopa (**DOPA**) *n.* 3,4-*d*ihydr*o*xy*p*henyl*a*lanine, the naturally occurring (levorotatory) form of which—L-dopa—is a precursor to DOPAMINE and other catecholamines. As a drug, L-dopa is used to treat Parkinson's disease (see LEVODOPA).

dopac (**DOPAC**) *n.* *d*ihydr*o*xy*p*henyl*ac*etic acid: the major metabolite of DOPAMINE. It is analyzed as an index of dopamine activity in regions of the brain.

dopa decarboxylase the intermediate enzyme in the metabolism of catecholamines from the dietary amino acid tyrosine. Tyrosine is transformed to L-DOPA by TYROSINE HYDROXYLASE. L-Dopa is in turn converted to DOPAMINE by dopa decarboxylase, which also transforms a number of other aromatic amino acids. Dopamine is the final product in DOPAMINERGIC NEURONS; in ADRENERGIC NEURONS, dopamine is transformed by the enzyme dopamine beta-hydroxylase to NOREPINEPHRINE and subsequently—in specialized cells in the adrenal medulla and other sites, via the action of the enzyme phenylethanolamine *N*-methyltransferase—to EPINEPHRINE. Also called **aromatic L-amino acid decarboxylase**.

dopamine (**DA**) *n.* a CATECHOLAMINE neurotransmitter that has an important role in motor behavior and is implicated in numerous mental conditions (see CATECHOLAMINE HYPOTHESIS; DOPAMINE HYPOTHESIS). It is found in DOPAMINERGIC NEURONS in the brain and elsewhere. Dopamine is synthesized from the dietary amino acid tyrosine, which in the first, rate-limiting stage of the reaction is converted to L-dopa (3,4-dihydroxy-L-phenylalanine; see LEVODOPA) by the enzyme TYROSINE HYDROXYLASE. L-Dopa is then transformed into dopamine by the enzyme DOPA DECARBOXYLASE. In nondopaminergic neurons and the adrenal medulla, dopamine is further metabolized to form norepinephrine and epinephrine, respectively. Destruction of the dopaminergic neurons in the SUBSTANTIA NIGRA is responsible for the symptoms of Parkinson's disease (e.g., rigidity, tremor). Blockade of the actions of dopamine in other brain regions accounts for the therapeutic activities of antischizophrenic drugs.

dopamine hypothesis the theory that schizophrenia is caused by an excess of dopamine in the brain, due either to an overproduction of dopamine or a deficiency of the enzyme needed to convert dopamine to norepinephrine (adrenaline). Although this hypothesis is still widely discussed and promoted, it has not been empirically supported. See also GLUTAMATE HYPOTHESIS.

dopamine receptor a receptor molecule that is sensitive to DOPAMINE and chemically related compounds. Dopamine receptors are located in parts of the nervous system, such as the BASAL GANGLIA, and also in blood vessels of the kidneys and mesentery, where binding of dopamine to its receptors results in widening (dilation) of the arteries. There are several subtypes of dopamine receptors, designated D1, D2, and so on.

dopamine-receptor agonists drugs or other agents that bind to and directly activate DOPAMINE RECEPTORS, producing physiological effects that mimic those of the neurotransmitter DOPAMINE. BROMOCRIPTINE is an example. Because PARKINSONISM is associated with a deficiency of dopamine in the brain, drugs that help to maintain adequate levels of dopamine are valuable in treating the disorder. Dopamine-receptor agonists are used to manage some of the drug-induced parkinsonian symptoms associated with use of antipsychotic drugs; they are also used in the treatment of Parkinson's disease, GALACTORRHEA, and prolactin-secreting tumors of the pituitary gland. Also called **dopaminergic agents**. Compare DOPAMINE-RECEPTOR ANTAGONISTS.

dopamine-receptor antagonists substances that reduce the effects of the neurotransmitter DOPAMINE by competitively binding to, and thus blocking, DOPAMINE RECEPTORS. Classically, the clinical use of dopamine antagonists in mental health has been to modulate the symptoms of schizophrenia and other psychotic conditions. Most conventional (typical or first-generation) ANTIPSYCHOTIC drugs are thought to act via antagonism of the postsynaptic dopamine D2 receptor. Most second-generation (atypical) antipsychotics possess some degree of antagonistic activity at that receptor. Other dopamine-receptor antagonists are used to prevent or treat nausea and vomiting. Compare DOPAMINE-RECEPTOR AGONISTS.

dopaminergic agents see DOPAMINE-RECEPTOR AGONISTS.

dopaminergic neuron any neuron in the brain and other parts of the central nervous system for which DOPAMINE serves as the principal neurotransmitter. Three major tracts of dopamine-containing neurons are classically described: the mesolimbic–mesocortical tract (see MESOCORTICAL SYSTEM; MESOLIMBIC SYSTEM), in which excess dopamine activity is hypothesized to be associated with positive and negative symptoms of schizophrenia; the NIGROSTRIATAL TRACT, which is involved in motor functions and Parkinson's disease; and the tuberoinfundibular pathway, a local circuit in the hypothalamus that is involved in the regulation of the pituitary hormone prolactin.

dopaminergic pathway a NEURAL PATHWAY consisting of DOPAMINERGIC NEURONS. These pathways include the mesostriatal system, from the SUBSTANTIA NIGRA to the BASAL GANGLIA, whose dysfunction results in PARKINSON'S DISEASE; and the mesolimbocortical system (see MESOCORTICAL SYSTEM; MESOLIMBIC SYSTEM).

Dopar *n.* a trade name for LEVODOPA.

Doppelganger phenomenon the delusion that one has a double or twin, who looks and acts the same as oneself (German, "double walker"). See also AUTOSCOPY.

Doppler effect the apparent increase or decrease in wavelength or frequency observed when a source of electromagnetic radiation or sound approaches or recedes from the observer or listener, producing a change in hue or pitch. The **total Doppler effect** may result from motion of both the observer or listener and the source. [Christian Andreas **Doppler** (1803–1853), Austrian mathematician]

Dora case one of Sigmund FREUD's earliest and most celebrated cases, reported in *Fragment of an Analysis of a Case of Hysteria* (1905). The study of this woman's multiple symptoms (headaches, loss of speech, suicidal thoughts, amnesic episodes) contributed to his theory of REPRESSION and the use of DREAM ANALYSIS as an analytic tool.

Doral *n.* a trade name for QUAZEPAM.

Doriden *n.* a trade name for GLUTETHIMIDE.

dorsal *adj.* pertaining to the back (posterior side) of the body or to the upper (superior) surface of the brain. Compare VENTRAL. **—dorsally** *adv.*

dorsal column any of various tracts of sensory nerve fibers that run through the white matter of the SPINAL CORD on its dorsal side. See CUNEATE FASCICULUS; GRACILE FASCICULUS. See also DORSAL COLUMN SYSTEM; LEMNISCAL SYSTEM.

dorsal column system a SOMATOSENSORY SYSTEM that transmits most touch information via the DORSAL COLUMNS of the spinal cord to the brain.

dorsal horn either of the regions of GRAY MATTER in the posterior SPINAL CORD that extend toward the DORSAL ROOTS. They mainly serve sensory mechanisms. Also called **posterior horn**. See also CENTRAL GRAY. Compare ANTERIOR HORN.

dorsal root any of the SPINAL ROOTS that convey sensory nerve fibers and enter the spinal cord dorsally on each side. Also called **posterior root**; **sensory root**. Compare VENTRAL ROOT. See also BELL–MAGENDIE LAW.

dorsal stream a neural system that projects dorsally from the primary visual cortex (visual area 1; see V1) into the parietal lobe (visual area MT) and is involved in processing object motion and location in space. It is known informally as the "where" or "how" pathway. Compare VENTRAL STREAM.

dorsal tegmental bundle a bundle of nerve fibers from the LOCUS CERULEUS that, together with the central tegmental tract, forms the MEDIAL FOREBRAIN BUNDLE.

dorsiflexion *n.* flexing the ankle or wrist so that the foot or hand moves toward its upper (dorsal) surface.

dorsolateral *adj.* located both dorsally (toward the back) and laterally (toward the side). **—dorsolaterally** *adv.*

dorsolateral column a tract of motor fibers that descend in the dorsolateral part of the spinal cord, terminating on motor neurons. The CELL BODIES of these fibers lie in the MOTOR CORTEX, and the fibers descend on the same side until they cross over (decussate) at the PYRAMIDS of the medulla oblongata.

dorsolateral prefrontal cortex (DLPFC) a region of the brain located near the front and to both sides of the PREFRONTAL CORTEX (BRODMANN'S AREAS 9 and 46) in mammals, involved in WORKING MEMORY and attentional control. Damage to this region in humans results in an inability to select task-relevant information and to shift attention based on external cues.

dorsomedial nucleus a mass of tissue projecting from the THALAMUS to the FRONTAL LOBES. It is mainly implicated in memory function but is also associated with the emotional expressions of anxiety and fear. Also called **mediodorsal nucleus**.

dorsoventral *adj.* oriented or directed from the back (posterior) of the body to the front (anterior). Compare VENTRODORSAL.

dose–response relationship a principle relating the potency of a drug to the efficacy of that drug in affecting a target symptom or organ system. **Potency** refers to the amount of a drug necessary to produce the desired effect; **efficacy** refers to the drug's ability to act at a target receptor or organ to produce the desired effect. Dose–response curves may be graded, suggesting a continuous relationship between dose and effect, or quantal, where the desired effect is an either–or phenomenon, such as prevention of arrhythmias. There is considerable variability among individuals in response to a given dose of a particular drug.

dotage *n.* the state of DEMENTIA in old age, particularly, the childlike behavior often associated with this condition.

dot figure an arrangement of dots that is interpreted as forming a structure that changes shape over time, depending on which dots are seen as grouped together.

dotting test a pencil-and-paper motor test in which the participant makes as many dots as possible in a given time period, either randomly (**tapping test**) or within small circles (**aiming test**).

double *n.* in PSYCHODRAMA, an individual, one of the AUXILIARY EGOS, who speaks or acts out the presumed inner thoughts of the PROTAGONIST (i.e., the person presenting the problem to be explored). The technique is known as **doubling**.

double-agentry *n.* the situation in which the therapist's allegiance to the patient is in conflict with demands from the institution or from other professionals. See CONFLICT OF INTEREST.

double alternation in experimental research, a pattern in which two consecutive events of one kind alternate with two consecutive events of another kind. For example, in an OPERANT CONDITIONING experiment, two consecutive reinforced (R) trials may alternate with two consecutive nonreinforced (N) trials, yielding the pattern RRNNRRNN . . . . See also ALTERNATION.

double approach–avoidance conflict a complex conflict situation arising when a person is confronted with two goals or options that each have significant attractive and unattractive features. See also APPROACH–AVOIDANCE CONFLICT.

double-approach conflict see APPROACH–APPROACH CONFLICT.

double-aspect theory the position that mind and body are two attributes of a single substance (see MIND–BODY PROBLEM). This view is particularly associated with Dutch philosopher Baruch Spinoza (1632–1677), who held that there is one (and only one) infinite substance, which he identified as God (see PANTHEISM).

double-avoidance conflict see AVOIDANCE–AVOIDANCE CONFLICT.

double bind a situation in which an individual receives contradictory messages from another person or from two different people. For example, a parent may respond negatively when his or her child approaches or attempts to engage in affectionate behavior, but then, when the child turns away or tries to leave, reaches out to encourage the child to return. Double-binding communication was once considered a causative factor in schizophrenia. [proposed by British anthropologist Gregory Bateson (1904–1980)]

double blind describing an experimental procedure in which both experimenter and participants are unaware of the nature of the experiment, manipulation, or treatment administered. See also BLIND. Compare SINGLE BLIND; TRIPLE BLIND.

double consciousness a condition in which two distinct, unrelated mental states coexist within the same person. This may occur, for example, in an individual with a DISSOCIATIVE IDENTITY DISORDER. Also called **dual consciousness**.

double deception a deception embedded in what the research participant thinks is the official debriefing, which itself is a deception. See DECEPTION RESEARCH.

double dissociation a research process for demonstrating the action of two separable psychological or biological systems, such as differentiating between types of memory or the function of brain areas. One experimental variable is found to affect one of the systems, whereas a second variable affects the other. The differentiating variables may be task-related, pharmacological, neurological, or individual differences. For example, double dissociation has been used to separate DECLARATIVE MEMORY from PROCEDURAL LEARNING. [described by German-born U.S. psychologist Hans-Lukas Teuber (1916–1977)]

double entendre a word, phrase, or sentence that could be interpreted in two ways, especially when one of the possible meanings is a sexual one. See also AMBIGUITY; PUN. [French: "double meaning"]

double helix see DNA.

double image 1. a duplicate retinal image that occurs as a result of eye defects. **2.** a duplicate image of a distant object when fixating on near objects or of a near object when fixating on distant objects. See also DIPLOPIA; DOUBLE VISION.

double insanity see FOLIE À DEUX.

double personality see DUAL PERSONALITY.

double predestination see PREDESTINATION.

double-simultaneous stimulation a test used in studies of parietal-lobe lesions in which two sensory stimuli are presented to an individual simultaneously.

double-simultaneous tactile sensation the ability of a person to perceive that he or she has received two tactile sensations in different areas at the same time, for example, when touched simultaneously on the left and right hands or the right hand and left side of the face. An inability to perceive one or both of the simultaneous tactile sensations is referred to as **tactile extinction**. See also FACE–HAND TEST.

double standard the hypocritical belief that a code of behavior is permissible for one group or individual but not for another. For example, a double standard is held by the man who believes that free sexual expression is acceptable only for males, thus insisting on his daughter's virginity while encouraging or ignoring his son's philandering.

double technique in PSYCHODRAMA, a procedure in which one of the participants, usually the therapist, sits behind a member of the group and speaks for that member saying what he or she believes the person is thinking. Also called **priming-the-pump technique**.

double vision the perception of a single object as a separate image by each eye. Double vision is usually caused by STRABISMUS and can be manifest in several forms: (a) The image perceived by the right eye may appear to the left of the image perceived by the left eye, (b) there may be a binocular effect of two separate parallel images, or (c) the images may be vertically displaced so that one appears above the other. It may occur only when looking to the left or right rather than straight ahead. Double vision can also occur after injury to the posterior regions of the brain. See also DIPLOPIA; DOUBLE IMAGE.

double-Y condition see XYY SYNDROME.

doubling *n.* see DOUBLE.

doubt *n.* **1.** lack of confidence or uncertainty about something or someone, including the self. Doubt may center on everyday concerns (Can I accomplish this task?), issues of daily living (Can I change this ingrained habit?), or the very meaning of life itself (see EXISTENTIAL ANXIETY; EXISTENTIAL CRISIS). It is a perception, typically with a strong affective component, that is frequently a focus during psychotherapeutic intervention. **2.** in ERIKSON'S EIGHT STAGES OF DEVELOPMENT, see AUTONOMY VERSUS SHAME AND DOUBT.

doubting mania extreme and obsessive feelings of uncertainty about even the most obvious matters. Doubting mania is a common obsession associated with OBSESSIVE-COMPULSIVE DISORDER and often results in checking rituals (e.g., repeatedly looking to see if the door is locked) as a means of reducing doubt-related anxiety. Also called **doubting madness**; **folie du doute**; **maladie du doute**. [named by French psychiatrist Jean-Pierre Falret (1794–1870)]

downers *pl. n.* slang for SEDATIVE, HYPNOTIC, AND ANXIOLYTIC DRUGS.

down-regulation *n.* a decrease in the number of RECEPTOR molecules in a given area. Compare UP-REGULATION.

Down syndrome a chromosomal disorder characterized by an extra chromosome 21 (in some cases, 22) and manifested by a round flat face and eyes that seem to slant (the disorder was formerly known as **mongolism**). Brain size and weight are below average; affected individuals usually have mild to severe mental retardation and have been characterized as having docile, agreeable dispositions. Muscular movements tend to be slow, clumsy, and uncoordinated. In many cases growth is retarded, the tongue is thick, and the fingers are stubby. Affected individuals may have heart defects and respiratory insufficiencies or anomalies that are often corrected during infancy by surgery. However, lifespan is reduced compared to the general population, and affected individuals typically show early onset of ALZHEIMER'S DISEASE. Down syndrome is one of the most common organic causes of mental retardation. Also called **Down's syndrome**; **Langdon Down's disease**; **congenital acromicria**. See also AUTOSOMAL TRISOMY OF GROUP G; TRISOMY 21. [described in 1866 by John Langdon Haydon **Down** (1828–1896), British physician]

down through a technique for testing CLAIRVOYANCE in which the participant is asked to state the order of a stacked deck of ZENER CARDS from top to bottom. Compare UP THROUGH. See also BASIC TECHNIQUE; SCREENED TOUCH MATCHING.

downward communication the transmission of information from individuals who occupy relatively high-status positions within a group or organization to those who occupy subordinate positions. Such communications tend to be informational and directive, whereas UPWARD COMMUNICATIONS request information, provide factual information, or express grievances. Communication tends to flow downward in hierarchically organized groups. See CHANNELS OF COMMUNICATION; COMMUNICATION NETWORK.

downward drift hypothesis see DRIFT HYPOTHESIS.

downward mobility the movement of a person or group to a lower social class. See also SOCIAL MOBILITY. Compare UPWARD MOBILITY.

downward social comparison the self-protective tendency to compare oneself with those who are less well off. For example, people who are ill might feel better about their condition by comparing themselves with others who are even sicker.

dowry *n.* in some cultures, money or assets bestowed on the groom or his family by the bride's family on marriage. Compare BRIDE PRICE.

dowsing *n.* a purported technique for finding sites to dig for water or minerals. A forked stick, called a **divining rod**, is held by a person acting as a **dowser** in such a way that a downward movement of the stick indicates a likely site. See also RHABDOMANCY. **—dowse** *vb.*

doxepin *n.* a TRICYCLIC ANTIDEPRESSANT, among the most sedating and most anticholinergic of these agents. Although it currently has little use as an antidepressant, it may be used in relatively low doses as a hypnotic or in the management of neuromuscular or musculoskeletal pain. It is also available as a topical treatment for management of dermatologic conditions. U.S. trade name (among others): **Sinequan**.

doxylamine *n.* an ethanolamine antihistamine (see HISTAMINE ANTAGONISTS) with significant sedative properties, which is included in numerous nonprescription sleep aids. Like all antihistamines, it may lose its efficacy with repeated use. Overdose is characterized by symptoms of anticholinergic toxicity, including raised temperature, a rapid heart rate, and delirium.

DPE abbreviation for DELIBERATE PSYCHOLOGICAL EDUCATION.

d prime (symbol: d′) a measure of an individual's ability to detect signals; more specifically, a measure of sensitivity or discriminability derived from SIGNAL DETECTION THEORY that is unaffected by response biases. It is the difference (in standard deviation units) between the means of the NOISE and signal+noise distributions. The assumptions underlying the validity of d′ as a bias-free measure are that the probability distributions upon which decisions are based are Gaussian (normal) and have equal variances. If this is true, then d′ completely describes the RECEIVER-OPERATING CHARACTERISTIC CURVE. In practice, d′ has proved to be sufficiently bias-free to be the "best" measure of psychophysical performance. It is essentially a STANDARD SCORE and is computed as the difference between the (Gaussian) standard scores for the FALSE-ALARM rate and the HIT RATE. A value of $d' = 3$ is close to perfect performance; a value of $d' = 0$ is chance ("guessing") performance.

DQ abbreviation for DEVELOPMENTAL QUOTIENT.

DRA abbreviation for DIFFERENTIAL REINFORCEMENT OF ALTERNATIVE BEHAVIOR.

Dramamine *n.* a trade name for DIMENHYDRINATE.

drama therapy in GROUP PSYCHOTHERAPY, the use of theater techniques to gain self-awareness and increase self-expression. See also PSYCHODRAMA.

dramatics *n.* **1.** the art or practice of stagecraft and theatrical performance. **2.** the use of drama as a rehabilitation technique, using published or original scripts with patients as performers. See also PSYCHODRAMA. **3.** see CREATIVE DRAMATICS.

dramatization *n.* **1.** the use of ATTENTION-GETTING behavior as a defense against anxiety. An example of dramatization is the exaggeration of the symptoms of an illness to make it appear more important than the occurrence of the same illness in another person. **2.** in psychoanalytic theory, the expression of repressed wishes or impulses in dreams. **—dramatize** *vb.*

dramatized coping the overt practice of methods to be used to cope with pain. See PAIN MANAGEMENT.

drawing disability see CONSTRUCTIONAL DYSPRAXIA.

DRC abbreviation for DAMAGE-RISK CRITERIA.

dread *n.* **1.** intense fear or fearful anticipation. **Existential dread** (see EXISTENTIALISM) refers to a profound, deep-seated psychic or spiritual condition of insecurity and despair in relation to the human condition and the meaning of life. See also ANGST. **2.** in psychoanalysis, anxiety elicited by a specific threat, such as going out on a dark night, as contrasted with anxiety that does not have a specific object.

dream *n.* a mental state that occurs in sleep and is characterized by a rich array of sensory, motor, emotional, and cognitive experiences. Dreams occur most often, but not exclusively, during periods of REM SLEEP. They are characterized by (a) vivid imagery, especially visual imagery, and a strong sense of movement; (b) intense emotion, especially fear, elation, or anger; (c) delusional acceptance of the dream as a waking reality; and (d) discontinuity in time and space and incongruity of character and plot. Despite the vivid intensity of dreams, it can be difficult to remember them to any extent unless promptly awakened from REM sleep, but even then much content cannot be accurately retrieved.

Because the reports of dream content have little apparent relation to the physical or mental stimuli impinging on the sleeper and few dream events seem ever to have occurred, as it were, in vivo, the research tools of experimental psychology cannot be used effectively to study the phenomenon. Thus, assumptions about how a dream is produced and what it means are strongly dependent on theories about waking cognitive events and processes. Diverse theories have arisen from varied sources throughout history, including certain cultural beliefs in communication with the supernatural; the suggestion of Greek physician Hippocrates (c. 460–c. 377 BCE) that dreams provide early evidence of disease; FREUD's interpretation of dreams as a struggle in which the part of the mind representing social strictures (the SUPEREGO) plays out a conflict with the sexual impulses (the LIBIDO) while the rational part of the mind (the EGO) is at rest; JUNG's view that dreams provide evidence of the biological inheritance of universal symbols (ARCHETYPES); and ADLER's view that inferiority feelings are played out in dreams. The discovery in the early 1950s of REM sleep initiated the scientific study of dreaming as a neurocognitive process, a recent product of which is the ACTIVATION–SYNTHESIS HYPOTHESIS. See also DREAM CENSORSHIP; DREAM STATE; DREAM-WORK; LATENT CONTENT; MANIFEST CONTENT; NIGHTMARE. **—dreamlike** *adj.* **—dreamy** *adj.*

dream analysis a technique, originally used in psychoanalysis but now also used in other psychotherapies, in which the content of dreams is interpreted to reveal underlying motivations or symbolic meanings and representations (i.e., LATENT CONTENT). Dream analysis is aided by such techniques as FREE ASSOCIATION. Also called **dream interpretation**.

dream anxiety disorder see NIGHTMARE DISORDER.

dream censorship in psychoanalytic theory, the disguising in dreams of unconscious wishes that would be disturbing to the EGO if allowed conscious expression. According to the classic psychoanalytic theory of Sigmund FREUD, the thoroughness of dream disguise varies directly with the strictness of the censorship. See CENSOR.

dream content the images, ideas, and impulses expressed in a dream. See LATENT CONTENT; MANIFEST CONTENT.

dream deprivation a technique used in research in which participants are awakened frequently to minimize the amount of REM SLEEP—and hence time for dreaming—they have during the night. Participants will spontaneously compensate by having longer periods of REM sleep on subsequent nights, a finding often taken to be evidence for the homeostatic nature of dream regulation.

dream ego in the ANALYTIC PSYCHOLOGY of Carl JUNG, a fragment of the conscious EGO that is active during the dream state.

dream function the purpose or function of dreaming. In the classical psychoanalytic theory of Sigmund FREUD, the dream functions as a disguised fulfillment of a repressed WISH or as mastery of a traumatic experience. In the ANALYTIC PSYCHOLOGY of Carl JUNG, it is a reflection of fundamental personality tendencies and may have either a transient or a continuous significance. With the advent of modern neuroscience and the association of dreams with REM SLEEP cycles, theories that dreams are initiated by basic biological and social conflicts have been largely negated, if not obliterated.

dream imagery endogenous visual experiences during dreams, sometimes taken to represent daytime experiences or dilemmas.

dream incorporation the integration of an ACCIDENTAL STIMULUS in the content of a dream.

dream induction see DREAM SUGGESTION.

dream interpretation see DREAM ANALYSIS.

dream state (**D-state**) the state of sleep during which dreaming takes place most often, characterized by rapid eye movements (see REM SLEEP) and patterns on the electroencephalogram that most closely resemble those of wakefulness. It usually occurs four or five times during the night and is physiologically distinct from DEEP SLEEP and wakefulness. Studies indicate that about 20% of sleeping time is spent in the dream state and that there is probably a basic need for dreaming. The lower brainstem appears to be the area most involved in originating the dream state, under the control of genetically and light-regulated diurnal rhythms (see PGO SPIKES; PONTINE SLEEP). See also TWILIGHT STATE.

dream stimulus any of the stimuli that may initiate a dream, such as external stimulation, internal sensory stimulation, mental images, feelings, or memories. Compare ACCIDENTAL STIMULUS.

dream suggestion a specialized hypnotic technique in which the client is instructed to dream about a problem or its source, either during the hypnotic state or posthypnotically, during natural sleep. The technique is sometimes used as an aid in HYPNOTHERAPY. Also called **dream induction**.

dream-work *n.* in psychoanalytic theory, the transformation of the LATENT CONTENT of a dream into the MANIFEST CONTENT experienced by the dreamer. This transformation is effected by such processes as CONDENSATION, SYMBOLISM, DISPLACEMENT, and DRAMATIZATION.

dreamy state a brief altered state of consciousness similar to a dream, during which the individual experiences visual, olfactory, or auditory hallucinations.

dressing aid an ASSISTIVE TECHNOLOGY device that helps people with disabilities to dress independently. Dressing aids include buttonhooks, specially designed fasteners (e.g., Velcro strips), grabbers, and other devices.

dressing apraxia an inability to dress onself normally, sometimes associated with brain damage. For example, an individual may put on his or her clothing so that it covers only the right side of the body, neglecting the left side.

dressing behavior dressing in accordance with social expectations for one's gender, which is an important factor in GENDER IDENTITY. Studies of transvestites and transsexuals indicate that they often cross-dressed (or were cross-dressed) in childhood and adolescence. See CROSS-DRESSING.

DRGs abbreviation for DIAGNOSIS-RELATED GROUPS.

DRH abbreviation for DIFFERENTIAL REINFORCEMENT OF HIGH RATE.

drift hypothesis a sociological concept purporting to explain the higher incidence of schizophrenia in urban poverty centers, suggesting that during the preclinical phase people tend to drift into poverty and social isolation. Also called **downward drift hypothesis**.

drifting attention a disorder marked by a tendency to maintain attention for a short period, when alerted, but then to drift back to a somnolent state. It is caused by disturbance of the subcortical ALERTING MECHANISMS, which usually indicates pathological involvement of the midbrain or thalamic portion of the RETICULAR ACTIVATING SYSTEM. See also WANDERING ATTENTION.

drill *n.* the methodical repetition or systematic practice of a physical or mental response or response sequence for the purpose of learning. Drill may be necessary when the material to be learned does not yet represent to the student an integrated or internally coherent entity. For example, an individual learning a foreign language may need to use drill. Drill is also necessary to produce AUTOMATIZATION of a behavior or skill.

drinking aid an ASSISTIVE TECHNOLOGY device that permits an individual with a disability to ingest liquids without the aid of another person. Drinking aids include terry-cloth tumbler jackets, wooden or metal glass holders, various built-in and flexible sipping straws, coasters with suction-cup attachments, and cups designed for drinking while lying down.

drinking bouts see EPSILON ALCOHOLISM.

drinkometer *n.* a device used in animal experiments to record the number of times an animal licks a drinking tube. Also called **lickometer**.

drive *n.* **1.** a generalized state of READINESS precipitating or motivating an activity or course of action. Drive is hypothetical in nature, usually created by deprivation of a needed substance (e.g., food), the presence of negative stimuli (e.g., pain, cold), or the occurrence of negative events. Drive is said to be necessary for the stimuli or events to serve as REINFORCERS. **2.** in the psychoanalytic theory of Sigmund FREUD, a concept used to understand the relationship between the psyche and the soma (mind and body); drive is conceived as a having a somatic source but creating a psychic effect. Freud identified two separate drives as emerging from somatic sources: LIBIDO and AGGRESSION. See also MOTIVATION; OBJECT RELATIONS.

drive discrimination the ability of an organism to differentiate between various psychological, emotional, and physiological needs and to direct responses accordingly, for example, drinking when thirsty, eating when hungry. [defined by Edward C. TOLMAN]

drive displacement the activation of one drive when another drive is thwarted; for example, eating chocolate when one is prohibited from smoking a cigarette.

drive-induction theory the theory that REINFORCEMENT is the degree of drive induced by a given reinforcer. According to this theory, it is the arousal or excitement produced by consummating a reinforcer (e.g., eating, drinking, mating) that produces reinforcement of behavior, and not the reduction of the drive state that the reinforcer may produce. Drive-induction theory was proposed as an alternative to HULL'S DRIVE-REDUCTION THEORY. Also called **consummatory response theory of reinforcement**. [introduced by U.S. learning theorist Frederick Sheffield (1914–1994)]

drive-reduction theory a theory of learning in which the goal of motivated behavior is a reduction of a drive state. It is assumed that all motivated behavior arises from drives, stemming from a disruption in homeostasis, and that responses that lead to reduction of those drives tend to be reinforced or strengthened. See also HULL'S MATHEMATICO-DEDUCTIVE THEORY OF LEARNING. Compare DRIVE-INDUCTION THEORY. [proposed by Clark HULL]

driver training in rehabilitation, the training of individuals with disabilities to operate an automobile, which may be equipped with ASSISTIVE TECHNOLOGY devices, such as customized or adapted controls. For example, a previously trained driver may have to learn to operate a vehicle with hand-operated accelerator and brakes or a gearshift extension for left-hand rather than right-hand use.

drive state see DRIVE.

drive stimulus in Clark HULL's theories of learning, any of the hypothetical nerve impulses produced by a drive state. Behaviors that reduce these impulses are reinforced or strengthened. See DRIVE-REDUCTION THEORY; HULL'S MATHEMATICO-DEDUCTIVE THEORY OF LEARNING.

drive strength the intensity of a drive, particularly as quantified in HULL'S MATHEMATICO-DEDUCTIVE THEORY OF LEARNING as the number of hours of deprivation of a need.

drive theory see CLASSICAL PSYCHOANALYSIS.

DRL abbreviation for DIFFERENTIAL REINFORCEMENT OF LOW RATE.

DRO abbreviation for DIFFERENTIAL REINFORCEMENT OF OTHER BEHAVIOR.

dromomania *n.* an abnormal drive or desire to travel that involves spending beyond one's means and sacrificing job, partner, or security in the lust for new experiences. People with dromomania not only feel more alive when traveling but also start planning their next trip as soon as they arrive home. Fantasies about travel occupy many of their waking thoughts and some of their dreams. The condition was formerly referred to as **vagabond neurosis**.

dronabinol *n.* see TETRAHYDROCANNABINOL.

droperidol *n.* an antipsychotic agent of the BUTYROPHENONE class that is used in premedication for surgery and to maintain surgical anesthesia. It is occasionally used for the emergency treatment of acute psychotic agitation. Because of its extremely rapid onset of action, it has few other mental health applications. U.S. trade name: **Inapsine**.

drop-in center a facility, often associated with a substance-abuse program, where professional support and advice can be obtained without an advance appointment. A drop-in center also serves as a gathering place providing social, educational, and recreational activities.

dropout *n.* **1.** a student who leaves school before graduating. **2.** a patient or client who terminates treatment before it is completed.

Drosophila *n.* a genus of small fruit flies consisting of about a thousand species commonly known as vinegar flies. The species *Drosophila melanogaster* is used extensively in genetic investigations.

drowsiness *n.* a state of low alertness in which the BRAIN WAVE pattern found during waking alternates with DELTA WAVES. See also HYPERSOMNIA; SOMNOLENCE.

DRS 1. abbreviation for DEMENTIA RATING SCALE. **2.** abbreviation for DISABILITY RATING SCALE.

drug *n.* **1.** any substance, other than food, that is administered for experimental, diagnostic, or treatment purposes. **2.** any substance that is used recreationally for its effects on motor, sensory, or cognitive activities.

drug abuse see SUBSTANCE ABUSE.

drug abuse treatment see SUBSTANCE ABUSE TREATMENT.

drug addiction see SUBSTANCE DEPENDENCE.

drug culture the activities and way of life of those people who habitually use one or more kinds of drugs of abuse, usually illicit drugs such as hashish, cocaine, heroin, LSD, or other substances that produce altered states of consciousness.

drug dependence see SUBSTANCE DEPENDENCE.

drug discrimination the ability of an organism to distinguish between the internal states produced by different drugs (or by a particular drug and saline). In a typical experimental procedure, an animal is injected with one drug, and a certain response (e.g., pressing the left-hand lever in a two-lever apparatus) is reinforced. When injected with a different drug (or with saline), a different response (e.g., pressing the right-hand lever) is reinforced. Thus, the animal must discriminate between the internal cues produced by the drugs in order to make the correct response.

drug education the process of informing individuals or groups about the effects of various chemical agents on the human body, usually with a special emphasis on the effects of mind-altering substances.

drug holiday discontinuance of a therapeutic drug for a limited period in order to control dosage and side effects and to evaluate the patient's behavior with and without it. Formerly commonly recommended for children taking METHYLPHENIDATE, drug holidays on weekends or school vacations were thought to prevent growth suppression that was tentatively associated with this agent. Drug holidays are infrequent in modern clinical practice.

drug-induced lactation see GALACTORRHEA.

drug-induced parkinsonism see PARKINSONISM.

drug-induced psychosis a psychotic state resulting from use or abuse of a variety of therapeutic or illicit substances. Well-described drug-induced psychoses may result from excessive or chronic use of amphetamines, cocaine, or other stimulants; cannabis; LSD, PCP (phencyclidine), or other hallucinogens; and other illicit substances. A variety of medications may produce psychotic symptoms, including anticholinergic drugs at therapeutic doses in susceptible individuals. In *DSM–IV–TR*, it is categorized as SUBSTANCE-INDUCED PSYCHOTIC DISORDER.

drug interactions the effects of administering two or more drugs concurrently, which alters the pharmacological action of one or more of them. Pharmacokinetic interactions alter the absorption, distribution, metabolism, and excretion of the drugs; they may induce or inhibit the elimination of drugs, leading to unexpected increases or decreases in their concentrations in the body. Pharmacodynamic interactions affect the drugs' activities at target organs or receptor sites; they may be synergistic, enhancing the effectiveness of a drug at a target receptor or organ (see DRUG SYNERGISM), or antagonistic, in which the presence of one drug reduces the effectiveness of another (see ANTAGONIST).

drug metabolism the process by which a drug is transformed in the body (in the liver and other organs), usually from a more lipid-soluble form, which makes it more readily absorbed into the body, to a more water-soluble form, which facilitates its excretion. Two phases of drug metabolism are recognized. In **Phase I metabolism**, the drug is oxidized, reduced, or hydrolyzed—that is, oxygen is added, oxygen is removed, or hydrogen is added, respectively (see CYTOCHROME P450). In **Phase II metabolism**, functional groups (specific clusters of atoms) are added to drug molecules (e.g., by GLUCURONIDATION).

drug screening instrument a brief interview, such as CAGE, or a brief self-report instrument, such as MAST, that is designed to identify individuals who should be assessed thoroughly for the possibility of substance abuse.

drug synergism an enhancement of efficacy occurring when two or more drugs are administered concurrently, so that their combined pharmacological or clinical effects are greater than those occurring when the drugs are administered individually. Drug synergism can be metabolic, when the administration of one agent interferes with the metabolism of another, or it can be pharmacological, when the administration of two or more agents results in enhanced receptor binding or other activity at target sites. The enhanced antimicrobial activity of two antibiotics administered together is an example of positive synergism; negative synergism can be seen when the administration of a nontoxic agent with a toxic drug worsens the toxicity of the latter.

drug therapy see PHARMACOTHERAPY.

drug tolerance see TOLERANCE.

drug withdrawal see SUBSTANCE WITHDRAWAL.

dry eyes see XEROPHTHALMIA.

D sleep abbreviation for dreaming sleep (see DREAM STATE) or desynchronized sleep, that is, REM SLEEP. Compare S SLEEP.

DSM–IV–TR the text revision of the fourth edition of the *Diagnostic and Statistical Manual of Mental Disorders*, prepared by the Task Force on *DSM–IV* of the American Psychiatric Association and published in 2000. The classification presents descriptions of diagnostic categories (which appear as entries in this dictionary) without favoring any particular theory of etiology. It is largely modeled on the INTERNATIONAL CLASSIFICATION OF DISEASES (9th edition, 1978), developed by the World Health Organization and modified for use in the United States (*ICD–9–CM*), but contains greater detail and recent changes, as well as a method of coding on different axes (see AXIS; MULTIAXIAL CLASSIFICATION). Previous editions were published in 1952 (*DSM–I*), 1968 (*DSM–II*), 1980 (*DSM–III*), and 1994 (*DSM–IV*). Over that period, the number of identified disorders has increased from about 100 to more than 300.

DST abbreviation for DEXAMETHASONE SUPPRESSION TEST.

D-state abbreviation for DREAM STATE, as opposed to the S-state (sleeping state) and the W-state (waking state).

DT→PI model *d*iagnostic *t*esting to *p*rescriptive *i*nstruction model: a style of teaching developed by the Center for Talented Youth (CTY) of Johns Hopkins University to address the needs of individual schools, both public and private. This model of instruction takes into consideration the prior knowledge, ability, learning style, and motivation of individual students, tailoring instructional strategies to their specific needs. The style is appropriate for a broad spectrum of students, including the most able.

DTPS abbreviation for DIFFUSE THALAMIC PROJECTION SYSTEM.

D trisomy see CHROMOSOME-13 TRISOMY.

DTs abbreviation for DELIRIUM TREMENS.

dual-action antidepressants see MIXED-FUNCTION ANTIDEPRESSANTS.

dual-aspect physicalism a theoretical solution to the MIND–BODY PROBLEM claiming that there are two aspects of reality—physical and subjective—but that the more fundamental aspect is physical.

dual attitudes two contradictory attitudes about the same object that are held simultaneously by the same individual. One attitude is usually held explicitly, and the other held implicitly.

dual careers the situation in which both spouses or partners in a family or other domestic unit are committed to their careers, rather than one being regarded as the main breadwinner and the other as the main homemaker.

dual coding theory 1. the theory that linguistic input can be represented in memory in both verbal and visual formats. CONCRETE WORDS that readily call to mind a picture, such as *table* or *horse*, are remembered better than ABSTRACT WORDS, such as *honesty* or *conscience*, which do not readily call to mind a picture, because the concrete words are stored in two codes rather than one. [proposed by Canadian cognitive psychologist Alan U. Paivio (1925–)] **2.** the theory that linguistic knowledge in bilingual people is stored in two distinct codes. See COORDINATE BILINGUAL. **3.** a theory for explaining the relationship between IMAGERY and performance that suggests there are two ways of gaining information about a skill: the motor channel for encoding human actions and the verbal channel for encoding speech. Using auditory imagery linked with visual imagery is suggested to be the most effective in PERFORMANCE ENHANCEMENT.

dual consciousness see DOUBLE CONSCIOUSNESS.

dual diagnosis the identification of two distinct disorders that are present in the same person at the same time, for example, the coexistence of depression or anxiety disorder and a substance-abuse disorder (e.g., alcohol or drug dependence). See also COMORBIDITY.

dual encoding see DUAL REPRESENTATION.

dual instinct theory in psychoanalytic theory, the view that human life is governed by two antagonistic forces: the LIFE INSTINCT, or EROS, and the DEATH INSTINCT, or THANATOS. This was a late theoretical formulation by Sigmund FREUD, who held that "the interaction of the two basic instincts with or against each other gives rise to the whole variegation of the phenomena of life" (*Beyond the Pleasure Principle*, 1920).

dualism *n.* the position that reality consists of two separate substances, defined by French philosopher René Descartes (1596–1650) as thinking substance (mind) and extended substance (matter). In the context of the MIND–BODY PROBLEM, dualism is the position that the mind and the body constitute two separate realms or substances. Dualistic positions raise the question of how mind and body interact in thought and behavior. Compare MONISM. See also CARTESIAN DUALISM. **—dualist** *adj., n.* **—dualistic** *adj.*

duality of language the concept that language can be represented at two levels: (a) PHONOLOGY, which is the sound that a speaker produces; and (b) meaning, which is a function of SYNTAX and SEMANTICS.

dual-leadership therapy see COTHERAPY.

dual memory theory see DUAL-STORE MODEL OF MEMORY.

dual orientation see DUAL REPRESENTATION.

dual personality a condition in which the personality is divided into two relatively independent and generally contrasting systems. See DISSOCIATIVE IDENTITY DISORDER.

dual process models of persuasion persuasion theories postulating that ATTITUDE CHANGE can occur as a result of strategies for processing attitude-relevant information that involve either a very high degree of effort or very little effort. The most prominent theories of this type are the ELABORATION-LIKELIHOOD MODEL and the HEURISTIC-SYSTEMATIC MODEL.

dual process theory **1.** the theory that the response made by an individual to a stimulus that permits behavioral control involves two stages: (a) a decision as to whether or not to respond and (b) a choice between alternative responses. **2.** in theories of memory, the operation of two different cognitive processes (for example, recollection and familiarity) in recognition memory.

dual process theory of color vision see OPPONENTS THEORY OF COLOR VISION.

dual relationship see MULTIPLE RELATIONSHIP.

dual representation the ability to comprehend an object simultaneously as the object itself and as a representation of something else. For example, a photograph of a person can be represented both as the print itself and as the person it depicts. Also called **dual encoding**; **dual orientation**.

dual-store model of memory the concept that memory is a two-stage process, comprising SHORT-TERM MEMORY, in which information is retained for a few seconds, and LONG-TERM MEMORY, which permits the retention of information for hours to many years. William JAMES called these stages PRIMARY MEMORY and SECONDARY MEMORY, respectively. Also called **dual memory theory**. See also MODAL MODEL OF MEMORY; MULTISTORE MODEL OF MEMORY.

dual-task competition a phenomenon observed in experimental techniques examining DUAL-TASK PERFORMANCE, in which participants are asked to perform two tasks (e.g., speeded reaction time and mental arithmetic) simultaneously. Such tasks require effort (see EFFORTFULNESS) and tend to compete against each other (see RESOURCE COMPETITION), so that their performances degrade. The decrease in performance is often taken as a measure of mental capacity limits (see CENTRAL LIMITED CAPACITY).

dual-task performance the concurrent performance of two tasks, an activity that—especially in the study of attention—is examined to explore the nature of processing limitations and the strategies used to coordinate performance. See DUAL-TASK COMPETITION.

dual thresholds a threshold theory in which high and low thresholds are postulated. When the lower threshold is exceeded, the observer may believe a stimulus is present, but is not sure. When the higher threshold is exceeded, the observer is certain that the stimulus is present.

dual trace hypothesis a restatement of the PERSEVERATION–CONSOLIDATION HYPOTHESIS of memory formation specifying that short-term memory is represented neurally by activity in reverberating circuits and that stabilization of these circuits leads to permanent synaptic change, reflecting the formation of long-term memory. See HEBBIAN SYNAPSE. [proposed in 1949 by Donald O. HEBB]

Duchenne muscular dystrophy see MUSCULAR DYSTROPHY. [Guillaume Benjamin Armand **Duchenne** (1806–1875), French neurologist]

Duchenne smile a smile characterized by bilaterally symmetrical upturning of the lips and activation of the orbicularis oculi muscles surrounding the eyes, which creates a crow's-foot effect at the corners of the eyes. Duchenne smiles are believed to be authentic smiles, as opposed to posed, voluntary smiles that lack the orbicularis oculi component. [Guillaume **Duchenne**]

duct *n.* in anatomy, a tubular canal or passage, especially one that transports a secretion, such as a bile duct or tear duct. Glands with ducts are called EXOCRINE GLANDS. **—ductal** *adj.*

ductless gland see ENDOCRINE GLAND.

ductus deferens see VAS DEFERENS.

due process the administration of the law according to established and accepted principles, especially those upholding natural justice and the rights of the accused. In the United States, due process of law is guaranteed by the 5th and 14th amendments to the U.S. Constitution. Also called **due process rights**.

due process model a view of legal process that places a premium on the rights of the accused and the maintenance of fair procedures by which such people are processed within the criminal justice system. Compare CRIME CONTROL MODEL.

dull normal see BELOW AVERAGE.

dummy *n.* in DOUBLE-BLIND drug trials, a PLACEBO that appears identical in all aspects (e.g., dosage form, method of administration) to the active drug under investigation, thereby helping to preserve experimental blinds for both patients and clinical investigators.

dummy variable coding a method of assigning numerical values (often 0 and 1) to a CATEGORICAL VARIABLE in such a way that the variable reflects class membership.

dummy variables variables, often in a logic-based representation, that can stand for or be bound to any element from their domain.

Duncan multiple-range test a post hoc MULTIPLE COMPARISON procedure used to determine which mean, among a set of means, can be said to be significantly different, while controlling the Type I comparison-wise error rate (see TYPE I ERROR) at α (the criterion value: see SIGNIFICANCE LEVEL). [David Beattie **Duncan** (1916–), Australian-born U.S. statistician]

Dunnett's multiple comparison test a MULTIPLE COMPARISON method for comparing all groups with a single control group mean in such a way that the SIGNIFICANCE LEVEL for the set of comparisons is controlled at α (the criterion value). [Charles W. **Dunnett** (1921–), Canadian statistician]

Dunn's multiple comparison test see BONFERRONI T TEST.

duplex theory the theory that vision depends on the activity of two types of receptors: the RETINAL RODS, which are active in dim light; and the RETINAL CONES, which are active in brighter light. Also called **duplicity theory**.

durable power of attorney a legal document that designates someone to make health care decisions, financial decisions, or both for an individual if that person becomes incapacitated or otherwise incapable of making decisions on his or her own.

Duragesic *n.* a trade name for FENTANYL.

dura mater the outermost and strongest of the three layers of membranes (MENINGES) that cover the brain and spinal cord.

duration of untreated illness in schizophrenia, the length of time that the illness is present before antipsychotic drug treatment or other forms of therapy are initiated. Such periods are studied to determine the effect of untreated schizophrenia on symptom severity and the likelihood that specific treatments will be effective.

duress *n.* acts or threats (e.g., the threat of confinement) that compel people to act or speak against their will (e.g., to make a COERCED CONFESSION).

Durham rule a 1954 ruling by the U.S. Court of Appeals in a case involving a defendant named Durham. It stated that "an accused is not criminally responsible if his unlawful act was the product of mental disease or mental defect." This rule has been replaced by the AMERICAN LAW INSTITUTE MODEL PENAL CODE INSANITY TEST. Also called **Durham decision**; **Durham test**; **product rule**.

Dusky standard an influential 1960 U.S. Supreme Court ruling establishing that defendants' COMPETENCY TO STAND TRIAL must be related to their ability to understand and appreciate the criminal proceedings against them and to whether they can reasonably assist their own counsel by making choices among available options (e.g., pleas).

Duso program *D*eveloping *u*nderstanding of *s*elf and *o*thers: an educational program developed by the American Guidance Services to provide therapy for emotionally disturbed children. The program is one of several similar methods of providing a curriculum environment in which children can explore their feelings and understand how these affect their friends and family.

dustbowl empiricism an approach to science and the social sciences that consists primarily of making empirical observations and collecting data rather than establishing a theoretical framework. The "dustbowl" refers to certain campuses in the center of the United States, where this approach was once considered to be widespread.

duty to protect the obligation of mental health professionals to protect third parties from harm or violence that may result from the actions of their clients. This obligation may involve, but is not necessarily restricted to, a DUTY TO WARN. See TARASOFF DECISION.

duty to warn the obligation of mental health professionals to warn third parties whom their clients intend to harm. See also DUTY TO PROTECT; TARASOFF DECISION.

DV abbreviation for DEPENDENT VARIABLE.

Dvorak keyboard a keyboard layout based upon the frequency with which letters appear in the English language. Keys are placed such that the most frequently occurring keys are all in the main or home row (the row upon which the fingers rest) and are therefore the easiest to reach. Also called **Dvorak simplified keyboard**. See also CHORD KEYBOARD. [invented in 1936 by August **Dvorak** (1894–1975), U.S. educator]

DVT abbreviation for DEEP VEIN THROMBOSIS.

dwarfism *n.* a condition of underdeveloped body structure due to a developmental defect, a hereditary trait, hormonal or nutritional deficiencies, or diseases. The proportions of the body to the head and limbs may be normal or abnormal. A perfectly proportioned dwarf is called a **midget**, although this is now considered an offensive term. Some forms of dwarfism, such as that due to thyroid-hormone deficiency, are associated with mental retardation. Individuals with achondroplastic dwarfism (see ACHONDROPLASIA) usually have normal intelligence. See also PSEUDOACHONDROPLASIA; PYGMYISM.

Dx abbreviation for DIAGNOSIS.

dyad (**diad**) *n.* **1.** a pair of individuals in an interpersonal situation, such as mother and child, husband and wife, cotherapists, or patient and therapist. **2.** two individuals who are closely interdependent, particularly on an emotional level (e.g., twins reared together, mother and infant, or a very close married couple). See also SOCIAL DYAD. **—dyadic** *adj.*

dyadic effect that part of the behavior of two interacting individuals that is due to their particular interaction, as distinct from the way in which each characteristically relates to others.

dyadic relationship 1. any committed, intimate two-person relationship. **2.** in psychotherapy and counseling, the working relationship between therapist and patient or counselor and client.

dyadic session a meeting of a therapist with only one particular client, as opposed to a couple or a family.

dyadic therapy see INDIVIDUAL THERAPY.

dying phobia see THANATOPHOBIA.

dying process a progressive and nonreversible loss of vital functions that results in the end of life. The transition from health to death can be swift or extended, predictable or unpredictable, depending on the specific life-threatening condition, the vigor of the patient, and the treatment available (see also END OF LIFE; TRAJECTORIES OF DYING). See also STAGES OF DYING.

dynamic *adj.* **1.** pertaining to force. **2.** continuously changing or in flux. **3.** describing systems of psychology that emphasize motivation, mental processes, and the complexities of force and interaction. See also DYNAMIC PSYCHOLOGY; PSYCHODYNAMICS.

dynamic anthropometry design practice that takes into account the actions and movements expected of product or system users, with the goal of shifting adjustment demands from the user to the product, so that, for example, the angle of a backrest changes automatically when the user moves. See ANTHROPOMETRY.

dynamic assessment 1. an approach to CLINICAL ASSESSMENT that follows the same basic principles as DYNAMIC TESTING, including not only tests but also other forms of assessment, such as projects, essays, and performances. **2.** an assessment that has the goal of elaborating on the complex reasons for dysfunctions, especially with regard to conflicts.

dynamic calculus a model of motivation based on measurements of innate drives (ERGS) and sentiments. [proposed by British-born U.S. psychologist Raymond B. Cattell (1905–1998)]

dynamic core a theoretical construct involving a subset of neurons in the THALAMOCORTICAL SYSTEM of the brain that support conscious experience. The specific subset of neurons involved may vary dynamically from moment to moment, but the dynamic core always maximizes high integration and differentiation of information. See COMPLEXITY HYPOTHESIS. [proposed by U.S. neuroscientist Gerald M. Edelman (1929–) and Italian–U.S. psychologist Giulio Tononi (1960–)]

dynamic effect law the theory that GOAL-DIRECTED BEHAVIORS become habitualized as they effectively attain the goal. [proposed by British-born U.S. psychologist Raymond B. Cattell (1905–1998)]

dynamic equilibrium the state of a system in which

different (often opposing) reactions or other processes occur at the same rate and thus balance each other, such that there is no net change to the overall system. See also DYNAMIC SYSTEM.

dynamic formulation the ongoing attempt to organize the clinical material elicited about a client's behavior, traits, attitudes, and symptoms into a structure that helps the therapist understand the client and plan his or her treatment more effectively.

dynamic interactionism a model of personality and behavior in which individual development depends upon continuous, reciprocal interaction with the environment.

dynamic kinesthetic imagery see KINESTHETIC IMAGERY.

dynamic model in psychoanalytic theory, the view that the psyche can be explained in terms of underlying, unconscious drives and instincts that mold the personality, motivate behavior, and produce emotional disorder. Compare ECONOMIC MODEL; TOPOGRAPHIC MODEL. See also METAPSYCHOLOGY.

dynamic psychology **1.** any system of psychology that emphasizes MOTIVATION or DRIVE. **2.** a theory of psychology emphasizing causation and motivation in relation to behavior, specifically the stimulus–organism–response chain in which the stimulus–response relationship is regarded as the mechanism of behavior and the drives of the organism are the mediating variable. See S–O–R PSYCHOLOGY.

dynamic psychotherapy any form or technique of psychotherapy that focuses on the underlying motivational or defensive factors (e.g., unconscious conflicts, interpersonal patterns) that determine a person's behavior and adjustment. See also DEPTH THERAPY.

dynamic resignation see NEUROTIC RESIGNATION.

dynamics *n.* **1.** the study of motion in terms of the forces involved. **2.** the forces that bring about motion. See also KINEMATICS.

dynamic self-distribution in GESTALT PSYCHOLOGY, the tendency of the constituents of a whole to arrange themselves in a way that is influenced by the totality and the role of each part in that totality. [attributed to Wolfgang KÖHLER]

dynamic skill theory see SKILL THEORY.

dynamic social impact theory an extension of SOCIAL IMPACT THEORY that seeks to explain the changes in physiological states, subjective feelings, emotions, cognitions, and behavior that occur as a result of SOCIAL INFLUENCE. The model assumes that influence is a function of the strength, immediacy, and number of people (or, more precisely, sources) present, and that this influence results in consolidation (growth of the majority), clustering (the emergence of small groups whose members hold similar opinions), correlation (the convergence of group members' opinions on a variety of issues), and continuing diversity (the maintenance of the beliefs of the members of the minority) in groups that are spatially distributed and interacting repeatedly over time. [developed by U.S. social psychologist Bibb Latané (1937–)]

dynamic system a system in which a change in one part influences all interrelated parts. Such a system is described by a set of quantitative variables changing continuously and interdependently in time in accordance with laws captured by some set of equations. The motion on a pendulum is a simple example. Dynamic system models provide an important alternative to symbolic models as a way to understand many psychological phenomena (e.g., coordinated movements, developmental phenomena, and decision making).

dynamic systems theory a theory, grounded in NONLINEAR systems principles, that attempts to explain behavior and personality in terms of constantly changing, self-organizing interactions among multiple organismic and environmental factors that operate on multiple timescales and multiple levels of analysis. It is closely related to CHAOS THEORY.

dynamic testing a psychometric approach that attempts to measure not only the products or processes of learning but also the potential to learn. It focuses on the difference between actual ability and potential, that is, the extent to which developed abilities reflect latent capacity. It attempts to quantify the process of learning rather than the products of that process. This is done by presenting progressively more challenging tasks and providing continuous feedback on performance in an atmosphere of teaching and guidance toward the right answer. [introduced by Lev VYGOTSKY]

dynamic touch the perception of the characteristics of an object by wielding and manipulating it. People can perceive length and shape by dynamic touch.

dynamic trait a personality trait that involves motivation or putting the individual into action. It is one of three classes of SOURCE TRAITS in CATTELL'S FACTORIAL THEORY OF PERSONALITY, the others being ABILITY TRAITS and TEMPERAMENT TRAITS.

dynamic unconscious see UNCONSCIOUS. Compare COGNITIVE UNCONSCIOUS.

dynamic visual display in ergonomics, a visual display that is designed to present fluctuating information, such as changes in temperature, speed, or volume.

dynamogenesis *n.* **1.** the development of force, especially in the muscles or nerves. **2.** the SENSORIMOTOR principle that changes in motor responses are correspondent and proportional to changes in sensory activities. **3.** the idea that motor responses are evoked by sensory stimulation. Also called **dynamogeny**.

dynamometer *n.* an instrument for measuring force or power, especially muscular effort or strength of humans or animals. A dynamometer usually consists of a spring that can be compressed by the force applied. **—dynamometric** *adj.*

dynorphin *n.* see ENDOGENOUS OPIOID.

dys- *prefix* **1.** diseased or abnormal (e.g., DYSGEUSIA). **2.** painful or difficult (e.g., DYSMENORRHEA).

dysacusis *n.* a distressing subjective, rarely objective, sensation of tones or noises of peripheral origin, such as TINNITUS from cochlear or tympanic disease. Also called **dysacousia**; **dysacusia**. **—dysacusic** *adj.*

dysaesthesia *n.* see DYSESTHESIA.

dysarthria *n.* any of a group of MOTOR SPEECH DISORDERS caused by impairment originating in the central or peripheral nervous system. Respiration, articulation, phonation, resonance, and prosody may be affected. There are four main types: dyskinetic, spastic, peripheral, and mixed. **Dyskinetic dysarthria** includes **hypokinetic dysarthria**, in which prosody is affected in terms of rate and rhythm, and **hyperkinetic dysarthria**, in which articulation is poor due to difficulties in controlling the rate and range of movement in ongoing speech. In **spastic dysarthria**, all speech parameters are affected, respiration is poor, intonation patterns are restricted, and spasticity in the vocal cords causes hoarseness. **Peripheral dysarthria** is characterized by continual breathiness during phonation, with audible inspiration, distortion of consonants, and, often, a need to speak in short phrases. **Mixed dysarthria** occurs in those who have impairment in more than one motor system, possibly caused by tumors, degenerative conditions, or trauma. —**dysarthric** *adj.*

dysautonomia *n.* dysfunction of the autonomic nervous system, including impairment, failure, or overactivity of sympathetic or parasympathetic functioning. The dysfunction may be local or generalized, acute or chronic, and is associated with a number of disorders. Also called **autonomic dysfunction**; **autonomic neuropathy**. See also FAMILIAL DYSAUTONOMIA.

dysbasia *n.* distorted or difficult walking due to either neurological disease or psychological disorder.

dysbulia *n.* **1.** difficulty in thinking, maintaining attention, or maintaining a train of thought. **2.** lack of will power or weakness of volition.

dyscalculia *n.* see ACALCULIA.

dyschromatopsia *n.* **1.** a congenital or acquired defect in the discrimination of colors. **2.** see CHROMATOPSIA; CEREBRAL DYSCHROMATOPSIA. **3.** see VISUAL ILLUSION.

dysconjugate gaze a condition in which the motion of the two eyes is uncoordinated.

dyscontrol *n.* an impaired ability to direct or regulate one's functioning in volition, emotion, behavior, cognition, or some other area, which often entails inability to resist impulses and leads to abnormal behaviors without significant provocation.

dysdiadochokinesis *n.* loss of ability to perform rapid alternating movements (e.g., repeatedly slapping one's palm and then the back of one's hand against the knee). Also called **adiadochokinesis**; **adiadochokinesia**; **dysdiadochokinesia**.

dyseidetic dyslexia a type of dyslexia that is marked by difficulty recognizing whole words and thus an overreliance on sounding out words each time they are encountered. It is supposedly due to deficits in VISUAL MEMORY and VISUAL DISCRIMINATION. There is, however, no reliable empirical evidence for this form of dyslexia. See also DYSPHONETIC DYSLEXIA. [proposed in 1973 by U.S. psychologist Elena Boder (1907–1995)]

dysesthesia (**disesthesia**; **dysaesthesia**) *n.* abnormalities of the sense of touch. These somatosensory distortions may manifest as pain, itching, tingling, temperature variations, or other sensations. Also called **dysesthesia syndrome**.

Dysexecutive Questionnaire see DYSEXECUTIVE SYNDROME.

dysexecutive syndrome (**DES**) a collection of symptoms that involve impaired executive control of actions (see EXECUTIVE DYSFUNCTION), caused by damage to the frontal lobes of the brain. Individuals can perform routine tasks but cannot deal with new tasks or situations. They have difficulty in initiating and switching actions; for example, they cannot prevent an inappropriate but highly automated action from occurring or change their actions to appropriate ones. A questionnaire called the **Dysexecutive Questionnaire** (**DEX**) can be used to assess the severity of the impairment.

dysfluency *n.* any disturbance in the normal flow or patterning of speech, marked by repetitions, prolongations, and hesitations. See also STUTTERING.

dysfunction *n.* any impairment, disturbance, or deficiency in behavior or functioning. —**dysfunctional** *adj.*

dysfunctional family a family in which relationships or communication are impaired and members are unable to attain closeness and self-expression. Members of a dysfunctional family often develop symptomatic behaviors, and often one individual in the family presents as the IDENTIFIED PATIENT.

dysfunctions associated with sleep, sleep stages, or partial arousals one of four basic types of SLEEP DISORDERS, differentiated from the other types by the presence of physiological activations at inappropriate times during sleep rather than abnormalities in the mechanisms involved in the timing of sleep and wakefulness. This type of sleep disorder includes NIGHTMARE DISORDER, SLEEP TERROR DISORDER, and SLEEPWALKING DISORDER; in *DSM–IV–TR* these are classified as PARASOMNIAS.

dysgenic *adj.* describing a factor or influence that may be detrimental to heredity. Compare EUGENIC.

dysgenic pressure a theoretical cause of reduction in intelligence of a population that is attributed to changes in the GENE POOL. For example, one theory of dysgenic pressure is that people with lower IQs tend to reproduce more than people with higher IQs, resulting in increased dispersion of genes associated with low IQ in comparison with genes associated with high IQ. This theory has not held up well so far, partly because people with very low IQs tend not to reproduce at all and partly because intelligence has environmental as well as genetic components. See FLYNN EFFECT.

dysgeusia *n.* abnormalities of the sense of taste. These gustatory distortions may occur during pregnancy, prior to an epileptic seizure, or as a symptom of psychosis or an eating disorder. See also HYPOGEUSIA.

dysglossia *n.* see AGLOSSIA.

dysgnosia *n.* a mild form of AGNOSIA.

dysgrammatism *n.* a persistent use of incorrect grammar as a symptom of APHASIA rather than educational impoverishment. See AGRAMMATISM.

dysgraphia *n.* a type of APHASIA in which a person is unable to perform the motor movements needed for handwriting.

dyskinesia *n.* distorted voluntary movements, such as tics, spasms, CHOREA, BALLISM, and MYOCLONIC MOVEMENTS. See EXTRAPYRAMIDAL DYSKINESIA; OROFACIAL DYSKINESIA; TARDIVE DYSKINESIA. —**dyskinetic** *adj.*

dyskinetic dysarthria see DYSARTHRIA.

dyslalia *n.* an obsolescent name for impaired articulation for which no physiological cause can be determined.

dyslexia *n.* a neurologically based learning disability manifested as severe difficulties in reading, spelling, and writing words and sometimes in arithmetic. Dyslexia is characterized by impairment in the ability to process sounds, that is, to make connections between written letters and their sounds; written work is often characterized by REVERSAL ERRORS. It can be either acquired (see ALEXIA) or developmental (see DEVELOPMENTAL DYSLEXIA), is independent of intellectual ability, and is unrelated to disorders of speech and vision that may also be present. It is not the result of lack of motivation, sensory impairment, inadequate instructional or environmental opportunities, emotional disturbances, or other such factors. Investigators have proposed various subtypes of dyslexia—DEEP DYSLEXIA, SURFACE DYSLEXIA, WORD-FORM DYSLEXIA, PHONOLOGICAL DYSLEXIA, and NEGLECT DYSLEXIA, among others—but there is no universally accepted system of classification. See also READING DISABILITY; READING DISORDER. —**dyslexic** *adj.*

dyslogia *n.* see ALOGIA.

dysmenorrhea *n.* difficult or painful menstruation. The cause may be an obstruction in the cervix or vagina that traps menstrual blood, or the condition may be secondary to an infection or tumor. More than three fourths of cases are a primary, or functional, form of the disorder for which no organic cause can be found. Dysmenorrhea may be characterized by cramplike pains in the lower abdomen, headache, irritability, depression, and fatigue. Kinds of dysmenorrhea include **congestive dysmenorrhea**, marked by congestion of the uterus; **inflammatory dysmenorrhea**, associated with inflammation; **membranous dysmenorrhea**, marked by loss of membrane tissue from the uterus; **obstructive dysmenorrhea**, associated with mechanical interference of menstrual flow; and **essential dysmenorrhea**, for which there is no obvious cause. **—dysmenorrheic** *adj.*

dysmetria *n.* an impaired ability to control the distance, speed, or power of one's body movements. It is a key sign of cerebellar damage.

dysmetropsia *n.* impairment in the ability to judge the size or shape of objects, although the objects may be recognized for what they are. Compare VISUAL FORM AGNOSIA.

dysmnesia *n.* an impairment of memory, which may occur as a discrete episode or persist as a chronic condition and may be caused by any of a number of problems, such as DELIRIUM, acute or chronic brain disorders, or brain injury. Also called **dysmnesic syndrome**. **—dysmnesic** *adj.*

dysmorphism *n.* an abnormality in the shape or structure of some part of the body.

dysmorphophobia *n.* see BODY DYSMORPHIC DISORDER.

dysnomia–auditory retrieval disorder a speech and language disorder marked by problems in object naming and word retrieval and deficits in AUDITORY MEMORY. Affected children may have difficulty remembering meaningful information (expressed, for example, as sentences or stories) in a sequential fashion, even though they may have good language skills and normal or high verbal output. The memory deficit may mimic some forms of ATTENTION-DEFICIT/HYPERACTIVITY DISORDER, but behavior is rarely a problem (although frustration may be seen). Although increasingly supported by the research literature, the disorder is not classified in *DSM–IV–TR*.

dysorexia *n.* any distortion of normal appetite or disturbance in normal eating behavior. See also EATING DISORDER.

dysorthographia *n.* an impairment in the ability to spell.

dysosmia *n.* any disorder or disability in the sense of smell, either organic or psychogenic in origin. See ANOSMIA; HYPEROSMIA; HYPOSMIA; MICROSMIA; PAROSMIA; PHANTOSMIA; TROPOSMIA.

dysostosis *n.* the defective development of the skeleton of an individual, either because of hereditary factors or because of improper care following birth. The genetic causes are usually expressed in faulty development of the bones of the face and skull. Examples of dysostosis include CROUZON'S SYNDROME and TREACHER COLLINS SYNDROME.

dyspareunia *n.* PAINFUL SEXUAL INTERCOURSE, particularly in women. The term is sometimes used for inability to enjoy intercourse, but *DSM–IV–TR* treats lack of enjoyment of intercourse without pain as FEMALE SEXUAL AROUSAL DISORDER or male erectile disorder (see IMPOTENCE). If there are no medical causes for the pain, the diagnosis is FUNCTIONAL DYSPAREUNIA.

dyspepsia *n.* abdominal pain or discomfort that may be caused by ULCERS, gastroesophageal reflux (acid reflux) disease, gallstones, and, rarely, stomach or pancreatic cancer, although in a majority of cases the cause is unknown. **Functional** (or **nonulcer**) **dyspepsia** describes the condition when other medical illnesses with similar symptoms have been excluded; it may be experienced, for example, after eating too much or too quickly or eating during stressful situations. In common parlance, dyspepsia is known as **indigestion**. See also GASTRODUODENAL ULCERATION.

dysphagia *n.* an impaired ability to swallow. It may be due to damage to the cranial nerves or to muscle problems.

dysphagia spastica a somatic or, more often, psychological symptom in which the act of swallowing is painful or difficult because of throat-muscle spasms. In psychological cases, it is a symptom of SOMATIZATION DISORDER.

dysphasia *n.* an inability to communicate clearly with speech, usually because of damage to the cerebral cortex. The condition is often identified by the person's difficulty in arranging a series of spoken words in a meaningful pattern. In some contexts dysphasia and APHASIA are used synonymously. See also DYSARTHRIA. **—dysphasic** *adj.*

dysphemia *n.* a disorder of phonation, articulation, or hearing associated with emotional or mental disturbance and, frequently, a predisposition to a neurological disorder. **—dysphemic** *adj.*

dysphonetic dyslexia a type of dyslexia that is marked by an inability to sound out the individual letters and syllables of words (see PHONICS) and is supposedly due to difficulty with sound–symbol correspondences. There is, however, no reliable empirical evidence for this form of dyslexia. See also DYSEIDETIC DYSLEXIA. [proposed in 1973 by U.S. psychologist Elena Boder (1907–1995)]

dysphonia *n.* any dysfunction in the production of sounds, especially speech sounds (see PHONATION; VOCALIZATION), which may affect pitch, intensity, or resonance. See also SPASMODIC DYSPHONIA; VOICE DISORDER.

dysphoria *n.* a mood characterized by sadness, discontent, and sometimes restlessness. **—dysphoric** *adj.*

dysphoria nervosa 1. a less common name for PSYCHOMOTOR AGITATION. **2.** convulsive or spasmodic muscle contractions.

dysphrasia *n.* an older, less common name for DYSPHASIA.

dysplastic type the disproportioned type of an individual who, according to KRETSCHMER TYPOLOGY, presents a combination of traits but frequently tends toward the introversive, seclusive temperament. See also CONSTITUTIONAL TYPE.

dyspnea *n.* shortness of breath or difficulty in breathing. When not accounted for by high altitude, exertion, or any identifiable organic cause, the condition is referred to as **functional dyspnea**.

dysponesis *n.* in biofeedback, a state of habitual tension that generates hypertension, migraine headaches, bruxism (teeth grinding), or related disorders.

dyspraxia *n.* an impaired ability to perform skilled, coordinated movements that is neurologically based and not due to any muscular or sensory defect. See ACQUIRED DYSPRAXIA; CONSTRUCTIONAL DYSPRAXIA; DEVELOPMENTAL DYSPRAXIA. See also APRAXIA. **—dyspraxic** *adj.*

dysprosody *n.* unusual or abnormal alteration in the pattern of stress, rate, intonation, or rhythm of speech.

dysrhythmia *n.* any rhythmic abnormality, as might be detected in speech or in brain waves.

dyssocial behavior a former name for behavior associated with delinquent or criminal activities, such as gangsterism, racketeering, prostitution, or illegal gambling. Also called **sociopathic behavior**, it was attributed to distorted moral and social influences, frequently aggravated by a broken home or a deprived environment. Such behavior is now regarded as an aspect of ANTISOCIAL PERSONALITY DISORDER.

dyssocial personality an obsolete name for ANTISOCIAL PERSONALITY DISORDER.

dyssomnia *n.* any of various SLEEP DISORDERS marked by abnormalities in the amount, quality, or timing of sleep. In *DSM–IV–TR* dyssomnias include PRIMARY INSOMNIA, PRIMARY HYPERSOMNIA, NARCOLEPSY, CIRCADIAN RHYTHM SLEEP DISORDER, BREATHING-RELATED SLEEP DISORDER, and **dyssomnia not otherwise specified**, which may be due to excessive noise, light, or other environmental factors, ongoing sleep deprivation, EKBOM'S SYNDROME, or NOCTURNAL MYOCLONUS.

dysspermia *n.* an impairment in the structure or functioning of the spermatozoa.

dystaxia *n.* a mild degree of ATAXIA, marked by difficulty in performing coordinated muscular movements.

dysthymia *n.* **1.** see DYSTHYMIC DISORDER. **2.** any depressed mood that is mild or moderate in severity. **—dysthymic** *adj.*

dysthymic disorder a DEPRESSIVE DISORDER characterized by a depressed mood for most of the day, occurring more days than not, that persists for at least 2 years (1 year in children or adolescents). During this depressed mood, at least two of the following must also be present: increased or decreased appetite, insomnia or hypersomnia, diminished energy, low self-esteem, difficulty in concentrating or making decisions, and hopelessness. It is distinguished from MAJOR DEPRESSIVE DISORDER in that the symptoms are less severe but more enduring: There are no MAJOR DEPRESSIVE EPISODES during the first 2 years (or, in children or adolescents, 1 year) of the disorder. Also called **dysthymia**.

dystocia *n.* abnormal labor or childbirth.

dystonia *n.* abnormal, involuntary tension or contraction of the muscles resulting in distorted postures, such as twisting of the neck (TORTICOLLIS) or arching of the back. See EXTRAPYRAMIDAL EFFECTS; TARDIVE DYSKINESIA. **—dystonic** *adj.*

dystopia *n.* see UTOPIA. **—dystopian** *adj.*

dystrophia myotonica see MYOTONIC MUSCULAR DYSTROPHY.

dystrophin *n.* a protein that is needed for normal muscle function. Dystrophin is deficient or lacking in some forms of MUSCULAR DYSTROPHY.

dystrophy *n.* **1.** any degenerative disorder arising from faulty or defective nutrition. **2.** any disorder involving ATROPHY (wasting) and weakening of the muscles. See MUSCULAR DYSTROPHY.

dysuria *n.* difficult or painful urination. A frequent cause is a bacterial infection that produces irritation or inflammation of the urethra or the neck of the bladder.

DZ twins abbreviation for DIZYGOTIC TWINS.

Ee

EA abbreviation for EDUCATIONAL AGE.

EAHCA abbreviation for EDUCATION FOR ALL HANDICAPPED CHILDREN ACT.

EAP abbreviation for EMPLOYEE ASSISTANCE PROGRAM.

ear *n.* **1.** the organ of hearing. In humans and other mammals the ear is divided into an EXTERNAL EAR, MIDDLE EAR, and INNER EAR. **2.** the projecting part of the external ear (see PINNA). See also AUDITORY SYSTEM.

ear canal see EXTERNAL AUDITORY MEATUS.

eardrum *n.* see TYMPANIC MEMBRANE.

Early and Periodic Screening, Diagnosis, and Treatment (**EPSDT**) surveillance or search for indications or early manifestations of a disease or disorder, regularly carried out at specific intervals. In the United States, an EPSDT program of preventive health care services (e.g., for vision, hearing, and dental problems) and mental health and behavioral screenings (e.g., for such issues as substance abuse) is provided for children and young adults insured through Medicaid.

early bilingualism a state of BILINGUALISM attained early in life, either through the simultaneous acquisition of two languages at home or through early exposure to a second language before the completion of first-language acquisition at around age 5. This is often contrasted with **late bilingualism**, which refers to second-language acquisition after age 5 (or, in some definitions, after the onset of puberty). Early bilingualism is more likely to result in a nativelike command of phonology and grammar than is late bilingualism.

early experience experience acquired in the first 5 years of life, which is believed to have a significant influence on a child's subsequent cognitive, social, and emotional development. Whereas theorists in the early and middle part of the 20th century believed that early experience permanently determined a child's development, more recent research indicates that later experience can modify the effects of early experience.

early infantile autism see AUTISTIC DISORDER.

early intervention services provided to or actions taken on behalf of individuals who appear to be at risk for, or are in the early stages of, a developmental, behavioral, or other condition in order to prevent the condition from developing or to minimize the impact of the condition on the person in the future.

early intervention program see INFANT DEVELOPMENT PROGRAM.

early memory adult recollection of childhood events, which typically goes back only to the age of 3 or so, even though the capacity to learn is present at birth. The absence of earlier childhood memories, referred to as CHILDHOOD AMNESIA, has been noted since the time of Sigmund FREUD. Explanations include neural immaturity, absence of language or adult SCHEMAS to organize event memory, or different coding dimensions in infancy.

early-selection theory any theory of attention proposing that an attentional filter blocks out unattended messages early in the processing stream, prior to stimulus identification. See ATTENUATION THEORY; FILTER THEORY. Compare LATE-SELECTION THEORY.

early transient incapacitation (**ETI**) incapacitation (i.e., nonresponse) as a result of radiation. The radiological factors on which it depends include dose, rate of exposure, nature of the radiation, and the body size of the organism. Gamma photons are more effective in producing ETI than either high-energy neutrons or fission-spectrum neutrons.

ear ossicles see OSSICLES.

earwax *n.* see CERUMEN.

Easterbrook hypothesis the hypothesis that the range of cues attended to is inversely related to the degree of arousal, that is, in a state of increased arousal, attention narrows and fewer environmental stimuli are focused on. The hypothesis was proposed as an explanation of YERKES–DODSON LAW, which describes the relationship between arousal and performance. [proposed in 1959 by J. A. **Easterbrook**, 20th-century Canadian psychologist]

eating aid an ASSISTIVE TECHNOLOGY device that can be used by people with disabilities to feed themselves independently. Eating aids include metal or plastic devices for holding sandwiches; nonslip place mats, bowls, and dishes with suction cups attached to the bottom; handles that can swivel, are angled, or have extensions; and combination eating devices, such as knife–fork or fork–spoon combinations.

eating behavior any behavior related to the act of eating, including patterns of eating that may be abnormal. See also EATING DISORDER.

eating compulsion an irresistible impulse leading to abnormal eating behavior. This is a primary symptom of a number of eating disorders, such as BULIMIA NERVOSA, KLÜVER–BUCY SYNDROME, and FOOD ADDICTIONS. See also COMPULSIVE EATING.

eating disorder any disorder characterized primarily by pathological eating behavior. *DSM–IV–TR* categorizes eating disorders as ANOREXIA NERVOSA, BULIMIA NERVOSA, or **eating disorder not otherwise specified**, which does not meet the diagnostic criteria for either of the specific eating disorders and includes BINGE-EATING DISORDER. Other eating-related disorders include PICA and RUMINATION DISORDER, which are usually diagnosed in infancy or early childhood and in *DSM–IV–TR* are classified as FEEDING AND EATING DISORDERS OF INFANCY OR EARLY CHILDHOOD.

Ebbinghaus, Hermann (1850–1909) German psychologist. Ebbinghaus received his doctorate in philosophy at Bonn University in 1873. At Berlin University he subsequently completed a second dissertation that became the basis for his famous book *On Memory* (1885). Ebbinghaus was the first to apply quantitative psychophysiological methods to the study of higher mental processes. His early experiments on memory employed NONSENSE SYLLABLES in order to reduce the effects of meaning on memorization. He performed systematic studies of memory and forgetting that yielded important results for our knowledge of such phenomena as memory span, overlearning, and spaced versus massed learning. Ebbinghaus's work had a lasting effect in establishing experimental psychology as a scientific discipline.

Ebbinghaus's curve of retention a graphic depiction of the amount of forgetting over time after learning has taken place. In his studies of forgetting lists of nonsense syllables, Hermann EBBINGHAUS showed there was a sudden drop in retention shortly following learning, but a more gradual decline thereafter.

Ebbinghaus test a test that uses NONSENSE SYLLABLES as a means of studying memory processes that are relatively free from prior associations. [Hermann EBBINGHAUS]

Ebonics *n.* see BLACK ENGLISH.

EBV abbreviation for EPSTEIN–BARR VIRUS.

ECA Survey abbreviation for EPIDEMIOLOGIC CATCHMENT AREA SURVEY.

eccentric projection see REFERRED SENSATION.

eccyesis *n.* see ECTOPIC PREGNANCY.

ECF abbreviation for extended care facility. See EXTENDED CARE.

ECG abbreviation for ELECTROCARDIOGRAM.

echinacea *n.* an herbal agent derived from any of nine related plant species native to the United States and southern Canada, with *Echinacea purpurea* being the most commonly used and perhaps the most potent. Echinacea traditionally has been used in the belief that it stimulates the immune system. It is approved by Commission E, a committee of 24 interdisciplinary health care professionals formed in 1978 by the German Federal Institute for Drugs and Medical Devices, for use in the treatment or prevention of fevers and colds, cough and bronchitis, urinary tract and other infections, inflammation of the mouth and pharynx, and—as an external application—to promote healing of wounds and burns. Some studies have shown, however, that taking echinacea has no clinical or significant effects on whether people become infected with a cold or, in those who develop colds, on the severity or duration of their symptoms. Although echinacea is generally considered safe and there are no known reports of toxicity, some people may experience hypersensitivity reactions to echinacea, such as rashes, increased asthma, and ANAPHYLAXIS. More commonly, side effects of use may include headache, dizziness, nausea, and constipation. Also, continual long-term use is not recommended as echinacea appears to lose its effectiveness over time, and people with autoimmune disorders (see AUTOIMMUNITY), leukemia, multiple sclerosis, tuberculosis, and HIV infection should not take echinacea at all. Concurrent use with immunosuppressant agents should be avoided, and, as echinacea is believed to be metabolized by the CYTOCHROME P450 3A4 enzyme, it accordingly has numerous potential interactions with psychotropic drugs metabolized via the same enzyme (e.g., clonidine, nefazodone, St. John's wort).

echo *n.* a reflected sound wave that is distinct from that directly transmitted from the source.

echocardiography *n.* the production of a graphic record or image (**echocardiogram**) of the internal structures of an individual's heart with an ultrasound device that uses sonarlike reflections. Echocardiography enables the visualization and measurement of all the chambers and valves of the heart as well as the pumping efficiency of the organ.

écho des pensées an AUDITORY HALLUCINATION in which an individual hears his or her own thoughts repeated in spoken form. Also called **thought echoing**.

echoencephalography *n.* a method of mapping the inside of the head for diagnostic purposes by using ultrasonic waves. The waves are beamed through the head from both sides, using an instrument called an **echoencephalograph**, and echoes of the waves from midline structures are recorded as visual images. Any variation in reflections from the midline may indicate an abnormality in the brain structure. The recording is called an **echoencephalogram**.

echographia *n.* pathological writing that involves copying words and phrases without understanding them.

echoic memory the persistence of auditory stimulation in the nervous system for a brief period (2–3 s) after the end of the stimulus. Also called **auditory sensory memory**. See also PRECATEGORICAL ACOUSTIC STORAGE.

echolalia *n.* mechanical repetition of words and phrases uttered by another individual. Echolalia occurs in some individuals with catatonic schizophrenia, autism, LATAH, TOURETTE'S DISORDER, or degenerative neurological disorders. Also called **echophrasia**; **echo-speech**.

echolocation *n.* the ability to judge the direction and distance of objects or obstacles from reflected echoes made by acoustic signals, such as footsteps, the tapping of a cane, or traffic noises. People with visual impairment can learn to develop this ability to find their way and avoid obstacles. Among animals, both bats and marine mammals (e.g., dolphins) can locate objects by emitting high-pitched sounds that are reflected from features of the physical environment and prey objects. High-pitched sounds provide better spatial resolution of an object than sounds of lower pitch but require more energy to travel the same distance. Thus a bat can locate a mosquito, but only at a short range. See also ULTRASONIC COMMUNICATION.

echomatism *n.* see ECHOPRAXIA.

echomimia *n.* see ECHOPRAXIA.

echopathy *n.* any pathological, automatic copying and repetition of another's movements (ECHOPRAXIA) or speech (ECHOLALIA).

echo phenomenon ECHOLALIA, ECHOPRAXIA, or both. See ECHOPATHY. [first described by German psychiatrist Emil Kraepelin (1856–1926)]

echophrasia *n.* see ECHOLALIA.

echopraxia *n.* automatic imitation of another person's movements or gestures. It is sometimes seen in association with ECHOLALIA. Also called **echomatism**; **echomimia**.

echovirus *n.* *e*nteric *c*ytopathic *h*uman *o*rphan *virus*: any of more than 30 types of small viruses that tend to produce respiratory, gastrointestinal, and poliolike symptoms during the summer and fall. When first discovered, the viruses were not a part of any known family of infectious agents (hence "orphan").

eclampsia *n.* convulsions that occur in patients who have experienced PREECLAMPSIA. This serious condition occurs only in pregnant women and is not associated with epilepsy or other cerebral disorders. The convulsions, which can occur before, during, or after delivery of the child, are usually followed by coma. **—eclamptic** *adj.*

eclectic behaviorism an approach to BEHAVIOR THERAPY that does not adhere to one theoretical model but applies, as needed, any of several techniques, including PAVLOVIAN CONDITIONING, MODELING, OPERANT CON-

DITIONING, self-control mechanisms, and COGNITIVE RESTRUCTURING.

eclectic counseling any COUNSELING theory or practice that incorporates and combines doctrines, findings, and techniques selected from diverse theoretical systems.

eclecticism *n.* a theoretical or practical approach that blends, or attempts to blend, diverse conceptual formulations or techniques into an integrated approach. See also BENEVOLENT ECLECTICISM. **—eclectic** *adj.*

eclectic psychotherapy any PSYCHOTHERAPY that is based on a combination of theories or approaches or uses concepts and techniques from a number of different sources, including the integrated professional experiences of the therapist. The more formalized **prescriptive eclectic psychotherapy** involves the use of a combination of psychotherapy approaches that is specifically sequenced in terms of formats, methods, and processes in order to improve outcome.

eclima *n.* increased appetite or insatiable hunger, often associated with BULIMIA NERVOSA. Also called **eclimia**. See also HYPEROREXIA; HYPERPHAGIA.

ECM abbreviation for EXTERNAL CHEMICAL MESSENGER.

ecobehavioral assessment an assessment used in APPLIED BEHAVIOR ANALYSIS to measure moment-to-moment effects of multiple environmental events on an individual's specific behaviors. These events include the behavior of others, task demands, time of day, and situational changes.

ECochG abbreviation for electrocochleography. See ELECTROPHYSIOLOGIC AUDIOMETRY.

ecofeminism *n.* a position that combines FEMINISM with a commitment to environmentalism and environmental activism. It emphasizes a concomitance between the exploitation of nature and the exploitation of women, suggesting that there is a set of social, political, and philosophical attitudes that give rise to and maintain both. **—ecofeminist** *n.*

ECoG abbreviation for ELECTROCORTICOGRAM.

ecological niche 1. the function or position of an organism or a population within a physical and biological environment. **2.** the particular area within a habitat occupied by an organism or a population.

ecological perception an organism's detection of the AFFORDANCES and INVARIANCES within its natural, real-world environment (i.e., its ecology as opposed to a laboratory setting), as mediated and guided by the organism's immersion in and movement through that environment. J. J. GIBSON proposed that ecological perception is holistic (the organism and environment are a single inseparable system), that environmental properties are perceived as meaningful entities, and that perceptual patterns may be direct rather than concepts that require interpretation by higher brain centers from visual or other cues. See DIRECT PERCEPTION.

ecological perspective a concept of COMMUNITY PSYCHOLOGY in which a community (or any other social entity) is viewed in terms of the interrelations between people, roles, organizations, local events, resources, and problems. It accounts for complex reciprocal interactions of individuals and their environment. The premise of the ecological perspective is that intervention should contribute to the development of the entire community.

ecological psychology the analysis of BEHAVIOR SETTINGS with the aim of predicting patterns of behavior that occur within certain settings. The focus is on the role of the physical and social elements of the setting in producing the behavior. According to behavior-setting theory, the behavior that will occur in a particular setting is largely prescribed by the roles that exist in that setting and the actions of those in such roles, irrespective of the personalities, age, gender, and other characteristics of the individuals present. In a place or worship, for example, one or more individuals have the role of leaders (the clergy, who preach and direct prayers), while a larger number of participants function as an audience (the congregation). Other factors that shape behavior are the size of the setting, the number of roles required to maintain it, its permeability (i.e., openness to outside influence or nonmembers), and the explicitness of rules and regulations relating to expected behavior there.

ecological studies 1. research into the mutual relations between organisms and their environments. See ECOLOGY. **2.** in psychology, research that evaluates the influence of environmental factors on individual behavior and mental health. See HUMAN ECOLOGY; SOCIAL ECOLOGY; URBAN ECOLOGY.

ecological systems theory an evolving body of theory and research concerned with the processes and conditions that govern the course of human development in the actual environments in which human beings live. Generally, ecological systems theory accords equal importance to the concept of environment as a context for development (in terms of nested systems ranging from micro- to macro-) and to the role of biopsychological characteristics of the individual person. The current, still evolving, paradigm is now referred to as the BIOECOLOGICAL MODEL. See also ECOSYSTEMIC APPROACH. [originally conceptualized by Russian-born U.S. developmental psychologist Urie Bronfenbrenner (1917–2005)]

ecological validity 1. the degree to which results obtained from research or experiment are representative of conditions in the wider world. For example, psychological research carried out exclusively among university students might have a low ecological validity when applied to the population as a whole. Ecological validity may be threatened by EXPERIMENTER BIAS or by naive sampling strategies that produce an unrepresentative selection of participants. See also VALIDITY. [defined by Austrian-born U.S. psychologist Martin T. Orne (1927–2000) on the basis of work by Hungarian-born U.S. psychologist Egon Brunswik (1903–1955)] **2.** in perception, the degree to which a PROXIMAL STIMULUS (i.e., the stimulus as it impinges on the receptor) covaries with the DISTAL STIMULUS (i.e., the actual stimulus in the physical environment). [originated by Egon Brunswik (see above)]

ecology *n.* the study of relationships between organisms and their physical and social environments. BEHAVIORAL ECOLOGY is a subfield that examines how the behavior of animals is affected by physical and social factors. **—ecological** *adj.* **—ecologist** *n.*

ecomania *n.* a morbid preoccupation with and pathological attitude toward members of one's family, characterized by irritable and domineering behavior. It is often a factor in DOMESTIC VIOLENCE and the CYCLE OF VIOLENCE. Also called **oikomania**.

economic model in psychoanalytic theory, the view that the psyche can be explained in terms of the amounts and distributions of PSYCHIC ENERGY associated with particular mental states and processes. Compare DYNAMIC MODEL; TOPOGRAPHIC MODEL.

Economo's disease see ENCEPHALITIS LETHARGICA. [Constantin von **Economo** (1876–1931), Austrian neurologist]

economy *n.* **1.** any system of rules and regulations by which something is managed; for example, a token economy is one in which a behavioral system is managed according to the disbursement of tokens as rewards. **2.** management of resources in order to maximize efficiency or returns and avoid waste.

economy of effort the tendency of an organism to act efficiently and minimize the expenditure of energy, for example by avoiding any unnecessary movements.

economy principle see LAW OF PARSIMONY. See also ELEGANT SOLUTION; OCCAM'S RAZOR.

ecopathology *n.* the identification of people as abnormal by other members of their community. Behavior considered normal in some communities (i.e., conforming to the attitudes and beliefs of community members) may be regarded as eccentric or even psychotic in other communities.

ecosystem *n.* the dynamic and interactive balance maintained among individuals of different species within an environment. The behavior of any one species or population must be understood in the context of competing and supportive species within the environment. There is an interdependent balance of predators, prey, food resources, and substrates such that a change in any one component is often followed by commensurate changes in the other components.

ecosystemic approach an approach to therapy that emphasizes the interaction between the individual or family and larger social contexts, such as schools, workplaces, and social agencies. The approach emphasizes interrelatedness and interdependency and derives from diverse fields, including psychology, sociology, anthropology, economics, and political science. FAMILY THERAPY, in particular, has made use of this approach in designing interventions for complex families and systems. See also ECOLOGICAL SYSTEMS THEORY. [developed in psychology by Russian-born U.S. developmental psychologist Uri Bronfenbrenner (1917–2005)]

ecphoria *n.* **1.** the activation of a memory, which involves the RETRIEVAL of a memory by a CUE. A retrieval cue that matches information stored in memory results in access to that memory. Cues or conditions that were present when the memory was formed are stored with the memory, therefore those same conditions need to be reinstated at retrieval to provoke ecphoria. **2.** the process in which a memory, emotion, or the like is revived in the mind by a stimulus. Also called **ecphory**. [defined by German biologist Richard Semon (1859–1918)] **—ecphoric** *adj.*

ECS abbreviation for electroconvulsive shock (see ELECTROCONVULSIVE THERAPY).

ecstasy *n.* a state of intense pleasure and elation, including some mystical states, orgasm, aesthetic experiences, and drug-induced states. Such extreme euphoria also occasionally occurs in the context of a HYPOMANIC EPISODE or a MANIC EPISODE. Also called **ecstatic state**. **—ecstatic** *adj.*

Ecstasy *n.* the popular name for MDMA.

ecstatic trance a TRANCE-like state of joy and happiness, which is often associated with various religious practices, such as intense meditation or certain emotional styles of worship. See also ALTERED STATE OF CONSCIOUSNESS; MYSTICISM; VOODOO.

ECT 1. abbreviation for ELECTROCONVULSIVE THERAPY. **2.** abbreviation for ELEMENTARY COGNITIVE TASK.

ECT-induced amnesia amnesia that is a by-product of ELECTROCONVULSIVE THERAPY (ECT). Although ECT is effective in the relief of depression, memory deficits often arise, especially when the current is applied to both sides of the brain. Memory can be severely compromised in the hours or days following treatment, but new learning typically returns to normal by 6 months after treatment. Some impairment in the retrieval of events that occurred close to the time of treatment may remain.

ecto- *combining form* outer or outside.

ectoderm *n.* the outermost of the primary GERM LAYERS of a developing embryo. Structures derived from ectoderm include skin and nails, hair, glands, mucous membranes, the nervous system, and external sense organs (e.g., ears, eyes). **—ectodermal** *adj.*

ectohormone *n.* see PHEROMONE.

ectomorph *n.* a constitutional type (SOMATOTYPE) in SHELDON'S CONSTITUTIONAL THEORY OF PERSONALITY characterized by a thin, long, fragile physique, which—according to this theory—is highly correlated with CEREBROTONIA. Also called **ectomorphic body type**. **—ectomorphic** *adj.* **—ectomorphy** *n.*

-ectomy *combining form* surgical removal of a part of the body (e.g., LOBECTOMY). See also -TOMY.

ectopia *n.* displacement or abnormal positioning of part of the body. For example, neurons are seen in unusual positions in the cerebral cortex of people with dyslexia. **—ectopic** *adj.*

ectopic pregnancy a pregnancy that develops outside the uterus, most commonly in a fallopian tube (a TUBAL PREGNANCY). Also called **eccyesis**; **extrauterine pregnancy**; **paracyesis**.

ectopic testis a testis that descended improperly from the abdominal cavity and became lodged outside the scrotum. It may be located beneath the outer tissue layers of the thigh or in the perineum.

ectoplasm *n.* **1.** the relatively more dense CYTOPLASM found at the periphery of a cell. Compare ENDOPLASM. **2.** in SPIRITUALISM, a viscous substance said to emanate from a medium's body during a seance and to adopt the face or form of a dead human being. Also called **teleplasm**. See also MATERIALIZATION. **—ectoplasmic** *adj.*

ectotherm *n.* an animal whose body temperature is largely regulated by the environment, which is the source of most of its heat. Examples include snakes and bees. Such animals, formerly called **poikilotherms**, are popularly described as cold-blooded. Compare ENDOTHERM. **—ectothermic** *adj.*

ED_{50} (**ED-50**) abbreviation for effective dose 50 (see EFFECTIVE DOSE). See also THERAPEUTIC RATIO.

edema *n.* an excess accumulation of fluid in body cells, organs, or cavities. The cause may be a loss of fluid through the walls of the blood vessels as a symptom of a circulatory disorder or the interruption of flow of cerebrospinal fluid due to blockage of a passageway or failure of tissues to absorb the excess. See also CEREBRAL EDEMA. **—edematous** *adj.*

edge *n.* **1.** the border of an object. **2.** the border between two elements in an image.

edge detectors cells in the visual system or hypothetical processors in models of vision that respond best to a dark–light border or edge.

edge theory a theory proposing that DEATH ANXIETY has a survival function that emerges when individuals perceive themselves to be in life-threatening situations. The theory attempts to resolve the apparent discrepancy between claims that death anxiety is a major motivational force and empirical studies that reveal only low to moderate levels of death anxiety in the general population. It suggests that death anxiety is the subjective or experiential side of a holistic preparation to deal with danger (symbolic of standing at the edge of the void). Heightened arousal is turned on by anxiety surges in emergency situations; difficulties arise when the emergency response has permeated the individual's everyday functioning. See also TERROR MANAGEMENT THEORY. [introduced by U.S. psychologist Robert J. Kastenbaum]

Edinger–Westphal nucleus a collection of small nerve cells in the midbrain: part of the PARASYMPATHETIC NERVOUS SYSTEM pathway to the ciliary muscle and the pupillary sphincter of the eye, which play a role in visual accommodation. [Ludwig **Edinger** (1855–1918), German neuroanatomist; Karl Friedrich Otto **Westphal** (1833–1890), German neurologist]

EDR abbreviation for electrodermal response. See GALVANIC SKIN RESPONSE.

edrophonium *n.* an anticholinesterase (see CHOLINERGIC DRUGS) characterized by a rapid onset and short duration of action. It is the drug of choice in the diagnosis of myasthenia gravis, and it may also be used in surgical anesthesia to reverse the effects of neuromuscular blocking agents. U.S. trade names: **Enlon**; **Reversol**.

educable *adj.* having the potential for academic learning. **—educability** *n.*

educable mentally retarded (**EMR**) formerly, describing people with mild or high-moderate mental retardation (IQ 50 to 70 or 80), who are capable of achieving approximately a fifth-grade academic level.

education *n.* **1.** the process of teaching or acquiring knowledge, skills, and values. **2.** a field of advanced teacher preparation study that involves the practice of methods for teaching and learning. **—educational** *adj.*

educational acceleration educational progress at a rate faster than usual through a variety of measures, such as strengthening or compacting the curriculum, accelerating instruction in particular subject areas, or grade skipping. These measures are designed to provide intellectually gifted students with work more ideally suited to their abilities. Grade acceleration is thought by some to represent a potential disadvantage if the student's social and emotional development is lagging behind his or her intellectual development. Careful assessment of intellectual, achievement, social, emotional, and physical development as well as adjustment to flexibility is absolutely essential prior to acceleration of one or more grades. Also called **scholastic acceleration**.

educational age (**EA**) the optimal age level at which a student is capable of performing. A student's educational age may be higher or lower than his or her chronological age. In such cases, the appropriate objective would be to offer a curriculum appropriate to the student's educational age rather than to his or her chronological age.

educational attainment level 1. the status of learning that has been achieved by a student or group of students. **2.** the set of standards for acquired knowledge that a student must master before being considered for the next educational step, level, or grade. **3.** the highest level of schooling completed. Research has linked educational attainment level to resulting income level, self-worth, happiness, and other positive outcomes.

educational counseling the COUNSELING specialty concerned with providing advice and assistance to students in the development of their educational plans, choice of appropriate courses, and choice of college or technical school. Counseling may also be applied to improve study skills or provide assistance with school-related problems that interfere with performance, for example, learning disabilities. Educational counseling is closely associated with VOCATIONAL COUNSELING because of the relationship between educational training and occupational choice. Also called **educational guidance**; **student counseling**. See also COUNSELING PSYCHOLOGY.

educational diagnosis 1. the process of analytically examining a learning problem, which may involve cognitive, perceptual, emotional, and other factors that influence academic performance or school adjustment. **2.** the conclusion reached as a result of the analytical examination of a learning problem.

educational guidance 1. see EDUCATIONAL COUNSELING. **2.** advice given to students to assist them in making suitable decisions regarding their educational needs (e.g., school program planning, course selection, academic specialization, etc.).

educational linguistics a broad field of study concerned with language in education, particularly the use of linguistic theory in developing instructional methods and broader educational policy.

educational measurement the development and application of tests used to measure student abilities.

educational pacing 1. the rate or speed of the learning process. **2.** the control and monitoring of student work speed by a teacher, supervisor, or discussion leader. **3.** the rate at which a whole class of students moves through a specific curriculum. This is determined by multiple factors, such as number of students in the class, student ability and interest, teacher philosophy, and teacher competence.

educational placement the act of matching students with the appropriate educational program or environment for their age, abilities, and needs. Standardized tests, classroom test data, interviews, and past student performance may all be taken into account in arriving at this decision.

educational program accreditation the certification by a supervisory organization of the minimum standards that must exist in a given institution of learning.

educational psychology a branch of psychology dealing with the application of principles and theories of psychology to methods of learning. Educational psychology also addresses the wide array of psychological problems that can arise in educational systems. Educational psychologists often hold applied as well as academic positions, spending their time in a variety of teaching, research, and applied pursuits.

educational quotient (**EQ**) a ratio of EDUCATIONAL AGE to CHRONOLOGICAL AGE times 100.

educational retardation 1. slowness or delay of student progress in acquiring knowledge due to a physical, emotional, intellectual, or mental disability. **2.** a slowness or delay that is specific to a certain subject or educational setting.

educational sport psychologist an individual educated and trained in the nonclinical psychology of human movement as it relates to sport. Education and training may be achieved through areas of psychology, SPORT SCIENCE, physical education, or KINESIOLOGY. Educational sport psychologists assist participants in sport to optimize PERFORMANCE ENHANCEMENT by helping them to deal with such issues as anxiety, self-confidence, use of IMAGERY, and ATTENTIONAL FOCUS. Compare CLINICAL SPORT PSYCHOLOGIST. See SPORT PSYCHOLOGY.

Educational Testing Service (**ETS**) a nonprofit organization, founded in 1947, whose mission is to help advance quality and equity in education by providing fair and valid assessments, research, and related services. The

SCHOLASTIC ASSESSMENT TEST and GRADUATE RECORD EXAMINATIONS are well-known tests developed by ETS.

educational tests see DIAGNOSTIC EDUCATIONAL TESTS.

educational therapy individualized treatment interventions for individuals with learning disabilities or emotional or behavioral problems that significantly interfere with learning. Educational therapy integrates educational techniques and therapeutic practices to promote academic achievement and the attainment of basic skills while building self-esteem and confidence, fostering independence, and aiding personal development. It is usually conducted by a professionally trained **educational therapist**.

Education for All Handicapped Children Act (**EAHCA**; **EHA**) an act passed by the U.S. Congress in 1975 guaranteeing all children equal access to education in the LEAST RESTRICTIVE ENVIRONMENT, which led to the promotion of programs for admitting children with disabilities into the general population of students. This act has since been replaced by the INDIVIDUALS WITH DISABILITIES EDUCATION ACT.

eduction *n.* the comprehension of relations, or the comprehension of correlates, or both, in an analogy. **Eduction of relations** involves understanding the relationship between the first two terms of an analogy, while **eduction of correlates** involves the application of this understanding to the third term in the analogy, in order to find the solution. For example, in the analogy tall : short; heavy : ?, eduction of relations would be used to infer the relation between *tall* and *short,* and eduction of correlates would be used to apply the relation to produce *light* as a solution. [defined in the early 20th century by British psychologist Charles Spearman (1863–1945)]

Edwards Personal Preference Schedule (**EPPS**) a personality inventory for college students and adults in which the strength of 15 "manifest needs" is assessed on a forced-choice basis. The needs are: achievement, order, deference, autonomy, exhibition, affection, succorance, sympathy, change, endurance, heterosexuality, aggression, intraception, abasement, and affiliation. [developed in the 1950s by Allen L. **Edwards** (1914–1994), U.S. psychologist, based on the needs described in the personality theory of U.S. psychologist Henry A. Murray (1893–1988)]

Edwards syndrome see TRISOMY 17–18. [John Hilton **Edwards** (1928–), British geneticist]

EE abbreviation for EXPRESSED EMOTION.

EEG abbreviation for ELECTROENCEPHALOGRAPHY, electroencephalograph, or electroencephalogram.

EEG measures of intelligence measures of intelligence that are extracted from electroencephalographic assessments of sites in the brain. These measures are apparently more accurate when participants are asked to do nothing in particular while they are being measured than when they are asked to engage in a particular cognitive task. However, while some investigators have found significant and substantial correlations between EEG measures of intelligence and psychometric test scores, other investigators have often failed to replicate their findings. These measures have therefore now largely been superseded by more precise EVENT-RELATED POTENTIALS (see ERP MEASURES OF INTELLIGENCE).

EEOC abbreviation for EQUAL EMPLOYMENT OPPORTUNITY COMMISSION.

effectance *n.* the state of having a causal effect on objects and events in the environment, commonly used in the term **effectance motivation**.

effective dose the minimum dose of a drug that is required to produce a specified effect. It is usually expressed in terms of **median effective dose**, or **effective dose 50** (**ED_{50}**, **ED-50**), the dose at which 50% of patients have a positive response (see also THERAPEUTIC RATIO). In psychotherapy, this criterion is also used to express the number of sessions that are needed for 50% of patients to show a clinically significant change.

effectiveness evaluation the assessment of the degree of success of a program in achieving a project's goals. The process requires the determination of EVALUATION OBJECTIVES, methods, and CRITERIA OF EVALUATION and the presentation of findings. See also IMPACT ANALYSIS; PROGRAM OUTCOME.

effective stimulus in stimulus–response experiments, the stimulus that actually produces a particular effect on the organism. This may be different from the NOMINAL STIMULUS as defined by the experimenter. For example, if an experimenter presents a tone as a nominal stimulus, the effective stimulus may be the combination of tone and the chamber in which the tone is presented. Also called **functional stimulus**.

effect law see LAW OF EFFECT.

effector *n.* **1.** an organ, such as a muscle or a gland, that produces an effect. **2.** a motor nerve ending that triggers activity in tissue cells, such as causing a muscle to contract or a gland to secrete. **3.** in motor control, the part of the body that interacts with the environment during an action (e.g., the hand during a reaching movement).

effect size the magnitude, often in standardized units, of an effect in a study. It is often an indicator of the strength of a relationship, the magnitude of mean differences among several groups, or the like. See also COMBINING EFFECT SIZES; STATISTICAL SIGNIFICANCE.

effect-size correlation (symbol: $r_{\text{effect size}}$) the correlation between scores on the DEPENDENT VARIABLE and the contrast weights (i.e., predicted values) without removing any other sources of variation in the data.

effect spread see GENERALIZATION.

effeminacy *n.* female behavior or appearance in a male, which is regarded as not fitting the male GENDER ROLE expectations of society. —**effeminate** *adj.*

efference copy see COROLLARY DISCHARGE.

efferent *adj.* conducting or conveying away from a central point. For example, EFFERENT NERVE FIBERS conduct impulses away from the brain or spinal cord. Compare AFFERENT.

efferent motor aphasia a form of EXPRESSIVE APHASIA marked by difficulty in articulating sound and speech sequences, resulting from lesions in the lower part of the left PREMOTOR AREA of the brain.

efferent nerve fiber a nerve fiber that carries impulses from the central nervous system to the periphery. Compare AFFERENT NERVE FIBER.

efferent neuron a neuron, such as a MOTOR NEURON, whose axon carries impulses away from the central nervous system toward an EFFECTOR.

efferent pathway a NEURAL PATHWAY that carries impulses away from a particular region of the central nervous system toward an EFFECTOR. Examples are MOTOR PATHWAYS. Compare AFFERENT PATHWAY.

Effexor *n.* a trade name for VENLAFAXINE.

efficacy *n.* **1.** competence in behavioral performance, especially with reference to a person's perception of his or her performance capabilities, or PERCEIVED SELF-EFFICACY. **2.** in pharmacology, see DOSE–RESPONSE RELATIONSHIP.

efficiency *n.* **1.** a measure of the ability of an organization, work unit, or individual employee to produce the maximum output with a minimum investment of time, effort, and other inputs. Given the same level of output, efficiency increases as the time, effort, and other inputs taken to produce that level decrease. Also called **industrial efficiency**; **organizational efficiency**. See also ORGANIZATIONAL EFFECTIVENESS. **2.** in statistics, the degree to which an ESTIMATOR uses all the information in a sample to estimate a particular parameter. **—efficient** *adj.*

efficient cause in the doctrine of the four CAUSES stated by Greek philosopher Aristotle (384–322 BCE), the agent that initiates a causal process by bringing together the material cause (matter), the formal cause (form), and the final cause (purpose) of a particular effect. One of Aristotle's examples of an efficient cause was a skilled craftsman who creates an artifact; another was a father who begets a child. More generally, the term is used to mean that which produces a given effect by a causal process.

effluvium *n.* a supposed flow of physical particles too subtle to be perceived by ordinary sensory mechanisms that is sometimes cited as an explanation for various paranormal and spiritualistic phenomena (Latin, "flowing out"). In the 18th century, the term was widely used to explain such phenomena as magnetism and electricity and later became associated with the idea of ANIMAL MAGNETISM. In spiritualism and parapsychology it is often linked with the notion that people and things have an invisible AURA. See also REICHENBACH PHENOMENON.

effort *n.* the activation of physical or mental power.

effort after meaning the persistent effort to put unfamiliar ideas into more familiar terms in an attempt to comprehend ambiguous or unfamiliar material. See BARTLETT TECHNIQUE. [defined by British psychologist Sir Frederic Charles Bartlett (1886–1969)]

effortfulness *n.* a sense of effort, or consciousness of effort: a feature of many psychological tasks that can be judged reliably by participants. Effortful tasks compete against each other under dual-task conditions (see DUAL-TASK COMPETITION; DUAL-TASK PERFORMANCE), indicating that effortfulness correlates with demands on mental resources. Novel skills often begin in an effortful and conscious way and become less effortful and more automatic with practice. Because the sense of effort lacks conscious sensory qualities, it can be considered an experience of FRINGE CONSCIOUSNESS. It is believed to involve increased brain activity in the DORSOLATERAL PREFRONTAL CORTEX. **—effortful** *adj.*

effortful processing mental activity that requires deliberation and control and involves a sense of EFFORT, or overcoming resistance. Compare AUTOMATICITY. See also MENTAL EFFORT.

effort justification a phenomenon whereby people come to evaluate a particular task or activity more favorably when it involves something that is difficult or unpleasant. The effect is most likely to occur when there are no obvious reasons for performing the task. Because expending effort to perform a useless or unenjoyable task, or experiencing unpleasant consequences in doing this, is cognitively inconsistent (see COGNITIVE DISSONANCE), people are assumed to shift their evaluations of the task in a positive direction to restore consistency. See also COGNITIVE DISSONANCE THEORY; DISSONANCE REDUCTION.

effort syndrome the former name for an anxiety reaction now classified as PANIC DISORDER: The symptoms are those of a PANIC ATTACK. This syndrome has been given many names, including cardiac neurosis, hyperkinetic heart syndrome, irritable heart, soldier's heart, Da Costa's syndrome, neurocirculatory asthenia, and hyperventilation syndrome.

EFPPA abbreviation for EUROPEAN FEDERATION OF PROFESSIONAL PSYCHOLOGISTS' ASSOCIATIONS.

EFT abbreviation for EMBEDDED FIGURES TEST.

egersis *n.* intense or extreme wakefulness.

egg cell see OVUM.

ego *n.* **1.** the SELF, particularly the conscious sense of self (Latin, "I"). In its popular and quasi-technical sense, ego refers to all the psychological phenomena and processes that are related to the self and that comprise the individual's attitudes, values, and concerns. **2.** in psychoanalytic theory, the component of the personality that deals with the external world and its practical demands. More specifically, the ego enables the individual to perceive, reason, solve problems, test reality, and adjust the instinctual impulses of the ID to the behests of the SUPEREGO. See also ANTILIBIDINAL EGO; BODY EGO; SUPPORTIVE EGO.

ego-alien *adj.* see EGO-DYSTONIC.

ego analysis psychoanalytic techniques directed toward discovering the strengths and weaknesses of the EGO and uncovering its DEFENSES against unacceptable impulses. Ego analysis is a short form of psychoanalysis: It does not attempt to penetrate to the ultimate origin of impulses and repressions. See also EGO STRENGTH; EGO WEAKNESS.

ego anxiety in psychoanalytic theory, anxiety caused by the conflicting demands of the EGO, ID, and SUPEREGO. Thus, ego anxiety refers to internal, rather than external demands. Compare ID ANXIETY. See also SIGNAL ANXIETY.

ego boundary **1.** the concept that individuals are able to distinguish between self and not-self. Someone who is said to lack clear ego boundaries blurs the distinction between himself or herself and others by identifying with them too easily and too much. **2.** in psychoanalysis, the boundary between the EGO and the ID (the INTERNAL BOUNDARY) or between the ego and external reality (the EXTERNAL BOUNDARY).

ego-boundary loss a condition in which the person lacks a clear sense of where his or her own body, mind, and influence end and where these characteristics in other animate and inanimate objects begin.

ego cathexis in psychoanalytic theory, the concentration of PSYCHIC ENERGY onto the self, taking one's own ego as a LOVE OBJECT. Ego cathexis is thus a form of NARCISSISM. Also called **ego libido**. See CATHEXIS. Compare OBJECT CATHEXIS.

ego-centered network see GROUP NETWORK.

egocentric predicament a problematic condition arising from the assumption that each person's experience is essentially private. The problem is commonly expressed in terms of one or more of the following propositions: (a) It is difficult to explain how any person could know anything about another person's experience; (b) it is likewise difficult to understand how general knowledge of the external world is possible apart from one's individual experience; and (c) given that experience is essentially private, it is difficult to understand how genuine communication between two people might be possible, since both the content and symbols of any communication will be similarly private. The egocentric predicament is often said to be an unavoidable consequence of the CARTESIAN SELF. See also SOLIPSISM.

egocentric speech speech that is apparently not directed to others or in which there is no attempt to exchange thoughts or take into account another person's point of view. According to Jean PIAGET, a child's use of egocentric speech prevails until the 7th or 8th year of age and then disappears as the child develops SOCIAL SPEECH geared to others' needs. According to Lev VYGOTSKY, however, egocentric speech is in part vocalized social speech geared to solving problems and develops into INNER LANGUAGE. Also called **private speech**.

egocentrism *n.* **1.** the tendency to emphasize one's personal needs and focus on one's individual concerns rather than those of the social unit or group to which one belongs. Also called **egocentricity**. See also EGOMANIA; IDIOCENTRIC. Compare SOCIOCENTRISM. **2.** in Jean PIAGET's theory of cognitive development, the tendency to perceive the situation from one's own perspective, believing that others see things from the same point of view as oneself and that events will elicit the same thoughts, feelings, and behavior in others as in oneself. **—egocentric** *adj.*

ego control a personality characteristic consisting of the tendency to inhibit the expression of emotional and motivational impulses, ranging from undercontrol to overcontrol of such impulses.

ego-coping skills adaptive techniques developed by an individual to deal with personal problems and environmental stresses.

ego defect in psychoanalytic theory, the absence of limitation of an EGO FUNCTION. The prime function of the ego is perception of reality and adjustment to it. An ego defect can be either the target of treatment or a deficiency that slows recovery.

ego defense in psychoanalytic theory, protection of the EGO from anxiety arising from threatening impulses and conflicts as well as external threats through the use of DEFENSE MECHANISMS.

ego-defensive function of an attitude the role an attitude can play in enhancing or maintaining the self-esteem of the person holding that attitude. For example, people may hold very positive attitudes toward social groups to which they belong as a means of maintaining their positive self-regard.

ego depletion a state marked by reduction in the self's capacity for VOLITION (initiative, choice, and SELF-REGULATION), especially in the context of SELF-REGULATORY RESOURCES THEORY. Ego depletion is typically temporary and is restored by rest or other means.

ego development 1. the infant's emerging consciousness of being a separate individual distinct from others, particularly the parents. **2.** in classical psychoanalytic theory, the process in which a part of the ID is gradually transformed into the EGO as a result of environmental demands. It involves a preconscious stage, in which the ego is partly developed, and a subsequent conscious stage, in which such ego functions as reasoning, judging, and reality testing come to fruition and help to protect the individual from internal and external threats. Also called **ego formation**. See also ID-EGO.

ego-dystonic *adj.* in psychoanalytic theory, describing impulses, wishes, or thoughts that are unacceptable or repugnant to the EGO or self. Also called **ego-alien**. Compare EGO-SYNTONIC.

ego-dystonic homosexuality the condition of being distressed about an inability to be aroused by the opposite sex. There is a sustained pattern of same-sex arousal that the person explicitly states has been unwanted and persistently distressing. The condition is frequently accompanied by feelings of loneliness, shame, anxiety, and depression. In *DSM–IV–TR* it is categorized as a SEXUAL DISORDER NOT OTHERWISE SPECIFIED.

ego formation see EGO DEVELOPMENT.

ego functions in psychoanalytic theory, the various activities of the EGO, including perception of the external world, self-awareness, problem solving, control of motor functions, adaptation to reality, memory, and reconciliation of conflicting impulses and ideas. The ego is frequently described as the executive agency of the personality, working in the interest of the REALITY PRINCIPLE. See also SECONDARY PROCESS.

ego-ideal *n.* in psychoanalytic theory, the part of the EGO that is the repository of positive identifications with parental goals and values that the individual genuinely admires and wishes to emulate, such as integrity and loyalty, and which acts as a model of how he or she wishes to be. As new identifications are incorporated in later life, the ego-ideal may develop and change. In his later theorizing, Sigmund FREUD incorporated the ego-ideal into the concept of the SUPEREGO. Also called **self-ideal**.

ego identity 1. in psychoanalytic theory, the experience of the self as a recognizable, persistent entity resulting from the integration of one's unique EGO-IDEAL, life roles, and ways of adjusting to reality. **2.** the gradual acquisition of a sense of continuity, worth, and integration that Erik ERIKSON believed to be the essential process in personality development. See ERIKSON'S EIGHT STAGES OF DEVELOPMENT. See also IDENTITY.

ego instincts in psychoanalytic theory, instincts, such as hunger, that are directed toward self-preservation. In Sigmund FREUD's early theory, the energy of the ego instincts is used by the EGO to defend against the SEXUAL INSTINCTS.

ego integration in psychoanalytic theory, the process of organizing the various aspects of the personality, such as drives, attitudes, and aims, into a balanced whole.

ego integrity versus despair see INTEGRITY VERSUS DESPAIR.

ego involvement the extent to which an ATTITUDE OBJECT is perceived as psychologically significant or important. It is presumed to be a determinant of the STRENGTH OF AN ATTITUDE. Also called **attitudinal involvement**; **personal involvement**; **self-relevance**. See also CENTRALITY OF AN ATTITUDE; IMPORTANCE OF AN ATTITUDE.

egoism *n.* a personality characteristic marked by selfishness and behavior based on self-interest with disregard for the needs of others. See also EGOTISM. **—egoistic** *adj.*

egoistic helping a form of HELPING BEHAVIOR in which the goal of the helper is to increase his or her positive feelings or to receive some other benefit. See also ALTRUISTIC BEHAVIOR.

egoistic relative deprivation see RELATIVE DEPRIVATION.

egoistic suicide an obsolescent concept in which suicide is associated with an extreme sense of alienation. [associated with the work of French sociologist Émile Durkheim (1858–1917)]

ego libido see EGO CATHEXIS.

egomania *n.* extreme, pathological preoccupation with oneself, often characterized by an exaggerated sense of one's abilities and worth. This includes the tendency to be totally self-centered, callous with regard to the needs of others, and interested only in the gratification of one's own impulses and desires. See also EGOPATHY. Compare EGOCENTRISM. **—egomaniac** *n.*

ego orientation a motivational focus on winning a game or achieving superior status in a social comparison.

Ego orientation is a component of ACHIEVEMENT GOAL THEORY.

egopathy *n.* hostile attitudes and actions stemming from an exaggerated sense of self-importance, often manifested by a compulsion to deprecate others. See also EGOMANIA.

ego psychology in psychoanalysis, an approach that emphasizes the functions of the EGO in controlling impulses and dealing with the external environment. This is in contrast to ID PSYCHOLOGY, which focuses on the primitive instincts of sex and hostility. Ego psychology differs from CLASSICAL PSYCHOANALYSIS in proposing that the ego contains a CONFLICT-FREE SPHERE of functioning and that it has its own store of energy with which to pursue goals that are independent of instinctual wishes.

Ego psychology theories extend beyond classic psychoanalytic drive theory by combining a biological and psychological view of the individual's development with a recognition of the complex influences of sociocultural dimensions on individual functioning. The scope of psychoanalysis is thereby broadened from the study of unconscious events and psychopathology to exploration of adaptive processes within the matrix of interpersonal, familial, and sociocultural forces.

ego resiliency a personality characteristic consisting of the ability to vary, in an adaptive manner, the degree to which one inhibits or expresses emotional impulses, depending on social demands.

ego resistance see REPRESSION-RESISTANCE.

ego-splitting *n.* **1.** in psychoanalytic theory, the EGO's development of opposed but coexisting attitudes toward a phenomenon, whether in the normal, neurotic, or psychotic person. In the normal context, ego-splitting can be seen in the critical attitude of the self toward the self; in neuroses, contrary attitudes toward particular behaviors are fundamental; and in psychoses, ego-splitting may produce an "observing" part of the individual that sees and can report on delusional phenomena. **2.** in the OBJECT RELATIONS THEORY of Melanie KLEIN, fragmentation of the EGO in which parts that are perceived as bad are split off from the main ego.

ego state in psychoanalytic theory, an integrated state of mind that determines the individual's relationships to the environment and to other people.

ego strength in psychoanalytic theory, the ability of the EGO to maintain an effective balance between the inner impulses of the ID, the SUPEREGO, and outer reality. An individual with a **strong ego** is thus one who is able to tolerate frustration and stress, postpone gratification, modify selfish desires when necessary, and resolve internal conflicts and emotional problems before they lead to NEUROSIS. Compare EGO WEAKNESS.

ego stress any situation, external or internal, that challenges the individual and produces stress (tension, anxiety, etc.) requiring adaptation by the EGO. Ego stress is sometimes expressed as such defensive reactions as DISSOCIATION, SOMATIZATION, or panic.

ego structure in psychoanalytic theory, the organization of the EGO.

ego suffering in psychoanalytic theory, the guilt feelings produced in the EGO by the aggressive forces in the SUPEREGO when it disapproves of the ego.

ego-syntonic *adj.* compatible with the ego or conscious SELF-CONCEPT. Thoughts, wishes, impulses, and behavior are said to be ego-syntonic when they form no threat to the ego and can be acted upon without interference from the superego. Compare EGO-DYSTONIC. [first described in 1914 by Sigmund FREUD]

egotheism *n.* identification of oneself with a deity. See also JEHOVAH COMPLEX; MESSIAH COMPLEX.

egotism *n.* excessive conceit or excessive preoccupation with one's own importance. See also EGOISM. **—egotistic** *adj.*

ego transcendence the feeling that one is beyond concern with the self and is thus able to perceive reality with less egocentric bias and greater objectivity.

ego weakness in psychoanalytic theory, the inability of the EGO to control impulses and tolerate frustration, disappointment, or stress. The individual with a **weak ego** is thus one who suffers from anxiety and conflicts, makes excessive use of DEFENSE MECHANISMS or uses immature defense mechanisms, and is likely to develop neurotic symptoms. Compare EGO STRENGTH.

EHA abbreviation for EDUCATION FOR ALL HANDICAPPED CHILDREN ACT.

eidetic image a mental image of a visual scene that is retained for a period (minutes to months) after the event. As with a real-time image, an eidetic image can be reviewed to report on its details and their relation to one another. Individuals who experience eidetic imagery are called **eidetikers**. This type of imagery is more common in children than in adults.

eigenvalue *n.* in linear algebra, the degree of stretching or shrinkage that an EIGENVECTOR of *A* undergoes as a result of the TRANSFORMATION *A* being applied to the *p*-dimensional vector space. Also called **characteristic value**.

eigenvector *n.* in linear algebra, any VECTOR in a *p*-dimensional space that is associated with a given transformation and is left invariant (except for stretching or shrinking) by the transformation. Eigenvectors are of basic importance in MULTIVARIATE statistics. Also called **characteristic vector**.

Eigenwelt *n.* in the thought of German philosopher Martin Heidegger (1889–1976), that aspect of DASEIN (human being-in-the-world) that is constituted by a person's relationship to the self. The term was introduced into the vocabulary of psychology chiefly through the work of Swiss existential psychologist Ludwig Binswanger (1881–1966). Compare MITWELT; UMWELT. [German, literally: "own world"]

eighth cranial nerve see AUDITORY NERVE; VESTIBULOCOCHLEAR NERVE.

80:20 rule see PARETO PRINCIPLE.

eikonometer *n.* **1.** an instrument for determining the magnifying power of a microscope or the size of a microscopic object. **2.** an instrument for determining the degree of ANISEIKONIA in an individual.

Einfühlung *n.* German for EMPATHY.

Einstellung *n.* **1.** a relatively inflexible mental attitude. **2.** a tendency to respond to a situation in a preconceived, stereotypical way, for example, by attempting to apply formerly successful techniques to the solution of a new problem. See also AUFGABE; DETERMINING TENDENCY; MENTAL SET; SET. [German: "attitude"]

either–or fallacy a type of informal FALLACY or persuasive technique in which an argument is constructed so as to imply the necessity of choosing one of only two alternatives. This ignores the possibility that (a) the alternatives may not be mutually exclusive and (b) there may be other equally viable alternatives. For example, the argument that the cause of behavior is either nature or nurture ignores the possibility that both might play a causal role or that human agency might also be part of the explanation.

either–or thinking a less common name for DICHOTOMOUS THINKING.

ejaculation *n.* the automatic expulsion of semen and seminal fluid through the penis resulting from involuntary and voluntary contractions of various muscle groups. See ORGASM. See also PREMATURE EJACULATION; RETROGRADE EJACULATION. **—ejaculatory** *adj.*

ejaculatio retardata excessively delayed ejaculation during sexual intercourse, usually due to psychogenic factors, aging, or the use of drugs, but also voluntary. Also called **male continence**.

ejaculatory duct a duct on either side of the prostate gland, formed by union of the VAS DEFERENS and the efferent duct of the SEMINAL VESICLE. The ejaculatory ducts converge in the prostate gland and empty into the urethra at a point below the urinary bladder.

Ekbom's syndrome a sense of uneasiness, twitching, or restlessness that occurs in the legs when at rest (i.e., sitting or lying) or after retiring for the night. The cause is unknown but it has been associated with a deficiency of iron, vitamin B_{12}, or folic acid; nerve damage associated with rheumatoid arthritis, kidney failure, or diabetes; and the use of such drugs as lithium, anticonvulsants, antidepressants, and beta blockers. Also called **restless-legs syndrome**; **tachyathetosis**; **Wittmaack–Ekbom syndrome**. [Karl-Axel **Ekbom** (1907–1977), Swedish physician]

EKG abbreviation for ELECTROCARDIOGRAM. [from German *Elektrokardiogram*]

elaborated code a linguistic REGISTER typically used in formal situations (e.g., academic discourse), characterized by a wide vocabulary, complex constructions, and unpredictable collocations of word and idea. This contrasts with the **restricted code** used in much informal conversation, which is characterized by a narrow vocabulary, simple constructions, and predictable ritualized forms, with much reliance on context and nonverbal communication to convey meaning.

elaboration *n.* **1.** the process by which information to be remembered is linked or related to information already known. See ELABORATIVE REHEARSAL. **2.** the process of developing an idea by incorporating details or relationships that amplify the original concept or by relating it to other information in memory. The LEVELS-OF-PROCESSING MODEL OF MEMORY holds that the level of elaboration applied to information as it is processed affects both the length of time that it can be retained in memory and the ease with which it can be retrieved. See ACTIVATION–ELABORATION. See also CHUNKING; DEEP PROCESSING; RECODING. **3.** the process of scrutinizing and thinking about the central merits of attitude-relevant information. This process includes generating inferences about the information, assessing its validity, and considering the implications of evaluative responses to the information. See also CENTRAL ROUTE TO PERSUASION; COGNITIVE RESPONSE; ELABORATION-LIKELIHOOD MODEL; PERIPHERAL ROUTE TO PERSUASION. **—elaborate** *vb.*

elaboration-likelihood model (**ELM**) a theory of PERSUASION postulating that attitude change occurs on a continuum of elaboration and thus, under certain conditions, may be a result of relatively extensive or relatively little scrutiny of attitude-relevant information. The theory postulates that the STRENGTH OF AN ATTITUDE depends on the amount of elaboration on which the attitude is based and proposes four possible mechanisms by which a variable may influence the persuasion process (i.e., serving as an ARGUMENT, BIASING FACTOR, DETERMINANT OF ELABORATION, or PERIPHERAL CUE). [first proposed by U.S. psychologists Richard E. Petty and John T. Cacioppo (1951–)]

elaborative rehearsal an ENCODING STRATEGY to facilitate the formation of memory by linking new information to what one already knows. For instance, when trying to remember that someone is named George, one might think of five other things one knows about people named George. See DEPTH-OF-PROCESSING HYPOTHESIS; ELABORATION.

élan vital in the thought of French philosopher Henri Bergson (1859–1941), a vital force or energy that animates living organisms, including humans, and propels life toward some end through the process of evolution. Also called **life force**. See VITALISM. [French, literally: "vital impetus"]

elation *n.* a state of extreme joy, exaggerated optimism, and restless excitement. In extreme or prolonged forms, it is a symptom of a number of disorders; in particular, it may be drug-induced or a symptom of acute MANIA, but it is also found in GENERAL PARESIS, schizophrenia, and psychosis with brain tumor. **—elated** *adj.*

Elavil *n.* a trade name for AMITRIPTYLINE.

Eldepryl *n.* a trade name for SELEGILINE.

elder abuse harm to an older adult caused by another individual. The harm can be physical (violence), sexual (nonconsensual sex), psychological (causing emotional distress), material (improper use of belongings or finances), or neglect (failure to provide needed care).

elder care the provision, often via specialized programs or facilities, of assistance to an older adult with physical, medical, mental, or functional impairments. See CAREGIVER.

elderly housing accommodation appropriate for older adults, designed to take into account the cognitive and physical changes associated with aging. Key housing features include those that enhance independence, prevent falls and other accidents, provide good lighting, and ensure ease of maintenance and care. The impact of the type and quality of housing on the satisfaction and well-being of older residents is becoming a major social concern as the number of older adults increases.

elder neglect the failure of a responsible caregiver to provide needed care to an older adult. Extreme neglect in the form of abandonment can occur when the caregiver deserts the older adult in need. See ELDER ABUSE.

elderspeak *n.* adjustments to speech patterns, such as speaking more slowly, shortening sentences, or using limited or less complex vocabulary, that are sometimes made by younger people when communicating with older adults. These simplified speech patterns are implicitly based on the assumption that older adults are cognitively impaired or incapable of understanding normal speech.

elective *n.* an educational course, chosen from a number of alternatives, that is not required for a particular program of study. Electives are optional courses that students are permitted to choose beyond their core and major requirements and typically include the fine arts, physical education, and courses from core areas outside the student's primary focus of study.

elective abortion the planned, premature termination of a pregnancy by removal of the fetus, either through surgery or the use of medication. See also ABORTION.

elective affinity a feeling of sympathy, attraction, or

connection to a particular person, thing, or idea. The term was originally used to refer to certain chemical processes but took on a new figurative sense after the publication in 1809 of *The Elective Affinities*, a novel by Johann Wolfgang von Goethe. It is often used to mean those preferences and common feelings that constitute a cultural or national identity or that distinguish groups and subgroups from one another.

elective bilingualism see ELITE BILINGUALISM.

elective mutism see SELECTIVE MUTISM.

Electra complex the female counterpart of the OEDIPUS COMPLEX, involving the daughter's love for her father, jealousy toward the mother, and blame of the mother for depriving her of a penis. Although Sigmund FREUD rejected the phrase, using the term "Oedipus complex" to refer to both boys and girls, many modern textbooks of psychology propagate the mistaken belief that Electra complex is a Freudian term. The name derives from the Greek myth of Electra, daughter of Agamemnon and Clytemnestra, who seeks to avenge her father's murder by persuading her brother Orestes to help her kill Clytemnestra and her lover Aegisthus. [defined by Carl JUNG]

electrical activity of the brain spontaneous or evoked changes in electrical brain potentials. Spontaneous electrical activity of the brain was discovered by British physiologist Richard Caton (1842–1926) and others around 1875 but not explored in detail until the development of sophisticated electronic recording devices in the 1930s. The oscillations may vary in frequency from 1 to more than 50 Hz, and from 50 to 200 mV in amplitude, as recorded by electrodes attached to the scalp. See also BRAIN WAVES.

electrical brain stimulation see INTRACRANIAL STIMULATION.

electrical intracranial stimulation see INTRACRANIAL STIMULATION.

electrical self-stimulation of the brain (**ESSB**) see INTRACRANIAL SELF-STIMULATION.

electrical stimulation the stimulation of brain areas, sensory receptors, or sensory or motor neurons by electrical or electronic devices. This is usually accomplished with the use of an electrode on a research animal but also occasionally on human volunteers undergoing brain surgery.

electrical stimulation of the cortex the use of electric charges introduced through ELECTRODES implanted in the brain cells of the cerebral cortex to produce a desired effect. In animal experiments, a reward or punishment effect depends upon the site of the electrodes and the intensity of the stimulation. Electrical stimulation of the cortex has also been used to promote recall and as therapy.

electrical synapse a type of SYNAPSE in which the presynaptic and postsynaptic membranes are not separated by a cleft but instead are joined by a GAP JUNCTION so that the nerve impulse is transmitted to the postsynaptic membrane without first being translated into a chemical message.

electrical transcranial stimulation see ELECTROSLEEP THERAPY.

electric ophthalmia see OPHTHALMIA.

electric sense the ability of some species to generate and sense electric fields within their environment. Specialized muscle cells can be coupled to generate a significant electric field, and specialized neural receptors or other organs can detect changes in electric fields. Sea lampreys and eels generate an electric current that is used to stun and disable their prey, but these animals do not appear to sense electric fields. Dogfish sharks hide in the sand and detect electric currents generated by prey using specialized receptors called **Lorenzini ampullae**. Several families of fish found in the tropics both generate and detect electric signals, adjusting signal production to avoid jamming with nearby fish and changing discharge rates to communicate aggression or reproductive status.

electric shock method the use of electricity in treating humans. See ELECTROCONVULSIVE THERAPY; ELECTROTHERAPY.

electric sink a device or region that collects or dissipates electrical energy: the opposite of an electric source.

electrocardiogram (**ECG**; **EKG**) *n.* a wavelike tracing, either printed or displayed on a monitor, that represents the electrical impulses of the conduction system of the heart muscle as it passes through a typical cycle of contraction and relaxation. The electrical currents are detected by electrodes attached to specific sites on the patient's chest, legs, and arms and recorded by an instrument, the **electrocardiograph**. In the procedure, which is called **electrocardiography**, the wave patterns of the electrocardiogram reveal the condition of the heart chambers and valves to provide an indication of cardiac problems.

electrocardiographic effect a change in the electrical activity of the heart as recorded by an electrocardiogram, especially one associated with administration of a drug. Prolongation of segments of the cardiac cycle, particularly the Q-T interval (the period of ventricular contraction), may be observed with excess doses of numerous antipsychotics and tricyclic antidepressants. A malignant form of electrocardiographic change is an arrhythmia known as **torsades de pointes** (French, literally "twisting of the points"), so called because of its characteristic outline on an electrocardiograph tracing. Torsades de pointes syndrome may result from drug interactions increasing the serum concentration of certain drugs or from an abnormal reaction to single drugs (e.g., pimozide) in susceptible individuals.

electrocochleography (**ECochG**) *n.* see ELECTROPHYSIOLOGIC AUDIOMETRY.

electroconvulsive therapy (**ECT**) a controversial treatment in which a seizure is induced by passing controlled, low-dose electric currents through one or both temples. The patient is prepared by administration of an anesthetic and injection of a muscle relaxant. An electric current is then applied for a fraction of a second through electrodes placed on the temples and immediately produces a two-stage seizure (tonic and clonic). ECT may be bilateral or unilateral (usually of the right hemisphere). Now a somewhat rare procedure, it is sometimes used with patients with severe endogenous depression who fail to respond to antidepressant drugs. Benefits are temporary, and the mechanisms of therapeutic action are unknown. Also called **electroconvulsive shock** (**ECS**); **electroconvulsive shock therapy** (**EST**); **electroshock therapy** (**EST**). See also BRIEF STIMULUS THERAPY; ECT-INDUCED AMNESIA. [introduced in 1938 by Italian psychiatrists Ugo Cerletti (1877–1963) and Lucio Bini (1908–1964)]

electrocorticogram (**ECoG**) *n.* a record of the electrical activity of the brain produced by placing electrodes directly on the cerebral cortex of the brain, rather than on the skull as in ELECTROENCEPHALOGRAPHY.

electrode *n.* an instrument with a positive-pole cathode and a negative-pole anode used to electrically stimulate biological tissues or record electrical activity in these tissues. Also called **bipolar electrode**. See also MICROELECTRODE.

electrode placement the positioning of ELECTRODES on the scalp or in NEURONS to record changes of electric potential caused by neural activity. In animal research studies and some human studies, needlelike MICROELECTRODES are placed in specific brain cells.

electrodermal changes changes in the skin that alter its electrical conductivity. See GALVANIC SKIN RESPONSE; SKIN CONDUCTANCE.

electrodermal response (**EDR**) see GALVANIC SKIN RESPONSE.

electrodiagnosis *n.* **1.** the use of electrical techniques, such as ELECTROENCEPHALOGRAPHY and ELECTROMYOGRAPHY, as diagnostic tools. **2.** the application of an electric current to nerves and muscles for diagnostic purposes.

electroencephalic audiometry see ELECTROENCEPHALOGRAPHIC AUDIOMETRY; ELECTROPHYSIOLOGIC AUDIOMETRY.

electroencephalographic audiometry the measurement of hearing sensitivity with the use of ELECTROENCEPHALOGRAPHY. Gross measures are obtained from changes in brain-wave patterns when above-threshold sound stimuli are introduced.

electroencephalography (**EEG**) *n.* a method of studying BRAIN WAVES using an instrument (**electroencephalograph** [EEG]) that amplifies and records the electrical activity of the brain through electrodes placed at various points on the skull. The resulting record (**electroencephalogram** [EEG]) of the brain-wave patterns is frequently used in studying sleep, monitoring the depth of anesthesia, diagnosing epilepsy and other brain disorders or dysfunction, and studying normal brain function. Also called **cognitive electrophysiology**. See also ELECTRICAL ACTIVITY OF THE BRAIN.

electrolyte imbalance abnormal levels of one or more **electrolytes**, the ions of chemicals that play a vital role in fluid balance, acid-base balance, and other functions of body cells. Electrolytes that may be affected include sodium, which is needed for water regulation and normal nerve and muscle function; potassium, which is necessary for acid-base balance; and calcium, which is essential for normal blood and muscle functions.

electromagnetic senses see ELECTRIC SENSE; MAGNETIC SENSE.

electromagnetic spectrum the range of wavelengths of electromagnetic radiation from gamma rays (very short waves) to radio waves (very long waves). The human eye is sensitive to only a narrow range of wavelengths of approximately 400–700 nm. See SPECTRUM.

electromyography (**EMG**) *n.* the recording (via an instrument called an **electromyograph**) of the electrical activity of muscles through electrodes placed in or on different muscle groups when they are relaxed or performing various activities. This procedure is used in the diagnosis and study of neuromuscular diseases, such as muscular dystrophy, myasthenia gravis, and spasmodic torticollis. A record of the electric potentials is called an **electromyogram**.

electronarcosis *n.* a form of ELECTROTHERAPY in which the amount of electricity, the duration of the shock, or both is sufficient to generate the tonic phase of a seizure but either limits or prevents the clonic phase. Electronarcosis is a generally less effective alternative to standard ELECTROCONVULSIVE THERAPY (ECT) and more likely to cause side effects. The technique has also been used to induce relaxation and sleep. See ELECTROSLEEP THERAPY.

electronic aid to daily living see ENVIRONMENTAL CONTROL DEVICE.

electronic brainstorming using computer-based procedures, such as online discussions and real-time e-mail communication, to generate unique ideas and solutions to problems. If such sessions are to adhere to the principles of BRAINSTORMING used in face-to-face groups, then they will explicitly encourage expressiveness, building on others' ideas and maximizing the number of ideas generated, and will discourage evaluation of any idea that is offered.

electronic bulletin board an electronic representation of a physical bulletin board viewed on a computer screen and accessed by a COMPUTER NETWORK. Messages can be posted and read on a specific board by anyone who has access to it. Generally messages are posted that would be considered of interest to the community using a given board. Another common use is for the posting of "Does anybody know . . . ?" questions.

electronic nose a device that is capable of sensing gases, especially odors. Electronic noses are used commercially to detect malodorous foodstuffs, for example, and scientifically in modeling the olfactory system.

electronystagmography *n.* a neurological test that measures movements of the eye muscles, used to confirm the presence of NYSTAGMUS. A graphical recording of eye movements is generated and is used to evaluate dizziness, vertigo, and the function of the AUDITORY NERVE and the SEMICIRCULAR CANALS.

electrooculogram (**EOG**) *n.* a graphic representation of the difference in electric potential that exists between the front and back of the eye as fixation moves between two points. The process of recording the potentials is **electrooculography**.

electroolfactogram (**EOG**) *n.* a recording of the response of olfactory nerve endings to various stimulating ODORANTS. It can be used to diagnose olfactory disorders, such as ANOSMIA, after injury or disease affecting the olfactory receptors.

electrophysiologic audiometry a large class of procedures for measuring auditory function that use electrical responses evoked by sound stimulation. Included in this class of procedures are averaged ELECTROENCEPHALOGRAPHIC AUDIOMETRY and **electrocochleography** (ECochG); responses used include the **auditory brainstem response** (ABR) and the **brainstem evoked response** (BSER).

electrophysiology *n.* the study of the electrical properties and processes of tissues. This includes such specialized subfields as electrocardiography, ELECTROENCEPHALOGRAPHY, ELECTROMYOGRAPHY, electrooculography, and electroretinography. **—electrophysiologic** or **electrophysiological** *adj.*

electroplethysmography *n.* a test or testing procedure based on the measurement of blood volume or volume changes in organs, organ systems, or circulation.

electroretinogram (**ERG**) *n.* a recording of the electrical activity of the retina during visual stimulation using electrodes placed on the anesthetized surface of the eye. Different segments of the recorded waveform correspond to activity in the different cells and layers of the retina. The process of obtaining the recording is called **electroretinography**.

electroshock therapy (**EST**) see ELECTROCONVULSIVE THERAPY; REGRESSIVE ELECTROSHOCK THERAPY.

electrosleep therapy a former treatment for depression, chronic anxiety, and insomnia by inducing a state of relaxation or sleep through low-voltage **electrical transcranial stimulation (ETS**; or **cranial electrical stimulation, CES**), a technique developed in the Soviet Union in the 1940s.

electrostimulation *n.* an aversive, or negative-reinforcement, technique involving administration of an electric shock. See also AVERSION THERAPY.

electrostimulation of the brain (ESB) electrical stimulation of a specific area of the brain to determine the functions served by that area.

electrostimulator *n.* an instrument that delivers controlled electrical stimulation to a specific area of the body.

electrotactile aid see TACTILE SENSORY AID.

electrotherapy *n.* any therapeutic measure that involves the application of an electric current to the central nervous system. See also ELECTROCONVULSIVE THERAPY.

electrotonic conduction the passive, decremental conduction of a charge along a nerve or muscle membrane. It contrasts with an actively propagated ACTION POTENTIAL. Also called **tonic conduction**. See also CABLE PROPERTIES; CONDUCTION WITH DECREMENT.

electrotonus *n.* the change in the excitability, conductivity, or electrical status of a nerve or muscle following application of an electric current.

elegant solution a solution to a question or a problem that achieves the maximally satisfactory effect with minimal effort, materials, or steps. In terms of theories or models of behavior, an elegant solution would be one that satisfies the requirements of the LAW OF PARSIMONY. See also OCCAM'S RAZOR.

element *n.* **1.** a subunit or constituent part of something, often with the connotation that it cannot be reduced further. **2.** a member of a set, class, or group. For example, in the set of all PhD-conferring American universities, any one of those American universities that confer the PhD is an element of the set. See also SET THEORY. **3.** one of the 116 officially identified chemical substances, of which 92 occur naturally, that cannot be reduced to simpler fragments by chemical means alone.

elementarism *n.* **1.** in scientific theory, the procedure of explaining a complex phenomenon by reducing it to simple, elemental units. **2.** the belief that such a procedure is appropriate to a science dealing with psychological phenomena, which are explained by reduction to simple elements, such as basic sensations or elementary reflexes. Both psychological STRUCTURALISM and BEHAVIORISM have been described as elementarist approaches. Also called **elementalism**; **elementism**. See also ATOMISM; MOLECULAR APPROACH. **—elementarist** *adj.*

elementary anxiety see PRIMORDIAL PANIC.

elementary cognitive task (ECT) a simple laboratory test designed to measure participants' response times as they perform very easy tasks and make what are presumed by the researchers to be simple decisions. Examples of elementary cognitive tasks include selecting the "odd man out" among three or more alternatives, identifying whether a single presented number (or letter) was or was not part of a previously presented set, and indicating whether or not a statement agrees with a pictorial representation. The low-level, or basic, processes measured by elementary cognitive tasks are believed to be closely related to physiological functioning and thus primarily under the influence of endogenous, inherited factors.

elementary event in probability theory, the fundamental outcome of an experiment of chance. For example, in selecting an individual from a list of eligible job candidates, the individuals who might be drawn from the list are the elementary events of the experiment.

Elementary Perceiver and Memorizer (EPAM) a computer program that reflects or models the rote learning of nonsense syllables by human beings. [created in 1963 by U.S. computer scientist Edward A. Feigenbaum (1936–)]

element-level compatibility effect see STIMULUS–RESPONSE COMPATIBILITY.

Elephant Man's disease see VON RECKLINGHAUSEN'S DISEASE.

elevated mood a heightened mood characterized by feelings of EUPHORIA, ELATION, and well-being.

elevated plus maze an apparatus used as a test of anxiety in laboratory rats and mice. It is a cross-shaped maze that is raised from the ground and has two enclosed arms and two open arms. Because of a natural fear of heights, rodents typically spend more time in the enclosed arms than in the open arms. However, if injected with anxiolytic (antianxiety) drugs, rodents will increase the amount of time they spend in the open arms.

elevation *n.* the overall level or trend of an individual's test profile.

elevator phobia a persistent and irrational fear of elevators, which may represent fear of height (ACROPHOBIA), fear of being enclosed (CLAUSTROPHOBIA), or fear of having panic symptoms in people with AGORAPHOBIA.

eleventh cranial nerve see ACCESSORY NERVE.

elfin facies see HYPERCALCEMIA SYNDROME.

elicitation *n.* the reliable production of a particular response by a stimulus. For example, salivation following food in the mouth is an example of elicitation. **—elicit** *vb.*

elicited behavior see RESPONDENT BEHAVIOR.

elimination by aspects a theory of decision making holding that a choice is reached through a series of eliminations. At each stage, the decision maker selects an attribute or aspect perceived to be important and eliminates alternatives lacking that attribute. The next most important attribute is then selected, and the process continues until only one alternative is left. [introduced in 1972 by Israeli psychologist Amos Tversky (1937–1996)]

elimination disorder any disorder related to defecation or urination, usually occurring in children (or individuals of equivalent mental age), that is not due to the use of substances or a general medical condition. In *DSM–IV–TR*, this class of disorders includes ENCOPRESIS and ENURESIS.

elimination drive the urge to expel feces or urine from the body. Psychological factors have considerable effects on these drives; for example, tension and fright may precipitate involuntary voiding of both the bladder and bowel. See BLADDER CONTROL; BOWEL CONTROL; DEFECATION REFLEX; ENCOPRESIS; ENURESIS; MICTURITION REFLEX.

eliminativism *n.* the view that mental states, such as beliefs, feelings, and intentions, are not necessary to a scientific account of human behavior. These are regarded as the stuff of FOLK PSYCHOLOGY, informal and intuitive concepts by which human beings offer accounts of their behaviors. According to the eliminativist view, when truly scientific psychology progresses far enough to replace folk psychology, the explanatory language of mental states will probably be replaced by a language of biological states. Also called **eliminative materialism**. See also IDENTITY THEORY; REDUCTIONISM. Compare CONSCIOUS MENTALISM; MENTALISM. **—eliminativist** *adj.*

elision *n.* in speech, the omission of certain sounds in particular phonological environments, as when an unstressed vowel occurs at the beginning or end of a word (e.g., *How d'you do*).

elite athlete an athlete who competes at a national, international, or professional level.

elite bilingualism a type of BILINGUALISM attained through formal study of the second language, which involves literacy in that language and is considered a sign of high social status and education. Also called **elective bilingualism**. Compare FOLK BILINGUALISM. [first described by U.S. sociolinguist Joshua A. Fishman (1926–)]

ellipsis *n.* **1.** a linguistic structure in which a word or words normally needed for reasons of grammar or logic are omitted. This may be done for the sake of brevity, emphasis, or both, as, for example, in the reply *Gone* to the question *Where is she?* See also DELETION. **2.** in psychoanalysis, a form of PARAPRAXIS involving the omission of significant ideas in FREE ASSOCIATION or DREAMS. Efforts are made to recover these ideas during analysis. **—elliptical** *adj.*

Ellis–van Creveld syndrome an AUTOSOMAL RECESSIVE disorder marked by polydactyly (extra fingers or toes), poorly formed hair, teeth, and nails, and skeletal anomalies. Associated abnormalities may include genital anomalies and mental retardation. A high incidence of the disorder is seen among the Old Order Amish of Pennsylvania. Also called **chondroectodermal dysplasia**. [Richard White Bernard **Ellis** (1902–1966), British physician; Simon **van Creveld** (1894–1971), Dutch pediatrician]

ELM abbreviation for ELABORATION-LIKELIHOOD MODEL.

elopement *n.* **1.** the act of secretly leaving home to marry without parental consent. **2.** the departure of a patient from a psychiatric hospital or unit without permission. **3.** in law enforcement, slang for the escape of an inmate.

ELSI Program the *E*thical, *L*egal, and *S*ocial *I*mplications Program of the HUMAN GENOME PROJECT. This program aims to advance the study of social, psychological, and cultural issues and problems raised by advances in the understanding of the human genome and related changes in the diagnosis and treatment of inherited susceptibility to illness. Five percent of the budget of the Human Genome Project is devoted to research in these areas.

e-mail *n.* an electronic analogue of conventional mail with such added capabilities as instant delivery, multiple addressees for the same message, electronic forwarding, and so forth. Messages are sent from one computer user to another or others, via a COMPUTER NETWORK (especially the Internet). It is also common to attach other data, such as documents and illustrations, to the message.

emancipated minor an individual who has not yet reached the legal age of adulthood (18 in most states) but who is self-supporting and exercises general control over his or her life and may claim the legal rights of an adult.

emancipation disorder a disorder of early adulthood in which the individual experiences conflict between a desire for freedom from parental control and the responsibilities of independence. Symptoms may include indecisiveness, homesickness, excessive dependence on peers, and paradoxical overdependence on parental advice. Also called **emancipation disorder of adolescence and early adulthood**.

emancipatory striving efforts to free oneself from the influence or domination of parents and to achieve a sense of independence and self-dependence. Emancipatory striving is particularly evident during adolescence.

emasculation *n.* castration or, by extension, the reduction or removal of a man's sense of MASCULINITY, as by depriving him of a culturally sanctioned male role. **—emasculate** *vb.*

embarrassment *n.* a SELF-CONSCIOUS EMOTION in which a person feels awkward or flustered in other people's company or because of the attention of others, as, for example, when being observed engaging in actions that are subject to mild disapproval from others. It often has an element of self-deprecating humor and is typically characterized by nervous laughter, a shy smile, or blushing. **—embarrassed** *adj.*

embedded figure a type of AMBIGUOUS FIGURE in which one or more images blend into a larger pattern and so are not immediately obvious. With repeated viewing the embedded figure usually becomes obvious more rapidly.

Embedded Figures Test (**EFT**) a test that consists of finding and tracing a simple form embedded within a complex figure, in some cases further complicated by an irregularly colored background. The test, for use with individuals aged 10 years and over, was designed to evaluate cognitive style, particularly FIELD DEPENDENCE and FIELD INDEPENDENCE: Those demonstrating ability in the test are defined as field-independent people, who tend to follow active, participant approaches to learning, whereas those who have difficulties in performing the test are defined as field-dependent people, who often use spectator approaches and are also more open and responsive to other people's behavior. The EFT is also employed in neuropsychological contexts, as poor performance on the test may indicate a lesion or injury in the cerebral cortex. Also called **Hidden Figures Test**. [originally developed in 1950 by U.S. psychologist Herman Allen Witkin (1916–1979)]

embeddedness of an attitude the extent to which an attitude is linked to or associated with other cognitive structures in memory. Such structures could include other attitudes, values, and BELIEFS. See also ATTITUDE SYSTEM; BELIEF SYSTEM; INTERATTITUDINAL CONSISTENCY.

embedded sentence in TRANSFORMATIONAL GENERATIVE GRAMMAR, a subordinate CLAUSE in a COMPLEX SENTENCE. According to this analysis, the complex sentence *The dog chased the squirrel that stole the peanut* has a DEEP STRUCTURE consisting of two sentences, *The dog chased the squirrel* and *The squirrel stole the peanut*. In its SURFACE STRUCTURE, the second sentence is embedded within the first.

emblem *n.* a bodily GESTURE that substitutes for a spoken word or phrase and that can be readily comprehended by most individuals in a culture. Examples are shaking the head back and forth to signify *no* and nodding the head up and down to indicate *yes*. See also NONVERBAL LANGUAGE. **—emblematic** *adj.*

embodied cognition a theory of human problem solving in which intelligent human behavior is seen as the action of a physical and emotional body-based AGENT operating in a concrete world of objects, goals, and expectations. This approach was contrasted with the more rationalist viewpoint of intelligence as an abstract power.

See SCAFFOLDING. [proposed in the 1980s by J. Lave and others]

embodiment *n.* the claim that much human thinking is a metaphorical extension of experiences of the body and its immediate surroundings. [attributable to U.S. cognitive linguist George Philip Lakoff (1941–)]

embolic stroke a STROKE caused by a blood clot, cholesterol, fibrin, or other material breaking away from the wall of an artery or the heart and traveling up the arterial tree to lodge suddenly in a smaller cerebral artery (see CEREBRAL EMBOLISM). Embolic strokes account for approximately 30% of all strokes and are abrupt in onset.

embolism *n.* the interruption of blood flow due to blockage of a vessel by an **embolus** (obstructing material) carried by the bloodstream. The embolus may be a blood clot, air bubble, fat droplet, or other substance, such as a clump of bacteria or tissue cells. An embolus usually occurs at a point where a blood vessel branches or narrows. The symptoms are those associated with a disruption of the normal flow of fresh blood to a part of an organ and include pain, numbness, and loss of body warmth in the affected area. An embolus in a coronary artery may cause a fatal heart attack, whereas in the brain the result is an EMBOLIC STROKE.

embolus *n.* see EMBOLISM; THROMBUS.

embryo *n.* an animal in the stages of development between CLEAVAGE of the fertilized egg and birth or hatching. In human prenatal development, the embryo comprises the products of conception during the first 8 weeks of pregnancy; thereafter it is called a FETUS. See EMBRYONIC STAGE. **—embryonic** *adj.*

embryology *n.* the branch of biology that studies the formation, early growth, and development of organisms. **—embryological** or **embryologic** *adj.* **—embryologist** *n.*

embryonic stage in human prenatal development, the roughly 6-week period in which the three-layered embryo (GASTRULA) develops. The embryonic stage follows the 2-week GERMINAL STAGE and precedes the FETAL STAGE, which begins in the 3rd month of pregnancy.

embryonic stem cell a type of cell, produced in the embryo during the BLASTOCYST stage of development, that has the potential to develop into any type of tissue cell. Because of this capability, many researchers believe that embryonic stem cells hold greater potential in the development of therapeutic treatments than do adult tissue STEM CELLS, which are limited in the range of cell types into which they can develop.

embryo transfer the process in which an ovum fertilized in vitro is transferred to the uterus of the woman from whom it was originally removed or to the uterus of another woman.

EMDR abbreviation for eye-movement desensitization and reprocessing (see EYE-MOVEMENT DESENSITIZATION THERAPY).

emergence *n.* **1.** in philosophy of mind, the notion that conscious experience is the result of, but cannot be reduced to, brain processes. **2.** the idea that higher order phenomena are derived from lower order phenomena but exhibit characteristics not predictable from those lower order phenomena. See EPIGENETIC THEORY.

emergency call system a portable device that summons immediate assistance for an individual who may not be able to reach a telephone in an emergency due to illness or an impairment. Such devices may be worn (e.g., on the wrist) or carried and are often used in hospitals, long-term care institutions, ASSISTED LIVING FACILITIES, and private residences. An emergency call system is generally a portable noisemaker, a one-way alerting device (e.g., an alarm), or an intercom that may be used to contact a neighbor, family member, or 24-hour monitoring station staffed by trained personnel.

emergency intervention immediate action undertaken to minimize or eliminate the harm caused by a sudden and (usually) unforeseen occurrence.

emergency psychotherapy psychological treatment of individuals who have undergone a traumatic experience (e.g., a road accident) and are in a state of acute anxiety, panic, or shock or are suicidal. Therapists may call on a very broad range of techniques depending on the immediate needs of the client. See also CRISIS INTERVENTION.

emergency reaction see FIGHT–FLIGHT REACTION.

emergency services in health care, services provided to an individual in response to perceived need for immediate medical or psychological treatment.

emergency syndrome see FIGHT–FLIGHT REACTION.

emergency theory of emotions the theory that the emotional and visceral changes controlled by the AUTONOMIC NERVOUS SYSTEM are designed to prepare individuals for fight or flight during an emergency (see FIGHT–FLIGHT REACTION). It originated as part of the CANNON–BARD THEORY of emotion. Also called **emergency theory**.

emergent evolution the theory that new phenomena evolve from an interaction of ancestral events but cannot be reduced to them.

emergent features the interaction of small or simple elements (e.g., short line segments) in the visual system to produce an entity that is more salient to human perception (e.g., a polygon) than are the elements themselves. In ergonomics, OBJECT DISPLAYS are usually designed to make use of emergent features; the display configurations yield an overall image (e.g., a rectangle or pentagon) that can be perceived holistically by the operator and therefore rapidly analyzed to assess the state of the system. When a component of the system is not in the appropriate or normal state, the image will be distorted, alerting the operator to potential problems.

emergentism *n.* the view that complex phenomena and processes have EMERGENT PROPERTIES that arise from interactions of the more basic processes that underlie them but cannot be deduced or explained from the nature and logic of these processes. Compare REDUCTIONISM.

emergent leader an individual who becomes the leader of an initially leaderless group, not by appointment or by election but gradually and implicitly as the members allow that individual to assume the responsibilities of the leadership role. See also LEADERSHIP EMERGENCE.

emergent literacy the skills, knowledge, and attitudes that are presumed to be developmental precursors to conventional forms of reading and writing. Emergent literacy begins before the child receives formal instruction in reading and writing and occurs in environments that support these developments, as when, for example, the child is being read to.

emergent-norm theory an explanation of COLLECTIVE BEHAVIOR suggesting that the uniformity in behavior often observed in such collectives as CROWDS and CULTS is caused by members' conformity to unique standards of behavior (norms) that develop spontaneously in those groups. See CONTAGION; UNIVERSALITY.

emergent property a characteristic of a complex system that is not implicit in or predictable from an analysis of the components or elements that make it up. For example, it has been said that the fluid state of water is an emergent property not predicted from the gaseous states of its two components, hydrogen and oxygen, and that conscious experience is not explicable by analysis of the brain.

emetic therapy the use of drugs that produce aversive states when combined with problem behaviors or stimuli. Side effects of the drugs used and other issues with regard to this form of treatment limit its application. See AVERSION THERAPY.

EMG abbreviation for ELECTROMYOGRAPHY.

emic *adj.* **1.** denoting an approach to the study of human cultures that interprets behaviors and practices in terms of the system of meanings created by and operative within a particular cultural context. Such an approach would generally be of the kind associated with ETHNOGRAPHY rather than ETHNOLOGY. Compare ETIC. [introduced by U.S. linguist Kenneth Pike (1912–2000); first used in anthropology by U.S. cultural anthropologist Marvin Harris (1927–2001)] **2.** denoting an approach to the study of language based on PHONEMICS (i.e., the study of the system of speech sounds that creates distinctions of meaning in a particular language) as opposed to PHONETICS (i.e., the study of human speech sounds generally).

emic–etic distinction 1. a distinction between two fundamentally different approaches to language analysis, one characteristic of PHONEMICS and the other of PHONETICS. An **emic analysis** puts primacy on the characterization of a particular language through close attention to those features that have a meaningful structural significance within it. By contrast, an **etic analysis** concentrates on universal features of language, particularly the acoustic properties of speech sounds and the physiological processes involved in making them. To illustrate the point, an emic analysis of English speech sounds would show interest in the difference between the sounds /r/ and /l/ because this is used to make meaningful distinctions (e.g., it differentiates the words *rash* and *lash*); an emic analysis of Japanese, however, would disregard this difference in sounds, as it is not a meaningful contrast in that language. An etic analysis would show the same interest in this feature in both languages. See also MINIMAL PAIR. **2.** the distinction between EMIC and ETIC approaches in anthropology and related disciplines.

emitted behavior a natural response to a circumstance, that is, behavior that is not influenced by, or dependent on, any external stimuli. Compare RESPONDENT BEHAVIOR.

Emmert's law the principle that the size of an afterimage or eidetic image increases with the distance between the image and the ground on which it is projected. [Emil **Emmert** (1844–1913), German physiologist]

emmetropism *n.* the state of the eye's normal optical system, in which distant objects are sharply focused on the retina by the curvature of the cornea and the lens. This normal optical system is said to be **emmetropic**. Also called **emmetropia**. Compare HYPEROPIA; MYOPIA.

emotion *n.* a complex reaction pattern, involving experiential, behavioral, and physiological elements, by which the individual attempts to deal with a personally significant matter or event. The specific quality of the emotion (e.g., FEAR, SHAME) is determined by the specific significance of the event. For example, if the significance involves threat, fear is likely to be generated; if the significance involves disapproval from another, shame is likely to be generated. Emotion typically involves FEELING but differs from feeling in having an overt or implicit engagement with the world. **—emotional** *adj.*

emotional abuse nonphysical abuse. This may involve verbal abuse, demeaning or shaming the victim, emotional control, or withholding of affection or financial support, or any combination of these. Also called **psychological abuse**.

emotional adjustment the ability to maintain a balance in the emotional aspects of life, to exert reasonable control over one's emotions, and to express emotions that are appropriate to a given situation.

emotional blocking the inhibition of thought, speech, or other responses due to extreme emotion, often associated with extreme fear. See also BLOCKING.

emotional charge strong emotion, such as anger, conceived as being bottled up under pressure and ready to explode. The concept also involves the idea that emotions are negatively or positively charged.

emotional cognition the ability to recognize and interpret the emotions of others, notably from such cues as facial expression and voice tone, and to interpret one's own feelings correctly. Impairment of emotional cognition is associated with a range of psychological conditions, notably ASPERGER'S DISORDER.

emotional conflict a state of disharmony between incompatible intense emotions, such as love and hate or the desire for success and fear of failure, that causes distress to the individual.

emotional contagion the rapid spread of an emotion from one or a few individuals to others. For example, fear of catching a disease can spread rapidly through a community. See also BEHAVIORAL CONTAGION; CONTAGION; MASS CONTAGION.

emotional content themes or characteristics of feelings that tend to elicit strong emotions, especially as they are portrayed in various forms of communication (reading material, motion pictures, etc.) or as they are manifested in specific situations.

emotional control self-regulation of the influence that one's emotions have on one's thoughts and behavior.

emotional dependence dependence on others for emotional support, comfort, and nurturance.

emotional deprivation lack of adequate warmth, affection, and interest, especially on the part of the primary caregiver during a child's developmental years. It is common in situations involving separation from the primary caregiver, CHILD NEGLECT, CHILD ABUSE, and INSTITUTIONALIZATION.

emotional deterioration an emotional state characterized by carelessness toward oneself, indifference to one's surroundings, including other people, and inappropriate emotional reactions.

emotional development a gradual increase in the capacity to experience, express, and interpret the full range of emotions. For example, infants begin to smile and frown around 8 weeks of age and to laugh around 3 or 4 months. Expressions of delight, fear, anger, and disgust are evident by 6 months of age, and fear of strangers from 8 months. Expressions of affection and jealousy are seen between 1 and 2 years of age, and expressions of rage in the form of temper tantrums appear a year or so later. Cortical control, imitation of others, hormonal influences, home atmosphere, and conditioning play major roles in emotional development. Also called **affective development**.

emotional disorder 1. any psychological disorder

characterized primarily by maladjustive emotional reactions that are inappropriate or disproportionate to reality. Also called **emotional illness**. See also AFFECTIVE DISORDER; MOOD DISORDER. **2.** loosely, any mental disorder.

emotional disposition a tendency to have a particular type or class of affective experience (e.g., POSITIVE AFFECT or NEGATIVE AFFECT).

emotional dissemblance lack of correspondence between an individual's internal AFFECTIVE STATE and its outward expression. There are two broad categories of emotional dissemblance: culturally acceptable DISPLAY RULES and nonverbal or verbal deception.

emotional divorce a marital relationship in which the partners live separate lives, with an absence of normal interaction between them.

emotional engineering see KANSEI ENGINEERING.

emotional expression 1. an outward manifestation of an intrapsychic state. For example, a high-pitched voice is a sign of AROUSAL, blushing is a sign of EMBARRASSMENT, and so on. See also AFFECT DISPLAY. **2.** an emotional response in which the individual attempts to influence his or her relation to the world through the intermediacy of others, rather than directly. For example, a sad face and slumped posture elicit nurturing from others. Expressions differ from ACTION TENDENCIES, which influence the world directly, and from FEELINGS, which are intrapsychic experiences of the significance of a transaction.

emotional flatness see FLAT AFFECT.

emotional flooding a lay term, not used in current psychological or medical literature, for an influx of great and uncontrollable emotion that may be overwhelming to the person who experiences it.

emotional handicap a learning or behavioral disorder grounded in fears and anxieties that prevent a child from functioning socially or academically in a regular classroom setting.

emotional illness see EMOTIONAL DISORDER.

emotional immaturity 1. a tendency to express emotions without restraint or disproportionately to the situation. Compare EMOTIONAL MATURITY. **2.** a lay term for MALADJUSTMENT.

emotional incest a form of child SEXUAL ABUSE consisting of nonphysical sexualized interactions between parent figures and a child in their care. Emotional incest may involve the parent commenting on the child's sexual attractiveness, the parent's own arousal to the child, or the size or shape of the child's secondary sexual characteristics (e.g., breasts, pubic hair), or implying that the child is sexually active (e.g., calling a child a slut).

emotional inoculation the imagining, practicing, or COGNITIVE REHEARSAL of an anxiety-producing experience. Rehearsal lowers anxiety by allowing the individual to anticipate reactions and plan responses.

emotional insight 1. an awareness of one's own emotional reactions or those of others. **2.** in PSYCHOTHERAPY, the client's awareness of the emotional forces, such as internal conflicts or traumatic experiences, that underlie his or her symptoms. This form of insight is considered a prerequisite to change in many therapeutic approaches.

emotional instability a tendency to exhibit unpredictable and rapid changes in emotions. See AFFECTIVE LABILITY.

emotional insulation a defense mechanism characterized by seeming indifference and detachment in response to frustrating situations or disappointing events. The extreme of emotional insulation is found in states of complete apathy and catatonic stupor; in lesser forms it appears as **emotional isolation**.

emotional intelligence a type of intelligence that involves the ability to process emotional information and use it in reasoning and other cognitive activities, proposed by U.S. psychologists Peter Salovey (1958–) and John D. Mayer (1953–). According to Mayer and Salovey's 1997 model, it comprises four abilities: to perceive and appraise emotions accurately; to access and evoke emotions when they facilitate cognition; to comprehend emotional language and make use of emotional information; and to regulate one's own and others' emotions to promote growth and well-being. Their ideas were popularized in a best-selling book by U.S. psychologist and science journalist Daniel J. Goleman (1946–), who also altered the definition to include many personality variables. See also EMOTIONAL INTELLIGENCE QUOTIENT.

emotional intelligence quotient an index of EMOTIONAL INTELLIGENCE. Popular writers and the media sometimes abbreviate the term to **EQ** (for emotional quotient, nominally similar to IQ).

emotional isolation see EMOTIONAL INSULATION.

emotionality *n.* the degree to which an individual experiences and expresses emotions, irrespective of the quality of the emotional experience.

emotionally based persuasion see AFFECTIVELY BASED PERSUASION.

emotional maturity a high and appropriate level of emotional control and expression. Compare EMOTIONAL IMMATURITY.

emotional quotient see EMOTIONAL INTELLIGENCE QUOTIENT.

emotional reeducation PSYCHOTHERAPY focused on modifying the client's attitudes, feelings, and reactions by helping the client gain greater insight into emotional conflicts and self-defeating behavior arising from affective disturbance or disorder. Typical objectives are an increase in self-confidence, sociability, and self-reliance. The methods used include group discussions, personal counseling, relationship therapy, and self-exploration.

emotional regulation the ability of an individual to modulate an EMOTION or set of emotions. Techniques of conscious emotional regulation can include learning to construe situations differently in order to manage them better, changing the target of an emotion (e.g., anger) in a way likely to produce a more positive outcome, and recognizing how different behaviors can be used in the service of a given emotional state. Emotional regulation typically increases across the life span.

emotional release the CATHARSIS or sudden outpouring of emotions that have been pent up or suppressed.

emotional response an emotional reaction, such as happiness, fear, or sadness, to a given stimulus.

emotional security the feeling of safety, confidence, and freedom from apprehension. In the approach of German-born U.S. psychoanalyst Karen D. Horney (1885–1952), the need for emotional security is the underlying determinant of personality and behavior; in the approach of U.S. psychoanalyst Harry Stack Sullivan (1892–1949), it is itself determined primarily by interpersonal relations. See also SECURITY OPERATIONS.

emotional stability predictability and consistency in emotional reactions, with absence of rapid mood changes. Compare AFFECTIVE LABILITY.

emotional stress the feeling of psychological strain

and uneasiness produced by situations of danger, threat, and loss of personal security or by internal conflicts, frustrations, loss of self-esteem, and grief. Also called **emotional tension**.

emotional stupor a form of affective stupor marked by depression or intense anxiety and accompanied by mutism.

emotional support reassurance, encouragement, understanding, empathy, and approval received from an individual or group. It may be a major factor contributing to the effectiveness of SELF-HELP GROUPS, within which members both provide and receive emotional support.

emotional tension see EMOTIONAL STRESS.

emotion-focused coping a type of COPING STRATEGY that focuses on regulating negative emotional reactions to a stressor, as opposed to taking actions to change the stressor. Emotion-focused coping may include social withdrawal, disengagement, and acceptance of the situation. Also called **passive coping**. See also SECONDARY COPING. Compare PROBLEM-FOCUSED COPING.

emotion-focused couples therapy a form of COUPLES THERAPY that is based on the premise that relationship problems are most often due to thwarted fulfillment of emotional needs, particularly the need for attachment. This intervention involves isolating the conflict regarding thwarted needs, interrupting the negative interaction cycle, reframing the conflict, and accepting the emotional experience of one's partner as valid.

emotion-focused therapy an integrative INDIVIDUAL THERAPY that focuses on emotion as the key determinant of personality development and of psychotherapeutic change. In sessions, the therapist helps the client to become aware of, accept, make sense of, and regulate emotions as a way of resolving problems and promoting growth. Techniques are drawn from CLIENT-CENTERED THERAPY, GESTALT THERAPY, and COGNITIVE BEHAVIOR THERAPY. A principal proponent of this approach is South African-born Canadian psychologist Leslie S. Greenberg (1945–).

emotive *adj.* related to or arousing emotion.

emotive imagery in behavior therapy and cognitive behavior therapy, a procedure in which the client imagines emotion-arousing scenes while relaxing in a comfortable, protective setting. See RECIPROCAL INHIBITION.

emotive technique any of various therapeutic techniques designed to encourage clients to express their thoughts and feelings in an intense and animated manner so as to make these more obvious and available for discussion in therapy. Emotive techniques are used, for example, in RATIONAL EMOTIVE BEHAVIOR THERAPY in attempts to dispute irrational beliefs in order to move from intellectual to emotional insight.

empathy *n.* understanding a person from his or her frame of reference rather than one's own, so that one vicariously experiences the person's feelings, perceptions, and thoughts. Empathy does not, of itself, entail motivation to be of assistance, although it may turn into SYMPATHY or personal distress, which may result in action. In psychotherapy, therapist empathy for the client can be a path to comprehension of the client's cognitions, affects, or behaviors. **—empathic** or **empathetic** *adj.* **—empathize** *vb.*

empathy–altruism helping a theory that explains ALTRUISTIC BEHAVIORS as resulting from feelings of empathy and compassion toward others.

empathy training 1. a systematic procedure to increase empathetic feeling and communications in an individual. **2.** help given to convicted abusers to enable them to envision their victims' feelings and become sensitive to the pain they have caused, with the aim of decreasing the likelihood that they will commit similar crimes in the future.

empirical *adj.* **1.** derived from or denoting experimentation or systematic observations as the basis for conclusion or determination, as opposed to speculative, theoretical, or exclusively reason-based approaches. **2.** based on experience.

empirical construct see CONSTRUCT.

empirical-criterion keying a method used in selecting questions for personality inventories, in which the items are chosen and weighted according to an external criterion, such as the responses of individuals who belong to identifiable groups (e.g., patients with mental illness, people having the same occupation) as compared to a standardization sample.

empirical grounding the practice or procedure of anchoring theoretical terms to scientifically measurable or observable events. The extent to which this is possible for a particular theory is a measure of the value of that theory. See OPERATIONAL DEFINITION.

empirical knowledge 1. in philosophy, knowledge gained from experience, rather than from INNATE IDEAS or DEDUCTIVE REASONING. **2.** in the sciences, knowledge gained from experiment and observation rather than from theory. See EMPIRICISM.

empirical law a law that is based on facts, experimental evidence, or systematic observations and expresses a general relationship between variables, as opposed to a law based only on theory.

empirically derived test a test developed using content, criterion, or construct validation procedures or a combination of these.

empirically keyed test a test in which answers are coded in such a way as to maximize CRITERION VALIDITY, CONSTRUCT VALIDITY, or both. See also EMPIRICAL-CRITERION KEYING.

empirical method any method of conducting an investigation that relies upon experimentation and systematic observations rather than theoretical speculation.

empirical psychology an approach to the study and explanation of psychological phenomena that emphasizes objective observation (see OBSERVATIONAL METHOD) and the EXPERIMENTAL METHOD as the source of information about the phenomena under consideration. Compare RATIONAL PSYCHOLOGY. See also EXPERIMENTAL PSYCHOLOGY.

empirical-rational strategy in social psychology, the idea that societal and institutional change can be brought about if the public receives enough convincing factual evidence. The concept holds that reason alone can motivate people to change their attitudes. See also NORMATIVE-REEDUCATIVE STRATEGY; POWER-COERCIVE STRATEGY.

empirical self the SELF that is known by the self, rather than the self as knower. In the psychology of William JAMES, the empirical self is held to consist of the **material self** (everything material that can be seen as belonging to the self), the SOCIAL SELF (the self as perceived by others), and the **spiritual self** (the self that is closest to one's core subjective experience of oneself). The empirical self (or "me") is contrasted with the NOMINATIVE SELF (or "I").

empirical test the test of a hypothesis by means of experiments or other systematic observations.

empirical validity VALIDITY based on experimentation and systematic observation rather than on theory alone.

empiricism *n.* **1.** an approach to EPISTEMOLOGY holding that all knowledge of matters of fact either arises from experience or requires experience for its validation. In particular, empiricism denies the possibility of INNATE IDEAS, arguing that the mind at birth is like a blank sheet of paper (see TABULA RASA CONCEPT). During the 17th and 18th centuries, empiricism was developed as a systematic approach to philosophy in the work of such British philosophers as John Locke (1632–1704), George Berkeley (1685–1753), and David Hume (1711–1776). These thinkers also developed theories of ASSOCIATIONISM to explain how even the most complex mental concepts can be derived from simple sense experiences. Although there is a strong emphasis on empiricism in psychology, this can take different forms. Some approaches to psychology hold that sensory experience is the origin of all knowledge and thus, ultimately, of personality, character, beliefs, emotions, and behavior. BEHAVIORISM is the purest example of empiricism in this sense. Advocates of other theoretical approaches to psychology, such as PHENOMENOLOGY, argue that the definition of experience as only sensory experience is too narrow; this enables them to reject the position that all knowledge arises from the senses, while also claiming to adhere to a type of empiricism. **2.** the view that experimentation is the most important, if not the only, foundation of scientific knowledge and the means by which individuals evaluate truth claims or the adequacy of theories and models. **3.** in philosophy, the position that all linguistic expressions that are not tautologous must be empirically verifiable if they are to be deemed valid or meaningful. This principle was essential to the philosophy of LOGICAL POSITIVISM. See also POSITIVISM; VERIFICATION. **—empiricist** *adj., n.*

empiric-risk figure in genetic counseling, a percentage representing the risk for common disorders, such as schizophrenia and depression, when there is evidence of genetic factors of unknown mechanism. The figure is based upon reports of frequency of occurrence in large series of families (in addition to the approximately 3% risk of mental retardation or birth defects that every couple takes when having a child).

employee appraisal see EMPLOYEE EVALUATION.

employee assistance program (EAP) a designated formal function within an organization that is responsible for helping individual employees with personal problems that affect their job performance (e.g., substance abuse, family difficulties, or emotional problems). EAPs usually refer employees to outside consultants who provide the services required to deal with these problems.

employee comparison technique any method of EMPLOYEE EVALUATION in which the performance of one employee is compared with that of others, rather than considered in absolute terms. Examples include the RANKING METHOD, the FORCED DISTRIBUTION method, and the PAIRED COMPARISON method.

employee evaluation the judgment of an employee's overall JOB PERFORMANCE and of certain related personal characteristics (e.g., ability to get on with colleagues) that may be relevant. Employee evaluation is usually performed by a superior or consultant. Also called **employee appraisal**; **work evaluation**. See CRITERION DIMENSIONS; JOB CRITERION; PERFORMANCE REVIEW.

Employee Retirement Income Security Act (ERISA) a federal act, passed in 1974, that established new standards for qualified, private-sector, employer-funded pension and welfare benefits plans within the United States, providing protection for beneficiaries.

employee training see PERSONNEL TRAINING.

employment counseling counseling designed to help an individual with issues related to work, such as job seeking, work compatibility, outside pressures interfering with job performance, termination of employment, and work efficiency. Within an organization, employment counseling is often provided through an EMPLOYEE ASSISTANCE PROGRAM.

employment discrimination an employer's use of a person's ethnicity, color, age, religion, gender, sexual orientation, national origin, disability, or other variable unrelated to job qualifications or performance as a factor in differential pay, hiring practices, termination of employment, or working conditions.

employment interview an interview with an applicant for a job, in which a personnel worker, executive, or supervisor (a) imparts information and answers questions about the company, including its products, working conditions, and benefits offered, (b) describes the job or jobs in which the applicant is interested, and (c) obtains information about the applicant that will contribute to a judgment of his or her suitability for a job or jobs. The information obtained will usually include an impression of the candidate's personality, motivation level, and verbal, interpersonal, and other skills as demonstrated in the interview. See PATTERNED INTERVIEW; STRUCTURED INTERVIEW; UNSTRUCTURED INTERVIEW. Also called **job interview**.

employment psychology see INDUSTRIAL AND ORGANIZATIONAL PSYCHOLOGY.

employment test an instrument used to assess the KNOWLEDGE, SKILLS, ABILITIES, AND OTHER CHARACTERISTICS of applicants so as to predict their performance in a job. A test, as opposed to an inventory, has right and wrong answers and can be used to measure a variety of attributes such as intelligence, mechanical aptitude, sensory and motor abilities, and physical abilities. See SELECTION TEST. See also INTEGRITY TESTING; OCCUPATIONAL TEST; PERSONNEL TEST; WORK-SAMPLE TEST.

empowerment *n.* **1.** the promotion of the skills, knowledge, and confidence necessary to take greater control of one's life, as in certain educational or social schemes. In psychotherapy, the process involves helping clients become more active in meeting their needs and fulfilling their desires. Empowerment provides a client with a sense of achievement and realization of his or her own abilities and ambitions. See also ENABLING. **2.** the delegation of increased decision-making powers to individuals or groups in a society or organization. **—empower** *vb.*

empowerment evaluation see PARTICIPATORY EVALUATION.

empty-chair technique a technique originating in GESTALT THERAPY in which the client conducts an emotional dialogue with some aspect of himself or herself or some significant person in his or her life (e.g., a parent), who is imagined to be sitting in an empty chair during the session. The client then exchanges chairs and takes the role of that aspect or of that other person. This technique is now sometimes also referred to as the **two-chair technique**.

empty nest the family home after the children have reached maturity and left, often creating an emotional void (**empty nest syndrome**) in the lives of the parents (**empty nesters**).

empty organism psychology a behavioral psychology that attempts to predict and control behavior on the basis of external, observable stimulus and reinforcement conditions. Empty organism psychologies are so named because they do not hypothesize internal processes or theoretical constructs to explain behavior.

empty set a SET with no elements. Also called **null set**.

empty speech fluent speech that lacks information or meaningful content.

empty word see FUNCTION WORD.

empyreumatic *adj.* in the ZWAARDEMAKER SMELL SYSTEM, denoting an odor quality that is smelled in roasted coffee and creosote.

EMR abbreviation for EDUCABLE MENTALLY RETARDED.

emulation *n.* the ability to comprehend the goal of a model and engage in similar behavior to achieve that goal, without necessarily replicating the specific actions of the model. Emulation facilitates SOCIAL LEARNING.

enabler *n.* a person, often an intimate partner or good friend, who passively permits or unwittingly encourages negative behavior in an individual, such as abusing a child or maintaining an addiction. Often, the enabler is aware of the destructiveness of the negative behavior but feels powerless to prevent it.

enabling *n.* **1.** the process of encouraging or allowing individuals to meet their own needs and achieve desired ends. A therapist attempts to enable clients to believe in themselves, have the confidence to act on their desires, and affirm their ability to achieve. See also EMPOWERMENT. **2.** a process whereby someone unwittingly or knowingly contributes to continued maladaptive or pathological behavior in another person, such as one with substance dependence. See also ENABLER.

enaction *n.* the process of putting something into action. The word is preferred to terms like execution, which have computing or machine-based connotations. Enaction thus involves guidance and support; it does not imply complete automation. Much of the literature on process modeling states that models should be **enactable**.

enactive mode the way in which a child first comes to know his or her environment through physical interaction (e.g., touching and manipulating objects, crawling). The enactive mode is knowing through doing, whereas the ICONIC MODE is knowing through mental images, and the SYMBOLIC MODE is knowing through language and logic. Also called **enactive stage**. [proposed by U.S. developmental psychologist Jerome Seymour Bruner (1915–)]

enactive representation representation of objects and events through action and movement, which is characteristic of infants and small children. That is, the child understands things in terms of how they can be manipulated, used, or acted upon. See ENACTIVE MODE. [proposed by U.S. developmental psychologist Jerome Seymour Bruner (1915–)]

enactive stage see ENACTIVE MODE.

enactment *n.* the acting out of an important life event, rather than expressing it in words. See also PSYCHODRAMA.

enantiodromia *n.* **1.** the conception of Greek philosopher Heraclitus (c. 535–c. 475 BCE) that all things eventually turn into, or are replaced by, their opposite. **2.** in the approach of Carl JUNG, the "necessary opposition" that governs psychic life, as in the interplay between conscious and unconscious, introverted and extraverted tendencies, and the EGO and SHADOW.

encapsulated delusion a delusion that does not significantly affect the person's functioning or everyday behavior.

encapsulated end organ the terminal portion of a sensory nerve fiber, usually located in peripheral tissue, such as the skin, and enclosed in a membranous sheath. Kinds of encapsulated end organs include MEISSNER'S CORPUSCLES, which are sensitive to touch; and PACINIAN CORPUSCLES, which are sensitive to pressure.

encapsulation *n.* **1.** the process of separating or keeping separate, particularly the ability of some people experiencing delusions to maintain high levels of functioning and prevent their delusions from pervading everyday behavior and cognitive states. **2.** enclosure, as in a sheath or other covering.

encéphale isolé an animal whose brainstem has been transected in the region where the spinal cord meets the brain. Such an animal is alert but paralyzed. See also CERVEAU ISOLÉ. [French, "isolated brain"]

encephalitis *n.* inflammation of the brain, typically caused by viral infection. The symptoms may be mild, with influenza-like characteristics, or severe and potentially fatal, with fever, vomiting, confusion or disorientation, drowsiness, seizures, and loss of consciousness or coma. See also ENCEPHALITIS LETHARGICA; HERPES-SIMPLEX ENCEPHALITIS; MENINGOENCEPHALITIS; POLIOENCEPHALITIS. **—encephalitic** *adj.*

encephalitis lethargica an epidemic form of ENCEPHALITIS that was observed globally between 1915–1926 and believed to be of viral origin (it appeared following an influenza pandemic of 1914–1918). Symptoms include pathological sleepiness and drowsiness, apathy, and ocular paralysis. Also called **Economo's disease**; **von Economo's disease**.

encephalization *n.* the transfer of cognitive functions from phylogenetically more primitive brain areas to cerebral centers during evolution; that is, the increased control of neural functions by the CEREBRAL CORTEX in the most recently evolved animals, which have larger brains. Also called **corticalization**. See EVOLUTION OF THE BRAIN.

encephalocele *n.* a congenital hernia (see HERNIATION) of the brain, which protrudes through a cleft in the skull.

encephalofacial angiomatosis see STURGE–WEBER SYNDROME.

encephalomalacia *n.* softening of the brain, usually due to tissue deterioration resulting from an inadequate blood supply to the area.

encephalomyelitis *n.* inflammation of the brain and spinal cord. As with ENCEPHALITIS, it is most often caused by viral infection.

encephalon *n.* see BRAIN.

encephalopathy *n.* any of various diffuse disorders or diseases of the brain that alter brain function or structure and are characterized primarily by altered mental states, especially confusion.

encephalopsy *n.* a condition in which one associates colors with numbers, letters, smells, or other dimensions.

encoding *n.* **1.** the conversion of a sensory input into a form capable of being processed and deposited in memory. Encoding is the first stage of memory processing, followed by RETENTION and then RETRIEVAL. **2.** in communications, the conversion of messages or data into codes or signals capable of being carried by a communication channel.

encoding specificity principle the principle that RETRIEVAL of memory is optimal when the retrieval conditions (such as context or cues present at the time of retrieval) duplicate the conditions that were present when the memory was formed. [proposed in 1983 by Estonian-born Canadian psychologist Endel Tulving (1927–)]

encoding strategy a mental or behavioral strategy that one may use to ensure learning or remembering, such as ELABORATIVE REHEARSAL, mental imagery, or a MNEMONIC STRATEGY.

encopresis *n.* repeated voluntary or involuntary defecation in inappropriate places (clothing, floor, etc.) that occurs after the age of 4 (or the equivalent MENTAL AGE) and is not due to a substance (e.g., a laxative) or to a general medical condition. Encopresis may or may not be accompanied by constipation and is often associated with poor toilet training and stressful situations. Also called **functional encopresis**. Compare FECAL INCONTINENCE.

encounter *n.* a direct confrontation or other emotional involvement of one individual with another or between several members of a group.

encounter group a group of individuals in which constructive insight, sensitivity to others, and personal growth are promoted through direct interactions on an emotional and social level. The leader functions as a catalyst and facilitator rather than a therapist and focuses on here-and-now feelings and interaction, rather than on theory or individual motivation.

encounter movement a trend toward the formation of small groups in which various techniques, such as CONFRONTATION, GAMES, and REENACTMENT, are used to stimulate awareness, personality growth, and productive interactions. The movement gained popularity in the 1960s but diminished at the end of the 20th century.

encourager *n.* see RELATIONSHIP ROLE.

enculturation *n.* **1.** the processes, beginning in early childhood, by which particular cultural values, ideas, beliefs, and behavioral patterns are instilled in the members of a society. Compare ACCULTURATION. See also CULTURAL HERITAGE; SOCIAL TRANSMISSION. **2.** in anthropology, the rearing of great apes in an environment that includes frequent contact with humans and their artifacts and, usually, human–ape interactions, such as direct teaching, the use of language, and JOINT ATTENTION. Some investigators have suggested that enculturated great apes may show aspects of social cognitive development that are more like those of children than of mother- or nursery-reared apes. **—enculturate** *vb.*

endarterectomy *n.* a surgical procedure in which atherosclerotic plaque is removed from an artery, most commonly the carotid artery at the level of bifurcation in the neck. By removing the plaque, the bore of the artery is enlarged, allowing a greater flow of blood to the brain and thus decreasing the risk of stroke.

end brush the finely branched terminal of an axon (see AXON TERMINAL). Also called **telodendron**.

end button see TERMINAL BUTTON.

endemic *adj.* peculiar to a specific region, nation, or people. The term often denotes a disease, but is also applied to customs or folkways. Compare EPIDEMIC; PANDEMIC.

end feet the terminal processes of an AXON or an ASTROCYTE.

endo- (**end-**) *combining form* inside or internal.

endocarditis *n.* inflammation of the **endocardium**, the inner lining of the heart, often involving the valves. Causes include bacterial or fungal infections (e.g., syphilis, tuberculosis, staphylococcus) and occasionally a rickettsial invasion of the heart valves following an infection of Q fever. See also BACTERIAL ENDOCARDITIS.

endocast *n.* a cast of the cranial cavity of a skull. It is especially useful for studying the size and form of brains of fossils of extinct species.

endocathection *n.* the inward focusing of PSYCHIC ENERGY and withdrawal from external pursuits. Compare EXOCATHECTION. See CATHEXIS. [defined by U.S. psychologist Henry Alexander Murray (1893–1988)]

endocochlear potential see ENDOLYMPHATIC POTENTIAL.

endocrine *adj.* describing or relating to a type of chemical signaling in which a chemical messenger is released by a cell and is carried (e.g., via the bloodstream) to a distant target cell, on which it exerts its effect. Compare AUTOCRINE; PARACRINE.

endocrine gland a gland that secretes HORMONES directly into the bloodstream to act on distant targets. Such glands include the PITUITARY GLAND, ADRENAL GLAND, THYROID GLAND, gonads (TESTIS and OVARY), and ISLETS OF LANGERHANS. Also called **ductless gland**. Compare EXOCRINE GLAND.

endocrine system the set of ENDOCRINE GLANDS, which synthesize and secrete HORMONES into the bloodstream.

endocrinology *n.* the study of the morphology, physiology, biochemistry, and pathology of the ENDOCRINE GLANDS. See also NEUROENDOCRINOLOGY. **—endocrinological** *adj.* **—endocrinologist** *n.*

endoderm *n.* the innermost of the three primary GERM LAYERS of a developing embryo. It gives rise to the gastrointestinal and respiratory tracts and some glands. **—endodermal** *adj.*

end of life the variable period during which individuals and their families, friends, and caregivers face issues and decisions related to the imminent prospect of death. The end-of-life concept is a way of considering the total context of an approaching death, rather than medical factors only. End-of-life issues include decisions relating to the nature of terminal care (hospice or traditional), whether or not to resuscitate, the distribution of property and assets, funeral and memorial arrangements, and leave taking and possible reconciliations with family and friends. See also ADVANCE DIRECTIVE; INFORMED CONSENT.

endogamy *n.* the custom or practice of marrying within one's KINSHIP NETWORK, CASTE, or religious or social group. Compare EXOGAMY. **—endogamous** *adj.*

endogenous *adj.* originating within the body as a result of normal biochemical or physiological processes (e.g., ENDOGENOUS OPIOIDS) or of predisposing biological or genetic influences (e.g., ENDOGENOUS DEPRESSION). Compare EXOGENOUS. **—endogenously** *adv.*

endogenous cue a CUE, such as a centered arrow, that instructs a participant in a task to direct attention to a particular location but does not automatically draw attention to that location. Compare EXOGENOUS CUE.

endogenous depression depression that occurs in the absence of an obvious psychological stressor and in which a biological or genetic cause is implied. Compare REACTIVE DEPRESSION.

endogenous opioid a substance produced in the body that has the analgesic and euphoric effects of morphine. Three families of endogenous opioids are well known: the **enkephalins**, BETA-ENDORPHINS, and **dynorphins**. All are NEUROPEPTIDES that bind to OPIOID RECEPTORS in the central nervous system; they are mostly inhibitory, acting like opiates to block pain. They bind relatively nonselectively to opioid receptors, although enkephalins bind preferentially to the delta opioid receptors and dynorphins to kappa receptors. Recently, three other endogenous opioid peptides have been identified: **orphanin** (**nociceptin**) and **endomorphins 1** and **2**. Also called **opioid neurotransmitter**.

endogenous oscillator a NEURAL CIRCUIT that generates regularly repeating sequences of neural activity or behavior. In the context of chronobiology, it refers to the BIOLOGICAL CLOCK. See also CIRCADIAN OSCILLATOR.

endogenous rhythm see BIOLOGICAL RHYTHM.

endogenous smile a spontaneous or reflexive smile that is observed when an infant, early in life, is in a state of REM SLEEP. Characterized by a simple turning up of the corners of the mouth, such smiles are seen from birth and are not elicited by social stimulation.

endogenous thyrotoxicosis see THYROTOXICOSIS.

endolymph *n.* the fluid contained in the membranous labyrinth of the inner ear, that is, within the SCALA MEDIA, SEMICIRCULAR CANALS, SACCULE, and UTRICLE. —**endolymphatic** *adj.*

endolymphatic potential a DC electric potential of approximately 80 mV measurable with electrodes inserted into the endolymph in the scala media. Also called **endocochlear potential**.

endometrium *n.* the layer of cells lining the UTERUS. It varies in thickness during the MENSTRUAL CYCLE, reaching a peak of cellular proliferation approximately 1 week after ovulation, in preparation for implantation of a fertilized ovum, and sloughing off as menstrual flow 2 weeks after ovulation if the ovum is not fertilized. —**endometrial** *adj.*

endomorph *n.* a constitutional type (SOMATOTYPE) in SHELDON'S CONSTITUTIONAL THEORY OF PERSONALITY characterized by a soft, round physique, which—according to this theory—is highly correlated with VISCEROTONIA. Also called **endomorphic body type**. —**endomorphic** *adj.* —**endomorphy** *n.*

endomusia *n.* literally, inner music (Greek): the reproduction of a tune or piece of music in the mind.

endophasia *n.* literally, inner speech (Greek): the reproduction of spoken language in the mind. See also COVERT SPEECH.

endophenotype *n.* BIOLOGICAL MARKERS that are simpler to detect than genetic sequences, that may be useful in researching vulnerability to a wide range of psychological and neurological disorders, and that may be a useful link between genetic sequences and their external emotional, cognitive, or behavioral manifestations.

endoplasm *n.* the relatively less dense CYTOPLASM that fills the bulk of a cell, away from the periphery and excluding the nucleus. Compare ECTOPLASM. —**endoplasmic** *adj.*

endoplasmic reticulum (**ER**) a network of membranous tubules and sacs extending from the nucleus to the outer membrane of a typical animal or plant cell. It is responsible for the processing and modification of proteins and lipids, both for distribution within the cell and for secretion.

endopsychic *adj.* pertaining to unconscious material or intrapsychic processes (i.e., processes occurring within the mind). Compare EXOPSYCHIC.

endopsychic structure in psychoanalysis, the internal structure of the mind or psyche. In Sigmund FREUD'S formulation the mind is divided into three components: the ID, EGO, and SUPEREGO. See STRUCTURAL MODEL.

endoradiosonde *n.* a miniature instrument consisting of recording devices and a radio transmitter that is implanted in or ingested by an animal in order to study internal reactions or behaviors.

end organ the structure associated with a nerve ending, such as a muscle END PLATE or a sensory receptor. See also ENCAPSULATED END ORGAN.

endorphins *pl. n.* a class of NEUROPEPTIDES, found mainly in the pituitary gland, that function as ENDOGENOUS OPIOIDS. The best known is BETA-ENDORPHIN; the others are **alpha-endorphin** and **gamma-endorphin**. The production of endorphins during intense physical activity is one explanation for the RUNNER'S HIGH or EXERCISE HIGH, as well as for an athlete's ability to feel little or no pain during a competition.

endosomatic current an electrical current produced by a living organism.

endotherm *n.* an animal whose BODY TEMPERATURE is regulated chiefly by internal metabolic processes. The only true endotherms are mammals and birds. Such animals, formerly called **homeotherms**, are popularly described as warm-blooded. Compare ECTOTHERM. —**endothermic** *adj.* —**endothermy** *n.*

endowment effect the tendency of people to place a higher value on items once they own them or once these have been associated with the self in some other way. The endowment effect is characterized by increased positive emotions toward the object.

end plate a specialized region of a muscle-cell membrane that faces the terminus of a motor neuron within a NEUROMUSCULAR JUNCTION. See also END-PLATE POTENTIAL.

end-plate potential (**EPP**) the depolarization that is induced at the END PLATE of a muscle cell when stimulated by neurotransmitter released from the adjacent motor neuron terminus.

end spurt the increased productivity or gain in performance frequently noted near the end of a task, series of trials, or day's work. It is also commonly observed in athletic endeavors, for example, in long-distance running. Compare INITIAL SPURT. See SPURT.

end-stage renal disease the terminal stage of chronic kidney failure, indicating the necessity for the individual with the disease to undergo replacement therapy (hemodialysis, peritoneal dialysis, or kidney transplant) in order to survive. The psychological effects of living with the condition and its treatment can include depression arising from a sense of lost or limited personal control due to dependence on a dialysis machine, to dialysis-related diet restrictions, and the like. Body-image problems caused by transplantation can develop as well.

end-stopped cell a neuron in any VISUAL AREA of the cerebral cortex that is maximally responsive to a line of a certain length or to a corner of a larger stimulus. Such neurons have a reduced response when the line or corner is extended beyond a certain point. End stopping is a characteristic of HYPERCOMPLEX CELLS in striate cortex.

endurance activity a physical activity that depends on aerobic capacity, that is, the ability to produce energy for muscles by using oxygen for long periods of time. Sport performances that are endurance activities include marathons, runs over 10,000 m, and triathlons. Also called **aerobic activity**. See AEROBIC EXERCISE; ANAEROBIC EXERCISE.

enelicomorphism *n.* see ADULTOMORPHISM.

enema *n.* the injection of a liquid into the rectum via the anus. It is used for introducing radiopaque contrast media into the bowel for radiography and also for AD-

MINISTRATION of certain drugs in solution for absorption through the rectal mucosa.

enema addiction a dependence upon enemas to empty the bowel. Enema addiction may develop through the repeated use of enemas, which reduce rectal sensitivity to the presence of feces in the bowel. This condition is often associated with EATING DISORDERS in which enemas are routinely used for purging. See also KLISMAPHILIA; LAXATIVE ADDICTION.

energization theory the theory that the subjective perception of a GOAL's value or attainability corresponds to the level of energy expended to reach that goal. [proposed by U.S. social psychologist Jack W. Brehm (1928–) and colleagues]

energizing *n.* the mental skill of revitalization when an individual is beginning to feel fatigued. Energizing is a technique of overcoming the mental state of fatigue before it becomes a physiological state.

energy-flow system any system in which the component organisms or entities convert energy into forms that can be used by the other organisms or entities, such that there is a constant energy flow through the entire system. An ECOSYSTEM is perhaps the clearest example of an energy-flow system. In psychology, Sigmund FREUD's early models of the psyche were essentially energy-flow models, in which LIBIDO was employed by the instincts to bring thoughts to consciousness while simultaneously employed by other parts of the psyche to keep them out of consciousness. More recently a field known as **energy psychology** has emerged, which attempts to treat trauma and emotional problems by intervening in the energy flow of the body.

enervate *vb.* **1.** to weaken or deprive of energy. **2.** to surgically remove a nerve or a part of a nerve. **—enervation** *n.*

enforced treatment see FORCED TREATMENT.

engendering psychology the project of developing an approach to psychological issues that is sensitive to questions of gender. See FEMINIST PSYCHOLOGY; WOMAN-CENTERED PSYCHOLOGY. [introduced by U.S. psychologist Florence L. Denmark (1932–)]

engineering anthropometry measurement of the static and dynamic features of the human body, including dimensions, movements, and center of gravity, and the application of these data to the design and evaluation of equipment for human use. See ANTHROPOMETRY. See also HUMAN ENGINEERING; HUMAN FACTORS ENGINEERING.

engineering controls the avoidance of hazards through redesign of machinery or equipment (e.g., by using guards, ventilation systems, and radiation shields) and the replacement or removal of unsafe systems or practices. Engineering controls are considered the first resort in the creation of a safe working environment, followed by ADMINISTRATIVE CONTROLS and the use of PERSONAL PROTECTIVE EQUIPMENT. See also HAZARD-CONTROL PROTOCOL.

engineering model a belief or hypothesis that living organisms, including humans, can be viewed mechanistically, that is, as machines. See MEDICAL MODEL.

engineering psychology a field concerned with identifying the psychological principles that govern human interaction with environments, systems, and products and applying these principles to issues of engineering and design. A computer, for example, should not be designed for engineering efficiency alone, but in such a way that it is adapted to the physical and psychological needs of the user. This term is often used synonymously with HUMAN FACTORS PSYCHOLOGY. See HUMAN ENGINEERING; HUMAN FACTORS ENGINEERING; USABILITY ENGINEERING. See also EQUIPMENT DESIGN; TOOL DESIGN; WORKSPACE DESIGN.

English as a second language (**ESL**) education in English for students who are not native English speakers, most often with an emphasis on language proficiency. When English language proficiency is achieved, the use of English can be applied to the broader curriculum. It was formerly known as **English as a foreign language** (**EFL**).

engram *n.* the hypothetical MEMORY TRACE that is stored in the brain. The nature of the engram, in terms of the exact physiological changes that occur to encode a memory, is as yet unknown. The term was introduced by German biologist Richard Semon (1859–1918) in the early 1900s and was popularized by K. S. LASHLEY in his 1950 paper "In Search of the Engram." Also called **mneme**; **mnemonic trace**; **neurogram**.

engulfment *n.* **1.** extreme distress and anxiety related to feelings of being taken over by an external force. **2.** fear of close interpersonal relationships because of a perceived loss of independence and selfhood. This fear is common in those with feelings of personal insecurity, who experience relationships as overwhelming threats to personal identity. It may also be associated with BORDERLINE PERSONALITY DISORDER. [first described by British psychiatrist R. D. Laing (1927–1989)]

enhancement *n.* the use of genetic technology to produce superior offspring.

enjoyment *n.* a perception of great pleasure and happiness brought on by success or satisfaction in an activity.

enkephalin *n.* see ENDOGENOUS OPIOID.

Enlon *n.* a trade name for EDROPHONIUM.

enmeshed family a family in which the members are involved in each other's lives to an excessive degree, thus limiting or precluding healthy functioning of the unit, or system, and compromising individual AUTONOMY.

enriched environment an environment that offers many opportunities to engage in activity and provides plenty of sensory and intellectual stimulation. See ENRICHMENT.

enrichment *n.* **1.** enhancement or improvement by the addition or augmentation of some desirable property, quality, or component. For example, the INSTRUMENTAL ENRICHMENT program was originally designed to help pupils with mental retardation improve their metacognitive and cognitive skills; JOB ENRICHMENT policies are designed to enhance QUALITY OF WORKLIFE and thus employees' interest in and attitude toward work tasks; and MARRIAGE-ENRICHMENT GROUPS are intended to enhance the interpersonal relationships of married couples. **2.** the provision of opportunities to increase levels of behavioral or intellectual activity in an otherwise unstimulating (i.e., impoverished) environment. For example, the provision of play materials and opportunities for social contacts has been shown to enhance the development of young children. In laboratory studies of animal behavior, the addition of physical features or task requirements to an environment elicits a more natural behavioral repertoire from the animals. Devices, such as puzzle boxes and complex feeders, are used to reduce boredom and STEREOTYPY. Environmental enrichment has been shown in rats to induce greater brain neuronal growth and complexity compared with standard caging environments. Also called **environmental enrichment**. **3.** in education, the intellectual stimulation, often by means of special preschool programs, of children who are believed to be culturally or economically disadvantaged or are otherwise thought not to have adequate intellectual stimulation in their homes.

enrichment program an educational program designed to broaden the potential and forestall the boredom of very bright or gifted children by providing them with an expanded curriculum. The enrichment program may be individually applied to students in regular classes or applied to an entire class of gifted students. Enrichment programs most often focus on expanding the horizons of learning for gifted students with auxiliary instruction, rather than by providing accelerated instruction in the regular curriculum.

entelechy *n.* in philosophy and metaphysics, actuality or realization as opposed to potentiality. Greek philosopher Aristotle (384–322 BCE) used the word to refer to the soul (psyche), seen as that form within the material being by virtue of which it achieves the actuality of its nature (see ACTUAL). Later philosophers employed the term in a similar vein. German philosopher Gottfried Wilhelm Leibniz (1646–1716) referred to MONADS as being entelechy, or having entelechy, this being the power to perfect their given nature (see NISUS). In certain vitalist philosophies and theories, entelechy refers to the vital force within an organism that allows for life, development, and self-fulfillment (see ÉLAN VITAL; VITALISM).

enteric virus infection a disease produced by one of the polio, Cocksackie, or echoviruses (called **enteroviruses**), which are members of the picornavirus family. Such infections include poliomyelitis, aseptic meningitis, herpangina, and myocarditis. The viruses have been classed as enteric because they multiply in the human gastrointestinal tract. Also called **enteroviral infection**.

enterogastrone *n.* a hormone secreted by the small intestine that inhibits the secretion of gastric juice by the stomach. It is released when the stomach contents pass into the small intestine.

enthusiasm *n.* a feeling of excitement or passion for an activity, cause, or object. **—enthusiastic** *adj.*

entitativity *n.* the extent to which a group or collective is considered by others to be a real entity rather than a set of independent individuals. In general, groups whose members share a common fate, are similar to one another, and are located close together are more likely to be considered a group rather than a mere AGGREGATION. Also called **entitivity**. [first described by Donald CAMPBELL]

entitlement *n.* **1.** rights or benefits legally bestowed on a person or group, for example, by legislation or contract. **2.** unreasonable claims to special consideration, especially as a disturbance of self-concept in NARCISSISTIC PERSONALITY DISORDER. The exploitiveness–entitlement dimension of narcissism may be particularly useful for explaining why people with narcissistic personality disorder report higher rates of interpersonal transgressions in their daily lives.

entitlement program a program of the U.S. government that provides financial assistance and welfare benefits to individuals who meet requirements set by law, for example, people with mental or physical disabilities. Entitlement programs are administered through MEDICARE, MEDICAID, SOCIAL SECURITY disability insurance, and similar funding sources.

entity theory the belief that psychological attributes, such as level of intelligence, are fixed, essential qualities rather than attributes that develop gradually. [formulated by U.S. personality psychologist Carol S. Dweck (1946–) in her analysis of cognition, personality, and motivation]

entoptic *adj.* denoting visual sensations caused by stimulation originating within the eyeball itself. See ENTOPTIC PHENOMENA.

entoptic phenomena visual sensations that arise from stimulation within the eyeball. A classic example is seeing faint dark specks moving through the visual field when gazing at a clear, blue sky with one eye. These are shadows caused by blood cells moving through the vasculature on the surface of the retina.

entorhinal cortex a region of cerebral cortex in the ventromedial portion of the TEMPORAL LOBE. It has reciprocal connections with the HIPPOCAMPAL FORMATION and various other cortical and subcortical structures and is an integral component of the medial temporal lobe memory system.

entorhinal-cortex lesion damage to the entorhinal cortex. Lesions in this area are used to study neural plasticity and working memory; they are also seen in temporal lobe epilepsy and the early stages of Alzheimer's disease.

entrainment *n.* the process of activating or providing a timing cue for a BIOLOGICAL RHYTHM. For example, the production of gonadal hormones in seasonally breeding animals can be a result of entrainment to increasing day length. The timing of CIRCADIAN RHYTHMS can be due to entrainment to either sunrise or sunset.

entropy *n.* **1.** a thermodynamic quantity providing a measure of the unavailability of the energy of a closed system to do work. **2.** in statistics, a measure of the disorder of a closed system. **3.** in information theory, a measure of the efficiency with which a system transmits information.

entry behavior see READINESS.

enucleation *n.* **1.** the removal of an entire organic structure, such as a tumor or a bodily organ, without damaging the structure. Enucleation often refers to the removal of an eyeball in which the optic nerve and connective eye muscles have been severed so that the eye can be removed wholly and cleanly. See also AUTOENUCLEATION. **2.** the destruction or removal of the nucleus of a cell.

enumeration *n.* the process of counting or listing people, events, or objects.

enuresis *n.* repeated involuntary urination in inappropriate places (clothing, floor, etc.) that occurs after the chronological age or equivalent MENTAL AGE when continence is expected and is not due to a substance (e.g., a diuretic) or to a general medical condition. Enuresis may occur during the day (**diurnal enuresis**), night (**nocturnal enuresis**), or both and is frequently associated with delayed bladder development, poor toilet training, and stressful situations. Also called **functional enuresis**. See also BED-WETTING. Compare URINARY INCONTINENCE.

envelope *n.* in acoustics, a slowly varying or "smoothed" change in amplitude. Usually it refers to temporal changes, such as those produced by amplitude MODULATION or BEATS, but it can also refer to the shape of a spectrum, as in a **spectral envelope**, or to spatial changes, as in the envelope of the TRAVELING WAVE. "Slowly varying" is not precisely defined, but generally refers to fluctuations whose rate is much less, by a factor of at least 0.5, than the highest rates in the temporal, spectral, or spatial representations. For example, the beats created by adding 1000-Hz and 1005-Hz tones have a quasi-sinusoidal envelope with a periodicity of 5 Hz, but there is no envelope created by the addition of 1000 Hz and

2005 Hz. Temporal and spectral envelopes are important in auditory perception.

environment *n.* the aggregate of external agents or conditions—physical, biological, social, and cultural—that influence the functions of an organism. The physical environment may be measured in terms of temperature, air pressure, noise, vibration, atmosphere, or sources of nutrients, which in turn may be specified by a range of values (e.g., a temperature scale). See also ECOLOGY. **—environmental** *adj.*

environmental aesthetics analysis of the role of environmental characteristics in judgments of beauty, scenic quality, or visual preference. Aesthetic judgments may be heightened by moderate levels of complexity as conveyed, for example, by moving water, views from a height, and the element of mystery (i.e., the suggestion that greater information will be available through additional exploration of the environment). The validity of simulations of the real-world environment (e.g., photography, computer images, virtual reality) is also taken into account in the study of environmental aesthetics.

environmental agnosia 1. the inability of brain-injured individuals to recognize familiar places and surroundings, including their homes and neighborhood. **2.** loss of topographical familiarity. See also TOPOGRAPHAGNOSIA.

environmental approach a therapeutic approach in which efforts are directed either toward reducing external pressures (e.g., employment or financial problems) that contribute to emotional difficulties or toward modifying aspects of the individual's living or working space to improve functioning.

environmental assessment the evaluation of situational and environmental variables that have an influence on behavior, based on the theory that disordered functioning may be rooted partly in the social system, or particular social context, rather than wholly in the individual and his or her personal characteristics. In an organizational context, for example, measures of manager support and availability of resources to accomplish a job would likely be used in the environmental assessment of employee job satisfaction.

environmental attitudes the beliefs and values of individuals or societies with respect to nature, ecology, or environmental issues. Research in this area examines how such factors as age, gender, and politics relate to people's environmental attitudes, the influence of ENVIRONMENTAL EDUCATION on attitudes, and the role of attitudes in PROECOLOGICAL BEHAVIOR.

environmental attribution see SITUATIONAL ATTRIBUTION.

environmental cognition information processing in real-world settings, often with regard to memory for geographic location and way finding. See COGNITIVE MAP; LANDMARK.

environmental constraint any circumstance of a person's situation or environment that discourages the development of skills and abilities, independence, social competence, or ADAPTIVE BEHAVIOR or inhibits the display of skills previously acquired. For example, living in a COMMUNITY RESIDENCE where staff prepare all the meals would act as an environmental constraint for someone who has learned how to make sandwiches, since it would provide no opportunity to display this ability.

environmental control device an ASSISTIVE TECHNOLOGY device with the capacity to regulate or manipulate aspects of a person's physical surroundings. Examples include devices that turn on lights, open doors, and operate appliances. Also called **electronic aid to daily living**; **environmental control unit**. See also SWITCH DEVICE; CONTROL DEVICE; FEEDBACK DEVICE; TARGET DEVICE.

environmental deprivation an absence of conditions that stimulate intellectual and behavioral growth and development, such as educational, recreational, and social opportunities. Environmental deprivation is often associated with social isolation and may be so severe that it causes PSEUDORETARDATION.

environmental design the creative planning of living and working areas to enhance their HABITABILITY. Environmental design may also be applied to the enhancement of recreational areas. Habitability factors range from simple shelter needs to complex and sophisticated environmental aesthetics and conformance factors, for example, the use of specific colors of paint or levels of illumination for the optimum performance of tasks.

environmental determinism a philosophical position that attributes INDIVIDUAL DIFFERENCES largely or completely to environmental factors, that is, to nurture as opposed to nature. Compare BIOLOGICAL DETERMINISM; GENETIC DETERMINISM. See DETERMINISM; NATURE–NURTURE CONTROVERSY.

environmental education the development of principles and materials to raise awareness and change behaviors with respect to environmental problems. See ENVIRONMENTAL ATTITUDES; PROECOLOGICAL BEHAVIOR; SOCIAL TRAP.

environmental enrichment see ENRICHMENT.

environmental field in GESTALT PSYCHOLOGY, the entire context in which an event takes place and with which the components of the event interact.

environmental hazards environmental factors that pose some danger to an organism or community, for example, exposed electrical wiring in a home or workplace and nuclear reactors or lead smelters in a community. Chronic exposure to environmental hazards is linked to both psychological and physiological indicators of STRESS.

environmentalism *n.* **1.** the concept that the environment and learning are the chief determinants of behavior. They are, therefore, the major cause of interpersonal variations in ability and adjustment; accordingly, behavior is largely modifiable. Compare HEREDITARIANISM. See also NATURE–NURTURE CONTROVERSY. **2.** a policy that emphasizes the ecological relationship between humans and the natural environment and strives to protect the environment as an essential resource. **—environmentalist** *n.*

environmental justice fair and impartial treatment with respect to the distribution of environmental hazards in the general population, such that no single group is exposed disproportionately to suboptimal environmental conditions at home, work, or school.

environmental load theory the theory that humans have a limited ability to handle environmental stimuli. The limit is determined by the amount of information inputs that can be processed by the central nervous system. When the environmental load exceeds the individual's capacity for processing, the central nervous system reacts by ignoring some of the inputs. See also COGNITIVE OVERLOAD; INFORMATION OVERLOAD; SENSORY OVERLOAD; STIMULUS OVERLOAD.

environmental manipulation a method of improving the well-being of people by changing their living conditions, for example, by placing an abused or delinquent child in a foster home or by transferring an adult patient from a mental institution to an ADULT HOME or a HALFWAY HOUSE.

environmental modifications changes in the home environment (such as installing ramps, grab bars, etc.) to accommodate an individual's disabilities and enable him or her to live more independently.

environmental noise see DIFFERENTIATION THEORY; NOISE.

environmental press a stimulus or situation in the environment that arouses a NEED, especially a need for adaptation. See also ENVIRONMENTAL PRESS–COMPETENCE MODEL.

environmental press–competence model a model of stress and adaptation in which adaptive functioning in the environment depends on the interaction between external demands (ENVIRONMENTAL PRESS) and an individual's competence in meeting these demands. [proposed by U.S. gerontological psychologist M. Powell Lawton (1923–2001)]

environmental psychology a branch of psychology that emphasizes the effects of the physical environment on human behavior and welfare. Influences may include environmental stressors (e.g., noise, CROWDING, air pollution, temperature), design variables (e.g., lighting and illumination), the design of technology (see ERGONOMICS), and larger, more ambient qualities of the physical environment, such as floorplan layouts, symbolic elements, the size and location of buildings, and proximity to nature.

environmental psychophysics the application of psychophysical methods to problems in real-world environments, such as investigating the magnitude of odor created by a processing plant.

environmental stress any kind of STRESS caused by factors in the environment.

environmental stress theory the concept that autonomic and cognitive factors combine to form an individual's appraisal of STRESSORS in the environment as threatening or nonthreatening. Stressors perceived as threatening may lead to stress reactions involving physiological, emotional, and behavioral elements, which in turn may elicit strategies designed to cope with and potentially adapt to the threat.

environmental therapy therapy that includes and addresses the client's interaction with his or her physical or social surroundings (or both) in an effort to promote greater cognitive, affective, and behavioral health. See MILIEU THERAPY; THERAPEUTIC COMMUNITY.

envy 1. *n.* a NEGATIVE EMOTION of discontent and resentment generated by desire for the possessions, attributes, qualities, or achievements of another (the target of the envy). Unlike JEALOUSY, with which it shares certain similarities and with which it is often confused, envy need involve only two individuals: the envious person and the person envied. **2.** *vb.* to feel such discontent or resentment. **—envious** *adj.*

enzyme *n.* a protein that acts as a biological catalyst, thereby speeding up the rate of a biochemical reaction without itself becoming a part of the end product. Many enzymes require other organic molecules (COENZYMES) or inorganic ions (cofactors) to function normally. Most enzymes are named according to the type of reaction they catalyze; for example, glucosidases convert glucosides to glucose; ACETYLCHOLINESTERASE splits and inactivates molecules of the neurotransmitter acetylcholine.

enzyme induction the ability of drugs or other substances to increase the activity of enzymes, especially hepatic (liver) enzymes, that are responsible for the metabolism of those drugs or other substances. The CYTOCHROME P450 hepatic enzymes, which are responsible for the metabolism of numerous psychotropic compounds, are susceptible to induction. Barbiturates, some anticonvulsants, and steroids may induce hepatic enzymes, usually resulting in a decrease in activity of the drug or other substances metabolized via the same enzyme system. Substances contained in cigarette smoke, charbroiled meat, and environmental pollutants are also capable of enzyme induction.

enzyme inhibition the ability of drugs or other substances to impair or arrest the ability of enzymes, especially liver (hepatic) enzymes, to metabolize those drugs or other substances. The CYTOCHROME P450 enzymes that are responsible for the metabolism of numerous psychotropic drugs are susceptible to inhibition by psychotropics or other substances. Many of the SSRIs (selective serotonin reuptake inhibitors) inhibit the activity of enzymes for which they are SUBSTRATES, leading to increased concentrations of the SSRIs or other drugs that are metabolized by the same enzyme. Enyzme inhibition can be competitive, when a drug partially inhibits an enzyme by competing for the same binding site as the substrate, or irreversible, when a drug binds so completely to an enzyme that it fundamentally alters the enzyme and even partial metabolism of other substances cannot take place.

EOG 1. abbreviation for ELECTROOCULOGRAM. **2.** abbreviation for ELECTROOLFACTOGRAM.

eonism *n.* the adoption by a male of a female role, or vice versa, as in TRANSVESTISM. Eonism is named for Charles Eon de Beaumont, a French political adventurer, who died in 1810 after posing as a woman for many years.

EP abbreviation for EVOKED POTENTIAL.

EPAM abbreviation for ELEMENTARY PERCEIVER AND MEMORIZER.

epena *n.* a hallucinogenic snuff prepared from the bark of South American trees of the genus *Virola* and used in Colombia, Brazil, and Venezuela. The bark is scraped from the trees and boiled to extract a red resin that is dried, ground, and mixed with wood ash. The active agents, which include dimethyltryptamine (see DMT), produce effects that are comparable to those of LSD. Also called **nyakwana**; **parica**; **yakee**.

ependyma *n.* the membrane lining the brain VENTRICLES and the CENTRAL CANAL of the spinal cord. It produces neurons, especially early in development, and **ependymal cells** (a type of NEUROGLIA) throughout life. **—ependymal** *adj.*

ephebophilia *n.* sexual attraction to and arousal by adolescent children, usually early adolescents who are just going through puberty.

ephedra *n.* a bushy shrub (*Ephedra sinica*), known to Chinese herbalists as ma huang, that is indigenous to arid regions of the world, particularly Mongolia and northern China. The leaves contain significant amounts of the alkaloid stimulants **ephedrine** and **pseudephedrine** and are traditionally made into a tisane and drunk as a stimulating beverage. Both ephedrine and pseudephedrine are strong sympathomimetic agents and therefore increase blood pressure, alertness, and anxiety, as well as causing peripheral symptoms of sympathetic activity (e.g., tremor, sweating). These agents also relax smooth muscle, hence the plant and its active components have often been used as a remedy for asthma or other respiratory complaints. In addition, ephedra has been combined into many dietary supplements that are reputed to aid weight loss, increase energy, and enhance athletic performance.

There is, however, little evidence of ephedra's effectiveness for these uses except for modest, short-term weight loss without any clear health benefit. It is toxic and potentially fatal, particularly in high doses or when combined with other stimulants, such as CAFFEINE; reported adverse events include headaches, insomnia, rapid or irregular heartbeat, nerve damage, muscle injury, psychosis, memory loss, heart attack, stroke, seizure, and death. In 2004 the U.S. Food and Drug Administration banned the sale of products containing ephedra, the first U.S. government ban of a dietary supplement.

ephedrine *n.* see EPHEDRA.

ephemeral *adj.* fleeting, transient, or short-lived. The term literally means "lasting only one day." **—ephemera** *n.*

EPI 1. abbreviation for extrapyramidal involvement. See EXTRAPYRAMIDAL EFFECTS. **2.** abbreviation for EYSENCK PERSONALITY INVENTORY.

epi- *prefix* upon, above, or over.

epicritic sensation a cutaneous sensation, such as pressure or temperature, that is detected at a very low threshold of sensitivity. It was proposed by British neurologist Sir Henry Head (1861–1940) in 1920 that lower animals may be less sensitive than humans to cutaneous stimuli.

epicritic sensibility see GNOSTIC FUNCTION.

epicritic system one of the two divisions of the SOMATOSENSORY SYSTEM, the other being the PROTOPATHIC SYSTEM. The epicritic system has receptors that are sensitive to joint movement, light touch, and deep pressure. Impulses from these receptors feed into the SOMATOSENSORY AREA of the brain.

epidemic 1. *adj.* generally prevalent, widespread: usually applied to a disease. **2.** *n.* an epidemic disease. Compare ENDEMIC; PANDEMIC.

epidemic catalepsy a situation in which CATALEPSY occurs in a number of individuals at the same time as a result of identification or imitation.

epidemic hysteria an old term, no longer in professional use, for an outbreak of seemingly uncontrollable emotion, such as fear, panic, laughter, or violence, in a large segment of a population. The term reflects the former belief that such emotions were passed from one person to another through direct contact, like a contagious disease (see CONTAGION). See COLLECTIVE HYSTERIA.

Epidemiologic Catchment Area Survey (**ECA Survey**) a telephone survey of mental disorders carried out in two waves from 1980 to 1985 using *DSM–III* and the DIAGNOSTIC INTERVIEW SCHEDULE (DIS). More than 20,000 people were surveyed in households, group homes, and long-term care institutions across the United States to obtain information on the prevalence and incidence of mental disorders, the use of services for mental health problems, and the extent to which those with mental disorders are underserved.

epidemiology *n.* the study of the incidence and distribution of specific diseases and disorders. The **epidemiologist** also seeks to establish relationships to such factors as heredity, environment, nutrition, or age at onset. Results of epidemiological studies are intended to find clues and associations rather than necessarily to show causal relationships. See also INCIDENCE; RELATIVE RISK. **—epidemiologic** or **epidemiological** *adj.*

epidermis *n.* **1.** the outer, protective, nonvascular layer of the SKIN of vertebrates. **2.** the outer layer of cells of various invertebrates. **3.** the outermost layer of cells covering the leaves and young parts of plants.

epididymis *n.* (*pl.* **epididymides**) an elongated tubule running along the top and back of the testis that stores spermatozoa received from seminiferous tubules within the testis. It empties into the VAS DEFERENS. **—epididymal** *adj.*

epidural hematoma an accumulation of blood (see HEMATOMA) in the space above the DURA MATER caused by rupture of a blood vessel (see EXTRADURAL HEMORRHAGE), typically due to trauma.

epigastric reflex a SPINAL REFLEX that draws in the upper central region of the abdominal wall, elicited by a quick stroke with a pin from the nipple downward.

epigenesis *n.* **1.** the theory that characteristics of an organism, both physical and behavioral, arise from an interaction between genetic and environmental influences rather than from one or the other. See also NATURE–NURTURE CONTROVERSY. **2.** in genetics, the occurrence of a heritable change in gene function that is not the result of a change in the base sequence of the organism's DNA. **3.** in the theory of Erik ERIKSON, the emergence of dif-ferent goals at each stage of ego and social development. See ERIKSON'S EIGHT STAGES OF DEVELOPMENT. **—epigenetic** *adj.*

epigenetic landscape a visual metaphor that depicts development as a hill with valleys of various depths and steepness, to convey the idea that some aspects of development are directed along certain general pathways and likely to occur under most circumstances but that the exact sequence of paths varies across individuals and can be altered by sudden environmental or genetic change. [proposed by British biologist Conrad Hall Waddington (1905–1975)]

epigenetic theory the concept that mind and consciousness developed when living organisms reached a high level of complexity. See EMERGENCE.

epilepsy *n.* a group of chronic brain disorders associated with disturbances in the electrical discharges of brain cells and characterized by recurrent SEIZURES, with or without clouding or loss of consciousness. **Symptomatic epilepsy** is due to known conditions, such as brain inflammation, brain tumor, vascular disturbances, structural abnormality, brain injury, or degenerative disease; **idiopathic epilepsy** is of unknown origin or is due to nonspecific brain defects. Types of seizure vary depending on the nature of the abnormal electrical discharge and the area of the brain affected (see ABSENCE SEIZURE; GENERALIZED SEIZURE; PARTIAL SEIZURE; TONIC–CLONIC SEIZURE). Epilepsy was formerly known as **falling sickness**. Also called **seizure disorder**. See also STATUS EPILEPTICUS; TEMPORAL LOBE EPILEPSY. **—epileptic** *adj.*

epilepsy surgery neurosurgery to remove a part of the brain, often the anterior temporal lobe, that is the focus for intractable (uncontrollable) epileptic seizures. The goal of the surgery is to reduce or eliminate seizures.

epileptic aura see AURA.

epileptic cry a momentary cry produced by sudden contraction of the chest and laryngeal muscles during the tonic phase of a TONIC–CLONIC SEIZURE. Also called **initial cry**.

epileptic furor see FUROR.

epileptiform seizure an episode that resembles an epileptic seizure but is unrelated to epilepsy. See also NONEPILEPTIC SEIZURE.

epileptogenic *adj.* describing any factor or agent that causes epileptic SEIZURES.

epileptogenic focus a discrete area of the brain in

which originate the electrical discharges that give rise to seizure activity.

epileptogenic lesion an area of tissue damage in the brain that results in epileptic seizures. Epilepsy may result from various brain lesions, for example, head injury, laceration, tumor, or hemorrhage, arising either immediately after the injury or, in some cases, months or years later.

epileptoid *adj.* resembling epilepsy or occurring in sudden spasms. Also called **epileptiform**.

epileptoidism *n.* see EPILEPTOID PERSONALITY.

epileptoid personality a personality pattern that includes such traits as irritability, selfishness, uncooperativeness, and aggressiveness. This personality pattern is believed by some to be associated with epilepsy. Also called **epileptoidism**.

epimenorrhagia *n.* see MENORRHAGIA.

epinephrine *n.* a CATECHOLAMINE neurotransmitter and adrenal hormone that is the end product of the metabolism of the dietary amino acid tyrosine. It is synthesized primarily in the adrenal medulla by methylation of norepinephrine, which itself is formed from DOPAMINE by the action of the enzyme dopamine β-hydroxylase. As a hormone, it is secreted in large amounts when an individual is stimulated by fear, anger, or a similar stressful situation. As a neurotransmitter, it is the primary stimulant of both ALPHA and BETA ADRENORECEPTORS. Thus it increases the heart rate and force of heart contractions, relaxes bronchial and intestinal smooth muscle, and produces varying effects on blood pressure as it acts both as a vasodilator and vasoconstrictor. Also called **adrenaline**.

epiphany *n.* a sudden perception of the essential nature of oneself, others, or reality.

epiphenomenalism *n.* the position that bodily (physical) events produce mental events, such as thoughts and feelings, but that mental events do not have causal power to produce bodily (physical) events. Thus, causality between the mental and the physical proceeds in one direction only. A more radical form of the same position would add that mental events lack causal efficacy to produce anything, including other mental events. An example of this radical position is the claim that consciousness is merely a side effect of the functioning of the brain, with no causal connection to it. See EPIPHENOMENON. See also MIND–BODY PROBLEM; REDUCTIONISM. [coined by British philosopher and psychologist James Ward (1843–1925)]

epiphenomenon *n.* a mere by-product of a process that has no effect on the process itself. The term is used most frequently to refer to mental events considered as products of brain processes. Thus, while mental events are real in some sense, they are not real in the same way that biological states and events are real, and not necessary to the explanation of mental events themselves. Epiphenomena are conceived of as having no causal power. In some Marxist theories, cultural and intellectual movements are seen as mere epiphenomena produced by the process of DIALECTICAL MATERIALISM. See EPIPHENOMENALISM. **—epiphenomenal** *adj.*

epiphora *n.* excessive secretion of tears, which is most commonly due to an organic condition causing an insufficient drainage of tears but may be associated with emotional stress, such as chronic anxiety or fear.

epiphysis cerebri see PINEAL GLAND.

episode *n.* a noteworthy isolated event or series of events. An episode of an illness is an isolated occurrence, which may be repeated.

episodic amnesia a loss of memory only for certain significant events. Episodic amnesia may also involve a transient ability to recall an event followed by periods of inability to access the memory.

episodic disorder any disorder characterized by the appearance of symptoms in discrete, often brief, periods or episodes.

episodic memory memory for specific, personally experienced events that happened at a particular time or place. Retrieval from episodic memory involves using cues based on the context associated with the original experience (time and place). Episodic memory supplements SEMANTIC MEMORY and may decline with normal aging. See also AUTOBIOGRAPHICAL MEMORY; AUTONOETIC MEMORY; DECLARATIVE MEMORY.

epistemic *adj.* of or relating to knowledge or to EPISTEMOLOGY. The epistemic DRIVE, created by the desire for knowledge, is often considered a fundamental drive. See NEED FOR COGNITION.

epistemic value 1. the extent to which a belief, theory, or explanatory model is capable of providing accurate knowledge. **2.** the extent to which a cognitive process, such as a sense perception or memory, is considered capable of providing such knowledge. **3.** a specific attribute of a theory or cognitive process that is considered to be a sign of its ability to convey accurate knowledge. For example, FALSIFIABILITY and EMPIRICAL GROUNDING are important epistemic values in science; consistency and clarity might be considered epistemic values in relation to memory.

epistemological loneliness a profound sense of alienation or separation from others.

epistemology *n.* the branch of philosophy concerned with the nature, origin, and limitations of knowledge. It is also concerned with the justification of truth claims. Mainly owing to the work of French philosopher and mathematician René Descartes (1596–1650), epistemology has been the dominant question in philosophy since the 17th century (see CARTESIANISM; CARTESIAN SELF; MODERNISM). In psychology, interest in epistemology arises from two principal sources. First, as the study of the behavior of human beings, psychology has long had interest in the processes of knowledge acquisition and learning of all sorts. Second, as a science, psychology has an interest in the justification of its knowledge claims. In connection with this concern, most work on epistemology in psychology has concentrated on scientific method and on the justification of scientifically derived knowledge claims. In general, the guiding epistemology of psychology has been EMPIRICISM, although some approaches to the subject, such as PSYCHOANALYSIS, the developmental psychology of Jean PIAGET, and the HUMANISTIC PSYCHOLOGY of Carl ROGERS, are heavily influenced by RATIONALISM. **—epistemological** *adj.*

epistemophilia *n.* the love of knowledge: the impulse to investigate and inquire. See also CURIOSITY.

epithalamus *n.* a portion of the DIENCEPHALON that is immediately above and behind the THALAMUS. It includes the PINEAL GLAND and the POSTERIOR COMMISSURE.

epithelioma *n.* any tumor that originates in cells of the epithelium. A skin cancer may begin as an epithelioma.

epithelium *n.* (*pl.* **epithelia**) the cellular layer covering the outer surface of the body and lining body cavities, such as the lungs and gastrointestinal tract. **—epithelial** *adj.*

EPP abbreviation for END-PLATE POTENTIAL.

EPPS abbreviation for EDWARDS PERSONAL PREFERENCE SCHEDULE.

EPQ abbreviation for Eysenck Personality Questionnaire. See EYSENCK PERSONALITY INVENTORY.

EPS abbreviation for extrapyramidal symptoms or syndrome (see EXTRAPYRAMIDAL EFFECTS).

EPSDT abbreviation for EARLY AND PERIODIC SCREENING, DIAGNOSIS, AND TREATMENT.

epsilon alcoholism the fifth stage of alcoholism. It is characterized by periodic drinking bouts or binges interspersed with dry periods lasting weeks or months. During the binges, the alcoholic drinks heavily day after day until he or she can drink no more. See also ALPHA ALCOHOLISM; BETA ALCOHOLISM; GAMMA ALCOHOLISM; DELTA ALCOHOLISM. [defined by U.S. physician Elvin M. Jellinek (1890–1963)]

epsilon movement the perception of motion occurring when a white line on a black background is changed to a black line on a white background. Also called **epsilon motion**.

EPSP abbreviation for EXCITATORY POSTSYNAPTIC POTENTIAL.

Epstein–Barr virus (**EBV**) a herpes virus that is the cause of infectious mononucleosis. It is commonly found in the extracellular oral fluids of those who have been exposed to the disease. The virus has also been isolated from the cells of patients with certain cancers (e.g., Burkitt's lymphoma). [Michael Anthony **Epstein** (1921–) and Yvonne M. **Barr** (1932–), British pathologists]

EQ 1. abbreviation for EDUCATIONAL QUOTIENT. **2.** see EMOTIONAL INTELLIGENCE QUOTIENT.

equal-and-unequal-cases method see METHOD OF EQUAL AND UNEQUAL CASES.

equal-appearing-intervals method see METHOD OF EQUAL-APPEARING INTERVALS.

Equal Employment Opportunity Commission (**EEOC**) a U.S. federal agency, created by the 1964 Civil Rights Act, that has the responsibility of enforcing the laws and regulations prohibiting discrimination on the basis of race, sex, age, disability, ethnicity, religion, and national origin. See EQUAL OPPORTUNITY. See also AFFIRMATIVE ACTION; UNIFORM GUIDELINES FOR EMPLOYEE SELECTION PROCEDURES.

equal-interval scale see INTERVAL SCALE.

equality law see LAW OF EQUALITY.

equality stage see DISTRIBUTIVE JUSTICE.

equal loudness contour the function relating DECIBELS sound-pressure level (dB SPL) to frequency for PURE TONES that have a loudness equal to that of a 1-kHz tone at a fixed level. For example, a 100-Hz tone presented at 70 dB SPL is as loud as a 1-kHz tone presented at 60 dB SPL. This is a point on the equal loudness contour for a 60-phon reference. This function has been incorporated in audio circuitry as "loudness compensation," primarily in an attempt to correct for the decreased loudness of low frequencies when listening at low levels. See LOUDNESS.

equally noticeable difference see DIFFERENCE THRESHOLD.

equal opportunity under U.S. federal law, the principle that all individuals should have the opportunity to find employment and to succeed in their jobs regardless of race, age, color, religion, sex, disability, and national origin. The principle of equal opportunity also applies to education, health care, and social and other services, and in some states and municipalities has been extended to include sexual orientation. See also AFFIRMATIVE ACTION; AGE DISCRIMINATION IN EMPLOYMENT ACT; AMERICANS WITH DISABILITIES ACT; FOUR-FIFTHS RULE; POSITIVE DISCRIMINATION; UNIFORM GUIDELINES FOR EMPLOYEE SELECTION PROCEDURES.

equal rights amendment (**ERA**) a proposed amendment to the U.S. Constitution that would guarantee equal rights under the law for both sexes. First proposed in 1923, it was approved by Congress in 1972 but failed to achieve ratification in 1982.

equal sense-difference method see METHOD OF EQUAL-APPEARING INTERVALS.

equal steps in a series of stimuli differing in intensity, increments that are equal physically or perceptually.

equal weighting see WEIGHTING.

equated score the score distribution from measure B transformed to match the distribution of measure A in one or more features. See TRANSFORMATION.

equilibration *n.* the process by which an individual uses ASSIMILATION and ACCOMMODATION to restore or maintain a psychological equilibrium, that is, a cognitive state devoid of conflicting SCHEMAS. [postulated by Jean PIAGET]

equilibratory sense see SENSE OF EQUILIBRIUM.

equilibrium *n.* **1.** a state of physical or mental balance or stability, for example in posture, physiological processes, or psychological adjustment. See HOMEOSTASIS; SENSE OF EQUILIBRIUM; VESTIBULAR SYSTEM. **2.** a state of stability in any other system. See also DYNAMIC EQUILIBRIUM.

equilibrium model of group development in general, any conceptual analysis that assumes that the processes contributing to GROUP DEVELOPMENT fluctuate around, but regularly return to, a resting point where opposing forces are balanced or held in check. For example, U.S. social psychologist Robert Freed Bales (1916–) suggested that groups, over time, fluctuate in the extent to which they stress the accomplishment of group tasks relative to the improvement of interpersonal relationships among group members.

equilibrium-point model a model of limb control in which the target of a movement is specified as an equilibrium point between the AGONIST and ANTAGONIST muscle groups acting on the limb. Variants of this model are called the **mass-spring model** and the **lambda (λ) model**. See also IMPULSE-TIMING MODEL.

equilibrium potential the state in which the tendency of ions to flow across a membrane from regions of high concentration is exactly balanced by the opposing potential difference across the membrane.

equipercentile method a method of equating two measures such that a shared value of X on the two measurements implies that the probability of a subject drawn at random will have a score greater than X is the same for both measures.

equipment automation the extent to which equipment can operate without human intervention. For example, progress from manual feeds to fully automated feeds reflects an increasing degree of equipment automation.

equipment design an area of HUMAN ENGINEERING concerned with the design of work tools, home appliances, and machines of all kinds, including their displays and controls. One particularly important application is the design of transport systems, such as roads, road signs, and the vehicles that use them. The major goal is to see that the equipment is designed with HUMAN FACTORS in mind, such as safety, fatigue, convenience, comfort, and efficiency. See TOOL DESIGN; WORKSPACE DESIGN. See also ENGINEERING PSYCHOLOGY; ERGONOMICS.

equipotentiality *n.* **1.** equal potential, such as the capacity of one part of the brain to be trained or conditioned to perform a function previously performed by another part of the brain. **2.** see LAW OF EQUIPOTENTIALITY.

equipotentiality in memory the hypothesis that the cortex is relatively nonspecific in learning and that many parts of the brain contribute to the formation of memory, rather than memory being localized to specific areas of the brain. It is derived from experiments by K. S. LASHLEY on the effects of various brain lesions on maze learning in rats (see LAW OF EQUIPOTENTIALITY). See also LAW OF MASS ACTION.

equity stage see DISTRIBUTIVE JUSTICE.

equity theory a theory of justice regarding what individuals are likely to view as a fair return from activities involving themselves and a number of other people. The theory posits that people compare the ratio of the outcome of the activity, that is, the benefits they receive from it (e.g., pay, fringe benefits, intrinsic gratifications, recognition) to their input (e.g., effort, seniority, skills, social status) with the outcome-to-input ratios of those engaged in a comparable activity. See EXTERNAL INEQUITY; INTERNAL INEQUITY; OVERPAYMENT INEQUITY; UNDERPAYMENT INEQUITY.

equivalence *n.* a relationship between two or more items (e.g., stimuli or variables) that permits one to replace another.

equivalence class a stimulus group whose members exhibit reflexivity, symmetry, and transitivity in the context of CONDITIONAL DISCRIMINATIONS. That is, the members demonstrate STIMULUS EQUIVALENCE and hence may substitute for one another.

equivalency test an assessment of one's educational level regardless of whether one has completed a specific course of study. For example, by taking the appropriate equivalency test, one may obtain a high school diploma without completing high school state requirements.

equivalent form an alternative form of a test that has the same psychometric properties as the original.

equivalent groups see MATCHED-GROUP DESIGN.

equivalents method see METHOD OF ADJUSTMENT.

equivalent stimulus see STIMULUS EQUIVALENCE.

equivocal sign see SOFT SIGN.

ER abbreviation for evoked response (see EVOKED POTENTIAL).

ERA abbreviation for EQUAL RIGHTS AMENDMENT.

erect *adj.* **1.** upright or vertical. See PILOERECTION; POSTURE. **2.** tumescent, as an erect penis (see TUMESCENCE).

erectile dysfunction the lack or loss of ability to achieve an erection. Causes of erectile dysfunction may be psychological or physical, including the effects of medications or drug abuse. If a man normally experiences a nocturnal erection or is able to induce an erection by masturbation, but cannot achieve or maintain an erection during sexual intercourse, the dysfunction is assumed to be due largely or solely to psychological factors and in *DSM–IV–TR* is called MALE ERECTILE DISORDER. See also PRIMARY ERECTILE DYSFUNCTION; SECONDARY ERECTILE DYSFUNCTION.

eremophilia *n.* a pathological desire to be alone.

erethism *n.* **1.** an abnormally high degree of sensitivity to sensory stimulation in some or all parts of the body. It is associated with a number of conditions and is a major symptom of mercury poisoning. See also MAD HATTER'S DISEASE. **2.** any abnormally high degree of sensitivity, excitability, or irritability in response to stimulation, such as emotional erethism.

ERF abbreviation for EVENT-RELATED MAGNETIC FIELD.

erg *n.* **1.** a specific, innate DRIVE directed toward a goal. See DYNAMIC CALCULUS. [defined by British-born U.S. psychologist Raymond B. Cattell (1905–1998)] **2.** in physics, a unit of work or energy.

ERG abbreviation for ELECTRORETINOGRAM.

ergasiology *n.* see PSYCHOBIOLOGY.

ergative *n.* in English and some other languages, a verb that can be used either transitively or intransitively with the same noun to describe the same action. An example is *close* in *I closed the door* or *the door closed*: The direct object of the transitive verb (here *door*) becomes the subject of the intransitive verb. Such constructions are of great interest in CASE GRAMMAR and GENERATIVE GRAMMAR.

ergic trait a dynamic trait that motivates an individual to achieve an objective.

ergogram *n.* the output of an ERGOGRAPH, indicating the amount of work done or the physical exertion of the muscles.

ergograph *n.* a device used to record the work capacity or FATIGUE of a muscle or muscle group.

ergomania *n.* a compulsion to work and keep busy. Also called **workaholism**. See WORKAHOLIC.

ergometry *n.* the measurement of physical work performed by muscles under various task demands. **—ergometric** *adj.*

ergonomics *n.* the discipline that applies a knowledge of human abilities and limitations drawn from physiology, BIOMECHANICS, ANTHROPOMETRY, and other areas to the design of systems, equipment, and processes for safe and efficient performance. Speciality areas include COGNITIVE ERGONOMICS, COMMUNICATION ERGONOMICS, CULTURAL ERGONOMICS, INDUSTRIAL ERGONOMICS, MACROERGONOMICS, and OCCUPATIONAL ERGONOMICS. This term is often used synonymously with HUMAN FACTORS ENGINEERING. **—ergonomic** *adj.*

ergonomic traps components of a design that contribute to the probability of accidents and HUMAN ERROR. Designs that are not intuitive or that violate normal human tendencies in terms of behavior and mental processing contain ergonomic traps. See BEHAVIOR-BASED SAFETY.

ergonomist *n.* a person who studies or practices ERGONOMICS.

ergonovine *n.* see ERGOT DERIVATIVES; OXYTOCICS.

ergot alkaloids pharmacologically active substances derived from the parasitic fungus *Claviceps purpurea*, which grows naturally on rye and other grains. Although highly toxic, ergot alkaloids have been used for centuries by midwives to induce abortion or labor. A number have been isolated, including lysergic acid, and the compounds are sometimes utilized as adrenoreceptor blocking agents (see ERGOT DERIVATIVES). Epidemics of ergot poisoning (**ergotism**) were widespread until relatively modern times in Europe; symptoms included peripheral vasoconstriction (rarely gangrene) and changes in mental functioning, including visual hallucinations. Because of the pharmacological relationship between ergot and LSD (lysergic acid diethylamide), the hallucinogenic effects are similar to those of LSD.

ergotamine *n.* an alkaloid drug (an ERGOT DERIVATIVE) used in the treatment of vascular headaches, including migraines. The exact nature of its therapeutic action is unknown, but ergotamine is believed to constrict the dilated cranial blood vessels responsible for the headache symptoms. U.S. trade name (among others): **Cafergot**.

ergot derivatives a group of ADRENORECEPTOR BLOCKING AGENTS with selective inhibitory activity, derived from ERGOT ALKALOIDS. Ergot derivatives act on the central nervous system in a complex manner and, in various forms and doses, can both stimulate and depress higher brain centers. A circulatory effect is vasoconstriction. Some of these agents, including ERGOTAMINE, are used in the control of migraine headaches, sometimes combined with other drugs (e.g., caffeine). The derivative ergonovine is used as an OXYTOCIC.

ergotherapy *n.* treatment of disease by muscular exercise. This term is used in Europe; it is not common in the United States.

ergotropic *adj.* related to or concerning a capacity or propensity for expenditure of energy, that is, for activity, effort, or work. Compare TROPHOTROPIC.

ERG theory abbreviation for EXISTENCE, RELATEDNESS, AND GROWTH THEORY.

Erhard Seminar Training (**est**; **EST**) a controversial group therapy technique and personal development training system introduced in 1971. It purports to be consciousness-expanding, borrowing from business-world motivation techniques and various theories of psychology. It was renamed **Landmark Forum** in 1985. [Werner **Erhard** (born John Paul Rosenberg; 1935–), U.S. consultant and lecturer]

Erichsen's disease a disorder characterized by back pain and other spinal symptoms that was first identified in 1866 (at a time when railroad transportation was becoming increasingly popular) and was believed to be a result of railroad accidents. As the state of medicine advanced, it was realized that these symptoms were not of organic origin but indicated a functional disorder that may have been a precursor to POSTTRAUMATIC STRESS DISORDER. Also called **railway spine**. [John Eric **Erichsen** (1818–1896), British surgeon]

Ericksonian psychotherapy a form of psychotherapy in which the therapist works with the client to create, through hypnosis (specifically through indirect suggestion) and suggestive metaphors, real-life experiences intended to activate previously dormant, intrapsychic resources. Also called **Ericksonian hypnotherapy**. [Milton H. **Erickson** (1902–1980), U.S. psychiatrist and psychologist]

Eriksen flankers task a task in which stimuli are assigned one of two responses and the participant is required to respond to the target stimulus when this is flanked by other stimuli. The stimuli are presented at a known location (usually at fixation), and the flanking stimuli are associated with a response that is either the same as or different from that assigned to the target. Reaction time is slower if the stimuli flanking the target are assigned the alternative response than if they are assigned the same response as the target. This is known as the **Eriksen flanker compatibility effect.** [Charles **Eriksen**]

Erikson, Erik H. (1902–1994) German-born U.S. psychologist. Originally called Erik Homburger, he lived from 1927 to 1933 in Vienna, where he underwent training in PSYCHOANALYSIS with Anna FREUD for 3 years. When the Nazis rose to power, Erikson emigrated with his wife Joan to the United States, where he spent the bulk of his career at Harvard University. Erikson is best known as a personality theorist and preeminent figure in the field of EGO PSYCHOLOGY. His theory of the eight stages of the life cycle (see ERIKSON'S EIGHT STAGES OF DEVELOPMENT) contained the development of self-identity as its central theme; he coined the term IDENTITY CRISIS to describe the crucial developmental process of ADOLESCENCE. Erikson argued for the importance of researching individual life histories in personality theory, opposing the trend toward the use of aggregate statistics in his field. Erikson's most influential works include *Childhood and Society* (1950) and *Identity: Youth and Crisis* (1968), as well as two psychobiographies, *Young Man Luther* (1958) and *Ghandi's Truth* (1969). See also EPIGENESIS; PSYCHOBIOGRAPHY; PSYCHOHISTORY.

Erikson's eight stages of development the theory of psychosocial development proposed by Erik ERIKSON, in which EGO IDENTITY is gradually achieved by facing positive goals and negative risks during eight stages of development across the lifespan. The stages are: (a) infancy: TRUST VERSUS MISTRUST; (b) toddler: AUTONOMY VERSUS SHAME AND DOUBT; (c) preschool age: INITIATIVE VERSUS GUILT; (d) school age: INDUSTRY VERSUS INFERIORITY; (e) adolescence: IDENTITY VERSUS ROLE CONFUSION; (f) young adulthood: INTIMACY VERSUS ISOLATION; (g) middle age: GENERATIVITY VERSUS STAGNATION; and (h) older adulthood: INTEGRITY VERSUS DESPAIR.

ERISA acronym for EMPLOYEE RETIREMENT INCOME SECURITY ACT.

erogenous zone an area or part of the body sensitive to stimulation that is a source of erotic or sexual feeling or pleasure. Any area of the body might be considered erogenous depending on the individual's perception, but among the primary zones are the genitals and adjacent areas, the breasts (especially the nipples), the buttocks and anus, and the mouth. Also called **erotogenic zone**.

Eros *n.* the god of love in Greek mythology (equivalent to the Roman Cupid), whose name was chosen by Sigmund FREUD to designate a theoretical set of strivings oriented toward sexuality, development, and increased life activity (see LIFE INSTINCT). In Freud's DUAL INSTINCT THEORY, Eros is seen as involved in a dialectic process with THANATOS, the striving toward reduced psychical tension and life activity (see DEATH INSTINCT). See also LIBIDO.

erosion *n.* the deterioration or corrosion of a physical setting from climatic effects and from use by organisms, including human beings. For example, the degree of wear evident in footpaths or trails in a woodland may be taken as an indication of their degree of use. Compare ACCRETION.

erotica *pl. n.* literature, illustrations, motion pictures or other artistic material likely to arouse sexual response. The term is sometimes used interchangeably with PORNOGRAPHY. However, the distinction is often made that erotica, unlike pornography, does not involve violence, coercion, or exploitative sexuality, instead depicting sexuality in a positive manner.

erotic-arousal pattern the sequence of actions or stimuli that produces sexual response. The actions or stimuli vary with different species: In humans they may involve dress, perfume, music, and foreplay.

erotic asphyxiation sexual pleasure associated with restriction of breathing during sexual activity. See ASPHYXOPHILIA, AUTOEROTIC ASPHYXIATION.

erotic delusion the false perception or belief that one is loved by or has had a sexual affair with a public figure or other individual. Also called **erotomanic delusion**. See CLÉRAMBAULT'S SYNDROME; DELUSIONAL DISORDER; EROTIC PARANOIA; SIMENON'S SYNDROME.

erotic feminism a type of FEMINISM that emphasizes female sexuality and its expression as a means of opposing the exploitation of women and escaping male domination. This contrasts with some other tendencies in mainstream feminism, which can appear wary or even dismissive in their approach to erotic expression.

erotic instinct **1.** in psychoanalytic theory, the sex drive or LIBIDO. **2.** EROS, or the LIFE INSTINCT.

eroticism *n.* **1.** the quality of being sexually arousing or pleasurable or the condition of being sexually aroused. **2.** a preoccupation with or susceptibility to sexual excitement. **3.** the use of sexually arousing themes, images, or suggestions in entertainment or the arts. **4.** in psychoanalytic theory, the pleasurable sensations associated not only with stimulation of the genitals but also with nongenital parts of the body, such as the mouth or anus (see ANAL EROTICISM; ORAL EROTICISM). Also called **erotism**. See also AUTOEROTICISM; EROTIZATION. **—erotic** *adj.*

eroticization *n.* see EROTIZATION.

erotic love a type of LOVE, identified in certain classifications of love, that is characterized by strong sexual arousal. See also LIMERENCE; PASSIONATE LOVE.

erotic paranoia a disorder in which the individual experiences EROTIC DELUSIONS. Also called **erotomanic-type delusional disorder**. See DELUSIONAL DISORDER. See also CLÉRAMBAULT'S SYNDROME; SIMENON'S SYNDROME.

erotic plasticity the degree to which sexual desire and sexual behavior are shaped by social, cultural, and situational factors. See BEHAVIORAL PLASTICITY.

erotic pyromania see PYROLAGNIA.

erotic type see LIBIDINAL TYPES.

erotism *n.* see EROTICISM.

erotization *n.* the investment of bodily organs and biological functions or other not specifically sensual or sexual activities with sexual pleasure and gratification. Common examples are the erotization of certain areas of the body, such as the oral or anal EROGENOUS ZONES; organs, such as the nipple or skin; functions, such as sucking, defecation, urination, or scopophilic activities (looking at nudity or sexual activity); and olfactory sensations associated with sex. Theoretically, almost any interest or activity can be erotized by the individual; for example, activities such as dancing and eating are not infrequently seen as erotic or as having erotic components. Also called **eroticization**; **libidinization**; **sexualization**. **—erotize** *vb.*

erotogenesis *n.* in psychoanalytic theory, the origination of erotic impulses from sources that may include the anal, oral, and genital zones. See EROTIZATION.

erotogenic *adj.* denoting or relating to any stimulus that evokes or excites sexual feelings or responses. Also called **erotogenetic**.

erotogenic masochism see PRIMARY MASOCHISM.

erotogenic zone see EROGENOUS ZONE.

erotographomania *n.* an obsession with erotic writing that is accompanied by a pathological compulsion to write about sexual matters or draw sexual images, typically expressed through anonymous love letters or graffiti.

erotolalia *n.* speech that contains sexual obscenities, particularly as used to enhance gratification during sexual intercourse.

erotomania *n.* **1.** a preoccupation with sexual activities, thoughts, and fantasies. **2.** the false belief that one is loved by another person. See EROTIC DELUSION. **3.** compulsive, insatiable sexual activity with the opposite sex. Also called **aidoiomania**. See DON JUAN; NYMPHOMANIA; SATYRIASIS. **—erotomanic** *adj.*

erotomanic delusion see EROTIC DELUSION.

erotophonophilia *n.* see LUST MURDER.

ERP abbreviation for EVENT-RELATED POTENTIAL.

ERP measure of attitudes see EVENT-RELATED-POTENTIAL MEASURE OF ATTITUDES.

ERP measures of intelligence measures of intelligence elicited by observing EVENT-RELATED POTENTIALS (ERPs) in the brain in response to various kinds of stimuli. These measures show reliable correlations with traditional measures of intelligence, with the level of the correlation depending on the particular potential being measured. For example, P300, a positive potential observed roughly 300 milliseconds after presentation of a stimulus, tends to be related to effectiveness in coping with novelty and appears to be related to intelligence.

error *n.* **1.** a deviation from true or accurate information (e.g., a wrong response or a mistaken belief). **2.** in experimentation, any change in a DEPENDENT VARIABLE not attributable to the manipulation of an INDEPENDENT VARIABLE. **3.** in psychometrics, a deviation from a true score, where true score is often defined by the MEAN of the particular group or condition in which the score being assessed for error occurs. **4.** in statistics, a deviation of an observed score from the score predicted by a statistical model.

error analysis **1.** the study of HUMAN FACTORS and engineering-design factors that may result in production or operation errors. See also ACCIDENT ANALYSIS; FAILURE MODES AND EFFECTS ANALYSIS; FAULT-TREE ANALYSIS; JOB-SAFETY ANALYSIS. **2.** a systematic analysis of the language corpus obtained from second-language learners to identify ways in which the linguistic forms systematically deviate from target-language norms and to make inferences about the learner's state of second-language development. See FOSSILIZATION; INTERLANGUAGE; LANGUAGE TRANSFER.

errorless learning a method of learning whereby errors are eliminated through training. Specifically, learning occurs across several sessions, but memory is not tested until the last session. This method prevents the production of incorrect answers during the learning period. It is thought to be more efficient than standard trial-and-error learning for individuals with memory impairment because it eliminates interference.

error method see METHOD OF ADJUSTMENT.

error of anticipation in the METHOD OF LIMITS, an error in which the participant incorrectly changes his or her response of "target present" to "target absent," or vice versa, based on the knowledge that the stimuli are being presented in an ascending or descending order.

error of commission a category of HUMAN ERROR in which an operator performs an incorrect or additional action, such as pressing a control button twice, leading to inappropriate or duplicate performance of a function. Compare ERROR OF OMISSION.

error of expectation an error arising because of a preconceived idea of the nature of the stimulus to be presented or the timing of the presentation.

error of habituation in the METHOD OF LIMITS, a tendency to continue with the previous response (either "target present" or "target absent") beyond the point at which a transition in judgments should occur.

error of measurement any deviation or departure of a measurement from its true value.

error of omission a category of HUMAN ERROR in which an operator fails to perform a necessary step or action, such as failing to press a control button, leading to the failure of a function. Compare ERROR OF COMMISSION.

error of refraction a defect in the eye such that it does not refract, or bend, incident light into perfect focus on the retina, so that visual acuity is reduced. Correction requires the use of spectacles, contact lenses, or surgery. Also called **refractive error**; **refractive disorder**. See also MYOPIA; HYPEROPIA.

error rate the rate at which errors are made, for example, the proportion of an experimenter's data recordings that are wrong.

error score in CLASSICAL TEST THEORY, the difference between a person's observed measurement or score and his or her expected measurement or score.

error term the element of a statistical equation that indicates what is unexplained by the INDEPENDENT VARIABLES. Also called **disturbance term**; **residual term**.

error variance variability in a score that is not systematic or controlled, not produced by the INDEPENDENT VARIABLE, or not associated with variance in scores predicted by a statistical model.

erythema multiforme major see STEVENS–JOHNSON SYNDROME.

erythro- (**erythr-**) *combining form* red.

erythropoietin *n.* a protein produced by the kidneys and liver that stimulates the production of red blood cells (erythrocytes) in the bone marrow and maintains erythrocytes in the circulation at an optimal level.

erythropsia *n.* see CHROMATOPSIA.

Esalen Institute an alternative educational center in California, founded in 1962, where enhancement of well-being is approached through a number of meditative and new-age therapies. Therapists and members of the general public participate in seminars, workshops, experiential programs, and other events that are designed to promote self-exploration and enhance relationships with others.

ESB abbreviation for ELECTROSTIMULATION OF THE BRAIN.

escalation of aggression the increase of intensity or severity of hostile or destructive behavior, often to the point of violence. This process is often associated with assaultive behavior, DOMESTIC VIOLENCE, and the CYCLE OF VIOLENCE.

escalation of commitment continued commitment and increased allocation of resources to a failing course of action, often in the hope of recouping past losses associated with that course of action. It is often associated with expenditures and decision making in the development of new products, when a company increases the allocation of resources to a failing product, regardless of the low probability of its success, in an attempt to recover some of its initial investment. Also called **creeping commitment**.

escape behavior any response designed to move away from or eliminate an already present aversive stimulus. Escape behavior may be mental (through fantasy or daydreams) or behavioral (physical withdrawal from a noxious stimulus or a conditioned response, as when an animal taps a lever in order to terminate a shock). See also ESCAPE LEARNING. Compare AVOIDANCE BEHAVIOR.

escape from freedom a false solution to the individual's problems of loneliness and isolation, in which he or she seeks refuge in social conformity. See also IDENTITY NEED. [defined by Erich FROMM]

escape from reality a defensive reaction involving the use of fantasy as a means of avoiding conflicts and problems of daily living. See also FLIGHT FROM REALITY.

escape into illness see FLIGHT INTO ILLNESS.

escape learning a type of learning in which a subject acquires a response that results in the termination of an aversive stimulus. For example, if a monkey learns that pulling a string frequently results in the elimination of a loud noise, escape learning has occurred. The principle is identical to that of NEGATIVE REINFORCEMENT. The actual process of training an organism to terminate an aversive stimulus is known as **escape conditioning**. See also AVOIDANCE CONDITIONING; ESCAPE BEHAVIOR.

escape mechanism see DEFENSE MECHANISM.

escape titration a procedure in which an animal, presented with an AVERSIVE STIMULUS that increases in intensity over time, can by responding decrease the stimulus intensity by some fixed (usually small) amount. By responding, therefore, the subject can control the intensity of the stimulus at virtually any level within the range set by the experimenter. Also called **fractional escape**.

escapism *n.* the tendency to escape from the real world to the delight or security of a fantasy world. Escapism may reflect a periodic, normal, and common impulse, as might be seen in harmless DAYDREAMS, or it may be evidence of or accompany other symptoms of neurosis or more serious mental pathology. **—escapist** *adj.*

Eskalith *n.* a trade name for LITHIUM.

ESL abbreviation for ENGLISH AS A SECOND LANGUAGE.

esophageal speech a type of phonation, not involving the larynx, in which air supply originates in the narrow upper portion of the esophagus, with the pharyngoesophageal segment (the sphincter-like muscle at the junction of the LARYNGOPHARYNX and the esophagus) acting as a neoglottis (vibratory apparatus).

esophoria *n.* an inward deviation of one eye that is due to a muscular imbalance and that interferes with binocular vision. Esophoria is a form of HETEROPHORIA. See also PHORIA.

esotropia *n.* see CROSS-EYE; STRABISMUS.

ESP abbreviation for EXTRASENSORY PERCEPTION.

espanto *n.* see SUSTO.

ESP forced-choice test in parapsychology experiments, a technique in which a participant's "calls" or guesses are restricted to a predetermined set of TARGETS, as with ZENER CARDS. The main advantages of this procedure are that the success or failure of the participants' calls should be (a) unambiguous, and (b) statistically measurable, enabling them to be compared with chance expectations. Compare ESP FREE-RESPONSE TEST.

ESP free-response test in parapsychology experiments, a technique in which a participant's "calls" or guesses are not restricted to a predetermined set of TARGETS. The calls are then correlated to possible targets by a process of PREFERENTIAL MATCHING. Compare ESP FORCED-CHOICE TEST.

esprit de corps a feeling of unity, commitment, purpose, and COLLECTIVE EFFICACY shared by most or all of the members of a cohesive group or organization. Members of groups with esprit de corps feel close to one another, are committed to the group and its goals, and are in some cases willing to sacrifice their own individual desires for the good of the group. Unlike GROUP MORALE, which can be low when members are dissatisfied or indifferent, esprit de corps implies confidence and enthusiasm for the group. See also COHESION; COMMUNAL FEELING; COMMUNAL SPIRIT; GROUP SOLIDARITY.

ESS abbreviation for EVOLUTIONARILY STABLE STRATEGY.

essay test an examination in which examinees answer questions by writing sentences, paragraphs, or pages. The reliability of grading such tests is usually lower than that of OBJECTIVE EXAMINATIONS, but the validity may be higher.

ESSB abbreviation for electrical self-stimulation of the brain. See INTRACRANIAL SELF-STIMULATION.

essence *n.* in philosophy, the presumed ontological reality at the core of something that makes it what it is and not something else. There have been various philosophical attempts to define the difference between what something necessarily is, and what it merely coincidentally is (see ACCIDENTAL PROPERTY; ESSENTIAL PROPERTY). In psychology, the concept of essence is relevant to discussions of personhood, including questions of human agency and of the SELF. It is thus important for personality theories. The view that human beings have certain important essential characteristics is known as ESSENTIALISM. **—essential** *adj.*

essential dysmenorrhea see DYSMENORRHEA.

essential hypertension high blood pressure (see HYPERTENSION) that is not secondary to another disease and for which no obvious cause can be found. It accounts for at least 85% of all cases of hypertension; predisposing factors include obesity, cigarette smoking, genetic factors, and psychological influences (e.g., an aggressive personality or stressful environment). See also TYPE A PERSONALITY.

essentialism *n.* in philosophy, the position that things (or some things) have ESSENCES; that is, they have certain necessary properties without which they could not be the things they are. In MARXISM, POSTMODERNISM, POSTSTRUCTURALISM, and certain feminist perspectives, essentialism is the rejected position that human beings have an essential nature that transcends such factors as social class, gender, and ethnicity. See also UNIVERSALISM.

essential property a characteristic of an idea or entity that is essential to its nature or existence. For example, being female is an essential property of mothers, whereas being tired is an ACCIDENTAL PROPERTY.

essential tremor a fine TREMOR of the hands, head, and voice that appears to be hereditary and is not associated with any pathology of the nervous system, such as Parkinson's disease. Also called **benign hereditary tremor**; **familial tremor**.

est (**EST**) abbreviation for ERHARD SEMINAR TRAINING.

EST 1. abbreviation for electroshock therapy or electroconvulsive shock therapy. See ELECTROCONVULSIVE THERAPY. **2.** see EST.

establishing operation any event or procedure that changes the efficacy of a stimulus as a reinforcer or punisher. For example, in an operant-conditioning study where food is used to positively reinforce behavior, the establishing operation may be food deprivation, which sets up food as a rewarding and reinforcing stimulus.

estazolam *n.* a high-potency, intermediate-acting BENZODIAZEPINE used for the short-term treatment of insomnia (see HYPNOTIC). U.S. trade name: **ProSom**.

esteem needs in MASLOW'S MOTIVATIONAL HIERARCHY, the fourth level in his hierarchy of needs, characterized by striving for a sense of personal value derived from achievement, reputation, or prestige. In this level of development, the admiration and approval of others leads to the development of SELF-ESTEEM.

Estes, William Kaye (1919–) U.S. psychologist. Estes was awarded his doctorate in psychology in 1943 from the University of Minnesota, where he studied with B. F. SKINNER. His career was spent at various institutions, including Indiana University, Stanford University, Rockefeller University, and Harvard University. Estes is a founding figure of MATHEMATICAL PSYCHOLOGY and a major figure in cognitive psychology. His classic 1950 paper, "Toward a Statistical Theory of Learning," demonstrated the potential of applying mathematics to problems of animal and human learning. Throughout his career he contributed to the theoretical and empirical advance of cognitive psychology in such areas as learning, memory, categorization, and choice. Together with Skinner, Estes pioneered the widely used technique of CONDITIONED EMOTIONAL RESPONSE for the experimental study of fear and anxiety. Among his works are the advanced textbook *Statistical Models in Behavioral Research* (1991) and the six-volume *Handbook of Learning and Cognitive Processes* (1975–1978), which he edited. Estes's honors include election to the National Academy of Sciences and the American Academy of Arts and Sciences and receipt of the Distinguished Research Contribution Award of the American Psychological Association, the American Psychological Foundation's Gold Medal for Lifetime Achievement in Psychological Science, and the National Medal of Science. See also STIMULUS SAMPLING THEORY.

Estes–Skinner procedure a procedure in which PAVLOVIAN CONDITIONING trials are superimposed on a BASELINE of operant responding (usually maintained by a schedule of INTERMITTENT REINFORCEMENT). It is used to examine emotion-inducing operations. See also CONDITIONED SUPPRESSION. [William K. ESTES and B. F. SKINNER]

esthesiometer (**aesthesiometer**) *n.* a compasslike device used to measure tactile sensitivity, either absolute sensitivity or spatial sensitivity (see TWO-POINT THRESHOLD). See also ESTHESIOMETRY; FREY ESTHESIOMETER.

esthesiometry (**aesthesiometry**) *n.* the measurement of sensitivity to touch. Classically, an ESTHESIOMETER, a compasslike device, has been used to measure TWO-POINT DISCRIMINATION on the skin. More sophisticated techniques have now been developed.

estimable function a function of the parameters of a model that can be uniquely estimated from the data. The estimable function is important in GENERAL LINEAR MODEL applications.

estimate 1. *n.* a best guess of the value of a parameter of a DISTRIBUTION on the basis of a set of empirical observations. **2.** *vb.* to assign a value to a parameter in this way.

estimator *n.* a quantity calculated from the values in a sample according to some rule and used to give an estimate of the value in a population. For example, the sample mean is an estimator for the population mean; the value of the sample mean is the estimate.

estimators *pl. n.* the mental processes involved in judging quantity, as in the ability to recognize that a given set contains six elements rather than five or seven. Compare OPERATORS. [defined in this sense by U.S. statistician Andrew Gelman]

estradiol *n.* a naturally occurring steroid hormone that is the most potent of the ESTROGENS. It is secreted mainly by the ovary but also by the placenta and testes.

estrangement *n.* **1.** a state of increased distance or separation from oneself or others. See ALIENATION. **2.** a significant decrease or discontinuation of contact with individuals with whom one formerly had close relationships, such as a spouse or family member, due to apathy or antagonism. **—estranged** *adj.*

estriol *n.* see ESTROGEN.

estrogen *n.* any of a class of STEROID HORMONES that are produced mainly by the ovaries and act as the principal female SEX HORMONES, inducing estrus in female mammals and secondary female sexual characteristics in humans. The estrogens occurring naturally in humans are ESTRADIOL, ESTRONE, and **estriol**, secreted by the ovarian follicle, corpus luteum, placenta, testes, and adrenal cortex. Estrogens are also produced by certain plants; these **phytoestrogens** may be used in the manufacture of synthetic steroid hormones. Estrogens are used therapeutically in ESTROGEN REPLACEMENT THERAPY and oral contraceptives and to treat certain menstrual disorders and some types of breast and prostate cancers.

estrogen antagonist see ANTIESTROGEN.

estrogen replacement therapy the administration of natural or synthetic estrogens, such as estradiol or ethinyl estradiol, for the relief of symptoms associated with menopause, surgical removal of the ovaries, or failure of the ovaries to develop. Although estrogen replacement therapy is an extremely common therapy in menopausal women, recent studies have questioned its material long-term benefits. See HORMONE REPLACEMENT THERAPY.

estrone *n.* an ESTROGEN produced by ovarian follicles and other tissues. It is used therapeutically in the treatment of menopausal and other estrogen-deficiency disorders (see ESTROGEN REPLACEMENT THERAPY) and in certain cases of vaginitis.

estrous behavior a behavior pattern observed in nonhuman females during ESTRUS, the phase of their ESTROUS CYCLE when they are more likely to mate. Estrous behavior can be divided into PROCEPTIVITY and RECEPTIVITY. Also called **heat**.

estrous cycle the cyclical sequence of reproductive activity shown by most female mammals (except humans and other primates; see MENSTRUAL CYCLE). Animals that experience one estrous cycle per year are called **monestrous**; those that have multiple estrous cycles annually are **polyestrous**. See also DIESTRUS; ESTRUS; PROESTRUS.

estrus *n.* the stage in the ESTROUS CYCLE when a female animal is receptive to the male and willing to mate. Also called **heat**. See also ESTROUS BEHAVIOR. **—estrous** *adj.*

eta (symbol: η) *n.* a coefficient of nonlinear correlation. See CORRELATION RATIO.

ethanol *n.* a substance formed naturally or synthetically by the fermentation of glucose and found in alcoholic beverages, such as beers, wines, and distilled liquors. It is the second most widely used PSYCHOACTIVE DRUG (after caffeine). The ethanol content of alcoholic beverages ranges from as low as 2% in beers to as much as 60% in some distilled products. The effects of ingesting ethanol differ across individuals and in the same person at different times. In small doses, it can produce feelings of warmth, well-being, and confidence in one's mental and physical powers. As more is consumed, there is a gradual loss of self-control, excitement is increased, and speech and control of limbs become difficult; at high consumption levels, nausea and vomiting, loss of consciousness, and even fatal respiratory arrest may occur. Ethanol is a CNS DEPRESSANT and was formerly used as an anesthetic agent. It has been mistakenly identified as a stimulant, since its stimulating effect derives from an associated loss of cortical inhibition. Its predominant depressant effect begins in the cortex and gradually spreads to lower centers as dosage increases. Also called **ethyl alcohol**. See also ALCOHOL ABUSE; ALCOHOL DEPENDENCE; ALCOHOL INTOXICATION.

ethchlorvynol *n.* an ALCOHOL DERIVATIVE introduced in the 1950s as a nonbarbiturate sedative. Ethclorvynol is an effective, rapidly acting hypnotic, but because of its toxicity in overdose, as well as its ability to induce enzymes involved in drug metabolism (see ENZYME INDUCTION) and its association with blood disorders, it has become clinically obsolete. It is at times a substance of abuse. U.S. trade name: **Placidyl**.

ether *n.* a drug introduced into medicine as a general anesthetic in the mid-1800s. The effects of ether include a progressive series of physical and psychological reactions, beginning with a feeling of suffocation, bodily warmth, visual and auditory aberrations, and a feeling of stiffness and inability to move the limbs. A second stage may be marked by some resistance to the sense of suffocation of the anesthetic, but the muscles relax, blood pressure and pulse increase, and pupils dilate. In the third stage, pulse and blood pressure return to normal, pupils contract, and reflexes are absent. If additional ether is administered beyond the third stage, there is danger of paralysis of the medullary centers, followed by shock and death. In clinical practice, ether has been replaced by safer anesthetics.

e-therapy *n.* an Internet-based form of DISTANCE THERAPY used to expand access to clinical services typically offered face-to-face. This therapy can be conducted in real-time messaging, in chat rooms, and in e-mail messages. Also called **online therapy**.

ethereal *adj.* **1.** in the ZWAARDEMAKER SMELL SYSTEM, denoting an odor quality that is smelled in fruits and wines. **2.** denoting one of the seven classes of odorants in the STEREOCHEMICAL SMELL THEORY.

ethical conflict see BOUNDARY ISSUES; CONFLICT OF INTEREST; DOUBLE-AGENTRY.

ethical determinism the position, stated definitively by Greek philosopher Plato (c. 427–c. 347 BCE), that one who knows the good will (necessarily) do the good. It is implied that a sense of obligation is the defining feature of knowledge of the good, and that this sense will be strong enough to compel, rather than merely suggest, action. This position assumes the essential rationality of human beings. Later modifications of the position have argued that a person will necessarily act in accordance with what he or she perceives to be good, whether or not it really is good, or that a person will act consistently with what he or she perceives to be good, where what is good is what is in that person's self-interest (see EUDEMONISM). Also called **moral determinism**.

ethical dilemma a situation in which two moral principles conflict with one another. Fictional or hypothetical dilemmas of this kind are often used to assess the moral beliefs or moral reasoning skills of individuals. See HEINZ DILEMMA; KOHLBERG'S THEORY OF MORAL DEVELOPMENT.

ethical imperative a principle or practice taken to be ethically required of one. The binding character of the principle or behavior may result from a perceived logical or rational necessity, as in the CATEGORICAL IMPERATIVE defined by German philosopher Immanuel Kant (1724–1804), or it may seem to arise from some set of empirical facts; for example, energy conservation may seem to be an ethical imperative given that one accepts the evidence of global warming.

ethical judgment 1. a moral decision made by an individual, especially a difficult one made in the context of a real or hypothetical ETHICAL DILEMMA. Such judgments often reveal the beliefs that an individual applies in discriminating between right and wrong and the attitudes that comprise his or her basic moral orientation. **2.** the faculty of making moral distinctions. Also called **moral judgment**.

ethical nihilism see MORAL NIHILISM.

ethics *n.* **1.** the branch of philosophy that investigates both the content of moral judgments (i.e., what is right and what is wrong) and their nature (i.e., whether such judgments should be considered objective or subjective). The study of the first type of question is sometimes termed **normative ethics** and that of the second **metaethics**. Also called **moral philosophy**. **2.** the principles of morally right conduct accepted by a person or a group or considered appropriate to a specific field (e.g., medical ethics). See CODE OF ETHICS; PROFESSIONAL ETHICS. **—ethical** *adj.*

ethics of animal research the complex set of issues relating to the ethics of manipulating animals experimentally, holding them in captivity, and sacrificing them for the purpose of research. Some argue that any animal research is unethical because animals cannot give informed consent. Others see value in animal research if the animals are well cared for and treated humanely. See ANIMAL CARE AND USE; INSTITUTIONAL ANIMAL CARE AND USE COMMITTEE.

ethmocephaly *n.* a birth defect involving the olfactory system and often marked by a rudimentary proboscis-shaped nose, which may have imperforate nostrils. The condition is sometimes associated with CEBOCEPHALY and tends to occur as part of CHROMOSOME-13 TRISOMY.

ethmoid fossa see FOSSA.

ethnic *adj.* denoting or referring to a group of people having a shared social, cultural, linguistic, religious, and usually racial background. ETHNIC IDENTITY is usually considered to be a complex construct involving some or all of these factors but identical with none of them.

ethnic cleansing the methodical removal, detention, or GENOCIDE of an ethnic group or groups in order to produce an ethnically homogeneous territory or society.

ethnic drift 1. the process by which people belonging to an ethnic minority tend to lose, alter, or redefine their sense of ETHNIC IDENTITY over time, generally as a result of assimilation with the dominant culture, intermarriage, or loss of contact with their culture of origin. See also CULTURAL DRIFT. **2.** the tendency for people of the same ethnicity to gather in or be assigned to the same formal or informal groups, whether as a result of voluntary association or the conscious or unconscious policies of others. At work, for example, people of the same ethnicity are often assigned to the same work team or supervisor.

ethnic group any major social group that possesses a common ETHNIC IDENTITY based on history, culture, language, and, often, religion. Members are likely to be biologically related, but an ethnic group is not equivalent to a RACE.

ethnic identity an individual's sense of being a person who is defined, in part, by membership in a specific ethnic group.

ethnicity *n.* a social categorization based on an individual's membership of or identification with a particular ETHNIC GROUP. See also ETHNIC IDENTITY.

ethnocentrism *n.* the tendency to reject and malign other ethnic groups and their members while glorifying one's own group and its members. Just as EGOCENTRISM is the tendency to judge oneself as superior to others, so ethnocentrism is the parallel tendency to judge one's group as superior to other groups. See also INGROUP BIAS; RACISM. **—ethnocentric** *adj.*

ethnographic approach a strategy frequently used by anthropologists for studying a community as a way of life. The method requires extensive residence in the community, fluency in the local languages, and active participation in community life in order to develop insight into its total culture.

ethnography *n.* the descriptive study of cultures or societies based on direct observation (see FIELD WORK) and (ideally) some degree of participation. Compare ETHNOLOGY. See also EMIC. **—ethnographer** *n.* **—ethnographic** *adj.*

ethnolinguistics *n.* the investigation of language within the context of human cultures or societies, paying attention to cultural influences and incorporating the principles of anthropology and ethnography. See also ANTHROPOLOGICAL LINGUISTICS.

ethnology *n.* the comparative, analytical, or historical study of human cultures or societies. Compare ETHNOGRAPHY. See also ETIC. **—ethnological** *adj.* **—ethnologist** *n.*

ethnomethodology *n.* the analysis of the underlying conventions and systems of meaning that people use to make sense of commonplace social interactions and experiences. [introduced by U.S. sociologist Harold Garffinkel (1917–)] **—ethnomethodological** *adj.* **—ethnomethodologist** *n.*

ethnopsychology *n.* see CROSS-CULTURAL PSYCHOLOGY.

ethnopsychopharmacology *n.* the branch of pharmacology that deals with issues related to ethnic and cultural variations in the use of and response to psychoactive agents across divergent groups, as well as the mechanisms responsible for such differences. **—ethnopsychopharmacological** *adj.*

ethnotherapy *n.* therapy sensitive to the distinct cultural features of a client from an ethnic minority and the various ways in which the client relates to others, expresses him- or herself, and deals with problems. See also MULTICULTURAL COUNSELING.

ethogram *n.* a detailed listing and description of the behavior patterns of an animal in its natural habitat. The description is objective rather than interpretative. For example, a vocalization given in response to a predator would be described in terms of its acoustic properties rather than its apparent function of alarm call. An ethogram can be used to determine categories for a BEHAVIOR RECORD and is a prerequisite for observational research. See ETHOLOGY.

ethologically oriented universal see PSYCHOLOGICAL UNIVERSAL.

ethology *n.* the comparative study of the behavior of animals, typically in their natural habitat but also involving experiments both in the field and in captivity. Ethology was developed by behavioral biologists in Europe and is often associated with connotations of innate or species-specific behavior patterns, in contrast with COMPARATIVE PSYCHOLOGY. The theory and methods from both areas are now closely interrelated, and ANIMAL BEHAVIOR is a more neutral and more broadly encompassing term. **—ethological** *adj.* **—ethologist** *n.*

ethos *n.* the distinctive character or spirit of an individual, group, culture, nation, or period, as revealed particularly in its attitudes and values. See also ORTGEIST; ZEITGEIST.

ethosuximide *n.* see SUCCINIMIDES.

ethotoin *n.* see HYDANTOINS.

ethyl alcohol see ETHANOL.

ETI abbreviation for EARLY TRANSIENT INCAPACITATION.

etic *adj.* **1.** denoting an approach to the study of human cultures based on concepts or constructs that are held to be universal and applicable cross-culturally. Such an approach would generally be of the kind associated with ETHNOLOGY rather than ETHNOGRAPHY. The term is sometimes used in a critical sense of studies or perspectives that aspire to objectivity but succeed only in defining social behaviors in terms of the researcher's own cultural values. Compare EMIC. [introduced by U.S. linguist Kenneth Pike (1912–2000); first used in anthropology by U.S. cultural anthropologist Marvin Harris (1927–2001)] **2.** denoting an approach to the study of language based on PHONETICS (i.e., the study and classification of human speech sounds) rather than PHONEMICS (i.e., the study of the significance of speech sounds within a particular language). See EMIC–ETIC DISTINCTION.

etiology *n.* **1.** the causes and progress of a disease or disorder. **2.** the branch of medical and psychological science concerned with the systematic study of the causes of physical and mental disorders. **—etiological** *adj.*

Etrafon *n.* a trade name for a combination of the tricyclic antidepressant AMITRIPTYLINE and the antipsychotic PERPHENAZINE, used for the treatment of concurrent anxiety and depression.

E trisomy see TRISOMY 17–18.

ETS 1. abbreviation for EDUCATIONAL TESTING SERVICE. **2.** abbreviation for electrical transcranial stimulation. See ELECTROSLEEP THERAPY.

etymology *n.* the study of the origins and historical development of words and MORPHEMES. **—etymological** *adj.*

eu- *combining form* **1.** normal or good (e.g., EUPHORIA). **2.** easy (e.g., EUTHANASIA).

eudemonia (**eudaemonia**) *n.* happiness considered as a criterion for what is moral and as a motivation for human action. Modern versions of eudemonia, such as those found in psychology, have most often emphasized its individualist and pleasure-seeking aspects; more ancient theories, particularly that of Greek philosopher Aristotle (384–322 BCE), have given greater emphasis to the notion of one's being drawn by nature toward a higher good or a "flourishing life" as the source of genuine happiness.

eudemonism (**eudaemonism**) *n.* **1.** the position that happiness or EUDEMONIA is the ultimate ground of morality, so that what is good is what brings happiness. Debate then centers on whose happiness is achieved and whether certain means of achieving happiness are immoral. UTILITARIANISM is a eudemonism. **2.** the position that humans will naturally act in ways that bring them happiness. Psychoanalytic, behavioristic, and modern humanistic psychologies can all be seen as modern eudemonisms. Debate centers on whether humans are compelled to act so as to maximize their happiness, as HEDONISM would suggest, or whether the association between happiness and behavior is more subtle. Older versions of eudemonism suggested that the motives for human action included some altruistic impulses, such that the achievement of the happiness of others or a greater good could also be the cause or source of behaviors.

euergasia *n.* normal mental or psychobiological functioning. Also called **orthergasia**. [defined by U.S. psychiatrist Adolf Meyer (1866–1950)]

eugenic *adj.* describing a factor or influence that is favorable to heredity. Compare DYSGENIC.

eugenics *n.* a social and political philosophy, based loosely on the evolutionary theory of Charles Darwin (1809–1882) and the research on hereditary genius of Francis Galton (1822–1911), that seeks to eradicate genetic defects and improve the genetic makeup of populations through selective human breeding. **Positive eugenics** is directed toward promoting reproduction by individuals with superior traits, whereas **negative eugenics** is directed toward preventing reproduction by individuals with undesirable traits. The eugenic position is groundless and scientifically naive, in that many conditions associated with disability or disorder, such as syndromes that increase risk of MENTAL RETARDATION, are inherited recessively and occur unpredictably. Nevertheless, the philosophy gained popularity in the United Kingdom and United States, where eugenic policies, such as sterilization of women with mental retardation, persisted into the latter half of the 20th century. Attitudes toward genetics in the 21st century are often influenced by individual and community concerns about prior eugenic abuses.

eumorphic *adj.* denoting a constitutional body type characterized by normal shape and structure and roughly equivalent to the NORMOSPLANCHNIC TYPE.

eunuch *n.* a male who has been castrated before puberty and who therefore develops the secondary SEX CHARACTERISTICS of a female, such as a higher voice and absence of facial hair. See also CASTRATION.

euphemism *n.* the substitution of a neutral, inoffensive, or evasive term for one considered offensive or unpleasantly direct. **—euphemistic** *adj.*

euphenics *n.* interventions that aim to improve the outcome of a genetic disease by altering the environment to minimize expression of the disease. For example, people with PHENYLKETONURIA can reduce or prevent its expression by eliminating major sources of phenylalanine (e.g., soft drinks sweetened with aspartame) from their diet.

euphoria *n.* an elevated mood of well-being and happiness. An exaggerated degree of euphoria that does not reflect the reality of one's situation is a frequent symptom of MANIC EPISODES and HYPOMANIC EPISODES. **—euphoric** *adj.*

euphoriant *n.* a substance capable of inducing a subjective sense of well-being and happiness.

euphorogenic *adj.* describing an event or medication that generates a state of EUPHORIA.

eureka task a problem-solving task designed to investigate the phenomenon of sudden INSIGHT into a problem's solution. The route to solving the problem is usually not obvious, and usually requires a mental leap of some kind beyond the sorts of solutions used for everyday problems. See also AHA EXPERIENCE; DISCONTINUITY HYPOTHESIS.

European Federation of Professional Psychologists' Associations (**EFPPA**) a federation of national psychology associations founded in 1981 to provide a forum for European cooperation in a wide range of fields of academic training, psychology practice, and research.

European Federation of the Psychology of Sport and Physical Activity a European federation of national organizations in the area of SPORT AND EXERCISE PSYCHOLOGY. The organization is usually called **FEPSAC**, an acronym of its French name (Fédération Européenne de Psychologie des Sports et des Activités Corporelles).

eurymorph *n.* see BODY-BUILD INDEX.

euryplastic *adj.* denoting a constitutional body type that is roughly equivalent to the PYKNIC TYPE in

KRETSCHMER TYPOLOGY and to the HYPERVEGETATIVE TYPE.

eusociality *n.* a social structure among animals in which there is a marked division of labor, with only a few individuals that reproduce and many more nonreproductive individuals that guard the nest, gather food and nest materials, or help to care for the young. Eusociality is a common form of social structure in colonial species of bees and wasps (see SOCIAL INSECTS): The HAPLODIPLOIDY mode of inheritance helps to explain the adaptiveness of nonreproductive helpers caring for the young of the queen. —**eusocial** *adj.*

eustachian tube a slender tube extending from the middle ear to the pharynx, with the primary function of equalizing air pressure on both sides of the tympanic membrane (eardrum). [Bartolommeo **Eustachio** (1524–1574), Italian anatomist]

eusthenic *adj.* denoting a constitutional body type that is equivalent to the ASTHENIC TYPE and close to the ATHLETIC TYPE in KRETSCHMER TYPOLOGY.

eustress *n.* a type of stress that results from being overwhelmed by multiple enjoyable or worthwhile tasks. It has a beneficial effect by generating a sense of fulfillment or achievement. [first described by Canadian physician Hans Selye (1907–1982)]

euthanasia *n.* the act or process of terminating a life to prevent further suffering. Voluntary euthanasia requires the consent of a competent person who has established a valid ADVANCE DIRECTIVE or made his or her wishes otherwise clearly known. Euthanasia is distinguished from the much more widely accepted practice of forgoing invasive treatments, as permitted under natural-death laws throughout the United States. See also ACTIVE EUTHANASIA; ASSISTED DEATH; END OF LIFE; INFORMED CONSENT; MERCY KILLING; PASSIVE EUTHANASIA.

euthymia *n.* **1.** a mood or state of well-being and tranquillity. **2.** a phase or state in patients with a bipolar disorder that is neither manic nor depressive but in between, close to normal functioning. —**euthymic** *adj.*

evaluability assessment see EVALUABILITY-ASSESSMENT DATA.

evaluability-assessment data information sought to identify problematic areas of PROGRAM EVALUATION. **Evaluability assessment** comprises a review of expectations for program performance and questions to be answered by evaluation data, followed by a study of program implementation to identify designs, measurements, and analyses that are possible.

evaluation *n.* **1.** a careful examination or overall appraisal of something to determine its worth, value, or desirability. **2.** a determination of the success of something (e.g., a therapeutic technique or a newly implemented program) in achieving defined goals. **3.** the interpretation of test results and experimental data.

evaluation apprehension uneasiness or worry about being judged by others, especially feelings of worry experienced by participants in an experiment as a result of their desire to be evaluated favorably by the experimenter. Participants experiencing evaluation apprehension may inhibit reactions (e.g., the display of aggression) that they believe will lead the experimenter to regard them as psychologically unhealthy.

evaluation interview an interview conducted as part of an EMPLOYEE-EVALUATION program. An evaluation interview may be a routine or periodic discussion of a subordinate's JOB PERFORMANCE (see PERFORMANCE REVIEW) or may arise from specific circumstances. In some cases it may involve psychological incentives, such as suggesting that the subordinate present a set of personal goals to be reviewed by management.

evaluation objective any of the purposes of an evaluation of a program. For example, the purpose of FORMATIVE EVALUATIONS is to consider implementation problems, program integrity, and program monitoring, whereas the purpose of SUMMATIVE EVALUATIONS is to focus on program impact, program effectiveness, and cost analysis.

evaluation of training a review of PERSONNEL TRAINING programs to determine their effectiveness. Training evaluations can focus on trainee attitudes and reactions to the training, trainee knowledge of the information disseminated in the program, or changes in the behavior of the trainee or the effectiveness of the group or organization. Also called **training evaluation**. See TRAINING VALIDITY.

evaluation research the application of scientific principles, methods, and theories to identify, describe, conceptualize, measure, predict, change, and control those factors that are important to the development of effective HUMAN SERVICE DELIVERY SYSTEMS. See PROGRAM EVALUATION.

evaluation utilization an effort to act on the findings of an evaluation program. It involves managing disparate evaluation outcomes as well as generalizing solutions for the problems brought to light by the evaluation process.

evaluative ratings the ranking of judgments of the aesthetic or other qualities of a group of objects. Evaluative ratings may be based on hedonic values, such as the relative pleasantness of a set of paintings, on the relative complexity of a series of problems, or on other factors.

evaluative reasoning a form of CRITICAL THINKING that involves appraisal of the effectiveness, validity, meaning, or relevance of any act, idea, feeling, technique, or object.

evaluative semantic priming measure of attitudes an IMPLICIT ATTITUDE MEASURE based on the phenomenon that the speed of evaluating some target ATTITUDE OBJECT is facilitated by a prime (i.e., the prior presentation of another attitude object) that is evaluatively consistent with the target and inhibited by a prime that is evaluatively inconsistent with the target. For example, if the name of a product is presented as a prime immediately prior to a target word likely to be negative to most people (e.g., cockroach), evaluation of the target should be faster if the attitude toward the product is negative and slower if the attitude toward the product is positive. A measure of attitudes toward the prime (i.e., the product) can be created by computing the relative difference in speed of evaluating a negative target paired with the prime versus a positive target paired with the prime. Also called **bona fide pipeline measure of attitudes**. See also DIRECT ATTITUDE MEASURE; EXPLICIT ATTITUDE MEASURE; INDIRECT ATTITUDE MEASURE. [originally developed by U.S. psychologist Russell H. Fazio (1952–)]

evaluator *n.* an individual whose role is to evaluate and provide advice about the progress of a therapy or sensitivity group, a project team, an institution, or an individual. See also EXTERNAL EVALUATOR; INTERNAL EVALUATOR.

evaluator credibility the extent to which the evaluator of a program is viewed by the STAKEHOLDERS as trustworthy, technically competent, and knowledgeable enough to execute the evaluation in a fair and responsible manner.

evasion *n.* **1.** a form of PARALOGIA in which an idea that is logically next in a chain of thought is replaced by another idea closely but not accurately or appropriately related to it. **2.** elusion or avoidance.

evasive action see ANTIPREDATOR BEHAVIOR.

evenly hovering attention see FREE-FLOATING ATTENTION.

event *n.* **1.** any occurrence or phenomenon that has a definite beginning and end and that involves or produces change. **2.** in probability theory, any of the namable things that can be said to result from a single trial of an experiment of chance. For example, in the roll of a single die, the events could include (among others) any of the six individual numbers, any even number, and any odd number.

event history analysis see SURVIVAL ANALYSIS.

event memory memory for everyday events, which is a form of EPISODIC MEMORY.

event-related magnetic field (**ERF**) a change in the magnetic field of the brain, detected at the scalp in a magnetoencephalogram (see MAGNETOENCEPHALOGRAPHY), that is elicited by an event, such as stimulus presentation or response initiation. ERFs allow more accurate localization of function than do EVENT-RELATED POTENTIALS because they are less influenced by the surrounding brain structures.

event-related potential (**ERP**) an electrical brain potential elicited by an event, such as stimulus presentation or response initiation. There are a number of different ERP components, which indicate different aspects of processing. See N1 ATTENTION EFFECT; P1 ATTENTION EFFECT; P3 COMPONENT.

event-related-potential measure of attitudes (**ERP measure of attitudes**) a physiological measure of attitudes based on electrocortical activity. The procedure makes use of the phenomenon that one component of EVENT-RELATED POTENTIALS, the late positive potential (or P300), varies as a function of categorization of stimuli. This component is large when a target stimulus is judged to be inconsistent with the context in which it is encountered and small when it is judged to be consistent with the context. To assess attitudes, the target ATTITUDE OBJECT is evaluated as part of a series of objects that are either positive or negative in nature. If a large late positive potential is produced when the attitude object is evaluated in the negative context and a small positive potential is produced when it is evaluated in the positive context, this indicates a positive attitude. The reverse pattern indicates a negative attitude. [originally developed by U.S. psychologists John T. Cacioppo (1951–), Stephen L. Criters, Jr., and their associates]

event sampling a type of SAMPLING in which the SAMPLING FRAME consists of events or behaviors, such as going to a party or experiencing symptoms of a disorder. The sample that is drawn is a sample of these events for a randomly determined group of participants in the study.

eversion theory of aging the concept that aging results from functional deterioration of body tissues due to changes in the molecular structure of COLLAGEN. Also called **cross-linkage theory**.

everyday intelligence the intelligence used in everyday living. Everyday intelligence refers not to a psychometrically validated construct but to a loosely conceptualized kind of intelligence relevant to the problems people face on a daily basis.

everyday racism differential treatment of individuals on the basis of their racial group that occurs in common, routine social situations. Examples include a White teacher ignoring the question asked by an African American student and a White store clerk watching African American shoppers more closely than White shoppers. See RACISM.

evil eye a folk belief in the supernatural powers of a malevolent stare or hostile gaze, which is believed to cause adversity, illness, injury, or destruction to the recipient. The term is specifically applies to a culture-bound syndrome in Mediterranean countries and other regions (see MAL DE OJO). Also called **fascinum**. See also WITCHCRAFT.

eviration *n.* **1.** castration or emasculation. **2.** the delusion of a man that he has been turned into a woman.

evocative therapy therapy based on the idea that behavior is aroused by underlying factors. Once the factors underlying a maladaptive or unwanted behavior have been identified, dispositional and environmental changes can be made to affect those factors and therefore alter the behavior. [originated by U.S. psychologist Jerome D. Frank (1910–2005)]

evoked potential (**EP**) electric activity observed in a particular part of the nervous system, especially the brain, in response to stimulation. For example, a flash of light will produce an evoked potential in the visual cortex, whereas a tone will result in an evoked potential in the auditory cortex. Evoked potentials differ from ordinary BRAIN WAVES in that the activity occurs at the time of stimulation rather than spontaneously and also occurs in a sensory area associated with the appropriate nerve tract. The evoked potential is predictable and reproducible. Also called **evoked response** (**ER**).

evoked response see EVOKED POTENTIAL.

evolution *n.* **1.** the process of gradual change in the appearance of populations of organisms that has taken place over generations. Such changes are widely held to account for the present diversity of living organisms originating from relatively few ancestors since the emergence of life on Earth. Also called **organic evolution**. See EVOLUTIONARY THEORY. See also CONVERGENT EVOLUTION; DIVERGENT EVOLUTION. **2.** any other process of gradual change. **—evolutionary** *adj.*

evolutionarily stable strategy (**ESS**) a state of equilibrium between two different adaptive strategies that allows both strategies to be maintained within a population. For example, shy animals are less likely than bold animals to behave in a way that attracts predators, but bold animals are more likely to find new food resources or secure additional mates. Within a population, therefore, there will be an optimal balance of costs and benefits for both shy and bold animals so that members of both types can survive. Evolutionarily stable strategy is a mechanism that accounts for the maintenance of diversity within a population.

evolutionary aesthetics the concept that art evolves due to intrinsic forces rather than changing to reflect extra-artistic forces.

evolutionary developmental psychology the application of the basic principles of Darwinian evolution, particularly NATURAL SELECTION, to explain contemporary human development. Evolutionary developmental psychology involves the study of the genetic and environmental mechanisms that underlie the universal development of social and cognitive competencies and the evolved epigenetic processes (GENE–ENVIRONMENT INTERACTIONS) that adapt these competencies to local conditions. It assumes that not only are behaviors and cognitions that characterize adults the product of selection pressures operating over the course of evolution, but so also are characteristics of children's behaviors and minds. [proposed in 2002 by U.S. developmental psychologists David Bjorklund (1949–) and Anthony D. Pellegrini (1949–)]

evolutionary epistemology any of a number of approaches to EPISTEMOLOGY that seek to explain the origins and development of human knowledge in terms of biological, chiefly Darwinian, evolution. One form suggests that ideas and explanations evolve in a way analogous to the evolution of organisms; that is, they survive as they show themselves to be "fit," or useful. Another form suggests that there is a literal biological origin of ideas and that certain ideas, such as the rules of logic, have enhanced the survival of those in whom they evolved: Thus the ideas themselves tend to survive and take on importance.

evolutionary psychology an approach to psychological inquiry that views human cognition and behavior in a broadly Darwinian context of adaptation to evolving physical and social environments and new intellectual challenges. It differs from SOCIOBIOLOGY mainly in its emphasis on the effects of NATURAL SELECTION on INFORMATION PROCESSING and the structure of the human mind.

evolutionary theory any theory to account for the EVOLUTION of organisms over successive generations. One early and influential example was Lamarck's theory of evolution by use or disuse (see LAMARCKISM). Nowadays, the most widely accepted is an updated version of Darwin's theory of evolution through NATURAL SELECTION, called neo-Darwinism (see DARWINISM). Theories concerning specific aspects of evolution include COEVOLUTION, EXAPTATION, NEOTENY, PUNCTUATED EQUILIBRIUM, and RECAPITULATION THEORY. Opposed to all theories of evolution is the doctrine of CREATIONISM.

evolution of consciousness the process by which CONSCIOUSNESS arose and developed in the animal kingdom. The development of consciousness in mammals is associated with the evolution of the THALAMOCORTICAL SYSTEM of the brain over the past 100 million years. Sensory consciousness in humans depends on activity in the posterior SENSORY AREA and its gateway, the THALAMUS. It is possible, however, that nonmammalian species may have evolved other brain bases of conscious sensation. Humanistic and transpersonal psychologists assert that human consciousness continues to evolve through the medium of culture.

evolution of intelligence the process by which intelligence has developed from earlier and generally simpler species to later and generally more complex species. There are many theories of how intelligence has evolved, but most emphasize some kind of Darwinian natural-selection process, in which evolution favored skills that were more useful over the eons for adaptation to environments over skills that were less useful.

evolution of the brain the concept that the brains of complex animals have evolved over many millions of years from a network of simple NERVE FIBERS connecting various body areas, as in primitive multicellular animals. At a more advanced stage, a neural axis developed to connect and integrate neurons serving the periphery and to house cell bodies; this axis became a spinal cord. Still later, collections of neurons with control functions developed at the head end of the spinal cord, as in the brains of higher invertebrates, birds, fish, and reptiles. From those concentrations of brain tissue evolved the FOREBRAIN, with its highly convoluted CEREBRAL CORTEX, of mammals, especially prominent in whales, great apes, and *Homo sapiens*. See also CEPHALIZATION; ENCEPHALIZATION.

evolved mechanism a subsystem of the brain (or mind) that is a product of natural selection and is generally seen as having evolved as a result of its success in solving a problem related to survival or reproduction during the evolution of a species. For example, the elements of the brain's visual system that enable organisms to perceive objects in three-dimensional space (despite the fact that vision involves the projection of light onto a two-dimensional surface, the retina) would be seen as an evolved mechanism that solved the problem of determining the distance between oneself and objects in the environment.

ex- *prefix* see EXO-.

exacerbation *n.* an increase in the severity of a disease or disorder or of its symptoms.

exact replication repetition of an experiment in which the goal is to duplicate as closely as possible the conditions of the original experiment. See REPLICATION.

exaggeration *n.* the act of embellishing or overstating a quality or characteristic of a person, thing, or situation. It is often a defensive reaction in which the individual justifies questionable attitudes or behavior through overstatement, such as dramatizing the oppressive acts of a parent as a means of justifying rebellious behavior.

exaltation *n.* an extreme state of EUPHORIA and PSYCHOMOTOR AGITATION, accompanied by a lack of restraint. It occurs in some MANIC EPISODES.

examination *n.* a test, observation, or other means of investigation carried out on a patient to evaluate physical or mental health or detect the presence or absence of signs or symptoms of diseases, disorders, or conditions. See also MENTAL EXAMINATION; NEUROLOGICAL EVALUATION; PSYCHOLOGICAL EXAMINATION.

examination anxiety see TEST ANXIETY.

exaptation *n.* a trait that, having evolved to serve one function, is later used for another. For example, feathers may have evolved as cooling or insulating mechanisms and later aided in flying. Whether such traits exist is controversial. Also called **spandrel**. [proposed by U.S. zoologist Stephen Jay Gould (1941–2002)]

exceptional child a child who is substantially above or below the average in some significant respect. Often applied to a child who shows marked deviations in intelligence, the term may also be used to indicate the presence of a special talent or an unusual emotional or social difficulty. See also GIFTEDNESS; SLOW LEARNER.

exceptional creativity the capability of individuals to make unique and important contributions to society through their work and the products of their work. Exceptional creativity, as measured by creative output, seems to peak at different points in the adult life span depending on the field of activity. Also called **creative genius**. Compare ORDINARY CREATIVITY.

exchange relationship see COMMUNAL RELATIONSHIP.

exchange theory see SOCIAL EXCHANGE THEORY.

excitability *n.* **1.** the tendency of some individuals to be readily aroused to emotional responses. **2.** the property of a neuron in reacting to stimulation, marked by an electrical or chemical response. Whereas all living cells display IRRITABILITY, neurons and some muscle cells show responses in the form of excitability, which is characterized by a sudden, transient increase in their ionic permeability and a change in the electric potential across their cell membrane. See ACTION POTENTIAL. **—excitable** *adj.*

excitant *n.* an agent capable of eliciting a response.

excitation *n.* the activity elicited in a nerve or muscle when it is stimulated.

excitation gradient the principle that the more similar two stimuli are, the more likely they are to elicit similar responses. Also called **generalization gradient**.

excitation pattern a spatial pattern of responses to sound in the auditory system. It usually refers to the ENVELOPE of the displacement pattern on the BASILAR MEMBRANE or its representation in the auditory nerve. See TONOTOPIC ORGANIZATION; TUNING CURVE.

excitation-transfer theory the theory that aggressive responses can be intensified by AROUSAL from other stimuli not directly related to the stimulus that originally provoked the aggression. According to this theory, which has since also been applied to other emotional responses, when a person becomes aroused physiologically, there is a subsequent period of time when the person will experience a state of residual arousal yet be unaware of it. If additional arousing stimuli are presented during this time, the individual will experience more arousal, and thus greater response, to those succeeding stimuli than if there had been no residual arousal. See also AROUSAL TRANSFER; MISATTRIBUTION OF AROUSAL. [originally proposed in 1971 by psychologist Dolf Zillman]

excitatory conditioning direct PAVLOVIAN CONDITIONING, that is, conditioning in which a conditioned stimulus acts as a signal that a particular unconditioned stimulus will follow.

excitatory field an area of the brain surrounding and sharing the response of an excited sensory area.

excitatory–inhibitory processes 1. processes in which the transmission of neuronal signals is activated or inhibited by the effects of neurotransmitters on the postsynaptic membrane. **2.** antagonistic functions of the nervous system defined by Ivan Petrovich PAVLOV. **3.** the stimulation of the cortex and the subsequent facilitation of the processes of learning, memory, and action (excitatory processes) and central nervous system processes that inhibit or interfere with perceptual, cognitive, and motor activities (inhibitory processes). Individuals with predominant inhibitory processes are theorized to be predisposed to a higher degree of INTROVERSION, whereas individuals with predominant excitatory processes are theorized to be predisposed to a higher degree of EXTRAVERSION. [proposed by Hans EYSENCK]

excitatory postsynaptic potential (**EPSP**) a depolarizing potential in a POSTSYNAPTIC neuron that is caused by excitatory presynaptic impulses. EPSPs increase the probability that the postsynaptic neuron will initiate an ACTION POTENTIAL and hence fire a nerve impulse. See also FACILITATION; SPATIAL SUMMATION; TEMPORAL SUMMATION. Compare INHIBITORY POSTSYNAPTIC POTENTIAL.

excitatory synapse a SYNAPSE at which the firing of the presynaptic fiber causes an EXCITATORY POSTSYNAPTIC POTENTIAL in the postsynaptic neuron, increasing the probability that the postsynaptic neuron will fire a nerve impulse. Compare INHIBITORY SYNAPSE.

excitatory threshold the stimulus intensity that is just sufficient to trigger a NERVE IMPULSE.

excitement *n.* an emotional state marked by enthusiam, eagerness or anticipation, and general arousal. Compare EXCITATION.

excitement phase see SEXUAL-RESPONSE CYCLE.

excitotoxicity *n.* the property that causes neurons to die when overstimulated, for example by large amounts of the excitatory neurotransmitter GLUTAMATE.

excitotoxic lesion a lesion caused by paroxysmal overactivity of neurons, which may be associated with seizures or occur after stroke. This is most commonly caused by overstimulation of neurons by excitatory amino acids (see EXCITOTOXICITY).

excluded middle principle in logic and philosophy, the principle that either a statement or its negation must be true. For example: Either behaviour X is a free act or it is not a free act. This is related to, but not identical with, the principle of BIVALENCE. Also called **principle of the excluded middle**. See also CONTRADICTION PRINCIPLE.

exclusion design tools or systems that have been designed so as to virtually exclude the possibility of HUMAN ERROR. Error triggers or ERGONOMIC TRAPS are first identified and then designed out of the system. See ENGINEERING CONTROLS. See also FAIL-SAFE; PREVENTION DESIGN.

excrement *n.* see FECES.

exculpatory evidence evidence supporting a defendant's claim of innocence.

executive *n.* in cognitive psychology, a process or stage of mental activity that organizes and controls other mental activity. For example, the executive may initiate a REHEARSAL process as a means of remembering a list of stimuli. See also COGNITIVE CONTROL; CONTROL PROCESSES. Also called **supervisory attentional system**.

executive area a region of the brain hypothesized to account for higher order brain functions, such as thinking and reasoning (see EXECUTIVE FUNCTION). The FRONTAL LOBE is commonly referred to as an executive area.

executive coaching one-on-one personal counseling and feedback provided to managers in an organization to develop their interpersonal and other managerial skills. See MANAGEMENT DEVELOPMENT.

executive control structures theoretical problem-solving mental structures that involve a representation of the problem situation, a representation of the objectives of the task, and a representation of the particular strategy or procedures for solving the problem. [proposed by Canadian developmental psychologist Robbie Case (1944–2000)]

executive dysfunction impairment in the ability to think abstractly and to plan, initiate, sequence, monitor, and stop complex behavior. Related especially to disorders of the frontal lobe or associated subcortical pathways, it is one of the multiple COGNITIVE DEFICITS characteristic of ALCOHOL-INDUCED PERSISTING DEMENTIA and SUBSTANCE-INDUCED PERSISTING DEMENTIA. Also called **disturbance in executive functioning**.

executive function higher level cognitive processes that organize and order behavior, including (but not limited to) logic and reasoning, abstract thinking, problem solving, planning, and carrying out and terminating goal-directed behavior. In schizophrenia, specific cognitive abilities, such as selecting goals or task-relevant information and eliminating extraneous information, are believed to be major deficits and are a focus of neurorehabilitative treatment. Also called **central processes**; **executive functioning**; **higher order processes**.

executive leadership LEADERSHIP exerted by those occupying the highest level positions of power and authority in an organization.

executive organ the body organ that plays the major role in responding to a stimulus. For example, when the stimulus instigates touching an object, the hand becomes the executive organ. Other organs often play subsidiary roles; for example, the eye that helps direct the hand serves as an **auxiliary organ**.

executive self the AGENT to which voluntary actions are ordinarily attributed. The concept of an executive self has acquired considerable scientific plausibility, being associated with well-studied functions of the PREFRONTAL CORTEX of the brain. However, there is a class of false attributions of executive control (see ILLUSION OF AGENCY).

executive stress strain experienced by management personnel who are responsible for major decisions, the effectiveness of subordinates, and the success of the company as a competitive organization. See BURNOUT; OCCUPATIONAL STRESS; STRESS.

Exelon *n.* a trade name for RIVASTIGMINE.

exemplar theory see INSTANCE THEORY.

exemplification *n.* in SELF-PRESENTATION theory, a strategy that involves inducing other people to regard one as a highly moral, virtuous person whose actions are consistent with positive, shared values.

exercise *n.* a form of physical activity that is planned, repetitive in nature, and designed to enhance or maintain physical condition. Physical exercise may also be used as an adjunct to mental health therapy. See also EXERCISE ADHERENCE; EXERCISE PSYCHOLOGY; TIME-OUT THEORY; WALK–TALK COUNSELING SESSION.

exercise addiction the condition of being dependent on or devoted to physical exercise. Stopping exercise will cause the addicted person to experience withdrawal symptoms. Also called **exercise dependence**. See NEGATIVE EXERCISE ADDICTION; POSITIVE EXERCISE ADDICTION.

exercise adherence a combination of attendance at an exercise program and achieving the set intensity and duration of exercise in the program. Also called **exercise compliance**.

exercise–behavior model an adaptation of the HEALTH–BELIEF MODEL that identifies the relationships of the following to likelihood of exercising: (a) personal predispositions, (b) sociodemographic variables, and (c) the perceptions of cost and benefits of exercising.

exercise compliance see EXERCISE ADHERENCE.

exercise high a feeling of euphoria during or immediately after a bout of physical exercise. See RUNNER'S HIGH.

exercise obsession see NEGATIVE EXERCISE ADDICTION.

exercise play a type of LOCOMOTOR PLAY that involves gross locomotor movements, such as running or jumping. It is physically vigorous and may or may not be social.

exercise psychology a combination of exercise science and psychology used to study the psychological circumstances and consequences of involvement in exercise.

exercise therapy the adjunctive treatment of psychological disorders, or medical disorders with underlying psychological causes, using physical exercise. This type of therapy is most beneficial when individuals become actively involved in vigorous motion as often and with as much enjoyment and satisfaction as possible. See also ADJUNCTIVE THERAPY.

exhaustion *n.* a state of extreme tiredness. See FATIGUE.

exhaustion death see LETHAL CATATONIA.

exhaustion delirium a DELIRIOUS STATE occurring under conditions of extreme fatigue resulting from prolonged and intense overexertion, particularly when coupled with other forms of stress, such as prolonged insomnia, starvation, excessive heat or cold, or toxic states. It is typically associated with the extreme physical effort required of mountain climbers, long-distance swimmers, explorers, and others facing extreme environmental conditions as well as with individuals suffering from advanced cancer or other debilitating diseases. See DELIRIUM.

exhaustion stage see GENERAL ADAPTATION SYNDROME.

exhaustive search any SEARCH process in which every item of a set is checked before a decision is made about the presence or absence of a target item. This may be a search for particular items in memory, a VISUAL SEARCH, or any problem-solving exercise that involves choosing the best path to a solution from a number of alternative paths. Compare SELF-TERMINATING SEARCH. See also ALGORITHM; HEURISTIC SEARCH.

exhibitionism *n.* **1.** the disposition or tendency to draw attention to oneself, particularly through conspicuous behavior. See also ATTENTION-GETTING. **2.** a PARAPHILIA in which the genitals are repeatedly exposed to unsuspecting strangers as a means of achieving sexual excitement, but without any attempt at further sexual activity with the stranger. **—exhibitionist** *n.*

existence *n.* **1.** being: the quality by virtue of which something is, and which distinguishes it from what is not. **2.** in EXISTENTIALISM, the concrete lived experience of human beings rooted in a concrete world, as opposed to a more abstract concept of a human being, such as an ESSENCE. **—existent** *adj.*

existence needs see EXISTENCE, RELATEDNESS, AND GROWTH THEORY.

existence, relatedness, and growth theory (ERG theory) a variation of MASLOW'S MOTIVATIONAL HIERARCHY as applied in industrial and organizational psychology. The model recognizes three main categories of WORK MOTIVATION: **existence needs**, relating to the physical needs of the organism (food, clothing, shelter); **relatedness needs**, involving interpersonal relations with others on and off the job; and **growth needs**, in the form of personal development and improvement. [proposed by U.S. organizational psychologist Clayton P. Alderfer (1940–)]

existential analysis a type of psychoanalysis, or a phase in EXISTENTIAL PSYCHOTHERAPY, that places an emphasis on conscious perception and experience over unconscious motivation and drive in the search for meaning. The therapist typically takes an active, often confrontational, role by posing difficult questions and noting maladaptive decision making. The approach to "being" is future- or growth-oriented, and the goal is the development and encouragement of highly conscious decision making on the part of the client. Also called **existential psychoanalysis**.

existential anxiety **1.** a general sense of apprehension and ANGST associated with the feeling that life is ultimately meaningless and futile and that we are alienated not only from other people but from ourselves. **2.** the feeling of fear, even of dread, that can accompany a choice involving unknowns. Also called **existential anguish**.

existential crisis **1.** in EXISTENTIALISM, a crucial stage or turning point at which an individual is faced with finding meaning and purpose in life and taking responsibility for his or her choices. See EXISTENTIAL NEUROSIS; EXISTENTIAL VACUUM. **2.** more generally, any psychological or moral crisis that causes an individual to ask fundamental questions about human existence.

existential–humanistic therapy a form of psychotherapy that focuses on the entire person, rather than just behavior, cognition, or underlying motivations. Emphasis is placed on the client's subjective experiences, free will, and ability to decide the course of his or her own life. Also called **humanistic–existential therapy**.

existential intelligence a kind of intelligence proposed as a "candidate" intelligence in the MULTIPLE-INTELLIGENCES THEORY. It is involved in understanding larger fundamental questions of existence and the role and place of humans in the universe. At present, there are no developed measures of existential intelligence.

existentialism *n.* a philosophical and literary movement that emerged in Europe in the period between the two World Wars and became the dominant trend in Continental thought during the 1940s and 1950s. Existentialism is notoriously difficult to sum up in a single definition—partly because many who might be identified with the movement reject the label, and partly because the movement is itself, in many ways, a rejection of systematization and classification. The origins of existentialism have been traced to a range of thinkers, including French philosopher and mathematician Blaise Pascal (1623–1662), Danish philosopher Søren Kierkegaard (1813–1855), German philosopher Friedrich Nietzsche (1844–1900), and Russian novelist Fyodor Dostoevsky (1821–1881). However, the first fully developed philosophy of existentialism is usually taken to be the EXISTENTIAL PHENOMENOLOGY elaborated by German philosopher Martin Heidegger (1889–1976) in the 1910s and 1920s. Heidegger's concept of DASEIN was a key influence on the work of the French philosopher and author Jean-Paul Sartre (1905–1980), who is usually seen as the existentialist thinker *par excellence*. In the immediate postwar years Sartre popularized both the term "existentialism" and most of the ideas now associated with it. Existentialism represents a turning away from systematic philosophy, with its emphasis on metaphysical absolutes and principles of rational certainty, and toward an emphasis on the concrete existence of a human being "thrown" into a world that is merely "given" and contingent. Such a being encounters the world as a subjective consciousness, "condemned" to create its own meanings and values in an "absurd" and purposeless universe. The human being must perform this task without benefit of a fixed ESSENCE or inherent nature, and in the absence of any possibility of rational certainty. However, by accepting the burden of this responsibility, and refusing the "bad faith" of religion and other spurious rationalizations, he or she can achieve AUTHENTICITY. Various forms of EXISTENTIAL PSYCHOLOGY have taken up the task of providing explanations, understandings of human behavior, and therapies based on existentialist assumptions about human existence. They have emphasized such constructs as ALIENATION, authenticity, and freedom, as well as the difficulties associated with finding meaning and overcoming anxiety. **—existential** *adj.* **—existentialist** *n.*, adj.

existential judgment in philosophy, a judgment having to do with the EXISTENCE, origin, or nature of a thing (i.e., its factual status), as contrasted with a judgment as to the meaning, value, or importance of a thing.

existential living the capacity to live fully in the present and respond freely and flexibly to new experience without fear. Existential living is considered to be a central feature of the FULLY FUNCTIONING PERSON. [defined in psychology by Carl ROGERS]

existential neurosis NEUROSIS characterized by feelings of despair and anxiety that arise from living inauthentically, that is, from failing to take responsibility for one's own life and to make choices and find meaning in living. See AUTHENTICITY; EXISTENTIAL CRISIS; EXISTENTIAL VACUUM.

existential phenomenology a philosophical development from the PHENOMENOLOGY of German thinker Edmund Husserl (1859–1938) that can be seen most clearly in the work of German philosopher Martin Heidegger (1889–1976) and French philosopher Maurice Merleau-Ponty (1908–1961). Phenomenology originally sought to achieve immediate and direct apprehension of phenomena at the most fundamental level, the level of that which manifests itself to pure consciousness. Heidegger's contribution was to turn the phenomenological method toward the existential, or lived experience, rather than mere objects of consciousness. Thus existential phenomenology seeks to get at the meaning of lived experience through the careful and systematic analysis of lived experience itself. In its fundamental project and subject matter, Heidegger's work of the 1910s and 1920s anticipated the French EXISTENTIALISM of the postwar era. See BEING-IN-THE-WORLD; DASEIN.

existential psychoanalysis see EXISTENTIAL ANALYSIS.

existential psychology a general approach to psychological theory and practice that derives from EXISTENTIALISM. It emphasizes the subjective meaning of human experience, the uniqueness of the individual, and personal responsibility reflected in choice. Such an approach was pioneered by Swiss psychologist Ludwig Binswanger (1881–1966). See BEING-IN-THE-WORLD; WORLD DESIGN. See also HUMANISTIC PSYCHOLOGY.

existential psychotherapy a form of psychotherapy that deals with the HERE AND NOW of the client's total situation rather than with the client's past or underlying dynamics. It emphasizes the exploration and development of meaning in life, focuses on emotional experiences and decision making, and stresses a person's responsibility for his or her own existence. See also LOGOTHERAPY.

existential vacuum the inability to find or create meaning in life, leading to feelings of emptiness, alienation, futility, and aimlessness. Most existentialists have considered meaninglessness to be the quintessential symptom or ailment of the modern age. See EXISTENTIAL CRISIS; EXISTENTIAL NEUROSIS. See also LOGOTHERAPY. [introduced by Austrian existential psychologist Viktor E. Frankl (1905–1997)]

exit interview 1. a meeting between a student and a school counselor before the student leaves to begin high school, college, technical school, a vocational program, or a job. Future plans, the future course of study, and the student's degree of preparation are discussed. **2.** an employee's final meeting with his or her supervisor or personnel staff prior to termination of employment. Information from such interviews can be used to reduce staff TURNOVER and improve JOB SATISFACTION.

exo- (ex-) *prefix* outside or external.

exocathection *n.* a concentration of PSYCHIC ENERGY on practical, worldly affairs rather than personal matters. Compare ENDOCATHECTION. See CATHEXIS. [defined by U.S. psychologist Henry Alexander Murray (1893–1988)]

exocrine gland any gland that secretes a product through a duct, for example, the LACRIMAL GLAND. Compare ENDOCRINE GLAND.

exogamy *n.* in anthropology, the practice of marrying outside the family, CLAN, or social unit. Compare ENDOGAMY. See also INTERMARRIAGE; MISCEGENATION; OUTBREEDING. **—exogamous** *adj.*

exogenous *adj.* originating outside the body: referring, for example, to drugs (exogenous chemicals) or to phenomena, conditions, or disorders resulting from the influence of external factors (e.g., EXOGENOUS STRESS). Compare ENDOGENOUS. **—exogenously** *adv.*

exogenous cue a CUE, usually the onset of a stimulus in the peripheral visual field, that draws attention automatically to the location of the stimulus. Compare ENDOGENOUS CUE.

exogenous depression see REACTIVE DEPRESSION.

exogenous stress stress arising from external situations, such as natural catastrophes, excessive competition at work, or climbing a precipitous mountain.

exon *n.* a sequence of DNA within a gene that encodes a part or all of the gene's product or function. Exons are separated by noncoding sequences (see INTRON).

exophoria *n.* deviation of one eye in an outward direction. See also PHORIA.

exophthalmos *n.* abnormal protrusion of the eyeball, a condition commonly associated with hyperthyroidism. Exophthalmos combined with a goiter, a swelling in the neck due to an enlarged thyroid gland (**exophthalmic goiter**), is a prominent feature of GRAVES' DISEASE. Exophthalmos may also be the result of a tumor or infection involving the eye. It is often characterized by the appearance of a fixed stare. **—exophthalmic** *adj.*

exopsychic *adj.* characterizing mental activity that purportedly produces effects outside the individual. Compare ENDOPSYCHIC.

exorcism *n.* the act or practice in which supposed evil spirits are expelled from a person believed to be possessed, or a place thought to be haunted, by means of certain rites, ceremonies, prayers, and incantations. It was formerly widely believed that such spirits were the major cause of mental disease and other disorders and that exorcism was therefore a suitable form of treatment. The Roman Catholic Church still makes use of ritual exorcism in certain very restricted circumstances. See also INHABITANCE. **—exorcise** *vb.* **—exorcist** *n.*

exosomatic method a technique used in psychogalvanic-response studies in which skin resistance to a small electric current from an external source is measured. See GALVANIC SKIN RESPONSE.

exosystem *n.* in ECOLOGICAL SYSTEMS THEORY, those societal structures that function largely independently of the individual but which nevertheless affect the immediate context within which he or she develops. They include the government, the legal system, and the media. Compare MACROSYSTEM; MESOSYSTEM. [introduced by Russian-born U.S. psychologist Urie Bronfenbrenner (1917–2005)]

exotic psychosis see HYSTERICAL PSYCHOSIS.

exotropia *n.* the permanent outward deviation of one eye. Also called **divergent strabismus**; **walleye**. See also STRABISMUS; TROPIA.

expanded consciousness a purported sensory effect of meditation or mind-altering drugs that causes the individual to feel that his or her mind has been opened to a new kind of awareness or to new concepts. See also ALTERED STATE OF CONSCIOUSNESS; COSMIC CONSCIOUSNESS.

expansive delusion a less common name for a DELUSION OF GRANDEUR.

expansive mood a mood that reflects feelings of GRANDIOSITY.

expansiveness *n.* a personality trait manifested by loquaciousness, overfriendliness, hyperactivity, and lack of restraint.

ex-patient club in psychiatry, an ongoing group organized by a former mental patient or by a hospital as part of its aftercare program. The objective is to provide social and recreational experience, to promote readjustment and rehabilitation, and to maintain improvement through group support and, in some cases, group therapy. See also MENTAL PATIENT ORGANIZATION.

expectancy *n.* **1.** in behavioral psychology, a state or condition in which an organism anticipates a given stimulus or event on the basis of its previous experience with related stimuli or events. Physical signs of expectancy include attention and muscular tension. **2.** in cognitive psychology, an attitude or MENTAL SET that determines the way in which a person approaches a situation. See also AUFGABE; SET. **3.** in MOTIVATION theory, an individual's belief that his or her actions can produce a particular outcome (e.g., attainment of a goal or performance target). **4.** in statistics, the expected value of a random variable or one of its functions as derived by mathematical calculation. **—expectant** *adj.*

expectancy control design an experimental design in which the EXPERIMENTER EXPECTANCY EFFECT operates separately from the INDEPENDENT VARIABLE of primary substantive interest.

expectancy effect the effect of one person's expectation about the behavior of another person on the actual behavior of that other person (**interpersonal expectancy effect**) or the effect of a person's expectation about his or her own behavior on that person's actual subsequent behavior (**intrapersonal expectancy effect**). See also EXPERIMENTER EXPECTANCY EFFECT.

expectancy theory **1.** a theory that cognitive learning involves acquired expectancies and a tendency to react to certain objects as signs of other objects previously associated with them. PURPOSIVE BEHAVIORISM is a specific form of expectancy theory. **2.** a motivational theory that the greater the likelihood of a particular activity having a positive outcome, the more likely it is that the activity will occur.

expectancy-value model the concept that motivation for an outcome depends on the significance of that outcome and the probability of achieving it.

expectancy wave see CONTINGENT NEGATIVE VARIATION.

expectant analysis the orthodox technique of psychoanalysis, in which the analyst awaits the gradual, free-floating unfolding of the patient's psyche. Compare FOCUSED ANALYSIS.

expectation *n.* a state of tense, emotional anticipation.

expectation-states theory an explanation of status differentiation in groups proposing that group members allocate status not only to those who possess qualities suggesting competence at the task in question (SPECIFIC-STATUS CHARACTERISTICS) but also to those who have qualities that the members (mistakenly) think are indicators of competence and potential, such as sex, age, wealth, and ethnicity (DIFFUSE-STATUS CHARACTERISTICS). See also STATUS GENERALIZATION.

expected frequency 1. a frequency predicted from a theoretical model and contrasted with an observed frequency. **2.** a frequency that would occur on the basis of chance alone.

expected value the central value of a RANDOM VARIABLE. Also called **first moment**; **population mean**.

experience *n.* **1.** a conscious event: an event that is lived through, or undergone, as opposed to one that is imagined or thought about. **2.** the present contents of CONSCIOUSNESS. **3.** events that result in learning. **—experiential** *adj.*

experience-dependent process a process whereby SYNAPSES are formed and maintained as a result of the unique experiences of an individual. Also called **experience-dependent synaptogenesis**.

experience-expectant process a process whereby SYNAPSES are formed and maintained when an organism has species-typical experiences. As a result, such functions as vision will develop for all members of a species, given species-typical environmental stimulation (e.g., light). Also called **experience-expectant synaptogenesis**.

experiencer *n.* in CASE GRAMMAR, the entity that experiences the effect of the action, state, or process described in a sentence, for example, *John* in *John sees Mary, The wind felt soft to John, The walk invigorated John*. Note that experiencer case is independent of the grammatical role of *John* in the sentence. The category, which overlaps with that of PATIENT, is usually reserved for ANIMATE NOUNS capable of sensory or emotional experience. See also AGENT; INSTRUMENTAL.

experiential family therapist a therapist who emphasizes intuition, feelings, and underlying processes in treating families and who deemphasizes theoretical frameworks. The work is often characterized by the use of the therapist's own feelings and self-disclosures in interactions with clients. Notable experiential family therapists have included U.S. psychiatrists Carl A. Whitaker (died 1995) and Virginia M. Satir (1916–1988).

experiential history the social, environmental, and behavioral components of an individual's background from birth to death.

experiential knowledge understanding and expertise that emerge from life experience, rather than from professional training. Members of SELF-HELP GROUPS draw upon experiential knowledge in supporting and helping each other.

experiential learning learning that occurs by actively performing and participating in an activity.

experiential psychotherapy a broad family of psychotherapies originating in the 1950s and 1960s and falling under the umbrella of existential–humanistic psychology. A core belief of the approach is that true client change occurs through direct, active "experiencing" of what the client is undergoing and feeling at any given point in therapy, both on the surface and at a deeper level. Experiential therapists typically engage clients very directly with regard to accessing and expressing their inner feelings and experiencing both present and past life scenes, and they offer clients perspectives for integrating such experiences into realistic and healthy self-concepts. Experiential psychotherapy has its antecedents in the work of U.S. psychiatrists Carl A. Whitaker (died 1995) and Thomas P. Malone (died 2000), U.S. psychologist Carl ROGERS, U.S. philosopher and psychologist Eugene T. Gendlin (1926–), and others.

experiential subtheory a subtheory in the TRIARCHIC THEORY OF INTELLIGENCE specifying the kinds of experience to which the components of intelligence (specified in the COMPONENTIAL SUBTHEORY) are applied. According to the experiential subtheory, people are creatively intelligent to the extent that they can cope with relative novelty and automatize routine aspects of tasks so as to devote more resources to novel stimuli in their environment.

experiment *n.* a series of observations conducted under controlled conditions to study a relationship with the purpose of drawing causal inference about that relationship. Experiments typically involve the manipulation of an INDEPENDENT VARIABLE, the measurement of a DEPENDENT VARIABLE, and the exposure of various participants to one or more of the conditions being studied. **—experimental** *adj.*

experimental aesthetics the use of techniques of experimental psychology in the study of natural objects or art forms and their components. Studies in experimental aesthetics may also involve the use of Gestalt and other concepts in analyzing emotional effects and preferences for colors and patterns.

experimental analysis of behavior an approach to experimental psychology that emphasizes behavior as the subject matter, rather than as an indicator of internal processes. The relationships between particular experiences and changes in behavior are explored, and emphasis is placed on the behavior of individuals rather than on group averages.

experimental attrition see ATTRITION.

experimental control see CONTROL.

experimental design an outline or plan of the procedures to be followed in scientific experimentation in order to reach valid conclusions. Also called **research design**.

experimental epilepsy induction of an epileptic attack in an animal through the use of electrical or chemical brain stimulation.

experimental ethics see RESEARCH ETHICS.

experimental group a group of participants exposed to a particular level of the INDEPENDENT VARIABLE in an experiment. The responses of the experimental group are compared to the responses of a CONTROL GROUP, other experimental groups, or both.

experimental hypothesis a premise that describes what a researcher in a scientific study hopes to demonstrate if certain experimental conditions are met.

experimental introspection contemplation of one's own experience under controlled conditions.

experimental method a system of scientific investigation, usually based on a design to be carried out under controlled conditions, that is intended to test a hypothesis and establish a causal relationship between independent and dependent variables.

experimental neurosis a disordered behavioral or emotional state, characterized by high levels of anxiety, that is produced artificially in an animal (e.g., a dog, chimpanzee, or pig) during conditioning experiments in which the animal is required but unable to solve problems or discriminate between highly similar sounds, shapes, or other stimuli. Each failure is followed by punishment or loss of reinforcement, which may give rise to such symptoms as stereotyped behavior, compulsivity, disorganized responses, extreme emotional display, and emotional apathy. Also called **artificial neurosis**.

experimental philosophy 1. in the late 17th and 18th centuries, a name for the new discipline of experimental science then emerging. Use of the term often went with an optimism about the ability of experimental science to answer the questions that had been posed but unsolved by "natural philosophy." The systematic work of British physicist Isaac Newton (1642–1727) is often given as a defining example of the experimental philosophy. **2.** a late 20th-century movement holding that modern experimental science, particularly neuroscience, will ultimately uncover the biological foundations of thought and thereby provide a material answer to the questions of EPISTEMOLOGY. In other words, experimental philosophy holds that answers to philosophical questions regarding the mind and its activities can, and likely will be, reduced to questions of how the brain functions. See REDUCTIONISM.

experimental psychology the scientific study of behavior, motives, or cognition in a laboratory or other experimental setting in order to predict, explain, or control behavior or other psychological phenomena. Experimental psychology aims at establishing quantified relationships and explanatory theory through the analysis of responses under various controlled conditions and the synthesis of adequate theoretical accounts from the results of these observations. See also EMPIRICAL PSYCHOLOGY.

experimental realism the extent to which an experimental situation is psychologically realistic and elicits valid emotional responses from the participants. Deception may be used to achieve greater experimental realism (see ACTIVE DECEPTION; PASSIVE DECEPTION). See also MUNDANE REALISM.

experimental replication see REPLICATION.

experimental research research based on randomized EXPERIMENTS with the objective of drawing causal inference.

experimental series the trials administered to an EXPERIMENTAL GROUP in an experiment, as opposed to those administered to the CONTROL GROUP.

experimental treatment 1. in research, the conditions applied to one or more groups that are expected to cause change in some outcomes. **2.** a treatment or regimen that has shown some promise as a cure or ameliorative for a disease or condition but is still being evaluated for efficacy, safety, and acceptability. See also TREATMENT COMBINATION; TREATMENT LEVEL.

experimental unit the unit to which an experimental manipulation is applied. For example, if the experimental treatment is applied to a classroom of students, the classroom (not the individual students) is the experimental unit. The experimental unit is usually the unit of analysis.

experimental variable a variable under investigation, usually manipulated by the experimenter, to determine its relationship to or influence upon some DEPENDENT VARIABLE. See INDEPENDENT VARIABLE.

experimentation *n.* the carrying out of EXPERIMENTS.

experimentee *n.* a research participant, that is, a person who is studied in an experiment by the EXPERIMENTER.

experimenter *n.* the party who devises tasks for the EXPERIMENTEE to perform, determines the conditions under which the performance will take place, and monitors and interprets the results.

experimenter bias systematic experimenter error manifested by errors of observation, interpretation, or computation or by EXPERIMENTER EXPECTANCY EFFECTS. Such bias may threaten the ECOLOGICAL VALIDITY of the research.

experimenter biosocial effect an unintended effect on participants' responses that is associated with individual differences among the biological or social characteristics of the experimenters.

experimenter drift a gradual systematic change in the way an experimenter conducts an experiment.

experimenter effect either of two types of experimental bias: (a) errors on the part of the experimenter caused by his or her expectations about the results of the research or (b) bias resulting from the effects on the participants of the personal characteristics of the experimenter, such as age, sex, race, or linguistic features. See EXPERIMENTER BIAS; EXPERIMENTER EXPECTANCY EFFECT.

experimenter expectancy effect a type of EXPERIMENTER EFFECT in which experimental findings are distorted as a result of the influence of an experimenter's expectations on a participant's responses. The experimenter's body movements, gestures, facial expressions, and tone of voice have all been found to unintentionally influence participants' responses. The term is often used synonymously with ROSENTHAL EFFECT. See also EXPERIMENTER BIAS.

experimenter interpreter effect a systematic error that results when a researcher's interpretation of the observed data is biased (e.g., by the researcher's expectation).

experimenter modeling effect a systematic error that results in participants responding to a task in a way that is too similar to the way in which the experimenter would respond to the task.

experimenter observer effect a systematic error by an investigator in the perception or recording of data. This is often predictable from a knowledge of the investigator's expectation.

experimenter psychosocial effect an unintended effect on participants' responses associated with individual differences among the psychological or social characteristics of the experimenters.

experiment of nature see NATURAL EXPERIMENT.

expert authority see AUTHORITY.

expert fallacy the paradoxical finding that experts are poor reporters of their special skills or knowledge and may feel as if they have nothing to say within their fields of expertise. It is presumed that this expert knowledge has become automatized and hence less accessible to introspection and report.

expertise *n.* a high level of domain-specific knowledge and skills accumulated through age or experience.

expert–novice differences the ways in which the performance of those skilled in a particular domain will typically differ from that of those who have no experience in that domain.

expert power the capacity to influence others that derives from their assumption that the influencer possesses superior skills and abilities in a given domain. See POWER.

expert system a program, often mimicking human expert problem-solving performance, that uses the explicit representation of human knowledge, usually in the form of "if → then" rules. The expert system often employs a certainty-factor algebra to support reasoning in uncertain situations, in which there are missing or vague data or unclear alternatives. Expert systems are used in such fields as medical diagnosis and financial prediction. Also called **knowledge-based system** (**KBS**).

expert testimony evidence given in court by an EXPERT WITNESS. Unlike other testimony, this evidence may include the witness's opinions about certain facts in order to help the TRIER OF FACT to make a decision. See OPINION TESTIMONY; ULTIMATE OPINION TESTIMONY.

expert witness an individual who is qualified to testify regarding scientific, technical, or professional matters and provide an opinion concerning the evidence or facts presented in a court of law. Eligibility to testify as an expert witness is based on the person's special skills or knowledge as judged by the court. In U.S. federal courts, eligibility criteria are established by the Federal Rules of Evidence 702–706. See DAUBERT TEST; DAUBERT V. MERRELL DOW PHARMACEUTICALS INC.

expiation *n.* atonement for wrongdoing that represents acknowledgment, relieves or reduces feelings of guilt, and moves toward righting the situation.

expiatory punishment a punishment in which the wrongdoer is made to suffer in proportion to the severity of the wrongdoing, but not necessarily in a way that reflects the nature of the transgression. Compare RECIPROCAL PUNISHMENT.

explanation *n.* an account that provides a meaning for some phenomenon or event in terms of causal conditions, a set of beliefs or assumptions, or a metaphor that relates it to something already understood. See SCIENTIFIC EXPLANATION. —**explanatory** *adj.*

explanatory style an individual's unique style of describing and explaining some phenomenon, event, or personal history.

explicit attitude an attitude of which a person is consciously aware. Compare IMPLICIT ATTITUDE.

explicit attitude measure an ATTITUDE MEASURE in which a person is consciously aware of the fact that his or her attitude toward a particular ATTITUDE OBJECT is being assessed. Measures of this type are generally DIRECT ATTITUDE MEASURES. Compare IMPLICIT ATTITUDE MEASURE; INDIRECT ATTITUDE MEASURE.

explicit behavior see OVERT BEHAVIOR.

explicit memory memory that can be consciously recalled, either in the form of memory for personal events or general knowledge. Tests of this type of memory explicitly ask for recollection, in contrast to tests of IMPLICIT MEMORY, which indirectly assess remembering. See DECLARATIVE MEMORY.

explicit prejudice a PREJUDICE against a specific social group that is consciously held, even if not expressed publicly. Compare IMPLICIT PREJUDICE.

explicit process 1. a cognitive event that can be described accurately and that is available to introspection, especially one that involves a defined meaning. **2.** an occasional synonym for CONSCIOUS PROCESS. Compare IMPLICIT PROCESS.

exploitative orientation in the existential psychoanalysis of Erich FROMM, a character pattern marked by the use of stealth, deceit, power, or violence to obtain what the individual wants. The character type is plagiaristic rather than spontaneously or resourcefully creative. Also called **exploitative character**. Compare HOARDING ORIENTATION; MARKETING ORIENTATION.

exploratory behavior the movements made by human beings or other animals in orienting to new environments. Exploratory behavior occurs even when there is no obvious biological reward associated with it. A lack of such behavior in a new environment is often used as a measure of fearfulness or emotionality. See also DIVERSIVE EXPLORATION; INSPECTIVE EXPLORATION.

exploratory data analysis data analysis designed to generate new research questions or insights rather than to address specific preplanned research questions. Compare CONFIRMATORY DATA ANALYSIS.

exploratory drive the motivation that compels an organism to examine its environment. The exploratory drive may be secondary to other drives, such as fear or hunger leading to exploration. Alternatively, EXPLORATORY BEHAVIOR may be a separate and independent drive. Also called **exploration drive**. See also CURIOSITY.

exploratory experiment an experiment designed to give preliminary indications as to possible relationships among variables and possible procedures to employ in subsequent, more definitive experiments, rather than to provide clear answers to precisely formulated questions.

exploratory factor analysis a set of data-analytical techniques, applied to a covariance or correlation matrix, that allegedly reveals the structure underlying the set of coefficients. The techniques do not yield a unique solution: Although points (usually tests) are fixed in a multidimensional space of underlying factors, the axes according to which one should interpret the factors are not fixed and are infinite in number. These axes may be either orthogonal (producing uncorrelated factors) or oblique (producing correlated factors). Two frequently used configurations are unrotated axes, which tend to maximize the amounts of individual-differences variation packed into each successive factor (and which tend to yield a general factor of intelligence), and axes rotated to simple structure, which tend to produce factors on which particular tests show either relatively high or relatively low loadings, but few loadings of intermediate value.

exploratory procedures methods used by people for feeling the surfaces of objects. People tend to modify their use of touch to optimize the acquisition of information. Thus, they may push on a surface to judge its hardness or stroke it with the index finger to perceive texture. [described in 1987 by Canadian psychologist Susan J. Lederman and U.S. psychologist Roberta L. Klatzky (1947–)]

explosive disorder see INTERMITTENT EXPLOSIVE DISORDER; ISOLATED EXPLOSIVE DISORDER.

explosive personality a personality with a pattern of frequent outbursts of uncontrolled anger and hostility out of proportion to any provocation. See INTERMITTENT EXPLOSIVE DISORDER.

exponential distribution one of the basic distributions useful in psychological research. The probability distribution function is given by

$$(1/\beta)\exp[-(x - \alpha)/\beta],\ x \geq \alpha,\ \beta > 0,$$

where α is a location parameter determining the position of the distribution curve and β is a scale parameter determining how much the curve is stretched.

exponential function a FUNCTION of the type $y = a^x$, where a is a constant. A particular type has the form $y = e^x$, where e is a fundamental mathematical constant that is the base of natural logarithms (with the value 2.718...). Often, functions of this type (e.g., e^{x+a}) are written as $\exp(x + a)$.

ex post facto evaluation see SUMMATIVE EVALUATION.

ex post facto research research that either begins with data that have already been collected or is conducted after the experimental treatments have been administered. [from Latin *ex post facto*, "after the event"]

exposure deafness loss of hearing due to prolonged exposure to loud sounds. The condition may be temporary or permanent, depending upon the loudness, length of exposure, and sound frequencies. See also AUDITORY FATIGUE.

exposure therapy a form of BEHAVIOR THERAPY that is effective in treating anxiety disorders. Exposure therapy involves systematic confrontation with a feared stimulus, either in vivo (live) or in the imagination. It works by (a) HABITUATION, in which repeated exposure reduces anxiety over time by a process of EXTINCTION; (b) disconfirming fearful predictions; (c) deeper processing of the feared stimulus; and (d) increasing feelings of SELF-EFFICACY and mastery. Exposure therapy may encompass any of a number of behavioral interventions, including systematic DESENSITIZATION, FLOODING, IMPLOSIVE THERAPY, and extinction-based techniques.

expressed emotion (**EE**) negative feelings, such as those indicating criticism, hostility, and emotional overinvolvement, expressed by family members toward a person with an emotional or mental disorder. This negativity is associated with a high rate of relapse of the disorder in the individual. [first described in a study (1972) by British psychiatrists George W. Brown, Jim L. T. Birley, and John K. Wing]

expression *n.* the communication of a thought, behavior, or emotion. See also EMOTIONAL EXPRESSION; FACIAL EXPRESSION.

expressionism factor in psychological aesthetics, the components of artistic style that emphasize the artist's emotional experience and feelings of tension. According to British-born Canadian psychologist Daniel E. Berlyne (1924–1976), the expressionism factor is based on stylistic ratings that are high on such scales as tense–tranquil.

expressive amimia see AMIMIA.

expressive amusia see AMUSIA.

expressive aphasia a type of APHASIA in which the ability to speak, write, or use gestures is lost or impaired. The condition is often associated with a lesion in BROCA'S AREA of the brain. Also called **cortical motor aphasia**; **expressive dysphasia**; **speech aphasia**; **verbal aphasia**; **word dumbness**. Compare RECEPTIVE APHASIA.

expressive dysphasia see EXPRESSIVE APHASIA.

expressive language the language produced by a speaker or writer, as opposed to that received by a listener or reader (see RECEPTIVE LANGUAGE). Also called **productive language**.

expressive language disorder in *DSM–IV–TR*, a COMMUNICATION DISORDER characterized by impairment in the ability to use expressive language (speaking, writing, or gesturing) effectively for communicating with others. In the most common, developmental, form of the disorder, the impairment is usually apparent by the age of 3 years, and most children have achieved near-normal expressive language abilities by late adolescence. The less common acquired form occurs after a period of normal language development as a result of a neurological or other disorder or injury.

expressive therapy **1.** a form of PSYCHOTHERAPY in which the client is encouraged to talk through his or her problems and to express feelings openly and without restraint. Compare SUPPRESSIVE THERAPY. **2.** any of a variety of therapies that rely on nonverbal methods (e.g., art, dance, movement) to facilitate change.

extended care a health care service provided at a residential facility where 24-hour nursing care and rehabilitation therapy are available, usually following an acute hospitalization. A facility that provides such a service is known as an **extended care facility** (**ECF**). See also CONTINUING CARE UNIT; CONVALESCENT CENTER; SKILLED NURSING FACILITY.

extended family **1.** a family unit consisting of parents and children living in one household with certain other individuals united by kinship (e.g., grandparents, cousins). **2.** in modern Western societies, the NUCLEAR FAMILY together with various other relatives with whom it keeps in regular touch but does not live.

extended-family therapy GROUP PSYCHOTHERAPY involving not only the nuclear family but also other family members, such as aunts, uncles, grandparents, and cousins. See also FAMILY THERAPY.

extended-release preparation see SLOW-RELEASE PREPARATION.

extended-stay review a review of a continuous hospital stay that has equaled or exceeded the period defined by a hospital or third-party UTILIZATION REVIEW. See also CONTINUED-STAY REVIEW.

extended suicide MURDER–SUICIDE in which both the murder and the suicide reflect the suicidal process. The individual first kills those perceived as being a part of his or her identity or extended self and then commits suicide.

extensional meaning the meaning of a word or phrase as established by a list of the individual instances to which it applies. So, for example, the extensional meaning of *cardinal points of the compass* is "north, south, east, and west." Compare INTENSIONAL MEANING.

extension reflex any reflex action that causes a limb or part of a limb to move away from the body. Extension reflexes include the EXTENSOR THRUST, STRETCH REFLEXES, and CROSSED-EXTENSION REFLEXES. Compare FLEXION REFLEX.

extensor motor neuron a MOTOR NEURON whose fibers connect with extensor effectors, that is, muscles that extend a part of the body by contracting (see EXTENSOR MUSCLE).

extensor muscle a muscle whose contraction extends a part of the body; for example, the triceps muscle group extends, or straightens, the arm. Compare FLEXOR MUSCLE.

extensor posturing see DECEREBRATE RIGIDITY.

extensor rigidity rigid contractions of extensor muscles. The kind of rigidity sometimes indicates the site of the motor neuron lesion associated with the disorder. Injury to the cerebellum produces increased tone of extensor muscles, called **cerebellar rigidity**. See also DECEREBRATE RIGIDITY.

extensor thrust a reflex extension of the leg caused by applying a stimulus to the sole of the foot. The reflex normally occurs each time a person takes a step in walking or running, signaling a need for body support and providing the thrust for taking the next step. See also STRETCH REFLEX.

exteriorization *n.* **1.** the act of relating one's inner feelings and attitudes to external, objective reality. **2.** the outward expression of one's private and personal ideas.

external aim see OBJECT OF INSTINCT.

external attribution see SITUATIONAL ATTRIBUTION.

external auditory meatus the canal that conducts sound through the external ear, from the pinna to the tympanic membrane (eardrum). Also called **auditory canal**; **ear canal**.

external boundary in psychoanalytic theory, the boundary between the EGO and external reality, as opposed to the INTERNAL BOUNDARY between ego and ID. Also called **outer boundary**.

external capsule a thin, flat layer of tissue separating the CLAUSTRUM from the PUTAMEN, near the midline of the human brain. It consists of white fibers from the anterior WHITE COMMISSURE and subthalamic region, and is continuous with the INTERNAL CAPSULE. Also called **capsula externa**.

external chemical messenger (**ECM**) an ODORANT or other substance that is secreted or released by an organism and influences other organisms. PHEROMONES are examples.

external control the belief that one's experiences and behavior are determined by circumstances, luck, other people, or other external factors. See EXTERNALIZERS; LOCUS OF CONTROL. Compare INTERNAL CONTROL.

external ear the part of the ear consisting of the PINNA, the EXTERNAL AUDITORY MEATUS, and the outer surface of the eardrum (see TYMPANIC MEMBRANE). Also called **outer ear**.

external evaluator an individual who conducts an evaluation of a program and who is not a regular full-time employee of the program being evaluated. Such an evaluation is considered more objective and potentially less biased than one produced by an INTERNAL EVALUATOR. External agents are often preferred for SUMMATIVE EVALUATIONS, with possible highly visible consequences, to ensure the validity and credibility of the results.

external fertilization see FERTILIZATION.

external granular layer see CORTICAL LAYERS.

external hair cells the outer hair cells of the ear. See HAIR CELLS.

external inequity the situation in which employers compensate employees at levels that are unfair in relation to the levels of compensation they would receive from other comparable employers. Compare INTERNAL INEQUITY. See EQUITY THEORY.

externality effect the tendency of very young infants to direct their attention primarily to the outside of a figure and to spend little time inspecting internal features. The externality effect appears to diminish after the age of 1 month.

externalization *n.* **1.** a DEFENSE MECHANISM in which one's own thoughts, feelings or perceptions are attributed to the external world. A common expression of this is PROJECTION. **2.** the process of learning to distinguish between the self and the environment during childhood. **3.** the process by which a drive, such as hunger, is aroused by external stimuli, such as food, rather than by internal stimuli. **4.** the perception that particular aspects of one's behavior are attributable to the external world and are independent of oneself or one's own experiences.

externalizers *pl. n.* people who believe that their behavior and reactions to conditions or situations around them are determined largely or entirely by events beyond their control, that is, they have an external LOCUS OF CONTROL. Compare INTERNALIZERS.

externalizing behavior see EXTERNALIZING–INTERNALIZING.

externalizing–internalizing 1. a broad classification of children's behaviors and disorders based on their reactions to stressors. Externalizing behaviors and disorders are characterized primarily by actions in the external world, such as acting out, antisocial behavior, hostility, and aggression. Internalizing behaviors and disorders are characterized primarily by processes within the self, such as anxiety, SOMATIZATION, and depression. [proposed by U.S. psychologist Thomas M. Achenbach (1940–)] **2.** see EXTERNALIZATION; INTERNALIZATION.

external locus of control see LOCUS OF CONTROL.

external pyramidal layer see CORTICAL LAYERS.

external rectus see LATERAL RECTUS.

external sense a sensory system that depends on external stimulation (e.g., vision). See EXTEROCEPTOR.

external stigmata physical marks or peculiarities that aid in the identification of a condition.

external validity the extent to which the results of research or testing can be generalized beyond the sample that generated the results to other individuals or situations. For example, if research has been conducted only with male participants, it cannot be assumed that similar results will apply to female participants. The more specialized the sample, the less likely will it be that the results are highly generalizable.

external world the world of real existing things external to and independent of human consciousness. The question of how one can have knowledge of such a world, or even be sure that such a world exists, has been fundamental to philosophy since the time of French philosopher René Descartes (1596–1650). See ABSOLUTE REALITY; OBJECTIVE REALITY. See also CARTESIAN SELF; EGOCENTRIC PREDICAMENT; SOLIPSISM.

exteroception *n.* input of information from EXTEROCEPTORS about stimuli that are outside the body (e.g., from objects or events in the world). Compare INTEROCEPTION.

exteroceptive stimulus a stimulus that arises in the external world and is sensed by an organism through any of the five senses, namely, sight, smell, hearing, touch, or taste. Compare INTEROCEPTIVE STIMULUS; PROPRIOCEPTIVE STIMULUS.

exteroceptor *n.* a sensory nerve ending, as in the skin or mucous membranes, that receives stimulation from outside the body. Compare INTEROCEPTOR.

extinction *n.* **1.** in biology, the loss of a species or subspecies either completely or within a particular environment. For example, the passenger pigeon is globally extinct, and condors and whooping cranes were extinct in many places where previously they had been found but have been reintroduced after successful captive breeding. **2.** in neurophysiology, a progressive decrease in EXCITABILITY of a nerve to a previously above-threshold stimulus as stimulation continues. **3.** see PERCEPTUAL EXTINCTION. **4.** in PAVLOVIAN CONDITIONING: (a) a procedure in which PAIRING of stimulus events is discontinued, either by presenting the CONDITIONED STIMULUS alone or by presenting the conditioned stimulus and the UNCONDITIONED STIMULUS independently of one another; or (b) the result of this procedure, which is a gradual decline in the probability and magnitude of the CONDITIONED RESPONSE. **5.** in OPERANT CONDITIONING: (a) a procedure in which reinforcement is discontinued, that is, the reinforcing stimulus is no longer presented; or (b) the result of this procedure, which is a decline in the rate of the formerly reinforced response. **—extinguish** *vb.*

extirpation *n.* see ABLATION.

extra- (**extr-**) *prefix* outside of or beyond (e.g., EXTRASENSORY PERCEPTION).

extracellular space the fluid-filled space in an organism that lies outside the plasma membrane of cells.

extraception *n.* an attitude of skepticism, objectivity, and adherence to the facts. [defined by U.S. psychologist Henry Alexander Murray (1893–1988)]

extrachance *adj.* in parapsychology experiments, describing test results that depart radically from chance expectations.

extradural hemorrhage bleeding that occurs outside the dura mater, the outermost of the three protective membranes (meninges) that cover the brain. It usually involves a ruptured artery resulting from a severe head injury, such as a skull fracture. There may be a brief lucid period after the injury, then severe headaches, dizziness, confusion, loss of consciousness, and finally death if the hemorrhage is not controlled.

extrafusal fiber any of the muscle fibers that lie outside MUSCLE SPINDLES and provide most of the force for muscle contraction. Compare INTRAFUSAL FIBER.

extraneous variable a variable that is not relevant to the relationship under investigation in an experiment but may have an unplanned effect on the DEPENDENT VARIABLE.

extrapair mating in socially monogamous species, mating that occurs with individuals other than the mate. In many monogamous bird species genetic evidence of paternity suggests extensive extrapair mating, with the result that many chicks are not sired by the male that cares for them. Extrapair mating might also occur at times when conception is not possible, either to test other potential mates or to strengthen social relationships with others. See also CUCKOLDRY.

extrapsychic *adj.* pertaining to that which originates outside the mind or that which occurs between the mind and the environment.

extrapsychic conflict CONFLICT arising between the individual and the environment, as contrasted with INTRAPSYCHIC CONFLICT.

extrapunitive *adj.* **1.** describing a reaction to frustration or distress in which anger or aggression is directed at the person or situation perceived to be the source of the frustration. **2.** relating to the outward direction of hostility or a tendency to regard external factors as the cause of one's frustrations.

extrapyramidal dyskinesia any of various distortions of voluntary movement (DYSKINESIAS), such as tremors, spasms, tics, rigidity, or gait disturbances, associated with some lesion of the EXTRAPYRAMIDAL TRACT. These dyskinesias can occur in neurological disorders or as a side effect of antipsychotic drugs, which produce such conditions as AKATHISIA, ACUTE DYSTONIA, and TARDIVE DYSKINESIA.

extrapyramidal effects adverse drug reactions that involve the EXTRAPYRAMIDAL TRACT of the central nervous system, which are responsible for the regulation of movement. They include drug-induced parkinsonism (e.g., slowness of voluntary movements, lack of facial expression, rigidity of the limbs, tremor), dystonia (abnormal facial and body movements), and AKATHISIA (restlessness). Extrapyramidal effects are among the most common side effects of the HIGH-POTENCY ANTIPSYCHOTICS and have also been reported with use of other drugs (e.g., SSRIS). Also called **extrapyramidal symptoms** (**EPS**); **extrapyramidal syndrome** (**EPS**).

extrapyramidal tract a motor portion of the central nervous system that excludes the motor cortex, motor neurons, and corticospinal tract (see PYRAMIDAL TRACT). It includes the BASAL GANGLIA and some closely related structures (e.g., the SUBTHALAMIC NUCLEI) and descending pathways to the midbrain. Its functions are the regulation of muscle tone and body posture and the coordination of opposing sets of skeletal muscles and movement of their associated skeletal parts. Also called **extrapyramidal motor system**; **extrapyramidal system**.

extrasensory perception (**ESP**) alleged awareness of external events by other means than the known sensory channels. It includes TELEPATHY, CLAIRVOYANCE, PRECOGNITION, and, more loosely, PSYCHOKINESIS. Despite considerable research, the existence of any of these modalities remains highly controversial. Also called **paranormal cognition**. See PARAPSYCHOLOGY.

extra-small acrocentric chromosome syndrome see CAT'S-EYE SYNDROME.

extraspective perspective a methodological approach based on objective, empirical observation of actions and reactions, as contrasted with an introspective, first-person account of experience. The approach of BEHAVIORISM is based on an extraspective perspective.

extraspectral hue a hue composed of a mixture of wavelengths, and thus not falling along the visible spectrum (compare SPECTRAL COLOR). Two examples are purple and white: Purple is a mixture of long and short wavelengths, whereas white is a mixture of all wavelengths. Also called **nonspectral hue**.

extrastriate cortex see PRESTRIATE CORTEX.

extrastriate visual areas visually responsive regions of cerebral cortex that are located outside the primary visual cortex (striate cortex), that is, in the PRESTRIATE CORTEX. Extrastriate visual areas include V2, V4, and V5.

extra sum of square principle a basic approach for model comparison significance testing in the GENERAL LINEAR MODEL in which the value of an additional parameter in the model is assessed in terms of the reduction in the SUM OF SQUARES error that its addition accomplishes.

extraterrestrial kidnapping see ALIEN ABDUCTION.

extrauterine pregnancy see ECTOPIC PREGNANCY.

extraversion (**extroversion**) *n.* **1.** an orientation of one's interests and energies toward the outer world of people and things rather than the inner world of subjective experience. Extraversion is a broad personality trait and, like INTROVERSION, exists on a continuum of attitudes and behaviors. Extroverts are relatively more outgoing, gregarious, sociable, and openly expressive. [concept originated by Carl JUNG for the study of personality types] **2.** one of the elements of the FIVE-FACTOR PERSONALITY MODEL and the BIG FIVE PERSONALITY MODEL, characterized by POSITIVE AFFECT and sociability. **3.** one of the three personality dimensions, along with PSYCHOTICISM and NEUROTICISM, of EYSENCK'S TYPOLOGY. See also FACTOR THEORY OF PERSONALITY. **—extraversive** *adj.* **—extraverted** *adj.* **—extravert** *n.*

extreme environments extreme living conditions (e.g., space habitats, polar regions, offshore oil platforms) as they affect human health and well-being. Salient issues in the analysis of extreme environments include PRIVACY, CROWDING, social support, and levels of stimulation.

extremity of an attitude the extent to which a person's evaluation of an ATTITUDE OBJECT deviates from neutrality. Extremity is related to the STRENGTH OF AN ATTITUDE.

extrinsic eye muscles see EYE MUSCLES.

extrinsic interest engagement in a task or behavior stimulated by the belief that performing it effectively will secure some reward or prevent a punishment, rather than by the intrinsic satisfaction of performing the task for its own sake. For example, those with an extrinsic interest in studying music hope to use their musical skills to earn money, whereas those with an **intrinsic interest** study music for its own sake.

extrinsic motivation an external incentive to engage in a specific activity, especially motivation arising from the expectation of punishment or reward. An example of extrinsic motivation for studying is fear of failing an examination. Compare INTRINSIC MOTIVATION.

extrinsic reinforcer a REINFORCER that has an arbitrary relation to the response that produces it. For example, a food pellet is an extrinsic reinforcer for a lever press. **Extrinsic reinforcement** denotes both the reward itself and the actual process or procedure of providing that reward. Compare INTRINSIC REINFORCER.

extrinsic religion a religious orientation in which RELIGIOSITY is largely a means to other ends, such as social morality or individual well-being, rather than an end in itself. Compare INTRINSIC RELIGION. [introduced by Gordon W. ALLPORT]

extrinsic reward a reward for behavior that is not a natural consequence of that behavior. For example, winning a trophy for finishing first in a race and receiving praise or money in the work setting are extrinsic rewards. Compare INTRINSIC REWARD.

extroversion *n.* see EXTRAVERSION.

eye *n.* the organ of sight. The human eye is a layered, globular structure whose shape is maintained by fluid filling its interior. There are three layers: (a) the outer corneoscleral coat, which includes the transparent CORNEA in front and continues as the fibrous SCLERA over the rest of the globe; (b) the middle layer, called the **uveal tract**, which includes the IRIS, the CILIARY BODY, and the CHOROID LAYER; and (c) the innermost layer, the RETINA, which is sensitive to light. RETINAL GANGLION CELLS within the retina communicate with the central nervous system through the OPTIC NERVE, which leaves the retina at the OPTIC DISK. The eye has three chambers. The **anterior chamber**, between the cornea and the iris, and the **posterior chamber**, between the ciliary body, LENS, and posterior aspect of the iris, are filled with a watery fluid, the AQUEOUS HUMOR. The anterior and posterior chambers are in continuity through the PUPIL. The third chamber, the **vitreous body**, is the large cavity between the lens and the retina filled with VITREOUS HUMOR. See also EYE MUSCLES; VISUAL SYSTEM.

eyeballing *n.* slang for a preliminary casual look at research results, usually prior to a more formal analysis of the data.

eye bank a repository for corneas or other parts of the human eye to be used for surgical transplantation in medically and immunologically appropriate recipients.

eye contact the act of looking into the eyes of the person with whom one is communicating. Maintaining eye contact is considered essential to communication between therapist and client during face-to-face interviews. This communication behavior is used as a variable in some social-psychological studies to represent the degree of interpersonal intimacy. Social-psychological studies of eye contact generally find that people typically look more at the other person when listening to that person than when they themselves are talking, that they tend to avoid eye contact when they are embarrassed, that women are apt to maintain more eye contact than are men, and that the more intimate the relationship, the greater is the eye contact. Also called **mutual gaze**.

eye dominance a preference for using one eye rather than the other. Preference is often for the right eye and is caused mainly by the differential acuity of the two eyes.

eyeglasses *pl. n.* see CORRECTIVE LENS.

eye–hand coordination the harmonious functioning of eyes and hands in grasping and exploring objects and performing specific tasks. By 6 months of age, most infants can grasp an object within reach, although full use of the thumb develops later, between 8 and 12 months.

eyelash sign a reaction of eyelid movement to the stimulus of stroking the eyelashes. It can be used as part of a diagnostic test for LOSS OF CONSCIOUSNESS due to a functional or psychogenic disorder. If the loss of consciousness is due to a neurological disease or injury, the reflex will not occur.

eyelid conditioning a procedure for studying PAVLOVIAN CONDITIONING in which the UNCONDITIONED STIMULUS (usually an electrical stimulus or a puff of air) elicits an eyeblink.

eye-movement camera a research device that photographs eye movements, used to study visual sequences in performing perceptual or cognitive operations. See also EYE TRACKER.

eye-movement desensitization therapy a treatment methodology used to reduce the emotional impact of trauma-based symptomatology associated with anxiety, nightmares, flashbacks, or intrusive thought processes. The therapy incorporates simultaneous visualization of the traumatic event while concentrating, for example, on the rapid lateral movements of a therapist's finger. Also called **eye-movement desensitization and reprocessing** (**EMDR**). [developed in the late 1980s by U.S. psychologist Francine Shapiro]

eye movements movements of the eyes caused by contraction of the extrinsic EYE MUSCLES. These include movements that allow or maintain the FIXATION of stationary targets; SMOOTH-PURSUIT MOVEMENTS; VERGENCE movements; and reflexive movements of the eyes, such as the OPTOKINETIC REFLEX and VESTIBULAR NYSTAGMUS.

eye muscles 1. (**extrinsic eye muscles**) the muscles that move the eye within the eye socket. There are three pairs: (a) the SUPERIOR RECTUS and INFERIOR RECTUS, (b) the LATERAL RECTUS and MEDIAL RECTUS, and (c) the SUPERIOR OBLIQUE and INFERIOR OBLIQUE. **2.** (**intrinsic eye muscles**) the muscles that move structures within the eye itself. They include the CILIARY MUSCLES, which alter the shape of the lens during ACCOMMODATION, and the muscles of the IRIS, which change the size of the PUPIL.

eye preference see EYE DOMINANCE.

eye-roll sign a physiological index believed to show susceptibility to hypnosis. The participant is directed to roll his or her eyes upward as far as possible and at the same time lower the eyelids slowly. Hypnotizability or depth of hypnosis is believed to be a function of the amount of white sclera that becomes visible below the cornea.

eye span see READING SPAN.

eye structure see EYE.

eye tracker a device that measures the successive locations of an individual's visual fixation point as he or she observes displays. See also EYE-MOVEMENT CAMERA.

eye–voice span when reading aloud, the distance in terms of characters between the word being spoken and the word the eye is focused on. See also READING SPAN.

eyewitness memory an individual's memory of an event, often a crime or accident of some kind, that he or she personally saw or experienced. The reliability of EYEWITNESS TESTIMONY is a major issue in FORENSIC PSYCHOLOGY.

eyewitness testimony evidence given under oath in a court of law by an individual who claims to have witnessed the facts under dispute. See also EYEWITNESS MEMORY.

Eysenck, Hans Jurgen (1916–1997) German-born British psychologist. An emigré from Germany because of his unwillingness to join the Nazi party, Eysenck earned his doctorate in psychology at University College, London, in 1940. He founded the Department of Psychology at the Institute of Psychiatry, Maudsley Hospital, University of London, where he remained throughout his career. He is best known for contributions to personality theory, popularizing the terms "introvert" and "extravert" (see EYSENCK'S TYPOLOGY), and developing a number of personality tests, such as the EYSENCK PERSONALITY INVENTORY. Eysenck was often controversial, most notably for his claim that patients undergoing Freudian psychoanalysis and other psychodynamic therapies were no more likely to improve than patients who had no therapy. He favored behavioral treatments for emotional and behavioral disorders. Eysenck also advocated the controversial view that racial differences in intelligence are genetically based, publishing *Race, Intelligence, and Education* in 1971; in later years, however, he acknowledged the mitigating influences of environment.

Eysenck Personality Inventory (**EPI**) a self-report personality test for use with adolescents and adults. It comprises 57 yes–no questions that are designed to measure two major personality dimensions of EYSENCK'S TYPOLOGY—introversion–extraversion and neuroticism—and includes a Lie scale intended to detect response distortion. It was a modification and replacement of the **Maudsley Personality Inventory** (**MPI**), a personality test containing 24 items measuring neuroticism and 24 measuring extraversion that was developed in 1959 by Hans EYSENCK while working at the Maudsley Hospital, London, England. The EPI has been revised and expanded since its initial publication in 1963 to become the **Eysenck Personality Questionnaire** (**EPQ**), the most recent version of which (the **EPQ–R**) includes 90 questions and measures the additional personality dimension of PSYCHOTICISM. [Hans Eysenck and British psychologist Sybil B. G. **Eysenck**]

Eysenck's typology a system for classifying personality types in which individual differences are described according to three dimensions: PSYCHOTICISM, EXTRAVERSION, and NEUROTICISM (referred to as **PEN**). Also called **PEN typology**. See also FACTOR THEORY OF PERSONALITY. [Hans EYSENCK]

Ff

F_1 abbreviation for first FILIAL GENERATION.

fables test a test in which an individual is asked to interpret fables. It is used, although relatively infrequently, in intelligence and projective tests.

fabrication *n.* **1.** the act of concocting or inventing a whole or part of a story, often with the intention to deceive. **2.** a story concocted in this way.

fabulation *n.* random speech that includes the recounting of imaginary incidents by a person who believes these incidents are real. See also DELUSION. [first described by Swiss-born U.S. psychiatrist Adolf Meyer (1866–1950)]

face–hand test a test of tactile extinction (see DOUBLE-SIMULTANEOUS TACTILE SENSATION) in which the examiner touches the individual's face and the back of his or her hand at the same time.

face-ism *n.* the alleged tendency for advertisements and other visual media to represent men by their faces (symbolizing their intellectual nature) but women by their whole bodies (symbolizing their sensual nature). It is thus a form of SEXISM. **—face-ist** *adj.*

face perception the sum of the sensory, neurological, and cognitive processes involved in the interpretation of FACIAL EXPRESSION and in FACE RECOGNITION. There is much research in this area as faces are extensively represented in different areas of the brain. See also FACIAL ACTION CODING SYSTEM.

face recognition the identification of an individual by perceiving his or her face. The existence of a specific face-recognition area in the brain is indicated by brain imaging and evidenced by PROSOPAGNOSIA, a sudden-onset failure to recognize previously familiar faces, which can be caused by brain injury.

face-saving behavior an act in which one attempts to uphold one's dignity, as by redressing a social blunder or compensating for a poor impression one has made. Face-saving behavior is an aspect of IMPRESSION MANAGEMENT. See also FACEWORK.

face-to-face group any group whose members are in personal contact and, as a result, are able to perceive each other's needs and responses and carry on direct interaction. Examples include T-GROUPS and psychotherapy groups. Also called **direct-contact group**.

face-to-face interaction a direct encounter between two or more individuals, as opposed to one involving communication by writing, telephone, or some other medium, or intercession by third parties.

face validity the extent to which the items or content of a test appear to be appropriate for measuring something, regardless of whether they really are. A test with face validity, however, may lack EMPIRICAL VALIDITY.

facework *n.* **1.** in social interactions, a set of strategic behaviors by which people maintain both their own dignity ("face") and that of the people with whom they are dealing. Facework strategies include politeness, deference, tact, avoidance of difficult subjects, and the use of half-truths and "white lies." The conventions governing facework differ widely between cultures. **2.** formal FACE-TO-FACE INTERACTIONS between people engaged in business, politics, diplomacy, and other goal-directed activities. Such interactions may involve a certain amount of small talk and personal conversation as well as discussion of the official agenda.

facial action coding system (**FACS**) a coding system for classifying facial expressions in terms of the movements of particular facial muscles, such as the orbicularis oculi (the muscle encircling each eye) and the zygomaticus major (the muscle pulling the corners of the lips upward). Later elaborations of this system have been used in attempts to identify the emotional state of a person. True enjoyment, for example, is said to be indicated by contraction of the orbicularis oculi muscle, which is not under conscious control. See also FACIAL EXPRESSION. [first published in 1978 by U.S. psychologists Paul Ekman (1934–) and Wallace V. Friesen (1933–)]

facial-affect program a hypothetical set of central nervous system structures that accounts for the patterning of universal, basic facial expressions of emotion in humans. Such a program could provide the link between a specific emotion and a given pattern of facial muscular activity.

facial angle any of various angles that quantify facial protrusion, established by using a set of craniometric reference points, such as the juncture of the frontal and nasal bones, the foremost projection point of the chin, and the horizontal eye–ear plane.

facial disfigurement any distortion, malformation, or abnormality of the facial features due to injury, disease, or congenital anomaly. Because of a common tendency to assign traits to individuals on the basis of facial features, people with facial disfigurements are particularly vulnerable to social, psychological, and economic discrimination and unfavorable stress effects. See DISFIGUREMENT.

facial display see FACIAL EXPRESSION.

facial electromyography a technique for measuring the endogenous electrical activity of any muscle or muscle group in the face by the appropriate placement of electrodes (see ELECTROMYOGRAPHY). This procedure is usually carried out to detect implicit, invisible facial movements related to emotion or speech.

facial expression a form of nonverbal signaling using the movement of facial muscles. As well as being an integral part of communication, facial expression also reflects an individual's emotional state. British biologist Charles Darwin (1809–1882) suggested that facial expressions are innate reactions that possess specific survival value; for example, a baby's smile evokes nurturing responses in parents. Although controversial, this theory has been supported by cross-cultural research and studies of blind children, which indicate that certain facial expressions are spontaneous and universally correlated with such primary emotions as surprise, fear, anger, sadness, and happiness; DISPLAY RULES, however, can modify or even inhibit these expressions. Physical conditions can produce characteristic facial expressions, such as the masklike countenance in parkinsonism, and the face can be a mirror of emotional disorder, as evidenced by the anguished look of those who are depressed.

facial feedback hypothesis the hypothesis that AFFERENT information from facial muscle movements is a major determinant of intrapsychic feeling states, such as fear, anger, joy, contempt, and so on. This idea was introduced by British naturalist Charles Darwin (1809–1882) and developed by U.S. psychologists Sylvan S. Tomkins (1911–1991) and Carroll E. Izard (1923–).

facial muscle any one of the numerous muscles in the human face that control not only functional movements (e.g., biting and chewing) but also a variety of FACIAL EXPRESSIONS.

facial nerve the seventh CRANIAL NERVE, which innervates facial musculature and some sensory receptors, including those of the external ear and the tongue. Also called **cranial nerve VII**. See GREATER SUPERFICIAL PETROSAL NERVE.

-facient *suffix* making or causing.

facies *n.* FACIAL EXPRESSION, which is often considered to be a guide to an individual's emotions or state of health.

facilitated communication 1. communication that is made more effective or efficient (e.g., easier to understand or faster), often with the aid of a technological device or process. Examples include the captioning of TV broadcasts for the benefit of viewers with hearing loss (see CLOSE-CAPTIONED TELEVISION) and the use of SPEECH SYNTHESIZERS by people who are unable to talk. See also AUGMENTATIVE COMMUNICATION. **2.** a controversial method of communication in which a person with a severe developmental disability (e.g., AUTISM) is assisted by a **facilitator** in typing letters, words, phrases, or sentences using a typewriter, computer keyboard, or alphabet facsimile. Facilitated communication involves a graduated manual prompting procedure, with the intent of supporting a person's hand sufficiently to make it more feasible to strike the keys he or she wishes to strike, without influencing the key selection. The procedure is often claimed to produce unexpected literacy, revealed through age-normative or superior communication content, syntax, and fluency. Scientific research findings, however, indicate that the content of the communication is being determined by the facilitator via nonconscious movements. [developed in the 1970s by Australian educator Rosemary Crossley (1945–)]

facilitation *n.* **1.** the strengthening or increased occurrence of a response resulting from environmental support for the response. See also SOCIAL FACILITATION. **2.** in neuroscience, the phenomenon in which the threshold for propagation of the action potential of a neuron is lowered due to repeated signals at a SYNAPSE or the SUMMATION of subthreshold impulses. **—facilitate** *vb.*

facilitative anxiety a level of anxiety that an individual (e.g., an athlete) perceives as assisting performance, for example, being psyched up (see PSYCHING UP) or "in the zone."

facilitator *n.* **1.** a professionally trained or lay member of a group who fulfills some or all of the functions of a group leader. The facilitator encourages discussion among all group members, without necessarily entering into the discussion. **2.** *see* facilitated communication.

FACM abbreviation for FUNCTIONAL ANALYTIC CAUSAL MODEL.

FACS acronym for FACIAL ACTION CODING SYSTEM.

fact finder see TRIER OF FACT.

fact giver a person who assumes the role of providing information during a GROUP PSYCHOTHERAPY discussion of a particular topic.

factitious disorder in *DSM–IV–TR*, any of a group of disorders in which the patient intentionally produces or feigns physical or psychological symptoms solely so that he or she may assume the SICK ROLE (compare MALINGERING). Four subtypes are recognized: **factitious disorder with predominantly psychological signs and symptoms** (e.g., depression, suicidal thoughts following the [unconfirmed] death of a spouse, hallucinations, delusions), in which the symptoms often become aggravated if the individual is aware of being observed and very often do not respond to treatment or follow traditional courses; **factitious disorder with predominantly physical signs and symptoms** (e.g., pain, vomiting, blackouts, seizures, infections), the most severe form of which is MUNCHAUSEN SYNDROME; **factitious disorder with combined psychological and physical signs and symptoms**; and FACTITIOUS DISORDER NOT OTHERWISE SPECIFIED.

factitious disorder not otherwise specified in *DSM–IV–TR*, a FACTITIOUS DISORDER that does not meet the criteria for one of the four specific subtypes. An example is **factitious disorder by proxy** (commonly known as MUNCHAUSEN SYNDROME BY PROXY), in which a caretaker, very often a mother, will intentionally produce symptoms (usually physical) in the person being cared for, solely to play a role in the illness, its treatment, or both (i.e., to assume the sick role by proxy).

fact memory memory for facts or specific items of knowledge (see FACTUAL KNOWLEDGE). Compare SOURCE MEMORY.

factor *n.* **1.** anything that contributes to a result or has a causal relationship to a phenomenon, event, or action. **2.** an underlying influence that accounts in part for variations in individual behavior. **3.** in ANALYSIS OF VARIANCE, an independent variable. **4.** in FACTOR ANALYSIS, an underlying, unobservable LATENT VARIABLE thought (together with other factors) to be responsible for the interrelations among a set of variables. **5.** in mathematics, a number that divides without remainder into another number.

factor analysis a mathematical procedure for reducing a set of intercorrelations (see MANIFEST VARIABLE) to a small number of descriptive or explanatory concepts (see LATENT VARIABLE). For example, a number of tests of mechanical ability might be intercorrelated to enable factor analysis to reduce them to a few factors, such as fine motor coordination, speed, and attention.

factor-comparison method a method of evaluating jobs for the purpose of setting wage or salary levels in which jobs are compared to certain BENCHMARK JOBS in terms of COMPENSABLE JOB FACTORS. The factors usually include mental requirements, skill requirements, physical requirements, responsibility, and working conditions. Compare CLASSIFICATION METHOD; HAY METHOD; JOB-COMPONENT METHOD; POINT METHOD; RANKING METHOD. See JOB EVALUATION.

factorial design an experimental design in which two or more independent variables are simultaneously manipulated or observed in order to study their joint and separate influences on a dependent variable. See also INCOMPLETE FACTORIAL DESIGN; SIMPLE FACTORIAL DESIGN; TWO-BY-TWO FACTORIAL DESIGN; TWO-FACTOR DESIGN.

factorial invariance the concept that factors in a FACTOR ANALYSIS remain identical from sample to sample.

factoring *n.* **1.** in factor analysis, the process of extracting factors. **2.** in mathematics, the subdivision of a target number into a series of numbers whose product is the target number.

factor loading the correlation between a MANIFEST VARIABLE and a LATENT VARIABLE (factor) in factor analysis. The factor loading reflects the degree to which a manifest variable is said to be "made up of" the factor whose loading is being examined.

factor method the method by which factors are extracted in FACTOR ANALYSIS.

factor of uniform density see COMMON FATE.

factor pattern matrix in factor analysis, a matrix of regression-like WEIGHTS that indicate the composition of the MANIFEST VARIABLE in terms of the factors.

factor reflection a change of the signs of a set of FACTOR LOADINGS from positive to negative, or vice versa.

factor rotation in FACTOR ANALYSIS, the repositioning of FACTORS to a new, more interpretable configuration by a set of mathematically specifiable TRANSFORMATIONS.

factor score an estimate of the score that an individual would have on a factor after the factor is determined through FACTOR ANALYSIS.

factor structure matrix in factor analysis, a matrix containing the FACTOR LOADINGS.

factor theory of intelligence a theory postulating that intelligence consists of a number of distinct factors, and it is the individual's ability in these factors that underpins his or her test scores. For example, a factor theory of intelligence might hold that underlying scores on the many different tests of intelligence are verbal and nonverbal factors. These factors are hypothetical constructs whose existence is proposed on the basis of a psychometric procedure referred to as FACTOR ANALYSIS, which analyzes alleged sources of individual differences underlying test scores.

factor theory of personality an approach to the discovery and measurement of personality components through FACTOR ANALYSIS. The components are identified primarily by a statistical study of the differences between people as revealed by tests covering various aspects of behavior. The factor-analytic method is central to such personality models as the BIG FIVE PERSONALITY MODEL, CATTELL'S FACTORIAL THEORY OF PERSONALITY, and EYSENCK'S TYPOLOGY.

fact retrieval the retrieval of a fact directly from long-term memory without using great mental effort.

fact seeker a person who takes the role of seeking further information in relation to specific topics, for example, during a GROUP PSYCHOTHERAPY discussion.

factual knowledge knowledge of specific factual items of information, without memory of when each fact was learned. Factual knowledge is technically referred to as SEMANTIC KNOWLEDGE or generic knowledge.

facultative polyandry see POLYANDRY.

faculty *n.* **1.** in cognitive psychology, see COGNITIVE FACULTY. **2.** more generally, any intrinsic mental or physical power, such as reason, sight, or will. **3.** the body of the teaching, research, and administrative staff of an educational institution.

faculty psychology any approach to psychological issues based on the idea that mental processes can be divided into separate specialized abilities or powers, which can be developed by mental exercises in the same way that muscles can be strengthened by physical exercises. Faculty psychology was formulated in the 18th century by Scottish philosophers Thomas Reid (1710–1796) and Dugald Stewart (1753–1828), who held that will, judgment, perception, conception, memory, and so forth could be explained simply by referring to their active powers; for example, individuals remember because they possess the faculty of memory.

fad *n.* an abrupt but short-lived change in the opinions, behaviors, or lifestyles of a large number of widely dispersed individuals. Preoccupations with new products, dances, television programs, and fashions can be considered fads when many people quickly embrace the trend but then lose interest just as rapidly. Fads often pertain to relatively trivial matters, and so disappear without leaving any lasting impact on society. Extremely irrational, expensive, or widespread fads are termed **crazes**.

fading *n.* in conditioning, the gradual changing of one stimulus to another, which is often used to transfer STIMULUS CONTROL. Stimuli can be faded out (gradually removed)—as in, for example, the gradual removal of extrinsic feedback so that an athlete becomes more dependent on sensory feedback while learning a skill—or faded in (gradually introduced).

FAE abbreviation for fetal alcohol effects (see FETAL ALCOHOL SYNDROME).

fail-safe *adj.* **1.** of a machine or work system, incorporating a feature by means of which the failure of a component or subsystem results in automatic shutdown or switch to a safer mode of operation. This **fail-safe design** reduces the chance that an operator will be exposed to hazards related to the malfunction or that machinery will be damaged. Fail-safe designs do not, however, reduce the likelihood of an accident or failure. See also EXCLUSION DESIGN; PREVENTION DESIGN. **2.** more generally, having no or an extremely low probability of failure.

failure modes and effects analysis (**FMEA**) a method of qualitative safety analysis in which the components of a system are listed along with the possible safety consequences that may occur should each of them fail or should the system as a whole go into failure mode. See also ACCIDENT ANALYSIS; ACCIDENT-PATH MODEL; FAULT-TREE ANALYSIS; JOB-SAFETY ANALYSIS.

failure to grow see FAILURE TO THRIVE.

failure-to-inhibit hypothesis a theory of COGNITIVE AGING that attributes attention and memory problems of older adults to their increasing inability to select relevant information and suppress irrelevant information when performing a cognitive task. [developed by U.S.-born Canadian psychologist Lynn Ann Hasher (1944–) and U.S. psychologist Rose T. Zacks (1941–)]

failure to thrive (**FTT**) significantly inadequate gain in weight or a significant decline in the rate of weight gain in a child under the age of 2, accompanied by progressive decline in responsiveness, poor appetite, and slowdown in physical and emotional development. It reflects a degree of growth failure due to inadequate release of GROWTH HORMONE and appears to be related in some cases to parental neglect and emotional deprivation. Secretion of the hormone often returns to normal following a period of emotionally supportive caregiving and interpersonal bonding.

fainting *n.* see SYNCOPE.

faintness *n.* **1.** absence of loudness, distinctness, or intensity, especially with reference to auditory stimuli. **2.** a sudden sensation of dizziness and weakness. See SYNCOPE.

Fairbairnian theory the psychoanalytic approach of British psychoanalyst W. Ronald D. Fairbairn (1889–1964), which forms a part of OBJECT RELATIONS THEORY. Fairbairn saw personality structure developing in terms of object relationships, rather than in terms of Sigmund FREUD'S ID, EGO, and SUPEREGO. Fairbairn proposed the existence of an ego at birth, which then splits apart during the PARANOID-SCHIZOID POSITION to form the structures of personality. In response to frustrations and excitement experienced in the relationship with the mother, the ego is split into (a) the central ego, which corresponds to Freud's concept of the ego; (b) the libidinal ego, which corresponds to the id; and (c) the ANTILIBIDINAL EGO, which corresponds to the superego.

fairness *n.* **1.** equity of opportunity for education regardless of racial, gender-related, social, cultural, economic, or geographical considerations. **2.** lack of bias in scoring tests and measuring achievement, while following a set of prescribed rules that are understood by those taking and scoring the tests. **3.** accuracy in test results, particularly concerning specific questions that are considered racially, socially, economically, or geographically exclusionary.

faith *n.* unwavering loyalty, belief, and trust. See also RELIGIOUS FAITH. **—faithful** *adj.*

faithful participant a research participant who cooperates fully with the explicit and implicit wishes of the experimenter. Also called **faithful subject**.

faith healing **1.** the treatment of physical or psychological illness by means of religious practices, such as prayer or "laying on of hands." Believers hold that this may be effective even when those being prayed for have no knowledge of the fact and no faith themselves. Also called **faith cure**; **religious healing**; **spiritual healing**. **2.** any form of unorthodox medical treatment the efficacy of which is said to depend upon the patient's faith in the healer or the healing process (see PLACEBO EFFECT). In such cases any beneficial effects may be attributed to a psychosomatic process rather than a paranormal or supernatural one. See also MENTAL HEALING; PSYCHIC HEALING.

faking *n.* the practice of some participants in an evaluation or psychological test who either (a) "fake good" by choosing answers that create a favorable impression, as may occur, for example, when an individual is applying for a job or admission to an educational institution; or (b) "fake bad" by choosing answers that make them appear disturbed or incompetent, as may occur, for example, when an individual wishes to be exempted from military service or exonerated in a criminal trial. **—fake** *vb.*

fallacy *n.* **1.** an error in reasoning or argument that leads to a conclusion that may appear valid but is actually invalid. A fallacy may be formal or informal. A **formal fallacy** involves a violation of a principle of formal logic, as in AFFIRMING THE CONSEQUENT or DENYING THE ANTECEDENT. An **informal fallacy** leads to an invalid conclusion because it is misleading in its language, as in AMPHIBOLY, or appears to apply to a situation when it does not really apply, as in an AD HOMINEM argument. See also EITHER–OR FALLACY; FALSE ANALOGY; FALSE AUTHORITY; FALSE CAUSE; HISTORICAL FALLACY. **2.** more generally, any mistaken idea. **—fallacious** *adj.*

fallectomy *n.* a sterilization procedure in which the fallopian tubes are cut, tied off, or both. See SALPINGECTOMY; TUBAL LIGATION.

falling out a CULTURE-BOUND SYNDROME found in the United States and the Caribbean. Symptoms include sudden collapse, sometimes preceded by feelings of dizziness or "swimming" in the head. Although their eyes are usually open, patients claim to be unable to see; they usually hear and understand what is occurring around them but feel powerless to move. The condition may correspond to CONVERSION DISORDER or DISSOCIATIVE DISORDER. Also called **blacking out**.

falling sickness see EPILEPSY.

fallopian tube either of the slender fleshy tubes in mammals that convey ova (egg cells) from each ovary to the uterus and where fertilization may occur. [Gabriele **Fallopius** (1523–1562), Italian anatomist]

fallopian-tube pregnancy see TUBAL PREGNANCY.

false alarm in signal detection tasks, an incorrect observation by the participant that a signal is present in a noise trial when in fact it is absent. The **false-alarm rate** is the proportion of incorrect "yes" responses in such a task. See also SIGNAL DETECTION THEORY. Compare MISS.

false analogy a type of informal FALLACY or a persuasive technique in which the fact that two things are alike in one respect leads to the invalid conclusion that they must be alike in some other respect. For example: *The brain is in some respects like a computer: Computers receive and store input in discrete bits: Therefore, ideas in the brain are formed from discrete bits of information.* See ANALOGY.

false authority a type of informal FALLACY or a persuasive technique in which it is assumed that the opinions of a recognized expert in one area should be heeded in another area. For example: *Mr. X should know how to deal with government deficits because he is a successful businessman.* See also AD VERECUNDIAM.

false belief an internal cognitive representation that has no basis in reality.

false-belief task a type of task used in THEORY-OF-MIND studies in which children must infer that another person does not possess knowledge that they possess. For example, children shown that a candy box contains pennies rather than candy are asked what someone else would expect to find in the box. Children of about 3 or younger would say pennies, whereas older children would correctly reply candy.

false cause a type of informal FALLACY or persuasive technique in which a temporal sequence of events is assumed to be a causal sequence of events. Thus, since B follows A, A is the cause of B. For example: *Since Smith became angry after being frustrated, Smith's frustration caused Smith's anger.* In statistics and experimental design, this is referred to as a **post hoc fallacy**. Also called **post hoc ergo propter hoc**. See also CAUSAL ORDERING; REVERSE CAUSALITY.

false consensus an opinion or belief that is mistakenly thought to be held by all or nearly all the people in a given group, whereas in fact there is significant dissent. See CONSENSUS.

false-consensus effect the tendency to assume that one's own opinions, beliefs, attitudes, values, or behavioral inclinations are more widely shared than is actually the case. Compare FALSE-UNIQUENESS EFFECT.

false dementia a condition that mimics the symptoms of DEMENTIA but is a normal response to certain environmental conditions, such as sensory deprivation, restricted movement, or institutionalization with prolonged medication.

false detection the incorrect detection of a signal in the presence of NOISE. See also FALSE ALARM.

false memory a falsification or distortion of memory, as in the conviction that we have actually witnessed events that have only been described to us or the illusion that we have already viewed a scene that is actually new to us. Also called **illusory memory**; **paramnesia**. See also CONFABULATION; REDUPLICATIVE PARAMNESIA.

false memory syndrome (**FMS**) the false recollection

of having been sexually or physically abused during childhood. The label is controversial, as is the evidence for and against recovery of abuse memories; false memory syndrome is not an accepted diagnostic term, and some have suggested using the more neutral phrase RECOVERED MEMORY.

false negative a case that is incorrectly excluded from a group by the test used to determine inclusion. In diagnostics, for example, a false negative is an individual who, in reality, has a particular condition but whom the diagnostic instrument indicates does not have the condition.

false positive a case that is incorrectly included in a group by the test used to determine inclusion. In diagnostics, for example, a false positive is an individual who, in reality, does not have a particular condition but whom the diagnostic instrument indicates does have the condition.

false pregnancy a condition in which a woman shows many or all of the usual signs of PREGNANCY when conception has not taken place. In some cases the condition is psychogenic, while in others it is due to a medical condition (e.g., a tumor or an endocrine disorder). Also called **pseudocyesis**; **pseudopregnancy**.

false rejection the inability to detect a signal when it is presented with NOISE. In SIGNAL DETECTION THEORY false rejection is known as a MISS. Compare FALSE ALARM.

false self in the OBJECT RELATIONS THEORY of British psychoanalyst Donald Winnicott (1896–1971), the self that develops as a defense against IMPINGEMENTS and in adaptation to the environment. This contrasts with the TRUE SELF, which develops in an environment that adapts to the infant and allows him or her to discover and express his or her true impulses.

falsetto *n.* a thin, high-pitched voice in which vocal register is extended upward beyond the normal range when a reduced surface of the expanded and separated vocal cords is activated by the airstream. In men, this quality of vocal resonance can be used to extend the normal range of their singing voice.

false-uniqueness effect the tendency to underestimate the extent to which others possess the same talents or positive traits as oneself. Compare FALSE-CONSENSUS EFFECT.

falsifiability *n.* the condition of admitting falsification. In science, a statement, such as a hypothesis or theory, is considered falsifiable if there exists a specifiable set of observations that would justify a conclusion that the statement is false. The most important properties that make a statement falsifiable in this way are (a) that it makes a prediction about an outcome or a universal claim of the type "All Xs have property Y" and (b) that what is predicted or claimed is observable. Austrian-born British philosopher Karl Popper (1902–1994) argued that falsifiability is an essential characteristic of any genuinely scientific hypothesis. Also called **disconfirmability**; **refutability**. See RISKY PREDICTION. **—falsifiable** *adj.*

falsificationism *n.* the position that (a) falsification, rather than verification, of hypotheses is the basic procedure of scientific investigation and the chief means by which scientific knowledge is advanced; and (b) that FALSIFIABILITY is the property that distinguishes scientific claims from truth claims of other kinds, such as those of metaphysics or political ideology. [introduced by Austrian-born British philosopher Karl Popper (1902–1994)] **—falsificationist** *adj.*

familial dysautonomia an AUTOSOMAL RECESSIVE disorder affecting nerve function throughout the body and characterized by insensitivity to pain, feeding difficulties, seizures, deficient tear production, excessive sweating, drooling, and blotchy skin. Mental impairment may be associated with the disorder, but most patients have normal intelligence. Also called **Riley–Day syndrome**.

familial factor an element or condition in a family that accounts for a certain disease, disorder, or trait.

familial hormonal disorder a syndrome associated with mental deficiency, deafness, and ataxia. Urinary gonadotropins, estrogen, pregnandiol, and 17-ketosteroids are markedly reduced in the patients, who seldom exceed a mental age of 5 years. Development of genitalia is impaired, and female patients may never experience menstruation. The disease is believed to be hereditary. [first observed in 1919 by W. Koennicke]

familial microcephaly see MICROCEPHALY.

familial Portuguese polyneuritic amyloidosis see ANDRADE'S SYNDROME.

familial retardation see CULTURAL-FAMILIAL MENTAL RETARDATION.

familial study of intelligence a study in which some measure or measures of intelligence among people of a known genetic relationship are correlated. The extent to which performance on a given measure varies as a function of genetic similarity is used as an indication of the HERITABILITY of that measure.

familial tremor see ESSENTIAL TREMOR.

familial Turner syndrome see NOONAN'S SYNDROME.

familiar *n.* in folklore and DEMONOLOGY, a supernatural spirit that supposedly lives with somebody and acts as his or her servant, often taking the form of an animal (e.g., a witch's cat).

familiarity *n.* a form of remembering in which a situation, event, place, person, or the like provokes a subjective feeling of recognition and is therefore believed to be in memory, although it is not specifically remembered. Also called **feeling of familiarity**.

familism *n.* a cultural value common in collectivist or traditional societies that emphasizes strong interpersonal relationships within the EXTENDED FAMILY together with interdependence, collaboration, and the placing of group interests ahead of individual interests. **—familistic** *adj.*

family *n.* **1.** a kinship unit consisting of a group of individuals united by blood or by marital, adoptive, or other intimate ties. Although the family has been the fundamental social unit of most human societies, its form and structure have varied widely. See BIOLOGICAL FAMILY; BLENDED FAMILY; EXTENDED FAMILY; NUCLEAR FAMILY; PATRIARCHY; PERMEABLE FAMILY; STEPFAMILY. **2.** in BIOLOGICAL TAXONOMY, a main subdivision of an ORDER, consisting of a group of similar, related genera (see GENUS). **—familial** *adj.*

family constellation the total set of relationships within a particular family, as characterized by such factors as the number and birth order of members and their ages, roles, and patterns of interaction. The term is associated with Alfred ADLER.

family counseling counseling of parents or other family members by psychologists, social workers, licensed counselors, or other professionals, who provide information, emotional support, and practical guidance on problems faced in the family context, such as raising a child with visual or hearing impairment, adoption, public assistance, family planning, and substance abuse. See also GENETIC COUNSELING.

family group psychotherapy therapeutic methods that treat a family as a system rather than concentrating on individual family members. The various approaches include psychodynamic, behavioral, systemic, and structural, but all regard the interpersonal dynamics within the family as more important than individual intrapsychic factors. See also FAMILY THERAPY.

family interaction method a study technique for investigating family behavior by observing the interaction of its members in a controlled situation, such as a clinic or laboratory.

family life cycle the series of steps or stages that occur in the life history of any given family, the stages typically including marriage (or coupling), raising children to independent young adulthood, and retirement.

family mediation a structured process in which a neutral third party, typically an attorney or a mental health practitioner with training in negotiation, helps individuals or families to resolve conflicts and reach agreements in such areas as divorce and child custody.

family method in behavior genetics, the study of the frequency of a trait or disorder by determining its occurrence in relatives who share the same genetic background.

family of origin the family in which an individual was raised, which may or may not be his or her BIOLOGICAL FAMILY.

family pattern a characteristic quality of the relationship between the members of a particular family (e.g., between parents and children). Family patterns vary widely in emotional tone and in the attitudes of the members toward each other. Some families are warm, others cool; some are extremely close and symbiotic, in others the members keep each other at a distance; some are open to friends and relatives, others are not; in some, one or more children are accepted and loved, in others one or more children are distanced or otherwise rejected. Such patterns or elements of such patterns may range from unconscious to fully realized. See also PATHOGENIC FAMILY PATTERN.

family planning controlling the size of the family, especially through the use of BIRTH-CONTROL measures for determining the number and spacing of children. See also POPULATION RESEARCH.

family psychology a basic and applied specialty in psychology that focuses on interactions within the family and developmentally influential contexts (neighborhood, schools, etc.). Research and clinical intervention in this specialty are taught in doctoral psychology programs, either within a specified family curriculum or more often within broader programs, such as clinical research and applied clinical and counseling programs.

family resemblance in studies of CATEGORIZATION, the idea that a set of instances may form a category or give rise to a concept even though there is no single attribute common to all the instances: It is sufficient that each instance should have one or more attributes in common with one or more other instances. The members of the category that have the most attributes in common with other members are said to have the highest family resemblance. The category PROTOTYPE will be based on those members with the highest family resemblance and the lowest resemblance to members of other categories. See also DISJUNCTIVE CONCEPT.

family romance a common childhood fantasy in which a child imagines that he or she is not the child of his or her biological parents but the offspring of a noble or royal personage. Sigmund FREUD saw this as rooted in the OEDIPUS COMPLEX. See FOSTER-CHILD FANTASY.

family sculpting a technique in FAMILY THERAPY in which the therapist asks one or more members of the family to physically arrange the other family members (and lastly themselves) in relation to one another in terms of posture, space, and attitude so as to portray the arranger's perception of the family, either in general or with regard to a particular situation or conflict. This technique often reveals family dynamics visually in a way that may not be adequately captured in verbal descriptions by family members.

family support services partial, periodic, or intermittent services provided to one or more family members of a person with a developmental disability for the purpose of enhancing their ability to care for the person or alleviating stress associated with family living. Examples include day and overnight respite (see RESPITE SERVICES), parent training, behavioral consultation, parent education, transportation to appointments, and sibling services (e.g., counseling).

family systems theory a broad conceptual model underlying various family therapies. Family systems theory focuses on the relationships between and among interacting individuals in the family and combines core concepts from GENERAL SYSTEMS THEORY, CYBERNETICS, family development theory, OBJECT RELATIONS theory, and SOCIAL LEARNING THEORY. Family systems theory stresses that therapists cannot work only with individual family members to create constructive family changes but must see the whole family to effect systemic and lasting changes. Also called **Bowen family systems theory; family systems model**. [developed by U.S. psychiatrist Murray Bowen (1913–1990)]

family therapy a form of PSYCHOTHERAPY that focuses on the improvement of interfamilial relationships and behavioral patterns of the family unit as a whole, as well as among individual members and groupings, or subsystems, within the family. Family therapy includes a large number of treatment forms with diverse conceptual principles, processes and structures, and clinical foci. Some family therapy approaches (e.g., OBJECT RELATIONS therapy) reflect extensions of models of psychotherapy with individuals in the interpersonal realm, whereas others (e.g., STRUCTURAL FAMILY THERAPY) evolved in less traditional contexts. Most approaches emphasize contexts in which clinical problems arise. This accompanying systemic view potentially allows clinical attention to all levels of the organization of behavior, for example from individual unconscious and conscious dynamics, to the family, and to the community. Family therapy models vary enormously in terms of length, past versus present orientation, techniques used, and treatment goals. See also CONJOINT THERAPY; COUPLES THERAPY; FAMILY GROUP PSYCHOTHERAPY; FAMILY SYSTEMS THEORY.

family values moral and social values attributed to the traditional NUCLEAR FAMILY, typically including discipline, respect for authority, and sexual abstinence outside marriage. The term is now primarily associated with political or religious conservatism.

fanaticism *n.* excessive and often irrational zeal or devotion, for example, to a cause or a set of extreme beliefs. **—fanatic** *adj., n.*

fan effect the finding that as the number of relations between one concept and others increases, the time required to make a decision about one of those relations increases. For example, if John has one brother and Bill has six, it would take longer to verify that Joe is Bill's brother than it would to verify that Ted is John's brother.

fantasy *n.* **1.** any of a range of mental experiences and processes marked by vivid imagery, intensity of emotion, and relaxation or absence of logic. These experiences may be conscious (thus, under the control of the fantasizing individual) or unconscious to varying degrees. Fantasizing is normal and common and often serves a healthy purpose of releasing tension, giving pleasure and amusement, or stimulating creativity. It can also be indicative of pathology, as in delusional thinking or significant disconnection from reality. **2.** in psychoanalytic theories, a figment of the imagination: a mental image, night DREAM, or DAYDREAM in which a person's conscious or unconscious wishes and impulses are fulfilled (see WISH-FULFILLMENT). Followers of Melanie KLEIN use the spelling PHANTASY to denote specifically unconscious wishes. **—fantasize** *vb.*

fantasy play pretend or make-believe play that includes an as-if orientation to actions, objects, and peers. It often involves playing a distinct role, such as mother, teacher, or doctor. Fantasy play involves taking a stance that is different from reality and using a mental representation of a situation as part of an enactment. See also SYMBOLIC PLAY.

FAP abbreviation for FIXED-ACTION PATTERN.

FAR abbreviation for FETUS AT RISK.

Farber's lipogranulomatosis a disorder of lipid metabolism characterized by the development of nodules and pigmentation of the skin. The upper extremities are affected, with arthritic swelling and erosion of the bones. Normal body tissues are infiltrated and replaced by foam cells. Respiratory distress and mental retardation appear at a very early age. [Sydney **Farber** (1903–1973), U.S. pediatric pathologist]

far point the farthest point at which an object can be seen clearly under conditions of relaxed ACCOMMODATION. Compare NEAR POINT.

farsightedness *n.* see HYPEROPIA.

fartlek training a form of athletic training or exercise characterized by alternating intervals of intense activity (e.g., running) followed by periods of less intense activity (e.g., walking). The length and speed of each interval are determined by the individual according to his or her perceived endurance and needs. [Swedish *fartlek,* "speed play"]

FAS abbreviation for FETAL ALCOHOL SYNDROME.

fascia *n.* (*pl.* **fasciae**) a sheet or band of fibrous connective tissue covering, separating, or binding together muscles, organs, and other soft-tissue structures of the body. Also called **fascial tissue**. **—fascial** *adj.*

fasciculus *n.* (*pl.* **fasciculi**) a bundle of nerve fibers, muscle fibers, or tendon fibers. **—fascicular** *adj.*

fasciculus cuneatus see CUNEATE FASCICULUS.

fasciculus gracilis see GRACILE FASCICULUS.

fascination *n.* **1.** profound interest in, attraction to, or enchantment with a person, object, activity, or phenomenon. **2.** in psychoanalytic theory, an infant's primitive attempt to master what is perceived (e.g., a light) by identifying with it. **—fascinate** *vb.*

fascinum *n.* see EVIL EYE.

fasciolus gyrus a brain convolution that is a part of the HIPPOCAMPAL FORMATION, appearing as a delicate band of tissue that communicates with a thin sheet of gray matter, the indusium griseum, on the surface of the corpus callosum. It is associated with olfactory functions. Also called **gyrus fasciolaris**.

fashion *n.* the styles of artistic and cultural expression, garments, manners, and customs prevalent in a particular time and place. Fashion may be transient and irrational but often reflects the ZEITGEIST or mood of society.

FAS Test see CONTROLLED ORAL WORD ASSOCIATION.

fastigial nucleus a NUCLEUS deep in the cerebellum that projects to the VESTIBULAR NUCLEI and the RETICULAR FORMATION of the pons and midbrain.

fast mapping the ability of young children to learn new words quickly on the basis of only one or two exposures to these words.

fast muscle fiber a type of muscle fiber found in SKELETAL MUSCLE that contracts rapidly but fatigues readily. Compare SLOW MUSCLE FIBER.

fat *n.* a mixture of lipids, mainly triglycerides, which is typically solid at room temperature. In mammals (including humans) it serves as the most concentrated store of food energy and is deposited primarily beneath the skin and around certain organs. In many animals it also serves as a primary source of insulation. See ADIPOSE TISSUE; BROWN FAT; FAT METABOLISM.

fatal familial insomnia a genetic (AUTOSOMAL DOMINANT) disorder caused by a mutation of the PRION protein in the brain. It affects the thalamus, causing progressive insomnia and eventually dementia; death occurs about 18 months after onset of symptoms.

fat cell see ADIPOCYTE.

fate neurosis in psychoanalytic theory, a compulsive, unconscious, and self-punitive need to arrange life experiences in such a way that failure and defeat are inevitable. Also called **destiny neurosis**.

father–daughter incest sexual relations between father and daughter, which is the most common form of INCEST.

father figure see FATHER SURROGATE.

father fixation in psychoanalytic theory, an abnormally strong emotional attachment to the father. See FIXATION.

father-ideal *n.* in psychoanalytic theory, the father component of the EGO-IDEAL, which is formed through identification with the parents.

father surrogate a substitute for a father, who performs typical paternal functions and serves as an object of identification and attachment. Also called **father figure**; **surrogate father**.

fatigability *n.* the susceptibility of an organ or an individual to fatigue, as compared with other organs or individuals.

fatigue *n.* **1.** a usually transient state of discomfort and loss of efficiency as a normal reaction to emotional strain, physical exertion, boredom, or lack of rest. Abnormal precipitating factors may include emotional stress, improper diet, or a debilitating disease. Fatigue may be localized, involving only certain muscles. See also FATIGUE CHECKLIST. **2.** reduced response of a sensory system, such as hearing, resulting from overexposure to a stimulus. See SENSORY OVERLOAD.

fatigue checklist a list of the symptoms of fatigue, including (a) an increased need to sleep, (b) trouble finding the energy to start new tasks, (c) poor endurance for completing a task that has been started, (d) difficulty in concentrating on any task, and (e) weakness or fatigability of muscles during physical effort.

fatigue effect a decline in performance on a task over time that is generally attributed to the participant becoming tired or bored with the task.

fatigue studies research on factors that cause both mental and physical fatigue. Physiological and psychological studies are conducted in numerous and varied contexts, such as job stress, caregiving, chronic illness, and ergonomic design.

fat metabolism all the biochemical processes involved in the breakdown, manufacture, or storage of fat in the body. Excess dietary carbohydrate (in the form of glucose) can be converted to fat (in the form of glycerides) and stored in specialized ADIPOSE TISSUE at sites distributed around the body. Excess dietary fat is also stored in this way. Following a meal, uptake of glucose into fat cells (ADIPOCYTES) and manufacture of fat is promoted by the hormone INSULIN. Mobilization of fat occurs during fasting, exercise, and in response to stress and is triggered by the hormone EPINEPHRINE and by norepinephrine released by nerve endings of the sympathetic nervous system. Stored fat is mobilized by being broken down to its constituents—FATTY ACIDS and glycerol—which are released into the bloodstream to provide fuel for other tissues, especially liver and muscle. Here, the fatty acids are converted into the energy carrier ATP by a process called beta oxidation. However, fatty acids cannot be converted (at least in appreciable amounts) into glucose, which is the fuel required by the brain.

fatty acid an organic acid with a long, usually unbranched hydrocarbon chain and an even number of carbon atoms. Fatty acids are the fundamental constituents of many important lipids, including triglycerides. Some fatty acids can be synthesized by the body, but others—the **essential fatty acids**, such as linoleic acid—must be obtained from the diet. See FAT METABOLISM.

fault-tree analysis a method of qualitative or quantitative safety analysis in which logic symbols are used to analyze the possible factors contributing to an accident or hazardous system state. The accident or hazardous state forms the "root" of the tree, and the logic symbols representing the possible contributing factors form the "branches." See also ACCIDENT ANALYSIS; ACCIDENT-PATH MODEL; FAILURE MODES AND EFFECTS ANALYSIS; JOB-SAFETY ANALYSIS.

F distribution the PROBABILITY DISTRIBUTION of the ratio of two independent chi-square random variables each divided by its DEGREES OF FREEDOM. See CHI-SQUARE DISTRIBUTION.

fear *n.* an intense emotion aroused by the detection of imminent threat, involving an immediate alarm reaction that mobilizes the organism by triggering a set of physiological changes. These include rapid heartbeat, redirection of blood flow away from the periphery toward the gut, tensing of the muscles, and a general mobilization of the organism to take action (see FEAR RESPONSE; FIGHT–FLIGHT REACTION). According to some theorists, fear differs from ANXIETY in that it has an object (e.g., a predator, financial ruin) and is a proportionate response to the objective threat, whereas anxiety typically lacks an object or is a more intense response than is warranted by the perceived threat. See also FRIGHT.

fear appeal a persuasive message that is designed to alter attitudes by producing fear in the recipient. Such messages are most effective when they provide compelling arguments for the likelihood of negative outcomes if the advocacy is not adopted, and the arguments make a strong case that adopting the advocacy will eliminate the threat. See also AFFECTIVELY BASED PERSUASION.

fear drive in the TWO-FACTOR THEORY of avoidance learning, the learned aversion to a situation or other stimulus that acts as a drive to motivate escape from or avoidance of the stimulus.

feared self in analyses of self-concept, a mental representation of psychological attributes that one might possess in the future, in which thoughts about the acquisition of these attributes elicits a sense of anxiety or dread.

fearful attachment an adult attachment style characterized by a negative INTERNAL WORKING MODEL OF ATTACHMENT of oneself and of others. Individuals with fearful attachment doubt both their own and others' competence and efficacy and are presumed not to seek help from others when distressed. Compare DISMISSIVE ATTACHMENT; PREOCCUPIED ATTACHMENT; SECURE ATTACHMENT.

fear-induced aggression a form of ANIMAL AGGRESSION in which an animal attacks only after it has been severely threatened or cornered.

fear of commitment feelings of anxiety and uncertainty related to the decision to become bound to a course of action. Such feelings are commonly aroused by the decision to become emotionally or legally committed to a long-standing relationship with another person and often stem from problems with intimacy and attachment; in an extreme form, fear of commitment may lead to social maladjustment.

fear of darkness normal or pathological fear of darkness or night. Fear of darkness is associated with feelings of helplessness and a sense of unfamiliarity because things look different in the dark. The fear first occurs at about 3 years of age but may develop into a SPECIFIC PHOBIA in which darkness is associated with danger and threat (this phobia is also known variously as **achluophobia**, **nictiphobia**, **noctiphobia**, **nyctophobia**, and **scotophobia**, although these names are now seldom used).

fear of failure persistent and irrational anxiety about failing to measure up to the standards and goals set by oneself or others. This may include anxiety over academic standing, losing a job, sexual inadequacy, or loss of face and self-esteem. Fear of failure may be associated with PERFECTIONISM and is implicated in a number of psychological disorders, including some ANXIETY DISORDERS and EATING DISORDERS. A pathological fear of failure has been called **kakorrhaphiophobia**, but this name is now seldom used.

fear of flying a persistent and irrational fear of flying in an airplane or other airborne vehicle, also called **aviophobia** (although this name is now seldom used). In *DSM–IV–TR*, fear of flying is classified as a SPECIFIC PHOBIA, situational type.

fear of public speaking see SOCIAL PHOBIA.

fear of rejection a persistent and irrational fear of being socially excluded or ostracized, which is often a feature of SOCIAL PHOBIA.

fear of strangers see STRANGER ANXIETY.

fear of success a fear of accomplishing one's goals or succeeding in society, or a tendency to avoid doing so. Fear of success was originally thought to be experienced primarily by women, because striving for success was held to place a woman in conflict between a general need for achievement and social values that tell her not to achieve "too much." It is now thought that men and women are equally likely to experience fear of success. Also called **fear of success syndrome**; **Horner effect**. See also JONAH COMPLEX. [first proposed in 1969 by U.S. psychologist Matina Horner (1939–)]

fear response a response to a threat in which the threatened organism attempts to guard vulnerable vital organs and to protect the integrity of the self. In addition to these protective functions, the fear response is aimed at removing the person or animal from the threatening situation, either by overt withdrawal or by coping behaviors, such as shutting the eyes to avoid seeing the fear stimulus. Physiological responses vary depending on the situation and the proximity of the threat. See also FIGHT–FLIGHT REACTION.

Fear Survey Schedule (**FSS**) a questionnaire designed to measure fear, phobic behavior, and generalized anxiety. It is currently available in numerous versions, with the 72-item **FSS–III** being the most commonly used, particularly in SYSTEMATIC DESENSITIZATION. These items consist of fear- or anxiety-producing objects or situations, grouped into six classes (animal fears, social fears, etc.), to which participants respond on a scale from 0 ("Not at all") to 4 ("Very much") regarding their degree of discomfort. [originally published in 1964 by South African-born U.S. psychologist Joseph Wolpe (1915–1997) and U.S. clinical psychologist Peter J. Lang (1930–)]

feasibility standards criteria used to judge the practical, feasible, and cost-effective nature of any enterprise or project. For example, the feasibility of an evaluation research study is determined on the basis of its pragmatic implementation, its political viability among various STAKEHOLDERS, and the cost of the resources necessary to carry out the research. See also ACCURACY STANDARDS; PROPRIETY STANDARDS; UTILITY STANDARDS.

feasibility test an investigation conducted prior to a study in order to establish properties of response measures and to determine the successfulness of the study's designs. It is used to establish the validity of response measures, to provide early information on the probable level of effects, or to try out new methodologies. See also EVALUABILITY-ASSESSMENT DATA; FEASIBILITY STANDARDS.

feature *n.* **1.** an attribute of an object or event that plays an important role in distinguishing it from other objects or events and in the formation of category judgments. For example, a particular nose is a feature of one person's face, wings are a feature of the category "bird," particular lines and angles are features of a particular shape, line segments of various types are features of letters, and so on. **2.** in phonemics, an attribute of a speech sound, such as whether or not it is VOICED, that plays a critical role in distinguishing one PHONEME from another. See BINARY FEATURE; MINIMAL PAIR.

feature abstraction a hypothetical process by which people learn from their experience with exemplars of different categories which features might be used to define membership in these categories. See CATEGORIZATION; CONCEPT FORMATION.

feature detection theory the theory that all complex stimuli can be broken down into individual parts (features) each of which is analyzed by a specific FEATURE DETECTOR.

feature detector any of various hypothetical or actual mechanisms within the human information-processing system that respond selectively to specific distinguishing FEATURES. For example, the visual system has feature detectors for lines and angles of different orientations or even for more complex stimuli, such as faces (see BOUNDARY DETECTOR; CONTRAST DETECTOR; MOVING-EDGE DETECTOR). Feature detectors are also thought to play an important role in speech perception, where their function would be to detect those BINARY FEATURES (e.g., voiced or unvoiced speech sounds) that distinguish one PHONEME from another. Also called **feature analyzer**.

feature indicator any aspect of an object that provides visual cues to FEATURE DETECTORS in the visual cortex. Examples of feature indicators include boundaries between dark and light regions, straight or curved edges or surfaces, and connecting features (e.g., crossbars).

feature-integration theory (**FIT**) a two-stage theory of VISUAL ATTENTION. In the first (preattentive) stage, basic features (e.g., color, contrast, location in space, and shape) are processed automatically, independently, and in parallel. In the second (attentive) stage, other properties, including relations between features of an object, are processed in series, one object (or group) at a time, and "bound" together to create a single object that is perceived. Also called **feature-integration hypothesis**. See BINDING HYPOTHESIS. See also TEXTONS. [proposed in 1980 by British psychologist Anne Marie Treisman (1935–)]

feature model a model of general knowledge or SEMANTIC MEMORY suggesting that information can be described as sets of features (e.g., the features that define "bird").

feature-negative discrimination a GO/NO-GO discrimination procedure, based on a distinctive feature of one of two similar stimuli, in which the feature is part of the negative, or no-go, stimulus, that is, the stimulus associated with EXTINCTION.

feature-positive discrimination a GO/NO-GO discrimination procedure, based on a distinctive feature of one of two similar stimuli, in which the feature is part of the positive stimulus, that is, the stimulus associated with REINFORCEMENT.

febrile delirium DELIRIUM associated with or caused by fever.

febrile seizure a seizure, most often occurring in children, arising from a high fever and without evidence of brain infection or damage. Febrile seizures are not associated with epilepsy.

fecal incontinence the involuntary passage of flatus and feces in inappropriate places (clothing, floor, etc.) resulting from loss of bowel control and due to an injury or organic condition. Also called **bowel incontinence**. Compare ENCOPRESIS.

feces *n.* waste matter expelled from the bowels. In psychoanalytic theory, a child's interest in feces is one of the earliest expressions of curiosity and withholding feces is one of the earliest expressions of the drive for aggression and independence. Also called **excrement**; **fecal matter**. See also ANAL-EXPULSIVE PHASE; ANAL-RETENTIVE PHASE; ANAL PERSONALITY; ANAL-SADISTIC PHASE; SPHINCTER CONTROL. —**fecal** *adj.*

Fechner, Gustav Theodor (1801–1887) German physician and philosopher. Although trained as a physician at the University of Leipzig, Fechner never practiced medicine, instead devoting his life to the study of natural philosophy. Early in his career he made contributions to the field of experimental physics, then fell seriously ill and underwent a spiritual crisis. After recovering, he turned his attention to advancing his philosophical belief that the mental and the physical are merely different aspects of the same underlying reality. He used rigorous experimental methods to show the relationship between physical and psychological events through investigations on such subjects as sensations, AFTERIMAGES, and AESTHETICS, thus establishing the psychophysical approach. He developed scientific methods still in use today for studying subjective sensations: the METHOD OF JUST NOTICEABLE DIFFERENCES, the METHOD OF CONSTANT STIMULI, and the METHOD OF ADJUSTMENT. Using these methods, he developed what is now called FECHNER'S LAW. His psychophysical law and methods were extremely important in establishing psychology as an empirical science. See also DUALISM; FECHNER'S PARADOX; MONISM.

Fechner's colors illusory sensations of color that arise when a disk with black and white sectors is spun about its axis. Also called **subjective colors**. [Gustav Theodor FECHNER]

Fechner's law a law that relates subjective experience to changes in stimulus intensity. This psychophysical formula proposes that the sensation experienced is proportional to the logarithm of the stimulus magnitude. See also STEVENS LAW; WEBER'S LAW. [Gustav Theodor FECHNER]

Fechner's paradox the apparent increase in brightness of a figure caused by closing one eye after viewing the figure with both eyes open. [Gustav Theodor FECHNER]

fecundity *n.* **1.** in biology, a measure of the number of offspring produced by an individual organism over a given time. **2.** in demography, the general capacity of a human population to have offspring. A below-average capacity is termed **subfecundity**. Compare BIRTH RATE; FERTILITY. **—fecund** *adj.*

Federation of Behavioral, Psychological, and Cognitive Sciences an association of scientific societies with interests in basic research on problems of behavior, psychology, language, education, and knowledge systems and their psychological, behavioral, and physiological bases. The federation was incorporated in 1980; its efforts focus on legislative and regulatory advocacy, education, and the communication of information to scientists.

feeblemindedness *n.* an obsolete name for MENTAL RETARDATION, MENTAL DEFICIENCY, or LEARNING DISABILITY.

feedback *n.* **1.** the process whereby any element of an interaction sustains, amplifies, or modifies the interaction. NEGATIVE FEEDBACK sustains or stabilizes patterns of interaction, whereas POSITIVE FEEDBACK amplifies or reorganizes them. **2.** the process of receiving visual input or afferent impulses from the PROPRIOCEPTORS, which enables individuals to make accurate movements (e.g., reaching for a pencil). **3.** information provided to a person or group regarding their behavior or performance, especially with the aim of modifying or improving it. The feedback may be accompanied by suggestions. Feedback provided to trainees is important in supervision during training; it is also relevant to individuals who have difficulty perceiving how their behavior will be interpreted by others. **4.** the reception of appropriate signals by a regulator, such as a thermostat (see CLOSED-LOOP SYSTEM). See also AUDITORY FEEDBACK; BIOFEEDBACK; DEVIATION-AMPLIFYING FEEDBACK; INFORMATION FEEDBACK; SOCIAL FEEDBACK. Compare FEED-FORWARD.

feedback device a device that presents a visual, auditory, or tactile signal to communicate to the operator of an ENVIRONMENTAL CONTROL DEVICE the status of actions taken. See also CONTROL DEVICE; SWITCH DEVICE; TARGET DEVICE.

feedback evaluation see FORMATIVE EVALUATION.

feedback loop in CYBERNETIC THEORY, a self-regulatory model that determines whether the current operation of a system is acceptable and, if not, attempts to make the necessary changes. Its operation is summarized by the acronym TOTE (*t*est, *o*perate, *t*est, *e*xit). The two test phases compare the current reality against the goal or standard. Operate refers to any processes or interventions designed to resolve unacceptable discrepancies between the reality and the standard. Exit refers to the closing down of the supervisory feedback loop because the circumstances have been brought into agreement with the standard. Also called **TOTE model**. See also NEGATIVE FEEDBACK.

feedback system a circuit in which output information (e.g., biological or mechanical) is used to modulate the input to the same circuit. In a NEGATIVE FEEDBACK system the output is used to reduce the input; such systems play important roles in maintaining equilibrium of processes within organisms. See HOMEOSTASIS; POSITIVE FEEDBACK.

feed-forward *n.* **1.** information or control signals sent to a part of the body or other system in order to prepare it for future motor activity or expected sensory input. **2.** information that can be used to forecast the performance of a person, group, product, or system so that adjustments can be made to avoid problems before they occur. Compare FEEDBACK.

feeding and eating disorders of infancy or early childhood in *DSM–IV–TR*, a category of disorders characterized by pathological feeding or eating behaviors that are usually first diagnosed in infancy, childhood, or adolescence. They include PICA, RUMINATION DISORDER, and FEEDING DISORDER OF INFANCY OR EARLY CHILDHOOD.

feeding behavior the behavior involved in taking nourishment. In humans, the development of feeding behavior includes (a) stimulation and coordination of the sucking and swallowing reflexes in early infancy, (b) adaptation to breast or bottle and to scheduled or self-demand feeding (see SELF-DEMAND SCHEDULE), (c) biting at about the 4th month, (d) anticipatory chewing movements, (e) actual chewing when the teeth are developed, and (f) transferring from finger feeding to the use of various utensils.

feeding center a traditional name for the region of the LATERAL HYPOTHALAMUS in the brain that, when stimulated, produces eating behavior. Also called **hunger center**.

feeding disorder of infancy or early childhood in *DSM–IV–TR*, a disorder with an onset before the age of 6 (but typically within the 1st year following birth) characterized by persistent failure to eat adequately that results in significant failure to gain weight or significant loss of weight over a period of 1 month or more. There is no apparent cause.

feeding problem a form of behavior disorder in children that is characterized by refusal to eat, persistent failure to eat adequate amounts or types of food, or failure to hold down the food ingested. It is not due to a gastrointestinal or other medical condition or lack of available food, and it is not an EATING DISORDER. Also called **feeding disturbance**. See also RUMINATION DISORDER.

feeding technique the manner in which an infant is fed, specifically via breast or bottle.

fee-for-service *adj.* denoting the traditional method of payment for health care services, in which physicians or other providers set their own fees for services, and patients or insurance companies pay all or a percentage of these charges. This is the system of reimbursement used by indemnity insurance plans.

feeling *n.* **1.** a self-contained phenomenal experience. Feelings are subjective, evaluative, and independent of the sensory modality of the sensations, thoughts, or images evoking them. They are inevitably evaluated as pleasant or unpleasant but they can have more specific intrapsychic qualities, so that, for example, the AFFECTIVE TONE of fear is experienced as different from that of anger. The core characteristic that differentiates feelings from cognitive, sensory, or perceptual intrapsychic experiences is the link of AFFECT to APPRAISAL. Feelings differ from EMOTIONS in being purely mental, whereas emotions are designed to engage with the world. **2.** any experienced sensation, particularly a tactile or temperature sensation (e.g., pain or coldness).

feeling of knowing a sense of conviction about an event, which can be quite accurate and distinct although it is not experienced as a result of sensory stimulation. It is a classic experience of FRINGE CONSCIOUSNESS.

feeling of reality a sense that the world is tangible, which may be lost in mild dissociative conditions (e.g., derealization) and in more serious disorders (e.g., posttraumatic stress disorder, psychosis). It is a feature of imaginative identification in fiction and art.

feeling of unreality see DEPERSONALIZATION.

feeling theory of three dimensions the theory that feelings can vary along three dimensions: pleasantness–unpleasantness (hedonic quality), excitement–calmness, and arousal–relaxation. Elementary feelings combine into complex ones. The theory is used to define different emotions as characterized by different combinations and successions of feelings and by the specific course of change of the feelings along each of the three dimensions. Also called **tridimensional theory of feeling**; **Wundt's tridimensional theory of emotion**. [introduced by Wilhelm WUNDT]

feeling tone see AFFECTIVE TONE.

feeling type in Carl JUNG'S ANALYTIC PSYCHOLOGY, a FUNCTIONAL TYPE characterized by a dominance of feeling or affects. Feeling types evaluate their experiences and the world in terms of how these make them feel. The feeling type is one of Jung's two RATIONAL TYPES, the other being the THINKING TYPE. See also INTUITIVE TYPE; SENSATION TYPE.

felbamate *n.* an ANTICONVULSANT drug, structurally related to MEPROBAMATE, that is thought to work by both enhancing the effects of the inhibitory neurotransmitter GAMMA-AMINOBUTYRIC ACID (see GABA AGONISTS) and inhibiting the effects of the excitatory amino acid GLUTAMATE (see NMDA RECEPTOR). Due to the increased incidence of aplastic anemia and hepatitis associated with this drug, it is less commonly used than other anticonvulsants; it is generally reserved for patients with severe epilepsy who respond inadequately to other treatments. U.S. trade name: **Felbatol**.

Feldenkrais method a process of body movements that are designed to enhance psychological functioning. The method is used by certified practitioners and may be interpreted in numerous ways, but always involves a dynamic interaction between bodily movements and psychological awareness. [Moshe **Feldenkrais** (1904–1984), physicist and engineer]

fellatio *n.* the use of the mouth in sexual stimulation of the penis. Also called **fellation**; **oral coitus**; **penilingus**. See also OROGENITAL ACTIVITY. **—fellate** *vb.*

felt need a consciously experienced need that may relate to a sense of deprivation or a discrepancy with an affective ideal.

felt sense in FOCUSING therapy, the subjective qualities of the contents of CONSCIOUSNESS. See FRINGE CONSCIOUSNESS. [defined by Austrian-born U.S. psychologist Eugene T. Gendlin (1926–)]

female choice the selectivity displayed by females in choosing a mate. Because ova are typically larger than sperm and because females often expend much more energy than males in the production and care of the young, females are thought to be more careful than males in choosing their mates. See also CRYPTIC FEMALE CHOICE; MATE SELECTION; MULTIPLE MATING.

female circumcision see CLITORIDECTOMY; FEMALE GENITAL MUTILATION.

female–female competition see MALE–MALE COMPETITION.

female genital mutilation a procedure performed on the genital organs of prepubertal or pubertal girls in some African and Asian cultures. Female genital mutilation occurs as a means of ensuring that the girl will not engage in premarital sex, which in some cultures would end her chance for a "good marriage" or reduce the bride price her future husband's family will pay to her family. In some cultures the clitoral hood only is removed, but in others the entire clitoris is lost, and the labia are sewn shut with only a small hole left to allow for menstruation (see CLITORIDECTOMY; INFIBULATION). Female genital mutilation is sometimes called **female** (or **clitoral**) **circumcision**, a term that downplays the adverse effects of the practice. It significantly interferes with sexual functioning—most women who have had this procedure are unable to reach orgasm—and many girls die each year from infections, since the procedure is performed by individuals who are not physicians, without the use of sterile instruments or antiseptics.

femaleness *n.* the quality of being female in the anatomical and physiological sense by virtue of possessing the female complement of a pair of X CHROMOSOMES. Compare FEMININITY.

female orgasmic disorder in *DSM–IV–TR*, absence of female orgasm following normal sexual stimulation. This may be a lifelong problem or it may have developed after a period of normal response (**acquired type**). The woman may be unable to have an orgasm in any form of sexual activity (**generalized type**) or she may be able to achieve orgasm only in certain ways (**situational type**).

female sexual arousal disorder in *DSM–IV–TR*, failure in a woman to attain or maintain an adequate response in the excitement (arousal) phase of the SEXUAL-RESPONSE CYCLE (e.g., vaginal lubrication and swelling).

female sperm spermatozoa that bear an X CHROMOSOME and therefore determine that an ovum they fertilize will become a female embryo.

femininity *n.* possession of social-role behaviors that are presumed to be characteristic of a girl or woman, as contrasted with FEMALENESS, which is genetically determined. **—feminine** *adj.*

femininity complex in psychoanalytic theory, a man's envy of women's procreative powers that has its roots in the young boy's envy of the mother's body. Some psychoanalysts see the femininity complex as the male counterpart to the female CASTRATION COMPLEX and PENIS ENVY. [first used in 1930 by German psychoanalyst Felix Boehm (1881–1958)]

femininity phase in the OBJECT RELATIONS THEORY of Melanie KLEIN, a period during the early phases of the OEDIPUS COMPLEX in which both boys and girls are posited to adopt a feminine attitude toward the father and desire a child by him. Klein saw this as turning to the father as an object of desire and away from the mother as the child's first object.

feminism *n.* **1.** any of a number of perspectives that take as their subject matter the problems and perspectives of women, or the nature of biological and social phenomena related to GENDER. Feminism has evolved from a largely political movement in the 19th century, focused (in the United States) on women's suffrage and political and economic opportunities, into broader and more comprehensive academic, philosophical, and social movements. Although some feminist perspectives continue to focus on issues of fairness and equal rights, other approaches emphasize what are taken to be inherent and systematic gender inequities in Western society (see PATRIARCHY). In psychology, feminism has focused attention on the nature and origin of gender differences in psychological processes. See WOMEN'S LIBERATION MOVEMENT. See also ECOFEMINISM; EROTIC FEMINISM; INDIVIDUALIST FEMINISM; LESBIAN FEMINISM; MARXIST FEMINISM; MATERIAL FEMINISM; RADICAL FEMINISM. **2.** the appearance of female physical and psychological characteristics in a male. This usage is now archaic. **—feminist** *adj., n.*

feminist family therapy an intervention model, informed by FEMINIST THERAPY, used by therapists to reorganize the family so that no one is entrapped in dysfunctional roles or patterns of interaction that are based on the politics of power, particularly with regard to patriarchal roles.

feminist psychology an approach to psychological issues that emphasizes the role of the female perspective in thought, action, and emotion in the life of the individual and in society. It is seen by its proponents as an attempt to counterbalance traditional male-oriented and male-dominated psychology, as well as a model for similar approaches for other less represented groups. See also ENGENDERING PSYCHOLOGY; WOMAN-CENTERED PSYCHOLOGY.

feminist therapy an eclectic approach to psychotherapy based conceptually in feminist political analyses and feminist scholarship on the psychology of women and gender. In this orientation, the ways in which gender and gendered experiences inform people's understanding of their lives and the development of the distress that serves as a catalyst for seeking therapy are central. Race, class, sexual orientation, age cohort, and ability, as they interact with gender, are explored. Feminist therapy attempts to create an egalitarian therapy relationship in which intentional efforts are made by the therapist to empower the client and define the client as an authority equal in value to the therapist. Feminist therapy can be indicated for both female and male clients.

feminization *n.* the process of acquiring FEMININITY, regardless of the sex of the individual. **—feminize** *vb.*

feminization of poverty the trend for a disproportionate number of the poorest people in Western societies to be women. This can be attributed to a range of factors, including the growing number of families that are headed by a single female parent, often with no financial support from the father, and the continuing tendency for occupations with a largely female workforce to pay lower wages. See also UNDERCLASS.

feminizing testes syndrome see ANDROGEN-INSENSITIVITY SYNDROME.

fenestration *n.* the surgical creation of an opening, as in the procedure, now rarely used, in which an opening is formed in the bony wall of the middle ear and into the semicircular canal in order to improve hearing loss caused by OTOSCLEROSIS.

fenfluramine *n.* a sympathomimetic agent, structurally related to the AMPHETAMINES, that functions as a SEROTONIN-RECEPTOR AGONIST and was formerly used for management of obesity (see APPETITE SUPPRESSANTS). It was withdrawn from the U.S. market in 1997 due to the incidence of heart-valve abnormalities associated with its use.

fentanyl *n.* a highly potent OPIOID ANALGESIC that is used for anesthesia during surgery, for the management of severe cancer pain in patients resistant to other opioids, and (as a lozenge or sucker) for the relief of severe anxiety in children prior to surgical procedures. Its toxicity is similar to that of other opioids, with respiratory and circulatory depression predominating. It is known as **China white** in illicit use. Analogs of fentanyl in current use include SUFENTANIL, **alfentanil** (U.S. trade name: **Alfenta**), and **remifentanil** (U.S. trade name: **Ultiva**). U.S. trade names: **Sublimaze** (injectable form); **Actiq** and **Oralet** (oral forms); **Duragesic** (transdermal form, i.e., applied to the skin).

FEPSAC see EUROPEAN FEDERATION OF THE PSYCHOLOGY OF SPORT AND PHYSICAL ACTIVITY.

feral children children that reportedly have been raised by wild animals and isolated from human contact. Famous examples include the WILD BOY OF AVEYRON and the WOLF CHILDREN of India.

Féré phenomenon see GALVANIC SKIN RESPONSE. [Charles S. **Féré** (1852–1907), French neurologist]

Fernald method an approach to reading based on the idea that students learn best when material is presented to several different senses. These methods, which employ tracing, hearing, writing, and seeing, are often referred to as **VAKT** (visual, auditory, kinesthetic, tactile). The Fernald method teaches whole words. [Grace **Fernald** (1879–1950), U.S. psychologist]

Ferree–Rand double broken circles a figure used to test simultaneously for VISUAL ACUITY and ASTIGMATISM. Outlines of circles are interrupted by two small gaps, 90° apart, and the minimum gap size that can be detected is a measure of acuity (similar to LANDOLT CIRCLES). If one gap is more detectable than the other, it suggests that astigmatism is present. [Clarence **Ferree** (1877–1942) and Gertrude **Rand** (1886–1970), U.S. psychologists]

Ferry–Porter law see PORTER'S LAW.

fertility *n.* **1.** in biology, the potential of an individual to have offspring. Although most frequently applied to females, it may also refer to reproductive capacity in males. **2.** in demography, the number of live children born to an individual or a population. Compare FECUNDITY.

fertilization *n.* the fusion of a sperm and an egg cell to produce a ZYGOTE. External fertilization occurs outside the female's body, as in fish and amphibians. Mammals, birds, and reptiles have internal fertilization (i.e., within the body of the female). In humans, fertilization occurs in a FALLOPIAN TUBE.

FES abbreviation for FUNCTIONAL ELECTRIC STIMULATION.

festinating gait a gait disturbance often seen in individuals with PARKINSON'S DISEASE, marked by short, shuffling steps that begin slowly but increase in rapidity until the walk becomes a half run. The body leans stiffly forward to maintain balance, and there is an associated risk of falling. Also called **festination**; **propulsive gait**.

Festinger, Leon (1919–1989) U.S. psychologist. Festinger earned his doctorate at the University of Iowa under Kurt LEWIN in 1942. He was hired as a statistician for the remainder of World War II and was involved in the training and selection of Air Force pilots. After the war he held brief appointments at the Massachusetts Institute of Technology, the University of Michigan, and the University of Minnesota before settling at Stanford University in 1955 for 13 years; he completed his career at the New School for Social Research in New York City. Festinger's research interests in SOCIAL PSYCHOLOGY included such phenomena as group COHESION, CONFORMITY, and SOCIAL COMPARISON THEORY. He is best known, however, for his series of experiments that tested his COGNITIVE DISSONANCE THEORY. Festinger argued that DISSONANCE REDUCTION was capable of explaining phenomena that traditional behaviorist theories of reinforcement could not, such as why low or infrequent rewards could result in persistent behavior. His most influential writings include his books, *A Theory of Cognitive Dissonance* (1957) and *Conflict, Decision, and Dissonance* (1964). Festinger was elected to the National Academy of Sciences and the American Academy of Arts and Sciences and received the Distinguished Scientific Contribution Award of the American Psychological Association in 1959.

fetal activity the activity level of the fetus during intrauterine development, for example, kicking or other movements.

fetal age see GESTATIONAL AGE.

fetal alcohol syndrome (**FAS**) a condition associated with extreme maternal alcohol intake during pregnancy. It is characterized by low birth weight and retarded growth, craniofacial anomalies (e.g., microcephaly), and neurobehavioral problems (e.g., hyperactivity); mental retardation may be present. Children showing some (but not all) features of this syndrome are described as having **fetal alcohol effects** (**FAE**).

fetal cephalometry see CEPHALOMETRY.

fetal distress the condition of a fetus whose life or health is threatened by the effects of a disease or other disorder originating in the organ systems of the mother. The most common cause of fetal distress is an inadequate supply of oxygen via the placenta. See also FETAL INFECTION; FETUS AT RISK.

fetal hypoxia a significant reduction in oxygen to the human fetus, which is believed to be a risk factor for severe mental illness, such as schizophrenia. See also HYPOXIA.

fetal infection any disease that may affect a fetus as a result of the infectious agent being transmitted from the mother via the placenta. Fetal infections are usually caused by viruses; other agents may include tuberculosis bacteria, the syphilis spirochete, or the toxoplasmosis protozoa. Rubella is a common viral fetal infection, resulting in various congenital defects (see CONGENITAL RUBELLA SYNDROME).

fetal–maternal exchange the exchange of substances between mother and fetus, via the PLACENTA, during gestation. The fetus is thereby supplied with nutrients and oxygen, and its waste products (e.g., carbon dioxide, urea) are eliminated. Substances of low molecular weight cross the placental barrier easily, but large molecules (e.g., proteins) do not, therefore the fetus manufactures its own proteins from amino acids supplied by the mother. Some drugs (e.g., alcohol, opioids) as well as disease agents (e.g., the rubella virus) may cross the placental barrier and produce congenital defects.

fetal monitoring measurement of the physiological characteristics (e.g., heart rate) of a fetus. Fetal monitoring is used to assess the well-being of the fetus before and during childbirth.

fetal presentation the way the fetus is oriented during the birth process, specifically whether the fetus is exiting the birth canal head first or not. If the fetus is oriented so that it will be delivered buttocks first, this is known as a **breech presentation**; breech births are associated with risks to mother and baby (see BIRTH INJURY).

fetal response a response of a fetus to environmental conditions. For example, there is an increase in the fetal heart rate when the mother smokes, and some investigators claim that there is an increase in activity when the mother is undergoing severe emotional stress. See PRENATAL INFLUENCE.

fetal stage the final stage of human prenatal development, from the 8th or 9th week after fertilization to the time of birth. It is preceded by the EMBRYONIC STAGE.

fetal tobacco syndrome a condition in infants born to mothers who smoked excessively during pregnancy, marked by low birth weight.

fetation *n.* see PREGNANCY.

feticide *n.* destruction of the embryo or fetus in the uterus. See also ABORTION.

fetish *n.* **1.** a nonsexual object (e.g., a glove, shoe, or handkerchief) or part of the body (e.g., a foot, lock of hair, or ear) that arouses sexual interest or excitement by association or symbolization. Gratification is achieved by fondling, kissing, or licking the object or by masturbation while looking at the object. **2.** behavior involving FETISHISM. See OBJECT FETISH. **3.** in anthropology, an object, such as a talisman or amulet, that is believed to embody a supernatural spirit or exert magical force. **4.** an idea, goal, or mode of behavior that elicits special devotion, for example, the single-minded pursuit of success.

fetishism *n.* a PARAPHILIA in which fetishes are repeatedly or exclusively used in achieving sexual excitement. Objects designed for use in stimulating the genitals (e.g., vibrators) are not considered to be involved in fetishism. See also PARTIALISM. —**fetishistic** *adj.*

fetoscopy *n.* a procedure for observing the fetus in the uterus in which a viewing instrument (**fetoscope**) is passed through a pregnant woman's abdomen and into the amniotic sac.

fetus *n.* a human EMBRYO in the later stages of development, that is, from 8 or 9 weeks after fertilization until birth. —**fetal** *adj.*

fetus at risk (**FAR**) a fetus that has a significant risk of being born with a mental or physical disorder because of known influences from the parents or other family members (e.g., a mother with diabetes or hypertension). The risk of a mental disorder in a child born into a family with no history of mental disorder is relatively small, but the risk may be as much as 50% in certain cases, for example, if the disorder is a SEX-LINKED recessive trait inherited from the mother's side of the family and the parents are related. See also FETAL DISTRESS.

FFDE abbreviation for FITNESS FOR DUTY EVALUATION.

FFM abbreviation for FIVE-FACTOR PERSONALITY MODEL.

FI abbreviation for fixed interval (see FIXED-INTERVAL SCHEDULE).

fiat *n.* in IDEOMOTOR THEORY, the sense of allowing an action to proceed when one is ready to perform the action. [from Latin: "let it be done" or "let it happen"; originally defined by William JAMES]

fiat equivalence classification see IDIOSYNCRATIC CLASSIFICATION.

fibril *n.* any small anatomical fiber or threadlike structure.

fibrillation *n.* a small, local, involuntary muscular contraction due to spontaneous activation of single muscle cells or fibers, especially the rapid, abnormal contraction of individual muscle fibers of the heart. See also ARRHYTHMIA.

fibromyalgia syndrome a syndrome of uncertain origin that is characterized by widespread musculoskeletal pain and chronic fatigue. Pain may be triggered by pressure on numerous tender points on the body. Other commonly associated symptoms are muscle stiffness, headaches, sleep disturbance, and depression. Symptoms overlap with those of CHRONIC FATIGUE SYNDROME, and fibromyalgia syndrome often occurs simultaneously with other disorders, such as IRRITABLE BOWEL SYNDROME and migraine. The condition was formerly called **fibromyositis–fibromyalgia syndrome**. See also CHRONIC MYOFASCIAL PAIN.

fiction *n.* **1.** in psychology, an unproven or imaginary concept that may be accepted by an individual as if it were true for pragmatic reasons. See ALS OB; AS-IF HYPOTHESIS. **2.** see GUIDING FICTION. **—fictional** *adj.*

fictional finalism in the psychoanalytic theory of Alfred ADLER, the belief that human beings are more strongly motivated by the goals and ideals—realizable or unattainable—that they create for themselves and more influenced by future possibilities, than by past events such as childhood experiences. This is in strong contrast to the emphasis of classical Freudian psychoanalytic theory. See also GUIDING FICTION; INDIVIDUAL PSYCHOLOGY.

fidelity *n.* **1.** faithfulness to a person, group, belief, or the like. **2.** the degree of accuracy of a measuring instrument. **3.** the degree of accuracy of sound or visual reproduction in an electronic device (e.g., a sound system or television).

fidgetiness *n.* a state of increased motor activity, which is associated with anxiety, tics, chorea, or boredom.

fiduciary 1. *adj.* describing a relationship in which one person holds a position of trust in relation to another and is required to apply his or her skill and effort in the best interests of that other. A psychologist and client have a fiduciary relationship in that the psychologist is assumed to place the welfare and best interests of the client above all else. **2.** *n.* a person who holds a position of trust in a fiduciary relationship.

field *n.* **1.** a defined area or region of space, such as the VISUAL FIELD. **2.** a complex of personal, physical, and social factors within which a psychological event takes place. See FIELD THEORY. **3.** an area of human activity or knowledge or a division of such an area. **4.** somewhere other than a laboratory, library, or academic setting in which experimental work is carried out or data collected. See FIELD EXPERIMENT.

field defect see VISUAL FIELD DEFECT.

field dependence a COGNITIVE STYLE in which the individual consistently relies more on external referents (environmental CUES) than on internal referents (bodily sensation cues). Field-dependent people tend to be susceptible to deceptive environmental cues, particularly in tasks requiring the performance of simple actions or the identification of familiar elements in unfamiliar contexts. Compare FIELD INDEPENDENCE.

field experiment an experiment that is conducted outside the laboratory in a "real-world" setting. Participants are exposed to one of two or more levels of an independent variable and observed for their reactions; they are likely to be unaware of the experiment.

field independence a COGNITIVE STYLE in which the individual consistently relies more on internal referents (body sensation CUES) than on external referents (environmental cues). Field-independent people tend to be able to disregard deceptive environmental cues, particularly in tasks requiring the performance of simple actions or the identification of familiar elements in unfamiliar contexts. Compare FIELD DEPENDENCE.

field notes notes on observations made in natural settings (i.e., the field) rather than in laboratories.

field of consciousness the total awareness of an individual at a given time. See CONSCIOUSNESS.

field of regard the total space and all the objects within that space that can be seen at one time by the moving eye.

field properties the environmental factors that surround and influence a living organism.

field research research conducted outside the laboratory, in a natural, social, or other real-world setting. Field research has the advantages of ECOLOGICAL VALIDITY and the opportunity to understand how and why behavior occurs in a natural social environment; it has the disadvantages of loss of environmental control and ability to do experimental manipulations.

field structure in Kurt LEWIN'S FIELD THEORY, the pattern, distribution, or hierarchy of parts within a psychological FIELD. See also LIFE SPACE.

field theory 1. in physics, the theory that forces acting at a distance between bodies not in contact do so by means of a field of force that fills the space between them. See ACTION AT A DISTANCE. **2.** in psychology, a systematic approach describing behavior in terms of patterns of dynamic interrelationships between individuals and the psychological, social, and physical situation in which they exist. This situation is known as the **field space** or LIFE SPACE, and the dynamic interactions are conceived as forces with positive or negative VALENCES. [proposed by Kurt LEWIN]

field theory of personality a theory in which personality is understood in terms of dynamic interrelations among a field of intrapsychic forces. See FIELD THEORY. [devised by Kurt LEWIN]

field verification research to assess the effectiveness of product packaging and other marketing-related activities in the consumer's own environment. Field studies provide validation of focus-group studies and other initial research by showing whether people are engaging in the behavior predicted by that research.

field work research or practice carried out in everyday, real-world settings rather than in the laboratory or classroom. In clinical social work education, field work is a practicum in which the student supplements and applies classroom theory by taking responsibility for actual cases under the tutelage of experienced, qualified supervisors.

fifth cranial nerve see TRIGEMINAL NERVE.

fight–flight reaction an emotional and visceral response to an emergency that is designed to mobilize energy for attacking or avoiding the offending stimulus. It is characterized by a pattern of physiological changes elicited by activity of the SYMPATHETIC NERVOUS SYSTEM in response to stress that leads to mobilization of energy for physical activity (e.g., attacking or avoiding the offending stimulus), either directly or by inhibiting physiological activity that does not contribute to energy mobilization. Specific sympathetic responses involved in the reaction include (a) energy supply to smooth muscles, metabolism, and thermoregulation; (b) energy conservation; and (c) increased heart rate, respiratory rate, sweat gland activity, and blood glucose level. These are followed by regulatory responses of the PARASYMPATHETIC NERVOUS SYSTEM in the body's physiological effort to control and suppress the initial responses to stress. In the EMERGENCY THEORY OF EMOTIONS, such changes are the basis of all human emotions. Also called **emergency reaction**; **emergency syndrome**. See also CANNON–BARD THEORY. [first described by U.S. psychologist Walter B. Cannon (1871–1945)]

fighting *n.* direct physical AGGRESSION between two individuals. In animals much aggression can be communicated through THREAT DISPLAYS and SUBMISSIVE SIGNALS; fighting typically occurs only when signals alone do not resolve the encounter.

figural aftereffect a gestalt-perceptual phenomenon in which a shift of vision from a first figure superimposes its image on a second figure.

figural cohesion a principle of GESTALT PSYCHOLOGY describing the tendency for parts of a figure to be perceived as a whole figure even if the parts are disjointed. See also CLOSURE.

figural fluency test see DESIGN FLUENCY TEST.

figural synthesis the creation of a meaningful figure from the synthesis of selected portions of the incoming stimulus input. [proposed in 1967 by U.S. cognitive psychologist Ulric Neisser (1928–)]

figurative knowledge knowledge acquired by attending to and remembering specific perceptual features, words, or facts, for example, the ability to recall vocabulary, dates, colors, shapes, impressions, and other details. Compare OPERATIVE KNOWLEDGE. [first described by Jean PIAGET]

figurative language use of language in which meaning is extended by analogy, METAPHOR, or personification or emphasized by such devices as antithesis, alliteration, and so forth. Figurative language is most important in poetry and rhetoric but extends into almost all areas of language use.

figure-drawing test any test in which the participant draws a human figure, used as a measure of intellectual development or as a projective technique. See MACHOVER DRAW-A-PERSON TEST.

figure–ground *adj.* relating to the principle that perceptions have two parts: a figure that stands out in good contour and an indistinct, homogeneous background.

figure–ground distortion the interference of an object's setting with the perception of the object itself, rendering the viewer unable to focus on the object.

figure–ground perception the ability to discriminate properly between an object and the background in a visual field presentation. An impairment in this perceptual skill can seriously affect a child's ability to learn.

file-drawer analysis a statistical procedure for addressing the FILE-DRAWER PROBLEM by computing the number of unretrieved studies, averaging an EFFECT SIZE of .00, that would have to exist in file drawers before the overall results of a meta-analysis would become nonsignificant at $p \geq .05$, that is, would exceed an acceptable probability level (.05) of occurring by chance.

file-drawer problem the fact that a large proportion of all studies actually conducted are not available for review because they remain unpublished in "file drawers." See also FILE-DRAWER ANALYSIS.

filial anxiety fear and apprehension in children caused by their relationships with their parents, often in anticipation of caregiving responsibility by adult children of older parents.

filial generation any of the successive generations of descent from an original parental generation. The immediate descendants of the initial parents are the **first filial generation** (denoted F_1), their descendants are the **second filial generation** (denoted F_2), and so on.

filial imprinting a learning process in which a young animal becomes attached to its parent (see IMPRINTING).

filial maturity a mutual caring relationship between adult children and older parents, involving an understanding of each other's needs, responsibilities, and desires.

filial responsibility a sense of duty toward family members, with particular reference to child–parent obligations. Also called **filial duty**.

filicide *n.* the intentional killing of one's children, a very rare event that is sometimes thought to be caused by severe MAJOR DEPRESSIVE DISORDER.

filiform papillae the most common of the four types of PAPILLAE, covering most of the surface of the human tongue and giving that organ its rough surface. They have no TASTE BUDS and are not involved in gustation.

filled-space illusion a source of distortion in estimating distance: Estimates increase as a linear function of the number of intervening points (as on a map).

fill-in questions a testing method in which students are provided with incomplete sentences relating to concepts or terms and are required to supply the missing words or phrases.

film color a filmlike, texture-free soft color that lacks localization, as contrasted with the color of a surface, which is an example of OBJECT COLOR.

filopodium *n.* (*pl.* **filopodia**) a very fine, tubular outgrowth from a cell, for example, from the GROWTH CONE of a neuron.

filter *n.* **1.** a device or material that allows some elements of a mixture (e.g., of light, a liquid, or a gas) to pass through but not others. **2.** a hypothetical construct applied to cognitive channels of information that allow only certain aspects of a stimulus to pass into sensory consciousness. Filters are often used in discussions of ATTENTION to explain the ability to focus selectively on aspects of the environment (e.g., a conversation in a noisy room). See FILTER THEORY. **3.** in acoustics, a device, procedure, or process that alters the spectral composition of its input. A **low-pass filter** passes low frequencies with greater ease than high frequencies, that is, high frequencies are attenuated relative to low frequencies. A **high-pass filter** attenuates low frequencies, and a **bandpass filter** attenuates frequencies both above and below its **passband**.

filtered speech words that have been filtered to allow only specific frequency bands to pass through. Filtered speech is presented to the ear at a comfortably loud level to measure auditory processing abilities. See also DISTORTED SPEECH TEST.

filter theory 1. an early theory of attention proposing that unattended channels of information are filtered prior to identification. This theory continues to be influential in the form of its successor, the ATTENUATION THEORY. See also EARLY-SELECTION THEORY. [proposed in 1958 by Donald BROADBENT] **2.** any explanation of MATE SELECTION that postulates a series of steps that rule out more and more potential mates until only one is left.

FIM abbreviation for FUNCTIONAL INDEPENDENCE MEASURE.

fimbria *n.* (*pl.* **fimbriae**) **1.** a structure that resembles a fringe. **2.** the band of WHITE MATTER along the medial edge of the ventricular surface of the HIPPOCAMPUS. Also called **fimbria hippocampi**.

final cause see CAUSE.

final common path see MOTOR NEURON.

final free recall an unexpected test of memory given at the end of a memory assessment session, asking the individual to recall all of the materials that were studied and tested in the session.

finasteride *n.* see ANTIANDROGEN.

fine motor describing activities or skills that require coordination of small muscles to control small, precise movements, particularly in the hands and face. Examples of **fine motor skills** include handwriting, tracing, speaking, visual tracking, catching, cutting, and manipulating small objects with the hands and fingers. Compare GROSS MOTOR.

fine tremor see TREMOR.

finger agnosia a form of AGNOSIA characterized by difficulty in discriminating between different kinds of tactual stimuli applied to the fingers as well as an inability to recognize, name, or point to one's own or another person's fingers. If the fingers are touched in two places, for example, an individual may be unable to judge without visual clues whether the sensations come from the same finger or from two different fingers.

Finger Localization Test a 60-item NEUROPSYCHOLOGICAL TEST consisting of three parts: (1) The participant is asked to identify which finger is touched by the examiner; (2) the participant is blindfolded or otherwise prevented from using vision and then asked to identify which finger is touched; and (3) the participant again is blindfolded or otherwise prevented from using vision and then asked to identify which two fingers are simultaneously touched. Each hand is tested in each part of the test, which is scored for the number of correct identifications and currently appears in a variety of forms and as part of several neuropsychological test batteries. Also called **Tactile Finger Recognition**. [originally developed in 1983 by U.S. neuropsychologist Arthur Lester Benton (1909–) and colleagues]

Finger Oscillation Test see FINGER TAPPING TEST.

finger spelling the representation of the letters of the alphabet by shapes formed with the hand. Finger spelling is used in conjunction with SIGN LANGUAGE to spell names and other words for which conventional signs do not exist.

Finger Tapping Test a measure of fine motor speed in which the individual taps an index finger as quickly as possible against a response key. The test is part of the HALSTEAD–REITAN NEUROPSYCHOLOGICAL BATTERY. It was originally called the **Finger Oscillation Test**.

finite-state grammar a simple model of GENERATIVE GRAMMAR discussed by Noam CHOMSKY in his *Syntactic Structures* (1957). In this model it is supposed that the grammar generates sentences one unit at a time in strict linear sequence (i.e., working from left to right); once the first unit has been selected, the choice of subsequent units will be circumscribed at each stage by the sum of the previous choices. Chomsky presented this model, with its obvious inadequacy as an account of sentence generation, to demonstrate the need for the more complex explanations provided by PHRASE-STRUCTURE GRAMMAR and (especially) TRANSFORMATIONAL GENERATIVE GRAMMAR. Psychological interest in finite-state grammar stems largely from its similarity to certain principles of BEHAVIORISM and OPERATIONISM.

fire-setting behavior a tendency to set fires. Compare PYROMANIA.

firewall *n.* a program or hardware device designed to keep unwanted data or codes (e.g., a VIRUS) from entering a protected computer. Firewalls are often built into newer computers, but they can also be purchased as separate software or hardware add-ons. The problem in designing firewalls is to block unwanted data without also blocking data the user wishes to receive.

FIRO theory acronym for FUNDAMENTAL INTERPERSONAL RELATIONS ORIENTATION THEORY.

first admission a patient admitted for the first time to a mental institution.

first cranial nerve see OLFACTORY NERVE.

first-degree relative a parent, sibling, son, or daughter. Compare SECOND-DEGREE RELATIVE.

first-episode schizophrenia the first time that the criteria for a diagnosis of SCHIZOPHRENIA are met in an individual, a situation that poses a number of specific treatment challenges that the practitioner must address, such as denial and grief in the patient and his or her family. It is helpful to study specific impairments, underlying neurological deficits, and course of treatment response in such patients, since there is hypothetically no confounding of results due to previous administration of antipsychotic drugs.

first-generation antipsychotics see ANTIPSYCHOTICS.

first impression one's initial perception of another person, typically involving a positive or negative evaluation as well as a sense of physical and psychological characteristics. Such impressions are based on the earliest information received about a person, often through a direct encounter, and tend to persist, even in the face of later information that outside observers would consider inconsistent with the initial perception. That is, there is a PRIMACY EFFECT in the impression formation. Some theoretical analyses account for this effect by holding that the first received information is given greater weight in the perceiver's mind than is the later information; others propose that the initial information shapes the meaning subsequently given to the later information.

first-impression bias see PRIMACY EFFECT.

first-line medication a drug that is the first choice for treating a particular condition, because it is considered a very effective treatment for that condition with the least likelihood of causing side effects. A first-line medication may be a class of drugs (e.g., SSRIS for depression) as well as a single drug.

first moment see EXPECTED VALUE.

first-order factor in FACTOR ANALYSIS, any of the factors that are derived from the correlation (or covariance) among the MANIFEST VARIABLES, as opposed to SECOND-ORDER FACTORS, which are determined from the correlation (or covariance) among the factors.

first-order neuron the first neuron in a chain or tract of neurons. For example, in the somatosensory system, a first-order neuron receives peripheral input (e.g., sensations from the skin) and transmits it to the spinal cord. See also SECOND-ORDER NEURON.

first-person perspective the point of view of the subjective observer. Compare SECOND-PERSON PERSPECTIVE; THIRD-PERSON PERSPECTIVE.

first-rank symptoms symptoms, divided into five categories, originally proposed for the differential diagnosis of schizophrenia. The categories include hallucinations, changes in thought process, delusional perceptions, somatic passivity (experiencing external forces as influencing or controlling one's body), and other external impositions. Nearly 60% of all the patients diagnosed with schizophrenia in the INTERNATIONAL PILOT STUDY OF SCHIZOPHRENIA demonstrated first-rank symptoms. It is now known that these symptoms can also occur in other psychotic disorders, in mood disorders, and in neurological disorders. [first described by German psychiatrist Kurt Schneider (1887–1967)]

fishbone diagram see CAUSE-AND-EFFECT DIAGRAM.

fishbowl technique a procedure used in a GROWTH GROUP in which participants form two concentric circles.

The individuals in the inner group engage in a discussion or other form of interaction while the members of the outer group observe. When the interaction has concluded, the outer group provides information and feedback to the inner group. Later, the groups may exchange places and repeat the exercise.

Fisher exact test a statistical test giving the exact probability of departure from chance for data in a fourfold CONTINGENCY TABLE. [Sir Ronald Aylmer **Fisher** (1890–1962), British statistician and geneticist]

Fisher's r to Z transformation a mathematical transformation of the PRODUCT–MOMENT CORRELATION coefficient (*r*) to a new statistic (*Z*) whose sampling distribution is the normal distribution. It is used for testing hypotheses about correlations and constructing CONFIDENCE INTERVALS on correlations. [Sir Ronald Aylmer **Fisher**]

fission *n.* **1.** in biology, the reproduction of a cell or unicellular organism by splitting into two independent parts. **2.** in audition, the separation of two simultaneous sounds into separate perceptual **streams** or **auditory objects**. When two streams are perceived as one, **auditory fusion** is said to occur (see also FUSION).

fissure *n.* a cleft, groove, or indentation in a surface, especially any of the deep grooves in the CEREBRAL CORTEX, which increase the surface area of the brain. See also SULCUS.

fissure of Rolando see CENTRAL SULCUS. [Luigi **Rolando** (1773–1831), Italian anatomist]

fissure of Sylvius see LATERAL SULCUS. [Franciscus **Sylvius** (1614–1672), Dutch physician and anatomist]

fistula *n.* an abnormal passageway between two internal organs or between an internal organ and the outside of the body. A fistula may develop as a result of an injury (e.g., a gunshot wound), as a congenital defect, as an effect of an abscess, or as a result of a surgical procedure. A **craniosinus fistula** is marked by loss of cerebrospinal fluid through a sinus into the nose.

fit 1. *n.* the degree to which values predicted by a model correspond with empirically observed values. **2.** *n.* a lay term for an epileptic SEIZURE. **3.** *n.* a colloquial name for an emotional outburst. **4.** *adj.* see FITNESS.

FIT abbreviation for FEATURE-INTEGRATION THEORY.

fitness *n.* **1.** a set of attributes that people have or are able to achieve relating to their ability to perform physical work and to carry out daily tasks with vigor and alertness, without undue fatigue, and with ample energy to enjoy leisure pursuits. **2.** in biology, the extent to which an organism or population is able to produce viable offspring in a given environment or ECOLOGICAL NICHE, which is a measure of that organism's or population's adaptation to that environment. See DARWINIAN FITNESS; INCLUSIVE FITNESS; REPRODUCTIVE SUCCESS. **—fit** *adj.*

fitness for duty evaluation (**FFDE**) a psychological assessment of an employee's present mental state and functioning to estimate the employee's future functioning and determine whether that individual is able to safely and effectively perform his or her job duties. An FFDE is also used to determine if mental illness or emotional stress experienced by a person has interfered with his or her job performance. It is routinely conducted on police officers after they have had a traumatic experience in the line of duty. Also called **fit for duty evaluation**.

fitness for trial see COMPETENCY TO STAND TRIAL.

Fit to Win Health Promotion Program a U.S. Department of Defense educational program designed to promote health by reducing behavioral risk factors, such as smoking, excessive alcohol intake, and overconsumption of fatty foods.

Fitts law the principle of motor control that activities that are performed more quickly tend to be done less accurately (see SPEED–ACCURACY TRADEOFF). It is formulated as $MT = a + b\,f(DW)$, observed under a wide array of conditions to relate movement time (MT) linearly to a function $f(DW)$ of the ratio of movement distance (D) and target size (W) under conditions described by the FITTS MOVEMENT TASK. [Paul Morris **Fitts** (1912–1965), U.S. psychologist]

Fitts movement task a motor-skills test that illustrates the relationship between speed and accuracy of movement. If a participant is asked to tap a pencil 20 times within the outline of a circle (the discrete version), more pencil marks will fall outside the circle when the participant is asked to do the task quickly than when urged to be accurate. If a participant is asked to tap a pencil 20 times alternating between two circular outlines a fixed distance apart (the continuous version), accuracy will be similarly decreased. In current practice, the discrete version is almost always used in basic research, because the modeling issues are more straightforward, and the continuous version is usually used in neuropsychological testing and other more applied settings. The relationship between speed and accuracy for movement is formalized as FITTS LAW. [Paul Morris **Fitts**]

five-factor personality model (**FFM**) a model of personality in which five dimensions of individual difference—EXTRAVERSION, NEUROTICISM, CONSCIENTIOUSNESS, AGREEABLENESS, and OPENNESS TO EXPERIENCE—are viewed as core personality structures. Unlike the BIG FIVE PERSONALITY MODEL, which views the five personality dimensions as descriptions of behavior and treats the five-dimensional structure as a taxonomy of individual differences, the FFM also views the factors as psychological entities with causal force. The two models are frequently and incorrectly conflated in the scientific literature, without regard for their distinctly different emphases. [proposed by U.S. psychologists Robert R. McCrae (1949–) and Paul T. Costa, Jr.]

five-number summary in EXPLORATORY DATA ANALYSIS, the characterization of a batch of data through the use of five summary statistics: the two extreme scores, the upper and lower HINGES, and the MEDIAN.

five-to-seven shift the striking progress in many aspects of children's development between the ages of 5 and 7, when very significant advances in physical growth, motor coordination, reasoning capacity, linguistic ability, and socioemotional development occur. Among the many observable changes are a decline in egocentrism, the emerging ability to adopt the perspective of others, and a vastly improved competence in communication.

fixation *n.* **1.** an obsessive preoccupation with a single idea, impulse, or aim, as in an IDÉE FIXE. **2.** in psychoanalytic theory, the persistence of an early psychosexual stage (see PSYCHOSEXUAL DEVELOPMENT) or inappropriate attachment to an early psychosexual object or mode of gratification, such as anal or oral activity. **3.** in vision, focusing both eyes on a single target by rapid EYE MOVEMENTS, such as SACCADES, or by reflexes that allow the eyes to stay focused on a target when the observer moves (see OPTOKINETIC REFLEX; VESTIBULO-OCULAR REFLEX). **4.** the process of strengthening a habit until it becomes "fixed." **—fixate** *vb.*

fixation pause a period during which the eyes are focused directly on an object.

fixation point the point in space on which the eyes are

focused. In experimental studies of visual perception, a specific fixation point is often provided while vision is tested in some other location in the visual field.

fixation reflex a reflexive orienting of the eyes to maintain fixation on a target. It involves cortical and subcortical regions. Also called **fixation response**. See OPTOKINETIC REFLEX; VESTIBULO-OCULAR REFLEX.

fixed-action pattern (**FAP**) in classical ethology, a stereotyped, genetically preprogrammed, species-specific behavioral sequence that is evoked by a particular stimulus (see RELEASER) and is carried out without sensory feedback. See INNATE RELEASING MECHANISM. See also MODAL ACTION PATTERN.

fixed-alternative question see CLOSED-ENDED QUESTION.

fixed belief see IDÉE FIXE.

fixed class society a society with very little or no SOCIAL MOBILITY, as in the Hindu CASTE system. Compare OPEN CLASS SOCIETY.

fixed-effects model a statistical model in which the statistical parameters that index the effectiveness of treatments are treated as fixed parameters (numerical constants) rather than as random variables. See also FIXED FACTOR; RANDOM-EFFECTS MODEL.

fixed factor a factor (INDEPENDENT VARIABLE) in an experimental design whose levels are specified by the researcher rather than randomly generated within some range of permissible values. As a rule, one should not generalize results of studies of this type beyond the specific levels of the factors used in the experiment.

fixed idea see IDÉE FIXE.

fixed-interval schedule (**FI schedule**) a SCHEDULE OF REINFORCEMENT, formerly known as **periodic reinforcement**, in which the first response after a set interval has elapsed is reinforced. "FI 3 min" means that reinforcement is given to the first response occurring at least 3 min after a previous reinforcement (or some other time marker). Often, experience with FI schedules results in a temporal pattern of responding, characterized by little or no responding at the beginning of the interval, followed by an increased rate later on as reinforcement becomes more imminent. This pattern is often referred to as the **fixed-interval scallop**. Compare PROGRESSIVE-INTERVAL SCHEDULE.

fixed model see FIXED-EFFECTS MODEL; FIXED FACTOR.

fixedness *n.* in problem solving, see FUNCTIONAL FIXEDNESS.

fixed-ratio schedule (**FR schedule**) a SCHEDULE OF REINFORCEMENT in which reinforcement is given after a specified number of responses. "FR 1" means that reinforcement is given after each response; "FR 50" means that reinforcement is given after 50 responses. Compare PROGRESSIVE-RATIO SCHEDULE.

fixed-time schedule in conditioning, circumstances under which the event (e.g., stimulus, reinforcer) is delivered, independently of other events (including behavior), at fixed time intervals. See NONCONTINGENT REINFORCEMENT.

FJA abbreviation for FUNCTIONAL JOB ANALYSIS.

flaccid paralysis a type of paralysis marked by loss of muscle tone and absence of reflexes, producing a weak, flabby condition in the affected areas. Compare SPASTIC PARALYSIS.

flagellation *n.* whipping another person or oneself or submitting to whipping. Flagellation may be a form of penitence (as a religious ritual) or a means of achieving sexual excitement. Flagellation is a common practice among those who engage in BONDAGE AND DISCIPLINE. Also called **flagellantism**.

flapping tremor see ASTERIXIS.

flashback *n.* **1.** the reliving of a traumatic event after the initial adjustment to the trauma appears to have been made. Flashbacks are part of POSTTRAUMATIC STRESS DISORDER: Forgotten memories are reawakened by words, sounds, smells, or scenes that are reminiscent of the original trauma (e.g., when a backfiring car elicits the kind of anxiety that a combat veteran experienced when he or she was the target of enemy fire). **2.** the spontaneous recurrence, after a drug-free period, of predominantly visual hallucinations similar to those experienced following ingestion of CANNABIS or a HALLUCINOGEN. These hallucinations most often follow repeated ingestion of LSD and may occur months after the last use. See also ACID FLASHBACK.

flashbulb memory the memory associated with a personally significant and emotional event. Such memories have the quality of a photograph taken the moment the individual experienced the emotion, including such details as where the individual was or what he or she was doing. [first described in 1977 by U.S. psychologists Roger BROWN and James Kulick (1940–) in their study of people's recollection of public events, such as U.S. President John F. Kennedy's assassination]

flash card one of a series of small pieces of cardboard or paper with definitions or questions and answers written or printed on them, used as a learning aid. Often a question is on the front of the flash card with the answer on the back. A student reads the question, gives an answer, and then is able to turn the card over to see the correct answer. Flash cards are commonly used in rapid succession, in order to aid memorization and to facilitate learning of a fact or concept.

flat affect absence or apparent absence of emotional response to any situation or event. Also called **emotional flatness**; **flattened affect**; **flattening of affect**; **flatness of affect**. See also SHALLOW AFFECT.

flat organizational structure an organizational structure in which there are relatively few levels of management. In recent decades there has been a general trend in favor of such structures in the business world.

flavor *n.* a sensation produced by a combination of aroma, taste, texture, and temperature and involving olfactory, gustatory, and tactile sense organs.

fleeting present the ever-changing present moment of conscious experience. [defined by William JAMES]

flehmen *n.* a distinctive posture of animals in which the head is raised and lips curled (from German, "to bare the upper teeth"), often accompanied by a snort or deep inhalation of air. Flehmen serves to deliver chemical cues to the VOMERONASAL SYSTEM, an accessory olfactory organ that appears specialized to process species-specific olfactory cues. Flehmen is often seen in male ungulates inspecting female urine to determine if the female is in ESTRUS.

Flesch index a system used for evaluating readability and reading level of a document by examining word and sentence length, vocabulary, and phrases. [Rudolph **Flesch** (1911–1986), U.S. philologist and psychologist]

Flexeril *n.* a trade name for CYCLOBENZAPRINE.

flexibilitas cerea see CATALEPSY.

flexion *n.* the bending of a joint in a limb (e.g., the elbow joint), brought about by a FLEXOR MUSCLE, so that two parts of the limb (e.g., the forearm and upper arm) are brought toward each other.

flexion reflex the abrupt withdrawal of a limb in response to painful stimulation. Compare EXTENSION REFLEX.

flexor muscle a muscle whose contraction causes bending of a limb, such as the biceps muscle of the upper arm. Compare EXTENSOR MUSCLE.

flextime *n.* an arrangement that gives employees a certain amount of discretion over when they arrive at and leave work, provided that an agreed period of **core hours** is spent in the workplace. Flextime allows workers to adjust their work schedules to nonwork demands, such as parental responsibilities. Also called **flexitime**.

flicker discrimination the ability to perceive a change in brightness of a light source. The ability varies with the frequency of alternating changes in brightness until CRITICAL FLICKER FREQUENCY is reached, when the observer sees an apparently steady level of brightness.

flicker fusion the sensation produced by a flickering light source when the rate of flickering is so rapid that the light pulses seem to fuse into a continuous illumination. See CRITICAL FLICKER FREQUENCY.

flicker stimulus a periodically changing visual or auditory stimulus that produces a rapidly alternating sensation.

flight *n.* **1.** a form of LOCOMOTION that allows some animals (notably birds, bats, and insects) to become airborne and travel varying distances. It has several forms: active flight, gliding, and hovering. Bones of flying vertebrates must be light and rigid. Flight is used for escaping danger, locating food, and migrating from one location to another as seasons change (see MIGRATION BEHAVIOR). **2.** rapid departure as a means of escape from danger, whether by flying or some other form of locomotion. See also FIGHT–FLIGHT REACTION.

flight from reality a defensive reaction involving withdrawal into inactivity, detachment, or fantasy as an unconscious defense against anxiety-provoking situations. This may be expressed as a number of defensive behaviors, such as RATIONALIZATION, daydreaming, or substance abuse. It may include a retreat into psychotic behavior as a means of avoiding real or imagined problems. Also called **retreat from reality**. See also ESCAPE FROM REALITY. Compare FLIGHT INTO FANTASY; FLIGHT INTO REALITY.

flight into disease see FLIGHT INTO ILLNESS.

flight into fantasy a defensive reaction in which individuals experiencing disturbing thoughts and impulses retreat into fantasy (e.g., through DAYDREAMS) as a means of avoiding harming themselves or others by acting on these impulses. In this way they can maintain control over their impulses. Compare FLIGHT FROM REALITY; FLIGHT INTO REALITY.

flight into health in psychotherapy, an abrupt "recuperation" by a prospective client after or during intake interviews and before entry into therapy proper or, more commonly, by a client in ongoing therapy in order to avoid further confrontation with cognitive, emotional, or behavioral problems. Psychoanalytic theory interprets the flight into health as an unconscious DEFENSE MECHANISM. Also called **transference cure**; **transference remission**.

flight into illness **1.** a tendency to focus on or exaggerate minor physical complaints as an unconscious means of avoiding stressful situations and feelings. **2.** in psychotherapy, the sudden development of neurotic or physical symptoms by a client or prospective client. Psychoanalytic theory interprets this as an unconscious DEFENSE MECHANISM that is used to avoid examination of a deeper underlying conflict. Also called **escape into illness**; **flight into disease**.

flight into reality a defensive reaction in which an individual becomes overinvolved in activity and work as an unconscious means of avoiding threatening situations or painful thoughts and feelings. Compare FLIGHT FROM REALITY; FLIGHT INTO FANTASY.

flight of colors an AFTERIMAGE consisting of a succession of colors following exposure to a brief intense flash of light.

flight of ideas a disturbance in thinking consisting of a rapid, continuous succession of related ideas, evidenced by speech that shifts rapidly from one topic to another. This is observed primarily in ACUTE MANIA but may also occur in schizophrenia and other disorders. Also called **topical flight**. See also PRESSURED SPEECH.

flippancy *n.* inappropriate levity when addressing a serious problem or an anxiety-provoking subject, often as a defensive strategy for limiting discussion. Compare GALLOWS HUMOR. **—flippant** *adj.*

floaters *pl. n.* see DETACHED RETINA.

floating-limb response in standard hypnotic inductions, a positive response to the suggestion to allow the hand and arm to float upward. See also KOHNSTAMM TEST.

floccillation *n.* aimless grasping and plucking at clothing or bedding, typically associated with dementia, delirium, and high fever. It is sometimes a sign of extreme exhaustion and is considered a serious symptom, often associated with a poor prognosis. Also called **carphology**.

flocculonodular lobe one of the divisions of the CEREBELLUM, lying below the posterior lobe. The flocculonodular lobe projects to the VESTIBULAR NUCLEI of the brainstem and is mainly involved with vestibular functions (posture and eye movements).

flocking *n.* the grouping of birds due to social attraction and interaction. It is related to COLONIAL NESTING and contrasts with AGGREGATION, which is due to some independent factor. The equivalent of flocking in mammals is known as **herding** (see HERD INSTINCT).

flooding *n.* a BEHAVIOR-THERAPY technique in which the individual is exposed directly to a maximum-intensity anxiety-producing situation or stimulus, either in the imagination (see IMAGINAL FLOODING) or in reality (see IN VIVO DESENSITIZATION). Flooding techniques aim to diminish or extinguish the undesired behavior and are used, for example, in the treatment of individuals with phobias. See also IMPLOSIVE THERAPY. Compare SYSTEMATIC DESENSITIZATION.

floor effect the inability of a test to measure or discriminate below a certain point, usually because its items are too difficult. Compare CEILING EFFECT.

floral *adj.* denoting one of the seven classes of odorants in the STEREOCHEMICAL SMELL THEORY.

flourishing *n.* a condition denoting good mental and physical health: the state of being free from illness and distress but, more important, of being filled with vitality and functioning well in one's personal and social life. Compare LANGUISHING. **—flourish** *vb.*

flow *n.* a state of optimal experience arising from intense involvement in an activity that is enjoyable, such as playing a sport, engaging in an art form, or reading a good book. Flow arises when one's skill is equal to the demands of the task, intrinsic motivation is at a peak, maximum performance is achieved, and one has a sense of total control, effortless movement, and complete concentration.

flower-spray ending a type of nerve-fiber ending at the thin ends of a MUSCLE SPINDLE in which the fiber branches out across the surface of the spindle. Also called **secondary sensory ending**. Compare ANNULOSPIRAL ENDING.

flowery *adj.* denoting one of the primary odor qualities in HENNING'S ODOR PRISM.

flowing consciousness the pleasurable sense of FLOW and effortlessness that accompanies skilled, nonconflictual activities.

flow pattern the aggregate movement of elements in a visual scene as an observer moves through the scene.

fluctuating asymmetry the degree to which the symmetry of body parts of individuals varies from the norm for a given species. This provides information to others about the relative health or well-being of an individual: It is assumed that those with more symmetrical bodies are healthier and more vigorous than those with more asymmetry. Thus, fluctuating asymmetry is an important cue in MATE-SELECTION decisions.

fluctuation of attention the changing of sensory clarity even though stimulation is constant.

fluctuation of perception a tendency for perception to alternate between competing stimuli that cannot be integrated or synthesized. See BISTABLE PERCEPTUAL EVENTS.

fluency *n.* **1.** in cognitive psychology, the ability to generate ideas, words, mental associations, or potential solutions to a problem with ease and rapidity. It is usually considered to be an important dimension of CREATIVITY. See ASSOCIATIVE FLUENCY. **2.** facility in speaking or writing, especially in a language that is not one's native language. **—fluent** *adj.*

fluent aphasia a form of APHASIA in which the individual can speak fluently but has difficulties in, for instance, naming objects, understanding language, or repeating words. WERNICKE'S APHASIA is a classic example. Compare NONFLUENT APHASIA.

fluent speech speech that is essentially normal in quantity, stress, pitch, rhythm, and intonation.

fluid abilities abilities, such as memory span and mental quickness, that are functionally related to physiological condition and maturation. Fluid abilities appear to increase during childhood and to deteriorate, to some extent, in old age. Compare CRYSTALLIZED ABILITIES. See also FLUID–CRYSTALLIZED INTELLIGENCE THEORY.

fluid–crystallized intelligence theory the theory that intelligence tends to be of two kinds, fluid and crystallized. FLUID INTELLIGENCE is used in coping with new kinds of problems and situations, and CRYSTALLIZED INTELLIGENCE is used in applying one's cultural knowledge to problems.

fluid intelligence the form of intelligence that comprises FLUID ABILITIES. See FLUID–CRYSTALLIZED INTELLIGENCE THEORY.

flumazenil *n.* a drug used for the emergency reversal of symptoms of BENZODIAZEPINE overdose and in anesthesia to reverse benzodiazepine-induced sedation. It acts by displacing benzodiazepine (which acts as a GABA AGONIST) from binding sites on the GABA receptor complex (see BENZODIAZEPINE ANTAGONISTS; $GABA_A$ RECEPTOR). Because it is a short-acting agent, multiple doses may be required. It is not effective in managing benzodiazepine dependence, because its rapid action may precipitate a sudden withdrawal syndrome, nor does it antagonize the central nervous system effects of other GABA agonists (e.g., barbiturates) or reverse their effects. U.S. trade name: **Romazicon**.

flunitrazepam *n.* a BENZODIAZEPINE that is legally prescribed in some countries (but not the United States) for the short-term treatment of insomnia and as a preanesthetic medication. It is also used as a drug of abuse for its sedating and disinhibiting effects. When combined with alcohol, like many other CNS DEPRESSANTS, it can cause serious problems (see DATE-RAPE DRUG). Trade name: **Rohypnol**.

fluorescein angiography a diagnostic procedure used to examine the retinal vasculature. A fluorescent compound, fluorescein, is injected into the systemic circulation; as it flows through the blood vessels on the surface of the retina, these are photographed with a special camera.

fluoxetine *n.* an antidepressant that is the prototype of the SSRIS (selective serotonin reuptake inhibitors). It acts by inhibiting the serotonin TRANSPORTER, preventing reuptake of serotonin into the TERMINAL BUTTON of the presynaptic neuron. This presumably results in higher levels of available neurotransmitter to interact with postsynaptic receptors. Fluoxetine differs from other SSRIs in that it and its biologically active metabolic product, norfluoxetine, have a prolonged HALF-LIFE of 5–7 days after a single dose; thus it takes around 30 days (20–35 days) for the drug to reach steady-state concentrations. Like other SSRIs, it should not be used with monoamine oxidase inhibitors. U.S. trade names: **Prozac**; **Sarafem**.

fluphenazine *n.* a HIGH-POTENCY ANTIPSYCHOTIC of the piperazine PHENOTHIAZINE class. It is as potent as HALOPERIDOL and has similar side effects, with neuromuscular and extrapyramidal symptoms predominating. Like haloperidol, it is also available in an oil-based injectable form. These so-called depot preparations are injected intramuscularly and are very slowly absorbed, allowing periods of several weeks between doses. U.S. trade name: **Prolixin**.

flurazepam *n.* a BENZODIAZEPINE derivative used in the short-term treatment of insomnia. U.S. trade name: **Dalmane**.

flutamide *n.* see ANTIANDROGEN.

flutter *n.* see ROUGHNESS.

flutter dysmetria see OCULAR FLUTTER.

fluttering hearts a visual illusion in which figures of one color (typically red), presented on a background of the same brightness but a different color (typically blue), will appear to dance when the whole image is moved. The different response speeds of the RETINAL CONES encoding the two colors is thought to be the basis of this illusion.

fluvoxamine *n.* a potent SSRI (selective serotonin reuptake inhibitor). Although its mechanism of action and antidepressant efficacy match those of other SSRIs, it is marketed largely as an agent for treating obsessive-compulsive disorder (see also CLOMIPRAMINE). U.S. trade name: **Luvox**.

fly agaric the highly poisonous mushroom *Amanita muscaria*, so called because it was once used as an insecticide to kill flies. MUSCARINE was the first active ingredient to be identified, but it is now known that IBOTENIC ACID and its metabolite **muscimol**, which is similar in structure to the inhibitory neurotransmitter GAMMA-AMINOBUTYRIC ACID (GABA) and acts as a GABA AGONIST, are the principal active components. Effects on humans are initially stimulating, ranging from euphoria through hallucinations to hyperactivity or excitement, and then sedating, inducing deep sleep. Symptoms of poisoning include dizziness, abdominal pains, vomiting, muscle cramps, and movement difficulties; at higher doses these symptoms may be followed by unconsciousness, asphyxiation, coma, and potentially death. Fly agaric has been variously identified as the substance taken by Norse berserkers before battle, as the plant SOMA worshipped in ancient times, and, in fiction, as the mushroom eaten by Alice before she perceived objects larger than life in Lewis Carroll's *Alice in Wonderland*.

flying flies see MUSCAE VOLITANTES.

Flynn effect the gradual rise of IQ level that has been observed since the time when records of IQs first were kept. Although the average IQ remains 100 due to periodic renorming of IQ tests, RAW SCORES have been rising. These increases have been roughly 9 points per generation (i.e., 30 years). The gains have been unequally distributed across the different kinds of abilities, with FLUID ABILITIES showing substantially greater gains than CRYSTALLIZED ABILITIES. [James **Flynn** (1934–), New Zealand philosopher who first documented its occurrence]

FMEA abbreviation for FAILURE MODES AND EFFECTS ANALYSIS.

fMRI abbreviation for FUNCTIONAL MAGNETIC RESONANCE IMAGING.

fMRI measures of intelligence measures of intelligence yielded by FUNCTIONAL MAGNETIC RESONANCE IMAGING methods, which enable investigators to obtain relatively precise indications of which part or parts of the brain are being utilized in the solution of a given cognitive task. Thus, the typical goal is to pinpoint that part of the brain in which processing is taking place for a given task at a given point in information processing for that task.

FMS abbreviation for FALSE MEMORY SYNDROME.

focal attention attention that is focused on specific stimuli while ignoring other stimuli. Information that is within one's ATTENTION SPAN is said to be in focal attention. Much research is devoted to determining the information capacity of focal attention and to understanding how it interacts with various memory systems after its capacity is exceeded. Also called **focused attention**.

focal consciousness the clearest contents of consciousness. See FRINGE–FOCUS STRUCTURE. Compare FRINGE CONSCIOUSNESS.

focal degeneration the development of a lesion or dysfunction in a specific area of the brain due to a degenerative process, such as dementia. The lesion may remain limited in focus or spread into neighboring regions.

focal length (symbol: *f*) the distance between the surface of a lens and the point at which it focuses the light passing through the lens.

focal lesion a lesion that is restricted to a specific area (of the brain, for example).

focal motor seizure a simple PARTIAL SEIZURE that results in motor abnormalities and is due to localized seizure activity in brain areas important for movement.

focal pathology the study of changes in body tissues and organs involved in a disease at the focal point of the diseased area.

focal psychotherapy SHORT-TERM THERAPY aimed at the relief of a single symptom, such as a phobic anxiety or feelings of guilt, and not involving a DEPTH THERAPY approach.

focal seizure see PARTIAL SEIZURE.

focal symptoms symptoms limited to a specific area.

focal therapy see FOCUSED ANALYSIS.

focus *n.* the concentration or centering of attention on a stimulus.

focused analysis a modification of orthodox psychoanalysis in which interpretations are focused on a specific area of the patient's problem or pathology (e.g., a particular symptom, a particular aspect of the TRANSFERENCE). Also called **directed analysis**; **focal therapy**. Compare EXPECTANT ANALYSIS.

focused attention see FOCAL ATTENTION.

focus gambling in a task that requires the generation of hypotheses about what combination of FEATURES defines a concept, a strategy in which the participant changes more than one feature from one hypothesis to the next. Focus gambling contrasts with the more conservative strategy of varying one feature at a time to determine its relevance to the concept. See CONCEPT-DISCOVERY TASK.

focus group a small group of people, typically 8–12 in number, who share common characteristics (e.g., working parents with 5- to 8-year-old children) and are selected to discuss a topic of which they have personal experience (e.g., their children's reading abilities and school performance). A leader conducts the discussion and keeps it on target. Originally used in marketing to determine consumer response to particular products, focus groups are now used for determining typical reactions, adaptations, and solutions to any number of issues, events, or topics.

focusing *n.* in EXPERIENTIAL PSYCHOTHERAPY, a process in which the therapist guides a client to focus silently on his or her body-centered experience of a problem or symptom in a relaxed and nonjudgmental way, often with eyes closed. The client then invites his or her mind to explore intuitively what the issue is about, without attempting to analyze or control thought processes. The method is believed to lead the client to deeper feelings and greater insight about and peace with the problem or symptom. [developed by Austrian-born U.S. psychologist Eugene T. Gendlin (1926–)]

focusing effect in studies of EXTRASENSORY PERCEPTION and PSYCHOKINESIS, the ostensible phenomenon in which performance is better for trials in which the TARGET is the object of special attentional focus (perhaps because it has particular significance for the participant). See also DECLINE EFFECT; DIFFERENTIAL EFFECT; POSITION EFFECT; PREFERENTIAL EFFECT; SHEEP–GOAT EFFECT; ZENER CARDS.

focusing mechanism the system of CILIARY MUSCLES, lens elasticity, and ocular-fluid pressure that enables the eye to focus an image sharply on the retina. The natural shape of the lens is spherical, which is required to focus near objects. When focusing distant objects the lens is flattened by tension exerted on the ZONULES as the ciliary muscles are relaxed and by fluid pressure within the eye.

focusing power the degree to which a converging lens causes parallel rays of light to be refracted (see REFRACTION). A high focusing power will cause light to be focused to a point close to the lens; a low focusing power causes the light to be focused farther from the lens. The focusing power of a lens is measured in DIOPTERS. The **magnification power** of a lens indicates how many times an object is enlarged when viewed through the lens; for example, a 4× lens will produce an image four times larger than the object.

focus of attention that aspect of an internal or external event to which attention is directed.

focus of convenience in the personality theory of U.S.

psychologist George A. Kelly (1905–1967), the set of phenomena to which a given theory best applies.

foliate papillae swellings along the lateral margins (sides) of the tongue, in humans numbering 5–7 on each side, each shaped like a leaf. The groove between each pair of papillae contains about 100 TASTE BUDS. See also PAPILLA.

folie à cinq a rare psychotic disorder in which five people, usually members of the same family, share similar or identical delusions (French, "insanity of five"). It is an example of SHARED PSYCHOTIC DISORDER.

folie à deux a rare psychotic disorder in which two intimately related individuals simultaneously share similar or identical delusions (French, "double insanity"). It is the most common form of SHARED PSYCHOTIC DISORDER.

folie à groupe irrational but consensually validated phenomena, such as bigotry shared by massive numbers of people. [defined by Erich FROMM]

folie à quatre a rare psychotic disorder in which four people, usually members of the same family, share similar or identical delusions (French, "insanity of four"). It is an example of SHARED PSYCHOTIC DISORDER.

folie à trois a rare psychotic disorder in which three intimately related people simultaneously share similar or identical delusions (French, "triple insanity"). It is an example of SHARED PSYCHOTIC DISORDER.

folium *n.* (*pl.* **folia**) a leaflike structure, especially one of the leaflike folds of the CEREBELLAR CORTEX.

folk bilingualism a type of BILINGUALISM associated mainly with working-class immigrant communities, in which the native language is primarily oral and its use is unsupported by formal education. Bilingual proficiency of this kind is not considered a sign of status and may well be a social stigma. Also called **circumstantial bilingualism**. Compare ELITE BILINGUALISM.

folklore *n.* the traditions, beliefs, legends, tales, and songs that have endured in a specific culture owing to transmission from generation to generation.

folk psychology 1. the everyday, common-sense, implicit knowledge that enables the prediction or explanation of the behavior of others (and of oneself) by reference to the mental states involved. Although such an understanding is accepted in much of social and personality psychology, there are those who view it as illusory or mythological and hold its tenets unworthy of scientific consideration. In ELIMINATIVISM the term "folk psychology" is used pejoratively for any explanatory language that refers to mental states, such as beliefs and intentions, rather than to biological states. See also COMMONSENSE PSYCHOLOGY; POPULAR PSYCHOLOGY. **2.** an obsolete name for a branch of psychology that deals with the influence of specific cultural experiences (e.g., legends, religious rituals, indigenous healing practices, etc.) on human behavior and psychological constructs. It is essentially equivalent to modern CROSS-CULTURAL PSYCHOLOGY. **3.** a branch of the psychological system of Wilhelm WUNDT, who believed that an understanding of higher mental processes could be deduced from the study of such cultural products as language, history, myths, art, government, and customs. As such, it is the historical predecessor to modern CULTURAL PSYCHOLOGY.

folk soul in the FOLK PSYCHOLOGY of Wilhelm WUNDT, a group's perpetual and fundamental characteristics, moralities, norms, and values, which cannot be explained solely in terms of the characteristics of the individual members of the group. Belief in a folk soul is usually seen as an example of the GROUP FALLACY. See also GROUP MIND.

folkways *n.* the traditional modes of behavior in a particular culture, society, or group.

follicle *n.* a cluster of cells enclosing, protecting, and nourishing a cell or structure within, such as a HAIR FOLLICLE or a GRAAFIAN FOLLICLE. See also FOLLICLE-STIMULATING HORMONE. **—follicular** *adj.*

follicle-stimulating hormone (**FSH**) a GONADOTROPIN released by the anterior pituitary gland that, in females, stimulates the development in the ovary of GRAAFIAN FOLLICLES (see MENSTRUAL CYCLE). The same hormone in males stimulates SERTOLI CELLS in the testis to produce spermatozoa. Also called **follitropin**.

follicular phase see MENSTRUAL CYCLE.

following behavior a species-specific trait of certain young animals that run or swim after a parent or surrogate parent. It is a manifestation of IMPRINTING.

follow-up counseling 1. the measures taken by a counselor or clinician in helping a client with ongoing problems or new manifestations of the original problems. **2.** an evaluation of a client's progress and the effectiveness of counseling to date.

follow-up history see CATAMNESIS; POSTTREATMENT FOLLOW-UP.

follow-up study a long-term study designed to examine the degree to which effects seen shortly after the imposition of a therapeutic intervention persist over time. Follow-up studies are also used for the long-term study of participants in a laboratory experiment to examine the degree to which effects of the experimental conditions are lasting.

Folstein Mini-Mental State Examination see MINI-MENTAL STATE EXAMINATION.

fontanel (**fontanelle**) *n.* a soft, membrane-covered area in the incompletely ossified skull of a newborn infant. Fontanels typically close before the 2nd year of life, as the skull bones gradually fuse. Also called **soft spot**.

food addiction an eating disturbance characterized by a preoccupation with one's body image and weight, obsessive thoughts about food, the use of food as a source of pleasure, and COMPULSIVE EATING. In addition, the individual may experience symptoms of withdrawal during attempts to reduce food intake or abstain from particular types of food. See also BINGE-EATING DISORDER; BULIMIA NERVOSA.

food caching the hiding or storing of food by an animal for later use. Clark's nutcracker, a bird of the southwestern United States, is said to cache up to 30,000 pine nuts each year and to retrieve enough of these to survive over winter. Food-caching birds have good SPATIAL MEMORY and an enlarged HIPPOCAMPUS. See HOARDING.

food faddism a dietary practice based on exaggerated and often incorrect beliefs about the effects of food or nutrition on health, particularly for the prevention or cure of illness. This is often expressed as strange or inappropriate eating habits and the adoption of cult diets; it may lead to unhealthy weight loss or side effects arising from poor nutrition. It is sometimes associated with eating disorders, such as ANOREXIA NERVOSA.

food-intake regulation the ability to adjust daily intake of calories and other nutrients according to the temperature of the environment, energy expended at various tasks, and other factors, so that calorie intake and calorie loss, as well as other nutritional components (e.g., proteins, fats, vitamins, minerals), are constantly in balance. Food-intake regulation is one example of HOMEOSTASIS.

foot anesthesia see STOCKING ANESTHESIA.

foot-candle (**fc**) *n.* a former unit of illuminance now replaced by the LUX (1 foot-candle = 10.764 lux). Average street lights are approximately 1 foot-candle.

foot drop a characteristic of certain neuromuscular disorders in which the muscles that control movement of the foot or toes are weakened or paralyzed. The affected foot may fall toward and slap against the floor or ground, or the affected toes may tilt forward and drag along the floor or ground.

footedness *n.* preferential use of one foot rather than the other, for example, in kicking. See HANDEDNESS; LATERALIZATION.

foot fetishism see RETIFISM.

foot-in-the-door technique a two-step procedure for enhancing COMPLIANCE in which a minor initial request is presented immediately before the more substantial target request. Agreement to the initial request makes people more likely to agree to the target request than would have been the case if the latter had been presented on its own. See also DOOR-IN-THE-FACE TECHNIQUE; LOW-BALL TECHNIQUE; THAT'S-NOT-ALL TECHNIQUE.

foraging *n.* the process of searching for, locating, capturing, and processing food for ingestion or for provisioning young. For example, fruit-eating animals must locate trees containing fruit ripe enough to eat and often process the fruit by removing husks or seeds prior to ingestion. OPTIMAL FORAGING THEORY provides a framework for predicting the costs and benefits of different decisions about where to forage and for how long.

foramen *n.* (*pl.* **foramina**) an anatomical opening or hole, particularly in a bone, such as the foramen magnum.

foramen magnum a large opening at the base of the skull through which the spinal cord and the left and right vertebral arteries, as well as other tissues, pass between the neck and the interior of the skull.

foramen of Monro see INTERVENTRICULAR FORAMEN. [Alexander **Monro**, Jr. (1733–1817), Scottish anatomist]

foraminotomy *n.* the surgical enlargement of one of the foramina (openings) between adjacent vertebrae through which a spinal nerve passes, usually by enlarging the opening above the nerve root. The procedure is done for the relief of nerve pressure, such as that causing lower back pain.

forced-choice test 1. see FORCED-RESPONSE TEST. **2.** in signal detection tasks, a test in which two or more intervals are presented, one of which contains the signal. The observer must choose the interval in which the signal was presented.

forced compliance effect the tendency of a person who has behaved in a way that contradicts his or her attitude to subsequently alter the attitude to be consistent with the behavior. It is one way of reducing COGNITIVE DISSONANCE. Also called **induced compliance effect**. See also DISSONANCE REDUCTION.

forced copulation copulation of a male with a female against her choice. In scorpion flies males have several tactics for obtaining mates: Larger males can monopolize resources and offer food to females that accept copulation; smaller males without access to food use forced copulation, which leads to much less REPRODUCTIVE SUCCESS. See also RAPE.

forced distribution a rating system in which raters must use a prescribed number of entries for each level of the rating scale used. For example, given 25 statements that describe a person, the rater might be asked to sort the statements into seven piles ranging from least to most characteristic of that person. The number of characterizations assigned to each of the seven piles might, for example, be set at 1, 3, 5, 7, 5, 3, 1.

forced-response test an examination that provides participants with fixed responses from which they must choose an answer (e.g., a multiple-choice or matching test). This type of test is sometimes described as an OBJECTIVE TEST. Also called **forced-choice test**. Compare FREE-RESPONSE TEST.

forced treatment therapy administered to an individual against his or her will. Forced treatment refers particularly to unusual or hazardous treatment, such as lobotomy, aversive-reinforcement conditioning, or electroconvulsive therapy. Also called **coercive treatment**; **enforced treatment**. See also CONSUMERISM; RIGHT TO REFUSE TREATMENT.

force field in FIELD THEORY, the totality at any instant of coexisting factors that influence change (e.g., behavioral change).

forceps injury a congenital defect, temporary or permanent, induced by the use of forceps to extract a newborn infant from the mother's uterus during labor. Forceps injury is one of the causes of cerebral palsy, a disorder in which 85% of the cases are due to neurological damage during gestation or delivery.

forebrain *n.* the part of the brain that develops from the anterior section of the NEURAL TUBE in the embryo, containing the CEREBRAL HEMISPHERES, BASAL GANGLIA, AMYGDALA, and HIPPOCAMPUS. The THALAMUS and HYPOTHALAMUS are sometimes also included (see DIENCEPHALON). Also called **prosencephalon**.

foreclosure *n.* in development, commitment to an IDENTITY, which typically occurs during adolescence. See IDENTITY FORECLOSURE. See also IDENTITY VERSUS ROLE CONFUSION.

foreconscious *n.* see PRECONSCIOUS.

foreground–background in perception, the distinction between the object of attention, which is foreground, and details in the background, which are less likely to receive individual attention.

foregrounding *n.* the process or technique of highlighting certain aspects of a complex stimulus to make them the focus of attention. Foregrounding occurs, for example, when a speaker or writer gives prominence to some elements in a communication rather than others. This is usually achieved by a combination of word order, sentence construction, and more explicit verbal pointers (*Mark my words, Most importantly*, etc.); in speech, it is reinforced by stress, pausing, and body language. DISCOURSE ANALYSIS is much concerned with the ways in which speakers and writers tend unconsciously to foreground certain categories of information (see GIVEN–NEW DISTINCTION).

foreigner talk a speech REGISTER commonly adopted when speaking to those perceived as foreigners not competent in the language being used, typically characterized by short sentences, simplified grammar and vocabulary, and slow, loud delivery.

foreign hull in Kurt LEWIN'S FIELD THEORY, all tangible things beyond the LIFE SPACE, which can potentially permeate the life space.

forensic assessment evaluation of the mental state of a defendant, witness, or offender for the purpose of informing the court. Using a variety of techniques (e.g., interviews, standardized testing instruments) administered by mental health practitioners, it focuses on such issues as COMPETENCY TO STAND TRIAL, CRIMINAL RESPONSIBILITY, RISK ASSESSMENT, and potential for sexual abuse.

forensic neuropsychology the application of CLINICAL NEUROPSYCHOLOGY to issues of both civil and criminal law, particularly those relating to claims of brain injury.

forensic psychiatry the branch of psychiatry concerned with abnormal behavior and mental disorders as they relate to legal issues, hearings, and trials. Major areas of concern include insanity pleas (see INSANITY DEFENSE) and the legal definition of INSANITY, procedures to commit individuals to mental hospitals, and questions of CRIMINAL RESPONSIBILITY, COMPETENCY TO STAND TRIAL, GUARDIANSHIP, conservatorship (see CONSERVATOR), and confidentiality. Also called **legal psychiatry**.

forensic psychology the application of psychological principles and techniques to situations involving the law or legal systems (both criminal and civil). Its functions include assessment, diagnosis, and treatment of offenders and others, provision of ADVOCACY and EXPERT TESTIMONY, and research and policy analysis. Also called **legal psychology**. See also CORRECTIONAL PSYCHOLOGY.

forensic social work the application of social work principles and techniques to legal issues or situations involving the law or legal systems (both criminal and civil). Its functions include providing consultation, education, or training to various individuals within the legal and correctional systems; making recommendations regarding CHILD CUSTODY and other related issues; providing EXPERT TESTIMONY and ADVOCACY; and conducting research and policy analysis.

foreperiod *n.* in reaction-time experiments, the pause between the ready signal and the presentation of the stimulus.

foreplay *n.* activity engaged in prior to COITUS, marked by psychological as well as physical stimulation. The purpose of foreplay, which includes kissing, stroking, fantasizing, and similar activities, is to encourage sexual arousal in the participants. It may last from a few minutes to several hours.

foreshortening *n.* the illusion that the length of a line appears shorter when viewed lengthwise.

foreskin *n.* a loose fold of skin that normally covers the GLANS PENIS but can retract during erection or coitus. It is a continuation of the skin covering the rest of the penis. Also called **prepuce**; **preputium penis**. See also CIRCUMCISION.

forethought *n.* the ability of an individual to anticipate the consequences of his or her actions and the actions of others. According to Albert BANDURA's SOCIAL-COGNITIVE THEORY, forethought is a key element in learning behavior.

forewarning of persuasive intent the receipt of information that a subsequent communication is intended to change the attitude of the recipient. This tends to decrease ATTITUDE CHANGE as a result of biasing ELABORATION against what is advocated in the message. See also BIASED ELABORATION; BIASING FACTOR.

forewarning of persuasive position the receipt of information that a subsequent communication will contain arguments for a particular attitudinal position. Forewarning that a communication will be a COUNTERATTITUDINAL ADVOCACY tends to decrease ATTITUDE CHANGE by biasing ELABORATION against the message. See also BIASED ELABORATION; BIASING FACTOR.

forgetting *n.* the inability to remember something that was once recallable or that one believes should be recallable. See DECAY THEORY; INTERFERENCE THEORY; MOTIVATED FORGETTING; RETROACTIVE INTERFERENCE.

forgiveness *n.* willfully putting aside feelings of resentment toward an individual who has committed a wrong, been unfair or hurtful, or otherwise harmed one in some way. Forgiveness is not equated with reconciliation or excusing another, and it is not merely accepting what happened or ceasing to be angry. Rather, it involves a voluntary transformation of one's feelings, attitudes, and behavior toward the individual, so that one is no longer dominated by resentment and can express compassion, generosity, or the like toward the individual. Forgiveness is often considered an important process in psychotherapy or counseling.

formal cause see CAUSE.

formal discipline a concept that certain subjects (e.g., mathematics and foreign languages) should be studied for the primary purpose of exercising and developing the mind.

formal fallacy see FALLACY.

formal grammar a description of language in terms of its form and structure as opposed to its function and meaning. Compare FUNCTIONAL GRAMMAR. See FORM–FUNCTION DISTINCTION.

formal group any group that is deliberately formed by its members or an external authority for some purpose. Unlike an ACCIDENTAL GROUP, a formal group is likely to use explicit terms to define its membership criteria, operating procedures, role structure, and goals.

formalism *n.* the study of the outward form of works of art and literature, as opposed to their content or meaning. **—formalist** *n.* **—formalistic** *adj.*

formal language see ARTIFICIAL LANGUAGE.

formal logic a system of prescribed rules for generating valid conclusions or predictions from initial axiomatic assumptions or knowledge. It is often contrasted with more intuitive forms of thought, such as common sense. See DEDUCTIVE REASONING; LOGIC; SYMBOLIC LOGIC.

formal operations in Jean PIAGET's theory of cognitive development, completely developed intellectual functions, such as abstract thinking, logical processes, conceptualization, and judgment. These capacities develop during the **formal operational stage**, the fourth major period in Piaget's theory, which begins at about age 11. See also IDENTITY, NEGATION, RECIPROCAL, AND CORRELATIVE OPERATIONS.

formal organizational structure the official patterns of coordination and control, workflow, authority, and communication that channel the activity of members of an organization. The formal structure is embedded in the design of the organization and is seen as the pattern that should be followed by employees. It can be contrasted with the informal structure, which is defined by patterns that are not officially recognized but that emerge from the daily interactions of employees. See ORGANIZATIONAL STRUCTURE.

formal parallelism a comparative approach to the concept of development that relates multiple modes of functioning (i.e., different modes of animal life, different kinds of sociocultural organization, or different types of consciousness) to different levels of organization and integration, rather than relating them to a single line of chronological development, as in the RECAPITULATION THEORY. [proposed by German-born U.S. psychologist Heinz Werner (1890–1964)]

formal reasoning reasoning that entails the use of formal logical operations. See DEDUCTIVE REASONING; LOGIC.

formal thought disorder a type of thought disturbance characterized by disruptions in the form or structure of thinking. Examples include DERAILMENT and TANGENTIALITY. It should be distinguished from THOUGHT DISORDER, in which the disturbance relates to thought content. See also SCHIZOPHRENIC THINKING.

formal universal see LANGUAGE UNIVERSAL.

formants *pl. n.* the frequency bands of sounds produced by the vocal cords and other physical features of the head and throat in speaking. A simple sound, such as the vowel /a/, may span several kilohertz of frequencies when recorded by a SOUND SPECTROGRAPH.

formative evaluation a process that is concerned with helping to improve or guide the development of a program through the use of qualitative or quantitative research methodology. Ideally, the formative evaluator will repeatedly interact, often informally, with the program personnel from the outset of the work to clarify goals, monitor implementation, and assess staff and resource requirements. Also called **feedback evaluation**. See also PROCESS EVALUATION; SUMMATIVE EVALUATION.

formative spirituality see TRANSCENDENCE THERAPY.

formative tendency the general drive toward self-improvement, growth, and SELF-ACTUALIZATION hypothesized by Carl ROGERS in his CLIENT-CENTERED THERAPY.

formboard test a performance test in which the individual fits blocks or cut-outs of various shapes into depressions in a board.

form discrimination the ability to use one's senses, primarily vision and touch, to judge the shape, size, texture, and other features of an object.

form distortion a change in an image that results from the optical qualities of the eye or an artificial lens, so that the image appears different from the stimulus that gave rise to it.

formes frustes indefinite or atypical symptoms or types of a disease. [French, "coarse forms"]

form–function distinction a distinction between two fundamentally different ways of analyzing language, one with respect to its structural properties (**form**) and the other with respect to its communicative properties (**function**). So, for example, a formal analysis of the utterance *Where are the pretzels?* would point to the use of *where* and the auxiliary verb *be* to frame a *wh-* question and the agreement between that verb and the subject *pretzels*; a functional analysis would need to judge whether the utterance is a request for information or a request for action. See FORMAL GRAMMAR; FUNCTIONAL GRAMMAR.

formication *n.* an acutely distressing sensation of ants or other insects crawling on the skin. It is a tactile (haptic) hallucination that occurs in cocaine abuse and delirious states associated with acute alcoholic hallucinosis, meningitis, rheumatic fever, scarlet fever, diphtheria, and other infectious disorders. See also ACAROPHOBIA.

formicophilia *n.* sexual interest and pleasure derived from small animals, insects, or snails, which sometimes involves having these creatures placed on the genitals.

form perception the perception of two-dimensional retinal images as coherent three-dimensional forms and entities, such that elements of an object are bound together into a coherent percept that stands apart from the background and from other objects. See GESTALT.

form quality in GESTALT PSYCHOLOGY, the emergent character of a gestalt, or whole, that makes it recognizable even after transformations. For example, a musical chord remains recognizable even after being transposed to a different key.

forms of address conventional verbal formulas by which individuals address one another in written or spoken communication, for example, *Sir, Your Excellency, Mrs. Jones, Darling.* The forms used will reflect the relationship of those using them in various ways: for example, whether they are of equal or unequal status; whether they are strangers, acquaintances, or intimates; and whether they wish to signal warmth, politeness, or displeasure. Certain forms of address may also be prescribed in specific situations, such as a courtroom. Very hierarchical and conservative societies (or parts of society) will often have elaborate conventions about the correct form to use when addressing those holding particular ranks or offices. In some languages, such as French and German, the form of the second person pronoun used (*tu* or *Du* as opposed to *vous* or *Sie*) will also be significant.

fornication *n.* voluntary sexual intercourse between any two people who are not married to each other. The legal definition varies in different areas.

fornix *n.* (*pl.* **fornices**) a long tract of nerve fibers in the brain that forms an arch between the HIPPOCAMPUS and the HYPOTHALAMUS. It is an efferent pathway of the hippocampus, projecting chiefly to the MAMMILLARY BODIES.

FORTRAN *n.* FOR(mula) TRAN(slation) (language): a computer programming language, begun in the late 1950s, that is used primarily for mathematical modeling and problem solving.

forward association the formation of an associative link between one item and an item that follows it in a series or sequence. Compare BACKWARD ASSOCIATION.

forward conditioning in PAVLOVIAN CONDITIONING, the PAIRING of two stimuli such that the conditioned stimulus is presented before the unconditioned stimulus. Also called **forward pairing**. Compare BACKWARD CONDITIONING.

forward-conduction law see LAW OF FORWARD CONDUCTION.

forward displacement in parapsychology experiments using ZENER CARDS or similar targets, a result in which the participant's "call" or guess matches the outcome of the next trial in the series, rather than the current one. If this occurs consistently, it may be cited as evidence of PRECOGNITION. Compare BACKWARD DISPLACEMENT.

forward masking see MASKING.

forward pairing see FORWARD CONDITIONING.

forward selection a variable selection (model building) technique used in MULTIPLE REGRESSION in which variables are added to the model in the order of their predictive power. Also called **forward stepwise regression**.

fossa *n.* (*pl.* **fossae**) a hollow or depressed area. In neuroanatomy, fossae range from relatively large areas, such as the **anterior fossa**, **middle fossa**, and **posterior fossa** in the base of the cranium for the lobes of the brain, to small regions, such as the **ethmoid fossa** for the OLFACTORY BULB and the **hypophyseal fossa** for the pituitary gland.

fossil *n.* the remains or traces of an organism that lived in the past, often the remote past. Usually only the hard parts of organisms become fossilized (e.g., bones, shells, or wood), but under certain circumstances an entire organism is preserved. In some cases the organism has been turned into stone, a process called **petrification**.

fossilization *n.* in second-language acquisition, an intermediate state at which the learner's development ceases short of the attainment of full nativelike proficiency. See also IDIOLECT; INTERLANGUAGE; LANGUAGE TRANSFER. **—fossilize** *vb.*

foster care temporary care provided to children in settings outside their family of origin and by individuals other than their natural or adoptive parents. For example, a child might be placed in foster care while awaiting adoption or while a single parent is hospitalized or incarcerated. Typically, a child is placed with a family approved for this purpose by a public child welfare agency. See also ADULT FOSTER CARE.

foster-child fantasy the childhood belief or fantasy that the parents are actually adoptive or foster parents. See FAMILY ROMANCE.

foster home 1. a home for the temporary placement of children whose parents are unavailable or incapable of proper care. **2.** a home in which a person with a mental or physical impairment is placed by a social agency for purposes of care and sustenance. The foster family is usually paid by the agency, and the placement may be temporary or permanent. See ADULT FOSTER CARE.

fostering *n.* the process of providing care in a family environment to children or others to whom one is not related. See ADULT FOSTER CARE; FOSTER CARE.

foster placement see FOSTER CARE.

foul *adj.* **1.** denoting an odor quality that in the ZWAARDEMAKER SMELL SYSTEM is associated with bedbugs and French marigolds. **2.** denoting one of the primary odor qualities in HENNING'S ODOR PRISM.

founder effect the occurrence of a mutation at increased frequency in a population because of the presence of that mutation in the population's ancestral founders. The presence of a founder effect gives a characteristic genetic makeup and can allow for tracing of the migration of a particular ethnic group or population over time. Founder effects have been found for mutations predisposing to breast, ovarian, and colon cancer among Eastern European Jewish groups and Scandinavian and Icelandic populations, for example.

Four As see FUNDAMENTAL SYMPTOMS.

four-card selection problem a problem-solving task involving four cards, each with a letter on one side and a number on the other, and a rule that is supposed to govern their correlation (e.g., if the letter is a vowel, then the number should be even). One side of each card is shown (e.g., the cards might show E D 3 8), and the solver is asked which cards must be turned over to determine if the rule has been followed. The great majority of participants fail to realize that the only way to confirm the rule is to check those instances in which it could have been breached (i.e., in the example given, by turning over E and 3). See CONFIRMATION BIAS. Also called **Wason task**. [developed by British psychologist Peter Cathcart Wason (1924–2003)]

four-day week a work schedule that arranges, for example, a standard 40-hour employment week into four 10-hour days rather than five 8-hour days.

four-fifths rule an arbitrary rule of thumb for determining a prima facie case of discrimination, as set forth in the UNIFORM GUIDELINES FOR EMPLOYEE SELECTION PROCEDURES. If the employer hires a protected group (e.g., an ethnic minority, women) at a rate that is less than four-fifths the rate at which the majority group (i.e., White males) is hired, the company must justify its hiring procedures by showing that they are job-related or of business necessity. If justification cannot be provided, the employer may be open to a charge of violating civil-rights laws. See also ADVERSE IMPACT; AFFIRMATIVE ACTION; EQUAL EMPLOYMENT OPPORTUNITY COMMISSION; EQUAL OPPORTUNITY.

fourfold table a 2 × 2 CONTINGENCY TABLE.

four goals of education a passion for learning, a passion for living, compassion for a larger society, and willingness to develop the unique aspects of one's own personality. [as stated by U.S. educator Marilyn Wherry]

Fourier analysis the mathematical analysis of complex waveforms using the fact that they can be expressed as an infinite sum of sine and cosine functions (a **Fourier series**). A **Fourier transform** is a mathematical operation that analyzes any waveform into a set of simple waveforms with different frequencies and amplitudes. The reconstruction of complex waveforms from simple components is called **Fourier synthesis**. Fourier analysis is particularly important in the study of sound (see SOUND SPECTRUM), and Fourier analysis and synthesis are important for the theoretical understanding of visual analysis. [Jean Baptiste Joseph **Fourier** (1768–1830), French mathematician and physicist]

Fourier spectrum a graph of amplitude as a function of frequency for all the sine waves that comprise a FOURIER ANALYSIS of an image. [Jean Baptiste Joseph **Fourier**]

fourth cranial nerve see TROCHLEAR NERVE.

fourth ventricle see VENTRICLE.

fovea centralis a small depression in the retina on which the lens normally focuses an image most clearly. It is also the portion of the retina in which RETINAL CONE cells are most concentrated. Also called **fovea**. **—foveal** *adj.*

foveal sparing see VISUAL FIELD SPARING.

foveal vision see CENTRAL VISION.

FR abbreviation for fixed ratio (see FIXED-RATIO SCHEDULE).

fractional antedating goal response a reaction that develops progressively earlier in conditioning a series of responses and may become a CONDITIONED STIMULUS for subsequent responses.

fractional escape see ESCAPE TITRATION.

fractional factorial design an experimental design in which some higher order interactions are intentionally confounded with lower order interactions in order to reduce the total number of CELLS in the design. See CONFOUNDS.

fractional replication design an experimental design in which every level of each factor (INDEPENDENT VARIABLE) is not assessed in combination with every level of every other factor. There is intentional confounding in order to make the design more economical. However, the pattern of combinations not assessed is carefully specified so that all confounding can be identified. A LATIN SQUARE design is a common example of a fractional replication design. See also CONFOUNDS.

fractionation *n.* a psychophysical procedure to scale the magnitude of sensations. A participant might be asked to adjust a light so that it seems half as bright as a comparison light, that is, to bisect it. This particular type of fractionation, in which an observer adjusts a variable stimulus to be half that of a standard stimulus, is called the **halving method**.

fragile X chromosome a genetic defect that affects mostly male offspring and is associated with mental retardation. The disorder is so named because of the tendency of the long arm of the X chromosome to break when the defect is present, entailing alteration in the *FMR1* gene, at locus Xq27. Fragile X chromosome is the second most prevalent cause, after DOWN SYNDROME, of mental retardation among males. There are no definitive physical characteristics, and diagnosis requires molecular genetic testing. Also called **fragile X syndrome**.

fragmentary delusion a disorganized, undeveloped DELUSION or a series of disconnected delusions that is inconsistent and illogical. Also called **unsystematized delusion**. Compare SYSTEMATIZED DELUSION.

fragmentation *n.* division or separation into pieces or fragments, particularly a psychological disturbance in which thoughts or actions that are normally integrated are split apart, as in LOOSENING OF ASSOCIATIONS, vagueness of ideas, or bizarre actions.

fragmentation of thinking a disturbance of association that is considered by some authorities to be a primary symptom of schizophrenia. The thinking processes become confused to the point that complete actions or ideas are not possible. In a mild form, the individual may give general rather than specific answers to questions.

fragrant *adj.* **1.** in the ZWAARDEMAKER SMELL SYSTEM, denoting an odor quality that is smelled in flowers and vanilla. **2.** denoting one of the four primary odor qualities in the CROCKER–HENDERSON ODOR SYSTEM.

frame *n.* **1.** in artificial intelligence, a KNOWLEDGE REPRESENTATION scheme, much like an object system, used to represent and structure knowledge for a computational system. [first proposed in 1981 by U.S. mathematician and computer scientist Marvin Minsky (1927–)] **2.** in education, see PROGRAMMED INSTRUCTION; LINEAR PROGRAM.

frame-of-orientation need the need to develop or synthesize one's major assumptions, ideas, and values into a coherent worldview. The term was introduced by Erich FROMM, who distinguished between frames of reference based on reason and those based on subjective distortions, superstition, or myth.

frame of reference 1. in social psychology, the set of assumptions or criteria by which a person or group judges ideas, actions, and experiences. A frame of reference can often limit or distort perception, as in the case of PREJUDICE and STEREOTYPES. **2.** in cognitive psychology, a set of parameters defining either a particular mental SCHEMA or the wider COGNITIVE STRUCTURE by which an individual perceives and evaluates the world. See also CONCEPTUAL SYSTEM; PERCEPTUAL SET.

frame-of-reference training training provided to those responsible for EMPLOYEE EVALUATION with the aim of improving the accuracy of their performance ratings. It involves providing raters with (a) a common reference standard to be used in performing evaluations and (b) practice in identifying good, average, and poor performances as defined by this standard.

frame problem a technical difficulty arising in ARTIFICIAL INTELLIGENCE and COMPUTATIONAL MODELS of human cognition involving the specification of the persistence of states that form the context in which thought takes place. The frame problem is essentially a question of how to use FORMAL LOGIC to specify or describe efficiently what remains unchanged in a given situation involving change, that is, what are the non-effects of a particular action on the properties of a situation (e.g., painting an object will not alter its position). In COGNITIVE PSYCHOLOGY and COGNITIVE SCIENCE, the term has been extended to the difficulty of modeling the human ability to quickly generate reasonable hypotheses making sense of events in the environment and to respond sensibly to incoming information, using relevant knowledge to guide the formation of new beliefs. [described by U.S. philosopher and psychologist Jerry Alan Fodor (1935–)]

framing *n.* the process of defining the context or issues surrounding a question, problem, or event in a way that serves to influence how the context or issues are perceived and evaluated. Also called **framing effect**. See also REFRAMING.

framing effect 1. see ATMOSPHERE EFFECT. **2.** see FRAMING.

Framingham Heart Study a large-scale, long-range survey focused on understanding, preventing, and treating cardiovascular disease. Conducted for over 50 years, the study has involved data collection from three generations of residents of the town of Framingham, Massachusetts. The data have identified primary risk factors involved with heart disease and stroke, such as cigarette smoking, physical inactivity, obesity, high cholesterol levels, diabetes, and hypertension. The study is regarded as one of the most reliable of its kind because it is of prospective design; that is, it enrolled people who were originally free of heart disease and recorded the dietary and other habits of the participants before signs of heart disease appeared.

Franschetti–Zwahlen–Klein syndrome see TREACHER COLLINS SYNDROME. [Adolphe **Franschetti** (1896–1968), Swiss ophthalmologist]

Fraser syndrome (**Fraser–François syndrome**) see CYCLOPIA. [George R. **Fraser** (1932–), British geneticist; Jules **François** (1907–1984), Belgian ophthalmologist]

fraternalistic relative deprivation see RELATIVE DEPRIVATION.

fraternal twins see DIZYGOTIC TWINS.

F ratio (symbol: *F*) in an ANALYSIS OF VARIANCE or a MULTIVARIATE ANALYSIS OF VARIANCE, the ratio of explained to unexplained variance; that is, the ratio of BETWEEN-GROUPS VARIANCE to WITHIN-GROUP VARIANCE. Also called **F statistic**; **F value**.

free and appropriate public education provisions of U.S. educational law requiring that SPECIAL EDUCATION and related services will be provided to each student with a disability at no cost to the student or parents. The services provided must meet standards established by the student's state of residence and be consistent with decisions that are made at an INDIVIDUALIZED EDUCATION PROGRAM (IEP) meeting and specified in a written IEP.

free association a basic process in PSYCHOANALYSIS and other forms of PSYCHODYNAMIC PSYCHOTHERAPY, in which the patient is encouraged to verbalize freely whatever thoughts come to mind, no matter how embarrassing, illogical, or irrelevant, without censorship or selection by the therapist. The object is to allow unconscious material, such as traumatic experiences or threatening impulses, and otherwise inhibited thoughts and emotions to come to the surface where they can be interpreted. Free association is also posited to help the patient discharge some of the feelings that have given this material excessive control over him or her. See BASIC RULE; VERBALIZATION.

free-association test a test in which participants are offered a stimulus word and are expected to respond as quickly as possible with a word they associate with the stimulus.

freebase 1. *n.* a highly concentrated, chemically altered form of COCAINE that is prepared by treating cocaine with ether. It is ingested by smoking. **2.** *vb.* to smoke this form of cocaine.

Freedom from Distractibility Index an index calculated on the WECHSLER ADULT INTELLIGENCE SCALE and other Wechsler tests that measures short-term attention and concentration.

freedom to withdraw the right of a research participant to drop out of an experiment at any time.

free energy in psychoanalytic theory, PSYCHIC ENERGY that is located in the ID, is mobile, and is associated with PRIMARY PROCESSES. Compare BOUND ENERGY.

free feeding see AD LIB.

free-feeding weight the body weight achieved by laboratory animals when given unrestricted access to food and water for an extended period.

free field in acoustics, a sound field that has no reflective boundaries.

free-floating anxiety 1. a diffuse, chronic sense of uneasiness and apprehension not directed toward any specific situation or object. It may be a characteristic of a number of anxiety disorders, in particular GENERALIZED ANXIETY DISORDER. **2.** in psychoanalysis, general feelings of distress that have been set free from the original circumstances that caused them.

free-floating attention in psychoanalysis and in other forms of psychodynamic psychotherapy, the analyst's or therapist's state of evenly suspended attention during the therapeutic session. This attention does not focus on any one thing the client says, but allows the analyst or therapist to listen to all the material being presented and tune into the client's affects and unconscious ideas. Also called **evenly hovering attention**.

free-floating emotion a diffuse, generalized emotional state that does not appear to be associated with any specific cause. A common example is FREE-FLOATING ANXIETY.

free-floating fear a generalized sense of fear that is not directed toward a particular object or situation.

free love the practice of engaging in sexual relationships without legal ties or any other commitment to fidelity or permanence. Advocates of free love emphasize the individual's right to sexual expression and have sometimes argued for alternative forms of marriage and family relationships.

free morpheme in linguistics, a MORPHEME that can stand alone, as a word in its own right. Free morphemes are contrasted with BOUND MORPHEMES, such as the plural *-s*, which can only appear in combination.

free nerve ending a branched ending of an afferent neuron found in the skin and believed to be a pain or temperature receptor.

free operant a response to a situation that occurs freely at any time. See OPERANT.

free-operant avoidance see SIDMAN AVOIDANCE SCHEDULE.

free play play that is not controlled or directed by a group leader, teacher, or play therapist. Compare ORGANIZED PLAY.

free recall a type of memory experiment in which a list of items is presented one at a time and participants attempt to remember them in any order. The first and last items presented are best remembered: Proponents of the DUAL-STORE MODEL OF MEMORY attribute this to the fact that the last items are still in SHORT-TERM MEMORY, and hence recoverable, while the first items received the most REHEARSAL and were transferred to LONG-TERM MEMORY. Compare RECOGNITION METHOD.

free-response test a type of examination in which answers are constructed by the student. SHORT-ANSWER TESTS and ESSAY TESTS are examples. This type of test is sometimes described as a SUBJECTIVE TEST. Compare FORCED-RESPONSE TEST.

free rider an individual who contributes little or nothing to a joint endeavor but nonetheless garners the same benefits as members who contribute their fair share. The resentment caused by free riders can hamper the efficiency of a group working on a collective task.

free-running rhythm a cycle of behavior or physiological activity that occurs if external stimuli do not provide ENTRAINMENT. See also BIOLOGICAL RHYTHM.

free variation in linguistics, the state in which variant forms of the same linguistic unit appear on an apparently random basis. The term is most often used in phonology. For example, in colloquial speech many speakers will articulate or not articulate the final stop consonant of the past-tense morpheme *-ed* (as in *walked, stalked,* etc.) in an entirely arbitrary way. Compare COMPLEMENTARY DISTRIBUTION.

free will the power or capacity of a human being for self-direction. The function of the WILL is to be inclined or disposed toward an idea or action. The concept of free will thus suggests that inclinations, dispositions, thoughts, and actions are not determined entirely by forces over which people have no independent directing influence. Free will is generally seen as necessary for moral action and responsibility and is implied by much of our everyday experience, in which we are conscious of having the power to do or forbear (see PARADOX OF FREEDOM). However, it has often been dismissed as illusory by advocates of DETERMINISM, who hold that all occurrences, including human actions, are predetermined. See also AGENT; VOLITION.

freezing behavior a form of passive avoidance in which the individual remains motionless and makes no effort to run or hide. The behavior is most often observed as a severe reaction to a threatening situation. Freezing behavior occurs in wild animals in response to ALARM CALLS signifying the approach of a predator or other risk. See also IMMOBILITY.

Fregoli's phenomenon a MISIDENTIFICATION SYNDROME in which an individual identifies a persecutor successively in different people known to him or her (e.g., a neighbor, doctor, attendant), on the delusional assumption that the persecutor is capable of changing faces. [first identified in 1927 and named for Italian actor Leopoldo **Fregoli** (1867–1936), who was renowned for his ability to alter his appearance]

French kiss a type of sexual arousal in which the participants kiss with their mouths open so that their tongues can touch. Also called **soul kiss**; **tongue kiss**.

frenulum *n.* (*pl.* **frenula**) any membranous fold that supports or restrains an anatomical part, for example, the membrane under the tongue (**lingual frenulum** or **frenum**) or the fold of tissue that limits the backward movement of the FORESKIN. Also called **frenum**.

frenzy *n.* a temporary state of wild excitement and mental agitation, at times including violent behavior. It has been associated with MANIA and is sometimes considered synonymous with this term.

frequency *n.* the number of repetitions of a periodic

waveform in a given unit of time. In acoustics, the frequency of a PURE TONE is the number of cycles of a sinusoidal pressure variation that occur in one second. The standard measure of frequency is the hertz (Hz); this replaces, and is equivalent to, cycles per second (cps). For complex periodic waveforms, that is, those consisting of more than one frequency component (e.g., a square wave), the "frequency" is the rate of repetition of the waveform and is more appropriately called the **fundamental frequency** (or **fundamental tone**, or simply the **fundamental**). The **period** of a waveform is the time to complete one repetition and is the reciprocal of the frequency (or fundamental frequency). For waveforms that are not periodic, such as white NOISE, the frequency is undefined. In such cases the spectral characteristics should be described. See also SOUND SPECTRUM.

frequency analysis analysis of the frequency changes in EVENT-RELATED POTENTIALS (ERPs).

frequency curve a smoothed curve, derived from empirical data, that represents the DENSITY FUNCTION of the population from which the sample was drawn.

frequency discrimination the ability to detect a change in the frequency of a PURE TONE. See also PITCH DISCRIMINATION.

frequency distribution a plot of the frequency of occurrence of scores of various sizes, arranged from lowest to highest score.

frequency judgment a participant's judgment of how many times a particular stimulus was presented during a test. Such judgments are used in research on memory and sensory thresholds. See also WORD-FREQUENCY STUDY.

frequency law see LAW OF FREQUENCY.

frequency modulation see MODULATION.

frequency of response the number of countable responses per unit of time. For example, if an individual pressed a telegraph key 500 times in 5 min, the frequency of response would be 100 per minute.

frequency polygon a graph depicting a statistical distribution, made up of lines connecting the peaks of adjacent intervals.

frequency principle the principle that the greater the intensity of stimulation, the greater the frequency of nerve impulses elicited, and the more intense the response of the organism.

frequency selectivity the property of a system that enables it to be "tuned" to respond better to certain frequencies than to others. The degree of selectivity of such filtering is sometimes specified as Q, which is the center or best frequency of a filter divided by its bandwidth: Higher values of Q correspond to higher frequency selectivity. The frequency selectivity of the auditory system is a fundamental aspect of hearing and has been a major research theme for many decades. Also called **bandwidth selectivity**. See AUDITORY FILTER; CRITICAL BAND; TONOTOPIC ORGANIZATION; TUNING CURVE.

frequency table a numerical summary of the frequency of occurrences of particular values of a measurement.

Freud, Anna (1895–1982) Austrian-born British psychoanalyst. The youngest daughter of Sigmund FREUD, Anna Freud trained first as an elementary school teacher and then as a psychoanalyst in Vienna. She made many original contributions to both the theory and practice of psychoanalysis, particularly through her studies of DEFENSE MECHANISMS (*The Ego and the Mechanisms of Defense*, 1936). She was a pioneer in the field of CHILD ANALYSIS, especially through her work at the Hampstead Clinic in England, to which she moved after the Nazis invaded Austria in 1938. Although an orthodox psychoanalyst in many respects, she devoted more attention than most to the topic of normal development; this research resulted in her 1965 book, *Normality and Pathology in Childhood*. Anna Freud held numerous administrative posts during her career; among them, she served as chair of the prestigious Vienna Psychoanalytic Society in the 1920s and 1930s, until it disbanded at the time of the Nazi invasion. See also METAPSYCHOLOGICAL PROFILE.

Freud, Sigmund (1856–1939) Austrian neurologist and psychiatrist, who invented the technique of PSYCHOANALYSIS. Freud earned a doctorate in medicine in 1881 from the University of Vienna, where he studied under psychologist Franz Brentano (1838–1917) and physiologist Ernst Brücke (1819–1892). He began his professional life as a neurologist, making significant contribu-tions to that field, but turned his full attention to the psychological approach to mental disorders, such as hysteria, after witnessing demonstrations of hypnosis in Paris by French physician Jean-Martin Charcot (1825–1893). After discarding hypnosis as a technique limited to removal of symptoms, Freud developed the method of FREE ASSOCIATION, which led to recognition of UNCONSCIOUS sexual conflicts and REPRESSIONS as the major factors in neuroses. These concepts became the cornerstones of the new discipline that he called psychoanalysis. This discipline focused on such procedures as (a) the interpretation of dreams in terms of hostile or sexual feelings stemming from childhood, (b) analysis of resistances and the relationship between therapist and patient, and (c) a study of the patient's present symptomatology in terms of psychosexual development and early experiences. The goal of this process, which takes many months or years, was not merely to eliminate symptoms, but to restructure the patient's entire psyche. Freud also applied his psychoanalytic method to the study of historical figures, such as Leonardo da Vinci, and to the exploration of primitive cultures, drawing a parallel between the childhood of the individual and the "childhood" of the human race. To disseminate his views, which were regarded as highly controversial at the time (and have remained so), he taught many disciples, was instrumental in establishing the first psychoanalytic association, and published a series of books, including *The Interpretation of Dreams* (1900), *Three Essays on the Theory of Sexuality* (1905), *Totem and Taboo* (1913), *Beyond the Pleasure Principle* (1920), and *The Ego and the Id* (1923). See also FREUDIAN THEORY OF PERSONALITY; NEO-FREUDIAN. —**Freudian** *adj.*

Freudian approach (**Freudianism**) see PSYCHOANALYSIS.

Freudian slip in the popular understanding of psychoanalytic theory, an unconscious error or oversight in writing, speech, or action that is held to be caused by unacceptable impulses breaking through the EGO's defenses and exposing the individual's true wishes or feelings. See PARAPRAXIS; SLIP OF THE TONGUE; SYMPTOMATIC ACT. [Sigmund FREUD]

Freudian theory of personality the general psychoanalytic concept that character and personality are the product of experiences and FIXATIONS stemming from the early stages of PSYCHOSEXUAL DEVELOPMENT. See PSYCHOANALYSIS. [Sigmund FREUD]

Frey esthesiometer a device used to measure the minimum intensity of a pressure stimulus required to produce a sensation in the skin. It consists of bristles of different lengths and thicknesses (called **von Frey hairs**) that are applied to different regions of the skin with just enough force to bend the bristle.[Maximilian von **Frey** (1852–1932), German physiologist]

fricative 1. *adj.* denoting a speech sound made by forcing a stream of air through a narrow opening of the vocal tract against one or more surfaces, particularly the hard palate, ALVEOLAR RIDGE, teeth, or lips. A fricative has high-frequency vibrations. It may be VOICED (e.g., [v], [z], [th]) or UNVOICED (e.g., [f], [s], [sh]). **2.** *n.* a fricative speech sound.

Friedman test a nonparametric test of the equality of medians in *J* repeated measures of a matched group. [Herbert **Friedman**, 21st-century U.S. psychologist]

Friedreich's ataxia a hereditary, progressive syndrome of muscular incoordination (see ATAXIA) that results from the degeneration of nerve tissue in the spinal cord and of nerves that control muscle movement in the arms and legs. It is an AUTOSOMAL RECESSIVE condition that first affects the legs and then the arms and trunk. Initial symptoms typically appear in childhood or early adolescence and include difficulty in walking, an unsteady gait, and loss of reflexes. These symptoms are often accompanied by foot deformities, spinal curvature (kyphoscoliosis), involuntary, rapid eye movements (see NYSTAGMUS), and speech difficulties. Individuals with Friedreich's ataxia are usually confined to a wheelchair within 15–20 years after symptom onset, and most die in early adulthood. Also called **hereditary ataxia**. [Nikolaus **Friedreich** (1825–1882), German neurologist]

friendship *n.* a voluntary relationship between two or more people that is relatively long-lasting and in which those involved tend to be concerned with meeting the others' needs and interests as well as satisfying their own desires. Friendships frequently develop through shared experiences in which the people involved learn that their association with one another is mutually gratifying.

friendship network the interconnected relationships among a group of friends who provide social and emotional support for each other.

fright *n.* the emotional reaction that arises in the face of a dangerous or potentially dangerous situation or encounter. Fright differs from FEAR in that the danger is usually immediate, physical, concrete, and overwhelming. Physiological changes in the body associated with fright include trembling, widening of the eyes, and drawing away from the fear-producing stimulus.

frigidity *n.* impairment of sexual desire or inability to achieve full sexual gratification in a woman. The term is applied to a wide range of conditions, including mild disinterest in sexual relations, sexual interest without orgasm, and active aversion to sexual activity. See DYSPAREUNIA; HYPOACTIVE SEXUAL DESIRE DISORDER; SEXUAL AVERSION DISORDER; VAGINISMUS. **—frigid** *adj.*

fringe consciousness aspects of experience that lack focal perceptual qualities (e.g., color, texture, taste) but are nevertheless reported with a high degree of confidence and accuracy. Fringe experiences vary widely, from feelings of EFFORTFULNESS, TIP-OF-THE-TONGUE PHENOMENA, and FEELINGS OF KNOWING to mystical feelings.

fringe–focus structure a model of consciousness in which the conscious contents typically have a focal component, with clear and discriminable sensory features, and a "fringe-conscious" component, such as FEELINGS OF KNOWING (see FRINGE CONSCIOUSNESS).

fringe of consciousness see FRINGE CONSCIOUSNESS.

fringer *n.* a person on the margins of a social group, who is neither genuinely accepted nor clearly excluded.

Fröbelism *n.* a method of education developed by German educator Friedrich Fröbel (1782–1852), the originator of the kindergarten system. He believed that it was important for a child's development to have an open environment that encouraged learning and physical activity.

Fröhlich's syndrome a disorder caused by underfunctioning of the anterior lobe of the pituitary gland (**hypopituitarism**). Major symptoms are underdeveloped genital organs and secondary sexual characteristics, general sluggishness, obesity, and in some cases polyuria (frequent urination), polydipsia (frequent consumption of liquids), and mild mental retardation. Also called **adiposogenital dystrophy**; **adiposogenitalism**; **Launois–Cleret syndrome**. [Alfred **Fröhlich** (1871–1953), Austrian neurologist]

Fromm, Erich (1900–1980) German psychoanalyst. Fromm earned a doctorate at the University of Heidelberg in 1922 before training as a psychoanalyst in Berlin and Munich. The bulk of his career was spent in the United States. Fromm developed a broad cultural, yet personal, approach focused on (a) the search for meaning, (b) the development of personality and socially productive relationships, and (c) the enrichment of life through character, the need to belong, the development of individuality, and the replacement of a commercial MARKETING ORIENTATION with a sane society. This enrichment of life, he believed, should be built around cooperation, caring, and the ability to love. These concepts were vividly expressed in such books as *Man for Himself* (1947), *The Sane Society* (1955), and *The Art of Loving* (1956).

frontal *adj.* **1.** pertaining to the front, or anterior, side or aspect of the body or of an organ, such as the brain. **2.** pertaining to the frontal bone of the skull, or forehead.

frontal association area see PREFRONTAL CORTEX.

frontal cortex the most anterior part of the CEREBRAL CORTEX. See also PREFRONTAL CORTEX.

frontal eye-field lesion a lesion, produced surgically or by injury, in a region of the brain anterior to the motor area involved in head and eye movements. Such a lesion may result in unilateral blindness with the effect observed on the side opposite the lesion.

frontalis muscle a muscle that covers the scalp beneath the skin of the forehead.

frontal lisp see LISP.

frontal lobe one of the four main lobes of each cerebral hemisphere of the brain, lying in front of the CENTRAL SULCUS. It is concerned with motor and higher order EXECUTIVE FUNCTIONS. See CEREBRUM.

frontal lobe syndrome a mental disorder due to lesions in the frontal lobe, characterized by such symptoms as impairment of purposeful behavior, emotional lability, impairment in social judgment, perseveration, and impulse control, difficulty with abstract thinking, and apathy. The symptoms vary with the size and location of the lesion.

frontal lobotomy a surgical procedure in which nerve fibers connecting the frontal lobes with the rest of the brain are cut or portions of the frontal lobe are removed. The procedure was formerly used to treat depression, aggression, anxiety, schizophrenia, and severe pain but has been discredited since the 1950s. Also called **lobotomy**. See also LEUKOTOMY.

frontal plane see CORONAL PLANE.

frontal release signs the appearance in adults with frontal lobe lesions of certain primitive reflexes that are normally present only in infants and disappear within the first few months of life. These reflexes include the grasp, rooting, and sucking reflexes.

frontal section see CORONAL SECTION.

front-clipping *n.* see CLIPPING.

frotteurism *n.* in *DSM–IV–TR*, a PARAPHILIA in which an individual deliberately and persistently seeks sexual excitement by rubbing against other people. This may occur as apparently accidental contact in crowded public settings, such as elevators or lines. The person displaying this type of behavior is called a **frotteur** or a **rubber**. Also called **frottage**.

frozen form see IDIOM.

frozen noise a recorded sample of NOISE.

fruity *adj.* denoting one of the primary odor qualities in HENNING'S ODOR PRISM.

frustration *n.* **1.** the thwarting of impulses or actions that prevents individuals from obtaining something they have been led to expect based on past experience, as when a hungry animal is prevented from obtaining food that it can see or smell or when a child is prevented from playing with a visible toy. Internal forces can include motivational conflicts and inhibitions; external forces can include the actions of other individuals, admonitions of parents or others, and the rules of society. **2.** the emotional state an individual experiences when such thwarting occurs. **3.** in psychoanalytic theory, the damming up of PSYCHIC ENERGY, which then seeks an outlet in wish-fulfilling fantasies and dreams or in various neurotic symptoms. **—frustrate** *vb.*

frustration–aggression hypothesis the theory, advanced in 1939 by U.S. social scientist John Dollard (1900–1980) and colleagues, that (a) frustration always produces an aggressive urge and (b) aggression is always the result of prior frustrations. U.S. psychologist Neal MILLER, one of the proponents of this theory, later noted that frustration can lead to several kinds of actions, but maintained that the urge to aggression will become more dominant as the thwarting continues. In 1989 U.S. psychologist Leonard Berkowitz (1926–) proposed that the frustration must be decidedly unpleasant in order to evoke an aggressive urge. Also called **aggression–frustration hypothesis**.

frustration–regression hypothesis the theory that frustration often leads to behavior characteristic of a much earlier period of life (see REGRESSION). [proposed in 1941 by U.S. psychologists Roger G. Barker (1903–1990), Tamara Dembo (1902–1993), and Kurt LEWIN]

frustration tolerance the ability of an individual to endure tension, to preserve relative equanimity on encountering obstacles, and to delay gratification. The growth of adequate frustration tolerance is a feature of normal cognitive and affective development; poor frustration tolerance typically indicates developmental weaknesses or deteriorations and losses in more adaptive levels that may be strengthened or revived through therapeutic intervention.

frustrative nonreward hypothesis the proposition that consistently withholding REINFORCEMENT of responses during operant or instrumental conditioning leads to an internal state of frustration manifested in a variety of emotional responses, such as an aggressive attitude toward further stimuli.

Frye test a test for the admissibility in U.S. courts of scientific evidence, derived from the case *Frye v. United States* (1923) in which an early form of lie-detector evidence (see POLYGRAPH) was ruled inadmissible because it had not yet "gained general acceptance in the field in which it belongs." This "general acceptance" test became the chief standard for ruling on admissibility of scientific evidence in both state and federal courts until 1993, when it was replaced by the DAUBERT TEST.

FSH abbreviation for FOLLICLE-STIMULATING HORMONE.

FSS abbreviation for FEAR SURVEY SCHEDULE.

F statistic see F RATIO.

F_{max} statistic a statistic used for testing the hypothesis of HOMOGENEITY OF VARIANCE in k independently sampled populations.

F test any hypothesis test that relies on the sampling distribution, under the NULL HYPOTHESIS, being distributed as the F DISTRIBUTION, which results in an F RATIO.

FTT abbreviation for FAILURE TO THRIVE.

fugitive literature research findings that have not been published in archival sources, such as dissertations, papers presented at meetings, papers either not submitted or rejected for publication, and technical reports.

fugue *n.* **1.** see DISSOCIATIVE FUGUE. **2.** a brief period in which an individual appears to be in a semiconscious state, sometimes engaging in routine activity, and subsequently has no memory for events during that period. This condition is typically associated with epilepsy but may occur in other conditions, such as alcohol intoxication and catatonic excitement.

fulfillment *n.* the actual or felt satisfaction of needs and desires, or the attainment of aspirations. See also WISH-FULFILLMENT. **—fulfill** *vb.*

fulfillment model a basic type of personality theory based on the assumption that the primary motivation for behavior is self-fulfillment, as manifest in a drive to fulfill one's innate potential. Humanistic approaches to psychology, as exemplified by the work of Abraham MASLOW and Carl ROGERS, are prominent examples of the fulfillment model. [introduced by U.S. psychologist Salvatore R. Maddi (1933–)]

Fullerton–Cattell law a generalization that errors of observation and DIFFERENCE THRESHOLD are proportional to the square root of the magnitude of the stimulus. The Fullerton–Cattell law was proposed as a replacement for WEBER'S LAW. [George S. **Fullerton** (1859–1925), U.S. philosopher; James McKeen CATTELL]

full inclusion the practice of providing children with disabilities (intellectual, physical, or behavioral) with services in their home school and of placing them in a regular classroom on a full-time basis. See also COMMUNITY INCLUSION; LEAST RESTRICTIVE ENVIRONMENT; MAINSTREAMING.

fully functioning person a person with a healthy personality, who experiences freedom of choice and action, is creative, and exhibits the qualities of EXISTENTIAL LIVING. [as defined in the CLIENT-CENTERED THERAPY of Carl ROGERS]

fun *n.* a perception of pleasure and happiness brought on by achieving one's desires from an activity.

function *n.* **1.** the use or purpose of something. **2.** in biology, an activity of an organ or an organism that contributes to the organism's FITNESS, such as the secretion of a sex hormone by a gonad to prepare for reproduction or the defensive behavior of a female with young toward an intruder. **3.** (symbol: f) a mathematical procedure that relates one number, quantity, or entity to another according to a defined rule. For example, if $y = 2x + 1$, y is said to be a function of x. This is often written $y = f(x)$. Here y is the dependent variable and x is the independent variable.

functional *adj.* **1.** in psychology, denoting or referring to a disorder in which normal behavior changes without an observable organic or structural cause. See PSYCHOGENIC. **2.** more generally, based on or relating to use rather than structure.

functional activities actions associated with basic daily home and work requirements (e.g., mobility, cooking and eating, bathing, dressing, conversing, and operating simple types of equipment). Skills in performing such actions must sometimes be retaught or improved in people who have experienced neurological damage or disease. See also ACTIVITIES OF DAILY LIVING; INSTRUMENTAL ACTIVITIES OF DAILY LIVING.

functional age an individual's age as determined by measures of functional capability indexed by age-normed standards. Functional age is distinct from CHRONOLOGICAL AGE and represents a combination of physiological, psychological, and social age. In older adults it is calculated by measuring a range of variables that correlate closely with chronological age, such as eyesight, hearing, mobility, cardiopulmonary function, concentration, and memory. Following the passing of the AGE DISCRIMINATION IN EMPLOYMENT ACT, functional age, rather than chronological age, has been made a criterion for employment in some jobs. The functional age of a child is measured in terms of the developmental level he or she has reached. It may be compared with his or her chronological age as a means of gauging the existence and extent of any impairment or developmental problem.

functional amblyopia poor vision that occurs in an otherwise normal eye because of disuse or improper use of the eye during early life. Causes of functional amblyopia include STRABISMUS, ANISOMETROPIA, and sensory deprivation, when no image is allowed to reach the eye (e.g., in unilateral cataract).

functional amnesia a psychiatric disorder characterized by amnesia for autobiographical events, that is, events one has personally experienced. While loss of EPISODIC MEMORY about oneself is the hallmark of functional amnesia, in some cases SEMANTIC MEMORY about the self may also be lost, as when a person forgets who he or she is. Functional amnesia is thought to arise as a defense against anxiety and distress or as a way of escaping from specific situations. Also called **affective amnesia**.

functional analysis 1. the detailed analysis of a behavior to identify contingencies that sustain the behavior. **2.** a synthesis of a client's behavior problems and the variables that are associated with or hypothesized to cause them.

functional analytic causal model (FACM) a vector diagram of a functional analysis of an individual client that visually presents a clinician's conjectures or theories about the client's maladaptive behaviors, the objectives of those behaviors, and the variables affecting them. Use of FACM graphically organizes and elucidates contingencies affecting the design of therapeutic interventions and provides an alternative or supplement to clinical case conceptualization.

functional approach to attitudes a theoretical perspective postulating that attitudes are formed to serve one or more different functions and that these functions can influence such processes as ATTITUDE CHANGE and ATTITUDE–BEHAVIOR CONSISTENCY. See also EGO-DEFENSIVE FUNCTION OF AN ATTITUDE; KNOWLEDGE FUNCTION OF AN ATTITUDE; SOCIAL-ADJUSTIVE FUNCTION OF AN ATTITUDE; UTILITARIAN FUNCTION OF AN ATTITUDE; VALUE-EXPRESSIVE FUNCTION OF AN ATTITUDE.

functional asymmetry perceptual superiority of the eye or ear on one side of the body for certain kinds of stimuli. Studies show, for example, that the right ear usually is superior for receiving verbal material or the human voice, whereas the left ear is superior for pitch patterns, melodies, and environmental sounds. In visual asymmetry, the right half-field has superiority for verbal material, while the left half-field is superior for recognition of faces and shapes and for slope of line and depth perception.

functional autonomy the tendency for drive-motivated behavior to develop derivative drives, such that behavior may become independent of the original drive. For example, studying motivated by the need for approval may be gradually replaced by the desire for (and therefore pursuit of) knowledge for its own sake. Also called **autonomy of motives**; **functional autonomy principle**. [concept introduced by Gordon Willard ALLPORT]

functional behavioral assessment 1. an assessment approach that identifies the circumstances and consequences associated with the occurrence of a particular behavior. The circumstances (called antecedents), behavior, and consequences are typically defined in measurable terms, and combinations of particular types of antecedents and consequences may be presented systematically as part of the assessment. Thus circumstances and consequences (i.e., motivational factors) associated with increases or decreases in the particular behavior can be identified. Results of these assessments provide information of immediate utility in designing interventions or treatments to address the behavior. **2.** any of a wide variety of assessment methods used in APPLIED BEHAVIOR ANALYSIS.

functional blindness visual deterioration without any apparent change or disease affecting the structural integrity of the visual system: one of the most frequent symptoms in SOMATIZATION DISORDER. In addition to loss of acuity, visual functional phenomena may include photophobia, burning eyes, painful eyes, tired eyes, monocular diplopia (double vision), PTOSIS, BLEPHAROSPASM, CONVERGENCE problems, and severe concentric visual field constriction in one or both eyes. Despite the symptoms, the pupils continue to react to light, and the patient automatically avoids objects that would cause injury. Complete functional blindness is rare; functional AMBLYOPIA is more common, and occasionally functional HEMIANOPIA can be present. The condition was formerly known as **hysterical blindness** or **psychic blindness**.

functional brain imaging the use of BRAIN IMAGING techniques to localize areas of cognitive activation. See FUNCTIONAL MAGNETIC RESONANCE IMAGING; POSITRON EMISSION TOMOGRAPHY.

functional classification see COMPLEMENTARY CLASSIFICATION.

functional communication training a BEHAVIOR THERAPY technique used with children and adults diagnosed with developmental impairments, such as autism or mental retardation, who are exhibiting aggressive, self-injurious, or highly disruptive behavior. The technique assesses the function that the negative behavior serves and uses positive reinforcement to replace it with more appropriately adaptive communication or behavior that meets the same need.

functional conformance in ENVIRONMENTAL DESIGN, the provision of the objects and equipment required to adapt an environment to a given set of functional uses, as, for example, by furnishing a study with a desk, lights, and a comfortable chair.

functional deafness loss of hearing that is not associated with any known structural abnormality.

functional disorder a disorder for which there is no known organic basis. In psychology and psychiatry, functional disorders are improperly considered equivalent to PSYCHOGENIC DISORDERS.

functional distance the degree to which the arrangement or configuration of residential facilities influences the probability of unplanned social interaction. Physical distance can affect functional distance, as can the juxtaposition of entrances and proximity to gathering points (e.g., a lounge, common mailboxes, the intersection of paths).

functional dysmenorrhea see DYSMENORRHEA.

functional dyspareunia a sexual dysfunction of men or women in which there is recurrent and persistent genital pain during coitus. It does not include conditions caused exclusively by a physical disorder or due to lack of lubrication, FUNCTIONAL VAGINISMUS, or another mental disorder.

functional dyspepsia see DYSPEPSIA.

functional dyspnea see DYSPNEA.

functional electric stimulation (**FES**) the application of electric current to peripheral nerves through the use of electrodes in order to generate muscle contractions as a response. When multiple FES electrodes are used, the muscle contractions can create functional movements in the extremities of an individual. For example, FES has been used to enable individuals with PARAPLEGIA to pedal adapted exercise bicycles or, in combination with custom leg braces, to walk.

functional encopresis see ENCOPRESIS.

functional enuresis see ENURESIS.

functional family therapy a type of FAMILY THERAPY that focuses on both family interaction patterns and on the benefits family members may derive from problem behavior. Using reframing and COGNITIVE BEHAVIOR THERAPY methods, functional family therapy focuses primarily on at-risk and behaviorally troubled youth and their families.

functional fixedness in problem solving, the tendency to cling to set patterns and overlook possible new approaches. For example, one may overlook new and different uses for an object (see ALTERNATE-USES TEST). Compare CREATIVE THINKING; DIVERGENT THINKING.

functional grammar an approach to GRAMMAR using categories that reflect nonlinguistic factors, such as intention and social context, rather than categories based solely on a formal linguistic analysis. Compare FORMAL GRAMMAR. See also FORM–FUNCTION DISTINCTION; PRAGMATICS.

functional hearing disorders auditory impairments for which there is no known biological cause.

functional hyperinsulinism see HYPOGLYCEMIA.

Functional Independence Measure (**FIM**) an instrument used in rehabilitation to evaluate specific routine motor, cognitive, and self-care skills and provide a measure of FUNCTIONAL STATUS. It consists of 18 items related to eating, grooming, bathing, dressing, toileting, bladder and bowel management, transfers, locomotion, comprehension, expression, social interaction, problem solving, and memory that are each rated on a 7-point scale ranging from "dependent" to "independent."

functional invariant in Jean PIAGET's theory, any of the processes of ORGANIZATION and ADAPTATION that characterize biological systems and operate throughout the life span. See ACCOMMODATION; ASSIMILATION.

functionalism *n.* a general psychological approach that views mental life and behavior in terms of active adaptation to environmental challenges and opportunities. Functionalism was developed at the University of Chicago by psychologists John DEWEY, James R. ANGELL, and Harvey A. Carr (1878–1954) at the beginning of the 20th century as a revolt against the atomistic point of view of STRUCTURALISM, which limited psychology to the dissection of states of consciousness and the study of mental content rather than mental activities. This focus reveals the debt of functionalism to evolutionary concepts, to the ACT PSYCHOLOGY of German psychologist Franz Brentano (1838–1917), and to the approach detailed by William JAMES. Functionalism emphasized the causes and consequences of human behavior; the union of the physiological with the psychological; the need for objective testing of theories; and the applications of psychological knowledge to the solution of practical problems, the evolutionary continuity between animals and humans, and the improvement of human life. Also called **functional psychology**. See also CHICAGO SCHOOL.

functional job analysis (**FJA**) a form of JOB ANALYSIS in which tasks are rated on the degree of complexity they entail in dealing with people, data, and things. Such an analysis is commonly used in drawing up PERSONNEL SPECIFICATIONS and JOB DESCRIPTIONS. See also WORK FUNCTION SCALE.

functional leader any member of a group, whether a designated leader or not, who performs the activities associated with a leadership role, particularly by satisfying interpersonal needs (boosting morale, increasing COHESION, reducing interpersonal conflict, establishing rapport) and by guiding the group in the direction of successful goal attainment (defining problems, establishing communication networks, planning, motivating action, coordinating members' actions). Compare NOMINAL LEADER.

functional level see OPTIMAL LEVEL.

functional limitation restriction or lack of ability in performing an action or activity.

function allocation the systematic process of applying a knowledge of HUMAN FACTORS and ERGONOMICS to determine those system functions that can be performed by human operators and those that require automation, or that require an interaction between the human operator and the equipment. Function allocation is carried out early in the system DEVELOPMENT CYCLE. See also ADAPTIVE TASK ALLOCATION; CLUMSY AUTOMATION.

functional magnetic resonance imaging (**fMRI**; **functional MRI**) a form of MAGNETIC RESONANCE IMAGING used to localize areas of cognitive activation, based on the correlation between brain activity and blood property changes linked to local changes in blood flow to the brain. During periods of cognitive activation, blood flow is always increased to a greater extent than oxygen extraction. In consequence, the proportion of oxygenated hemoglobin in the red blood cells transiently increases in an active region, leading to a local increase in the signal detected by fMRI.

functional measurement a procedure that measures functional experience of stimuli as that experience changes across different contexts. When two or more stimuli are combined, their impressions on the observer are rated and integrated according to a psychological law that obeys simple arithmetic rules (e.g., addition). The law is discovered by examining the way in which the observer's ratings change when the combination of stimuli is changed.

functional moneme see FUNCTION WORD.

functional operant the class of responses whose probability is changed by the imposition of an OPERANT contingency. For example, lever presses with a force greater than 0.2 N may be required for reinforcement. Presses with forces greater than 0.2 N will increase in frequency, as will the frequency of presses just (but not far) below that value. These latter presses are part of the functional operant class. Compare DESCRIPTIVE OPERANT.

functional pain pain with no known organic cause.

functional plasticity 1. an adaptive change, often one that occurs relatively rapidly. **2.** the ability of one part of the brain to adapt to the loss of another part by carrying on most of the functions of both. Functional plasticity is observed in cases of infantile HEMIPLEGIA when one of the cerebral hemispheres has been removed surgically to control the symptoms of the disorder and the remaining hemisphere takes over many of the functions normally performed by both. See also SPLIT BRAIN.

functional plateau a relatively stable level of physical or psychological functioning, characteristic of a person in a given developmental state or set of environmental circumstances.

functional psychology see FUNCTIONALISM.

functional psychosis 1. a psychotic state for which no specific neurological or other physical pathology has been demonstrated. **2.** an obsolete name for any severe mental disorder for which no specific neurological or other physical pathology has been demonstrated.

functional reorganization changes that occur after a brain injury to enable other areas of the brain to take over all or part of the functions performed by the injured area. See also FUNCTIONAL RESERVE.

functional reserve the degree to which the brain is able to adapt functionally to a brain injury. This is thought to depend on such factors as age, preexisting intellect, education, and physical status of the brain. See FUNCTIONAL REORGANIZATION.

functional selection the survival, over time, of capacities that are more useful to the individual coupled with the disappearance of capacities that are less useful.

functional skills activities that develop from aptitudes, such as mechanical ability, artistic talent, and writing.

functional status a measure of an individual's ability to perform ACTIVITIES OF DAILY LIVING independently. Functional status may be used as an assessment of the severity of an individual's disability.

functional stimulus see EFFECTIVE STIMULUS.

functional types in Carl JUNG'S ANALYTIC PSYCHOLOGY, four personality types based on functions of the ego. Jung identified four functions, one of which typically dominates the conscious ego while the others remain unconscious. The individuated person (see INDIVIDUATION) will have integrated all the functions into his or her conscious personality. The functional types are: (a) the FEELING TYPE; (b) the THINKING TYPE; (c) the SENSATION TYPE; and (d) the INTUITIVE TYPE. See QUATERNITY. See also ATTITUDINAL TYPES.

functional unity the state or condition in which a set of parts, traits, or processes work together as an integrated unit.

functional universal see PSYCHOLOGICAL UNIVERSAL.

functional vaginismus a sexual dysfunction characterized by recurrent and persistent involuntary spasms of the musculature of the outer third of the vagina, which interfere with coitus and are not caused exclusively by a physical disorder or due to another mental disorder.

function pleasure the pleasure that results from doing something well and that motivates people to do their best at a task even when there is no other reward. See also ACTIVITY PLEASURE.

function word in a language, a word that has little or no meaning of its own but plays an important grammatical role: Examples include the articles (*a*, *the*, etc.), prepositions (*in*, *of*, etc.), and conjunctions (*and*, *but*, etc.). Function words are of high frequency, are typically short, and do not generally admit new members (see CLOSED-CLASS WORDS). The distinction between function words and CONTENT WORDS is of great interest to the study of language disorders, LANGUAGE ACQUISITION, and psycholinguistic processing. Psycholinguists are especially interested in function words because of their role in facilitating sentence parsing. In combination with nonsense words, they can be used to create sentence frames whose GRAMMATICALITY can be recognized but whose content is meaningless, such as *He zibbed from the fluv by sibbing the flix*. Also called **empty word**; **functional moneme**; **functor**; **relational word**; **structure word**.

functor *n*. see FUNCTION WORD.

fundamental attribution error in ATTRIBUTION THEORY, the tendency to overestimate the degree to which an individual's behavior is determined by his or her abiding personal characteristics, attitudes, or beliefs and, correspondingly, to minimize the influence of the surrounding situation on that behavior (e.g., financial or social pressures). There is evidence that this tendency may be more common in some societies (e.g., the United States) than in others (e.g., Hindu India), so it is questionable whether it is indeed fundamental. Also called **correspondence bias**; **overattribution bias**. See also ACTOR–OBSERVER EFFECT; CORRESPONDENCE; DISPOSITIONAL ATTRIBUTION; SITUATIONAL ATTRIBUTION. [identified by U.S. psychologist Lee D. Ross]

fundamental frequency see FREQUENCY.

fundamental interpersonal relations orientation theory (**FIRO theory**) a theory explaining the pattern of interactions among members of a group in terms of three interpersonal needs of the group members: the need for inclusion (i.e., to belong to and be accepted by the group), the need for control (i.e., to direct the group's activities), and the NEED FOR AFFECTION. [proposed by U.S. psychologist William Schutz (1925–2002)]

fundamental lexical hypothesis see LEXICAL HYPOTHESIS.

fundamental need see BASIC PHYSIOLOGICAL NEED.

fundamental rule see BASIC RULE.

fundamental skill 1. the ability that is necessary in order to perform a task or understand an idea because it is a foundation for other concepts, skills, or ideas. **2.** a basic ability usually considered necessary for competent functioning in our society (e.g., reading, basic mathematics, essential communication skills).

fundamental symptoms according to Swiss psychiatrist Eugen Bleuler (1857–1939), the four primary symptoms of SCHIZOPHRENIA: abnormal *a*ssociations in thinking, *a*utistic behavior and thinking, abnormal *a*ffect (including flat and inappropriate affect), and *a*mbivalence. These symptoms are also known as the **Four As**. Compare SECONDARY SYMPTOMS.

fundamental tone see FREQUENCY.

fungiform papillae swellings on the anterior surface (front) of the tongue, in humans numbering about 200 and each shaped like a mushroom. About half the fungiform papillae lack TASTE BUDS; the others each contain from 1 to 36 taste buds, with a mean of 3. Receptors in fungiform papillae are particularly sensitive to SALTY and SWEET chemicals. See also PAPILLA.

funnel interview see AIDED RECALL.

funnel sequence a method for structuring the order of questions in surveys and interviews that starts with general items and gradually narrows the focus to more specific items.

furor *n.* a sudden outburst of rage or excitement during which an irrational act of violence may be committed. In rare cases of epilepsy, the occurrence of furor takes the place of a tonic–clonic or complex partial seizure; this is known as **furor epilepticus** or **epileptic furor**. See also EXPLOSIVE PERSONALITY; INTERMITTENT EXPLOSIVE DISORDER; ISOLATED EXPLOSIVE DISORDER.

fusiform gyrus a ridge on the inferior (lower) surface of each TEMPORAL LOBE in the brain. It lies between the inferior temporal gyrus and the PARAHIPPOCAMPAL GYRUS and is involved in high-level visual perception.

fusion *n.* **1.** in perception, the blending into one unified whole of two or more stimulus components or elements, for example, of colors (**color fusion**), of sounds received by the two ears (**binaural fusion**), or of images falling on the two retinas (**binocular fusion**). See also FLICKER FUSION. **2.** a state in which the normal differentiation between the self and the environment may seem to recede or disappear while the individual experiences a sense of merging, fusing, or uniting with other individuals, objects, nature, or the universe. Also called **unity**. See also MYSTIC UNION. **3.** in psychoanalytic theory, the merging of different INSTINCTS, as in the union of sexual and aggressive drives in SADISM. In Sigmund FREUD's view, the instincts of life and death are normally fused and it is only in pathology that they operate singly. Also called **instinctual fusion**. Compare DEFUSION. **—fuse** *vb.*

fusional language in LINGUISTIC TYPOLOGY, a language that forms words by the fusion (rather than the AGGLUTINATION) of MORPHEMES, so that the constituent elements of a word are not kept distinct. Fusional languages, such as Latin and Greek, tend to have numerous grammatical inflections, with each form serving several distinct functions. Also called **synthetic language**. Compare AGGLUTINATIVE LANGUAGE; ISOLATING LANGUAGE.

fusion frequency see CRITICAL FLICKER FREQUENCY; FLICKER FUSION.

future lives in perspectives deriving from a belief in REINCARNATION, those of a human being's multiple lives that have yet to be lived. See also METEMPSYCHOSIS.

future-mindedness *n.* the ability to engage in means–ends thinking about the future, that is, to think ahead to what the future may hold and how it might come to pass.

future orientation a time perspective that is focused on the future, especially on how to achieve one's future goals.

future shock the personal confusion and social disorientation that accompany very rapid technological and social change. [defined by U.S. futurist Alvin Toffler (1928–)]

futuristics *n.* inquiry into possible or predicted developments within a particular field or discipline, such as expected future patterns of technological, economic, and social organization. Futuristics aims to enhance future society and promote better decision making by, for example, identifying significant problems that may arise and proposing solutions.

fuzzy logic a logic-based KNOWLEDGE REPRESENTATION scheme founded on the axiom that set membership is based on a probability distribution (as opposed to traditional set theory, in which an element is either in a set or not in that set). An example of fuzzy logic is that a certain person can be a member of the set of tall people with confidence .75 and also be a member of the set of short people with confidence .05. Fuzzy logic also breaks the assumption of the excluded middle in philosophy, in that an element can be a member of both a set and the opposite of that set at the same time. Fuzzy logic is often used to support the design of EXPERT SYSTEMS as well as control algorithms. [first proposed in 1965 by Romanian-born computer engineer Lotfi A. Zadeh]

fuzzy trace an imprecise memory representation. According to FUZZY TRACE THEORY, such representations are more easily accessed, generally require less effort to use, and are less susceptible to interference and forgetting than VERBATIM TRACES.

fuzzy trace theory a theory proposing that information is encoded on a continuum from precise VERBATIM TRACES to gistlike FUZZY TRACES and that developmental differences in many aspects of cognition can be attributed to age differences in encoding and to differences in sensitivity to OUTPUT INTERFERENCE. [proposed by U.S. psychologists Charles Brainerd (1944–) and Valerie Reyna (1955–)]

F value see F RATIO.

Gg

g symbol for GENERAL FACTOR.

GA abbreviation for GAMBLERS ANONYMOUS.

GABA abbreviation for GAMMA-AMINOBUTYRIC ACID.

GABA agonists compounds that exert an agonistic (augmentative) effect at gamma-aminobutyric acid (GABA) receptor sites (see $GABA_A$ RECEPTOR; $GABA_B$ RECEPTOR) or on the action of GABA. Several classes of GABA receptor agonists exist. Direct GABA agonists (e.g., muscimol) act at the GABA binding-site on the receptor; indirect GABA agonists facilitate, in various ways, the release or activity of GABA. Of the indirect GABA agonists, the BENZODIAZEPINES, which act as allosteric modulators (see ALLOSTERIC MODULATION) at the GABA receptor complex, are in the most common clinical use.

GABA antagonists substances that exert an antagonistic (inhibitive) effect at gamma-aminobutyric acid (GABA) receptor sites (see $GABA_A$ RECEPTOR; $GABA_B$ RECEPTOR) or on the action of GABA. Like GABA AGONISTS, GABA antagonists can be direct or indirect. Direct GABA antagonists block the GABA receptor; the best known of these is BICUCULLINE, which acts as a competitive antagonist for GABA at its receptor site. Indirect GABA antagonists include PICROTOXIN, which is a noncompetitive antagonist at the $GABA_A$ receptor complex and blocks the effects of GABA on the receptor complex.

gabapentin *n.* a drug used for the treatment of seizures (see ANTICONVULSANTS) and for the relief of pain associated with shingles (see HERPETIC NEURALGIA). Its mechanism of action is unknown: It is a chemical analog of the neurotransmitter gamma-aminobutyric acid (GABA) and may be involved in the increased synthesis or release of GABA. Gabapentin is currently being investigated for the treatment of certain psychological disorders: It may be of some use in managing mania associated with BIPOLAR DISORDERS, but this has not yet been conclusively established and gabapentin has been reported to induce excitation or increase the frequency of episodes in bipolar disorders. Side effects are primarily sedation, dizziness, ATAXIA, and fatigue; abrupt withdrawal may precipitate seizures. U.S. trade name: **Neurontin**.

$GABA_A$ receptor one of the two main types of receptor protein that bind the neurotransmitter GAMMA-AMINOBUTYRIC ACID (GABA), the other being the $GABA_B$ RECEPTOR. It is located at most synapses of most neurons that use GABA as a neurotransmitter. The predominant inhibitory receptor in the central nervous system (CNS), it functions as a chloride channel (see ION CHANNEL). GABA AGONISTS, such as the barbiturates and benzodiazepines, enhance the binding of GABA to $GABA_A$ receptors, allowing for increased conductance of chloride through the ion channel and thereby hyperpolarizing the neuron and inhibiting its activity. GABA ANTAGONISTS, such as bicuculline and picrotoxin, block the inhibitory effects of GABA at this receptor. Many other substances, including alcohol (ethanol), are thought to exert at least part of their effect via interaction at the $GABA_A$ receptor.

$GABA_B$ receptor one of the two main types of receptor protein that bind the neurotransmitter GAMMA-AMINOBUTYRIC ACID (GABA), the other being the $GABA_A$ RECEPTOR. $GABA_B$ receptors, which are G PROTEIN-coupled receptors, are less plentiful in the brain than $GABA_A$ receptors and do not have binding sites for benzodiazepine or barbiturate GABA agonists. Activation of $GABA_B$ receptors results in relatively long-lasting neuronal inhibition, but few psychotropic substances exert their effect at these receptors: BACLOFEN is a relatively selective agonist at $GABA_B$ receptors and is used clinically as a skeletal-muscle relaxant.

Gabriel's simultaneous test procedure (**Gabriel's STP**) one of several approaches for controlling the TYPE I ERROR rate by adjusting significance levels in multiple post hoc comparisons.

GAD abbreviation for GENERALIZED ANXIETY DISORDER.

GAF scale abbreviation for GLOBAL ASSESSMENT OF FUNCTIONING SCALE.

GAG abbreviation for glycosaminoglycan. See MUCOPOLYSACCHARIDOSIS.

GAI abbreviation for GUIDED AFFECTIVE IMAGERY.

Gaia hypothesis the hypothesis that the earth, its living things, and its physical environments constitute a single self-regulating entity. In contrast to Darwinian theories of evolution, which hold that living things adapt themselves to the extant environment, the hypothesis suggests that the earth has adapted to, and been transformed by, the living things that are a part of it. This perspective has been influential in modern ecological movements but is rejected by mainstream scientists. The hypothesis is named for Gaia, the Earth, a primordial Greek goddess who emerged from Chaos. [formulated and named by British scientist James E. Lovelock (1919–)]

gain–loss theory of attraction a theory of interpersonal attraction stating that people's like (or dislike) for another person is more strongly affected by the degree to which they believe they have gone up (or down) in that individual's estimation than by the unvarying degree to which they think they are attractive (or unattractive) to that person. [first studied by U.S. psychologists Elliot Aronson (1932–) and Darwyn E. Linder (1939–)]

gainsharing *n.* a reward system in which employees are provided with monetary incentives in the form of bonuses that are tied to the performance of a business unit or organization. See INCENTIVE SYSTEM; SCANLON PLAN. See also AGENCY THEORY.

gait *n.* a manner of walking.

gait apraxia see APRAXIA OF GAIT.

galactorrhea *n.* abnormal expression of breast milk, which may occur either in women at times other than when nursing or in men. Lactation is stimulated by the pituitary hormone PROLACTIN, and the neurotransmitter dopamine normally acts to inhibit the release of prolactin. Therefore administration of DOPAMINE-RECEPTOR ANTAGONISTS (e.g., conventional antipsychotics), which inhibit the effects of dopamine, may cause galactorrhea. Pituitary tumors or injury to the pituitary gland, causing excessive secretion of prolactin, may also result in gallactorrhea. The dopamine-receptor agonist BROMOCRIPTINE may be used to treat the condition.

galactosemia *n.* an autosomal recessive disease in which the body is unable to metabolize the sugar galactose, which therefore accumulates in the blood. Untreated, this results in cataracts, jaundice, lethargic and hypotonic behavior, and mental retardation; the condition is associated with a high infant death rate. Treatment is based on restricted intake of dietary galactose.

galanin *n.* a NEUROPEPTIDE that is implicated in a variety of functions, including normal growth of the nervous system, recovery of function after nerve injury, and regulation of appetite.

galantamine *n.* an inhibitor of the enzyme acetylcholinesterase that is used for the treatment of mild to moderate Alzheimer's disease (see NOOTROPIC DRUGS). Although galantamine and other ACETYLCHOLINESTERASE INHIBITORS do not reverse symptoms of dementia, they have been demonstrated to temporarily slow progression of the disease. U.S. trade name: **Reminyl**.

Galilean method an approach to knowledge emphasizing an understanding of the individual case, analyzing dynamic causal interaction in the present, and making specific predictions about an individual. Compare ARISTOTELIAN METHOD. [**Galileo** Galilei (1564–1642), Italian mathematician, physicist, and astronomer]

gallows humor humor or comical behavior that is inappropriately displayed at a time of death or disaster. Compare FLIPPANCY.

Galton bar an instrument that measures the DIFFERENCE THRESHOLD (just noticeable difference) for visual linear distances. [Francis **Galton** (1822–1911), British scientist]

Galton's questionary a set of questions sent by British scientist Francis Galton (1822–1911) to 200 eminent men of science in Britain. The recipients were asked about matters ranging from their physiology (e.g., hat size) to their religious and political background and their reasons for undertaking a career in science. This study, published in 1874 as *English Men of Science*, is acknowledged as the first use of a questionnaire for psychological research.

galvanic skin response (**GSR**) a response to certain stimuli in the form of a change in electrical resistance of the skin, particularly on the palms or other areas lacking hair. The effect is produced by activity of the sweat glands and may occur as a reaction to both pleasant and unpleasant stimuli, to emotional arousal and stress, and even to a novel stimulus or a conditioned neutral stimulus. Also called **electrodermal response** (**EDR**); **Féré phenomenon**; **psychogalvanic reflex** (**PGR**); **Tarchanoff phenomenon**. See also POLYGRAPH; SKIN CONDUCTANCE.

galvanotropism *n.* an orienting response of an organism toward electrical stimulation. It is distinct from **galvanotaxis**, which is active, directed movement of an organism in response to electrical stimulation. **—galvanotropic** *adj.*

Gamblers Anonymous (**GA**) an organization of men and women who share experiences, strength, and hope with each other to recover from compulsive gambling, following the TWELVE-STEP PROGRAM. See PATHOLOGICAL GAMBLING.

gambler's fallacy a failure to recognize the independence of chance events, leading to the mistaken belief that one can predict the outcome of a chance event on the basis of the outcomes of past chance events. For example, a person might think that the more often a tossed coin comes up heads, the more likely it is to come up tails in subsequent tosses, although each coin toss is independent of the other, and the true probability of the outcome of any toss is still just 0.5.

gambling *n.* see PATHOLOGICAL GAMBLING.

game *n.* **1.** a social interaction, organized play, or transaction with formal rules. See ZERO-SUM GAME. **2.** in psychotherapy, a situation in which members of a group take part in some activity designed to elicit emotions or stimulate revealing interactions and interrelationships. In PLAY THERAPY games are often used as a projective or observational technique. **3.** in TRANSACTIONAL ANALYSIS, a recurrent and often deceitful ploy adopted by an individual in his or her dealings with others. **4.** in GESTALT THERAPY, an exercise or experiment designed to increase self-awareness, for example, acting out frightening situations or participating in the HOT-SEAT TECHNIQUE. See also RULES OF THE GAME.

game reasoning the reasoning that governs acceptable behavior within a sporting context. As sport is deemed to be outside real life, the level of morality applied to behavior in sport is different from and usually lower than that applied to behavior in real life. See BRACKETED MORALITY.

gamete *n.* either of the female or male reproductive cells that take part in fertilization to produce a zygote. In humans and other animals, the female gamete is the OVUM and the male gamete is the SPERMATOZOON. Gametes contain the HAPLOID number of chromosomes rather than the DIPLOID number found in body (somatic) cells. See also GERM CELL.

gamete intrafallopian transfer (**GIFT**) an alternative to IN VITRO FERTILIZATION in which ova and sperm are introduced directly into the fallopian tubes, where fertilization takes place. Compare ZYGOTE INTRAFALLOPIAN TRANSFER.

game theory a model or paradigm for understanding the dynamics of interpersonal conflict. Game theory likens conflict situations to the relationship of two players in a game, where each party stands to win or lose. Game theory is often used in both theoretical modeling and empirical studies of cooperation and competition.

gametogenesis *n.* the process resulting in the formation of GAMETES from GERM CELLS, which normally involves MEIOSIS. In mammals, gametogenesis in the female is known as OOGENESIS and occurs in the ovaries; in the males it is called SPERMATOGENESIS and occurs in the testes.

gamma (symbol: γ) *n.* the distance of a stimulus from the threshold.

gamma alcoholism the third and most serious stage of alcoholism. It is characterized by increasing tolerance, physiological adaptation, loss of control, and, if drinking is suspended, a withdrawal or abstinence syndrome that can include powerful cravings for alcohol, convulsions, and DELIRIUM TREMENS. See also ALPHA ALCOHOLISM; BETA ALCOHOLISM; DELTA ALCOHOLISM; EPSILON ALCOHOLISM. [defined by U.S. physician Elvin M. Jellinek (1890–1963)]

gamma-aminobutyric acid (**GABA**) a major inhibitory NEUROTRANSMITTER in the mammalian nervous system and found widely distributed in both invertebrate and vertebrate nervous systems. It is synthesized from the amino acid GLUTAMIC ACID. See also $GABA_A$ RECEPTOR; $GABA_B$ RECEPTOR.

gamma-aminobutyric acid agonists see GABA AGONISTS.

gamma-aminobutyric acid antagonists see GABA ANTAGONISTS.

gamma coherence see GAMMA SYNCHRONY.

gamma-cystathionase deficiency see CYSTATHIONINURIA.

gamma efferent neuron a motor neuron that controls MUSCLE SPINDLE sensitivity. Compare ALPHA MOTORNEURON.

gamma-endorphin *n.* see ENDORPHINS.

gamma-hydroxybutyrate *n.* see GHB.

gamma motor neuron (**gamma motoneuron**) any of a category of motor neurons that control the sensitivity of MUSCLE SPINDLES. Also called **intrafusal motor neuron**.

gamma movement a form of apparent movement in which an object appears to expand when it is suddenly presented and contract when it is withdrawn. When the intensity of a light is suddenly increased, the light appears to expand and approach the observer; when its intensity is suddenly decreased, it appears to shrink and recede. Also called **gamma motion**.

gamma synchrony a pattern of electrical activity in the brain, as recorded on an electroencephalogram (EEG), that is predominant in active mental states, such as waking and dreaming. It is characterized by spatially correlated GAMMA WAVES with zero phase lag. **Gamma coherence** is a similar pattern but distinguished by a brief phase lag.

gamma wave in electroencephalography, a type of BRAIN WAVE that tends to be irregular, low in amplitude, and fast, ranging from 20 to 70 Hz and with power peaking near 40 Hz. Gamma waves appear to reflect active mental processes.

gamonomania *n.* an abnormally strong desire or urge to marry.

-gamy *suffix* marriage (e.g., POLYGAMY).

gang *n.* a social group composed of members with a high degree of personal contact who share common interests and standards of behavior, which in some cases (e.g., street gangs) are antisocial.

ganglion *n.* (*pl.* **ganglia**) a collection of CELL BODIES of neurons that lies outside the central nervous system. Many invertebrates have only distributed ganglia and no centralized nervous system. Compare NUCLEUS. **—ganglionic** *adj.*

ganglion cells see RETINAL GANGLION CELLS.

ganglionic blocking agents drugs that inhibit the action of the neurotransmitter ACETYLCHOLINE at synapses in the AUTONOMIC GANGLIA. Among other effects, this causes a decrease in heart rate and a lowering of blood pressure, and these drugs were formerly widely used in the treatment of hypertension. However, because of the severity of their side effects, this use is now rare. See MECAMYLAMINE.

ganglionic layer see CORTICAL LAYERS.

ganglioside *n.* any of a group of glycosphingolipids (sugar-containing lipids) that occur mainly in the tissues of the central nervous system. **—gangliosidic** *adj.*

gangliosidosis *n.* a disorder of lipid metabolism marked by the excessive accumulation of GANGLIOSIDES in the nervous system. Gangliosidosis occurs in a number of different forms, each associated with a specific ganglioside; TAY–SACHS DISEASE is one type of gangliosidosis.

ganja *n.* one of the more potent forms of CANNABIS, made from the dried flowering tops of female plants. Smokers of this substance reportedly experience respiratory disorders at a rate twice that of the average for cannabis smokers.

Ganser syndrome a condition in which psychotic illness is simulated or a DISSOCIATED STATE occurs purportedly as a result of an unconscious effort by the individual to escape from an intolerable situation. It is typically seen in psychiatric hospitals and, historically, in prisons (it is referred to in the older literature as **prison psychosis**). The most prominent feature is the giving of approximate answers to simple or familiar questions (e.g., "3 + 3 = 7"; "a horse has five legs"). Other features include clouding of consciousness, inattentiveness or drowsiness, conversion symptoms (e.g., CONVERSION PARALYSIS), hallucinations, and, frequently, loss of memory for events subsequent to the episode. The syndrome has been variously categorized as a MALINGERING process, a psychotic disorder, and a consequence of a head injury. In *DSM–IV–TR*, it is classified as a DISSOCIATIVE DISORDER NOT OTHERWISE SPECIFIED. Also called **pseudodementia**. [first described in 1898 by Sigbert **Ganser** (1853–1931), German psychiatrist]

Ganzfeld *n.* **1.** a homogeneous visual field, without any particular point or area of stimulation. In an experiment, participants looked into white spheres: When colors were introduced, the colors tended to disappear, indicating that registration of color (and likewise of form) requires stimulus change. **2.** in parapsychology experiments, a technique in which the participant is isolated from the sensory environment (e.g., by covering the eyes and placing headphones over the ears). [German, "whole field"]

gap detection the detection of a temporal interruption in a quasi-continuous sound. In individuals with normal hearing in laboratory situations, a gap of approximately 3 ms is just detectable.

gap junction a type of intercellular junction consisting of a gap of about 2–4 nm between the plasma membranes of two cells, spanned by protein channels that allow passage of chemical substances or electrical signals. See ELECTRICAL SYNAPSE.

Garcia effect a CONDITIONED TASTE AVERSION achieved rapidly by a single pairing of illness (e.g., nausea) with consumption of a specific food. [John **Garcia** (1917–), U.S. psychologist]

garden-path sentence a sentence in which structural cues, lexical ambiguity, or a combination of both mislead the reader or listener into an incorrect interpretation until a disambiguating cue appears later in the sentence. For example, in the sentence *As the car drove past the church clock could be heard striking*, the appearance of the verb phrase *could be heard* indicates that a parsing of the sentence in which *past* is interpreted as governing *the church* must be erroneous. Such sentences have proved useful in psycholinguistic research into the role of memory in sentence parsing.

Gardner–Diamond syndrome a condition in which an individual bruises easily (purpura simplex) and the black and blue patches (ecchymoses) tend to enlarge and result in pain in the affected tissue. Also called **autoerythrocyte sensitization syndrome**; **painful bruising syndrome**; **psychogenic purpura**. [Louis Klein **Diamond** (1902–1995) and Frank H. **Gardner** (1919–), U.S. physicians]

gargoylism *n.* the facial appearance of people with HURLER'S SYNDROME. The features include an abnormally long and narrow skull due to premature closure of the sagittal suture, a broad nose bridge, an open mouth with a large protruding tongue, thick lips, and clouded corneas.

GAS abbreviation for GENERAL ADAPTATION SYNDROME.

gas chromatography a method of chemical analysis used to separate and identify the components of a mixture. The substance being tested is placed at one end of a long tube, and its components are volatilized by an inert gas injected into the tube. Components can be identified by the time they take to pass through the tube. The technique is used to separate and quantify barbiturates, steroids, and fatty acids.

gasoline intoxication a euphoric reaction induced by inhalation of gasoline vapor. It also results in headache, weakness, depression of the central nervous system, confusion, nausea, and respiratory disorders. See INHALANT; INHALANT ABUSE.

gastric motility movements of the stomach muscles, particularly those caused by digestive processes. Such movements may also occur in the absence of food in the stomach, as in the reaction of a patient to stress.

gastric neuropathy a form of DIABETIC GASTROPATHY marked by delayed emptying of the stomach and irregular food absorption.

gastrin *n.* a hormone, synthesized in the **G cells** of the stomach wall, that regulates the release of gastric juice by the stomach. See also SECRETIN.

gastro- (**gastr-**) *combining form* stomach.

gastrocolic reflex the reflex wave of contraction that passes along the colon when food enters a fasting stomach or even in anticipation of a meal.

gastroduodenal ulceration ulceration of the mucosa lining the stomach and duodenum caused by the action of hydrochloric acid and the digestive enzyme pepsin, which are secreted by the stomach. Gastric (stomach) ulcers tend to develop later in life and are less likely to be associated with increased acid secretion than duodenal ulcers. Although in some cases gastroduodenal ulceration is due to secretion of excess acid, in many others secretion is normal, and the mucosa seems to be more susceptible to attack by gastric acid. Factors implicated as being responsible for this increased susceptibility include infection with *Helicobacter pylori* bacteria and long-term use of NSAIDS (nonsteroidal anti-inflammatory agents; e.g., aspirin, ibuprofen); there may also be a familial or genetic factor. See also DYSPEPSIA; ULCER.

gastroenteritis *n.* inflammation of the lining of the stomach and intestines. The causes may be food poisoning, infectious diseases, allergic reactions, or psychological factors, such as fear, anger, or other emotional disturbance. Symptoms may include headache, nausea and vomiting, diarrhea, and gas pain.

gastrointestinal motility the involuntary forward movement of the contents of the gastrointestinal tract, which are propelled mainly by the alternate contraction and relaxation of the bands of circular and longitudinal muscle fibers that form the walls of the tract.

gastrointestinal problems disorders associated with dysfunctions of the gastrointestinal tract, such as diarrhea, malabsorption syndrome, colitis, flatulence, dysphagia, gastroenteritis, and peptic ulcer.

gastrula *n.* an early embryo showing differentiation of cells into the three GERM LAYERS that will give rise to all of the major tissue systems in the adult animal.

gastrulation *n.* a stage of embryonic development in which the BLASTULA—essentially a hollow ball of cells—is reorganized to form the GASTRULA, which contains the basic plan of the future organism.

gate *n.* a device or circuit (e.g., an ION CHANNEL or a neural circuit) that controls the passage of a substance or signal. See GATE-CONTROL THEORY OF PAIN; GATED CHANNEL; LIGAND-GATED ION CHANNEL; VOLTAGE-GATED ION CHANNEL.

gate-control theory of pain the hypothesis that the spinal cord regulates the amount of perceived pain reaching the brain by opening or closing gates for the flow of pain impulses. See SPINAL GATE. [first proposed in 1965 by Canadian psychologist Ronald Melzack (1929–) and British neuroscientist Patrick D. Wall (1925–2001)]

gated channel a channel in a cell membrane that can open or close to regulate the passage of certain ions or molecules.

gatekeeper *n.* **1.** a health care professional, usually a PRIMARY CARE PROVIDER associated with a MANAGED CARE organization, who determines a patient's access to health care services and whose approval is required for referrals to specialists. **2.** in the psychology of groups, see RELATIONSHIP ROLE.

gatekeeper role the responsibility of judges to determine the admissibility in court of both scientific and nonscientific expert testimony according to criteria relevant to reliability. See also DAUBERT V. MERRELL DOW PHARMACEUTICALS INC.; KUMHO TIRE CO. V. PATRICK CARMICHAEL.

gating *n.* the inhibition or blocking of one set of sensory stimuli or one sensory channel when attention is focused on another channel or set of stimuli. That is, while attending to one sensory channel, other channels are either "turned off" or processed at the periphery of awareness. Also called **sensory gating**.

gating mechanism see SPINAL GATE.

Gaussian distribution see NORMAL DISTRIBUTION. [Karl Friedrich **Gauss** (1777–1855), German mathematician]

Gaussian noise see NOISE. [Karl Friedrich **Gauss**]

Gauss–Markov theorem a fundamental theorem of mathematical statistics that deals with the generation of linear unbiased ESTIMATORS with minimum variance in the GENERAL LINEAR MODEL. It is one of the basic theorems in the ANALYSIS OF VARIANCE. [Karl Friedrich **Gauss**; Andrei **Markov** (1856–1922), Russian mathematician]

gay 1. *adj.* denoting individuals, especially males, who are sexually attracted to and aroused by members of their own sex. **2.** *n.* a gay individual. See also HOMOSEXUALITY.

gay bashing see HOMOPHOBIA.

gay liberation a social movement seeking to redress legal, social, and economic discrimination against homosexuals by advocating equal rights for gay and lesbian people and promoting acceptance of homosexuality. Gay liberation emerged from the radicalism and social turmoil of the late 1960s but has since evolved into a broad movement with a number of different tendencies. One division is between those who look for the complete integration of gays and lesbians into mainstream society and its institutions (e.g., through legalization of same-sex marriage) and those who stress the essential difference of homosexual experience, culture, and identity. Also called **gay lib**; **gay rights movement**; **homosexual rights movement**.

gay-related immune deficiency (**GRID**) a former name for AIDS, reflecting the (erroneous) belief that it was restricted to gay and bisexual men.

gaze 1. *vb.* to maintain the direction of the eyes toward a FIXATION POINT. **2.** *n.* the act or process of gazing. See also EYE CONTACT. **3.** *n.* the orientation of the eyes within the face, which can be used by others to interpret where an individual is looking. Gaze direction is an effective way of communicating the location of hidden objects and is functionally similar to pointing. There is some controversy over whether nonhuman animals can understand the function of gaze direction.

gaze palsy an inability to move the eyes, either by SACCADES or SMOOTH-PURSUIT MOVEMENTS, past midposition in a particular direction, although the eye muscles are capable of contraction. Typical forms are vertical gaze palsy (affecting up–down movements) and horizontal gaze palsy (affecting left–right movements); in complete gaze palsy, gaze shifts are restricted in all directions. Gaze palsy can be caused by injury to the brainstem, thalamus, or posterior occipitotemporal, parietal, or frontal cortex. It leads to a restriction of the FIELD OF REGARD. Also called **gaze paresis**.

GBBB syndrome see TELECANTHUS-HYPOSPADIAS SYNDROME.

GBMI abbreviation for GUILTY BUT MENTALLY ILL.

GCS abbreviation for GLASGOW COMA SCALE.

GDS 1. abbreviation for GERIATRIC DEPRESSION SCALE. **2.** abbreviation for GLOBAL DETERIORATION SCALE. **3.** abbreviation for GORDON DIAGNOSTIC SYSTEM.

GDSS abbreviation for GROUP DECISION SUPPORT SYSTEMS.

Gegenhalten *n.* in neurology, involuntary resistance to passive movement of the extremities. [German, "resisting"]

Geisser–Greenhouse correction an adjustment technique in repeated measures ANALYSIS OF VARIANCE that corrects for violations of the SPHERICITY assumption. [Seymour **Geisser** (1924–2004) and Samuel W. **Greenhouse** (1918–2000), U.S. statisticians]

Geisteswissenschaftliche Psychologie one of two branches of the subject matter of psychology as defined by German academics in the 19th century. Variously translated, the term literally means a psychology dealing with the science of the mind or spirit; as such it was intended to encompass the moral, spiritual, historical, and human aspects of behavior now known as SOCIAL SCIENCE. Compare NATURWISSENSCHAFTLICHE PSYCHOLOGIE. See also VERSTEHENDE PSYCHOLOGIE.

gelasmus *n.* spasmodic laughter in individuals with certain psychogenic disorders, schizophrenia, and some diseases of the brain (especially of the medulla oblongata). When occurring as an aspect of a psychomotor seizure, this type of spasmodic laughter is termed **gelastic epilepsy**.

gel electrophoresis a method of separating molecules of differing size or electrical charge by forcing them to flow through a gel under the influence of an electric field.

gematria *n.* an occult practice in which the numerical values of letters, words, and phrases are calculated and these values used to uncover "hidden" significances in words, names, or texts (most often the Hebrew scriptures). It is a form of NUMEROLOGY.

Gemeinschaft *n.* a type of society or social group based on a community of feeling resulting from shared life experiences and similar beliefs and values (from German, "community"). Familial and kinship relations are an example, although the term can also apply to friendship networks and neighborhood relations. Compare GESELLSCHAFT. [first described by German sociologist Ferdinand Julius Tönnies (1855–1936)]

Gemeinschaftsgefühl *n.* SOCIAL INTEREST or community spirit (German, literally: "feeling for community"): a spirit of equality, belonging, and unity.

gemellology *n.* the study of twins and the phenomenon of twinning.

-gen *suffix* producing (e.g., ALLERGEN).

gender *n.* the condition of being male, female, or neuter. In a human context, the distinction between gender and sex reflects usage of these terms: Sex usually refers to the biological aspects of maleness or femaleness, whereas gender implies the psychological, behavioral, social, and cultural aspects of being male or female (i.e., masculinity or femininity). See also SEX ROLE.

gender assignment classification of an infant at birth as either male or female. Children born with AMBIGUOUS GENITALIA are usually assigned a gender by parents or physicians. See also GENDER REASSIGNMENT.

gender bias any one of a variety of biases relating to the differential treatment of females and males. These biases may include unwarranted assumptions expressed linguistically, such as *physicians and their wives* (instead of *physicians and their spouses*, which avoids the implication that physicians must be male) or the use of *he* when people of both sexes are under discussion, and omitting women from medical research on heart disease.

gender coding assigning particular traits or behaviors exclusively or predominantly to males or females.

gender concept an enculturated idea of GENDER ROLE. It has been theorized that gender is a socially constructed concept, based on biological sex but also including the roles and expectations for males and females of a culture. Children's concept of gender, particularly how they view themselves as a male or female in their culture, develops over childhood. See GENDER-ROLE SOCIALIZATION.

gender consistency the understanding that one's own and other people's sex is fixed across situations, regardless of superficial changes in appearance or activities. See GENDER CONSTANCY.

gender constancy a child's emerging sense of the permanence of being a boy or a girl, an understanding that occurs in a series of stages: GENDER IDENTITY, GENDER STABILITY, and GENDER CONSISTENCY.

gender differences typical differences between men and women, often specific to a particular culture, in such domains as careers, communication, health, social awareness, and orientation to the environment.

gender discrimination see SEX DISCRIMINATION.

gender dysphoria discontent with the physical or social aspects of one's own sex. See also DYSPHORIA; GENDER IDENTITY DISORDER.

gender identification the process of identifying oneself as male or female and adopting the roles and values of that gender. See also GENDER CONCEPT; GENDER-ROLE SOCIALIZATION; GENDER SCHEMA.

gender identity a recognition that one is male or female and the internalization of this knowledge into one's self-concept. This sense of maleness or femaleness typically results from a combination of biological and psychic influences, including the environmental effects of family and cultural attitudes. The main biological factor is the influence of the Y CHROMOSOME on the production of male hormones, which appears to affect brain development, resulting in masculine behavior. Female gender identity is the state resulting from absence of this Y-chromosome influence. See GENDER CONSISTENCY. See also GENDER ROLE; ROLE CONFUSION.

gender identity disorder in *DSM–IV–TR*, a disorder characterized by clinically significant distress or impairment of functioning due to cross-gender identification (i.e., a desire to be or actual insistence that one is of the opposite sex) and persistent discomfort arising from the belief that one's sex or gender is inappropriate to one's true self (see TRANSSEXUALISM). The disorder is distinguished from simple dissatisfaction or nonconformity with gender roles. In children, the disorder is manifested as aversion to physical aspects of their sex and rejection of traditional gender roles. In adolescents and adults, it is manifested as the persistent belief that one was born the wrong sex and preoccupation with altering primary and secondary sex characteristics. The category **gender identity disorder not otherwise specified** is used to classify gender-related disorders distinct from gender identity disorder, such as GENDER DYSPHORIA related to congenital INTERSEXUALITY, stress-related cross-dressing behavior (see TRANSVESTISM), or preoccupation with castration or penectomy (removal of the penis).

gender nonconformity behavior that differs from that of others of the same sex or from cultural expectations of male and female behavior.

gender orientation see SEXUAL ORIENTATION.

gender reassignment **1.** the changing of an individual's gender label because of incorrect gender assignment at birth, due to the presence of anomalous genitalia (as in INTERSEXUALITY). **2.** the process, involving hormone treatment, surgery, or both, in which a person's sex characteristics are changed to conform to that person's sense of his or her own GENDER IDENTITY. Also called **sex reassignment; sexual reassignment**. See GENDER DYSPHORIA; GENDER IDENTITY DISORDER; SEX REVERSAL; TRANSSEXUALISM.

gender role the pattern of behavior, personality traits, and attitudes that define masculinity or femininity in a particular culture. The gender role is largely determined by upbringing and may or may not conform to the individual's GENDER IDENTITY. See also ROLE CONFUSION.

gender-role socialization the conditioning of individuals to the roles, expectations, and behaviors that society prescribes for males and females.

gender schema the organized set of beliefs and expectations that guides one's understanding of gender or sex.

gender script a temporally organized, gender-related sequence of events. Stereotypically female gender scripts may include doing laundry or preparing dinner in the kitchen, whereas stereotypically male scripts may include building a birdhouse or barbecuing. See also SCRIPT.

gender stability the understanding that one's own or other people's sex does not change over time. See GENDER CONSTANCY.

gender stereotypes relatively fixed, overgeneralized attitudes and behaviors considered normal and appropriate for a person in a particular culture, based on his or her biological sex. Research indicates that these STEREOTYPES are prescriptive as well as descriptive. Gender stereotypes often support the social conditioning of gender roles.

gender typing expectations about people's behavior that are based on their biological sex.

gene *n.* the basic unit of heredity, responsible for storing genetic information and transmitting it to subsequent generations. The observable characteristics of an organism (i.e., its PHENOTYPE) are determined by numerous genes, which contain the instructions necessary for the functioning of the organism's constituent cells. Each gene consists of a section of DNA, a large and complex molecule that, in higher organisms, is arranged to form the CHROMOSOMES of the cell nucleus. Instructions are embodied in the chemical composition of the DNA, according to the GENETIC CODE. In classical genetics, a gene is described in terms of the trait that it determines and is investigated largely by virtue of the variations brought about by its different forms, or ALLELES. At the molecular level, most genes encode proteins, which carry out the functions of the cell or act to regulate the expression of other genes. A minority encode vital components of the cell's protein-assembling apparatus, such as ribosomes. Recent advances in genetic technology and the work of the HUMAN GENOME PROJECT have done much to illuminate the mechanism of gene action and have pinpointed genes responsible for various inherited diseases. This will greatly enhance knowledge of physical and mental disease in coming decades. See also DOMINANT ALLELE; RECESSIVE ALLELE.

genealogy *n.* the study of the ancestry of an individual or group with emphasis on family history and relationships rather than hereditary traits. **—genealogical** *adj.* **—genealogist** *n.*

gene–environment interaction an interaction between one or more genes and factors in the environment, such as may be needed to trigger the onset of a disease, condition, or characteristic.

gene–gene interaction an interaction between two or more genes, such as may be responsible for the development of a disease, condition, or characteristic.

gene imprinting the phenomenon in which the expression of a gene is different depending on whether it was inherited from the mother or the father.

gene knockout the deliberate inactivation of a particular gene in order to understand better the function of that gene. Using GENETIC ENGINEERING, scientists replace a normal gene (in an organism such as a mouse) with a defective gene and assess the impact of the defect on the organism.

gene linkage the tendency for genes or GENETIC MARKERS that are located physically close to each other on a chromosome to be inherited together. Linkage data can provide high-risk family members with estimates of their individual risk for the disease or condition conveyed by the gene.

gene mosaicism the presence in an individual of two or more cell lines that are distinct in respect to their genetic and chromosomal makeup and are derived from a single zygote.

gene mutation see MUTATION.

gene pool the total number of genes and their variants (ALLELES) that occur within a given population of a species at a particular time.

genera *pl. n.* see GENUS.

general ability a measurable ability believed to underlie skill in handling all types of intellectual tasks. See also GENERAL FACTOR.

general ability tests tests designed to measure the GENERAL FACTOR of intelligence. They usually require, among other things, understanding and applying relations among relatively abstract stimuli, such as geometric forms.

general adaptation syndrome (**GAS**) the physiological consequences of severe stress. The syndrome has three stages: alarm, resistance, and exhaustion. The first stage, the **alarm reaction** (or **alarm stage**), comprises two substages: the **shock phase**, marked by a decrease in body temperature, blood pressure, and muscle tone and loss of fluid from body tissues; and the **countershock phase**, during which the sympathetic nervous system is aroused and there is an increase in adrenocortical hormones, triggering a defensive reaction, such as the FIGHT–FLIGHT REACTION. The **resistance stage** (or **adaptation stage**) consists of stabilization at the increased physiological levels. High blood pressure can develop into hypertension, with risk of cardiovascular disturbance. Resources may be depleted, and permanent organ changes produced. The **exhaustion stage** is characterized by breakdown of acquired adaptations to a prolonged stressful situation; it is evidenced by sleep disturbances, irritability, severe loss of concentration, restlessness, trembling that disturbs motor coordination, fatigue, jumpiness, low startle threshold, vulnerability to anxiety attacks, depressed mood, and crying spells. [first described by Austrian-born Canadian physician Hans Seyle (1907–1982)]

general anesthetics see ANESTHETIC.

general aptitude see APTITUDE.

general arousal level of energy expenditure, proposed as one of the two dimensions in terms of which all human behavior can be explained (see AROUSAL), the other being approach–withdrawal.

general behavior theory see BEHAVIOR THEORY.

general consciousness see GROUP MIND.

general drive see NONREGULATORY DRIVE.

general extrasensory perception (**GESP**) in parapsychology, a paranormal outcome that cannot be assigned to any specific process of EXTRASENSORY PERCEPTION. For example, in an experiment with ZENER CARDS, it may be impossible to determine whether the RECEIVER has perceived the contents of the deck directly through CLAIRVOYANCE, received the thoughts of the SENDER through TELEPATHY, or controlled the original shuffling of the cards through PSYCHOKINESIS.

general factor (symbol: *g*) a hypothetical source of individual differences in GENERAL ABILITY, which represents individuals' abilities to perceive relationships and to derive conclusions from them. The general factor is said to be a basic ability that underlies the performance of different varieties of intellectual tasks, in contrast to SPECIFIC ABILITIES, which are alleged each to be unique to a single task. Even theorists who posit multiple mental abilities have often suggested that a general factor may underlie these (correlated) mental abilities. See TWO-FACTOR THEORY. Compare SPECIAL FACTOR. [postulated in 1904 by British psychologist Charles Spearman (1863–1945)]

general genetic law of cultural development the idea that a child's development, as a process embedded in culture, occurs on two planes: first the social, between individuals, and later the psychological, as thought is internalized by the child. [proposed by Lev VYGOTSKY]

general intelligence intelligence that is applicable to a very wide variety of tasks. See GENERAL FACTOR.

generalizability *n.* the accuracy with which results or findings can be transferred to situations or people other than those originally studied.

generalization *n.* **1.** the process of deriving a concept, judgment, principle, or theory from a limited number of specific cases and applying it more widely, often to an entire class of objects, events, or people. See INDUCTIVE REASONING. **2.** a judgment or principle derived and applied in this way. **3.** in conditioning, the process by which a CONDITIONED RESPONSE comes to be evoked by stimuli similar to those used in the original conditioning procedure. For example, a dog conditioned to bark when a particular bell sounds tends to bark to bells of any pitch. Also called **effect spread**; **spread of effect**. See INDUCTION; STIMULUS GENERALIZATION. **—generalize** *vb.*

generalization gradient see EXCITATION GRADIENT.

generalized anxiety disorder (**GAD**) excessive anxiety and worry about a range of events and activities (e.g., world events, finances, health, appearance, activities of family members and friends, work, or school) accompanied by such symptoms as restlessness, fatigue, impaired concentration, irritability, muscle tension, and disturbed sleep. The anxiety occurs on more days than not and is experienced as difficult to control.

generalized imitation imitation of forms of behavior that, until presented by a model, had been previously unseen. Presumably this results from a history of reinforcement for imitating.

generalized matching law in behavioral studies, a formula, in the form of a power function ($y = ax^b$), that describes the choice between two alternatives in terms of the ratio (y) of rates of occurrence of (or time spent in) each alternative and the ratio (x) of the rates of reinforcement of the two alternatives. The exponent (b) of the function indexes sensitivity to reinforcement rates, and the coefficient (a) indexes inherent bias for one of the alternatives. When both a and b are equal to 1.0, the formula makes the same prediction as the MATCHING LAW.

generalized motor program the hypothesized, abstract form of a MOTOR PROGRAM whose expression can be varied depending on the concurrent choice of parameters, such as overall extent or speed.

generalized other in SYMBOLIC INTERACTIONISM, the aggregation of other people's viewpoints. It is distinguished from specific other people and their individual views.

generalized seizure a seizure in which abnormal electrical activity involves the entire brain rather than a specific focal area. The two most common forms are ABSENCE SEIZURES and some TONIC–CLONIC SEIZURES.

generalizing assimilation in Jean PIAGET's theory of SENSORIMOTOR INTELLIGENCE, the incorporation of increasingly varied objects into a reflex SCHEME, as, for example, when an infant generalizes a sucking scheme to his or her hand, a blanket, or a toy.

general language disability any language difficulty in children characterized by delayed speech, prolonged use of infantile speech and grammar, and difficulty with reading and spelling.

general linear model a large class of statistical techniques, including REGRESSION ANALYSIS, ANALYSIS OF VARIANCE, and correlational analysis, that describe the relationship between a DEPENDENT VARIABLE and one or more INDEPENDENT VARIABLES. Most statistical techniques employed in the behavioral sciences can be subsumed under the general linear model.

general medical condition a disorder that has known physical causes and observable physical psychopathology. Examples include hypertension and diabetes. Such disorders are classified on Axis III of the *DSM–IV–TR* (see AXIS).

General Neuropsychological Deficit Scale a scale that combines a series of tests from the HALSTEAD–REITAN NEUROPSYCHOLOGICAL BATTERY to generate an overall estimate of cognitive impairment: The higher the score, the greater the impairment.

general paresis dementia associated with advanced neurosyphilitic infection of the brain (see NEUROSYPHILIS), a condition that is now extremely rare because syphilis is usually diagnosed and treated in its early stages. The first symptoms of general paresis appear 5–30 years after the primary infection. Psychological signs are irritability, confusion, fatigue, and forgetfulness, followed by headaches, confabulation, and deterioration in behavior and judgment. If untreated with antibiotics, physical signs gradually develop, including ARGYLL ROBERTSON PUPILS, sagging facial muscles, vacant expression, slurred speech, poor handwriting, and LOCOMOTOR ATAXIA, followed by inability to dress, paralysis, convulsions, loss of bladder and bowel control, and gradual deterioration to a vegetative state. General paresis was formerly known as **general paralysis of the insane, dementia paralytica, paralytic dementia**, and **paretic psychosis**. Also called **general paralysis**.

General Problem Solver (**GPS**) a computer program so named because its approach to problem solving using MEANS–ENDS ANALYSIS was intended to address many different problems and problem types. It employs a general recursive goal-reduction search procedure that looks to a problem-specific table of connections for goal and subgoal solution formulas. [built in 1961 by U.S. cognitive and computer scientist Allen Newell (1927–1992) and Herbert A. SIMON]

general psychology the study of the basic principles, problems, and methods underlying the science of psychology, including such areas as the physiological basis of behavior, human growth and development, emotions, motivation, learning, the senses, perception, thinking processes, memory, intelligence, personality theory, psychological testing, behavior disorders, social behavior, and mental health. The study is viewed from various perspectives, including physiological, historical, theoretical, philosophical, and practical.

general semantics an early attempt in the philosophy of language to establish the relationship between words and REFERENTS on a scientific basis. It proved influential in a number of disciplines in the 1930s and 1940s. See SEMANTICS; SEMIOTICS. [introduced by Polish-born U.S. philosopher and scientist Alfred Korzybski (1879–1950) in his *Science and Sanity* (1933)]

general slowing an explanation of COGNITIVE AGING that attributes poorer cognitive performance of older adults on a variety of cognitive tasks to reduced speed of COGNITIVE PROCESSING.

general systems theory an interdisciplinary conceptual framework focusing on wholeness, pattern, relationship, hierarchical order, integration, and organization. It was designed to move beyond the reductionistic and mechanistic tradition in science (see REDUCTIONISM) and integrate the fragmented approaches and different classes of phenomena studied by contemporary science into an organized whole. An entity or phenomenon should be viewed holistically as a set of elements interacting with one another (i.e., as a system), and the goal of general systems theory is to identify and understand the principles applicable to all systems. The impact of each element in a system depends on the role played by other elements in the system and order arises from interaction among these elements. Also called **systems theory**. [formulated by Austrian biologist Ludwig von Bertalanffy (1901–1972)]

general transfer the transfer of general skills or principles acquired in one task or situation to problems in a totally different field: for example, applying the capacity for logical thought acquired in a philosophy course to problems arising in business (see TRANSFER OF TRAINING). Also called **transfer by generalization**; **transfer of principles**. Compare SPECIFIC TRANSFER. See also COGNITIVE GENERALIZATION.

general will aims and intentions of a population regarding a particular issue or possible future course of action, arising through interaction and expressed through some social process or institution. The term was introduced by Swiss-born philosopher Jean-Jacques Rousseau (1712–1778), who argued that the general will is infallible and that every individual member of a society should submit his or her particular will to its dictates. See SOCIAL CONTRACT.

generate–recognize model see TWO-PROCESS MODEL OF RECALL.

generation *n.* **1.** the act or process of reproduction or creation. **2.** all of the offspring that are at the same stage of descent from a common ancestor. See also FILIAL GENERATION. **3.** the average time interval between the birth of parents and the birth of their offspring.

generation effect the fact that memory for items to be remembered in an experiment is enhanced if the participants help to generate the items. For example, the word *hot* will be better remembered if the studied item is "Opposite of COLD: H_ _" than if the word *hot* is simply read.

generation gap the differences in values, morals, attitudes, and behavior apparent between younger and older people in a society. The term was first used with reference to the burgeoning YOUTH CULTURE of the late 1960s. See also COHORT EFFECT.

generative grammar an approach to linguistics whose goal is to account for the infinite set of possible grammatical sentences in a language using a finite set of generative rules. Unlike earlier inductive approaches that set out to describe and draw inferences about grammar on the basis of a corpus of natural language, the theories of generative grammar developed by Noam CHOMSKY in the 1950s and 1960s took for their basic data the intuitions of native speakers about what is and is not grammatical (see COMPETENCE; GRAMMATICALITY). In taking this mentalist approach, Chomsky not only repudiated any behaviorist account of language use and acquisition but also revolutionized the whole field of linguistics, effectively redefining it as a branch of COGNITIVE PSYCHOLOGY. Much research in PSYCHOLINGUISTICS has since focused on whether the various models suggested by generative grammar have psychological reality in the production and reception of language. See also FINITE-STATE GRAMMAR; GOVERNMENT AND BINDING THEORY; PHRASE-STRUCTURE GRAMMAR; TRANSFORMATIONAL GENERATIVE GRAMMAR.

generativity versus stagnation the seventh stage of ERIKSON'S EIGHT STAGES OF DEVELOPMENT. Generativity is the positive goal of middle adulthood, interpreted in terms not only of procreation but also of creativity and fulfilling one's full parental and social responsibilities toward the next generation, in contrast to a narrow interest in the self, or self-absorption. Also called **generativity versus self-absorption**.

generator potential see RECEPTOR POTENTIAL.

generic knowledge see SEMANTIC KNOWLEDGE.

generic name the nonproprietary name for a pharmaceutical compound. In the United States, the name is adopted by the United States Adopted Name Council and, if recognized by the United States Pharmacopoeia (USP), becomes the official name of the compound. Compare PROPRIETARY DRUG; TRADEMARK.

generosity *n.* the quality of freely giving one's support or resources to others in need. See also KINDNESS. —**generous** *adj.*

-genesis *suffix* creation, origin, or development (e.g., PARTHENOGENESIS).

gene splicing the technique of inserting genetic material, in the form of DNA, into an existing DNA molecule. This is commonly performed in GENETIC ENGINEERING when genetic material from one organism is introduced into another organism, usually of a different species. The resultant RECOMBINANT DNA may create new sources of drugs or similar organic substances from microorganisms or correct genetic defects in organisms.

genetic *adj.* relating to GENES or GENETICS.

genetic algorithm a search procedure from ARTIFICIAL INTELLIGENCE in which populations of solutions of a problem (usually encoded in strings of BITS) are combined to make new possible solutions for the problem. A fitness measure is used to determine which solutions are suitable for making the new populations of solutions. Genetic operators, such as crossover (where sections of two solutions are interchanged) and mutation (where various bits in a solution are switched), are used to produce the new generations of solutions. This approach to creating problem solutions is intended to be an analogue of the survival of the fittest in actual evolutionary processes.

genetic bases of intelligence theoretical predispositions toward greater or lesser intelligence as a function of one's genetic makeup. Some investigators currently are seeking to identify the precise genes involved in generating individual differences in intelligence, and some research groups, such as that of British behavioral geneticist Robert Plomin (1948–), have already isolated genes that they believe are related to these differences.

genetic code the instructions in genes that "tell" the cell how to make specific proteins. The code resides in the sequence of bases occurring as constituents of the genetic material, DNA or RNA. These bases are represented by the letters A, T, G, and C (which stand for ADENINE, THYMINE, GUANINE, and CYTOSINE, respectively). In messenger RNA, URACIL (U) replaces thymine. Each unit, or CODON, of the code consists of three consecutive bases. Hence, there are 64 possible triplet combinations of the four bases, which specify the amino acids that make up each protein molecule.

genetic constraints on learning the concept, prominent from the 1960s to the early 1980s, that species-typical factors restrict the kinds of learning that a species can accomplish readily.

genetic counseling an interactive method of educating individuals about genetic risks, benefits and limitations of genetic testing, reproductive risks, and options for surveillance and screening related to diseases with potentially inherited causes. Genetic counseling is most often provided by geneticists or **genetic counselors**, who are trained to discuss hereditary disease with individuals, take PEDIGREES, and help individuals and families make decisions about the options open to them with regard to genetic disease. Genetic testing may or may not be a part of genetic counseling. Genetic counselors also assess the psychological implications of risk notification to the individual being counseled and the need for further psychological counseling following disclosure of test results. Also called **genetic guidance**. See also PRETEST COUNSELING; POSTTEST COUNSELING.

genetic defect any physical or mental illness, condition, or abnormality in an offspring that is due to a MUTATION in a gene or a chromosome. Generally, these genetic changes are expressed in a failure to synthesize a normally functioning enzyme that is required for a specific step in building a certain body cell or for a vital stage in the metabolism of a food element.

genetic determinism the doctrine that human and nonhuman animal behavior and mental activity are largely (or completely) controlled by the genetic constitution of the individual and that responses to environmental influences are for the most part innately determined. See BIOLOGICAL DETERMINISM; DETERMINISM; NATURE–NURTURE CONTROVERSY.

genetic disorder any disease or condition that is due to an abnormality of a gene or chromosome (see MUTATION). Also called **inherited disorder**.

genetic dominance see DOMINANT ALLELE.

genetic engineering techniques by which the genetic contents of living cells or viruses can be deliberately altered, either by modifying the existing genes or by introducing novel material (e.g., a gene from another species). This is undertaken for many different reasons, including basic research on genetic mechanisms, the large-scale production of particular gene products (e.g., medically useful proteins), and the genetic modification of crop plants. There have also been attempts to modify defective human body cells in the hope of treating certain genetic diseases. However, considerable public concern focuses on the effects and limits of genetic engineering of plants and animals, including humans. See also GENE SPLICING; RECOMBINANT DNA.

genetic epistemology the experimental study of the development of knowledge, originated by Jean PIAGET.

genetic error an error in the DNA code of a single gene. The genetic error may be due to a mutation that is spontaneous or caused by an environmental hazard, such as radiation that alters the gene's ability to provide the proper instructions for cellular manufacture of an enzyme required to metabolize an important amino acid. A genetic error that becomes hereditary usually is not lethal to the embryo or fetus; the individual is able to survive birth and become a fertile adult and thus able to transmit the genetic error to another generation of individuals. Some genetic errors, however, may result in fetal death or mortality for the individual before maturity. More than 2,000 kinds of genetic errors have been cataloged.

genetic guidance see GENETIC COUNSELING.

geneticism *n.* the concept that behavior is inborn, as in Sigmund FREUD's theory of instincts and psychosexual development. See also GENETIC DETERMINISM.

geneticist *n.* a health professional who specializes in the study of GENETICS. A geneticist may be a member of the staff of a medical services department of a hospital, medical college, or research institution.

genetic linguistics an approach to linguistics in which languages are classified according to their historical "family" relationships. The world's 4,000 or so languages are conventionally divided into some 18 families, each of which is presumed to have developed from a common ancestral PROTOLANGUAGE. The larger families, such as Indo-European, are further divided into subfamilies, such as Celtic, Germanic, Aryan, and so on. Compare AREAL LINGUISTICS; LINGUISTIC TYPOLOGY. See COMPARATIVE LINGUISTICS; SYNCHRONIC LINGUISTICS.

genetic linkage see GENE LINKAGE.

genetic map a chromosome map of a species that shows the position of its known genes, GENETIC MARKERS, or both relative to each other. In humans, genetic mapping entails examining the pattern of inheritance of numerous traits or other markers, over many generations, to establish the degree of GENE LINKAGE. See also MAPPING OF GENES.

genetic marker a gene or segment of DNA with an identifiable location on a chromosome and whose inheritance can be readily tracked through different generations. Because DNA segments that lie near each other on a chromosome tend to be inherited together, markers are often used to determine the inheritance of a gene that has not yet been identified but whose approximate location is known.

genetic method the study of psychological processes in terms of hereditary origins and developmental history, with an emphasis on the role of genes as explanatory devices.

genetic monogamy see MONOGAMY.

genetic predisposition a tendency for certain physical or mental traits to be inherited, including physical and mental conditions and disorders. Schizophrenia, for example, is a mental disorder with a genetic predisposition that affects less than 1% of the general population but increasingly larger percentages of distant relatives, siblings, and identical twins of individuals affected. Also called **hereditary predisposition**.

genetic programming a search process for generating problem solutions based on research in GENETIC ALGORITHMS. In this situation, problem solutions are represented by computer code. Genetic operators, including the exchange of components of code between two solutions as well as the mutation of pieces of a solution code, are used to produce new solutions. A fitness metric is used to determine which solutions are most appropriate for use in producing each new generation of solutions.

genetic psychology the study of genetic and early environmental factors that influence child development. In the 19th and early 20th centuries, genetic psychology was synonymous with DEVELOPMENTAL PSYCHOLOGY.

genetics *n.* the branch of biology that is concerned with the mechanisms and phenomena of heredity and the laws that determine inherited traits. See also BEHAVIOR GENETICS; BIOGENESIS; POLITICAL GENETICS; SOCIOGENETICS.

genetic sequence the order of base pairs along a particular strand or segment of a DNA or MESSENGER RNA molecule.

genetic theory **1.** the view that behavior can be explained in hereditary and developmental terms. **2.** the theoretical principles accepted in the science of genetics.

genetic underclass see UNDERCLASS.

genetic variation the basis for individual differences (see VARIATION) and for NATURAL SELECTION. Within any population or species there is usually considerable genetic variation. In some conditions those with certain genetic features will be favored and have higher REPRODUCTIVE SUCCESS, but if conditions change, then individuals with other genetic features might be favored.

genetotropic disease any disease due to an inherited enzyme defect or deficiency. Phenylketonuria and other inborn errors of metabolism are examples of such disorders.

Geneva school of genetic psychology those who adhere to Jean PIAGET's theory of developmental psychology.

-genic *suffix* produced by or producing (e.g., PSYCHOGENIC).

geniculate nucleus any of several clusters of nerve cell bodies (see NUCLEUS) on the surface of the THALAMUS in the brain. There are two pairs—the LATERAL GENICULATE NUCLEI and the MEDIAL GENICULATE NUCLEI—with one of each pair on either lobe of the thalamus; these relay, respectively, visual impulses and auditory impulses to the cerebral cortex. Also called **geniculate body**.

genital *adj.* relating to the sex organs. The external genital organs are the penis and scrotum for men and the VULVA for women. The internal genital organs are the vagina, uterus, and ovaries for women and the testicles and prostate for men.

genital arousal in sleep penile erection in men and clitoral enlargement and vaginal lubrication in women that occur during REM SLEEP (in which dreams occur). It is the result of an increase in pelvic blood flow and occurs with all dream content; it is not associated only with sexual dreams. The phenomenon is used as part of the diagnostic procedures for male erection problems, as absence of nocturnal penile tumescence is a measure of physical problems involved in ERECTILE DYSFUNCTION.

genital character see GENITAL PERSONALITY.

genital eroticism the arousal of sexual excitement by stimulation of the genital organs.

genital herpes a HERPES INFECTION that involves the genitals, caused by herpes simplex Type 2. Although genital herpes is usually transmitted by sexual contact, some epidemiologists believe that because of extreme human susceptibility to the virus it is possible for transmission to occur through other means (e.g., hand-to-hand contact), especially in cities or other areas of high population density.

genitalia *pl. n.* the reproductive organs of the male or female. The **male genitalia** include the penis, testes and related structures, prostate gland, seminal vesicles, and bulbourethral glands. The **female genitalia** consist of the vagina, uterus, ovaries, fallopian tubes, and related structures. The **external genitalia** comprise the VULVA in females and the penis and testicles in males. Also called **genitals**. See also AMBIGUOUS GENITALIA.

genital intercourse sexual intercourse involving insertion of the penis into the vagina, as opposed to other forms of sexual activity.

genitality *n.* the capacity to experience erotic sensation in the genital organs, starting with childhood masturbation and culminating in adult sexuality.

genitalization *n.* **1.** in psychoanalytic theory, the focusing of the genital libido on nonsexual objects that resemble or symbolize the sex organs, such as knives, shoes, or locks of hair. See also FETISH. **2.** in psychoanalytic theory, the achievement of a GENITAL PERSONALITY. **—genitalize** *vb.*

genital love in psychoanalytic theory, sexually mature love of another person achieved during the GENITAL STAGE of PSYCHOSEXUAL DEVELOPMENT. See also GENITAL PERSONALITY.

genital mutilation the destruction or physical modification of the external genitalia. This may be (a) an aspect of a cultural or religious ritual, such as CIRCUMCISION or FEMALE GENITAL MUTILATION; (b) a self-injurious behavior, typically associated with psychosis; or (c) a violent act inflicted on others, such as castration of enemy soldiers in wartime.

genital personality in psychoanalytic theory, the sexually mature, adult personality that ideally develops during the last stage (the GENITAL STAGE) of PSYCHOSEXUAL DEVELOPMENT. Individuals who have reached this stage of development are posited to have fully resolved their OEDIPUS COMPLEX and to exhibit a mature sexuality that involves true intimacy and expresses equal concern for their own and their partner's satisfaction. Also called **genital character**. See also GENITAL LOVE.

genital stage in psychoanalytic theory, the final stage of PSYCHOSEXUAL DEVELOPMENT, ideally reached in puberty, when the OEDIPUS COMPLEX has been fully resolved and erotic interest and activity are focused on intercourse with a sexual partner. Also called **genital phase**. See also GENITAL LOVE; GENITAL PERSONALITY.

genital stimulation a complex set of factors associated with sexual arousal in mammals, including integration of male and female genital reflexes, odors, hormone secretions, sights, sounds, and tactile and kinesthetic cues. Each factor contributes to genital stimulation, which still may occur in the absence of one or more of the cues.

genital zones the external reproductive organs and adjacent areas that are capable of producing genital sensations. See also EROTOGENOUS ZONE.

genitive *n.* a CASE of nouns, pronouns, and noun phrases that expresses a possessor–possessed relation. In English, unlike more inflected languages, the genitive case is apparent only in the possessive pronouns (*my/mine, your/yours, our/ours,* etc.) and the use of the noun ending *-'s* or *-'* to indicate possession. Compare ACCUSATIVE; DATIVE; NOMINATIVE.

genitofemoral nerve a nerve that receives sensory impulses from the genitalia and the leg. It divides into femoral and genital branches. In men the genital branch innervates the cremaster muscle and skin of the scrotum; in women it accompanies one of the ligaments of the uterus. The femoral branch subdivides into other smaller nerves of the leg.

genius *n.* **1.** an extreme degree of creative or other abilities, usually demonstrated by exceptional achievement. **2.** a person who possesses this ability. British scientist Francis Galton (1822–1911), the first to investigate genius systematically, mistakenly based his conclusions on the genealogy of eminent individuals (1869) and concluded that genius was inherited. James M. CATTELL favored an environmental explanation for the emergence of genius. Lewis M. TERMAN originally applied the term to children with an IQ of 140 or more; however, although he followed up a large group of such children until they were over 50, he found few geniuses among them. Alfred ADLER attributed exceptional achievement to overcompensation for feelings of inferiority, while Sigmund FREUD held that geniuses are born with extraordinary ability but are basically conflicted and frustrated individuals who solve their emotional problems by expressing themselves in works of art or science, a theory that has not been widely accepted. In general, genius is seen to emerge as a joint product of heredity and environment and to require a great deal of very hard and dedicated work to achieve.

genocide *n.* the intentional and systematic annihilation of a racial, ethnic, national, or religious group. Thus defined, genocide was declared an international crime by the United Nations Genocide Convention of 1948. See also ETHNIC CLEANSING. **—genocidal** *adj.*

genocopy *n.* see GENOTYPE.

genogram *n.* a diagrammatic representation of a family that includes not only PEDIGREE information, that is, individual histories of illness and death, but also incorporates aspects of the interpersonal relationships between the family members.

genome *n.* all of the genetic material contained in an organism or cell. Mapping of the human genome was the work of the HUMAN GENOME PROJECT.

genotype *n.* **1.** the full set of genes of an individual organism. The human genotype includes about 30,000 genes. An individual whose genotype appears to be identical to that of another is called a **genocopy**. **2.** the combination of ALLELES present at one or more genetic loci. Compare PHENOTYPE. **—genotypic** *adj.*

genotype–environment effects the effects of genetic constitution on experience, based on the proposal that an individual's GENOTYPE influences which environments he or she encounters and the type of experiences he or she has. Three types of genotype–environment effects are proposed: passive (through environments provided by biologically related parents); evocative (through responses elicited by individuals from others); and active (through the selection of different environments by different individuals). [proposed by U.S. psychologists Sandra Scarr (1936–) and Kathleen McCartney (1955–)]

genotype–phenotype correlation a correlation between the location or nature of a mutation in a gene and the expression of that mutation in the individual, based on observations of affected individuals and their genotypes. Attempts at such correlations are made to elucidate which characteristics of a mutation affect the age of onset or severity of diseases with a genetic etiology.

gentrification *n.* the physical upgrading of neighborhoods and housing accompanying an influx of wealthier residents. It is theorized that an important adverse effect of gentrification is the displacement of many long-term residents who can no longer afford to live in the gentrified area. **—gentrify** *vb.*

genu *n.* (*pl.* **genua**) **1.** the knee, or an anatomical structure that resembles a knee. **2.** the anterior portion of the CORPUS CALLOSUM as it bends forward and downward.

genus *n.* (*pl.* **genera**) in BIOLOGICAL TAXONOMY, a main subdivision of a FAMILY, containing a group of similar, related SPECIES.

geocentric theory the theory, attributed to Alexandrian astronomer, geographer, and mathematician Ptolemy (2nd century CE), that the earth is the center of the universe and that the heavenly bodies move around it. Also called **Ptolemaic theory**. Compare HELIOCENTRIC THEORY.

Geodon *n.* a trade name for ZIPRASIDONE.

geographical mobility the capacity or facility of individuals to move from one geographic region to another. See also HORIZONTAL MOBILITY; MOBILITY; SOCIAL MOBILITY.

geographic segmentation the division of consumers into different groups based on where they live (determined, e.g., through postal codes). Geographic segmentation is usually combined with demographic information, in which case it is often called **geodemographic segmentation**.

geometrical illusion a figure made of straight or curved lines in which the lines or their interrelationships are misinterpreted by the visual system. Examples of such illusions are the MÜLLER-LYER ILLUSION and the ZÖLLNER ILLUSION.

geometric distribution the PROBABILITY DISTRIBUTION of the number of failed trials before the first success in a series of BERNOULLI TRIALS.

geometric mean a measure of CENTRAL TENDENCY. The geometric mean of k numbers $x_1 \ldots x_k$ is $(x_1 x_2 x_3 \ldots x_k)^{1/k}$.

geon *n.* a simple three-dimensional element (e.g., a sphere or cube) regarded as a fundamental component in the perception of a more complex object. See RECOGNITION BY COMPONENTS THEORY. [first proposed by U.S. psychologist Irving Biederman (1939–)]

geophagy *n.* the eating of dirt or clay. It is most commonly seen in individuals with mental retardation, young children, and occasionally in pregnant women. It is usually a symptom of PICA but in some cultures it is an accepted practice.

geotaxis *n.* the involuntary movement of an organism

that helps it maintain a postural orientation related to the force of gravity. See TAXIS.

Geriatric Depression Scale (**GDS**) an assessment instrument specifically designed for use with adults aged 65 years and over. It is self-administered and comprises a series of 30 yes–no questions (e.g., "Do you often get bored?", "Is it easy for you to make decisions?", "Do you enjoy getting up in the morning?") about depressive symptoms that excludes somatic disturbances often experienced by older adults. [originally developed in 1982 by psychologist T. L. Brink (1949–), psychiatrist Jerome A. Yesavage, and colleagues]

geriatric disorder a chronic physical or mental disease or disorder that occurs commonly, but not exclusively, among older people. Examples of geriatric disorders include glaucoma, cataract, arthritis, rheumatism, and Alzheimer's disease.

geriatrician *n.* a physician, psychologist, or other health care provider who specializes in the biopsychosocial treatment and management of older adults. See also GERIATRICS.

geriatric psychology see GEROPSYCHOLOGY.

geriatric psychopharmacology the branch of pharmacology that deals with issues related to the use of and response to psychoactive agents in older adults, as well as the mechanisms responsible. Metabolic changes associated with aging can affect a drug's biological activity and may increase the sensitivity of the patient's central nervous system to drugs.

geriatric psychotherapy the use of therapy to treat the mental disorders of older adults. Geriatric psychotherapy requires an understanding of age-related and cohort-related differences (see COHORT EFFECT) in symptoms and behavior.

geriatric rehabilitation the restoration of mobility and the ability to live independently in people with GERIATRIC DISORDERS. Gerontologists generally do not regard infirmities of aging as inevitable and agree that many of the diseases associated with aging are preventable and controllable when individuals seek early treatment.

geriatrics *n.* the branch of medicine that deals with old age and the treatment of physical and mental disorders in older adults. See GEROCOMY. **—geriatric** *adj.*

geriatric screening a program or system administered by a hospital, community center, county health center, or other such agency to provide qualified staff who evaluate the needs of older adults by providing physical examinations and care, psychological evaluations, and financial counseling.

geriopsychosis *n.* an outdated term for any manifestation of brain deterioration and severe mental disorder associated with aging.

German measles a disease caused by the rubella virus, which produces symptoms similar to measles, although it is less contagious. A woman who develops German measles during pregnancy has a 25% chance of giving birth to a child with congenital rubella. The rate of malformation in the fetus ranges from a low of 6% if the virus is contracted during the third month of pregnancy to as high as 50% in the first month. The birth defects include malformations of the eyes, ears, and central nervous system (see CONGENITAL RUBELLA SYNDROME). Also called **rubella**.

germ cell any of the cells in the gonads that give rise to the GAMETES by a process involving growth and MEIOSIS. See OOGENESIS; SPERMATOGENESIS.

germinal stage 1. in humans, the first 1 to 2 weeks of prenatal life after fertilization, in which the fertilized egg (zygote) migrates to the uterus and becomes implanted in the ENDOMETRIUM. The EMBRYONIC STAGE follows the germinal stage. **2.** in plants, the season during which germination occurs.

germ layer any of the three layers of cells in an animal embryo at the GASTRULA stage, from which the various organs and tissues develop. The outermost layer is the ECTODERM, the middle layer is the MESODERM, and the inner layer is the ENDODERM.

germ line the line of cells that gives rise to the reproductive cells—the ova and spermatozoa—and is thereby continued between successive generations of organisms. Hence germ-line mutations, unlike somatic mutations (i.e., mutations in body cells), are transmitted to offspring and may cause predisposition to disease or other traits.

germ plasm 1. the region of cytoplasm in an egg cell that is destined to give rise to the GERM CELLS during subsequent embryological development. **2.** the hereditary material that, according to German cytologist August Weismann (1834–1914) in his germ plasm theory (also known as **continuity of germ plasm** or **Weismannism**), passes unchanged from generation to generation in the germ cells. It is now identified as DNA.

germ theory the doctrine that infectious diseases are caused by the presence and activity in body tissues of microorganisms, such as bacteria, viruses, or fungi.

gerocomy *n.* the medical care of aging individuals. See GERIATRICS.

geromorphism *n.* the condition of appearing older than one's actual chronological age.

geront- (**gero-**) *combining form* old age.

gerontological psychology see GEROPSYCHOLOGY.

gerontology *n.* the scientific interdisciplinary study of old age and the aging process. Those involved in gerontology include psychologists, biologists, sociologists, medical scientists, medical practitioners, geriatric service providers, and scholars from the humanities and social sciences. See also SOCIAL GERONTOLOGY. **—gerontological** *adj.* **—gerontologist** *n.*

gerophilia *n.* sexual attraction to much older partners. Also called **gerontophilia**.

geropsychology *n.* a branch of psychology dealing with the mental health of older adults and the study of the process of aging. Also called **geriatric psychology**; **gerontological psychology**. **—geropsychological** *adj.* **—geropsychologist** *n.*

Gerstmann's syndrome a set of symptoms of a neurological disorder marked by DYSGRAPHIA, FINGER AGNOSIA, ACALCULIA, and RIGHT–LEFT DISORIENTATION. [Josef G. **Gerstmann** (1887–1969), Austrian neurologist]

Gesamtvorstellung *n.* the act of holding in mind the entire content of a sentence before the first word is spoken. [German, literally: "complete concept"; coined by Wilhelm WUNDT]

Geschwind's theory the hypothesis that excessive intrauterine exposure to ANDROGENS inhibits development of the THYMUS gland and left cerebral hemisphere, explaining why autoimmune disorders tend to be associated with learning disabilities (including DYSLEXIA) and are more frequent in males than in females. [proposed in 1984 by U.S. neuroscientists Norman **Geschwind** (1926–1984) and Albert Galaburda (1948–)]

Gesellschaft *n.* a type of society (the literal meaning of this German word) or social group in which people feel relatively isolated from each other. Their relationships are primarily contractual in nature, being guided chiefly by rational self-interest and the logic of the marketplace. Compare GEMEINSCHAFT. [first described by German sociologist Ferdinand Julius Tönnies (1855–1936)]

GESP abbreviation for GENERAL EXTRASENSORY PERCEPTION.

gestalt *n.* an entire perceptual configuration (from German: "shape," "configuration," "totality," "form"), made up of elements that are integrated and interactive in such a way as to confer properties on the whole configuration that are not possessed by the individual elements. See PERCEPTUAL ORGANIZATION. See also GESTALT PRINCIPLES OF ORGANIZATION; GESTALT PSYCHOLOGY.

gestalt completion test a visual-perceptual task in which the participant is required to synthesize elements from fragmented, ambiguous pictures of items to form a "whole." Poor performance on this test (i.e., inability to report complete objects) may indicate impairment of right-hemisphere brain function. This testing technique was initially developed in 1931 by U.S. psychologist Roy F. Street but has since been adapted by others. The original **Street Gestalt Completion Test** (also known as the **Street Gestalt test** or **Street test**) consists of 13 incomplete silhouettes of common objects.

gestalt grouping factor a condition (e.g., proximity) that favors perception of a GESTALT figure, that is, of wholeness or entirety.

gestalt homology in GESTALT PSYCHOLOGY, the notion that components of two different structures can have the same role in their respective structures and be defined by that role. For example, a hypotenuse has the same function in any right triangle and is defined by its relationship to the other two sides and the right angle opposite.

gestaltism *n.* the belief system of GESTALT PSYCHOLOGY.

gestalt principles of organization principles of perception, derived by the Gestalt psychologists, that describe the tendency to perceive and interpret certain configurations at the level of the whole, rather than in terms of their component features. They include the **laws of grouping** identified by German psychologist Max WERTHEIMER in 1923: the law of CLOSURE, the law of COMMON FATE, the LAW OF CONTINUITY, the LAW OF PROXIMITY, the LAW OF SIMILARITY, and the LAW OF SYMMETRY. Also called **gestalt laws of organization**. See also GOODNESS OF CONFIGURATION; PRINCIPLE OF PRÄGNANZ.

Gestalt psychology a psychological approach that focuses on the dynamic organization of experience into patterns or configurations (from German *Gestalt* [pl. *Gestalten*]: "shape," "form," "configuration," "totality"). This view was espoused by German psychologists Wolfgang KÖHLER, Kurt KOFFKA, and Max WERTHEIMER in the early 20th century as a revolt against STRUCTURALISM, which analyzed experience into static, atomistic sensations, and also against the equally atomistic approach of BEHAVIORISM, which attempted to dissect complex behavior into elementary conditioned reflexes. Gestalt psychology holds, instead, that experience is an organized whole of which the pieces are an integral part. A crucial demonstration (1912) is that of Wertheimer with two successively flashed lights, which gave the illusion of motion between them rather than of individually flashing lights. Later experiments gave rise to principles of perceptual organization (see, for example, CLOSURE; PRINCIPLE OF PRÄGNANZ; LAW OF PROXIMITY), which were then applied to the study of learning, insight, memory, social psychology, and art.

gestalt therapy a form of PSYCHOTHERAPY in which the central focus is on the totality of the client's functioning and relationships in the HERE AND NOW, rather than on investigation of past experiences and developmental history. One of the themes of gestalt therapy is that growth occurs by assimilation of what is needed from the environment and that psychopathology arises as a disturbance of contact with the environment. Gestalt techniques, which can be applied in either a group or an individual setting, are designed to bring out spontaneous feelings and self-awareness and promote personality growth. Examples of such techniques are ROLE PLAY, the EMPTY-CHAIR TECHNIQUE, and the HOT-SEAT TECHNIQUE. [first proposed in the 1940s by German-born U.S. psychiatrist Frederick (Fritz) S. Perls (1893–1970)]

gestation *n.* the development of the embryo and fetus in the uterus until birth. See PREGNANCY. **—gestational** *adj.*

gestational age the age of a fetus calculated from the date of conception. Also called **fetal age**. See also MENSTRUAL AGE.

gestational surrogate a woman in whom is implanted an embryo produced by IN VITRO FERTILIZATION using the ova and sperm of another couple.

gestation period the period of pregnancy, or carrying the offspring in the uterus of the mother. Gestation periods range from 20 days for the shrew to 550 days for the African rhinoceros and 22 months for the elephant. In human beings, the expected date of birth is usually calculated as 280 days or 9 calendar months from the beginning of the woman's last menstruation.

gestural communication nonverbal transmission and reception of messages (ideas, feelings, signals) by means of body movements.

gestural-postural language nonverbal language in which communication is limited to gestures and postures.

gesture *n.* **1.** a movement, such as the clenching of a fist, the waving of a hand, or the stamping of a foot, that communicates a particular meaning or indicates the individual's emotional state or attitude. See EMBLEM; ICONIC GESTURE. See also NONVERBAL BEHAVIOR. **2.** a statement or act, usually symbolic, that is intended to influence the attitudes of others (as in a *gesture of goodwill*). **—gestural** *adj.*

G_{M2} gangliosidosis see TAY-SACHS DISEASE.

GH abbreviation for GROWTH HORMONE.

GHB *g*amma-*h*ydroxy*b*utyrate: a potent CNS DEPRESSANT that is a metabolic product of the inhibitory neurotransmitter GAMMA-AMINOBUTYRIC ACID (GABA). It is currently used for treatment of narcolepsy and management of alcohol withdrawal, and in some countries (although not the United States) has been used as an intravenous general anesthetic. It is commonly encountered as a drug of abuse that produces euphoria and sedation and purportedly enhances sexual arousal. Its ability to induce amnesia or unconsciousness has led it to be characterized as a DATE-RAPE DRUG. Signs of severe toxicity may occur at levels greater than 40–60 mg/kg, and deaths have been reported, usually when the substance is mixed with alcohol. Withdrawal syndromes, characterized by anxiety, tremor, confusion, and rarely seizures, have also been reported. U.S. trade name: **Xyrem**.

Gheel colony a colony of people with serious mental illness at Gheel in Belgium, a town of refuge where they are given shelter in individual homes and employed in various capacities. This practice dates from the 13th century and is associated with the legend of St. Dymphna, who was martyred at Gheel and became the patron saint of mental illness, incest victims, and runaways. The colony became a government institute in 1850. See SAINT DYMPHNA'S DISEASE.

ghost image any APPARITION of a disembodied figure that retains some general bodily characteristics of a previously living person. Ghost images are rarely "seen" by more than one individual at a time, even when others are present, and tend to be perceived in periods of emotional crisis. The image often includes some implausible physical factors; for example, the ghost wears clothing, rides a horse, or carries a heavy object despite its disembodied nature. See also VERIDICAL HALLUCINATION.

ghost in the machine a phrase used to emphasize the problems associated with CARTESIAN DUALISM, in which the mind is seen as a nonphysical entity (a "ghost") that somehow inhabits and interacts with a mechanical body (the "machine"). See DUALISM; MIND–BODY PROBLEM. [coined by British philosopher Gilbert Ryle (1900–1976)]

ghost sickness a CULTURE-BOUND SYNDROME found in Native American communities. Symptoms include preoccupation with death and the deceased (sometimes associated with witchcraft), bad dreams, weakness, feelings of danger, loss of appetite, fainting, dizziness, fear, anxiety, hallucinations, loss of consciousness, confusion, feelings of futility, and a sense of suffocation.

ghrelin *n.* a peptide secreted by endocrine cells in the stomach that binds to growth hormone receptors in the hypothalamus and anterior pituitary, stimulating appetite and the release of growth hormone.

giant cell arteritis see ARTERITIS.

gibberish *n.* language that is incoherent and unintelligible and of a type observed in some individuals with schizophrenia.

Gibson, Eleanor Jack (1910–2002) U.S. psychologist. Gibson married experimental psychologist James Jerome GIBSON, one of her undergraduate teachers at Smith College, and subsequently (1938) earned her PhD at Yale University under Clark Leonard HULL. She is best known for her research on the VISUAL CLIFF, which demonstrated the existence of DEPTH PERCEPTION in infants. This work was part of her larger body of research on PERCEPTUAL LEARNING, that is, how perception is affected by experience. Her book *Principles of Perceptual Learning and Development* (1969) was important in providing both theories and methods for studying perception in preverbal children. Another major focus for Gibson was the psychology of reading, a field that she and colleagues helped to revive with the publication of *The Psychology of Reading* (1975, coauthored by Harry Levin). Gibson's contributions were recognized through such awards as the American Psychological Association's Distinguished Scientific Contribution Award (1968) and Gold Medal Award (1968) and the National Medal of Science (1992).

Gibson, James Jerome (1904–1979) U.S. psychologist. Gibson earned his doctorate at Princeton University in 1928 under Herbert S. Langfeld (1879–1958). He married Eleanor Jack GIBSON, who subsequently earned a doctorate and became a respected experimental psychologist in her own right. During World War II he served as a captain in the Air Force, studying flight-related aspects of visual perception. He later developed the influential theory of ECOLOGICAL PERCEPTION, in which he argued, among other things, that organisms can directly perceive the adaptive value of objects and events in the environment. His most important works include *The Perception of the Visual World* (1950), *The Senses Considered as Perceptual Systems* (1966), and *The Ecological Approach to Visual Perception* (1979).

GIFT acronym for GAMETE INTRAFALLOPIAN TRANSFER.

giftedness *n.* the state of possessing a great amount of natural ability, talent, or intelligence, which usually becomes evident at a very young age. Giftedness in intelligence is often categorized as an IQ of two standard deviations above the mean or higher (130 for most IQ tests), obtained on an individually administered IQ test. Many schools and service organizations now use a combination of attributes as the basis for assessing giftedness, including one or more of the following: high intellectual capacity, academic achievement, demonstrable real-world achievement, creativity, task commitment, proven talent, leadership skills, and physical or athletic prowess. The combination of several attributes, or the prominence of one primary attribute, may be regarded as a threshold for the identification of giftedness. Unfortunately, many schools and program administrators have created policies that require multiple indicators for identifying and teaching gifted individuals, and—as a group—these people have received less attention and fewer special services than individuals with disabilities who require SPECIAL EDUCATION. **—gifted** *adj.*

gigantism *n.* an abnormally large body size due to excessive secretion of growth hormone by the pituitary gland: the term is sometimes applied to individuals more than 205 cm (81 in) in height. See also ACROMEGALY.

gigolo *n.* a man who is paid to be a woman's social companion or escort, or to provide sexual services for her, or both.

Gilles de la Tourette's syndrome see TOURETTE'S DISORDER.

Gillespie syndrome see ANIRIDIA-OLIGOPHRENIA-CEREBELLAR ATAXIA SYNDROME. [described in 1965 by F. D. **Gillespie** (1927–), U.S. ophthalmologist]

Gindler method a series of exercises involving breathing, gentle touch, and posturing intended to foster personal growth and enhance sensory awareness. [Elsa **Gindler** (1885–1961), German gymnastics teacher]

ginkgo *n.* a tree, *Ginkgo biloba*, that is indigenous to Asia but now cultivated widely. An extract of the leaves has been used for centuries by Chinese herbalists and is reputed to possess medicinal and psychotropic properties. It is also a popular dietary supplement primarily used to improve mental acuity, although clinical evidence supporting this effect is largely lacking. The active compounds in ginkgo extract have anticoagulant properties, and ginkgo has been investigated as a treatment for vascular disorders, both peripheral and cerebral (e.g., vascular dementia), the latter with equivocal results. Gingko may also have neuroprotective properties and currently is under investigation as a treatment for the symptoms of Alzheimer's disease, with results suggesting a potential cognition stabilizing effect. Side effects of ginkgo use are rare and may include headaches or mild gastrointestinal disturbances. Data, however, suggest continual long-term use of ginkgo may be associated with excessive bleeding or spontaneous hemorrhage. Additionally, there are several known and potential interactions of ginkgo with other agents, including anticoagulants, anticonvulsants, MONOAMINE OXIDASE INHIBITORS, and NSAIDS. Ginkgo may also lower seizure thresholds and should not be used by people who have a history of seizures.

ginseng *n.* the root of various plants of the genus *Panax*, valued for its medicinal properties, particularly in Oriental cultures. It has a reputation as an aphrodisiac and is also used to enhance overall physical and mental well-being, enhance strength, boost energy, and relieve stress, but there is little clinical evidence supporting its effectiveness for any of these purposes. Some studies, however, have suggested that ginseng may help regulate blood glucose levels, which has prompted investigation of its potential use as a treatment for diabetes, and may improve immune function. Side effects of ginseng use are infrequent but may include nausea and vomiting, diarrhea, insomnia, headaches, nosebleeds, and blood pressure abnormalities. Additionally, ginseng may interact with anticoagulants, caffeine, MONOAMINE OXIDASE INHIBITORS, and oral hypoglycemics.

girdle sensation the sensation of feeling a tight band around the trunk, sometimes experienced in MULTIPLE SCLEROSIS.

give-and-take process see INTERPERSONAL ACCOMMODATION.

given–new distinction in a sentence or other linguistic structure, the distinction made between information that is probably new to the recipient and that which is probably already known (or can be regarded as given by the context). A speaker's or writer's assumptions about which information falls into which category will usually affect word order, stress, and other observable features of language. The distinction is important in PRAGMATICS and DISCOURSE ANALYSIS. See FOREGROUNDING.

glabrous skin the tough, thick hairless skin that is found on the soles of the feet and the palms of the hands.

gland *n.* an organ that secretes a substance needed for some bodily function or for discharge from the body. EXOCRINE GLANDS discharge substances (e.g., tears, sweat) outside the body or into the gastrointestinal tract, whereas ENDOCRINE GLANDS discharge their products (hormones) into the bloodstream. Exocrine glands generally release their product through a duct, whereas endocrine glands are ductless.

glans penis the roughly mushroom-shaped cap at the tip of the penis. It consists of the expanded extremity of the CORPUS SPONGIOSUM associated with connective tissue and covered in skin (see FORESKIN).

glare *n.* a quality of intense brightness, due either to a reflection from a glass or metallic surface or to any strong and harsh light that hinders visual acuity (e.g., high-beam headlights). See also DIRECT GLARE.

Glasgow Coma Scale (**GCS**) a rating scale, with scores ranging from 3 to 15, that is used to assess levels of consciousness following a head injury. It is the sum of three ratings: eye-opening response (graded 1–4), motor response (1–6), and verbal response (1–5). Scores of 8 or below are indicative of severe brain injury and coma, scores of 9 to 12 are indicative of moderate injury, and scores of 13 or higher are indicative of mild injury. [originally developed in 1974 by neurologists Graham M. Teasdale and Bryan J. Jennett at the University of Glasgow, Scotland]

Glasgow Outcome Scale (**GOS**) a rating scale to assess social activity and independent functioning after traumatic brain injury. The five categories of the original scale are death, persistent vegetative state, severe disability, moderate disability, and good recovery. An extended GOS that divides each of the latter three levels into an upper and lower degree of disability is also available. [originally developed in 1975 by neurologist Bryan J. Jennett and psychiatrist Michael R. Bond at the University of Glasgow, Scotland]

glass ceiling an invisible barrier that prevents able and ambitious women from rising to positions of authority in many organizations. See SEX DISCRIMINATION; SEXISM.

glaucoma *n.* a common eye disease marked by raised INTRAOCULAR PRESSURE in one or both eyes and, in uncontrolled glaucoma, severe peripheral visual field loss. Age, myopia, and vascular disease are among the risk factors for glaucoma, and there is a higher incidence of the disease among those of African ancestry than in those of other groups. The acute form causes pain and abrupt reduction of visual acuity, visual blurring, and (if untreated) severe VISUAL IMPAIRMENT. Chronic glaucoma is characterized by progressive visual failure without accompanying pain. See also CONGENITAL GLAUCOMA; TUNNEL VISION.

glial cells see NEUROGLIA.

glioblastoma *n.* a fast-growing, malignant brain tumor derived from support cells of the central nervous system. It is a type of ASTROCYTOMA that results in widespread cognitive damage and often death. The most malignant form is **glioblastoma multiforme** (or **anaplastic astrocytoma**), consisting of poorly differentiated cells.

glioma *n.* the most malignant form of brain tumor, which develops from support cells (NEUROGLIA) of the central nervous system (CNS). There are three main types, grouped according to the form of support cell involved: ASTROCYTOMA (from astrocytes), oligodendroglioma (from OLIGODENDROCYTES), and ependymoma (from ependymal cells; see EPENDYMA). Glioma is usually a primary tumor and rarely metastasizes beyond the CNS. It is the most common type of brain cancer and accounts for about a quarter of spinal cord tumors. Also called **neuroglioma**.

gliosis *n.* an excess of ASTROCYTES in a damaged area of the central nervous system. Gliosis is a prominent feature of some neurological diseases, including stroke.

glittering generalities vague but catchy phrases and slogans frequently used in propaganda and political campaigns to elicit favorable reactions. Examples are "good, clean government" and "our noble heritage."

global amnesia amnesia that encompasses verbal and nonverbal information and occurs regardless of the modality in which information is presented. See also TRANSIENT GLOBAL AMNESIA.

global analysis see MOLAR ANALYSIS.

global aphasia a complete loss of expressive and receptive language skills. Also called **total aphasia**. See SENSORIMOTOR APHASIA.

Global Assessment of Functioning scale (**GAF scale**) a scale used for treatment planning and outcome evaluation on Axis V of *DSM–IV–TR*'s multiaxial evaluation system. Scores (1–100) reflect the clinician's judgment of a patient's overall level of psychological, social, and occupational functioning at the time of assessment. The GAF scale is also used to measure the highest level of such functioning in the past year.

Global Deterioration Scale (**GDS**) a seven-point scale used to indicate the severity of a primary degenerative DEMENTIA, such as ALZHEIMER'S DISEASE, in an older adult, based on caregivers' observations of behaviors in the individual. The scale ranges from no cognitive decline (1) to very severe cognitive decline (7). [developed in 1982 by U.S. geriatric psychiatrist Barry Reisberg (1947–)]

global intelligence verbal and nonverbal intelligence, especially as measured by the verbal and performance subtests in various WECHSLER scales. It is sometimes used synonymously with GENERAL INTELLIGENCE.

globalization *n.* the process by which many commercial organizations have moved from a local model of production and distribution to an international or global model, largely owing to technological advances and the internationalization of trade, finance, media, and travel. The globalization of a company's activities requires attention to organizational and cultural differences that may impact efficiency and safety. See CULTURAL ERGONOMICS. **—globalize** *vb.*

global memory model a mathematical model of the structure and organization of memory that is intended to explain data from a range of experimental tasks and manipulations, as opposed to more restricted models of single phenomena. See also MINERVA 2; SEARCH OF ASSOCIATIVE MEMORY (SAM).

global perception overall perception of an object or a situation focusing on the totality rather than the parts.

global rating a rating based upon the rater's integration of many attributes into a single unified rating. Global ratings are, as a rule, vague in their definitions.

global workspace theory a theory suggesting that consciousness involves the global distribution of focal information to many parts of the brain. [originated by U.S. psychologist Bernard Joseph Baars (1946–)]

globus pallidus one of the BASAL GANGLIA. It is the main output region of the basal ganglia: Its output neurons terminate on thalamic neurons, which in turn project to the cerebral cortex.

globus pharyngeus a sensation of having a lump in the throat for which no medical cause can be identified. It can be a symptom of CONVERSION DISORDER and was formerly called **globus hystericus**.

G-LOC abbreviation for GRAVITY-INDUCED LOSS OF CONSCIOUSNESS.

glomerulus *n.* (*pl.* **glomeruli**) **1.** a small tuft or cluster in which OLFACTORY NERVE fibers terminate in part of the OLFACTORY BULB. **2.** a small tuft or cluster of blood capillaries enclosed in a kidney capsule. **—glomerular** *adj.*

glosso- (**gloss-**) *combining form* **1.** tongue (e.g., GLOSSOPHARYNGEAL NERVE). **2.** speech (e.g., GLOSSOLALIA).

glossodynia *n.* a feeling of pain in the tongue, or in the tongue and buccal mucous membranes, without any observable cause. Also called **glossalgia**.

glossolalia *n.* unintelligible utterances that simulate coherent speech. It is found in religious ecstasy ("speaking in tongues"), hypnotic or mediumistic trances, and occasionally in schizophrenia. See NEOLOGISM.

glossopharyngeal nerve the ninth CRANIAL NERVE, which supplies the pharynx, soft palate, and posterior third of the tongue, including the taste buds of that portion. It is responsible for the swallowing reflex, stimulation of parotid gland secretions, and reflex control of the heart through innervation of the carotid sinus. Also called **cranial nerve IX**.

glossosynthesis *n.* the creation of nonsense words.

glottal 1. *adj.* pertaining to or involving the glottis or larynx. **2.** *n.* a speech sound produced by constriction of the glottis, as in the [h] sound in *hobble.*

glottal stop a PLOSIVE speech sound produced by complete closure of the glottis followed by sudden release of the breath stream. Although this is a standard speech sound in some languages, in English it occurs mostly in certain dialects, as in the Cockney pronunciation of the *t* in *daughter*, or in certain words "loaned" from other languages, such as the native pronunciation of *Hawai'i*, in which the stop is indicated by the single quote.

glottis *n.* the opening between the VOCAL CORDS or, by extension, the vocal cords themselves or elements (collectively) of the larynx that are involved in voice production.

glove anesthesia a SENSORY CONVERSION SYMPTOM in which there is a functional loss of sensitivity in the hand and part of the forearm (i.e., areas that would be covered by a glove). See also STOCKING ANESTHESIA.

glucagon *n.* a polypeptide hormone, secreted by the A cells of the ISLETS OF LANGERHANS, that increases the concentration of glucose in the blood. It opposes the effects of INSULIN by promoting the breakdown of glycogen and fat reserves to yield glucose. Glucagon is administered therapeutically to relieve symptoms of HYPOGLYCEMIA.

glucocorticoid *n.* any CORTICOSTEROID hormone that acts chiefly on carbohydrate metabolism. Glucocorticoids include CORTISOL, CORTICOSTERONE, and CORTISONE.

glucoreceptor *n.* any of certain cells in the HYPOTHALAMUS that detect levels of circulating glucose and convey this information to brain areas. Also called **glucodetector**; **glucostat**.

glucose *n.* a soluble sugar, abundant in nature, that is a major source of energy for body tissues. The brain relies almost exclusively on glucose for its energy needs. Glucose is derived from the breakdown of carbohydrates, proteins, and—to a much lesser extent—fats. Its concentration in the bloodstream is tightly controlled by the opposing actions of the hormones INSULIN and GLUCAGON. See also BLOOD SUGAR.

glucose transporter a molecule that spans the plasma membrane of a cell and transports glucose molecules across the membrane.

glucostat *n.* see GLUCORECEPTOR. **—glucostatic** *adj.*

glucostatic theory the theory that short-term regulation of food intake is governed by the rate of glucose metabolism (i.e., utilization), rather than by overall blood levels of glucose. See also LIPOSTATIC HYPOTHESIS. [proposed in the 1950s by French-born U.S. nutritionist Jean Mayer (1924–1993)]

glucuronidation *n.* a metabolic process by which drugs or other substances are combined with glucuronic acid to form more water-soluble compounds, which are more readily excreted by the kidneys or in bile. Glucuronidation is the most prevalent of the Phase II reactions of DRUG METABOLISM.

glue sniffing a form of substance abuse in which the fumes of certain adhesives, particularly plastic model glue, are inhaled for their stimulant effect and euphoria. TOLUENE is the ingredient with psychoactive effects; other hydrocarbons used for this purpose include XYLENE and BENZENE. See INHALANT; INHALANT ABUSE.

glutamate *n.* a salt or ester of the amino acid GLUTAMIC ACID that serves as the predominant excitatory NEUROTRANSMITTER in the brain. Glutamate plays a critical role in cognitive, motor, and sensory functions; its role in the pathogenesis of schizophrenia is the subject of investigation. It exerts its effects by binding to GLUTAMATE RECEPTORS on neurons. Excessive activity of glutamate at these receptors is associated with damage to nerve tissue (neurotoxicity) and cell death (see EXCITOTOXICITY), possibly the result of calcium ions flooding into the cell following overstimulation of NMDA RECEPTORS.

glutamate hypothesis the theory that decreased activity of the excitatory neurotransmitter glutamate is responsible for the clinical expression of schizophrenia. The hypothesis developed from the observation that psychotic symptoms induced by PCP (phencyclidine) and related agents, which act as antagonists at the NMDA RECEPTOR, closely resemble both POSITIVE SYMPTOMS and NEGATIVE SYMPTOMS of schizophrenia. See also DOPAMINE HYPOTHESIS.

glutamate receptor any of various receptors that bind and respond to the excitatory neurotransmitter glutamate. Glutamate receptors are found on the surface of most neurons. There are two main divisions of glutamate receptors: the IONOTROPIC RECEPTORS and the METABOTROPIC RECEPTORS. Ionotropic glutamate receptors are further divided into three classes: NMDA RECEPTORS, AMPA RECEPTORS, and KAINATE RECEPTORS. Metabotropic glutamate receptors (mGlu or mGluR) are subdivided into several classes denoted by subscript numbers (i.e., $mGlu_1$, $mGlu_2$, etc.).

glutamic acid an AMINO ACID that is regarded as nonessential in diets but is important for normal brain function. It is converted into GAMMA-AMINOBUTYRIC ACID in a reaction catalyzed by the enzyme glutamic acid decarboxylase and requiring pyridoxal phosphate, formed from vitamin B_6 (pyridoxine), as a coenzyme.

glutamic acid decarboxylase the enzyme responsible for the formation of the neurotransmitter GAMMA-AMINOBUTYRIC ACID (GABA) from GLUTAMIC ACID.

glutamic–oxaloacetic transaminase see ASPARTATE AMINOTRANSFERASE.

glutaminergic *adj.* describing neurons that use GLUTAMATE as a neurotransmitter.

glutethimide *n.* one of the nonbarbiturate sedatives introduced in the early 1950s. Structurally similar to and pharmacologically interchangeable with the BARBITURATES, glutethimide offered no advantages for treatment of anxiety or insomnia. Now rarely used clinically, it is sometimes encountered as a drug of abuse. U.S. trade name: **Doriden**.

glycine *n.* an AMINO ACID that serves as one of the two major inhibitory neurotransmitters in the central nervous system (particularly the spinal cord), the other being GAMMA-AMINOBUTYRIC ACID (GABA). Glycine synthesis occurs via two different pathways; in the most important of these, glycine is synthesized from the amino acid serine in a single reaction catalyzed by the enzyme serine hydroxymethyltransferase. Also called **aminoacetic acid**.

glycogen *n.* a polysaccharide formed in the liver from GLUCOSE and stored in the liver and other body tissues as a primary source of chemical energy. It is easily broken down into glucose molecules as needed for energy. Also called **animal starch**.

glycosaminoglycan *n.* see MUCOPOLYSACCHARIDOSIS.

gnostic function the ability to make fine spatial judgments with the skin senses by discriminating light touch sensations that stimulate the cutaneous receptors. Also called **epicritic sensibility**; **gnostic sensation**. See also EPICRITIC SYSTEM.

gnothi se auton know thyself (Greek). These words, which were inscribed over the portico of the temple of Apollo at Delphi in ancient Greece, have been ascribed to various sources. The pursuit of self-knowledge, or knowledge of the psyche, became a key element in the philosophical project of Greek thinker Socrates (469–399 BCE). In a sense, this project is the fundamental undertaking of psychology.

GnRH abbreviation for GONADOTROPIN-RELEASING HORMONE.

goal *n.* **1.** the end state toward which a human or nonhuman animal is striving: the purpose of an activity or endeavor. It can be identified by observing that an organism ceases or changes its behavior upon attaining this state. **2.** a target of proficiency in a task to be achieved within a set period of time. See GOAL SETTING.

goal-attainment model a process that focuses on the achievement of a particular time-limited goal and measures the degree to which that goal has been achieved (e.g., by a program).

goal-based evaluation an evaluation that determines the extent to which a program has achieved its goals or EVALUATION OBJECTIVES. This approach relies heavily on stated program goals and objectives, and as such it might overlook other merits of the program. Compare GOAL-FREE EVALUATION. See also QUANTITATIVE EVALUATION.

goal difficulty the degree of ability, effort, and time commitment needed to achieve a goal.

goal-directed behavior behavior that is oriented toward attaining a particular goal. It is typically identifiable by observing that the animal or person ceases search behavior and engages in detour behavior when it encounters obstacles to the goal.

goal-free evaluation an evaluation of a program that is conducted without special knowledge of the program's stated goals or EVALUATION OBJECTIVES and is therefore less subject to the preconceptions or biases of the researcher. Instead, the evaluation attempts to assess the program's actual effects on its clients, their real needs, and, importantly, any unintended negative side effects emerging from the program. Also called **value-free evaluation**. Compare GOAL-BASED EVALUATION. See also QUALITATIVE EVALUATION.

goal gradient systematic changes in behavior that occur as a function of spatial or temporal distance from a REINFORCER.

goal-limited adjustment therapy see SECTOR THERAPY.

goal model of evaluation a system of assessing organizational effectiveness by focusing on the organization's public goals or expectations rather than its private goals. See also GOAL-BASED EVALUATION; GOAL-FREE EVALUATION.

goal object that which an individual is seeking to attain, particularly the final, ultimate goal following a series of subgoals.

goal orientation 1. the tendency to physically or mentally position oneself toward a goal. **2.** the characteristic of individuals who tend to direct their behaviors toward attaining goals, particularly long-term goals.

goal response 1. in HULL'S MATHEMATICO-DEDUCTIVE THEORY OF LEARNING, the unconditioned response elicited by a GOAL STIMULUS. **2.** more generally, the final response in a chain of behavior directed toward obtaining a goal. In conditioning, it specifically refers to the response given to a positive reinforcing stimulus. See also CONSUMMATORY RESPONSE.

goal setting a process that establishes specific, time-based behavior targets that are measurable, achievable, and realistic. In work-related settings, for example, this practice usually provides employees with both (a) a basis for motivation, in terms of effort expended, and (b) guidelines or cues to behavior that will be required if the goal is to be met. Goal setting is effective only if individuals concerned are aware of what is to be accomplished and accept the goals for themselves, believing in their attainability. See also LOCKE'S THEORY OF GOAL SETTING; OUTCOME GOAL; PERFORMANCE GOAL; PROCESS GOAL.

goal specificity the degree to which the target behavior of a goal is defined.

goal stimulus 1. in HULL'S MATHEMATICO-DEDUCTIVE THEORY OF LEARNING, a desired object or goal. **2.** more generally, a proprioceptive or other interoceptive stimulus arising from GOAL-DIRECTED BEHAVIOR.

go-around *n.* a technique used in group psychotherapy in which each member in turn is requested to react to another member, a discussion theme, or a described or enacted situation.

goblet figure see RUBIN'S FIGURE.

Goddard, Henry Herbert (1866–1957) U.S. psychologist. Goddard earned his doctorate under G. Stanley HALL at Clark University in 1899. He taught psychology at a State Normal School in Pennsylvania before becoming director of the psychology laboratory at a school for children with mental retardation (at that time called feebleminded) in Vineland, New Jersey, in 1906. Goddard remained at Vineland until 1918, when he became director of the Ohio Bureau of Juvenile Research; in 1922 he became professor of abnormal and clinical psychology at Ohio State University. Working in the fields of SPECIAL EDUCATION and mental retardation, Goddard is best known as one of the founders of intelligence testing in the United States. He sought new methods in Europe (1908) to diagnose and care for children institutionalized as feebleminded and persuaded U.S. physicians to adopt both the new intelligence tests developed by Alfred BINET and Binet's classification system for those of subnormal intelligence. He also coined the word "moron" to denote the highest functioning level of these children (who would now be described as having MILD MENTAL RETARDATION). Goddard applied the Binet tests in the public school system for the first time and advocated their use in classroom placement; he was also a central figure in designing the ARMY TESTS in World War I. Goddard's most famous book was his hereditarian study, *The Kallikak Family* (1912; see KALLIKAK). His early hereditarian views and eugenicist beliefs were controversial and largely retracted by Goddard himself in his later years.

Gödel's proof a proof that in any logic system at least as powerful as arithmetic it is possible to state theorems that can be proved to be neither true nor false, using only the proof rules of that system. Published in 1931, this incompleteness result was very challenging to the mathematics of the time. Alan Turing (1912–1954), with his proof of the undecidability of the halting problem, extended this result to computation (see TURING MACHINE). [Kurt **Gödel** (1906–1978), Austrian-born U.S. mathematician]

godemiche *n.* see DILDO.

goiter *n.* a swelling in the front part of the neck caused by enlargement of the thyroid gland. See EXOPHTHALMOS; GRAVES' DISEASE; THYROTOXICOSIS.

Golden Rule the principle of reciprocity in ethics. In the Christian tradition it is usually expressed as "Do unto others as you would have them do unto you," but versions are found in most world religions and many ethical systems. German philosopher Immanuel Kant (1724–1804) proposed a similar principle in the CATEGORICAL IMPERATIVE.

goldenseal *n.* a shrub, *Hydrastis canadensis*, with medicinal properties. Indigenous to the eastern United States, it has a long history as a folk remedy to control uterine bleeding, and its leaves are commonly used as a poultice and antibacterial agent. There are few clinical studies evaluating the efficacy of goldenseal but its active ingredients, the alkaloids **berberine** and **hydrastine**, have been studied extensively. Berberine has been shown to have antimicrobial properties and may also be effective in preventing the growth of cancer cells. Hydrastine has vasoconstrictive and abortifacient effects and has been shown to induce labor in pregnant women when taken orally. At recommended doses, goldenseal appears to have minimal adverse effects (e.g., irritation of the mouth, throat, and stomach; tingling of the skin) but at higher doses it may cause hypertension and increase heart rate; it has also been associated with seizures and other evidence of overstimulation of the central nervous system, and at very high doses may be toxic, potentially causing paralysis, respiratory failure, and death. Chronic long-term use may inhibit vitamin B absorption. Additionally, goldenseal may interact with other agents, including anticoagulants, antihypertensives, and drugs metabolized by the CYTOCHROME P450 3A4 enzyme (e.g., clonidine, nefazodone, St. John's wort).

golden section the division of a line or area so that the ratio of the smaller to the larger portion is equal to the ratio of the larger portion to the whole line or area. Since classical times this ratio has been regarded as having aesthetic value. Also called **golden mean**.

golem *n.* in medieval Jewish folklore, a being created from inanimate material, specifically clay, and used as a servant by its creator. In spite of such disadvantages as an inability to speak or think and act on their own, golems were often associated with holiness, wisdom, and magical powers. More recently, the term has come to signify a brainless, clumsy oaf or an automaton.

Golgi apparatus an irregular network of membranes and vesicles within a cell that is responsible for modifying, sorting, and packaging proteins produced within the cell. [Camillo **Golgi** (1843–1926), Italian histologist]

Golgi tendon organ a receptor in muscle tendons that sends impulses to the central nervous system when a muscle contracts. When tension in the tendon becomes high enough to cause damage to tissues, Golgi tendon organs send inhibitory messages to the motor neurons of the attached muscle. Also called **Golgi corpuscle**. [Camillo **Golgi**]

Golgi Type I neuron see PROJECTION NEURON. [Camillo **Golgi**]

Golgi Type II neuron see LOCAL CIRCUIT NEURON. [Camillo **Golgi**]

Goltz syndrome a congenital disorder marked by eye anomalies, absent or extra digits, and skin lesions, particularly nodules of herniated subcutaneous fat in thin skin areas. About 5% of affected individuals tested have been found to have mental retardation. Also called **focal dermal hypoplasia**; **Goltz–Gorlin syndrome**. [Robert William **Goltz** (1923–) and Robert James **Gorlin** (1923–), U.S. physicians]

Gompertz hypothesis a hypothesis suggesting that the probability of human mortality increases exponentially with age in a geometric proportion, doubling every 8 years, between the ages of 20 and 80. Also called **Gompertz equation**. [Benjamin **Gompertz** (1779–1865), British actuary]

gonad *n.* either of the primary male and female sex organs, that is, the TESTIS or the OVARY. **—gonadal** *adj.*

gonadal dysgenesis see TURNER'S SYNDROME.

gonadal hormones the primary male and female SEX HORMONES.

gonadopause *n.* the cessation of endocrine-related reproductive function that occurs with age in either sex. See also CLIMACTERIC; MALE CLIMACTERIC.

gonadostat theory a mechanism, associated with the initiation of puberty, by which ovarian or testicular hormones regulate hypothalamic and pituitary secretions. [proposed in 1955 by neuroendocrinologist Geoffrey Wingfield Harris (1913–1971)]

gonadotropin *n.* any of several hormones that stimulate functions of the gonads. Gonadotropins include FOLLICLE-STIMULATING HORMONE and LUTEINIZING HORMONE, produced by the anterior PITUITARY GLAND in response to GONADOTROPIN-RELEASING HORMONE, and chorionic gonadotropin, which is produced by the placenta (see HUMAN CHORIONIC GONADOTROPIN). Also called **gonadotropic hormone**. See also HUMAN MENOPAUSAL GONADOTROPIN. **—gonadotropic** *adj.*

gonadotropin-releasing hormone (**GnRH**) a HYPOTHALAMIC HORMONE that controls the release of LUTEINIZING HORMONE and FOLLICLE-STIMULATING HORMONE from the anterior pituitary gland. See also RELEASING HORMONE.

goniometer (**goneometer**) *n.* **1.** an instrument for measuring angles, particularly the arc or range of motion of a joint. Also called **arthrometer**. **2.** an instrument for measuring balance, consisting of a gradually raised plank. It is used to test for disease of the vestibular system.

go/no-go in CONDITIONING, denoting two-stimulus DISCRIMINATION procedures in which a particular action is reinforced in the presence of one stimulus (the go stimulus) and not reinforced in the presence of the other (the no-go stimulus). In neurological assessment, a **go/no-go task** assesses the ability to inhibit a simple motor response after it has been established. A common go/no-go task requires the participant to display two fingers when the examiner presents one finger (go) and to display no fingers when the examiner presents two fingers (no-go). Performance on these tasks is generally impaired following frontal lobe damage.

gonorrhea *n.* a sexually transmitted disease caused by the bacterium *Neisseria gonorrhoeae* (the gonococcus). The primary focus of infection is the genital tract; untreated, it can lead to sterility. The bacterium can later infect the eyes and cause **gonococcal conjunctivitis**, a serious condition that can lead to blindness. See also URETHRITIS.

good-and-evil test a variation of the right-and-wrong test (see MCNAUGHTEN RULE) employed in CRIMINAL RESPONSIBILITY evaluations to determine whether the person accused was aware of the differences between right and wrong behaviors at the time of committing the act with which he or she is charged.

good-boy-nice-girl orientation see INTERPERSONAL CONCORDANCE.

good breast in the psychoanalytic theory of Melanie KLEIN, the internalized representation (see INTROJECTION) of the mother's breast as nourishing and satisfying. According to Klein, the infant first experiences the mother and the nourishing breast as PART-OBJECTS with positive qualities—the good breast—and negative qualities—the BAD BREAST.

good continuation the principle of perception that a perceived line tends to maintain its direction. See GESTALT PRINCIPLES OF ORGANIZATION.

good enough mother in the OBJECT RELATIONS THEORY of British psychoanalyst Donald Winnicott (1896–1971), the ordinary, devoted mother who provides an adequate or good enough environment for the growth of the infant's ego to express its TRUE SELF. The good enough mother begins mothering by adapting entirely to the infant and providing an environment free of IMPINGEMENTS, but later gradually creates small failures of adaptation to teach the infant to tolerate the frustrations of reality.

good enough parent a parent who cares for his or her child in any way that is adequate for proper development. [proposed by U.S. psychologist Sandra Scarr (1936–)]

good-faith bargaining under the NATIONAL LABOR RELATIONS ACT of the United States, the principle that employers recognizing a union as the representative of their employees must treat that union as the exclusive representative of the employees and agree to bargain with that union in an honest, open manner over the terms and conditions of employment. See COLLECTIVE BARGAINING.

good figure see LAW OF GOOD FIGURE.

good genes hypothesis a hypothesis of female mate selection arguing (a) that GENETIC VARIATION in males is correlated with reproductive success, (b) that there are features of male behavior and body structure that provide information about this variation, and (c) that females respond to this variation by choosing males with good genes as mates. Compare RUNAWAY SELECTION.

good gestalt the quality possessed by an arrangement of stimuli that is complete, orderly, and clear with a high degree of GOODNESS OF CONFIGURATION. Although this is related to the PRINCIPLE OF PRÄGNANZ, it is distinct in that the arrangement of stimuli need not be the simplest one possible. See also GESTALT; GESTALT PRINCIPLES OF ORGANIZATION.

good me in the SELF-SYSTEM theory of U.S. psychoanalyst Harry Stack Sullivan (1892–1949), the child's PERSONIFICATION of behaviors and impulses that meet with the approval of the parents. The good me is posited to develop as a part of the socialization process and to protect the child from anxiety about himself or herself. Compare BAD ME. See also NOT ME.

goodness of configuration the quality of a shape or form that has high levels of simplicity, regularity, symmetry, or continuity. Gestalt psychologist Wolfgang KÖHLER speculated that the mind tends to perceive more goodness of configuration than may actually exist in a shape. See also CLOSURE; GESTALT PRINCIPLES OF ORGANIZATION; PRINCIPLE OF PRÄGNANZ.

goodness of fit any index that reflects the degree to which values predicted by a model agree with empirically observed values.

good object in the OBJECT RELATIONS THEORY of Melanie KLEIN, an introjected PART-OBJECT that is perceived as benevolent and satisfying (see INTROJECTION). It is an early object representation that derives from SPLITTING of the object into parts containing positive and negative qualities. The good object forms the core of the infant's immature ego. Compare BAD OBJECT.

good shape a principle of perception identified in 1923 by German psychologist Max WERTHEIMER and associated with GESTALT PSYCHOLOGY. It states that people tend to perceive figures as the most uniform and stable forms possible. Also called **law of good shape**; **principle of good shape**. See GESTALT PRINCIPLES OF ORGANIZATION.

goose bumps (**goose flesh**; **goose pimples**; **goose skin**) see PILOERECTION.

Gordon Diagnostic System (**GDS**) an assessment device that aids in the diagnosis of attention deficits. It provides information about an individual's ability to sustain attention and exert self-control on a continuous performance test. The GDS is a microprocessor-based, portable unit that administers a series of tasks in the form of games. [Michael **Gordon** (1952–), U.S. psychologist]

GOS abbreviation for GLASGOW OUTCOME SCALE.

go-slow *n.* see SLOWDOWN.

gossip 1. *n.* idle personal talk or communication of often unsubstantiated information. Gossip may be scandalous in content or malicious in intention. **2.** *vb.* to engage in such talk.

government and binding theory an enhanced version of GENERATIVE GRAMMAR involving multiple levels of abstraction that seeks to explain, among other things, the relation between universals and particulars that accounts for the generativity of all human languages.

G-protection device a device to counter the effects of gravity during flight. The faster the speed, the greater the acceleration due to gravity (acceleration of free fall). Inflatable pressure cuffs in the flight suit help counter some of the gravity effects in order to keep the pilot from losing consciousness.

G protein any of a class of proteins that are coupled to the intracellular portion of a type of membrane RECEPTOR (**G-protein-coupled receptors**) and are activated when the receptor binds an appropriate ligand (e.g., a neurotransmitter) on the extracellular surface. G proteins thus have a role in signal transduction, being involved, for example, in indirect chemical NEUROTRANSMISSION. They work in conjunction with the nucleotides guanosine diphosphate (GDP) and guanosine triphosphate (GTP) and serve to transmit the signal from the receptor to other cell components (e.g., ion channels) in various ways, for example by controlling the synthesis of SECOND MESSENGERS within the cell.

GPS abbreviation for GENERAL PROBLEM SOLVER.

graafian follicle a small pouchlike cavity in an ovary in which an ovum develops (see OOGENESIS). At ovulation, one of the follicles ruptures and releases a mature ovum into a FALLOPIAN TUBE, where it may be fertilized. The ruptured follicle becomes the site of the CORPUS LUTEUM. Also called **ovarian follicle**. [Reijner de **Graaf** (1641–1673), Dutch histologist]

graceful degradation a property of cognitive networks in which damage to a portion of the network produces relatively little damage to overall performance, because performance is distributed across the units in the network and no one unit is solely responsible for any aspect of processing. It is a property of the NEURAL NETWORK model of cognition and of models derived from the PARALLEL DISTRIBUTED PROCESSING hypothesis. See also DISTRIBUTED PROCESSING.

gracile fasciculus the medial portion of either of the DORSAL COLUMNS of the spinal cord, composed of ascending fibers that terminate in the NUCLEUS GRACILIS of the medulla oblongata. Also called **fasciculus gracilis**. See also CUNEATE FASCICULUS.

gracile nucleus see NUCLEUS GRACILIS.

gracile tubercle an elongated swelling on the upper end of the GRACILE FASCICULUS in the medulla oblongata. The tubercle contains the NUCLEUS GRACILIS, which receives DORSAL ROOT fibers from sensory receptors in the leg. Also called **clava**.

gradation method the psychophysical technique of measuring change in small equal units.

graded potential a neural potential that is not propagated but declines with distance from the source. Kinds of graded potential include receptor potentials, POSTSYNAPTIC POTENTIALS, and SUBTHRESHOLD POTENTIALS. Compare ACTION POTENTIAL.

grade equivalent a test score expressed in terms of a GRADE NORM. For example, if a third-grader's score in the 99th percentile conforms to fifth-grade norms, the grade equivalent is expressed as five.

Grade II astrocytoma see ASTROBLASTOMA.

grade inflation a trend that results in higher grades being awarded for lower levels of scholarship. Also called **upward grade homogenization**.

grade norm the standard score or range of scores that represent the average achievement level of a specified group of people. For example, the mean achievement of all fifth-graders in Wisconsin might be taken to constitute a fifth-grade norm for that state. See also GRADE EQUIVALENT.

grade-point average see POINT–HOUR RATIO.

grade points 1. numbers equivalent to letter-grade assignments for academic coursework. Usually, A = 4, B = 3, C = 2, D = 1, and F = 0. The resulting average allows the appropriate reward to be given, or disciplinary action to be taken, on the basis of academic performance. **2.** letter grades converted to a numerical value, typically as follows: A = 90–100 (superior work that is clearly above average); B = 80–89 (good work, meeting all requirements and eminently satisfactory); C = 70–79 (competent work, meeting requirements); D = 60–69 (fair work, minimally acceptable); F = 59 and below (failing work). See also POINT–HOUR RATIO.

grade scale a standardized scale with scores expressed in terms of the GRADE NORM.

grade skipping see EDUCATIONAL ACCELERATION.

gradient *n.* **1.** the slope of a line or surface. **2.** a measure of the change of a physical quantity (e.g., temperature). **3.** in motivational psychology, a graduated change in the strength of a DRIVE resulting from a change in the environment, such as time interval, distance from a situation, and degree of conflict. See also APPROACH GRADIENT; AVOIDANCE GRADIENT.

gradient of effect the principle that, in a stimulus–response sequence in which one of the responses is reinforced, the responses closely preceding or following the reinforced response are likely to show the effects of the reinforcement procedure to a greater extent than those that are remote from that response.

gradient of reinforcement the generalization that the closer in time a response is to REINFORCEMENT, the stronger it will be.

gradient of texture the progressively finer appearance of textures and surface grains of objects as the viewer moves away from them. See also VISUAL TEXTURE.

grading *n.* the process by which an instructor assigns a performance rank to a student's work. A definitive way of portraying a student's acquired knowledge, grading is usually based on both quantitative achievements (e.g., test results, essay completion, attendance) and qualitative considerations (e.g., class participation, teacher's perception).

Graduated and Reciprocated Initiatives in Tension Reduction (**GRIT**) an approach to intergroup conflict reduction that encourages the parties to communicate cooperative intentions, engage in behaviors that are consistent with these intentions, and initiate cooperative responses even in the face of competition. GRIT is usually recommended when disputants have a prolonged history of conflict, misunderstanding, misperception, and hostility.

Graduate Record Examinations (**GRE**) a collection of aptitude tests used in the graduate school admissions process to make decisions regarding applicants. The GRE General Test, currently consisting of two essay writing tasks and approximately 60 multiple-choice questions, evaluates critical thinking, analytical writing, verbal reasoning, and quantitative reasoning abilities. The eight GRE Subject Tests (biochemistry, biology, chemistry, computer science, literature in English, mathematics, physics, psychology), currently consisting of between 66 and 230 multiple-choice questions, evaluate knowledge specific to particular disciplines.

Graeco-Latin square a variant of a LATIN SQUARE that superimposes one orthogonal Latin square upon another to allow for three-way control of variation (e.g., to minimize or eliminate the influence of other variables that are unrelated to the experiment). A Graeco-Latin square is an example of a FRACTIONAL REPLICATION DESIGN involving four factors, or INDEPENDENT VARIABLES.

Graefenberg spot (**G-spot**) an area on the anterior wall of the vagina, about 4 cm (1–2 in.) into the vagina. Some women experience pleasure from stimulation of this area and may have an ejaculation from a gland there. However, it is not clear how many women have this gland, or find this area to be especially responsive during sexual activity, and some research suggests that the ejaculation may be urine, expelled from the bladder. [Ernst **Graefenberg** (1881–1957), German gynecologist]

grammar *n.* in linguistics, an abstract system of rules that describes how a language works. Although it is traditionally held to consist of SYNTAX (rules for arranging words in sentences) and MORPHOLOGY (rules affecting the form taken by individual words), PHONOLOGY and SEMANTICS are also included in some modern systems of grammar. **—grammatical** *adj.*

grammaticality *n.* the quality of adhering to the rules of grammar. In the linguistics of Noam CHOMSKY, the grammaticality (or otherwise) of a sentence can be intuited by native speakers and explained by the rules of FORMAL GRAMMAR. A sentence can be recognized as grammatical even when it is otherwise meaningless, as in the case of Chomsky's famous example *Colorless green ideas sleep furiously*.

grandiose delusion see DELUSION OF GRANDEUR.

grandiosity *n.* an exaggerated sense of one's greatness, importance, or ability. In extreme form, it may be regarded as a DELUSION OF GRANDEUR.

grand mal see TONIC–CLONIC SEIZURE.

grand mean a mean of a group of means.

grandmother cells feature-detector cells in the VISUAL ASSOCIATION CORTEX that are stimulated by only certain objects in the visual field, such as a moving insect or the outline of a hand. The name refers to hypothetical cells that would be stimulated only by the features of one's grandmother.

grandmother hypothesis the proposition, based on evolutionary theory, that the contribution of grandparents (particularly grandmothers) to the care of their grandchildren has been a factor in extending the human life span.

Grandry–Merkel corpuscle see MERKEL'S TACTILE DISK.

Granit theory of color vision a theory that the perception of color relies on the activation of three types of cells: (a) **scotopic dominators**, which are RETINAL RODS most sensitive to wavelengths of 500 nm; (b) **photopic dominators**, which are RETINAL CONES most sensitive to wavelengths of 560 nm; and (c) **photopic modulators**, other cones sensitive to very narrow frequency ranges. [Ragnar Arthur **Granit** (1900–1991), Finnish-born Swedish physiologist]

granular cortex the portion of the cerebral cortex that contains GRANULE CELLS, which are located in layers II and IV of the cortex (see CORTICAL LAYERS). The term refers particularly to primary sensory cortex, in which layer IV (the major input area) is very thick. Compare AGRANULAR CORTEX.

granule cell a type of small, grainlike nerve cell found in certain layers of the cerebral cortex (see CORTICAL LAYERS) and cerebellar cortex.

grapevine *n.* the unofficial channel of communication in which information, especially rumors and gossip, is passed informally from person to person.

graph *n.* **1.** a visual representation of the relationship between numbers or quantities, which are plotted on a drawing with reference to axes at right angles (see X-AXIS; Y-AXIS) and linked by lines, dots, or the like. **2.** in computer programming, a data structure consisting of a set of nodes (not necessarily finite in number) and a set of arcs that connect pairs of nodes. In a **directed graph** the arcs have a unique direction from one node (the parent) to the other node (the child). The set of child nodes of one parent are called siblings of each other. A path is a sequence of connected parent–child arcs, in which each child in the sequence is also a parent of the next state in the sequence. A **rooted graph** has a unique node from which all paths in the graph originate. A **tip node** or **leaf node** in the graph is a node without children. The graph structure is often used for representing SEARCH in games or other situations of problem solving or for capturing relationships, as in SEMANTIC NETWORKS. See also TREE.

graph- *combining form* writing or drawing.

graphanesthesia *n.* inability to recognize numbers or letters traced or written on the skin, for example with finger movements or with a dull pointed object. See also GRAPHESTHESIA.

grapheme *n.* a minimal meaningful unit in the writing system of a particular language. It is usually a letter or fixed combination of letters corresponding to a PHONEME in that language. **—graphemic** *adj.*

graphesthesia *n.* the recognition of numbers or letters that are spelled out on the skin, for example with finger movements or a dull pointed object. This form of PASSIVE TOUCH has been used as a diagnostic tool for brain damage. People with both visual and hearing impairment are taught to communicate with those who are unfamiliar with sign language by digitally spelling out words on the skin. See also GRAPHANESTHESIA.

graphical user interface an interface that enables a user to operate a computer system using visual devices such as windows, icons, and pull-down menus. Compare PERCEPTUAL USER INTERFACE; TANGIBLE USER INTERFACE.

graphic method the use of visual displays in the recording, presentation, and interpretation of data.

graphoanalysis *n.* see GRAPHOPATHOLOGY.

graphology *n.* the analysis of the physical characteristics of handwriting, particularly as a means of inferring the writer's stable personality characteristics or psychological state at the time of writing. Also called **handwriting analysis**. **—graphological** *adj.* **—graphologist** *n.*

graphomania *n.* a pathological impulse to write. In its most severe form, it may degenerate into GRAPHORRHEA.

graphomotor apraxia inability to perform the motor

activities involved in writing or drawing despite normal capacity to hold and manipulate a writing implement. Also called **apraxic agraphia**.

graphopathology *n.* the interpretation of personality disorders by studying handwriting. Also called **graphoanalysis**.

graphorrhea *n.* the writing of long lists of incoherent, meaningless words, which sometimes occurs in the context of a MANIC EPISODE.

graphospasm *n.* a rare name for WRITER'S CRAMP.

graph theory the study of the use of visual representations (graphs) to describe relationships, structures, and dynamics. Applications in psychology include BALANCE THEORY, SOCIOMETRY, and analyses of SOCIAL NETWORKS and LIFE SPACE.

grasp reflex an involuntary reaction in which an individual automatically grasps whatever touches the palm. In infants this reaction is normal; later, it may be a sign of injury to the frontal lobe (see FRONTAL RELEASE SIGNS). The grasp reflex is observed mainly in human infants and young monkeys before the cerebral cortex has matured. Also called **grasping reflex**.

gratification *n.* the state of satisfaction following the fulfillment of a desire or the meeting of a need. See DELAY OF GRATIFICATION; IMMEDIATE GRATIFICATION.

gratification of instincts see SATISFACTION OF INSTINCTS.

grating *n.* in vision, a stimulus that consists of parallel light and dark bars.

gratitude *n.* a sense of thankfulness and happiness in response to receiving a gift, either a tangible benefit (e.g., a present or favor) given by someone or a fortunate happenstance (e.g., a beautiful day).

Graves' disease a disorder characterized by enlargement and overactivity of the thyroid gland and marked by exophthalmic goiter (see EXOPHTHALMOS), reddish nodules on the legs, muscle weakness, and other symptoms of THYROTOXICOSIS. Autoimmunity and emotional distress are often associated with the condition, which mainly affects women between the ages of 30 and 50; many physicians report an apparent emotional trauma linked to the onset of symptoms (e.g., death of a loved one, divorce). Also called **Parry's disease**. [Robert J. **Graves** (1796–1853), Irish physician]

gravida *n.* a pregnant woman. The use of a Roman numeral after the term indicates the number of pregnancies a particular woman has undergone (e.g., **gravida IV** indicates a woman in her fourth pregnancy). See also PRIMIGRAVIDA.

gravidity *n.* see PREGNANCY.

gravireceptor (**graviceptor**) *n.* any of various specialized nerve endings and receptors located in the inner ear, joints, muscles, and tendons that provide the brain with information regarding body position, equilibrium, and gravitational forces.

gravity-induced loss of consciousness (**G-LOC**) loss of consciousness associated with g-forces resulting from acceleration. When acceleration is of high value and rapid onset, loss of consciousness may occur suddenly and without warning, before any other physiological symptoms are noticed. See ACCELERATION EFFECTS.

gray *n.* a visual sensation that has neither hue (color) nor saturation and can vary from black to white.

gray commissure a bundle of nerve fibers that surrounds the central canal of the spinal cord and connects the anterior and dorsal horns of GRAY MATTER in each half of the cord.

gray matter any area of neural tissue that is dominated by CELL BODIES and is devoid of myelin, such as the CEREBRAL CORTEX and the H-shaped CENTRAL GRAY of the spinal cord (see also ANTERIOR HORN; DORSAL HORN). Compare WHITE MATTER.

gray-out *n.* partial loss of consciousness due to deficiency of oxygen in the blood (hyoxemia) resulting in HYPOXIA, which occasionally occurs in mountain climbers and high-flying pilots. Major symptoms are a dulling of sensory, motor, and mental capacities and impairment in judgment, memory, and time sense.

gray ramus a short nerve in the autonomic nervous system that carries unmyelinated postganglionic fibers from a SYMPATHETIC GANGLION to an adjacent spinal nerve. The fibers within a gray ramus are called **gray rami communicantes**.

Graz school of psychology see AUSTRIAN SCHOOL.

GRE abbreviation for GRADUATE RECORD EXAMINATIONS.

great chain of being a construction, attributed to Greek philosopher Plato (c. 429–347 BCE) and elaborated by many later philosophers, that sees creation as a continuous linked hierarchy descending from God at the top, through heavenly beings, humans, animals, and plants to nonliving matter. The classic work on the history of this idea is the 1936 study by U.S. philosopher Arthur O. Lovejoy (1873–1963).

great commissure 1. in vertebrate brains, the CORPUS CALLOSUM, so called because it is by far the largest COMMISSURE that connects the two cerebral hemispheres. **2.** in insect brains, the commissure that connects the two lateral protocerebra.

greater superficial petrosal nerve (**GSP nerve**) the sensory nerve that carries taste information from the soft palate. The GSP nerve merges with the **chorda tympani** (the nerve that innervates TASTE BUDS on the front of the tongue) to form the **intermediate nerve** (or **nerve of Wrisberg**), the sensory component of the predominantly motor FACIAL NERVE (seventh cranial nerve).

great imitator 1. slang for LUPUS ERYTHEMATOSUS, LYME DISEASE, and other diseases that are difficult to diagnose correctly. **2.** a former colloquial name for SYPHILIS, because the rash of secondary syphilis may mimic many other diseases.

great man theory a view of political leadership and historical causation that assumes that history is driven by a small number of exceptional individuals with certain innate characteristics that predispose them for greatness. A ZEITGEIST (spirit of the times) view of history, in contrast, supposes that history is largely determined by economics, technological development, and a broad spectrum of social influences. [associated with British historian Thomas Carlyle (1795–1881)]

Great Mother see MAGNA MATER.

Greek cross a simple figure resembling an equal-armed cross (+), the drawing of which is used to measure basic constructional ability.

greeting behavior a form of ATTACHMENT BEHAVIOR that in humans begins to manifest itself clearly at about 6 months of age, when the infant responds to the arrival of a parent or caregiver.

gregariousness *n.* the tendency for human beings to associate with others in groups, organizations, and activities, in order to enjoy social life for its own sake. The drive is probably not instinctual but develops slowly out of the child's helplessness and dependence; gregariousness gives the child security, companionship, acceptance, and a sense of belonging. In nonhuman animals, gregariousness is seen in the tendency to congregate in herds or flocks. See AFFILIATIVE DRIVE; SOCIAL INSTINCT. **—gregarious** *adj.*

Greig syndrome see HYPERTELORISM. [David M. **Greig** (1864–1936), Scottish physician]

grid organizational development (grid OD) a comprehensive ORGANIZATIONAL DEVELOPMENT intervention based on the BLAKE–MOUTON MANAGERIAL GRID. The aim is to increase managers' concerns for both production and people, thereby improving ORGANIZATIONAL EFFECTIVENESS. It consists of six phases conducted in the following order: (a) a seminar on the Blake–Mouton grid, (b) teamwork development, (c) intergroup development, (d) development of an ideal strategic corporate model, (e) implementation of the ideal strategic model, and (f) systematic critique. [designed by U.S. psychologists Robert R. Blake (1918–) and Jane S. Mouton (1930–)]

grief *n.* the anguish experienced after significant loss, usually the death of a beloved person. Grief is often distinguished from BEREAVEMENT and MOURNING. Not all bereavements result in a strong grief response; nor is all grief given public expression (see DISENFRANCHISED GRIEF). Grief often includes physiological distress, SEPARATION ANXIETY, confusion, yearning, obsessive dwelling on the past, and apprehension about the future. Intense grief can become life-threatening through disruption of the immune system, self-neglect, and suicidal thoughts. Grief may also take the form of regret for something lost, remorse for something done, or sorrow for a mishap to oneself.

grief counseling the provision of advice, information, and psychological support to help individuals whose ability to function has been impaired by someone's death, particularly that of a loved one or friend. It includes counseling for the grieving process and practical advice concerning arrangements for the funeral and burial of the loved one. Grief counseling is sometimes offered by staff in specialized agencies (e.g., hospices) or it may be carried out in the context of other counseling. See also BEREAVEMENT THERAPY.

griefwork *n.* the slow process through which bereaved people gradually reduce their emotional connection to the person who has died and thereby regain involvement in their own ongoing lives. According to griefwork theory, this activity will gradually transfer CATHEXIS from the past relationship to their ongoing lives. A more recent perspective holds that it is not necessary to sever all emotional connections with the dead person. Instead, this relationship can be transformed symbolically as a CONTINUING BOND that provides a sense of meaning and value conducive to forming new relationships.

grievance *n.* **1.** a feeling of resentment arising from a sense of having been unjustly treated. **2.** in industrial and organizational psychology, a complaint filed by an employee according to rules and procedures set forth by the management of the organization or in a contract negotiated with the union representing that employee.

Griggs v. Duke Power Co. a case resulting in an influential 1971 ruling by the U.S. Supreme Court regarding discrimination in hiring practices. The ruling established that proof of discrimination does not require the plaintiff to show the defendant had intention or motives to discriminate if the selection practices had ADVERSE IMPACT on a particular group (e.g., those defined by ethnicity, age, or sex).

Grip Strength Test a test in which the strength of hand grip is assessed with a dynamometer. It is part of the HALSTEAD–REITAN NEUROPSYCHOLOGICAL BATTERY. Also called **Hand Dynamometer Test**.

grisi siknis a CULTURE-BOUND SYNDROME found in Nicaragua and characterized by headache, anxiety, anger, and the sudden onset of an episode of hyperactivity and potentially dangerous behavior in the form of running or fleeing. There is ensuing exhaustion, sleep, and amnesia for the episode. The syndrome, which has some similarities to PIBLOKTO, is usually classified as a DISSOCIATIVE TRANCE DISORDER.

GRIT acronym for GRADUATED AND RECIPROCATED INITIATIVES IN TENSION REDUCTION.

grooming *n.* a basic function of self-care that includes cleaning and maintaining one's body, hair, clothes, and general appearance. In animals, grooming has both hygienic functions, such as picking parasites or dirt from the fur, and social functions, including the provision of reward through activation of ENDOGENOUS OPIOIDS in the recipients (see ALLOGROOMING; ANIMAL GROOMING BEHAVIOR). Training or retraining in grooming can be a central aspect in the rehabilitation of individuals with mental or physical impairments.

gross motor describing activities or skills that use large muscles to move the trunk or limbs and to control posture to maintain balance. Examples of **gross motor skills** include waving an arm, walking, hopping, and running. Compare FINE MOTOR.

ground *n.* the relatively homogeneous and indistinct background of FIGURE–GROUND perceptions.

ground bundle a short tract within the spinal cord that connects different or neighboring levels of the cord. Also called **intersegmental tract**.

grounded theory **1.** a theory based on qualitative data. **2.** procedures for the systematic analysis of unstructured qualitative data.

ground rules in psychotherapy, the elements of the contract for therapy, including but not limited to the fee; the time, location, and frequency of the sessions; and therapist confidentiality.

ground truth the truth regarding whether or not an individual actually committed the act with which he or she is accused. The concept is often used in the context of lie detection. Because ground truth is generally not known in field studies using the POLYGRAPH test, the true error rate of this test is difficult to determine.

group *n.* **1.** any collection or assemblage, particularly of items or individuals. **2.** in social psychology, two or more interdependent individuals who influence one another through social interaction. Common features of groups include joint activities that either focus on the task at hand or concern the interpersonal relations between group members, structures involving roles and norms, a degree of cohesiveness, and shared goals. Also called **social group**. **3.** in animal behavior, an organized collection of individuals that moves together or otherwise acts to achieve some common goal (e.g., reproduction and care of young, defense of resources, or protection against predators) that would be less effectively achieved by individual action. Compare AGGREGATION. **4.** a collection of participants in a research study whose responses are to be compared to the responses of one or more other collections of research participants. Participants in a particular group all experience the same experimental conditions or receive the same treatment, which differs from the experimental conditions or treatments participants in other groups experience or receive. **5.** in the psychology of perception, a configuration of individual objects that are perceived to form a unified whole, or GESTALT.

group abilities abilities, such as verbal-comprehension abilities, spatial abilities, and memory abilities, that are sources of individual differences in some groups of intelligence tests.

group acceptance the degree to which group members approve of a new, prospective, or potential member as reflected in his or her admission to the group and relative status and role within it.

group analysis the study of the pathological behavior of a group.

group-analytic psychotherapy a type of group psychotherapy that focuses on the communication and interaction processes taking place in the group as a whole. Interventions make use of group rather than individual forces as the principal therapeutic agent. Also called **therapeutic group analysis**. [originated in the 1940s by Sigmund Heinrich Foulkes (1898–1976)]

group attribution error the tendency for perceivers to assume that a specific group member's personal characteristics and preferences, including beliefs, attitudes, and decisions, are similar to the preferences of the group to which he or she belongs. For example, observers may assume that the individual who is a member of a group that publicly announces its opposition to an issue also opposes the issue, even though the group's decision to take the stated position may not have been unanimous. See also GROUP FALLACY; OUTGROUP HOMOGENEITY BIAS.

group behavior actions performed by a group as a whole or by individuals when part of a group. In the latter case it applies particularly to those actions that are influenced (either directly or indirectly) by the group and are atypical of actions performed by the same individuals when alone.

group boundary the implicit and explicit standards that set limits on aspects of the group, including who can be members, the expected duties of members, and the types of actions that the group will permit members to perform.

group-centered leader in general, an individual who adopts a LEADERSHIP STYLE based on the sharing of the traditional duties and powers of the leader with other group members. In therapeutic groups, a group-centered leader avoids guiding the course of the interaction by asking the group members to identify topics and goals, provide interpretations, and set their own limits. Compare DIRECTIVE LEADER.

group climate the relative degree of acceptance, tolerance, and freedom of expression that characterizes the relationships within a counseling or therapy group. Interpersonal behavioral boundaries are generally freer and broader than in social contexts, and the meaning of interpersonal behavior is often the specific focus of group discussion.

group cohesion see COHESION.

group consciousness 1. the awareness of the group, its members, and their commonalities exhibited by individual members of the group. Just as SELF-CONSCIOUSNESS pertains to awareness of the self, so group consciousness pertains to awareness of the collective. **2.** a group's total awareness of itself, suggested in some cases to be greater than the sum of individual members' awareness. **3.** see GROUP MIND.

group contagion see CONTAGION.

group counseling a method of providing guidance and support for clients organized as a group, as opposed to individual counseling. Group counseling can be used, for example, to assist high school students in choosing a college or to assist employees of an organization in stating dissatisfactions and proposing solutions to managers and employers.

group decision support systems (**GDSS**) technology used to improve the quality, speed, and efficiency of group decision making and to help the group avoid common sources of error, such as pressures to conformity. GDSS most often comes in the form of computer software modules that help the group to communicate freely about an issue, identify key stakeholders and their assumptions, formulate ideas, and evaluate and vote on alternatives.

group development 1. naturally occurring patterns of growth and change that unfold across the life span of a group. The term usually implies a progressive movement toward a more complete or advanced state, with different theorists characterizing this movement as (a) discontinuous and occurring in distinct stages rather than continuous and incremental and (b) incremental and irreversible rather than cyclical and repetitious. See also EQUILIBRIUM MODEL OF GROUP DEVELOPMENT. **2.** a strategic intervention designed to alter the processing and functioning of a group; this usually involves assessing the group's current level of development, helping to clarify its mission and goals, and reviewing its operating procedures. See also TEAM BUILDING.

group difference any observed difference between groups of participants in an experiment who experienced different treatments based upon the group to which they were assigned.

group dynamics 1. the dynamic rather than static processes, operations, and changes that occur within social groups, which affect patterns of affiliation, communication, conflict, conformity, decision making, influence, leadership, norm formation, and power. The term, as used by Kurt LEWIN, emphasizes the power of the fluid, ever-changing forces that characterize interpersonal groups. Also called **group process**. See also INTERGROUP DYNAMICS. **2.** the field of psychology devoted to the study of groups and group processes. **3.** a conceptual and clinical orientation in group psychotherapy that explicitly recognizes and explores group-level processes in the treatment group.

group experience in group psychotherapy and group counseling, the interactions that give the client an opportunity to gain insight into his or her problems by sharing with and learning from other members. The group experience is particularly valuable in helping clients understand how they are perceived by other people. When group therapy or counseling is given in addition to individual intervention, it allows the therapist or counselor to observe the client's emotional difficulties as revealed in group interactions.

group experiment an experiment in which groups serve as the unit of analysis. For example, the performance of groups under conditions of autocratic and democratic leadership may be compared.

group factors the psychometric entities underlying GROUP ABILITIES.

group fallacy 1. the assumption, regarded as erroneous, that groups possess emergent, supervening qualities that cannot be understood completely through the analysis of the qualities of the individual members. See CROWD MIND; FOLK SOUL; GROUP MIND. **2.** the mistaken assumption that a group is totally uniform, whereas in fact members differ from one another in many respects. Such a fallacy is involved in many forms of prejudice and usually lies behind ideas of COLLECTIVE GUILT.

group feeling the desire of the members of a group to

associate with each other, to participate in joint activities, and to seek the general good of the group.

group G monosomy a rare chromosomal disorder involving the absence of all or part of a G-group chromosome (i.e., chromosome 21 or 22). Affected individuals have short spadelike hands and severe mental retardation. Because of varied effects, more than one chromosomal defect may be involved. Chromosome 21 is often involved in translocations and aberrations related to DOWN SYNDROME.

group harmony the extent to which group interactions are friendly, congruous, and conflict-free.

group health plan see INDEMNITY PLAN.

group home a residential facility that offers housing and personal care services, such as meals, supervision, and transportation. Also called **group residence**.

group hypnosis see COLLECTIVE HYPNOTIZATION.

group hysteria see COLLECTIVE HYSTERIA.

group identification 1. the act or process of associating oneself so strongly with a group and its members that one imitates and internalizes the group's distinctive features (actions, beliefs, standards, objectives, etc.). This process can lead not only to an enhanced sense of group belonging, group pride, and group commitment but also to AUTOSTEREOTYPING, in which one accepts as self-descriptive certain stereotypical qualities attributed to the group as a whole, and a reduced sense of individuality (see DEINDIVIDUATION). **2.** in the psychoanalytic theory of Sigmund FREUD, the process by which individuals become emotionally attached to social groups. Just as children bond with and imitate their parents, adults bond with, and take on the characteristics of, their groups. **3.** more rarely, the act of considering another group's perspective or outlook even though one is not a member of that group.

grouping *n.* **1.** in education, the process of assigning pupils to grades, classes, or subgroups. **2.** in statistics, the process of arranging scores in categories, intervals, classes, or ranks.

group intelligence test an intelligence test administered simultaneously to all the individuals in a group. Such tests are contrasted with **individual intelligence tests**, which are administered to one person at a time.

group interview a conference or meeting in which one or more questioners elicit information from two or more respondents in an experimental or real-life situation. This method encourages the interviewees to interact with one other in responding to the interviewer. Group interviews are often employed in motivation research because the participation of a number of people, particularly if they are acquainted with each other as members of a club or similar group, is believed to yield more informative responses than are typically obtained by interviewing individuals separately.

group justification reasons, explanations, and accounts offered by a group to defend its actions and interests and to enhance its collective self-esteem. This may often involve denigration and stereotyping of an OUTGROUP. See GROUP-SERVING BIAS; INGROUP BIAS; SOCIAL IDENTITY THEORY.

group marriage a family pattern found in some indigenous cultures and certain minority religious groups in which several men and women live together, sharing the burdens of the household, the rearing of children, and a common sexual life. See also COMMUNE; POLYGAMY.

group medical practice the practice of medicine by a group of physicians, typically various specialists, associated not only for administrative reasons but also for such clinical purposes as cooperative diagnosis, treatment, and prevention. Also called **group practice**.

group mind a hypothetical, transcendent consciousness created by the fusion of the individual minds in a collective, such as a nation or race. This controversial idea, often seen as a prime example of the GROUP FALLACY, assumes that the group mind is greater than the sum of the psychological experiences of the individuals and that it can become so powerful that it can overwhelm the will of the individual. Also called **collective consciousness**; **collective mind**; **general consciousness**; **group consciousness**. Compare CROWD MIND. See also FOLK SOUL. [first described by French psychologist Gustave Le Bon (1841–1931)]

group mission a mission undertaken by a military unit, in which group COHESION is a major factor in ensuring its successful accomplishment.

group morale group members' overall level of enthusiasm (confidence, dedication, zeal, ESPRIT DE CORPS) for the group, its tasks, and its goals.

group network the relatively organized system of connections linking members of a group, unit, or collective, including social or interpersonal evaluations (e.g., friendship, acquaintanceship, dislike), communication, transfer of resources, and formal role relationships (e.g., supervisor–subordinate). In so-called **standard networks** all members of the network can relate to and interact with each other. **Ego-centered networks** consist of a central member, or ego, and the set of others who are linked to the ego. **Perceptual networks** are the relational ties among members as perceived by a given individual or ego.

group norms see SOCIAL NORMS.

group personal space see GROUP SPACE.

group polarization the tendency for members of a group discussing an issue to move toward a more extreme version of the positions they held before the discussion began. As a result, the group as a whole tends to respond in more extreme ways than one would expect given the sentiments of the individual members prior to deliberation. Polarization is sustained by social comparison (see SOCIAL COMPARISON THEORY), exposure to other members' relatively extreme responses (see PERSUASIVE ARGUMENTS THEORY), and by groups' implicit SOCIAL-DECISION SCHEMES. See CHOICE-SHIFT EFFECT; RISKY SHIFT.

group practice see GROUP MEDICAL PRACTICE.

group pressure direct or indirect SOCIAL PRESSURE exerted by a group on its individual members to influence their choices. Such pressure may take the form of rational argument and persuasion (INFORMATIONAL INFLUENCE), calls for conformity to group norms (NORMATIVE INFLUENCE), or more direct forms of influence, such as demands, threats, personal attacks, and promises of rewards or social approval (INTERPERSONAL INFLUENCE).

group problem solving the use of a social group to resolve matters that involve doubt, uncertainty, or unknown difficulties. The typical stages involved in group problem solving include (a) identification of the problem and the process to use in solving it, (b) gathering of information and evaluation of alternatives through discussion, (c) selection of the solution, and (d) implementation of the solution.

group process 1. see GROUP DYNAMICS. **2.** the interpersonal component of a group session, in contrast to the content (such as decisions or information) generated during the session.

group psychotherapy treatment of psychological problems in which two or more participants interact with each other on both an emotional and a cognitive level, in the presence of one or more psychotherapists who serve as catalysts, facilitators, or interpreters. The approaches of groups vary, but in general they aim to provide an environment in which problems and concerns can be shared in an atmosphere of mutual respect and understanding. Group psychotherapy seeks to enhance self-respect, deepen self-understanding, and improve interpersonal relationships. Also called **group therapy**.

group relations theory the view that behavior is influenced not only by one's unique pattern of traits but also by one's need to conform to social demands and expectations. Social determinants become particularly evident in group therapy, which tends to challenge attitudes, such as prejudices, that are based on conformity and restricted thinking. [proposed by Gordon W. ALLPORT]

group residence see GROUP HOME.

group risk taking embarking on a hazardous, dangerous, or uncertain course of action as a social group. Studies of GROUP POLARIZATION and the CHOICE-SHIFT EFFECT indicate that group decisions tend toward greater extremity or risk than individual decisions. See RISKY SHIFT.

group roles coherent sets of behaviors expected of people in specific positions within a group. In addition to the basic roles of leader and follower, groups usually allocate TASK ROLES pertaining to the group's tasks and goals and RELATIONSHIP ROLES that focus on the group members' interpersonal and emotional needs. When the behaviors associated with a particular role are poorly defined, ROLE AMBIGUITY may occur; similarly, when group members occupy two or more roles that call for incompatible behaviors, the result may be ROLE CONFLICT.

group selection the concept that social groups can act as adaptive units in NATURAL SELECTION. See KIN SELECTION. Compare INDIVIDUAL SELECTION.

group-serving bias any one of a number of cognitive tendencies that contribute to an overvaluing of one's group, particularly the tendency to credit the group for its successes but to blame external factors for its failures (the **ultimate attribution error**). Compare SELF-SERVING BIAS. See also ATTRIBUTION ERROR; INGROUP BIAS; SOCIOCENTRISM.

group sex sexual activity among a group of heterosexual people, gay men, or lesbians, who usually meet with the express purpose of obtaining maximum satisfaction through such means as observing each other, experimenting with different techniques, and exchanging partners.

group socialization 1. the process of interaction between an individual and a group that begins when he or she first considers joining the group and ends when he or she leaves it. **2.** the SOCIALIZATION of an individual, from infancy onward, through interaction with and observation of others in a group context.

group socialization theory a theory of personality development proposing that children are primarily socialized by their peers and that the influences of parents and teachers are filtered through children's peer groups. According to this theory, children seek to be like their peers rather than like their parents. [proposed by U.S. developmental psychologist Judith Rich Harris (1938–)]

group solidarity a sense of fellowship and community displayed by members of a collective who are united by shared purposes, responsibilities, and interests. See also COHESION; COMMUNAL FEELING; COMMUNAL SPIRIT; ESPRIT DE CORPS.

group space space defined by the temporary boundary that forms around interacting groups and serves as a barrier to unwanted intervention by nonmembers. Also called **group personal space**; **interactional territory**.

group structure the complex of processes, forms, and systems that organizes and regulates interpersonal phenomena in a group. Group structure defines the positions and roles in a group and the network of authority, attraction, and communication relations linking members. Such relations may be explicitly designated within the group, as in the case of FORMAL GROUP structure, or only tacitly acknowledged by the group, as in the case of ACCIDENTAL GROUP structure. See also SOCIAL STRUCTURE.

group superego in psychoanalytic theory, the portion of the SUPEREGO acquired from peer groups as opposed to the part derived from parental IDENTIFICATIONS.

group territorial behavior the tendency for ethnic and other groups to establish and defend areas as separate or shared territories. Such behavior can be observed, for instance, in the neighborhoods of large cities and in the activities of city street gangs. A form of **intragroup territorial behavior** is often seen in family settings and workplaces, where individuals may regard certain rooms or areas or even certain chairs as their personal territory.

group test a test administered to several individuals simultaneously. Compare INDIVIDUAL TEST.

group therapy see GROUP PSYCHOTHERAPY.

groupthink *n.* a strong CONCURRENCE-SEEKING tendency that interferes with effective group decision making. Symptoms include apparent unanimity, illusions of invulnerability and moral correctness, biased perceptions of the OUTGROUP, interpersonal pressure, self-censorship, and defective decision-making strategies. Causes are thought to include group COHESION and isolation, poor leadership, and the stress involved in making decisions. [identified by U.S. psychologist Irving Janis (1918–1990)]

groupware *n.* computer software associated with collaborative work (i.e., among several people on the same project) and GROUP DECISION SUPPORT SYSTEMS (GDSS).

GROW, INC. a mutual-help organization developed to provide help for individuals with depression, anxiety, and other mental health problems. Using a TWELVE-STEP PROGRAM, it offers a "caring and sharing" community to help members attain emotional maturity, personal responsibility, and recovery from mental illness. GROW, INC., originated in Australia.

growth *n.* **1.** the series of physical changes that occur from conception through maturity. **2.** the development of any entity toward its mature state.

growth cone the growing tip of an AXON or a DENDRITE.

growth curve 1. a graphic representation of the growth rate of an organism. **2.** a graphic representation of the increase in learning of an individual or group. See LEARNING CURVE.

growth function the relationship between a DEPENDENT VARIABLE and several levels of an INDEPENDENT VARIABLE defined in units of time (e.g., days, weeks, months, or years) or in other developmental indexes (e.g., lexical size).

growth group a group that focuses on the growth and

development of its individual members. See also ENCOUNTER GROUP; MARATHON GROUP; T-GROUP.

growth hormone (**GH**) a hormone, secreted by the anterior PITUITARY GLAND, that promotes the growth of cells and tissues. It stimulates protein synthesis, bone growth in early life, mobilization of fat stores, and carbohydrate storage. In humans, excessive secretion of growth hormone results in GIGANTISM in children and ACROMEGALY in adults. Also called **somatotropic hormone**; **somatotropin**. See also SOMATOMEDIN.

growth motivation see METAMOTIVATION.

growth needs see EXISTENCE, RELATEDNESS, AND GROWTH THEORY.

growth principle the concept that in an atmosphere free of coercion and distortion an individual's creative and integrative forces will lead to fuller adaptation, insight, self-esteem, and realization of potential. [formulated by Carl ROGERS]

growth spurt any period of accelerated physical development, especially the PUBESCENT GROWTH SPURT.

GSP nerve abbreviation for GREATER SUPERFICIAL PETROSAL NERVE.

G-spot abbreviation for GRAEFENBERG SPOT.

GSR abbreviation for GALVANIC SKIN RESPONSE.

G-tolerance limits the maximum gravitation effects (g-forces) that an individual can withstand before blacking out as a result of acceleration drawing blood out of the head toward the feet (the +Gz direction). Pilots of high-performance aircraft can tolerate +9 Gz with use of G-suits and straining maneuvers. The duration of G-exposure and the type of safety protection used are important in determining whether or not blackout will occur.

guanfacine *n.* a drug used for the treatment of hypertension. It acts as an agonist at ALPHA ADRENORECEPTORS, directly stimulating α_2-adrenoreceptors to restrict the flow of impulses in peripheral sympathetic nerves supplying the arteries, thus causing them to relax (widen); most of the other commonly prescribed antihypertensive drugs act as beta blockers or as diuretics. Guanfacine is also a sedating agent that is occasionally used as an adjunct in the treatment of attention-deficit/hyperactivity disorder and similar behavior disorders in children, although it is not officially approved by the U.S. Food and Drug Administration for these conditions and may cause excess sedation and hypotension (low blood pressure). The drug has also been investigated for the management of posttraumatic stress disorder, Tourette's disorder, and Alzheimer's disease. U.S. trade name: **Tenex**.

guanine (symbol: G) *n.* a purine compound that occurs in nucleotides and is one of the four bases in DNA and MESSENGER RNA. It is one of the elements of the GENETIC CODE.

guarana *n.* a shrub (*Paullinia cupana*) indigenous to the Brazilian Amazon, the seeds of which were originally thought to contain **guaranine**, a METHYLXANTHINE compound that is essentially indistinguishable from CAFFEINE. It is now known that guarana in fact contains a significant amount of caffeine, which is its primary active ingredient, as well as lesser amounts of the methylxanthines **theophylline** (the active ingredient in tea) and THEOBROMINE. Used as a stimulant and appetite suppressant, guarana is available in many over-the-counter preparations in the United States and other Western nations. At recommended doses it appears to have the same mild adverse effects known to be associated with other sympathomimetic stimulants (e.g., restlessness, increased urination, gastrointestinal distress) but may interact with medications, particularly MONOAMINE OXIDASE INHIBITORS. Additionally, additive effects and potential toxicity may occur when guarana is combined with other caffeine-containing products, and there is growing concern that use of guarana-containing products may cause such serious adverse events as chest pain, irregular heartbeat, seizures, coma, and possibly death.

guardian ad litem an individual appointed by the court to represent in a lawsuit someone who is incapacitated, either by age or by mental or physical disability. The individual's status as guardian ad litem is temporary and is dissolved upon resolution of that lawsuit.

guardianship *n.* a legal arrangement that places the care of a person and his or her property in the hands of another. When people are deemed incompetent by the court, and therefore unable to make decisions about their own care or to manage their own affairs, a **guardian** is appointed by the court to manage their property, make personal decisions on their behalf, and provide for their care and well-being. See also CONSERVATOR.

guess-who technique a type of personality rating device used chiefly in schools. Students, given short word pictures depicting a variety of personality types, are directed to identify the classmates whose personalities seem to correspond most closely to those descriptions.

guidance *n.* direction, advice, and counseling provided in cooperation with the client, often using personal data and interviews as important auxiliary tests.

guidance program the cumulative resources of staff and techniques used by a school to assist students in resolving scholastic or social problems. A specialized approach will include professionally trained counselors, social workers, and test administrators who each have specified functions within the overall program. In some programs, the use of specialists may be minimized, with teachers and administrators filling guidance functions.

guidance specialist an individual who has been trained in a counselor education program or whose credentials and experience are adequate to provide guidance.

guided affective imagery (**GAI**) in psychotherapy, the drawing out of emotional fantasies, or waking dreams, a technique used to ease CATHARSIS and work on emotions that are present but painful for the client to discuss. The therapist suggests concentration on past images that would bring up the emotional state or, in some cases, images of desired future successes. The technique is often used in SHORT-TERM THERAPY and GROUP PSYCHOTHERAPY. Also called **guided imagery**. See also VISUALIZATION.

guided participation a process in which the influences of social partners and sociocultural practices combine in various ways to provide children and other learners with direction and support, while the learners themselves also shape their learning engagements. It occurs not only during explicit instruction but also during routine activities and communication of everyday life. See SOCIOCULTURAL PERSPECTIVE. [proposed in the early 1980s by U.S. developmental psychologist Barbara Rogoff (1950–   )]

guided performance the process in which a learner is assisted by being given information or guidance to minimize errors, for example, by having a teacher guide the learner's movements or steps in solving a problem.

guiding fiction in the psychoanalytic theory of Alfred ADLER, a personal principle that serves as a guideline by which an individual can understand and evaluate his or her experiences and determine his or her lifestyle. In individuals considered to be in good or reasonable mental health, the guiding fiction is assumed to approach reality and be adaptive. In those who are not, it is assumed to be largely unconscious, unrealistic, and nonadaptive.

Guilford, Joy Paul (1897–1987) U.S. psychologist. Guilford received his doctorate in psychology from Cornell University, studying under Edward B. TITCHENER, Karl Dallenbach (1887–1971), and Gestalt psychologists Kurt KOFFKA and Harry Helson (1898–1977). After teaching at the University of Nebraska, he moved in 1940 to the University of Southern California, where he remained for the rest of his career. Guilford is best known for his contributions to psychometrics, publishing the first edition of the widely used *Psychometric Methods* in 1936, and also for his use of FACTOR ANALYSIS in studying personality and intelligence. Important works on these topics include *Personality* (1959) and *The Nature of Human Intelligence* (1967). Countering the view that intelligence could be characterized by a single, immutable rating, such as the IQ, Guilford argued that intelligence was multifaceted and that its components could be improved through education. He developed an important model, known as the STRUCTURE OF INTELLECT MODEL, to classify the many components of intelligence that he and other researchers had named. Among his honors were the Distinguished Scientific Contributions Award from the American Psychological Association and the Gold Medal of the American Psychological Foundation.

Guilford dimensions of intelligence three dimensions of intelligence postulated to underlie individual differences in scores on intelligence tests, namely, contents, operations, and products. Each mental ability represents a combination of these three facets. For example, a verbal-analogies test would represent a combination of cognition (operation) of verbal (content) relations (product). The number of mental abilities initially proposed by Guilford was 120; this was later increased to 150. The validity of this theory has been called into question by the work of U.S. psychologist John L. Horn (1928–), which has suggested that the existence of the proposed factors is not supported by research results. See also STRUCTURE OF INTELLECT MODEL. [Joy Paul GUILFORD]

Guilford–Zimmerman Temperament Survey (**GZTS**) a personality inventory for use with individuals aged 16 years and over, measuring 10 traits identified by FACTOR ANALYSIS: ascendance, sociability, friendliness, thoughtfulness, personal relations, masculinity, objectivity, general activity, restraint, and emotional stability. It comprises 300 descriptive statements (e.g., "You tend to lose your temper") to which participants respond "yes," "no," or "?". [originally developed in 1949 by U.S. psychologists Joy Paul GUILFORD and Wayne S. **Zimmerman** (1916–)]

Guillain–Barré syndrome an acute, progressive, demyelinating type of PERIPHERAL NEUROPATHY that starts with muscular weakness and loss of normal sensation in the extremities, spreading inward as the disease progresses. The condition often begins in the feet and ascends toward the head. These symptoms can increase in intensity until the muscles cannot be used at all and the individual is almost totally paralyzed, in which case the disorder is life threatening. Because the syndrome often develops after an infection, it may result from an immune reaction. [Georges **Guillain** (1876–1961) and Jean **Barré** (1880–1967), French neurologists]

guilt *n.* a SELF-CONSCIOUS EMOTION characterized by a painful sense of having done (or thought) something that is wrong and often by a readiness to take action designed to undo or mitigate this wrong. **—guilty** *adj.*

guilt by association responsibility for a misdeed ascribed to an innocent person solely because he or she has some connection with the perpetrator (or perpetrators) of the wrong. The observer's negative attitude toward the wrongdoer generalizes to the associated person.

guilt culture a trend or organizing principle in a society characterized by the use of guilt to promote socially acceptable behavior. Compare SHAME CULTURE.

guilty but mentally ill (**GBMI**) a court judgment that may be made in some states when defendants plead insanity (see INSANITY DEFENSE). Defendants found guilty but mentally ill are treated in a mental hospital until their mental health is restored; they then serve the remainder of their sentence in the appropriate correctional facility.

guilty knowledge test a form of lie detection in which knowledge about the details of a crime is tested. A POLYGRAPH examiner presents examinees with multiple-choice questions concerning the crime, to which only the guilty party should know the correct answers; it is assumed that innocent examinees will see all options as equally plausible. The polygraph examiner measures the examinees' physiological arousal as each option is presented and identifies which option produces the highest physiological response. Over a series of questions, if an individual consistently shows the greatest response to the correct option, the examiner may identify that person as untruthful in his or her denial of knowledge of the details of the crime. See also CONTROL QUESTION TEST; RELEVANT–IRRELEVANT TEST.

Gulf War syndrome a collection of unexplained symptoms experienced by some veterans of the 1991 Gulf War. Symptoms may include headaches, fatigue, joint pain, skin rashes, and memory loss.

Günther's disease a congenital form of PORPHYRIA in which excess porphyrin is formed in the bone marrow. Psychological and neurological changes often accompany pain, nausea, and other symptoms. [Hans **Günther** (1884–1929), German physician]

guru *n.* **1.** in Hinduism and Sikhism, a spiritual teacher or leader, specifically one charged with keeping alive the oral teachings. **2.** in general usage, any teacher, counselor, or intellectual leader, especially one regarded as having special knowledge. [Sanskrit, literally: "teacher"]

gustation *n.* the sense of TASTE. Taste is at the threshold between the external (chemical) and internal (biochemical) worlds; it serves an organism's nutritional needs and protects it from poisons. **—gustatory** *adj.*

gustatory agnosia the inability to identify or categorize gustatory (taste) stimuli, despite the capacity to experience them.

gustatory hallucination a false and enduring taste sensation, usually of bitterness or sourness. It is often attributable to tonic stimulation of TASTE CELLS or of the peripheral taste nerves.

gustatory nerve see LINGUAL NERVE.

gustatory neuron types categories into which taste neurons of the peripheral and central nervous system can be grouped according to their sensitivities to PRIMARY TASTE qualities. About 40% of the taste neurons in primates are most responsive to sweet stimuli, 35% to those that are salty, 20% to bitter chemicals, and 5% to acids. Therefore some 75% of neurons are devoted to detecting nutrients, and 25% to avoiding toxins.

gustatory qualities the range of taste sensations to

which humans are sensitive. These are often categorized into basic, or primary, tastes—thought to be SWEET, SALTY, UMAMI, SOUR, and BITTER—although the full range of taste perceptions may exceed these categories.

gustatory stimulus a chemical capable of activating TASTE CELLS. Gustatory stimuli include sugars (SWEET), salts of sodium (SALTY) and heavier elements (BITTER or rarely sweet), acids (SOUR), alkaloids (bitter), and monosodium glutamate (UMAMI), among others. Also called **sapid stimulus**; **taste stimulus**.

gustatory system the primary structures and processes involved in an organism's detection of and responses to GUSTATORY STIMULI. The gustatory system includes lingual PAPILLAE, TASTE BUDS and TASTE CELLS, TASTE TRANSDUCTION, neural impulses and pathways (see GREATER SUPERFICIAL PETROSAL NERVE), and associated brain areas and their functions (see PRIMARY TASTE CORTEX; SECONDARY TASTE CORTEX; SOLITARY NUCLEUS; THALAMIC TASTE AREA). The responses of this system can be modified to an extent by an organism's physiology, its immediate needs, and its experiences. Also called **taste system**.

gustatory transduction see TASTE TRANSDUCTION.

gustometer *n.* an instrument used to deliver a predetermined volume and concentration of a taste (gustatory) stimulus to the tongue over a specified period of time.

gut hormone any hormone that is released by the stomach or intestines, sometimes in response to food.

Guthrie, Edwin Ray (1886–1959) U.S. psychologist. After earning his doctorate in philosophy at the University of Pennsylvania in 1912, he moved to the University of Washington, where he remained for the rest of his career. Guthrie is best known for his stimulus–response (S–R) CONTIGUITY LEARNING THEORY, a variant of behaviorist theory. According to this theory, temporal contiguity rather than drive (as in HULL's theory) or reinforcement (as in SKINNER's theory) was the critical element for learning new behaviors. His best known work was *The Psychology of Learning* (1935; revised 1952). Guthrie also pioneered the use of teaching evaluations for college faculties. He served as president of the American Psychological Association (1945). See also BEHAVIORISM.

Guttman scale see CUMULATIVE SCALE.

gutturophonia *n.* a form of DYSPHONIA characterized by a throaty or low-pitched voice.

gymnemic acid an extract of the Indian plant *Gymnema sylvestris*, noted for its capacity to block sweet taste. It is one of a family of triterpene saponins (plant glucosides producing a soapy lather) that also includes ziziphin, gurmarin, and hodulcin.

gynandromorph *n.* an organism with both male and female physical characteristics. In most instances male characteristics occur on one side of the body, and female on the other; in a few cases the head is female, and the rest of the body is male. Also called **gynander**. See also ANDROGYNY. **—gynandromorphism** *n.*

gynecology *n.* the branch of medicine concerned with diseases and disorders of the reproductive organs of women. **—gynecological** *adj.* **—gynecologist** *n.*

gynecomastia *n.* abnormal development of breast tissue in males. In young men the condition usually occurs on both sides, whereas in men over 50, gynecomastia tends to be unilateral. Gynecomastia may occur as a result of hormonal imbalance related to a tumor or as a side effect of therapy with ANTIANDROGENS or with DOPAMINE-RECEPTOR ANTAGONISTS, which include many antipsychotic drugs. Dopamine inhibits the release from the anterior pituitary of the hormone PROLACTIN; therefore, inhibition of dopaminergic activity may result in excess secretion of prolactin, leading to engorgement of breast tissue and possibly expression of breast milk (see GALACTORRHEA). Gynecomastia may also be observed (though rarely) with administration of SSRIS.

gynecomimesis *n.* sexual interest and arousal obtained by a man from impersonating a woman.

gynemimetophilia *n.* sexual interest in and arousal by men who are cross-dressing and playing the role of women.

gynetresia *n.* the condition of having imperforate female genitalia (i.e., lacking an opening).

gyno- (**gyn-**) *combining form* women or female.

gyrator treatment a form of alternative psychiatric treatment used in the late 18th and early 19th centuries for patients diagnosed as "torpid and melancholic" and whose condition was attributed to depletion of blood in the brain. The patient was placed in a revolving device in the belief that the rotation would drive out the illness by inducing vertigo, perspiration, and nausea and would restore the blood supply to the brain by centrifugal force. Also called **rotation treatment**. [devised by U.S. physician Benjamin Rush (1745–1813)]

gyrus *n.* (*pl.* **gyri**) a ridged or raised portion of a convoluted brain surface. Compare SULCUS.

gyrus cinguli see CINGULATE GYRUS.

gyrus fasciolaris see FASCIOLUS GYRUS.

GZTS abbreviation for GUILFORD–ZIMMERMAN TEMPERAMENT SURVEY.

Hh

H_0 symbol for NULL HYPOTHESIS.

H_1 symbol for ALTERNATIVE HYPOTHESIS.

Haab's pupillary reflex the normal contraction of both pupils when the eyes focus on a bright object in a darkened room. [Otto **Haab** (1850–1931), Swiss ophthalmologist]

habeas corpus a writ requiring a court to determine whether or not there is sufficient cause to hold someone in a correctional or other facility (Latin, literally: "you may have the body"). In the context of forensic psychology, it is typically used to determine whether confinement to a mental institution has been carried out with DUE PROCESS.

habilitation *n.* the process of enhancing the independence, well-being, and level of functioning of an individual with a disability or disorder by providing appropriate resources, such as treatment or training, to enable that person to develop skills and abilities he or she had not had the opportunity to acquire previously. Compare REHABILITATION.

habit *n.* a well-learned behavior or automatic sequence of behaviors that is relatively situation-specific and over time has become motorically reflexive and independent of motivational or cognitive influence, that is, it is performed with little or no conscious intent. For example, the habit of hair twirling may eventually occur without the individual's conscious awareness. **—habitual** *adj.*

habitability *n.* the degree to which a specific environment meets the functional and aesthetic requirements of its occupants. See also ENVIRONMENTAL DESIGN.

habitat *n.* the external environment in which an organism lives. Animals are assumed to select habitats that provide optimal features for survival and reproduction. An organism's habitat includes other animal and plant species that are important to it, as well as the physical aspects of the environment, including soil, substrate, and climate.

habit deterioration a tendency to regress in social behavior to less integrated patterns as a result of mental or physical illness.

habit disorder any repetitive maladaptive behavior that may interfere with social, educational, or other important areas of functioning. In *DSM–IV–TR*, this has been subsumed under the diagnostic category of STEREOTYPIC MOVEMENT DISORDER.

habit family hierarchy the concept that several different routes to the same goal—or more generally, responses to the same stimulus—are available, each having a particular strength that determines its arrangement in a preferential order and hence its potential for expression. Also called **habit hierarchy**. [developed by Clark L. HULL]

habit formation the process by which, through repetition or conditioning, animals or humans acquire a behavior that becomes regular and increasingly easy to perform.

habit-forming drug a drug with ABUSE POTENTIAL.

habit hierarchy 1. see HABIT FAMILY HIERARCHY. **2.** the arrangement of simple habits into progressively more complex habit patterns.

habit regression the act of returning to a previously discontinued habit or pattern of behavior, often as a result of emotional distress.

habit reversal a technique of BEHAVIOR THERAPY in which the client must learn a new correct response to a stimulus and stop responding to a previously learned cue. Habit reversal is used in behavioral conditioning, for example, to control such unwanted habits as overeating, smoking, hair pulling (trichotillomania), and nail biting.

habit strength a hypothetical construct said to reflect learning strength, which varies with the number of reinforcements, the amount of reinforcement, the interval between stimulus and response, and the interval between response and reinforcement. [proposed in 1943 by Clark L. HULL]

habit tic a brief, recurrent movement of a psychogenic nature, as contrasted with TICS of organic origin. Examples are grimacing, blinking, and repeatedly turning the head to one side.

habituation *n.* **1.** in general, the process of growing accustomed to a situation or pattern of behavior. **2.** the weakening of a response to a stimulus, or the diminished effectiveness of a stimulus, following repeated exposure to the stimulus. Compare DISHABITUATION. **3.** the process of becoming psychologically dependent on the use of a particular drug, such as cocaine, but without the increasing tolerance and physiological dependence that are characteristic of addiction. **4.** the elimination of extraneous responses that interfere with learning a skill, through repetition and practice.

habitus *n.* **1.** a susceptibility to certain types of physical disorders associated with particular SOMATOTYPES. **2.** the general appearance of the body.

habitus apoplecticus see APOPLECTIC TYPE.

habitus phthisicus a tendency or susceptibility of a patient to develop pulmonary tuberculosis. In constitutional typologies, the habitus phthisicus person would have a slender, flat-chested physique.

hacker *n.* a colloquial name for a highly skilled computer programmer, especially one who is able to break into protected computer systems or files for dishonest purposes.

haemo- *combining form* see HEMO-.

hair cells 1. the sensory receptors for hearing, located in the ORGAN OF CORTI within the cochlea of the inner ear. They respond to vibrations of the BASILAR MEMBRANE via movement of fine hairlike processes (**stereocilia**) that protrude from the cells. In humans there are 12,000 **outer hair cells** and 3,500 **inner hair cells**. Almost all auditory nerve fibers communicate only with inner hair cells. The outer hair cells appear to be capable of movement and may provide amplification of the vibration that stimulates the inner hair cells. **2.** the sensory receptors for balance, similar in structure to the cochlear hair cells. They are located in the inner ear within the ampullae of the SEMICIRCULAR CANALS (forming part of the CRISTA) and within the SACCULE and UTRICLE (forming part of the MACULA).

hair esthesiometer a device used to measure sensitivity to pressure. See also FREY ESTHESIOMETER.

hair follicle the protective casing of the root of a hair. Inside the follicle, the end of the hair shaft is surrounded by a FLOWER-SPRAY ENDING, one of the basic types of somatosensory receptors. In defense behavior, a follicular nerve ending stimulates muscle fibers that contract and cause PILOERECTION.

hair pulling see TRICHOTILLOMANIA.

halazepam *n.* a BENZODIAZEPINE used for the management of anxiety disorders and the short-term treatment of insomnia. As with most of the long-acting benzodiazepines, halazepam is metabolized to the active intermediate compound, desmethyldiazepam (nordiazepam), which has a very long HALF-LIFE (and therefore duration of action). This allows halazepam to be taken only once a day but also is associated with its accumulation in older adults and others with reduced ability to metabolize the long-acting benzodiazepines. U.S. trade name: **Paxipam**.

Halcion *n.* a trade name for TRIAZOLAM.

Haldol *n.* a trade name for HALOPERIDOL.

half-life (symbol: $t_{1/2}$) *n.* in pharmacokinetics, the time necessary for the concentration in the blood of an administered drug to fall by 50%. Half-life is a function of the rate of CLEARANCE of a drug and its VOLUME OF DISTRIBUTION in various body systems; it is expressed by the equation $t_{1/2}$ = (0.7 × volume of distribution)/clearance. Clinically, half-life varies among individuals as a result of age, disease states, or concurrent administration of other drugs. Half-life is useful in predicting the duration of effect of a drug and the time required for a drug to reach a state of equilibrium (steady state) in the body, that is, when the amount of drug administered is equal to that excreted. Generally, steady state is predicted to be achieved after 4–5 half-lives of a drug; for example, if a drug has a measured half-life of 8 hours (and its dosing schedule remains the same), steady state would be anticipated within 32–40 hours.

half-show *n.* a form of child psychotherapy in which a psychological problem is presented as a puppet-show drama, which is stopped at a crucial moment. The child is then asked to suggest how the story should end.

halfway house a transitional living arrangement for formerly institutionalized people, such as individuals recovering from alcohol or substance abuse, who have completed treatment at a hospital or rehabilitation center but still require support to assist them in restructuring their lives.

Hall, Granville Stanley (1844–1924) U.S. psychologist. Hall is best known as a founder and organizer of psychology in the United States. He received what was probably the first PhD in psychology in America (Harvard, 1878). He founded the first U.S. psychology journal, the *American Journal of Psychology* (1887), as well as several other journals, and became the first president of the American Psychological Association, which he helped to organize, in 1892. As an early advocate of child study, he gathered information on children's interests and attitudes through the use of questionnaires, stimulated interest in child guidance, and published widely read texts on *Adolescence* (1904), human development, and educational problems. His research was underpinned throughout by an interest in evolutionary theory and a belief that the development of individual humans recapitulated the development of the human race (see RECAPITULATION THEORY). He became the first president of the newly founded Clark University in 1889, but maintained an active research and writing career and was mentor to a number of graduate students who rose to prominence within psychology. As a side interest, Hall introduced Sigmund FREUD, Carl JUNG, and other leading European psychoanalysts to the American public by inviting them to a special conference celebrating Clark University's 20th anniversary in 1909. See also STORM-AND-STRESS PERIOD.

Hallermann–Streiff syndrome a congenital disorder marked by craniofacial anomalies, including a small, beaked nose, small eyes, and low-set ears. In many affected individuals, the skull sutures are slow to close and may remain open into puberty. Mental retardation is present in about 15% of these individuals. [reported in 1948 by Wilhelm **Hallermann** (1901–1976), German physician, and in 1950 by Enrico Bernardo **Streiff** (1908–), Swiss ophthalmologist]

hallucination *n.* a false sensory perception that has a compelling sense of reality despite the absence of an external stimulus. It may affect any of the senses, but AUDITORY HALLUCINATIONS and VISUAL HALLUCINATIONS are most common. Hallucination is typically a symptom of PSYCHOSIS, although it may also result from substance use or a medical condition, such as epilepsy, brain tumor, or syphilis. Compare DELUSION; ILLUSION.

hallucinogen *n.* a substance capable of producing a sensory effect (visual, auditory, olfactory, gustatory, or tactile) in the absence of an actual stimulus. Because they produce alterations in perception, cognition, and mood, hallucinogens are also called **psychedelic drugs** (from the Greek, meaning "mind-manifesting"). Hallucinogens are a group of heterogeneous compounds, many of which are naturally occurring; others are produced synthetically. Many hallucinogens are structurally similar to one of several neurotransmitters, which may be used as a mechanism of categorization. For example, serotonin-like hallucinogens include the indolealkylamines, exemplified by lysergic acid diethylamide (see LSD), PSILOCIN, DMT, DET, and BUFOTENIN; catecholamine-like hallucinogens include the PHENYLETHYLAMINES and their derivatives, such as MESCALINE, DOM, MDA, and MDMA. Both classes in general produce visual hallucinations via activity on subtypes of SEROTONIN RECEPTORS. Other hallucinogens include PCP and various natural substances, including AYAHUASCA. See HALLUCINOGEN ABUSE; HALLUCINOGEN DEPENDENCE. **—hallucinogenic** *adj.*

hallucinogen abuse in *DSM–IV–TR*, a pattern of HALLUCINOGEN use manifested by recurrent significant adverse consequences related to the repeated ingestion of hallucinogens. This diagnosis is preempted by the diagnosis of HALLUCINOGEN DEPENDENCE: If the criteria for hallucinogen abuse and hallucinogen dependence are both met, only the latter diagnosis is given. See also SUBSTANCE ABUSE.

hallucinogen-affective disorder see HALLUCINOGEN-INDUCED MOOD DISORDER.

hallucinogen dependence in *DSM–IV–TR*, a cluster of cognitive, behavioral, and physiological symptoms indicating continued use of hallucinogens despite significant hallucinogen-related problems. There is a pattern of repeated hallucinogen ingestion resulting in tolerance, withdrawal symptoms (agitation, mood lability, and craving) if use is suspended, and an uncontrollable drive to continue use. See also HALLUCINOGEN ABUSE; SUBSTANCE DEPENDENCE.

hallucinogen hallucinosis see HALLUCINOGEN-INDUCED PSYCHOTIC DISORDER.

hallucinogen-induced mood disorder a prominent and persistent disturbance of mood experienced during and after HALLUCINOGEN INTOXICATION. It may be characterized by depression or anxiety, self-reproach, feelings of guilt, and tension. Also called **hallucinogen-affective disorder**.

hallucinogen-induced psychotic disorder prominent hallucinations, delusions, or both due to HALLUCINOGEN INTOXICATION that are not recognized by the individual as having been induced by hallucinogens. The hallucinations and delusions exceed those usually associated with such intoxication, being sufficiently severe to warrant clinical attention. Also called **hallucinogen hallucinosis**.

hallucinogen intoxication a reversible syndrome due to the recent ingestion of a specific hallucinogen. Clinically significant behavioral or psychological changes include marked anxiety or depression, DELUSIONS OF REFERENCE, difficulty focusing attention, fear of losing one's mind, paranoia, and impaired judgment. These are accompanied by one or more signs of physiological involvement, for example, subjective intensification of perceptions, hallucinations, SYNESTHESIAS, pupillary dilation, increased heart rate, sweating, palpitations, blurring of vision, tremors, or incoordination. See also SUBSTANCE INTOXICATION.

hallucinosis *n.* see SUBSTANCE-INDUCED PSYCHOTIC DISORDER.

halo effect the tendency for a general evaluation of a person, or an evaluation of a person on a specific dimension, to be used as a basis for judgments of that person on other specific dimensions. For example, a person who is generally liked might be judged as more intelligent, competent, and honest than a person who is generally disliked.

haloperidol *n.* a HIGH-POTENCY ANTIPSYCHOTIC of the BUTYROPHENONE class, in use in Europe in the 1950s and in the United States from 1965. Haloperidol and other high-potency antipsychotics were preferred over lower potency PHENOTHIAZINES because of their lack of cardiovascular and ANTICHOLINERGIC EFFECTS; however, they were associated more with EXTRAPYRAMIDAL EFFECTS and TARDIVE DYSKINESIA than lower potency agents. The increased safety profile of the second-generation ATYPICAL ANTIPSYCHOTICS has led to a decline in use of haloperidol, although it is still used individually and in conjunction with newer agents. Some argue that few differences exist between the newer agents and haloperidol if the latter is used in much lower doses than has been customary. U.S. trade name: **Haldol**.

Halstead Category Test see CATEGORY TEST.

Halstead–Reitan Impairment Index see IMPAIRMENT INDEX. [Ward C. **Halstead** (1908–1969) and Ralph M. **Reitan** (1922–), U.S. psychologists]

Halstead–Reitan Neuropsychological Battery (**HRNB**) a set of tests designed to diagnose and localize brain damage by providing a comprehensive assessment of cognitive functioning. The battery includes five core subtests (CATEGORY TEST, TACTUAL PERFORMANCE TEST, SEASHORE RHYTHM TEST, SPEECH-SOUNDS PERCEPTION TEST, FINGER TAPPING TEST) and five optional subtests (TRAIL MAKING TEST, REITAN INDIANA APHASIA SCREENING TEST, REITAN–KLOVE SENSORY PERCEPTUAL EXAMINATION, GRIP STRENGTH TEST, Lateral Dominance Examination) purportedly measuring elements of language, attention, motor dexterity, sensory–motor integration, abstract thinking, and memory. Additionally, the MINNESOTA MULTIPHASIC PERSONALITY INVENTORY and either the WECHSLER ADULT INTELLIGENCE SCALE or the WECHSLER INTELLIGENCE SCALE FOR CHILDREN are often administered as well. There is a version of the HRNB for adults, for children aged 5 to 8 years, and for children aged 9 to 14 years. [Ward C. **Halstead** and Ralph M. **Reitan**]

halving method see FRACTIONATION.

Hamilton Rating Scale for Depression (**HAM-D**; **HRSD**) an interview-based, clinician-administered measure of the severity of depressive symptoms, such as DYSPHORIA, insomnia, and weight loss. It is the most widely used measure of the effectiveness of antidepressant medication in clinical trials, and its use is most appropriately restricted to individuals in whom depression has been diagnosed, rather than as a general measure of depressive symptoms. A 38-item self-report version, the **Hamilton Depression Inventory** (**HDI**), was developed in 1995. Also called **Hamilton Depression Scale**. [originally published in 1960 by Max **Hamilton** (1912–1988), British psychiatrist]

hammer *n.* see OSSICLES.

hand–arm vibration syndrome (**HAVS**) an occupational disorder caused by excessive exposure to vibration from equipment. It is a form of RAYNAUD'S DISEASE. Also called **vibration white finger**.

Hand–Christian–Schüller syndrome a rare disturbance of lipid metabolism marked by the presence of large phagocytic blood cells and an accumulation of cholesterol plus a triad of symptoms: membranous bone defects, diabetes insipidus, and protrusion of the eyes. Growth and mental development are retarded in half of affected individuals. Also called **Schüller–Christian–Hand disease**. [Alfred **Hand** (1868–1949), U.S. pediatrician; Henry A. **Christian** (1876–1951), U.S. physician; Arthur **Schüller** (1874–1958), Austrian neurologist]

hand dominance see HANDEDNESS.

hand dynamometer a device for measuring grip strength in each hand.

Hand Dynamometer Test see GRIP STRENGTH TEST.

handedness *n.* a tendency to prefer using one hand rather than the other to perform certain tasks. The preference usually is related to a DOMINANCE effect of the MOTOR CORTEX on the opposite side of the body. Also called **hand dominance**. See CEREBRAL DOMINANCE; LATERALITY; LEFT-HANDEDNESS; RIGHT-HANDEDNESS.

handicap 1. *n.* an inability to perform one or more educational, physical, or social tasks, or consistent underperformance in such tasks, as a result of a physical or nonphysical obstacle or hindrance. For example, a nonaccessible entry or exit for a person in a wheelchair would be a physical obstacle, whereas discrimination with regard to employment would be a nonphysical hindrance. See also DISABILITY; EMOTIONAL HANDICAP. **2.** *vb.* to place an individual or group of individuals at a disadvantage, or to hinder or impede progress. **—handicapped** *adj.*

handicapping strategy see SELF-HANDICAPPING.

handicap principle the idea that animals use high-cost HONEST SIGNALS in order to demonstrate their potential as mates. The long, loud, continuous song of songbirds, the tails of peacocks, and the loud roars of howler monkeys are all energetically costly and make the caller conspicuous to predators. However, if these "handicaps" provide accurate information about the condition or quality of the animal, high-quality individuals will become preferred mates, and the conspicuous and costly traits will be maintained in future generations.

hand-tool dexterity test a test of ability to use hand tools effectively.

hand-washing obsession a persistent and irrational preoccupation with washing the hands, also called **ablutomania** (although this name is now seldom used). It is characteristic of OBSESSIVE-COMPULSIVE DISORDER. See OBSESSION.

handwriting analysis see GRAPHOLOGY.

Hans *n.* see CLEVER HANS; LITTLE HANS.

haphalgesia *n.* an extreme and rare sensitivity of cutaneous pain receptors to normally harmless or painless tactile stimuli. It may be of psychogenic origin, as observed by reactions to specific substances that appear to have special significance for the individual; for example, the thought of touching porcelain may cause intense pain and a burning sensation.

haphazard sampling a method of selecting research participants that is neither random nor systematic.

haplodiploidy *n.* the state in which individuals of one sex have only one set of chromosomes (i.e., are HAPLOID), because they have developed from an unfertilized egg, and individuals of the other sex have two sets of chromosomes (i.e., are DIPLOID). Haplodiploidy is common in bees and wasps, in which males are haploid. Female offspring inherit identical paternal genes and thus share 75% of their genes (siblings of diploid parents share only 50% of their genes). This provides a genetic basis for EUSOCIALITY. **—haplodiploid** *adj.*

haploid *adj.* describing a nucleus, cell, or organism that possesses only one representative of each chromosome, as in a sperm or egg cell. In most organisms, including humans, fusion of the haploid sex cells following fertilization restores the normal DIPLOID condition of body cells, in which the chromosomes occur in pairs. Hence for humans, the **haploid number** is 23 chromosomes, that is, half the full complement of 46 chromosomes.

haplology *n.* the omission of identical or similar syllables that immediately precede or follow one another during speech. It is common in PRESSURED SPEECH.

happiness *n.* an emotion of joy, gladness, satisfaction, and well-being. **—happy** *adj.*

happy-puppet syndrome see ANGELMAN SYNDROME.

haptic *adj.* relating to the sense of touch or contact and the cutaneous sensory system in general. It typically refers to ACTIVE TOUCH, in which the individual intentionally seeks sensory stimulation, moving the limbs to gain information about an object or surface.

haptic hallucination see TACTILE HALLUCINATION.

haptic horizontal–vertical illusion an illusion in touch in which verticals may be judged as different in length from horizontals. The illusion depends upon figural characteristics and is especially strong when one feels inverted T shapes.

haptic illusion an illusion in touch perceived by voluntary, directed contact with the object or objects (see ACTIVE TOUCH). The HAPTIC MÜLLER-LYER ILLUSION is an example. Compare TACTILE ILLUSION.

haptic map a tactile map that can be felt by people with visual impairment. Such maps may be two-dimensional, comprising raised lines, or they can use three-dimensional landmarks.

haptic Müller-Lyer illusion an illusion in touch in which tangible lines that end in a pattern with arrowheads that face toward each other are judged as longer than lines that end with arrowheads that face away from each other. See also HAPTIC ILLUSION. [Franz **Müller-Lyer** (1857–1916), German experimental psychologist]

haptic perception perception by ACTIVE TOUCH and intentional exploration of objects and surfaces. See also TOUCH SENSE.

haptic picture a picture produced with raised lines so that it can be felt by people with visual impairment.

haptics *n.* the study of touch, particularly as a means of actively exploring and gaining information about the environment, and the applications of this study in communication systems.

hard colors yellows and reds.

hard determinism the doctrine that human actions and choices are causally determined by forces and influences over which a person exercises no meaningful influence. The term can also be applied to nonhuman events, implying that all things must be as they are and could not possibly be otherwise. Compare SOFT DETERMINISM. See DETERMINISM.

hard drug a colloquial name for a drug of abuse, especially one that produces PHYSICAL DEPENDENCE. See SUBSTANCE ABUSE; SUBSTANCE DEPENDENCE.

hardiness *n.* an ability to adapt easily to unexpected changes combined with a sense of purpose in daily life and of personal control over what occurs in one's life. Hardiness dampens the effects of a stressful situation through information gathering, decisive actions, and learning from the experience. A hardy athlete, for example, is less prone to MORBIDITY or injury. **—hardy** *adj.*

hard of hearing having difficulty in distinguishing sounds at normal levels of intensity.

hard palate the bony anterior portion of the roof of the mouth, covered above and below, respectively, by the mucous membranes of the nasal and oral cavities. Also called **palatum durum**. Compare SOFT PALATE.

hard problem in philosophy of mind, the claim that the relation between subjectivity and the brain is inherently difficult or impossible to explain. [proposed by Australian philosopher David Chalmers (1966–)]

hard psychology a colloquial name for EXPERIMENTAL PSYCHOLOGY in contradistinction to so-called SOFT PSYCHOLOGY, which is seen as having a more subjective, less rigorous approach.

hard sell the selling of a product or service by using strong persuasive or compliance techniques, including setting artificial deadlines or offering special deals to encourage potential buyers to commit themselves to a purchase. A hard sell can be compared to a **soft sell**, in which little pressure is placed on the consumer to make an immediate decision.

hardware *n.* the physical equipment in which an information-processing program is implemented, such as the physical components of a computer system or the brain.

hard-wired *adj.* **1.** referring to electrical or electronic circuits in which the connections among components are permanently established and which are usually designed to perform a specific function. **2.** in neurophysiology, referring to fixed, inflexible NEURAL NETWORKS or NEURAL CIRCUITS.

Hardy–Rand–Rittler pseudoisochromatic plates (**H–R–R plates**) embedded figures composed of small elements that can be distinguished from identical small background elements only on the basis of hue. The figures are used to test for color blindness. Also called **American optical H–R–R plates**. See also ISHIHARA TEST FOR COLOR BLINDNESS. [developed in the 1950s by LeGrand H. **Hardy** (1895–1954), U.S. ophthalmologist; Gertrude **Rand** (1886–1970), U.S. experimental psychologist; and M. Catherine **Rittler** (1905–1987)]

harem *n.* in animal behavior, a group of females controlled by or associated with one or two males in a highly polygynous species. See POLYGYNY.

Harlow, Harry Frederick (1905–1981) U.S. psychologist. Born Harry Israel, Harlow earned his doctorate in 1930 at Stanford University, where he studied with Lewis TERMAN and Walter Miles (1885–1978), a comparative psychologist. He changed his name to Harlow on the advice of Terman, who felt that the name Israel would be a handicap in a job market that discriminated against Jews, even though Harlow was not Jewish. Harlow spent his career at the University of Wisconsin, where he specialized in primate research. He is best known for two different bodies of work: on LEARNING SETS (learning to learn) and on MOTHERING. He found that primates are able to learn how to solve particular types of problems, so that performance on new instances of a type of problem is superior to performance on earlier problems of the same type. Prior to Harlow's work, few had believed that nonhuman animals were capable of these higher levels of INFORMATION PROCESSING or METACOGNITION. Perhaps even better known is a series of famous experiments on social development in rhesus monkeys, in which Harlow documented that the presence of a mother or a MOTHER SURROGATE was crucial to proper emotional and social development in young monkeys. It was the CONTACT COMFORT, rather than mother's milk (as had been suggested by previous reinforcement theories), that was the critical element. Harlow received numerous awards for his work, including the National Medal of Science (1967) and the Gold Medal Award of the American Psychological Foundation (1973). He served as president of the American Psychological Association in 1958.

harmaline *n.* see AYAHUASCA.

harmine *n.* a naturally occurring hallucinogen derived from the plant *Peganum harmala*, native to the Middle East, and *Banisteriopsis caapi*, native to the South American tropics. Harmine is a potent MONOAMINE OXIDASE INHIBITOR and is a principal ingredient in AYAHUASCA, a psychoactive beverage.

harmonic *n.* a PURE-TONE component whose frequency is an integer multiple of the fundamental FREQUENCY. For example, the third harmonic of 500 Hz is 1500 Hz. An **overtone** is a harmonic, but the numbering is different: 1500 Hz is the second overtone of 500 Hz. Harmonic is the preferred term.

harmonic mean a measure of CENTRAL TENDENCY. It is computed for *n* scores as $n/\Sigma(1/x_i)$, that is, *n* divided by $1/x_1 + 1/x_2 + \ldots 1/x_n$.

harmonizer *n.* in the social psychology of groups, the RELATIONSHIP ROLE adopted by a group member who plays the role of diplomat and facilitates group unity by mediating between opposing points of view and reducing interpersonal tension.

harmony *n.* **1.** friendly or cooperative relations among people. **2.** in a design, work of art, or the like, an arrangement of parts (e.g., lines or musical tones) into a whole pattern that is considered to be balanced and pleasing. —**harmonious** *adj.*

harm reduction a theoretical approach in programs designed to reduce the adverse effects of risky behaviors (e.g., alcohol use, drug use, indiscriminate sexual activity), rather than to eliminate the behaviors altogether. Programs focused on alcohol use, for example, do not advocate abstinence but attempt instead to teach people to anticipate the hazards of heavy drinking and learn to drink safely.

Harrisburg Seven seven Vietnam War protesters who were arrested and tried in Harrisburg, Pennsylvania, in 1972 for various antiwar activities. The trial was one of the earliest occasions of the use of social science methods (see SCIENTIFIC JURY SELECTION) to help attorneys select jurors.

Harris v. Forklift Systems Inc. a case resulting in a 1993 U.S. Supreme Court ruling that in SEXUAL HARASSMENT cases the victim is not required to show psychological injury as a consequence of the offensive behavior and that a REASONABLE PERSON STANDARD should be used to judge the offensiveness of the conduct. See also HOSTILE WORK ENVIRONMENT.

hashish *n.* the most potent CANNABIS preparation. It contains the highest concentration of delta-9-TETRAHYDROCANNABINOL (THC) because it consists largely of pure resin from one of the species of the *Cannabis* plant from which it is derived.

hassle *n.* any circumstance or situation that is mildly troublesome to an individual and considered a bother or annoyance.

hassles and uplifts small, frustrating events and small, pleasant events occurring throughout the day.

hasty generalization see CONVERSE ACCIDENT.

hate *n.* a hostile emotion combining feelings of detestation, anger, and a desire to retaliate for real or imagined harm. Also called **hatred**.

hate crime a crime of violence that is motivated by bias or hatred against the group to which the victims of the crimes belong. Examples of hate crimes are killing a man because he is (or is thought to be) gay and bombing a place of worship of a religious minority.

haunted swing illusion an illusory perception of movement that occurs when an individual is seated on a stationary swing and the surrounding environment is moved.

HAVS abbreviation for HAND–ARM VIBRATION SYNDROME.

Hawthorne effect the effect on the behavior of individuals of knowing that they are being observed or are taking part in research. The Hawthorne effect is typically positive and is named after the Western Electric Company's Hawthorne Works plant in Cicero, Illinois, where the phenomenon was first observed during a series of studies on worker productivity conducted from 1924 to 1932. These **Hawthorne Studies** began as an investigation of the effects of ILLUMINATION CONDITIONS, monetary incentives, and rest breaks on productivity, but evolved into a much wider consideration of the role of worker attitudes, supervisory style, and GROUP DYNAMICS. The HUMAN RELATIONS THEORY of management is usually considered to have developed from these studies.

Hay method a method of job evaluation used in determining the pay structure in an organization. Jobs are evaluated on the extent to which they require know-how, problem solving, and accountability, and compensated accordingly. The method combines elements of the FACTOR-COMPARISON METHOD and the POINT METHOD. [Edward N. **Hay**, 20th-century U.S. management expert]

hazard *n.* a potential source of injury, illness, or equipment damage. —**hazardous** *adj.*

hazard-assessment matrix see RISK-ASSESSMENT MATRIX.

hazard control the process of identifying, evaluating, and eliminating hazards from an environment, system, or product (ENGINEERING CONTROLS) or of protecting users and workers from exposure to hazards where these cannot be completely eliminated (ADMINISTRATIVE CONTROLS). See also SAFETY ENGINEERING.

hazard-control protocol the order of priority that applies in the process of eliminating or protecting against hazards. The protocol is: design out, guard against, warn, and train. See ADMINISTRATIVE CONTROLS; ENGINEERING CONTROLS.

hazard function a mathematical function that describes the relationship between the risk of a particular event occurring and time. It is one element of SURVIVAL ANALYSIS.

hazard prevention the use of ENGINEERING CONTROLS to prevent the occurrence of hazards by eliminating their sources.

Hb abbreviation for HEMOGLOBIN.

HCBS abbreviation for HOME AND COMMUNITY-BASED SERVICES.

HCFA abbreviation for HEALTH CARE FINANCING ADMINISTRATION.

HD abbreviation for HUNTINGTON'S DISEASE.

HDI abbreviation for Hamilton Depression Inventory. See HAMILTON RATING SCALE FOR DEPRESSION.

headache *n.* a pain in the head from any cause, for example, a CLUSTER HEADACHE, MIGRAINE, or TENSION HEADACHE.

head banging the act or habit of repeatedly striking the head on a crib, wall, or other object, observed in infants and young children as a stereotyped behavior (see STEREOTYPY) or during a temper tantrum. See also STEREOTYPIC MOVEMENT DISORDER.

head injury any injury to the head or any brain damage that may result from such an injury. Head injuries are usually caused by a blow but may result from significant acceleration or deceleration in the absence of a blow (see ACCELERATION–DECELERATION INJURY). They are commonly classified as either CLOSED HEAD INJURIES or OPEN HEAD INJURIES. Also called **head trauma**.

head nystagmus the slow movement of the head in the opposite direction after an individual is rotated, followed by a rapid movement of the head in the direction of rotation.

head-of-the-table effect the propensity for group members to associate the leadership role and its responsibilities with the seat located at the head of the table. As a result, individuals who occupy such positions tend to emerge as leaders in groups without designated leaders. Compare STEINZOR EFFECT.

head-related transfer function (**HRTF**) a function that describes the spectral characteristics of sound measured at the TYMPANIC MEMBRANE when the source of the sound is in three-dimensional space. It is used to simulate externally presented sounds when the sounds are presented through headphones. The HRTF is a function of frequency, azimuth, and elevation and is determined primarily by the acoustical properties of the external ear, the head, and the torso. HRTFs can differ substantially across individuals but, because measurement of an individual HRTF is expensive, an averaged HRTF is often used.

head retraction reflex withdrawal of the head when receptors in the nasal cavities are sharply irritated.

head rolling repeated movements of the head from side to side as manifested by some children before going to sleep. The condition has been attributed to inhibition of movement in the crib, lack of stimulating play, and possibly fetal passivity during intrauterine life. Also called **jactatio capitis nocturnis**.

headshrinking *n.* the shrinking of severed heads, usually human, through the application of heat or herbal liquids, as practiced among various indigenous societies, mainly in southeast Asia and South America. The heads are used for various ritual purposes, including healing rituals. The slang SHRINK (short for **headshrinker**), meaning a psychiatrist or psychologist, is probably derived from this practice.

head-slaved *adj.* describing a VIRTUAL REALITY environment in which head movements by the user produce corresponding changes in the virtual scene. See also PERCEPTUAL USER INTERFACE.

Head Start see PROJECT HEAD START.

headstick *n.* a type of PHYSICAL EXTENSION DEVICE used by individuals with disabilities who have adequate head function. The stick is mounted on a headpiece and can be used to press against, grasp, pull, or point to an object.

head trauma see HEAD INJURY.

head-up display (**HUD**) a type of machine display in which critical information is presented within the forward view of the operator, as, for example, on the windshield of a vehicle. Head-up displays are used to reduce the need for the operator to look away from the forward field. See also LOOK ANGLE.

head voice the upper reaches, or higher range, of the speaking or singing voice, in which tone resonates primarily in the mouth, nasal cavity, and bones of the skull. An excited or anxious speaking tone is generally produced in a head voice. Compare CHEST VOICE.

healing group broadly, any of a variety of groups formed for the purpose of improving or promoting the mental and emotional health and well-being or interpersonal relationships of the members, as in GROUP PSYCHOTHERAPY, SELF-HELP GROUPS, ENCOUNTER GROUPS, and CONSCIOUSNESS-RAISING groups.

health activities questionnaire any questionnaire designed to measure an individual's current repertoire of health-related behaviors. There is an increased emphasis on prevention in health care, and many inventories exist to measure an individual's compliance with physical activity, dietary control, preventive inoculations, and screening for potential health problems, such as mammography and prostate or colon cancer testing.

health anxiety excessive or inappropriate anxiety about one's health, based on misinterpretation of symptoms (e.g., pain, gastrointestinal distress) as indicative of serious illness. Health anxiety is regarded as a less severe form of HYPOCHONDRIASIS.

health–belief model a model that identifies the relationships of the following to the likelihood of taking preventive health action: (a) individual perceptions about susceptibility to and seriousness of a disease, (b) sociodemographic variables, (c) environmental cues, and (d) perceptions of the benefits and costs. See also EXERCISE–BEHAVIOR MODEL.

health care services and delivery related to the health and well-being of individuals and communities, including preventive, diagnostic, therapeutic, rehabilitative, maintenance, monitoring, and counseling services. In its broadest sense, health care relates to both physical and mental health and is provided by medical and mental health professionals. See also MENTAL HEALTH CARE; MENTAL HEALTH SERVICES.

Health Care Financing Administration (**HCFA**) see CENTERS FOR MEDICARE AND MEDICAID SERVICES.

health education **1.** instruction in the care and hygiene of the human body, with emphasis on how to prevent illness. **2.** any type of education regarding physical, mental, and emotional health. Conducted in school, institutional, and community settings, this education may cover stress management, smoking cessation, nutrition and fitness, reproductive health, self-esteem, relationship issues, health risks, personal safety (e.g., self-defense and rape prevention), and minority health issues.

health insurance a contractual relationship in which an insurance company undertakes to reimburse the insured for health care expenses in exchange for a premium. Such payment protections might include, for example, medical expense, outpatient mental health, accident, dental, disability income, and accidental death and dismemberment insurances.

health locus of control the perceived source of control over health, that is, either personal behaviors or external forces.

health maintenance organization see HMO.

Health Opinion Survey see KRANTZ HEALTH OPINION SURVEY.

health plan an organized program that provides a defined set of health care benefits. Health plans may be HMOs, PPOs, insured plans, self-insured plans, or other plans that cover health care services.

Health Plan Employer Data and Information Set (**HEDIS**) a set of performance measures for health plans developed for the NATIONAL COMMITTEE FOR QUALITY ASSURANCE (NCQA) in 1991 and designed to standardize the way health plans report data to employers. HEDIS measures five major areas of health plan performance: quality, access and patient satisfaction, membership and utilization, finance, and descriptive information on health plan management.

health professional an individual who has received advanced training or education in a health-related field, such as direct patient care, administration, or ancillary services.

health psychology the subfield of psychology that focuses on (a) the examination of the relations between behavioral, cognitive, psychophysiological, and social and environmental factors and the establishment, maintenance, and detriment of health; (b) the integration of psychological and biological research findings in the design of empirically based interventions for the prevention and treatment of illness; and (c) the evaluation of physical and psychological status before, during, and after medical and psychological treatment.

health risk appraisal the perception by individuals of the extent to which they believe that they are susceptible to a health threat. See also PERCEIVED RISK; PERCEIVED SUSCEPTIBILITY.

health visitor a health professional, usually associated with a VISITING NURSE association, who visits families where health supervision is needed, for example, to ensure that children are not abused or neglected.

hearing *n.* the ability of an organism to sense sound and to process and interpret the sensations to gain information about the source and nature of the sound. In humans hearing refers to the perception of sound. Also called **audition**.

hearing aid an electronic device that amplifies sounds for people with hearing loss. The basic parts of a hearing aid include a microphone to collect sounds, a replenishable battery power supply, an amplifier to increase the volume of sounds, and a receiver to transmit the amplified sounds to the ear. Hearing aids are available in four different styles (behind-the-ear, in-the-ear, in-the-canal, and completely-in-the-canal) and four different types: (a) conventional, which is the most basic and amplifies all sounds; (b) programmable, which adjusts the level of amplification of sounds according to a customized listening program; (c) digital, which automatically adjusts amplification and volume, is freer from distortion, and provides enhanced sound clarity and improved selective listening in noisy environments; and (d) disposable, which is comparable to a conventional hearing aid but must be replaced entirely once the battery wears out. See also ASSISTIVE LISTENING DEVICE; COCHLEAR IMPLANT.

hearing disorder any disease, injury, or congenital condition resulting in HEARING LOSS or DEAFNESS.

hearing level see AUDIOGRAM.

hearing loss the inability to hear a normal range of tone frequencies, a normally perceived level of sound intensity, or both.

hearing mute an obsolescent and pejorative name for an individual who is unable or unwilling to speak but is able to hear.

hearing protection a device or method used to control noise exposure by reducing the intensity of noise reaching the ear. Techniques range from simple barrier methods (e.g., earplugs) to ACTIVE NOISE PROTECTION.

hearing theories theories related to the sensation and perception of sound. Until the 1960s such theories related almost exclusively to sound processing in the inner ear; they include PLACE THEORY, **telephone theory**, VOLLEY THEORY, and **traveling wave theory**. Contemporary theories and models relate to various aspects of hearing, including pitch perception, intensity coding, and BINAURAL hearing.

heart attack sudden, severe chest pain that occurs when one of the coronary arteries becomes blocked. The condition may result in a myocardial infarction (i.e., death of a section of heart muscle), depending upon the extent of damage to the surrounding muscle.

heart block see ARRHYTHMIA.

heart rate in emotion changes in heart rate associated with particular emotional states. It is usually held that heart rate increases in states of fear, anger, and scorn and decreases in states of attentiveness, positive emotional reaction, and interest. However, the actual relation between heart rate and emotion is complex and largely mediated by the energy demands of the bodily musculature of the organism in an emotional state. Thus, a frightened animal that reacts with tonic immobility (death feigning) and limpness will show a reduction in heart rate in its reaction to a threat, whereas an animal that is immobile but poised for flight typically shows acceleration of heart rate. States of laughter, although pleasurable, are typically associated with an accelerated heart rate owing to the involvement of large muscle groups in the act of laughing.

heat *n.* **1.** a thermal sensation produced by a stimulus that is above body temperature. **2.** in animal behavior, see ESTROUS BEHAVIOR.

heat dolorimeter a device for the measurement of heat-induced pain.

heat effects changes in mental or physical conditions due to perceived or actual ambient temperatures above the normal comfort range. Perceived heat may be affected by humidity or individual cognition factors; high humidity usually makes excessive heat less tolerable. The main physiological heat effects are HEAT-INDUCED ASTHENIA, HEATSTROKE, HEAT EXHAUSTION, and severe circulatory disorders (e.g., heart attacks) caused by excessive demands on the cardiovascular system to circulate blood near external surfaces for a cooling effect. Because of variable perceived heat effects, studies of psychological effects are less conclusive, although performance appears to improve with increasing ambient temperatures up to a level of around 32 °C (90 °F), after which arousal and performance decline. High temperatures can have adverse effects on feelings and emotions and can influence aggression, although no consensus exists in the scientific literature on the exact degree of this influence. Some believe that aggression increases with temperature, whereas others hold that moderately high temperatures produce the most negative outcomes, arguing that under very high temperatures motivation for escape or relief predominates, precluding aggression. See ACCLIMATIZATION; OVERHEATING.

heat exhaustion a disorder marked by circulatory collapse and a comatose condition after exposure to excessive heat. The symptoms result from an inability of the circulatory system to adjust to the dilation of blood vessels in the skin. Excessive sweating, dehydration, alcohol drinking, or diarrhea can be precipitating factors. The symptoms may resemble those of a drug overdose, but the patient usually responds rapidly to treatment.

heat hyperpyrexia see HEATSTROKE.

heat-induced asthenia a condition associated with prolonged exposure to heat and characterized by general physical and mental impairment, fatigue, lethargy, irritability, insomnia, headache, and possible loss of appetite.

heat stress any stress effect on an organism that results from exposure to excessive ambient temperatures, particularly the physiological disorders that include HEAT-INDUCED ASTHENIA, HEAT EXHAUSTION, and HEATSTROKE.

heatstroke *n.* a physiological heat-stress effect caused by a breakdown of the body's ability to cope with heat by sweating. Symptoms include weakness, headaches, anorexia, nausea, and in some cases cramps and muscle twitches. Since body heat cannot be reduced by sweating, the skin feels hot and dry. The trapped heat may cause brain damage. Emergency treatment involving cooling the patient must be started immediately. Also called **heat hyperpyrexia**; **thermic fever**.

Hebb, Donald Olding (1904–1985) Canadian psychobiologist. Hebb earned his doctorate from Harvard University in 1936, studying under Karl LASHLEY. He held positions at the Montreal Neurological Institute and Queen's University in Kingston, Ontario, before working with Lashley once again (1942–1947) at the Yerkes Laboratories of Primate Biology in Florida. He then moved to McGill University in Montreal, where he spent the bulk of his career. Hebb made important contributions to our understanding of the relationship between the brain and behavior in an era dominated by the behaviorist argument that the brain and nervous system could simply be treated as an unknown, or black box. Hebb's most important theoretical statement is contained in his book, *The Organization of Behavior* (1949). In it, he suggested that networks of nerve cells (neurons), called CELL ASSEMBLIES, could develop in response to visual experience. When a similar visual stimulus is experienced, the cell assembly is activated in a phase sequence. He postulated permanent synaptic changes that were not detectable in his day but have become testable with the development of new technologies. Hebb served as president of the American Psychological Association in 1960. See also LOCALIZATION OF FUNCTION.

Hebbian synapse a SYNAPSE that is strengthened when it successfully fires the POSTSYNAPTIC cell. See DUAL TRACE HYPOTHESIS. [Donald O. HEBB]

Hebb's theory of perceptual learning a learning theory that assumes that perception has both innate components, such as perceiving depth, and learned components, such as distinguishing shapes. [Donald O. HEBB]

hebephrenia *n.* see DISORGANIZED SCHIZOPHRENIA.

hebetude *n.* a state of severe emotional dullness, lethargy, and lack of interest, which is observed in some individuals with schizophrenia who not only withdraw from the environment but withdraw from themselves, becoming apathetic and listless.

Hecht's theory of vision the theory that incremental discrimination of light intensity results from incremental changes in the photochemical materials, such as RHODOPSIN, present in the photoreceptors. [proposed in 1934 by Selig **Hecht** (1892–1947), Polish-born U.S. biophysicist]

hedge *n.* a statement in which the speaker qualifies its apparent meaning or uses various linguistic devices to make it evasive or noncommittal.

HEDIS acronym for HEALTH PLAN EMPLOYER DATA AND INFORMATION SET.

hedonic contingency hypothesis a theory of affect and information processing postulating that people consider the hedonic implications of information when determining whether to elaborate information. When people are in positive mood states, they tend to be highly attentive to the impact information will have on their mood. If the information is seen as uplifting, they will engage in extensive ELABORATION to maintain their positive mood, but if it is seen as unpleasant, they will engage in little elaboration. When people are in negative mood states, they tend to elaborate information with little attention to its hedonic consequences because such information is unlikely to make their mood more negative and might make it more positive. [originally proposed by U.S. social psychologists Duane T. Wegener (1966–) and Richard E. Petty (1951–)]

hedonic contrast the concept that preference for a beautiful stimulus is enhanced if it is preceded or accompanied by a less pleasing stimulus. Hedonic contrast is only found when the two stimuli are extremely similar (e.g., shades of the same hue).

hedonic level the degree of pleasantness or unpleasantness aroused by an interaction or a thought. See HEDONIC THEORY.

hedonic psychology a psychological perspective that focuses on the spectrum of experiences ranging from pleasure to pain and includes biological, social, and phenomenological aspects and their relationship to motivation and action. See HEDONISM.

hedonic relevance the extent to which a situation or activity has bearing on the attainment or maintenance of a positive mood. According to the HEDONIC CONTINGENCY HYPOTHESIS, happy people consider the hedonic relevance of an activity they might carry out before actually engaging in that behavior, because they want to maintain their good mood.

hedonics *n.* the branch of psychology concerned with the study of pleasant and unpleasant sensations and thoughts, especially in terms of their role in human motivation.

hedonic theory the view that a fundamental motivational principle in human beings and nonhuman animals is the level of pleasantness or unpleasantness aroused by an interaction or thought. See also HEDONISM. [proposed by U.S. psychologist Paul Thomas Young (1892–1978)]

hedonic time-order error preference for one of two

otherwise equally preferred stimuli, which depends upon the interval that separates their presentation.

hedonic tone a property of a sensory or other experience relating to its pleasantness or unpleasantness.

hedonism *n.* **1.** in philosophy, the doctrine that pleasure is an intrinsic good and the proper goal of all human action. One of the fundamental questions of ethics has been whether pleasure can or should be equated with the good in this way. **2.** in psychology, any theory that suggests that pleasure and the avoidance of pain are the only or the major motivating forces in human behavior. Hedonism is a foundational principle in psychoanalysis, in behaviorism, and even in theories that stress self-actualization and need-fulfillment. To the extent that human beings are hedonistic, it is difficult to admit the possibility of genuine ALTRUISM. Also called **hedonistic psychology**. See EUDEMONISM; HEDONIC PSYCHOLOGY. **—hedonistic** *adj.*

heft 1. *vb.* to lift an object in order to judge its weight. **2.** *n.* the weight or inertia of an object.

hegemony *n.* the dominance of one individual, group, or state over others. In some 20th-century Marxist writings the term refers particularly to the success of the dominant social class in imposing its ideology on other classes, so that this comes to seem part of the "natural" order of things. See DOMINANT IDEOLOGY THESIS. **—hegemonic** *adj.*

height phobia see ACROPHOBIA.

Heinz dilemma a story about an ethical dilemma faced by a character named Heinz that was used by Lawrence KOHLBERG to assess the moral reasoning skills of those he asked to respond to it. Having exhausted every other possibility, Heinz must decide whether or not to steal the expensive drug that offers the only hope of saving his dying wife. See KOHLBERG'S THEORY OF MORAL DEVELOPMENT.

Heisenberg principle see UNCERTAINTY PRINCIPLE.

helicotrema *n.* a small opening at the apex of the cochlea where the SCALA VESTIBULI and SCALA TYMPANI communicate. This opening limits the ability of the BASILAR MEMBRANE to vibrate in response to sounds of very low frequency.

heliocentric theory the cosmological theory that the sun is the center of the solar system and that the earth and other heavenly bodies orbit around it. The theory, which originated in ancient Greece, was revived by Polish astronomer Nicolaus Copernicus (1475–1543) and elaborated by Italian physicist and astronomer Galileo Galilei (1564–1642). It was controversial in the 16th and 17th centuries because it opposed the traditional doctrine of the Catholic Church that the earth was stationary at the center of the universe (see GEOCENTRIC THEORY). Also called **Copernican theory**.

heliotropism *n.* see TROPISM.

hellebore *n.* any plant of the genus *Veratrum* but particularly *Veratrum viride*, a poisonous plant indigenous to North America that has a history of use by Native Americans for various medicinal purposes. It contains more than 20 alkaloids, including **veratrine**, which has analgesic properties when used topically but produces prolonged muscle contractions when ingested. The hellebore alkaloids were also used medicinally in England as well as America in the 18th and 19th centuries in the treatment of numerous conditions, including seizures, neuralgia, headaches, and respiratory problems. They have been used more recently to lower blood pressure but generally are avoided because of their potential toxicity.

The name "hellebore" is also given to poisonous ornamental plants of the Eurasian genus *Helleborus*.

Helmert contrast a procedure in the ANALYSIS OF VARIANCE of longitudinal data in which each level of a repeated measure is compared with the mean of the remaining levels. [Friedrich Robert **Helmert** (1843–1917), German mathematician]

Helmholtz chessboard see CHESSBOARD ILLUSION. [Hermann Ludwig Ferdinand von **Helmholtz** (1821–1894), German physiologist and physicist]

Helmholtz color mixer a device that enables the intensity and wavelength of two light sources to be independently adjusted, mixed, and presented by means of a prism as a single homogeneous field to an observer, who views the field through a modified telescope. [Hermann von **Helmholtz**]

Helmholtz theory in audition, the still-controversial theory that pitch is determined by the place of stimulation along the BASILAR MEMBRANE. The theory is clearly flawed in certain aspects, such as its inability to account for the pitch of a missing fundamental (see VIRTUAL PITCH), but the essential notion remains viable. See PLACE THEORY. [Hermann von **Helmholtz**]

helper *n.* in animal behavior, see ALLOPARENTING.

helping behavior a type of PROSOCIAL BEHAVIOR that involves one or more individuals acting to improve the status or well-being of another or others. Although much helping behavior is typically in response to a small request that involves little individual risk, all helping behavior incurs some cost to the individual providing it. Also called **helpfulness**. See also ALTRUISM; ALTRUISTIC BEHAVIOR; EGOISTIC HELPING.

helping model a broadly based educational approach that has much in common with humanistic models in its emphasis on the development of the complete individual and the realization of the student's full potential. The helping model is concerned with motor development, perceptual skills, cognitive development, emotional maturity, interpersonal skills, expression, creativity, and ethical values.

helping professions those professions that provide health and education services to individuals and groups, including occupations in the fields of psychology, psychiatry, counseling, medicine, nursing, social work, physical and occupational therapy, teaching, and education.

helping relationship a relationship in which at least one of the parties intends to promote the growth, development, maturity, or improved functioning of the other. The parties may be either individuals or groups. [defined in 1961 by Carl ROGERS]

helplessness *n.* a state of incapacity, vulnerability, or powerlessness defined by low problem-focused COPING POTENTIAL and low future expectancy. It results from the realization that one cannot do much to improve a negative situation and that the situation is not going to get better on its own; it often involves anxiety and dependence on others. A recognition of one's helplessness in a situation can lead one to withdraw and become sad or demoralized. See also LEARNED HELPLESSNESS. **—helpless** *adj.*

helplessness theory the theory that LEARNED HELPLESSNESS explains the development of or vulnerability to depression. According to this theory, people repeatedly exposed to stressful situations beyond their control develop an inability to make decisions or engage effectively in purposeful behavior.

help-seeking behavior actions directed toward searching for or requesting help from others via formal or informal mechanisms, especially through mental health services. See TREATMENT-SEEKING BEHAVIOR.

hem- *combining form* see HEMO-.

hematoma *n.* an abnormal accumulation of blood as a result of vessel leakage or rupture. In the brain, hematomas can cause substantial behavioral deficits, and even death, by increasing INTRACRANIAL PRESSURE. Although some may spontaneously reabsorb and disappear, others must be surgically evacuated. See EPIDURAL HEMATOMA; SUBDURAL HEMATOMA.

hemeralopia *n.* **1.** a form of DAY BLINDNESS in which the individual has difficulty seeing in bright light but has good vision in dim light. **2.** a less common name for NIGHT BLINDNESS. Also called **hemeralopsia**. See also DARK ADAPTATION.

hemeraphonia *n.* a psychogenic speech disorder in which the person is unable to vocalize during the day but may be able to speak normally at night.

hemi- *prefix* half.

hemiachromatopsia *n.* a VISUAL FIELD DEFECT that occurs after injury to the occipitotemporal region of the brain and is characterized by the selective loss of color vision in the CONTRALATERAL half of the visual field in each eye.

hemiamblyopia *n.* a VISUAL FIELD DEFECT characterized by loss of color and form vision and depressed light vision in the same half of the visual field in each eye. It is caused by injury to the posterior region of the brain. See CEREBRAL AMBLYOPIA.

hemianalgesia *n.* a loss of pain sensation on one side of the body.

hemianesthesia *n.* a loss of sensitivity to stimuli on one side of the body.

hemianopia *n.* a VISUAL FIELD DEFECT marked by loss of vision in half the normal visual field. Hemianopia may result from a lesion in the OPTIC CHIASM or the OPTIC RADIATIONS. Also called **hemianopsia**; **hemiopia**. See also BINASAL HEMIANOPIA; BITEMPORAL HEMIANOPIA; HETERONYMOUS HEMIANOPIA; HOMONYMOUS HEMIANOPIA. —**hemianopic** *adj.* —**hemianoptic** *adj.*

hemianopic dyslexia see PARACENTRAL SCOTOMA.

hemiasomatognosia *n.* lack of sensory awareness of one side of one's body. See ASOMATOGNOSIA.

hemiballismus *n.* a type of involuntary movement characterized by throwing or flinging of the arm or leg on one side of the body. The condition is often associated with lesions of the extrapyramidal tract. Also called **hemiballism**. See BALLISM.

hemichorea *n.* a disorder involving choreic movements on only one side of the body. See CHOREA.

hemicrania *n.* pain or aching on only one side of the head, characteristic of a typical migraine.

hemidecortication *n.* surgical removal of the CEREBRAL CORTEX from one of the sides of the CEREBRUM of the brain.

hemineglect *n.* see UNILATERAL NEGLECT.

hemiopia *n.* see HEMIANOPIA.

hemiparesis *n.* weakness or partial paralysis affecting one side of the body. See SPASTIC HEMIPARESIS.

hemiplegia *n.* complete paralysis that affects one side of the body, most often as a result of a STROKE. The paralysis is typically opposite (contralateral) to the side of the brain affected. —**hemiplegic** *adj.*

hemispheral roles in emotion the different roles of the left and right hemispheres of the brain in the generation and regulation of emotions. In particular, the frontal lobe of the left hemisphere is believed to control positive emotions: Injury or damage to this region results in loss of POSITIVE AFFECT. By contrast, the frontal lobe of the right hemisphere is believed to control negative emotions (e.g., sadness, fear), with lesions to this portion of the brain resulting in loss of NEGATIVE AFFECT. Alternatively, the left frontal region is regarded as controlling emotions involving approach, and the right frontal region as controlling emotions involving avoidance.

hemisphere *n.* either of the symmetrical halves of the cerebrum (see CEREBRAL HEMISPHERE) or the CEREBELLUM. —**hemispheric** or **hemispherical** *adj.*

hemispherectomy *n.* surgical removal of either one of the cerebral hemispheres of the brain.

hemispheric asymmetry the idea that the two cerebral hemispheres of the brain are not identical but differ in size, shape, and function. The functions that display the most pronounced asymmetry are language processing in the left hemisphere and visuospatial processing in the right hemisphere.

hemispheric communication the continuous exchange of neural signals between the two cerebral hemispheres, either directly through the CORPUS CALLOSUM or through intermediate stations, such as the BASAL GANGLIA and the THALAMUS.

hemispheric dominance see HEMISPHERIC LATERALIZATION.

hemispheric encoding–retrieval asymmetry (**HERA**) the hypothesis that the LEFT HEMISPHERE of the cerebrum is especially active during the ENCODING of a memory, whereas the RIGHT HEMISPHERE is especially active during the RETRIEVAL of the memory. [proposed by Estonian-born Canadian psychologist Endel Tulving (1927–)]

hemispheric lateralization the processes whereby some functions, such as HANDEDNESS or language, are controlled or influenced more by one cerebral hemisphere than the other and each hemisphere is specialized for particular ways of working. Researchers now prefer to speak of hemispheric lateralization or **hemispheric specialization** for particular functions, rather than **hemispheric dominance** or **lateral dominance** (see DOMINANCE).

hemlock *n.* see SORCERY DRUGS.

hemo- (**hem-**; **haemo-**; **haem-**) *combining form* blood.

hemoglobin (**Hb**) *n.* an iron-rich pigment of red blood cells that transports oxygen molecules and is responsible for the color of blood. When saturated with oxygen, the pigment becomes bright red.

hemoglobinopathy *n.* any of various inherited disorders associated with genetic defects in the characteristics of hemoglobin. A common effect of hemoglobinopathies is anemia, which may be severe in HOMOZYGOUS individuals and mild in HETEROZYGOUS carriers. Sickle-cell anemia and Cooley's anemia are examples of hemoglobinopathies.

hemorrhage *n.* bleeding; any loss of blood from an artery or vein. A hemorrhage may be external, internal, or within a tissue, such as the skin; a bruise is a sign of bleeding within the skin. A hemorrhage from a ruptured artery is bright red in color and erupts in spurts that coincide with heart contractions; it is generally more serious than hemorrhage from a vein, which shows as a relatively slow, steady flow of dark red blood. Brain hemorrhages may arise from head injuries or ANEURYSMS, causing widespread damage in some cases (see CEREBRAL HEMORRHAGE). —**hemorrhagic** *adj.*

hemorrhagic stroke a STROKE resulting from rupture of a cerebral vessel, causing intracranial bleeding. Intracerebral hemorrhage accounts for approximately 10% of strokes and tends to occur deep in the BASAL GANGLIA, INTERNAL CAPSULE, and brainstem.

hemothymia *n.* a lust for blood and a morbid desire to commit murder. See also HOMICIDOMANIA.

hemp *n.* see CANNABIS.

henbane *n.* a poisonous plant, *Hyoscyamus niger*, native to the Mediterranean and southern Europe and a source of the anticholinergic alkaloids ATROPINE, hyoscyamine, and SCOPOLAMINE. Although traditionally used in small doses as an analgesic, sedative, and smooth muscle relaxant, henbane in larger quantities is highly toxic, producing effects similar to those of poisoning with BELLADONNA ALKALOIDS, including delirium, hallucinations, convulsions, coma, and possibly death. It has long been associated in folklore with witchcraft and magic and even enjoyed a reputation for a time as an aphrodisiac.

Henle fiber the cytoplasmic extension that allows a RETINAL CONE in the region of the FOVEA CENTRALIS to reach one of the RETINAL BIPOLAR CELLS, all of which are laterally displaced from the fovea. [Friedrich Gustav Jakob **Henle** (1809–1885), German anatomist]

Henning's odor prism a prism-shaped graphic representation of six PRIMARY ODORS and their relationships. Burnt, spicy, resinous, foul, fruity, and flowery are the primaries that occupy the corners of the prism, and each surface represents the positions of odors that are similar to the primaries at the corners of that surface. Also called **Henning's smell prism**. [Hans **Henning** (1885–1946), German psychologist]

Henning's taste tetrahedron an arrangement to represent four putative PRIMARY TASTES: sweet, salty, sour, and bitter. These basic tastes are at the apices of the tetrahedron; a combination of two qualities, such as salty–bitter (e.g., the taste of potassium chloride), are along the edges; tastes combining three qualities, such as salty–sweet–bitter (e.g., the taste of sodium saccharin), are on the faces. The tetrahedron is hollow because Henning believed no chemical could generate all four basic tastes. [proposed in 1927 by Hans **Henning**]

heparitinuria *n.* see SANFILIPPO'S SYNDROME.

hepatic encephalopathy a metabolic brain disorder marked by tremors with increased muscle tone, mental status changes, and disturbances in personality, mood, and behavior. It is associated with liver disease and an accumulation of ammonia products in the blood and other tissues. Also called **portal-systemic encephalopathy**.

hepatitis *n.* inflammation of the liver, marked by diffuse or patchy areas of dead liver cells in the liver lobules. Symptoms range from mild, flulike symptoms to liver failure, which can be fatal. JAUNDICE and BILIRUBIN coloring of the urine are usual signs. The causes include viruses, alcohol and drug abuse, infectious mononucleosis, and other infectious agents. The different forms of viral hepatitis are identified by letters, indicating the virus responsible. **Hepatitis A** is contracted by ingesting contaminated food or water, while **hepatitis B** is usually transmitted by transfusions of contaminated blood, through group use of dirty hypodermic needles, or by sexual contact with an infected person. The **hepatitis C** virus (HCV) is one of the most important causes of chronic liver disease in the United States, having similar modes of transmission to hepatitis B.

HERA abbreviation for HEMISPHERIC ENCODING–RETRIEVAL ASYMMETRY.

herbal Ecstasy an over-the-counter stimulant purchased through mail-order catalogs and often confused with MDMA.

herd instinct a drive in animals to congregate in flocks and in humans to form social groups. See GREGARIOUSNESS. [defined by British-born U.S. psychologist William McDougall (1871–1938)]

here and now the immediate situation. In psychotherapy, it comprises the cognitive, affective, and behavioral material arising at any given point in a session, as well as the relationship between the therapist and client at the corresponding point in time. When the **here-and-now approach** is used in psychotherapy, the emphasis is placed on understanding present feelings and interpersonal reactions as they occur in an ongoing treatment session, with little or no emphasis on or exploration of past experience or underlying reasons for the client's thoughts, emotions, or behavior. The approach is often used in PSYCHODYNAMIC PSYCHOTHERAPY with regard to the therapeutic relationship, GESTALT THERAPY, and many forms of FAMILY THERAPY to heighten the client's awareness.

hereditarianism *n.* the view that genetic inheritance is the major influence on behavior. Opposed to this view is the belief that environment and learning account for the major differences between people. The question of heredity versus environment or "nature versus nurture" continues to be controversial, especially as it applies to human intelligence. See GENETIC DETERMINISM; NATURE–NURTURE CONTROVERSY. —**hereditarian** *adj.*

hereditary ataxia see FRIEDREICH'S ATAXIA.

hereditary hyperuricemia (**hereditary choreoathetosis**) see LESCH–NYHAN SYNDROME.

hereditary myopathy see MYOPATHY.

hereditary predisposition see GENETIC PREDISPOSITION.

heredity *n.* **1.** the transmission of traits from parents to their offspring. Study of the mechanisms and laws of heredity is the basis of the science of GENETICS. Heredity depends upon the character of the genes contained in the parents' CHROMOSOMES, which in turn depends on the particular GENETIC CODE carried by the DNA of which the chromosomes are composed. **2.** loosely, the sum of the characteristics transmitted from parents to their offspring.

heredity–environment controversy see NATURE–NURTURE CONTROVERSY.

Hering–Breuer reflex a nervous mechanism involved in normal breathing, with stimuli from sensory endings in lung tissue limiting inspiration and expiration. [Heinrich Ewald **Hering** (1834–1918), German physiologist and psychologist; Josef **Breuer** (1842–1925), Austrian physician]

Hering grays a set of 50 gray papers ranging in subjectively equal steps from extreme white to extreme black. [Ewald **Hering**]

Hering illusion a misperception that occurs when two parallel straight lines are superimposed on a pattern of lines that radiate from a central point. When the two lines are placed equidistant from one another, on opposite sides of the center point, they appear to be bowed outward from the center, rather than straight. [Ewald **Hering**]

Hering's afterimage a positive aftersensation of the same hue and saturation as the original stimulus. [Ewald **Hering**]

Hering theory of color vision a theory of color vision postulating that there are three sets of receptors, one of which is sensitive to white and black, another to red and green, and the third to yellow and blue. The breaking down (catabolism) of these substances is supposed to yield one member of these pairs (white, red, or yellow), while the building up (anabolism) of the same substances yields the other (black, green, or blue). Color blindness results from the absence of one or more of the chromatic processes. See OPPONENTS THEORY OF COLOR VISION. [proposed in 1875 by Ewald **Hering**]

heritability *n.* **1.** the capacity to be inherited. **2.** an estimate of the contribution of inheritance to a given trait or function. Heritabilities can range from 0, indicating no contribution of heritable factors, to 1, indicating total contribution of heritable factors. The heritability of intelligence is believed to be roughly .5, although research indicates that heritability tends to increase with age and may rise to .7 or above in adulthood. Heritability is determined using a variety of behavior-genetic methods, such as studies of identical twins raised apart or ADOPTION STUDIES in which IQs of children are compared to the IQs of both their biological and their adoptive parents. Heritability is not the same as genetic contribution, because heritability is sensitive only to sources of individual differences. Moreover, a trait can be heritable and yet modifiable. For example, intelligence is heritable in some degree, but also has risen in recent generations. Also called **heritability estimate**. See FLYNN EFFECT.

heritage *n.* **1.** anything inherited from preceding generations, including physical or mental traits, property, or cultural traditions. **2.** artworks, historic buildings or monuments, and natural landscapes that are regarded as having special value and accordingly preserved for future generations. See CULTURAL HERITAGE; SOCIAL HERITAGE. See also CULTURAL CONSERVE.

hermaphrodite *n.* an organism possessing both male and female sex organs (in the human species, for example, possessing both ovarian and testicular tissue). The true hermaphrodite may have either male or female sex chromosome combinations or show CHROMOSOME MOSAICISM, with XX chromosomes in ovarian tissues and XY chromosomes in testicular cells. True hermaphroditism occurs more rarely than PSEUDOHERMAPHRODITISM. See also AMBIGUOUS GENITALIA; ANDROGYNY; INTERSEXUALITY. **—hermaphroditism** *n.*

hermeneutics *n.* the theory or science of interpretation. Hermeneutics is concerned with the ways in which humans derive meaning from language or other symbolic expression. Originally, the term was confined to the interpretation of Scripture, with an emphasis on deriving methods of interpretation that would yield the correct meaning of the text. Subsequently, two main strains of hermeneutic thought developed. One begins in the work of German philosopher Friedrich Schleiermacher (1768–1834), who broadened hermeneutics by applying it to the interpretation of texts in general rather than to religious texts in particular. This project was expanded by German philosopher Wilhelm Dilthey (1833–1911) into the interpretation of all forms of cultural expression, including artworks, institutions, and historical events. A key concept in this tradition of hermeneutics is the so-called **hermeneutic circle**—the notion that interpretation is always circular, in that particulars will necessarily be interpreted in the light of one's understanding of the whole, and the understanding of the whole will be altered by the understanding of the particulars. Another key assumption is the need to gain insight into the mind of the person or people whose expression is the subject of interpretation. This approach has been criticized on the grounds that such insight is impossible, because there is no access to the mind of another; thus, the methods of hermeneutics will always be imprecise and their results relativistic.

A second, more radical, strain of hermeneutics derives from the PHENOMENOLOGY of Edmund Husserl (1859–1938) and the work of German philosopher Martin Heidegger (1889–1976). Heidegger expanded the project of interpretation to include DASEIN or human being itself. This suggests that all human behavior can be understood as meaningful expression, much as one would understand a written text. It also turns the process of interpretation back on the interpreter, as the understanding of the being of human beings entails interpretations of interpretive acts. This move has given rise to a broad movement within philosophy, psychology, and literary criticism in which richness of interpretation is considered more valuable than consistent methodology or arriving at the "correct" interpretation. Such an approach is a clear alternative to a natural scientific psychology. This type of hermeneutics has informed other contemporary movements, notably EXISTENTIALISM, POSTMODERNISM, and POSTSTRUCTURALISM. **—hermeneutic** *adj.*

herniation *n.* the abnormal protrusion of an organ or other bodily structure through an opening in a membrane, muscle, or bone.

hero *n.* in PSYCHODRAMA, the person (PROTAGONIST) who is portraying a problem.

heroin *n.* a highly addictive OPIOID that is a synthetic analog of MORPHINE and three times more potent. In many countries, including Great Britain and Canada, it is used clinically for pain management (see DIACETYLMORPHINE), but it is not legally available in the United States due to concerns about its potential for abuse. Its rapid onset of action leads to an intense initial high, followed by a period of euphoria and a sense of well-being. As a street drug, heroin is commonly injected intravenously or subcutaneously ("skin popping"). Injection using shared needles is a common mechanism of transmission of HIV, hepatitis, and other disease agents. It can also be insufflated (snorted) or smoked.

heroin abuse in *DSM–IV–TR*, a pattern of heroin use manifested by recurrent significant adverse consequences related to the repeated ingestion of the substance. This diagnosis is preempted by the diagnosis of HEROIN DEPENDENCE: If the criteria for heroin abuse and heroin dependence are both met, only the latter diagnosis is given.

heroin dependence in *DSM–IV–TR*, a cluster of cognitive, behavioral, and physiological symptoms indicating continued use of heroin despite significant heroin-related problems. There is a pattern of repeated heroin ingestion resulting in tolerance, characteristic withdrawal symptoms if use is suspended (see OPIOID WITHDRAWAL), and an uncontrollable drive to continue use.

heroin overdose the ingestion of an amount of heroin sufficient to produce pronounced intoxication, characterized by apathy, PSYCHOMOTOR RETARDATION, drowsiness, slurred speech, and impaired attention or memory. If untreated, this progresses to shock, coma, pinpoint pupils, and depressed respiration, with the possibility of death from respiratory arrest.

herpes infection a disease produced by one of the strains of herpes virus. A herpes infection may be manifested as chicken pox, cold sores, shingles, ulceration of the cornea, encephalitis, stomatitis, or vulvovaginitis (GENITAL HERPES). The major strains are **herpes varicella-zoster**, which causes both chicken pox and shingles; **her-**

pes simplex Type 1, the cause of cold sores, and **herpes simplex Type 2**, the cause of genital herpes. See also PERINATAL HERPES-VIRUS INFECTION.

herpes-simplex encephalitis a form of ENCEPHALITIS (inflammation of the brain) caused by infection with the herpes-simplex virus. Seizures occur repeatedly early in the course of the disease, and there may be serious memory impairment. The virus tends to affect the temporal and frontal lobes.

herpetic neuralgia pain associated with shingles, caused by reactivation of the herpes varicella-zoster virus (see HERPES INFECTION). Following an attack of chicken pox, the virus lies dormant in a dorsal nerve root and ganglion of the spinal cord; when reactivated, it spreads down the sensory nerve, causing vesicle formation and severe, burning, lancinating pain. This acute pain typically resolves in 3–5 weeks, but patients often develop the chronic, debilitating pain known as **postherpetic neuralgia**.

hertz (symbol: Hz) *n.* the unit of FREQUENCY equal to one cycle per second. [Heinrich Rudolf **Hertz** (1857–1894), German physicist]

Heschl's gyrus one of several transverse ridges on the upper side of the TEMPORAL LOBE of the brain that are associated with the sense of hearing. [Richard **Heschl** (1824–1881), Austrian pathologist who first traced the auditory pathways of humans to this convolution]

hetaeral fantasy a fantasy in which a woman plays the role of a courtesan. In the male version of the fantasy, the man possesses a courtesan. Also called **courtesan fantasy**.

hetero- *combining form* other or different.

heterochromic iridocyclitis see IRIDOCYCLITIS.

heterochrony *n.* **1.** a difference in the rate of two processes, such as the conduction of nerve impulses. **2.** any evolutionary change in the relative time of appearance of maturational features or events or the rate of development of an organism. Also called **heterochronia**.

heteroeroticism *n.* an attraction toward the opposite sex, as in heterosexuality. Compare HOMOEROTICISM. Also called **heteroerotism**. **—heteroerotic** *adj.*

heterogametic *adj.* referring to the sex that has two dissimilar SEX CHROMOSOMES, such as the male sex in mammals and the female sex in birds. Compare HOMOGAMETIC.

heterogeneity of variance the situation in which populations or CELLS in a experimental design have unequal variances. Compare HOMOGENEITY OF VARIANCE.

heterogeneous *adj.* composed of diverse elements. Compare HOMOGENEOUS.

heterogeneous group an aggregate of individuals or other elements that are different from one another in a number of significant respects. In a social context, for example, a heterogeneous group might range in age, socioeconomic background, values, work experience, education, and so on. In an educational context, heterogeneous groups may be entire classes or smaller groups of students of varying ability who work together in a specific area, such as art or reading. Compare HOMOGENEOUS GROUP.

heterohypnosis *n.* a state of suggestibility induced in one person by another. Compare AUTOHYPNOSIS.

heterolalia *n.* see HETEROPHEMY.

heteromorphosis *n.* **1.** abnormal shape or structure. **2.** the development of a regenerated organ or structure that is different from the one that was lost.

heteronomous *adj.* under the control of or influenced by various external factors. Compare AUTONOMOUS.

heteronomous stage in Jean PIAGET's theory of moral development, the stage at which the child, approximately 6 to 10 years of age, equates morality with the rules and principles of his or her parents and other authority figures. That is, the child evaluates the rightness or wrongness of an act only in terms of adult sanctions for or against it and of the consequences or possible punishment it may bring. Also called **heteronomous morality**. See also IMMANENT JUSTICE; MORAL ABSOLUTISM; MORAL REALISM. Compare AUTONOMOUS STAGE; PREMORAL STAGE.

heteronomous superego in psychoanalytic theory, a SUPEREGO that demands that the individual behave in whatever manner is expected at the moment in order to secure the approval of others.

heteronomy *n.* **1.** a state in which a person is emotionally or physically dependent on others and unable to regulate his or her behavior. **2.** a child's or a childlike person's dependence on another's ideas or values, as in Jean PIAGET'S HETERONOMOUS STAGE. Compare AUTONOMY.

heteronymous hemianopia a VISUAL FIELD DEFECT in which vision in either the left or right half of both eyes is absent, due to a lesion in the optic chiasm. See HEMIANOPIA.

heteronymous reflex a reflex elicited by stimulation in one muscle of a synergistic group that results in contraction of another muscle in the same group. Compare HOMONYMOUS REFLEX.

heterophemy *n.* the act of saying or writing a word or phrase other than the words intended. Often, the substitution conveys the opposite meaning to what the individual intended. Also called **heterolalia**; **heterophasia**; **heterophemia**. See also FREUDIAN SLIP; SLIP OF THE TONGUE.

heterophilia *n.* love of, or attraction to, members of the opposite sex.

heterophily *n.* **1.** any tendency for individuals who differ from one another in some way to make social connections. It is less common than HOMOPHILY. COMPLEMENTARITY, which occurs when people with different but complementary characteristics form a relationship, is an example of heterophily. **2.** the degree of dissimilarity between individuals who share social ties.

heterophoria *n.* the deviation of an eye because of an imbalance in the extrinsic EYE MUSCLES.

heteroscedasticity *n.* the situation in which $\mathrm{Var}(Y|X)$ is not the same for all values of X, that is, the variance in Y is a function of the variable X. Compare HOMOSCEDASTICITY. **—heteroscedastic** *adj.*

heterosexism *n.* prejudice against any nonheterosexual form of behavior, relationship, or community, in particular the denigration of gay men and lesbians. Whereas HOMOPHOBIA generally refers to an individual's fear or dread of gay men or lesbians, heterosexism denotes a wider system of beliefs, attitudes, and institutional structures that attach value to heterosexuality and denigrate same-sex behavior and orientation.

heterosexual anxiety persistent and irrational anxiety that is related to heterosexual relationships, for example, a feeling that one is not sexually attractive in appearance or performance.

heterosexuality *n.* **1.** sexual attraction to members of the opposite sex. **2.** the developmental stage in which sexual attraction to or intercourse with members of the opposite sex occurs. **—heterosexual** *adj.*

heterosis *n.* see HYBRID VIGOR.

heterosociality *n.* relationships on a social (rather than a sexual or romantic) level between people of opposite sexes.

heterostasis *n.* an organism's seeking of maximal stimulation. [defined by A. Harry Klopf]

heterotopia *n.* the congenital development of gray matter in the area of the brain and spinal cord normally consisting of white matter.

heterotropia *n.* see STRABISMUS.

heterozygous *adj.* possessing two different forms of a gene (i.e., different ALLELES) at a given genetic locus on each of a pair of HOMOLOGOUS chromosomes. One allele is inherited from the mother, and the other from the father. In such individuals, the DOMINANT ALLELE is expressed, and the RECESSIVE ALLELE is not. Compare HOMOZYGOUS. **—heterozygote** *n.*

heuristic *n.* **1.** in cognition, a strategy for solving a problem or making a decision that provides an efficient means of finding an answer but cannot guarantee a correct outcome. By contrast, an ALGORITHM guarantees a solution to a problem (if there is one) but may be much less efficient. Also called **cognitive heuristic**. See also AVAILABILITY HEURISTIC; REPRESENTATIVENESS HEURISTIC. **2.** in the social sciences, a conceptual device, such as a model or working hypothesis, that is intended to explore or limit the possibilities of a question rather than to provide an explanation of the facts. See also AS-IF HYPOTHESIS; CONSTRUCT. **3.** in ergonomics, a procedure in which several experts, working independently, evaluate a product or system according to established usability guidelines and produce structured reports noting any failings. The advantage of this type of evaluation is that it is relatively simple and cheap. The chief disadvantage is that it does not involve testing among target users and so may not identify problems experienced by particular groups (e.g., those with a different cultural background). Compare TASK ANALYSIS.

heuristic search a search through a PROBLEM SPACE that is optimized by the use of strategies that reduce the number of possible paths to a solution that need to be attempted. See BEST-FIRST SEARCH. Compare EXHAUSTIVE SEARCH.

heuristic-systematic model (**HSM**) a theory of persuasion postulating that the validity of a persuasive message can be assessed in two different ways. **Systematic processing** involves the careful scrutiny of the merits of attitude-relevant information in the message. **Heuristic processing** involves the use of a subset of information in the message as a basis for implementing a simple decision rule to determine if the message should be accepted (e.g., judging a message to be valid because its source is highly credible). See also DUAL PROCESS MODELS OF PERSUASION. [first proposed and subsequently developed by U.S. psychologists Shelly Chaiken (1949–) and Alice H. Eagly (1938–)]

heuristic value the potential to stimulate or encourage further thinking.

Heymans's law the generalization that sensitivity to one stimulus decreases with increases in the intensity of another, concurrent, stimulus. [Corneille **Heymans** (1892–1968), Belgian physiologist]

HGPRT abbreviation for HYPOXANTHINE–GUANINE PHOSPHORIBOSYLTRANSFERASE.

5-HIAA abbreviation for 5-HYDROXYINDOLEACETIC ACID.

hibernation *n.* a period of inactivity accompanied by a significant decrease in body temperature that occurs in certain warm-blooded vertebrates in temperate or arctic environments during winter. The body temperature may drop to within a few degrees of freezing. Activity of endocrine glands decreases during this period, but no single gland has been found to control hibernation. Some species (e.g., bears) consume large quantities of food before hibernation and maintain bodily functions with energy from fat deposits, but others (e.g., golden hamsters) store food and leave hibernation periodically to feed. Cold-blooded animals become dormant in cold temperatures. **—hibernate** *vb.*

Hick's law in experiments or tasks involving CHOICE REACTION TIME, the finding that the time required to classify a stimulus as being from a particular set increases proportionally with the number of stimuli in the set. Also called **Hick–Hyman law**. [William Edmund **Hick** (1912–1974), British psychologist; Ray **Hyman** (1928–), U.S. cognitive psychologist]

hidden agenda an undisclosed intention or motive that is concealed within an overt action, policy, or statement.

hidden-clue test a test in which the participant must discover a particular feature of the stimulus situation that is the clue to a reward.

Hidden Figures Test see EMBEDDED FIGURES TEST.

hidden grief see DISENFRANCHISED GRIEF.

hidden observer the phenomenon whereby highly hypnotizable people (see HYPNOTIC SUSCEPTIBILITY) who are asked to block certain stimuli (e.g., pain) can sometimes register the blocked pain or other sensation via hand signals, as if a dissociated observer is simultaneously taking in events that are disavowed by the dominant observer. Such individuals can later recall auditory, visual, or tactile stimuli to which they appeared oblivious at the time.

hidden variable an undiscovered causative variable. When a relationship is found between variables *A* and *B*, variable *A* may erroneously be thought to be the cause of *B*. However, the cause of *B* may be a hidden variable *C* (sometimes called a third variable) that is correlated with variable *A*.

hierarchically nested design a research design in which two or more levels of sampling units are nested within higher order sampling units, for example, students (A), nested within classrooms (B), nested within schools (C), nested within school systems (D). Analysis of the data of such designs depends on whether the different levels are regarded as fixed or random factors.

hierarchical model of personality a model of either within-person psychology dynamics or individual differences in personality in which some psychological constructs are viewed as high-level variables that organize or govern the functioning of lower-level variables. For example, a hierarchical model of personality traits might view the construct SOCIABILITY as being at a lower level in a hierarchy than the construct EXTRAVERSION: Sociability would be seen as a form or example of the higher level trait of extraversion.

hierarchical theories of intelligence theories of intelligence postulating that the abilities constituting intelligence are arranged in a series of levels (of a hierarchy) ranging from general to specific. Many of these theories are based on recognizing three levels of factors, first proposed by U.S. psychologist Karl J. Holzinger (1892–1954): (a) the general factor, applying to all intellectual tasks; (b) group factors, which apply to some but not all intellectual tasks; and (c) specific factors, applying to individual tasks. Examples of such theories are the THREE-

STRATUM MODEL OF INTELLIGENCE and the CATTELL–HORN THEORY OF INTELLIGENCE.

hierarchization *n.* in Jean PIAGET's theory of cognitive development, the process whereby each current cognitive structure can be traced to earlier, more primitive structures, which were necessary for the attainment of the more advanced structure.

hierarchy *n.* **1.** a clear ordering of individuals on some behavioral dimension, such as dominance–submission. A linear hierarchy occurs when all individuals can be arrayed in a strict transitive order along a continuum (see DOMINANCE HIERARCHY; ORGANIZATIONAL HIERARCHY). Often, however, a hierarchy is more complex, with some individuals having equal status or acting in COALITIONS or with ordering based on different factors (see ANIMAL DOMINANCE). **2.** in neuroscience, an organization of control systems such that one area of the brain controls another, which in turn may control neuromuscular action.

hierarchy of motives (**hierarchy of needs**) see MASLOW'S MOTIVATIONAL HIERARCHY.

hierarchy of response see RESPONSE HIERARCHY.

high *n.* slang for the subjective feelings of intoxication experienced following ingestion of psychoactive drugs.

high-altitude cerebral edema see ACUTE MOUNTAIN SICKNESS.

high blood pressure see HYPERTENSION.

higher brain center loosely, any part of the cerebrum associated with cognitive processes, such as learning and memory.

higher level skill a work method or skill that can be applied to many tasks rather than one particular task.

higher mental process any of the more complex types of cognition, such as thinking, judgment, imagination, memory, and language. See also MENTAL FUNCTION.

higher order conditioning in PAVLOVIAN CONDITIONING, a procedure in which the CONDITIONED STIMULUS of one experiment acts as the UNCONDITIONED STIMULUS of another, for the purpose of conditioning a NEUTRAL STIMULUS. For example, after pairing a tone with food, and establishing the tone as a conditioned stimulus that elicits salivation, a light could be paired with the tone. If the light alone comes to elicit salivation, then higher order conditioning has occurred.

higher order consciousness a type of CONSCIOUSNESS that goes beyond sensory contents (see SENSORY CONSCIOUSNESS) to include abstract ideas, language-dependent thinking, and self-consciousness. [proposed by U.S. neuroscientist Gerald M. Edelman (1929–) and others]

higher order construct any large, coherent construct that is used to organize information and to integrate it into one's general knowledge.

higher order interaction in the ANALYSIS OF VARIANCE, the joint effect of three or more independent variables on the dependent variable.

higher order processes see EXECUTIVE FUNCTION.

higher response unit any integration of simple responses into a more complex response.

higher states of consciousness see TRANSPERSONAL PSYCHOLOGY.

high-involvement management an approach to managing organizations that attempts to tap the potential of employees by obtaining input from them on decisions, sharing information about the business with them, providing training to enhance their skills, and providing incentives for becoming skilled and committed. [described by U.S. management theorist Edward E. Lawler III (1938–)]

high Machs see MACH SCALE.

high-pass filter see FILTER.

high-potency antipsychotics conventional ANTIPSYCHOTICS that have either a relatively high degree of affinity for the dopamine D2 receptor or significant EXTRAPYRAMIDAL EFFECTS. High-potency antipsychotics include FLUPHENAZINE, HALOPERIDOL, thiothixene (see THIOXANTHENES), TRIFLUOPERAZINE, and PIMOZIDE.

high resolution the ability to distinguish as separate entities two stimuli that are very close to one another in some dimension.

high-risk participant studies research on vulnerable, or "high-risk," participants, who may be predisposed to social, physical, or psychiatric pathology by reason of genetic, constitutional, or environmental factors. The object of these studies is both to identify specific factors that differentiate between those who ultimately develop disorders and those who do not and to establish the statistical probability of different types of pathology.

high-technology assistive device a device using complex electronics, such as a computerized communications system or a motorized wheelchair, to enhance the functional capabilities of individuals with disabilities. The device may require individualized adaptation and training. See ASSISTIVE TECHNOLOGY.

high threshold a threshold that is never exceeded unless a signal is present. Classical psychophysics assumes a high threshold, although some psychophysical models combine high thresholds with **low thresholds**, which can be exceeded by random NOISE.

highway hypnosis a colloquial name for accident proneness resulting from a state of drowsy inattention experienced during long-distance driving on monotonous roads.

Hilgard, Ernest R. (1904–2001) U.S. psychologist. Hilgard earned his doctorate in psychology in 1930 from Yale University, where he studied under Raymond Dodge (1871–1942). He taught at Yale until 1933, when he accepted a joint appointment in psychology and education at Stanford University. Throughout his career Hilgard was a masterful synthesizer and organizer of research in the fields of conditioning, learning theory, and hypnosis. His early research on EYELID CONDITIONING led to publication of the classic text *Conditioning and Learning* (1940) with Donald G. Marquis (1908–1973). Hilgard's subsequent *Theories of Learning* (1948) also became a standard text in the field. Later in his career Hilgard's research interests focused on hypnosis, culminating in a number of books including *Hypnotic Susceptibility* (1965) and *Divided Consciousness* (1977). After his retirement, Hilgard became increasingly interested in the history of psychology and published *Psychology in America: A Historical Survey* (1987). His many honors included the Award for Distinguished Scientific Contributions from the American Psychological Association, the Gold Medal Award from the American Psychological Foundation, and membership in the National Academy of Sciences, the American Academy of Arts and Sciences, and the American Philosophical Society.

hindbrain *n.* the posterior of three bulges that appear in the embryonic brain as it develops from the NEURAL TUBE. The bulge eventually becomes the MEDULLA OBLONGATA, PONS, and CEREBELLUM. Also called **rhombencephalon**.

hindsight bias the tendency, after an event has occurred, to overestimate the extent to which the outcome could have been foreseen.

Hindu caste system see CASTE.

Hinduism *n.* the name, invented by Europeans, for the religion of the majority of the inhabitants of the Indian subcontinent. Indians who are not followers of the distinct teachings of Islam, Jainism, or Sikhism are generally referred to as **Hindus**. In India, the religious complex of such people is called *sanatana-dharma*, "the eternal religion," because it has incorporated all aspects of truth for many centuries. As a religion based on mythology, it has neither a founder nor a fixed canon. Myriad local cults and traditions of worship or belief can be distinguished. Common to all Hindus, however, is the teaching of the law of KARMA. The three most significant devotional movements in present-day Hinduism are Vaishnavism, devoted to the god Vishnu; Shaivism, devoted to the god Shiva; and Tantrism, or Shaktism, devoted to the goddess Shakti. Tantrism is of particular interest in psychology in that Shakti is the personification of the fundamental creative force whose primary expression is the sexual energy that unites the polarity of male and female and brings forth new life.

hinge *n.* in EXPLORATORY DATA ANALYSIS, either of the scores in a batch of data that divide the lower 25% of cases (the lower hinge) and the upper 25% of cases (the upper hinge) from the remainder of the cases.

hippie (**hippy**) *n.* a member of a 1960s and 1970s SUBCULTURE of mainly young people who rejected mainstream Western society and its values of work, consumerism, and material success in favor of an alternative lifestyle characterized by free love, communal living arrangements, and recreational drug use. The hippie philosophy was essentially one of hedonism, pacifism, and anarchism. See also COUNTERCULTURE; DRUG CULTURE; YOUTH CULTURE.

hippocampal commissure see COMMISSURE.

hippocampal formation a region of the brain located in the medial temporal lobe and concerned with the consolidation of long-term memory. It comprises the DENTATE GYRUS, HIPPOCAMPUS, and SUBICULUM and communicates with areas of neocortex via the ENTORHINAL CORTEX.

hippocampal gyrus see SUBICULUM.

hippocampus *n.* (*pl.* **hippocampi**) a seahorse-shaped part of the forebrain, in the basal medial region of the TEMPORAL LOBE, that is important for DECLARATIVE MEMORY and learning. Because of its resemblance to a ram's horn, 19th-century neuroanatomists named it **Ammon's horn** (**cornu ammonis**; CA) for the horn of the ram that represented the Egyptian deity Ammon. Parts of the hippocampus were then labeled **CA1**, **CA2**, **CA3**, and **CA4**; these designations are still used for the different regions of the hippocampus. See HIPPOCAMPAL FORMATION; PAPEZ CIRCUIT. —**hippocampal** *adj.*

hircine *adj.* in the ZWAARDEMAKER SMELL SYSTEM, denoting an odor quality that is smelled in goaty odors and rancid fat. See also CAPRYLIC.

hired gun a colloquial name for an expert witness who testifies in a manner that best suits his or her client, with little regard for any inaccuracies or misrepresentations of fact that might occur.

histamine *n.* a compound that is synthesized from the amino acid histidine by the enzyme histidine decarboxylase. Most histamine in humans is localized in peripheral tissues, where it is involved in allergic reactions or the inflammatory response to injury, causing dilation of blood vessels. In the brain, histamine acts as a neurotransmitter to modulate such functions as arousal, appetite, and regulation of autonomic functions. **Histamine receptors** can be divided into three categories, designated H_1, H_2, and H_3 receptors. Many antidepressants and antipsychotics may block histamine receptors in the brain, causing sedation and other side effects.

histamine antagonists drugs or other agents that inhibit the effects of HISTAMINE at central or peripheral histamine receptors. Many of these agents have a role in medicine and mental health. Antagonists at the H_1 receptor (more commonly called **antihistamines**) may have sedative effects and are a common component of over-the-counter sleeping aids; an example is DOXYLAMINE. Others (e.g., DIPHENHYDRAMINE, DIMENHYDRINATE) are used in the treatment of allergic reactions and as sedatives or in the management of motion sickness, and some (e.g., diphenhydramine) function as ANTIPARKINSONIAN AGENTS (see also CYPROHEPTADINE; HYDROXYZINE). The so-called **nonsedating antihistamines** have less ability to cross the BLOOD–BRAIN BARRIER and are used solely in the management of allergic responses. The older nonsedating antihistamines terfenadine and astemizole are potent inhibitors of the CYTOCHROME P450 3A4 enzyme and, when administered with other inhibitors of this enzyme (e.g., the antidepressants nefazodone, fluoxetine, and fluvoxamine), can cause disturbances of heart rhythm that can be fatal. Terfenadine has been withdrawn from the U.S. market because of its association with the dangerous arrhythmia torsades de pointes (see ELECTROCARDIOGRAPHIC EFFECT). H_2-receptor antagonists block the histamine-mediated production of gastric acid and are widely used as antacid compounds and in the treatment of gastric and peptic ulcers. H_3 antagonists do not presently have a defined clinical use.

histamine headache a headache caused by a release of HISTAMINE from body tissues. It usually involves only one side of the head and is often associated with common cold symptoms.

histo- (**hist-**) *combining form* tissue.

histogenesis *n.* the formation of body tissues.

histogram *n.* a graphical depiction of continuous data using bars of varying length or height, similar to a BAR GRAPH, but with data on the *x*-axis split into equal blocks that adjoin so as to denote their continuous nature. For example, to display the relationship between individuals' weight and height, groups of individuals might be represented by blocks consisting of ranges of 10 pounds (lb): under 100 lb, 100–109 lb, 110–119 lb, 120–129 lb, and so on.

histology *n.* the scientific study of the structure and function of tissues. —**histological** *adj.* —**histologist** *n.*

historical control group a comparison group in which the participants are selected to be similar to those in the treatment group but for whom the data for comparison with the treatment group were collected some time in the past.

historical fallacy an error in interpreting a process in which one reads into the process itself, either as a cause or an essential element, what only comes about as the result of the process. For example, a man has lost his wallet but can think of several places where he might have left it. When he finds it in the first place that he looks, he assumes quite falsely that he knew where the wallet was all along. His error is to suppose that a state of affairs arising from the process of looking (knowing where the wallet is) was in fact the cause of the process. Errors of this kind are easily made in interpreting our own and others' behaviors. The term "historical fallacy" was introduced into psychology by John DEWEY in his classic paper "The Reflex Arc Concept in Psychology" (1896); here he argued that contemporary psychology was committing this fallacy in its attempts to isolate one set of events termed "responses" from another set termed "stimuli" and to show that the former result from the latter. See also REVERSE CAUSALITY.

historical linguistics the study of historical change in language. See DIACHRONIC LINGUISTICS; PHILOLOGY.

historical method the technique of analyzing, counseling, or otherwise offering therapy by focusing on a client's personal history.

historical psychoanalysis see PSYCHOHISTORY.

historicism *n.* **1.** the doctrine that the study of history can reveal general laws governing historical events and social and cultural phenomena and that these laws may allow for predictions of the future. **2.** the doctrine that beliefs, values, and cultural products are determined by their historical context and can only be understood in this context.

history taking the process of compiling the history of a patient or research participant from the individual directly and from other sources, such as the patient's family, hospitals or clinics, psychiatrists or psychologists, neurologists, social workers, and others who have direct knowledge of the individual. See ANAMNESIS.

histrionic personality disorder in *DSM–IV–TR*, a personality disorder characterized by a pattern of long-term (rather than episodic) self-dramatization in which individuals draw attention to themselves, crave activity and excitement, overreact to minor events, experience angry outbursts, and are prone to manipulative suicide threats and gestures. Such individuals appear to others to be shallow, egocentric, inconsiderate, vain, demanding, dependent, and helpless. The disorder was formerly known as **hysterical personality disorder**.

hit *n.* **1.** the accurate identification of a signal in a signal detection task. Compare MISS. **2.** in computing, a single instance of a website being viewed by a visitor. In advertising, the number of hits is sometimes regarded as a measure of promotional success.

hit rate in signal detection tasks, the proportion of trials in which a signal is present and the participant correctly responds that it is.

HIV *h*uman *i*mmunodeficiency *v*irus: the agent responsible for AIDS. Infection can occur by various routes, including unprotected sexual intercourse or administration of contaminated blood products. However, among those who abuse drugs infection is often acquired by the sharing of contaminated needles and syringes, used to inject drugs intravenously. HIV infection is characterized by a gradual deterioration of immune function that can progress to AIDS. The virus binds to an antigen, CD4, found on the surface of helper T cells (or CD4+ cells), a class of lymphocytes with a crucial role in the immune response. Once bound to a target cell, the virus releases its genetic material (RNA) into the cell and replicates. Helper T cells are disabled and killed during the typical course of infection. The diagnosis of HIV infection can result in considerable emotional stress and social ostracism.

HIV/AIDS counseling see AIDS COUNSELING.

hives *n.* a temporary inflammation of the skin marked by sudden outbreaks of burning and itching swellings. The condition may be caused by psychogenic factors or by an allergy, such as a food allergy. Also called **urticaria**.

Hi-Wa itck a CULTURE-BOUND SYNDROME found in Mohave American Indian populations that would be categorized as a mood disorder by *DSM–IV–TR* standards. Symptoms include depression, insomnia, loss of appetite, and sometimes suicide associated with unwanted separation from a loved one; it generally affects the young wife of an older Mohave male.

HM the initials of a patient who became amnesic after undergoing bilateral temporal lobectomy in 1953 for the relief of intractable seizures. The case of HM, who was a patient of U.S. neurologist William Beecher Scoville (1906–1984), demonstrated the critical role of the HIPPOCAMPUS and surrounding structures in the process of memory formation and storage. The analysis of his memory disorder has also contributed greatly to understanding of the existence of various forms of memory mediated by distinct neural systems.

hMG abbreviation for HUMAN MENOPAUSAL GONADOTROPIN.

HMO health maintenance organization: a health plan that offers a range of services through a specified network of health professionals and facilities to subscribing members for a fixed fee. Members select a PRIMARY CARE PROVIDER who coordinates all care and is required to use approved providers for all services. Services may need further approval from the HMO utilization program. The HMO is reimbursed through fixed, periodic prepayments (capitated rates) by, or on behalf of, each member for a specified period of time. HMOs may subcapitate, or CARVE OUT, certain services, such as mental health, to other groups. See CAPITATION.

hoarding *n.* **1.** the carrying and storing of food or other items believed necessary for survival, which has been identified as either instinctive or learned behavior, or both. For example, hoarding by rodents varies with the environmental temperature, increasing when the temperature falls and decreasing as the temperature rises. See FOOD CACHING. **2.** a COMPULSION, characteristic of OBSESSIVE-COMPULSIVE DISORDER, that involves the persistent collection of useless or trivial items (e.g., old newspapers, garbage, magazines) and an inability to organize or discard these. The accumulation of items (usually in piles) leads to the obstruction of living space, causing distress or impairing function. Any attempt or encouragement by others to discard hoards causes extreme anxiety. See also COLLECTING MANIA. **—hoard** *vb., n.*

hoarding orientation in the existential psychoanalysis of Erich FROMM, a character pattern in which the individual doubts that personal needs can ever be completely satisfied and bases his or her sense of security on what he or she can save and own. The character is thought to be rigid, stubborn, and obsessively orderly. Also called **hoarding character**. See also ANAL PERSONALITY. Compare EXPLOITATIVE ORIENTATION; MARKETING ORIENTATION.

hoarseness *n.* an abnormally rough, harsh, or strained quality in the voice that may be produced by any interference with optimal adduction of the vocal cords, including that caused by overuse of the voice, damage to the larynx, or such disorders as gastric reflux and thyroid disease.

Hoffmann's sign a sign of brain disease in individuals with hemiplegia: Flicking or nipping the nail of the second, third, or fourth finger will, if the reflex is present, cause a flexion in these fingers and the thumb. Also called **Hoffmann's reflex**. [Johann **Hoffmann** (1857–1919), German neurologist]

hol- *combining form* see HOLO-.

hold functions cognitive abilities—such as those involved in vocabulary and verbal knowledge, object assembly, and picture completion—that typically remain stable or improve with adult aging as observed on intellectual or cognitive tests (e.g., the WECHSLER ADULT INTELLIGENCE SCALE).

holding environment in the OBJECT RELATIONS THEORY of British psychoanalyst Donald Winnicott (1896–1971), that aspect of the mother experienced by the infant as the environment that literally—and figuratively, by demonstrating highly focused attention and concern—holds him or her comfortingly during calm states. This is in contrast to the mother who is experienced as the object of the infant's excited states.

holiday syndrome feelings of dejection and psychic pain that tend to occur during major holiday periods as a result of nostalgic reminiscence and unmet emotional needs. Severe depression, serious injuries, suicides, and fatal accidents tend to increase during the holiday season. Also called **holiday blues**.

holism *n.* any approach or theory holding that a system or organism is a coherent, unified whole that cannot be fully explained in terms of individual parts or characteristics. The system or organism may have properties, as a complete entity or phenomenon, in addition to those of its parts. Thus, an analysis or understanding of the parts does not provide an understanding of the whole. **—holistic** *adj.*

holistic education a form of psychotherapy, derived from the approach of HOLISTIC MEDICINE, in which the therapist serves as a teacher and the client as student. The therapist aims to create conditions within which the student may choose to learn. For maximum growth, all aspects of the client's physical, spiritual, emotional, and intellectual life should be explored and developed. [developed by U.S. psychologist William C. Schutz (1925–2002)]

holistic healing a health care concept based on the premise that body, mind, and spirit function as a harmonious unit and that an adverse effect on one also adversely affects the others, requiring treatment of the whole to restore the harmonious balance.

holistic medicine a branch of medicine that, in the prevention and treatment of disease, focuses on the whole person—including physical, mental, spiritual, social, and environmental aspects—rather than on disease symptoms alone. Major features of holistic medicine include patient education about behavioral and attitudinal changes that promote and maintain good health and well-being, and patient self-help and participation in the healing process through diet, exercise, and other measures. It is often practiced in tandem with both conventional medicine (e.g., medication, surgery) and with COMPLEMENTARY AND ALTERNATIVE MEDICINE.

holistic psychology an approach to psychology based on the view that psychological phenomena must be studied as wholes, or that individuals are biological, psychological, and sociocultural totalities that cannot be fully explained in terms of individual components or characteristics. Holistic psychology is not a specific school but a perspective that informs the theories, methodologies, and practice of certain approaches, such as HUMANISTIC PSYCHOLOGY and CLIENT-CENTERED THERAPY.

Hollingshead scales several measures of individual socioeconomic status based on education and occupation. They include the Hollingshead Four-Factor Index of Social Status and the earlier Hollingshead Two-Factor Index of Social Position. [August B. **Hollingshead**, U.S. sociologist]

Hollingworth, Harry L. (1880–1956) U.S. psychologist. Hollingworth completed his doctorate at Columbia University in 1909, having studied under James McKeen CATTELL, Edward L. THORNDIKE, and Robert S. WOODWORTH. He took a faculty position at Barnard College in New York City and remained there until his retirement. Hollingworth was a pioneer in the field of APPLIED PSYCHOLOGY. In 1917 he published, with Albert T. Poffenberger (1885–1977), the first textbook in the field, *Applied Psychology*. He is particularly known for his work in ADVERTISING PSYCHOLOGY, publishing an influential book, *Advertising and Selling: Principles of Appeal and Response* (1913). He also contributed to the fields of vocational psychology, educational psychology, and abnormal psychology. Hollingworth's best known empirical study involved the behavioral and cognitive effects of drinking Coca Cola. The research, sponsored by the Coca Cola company and viewed as a model of scientific rigor, demonstrated that psychological research tools could prove valuable in the marketplace as well as in research universities. Hollingworth was elected president of the American Psychological Association in 1927. He was married to Leta Stetter HOLLINGWORTH.

Hollingworth, Leta Stetter (1886–1939) U.S. psychologist. Hollingworth earned her doctorate from Columbia University in 1916, studying under Edward L. THORNDIKE. While completing her graduate studies she became the first psychologist in New York to be licensed by the civil service to administer Binet intelligence tests. Upon completing her doctorate she accepted a faculty position at Columbia University's Teachers College, remaining there for the rest of her career. Hollingworth's main contributions to psychology lie in three fields: educational psychology, clinical psychology, and the psychology of women. For her dissertation, she studied women's intellectual performance throughout the menstrual cycle, debunking widespread beliefs that women were incapacitated mentally and physically during the menstrual period. Countering the biologically based arguments of many scientists, she made persuasive arguments for the social and economic causes of women's historic lack of achievement. In educational psychology, Hollingworth studied children at opposite ends of the spectrum of intelligence, from the gifted to those with mental retardation, publishing *The Psychology of Subnormal Children* (1920) and *Special Talents and Defects* (1923). She performed pathbreaking longitudinal studies of the intellectually gifted, resulting in her classic *Gifted Children* (1926). Her book *The Psychology of the Adolescent* (1928) was a leading textbook for two decades. Finally, she was a leader in professionalizing clinical psychology, arguing for the need to set standards for the field and helping the American Psychological Association to establish a clinical section in 1918. See also HOLLINGWORTH, HARRY L.

hollow-square puzzle an exercise sometimes used in team-building interventions designed to enhance collaboration and communication. The task requires the group to assemble a model from various constituent pieces, some of which are shared among the group and some of which are held by individual group members.

Holmes's phenomenon see REBOUND PHENOMENON. [Gordon M. **Holmes** (1876–1965), British neurologist]

Holmgren Test for Color Blindness one of the first standardized tests for color blindness, which required the participant to match skeins of colored yarns with standard skeins. [devised in 1879 by A. Frithiof **Holmgren** (1831–1897), Swedish physiologist]

holo- (**hol-**) *combining form* entire or complete.

hologram *n.* an interference pattern that appears as a three-dimensional image of an object.

holographic brain theory a brain theory suggesting that neuronal processes operate by means of fieldlike states of wave interference similar to holograms. Also called **holonomic brain theory**. [originated by Austrian-born U.S. neurophysiologist Karl Harry Pribram (1919–)]

holography *n.* a method of producing three-dimensional images by using interference patterns made by light waves. The technique is used in photography and has been suggested as an explanation for the process by which images may be formed in the mind. **—holographic** *adj.*

holonomic brain theory see HOLOGRAPHIC BRAIN THEORY.

holophrase *n.* one of the single-word utterances characteristic of children in the early stages of LANGUAGE ACQUISITION, such as *dada* or *yes*. These are considered to involve a SPEECH ACT going beyond the literal meaning of the single word so that, for example, *biscuit* means *I want a biscuit now*. See RICH INTERPRETATION. **—holophrastic** *adj.*

holophrastic stage see ONE-WORD STAGE.

holy anorexia see ANOREXIA MIRABILIS.

hom- *combining form* see HOMO-.

HOME abbreviation for HOME OBSERVATION FOR MEASUREMENT OF THE ENVIRONMENT.

home advantage 1. the increased likelihood that an individual or group will be victorious in a competitive event that is held on its home territory. This can be explained by (a) the familiarity with, and comfort of playing in, the home venue; (b) the likely backing of a majority of the spectators; and (c) the increased confidence that follows from a sense of having an advantage over the competition. **2.** the extent to which a team wins more home games than away games against the same opponent. Also called **home-field advantage**.

home and community-based services (**HCBS**) care or services provided in a patient's place of residence or in a noninstitutional setting located in the community. The aim is to help individuals of all ages with disabilities to live in the community, thereby avoiding more costly residential placements. In the United States, the primary means by which such services are funded is the **Home and Community-Based Services Waiver** (or **Medicaid Waiver**) program. Through this waiver, the federal government reimburses states for a percentage of their spending on designated community services, such as DAY HABILITATION, RESIDENTIAL HABILITATION, and service coordination. These services are defined in a flexible manner; they can be tailored to the specific needs of individuals enrolled in the waiver, allowing appropriate services to be provided to people with greatly varying requirements.

home cage a cage in which a nonhuman animal is housed when it is not engaged in an experimental session.

home care patient care in the home for people with physical or mental disabilities, including older adults with dementia or physical infirmity. Home care is an alternative to institutionalization, enabling the patient to live in familiar surroundings and preserve family ties. Such services as nursing care, administration of medication, therapeutic baths, physical therapy, and occupational therapy are provided by visiting professionals or paraprofessionals connected with clinics, hospitals, or health agencies. Also called **home health care**.

home health aide a specially trained person who works with a SOCIAL SERVICES agency or a local VISITING NURSE association to provide personal care services, such as bathing, light meal preparation, and dressing, to people with disabilities. See also HOMEMAKER HOME HEALTH AIDE.

home health care see HOME CARE.

homemaker home health aide a HOME HEALTH AIDE who assists people with disabilities in homemaking tasks, personal care, and rehabilitation routines in their own homes, whether through a private or public agency.

homeo- *combining form* similar or like.

Home Observation for Measurement of the Environment (**HOME**) a measure of the quality and extent of stimulation available to a child in the home environment. It is available in four versions: infant/toddler (birth to 3 years), early childhood (3 to 6 years), middle childhood (6 to 10 years), and early adolescent (10 to 15 years). Each version contains both observational and parent-reported items that provide a detailed analysis of characteristics of the home (parental responsiveness, play materials, etc.) that are hypothesized to be associated with a child's cognitive development. Originally published in 1967, the HOME was revised in 1984. [developed by 21st-century U.S. childcare specialist Bettye M. Caldwell and U.S. educational psychologist Robert H. Bradley (1946–)]

homeopathy *n.* a system of medicine based on the belief that "like cures like," that is, small, highly diluted quantities of medicinal substances are given to cure symptoms, when the same substances given at higher or more concentrated doses would actually cause those symptoms. Also called **homeopathic medicine**. See also COMPLEMENTARY AND ALTERNATIVE MEDICINE. Compare ALLOPATHY. [first given practical application by German physician Christian Friedrich Samuel Hahnemann (1755–1843)] **—homeopathic** *adj.*

homeostasis *n.* **1.** the regulation by an organism of all aspects of its INTERNAL ENVIRONMENT, including body temperature, salt–water balance (see OSMOREGULATION), acid–base balance (see HYDROGEN-ION CONCENTRATION), and blood sugar level. This involves monitoring changes in the external and internal environments by means of RECEPTORS and adjusting bodily processes accordingly. [first described by U.S. physiologist Walter Bradford Cannon (1871–1945)] **2.** maintenance of a stable balance, evenness, or symmetry. **—homeostatic** *adj.*

homeostatic model in social psychology, a model that assumes that all people are motivated by the **homeostatic principle**, that is, the need to maintain or restore their optimal level of environmental, interpersonal, and psychological stimulation. According to this theory, insufficient or excessive stimulation causes tension and often prompts the behavior required to achieve optimal stimulation levels.

homeotherm (**homoiotherm**) *n.* see ENDOTHERM. **—homeothermic** *adj.* **—homeothermy** *n.*

home page a site (address) on the WORLD WIDE WEB containing information about an organization (professional, business, educational, religious, or governmental) or an individual, usually created and maintained by the organization or individual concerned. The information provided depends on the intentions of the provider. Home pages may have links to other sites, where related information can be found.

home range the entire space through which an animal moves during its normal activities. The space may or may not be defended from other members of the same species. The part of the home range in which the greatest activity occurs is known as the CORE AREA. Home range (or **secondary territory**) differs from primary territory (see TERRITORIALITY), which is an actively defended specific area, and from PERSONAL SPACE, which is the defended space that moves with an individual.

home schooling 1. formal instruction of a student in his or her home or other private setting, often by one or both parents or by a tutor. Instruction must meet the preset requirements of a school district, a state, or both. Home schooling is often used for gifted students or for students with special needs, chronic illness, atypical learning styles, or behavior problems. **2.** education in a home environment of one family's children or a group of unrelated children.

home-service agency a group, which may be a public health, social service, or voluntary organization, that provides HOME HEALTH AIDES or HOMEMAKER HOME HEALTH AIDES for people with mental or physical disabilities. The personnel generally are paraprofessionals who are recruited, trained, and supervised by another agency, such as the VISITING NURSE association or a hospital with a home-care unit.

homesickness *n.* a feeling of intense sadness and longing caused by absence from one's home or native land. See also NOSTALGIA. **—homesick** *adj.*

home visit a visit to an individual at home by a professional or paraprofessional, such as a psychologist, physician, nurse, social worker, or rehabilitation therapist, for crisis intervention, aftercare, or other assistance in solving personal problems.

homework *n.* **1.** tasks assigned to a client to be performed between sessions of therapy. Assignments may require reading, research, or practicing new behaviors (e.g., attending a lecture, speaking to a specific person). **2.** schoolwork that is to be completed away from school or outside the classroom, most often at the student's home or dormitory room and in the student's private time. The assignments are designed to enhance the student's basic knowledge, which can then be used more effectively in the classroom. Also called **homework assignments**.

homicide *n.* the killing of one person by another person. In a legal context, homicide is often subdivided into **excusable homicide** (as in self-defense or resulting from an accident), **justifiable homicide** (as in carrying out a death sentence), and **felonious homicide** (as in murder or manslaughter). **—homicidal** *adj.*

homicidomania *n.* a mental or emotional disturbance characterized by a desire to kill others, often including actual attempts to do so.

homicidophilia *n.* sexual interest and arousal obtained from murder. In the extreme form, this PARAPHILIA results in what are called LUST MURDERS, or cases of murder and rape. Less extreme cases may consist of the use of murder fantasies or murder-related pornographic materials during masturbation.

homing *n.* the ability of individuals to return to an original home after traveling or being transported to a point that is a considerable distance from the home and that lacks most visual clues as to its location. In an ANIMAL-HOMING experiment, banded Manx shearwaters were transported 3,050 miles from their native Isle of Man, off the west coast of England, to North America: Released separately, they returned within 13 days to their burrows on the island. See also NAVIGATION.

hominid *n.* a primate of the family Hominidae, of which humans (*Homo sapiens*) are the only living species.

homo- (**hom-**) *combining form* **1.** same or like. [from Greek *homos,* "one and the same"] **2.** human being. [from Latin *homo,* "man"]

homocystinuria *n.* a genetic metabolic disorder characterized by a deficiency of an enzyme needed to convert L-homocystine to L-cystathionine. Mental retardation often occurs, along with a shuffling, ducklike gait and, in some instances, seizures or hemiplegia. Brain abnormalities are often due to arterial or venous thromboses. Also called **cystathionine synthetase deficiency**.

homoeroticism *n.* an erotic desire for people of one's own sex. Also called **homoerotism**. **—homoerotic** *adj.*

homogametic *adj.* referring to the sex that has two similar SEX CHROMOSOMES, such as the female sex in mammals and the male sex in birds. Compare HETEROGAMETIC.

homogeneity *n.* see LINEAR SYSTEM.

homogeneity of cognitive function in stage theories of cognitive development, such as Jean PIAGET's, the assumption that a child's mental processes (e.g., problem solving) are relatively homogeneous, or similar, across different tasks and contexts.

homogeneity of variance the condition in which multiple populations, or CELLS in an experimental design, have the same variance: a basic assumption of many statistical procedures. Compare HETEROGENEITY OF VARIANCE.

homogeneous *adj.* having the same, or relatively similar, composition throughout. Compare HETEROGENEOUS.

homogeneous group an aggregate of individuals or other elements that are similar to one another in a number of significant respects. In a social context, for example, a homogeneous group might include members who are the same age or have the same socioeconomic background, values, work experience, education, and so on. In educational contexts, a homogeneous group may be an entire class or a smaller group formed within a class and based on similar ability in a specific area (e.g., mathematics). Compare HETEROGENEOUS GROUP.

homogenitality *n.* an interest in the genitalia of one's own sex.

homograph *n.* one of two or more words that are written in exactly the same way but have unrelated meanings. For example, *row* meaning "linear arrangement" and *row* meaning "argument" are homographs. Compare HOMONYM; HOMOPHONE. **—homographic** *adj.*

homolateral *adj.* on the same side of the body. **—homolaterally** *adv.*

homologous *adj.* **1.** exhibiting resemblance based on common ancestry (see HOMOLOGY). **2.** describing chromosomes that are identical in terms of their visible structure and location of gene segments, although they may carry different ALLELES. DIPLOID organisms, such as humans, possess homologous pairs of chromosomes (see AUTOSOME) in the nuclei of their body cells. See also RECOMBINATION. **3.** describing any segment of a nucleic acid (DNA or RNA) or protein whose sequence of, respectively, bases or amino acids is similar to that of another segment.

homology *n.* a resemblance based on common ancestry, such as the similarity in forelimb structures of vertebrates. Homology suggests evolution of different species from a common ancestor. Compare ANALOGY; HOMOPLASY.

homonym *n.* one of two or more words that are written or pronounced (or both) in the same way but are unrelated in meaning. For example, *cape* meaning "promontory" and *cape* meaning "garment" are homonyms. Compare HOMOGRAPH; HOMOPHONE.

homonymous hemianopia the loss of sight in the same half of the visual field of each eye (i.e., the left half of the visual field of both the left and right eyes, or vice versa) caused by injury to the postchiasmatic visual system (see POSTCHIASMATIC VISUAL DEFICIT). See also HEMIANOPIA.

homonymous paracentral scotoma see PARACENTRAL SCOTOMA.

homonymous quadranopia see QUADRANOPIA.

homonymous reflex a reflex in which stimulation of a muscle produces a contraction of the same muscle. Compare HETERONYMOUS REFLEX.

homophile *n.* a person who loves others of his or her own sex, that is, a gay man or a lesbian.

homophily *n.* **1.** the tendency for individuals who are socially connected in some way to display certain affinities, such as similarities in demographic background, attitudes, values, and so on. **2.** the degree of similarity between individuals who share social ties. See also BIRDS-OF-A-FEATHER PHENOMENON. Compare HETEROPHILY.

homophobia *n.* hatred and fear of gay men and lesbians, associated with prejudice and anger focused on them. This results in discrimination on such issues as employment, housing, and legal rights and may also lead to violence (**gay bashing**). Extreme homophobia may lead to murder.

homophone *n.* one of two or more words that are pronounced in exactly the same way but have unrelated meanings and may or may not have different spellings. For example, *whole* and *hole* are homophones. Compare HOMOGRAPH; HOMONYM. **—homophonic** *adj.*

homoplasy *n.* the resemblance of features in species that are not descended from a common ancestor (e.g., the body forms of a tuna and a dolphin). This superficial similarity often arises through the process of CONVERGENT EVOLUTION because the species live in the same environment. Compare HOMOLOGY. **—homoplastic** *adj.*

homoscedasticity *n.* the situation in which $\text{Var}(Y|X) = \text{Var}(Y)$, that is, the variance of variable Y is unrelated to the value of another variable X. Homoscedasticity is a basic assumption in some forms of REGRESSION ANALYSIS. Compare HETEROSCEDASTICITY. **—homoscedastic** *adj.*

homosexual behavior 1. sexual impulses, feelings, or relations directed toward members of one's own sex. **2.** sexual acts, such as mutual genital caressing, cunnilingus, fellatio, and anal intercourse, that are practiced by gay men and lesbians but also may be practiced by heterosexual couples.

homosexual community the gay and lesbian people in a particular country, region, or city, especially when regarded as having their own meeting places, customs, linguistic expressions, organizations, and so on.

homosexuality *n.* sexual attraction or activity between members of the same sex. Although the term can refer to such sexual orientation in both men and women, current practice distinguishes between gay men and lesbians, and homosexuality itself is now commonly referred to as same-sex sexual orientation or activity. **—homosexual** *adj., n.*

homosexual love a sexual relationship with a member of one's own sex involving the full range of erotic, emotional, and sexual feelings.

homosexual marriage see SAME-SEX MARRIAGE.

homosexual panic a sudden, acute anxiety attack precipitated by (a) the unconscious fear that one might be gay or lesbian or will act out gay or lesbian impulses, (b) the fear of being sexually attacked by a person of the same sex, or (c) loss of or separation from a same-sex partner.

homosexual rights movement see GAY LIBERATION.

homovanillic acid (**HVA**) the end product of the catabolism of the neurotransmitter dopamine, produced by the action either of catechol-*O*-methyltransferase (COMT) on 3,4-dihydroxyphenylacetic acid (DOPAC) or of aldehyde dehydrogenase on 3-methoxy-4-hydroxyphenylacetaldehyde (MHPA). Levels of homovanillic acid are typically reduced in individuals with Parkinson's disease.

homozygous *adj.* possessing identical forms of a gene (i.e., identical ALLELES) at a given genetic locus on each of a pair of HOMOLOGOUS chromosomes. Either AUTOSOMAL DOMINANT or AUTOSOMAL RECESSIVE conditions are expressed when the individual is homozygous for that condition. Compare HETEROZYGOUS. **—homozygote** *n.*

homunculus *n.* (*pl.* **homunculi**) **1.** a putative process or entity in the mind or the nervous system whose operations are invoked to explain some aspect of human behavior or experience. The problem with such theories is that the behavior or experience of the homunculus usually requires explanation in exactly the same way as that of the person as a whole. As a result, homunculus theories tend to end in CIRCULAR REASONING or to involve an INFINITE REGRESSION of homunculi. For example, to explain its theory that certain ideas are kept from conscious awareness because they are threatening to the person, psychoanalysis must posit some specialized part of the person that is aware of the ideas, and knows that they are threatening. Similarly, some information-processing theories invoke a "decision-making process" to explain the making of decisions. Both theories invoke a sophisticated level of inner awareness or processing in an attempt to explain another outward level of awareness or processing. For this reason critics would say that they require homunculi, or that they commit the **homunculus fallacy**. **2.** in neuroanatomy, a figurative representation, in distorted human form; of the relative sizes of motor and sensory areas in the brain that correspond to particular parts of the body. For example, the brain area devoted to the tongue is much larger than the area for the forearm, so the homunculus has a correspondingly larger tongue. See MOTOR-FUNCTION HOMUNCULUS; SENSORY HOMUNCULUS. **3.** a completely formed minute human figure (Latin, "little man") thought by some 16th- and 17th-century theorists to exist in the spermatozoon and simply to expand in size in the transition from zygote to embryo to infant to adult. This idea is an example of PREFORMISM and is contrary to the epigenetic principle of cumulative development and successive differentiation. **—homuncular** *adj.*

honestly significant difference (**HSD**) see TUKEY'S HONESTLY SIGNIFICANT DIFFERENCE TEST.

honest signal in animal communication, a signal that provides accurate information about an individual's internal state or its intentions. Although some theorists argue that communication should be deceptive or manipulative to ensure survival, honest signals have value if they are highly correlated with a physical trait (e.g., body size) that might, for example, provide important information for mate selection or if they are used within a stable social group where DISHONEST SIGNALS can be detected and "cheaters" punished. See HANDICAP PRINCIPLE.

honesty *n.* **1.** in general, truthfulness, uprightness, and integrity. **2.** in psychotherapy, the ability of an individual to express true feelings and communicate immediate experiences, including conflicting, ambivalent, or guilt-ridden attitudes. **—honest** *adj.*

honesty test see INTEGRITY TESTING.

ho'oponopono *n.* in Hawaiian culture, a type of group process, similar to family therapy, in which the 'OHANA or a similar group addresses its personal and family problems in order to restore harmony within the group.

Hoover's sign a diagnostic test for neurological (as distinct from psychological) hemiplegia in which the individual in a reclining position attempts to raise the paralyzed leg: An individual with true hemiplegia reflexively presses down the heel of the healthy leg during the test. The absence of the downward movement is a positive Hoover's sign and suggests psychogenic PARESIS or malingering. [Charles Franklin **Hoover** (1865–1927), U.S. physician]

hope *n.* an emotion characterized by the expectation that one will have positive experiences (or that a potentially threatening or negative situation will not materialize or will ultimately result in a favorable state of affairs) and by the belief that one can influence one's experiences in a positive way. See also OPTIMISM.

hopelessness *n.* the feeling that one will not experience positive emotions or an improvement in one's condition. Hopelessness is common in severe MAJOR DEPRESSIVE EPISODES and other DEPRESSIVE DISORDERS and is often implicated in attempted and completed suicides. **—hopeless** *adj.*

Hopkins Symptom Checklist (**HSCL**) a 58-item self-report inventory designed to identify symptom patterns along five dimensions that yield a total distress score: obsessive-compulsive behavior, anxiety, depression, somatization, and interpersonal sensitivity. Developed at Johns Hopkins University in the 1970s, the HSCL provided a much-needed standard for self-report measurement of psychological distress and, ultimately, provided a sound foundation for the development of more comprehensive and sophisticated outcome measures that followed. See also SYMPTOM CHECKLIST-90-R.

Hopkins Verbal Learning Test (**HVLT**) a standardized brief INDIVIDUAL TEST used to assess verbal learning and memory (specifically, immediate recall, delayed recall, and delayed recognition) in individuals aged 16 years and over. The examiner reads aloud 12 nouns, and participants must first repeat them (both immediately and 25 min following their presentation) and then identify them from among a verbally presented list of DISTRACTOR words. Originally published in 1991, the HVLT subsequently was revised in 2001 (**HVLT–R**). [developed by U.S. medical psychologist Jason Brandt (1954–) and U.S. clinical psychologist Ralph H. B. Benedict (1960–) at Johns Hopkins University, Baltimore]

horde *n.* a large, usually mobile group, particularly a nomadic CLAN.

horizontal career move a career move involving a change in functional area or expertise but not a promotion to a higher level of authority.

horizontal cells see RETINAL HORIZONTAL CELLS.

horizontal communication the exchange of messages, written or spoken, among employees occupying positions at the same level of authority in the organization. Compare DOWNWARD COMMUNICATION; UPWARD COMMUNICATION.

horizontal décalage in Jean PIAGET's theory of cognitive development, the invariant order in which accomplishments occur within a particular stage of development. For example, an understanding of CONSERVATION of quantity is always achieved before understanding conservation of weight, which is achieved before understanding conservation of volume. Compare VERTICAL DÉCALAGE.

horizontal group a group composed of people from the same SOCIAL CLASS. Compare VERTICAL GROUP.

horizontal job enlargement see JOB ENLARGEMENT.

horizontal loading see JOB ENLARGEMENT.

horizontal mobility the movement of individuals or groups from one position or role to another within the same SOCIAL CLASS. Compare VERTICAL MOBILITY. See also GEOGRAPHICAL MOBILITY; MOBILITY; SOCIAL MOBILITY.

horizontal plane the plane that divides the body or brain into upper and lower parts. Also called **transverse plane**.

horizontal section 1. in imaging, a theoretical "slice" of a body or an organ (e.g., the brain) in a plane perpendicular to the dorsal–ventral axis. **2.** a thin slice of tissue for microscopic study that has been cut at an angle perpendicular to the dorsal–ventral axis of the organ. See SECTION.

horizontal transmission host-to-host transmission of infection, as contrasted with **vertical** (or **transplacental**) **transmission**, in which the infection is passed from one generation to the next.

horizontal–vertical illusion the misperception that vertical lines are longer than horizontal lines when both are actually the same length. The vertical element of an upper case letter T looks longer than the cross bar, even when the lengths are identical.

hormic psychology a school of psychology, originating in the 1920s, that emphasizes goal seeking, striving, and foresight, with the instincts serving as the primary motivation for behavior. It is particularly concerned with explaining social psychological phenomena in terms of INSTINCTIVE BEHAVIOR. See also PURPOSIVE PSYCHOLOGY; SOCIOBIOLOGY; TELEOLOGY. [introduced by British-born U.S. psychologist William McDougall (1871–1938)]

hormone *n.* a substance secreted into the bloodstream by an ENDOCRINE GLAND or other tissue or organ to regulate processes in distant target organs and tissues. These secretions include the posterior and ANTERIOR PITUITARY HORMONES (see PITUITARY GLAND); the CORTICOSTEROIDS and EPINEPHRINE, secreted by the adrenal glands; and the SEX HORMONES released by the reproductive glands. Other organs that secrete hormones include the hypothalamus (see HYPOTHALAMIC HORMONE) and the stomach, which secretes at least five: CHOLECYSTOKININ, ENTEROGASTRONE, GASTRIN, GHRELIN, and SECRETIN. **—hormonal** *adj.*

hormone feedback a FEEDBACK SYSTEM in which the output of hormones is regulated by other, circulating hormones, which have positive or negative feedback effects. During the follicular phase of the MENSTRUAL CYCLE, for example, estrogen has a positive effect on the hypothalamus, increasing the secretion of GONADOTROPIN-RELEASING HORMONE, and hence the secretion of pituitary GONADOTROPINS, which stimulate ovulation.

hormone replacement therapy (**HRT**) **1.** the administration of female sex hormones—usually an estrogen (see ESTROGEN REPLACEMENT THERAPY) or a combined estrogen–progestin preparation—to postmenopausal women to relieve menopausal symptoms. The use of HRT for other purposes is controversial, since long-term use may increase the risk of breast cancer, cardiovascular disease, stroke, and other conditions associated with the aging process. **2.** the administration of any other hormone to treat a hormone deficiency, for example, thyroid hormone to treat hypothyroidism.

Horner effect see FEAR OF SUCCESS. [Matina **Horner** (1939–), U.S. psychologist]

Horner's law the principle that red–green color blindness is a genetic disorder transmitted indirectly from male to male through a female. [Johann Friedrich **Horner** (1831–1886), Swiss ophthalmologist]

Horner's syndrome a condition characterized by partial ptosis (drooping of the upper eyelid), miosis (excessive constriction of the pupil), and often anhidrosis (absence of sweating) on the same half of the face. Congenital or acquired, it is caused by damage to the PONS region of the brainstem. There may be lack of coordination in eye movements (SACCADES and SMOOTH-PURSUIT MOVEMENTS). Also called **oculosympathetic paralysis**. [Johann **Horner**]

horopter *n.* the location in space occupied by points that fall on corresponding locations on the two retinas. See also PANUM'S FUSIONAL AREA; VIETH–MÜLLER CIRCLE.

horoscope *n.* **1.** in ASTROLOGY, a chart showing the relative position of the planets and the signs of the zodiac at the time of a person's birth, used to infer that person's character and to predict his or her future. **2.** a short-term forecast of a person's future based on the current position of the planets relative to his or her sign of the zodiac, especially as published in newspapers and magazines.

horseradish peroxidase (**HRP**) an enzyme found in horseradish and other plants that is used as a tracer, for example, to determine the neurons from which a particular set of axons originates.

horseshoe crab a marine arthropod with very large COMPOUND EYES useful for experimental investigations of the physiology of vision because their neurons are large and activity is easily recorded. Also called **limulus**.

horticultural therapy the use of gardening as an auxiliary intervention for therapeutic or rehabilitational purposes. It is typically used for individuals with physical or mental illness or disability but may also be used to improve the social, educational, psychological, and physical well-being of older adults as well as those recovering from injury. Also called **horticulture therapy**.

HOS abbreviation for Health Opinion Survey (see KRANTZ HEALTH OPINION SURVEY).

hospice *n.* a place or form of care for terminally ill individuals, often those with life expectancies of less than a year as determined by medical personnel. Instead of curing disease and prolonging life, the emphases of the hospice concept are patient comfort, psychological well-being, and pain management. Care is provided by medical, volunteer, and family caregivers, either in special facilities or in the patient's home. See also TERMINAL CARE.

hospitalitis *n.* the state of mind of patients who are so dependent psychologically on hospital life that their symptoms suddenly recur when they learn that they are about to be discharged.

hospital phobia a persistent and irrational fear of hospitals. In *DSM–IV–TR*, hospital phobia is classified as a form of SPECIFIC PHOBIA, situational type.

hostage negotiation the techniques used to bring about the safe release of hostages.

hostile aggression see AGGRESSION.

hostile–detached marriage an unstable marriage in which there are short but hostile disagreements between the partners.

hostile–engaged marriage an unstable marriage in which the partners have long and frequent arguments without the balance of love and humor found in long-lasting VOLATILE MARRIAGES.

hostile witness an individual who is either unwilling to testify in court or exhibits hostility or bias against the party conducting the direct examination. If the court recognizes a person to be a hostile witness, the counsel conducting the examination is permitted to ask leading questions. See also ADVERSE WITNESS.

hostile work environment a situation in which the workplace is made intimidating, abusive, or offensive to an employee as a consequence of another's conduct within it (e.g., inappropriate comments, remarks, or gestures, unwanted sexual attention) or characteristics of the setting (e.g., displays of distasteful, insulting, or otherwise inappropriate material). See also MERITOR SAVINGS BANK V. VINSON; QUID PRO QUO; SEXUAL HARASSMENT.

hostility *n.* the expression of unfriendliness or antagonism in action, feeling, or attitude. **—hostile** *adj.*

hostility displacement the direction of hostility or aggression to a target (sometimes called a scapegoat) other than the agent responsible for provoking this behavior. The causes are complex. Conventional accounts typically state that the target is selected because there is no anticipation of punishment for the attack. According to the classic analysis of Neal MILLER, the strength of the urge to displace hostility is related to the target's association with the perceived source of provocation. It has also been suggested that the selected target may have an association with prior victims of aggression. See SCAPEGOAT THEORY.

hot cognition an enlightened comprehension of the self, others, and events that engenders strong emotional reactions. See also ABREACTION.

Hotelling's T² a statistical technique used in MULTIVARIATE ANALYSIS for testing the equality of two populations with regard to their mean VECTORS. It is the multivariate generalization of the two-group T TEST. [Harold **Hotelling** (1895–1973), U.S. economist and statistician]

hot flash a typical menopausal symptom, caused by decreased levels of estrogen, experienced as a sudden rush of heat to the neck, face, and possibly other parts of the body that may last from 30 s to 5 min. It may begin with a sudden tingling in the fingers, toes, cheeks, or ears, and in some women it is followed by a sensation of cold. Fifty percent of women experience hot flashes around the time of menopause.

hothousing *n.* the acceleration of young children's academic skills through instruction designed to increase academic achievement. Some theorists believe that hothousing is equivalent to hurrying children and that it is therefore maladaptive to normal development.

hotline *n.* a telephone line maintained by trained personnel for the purpose of providing a crisis intervention service. See TELEPHONE COUNSELING.

hot plate an apparatus used in studies of heat or pain sensitivity. A nonhuman animal (usually a rat or a mouse) is placed on top of an electrically heated plate, the temperature of which is controlled by the experimenter. The time that elapses before the animal raises its front paws off the plate at a given temperature is used as an index of sensitivity to heat or pain.

hot-seat technique a technique of GESTALT THERAPY in which a client sits in a chair next to the therapist, who encourages the client through direct prompting and questioning to relive stressful experiences and openly express feelings of discomfort, guilt, or resentment. The technique aims to generate a new, more vivid awareness, which leads the client to find his or her own solutions to problems or emotional difficulties. In a GROUP PSYCHOTHERAPY variation of the hot-seat technique, an individual member expresses to the therapist his or her interest in dealing with a particular issue, and the focus moves away from the group into an extended interaction between the group member and group leader for a limited period of time. During the one-on-one interaction, the other group members remain silent; afterward, they give feedback on how they were affected, what they observed, and how their own experiences are similar to those on which the individual member worked. Compare EMPTY-CHAIR TECHNIQUE.

Hottentot apron an overgrowth of the labia minora, so named because it is commonly seen in members of the Khoikhoi of southern Africa, formerly known as Hottentots.

houselight *n.* a small light bulb or bulbs used to provide continuous low-level illumination of a CONDITIONING APPARATUS.

Hovland model see MESSAGE-LEARNING APPROACH.

HPA abbreviation for HYPERPHENYLALANINEMIA.

HPA system abbreviation for HYPOTHALAMIC–PITUTARY–ADRENOCORTICAL SYSTEM.

HRNB abbreviation for HALSTEAD–REITAN NEUROPSYCHOLOGICAL BATTERY.

HRP abbreviation for HORSERADISH PEROXIDASE.

H–R–R plates abbreviation for HARDY–RAND–RITTLER PSEUDOISOCHROMATIC PLATES.

HRSD abbreviation for HAMILTON RATING SCALE FOR DEPRESSION.

HRT abbreviation for HORMONE REPLACEMENT THERAPY.

HRTF abbreviation for HEAD-RELATED TRANSFER FUNCTION.

HSCL abbreviation for HOPKINS SYMPTOM CHECKLIST.

HSD abbreviation for honestly significant difference. See TUKEY'S HONESTLY SIGNIFICANT DIFFERENCE TEST.

hsieh-ping *n.* a CULTURE-BOUND SYNDROME observed in China and Taiwan, characterized by temporary trancelike states in which the individual supposedly becomes possessed by ancestral spirits. It is often accompanied by tremors, DISORIENTATION, DELIRIUM, and visual or auditory hallucinations.

HSM abbreviation for HEURISTIC-SYSTEMATIC MODEL.

5-HT abbreviation for 5-hydroxytryptamine (see SEROTONIN).

hubris *n.* arrogant pride or presumption. In Greek tragedy, hubris is specifically the overweening pride that leads to the destruction of the protagonist. —**hubristic** *adj.*

HUD abbreviation for HEAD-UP DISPLAY.

hue *n.* the subjective quality of color, which is determined primarily by wavelength and secondarily by amplitude.

Hull, Clark Leonard (1884–1952) U.S. psychologist. Hull earned his doctorate in 1918 at the University of Wisconsin under Joseph Jastrow (1863–1944). He was the originator of the influential DRIVE-REDUCTION THEORY, which states that all behavior, including conditioning and learning, is initiated by needs and directed to need reduction. Activities that reduce need reinforce specific responses called habits; for example, when a hungry rat obtains food by inadvertently pushing a lever, it learns to repeat that response. Hull's most important work was his widely cited *Principles of Behavior: An Introduction to Behavior Theory* (1943). Together with B. F. SKINNER and Edward Chace TOLMAN, he is considered one of the founders of NEOBEHAVIORISM. He spent the bulk of his career at Yale University, where he was mentor to numerous graduate students who became prominent psychologists.

Hull's mathematico-deductive theory of learning a mathematical system of learning based on Pavlovian and instrumental conditioning with numerous postulates and corollaries to explain various behaviors. There is major emphasis on NEED REDUCTION as a condition of learning, the building up of HABIT STRENGTH by contiguous reinforcement, EXTINCTION brought about by nonreinforced repetition of responses, and forgetting as a process of decay with the passage of time. [Clark L. HULL]

human channel capacity the limit on the amount of information that may be processed simultaneously by the human information-processing system.

human chorionic gonadotropin a hormone, produced by the human placenta, that maintains the activity of the CORPUS LUTEUM during pregnancy. Its presence or absence in the urine is used as a basis for pregnancy testing. See also GONADOTROPIN.

human courtship the process by which couples develop mutual commitment, traditionally having marriage as its goal. Patterns and norms of courtship vary greatly between cultures. See COURTSHIP BEHAVIOR.

human ecology in sociology, the study of the relationship between human beings and their physical and social environments. See ECOLOGY. See also ECOLOGICAL STUDIES; ECOLOGICAL SYSTEMS THEORY; SOCIAL ECOLOGY; URBAN ECOLOGY.

human engineering the design of environments and equipment that promote optimum use of human capabilities and optimum safety, efficiency, and comfort. See also ENGINEERING PSYCHOLOGY; HUMAN FACTORS ENGINEERING.

human error an error in the operation of a HUMAN–MACHINE SYSTEM resulting from human action or inaction (see ERROR OF COMMISSION; ERROR OF OMISSION), as opposed to mechanical failures or faults in product or system design. Although human error can never be entirely eradicated, good design will minimize both its occurrence and its consequences (see EXCLUSION DESIGN; FAIL-SAFE).

human factors **1.** in ERGONOMICS, the impact of human beings, with their characteristic needs, abilities, and limitations, on system function. **2.** the considerations to be made when designing, evaluating, or optimizing systems for human use, especially with regard to safety, efficiency, and comfort. **3.** particularly in the United States, a common synonym of ERGONOMICS.

human factors engineering an interdisciplinary field concerned with the design, maintenance, operation, and improvement of operating systems in which human beings are components, such as industrial equipment, automobiles, health care systems, transportation systems, recreational facilities, consumer products, and the general living environment. This term is often used synonymously with ERGONOMICS. See also ENGINEERING ANTHROPOMETRY; ENGINEERING PSYCHOLOGY; HUMAN ENGINEERING; SYSTEMS ENGINEERING.

human factors psychology a branch of psychology that studies the role of HUMAN FACTORS in operating systems, with the aim of redesigning environments, equipment, and processes to fit human abilities and characteristics. This term is often used synonymously with ENGINEERING PSYCHOLOGY. See HUMAN ENGINEERING. See also ERGONOMICS; SOCIOTECHNICAL SYSTEMS APPROACH.

Human Genome Project an international project to map each human gene and determine the complete sequence of base pairs in human DNA. The project began in 1990 and was completed in 2003. It has yielded vast amounts of valuable information about the genes responsible for various diseases, which may lead to the development of effective genetic screening tests and, possibly, treatments. However, controversy surrounds the attempts by some biotechnology companies to patent certain human DNA sequences with the potential for commercial exploitation. See also ELSI PROGRAM.

human-growth movement see HUMAN-POTENTIAL MOVEMENT.

human immunodeficiency virus see HIV.

human information storage the process in which the mind, which is conceived as being analogous to a computer, codes external information into a form that can be remembered, manipulated, and retrieved.

humanism *n.* **1.** a perspective that begins with a presumption of the inherent dignity and worth of humankind and, as a scholarly or artistic discipline, focuses attention on the study and representation of human beings and human experiences. The roots of Western humanism lie in the Renaissance period, when those who studied the classical Greek and Roman languages and writings became known as humanists. **2.** any position taken in opposition to religious belief or other forms of supernaturalism. See SECULAR HUMANISM. **3.** in psychology, any perspective that seeks to uphold human values and to resist the reduction of human beings and behaviors to merely natural objects and events. In this spirit, HUMANISTIC PSYCHOLOGIES have resisted not only natural scientific psychology, but also theories that emphasize the negative and pathological aspects of human nature. In contemporary psychology, the term humanism is often applied to theories and perspectives in the tradition of Carl ROGERS and Abraham MASLOW or to those inspired by PHENOMENOLOGY and EXISTENTIALISM. **—humanist** *adj., n.* **—humanistic** *adj.*

humanistic communitarian socialism an ideal political system proposed by Erich FROMM in which humane values would underlie the socioeconomic structure. The goal of humanistic communitarian socialism is a nonexploitative society, composed of small communities rather than large governmental or corporate entities, in which all members develop to their maximum ability, are self-regulating, and contribute fully as individuals and citizens.

humanistic conscience the type of conscience that is guided by individual standards and not by fear of external authority. Compare AUTHORITARIAN CONSCIENCE. [defined by Erich FROMM]

humanistic–existential therapy see EXISTENTIAL–HUMANISTIC THERAPY.

humanistic perspective the assumption in psychology that people are essentially good and constructive, that the tendency to self-actualize is inherent, and that, given the proper environment, human beings will develop to their maximum potential. The humanistic perspective arose from the contributions of Gordon ALLPORT, Abraham MASLOW, and Carl ROGERS, who advocated a personality theory based on the study of healthy individuals as opposed to people with mental disorders. See HUMANISM; SELF-ACTUALIZATION.

humanistic psychology an approach to psychology that flourished particularly in academia between the 1940s and the early 1970s and that is most visible today as a family of widely used approaches to psychotherapy and counseling. It derives largely from ideas associated with EXISTENTIALISM and PHENOMENOLOGY and focuses on individuals' capacity to make their own choices, create their own style of life, and actualize themselves in their own way. Its approach is holistic, and its emphasis is on the development of human potential through experiential means rather than analysis of the unconscious or behavior modification. Leading figures associated with this approach include Abraham MASLOW, Carl ROGERS, and Rollo MAY. Also called **humanistic theory**. See also FULFILLMENT MODEL; HUMAN-POTENTIAL MOVEMENT.

humanistic therapy any of a variety of psychotherapeutic approaches that reject psychoanalytic and behavioral approaches; seek to foster personal growth through direct experience; and focus on the development of human potential, the HERE AND NOW, concrete personality change, responsibility for oneself, and trust in natural processes and spontaneous feeling. Some examples of humanistic therapy are CLIENT-CENTERED THERAPY, GESTALT THERAPY, EXISTENTIAL PSYCHOTHERAPY, and EXPERIENTIAL PSYCHOTHERAPY.

humanity *n.* compassion in one's personal relations with specific others, shown by kindness, nurturance, charity, and love.

human–machine system in ergonomics, any system with interdependencies between human operators, machines, and processes. Also called **man–machine system**; **person–machine system**.

human menopausal gonadotropin (hMG) a mixture of FOLLICLE-STIMULATING HORMONE and LUTEINIZING HORMONE extracted from the urine of postmenopausal women for stimulating ovulation, either in women undergoing assisted conception or as a treatment for infertility due to deficiency of pituitary GONADOTROPINS. In postmenopausal women the concentrations of these gonadotropins are high in response to decreased output of estrogens at menopause.

human nature the generally innate but flexible characteristics of humankind as a whole, comprising the set of behaviors, attitudes, and dispositions that typify the human race. The concept of human nature has been rejected by several schools of modern thought, notably MARXISM, FEMINISM, and POSTMODERNISM. See also ESSENTIALISM; UNIVERSALISM.

human operator modeling the practice of using qualitative or quantitative tools to illustrate the behavior, mental processes, or both of human operators when performing tasks. The use of physical or computer models for this purpose is known as **human operator simulation**. Physical simulations involve the use of robotic or remote-controlled operators in actual or realistic task environments. Computer simulations use a variety of parameters to test different scenarios and explore outcomes. Human operator modeling is used to describe, explain, or predict behavior under a variety of task and environmental conditions. See also MODEL HUMAN PROCESSOR.

human-potential model a psychological approach in education that emphasizes the importance of helping learners to achieve the maximum development of their potential in all aspects of their functioning. It is derived from the basic tenets of HUMANISTIC PSYCHOLOGY. See also HUMANISTIC PERSPECTIVE.

human-potential movement an approach to psychotherapy and psychology based on the quest for personal growth, development, interpersonal sensitivity, and greater freedom and spontaneity in living. The ideas of German-born U.S. psychiatrist Frederick (Fritz) S. Perls (1893–1970) were an influential force in the development of the human-potential movement, which derives its general perspective from HUMANISTIC PSYCHOLOGY. GESTALT THERAPY, SENSITIVITY TRAINING, and ENCOUNTER GROUPS are representative of this approach. Also called **human-growth movement**.

human relations see INTERPERSONAL RELATIONS.

human relations theory a general approach to management that emphasizes the importance of employee attitudes, interpersonal relationships, GROUP DYNAMICS, and LEADERSHIP STYLES in achieving ORGANIZATIONAL EFFECTIVENESS. In human relations theory, considerate, participative leaders who are skilled in communicating with employees are held to achieve better results than authoritarian leaders. See HAWTHORNE EFFECT.

human relations training techniques designed to promote awareness in an individual of the feelings and needs of others and to promote constructive interactions. See also SENSITIVITY TRAINING; T-GROUP.

human resources 1. the individuals and groups whose KNOWLEDGE, SKILLS, ABILITIES, AND OTHER CHARACTERISTICS enable an organization to achieve its objectives. **2.** the department of an organization concerned with recruiting, training, and appraising employees and with any issues relating to their welfare. Also called **personnel**.

human service delivery system a complex, interrelated set of services aimed at providing physical and mental health programs.

human strength see CHARACTER STRENGTH.

human–system coupling in ergonomics, the extent to which operator and system are interdependent. A highly automated system requires a lower degree of coupling than a manual system.

human–vehicle interface the junction between the human operator and the functions of a vehicle. It includes all components of the control panel.

humidity effects the effects of the amount of moisture in the air on one's perception of ambient temperature. High humidity makes hot weather uncomfortable because it diminishes the cooling efficiency of air movement to evaporate heat from the body.

humiliation *n.* a feeling of shame due to being disgraced or deprecated. The feeling sometimes leads to severe depression and deterioration of the individual's sense of SELF-ESTEEM. Humiliation of the partner is frequently found in sexual sadism and sexual masochism.

humility *n.* the quality of being humble, characterized by a low focus on the self, an accurate (not over- or underestimated) sense of one's accomplishments and worth, and an acknowledgment of one's limitations, imperfections, mistakes, gaps in knowledge, and so on.

humor *n.* **1.** the capacity to perceive or express the amusing aspects of a situation. There is little agreement about the essence of humor and the reasons one laughs or smiles at jokes or anecdotes. Among philosophers, both Plato (c. 427–c. 347 BCE) and Thomas Hobbes (1588–1679) claimed that individuals laugh at people and situations that make them feel superior, whereas Immanuel Kant (1724–1804) emphasized surprise and anticlimax: "the sudden transformation of a strained expectation to nothing." U.S. writer Max Eastman (1883–1969) saw humor as "playful pain," a way of taking serious things lightly and thereby triumphing over them. Sigmund FREUD called attention to the many jokes (especially those having to do with sex and hostility) that enable individuals to give free expression to forbidden impulses and explained laughter in terms of a release of the energy normally employed in keeping them out of consciousness. See also INCONGRUITY THEORY OF HUMOR; RELEASE THEORY OF HUMOR. **2.** the semifluid substance that occupies the spaces in the eyeball. See AQUEOUS HUMOR; VITREOUS HUMOR. **3.** anciently, one of four bodily fluids (blood, black bile, yellow bile, and phlegm) that were thought to be responsible for a person's physical and psychological characteristics (see HUMORAL THEORY). This belief accounts for the use of the word "humor" to mean "mood," as in *good humor*, or "whim," as in *It is her humor*. **—humoral** *adj.* **—humorous** *adj.*

humoral immunity see IMMUNE RESPONSE.

humoral reflex a REFLEX that involves secretion of a hormone.

humoral theory a former theory that explained physical and psychological health or illness in terms of the state of balance or imbalance of various bodily fluids. According to Greek physician Hippocrates (5th century BCE), health was a function of the proper balance of four humors: blood, black bile, yellow bile, and phlegm (the **classical humors** or **cardinal humors**). This idea was also used to explain temperament: A predominance of blood was associated with a SANGUINE TYPE; black bile with a MELANCHOLIC TYPE; yellow bile or choler with a CHOLERIC TYPE; and phlegm with a PHLEGMATIC TYPE. Roman physician Galen (129–199) did much to preserve and promulgate this explanatory approach, which survived well into the 17th century. Humoral theory provides psychology with its earliest personality typology, as well as an early model of the relation between bodily and psychological states.

hunger center see FEEDING CENTER.

hunger drive a DRIVE or arousal state induced by food deprivation, precipitating food-seeking behavior. See also SPECIFIC HUNGER.

hunger strike a refusal to eat for an extended period of time as a method of social or political protest.

Hunter's syndrome an X-linked recessive disease, the most common MUCOPOLYSACCHARIDOSIS. As in HURLER'S SYNDROME, there is an excess of mucopolysaccharides in the tissues. The child shows normal development until the 2nd year and may learn some words and sentences and achieve toilet training. Hyperkinetic behavior and a clumsy gait develop after the age of 2; physical activity slows down around the age of 5. Mental retardation appears in the 2nd year. Also called **mucopolysaccharidosis Type II**. [Charles **Hunter** (1872–1955), U.S. physician]

hunting behavior the pursuit of other animals for food or sport. Hunting behavior may include other forms of behavior, such as stalking, running after moving objects, or use of concealment or camouflage. In chimpanzees and social carnivores (e.g., wolves and lions) there is evidence of cooperative hunting behavior, which appears to be coordinated among several individuals.

Huntington's disease (**HD**) a progressive hereditary disease characterized by degeneration of nerve cells in the brain, marked personality changes, affective disorders, DEMENTIA, involuntary jerking motions (see CHOREA), motor incoordination, and disorders of gait and posture. Brain imaging reveals atrophy of the CAUDATE NUCLEUS and PUTAMEN and general loss of cerebral neurons. The age of onset is usually between 30 and 50, but there is a juvenile form of the disease in which symptoms first appear before the age of 20. Huntington's disease is inherited as an AUTOSOMAL DOMINANT trait; the single gene responsible is located on chromosome 4. Also called **Huntington's chorea**. [George **Huntington** (1850–1916), U.S. physician]

Hurler's syndrome an autosomal recessive disease marked by mucopolysaccharide levels in tissues more than 10 times normal (see MUCOPOLYSACCHARIDOSIS), combined with elevated levels of polysaccharides and GARGOYLISM. Mental development begins normally but slows after the early months and reaches a plateau around 2 years of age. The child may learn a few words, but not sentences, and toilet training is seldom achieved. Also called **Pfaundler–Hurler syndrome**; **mucopolysaccharidosis Type I**. [Gertrud **Hurler** (1889–1965), Austrian pediatrician]

HVA abbreviation for HOMOVANILLIC ACID.

HVLT abbreviation for HOPKINS VERBAL LEARNING TEST.

hwa-byung *n.* a CULTURE-BOUND SYNDROME specific to Korea and characterized by a range of symptoms that are attributed to the suppression of anger (Korean, literally "anger disease"). Symptoms include a feeling of a mass in the throat, chest, or abdomen, a sensation of heat in the body, headaches, palpitations, indigestion, insomnia, fatigue, panic, dysphoria, fear of impending death, anorexia, generalized aches and pains, and poor concentration. Also called **suppressed anger syndrome**; **wool-hwa-byung**.

hyaline membrane disease see RESPIRATORY DISTRESS SYNDROME.

hyalophagia *n.* the eating of glass, typically a symptom of PICA.

hybrid *n.* **1.** in genetics, the product of crossbreeding genetically dissimilar plants or animals. See HYBRIDIZATION. **2.** in molecular biology, a double helix formed of NUCLEIC ACIDS from different sources.

hybridization *n.* the interbreeding of individuals with different genetic traits. Depending on the nature of the genes involved, HYBRIDS might display traits of one or the other parent or some combination of parental traits. Hybridization is used in animal behavior studies as a method to evaluate genetic transmission of behavior. **—hybridize** *vb.*

hybrid vigor increased vigor or other favorable qualities arising from crossbreeding genetically different plants or animals. Also called **heterosis**.

hybristophilia *n.* sexual interest in and attraction to those who commit crimes. In some cases, this may be directed toward people in prison for various types of criminal activities.

hydantoins *pl. n.* a group of drugs developed primarily to control epileptic seizures. They were introduced in 1938 after careful studies of chemicals capable of suppressing electroshock convulsions without also causing adverse effects on the central nervous system. Hydantoin molecules are similar in structure to barbiturates but have the advantage of not altering the threshold for minimal seizures. The prototype of the hydantoins is PHENYTOIN (previously called diphenylhydantoin). Other hydantoins include **mephenytoin** (U.S. trade name: Mesantoin) and **ethotoin** (U.S. trade name: Peganone), but these are rarely used.

hydration *n.* the act or process of accumulating or combining with water. For example, hydration occurs in body cells when sodium intake increases. Compare DEHYDRATION.

hydraulic model any physiological or psychological model based on the analogy of fluid flowing through a system under pressure, such that pressure may build up in the system and seek release. Sigmund FREUD's model of the LIBIDO as an energy that can build pressure and seek release (CATHARSIS) is a notable example. A more literal use of the hydraulic model was the erroneous concept of the nervous system introduced in the early 17th century by French philosopher René Descartes (1596–1650), who believed that nerves were tubes through which ANIMAL SPIRITS flowed from the brain to the muscles. According to this model, habits were formed when repeated use of the nerve tubes caused them to become distended and blocked.

hydro- (**hydr-**) *combining form* water or fluid.

hydrocephalus *n.* a condition caused by excessive accumulation of cerebrospinal fluid in the ventricles of the brain, resulting in raised INTRACRANIAL PRESSURE, with such symptoms as headache, vomiting, nausea, poor coordination, gait imbalance, urinary incontinence, slowing or loss of development, lethargy, drowsiness, or irritability or other changes in personality or cognition, including memory loss. Hydrocephalus commonly occurs due to obstruction of cerebrospinal fluid from head injury, brain tumor, or hemorrhage. The pressure can sometimes be relieved by surgery, in which the excess fluid is shunted into the bloodstream. In infants, hydrocephalus often produces enlargement of the skull. Also called **hydrocephaly**. **—hydrocephalic** *adj.*

hydrocodone *n.* a mild to moderately potent, orally administered OPIOID ANALGESIC used in the treatment of moderate to moderately severe pain. It is more effective when combined with ACETAMINOPHEN or an NSAID (e.g., aspirin) and is generally marketed in combination with such agents. It is also often marketed in combination with a cough suppressant for the symptomatic relief of cough due to colds or nasal congestion. U.S. trade names (among others): **Detussin** (in combination with pseudephedrine); **Vicadin** (in combination with acetaminophen).

hydrocortisone *n.* see CORTISOL.

hydrogen-ion concentration a measure of the **acidity** or **alkalinity** of a substance. When acid and alkaline substances dissociate in water, hydrogen ions (H^+) and hydroxyl ions (OH^-) are released. Acidity or alkalinity is associated with an excess of one or the other kind of ion. The hydrogen-ion concentration can be measured on the **pH scale**, on which values represent the negative logarithm of the H^+ ion concentration: Thus the greater the excess of H^+ ions, the lower the pH value. A pH of 0 represents the greatest possible excess of H^+ ions, or a "pure" acid. At the other extreme, a pH of 14 represents the maximum degree of alkalinity. A pH of 7 represents a neutral solution. Human body fluids have an average pH of about 7.4, that is, slightly alkaline. If the pH rises above 7.8 or falls below 6.8, enzymes and other biochemical substances in the body malfunction (see ACIDOSIS; ALKALOSIS). See also HOMEOSTASIS.

hydrophobia *n.* **1.** a persistent and irrational fear of water. **2.** see RABIES. **—hydrophobic** *adj.*

hydrotherapy *n.* the use of water, internally or externally, to treat illness, injury, or some other condition or to promote a sense of well-being. Hydrotherapy includes such treatments as BATH THERAPY, hygienic douches, and aquatic sports or exercise for auxiliary therapy and physical rehabilitation. At one time, it was also used as a psychiatric treatment to calm delirious or agitated patients, in the form of **wet packs** (wet sheets wrapped around the patient's body) and **continuous bath treatment** (in which patients were placed in a continuously flowing tub of warm water kept at body temperature).

6-hydroxydopamine (6-OHDA) *n.* a dopamine analog used in nonhuman animal studies for its ability to destroy catecholamine-containing nerve cell bodies. 6-OHDA does not cross the blood–brain barrier, but when administered into the central nervous system it causes permanent degeneration of catecholamine-containing neurons. Destruction of dopamine-containing neurons in the NIGROSTRIATAL TRACT with 6-OHDA results in symptoms that clinically resemble Parkinson's disease.

5-hydroxyindoleacetic acid (5-HIAA) the main metabolic product of SEROTONIN. Some individuals with depression have low levels of 5-HIAA in the cerebrospinal fluid and exhibit a preferential response to CLOMIPRAMINE.

5-hydroxytryptamine (5-HT) *n.* see SEROTONIN.

5-hydroxytryptophan (5-HTP) *n.* a naturally occurring precursor of the neurotransmitter SEROTONIN. It is produced from the essential amino acid tryptophan (see TRYPTOPHAN HYDROXYLASE) and is converted in the brain to 5-hydroxytryptamine, or serotonin. Administration of 5-HTP increases the production of serotonin in the brain, and the agent is being investigated for potential use in the treatment of certain forms of MYOCLONUS (severe muscle spasms). 5-HTP is currently available as a dietary supplement for the relief of (among other conditions) headache, depression, fibromyalgia, and CEREBELLAR ATAXIA (causing difficulty in standing and walking) and for appetite suppression. However, reports of a serious, potentially fatal reaction (eosinophilia-myalgia syndrome) have led to cautions regarding its use as a natural remedy.

hydroxyzine *n.* a sedating antihistamine of the DIPHENYLMETHANE class. It is used for the relief of pre- and postoperative pain, obstetric pain, anxiety, dermatitis, and emesis (vomiting). Although also appropriate for the management of alcohol withdrawal, it is rarely used for this purpose in modern clinical practice. Hydroxyzine has significant ANTICHOLINERGIC EFFECTS. U.S. trade names: **Atarax**; **Vistaril**.

hygiene *n.* **1.** the science of health and how to maintain it. **2.** a condition or practice that promotes cleanliness and good health. **—hygienic** *adj.* **—hygienist** *n.*

hygiene factors in the two-factor theory of WORK MOTIVATION proposed by U.S. clinical psychologist Frederick Herzberg (1923–2000), certain aspects of the working situation that can produce discontent if they are poor or lacking but that cannot by themselves motivate employees to improve their job performance. These include pay, relations with peers and supervisors, working conditions, and benefits. Compare MOTIVATORS.

hylozoism *n.* the view that all material objects have some degree or quality of life. Some equate this view with PANPSYCHISM, which holds that all matter possesses some attributes of psyche. Others make the distinction that to possess the quality of life is not necessarily to be possessed of soul or sentience.

hymen *n.* a thin membrane that normally partly covers the opening to the vagina at birth. Although the hymen is sometimes not broken until the first experience of sexual intercourse, it normally ruptures at or before puberty; thus its absence is not a reliable sign of loss of virginity. **—hymenal** *adj.*

hyoscine *n.* see SCOPOLAMINE.

hyp- *combining form* see HYPO-.

hypacusia *n.* see HYPOACUSIA.

hypalgesia *n.* see HYPOALGESIA.

hyper- *prefix* **1.** above or beyond (e.g., HYPERCOLUMN). **2.** extreme or excessive (e.g., HYPERESTHESIA).

hyperactive child syndrome an old name for ATTENTION-DEFICIT/HYPERACTIVITY DISORDER.

hyperactivity *n.* a condition characterized by spontaneous gross motor activity or restlessness that is excessive for the age of the individual. Although a prominent feature of ATTENTION-DEFICIT/HYPERACTIVITY DISORDER, it is not diagnostic of any particular entity and must be correlated with other findings to identify the appropriate diagnosis. See also DEVELOPMENTAL HYPERACTIVITY; PURPOSELESS HYPERACTIVITY. **—hyperactive** *adj.*

hyperacusis *n.* unusually acute hearing and a lowered tolerance for loud sounds. Also called **hyperacusia**.

hyperadrenal constitution a body and personality type associated with overactivity of the adrenal gland. It is characterized by muscular strength and development, hyperglycemia, a tendency toward hypertension, and a personality marked by euphoria and by moral and intellectual energy.

hyperaggressivity *n.* an increased tendency to express anger and hostility in action, as in violent and assaultive behavior. See also EXPLOSIVE PERSONALITY.

hyperalgesia *n.* an abnormal sensitivity to pain. The effect occasionally results from development of new nerve endings in skin areas that have been severely injured. Also called **hyperalgia**.

hyperbulimia *n.* inordinate appetite and excessive intake of food. It is observed, for example, in certain psychological disorders and in patients with hypothalamic lesions. See also BULIMIA; HYPERPHAGIA. **—hyperbulimic** *adj.*

hypercalcemia syndrome an autosomal dominant hereditary disorder caused by deletion of a segment of chromosome 7 and marked by failure to thrive, high concentrations of calcium in the blood, an elfin facial appearance, and mental retardation. Aortic stenosis (narrowing of the aorta, restricting blood flow from the heart) occurs in most cases. Some affected children have average intelligence, but the majority have IQs between 40 and 70. Most children with this condition are sociable and have superior verbal (compared to nonverbal) skills, many with evidence of the CHATTERBOX EFFECT. Muscular hypotonia (weakness) in infancy occurs in some cases. Also called **elfin facies**; **Williams–Barratt syndrome**; **Williams–Beuren syndrome**; **Williams syndrome**.

hypercathexis *n.* in psychoanalytic theory, an excess of PSYCHIC ENERGY invested in an OBJECT. Compare HYPOCATHEXIS. See CATHEXIS.

hypercholesterolemic xanthomatosis see XANTHOMATOSIS.

hypercolumn *n.* a repeating subdivision of STRIATE CORTEX (primary visual cortex) that contains a full set of ORIENTATION COLUMNS and a pair of OCULAR DOMINANCE COLUMNS. Thus the population of neurons in one hypercolumn includes those responsive to all orientations, as viewed through either eye. A hypercolumn occupies an area of about 1 mm^2 on the cortical surface.

hypercompensatory type a constitutional type characterized by overdevelopment of blood and lymph vessels, digestive tract, and endocrine glands. The hypercompensatory characteristic is expressed in the form of symptoms of paranoid or bipolar reactions.

hypercomplex cell a neuron in the visual cortex for which the optimal stimulus is a moving line of specific length or a moving corner. See also END-STOPPED CELL. [first described in 1965 by U.S. scientist David Hubel (1926–) and Swedish scientist Torsten Wiesel (1924–)]

hypercorrection *n.* in linguistics, the use of an incorrect form or pronunciation in a mistaken belief that this is more formal or correct than the one generally used. Hypercorrection usually arises from false analogy, half-remembered rules learned in childhood, or an exaggerated fear of using nonstandard or lower-class forms. Common examples in English are the use of *whom* rather than *who* in, for example, *Whomever is responsible for this*, and the use of *I* rather than *me* in, for example, *She was referring to you and I.*

hypercritical *adj.* having an excessive tendency to scrutinize and find fault.

hyperemia *n.* the presence of an increased amount of blood in a part of the body. In some parts, this condition causes a flushed appearance. See also BLUSHING.

hyperesthesia *n.* extreme sensitivity in any of the senses, especially abnormal sensitivity to touch. **—hyperesthetic** *adj.*

hyperexcitability *n.* a tendency to overreact to stimuli, often occurring during a MANIC EPISODE. **—hyperexcitable** *adj.*

hyperfunction *n.* excessive activity of a body function, part, or organ.

hypergenitalism *n.* an excessive development of the genital system.

hypergenital type a constitutional type characterized by premature and exaggerated development of sexual characteristics, relatively short extremities, and a large chest and skull. The female hypergenital type also shows extremely sensitive breasts and genitalia and experiences an unusually early menarche. [defined by Italian endocrinologist Nicola Pende (1880–1970)]

hypergeometric distribution a discrete PROBABILITY DISTRIBUTION that is used to model sampling without replacement, a situation when each selection or trial changes the probability of the outcome of the next (see SAMPLING WITH REPLACEMENT).

hypergeusia *n.* a heightened sensitivity to taste. See SUPERTASTER.

hyperglycemia *n.* an excess of glucose in the blood. In DIABETES MELLITUS, hyperglycemia results from a relative or absolute lack of insulin needed to remove the excess glucose from the blood. Signs range from pain or sensory loss to failure of reflexes and coma. **—hyperglycemic** *adj.*

hyper-Graeco-Latin square a GRAECO-LATIN SQUARE on which an orthogonal LATIN SQUARE has been superimposed. Thus a hyper-Graeco-Latin square is to a Graeco-Latin square as a Graeco-Latin square is to a Latin square: One orthogonal dimension has been added.

hyperhedonia *n.* a pathological increase in the feeling of pleasure derived from any act or event. Compare ANHEDONIA; HYPHEDONIA.

hyperhidrosis *n.* excessive sweating, which may occur under various circumstances and is not necessarily related to environmental, physical, or psychological factors. In severe cases, the skin in the affected areas may become macerated and vulnerable to infections. Also called **hyperidrosis**.

hypericin *n.* a psychoactive compound that is thought to be the most pharmacologically active agent in ST. JOHN'S WORT.

hyperingestion *n.* excessive intake of food, fluid, or drugs through the mouth, particularly when intake is greater than the maximum safe level.

hyperkinesis *n.* **1.** excessive muscular activity. **2.** restlessness or HYPERACTIVITY. **—hyperkinetic** *adj.*

hyperkinesthesia *n.* a high level of sensitivity in the SOMATOSENSORY SYSTEM (e.g., to touch, weight, pressure, and motion and position of the body). See also KINESTHESIS; PROPRIOCEPTION. Compare HYPOKINESTHESIA.

hyperkinetic-impulse disorder an old name for ATTENTION-DEFICIT/HYPERACTIVITY DISORDER.

hyperkinetic syndrome an old name for ATTENTION-DEFICIT/HYPERACTIVITY DISORDER.

hyperlexia *n.* the development of extremely good reading skills at a very early age, well ahead of word comprehension or cognitive ability. Children with hyperlexia often start to recognize words without instruction and before any expressive language develops. Hyperlexia is usually found in the context of cognitive and language deficits or certain developmental disorders; some children with AUTISTIC DISORDER, for example, may show hyperlexia. [first defined in 1967 by Norman E. Silberberg and Margaret C. Silberberg] **—hyperlexic** *adj.*

hyperlipidemia *n.* the presence in the blood of excessive amounts of lipids (e.g., cholesterol, triglycerides), which may predispose to atherosclerosis.

hyperlogia *n.* see LOGORRHEA.

hypermania *n.* an extreme manic state marked by constant activity, erratic behavior, DISORIENTATION, and incoherent speech. See also LETHAL CATATONIA. **—hypermanic** *adj.*

hypermetamorphosis *n.* a strong tendency to react excessively or devote an inordinate amount of attention to any visual stimulus.

hypermetria *n.* overreaching an object during voluntary motor activity. This can be caused by impaired visual localization, defective visuomotor coordination, or a disorder in the execution of eye or hand movements. See also DYSMETRIA; OCULAR DYSMETRIA. Compare HYPOMETRIA.

hypermnesia *n.* **1.** remembering more over time rather than less, in contrast to forgetting. See REMINISCENCE. **2.** an extreme degree of retentiveness and recall, with unusual clarity of memory images. In forensic contexts, eyewitnesses have demonstrated increased recall after undergoing hypnotic induction to help retrieve memories, but such memories have been ruled inadmissible in some U.S. courts (see STATE V. MACK). See also CIRCUMSTANTIALITY.

hypermobile testes testes that move between the scrotum and the abdominal cavity, usually because of an inguinal hernia that has not been corrected. The testes may descend into the scrotum when the environment is warm, as when taking a hot bath, but retract into the abdominal cavity when the body is exposed to cold.

hypermotility *n.* abnormally increased or excessive activity in a body function, particularly that of the digestive tract. The cholinergic nervous system dominates the upper portion of the gastrointestinal tract, while the adrenergic system controls the lower portion. Gastrin and serotonin stimulate digestive-tract motility, while secretin and glucagon inhibit contractions. Hypermotility is associated with gastric neuropathy, colitis, and IRRITABLE BOWEL SYNDROME.

hyperobesity *n.* a state of being extremely overweight, sometimes defined as weighing in excess of 45 kg (100 lb) above the accepted ideal body weight for one's height, age, and body build. See also MORBID OBESITY. **—hyperobese** *adj.*

hyperopia *n.* farsightedness. Hyperopia is an ERROR OF REFRACTION due to an abnormally short eyeball, in which the image is blurred because the focal point of one or both eyes lies behind, rather than on, the retina.

hyperorexia *n.* a pathologically increased appetite. See also BULIMIA. Compare HYPOPHAGIA.

hyperosmia *n.* abnormally acute sensitivity to ODORANTS. Compare HYPOSMIA.

hyperphagia *n.* a tendency to overeat, which may be due to a metabolic disorder or to a brain lesion in the AMYGDALA, TEMPORAL LOBE, or VENTROMEDIAL NUCLEUS of the hypothalamus. See also BULIMIA.

hyperphenylalaninemia (**HPA**) *n.* an abnormally high level of phenylalanine metabolites in the blood, which is characteristic of individuals with PHENYLKETONURIA and may be present even after successful dietary management of this disorder. See also MATERNAL PKU.

hyperphilia *n.* sexual arousal by and response to a particular activity or type of stimulus that is above the normal range.

hyperphoria *n.* deviation of one eye in an upward direction. See also PHORIA.

hyperphrasia *n.* see LOGORRHEA.

hyperphrenia *n.* an obsolescent name for a state of increased mental activity combined with concentration difficulty and distractibility, a common pattern in MANIC EPISODES.

hyperpituitary constitution a body and personality type associated with overactivity of the pituitary gland near or after the end of the normal growth period. The physical characteristics resemble those of the ATHLETIC TYPE in KRETSCHMER TYPOLOGY, with a hypervigilant attitude and a tendency to control emotions through intellectualization.

hyperplasia *n.* an abnormal increase in the size of an organ or tissue caused by the growth of an excessive number of new, normal cells. Hyperplasia may be induced by viruses, as in the growth of warts; by drugs (such as phenytoin, which is prescribed for epilepsy patients); or by bodily changes associated with aging, as in benign prostatic hyperplasia. **—hyperplastic** *adj.*

hyperpnea *n.* an abnormal increase in the rate and depth of breathing, which may be deep, labored, and rapid.

hyperpolarization *n.* an increase in MEMBRANE POTENTIAL such that the inner surface of the cell membrane (e.g., of a neuron) becomes more negative in relation to the outer surface. It is caused by inhibitory neural messages. Compare DEPOLARIZATION.

hyperpraxia *n.* a less common name for PSYCHOMOTOR AGITATION.

hyperprosexia *n.* an exaggerated fixation of attention on an idea or stimulus (e.g., the creaking of a door) to the exclusion of other stimuli. Hyperprosexia is a feature of COMPULSIVE DISORDERS. Also called **hyperprosessis**.

hypersensitivity reactions severe allergylike reactions that may occur after exposure to various drugs in susceptible individuals. Hypersensitivity reactions may be immediate, involving an acute allergic reaction leading to ANAPHYLAXIS. Autoimmune drug reactions are more delayed, involving dangerous and sometimes fatal reductions in the number of certain white blood cells (see AGRANULOCYTOSIS) in response to treatment with some antipsychotic drugs (CLOZAPINE is a classic example). Drug hypersensitivity can also result in serum-sickness-type reactions or in an immune vasculitis, such as STEVENS–JOHNSON SYNDROME, as seen after administration of some ANTICONVULSANT drugs.

hypersexuality *n.* extreme frequency of sexual activity, or an inordinate desire for sexual activity. Hypersexuality may be associated with lesions of the AMYGDALA or HIPPOCAMPUS as demonstrated in nonhuman animal experiments, but direct proof of this in humans is lacking. See NYMPHOMANIA; SATYRIASIS. **—hypersexual** *adj.*

hypersomnia *n.* excessive sleepiness during daytime hours or abnormally prolonged episodes of nighttime sleep. This can be a feature of certain DYSSOMNIAS (e.g., NARCOLEPSY) or other sleep or mental disorders, or it can be associated with neurological dysfunction or damage, with a general medical condition, or with substance use. Hypersomnia may, however, occur in the absence of any known cause or of an association with another condition (see PRIMARY HYPERSOMNIA). See also DISORDERS OF EXCESSIVE SOMNOLENCE. Compare HYPOSOMNIA.

hypersthenia *n.* a condition of excessive strength and tension associated with hyperactivity of the lymphatic system. **—hypersthenic** *adj.*

hypertelorism *n.* an abnormally large distance between two body organs or areas. **Ocular hypertelorism** (**Greig's syndrome**), in which the eyes are farther apart than normal, is often associated with mental retardation or other neurological conditions involving cranial anomalies. See also MEDIAN-CLEFT-FACE SYNDROME.

hypertension *n.* high blood pressure: a circulatory disorder characterized by persistent arterial blood pressure that exceeds readings higher than an arbitrary standard, which usually is 140/90. In the majority of cases there is no obvious cause (see ESSENTIAL HYPERTENSION). In a few people high blood pressure can be traced to a known cause, such as tumors of the adrenal gland, chronic kidney disease, hormone abnormalities, the use of oral contraceptives, or pregnancy. This is called **secondary hypertension**; it is usually cured if its cause is removed or is corrected. **—hypertensive** *adj.*

hypertensive crisis a sudden extreme rise in blood pressure.

hyperthymia *n.* emotional response that is disproportionate to the stimulus, frequently occurring in MANIC EPISODES and HYPOMANIC EPISODES.

hyperthyroid constitution a constitutional type associated with overactivity of the thyroid gland, characterized by youthfulness, well-developed sexual characteristics, hyperemotivity, and instability. It roughly corresponds to the ASTHENIC TYPE in KRETSCHMER TYPOLOGY.

hyperthyroidism *n.* overactivity of the thyroid gland, resulting in excessive production of thyroid hormones. This can lead to confusion, paranoia, hyperactivity, and physical problems, such as weight loss. See APATHETIC HYPERTHYROIDISM; THYROTOXICOSIS.

hypertonia *n.* a state of increased muscle tension or tonicity. Also called **hypertonicity**. **—hypertonic** *adj.*

hypertonic type a constitutional type characterized by

a high degree of muscle tone and corresponding to the ATHLETIC TYPE in KRETSCHMER TYPOLOGY. [defined by Italian endocrinologist Nicola Pende (1880–1970)]

hypertrophy *n.* overgrowth of an organ or part due to an increase in the size of its constituent cells. **—hypertrophic** *adj.*

hypertropia *n.* see STRABISMUS.

hypervegetative type a constitutional type that corresponds roughly to the PYKNIC TYPE and more closely to the megalosplanchnic type (prominent belly) and the brachymorphic type (see BRACHYMORPH).

hyperventilation *n.* abnormally rapid and deep breathing, usually due to anxiety or emotional stress. This lowers the carbon dioxide level of the blood and produces such symptoms as light-headedness, palpitation, numbness and tingling in the extremities, perspiration, and in some cases fainting (these features are known as **hyperventilation syndrome**). Also called **overbreathing**.

hypervigilance *n.* a state of heightened alertness, usually with continual scanning of the environment for signs of danger.

hypesthesia (**hypaesthesia**) *n.* severely diminished sensitivity in any of the senses, especially the touch sense. Also called **hypoesthesia** (**hypoaesthesia**).

hyphedonia *n.* a pathological diminution in pleasure from experiences that normally would produce pleasure. Compare HYPERHEDONIA.

hyphenophilia *n.* sexual interest and arousal derived from touching skin, fur, hair, leather, or fabrics.

hypn- *combining form* see HYPNO-.

hypnagogic *adj.* describing or relating to a state of drowsiness or light sleep that occurs just before falling fully asleep.

hypnagogic hallucination a hallucination experienced while falling asleep. Such hallucinations are ordinarily not considered pathological.

hypnagogic imagery vivid imagery occurring during the drowsy state between wakefulness and full sleep.

hypnagogic reverie 1. dream activity or fantasies occuring during the period of drowsiness and fading awareness that immediately precedes the onset of sleep. **2.** the state of being hypnotized.

hypnagogic state the drowsy period between waking and sleep during which transient, dreamlike fantasies and hallucinations may appear.

hypnalgia *n.* literally, dream pain: pain experienced during sleep or in a dream.

hypno- (**hypn-**) *combining form* sleep.

hypnoanalysis *n.* a modified and shortened form of psychoanalytic treatment, or a technique incorporated into full analysis, in which hypnosis is used (a) to help patients overcome RESISTANCES, (b) to enhance the TRANSFERENCE process, and (c) to recover memories and release repressed material. The material so brought forth is meant to be incorporated into the patient's consciousness for exploration and, ultimately, for interpretation by the therapist. However, this form of therapy is controversial because many psychologists and psychoanalysts question the veracity of repressed memories recovered during a hypnotic state.

hypnodontics *n.* the use of HYPNOSUGGESTION in dentistry as a means of relaxing tense patients, relieving anxiety, reinforcing or replacing anesthesia, and correcting such habits as bruxism (grinding the teeth).

hypnodrama *n.* a technique of PSYCHODRAMA in which a hypnotic state is induced and the client, or PROTAGONIST, is encouraged to act out his or her relationships and traumatic experiences with the aid of AUXILIARY EGOS. Hypnodrama might be used to overcome a client's resistance to dramatizing his or her problems in conscious psychodrama and to stimulate the revival of past incidents and emotional scenes in their full intensity. The technique is rarely used now. [introduced in 1959 by Austrian-born U.S. psychiatrist Jacob Levi Moreno (1889–1974)]

hypnogenic *adj.* **1.** sleep-producing. **2.** hypnosis-inducing.

hypnogenic spot a putative point on the body that, when touched, may induce hypnosis if the individual is highly susceptible. Such an effect is probably the result of AUTOSUGGESTION.

hypnoid state 1. a state of light hypnosis. **2.** a state resembling hypnosis. Also called **hypnoidal state**.

hypnonarcosis *n.* a sleeplike state induced by hypnosis.

hypnophrenosis *n.* any type of sleep disturbance. See also SLEEP DISORDER.

hypnopompic *adj.* relating to the drowsy, semiconscious state between deep sleep and waking.

hypnopompic hallucination a false sensory perception occurring in the period between sleeping and full wakefulness.

hypnosis *n.* (*pl.* **hypnoses**) the procedure, or the state induced by that procedure, whereby a hypnotist suggests that a subject experience various changes in sensation, perception, cognition, emotion, or control over motor behavior. Subjects appear to be receptive, to varying degrees, to suggestions to act, feel, and behave differently than in a normal waking state. The exact nature of the psychological state and of the use and effectiveness of hypnotic procedures as therapy remain the subject of much debate and, consequently, of ongoing psychological research. As a specifically psychotherapeutic intervention, hypnosis is referred to as HYPNOTHERAPY. See also ALTERED STATE OF CONSCIOUSNESS; AUTOHYPNOSIS; HETEROHYPNOSIS; POSTHYPNOTIC SUGGESTION; SELF-HYPNOSIS; WAKING HYPNOSIS.

hypnosuggestion *n.* the application of direct hypnotic suggestion in therapy. It is used to relieve such problems as insomnia, intractable pain, cigarette smoking, anorexia nervosa, and various types of crises (e.g., combat situations, panic, and dissociative amnesia).

hypnotherapy *n.* the use of hypnosis in psychological treatment, either in SHORT-TERM THERAPY directed toward alleviation of symptoms and modification of behavior patterns or in long-term RECONSTRUCTIVE PSYCHOTHERAPY aimed at personality adaptation or change. Hypnotherapy may use one or a combination of techniques, typically involving the administration by a properly trained professional of therapeutic suggestions to patients or clients who have been previously exposed to a HYPNOTIC INDUCTION procedure. Although discussions of its clinical applications engender controversy, there has been scientific evidence that hypnotherapy can be applied with some success to a wide range of clinical problems (e.g., hypertension, asthma, insomnia, bruxism); chronic and acute pain management; habit modification (e.g., anorexia nervosa, overeating, smoking); mood and anxiety disorders (e.g., some phobias); and personality disorders. There is also some positive evidence demonstrating the effectiveness of hypnosis as an ADJUNCTIVE THERAPY. See also AGE REGRESSION; AUTOMATIC WRITING; DIRECT SUGGESTION; DREAM SUGGES-

TION; ERICKSONIAN PSYCHOTHERAPY; HYPNOANALYSIS; HYPNOTIC REGRESSION.

hypnotic **1.** *n.* a drug that helps induce and sustain sleep by increasing drowsiness and reducing motor activity. In general, hypnotics differ from SEDATIVES only in terms of the dose administered, with higher doses used to produce sleep or anesthesia and lower doses to produce sedation or relieve anxiety. BENZODIAZEPINES are among the most widely prescribed hypnotics; antihistamines and other agents are used to lesser degrees. Newer, nonbenzodiazepine hypnotics, such as ZOPICLONE, ZOLPIDEM, and ZALEPLON, are achieving clinical currency because of their relative infrequency of adverse side effects. **2.** *adj.* pertaining to hypnosis or sleep.

hypnotic amnesia suggested forgetfulness for designated events. In highly hypnotizable individuals (see HYPNOTIC SUSCEPTIBILITY), there can be spontaneous forgetfulness for the entire hypnotic experience.

hypnotic analgesia unresponsiveness or substantially reduced sensitivity to pain under hypnotic suggestion.

hypnotic induction a process by which an individual comes under the influence of verbal suggestions, or any other stimuli that are believed by the individual to induce suggestibility, during HYPNOSIS. The process depends on the individual's HYPNOTIC SUSCEPTIBILITY and often involves fixation of attention and relaxation.

hypnotic regression a technique of HYPNOTHERAPY in which an individual under hypnosis is induced to relive a past experience that has been forgotten or inhibited but may be contributing to an emotional conflict.

hypnotic rigidity a condition of apparent muscular rigidity induced by suggestion during hypnosis.

hypnotic susceptibility the degree to which an individual is able to enter into HYPNOSIS. Although many individuals can enter at least a light trance, people vary greatly in their ability to achieve a moderate or DEEP TRANCE. Also called **hypnotizability**. See also STANFORD HYPNOTIC SUSCEPTIBILITY SCALE.

hypnotic trance see TRANCE.

hypnotism *n.* **1.** the act of inducing HYPNOSIS. **2.** the state of hypnosis.

hypnotizability *n.* see HYPNOTIC SUSCEPTIBILITY. —**hypnotizable** *adj.*

hypo- (**hyp-**) *combining form* **1.** under or below (e.g., HYPOSPADIAS). **2.** less than normal, deficient (e.g., HYPOGLYCEMIA).

hypoactive sexual desire disorder in *DSM–IV–TR*, persistent deficiency or absence of sexual interest and desire to engage in sexual activity. This may be global, involving all forms of sexual activity, or situational, limited to one partner or one type of sexual activity. It also may be lifelong or result from some life event or relationship issue. Frequency of sexual activity cannot be used as the sole basis for diagnosis of the disorder, as the person may engage in sex under pressure from the partner.

hypoactivity *n.* see PSYCHOMOTOR RETARDATION.

hypoacusia *n.* a state of reduced hearing sensitivity. Also called **hypacusia**; **hypacusis**; **hypacousia**. —**hypoacusic** *adj.*

hypoadrenal constitution a constitutional type associated with underactivity of the adrenal gland. Such individuals are lean and slender-boned, with developmental deficiency of skeletal and smooth muscles, and exhibit a tendency toward depression and average or above average intelligence. [defined by Italian endocrinologist Nicola Pende (1880–1970)]

hypoaffective type a constitutional body type distinguished by an absence of emotional reactivity.

hypoageusia *n.* see HYPOGEUSIA.

hypoalgesia *n.* diminished sensitivity to pain. Also called **hypalgesia**.

hypobaropathy *n.* see ALTITUDE SICKNESS.

hypocathexis *n.* in psychoanalytic theory, an abnormally low investment of PSYCHIC ENERGY in an OBJECT. Compare HYPERCATHEXIS. See CATHEXIS.

hypochondria *n.* morbid concern with the state of one's health, including unfounded beliefs of ill health. If severe and disabling, this preoccupation is classified as a mental disorder (see HYPOCHONDRIASIS). —**hypochondriac** or **hypochondriacal** *adj.* —**hypochondriac** *n.*

hypochondriasis *n.* in *DSM–IV–TR*, a SOMATOFORM DISORDER characterized by a preoccupation with the fear or belief that one has a serious physical disease based on the incorrect and unrealistic interpretation of bodily symptoms. This fear or belief persists for at least 6 months and interferes with social and occupational functioning in spite of medical reassurance that no physical disorder exists.

hypodermic injection see SUBCUTANEOUS INJECTION.

hypodontia *n.* see RIEGER'S SYNDROME.

hypoesthesia (**hypoaesthesia**) *n.* see HYPESTHESIA.

hypofrontality *n.* a condition of reduced activation or inadequate functioning of the cortex of the frontal lobes of the brain. In theory, this is a factor in schizophrenia but it is not well established, either as a characteristic phenomenon or as a cause.

hypofunction *n.* reduced function or activity, especially of an organ, such as a gland.

hypogastric nerve either of a pair of single large nerves, or sets of smaller parallel nerves, that extend into the pelvic region and carry postganglionic fibers that innervate the bladder, rectum, and genitalia.

hypogenital type a constitutional body type in which the lower extremities are abnormally long and development of genitalia and other sexual characteristics is delayed. An attenuated form of the hypogenital type is identified as a **hypogenital temperament**. [defined by Italian endocrinologist Nicola Pende (1880–1970)]

hypogeusia *n.* diminished sensitivity to taste. Also called **hypoageusia**.

hypoglossal nerve the 12th cranial nerve, a sensory nerve that originates in a NUCLEUS on the floor of the fourth VENTRICLE within the brain and innervates the tongue, lower jaw, and areas of the neck and chest. Also called **cranial nerve XII**.

hypoglycemia *n.* the condition of having a low blood-sugar level, due to interference with the formation of sugar in the blood or excessive utilization of sugar. In infants the major symptoms are tremors, cyanosis, seizures, apathy, weakness, respiratory problems, and failure to develop intellectually; the infantile idiopathic form may be due to a single recessive gene. In adults the major symptoms are debility, profuse sweating, nervousness, and dizziness. The adult form may be a psychophysiological reaction (**functional hyperinsulinism**) or it may result from inadequate intake of carbohydrates or insulin overdosage in those with DIABETES MELLITUS. —**hypoglycemic** *adj.*

hypogonadism *n.* decreased functional activity of the gonads, with retardation of growth and sexual development.

hypokinesis *n.* see PSYCHOMOTOR RETARDATION.

hypokinesthesia *n.* a diminished level of sensitivity in the SOMATOSENSORY SYSTEM (e.g., to touch, weight, pressure, and motion and position of the body). See also KINESTHESIS; PROPRIOCEPTION. Compare HYPERKINESTHESIA.

hypolipemia *n.* the presence in the blood of an abnormally low level of lipids.

hypomania *n.* see HYPOMANIC EPISODE. **—hypomanic** *adj.*

hypomanic episode a period of elevated, expansive, or irritable mood lasting at least 4 days and accompanied by at least three of the following (four if the mood is irritable): inflated self-esteem, a decreased need for sleep, increased speech, racing thoughts, distractibility, increase in activity or PSYCHOMOTOR AGITATION, and increased involvement in risky activities (e.g., foolish investments, sexual indiscretions), all of which affect functioning and are noticeable by others but do not cause marked impairment. One or more hypomanic episodes are characteristic of bipolar II disorder (see BIPOLAR DISORDERS), and hypomanic symptoms are a feature of CYCLOTHYMIC DISORDER. Also called **hypomania**.

hypomenorrhea *n.* a condition of diminished menstrual flow or menstruation of abnormally short duration.

hypometria *n.* underreaching an object during voluntary motor activity. This can be caused by impaired visual localization, defective visuomotor coordination, or a disorder in the execution of eye or hand movements. See also DYSMETRIA; OCULAR DYSMETRIA. Compare HYPERMETRIA.

hypomotility *n.* see PSYCHOMOTOR RETARDATION.

hyponasality *n.* lack of nasal resonance as a result of partial or complete obstruction in the nasal tract. Also called **denasality**.

hypoparathyroid constitution a constitutional type associated with deficient activity of the parathyroid gland, marked by hyperflexia and hyperkinesis of the skeletal and smooth muscles and a tendency toward rickets or other disorders of calcium metabolism.

hypophagia *n.* a pathologically diminished appetite. See also ANOREXIA. Compare HYPEROREXIA.

hypophilia *n.* sexual arousal by and response to a particular activity or type of stimulus that is below the normal range.

hypophonia *n.* a dysfunction in the production of sounds in which poor or absent coordination of speech muscles causes an abnormally weak voice, characterized by the need to whisper rather than speak aloud. Also called **microphonia**. See DYSPHONIA.

hypophoria *n.* deviation of one eye in a downward direction. See also PHORIA.

hypophrasia *n.* impaired or slow speech, a feature of severe PSYCHOMOTOR RETARDATION that sometimes occurs in a MAJOR DEPRESSIVE EPISODE.

hypophyseal cachexia a disease caused by total failure of the pituitary gland, resulting in secondary atrophy of the adrenal cortex, thyroid gland, and gonads. Sexual glands and breasts atrophy, teeth and hair fall out, and anorexia, diabetes insipidus, hypoglycemia, and mental changes develop. The disease occurs in two forms: **Sheehan's syndrome**, which affects women after childbirth; and SIMMONDS' DISEASE, which affects both sexes. Also called **pituitary cachexia**.

hypophyseal fossa see FOSSA.

hypophysectomy *n.* surgical removal of the pituitary gland (hypophysis). Also called **pituitectomy**.

hypophysis (**hypophysis cerebri**) *n.* see PITUITARY GLAND.

hypopituitarism *n.* see FRÖHLICH'S SYNDROME.

hypopituitary constitution a constitutional type associated with deficient activity of the pituitary gland, low blood pressure, slow pulse, diminished sexual desire, and mental lethargy or inactivity.

hypoplasia *n.* underdevelopment of an organ, tissue, or organism, usually due to an inadequate number of cells or diminished size of cells forming the structure. When applied to an entire body, hypoplasia usually refers to a dwarf of the species. **—hypoplastic** *adj.*

hypoprosexia *n.* an abnormal lack of attentive ability. Also called **hypoprosessis**.

hyposexuality *n.* an abnormally low level of sexual behavior. Hyposexual individuals may show no sex drive or interest in sexual activity. **—hyposexual** *adj.*

hyposmia *n.* decreased sensitivity to some or all ODORANTS. Individuals with this condition are described as **hyposmic**. See also MICROSMIA.

hyposomnia *n.* a reduction in a person's sleep time, often as a result of INSOMNIA or some other sleep disturbance. See also SLEEP DISORDER. Compare HYPERSOMNIA.

hypospadias *n.* a congenital anomaly in which the urethra opens below its normal anatomical position. In males, hypospadias is usually manifested by a urethral opening on the underside of the penis. In females, the urethra may open into the vagina.

hypotaxia *n.* a state of poor motor coordination or lack of movement. **—hypotaxic** *adj.*

hypotension *n.* abnormally low blood pressure, causing dizziness and fainting. See also ORTHOSTATIC HYPOTENSION. **—hypotensive** *adj.*

hypothalamic hormone any hormone secreted by neurons of the HYPOTHALAMUS. Neuroendocrine cells in the hypothalamus produce the hormones OXYTOCIN and VASOPRESSIN. The axons of these cells pass through the pituitary stalk (infundibulum) to the posterior pituitary, where they are released into the bloodstream. Other neuroendocrine cells in the hypothalamus produce either RELEASING HORMONES, which stimulate secretion of anterior pituitary hormones, or inhibiting hormones, which prevent secretion of anterior pituitary hormones. These hormones travel to the anterior pituitary through the HYPOTHALAMIC–PITUITARY PORTAL SYSTEM.

hypothalamic hyperphagia see VENTROMEDIAL HYPOTHALAMIC SYNDROME.

hypothalamic–hypophyseal portal system see HYPOTHALAMIC–PITUITARY PORTAL SYSTEM.

hypothalamic–pituitary–adrenocortical system (**HPA system**) a neuroendocrine system that is involved in the physiological response to stress. Outputs from the amygdala to the hypothalamus stimulate the release of CORTICOTROPIN-RELEASING HORMONE (CRH) into the HYPOTHALAMIC–PITUITARY PORTAL SYSTEM. CRH elicits the release from the anterior pituitary of ADRENOCORTICOTROPIC HORMONE, which in turn regulates the production and release of stress hormones (e.g., cortisol) from the adrenal cortex into the bloodstream.

hypothalamic–pituitary portal system a system of blood capillaries that transports RELEASING HORMONES from the hypothalamus to the anterior pituitary. Also called **hypothalamic–hypophyseal portal system**. See also HYPOTHALAMIC–PITUITARY–ADRENOCORICAL SYSTEM.

hypothalamic syndrome any of various disorders arising from injuries to the HYPOTHALAMUS. These may involve disturbances of eating, drinking, sleep, water balance, and temperature or development of secondary sexual characteristics. See LATERAL HYPOTHALAMIC SYNDROME; VENTROMEDIAL HYPOTHALAMIC SYNDROME.

hypothalamic theory of Cannon see CANNON–BARD THEORY. [Walter B. **Cannon** (1871–1945), U.S. physiologist]

hypothalamus *n.* (*pl.* **hypothalami**) part of the DIENCEPHALON of the brain, lying ventral to the THALAMUS, that contains nuclei with primary control of the autonomic (involuntary) functions of the body. It also helps integrate autonomic activity into appropriate responses to internal and external stimuli. See also HYPOTHALAMIC HORMONE; LATERAL HYPOTHALAMUS. **—hypothalamic** *adj.*

hypothermia *n.* the state of having an abnormally low body temperature. It can be caused by absence of normal reflexes such as shivering, sometimes associated with disease or a disorder of the brain, or by exposure to extreme cold. **Accidental hypothermia** is most likely to affect older people, who are less able to cope with the cooling effect of environmental temperatures in the winter months. Symptoms include listlessness, drowsiness, apathy, and indifference to progressive frostbite, progressing (if untreated) to coma and death. See also INDUCED HYPOTHERMIA. **—hypothermic** *adj.*

hypothesis *n.* (*pl.* **hypotheses**) an empirically testable proposition about some fact, behavior, relationship, or the like, usually based on theory, that states an expected outcome resulting from specific conditions or assumptions.

hypothesis behavior a pattern of behavior displayed by an organism when one particular cue or response is chosen consistently from a number of alternatives.

hypothesis testing the process of using any of a collection of STATISTICAL TESTS to assess the likelihood that an experimental result might have been the result of a chance or random process.

hypothetical construct see CONSTRUCT.

hypothetical imperative in the moral teaching of German philosopher Immanuel Kant (1724–1804), a maxim of the type "If you would achieve end X, take action Y." Such maxims of skill or prudence differ from the CATEGORICAL IMPERATIVE of morality in that (a) they are aimed at particular material ends rather than absolute and unconditional ends and (b) they cannot be defended as a universal and transituational law. See also UNIVERSALIZABILITY.

hypothetico-deductive method a method of examining the accuracy of predictions made on the basis of some theory, in which the theory gains credibility as more predictions are found to be accurate. Also called **mathematico-deductive method**.

hypothetico-deductive reasoning the abstract logical reasoning that, according to Jean PIAGET's theory of cognitive development, emerges in early adolescence and marks the period of FORMAL OPERATIONS. Hypothetico-deductive reasoning is distinguished by the capacity for abstract thinking and hypothesis testing, which frees the adolescent from total reliance on concrete thinking and immediate perception.

hypothymia *n.* an obsolescent name for a restricted range of affect, occurring in severe cases of MAJOR DEPRESSIVE EPISODE.

hypothyroid constitution a constitutional body type associated with deficient activity of the thyroid gland. It corresponds roughly to the PYKNIC TYPE in KRETSCHMER TYPOLOGY but with the added features of fatty deposits about the face and neck, short, stubby hands, low basal metabolism, and mental lethargy or inactivity.

hypothyroidism *n.* underactivity of the thyroid gland. In adults, it is marked by decreased metabolic rate, tiredness, and lethargy (see MYXEDEMA). See also CONGENITAL HYPOTHYROIDISM.

hypotonia *n.* decreased muscle tone or strength. **—hypotonic** *adj.*

hypotropia *n.* see STRABISMUS.

hypovegetative type a constitutional type in which the body features correspond to the ASTHENIC TYPE in KRETSCHMER TYPOLOGY.

hypovolemic thirst thirst caused by depletion of the volume of extracellular fluid, caused, for example, by blood loss (i.e., hypovolemia) or vomiting. Also called **volumetric thirst**. Compare OSMOMETRIC THIRST.

hypoxanthine–guanine phosphoribosyltransferase (**HGPRT**) an enzyme whose deficiency in the human body leads to symptoms of LESCH–NYHAN SYNDROME. It was the first enzyme found to be associated with an inherited disorder involving maladaptive behavior and mental retardation. Also called **hypoxanthine phosphoribosyltransferase**.

hypoxemia *n.* a deficiency of oxygen in the blood. The most reliable method for measuring the degree of hypoxemia is blood gas analysis to determine the partial pressure of oxygen in the arterial blood. Insufficient oxygenation of the blood may lead to HYPOXIA. Compare ANOXEMIA.

hypoxia *n.* diminished availability of oxygen to the body tissues. This can result in widespread brain injury depending on the degree of oxygen deficiency and its duration. Its many causes include (a) a deficiency of oxygen in the atmosphere, as in ALTITUDE SICKNESS; (b) pulmonary disorders that interfere with adequate ventilation of the lungs; (c) anemia or circulatory deficiencies, leading to inadequate transport and delivery of oxygen to the tissues; and (d) EDEMA or other abnormal conditions of the tissues themselves that impair the exchange of oxygen and carbon dioxide between capillaries and tissues. Signs and symptoms of hypoxia vary according to its cause. Generally they include DYSPNEA, rapid pulse, SYNCOPE, and mental disturbances (e.g., delirium, euphoria). Compare ANOXIA. **—hypoxic** *adj.*

hypoxic hypoxia hypoxia due to insufficient oxygen reaching the blood, as at the decreased barometric pressures of high altitudes. See ALTITUDE SICKNESS.

hypoxyphilia *n.* erotic self-strangulation. See ASPHYXOPHILIA; AUTOEROTIC ASPHYXIATION.

hysterectomy *n.* the surgical removal of the uterus. It may be **total hysterectomy**, including excision of the cervix; **subtotal hysterectomy**, in which only the uterus above the cervix is removed; or **radical hysterectomy**, with excision of a part of the vagina with the uterus and cervix.

hysteresis *n.* **1.** an effect in which the perception of a stimulus is influenced by one's immediately preceding perceptions. It can be demonstrated in experiments that involve making successive changes to a stimulus that varies along some dimension and asking a participant to describe his or her perception. When values along the dimension are steadily increased, there comes a point at which the participant will begin to place the percept in a different category (e.g., a sound is "loud" rather than "quiet"). However, when values along the dimension are decreased, the crossover point will occur at a different point along the dimension. **2.** in vision, the tendency for a perceptual state to persist under gradually changing conditions. For example, stereoscopic fusion can persist, producing the appearance of depth even when RETINAL DISPARITY between the two images becomes so great that they would normally not be able to be fused. **—hysteretic** *adj.*

hysteria *n.* the historical name for the condition classified in *DSM–IV–TR* as SOMATIZATION DISORDER. Although technically outdated, it is often used as a lay term for any psychogenic disorder characterized by such symptoms as paralysis, blindness, loss of sensation, and hallucinations and often accompanied by suggestibility, emotional outbursts, and histrionic behavior. Sigmund FREUD interpreted hysterical symptoms as defenses against guilty sexual impulses (e.g., a paralyzed hand cannot masturbate), but other conflicts are now recognized. Freud also included dissociative conditions in his concept of hysteria, but these are now regarded as separate disorders. The name derives ultimately from the Greek *husteros*, "uterus," based on the early and erroneous belief that such disorders were unique to women and originated in uterine disorders. **—hysterical** *adj.*

hysterical amnesia an older name, now rarely encountered, for a disorder characterized by inability to recall traumatic or anxiety-provoking events, such as experiences associated with guilt, failure, or rejection. See DISSOCIATIVE AMNESIA.

hysterical blindness see FUNCTIONAL BLINDNESS.

hysterical disorder an outdated name for any disorder characterized by involuntary psychogenic dysfunction of the sensory, motor, or visceral activities of the body. See CONVERSION DISORDER; SOMATIZATION DISORDER.

hysterical paralysis a former name for CONVERSION PARALYSIS.

hysterical personality disorder see HISTRIONIC PERSONALITY DISORDER.

hysterical psychosis an old name for a condition in which psychotic symptoms (e.g., hallucinations, delusions, and bizarre and sometimes violent behavior) appear suddenly in a person with HISTRIONIC PERSONALITY DISORDER (formerly referred to as hysterical personality disorder), usually in response to a stressful precipitating life event. Symptoms are of short duration, lasting 2 weeks or less, and there is a full return to the previous level of functioning. In *DSM–III*, hysterical psychosis was subsumed under the diagnostic category of brief reactive psychosis (see BRIEF PSYCHOTIC DISORDER). Currently, however, hysterical psychosis is not widely considered a distinct clinical entity; it is not listed in the *DSM–IV–TR*. Also called **dissociative psychosis**.

hysteriform *adj.* characterized by symptoms that resemble those associated with HYSTERIA. The term is not in current usage.

hystero- (**hyster-**) *combining form* uterus.

Hz symbol for HERTZ.

Ii

I *pron.* the nominative pronoun referring to the self. In William JAMES's psychology, the "I" is the NOMINATIVE SELF.

IAAP abbreviation for INTERNATIONAL ASSOCIATION OF APPLIED PSYCHOLOGY.

IACUC acronym for INSTITUTIONAL ANIMAL CARE AND USE COMMITTEE.

IADLs abbreviation for INSTRUMENTAL ACTIVITIES OF DAILY LIVING.

-iasis (**-asis**) *suffix* disease or diseased (e.g., HYPOCHONDRIASIS).

IAT abbreviation for IMPLICIT ASSOCIATION TEST.

iatro- *combining form* physician or medicine.

iatrochemical school of thought a school of thought, active from the early 16th to the mid-17th centuries, which held that disease resulted from chemical imbalances in the body and that, conversely, health and longevity resulted from the proper balance of chemicals. It also held that disease was to be treated chemically and that drugs could be chemically produced. This view was heavily influenced by the work of Swiss chemist and physician Paracelsus (1493–1541) and developed in opposition to the theories of Roman physician Galen (129–215), still prevalent at that time, holding that diseases resulted from an imbalance of bodily HUMORS. The iatrochemical school provided the impetus for the development of modern pharmaceutical laboratories and modern chemotherapy. See also IATROPHYSICAL SCHOOL OF THOUGHT.

iatrogenesis *n.* the process of producing an IATROGENIC ILLNESS. Also called **iatrogeny**.

iatrogenic *adj.* denoting or relating to a disease or pathological condition that is caused inadvertently by treatment.

iatrogenic addiction dependence on a substance, most often a painkiller, originally prescribed by a physician to treat a physical or psychological disorder.

iatrogenic illness a disorder that is induced or aggravated by the attending clinician, therapist, or physician. It may be due to the behavior of the clinician (e.g., his or her comments or expressions, the manner in which the patient is examined) or a result of the treatment given (e.g., an infection acquired during the course of the treatment).

iatrogenic schizophrenia see TARDIVE DYSMENTIA.

iatrogeny *n.* see IATROGENESIS.

iatrophysical school of thought a 17th-century school of thought that sought to apply the principles of mathematics and mechanics to medicine. Early examples include the development of the thermometer as an instrument of medical diagnosis and the invention of other mechanical and measurement devices to give knowledge of physiological processes. This view, at least in its early development, was based on the Cartesian view that the physical body is essentially a machine (see CARTESIAN DUALISM). Many early proponents of this school also practiced iatrochemistry (see IATROCHEMICAL SCHOOL OF THOUGHT). Also called **iatromathematics; iatromechanism**.

-iatry (**-iatrics**) *suffix* medical care or treatment (e.g., PSYCHIATRY).

ibogaine *n.* a hallucinogenic agent found in the root of the African forest plant *Tabernanthe iboga*. It is used mainly by adherents of the Bwiti (or Bouiti) religion in rituals or as a stimulant, although data suggest that ibogaine may have potential clinical use in the treatment of substance dependence and management of withdrawal symptoms. Although its mechanism of action is unknown, ibogaine may function as a low-affinity blocker of the ion channels associated with NMDA RECEPTORS.

ibotenic acid an agent that enhances the action of the excitatory neurotransmitter GLUTAMATE: It is an agonist at NMDA RECEPTORS. Ibotenic acid and its metabolic product, muscimol (a GABA AGONIST), are found in some mushrooms of the genus *Amanita* (see FLY AGARIC).

IBS abbreviation for IRRITABLE BOWEL SYNDROME.

ICA-90 abbreviation for INSTRUMENT COORDINATION ANALYZER-90.

ICD abbreviation for INTERNATIONAL CLASSIFICATION OF DISEASES.

ice *n.* slang for illicitly manufactured METHAMPHETAMINE, a common drug of abuse, especially the free-base, concentrated, smokable form of methamphetamine. It has an intense, persistent action; chronic use may lead to serious psychiatric, metabolic, cardiovascular, and neuromuscular changes.

iceberg metaphor the notion that conscious events represent only a small and accessible aspect of a larger domain of unconscious psychological functioning.

iceberg principle the principle that the observed reasons or explanations for a behavior or opinion are incomplete: Much of the real explanation lies below the surface, requiring extensive interviews or other research techniques to uncover.

iceberg profile a pattern of response to the PROFILE OF MOOD STATES questionnaire in which VIGOR scores are above the 50th T SCORE and all other scales (tension, depression, anger, fatigue, and confusion) are below that level. Successful ELITE ATHLETES have been shown to exhibit this mental health profile.

iceblock theory a concept of behavior change associated with SENSITIVITY TRAINING and similar group therapeutic processes in which existing attitudes and behavior are unfrozen, new attitudes and behavior are explored, and the latter are then frozen into new habit patterns. [conceived by Kurt LEWIN]

icebreaker *n.* a brief but relatively engaging dyadic or group activity that promotes social interaction and alleviates feelings of discomfort and tension, especially when the two individuals or the group members are unfamiliar with each other or with the activity.

ICF abbreviation for INTERMEDIATE CARE FACILITY.

icon (**ikon**) *n.* **1.** an image, picture, or pictorial representation of something. **2.** an aftersensation representing something previously seen or experienced. **3.** a picture or symbol used in a computer display to represent an action the user can select by pointing to and clicking on it with a mouse. Icons are also used on some computer-controlled displays to represent alternatives that can be selected by simply touching them with a finger. **—iconic** or **ikonic** *adj.*

iconic content mental images or pictures of particular aspects of reality, such as a child's mental representation of a doll. See ICONIC MODE. [first described by U.S. developmental psychologist Jerome Seymour Bruner (1915–)]

iconic gesture a gesture that has some physical resemblance to the meaning or idea that it stands for, such as holding up the hand with the thumb and forefinger very close together to signify that something is very small.

iconicity *n.* an association between form and meaning in which a resemblance between two objects, images, or events allows one to be a sign or symbol for the other.

iconic memory the perceptual experience of briefly retaining an image of a visual stimulus beyond cessation of the stimulus. This iconic image usually lasts less than a second. In a MULTISTORE MODEL OF MEMORY, iconic memory (more formally referred to as the **visual sensory store**) precedes SHORT-TERM MEMORY.

iconic mode a way of acquiring knowledge in which objects and experiences are represented by images based on sensory impressions (see ICONIC REPRESENTATION). The iconic mode begins to develop in early infancy and is dominant in the preschool years. Also called **iconic stage**. Compare ENACTIVE MODE; SYMBOLIC MODE. [proposed by U.S. developmental psychologist Jerome Seymour Bruner (1915–)]

iconic representation the MENTAL REPRESENTATION of visual stimuli in raw, unprocessed form.

iconic symbol a linguistic sign (written or spoken word) that has a physical resemblance, rather than an arbitrary relation, to its referent. Examples include onomatopoeic coinages, such as *choo-choo* (train), and the signs used in pictographic languages. With these few exceptions, linguistic signs are held to be arbitrary in most modern thinking on language. The contrary view, which holds that there is a general if hidden correspondence between the sounds of words and their referents, is known as the theory of PHONETIC SYMBOLISM. Compare ARBITRARY SYMBOL.

iconoclast *n.* **1.** one who challenges or seeks to overthrow established ideas, traditions, or practices. **2.** in religion, one who opposes iconolatry or (more generally) the use of physical images in worship. **—iconoclastic** *adj.*

iconolatry *n.* the veneration of certain holy images as channels of the divine, as practiced by the Orthodox and Eastern Catholic (Uniate) Churches. This should be distinguished from worship of the images themselves, which would be idolatry.

iconomania *n.* a pathological impulse to collect and worship images.

ICP abbreviation for INTRACRANIAL PRESSURE.

ICS abbreviation for INTRACRANIAL STIMULATION.

ICSH abbreviation for interstitial cell-stimulating hormone. See LUTEINIZING HORMONE.

icterus *n.* see JAUNDICE.

ictus *n.* a sudden event, particularly a seizure.

ICU abbreviation for INTENSIVE CARE UNIT.

id 1. *n.* in psychoanalytic theory, the component of the personality that contains the instinctual, biological drives that supply the psyche with its basic energy or LIBIDO. Sigmund FREUD conceived of the id as the most primitive component of the personality, located in the deepest level of the unconscious; it has no inner organization and operates in obedience to the PLEASURE PRINCIPLE. Thus the infant's life is dominated by the desire for immediate gratification of instincts, such as hunger and sex, until the EGO begins to develop and operate in accordance with reality. See also PRIMARY PROCESS; STRUCTURAL MODEL. **2.** abbreviation for *i*ntra*d*ermal.

id anxiety in psychoanalytic theory, anxiety deriving from instinctual drives. This is the main cause of PRIMARY ANXIETY (automatic anxiety). Compare EGO ANXIETY.

idea *n.* **1.** in cognitive psychology, a mental image or cognition that is ultimately derived from experience but that may occur without direct reference to perception or sensory processes. **2.** in the writings of French philosopher René Descartes (1596–1650) and the British empiricist philosophers (see EMPIRICISM), a mental event that may correspond to something outside the mind but that is itself the immediate object of thought or perception. Descartes made a celebrated and much disputed distinction between DERIVED IDEAS and INNATE IDEAS. See also ASSOCIATION OF IDEAS. **3.** in the thought of Greek philosopher Plato (c. 427–c. 347 BCE), the abstract or intellectual form of something regarded as its true reality. See PLATONIC IDEALISM; THEORY OF FORMS.

IDEA abbreviation for INDIVIDUALS WITH DISABILITIES EDUCATION ACT.

idealism *n.* **1.** in philosophy, the position that reality, including the natural world, is not independent of mind. Positions range from strong forms, holding that mind constitutes the things of reality, to weaker forms holding that reality is correlated with the workings of the mind. There is also a range of positions as to the nature of mind, from those holding that mind must be conceived of as absolute, universal, and apart from nature itself to those holding that mind may be conceived of as individual minds. See ABSOLUTE IDEALISM; IDEALISTIC MONISM; SUBJECTIVE IDEALISM. See also MIND–BODY PROBLEM. **2.** commitment to moral, political, or religious ideals. **3.** see PLATONIC IDEALISM. Compare MATERIALISM. **—idealist** *n.* **—idealistic** *adj.*

idealistic monism the position that all reality consists of a single SUBSTANCE, that substance being mind or spirit. See IDEALISM; MONISM. Compare NATURAL MONISM. See also MIND–BODY PROBLEM.

idealization *n.* **1.** the exaggeration of the positive attributes and minimization of the imperfections or failings associated with a person, place, thing, or situation, so that it is viewed as perfect or nearly perfect. **2.** in psychoanalytic theory, a DEFENSE MECHANISM that protects the individual from conscious feelings of ambivalence toward the idealized OBJECT. Idealization of the parents and other important figures plays a role in the development of the EGO-IDEAL. **—idealize** *vb.*

ideal observer a hypothetical person whose sensory and perceptual systems operate without error or bias. The concept of the ideal observer is used most commonly within the context of psychophysical testing, particularly SIGNAL DETECTION THEORY. Performance of the ideal observer can be simulated and compared with actual human performance.

ideal performance state (**IPS**) the state of cognitive and physiological activation that permits optimal performance for an individual. See ZONE OF OPTIMAL FUNCTIONING.

ideal self in models of self-concept, a mental representation of an exemplary set of psychological attributes that may or may not be part of one's ACTUAL SELF.

idea of influence see DELUSION OF INFLUENCE.

idea of reference the sense that events or the actions of others (e.g., talking, whispering, or smiling) relate particularly to oneself. In an extreme degree, it is a DELUSION OF REFERENCE.

ideation *n.* the process of forming IDEAS and IMAGES. **—ideate** *vb.* **—ideational** *adj.*

ideational agnosia a form of AGNOSIA characterized by an inability to form an association between the idea or purpose of an object and the object itself.

ideational apraxia loss or impairment of the ability to perform a series of actions because of failure to conceive the sequence or plan as a whole. Both perceptual and motor tasks of action sequencing are impaired, but the ability to imitate gestures or to produce movements on command is unaffected. For instance, this deficit would be apparent on a task in which an individual would need to fill and then light a pipe.

idée fixe 1. a firmly held, irrational idea or belief that is maintained despite evidence to the contrary. It may take the form of a delusion and become an obsession. Also called **fixed belief**; **fixed idea**. **2.** a subconscious unit of mental processing (see AUTOMATISM) that has become split off or dissociated from consciousness and, as a result, interferes with the normal processing of information. In some theories, this is considered a primary mechanism for the symptoms of HYSTERIA. [proposed by French psychologist Pierre Janet (1859–1947)]

id-ego *n.* in psychoanalytic theory, the undifferentiated structure of the infant's personality before the EGO develops enough maturity to separate from the ID. The concept is based on Sigmund FREUD's view that the newborn infant is all id and the ego develops out of it in response to the demands of reality. See EGO DEVELOPMENT.

idempotent matrix a matrix (X) with the property that $X = X^2$.

identical elements theory the concept that the ability to learn a new task is enhanced if it contains elements of previously mastered tasks. Also called **identical components theory**.

identical points points on the retinas of the left and right eyes that receive identical images from the same object at a specified distance.

identical twins see MONOZYGOTIC TWINS.

identifiable neuron a large neuron that is similar from one individual to the next, enabling investigators to recognize it and give it a code name. Identifiable neurons are common in invertebrates but uncommon in vertebrates.

identification *n.* **1.** the process of associating the self closely with other individuals and their characteristics or views. This process takes many forms: The infant feels part of his or her mother; the child gradually adopts the attitudes, standards, and personality traits of the parents; the adolescent takes on the characteristics of the peer group; the adult identifies with a particular profession or political party. Identification operates largely on an unconscious or semiconscious level. **2.** in psychoanalytic theory, a DEFENSE MECHANISM in which the individual incorporates aspects of his or her OBJECTS inside the EGO in order to alleviate the anxiety associated with OBJECT LOSS or to reduce hostility between himself or herself and the object.

identification test a verbal intelligence test in which the participant identifies objects or parts of objects in a picture.

identification transference in GROUP PSYCHOTHERAPY, the client's identification with other members of the group and desire to emulate them. [first described by 20th-century Russian-born U.S. psychotherapist Samuel Richard Slavson]

identification with the aggressor an unconscious mechanism in which an individual identifies with someone who poses a threat or an opponent who cannot be mastered. The identification may involve adopting the aggression, or emulating other characteristics, of the aggressor. This has been observed in cases of hostage taking and in other extreme situations, such as concentration camps. In psychoanalytic theory, it occurs on a developmental level when the male child identifies with his rival, the father, toward the end of the OEDIPAL PHASE. It was first described by Anna FREUD in 1936. See also STOCKHOLM SYNDROME.

identified patient a member of a structured group (especially a family) who exhibits the symptoms of a mental disorder and for whom treatment may be sought by the other group members. Clinical investigation may reveal that there is a complex and seriously maladaptive behavioral pattern among members of the group as a whole but that the psychological stigma has fallen primarily on one person, the identified patient. Also called **symptom bearer**; **symptom wearer**. See also DYSFUNCTIONAL FAMILY.

identity *n.* **1.** an individual's sense of self defined by (a) a set of physical and psychological characteristics that is not wholly shared with any other person and (b) a range of social and interpersonal affiliations (e.g., ethnicity) and social roles. Identity involves a sense of continuity: the feeling that one is the same person today that one was yesterday or last year (despite physical or other changes). Such a sense is derived from one's body sensations, one's body image, and the feeling that one's memories, purposes, values, and experiences belong to the self. Also called **personal identity**. **2.** in cognitive development, awareness that an object remains the same even though it may undergo many transformations. For example, a piece of clay may be made to assume various forms but is still the same piece of clay.

identity confusion uncertainty regarding one's identity, which often occurs during adolescence but may also occur at a later stage of life. See IDENTITY VERSUS ROLE CONFUSION.

identity crisis a phase of life marked by role experimentation, changing, conflicting, or newly emerging values, and a lack of commitment to one's usual roles in society (especially in work and family relationships). Erik ERIKSON claimed that it is natural and desirable for adolescents to go through a period of identity crisis and that greater maturity results from the experience. The concept has been expanded to refer to adult MIDLIFE CRISES and other periods marked by change or experimentation with the SELF. See EGO IDENTITY.

identity diffusion 1. lack of stability or focus in the view of the self or in any of the elements of an individual's IDENTITY. **2.** in the EGO PSYCHOLOGY of Erik ERIKSON, a possible outcome of the IDENTITY VERSUS ROLE CONFUSION stage in which the individual emerges with an uncertain sense of identity and confusion about his or her wishes, attitudes, and goals.

identity disorder 1. in *DSM–III*, a chronic disturbance, usually of late adolescence, in which feelings of uncertainty and distress are generated by such identity issues as long-term goals, career choice, sexual orientation and behavior, group loyalty, moral values, and religious identification. In *DSM–IV–TR*, this is categorized as an **identity problem** within the section **Other Conditions that May Be a Focus of Clinical Attention**. **2.** see DISSOCIATIVE IDENTITY DISORDER; GENDER IDENTITY DISORDER.

identity foreclosure in the development of identity, the unquestioning acceptance by individuals (usually adolescents) of the role, values, and goals that others (e.g., parents, close friends, teachers, athletic coaches) have chosen for them. The individual's commitment to the foreclosed identity—for example, that of an athlete—occurs without exploring its value or contemplating alternative roles that might be more appropriate for him or her. See also SEPARATION–INDIVIDUATION.

identity matrix (symbol: I) a square matrix with ones along its main diagonal and zeros elsewhere. The identity matrix has the property that for any matrix A, $AI = A$; that is, it serves as the identity for multiplication in matrix algebra.

identity need in the theory of Erich FROMM, the need to achieve a sense of uniqueness, individuality, and selfhood. Psychological autonomy and the severing of INCESTUOUS TIES are considered essential for healthy individuality. Unhealthy, spurious individuality is expressed in conformity, a manifestation of the ESCAPE FROM FREEDOM. Compare ROOTEDNESS.

identity, negation, reciprocal, and correlative operations (**INRC group**) in Jean PIAGET's theory of cognitive development, a group of four logical FORMAL OPERATIONS that are applied to new pieces of information before they become knowledge. These operations can be illustrated by considering a dime and a penny both showing heads. The identity (I) operation leaves the situation unchanged: Both coins remain heads up. The negation (N) operation negates the situation: If the dime has been turned over once, an N operation would be turning the dime back over. The reciprocal (R) operation reciprocates an earlier operation: If the previous operation was turning the penny over, the R operation would be turning the dime over. The correlative (C) operation is the inverse of the reciprocal operation: If the R operation was turning the dime over, the C operation would be turning both the dime and penny over. Piaget asserted that these logical operations were in fact cognitive operations that formal operational thinkers apply to solve problems.

identity politics 1. political activity or theorizing that derives from individuals' sense of belonging to particular ethnic, sexual, or other identity-based groups, rather than from traditional party or ideological commitments. **2.** the interpersonal processes involved in establishing, maintaining, and negotiating both one's own personal and social identity and the identities of others in the social setting.

identity principle 1. in logic, the principle that where X is known to be identical to Y, any statement about X (or Y) will have the same meaning and truth value as the same statement about Y (or X). So, for example, any statement made about "Paris" will have the same meaning, and be equally true or false, as the same statement made about "the capital of France." Compare CONTRADICTION PRINCIPLE. See also LAWS OF THOUGHT. **2.** in the theory of Jean PIAGET, the principle underlying a child's awareness of the CONSERVATION of physical quantities.

identity theory the theory that mental states are identical with brain states. In **token identity theory**, identical mental and brain states occur within the individual. **Type identity theory** extends this to theorize that when two or more people share a mental state (e.g., the belief that ice is cold) they also have the same brain state. Also called **central state theory**; **identity theory of the mind**. See also ELIMINATIVISM; EPIPHENOMENALISM; MATERIALISM; MIND–BODY PROBLEM; PHYSICALISM; REDUCTIONISM.

identity versus role confusion the fifth of ERIKSON'S EIGHT STAGES OF DEVELOPMENT, marked by an identity crisis that occurs during adolescence. During this stage the individual may experience a psychosocial MORATORIUM, a period of time that permits experimentation with social roles. The individual may "try on" different roles and identify with different groups before forming a cohesive, positive identity that allows him or her to contribute to society; alternatively, the individual may identify with outgroups to form a negative identity, or may remain confused about his or her sense of identity, a state Erikson calls IDENTITY DIFFUSION.

ideogram *n.* a picture or symbol used to represent an object or idea. Ideograms are often used in computer interfaces to represent actions that can be selected by pointing to and clicking on them with a mouse. In this context they are usually referred to as ICONS. Also called **ideograph**. See also LOGOGRAPHIC.

ideology *n.* **1.** a systematic ordering of ideas with associated doctrines, attitudes, beliefs, and symbols that together form a more or less coherent philosophy or WELTANSCHAUUNG for a person, group, or sociopolitical movement. **2.** in MARXISM, any philosophy or set of ideas regarded as false and distorting, usually because it ignores or tries to disguise the material basis of society. **—ideological** *adj.*

ideomotor activity movement, in some cases elaborate, related to ongoing thoughts but produced without volition. Ideomotor activity explains a variety of phenomena, including nonverbal gestures during conversations and various spiritualist phenomena, such as may be experienced with the Ouija board. Also called **ideomotor action**. [first identified in 1852 by British physiologist and psychologist William B. Carpenter (1813–1885)]

ideomotor apraxia loss or impairment of the ability to make gestures or use objects appropriately. For instance, this deficit would be apparent on a task in which an individual would need to pretend to be using a screwdriver or to imitate someone using a screwdriver. Ideomotor apraxia is most commonly caused by parietal damage in the dominant hemisphere of the brain. See also CONCEPTUAL APRAXIA.

ideomotor compatibility the extent to which stimuli resemble the sensory feedback from their assigned responses. For example, if the stimulus is the speech sound [a] and the response is to say the letter aloud, stimulus and response have high ideomotor compatibility. Ideomotor compatibility minimizes the difficulty of RESPONSE SELECTION, possibly allowing the normal response-selection process to be bypassed.

ideomotor principle see MOTOR PROCESS THEORY OF IMAGERY.

ideomotor theory the hypothesis that actions are evoked impulsively by mental images and are carried out spontaneously in the absence of inhibitory events. Hence, it claims that images have motivational power. [proposed by William JAMES]

idio- *combining form* distinct or private.

idiocentric 1. *adj.* describing a person who is oriented toward individual, rather than group, goals. **2.** *n.* an individual who is dispositionally predisposed to put his or her personal interests and motivations before the interests and goals of other people and other groups. Just as societies based on INDIVIDUALISM stress the rights of the individual over the group, so idiocentrics emphasize their personal needs and are emotionally detached from groups and communities. They are more likely to describe themselves in terms of personal qualities and traits rather than memberships and roles. See also EGOCENTRISM; INDIVIDUALISM. Compare ALLOCENTRIC. **—idiocentrism** *n.*

idiocy *n.* an obsolete name for PROFOUND MENTAL RETARDATION.

idiodynamics *n.* the concept that the individual is primarily responsible for selecting stimuli and organizing responses. Individuals attend to those aspects of the environment they deem relevant, rather than responding to whatever stimuli are present and detectable.

idiogamist *n.* a person who is capable of full sexual response only with his or her spouse and is sexually incapable or inadequate with other partners. An idiogamist is usually a man who cannot obtain or maintain penile erection with any partner other than his wife (or, sometimes, women who resemble his wife).

idiogenesis *n.* origin without evident cause, particularly the origin of an IDIOPATHIC disease.

idioglossia *n.* the omission, substitution, and distortion of so many sounds that speech is rendered unintelligible. It is often associated with mental retardation. Also called **idiolalia**.

idiographic *adj.* relating to the description and understanding of an individual case, as opposed to the formulation of NOMOTHETIC general laws describing the average case. U.S. psychologists Kenneth MacCorquadale (1919–1986) and Paul MEEHL identified these as two contrasting traditions in explaining psychological phenomena. An **idiographic approach** involves the thorough, intensive study of a single person or case in order to obtain an in-depth understanding of that person or case, as contrasted with a study of the universal aspects of groups of people or cases. In those areas of psychology in which the individual person is the unit of analysis (e.g., in personality, developmental, or clinical psychology), the idiographic approach has appeal because it seeks to characterize a particular individual, emphasizing that individual's characteristic traits (see IDIOGRAPHIC TRAIT) and the uniqueness of the individual's behavior and adjustment, rather than to produce a universal set of psychological constructs that might be applicable to a population.

idiographic trait a personality trait that is observed in only one individual or one member of a population or that is seldom found in the same form among individuals or members. Also called **unique trait**.

idiolalia *n.* see IDIOGLOSSIA.

idiolect *n.* a DIALECT spoken at the level of an individual. In one sense, all speakers have an idiolect because no two people use their native language in exactly the same way. In another, the term is reserved for the most idiosyncratic forms of personal language use, especially those involving eccentricities of construction or vocabulary. An idiolect of this kind may be developed by a person who acquires a second language unsystematically, especially if this occurs in an unusual or isolated learning environment (see INTERLANGUAGE; FOSSILIZATION). Some poets and writers also develop distinctive idiolects in their writings. **—idiolectal** *adj.*

idiom *n.* a fixed phrase established by usage whose meaning cannot be deduced from the meanings of its individual words, such as *to kick the bucket*, meaning "to die." Idioms are sometimes known as **frozen forms** because they have a fixed structure that cannot be varied according to the usual grammatical rules. So, for example, *The old man kicked the bucket* cannot be changed to *The bucket was kicked by the old man* without losing the idiomatic sense.

idiopathic *adj.* without known cause or of spontaneous origin: usually denoting diseases, such as some forms of epilepsy, whose ETIOLOGY is obscure.

idiopathic epilepsy see EPILEPSY.

idiophrenic *adj.* denoting a mental disorder that is caused by a disease of the brain.

idioretinal light an illusion of shades of gray observed in a dark environment. The effect is caused by chemical changes in the retina or brain cells rather than the wavelength of visible light.

idiosyncrasy *n.* **1.** a habit or quality of body or mind peculiar to an individual. **2.** abnormal susceptibility to an agent (e.g., a drug) peculiar to an individual. **—idiosyncratic** *adj.*

idiosyncrasy-credit model an explanation of the leniency that groups sometimes display when high-status members violate group norms. This model assumes that such individuals, by contributing to the group in significant ways and expressing loyalty to it, build up **idiosyncrasy credits**, which they "spend" whenever they make errors or deviate from the group's norms. So long as their actions do not completely deplete their supply of credits, their infractions will not undermine their status in the group. [developed by U.S. psychologist Edwin P. Hollander (1927–)]

idiosyncratic classification in classification tasks, the grouping together of items that do not appear to share physical or conceptual characteristics. Also called **fiat equivalence classification**; **random classification**. Compare COMPLEMENTARY CLASSIFICATION; CONCEPTUAL CLASSIFICATION; PERCEPTUAL CLASSIFICATION.

idiosyncratic intoxication a condition characterized by sudden and extreme changes in personality, mood, and behavior following the ingestion of an amount of alcohol usually considered to be too little to account for the degree of the changes. It may include extreme excitement, impulsive and aggressive behavior (at times to the point of extreme violence), persecutory ideas, disorientation, and hallucinations. The episode ends when the individual falls into a deep sleep, after which there is often complete loss of memory for it. Some researchers believe that the condition may be related to stress or may be due in part to a psychomotor seizure triggered by alcohol. Also called **mania a potu**; **pathological intoxication**. See also FUROR.

idiosyncratic reaction an unexpected reaction to a drug resulting in effects that may be contrary to the anticipated results. Idiosyncratic reactions can result in various symptoms, but generally refer to an extreme sensitivity or an extreme insensitivity to a particular agent. Such reactions may be genetically mediated.

idiot *n.* an obsolete name for a person with PROFOUND MENTAL RETARDATION. **—idiotic** *adj.*

idiot savant (*pl.* **idiot savants** or **idiots savants**) a person with mental retardation who possesses a remarkable, highly developed ability or talent in one area, such as rapid calculation, expertise in playing music, or feats of memory. Such people are rare, and this ability usually occurs in those with mild or moderate mental retardation, with or without AUTISTIC SPECTRUM DISORders. See also CALENDAR CALCULATION. [French, "learned idiot"]

idioverse *n.* in postmodern discourse (see POSTMODERNISM), the totality of a person's unique sensations, perceptions, and understandings, that is, a person's unique lived world.

id psychology in psychoanalysis, an approach that focuses on the unorganized, instinctual impulses contained in the ID that seek immediate pleasurable gratification of primitive needs. The id is believed to dominate the lives of infants and is frequently described as blind and irrational until it is disciplined by the other two major components of the personality: the EGO and the SUPEREGO. Compare EGO PSYCHOLOGY.

IDRA abbreviation for INSANITY DEFENSE REFORM ACT.

id resistance in psychoanalysis, a form of RESISTANCE to therapy that is motivated by unconscious ID impulses, whose underlying motive is the REPETITION COMPULSION. Compare REPRESSION-RESISTANCE; SUPEREGO RESISTANCE.

IDS abbreviation for INTEGRATED DELIVERY SYSTEM.

IE abbreviation for INDIVIDUAL EDUCATION.

IEP 1. abbreviation for individualized educational planning (see INDIVIDUAL EDUCATION). **2.** abbreviation for INDIVIDUALIZED EDUCATION PROGRAM.

I/E ratio abbreviation for INSPIRATION–EXPIRATION RATIO.

IFSP abbreviation for INDIVIDUAL FAMILY SERVICE PLAN.

if . . . then profiles a methodology for describing personal dispositions in which within-person variations across social contexts are charted in terms of the behaviors evoked by particular situations. [developed by U.S. personality psychologists Walter Mischel (1930–) and Yuichi Shoda]

ignoratio elenchi a type of informal FALLACY or a persuasive technique in which a person mounts an argument that may be valid on its own terms but is irrelevant to the point at issue. It is sometimes referred to colloquially as "missing the point." Also called **irrelevant argument**. [Latin: "ignorance of the refutation"]

IHS abbreviation for INDIAN HEALTH SERVICE.

iich'aa *n.* a CULTURE-BOUND SYNDROME found in Navaho communities, with symptoms similar to those of AMOK.

I–It *adj.* describing a relationship in which a subject ("I") treats something or someone else exclusively as an impersonal object ("It") to be used or controlled. German Jewish philosopher Martin Buber (1878–1965), who originated the term, maintained that this type of relationship between people stands in the way of human warmth, mutuality, trust, and group cohesiveness. Compare I–THOU.

IKBS abbreviation for INTELLIGENCE KNOWLEDGE-BASED SYSTEM.

ikonic representation see ICONIC REPRESENTATION.

ikota *n.* see MYRIACHIT.

ILD abbreviation for interaural level differences. See BINAURAL CUES.

iliohypogastric nerve one of the nerves that extend from the spinal cord in the lumbar region, with branches that innervate the skin of the gluteal and lower abdominal regions.

ilioinguinal nerve a nerve with branches that extend into the genitalia. In the male, the ilioinguinal nerve follows the spermatic cord through the inguinal ring and sends branches into the penis and scrotum. In the female, this nerve extends to the mons pubis and the labia majora.

illegitimacy *n.* **1.** the status of a child whose parents were unmarried at the time of birth. In Western societies, the term has fallen into virtual disuse with changing family structures (e.g., the large numbers of children now born to cohabiting but unmarried parents), the fading of the stigma formerly attached to illegitimacy, and the disappearance of most legal distinctions between legitimate and illegitimate children. **2.** the state of being unlawful, improper, or contrary to reason and logic. **—illegitimate** *adj.*

illicit *adj.* illegal: often referring to widely abused psychoactive drugs for which there are few or no legitimate medical uses.

Illinois Test of Psycholinguistic Abilities (ITPA) a norm-referenced test for children aged 5–13 years and designed to measure spoken and written linguistic abilities considered important in communication and learning disorders. It currently consists of 12 subtests: spoken analogies, spoken vocabulary, morphological closure, syntactic sentences, sound deletion, rhyming sequences, sentence sequencing, written vocabulary, sight decoding, sound decoding, sight spelling, and sound spelling. First published in 1961 as an experimental edition, the ITPA is now in its third edition (published in 2001). [originally developed by U.S. psychologists Samuel Alexander Kirk (1904–1996) and James Jerome McCarthy (1927–) at the University of Illinois]

illiteracy *n.* **1.** an inability to read, write, or both. **2.** a lack of education or knowledge in a particular field of education, or, more generally, evidence of social and educational ineptitude. **—illiterate** *adj.*

illness *n.* the experience of sickness or lack of well-being of body or mind.

illness behavior behaviors, attitudes, and emotions exhibited by individuals during the course of a physical or mental illness. It includes the perception of feeling ill, the expression of illness-related concerns to others, changes in functioning, and utilization of health care services.

illocutionary act in the theory of SPEECH ACTS, the act that is performed by saying something (such as asking, ordering, or threatening), as opposed to the act of speaking itself (the **locutionary act**) or the act of causing a particular effect on others (such as persuading, amusing, or inspiring) as a result of speech (the **perlocutionary act**). In practice, most utterances involve the performance of all three acts simultaneously. See also PERFORMATIVE. [first described by British philosopher John Longshaw Austin (1911–1960)]

illogicality *n.* a tendency to make unwarranted or faulty inferences, often characteristic of delusional thinking and speech. **—illogical** *adj.*

illuminance *n.* (symbol: *E*) the light (luminous flux) falling on a unit area of a surface. The standard unit of illuminance is the LUX.

illumination *n.* **1.** the act of lighting or casting light or the state of being lighted. **2.** a moment of insight, for example into the nature and processes of an interpersonal relationship, the solution to a problem, or understanding of an event. See also AHA EXPERIENCE; EPIPHANY.

illumination conditions the types of illumination, taking into account such factors as intensity and absence of glare, available within an environment, particularly as related to suitability for certain tasks and the comfort of those performing them.

illumination standards the amounts of illumination

recommended for effective performance of certain tasks, as determined by the Illuminating Engineering Society of North America. The illumination standards were formerly expressed in foot-candles, but are now expressed in lux.

illumination unit formerly, the amount of light produced by one FOOT-CANDLE: now replaced by the LUX.

illuminism *n.* an exalted hallucinatory state in which the person carries on conversations with imaginary, often supernatural, beings.

illusion *n.* **1.** a false perception. Illusions of the senses, such as visual (or optical) illusions, result from the misinterpretation of sensory stimuli. For example, parallel railroad tracks appear to meet in the distance (see ALLEY PROBLEM; LINEAR PERSPECTIVE). Other examples of visual illusions are APPARENT MOVEMENT, CONTRAST ILLUSIONS, distortion illusions (such as the HERING ILLUSION, MÜLLER-LYER ILLUSION, POGGENDORF ILLUSION, PONZO ILLUSION, and ZÖLLNER ILLUSION), and the PANUM PHENOMENON. Illusions involving other senses include ARISTOTLE'S ILLUSION. All these illusions are quite normal occurrences, although they may also occur in delirium, schizophrenia, and in those taking mind-altering drugs. VISUAL ILLUSIONS may also occur as a result of a pathological condition. **2.** a distortion in memory (see MEMORY ILLUSION), such as DÉJÀ VU. **—illusory** *adj.*

illusion of agency the illusion of controlling an action that is not actually under one's control. Also called **illusion of will**. [defined by U.S. psychologist Daniel M. Wegner (1948–)]

illusion of control a false belief that external events result from or are governed by one's own actions or choices. See POSITIVE ILLUSION.

illusion of doubles see CAPGRAS SYNDROME.

illusion of group productivity the impression that a work group is producing more than it actually is.

illusion of orientation misidentification of environmental or other stimuli, such as confusion about one's location or the identity of people, due to impaired consciousness, for example, during DELIRIUM.

illusion of unique invulnerability the false belief that the SELF is somehow safeguarded from the dangers and misfortunes that afflict other people. The illusion may cause people to disregard such safety measures as seat belts or condoms.

illusion of will see ILLUSION OF AGENCY.

illusory conjunction the attribution of a characteristic of one stimulus to another stimulus when the stimuli are presented only briefly. Illusory conjunctions are most common with visual stimuli when, for example, the color of one form can be attributed to a different form. However, illusory conjunctions can also occur for other sensory stimuli.

illusory contour see SUBJECTIVE CONTOUR.

illusory correlation **1.** the appearance of a relationship that in reality does not exist. **2.** an overestimation of the degree of relationship (i.e., correlation) between two variables. For example, if an unusual action occurred at the same time that an adolescent was present, the assumption that the action was carried out by the adolescent would be an illusory correlation.

illusory covariation an apparent predictable or systematic correlation between two phenomena (objects or events) that in fact does not exist. See CO-OCCURRENCE; COVARIATION.

illusory memory see FALSE MEMORY.

illusory movement see APPARENT MOVEMENT.

iloperidone *n.* an ATYPICAL ANTIPSYCHOTIC agent of the benzisoxazole class that is active at a range of receptors. It acts as an antagonist at postsynaptic serotonin 5-HT_{2A} receptors as well as at dopamine D2 receptors. It is thought also to act as a PARTIAL AGONIST at postsynaptic dopamine D2 receptors. This blend of agonist and antagonist properties, plus its wide-ranging receptor activity, is thought to confer antipsychotic activity without the negative side effects commonly associated with antipsychotics. U.S. trade name: **Zomaril**.

im abbreviation for *i*ntra*m*uscular.

image *n.* **1.** in cognitive psychology, a likeness or representation of an earlier sensory experience recalled without external stimulation. For example, imagining the shape of a horse or the sound of a jet airplane brings to mind an image derived from earlier experiences with these stimuli. **2.** a representation of an object produced by an optical system. See also RETINAL IMAGE.

imageless thought thinking that occurs without the aid of IMAGES or sensory content. The WÜRZBURG SCHOOL upheld the existence of imageless thought on the basis of introspective reports, for example, experimental participants' stated ability to name a piece of fruit without picturing it. Edward Bradford TITCHENER and others in the structural school opposed this view (see STRUCTURALISM). See BEWUSSTSEINSLAGE.

imagery *n.* **1.** cognitive generation of sensory input from the five senses, individually or collectively, which is recalled from experience or self-generated in a nonexperienced form. **2.** mental IMAGES considered collectively, or the particular type of imagery characteristic of an individual, such as VISUAL IMAGERY. See IMAGERY CUE; IMAGERY TRAINING; KINESTHETIC IMAGERY.

imagery code the ENCODING of an object, idea, or impression in terms of its visual imagery. For example, the item "typewriter" might be remembered as a mental picture of a typewriter, rather than as the word *typewriter*. Compare SEMANTIC CODE.

imagery cue a cognitively created signal used to direct behavior. Examples are mental images of a stop sign when one has negative thoughts or of a butterfly when one wants to exhibit delicate, free-flowing motion in a skating routine. See also THOUGHT STOPPING.

imagery technique the use of imagined scenes as a therapeutic technique, often in HYPNOTHERAPY but also in therapies that use breathing and relaxation techniques to reduce anxiety. For example, an anxious client may be directed to imagine a placid scene recalled from memory, such as sitting, relaxed and calm, on a beach. The technique may be used by an individual in stressful situations, for example, by a nervous passenger in an aircraft. See also GUIDED AFFECTIVE IMAGERY.

imagery training a series of exercises to improve the clarity, vividness, and controllability of the images from the five senses, first individually, then in combination. See VIVIDNESS TRAINING.

imaginal flooding a type of EXPOSURE THERAPY used for treating individuals with obsessive, hypochondriacal, or phobic conditions or posttraumatic stress disorder. Vivid imagery evoked through speech is used by the therapist to expose the client mentally to an anxiety-evoking stimulus. See also FLOODING.

Imaginary *n.* the realm of images: one of three aspects of the psychoanalytic field defined by French psychoanalyst Jacques Lacan (1901–1981). The Imaginary is that state of being in which the infant has no sense of being a subject distinct from other people or the external world and no sense of his or her place in human culture. After the infant's entry into the SYMBOLIC (the world of language, culture, and morality), he or she can return to the wholeness of the Imaginary only in fantasy. See also REAL.

imaginary audience the nonexistent audience believed by the adolescent to be constantly focusing attention on him or her. It is an early adolescent construct reflective of acute self-consciousness and is considered an expression of ADOLESCENT EGOCENTRISM.

imaginary companion a fictitious person, animal, or object created by a child or adolescent. The individual gives the imaginary companion a name, talks, shares feelings, and pretends to play with it, and may use it as a scapegoat for his or her misdeeds. The phenomenon is considered an elaborate but common form of SYMBOLIC PLAY. Also called **invisible playmate**.

imagination *n.* the faculty that produces IDEAS and IMAGES in the absence of direct sensory data, often by combining fragments of previous sensory experiences into new syntheses. See also CREATIVE IMAGINATION. **—imaginary** *adj.* **—imagine** *vb.*

imagination inflation the increased likelihood of a person judging that an event has actually occurred (e.g., during that person's childhood) when the person imagines the event before making such a judgment.

imaging *n.* **1.** the process of scanning the brain or other organs or tissues to obtain an optical image. Techniques used include COMPUTED TOMOGRAPHY, POSITRON EMISSION TOMOGRAPHY (PET), anatomical MAGNETIC RESONANCE IMAGING (aMRI), and FUNCTIONAL MAGNETIC RESONANCE IMAGING (fMRI). The imaging may be either static or dynamic. See also BRAIN IMAGING; NUCLEAR IMAGING. **2.** in therapy, the use of suggested mental images to control body function, including the easing of pain. See also IMAGERY TECHNIQUE; VISUALIZATION.

imago *n.* an unconscious mental image of another person, especially the mother or father, that influences the way in which an individual relates to others. The imago is typically formed in infancy and childhood and is generally an idealized or otherwise not completely accurate representation. The term was originally used by Sigmund FREUD and the early psychoanalysts, and its meaning has carried over into other schools of psychology and psychotherapy.

imago therapy a type of therapy for relationship problems based on the theory that people carry unconscious composite images (see IMAGO) of the character traits and behaviors of their primary childhood caretakers that impel them to select certain partners and to behave in ways that are meant to heal earlier emotional wounds but that actually create relationship problems. Structured exercises, either in groups (for individuals or couples) or in COUPLES THERAPY, reveal the imago and help individuals learn to become less defensive and more compassionate toward partners as well as themselves.

imbecility *n.* formerly, a low to moderate level of intellectual disability characterized by an IQ between 25 and 50–55 and social and practical skills similar to those of 2- to 7-year-olds. This level of intellectual disability is now described as SEVERE MENTAL RETARDATION or MODERATE MENTAL RETARDATION (depending on the degree).

imipramine *n.* a TRICYCLIC ANTIDEPRESSANT (TCA) with a tertiary amine molecular structure. It was originally synthesized in the hopes of creating an effective antipsychotic, but was observed to be ineffective in reducing psychotic symptoms. It did, however, seem to help individuals with severe depression and was subsequently marketed as an antidepressant. It is considered the prototype TCA and, like all tricyclic agents, its use as an antidepressant has been largely supplanted by less toxic drugs. It continues, however, to have a therapeutic role as a sedative and adjunct in the management of neuromuscular or musculoskeletal pain. U.S. trade name: **Tofranil**.

imitation *n.* the process of copying the behavior of another person, group, or object, intentionally or unintentionally. It is a basic form of learning that accounts for many human skills, gestures, interests, attitudes, role behaviors, social customs, and verbal expressions, but can also take pathological form, as in ECHOLALIA and ECHOPRAXIA. Some theorists propose that true imitation requires that an observer be able to take the perspective of the model. This contrasts with other forms of SOCIAL LEARNING, such as EMULATION, LOCAL ENHANCEMENT, and MIMICRY. There is controversy concerning whether true imitation occurs in nonhuman animals or whether they either merely emulate the actions of others or are attracted to the location of others and by chance appear to show imitation. **—imitate** *vb.*

imitative learning the first stage of CULTURAL LEARNING, which occurs when the learner internalizes aspects of the model's behavioral strategies and intentions for executing the behavior. According to cultural learning theory, imitative learning is followed by INSTRUCTED LEARNING and COLLABORATIVE LEARNING. [proposed by U.S. psychologist Michael Tomasello (1950–) and colleagues]

immanent justice the belief that rules are fixed and immutable and that punishment automatically follows misdeeds regardless of extenuating circumstances. Children up to the age of 8 equate the morality of an act only with its consequences; not until later do they develop the capacity to judge motive and subjective considerations. See MORAL ABSOLUTISM; MORAL REALISM. Compare DISTRIBUTIVE JUSTICE. [postulated by Jean PIAGET]

immaterialism *n.* the philosophical position that denies the independent existence of matter as a substance in which qualities (see PRIMARY QUALITY; SECONDARY QUALITY) might inhere. Sensible objects are held to exist as the sum of the qualities they produce in the perceiving mind, with no material substratum. The best known philosophy of this kind is that of Anglo-Irish philosopher George Berkeley (1685–1753). It is difficult to distinguish such a position from IDEALISM, which holds that mind is the essential to all reality and that things and qualities exist only as perceived.

immature science a science that has not advanced to the stage of development characteristic of a PREPARADIGMATIC SCIENCE or a NORMAL SCIENCE. [proposed by U.S. philosopher of science Thomas Kuhn (1922–1996)]

immediacy behavior any action, movement, or physical stance that indicates comfort, intimacy, or a close relationship between two people, for example, EYE CONTACT or touching.

immediate experience current experience and impressions of that experience without any analysis (see MEDIATE EXPERIENCE). See also CONTEMPORANEITY.

immediate gratification the experience of satisfaction or receipt of reward as soon as a response is made. See also PLEASURE PRINCIPLE. Compare DELAY OF GRATIFICATION.

immediate memory a type or stage of memory in which an individual recalls information recently presented, such as a street address or telephone number, although this information may be forgotten after its immediate use. Immediate memory is frequently tested in assessing intelligence or cerebral impairment. See also SHORT-TERM MEMORY.

immediate recall test a test in which the participant is tested for recall (reproduction) of stimuli immediately after the stimuli are presented.

immobility *n.* a condition in which an organism shows no signs of motion, as in DEATH FEIGNING or FREEZING BEHAVIOR. This may occur in response to sudden stimuli that might be associated with a predator or it may be elicited in a fear-conditioning study as a learned response to an aversively conditioned signal. **—immobile** *adj.*

immobilizing activity see LIBIDO-BINDING ACTIVITY.

immune response the response of the IMMUNE SYSTEM to invasion of the body by foreign substances (ANTIGENS), such as viruses, bacteria, or tissues of other organisms. Nonspecific immune responses include inflammation (with the release of HISTAMINE) and PHAGOCYTOSIS of invading microbes, tissues, and so forth by various types of LEUKOCYTE (white blood cells). The two types of specific immune response are **humoral immunity**, in which B LYMPHOCYTES produce ANTIBODIES that either directly destroy antigens or enhance the destruction of antigens by other cells; and **cell-mediated immunity**, mediated by T lymphocytes, which attack antigens directly and specifically. See also ANTIGEN–ANTIBODY REACTION.

immune system a complex system in vertebrates that helps protect the body against pathological effects of foreign substances (ANTIGENS), such as viruses and bacteria. The organs involved include the bone marrow and THYMUS, in which LYMPHOCYTES—the principal agents responsible for specific IMMUNE RESPONSES—are produced, together with the spleen, lymph nodes, and other lymphoid tissues and various chemicals (e.g., CYTOKINES) that mediate the immune response. The immune system interacts with both the nervous system and the endocrine system. See also PSYCHONEUROIMMUNOLOGY.

immunity *n.* the ability of the body to resist infection, afforded by the actions of the IMMUNE SYSTEM in mounting IMMUNE RESPONSES. **Active immunity** arises when immune cells (see LYMPHOCYTE) produce, and remain able to produce, appropriate antibodies following infection or deliberate stimulation (IMMUNIZATION). **Passive immunity** is conferred by the introduction of antibodies from another organism (e.g., via COLOSTRUM). **Innate immunity** does not require prior contact with invading microorganisms or tissues and involves nonspecific immune responses. See also ANTIGEN–ANTIBODY REACTION.

immunization *n.* the process of conferring immunity by other than natural means. Active immunity is acquired by inoculation or vaccination, which involves the injection of a specific, prepared antigen to induce the production of natural antibodies by the body's immune system. Passive immunity, which is short-lived (1–6 months), is acquired by the injection of prepared antibodies obtained from an animal or human already immune to the disease in question.

immunocytochemistry *n.* techniques that use labeled antibodies specific to particular proteins to localize those proteins in cells or tissues. The label creates a visible mark, thus enabling visualization and localization of the component. Also called **immunohistochemistry**.

immunology *n.* the branch of medicine that specializes in the study of IMMUNITY and immune reactions (e.g., allergies and hypersensitivities). **—immunological** *adj.* **—immunologist** *n.*

Imodium *n.* a trade name for LOPERAMIDE.

impact analysis a quantitative analytic procedure used to assess the net success or failure of a program, usually through controlled experimentation. It is appropriate only if the program's objectives are specifiable and measurable, the program is well implemented for its intended participants, and the outcome measures are reliable and valid. Also called **impact assessment**. See also OUTCOME EVALUATION; SUMMATIVE EVALUATION.

impaired judgment difficulty in forming evaluative opinions or reaching conclusions concerning available evidence, often about events and people. Impaired judgment may lead to seemingly irrational actions and risk-taking behaviors.

impairment *n.* any departure from the body's typical structure or physiological or psychological functioning.

impairment index a measure of impairment on a series of cognitive tests. The best known such index is the **Halstead–Reitan Impairment Index**, which reflects the percentage of tests in the impaired range; the higher the percentage, the greater the likelihood of brain damage.

impairment in new learning see ANTEROGRADE AMNESIA.

impeachment evidence evidence used to attack or discredit testimony given by an individual in court.

impenetrability *n.* the state of certain cognitive capacities, such as syntax, that are claimed to be inherently walled off from conscious access and not available to introspective analysis.

imperative *n.* **1.** any demand that is critical or pressing. See CATEGORICAL IMPERATIVE; ETHICAL IMPERATIVE. **2.** in psychoanalytic theory, a demand of the SUPEREGO that represents the commanding voice of parental or social rule, and operates on an unconscious level to direct the behavior of the individual. **3.** in linguistics, the MOOD of a verb used to issue commands or make requests, as in *Get off!* or *Please come back*. Compare INDICATIVE; INTERROGATIVE; SUBJUNCTIVE.

imperceptible difference a physical difference between two stimulus events that is below an observer's DIFFERENCE THRESHOLD. This results in the two events being judged as the same psychologically when they are not the same physically.

impersonation *n.* **1.** the deliberate assumption of another person's identity, usually as a means of gaining status or other advantage. See also IMPOSTOR SYNDROME. **2.** the imitation of another person's behavior or mannerisms, which is sometimes done for its corrective or therapeutic effect on one's own behavior (e.g., to gain insight).

impingement *n.* **1.** in the OBJECT RELATIONS THEORY of British psychoanalyst Donald Winnicott (1896–1971), an experience in the infant's maternal environment that is felt to be disturbing. Such experiences are posited to lead to the development of a FALSE SELF because the infant may develop through a series of reactions to impingements rather than becoming aware of his or her true tendencies and capacities by discovering the environment on his or her own terms. **2.** in perception, impact or contact with a sensory receptor. **—impinge** *vb.*

implantation *n.* **1.** the attachment of a fertilized ovum to the uterine wall at the BLASTOCYST stage of development, 6–8 days after ovulation. **2.** the placing of a drug (e.g., a subcutaneous implant) or an object (e.g., an artificial pacemaker) within the tissues of the body.

implanted memory the apparent recollection of an event that never occurred because someone has convinced the person that it did occur. There have been allegations that some psychotherapists have implanted memories in their clients by leading questioning. See FALSE MEMORY SYNDROME.

implementation evaluation an evaluation approach that focuses on the way a program was delivered and whether it reached its intended recipients.

implementation stage in a normative model of GROUP PROBLEM SOLVING, the application of the proposed solution or decision after group deliberation and identification of the favored alternative.

implicature *n.* in linguistics, a PROPOSITION that is not stated explicitly in an utterance and is not a condition for its truth but can nevertheless be inferred from it. The types of implicature recognized in PRAGMATICS and DISCOURSE ANALYSIS go beyond those recognized as valid in formal logic. For example, the statement *Mary is my dad's wife* would imply in most contexts "Mary is not my mother," even though the first proposition cannot be said to entail the second. Compare PRESUPPOSITION. See also CONVERSATIONAL INFERENCE; INDIRECT SPEECH ACT. —**implicative** *adj.*

implicit association test (**IAT**) an IMPLICIT ATTITUDE MEASURE in which participants perform a series of categorization tasks on computer for a set of words representing an ATTITUDE OBJECT (e.g., words such as *ant, fly,* and *grasshopper* representing the attitude object of insects). Attitudes are assessed by having participants perform a joint categorization task in which they must judge if the target words are members of a specified category (e.g., insects) as well as if a second set of intermixed words, selected to be highly evaluative in nature, are positive or negative. In one phase of the test, the computer response key used to indicate membership in the specified category is the same as that used to indicate a positive word. In a different phase, the key used to indicate membership in the specified category is the same as that used to indicate a negative word. If attitudes are positive, judging the target words should be faster when the same response key is used for category membership and positive words than when the same response key is used for category membership and negative words. Negative attitudes produce the opposite pattern. [originally developed by U.S. psychologist Anthony G. Greenwald (1939–) and his colleagues]

implicit attitude an ATTITUDE of which a person has little or no conscious awareness. Compare EXPLICIT ATTITUDE.

implicit attitude measure an ATTITUDE MEASURE in which a person is not consciously aware of the fact that his or her attitude toward a particular ATTITUDE OBJECT is being assessed. Measures of this type are generally INDIRECT ATTITUDE MEASURES. See also DIRECT ATTITUDE MEASURE. Compare EXPLICIT ATTITUDE MEASURE.

implicit behavior 1. behavior that cannot be observed directly, such as a cognitive process or emotional reaction. **2.** behavior that cannot be observed without the aid of instruments, such as subtle physiological responses. **3.** behavior of which the individual is not consciously aware.

implicit causality the property of VERBS such that causality is implicit either in the AGENT or the PATIENT of the verb.

implicit cognition an idea, perception, or concept that may be influential in the cognitive processes or the behavior of an individual, even though the person is not explicitly aware of it. See COGNITION.

implicit knowledge see TACIT KNOWLEDGE.

implicit leadership theories perceivers' general assumptions about the traits, characteristics, and qualities that distinguish leaders from the people they lead. Like the LEADERSHIP THEORIES developed by psychologists, these cognitive frameworks tend to include lawlike generalities about leadership and more specific hypotheses about the types of qualities that characterize most leaders. However, unlike scientific theories, they are based on intuition and personal experience and are usually not stated explicitly. See also ATTRIBUTION THEORY OF LEADERSHIP; LEADER-CATEGORIZATION THEORY; LEADER PROTOTYPE.

implicit learning learning of a cognitive or behavioral task that occurs without intention to learn or awareness of what has been learned. Implicit learning is evidenced by improved task performance rather than as a response to an explicit request to remember. See also IMPLICIT MEMORY. Compare EXPLICIT MEMORY.

implicit measures of personality measures that do not ask people to report explicitly on their psychological characteristics but instead employ subtle indices capable of tapping mental content that individuals may not wish to express or perhaps are not even aware they possess because the mental content is not explicitly represented in consciousness. Measures of the time it takes individuals to answer questions, irrespective of the content of their answers, are one commonly employed implicit measure.

implicit memory memory for a previous event or experience that is produced indirectly, without an explicit request to recall the event and without awareness that memory is involved. For instance, after seeing the word *store* in one context, a person would complete the word fragment *st_r_* as *store* rather than *stare,* even without remembering that *store* had been recently encountered. Implicit memory can exist when conscious or EXPLICIT MEMORY fails, as occurs in amnesia and brain disease.

implicit personality theories tacit assumptions about the interrelations of personality traits, used in everyday life when people infer the presence of one trait on the basis of observing another.

implicit prejudice a prejudice against a specific social group that is not consciously held. Compare EXPLICIT PREJUDICE.

implicit process 1. a cognitive event that cannot be described accurately, even under optimal conditions. **2.** an occasional synonym for UNCONSCIOUS PROCESS. Compare EXPLICIT PROCESS.

implicit response see COVERT RESPONSE.

implosive therapy a technique in BEHAVIOR THERAPY in which the client is repeatedly encouraged to imagine an anxiety-arousing situation, or to recall the incident that led to trauma, and to experience anxiety as intensely as possible while doing so. Since there is no actual danger in the situation, the anxiety response is not reinforced and therefore is gradually extinguished. Also called **implosion therapy**. See also FLOODING; PARADOXICAL INTENTION. [developed by U.S. psychologists Thomas G. Stampfl (1923–) and Donald J. Levis (1936–)]

importance of an attitude the extent to which an individual personally cares about an ATTITUDE OBJECT or attaches psychological significance to it. Importance is related to the STRENGTH OF AN ATTITUDE. See also CENTRALITY OF AN ATTITUDE; EGO INVOLVEMENT.

impossible figure a shape or form in which different components produce conflicting and mutually exclusive interpretations.

impostor syndrome 1. the tendency to attribute achievements and success to external factors rather than internal factors, associated with a persistent belief in one's lack of ability despite consistent objective evidence to the contrary. As a result, the individual may feel like a fraud and have low self-esteem and identity problems. Also called **impostor phenomenon**. **2.** a personality pattern characterized by PATHOLOGICAL LYING, which takes the form of fabricating an identity or a series of identities in an effort to gain recognition and status. See IMPERSONATION.

impotence *n.* the inability of a man to complete the sex act due to partial or complete failure to achieve or maintain erection. This condition is called MALE ERECTILE DISORDER in *DSM–IV–TR* and ERECTILE DYSFUNCTION in clinical contexts. The most common causes of drug-induced impotence are antidepressants and antihypertensives. It is not clearly understood how the use of antidepressants results in impotence and other forms of sexual dysfunction: Possible mechanisms include inhibition of NITRIC OXIDE or effects on serotonin (particularly the 5-HT_2 SEROTONIN RECEPTOR), dopamine, acetylcholine, and norepinephrine. Impotence may also denote premature ejaculation, limited interest in sex, orgasm without pleasure, or coitus without ejaculation. See also ORGASTIC IMPOTENCE; PRIMARY ERECTILE DYSFUNCTION; SECONDARY ERECTILE DYSFUNCTION. **—impotent** *adj.*

impoverished *adj.* **1.** describing a stimulus that is lacking in complexity or information value. **2.** deficient in or deprived of qualities or lacking in richness because something essential is missing. An **impoverished environment** offers few opportunities to engage in activity and does not provide adequate sensory and intellectual stimulation. See also INTELLECTUAL IMPOVERISHMENT. **—impoverishment** *n.*

impression *n.* **1.** the presumed effect on the brain of stimulation. **2.** a vague or unanalyzed judgment or reaction.

impression formation the process in which an individual develops a PERCEPTUAL SCHEMA of some object, person, or group. Early research on impression formation demonstrated that the accuracy of impressions was frequently poor; more recent studies have focused on the roles played in the process by such factors as the perceiver's cognitive processes (e.g., how readily some types of ideas come to mind) and feelings (e.g., anger can predispose the perceiver to stereotype an individual).

impressionism factor the quality of a style of art characterized by blurred outlines and emphasis on surface qualities and textures. The style was popular with impressionist painters of the 19th century. In studies of perceptions of art by British-born Canadian psychologist Daniel E. Berlyne (1924–1976), the impressionism factor is reflected in evaluation ratings that are highly positive for surface qualities and highly negative for beliefs, imagination, and lines.

impression management behaviors that are designed to control how others perceive one's SELF, especially by guiding them to attribute desirable traits to the self. Typically, it is assumed that people attempt to present favorable images of themselves as a means of obtaining social rewards and enhancing self-esteem. Impression management has been offered as an alternative explanation for some phenomena that have traditionally been interpreted in terms of COGNITIVE DISSONANCE THEORY. Some psychologists distinguish impression management from SELF-PRESENTATION by proposing that impression management involves only deliberate, conscious strategies.

impression method a procedure in which the participants make introspective reports on stimuli in terms of their feelings (e.g., pleasant or unpleasant).

impression of universality see UNIVERSALITY.

impressive aphasia see RECEPTIVE APHASIA.

imprinting *n.* **1.** a simple yet profound and highly effective learning process that occurs during a CRITICAL PERIOD in the life of some animals. It was first described in 1873 by British naturalist Douglas A. Spalding (1840–1877) when he observed that newly hatched chicks tended to follow the first moving object, human or animal, that caught their attention. The term itself was introduced by Austrian ethologist Konrad Lorenz (1903–1989) in 1937. Some investigators believe that such processes are instinctual; others regard them as a form of PREPARED LEARNING. **2.** in conditioning, the process of establishing a stimulus as a REINFORCER by presenting it in the appropriate context. The stimulus thus established is called an **imprinted stimulus**.

improvement rate see DISCHARGE RATE.

improvisation *n.* in PSYCHODRAMA, the spontaneous acting out of problems and situations without prior preparation.

IMPS abbreviation for INPATIENT MULTIDIMENSIONAL PSYCHIATRIC SCALE.

impuberism *n.* **1.** a state of not having reached puberty because of age or delayed development. **2.** the continuation of childhood characteristics into adolescence or adulthood. Also called **impuberty**.

impulse *n.* **1.** a sudden and compelling urge to act immediately, often resulting in action without deliberation for a purpose that cannot be recalled. Also called **impulsion**. See also IMPULSE-CONTROL DISORDER; IMPULSIVE. **2.** see NERVE IMPULSE. **3.** in psychoanalytic theory, the movement of PSYCHIC ENERGY associated with instinctual drives, such as sex and hunger.

impulse control the ability to resist an impulse, desire, or temptation and to regulate its translation into action. See also IMPULSE-CONTROL DISORDER.

impulse-control disorder a disorder characterized by a failure to resist impulses, drives, or temptations to commit acts that are harmful to oneself or to others. Impulse-control disorders include those in the *DSM–IV–TR* category IMPULSE-CONTROL DISORDERS NOT ELSEWHERE CLASSIFIED. Other disorders that may involve problems of impulse control include substance-use disorders, paraphilias, conduct disorders, and mood disorders.

impulse-control disorders not elsewhere classified in *DSM–IV–TR*, a class of IMPULSE-CONTROL DISORDERS not classified in other categories (such as substance-use disorders). This class includes PATHOLOGICAL GAMBLING, KLEPTOMANIA, PYROMANIA, INTERMITTENT EXPLOSIVE DISORDER, and TRICHOTILLOMANIA, all of which have their own specific sets of diagnostic criteria, together with **impulse-control disorders not otherwise specified**, which do not meet the criteria for any of the specific disorders. All these disorders have the following common features: (a) failure to resist an impulse or a drive or a temptation to perform an act that is harmful to the individual or others; (b) mounting tension before committing the act; and (c) pleasure or relief during the act, with or without regret and self-reproach afterward.

impulse-timing model a model for the organization of a MOTOR PROGRAM in which the movement TRAJECTORY is determined by the amplitude and timing of force impulses produced by the AGONIST and ANTAGONIST muscles. See also EQUILIBRIUM-POINT MODEL.

impulsion *n.* see IMPULSE.

impulsive *adj.* describing or displaying behavior characterized by little or no forethought, reflection, or consideration of the consequences, which may involve taking risks. Compare REFLECTIVE. See also REFLECTIVITY–

IMPULSIVITY; SELF-CONTROL. **—impulsiveness** or **impulsivity** *n.*

impulsive character a personality pattern marked by a tendency to act hastily and without due reflection.

imu *n.* a CULTURE-BOUND SYNDROME resembling LATAH, observed among the Ainu and Sakhalin women of Japan. It is characterized by an extreme STARTLE RESPONSE involving automatic movements, imitative behavior, infantile reactions, and obedience to command. See also JUMPING FRENCHMEN OF MAINE SYNDROME; MYRIACHIT.

Imuran *n.* a trade name for AZATHIOPRINE.

in absentia denoting legal proceedings against people that are conducted in their absence.

inaccessibility *n.* **1.** the state of being impossible to reach, approach, or use. **2.** unresponsiveness to external stimuli, most commonly associated with the state of withdrawal sometimes seen in autism and schizophrenia. **—inaccessible** *adj.*

inanimate noun see ANIMATE NOUN.

inappetence *n.* impaired appetite or desire, a frequent symptom of depression.

inappropriate affect emotional responses that are not in keeping with the situation or are incompatible with expressed thoughts or wishes, for example, smiling when told about the death of a friend. Extreme inappropriate affect is a defining characteristic of DISORGANIZED SCHIZOPHRENIA.

inappropriate stimulus a stimulus or condition that elicits a response not normally triggered by that stimulus. For example, pressing against one's closed eyelid elicits perception of lights; that is, a mechanical stimulus elicits a response in PHOTORECEPTORS that typically respond to light.

Inapsine *n.* a trade name for DROPERIDOL.

inattention *n.* a state in which there is a lack of concentrated or focused attention or in which attention drifts back and forth. See also SELECTIVE INATTENTION; PERCEPTUAL EXTINCTION.

inattentional blindness failure to notice and remember otherwise perceptible stimuli in the visual background while the focus of attention is elsewhere. Research into inattentional blindness has led some to conclude that there is no conscious perception of the world without attention. See also CHANGE BLINDNESS; PERCEPTUAL SET; SELECTIVE PERCEPTION. [defined by U.S. psychologists Arien Mack (1931–) and Irvin Rock (1922–1995)]

in-basket test a WORK-SAMPLE TEST used in management training and selection. The participant is given an assortment of items (letters, memos, reports) that might be found in a typical office in-basket and must take action on them as if he or she were on the job.

inborn *adj.* see INNATE.

inborn error of metabolism any biochemical disorder caused by a genetic defect. It is often expressed as a defect or deficiency in the structure or enzymatic function of a protein molecule or in the transport of a vital substance across a cell membrane. Examples of such errors include diabetes mellitus, gout, phenylketonuria, and Tay–Sachs disease. Also called **metabolic anomaly**.

inbreeding *n.* the mating of individuals that are closely related, usually for the purpose of preserving certain preferred traits while preventing the acquisition of unwanted traits in the offspring. Inbreeding increases the risk of perpetuating certain genetic defects in the family, as in consanguineous marriages. Inbreeding within small populations, such as ethnic minorities or geographically isolated populations, leads to increased frequency of particular mutations within such groups. This fact has been used to demonstrate the FOUNDER EFFECT for certain cancers and other disorders. Such studies have contributed to our ability to identify and test for mutations predisposing to disease in some groups of people.

inbreeding avoidance the avoidance of breeding with close relatives in order to maintain genetic diversity. Several mechanisms that promote inbreeding avoidance have been identified. In some species olfactory or vocal signals may provide information about genetic relatedness, but most often individuals simply avoid breeding with those who are most familiar. Some studies of MATE SELECTION provide evidence of **optimal outbreeding**: Neither closely related individuals nor those that differ greatly are chosen; those that are different enough to avoid inbreeding but not too different are regarded as optimal mates.

incantation *n.* ritualistic chanting, singing, or speaking. The incantation of certain prescribed phrases forms an important part of many religious and magical RITUALS. **—incant** *vb.*

incendiarism *n.* compulsive or intentional fire setting. See FIRE-SETTING BEHAVIOR; PYROMANIA.

incentive *n.* an external stimulus, such as a condition or an object, that enhances or serves as a motive for behavior.

incentive motivation 1. in HULL'S MATHEMATICO-DEDUCTIVE THEORY OF LEARNING, an inducement, such as the expectation of a reward or punishment, that serves as an INTERVENING VARIABLE to influence response strength. See also STIMULUS-INTENSITY DYNAMISM. **2.** more generally, any motivation induced by a positive reinforcer.

incentive system in organizational settings, a set of rewards and rules for their disbursement that is designed to influence future performance. Incentives vary in motivating power from group to group. As well as increased pay, common incentives include such items as hospital insurance, pensions, GAINSHARING schemes, performance-related bonuses, employee stock shares, gym membership, and corporate entertainment (e.g., tickets for sports events). See also DISINCENTIVE; WORK MOTIVATION.

incentive theory the theory that motivation arousal depends on the interaction between environmental incentives (i.e., STIMULUS OBJECTS)—both positive and negative—and an organism's psychological and physiological states (e.g., DRIVE states). Compare DRIVE-REDUCTION THEORY.

incentive value the perceived value of a motivating stimulus or condition, which varies among individuals.

incest *n.* sexual activity between people of close blood relationship (e.g., brother and sister) that is prohibited by law or custom. In some societies sexual intercourse between cousins, uncles and nieces, or aunts and nephews is prohibited; in others it is permitted. Incest taboos of some kind are found in practically every society. **—incestuous** *adj.*

incest barrier in psychoanalytic theory, an EGO DEFENSE against incestuous impulses and fantasies. The barrier is the result of the INTROJECTION of social laws and customs. These internal and external prohibitions free the LIBIDO to make an external OBJECT CHOICE.

incest taboo social prohibition against sexual intercourse between people of close blood relationship. See INCEST.

incestuous ties in psychoanalytic theory, the condition in which an individual remains psychologically dependent on the mother, family, or symbolic substitute to the extent that healthy involvement with others and with society is inhibited or precluded. According to Erich FROMM, who introduced the term, incestuous ties represent the negative resolution of the search for ROOTEDNESS. See also IDENTITY NEED.

incidence *n.* the rate of occurrence of new cases of a given event or condition, such as a disorder, disease, symptom, or injury, in a particular population in a given period. An **incidence rate** is normally expressed as the number of cases per 100,000 population per year. See also PREVALENCE.

incidental learning learning that is not premeditated, deliberate, or intentional and that is acquired as a result of some other, possibly unrelated, mental activity. Some theorists believe that much learning takes place without any intention to learn, occurring incidentally to other cognitive processing of information. Also called **nonintentional learning**. See also LATENT LEARNING. Compare INTENTIONAL LEARNING.

incidental memory a memory that is acquired without conscious effort or intention to remember.

incidental stimulus an unintentional or coincidental stimulus that may occur during an experiment or in another situation, which may elicit an unplanned response from the participants or result in the distortion of research findings.

incident process 1. a systematic sequence of actions or steps that are approved for use in a potentially dangerous situation, such as fire, severe weather, or the presence of bombs or guns. In a school setting, these procedures are often practiced as a drill, in order to familiarize students with the appropriate procedure. **2.** a system in which learners begin with inadequate data and ask questions to gain additional information. The instructor has all the data and reveals a limited amount at the beginning, then reveals more in response to specific questions, so that the group can reach decisions. The system is designed to teach the skills of analysis, synthesis, and interrogation that are relevant to problem solving and investigative techniques.

inclusion *n.* in education, the practice of teaching students with disabilities and low ability, including all ranges of intelligence except those below a certain minimum level, in the same classroom as other students and in a way that meets the needs of all students.

inclusion–exclusion criteria in clinical research, criteria used for determining which individuals are eligible to participate in a particular study. Inclusion criteria might specify, for example, age range, whereas exclusion criteria might specify, for example, the existence of more than one illness or psychological disorder.

inclusive fitness the REPRODUCTIVE SUCCESS not only of an individual but of all that individual's relatives in proportion to their COEFFICIENT OF RELATEDNESS. In calculating estimates of reproductive success, it is assumed that parents, offspring, and siblings have an average of 50% of their genes in common, grandparents and grandoffspring, and uncles and nieces, share 25% of genes, and so forth.

inclusiveness *n.* one of the gestalt laws of grouping that describes the tendency to perceive only the larger figure when a smaller figure is completely encompassed within it. Also called **principle of inclusiveness**.

incoherence *n.* inability to express oneself in a clear and orderly manner, most commonly manifested as disjointed and unintelligible speech. This may be an expression of disorganized and impaired thinking. **—incoherent** *adj.*

incommensurable *adj.* unable to be compared. For example, two or more characteristics or variables that are not measured in the same units and thus cannot be compared in terms of the same scale or standard would be described as incommensurable.

incompatibilism *n.* the position that FREE WILL and DETERMINISM are incompatible and cannot coexist in any form or sense. Compare COMPATIBILITY. See also HARD DETERMINISM; SOFT DETERMINISM.

incompatibility *n.* the state of affairs in which two or more people are unable to interact harmoniously with each other. Compare COMPATIBILITY. **—incompatible** *adj.*

incompatible response a response or action that conflicts with another or occurs simultaneously with another. For example, a state of anxiety is incompatible with a state of relaxation.

incompatible response method a technique used to break bad habits in which an undesirable response is replaced by a more acceptable one that cannot coexist with the undesirable response.

incompetence *n.* **1.** the inability to carry out a required task or activity adequately. **2.** in law, the inability of a defendant to participate meaningfully in criminal proceedings, which include all elements of the criminal justice system, from initial interrogation to sentencing. Defendants who do not have the ability to communicate with attorneys or understand the proceedings may be ruled incompetent to stand trial (see COMPETENCY TO STAND TRIAL). See also DUSKY STANDARD. **3.** in law, the inability to make sound judgments regarding one's transactions or personal affairs. See LEGAL CAPACITY. Also called **incompetency**. **—incompetent** *adj.*

incompetency plea the plea, in a court of law, that the defendant, because of mental illness, mental defect, or other reasons, does not understand the nature and object of the proceedings, cannot appreciate or comprehend his or her own condition in relation to the proceedings, or is unable, for some other reason, to assist the attorney in his or her own defense. See also COMPETENCY TO STAND TRIAL.

incomplete block design an experimental design in which selected higher order interactions and main effects are intentionally confounded in order to keep the total number of CELLS in the design relatively small. See BLOCK DESIGN; CONFOUNDS.

incomplete factorial design a FACTORIAL DESIGN in which every level of every factor (INDEPENDENT VARIABLE) does not occur together with every level of every other factor, as it would in a complete factorial design. An example is the LATIN SQUARE.

incomplete-pictures test a test of visual recognition and interpretation in which drawings in varying degrees of completion are presented, and the participant attempts to identify the object as early in the series as possible. See also PICTURE-COMPLETION TEST.

incomplete-sentence test see SENTENCE-COMPLETION TEST.

incomplete spinal cord injury damage to the spinal cord that results in partial loss of motor or sensory function below the site of the injury. See also SPINAL CORD INJURY.

incongruence *n.* lack of consistency or appropriateness, as in INAPPROPRIATE AFFECT or as when one's subjective evaluation of a situation is at odds with reality. **—incongruent** *adj.*

incongruity *n.* the quality of being inconsistent, incompatible, not harmonious, or otherwise in disagreement with an accepted mode or standard. Perception experiments may include tests of incongruity in which, for example, a deck of playing cards may contain incongruous colors and suits, such as black hearts or purple spades.

incongruity theory of humor an explanation of the ability of HUMOR to elicit laughter that emphasizes the juxtaposition of incompatible or contradictory elements. For example, British-born U.S. comedian Bob Hope (1903–2003) once quipped in regard to a place he was visiting: "The mosquitoes here are huge. Last night I shot one in my pajamas. They were tight on him too." Such theories have roots in the work of German philosophers Immanuel Kant (1724–1804) and Arthur Schopenhauer (1788–1860), British philosopher Herbert Spencer (1820–1903), and Sigmund FREUD. See also RELEASE THEORY OF HUMOR.

incontinence *n.* **1.** an inability to control basic body functions, particularly urination and defecation (see FECAL INCONTINENCE; URINARY INCONTINENCE). Incontinence is often caused by bodily and neurological injury or damage or organic abnormalities and changes. **2.** an inability to restrain sexual impulses. **—incontinent** *adj.*

incoordination *n.* a lack of harmony or coordination of movement.

incorporation *n.* in psychoanalytic theory, the fantasy that one has ingested an external OBJECT, which is felt to be physically present inside the body. According to the theory, it first occurs in the ORAL STAGE, when the infant fantasizes that he or she has ingested the mother's breast. Incorporation is often confused with IDENTIFICATION and INTROJECTION. **—incorporate** *vb.*

incorporation dream a dream whose content is wholly or partially taken in from concurrent sensory stimulation. See ACCIDENTAL STIMULUS.

incremental *adj.* describing or relating to changes that take place in small, cumulative steps rather than in large jumps.

incremental validity an increase in the accuracy level of decisions made on the basis of a test over the level of accuracy obtained had the test not been employed.

incubation *n.* **1.** the provision of warmth and protection for eggs that develop outside the female's body. In birds, incubation can be undertaken by either or both parents and is essential for hatching of the eggs. **2.** the gradual generation of a solution to a problem at an unconscious or semiconscious level, often after an attempt at a conscious, deliberate solution has failed. **3.** in microbiology, the growth of cultures in a controlled environment. **4.** the maintenance of an artificial environment for a premature or hypoxic infant. **5.** the asymptomatic stage of development of an infection. **—incubate** *vb.* **—incubator** *n.*

incubation of anxiety the increase in a conditioned anxiety response that occurs with repeated unreinforced presentation of a CONDITIONED STIMULUS. For example, a person with a spider phobia might become more afraid of spiders each time he or she encounters one, even if no encounter is paired with a traumatic event, such as the spider biting. [first proposed by Hans EYSENCK as the basis of his conditioning theory of neurosis]

incubus *n.* **1.** a demon or evil spirit in male form believed to have sexual intercourse with sleeping women. Compare SUCCUBUS. **2.** a nightmare. **3.** a person or thing that is oppressive or an encumbrance.

incus *n.* see OSSICLES.

indecency *n.* behavior considered offensive, obscene, improper, or immoral according to the norms of a particular culture, especially in relation to sexual matters. **—indecent** *adj.*

indefinite article in linguistics, an ARTICLE (*a* or *an* in English) used with a noun phrase to indicate a nonspecific entity or one not previously defined, as in *A dog is a wonderful companion* or *A dog started barking*. Compare DEFINITE ARTICLE.

indemnity plan a system of HEALTH INSURANCE in which the insurer pays for the costs of covered services after care has been given. Such plans typically offer participants considerable freedom to choose their own health care providers and are contrasted with **group health plans**, which provide service benefits through GROUP MEDICAL PRACTICES.

independence *n.* **1.** freedom from the influence or control of other individuals or groups. **2.** complete lack of relationship between two or more events, sampling units, or variables such that none is influenced by any other and that changes in any one have no implication for changes in any other. **3.** in probability theory, the condition in which the probability of an event does not depend on the probability of some other event. If A and B are independent events, then $\Pr(A/B) = \Pr(A)$. **—independent** *adj., n.*

independent events either of two events whose occurrence does not influence the occurrence of the other.

independent living 1. the ability of an individual to perform—without assistance from others—all or most of the daily functions typically required to be self-sufficient, including those tasks essential to personal care (see ACTIVITIES OF DAILY LIVING) and to maintaining a home and job. **2.** a philosophy and civil reform movement promoting the rights of people with disabilities to determine the course of their lives and be full, productive members of society with access to the same social and political freedoms and opportunities as individuals without disabilities. Central to the philosophy are the concepts of self-determination and self-worth, peer support, consumer-controlled assistance and support services, and political and social reform. **Centers for Independent Living** (**CILs**), nonresidential, nonprofit organizations that are staffed and operated by individuals with disabilities, encourage self-sufficiency and self-determination in all aspects of life for individuals with disabilities by providing information and referral services, peer counseling, and independent living training (e.g., assistance with such things as ASSISTIVE TECHNOLOGY, budgeting, meal preparation, transportation arrangements, employment searches, and access to housing and health care). CILs also advocate on behalf of individuals with disabilities to achieve legislative and social change.

independent-living aid see ASSISTIVE TECHNOLOGY.

independent-living program 1. a system of community-based services and support designed to help individuals with disabilities achieve their highest level of personal functioning without the need to depend on others. Independent-living programs are administered by state vocational rehabilitation agencies. See also INDEPENDENT LIVING. **2.** a federally funded, state-administered program to prepare foster care youth who are 16–21 years old for the transition to independence.

independent measures measures that are unrelated to each other.

independent phenomena in parapsychology, any paranormal phenomena that appear to occur independently of any human AGENT, so that they cannot be ascribed to TELEPATHY or PSYCHOKINESIS. This might include video or audio recordings of POLTERGEIST activity made in an empty house.

independent practice association (**IPA**) an organized form of prepaid medical practice in which a group of private physicians join together in an association and are reimbursed on a FEE-FOR-SERVICE basis or a CAPITATION basis.

independent self-construal a view of the self (SELF-CONSTRUAL) that emphasizes one's unique traits and accomplishments and downplays one's embeddedness in a network of social relationships. Compare INTERDEPENDENT SELF-CONSTRUAL.

independent variable (**IV**) the variable in an experiment that is specifically manipulated or is observed to occur before the occurrence of the dependent, or outcome, variable. Independent variables may or may not be causally related to the DEPENDENT VARIABLE. In statistical analysis, an independent variable is likely to be referred to as a PREDICTOR VARIABLE. See also TREATMENT.

Inderal *n.* a trade name for PROPRANOLOL.

indeterminacy *n.* **1.** the inability to uniquely determine the form or magnitude of a relationship. **2.** the inability to arrive at a unique solution to a problem or mathematical form. **3.** in FACTOR ANALYSIS, the inability to form a unique representation of the factor structure.

indeterminacy principle see UNCERTAINTY PRINCIPLE.

indeterminate sentencing a punishment in which the judge mandates confinement of an offender over a time range (e.g., between 5 and 10 years), rather than a fixed period (e.g., 7 years). This practice allows greater discretion to the parole board to establish the specific time of release.

indeterminism *n.* **1.** in psychology, the doctrine that humans have FREE WILL and are able to act independently of antecedent or current situations, as in making choices. Compare DETERMINISM. See also HARD DETERMINISM; SOFT DETERMINISM. **2.** in philosophy, the position that events do not have necessary and sufficient causes. **—indeterminist** *adj.*

index 1. *n.* a reference point, standard, or indicator. **2.** *n.* a variable that is employed to indicate the presence of another phenomenon or event. **3.** *vb.* to act as an index of.

index adoptees see CROSS-FOSTERING.

index case see PROBAND.

index of discrimination an index of the sensitivity of a test or test item to differences between individuals. Also called **discrimination index**.

index of reliability an estimate of the linear relationship between observed test scores and their corresponding theoretical true scores.

index of validity see VALIDITY.

index of variability see VARIANCE.

index variable a variable that is not a determinant or true causal factor but represents or symbolizes the complex process or processes under study.

Indian Health Service (**IHS**) the principal federal health care provider and health advocate for Native Americans, providing services to approximately 1.5 million American Indians and Alaska Natives belonging to more than 557 federally recognized peoples in 35 states. It is an agency within the U.S. Department of Health and Human Services.

indicative *n.* in linguistics, the MOOD of a verb used to make ordinary DECLARATIVE statements, rather than commands, questions, and so on. Compare IMPERATIVE; INTERROGATIVE; SUBJUNCTIVE.

indicator variable a variable used with the GENERAL LINEAR MODEL for quantitatively indicating the class of a qualitative attribute.

indictment *n.* a formal accusation of criminal wrongdoing brought before the court by a grand jury, the group responsible for reviewing complaints of wrongdoing in order to determine whether a trial is warranted. **—indict** *vb.*

indifference of indicator the observation that, although items on tests of intelligence differ widely in appearance, almost all of them seem to measure GENERAL ABILITY to a greater or lesser extent. The term *indifference* is used to signify that the items measure the same thing without regard to their specific appearance.

indifference point the intermediate region between experiential opposites. For example, on the pleasure–pain dimension, it is the degree of stimulation that provokes an indifferent or neutral response.

indifferent stimulus a stimulus that has not yet elicited the reaction being studied.

indigenous researcher in ergonomics, a researcher who originates from the same environment or community as the target users for a specific system or product design. Indigenous researchers are employed in TASK ANALYSIS and USABILITY ENGINEERING among different ethnic and cultural groups. See also CULTURAL ERGONOMICS; POPULATION STEREOTYPE.

indirect agonist a substance that acts to increase the activity of an AGONIST at a receptor in ways other than direct action at the receptor site. Indirect agonists may exert their effect by increasing the metabolism or release of agonist compounds or by displacing other substances that impair full binding of an agonist to its receptor site.

indirect associations a symptom of schizophrenia in which the association between ideas is not apparent and not expressed, such that the person's statements seem bizarre and incoherent to others. See also LOOSENING OF ASSOCIATIONS.

indirect attitude measure any procedure for assessing attitudes that does not require a person to provide a report of his or her attitude. Nontraditional approaches to attitude measurement, such as the LOST LETTER PROCEDURE and the INFORMATION-ERROR TECHNIQUE, are examples of indirect attitude measures. See also EXPLICIT ATTITUDE MEASURE; IMPLICIT ATTITUDE MEASURE. Compare DIRECT ATTITUDE MEASURE.

indirect method of therapy a method of conducting therapy, particularly exemplified by CLIENT-CENTERED THERAPY, in which the therapist does not attempt to direct the client's communication or evaluate the client's remarks, although he or she may refer back to the client's remarks or restate them (see RESTATEMENT).

indirect object see OBJECT.

indirect odor effect see DIRECT ODOR EFFECT.

indirect scaling see DIRECT SCALING.

indirect speech act a SPEECH ACT whose purpose does not appear explicitly from the form or content of the utterance but must be inferred. For example, the apparent observation *It's so cold in here!* may well be intended as a request that someone close the window. See CONVERSA-

TIONAL INFERENCE; FORM–FUNCTION DISTINCTION; IMPLICATURE.

individual accountability the extent to which a particular person can be held responsible for his or her actions and the consequences of those actions. In groups, ACCOUNTABILITY is influenced by anonymity and the extent to which the contributions of each member of the group are clearly identifiable.

individual difference a trait or other characteristic by which one individual may be distinguished from others.

individual education (IE) 1. a plan that identifies the special educational needs of a particular student. It is created by the student's instructors, school administrators, parents, and other professionals to form supplementary or unique educational opportunities that will attempt to meet the student's needs. **2.** a detailed statement of goals and objectives for incremental learning of a particular student over a set period. The plan takes into account ability level, motivation, behavior, and variations in mood, energy, and attention. Also called **individualized educational planning (IEP)**.

Individual Family Service Plan (IFSP) a plan of services and supports for children up to 3 years of age and their families. Under the U.S. requirements for early intervention programs, the IFSP content must address the child's developmental status and the concerns of parents, define services to be provided and their desired outcomes, and (if appropriate) contain transition steps to preschool services. Also called **Individualized Family Service Plan**.

individualism *n.* **1.** a social or cultural tradition, ideology, or personal outlook that emphasizes the individual and his or her rights, independence, and relationships with other individuals. Compare COLLECTIVISM. **2.** in ethical and political theory, the view that individuals have intrinsic value. Once granted, this implies that the unique values, desires, and perspectives of individuals should also be valued in their own right. Thus, individualism often manifests itself as an approach to life that emphasizes the essential right to be oneself and to seek fulfillment of one's own needs and desires. **—individualist** *n.* **—individualistic** *adj.*

individualist feminism a perspective within feminist thought that is closely related to INDIVIDUALISM. The position values female autonomy, emphasizes individual rights and freedom of action, and upholds diversity as an inherent good. See FEMINISM.

individualistic reward structure a performance setting structured in such a way that rewards are assigned on the basis of individual achievement and the success or failure of each person is independent of the success or failure of any other individual. Compare COMPETITIVE REWARD STRUCTURE; COOPERATIVE REWARD STRUCTURE.

individuality *n.* the uniqueness of each individual's personality.

individualization *n.* any process in which an individual becomes distinguishable from one or more other members of the same species, sex, or other category. **—individualize** *vb.*

individualized education program (IEP) a plan for providing specialized educational services and procedures that meet the unique needs of a child with a disability. Each IEP must be documented in writing, tailored to a particular child, and implemented in accordance with the requirements of U.S. federal law. The IEP must be created by a team of individuals that includes, but is not restricted to, parents, teachers, a representative of the school system, and an individual who will evaluate the child's needs and monitor progress. Additionally, the IEP must contain certain information, such as the child's current academic performance, annual achievement objectives for the child, a discussion of the particular special education and related services that will be provided for the child and their duration and location, and a means of measuring and informing the parents of the child's progress. See also FREE AND APPROPRIATE PUBLIC EDUCATION.

individualized instruction an instructional method that permits students to work separately at their own pace. Teachers assist students in identifying skills that need development or knowledge that needs to be acquired. Group projects are also incorporated in the program.

individualized reading a method of teaching reading that makes use of the child's interests and of a variety of books specifically focused on the child's level of skills.

individual program an instructional method in which the student is responsible for developing and carrying out his or her own program. This method is most often used for children who possess a high level of motivation and cognitive development. Compare COMMAND STYLE.

individual psychology 1. the psychological theory of Alfred ADLER, which is based on the idea that throughout life individuals strive for a sense of mastery, completeness, and belonging and are governed by a conscious drive to overcome their sense of inferiority by developing to their fullest potential, obtaining their life goals, and creating their own styles of life, as opposed to the view that human beings are dominated by "blind," irrational instincts operating on an unconscious level. Also called **Adlerian psychology**. **2.** historically, a synonym for DIFFERENTIAL PSYCHOLOGY.

individual psychotherapy see INDIVIDUAL THERAPY.

individual response the response of an individual to an item on a test of intelligence or some other construct.

individual response stereotypy see AUTONOMIC REACTIVITY.

individual selection an aspect of NATURAL SELECTION in which those traits of an individual that lead to increased REPRODUCTIVE SUCCESS are more likely to appear in subsequent generations. The focus of individual selection is on the direct benefits to the individual; this contrasts with KIN SELECTION, in which those who assist their relatives receive indirect benefits.

Individual Service Plan (ISP) the core plan of services and supports for a person with a developmental disability, constructed by professionals, paraprofessionals, the focal person (depending on his or her abilities), and others concerned (e.g., parents and advocates). The ISP incorporates relevant comprehensive functional assessment findings, stipulates desired and preferred outcomes, and identifies the full range of services and supports to be provided in order to achieve each outcome. In certain instances ISPs may be drawn up for individuals with psychiatric conditions, emotional disturbances, or behavior disorders.

Individuals With Disabilities Education Act (IDEA) legislation passed by the U.S. Congress in 1990 and amended in 1997 that provides public funding for special educational services and mandates that such services be provided in the LEAST RESTRICTIVE ENVIRONMENT. It consolidated and replaced the EDUCATION FOR ALL HANDICAPPED CHILDREN ACT.

individual test a test administered to a single examinee at a time, usually by a trained examiner. Compare GROUP TEST.

individual therapy psychotherapy conducted on a one-to-one basis (i.e., one therapist to one client). Also called **dyadic therapy**; **individual psychotherapy**. Compare GROUP PSYCHOTHERAPY.

individuation *n.* **1.** in psychology, the physiological, psychological, and sociocultural processes by which a person attains status as an individual human being and exerts him- or herself as such in the world. **2.** in the psychoanalytic theory of Carl JUNG, the gradual development of a unified, integrated personality that incorporates greater and greater amounts of the UNCONSCIOUS, both personal and collective, and resolves any conflicts that exist, such as those between introverted and extraverted tendencies. Also called **self-realization**. **3.** a phase of development, occurring between the 18th and 36th months, in which infants become less dependent on their mothers and begin to satisfy their own wishes and fend for themselves. [postulated by Hungarian-born U.S. psychiatrist Margaret Schonberger Mahler (1897–1985)]

indoctrination *n.* the social inculcation of beliefs, especially by those in positions of power or authority. Such beliefs are characterized by their inflexibility. **—indoctrinate** *vb.*

indole *n.* an organic molecule that is the basis of many substances involved in nervous system activity, including LSD (lysergic acid diethylamide), serotonin, melatonin, and tryptophan. Also called **2,3,-benzopyrrole**.

indolealkylamines *pl. n.* see HALLUCINOGEN.

indoleamine *n.* any of a class of MONOAMINES formed by an indole molecule, which is produced as a breakdown metabolite of tryptophan, and an amine group. Serotonin and melatonin are indoleamines.

induced abortion the deliberate, premature removal of the fetus from the uterus prior to the stage of viability (ability to live outside the uterus) by artificial means, such as drugs or mechanical devices. See also ABORTION; THERAPEUTIC ABORTION.

induced aggression a state of violence or hostile behavior caused by drugs, electrical stimulation of a brain area, or aversive stimuli.

induced color a color change in a visual field resulting from stimulation of a neighboring area, rather than from stimulation of the part of the field in which the change appears.

induced compliance effect see FORCED COMPLIANCE EFFECT.

induced hallucination a hallucination that is evoked in one individual by another, typically by hypnotic suggestion in highly susceptible individuals.

induced hypothermia the gradual reduction of body temperature by artificial means, usually for medical reasons. It is used, for example, in some surgical procedures (especially those involving the heart), to decrease the body's need for oxygen, and in the treatment of neurological diseases causing a fever.

induced movement an illusion of movement that occurs when a small stationary stimulus is surrounded by a large moving stimulus. The small object appears to move, while the large object appears to be still.

induced psychotic disorder see SHARED PSYCHOTIC DISORDER.

induced tonus a muscle tonus (sustained tension) brought about by a movement of another body part.

induction *n.* **1.** a general conclusion, principle, or explanation derived by reasoning from particular instances or observations. See INDUCTIVE REASONING. Compare DEDUCTION. **2.** the process of inductive reasoning itself. **3.** in conditioning, the phenomenon in which REINFORCEMENT of some forms of behavior results in an increased probability not only of these forms but also of similar but nonreinforced forms. For example, if lever presses with forces between 0.2 and 0.3 N are reinforced, presses with forces less than 0.2 N or greater than 0.3 N will increase in frequency although they are never explicitly reinforced. Also called **response generalization**. **4.** in developmental biology, the process by which one set of cells influences the fate of neighboring cells, usually by secreting a chemical factor that changes gene expression in the target cells. **5.** the act or process of producing or causing to occur. **—inductive** *adj.*

induction test a series of test items in which the participant must apply INDUCTIVE REASONING to derive or formulate a general law, rule, or principle based on several relevant facts or cases.

inductive problem solving a learning technique in which the student is asked to identify relevant relationships between given facts and events and explain the general principles that underlie these relationships.

inductive reasoning the form of reasoning in which inferences and general principles are drawn from specific observations and cases. Inductive reasoning is a cornerstone of the scientific method (see BACONIAN METHOD) in that it underlies the process of developing hypotheses from particular facts and observations. See also BOTTOM-UP ANALYSIS; GENERALIZATION. Compare DEDUCTIVE REASONING.

inductive teaching model an approach in education that strongly emphasizes the role of inductive reasoning and INDUCTIVE PROBLEM SOLVING in cognitive development. Also called **inquiry training model**.

industrial and organizational psychology (**I/O psychology**) the branch of psychology that studies human behavior in the work environment and applies general psychological principles to work-related issues and problems, notably in such areas as PERSONNEL SELECTION, PERSONNEL TRAINING, EMPLOYEE EVALUATION, working conditions, ACCIDENT PREVENTION, JOB ANALYSIS, JOB SATISFACTION, leadership, team effectiveness, and WORK MOTIVATION. I/O psychologists conduct empirical research aimed at understanding individual and group behavior within organizations and use their findings to improve ORGANIZATIONAL EFFECTIVENESS and the welfare of employees. Also called **business psychology**; **employment psychology**; **industrial psychology**; **management psychology**; **occupational psychology**; **organizational psychology**; **work psychology**. See also OCCUPATIONAL HEALTH PSYCHOLOGY; PERSONNEL PSYCHOLOGY.

industrial democracy a system of managing an organization in which employees participate in important decisions. An example would be the use of autonomous work groups in which employees determine their work procedures and assignments and are responsible for evaluating and rewarding performance. See also PARTICIPATIVE DECISION-MAKING; QUALITY CIRCLE; SCANLON PLAN.

industrial efficiency see EFFICIENCY.

industrial ergonomics a specialty area of ERGONOMICS that applies knowledge of human physical capabilities and limitations to the design of industrial WORK SYSTEMS, including work processes.

industrial psychology see INDUSTRIAL AND ORGANIZATIONAL PSYCHOLOGY.

industrial psychopath an individual in a work setting who displays a pattern of behavior regarded as typical of ANTISOCIAL PERSONALITY DISORDER. Such individuals act without regard for others and use manipulation to effectively manage both supporters and detractors, often resulting in career advancement. This type of individual is most likely to find success in organizations undergoing rapid changes.

industrial relations see LABOR RELATIONS.

industriousness *n.* see PERSISTENCE.

industry versus inferiority the fourth of ERIKSON'S EIGHT STAGES OF DEVELOPMENT, covering the Freudian LATENCY STAGE of ages 6 to 11 years, during which the child learns to be productive and to accept evaluation of his or her efforts. If the child is not encouraged to be industrious, the risk is that he or she will feel inferior or incompetent.

ineffability *n.* **1.** the quality of certain kinds of feelings or experiences that are difficult to describe explicitly. The sense of something being ineffable is often attributed to spiritual, aesthetic, or affective states. **2.** an irrepressible sense of well-being that is difficult to convey to others, often described by patients experiencing a MANIC EPISODE. **—ineffable** *adj.*

inertia principle see PRINCIPLE OF INERTIA.

infancy *n.* the earliest period of postnatal life, roughly the first 2 years, during which the child is helpless and dependent on parental care. **—infant** *n.*

infant and preschool tests individually administered tests designed to assess the development of infants (from birth to 18 months) and preschool children (from 18 to 60 months). Important tests include the BAYLEY SCALES OF INFANT AND TODDLER DEVELOPMENT, the MCCARTHY SCALES OF CHILDREN'S ABILITIES, and the WECHSLER PRESCHOOL AND PRIMARY SCALE OF INTELLIGENCE.

infant at risk an infant whose development may be threatened by complications at the time of birth, such as conditions that reduce the supply of oxygen to brain tissue, or by conditions after birth, such as malnutrition during the first months of life.

Infant Behavior Record the former name for the Behavior Rating scale. See BAYLEY SCALES OF INFANT AND TODDLER DEVELOPMENT.

infant consciousness sensory and higher order awareness as developed early in life, including prenatally. See ONTOGENY OF CONSCIOUS EXPERIENCE.

infant development program a coordinated program of stimulatory, social, therapeutic, and treatment services provided to children from birth to 3 years of age with identified conditions placing them at risk of developmental disability or with evident developmental delays. Younger children are more likely to have syndromes posing risk of mental retardation or physical and sensory disability, whereas older children are likely to have developmental delays identified by the age of 1½ to 2 years. Services can include assessment, stimulation, parent or family training, and assistance to families in identifying and accessing appropriate community services. Also called **early intervention program**.

infant-directed speech the specialized style of speech that adults and older children use when talking specifically to infants, which usually includes much inflection and repetition. See also CHILD-DIRECTED SPEECH.

infanticide *n.* the killing of an infant or child. Although now predominantly considered both immoral and criminal, in the past infanticide was an accepted practice in some societies, often as a response to scarcity or overpopulation or as a means of eliminating offspring deemed unfit. Infants (particularly female infants) are still at risk in some cultures. Infanticide has been observed in many animal species. It is thought to be advantageous for a new male taking over a group, which thus avoids the need to care for unrelated young; moreover, females that lose offspring will stop lactation and be able to reproduce sooner. Infanticide has also been observed in COOPERATIVE-BREEDING species when two females give birth at around the same time and there is competition for helpers to provide care of the young. **—infanticidal** *adj.*

infantile amnesia the inability to remember clearly or accurately the first years of life (from infancy through about 5 years of age).

infantile autism see AUTISTIC DISORDER.

infantile myxedema see BRISSAUD'S INFANTILISM.

infantile osteopetrosis a rare hereditary disorder in which the bones, including the skull bones, are abnormally dense and brittle. It is sometimes accompanied by retinal degeneration and cranial-nerve palsy. Mental retardation has been reported in more than 20% of affected children, with sensory deprivation a possible contributing factor.

infantile sexuality in psychoanalytic theory, the concept that PSYCHIC ENERGY or LIBIDO concentrated in various organs of the body throughout infancy gives rise to erotic pleasure. This is manifested in sucking the mother's breast during the ORAL STAGE of development, in defecating during the ANAL STAGE, and in self-stimulating activities during the early GENITAL STAGE. The term and concept, first enunciated by Sigmund FREUD, proved highly controversial from the start, and it is more in line with subsequent thought to emphasize the sensual nature of breast-feeding, defecation, and discovery of the body in childhood and the role of the pleasurable feelings so obtained in the origin and development of sexual feelings.

infantile speech speech or verbalizations using the sounds and forms characteristic of infants or very young children beyond the stage when such speech is normal.

infantile spinal muscular atrophy see SPINAL MUSCULAR ATROPHY.

infantilism *n.* behavior, physical characteristics, or mental functioning in older children or adults that is characteristic of that of infants or young children. See REGRESSION.

infantilization *n.* the encouragement of infantile or childish behavior in a more mature individual.

infant massage therapy the systematic gentle touching, stroking, and kneading of the body of a baby. Therapeutic benefits include helping the baby relax and inducing sounder, longer sleep.

infantry-type duties the basic tasks and skills required by a foot soldier, which include rifle marksmanship, hand-grenade qualification, and physical training.

infant states of arousal the behavioral states experienced by infants in fairly even alternation, including (a) regular, periodic, and irregular sleep; (b) crying; (c) waking activity; and (d) ALERT INACTIVITY.

infant test see INFANT AND PRESCHOOL TESTS.

infarction *n.* **1.** an area of dead tissue resulting from obstruction of a supplying artery. Infarction of brain tissue can have effects ranging from mild to severe, depending on the extent of the dead tissue and its location in the brain (see CEREBRAL INFARCTION). A **myocardial infarction** (heart attack) involves death of a segment of the heart muscle, usually due to obstruction of a coronary artery, and is a common cause of death. **2.** a sudden shortfall in the blood supply to a particular tissue, organ, or part resulting from obstruction of a supplying artery, due, for example, to THROMBOSIS or EMBOLISM. Also called **infarct**. See STROKE.

infecundity *n.* inability to produce offspring.

inference *n.* **1.** a CONCLUSION deduced from an earlier premise or premises according to valid RULES OF INFERENCE, or the process of drawing such a conclusion. Some hold that an inference, as contrasted with a mere conclusion, requires that the person making it actually believe that the inference and the premises from which it is drawn are true. Also called **logical inference**. **2.** in statistical analysis, the process of drawing conclusions about a population based on a sample. The most common example of this type of inference is statistical hypothesis testing. **—inferential** *adj.*

inferential statistics a broad class of statistical techniques that allows inferences about characteristics of a population to be drawn from a sample of data from that population while controlling (at least partially) the extent to which errors of inference may be made. These techniques include approaches for testing hypotheses and estimating the value of parameters.

inferential validity the extent to which causal inferences made in a laboratory setting are applicable to the real-life experiences they are meant to represent.

inferior *adj.* in anatomy, lower, below, or toward the feet. Compare SUPERIOR.

inferior colliculus either of the caudal pair of COLLICULI. They receive and process auditory nerve impulses and relay these to the MEDIAL GENICULATE NUCLEI.

inferior function in the ANALYTIC PSYCHOLOGY of Carl JUNG, one of the three nondominant, unconscious functions of the personality that are dominated by the SUPERIOR FUNCTION in a particular FUNCTIONAL TYPE.

inferiority *n.* in ERIKSON'S EIGHT STAGES OF DEVELOPMENT, see INDUSTRY VERSUS INFERIORITY.

inferiority complex a basic feeling of inadequacy and insecurity, deriving from actual or imagined physical or psychological deficiency, that may result in behavioral expression ranging from the "withdrawal" of immobilizing timidity to the overcompensation of excessive competition and aggression. See also SUPERIORITY COMPLEX.

inferior longitudinal fasciculus a bundle of association fibers that extends from the occipital to the temporal pole of each CEREBRAL HEMISPHERE.

inferior oblique the extrinsic EYE MUSCLE that rotates the eyeball upward if it contracts when the eye is pointing toward the nose and contributes to upward motion (together with the INFERIOR RECTUS) if it contracts when the eye is pointing straight ahead.

inferior rectus the extrinsic EYE MUSCLE that rotates the eyeball upward if it contracts when the eye is pointing toward the side of the head and contributes to upward motion (together with the INFERIOR OBLIQUE) if it contracts when the eye is pointing straight ahead.

inferotemporal cortex (**IT cortex**) a region of the brain on the inferior portion of the temporal lobe that is particularly involved in the perception of form. This VISUAL ASSOCIATION CORTEX contains neurons with very complicated stimulus requirements; lesions in this area impair form and object perception even though visual discrimination thresholds are unchanged (see VISUAL FORM AGNOSIA). See also GRANDMOTHER CELLS.

infertility *n.* inability to produce offspring due to a low fertility level in the male partner (about 40% of cases), the female partner (about 60% of cases), or both. Infertility is caused by physical problems: No evidence clearly shows a psychological cause, although maternal stress has been suggested as a factor. Many patients can be treated successfully. See also ARTIFICIAL INSEMINATION; IN VITRO FERTILIZATION. **—infertile** *adj.*

infibulation *n.* the sewing together of the lips of the vulva in order to prevent coitus, leaving a small opening for menstruation. It is practiced in some cultures as the most extreme form of FEMALE GENITAL MUTILATION, usually being done in early childhood or in the prepubertal years. When the girl grows up and begins sexual activity, intercourse is difficult and painful and may be impossible until the opening is enlarged by cutting.

infinite regression a line of reasoning in which the supposed explanation for something itself requires a similar explanation, and so on endlessly. An example is an explanation of consciousness that assumes the existence of a HOMUNCULUS inside the mind that observes conscious experience, which requires another homunculus to observe the mind of the first homunculus, and so on.

infinite-valued logic a system of logic that differs from classical logic, which permits only two truth categories to be assigned to a proposition (true or false), by allowing for multiple categories or degrees of truthfulness. For example, whereas the statement *Smith is a professor* is either true or false, the statement *Smith is depressed* might have varying degrees of truthfulness. Thus, the intersection of the categories "Smith" and "depressed" has "fuzzy" as opposed to "crisp" boundaries. Infinite-valued logic is related to FUZZY LOGIC. See also BIVALENCE.

infix *n.* an element inserted medially within a word to modify the word's meaning. The only known examples in English are swearwords, as in *fan-fucking-tastic*. Compare PREFIX; SUFFIX.

inflammatory dysmenorrhea see DYSMENORRHEA.

inflection *n.* in linguistics, a change in the form of a word, often by the addition of a SUFFIX, that signals a change in tense, person, number, or case. Common inflections in English are the addition of *-ed* or *-ing* to signal the past tense or present participle of a verb and the addition of *-s* or *-'s* to signal the plural or possessive form of a noun. See MORPHOLOGY. **—inflectional** *adj.*

influence analysis a set of statistical techniques that allows one to determine the degree to which one or a small number of cases affect the overall result of an analysis, particularly in the GENERAL LINEAR MODEL.

influence tactics the specific actions taken by one person to change the behavior or attitudes of another.

influencing machine the subject of a DELUSION OF PERSECUTION in which the individual feels controlled by a machine that serves as the instrument of persecution.

infomercial *n.* see COMMERCIAL.

informal communications in organizational settings, communications among employees that do not occur through the formally prescribed CHANNELS OF COMMUNICATION. Even informal communications, such as GOSSIP and RUMORS, often serve important functions that are instrumental to achieving organizational objectives.

informal fallacy see FALLACY.

informal test a nonstandardized test that is graded intuitively, without norms.

informant *n.* an expert who is consulted in ethnographic and related research. The researcher obtains information from the informant about the individual, group, and cultural characteristics and behaviors of the unit (e.g., group, tribe, society) about which the informant has knowledge.

information *n.* **1.** in communication theory, the reduction in uncertainty provided in a message; that is, information tells us something we do not already know. The BIT is the common unit of information in INFORMATION THEORY. **2.** knowledge about facts or ideas gained through investigation, experience, or practice.

informational influence 1. those interpersonal processes that challenge the correctness of an individual's beliefs or the appropriateness of his or her behavior, thereby promoting change. Such influence may occur directly, as a result of communication and persuasion, or indirectly, through exposure to information and comparison of oneself with others (see SOCIAL COMPARISON THEORY). Also called **informational social influence**. Compare INTERPERSONAL INFLUENCE; NORMATIVE INFLUENCE. **2.** the degree to which a person's judgments or opinions about an unclear situation are accepted by others as correct, that is, as reflecting the reality of that situation.

informational power see POWER.

information-error technique an INDIRECT ATTITUDE MEASURE that consists of a series of objective-knowledge multiple-choice questions about an ATTITUDE OBJECT. These questions are constructed so that people are unlikely to know the true answers, but with response options that imply positive or negative evaluations of the attitude object. For example, an information-error measure of attitudes toward capital punishment might include questions about the percentage of people falsely convicted for capital crimes and the percentage difference in the number of violent crimes in states with and without capital punishment. The procedure is based on the assumption that participants will use their attitudes as a basis for guessing, that is, they will tend to select answers that support their attitudes. Attitudes are assessed by computing the number of positive response options selected relative to the number of negative response options selected.

information feedback responses that inform an individual about the correctness, physical effect, or social or emotional impact of his or her behavior or thinking. The concept is similar to the principle behind KNOWLEDGE OF RESULTS, namely, that immediate feedback is beneficial to learning. In interpersonal relations and psychotherapy, information feedback gives an individual insight into other people's experience of him or her. In BEHAVIOR THERAPY, information feedback is intended to help change and shape behavior directly.

information giver see OPINION GIVER.

information hypothesis the theoretical claim that conscious sensory processes may be modeled and explained by reference to the formal concepts of INFORMATION THEORY.

information overload the state that occurs when the amount or intensity of environmental stimuli exceeds the individual's processing capacity, thus leading to an unconscious or subliminal disregard for some environmental information.

information processing (IP) 1. the manipulation of data by computers to accomplish some goal, such as problem solving or communication. **2.** in cognitive psychology, the flow of INFORMATION through the human nervous system, involving the operation of perceptual systems, memory stores, decision processes, and response mechanisms. **Information processing psychology** is the approach that concentrates on understanding these operations. See also INFORMATION THEORY.

information science the field of study concerned with the representation, storage, retrieval, and transmission of information. Information science usually includes computer science and communication science. See INFORMATION THEORY.

information seeker see OPINION SEEKER.

information systems technology used to collect, organize, manage, store, and report data. An example of such technology is a computerized database of records for a HUMAN SERVICE DELIVERY SYSTEM. Reports generated from the client data collected by the database can serve to document and account for many program services, costs, and outcomes.

information technology (IT) the application of INFORMATION SCIENCE to practical objectives. Information technology subsumes computer and communication technologies.

information test a test that measures the subject's general knowledge in different areas and at different levels of complexity.

information theory the principles relating to the communication or transmission of INFORMATION, which is defined as any message that reduces uncertainty. These principles deal with such areas as the ENCODING and DECODING of messages, types of CHANNELS OF COMMUNICATION and their capacity to throughput information, the application of mathematical methods to the process, the problem of noise (distortion), and the relative effectiveness of various kinds of FEEDBACK. See also INFORMATION PROCESSING.

informed consent voluntary agreement to participate in a research or therapeutic procedure on the basis of the participant's or patient's understanding of its nature, its potential benefits and possible risks, and available alternatives. Supported by court decisions, the principle of informed consent has provided a foundation for do not resuscitate (DNR) orders, ADVANCE DIRECTIVES, and the natural-death acts that have been passed into law throughout the United States.

infra- *prefix* below or within.

infradian rhythm any periodic variation in physiological or psychological function (see BIOLOGICAL RHYTHM) recurring in a cycle of less than 24 hours, for example, the breathing rhythm. Compare CIRCADIAN RHYTHM; ULTRADIAN RHYTHM.

infrahuman *adj.* an obsolete term describing all species "below" humans, that is, nonhumans. This reflects the earlier concept of a "chain of being" that culminates in humans.

infrared *n.* that part of the electromagnetic spectrum with wavelengths between about 0.8 μm and 1 mm. The **near-infrared** part of the range (0.8–3 μm) is experienced as heat. **Infrared cameras** are sensitive to thermal emission from objects and can therefore produce photography in the dark.

infrared theory of smell a theory that the olfactory sense organ functions as an infrared spectrometer. It assumes that ODORANTS each have a unique infrared absorption spectrum, which produces transient cooling of the cilia in the OLFACTORY EPITHELIUM. The theory is called into question by the fact that isomers of some odorants have identical infrared absorption spectrums but produce different odors. See also SMELL MECHANISM.

infrasonic communication the use of sound frequencies below the range of human hearing (i.e., below 20 Hz) for ANIMAL COMMUNICATION. Both elephants and whales use infrasonic communication extensively. The low frequencies have very long wavelengths that are transmitted for very long distances: They have been shown to coordinate activity between individuals over distances of several kilometers. Compare ULTRASONIC COMMUNICATION.

infundibulum *n.* (*pl.* **infundibula**) a funnel-shaped anatomical structure, in particular the stalk of the PITUITARY GLAND, situated just below the THIRD VENTRICLE of the brain and above the sphenoid sinus at the base of the skull.

ingenuity *n.* cleverness at solving routine problems of daily life (at work, home, etc.): everyday CREATIVITY. **—ingenious** *adj.*

ingratiation *n.* efforts to win the liking and approval of other people, especially by deliberate IMPRESSION MANAGEMENT. Ingratiation is usually regarded as consisting of illicit or objectionable strategies, especially for manipulative purposes, which distinguish it from sincere efforts to be likable. **—ingratiate** *vb.*

ingroup *n.* **1.** in general, any group to which one belongs or with which one identifies, but particularly a group judged to be different from, and often superior to, other groups (OUTGROUPS). **2.** a group characterized by intense bonds of AFFILIATION such that each member feels a sense of kinship and some degree of loyalty to other members by virtue of their common group membership. Also called **we-group**. [defined by U.S. sociologist William G. Sumner (1840–1910)]

ingroup bias the tendency to favor one's own group, its members, its characteristics, and its products, particularly in reference to other groups. The favoring of the ingroup tends to be more pronounced than the rejection of the OUTGROUP, but both tendencies become more pronounced during periods of intergroup contact. At the regional, cultural, or national level, this bias is often termed ETHNOCENTRISM. Also called **ingroup favoritism**. See also GROUP-SERVING BIAS.

ingroup extremity effect the tendency to describe and evaluate INGROUP members, their actions, and their products in exaggeratedly positive ways. Compare OUTGROUP EXTREMITY EFFECT. See also INGROUP BIAS.

inguinal *adj.* referring to the groin (inguen).

INH abbreviation for isonicotinic acid hydrazide. See ISONIAZID.

inhabitance *n.* the idea that ghosts or SPIRITS can occupy particular locations, as in hauntings, or take control of people, animals, or things, as in cases of alleged possession. See EXORCISM.

inhalant *n.* any of a variety of volatile substances that can be inhaled to produce intoxicating effects. Anesthetic gases (e.g., ether, chloroform, NITROUS OXIDE), industrial solvents (e.g., TOLUENE, gasoline, trichloroethylene, various aerosol propellants), and organic nitrites (e.g., AMYL NITRITE) are common inhalants. Anesthetic gases may cause asphyxiation, and chloroform has been associated with damage to the liver and kidneys. Industrial solvents are generally toxic, being associated with damage to the kidneys, liver, and both central and peripheral nervous systems. Organic nitrites are less toxic but may cause ARRHYTHMIAS in individuals with heart conditions. See also INHALATION OF DRUGS.

inhalant abuse in *DSM–IV–TR*, a pattern of inhalant use manifested by recurrent significant adverse consequences related to the repeated ingestion of these substances. This diagnosis is preempted by the diagnosis of INHALANT DEPENDENCE: If the criteria for inhalant abuse and inhalant dependence are both met, only the latter diagnosis is given. See also SUBSTANCE ABUSE; SUBSTANCE DEPENDENCE.

inhalant dependence in *DSM–IV–TR*, a cluster of cognitive, behavioral, and physiological symptoms indicating continued use of inhalants despite significant inhalant-related problems. There is a pattern of repeated inhalant ingestion resulting in tolerance, withdrawal symptoms if use is suspended, and an uncontrollable drive to continue use. See INHALANT ABUSE. See also SUBSTANCE ABUSE; SUBSTANCE DEPENDENCE.

inhalant intoxication a reversible syndrome resulting from the recent ingestion of inhalants. It includes clinically significant behavioral or psychological changes (e.g., confusion, belligerence, assaultiveness, apathy, impaired judgment, and impaired social or occupational functioning), as well as one or more signs of physiological involvement (e.g., dizziness, visual disturbances, involuntary eye movements, incoordination, slurred speech, unsteady gait, tremor). At higher doses, lethargy, PSYCHOMOTOR RETARDATION, generalized muscle weakness, depressed reflexes, stupor, or coma may develop. See also SUBSTANCE INTOXICATION.

inhalation of drugs a means of administering a drug—in the form of a gas or aerosol—via the mouth or the nose (insufflation), enabling it to reach the body tissues rapidly. Anesthetics for major surgery are administered by inhalation, which permits almost instant contact with the blood supplying the alveoli (air sacs) of the lungs. Inhalation (oral or nasal) is also a means of self-administration of abused substances, including cannabis, nicotine, cocaine, and volatile hydrocarbons (see INHALANT). Oral inhalation is used for nicotine (smoking) and amyl or butyl nitrite, and the nasal route ("snorting") for cocaine, heroin, amphetamines, and other street drugs.

inheritance *n.* the transmission of physical or psychological traits from parents to their offspring. See also MENDELIAN INHERITANCE; MULTIFACTORIAL INHERITANCE.

inherited disorder see GENETIC DISORDER.

inhibited female orgasm in *DSM–III*, the dysfunction now called FEMALE ORGASMIC DISORDER.

inhibited male orgasm in *DSM–III*, the dysfunction now called MALE ORGASMIC DISORDER.

inhibitedness *n.* the tendency to constrain one's actions and emotional experiences, particularly in social settings, or to withdraw entirely from social interactions in such settings. **—inhibited** *adj.*

inhibited sexual desire in *DSM–III*, the dysfunction now called HYPOACTIVE SEXUAL DESIRE DISORDER.

inhibited sexual excitement in *DSM–III*, a psychosexual disorder characterized by recurrent and persistent inhibition of sexual excitement during sexual activity that is judged to be adequate in focus, intensity, and duration. In *DSM–IV–TR* this general diagnosis was replaced by FEMALE SEXUAL AROUSAL DISORDER and MALE ERECTILE DISORDER.

inhibition *n.* **1.** the process of restraining one's impulses or behavior, either consciously or unconsciously, due to such factors as lack of confidence, fear of consequences, or moral qualms. **2.** in RESPONSE SELECTION, the suppression of COVERT RESPONSES in order to prevent incorrect responses. **3.** in conditioning, the active blocking or delay of a response to a stimulus. **4.** in psychoanalysis, an unconscious mechanism in which the SUPEREGO controls instinctive impulses that would threaten the EGO if allowed conscious expression. For example, inhibited sexual desire may result from unconscious feelings of guilt implanted by parents. See also REACTIVE INHIBITION; RECIPROCAL INHIBITION. —**inhibit** *vb.* —**inhibited** *adj.*

inhibition mechanisms a series of neural mechanisms that restrict the flow of excitatory impulses. They include presynaptic and postsynaptic influences and HYPERPOLARIZATION of cells.

inhibition of delay in DELAY CONDITIONING, a reduction in the magnitude of the conditioned response (CR) during the early part of the conditioned stimulus (CS). For example, if a 15-s tone (the CS) precedes delivery of food (the unconditioned stimulus) to a dog, salivation (the CR) will eventually occur only after the tone has been on for a few seconds, not when it first comes on. See also TEMPORAL DISCRIMINATION.

inhibition of return (**IOR**) difficulty in returning attention to a previously attended location. When attention has been directed to a location for a period of time, it is more difficult to redirect attention to that location than to direct it to another location. Also called **inhibitory aftereffect**.

inhibitor *n.* a mechanism or stimulus that slows or suppresses an activity, process, or behavior.

inhibitory aftereffect see INHIBITION OF RETURN.

inhibitory postsynaptic potential (**IPSP**) a hyperpolarizing potential (see HYPERPOLARIZATION) in a POSTSYNAPTIC neuron that is caused by a volley of impulses over an inhibitory pathway. IPSPs decrease the probability that the postsynaptic neuron will fire a NERVE IMPULSE. See INHIBITORY SYNAPSE. Compare EXCITATORY POSTSYNAPTIC POTENTIAL.

inhibitory potential a hypothesized temporary state in which REACTIVE INHIBITION and CONDITIONED INHIBITION result from responding to a stimulus, causing a reduction in the potential of recurrence of that response. [proposed by Clark Leonard HULL]

inhibitory process any phenomenon in human or animal behavior that prevents or blocks actions that are problematic for the individual. See EXCITATORY–INHIBITORY PROCESSES.

inhibitory synapse a synapse where a nerve impulse arriving at the PRESYNAPTIC terminal causes HYPERPOLARIZATION in the POSTSYNAPTIC cell, that is, an INHIBITORY POSTSYNAPTIC POTENTIAL.

in-home respite see RESPITE SERVICES.

in-house evaluation an organization's internal program assessments, conducted by an INTERNAL EVALUATOR, as opposed to evaluation conducted by an EXTERNAL EVALUATOR.

initial cry see EPILEPTIC CRY.

initial insomnia difficulty in falling asleep, usually due to tension, anxiety, or depression. Some people with INSOMNIA due to anxiety become so worried about being unable to fall asleep or about the effects of loss of sleep that they cannot relax sufficiently to induce sleep. Initial insomnia may be a symptom of a MAJOR DEPRESSIVE EPISODE. Compare MIDDLE INSOMNIA; TERMINAL INSOMNIA.

initial interview in psychotherapy, the first interview with a client, which has some or all of the following goals: to establish a positive relationship; to listen to the client's problem described in his or her own words; to make a tentative diagnosis; and to formulate a plan for diagnostic tests, possible treatment, or referral.

initialism *n.* see ACRONYM.

initial spurt the high productivity or performance frequently noted at the start of a job, task, or series of trials. The initial spurt is more common with new tasks than tasks already familiar to the individual. Compare END SPURT.

Initial Teaching Alphabet (**ITA**) a near-phonetic alphabet of 44 characters, each with a single sound. It has been used since the early 1960s, with varying success, in teaching English-speaking children to read. The system was originally called **Augmented Roman**. [devised by British educator and publisher Sir James Pitman (1901–1985)]

initial values law see LAW OF INITIAL VALUES.

initiating structure a function of effective leadership that involves organizing the group for its work, typically by setting standards and objectives, identifying roles and positioning members in those roles, developing standard operating procedures, criticizing poor work, and defining the relationship between leaders and subordinates. Compare CONSIDERATION.

initiation deficit see ABULIA.

initiative versus guilt the third of ERIKSON'S EIGHT STAGES OF DEVELOPMENT, which occurs during the child's 3rd through 5th years. Central to this stage is the child's feeling of freedom in planning, launching, and initiating all forms of fantasy, play, and other activity. If resolution of the two earlier stages was unsuccessful, or if the child is consistently criticized or humiliated, guilt and a feeling of not belonging will develop in place of initiative.

initiator *n.* the TASK ROLE adopted by a group member who defines problems, sets goals, and helps to launch specific courses of action. [identified in 1948 by U.S. educational theorist Kenneth D. Benne (1908–1992) and U.S. social psychologist Paul Sheats, following studies of discussion groups conducted at the National Training Laboratories]

injection *n.* see ADMINISTRATION; INTRAMUSCULAR INJECTION; INTRAVENOUS INJECTION; SUBCUTANEOUS INJECTION.

injunctive norms socially determined consensual standards (SOCIAL NORMS) that describe how people should act, feel, and think in a given situation, irrespective of how people typically respond in the setting. Individuals who violate these standards are often judged negatively. Also called **prescriptive norms**. Compare DESCRIPTIVE NORMS.

injury deceitfulness in sport, failure to disclose the presence of an injury in order to join or retain one's position on a team, to exercise, or to avoid benching or some other consequence.

injury denial failure to acknowledge the existence or severity of an injury.

injury feigning behavior suggesting that an animal is hurt or disabled, often used by birds to lure potential predators away from a nest. The bird feigns injury at some distance from the nest and flies away as the predator approaches.

inkblot test see RORSCHACH INKBLOT TEST.

INL abbreviation for INNER NUCLEAR LAYER.

innate *adj.* **1.** denoting a capability or characteristic existing in an organism from birth, that is, belonging to the original or essential constitution of the body or mind. Innate processes should be distinguished from those that develop later in infancy and childhood under maturational control. **2.** in philosophy, denoting an idea that is knowable by reason alone and that does not need to be established or confirmed by experience. Also called **inborn**; **native**; **natural**.

innate behavior behavior that appears to be developed and expressed with no specific training or experience and thus has a strong genetic basis. It is generally accepted that most behavior is neither purely innate nor purely due to learning or experience. See EPIGENESIS; NATURE–NURTURE CONTROVERSY.

innate ideas ideas that are held to be present in the mind prior to any experience. Innate ideas are usually taken to be those ideas that are so intuitively obvious as to require no proof, such as the AXIOMS of geometry or the CONTRADICTION PRINCIPLE (X is not non-X) in logic. For French philosopher René Descartes (1596–1650), who is often cited as the originator of the concept, innate ideas referred not so much to particular ideas as to the capacities and processes of rationality that allow such ideas to be immediately intuited as true. The notion of innate ideas later came under attack from English philosopher John Locke (1632–1704) and other thinkers in the empiricist tradition (see EMPIRICISM). Compare DERIVED IDEAS.

innate releasing mechanism (**IRM**) in ethology, the hypothesized means by which instinctive behaviors are inhibited until an appropriate RELEASER (sign stimulus) evokes a FIXED-ACTION PATTERN. For example, the zigzag dance is performed by a male three-spined stickleback fish only when it sees another fish with a swollen abdomen.

inner audience the imaginary hearer of silent, spontaneous inner speech, often associated in psychoanalytic and psychodynamic theory with parental figures.

inner boundary see INTERNAL BOUNDARY.

inner conflict see INTRAPSYCHIC CONFLICT.

inner dialogue a mental debate that an individual may engage in about any issue. In some systems of psychotherapy, clients are encouraged to express the inner dialogue aloud in words during sessions.

inner-directed *adj.* describing or relating to an individual who is self-motivated and not easily influenced by the opinions, values, or pressures of other people. Compare OTHER-DIRECTED; TRADITION-DIRECTED. [introduced by U.S. sociologist David Riesman (1909–2002)]

inner ear the part of the ear that comprises the bony and membranous LABYRINTHS and contains the sense organs responsible for hearing and balance. For hearing the major structure is the COCHLEA (see also AUDITORY LABYRINTH). For the sense of balance, the major structures are the SEMICIRCULAR CANALS, SACCULE, and UTRICLE (see also VESTIBULAR APPARATUS).

inner estrangement the feeling that external objects are unfamiliar and unreal. [defined by Austrian psychoanalyst Paul Federn (1871–1950)]

inner hair cells see HAIR CELLS.

inner language 1. the visual, auditory, and kinesthetic mental imagery of words and concepts. **2.** speech spoken to oneself without vocalization. According to Lev VYGOTSKY, inner language follows EGOCENTRIC SPEECH and represents the child's recruitment of language in his or her reasoning efforts. Also called **inner speech**. See also INTERNALIZED SPEECH; VERBAL THOUGHT.

inner nuclear layer (**INL**) the layer of retinal cell bodies interposed between the photoreceptors and the RETINAL GANGLION CELLS. The inner nuclear layer contains AMACRINE CELLS, RETINAL HORIZONTAL CELLS, RETINAL BIPOLAR CELLS, and MÜLLER FIBERS.

inner plexiform layer (**IPL**) the synaptic layer in the retina in which contacts are made between the dendrites of RETINAL GANGLION CELLS, BIPOLAR NEURONS, and AMACRINE CELLS.

inner psychophysics a systematic attempt to relate experience in the mind to states of excitation in the sensory apparatus. Compare OUTER PSYCHOPHYSICS. See PSYCHOPHYSICAL LAW. [introduced by Gustav FECHNER]

inner speech see INNER LANGUAGE.

innervation *n.* the supply of nerves or nerve fibers to an organ (e.g., muscle or gland) or a body region. **—innervate** *vb.*

innervation ratio the ratio expressing the number of muscle fibers innervated by a single motor axon. It may vary from 3 muscle fibers per axon for small muscles in the fingers to 150 muscle fibers per axon for large muscle bundles of the arms and legs. The lower the ratio, the finer is the control of movements.

innovation *n.* in the psychology of groups, a change in some aspect of the group, such as its operating procedures or general orientation, away from a long-held or unquestioned position to a novel, and in many cases previously unpopular, position. Studies suggest that innovation is most often generated by a minority within a group arguing consistently for change and not by the majority, which tends to favor consensus and conformity. See MAJORITY INFLUENCE; MINORITY INFLUENCE.

innovation diffusion the gradual spread of a new technology to populations or population segments. Rates of diffusion are determined by adoption of, and successful use of, the technology. Innovation includes both tangible technologies, such as computer-based systems, and intangible technologies, such as processes or ways of thinking. See also PRODUCT CHAMPION.

innovative therapies loosely, psychological treatments that are new and different from traditional therapies. Relatively current examples include the EMPTY-CHAIR TECHNIQUE and PARADOXICAL TECHNIQUES.

inoculation effect the finding that exposure to and arguing against a weak persuasive message make people more resistant to a subsequent strong persuasive message than would otherwise have been the case. See also INOCULATION THEORY. [originally demonstrated by U.S. psychologist William J. McGuire (1925–)]

inoculation theory a theory postulating that resistance to PERSUASION can be created by exposing people to weak persuasive attacks that are easily refuted. This helps people to practice defending their attitudes, as well as making them aware that their attitudes can be challenged, and thereby creates resistance to subsequent stronger messages. See also INOCULATION EFFECT. [originally proposed by U.S. psychologist William J. McGuire (1925–)]

Inocybe *n.* a genus of mushrooms, some species of which are poisonous because they contain the toxic alkaloid MUSCARINE. Symptoms of poisoning include salivation, perspiration, and lacrimation (tears); at higher doses these symptoms may be followed by abdominal pains, severe nausea and vomiting, diarrhea, visual disturbances, labored breathing, and bradycardia (slowed heart rate), which may potentially result in death from cardiac or respiratory failure. Treatment is with ATROPINE.

inositol *n.* a compound (similar to glucose) that occurs in many foods and is sometimes classed as a vitamin. It is a component of cell-membrane phospholipids and plasma lipoproteins, and phosphorylated derivatives (see INOSITOL PHOSPHATES) function as SECOND MESSENGERS in cells.

inositol phosphates derivatives of INOSITOL that contain one or more phosphate groups, some of which are SECOND MESSENGERS in cells, serving to relay signals from receptors at the cell surface to other parts of the cell. The most studied of these second messengers is **inositol 1,4,5-trisphosphate** (**IP_3**). The action of LITHIUM salts, used to treat bipolar disorders, may be linked to their inhibition of the enzyme **inositol monophosphatase**, which is involved in the recycling of inositol from the inositol phosphates. It has been hypothesized that this inhibition thus leads to a deficiency of inositol and a corresponding excess of inositol phosphates.

inpatient *n.* a person who has been formally admitted to a hospital for a period of at least 24 hours for observation, care, diagnosis, or treatment, as distinguished from an OUTPATIENT or an emergency-room patient.

Inpatient Multidimensional Psychiatric Scale (**IMPS**) an interview-based rating instrument used to assess attitudes and behaviors of individuals with psychoses, typically administered on admission to mental institutions. It yields information on symptom severity and is used to classify patients into psychotic types, such as hostile–paranoid, excited–hostile, excited–grandiose, and so forth. The scale was originally published in 1962 as a revision of the 1953 **Multidimensional Scale for Rating Psychiatric Patients**. [developed by U.S. psychometrician Maurice Lorr (1910–) and U.S. psychologists C. James Klett (1926–), Douglas M. McNair (1927–), and Julian J. Lasky (1918–)]

inpatient services diagnostic and treatment services available to hospitalized patients and usually unavailable or only partially available in outpatient facilities. Examples are continuous supervision; medical treatment and nursing care; and specialized treatment techniques, such as rehabilitational, occupational, movement, or recreation therapy, as well as social-work services.

input *n.* the signals fed into a communication channel together with the energy put into a system. In the context of the interaction between a person and a computer, input usually refers to data or instructions fed into the computer. Compare OUTPUT.

input–output mechanism a simple model of INFORMATION PROCESSING in which a given input automatically produces a given output. An input–output mechanism is a closed system in which information is subjected to a fixed sequence of preset operations and there is no interaction with the environment during throughput. Some behaviorist theories have been criticized as reducing the human organism to an input–output mechanism.

inquiry training model see INDUCTIVE TEACHING MODEL.

inquisitorial system see ADVERSARIAL SYSTEM.

INRC group abbreviation for IDENTITY, NEGATION, RECIPROCAL, AND CORRELATIVE OPERATIONS.

in re Gault a U.S. Supreme Court decision in 1967 that fundamentally changed the rights of juveniles in legal proceedings by establishing that MINORS have many of the same DUE PROCESS rights as adults.

insane asylum a former (19th-century) name for a residential institution for the treatment of people with severe mental illness. Also called **lunatic asylum**. See ASYLUM.

insanity *n.* in law, a condition of the mind that renders a person incapable of being responsible for his or her criminal acts. Defendants who are found to be NOT GUILTY BY REASON OF INSANITY therefore lack CRIMINAL RESPONSIBILITY for their conduct. Whether a person is insane, in this legal sense, is determined by judges and juries, not psychologists or psychiatrists. Numerous legal standards for determining criminal responsibility, the central issue in an INSANITY DEFENSE, have been used at various times in many jurisdictions. These include the DURHAM RULE, the AMERICAN LAW INSTITUTE MODEL PENAL CODE INSANITY TEST, and the MCNAUGHTEN RULE. See also PARTIAL INSANITY. **—insane** *adj.*

insanity defense in criminal law, the defense plea that an individual lacks CRIMINAL RESPONSIBILITY for his or her conduct. See also AMERICAN LAW INSTITUTE MODEL PENAL CODE INSANITY TEST; DIMINISHED RESPONSIBILITY; DURHAM RULE; MCNAUGHTEN RULE.

Insanity Defense Reform Act (**IDRA**) legislation passed by the U.S. Congress in 1984 that modified existing laws relating to INSANITY DEFENSE cases. One modification involved removing the volitional component of the AMERICAN LAW INSTITUTE MODEL PENAL CODE INSANITY TEST, so that "conforming one's conduct to the requirements of the law" was no longer a factor in judging insanity. Another modification involved shifting the burden of proof (responsibility for convincing the court beyond a reasonable doubt of the truth of an allegation) in insanity defense cases from the prosecution to the defense.

insect phobia see ACAROPHOBIA; ANIMAL PHOBIA; SPECIFIC PHOBIA.

insecure attachment in the STRANGE SITUATION, one of several patterns of generally negative parent–child relationship in which the child fails to display confidence when the parent is present, sometimes shows distress when the parent leaves, and reacts to the returning parent by avoidance (see AVOIDANT ATTACHMENT) or with ambivalence (see AMBIVALENT ATTACHMENT). See also ANXIOUS–AVOIDANT ATTACHMENT; ANXIOUS–RESISTANT ATTACHMENT; DISORGANIZED ATTACHMENT.

insecurity *n.* a feeling of inadequacy, lack of self-confidence, and inability to cope, accompanied by general uncertainty and anxiety about one's goals, abilities, or relationships with others. **—insecure** *adj.*

insemination *n.* the deposition of semen within the vagina, either during coitus or by artificial means (see ARTIFICIAL INSEMINATION). Also called **semination**.

insensible *adj.* **1.** denoting or relating to a state of nonresponsiveness and unconsciousness. **2.** lacking emotional response. **—insensibility** *n.*

insert headphone a device for presenting sound in a sealed ear canal. Typically, the transducer is located remotely, and sound is routed via a thin tube, which is embedded at its terminus in a soft foam plug; the earplug and tube are inserted in the ear canal. Such a system provides better acoustic isolation than do typical headphones and perhaps better control of the sound impinging on the tympanic membrane.

insight *n.* **1.** the clear and often sudden discernment of a solution to a problem by means that are not obvious and may never become so, even after one has tried hard to work out how one has arrived at the solution. There are many different theories of how insights are formed and of the kinds of insights that exist. For example, in the 1990s, U.S. psychologists Robert Sternberg (1949–) and Janet Davidson proposed a theory in which there are three main kinds of insights: (a) selective encoding insights, which are used to distinguish relevant from irrelevant information; (b) selective comparison insights, which are used to distinguish what information already stored in long-term memory is relevant for one's purposes; and (c) selective combination insights, which are used to put together the information available so as to formulate a solution to a given problem. **2.** in psychotherapy, an awareness of underlying sources of emotional, cognitive, or behavioral difficulty in oneself or another person. See also AHA EXPERIENCE; EPIPHANY.

insightful learning a cognitive form of learning involving the mental rearrangement or restructuring of the elements in a problem to achieve an understanding of the problem and arrive at a solution. Insightful learning was described by Wolfgang KÖHLER in the 1920s, based on his observations of apes stacking boxes or using sticks to retrieve food, and was offered as an alternative to learning based on conditioning.

insight therapy any form of psychotherapy based on the theory that deep and lasting personality changes cannot be brought about unless the client understands the origin of his or her distorted attitudes and defensive measures. This approach (characteristic, for example, of PSYCHOANALYSIS and PSYCHODYNAMIC PSYCHOTHERAPY) contrasts with therapies directed toward removal of symptoms or behavior modification.

in situ hybridization a method for detecting particular NUCLEOTIDE sequences within DNA or RNA in tissue sections by providing a labeled nucleotide probe that is complementary to, and will therefore hybridize with, the sequence of interest.

insomnia *n.* difficulty in initiating or maintaining a restorative sleep that results in fatigue, the severity or persistence of which causes clinically significant distress or impairment in functioning. Such sleeplessness may be caused by a transient or chronic physical condition or psychological disturbance. Also called **agrypnia**; **ahypnia**; **ahypnosia**; **anhypnia**. See DISORDERS OF INITIATING AND MAINTAINING SLEEP; FATAL FAMILIAL INSOMNIA; INITIAL INSOMNIA; INTERMITTENT INSOMNIA; MIDDLE INSOMNIA; PRIMARY INSOMNIA; PSEUDOINSOMNIA; TERMINAL INSOMNIA. **—insomniac** *n.*

inspectionalism *n.* see VOYEURISM.

inspection time (**IT**) in DISCRIMINATION LEARNING, the amount of time it takes an individual to make simple visual discriminations, such as which of two lines is longer, under specific experimental conditions. Inspection time is found to be correlated with IQ.

inspective exploration EXPLORATORY BEHAVIOR used as a means of reducing anxiety, fear, or uncertainty associated with novel stimuli and thus decreasing arousal. Also called **specific exploration**. Compare DIVERSIVE EXPLORATION. [defined by British-born Canadian psychologist Daniel E. Berlyne (1924–1976)]

inspiration *n.* **1.** the act of drawing air into the lungs. **2.** in cognitive psychology, a sudden INSIGHT or leap in understanding that produces new, creative ideas or approaches to a problem. See AHA EXPERIENCE; DISCONTINUITY HYPOTHESIS. See also CREATIVE IMAGINATION; CREATIVE THINKING; DIVERGENT PRODUCTION. **3.** the process of being aroused or stimulated to do something, or the quality of being so aroused, as in *Her speech gave us the inspiration we needed.* **—inspirational** *adj.* **—inspire** *vb.* **—inspired** *adj.*

inspirational motivation a goal-directed state aroused by exposure to high-performing, successful, or admired models.

inspiration–expiration ratio (**I/E ratio**) the ratio of the duration of the inspiration phase of the respiratory cycle to the duration of the exhalation phase, that is, the time taken to breathe in divided by the time taken to breathe out. This ratio is typically used in studies of emotion: Fearful states have high I/E ratios, whereas nonfearful attentive states have low I/E ratios.

instability *n.* in psychology, a tendency toward lack of self-control, erratic behavior, and rapidly changing or excessive emotions. Also called **lability**. **—unstable** *adj.*

instance theory the hypothesis that CATEGORIZATION depends on specific remembered instances of the category, as opposed to an abstract PROTOTYPE or a FEATURE-based rule that defines category membership. Instance theory has also been applied to questions of attention, skill acquisition, and social decision making, among other problems. Instance theories of prejudice, for example, suggest that stereotypes are not just abstractions about the typical characteristics of members of a particular group but are instead based on the perceiver's memories of specific individual group members. Also called **exemplar theory**.

instant gratification the meeting or satisfying of one's needs or wishes without delay. Therapy may be important to help reduce the desire for instant gratification when postponing needs and tolerating delays would be realistic or in the best interests of the client.

instigation therapy BEHAVIOR THERAPY in which the therapist provides a positive model and reinforces the client's progress toward self-regulation and self-evaluation.

instinct *n.* **1.** an innate, species-specific biological force that impels an organism to do something, particularly to perform a certain act or respond in a certain manner to specific stimuli (see INSTINCTIVE BEHAVIOR). See also HERD INSTINCT; HORMIC PSYCHOLOGY. **2.** in psychoanalytic theory, a basic biological drive (e.g., hunger, thirst, sex, or aggression) that must be fulfilled in order to maintain physical and psychological equilibrium. Sigmund FREUD classified instincts into two types: those derived from the LIFE INSTINCT and those derived from the DEATH INSTINCT. See also COMPONENT INSTINCT; DESTRUDO; EROTIC INSTINCT; LIBIDO; SATISFACTION OF INSTINCTS; SEXUAL INSTINCT. **3.** in popular usage, any inherent or unlearned predisposition (behavioral or otherwise) or motivational force. **—instinctive** or **instinctual** *adj.*

instinct doctrine the belief that behavior is largely determined by instincts.

instinctive behavior stereotyped, unlearned, largely stimulus-bound adaptive behavior limited in its expression by the inherent properties of the nervous system and genetic factors. It is species-specific and involves complex activity patterns rather than simple reflexes. See FIXED-ACTION PATTERN; INNATE RELEASING MECHANISM; INSTINCT; MODAL ACTION PATTERN; RELEASER.

instinctive drift the tendency of learned, reinforced behavior to gradually return to a more innate behavior. For example, racoons trained to drop coins into a container will eventually begin to dip the coins into the container, pull them back out, rub them together, and dip them in again. The learned behavior of dropping coins becomes more representative of the innate behavior of food washing. Also called **instinctual drift**. [proposed in 1961 by U.S. psychologists Keller Breland (1915–1965) and Marian Breland (1920–2001)]

instinctive knowledge unlearned and generally unalterable behavior, observable when a new stimulus (i.e., one not previously encountered) elicits an affective response indicative of genetic influences. An example is fear of and flight from certain predators in the absence of previous exposure to these animals.

instinctual aim see AIM OF THE INSTINCT.

instinctual drive see INSTINCT.

instinctual fusion see FUSION.

instinctual impulse see INSTINCT. See also IMPULSE.

instinctualization of smell 1. the capacity of smell to play a part in COPROPHILIA or anal fixations. **2.** the role of body odors as arousal factors in sexual foreplay. See also COMPONENT INSTINCT.

institution *n.* **1.** an established practice, tradition, behavior, or system of roles and relationships, such as marriage, that is considered normative within a society. Sociologists usually distinguish between four main types of institution: political institutions (e.g., monarchy), economic institutions (e.g., capitalism), cultural institutions (e.g., religion and accepted forms of artistic expression), and kinship institutions (e.g., the extended family). **2.** a large, often publicly funded organization, such as a university, museum, or charitable foundation, or the building that houses such an organization. **3.** a building or building complex in which individuals are cared for or confined for extended periods of time, especially a psychiatric hospital or a prison. **—institutional** *adj.*

Institutional Animal Care and Use Committee (IACUC) a committee that is responsible for overseeing an institute's ANIMAL CARE AND USE program and research protocols involving animals. The primary responsibility of the IACUC is to ensure the humane treatment of the animals and compliance of the research program and procedures with established regulations. U.S. federal law mandates that any institute conducting research with laboratory animals must establish an IACUC, and any member of the institution who plans to conduct an experiment or undertake activities that involve animals must submit a proposal to the IACUC for review.

institutional care medical or mental health care services received by an inpatient in a hospital, nursing home, or other residential institution.

institutionalism *n.* see SOCIAL BREAKDOWN SYNDROME.

institutionalization *n.* **1.** placement of an individual in an institution for therapeutic or correctional purposes. **2.** an individual's gradual adaptation to institutional life over a long period, especially when this is seen as rendering him or her passive, dependent, and generally unsuited to life outside the institution. **—institutionalize** *vb.*

institutionalized racism differential treatment of individuals on the basis of their racial group by social INSTITUTIONS, including religious organizations, governments, businesses, the media, and educational institutions. Examples include DISCRIMINATION in hiring, promotion, and advancement at work, restrictive housing regulations that promote segregation, unfair portrayal of minority members in newspapers and magazines, and legal statutes that restrict the civil liberties of the members of specific racial categories. Also called **institutional racism**. See RACISM.

institutional neurosis see SOCIAL BREAKDOWN SYNDROME.

institutional review board (IRB) a committee named by an agency or institution to review research proposals originating within that agency for ethical acceptability.

institutional sales promotion an aspect of business-to-business marketing in which large industrial buyers are typically encouraged to buy in large quantities or to sign contracts for long-term relationships in exchange for special pricing or services.

instructed learning the second stage of CULTURAL LEARNING, in which a more accomplished person instructs a less accomplished person. The process requires that learners grasp the instructor's understanding of the task and then compare it with their own understanding. Compare COLLABORATIVE LEARNING; IMITATIVE LEARNING. [proposed by U.S. psychologist Michael Tomasello (1950–) and colleagues]

instructional set the attitude toward a task or test that is communicated (intentionally or unintentionally) by the experimenter to the participants. It conveys information on how they should approach the task or test, for example, that speed is more (or less) important than accuracy.

instructional theory of development the theory that the development of unorganized neural elements into differentiated neural structures is shaped by environmental factors.

instructional treatments educational interventions that have been designed, implemented, and evaluated by an instructor to increase learning or various kinds of performance.

instrument *n.* **1.** any tool or device used in measuring, recording, testing, or similar functions. **2.** in general, an implement used in performing specific operations, such as cutting or writing.

instrumental *n.* in some languages, such as Sanskrit, a CASE of nouns, pronouns, and noun phrases identifying entities that are used by the AGENT to perform the action of a verb. The instrumental is also used as a category in CASE GRAMMAR; in *The crowbar pried open the door*, for example, the inanimate noun *crowbar* is said to be the instrument rather than the agent (here unidentified). See also EXPERIENCER; PATIENT.

instrumental activities of daily living (IADLs) activities essential to an individual's ability to function autonomously, including preparing meals, using the telephone, managing money, shopping, getting to places beyond walking distance, and the like. See also ACTIVITIES OF DAILY LIVING.

instrumental aggression see AGGRESSION; ANIMAL AGGRESSION.

instrumental behavior 1. behavior that is learned and elicited via positive or negative reinforcement of target (rather than instinctive) responses. The term is used synonymously with OPERANT BEHAVIOR, usually for describing behavior during CONDITIONING procedures that involves long sequences of activity, such as solving a puzzle box. **2.** actions that directly affect or manage the behavior of others. A subordinate animal may engage in infantile behavior to inhibit threatening or aggressive actions, even though the subordinate is not an infant. Some animals use ALARM CALLS to distract other group members so they can make use of a valued resource without interference.

instrumental conditioning any form of CONDITIONING in which the correct response is essential for REINFORCEMENT. Instrumental conditioning is similar to OPERANT CONDITIONING and usually involves complex activities in order to reach a goal, such as when a rat is trained to navigate a maze to obtain food. It contrasts with PAVLOVIAN CONDITIONING, in which reinforcement is given regardless of the response. Also called **instrumental learning**; **Type II conditioning**; **Type R conditioning**.

instrumental dependence the tendency to rely on others for accomplishing tasks.

Instrumental Enrichment a program for helping people to improve their intellectual performance by developing the metacognitive and cognitive skills essential to successful performance of intellectual tasks. The program is taught as a course or series of modules separately from regular instruction in school. First used for pupils with mental retardation, it was later applied to performers at all intellectual levels. The program involves solving puzzles, some of which are similar to the kinds of problems found on conventional intelligence tests, as well as bridging, which involves relating performance on these puzzles to the solution of real-world problems. Results of evaluations are mixed, but suggest at least some benefits for performers with mental retardation (who tend to be weak in metacognitive skills) and for teachers using the program. [formulated in the 1970s by Romanian-born psychologist Reuven Feuerstein (1921–) and his collaborators]

instrumentalism *n.* **1.** in the philosophy of science, the position that theories are not to be considered as either true or false but as instruments of explanation that allow observations of the world to be meaningfully ordered. This view is related to MACHIAN POSITIVISM. **2.** a theory of knowledge that emphasizes the pragmatic value, rather than the truth value, of ideas. In this view, the value of an idea, concept, or judgment lies in its ability to explain, predict, and control one's concrete functional interactions with the experienced world. This view is related to PRAGMATISM. [developed by John DEWEY] **3.** the view or attitude that the primary motivation for social interaction is the attaining of some positive advantage or good for the self, such that others are regarded and used as instruments in attaining such advantage. **—instrumentalist** *adj., n.*

instrumentality theory the theory that a person's attitude toward an event will depend on his or her perception of its function as an instrument in bringing about desirable or undesirable consequences. See also VALENCE–INSTRUMENTALITY–EXPECTANCY THEORY.

instrumental learning see INSTRUMENTAL CONDITIONING.

instrumental orientation the tendency of an individual or group to focus on assigned tasks and goals and the tangible benefits of achieving them (e.g., increased pay) rather than on the interpersonal relationships involved in achieving them. See also TASK-MOTIVATED; TASK-ORIENTED GROUP.

instrumental-relativist orientation see NAIVE HEDONISM.

instrumental response any response that achieves a goal or contributes to its achievement, such as a response that is effective in gaining a reward or avoiding pain (e.g., a rat's bar pressing to obtain food).

instrumentation *n.* the creation and use of equipment and devices (including psychological tests) for the measurement of some attribute or the control of experiments (e.g., automation of stimulus presentation and data collection).

Instrument Coordination Analyzer-90 (**ICA-90**) a German table-top computer cockpit simulator for flight simulation.

instrument drift changes in an INSTRUMENT, usually gradual and often predictable, that can threaten the validity of conclusions drawn from the data obtained with that instrument. Examples include the stretching of spring scales and the fatiguing of human observers. Also called **instrument decay**.

insula *n.* (*pl.* **insulae**) a region of the cerebral cortex of primate brains that is buried in a cleft near the lower end of the LATERAL SULCUS. Also called **central lobe**; **island of Reil**.

insulin *n.* a hormone, secreted by the B cells of the ISLETS OF LANGERHANS in the pancreas, that facilitates the transfer of glucose molecules through cell membranes. Together with GLUCAGON, it plays a key role in regulating BLOOD SUGAR and carbohydrate metabolism. In the absence of sufficient concentrations of insulin, glucose accumulates in the blood and is excreted, as in DIABETES MELLITUS (see also HYPERGLYCEMIA). Excessive concentrations of insulin (resulting, for example, from insulin overdosage or an insulin-secreting tumour) give rise to HYPOGLYCEMIA.

insulin-coma therapy see COMA THERAPY.

insulin lipodystrophy see LIPODYSTROPHY.

insulin-shock therapy see COMA THERAPY.

intake interview **1.** the initial interview with a client by a therapist or counselor to obtain both information regarding the issues or problems that have brought the client into therapy or counseling and preliminary information regarding personal and family history. **2.** the initial interview with a patient who is being admitted into a psychiatric hospital, day treatment, or inpatient substance abuse facility. Intake interviews are also common in government-funded mental health services, such as those provided at community mental health centers, in determining eligibility and appropriateness of the client for services offered. An intake interview may be carried out by a specialist who may not necessarily treat the patient, but the information obtained is used to determine the best course of treatment and the appropriate therapist to provide it.

integrated delivery system (**IDS**) a health care provider organization that is completely integrated operationally and clinically and that offers a full range of health care services, including physician, hospital, and adjunct services. IDSs began to develop in the early 1980s and multiplied rapidly in the 1990s. They come in varying formats, one of the more typical being an alliance between hospitals and individual physicians or GROUP MEDICAL PRACTICES. An IDS is a MANAGED CARE organization.

integrated display in ergonomics, a machine display designed on the principle that similar categories of information should be grouped together. Compare SEPARATED DISPLAY.

integrated model in evaluation research, an administrative relationship, used in FORMATIVE EVALUATION, between the program director and multiple production units, each made up of writers, designers, and evaluators who are all involved in program development as well as program evaluation. Members of these units do not necessarily share equal importance or equal access to the program director. Also called **dependent model**. Compare SEGREGATED MODEL.

integrated personality a personality in which the constituent traits, behavioral patterns, motives, and so forth are used effectively and with minimal effort or without conflict. Those with integrated personalities are thought essentially to know themselves and to be able to enjoy and live life fully. Also called **well-integrated personality**.

integrated system a program allowing individuals with disabilities to control computer functions, their environments, telephone communication, and powered mobility through a central control.

integrated therapy see INTEGRATIVE PSYCHOTHERAPY.

integration *n.* **1.** in general, the coordination or unification of parts into a totality. **2.** the developmental process in which separate drives, experiences, abilities, values, and personality characteristics are gradually brought together into an organized whole.

integrative bargaining a form of BARGAINING in which the parties work together to achieve outcomes that benefit both sides.

integrative behavioral couples therapy couples therapy that uses techniques of BEHAVIORAL COUPLES THERAPY but also focuses on each person's emotional acceptance of his or her partner's genuine incompatibilities, which may or may not be amenable to change. It is based on the conviction that focusing on changing incompatibilities leads to a resistance to change when change is possible or that this focus results in unnecessary frustration for both partners when change is not possible.

integrative complexity the extent to which an ATTITUDE OBJECT is seen as having both positive and negative features and the extent to which these features are seen as related to one another. Low integrative complexity occurs when an attitude object is seen exclusively in positive or negative terms. Moderate integrative complexity occurs when the object is seen as having both positive and negative features, but these features are seen as having little relation to one another. High integrative complexity occurs when the positive and negative features are seen as related to one another.

integrative learning the process of learning tasks that involve simultaneous or successive functioning of several modalities, as in reading and writing.

integrative medicine the combination of conventional medical treatments and complementary therapies that have demonstrated scientific merit with regard to safety and efficacy. See also COMPLEMENTARY AND ALTERNATIVE MEDICINE.

integrative psychotherapy psychotherapy that selects models or techniques from various therapeutic schools to suit the client's particular problems. For example, PSYCHODYNAMIC PSYCHOTHERAPY and GESTALT THERAPY may be combined through the practice of INTERPRETATION of material in the HERE AND NOW. The Society for the Exploration of Psychotherapy Integration (SEPI), founded in 1983, reflects the growing interest in, and the rapid development and use of, such combined therapeutic techniques. Also called **integrated therapy**; **psychotherapy integration**. See also ECLECTIC PSYCHOTHERAPY.

integrity *n.* the quality of moral consistency, honesty, and truthfulness with oneself and others.

integrity group psychotherapy a type of GROUP PSYCHOTHERAPY in which openness and honesty are expected from all participants, and experienced members of the group serve as models of sincerity and involvement. [developed by O. Hobart MOWRER]

integrity testing procedures used to determine whether employees or applicants for employment are likely to engage in counterproductive behavior in an organization. **Overt integrity tests** are paper-and-pencil inventories that ask people about their past behaviors and their attitudes toward unethical, illegal, and counterproductive behavior. **Personality-based integrity tests** are inventories measuring the character traits thought to be related to unethical, illegal, and counterproductive behavior. Integrity tests are sometimes called **honesty tests**.

integrity versus despair the eighth and final stage of ERIKSON'S EIGHT STAGES OF DEVELOPMENT, which occurs during old age. In this stage the individual reflects on the life he or she has lived and may develop either integrity—a sense of satisfaction in having lived a good life and the ability to approach death with equanimity—or despair—a feeling of bitterness about opportunities missed and time wasted, and a dread of approaching death. Also called **ego integrity versus despair**.

intellect *n.* **1.** the INTELLECTUAL FUNCTIONS of the mind considered collectively. **2.** an individual's capacity for abstract, objective reasoning, especially as contrasted with his or her capacity for feeling, imagining, or acting. —**intellectual** *adj.*

intellectual detachment see DETACHMENT.

intellectual disability see MENTAL RETARDATION.

intellectual function any of the mental functions involved in acquiring, developing, and relating ideas, concepts, and hypotheses. Memory, imagination, and judgment can also be considered intellectual functions. See HIGHER MENTAL PROCESS. Also called **intellectual operation**.

intellectual impoverishment diminished intellectual capacity, such as problem-solving ability and concentration. This condition is observed in many people with chronic schizophrenia, senility, or depression and in individuals living in a deprived, unstimulating environment. See also POVERTY OF IDEAS.

intellectual insight in psychotherapy, an objective, rational awareness of experiences or relationships. Some theorists posit that intellectual insight by itself does not advance the therapeutic process and may even impede it because little or no feeling (i.e., emotional content) is involved.

intellectualism *n.* **1.** in philosophy, a position consistent with IDEALISM OR RATIONALISM that emphasizes the preeminence of mind or idea. **2.** in psychology, the doctrine that cognitive functions are preeminent, such that emotive and motivational experiential states can be explained by, or originate from, more fundamental cognitive states. **3.** in general language, a tendency to place an exaggerated value or dependence on the intellect. —**intellectualist** *adj.*

intellectual maturity the adult stage of intellectual development, in which the individual typically has a high level of good judgment, often combined with WISDOM.

intellectual operation see INTELLECTUAL FUNCTION.

intellectual plasticity the extent to which an individual's intellectual abilities are modifiable and thus subject to various kinds of change.

intellectual stimulation 1. the enhancement of cognitive processing—including creativity, discernment, and insight—that occurs when individuals exchange ideas and opinions during interpersonal or group discussion. **2.** the pleasurable sense of being challenged and provoked that can arise from an encounter with new, difficult, or interesting ideas.

intellectual subaverage functioning an IQ more than two standard deviations below the test mean obtained on an intelligence test. Also called **significantly subaverage intellectual functioning**.

intelligence *n.* the ability to derive information, learn from experience, adapt to the environment, understand, and correctly utilize thought and reason. There are many different definitions of intelligence, including an operational one, proposed by Edwin BORING, that intelligence is what is tested by INTELLIGENCE TESTS. There is currently much debate, as there has been in the past, over the exact nature of intelligence. —**intelligent** *adj.*

intelligence knowledge-based system (**IKBS**) a system used in the United Kingdom for reasoning and decision making. It was developed from artificial intelligence, using a KNOWLEDGE REPRESENTATION system (symbolic, quantitative, or both) in a field to provide either a solution to some problem or an aid to decision making.

intelligence quotient see IQ.

intelligence quotient stability see CONSTANCY OF THE IQ.

intelligence test an individually administered, standardized test used to determine a person's level of intelligence by measuring his or her ability to solve problems, form concepts, reason, acquire detail, and perform other intellectual tasks. It comprises mental, verbal, and performance tasks of graded difficulty that have been standardized by use on a representative sample of the population. Examples of intelligence tests include the STANFORD–BINET INTELLIGENCE SCALE and the WECHSLER ADULT INTELLIGENCE SCALE. Also called **intelligence scale**. See IQ.

intelligent design a theoretical position, developed by opponents of EVOLUTION, that the universe with all its diversity is so ingeniously and complexly constructed and interrelated that it could only have been created by some intelligent force and that complex biological organisms could not have emerged through NATURAL SELECTION. In some contexts, the term has become synonymous with CREATIONISM.

intensional meaning the meaning of a word or phrase as defined by listing the essential or salient properties of the thing or concept referred to. For example, the intensional meaning of *sister* is "female sibling." Compare EXTENSIONAL MEANING.

intensity *n.* **1.** the quantitative value of a stimulus or sensation. **2.** the strength of any behavior, such as an impulse or emotion. **3.** the strength of an individual's performance in some activity or field with reference to one or more of the following attributes: arousal, commitment, effort, assertiveness, and attentional focus. Also called **performance intensity**. See also OPTIMAL INTENSITY. **—intense** *adj.*

intensive care syndrome a type of psychotic condition observed in some individuals in intensive care who are immobilized in an isolated, unfamiliar environment that may have the effect of sensory deprivation. Variable factors may include the mental and physical condition of the individual prior to the need for intensive care, the age of the individual, medical or surgical complications, and behavioral effects of drugs administered.

intensive care unit (**ICU**) a hospital unit in which critically ill patients receive intensive and continuous nursing, medical care, and supervision that includes the use of sophisticated monitoring and resuscitative equipment. ICUs are often organized for the care of specific groups of patients, such as neonatal ICUs or pulmonary ICUs. Also called **critical care unit** (**CCU**). Compare CONTINUING CARE UNIT.

intensive psychotherapy broad, thorough, and prolonged psychological treatment of an individual's concerns and problems. The qualifier "intensive" indicates both the nature of the discussions, which typically involve extensive examination of the individual's life history and conflicts, and the duration of the therapy. Compare COUNSELING; SHORT-TERM THERAPY.

intent analysis analysis of social interaction in which verbal content is classified according to intent (providing support, seeking approval, etc.).

intention *n.* **1.** a conscious decision to perform a behavior. See also THEORY OF PLANNED BEHAVIOR; THEORY OF REASONED ACTION. **2.** a resolve to act in a certain way, or an impulse for purposeful action. In experiments, intention is often equated with the goals defined by the task instructions. **—intentional** *adj.*

intentional accident see PURPOSIVE ACCIDENT.

intentional behavior goal-oriented behavior in which an individual uses strategies to achieve various ends or effects. According to Jean's PIAGET's theory of cognitive development, intentional behavior emerges in human infants between 8 and 12 months of age.

intentional forgetting inaccessibility of a memory that is due to REPRESSION or to an unconscious wish to forget. See also FORGETTING.

intentional inexistence in ACT PSYCHOLOGY and PHENOMENOLOGY, the principle that the object of perception or thought (the intentional object) exists within the act of perceiving or thinking. See INTENTIONALITY. [developed by German philosopher and psychologist Franz Brentano (1838–1917)]

intentionality *n.* a characteristic of an individual's acts that requires the individual (a) to have goals, desires, and standards; (b) to select behaviors that are in the service of attaining the goal (e.g., means to an end); and (c) to call into conscious awareness a desired future state. Investigators differ as to whether (a) alone, (a) and (b) but not (c), or (a), (b), and (c) are required for intentionality to be attributable to an individual. The concept of intentionality, as developed by German philosopher and psychologist Franz Brentano (1838–1917), has been very influential in ACT PSYCHOLOGY, PHENOMENOLOGY, and related approaches in HERMENEUTICS.

intentional learning learning that is planned or deliberate and therefore consciously employs MNEMONIC STRATEGIES. Compare INCIDENTAL LEARNING.

intentional stance a strategy for interpreting and predicting behavior that views organisms as rational beings acting in a reasonable manner according to their beliefs and desires (i.e., their intentions). [proposed by U.S. philosopher Daniel C. Dennett (1942–)]

intention movement a physical behavior that precipitates another physical response, such that the first behavior may signal the second. For example, when two people are talking, one may exhibit certain postural behaviors (e.g., changing stance, shifting weight) predictive of terminating the interaction, before actually ending the conversation and walking away.

intention tremor an ACTION TREMOR that is associated with a directed, voluntary movement, such as attempting to touch something, and increases as the movement progresses, as when the hand approaches the target object. It occurs in cerebellar disease.

interaction *n.* **1.** a relationship between two or more systems, people, or groups that results in mutual or reciprocal influence. See also SOCIAL INTERACTION. **2.** see INTERACTION EFFECT. **—interact** *vb.*

interactional model of anxiety a model of anxiety proposing that STATE ANXIETY is determined by the interaction of factors relating to the situation (**situational factors**) and factors relating to the individual (**person factors**).

interactional synchrony see SYNCHRONY.

interactional territory see GROUP SPACE.

interaction analysis a variety of methods used to describe, categorize, and evaluate instances of person–person interaction, person–system interaction, or team and group interaction. Interaction analysis is used in specialties such as HUMAN FACTORS ENGINEERING, human–

computer interaction, cultural studies, and communication studies.

interaction effect in the ANALYSIS OF VARIANCE, the joint effect of two or more independent variables on a dependent variable above and beyond the sum of their individual effects. See MAIN EFFECT.

interactionism *n.* **1.** the position that mind and body are distinct, incompatible substances that nevertheless interact, so that each has a causal influence on the other. This position is particularly associated with French philosopher René Descartes (1596–1650). See CARTESIAN DUALISM; MIND–BODY PROBLEM. **2.** a set of approaches, particularly in personality psychology, in which behavior is explained not in terms of personality attributes or situational influences but by references to interactions that typify the behavior of a certain type of person in a certain type of setting. **—interactionist** *adj.*

interactionist view of intelligence the view that intelligence always develops as an interaction between biological dispositions and environmental conditions and that it is difficult or impossible to separate the contributions of these two factors. Interactionists point out that genes always express themselves (manifest their effects in an individual) through a given set of environments and that the expression of the genes may be different as a function of the environment(s) in which they are expressed.

interaction-process analysis (**IPA**) a technique used to study the emotional, intellectual, and behavioral interactions among members of a group, for example, during GROUP PSYCHOTHERAPY. It requires observers to classify every behavior displayed by a member of a group into one of 12 mutually exclusive categories, such as "asks for information" or "shows tension." See also CATEGORY-SYSTEM METHOD; STRUCTURED OBSERVATIONAL MEASURES. [developed by U.S. social psychologist Robert Freed Bales (1916–)]

interaction territory in social psychology, a space around two or more people while they converse. It is recognized by outsiders that the interaction territory should not be invaded while the conversation is in progress. See also GROUP SPACE; PROXEMICS.

interactive advertising the process, used in Internet marketing, of consumers answering questions or interacting with a website in order to see an advertisement or promotion.

interactive group psychotherapy see INTERPERSONAL GROUP PSYCHOTHERAPY.

interactive sport a sport that requires the participants to integrate and coordinate their actions. Football and basketball are examples of interactive sports. Compare COACTIVE–INTERACTIVE SPORT; COACTIVE SPORT.

Interamerican Society of Psychology a professional organization founded in 1951 to promote communication and research among psychologists in North, Central, and South America.

interattitudinal consistency the extent to which attitudes in an ATTITUDE SYSTEM are evaluatively consistent with one another. High consistency occurs when each attitude implies the other attitudes in the system. Low consistency occurs when some attitudes in the system imply the opposite of others.

interaural differences see BINAURAL CUES.

interaural rivalry the competition within the auditory system to comprehend conflicting inputs received simultaneously in both ears. Interaural rivalry has been employed in the study of temporal lobe lesions: Patients typically recall less of the information heard in the left ear if a lesion is on the right side, and vice versa.

interbehavioral psychology a system of psychology concerned with interactions between an organism and its environment. The focus is on the interaction of stimulus functions (the use or role of a stimulus) and response functions (the purpose served by a response) and how context and experience shape those interactions. Also called **interbehaviorism**. [proposed by U.S. psychologist Jacob Robert Kantor (1888–1984)]

interblobs *pl. n.* the regions of striate cortex that exist between the CYTOCHROME OXIDASE BLOBS. Neurons in the interblobs are less sensitive to wavelength than neurons in the blobs.

intercept *n.* the intersection of an axis of a graph by a line at a particular point, for example, the value of Y when $X = 0$ in an equation of the form $Y = a + bX$.

intercerebral fiber see COMMISSURAL FIBER.

intercorrelation *n.* the correlation between each variable and every other variable in a group of variables.

intercourse *n.* see COITUS.

interdental 1. *adj.* denoting a speech sound made with the tongue placed between the upper and lower front teeth (e.g., [th]). **2.** *n.* an interdental speech sound.

interdental lisp see LISP.

interdependence *n.* **1.** dependence of two or more people, things, situations, or other entities on each other. See CONTRIENT INTERDEPENDENCE; OUTCOME INTERDEPENDENCE; POSITIVE INTERDEPENDENCE. **2.** a state in which factors rely on or react with one another such that one cannot change without affecting the other. Also called **interdependency**. **—interdependent** *adj., n.*

interdependence theory an approach to analyzing social interactions and relationships that focuses on how each person's outcomes depend on the actions of others. See OUTCOME INTERDEPENDENCE.

interdependent self-construal a view of the self (SELF-CONSTRUAL) that emphasizes one's embeddedness in a network of social relationships and downplays one's unique traits or accomplishments. Compare INDEPENDENT SELF-CONSTRUAL.

interdisciplinary approach a manner of dealing with psychological, medical, or other scientific questions in which individuals from different disciplines or professions collaborate to obtain a more thorough, detailed understanding of the nature of the questions and consequently develop more comprehensive answers. For example, an interdisciplinary approach to the treatment or rehabilitation of an individual who is ill, disabled, or experiencing distress or pain uses the talents and experiences of therapists from a number of appropriate medical and psychological specialties. Also called **multidisciplinary approach**.

interdisciplinary team a health care team that consists of professionals from different therapeutic disciplines, paraprofessionals, a focal person, and concerned family members. Teams establish treatment priorities and goals and plan and provide treatment. Effective teams increase treatment benefits by conducting comprehensive assessment, sharing information, and adopting complementary treatment approaches.

interest *n.* an attitude characterized by a need to give SELECTIVE ATTENTION to something that is significant to the individual, such as an activity, goal, or research area.

interest factors in VOCATIONAL GUIDANCE and PERSONNEL SELECTION, an individual's interests or preferences regarded as indicators of personality traits and therefore of suitability for a particular job or type of employment. Interest factors can be derived from SELF-REPORT INVENTORIES (see INTEREST TEST) or from hobbies, leisure-time activities, and previous jobs.

interestingness *n.* in psychological aesthetics, the quality in a work of art that arouses interest rather than pleasure. Interestingness tends to increase with levels of complexity and uncertainty of the work.

interest test a SELF-REPORT INVENTORY in which the participant is required to express likes or dislikes for a range of activities and attitudes. These are then compared with the interest patterns of successful members of different occupations as a means of assessing the participant's suitability for different types of work. Important examples are the KUDER PREFERENCE RECORD and the STRONG INTEREST INVENTORY. Also called **interest inventory**; **occupational interest measure**.

interface 1. *n.* a point or means of interaction between two systems, disciplines, individuals, groups, or components. **2.** *vb.* to interact or form an interconnection. The term is commonly used in computer science, but its use in other fields is often considered jargon.

interfemoral sex see COITUS.

interference *n.* **1.** the blocking of learning or recall by the learning or remembering of other, conflicting material. Interference has many sources, including prior learning (see PROACTIVE INTERFERENCE), subsequent learning (see RETROACTIVE INTERFERENCE), competition during recall (see OUTPUT INTERFERENCE), and presentation of other material (see INTERPOLATED TASK). **2.** the mutual effect on meeting of two or more light, sound, or any other waves, the overlap of which produces a new pattern of waves. The term is used most frequently with reference to waves of the same or similar frequency, whose interference may be either constructive or destructive. In the former, the waves are in phase and the wave motions are reinforced, which results in alternating areas of increased and decreased wave amplitude (e.g., as light and dark lines or louder and softer sound); in the latter, the waves are out of phase and the wave motions are decreased or cancelled. **3.** the distortion of a signal due to the presence of NOISE. **4.** see LANGUAGE TRANSFER.

interference effects see INTERFERENCE.

interference sensitivity see RESISTANCE TO INTERFERENCE.

interference theory the hypothesis that forgetting is due to competition from other learning or other memories. INTERFERENCE could be produced by information acquired previously (see PROACTIVE INTERFERENCE) or information presented after the target memory was acquired (see RETROACTIVE INTERFERENCE).

intergluteal sex coitus in which the penis is placed between the cheeks of the buttocks, without entry into the vagina or anus.

intergroup competition see COMPETITION.

intergroup conflict disagreement or confrontation between two or more groups and their members. This may involve physical violence, interpersonal discord, or psychological tension. Compare INTRAGROUP CONFLICT.

intergroup-contact hypothesis see CONTACT HYPOTHESIS.

intergroup culture conflict see CULTURE CONFLICT.

intergroup dynamics the dynamic rather than static processes that influence the ever-shifting relationships between groups, including intergroup stereotyping, competition, conflict, and INGROUP BIAS. See GROUP DYNAMICS.

intergroup problem solving resolving matters of conflict, doubt, and uncertainty using procedures that involve two or more groups.

interhemispheric fissure see LONGITUDINAL FISSURE.

interhemispheric transfer the transfer of MEMORY TRACES or learning experiences from one cerebral hemisphere to the other. Interhemispheric transfer can be demonstrated in humans when information presented to one visual field (and therefore one hemisphere) is known by the other hemisphere.

interim behavior behavior that occurs generally midway in time between successive stimuli. Compare ADJUNCTIVE BEHAVIOR; COLLATERAL BEHAVIOR; MEDIATING BEHAVIOR.

interindividual differences the variations between individuals in one or more traits, behaviors, or characteristics (e.g., variations in intelligence). Compare INTRAINDIVIDUAL DIFFERENCES.

interitem interval the time interval between the presentation of items in a sequence. For instance, in a memory experiment, words in a list may be presented five seconds apart.

interitem reliability INTERNAL CONSISTENCY reliability of a set of items. It is indexed in two ways: (a) the average INTERCORRELATION (*r*) of each item with every other item and (b) the reliability of the sum or mean of all the items taken together. The latter reliability can be expressed in various ways, including Spearman–Brown upward adjustment, CRONBACH'S ALPHA, K–R 20 (see KUDER–RICHARDSON FORMULAS), and ARMOR'S THETA. The reliability of the sum or mean of items is often dramatically higher than the reliability of individual items.

interjudge reliability see INTERRATER RELIABILITY.

interlanguage *n.* in second-language acquisition, a state in which the learner has developed an internally consistent grammatical system with properties of both the native language and the target language. See FOSSILIZATION; IDIOLECT; LANGUAGE TRANSFER.

interlocking pathologies unconscious and dysfunctional ways of acting that are present in a couple or other intimate dyad or in a family or other close social unit.

interlocking reinforcement schedule a schedule of INTERMITTENT REINFORCEMENT in which the requirements of one schedule change depending on progress in another schedule. For example, in an interlocking fixed-interval, fixed-ratio schedule, reinforcement is given after a fixed number of responses and a fixed time, but this could be changed so that the number of responses required for reinforcement decreases as the interval between responses and reinforcement increases.

intermale aggression ANIMAL AGGRESSION occurring between males, usually to develop, maintain, or challenge dominance relationships between those males.

intermarriage *n.* **1.** marriage between two individuals belonging to different racial, ethnic, or religious groups. See EXOGAMY; MISCEGENATION; OUTBREEDING. **2.** marriage between two closely related individuals, as in a consanguineous marriage. See INBREEDING. **—intermarry** *vb.*

intermediate care facility (**ICF**) a facility providing an appropriate level of nursing and other medical care to individuals who do not require the degree of care and treatment provided by a hospital or SKILLED NURSING FACILITY but need more than room and board.

intermediate cell see TYPE III CELL.

intermediate need in MASLOW'S MOTIVATIONAL HIER-

ARCHY, a DEFICIENCY NEED that is psychologically based, such as the need for self-esteem, love, or security.

intermediate nerve see GREATER SUPERFICIAL PETROSAL NERVE.

intermediate precentral area see PREMOTOR AREA.

intermetamorphosis syndrome a MISIDENTIFICATION SYNDROME characterized by delusions that particular people have been transformed both physically and psychologically into other people.

intermission *n.* an asymptomatic period, for example, between MANIC EPISODES, MAJOR DEPRESSIVE EPISODES, or both.

intermittent explosive disorder an impulse-control disorder consisting of multiple episodes in which the individual fails to resist aggressive impulses and commits assaultive acts or destroys property. These aggressive acts are significantly out of proportion to any precipitating factors, are not caused by any other mental disorder or a general medical condition, and are not substance-induced. In *DSM–IV–TR* this disorder is included in the category IMPULSE-CONTROL DISORDERS NOT ELSEWHERE CLASSIFIED. Compare ISOLATED EXPLOSIVE DISORDER.

intermittent insomnia periods of INSOMNIA occurring several times a night.

intermittent processing see SERIAL PROCESSING.

intermittent reinforcement in operant or instrumental conditioning, any pattern of REINFORCEMENT in which only some responses are reinforced. Also called **partial reinforcement**; **partial schedule of reinforcement**.

intermodal integration the coordination or integration of information from two or more senses, such as touch and vision.

intermodal matching the ability to recognize an object initially inspected with one modality (e.g., touch) via another modality (e.g., vision). Also called **cross-modal matching**.

internal aim see OBJECT OF INSTINCT.

internal attribution see DISPOSITIONAL ATTRIBUTION.

internal boundary in psychoanalytic theory, the boundary between EGO and ID. Also called **inner boundary**. Compare EXTERNAL BOUNDARY.

internal capsule a large band of nerve fibers in the CORPUS STRIATUM that extends between the CAUDATE NUCLEUS on its medial side and the GLOBUS PALLIDUS and PUTAMEN on its lateral side. It contains afferent and efferent fibers from all parts of the cerebral cortex as they converge near the brainstem. See also EXTERNAL CAPSULE.

internal carotid artery one of the main arteries supplying blood to the neck and head. It begins as a bifurcation of the common CAROTID ARTERY at about the level of the thyroid cartilage in the neck, on either side of the body, and enters the skull at about the level of the eye. Inside the skull, the internal carotid artery branches into the ANTERIOR CEREBRAL ARTERY and the MIDDLE CEREBRAL ARTERY.

internal clock see BIOLOGICAL CLOCK.

internal conflict see INTRAPSYCHIC CONFLICT.

internal consistency the degree to which all the items on a test measure the same thing. See INTERITEM RELIABILITY; INTERRATER RELIABILITY.

internal control the belief that one is responsible for the consequences of one's behavior and that one can take action to deal with any problems, threats, or challenges. Higher internal control is thought to be associated with better mental health. See INTERNALIZERS; LOCUS OF CONTROL. Compare EXTERNAL CONTROL.

internal culture conflict see CULTURE CONFLICT.

internal environment the conditions within the body, including body temperature, blood pressure, blood-sugar level, and acid–base balance, as opposed to those in the external environment. The internal environment is maintained in a constant state, which is required for the normal functioning of the body's tissues and organs, by mechanisms of HOMEOSTASIS. [proposed by French physiologist Claude Bernard (1813–1878)]

internal evaluator an individual who conducts an evaluation of a service delivery program and is also a regular full-time staff member of the program being evaluated. Compare EXTERNAL EVALUATOR.

internal fertilization see FERTILIZATION.

internal frustration in psychoanalytic theory, denial of gratification of instinctual impulses due to internal factors (e.g., the SUPEREGO), as opposed to external factors.

internal granular layer see CORTICAL LAYERS.

internal grouping any subgroup of individuals, such as a CLIQUE or a COALITION, within a larger group.

internal inequity the situation in which employers compensate certain employees at levels that are unfair relative to other employees in the same organization. Compare EXTERNAL INEQUITY. See EQUITY THEORY.

internalization *n.* **1.** the unconscious mental process by which the characteristics, beliefs, feelings, or attitudes of other individuals or groups are assimilated into the self and adopted as one's own. **2.** in psychoanalytic theory, the process of incorporating an OBJECT relationship inside the psyche, which reproduces the external relationship as an intrapsychic phenomenon. For example, through internalization the relationship between father and child is reproduced in the relationship between SUPEREGO and EGO. Internalization is often mistakenly used as a synonym for INTROJECTION. **—internalize** *vb.*

internalized speech silent speech in which one argues with oneself over a course of action, rehearses what one is going to do, or reassures oneself when feeling threatened. See also INNER LANGUAGE; SELF-TALK.

internalizers *pl. n.* people who assume that the LOCUS OF CONTROL over their lives is within themselves (i.e., under their own control) and who characteristically try harder to change themselves and their environment. This involves being more perceptive, gathering more information and remembering it better, and using more facts and care in making decisions about how to cope. Internalizers may be less likely to follow orders blindly; they are more likely to realize there are choices to be made and to rely on their own judgment. Compare EXTERNALIZERS.

internalizing behavior see EXTERNALIZING–INTERNALIZING.

internal locus of control see LOCUS OF CONTROL.

internal object an image or representation of a person (particularly someone significant to the individual, such as a parent) that is experienced as an internalized "presence" within the mind. In her development of OBJECT RELATIONS THEORY, Melanie Klein saw the psyche as being made up of internal objects whose relations to each other and to the individual determine his or her personality and symptoms. See also PART-OBJECT.

internal rhythm see BIOLOGICAL RHYTHM.

internal saboteur see ANTILIBIDINAL EGO.

internal senses the interoceptive and proprioceptive systems within the body. See INTEROCEPTION; PROPRIOCEPTION.

internal-state ratings one of several methods of evaluating a person's reactions to a work of art. Internal-state ratings are based on the person's mood while exposed to a pattern. Other types of rating scales include descriptive ratings and EVALUATIVE RATINGS. See STYLISTIC RATINGS.

internal validity the degree to which a study or experiment is free from flaws in its internal structure and its results can therefore be taken to represent the true nature of the phenomenon.

internal working model of attachment a cognitive construction or set of assumptions about the workings of relationships, such as expectations of support or affection. The earliest relationships may form the template for this internal model, which may be positive or negative. See also ATTACHMENT THEORY. [originally proposed by John BOWLBY]

International Association of Applied Psychology (IAAP) the oldest international association of professional psychologists, founded in 1920 to promote the science and practice of applied psychology and to facilitate interaction and communication among those who work in applied psychology around the world.

International Classification of Diseases (ICD) a system of categories of disease conditions compiled by the World Health Organization (WHO) in conjunction with 10 WHO collaborating centers worldwide. Based on a formal classification system developed in 1893 that was known as the *Bertillon Classification or International List of Causes of Death,* the ICD is now in its 10th revision. The **ICD-10**, published in 1992 as the *International Statistical Classification of Diseases and Related Health Problems*, uses a four-character alphanumeric coding system to classify diseases and disorders and their subtypes. Such standardization permits international statistical analyses and comparisons of mortality data, although the ICD is often used in epidemiological studies and by systems of payment for health care. See also DSM-IV-TR.

International Council of Psychologists a professional organization founded in 1941 to advance psychology and its applications by facilitating communication and strengthening bonds between psychologists worldwide. In 1981, ICP was recognized as a nongovernmental organization in consultative status with the United Nations Economic and Social Council.

International Military Testing Association an organization that, since 1959, has held conferences to discuss areas of common interest in the field of job proficiency evaluation. Originally called the **Military Testing Association**, the organization changed its name in 1993 to reflect the increasing involvement of countries around the world. Participants include civilian as well as uniformed researchers and practitioners. Research areas include aptitude and job proficiency testing, training, occupational analysis, leadership, organizational behavior, human factors, personnel trends, and manpower analysis.

International Phonetic Alphabet (IPA) a system of written symbols devised by the International Phonetic Association to enable the phonetic transcription of any spoken language. It is based on the Roman alphabet, with various additional symbols.

International Pilot Study of Schizophrenia (IPSS) a 1973 diagnostic study sponsored by the World Health Organization, involving psychiatrists in 9 countries and a total of 1,119 patients assigned to a schizophrenic or nonschizophrenic category. The most discriminating of 13 symptoms were lack of insight, auditory hallucinations, verbal hallucinations, ideas of reference, and delusions of reference. The project used the PRESENT STATE EXAMINATION. See also FIRST-RANK SYMPTOMS.

International Society for Sport Psychology (ISSP) an international society of individuals and national organizations interested in SPORT AND EXERCISE PSYCHOLOGY.

International Standard Manual Alphabet a means of communication for those with impaired hearing or vision in which the speaker traces block capital letters with his or her finger on the palm of the listener. See also AMERICAN MANUAL ALPHABET.

International Union of Psychological Science (IUPsyS) an affiliation of professional psychological organizations, founded in 1951 to develop the exchange of ideas and scientific information between psychologists of different countries and, in particular, to organize international congresses and other meetings on subjects of general or special interest in psychology. The union evolved from the International Congress of Psychology, first held in Paris in 1889.

interneuron *n.* any neuron that is neither sensory nor motor but connects other neurons within the central nervous system. Also called **connector**; **connector neuron**; **internuncial neuron**.

interoception *n.* input of information from INTEROCEPTORS within the body (e.g., from the viscera). Compare EXTEROCEPTION.

interoceptive conditioning PAVLOVIAN CONDITIONING that requires direct access to internal organs, through fistulas, balloons inserted into the digestive tract, or implanted electrical devices, to present the conditioned stimulus.

interoceptive stimulus any stimulus arising from inside an organism. Examples include headache, stomach ache, and hunger pangs. Compare EXTEROCEPTIVE STIMULUS; PROPRIOCEPTIVE STIMULUS.

interoceptive system the totality of sensory receptors and nerves that gather information from within the body.

interoceptor *n.* any receptor that responds to stimuli within the body, such as changes in temperature or blood acidity, or the stretching of muscles. **—interoceptive** *adj.*

interocular distance the distance between the pupils of the left and right eyes when the eyes are in normal FIXATION.

interocular transfer the ability of an aftereffect to be produced by stimulation through only one eye but to be experienced by looking only through the other eye. The presence of interocular transfer implies that the afterimage is mediated by a postretinal structure, such as the cerebral cortex, since the two eyes have no direct communication prior to the activation of BINOCULAR CELLS in the striate cortex.

interpersonal *adj.* pertaining to actions, events, and feelings between two or more individuals.

interpersonal accommodation the "give-and-take" process that is involved in developing satisfactory interpersonal relationships.

interpersonal attraction the interest in and liking of one individual by another, or the mutual interest and liking between two or more individuals. Interpersonal attraction may be based on shared experiences, physical appearances, internal motivation (e.g., loneliness), or some combination of these. See also ATTRACTION.

interpersonal competition see COMPETITION.

interpersonal concordance in KOHLBERG'S THEORY OF MORAL DEVELOPMENT, the first of two stages in the CONVENTIONAL LEVEL, in which the idea of motive and underlying intention emerge, and moral behavior is that which wins approval. Also called **good-boy-good-girl stage**; **good-boy-nice-girl orientation**. Compare LAW-AND-ORDER ORIENTATION.

interpersonal conflict disagreement or discord between people with respect to goals, values, or attitudes. See also EXTRAPSYCHIC CONFLICT.

interpersonal distance the distance that individuals choose to maintain between themselves and others (see BUBBLE CONCEPT OF PERSONAL SPACE). Studies show that most individuals maintain a smaller interpersonal distance for friends than for strangers. See also PROXEMICS.

interpersonal group psychotherapy a group approach to the treatment of psychological, behavioral, and emotional problems that emphasizes the curative influence of interpersonal learning, including the analysis of group events, experiences, and relationships, rather than the review of issues that are external to the group. Also called **interactive group psychotherapy**.

interpersonal influence direct SOCIAL PRESSURE exerted on a person or group by another person or group in the form of demands or threats on the one hand or promises of rewards or SOCIAL APPROVAL on the other. Compare INFORMATIONAL INFLUENCE; NORMATIVE INFLUENCE.

interpersonal intelligence in the MULTIPLE-INTELLIGENCES THEORY, the intelligence involved in understanding and relating to other people. Interpersonal intelligence is alleged to be relatively independent of other intelligences posited by the theory.

interpersonal learning group any group formed to help individuals extend their self-understanding and improve their relationships with others, such as an experiential group, T-GROUP, or GROWTH GROUP. See also STRUCTURED LEARNING GROUP.

interpersonal perception see SOCIAL PERCEPTION.

interpersonal process recall (**IPR**) a method used for understanding the processes of psychotherapy and for the training of counselors and therapists. It involves videotaping or audiotaping counseling or psychotherapy sessions, which are later reexperienced and analyzed by the counselor or therapist in the presence of a supervisor, who questions and discusses the thoughts and feelings of the counselor or therapist and client. [developed by U.S. counseling psychologist Norman I. Kagan (1931–1994)]

interpersonal psychotherapy (**IPT**) a form of psychotherapy, originally based on the INTERPERSONAL THEORY of U.S. psychiatrist Harry Stack Sullivan (1892–1949), positing that relations with others constitute the primary force motivating human behavior. A central feature of IPT is the clarification of the client's interpersonal interactions with significant others, including the therapist. The therapist helps the client explore current and past experiences in detail, relating not only to interpersonal reaction but also to environmental influences generally on personal adaptive and maladaptive thinking and behavior.

interpersonal reconstructive psychotherapy an INTEGRATIVE PSYCHOTHERAPY and method of symptom analysis that blends psychodynamic and cognitive behavior techniques and focuses on presenting problems and symptoms as they relate to long-term interpersonal difficulties. Interventions are active and focused on attachment-based factors that maintain current problems. [approach developed by U.S. clinical psychologist Lorna Smith Benjamin]

interpersonal relations 1. the connections and interactions, especially ones that are socially and emotionally significant, between two or more people. **2.** the pattern or patterns observable in an individual's dealings with other people.

interpersonal skill an aptitude enabling a person to carry on effective relationships with others, such as an ability to cooperate, to communicate thought and feeling, to assume appropriate social responsibilities, or to exhibit adequate flexibility.

interpersonal theory in psychoanalysis, the theory of personality developed by U.S. psychoanalyst Harry Stack Sullivan (1892–1949), which is based on the belief that people's interactions with other people, especially SIGNIFICANT OTHERS, determine their sense of security, sense of self, and the dynamisms that motivate their behavior. For Sullivan, personality is the product of a long series of stages in which the individual gradually develops "good feeling" toward others and a sense of a GOOD ME toward himself or herself. The individual also learns how to ward off anxiety and correct distorted perceptions of other people; learns to verify his or her ideas through CONSENSUAL VALIDATION; and above all seeks to achieve effective interpersonal relationships on a mature level.

interpersonal trust the confidence a person or group of people has in the reliability of another person or group, specifically the degree to which people feel they can depend on others to do what they say they will do. The key factor is not the intrinsic honesty of the other people but their predictability.

interpersonal zone see DISTANCE ZONE.

interphase *n.* the interval between cell divisions, when the nucleus has finished dividing, particularly in rapidly dividing tissues or during embryonic growth.

interpolated task an activity that is presented between two experimental tasks to fill time or to disguise the connection between the two critical tasks. For instance, an interpolated arithmetic task might be given between the study phase and test phase of a memory experiment. See also INTERFERENCE.

interposition *n.* a monocular DEPTH CUE occurring when two objects are in the same line of vision and the closer object, which is fully in view, partly conceals the farther object. Also called **relative position**.

interpret *vb.* **1.** to translate orally from one language into another. A distinction is sometimes made between interpreting, in which it is sufficient to convey the sense of the original, and TRANSLATION, in which some attempt to replicate form and style will also usually be made. **2.** in psychotherapy, to provide an interpretation. **—interpreter** *n.*

interpretation *n.* **1.** in psychotherapy, explanation by the therapist in terms that are meaningful to the client of the client's issues, behaviors, or feelings. Interpretation typically is made along the lines of the particular conceptual framework or dynamic model of the form of therapy. In psychoanalysis, for example, the analyst uses the constructs of psychoanalytic theory to interpret the patient's early experiences, dreams, character defenses, and resistance. Although interpretation exists to some extent in almost any form of therapy, it is a critical procedural step in psychoanalysis and in other forms of PSYCHO-

DYNAMIC PSYCHOTHERAPY. **2.** an oral translation (*see* interpret).

interpretive response a reply by a therapist intended to summarize or illuminate the essential meaning of or motive underlying a statement made by a client during therapy. See also INTERPRETATION.

interpretive therapy any form of active, directive psychotherapy in which the therapist elicits the client's conflicts, repressions, dreams, and resistances, which are then interpreted or explained to the client in the light of his or her experiences. See also INTERPRETATION.

interquartile range an index of the dispersion within a batch of scores: the difference between the 75th and 25th percentile scores within a distribution.

interrater agreement the degree to which a group of raters (people, instruments, tests) rate an attribute in the same way (e.g., assign the same score or category to the same case). Although often used synonymously with INTERRATER RELIABILITY, interrater agreement refers only to the degree to which raters agree on (typically) categorical assignments.

interrater reliability the consistency with which different examiners produce similar ratings in judging the same abilities or characteristics in the same target person or object. Although often used synonymously with INTERRATER AGREEMENT, this is a more specific term linked conceptually with CLASSICAL TEST THEORY and possessing an underlying TRUE SCORE sense. It usually refers to continuous measurement assignments. Also called **interjudge reliability**.

interresponse time (**IRT**) the time between successive responses, especially between successive responses of the same type.

interrogative *n.* in linguistics, the form of a sentence used to pose a question rather than to make a statement, issue a command, and so on, or the MOOD of the verb used in such constructions. In English there are two main types of interrogative: yes/no questions (e.g., *Are you going?*) and *wh-* questions using *what, when, where, who, how,* and so on (e.g., *Where are you going?*). Both types require the use of an AUXILIARY VERB (usually *be, have,* or *do*). The structural relationships between the DECLARATIVE and interrogative forms of a sentence are of major interest in GENERATIVE GRAMMAR and PSYCHOLINGUISTICS (see AUXILIARY INVERSION). Compare IMPERATIVE; INDICATIVE; SUBJUNCTIVE.

interrogative suggestibility the degree to which an individual is susceptible to suggestive questioning. The level of suggestibility may be assessed in two ways: (a) yield, or the degree to which an individual will respond affirmatively to leading questions; and (b) shift, or the tendency to alter previous responses when receiving negative feedback.

interrogatories *pl. n.* formal written questions prepared for an official pretrial questioning of an individual who possesses information relevant to a case or used in the judicial examination of an individual or party.

interrole conflict the form of ROLE CONFLICT that occurs when individuals have more than one role within a group and the expectations and behaviors associated with one role are not consistent with the expectations and behaviors associated with another. Compare INTRAROLE CONFLICT. See GROUP ROLES.

interrupted-time-series design an experimental design in which the effects of an intervention are evaluated by comparing outcome measures obtained at several time intervals before, and several time intervals after, the intervention was introduced.

interscorer reliability INTERNAL CONSISTENCY reliability among two or more individuals scoring responses of examinees. See also INTERITEM RELIABILITY.

intersegmental arc reflex a REFLEX ARC formed by fibers of sensory neurons or interneurons that travel from one spinal segment to another to communicate with motor neurons.

intersegmental tract see GROUND BUNDLE.

intersensory perception 1. the perception of information presented through separate modalities as an integrated experience. **2.** the transmission of information from one sensory source into the ASSOCIATION CORTEX, where it can be integrated with information from another sensory source. Intersensory perception is required in tasks that coordinate two or more sensorimotor activities, such as playing a musical instrument according to the pattern of notes on a page of sheet music. Also called **cross-modal perception**. See PERCEPTUAL SYNTHESIS; SENSORY INTERACTION.

intersexuality *n.* the condition of possessing the sexual characteristics of both sexes, particularly secondary characteristics and in some cases partial development of the internal or external sex organs. An individual who exhibits such characteristics is called an **intersex**. Also called **intersexualism**. See also HERMAPHRODITE; PSEUDOHERMAPHRODITISM. **—intersexual** *adj.*

interspecies interaction all forms of interaction between species. Long-term interactions include PARASITISM, in which one species lives on or in another at a cost to the host; MUTUALISM, in which both species benefit from the interaction; and COMMENSALISM, in which the species coexist with neither cost nor benefit. Shorter term interspecies interactions include predator–prey relationships and the mixed FLOCKING of birds to feed and give ALARM CALLS together.

interstimulus interval (**ISI**) the time between stimulus presentations, usually timed from the end of one stimulus presentation to the beginning of the next.

interstitial cell any of the cells that fill the spaces between other tissues and structures. The interstitial cells of the TESTIS surround the seminiferous tubules and secrete testosterone when stimulated by LUTEINIZING HORMONE.

interstitial cell-stimulating hormone (**ICSH**) see LUTEINIZING HORMONE.

interstripes *pl. n.* regions of PRESTRIATE CORTEX that have low levels of cytochrome oxidase activity. They are connected to the INTERBLOBS in the striate cortex and have similar response properties.

intersubjectivity *n.* **1.** empathic communication: the ability to share conscious experiences, for example, by shared gaze between infants and their caretakers. **2.** a philosophical view that all public, objective events are in actuality shared subjective experiences. See also FIRST-PERSON PERSPECTIVE; SECOND-PERSON PERSPECTIVE; THIRD-PERSON PERSPECTIVE. **—intersubjective** *adj.*

interthalamic adhesion a mass of GRAY MATTER that extends in most individuals across the midline of the THIRD VENTRICLE of the brain from the medial surfaces of the two halves of the thalamus. Although sometimes called the middle commissure, the interthalamic adhesion has no particular commissural (i.e., connecting) function. Also called **massa intermedia**.

intertrial interval (**ITI**) the time between successive presentations of the stimulus in a series of experimental trials.

interval *n.* in statistics, a range of scores or values. See CLASS INTERVAL; CONFIDENCE INTERVAL.

interval estimate an estimated range of likely values for a given population parameter. Compare POINT ESTIMATE.

interval of uncertainty the interval between the upper threshold (the stimulus just noticeably greater than the standard) and the lower threshold (the stimulus just noticeably less than the standard) when finding a DIFFERENCE THRESHOLD.

interval reinforcement the REINFORCEMENT of the first response to a stimulus after a predetermined interval has lapsed. Reinforcement may be given at uniform or variable intervals; the number of responses during the interval is irrelevant. Also called **interval-reinforcement schedule**. See also FIXED-INTERVAL SCHEDULE; RANDOM-INTERVAL SCHEDULE; VARIABLE-INTERVAL REINFORCEMENT SCHEDULE. Compare RATIO REINFORCEMENT.

interval scale a scale marked in equal intervals so that the difference between any two consecutive values on the scale is equivalent regardless of the two values selected, that is, the ratio of any two intervals is independent of the unit of measurement and of the zero point. Both the zero point and the units of measurement are arbitrary. Also called **equal-interval scale**. Compare NOMINAL SCALE; ORDINAL SCALE; RATIO SCALE.

interval timer an instrument that measures the time between two events.

intervening variable 1. a hypothetical entity that is influenced by an INDEPENDENT VARIABLE and that in turn influences a DEPENDENT VARIABLE. **2.** more specifically, an unseen process or event, inferred to occur within the organism between a stimulus event and the time of response, that affects the relationship between the stimulus and response. An example is INCENTIVE MOTIVATION in HULL'S MATHEMATICO-DEDUCTIVE THEORY OF LEARNING. Also called **mediating variable**; **mediator variable**.

intervention *n.* **1.** action on the part of a therapist to deal with the issues and problems of a client. The selection of the intervention is guided by the nature of the problem, the orientation of the therapist, the setting, and the willingness and ability of the client to proceed with the treatment. Also called **psychological intervention**. **2.** a technique in addictions counseling in which significant individuals in a client's life meet with him or her, in the presence of a trained counselor, to express their observations and feelings about the client's addiction and related problems. The session, typically a surprise to the client, may last several hours, after which the client has a choice of seeking a recommended treatment immediately (e.g., as an inpatient) or ignoring the intervention. If the client chooses not to seek treatment, participants state the interpersonal consequences; for example, a drug-abusing adult living at home may be requested to move out, or the client's employment may be terminated. **3.** a similar confrontation between an individual and family and friends, but outside of the formal structure of counseling or therapy, usually over similar issues and with the goal of urging the confronted individual to seek help with an attitudinal or behavioral problem.

interventionist *n.* a physician, behavioral scientist, therapist, or other professional who modifies the conditions or symptoms of a patient.

intervention program for children any of a number of types of program with the goal of providing intellectual, emotional, nutritional, or medical benefits to children believed to be at risk for inadequate development. Target children are usually preschoolers and are often from homes judged to be economically or culturally disadvantaged.

intervention research activities designed to measure how much better a situation is after a systematic modification has been imposed or to measure the effects of one type of intervention program as compared to those of another program.

interventricular foramen an opening that connects the THIRD VENTRICLE of the brain with either LATERAL VENTRICLE. It permits the flow of cerebrospinal fluid through the ventricles. Also called **foramen of Monro**.

interview *n.* a directed conversation in which a researcher, therapist, clinician, employer, or the like (the **interviewer**) intends to elicit specific information from an individual (the **interviewee**) for purposes of research, diagnosis, treatment, or employment. Interviews may be either highly structured, including set questions, or unstructured, varying with material introduced by the interviewee. See also CLINICAL INTERVIEW; EMPLOYMENT INTERVIEW.

interviewer effects the influence of an interviewer's attributes and behaviors on a respondent's answers. The interviewer's appearance, demeanor, training, age, sex, and ethnicity may all produce effects of this kind. The term **interviewer bias** refers more specifically to an interviewer's expectations, beliefs, and prejudices as they influence the interview process and the interpretation of the data it provides.

interviewer stereotype in employment, an interviewer's concept of the "ideal" job candidate, which becomes the standard against which actual job applicants are compared. Such a stereotype may obscure the genuine merits of applicants who deviate from it in some way. See also PROFILE MATCHING SYSTEM.

interviewer training instructional methods employed in training individuals to be effective interviewers. These may include group discussions, role play, and the use of videotapes of real or simulated interviews, in addition to instruction in the basic principles of interviewing.

interview group psychotherapy a type of GROUP PSYCHOTHERAPY for adolescents and adults. A balanced therapeutic group is selected on the basis of common problems and personal characteristics, and participants are encouraged to reveal their attitudes, symptoms, and feelings. See also ANALYTIC GROUP PSYCHOTHERAPY. [developed by 20th-century Russian-born U.S. psychotherapist Samuel Richard Slavson]

interview schedule a script containing the questions an interviewer will ask.

intestinal lipodystrophy see LIPODYSTROPHY.

in the closet see CLOSET HOMOSEXUAL.

intimacy *n.* an interpersonal state of extreme emotional closeness such that each party's PERSONAL SPACE can be entered by any of the other parties without causing discomfort to that person. Intimacy characterizes close, familiar, and usually affectionate or loving personal relationships and requires the parties to have a detailed knowledge or deep understanding of each other. **—intimate** *adj.*

intimacy problem difficulty in forming close relationships and becoming intimate with others, whether physically or psychologically, which might involve difficulties with sexual contact, self-disclosure, trust, or commitment to a lasting relationship. See also FEAR OF COMMITMENT.

intimacy versus isolation the sixth of ERIKSON'S EIGHT STAGES OF DEVELOPMENT, which extends from late adolescence through courtship and early family life to early middle age. During this period, individuals must learn to share and care without losing themselves; if they fail, they will feel alone and isolated. The development of a cohesive identity in the previous stage provides the opportunity to achieve true intimacy, but the development of DIFFUSION makes it harder for individuals to achieve a positive outcome at this stage.

intimate zone in social psychology, the small DISTANCE ZONE adopted by those in very close relationships, such as that of mother and infant. Compare PERSONAL DISTANCE ZONE; PUBLIC DISTANCE ZONE; SOCIAL ZONE. See also PROXEMICS.

intonation *n.* see TONE.

intoxicant *n.* a substance capable of producing transient alterations in mental function. The nature of the intoxication depends on the psychoactive properties of the intoxicant. In general, mild intoxication is marked by minor perceptual changes or a sense of euphoria or well-being; more pronounced intoxication involves such changes as behavioral disinhibition, perceptual distortions, hallucinations, or delirium; and severe intoxication is marked by loss of motor control and cognitive and autonomic function, possibly progressing to coma or death.

intoxication *n.* see INTOXICANT; SUBSTANCE INTOXICATION.

intoxication defense a defense that a crime was committed by a person who was intoxicated, which has been used to challenge a charge of CRIMINAL RESPONSIBILITY. If the intoxicant was taken involuntarily, it can negate criminal responsibility altogether. If the intoxicant was taken voluntarily, it may serve as a MITIGATING FACTOR in reducing the penalty imposed or it may be used to argue against PREMEDITATION in a first-degree murder charge. See DIMINISHED CAPACITY.

intraattitudinal consistency the extent to which evaluative responses underlying a single attitude are consistent with one another. Uniformly positive responses or uniformly negative responses constitute high consistency. The existence of both positive and negative responses reflects low consistency. See also AMBIVALENCE OF AN ATTITUDE.

intracarotid amobarbital procedure see WADA TEST.

intracarotid sodium Amytal test (**ISA**) see WADA TEST.

intracellular fluid the fluid within cells. Also called **cellular fluid**.

intracellular thirst see OSMOMETRIC THIRST.

intracerebral hemorrhage see CEREBRAL HEMORRHAGE.

intraclass correlation 1. an index of the homogeneity of members (people, items, etc.) within a group. **2.** the average intercorrelation among randomly formed pairs of cases within a group.

intraclass variance see WITHIN-GROUP VARIANCE.

intraconscious personality a phenomenon of DISSOCIATIVE IDENTITY DISORDER in which one personality functioning on a subconscious level is aware of the thoughts and outer world of another personality functioning on a conscious level.

intracranial *adj.* within the skull or CRANIUM.

intracranial hemorrhage bleeding within the skull. Hemorrhages of this type include CEREBRAL HEMORRHAGES and SUBARACHNOID HEMORRHAGES.

intracranial pressure (**ICP**) the pressure within the skull. Excessive intracranial pressure can cause brain damage and impede blood flow within the brain, with a range of effects that may include memory loss, balance problems, dementia, coma, and death. Causes of raised ICP include hydrocephalus, hemorrhage, hematomas, brain tumors, and head injuries.

intracranial self-stimulation stimulation of a brain region by implanted electrodes controlled by the individual being stimulated. In animal experiments, this is achieved by the animal performing an OPERANT RESPONSE, such as lever pressing. When the electrodes are placed in certain areas of the brain, animals will press the lever quite frequently, indicating that stimulation of these brain areas is rewarding. Also called **brain self-stimulation**. [originated in 1954 by U.S. psychologist James Olds (1922–1976) and Canadian psychologist Peter M. Milner]

intracranial stimulation (**ICS**) stimulation of the brain cells of a human or nonhuman animal by direct application of an electric current or a chemical stimulus (e.g., a hormone or neurotransmitter). See also INTRACRANIAL SELF-STIMULATION.

intrafamily dynamics the changes in the relationships among the members of a family within a period of time, together with the influences operating in their interactions with each other that bring about these changes.

intrafusal fiber a small muscle fiber, 2 to 12 of which are located within each MUSCLE SPINDLE. Intrafusal fibers are sensitive to stretching and muscle tension and are connected to the STRETCH RECEPTORS. Compare EXTRAFUSAL FIBER.

intrafusal motor neuron see GAMMA MOTOR NEURON.

intragroup competition see COMPETITION.

intragroup conflict disagreement or confrontation between two or more members of a single group. Compare INTERGROUP CONFLICT.

intragroup territorial behavior see GROUP TERRITORIAL BEHAVIOR.

intraindividual differences the variations between two or more traits, behaviors, or characteristics of a single person. For example, certain aptitude tests measure a testee's strengths in mathematical, verbal, and analytic abilities; differences among the three standardized scores represent intraindividual differences. Compare INTERINDIVIDUAL DIFFERENCES.

intralaminar nucleus any of certain NUCLEI located in the internal medullary lamina, a nearly vertical layer of white matter in the thalamus. The largest of these nuclei is the CENTER MEDIAN.

intralaminar system a diffuse system of thalamic nerve cells associated with sleep and wakefulness and believed to be a part of the RETICULAR FORMATION.

intramaze cue a CUE that is within a maze, such as floor texture, wall color, or a scent.

intramuscular injection (**im injection**) the injection of a substance into a muscle by means of a hypodermic syringe, usually into the muscle of the upper arm, thigh, or buttock. The choice of muscle area is important in order to avoid damage to a nerve or blood vessel. See ADMINISTRATION.

intransitivity *n.* the quality of a relationship among elements such that relationships do not transfer across elements (i.e., that relationships do not exhibit TRANSITIVITY). For example, a transitive relationship would be: Given that a > b, and b > c, it must be the case that a > c. An intransitive relationship would be one in which such a conclusion did not necessarily follow. Such relationships appear to be illogical and inconsistent but are often found in matters of personal preference or other subjective judgments. For example, a person might prefer the color blue over red, and red over green, but when given a choice prefer green over blue. **—intransitive** *adj.*

intraocular pressure (**IOP**) the pressure inside the eye. Intraocular pressure is measured by TONOMETRY; increased pressure may indicate GLAUCOMA, a disease in which the pressure inside the eye increases to the point at which it causes impaired vision and eventually blindness if untreated. Intraocular pressure may be raised by the use of drugs with anticholinergic effects (e.g., tricyclic antidepressants, antihistamines, or sympathomimetics) in patients with acute GLAUCOMA. Rarely, administration of such drugs may trigger an acute rise in intraocular pressure requiring immediate medical intervention to preserve sight.

intrapersonal *adj.* describing factors operating or constructs occurring within the person, such as attitudes, decisions, self-concept, self-esteem, or self-regulation.

intrapersonal conflict see INTRAPSYCHIC CONFLICT.

intrapersonal intelligence in the MULTIPLE-INTELLIGENCES THEORY, the intelligence involved in self-understanding and in reflecting upon oneself, one's skills, one's motives, etc. Intrapersonal intelligence is alleged to be relatively independent of other intelligences posited by the theory.

intrapsychic *adj.* pertaining to impulses, ideas, conflicts, or other psychological phenomena that arise or occur within the psyche or mind.

intrapsychic ataxia lack of coordination of feelings, thoughts, and volition (e.g., laughing when depressed). The concept was introduced in 1904 by Austrian psychiatrist Erwin Stransky (1878–1962) in association with schizophrenia, but it has subsequently been seen in other disorders as well. Also called **mental ataxia**. See also INAPPROPRIATE AFFECT.

intrapsychic conflict in psychoanalytic theory, the clash of opposing forces within the psyche, such as conflicting drives, wishes, or agencies. Also called **inner conflict**; **internal conflict**; **intrapersonal conflict; psychic conflict**.

intrarole conflict the form of ROLE CONFLICT caused by incompatibility among the behaviors and expectations associated with a single role. These inconsistencies may result from the inherent complexity of the role itself, the ambiguity of the role, or the group's lack of consensus in defining the role and its demands. Compare INTERROLE CONFLICT. See GROUP ROLES.

intrasubject replication design see SINGLE-CASE EXPERIMENTAL DESIGN.

intrauterine device (**IUD**) a device made of plastic or other material (e.g., copper or rubber) that is inserted into the cervix as a contraceptive device. Usually having a **coil** design or the shape of a T, Y, or other configuration, it interferes with implantation of an embryo in the wall of the uterus.

intravenous drug usage a form of drug use in which the drug is injected directly into a vein with a needle and syringe. The opioids, especially HEROIN, are often injected intravenously to enhance their effects. Poor hygiene results in dirty needles or syringes, use of which increases the risk of acquiring serious blood-borne disorders, including HEPATITIS and HIV infection.

intravenous injection (**iv injection**) the injection of a substance into a vein by means of a hypodermic syringe. This technique is used when rapid absorption of a drug is needed, when the substance would be irritating to the skin or to muscle tissue, or when it cannot be administered through the digestive tract. It is a dangerous route of administration because of its rapid onset of pharmacological action, which may cause a potentially fatal reaction. Slow intravenous injection, called **intravenous (iv) infusion**, is used for blood transfusions, parenteral administration of nutrients (i.e., directly into the bloodstream, bypassing the digestive tract), or continuous administration of drugs. See also ADMINISTRATION.

intraverbal *n.* a verbal response occasioned by a preceding verbal stimulus. It illustrates CHAINING in the domain of VERBAL BEHAVIOR.

intrinsic activity 1. the magnitude of a response to a drug regardless of dosage. **2.** a measure of the efficacy of a drug-receptor complex in producing a pharmacological effect. Also called **intrinsic efficacy**. **3.** the inborn readiness of babies to be inquisitive and to make contact with their environment. According to Jean PIAGET's theory of cognitive development, cognitive structures, by their very nature, seek to be active, predisposing the child to learn from experience with the environment.

intrinsic behavior 1. a type of behavior expressed through a specific organ (e.g., smiling, the knee-jerk reflex). **2.** behavior that is inherently rewarding. For example, reading a book is pleasurable for some individuals and so is intrinsically rewarding.

intrinsic eye muscles see EYE MUSCLES.

intrinsic interest see EXTRINSIC INTEREST.

intrinsic motivation an incentive to engage in a specific activity that derives from the activity itself (e.g., a genuine interest in a subject studied), rather than because of any external benefits that might be obtained (e.g., course credits). Compare EXTRINSIC MOTIVATION.

intrinsic reinforcer a REINFORCER that is naturally related to the response that produces it. For example, blowing on a harmonica naturally produces sounds. If the sounds serve to reinforce blowing on the harmonica, then the sounds are intrinsic reinforcers. Compare EXTRINSIC REINFORCER.

intrinsic religion a religious orientation in which religiosity is an end itself, rather than a means to other ends. Compare EXTRINSIC RELIGION. [introduced by Gordon W. ALLPORT]

intrinsic reward a positively valued outcome that is implicit in an activity, such as the pleasure or satisfaction gained from developing a special skill. Intrinsic rewards originate directly from the task performance and do not originate from other people. Compare EXTRINSIC REWARD.

introception *n.* a personality trait reflecting the extent to which a person is attentive to understanding the needs, motives, and experiences of him- or herself and others. **—introceptive** *adj.*

introitus *n.* an opening or entrance to a hollow organ or tube. For example, the anus is the introitus of the rectum, and the **introitus vaginae** is the entrance of the vagina.

introjection *n.* **1.** a process in which an individual unconsciously incorporates aspects of reality external to himself or herself into the self, particularly the attitudes, values, and qualities of another person or a part of another person's personality. Introjection may occur, for example, in the mourning process for a loved one. **2.** in psychoanalytic theory, the process of internalizing the qualities of an external OBJECT into the psyche in the form of an internal object or mental REPRESENTATION, which then has an influence on behavior. This process is posited to be a normal part of development, as when introjection of parental values and attitudes forms the SUPEREGO, but may also be used as a DEFENSE MECHANISM in situations that arouse anxiety. Compare IDENTIFICATION; INCORPORATION. **—introject** *vb.* **—introjective** *adj.*

introjective depression depression in which individuals have punitive and angry feelings toward themselves. Compare ANACLITIC DEPRESSION.

introjective personality according to some psychoanalytic theories, a line of personality development that is focused on achievement and evaluation and—if the personality fails to develop properly—may result in feelings of worthlessness, failure, and psychopathological self-criticism. Compare ANACLITIC PERSONALITY.

intromission *n.* the act of sending or putting in something, especially the insertion of the penis into the vagina. See also PENETRATION. **—intromissive** *adj.*

intron *n.* a sequence of DNA within a gene that does not encode any part of the gene's ultimate product. Such sequences are transcribed into MESSENGER RNA (mRNA) but then removed during formation of the mature mRNA, which instructs the cell to synthesize a protein. Compare EXON.

intropunitive *adj.* turning anger, blame, or hostility internally, against the self. See SELF-ACCUSATION. Compare EXTRAPUNITIVE. **—intropunitiveness** *n.*

introspection *n.* the process of attempting to access directly one's own internal psychological processes, judgments, perceptions, or states. **—introspective** *adj.*

introspectionism *n.* the doctrine that the basic method of psychological investigation is or should be INTROSPECTION. Historically, such an approach is associated with the school of psychological STRUCTURALISM. **—introspectionist** *adj.*

introspective method an approach to research in which participants describe their conscious experiences.

introversion *n.* orientation toward the internal private world of one's self and one's inner thoughts and feelings, rather than toward the outer world of people and things. Introversion is a broad personality trait and, like EXTRAVERSION, exists on a continuum of attitudes and behaviors. Introverts are relatively more withdrawn, retiring, reserved, quiet, and deliberate; they may tend to mute or guard expression of positive affect, adopt more skeptical views or positions, and prefer to work independently. See also INTROVERSION–EXTRAVERSION. [concept originated by Carl JUNG for the study of personality types] **—introversive** *adj.* **—introvert** *n.* **—introverted** *adj.*

introversion–extraversion the range, or continuum, of self-orientation from INTROVERSION, characterized by inward and self-directed concerns and behaviors, to EXTRAVERSION, characterized by outward and social-directed concerns and behaviors. See also EYSENCK'S TYPOLOGY; FIVE-FACTOR PERSONALITY MODEL. [concept originated by Carl JUNG for the study of personality types]

intrusion error in a memory test, the recall of an item that was not among the material presented for remembering. Intrusion errors can be informative about the nature of forgetting, for instance, if the intrusion is a synonym, rhyme, or associate of a correct item.

intrusive thoughts mental events that interrupt the flow of ongoing and task-related thoughts in spite of persistent efforts to avoid them. They are a common aspect of such disorders as posttraumatic stress and obsessive-compulsive disorder. Also called **TUITs** (task-unrelated images and thoughts).

intuition *n.* immediate insight or perception as contrasted with conscious reasoning or reflection. Intuitions have been characterized alternatively as quasi-mystical experiences or as the products of instinct, feeling, minimal sense impressions, or unconscious forces. **—intuit** *vb.* **—intuitive** *adj.*

intuitionism *n.* **1.** the belief that knowledge is obtained primarily by means of INTUITION. **2.** the tendency of people to prefer to think, reason, and remember by processing inexact memory representations rather than working logically from exact representations. See FUZZY TRACE THEORY. [proposed by U.S. psychologists Charles Brainerd (1944–) and Valerie Reyna (1955–)]

intuitive judgment a decision reached on the basis of subjective feelings that cannot easily be articulated and may not be fully conscious. See INTUITION.

intuitive knowledge knowledge that appears to be based on subjective judgment or gut feeling rather than on specific learning. Intuitive knowledge is probably based on nonconsciously recalled information, such as IMPLICIT MEMORY or PROCEDURAL MEMORY, both of which are forms of knowing that are not necessarily accompanied by verbal awareness of knowing.

intuitive sociogram see SOCIOGRAM.

intuitive stage in Jean PIAGET'S theory of cognitive development, the period during the PREOPERATIONAL STAGE, from about 4 to 7 years, in which children are able to think in terms of classes and to deal with number concepts, although their thinking is dominated by perception.

intuitive type in Carl JUNG'S ANALYTIC PSYCHOLOGY, a FUNCTIONAL TYPE characterized by an ability to adapt "by means of unconscious indications" and "a fine and sharpened perception and interpretation of faintly conscious stimuli." The intuitive type is one of Jung's two IRRATIONAL TYPES; the other is the SENSATION TYPE. See also FEELING TYPE; THINKING TYPE.

in utero in the uterus, that is, before birth.

invalid 1. *n.* a person with chronic illness or disability who is confined to the home or another environment. **2.** *adj.* lacking VALIDITY.

invalidate *vb.* to show the lack of VALIDITY of a proposition, hypothesis, or theory.

invalid conversion a type of informal FALLACY in logic or argument that results from overextending the meaning of a premise or, alternatively, taking it in too narrow a sense.

invariance *n.* **1.** the quality of remaining constant although the surrounding conditions may change. **2.** the tendency of an image or afterimage to retain its size despite variations in the distance of the surface upon which it is projected. **3.** in statistics, the property of being unchanged by a TRANSFORMATION. **—invariant** *adj.*

invariant feature a characteristic of an object that does not change when the object is viewed under different circumstances. Because invariant features are unaffected by manipulations of the object or the observer, they are powerful cues for object recognition by humans or machines. For example, when solid objects of different orientation are compared, the volume of the objects is an invariant feature.

invariant sequence in stage theories of development, such as Jean PIAGET's theory, the unchanging order in which the stages of development occur. Children must progress sequentially through these stages, none of which can be skipped.

invasive *adj.* **1.** denoting procedures or tests that require puncture or incision of the skin or insertion of an instrument or foreign material into the body. **2.** able to spread from one tissue to another, or having the capacity to spread, as in the case of an infection or a malignant tumor (see CANCER). Compare NONINVASIVE.

invention of new means through mental combination see MENTAL COMBINATION.

inventory *n.* a list of items, often in question form, used in describing and studying behavior, interests, and attitudes.

inventory test 1. in educational assessment, a type of achievement test that contains questions in the major areas of instruction so that an overview or profile of the individual's achievement may be obtained. **2.** in personality research, a test designed to provide a broad overview of personality patterns in a variety of areas.

inverse agonist an agent (e.g., a drug) that binds to the same receptor site as another agent but produces an opposite effect. For example, if drug X binds to receptor site A and potentiates the release of a neurotransmitter, drug X is an agonist at that receptor site. If drug Y also binds to receptor site A but inhibits the release of the neurotransmitter, drug Y is an inverse agonist at that receptor site.

inverse derivation see BACK-FORMATION.

inverse dynamics see INVERSE KINEMATICS.

inverse factor analysis see Q-TECHNIQUE FACTOR ANALYSIS.

inverse kinematics the transformation necessary to go from movement goals, typically specified in terms of positions or TRAJECTORIES in space, to the means of achieving those goals, described in terms of joint angles. **Inverse dynamics** describes this transformation in terms of the forces exerted by muscles. Because of the DEGREES OF FREEDOM PROBLEM, each of these transformations has many possible solutions for any particular movement.

inverse prediction the prediction of an *X* score from a *Y* score using a REGRESSION EQUATION. Compare REGRESSION OF Y ON X.

inverse relationship a negative relationship in which one variable decreases as the other variable increases, or vice versa.

inverse-square law any law of physics stating that one variable decreases or increases in proportion to the reciprocal of the square of another variable. For example, the intensity of a sound is inversely proportional to the square of the distance from the source.

Inversine *n.* a trade name for MECAMYLAMINE.

inversion *n.* **1.** in Jean PIAGET's theory of cognitive development, see NEGATION. **2.** in vision, a reversed image formed on the retina. **3.** in sexual psychology, an old name for same-sex sexual behavior or orientation or the assumption of the role of the opposite sex.

inversion of affect see REVERSAL OF AFFECT.

inversion relationship a change in the usual roles of members of a family or group, as, for example, when a child replaces a parent as the family breadwinner.

inverted Oedipus complex see NEGATIVE OEDIPUS COMPLEX.

inverted retina the vertebrate retina, with reference to the fact that light must pass through all the cell layers of the retina before it reaches the photosensitive region of the PHOTORECEPTORS, which is at the very back of the eye.

inverted-U hypothesis a proposed correlation between motivation (or AROUSAL) and performance such that performance is poorest when motivation or arousal is at very low or very high states. This function is typically referred to as the YERKES–DODSON LAW. Emotional intensity (motivation) increases from a zero point to an optimal point, increasing the quality of performance; increase in intensity after this optimal point leads to performance deterioration and disorganization, forming an inverted U-shaped curve. The optimal point is reached sooner (i.e., at lower intensities) the less well learned or more complex the performance; increases in emotional intensity supposedly affect finer skills, finer discriminations, complex reasoning tasks, and recently acquired skills more readily than routine activities. However, the correlation is considered weak; at best, the inverted U-function represents an entire family of curves in which the peak of performance takes place at different levels of arousal.

investigatory behavior exploration of a new object or other aspect of the environment. Investigatory behavior can be important in locating new food resources, detecting cryptic predators, extending HOME RANGE, or finding shelter. In laboratory studies, investigatory behavior independent of any external rewards is often observed. See also CURIOSITY.

investment *n.* see CATHEXIS. **—invest** *vb.*

invisible displacement see OBJECT PERMANENCE.

invisible playmate see IMAGINARY COMPANION.

in vitro referring to biological conditions or processes that occur or are made to occur outside the living body, usually in a laboratory dish (Latin, literally: "in glass"). Compare IN VIVO.

in vitro fertilization (**IVF**) a procedure in which an ovum (egg) is removed from a woman's body, fertilized externally with sperm, and then returned to the uterus. It is used to treat the most difficult cases of INFERTILITY, but success rates for the procedure are not high.

in vivo 1. referring to biological conditions or processes that occur or are observed within the living organism. Compare IN VITRO. **2.** denoting a condition or process that approximates a real-life environment, often created for an experiment or research study. [Latin, literally: "in life"]

in vivo desensitization a technique used in BEHAVIOR THERAPY, usually to reduce or eliminate phobias, in which the client is exposed to the stimuli that induce anxiety. The therapist, in discussion with the client, produces a hierarchy of anxiety-invoking events or items relating to the anxiety-producing stimulus or phobia. The client is then exposed to the actual stimuli in the hierarchy, rather than being asked to imagine them. Success depends on the client overcoming anxiety as the events or items are encountered. Compare COVERT DESENSITIZATION. See also SYSTEMATIC DESENSITIZATION. [first developed by U.S. psychologist Mary Cover Jones (1896–1987)]

in vivo exposure therapy BEHAVIOR THERAPY in which the client is exposed to anxiety-provoking situations or stimuli in real-world conditions in order to master anxiety and be able to function adequately in the presence of these situations or stimuli. For example, a client who fears flying could be accompanied by a therapist to the airport to simulate boarding a plane while practicing anxiety-decreasing techniques, such as deep breathing.

See also EXPOSURE THERAPY. Compare IN VIVO DESENSITIZATION.

involuntary attention attention that is captured by a prominent stimulus, for example in the peripheral visual field, rather than deliberately applied or focused by the individual.

involuntary civil commitment COMMITMENT of an individual to a mental facility against his or her wishes. For individuals to be committed in this way, it must be established in court that the individuals pose a threat to themselves or others.

involuntary confession see COERCED CONFESSION.

involuntary errors errors that are made in spite of one knowing that they are mistakes, for example, slips of the tongue and place-losing errors.

involuntary hospitalization the confinement of a person with a serious mental disorder or illness to a mental hospital by medical authorization and legal direction (as in INVOLUNTARY CIVIL COMMITMENT). Individuals so hospitalized may be considered dangerous to themselves or others, may fail to recognize the severity of their illness and the need for treatment, or may be unable to have their daily living and treatment needs otherwise met in the community or survive without medical attention. Compare VOLUNTARY ADMISSION.

involuntary intoxication defense see INTOXICATION DEFENSE.

involuntary movement a movement that occurs without intention or volition, such as a TIC or a MYOCLONIC MOVEMENT, or that is carried out in spite of an effort to suppress it.

involuntary muscle see SMOOTH MUSCLE.

involuntary nervous system a less common name for the AUTONOMIC NERVOUS SYSTEM, that is, the neural circuits and pathways involved in involuntary bodily functions.

involuntary response a response that is not under conscious control, such as the reflex contraction of the pupils in response to bright light.

involuntary treatment the treatment of people diagnosed with a mental illness against their will. See FORCED TREATMENT.

involuntary turnover the number of employees who leave an organization or unit involuntarily during a given period. A distinction is usually made between uncontrollable involuntary turnover, as by death, retirement, or reductions in the workforce, and controllable involuntary turnover, as by work-related accidents or illness or by dismissal for poor performance or disciplinary violations. A high rate of controllable involuntary turnover is almost always a sign of serious organizational problems. Compare VOLUNTARY TURNOVER. See TURNOVER.

involutional *adj.* **1.** describing the decline of the body or any of its parts from an optimal level of functioning as a result of increasing age. **2.** referring to phenomena occurring in the years of menopause. This usage is now largely obsolete. **—involution** *n.*

involutional depression a largely obsolete name for a MAJOR DEPRESSIVE EPISODE occurring during late middle age or menopause.

involved grandparent the type of grandparent who has a warm, loving relationship with his or her grandchildren and takes on some of the day-to-day responsibilities for them, such as after-school care or financial assistance. See also COMPANIONATE GRANDPARENT. Compare REMOTE GRANDPARENT.

involved shoppers shoppers who are more deliberate than others in their CONSUMER BEHAVIOR. They spend more time and effort in acquiring detailed knowledge about products by searching for product information and making product comparisons.

involvement *n.* in attitude psychology, see EGO INVOLVEMENT.

iodopsin *n.* any one of three PHOTOPIGMENTS found in the RETINAL CONES. Each consists of 11-*cis*-retinal combined with one of three different OPSINS, each of which confers a different wavelength sensitivity on the iodopsin. Also called **cone opsin**. See also RHODOPSIN.

ion *n.* an atom or molecule that has acquired an electrical charge by gaining or losing one or more electrons. **—ionic** *adj.*

Ionamin *n.* a trade name for PHENTERMINE.

ion channel a group of proteins forming a channel that spans a cell membrane, allowing the passage of ions between the extracellular environment and the cytoplasm of the cell. Ion channels are selective, allow passage of ions of a particular chemical nature, size, or electrostatic charge, and may be ungated (i.e., always open) or gated, opening and closing in response to chemical, electrical, or mechanical signals (see LIGAND-GATED ION CHANNEL; VOLTAGE-GATED ION CHANNEL). Ion channels are important in the transmission of neural signals between neurons at a SYNAPSE. The opening of **sodium channels** in the membrane of a postsynaptic neuron permits an influx of sodium ions (Na^+) into the neuron, which produces an EXCITATORY POSTSYNAPTIC POTENTIAL. The opening of **potassium channels** or **chloride channels** allows potassium ions (K^+) to leave the postsynaptic neuron or chloride ions (Cl^-) to enter it, either of which produces an INHIBITORY POSTSYNAPTIC POTENTIAL. See also CALCIUM CHANNEL.

ionotropic receptor a RECEPTOR protein that includes an ION CHANNEL that is opened when the receptor is activated. See GLUTAMATE RECEPTOR. Compare METABOTROPIC RECEPTOR.

ion pump 1. a protein molecule that carries out ACTIVE TRANSPORT of ions across a cell membrane. See also SODIUM PUMP. **2.** a type of high-vacuum pump that removes gas and reduces pressure by ionizing atoms or molecules, thus attracting them off onto a metal surface.

IOP abbreviation for INTRAOCULAR PRESSURE.

I/O psychology abbreviation for INDUSTRIAL AND ORGANIZATIONAL PSYCHOLOGY.

IOR abbreviation for INHIBITION OF RETURN.

Iowa Tests of Basic Skills (ITBS) an ACHIEVEMENT BATTERY providing tests for reading, language, mathematics, social studies, science, and sources of information for students in kindergarten through grade 8. It is divided into 10 skill levels (numbered 5 through 14) according to grade, with norms for the beginning, middle, and end of each academic year. The numerical label of each level reflects the approximate age of the children for which it is intended (e.g., level 9 is administered to students in grade 3, who are typically 9 years old). The various subtests of the ITBS are designed to measure the higher level cognitive functions considered basic to succeeding in school, such as interpretation, classification, comparision, and analysis. The ITBS, originally developed at the University of Iowa in 1935 as the **Iowa Every Pupil Test of Basic Skills**, was revised most recently in 2001.

ip abbreviation for *i*ntra*p*eritoneal.

IP abbreviation for INFORMATION PROCESSING.

IPA 1. abbreviation for INDEPENDENT PRACTICE ASSOCIATION. **2.** abbreviation for INTERACTION-PROCESS ANALYSIS. **3.** abbreviation for INTERNATIONAL PHONETIC ALPHABET.

IPL abbreviation for INNER PLEXIFORM LAYER.

IPR abbreviation for INTERPERSONAL PROCESS RECALL.

iproniazid *n.* a MONOAMINE OXIDASE INHIBITOR developed in the 1950s for the treatment of tuberculosis and later found to have therapeutic value in the treatment of mood disorders. Iproniazid was found to elevate the mood of tuberculosis patients, and clinical trials led to its widespread use as an antidepressant. However, it has now been replaced by other less toxic antidepressant drugs.

IPS abbreviation for IDEAL PERFORMANCE STATE.

ipsative *adj.* referring back to the self. In psychology, ipsative analyses of personal characteristics involve assessing multiple psychological attributes and conducting within-person analyses of the degree to which an individual possesses one attribute versus another (rather than between-person analyses of individual differences with respect to an attribute).

ipsative method a type of research procedure in which a person's responses are compared only to other responses of that person rather than to the responses of other people.

ipsative scale a scale in which the points distributed to all of the items in that scale must sum to a specific total. In such a scale, all participants will have the same total score but the distribution of the "points" among the various items within the scale will differ for each individual.

ipsative score a participant's score on a particular item in an IPSATIVE SCALE.

ipsilateral *adj.* on the same side of the body. Compare CONTRALATERAL. **—ipsilaterally** *adv.*

ipsilateral deficit a loss of normal function on the same side of the body as a brain lesion or brain damage. More usually, however, a lesion results in a **contralateral deficit**, that is, loss of a normal function on the opposite side of the body.

ipsilateral eye the eye located on the same side of the body as another structure or object. For example, layer 5 of the left LATERAL GENICULATE NUCLEUS receives input from the RETINAL GANGLION CELL axons that originate in the left (i.e., ipsilateral) eye. Compare CONTRALATERAL EYE.

IPSP abbreviation for INHIBITORY POSTSYNAPTIC POTENTIAL.

IPSS abbreviation for INTERNATIONAL PILOT STUDY OF SCHIZOPHRENIA.

IPT abbreviation for INTERPERSONAL PSYCHOTHERAPY.

IQ intelligence quotient: a standard measure of an individual's intelligence level based on psychological tests. In the early years of intelligence testing, IQ was calculated by dividing the MENTAL AGE by the CHRONOLOGICAL AGE and multiplying by 100 to produce a **ratio IQ**. This concept has now mostly been replaced by the DEVIATION IQ, computed as a function of the discrepancy of an individual score from the mean (or average) score. The mean IQ is customarily 100, with slightly more than two thirds of all scores falling within plus or minus 15 points of the mean (usually one standard deviation). More than 95% of all scores fall between 70 (two standard deviations below the mean) and 130 (two standard deviations above the mean).

Some tests yield more specific IQ scores, such as a VERBAL IQ, which measures VERBAL INTELLIGENCE, and **performance IQ**, which measures NONVERBAL INTELLIGENCE. Discrepancies between the two can be used diagnostically to detect learning disabilities or specific cognitive deficiencies. Additional data is often derived from IQ tests, such as performance speed, freedom from distractibility, verbal comprehension, and PERCEPTUAL ORGANIZATION indices.

There are critics who consider the concept of IQ (and other intelligence scales) to be flawed. They point out that the IQ test is more a measure of previously learned skills and knowledge than of underlying native ability and that many participants are simply not accustomed to sitting still and following orders (conditions that such tests require), although they function well in the real world. Critics also refer to cases of misrepresentation of facts in the history of IQ research. Nevertheless, these problems seem to apply to the interpretation of IQ scores rather than the validity of the scores themselves.

IQ stability see CONSTANCY OF THE IQ.

IRB abbreviation for INSTITUTIONAL REVIEW BOARD.

iridocyclitis *n.* inflammation of the iris and ciliary body of the eye. **Heterochromic iridocyclitis** is a form of the disorder that results in a loss of pigment in the iris.

iridology *n.* a highly controversial method of assessing health by examining the irises of an individual's eyes. Patterns, color variations, and other characteristics of the connective tissue of the iris are thought to be related to specific body parts and indicative of health, disorder, or disease. This method lacks sufficient supporting evidence and is not widely accepted among medical professionals.

iris *n.* a muscular disk that surrounds the pupil of the eye and controls the amount of light entering the eye by contraction or relaxation. The stroma of the iris, which faces the cornea, contains a pigment that gives the eye its coloration; the back of the iris is lined with a dark pigment that restricts light entry to the pupil, regardless of the apparent color of the iris.

iris coloboma a congenital defect of the iris that shows as a cleft or fissure (coloboma) extending outward from the edge of the pupil. A coloboma usually occurs in the lower portion of the iris. The defect may be one of several signs of a chromosomal anomaly.

iritic reflex a less common name for PUPILLARY REFLEX.

irkunii *n.* see MYRIACHIT.

IRM abbreviation for INNATE RELEASING MECHANISM.

ironic mental control the phenomenon whereby the attempt to suppress some mental content from consciousness results in an unexpectedly high level of awareness of that very content. [defined by U.S. psychologist Daniel M. Wegner (1948–)]

ironic monitoring process a component of mental processing that keeps suppressed mental content active and available outside of awareness.

irradiation *n.* **1.** exposure of the body to RADIATION, usually ionizing radiation. See RADIATION THERAPY. **2.** any outward diffusion of energy. **3.** an outmoded concept of I. P. PAVLOV that neural processes tend to spread across the cerebral cortex from one functional region to another. **—irradiate** *vb.*

irradiation effects a factor in the occurrence of ionizing radiation, based on evidence of rates of congenital malformation in geographic areas where natural background radiation is high. Examples of conditions that can be related to irradiation effects include anencephaly, microcephaly, Down syndrome, cerebral atrophy, and mental retardation. Irradiation effects on cells of the testes appear as abnormal cell divisions within 2 hours after exposure to radioactivity.

irradiation theory of learning the theory that each stimulus activates a specific set of cells in the brain, and this activation spreads (irradiates). Two stimuli become associated when their areas of activation overlap. Irradiation was hypothesized to be the neural basis for classical conditioning by Ivan PAVLOV.

irrational *adj.* **1.** lacking in reason or sound judgment: illogical or unreasonable. **2.** lacking in usual mental clarity.

irrational belief an illogical, erroneous, or distorted idea, firmly held despite objective contradictory evidence. See NONRATIONAL; RATIONAL. See also COGNITIVE DISTORTION. [attributed to U.S. psychologist Albert Ellis (1913–)]

irrationality *n.* the state, condition, or quality of lacking rational thought. The term is typically used in relation to cognitive behavior (e.g., thinking, decision making) that is illogical.

irrational type in Carl JUNG'S ANALYTIC PSYCHOLOGY, one of the two major categories of FUNCTIONAL TYPE: It comprises the INTUITIVE TYPE and the SENSATION TYPE. Compare RATIONAL TYPE.

irreflexive affect see AFFECT.

irregular *adj.* in linguistics, denoting a word or a form of a word that does not follow the usual patterns of INFLECTION in a language. For example, *go* has the irregular past tense *went* (not *go-ed*) and *sheep* has the irregular plural *sheep* (not *sheeps*). Compare REGULAR.

irrelevant argument see IGNORATIO ELENCHI.

irrelevant language a language composed of sounds, phrases, or words that are usually understood only by the speaker, as observed in some individuals with schizophrenia or autistic disorder.

irresistible impulse rule formerly, a rule commonly used in U.S. courts of law for determining INSANITY, according to which defendants were judged to be insane and therefore absolved of CRIMINAL RESPONSIBILITY if they were unable to control their conduct, even if they were aware that it was wrong. This rule is no longer used.

irreversible decrement model the view that physical and psychological changes associated with aging are caused by biological deterioration and thus are not amenable to training or intervention.

irritability *n.* **1.** a state of excessive, easily provoked anger, annoyance, or impatience. **2.** an abnormal sensitivity or excessive responsiveness, as of an organ or body part, to a stimulus. **3.** in neurophysiology, see NEURAL IRRITABILITY; SENSITIVITY. **—irritable** *adj.*

irritable bowel syndrome (**IBS**) a common functional disorder of the intestines characterized by abdominal pain or discomfort (e.g., bloating) and changes in bowel habits, with some people experiencing increased constipation, others increased diarrhea, and others alternating between the two. As yet there is no known cause (psychogenic or organic), though stress and emotional factors are currently thought to play a role. Also called **mucous colitis**.

IRT 1. abbreviation for INTERRESPONSE TIME. **2.** abbreviation for ITEM RESPONSE THEORY.

ISA abbreviation for intracarotid sodium Amytal test (see WADA TEST).

ischemia *n.* deficiency of blood in an organ or tissue, due to functional constriction or actual obstruction of a blood vessel. See CEREBRAL ISCHEMIA. **—ischemic** *adj.*

ischemic penumbra an area of moderate tissue damage surrounding a focus of primary damage due to inadequate blood supply (see ISCHEMIA). Tissues in the penumbra may be partly preserved due to collateral (alternative) blood flow from neighboring normal areas.

ischophonia *n.* an obsolescent name for STUTTERING.

Ishihara Test for Color Blindness a COLOR-BLINDNESS TEST using a series of plates (**Ishihara plates**) in which numbers or letters are formed by dots of a given color against a background of dots of varying degrees of brightness and saturation. A modification of the earlier STILLING COLOR VISION TEST, the Ishihara test was devised in 1916 for use by the Japanese army. It first became available commercially in late 1917 and reportedly is now the most widely used color-blindness test. [Shinobu **Ishihara** (1879–1963), Japanese ophthalmologist]

Ishikawa diagram see CAUSE-AND-EFFECT DIAGRAM.

ISI abbreviation for INTERSTIMULUS INTERVAL.

island deafness see TONAL GAP.

island of Reil see INSULA. [Johann **Reil** (1759–1813), German physician]

islands of knowledge the separate, small domains into which specialized knowledge may be organized. Such organization of knowledge is typically found among experts in such fields as engineering and medicine, who shift spontaneously between these islands of knowledge using visual images, metaphors, abstract formalisms, and intuitive rules of thumb.

islets of Langerhans clusters of ENDOCRINE cells within the PANCREAS. The A (or alpha) cells secrete GLUCAGON, the B (or beta) cells secrete INSULIN, and the D (or delta) cells secrete SOMATOSTATIN. Together these hormones play a key role in regulating BLOOD SUGAR and carbohydrate metabolism. [Paul **Langerhans** (1847–1888), German anatomist]

iso- *combining form* equal or alike.

isocarboxazid *n.* an irreversible MONOAMINE OXIDASE INHIBITOR (MAOI) whose use is limited by its unpleasant side effects (sedation, ORTHOSTATIC HYPOTENSION, weight gain, etc.) and potentially dangerous interactions with tyramine-containing foodstuffs (e.g., cheese). U.S. trade name: **Marplan**.

isochrony *n.* an observed regularity in which the components of continuous, complex movements (e.g., drawing, speech, handwriting, typing) are often produced at equal time intervals, even though the tasks being performed do not require this regularity. **—isochronal** *adj.* **—isochronous** *adj.*

isocortex *n.* see NEOCORTEX.

isogloss *n.* a line drawn on a map to indicate the geographical boundary between different linguistic usages, as in the distribution of certain dialect terms.

isohedonic trap the flaw in Daniel Berlyne's theory of aesthetic preference (see AROUSAL POTENTIAL) that stimuli producing equal amounts of arousal should be equally preferred. Given that equal amounts of arousal can be produced by pleasing or displeasing stimuli, this cannot be the case.

isolate 1. *n.* an individual who remains apart from others, either as a result of choosing to minimize his or her contact with others or through rejection and ostracism by other individuals or groups. **2.** *n.* in the psychology of groups, a group member with no, very few, or very superficial social and personal relations with other group members. **3.** *n.* in SOCIOMETRY, any individual who is infrequently or never mentioned when group members report on whom they like in their group. In measures of peer acceptance among children, an isolate (or **neglected child**) is a child who has low social impact and is usually referred to negatively but is not actively disliked by other children. Compare REJECTED CHILD; STAR. **4.** *vb. see* isolation.

isolated brain see CERVEAU ISOLÉ; ENCÉPHALE ISOLÉ.

isolated explosive disorder an IMPULSE-CONTROL DISORDER characterized by a single, discrete episode in which the individual commits a violent, catastrophic act, such as shooting strangers during a sudden fit of rage. The episode is out of all proportion to any precipitating stress, is not due to any other mental disorder or to a general medical condition, and is not substance-induced. Also called **catathymic crisis**. Compare INTERMITTENT EXPLOSIVE DISORDER.

isolate monkey a monkey that is separated from its mother at birth or at a very early age and raised in complete isolation.

isolating language a language in which each MORPHEME is typically a separate word, as in, for example, classical (but not modern) Chinese. Compare AGGLUTINATIVE LANGUAGE; FUSIONAL LANGUAGE.

isolating mechanism in evolution, a mechanism that prevents two populations from interbreeding so that the populations diverge enough to allow separate species to evolve. Isolating mechanisms are also important in preventing interbreeding between overlapping species. Geographic separation, behavioral differences, differences in physical features, and different seasons for reproduction all serve as isolating mechanisms.

isolation *n.* **1.** the condition of being separated from other individuals. See LONELINESS; SOCIAL ISOLATION. **2.** in psychoanalytic theory, a DEFENSE MECHANISM that relies on keeping unwelcome thoughts and feelings from forming associative links with other thoughts and feelings, with the result that the unwelcome thought is rarely activated. See also COMPARTMENTALIZATION. **3.** in ERIKSON'S EIGHT STAGES OF DEVELOPMENT, see INTIMACY VERSUS ISOLATION. **—isolate** *vb.*

isolation effect see VON RESTORFF EFFECT.

isolation experiment the removal of an animal from social or other contact with other members of its species in order to observe behavioral or other effects.

isolation of affect in psychoanalytic theory, a DEFENSE MECHANISM in which the individual screens out painful feelings by recalling a traumatic event without experiencing the emotion associated with it.

isomerization *n.* a change in the structural arrangement of a molecule without any change in its constituent atoms, which may change the properties of the molecule. When photons are absorbed by the photopigment RHODOPSIN, the 11-*cis* retinal component undergoes isomerization and triggers a biochemical cascade that ultimately results in a visual signal.

isomers *pl. n.* forms of molecules that are identical in chemical composition but differ in the spatial orientation of their atoms (i.e., they are **stereoisomers**). **Enantiomers** are stereoisomers that exist in pairs as mirror images. The two enantiomers of a pair rotate the plane of polarized light in opposite directions: L forms produce leftward or counterclockwise rotation (**levorotation**), while D forms produce rightward or clockwise rotation (**dextrorotation**). In general, L forms tend to have biological activity.

isometric contraction a type of muscle contraction in which tension develops but the muscle does not shorten, as when a weightlifter grasps a barbell. Compare ISOTONIC CONTRACTION.

isometric control in ergonomics, a control device, such as a lever or handle, that incorporates a degree of resistance, so that it can be activated only by the application of a certain level of force. Compare ISOTONIC CONTROL.

isomorphism *n.* **1.** a one-to-one structural correspondence between two or more different entities or their constituent parts. **2.** in cognition, the relationship between a perceived stimulus and the resulting verbal process, as in pronunciation of a printed word. **3.** the concept, especially in GESTALT PSYCHOLOGY, that there is a structural correspondence between perceptual experience and psychoneural activity in the brain. **—isomorph** *n.* **—isomorphic** *adj.*

isoniazid *n.* a drug of choice for the treatment of tuberculosis. Use of the drug can cause a form of neuritis by blocking the function of pyridoxine (vitamin B_6) in metabolizing glutamic acid to form the neurotransmitter GAMMA-AMINOBUTYRIC ACID. Isoniazid is a precursor of the monoamine oxidase inhibitor IPRONIAZID and was reputed to have some antidepressant activity, though it is not clinically used in this role. Also called **isonicotinic acid hydrazide (INH)**.

isophilia *n.* feelings of affection or affectionate behavior toward members of one's own sex, but without the genital component characteristic of same-sex sexual behavior. [first described by U.S. psychiatrist Harry Stack Sullivan (1892–1949)]

isopropyl alcohol an isomer of propyl alcohol used as an ingredient in cosmetics (e.g., hand lotion) as well as in medications for external use. It also may be used as an antiseptic. If ingested, it has initial effects similar to those of ETHANOL, but it is extremely toxic.

Isopto Carpine a trade name for PILOCARPINE.

Isopto Eserine a trade name for PHYSOSTIGMINE.

isosensitivity function see RECEIVER-OPERATING CHARACTERISTIC CURVE.

isotonic contraction a type of muscle contraction in which the muscle shortens and thickens, as when a person flexes the biceps muscle. Compare ISOMETRIC CONTRACTION.

isotonic control in ergonomics, a control device, such as a button or switch, that is activated by displacement of the control from a neutral point. Isotonic controls have no resistance and their activation is not dependent on the level of force applied. Compare ISOMETRIC CONTROL.

isotretinoin *n.* an analog of vitamin A used in the treatment of severe acne that is resistant to other therapies. It is highly TERATOGENIC and therefore should not be used in pregnancy. More controversially, the use of isotretinoin has been linked with psychological disturbances, such as depression, psychosis, and suicide. The mechanism responsible for these side effects is unknown. U.S. trade name (among others): **Accutane**.

ISP abbreviation for INDIVIDUAL SERVICE PLAN.

ISSP abbreviation for INTERNATIONAL SOCIETY FOR SPORT PSYCHOLOGY.

issue-relevant knowledge see ATTITUDE-RELEVANT KNOWLEDGE.

I statement a communication tool in which the first person pronoun is used in talking about relationship issues. Therapists may coach clients to use "I" instead of "you" in statements, for example, "I am bothered by your habit" rather than "You have a bad habit" (which is a **you statement**). I statements tend to reduce the negativity and blame directed toward the other person and put the ownership of the issue with the speaker, not the listener.

IT 1. abbreviation for INFORMATION TECHNOLOGY. **2.** abbreviation for INSPECTION TIME.

ITA abbreviation for INITIAL TEACHING ALPHABET.

ITBS abbreviation for IOWA TESTS OF BASIC SKILLS.

itch *n.* a cutaneous sensory experience related to pain. The associated nerve endings are the same as those sensitive to the prick-pain sensation (see PRICK EXPERIENCE): A rapidly repeated prick-pain sensation produces the itch reaction.

IT cortex abbreviation for INFEROTEMPORAL CORTEX.

ITD abbreviation for interaural time differences. See BINAURAL CUES.

item analysis a set of procedures used to evaluate the statistical merits of individual items comprising a psychological measure or test. These procedures may be used to select items for a test from a larger pool of initial items or to evaluate items on an established test.

item difficulty the difficulty of a test item for a particular group as determined by the proportion of individuals who correctly respond to the item.

item response theory (**IRT**) a psychometric theory of measurement based on the concept that the probability that an item will be correctly answered is a function of an underlying trait or ability that is not directly observable, that is, a latent trait (see LATENT TRAIT THEORY). Item response theory models differ in terms of the number of parameters contained in the model (as in the RASCH MODEL).

item scaling the assignment of a test item to a scale position on some dimension, often the dimension of difficulty level.

item selection the selection of test items for inclusion in a test battery based upon the final psychometric properties of the test battery, the ITEM RESPONSE THEORY parameters of the individual items, and the clarity and fairness of the individual items.

item-to-item reliability (symbol: r_{ii}) the correlation of responses to one particular item in a test or subtest with responses to another particular item in that test or subtest.

item validity the extent to which an individual item in a test or experiment measures what it purports to measure.

item weighting a numerical value assigned to a test item that expresses its percentage of the total score of the test. For example, an essay question may be assigned a value of 40, representing 40 out of 100 possible points.

iteration *n.* the repetition of a certain computational step until further repetition no longer changes the outcome or until the repetition meets some other predefined criterion.

iterative design in ergonomics, the practice of using results from prior testing or formative evaluation to make design changes during the DEVELOPMENT CYCLE of a new or improved product. The process of iteration continuously feeds previous results into the next design of the product, which is tested or evaluated in its turn, leading to further design changes, and so on.

I–Thou *adj.* denoting a relationship in which a subject ("I") treats someone or something else as another unique subject ("Thou") and in which there is complete personal involvement. German Jewish philosopher Martin Buber (1878–1965), who introduced the term, held that this type of relationship between individuals is characterized by mutual openness to, and recognition of, the unique personhood of the other. The I–Thou relationship is transformative for both people. Buber held that a person's relationship with God is the ultimate I–Thou relationship, because God is quintessentially Thou. In forms of EXISTENTIAL–HUMANISTIC THERAPY especially, I–Thou moments are prized and denote a significant contact and understanding between client and therapist. Compare I–IT.

ITI abbreviation for INTERTRIAL INTERVAL.

itinerancy *n.* see PEREGRINATION.

itinerant teacher a teacher who travels to several schools or classrooms, providing specialized instruction to children.

-itis *suffix* inflammation or diseased state (e.g., COLITIS).

ITPA abbreviation for ILLINOIS TEST OF PSYCHOLINGUISTIC ABILITIES.

IUD abbreviation for INTRAUTERINE DEVICE.

IUPsyS abbreviation for INTERNATIONAL UNION OF PSYCHOLOGICAL SCIENCE.

iv abbreviation for *i*ntra*v*enous. See INTRAVENOUS INJECTION.

IV abbreviation for INDEPENDENT VARIABLE.

IVF abbreviation for IN VITRO FERTILIZATION.

Jj

jabberwocky *n.* meaningless but grammatically correct writing or speech. [from a nonsense poem in *Through the Looking Glass* (1871) by British writer Lewis Carroll (1832–1898)]

jackknife *n.* an estimation procedure based on taking repeated subsamples from a batch of data. It is possible to estimate standard errors and confidence intervals, for example, through this procedure.

jacksonian march in a simple PARTIAL SEIZURE involving motor symptoms, an older name for clonic motor movements in one region or side of the body that start in one muscle group and then move systematically ("march") to adjacent motor groups. [John Hughlings **Jackson** (1835–1911), British neurologist]

Jackson's law the principle that when mental deterioration results from brain disease, the higher and more recently developed functions are lost first. [John **Jackson**]

Jacobson relaxation method see PROGRESSIVE RELAXATION.

Jacobson's organ see VOMERONASAL SYSTEM. [Ludvig Levin **Jacobson** (1835–1911), Danish anatomist]

jactatio capitis nocturnis see HEAD ROLLING.

jactitation *n.* extreme restlessness marked by frequent movements and tossing about. Also called **jactation**.

James, William (1842–1910) U.S. psychologist and philosopher. After earning his medical degree in 1868 from Harvard Medical School, James served as professor of physiology, philosophy, and psychology at Harvard University. Arguably the most influential psychologist of his time, he taught many students who contributed to the development of American psychology, including Mary Whiton CALKINS, G. Stanley HALL, Robert S. WOODWORTH, and Edward L. THORNDIKE. He also wrote a best-selling textbook, *Principles of Psychology* (1890), that helped shape the field of psychology in its early decades. Embracing Darwinian evolutionary theory, he promoted a functionalist approach to psychology, emphasizing the usefulness of psychological phenomena, such as habits, emotions, and consciousness, in helping organisms survive. James also made lasting contributions to the psychology of religion in his *Varieties of Religious Experience* (1902) and to psychical research as a means of uncovering unconscious factors in mental life. In addition, James is one of the founders, with John DEWEY and Charles S. Peirce (1839–1914), of PRAGMATISM, America's most important contribution to philosophy. See JAMES–LANGE THEORY; FUNCTIONALISM; SELF; STREAM OF ACTION; STREAM OF CONSCIOUSNESS.

James–Lange theory the theory that different feeling states stem from the feedback from the viscera and voluntary musculature to the brain. This theory hypothesizes that there are as many physiological responses as there are different intrapsychic feelings and that each of these responses precedes rather than follows the feeling. [William JAMES; Carl Georg **Lange** (1834–1900), Danish physiologist]

Janet's test a test of tactile sensibility in which participants simply answer in the affirmative or negative when asked if they feel the touch of the examiner's fingers. [Pierre **Janet** (1859–1947), French psychologist and neurologist]

Janis–Feyerabend hypothesis the notion that persuasive discourse will be more effective if one first refutes positive arguments on the other side of a question before answering negative attacks on one's own side. [Irving L. **Janis** (1918–1990), Austrian-born U.S. philosopher; Paul **Feyerabend** (1924–1994), U.S. psychologist]

Japanese management the style of management characteristic of many Japanese corporations, in which there is a stress on continuous improvement in quality, consensus decision-making, and just-in-time inventory systems. The economic success of Japan in the 1980s led to the adoption of similar practices in the United States and other Western nations. See also DEMING MANAGEMENT METHOD; THEORY Z; TOTAL QUALITY MANAGEMENT.

jargon *n.* **1.** the specialized words and forms of language used within a particular profession or field of activity. Although jargon is often unavoidable in dealing with technical or specialist subjects, inappropriate or unnecessary use can alienate outsiders, who find it unintelligible. **2.** in prelinguistic children, BABBLING that sounds like plausible speech but is incomprehensible.

jargon aphasia see WORD SALAD.

JAS abbreviation for JENKINS ACTIVITY SURVEY.

jaundice *n.* a condition, associated with a variety of disorders of the liver, gallbladder, and blood, marked by the deposition of bile pigments in the skin, eye surfaces, and excrement. The pigment, which is usually first observed in discoloration of the normally white areas of the eyes, is produced as BILIRUBIN, a breakdown product of the hemoglobin of red blood cells. Jaundice is associated with liver infections but may also occur as an adverse reaction to certain drugs; it is also a causative factor in neurological birth defects (see KERNICTERUS). Also called **icterus**.

jaw jerk a reflex test used in the diagnosis of lesions of the corticospinal tract: The examiner taps downward on the lower jaw while it hangs passively open; if the lesion is present, the jaw closes reflexively. Also called **chin reflex**; **jaw reflex**; **mandibular reflex**; **masseter reflex**.

JCAHO abbreviation for JOINT COMMISSION ON ACCREDITATION OF HEALTHCARE ORGANIZATIONS.

JDI abbreviation for JOB DESCRIPTIVE INDEX.

JDS abbreviation for JOB DIAGNOSTIC SURVEY.

jealousy *n.* a NEGATIVE EMOTION in which an individual resents a third party for appearing to take away (or likely to take away) the affections of a loved one. Jealousy requires a triangle of social relationships between three individuals: the one who is jealous, the partner with whom the jealous individual has or desires a relationship, and the rival who represents a preemptive threat to that relationship. Romantic relationships are the prototypic source of jealousy, but any significant relationship (with parents, friends, and so on) is capable of producing it. It differs from ENVY in that three people are always involved. See also DELUSIONAL JEALOUSY. **—jealous** *adj.*

Jehovah complex a form of MEGALOMANIA in which

the individual suffers from delusions of grandeur and identifies with qualities associated with God.

Jenkins Activity Survey (**JAS**) a self-administered, multiple-choice survey that attempts to duplicate the clinical assessment of the TYPE A BEHAVIOR pattern by means of an objective psychometric procedure. It measures characteristics of this behavior pattern, such as extreme competitiveness, striving for achievement and personal recognition, aggressiveness, haste, impatience, and explosiveness. [Carlyle David **Jenkins** (1928–), U.S. psychologist]

Jensenism *n.* the controversial theory that racial differences in IQ are at least partly heritable and that attempts to raise IQ through environmental interventions have been largely unsuccessful. [Arthur **Jensen** (1923–), U.S. psychologist]

jet lag a maladjustment of CIRCADIAN RHYTHMS that results from being transported through several global time zones within a short span of time. Rest, work, eating, body temperature, and adrenocortical-secretion cycles may require several days to adjust to local time. See also CIRCADIAN RHYTHM SLEEP DISORDER.

jiggle cage in experimental research, a box mounted on springs that records small oscillations caused by the enclosed animal.

jigsaw method a team-learning technique that was initially designed to alleviate prejudice and hostility among students in desegregrated schools. This technique is used to foster a cooperative learning environment, to reduce social isolation, and to improve academic achievement. Students work in groups on a content unit. The teacher assigns specific topics in the unit to each group member and allows students with the same topics to leave their group to study the topic with others who have that same assignment. The students then return to their original groups and teach their topics to the other members. Also called **jigsaw classroom**. [developed in the 1970s by U.S. experimental social psychologist Elliot Aronson (1932–) and his colleagues]

jimsonweed *n.* a poisonous annual weed, *Datura stramonium*, of the nightshade family that grows wild in temperate and subtropical areas of North America and the rest of the world and contains several potent anticholinergic agents, including the alkaloids SCOPOLAMINE and ATROPINE. It has been taken in small doses to treat asthma, whooping cough, muscle spasms, and other conditions and has also been applied externally for pain relief. Poisoning results in such symptoms as hyperthermia, flushing, dry mucous membranes, nausea and vomiting, rapid heartbeat, visual disturbances, hallucinations, delirium, coma, and potentially death; there is often amnesia for the period of intoxication. The name is a corruption of "Jamestown weed," the name given to the plant by early settlers of Virginia. Also called **devil's trumpet**.

jinjinia bemar see KORO.

jiryan *n.* a CULTURE-BOUND SYNDROME found in India, with symptoms similar to those of SHEN-K'UEI.

JND (**jnd**) abbreviation for just noticeable difference (see DIFFERENCE THRESHOLD).

job analysis the collection and analysis of information on a specific job. Data is obtained from those doing or supervising the job using interviews or written questionnaires (see POSITION ANALYSIS QUESTIONNAIRE), or through observation or audiovisual recordings of the jobs being performed. Important classes of job information include the behaviors, tools, working conditions, and skills involved in the job. Job analysis is the first step in developing effective PERSONNEL SELECTION, EMPLOYEE EVALUATION, JOB EVALUATION, and PERSONNEL TRAINING programs. Once data has been collected, the role of the **job analyst** is to use statistical techniques and subjective judgment to determine the primary dimensions of a job and to identify those positions that are sufficiently similar to be classified as the same job.

job-characteristics model a model that attempts to characterize the basic parameters of a job as they affect the psychological state of the employee, especially with regard to motivation. The five core **job dimensions** are identified as skill variety, TASK IDENTITY, TASK SIGNIFICANCE, autonomy, and feedback. The model holds that WORK MOTIVATION, JOB PERFORMANCE, and JOB SATISFACTION will all be improved if jobs are designed or redesigned to maximize these dimensions. See JOB DIAGNOSTIC SURVEY. See also JOB ENLARGEMENT; JOB ENRICHMENT. [proposed by U.S. psychologist J. Richard Hackman (1940–) and U.S. organizational behaviorist Greg R. Oldham (1947–)]

job-component method a JOB-EVALUATION technique based on the assumption that similarities in job content impose similar job demands on the employees and therefore warrant corresponding pay scales. The job-component method is often applied through a statistical analysis of data obtained from a POSITION ANALYSIS QUESTIONNAIRE. Compare CLASSIFICATION METHOD; FACTOR-COMPARISON METHOD; POINT METHOD; RANKING METHOD.

job-component validity a SYNTHETIC VALIDITY method of estimating the ability of a test battery to predict suitability for a particular job that involves use of the POSITION ANALYSIS QUESTIONNAIRE.

job context significant aspects of the work situation other than the work itself, such as the physical environment of the work, coworkers, supervisors, and technology.

job criterion the standard used to evaluate employees' performance on a specific dimension of performance in a job. The criteria usually consist of a supervisor's ratings of employee performance, but objective measures, such as quantity of productivity or absentee rates, may also be used. See CRITERION CUTOFF; CRITERION DATA; CRITERION DIMENSIONS. See also EMPLOYEE EVALUATION; JOB PERFORMANCE.

job description a formal description of a specific job, as supplied by an organization's personnel department to those holding or applying for the position. Although formats vary, a job description usually comprises three main elements: (a) identification information, including job title, location, and reporting structure (i.e., relations to superiors and subordinates); (b) a brief statement summarizing the purpose of the job; and (c) a more detailed description of JOB DIMENSIONS or of specific duties and responsibilities. The job description is usually compiled through a systematic process of JOB ANALYSIS and can be used in its turn as the basis for a PERSONNEL SPECIFICATION describing the attributes required to perform the job effectively. Also called **job profile**.

Job Descriptive Index (**JDI**) a 72-item instrument used to measure the attitudes of employees in such areas as work, supervision, pay, promotions, and coworkers. Each item is an adjective or short phrase (e.g., "boring," "good opportunities for promotion"), and the participant writes Y (yes), N (no), or ? (cannot decide) to indicate whether the item applies to his or her job. Originally published in 1969, the JDI was revised in 1985 and 1997. [developed by U.S. psychologist Patricia Cain Smith (1917–), 20th-century Canadian psychologist Lorne

M. Kendall, and U.S. organizational psychologist Charles L. Hulin (1936–)]

job design specification of the content (responsibilities and duties) of a given job with the goal of maximizing both JOB SATISFACTION and ORGANIZATIONAL EFFECTIVENESS. See also JOB REDESIGN.

Job Diagnostic Survey (JDS) a measure of the motivational components of a job, as identified by the JOB-CHARACTERISTICS MODEL of U.S. psychologist J. Richard Hackman (1940–) and U.S. organizational behaviorist Greg R. Oldham (1947–). The JDS is a self-report instrument in which employees' answers are used to score a job in terms of five core dimensions that are held to determine employee motivation (skill variety, TASK IDENTITY, TASK SIGNIFICANCE, autonomy, and feedback). If scores are low, a program of JOB ENLARGEMENT or JOB ENRICHMENT may be recommended.

job dimensions 1. the general categories of tasks or duties that define the nature of a particular job, for example, clerical duties, receptionist duties, or decision-making responsibilities. In compiling job descriptions it is now customary to define the key dimensions of a job instead of providing an exhaustive list of all the tasks that will be required. **2.** certain general areas of competence, personality traits, or attitudes that are thought to be essential to the performance of a job, such as ambition, attention to detail, or interpersonal skills. Such attributes may be included in PERSONNEL SPECIFICATIONS in addition to more specific skills and qualifications, such as directly related work experience or fluency in a particular language. **3.** see JOB-CHARACTERISTICS MODEL.

job enlargement the expansion of the responsibilities associated with a particular job. In **horizontal job enlargement** (or **horizontal loading**) the employee is required to perform a greater number and variety of subtasks of the same level of complexity as his or her existing duties; in **vertical job enlargement** (or **vertical loading**) he or she is required to perform more complex tasks and to assume increased responsibility and autonomy.

job enrichment the enhancement of employees' interest in and attitude toward work tasks by improving the "quality of life" on the job (see QUALITY OF WORKLIFE). Job enrichment methods include (a) reducing boredom by giving employees a variety of different tasks during a work schedule and (b) allowing employees to plan their own work activities.

job evaluation analysis and comparison of jobs for the purpose of determining the pay structure within an organization. Methods used in job evaluation include: (a) ranking jobs on the basis of a subjective estimation of their relative overall value to the company (see RANKING METHOD); (b) assigning jobs to certain predefined classifications on the basis of job description (see CLASSIFICATION METHOD); (c) comparing jobs to certain identified BENCHMARK JOBS in terms of the COMPENSABLE JOB FACTORS entailed; (d) assigning point values to jobs according to a series of defined criteria such as education, experience, and the initiative or effort needed (see POINT METHOD); and (e) ranking jobs according to a statistical analysis of job content, as revealed by employees' answers to a standard questionnaire (see JOB-COMPONENT METHOD).

job information the data relating to jobs and workers used in JOB ANALYSIS studies. This usually includes work activities required; general human behaviors required, such as communicating or making decisions; PERSONNEL SPECIFICATIONS; and types of materials processed and equipment used.

job interview see EMPLOYMENT INTERVIEW.

job inventory see TASK INVENTORY.

job involvement the degree to which a person psychologically identifies with his or her job. A person who has a high level of job involvement usually obtains major life satisfaction from the job. Job accomplishments lead to a strong sense of pride and self-esteem, whereas failures in the job lead to discontent and depression. See also JOB SATISFACTION.

job performance effectiveness of job-related behavior as measured against a specific criterion of success, such as quantity or quality of output, or against multiple CRITERION DIMENSIONS. See EMPLOYEE EVALUATION; JOB CRITERION; PERFORMANCE REVIEW.

job placement see PLACEMENT.

job-placement stage a level of rehabilitation and work-preparedness training at which a person with a disability is presumed to be ready to move into the competitive job market. Rehabilitation personnel may assist individuals with such tasks as filling out job applications and preparing for job interviews (see PLACEMENT COUNSELING).

job preview information provided to people applying for a position on what they can expect if they are hired to perform the job. A **realistic job preview (RJP)** will provide both positive and negative information in an attempt to avoid disillusionment and increase the JOB TENURE of those hired.

job redesign systematic efforts to improve work methods, equipment, and the working environment. Major approaches to job redesign include METHODS ANALYSIS, which focuses on the development of efficient work methods; HUMAN FACTORS ENGINEERING, which is primarily concerned with the design of equipment, facilities, and environments; and job enlargement or job enrichment, which aim to expand the variety, complexity, and responsibility of jobs.

job requirements the personal qualities or skills that are necessary for performing work tasks safely and effectively. Job requirements may include good verbal communication skills, the ability to drive a truck, or the ability to perform complex mathematical calculations. They are normally identified in the PERSONNEL SPECIFICATION for a job.

job rotation an employment practice in which workers are required to perform different duties on a regularly scheduled basis, usually as a means of increasing their motivation and developing their skills.

job-safety analysis a specialized form of TASK ANALYSIS used to identify and control operating hazards in the workplace. It involves defining the job, identifying required tasks, identifying hazards, and making recommendations to eliminate or control the hazards. Also called **job-hazard analysis**. See also ACCIDENT ANALYSIS; ACCIDENT-PATH MODEL; FAILURE MODES AND EFFECTS ANALYSIS; FAULT-TREE ANALYSIS.

job satisfaction the attitude of a worker toward his or her job, often expressed as a hedonic response of liking or disliking the work itself, the rewards (pay, promotions, recognition), or the context (working conditions, colleagues). See also JOB INVOLVEMENT.

job specification see PERSONNEL SPECIFICATION.

job tenure 1. the length of time an employee spends in a position. See TURNOVER. **2.** in certain professions, such as academia, a guarantee of life-long employment. Also called **tenure**.

Jocasta complex in psychoanalytic theory, an abnormally close or incestuous attachment of a mother to her son. It is named for Jocasta, the mother and wife of Oedipus in Greek mythology. Compare OEDIPUS COMPLEX.

Johari window a model used to evaluate the extent of open and authentic communications between individuals. It is an imaginary window with four panes that each represent a dimension of knowledge about a person: (a) The **open** pane contains information about the person that is known both to the person and to others, (b) the **blind** pane contains information about the person that is known only to others, (c) the **hidden** pane contains information about the person that is known only to the person, and (d) the **unknown** pane contains information about the person that is known neither to the person nor to others. The goal is to increase the amount of information about the self that is known both to the self and to others. [devised in the 1950s by 20th-century U.S. psychologist Joseph Luft and 20th-century U.S. physician Harrington V. Ingham]

John Henry effect an effect in which rivalry between a control group and an experimental group leads to competitive efforts that disturb the whole basis of the experiment. It is a particular danger in industrial psychology experiments that attempt to compare the outputs of groups working under different task conditions. The term derives from the legend of John Henry, a railroad steel driver who worked himself to death with a steam drill.

Johnson v. Louisiana a case resulting in an influential 1972 U.S. Supreme Court decision establishing that there is no constitutional requirement for states to require juries to be unanimous in their verdict for crimes that are not punishable by death. The court concluded that permitting a majority verdict does not violate DUE PROCESS rights.

joie de vivre a sense of enjoyment or pleasure in life that is absent in ANHEDONIA. [French, "joy of living"]

joint attention attention focused by two or more people on the same object, person, or action at the same time. Joint attention is an important developmental tool. Infants of around 9 months can follow their parents' gaze and begin to imitate what their parents do. Thus by focusing attention on an object as well as on the adult's reaction to it, children can learn about the world. This technique is also used in primate studies (see ENCULTURATION). Also called **shared attention**.

Joint Commission on Accreditation of Healthcare Organizations (JCAHO) a national, private, nonprofit organization, founded in 1951, whose purpose is to encourage the attainment of uniformly high standards of institutional medical care. The Joint Commission evaluates and accredits hospitals and health care organizations that provide MANAGED CARE (including HMOS, PPOS, and INTEGRATED DELIVERY SYSTEMS), HOME CARE, long-term care, behavioral health care, laboratory services, and ambulatory care services.

joint probability the probability that two events will occur simultaneously.

joke *n.* a story or remark that is intended to provoke laughter. See HUMOR; INCONGRUITY THEORY OF HUMOR.

joking mania see WITZELSUCHT.

Jonah complex in the humanistic psychology of Abraham MASLOW, inhibition of becoming fully self-actualized—that is, of fulfilling one's potential—for fear of facing new challenges and situations. It is named for the biblical prophet Jonah, who attempted to evade the mission imposed on him by God. See also FEAR OF SUCCESS.

Jonestown mass suicide the MASS SUICIDE in 1978 of over 900 members of the People's Temple Full Gospel Church. The group was initially based in San Francisco, but many emigrated with their church leader, Jim Jones, to a remote settlement in Guyana. When a small group of members attacked and killed members of a congressional fact-finding delegation from the United States, Jones ordered his followers to take their own lives by swallowing poison-laced Kool-Aid.

Jost's law the principle that the newer of two ASSOCIATIONS of equal strength will show more loss over time than will the older association. [Adolph **Jost** (1874–1920), German psychologist]

jouissance *n.* in the theory of French psychoanalyst Jacques Lacan (1901–1981), enjoyment or pleasure that goes beyond mere satisfaction of an INSTINCT. Such pleasure is seen as a subversive and destabilizing force. The term was later adopted by literary and philosophical critics in the traditions of DECONSTRUCTION and POSTSTRUCTURALISM. [French, literally: "enjoyment, pleasure"]

joy *n.* a feeling of extreme gladness, delight, or exultation of the spirit arising from a sense of well-being or satisfaction.

judge 1. *n.* a coder, rater, decoder, or other person who assists in describing, categorizing, or rating ongoing events or existing records of events. **2.** *vb.* to estimate, evaluate, or otherwise make a determination or form an opinion.

judge-made law see COMMON LAW.

judgment *n.* **1.** the capacity to recognize relationships, draw conclusions from evidence, and make critical evaluations of events and people. **2.** in psychophysics, the ability to determine the presence or relative magnitude of stimuli.

judgment sampling sampling based on personal opinion of what is representative of the population under study. Judgment sampling may be useful in pilot studies but does not generally result in warranted inference to any population of interest.

Juke *n.* pseudonym of a family in New York, seven generations of which were studied by U.S. social scientist Richard Lewis Dugdale (1841–1883), with findings reported in 1877. He claimed that the study showed relationships between prostitution and illegitimacy, with resulting neglected offspring, and between exhaustion and alcohol consumption, with resulting criminality and inability to make sound judgments. This study, which drew from and contributed to SOCIAL DARWINISM, stimulated many further studies throughout the early 20th century. These later studies erroneously claimed to identify linkages between immorality and mental retardation and ignored conclusions by Dugdale that environmental factors were significant.

jumping Frenchmen of Maine syndrome a CULTURE-BOUND SYNDROME resembling LATAH, observed in lumberjacks of French Canadian descent living in Quebec and Maine. It is characterized by an extreme STARTLE RESPONSE involving yelling, imitative speech and behavior, involuntary jumping, flinging of the arms, and command obedience. Also called **jumper disease of Maine; jumping disease**. See also IMU; MYRIACHIT.

jumping stand a type of apparatus formerly used to study DISCRIMINATIONS. Rats were placed on a stand and had to obtain food by jumping through doors on a platform some distance away. Usually two doors were present, each displaying a distinctive stimulus. Jumping through one door (designated as correct) led to food. Jumping toward the other door, which was locked, led to a fall into a net. The apparatus has been abandoned because too many variables were left uncontrolled.

juncture *n.* a set of phonological features (usually a combination of PAUSE and STRESS) that signals the boundary between words or word elements, so that, for example, *a nice cream van* can be distinguished from *an ice cream van.*

Jung, Carl Gustav (1875–1961) Swiss psychiatrist and psychoanalyst. Jung studied natural science and medicine at the University of Basel in Switzerland, earning a medical degree (c. 1899). He then moved to Zürich to work at the Bürghölzi Mental Hospital with the prominent Swiss physician Eugen Bleuler (1857–1939), who specialized in the schizophrenic disorders. A wide-ranging student of medicine, archeology, mysticism, and philosophy, Jung associated himself with the psychoanalytic school of Sigmund FREUD because it recognized the influence of the UNCONSCIOUS. However, after 5 years he broke with Freud over Freud's theories of infantile sexuality, his emphasis on instinctual impulses, and his limitation of mental contents to personal experiences. In contrast, Jung held that we are molded by our ancestral as well as personal history, and motivated by moral and spiritual values more than by psychosexual drives. On this basis he constructed a theory of ANALYTIC PSYCHOLOGY. An important aspect of this theory was its emphasis on personality dynamics, viewed in terms of opposing forces, such as conscious versus unconscious values, introversive versus extraversive tendencies, and rational versus irrational processes. For Jung, healthy personality development consisted in constructively resolving these conflicts between opposing forces and achieving a new integration. For conflicts that persist and generate emotional disturbances, Jung advocated a form of therapy aimed at eliciting unconscious forces to help individuals solve their problems and realize their potential. This process usually involves the study of dreams and drawings and the exploration of new activities that will express the individual's personality, but does not utilize the Freudian couch or the method of FREE ASSOCIATION. The popular MYERS–BRIGGS TYPE INDICATOR is based on Jungian principles. See also ANAMNESTIC ANALYSIS; ANIMA; ANIMUS; COMPLEX; FUNCTIONAL TYPES; INDIVIDUATION; INTROVERSION–EXTRAVERSION; SELF; SHADOW; TELEOLOGY. **—Jungian** *adj.*

Jungian psychology the psychoanalytical theory and approach to psychotherapy of Carl JUNG. See ANALYTIC PSYCHOLOGY.

Jungian typology a theory of personality that classifies individuals into types according to (a) attitudes of INTROVERSION and EXTRAVERSION (see ATTITUDINAL TYPES) and (b) the dominant functions of the psyche (see FUNCTIONAL TYPES). [Carl JUNG]

junkie *n.* slang for a drug addict, especially a heroin addict. See HEROIN DEPENDENCE.

junk science invalid research findings admitted into court. Junk science is a cause of concern because judges, attorneys, and juries often lack the scientific training to identify unsound research.

jurisprudential teaching model a teaching model that emphasizes the role of social interaction and uses law and the system of laws as a paradigm for information processing and evaluating social issues.

jury consultant see TRIAL CONSULTANT.

jury nullification a jury's decision to exonerate a defendant who has clearly committed a criminal act. This can occur when the members of the jury believe that to find the defendant guilty would be unfair or unjust or would demand a sentence (e.g., death penalty) with which the jurors do not wish to be associated.

justice *n.* the impartial and fair settlement of conflict and differences by legal process and the imposition of proportionate punishment. See also COMMONSENSE JUSTICE; PROCEDURAL JUSTICE; RESTORATIVE JUSTICE.

justification *n.* **1.** in ethics, the process of determining right actions and appropriate beliefs. **2.** in clinical psychology, the defensive intellectualization of behavior, as in making an excuse for an action, cognition, or affect that one knows to be or is considered to be wrong or indefensible. **3.** in epistemology, a concept of intellectual responsibility regarding the norms of belief about ideas, actions, emotions, claims, theories, and so forth.

just noticeable difference (**JND**; **jnd**) see DIFFERENCE THRESHOLD.

just-noticeable-differences method see METHOD OF JUST NOTICEABLE DIFFERENCES.

just noticeable duration the duration for a comparison stimulus that is just perceptibly shorter or longer than the duration of a standard stimulus. Also called **least perceptible duration**.

just-world phenomenon the belief that what happens to people is what they deserve. The just-world phenomenon is attributed to a universal psychological desire to believe that events proceed rationally and not by chance. Such an attitude may, for example, result in the belief that the innocent victim of an accident must somehow be responsible for, or deserve, it. Also called **just-world hypothesis**. [postulated by Canadian psychologist Melvin J. Lerner (1929–)]

juvenile delinquency illegal behavior by a minor (usually identified as a person under age 18), including behavior that would be considered criminal in an adult. Examples are vandalism, petty thievery, auto theft, rape, arson, drug abuse, and aggravated assault.

juvenile justice system the courts and other government entities involved in the ADJUDICATION of cases involving minors (usually identified as individuals aged under 18). Fundamentally, it differs from the criminal justice system for adults in its belief that young people are more amenable to treatment than adults. Consequently, there is greater emphasis on rehabilitation, and greater efforts are made than in the adult system to reduce the stigmatization associated with being labeled a criminal.

juvenile period the period when an animal is no longer dependent on its parents for survival but is not yet sexually active. In nonhuman mammals, this constitutes the time between the cessation of weaning (the end of infancy) and the onset of sexual activity.

juvenile spinal muscular atrophy see SPINAL MUSCULAR ATROPHY.

juvenile transfer hearing a formal presentation and assessment of facts during which the court decides whether a minor should be transferred to an adult court for ADJUDICATION.

juvenilism *n.* a sexual attraction to children or adolescents. See EPHEBOPHILIA; PEDOPHILIA.

Kk

k symbol for COEFFICIENT OF ALIENATION.

K-ABC abbreviation for KAUFMAN ASSESSMENT BATTERY FOR CHILDREN.

KAE abbreviation for KINESTHETIC AFTEREFFECT.

kainate receptor a type of GLUTAMATE RECEPTOR that binds kainic acid as well as glutamate. It is coupled to a LIGAND-GATED ION CHANNEL, which opens when the receptor is activated.

kainic acid a neuroexcitatory compound derived from the red seaweed *Digenea simplex*. It is commonly used in research to destroy brain tissue in experimental animals.

kairos *n.* in EXISTENTIAL PSYCHOLOGY, the moment of heightened awareness at which a person gains INSIGHT into the meaning of an important event. See also AHA EXPERIENCE; EPIPHANY. [from Greek, "fitness, opportunity, time"]

KAIT abbreviation for KAUFMAN ADOLESCENT AND ADULT INTELLIGENCE TEST.

Kalischer syndrome see STURGE–WEBER SYNDROME.

Kallikak *n.* pseudonym of a family, studied by Henry GODDARD in the early 1900s, that was purported to have one branch characterized as moral, upstanding, and productive and another as immoral, degenerate, and mentally retarded (then termed "feebleminded"). The study was claimed at the time to provide evidence of inheritance of moral traits and risk of moral degeneracy due to mental retardation. Goddard used these findings to support EUGENICS practices but later disavowed the argument that there was a linkage between morality and mental retardation. Moreover, subsequent reviews of the study have suggested that it was conducted in an unreliable manner, calling into question the findings it put forth.

Kallmann's syndrome a hereditary disorder characterized by HYPOGONADISM (sometimes in the form of underdeveloped male sexual organs), mental retardation, color blindness, complete ANOSMIA (absence of the sense of smell), and MOTOR OVERFLOW. Kallmann's syndrome is transmitted as an X-linked dominant trait. [Franz Josef **Kallmann** (1897–1965), German-born U.S. psychiatrist and geneticist]

kamikaze *n.* in World War II, a member of an elite military unit in the Japanese air force who carried out suicide attacks on the enemy by flying bomb-loaded aircraft into targets. The word is Japanese for "divine wind." See ALTRUISTIC SUICIDE.

Kamin effect see BLOCKING. [Leon J. **Kamin** (1924–), U.S. psychologist]

Kanizsa figure any one of several figures that induce the perception of illusory contours defining a shape that appears to be brighter than the background. The most common example is the **Kanizsa triangle**, which is induced by three black circles placed as the apexes of a triangle. Each circle has a 60° wedge removed so that these wedges become the angles of the illusory triangle. Even though nothing connects the circles, a strong impression of a triangle that is brighter than the background is perceived. [Gaetano **Kanizsa** (1913–), Italian psychologist]

Kanner's syndrome see AUTISTIC DISORDER. [Leo **Kanner** (1894–1981), Austrian-born U.S. child psychiatrist]

Kansas v. Hendricks a case resulting in a controversial 1997 U.S. Supreme Court decision that upheld the INVOLUNTARY CIVIL COMMITMENT of an offender after he had already completed his sentence for a sex crime. The court ruled that laws permitting confinement of sex offenders in mental hospitals after they have served their criminal sentences are not unconstitutional if the offender remains a threat.

kansei engineering an engineering and design practice that elicits and analyzes users' subjective feelings about aspects of a product or range of products and incorporates these findings into subsequent designs. Also called **affective engineering**; **emotional engineering**; **sensory engineering**. [Japanese: "psychological feeling"]

Kantianism *n.* the philosophical position of German philosopher Immanuel Kant (1724–1804), most notably that consciously experienced phenomena (see PHENOMENON) represent all that humans can know about essentially unknowable realities (see NOUMENON) and that these phenomena result from the application of certain intrinsic CATEGORIES OF THOUGHT to the material of sense experience. **—Kantian** *adj., n.*

kappa *n.* an index of INTERRATER AGREEMENT corrected for chance association. See COHEN'S KAPPA; WEIGHTED KAPPA.

kappa effect the interaction between the perceived duration of a stimulus and the spatial extent of the stimulus. When a small visual stimulus and a large visual stimulus are both flashed for the same length of time, the duration of the large stimulus is perceived as longer than that of the small stimulus. An analogous effect has been described for tactile sensations.

kappa receptor see OPIOID RECEPTOR.

kappa wave a type of BRAIN WAVE with a frequency similar to that of an ALPHA WAVE (10 Hz) but with a much weaker amplitude. Kappa waves normally occur while a person is reading, thinking, or dreaming.

karezza *n.* see CAREZZA.

karma *n.* **1.** in HINDUISM, a concept signifying (a) a mental or physical action, (b) the consequence of a mental or physical action, (c) the sum of all consequences of the actions of a person in this or some previous life, and (d) the chain of cause and effect in the world of morality. **2.** in BUDDHISM, the universal law of cause and effect. The effect of an action, which can be of the body, speech, or mind, is not primarily determined by the act itself but by the intention of the actor. When a deed cannot be done but the intention to do it exists, this still produces an effect. [Sanskrit, literally: "deed"] **—karmic** *adj.*

karyotype *n.* **1.** the chromosomal constitution of a cell, including the number of chromosomes, their structural features, and any abnormalities. **2.** a photograph of an individual's chromosomes, which shows them in an ordered, numbered array. **Karyotype testing** is a clinical test that allows scientists to look for chromosome alterations and mutations. It is also used for forensic comparison of genetic material from different sources. See also CHROMOSOMAL MAP.

kat *n.* see KHAT.

kata- *combining form* see CATA-.

katasexuality *n.* a sexual preference for dead people or human beings with animal-like characteristics. See NECROPHILIA.

Katz Index of Activities of Daily Living an observer-based measure of the FUNCTIONAL STATUS of older adults and individuals with chronic disorders. An individual is rated regarding the degree of assistance required to perform six basic functions: bathing, dressing, feeding, toileting, transferring, and continence. Baseline measurements provide useful feedback when compared to periodic or subsequent measurements. Also called **Katz Index of Independence in Activities of Daily Living**. [originally developed in 1963 by Sidney **Katz**, 20th-century U.S. physician and geriatrician]

Kaufman Adolescent and Adult Intelligence Test (**KAIT**) a test of intelligence based upon the theory of fluid and crystallized abilities, yielding scores that reflect these two kinds of abilities. Designed for use with individuals aged 11 to over 85 years, the KAIT may be administered in two forms: a standard battery of six core subtests or an expanded battery that includes four additional subtests. See FLUID–CRYSTALLIZED INTELLIGENCE THEORY; FLUID ABILITIES; CRYSTALLIZED ABILITIES. [Alan S. **Kaufman** (1944–) and Nadeen L. **Kaufman** (1945–), U.S. psychologists]

Kaufman Assessment Battery for Children (**K–ABC**) an intelligence test developed in 1983 based on the theory of Alexander LURIA, according to which intelligence comprises separate abilities for simultaneous and for successive processing. An example of a simultaneous ability test would be a test requiring solution of geometric matrix problems, in which one element of a geometric matrix is missing. An example of a successive ability test would be a test requiring solution of serial-recall problems, in which series of symbols are presented and individuals have to recall them in the order they were presented. Now in its second edition (published in 2004), the K–ABC has been expanded to allow for testing and interpretation of results in terms of the FLUID–CRYSTALLIZED INTELLIGENCE THEORY as well. It comprises 18 core and supplementary subtests and is designed for use with individuals aged 3 to 18 years. [Alan and Nadeen **Kaufman**]

kava *n.* an extract of the root of *Piper methysticum*, a shrub indigenous to certain southern Pacific islands, where it has an established use as a mild intoxicant, sedative, and analgesic agent. The primary active ingredients of the plant are kavain, dihydrokavain, methysticin, and dihydromethysticin—alkaloids that have anticonvulsant and muscle relaxant properties and also produce sedation without clouding of consciousness. Kava is now widely available in Western countries as an herbal supplement promoted for relaxation (e.g., to relieve stress, anxiety, and tension) and as a remedy for sleeplessness and menopausal symptoms, among other uses. However, the ability of these supplements to provide such benefits has not been definitively determined, and they have in fact been shown to be ineffective for treating menopausal symptoms. Additionally, in 2002 the U.S. Food and Drug Administration issued a consumer advisory warning of the potential risk of rare but serious reactions—including hepatitis, cirrhosis, and liver failure—associated with use of kava-containing supplements. Kava has also been associated with depression of the central nervous system or coma (particularly in combination with prescribed anxiolytics), and other less serious adverse reactions (e.g., skin rash) have been reported as well. There are several known and potential interactions of kava with other agents (see DRUG INTERACTIONS), including anticoagulants, MONOAMINE OXIDASE INHIBITORS, and drugs metabolized by the CYTOCHROME P450 3A4 enzyme (e.g., clonidine, nefazodone, St. John's wort). Also called **ava**; **kava kava**.

KBS abbreviation for knowledge-based system (see EXPERT SYSTEM).

K complex a characteristic brief, high-amplitude pattern of electrical activity recorded from the brain during the early stages of sleep. K complexes and SLEEP SPINDLES commonly occur during stage 2 sleep as a normal phenomenon (see SLEEP STAGES) but they may also be associated with nocturnal epileptic seizures.

Keeler polygraph see POLYGRAPH.

keep-awake pills a popular name for stimulant pills that contain CAFFEINE as the active ingredient and can be obtained without a doctor's prescription. A keep-awake pill usually contains approximately 100 mg caffeine, equivalent to the amount of caffeine in one cup of regular coffee or two cups of strong tea.

Kegel exercises exercises designed to help women build strength and gain control of the pelvic-floor muscles. These exercises are used in the treatment of VAGINISMUS and play a role in increasing sexual pleasure. The muscle increases abdominal pressure by contracting, drawing the anus toward the pubis, as when an individual tightens control of the urinary sphincter. The exercises are therefore also used in the treatment of stress incontinence. [developed in 1948 by A. H. **Kegel**, 20th-century U.S. gynecologist]

Keller plan **1.** a personalized system of education in which students work at their own pace, attending lectures and demonstrations, with emphasis on writing for student–instructor communication. **2.** a system of MASTERY LEARNING that uses multiple assessments of the same information until fundamental understanding of the content is demonstrated. Textbooks and written materials are primary resources for learning in this format. [Fred S. **Keller** (1899–1996), U.S. psychologist]

Kemadrin *n.* a trade name for PROCYCLIDINE.

Kendall's coefficient of concordance see COEFFICIENT OF CONCORDANCE. [Maurice George **Kendall** (1907–1983), British statistician]

Kendall's tau (symbol: τ) a nonparametric measure of association used with ordinal variables. [Maurice **Kendall**]

Kennard principle the idea that brain damage sustained early in life is less debilitating than brain damage sustained later in life, presumably because of the enhanced ability of the younger brain to reorganize. This principle is not always confirmed. [Margaret **Kennard** (1899–1976), U.S. psychologist]

keratitis *n.* inflammation of the cornea. Keratitis may be deep, when the infection causing it is carried in the blood or spreads to the cornea from other parts of the eye; or superficial, caused by bacterial or viral infection or by an allergic reaction. See also COGAN'S SYNDROME.

keratoconus *n.* the most common of a group of noninflammatory disorders that affect the central cornea of both eyes. The earliest symptom is loss of vision due to irregular corneal astigmatism.

keratometer *n.* an instrument used to measure the curvature of the cornea of the eye, used in the diagnosis of ASTIGMATISM. Also called **ophthalmometer**.

kernel-of-truth hypothesis the idea that STEREOTYPES, despite being exaggerated generalizations about a group of diverse individuals, sometimes contain elements that accurately describe the qualities of the stereotyped group.

kernel sentence in early versions of GENERATIVE GRAMMAR, a base version of a sentence upon which such operations as negation and interrogation are performed to produce variations of that base. So, for example, the kernel sentence *Jack kissed Jill* can be transformed into the sentences *Did Jack kiss Jill?*, *Jack did not kiss Jill*, *Jill was kissed by Jack*, and so forth. Psychological interest in this idea stems from its implications for the cognitive processes by which we form and interpret sentences. In later models of TRANSFORMATIONAL GENERATIVE GRAMMAR, as developed by Noam CHOMSKY, the transformational rules are seen as operating upon the DEEP STRUCTURES underlying sentences, rather than on any actual sentence.

kernicterus *n.* a congenital disorder associated with excessive levels of BILIRUBIN in the newborn infant. It is characterized by severe JAUNDICE and has the potential of causing severe damage to the central nervous system. Kernicterus is often a complication of RH BLOOD-GROUP INCOMPATIBILITY. See also BILIRUBIN ENCEPHALOPATHY.

Kernig's sign a reflex action that is a diagnostic sign for MENINGITIS. The test is positive if flexing the thigh at the hip while extending the leg at the knee results in resistance and pain. [Vladimir Michailovich **Kernig** (1840–1917), Russian physician]

ketamine *n.* a drug that is closely related to PCP (phencyclidine). It acts as an antagonist at NMDA RECEPTORS and was formerly used as a DISSOCIATIVE ANESTHETIC. Disorientation and perceptual distortions may result from its use, which have limited its utility in surgical anesthesia but have made it a sought-after and common drug of abuse. It is ingested (in the form of tablets, capsules, or powder) by drug users for its hallucinogenic effects. U.S. trade name: **Ketalar**.

ketoconazole *n.* an antifungal agent that has been suggested as a treatment for depression resistant to conventional drugs, due to its ability to inhibit the biosynthesis of steroids. No large-scale clinical data support this. Ketoconazole is a potent inhibitor of numerous CYTOCHROME P450 enzymes (particularly CYP3A4), and has significant interactions with psychotropic drugs that utilize this metabolic path. Its numerous interactions and propensity to cause liver damage limit its use. U.S. trade name: **Nizoral**.

key *n.* **1.** a set of symbols or concepts used in coding or decoding. **2.** a set of answers used in scoring a test.

keyboard *n.* a device that allows a user to input information to a computer by pressing specific alphanumeric, symbol, or function keys or key combinations. Many forms of specialized keyboards (e.g., enlarged, ergonomic, or reduced in size) are available and can be particularly useful to individuals with disabilities.

key-word method a technique sometimes used in learning foreign-language vocabulary. If the native language is English, the key word would consist of an English word associated with the sound of a foreign word and linked to the foreign word's meaning in a mental image. For example, the French word *livre* ("book") may remind an English speaker of the sound of *leaf*; the key word *leaf* can then be connected to "book" in a mental image, such as visualizing a leaf in a book as a bookmark. The key-word method is essentially a MNEMONIC STRATEGY.

khat (**chat**; **kat**; **qat**) *n.* an herbal CNS STIMULANT obtained from the leaves and other parts of an evergreen shrub, *Catha edulis*, indigenous to northeast Africa and the Arabian peninsula. The leaves are traditionally chewed to produce mild stimulant effects (e.g., mental alertness, suppression of appetite and the need for sleep, general sense of well-being); they can also be used to make a tea. The substance responsible for khat's psychoactive properties is **cathinone**, a compound that is structurally similar to amphetamine. As with amphetamines, physiological tolerance and dependence and a variety of adverse reactions (e.g., behavioral disorganization and psychosis) may occur with continued or high-dose use. The use of khat has spread beyond its traditional boundaries to the United States and other Western countries. In many of those places, however, khat is illegal; it is classified by the U.S. Drug Enforcement Administration as a Schedule I controlled substance (see SCHEDULED DRUGS).

KHOS abbreviation for KRANTZ HEALTH OPINION SURVEY.

kibbutz *n.* in Israel, a communal living arrangement, typically centered on agriculture, manufacturing, or tourism, with collective economic, social, and child-rearing practices. See also COMMUNE.

Kiddie Schedule for Affective Disorders and Schizophrenia (**KSADS**) see SCHEDULE FOR AFFECTIVE DISORDERS AND SCHIZOPHRENIA.

kids' culture the environments (e.g., playgrounds) and activities (e.g., games, rituals) that are unique to children and in which they create their own social structures separate from the adult world.

Kilner screen a special viewing apparatus that allegedly reveals the invisible AURAS emitted by human beings. It is essentially a light filter, consisting of two pieces of glass separated by a layer of cyanine (a blue dye used in photographic emulsions). Adherents claim that the inspection of human auras through such a screen can play a vital role in the early diagnosis of disease. Also called **Kilner goggles**. See also KIRLIAN PHOTOGRAPHY. [Walter J. **Kilner** (1847–1920), British physician]

kilobytophobia *n.* fear of, or discomfort with, computer technology, which sometimes accounts for a refusal or reluctance to use computer resources. See also COMPUTER ANXIETY.

kinase *n.* any of a class of enzymes that catalyze the addition of a phosphate group to a molecule (e.g., a protein).

kindling *n.* a phenomenon in which brain function is altered as a consequence of repeated minor electrical or chemical stimulation of the LIMBIC SYSTEM, culminating in the appearance of electrographic and fully generalized behavioral convulsions. It is often used as an experimental model for epilepsy.

kindness *n.* benevolent and helpful action intentionally directed toward another person. Kindness is motivated by the desire to help another, not to gain explicit reward or to avoid explicit punishment. See ALTRUISM. —**kind** *adj.*

kindred *n.* an extended family. The study in large kindreds of mutations that predispose to disease helps to identify the position and PENETRANCE of a particular gene mutation.

kinematics *n.* **1.** the study of motion of the body or parts of the body in terms of limb and joint position, velocity, and acceleration. In ergonomics, these are studied in the course of work activity. **2.** the patterns of movement of the limbs in motion. See also DYNAMICS. —**kinematic** *adj.*

kinesia *n.* see MOTION SICKNESS.

kinesialgia *n.* pain on muscular exertion.

kinesics *n.* the study of the part played by body movements, such as hand gestures, eye movements, and so on, in communicating meaning. See BODY LANGUAGE.

kinesics technique the analysis of the BODY LANGUAGE (e.g., facial expressions) of a person. The technique is used particularly during the interviewing of a suspect.

kinesimeter *n.* **1.** an instrument for measuring the extent of a movement. **2.** a 19th-century instrument for measuring the cutaneous sensation of the body.

kinesiology *n.* **1.** the study of the mechanics of body movement, especially their relationship to anatomical characteristics and physiological functions. **2.** a discipline that encompasses all the SPORT SCIENCES as well as the professional skills for the application of sport and exercise knowledge. **—kinesiological** *adj.* **—kinesiologist** *n.*

kinesiotherapy *n.* the application of progressive physical exercise and activities to treat individuals with FUNCTIONAL LIMITATIONS or to aid those interested in improving or maintaining general physical and emotional health, formerly called **corrective therapy**. A **kinesiotherapist** (formerly a **corrective therapist**) is a certified professional who develops a specific treatment plan for each individual, determining appropriate therapeutic exercises and physical-education activities and directing their implementation.

kinesis *n.* a type of movement in which an organism's response is related to the intensity of the stimulation but is not oriented in any spatial direction. An animal might be more or less active according to the amount of light, temperature, or humidity. Compare TAXIS; TROPISM.

kinesthesis *n.* the sense that provides information through receptors in the muscles, tendons, and joints, which enables humans and other animals to control and coordinate their movements, including walking, talking, facial expressions, gestures, and posture. Also called **kinesthesia**; **kinesthetic sense**; **movement sense**. See PROPRIOCEPTION. **—kinesthetic** *adj.*

kinesthetic aftereffect (**KAE**) any illusion involving the kinesthetic sense (see KINESTHESIS) in which one kinesthetic experience influences the next. For example, extended lifting of a heavy weight may cause a contrast illusion in which a new weight feels lighter than expected. This illusion may be the basis for the myth that performance in sport is improved by first practicing with a heavier than normal weight (e.g., swinging two bats before going to the plate in a baseball game).

kinesthetic feedback information about the position, movement, tension, and so forth of body parts provided by stretch receptors in the muscle spindles and tendons, as well as by receptors in the joints. See COROLLARY DISCHARGE; MUSCLE SENSATION.

kinesthetic hallucination a false perception of body movement.

kinesthetic imagery the cognitive re-creation of the feeling of movements, that is, of the sensations from the PROPRIOCEPTORS. **Dynamic kinesthetic imagery** is the cognitive creation of the feeling of movements while physically moving. For example, a figure skater may imagine the feeling of routine elements while walking through the pattern, or a skier may imagine the feel of the course while standing, shifting weight, and moving the shoulders.

kinesthetic receptor any of the sensory receptors that monitor the position and movement of muscles. These are found in muscles, tendons, and joints.

kinesthetics *n.* the ability to feel movement of the limbs or body.

kinesthetic sense see KINESTHESIS.

kinetic aftereffect see MOTION AFTEREFFECT.

kinetic depth effect the impression that a figure has three dimensions depending on the relative motions of the elements in the figure. See DEPTH FROM MOTION.

kinetic information in clinical assessment and therapy, the observed gestures, postures, and other body-language clues used in making an evaluation of a client or patient.

kingdom *n.* traditionally, the highest category used in BIOLOGICAL TAXONOMY, which contains related PHYLA. Modern classifications recognize five kingdoms—Bacteria, Protista (or Protoctista), Animalia, Fungi, and Plantae—which in some systems are grouped into DOMAINS.

kinkeeper *n.* the social role, usually assumed by women, of promoting and protecting relationships between family members.

kin recognition the ability to detect that another individual is closely related. A variety of cues—visual, auditory, and chemical—have been demonstrated to be effective. In many studies, kin recognition appears to be based on early social experience. That is, individuals recognize those they have interacted with during development but fail to recognize related individuals with whom they have never interacted. However, chimpanzees are able to recognize relationships, such as those between females and their male offspring, simply by observing similarities in photographs, even of chimpanzees they have never seen before. Kin recognition is important for directing support toward kin in KIN SELECTION.

kin selection a variation of NATURAL SELECTION that favors behavior by an individual that increases the chances of its relatives surviving and reproducing successfully (see ALTRUISM). Individuals share 50% of their genes with a parent or sibling, so if an individual risks its own ability to reproduce or survive but helps its parents or more than two siblings to survive or reproduce, the sacrificing individual will benefit indirectly by gaining INCLUSIVE FITNESS. Compare DIRECT SELECTION; INDIVIDUAL SELECTION.

Kinsey, Alfred (1894–1956) U.S. zoologist and sex researcher. Kinsey earned a doctorate of science at Harvard University in 1920 and then moved to Indiana University, where he remained for his entire teaching and research career, eventually serving as director of the Institute for Sex Research. His dissertation and early research involved studies of the gall wasp, but he is best known for his later scientific studies of human sexual behavior. Fifteen years of interviews with thousands of people culminated in two volumes that pioneered the field of SEXOLOGY: *Sexual Behavior in the Human Male* (1948) and *Sexual Behavior in the Human Female* (1953). These presented, for the first time, statistics on a range of human sexual behaviors, including such controversial issues as extramarital intercourse, masturbation, and homosexuality. Kinsey is also well known for developing what became known as the **Kinsey (Six) scale** (from 0 to 6), which provided an index of an individual's relative position on a continuum from homosexual to heterosexual.

Kinsey Institute for Research in Sex, Gender, and Reproduction a private nonprofit corporation affiliated with Indiana University whose mission is to promote interdisciplinary research and scholarship in the fields of human sexuality, gender, and reproduction.

It was founded in 1947 by Alfred KINSEY, who served as its first director and carried out much of his pioneering research into human sexual behavior there.

kinship *n.* the state of being related by birth, common ancestry, marriage, or adoption. Notions of who is and who is not kin may vary considerably from one culture to another. For example, in strongly patriarchal societies (see PATRIARCHY) some of one's mother's closest blood relatives may not be considered one's kin.

kinship migration **1.** a type of residence change among older adults, especially widows, that involves moving closer to family members. **2.** the movement of families, either all at once as a group or in phases as individual members or subgroups, from one geographic location to another.

kinship network the system of formal and informal relationships that make up an EXTENDED FAMILY in a given culture or society, typically based on blood ties, marriage, or adoption. The analysis of kinship networks and DESCENT GROUPS in preindustrial societies has been a major concern of cultural anthropology. See also RELATIONSHIP SYSTEM. Also called **kinship system**.

Kirlian photography a technique that ostensibly records on photographic film the AURA or "life force" emanating from a person, animal, plant, or object. It involves photographing subjects in a high-voltage electric field and produces images in which a colored halo or corona appears around the object. Supporters claim that changes in the quality of the aura can reflect changes in the health and emotional condition of the subject, making Kirlian photography of great potential benefit in medical diagnosis. Skeptics maintain that there is scant evidence for this. See also KILNER SCREEN; REICHENBACH PHENOMENON. [Semyon **Kirlian**, Armenian-born Russian inventor and electrician (1900–1980), and his wife Valentina **Kirlian**, Russian biologist]

Kirton Adaption–Innovation Inventory (**KAI**) a questionnaire, used chiefly in organizational settings, that is designed to measure creativity, cognitive style, and the degree to which individuals are adaptive, innovative, or a range of both in their approach to problem solving. It comprises 33 items (32 scored, 1 unscored) requiring participants to rate how difficult it is for them to be the person described (e.g., a person who is thorough) using a 17-point LIKERT SCALE format, ranging from "very hard" to "very easy." [originally developed in 1976 by Michael J. **Kirton**, British psychologist]

kissing behavior the activity of making contact with the lips, usually as a sign of friendship or affection. The kiss may involve lip contact with any part of the body and with varying degrees of pressure. Mouth-to-mouth kissing may include extension of the tongues (see FRENCH KISS). Kissing behavior possibly is related to the licking behavior manifested by animals. It is not observed in all cultures.

Kleeblattschädel syndrome a type of birth defect characterized by a three-lobed skull caused by upward and lateral bulging of the brain through skull sutures. Affected individuals also have hydrocephalus, severe mental retardation, and abnormally short limbs. Also called **cloverleaf skull**. [from German *Kleeblatt*, "cloverleaf," and *Schädel*, "skull"]

Klein, Melanie (1882–1960) Austrian-born British psychoanalyst. Although she had no formal medical education, Klein trained as a psychoanalyst in Budapest under Hungarian psychoanalyst Sandor Ferenczi (1873–1933). Klein was a pioneer in CHILD ANALYSIS. She was the first therapist to use play as an analytic and treatment technique; she also suggested that the OEDIPUS COMPLEX, paranoid attitudes, and the SUPEREGO originate in very early infancy. While Klein's ideas were not readily accepted by the psychoanalytic establishment on the European continent, they found fertile soil in England. Ernest Jones (1879–1958), president of the British Psycho-Analytical Society, invited her to England, where her work was sufficiently well received for her to remain there for the rest of her life. Klein's theories differed from those of Anna FREUD, another pioneer of child analysis. While Anna Freud emphasized the development of the child's ego, Klein emphasized oedipal conflicts and the primary object relationship with the mother (see OBJECT RELATIONS THEORY). She also developed controversial ideas about the similarities between infant mental life and adult neuroses and psychoses. Through her work on the PARANOID-SCHIZOID POSITION, she contributed to our knowledge of schizoid defense mechanisms. See also BAD BREAST; BAD OBJECT; DEPRESSIVE POSITION; EGO-SPLITTING; GOOD BREAST; GOOD OBJECT.

Kleine–Levin syndrome a rare disorder, primarily occurring in adolescent males, that is characterized by recurring episodes of excessive drowsiness and sleep (up to 20 hours per day). Symptoms, which may last for days to weeks, include excessive food intake, irritability, disorientation, lack of energy, and hypersensitivity to noise. It is possibly due to a malfunction of the hypothalamus, the part of the brain that governs appetite and sleep. [Willi **Kleine**, 20th-century German neuropsychiatrist; Max **Levin**, 20th-century U.S. neurologist]

Kleinian analysis psychotherapy in accordance with the theories and methods of the school of psychoanalysis founded by Melanie KLEIN, including such concepts as INTERNALIZATION, OBJECT RELATIONS, the DEPRESSIVE POSITION, IDEALIZATION, and the PARANOID-SCHIZOID POSITION.

kleptolagnia *n.* a morbid urge to steal, considered by some theorists to be associated with sexual excitement. However, this association is controversial, and many consider the urge to be unrelated to sexual issues.

kleptomania *n.* an impulse-control disorder characterized by a repeated failure to resist impulses to steal objects that have no immediate use or intrinsic value to the individual, accompanied by feelings of increased tension before committing the theft and either pleasure or relief during the act. The stealing is not done out of anger or in response to a delusion or hallucination and is not better accounted for by another disorder, such as conduct disorder or a manic episode. In *DSM–IV–TR*, kleptomania is included in the category IMPULSE-CONTROL DISORDERS NOT ELSEWHERE CLASSIFIED. **—kleptomaniac** *n.*

Klinefelter's syndrome a chromosomal disorder affecting males born with a karyotype of 47,XXY (i.e., they have an extra X chromosome), resulting in small testes, absence of sperm, enlarged breasts, and excretion of follicle-stimulating hormone. Mental retardation is uncommon, but many affected individuals have behavioral problems. Also called **XXY syndrome**. [Harry F. **Klinefelter** (1912–), U.S. physician]

klinotaxis *n.* see TAXIS.

Klippel–Feil syndrome a congenital condition characterized by a short neck, low hairline, and a reduced number of vertebrae, some of which may be fused into a single mass. The condition is often accompanied by deafness and mental retardation. [Maurice **Klippel** (1858–1942), French neurologist; André **Feil**, 20th-century French physician]

klismaphilia *n.* interest in, and arousal from, the use of enemas in sexual activity. See PARAPHILIA NOT OTHERWISE SPECIFIED.

Klonopin *n.* a trade name for CLONAZEPAM.

Klüver–Bucy syndrome a condition resulting from damage to both medial temporal lobes and marked by hypersexuality and a tendency to examine all objects by touch or by placing them in the mouth. Other symptoms may include visual agnosia (inability to visually recognize objects), decreased emotional responsivity (including loss of normal fear and anger responses), distractibility, and memory loss. The syndrome is observed in laboratory animals following temporal lobe ablation and, rarely, in humans following extensive bilateral temporal damage caused by HERPES-SIMPLEX ENCEPHALITIS or trauma. [Heinrich **Klüver** (1897–1975), German-born U.S. neurologist; Paul **Bucy** (1904–1992), U.S. neurosurgeon]

knee-jerk reflex a variant of the STRETCH REFLEX in which stretching or tapping the tendon beneath the knee causes an upward kick of the leg. The knee-jerk reflex is used in neurological examinations as a test of the integrity of the nervous system. Also called **patellar reflex**. See also PENDULAR KNEE JERK.

knockdown *n.* a laboratory animal in which specific genes are present but unexpressed, that is, their effects are not manifested.

knockout *n.* see GENE KNOCKOUT; KNOCKOUT ORGANISM.

knockout drops a popular name for a combination of CHLORAL HYDRATE (formerly in common use as a sedative but now rarely employed clinically) and alcohol, used surreptitiously to produce a sudden loss of consciousness. This combination was called **Mickey Finn** and might be considered an early example of a DATE-RAPE DRUG.

knockout organism an individual organism, or a line of organisms, in which a particular gene has been eliminated or inactivated (knocked out) by an experimenter (see GENE KNOCKOUT).

knowing *n.* see REMEMBER–KNOW PROCEDURE.

knowledge *n.* **1.** information and understanding of a specific topic or of the world in general, usually acquired by experience or by learning. **2.** an awareness of the existence of something.

knowledge base 1. an individual's general background knowledge, which influences his or her performance on most cognitive tasks. **2.** a repository of factual and heuristic information, usually in machine-processable form. **3.** the body of accumulated information (research, best practices, and so on) that guides an organization's approach to specific problems or challenges.

knowledge-based system (**KBS**) see EXPERT SYSTEM.

knowledge elicitation in ergonomics, a variety of methods used to educe the content and structure of users' knowledge or reasoning regarding a product or system. Methods used include CASE-BASED REASONING, CONVERSATION ANALYSIS, and TASK ANALYSIS. Knowledge elicitation should take account of EXPERT–NOVICE DIFFERENCES.

knowledge function of an attitude the role an attitude can play in helping to interpret ambiguous information or to organize information. For example, a positive attitude toward a friend may assist in attributing that person's negative behavior to situational factors rather than personal characteristics. See also EGO-DEFENSIVE FUNCTION OF AN ATTITUDE; FUNCTIONAL APPROACH TO ATTITUDES; SOCIAL-ADJUSTIVE FUNCTION OF AN ATTITUDE; UTILITARIAN FUNCTION OF AN ATTITUDE; VALUE-EXPRESSIVE FUNCTION OF AN ATTITUDE.

knowledge of performance (**KP**) verbalized (or verbalizable) information about the nature of the movement pattern that has been used to achieve a goal.

knowledge of results (**KR**; **KOR**) verbalized (or verbalizable) information about the outcome of a response in relation to the goal. Learning theory suggests that a learner profits most from immediate availability of this information (e.g., about the accuracy of responses on a test or quiz or the speed and accuracy of a movement or action sequence). Although knowledge of results is essential for guiding ACQUISITION, too much feedback can prevent the individual from forming an internal model of what is correct behavior.

knowledge representation the method used for encoding knowledge or semantic information in an artificial intelligence program. This is not (usually) the computer language employed but systematically developed structures encoded in that language. Examples of knowledge representation include the predicate calculus, CONCEPTUAL DEPENDENCIES, and FRAME.

knowledge, skills, abilities, and other characteristics (**KSAOs**) attributes of an employee or applicant for a position that are measured for such purposes as PERSONNEL SELECTION, personnel PLACEMENT, PERFORMANCE REVIEW, and PERSONNEL TRAINING. The KSAOs required of an employee performing a job should be identified on the basis of a thorough analysis of the tasks involved in the job. See JOB REQUIREMENTS; PERSONNEL SPECIFICATION. See also BONA FIDE OCCUPATIONAL QUALIFICATION.

know thyself see GNOTHI SE AUTON.

Kocher–Debré–Sémélaigne syndrome a disorder of infants and children marked by weakness and overgrowth of muscles associated with cretinism and mental retardation in some cases. Also called **Debré–Sémélaigne syndrome**. [reported in 1892 by Emil Theodor **Kocher** (1841–1917), Swiss surgeon, and in the 1930s by Robert **Debré** (1882–1978), French pediatrician, and Georges **Sémélaigne**, 20th-century French pediatrician]

Koffka, Kurt (1886–1941) German experimental psychologist. After obtaining his PhD at the University of Berlin in 1908 under Carl Stumpf (1848–1936), Koffka worked with Wolfgang KÖHLER and Max WERTHEIMER on studies that led to the founding of GESTALT PSYCHOLOGY. Following a number of research and teaching positions in Germany, in the mid-1920s Koffka took a series of teaching positions in the United States before settling into a research professorship at Smith College in Northampton, Massachusetts, in 1927. He spent the remainder of his career there, eventually becoming chief spokesperson for Gestalt psychology through articles and books that explained the theory and its applications. His most important writings include *Growth of the Mind* (1924) and *Principles of Gestalt Psychology* (1935). Koffka's research centered on visual perception, and his work contributed significantly to the understanding of visual phenomena, such as APPARENT MOVEMENT. More broadly, Gestalt psychology presented a holistic view of the mind that contrasted sharply with the reductionist view offered by BEHAVIORISM, another prominent and contemporaneous school of psychology. See also HOLISM; REDUCTIONISM.

Kohlberg, Lawrence (1927–1987) U.S. psychologist. Kohlberg earned his doctorate at the University of Chicago in 1958. He taught at Yale University and the University of Chicago before joining (in 1967) the faculty of Harvard University, where he remained throughout his career. His work was especially important to the fields of cognitive developmental psychology and education.

Kohlberg is best known for his studies of the development of moral reasoning in children, using LONGITUDINAL STUDIES and interviews in which he posed hypothetical moral dilemmas to children (see HEINZ DILEMMA). Influenced by both Jean PIAGET's theories of cognitive and moral development and *A Theory of Justice* (1971) by philosopher John Rawls (1921–), his research led to Kohlberg's theory of moral development. Like Piaget, Kohlberg believed that developmental stages are universal and their sequence is invariant, that is, children of all cultures develop moral reasoning in the same way. Among Kohlberg's most influential works are his *Essays on Moral Development* (1984) and, with Anne Colby (1946–), *The Measurement of Moral Judgment* (1987).

Kohlberg's theory of moral development the theory that the cognitive processes associated with moral judgment develop through a number of distinct stages. According to the theory, there are three main levels: the PRECONVENTIONAL LEVEL, the CONVENTIONAL LEVEL, and the POSTCONVENTIONAL LEVEL. Broadly speaking, the morally developed individual moves from a selfish concern with rewards and punishments, through a reliance on fixed rules and conventional attitudes, to a position of independent principled judgment. See also HEINZ DILEMMA. [Lawrence KOHLBERG]

Köhler, Wolfgang (1887–1967) German experimental psychologist. Köhler earned a doctorate at the University of Berlin in 1909, studying under the psychologist Carl Stumpf (1848–1936) and the physicist Max Planck (1858–1947). He subsequently joined Max WERTHEIMER and Kurt KOFFKA in developing GESTALT PSYCHOLOGY. In 1913 Köhler became director of the Anthropoid Station at Tenerife for 7 years. During this time he published his book *The Mentality of Apes* (1917), which included his famous studies of insight in nonhuman primates. He demonstrated persuasively that even chimpanzees can "get an idea" in order to solve a problem, such as piling up boxes or putting sticks together to retrieve a piece of fruit placed out of their reach (see INSIGHTFUL LEARNING). Köhler returned to Germany in 1920, ultimately becoming director of the Psychological Institute at Berlin, the most prestigious position for an experimental psychologist in Germany. When the Nazis came to power in the 1930s and began summarily dismissing Jewish and other professors from German universities, Köhler tried for 2 years to resist their policies within the institute but eventually gave up in frustration, moving to the United States. He became a professor at Swarthmore College in Pennsylvania for the remainder of his career. Apart from his book on apes, his most famous work includes *Gestalt Psychology* (1929) and *The Place of Value in the World of Facts* (1938). See also GOODNESS OF CONFIGURATION.

Köhler effect an increase in motivation that sometimes occurs among individuals working in groups on CONJUNCTIVE TASKS that require persistence but little coordination of effort. The effect is likely due to the increased effort expended by the less capable group members. Compare COMPENSATION EFFECT. [O. **Köhler**, early German researcher who confirmed the effect empirically]

Kohnstamm test a demonstration frequently used in preparing an individual for hypnosis. The participant is asked first to stand next to a wall and press an arm tightly against it for a minute or two, thus numbing it, and then to step away, whereupon the arm spontaneously rises (an occurrence known as **Kohnstamm's phenomenon**). This demonstrates to the participant how it feels to yield passively to an external force, as in hypnosis. [Oskar **Kohnstamm** (1871–1917), German physician]

Kohs Block Design Test a performance test of intelligence consisting of a set of 16 colored cubes that the participant must arrange into designs presented on 17 test cards. Although still available as a separate stand-alone instrument, the Kohs Block Design Test has been adapted for use as a component of various other assessment measures, most notably the intelligence scales devised by David WECHSLER. [developed in 1919 by Samuel C. **Kohs** (1890–1984), U.S. psychologist]

kola nut (**cola nut**) the seed of a tree, *Cola acuminata* or *Cola nitida*, that is native to tropical Africa and is cultivated in South America and the West Indies. The active ingredient is CAFFEINE, which comprises about 1.5% of the dry weight of the nut. Kola was discovered for the Western world in 1667 by a Congo missionary, Father Carli, who observed that local tribesmen chewed the nut before meals.

Kolmogorov–Smirnov test a nonparametric test of the distributional equivalence of two samples or of the fit of a sample to a theoretical distribution. [Andrei Nikolaevich **Kolmogorov** and Nikolai Vasilevich **Smirnov**, 20th-century Soviet mathematicians]

König bars a grating pattern of black and white bars used to assess visual acuity. [Karl Rudolf **König** (1832–1901), German-born French physicist]

Kopfermann cubes line drawings of cubes that are perceived as two-dimensional figures rather than as three-dimensional cubes. A hexagon equally divided into six triangles is one example. In this case gestalt principles of perception have been invoked to explain the compelling perception of two-dimensional triangles, rather than sides of a three-dimensional figure. [Hans **Kopfermann**, 20th-century German physicist and experimental psychologist]

kopro- *combining form* see COPRO-.

koprolagnia *n.* see COPROLAGNIA.

koprophemia *n.* see COPROPHEMIA.

KOR abbreviation for KNOWLEDGE OF RESULTS.

koro *n.* a CULTURE-BOUND SYNDROME observed primarily in males in China and southeast Asia. It is an acute anxiety reaction in which the male suddenly fears that his penis is shrinking and will disappear into his abdomen, bringing death. (In females, the fear is focused on the vulva and nipples.) Individuals may also experience shame if they associate the fear with immoral sexual behavior. Also called **jinjinia bemar**; **rok-joo**; **shook yong**; **shuk yang**; **suk-yeong**; **suo yang**.

Korsakoff's syndrome a syndrome occurring primarily in cases of severe, chronic alcoholism. It is caused by thiamine (vitamin B_1) deficiency and damage to the MAMMILLARY BODIES. Patients with Korsakoff's syndrome demonstrate dense ANTEROGRADE AMNESIA and RETROGRADE AMNESIA that are thought to be due to lesions in the anterior or DORSOMEDIAL NUCLEI (or both) of the thalamus. The selective and acute nature of the memory disorder in Korsakoff's syndrome sets it apart from alcoholic dementia (see ALCOHOL-INDUCED PERSISTING DEMENTIA), a syndrome characterized by more global impairments in intellectual functioning that evolve gradually over time. Korsakoff's syndrome often follows an episode of WERNICKE'S ENCEPHALOPATHY (see WERNICKE–KORSAKOFF SYNDROME). Also called **Korsakoff's disease**; **Korsakoff's psychosis**. [first described in 1887 by Sergei **Korsakoff** (1853–1900), Russian neurologist]

Korte's laws the laws describing the optimal conditions for the production of apparent motion that occurs when two or more stationary targets are presented in succession. The significant variables include the intensity of the stimuli, as well as their spatial separation, duration, and the interval between presentations. See also BETA MOVEMENT. [Adolf **Korte**, 20th-century German psychologist]

KP abbreviation for KNOWLEDGE OF PERFORMANCE.

KR abbreviation for KNOWLEDGE OF RESULTS.

K–R 20 abbreviation for KUDER–RICHARDSON FORMULA 20.

Kraepelin's disease a disorder that is characterized by depressive symptoms accompanied by psychotic features but does not meet the criteria for a MAJOR DEPRESSIVE EPISODE. [first described by Emil W. M. G. **Kraepelin** (1856–1926), German psychiatrist]

Kraepelin's theory the concept of DEMENTIA PRAECOX, the disorder now known as SCHIZOPHRENIA. Kraepelin's theory emphasized the progressive intellectual deterioration (dementia) and the early onset (praecox) of the disorder. [first presented in 1898 by Emil **Kraepelin**]

Krantz Health Opinion Survey (**KHOS**) a questionnaire to measure patient attitudes toward treatment and preferences for different approaches in health care. Participants indicate whether they agree or disagree with each of 16 statements (e.g., "I usually ask the doctor or nurse lots of questions about the procedures during a medical exam"), which are keyed so that high scores represent favorable attitudes toward self-directed care. Also called **Health Opinion Survey** (**HOS**). [developed in 1980 by David S. **Krantz** (1949–), U.S. medical psychologist, and colleagues at the Uniformed University of the Health Sciences, Bethesda]

Krause end bulb a specialized sensory nerve ending enclosed in a capsule in the skin. It is associated with temperature sensations. [Wilhelm **Krause** (1833–1910), German anatomist]

Kretschmer typology a controversial classification of individuals based on a "clear biological affinity" between specific physiques and specific personality tendencies. According to this classification, the short, stocky PYKNIC TYPE tends to be jovial and subject to mood swings; the frail ASTHENIC TYPE is likely to be introversive and sensitive; the muscular ATHLETIC TYPE is usually energetic and aggressive; and the disproportioned DYSPLASTIC TYPE presents a combination of traits but tends toward the asthenic. These tendencies were attributed to endocrine secretions. [formulated in the 1920s by German psychiatrist Ernst **Kretschmer** (1888–1964)]

Kruskal–Shepard scaling MULTIDIMENSIONAL SCALING applied to judgments of similarity or dissimilarity for pairs of items (e.g., cities). The dissimilarities are represented by distances between items in a high-dimensional space: Larger distances indicate greater dissimilarity. [William Henry **Kruskal** (1919–2005), U.S. statistician; Roger N. **Shepard** (1929–), U.S. experimental and cognitive psychologist]

Kruskal–Wallis test a *k*-group nonparametric method for determining statistical significance of the equality of centrality with ranked data. It is analogous to ONE-WAY ANALYSIS OF VARIANCE. [William **Kruskal** and Wilson Allen **Wallis** (1912–1998), U.S. statisticians]

KSADS abbreviation for Kiddie Schedule for Affective Disorders and Schizophrenia. See SCHEDULE FOR AFFECTIVE DISORDERS AND SCHIZOPHRENIA.

KSAOs abbreviation for KNOWLEDGE, SKILLS, ABILITIES, AND OTHER CHARACTERISTICS.

K-strategy *n.* a reproductive strategy that involves a high degree of PARENTAL INVESTMENT in a relatively small number of offspring over the individual's reproductive life, as in human beings and other primates. Populations of K-strategists expand to the maximum size that the habitat can support (its carrying capacity, or **K**). K-strategy implies that a constant, relatively small number of high-quality offspring is more likely to lead to REPRODUCTIVE SUCCESS than producing offspring at the maximum rate possible (see R-STRATEGY).

Kübler-Ross's stages of dying see STAGES OF DYING.

Kuder Preference Record a test used to assess participants' suitability for various fields of employment. Individuals are required to select their preferred activity from a series of three-choice items. The test yields percentile scores in ten vocational areas: clerical, computational, art, music, social service, outdoor, science, persuasive, literary, and mechanical. The **Kuder Occupational Interest Survey** is an updated version. [George Frederic **Kuder** (1903–2000), U.S. psychologist]

Kuder–Richardson formulas two psychometric methods, **Kuder–Richardson formula 20** (**K–R 20**) and **Kuder–Richardson formula 21** (**K–R 21**), for assessing the INTERNAL CONSISTENCY reliability of a test or subtest made up of binary items. [Frederic **Kuder** and Marion Webster **Richardson**, U.S. psychologists]

Kugelberg–Welander disease see SPINAL MUSCULAR ATROPHY. [Eric **Kugelberg** (1913–1983) and Lisa **Welander** (1909–), Swedish neurologists]

Kumho Tire Co. v. Patrick Carmichael a case resulting in a 1999 U.S. Supreme Court ruling that extended the GATEKEEPER ROLE of judges to cover both scientific expert testimony, as established in DAUBERT V. MERRELL DOW PHARMACEUTICALS INC., and nonscientific expert testimony.

Kundt's rules the principles that (a) distances divided by graduated lines appear larger than undivided distances and (b) when bisecting a horizontal line using one eye, the observer tends to place the midpoint too near the nasal side of the eye. [August **Kundt** (1839–1894), German physicist]

kurtosis *n.* the fourth CENTRAL MOMENT of a probability distribution.

kuru *n.* a progressive, ultimately fatal disease of the central nervous system that historically has affected the Fore people in the highlands of New Guinea. Symptoms include ataxia, tremors, difficulty in walking, and squint (strabismus). It is a PRION DISEASE, similar to CREUTZFELDT–JAKOB DISEASE, transmitted in cannibalistic rituals by eating the brains of individuals previously infected with the causative prion agent.

Kurzweil Personal Reader a computer system that reads print and outputs synthesized speech. It is intended for people who cannot read print (e.g., those with such disabilities as severe visual impairment and dyslexia). [Raymond **Kurzweil** (1948–), U.S. computer scientist and inventor]

kwashiorkor *n.* a form of malnutrition caused by inadequate intake of protein, usually observed in infants and small children who are deprived of essential amino acids during breast feeding (see PROTEIN DEFICIENCY). The symptoms include fluid accumulation in the tissues, liver disorders, impaired growth, distention of the abdomen, and pigment changes in the skin and hair. Normal cerebral development also may be impaired. The condition is usually found in developing countries. See also MARASMUS.

kymograph *n.* an instrument for recording temporal data in psychological or physiological research by tracing the variations of a particular parameter on a sheet of paper attached to a revolving drum. The resulting trace on the paper is a **kymogram**. Computer-output systems have largely replaced such instruments.

kyphosis *n.* an exaggerated curvature of the spine at the cervical (neck) level, producing a hunchback effect. The condition may result from trauma, developmental problems, or degenerative disease. See also LORDOSIS.

Ll

LAAM L-alpha-acetyl-methadol: a long-acting OPIOID AGONIST that is a chemical analog of METHADONE. A strong agonist at the mu OPIOID RECEPTOR, it is used in the management of opioid dependence. It has a longer HALF-LIFE (about 72 hours) than methadone and therefore needs to be taken only three times a week, which is a major advantage over methadone (which is taken daily). However, its possible adverse effects on heart rate and interactions with other drugs have limited its clinical use.

labeled lines nerve inputs to the brain conceptualized as each reporting only one particular type of information.

labeled-line theory of taste coding a theory postulating that each GUSTATORY NEURON TYPE comprises a private circuit through which is signaled the presence of its associated PRIMARY TASTE quality. The taste is perceived exclusively as a product of activity in that LABELED LINE; activity in neurons outside the labeled line contributes only NOISE. Compare PATTERNING THEORY OF TASTE CODING.

labeling *n.* in psychological assessment, classifying a patient according to a certain diagnostic category. Patient labeling may be incomplete or misleading, because not all cases conform to the sharply defined characteristics of the standard diagnostic categories.

labeling theory the sociological hypothesis that describing an individual in terms of particular behavioral characteristics may have a significant effect on his or her behavior, as a form of SELF-FULFILLING PROPHECY. For example, describing an individual as deviant and then treating him or her as such may result in mental disorder or delinquency. Also called **societal-reaction theory**. See also PRIMARY DEVIANCE.

la belle indifférence inappropriate lack of concern about the seriousness or implications of one's physical symptoms, seen in some people with CONVERSION DISORDER.

labia *pl. n.* (*sing.* **labium**) four folds of tissue forming part of the female external genitalia (see VULVA). The labia—comprising a larger, outer pair, the **labia majora** (*sing.* **labium majus**), and a thinner, inner pair, the **labia minora** (*sing.* **labium minus**)—enclose the clitoris and the openings of the urethra and vagina.

labial 1. *adj.* of or relating to the lips. **2.** *adj.* denoting a speech sound made with the lips, for example, [b], [p], [m], [w], [f], or [v]. If the sound is made with both lips, it is described as BILABIAL; if the sound is made with the lower lip and the upper teeth, it is termed LABIODENTAL. **3.** *n.* a labial speech sound.

labile *adj.* **1.** liable to change. **2.** lacking emotional stability. See AFFECTIVE LABILITY. **3.** describing the early stage of memory formation that can be easily disrupted by factors influencing brain activity. **—lability** *n.*

labile affect see AFFECTIVE LABILITY.

labio- *combining form* lips.

labiodental 1. *adj.* denoting a speech sound made with the lower lip touching or near the upper teeth, such as [f] or [v]. **2.** *n.* a labiodental speech sound. Also called **labial dental**. See LABIAL.

labor *n.* the first stage of childbirth, from the dilation of the cervix until the infant's head begins to emerge into the birth canal. See DELIVERY.

laboratory-method model an approach to education in which the role of social interaction is emphasized. The development of personal awareness and interpersonal skills is a major area of concern.

Labor Management Relations Act a series of amendments to the NATIONAL LABOR RELATIONS ACT that were passed in 1947 to adjust the power balance between unions and employers in the United States, the previous system being regarded as too restrictive of management. The act identified and prohibited certain UNFAIR LABOR PRACTICES of both unions and employers, created the Federal Mediation and Conciliation Service to aid in resolution of disputes, and provided a mechanism for dealing with strikes that create a national emergency. Sponsored by U.S. lawyer and politician Robert Alphonso Taft (1889–1953) and U.S. politician Fred Allan Hartley, Jr (1902–1969), it is also known as the **Taft–Hartley Act**.

labor relations 1. relations between employers and employees or between employers and unions, especially within the context of COLLECTIVE BARGAINING. **2.** a multidisciplinary field of study devoted to understanding and managing employee–employer or union–employer relations. Also called **industrial relations**.

labor turnover see TURNOVER.

labor union see UNION.

labyrinth *n.* in anatomy, the complex system of cavities, ducts, and canals within the temporal bone of the skull that comprises the inner ear. The **bony** (or **osseous**) **labyrinth** is a system of bony cavities that houses the **membranous labyrinth**, a membrane-lined system of ducts containing the receptors for hearing and balance. See also AUDITORY LABYRINTH.

labyrinthine sense see SENSE OF EQUILIBRIUM.

labyrinthitis *n.* infection or inflammation of the inner ear, which may result in dizziness, loss of balance, or partial or temporary loss of hearing.

lack of fit the degree to which the predicted values that are generated from a model diverge from the corresponding empirical values.

laconic speech see POVERTY OF SPEECH.

lacrimal gland (**lachrymal gland**) any of the glands that produce tears.

lacrimal reflex the secretion of tears in response to a variety of stimuli, including stimuli that irritate receptors in the nose.

lacrimation *n.* crying, especially excessive crying.

lactate dehydrogenase (**LDH**) any of a group of enzymes that catalyze reversibly the conversion of lactate to pyruvate. They are found especially in the liver, kidneys, skeletal muscles, and myocardium. Increased blood levels may indicate injury to or disease of these organs. Also called **lactic dehydrogenase**.

lacto- *combining form* milk.

lactogenic hormone see PROLACTIN.

lacuna *n.* (*pl.* **lacunae**) a gap or break, such as a gap in memory. **—lacunar** *adj.*

lacunar amnesia see LOCALIZED AMNESIA.

lacunar stroke a STROKE caused by small INFARCTIONS resulting from obstruction of small arterioles branching directly off large vessels in the brain. Lacunar strokes account for about 20% of all strokes.

LAD abbreviation for LANGUAGE ACQUISITION DEVICE.

Ladd-Franklin, Christine (1847–1930) U.S. psychologist and mathematician. Ladd completed the necessary work for a doctorate in mathematics and logic in 1882 at Johns Hopkins University, but was not awarded the doctorate because she was a woman. Her work in mathematics led to an article on a technical problem in BINOCULAR VISION in the first issue of the *American Journal of Psychology* (1887). Following postgraduate study in Germany in the early 1890s, Ladd-Franklin (now married) developed a theory of color vision (see LADD-FRANKLIN THEORY); after this she was regarded as an authority on vision and color theory. Her most important papers were published in the volume *Colour and Colour Theories* (1929). In part because she was a married woman, Ladd-Franklin never held a permanent academic position, although she taught courses periodically at both Johns Hopkins University and Columbia University, usually without pay. In 1926 Johns Hopkins University awarded her the doctorate she had earned 44 years earlier.

Ladd-Franklin theory a formerly influential but now superseded theory of color vision. It is based on the notion that light of certain wavelengths causes substances to be released from a highly developed photosensitive molecule in the retina and that these substances stimulate the retina, causing the perception of red, green, or blue. [introduced in 1929 by Christine LADD-FRANKLIN]

lag *n.* **1.** a delay between a stimulus and a response. **2.** a delay between the time a receptor is stimulated and the conscious awareness of the sensation.

lagophthalmos (**lagophthalmus**) *n.* a disorder marked by the inability to close the eyelids completely. The condition occurs in cases of leprosy.

laissez-faire group any group that exerts little or no control over members' activities, decisions, or interests.

laissez-faire leader the type of leader who provides little guidance for group activities, interacts only minimally with the group members, and provides input only when directly asked. Studies have found that groups with laissez-faire leaders show lower productivity, lower cohesiveness, and greater apathy than do groups with DEMOCRATIC LEADERS or with AUTHORITARIAN LEADERS. [defined by Kurt LEWIN and his colleagues in experimental studies of leadership styles]

laissez-faire parenting a parenting style in which parents intervene as little as possible in their children's development. Also called **permissive parenting**.

-lalia *suffix* abnormal or disordered speech (e.g., ECHOLALIA).

lalling *n.* an infantile form of speech characterized by the omission or substitution of sounds, particularly the substitution of the [l] sound for other sounds that are more difficult for the speaker to produce, for example, saying "lellow" for *yellow*. Lalling is considered a speech disorder when it persists beyond the age at which accurate articulation should have been acquired. See also PHONOLOGICAL DISORDER.

lalopathy *n.* any form of speech disorder.

Lamarckism *n.* the theory that changes acquired by an organism during its lifetime, for example, through use or disuse of particular parts, can be inherited by its offspring. Experiments have always failed to find evidence for such **inheritance of acquired characteristics**. Also called **use-and-disuse theory**. [Jean-Baptiste **Lamarck** (1744–1829), French natural historian] **—Lamarckian** *adj.*

Lamaze method a variation of the method of NATURAL CHILDBIRTH in which the mother learns about childbirth anatomy and physiology and practices pain management through relaxation, massage, and breathing exercises. The mother is aware and active during labor, guided by her partner, who shares in the birth experience (e.g., as a supportive coach). The method neither encourages nor discourages the use of medication during labor and delivery. See also LEBOYER TECHNIQUE. [Ferdinand **Lamaze** (1890–1957), French obstetrician]

lambda coefficient (symbol: λ) a less common name for CONTRAST WEIGHT.

lambda model (**λ model**) see EQUILIBRIUM-POINT MODEL.

Lambert's law the principle that the ILLUMINANCE of a surface lit by light falling on it perpendicularly from a point source is inversely proportional to the square of the distance between the surface and the source. [Johann Heinrich **Lambert** (1728–1777), French-born Prussian mathematician]

lamellipodium *n.* (*pl.* **lamellipodia**) a sheetlike extension of a cell, for example, of the GROWTH CONE of a neuron.

laminar organization the horizontal layering of cells found in some brain regions. See CORTICAL LAYERS.

lamotrigine *n.* an ANTICONVULSANT drug used as an adjunct in the treatment of adults with partial seizures and some generalized seizures and for maintenance treatment of bipolar disorder. Although ineffective in treating acute manic episodes, it has gained acceptance as a single-drug treatment for acute bipolar depression and rapid-cycling bipolar II disorder. Lamotrigine is presumed to exert its anticonvulsant and mood-stabilizing effects by inhibiting the release of GLUTAMATE from presynaptic neurons. Serious skin reactions, including STEVENS–JOHNSON SYNDROME, have been reported at the start of therapy, particularly in children. U.S. trade name: **Lamictal**.

LAMP abbreviation for LEARNING ABILITIES MEASUREMENT PROGRAM.

Landau–Kleffner syndrome a rare, childhood neurological disorder, of unknown cause, that is characterized by the sudden or gradual development of aphasia (inability to understand or express language) and an abnormal electroencephalogram (see ELECTROENCEPHALOGRAPHY). The syndrome usually occurs in children between the ages of 5 and 7 years, who develop normally but then lose their language skills for no apparent reason. Many children with the disorder experience seizures, which generally disappear by adulthood. [first described in 1957 by William M. **Landau** and Frank R. **Kleffner**]

Landau reflex a normal reaction observed in infants between the ages of 3 and 12 months: When the child is supported horizontally in the prone position, the head rises and the back arches. Absence of the reflex is a sign of a neurological disorder, such as cerebral palsy or motor neuron disease.

Land effect a demonstration used to develop the LAND THEORY OF COLOR VISION. To produce the effect, a multicolored scene is photographed with black and white film, once through a red filter and once through a blue–

green filter. When the resulting images are projected simultaneously onto a screen through the opposite filter used to photograph the image, the original multicolored scene is perceived. [Edwin Herbert **Land** (1909–1991), U.S. inventor]

landmark *n.* an external reference point that is a major component of a COGNITIVE MAP. The design and placement of landmarks can significantly affect way-finding behavior. See ENVIRONMENTAL COGNITION; LEGIBILITY.

Landmark Forum see ERHARD SEMINAR TRAINING.

Landolt circles a set of circles with gaps of varying size, used to test visual acuity. Also called **Landolt C's**. [Edmund **Landolt** (1846–1926), French ophthalmologist]

landscaped office a modification of the OPEN-OFFICE DESIGN in which emphasis is given to the interaction of people, such that the arrangement of work spaces is based on patterns of communication and facilitation of work flow. Landscaped offices typically place supervisors near workers and group people who communicate regularly with one another to perform their job duties in the same or adjacent spaces. Portable screens or partitions and other movable items, such as planters or cabinets, are used to separate areas and divide them into a variety of different yet easily accessible work spaces.

Land theory of color vision a theory based on the idea that color registration is carried out in the brain. Demonstrations, such as the LAND EFFECT, suggest that various wavelengths register on the color-sensitive components of the retina as a large number of color-separated "photos" (see RETINEX). The visual mechanism in the brain then acts as a computer, averaging together and comparing long-wave photos with the average of the shorter-wave photos; it then assigns different colors to them according to the ratios between them. Also called **retinex theory**. [Edwin Herbert **Land** (1909–1991), U.S. inventor]

Langdon Down's disease see DOWN SYNDROME.

Langerhans cells dendritic cells found in the epidermis. [Paul **Langerhans** (1847–1888), German anatomist]

language *n.* **1.** a system for expressing or communicating thoughts and feelings through speech sounds or written symbols. See NATURAL LANGUAGE. **2.** the communicative system used by a particular SPEECH COMMUNITY, with its distinctive vocabulary, grammar, and phonological system. **3.** any comparable nonverbal means of communication, such as SIGN LANGUAGE or the languages used in computer programming (see ARTIFICIAL LANGUAGE).

language acquisition the process by which children learn language. Although often used interchangeably with LANGUAGE DEVELOPMENT, this term is preferred by those who emphasize the active role of the child as a learner with considerable innate linguistic knowledge.

language acquisition device (**LAD**) a hypothetical faculty used to explain a child's ability to acquire language. In the early model proposed by U.S. linguist Benjamin Lee Whorf (1897–1941), the LAD is an inherited mechanism that enables children to develop a language structure from linguistic data supplied by parents and others. In Noam CHOMSKY's reinterpretation, however, the LAD contains significant innate knowledge that actively interprets the input: Only this can explain how a highly abstract COMPETENCE in language results from a relatively deprived input. See NATIVISTIC THEORY.

language acquisition support system (**LASS**) the processes whereby adults and older children help a young child to acquire language. It is suggested that adults and older children have learning devices that interact with the LANGUAGE ACQUISITION DEVICE of the younger child. [proposed by U.S. developmental psychologist Jerome Seymour Bruner (1915–)]

language arts the part of the school curriculum that incorporates the language skills of listening, speaking, reading, writing, spelling, and handwriting.

language center any area of the cerebral cortex, such as BROCA'S AREA or WERNICKE'S AREA, that is involved in spoken or written language.

language contact the sociolinguistic situation in which two or more language communities come into contact for reasons of commerce or politics, leading to mutual influence in lexical or structural features. See also CONTACT LANGUAGE.

language death the extinction of a language. The usual cause is a gradual shift to the use of another language in the younger generations of a SPEECH COMMUNITY, so that the original language dies out with the older generation. In the early 21st century it has been estimated that languages are dying out at a rate of two or three every month. See LANGUAGE SHIFT.

language deficit an absence, loss, or delay in the normal speech and language development of a child due to some neurological dysfunction.

language development the process by which children learn to use language. Although this term is often used interchangeably with LANGUAGE ACQUISITION, it is preferred by those who wish to emphasize the continuity of language development with cognitive and social development.

language disability any significant difficulty with or impairment of language development or function. See also GENERAL LANGUAGE DISABILITY.

language disorder any developmental disorder involving disabilities of reception, integration, recall, or production of spoken language, written language, or both. See also COMMUNICATION DISORDER.

language ESP in experiments testing EXTRASENSORY PERCEPTION (ESP), the ostensible phenomenon in which participants make an above-chance number of correct "calls" or guesses about TARGETS presented in an unknown foreign language. See also XENOGLOSSY.

language-experience approach to reading a method of teaching reading and other language skills based on children's experiences, using materials that may be suggested by the child to the teacher.

language localization the processing of various functions of spoken and written words in particular areas of the brain. Since 1861, when French physician Paul Broca (1824–1880) postulated that speech processing was localized near the third frontal convolution of the left hemisphere, research has identified numerous other cortical centers associated with visual and auditory language processing, as well as neural pathways linking these areas. See BROCA'S AREA; WERNICKE'S AREA.

language loyalty a strong preference for using a minority language demonstrated by a SPEECH COMMUNITY or any of its members.

language maintenance the continued use of the ethnic language by an immigrant or minority community across successive generations.

language-origin theory speculation about the origin and early development of language in the human species. The numerous early theories on this subject tend to fall into three main categories: (a) those that see language developing from conscious imitation by early humans of animal noises and other natural sounds; (b) those that see it emerging from the involuntary sounds produced by rage, pleasure, hunger, and so on; and (c) NATIVISTIC THEORIES that see the language faculty as innate to human beings and postulate an inherent relation between sound and meaning (see PHONETIC SYMBOLISM). Modern research tends to ask whether language is, in fact, a uniquely human capacity and if so, whether it evolved in response to various selective adaptations. See also SPECIES SPECIFICITY OF LANGUAGE.

language pathology see SPEECH AND LANGUAGE PATHOLOGY.

language planning a deliberate attempt by a government to change the way a language is used by a community. A policy of raising the status of a language (**status planning**) is often adopted in postcolonial situations, when the new government may take steps to promote the use of indigenous languages, rather than the colonial language, in government and education. This may be accompanied by **corpus planning**, which refers to attempts to "improve" a language, usually by standardizing its structures, expanding or "purifying" its vocabulary, and reforming (or, in some cases, creating) its writing system.

language retardation developmental lag in brain maturation resulting in delayed language skills, manifested by lisping, lalling, baby talk, congenital inability to recognize sounds (auditory agnosia), and word deafness. It does not apply to cases of language difficulty associated with mental retardation, impaired hearing, or structural abnormalities in the speech organs.

language shift a movement in the language preference of an immigrant or minority community from its ethnic language to the majority language, eventually resulting in monolingualism in the majority language. See LANGUAGE DEATH.

language socialization the process by which children are socialized into the language practices, such as particular DISCOURSE ROUTINES, of the family and community.

language transfer in second-language acquisition, the tendency to transfer the phonology, syntax, and semantics of the native language into the learning of the second language. **Negative transfer** (or **interference**) occurs when differences between the two languages' structures lead to systematic errors in the learning of the second language or to FOSSILIZATION. **Positive transfer** occurs when areas of similarity between the two languages facilitate learning. See CONTRASTIVE ANALYSIS; INTERLANGUAGE.

language universal **1.** a linguistic feature that is common to all known human languages, such as words, sentences, or (more specifically) a set of pronouns or a set of color words. Such **substantive universals** can be formulated on the basis of observations across multiple languages, yielding an empirically testable hypothesis that "all languages have X." **2.** in the linguistics of Noam CHOMSKY, a fundamental formal property that is built into the rule-structure of all or nearly all language systems. An example is the rule observed by U.S. linguist Joseph H. Greenberg (1915–2001) that "In declarative sentences with nominal subject and object, the predominant order is almost always one in which the subject precedes the object." Unlike substantive universals, these **formal universals** cannot be explained by universal features of human life or the physical environment. In Chomsky's view, they constitute a UNIVERSAL GRAMMAR that is innate to human beings and inseparable from the language faculty itself. Also called **linguistic universal**; **universal**.

languishing *n.* the condition of absence of mental health, characterized by ennui, apathy, listlessness, and loss of interest in life. Compare FLOURISHING. **—languish** *vb.*

Lansing (II) virus see LEON (III) VIRUS.

Lanterman Developmental Disabilities Act Californian legislation, introduced in 1969, that sets forth the rights and responsibilities of people with developmental disabilities and the structure of the system for planning, coordinating, and delivering services and supports to them. This act is noteworthy because, unlike similar statutes in most U.S. states, it has been interpreted judicially as establishing an entitlement to services. In a 1993 class action decision, reduction in the use of institutional settings and movement of institutional residents to community settings was ordered, as were specific changes to processes for individual planning of services and supports.

lapsus linguae see SLIP OF THE TONGUE.

Lariam *n.* a trade name for MEFLOQUINE.

Larodopa *n.* a trade name for LEVODOPA.

laryngeal cancer a malignant growth of the upper respiratory tract that affects mainly men over the age of 40 and accounts for about 4,200 deaths each year in the United States. The risk of laryngeal cancer increases with cigarette smoking, drinking alcoholic beverages, and living in urban areas; the incidence among cigarette smokers is approximately seven times that of the general population. Early symptoms include hoarseness or a feeling of soreness or a "lump" in the throat. As the cancer progresses, it interferes with breathing and swallowing. Treatment usually includes surgery or radiation, or both, the appropriate procedure depending upon the cancer site and the extent of its growth. If it is possible to correct the problem by excising only one vocal cord, the patient is trained to speak with the remaining vocal cord. If it is necessary to remove the entire larynx, the patient is trained to speak with the aid of an electronic device or by a technique of swallowing air into the esophagus and forcing it out again while the lips and teeth are manipulated to form speech sounds. However, the vocabulary of words that can be produced in this manner is limited. See LARYNGECTOMY.

laryngeal framework surgery see THYROPLASTY.

laryngeal neoplasm a cancerous or noncancerous growth or tumor on the larynx or any of its parts, which may affect breathing, swallowing, or speech. See LARYNGEAL CANCER. See also PHONOSURGERY.

laryngeal paralysis loss of use or feeling of one or both of the vocal cords caused by disease or injury to the nerves of the larynx.

laryngeal reflex the reaction to laryngeal irritation manifested by coughing.

laryngectomy *n.* the surgical removal of all or a part of the larynx, commonly because of LARYNGEAL CANCER.

laryngopharynx *n.* the portion of the PHARYNX that lies below the hyoid bone (a small, U-shaped bone below and supporting the tongue). **—laryngopharyngeal** *adj.*

larynx *n.* (*pl.* **larynges**) the muscular and cartilaginous structure at the top of the trachea (windpipe) and below the tongue that contains the VOCAL CORDS. Movements of the cartilages in the walls of the larynx, controlled by the laryngeal muscles, alter the tension of the vocal cords and change the frequency of the sound (thus, the pitch) emitted by the cords when they vibrate. **—laryngeal** *adj.*

Lashley, Karl Spencer (1890–1958) U.S. psychologist.

Lashley earned his PhD in zoology and genetics at Johns Hopkins University in 1914. His dominant influences were the zoologist Herbert S. Jennings (1868–1947), behaviorist John B. WATSON, and neuropsychologist Shepherd I. Franz (1874–1933). Lashley taught at a number of universities before joining the faculty of Harvard University, where he taught from 1935 until his retirement in 1955. From 1942 until 1955 he also served as director of the Yerkes Laboratories of Primate Biology in Florida. Lashley was most influential in the fields of animal learning, comparative psychology, and neurophysiology. Perhaps most famous is the work summarized in his classic *Brain Mechanisms and Intelligence* (1929). In it, he showed that if portions of a rat's brain were damaged (through lesions or partial ablations), any disruption in learning or ability was only temporary; in time the brain could recover its functions unless very large portions were damaged. In essence, healthy portions of the brain could adapt and take over the work of damaged portions. Lashley used his research to counter cerebral localization theory, which asserted that when specific portions of the brain were damaged, the disrupted functions were gone for good because brain function was extremely localized. Lashley's honors included election to the National Academy of Sciences and the American Academy of Arts and Sciences. See also LAW OF EQUIPOTENTIALITY; LAW OF MASS ACTION.

LASS acronym for LANGUAGE ACQUISITION SUPPORT SYSTEM.

Lasthenie de Ferjol syndrome a type of PATHOMIMICRY consisting of life-threatening hemorrhages caused by secretly self-inflicted wounds. It is linked with the pathology of mourning and introjection: Patients with this disorder have all experienced traumatic losses. The syndrome takes its name from a short story by French writer Jules Barbey D'Aurevilly (1808–1889).

latah (**lattah**) *n.* a CULTURE-BOUND SYNDROME first observed in Malaysia and Indonesia, although similar syndromes have been found in many other parts of the world. The condition primarily affects middle-aged women and is characterized by an exaggerated startle reaction. Its major symptoms, besides fearfulness, are imitative behavior in speech (see ECHOLALIA) and body movements (see ECHOPRAXIA), a compulsion to utter profanities and obscenities (see COPROLALIA), command obedience, and disorganization. See also IMU; JUMPING FRENCHMEN OF MAINE SYNDROME; MYRIACHIT.

latchkey children children who return after school to a home that is without adult supervision because their parents or caregivers work. The name alludes to the idea that the children have their own key with which to let themselves into the empty home after school. Also called **self-care children**.

late bilingualism see EARLY BILINGUALISM.

late luteal phase dysphoric disorder see PREMENSTRUAL DYSPHORIC DISORDER.

latency of response the time that elapses between the onset of a stimulus and the onset of a response, which may be used as an indicator of the strength of CONDITIONING. Also called **latency of reply**; **response latency**. See REACTION TIME.

latency stage in psychoanalytic theory, the stage of PSYCHOSEXUAL DEVELOPMENT in which overt sexual interest is sublimated and the child's attention focused on skills and peer activities with members of his or her own sex. This stage is posited to last from about the resolution of the OEDIPUS COMPLEX, at about age 6, to the onset of puberty during the 11th or 12th year. Also called **latency**; **latency period**; **latency phase**; **latent stage**.

latent addition period a brief time span when a second stimulus can add to the persisting effects of a preceding stimulus. The period varies with the size of the nerve and synaptic factors but lasts approximately 0.5 ms.

latent content 1. the hidden or disguised meanings, wishes, and ideas beneath the MANIFEST CONTENT of any utterance or other form of communication. **2.** in psychoanalytic theory, the unconscious wishes seeking expression in dreams or fantasies. This unconscious material is posited to encounter censorship (see CENSOR) and to be distorted by the DREAM-WORK into symbolic representations in order to protect the EGO. Through DREAM ANALYSIS, the latent content may be uncovered. See also DREAM CENSORSHIP.

latent goal an objective of a program or organization that is not publicly stated or that is unacceptable for public statement, although it may be known to the staff. The term is also applied to functions that result from the attempt to obtain MANIFEST GOALS but are not apparent or planned in advance.

latent homosexuality gay or lesbian tendencies that have never been expressed overtly and are usually unrecognized (i.e., repressed) and actively denied by the individual. Also called **unconscious homosexuality**.

latent inhibition retardation of PAVLOVIAN CONDITIONING as a result of prior exposures to the CONDITIONED STIMULUS before it is paired with an UNCONDITIONED STIMULUS. Also called **conditioned stimulus preexposure effect**.

latent learning learning that is acquired without conscious effort, awareness, intention, or reinforcement and is not manifested as a change in performance until a specific need for it arises. For example, a student writing an exam may be able to accurately cite a quotation encountered earlier without having made an effort previously to learn it. Among animals, a rat allowed to explore a maze without reward will later learn to find the goal more rapidly than a rat without prior exposure to the maze. See also INCIDENTAL LEARNING. [first described by Edward C. TOLMAN]

latent need a need that is assumed to be present in a person and determines behavior but is not in that person's conscious awareness.

latent stage see LATENCY STAGE.

latent trait theory a general psychometric theory contending that observed traits, such as intelligence, are reflections of more basic unobservable traits (i.e., latent traits). Several quantitative models (e.g., ITEM RESPONSE THEORY and FACTOR ANALYSIS) have been developed to allow for the identification and estimation of these latent traits from manifest observations.

latent variable a hypothetical, unobservable characteristic that is thought to underlie the observed, manifest attributes that are directly measurable. The values of latent variables are inferred from patterns of interrelationships among the MANIFEST VARIABLES. See also FACTOR ANALYSIS.

late-onset schizophrenia a psychotic state that starts after middle age (typically after age 45). It is believed that late-onset schizophrenia is distinct from early-onset schizophrenia.

late paraphrenia any delusional disorder with onset after age 60. Late paraphrenia is used as a diagnostic entity in Europe and Britain, but is not listed in the *DSM–IV–TR*. Also called **late-onset paraphrenia**.

lateral *adj.* toward the side of the body or of an organ. Compare MEDIAL. **—laterally** *adv.*

lateral bundle a bundle of nerve fibers in the dorsolateral spinal cord that carry impulses from pain- and temperature-sensory end organs.

lateral cervical nucleus a part of the LEMNISCAL SYSTEM, appearing as a small mass of gray matter beneath the MEDULLA OBLONGATA. Axons from the lateral cervical nucleus project to the MEDIAL LEMNISCI.

lateral confusion see MIXED LATERALITY.

lateral corticospinal tract the larger of the two subdivisions of the CORTICOSPINAL TRACT, the other being the anterior corticospinal tract. It originates on either side of the brain, in MOTOR AREAS of the cerebral cortex, and its fibers cross the midline at the PYRAMID of the medulla oblongata to descend laterally in the white matter on the contralateral sides of the spinal cord. The tract has an important influence on spinal motor neurons, especially those controlling fine movements of distal muscles.

lateral difference the difference between the two cerebral hemispheres in controlling various behaviors or serving cognitive functions.

lateral dominance see HEMISPHERIC LATERALIZATION.

lateral fissure see LATERAL SULCUS.

lateral geniculate nucleus (**LGN**) either of a pair of NUCLEI that protrude slightly from each side of the thalamus to the rear. Each LGN receives fibers originating from cone-rich areas of the retina and relays information to the VISUAL CORTEX via OPTIC RADIATIONS. Also called **lateral geniculate body**. See MAGNOCELLULAR SYSTEM; PARVOCELLULAR SYSTEM. See also MEDIAL GENICULATE NUCLEUS.

lateral gyrus a convolution in the surface of the brain located in the area of the CINGULATE GYRUS above the CORPUS CALLOSUM.

lateral hypothalamic syndrome a four-stage pattern of recovery from lesions of the LATERAL HYPOTHALAMUS induced in nonhuman animals. The first stage is marked by inability to eat and drink (aphagia and adipsia), and without assistance (including forced feeding) the animal is likely to die. The second stage includes a period of continued inability to drink and poor appetite for food (adipsia-anorexia), when only wet, palatable foods are accepted. In the third stage the animal will eat hydrated, dry food but continues to avoid water intake and may suffer dehydration. Recovery is the fourth stage, in which new, altered feeding and drinking habits are established and the animal maintains a stable, albeit lower, body weight. Compare VENTROMEDIAL HYPOTHALAMIC SYNDROME.

lateral hypothalamus (**LH**) the region of the HYPOTHALAMUS that may be involved in the regulation of eating. Lesions of the lateral hypothalamus in animals result in fasting and weight loss. Stimulation of that part of the brain increases food intake.

lateral inhibition in perception, a mechanism for detecting contrast in which a sensory neuron is excited by one particular receptor but inhibited by neighboring (lateral) receptors. In vision, for example, lateral inhibition is seen in neurons that respond to light at one position but are inhibited by light at surrounding positions.

laterality *n.* the preferential use of one side of the body for certain functions, such as eating, writing, and kicking. See also HANDEDNESS; MIXED LATERALITY.

lateralization *n.* **1.** the relationship between HANDEDNESS, EYE DOMINANCE, FOOTEDNESS, and HEMISPHERIC LATERALIZATION. Observed more frequently in humans than in other primates, lateralization is manifested in the way tasks are performed and can also be extrapolated from the effects of localized brain damage. DIRECTIONAL CONFUSION and DYSLEXIA are among disorders diagnosed through lateralization tests. See also SPEECH LATERALIZATION. **2.** in audition, see AUDITORY LOCALIZATION.

lateralized readiness potential an EVENT-RELATED POTENTIAL that is a measure of the difference in activation between the left and right motor areas of the brain. This potential is taken to indicate preparation to respond with one hand or the other, since each hand is controlled by the contralateral hemisphere.

lateral lemniscus a bundle of nerve fibers running from auditory nuclei in the brainstem upward through the PONS and terminating in the INFERIOR COLLICULUS and MEDIAL GENICULATE NUCLEUS. See also LEMNISCAL SYSTEM.

lateral-line system a sensory system, found in many kinds of fish and some amphibians, that informs the animal of water motion in relation to the body surface.

lateral lisp see LISP.

lateral olfactory tract a bundle of axons of MITRAL CELLS that forms the primary communication between the olfactory system and portions of the brain. See also OLFACTORY TRACT; TUFTED CELL.

lateral posterior nucleus a group of visually responsive neurons in the THALAMUS that are used for brightness discrimination. They project to several areas in the occipital and parietal lobes.

lateral rectus an extrinsic EYE MUSCLE that rotates the eyeball laterally (i.e., outward, away from the midline). Also called **external rectus**.

lateral specialization the development of specialized capabilities in either the right or the left cerebral hemisphere. Examples include the tendency for speech, writing, calculation, and language to be controlled more by the left hemisphere, and nonverbal ideation and spatial construction to be controlled more by the right hemisphere.

lateral spinothalamic tract see SPINOTHALAMIC TRACTS.

lateral sulcus a prominent groove that runs along the lateral surface of each CEREBRAL HEMISPHERE, separating the TEMPORAL LOBE from the FRONTAL LOBE and PARIETAL LOBE. Also called **fissure of Sylvius**; **lateral fissure**; **Sylvian fissure**.

lateral thalamic nucleus either of a pair of large masses of cell bodies, one on each side of the THALAMUS, that relay incoming sensory impulses. The lateral nuclei are the most recently evolved parts of the thalamus.

lateral thinking creative thinking that deliberately attempts to reexamine basic assumptions, to change perspective or direction, or to provide a fresh approach to solving a problem. See also DIVERGENT THINKING. [defined by British psychologist Edward de Bono (1933–)]

lateral ventricle a chamber of complex shape that lies within each cerebral hemisphere in the brain and serves as a reservoir of cerebrospinal fluid (see VENTRICLE). Each lateral ventricle communicates with the THIRD VENTRICLE at a point near the thalamus.

later life adjustment adaptation to stress caused by events associated with life as an older adult, including chronic disease, familial loss, and lifestyle changes.

lateropulsion *n.* a symptom of certain disorders of the central nervous system (e.g., parkinsonism) in which the individual makes involuntary sidewise movements.

lateroventral nucleus one of a group of relay nuclei

in the THALAMUS that transmit impulses from the cerebellum to the MOTOR CORTEX for coordination of muscular movements. Also called **ventral lateral nucleus**.

late-selection theory any theory of attention proposing that selection occurs after stimulus identification. According to late-selection theory, within sensory limits, all stimuli—both attended and unattended—are processed to the same deep level of analysis until stimulus identification occurs; subsequently, only the most important stimuli are selected for further processing. Compare EARLY-SELECTION THEORY.

Latin square an experimental design in which treatments, denoted by Latin letters, are administered in sequences that are systematically varied such that each treatment occurs equally often in each position of the sequence (e.g., first, second, third, etc.). For example, one group might receive treatments A, then B, and then C, while a second group receives them in sequence B, C, A, and a third group in sequence C, A, B. See also BALANCED LATIN SQUARE.

latitude of acceptance a range of attitudinal positions that includes a person's preferred position and the range of positions that he or she considers acceptable. It was first proposed as a part of SOCIAL JUDGMENT THEORY. See also LATITUDE OF NONCOMMITMENT; LATITUDE OF REJECTION.

latitude of noncommitment a range of attitudinal positions that a person considers to be neither acceptable nor objectionable. It was first proposed as part of SOCIAL JUDGMENT THEORY. See also LATITUDE OF ACCEPTANCE; LATITUDE OF REJECTION.

latitude of rejection a range of attitudinal positions that a person rejects. It was first proposed as part of SOCIAL JUDGMENT THEORY. See also LATITUDE OF ACCEPTANCE; LATITUDE OF NONCOMMITMENT.

lattah *n.* see LATAH.

laudanum *n.* a mixture of alcohol and opium once commonly used as an analgesic and anesthetic. The mixture was introduced around 1530 by German alchemist and physician Paracelsus (1493–1541) and was widely consumed as an intoxicating beverage in 18th-century England.

laughing gas see NITROUS OXIDE.

laughter *n.* vocal expression of the emotions of amusement, enjoyment, or derision, characterized by inspiratory and expiratory movements occurring in rapid succession. Laughter is pleasurable because it serves to release tension built up when people listen to an amusing story or watch an amusing event (see RELEASE THEORY OF HUMOR). Laughter may also result when states of threat occur in a safe context (see AROUSAL JAG) or from an abrupt resolution of a cognitive incongruity. In psychoanalytic theory, laughter may be viewed as a defense against crying or embarrassment. Unrestrained or paroxysmal **laughing spells** have been found to precipitate cataplectic attacks, to be a common manifestation in manias, and to be an occasional symptom of psychomotor seizure among children, termed gelastic epilepsy. Spasmodic laughter, or GELASMUS, is also found in schizophrenia, hysteria, and organic (especially bulbar and pseudobulbar) diseases of the brain, as well as in CHOREOMANIA. See also HUMOR. **—laugh** *vb.*

Launois–le Cleret syndrome see FRÖHLICH'S SYNDROME.

Laurence–Moon–Biedl syndrome an autosomal recessive disorder that may be characterized by some degree of obesity, extra fingers or toes, below average intelligence, and ocular abnormalities, particularly of the retina. A common finding is progressive cone and rod degeneration and night blindness. Hypogonadism (small testicles) and hearing difficulty are often associated with the disorder. More than 75% of affected individuals tested have mental retardation. Also called **Laurence–Moon–Biedl–Bardet syndrome**; **retinodiencephalic degeneration**. [John Zachariah **Laurence** (1830–1874), British ophthalmologist; Robert C. **Moon** (1844–1914), U.S. ophthalmologist; Artur **Biedl** (1869–1933), Austrian physician]

law *n.* **1.** a formal statement describing a regularity (e.g., of nature) to which no exceptions are known or anticipated. See CAUSAL LAW; NATURAL LAW. **2.** in science, mathematics, philosophy, and the social sciences, a theory that is widely accepted as correct and that has no significant rivals in accounting for the facts within its domain. **3.** a formally established rule regulating the conduct of people within a particular jurisdiction that must be obeyed in order to avoid legal sanctions.

law-and-order orientation in KOHLBERG'S THEORY OF MORAL DEVELOPMENT, the second of two stages in the CONVENTIONAL LEVEL, in which people make moral decisions based on maintaining the laws of society. Also called **social-order-maintaining morality**. Compare INTERPERSONAL CONCORDANCE.

law of advantage the principle that one of two or more incompatible or inconsistent responses has the advantage of being more beneficial or attractive and therefore occurs more frequently than the others.

law of assimilation 1. the principle that organisms respond to new situations in a manner similar to their reactions to familiar situations. See GENERALIZATION. **2.** see ASSIMILATION.

law of closure see CLOSURE.

law of combination the principle that stimuli occurring simultaneously or stimuli in close proximity may produce a combined response, or that two responses will occur together when a stimulus eliciting either of them is presented.

law of common fate see COMMON FATE.

law of constancy 1. the principle that visual stimuli retain a constant appearance despite alterations in stimulus conditions, such as the level of illumination (BRIGHTNESS CONSTANCY) or the angle subtended on the retina (SIZE CONSTANCY). **2.** in psychoanalytic theory, see PRINCIPLE OF CONSTANCY.

law of contiguity the principle that learning depends on the proximity of items (e.g., stimuli, responses, or ideas) in space or time. Contiguity is a principle of ASSOCIATIONISM. See also CONTIGUITY OF ASSOCIATIONS.

law of continuity a principle of perception identified in 1923 by German psychologist Max WERTHEIMER and associated with GESTALT PSYCHOLOGY. It states that when lines meet in a figure, the preferred interpretation is of two continuous lines. For example, a cross is interpreted as a vertical line and a horizontal line, rather than two right angles meeting at their vertices. Also called **principle of continuity**. See GESTALT PRINCIPLES OF ORGANIZATION.

law of contrast a principle of association stating that thinking about any thing or quality tends to remind one of its opposite. In later associationist doctrine, this principle was considered a special case of the LAW OF CONTIGUITY. Also called **principle of contrast**. See ASSOCIATIONISM; CONTRAST.

law of effect broadly, the principle that consequences of behavior act to modify the future probability of occurrence of that behavior. As originally postulated by Edward L. THORNDIKE, the law of effect stated that responses followed by a satisfying state of affairs are strengthened and responses followed by an unpleasant or annoying state of affairs are weakened. These ideas have been translated into contemporary notions of reward and punishment. Thorndike later revised the law to include only the response-strengthening effect of reinforcement; the original version of the law was called the **strong law of effect**, and the revised version was known as the **weak law of effect**.

law of equality a gestalt principle that parts of a figure perceived as equal tend to form a whole.

law of equipotentiality the principle that intact areas of ASSOCIATION CORTEX can take over some functions of areas that have been destroyed, that is, different areas can function virtually equivalently. Based on behavioral studies of rats with cortical lesions, the law has subsequently been challenged by research involving more specific behavioral tests, which has shown that areas of association cortex have relatively specific functions. Also called **principle of equipotentiality**. See also LAW OF MASS ACTION. [proposed in 1929 by Karl S. LASHLEY]

law of exercise the principle that repetition of some act makes that act more probable in the future. The law of exercise was first suggested, and then discarded, by Edward L. THORNDIKE.

law of filial regression the principle that inherited traits tend to revert toward the mean for the species; for example, very tall fathers tend to have sons shorter than themselves but taller than the population mean, and very short fathers tend to have sons taller than themselves but shorter than the population mean.

law of forward conduction the rule that under natural conditions nerve impulses always travel in the same direction, from the AXON HILLOCK, where the axon originates at the cell body, to the TERMINAL BUTTON of the axon. Also called **forward-conduction law**. Compare ANTIDROMIC CONDUCTION.

law of frequency the principle that the strength of learning increases with the amount of practice. Also called **law of repetition**; **law of use**.

law of good figure the PRINCIPLE OF PRÄGNANZ as applied to vision. It states that any pattern is perceived so that the resulting figure is as simple as possible.

law of good shape see GOOD SHAPE.

law of initial values the principle that the initial level of a physiological response is a major determinant of a later response in that system. Thus, if an individual's pulse rate is high, his or her cardiovascular response to an emotion-provoking stimulus will be weaker than if the initial pulse rate had been low. Also called **initial values law**; **rate dependence effect**; **Wilder's law of initial values**. See RATE DEPENDENCY. [proposed in 1957 by U.S. neuropsychiatrist Joseph Wilder (1895–1976)]

law of large numbers a mathematical principle indicating that as the sample size increases, the theoretical expectations of its statistical properties will be more and more closely realized.

law of least action see LEAST EFFORT PRINCIPLE.

law of mass action the theory that, although the brain has specific centers for sensory and motor function, large areas of the cortex function together in the learning process. If cortical lesions occur, a deficit in learning will be affected by the size of the injury rather than its specific location. The concept evolved from experiments in 1929 by Karl S. LASHLEY on the effects of different brain lesions on the ability of rats to escape from a problem box, which showed that the degree of learning deficit corresponded to the amount of tissue destruction. Also called **principle of mass action**. See LAW OF EQUIPOTENTIALITY.

law of neurobiotaxis the principle that DENDRITES of developing neurons grow in the direction of the AXONS of nearby active neurons. See NEUROBIOTAXIS.

law of parsimony the principle that the simplest explanation of an event or observation is the preferred explanation. Simplicity is understood in various ways, including the requirement that an explanation should (a) make the smallest number of unsupported assumptions, (b) postulate the existence of the fewest entities, and (c) invoke the fewest unobservable constructs. Also called **economy principle**; **principle of economy**. See ELEGANT SOLUTION; OCCAM'S RAZOR.

law of participation a principle used to characterize and account for types of thinking that do not conform to the CONTRADICTION PRINCIPLE and other LAWS OF THOUGHT basic to Western logic. This type of thinking has no difficulty in accepting that one thing can be some other logically incompatible thing in another time, place, or dimension and therefore lends itself to magic and mysticism (see MYSTICAL PARTICIPATION). Such thought is holistic, rather than differentiated, and is usually considered typical of "primitive" societies. [introduced by French philosopher and ethnologist Lucien Levy-Bruhl (1857–1939)]

law of Prägnanz see PRINCIPLE OF PRÄGNANZ.

law of precision in GESTALT PSYCHOLOGY, the principle that all percepts tend to become organized into regular, symmetrical forms with precise contours. The term is used occasionally as a synonym for the PRINCIPLE OF PRÄGNANZ.

law of primacy see PRIMACY EFFECT.

law of prior entry the principle that when two stimuli are presented simultaneously, one attended to and the other not, the attended stimulus will be perceived as having occurred before the other. See COMPLICATION EXPERIMENT.

law of proximity a principle of GESTALT PSYCHOLOGY stating that objects or stimuli that are close together, relative to others, will be perceived as a unity. For example, a series of notes is perceived as a melody, and a series of unconnected dots on a scoreboard is perceived as a number or letter. Also called **principle of proximity**. See GESTALT PRINCIPLES OF ORGANIZATION.

law of recency see RECENCY EFFECT.

law of repetition see LAW OF FREQUENCY.

law of segregation see MENDELIAN INHERITANCE.

law of similarity 1. a principle of perception identified in 1923 by German psychologist Max WERTHEIMER and associated with GESTALT PSYCHOLOGY. It states that perceivers will tend to organize objects with similar qualities into a perceptual group and interpret them as a whole. Also called **principle of similarity**. See GESTALT PRINCIPLES OF ORGANIZATION. **2.** a principle stating that like things produce like things or that an effect resembles its cause.

law of specific nerve energies the historical doctrine that the receptors and neural channels for the different sensory modalities are independent and can each produce only one particular kind of sensation. The name of this law seems odd since it is now known that nerve impulses are essentially the same throughout the nervous system. [first proposed in 1838 by German physiologist Johannes Müller (1801–1858)]

law of sufficient reason the proposition, introduced by German philosopher Gottfried Wilhelm Leibniz (1646–1716), that if something exists, it is necessarily the case that there is sufficient reason for its existence. The principle implies an inherent rationale for the universe. It is complemented by Leibniz's **law of insufficient reason**, which states that if there is not sufficient reason for the existence of something, it will not exist.

law of symmetry in GESTALT PSYCHOLOGY, the principle that regions bounded by symmetrical borders tend to be perceived as coherent figures. Also called **principle of symmetry**.

law of use see LAW OF FREQUENCY.

laws of grouping see GESTALT PRINCIPLES OF ORGANIZATION.

laws of learning principles that state the conditions under which learning occurs. The major laws are the LAW OF CONTIGUITY, the LAW OF EFFECT, the LAW OF FREQUENCY, the PRIMACY EFFECT, and the RECENCY EFFECT. Other principles and practices that enhance learning include PROGRESSIVE EDUCATION, DISTRIBUTED PRACTICE, MEANINGFUL LEARNING, ROTE LEARNING, OVERLEARNING, and ASSOCIATIVE LEARNING.

laws of thought certain principles of logic, such as the IDENTITY PRINCIPLE and the CONTRADICTION PRINCIPLE, that are deemed to be so essential to rational thought as to assume the character of law. Indeed, such principles define the very idea of logical thought. Which logical principles should be included in a set of such laws is, however, a matter of debate.

laxative addiction a dependence on the use of laxatives to induce bowel movements. The addiction is a vicious cycle, in which the use of laxatives gradually reduces bowel activity so that further use becomes the only way to avoid constipation. Laxative addiction is often associated with EATING DISORDERS in which laxatives are routinely used for purging. See also ENEMA ADDICTION; KLISMAPHILIA.

lay analysis psychoanalytic therapy performed by a person who has been trained in psychoanalytic theory and practice but is not a physician (i.e., a layperson). This is to be distinguished from psychoanalysis performed by a fully accredited PSYCHIATRIST.

layperson *n.* (*pl.* **laypersons** or **laypeople**) a person not belonging to or trained in a particular profession or who lacks specialized knowledge of a particular subject. This term is increasingly preferred over the older **layman**.

layperson theories see NAIVE PERSONALITY THEORIES.

lay psychology see NAIVE ANALYSIS OF ACTION.

lazy eye an eye that is healthy in all respects but has defective vision, even after the fitting of correcting lenses for a refractive error. See also AMBLYOPIA.

LCU abbreviation for LIFE-CHANGE UNIT.

LD 1. abbreviation for LEARNING DISABILITY. **2.** abbreviation for LEARNING DISORDER. **3.** abbreviation for LETHAL DOSE.

L data information about an individual's personality based on his or her *l*ife record or life history. See also O DATA; Q DATA; T DATA.

LDH abbreviation for LACTATE DEHYDROGENASE.

LE abbreviation for LUPUS ERYTHEMATOSUS.

leader *n.* **1.** an individual who guides others in their pursuits, often by organizing, directing, coordinating, and motivating their efforts. **2.** an individual of authority in a social group or organization, such as the head of a university department or a military commander. **3.** one who is thought to possess the qualities or characteristics associated with individuals who rise to positions of authority in groups and organizations. See also LEADERSHIP.

leader-categorization theory an information-processing model that assumes that perceivers automatically and spontaneously appraise the extent to which people, including themselves, can be classified as leaders. Such judgments are determined by IMPLICIT LEADERSHIP THEORIES that organize perceivers' general beliefs about the characteristics that most leaders possess. See also ATTRIBUTION THEORY OF LEADERSHIP; LEADER PROTOTYPE.

leaderless group 1. a group that has neither an explicitly appointed leader nor an EMERGENT LEADER. **2.** in studies of group productivity and LEADERSHIP EMERGENCE, a group with no identified leader among the participants, who are told to discuss or work together on a problem; as they do so, their behavior is observed and rated in order to evaluate specific interpersonal and leadership skills. Leaderless groups are sometimes set up to screen candidates for positions in business, social work, teaching, and the military.

leaderless group discussion (**LGD**) an exchange of opinions, ideas, and information related to some topic by the members of a leaderless group. Such discussions are used in training and educational settings to provide participants with insights into their own and others' behaviors in open, unstructured group situations.

leaderless group therapy a form of GROUP PSYCHOTHERAPY in which leaderless meetings are held either (a) on an occasional or regularly scheduled basis as an adjunct to the traditional therapist-led process or (b) on an entirely self-directed basis in which a group always meets without a designated leader.

leader match an approach to leadership training based on the CONTINGENCY THEORY OF LEADERSHIP of Austrian-born U.S. social psychologist Fred Fiedler (1922–). It proposes (a) that effective leadership is dependent on a match between the individual's LEADERSHIP STYLE and the particular group situation, (b) that individuals usually find it difficult to alter their established style of leadership, but (c) that leaders can be trained to diagnose a situation and alter it to fit their own style.

leader–member exchange theory (**LMX theory**) a dyadic, relational approach to leadership that assumes that (a) leaders develop exchange relationships with each one of their subordinates and (b) the quality of these leader–member exchange (LMX) relationships influences subordinates' responsibility, influence over decisions, access to resources, and performance. Those group members who are linked to the leader by a strongly positive LMX relationship are part of the unit's INGROUP, whereas those who have a low-quality LMX relationship are relegated to the OUTGROUP.

leader prototype a cognitive representation of an actual or abstract leader who is thought to possess features shared by most or all of the individuals in the category "leaders" and so to exemplify that category. See also ATTRIBUTION THEORY OF LEADERSHIP; LEADER-CATEGORIZATION THEORY.

leadership *n.* **1.** the processes involved in leading others, including organizing, directing, coordinating, and motivating their efforts toward achievement of certain group or organizational goals. Leadership tends to be reciprocal (leaders influence followers, and followers influence leaders), transactional (leaders and followers exchange their time, energies, and skills to increase their joint rewards), transformational (leaders inspire and motivate followers), cooperative rather than coercive (followers voluntarily accept the leader's suggestions), and goal-oriented (leaders organize and motivate members' attempts to attain personal and group goals). See TRANSACTIONAL LEADERSHIP; TRANSFORMATIONAL LEADERSHIP. **2.** the traits or behaviors characteristic of an effective leader. See LEADERSHIP THEORIES.

leadership emergence the process by which an individual is recognized (formally or informally, perceptually or behaviorally, implicitly or explicitly) as the leader of a formerly leaderless group. See EMERGENT LEADER.

leadership role 1. structurally, the position occupied by the person responsible for guiding others in their pursuits. **2.** behaviorally, a relatively coherent set of task and relationship behaviors expected of the individual who is formally or informally identified as a group's leader.

leadership style 1. the stable behavioral tendencies and methods displayed by a particular leader when guiding a group. Some common leadership styles are autocratic (see AUTOCRATIC LEADER), bureaucratic (see BUREAUCRATIC LEADER), charismatic (see CHARISMATIC LEADER), democratic (see DEMOCRATIC LEADER), and laissez-faire (see LAISSEZ-FAIRE LEADER). **2.** in style and contingency LEADERSHIP THEORIES, the extent to which the leader's approach can be characterized as TASK-MOTIVATED and RELATIONSHIP-MOTIVATED. Most such theories argue that effective leaders balance these two basic orientations in the groups they lead. See also LEAST PREFERRED COWORKER SCALE.

leadership substitute any aspect of the social setting, including the nature of the work task, the characteristics of the group members, or the qualities of the group or organization itself, that reduces or eliminates the need for a specific individual who performs such typical leadership behaviors as organizing, directing, coordinating, supporting, and motivating the group members.

leadership theories theories advanced to explain the effectiveness or ineffectiveness of leaders. The main types include TRAIT THEORIES OF LEADERSHIP, which focus on such characteristics as supervisory ability, intelligence, self-assurance, and decisiveness; **behavioral** (or **style**) **theories of leadership**, which focus on the task-based and relationship-based activities of the leader; CONTINGENCY THEORIES OF LEADERSHIP, which attempt to describe what type of leadership style is most effective in different situations; and **cognitive theories of leadership**, such as LEADER-CATEGORIZATION THEORY or the ATTRIBUTION THEORY OF LEADERSHIP, which describe the way subordinates' perceptions of their leaders influence leadership effectiveness. See also IMPLICIT LEADERSHIP THEORIES.

lead-pipe rigidity MUSCULAR RIGIDITY that produces a smooth, steady resistance to passive movement of the limbs of people with parkinsonism or cerebral palsy. Compare COGWHEEL RIGIDITY.

leaf switch a nonrigid, flexible LEVER SWITCH that is activated by a slight bending, enabling it to be operated by a user with a disability.

leakage *n.* the unintended revelation that a person has a feeling or motive different from the one intended to be communicated to others. It may be manifested, for example, by frequent speech pauses when a person describes an event untruthfully. See VERBAL LEAKAGE. See also DECEPTION CLUE.

lean medium see MEDIA RICHNESS.

learned autonomic control the individual's capacity to learn to regulate internal functions of the body, such as blood pressure and temperature, that are ordinarily under the control of the autonomic nervous system. The ability is accomplished primarily by the use of BIOFEEDBACK techniques and in some cases by the use of hypnosis (see HYPNOTHERAPY). Also called **visceral learning**.

learned helplessness lack of motivation and failure to act after exposure to unpleasant events or stimuli over which the individual has no control (e.g., noise, crowding. Individuals learn that they cannot control their environment, and this may lead them to fail to make use of any control options that are available. For example, animals exposed to inescapable electric shocks may later fail to learn to escape these shocks in situations when escape is possible. According to HELPLESSNESS THEORY, learned helplessness is a risk factor for depression. [first described in the mid-1960s by U.S. psychologist Martin E. P. Seligman (1942–)]

learned optimism a putative mechanism by which therapy ameliorates depression, by addressing LEARNED HELPLESSNESS.

learned taste aversion see CONDITIONED TASTE AVERSION.

learned treatise exception an exception to the hearsay rule (which states that evidence from statements by individuals other than the testifying individual is inadmissible in court) that allows expert witnesses to speak for others if they are reporting opinion shared by the experts in their field. Therefore, an expert may report findings contained in journal articles or similar published treatises for the purpose of informing the court of the general expert opinion concerning the matter in question. See also OPINION TESTIMONY.

learning *n.* the process of acquiring new and relatively enduring information, behavior patterns, or abilities, characterized by modification of behavior as a result of practice, study, or experience.

Learning Abilities Measurement Program (**LAMP**) a cognitive-assessment program, most often associated with the measurement of occupational work skills. It is exemplified by an information-processing model of assessment, such as that used by the British Army Recruitment Battery (BARB). LAMP assists in interpretive analysis of job- and task-ability clusters.

learning by doing see PROGRESSIVE EDUCATION.

learning curve a graphic representation of the course of learning of an individual or a group. A measure of performance (e.g., gains, errors) is plotted along the vertical axis; the horizontal axis plots trials or time. See NEGATIVE ACCELERATION; POSITIVE ACCELERATION.

learning difficulties in the United Kingdom, MENTAL RETARDATION or LEARNING DISABILITY.

learning disabilities specialist an individual, usually working within an interdisciplinary team of school professionals, who is trained to identify and assist students with problems associated with learning disabilities.

learning disability (**LD**) any of various conditions marked by substantial deficits in scholastic or academic skills, including LEARNING DISORDERS and learning difficulties due to perceptual disabilities, brain injury, or MINIMAL BRAIN DYSFUNCTION. Learning disabilities exclude learning problems that result from visual impairment or hearing loss, mental retardation, emotional disturbance, or environmental, cultural, or economic disadvantage. For diagnostic purposes, learning disability is the condition that exists when a person's actual performance on achievement testing is substantially (typically two standard deviations) below that expected for his or her established intelligence, age, and grade.

learning disorder (**LD**) in *DSM–IV–TR,* any disorder characterized by achievement that is substantially below the achievement expected for the age, education, and intelligence of that individual, as measured by standardized tests in reading, mathematics, and written material. In standard practice, a discrepancy of two standard deviations must exist between general intelligence testing scores (as measured by a standard normed IQ test) and achievement scores (as measured by a standard normed ACHIEVEMENT TEST). A discrepancy of between one and two deviations can be considered a learning disorder if some other special feature is present, such as a cognitive-processing disorder, a relevant mental disorder, a prominent medical disability, or exceptional absence from formal education. See DISORDER OF WRITTEN EXPRESSION; MATHEMATICS DISORDER; READING DISORDER.

learning disorder not otherwise specified in *DSM–IV–TR,* a learning disorder that does not meet the diagnostic criteria for any of the specific disorders of this category but nevertheless causes significant impairment of academic achievement, for example, because of problems in all three areas of reading, writing, and mathematics.

learning goal in the analysis of personality and goal-directed motivation of U.S. personality psychologist Carol Dweck (1946–), a goal to acquire mastery of a task or subject matter. Also called **mastery goal**.

learning model an approach to the study of human development and behavior that stresses the influence of environmental conditions on the physical, cognitive, interpersonal, and emotional functioning of the individual. According to the learning model, the child passively absorbs the relevant features of the environment in a continuous line of development. This contrasts with the cognitivist emphasis on development as an active construction of knowledge in specific stages characterized by distinct modes of organization and expression.

learning paradigm in abnormal psychology, the theory that abnormal behavior is learned through the same processes as other forms of behavior.

Learning Potential Assessment Device (**LPAD**) a test that dynamically assesses individuals' learning potential. First used primarily for individuals with mental retardation, it has since been used for participants displaying a wide variety of skill levels. The test exists in individual and group versions; it is dynamic in that the examinee receives feedback about his or her performance while actually taking the test. The LPAD is intended primarily for clinical use, yielding interpretive data to help the examiner understand the examinee's pattern of strengths and weaknesses. [devised in 1985 by Romanian-born psychologist Reuven Feuerstein (1921–) and colleagues]

learning set a form of DISCRIMINATION LEARNING in which the participant is given a succession of discriminations to learn, such as learning that one object contains a food reward and a different object does not. After a large number of such problems the participant acquires a rule or MENTAL SET for solving them, and successive discriminations are learned faster. See LEARNING TO LEARN. [introduced in 1949 by Harry F. HARLOW]

learning skills 1. the abilities involved in the gathering of knowledge through methods of study, classroom instruction, or both. **2.** activities that are used for acquiring knowledge or increasing understanding.

learning strategy a mental or behavioral strategy used to facilitate learning, such as forming a mental image, organizing items, searching for existing associations, or practicing RETRIEVAL.

learning style see COGNITIVE STYLE.

learning technologies applications of technology to learning. Examples of technologies used to facilitate learning include film, television, computer-assisted instruction, and—more recently—the Internet, Web-based instruction, and DISTANCE LEARNING.

learning theory a body of concepts and principles that seeks to explain the learning process. Learning theory actually encompasses a number of specific theories (e.g., HULL'S MATHEMATICO-DEDUCTIVE THEORY OF LEARNING and the PURPOSIVE BEHAVIORISM of Edward C. TOLMAN) whose common interest is the description of the basic LAWS OF LEARNING, usually derived from studies of Pavlovian and instrumental conditioning and verbal learning.

learning to learn repeated practice with one kind of task but learning different material each time, which facilitates the ability to learn new material. Harry F. HARLOW demonstrated learning to learn by teaching monkeys discriminations between pairs of objects. The animals eventually became skilled at rapidly learning new discriminations, sometimes in a single trial. See LEARNING SET.

learning trial a single presentation of the information to be learned in a learning experiment. Examples of learning trials are a single pairing of the conditioned stimulus and the unconditioned stimulus in Pavlovian conditioning and a single presentation of a word to be remembered in a memory experiment. The amount of learning is typically expressed as a function of the number of learning trials given, as in a LEARNING CURVE. Also called **acquisition trial**.

learning types individual differences in people's characteristic and preferred ways of organizing and processing information (see COGNITIVE STYLE). For example, some people may be better at remembering auditory information or at developing strategies to recall verbal information; others may prefer visual and imaginal coding of material.

learning without awareness learning that occurs without a person's conscious awareness. Evidence for such learning has been found in PAVLOVIAN CONDITIONING, PROCEDURAL LEARNING, IMPLICIT LEARNING, and SUBLIMINAL LEARNING. However, the critical data for assessing awareness depends on experimental participants' verbal reports that they are unable to describe the learning experience to which they were exposed.

least effort principle the basic behavioral hypothesis that an organism will choose a course of action that appears to require the smallest amount of effort or involve the least amount of resistance. Also called **law of least action**.

least noticeable difference see DIFFERENCE THRESHOLD.

least perceptible duration see JUST NOTICEABLE DURATION.

Least Preferred Coworker Scale (**LPC scale**) a measure of LEADERSHIP STYLE in which leaders are asked to think of the coworker with whom they have had the most difficulty in the past. They then rate this coworker on a series of bipolar adjective pairs (friendly–unfriendly, supportive–hostile, trustworthy–untrustworthy, etc.). The LPC score is the sum of these ratings, with higher scores indicating more positive ratings of the least preferred coworker. The measure assumes that leaders who rate least preferred coworkers relatively positively are RELATIONSHIP-MOTIVATED, whereas those who rate coworkers more negatively are TASK-MOTIVATED. The model predicts that leaders with low LPC scores (task-motivated) are most effective in extremely favorable or unfavorable group settings, whereas those with high LPC scores (relationship-motivated) are more effective in moderately favorable settings. See CONTINGENCY THEORIES OF LEADERSHIP. [developed by Austrian-born U.S. psychologist Fred Fiedler (1922–)]

least restrictive alternative the legal directive that less treatment rather than more (e.g., nursing home versus hospital) is the most desirable objective in treating involuntarily committed patients. The principal consideration is combining safety concerns with the minimum level of restrictions on the patient's freedom. This position was emphasized in two decisions of U.S. Court of Appeals Judge David L. Bazelon (1910–1993) in 1966: *Rouse v. Cameron* and *Lake v. Cameron.*

least restrictive environment (**LRE**) in the United States, an educational setting that gives a student with disabilities the opportunity to receive instruction within a classroom that meets his or her learning needs and physical requirements. According to the INDIVIDUALS WITH DISABILITIES EDUCATION ACT, students with disabilities should be educated with students who do not have disabilities to the maximum extent possible, depending on the nature or severity of their disabilities. See also FULL INCLUSION; MAINSTREAMING.

least significant difference (**LSD**) a criterion for the comparison of means in a multicelled experimental design that allows for TYPE I ERROR control at a prespecified level. It is one of several MULTIPLE COMPARISON methods.

least squares criterion the principle that one should estimate the values of the parameters of a model in such a way that will minimize the squared error of predictions from the model.

least squares regression see STEPWISE REGRESSION.

leaving the field the act of removing oneself from a situation when confronted with seemingly insurmountable obstacles, insoluble conflicts, or intensely frustrating problems. It may involve physical withdrawal, escape into PSYCHOGENIC illness, or some other behavior, such as distraction or changing the subject during a conversation.

Leber's disease a hereditary visual disorder characterized by slowly progressive optic atrophy with normal peripheral vision but blind areas of the retina toward the center. The genetic defect is transmitted by females, but males are most often affected, with symptoms beginning around the third decade of life. Also called **Leber's optic atrophy**. See also AMAUROSIS. [Theodor **Leber** (1840–1917), German ophthalmologist]

Leboyer technique a psychological approach to childbirth that focuses on the feelings and sensations of the baby. It advocates peace and quiet, dim lights, delay in severing the umbilical cord, body contact between newborn and parents, and an immediate warm bath that approximates to the conditions within the womb. See also LAMAZE METHOD. [Frédéric **Leboyer** (1918–), French obstetrician]

lecanomancy *n.* a system of divination in which a sensitive or clairvoyant looks into a basin of water and sees alleged visions of the future. **—lecanomancer** *n.*

lécheur *n.* a man or woman who performs CUNNILINGUS or FELLATIO. A female lécheur is more properly called a **lécheuse**. See also OROGENITAL ACTIVITY.

Lectopam *n.* a trade name for BROMAZEPAM.

lecture method the formal, verbal presentation of information or other material by an instructor to a group of students or other learners. The lecture method is used mainly when groups are large or time is limited (e.g., in personnel training). It can also be used to introduce other instructional methods, such as audiovisual presentations or role play, or to summarize material developed by other means.

Lee–Boot effect a prolonged DIESTRUS phase, induced by pheromones, that occurs when a female animal is housed with other females. [first reported in 1955 by S. van der **Lee** and L. M. **Boot**, Dutch biologists]

left-handedness *n.* the preferential use of the left hand for major activities, such as eating, writing, and throwing. See also LATERALITY; SINISTRALITY. Compare RIGHT-HANDEDNESS.

left hemisphere the left half of the cerebrum or cerebellum in the brain. The two CEREBRAL HEMISPHERES differ somewhat in function; for example, in most people the left hemisphere has greater responsibility for speech. See HEMISPHERIC ENCODING–RETRIEVAL ASYMMETRY; HEMISPHERIC LATERALIZATION. Compare RIGHT HEMISPHERE.

left-hemisphere consciousness the claim by U.S. cognitive neuropsychologist Michael Gazzaniga that the hemisphere of the brain that controls speech (the left hemisphere in most people) is the seat of consciousness. Others, including Roger SPERRY, have proposed that both hemispheres are independently conscious (see RIGHT-HEMISPHERE CONSCIOUSNESS).

legal blindness see BLINDNESS.

legal capacity the ability to acquire the knowledge and understanding necessary to make a rational choice regarding any issue that has legal implications (e.g., entering into contracts, making a will, standing trial). See also COMPETENCY TO STAND TRIAL.

legal psychiatry see FORENSIC PSYCHIATRY.

legal psychology see FORENSIC PSYCHOLOGY.

legal testimony evidence given by an individual in court under oath or affirmation, either orally or as a written statement of facts known as an affidavit. Written evidence that was obtained during a deposition (an official pretrial questioning of an individual) may also be presented as testimony.

legasthenia *n.* a controversial syndrome in which the primary symptom is difficulty in synthesizing letters into words and analyzing words into their component letters, despite adequate intellectual and perceptual ability.

legend *n.* **1.** a traditional story that has been passed down from an earlier period and may or may not contain elements of historical truth. Legends usually grow by a process of CHAIN REPRODUCTION. See also MYTHOLOGY. **2.** a caption or key that explains illustrations or symbols on a graph, map, or chart. **—legendary** *adj.*

legibility *n.* **1.** capability of being read or deciphered. **2.** the ease with which an environment can be cognitively represented, which determines one's ability to navigate or find one's way within an environment or setting. LANDMARKS, the overall shape or configuration of street grids, and building layout can significantly influence legibility. See also COGNITIVE MAP; ENVIRONMENTAL COGNITION. **—legible** *adj.*

legitimacy *n.* authority or rights derived from tradition or social convention. See LEGITIMATE POWER. **—legitimate** *adj.*

legitimacy knowledge in social psychology, the role played by an individual's major GROUP IDENTIFICATIONS in contributing to SELF-IMAGE and estimates of personal value. Legitimacy knowledge derives from the individual's perceptions of the culture's relative acceptance of his or her racial, sexual, ethnic, or religious group. It is often contrasted with COMPETENCE KNOWLEDGE, which is the component of self-image that derives from individual talents and accomplishments.

legitimate authority see AUTHORITY.

legitimate power a capacity to influence others that is based on the influencer's position or role in the group and members' recognition that an individual in such a position has the right to require and demand compliance with his or her directives. See POWER.

leisure lifestyle a way of life in which leisure and free time play a prominent role. Leisure activities (e.g., hobbies, recreation, self-selected activities) largely or entirely replace obligatory activities (e.g., work for pay), as is the case for people who have retired from full-time paid employment. It is assumed that a lifestyle that includes regular leisure activities is better for both physical and mental health.

Lejeune syndrome see CRI DU CHAT SYNDROME.

lek display a mating system in which several males congregate at one location during the mating season, forming small individual territories and competing with each other for mates by giving complex, elaborate visual and vocal displays. Females are attracted by these displays and move among the males to choose their mate. Typically, the males provide no parental care to resulting offspring.

lemma *n.* **1.** in logic, a subsidiary PROPOSITION used as a part of the proof of a subsequent proposition. The proof of the lemma may or may not be included in the argument. **2.** in linguistics, a word considered as the word in its basic dictionary form together with all its inflected forms. For example, the lemma *be* consists of *be* plus *am, are, is, was, were, being,* and *been.*

lemniscal system a system of long, ascending neural pathways projecting to the thalamus. It includes the MEDIAL LEMNISCUS, LATERAL LEMNISCUS, SPINOTHALAMIC TRACTS, and secondary trigeminal projections.

length of stay (**LOS**) the length of an inpatient's continuous stay in a hospital. A UTILIZATION REVIEW will normally compare the LOS under review with regional norms, as expressed by the average LOS for the relevant diagnosis.

leniency error a type of rating error in which the ratings are consistently overly positive, particularly as regards the performance or ability of the participants. It is caused by the rater's tendency to be too positive or tolerant of shortcomings and to give undeservedly high evaluations. Also called **leniency bias**. Compare SEVERITY ERROR.

lens *n.* in vision, a transparent, biconvex structure in the anterior portion of the eyeball that provides the fine, adjustable focus of the optical system. It is composed of tiny hexagonal prism-shaped cells, called lens fibers, fitted together in concentric layers. See ACCOMMODATION.

lens model a metaphorical model intended to characterize the fact that organisms do not perceive the environment directly and objectively, but instead use available cues to make inferences, judgments, or interpretations of the environment. A variety of cues are available, and the organism selects those it will use and then "focuses" them by assigning each a relative weight or importance in the interpretive process. [proposed by Viennese-born U.S. psychologist Egon Brunswik (1903–1955)]

lenticular nucleus the lens-shaped region in the BASAL GANGLIA that encompasses the GLOBUS PALLIDUS and the PUTAMEN. Also called **lentiform nucleus**.

Leonardo's paradox the apparent curvature of straight elements at the margins of a wide-angle scene containing linear perspective. [**Leonardo** da Vinci (1452–1519), Italian artist and scientist]

Leon (III) virus one of three enterovirus strains known to cause poliomyelitis in humans. The others are identified as **Brunhilde (I)** and **Lansing (II)** strains. Some primates and rodents can be infected with at least one of the three strains.

leprechaunism *n.* a familial disorder characterized by a large head with a small, emaciated body, large, wide-set eyes, long, low-set ears, and an abundance of hair at birth. The patients have poor psychomotor development and muscular hypotonia. The syndrome is believed to be due to an autosomal recessive gene that becomes manifested through consanguinity. Also called **Donohue's syndrome**.

leptin *n.* a protein, manufactured and secreted by fat cells, that may communicate to the brain the amount of body fat stored and may help to regulate food intake. Leptin is defective in obese mice.

leptokurtic *adj.* describing a frequency distribution that is more peaked than a comparison, such as the normal distribution. See also PLATYKURTIC; MESOKURTIC.

leptomorph *n.* see BODY-BUILD INDEX.

leptosome type see ASTHENIC TYPE.

LES abbreviation for LOCAL EXCITATORY STATE.

lesbian feminism a type of FEMINISM that emphasizes the sociopolitical meaning of lesbianism. Beyond the implications that lesbianism may have for women's right to control their own sexuality, it is suggested that lesbianism is the ultimate rejection of PATRIARCHY. See also LESBIAN SEPARATISM.

lesbianism *n.* female–female sexual orientation or behavior. The name is derived from Lesbos, an Aegean island where the poet Sappho (c. 600 BCE) wrote glowing accounts of erotic activities between women. Also called **Sapphism**. **—lesbian** *adj., n.*

lesbian separatism a radical form of LESBIAN FEMINISM arguing that feminist women should reject heterosexuality in order to effect a complete separation from patriarchal society and its institutions.

Lesch–Nyhan syndrome an X-linked recessive disorder associated with deficiency of the enzyme HYPOXANTHINE–GUANINE PHOSPHORIBOSYLTRANSFERASE, overproduction of uric acid, and a tendency to compulsions involving self-mutilation by biting the lips and fingers. Affected individuals have mental retardation, with IQs generally below 50. Motor development deteriorates after the first 6 to 8 months of life, marked by spasticity, chorea (involuntary jerky movements), and athetosis (sinuous involuntary movements). Also called **hereditary choreoathetosis**; **hereditary hyperuricemia**. [described in 1964 by Michael **Lesch** (1939–) and William L. **Nyhan** (1926–), U.S. pediatricians]

lesion *n.* any disruption of or damage to the normal structure or function of an organ or part of an organ due to injury, disease, or a surgical procedure. A lesion may be a wound, ulcer, tumor, cataract, or any other pathological change in tissue. See also TEMPORARY LESION.

less-is-more hypothesis the proposition that the cognitive limitations of infants and young children may serve to simplify the body of language they process, thus making it easier for them to learn the complicated syntactical system of any human language. The name is derived from the famous design dictum of German-born U.S. architect Ludwig Mies van der Rohe (1886–1969).

[proposed by 21st-century U.S. psychologist Elissa L. Newport]

lethal catatonia a form of acute maniacal excitement that in some cases leads to unexplained death. Also called **Bell's mania**; **deadly catatonia**; **exhaustion death**. See also HYPERMANIA. [first described in 1849 by U.S. physician Luther Vose Bell (1806–1862)]

lethal dose (**LD**) the dose of a drug that is required to cause death. It is generally expressed in terms of the **median lethal dose** (**LD_{50}**; **LD-50**), the dose required to cause death in 50% of nonhuman animals to which the drug is administered. See also EFFECTIVE DOSE; THERAPEUTIC RATIO.

lethality *n.* the degree of dangerousness or likelihood of death associated with a particular course of action. The word is often used when comparing methods of committing suicide. **—lethal** *adj.*

lethality scale a set of criteria used to predict the probability of a suicide or attempted suicide occurring. A variety of such scales exist, most including gender, prior suicide attempts, and psychiatric diagnosis and history.

lethargy *n.* low energy level and lack of motivated behavior, often occurring in depression. **—lethargic** *adj.*

letter-by-letter reading see PURE ALEXIA.

letter cancellation test any of a variety of tests that measure attention and UNILATERAL NEGLECT by requiring the participant to mark a specific letter out of long lines of random letters (e.g., the letter "e" embedded in random letters). Individuals with attention impairment respond inconsistently, whereas those with neglect perform worse or not at all on the side of their neglect (usually the left side).

Letter–Number Sequencing an attentional subtest on the WECHSLER ADULT INTELLIGENCE SCALE and the WECHSLER INTELLIGENCE SCALE FOR CHILDREN in which the participant must sequence a random order of numbers and letters. Specifically, the participant must first say the numbers in ascending order and then the letters in alphabetical order.

letting go discontinuing the struggle for life after a strenuous period of effort and suffering during the DYING PROCESS. See also ACCEPTANCE STAGE.

leuco- (**leuc-**; **leuko-**; **leuk-**) *combining form* white or colorless.

leucotomy *n.* see LEUKOTOMY.

leuko- *combining form* see LEUCO-.

leukocyte *n.* a type of blood cell that plays a key role in the body's defense against infection (see IMMUNE RESPONSE). Leukocytes include neutrophils, basophils, and eosinophils (known collectively as granulocytes because their cytoplasm contains granules), which ingest foreign particles by PHAGOCYTOSIS; and LYMPHOCYTES, which are involved in the production of antibodies and other specific immune responses. Also called **white blood cell**.

leukotomy (**leucotomy**) *n.* a former psychosurgical technique (see PSYCHOSURGERY) in which the frontal lobes of the brain were severed from the deeper centers underlying them. This technique was used in the early 20th century to relieve the symptoms of severe, chronic mental disorders. The development of antipsychotic drugs has reduced the need for psychosurgery, and this operation has been replaced by more sophisticated, stereotactic forms of neurosurgery that are less invasive and whose effects are more certain and less damaging. Also called **prefrontal lobotomy**. See also TRANSORBITAL LOBOTOMY.

leuprolide *n.* an analog of GONADOTROPIN-RELEASING HORMONE that opposes the action of androgens and estrogens through inhibition of GONADOTROPIN secretion. It is used for the treatment of uterine tumors, some forms of precocious puberty, and advanced prostate cancer. Because of its potent antiandrogen effects, it has been used controversially to perform CHEMICAL CASTRATION in repeat sex offenders. U.S. trade name (among others): **Lupron**.

level *n.* the quantity, magnitude, or category of the independent variable (or variables) in an experimental design.

Level I and Level II tests intelligence tests based on the theory that abilities can be viewed as being arranged hierarchically at two different levels. The first level is of associative processing, the second of more conceptual processing. According to this theory, different racial and ethnic groups tend to show minimal differences on Level I tests but more substantial differences on Level II tests. [developed by U.S. psychologist Arthur Jensen (1923–)]

level-of-aspiration theory in social psychology, a conceptual approach to group and individual performance that assumes that the emotional, motivational, and behavioral consequences of any particular performance will be determined not only by the absolute degree of success attained but also by the ideal outcome or goal envisioned prior to undertaking the task.

levels of consciousness levels of alertness or wakefulness, ranging from alert wakefulness, through relaxed wakefulness, drowsiness, sleep, and deep sleep to coma. Levels of consciousness can be indexed either behaviorally or by means of electroencephalographic or brain imaging methods.

levels of intelligence in theories proposing that intelligence can be envisaged as a series of levels, GENERAL ABILITY comes at the top of the hierarchy and successively narrower abilities come at lower levels in the hierarchy. In one variant, the top level comprises general ability, the second level major group factors, the third level minor group factors, and the fourth level specific factors. Major group factors are those that are measured by many (but not all) intelligence tests, whereas minor group factors are ones that are measured by smaller numbers of tests. Specific factors are measured only by single tests.

levels-of-processing model of memory the theory that ENCODING into memory, and therefore subsequent RETENTION, depends on the depth of cognitive ELABORATION that the information receives and that deeper encoding improves memory. In early critical experiments, depth was achieved by processing the meaning of to-be-remembered words rather than focusing on peripheral dimensions, such as the sound of the words. [formulated in 1972 by Canadian psychologist Fergus I. M. Craik (1935–) and Robert S. Lockhart]

Levene test a procedure for testing hypotheses about the HOMOGENEITY OF VARIANCE. [Howard **Levene** (1914–2003), U.S. statistician and geneticist]

leverage *n.* an index used in MULTIPLE REGRESSION to indicate the degree to which a particular case is outlying with respect to the full set of predictor variables (see OUTLIER). This index is often useful in identifying influential cases.

lever switch a switch mounted on a device at one end with the opposite end free to move within fixed or variable limits. The lever may be any length or shape. See also LEAF SWITCH.

Levinson's adult development theory a model of

human development in which adulthood is divided into early, middle, and late segments, each period consisting of (a) transitional, or entry, stages (e.g., age-30 transition, age-40 transition), which are often times of uncertainty, self-examination, exploration, and modification of the quality and significance of life commitments; and (b) intervening periods of relative stability, when individuals consolidate new interpretations, structures, and goals and move forward. The adaptations associated with transitional periods may be relatively smooth and uneventful or may be experienced as psychologically difficult and painful (e.g., as a MIDLIFE CRISIS). [proposed by Daniel **Levinson** (1920–1994), U.S. psychologist]

levitation *n.* an allegedly paranormal phenomenon in which a person or thing appears to ascend into the air and hover there without physical cause. Levitation is mainly associated with PSYCHOKINESIS and POLTERGEIST activity. A sensation of levitating is also common in dreams. **—levitate** *vb.*

levodopa (**L-dopa**) *n.* the naturally occurring form of dihydroxyphenylalanine (see DOPA), a precursor of the neurotransmitter dopamine. Levodopa is used in the treatment of Parkinson's disease (see DOPAMINE-RECEPTOR AGONISTS), usually in combination with carbidopa (see SINEMET). U.S. trade names: **Dopar**; **Larodopa**.

Levo-Dromoran *n.* a trade name for LEVORPHANOL.

levomepromazine *n.* see METHOTRIMEPRAZINE.

Levoprome *n.* a trade name for METHOTRIMEPRAZINE.

levorphanol *n.* an OPIOID ANALGESIC produced by manipulation of the morphine molecule. Levorphanol is approximately four to six times more potent as an analgesic than morphine and possesses similar risks of dependence and respiratory depression. U.S. trade name: **Levo-Dromoran**.

Lewin, Kurt (1890–1947) German-born U.S. psychologist. Lewin earned his PhD from the University of Berlin in 1916, studying under psychologist Carl Stumpf (1848–1936). He was heavily influenced by the nascent GESTALT PSYCHOLOGY as well as by the philosophy of Ernst Cassirer (1874–1945). The early part of Lewin's career was spent at the University of Berlin, but in 1933, with the rise of the Nazis in Germany, Lewin (a Jew) emigrated to the United States. He spent nearly a decade at the University of Iowa's Child Welfare Research Station, moving to the Massachusetts Institute of Technology's new Center for Group Dynamics in 1944. He was a founding member of the Society for the Psychological Study of Social Issues (SPSSI) and the Commission on Community Interrelations of the American Jewish Congress. Lewin is known for both his theoretical and experimental accomplishments. He developed a comprehensive and holistic FIELD THEORY, explaining human behavior as a function of various internal and external forces that together interact in a dynamic field. His book *Principles of Topological Psychology* (1936) attempted to formalize and mathematize field theory. His empirical studies have been even more influential. Particularly well known are his social psychological experiments on the styles of DEMOCRATIC LEADERS versus AUTHORITARIAN LEADERS, on frustration and regression in children, on GROUP COHESION, and on GROUP DYNAMICS, a term he coined in 1939. Opposing the trend to view science as value-free, Lewin promoted what he called ACTION RESEARCH, a type of socially engaged research, such as his research on intergroup relations with the Commission on Community Interrelations. See also LIFE SPACE; SENSITIVITY TRAINING; T-GROUP.

Lewy body dementia a specific type of DEMENTIA characterized by the presence of abnormal proteins called **Lewy bodies** in the brain on biopsy or autopsy. Symptoms can range from traditional parkinsonian effects, such as loss of spontaneous movement, muscular rigidity, tremor, and shuffling gait, to effects similar to those of Alzheimer's disease, such as acute confusion, loss of memory, and loss of or fluctuating cognition. Visual hallucinations are also common. [Frederich Heinrich **Lewy** (1885–1950), German neurologist]

lexical access in psycholinguistics, the process by which an individual produces a specific word from his or her MENTAL LEXICON or recognizes it when used by others. See PRODUCTIVE VOCABULARY; RECEPTIVE VOCABULARY.

lexical agraphia a disorder characterized by an impaired ability to spell irregular words (e.g., *yacht*) or ambiguous words. The ability to spell other words or nonwords is not affected. Also called **surface agraphia**.

lexical ambiguity the property of a word that has more than one possible meaning. See AMBIGUITY.

lexical decision a task in which the participant is presented with strings of letters, such as HOUSE or HOUPE, and is required to determine whether each string spells a word or not. The REACTION TIME required to make the decision is usually measured.

lexical hypothesis the supposition that any significant individual difference, such as a central personality trait, will be encoded into the natural-language lexicon, that is, there will be a term to describe it in any or all of the languages of the world. Also called **fundamental lexical hypothesis**.

lexical memory see MENTAL LEXICON.

lexical-selection rules in linguistics, rules governing which lexical items may appear in which sentence structures. For example, intransitive verbs, such as *smile* or *lie*, do not allow direct objects and are therefore incompatible with certain syntactic structures. The relationship between lexical selection and sentence structure is of major interest in GENERATIVE GRAMMAR.

lexical uncertainty **1.** in logic, the type of uncertainty that arises from the inherent imprecision of human language, and in particular from the attempt to describe and evaluate real-world situations using imprecise and often subjective linguistic categories (e.g., "successful," "ill"). FUZZY LOGIC is an attempt to solve the logical difficulties associated with lexical uncertainty. **2.** in psycholinguistics, any uncertainty about the meanings of particular words experienced by or observable in language users.

lexical word see CONTENT WORD.

lexicology *n.* the study of the meanings of words and their idiomatic combinations. Applied lexicology is called **lexicography**, the science and art of compiling dictionaries.

lexicon *n.* **1.** the vocabulary of a language. **2.** the lexical knowledge of an individual. See MENTAL LEXICON. See also PRODUCTIVE VOCABULARY; RECEPTIVE VOCABULARY.

LGD abbreviation for LEADERLESS GROUP DISCUSSION.

LGN abbreviation for LATERAL GENICULATE NUCLEUS.

LH **1.** abbreviation for LATERAL HYPOTHALAMUS. **2.** abbreviation for LUTEINIZING HORMONE.

liability *n.* see MULTIFACTORIAL MODEL.

liberation psychology a movement in psychology that emerged in South America with the intention of making psychology a force in the emancipation of peoples from poverty and injustice, rather than a force for maintaining the status quo. The movement was so named by analogy with the "liberation theology" that arose in Latin American churches in the late 1960s and early 1970s.

libidinal development see PSYCHOSEXUAL DEVELOPMENT.

libidinal stage in psychoanalytic theory, any of the various defined stages of PSYCHOSEXUAL DEVELOPMENT, principally the ORAL STAGE, the ANAL STAGE, the PHALLIC STAGE, and the GENITAL STAGE.

libidinal transference in psychoanalysis, the TRANSFERENCE of the patient's LIBIDO, or feelings of love, from his or her parents onto his or her therapist.

libidinal types in psychoanalytic theory, a personality classification based on the distribution of LIBIDO, or sexual energy, in the psyche. In the **erotic type** the libido remains largely in the ID and the main interest is in loving and being loved. In the **obsessional type** the libido is largely invested in the SUPEREGO and the individual is dominated by conscience. In the **narcissistic type** the libido is primarily invested in the EGO and the main interest is in self-preservation, with little concern for others or for the dictates of the superego. [devised by Sigmund FREUD]

libidinization *n.* see EROTIZATION.

libido *n.* **1.** in psychoanalytic theory, either the PSYCHIC ENERGY of the LIFE INSTINCT in general, or the energy of the SEXUAL INSTINCT in particular. In his first formulation, Sigmund FREUD conceived of this energy as narrowly sexual, but subsequently he broadened the concept to include all expressions of love, pleasure, and self-preservation. See also EROS. **2.** in the ANALYTIC PSYCHOLOGY of Carl JUNG, the general life force that provides energy for all types of activities: biological, sexual, social, cultural, and creative. **3.** more generally, sexual energy or desire. **—libidinal** *adj.* **—libidinize** *vb.* **—libidinous** *adj.*

libido-binding activity an activity in which members of a therapy group concentrate libidinal energies on a specific interest or occupation, rather than on activities that stimulate the libido. Also called **immobilizing activity**. [introduced by 20th-century Russian-born U.S. psychotherapist Samuel Richard Slavson]

Librium *n.* a trade name for CHLORDIAZEPOXIDE.

license *n.* permission granted by a government agency for an individual or organization to engage in a given occupation or business on the basis of examination, proof of education, or both rather than on measures of performance. See PROFESSIONAL LICENSING. **—licensed** *adj.* **—licensure** *n.*

licensed practical nurse (**LPN**) a graduate of an accredited school of practical nursing who has been legally authorized to practice as a nurse. Also called **licensed vocational nurse** (**LVN**).

licking behavior the licking by an animal of itself or another animal, particularly an offspring. Licking behavior appears to be part of the maternal behavior of many mammals; the pregnant female licks itself before giving birth, then licks the offspring, thereby establishing a means of identifying its own young. Licking of the offspring's urine may serve to maintain the female in fluid HOMEOSTASIS during lactation.

lickometer *n.* see DRINKOMETER.

lid apraxia see OCULOMOTOR APRAXIA.

lie *n.* a false statement or a false presentation, known to be untrue, that is made with the intention to deceive. See also FABRICATION; PATHOLOGICAL LYING. Compare CONFABULATION; FABULATION.

Liebmann effect the perceived merger of different visual stimuli that occurs when the border between them is defined only by hue. [Susanne E. **Liebmann** (1897–1990), German psychologist]

lie detector see POLYGRAPH.

lie scale a subtest or scale of a test (e.g., the MINNESOTA MULTIPHASIC PERSONALITY INVENTORY) used to help evaluate the general truthfulness of a person's responses on the test.

life age see CHRONOLOGICAL AGE.

life-change unit (**LCU**) a unit of measurement on the LIFE-EVENTS RATING SCALE, on which diverse life experiences are assigned numerical values in accordance with their stress-generating potential. For example, divorce and death of a spouse or significant other are ranked as high stress generators on the scale, retirement falls at about midscale, and moving to a new house and change in sleeping habits are ranked progressively lower. Some research indicates that individuals with a high cumulative LCU score (i.e., a high **potential-stress score**) show more health changes than other participants. See also LIFE CRISIS.

life coaching see COACHING.

life crisis a serious or significant life experience (e.g., divorce, marriage, career change, or death of a close family member) that produces stress and necessitates major adjustment. In studies relating health to life crises, individuals experiencing recent major stress-producing experiences are more likely than others to show significant alterations in mental and physical health status. See also LIFE-CHANGE UNIT; LIFE-EVENTS RATING SCALE.

life cycle **1.** the sequence of developmental stages through which an organism passes between a specified stage of one generation (e.g., fertilization, birth) and the same stage in the next generation. **2.** the series of stages that characterizes the life span of a group, institution, culture, or product.

life events important occasions throughout the life span that are either age-related and thus expected (e.g., marriage, retirement) or unrelated to age and unexpected (e.g., accidents, relocation). Contextual theories of personality often assume that personality is shaped by reactions to stress produced by CRITICAL LIFE EVENTS.

life-events rating scale a scale used to measure the relative impact of diverse stress-producing life experiences, changes, and crises. The derived score is expressed in LIFE-CHANGE UNITS. See also LIFE CRISIS.

life expectancy the number of years that a person can, on average, expect to live. Life expectancy is based on statistical probabilities and increases with improvements in medical care and hygiene.

life force see ÉLAN VITAL.

life goal in the individual psychology of Alfred ADLER, the individual's concept of what he or she could attain in life, seen as a means of compensating for real or imagined inferiority. See also LIFE PLAN.

life history in therapy and counseling, a systematic account of the client's development from birth to the present, including the meaningful aspects of the client's emotional, social, and intellectual development. The account is taken by the therapist or counselor directly from the client and may additionally be derived from autobiographical material.

life-history method a STRUCTURED INTERVIEW that attempts to summarize historical data about events that are relevant to evaluating the person's current functioning.

life instinct in psychoanalytic theory, the drive comprising the SELF-PRESERVATION INSTINCT, which is aimed at individual survival, and the SEXUAL INSTINCT, which is aimed at the survival of the species. In the DUAL INSTINCT THEORY of Sigmund FREUD, the life instinct, or EROS, stands opposed to the DEATH INSTINCT, or THANATOS. Also called **erotic instinct**.

life lie 1. the false conviction held by some individuals that their life plan is bound to fail due to other people or to circumstances beyond their control. This was postulated as a method of freeing oneself from personal responsibility. [defined by Alfred ADLER] **2.** any false belief around which an individual's life is built.

lifeline *n.* a therapeutic technique used in group or individual therapy in which each individual draws lines representing his or her life, marking past and future expected events with angles indicating even, upward, or downward progression of functioning, as well as specific dates and the affect surrounding these events. Discussion of this diagram with the therapist can enhance awareness and understanding of the individual's life patterns.

life plan in the individual psychology of Alfred ADLER, an individual's style of life and GUIDING FICTION as he or she strives to reach his or her LIFE GOAL.

life review the tendency of individuals, especially older adults, to reflect upon and analyze past life experiences. Life review, or analytical REMINISCENCE, is often made use of in counseling older adults showing symptoms of mild depression or people with terminal illness, sometimes as an adjunct to psychotherapy. [defined in 1961 by U.S. psychiatrist Robert N. Butler (1927–)]

life rhythm see BIOLOGICAL RHYTHM.

life satisfaction the extent to which a person finds life rich, meaningful, full, or of high quality. Numerous standardized measures have been developed to provide an index of a person's life satisfaction in comparison to various normative groups. Improved life satisfaction is often a goal of treatment, especially with older people. See also QUALITY OF LIFE.

life space in the FIELD THEORY of Kurt LEWIN, the "totality of possible events" for one person at a particular time, that is, a person's possible options together with the environment that contains them. The life space is a representation of the environmental, biological, social, and psychological influences that define one person's unique reality at a given moment in time. Contained within the life space are positive and negative valences, that is, forces or pressures on the individual to approach a goal or move away from a perceived danger.

life-space interview a form of CRISIS INTERVENTION involving techniques and strategies in which children in day and residential treatment are interviewed by staff members during moments of crisis or stress, for example, immediately after receiving an upsetting letter or after being attacked by another child. Efforts are made to convert these everyday events into therapeutic experiences by such means as restoring the children's belief in themselves and strengthening their ego. [originated by Austrian-born U.S. psychologist Fritz Redl (1902–1988)]

life span 1. the precise length of an individual's life. See also LIFE EXPECTANCY. **2.** the duration of existence of an entire species.

life-span contextualism a perspective on human development that views people as both products and producers of their own development, interacting throughout life with family, peers, and other social groups and institutions.

life-span developmental psychology the study of age-related psychological differences among individuals and age-related psychological change within the individual from birth through old age.

life-span perspective a general perspective emphasizing (a) that human development is a lifelong process of change; (b) that developmental change is multidimensional and multidirectional, involving both gain and loss—that is, both growth and decline—in one's performance (e.g., of cognitive tasks) as one ages; and (c) that there is plasticity in human behavior throughout the entire life span.

life stress severe strain produced by CRITICAL LIFE EVENTS or similar experiences, such as failure at work, marital separation, or loss of a loved one.

lifestyle *n.* **1.** the typical way of life or manner of living that is characteristic of an individual or group, as expressed by behaviors, attitudes, interests, and other factors. **2.** in the INDIVIDUAL PSYCHOLOGY of Alfred ADLER, an individual's characteristic way of overcoming or compensating for feelings of inadequacy. According to Adler, a lifestyle is first adopted in childhood, when the key factors informing it will be genetic endowment, upbringing, and interpersonal relations within the family.

lifetime personality the pattern of behavior that dominates a person's lifestyle between birth and death. [from the personality theory of U.S. psychologist Henry Alexander Murray (1893–1988)]

lifetime risk the odds of a person being diagnosed with a disease or condition during his or her lifetime (usually stated in terms of 70 to 85 years). It is often important for individuals undergoing GENETIC COUNSELING to differentiate lifetime risk from the risk of being diagnosed with the disease in the next 5 or 10 years.

ligand *n.* a molecule that binds to a specific site on another molecule, for example, a hormone binding to its receptor molecule at the surface of a cell.

ligand-gated ion channel an ION CHANNEL that opens or closes in response to the binding of a molecule (the ligand) to a receptor. An example is the IONOTROPIC RECEPTOR. Compare VOLTAGE-GATED ION CHANNEL.

light adaptation the changes in the eye that occur in response to stimulation by light. These include constriction of the pupil and a shift in the sensitivity of the retina so that the RETINAL CONES remain responsive to changes in illumination under lighting conditions that are too intense for the RETINAL RODS. Light adaptation enables the eye to function over a very wide range of illumination.

light cell see TYPE II CELL.

light–dark cycle the schedule according to which the lights are turned on and off in rooms housing nonhuman animals used for research. A 12-hour light–dark cycle, in which the lights are on for 12 consecutive hours and then off for 12 consecutive hours, is commonly used.

light induction the production or alteration of sensation in one part of the visual field by stimulation in an adjacent part of the field (e.g., INDUCED COLOR).

lightness constancy see BRIGHTNESS CONSTANCY.

lightning calculator an individual capable of extremely rapid mental calculations. While some of these individuals have a high IQ, most of them are people with a very well developed SPECIFIC ABILITY but not a particularly high IQ.

light pointer a form of HEADSTICK fitted with a light that can activate an ASSISTIVE TECHNOLOGY device.

light reflex see PUPILLARY REFLEX.

light sensitivity see PHOTOPHOBIA.

light therapy the use of natural or artificial light to

treat various ailments, primarily depressive and sleep disorders. See PHOTOTHERAPY.

light trance see TRANCE.

likelihood *n.* in statistics, the probability of obtaining a particular set of results given a set of assumptions about the distribution of the phenomena in the population and the parameters of that distribution.

likelihood principle in vision, the generality that the most likely interpretation of a visual stimulus is what will be perceived, rather than the simplest interpretation.

likelihood ratio the ratio of two probabilities, a/b, where a is the probability of obtaining the data observed if a particular research hypothesis (A) is true and b is the probability of obtaining the data observed when hypothesis B is true.

Likert scale a DIRECT ATTITUDE MEASURE that consists of statements reflecting strong positive or negative evaluations of an ATTITUDE OBJECT. Respondents indicate their reaction to each statement on a response scale ranging from "strongly agree" to "strongly disagree." Also called **Likert summated rating procedure**. [Rensis **Likert** (1903–1981), U.S. psychologist]

liking scale a measure of a person's degree of attraction to another individual, usually involving a willingness to be in the other's company as well as a positive evaluation of the other's personality characteristics. One such scale was published by U.S. social psychologist Zick Rubin (1944–) in 1973. Although Rubin distinguished between this measure and his LOVE SCALE, studies have shown that the two indices are usually positively correlated.

Lilliputian hallucination a VISUAL HALLUCINATION of objects, animals, or people greatly reduced in size, which may result from a number of conditions, such as DELIRIUM TREMENS, typhoid, or brain tumors in the temporal lobe. The name is derived from Jonathan Swift's *Gulliver's Travels* (1726), in which Gulliver journeys to the imaginary land of Lilliput, populated by tiny people. Also called **diminutive visual hallucination**; **microptic hallucination**. See also MICROPSIA.

limbic cortex the portions of the cerebral cortex, especially the CINGULATE GYRUS, that are associated with the LIMBIC SYSTEM.

limbic lobe a fifth subdivision of each cerebral hemisphere that is often distinguished in addition to the four main lobes (see CEREBRUM). It comprises the CINGULATE GYRUS, PARAHIPPOCAMPAL GYRUS, and HIPPOCAMPAL FORMATION.

limbic system a loosely defined, widespread group of brain nuclei that innervate each other to form a network that is involved in autonomic and visceral processes and mechanisms of emotion and learning. It includes portions of the cerebral cortex (see LIMBIC LOBE), thalamus, and certain subcortical structures, such as the AMYGDALA, HIPPOCAMPUS, and SEPTAL AREA.

Limbitrol *n.* a trade name for a combination of the tricyclic antidepressant AMITRIPTYLINE and the benzodiazepine CHLORDIAZEPOXIDE, appropriate for the treatment of concurrent anxiety and depression but not now commonly used.

limen *n.* see THRESHOLD.

limerence *n.* an intense sexual desire and a strong concern for the other person in a romantic relationship, accompanied by great sensitivity to how that other person is reacting to oneself. Limerence typically diminishes in intensity a month or two after the relationship is formed. See also PASSIONATE LOVE; ROMANTIC LOVE. [first described in 1979 by U.S. psychologist Dorothy Tennov (1928–)]

liminal *adj.* relating to the THRESHOLD of a sensation.

liminal sensitivity (**LS**) the degree of sensitivity to a stimulus property. The lower the threshold for an individual, the greater the sensitivity.

liminal stimulus a threshold-level stimulus that elicits a response half of the time.

limited competency a determination by a court that a person is competent with respect to some but not all activities. A limited guardian is appointed to assist the individual in exercising certain legal rights, such as the right to enter into contracts, get married, provide consent, obtain a driver's license, and vote.

limited guardianship a form of legal guardianship of a child or adult with a disability (e.g., mental retardation) in which a guardian has authority with respect to some areas of activity (e.g., legal, financial, health-related) in which the ward is not capable.

limited hold a feature that can be added to a SCHEDULE OF REINFORCEMENT in which the opportunity for REINFORCEMENT is limited to a fixed period. For example, if a FIXED-INTERVAL SCHEDULE in which reinforcement is given after 1 min had a 2-s limited hold, then only responses occurring within 2 s of the end of the 1-min interval would be reinforced.

limited responsibility see DIMINISHED RESPONSIBILITY.

limited symptom attack a discrete episode of intense fear or discomfort in the absence of real danger that meets all the criteria for a PANIC ATTACK but features fewer than four somatic or cognitive symptoms.

limited-term psychotherapy see TIME-LIMITED PSYCHOTHERAPY.

limophthisis *n.* the physical and mental signs of emaciation caused by severe undernourishment.

limulus *n.* see HORSESHOE CRAB.

linear causation the simplest type of causal relationship between events, usually involving a single cause that produces a single effect or a straightforward CAUSAL CHAIN. Linear causation is often contrasted with more complex models of causation involving multiple causes and effects (see CAUSAL AMBIGUITY; CAUSAL TEXTURE), FEEDBACK LOOPS, and indirect or REMOTE CAUSES.

linearity *n.* a relationship between two variables in which one variable is expressed as a linear function of the other variable, that is, all COEFFICIENTS are to the first power. Linear relationships are often, but not necessarily, straight-line relationships.

linear model any model for empirical data that is linear in its parameters; that is, a model that attempts to relate the values of the dependent variable to linear functions of the independent variables. Most commonly used statistical techniques (analysis of variance, regression analysis, etc.) can be represented as linear models. See also GENERAL LINEAR MODEL.

linear perspective the principle that the size of an object's visual image is a function of its distance from the eye. Thus, the same object looks smaller when removed to a distance. Two objects appear closer together as the distance from them increases, as seen in the tracks of a railroad that appear to converge on the horizon.

linear program a form of PROGRAMMED INSTRUCTION in which information is presented in small, discrete, step-by-step frames that usually become progressively more complex. Correct answers are given after each frame, thus eliminating the perpetuation of errors and providing immediate feedback and continuous reinforcement. Compare BRANCHING.

linear regression a REGRESSION ANALYSIS that assumes that the predictor (independent) variable is related to the criterion (dependent) variable through a linear function.

linear system a system in which the response to a complex input is the sum of the separate responses to the separate components of the input (this is the principle of **superposition**). In addition, another condition (**homogeneity**) is necessary: If an input is increased by a certain factor, the output must increase by the same factor.

linear transformation a transformation of X to Y by means of the equation $Y = a + bX$, where a and b are numerical constants.

linear type a body type characterized by a slender, narrow-chested, long-necked, long-nosed physique, sometimes equated with the ASTHENIC TYPE in KRETSCHMER TYPOLOGY.

line management a system of management in which individuals have authority over those immediately below them in the chain of command and are accountable to those immediately above. See UNITY OF COMMAND.

line of beauty an S-shaped curve said by the British painter William Hogarth (1697–1764) to possess maximal beauty.

line of fixation a straight line between the object of visual focus and the FOVEA CENTRALIS.

line of regard a straight line between an object being viewed and the center of rotation of the eye.

line spectrum see SOUND SPECTRUM.

lineup *n.* an identification procedure in which several individuals are presented to an eyewitness of a crime at the same time or in a sequence. The witness is asked to indicate if he or she recognizes one of the lineup members as the perpetrator of the crime.

lingam *n.* see DILDO.

lingering trajectory see TRAJECTORIES OF DYING.

lingua franca a common language used by people of different mother tongues for purposes of communication. Such a language may, but need not, be a hybrid of the mother tongues. Compare CREOLE; PIDGIN.

lingual *adj.* relating to the tongue or to speech and languages.

lingual frenulum see FRENULUM.

lingual gland any of the glands on the surface of the tongue whose seromucous secretions are thought to circulate tastants among the taste cells.

lingual gyrus a relatively short convolution of the cortical surface of the brain running from the occipital to temporal lobes along the inferior surface, medial to the FUSIFORM GYRUS.

lingual nerve a branch of the TRIGEMINAL NERVE (fifth cranial nerve) that supplies fibers to the anterior two thirds of the tongue, including the taste-bud papillae and mucous membrane. Also called **gustatory nerve**.

lingual papilla see PAPILLA.

linguist *n.* a scholar who specializes in the study of linguistics or any of its branches. Such a scholar may focus on the characteristics of a specific language or group of languages or on certain features of human language in general. A linguist will not necessarily have a command of multiple languages, the more precise term for such a person being a **polyglot**.

linguistic approach a method of teaching reading based on the assumption that children have mastery of oral language. Letters and sound equivalents taught in reading are embedded in meaningful words with regular spelling patterns.

linguistic awareness see METALINGUISTIC AWARENESS.

linguistic determinism the hypothesis, most commonly associated with the U.S. linguists Edward Sapir (1884–1939) and Benjamin Lee Whorf (1897–1941), that the semantic structure of a particular language determines the structure of mental categories among its speakers. Because languages differ in how they refer to basic categories and dimensions, such as time, space, and duration, native speakers of these languages are assumed to show corresponding differences in their ways of thinking. Also called **Sapir–Whorf hypothesis**; **Whorfian hypothesis**. Compare LINGUISTIC RELATIVITY. See also ANTHROPOLOGICAL LINGUISTICS; CONTRASTIVE RHETORIC.

linguistic intergroup bias the tendency to describe and evaluate positive behaviors by INGROUP members and negative behaviors by OUTGROUP members more abstractly than negative ingroup and positive outgroup behaviors. See INGROUP BIAS; OUTGROUP EXTREMITY EFFECT; OUTGROUP HOMOGENEITY BIAS.

linguistic–kinesic method the objective study of disordered behavior in terms of language and movement involved in interactions between individuals.

linguistic minority the group of individuals in a polity who are native speakers of a minority language.

linguistic relativity the observation that languages differ in the ways in which semantic space is identified and categorized. For example, the Native American language Hopi uses a completely different word for water in a natural setting and water in a vessel but has only one word for flying objects, which is applied to birds, insects, airplanes, and the like. Linguistic relativity is not to be equated with LINGUISTIC DETERMINISM, which is a theoretical commitment to the idea that these differences have cognitive consequences. See ANTHROPOLOGICAL LINGUISTICS.

linguistics *n.* the scientific study of the physical, structural, functional, psychological, and social characteristics of human language. See also PSYCHOLINGUISTICS; SOCIOLINGUISTICS.

linguistic typology the classification of languages with respect to their structural characteristics rather than their historical relationships (GENETIC LINGUISTICS) or geographical distribution (AREAL LINGUISTICS).

linguistic universal see LANGUAGE UNIVERSAL.

linkage *n.* see GENE LINKAGE.

link analysis in ergonomics, the analysis of operational sequences and the movements of workers or objects that these entail in order to determine the design of tools, equipment, jobs, and facilities that will best serve worker efficiency and safety.

linking verb see COPULA.

Lioresal *n.* a trade name for BACLOFEN.

liothyronine *n.* a pharmaceutical preparation of L-TRIIODOTHYRONINE, a naturally occurring thyroid hormone, used to treat conditions associated with thyroid deficiency. Occasionally it is used as an adjunct to standard antidepressant therapy in the management of depression that has not responded to standard therapy alone. U.S. trade name (among others): **Cytomel**.

lip biting habitual biting of the lips, which may be a nervous habit, a stereotyped behavior (see STEREOTYPY), or associated with a disorder, such as LESCH–NYHAN SYNDROME. Also called **morsicatio labiorum**.

lip eroticism the use of the lips to obtain sexual arousal or satisfaction.

lipid-metabolism disorders a group of metabolic anomalies characterized by abnormal levels of fatty substances in the blood or other tissues, resulting from genetic, endocrine, or external factors or organ failure. Lipid-metabolism disorders include NIEMANN–PICK DISEASE and TAY–SACHS DISEASE.

lipodystrophy *n.* any disorder of lipid metabolism. Kinds of lipodystrophy include **intestinal lipodystrophy**, in which a malabsorption of fats from the digestive tract may be associated with lesions in the central nervous system (as in **Whipple's disease**); and **progressive lipodystrophy**, marked by a symmetrical loss of subcutaneous fat deposits and abnormal deposits of fat around the kidney, heart, and abdominal cavity. No consistent neurological abnormalities are associated with the latter form of lipodystrophy, but nearly 20% of the patients in one study showed signs of mental retardation. The cause of progressive lipodystrophy is unknown. Lipodystrophy is also associated with diabetes mellitus in a form marked by loss of subcutaneous fat in areas injected with insulin; this is known as **lipotrophic diabetes mellitus** or **insulin lipodystrophy**. Manifestations of lipodystrophy are also often found in people living with HIV. See also PARTIAL LIPODYSTROPHY; TOTAL LIPODYSTROPHY.

lipostatic hypothesis a hypothesis stating that the long-term regulation of food intake is governed by the concentration in the blood of free fatty acids, which result from the metabolism of fat. High concentrations indicate the breakdown of fat, and food consumption increases accordingly; low concentrations are associated with reduction in consumption. Also called **lipostatic theory**. See also GLUCOSTATIC THEORY. [originally proposed in 1953 by Gordon C. Kennedy]

lipotrophic diabetes mellitus see LIPODYSTROPHY.

Lipps illusion theory a theory that explains the perception of a variety of visual illusions as visual distortions induced by the emotional state of the observer. [Theodor **Lipps** (1851–1914), German philosopher and psychologist]

lip pursing a facial contortion in which the lips protrude in a manner that resembles pouting or a snout. First described (as **Schnauzkrampf**) by German psychiatrist Karl Ludwig Kahlbaum (1828–1899), it is most commonly associated with CATATONIC SCHIZOPHRENIA.

lipreading *n.* a method used by some people with hearing loss to understand spoken words in which the listener interprets the speaker's lip movements. Some authorities claim that only about one third of speech sounds can be accurately "read" in this way and that attention to facial expression and general body language, with the additional use of SIGN LANGUAGE, assist significantly in better comprehension. Also called **speech reading**.

liquid 1. *adj.* in phonetics, denoting a frictionless speech sound produced when the SOFT PALATE is raised and the airstream is only partially obstructed, such as [l] or [r]. **2.** *n.* a liquid speech sound.

liquidation of attachment the process of freeing a patient from a painful situation by unraveling the ATTACHMENTS in which he or she is bound. [defined by French psychologist Pierre Janet (1859–1947)]

lisp 1. *n.* incorrect production of SIBILANT sounds caused by faulty tongue placement or abnormalities of the articulatory mechanism. Speech and language pathologists have described various types of lisps, including four primary forms: the **interdental** (or **frontal**) **lisp**, in which the tongue protrudes between the front teeth and airflow is directed forward and only partially obstructed; the **dental lisp**, in which the airflow is partially impeded by contact with the tongue as it rests on or pushes against the front teeth or ALVEOLAR RIDGE; the **lateral lisp**, in which airflow and saliva are pushed forward over the sides of the broadly extended tongue, creating a "wet" sound; and the **palatal lisp**, in which the airflow is partially disrupted by the middle area of the tongue touching the rear portion of the SOFT PALATE. See also SIGMATISM. **2.** *vb.* to speak using a lisp. **—lisping** *n.*

LISP *n.* LIS(t) P(rocessing): a computer language that was the primary language for writing artificial intelligence programs from the 1960s through the 1980s. The list is the primary data structure, and the basic unit of the language, the s-expression (symbol-expression), is defined recursively (if X is an s-expression, then so is the list of X). [created by U.S. computer scientist John McCarthy (1927–)]

lissencephaly *n.* the absence of convolutions (GYRI) in the cerebral cortex due to defective development. Symptoms may include unusual facial appearance, difficulty swallowing, muscle spasms, seizures, and severe PSYCHOMOTOR RETARDATION. The condition is characterized by an abnormally small head and is associated with severe to profound mental retardation. Also called **agyria**.

listening *n.* an essential activity in therapy and counseling that involves attending to the words and actions of the client as well as to the intentions conveyed by the words. See also ACTIVE LISTENING.

listening attitude 1. in a therapeutic setting, a therapist's openness to a client's personal experience, or a client's openness to his or her own personal experience. **2.** a behavior set in which a person expects and prepares to receive a message. Italian-born U.S. psychiatrist Silvano Arieti (1914–1982) claimed that a person with schizophrenia who is habitually prepared to experience a hallucination may learn to avoid it when made aware of this attitude.

listening strategy the tendency for listeners to pay more attention at the beginning and end of a talk than in the middle.

listwise deletion an approach to the problem of missing data in which one or more variables, for which there are substantial numbers of missing observations, are simply omitted from the analyses.

literacy *n.* **1.** the ability to read and write in a language. See also BILITERACY. **2.** the quality of being educated as well as knowledgeable. **3.** the quality of having a clear understanding of traditional and contemporary literature. **—literate** *adj.*

literacy test any test that examines the ability to read and write or an individual's understanding of literature.

literal alexia a form of ALEXIA in which a person cannot recognize individual letters or numerals and confuses such letters as *d* and *b*. Also called **literal dyslexia**.

literalism *n.* **1.** adherence to observable facts, as exhibited in Jean PIAGET's construct of OBJECTIVE RESPONSIBILITY. **2.** verbal or nonverbal answers of "yes" or "no," without cognitive elaboration, to questions during HYPNOSIS, asserted by some but strongly refuted by others to be a marker of hypnotic trance. **3.** adherence to the explicit meaning of a text or doctrine, as in biblical literalism.

literal paraphasia a type of speech disturbance in which PHONEMES are substituted in speech, making it difficult to comprehend what the individual is trying to say. For example *tar* may be used for *car*. See PARAPHASIA.

literary psychoanalysis the application of psychoanalysis and psychoanalytic theory to literary interpretation.

lithium *n.* an element of the alkali metal group whose salts are used in psychopharmacotherapy as MOOD STABILIZERS. Lithium salts were first used for the treatment of mania in the 1940s, but widespread use was limited by their toxicity. However, after further investigations into their role in treating bipolar depression, and better appreciation of the appropriate dosage, lithium salts entered broader clinical practice in the 1970s. Although its primary indication (appropriate use) is in managing bipolar disorder, lithium has some efficacy in managing acute manic phases and in reducing relapse. Its mechanism of action remains unclear; it most likely works via inhibition of the recycling of inositol from the INOSITOL PHOSPHATES, which are second messengers in cellular signaling. Toxic doses are no more than two to three times the therapeutic dose, and serum monitoring is required. Symptoms of acute toxicity include tremor, diarrhea, vomiting, and incoordination; at higher doses, disturbances of heart rhythm and neurological function leading to coma and death may occur. Long-term lithium use can cause thyroid and renal dysfunction in a small percentage of patients. Lithium has been associated with fetal cardiac malformation (Ebstein's malformation), and its use in pregnancy is not recommended. U.S. trade names (among others): **Eskalith**; **Lithobid**.

litigious paranoia a type of paranoid disorder characterized by constant quarreling, claims of persecution, and insistence that one's rights have been breached. The individual usually threatens to go to court—and frequently does so—to seek redress for exaggerated or fancied wrongs. Also called **paranoia querulans**; **paranoid litigious state**.

littering *n.* the strewing of trash, garbage, or other waste materials (**litter**) over the surface of an area, contributing to low ENVIRONMENTAL AESTHETICS.

Little Albert the name of a boy used by John B. WATSON and his graduate student Rosalie Rayner (1899–1935) to demonstrate Pavlovian fear conditioning in humans.

Little Hans a landmark case of Sigmund FREUD's, illustrating the OEDIPUS COMPLEX. Freud traced a child's phobia for horses to CASTRATION ANXIETY stemming from masturbation, to repressed death wishes toward the father, and to fear of retaliation owing to rivalry with the mother, with DISPLACEMENT of these emotions onto horses. Freud never actually met the boy but analyzed him through written communication with the father. The case was reported in "Analysis of a Phobia in a Five-Year-Old Boy" (1909).

living will a legal document clarifying a person's intentions and wishes with regard to ASSISTED DEATH or future medical care in the event of incurable illness, prepared at a time when he or she is still competent to make these known.

Lloyd Morgan's canon the principle that the behavior of an animal should not be interpreted in complex psychological terms if it can instead be interpreted with simpler concepts. Lloyd Morgan's canon, proposed in 1894, helped eliminate the older concept of ANTHROPOMORPHISM, or the endowment of animals with human traits, although some recent authors have argued that its application oversimplifies the abilities of animals. Also called **Morgan's canon**; **Morgan's principle**. [Conway **Lloyd Morgan** (1852–1936), British comparative psychologist]

LMX theory abbreviation for LEADER–MEMBER EXCHANGE THEORY.

LNNB abbreviation for LURIA–NEBRASKA NEUROPSYCHOLOGICAL BATTERY.

lobe *n.* a subdivision of an organ, such as the brain or the lungs. The four main lobes of each cerebral hemisphere of the brain are the FRONTAL LOBE, PARIETAL LOBE, TEMPORAL LOBE, and OCCIPITAL LOBE. There are also subdivisions of each of these lobes; for example, the temporal lobe comprises the inferior, middle, and superior temporal lobes. **—lobar** *adj.* **—lobate** *adj.*

lobectomy *n.* surgical removal of an entire lobe, or a portion of a lobe, in the brain. The most frequently performed lobectomy is done for seizure control and involves the anterior temporal lobe (see TEMPORAL LOBECTOMY). See also LEUKOTOMY.

lobotomy *n.* **1.** incision into a lobe in the brain. **2.** see FRONTAL LOBOTOMY.

LOC abbreviation for LOSS OF CONSCIOUSNESS.

local circuit see NEURAL CIRCUIT.

local circuit neuron a neuron with short processes that do not extend far from the CELL BODY. Also called **Golgi Type II neuron**. Compare PROJECTION NEURON.

local enhancement a form of SOCIAL LEARNING in which an individual observes one or more others engaging in some behavior with an object in a particular location. The observer may then interact with the same object or move to the particular location and, as a result, learns some specific behaviors. For example, several animals might be attracted to a specific location where, by chance of being at the same place at the same time (and not through any specific social interactions among themselves), individuals are able to obtain resources more efficiently.

local excitatory state (**LES**) the localized increase in negative potential on the surface of a neuron in response to a subthreshold electric potential. Also called **local excitatory potential**. See also LOCAL POTENTIAL.

local–global distinction the difference between perceiving a whole form and perceiving the subunits that make up that form. For example, if a large letter *S* is formed from an arrangement of small letter *p*s, perception is at the local level if it focuses on the *p*s, and at the global level if it focuses on the *S*.

localization *n.* **1.** the determination of the source (origin) or location of a stimulus, process, or other item. **2.** the assignment of cognitive and behavioral functions to particular regions of the nervous system. Thus, visual functions are associated with the eye, specific nerve tracts, and projection and association neurons of the visual cortex. See also VICARIOUS FUNCTION.

localization of function the concept that specific brain regions are mainly responsible for particular types of experience, behaviors, and psychological processes. Also called **cortical localization of function**. See also BRAIN LOCALIZATION THEORY.

localized amnesia a memory loss restricted to specific or isolated experiences. Also called **circumscribed amnesia**; **lacunar amnesia**.

local potential the phase of a GRADED POTENTIAL that precedes the ACTION POTENTIAL if the localized stimulation is above threshold level. Also called **local response**.

location constancy the tendency for a resting object and its setting to appear to have the same position even if the relationship between setting and observer is altered as the observer shifts position. See also OBJECT CONSTANCY.

location-invariant neurons neurons located in EX-

TRASTRIATE VISUAL AREAS, particularly those in the inferotemporal cortex of the temporal lobe, that respond regardless of the location of a stimulus in the receptive field. Because the receptive fields in these areas are so large, a stimulus may be located almost anywhere in the visual field. Many of these cells are also **size-invariant neurons**, which respond when presented with a particular object, regardless of its size.

loci *pl. n.* see LOCUS.

loci method see METHOD OF LOCI.

lock-and-key theory in the STEREOCHEMICAL SMELL THEORY, the proposition that the shapes of OLFACTORY RECEPTORS accommodate ODORANTS with a particular chemical structure. Molecules are assumed to fit the receptor site in a manner analogous to a key fitting a lock; thus, the molecule opens the lock and produces an odor. See SMELL MECHANISM.

locked-in syndrome a neurological condition, due to an injury to the brain at the level of the INTERNAL CAPSULE, in which the individual is conscious but completely paralyzed, unable to speak or move. Cognition is intact, and electroencephalograms (see ELECTROENCEPHALOGRAPHY) are normal.

locked ward a secured hospital unit in which patients with severe mental disorders are housed. The present trend is toward elimination of locked wards, since patients may feel they are being incarcerated and punished for being ill. Other factors leading to less frequent use of such wards are improvements in psychological interventions, the use of psychoactive drugs, an increase in the staff–patient ratio, and the concepts of the OPEN HOSPITAL and THERAPEUTIC COMMUNITY.

Locke's theory of goal setting a theory suggesting that (a) specific goals direct activity more effectively than do vague or general goals, (b) difficult or challenging goals produce better performance than do moderate or easy goals, and (c) short-term goals can be used to attain long-range goals. At least four mechanisms explain why GOAL SETTING improves performance: (a) It focuses and directs activities, (b) it regulates expenditure of energy, (c) it enhances persistence because the effort is continued until the goal or subgoal is reached, and (d) it can promote the development of new strategies for improving performance. Goal setting only works if there is timely feedback showing performance or progress in relation to the goal. Goals must be accepted to be effective, and their attainment is facilitated by a plan of action or strategy. Competition can be viewed as a form of goal setting. [Edwin A. **Locke** (1938–), U.S. industrial psychologist]

Lockhart v. McCree a case resulting in a 1986 U.S. Supreme Court decision that upheld the constitutionality of the death qualification process (see DEATH-QUALIFIED JURY) despite social science research indicating that this process produces a jury more likely to vote for conviction.

lockout *n.* a tactic used by an employer in negotiating a contract with a union in which employees are barred from entering the workplace and performing their jobs until they agree to the employer's terms.

locomotion *n.* movement of an organism from one place to another. Different species may have different typical modes of locomotion, such as crawling, swimming, flying, quadrupedal walking, and bipedal walking. **—locomotor** *adj.*

locomotor activity a form of general bodily activity involving movement from one area to another, as when an animal explores or chases. See also RESTLESSNESS.

locomotor arrest the inhibition of movement, which can be produced in animals by drugs or electrical stimulation of the HIPPOCAMPUS.

locomotor ataxia severe incoordination in walking, producing an unsteady gait. It involves degeneration of the DORSAL COLUMNS of the spinal cord and is seen in individuals with NEUROSYPHILIS. See GENERAL PARESIS. Also called **tabes dorsalis**.

locomotor play play that is physically vigorous, such as chasing, climbing, and wrestling. There are three distinctive forms of locomotor play: RHYTHMIC STEREOTYPY, EXERCISE PLAY, and ROUGH-AND-TUMBLE PLAY.

loco plant any of certain plants belonging to the genera *Astragalus* or *Oxytropis* that grow wild in western North America, particularly in the Rocky Mountains, and damage the nerve tissue of humans and animals that ingest them (*loco* is the Spanish word for "crazy"). The substances responsible include miserotoxin, swainsonine, and selenium. Symptoms of poisoning include muscular trembling or incoordination, staggering gait, and impairment of depth and other sensory perception. In sufficient doses, these toxins produce irreversible changes in the central nervous system, including brain lesions and eventual paralysis, and may cause coma or death. Also called **loco weed**.

locura *n.* a CULTURE-BOUND SYNDROME found among Latino groups in the United States and Latin America and attributed to hereditary vulnerability, the consequences of stressful and difficult life events, or a combination of the two. Symptoms include incoherence, agitation, auditory and visual hallucinations, inability to follow rules of social interaction, unpredictability, and possibly violence.

locus *n.* (*pl.* **loci**) **1.** the place or position of an anatomical or pathological entity (e.g., a hemorrhage in the brain, a butterfly rash on the skin). **2.** the position of a gene on a chromosome.

locus ceruleus (**locus coeruleus; locus caeruleus**) a small bluish-tinted NUCLEUS in the brainstem whose neurons produce NOREPINEPHRINE and modulate large areas of the forebrain.

locus of control a construct that is used to categorize people's basic motivational orientations and perceptions of how much control they have over the conditions of their lives. People with an **external locus of control** tend to behave in response to external circumstances and to perceive their life outcomes as arising from factors out of their control. People with an **internal locus of control** tend to behave in response to internal states and intentions and to perceive their life outcomes as arising from the exercise of their own agency and abilities. [introduced into psychology by U.S. psychologist Julian Rotter (1916–)]

locutionary act see ILLOCUTIONARY ACT.

LOD score *l*og of the *od*ds score: an estimate of whether or not data indicate that two gene loci are linked, that is, are likely to lie near each other on a chromosome and therefore are likely to be inherited together. A LOD score of 3 or more generally indicates that the two loci are close.

log- *combining form* see LOGO-.

logagnosia *n.* see RECEPTIVE APHASIA.

logamnesia *n.* see RECEPTIVE APHASIA.

logic *n.* **1.** the branch of EPISTEMOLOGY that is concerned with the forms of argument by which a valid conclusion may be drawn from accepted premises. As such it is also concerned with distinguishing correct from fallacious reasoning (see FALLACY). See also DEDUCTIVE REASON-

ING; INFERENCE. **2.** a particular rule-governed form of symbolic expression used to analyze the relations between propositions. See SYMBOLIC LOGIC. —**logical** *adj.*

logical error in rating an error in which judges give similar ratings for variables or traits that are related in the judges' minds but may not actually be related as applied to the ratee.

logical inference see INFERENCE.

logical-mathematical intelligence in the MULTIPLE-INTELLIGENCES THEORY, the set of skills used to solve problems requiring logical or mathematical thinking or both. These abilities are alleged to be relatively independent of the abilities involved in other multiple intelligences.

logical necessity a necessarily valid conclusion that follows from the operations of a system of FORMAL LOGIC on a set of premises or initial conditions.

logical paradox see PARADOX.

logical positivism a philosophical perspective that is committed to the principle of VERIFICATION, which holds that the meaning and truth of all nontautological statements is dependent on empirical observation. In the early 20th century, the positivists of the VIENNA CIRCLE sought to establish the essential unity of logic, philosophy, and science and to distinguish these disciplines from such others as metaphysics, ethics, and religion, which were dismissed for their speculative character. The positivist view of science was influential during the period in which psychology emerged as a science and has had a recognizable influence on the discipline. This is most pronounced in BEHAVIORISM and in psychology's commitment to empirical scientific methods. Logical positivism had waned by the middle of the century. See POSITIVISM. See also PHYSICALISM; POSTPOSITIVISM; REDUCTIONISM.

logical thinking thinking that is consistent with formal principles of LOGIC. See also DEDUCTIVE REASONING.

logicogrammatical disorder a manifestation of SEMANTIC APHASIA that affects individuals with lesions of the dominant PARIETAL LOBE. An individual uses the correct words, but in a sequence that gives a different meaning; for example, the words *plate* and *table* may be transposed in the sentence *The plate is on the table.*

logistic function a basic function of the form

$$y = c/(1 + a\exp(-bx)),$$

where y and x are variables, a, b, and c are constants, and exp is the EXPONENTIAL FUNCTION. The logistic function is used in describing growth rates and longitudinal data.

logistic regression a statistical technique for the prediction of a binary DEPENDENT VARIABLE from one or more continuous variables.

log–linear model a class of statistical techniques used to study the relationship among several CATEGORICAL VARIABLES. As compared with CHI-SQUARE TESTS, log–linear models use ODDS, rather than proportions (see PROPORTIONALITY), and they can be used to examine the relationship among several nominal variables in the manner of ANALYSES OF COVARIANCE.

log–log coordinate paper graph paper on which both ORDINATE and ABSCISSA are in logarithmic form. It is used especially for plotting psychophysical data.

Logo *n.* trademark for a computer programming language designed at the Massachusetts Institute of Technology's Artificial Intelligence Research Laboratory to encourage the development of problem-solving skills. Logo was directed primarily at children and is based on Jean PIAGET's research in the development of thinking.

logo- (**log-**) *combining form* speech or words.

logogen *n.* a theoretical memory unit corresponding to a word, letter, or digit, which when excited results in the output (recall, recognition, or reproduction) of the unit. For example, the logogen for *table* is activated by hearing or seeing the word or via associated words. [proposed by British psychologist John Morton (1933–)]

logographic *adj.* denoting or referring to writing systems that use a separate symbol (**logogram** or **logograph**) to represent each word or MORPHEME.

logopathy *n.* a speech disorder of any kind.

logopedics *n.* primarily in Britain, the study and treatment of speech disorders. See SPEECH AND LANGUAGE PATHOLOGY.

logorrhea *n.* rapid, uncontrollable, and incoherent speech, sometimes occurring as part of a MANIC EPISODE. It was formerly known as **hyperlogia** or **hyperphrasia**. Also called **verbomania**.

logotherapy *n.* an approach to psychotherapy that focuses on the "human predicament," helping the client to overcome crises in meaning. The therapeutic process typically consists of examining three types of values: (a) creative (e.g., work, achievement); (b) experiential (e.g., art, science, philosophy, understanding, loving); and (c) attitudinal (e.g., facing pain and suffering). Each client is encouraged to arrive at his or her own solution, which should incorporate social responsibility and constructive relationships. Also called **meaning-centered therapy**. See also EXISTENTIAL PSYCHOTHERAPY; EXISTENTIALISM. [developed in the 1950s and 1960s by Austrian psychiatrist Viktor E. Frankl (1905–1997)]

-logy (**-ology**) *suffix* field of study (e.g., PHONOLOGY).

Lokian personality a personality pattern characterized by the desire to cause distress to others, manipulative behavior, and deceit. The name is derived from Loki, the Norse god of mischief.

Lolita complex see NYMPHOLEPSY.

London syndrome explicit and constant resistance and refusal by hostages to do what captors expect during a hostage situation, first identified in 1981 after a hostage-taking incident in London. It may result in serious injury and death to the resistors.

loneliness *n.* affective and cognitive discomfort or uneasiness from being or perceiving oneself to be alone or otherwise solitary. Psychological theory and research offer multiple perspectives: Social psychology emphasizes the emotional distress that results when inherent needs for intimacy and companionship are not met; cognitive psychology emphasizes the unpleasant and unsettling experience that results from a perceived discrepancy (i.e., deficiency in quantity or quality) between an individual's desired and actual social relationships. Psychologists from the existential or humanistic perspectives may see loneliness as an inevitable, painful aspect of the human condition that, nevertheless, may contribute to increased self-awareness and renewal.

long-delay conditioning DELAY CONDITIONING in which the period during which the conditioned stimulus is presented is long enough to produce INHIBITION OF DELAY.

longevity *n.* **1.** long life. **2.** the actual length of an individual's life. See also LIFE EXPECTANCY.

longilineal *adj.* denoting a constitutional type of body that is long rather than broad and roughly equivalent to the ASTHENIC TYPE in KRETSCHMER TYPOLOGY.

longitudinal *adj.* **1.** in anatomy, referring to the long

AXIS of the body. **2.** in research, referring to the time dimension, that is, running over an extended period.

longitudinal design the study of a variable or group of variables in the same cases or participants over a period of time, sometimes of several years. An example of a longitudinal design is a comparative study of the same group of children in an urban and a suburban school over several years for the purpose of recording their cognitive development in depth. Compare CROSS-SECTIONAL DESIGN.

longitudinal fissure a FISSURE that marks the division between the left and right cerebral hemispheres of the brain. At the bottom of the fissure the hemispheres are connected by the CORPUS CALLOSUM. Also called **interhemispheric fissure**; **sagittal fissure**.

longitudinal stability the degree to which an individual's possession or expression of a psychological characteristic is consistent over a period.

long-term care facility an EXTENDED CARE institution, such as a NURSING HOME, that provides medical and personal services for patients who are unable to live independently but do not require the inpatient services of a hospital.

long-term depression (**LTD**) a long-lasting decrease in the amplitude of neuronal response due to persistent weak synaptic stimulation (in the case of the hippocampus) or strong synaptic stimulation (in the case of the cerebellum). Compare LONG-TERM POTENTIATION.

long-term memory (**LTM**) memory that endures for long periods of time, enabling one to perform a skilled task, recall events, or reproduce names and numbers long after they were originally learned. See also SECONDARY MEMORY. Compare SHORT-TERM MEMORY.

long-term potentiation (**LTP**) enhancement of synaptic transmission (see SYNAPSE), which can last for weeks, caused by repeated brief stimulations of one nerve cell that trigger stimulation of a succeeding cell. The capacity for potentiation has been best shown in hippocampal tissue. LTP is studied as a model of the neural changes that underlie memory formation and it may be a mechanism involved in some kinds of learning. Compare LONG-TERM DEPRESSION.

long-term therapy psychotherapy over a period of many months or years. Classic PSYCHOANALYSIS, which may last 2–5 years or longer, is a primary example.

long-wavelength pigment the PHOTOPIGMENT, present in one of the three populations of RETINAL CONES, that has maximum sensitivity to a light wavelength of 558 nm. The absence of the gene for the long-wavelength pigment causes PROTANOPIA (red color blindness). See also MEDIUM-WAVELENGTH PIGMENT; SHORT-WAVELENGTH PIGMENT.

look angle in ergonomics, the direction in which the operator looks during task performance. The goal is to design equipment and workstations in such a way that the viewing angle is central or forward, rather than requiring head movements or eye glances to the left or right. See also HEAD-UP DISPLAY.

looking-glass self a SELF-CONCEPT formed by learning how other people perceive and evaluate one. The term suggests a self that is a reflection of other people's impressions, reactions, and opinions. See REFLECTED APPRAISALS; SYMBOLIC INTERACTIONISM. [introduced by U.S. social thinker Charles Horton Cooley (1864–1929)]

look-say *n.* see WHOLE-WORD METHOD.

looming *n.* a type of space perception in which the retinal image of an object is magnified as the object approaches the observer. Reactions to looming vary: Chicks run away, kittens avert their heads, monkeys leap backward making alarm cries, and human infants attempt to withdraw their heads at 2 weeks and blink at 3 weeks.

loose culture a heterogeneous social group whose diverse members tend to value originality, risk-taking, and a flexible adherence to the collective norms of their culture or group. Compare TIGHT CULTURE. [coined by U.S. psychologist Harry C. Triandis (1926–)]

loosening of associations a mental disturbance in which thought and speech processes are disconnected and fragmented, and the individual jumps from one idea to another unrelated or indirectly related idea instead of following the usual lines of association. It is essentially equivalent to DERAILMENT. Also called **loose association**. See also COGNITIVE DERAILMENT; THOUGHT DERAILMENT.

loperamide *n.* an OPIOID that slows gastrointestinal motility and is used for the treatment of diarrhea. Because it is not effectively transported across the BLOOD–BRAIN BARRIER, it has few (if any) psychotropic effects and its abuse potential is low. U.S. trade name: **Imodium**.

lorazepam *n.* a highly potent BENZODIAZEPINE used for the treatment of anxiety, STATUS EPILEPTICUS, and nausea and vomiting and as premedication in surgical anesthesia. Unlike many other benzodiazepines, it has no active metabolic products and therefore requires minimal processing in the liver. This, together with its predictable duration of action, make it a favored drug in the management of alcohol withdrawal in patients with liver impairment. U.S. trade name (among others): **Ativan**.

lordosis *n.* **1.** an abnormal curvature of the spine that, when viewed from the side, shows a concavity in the lumbar and cervical regions. This posture is sometimes called **swayback** or **saddleback**. In extreme cases the condition is known as **hyperlordosis**. See also KYPHOSIS. **2.** in many rodents, a similar but normal posture that is assumed by females during periods of sexual receptivity and serves to facilitate copulation with a male. In the absence of lordosis males are physically unable to mate with the female. See PRESENTING.

Lorenzini ampullae see ELECTRIC SENSE.

LOS abbreviation for LENGTH OF STAY.

loser effect the reduced likelihood that an individual will compete in future contests over resources after repeated experiences of losing in such contests. Often physiological changes, such as increased glucocorticoids (e.g., cortisone, cortisol) or decreased testosterone, occur with the loser effect. Compare WINNER EFFECT.

loss of affect loss of the ability to respond emotionally, which results in FLAT AFFECT.

loss of consciousness (**LOC**) a state in which an organism capable of consciousness can no longer experience events or exert voluntary control. Examples of conditions associated with loss of consciousness include fainting (syncope), deep sleep, coma, general anesthesia, narcolepsy, and epileptic absence.

lost letter procedure an INDIRECT ATTITUDE MEASURE used at an aggregate group level. Two sets of stamped envelopes are created, one addressed to a group likely to adopt a particular attitudinal position on the target issue and the other addressed to a group likely to adopt the opposite position. Equal numbers of each version of the envelope are randomly distributed in a particular community. The procedure is based on the logic that a person finding a letter that has apparently been inadvertently dropped is more likely to place the letter in a mailbox if it is addressed to a group that shares his or her position.

The percentage of people in that community supporting the two positions is then inferred from the number of envelopes that are ultimately mailed to each address. Also called **lost letter technique**. [originally developed by Stanley MILGRAM]

loudness *n.* the subjective magnitude of sound. It is determined primarily by intensity but is also affected by other physical properties, such as frequency, spectral configuration, and duration. The unit of loudness is the **sone**: One sone is the loudness of a 1-kHz tone presented at 40 dB SPL (sound-pressure level). Loudness approximately doubles for each 10-dB increase in intensity. The **loudness level** is the level in decibels SPL of a 1-kHz tone that is judged equally loud to the test sound. The unit is the **phon**: A sound whose loudness level is 40 phons has a loudness equal to that of a 1-kHz tone presented at 40 dB SPL.

loudness summation a situation in which the LOUDNESS of different sounds presented together is the sum of their individual loudnesses. For example, if sound A at 40 dB SPL (decibels sound-pressure level) has a loudness of 1 sone, and sound B at 50 dB SPL has a loudness of 2 sones, then loudness summation is said to occur if the loudness of A and B presented together is 3 sones. Loudness summation depends on the frequency composition of the sounds. See also CRITICAL BAND.

Lou Gehrig's disease see AMYOTROPHIC LATERAL SCLEROSIS. [Henry (Lou) **Gehrig** (1903–1941), U.S. baseball player who died of the disease]

Louis-Bar syndrome see ATAXIA TELANGIECTASIA. [Denise **Louis-Bar** (1914–), French physician]

love *n.* a complex yet basically integrated emotion involving strong feelings of affection and tenderness for the love object, pleasurable sensations in his or her presence, devotion to his or her well-being, and sensitivity to his or her reactions to oneself. Although love takes many forms, including concern for one's fellow humans (brotherly love), parental love, EROTIC LOVE, SELF-LOVE, and identification with the totality of being (love of God), the TRIANGULAR THEORY OF LOVE proposes three essential components: passion, intimacy, and commitment. Social psychological research in this area has focused largely on PASSIONATE LOVE, in which passion (sexual desire and excitement) is predominant, and COMPANIONATE LOVE, in which passion is relatively weak and commitment is strong.

lovemap *n.* a person's mental image of the ideal lover, the ideal love relationship, and ideal sexual activity with that partner, expressed in fantasy and in actual sexual behavior. It incorporates issues of SEXUAL ORIENTATION and also of desire for deviant behaviors (see PARAPHILIA), which are called **altered lovemaps**. [developed by New Zealand-born psychologist John Money (1921–)]

love needs in the humanistic theory of Abraham MASLOW, the third level of the hierarchy of needs, characterized by the striving for affiliation and acceptance. Also called **belongingness and love needs**. See MASLOW'S MOTIVATIONAL HIERARCHY.

love object 1. the person in whom an individual invests the emotions of affection, devotion, and, usually, sexual interest. **2.** in psychoanalytic theory, the person who is loved by the individual's EGO, as opposed to the OBJECT that satisfies an INSTINCT.

love scale a measure of the strength of one person's feeling of love for another. Since love is a complex state occurring in many different forms, the various scales that have been devised do not always recognize the same components of this multifaceted emotion. As examples, the measure assessing PASSIONATE LOVE developed by U.S. social psychologist Elaine Hatfield (1937–) concentrates on items dealing with sexual desires as well as other, more cognitively oriented items, reflecting a preoccupation with the love object and idealization of this person, whereas the ROMANTIC LOVE scale devised by U.S. social psychologist Zick Rubin (1944–) involves elements of both passionate and COMPANIONATE LOVE and includes items dealing with willingness to confide in the loved person and the desire to be with him or her. See also LIKING SCALE.

love withdrawal a form of discipline in which parents threaten to withdraw their love and affection from children if they misbehave.

low-ball technique a procedure for enhancing compliance by first obtaining agreement to a request and then revealing the hidden costs of this request. Compliance to the target request is greater than would have been the case if these costs had been made clear at the time of the initial request. See also DOOR-IN-THE-FACE TECHNIQUE; FOOT-IN-THE-DOOR TECHNIQUE; THAT'S-NOT-ALL TECHNIQUE.

lower motor neuron any of the motor neurons in the cranial nerves or in the ANTERIOR HORN of the spinal cord, which receive input from UPPER MOTOR NEURONS and synapse directly on muscles. In cases of motor dysfunctions (see MOTOR NEURON DISEASE), neurologists attempt to determine whether the fault lies with lower or upper motor neurons.

Lowe's syndrome see OCULOCEREBRORENAL SYNDROME.

low Machs see MACH SCALE.

low normal see BELOW AVERAGE.

low-pass filter see FILTER.

low-pressure hydrocephalus see NORMAL-PRESSURE HYDROCEPHALUS.

low-technology assistive device a device using inexpensive, widely available technology to increase, maintain, or improve the functional capabilities of individuals with disabilities. An example is an eating utensil with a built-up handle. See ASSISTIVE TECHNOLOGY.

low threshold see HIGH THRESHOLD.

low vision reduction of visual capacity (especially visual acuity and visual field), regardless of the underlying cause, that cannot be corrected to the normal range with glasses, contact lenses, or medical or surgical treatment. Low vision causes problems with various aspects of visual performance (e.g., mobility, reading) and is often associated with a decline in quality of life, an increased risk of depression, and decreased functional status. **Low vision services** provided to those with this condition include assessment of an individual's residual vision and instruction in the use of high-powered optical devices (see VISION REHABILITATION). Also called **partial sight**. See also BLINDNESS; VISUAL IMPAIRMENT.

loxapine *n.* an ANTIPSYCHOTIC introduced into the U.S. market in the early 1970s. Loxapine differs from the traditional antipsychotics in that it binds strongly to serotonergic as well as dopaminergic receptors. Although its chemical structure (see DIBENZOXAZEPINE) is similar to that of the atypical antipsychotic CLOZAPINE, loxapine has the same antipsychotic, antiemetic, sedative, and extrapyramidal properties as the traditional antipsychotic agents. U.S. trade name: **Loxitane**.

loyalty *n.* faithfulness and allegiance to individuals or social groups. **—loyal** *adj.*

LPAD abbreviation for LEARNING POTENTIAL ASSESSMENT DEVICE.

LPC scale abbreviation for LEAST PREFERRED COWORKER SCALE.

LPN abbreviation for LICENSED PRACTICAL NURSE.

LRE abbreviation for LEAST RESTRICTIVE ENVIRONMENT.

LS abbreviation for LIMINAL SENSITIVITY.

LSD 1. lysergic acid diethylamide: a highly potent HALLUCINOGEN that structurally resembles the neurotransmitter SEROTONIN and presumably exerts its psychoactive effects by acting as a PARTIAL AGONIST at the 5-HT_{2A} serotonin receptor. It was originally synthesized from the ERGOT ALKALOID lysergic acid in 1938 by Swiss chemist Albert Hoffman, who then discovered its hallucinogenic effects on accidental ingestion in 1943. At very low doses it is capable of producing visual distortions (sharpened sense of color) or frank hallucinations, together with feelings of euphoria or arousal; it became a widely used and controversial recreational drug during the mid-1960s and early 1970s. The effects of LSD were the subject of research during the 1950s as a possible model for psychosis, and various attempts were made to use LSD as an aid to psychotherapy (see PSYCHEDELIC THERAPY), although they did not prove effective. Although the drug is usually taken orally, it has been known to be injected subcutaneously or intravenously. It can also be smoked, in which case intoxication is quite mild. **2.** abbreviation for LEAST SIGNIFICANT DIFFERENCE.

LSD psychotherapy an experimental technique, used in the 1960s, in which the drug LSD (lysergic acid diethylamide) was administered to patients with chronic alcoholism and serious mental disorders (e.g., schizophrenia) as a means of facilitating the process of uncovering and reliving memories and increasing the patients' ability to communicate their thoughts and feelings. Subsequent research not only failed to confirm therapeutic value but also revealed significant physiological, behavioral, and mental health risks in the therapeutic use of LSD, resulting in the abandonment of the technique. See HALLUCINOGEN; PSYCHEDELIC THERAPY.

LTD abbreviation for LONG-TERM DEPRESSION.

LTM abbreviation for LONG-TERM MEMORY.

LTP abbreviation for LONG-TERM POTENTIATION.

lucid dream a dream in which the sleeper is aware that he or she is dreaming and may be able to influence the progress of the dream narrative. Voluntary signaling of prespecified dream features is also possible.

lucid interval a period of mental clarity following a period of delirium, disorganization, or confusion brought on by a mental condition, such as a psychotic state.

lucidity *n.* a mental state in which a person may not have complete ability to reason or comprehend complex matters but has adequate mental powers to be legally responsible for his or her actions. **—lucid** *adj.*

ludes *n.* slang for METHAQUALONE.

ludic activity see PLAY.

Ludiomil *n.* a trade name for MAPROTILINE.

lues *n.* syphilis. The name may be combined with an anatomical or other term, for example, **lues nervosa** for syphilis of the nervous system. **—luetic** *adj.*

lumbar *adj.* referring to the lower part of the back or spinal cord.

lumbar nerve see SPINAL NERVE.

lumbar puncture a procedure used to obtain a sample of cerebrospinal fluid for diagnostic purposes or to measure the pressure of cerebrospinal fluid (see INTRACRANIAL PRESSURE) by inserting a hypodermic needle into the central canal of the spinal cord at a point between two lumbar vertebrae. Also called **spinal puncture**; **spinal tap**.

lumbosacral plexus a network of nerve fibers derived from the spinal roots of the fourth and fifth lumbar nerves and first through fourth sacral nerves (see SPINAL NERVE). It supplies the muscles of the leg and foot. The largest derivative of the lumbosacral plexus is the SCIATIC NERVE. Also called **lumbrosacral plexus**.

lumen (symbol: lm) *n.* the unit of LUMINOUS FLUX equal to the flux emitted by a uniform point source of 1 candela in a solid angle of 1 steradian.

Luminal *n.* a trade name for PHENOBARBITAL.

luminance *n.* the amount of light reflected or emitted from an object as measured in candelas per square meter.

luminosity *n.* the visual sensation of the brightness of a light source. It depends on the power emitted by the source and on the sensitivity of the eye to different wavelengths of light. Other factors can also influence the luminosity; for example, a light of a given LUMINOUS INTENSITY will appear brighter in a room with white walls than in a room with dark walls.

luminosity coefficient see COEFFICIENT OF VISIBILITY.

luminosity curve a graph of visual sensitivity (perceived luminosity) as a function of the wavelength of light.

luminous flux (symbol: Φ_v) the rate at which light is emitted from a source or reflected from a surface. It is measured in LUMENS by reference to a standard source.

luminous intensity (symbol: I_v) the LUMINOUS FLUX emitted per unit solid angle by a point source in a given direction, measured in candelas.

lunacy *n.* **1.** an obsolete name for any mental illness. **2.** in legal use, an obsolete name for mental incompetence or legal INSANITY. **3.** the theory that some forms of mental illness correspond with the phases of the moon. See also MOON-PHASE STUDIES. **—lunatic** *adj., n.*

lunatic asylum an obsolete name for a psychiatric hospital or a mental institution.

Lunesta *n.* a trade name for ZOPICLONE.

Lupron *n.* a trade name for LEUPROLIDE.

lupus erythematosus (**LE**) an autoimmune disorder of connective tissue occurring primarily in young women. Common symptoms are fatigue, fever, migratory joint pains, often a butterfly rash on the nose and cheeks, and scaly red patches on the skin. If the effects are disseminated throughout the body, the condition is known as **systemic lupus erythematosus** (**SLE**). A high prevalence of mild neuropsychiatric syndromes (e.g., mild cognitive dysfunction, headache, mild depression, anxiety) is associated with the disorder.

lure *n.* an incorrect item presented among correct items in testing memory, to serve as a DISTRACTOR.

Luria, Alexander R. (1902–1977) Russian neuropsychologist. Luria earned a degree in medicine in 1937 from the Moscow Medical School, having already worked in the field of psychology for over a decade. In the 1920s, before his medical training, Luria collaborated with Lev VYGOTSKY on the sociocultural theory of language. During World War II, Luria headed psychological services in a brain trauma hospital; following the war he became a faculty member in neuropsychology at Moscow University and head of the neuropsychological laboratory at the Burdenko Institute of Neurosurgery, from which he was forced to resign for political reasons. It is for his research and theories on brain trauma and brain function that Luria is perhaps best known. He developed a system of NEUROPSYCHOLOGICAL ASSESSMENT that aided in diagnosis, treatment, and rehabilitation of brain trauma patients. His assessment techniques also proved valuable in the cognitive assessment of children. Luria's work became influential outside Russia in the 1960s and 1970s. Some of his best known books include *The Working Brain* (1973), *Cognitive Development: Cultural and Social Foundations* (1976), *The Making of Mind* (1979), and *Language and Cognition* (1982).

Luria–Nebraska Neuropsychological Battery (LNNB) a set of tests to assess the cognitive functioning of individuals aged 15 years and older that is intended to represent a standardized, quantitative version of Alexander LURIA's neuropsychological testing procedures. The battery is available in two versions (Form I comprising 269 items and Form II comprising 279 items) and is used to diagnose general and specific cerebral dysfunction and to localize impaired brain areas. It includes 11 clinical scales, each representing different aspects of relevant skills: motor functions, tactile functions, visual functions, rhythm, receptive speech, expressive speech, writing, reading, arithmetic, memory, and intellectual processess; Form II also includes an intermediate-term memory scale. [originally developed in 1978 by U.S. clinical psychologists Charles J. Golden (1949–), Thomas A. Hammeke (1950–), and Arnold D. Purisch (1951–)]

Luria technique see COMBINED MOTOR METHOD. [Alexander **Luria**]

lust *n.* a very intense desire, usually associated with erotic excitement or arousal.

lust murder an extreme form of SEXUAL SADISM in which an individual experiences sexual arousal from the murder of a partner during the sexual act, often including elaborate staging of the act and mutilation of the victim's body. Also called **erotophonophilia**. See also HOMICIDOPHILIA.

luteal phase see MENSTRUAL CYCLE.

luteinizing hormone (LH) a GONADOTROPIN secreted by the anterior pituitary gland that, in females, stimulates the rapid growth of a GRAAFIAN FOLLICLE in the ovary until it ruptures and releases an ovum (see MENSTRUAL CYCLE). In males it stimulates the interstitial cells of the TESTIS to secrete androgens. Also called **interstitial cell-stimulating hormone (ICSH)**.

luteotropic hormone see PROLACTIN.

Luvox *n.* a trade name for FLUVOXAMINE.

lux *n.* the standard unit of ILLUMINANCE, equal to the illumination produced by a luminous flux of 1 lm (LUMEN) per square meter.

LVN abbreviation for licensed vocational nurse. See LICENSED PRACTICAL NURSE.

lycanthropy *n.* **1.** the supposed transformation, through witchcraft or magic, of a human being into a wolf or other animal (from Greek *lykos*, "wolf"). Belief in lycanthropy reached epidemic proportions in Europe during the 16th century, when 600 supposed lycanthropes were sentenced to death for having committed violent crimes in animal form. Also called **lycomania**; **zoanthropy**. **2.** a condition in which a person has delusions that he or she is, or can become, a wolf or other animal.

lygophilia *n.* an abnormal desire to be in dark or gloomy places.

Lyme disease a multisystemic illness caused by spirochete bacteria transmitted through the bite of an infected deer tick. Initial effects are a red rash around the site of the bite as well as flulike symptoms of fever, fatigue, headache, and body ache. If left untreated, the disease can result in ARTHRITIS, neurological symptoms (e.g., severe headache and temporary paralysis), and problems with memory loss, concentration, sleep, and mood changes. Its manifestation of physical, cognitive, and psychiatric symptoms makes it difficult to diagnose. The disease was first recognized in 1975 after a large number of children in Lyme, Connecticut, and nearby towns were initially diagnosed with rheumatoid arthritis.

lymphocyte *n.* a type of blood cell (see LEUKOCYTE) that plays a key role in specific IMMUNE RESPONSES. There are two main classes: B lymphocytes and T lymphocytes. **B lymphocytes** (or **B cells**), which develop and mature in the bone marrow, are responsible for humoral immunity: They produce circulating antibodies when they bind to an appropriate antigen and are costimulated by certain T cells. **T lymphocytes** (or **T cells**), which mature in the thymus, are responsible for cell-mediated immunity: They are characterized by the presence of particular cell-surface molecules and are capable of antigen recognition. There are two main subclasses: cytotoxic T cells, which release proteins that destroy invading cells; and helper T cells, which assist in this or other aspects of the immune response. See also NATURAL KILLER CELL. **—lymphocytic** *adj.*

lymphokine *n.* any of a group of proteins, secreted by lymphocytes, that have a role in cell-mediated immunity by inducing other cells of the immune system to divide. See CYTOKINE.

lynching *n.* an instance of a group or mob of vigilantes killing a person, especially by hanging. The lynch mob often justifies its actions by claiming that the victim is guilty of some crime and the group is administering an appropriate punishment. Most lynchings in the United States were racially motivated acts of violence perpetrated by White Americans against African Americans. The first documented U.S. lynching occurred in 1882, and by 1950 lynch mobs had killed over 3,000 people. **—lynch** *vb.*

lysergic acid diethylamide see LSD.

lysine *n.* an essential AMINO ACID that cannot be synthesized by the body and must be supplied in the diet. It is often added to human or nonhuman animal foods to improve their nutritive value.

lysinuria *n.* the presence of the amino acid lysine in the urine, due to deficiency of an enzyme involved in its metabolism. It is an inherited condition associated with muscle weakness and mental retardation.

lysis *n.* the gradual subsidence of the symptoms of a disease or disorder. Compare CRISIS.

-lysis *suffix* dissolution or breaking down (e.g., PARALYSIS).

Mm

M 1. abbreviation for memory. See PRIMARY ABILITIES. **2.** in statistics, symbol for MEAN.

MA abbreviation for MENTAL AGE.

mace *n.* an aromatic spice made from the fibrous seed coat of the NUTMEG. Mace has been associated with the euphoric effects produced by nutmeg intoxication, although the active ingredients of nutmeg are concentrated primarily in the oil of the nut.

Mach bands an example of a CONTRAST ILLUSION produced by two or more adjacent rectangular gray stimuli or bands that differ in lightness. The part of the light band that borders the dark band appears to be lighter than the rest of the light band, while the part of the dark band along the border between the two bands appears to be darker than the rest of the dark band. [Ernst **Mach** (1838–1916), Czech-born Austrian physicist]

Mach card a card used to demonstrate the factors that influence the perception of the brightness of a surface. A gray card is folded in half like a book, placed on a surface so that the convex side faces the observer, and then illuminated from either the left or the right. Even though the side closest to the illumination is physically brighter than the other side of the card, both sides appear roughly equal in brightness, an example of BRIGHTNESS CONSTANCY. However, the concave–convex nature of the card is ambiguous when viewed with one eye; when the card is perceived as concave, the side farther from the illumination suddenly appears darker than it does when the card is perceived as convex. [Ernst **Mach**]

Mach–Dvorak stereoillusion an illusion of perceived depth in the motion of a stimulus that actually moves only in two dimensions, such as a pendulum. The illusion is induced by allowing one eye to view the motion before the other eye and never allowing both eyes to view the motion at the same time. The delay between the from the two eyes is interpreted by the visual system as RETINAL DISPARITY, a normal DEPTH CUE. Compare PULFRICH EFFECT. [Ernst **Mach**; Vinko **Dvorak** (1848–1922), Czech physicist]

Machian positivism the subjectivist form of POSITIVISM developed by Czech-born Austrian physicist Ernst Mach (1838–1916). Mach held, with other positivists, that sensory experience is the touchstone of knowledge; however, unlike most other positivists, he held that sensations do not faithfully represent the reality of an EXTERNAL WORLD. Thus, from this antirealist perspective, empirical knowledge is subjective.

Machiavellian hypothesis the hypothesis that the evolution of intelligence, especially in its social aspects, was largely dependent on behavior characterized by a desire and striving for power. Individuals who were more Machiavellian in their behavior were more likely to be successful in adaptation and thus more likely to spread their genes to future generations. [Niccolò **Machiavelli** (1469–1527), Italian political theorist]

Machiavellianism *n.* a personality trait marked by a calculating attitude toward human relationships and a belief that ends justify means, however ruthless. A **Machiavellian** is one who views other people more or less as objects to be manipulated in pursuit of his or her goals, if necessary through deliberate deception. [Niccolò **Machiavelli**, who argued that an effective ruler must be prepared to act in this way]

machine consciousness replication of conscious functions via computers or robots.

Machover Draw-a-Person Test (**DAP test**) a projective technique based on the interpretation of drawings of human figures. The participant is given a sheet of blank paper and asked first to draw an entire person, without specification of details of age, sex, clothing, and so forth, and then to draw another person, without any specification other than that it must be of opposite sex from the first. The examiner, relying on his or her individual clinical experience, then interprets the drawings and any verbalizations the participant made while creating them in order to formulate a description of the participant's personality and identify signs of pathology. Various features of the drawings that are assessed include sequence of sex (whether a male or female is drawn first), the order in which body parts are drawn, distortions, omissions, size, and clothing, as well as more structural elements, such as direction of pencil strokes, shadings, and erasures. Analogous to this test is the **Machover Draw-a-House Test** (**DAH test**). [developed in 1949 by Karen **Machover** (1902–1996), U.S. psychologist]

Mach scale a measurement of the degree to which individuals condone, tolerate, or condemn the use of manipulation and deceit in pursuit of material or other aims. **Low Machs** affirm absolute ethical standards; **high Machs** reveal relative and shifting standards of behavior. "Mach" is an abbreviation for MACHIAVELLIANISM.

MacLean's theory of emotion an extension of PAPEZ'S THEORY OF EMOTION emphasizing the importance of all parts of the LIMBIC SYSTEM, especially the hippocampus and amygdala, in the control of emotional experience. Also called **Papez–MacLean theory of emotion**. See also CANNON–BARD THEORY. [Paul D. **MacLean** (1913–), U.S. neurologist]

macro- (**macr-**) *combining form* large or enlarged.

macrobiotics *n.* a theory of nutrition that is based on achieving balance and harmony between foods that are classified, according to the Chinese concept, as either yin or yang (see YIN AND YANG). **Macrobiotic diets** consist mainly of whole grains and vegetables, with fruit and occasional fish; animal products are avoided. Food is prepared and cooked in particular ways to preserve the yin and yang characteristics. [introduced to the West by Japanese educator George Ohsawa (1893–1966)]

macrocephaly *n.* a rare congenital defect involving gross enlargement of the head due to abnormal growth of the supporting tissue of the brain or to HYDROCEPHALUS. It can result in moderate to severe mental retardation with impaired vision and seizures. Also called **megalocephaly**. Compare MICROCEPHALY. **—macrocephalic** *adj.*

macroelectrode *n.* a conductor of electrical current usually with a diameter of a millimeter or more, used, for example, to stimulate or record from tissue. Compare MICROELECTRODE.

macroergonomics *n.* an approach to ERGONOMICS that examines any given WORK SYSTEM from a broad perspective in which all of its various elements—physical, organizational, environmental, and cognitive—are given due consideration. Compare MICROERGONOMICS. See also SOCIOTECHNICAL SYSTEMS APPROACH; SYSTEMS ENGINEERING.

macroglossia *n.* an abnormally large tongue, affecting the production of lingual sounds in speech.

macrogyria *n.* see PACHYGYRIA.

macromastia *n.* abnormally large breasts in a female.

macropsia *n.* a VISUAL ILLUSION in which an object appears to be larger than it is in reality. Also called **megalopsia**. See also METAMORPHOPSIA. Compare MICROPSIA.

macroskelic *adj.* denoting a constitutional type of body build in which the most prominent characteristic is abnormally long legs. The macroskelic individual would be classified as the ASTHENIC TYPE in KRETSCHMER TYPOLOGY.

macrosplanchnic type a body type in which the trunk is disproportionately large compared with the limbs. Also called **macrosplanchnic build**. [described by Italian physician Giacinto Viola (1870–1943)]

macrosystem *n.* in ECOLOGICAL SYSTEMS THEORY, the level of environmental influence that is most distal to the developing individual and that affects all other systems. It includes the values, traditions, and sociocultural characteristics of the larger society. See also EXOSYSTEM; MESOSYSTEM. [introduced by Russian-born U.S. psychologist Urie Bronfenbrenner (1917–2005)]

macula *n.* (*pl.* **maculae**) **1.** in hearing, a patch of sensory tissue in the UTRICLE and SACCULE of the inner ear that provides information about the position of the body in relation to gravity. The macula contains sensory HAIR CELLS whose processes (stereocilia) are embedded in a gelatinous matrix (**cupula**) containing calcareous particles (**otoliths**). When the orientation of the head changes, the relatively dense otoliths respond to gravity, causing the gelatinous mass to shift and the stereocilia to flex. This triggers nerve impulses in the hair-cell fibers, which act as signals to the brain. **2.** in vision, see MACULA LUTEA.

macula lutea a small spot in the retina that is in direct alignment with the optics of the eye. It contains a yellow pigment and a central depression, the FOVEA CENTRALIS. Also called **macula**.

macular degeneration dystrophy of the MACULA LUTEA, which affects both eyes and causes progressive loss of central vision. Macular degeneration occurs at various ages from birth to old age. **Age-related macular degeneration** is among the most common causes of VISUAL IMPAIRMENT in older people, with an incidence of about 5% in those aged 55–64 and up to about 45% in those aged 75–84. There are two types: **exudative** (or **wet**) **macular degeneration**, in which blood vessels grow under the retina and hemorrhage in the area of the macula; and **atrophic** (or **dry**) **macular degeneration**, in which one of the retinal layers degenerates or atrophies. Apart from age, other risk factors for the disease include exposure to ultraviolet light, smoking, hypertension, and possibly zinc deficiency in the diet.

macular sparing see VISUAL FIELD SPARING.

macular splitting see VISUAL FIELD SPARING.

maculopathy *n.* damage to the MACULA LUTEA, resulting in deterioration of visual acuity. It is caused by leakage from abnormal retinal capillaries, leading to the formation of hard exudate and edema.

MADD abbreviation for MOTHERS AGAINST DRUNK DRIVING.

Maddox rod test a test of eye-muscle balance. The individual views a light source through glass rods, which convert it into a line of light: The differential images perceived by the two eyes indicate the degree of HETEROPHORIA. [Ernest Edmund **Maddox** (1860–1933), British ophthalmologist]

Mad Hatter's disease a condition caused by chronic mercury poisoning and characterized by changes in mental status, emotional disturbance, gastrointestinal disturbances, and weakness or partial paralysis of the legs. The condition may also cause psychosis, behavioral changes, ERETHISM, and several other symptoms. Also called **Mad Hatter's syndrome**.

madness *n.* an obsolete name for mental illness or for legal INSANITY.

MAE 1. abbreviation for MULTILINGUAL APHASIA EXAMINATION. **2.** abbreviation for MOTION AFTEREFFECT.

MAF abbreviation for MINIMAL AUDIBLE FIELD.

magazine training in OPERANT CONDITIONING, the training needed to familiarize an experimental animal with the mechanism (usually a feeder) that delivers the REINFORCER.

magic *n.* **1.** a system of practices in which humans attempt to manipulate natural or supernatural forces through such means as rituals, incantations, and spells. Magic had an important social role in many prescientific societies, where its practitioners often held great power and authority. In the modern world, magical belief has survived most obviously as an underground esoteric tradition (see OCCULT) but also in many popular superstitions and "New Age" practices. Magical rituals can be said to differ from religious rituals in that they involve a direct attempt to control certain physical facts (e.g., the weather), as opposed to a supplication to a higher power or powers. **2.** in some individuals with OBSESSIVE-COMPULSIVE DISORDER, attempts to allay anxiety by invoking certain numbers or performing certain rituals. See also MAGICAL THINKING. **—magical** *adj.*

magical number see SEVEN PLUS OR MINUS TWO.

magical thinking the belief that events or the behavior of others can be influenced by one's thoughts, wishes, or rituals. Magical thinking is normal in children up to 4 or 5 years of age, after which reality thinking begins to predominate.

magic bone see VOODOO DEATH.

magic circle a group technique, usually used with children, who gather in a circle and disuss personal issues and concerns. A variation for use in school was developed by U.S. psychiatrist William Glasser (1925–) to increase motivation for learning.

magic mushroom see PSILOCIN.

magic omnipotence see COSMIC IDENTIFICATION.

Magna Mater Carl JUNG'S ARCHETYPE of the primordial mother image, based on the Great Mother of the Roman gods, Cybele. She represents that which is loving, sustaining, and fostering of growth and creativity. See also MOTHER ARCHETYPE. [Latin: "great mother"]

magnetic resonance imaging (MRI) a noninvasive diagnostic technique that uses the responses of hydrogen in tissue molecules to strong magnetic impulses to form a three-dimensional picture of body organs and tissues (e.g., the brain) with more accuracy than COMPUTED

TOMOGRAPHY. See also FUNCTIONAL MAGNETIC RESONANCE IMAGING.

magnetic sense the ability of an organism to orient itself according to the lines of force of a magnet or the magnetic fields of the earth. Some migrating birds tend to follow magnetic fields of the earth with the aid of a sensory apparatus that detects the force of magnetism. Homing pigeons use their magnetic sense as a backup system when solar cues for NAVIGATION are lacking, for example, on overcast days.

magnetoencephalography (**MEG**) *n.* the measurement of the magnetic signals arising from the electrical activity of the brain, using a device called a **magnetoencephalograph** (MEG). See also SUPERCONDUCTING QUANTUM INTERFERENCE DEVICE.

magnification factor in retinotopic mapping, see CORTICAL MAGNIFICATION FACTOR.

magnification power see FOCUSING POWER.

magnitude estimation subjective judgment of the magnitude of a stimulus by assigning it a numerical value along a scale. This might be required of a participant in a psychophysical experiment. See also METHOD OF CONSTANT STIMULI; METHOD OF LIMITS.

magnitude of effect see EFFECT SIZE.

magnitude of response see RESPONSE AMPLITUDE.

magnitude production a DIRECT SCALING procedure in which the observer is provided with a number representing the magnitude of a stimulus and is required to adjust the stimulus to produce a sensation that corresponds to this number, with reference to a standard stimulus to which a magnitude number has also been assigned. Also called **production method**.

magnitude scaling of attitudes a procedure for measuring attitudes and other constructs by representing them as physical stimuli. Participants indicate their attitudes by regulating some perceptual property of a stimulus, such as the brightness of a light, the length of a line, or the pitch of a tone. For example, they might indicate their evaluation of an object by turning a brightness dial on a light, with no light representing an extremely negative attitude and maximum brightness representing an extremely positive attitude. This procedure usually involves reporting the attitude on two different perceptual properties and then validating the measurement procedure by confirming that the mathematical relationship between these two modalities is close to established numerical values for the specific modalities. [primarily developed by U.S. psychologist Milton G. Lodge (1936–)]

magnocellular nucleus of the basal forebrain a collection of neurons in the BASAL FOREBRAIN that modulates the activity of many areas of the NEOCORTEX by providing CHOLINERGIC innervation. It is implicated in ALZHEIMER'S DISEASE. Also called **basal nucleus of Meynert**; **Meynert's nucleus**; **nucleus basalis magnocellularis**.

magnocellular system the part of the visual system that projects to or originates from large neurons in the two most ventral layers (the **magnocellular layers**) of the LATERAL GENICULATE NUCLEUS. It allows the rapid perception of movement, form, and changes in brightness but is relatively insensitive to stimulus location and color. See also M-CELLS. Compare PARVOCELLULAR SYSTEM.

Mahalanobis D^2 a measure of the distance between points in a multidimensional space. [Prasanta Chandra **Mahalanobis** (1893–1972), Indian statistician]

maieutic technique in psychotherapy, a commonly used form of SOCRATIC DIALOGUE in which pertinent questions are asked to achieve understanding on the part of the person being questioned. The questioner often already knows the answers. [from Greek *maieutikos*, literally: relating to midwifery or acting as a midwife]

main clause see CLAUSE.

main effect in the ANALYSIS OF VARIANCE, the consistent effect of a treatment (independent variable) over all other factors in the design, as contrasted with an INTERACTION EFFECT.

mainlining *n.* slang for taking illicit drugs by intravenous injection. See INTRAVENOUS DRUG USAGE. **—mainliner** *n.*

mainstreaming *n.* **1.** the placement of children with physical or cognitive impairments or CHALLENGING BEHAVIOR into regular classroom environments. The aim is to offer each child the opportunity to learn in an environment that has the highest probability of facilitating rehabilitation efforts and supporting academic growth. See also FULL INCLUSION; LEAST RESTRICTIVE ENVIRONMENT; REASONABLE ACCOMMODATIONS. **2.** the return of recovered or deinstitutionalized patients to the community, where they receive rehabilitative assistance directed toward helping them achieve as full and normal a life as possible.

maintaining cause an influence in a person's environment that tends to maintain and reinforce maladaptive behavior. An example is the required participation at cocktail parties of a professional person with alcoholism.

maintenance function any of the processes that keep an organism's physiological activities in HOMEOSTASIS.

maintenance rehearsal repeating items over and over to maintain them in SHORT-TERM MEMORY, as in repeating a telephone number until it has been dialed (see REHEARSAL). According to the LEVELS-OF-PROCESSING MODEL OF MEMORY, maintenance rehearsal does not effectively promote long-term retention because it involves little ELABORATION of the information to be remembered.

maintenance role see RELATIONSHIP ROLE.

maintenance therapy treatment or therapy designed to maintain patients in a stable condition and to promote gradual healing or prevent relapse. It usually (but not always) refers to **maintenance drug therapy** (**maintenance pharmacotherapy** or **prophylactic maintenance**). Drug therapy is generally divided into three phases—acute, continuation, and maintenance—roughly corresponding to intervals of 1 month, 6 months, and a year or longer. Patients who respond in the acute and continuation phases may be placed on maintenance pharmacotherapy in the hopes of preventing relapse. Drugs that may be used for maintenance include methadone (see METHADONE MAINTENANCE THERAPY), antipsychotics, lithium, and antidepressants. Prophylactic maintenance alone, however, does not eliminate relapse; for several conditions, evidence suggests that psychotherapy must also be included to minimize relapse. Although maintenance therapy is often continued indefinitely, patients should be periodically reassessed to determine if such treatment is still necessary.

major depressive disorder a DEPRESSIVE DISORDER in which the individual has experienced at least one MAJOR DEPRESSIVE EPISODE but has never experienced a MANIC EPISODE, MIXED EPISODE, or HYPOMANIC EPISODE. Also called **major depression**.

major depressive episode an episode of a MOOD DISORDER in which, for at least 2 weeks, the individual has either persistent depressed mood or ANHEDONIA as well as at least four other symptoms. These other symptoms include: poor or increased appetite with significant weight loss or gain; insomnia or excessive sleep; PSYCHOMOTOR AGITATION or PSYCHOMOTOR RETARDATION; loss of energy with fatigue; feelings of worthlessness or inappropriate guilt; reduced ability to concentrate or make decisions; and recurrent thoughts of death, SUICIDAL IDEATION, or ATTEMPTED SUICIDE. All of these symptoms cause significant distress or impair normal functioning (social, occupational, etc.). One or more major depressive episodes are a characteristic feature of MAJOR DEPRESSIVE DISORDER and bipolar II disorder and often occur in bipolar I disorder (see BIPOLAR DISORDERS).

major histocompatibility complex (**MHC**) a gene complex that regulates responses of the immune system protecting an organism from disease. The MHC varies greatly among individuals within a species and has been suggested as a basis for MATE SELECTION and KIN RECOGNITION. Mice prefer mates whose MHC differs from their own and can base this choice on differences in individual odors.

majority influence social pressure exerted by the larger portion of a group on individual members and smaller factions within the group. The majority tends to push for CONFORMITY and stability, and members usually respond to this either by accepting the majority's position as their own (CONVERSION) or by conforming publicly but retaining their own position privately (COMPLIANCE). Compare MINORITY INFLUENCE.

majority vote technique in parapsychology experiments, a technique in which the participant makes several "calls" or guesses about a single TARGET, the most frequent being considered the participant's only response.

major tranquilizers a name formerly applied to ANTIPSYCHOTICS to distinguish them from anxiolytic, sedative, and hypnotic drugs (which were called minor tranquilizers).

make-believe *n.* see SYMBOLIC PLAY.

mal- *prefix* **1.** bad or wrong (e.g., MALPRACTICE). **2.** diseased or abnormal (e.g., MALNUTRITION).

maladaptation *n.* a condition in which biological or psychological traits, behavior patterns, or defense mechanisms are detrimental, counterproductive, or otherwise interfere with optimal functioning in various domains, such as successful interaction with the environment and effectual coping with the challenges and stresses of daily life. **—maladaptive** *adj.*

maladjustment *n.* **1.** inability to maintain effective relationships, function successfully in various domains, or cope with difficulties and stresses. **2.** any emotional disturbance of a relatively minor nature. **—maladjusted** *adj.*

malaise *n.* a slight feeling of illness, discomfort, and uneasiness.

malapropism *n.* a linguistic error in which one word is mistakenly used for another having a similar sound, often to ludicrous effect, as in *She was wearing a cream casserole* (for *camisole*) or *I can't eat pasta without marzipan* (for *parmesan*). The term is named for Mrs. Malaprop, a character in Richard Brinsley Sheridan's play *The Rivals* (1775), whose speech is full of preposterous errors of this kind.

Malcolm horizon an improvement in flight instruments, based on ergonomic principles, in which the ground representation of the display is extended across the cockpit. This makes it easier to detect small angular motions. [Richard **Malcolm**, Canadian aviator]

mal de ojo a CULTURE-BOUND SYNDROME, reported in many Mediterranean regions, that is characterized by fever, sleep disturbances, and gastrointestinal problems. It most commonly affects children; the Spanish name translates to EVIL EYE.

mal de pelea a CULTURE-BOUND SYNDROME found in Puerto Rico that is similar to AMOK. Individuals experience a period of brooding and then suddenly become violent and attack others around them (the Spanish name literally means "fighting sickness"). Also called **Puerto Rican syndrome**.

maldevelopment *n.* the defective development of an individual because of genetic, dietary, or external factors that interfere with the normal rate of growth of tissues and bodily functions. A protein and calorie deficiency in children weaned prematurely, in particular in developing countries, may result in MARASMUS and KWASHIORKOR, which are marked by delayed physical and mental growth.

male chauvinism the belief that men are inherently superior to women. See CHAUVINISM; SEXISM.

male climacteric a hypothetical period in some men's lives that has been compared to female menopause (see CLIMACTERIC). Popularly known as **male menopause**, it occurs some 10 years later than in women and appears to be associated with declines in the levels of various hormones, such as testosterone. Symptoms, when they occur, include fatigue, problems with memory and concentration, decreased sexual desire, erectile dysfunction, and (in some cases) depression. Also called **andropause**; **male climacterium**. See also GONADOPAUSE.

male continence see EJACULATIO RETARDATA; COITUS RESERVATUS.

male erectile disorder in *DSM–IV–TR*, persistent or recurrent inability in a man to achieve or maintain an erection adequate to complete the sex act. It causes marked distress and impairment of interpersonal relations and is not due to the physiological effects of a physical disorder, medication, or a substance of abuse. The disorder may be lifelong or acquired and either situational (occurring only in certain situations or with certain partners) or generalized (occurring in all situations). See also ERECTILE DYSFUNCTION; IMPOTENCE.

male homosexual prostitution sexual contact between males for the financial or other gain of one of the participants. Studies indicate that a social hierarchy exists among male prostitutes, as in female prostitution. Lowest in status are the **street hustlers**, who are usually teenage boys and not necessarily gay themselves; next are the **bar hustlers**; and highest in prestige are the **call boys**, who do not solicit in public.

male–male competition in species in which the OPERATIONAL SEX RATIO leads to more reproductively active males than females, the rivalry that ensues as males compete over which will be able to mate with receptive females. In some species, such as COOPERATIVE-BREEDING mammals, male parental care is a limiting resource to female reproduction, and there is extensive **female–female competition**.

male menopause see MALE CLIMACTERIC.

maleness *n.* the quality of being male in the anatomical and physiological sense by virtue of possessing the XY combination of SEX CHROMOSOMES. Compare MASCULINITY.

male orgasmic disorder in *DSM–IV–TR*, persistent or recurrent delay in, or absence of, male orgasm during sexual stimulation that produces arousal. The man's age and the quality and duration of stimulation are considered in making this diagnosis, which does not apply if the condition is due only to the effects of drugs, medications, or medical conditions.

male sexual disorder any problem in sexual function experienced by males. See HYPOACTIVE SEXUAL DESIRE DISORDER; MALE ORGASMIC DISORDER; PREMATURE EJACULATION; PRIMARY ERECTILE DYSFUNCTION; SECONDARY ERECTILE DYSFUNCTION.

malevolent transformation the feeling that one lives among enemies and can trust no one. This attitude, purported to be the result of harsh or unfair treatment during childhood, has been posited to be the basis for social withdrawal, hostility, and, in some cases, mental disorder of a persecutory nature. [first described by U.S. psychiatrist Harry Stack Sullivan (1892–1949)]

malformation *n.* **1.** defective or abnormal structure. **2.** a DEFORMITY.

malfunction *n.* the failure of an organ or mechanical process to work properly.

malice aforethought the mental elements of PREMEDITATION and deliberation or extreme disregard for human life that are required for a person to be convicted of first-degree murder.

malignant *adj.* **1.** describing a disorder that gets progressively worse or is resistant to treatment, eventually causing death. **2.** describing a tumor that invades and destroys tissues and may also spread to other sites (i.e., undergo metastasis). See CANCER; NEOPLASM. Compare BENIGN.

mali-mali *n.* a CULTURE-BOUND SYNDROME found in the Philippines, with symptoms similar to those of LATAH.

malingering *n.* the deliberate feigning of an illness or disability to achieve a particular desired outcome (e.g., financial gain or escaping responsibility, punishment, imprisonment, or military duty). For example, it may take the form of faking mental illness as a defense in a trial, faking physical illness to win compensation, and, in sport, faking an injury or misinforming people of one's state of rehabilitation in order to avoid practicing or playing. Malingering is distinguished from FACTITIOUS DISORDER in that it involves a specific external factor as the motivating force. **—malingerer** *n.*

malleation *n.* a spasmodic tic in which the hands twitch in a hammering motion against the thighs.

malleus *n.* see OSSICLES.

malnutrition *n.* a state of health characterized by an improper balance of carbohydrates, fats, proteins, vitamins, and minerals in the diet with respect to energy needs as reflected in physical activity. Malnutrition may be due to excessive intakes of food categories, as in OBESITY and hypervitaminosis (see VITAMIN A TOXICITY; VITAMIN D TOXICITY), as well as inadequate levels. Dietary deficiencies are associated with many physical and psychological disorders. For example, nicotinic acid deficiency is marked by depression and other mental disturbances (see PELLAGRA). See also KWASHIORKOR; MARASMUS; THIAMINE; VITAMIN DEFICIENCY.

malpractice *n.* professional misconduct or negligent behavior on the part of a practitioner (e.g., a psychotherapist, psychiatrist, doctor, lawyer, or financial adviser) that may lead to legal action.

mal puesto see ROOTWORK.

Malthusian theory the doctrine proposed by British economist Thomas Malthus (1766–1834) that exponential increases in population growth would surpass arithmetical increases in food supply with dire consequences, unless population growth was arrested by such means as famine, war, or the control of reproduction through moral restraint. In the Western world, Malthus was proved wrong owing to increased prosperity from industrialization. However, his analysis has remained influential (see NEO-MALTHUSIAN). Also called **Malthusianism**; **Malthus theory**.

maltreatment *n.* ABUSE or NEGLECT of another person, which may involve emotional, sexual, or physical action or inaction, the severity or chronicity of which can result in significant harm or injury. Maltreatment also includes such actions as exploitation and denial of basic needs (e.g., food, shelter, medical attention).

malum *n.* a painful degenerative state of a joint as a result of aging.

malum in se in law, an action that is considered wrong because it is "evil in itself," such as murder. Compare MALUM PROHIBITUM.

malum prohibitum in law, an action that is considered wrong because it is against the law, such as driving without a valid license. Compare MALUM IN SE.

mammalingus *n.* the act of suckling the breast during sexual intercourse, particularly in terms of the concept, proposed by British psychoanalyst Ernest Jones (1879–1958), that the act represents a type of fellatio. Mammalingus is distinguished from the normal interest and pleasure derived from caressing or orally stimulating the breasts as a part of sexual activity.

mammary gland any of the glands in female mammals that secrete milk. In humans the mammary glands are called BREASTS.

mammillary body either of a pair of small, spherical NUCLEI at the base of the brain, slightly posterior to the infundibulum (pituitary stalk), that are components of the LIMBIC SYSTEM. Also called **corpus mammillare**.

mammillothalamic tract the TRACT that connects the MAMMILLARY BODIES to the thalamus at the base of the brain.

managed behavioral health organization (MBHO) a health maintenance organization (see HMO) that specializes in the management, administration, and provision of health care benefits with an emphasis on BEHAVIORAL HEALTH.

managed care any system of health care delivery that regulates the use of member benefits to contain expenses. The term originally referred to prepaid health plans (e.g., HMOs) but is now applied to many different kinds of reimbursement and UTILIZATION REVIEW mechanisms. It is also used to denote the organization of health care services and facilities into groups to increase cost-effectiveness. **Managed care organizations** (**MCOs**) include HMOs, PPOs (preferred provider organizations), point of service plans (POSs), exclusive provider organizations (EPOs), PHYSICIAN–HOSPITAL ORGANIZATIONS (PHOs), INTEGRATED DELIVERY SYSTEMS (IDSs), and INDEPENDENT PRACTICE ASSOCIATIONS (IPAs).

management by objectives (**MBO**) a type of ORGANIZATIONAL DEVELOPMENT program that focuses on the setting of goals and objectives and the evaluation of performance on the basis of their achievement. Such programs may also involve the introduction of new INCENTIVE SYSTEMS, PARTICIPATIVE DECISION-MAKING, and a process of JOB DESIGN.

management development programs used to improve the effectiveness with which people in managerial or executive positions perform their roles. Management development can involve a variety of interventions, including classroom training, counseling, mentoring, and EXECUTIVE COACHING as well as BUSINESS GAMES and other role play techniques. See also ORGANIZATIONAL DEVELOPMENT; PERSONNEL TRAINING.

management fashion management practices that are currently popular but not necessarily well-grounded in either theory or practice. [defined in 1996 by U.S. management theorist Eric Abrahamson (1958–)]

management information systems (**MIS**) systems that combine information technology, data, procedures for processing the data, and people who collect and use the data, with the objective of helping managers to make informed decisions.

management psychology see MANAGERIAL PSYCHOLOGY. See also INDUSTRIAL AND ORGANIZATIONAL PSYCHOLOGY.

managerial grid see BLAKE–MOUTON MANAGERIAL GRID.

managerial psychology the application of a knowledge of human behavior to issues that arise in the management of organizations, especially with regard to decision making, problem solving, leadership, and human relations in the workplace. Although often used synonymously with INDUSTRIAL AND ORGANIZATIONAL PSYCHOLOGY, the term suggests an approach that adopts the perspective of the employer. Also called **management psychology**.

mand *n.* in linguistics, a category of UTTERANCES in which the speaker makes demands on the hearer, as in *Listen to me* or *Pass the salt, please*. According to the behaviorist analysis of language, this form of VERBAL BEHAVIOR is reinforced by the compliance of the listener. See BEHAVIORISM. [coined by B. F. SKINNER from *command* and *demand*]

mandated reporting the legal requirement in the United States that psychologists and other human services personnel (e.g., social workers and nurses) report any suspected or known cases of child abuse or neglect. Those who fail to report such cases may be subject to legal and professional sanctions.

mandate phenomenon a tendency for leaders to overstep the bounds of their authority when they feel they have the overwhelming support of the group.

mandibular reflex see JAW JERK.

mandibulofacial dysostosis see TREACHER COLLINS SYNDROME.

mandrake *n.* the root or other parts of the plant *Mandragora officinarum*, traditionally used as an anesthetic, aphrodisiac, hallucinogen, and folk remedy for asthma, whooping cough, stomach ulcers, and other conditions. The name derives from the supposed resemblance of the root to the human form; *-drake* (from the Old English word for dragon) alludes to the alleged magical powers of the plant. A member of the nightshade family, it contains the anticholinergic alkaloids SCOPOLAMINE, mandragorine, and hyoscyamine, which are poisonous and potentially fatal. Symptoms of poisoning include flushing, pupillary dilation, dry mucous membranes, and dry mouth, progressing to visual disturbances, hallucinations, restlessness, agitation, delirium, and possibly death from respiratory failure.

mania *n.* **1.** a MANIC EPISODE or, sometimes, a HYPOMANIC EPISODE. **2.** excitement, overactivity, and PSYCHOMOTOR AGITATION, often accompanied by impaired judgment. **3.** excessive preoccupation with a particular activity or idea.

mania a potu see IDIOSYNCRATIC INTOXICATION.

maniac *n.* **1.** a lay term for a mentally or emotionally disturbed person, particularly one who is considered dangerous to others. **2.** an obsolete name for a person who experiences MANIA. See also MANIC.

manic 1. *adj.* relating to MANIA. **2.** *n.* an obsolete name for a person experiencing a MANIC EPISODE.

manic-depressive illness see BIPOLAR DISORDERS.

manic episode a period lasting at least 1 week characterized by elevated, expansive, or irritable mood with three or more of the following symptoms: an increase in activity or PSYCHOMOTOR AGITATION; talkativeness or PRESSURED SPEECH; FLIGHT OF IDEAS or racing thoughts; inflated self-esteem or grandiosity; a decreased need for sleep; extreme distractibility; and involvement in pleasurable activities that are likely to have unfortunate consequences, such as buying sprees, foolish investments, sexual indiscretions, or reckless driving. All of these symptoms impair normal functioning and relationships with others. One or more manic episodes are characteristic of bipolar I disorder (see BIPOLAR DISORDERS). See also MIXED EPISODE.

manic state a condition that meets all the criteria for a MANIC EPISODE or a HYPOMANIC EPISODE with regard to symptoms but not necessarily the duration required.

manifest anxiety in psychoanalysis, anxiety with overt symptoms that indicate underlying emotional conflict or repression.

Manifest Anxiety Scale see CHILDREN'S MANIFEST ANXIETY SCALE; TAYLOR MANIFEST ANXIETY SCALE.

manifestation *n.* an observable expression, indication, or sign of a physical or psychological condition.

manifest content 1. the matter that is overtly expressed and consciously intended in any utterance or other form of communication. **2.** in psychoanalytic theory, the images and events of a DREAM or FANTASY as experienced and recalled by the dreamer or fantasist, as opposed to the LATENT CONTENT, which is posited to contain the hidden meaning. See also DREAM ANALYSIS; DREAM CENSORSHIP; DREAM-WORK.

manifest goal in evaluation research, an openly stated, objectively defined goal or objective of an organization or program. Manifest goals are specified by indicators of success and assessed in an evaluation program.

manifest variable a variable that is directly observed or measured, as opposed to one whose value is inferred (see LATENT VARIABLE).

manipulandum *n.* (*pl.* **manipulanda**) an object designed to be manipulated in a psychological test or experiment.

manipulation *n.* conscious behavior designed to exploit or control others, such as weeping, throwing a tantrum, feigning illness, threatening suicide, and lying or scheming to gain special consideration or advantage. Also called **manipulative behavior**.

manipulation check a question or questions designed to help an experimenter evaluate the efficacy of the experimental manipulation, that is, to verify that the manipulation affected the participants as the experimenter intended.

manipulative behavior see MANIPULATION.

man–machine system see HUMAN–MACHINE SYSTEM.

mannerism *n.* a gesture, facial expression, or verbal habit peculiar to the individual.

manners *pl. n.* respectful, polite, and socially acceptable ways of behaving. Codes of manners vary greatly from one culture to another and may also vary between classes or subcultures in a society.

manning theory see STAFFING THEORY.

mannosidosis *n.* a rare and progressive disorder involving deficient activity of an enzyme (α-mannosidase) needed to metabolize the sugar mannose. Affected individuals have slow motor development, mental retardation, and hypotonic (flaccid) muscles, although these effects vary in magnitude. Laboratory tests may reveal brain and liver levels of mannose 8 to 10 times normal. It is thought to be an autosomal recessive trait.

Mann–Whitney U test a nonparametric statistical test of centrality for ranked data that contrasts scores from two independent samples in terms of the probabilities of obtaining the ranking distributions. [Henry Berthold **Mann** (1905–2000), Austrian-born U.S. mathematician; Donald Ransom **Whitney** (1915–), U.S. statistician]

manoptoscope *n.* a hollow cone used for measuring EYE DOMINANCE. The observer views a small target by placing the base of the cone up to the eyes and then viewing the target through the small end of the cone while closing first one eye and then the other. The eye through which the target is actually seen is the dominant eye.

MANOVA acronym for MULTIVARIATE ANALYSIS OF VARIANCE.

mantle layer in neuroanatomy, the middle layer of the embryonic NEURAL PLATE, which develops into cerebral GRAY MATTER.

man-to-man rating scale see PERSON-TO-PERSON RATING SCALE.

mantra *n.* **1.** in Hinduism and Buddhism, a sacred utterance, such as a syllable, phrase, or hymn (often in Sanskrit). **2.** any verbal formula used for spiritual, religious, or meditative purposes to help block out extraneous thoughts and induce a state of relaxation that enables the individual to reach a deeper level of consciousness. See also CONCENTRATIVE MEDITATION; TRANSCENDENTAL MEDITATION. Compare YANTRA.

manual arts therapy training in industrial arts, such as woodworking and metalworking, for therapeutic purposes as part of the rehabilitation process. See also OCCUPATIONAL THERAPY.

manual-assisted therapy see MANUALIZED THERAPY.

manual-based therapy see MANUALIZED THERAPY.

manual communication communication with the hands rather than by speech. Manual communication encompasses SIGN LANGUAGE and FINGER SPELLING and is used primarily with or between people with severe hearing impairment.

manual-control effects in the manual control of aircraft or spacecraft, the effects on human performance of the nature and complexity of the task, G forces (acceleration levels), and the aerodynamic characteristics of the vehicle.

manual dominance the tendency to favor one hand over the other and to use it more frequently in acts that require only one hand. See also HANDEDNESS.

manualism *n.* a method of instruction for people with severe hearing impairment that depends on the use of SIGN LANGUAGE and FINGER SPELLING for communication. Also called **manual method**.

manualized therapy interventions that are performed according to specific guidelines for administration, maximizing the probability of therapy being conducted consistently across settings, therapists, and clients. Also called **manual-assisted therapy**; **manual-based therapy**.

MAO abbreviation for MONOAMINE OXIDASE.

MAOIs (**MAO inhibitors**) abbreviation for MONOAMINE OXIDASE INHIBITORS.

MAP abbreviation for MINIMAL AUDIBLE PRESSURE.

maple-sugar urine disease (**MSUD**) a disorder of amino acid metabolism involving a deficiency of enzymes required for processing the amino acids leucine, isoleucine, valine, and alloisoleucine. The urine and sweat of affected individuals have a distinctive maple-syrup odor. Other characteristics include mental retardation, HYPERTONIA, altered reflexes, and convulsions. Special diets, dialysis, and transfusions are among the therapeutic measures needed. Also called **maple-syrup urine disease**.

mapping of genes the creation of a schematic representation of the arrangement of genes, genetic markers, or both as they occur in the genetic material of an organism. In humans and other higher organisms, three different types of map are made. A GENETIC MAP (or linkage map) shows the relative positions of genes along each chromosome. A PHYSICAL MAP shows the absolute physical distances between genes along the DNA molecule. A CYTOGENETIC MAP depicts the banded appearance of stained chromosomes; the bands can be correlated with the location of particular genes.

maprotiline *n.* a tetracyclic antidepressant closely related to the TRICYCLIC ANTIDEPRESSANTS. Like the tricylic agents, it can cause adverse ANTICHOLINERGIC EFFECTS and serious disturbances in heart rhythm; its use has therefore declined, and it is rarely encountered in modern clinical practice. U.S. trade name: **Ludiomil**.

map-tracing test a test of ability to visualize spatial relations and to orient oneself in space. It is used, for example, to test a pilot's ability to distinguish up from down when no obvious reference point, such as the horizon, is available.

marasmus *n.* a condition, usually occurring in infancy, that is characterized by apathy, withdrawal, and emaciation (from Greek *marasmos*, "consumption") resulting from severe protein–energy malnutrition. If left untreated, it can result in delayed physical and cognitive development and, in some cases, death. Marasmus tends to occur mostly in developing countries, often as a result of premature or abrupt weaning, famine, or vitamin insufficiency due to limitations in food variety. It can, however, occur in developed nations as well—for example, in children living in poor rural and urban areas, children with chronic disease, and children who are institutionalized. Also called **infantile atrophy**. See also KWASHIORKOR.

marathon group an ENCOUNTER GROUP that meets in seclusion for a long period, usually varying from 6 hours to several days. Marathon groups are based on the theory that a single, extended session will elicit more intense interactions, foster a greater sense of intimacy and sharing, and encourage a freer expression of feelings as the time elapses than a series of shorter, interrupted sessions. They are often organized around addressing a single issue or related set of issues. See also TIME-EXTENDED THERAPY.

Marbe's law in WORD-ASSOCIATION TESTS, the finding that the speed of making an association is proportional to the number of people who make that association. [Karl **Marbe** (1869–1953), German psychologist]

marche à petits pas a shuffling, progressively accelerating gait commonly seen in PARKINSON'S DISEASE. [French, literally: "walking in little steps"]

Marfan's syndrome an AUTOSOMAL DOMINANT disorder of the connective tissue in the body, affecting the blood vessels, skeleton, and eyes. Common symptoms of the disorder may include an unusually tall frame, long fingers and toes, loose-jointedness, curvature of the spine, protruding breastbone (pectus carinatum), and dislocation of the lens of the eye. The aorta of the heart may also be enlarged, and there may be leakage in the aortal valve. [Antoine Bernard-Jean **Marfan** (1858–1942), French pediatrician]

marginal 1. *adj.* describing an individual or a group (see MARGINAL GROUP) that has not been assimilated into the dominant group or culture and therefore remains on the periphery of a particular society. **2.** *adj.* describing an individual whose intelligence level is borderline or whose emotional adjustment is tenuous. **3.** *n.* in statistics, see MARGINAL FREQUENCY.

marginal consciousness the background contents of CONSCIOUSNESS that, although above the threshold of awareness, are not the center of attention. Marginal stimuli are not equivalent to subliminal stimuli (see SUBLIMINAL PERCEPTION).

marginal frequency the sum of any one of the rows or columns in a data matrix, such as a table of students classified by sex and area of study. In this example, the number of female students, regardless of area of study, would be one marginal frequency, and the number of students enrolled in a specific area of study, regardless of sex, would be another. Also called **marginal**.

marginal group in a relatively homogeneous country or community, a distinct group that is not assimilated into the social mainstream because it differs in one or more significant ways, as in its religious or cultural beliefs.

marginal individuals people who live on the fringe of their society, such as homeless people, or who are in a state of transition between two social worlds and not fully accepted in either, such as immigrants.

marginal intelligence an intelligence level between normal and mentally deficient.

marginalization *n.* a reciprocal process through which an individual or group with relatively distinctive qualities, such as idiosyncratic values or customs, becomes identified as one that is not accepted fully into the larger group. **—marginalize** *vb.*

marginal sulcus a branch of the CINGULATE SULCUS that turns upward between the paracentral lobule and superior frontal gyrus on the surface of each cerebral hemisphere. Also called **marginal branch of the cingulate sulcus**.

marginal value theorem a part of OPTIMAL FORAGING THEORY that predicts when an organism should leave one food patch and travel to the next. Decisions are based on the benefits and costs of staying in a location where food sources are known but declining compared with the costs and benefits of traveling to a new, unknown food patch. In experimental work, the time and effort needed to travel to a new patch appears to regulate how long animals remain foraging in the current patch.

marianismo *n.* in many Latin American or Hispanic cultures, an idealized traditional feminine gender role characterized by submissiveness, selflessness, chastity, hyperfemininity, and acceptance of machismo in males. Although clearly derived from the traditional ideal of the Virgin Mary, marianismo is not to be confused with a specific religious practice of the Roman Catholic Church.

marijuana (**marihuana**) *n.* see CANNABIS.

Marinesco–Sjögren syndrome an autosomal recessive hereditary disorder marked by cataracts, short stature, CEREBELLAR ATAXIA (incoordination of voluntary movements), and mental retardation. Affected individuals have cataracts in both eyes; some have very small heads (see MICROCEPHALY). Cerebellar ataxia is present at infancy, and mild to moderate mental retardation becomes evident. Affected individuals may live well past middle age but often lose their ability to walk because of progressive muscle weakness. [reported in the 1930s by Georges **Marinesco** (1864–1938), Romanian neurologist, and Torsten **Sjögren** (1896–1974), Swedish physician]

Marinol *n.* a trade name for dronabinol. See TETRAHYDROCANNABINOL.

marital adjustment the process by which individuals adapt successfully to the demands and opportunities of MARRIAGE. Especially important to marital adjustment are (a) the sharing of experiences, interests, and values; (b) respect for the partner's individual needs, aims, and temperament; (c) maintenance of open lines of communication and expression of feeling; (d) clarifying roles and responsibilities; (e) cooperation in decision making, problem solving, and rearing of children; and (f) attainment of mutual sexual gratification.

marital conflict open or latent antagonism between marriage partners. The nature and intensity of conflicts varies greatly, but studies indicate that the prime sources are often sexual disagreement, child-rearing differences, temperamental differences (particularly the tendency of one partner to dominate), and, to a lesser extent, religious differences, differences in values and interests, and disagreements over money management.

marital counseling see MARRIAGE COUNSELING.

marital schism a condition of open discord between marital partners, which puts a strain on the marriage and may lead to separation or divorce.

marital skew a defective family pattern in which the pathological behavior of the dominant partner is accepted by the other partner. See also COLLUSIONAL MARRIAGE.

marital subsystem the relationship between two spouses or partners in a family and their particular interactional rules for cooperation, conflict, and conflict resolution over marital issues (e.g., child rearing).

marital therapy COUPLES THERAPY when the couples are married. Also called **marriage therapy**.

marker *n.* **1.** see GENETIC MARKER. **2.** an item or article used to indicate territorial possession in a public setting, such as a coat or briefcase left on a seat in a waiting room.

marketing orientation in the existential psychoanalysis of Erich FROMM, a character pattern in which the individual regards people as commodities and evaluates personal worth in terms of salability. Attributes perceived as leading to business or social success are valued more than knowledge, creativity, integrity, or dedication. According to Fromm, the marketing orientation contributes to shallow relationships and alienation from self and society. Also called **marketing character**. See also EXPLOITATIVE ORIENTATION; HOARDING ORIENTATION.

market research research undertaken to understand the competitive challenges in a particular market by assessing the relative positions of various suppliers in the mind of consumers. For example, a comparison may be made between restaurants that are perceived to offer good service and high-quality food at a low price with those perceived to provide good service and high-quality food at a high price.

Markov chain a sequence consisting of a number of steps or events, with the same probability governing the transition between each pair of steps. [Andrei **Markov** (1856–1922), Russian mathematician]

Marlowe–Crowne Social Desirability Scale (**M–C**

SDS) a widely used research scale that attempts to assess the degree to which participants answer questions in such a manner as to present themselves in a favorable light. Test scores are often used in research where people might be inclined to bias their behavior in a socially desirable direction, rather than being perfectly frank. Although currently available in a variety of forms, the Marlowe–Crowne scale as it was originally developed in 1960 consisted of 33 self-descriptive statements (e.g., "I am sometimes irritated by people who ask favors of me") to which participants responded "true" or "false." [David **Marlowe** (1931–) and Douglas P. **Crowne** (1928–), U.S. psychologists]

Maroteaux–Lamy syndrome an inherited disorder of connective tissue and skeletal development: one of the MUCOPOLYSACCHARIDOSES. It is marked by dwarfism of the trunk and extremities and in some cases delayed closure of the cranial sutures and maldevelopment of the facial bones. Mental retardation and deafness often accompany the condition. Also called **mucopolysaccharidosis VI**; **systemic mucopolysaccharidosis**. [Pierre **Maroteaux** (1926–), French geneticist; Maurice **Lamy** (1895–1975), French physician]

Marplan *n.* a trade name for ISOCARBOXAZID.

marriage *n.* the social institution in which two (or, less frequently, more) people, usually but not always a man and a woman, commit themselves to a socially sanctioned relationship in which sexual intercourse is legitimated and there is legally recognized responsibility for any offspring as well as for each other. Although there are exceptions, the marital partners typically live together in the same residence. See also CLOSED MARRIAGE; COLLUSIONAL MARRIAGE; COMMON-LAW MARRIAGE; DOMESTIC PARTNERSHIP; GROUP MARRIAGE: NONTRADITIONAL MARRIAGE; OPEN MARRIAGE; SAME-SEX MARRIAGE; SYMBIOTIC MARRIAGE; SYNERGIC MARRIAGE; TRADITIONAL MARRIAGE. **—marital** *adj.*

marriage counseling COUPLES COUNSELING when the couples are married. Also called **marital counseling**.

marriage-enrichment group a support or therapy group in which married couples meet under the guidance of a professional or non-professional leader to discuss marriage-related problems and issues. See also COUPLES THERAPY.

marriage therapy see MARITAL THERAPY.

marsupial *n.* a nonplacental animal of the subclass Metatheria. Marsupials are born at a very early developmental stage and spend a prolonged period of development in the maternal pouch.

Marxism *n.* a philosophical position and economic theory drawn directly or indirectly from the works of German social theorist Karl Marx (1818–1883). Although there is much debate about the true nature of Marxism, there is general agreement that it emphasizes the role of economics (control of the means of production) in subtly determining other social institutions, the importance of labor as the foundation of all economies, the failings of capitalism as an economic system, and a utopian vision of social equality. Marxism has spawned, or been appropriated by, a number of social revolutionary and communitarian movements, including communism. See also CLASS THEORY; DIALECTICAL MATERIALISM. **—Marxist** *adj., n.*

Marxist feminism a branch of FEMINISM that locates the oppression of women in the context of a Marxist analysis of the oppression of the working class, thus viewing the oppression as systemic and ubiquitous. Marxist feminism concentrates on the economic aspects of women's oppression and advocates remedies largely consonant with Marxist principles. See MARXISM; RADICAL FEMINISM.

masculinity *n.* possession of social-role behaviors that are presumed to be characteristic of a man, as contrasted with MALENESS, which is genetically determined. **—masculine** *adj.*

masculinity–femininity test any test designed to measure the degree of masculinity or femininity in participants. The earliest was the Terman–Miles Attitude–Interest Analysis Test (1938); others, usually in inventory form, are the MINNESOTA MULTIPHASIC PERSONALITY INVENTORY, the GUILFORD–ZIMMERMAN TEMPERAMENT SURVEY, and the Gough Femininity Scale. The BEM SEX ROLE INVENTORY is one of the few masculinity–femininity tests to include androgyny.

masculinization *n.* see VIRILISM.

masked audiogram see MASKING PATTERN.

masked depression 1. a condition in which an individual experiencing a MAJOR DEPRESSIVE EPISODE complains of physical symptoms (e.g., headache, backache) rather than mood disturbance, and no organic cause of the physical symptoms can be found. **2.** a hypothesized state in which symptoms other than those normally associated with depression are held to be a result of underlying depression. This view has been difficult to test or verify and is no longer popular.

masked homosexuality theoretically, an unconscious form of same-sex sexual orientation in which a person seeks in heterosexual activities the pleasures presumed to be obtained only in same-sex acts, such as oral or anal intercourse. This hypothesized transposition, however, is essentially rendered meaningless because heterosexual couples may engage routinely in (for example) oral sex with no indication that such activities are exclusively related to gay or lesbian tendencies.

masking *n.* in perception, the partial or complete obscuring of one stimulus (the target) by another (the masker). The stimuli may be sounds (see AUDITORY MASKING), visual images (see VISUAL MASKING), tastes, odorants, or tactile stimuli. **Forward masking** occurs when the masker is presented a short time before the target stimulus, **backward masking** occurs when it is presented shortly afterward, and **simultaneous masking** occurs when the two stimuli are presented at the same instant. Also called **perceptual masking**. **—mask** *vb.*

masking level difference (**MLD**) a change in detection threshold for auditory stimuli produced by changes in the interaural characteristics of the masker or the signal (see AUDITORY MASKING). The typical reference is the signal threshold in the DIOTIC condition (N0S0), in which a pure-tone signal and noise masker are both presented in-phase at the ears. For a DICHOTIC condition, such as N0Sπ (noise in-phase, signal 180° out of phase), the detection threshold may be 15 dB lower. The MLD and related phenomena have provided valuable insights into the mechanisms involved in BINAURAL hearing and sound localization (see AUDITORY LOCALIZATION). Also called **binaural masking level difference** (BMLD).

masking pattern the detection thresholds as a function of frequency for a pure-tone signal masked by a sound whose spectral characteristics and level are fixed. The *y*-axis may be either the level of the signal at threshold (in DECIBELS sound-pressure level) or the amount of masking. Also called **masked audiogram**. See AUDITORY MASKING.

Maslach Burnout Inventory (**MBI**) a method for the evaluation of BURNOUT on three dimensions: emotional exhaustion, DEPERSONALIZATION, and reduced personal accomplishment. It consists of 22 statements about feelings and attitudes to which participants respond in terms of frequency on a 7-point scale ranging from "never" to "every day." [Christina **Maslach** (1946–), U.S. psychologist]

Maslow, Abraham Harold (1908–1970) U.S. psychologist. Maslow earned his PhD in 1934 from the University of Wisconsin, where he studied with the primatologist Harry HARLOW. Initially a behaviorist but frustrated by what he perceived as its limitations, Maslow broadened his orientation to include the subjective in human experience, so becoming a founder of HUMANISTIC PSYCHOLOGY. Maslow originated the concept of a hierarchy of needs that motivate all individuals (see MASLOW'S MOTIVATIONAL HIERARCHY): According to this concept, the ultimate goal of being human is SELF-ACTUALIZATION; only when a person's basic needs are met can self-actualization occur. His emphasis on self-fulfillment made him a leader in the HUMAN-POTENTIAL MOVEMENT of the 1960s and 1970s. Maslow's most influential works include his *Theory of Human Motivation* (1943), *Toward a Psychology of Being* (1968), and *The Farther Reaches of Human Nature* (1971). A founder of the American Association for Humanistic Psychology in 1962, and cofounder of the *Journal of Humanistic Psychology*, Maslow was elected president of the American Psychological Association in 1967. See also MASLOW'S THEORY OF HUMAN MOTIVATION; DEFICIENCY MOTIVATION; HUMANISTIC PERSPECTIVE; METAMOTIVATION; PERSONALITY STRUCTURE.

Maslow's being psychology see BEING PSYCHOLOGY.

Maslow's motivational hierarchy the hierarchy of human motives, or needs, as described by Abraham MASLOW, which he developed as a reaction against the determinism of the theories of Sigmund FREUD and B. F. SKINNER. PHYSIOLOGICAL NEEDS (air, water, food, sleep, sex, etc.) are at the base; followed by safety and security (the SAFETY NEEDS); then love, affection, and gregariousness (the LOVE NEEDS); then prestige, competence, and power (the ESTEEM NEEDS); and, at the highest level, aesthetic needs, the need for knowing, and SELF-ACTUALIZATION (the METANEEDS).

Maslow's theory of human motivation the humanistic view of motivation proposed by Abraham MASLOW, in which the higher human needs for understanding, aesthetic values, self-realization, and PEAK EXPERIENCES are emphasized. Maslow contrasted the METAMOTIVATION arising from such METANEEDS with the DEFICIENCY MOTIVATION arising from physical needs, insecurity, and alienation.

masochism *n.* **1.** a condition in which the individual derives pleasure from experiencing pain and humiliation inflicted by others or, in some cases, by himself or herself. It is named for Austrian writer Leopold Sacher-Masoch (1835–1895), whose stories include frequent scenes in which sexual gratification is associated with being whipped or other forms of domination. However, the term is also applied to experiences that do not obviously involve sex, such as martyrdom, religious flagellation, or asceticism. **2.** in psychoanalytic theory, the tendency to bring suffering and humiliation upon oneself. It is interpreted as resulting from the DEATH INSTINCT or from aggression turned inward because of excessive guilt feelings. See also MORAL MASOCHISM. **—masochist** *n.* **—masochistic** *adj.*

masochistic fantasies fantasies of being whipped, choked, or otherwise hurt or abused as an expression of masochistic tendencies, particularly as a means of achieving sexual excitement. See SEXUAL MASOCHISM.

masochistic personality disorder a personality disorder in which individuals persistently and characteristically obtain gratification or freedom from guilt feelings as a consequence of humiliation, self-derogation, self-sacrifice, wallowing in misery, and, in some instances, submitting to physically sadistic acts. This disorder was listed in *DSM–III–TR* as SELF-DEFEATING PERSONALITY DISORDER.

mass action the relative nonspecificity of the cerebral cortex in learning, the general mass of the cortex being involved in that function. See LAW OF MASS ACTION. See also EQUIPOTENTIALITY IN MEMORY.

massage *n.* the structured stroking or kneading of a body area or of the entire body by hand or by a mechanical or electrical device. Manual massage is usually administered for therapeutic and rehabilitative purposes because the hands can detect abnormalities, such as swellings or muscle spasms. Among the benefits of massage are improved circulation, the promotion of relaxation and healing from injury, and release from tension and psychological stress. Massage may also be performed in a fluid environment, as in a whirlpool bath.

massa intermedia see INTERTHALAMIC ADHESION.

mass contagion a form of CONTAGION in which behaviors, attitudes, or affect rapidly spread throughout large groups or populations, including those who are widely dispersed across a large area.

massed practice a learning procedure in which material is studied either in a single lengthy session or in sessions separated by short intervals. Massed practice is often found to be less effective than DISTRIBUTED PRACTICE.

massed repetition see REPETITION EFFECT.

masseter reflex see JAW JERK.

mass hysteria see COLLECTIVE HYSTERIA.

mass masochism the willingness of a population to endure sacrifices and suffering as demanded by a charismatic, dictatorial leader to whom people have surrendered their own power. See MASOCHISM. [coined by Austrian-born U.S. psychoanalyst Theodore Reik (1888–1969)]

mass media news and entertainment publications and broadcasts intended for the general public, notably newspapers, magazines, radio, and television. As their usage grows, the Internet and the WORLD WIDE WEB also serve increasingly as mass media.

mass murder the act of killing several to many people. The mass murder of an entire population (e.g., a racial or ethnic group) is called GENOCIDE. See also SPREE MURDER.

Masson disk a device for measuring the threshold of brightness vision. The disk is white with a black segmented line along one radius. When it is rotated, varying shades of gray are seen, the darkest at the center. The point at which the disk becomes indistinguishable from the background provides the required measurement. [Antoine-Philibert **Masson** (1806–1860), French physicist]

mass polarization a swing to extremes in consumer attitudes as a result of media information or other events. For example, negative attitudes may develop toward a particular model of car or brand of tire as a result of safety recalls.

mass psychology 1. the mental and emotional states and processes that occur in a large body of individuals who, although they may not share any common characteristics, are considered as a whole. **2.** the scientific study of these phenomena, including the study of mass movements, mass hysteria, and the effects of the mass media.

mass reflex **1.** an indiscriminate response of many body effectors to a single stimulus, as in "freezing" with fear. **2.** a life-threatening condition associated with spinal cord injury in which uncontrolled activation of both autonomic and somatic motor systems occurs.

mass-spring model see EQUILIBRIUM-POINT MODEL.

mass suicide the deliberate ending of the lives of all or most of the members of an intact social group or aggregate by the members themselves, either directly through self-injurious behavior or indirectly by choosing a course of action that will very likely be fatal. Examples include extremely hazardous missions undertaken by combat units (see ALTRUISTIC SUICIDE) and the suicides of nearly all the members of the People's Temple (see JONESTOWN MASS SUICIDE), the 70 members of the Order of the Solar Temple in Europe and Canada between 1994 and 1997, and the 39 Heaven's Gate followers of Marshall Applewhite in San Diego in 1997. Mass suicide often occurs at the command of a charismatic leader and may be provoked not by despair but by the desire to seek a "higher state of existence" promised by the leader. Also called **collective suicide**. Compare CLUSTER SUICIDES.

mass-to-specific development in fetal and infantile development, progression from gross, random movements involving the whole body to more refined movements of body parts.

MAST **1.** acronym for MICHIGAN ALCOHOLISM SCREENING TEST. **2.** acronym for MULTILEVEL ACADEMIC SURVEY TESTS.

master status a culturally defined aspect of one's identity, such as "mother" or "athlete," that serves to shape self-concept and to dominate others' perceptions of one's traits and behaviors, thereby possibly affecting one's life opportunities. A negative master status, such as "ex-convict," often carries a lasting stigma.

mastery goal see LEARNING GOAL.

mastery learning **1.** the process of gaining knowledge in a certain subject or domain, with the intent of understanding the full scope of that subject area. **2.** a theory of education in which students learn material in several different ways over a series of study sessions, until they understand the material well enough to teach it to others. **3.** the acquisition of material beyond basic recognition, recall, and understanding to a point of thorough cognitive integration at a conceptual level.

mastery orientation an adaptive pattern of achievement behavior in which individuals enjoy and seek challenge, persist in the face of obstacles, and tend to view their failings as due to lack of effort or poor use of strategy rather than to lack of ability.

mastery play play that leads to mastering new skills, such as language and intellectual abilities.

mastery tests assessments used to determine acquisition of the full scope of knowledge in a particular subject area or to evaluate ongoing progress and comprehension.

mastery training experimental or real-world training that prepares individuals for aversive situations or conflict by teaching them methods of assertion and constructive control over environmental conditions.

mastoid *n.* a projection from the anterior part of the temporal bone containing air spaces that communicate with the cavity of the middle ear. Also called **mastoid process**.

masturbation *n.* manipulation of one's own genital organs, typically the penis and clitoris, for purposes of sexual gratification. The act is usually accompanied by sexual fantasies or erotic literature, pictures, or videos. Masturbation may also include the use of mechanical devices (e.g., vibrators) or self-stimulation of other organs, such as the anus or nipples. **—masturbate** *vb.*

masturbation equivalents activities that have been identified by some theorists as psychological substitutes for MASTURBATION (e.g., gambling, nail biting, pulling on one's earlobe, twisting strands of one's hair). However, as the person performing such acts does not experience arousal or orgasm, and there are many other reasons for such behaviors (e.g., anxiety reduction), this concept is not widely accepted as valid.

MAT abbreviation for MILLER ANALOGIES TEST.

mata elap see AMOK.

matched-group design an experimental design in which experimental and control groups are matched on one or more background variables before being exposed to the experimental or control conditions. Results obtained in experiments using such **matched** (or **equivalent**) **groups** can therefore be attributed to manipulation of the INDEPENDENT VARIABLE rather than to any differences in the characteristics of the participants in the different groups. Compare RANDOMIZED-GROUP DESIGN.

matched samples two or more SAMPLES that are equivalent to one another with respect to certain relevant variables.

matching *n.* a research technique for ensuring comparability of participants by making sure that they all have similar background variables. The individuals in a CONTROL GROUP and in an EXPERIMENTAL GROUP might be matched, for example, on years of education, income, and marital status.

Matching Familiar Figures Test (**MFF**) a visual test in which the participant is asked to identify from among a group of six similar figures the one that matches a given sample. Items are scored for response time to first selection, number of correct first-choice selections, and number of errors. The test is used to measure CONCEPTUAL TEMPO, that is, the relative speed with which an individual makes decisions on complex tasks (see REFLECTIVITY–IMPULSIVITY). [originally published in 1965 by U.S. developmental psychologist Jerome Kagan (1929–)]

matching hypothesis the proposition that people tend to form relationships with individuals who have a similar level of physical attractiveness to their own. Research indicates that this similarity tends to be greater for couples having a romantic relationship than for friends; in the latter case, the matching hypothesis holds to some extent for men but not for women.

matching law in OPERANT CONDITIONING, a law that describes the distribution of responses when numerous task options are available. It states that the proportion of responses allocated to an alternative will match the proportion of reinforcement obtained from that alternative. For example, if a pigeon receives two thirds of its food allocation from alternative A and one third from alternative B, it will make two thirds of its responses (and give two thirds of its time) to alternative A. See also GENERALIZED MATCHING LAW.

matching patients the process of prescribing specific interventions or choosing specific therapists for particular patients or diagnostic groups of patients to improve compliance with or effectiveness of treatment. The process is based on the diagnoses, needs, problems, and characteristics of particular patients; on therapist variables, such as race, ethnicity, and experience levels; and on setting variables, such as inpatient or outpatient clinics. Also called **psychotherapy matching**.

matching test a test in which items selected from one list are matched with the appropriate items on another list.

matching to sample a CONDITIONAL-DISCRIMINATION procedure that involves both SUCCESSIVE DISCRIMINATION and SIMULTANEOUS DISCRIMINATION. Each trial begins with presentation of a sample stimulus. Once the organism responds to that stimulus, two or more additional stimuli (called comparison stimuli) appear, only one of which matches the first stimulus. Reinforcement is contingent on responding to the stimulus that matches. See also ARBITRARY MATCHING TO SAMPLE; DELAYED MATCHING TO SAMPLE; ODDITY FROM SAMPLE.

mate guarding a method of preventing a mate from reproducing with others. Immediately after copulation a male stays close to its mate and prevents other males from approaching or mating with the female until such time as additional mating will not result in fertilization. In some cases a **copulatory lock** literally keeps mates connected for several minutes or hours. See also SPERM COMPETITION.

material cause see CAUSE.

material feminism a movement in 19th-century and early 20th-century FEMINISM that concentrated on improving the material conditions of women's lives. Campaigners in this tradition sought to end women's legal, educational, and employment disabilities and to ease the burden of their domestic duties.

materialism *n.* **1.** the philosophical position that everything, including mental events, is composed of physical matter and is thus subject to the laws of physics. From this perspective, the mind is considered to exist solely as a set of brain processes (see MIND–BODY PROBLEM). Such philosophies can be traced back to ancient times but gained a new impetus from advances in the physical sciences beginning in the 17th century. A particular form of materialism is the DIALECTICAL MATERIALISM of classical MARXISM. **2.** a value system that emphasizes the pursuit and acquisition of material goods and luxuries, typically perceived by the individual as a measure of personal worth and achievement, often at the expense of moral, psychological, and social considerations. **3.** the position that the causes of behavior are to be found in the material of the body, particularly the nervous system. It is nearly always associated with HARD DETERMINISM. See also IDENTITY THEORY; PHYSICALISM. Compare IDEALISM; IMMATERIALISM. **—materialist** *adj., n.* **—materialistic** *adj.*

materialization *n.* in SPIRITUALISM, the alleged production of a spirit in bodily form during a seance, or of some other physical object by apparently supernatural means (see APPORT). See also ECTOPLASM. **—materialize** *vb.*

maternal aggression a form of ANIMAL AGGRESSION in which females defend their offspring against potential threats from intruders by means of THREAT DISPLAYS or ATTACK BEHAVIOR.

maternal attitudes attitudes of the mother toward her children, particularly those attitudes that play an important role in her children's health, character formation, emotional adjustment, and self-image, as well as in her own self-perception as a mother.

maternal behavior the actions associated with caring for the young, typically performed by the mother or a substitute mother (see also ALLOPARENTING). Some forms of maternal behavior in animals are impaired by hypothalamic lesions, and males of some species exhibit maternal behavior after receiving injections of PROLACTIN. See also ANIMAL MATERNAL BEHAVIOR; PARENTAL BEHAVIOR.

maternal deprivation lack of adequate nurturing for a young animal or child due to the absence or premature loss of, or neglect by, its mother or primary caregiver. See also FAILURE TO THRIVE; MARASMUS.

maternal drive the motivation of female animals to care for offspring.

maternal PKU a condition in women that is secondary to successful treatment of PHENYLKETONURIA through dietary intervention beginning at birth. Expectant mothers with high levels of blood phenylalanine—HYPERPHENYLALANINEMIA (HPA)—are at risk of giving birth to offspring with high rates of congenital heart defects, intrauterine growth retardation, mental retardation, and microcephaly (a small head). Treatment entails dietary management for the expectant mother before and during pregnancy to reduce blood levels of phenylalanine.

maternity blues see BABY BLUES.

mate selection the choice of an appropriate partner for reproduction. In species where female PARENTAL INVESTMENT is high, females are thought to be more careful in their choice of mates than males. However, in species where parental contribution to survival of offspring is more nearly equal, mate selection is shown by both sexes. Mate selection may be based on (a) behavioral traits, such as ability to defend a territory or to be dominant over others; (b) exaggerated signals of quality, such as bright tail plumage in the peacock; or (c) evaluations made during ANIMAL COURTSHIP. In species where females are smaller than males, females may mate with several males, either selectively keeping the sperm of only one or two or mating with the most dominant male at the time closest to possible conception (see CRYPTIC FEMALE CHOICE; SEXUAL AGGRESSION). See also SEXUAL SELECTION. Compare RANDOM MATING.

mathematical ability the ability used to solve various kinds of quantitative problems, such as mathematical word problems, computational problems, and number-concept problems. It is clear that mathematical ability comprises a number of distinct skills.

mathematical biology a branch of biology that deals with the development of mathematical models of biological phenomena, such as conditioning and nerve conduction.

mathematical learning theory a statistical learning model that makes assumptions about how an organism's probability of a correct response changes from trial to trial as a result of the outcome experienced on each trial. An important example is the STIMULUS SAMPLING THEORY.

mathematical model the representation of a psychological or physiological function, or other process, in mathematical terms, such as formulas or equations (e.g., FECHNER'S LAW).

mathematical psychology an approach to psychological phenomena that uses mathematical techniques to model the underlying processes and to make predictions of the outcomes of these processes.

mathematico-deductive method 1. the use of postulates and corollaries in mathematical form to develop a system or theory. **2.** see HYPOTHETICO-DEDUCTIVE METHOD.

mathematics disorder in *DSM–IV–TR*, a LEARNING DISORDER in which mathematical ability is substantially below what is expected given the person's chronological age, formal education experience, and measured intelligence. It may involve (among other problems) difficulties in counting, learning multiplication tables, understanding mathematical problems and performing mathematical operations, reading numerical symbols, and copying numbers.

mating behavior the activities that are involved in reproduction, including ANIMAL COURTSHIP, MATE SELECTION, and COPULATORY BEHAVIOR. Different species exhibit different MATING SYSTEMS, such as MONOGAMY, POLYGYNY, and POLYANDRY. Mating behavior varies with the species and may have several functions in addition to successful conception: preparing both mates physiologically, providing cues for mate selection, and coordinating behavior of mates for NEST BUILDING and subsequent care of young.

mating system the organization of typical mating patterns within a species. Mating systems include MONOGAMY, in which two individuals mate exclusively with each other; POLYGYNY, in which a male mates with multiple females; POLYANDRY, in which a female mates with multiple males; and POLYGYNANDRY, in which both sexes mate with multiple partners.

matriarchy *n.* **1.** a society in which descent and inheritance is **matrilineal**, that is, traced through the female only. See UNILATERAL DESCENT. See also DESCENT GROUP. **2.** more loosely, a family, group, or society in which women are dominant. Compare PATRIARCHY. **—matriarchal** *adj.*

matricide *n.* **1.** the killing of one's own mother. **2.** a person who kills his or her own mother. Compare PATRICIDE. **—matricidal** *adj.*

matrifocal *adj.* describing a family centered on the mother or a culture in which the role of the mother is central.

matrilineal *adj.* see MATRIARCHY.

matrilocal *adj.* denoting a living arrangement in which a married couple resides with or in close proximity to the wife's mother or relatives, or a culture in which this is the norm. Also called **uxorilocal**. Compare NEOLOCAL; PATRILOCAL.

matrix *n.* **1.** a context or environment within which something else is enclosed, embedded, originates, or develops. **2.** a rectangular ARRAY of numbers indexed by a row and column indicator.

matrix organization a complex type of organizational structure in which employees are grouped not only by the function they perform (e.g., marketing, production, research and development, engineering) but also by the product or project on which they are working. Employees working within a matrix organization report to both a functional boss and a product or project boss. Compare UNITY OF COMMAND.

maturation *n.* the process of becoming functional or fully developed.

maturational crisis a state of acute disorganization of behavior, mood, or emotions precipitated by a transition from one developmental phase to another, such as entering kindergarten, becoming engaged, getting married, becoming a parent, or retiring. Also called **developmental crisis; normative crisis**.

maturational lag slowness or delay in some aspects of neurological development that affects learning but does not involve specific brain damage.

maturation–degeneration hypothesis the principle that functions and abilities between birth and death can be plotted as a trajectory curve that reaches a peak in the early years and then gradually declines.

maturation hypothesis a generalization that some behaviors are solely hereditary but do not appear until appropriate organs and neural systems have matured.

maturity *n.* a state of completed growth or development, as in adulthood. See DEVELOPMENTAL LEVELS.

maturity rating an evaluation of behavior on a particular trait in comparison with a relevant peer-group norm.

matutinal insomnia a less common name for TERMINAL INSOMNIA.

Maudsley Personality Inventory see EYSENCK PERSONALITY INVENTORY.

maximin strategy in GAME THEORY, a strategy in which a player chooses the best of a set of worst possible outcomes or payoffs. Compare MINIMAX STRATEGY.

maximum likelihood an estimation technique in which estimates of the values of parameters of a distribution are based on the most likely sample of observations that one might have obtained from that population.

maximum-security unit a section of a mental institution reserved for patients who are likely to harm themselves or others.

Maxwell disks a series of slotted color disks on a rotating spindle, used as a COLOR MIXER. [James Clerk **Maxwell** (1831–1879), British physicist]

Maxwellian view an optical arrangement that causes a visual stimulus to be confined to the center of the pupil. The alternative, a **Newtonian view**, allows light to pass through all parts of the pupil. [James Clerk **Maxwell**]

May, Rollo (1909–1994) U.S. psychologist, psychoanalyst, and existentialist. May earned his PhD in clinical psychology at Columbia University in 1949 and spent the bulk of his career at the William Alanson White Institute in New York City, where he served as training analyst and president of the institute for many years. A broad-ranging thinker who incorporated classical, religious, and philosophical studies into his views on psychology and psychotherapy, May is best known as a proponent of HUMANISTIC PSYCHOLOGY and a spokesperson for the EXISTENTIAL PSYCHOLOGY movement. He was particularly concerned with combating feelings of emptiness, cynicism, and despair by emphasizing basic human values, such as love, free will, and self-awareness. Among his most influential writings are *Existence: A New Dimension in Psychiatry and Psychology* (1958, coauthored by Ernest Angel and Henri Ellenberger), *The Meaning of Anxiety* (1950), and *Love and Will* (1969).

maze *n.* a complex system of intersecting paths and blind alleys that must be navigated from an entrance to an exit. Various types of mazes are used in learning experiments for animals and humans. A common human maze is a printed paper pattern on which the participant traces the correct pathway with a pencil. See also MORRIS WATER MAZE; PORTEUS MAZE TEST; RADIAL MAZE; STYLUS MAZE; T MAZE.

maze-bright and maze-dull rats a group of rats that were artificially selected based on their performance in a standardized maze problem. Those that performed best were bred with each other, as were those that performed most poorly. Over relatively few generations, there was a complete separation in performance, with none of the maze-bright rats overlapping in scores with maze-dull rats. However, the selective breeding appeared to be specific to the maze tests that were used and did not affect learning ability more generally; moreover, maze-dull rats reared in an enriched environment (see ENRICHMENT) could perform as well as maze-bright rats.

maze learning learning to reach a certain objective by starting from a designated point and following a circuitous pathway that has more or less randomly placed blind alleys. The maze-learning process usually involves multiple trials and is regarded as successful when the participant can reach the goal in the most direct way and without errors on two successive trials.

maze task a measure of visual planning in which participants must trace a route through a series of progressively more complex mazes without entering blind alleys. An example of this type of test is the PORTEUS MAZE TEST.

MBD **1.** abbreviation for MINIMAL BRAIN DAMAGE. **2.** abbreviation for MINIMAL BRAIN DYSFUNCTION.

MBHO abbreviation for MANAGED BEHAVIORAL HEALTH ORGANIZATION.

MBI abbreviation for MASLACH BURNOUT INVENTORY.

MBO abbreviation for MANAGEMENT BY OBJECTIVES.

MBTI abbreviation for MYERS–BRIGGS TYPE INDICATOR.

McCarthy Scales of Children's Abilities a comprehensive instrument used to measure the cognitive and motor abilities of children between 2½ and 8½ years of age, comprising 18 subtests on 6 overlapping scales: Verbal, Perceptual-Performance, Quantitative, General Cognitive, Memory, and Motor. [developed in 1972 by Dorothea **McCarthy** (1906–1974), U.S. developmental psychologist]

McCarthy Screening Test (**MST**) an assessment that predicts the ability of a child to cope with schoolwork at an early age. It comprises six subtests (verbal memory, right–left orientation, leg coordination, draw-a-design, numeric memory, and conceptual grouping) designed to measure the cognitive and sensorimotor functions needed to successfully perform school tasks. Poor performance in this assessment may indicate the need for further evaluation and the possible presence of a learning disability. [originally developed in 1978 by Dorothea **McCarthy**]

McClelland, David (1917–1998) U.S. psychologist. McClelland was awarded his doctorate at Yale University in 1941. He taught at Connecticut College and Wesleyan University before joining the faculty at Harvard University, where he remained from 1956 until 1987. He then taught at Boston University until his death. McClelland is best known for his empirical and theoretical contributions to the study of personality and motivation. With John W. Atkinson (1923–) he developed a method of quantitatively scoring the THEMATIC APPERCEPTION TEST (TAT), using it to assess individual ACHIEVEMENT MOTIVATION. In later years he conducted research on power motivation. Representative writings include his classic *The Achieving Society* (1961), *Human Motivation* (1985), and *Power: The Inner Experience* (1975). McClelland received the American Psychological Association's Award for Distinguished Scientific Contributions in 1987 and was elected a fellow of the American Academy of Arts and Sciences. See also NEED FOR ACHIEVEMENT.

McCollough effect see CONTINGENT AFTEREFFECT. [Celeste **McCollough** (1926–), U.S. psychologist]

MCE abbreviation for MEDICAL CARE EVALUATION.

M-cells *pl. n.* large neurons in the two most ventral layers of the LATERAL GENICULATE NUCLEUS. M-cells are the origin of the MAGNOCELLULAR SYSTEM. The large RETINAL GANGLION CELLS that provide input to the M-cells of the lateral geniculate nucleus are called **M-ganglion cells**.

MCI abbreviation for MILD COGNITIVE IMPAIRMENT.

MCL abbreviation for MOST COMFORTABLE LOUDNESS.

MCMI abbreviation for MILLON CLINICAL MULTIAXIAL INVENTORY.

McNaughten rule (**McNaughton rule**; **M'Naghten rule**) a rule for defining INSANITY that focuses on the cognitive state of the defendant at the time of committing the act with which he or she is charged. It states that to plead insanity, the accused must be "laboring under such a defect of reason, from disease of the mind, as not to know the nature and quality of the act he was doing, or if he did know it, he did not know that what he was doing was wrong." The rule was established in 1843 by judges in England after the trial of Daniel McNaughten, who believed the government was persecuting him and killed prime minister Sir Robert Peel's secretary in mistake for the prime minister. Also called **right-and-wrong test**; **right-or-wrong test**. See also AMERICAN LAW INSTITUTE MODEL PENAL CODE INSANITY TEST; CRIMINAL RESPONSIBILITY; GOOD-AND-EVIL TEST; IRRESISTIBLE IMPULSE RULE; PARTIAL INSANITY.

McNemar test a test of equality of proportions in samples in which the observations are correlated, such as the proportion of cases exceeding a criterion in a PRETEST–POSTTEST DESIGN. [Quinn **McNemar** (1900–1986), U.S. psychologist]

MCO abbreviation for managed care organization (see MANAGED CARE).

MC4-R abbreviation for MELANOCORTIN-4 RECEPTOR.

M–C SDS abbreviation for MARLOWE–CROWNE SOCIAL DESIRABILITY SCALE.

MD abbreviation for MUSCULAR DYSTROPHY.

MDA *n.* 3,4-*m*ethylene*d*ioxy*a*mphetamine: a synthetic HALLUCINOGEN of the phenylisopropylamine family (see PHENYLETHYLAMINES). Because at low doses it acts as a CNS STIMULANT and euphoriant, MDA was once proposed as an aid to psychotherapy, but this use has not been supported. It is thought that MDA's psychostimulant properties occur through enhanced neurotransmission of norepinephrine and its hallucinogenic action through augmentation of serotonin transmission. MDA is a metabolite of MDMA and may be responsible for much of MDMA's action; there is some concern that these drugs and other synthetic amphetamine derivatives cause neuronal degeneration.

MDMA *n.* 3,4-*m*ethylene*d*ioxy*m*eth*a*mphetamine: a substituted PHENYLETHYLAMINE that, like its analog MDA, is a catecholamine-like HALLUCINOGEN with amphetamine-like stimulant properties that may produce visual disturbances and hallucinations at high doses. It is among the most commonly used illicit drugs, generally sold under the name **Ecstasy**. Taken orally, onset of effects is rapid; the high lasts several hours, and residual effects can be experienced for several days. Intoxication is characterized by euphoria, feelings of closeness and spirituality, and diverse symptoms of autonomic arousal. Widespread illicit use of MDMA as a "club drug" has caused increasing concern as nerve damage and serotonin dysfunction have been established as resulting from prolonged use. Persistent memory dysfunction and impaired decision making and self-control as well as depressed mood have been well documented. When used during periods of intense activity (as often occurs during rave parties), it may be toxic or fatal.

MDS abbreviation for MULTIDIMENSIONAL SCALING.

me *pron.* the objective pronoun referring to the self. In William JAMES's psychology, the "me" is the EMPIRICAL SELF.

mean (symbol: $\bar{X}$; *M*) *n.* the numerical average of a batch of scores (X_i): the most widely used statistic for describing CENTRAL TENDENCY. It is computed as:

$$\bar{X} = (\sum_i X_i)/n,$$

where *n* is the number of scores; that is, the scores are added up, and the total is divided by the number of scores. Also called **arithmetic mean**; **arithmetic average**. See also GEOMETRIC MEAN; HARMONIC MEAN.

mean deviation for a set of numbers, a measure of dispersion or spread equal to the average of the differences between each number and the mean value. It is given by $(\Sigma|x_i - \mu|)/n$, where μ is the mean value and *n* the number of values.

mean-gradation method see METHOD OF EQUAL-APPEARING INTERVALS.

meaning *n.* the cognitive or emotional significance of a word or sequence of words, or of a concept, sign, or symbolic act. This may include a range of implied or associated ideas (connotative meaning) as well as a literal significance (DENOTATIVE MEANING). The study of meaning in language is SEMANTICS, and that of meaning in symbolic systems generally is SEMIOTICS. **—mean** *vb.* **—meaningful** *adj.*

meaning-centered therapy see LOGOTHERAPY.

meaningful learning learning new material or information by relating it to the learner's experience or existing knowledge base, as contrasted with the ROTE LEARNING of material that has less relevance. See also READINESS.

meaninglessness *n.* a pervasive sense of the absence of significance, direction, or purpose in one's life, life in general, or the entire world. A sense of meaninglessness is sometimes a focal issue in psychotherapy. The perception of meaninglessness poses the central problem that the existential approach attempts to solve or accommodate. See also EXISTENTIALISM; LOGOTHERAPY; WILL TO MEANING.

mean length of utterance (**MLU**) a measure of language development in young children based on the mean length of UTTERANCES in their spontaneous speech. It is usually calculated by counting MORPHEMES rather than words, and is based on at least 100 successive utterances. [introduced in 1973 by Roger BROWN to characterize the different stages of early language development]

means–ends analysis 1. in ARTIFICIAL INTELLIGENCE, a technique to solve problems that sets up subgoals as means to achieve the goals (ends) and compares subgoals and goals using a recursive goal-reduction search procedure. See GENERAL PROBLEM SOLVER. **2.** more generally, any problem-solving strategy that assesses the difference between the current state and a desired end state and attempts to discover means to reduce that difference. Such a strategy would not discard means to the end that appeared blocked, but would consider possible ways to overcome any such intermediate problem.

means object in PURPOSIVE BEHAVIORISM, any object, response, event, or condition that contributes to an organism's progress toward a GOAL. Also called **means situation**.

mean square a SUM OF SQUARES divided by its DEGREES OF FREEDOM. The mean square is a variance ESTIMATOR.

measurement error a difference between an observed measurement and the true value of the parameter being measured that is attributable to flaws or biases in the measurement process.

measurement level the degree of specificity, accuracy, and precision reflected in a particular set of observations or measurements. Examples of common levels of measurement include NOMINAL SCALES, ORDINAL SCALES, INTERVAL SCALES, and RATIO SCALES.

measure of association any of various indices of the degree to which two or more variables are related.

measure of location any of a class of descriptive statistics that reflect the central point of a DISTRIBUTION (e.g., the mean or median).

measures of intelligence a series of norm-referenced tests used to determine an individual's ability to learn, reason, understand concepts, and acquire knowledge. See EEG MEASURES OF INTELLIGENCE; ERP MEASURES OF INTELLIGENCE; FMRI MEASURES OF INTELLIGENCE. See also ASSESSMENT OF INTELLIGENCE.

mecamylamine *n.* a GANGLIONIC BLOCKING AGENT formerly widely used in the treatment of hypertension. Because of the severity of its side effects, which include tremor, sedation, and movement disorders, this use is now rare. However, because mecamylamine has preferential antagonistic action at NICOTINIC RECEPTORS, it has been investigated as a possible antismoking agent. It has also been used in the treatment of TOURETTE'S DISORDER. U.S. trade name: **Inversine**.

mechanical aptitude an ability to comprehend and deal with machines or mechanisms and the principles underlying their construction and function.

mechanical-aptitude test any of various tests designed to measure abilities related to mechanical work, such as mechanical information, mechanical reasoning, spatial relations, perceptual skills, understanding of mechanical principles, mechanical assembly, and manual dexterity.

mechanical causality a construct that explains the causes of things and events, including behaviors, in terms of the causal relations among the parts of a machine. Such an explanation will nearly always be one of LINEAR CAUSATION. Mechanical causality is a type of HARD DETERMINISM. See MECHANISTIC THEORY. See also CAUSAL MECHANISM.

mechanical-comprehension test 1. an assessment that measures an individual's aptitude to learn mechanical skills. It requires a grasp of the principles underlying the operation and repair of complex devices. **2.** an assessment used to determine understanding of concepts relating to machinery or tools.

mechanical intelligence the mental ability to understand concrete objects and mechanical relationships.

mechanical-man concept the idea that human beings can be understood as living machines subject only to physical processes and not subject to nonphysical phenomena, such as consciousness. This is often cited as a model for the image of human beings proposed by BEHAVIORISM and similar deterministic and naturalistic theories. See also MECHANICAL CAUSALITY; MECHANISTIC THEORY.

mechanism *n.* **1.** in general, a device or physical property by which something is accomplished, or an explanation that relies on such a device or property. **2.** a philosophical position, similar to that of MATERIALISM, that provides explanations in terms of underlying physical properties. See MECHANICAL CAUSALITY; MECHANISTIC THEORY. **3.** the concept of the human being as a machine. See MECHANICAL-MAN CONCEPT. [credited to French physician and philosopher Julien Offroy de La Mettrie (1709–1751)] **4.** in psychodynamics, see MENTAL MECHANISM.

mechanistic approach see MECHANISTIC THEORY.

mechanistic interactionism a theory that considers both individual (dispositional) and situational variables in the determination of behavior. The relative weight assigned to dispositional and situational factors may be affected by certain moderating variables, for example, the nature of a situation: A highly structured situation may influence behavior more than will dispositional factors, and a highly ambiguous situation may allow dispositional factors to play a larger role in determining behavior.

mechanistic theory the assumption that psychological processes and behaviors can ultimately be understood in the same way that mechanical or physiological processes are understood. Its explanations of human behavior are based on the model or metaphor of a machine and invoke MECHANICAL CAUSALITY, reducing complex psychological phenomena to simpler physical phenomena. Also called **mechanistic approach**. See REDUCTIONISM.

mechanoreceptor *n.* a receptor that is sensitive to mechanical forms of stimuli. Examples of mechanoreceptors are the receptors in the ear that translate sound waves into nerve impulses, the touch receptors in the skin, and the receptors in the joints and muscles (see PROPRIOCEPTOR). Compare CHEMORECEPTOR.

Meckel's syndrome a congenital disorder marked by MICROCEPHALY, eye, ear, and olfactory abnormalities, and varying degrees of brain-tissue anomalies. Some affected children show premature closure of skull sutures. The patients either are stillborn or die in early infancy. [Johann Friedrich **Meckel** (1781–1833), German anatomist]

Medea complex a mother's wish to kill her children as a means of revenge against the father. The term is derived from Greek mythology, in which Medea killed her children fathered by Jason after he deserted her for a younger woman. See also FILICIDE.

medial *adj.* toward or at the middle of the body or of an organ. Compare LATERAL. **—medially** *adv.*

medial amygdala a portion of the AMYGDALA that receives olfactory and pheromonal information and participates in fear responses.

medial bundle a group of sensory fibers located in the medial portion of a body structure. For example, there is a medial bundle in the knee.

medial forebrain bundle a collection of nerve fibers passing through the midline of the forebrain to the hypothalamus. It includes tracts originating in the LOCUS CERULEUS, SUBSTANTIA NIGRA, and VENTRAL TEGMENTAL AREA and provides the chief pathway for reciprocal connections between the hypothalamus and the BIOGENIC AMINE systems of the brainstem.

medial geniculate nucleus either of a pair of NUCLEI in the THALAMUS, just medial to the LATERAL GENICULATE NUCLEUS, that receive, process, and relay auditory information. Each receives input from the INFERIOR COLLICULUS and sends output to the AUDITORY CORTEX. Also called **medial geniculate body**.

medial lemniscus either of a pair of somatosensory tracts in the midbrain carrying fibers from the spinal cord that communicate with the thalamus. They form part of the LEMNISCAL SYSTEM.

medial prefrontal cortex a region of the PREFRONTAL CORTEX of the brain that has a prominent role in the control of mood, having extensive connections throughout the LIMBIC SYSTEM.

medial preoptic area (mPOA) a region of the anterior HYPOTHALAMUS implicated in the regulation of many behaviors, including thermoregulation, sexual behavior, and gonadotropin secretion (see SEXUALLY DIMORPHIC NUCLEUS).

medial rectus an extrinsic EYE MUSCLE that rotates the eye medially (i.e., toward the midline).

medial sagittal see SAGITTAL.

medial temporal amnesia amnesia caused by damage to the MEDIAL TEMPORAL LOBE. Causes include infarction of the posterior cerebral artery, anoxia, encephalitis, temporal lobectomy, and trauma. See AMNESTIC DISORDER.

medial temporal lobe the medial region of the temporal lobe of each cerebral hemisphere. It contains the PYRIFORM AREA, the AMYGDALA, and the HIPPOCAMPUS.

median *n.* the score that divides a DISTRIBUTION into two equal-sized halves.

median-cleft-face syndrome a congenital disorder characterized by defective fusion of structures in the midline of the face. The cleft may involve the eyes, the tip of the nose, the palate, and the premaxilla. About 20% of affected individuals have some degree of mental retardation.

median effective dose see EFFECTIVE DOSE.

median nerve a nerve that supplies sensory and motor fibers to the arm and hand. Its fibers run through the BRACHIAL PLEXUS.

median test a nonparametric statistical procedure that tests the equality of the medians in two or more samples.

media richness the relative intensity and complexity of a communication channel. Face-to-face communication is a good example of a **rich medium**, as it involves a complex interaction of verbal and nonverbal cues; by contrast, communication exclusively via written messages is a **lean medium**. [proposed in 1984 by U.S. organizational and management theorists Richard L. Daft and Robert H. Lengel]

mediated generalization a type of STIMULUS GENERALIZATION in which a CONDITIONED RESPONSE is elicited by a new stimulus that is notably different from, but in some way associated with, the original CONDITIONED STIMULUS. For example, a person conditioned to feel anxious on hearing a bell may also become anxious on hearing the word "bell." See STIMULUS EQUIVALENCE.

mediated response a response that is elicited by a stimulus and is subsequently responsible for the initiation of a behavior.

mediate experience conscious awareness and interpretation of external events and stimuli. Mediate experience provides meaning and additional information not contained in the event or stimulus itself. It is contrasted with **immediate experience**: the elements or characteristics of the event or stimuli as perceived directly and without interpretation. INTROSPECTION makes use of immediate experience in analyzing the contents of mediate experience. [defined by Wilhelm WUNDT]

mediating behavior behavior that improves either the rate or probability of reinforcement of a target behavior for which reinforcement is arranged. Compare ADJUNCTIVE BEHAVIOR; COLLATERAL BEHAVIOR; INTERIM BEHAVIOR.

mediating variable see INTERVENING VARIABLE.

mediation *n.* in dispute resolution, use of a neutral outside person—the MEDIATOR—to help the contending parties communicate and reach a compromise. The process of mediation has gained popularity, for example for couples involved in separation or divorce proceedings (see DIVORCE MEDIATION).

mediational deficiency the inability of young children to use a strategy to benefit task performance even if it is taught to them. Compare PRODUCTION DEFICIENCY; UTILIZATION DEFICIENCY.

mediational learning a concept of learning that assumes the presence of MEDIATORS to bridge the association between two or more events that are not directly contiguous in space or time. The mediators are events or processes that serve as CUES.

mediation process any of the COGNITIVE PROCESSES that are presumed to occur in the mind between reception of a stimulus and initiation of a response. These may include interpretation of sense data, retrieval of stored information, judgments and evaluations, computations, reasoning, and other mental operations. See COGNITIVE MEDIATION.

mediation theory the hypothesis that stimuli affect behavior indirectly through an intervening process, as opposed to a simpler stimulus–response model. For example, cognitive therapists maintain that the effect an external event has on an individual is influenced by the individual's thoughts and perceptions of that event.

mediator *n.* **1.** a process or system that exists between a stimulus and a response, between the source and destination of a neural impulse, or between the transmitter and receiver of communications. **2.** a person—for example, a lawyer or psychologist—who helps contending parties communicate and reach a compromise. See also DIVORCE MEDIATION; MEDIATION. **3.** in statistical analyses of the interrelations among variables, a variable that accounts for an observed relation between two other variables.

mediator variable see INTERVENING VARIABLE.

Medicaid *n.* a joint federal and state program, instituted by law in 1965 (Title XIX of the Social Security Act), that provides medical benefits for people with low incomes and limited resources. Medicaid programs follow broad federal guidelines but each state determines specific benefits and amounts of payments.

Medicaid Waiver see HOME AND COMMUNITY-BASED SERVICES.

medical anthropology a subdiscipline in cultural ANTHROPOLOGY that applies anthropological theory and research methodology to the study of topics relating to health, healthcare, disease, and other medical areas.

medical audit a systematic evaluation of the effectiveness of diagnostic and treatment procedures. A **retrospective medical audit** is based on a review of a patient's charts after he or she has been discharged; a **concurrent medical audit** is conducted while the patient is still under treatment.

medical care evaluation (**MCE**) a health care review in which an assessment of the quality of care and its utilization is made. It will include an investigation of any suspected problems, analysis of the problems identified, and a plan for corrective action.

medical family therapy a form of psychotherapy that combines a BIOPSYCHOSOCIAL SYSTEMS approach with FAMILY SYSTEMS THEORY to help individuals and their families deal with the health problems of the individual. This therapy emphasizes collaboration with others—physicians, nurses, occupational therapists, nutritionists, and the like—in the individual's health care team.

medical history in psychology, the portion of the developmental history, or ANAMNESIS, that focuses on the patient's health throughout life, including congenital or acquired illnesses and disorders. The object is to uncover, where possible, clues to the cause of the patient's current psychological condition.

medical model 1. the concept that mental and emotional problems are analogous to biological problems, that is, they have detectable, specific, physiological causes (e.g., an abnormal gene or damaged cell) and are amenable to cure or improvement by specific treatment. **2.** in evaluation research, a systems-analysis approach to evaluation that considers the interrelatedness of all the factors that may affect performance and monitors possible side effects of treatment. The medical model is in contrast to the **engineering model**, which is a simple comparison of gains for different groups, some of which have been exposed to the program of interest.

medical psychology an area of applied psychology devoted to psychological questions arising in the practice of medicine, including emotional reactions to illness; attitudes toward terminal illness and impending death; psychological means of relieving pain (e.g., hypnotic suggestion); and reactions to disability.

medical psychotherapy psychotherapy that makes use of medication and other medical techniques in the treatment of mental illness.

medical rehabilitation the process of restoring to the fullest possible degree the physical functioning of an individual who has a physiological or anatomical impairment. See also REHABILITATION.

medical social worker a licensed SOCIAL WORKER, usually with a master's degree in social work, who assists patients and their families with health-related problems in such areas as employment, finances, living arrangements, marriage, child care, social life, and emotional adjustment.

Medicare *n.* a federal program of HEALTH INSURANCE operated by the Health Care Financing Administration of the U.S. Department of Health and Human Services for those over 65, certain younger people with disabilities, and people with end-stage renal disease. Monies from payroll taxes and premiums from subscribers are deposited in trust funds to meet the expenses of the insured. Medicare consists of two programs: Part A includes inpatient costs and Part B provides supplementary medical insurance.

medication *n.* PSYCHOACTIVE DRUGS that aid in the treatment of affective and behavioral disorders. Until recently, in the United States only medical physicians could legally prescribe psychoactive drugs, but prescription privileges have now been extended to psychologists in the military and to those in New Mexico. **Overmedication**—the taking of more than the prescribed dose of a drug or drugs—may occur when medication is not properly monitored. **Self-medication** is usually associated with individuals who use drugs or alcohol inappropriately to alleviate emotional problems.

medication-induced movement disorder any movement disorder that occurs as an adverse effect of medication. It may involve rigidity, tremor, hypertonia (increased muscle tone), and other motor symptoms and is commonly seen after treatment with antipsychotic drugs. See TARDIVE DYSKINESIA.

mediodorsal nucleus see DORSOMEDIAL NUCLEUS.

meditation *n.* profound and extended contemplation or reflection, sometimes in order to attain an ALTERED STATE OF CONSCIOUSNESS. Traditionally associated with spiritual and religious exercises, it is now increasingly also used to provide relaxation and relief from stress. See also CONCENTRATIVE MEDITATION; MINDFULNESS MEDITATION; TRANSCENDENTAL MEDITATION.

medium *n.* (*pl.* **media** or **mediums**) **1.** the state of being in the middle of or between two factors or conditions or midway on some scale. **2.** (*pl.* **media**) any means or agency through which messages are transmitted or information is diffused (e.g., the medium of television). **3.** (*pl.* **media**) a substance, such as air or water, that serves to transmit a physical effect, such as sound or light. **4.** (*pl.* **media**) a nutritive substance in which molds or other organisms are grown in a laboratory. **5.** (*pl.* **mediums**) in SPIRITUALISM, a person who functions as the instrument of alleged communication between the living and the dead or between spirits and humans. Some mediums claim more general paranormal abilities, such as CLAIRVOYANCE, ASTRAL PROJECTION, or powers of PSYCHIC HEALING.

medium trance see TRANCE.

medium-wavelength pigment the PHOTOPIGMENT, present in one of the three populations of RETINAL CONES, that has maximum sensitivity to a wavelength of 531 nm. The absence of the gene for the medium-wavelength pigment causes DEUTERANOPIA (red–green color blindness). See also LONG-WAVELENGTH PIGMENT; SHORT-WAVELENGTH PIGMENT.

medulla *n.* **1.** the central or innermost region of an organ, such as the ADRENAL MEDULLA. Compare CORTEX. **2.** see MEDULLA OBLONGATA. **—medullary** *adj.*

medulla oblongata the most inferior (lowest), or caudal (tailward), part of the HINDBRAIN. It contains many nerve tracts that conduct impulses between the spinal cord and higher brain centers, as well as autonomic nuclei involved in the control of breathing, heartbeat, and blood pressure. Also called **myelencephalon**.

medullary reticular formation the hindmost portion of the brainstem RETICULAR FORMATION, implicated in motor control and copulatory behavior.

medullary sheath see MYELIN SHEATH.

medullation *n.* see MYELINATION.

Meehl, Paul Everett (1920–2003) U.S. psychologist. Meehl received his PhD in psychology from the University of Minnesota and served on the faculty there for the remainder of his career. Both a practicing psychotherapist and an academic psychologist, Meehl made important contributions to research in the fields of clinical psychology and cliometrics, the use of mathematics and statistics to analyze historical data. In clinical psychology, his research focused on diagnosis and classification of mental disorders using quantitative methods that revolutionized the field by developing computerized scoring techniques for psychological tests. Meehl also applied his statistical expertise to problems in the history and philosophy of science, publishing many articles in those fields. Representative works include *Clinical versus Statistical Prediction: A Theoretical Analysis and a Review of the Evidence* (1954; reprinted 1996) and *Selected Philosophical and Methodological Papers* (1991). Among his many honors were the American Psychological Association's awards for Distinguished Scientific Contributions and for Outstanding Lifetime Contribution to Psychology, the American Psychological Foundation's Gold Medal Award for Life Achievement in the Application of Psychology, and membership of the National Academy of Sciences and the American Academy of Arts and Sciences.

mefloquine *n.* a chemical analog of quinine used in the treatment of malarial infections and prevention of malaria. It has been associated with seizures or psychological disturbances, including sleep disturbance, depression, panic attacks, and psychotic symptoms. Although such reactions are rare, mefloquine should not be taken by individuals with histories of depression, generalized anxiety disorder, psychosis, or seizure disorders. U.S. trade name: **Lariam**.

MEG abbreviation for MAGNETOENCEPHALOGRAPHY or magnetoencephalograph.

mega- *combining form* great or very large.

megadose pharmacotherapy a dosing strategy popular in the 1970s and 1980s in the United States and other countries, generally involving the rapid administration of very high doses of an antipsychotic drug in the hopes that this would hasten an antipsychotic response. It was based on the presumption that rapid blockade of postsynaptic dopamine D2 receptors would lead to faster resolution of psychotic symptoms. This strategy was largely ineffective in producing a more rapid response and had numerous adverse effects, such as severe movement disorders and death due to NEUROLEPTIC MALIGNANT SYNDROME. Research published in the late 1980s showed that lower doses were as effective as higher doses and had fewer adverse consequences. Because of the lack of clinical benefit and the high incidence of adverse side effects associated with megadose pharmacotherapy, it has fallen into disuse. Also called **rapid neuroleptization**.

megalocephaly *n.* see MACROCEPHALY. **—megalocephalic** *adj.*

megalomania *n.* a highly inflated conception of one's importance, power, or capabilities, as can be observed in many individuals with mania and paranoid schizophrenia. In the latter, megalomania is often accompanied or preceded by delusions of persecution. See DELUSION OF GRANDEUR.

megalopsia *n.* see MACROPSIA.

Megan's law U.S. legislation requiring that convicted but released sex offenders register with the authorities so that communities will be notified of their presence in a particular neighborhood. More formally known as the **Community Notification Act**, it was initially passed in New Jersey in 1994 after a repeat sex offender murdered a 7-year-old girl named Megan Nicole Kanka; it became a federal law in 1996.

megavitamin therapy the use of very high doses of vitamins and mineral supplements, particularly vitamin C (ascorbic acid), nicotinic acid (niacin), vitamin B_6 (pyridoxine), and magnesium, to treat certain mental disorders. Such an approach is not widely adopted, and effectiveness is uncertain.

meiosis *n.* a special type of division of the cell nucleus that occurs during the formation of the sex cells—ova and spermatozoa. During meiosis, a parental cell in the gonad produces four daughter cells that are all HAPLOID, that is, they possess only one of each chromosome, instead of the normal DIPLOID complement of homologous pairs of chromosomes. During the process of fertilization, the ova and spermatozoa undergo fusion, which restores the double set of chromosomes within the nucleus of the zygote thus formed.

Meissner's corpuscle a type of small, oval sensory-nerve ending that is sensitive to touch. Meissner's corpuscles are abundant in the fingertips, nipples, lips, and the tip of the tongue. [Georg **Meissner** (1829–1905), German anatomist and physiologist]

mel *n.* a unit for measuring PITCH. By definition the pitch of a 1000-Hz tone presented at 40 dB SPL (40 phons) is 1000 mels. A sound whose pitch is twice that of a 1000-mel tone has a pitch of 2000 mels, and so on.

melancholia *n.* an archaic name for depression. **—melancholic** *adj.*

melancholia agitata a 19th-century term for CATATONIC EXCITEMENT. It is occasionally still used for AGITATED DEPRESSION.

melancholic features features that may be associated with a MAJOR DEPRESSIVE EPISODE. These include loss of pleasure in most or all activities or inability to take pleasure in anything that normally elicits this feeling, together with three or more of the following: The depressed mood is experienced as quite distinct from normal sadness; it is worse in the morning; and there is early morning awakening, psychomotor agitation or retardation, loss of appetite or weight, or excessive guilt feelings.

melancholic type the morose personality type that Roman physician Galen (129–199 CE) attributed to an excess of black bile. See HUMORAL THEORY.

melano- (melan-) *combining form* black or dark.

melanocortin-4 receptor (MC4-R) a RECEPTOR that is activated by ALPHA-MELANOCYTE STIMULATING HORMONE. It may play a role in the regulation of eating and body weight.

melanocyte-stimulating hormone (MSH) a hormone secreted by the anterior pituitary gland that stimulates dispersal of melanin granules within pigment cells (melanophores) of the skin of certain vertebrates (e.g., amphibians) thereby darkening the skin. In mammals it may play a role in regulating eating behavior (see ALPHA-MELANOCYTE STIMULATING HORMONE).

melatonin *n.* an AMINE HORMONE, produced mainly by the PINEAL GLAND as a metabolic product of the neurotransmitter SEROTONIN, that helps to regulate seasonal changes in physiology and may also influence puberty. It is implicated in the initiation of sleep and in the regulation of the sleep–wake cycle. Melatonin has been investigated in clinical studies as a hypnotic and for the management of CIRCADIAN RHYTHM SLEEP DISORDERS. Although these studies are as yet inconclusive, melatonin is widely available as an over-the-counter medication.

melioration *n.* in behavioral studies, allocating time to two or more activities such that local rates of REINFORCEMENT (i.e., reinforcers obtained per unit of time for each activity) are equal.

melioristic *adj.* having a tendency to improve or an inclination or intent to make things better.

Mellaril *n.* a trade name for THIORIDAZINE.

melodic intonation therapy (MIT) speech therapy that uses melody to regain or improve speech in individuals with certain kinds of APHASIA, MOTOR SPEECH DISORDER, or EXPRESSIVE LANGUAGE DISORDER. Based on the theory of right-hemisphere dominance for music, MIT trains the speaker to intone, or "sing," text in pitches and rhythms that parallel natural spoken prosody. MIT is primarily an auxiliary to other forms of speech therapy.

membership group a social body or organization to which people belong as members, especially when they feel that the group has formally or informally accepted them into its ranks. Such groups, which include clubs, societies, cliques, teams, and political parties, often explicitly distinguish between individuals who belong to the group and those who do not. Compare ASPIRATIONAL GROUP; REFERENCE GROUP.

membrane potential a difference in electric potential across a membrane, especially the plasma membrane of a cell. See POLARIZED MEMBRANE; RESTING POTENTIAL.

membranous dysmenorrhea see DYSMENORRHEA.

memorandum as a whole see OBJECTIVE PSYCHOTHERAPY.

memorize *vb.* to commit to memory. Memorizing usually implies ROTE LEARNING or DRILL as the method of learning, although use of an active MNEMONIC STRATEGY is likely to be more effective. **—memorization** *n.*

memory *n.* **1.** the ability to retain information or a representation of past experience, based on the mental processes of learning or ENCODING, RETENTION across some interval of time, and RETRIEVAL or reactivation of the memory. **2.** specific information or a specific past experience that is recalled. **3.** the hypothesized part of the brain where traces of information and past experiences are stored (see MEMORY STORAGE; MEMORY SYSTEM). See also ASSOCIATIVE MEMORY; AUDITORY MEMORY; CONSTRUCTIVE MEMORY; EXPLICIT MEMORY; IMMEDIATE MEMORY; IMPLICIT MEMORY; LONG-TERM MEMORY; SHORT-TERM MEMORY.

memory abilities abilities involved in remembering information, as assessed by tests of FREE RECALL (recall of words in any order), SERIAL RECALL (recall of words in a fixed order), PAIRED-ASSOCIATES LEARNING (recall of a word paired with the word presented), and RECOGNITION memory (skill in stating correctly whether a presented word was previously presented on some list). Psychometric data suggest that, typically, various memory abilities are only weakly related to each other. Moreover, IMPLICIT MEMORY is largely independent of EXPLICIT MEMORY.

memory aid see MNEMONIC STRATEGY.

memory color any object's color as modified in memory. The quality of remembered color often differs substantially from the actual hue. Color perception is considered to be a compromise between the memory color and present sensory input.

memory consolidation see CONSOLIDATION; PERSEVERATION–CONSOLIDATION HYPOTHESIS.

memory curve see EBBINGHAUS'S CURVE OF RETENTION; RETENTION CURVE.

memory decay see DECAY THEORY.

memory disorders organic and psychogenic disorders of memory, including AMNESIA, HYPERMNESIA, and long- and short-term memory defects (see AMNESTIC DISORDER). Memory disorders may be partial or global, mild or severe, permanent or transitory, anterograde or retrograde. The cause may be medical conditions leading to structural lesions of the brain or metabolic disruption of brain function, aging, psychological trauma, fugue states, or intrapsychic conflicts. See also ANTEROGRADE AMNESIA; RETROGRADE AMNESIA.

memory distortion inaccurate or illusory recall or recognition. See DÉJÀ VU; FALSE MEMORY; MEMORY ILLUSION.

memory drum a device formerly used to present items in memory experiments. The drum turned at a given speed, allowing one item at a time to be seen through an opening. The memory drum has been replaced by presentation of items on a computer screen.

memory-enhancing drugs see NOOTROPIC DRUGS.

memory hardening an increased conviction, with the passage of time, that FALSE MEMORIES or PSEUDOMEMORIES are accurate. It is believed by some that such memory hardening can make eyewitnesses more resistant to cross-examination in court.

memory illusion a distortion in remembering, analogous to a perceptual illusion, in which one remembers inaccurately or remembers something that in fact did not occur. The DEESE PARADIGM is a memory illusion.

memory impairment the loss of memory associated with MEMORY DISORDERS.

memory loss see MEMORY IMPAIRMENT.

memory-operating characteristic curve (MOCC) a graphic representation of the proportion of items accurately remembered against the proportion mistakenly remembered (called false positives).

memory retraining strategies to help individuals with neurological deficits improve their ability to process information in WORKING MEMORY. These strategies are typically applied with patients with brain injury or Alzheimer's disease and those with HIV/AIDS who are experiencing memory problems.

memory span the number of items that can be recalled immediately after one presentation. Usually, the items consist of letters, words, numbers, or syllables that the participant must reproduce in order. A distinction may be drawn between **visual memory span** and AUDITORY MEMORY SPAN, depending on the nature of the presentation. See also DIGIT SPAN.

memory storage the retention of memories in an organism. Historically, explanations of this process have included the continuous operation or "reverberation" of loops of neurons in cell assemblies (see CELL ASSEMBLY; REVERBERATORY CIRCUIT), the growth of new nerve endings grouped in synaptic knobs, and the encoding of information in complex molecules, such as RNA. Contemporary biological research suggests changes in synaptic efficiency as the basis of memory storage, as postulated in the research of Austrian-born U.S. neuroscientist Eric Kandel (1929–).

memory system any of several different kinds of memory that are hypothesized to be located in separate brain areas and primarily employed in different sorts of memory tasks. Examples of hypothesized systems include WORKING MEMORY (a temporary store used in manipulating information), SEMANTIC MEMORY (general knowledge), EPISODIC MEMORY (memories of one's personal past), and PROCEDURAL MEMORY (habits and skills). See also PERCEPTUAL REPRESENTATION SYSTEM.

memory trace a hypothetical modification of the nervous system that encodes a representation of information or experience. See ENGRAM.

menacme *n.* the period of a woman's life cycle in which she experiences menstrual activity (i.e., from puberty to MENOPAUSE).

ménage à trois 1. a sexual relationship involving three people who are members of the same household, for example, a married couple and the husband's mistress sharing an apartment. **2.** three people having sex together (see TROILISM).

menarche *n.* the first incidence of MENSTRUATION in a female, marking the onset of puberty. The age at which menarche occurs varies among individuals and cultures: It tends to occur earlier in Western countries, possibly associated with better nutrition. **—menarcheal** *adj.*

mendacity *n.* **1.** the act of telling lies or falsehoods. **2.** a lie or falsehood. See PATHOLOGICAL LYING. **—mendacious** *adj.*

Mendelian inheritance a type of inheritance that conforms to the basic principles developed around 1865 by Austrian monk Gregor Mendel (1822–1884), regarded as the founder of genetics. Mendelian inheritance is essentially determined by genes located on chromosomes, which are transmitted from both parents to their offspring. It includes AUTOSOMAL DOMINANT, AUTOSOMAL RECESSIVE, and SEX-LINKED inheritance. Mendel proposed two principles. The **principle of segregation**, or **Mendel's first law**, states that RECESSIVE TRAITS are neither modified nor lost in future generations as both DOMINANT and RECESSIVE ALLELES are independently transmitted and so are able to segregate independently during the formation of sex cells. **Mendel's second law**, the **principle of independent assortment**, states that there is no tendency for genes of one parent to stay together in future offspring.

Ménière's disease a disorder of balance and hearing due to excessive fluid in the inner ear, resulting in dizziness, nausea, TINNITUS, and progressive DEAFNESS. See also ADULT SENSORINEURAL LESIONS. [Prosper **Ménière** (1799–1862), French physician]

meninges *pl. n.* (*sing.* **meninx**) the three membranous layers that provide a protective cover for the brain and spinal cord. They consist of a tough outer DURA MATER, a middle ARACHNOID MATER, and a thin, transparent PIA MATER, which fits over the various contours and fissures of the cerebral cortex.

meningioma *n.* a benign BRAIN TUMOR that develops in the arachnoid layer of the MENINGES, accounting for 15–25% of all tumors of the brain and spinal cord. Meningiomas are typically slow growing and cause damage mainly by pressure against the brain. Patients may complain of headaches or seizures as first symptoms.

meningitis *n.* inflammation of the meninges, the three membranous layers that cover the brain and spinal cord, usually due to infection by bacteria, viruses, or fungi. Symptoms include high fever, nausea, vomiting, stiff neck, and headache. BACTERIAL MENINGITIS includes meningococcal meningitis and TUBERCULOUS MENINGITIS. **Viral** (or **aseptic**) **meningitis** is a milder nonbacterial disease; causes include the mumps, poliomyelitis, herpes viruses, and the ECHOVIRUSES (which mainly affect young children during the summer). If untreated or not treated promptly, many types of meningitis can result in confusion, lethargy, coma, and eventually death.

meningocele *n.* a congenital herniation (protrusion) of the meninges (the three membranous layers that cover the brain and spinal cord) through an abnormal opening in the skull or spinal cord, with seepage of cerebrospinal fluid into the protrusion. The disorder is sometimes associated with HYDROCEPHALUS or other neurological defects, which reduces the chances of a favorable prognosis. If the herniation contains neural tissue, the condition is identified as an ENCEPHALOCELE.

meningococcal meningitis see BACTERIAL MENINGITIS.

meningoencephalitis *n.* inflammation of the brain and the meninges covering it.

meningomyelocele *n.* protrusion of the spinal cord and its covering meninges through a defect in the spinal column. This results in an external sac containing cerebrospinal fluid, poorly formed meninges, and a malformed spinal cord. See SPINA BIFIDA.

meningovascular syphilis see CEREBRAL SYPHILIS.

menkeiti *n.* see MYRIACHIT.

menopausal depression severe DYSPHORIA that occurs during the female CLIMACTERIC (menopause), particularly among women who have had a prior tendency to depression.

menopause *n.* the period during which menstruation ceases at the end of the reproductive cycle in women. See CLIMACTERIC. **—menopausal** *adj.*

menorrhagia *n.* excessive bleeding during menstruation. Also called **epimenorrhagia**.

Mensa *n.* an organization of individuals whose sole admission requirement is an IQ in the upper 2% of the population.

menses *pl. n.* see MENSTRUATION.

men's liberation movement a variety of social movements and positions united only by taking men and masculinity as their topic of interest. Some positions acknowledge the justice of feminist critiques of male dominance and recommend measures whereby men can overcome exploitation of women by men. Others aim to liberate men from stereotypical attitudes, particularly attitudes that prevent their expressing emotions and forming attachments to other men. A quite different type of movement seeks to help men rediscover traditional forms of masculinity and to become more responsible husbands and fathers. Yet another is essentially antifeminist, arguing that men are now subject to various injustices in education, employment, and the law (e.g., in divorce settlements and child-custody agreements). No one area of emphasis has become dominant under the rubric of men's liberation.

mens rea the malicious or blameworthy state of mind (Latin, "guilty mind") that must be proved in addition to the ACTUS REUS in order to establish CRIMINAL RESPONSIBILITY and secure a conviction. It involves a conscious disregard for the law, which is presumed to be known by the defendant. For some crimes the mens rea may be recklessness or negligence rather than a deliberate intention to bring about certain consequences. Also called **criminal intent**.

menstrual age the age of a fetus calculated from the beginning of the mother's last MENSTRUATION. At full term it is normally 280 days or 40 weeks, that is, usually 2 weeks longer than the GESTATIONAL AGE.

menstrual cycle a modified ESTROUS CYCLE that occurs in most primates, including humans (in which it averages about 28 days). The events of the cycle are dependent on cyclical changes in the concentrations of GONADOTROPINS secreted by the anterior pituitary gland, under the control of GONADOTROPIN-RELEASING HORMONE, and can be divided into two phases. In the follicular phase, FOLLICLE-STIMULATING HORMONE (FSH) and LUTEINIZING HORMONE (LH) stimulate development of an ovum and secretion of estrogen within the ovary, in a GRAAFIAN FOLLICLE, culminating in OVULATION, which occurs half way through the cycle. The estrogen stimulates thickening of the ENDOMETRIUM of the uterus in preparation to receive a fertilized ovum. The luteal phase begins immediately after ovulation, when the ruptured follicle becomes the CORPUS LUTEUM and secretes progesterone, which inhibits further secretion of releasing hormone (and hence of FSH and LH). If fertilization does not occur, this phase ends with menstruation and a repeat of the follicular phase.

menstrual synchrony the similar timing of menstrual cycles in women who live close together.

menstrual taboo any culture-bound tradition associated with menstruating women, typically involving physical separation from men, abstention from sexual intercourse, or the exclusion of women from certain daily activities (e.g., the preparation of food).

menstruation *n.* a periodic discharge of blood and endometrial tissue from the uterus through the vagina that occurs in fertile women as part of the MENSTRUAL CYCLE. Also called **menses**; **menstrual** (or **monthly**) **period**.

mental *adj.* **1.** of or referring to the MIND or to processes of the mind, such as thinking, feeling, sensing, and the like. **2.** phenomenal or consciously experienced. In contrast to physiological or physical, which refer to objective events or processes, mental denotes events known only privately and subjectively; it may refer to the COGNITIVE PROCESSES involved in these events, to differentiate them from physiological processes.

mental aberration 1. a pathological deviation from normal thinking. **2.** any mental or emotional disorder or an individual symptom of such a disorder.

mental abilities abilities as measured by tests of an individual in areas of spatial visualization, perceptual speed, number facility, verbal comprehension, word fluency, memory, inductive reasoning, and so forth, depending on the theory or test. See also PRIMARY ABILITIES.

mental age (**MA**) a numerical scale unit derived by dividing an individual's results in an intelligence test by the average score for other people of the same age. Thus, a 4-year-old child who scored 150 on an IQ test would have a mental age of 6 (the age-appropriate average score is 100; therefore, MA = (150/100) × 4 = 6). The MA measure of performance is not effective beyond the age of 14.

mental apparatus see PSYCHIC APPARATUS.

mental asthenia subjective loss of mental strength characterized by lack of energy or motivation for mental tasks, often expressed as **concentration difficulty**.

mental asymmetry an unbalanced relationship between mental processes, as in individuals with HYPERCALCEMIA SYNDROME (Williams syndrome), who may exhibit severe impairment in visuospatial abilities while possessing good to exceptional language abilities.

mental ataxia see INTRAPSYCHIC ATAXIA.

mental balance INTEGRATION of mental processes.

mental capacity inborn mental potential.

mental chemistry a concept proposed by British philosopher John Stuart Mill (1806–1873) as an alternative to the MENTAL MECHANICS described by his father, James Mill (1773–1836). The concept is modeled on a common phenomenon in physical chemistry, in which two chemical substances combine to form a compound with properties not present in either of the components. Similarly, Mill held that compound ideas were not merely combinations of simpler ideas but that they possessed other qualities not present in any of the constituent ideas. Thus, such an idea could be an essentially new one. See ASSOCIATIONISM; ASSOCIATION OF IDEAS.

mental chronometry see CHRONOMETRIC ANALYSIS.

mental claudication a temporary interruption of blood flow to a portion of the brain that results in brief episodes of mental status changes.

mental coaching in education, a field of teaching expertise, used mainly for counseling, business, and sports, that is focused on the direct cognitive features of behavior. It can improve overall performance, restore confidence, enhance motivation, reduce mental errors, and upgrade underperformance. It can also teach how to enhance concentration, overcome a slump or block in performance, focus better under pressure, and perform more consistently.

mental combination in Jean PIAGET's theory of cognitive development, a type of cognitive processing typical of the final subphase of the SENSORIMOTOR STAGE, in which children of 18 to 24 months of age begin to use mental images to represent objects and to engage in mental problem solving. It facilitates the transition between the action-oriented world of the infant and the symbol-oriented world of the child. Also called **invention of new means through mental combination**.

mental confusion see CONFUSION.

mental defective an obsolete name for a person with mental retardation, intellectual disability, or learning disability.

mental deficiency another (and now seldom used) name for mental retardation, sometimes referring to severe or profound mental retardation with known organic causes.

mental development the progressive changes in mental processes due to maturation, learning, and experience. See COGNITIVE DEVELOPMENT.

mental diplopia the experience of illusions, hallucinations, or false memories with concurrent awareness that these experiences are not real and are an abnormal occurrence.

mental disease an obsolete name for a MENTAL DISORDER.

mental disorder a disorder characterized by psychological symptoms, abnormal behaviors, impaired functioning, or any combination of these. Such disorders may cause clinically significant distress and impairment in a variety of domains of functioning and may be due to organic, social, genetic, chemical, or psychological factors. Specific classifications of mental disorders are elaborated in the American Psychiatric Association's *Diagnostic and Statistical Manual of Mental Disorders* (see DSM–IV–TR) and the World Health Organization's INTERNATIONAL CLASSIFICATION OF DISEASES. Also called **mental illness**; **psychiatric disorder**; **psychiatric illness**.

mental effort the amount of cognitive work or effort required by a given task. See also COGNITIVE LOAD; EFFORTFUL PROCESSING.

mental energy see PSYCHIC ENERGY.

mentalese *n.* a hypothetical language of thought that combines cognitive and semantic systems and operates on concepts and propositions.

mental examination a comprehensive evaluation of an individual's behavior, attitudes, and intellectual abilities for the purpose of establishing or ruling out pathology.

mental faculty see COGNITIVE FACULTY; FACULTY PSYCHOLOGY.

mental fog see CLOUDING OF CONSCIOUSNESS.

mental function any cognitive process or activity, such as thinking, sensing, or reasoning.

mental growth the increment in a mental function, usually intelligence, with increasing age.

mental handicap the condition of being unable to function independently in the community because of arrested or delayed cognitive development or any severe and disabling mental disorder. Also called **mental disability**.

mental healing the process of alleviating or attempting to alleviate mental or physical illness through the power of the mind, typically utilizing such methods as visualization, suggestion, and the conscious manipulation of energy flow. See also FAITH HEALING; PSYCHIC HEALING.

mental health a state of mind characterized by emotional well-being, good behavioral adjustment, relative freedom from anxiety and disabling symptoms, and a capacity to establish constructive relationships and cope with the ordinary demands and stresses of life. See also FLOURISHING; NORMALITY.

mental health care a category of health care service and delivery involving scientific and professional disciplines across several fields of knowledge and technology involved in psychological assessment and intervention (psychology, psychiatry, neurology, social work, etc.). This type of care includes but is not limited to psychological screening and testing, psychotherapy and family therapy, and neuropsychological rehabilitation. See also MENTAL HEALTH SERVICES.

mental health clinic an outpatient facility for the diagnosis and treatment of psychological and behavioral problems.

mental health counselor a certified mental health professional who provides counseling services either independently or as part of a treatment team.

mental health program a treatment, prevention, rehabilitation, or educational service offered by a community mental health center or other entity, for the purpose of maintaining or improving the mental health of an individual or community.

mental health services any interventions—assessment, diagnosis, treatment, or counseling—offered in private, public, inpatient, or outpatient settings that are aimed at the maintenance or enhancement of mental health or the treatment of mental or behavioral disorders in individual and group contexts.

mental health worker a member of a mental health treatment team who assists professional staff in a wide range of services.

mental history a record of information relating to a person's mental health (see CASE HISTORY). A mental history, which may be compiled by means of structured or unstructured INTERVIEWS, usually covers the history of both the client and family members.

mental hospital see PSYCHIATRIC HOSPITAL. See also MENTAL INSTITUTION; PRIVATE MENTAL HOSPITAL; PUBLIC MENTAL HOSPITAL.

mental housecleaning hypothesis an early hypothesis that dreams are an opportunity for reorganizing information acquired during the day, particularly to reduce "useless" or redundant information. [developed by U.S. psychologist J. Allan Hobson (1933–)]

mental hygiene a general approach aimed at maintaining mental health and preventing mental disorder through such means as educational programs, promotion of a stable emotional and family life, prophylactic and early treatment services (see PRIMARY PREVENTION), and public health measures. The term itself is now less widely used than formerly.

mental hygiene clinic a former name for a MENTAL HEALTH CLINIC or a COMMUNITY MENTAL HEALTH CENTER.

mental illness see MENTAL DISORDER.

mental imagery see IMAGERY.

mental institution a treatment-oriented facility in which patients with mental retardation or severe psychological disorder are provided with supervised general care and therapy by trained psychologists and psychiatrists as well as auxiliary staff. The patients of a mental institution will generally be those who are unable to function independently as outpatients when supported by psychoactive drugs. See also PSYCHIATRIC HOSPITAL.

mentalism *n.* a position that insists on the reality of explicitly mental phenomena, such as thinking and feeling. It holds that mental phenomena cannot be reduced to physical or physiological phenomena (see REDUCTIONISM). The term is often used as a synonym for IDEALISM, although some forms of mentalism may hold that mental events, while not reducible to physical substances, are nonetheless grounded in physical processes. Most modern cognitive theories are examples of this latter type of mentalism. Compare ELIMINATIVISM; IDENTITY THEORY. See also CONSCIOUS MENTALISM. **—mentalist** *adj.*

mentality *n.* the quality of mental or intellectual ability.

mental lexicon the set of words that a person uses regularly (see PRODUCTIVE VOCABULARY) or recognizes when used by others (see RECEPTIVE VOCABULARY). Psycholinguistics has proposed various models for such a lexicon, in which words are mentally organized with respect to such features as meaning, lexical category, frequency, length, and sound. Also called **lexical memory**.

mental load see COGNITIVE LOAD.

mentally defective an obsolete and pejorative descriptor for a person with mental retardation.

mental map 1. a mental representation of the world or some part of it based on subjective perceptions rather than objective geographical knowledge. Such a map will normally prioritize the individual's neighborhood, city, and nation and give prominence to more distant places according to personal experience (e.g., vacations), cultural connections (e.g., family history or language links), and the level of coverage in the mass media. The map will also incorporate the individual's negative or positive feelings about these places, which will often reflect conventional ideas or stereotypes. Research suggests that mental maps vary widely with nationality, region, ethnicity, gender, education, and socioeconomic class. **2.** any internal representation of two-dimensional or three-dimensional space. See COGNITIVE MAP.

mental maturity the fully developed mental functioning of an average adult.

mental measurement the use of quantitative scales and methods in measuring psychological processes. Also called **mental testing**. See PSYCHOMETRICS.

mental mechanics the concept, named and described by British philosopher James Mill (1773–1836) but common to most earlier associationist positions, that all complex ideas are merely agglomerations of simpler ideas combined according to the laws of association. Also called **mental physics**. Compare MENTAL CHEMISTRY. See also ASSOCIATIONISM; ASSOCIATION OF IDEAS.

mental mechanism in PSYCHODYNAMICS, the psychological functions, collectively, that help individuals meet environmental demands, protect the ego, satisfy inner needs, and alleviate internal and external conflicts and tensions. Among them are (a) language, which enables expression of thoughts; (b) memory, which stores information needed in solving problems; and (c) perception, which involves recognition and interpretation of phenomena. In addition, in psychoanalytic and psychodynamic theory, various defense mechanisms, such as RATIONALIZATION and COMPENSATION, help to prevent anxiety and protect self-esteem.

mental model any internal representation of the relations between a set of elements, as, for example, between workers in an office or department, the elements of a mathematics or physics problem, the terms of a syllogism, or the configuration of objects in a space. Such models may contain perceptual qualities and may be abstract in nature. They can be manipulated to provide dynamic simulations of possible scenarios and are thought to be key components in decision making. In the context of ergonomics, for example, a mental model of a system or product would include its various attributes, rules for operation and handling, and expectations regarding use and consequences and would be used to guide the individual's interactions with the system or product in question. See also TEAM MENTAL MODEL.

mental paper-folding test a test that requires the participant to indicate what sheets of paper, with directions for folding, will look like once folded to form a three-dimensional shape. The test measures three-dimensional spatial visualization ability.

mental patient organization a club or other organization established to provide social and recreational activities to former mental patients and to help them maintain their morale and readjust to community life. Many mental patient organizations are independent, but others are affiliated with clinics, hospitals, and mental health associations or centers. See EX-PATIENT CLUB.

mental practice the use of IMAGERY to practice a specific skill whereby the performance of a task (e.g., a double lutz in figure skating) is visualized but not carried out.

mental process any process that takes place in the mind. This term is often used synonymously with COGNITIVE PROCESS. See HIGHER MENTAL PROCESS.

mental rehearsal the use of IMAGERY to practice behavioral patterns or skills, for example, reacting without impatience to a request that seems unnecessary or performing a defensive play in basketball.

mental representation a hypothetical entity that is presumed to stand for a perception, thought, memory, or the like in the mind during cognitive operations. For example, when doing mental arithmetic, one presumably operates on mental representations that correspond to the digits and numerical operators; when one imagines looking at the reverse side of an object, one presumably operates on a mental representation of that object; when one repeats a phone number aloud while dialing, one presumably operates on mental representations of the names of the digits. However, there is no consensus yet as to what mental representations might be. See THINKING.

mental retardation (**MR**) in *DSM–IV–TR*, a disorder characterized by intellectual function that is significantly below average: specifically that of an individual with a measured IQ of 70 or below on tests with a standard deviation of 15, whose ADAPTIVE BEHAVIOR is impaired, and in whom the condition is manifested during the developmental period, defined variously as below the ages of 18 or 22. In infants, diagnosis is based on clinical judgment. Mental retardation may be the result of brain injury, disease, or genetic causes and is typically characterized by an impairment of educational, social, and vocational abilities. See MILD MENTAL RETARDATION; MODERATE MENTAL RETARDATION; PROFOUND MENTAL RETARDATION; SEVERE MENTAL RETARDATION; UNSPECIFIED MENTAL RETARDATION. Also called **intellectual disability**.

mental rotation a laboratory task in which people are asked to make judgments about stimuli that are rotated some degree clockwise or counterclockwise from their normal orientations. These judgments are assumed to require a mental rotation of the stimulus into its normal orientation. [developed by U.S. psychologist Roger Newland Shepard (1929–)]

Mental scale see BAYLEY SCALES OF INFANT AND TODDLER DEVELOPMENT.

mental set a temporary readiness to respond to a situation or to perform a psychological function, such as solving a problem in a particular way. It is often determined by instructions but need not be. See SET. See also AUFGABE; DETERMINING TENDENCY; EINSTELLUNG.

mental status the global assessment of an individual's cognitive, affective, and behavioral state as revealed by MENTAL EXAMINATION that covers such factors as general health, appearance, mood, speech, sociability, cooperativeness, facial expression, motor activity, mental activity, emotional state, trend of thought, sensory awareness, orientation, memory, information level, general intelligence level, abstraction and interpretation ability, and judgment.

mental status examination (**MSE**) a comprehensive WORK-UP of a patient, based on interviews, tests, and other sources of information and including details of mental status, personality characteristics, diagnosis, prognosis, and treatment options.

mental subnormality an obsolete name for MENTAL RETARDATION.

mental synthesis the process by which ideas and images are combined and formed into objects of thought, or by which objects of consciousness are brought together into meaningful wholes.

mental telepathy see TELEPATHY.

mental tension mental activity, usually involving unpleasant emotions.

mental test 1. any test that measures one or more of an individual's psychological traits. **2.** an intelligence test.

mental testing see MENTAL MEASUREMENT.

mental topography see TOPOGRAPHICAL PSYCHOLOGY.

mental workload see COGNITIVE LOAD.

mentation *n.* THINKING or mental activity in general.

mentor *n.* an experienced person who provides instruction, encouragement, guidance, advice, and other support to, and helps develop the skills of, a less experienced person.

mentoring *n.* the provision of instruction, encouragement, and other support to an individual (e.g., a student, youth, or colleague) to aid his or her overall growth and development or the pursuit of greater learning skills, a career, or other educational or work-related goals. Numerous **mentoring programs** exist today within occupational, educational, and other settings; they use frequent communication and contact between MENTORS and their respective protégés as well as a variety of other techniques and procedures to develop positive productive relationships.

meperidine *n.* a synthetic OPIOID used in the acute management of moderate to severe pain (see OPIOID ANALGESIC). It is an agonist at the mu OPIOID RECEPTOR and has the side effects of other opioid analgesics. Fatal reactions have resulted when meperidine is administered to patients taking monoamine oxidase inhibitors (MAOIs), and it should therefore not be used in patients who have taken MAOIs within 14 days. Patients taking phenothiazine antipsychotics or tricyclic antidepressants concurrently with meperidine may experience severe respiratory depression. Also called **pethidine**. U.S. trade name (among others): **Demerol**.

mephenytoin *n.* see HYDANTOINS.

meprobamate *n.* one of the drugs introduced into the U.S. market in the early 1950s as an alternative to the BARBITURATES. It was commonly and widely prescribed in the 1950s and 1960s for daytime sedation and the treatment of anxiety. Meprobamate is a less potent respiratory depressant than the barbiturates unless taken in combination with other CNS depressants, such as alcohol and OPIOIDS. Like the barbiturates, use of meprobamate has been almost completely supplanted by the benzodiazepines. U.S. trade name: **Miltown**. See also SEDATIVE, HYPNOTIC, AND ANXIOLYTIC DRUGS.

mercury switch an interface between a device and the user that comprises a glass tube containing mercury with electrodes at one end. The switch is activated when tilted from its neutral position; it can be attached to the hand, wrist, arm, or other body part of users with disabilities and activated by slight body movements.

mercy *n.* kindness, compassion, or leniency toward a transgressor, toward someone over whom one has power or authority, or toward someone in distress.

mercy killing a direct action intended to end what would otherwise be the prolonged agony of a dying person or animal. The concept has been known since ancient times: Warriors often were expected to kill a desperately wounded comrade or enemy. Severely injured animals are also put out of their misery by mercy killing. See also ASSISTED DEATH; EUTHANASIA.

mere-exposure effect the finding that individuals show an increased preference (or liking) for a STIMULUS OBJECT (e.g., a name, sound, or picture) as a consequence of repeated exposure to that stimulus. Research indicates that this effect is most likely to occur when there is no preexisting negative attitude toward the stimulus object, and that it tends to be strongest when the person is not consciously aware of the stimulus presentations. It has been suggested that the mere-exposure effect arises from a conditioning process in which the exposed stimulus is associated with the absence of an AVERSIVE STIMULUS. [identified in 1968 by U.S. social psychologist Robert Zajonc (1923–)]

mere-thought polarization the finding that merely thinking about an attitude can result in polarization in the direction of that attitude. For example, thinking about a moderately positive attitude can result in that attitude becoming extremely positive. [originally demonstrated by U.S. psychologist Abraham Tesser (1941–)]

Meridia *n.* a trade name for SIBUTRAMINE.

meridional amblyopia an abnormal condition, caused by ASTIGMATISM, in which contours of oblique orientation appear sharply focused whereas other orientations (vertical and horizontal) appear blurred, even when the astigmatism is optically corrected. This indicates that the astigmatism, prior to optical correction, altered ORIENTATION-selective mechanisms in the visual cortex in a direction favoring oblique over horizontal and vertical orientations. Presumably individuals with meridional amblyopia have a paucity of cortical cells tuned to vertical and horizontal orientations.

Merital *n.* a trade name for NOMIFENSINE.

meritocracy *n.* a political or social system in which rewards are given to individuals on the basis of their accomplishments. **—meritocratic** *adj.*

Meritor Savings Bank v. Vinson a case resulting in an influential 1986 U.S. Supreme Court ruling that a HOSTILE WORK ENVIRONMENT constitutes SEXUAL HARASSMENT and that victims do not bear the burden of demonstrating they were harmed by the harassment.

merit ranking the arrangement of people, data, or objects in order of size, value, or other characteristics. Also called **order-of-merit ranking**.

merit rating an evaluation of an individual's performance at a particular task.

Merkel's corpuscle see MERKEL'S TACTILE DISK.

Merkel's law the principle that equal suprathreshold

(above-threshold) differences in sensation correlate with equal differences in stimuli. [Julius **Merkel** (1834–1900), German psychologist]

Merkel's tactile disk a type of sensory-nerve ending in the GLABROUS SKIN of the hands and feet and in the hairy skin. Also called **Merkel's corpuscle**; **Grandry–Merkel corpuscle**.[Friedrich Siegmund **Merkel** (1845–1919), German anatomist; M. **Grandry**, 19th-century Belgian physician]

merycism *n.* see RUMINATION.

mescal buttons see PEYOTE.

mescaline *n.* a HALLUCINOGEN derived from the PEYOTE cactus and long used by indigenous peoples of the southwestern United States and central America. Its effects often include nausea and vomiting as well as visual hallucinations involving lights and colors; they have a slower onset than those of LSD and usually last 1–2 hours. Mescaline is the oldest classic hallucinogen known to Western science; its pharmacology was defined in 1896, and its structure was verified by synthesis in 1919. It is a substituted PHENYLETHYLAMINE, and its likely mechanism of action is via the 5-HT_2 SEROTONIN RECEPTOR. Mescaline is classified by the U.S. Drug Enforcement Administration as a Schedule I controlled substance (see SCHEDULED DRUGS).

mesencephalic nucleus one of the three nuclei of the TRIGEMINAL NERVE. It extends through the PONS into the lower part of the MIDBRAIN (mesencephalon), and its fibers innervate the muscles and joints of the head.

mesencephalic tegmentum a region of the dorsal MIDBRAIN (mesencephalon) with neural connections between the cerebrum, spinal cord, thalamus, and subthalamus, forming an indirect corticospinal tract.

mesencephalon *n.* see MIDBRAIN. **—mesencephalic** *adj.*

mesmerism *n.* an old name, used in the mid-18th through the mid-19th centuries, for HYPNOSIS. See ANIMAL MAGNETISM. [Franz Anton **Mesmer** (1733–1815), Austrian physician and an early proponent of hypnosis] **—mesmerist** *n.* **—mesmeric** *adj.*

mesmerize *vb.* an archaic word for hypnotize.

meso- (**mes-**) *combining form* middle or medium.

mesocephalic *adj.* having a head of medium breadth. See CEPHALIC INDEX. **—mesocephaly** *n.*

mesocortical system a network of DOPAMINERGIC NEURONS in the brain that consists of the medial PREFRONTAL CORTEX and the anterior CINGULATE GYRUS. It has connections to other parts of the limbic system, including the NUCLEUS ACCUMBENS, nuclei of the STRIA TERMINALIS, and AMYGDALA. It receives input from the VENTRAL TEGMENTAL AREA, and its activity is related to emotion, reward, and substance abuse.

mesoderm *n.* the middle of the three primary GERM LAYERS of an animal embryo at the GASTRULA stage, lying between the ectoderm and endoderm. It develops into cartilage and bone, connective tissue, muscle, blood vessels and blood cells, the lymphatic system, gonads, and the excretory system. **—mesodermal** *adj.*

mesokurtic *adj.* describing a statistical distribution that is neither flatter nor more peaked than a comparison, such as the normal distribution. See also PLATYKURTIC; LEPTOKURTIC.

mesolimbic system a network of DOPAMINERGIC NEURONS in the brain consisting of the NUCLEUS ACCUMBENS, AMYGDALA, and OLFACTORY TUBERCLE. It receives input from the VENTRAL TEGMENTAL AREA and its activity is related to emotion, reward, and substance abuse.

mesomorph *n.* a constitutional type (SOMATOTYPE) in SHELDON'S CONSTITUTIONAL THEORY OF PERSONALITY characterized by a muscular, athletic physique, which—according to this theory—is highly correlated with SOMATOTONIA. Also called **mesomorphic body type**. See also BODY-BUILD INDEX. **—mesomorphic** *adj.* **—mesomorphy** *n.*

mesontomorph *n.* a constitutional body type characterized by a broad, stocky body, roughly equivalent to a MESOMORPH. **—mesontomorphic** *adj.*

mesopic vision vision that involves aspects of both PHOTOPIC VISION and SCOTOPIC VISION, thus being mediated by both rods and cones.

mesoridazine *n.* a first-generation (typical or conventional) ANTIPSYCHOTIC of the piperidine PHENOTHIAZINE class. Mesoridazine is a low-potency agent that is a metabolic product of THIORIDAZINE. Like the latter drug, its use is associated with life-threatening disturbances in heart rhythm (prolongation of the Q-T interval potentially leading to torsades de pointes syndrome; see ELECTROCARDIOGRAPHIC EFFECT). It should not be administered to individuals taking other drugs that prolong the Q-T interval or who have a history of heart rhythm disturbances, and it is appropriate for the treatment of schizophrenia only in individuals who have not responded to other antipsychotic agents. U.S. trade name: **Serentil**.

mesoskelic *adj.* denoting a constitutional body type that is intermediate between brachyskelic (see BRACHYSKELETAL) and MACROSKELIC and roughly equivalent to the ATHLETIC TYPE in KRETSCHMER TYPOLOGY. [described by French physician L. P. Manouvrier (1850–1927)]

mesosomatic *adj.* denoting an individual whose body build is within one standard deviation of the mean after scores for height and chest measurements have been multiplied (see BODY-BUILD INDEX).

mesostriatal system a set of DOPAMINERGIC NEURONS whose axons arise from the midbrain and innervate the BASAL GANGLIA. It includes neurons connecting the substantia nigra to the striatum (see NIGROSTRIATAL TRACT).

mesosystem *n.* in the ecological theory of development of U.S. psychologist Urie Bronfenbrenner (1917–2005), the groups and institutions outside the home (e.g., day care, school, or a child's peer group) that influence the child's development and interact with aspects of the **microsystem** (e.g., relations in the home). See ECOLOGICAL SYSTEMS THEORY.

message factors characteristics of a persuasive message that can influence the effectiveness of the message itself. Such characteristics include whether the message is one-sided or two-sided (see ONE-SIDED MESSAGE) and whether or not it is a RHETORICAL-QUESTION MESSAGE.

message-learning approach a theory that conceptualizes ATTITUDE CHANGE as a type of learning process in which the extent of attitude change is determined by how well the ARGUMENTS in a persuasive message are learned. This process is seen as having five steps: exposure, attention, comprehension, yielding, and retention. The theory postulates that performance of these steps can be affected by four different types of variables: SOURCE FACTORS, MESSAGE FACTORS, CHANNEL FACTORS, and RECIPIENT FACTORS. Also called **Hovland model**; **Yale model**. [originally developed by U.S. psychologist Carl I. Hovland (1912–1961) and his colleagues at Yale University]

messenger RNA (**mRNA**) a type of RNA that carries instructions from a cell's genetic material (usually DNA) to the protein-manufacturing apparatus elsewhere in the cell and directs the assembly of protein components in precise accord with those instructions. The instructions are embodied in the sequence of bases in the mRNA, according to the GENETIC CODE.

Messiah complex the desire and compulsion to redeem or save others or the world. The individual may harbor the delusion of being divine. See also JEHOVAH COMPLEX.

Mestinon *n.* a trade name for PYRIDOSTIGMINE.

MET symbol for METABOLIC EQUIVALENT.

meta- (**met-**) *prefix* **1.** beyond or behind (e.g., METAPHYSICS). **2.** change or alteration (e.g., METABOLISM).

meta-analysis *n.* a quantitative technique for synthesizing the results of multiple studies of a phenomenon into a single result by combining the EFFECT SIZE estimates from each study into a single estimate of the combined effect size or into a distribution of effect sizes.

meta-attention *n.* awareness of the factors that influence one's attention.

metabolic anomaly see INBORN ERROR OF METABOLISM.

metabolic defect any deficiency in the structure or enzymatic function of protein molecules or in the transport of substances across cell membranes due to INBORN ERRORS OF METABOLISM or disturbances caused by toxic agents or dietary excesses (e.g., alcoholism or cholesterol-rich foods).

metabolic encephalopathy a form of ENCEPHALOPATHY arising from a metabolic disorder. Also called **toxic-metabolic encephalopathy**.

metabolic equivalent (symbol: MET) a unit of measurement of heat, or energy, produced by the body. 1 MET = 50 kcal/h/m^2 body surface. MET units are used to assess the expenditure of oxygen in a given activity; for example, 1 MET indicates that the body is at rest, 3–5 units would indicate light work, more than 9 units indicates heavy work.

metabolic–nutritional model a system of studying mental disorders in which the emphasis is on long-term assessments of the influence of such factors as toxins and deprivations in populations.

metabolic rate the rate of use of energy of an organism during a given period. It is measured in kilojoules or kilocalories per day. See also BASAL METABOLISM.

metabolic screening examination procedures used in predicting or diagnosing possible INBORN ERRORS OF METABOLISM (e.g., phenylketonuria). The procedures include routine blood tests for newborns, GENETIC COUNSELING of parents with known familial metabolic deficiencies, and AMNIOCENTESIS.

metabolic tolerance see PHARMACODYNAMIC TOLERANCE.

metabolism *n.* the physical and chemical processes within a living cell or organism that are necessary to maintain life. It includes **catabolism**, the breaking down of complex molecules into simpler ones, often with the release of energy; and **anabolism**, the synthesis of complex molecules from simple ones. See also BASAL METABOLISM; CARBOHYDRATE METABOLISM; FAT METABOLISM; PROTEIN METABOLISM. [term coined by German physiologist Theodor Schwann (1810–1882)] **—metabolic** *adj.*

metabolite *n.* a substance necessary for, involved in, or produced by METABOLISM.

metabotropic receptor a neurotransmitter RECEPTOR that does not itself contain an ION CHANNEL but may use a G PROTEIN to open a nearby ion channel. See GLUTAMATE RECEPTOR. Compare IONOTROPIC RECEPTOR.

metachromatic leukodystrophy an AUTOSOMAL RECESSIVE disorder characterized by deficiency or absence of the enzyme arylsulfatase A, which results in loss of myelin in the nervous system and accumulation of cerebroside sulfate (a type of myelin lipid) within the white matter of the central nervous system. Loss of motor function and deterioration in mental ability most commonly develop after the 1st year of life (late infantile form), but symptoms may also appear between 3 and 10 years of age (juvenile form) or around age 30 (adult form).

metacognition *n.* awareness of one's own cognitive processes, often involving a conscious attempt to control them. The so-called TIP-OF-THE-TONGUE PHENOMENON, in which one struggles to "know" something that one knows one knows, provides an interesting example of metacognition. **—metacognitional** *adj.*

metacommunication *n.* **1.** communication about the procedural aspects or the dynamics (rather than the actual content) of communication between two or more parties. **2.** auxiliary or covert messages, usually in the form of subtle gestures, movements, and facial expressions.

metacontrast *n.* a form of backward MASKING in which the perception of a visible stimulus (the target) is altered by the subsequent presentation of a second visual stimulus (the mask) in a different spatial location. The target is often a small dot, while the mask is a ring that surrounds it. Each stimulus is presented very briefly (10–100 ms), at intervals that are varied systematically, and the quality of the target's percept is measured. Compare PARACONTRAST.

metacriterion *n.* a suggested criterion for evaluating competing understandings of science proposed by Hungarian-born philosopher of science Imre Lakatos (1922–1974). Lakatos derived his metacriterion from the use of similar criteria in the evaluation of competing philosophical theories and proposed it as an alternative to both the FALSIFICATIONISM of Austrian-born British philosopher Karl Popper (1902–1994) and the historical theories of science of U.S. philosopher Thomas Kuhn (1922–1996). According to the metacriterion, a theory of science should be preferred to its competitors if it (a) makes more rational sense of the history of scientific practice and findings and (b) can be shown to lead to the discovery of more novel historical facts.

Metadate *n.* a trade name for METHYLPHENIDATE.

metaemotion *n.* one's awareness of and attitude toward one's own and others' emotions. For example, some people have negative attitudes toward anger in themselves or anyone else; others like to encourage anger. Some are ashamed of being too happy; others strive for such a state.

metaesthetic range the range of weak pain sensations just below the level of obvious, unmistakable pain.

metaethics *n.* see ETHICS.

metaevaluation *n.* in evaluation research, an attempt to make judgments on the worth of an evaluation process with regard to its value and usefulness and its reliance on accepted evaluation standards. This involves a systematic evaluation that focuses on assessing methodological rigor, utility, cost, relevance, scope, importance, credibility, timeliness, and pervasiveness of dissemination.

metagnomy *n.* the divination of knowledge of the past

or present by means other than the five senses, such as EXTRASENSORY PERCEPTION. Compare CLAIRVOYANCE.

metalanguage *n.* **1.** a language or set of symbols that is used to describe another language or set of symbols. Examples are English words used in teaching a foreign language, the instructions that accompany a computer program, and the use of mathematical symbols to analyze the logic of an argument (see SYMBOLIC LOGIC). Also called **second-order language**. **2.** any use of language to discuss or analyze language, as in formal linguistic study, literary criticism, or the attempts of speakers to make sure that they understand one another correctly (e.g., "When you said the book was unreadable, were you referring to the print quality or the author's style?").

metalinguistic awareness a conscious awareness of the formal properties of language as well as its functional and semantic properties. It is associated with a mature stage in language and metacognitive development (see METACOGNITION) and does not usually develop until around age 8. The arrival of metalinguistic awareness is often signaled by an interest in PUNS and word games. Also called **linguistic awareness**.

metamemory *n.* awareness of one's own memory processes, often involving a conscious attempt to direct or control them. It is an aspect of METACOGNITION.

metamorphopsia *n.* a visual disorder in which objects appear to be distorted in size (see MICROPSIA; MACROPSIA), contour (e.g., irregular wavy edges), position (e.g., tilted), distance (see TELEOPSIA), and color (e.g., fading of colors). Metamorphopsia can occur with migraine, temporal-lobe epilepsy, lesions of the PARIETAL LOBE, and MESCALINE intoxication; it may also be due to displacement of the retina. Also called **Alice in Wonderland effect**.

metamorphosis *n.* a change in form or structure, typically from one developmental stage to another. See also SEXUAL METAMORPHOSIS. **—metamorphose** *vb.*

metamotivation *n.* in the HUMANISTIC PSYCHOLOGY of Abraham MASLOW, those motives that impel an individual to "character growth, character expression, maturation, and development," that is, the motivation that operates on the level of SELF-ACTUALIZATION and transcendence in the hierarchy of needs (see MASLOW'S MOTIVATIONAL HIERARCHY). In Maslow's view, metamotivation is distinct from the motivation operating in the lower level needs, which he calls DEFICIENCY MOTIVATION, and it emerges after the lower needs are satisfied. Also called **being motivation**; **B-motivation**; **growth motivation**. See METANEEDS. See also MASLOW'S THEORY OF HUMAN MOTIVATION.

metaneeds *pl. n.* in the HUMANISTIC PSYCHOLOGY of Abraham MASLOW, the highest level of needs that come into play primarily after the lower level needs have been met. Metaneeds constitute the goals of self-actualizers and include the needs for knowledge, beauty, and creativity. In Maslow's view, the inability to fulfill them results in METAPATHOLOGY. Also called **being values**; **B-values**. See METAMOTIVATION. See also MASLOW'S THEORY OF HUMAN MOTIVATION.

metapathology *n.* in the HUMANISTIC PSYCHOLOGY of Abraham MASLOW, the state of vague frustration or discontent experienced by individuals who are unable to satisfy their METANEEDS (e.g., specific creative, intellectual, or aesthetic needs). See also METAMOTIVATION; MASLOW'S THEORY OF HUMAN MOTIVATION.

metaphor *n.* a figure of speech (see FIGURATIVE LANGUAGE) in which a word or phrase is applied to an object, person, or action that it does not literally denote (e.g., *the journey of life*) for the purpose of creating a forceful analogy. If the analogy is explicitly stated as such (e.g., *life is like a journey*), the figure is not a metaphor but a **simile**. **—metaphorical** or **metaphoric** *adj.*

metaphoric symbolism see CRYPTOPHORIC SYMBOLISM.

metaphor therapy a system that focuses on the symbolic meaning of language and the use of metaphors in therapy. It is theorized that metaphors may provide means for restructuring thinking and approaches to problem solving in treatment. [developed by U.S. psychotherapist Richard R. Kopp (1942–)]

metaphysics *n.* the branch of philosophy that deals with the question of the nature of ultimate reality; as such, it is considered to be the most abstract and speculative branch of philosophy. Metaphysics was the founding project of Greek philosophy and thus of the Western intellectual tradition as a whole. The term derives from the Greek meaning "above (or beyond) the physical." Early metaphysical philosophy, most notably that of Plato (c. 427–c. 347 BCE), suggested a reality above the physical world that accounts for and gives rise to physical reality (see PLATONIC IDEALISM). Later metaphysical conceptions have emphasized, as the ultimate foundation of reality, constructs as varied as mind, spirit, abstract principles, and physical matter. Since the time of French philosopher René Descartes (1596–1650), the main focus of Western philosophy has shifted from metaphysics to EPISTEMOLOGY, the study of the nature and limitations of knowledge; this is largely owing to a recognition that meaningful answers to questions of ultimate reality depend upon the working out of criteria (an epistemology) by which such answers can be judged as true. Nevertheless, any scholarly discipline, including psychology, that makes a claim of discovering or explaining the ultimate nature or origin of a phenomenon may be said to be engaged in metaphysics. **—metaphysical** *adj.*

metapsychics *n.* **1.** the study of purported mental phenomena and abilities that are beyond the limits of orthodox psychological understanding, such as TELEPATHY and the survival of the human psyche after death. The term has now been generally superseded by PARAPSYCHOLOGY. **2.** people who are or appear to be exceptionally gifted in one or more paranormal abilities. See PSYCHIC.

metapsychological profile in psychoanalysis, a systematic profile of a patient's intrapsychic functioning, in contrast to a mere list of symptoms; such a profile offers a picture of his or her entire personality. The technique was developed by Anna FREUD in 1965.

metapsychology *n.* the study of, or a concern for, the fundamental underlying principles of any psychology. The term was used by Sigmund FREUD to denote his own psychological theory, emphasizing its ability to offer comprehensive explanations of psychological phenomena on a fundamental level. Freud's criteria for a metapsychology were that it should explain a psychical phenomenon in terms of (a) its dynamics, (b) its topology, and (c) its economic aspects. Although these specific criteria apply most clearly to Freud's own theory, the notion of metapsychology as explanation at a fundamental and comprehensive level continues to be a useful construct. **—metapsychological** *adj.*

metastasis *n.* see CANCER.

metatheory *n.* a higher order theory about theories, allowing one to analyze, compare, and evaluate competing theories. The concept of a metatheory suggests that theories derive from other theories such that there are always prior theoretical assumptions and commitments behind any theoretical formulation. These prior assumptions and commitments are worthy of study in their own right, and an understanding of them is essential to a full understanding of derivative theories. **—metatheoretical** *adj.*

metathetic *adj.* **1.** denoting a stimulus dimension in which a change of magnitude can cause a qualitative change in the psychological sensation produced. For example, a faint smell may be quite pleasing, whereas an increase in intensity may cause revulsion. Compare PROTHETIC. **2.** relating to a change in place or condition, particularly the transposition of two PHONEMES in a word or the exchange of elements between chemical compounds to create different kinds of compounds. **—metathesis** *n.*

metempirical *adj.* describing or pertaining to knowledge that is not subject to verification by experience, and thus cannot be established by the methods of science. As described by British writer George Henry Lewes (1817–1878), the metempirical is roughly equivalent to the notion of the transcendent developed by German philosopher Immanuel Kant (1724–1804) (see NOUMENON; TRANSCENDENCE).

metempsychosis *n.* transmigration of the soul, whereby upon death a soul takes up residence in another body, human or animal. The belief is inherent in the doctrine of **samsara**, the cycle of birth, life, death, and rebirth, that is central to HINDUISM and BUDDHISM. An important and unanswerable issue attends the doctrine: the extent to which the reincarnated soul retains its memories and personality. In the ancient Western world, a similar belief in multiple lives was taught by Greek philosophers Pythagoras (c. 569–c. 475 BCE) and Empedocles (c. 493–c. 453 BCE). See also REINCARNATION.

metencephalon *n.* the portion of the BRAINSTEM that includes the PONS and CEREBELLUM. With the medulla oblongata, the metencephalon forms the HINDBRAIN. **—metencephalic** *adj.*

meth *n.* slang for METHAMPHETAMINE.

methadone *n.* a synthetic OPIOID ANALGESIC that is used for pain relief and as a substitute for heroin in METHADONE MAINTENANCE THERAPY. It is quite effective when orally ingested and has a long duration of action, both preventing withdrawal symptoms and blocking the reinforcing effects of heroin. U.S. trade name (among others): **Dolophine**.

methadone maintenance therapy a drug-rehabilitation therapy in which previously addicted heroin patients are prescribed a daily oral dose of METHADONE to blunt craving for opioid drugs. A controversial treatment, it is nonetheless widely considered the most effective approach to heroin addiction. See HEROIN DEPENDENCE.

Methadrine *n.* a trade name for METHAMPHETAMINE hydrochloride.

methamphetamine *n.* a CNS STIMULANT whose chemical structure is similar to that of amphetamine but that has a more pronounced effect on the central nervous system. It is used for treating attention-deficit/hyperactivity disorder in children and as a short-term aid to obesity treatment in adults. Like all AMPHETAMINES, methamphetamine is prone to abuse and dependence. It can be smoked, snorted, ingested orally, or injected. After the initial rush—it increases activity levels and induces a general sense of well-being—a state of high agitation that can lead to violence is experienced by some users. Long-term abuse is associated with nerve damage and behavioral and mental status changes, including psychosis. U.S. trade name: **Desoxyn**.

methaqualone *n.* a synthetic drug with sedative and hypnotic effects, unrelated chemically to other sedatives, and having a potency roughly equal to that of PENTOBARBITAL. It is used to treat patients who are unable to tolerate barbiturate drugs. In small doses, the drug depresses the sensory cortex; in larger doses, it affects the spinal reflexes. It has caused more deaths from overdose than such drugs as PCP and heroin. Trade name: **Quaalude**. See SEDATIVE, HYPNOTIC, AND ANXIOLYTIC DRUGS.

methocarbamol *n.* a member of a group of centrally acting MUSCLE RELAXANTS used as an adjunctive agent in the management of musculoskeletal pain. Because methocarbamol does not directly reduce skeletal muscle tension, its therapeutic action is thought to be due to its sedative or CNS DEPRESSANT properties. It is available in tablet and injectable forms. U.S. trade name: **Robaxin**.

method *n.* the procedures and system of analysis used in scientific investigation in general or in a particular research project.

method of absolute judgment a psychophysical procedure in which stimuli are presented in random order to a participant, whose task is to identify each stimulus by a unique response label. The results obtained can be analyzed using INFORMATION THEORY.

method of adjustment a psychophysical technique in which the participant adjusts a variable stimulus to match a constant or standard. For example, the observer is shown a standard visual stimulus of a specific intensity and is asked to adjust a comparison stimulus to match the brightness of the standard. Also called **adjustment method**; **error method**; **method of average error**; **method of equivalents**.

method of agreement the first of the five canons of empirical science laid down by British philosopher John Stuart Mill (1806–1873). It is meant to establish necessary conditions for a phenomenon. For example, if every instance of an effect E1 (E2, E3, etc.) had in common a particular condition C1, and it is observed that among all cases of E, only C1 and no other conditions (C2, C3, etc.) were common, it can be concluded that C1 is the necessary condition for E. See MILL'S CANONS.

method of agreement and difference the third of the five canons of empirical science laid down by British philosopher John Stuart Mill (1806–1873). It enables the discovery of necessary and sufficient conditions for a phenomenon by combining the first two of MILL'S CANONS: the METHOD OF AGREEMENT and the METHOD OF DIFFERENCE.

method of average error see METHOD OF ADJUSTMENT.

method of choice a psychophysical procedure in which the participant is presented with several arrays of stimuli, one of which contains the target stimulus. The participant's task is to choose the array that contains the target stimulus.

method of concomitant variation the fifth of the five canons of empirical science laid down by British philosopher John Stuart Mill (1806–1873). It is meant to establish the causal relationship between phenomena. It holds that if there is a functional relationship between a condition C1 and an effect E1, it may be inferred that there is a causal relationship between one or more of the elements that make up C1 and the resultant E1. Which element of C1 is causal can be established by implementing the rest of MILL'S CANONS. This strategy is essentially the foundation of modern approaches to experimentation in psychology and is directly related to the problems of inferring causality from correlation.

method of constant adjustment see METHOD OF LIMITS.

method of constant stimuli a psychophysical procedure for determining the sensory threshold by randomly presenting several stimuli known to be close to the threshold. The threshold is the stimulus value that was detected 50% of the time. Also called **constant stimulus method**; **method of right and wrong cases**. See also METHOD OF LIMITS.

method of difference the second of the five canons of empirical science laid down by British philosopher John Stuart Mill (1806–1873). It is meant to establish sufficient conditions for a phenomenon. For example, if under one condition, C1, an effect, E1, does not occur, and as C1 is changed to C2 the effect E1 does occur, it may be concluded that C2 is a sufficient cause of E1, and the alternative hypothesis, that C1 causes E1, can be eliminated. Thus the effect is attributed to the "difference" between conditions C1 and C2. Also called **difference canon**.

method of equal and unequal cases in psychophysics, a constant stimulus method (see METHOD OF CONSTANT STIMULI) requiring judgment of paired stimuli as equal or unequal.

method of equal-appearing intervals 1. a SCALING technique in which values are obtained for items on the assumption that the underlying intervals are equidistant. **2.** in psychophysics, a procedure in which magnitudes between pairs of stimuli are adjusted so that the differences between stimuli within each pair are perceived as equal. Also called **method of equal sense differences**; **method of mean gradations**.

method of equivalents see METHOD OF ADJUSTMENT.

method of exclusion a principle by which empirical observation can eliminate (or exclude) possible causes for a phenomenon and thereby reach conclusions about the true cause. The principle is attributed to English philosopher Francis Bacon (1561–1626), who proposed an inductive method (see INDUCTION) in which the observer lists both positive and negative instances of a phenomenon and then attempts to infer a common factor that is present in the positive instances and absent in the negative instances. Thus, the cause of the phenomenon is established by a method of exclusion of negative instances. See BACONIAN METHOD. See also MILL'S CANONS.

method of just noticeable differences a psychophysical procedure to determine the smallest difference between stimuli that can be perceived. A standard stimulus is presented together with a variable stimulus whose magnitude is increased in some trials and decreased in others until a just perceptible difference between the stimuli is reported. The average of the two series is taken, and the threshold is calculated at the point where the difference can be recognized 50% of the time. Also called **method of serial exploration**.

method of limits a psychophysical procedure for determining the sensory threshold by gradually increasing or decreasing the magnitude of the stimulus presented in discrete steps. That is, a stimulus of a given intensity is presented to a participant; if it is perceived, a stimulus of lower intensity is presented on the next trial, until the stimulus can no longer be detected. The threshold is the average of the stimulus values at which there is a detection-response transition (from "yes" to "no," or vice versa). An alternative procedure, the **method of constant adjustment**, allows the participant to adjust a stimulus continuously until it can no longer be perceived. See also METHOD OF CONSTANT STIMULI.

method of loci a MNEMONIC STRATEGY in which the items to be remembered are converted into mental images and associated with specific positions or locations. For instance, to remember a shopping list, each product could be imagined at a different location along a familiar street.

method of opposition see PROCESS-DISSOCIATION METHOD.

method of ratio estimation a psychophysical procedure in which two stimuli of different intensity are presented, and the observer estimates the ratio of the perceived intensities.

method of residues the fourth of the five canons of empirical science laid down by British philosopher John Stuart Mill (1806–1873). It is meant to establish sufficient conditions for a phenomenon through the elimination of alternative potential causes on the basis of previous experiment or already known laws. For example, if the phenomena E1 and E2 occur together having antecedents C1 and C2, and if it is known by prior research or established law that C1 cannot cause E2 but causes E1, one may conclude that C2 is the cause of E2. Also called **residue method**.

method of single stimuli any psychophysical procedure in which a series of single stimuli is presented, each of which requires a response.

method of successive approximations a method of shaping OPERANT BEHAVIOR by reinforcing responses similar to the desired behavior. Initially, responses roughly approximating the desired behavior are reinforced. Later, only responses closely approximating the desired behavior are reinforced. The process gradually leads to the desired behavior. Also called **successive-approximations method**.

method of successive intervals a variation of the METHOD OF EQUAL-APPEARING INTERVALS in which intervals are defined verbally or by the use of samples.

method of triads any psychophysical procedure in which three stimuli are presented, and the observer must choose one of the three based on some property (e.g., its dissimilarity from the other two).

methodological behaviorism a form of BEHAVIORISM that concedes the existence and reality of conscious events but contends that the only suitable means of studying them scientifically is via their expression in behavior. Compare RADICAL BEHAVIORISM. See NEOBEHAVIORISM.

methodological objectivism versus methodological subjectivism a prescriptive dimension along which psychological theories can be evaluated. Methodological objectivism is the position that methods of investigation can be, and should be able to be, repeated and verified by another investigator. Methodological subjectivism is the position that methods cannot be repeated and thus cannot be verified by another. See also CONTENTUAL OBJECTIVISM VERSUS CONTENTUAL SUBJECTIVISM. [introduced by U.S. psychologist Robert I. Watson (1909–1980)]

methodological pluralism the acceptance of the value of using more than one METHODOLOGY in approaching research.

methodological solipsism the adoption of SOLIPSISM as a philosophical position because of the belief that no other position is tenable.

methodological triangulation the use of multiple quantitative and qualitative methods to collect data.

methodology *n.* **1.** the science of method or orderly arrangement; specifically, the branch of logic concerned with the application of the principles of reasoning to scientific and philosophical inquiry. **2.** the system of methods, principles, and rules of procedure used within a particular discipline.

methods analysis in ergonomics, the development of improved ways of performing a task, through analysis of the particular operation and its component tasks, techniques, factors, and resources. This typically involves use of process charts and micromotion studies and application of the principles of MOTION ECONOMY. See also TASK ANALYSIS.

methotrimeprazine *n.* a low-potency antipsychotic of the aliphatic PHENOTHIAZINE class. In the United States, it is currently used only for the treatment of pain. Also called **levomepromazine**. U.S. trade name: **Levoprome**.

methyldopa *n.* a drug used for treating hypertension. It acts as an agonist at ALPHA ADRENORECEPTORS in brainstem centers that control the vascular system. When stimulated by methyldopa, these receptors, which act via an inhibitory feedback mechanism, slow the release of catecholamines from central neurons involved in the regulation of blood pressure. U.S. trade name: **Aldomet**.

3,4-methylenedioxyamphetamine *n.* see MDA.

3,4-methylenedioxymethamphetamine *n.* see MDMA.

methylphenidate *n.* a stimulant related to the AMPHETAMINES and with a similar mechanism of action. It is an INDIRECT AGONIST of catecholamine neurotransmission, blocking the reuptake of catecholamines from the synaptic cleft and stimulating presynaptic release of catecholamines. Unlike amphetamine, methylphenidate is more potent as a reuptake blocker than as a releasing agent. Methylphenidate is used as an adjunct to antidepressant therapy and to increase concentration and alertness in patients with brain injuries, brain cancer, or dementia. It is officially approved by the U.S. Food and Drug Administration for the treatment of attention-deficit/hyperactivity disorder (ADHD) and narcolepsy in both children and adults. In children with ADHD, methylphenidate increases attention and decreases impulsivity and physical overactivity, leading to improvement in academic and social functioning, at least while the drug is being administered. Potential long-term side effects in children include growth suppression, which may occur at least transiently in some children taking these drugs. It is not recommended to use methylphenidate or other stimulants in children without concurrent behavioral therapy or counseling. Methylphenidate is a drug of potential abuse; it is classified by the U.S. Drug Enforcement Administration as a Schedule II controlled substance (see SCHEDULED DRUGS). U.S. trade names (among others): **Concerta**; **Metadate**; **Ritalin**.

methylphenyltetrahydropyridine *n.* see MPTP.

methylxanthines *pl. n.* methylated derivatives of **xanthines** (stimulant plant alkaloids) with similar pharmacological actions. The most common are CAFFEINE (1,3,7-trimethylxanthine), the active ingredient in coffee; THEOBROMINE (3,7-dimethylxanthine), the active ingredient in cocoa; and **theophylline** (1,3-dimethylxanthine), the active ingredient in tea. At low doses methylxanthines cause CNS stimulation and arousal; at high doses, anxiety, agitation, and coma may result. Methylxanthines also relax bronchial muscles: Some (e.g., theophylline) have been used in the medical management of reactive airway disease, although they have now largely been supplanted by newer agents.

methysergide *n.* an ERGOT DERIVATIVE used in the treatment of migraine headaches. It reduces the frequency and intensity of migraine attacks in most individuals and is thought to act by opposing the action of serotonin (see SEROTONIN ANTAGONISTS). Methysergide is closely related to LSD and has similar effects at some tissue sites. Side effects of methysergide include lightheadedness or dizziness, nausea or vomiting, euphoria, insomnia, and unsteadiness. U.S. trade name: **Sansert**.

metonymic distortion a cognitive disturbance, observed in schizophrenia, in which related but inappropriate verbal expressions are used in place of the proper expression. For example, a person may say that he or she had three menus (instead of three meals) a day.

metonymy *n.* **1.** a figure of speech in which not the literal word but one associated with it is used, as *the sword* for *war*. **Synecdoche** is the form of metonymy in which a whole is represented by a part or vice versa, as in referring to a laborer as a *hand* or a police officer as *the police*. **2.** in speech pathology, a disturbance in which imprecise or inappropriate words and expressions are used. See METONYMIC DISTORTION. **—metonymic** *adj.*

Metrazol shock treatment a form of SHOCK THERAPY involving the intravenous injection of Metrazol, a trade name for pentylenetetrazol, a powerful CNS STIMULANT that induces convulsions and coma. Because the procedure produced intense feelings of dread, and the incidence of fatality was high, it is now rarely used. Also called **Metrazol therapy**; **Metrazol treatment**. [introduced in 1934 by Hungarian psychiatrist Ladislas von Meduna (1896–1964)]

metronomic pacing a technique of AUDITORY FEEDBACK to improve speaking performance, in which a portable device containing an electronic metronome is typically set between 50 and 150 beats per minute and the speaker receives pacing feedback through headphones as he or she speaks. Among those who benefit most are stutterers and those with MOTOR SPEECH DISORDERS.

Metropolitan Achievement Tests (**METROPOLITAN**) a test battery for students in kindergarten through grade 12 that measures progress in reading, writing, language, mathematics, science, and social studies. It is divided into 13 skill levels according to grade, with appropriate subtests for each level. Originally developed in 1931, the METROPOLITAN is now in its eighth edition (published in 2000); each new edition is intended to reflect material currently being taught in classrooms throughout the United States.

Meyer's loop see OPTIC RADIATIONS. [Adolf **Meyer** (1866–1950), Swiss-born U.S. psychiatrist]

Meyer's theory the theory of mental illness proposed by Swiss-born U.S. psychiatrist Adolf Meyer (1866–1950), who believed that mental disorders resulted from behavior patterns that developed as faulty responses to specific situations. He advocated a holistic approach (see PSYCHOBIOLOGY) to diagnosis and treatment of mental disorders.

Meynert's nucleus see MAGNOCELLULAR NUCLEUS OF THE BASAL FOREBRAIN. [Theodor H. **Meynert** (1833–1892), Austrian neurologist]

MFF abbreviation for MATCHING FAMILIAR FIGURES TEST.

MHC abbreviation for MAJOR HISTOCOMPATIBILITY COMPLEX.

MHV abbreviation for MILL HILL VOCABULARY SCALE.

mianserin *n.* an antidepressant with a mechanism of action similar to that of the related compound MIRTAZAPINE. Mianserin is marketed in several countries (e.g., under the trade name **Tolvon**) but not in the United States.

Michigan Alcoholism Screening Test (**MAST**) a widely used measure designed to provide a rapid screening for problematic alcohol consumption, alcohol abuse, and alcoholism. It comprises 25 yes–no questions, such as "Do you ever feel guilty about your drinking?" or "Are you able to stop drinking when you want to?". Various other forms of the instrument are available, including the 10-question **Brief Mast** (BMAST) and the 13-question **Short MAST** (SMAST). [developed in 1971 by U.S. psychiatrist Melvin L. Selzer at the University of Michigan, Ann Arbor]

Mickey Finn see KNOCKOUT DROPS.

micro- (**micr-**) *combining form* small.

microcephaly *n.* a condition in which the head is abnormally small in relation to the rest of the body. There are numerous causes and manifestations. Mental retardation ranging from moderate to profound often accompanies microcephaly. See also PRIMARY MICROCEPHALY; PURE MICROCEPHALY. Compare MACROCEPHALY. **—microcephalic** *adj.*

microdialysis *n.* a method for measuring the concentration of chemicals in a tissue or organ (e.g., a small region of brain) by allowing the chemicals to pass through a membrane into a small tube implanted in the interstitial space.

microelectrode *n.* an electrode with a tip no larger than a few micrometers in diameter, sometimes less than 1 μm, that can be inserted into a single cell. In the **microelectrode technique**, used in studies of neurophysiology and disorders of the nervous system, intracellular microelectrodes with tips less than 1 μm in diameter are able to stimulate and record activity within a single neuron (**single-cell** or **single-unit recording**).

microergonomics *n.* an approach to ERGONOMICS that focuses on the detailed examination of individual operator–machine interfaces or combinations. Compare MACROERGONOMICS.

microfilament *n.* a very small protein filament (7 nm in diameter) found within all cells. Microfilaments are key components of the cell's internal scaffolding (cytoskeleton) and help to determine cell shape.

microgenetic development the series of changes that occur over relatively brief periods of time—in seconds, minutes, or days—as distinct from the larger scale changes that are conventionally studied in ontogenetic development (see ONTOGENY). [postulated by Lev VYGOTSKY in his sociocultural theory]

microgenetic method a research methodology that looks at developmental change within a single set of individuals over relatively brief periods of time, usually days or weeks.

microgeny *n.* the series of small steps that lead up to a patient's symptoms or to an individual's specific behavior or mental processes. The term is used in the PSYCHODYNAMIC APPROACH.

microglia *n.* NEUROGLIA consisting of extremely small glial cells that remove cellular debris from injured or dead cells. Also called **microglial cells**. **—microglial** *adj.*

microglossia *n.* the condition of having an abnormally small tongue. Although relatively rare, the condition may occur during prenatal development and result in speech that sounds muffled.

micrographia *n.* a disorder characterized by very small, often unreadable, writing and associated most often with PARKINSON'S DISEASE.

micromastia *n.* abnormally small breasts in a female.

micromelia *n.* a developmental defect marked by abnormal shortness or smallness of the limbs, sometimes associated with mental retardation.

microorchidism *n.* abnormally small size of one or both testicles, as in KLINEFELTER'S SYNDROME. Also called **microrchidia**.

microphonia *n.* see HYPOPHONIA.

microphthalmos–corneal opacity–spasticity syndrome a presumably hereditary disorder of children born with MICROCEPHALY, small eyes with opaque corneas, spastic diplegia (spasticity in both legs or both arms), and mental retardation. Scissoring (crossing) of the legs is a common sign in such patients.

micropolygyria *n.* a condition of the brain in which small regions of the cerebral cortex are characterized by more gyri (ridges) than usual.

micropsia *n.* a VISUAL ILLUSION in which an object appears to be smaller than it is in reality. See also METAMORPHOPSIA. Compare MACROPSIA.

micropsychosis *n.* psychotic episodes of very brief duration (minutes to hours) that occur during times of stress. Micropyschoses have been observed primarily in BORDERLINE PERSONALITY DISORDER and PSEUDONEUROTIC SCHIZOPHRENIA, although the latter is no longer a valid diagnostic entity.

microptic hallucination see LILLIPUTIAN HALLUCINATION; MICROPSIA.

microsaccades *pl. n.* small rapid eye movements that occur during attempted fixation of a target and cease when fixation is achieved.

microscopic level an investigative approach that focuses on the smallest recognizable units of analysis. Microscopic psychology is sometimes associated with physiological psychology at the cellular level. See MOLECULAR ANALYSIS; MOLECULAR APPROACH.

microsleep *n.* a brief interval of dozing or loss of awareness that occurs during periods when a person is fatigued and trying to stay awake while doing monotonous tasks, such as driving a car, looking at a computer screen, or monitoring controls. Such periods of "nodding off" typically last for 2–30 s and are more likely to occur in the predawn and mid-afternoon hours. They increase the risk of accidents.

microsmia *n.* decreased sensitivity in the ability to smell. See also HYPOSMIA.

microsocial engineering a technique of conflict resolution among family members in which a BEHAVIORAL CONTRACT is established through a specific schedule of responsibilities, privileges, sanctions for violations, and bonuses for compliance.

microspectrophotometer *n.* a device that enables the absorption of light across the spectrum to be measured as the light passes through a small sample. A microspectrophotometer is used to determine the absorption spectrum of PHOTOPIGMENTS in retinal rods and cones.

microsplanchnic type a constitutional type characterized by a small abdomen and an elongated body. Also called **microsplanchnic build**. [described by Italian physician Giacinto Viola (1870–1943)]

microsystem *n.* see MESOSYSTEM.

microtome *n.* a device for cutting thin sections (slices) of tissue, used, for example, in preparing brain sections for microscopic examination.

microtubule *n.* a small, hollow, cylindrical structure (typically 20–26 nm in diameter), numbers of which occur in various types of cell. Microtubules are part of the cell's internal scaffolding (cytoskeleton) and form the spindle during cell division. In neurons, microtubules are involved in AXONAL TRANSPORT.

microvillus *n.* (*pl.* **microvilli**) in taste perception, the hairlike extension of each TASTE CELL that projects through the pore of a TASTE BUD to sample the environment. Although a microvillus accounts for only 3% of the surface area of a taste cell, it is studded with receptor proteins that recognize specific molecules and is the site of TASTE TRANSDUCTION.

micturition *n.* see URINATION. **—micturate** *vb.*

micturition reflex reflex contraction of the bladder in response to signals from its STRETCH RECEPTORS. During development, a child learns to suppress the micturition reflex and to control urination. Also called **bladder reflex**.

midazolam *n.* a highly potent, short-acting BENZODIAZEPINE used chiefly for the induction of anesthesia or conscious sedation for operative procedures. It is available in a form for intravenous or intramuscular administration and as a syrup for oral administration. Because of its potential to induce respiratory depression (particularly when used as a sedating agent in nonsurgical situations), its short HALF-LIFE, and the need for continuous monitoring of respiratory and cardiac function, midazolam has little, if any, application in mental health settings. It has reportedly been used as a DATE-RAPE DRUG. U.S. trade name: **Versed**.

midbrain *n.* a relatively small region of neural tissue lying between the FOREBRAIN and HINDBRAIN. It contains the inferior and superior COLLICULI, a portion of the RETICULAR FORMATION, sensory and motor tracts, and reflex centers. Also called **mesencephalon**.

middle cerebral artery the largest branch of the INTERNAL CAROTID ARTERY, running first through the LATERAL SULCUS and then upward on the surface of the INSULA. Here it divides into several branches, including the ANTERIOR CHOROIDAL ARTERY, which spread over the lateral surface of the cerebral hemispheres.

middle-child syndrome a hypothetical condition purported to be shared by all middle-born children, based on the assumption that middle children in a family develop personality characteristics that are different from first-born and later born children. Current research indicates that a child's birth order in a particular family may have small, subtle influences on personality and intelligence but not strong and consistent effects on psychological outcomes. See also BIRTH ORDER.

middle class a general socioeconomic class between the working class and the upper class. It is sometimes held to consist of an **upper middle class** of professionals, administrators, and middle-level executives and a **lower middle class** of shopkeepers, artisans, clerical staff, and service workers. The latter, although still relatively materially privileged, are often not positioned as advantageously in the power structure of a society. Also called **bourgeoisie**. See SOCIAL CLASS; SOCIOECONOMIC STATUS.

middle ear a membrane-lined cavity in the temporal bone of the skull. It is filled with air and communicates with the nasopharynx through the EUSTACHIAN TUBE. It contains the OSSICLES, which transmit sound vibrations from the outer ear and the tympanic membrane (eardrum) to the OVAL WINDOW of the inner ear. Also called **tympanic cavity**.

middle fossa see FOSSA.

middle insomnia a period of sleeplessness that occurs after falling asleep normally, with difficulty in falling asleep again. It is a common symptom of a MAJOR DEPRESSIVE DISORDER. Compare INITIAL INSOMNIA; TERMINAL INSOMNIA.

middle knowledge a floating cognitive state in which terminally ill people allow themselves to realize their mortal danger to a greater or lesser degree. Selective attention, denial, resistance, or some other protective strategy tends to be used more or less intensively depending on many factors, including physical condition, security within close relationships, and the ability to integrate the prospect of death into the overall evaluation of one's life.

midget *n.* see DWARFISM.

midget bipolar cell a RETINAL BIPOLAR CELL that connects to only one RETINAL CONE. Compare DIFFUSE BIPOLAR CELL.

midlife crisis a period of psychological distress occurring in some individuals during the middle years of adulthood, roughly from ages 45 to 60. Causes may include significant life events and health or occupational problems and concerns. See also AGE CRISIS. [term coined in 1965 by Canadian consulting organizational psychologist Elliot Jaques (1917–2003)]

midparent *adj.* describing an average measure of both parents with regard to height, intelligence, or other characteristics.

midpoint *n.* the point or value halfway between the highest and lowest values in a FREQUENCY DISTRIBUTION or CLASS INTERVAL.

midrange value a rough measure of CENTRAL TENDENCY gained by averaging the highest and lowest scores in a frequency distribution.

Mignon delusion a variation of the family-romance fantasy in which children believe that their parents are actually foster parents and their real families are of distinguished lineage. The name is derived from the child character in Goethe's novel *Wilhelm Meister's Apprenticeship* (1796).

migraine *n.* a headache that is recurrent, usually severe, usually limited to one side of the head, and likely to be accompanied by nausea, vomiting, and PHOTOPHOBIA. Migraine headaches may be preceded by an AURA of flickering or flashing light, blacking out of part of the visual field, or illusions of colors or patterns. They are much more common in women than in men. Also called **sick headache**.

Migranal *n.* a trade name for DIHYDROERGOTAMINE.

migration adaptation adjustment to a new community or area, which involves withstanding the stresses of geographic mobility (e.g., leaving familiar surroundings, adapting to unfamiliar surroundings and customs). Though stressful, such factors have not been proved to be a common source of mental illness.

migration behavior the behavior of animals who travel over relatively long distances to or from breeding areas. Migratory behavior is observed in birds, fish, and some mammals and insects (among others). In some species it is seasonal, involving movement from a breeding area to an overwintering area; in others, particularly the salmon, it is observed only once in the lifetime of an individual. Factors influencing migratory behavior include sensitivity to chemical cues, pituitary or other hormones, relative change in day length, and temperature. See also MIGRATORY RESTLESSNESS; NAVIGATION.

migration of nerve cells in the development of the nervous system, the movement of nerve cells from their origin in the ventricular zone to establish distinctive cell populations, such as brain nuclei and layers of the cerebral cortex.

migratory restlessness increased activity that occurs prior to the period of migration. Migratory restlessness in captive animals is an index of response to cues indicating ANNUAL CYCLES. Also called **Zugunruhe**.

MIH abbreviation for MÜLLERIAN-INHIBITING HORMONE.

mild cognitive impairment (**MCI**) a transitional condition between normal healthy aging and early DEMENTIA, characterized by a memory impairment greater than would be expected for age and education. Other cognitive functions are intact, and activities of daily living are normal. Individuals with MCI are at increased risk for developing ALZHEIMER'S DISEASE.

mild depression a mild form of depression, typically MINOR DEPRESSIVE DISORDER or a MAJOR DEPRESSIVE EPISODE with mild or few symptoms.

mild mental retardation a diagnostic and classification category applying to those with IQs of 50 to 69, comprising 80% of people with MENTAL RETARDATION. These individuals usually develop good communication skills and reach a sixth-grade level of academic performance in their late teens, but may not develop beyond the social skill levels typical of adolescents. Usually they are able to learn life and vocational skills adequate for basic self-support and independent living.

milestone *n.* see DEVELOPMENTAL MILESTONE; MOTOR MILESTONES.

Milgram, Stanley (1933–1984) U.S. social psychologist. Milgram received his PhD in 1960 from Harvard University (Department of Social Relations), where he studied with Gordon ALLPORT. His chief scientific influence was Solomon E. ASCH, who spent a year at Harvard as a visiting lecturer while Milgram was a graduate student. Milgram taught at Yale University and Harvard University before making his permanent career at the Graduate Center of the City University of New York. He created a number of original research methods for social psychology and pioneered the field of urban psychology, but is best known for his experiments on obedience to authority. In his BEHAVIORAL STUDY OF OBEDIENCE, Milgram demonstrated that a majority of normal adults would knowingly inflict punishment on another adult if asked to do so by a scientific authority; his experiments have been used to explain such phenomena as the Holocaust during World War II. They also raised ethical concerns about experimentation on humans and (together with a handful of other controversial experiments) led to federal standards for the protection of human subjects. Milgram's comprehensive account of the obedience experiments can be found in his book *Obedience to Authority: An Experimental View* (1974). See also DESTRUCTIVE OBEDIENCE; INFORMATION OVERLOAD; STIMULUS OVERLOAD.

milieu *n.* (*pl.* **milieux**) **1.** the environment in general. **2.** in psychology and psychiatry, the social environment, especially the atmosphere and character of the home, neighborhood, school, workplace, and so on as they affect the personality and adjustment of the individual.

milieu therapy psychotherapeutic treatment based on modification or manipulation of the client's life circumstances or immediate environment. Milieu therapy attempts to organize the social and physical setting in which the client lives or is being treated in such a way as to promote healthier, more adaptive cognitions, emotions, and behavior. See also ENVIRONMENTAL THERAPY; THERAPEUTIC COMMUNITY.

military environment factors that affect human performance in military operations. Performance may be compromised by exposure to extreme weather conditions (ranging from excessive heat to extreme cold); other factors include the effects of clothing and equipment in different environments, motivational and attitudinal factors, acclimatization, the size of the unit involved, and the quality of its leadership.

military human–machine system a HUMAN–MACHINE SYSTEM functioning in a military environment, in order to achieve a defined goal.

military officer selection the selection and assessment of military personnel considered suitable to carry the special responsibilities associated with being an officer. The assessment techniques used by applied psychologists involve evaluation of an individual's academic qualifications, use of psychological instruments in recognized assessment centers, and construct-oriented psychological assessment.

military peacekeeping military operations that, with the consent of the belligerent parties in a conflict, are conducted to maintain a negotiated truce and to facilitate a diplomatic resolution. Peacekeeping operations may include withdrawal and disengagement, ceasefire, prisoner-of-war exchanges, arms control, demilitarization, and demobilization. Military peacekeeping is frequently carried out on a multinational basis.

military performance the probability and ease of operational (combat) success. The object of military human-factors research and its applications is to improve performance.

Military Personnel Management a strategic global framework, proposed by the U.S. Department of Defense, with the object of achieving an accurate accounting of deployed personnel. It concentrates on identifying and eliminating waste, avoiding duplication, and reducing costs in military establishments.

military psychology the application of psychological principles, theories, and methods to the evaluation, selection, assignment, and training of military personnel, as well as to the design of military equipment. This field of applied psychology also includes the application of clinical and counseling techniques to the maintenance of morale and mental health in military settings and covers human functioning in a variety of environments during times of peace and war.

military service service by conscripts (draftees) or volunteers in the uniformed armed forces of a state.

military stress models models for assessing stress in military operations and strategies for coping with it. Factors affecting the number of military personnel that become STRESS CASUALTIES include the nature of the operation in which they are involved, the intensity of the conflict, the number of battle casualties occurring, and the size, cohesion, and leadership of the unit in which they are serving.

Military Testing Association see INTERNATIONAL MILITARY TESTING ASSOCIATION.

milk letdown reflex a reflex involving the release of maternal OXYTOCIN in response to suckling, or to stimuli associated with suckling, leading to the release of milk.

millenarianism *n.* **1.** belief in the imminent end of human history, to be followed by a thousand-year period of peace and blessedness (often associated with the Second Coming of Christ). Such beliefs were current in the early Christian church and appeared sporadically, primarily from the 11th through the 17th centuries, in periods of political or intellectual crisis and among marginalized groups. Some New Age groups proclaim similar beliefs but without the language and imagery of Christianity. **2.** by extension, any belief that rapid and violent change can lead to a golden age of justice and peace. **—millenarian** *adj.*

Miller, Neal Elgar (1909–2002) U.S. psychologist. Miller received his doctorate in psychology from Yale University in 1935, working with Walter Miles (1885–1978) and Clark HULL. After a postdoctoral year studying psychoanalysis in Vienna, he taught at Yale for 30 years before moving in 1966 to Rockefeller University, where he remained for the remainder of his career. Miller's abiding interest was in the motivational aspects of reward and drive reduction and in the applications of experimental work to clinical psychology. Much of his early research attempted to reconcile Sigmund FREUD's theories of psychopathology with Ivan PAVLOV's learning theory, through the laboratory study of experimentally induced pathological behavior. His work was fundamental to the fields of learning and motivation, clinical psychology, and especially the newer field of BEHAVIORAL MEDICINE, of which he is regarded as a founder. Among his books that are considered to be classics are *Social Learning and Imitation* (1941) and *Personality and Psychotherapy* (1950), both coauthored with John Dollard (1900–1980). Important early papers are collected in *Neal E. Miller: Selected Papers* (1971). His many honors included the National Medal of Science, the Gold Medal of the American Psychological Foundation, the American Psychological Association's Distinguished Scientific Contributions Award, and election to the National Academy of Sciences.

Miller Analogies Test (**MAT**) a test designed to measure ability to understand relationships between ideas and to think analytically. It has been used since 1926 to predict scholastic ability at the graduate school level as well as in hiring and promotion decisions in the workplace. The MAT is composed of 120 partial analogies that require knowledge in many different areas, including sciences, literature, the arts, history, and vocabulary. Participants complete the analogies, only 100 of which are scored, by choosing the appropriate answer from among four options. [Wilford Stanton **Miller**, 20th-century U.S. psychologist]

Miller–Mowrer shuttlebox an apparatus for studying escape and avoidance learning. It consists of a straight alley with a guillotine door at its midpoint and a grid floor that can be electrified independently in each half. The experimental animal can avoid the aversive stimulus (an electric shock) by moving to the opposite end of the box, but must do so within a given time. [Neal E. MILLER and O. Hobart MOWRER]

Mill Hill Vocabulary Scale (**MHV**) a measure of CRYSTALLIZED ABILITIES designed to be administered in conjunction with RAVEN'S PROGRESSIVE MATRICES. It consists of 88 words and is available in three forms: one requiring participants to define all words, one requiring participants to recognize the meanings of all words by choosing the correct synonym for each from among six options, and one requiring participants to define half of the words and choose synonyms for the rest. [originally developed in 1943 by British psychologist John C. Raven (1902–1970) at Mill Hill Emergency Hospital, London]

Milligan annihilation method a type of ELECTROCONVULSIVE THERAPY in which three treatments are administered the first day, followed by two treatments daily until the desired level of regression is achieved.

milling around the initial stage in an ENCOUNTER GROUP, during which participants discuss trivial topics in order to avoid exposing themselves to new people and new interpersonal processes.

milling crowd an AGGREGATION of individuals, usually gathered in a public area (e.g., a street or concourse), whose members seem to be moving restlessly or aimlessly about the area. See CROWD.

Millon Clinical Multiaxial Inventory (**MCMI**) a true–false questionnaire, consisting of 175 items, that is widely used to assess clinical conditions and personality disorders in psychiatric patients in the United States. First published in 1977, it has been revised twice; the most recent version, **MCMI–III**, includes 24 scales arranged into four groups: clinical personality patterns, severe personality pathology, clinical syndromes, and severe clinical syndromes. Additionally, there are four corrections scales to help detect random or dishonest responding. BASE RATE scores are used in interpreting results. [Theodore **Millon** (1929–), U.S. psychologist]

Mill's canons a set of five principles of sound experimental science proposed by British philosopher John Stuart Mill (1806–1873). These principles outline the logical conditions under which observations can establish necessary and sufficient causal relationships between events. Because each of the principles enables the observer to eliminate potential causes, the general approach is often referred to as eliminative induction. Mill's work in this area is related to both the METHOD OF EXCLUSION described by English philosopher Francis Bacon (1561–1626) and the work on the logic of causality of British philosopher David Hume (1711–1776). It also presages the FALSIFICATIONISM of Austrian-born British philosopher Karl Popper (1902–1994). Mill's five canons are (a) the METHOD OF AGREEMENT, (b) the METHOD OF DIFFERENCE, (c) the METHOD OF AGREEMENT AND DIFFERENCE, (d) the METHOD OF RESIDUES, and (e) the METHOD OF CONCOMITANT VARIATION.

Miltown *n.* a trade name for MEPROBAMATE.

mimetic *adj.* relating to imitation, for example, a young chimpanzee's imitation of its parent's actions or a parrot imitating the words of its owner. A **mimetic response** is a copying or imitative response. Mimetic can also refer to physical features, such as the pseudopenis of female spotted hyenas, which is an enlargement of the clitoris and vagina through which mating and birth are accomplished. See also MIMICRY. **—mimesis** *n.*

mimicry *n.* **1.** the presence of physical or behavioral traits in one species that so closely resemble those of another species that they confuse observers. This serves either to evade predators (see BATESIAN MIMICRY; MÜLLERIAN MIMICRY) or to attract prey (see AGGRESSIVE MIMICRY). **2.** a form of SOCIAL LEARNING that involves duplication of a behavior without any understanding of the goal of that behavior. Compare EMULATION; IMITATION; LOCAL ENHANCEMENT.

mind *n.* **1.** most broadly, all intellectual and psychological phenomena of an organism, encompassing motivational, affective, behavioral, perceptual, and cognitive systems; in other words, the organized totality of the MENTAL and PSYCHIC processes of an organism and the structural and functional cognitive components on which they depend. The term, however, is often used more narrowly to denote only cognitive activities and functions, such as perceiving, attending, thinking, problem solving, language, learning, and memory. The nature of the relationship between the mind and the body, including the brain and its mechanisms or activities, has been, and continues to be, the subject of much debate. See MIND–BODY PROBLEM; PHILOSOPHY OF MIND. **2.** the substantive content of such mental and psychic processes. **3.** consciousness or awareness, particularly as specific to an individual. **4.** a set of EMERGENT PROPERTIES automatically derived from a brain that has achieved sufficient biological sophistication. In this sense, the mind is considered more the province of humans and of human consciousness than of organisms in general. **5.** human consciousness regarded as an immaterial entity distinct from the brain. See CARTESIAN DUALISM; GHOST IN THE MACHINE. **6.** the brain itself and its activities: in this view, the mind essentially is both the anatomical organ and what it does. **7.** concentration or focused attention. **8.** intention or volition. **9.** opinion or point of view. **10.** the characteristic mode of thinking of a group, such as the criminal mind or the military mind.

mindblindness *n.* a deficit in THEORY OF MIND that is characteristic of people with autism. A person with mindblindness cannot "read the minds" of others, that is, understand their behavior in terms of BELIEF–DESIRE REASONING. [first described by British psychologist Simon Baron-Cohen (1958–)]

mind–body intervention therapeutic approaches that focus on harnessing the power of the mind to bring about change in the body or achieve reduction of symptoms of disease or disorder. The various techniques used include relaxation training (e.g., AUTOGENIC TRAINING, PROGRESSIVE RELAXATION), MEDITATION, prayer, and CREATIVE ARTS THERAPY. See also COMPLEMENTARY AND ALTERNATIVE MEDICINE.

mind–body problem the problem of accounting for and describing the relationship between mental and physical processes (psyche and soma). Solutions to this problem fall into six broad categories: (a) **interactionism**, in which mind and body are separate processes that nevertheless exert mutual influence (see CARTESIAN DUALISM); (b) PARALLELISM, in which mind and body are separate processes with a point-to-point correspondence but no causal connection (see OCCASIONALISM; PREESTABLISHED HARMONY); (c) IDEALISM, in which only mind exists and the soma is a function of the psyche; (d) DOUBLE-ASPECT THEORY, in which body and mind are both functions of a common entity (see NEUTRAL MONISM); (e) EPIPHENOMENALISM, in which mind is a by-product of bodily processes; and (f) MATERIALISM, in which body is the only reality and the psyche is nonexistent. Categories (a) and (b) are varieties of DUALISM; the remainder are varieties of MONISM. In the context of psychopathology, two central questions arising from the mind–body problem are which sphere takes precedence in the genesis and development of illness and how does each sphere affect the other. Also called **body–mind problem**.

mind control 1. an extreme form of social influence used to indoctrinate an individual in the attitudes and beliefs of a group, usually one that is religious or political in nature. See BRAINWASHING; COERCIVE PERSUASION. **2.** the control of physical activities of the body, particularly autonomic functions, by mental processes. See AUTOGENIC TRAINING; BIOFEEDBACK; TRANSCENDENTAL MEDITATION; YOGA. See also MIND–BODY INTERVENTION.

mind-cure movement a self-help movement in the 19th century that assumed that physical health was the product of "right" thinking, usually regarded as optimism, self-affirmation, and self-regulation of moods.

mindfulness *n.* full awareness of one's internal states and surroundings: the opposite of ABSENT-MINDEDNESS. The concept has been applied to various therapeutic interventions—for example, mindfulness-based COGNITIVE BEHAVIOR THERAPY, mindfulness-based stress reduction, mindfulness for addictions, and MINDFULNESS MEDITATION—to help people avoid destructive or automatic habits and responses by learning to observe their thoughts, emotions, and other present-moment experiences without judging or reacting to them. **—mindful** *adj.*

mindfulness meditation a type of MEDITATION in which thoughts, feelings, and sensations are experienced freely as they arise. Mindfulness meditation is intended to enable individuals to become highly attentive to sensory information and to focus on each moment as it occurs. See also MINDFULNESS; TRANSCENDENTAL MEDITATION. Compare CONCENTRATIVE MEDITATION.

mind reading a form of alleged EXTRASENSORY PERCEPTION in which an individual claims to have access to the thoughts in the mind of another person. With THOUGHT TRANSFERENCE it is one of the two main forms of TELEPATHY.

mind's eye the mind's capacity to recall or create IMAGES based on visual experience. See VISUAL IMAGERY.

mindsight *n.* a proposed mode of visual perception, hypothesized to work in parallel with everyday vision, in which a person registers a nonvisual sense of change in visual information before conscious awareness of the change through actually "seeing" it. Research on mindsight arises out of work on CHANGE BLINDNESS. [proposed by 21st-century Canadian psychologist and computer scientist Ronald A. Rensink]

mind stuff in the philosophy of British mathematician William K. Clifford (1845–1879), the single substance that constitutes reality; this consists internally of mind, but appears externally in the form of matter. His argument, from evolution, was that since consciousness exists in humankind, and humankind evolved from matter, matter must also possess consciousness. Clifford's position is often taken to be one of PANPSYCHISM.

mineralocorticoid *n.* a CORTICOSTEROID hormone that affects ion concentrations in body tissues and helps to regulate the excretion of salt and water. In humans the principal mineralocorticoid is ALDOSTERONE.

MINERVA 2 a GLOBAL MEMORY MODEL that describes, in mathematical form, memory for both individual experiences (see EPISODIC MEMORY) and abstract generic facts (see SEMANTIC MEMORY). The model postulates that each experience leaves a MEMORY TRACE, and repetition creates multiple copies rather than strengthening a single trace. Memory retrieval activates the sum of all relevant traces. [proposed by Douglas L. Hintzman (1941–)]

miniature end-plate potential a very small variation in END-PLATE POTENTIAL due to the random release of tiny amounts of neurotransmitter at an axon terminal.

miniature life situations procedures for the assessment and selection of personnel to be trained for espionage and sabotage, used by the Office of Strategic Services (OSS) during World War II. Personnel were evaluated for, among other things, the leadership and stress tolerance they showed when subjected to simulated real-life situations, some of them highly stressful.

miniature system the organized, integrated knowledge, including facts, assumptions, and theories or hypotheses, relating to a restricted area of study. An example is the theory that explains a particular perceptual phenomenon, such as the MÜLLER-LYER ILLUSION.

minimal audible field (MAF) the threshold for a tone presented in a sound field to a participant who is not wearing headphones. The participant faces the sound source, and the threshold intensity is measured at the midpoint of the head. In this procedure, the sound pressure is presented in an open space free of echoes, rather than directly at the eardrum. Also called **minimum audible field**.

minimal audible pressure (**MAP**) the level of a tone presented via headphones at the threshold of audibility. The level (in decibels sound-pressure level) is the inferred or measured pressure at the tympanic membrane. Also called **minimum audible pressure**.

minimal brain damage (**MBD**) **1.** a mild degree of brain damage that is presumed to exist because of the presence of a constellation of SOFT SIGNS, which may include short attention span, distractibility, impulsivity, hyperactivity, emotional lability, poor motor coordination, visual-perceptual disturbance, language difficulties, and learning problems. These symptoms occur among a number of conditions involving neurologically based disturbance, including ATTENTION-DEFICIT/HYPERACTIVITY DISORDER, LEARNING DISORDERS, COMMUNICATION DISORDERS, and DEVELOPMENTAL COORDINATION DISORDER. **2.** an old name for ATTENTION-DEFICIT/HYPERACTIVITY DISORDER.

minimal brain dysfunction (**MBD**) **1.** a relatively mild impairment of brain function that is presumed to account for a variety of SOFT SIGNS seen in certain learning or behavioral disabilities. These signs include hyperactivity, impulsivity, emotional lability, and distractibility. Also called **minimal cerebral dysfunction**. **2.** an old name for ATTENTION-DEFICIT/HYPERACTIVITY DISORDER.

minimal-change method an experimental technique for calculating thresholds in which a variable stimulus is presented in very small ascending and descending steps until the participant can no longer detect a change in the stimulus.

minimal cue the smallest measurable stimulus that will evoke a response.

minimal group 1. a nominal group that lacks the features typically found in social groups, such as interdependence, COHESION, shared characteristics, joint activities, and GROUP STRUCTURE. **2.** a temporary group of the kind studied by Polish-born British social psychologist Henri Tajfel (1919–1982) in his **minimal group paradigm**. Tajfel found that individuals in such groups responded in biased ways when allocating resources to INGROUP and OUTGROUP members, even though the groups were not psychologically or interpersonally meaningful. See MINIMAL INTERGROUP SITUATION.

minimal intergroup situation 1. any situation involving contact between two or more MINIMAL GROUPS, as when a group of individuals disembarking from a bus mingles with a group of individuals getting on the bus. **2.** a research procedure, used mainly in studies of INTERGROUP CONFLICT, that involves creating temporary groupings of anonymous people whose interdependence is virtually nil. [developed by Polish-born British social psychologist Henri Tajfel (1919–1982)]

minimal pair in linguistics, two forms that differ in just one phonological feature, thereby illustrating the critical contrastive role played by that feature. In English, for example, the spoken forms [pin] and [bin] are a minimal pair that serve to identify /p/ and /b/ as distinct PHONEMES. See BINARY FEATURE; EMIC–ETIC DISTINCTION.

minimax strategy in GAME THEORY, a strategy in which players attempt to minimize their maximum losses. Compare MAXIMIN STRATEGY.

Mini-Mental State Examination (**MMSE**) an instrument used extensively to provide a quick assessment of cognitive status as a tool for the diagnosis of dementia. The patient is asked simple questions relating to orientation (e.g., "What day is today?") and required to perform simple tasks (e.g., remember the names of three common objects, fold a piece of paper in half, write an intelligible sentence) assessing memory, attention and calculation, and language. Also called **Folstein Mini-Mental State Examination**. [devised in 1975 by U.S. psychiatrists Marshal F. Folstein (1941–), Susan E. Folstein (1944–), and Paul R. McHugh]

minimization *n.* COGNITIVE DISTORTION consisting of a tendency to present events to oneself or others as insignificant or unimportant. Minimization often involves being unclear or nonspecific, so the listener does not have a complete picture of all the details and may be led to draw inaccurate or incomplete conclusions. See also DENIAL.

minimum power theory an analysis of COALITION formation processes that assumes that (a) all members who control sufficient resources to turn a winning coalition into a losing one or a losing coalition into a winning one are equal in terms of power; and (b) individuals' expectations concerning the division of the coalition's payoff will conform to an equity norm (see EQUITY THEORY), but one based on power rather than resources. This theory predicts that the most likely coalition to form in a group will be one that wins but comprises the individuals with the smallest amounts of power consistent with this outcome. Compare MINIMUM RESOURCE THEORY.

minimum resource theory an analysis of COALITION formation processes that assumes that (a) people in group situations will behave hedonistically and will thus be motivated to maximize their power, outcomes, and payoffs by forming coalitions; and (b) individuals' expectations concerning the division of the coalition's payoff will conform to an equity norm (see EQUITY THEORY). The minimum resource theory predicts that the most likely coalition to form in a group will be the one that contains those individuals whose total, combined resources are the fewest needed to control the outcome of the entire group. Compare MINIMUM POWER THEORY.

minimum separable the minimum distance that can be detected between two adjacent high-contrast visual stimuli. This distance, 1 minute of arc at the fovea, is about 60 times greater than the minimum detectable width of a line that appears alone. Compare MINIMUM VISIBLE.

minimum visible the narrowest visual stimulus that can be detected when it appears alone in the visual field. Compare MINIMUM SEPARABLE.

Minnesota Multiphasic Personality Inventory (**MMPI**) a PERSONALITY INVENTORY first published in 1940 and now one of the most widely used SELF-REPORT tools for assessing personality. It has broad applications across a range of mental health, medical, substance abuse, forensic, and personnel screening settings as a measure of psychological maladjustment. The original inventory consisted of 550 true–false items grouped into nine scales reflecting common clinical problems: hypochondria, depression, hysteria, psychopathic deviate, masculine–feminine interest, paranoia, psychasthenia (i.e., anxiety), schizophrenia, and hypomania. The results were scored by the examiner or by computer to determine the participant's personality profile as well as any tendency to lie or to fake good or bad. The version currently in use, the **MMPI–2** (1989), features 567 true–false questions that assess symptoms, attitudes, and beliefs that relate to emotional and behavioral problems, including substantial revisions of the original items and the addition of new scales. The early 1990s saw the publication of a version of the instrument, the **MMPI–A**, with content items specifically relevant to adolescents aged 14–18. The instrument's 478 items help identify personal, social, and behavioral problems (e.g., family issues, eating disorders, chemical dependency). [originally developed by U.S. psychologist Starke Rosecrans Hathaway (1903–1984) and U.S. psychiatrist John Charnley McKinley (1891–1950) at the University of Minnesota]

Minnesota Satisfaction Questionnaire (**MSQ**) a measure of JOB SATISFACTION developed at the University of Minnesota in which employees rate the extent to which they are satisfied or dissatisfied with each of several intrinsic factors (e.g., the work itself) and extrinsic factors (e.g., pay) relating to the job.

minor *n.* a person who is not legally an ADULT. See also EMANCIPATED MINOR.

minor depressive disorder a mood disorder in which, for at least 2 weeks, the individual has either persistent depressed mood or ANHEDONIA as well as at least two of a range of other symptoms. These other symptoms include: poor or increased appetite with significant weight loss or gain; insomnia or excessive sleep; PSYCHOMOTOR AGITATION or PSYCHOMOTOR RETARDATION; loss of energy with fatigue; feelings of worthlessness or inappropriate guilt; reduced ability to concentrate or make decisions; and recurrent thoughts of death, SUICIDAL IDEATION, or ATTEMPTED SUICIDE. These symptoms do not meet the criteria for DYSTHYMIC DISORDER and, according to proposed formal diagnostic criteria, they must occur in an individual who has never had a MAJOR DEPRESSIVE EPISODE. However, in clinical practice, a diagnosis of minor depressive disorder is widely applied to people who have significant symptoms of, but fail to meet the full criteria for, MAJOR DEPRESSIVE DISORDER, regardless of their history of depression. See also DEPRESSIVE DISORDER NOT OTHERWISE SPECIFIED.

minority group a population subgroup with social, religious, ethnic, racial, or other characteristics that differ from those of the majority of the population. The term is sometimes extended to cover any group that is the subject of oppression and discrimination, whether or not it literally comprises a minority of the population. See also ETHNIC GROUP; SUBCULTURE.

minority influence SOCIAL PRESSURE exerted on the majority faction of a group by a smaller faction of the group. Studies suggest that minorities who argue consistently for change prompt the group to reconsider even long-held or previously unquestioned assumptions and procedures. MAJORITY INFLUENCE tends to be direct and results in CONFORMITY, but minority influence is indirect and instigates INNOVATION and CONVERSION as the members of the majority struggle to validate their judgments.

minor tranquilizers see ANXIOLYTICS.

min strategy an arithmetic strategy in which children faced with an addition problem start with the largest addend and count up from there. For example, for the problem, 3 + 2 = ?, a child would say "3... 4, 5."

minty *adj.* denoting one of the seven classes of odorants in the STEREOCHEMICAL SMELL THEORY.

miosis (**myosis**) *n.* contraction of the pupil of the eye. —**miotic** *adj.*

Miranda warning a warning given in the United States by police officers to suspects during an arrest to make them aware of their rights against self-incrimination. Suspects must be told they have the right to an attorney and the right to remain silent; they must also be informed that anything they say can be used as evidence against them in court. It is named for the defendant in *Miranda v. Arizona*, a case that was ultimately decided in 1966 by the U.S. Supreme Court.

mirror cell a type of cell in the brains of primates that responds in the same way to a given action (e.g., reaching out to grasp an object) whether it is performed by the primate itself or whether the primate has merely observed another primate (which may be a human) perform the same action. This phenomenon is known as **mirror imaging**. [named and described by 21st-century Russian-born Italian neurologist Giacomo Rizzolati]

mirror drawing a motor-skill test of ability to alter well-learned patterns of hand–eye coordination. In the test the participant traces an image while looking into a mirror that shows only the image and the pencil.

mirror imaging **1.** a type of reversed asymmetry of characteristics often found between twins, particularly MONOZYGOTIC TWINS. Examples include handedness, fingerprints, and hair whorls. **2.** see MIRROR CELL.

mirroring *n.* **1.** reflecting or emulating speech, affect, behavior, or other qualities in psychotherapeutic contexts. A therapist may adopt the movements, speech style, or locutions of a client, and vice versa, to indicate comprehension of what is being said or to reflect bonding, either unconsciously or with the intent of empathizing. **2.** in self psychology, the positive responses of parents to a child that are intended to instill internal self-respect. **3.** see MIRROR TECHNIQUE.

mirror phase the stage in development occurring around 6–18 months of age when the infant becomes able to imagine himself or herself as an autonomous ego in the image of the parent and also starts to recognize his or her reflection in a mirror. In sum, the child begins to acquire a self-image. French psychoanalyst Jacques Lacan (1901–1981), who introduced the phrase, saw this as marking the start of the infant's transition from the realm of the IMAGINARY to that of the SYMBOLIC. See also NAME-OF-THE-FATHER.

mirror reading **1.** reading in a pattern that is the reverse of that generally followed. See PALINLEXIA. **2.** a task in which a person must read words that are presented one at a time in mirror image. **3.** a preference for reading mirror-reversed rather than normally written words.

mirror sign **1.** the inability to recognize the reflection of oneself in a mirror. **2.** the tendency to look at oneself in a reflecting surface (window, mirror, etc.) frequently and for an extended period of time. [first described in 1927 by Paul Abely as an early symptom of schizophrenia]

mirror technique **1.** the conscious use of ACTIVE LISTENING by the therapist in psychotherapy, accompanied by reflection of the client's affect and body language in order to stimulate a sense of empathy and to further the development of the THERAPEUTIC ALLIANCE. **2.** in PSYCHODRAMA, a technique in which an AUXILIARY EGO imitates a client's behavior patterns to show that person how others perceive and react to him or her. Also called **mirroring**.

mirror transference in psychoanalysis, a TRANSFERENCE technique used in the treatment of NARCISSISTIC PERSONALITY DISORDERS in which the patients' grandiose selves are reactivated as a replica of the early phase of their lives when their mothers established their sense of perfection by admiring their exhibitionistic behavior.

This "reactivation process" helps to restore the patient's self-esteem.

mirror writing the production of individual letters and whole word strings in reverse direction. Mirror writing is characterized by an inversion of letters and words such that they appear reversed unless viewed in a mirror. It is related to STREPHOSYMBOLIA. Also called **palingraphia**; **retrography**.

mirtazapine *n.* an antidepressant whose mechanism of action differs from that of most other antidepressants. It is considered to be a MIXED-FUNCTION ANTIDEPRESSANT in that two separate actions result in increased neurotransmission of norepinephrine and serotonin. By binding to presynaptic α_2-adrenoreceptors (see ALPHA ADRENORECEPTOR; AUTORECEPTOR), it enables continued release of norepinephrine from presynaptic neurons. It also acts as a SEROTONIN-RECEPTOR AGONIST at postsynaptic 5-HT_1 receptors. Other actions of mirtazapine include potent antagonism of other serotonin receptors and histamine receptors, but it does not inhibit the reuptake of serotonin or norepinephrine. Sedation and weight gain are common adverse effects of mirtazapine, probably due to its potent ability to block the HISTAMINE H_1 receptor. Unlike many other antidepressants, in most patients mirtazapine does not cause sexual dysfunction. Rarely, AGRANULOCYTOSIS has been associated with its use. U.S. trade name: **Remeron**.

MIS 1. abbreviation for Müllerian-inhibiting substance (see MÜLLERIAN-INHIBITING HORMONE). **2.** abbreviation for MANAGEMENT INFORMATION SYSTEMS.

mis- *combining form* see MISO-.

misandry *n.* hatred or contempt for men. Compare MISOGYNY. **—misandrist** *n., adj.*

misanthropy *n.* a hatred, aversion, or distrust of all human beings. **—misanthrope** *n.* **—misanthropic** *adj.*

misarticulation *n.* **1.** faulty ARTICULATION, resulting in unclear, imprecise speech sounds and poorly understood speech. **2.** a poorly articulated sound or utterance.

misattribution of arousal an effect in which the arousal generated by one stimulus is mistakenly attributed to another source. See also EXCITATION-TRANSFER THEORY.

miscarriage *n.* the SPONTANEOUS ABORTION of a fetus before it is able to survive outside the womb, usually before the 28th week of pregnancy.

miscegenation *n.* marriage, sexual activity, or reproduction among individuals of different ethnicity, especially when this is emphasized by marked physical differences (e.g., skin color). The term has traditionally carried a heavy sense of disapproval and is now largely archaic and disfavored. See also EXOGAMY; INTERMARRIAGE; OUTBREEDING. **—miscegenational** *adj.*

miseducation *n.* teaching information, intentionally or in good faith, that is incorrect. The teaching of history is a common example of this, as historical material is prone to subjectivity, depending on the point of view of the writer and the period at which it was written.

misidentification *n.* **1.** failure to identify individuals correctly due to impaired memory or a confused state, as in dementia or alcoholic intoxication or sometimes in mania. **2.** failure to recognize people or objects due to a delusion that they have been transformed (**delusional misidentification**). See MISIDENTIFICATION SYNDROME.

misidentification syndrome a disorder characterized by the delusional MISIDENTIFICATION of oneself, other people, places, or objects. The misidentification may be expressed as the mistaken belief that a person has altered his or her identity in some way, either physically or psychologically, or that some place or object has undergone some aspect of transformation. Also called **delusional misidentification syndrome**. See also CAPGRAS SYNDROME; FREGOLI'S PHENOMENON; INTERMETAMORPHOSIS SYNDROME.

misinformation effect a phenomenon in which a person mistakenly recalls misleading information that an experimenter has provided, instead of accurately recalling the correct information that had been presented earlier. The misinformation effect is studied in the context of EYEWITNESS MEMORY.

miso- (**mis-**) *combining form* hatred.

misocainia (**misocainea**) *n.* see MISONEISM.

misogamy *n.* hatred of or aversion to marriage. **—misogamist** *n.*

misogyny *n.* hatred or contempt for women. Compare MISANDRY. **—misogynist** *n.* **—misogynistic** *adj.*

misologia *n.* an aversion to speaking or arguing. Also called **misology**.

misoneism *n.* an extreme resistance to change and intolerance of anything new, sometimes expressed as an obsessive desire to maintain routines and preserve the status quo. It is often associated with AUTISTIC DISORDER. Also called **misocainia**. **—misoneist** *n.*

misopedia *n.* a hatred of children. Also called **misopedy**.

misorientation effect difficulty recognizing an object when it appears in an orientation different from that in which it was initially learned. The effect is critical when navigating using visual images or maps that may be presented in different orientations, and usually results in slower recognition and lower accuracy.

miss *n.* in signal detection tasks, an incorrect indication by the participant that a signal is absent in a trial when it is actually present. See also FALSE REJECTION; SIGNAL DETECTION THEORY. Compare FALSE ALARM.

missing fundamental see VIRTUAL PITCH.

missing-parts test an intelligence test in which the participant is required to point out what is missing in a picture. It is frequently used as an observation test in IQ scales, such as the STANFORD–BINET INTELLIGENCE SCALE and the WECHSLER ADULT INTELLIGENCE SCALE.

missionaries and cannibals a problem often used in studies of problem solving. Three missionaries and three cannibals are on one side of a river and must cross to the other side in a canoe that will only hold two people. The missionaries on either bank must never be outnumbered by the cannibals, or they will be eaten, and the canoe must have at least one passenger each time it crosses the river. The solver must plan a series of moves that will get the group across the river in a way that meets these constraints.

mistress *n.* a woman with whom a married man has a continuing sexual relationship, usually without the knowledge of his wife. The man may provide for the woman, but the relationship is not one of prostitution.

mistrust *n.* see BASIC MISTRUST; TRUST VERSUS MISTRUST.

MIT abbreviation for MELODIC INTONATION THERAPY.

mitigating factor a fact relating to a crime or to a convicted defendant that supports the argument for a more lenient sentence. Examples of mitigating factors are the defendant's youth, personal or family circumstances, or DIMINISHED RESPONSIBILITY. Also called **mitigating circumstance**. Compare AGGRAVATING FACTOR.

mitochondrion *n.* (*pl.* **mitochondria**) an ORGANELLE that is the main site of energy production in cells. Mitochondria are most numerous in cells with a high level of metabolism. They also have their own DNA (mitochondrial DNA). **—mitochondrial** *adj.*

mitosis *n.* (*pl.* **mitoses**) the type of division of a cell nucleus that produces two identical daughter nuclei, each possessing the same number and type of chromosomes as the parent nucleus. It is usually accompanied by division of the cytoplasm, leading to the formation of two identical daughter cells. Compare MEIOSIS. **—mitotic** *adj.*

mitral cell any of the PYRAMIDAL CELLS that form a layer of the OLFACTORY BULB. Each mitral cell may receive signals from hundreds of olfactory receptors embedded in the OLFACTORY EPITHELIUM. See also LATERAL OLFACTORY TRACT.

mittelschmerz *n.* a pain experienced by some females about midway through the menstrual cycle, that is, at the time of OVULATION (from German, "midpain"). The pain is felt in the region of the ovary and is caused by the rupture of the ovarian follicle and bleeding into the peritoneum.

Mitwelt *n.* in the thought of German philosopher Martin Heidegger (1889–1976), that aspect of DASEIN (human being-in-the-world) that is constituted by a person's relationships and interactions with other people. It was introduced into psychology by Swiss existentialist psychologist Ludwig Binswanger (1881–1966). Compare EIGENWELT; UMWELT. [German, literally: "with world"]

mixed cerebral dominance a condition in which neither cerebral hemisphere clearly controls motor functions, possibly causing speech disorders or conflicts in HANDEDNESS.

mixed deafness see DEAFNESS.

mixed dysarthria see DYSARTHRIA.

mixed-effects model an analytic paradigm used in the ANALYSIS OF VARIANCE in which the experimenter regards one or more variables as fixed and one or more additional variables as random. Also called **mixed model**. See RANDOM-EFFECTS MODEL; FIXED-EFFECTS MODEL.

mixed emotions two or more emotions, differing in feeling quality and ACTION TENDENCY, elicited by the same event. For example, a father may be happy that his son is getting married but sorrowful if the marriage takes the son away from home; a person may become angry at an insult from a superior and also frightened by the implications for his or her employment. Also called **mixed feelings**. See AMBIVALENCE.

mixed episode an episode of a MOOD DISORDER lasting at least 1 week in which symptoms meeting criteria for both a MAJOR DEPRESSIVE EPISODE and a MANIC EPISODE are prominent over the course of the disturbance. One or more mixed episodes may be a feature of bipolar I disorder (see BIPOLAR DISORDERS).

mixed feelings see MIXED EMOTIONS.

mixed-function antidepressants antidepressants that act primarily via more than one major neurotransmitter system. The term is often applied to the SNRIS (e.g., VENLAFAXINE), which inhibit the reuptake of both norepinephrine and serotonin, to distinguish them from the SSRIS (selective serotonin reuptake inhibitors). Also called **dual-action antidepressants**.

mixed laterality the tendency to shift preference from the right side of the body to the left side when performing a particular activity, or to perform some acts with a preference for the right-hand side and others with a preference for the left. Also called **lateral confusion**.

mixed model see MIXED-EFFECTS MODEL.

mixed-motive game a simulation of social interaction that is structured so that players can reach their goals either by competing against others or by cooperating with others. Players in the PRISONER'S DILEMMA game, for example, will earn greater rewards in the short term if they compete against others, but if all players compete, rewards will be lower overall. See also SOCIAL DILEMMA; SOCIAL TRAP.

mixed neurosis in psychoanalysis, a condition in which a patient shows symptoms of two or more neuroses. The term is rarely used now.

mixed receptive-expressive language disorder in *DSM–IV–TR*, a communication disorder characterized by levels of language comprehension and expressive language development substantially below the expected level of verbal or nonverbal intellectual ability, as demonstrated by scores on standardized, individually administered measures of both receptive and expressive language development or functional assessment. The deficit interferes substantially with scholastic, academic, or occupational achievement or social interactions and is not due solely to mental retardation, motor speech disorders, sensory deficit, environmental deprivation, or a pervasive developmental disorder.

mixed reinforcement schedule a COMPOUND SCHEDULE OF REINFORCEMENT in which two or more schedules alternate. The same stimulus is used for all schedules, therefore no discriminative cues are available (see DISCRIMINATIVE STIMULUS).

mixed schizophrenia **1.** a form of schizophrenia in which either both negative and positive symptoms are prominent or neither is prominent. [defined in 1982 by U.S. psychiatrist Nancy C. Andreasen and Scott A. Olsen] **2.** historically, a form of schizophrenia that is manifested by symptoms of two or more of the four major types of schizophrenia described by German psychiatrist Emil Kraepelin (1856–1926) and Swiss psychiatrist Eugen Bleuler (1857–1939): simple, paranoid, catatonic, and hebephrenic (disorganized).

mixed serotonin and norepinephrine reuptake inhibitors see SNRIS.

mixed-standard scale a behavior-based rating procedure used in EMPLOYEE EVALUATION. Raters are presented with examples of good, average, and bad behaviors for a job and told to evaluate the performance of the employee in terms of whether it is better than, the same as, or poorer than each of the three behaviors. The performance rating is assigned on the basis of the pattern of responses, the highest score being given to employees rated "better than" on all three behaviors and the lowest rating being given to those rated "poorer than" on all three. Compare BEHAVIORALLY ANCHORED RATING SCALE; BEHAVIORAL OBSERVATION SCALE. See also CRITICAL-INCIDENT TECHNIQUE.

mixoscopia *n.* a form of VOYEURISM in which an orgasm is achieved by observing sexual intercourse between the person one loves and another person.

mixoscopia bestialis a type of sexual deviancy in which a person is excited or aroused by watching another individual have coitus with an animal.

MLD abbreviation for MASKING LEVEL DIFFERENCE.

MLH1 a germ-line mutation located on the short arm of chromosome 3 and associated with hereditary nonpolyposis colon cancer (HNPCC). See also MSH2.

MLU abbreviation for MEAN LENGTH OF UTTERANCE.

MMECT abbreviation for MULTIPLE MONITORED ELECTROCONVULSIVE TREATMENT.

MMPI abbreviation for MINNESOTA MULTIPHASIC PERSONALITY INVENTORY.

MMPI–2 abbreviation for the revised version of the MINNESOTA MULTIPHASIC PERSONALITY INVENTORY.

MMPI–A abbreviation for the version of the MINNESOTA MULTIPHASIC PERSONALITY INVENTORY designed for use with adolescents.

MMSE abbreviation for MINI-MENTAL STATE EXAMINATION.

MMT abbreviation for MULTIMODAL THERAPY.

M'Naghten rule see MCNAUGHTEN RULE.

mneme *n.* see ENGRAM.

mnemonic strategy any device or technique used to assist memory, usually by forging a link or association between the new information to be remembered and information previously encoded. For instance, one might remember the numbers in a password by associating them with familiar birth dates, addresses, or room numbers. Also called **mnemonic**; **mnemonic system**. See also KEY-WORD METHOD; METHOD OF LOCI; PEG-WORD MNEMONIC SYSTEM.

mnemonic trace see ENGRAM.

mnemonist *n.* an individual with exceptional ability to encode and retrieve information from memory. Some mnemonists have well-developed memory strategies that enable them to remember; others have exceptional memories in only certain domains (e.g., numbers or foreign words).

mnestic *adj.* related to memory.

mob *n.* a disorderly, unruly, and emotionally charged CROWD. Mobs tend to form when some event, such as a crime, a catastrophe, or a controversial action, evokes the same kind of mood and reaction in a substantial number of people. Early mob psychology argued that individuals in mobs were so overwhelmed by their emotions and the CROWD MIND that they could no longer control their actions: Unless the situation was diffused, mobs became volatile, unpredictable, and capable of violent action. Contemporary studies suggest that members of mobs may respond impulsively but rarely lose cognitive control, that mysterious social or psychological processes do not force them to behave abnormally in such situations, and that mobs tend to be organized and goal-directed rather than irrational and frenzied.

Moban *n.* a trade name for MOLINDONE.

mobbing behavior a response to a predator in which a group of animals join together to chase the predator away. Mobbing behavior, which is usually accompanied by loud, distinctive vocalizations, can be observed in many small birds and mammals.

mobility *n.* **1.** the capacity to move or be moved, for example, the ability of people to transport themselves between home and work or community facilities by such means as walking, driving a car, or traveling by public transportation. See also MOTILITY. **2.** in developmental psychology, the ability of an infant to creep, crawl, walk, or otherwise move through space. **3.** in sociology, the extent to which individuals are able to move between localities, occupations, or social classes. See GEOGRAPHICAL MOBILITY; SOCIAL MOBILITY. See also HORIZONTAL MOBILITY; VERTICAL MOBILITY. **—mobile** *adj.*

mob psychology CROWD PSYCHOLOGY, as applied to mobs.

MOCC abbreviation for MEMORY-OPERATING CHARACTERISTIC CURVE.

moclobemide *n.* an antidepressant drug that is a reversible MONOAMINE OXIDASE INHIBITOR (RIMA) and relatively selective for MONOAMINE OXIDASE A. It therefore lacks many of the food interactions that limit the use of irreversible, nonselective MAO inhibitors. Moclobemide has not yet been approved for use in the United States.

modafinil *n.* a CNS STIMULANT used for the treatment of narcolepsy. Its exact mechanism of action is unclear, but modafinil may exert its stimulant effects by decreasing GABA-mediated neurotransmission (see GAMMA-AMINOBUTYRIC ACID) and potentiating GLUTAMATE transmission. Modafinil may therefore serve as an alternative agent for patients who are intolerant of amphetamines and related stimulants, which have a different mechanism of action. Because it inhibits the CYTOCHROME P450 2C19 enzyme and induces the cytochrome P450 3A4 enzyme, it may have clinically significant interactions with drugs metabolized via those enzymes. U.S. trade name: **Provigil**.

modal action pattern the typical or most common behavioral pattern expressed in response to a RELEASER. In classical ETHOLOGY the term FIXED-ACTION PATTERN was used to describe behavioral responses, but this term obscures the variation in behavior typically seen within and between individuals. Modal action pattern conveys the variability of behavioral responses.

modality *n.* **1.** a particular therapeutic technique or process. **2.** a medium of sensation, such as vision or hearing. See SENSE.

modality effect the tendency for the final items of a list to be better recalled if the items are presented auditorily rather than visually. See RECENCY EFFECT.

modality profile in MULTIMODAL THERAPY, a list of problems and proposed treatments across the seven parameters (modalities) explored in the approach. The parameters, or dimensions (e.g., affect, sensation), are considered to be distinct yet interactive. The profiles are created specifically with clients for descriptive and therapeutic purposes.

modal model of memory a generic theory of memory incorporating assumptions common to most models. The modal model includes a SHORT-TERM MEMORY and a LONG-TERM MEMORY and provides details on how information is encoded and later retrieved from memory.

mode *n.* **1.** a characteristic manner of behavior or way of doing things, as in a technique. **2.** the most frequently occurring score in a batch of data, which is sometimes used as a measure of CENTRAL TENDENCY.

model *n.* **1.** a graphic, theoretical, or other type of representation of a concept (e.g., a disorder) or of basic behavioral or bodily processes that can be used for various investigative and demonstrative purposes, such as enhancing understanding of the concept, proposing hypotheses, showing relationships, or identifying epidemiological patterns. **2.** see MODELING.

model human processor a model of human INFORMATION PROCESSING that is used in evaluating the usability of products and systems. The model, which is derived from empirical findings, consists of three interacting subsystems—perceptual, motor, and cognitive. Estimates of processing capacity and of processing and decay times (see DECAY THEORY) can be used to quantify human performance under a variety of constraints. See also HUMAN OPERATOR MODELING. [developed in 1983 by U.S. psychologist Stuart K. Card (1943–), U.S. computer scientist Thomas P. Moran (1942–), and U.S. cognitive scientist Allen Newell (1927–1992)]

modeling *n.* **1.** a technique used in COGNITIVE BEHAVIOR THERAPY and BEHAVIOR THERAPY in which learning occurs through observation and imitation alone, without comment or reinforcement by the therapist. See also BEHAVIORAL MODELING. **2.** in DEVELOPMENTAL PSYCHOLOGY, the process in which one or more individuals or other entities serve as examples (**models**) that a child will emulate. Models are often parents, other adults, or other children, but may also be symbolic, for example, a book or television character. See also SOCIAL LEARNING THEORY.

modeling effect a type of EXPERIMENTER EFFECT in which a participant is unwittingly influenced to give responses similar to the responses the experimenter would give if the experimenter were a participant.

modeling theory the idea that changes in behavior, cognition, or emotional state result from observing someone else's behavior or the consequences of that behavior. See OBSERVATIONAL LEARNING; SOCIAL LEARNING THEORY.

model psychosis psychotic symptoms (e.g., delusions, hallucinations, disorientation, disorganized speech) deliberately produced by a PSYCHOTOMIMETIC drug, such as LSD, for purposes of research. This technique was particularly popular during the 1950s and 1960s.

models of evaluation different approaches or strategies in the conceptualization and methodological emphasis of PROGRAM EVALUATION. See also GOAL MODEL OF EVALUATION; UTILIZATION-FOCUSED EVALUATION.

moderate depression a MAJOR DEPRESSIVE EPISODE whose severity and number of symptoms do not meet the criteria for ACUTE DEPRESSION but exceed the criteria for MILD DEPRESSION.

moderate mental retardation a diagnostic and classification category applying to those with IQs of 35 to 49, comprising about 12% of people with MENTAL RETARDATION. These individuals rarely progress beyond the second grade in academic subjects. Although often poorly coordinated, they can learn to take care of themselves and to develop sufficient social and occupational skills to be able to perform unskilled or semiskilled work under supervision in sheltered and supportive environments, as well as in regular workplaces where accommodations are made.

moderator variable 1. in statistics, a variable that is unrelated to a criterion variable but is retained in a REGRESSION EQUATION because of its significant relationship to other predictor variables. **2.** a variable aspect of consumer behavior associated with different patterns of results. For example, consumer motivation might serve as a moderator of how individuals develop attitudes toward products. With high levels of motivation, consumers tend to base their attitudes on the quality of a product as assessed by detailed thinking about the product's features. With low levels of motivation, consumers tend to base their attitude toward a product on such factors as the attractiveness of the product endorser. Personality variables often serve as moderators of processes underlying consumer behavior.

modernism *n.* **1.** in philosophy, a set of general characteristics marking the whole period from the 17th century to the present day. Most historians of philosophy see the onset of modernity in the work of French philosopher René Descartes (1596–1650), with its attempt to establish a systematic account of reality on a radically new basis (see CARTESIANISM; CARTESIAN DUALISM; CARTESIAN SELF). Historically, modernism is inseparable from the Enlightenment of the 17th and 18th centuries and its complex legacy over the last 300 years. Its defining characteristics include a sense that religious dogma and classical metaphysics can no longer provide a sure foundation in intellectual matters and a quest for certain knowledge from other sources; the latter is sustained by confidence in absolutes in EPISTEMOLOGY and ETHICS and confidence in the new methods of EXPERIMENTAL PHILOSOPHY, or natural science. Traditional psychology can be seen to be the product of modernism to the extent that it is characterized by faith in scientific method, pursuit of control and prediction of behavior, explanation in terms of laws and principles, and the assumption that human behavior is ultimately rational as opposed to irrational. Some thinkers argue that modernism was superseded by POSTMODERNISM in the late 20th century, although others would dispute such a claim. **2.** a movement in the arts of the early 20th century characterized by the adoption of radically new techniques, forms, approaches, and subjects. Important developments associated with modernism include abstraction in the visual arts, free verse in poetry, and use of the 12-tone scale in music. Many writers and artists of the period were influenced by contemporary developments in psychology and psychoanalysis; a particular instance of this is the use of the STREAM OF CONSCIOUSNESS technique by novelists and poets, such as Irish writer James Joyce (1882–1941), British writer Virginia Woolf (1882–1941), French writer Marcel Proust (1871–1922), and others. In recent decades the concept of postmodernism in the arts has been much discussed. **—modernist** *adj., n.*

modernization *n.* the complex set of processes by which a largely rural and traditional society becomes a developed industrial society. Modernized societies are typically conceived as those societies that tend toward the secular and urbanized and that place a high value on science and technology, education, SOCIAL MOBILITY, acquired wealth, democratic government, and the rule of law. Modernization is often contrasted with the TRADITIONALISM of undeveloped or underdeveloped societies, which are often identified as religious and rural, with limited technology, low social mobility, weak political structures, and so forth. Other conceptualizations of this dichotomy are currently in debate, however, pointing to the highly variable social and psychological adjustments that occur in different societies as they respond to development. **—modernize** *vb.*

modern racism a contemporary form of PREJUDICE against members of other racial groups that is expressed indirectly and covertly, typically by condemning the cultural values of the OUTGROUP or by experiencing aversive emotions when interacting with its members but not acting on those negative emotions (see AVERSIVE RACISM). A modern racist, for example, expresses prejudice by condemning another group's cultural values or by avoiding any contact with members of that group. Changed social attitudes have brought about a decline in the direct expression of racial discrimination and hostility toward minority groups (**old-fashioned racism**), with a corresponding increase in the less blatant modern racism. See also RACISM.

modes of learning different sensory modalities through which information may be presented for learning and encoded into memory. For instance, one can learn through vision, hearing, or touch. See MOTOR LEARNING; VERBAL LEARNING; VISUAL LEARNING.

modesty *n.* **1.** absence of self-importance or conceit.

2. propriety in appearance, dress, demeanor, and social behavior. **—modest** *adj.*

MODE theory *M*otivation and *O*pportunity as *De*terminants theory: a theory of ATTITUDE–BEHAVIOR CONSISTENCY postulating that the process by which attitudes influence behavior differs according to the amount of deliberation involved. When people are motivated and able to deliberate about their actions, attitudes influence behavior in a manner similar to that postulated by the THEORY OF REASONED ACTION. When people are not motivated or able to deliberate about their actions, attitudes toward the target of the behavior can be activated in memory and affect the way the target is perceived. These perceptions in turn influence how people define the behavioral event (e.g., as a situation in which the target should be approached or avoided). The definition of the behavioral event in turn determines behavior. [originally developed by U.S. psychologist Russell H. Fazio (1952–)]

modified replication see REPLICATION.

Modified Rhyme Test (**MRT**) a test to evaluate auditory processing in which the participant listens to a single-syllable word and then identifies it from among several printed alternatives. The response choices are grouped into six-item lists within which the vowels in the words are held constant as either the initial or final consonants change (e.g., *beam, bead, beach, beat, beak, bean*). [developed in 1965 by Arthur S. House, Carl E. Williams, Michael H. L. Hecker, and psychoacoustician Karl D. Kryter (1914–)]

modifier *n.* **1.** in genetics, a gene that appears to have an effect of modifying other hereditary factors but has no significant effect when the main factor is absent. Some investigators believe modifier genes play a role in constitutional medical conditions. Many physical diseases and behaviors are thought to involve modifier genes as well as environmental triggers. **2.** in grammar, any word or phrase that qualifies or limits the meaning of another word or phrase.

modularity *n.* a theory of the human mind in which the various components of cognition are characterized as independent MODULES, each with its own specific domain and particular properties. It was first proposed by U.S. philosopher Jerry Fodor (1935–) in his book *The Modularity of Mind* (1983). A related notion had earlier been advanced by Noam CHOMSKY in his theory of the TASK SPECIFICITY OF LANGUAGE, which characterizes the human language faculty as a unique "mental organ" differing qualitatively from other aspects of cognition. More recently, evolutionary psychologists have shown interest in the idea that the various modules may be adaptive specializations. Compare COGNITIVE GRAMMAR.

modulation *n.* changes in some parameter of a waveform (e.g., amplitude, frequency, phase) so that the information contained by the variations of this parameter can be transmitted by the wave, which is known as the **carrier wave**. **Amplitude modulation** (AM) refers to changes in amplitude that are relatively slow compared to the usually sinusoidal variations in the carrier. In **frequency modulation** (FM) the frequency of the carrier is varied but its amplitude remains constant. In **phase modulation** the relative phase of the carrier wave is varied in accordance with the amplitude of the signal variations. For most modulated waveforms the frequency of modulation is much less than the frequency components in the carrier.

modulation threshold see TEMPORAL MODULATION TRANSFER FUNCTION.

modulatory role the role that some hormones play in maintaining the sensitivity of NEURAL CIRCUITS and other structures to hormonal influences.

modulatory site a site on a RECEPTOR molecule that, when bound by a ligand (e.g., a drug), alters the receptor's response on binding of its agonist (e.g., a neurotransmitter) to the usual site.

module *n.* **1.** in cognitive theory, a hypothetical center of information processing that is presumed to be relatively independent and highly specialized in its operations, such as a language module or face-processing module. **2.** in neuroscience, a unit of a region of the central nervous system. For example, regions of the NEOCORTEX in the brain are divided into CORTICAL COLUMNS of basically similar structure. **—modular** *adj.*

modus operandi a specific behavioral pattern that may typify a particular individual, especially with respect to criminal behavior.

modus ponens see AFFIRMING THE ANTECEDENT.

modus tollens see DENYING THE CONSEQUENT.

mogigraphia *n.* a rare name for WRITER'S CRAMP.

mogilalia *n.* difficulty or hesitancy in speaking (e.g., STUTTERING). Also called **molilalia**.

molar analysis the analysis of behavioral processes as holistic units, extended through time. Molar analyses consider overall relations between measures, such as average response rates to rates of reinforcement (e.g., food), of a large number of responses spread across a period of time. Also called **global analysis**. Compare MOLECULAR ANALYSIS.

molar approach any theory or method that stresses comprehensive concepts or overall frameworks or structures. Compare MOLECULAR APPROACH. See also HOLISM.

molar behavior a large but unified segment, or holistic unit, of behavior, such as kicking a ball. Compare MOLECULAR BEHAVIOR.

molecular analysis the analysis of behavioral processes that breaks them down into their component parts and examines them on a moment-by-moment basis and at the level of individual response-reinforcement sequences. Compare MOLAR ANALYSIS.

molecular approach any theory or method that stresses the components of a phenomenon, process, or system, making use of elemental units in its analysis (see MOLECULAR ANALYSIS). Compare MOLAR APPROACH. See also ATOMISM; ELEMENTARISM.

molecular behavior behavior that can be analyzed into smaller, more specific units, such as reflexes. Compare MOLAR BEHAVIOR.

molecularism *n.* see ATOMISM; MOLECULAR APPROACH.

molestation *n.* the act of making sexual advances toward a person who does not want them. Molestation generally implies sexual fondling or touching an individual "without lawful consent." When the victim of molestation is a child or a person who is mentally challenged, it may be assumed that he or she does not have the capacity to give lawful consent. See also SEX OFFENSE. **—molest** *vb.*

molilalia *n.* see MOGILALIA.

molimina *pl. n.* the unpleasant symptoms experienced by some women during the premenstrual or menstrual periods.

molindone *n.* a conventional (typical or first-generation) antipsychotic of the DIHYDROINDOLONE class. It is of intermediate potency and has few anticholinergic side effects. Until the advent of the atypical, or second-generation, antipsychotics, it was frequently used, usually in low doses, for the management of psychoses accompanying medical conditions (e.g., HIV-related dementia). U.S. trade name: **Moban**.

Molyneux's question the question posed by William Molyneux (1656–1698), a member of the Irish parliament, to English philosopher John Locke (1632–1704), who later discussed it in his *Essay Concerning Human Understanding* (1690). Molyneux's question was whether a man born blind but able to distinguish two distinct shapes by feeling them with his hands would be able to distinguish them by sight alone, without also touching them, if he were suddenly able to see. Locke's answer—and Molyneux's as well—was that the person would not be able to distinguish them by sight immediately because the sense modalities act independently and can be integrated only by experience.

moment *n.* the power to which the expected value of a RANDOM VARIABLE is raised. Thus, $E(x^k)$ is the *k*th moment of *x*. Moments are used for computing distribution measures, such as the MEAN, VARIANCE, SKEWNESS, and KURTOSIS.

moment about the mean see CENTRAL MOMENT.

mommy track a professional pathway associated with WORKING MOTHERS, typically characterized by flexible working conditions but limited career advancement.

mon- *combining form* see MONO-.

monad *n.* in the thought of German philosopher Gottfried Wilhelm Leibniz (1646–1716), one of the ultimate indivisible units of existence. Monads are independent of all other monads and have innately the power of action and direction toward some end (see NISUS). Although no monad in reality acts on any other, they work in a divinely PREESTABLISHED HARMONY so that an appearance of causal connection is maintained. The concept of the monad was intended, in part, to address the MIND–BODY PROBLEM arising from CARTESIAN DUALISM.

monaural *adj.* relating to or affecting one ear only. Compare BINAURAL; MONOTIC.

monestrous *adj.* see ESTRUS.

mongolism *n.* an obsolete name for DOWN SYNDROME.

moniliasis *n.* see CANDIDIASIS.

monism *n.* the position that reality consists of a single SUBSTANCE, whether this is identified as mind (IDEALISTIC MONISM), matter (NATURAL MONISM), or God (PANTHEISM). In the context of the MIND–BODY PROBLEM, monism is any position (such as NEUTRAL MONISM) that avoids DUALISM. **—monist** *adj., n.* **—monistic** *adj.*

monitoring *n.* the process of watching or overseeing individuals and their behavior or of checking machines at intervals to see how they are functioning.

mono- (**mon-**) *combining form* one, single, or alone.

monoamine *n.* an AMINE that contains only one amine group, $-NH_2$. Monoamines include neurotransmitters, such as the CATECHOLAMINES norepinephrine and dopamine and the INDOLEAMINE serotonin. See also MONOAMINE OXIDASE.

monoamine hormone see AMINE HORMONE.

monoamine hypothesis the theory that depression is caused by a deficit in the production or uptake of monoamines (serotonin, norepinephrine, and dopamine). This theory has been used to explain the effects of MONOAMINE OXIDASE INHIBITORS, but is now regarded as too simplistic.

monoamine neurotransmitter theory a theory that explains RUNNER'S HIGH as the result of an increase of the neurotransmitter monoamines NOREPINEPHRINE and SEROTONIN with exercise.

monoamine oxidase (**MAO**) an enzyme that breaks down and inactivates MONOAMINES, including several neurotransmitters. It is found in most tissues and, in humans, exists in two forms, MAO-A and MAO-B. MAO-B is the predominant enzyme in the brain, whereas MAO-A is found primarily in the gastrointestinal tract (it accounts for only 20 of brain monoamine oxidase). Drugs that inhibit MAO (see MONOAMINE OXIDASE INHIBITORS) are used to treat depression. There is some evidence that inhibition of MAO-A, which primarily degrades serotonin and norepinephrine, may lead to greater antidepressant effects than inhibition of MAO-B, which primarily degrades dopamine.

monoamine oxidase inhibitors (**MAOIs**; **MAO inhibitors**) a group of antidepressant drugs that function by inhibiting the activity of the enzyme MONOAMINE OXIDASE in presynaptic neurons, thereby increasing the amounts of monoamine neurotransmitters (serotonin, norepinephrine, and dopamine) available for release at the presynaptic terminal. There are two categories of MAOIs: irreversible and reversible inhibitors. **Irreversible MAOIs** bind tightly to the enzyme and permanently inhibit its ability to metabolize any monoamine. This may lead to dangerous interactions with foods and beverages containing the amino acid tryptophan or TYRAMINE, which are present in many foods, particularly those produced by enzymatic action or by aging (e.g., cheeses, preserved meats and fish). A hypertensive crisis (a potentially fatal rise in blood pressure) may result from these interactions, a phenomenon that is sometimes known as the "cheese effect." Irreversible MAOIs are of two classes: hydrazines related to isoniazid (see ISOCARBOXAZID; PHENELZINE), and nonhydrazines, of which **tranylcypromine** (U.S. trade name: Parnate) is the only agent used for mental disorders in the United States. **Reversible inhibitors of monoamine oxidase** (RIMAs) do not bind irreversibly to the enzyme, thereby freeing it to take part in the metabolism of amino acids and other amines. RIMAs may be less prone to producing a hypertensive crisis, which would obviate the need for dietary restrictions on tyramine-containing foods. Examples of RIMAs are MOCLOBEMIDE and BROFAROMINE, which are available in Europe but have not yet been approved for use in the United States. The availability of other effective antidepressants lacking the drug–food interactions of the MAOIs has led to a precipitous decline in their use, particularly of the irreversible agents.

monochorial twins a set of twins that, in utero, shared the same outermost embryonic membrane (CHORION). Monochorial twins are always identical twins (MONOZYGOTIC TWINS), but identical twins are not necessarily monochorial. Also called **monochorionic twins**. Compare DICHORIAL TWINS.

monochromatic light light of a single wavelength. Monochromatic light can be produced by a laser or by a **monochromator**, which uses a prism to refract the visible spectrum and a slit to restrict the light available to the viewer to a single wavelength.

monochromatism *n.* a form of color blindness in which the eye contains only one cone PHOTOPIGMENT and is therefore unable to discriminate color: Everything appears in various shades of gray. Also called **monochromasy**. See also ACHROMATISM.

monocular *adj.* referring to one eye. Also called **uniocular**.

monocular cells see BINOCULAR CELLS.

monocular cue a cue to the perception of distance or

depth that involves only one eye. The monocular cues include LINEAR PERSPECTIVE, relative position, relative movement, CHIAROSCURO, ACCOMMODATION, and ATMOSPHERIC PERSPECTIVE. Compare BINOCULAR CUE.

monocular deprivation the deprivation of light to one eye. Compare BINOCULAR DEPRIVATION.

monocular rearing an experimental paradigm in which an animal is raised from birth with vision restricted to one eye by suturing the eyelids closed or by inserting an opaque contact lens in one eye. Monocular rearing during the CRITICAL PERIOD has profound structural and functional consequences for the developing visual system, including a shift in the OCULAR DOMINANCE of cortical neurons to favor the nonoccluded eye and a broadening of the OCULAR DOMINANCE COLUMNS corresponding to the open eye.

monocular suppression the tendency of one eye to be dominant while the other is suppressed, resulting in a failure of binocular vision.

monocular vision the use of only one eye for sight.

monodrama *n.* in GROUP PSYCHOTHERAPY, a role-playing technique in which a member of the group acts out a scene alone. The member's behavior is then evaluated by the group.

monogamy *n.* **1.** a MATING SYSTEM in which two individuals mate exclusively with each other. Recent genetic studies of paternity indicate that some offspring of male–female pairs exhibiting monogamy are not related to the father, leading to a distinction between **social monogamy**, in which there is an appearance of a close PAIR BOND, and **genetic monogamy**, in which there is exclusive mating. Many species, including human beings, display **serial monogamy**, in which there is an exclusive social bond with each of a series of sexual partners at different times during the individual's life. Compare POLYANDRY; POLYGYNANDRY; POLYGYNY. **2.** traditionally, marriage to only one spouse at a time. Compare POLYGAMY. **—monogamous** *adj.*

monogenism *n.* the belief or theory that all human beings are descended from the same two ancestors. Also called **monogenesis**; **monogeny**.

monoideism *n.* obsessive preoccupation with a single idea to the exclusion of anything else.

monomania *n.* **1.** extreme enthusiasm or zeal for a single subject or idea, often manifested as a rigid, irrational idea. See also IDÉE FIXE. **2.** an obsolete name for a pattern of abnormal behavior with reference to a single subject in an otherwise apparently normally functioning individual. **—monomaniac** *n.*

monomorphic *adj.* describing or relating to a species in which both sexes are similar in body size, coloration, or other features. Also called **sexually monomorphic**. Compare SEXUAL DIMORPHISM.

monopediomania *n.* sexual interest in and arousal by people who have only one leg.

monophagism *n.* a pathological eating behavior in which the individual habitually eats only one type of food or only one meal a day.

monophasic sleep a sleep pattern in which sleeping occurs in one long period once a day, typically at night. Both it and biphasic sleep (see POLYPHASIC SLEEP) contribute to physical and emotional health and greater alertness. See also SLEEP–WAKE CYCLE.

monoplegia *n.* paralysis of a single part of the body, for example, one arm, one leg, or one digit. **—monoplegic** *adj.*

monorchidism *n.* the condition of having only one testis in the scrotum. The second testis may be undescended (see ARRESTED TESTIS). See also CRYPTORCHIDISM; ECTOPIC TESTIS. **—monorchid** *adj., n.*

monorhinic *adj.* relating to the presentation of an ODORANT to a single nostril via an OLFACTOMETER.

monosomy *n.* the condition in which one member of a HOMOLOGOUS pair of chromosomes is absent. Monosomy is the cause of several chromosomal disorders, including GROUP G MONOSOMY. **—monosomic** *adj.*

monosomy 5p see CRI DU CHAT SYNDROME.

monosymptomatic *adj.* denoting a disorder that is characterized by a single marked symptom.

monosymptomatic circumscription a mental disorder characterized by a single symptom.

monosynaptic arc a simple NEURAL ARC that involves just two neurons with a synapse between them, as in the case of a MONOSYNAPTIC STRETCH REFLEX. Also called **two-neuron arc**. Compare POLYSYNAPTIC ARC. See also REFLEX ARC.

monosynaptic stretch reflex a reflex in which there is muscle contraction in response to sudden stretching of a tendon, involving only a sensory neuron, a motor neuron, and the synapse connecting them in the spinal cord. The KNEE-JERK REFLEX is a monosynaptic stretch reflex. See also REFLEX ARC.

monosynaptic transmission the transmission of nerve impulses involving only a single synapse, as in a MONOSYNAPTIC ARC.

monotherapy *n.* the use of a single method or approach to treat a particular disorder or PRESENTING SYMPTOM, as opposed to the use of a combination of methods. An example is the use of only PHARMACOTHERAPY, instead of pharmacotherapy and psychotherapy in combination, to treat depression.

monotic *adj.* denoting or relating to the presentation of sound to one ear only. Compare DIOTIC; MONAURAL.

monotonic *adj.* denoting a variable that progressively either increases or decreases as a second variable increases or decreases but that does not change its direction. For example, a monotonically increasing variable is one that rises as a second variable increases.

monotonic relationship any relationship between two variables in which increase or decrease in one produces a corresponding increase or decrease in the other.

monozygotic twins (**MZ twins**) twins, always of the same sex, that develop from a single fertilized ovum (zygote) that splits in the early stages of MITOSIS to produce two individuals who carry exactly the same complement of genes; that is, they are clones, with identical DNA. For every 1,000 pregnancies there are, on average, 3–4 MZ twins. Also called **identical twins**. Compare DIZYGOTIC TWINS. See also TWIN STUDIES.

Montessori method an educational system that focuses on the self-education of preschool children through the development of initiative. This is achieved by means of freedom of action, sense-perception training with objects of different shapes and colors, and development of coordination through games and exercises. The system was developed in Italy, with the first American school established in 1913. [Maria **Montessori** (1870–1952), Italian educational reformer]

mood *n.* **1.** any short-lived emotional state, usually of low intensity (e.g., a cheerful mood, an irritable mood). **2.** a disposition to respond emotionally in a particular way that may last for hours, days, or even weeks, perhaps at a low level and without the person knowing what prompted the state. Moods differ from EMOTIONS in lacking an object; for example, the emotion of anger can be aroused by an insult, but an angry mood may arise when one does not know what one is angry about or what elicited the anger. Disturbances in mood are characteristic of MOOD DISORDERS. **3.** in linguistics, a category of a verb used to identify a clause or sentence as being a statement, question, command, expression of wish, and so on. See IMPERATIVE; INDICATIVE; INTERROGATIVE; SUBJUNCTIVE.

mood-altering drugs substances that change the affective state of the individual through pharmacological action, usually without clouding of consciousness. They include certain tranquilizing, sedating, and antidepressant agents.

mood-as-information theory a theory of affect and information processing postulating that a person often uses his or her current emotional state or mood as a piece of information when making social judgments. The theory also proposes that current affective states can influence the processing strategy that people adopt when making decisions. Specifically, negative affective states indicate something problematic in the current social situation and thus encourage careful and deliberative processing of social information. In contrast, positive affective states indicate that the current social situation is satisfactory and thus encourage less effort in deliberative processing of social information. [originally developed by U.S. psychologists Norbert Schwarz (1953–), Gerald L. Clore (1939–), and their colleagues]

mood-as-resource model a theory stating that positive moods are useful to individuals, making them better able to process goal-related information, better at coping with negative stimuli, and more flexible and constructive in dealing with situational demands.

mood-congruent psychotic features delusions or hallucinations that are thematically consistent with either depressed or manic mood and may occur in severe MAJOR DEPRESSIVE EPISODES, MANIC EPISODES, or MIXED EPISODES.

mood-dependent memory a condition in which memory for some event can be recalled more readily when one is in the same emotional mood (e.g., happy or sad) as when the memory was initially formed. See also CONTEXT-SPECIFIC LEARNING; STATE-DEPENDENT MEMORY.

mood disorder in *DSM–IV–TR*, a psychiatric disorder in which the principal feature is mood disturbance. Mood disorders include the DEPRESSIVE DISORDERS (e.g., MAJOR DEPRESSIVE DISORDER, DYSTHYMIC DISORDER), the BIPOLAR DISORDERS, MOOD DISORDERS DUE TO A GENERAL MEDICAL CONDITION, SUBSTANCE-INDUCED MOOD DISORDER, and **mood disorder not otherwise specified**, which does not meet the diagnostic criteria for any of the specific mood disorders. See also AFFECTIVE DISORDER.

mood disorder due to a general medical condition in *DSM–IV–TR*, significant and persistent mood disturbance (with depressive symptoms, manic symptoms, or both) associated with a medical condition and believed to be caused directly by the physiological effects of that condition. A variety of medical conditions may cause mood disturbance, including Parkinson's disease, Huntington's disease, stroke, hyper- or hypothyroidism, some infections (e.g., hepatitis, AIDS), and certain cancers (e.g., pancreatic cancer).

mood-incongruent psychotic features delusions or hallucinations whose content does not include manic or depressed themes. They may occur in severe MAJOR DEPRESSIVE EPISODES, MANIC EPISODES, or MIXED EPISODES.

mood induction any method for inducing a negative or positive change in mood, often by selectively reminding individuals of pleasant or unpleasant aspects of their lives.

moodiness *n.* an AFFECTIVE STATE characterized by irritability or DYSPHORIA combined with sensitivity to negative interpersonal cues. **—moody** *adj.*

mood stabilizers drugs used in the treatment of cyclic mood disorders (BIPOLAR DISORDERS and CYCLOTHYMIC DISORDER). Because they reduce the symptoms of mania or manic episodes, mood stabilizers are sometimes known as **antimanics**. LITHIUM is usually the FIRST-LINE MEDICATION for bipolar I disorder, but ANTICONVULSANTS, such as VALPROIC ACID, CARBAMAZEPINE, and oxcarbazine, are becoming more commonly used for this condition and are now preferred for other cyclic disorders. The CALCIUM-CHANNEL BLOCKER verapamil is also being investigated as a mood stabilizer. Mood stabilizers are occasionally used in the management of severe affective lability found in some personality disorders (e.g., borderline personality disorder). Because of the potential for self-injurious behavior in bipolar disorders and personality disorders, great caution must be taken when prescribing medications that are potentially lethal in overdose.

mood swings oscillations in mood, particularly between feelings of happiness and sadness, ranging in intensity from normal fluctuations to cyclothymia (see CYCLOTHYMIC DISORDER) or a BIPOLAR DISORDER.

moon illusion the change in the apparent size of the moon perceived when the moon is seen on the horizon compared to high in the sky. See SIZE–DISTANCE PARADOX.

moon-phase studies research into the possible relationship between the phases of the moon and episodes of violence or mental disorder. The relationship has long been expressed in folklore, folk medicine, and language itself (e.g., the words *lunacy* and *lunatic*). Methodologically sound studies of the effects of moon phase on behavior are infrequent.

moral *adj.* **1.** relating to the distinction between right and wrong behavior. **2.** describing a behavior that is considered ethical or proper, or a person or group who adheres to a MORAL CODE. See also MORALS.

moral absolutism 1. the belief that the morality or immorality of an action can be judged according to fixed standards of right and wrong. Compare MORAL RELATIVISM; SITUATION ETHICS. **2.** in Jean PIAGET's theory, the tendency of young children in the HETERONOMOUS STAGE of moral development to interpret laws and rules as absolute. See MORAL REALISM.

moral code a set of rules concerning right and wrong behavior accepted by a society or group as binding on all members or by an individual as binding on him- or herself.

moral conduct behavior that conforms to the accepted set of values, customs, or rules of a given society or group.

moral consistency a stable, predictable pattern of moral attitudes shown by the same individual in different settings and over time.

moral determinism see ETHICAL DETERMINISM.

moral development the gradual development of an individual's concepts of right and wrong, conscience, ethical and religious values, social attitudes, and behavior. Some of the major theorists in the area of moral development are Sigmund FREUD, Jean PIAGET, Erik ERIKSON, and Lawrence KOHLBERG.

moral dilemma see ETHICAL DILEMMA.

morale *n.* the state of mind that affects behavior and performance. The U.S. Army *Field Manual on Leadership* (FM 22-100) defines morale as the mental, emotional, and spiritual state of the individual: Essentially, it is how an individual feels.

moral independence the state an older child has achieved when he or she can recognize that an act's morality may be substantially determined by its motive and other subjective considerations, rather than by its consequences. Moral independence is a mark of the AUTONOMOUS STAGE of moral development. See also MORAL RELATIVISM. Compare MORAL REALISM. [proposed by Jean PIAGET]

morality *n.* a system of beliefs or set of values relating to right conduct, against which behavior is judged to be acceptable or unacceptable.

morality of constraint the morality of young children (up to roughly age 10), which consists of an unquestioning, unchallenging obedience to the rules laid down by parents. Obedience is based on fear and on the perception that rules established by parents are fixed, eternal, and sure to be valid. See RULES OF THE GAME. Compare MORALITY OF COOPERATION. [proposed by Jean PIAGET]

morality of cooperation the morality of children aged 10–11, characterized by the perception that rules are social conventions that can be challenged and modified when concerned parties agree. The child willingly accepts rules and adheres to them on the basis of reason and not on the basis of fear or in the spirit of unquestioning obedience. See RULES OF THE GAME. Compare MORALITY OF CONSTRAINT. [proposed by Jean PIAGET]

moral judgment see ETHICAL JUDGMENT.

moral masochism in psychoanalytic theory, the unconscious need for punishment by authority figures caused by unconscious guilt arising from the repressed OEDIPUS COMPLEX. It is a nonsexual form of MASOCHISM.

moral nihilism the assertion that there exist no valid moral principles. This position is distinct from moral RELATIVISM, which merely claims that there are no universally valid moral principles. Also called **ethical nihilism**.

moral philosophy see ETHICS.

moral realism the type of thinking characteristic of younger children, who equate good behavior with obedience just as they equate the morality of an act only with its consequences. For example, 15 cups broken accidentally would be judged to be a far worse transgression than 1 cup broken mischievously, because more cups are broken. Moral realism shapes the child's thinking until the age of about 8, when the concepts of intention, motive, and extenuating circumstances begin to modify the child's early MORAL ABSOLUTISM. Compare MORAL RELATIVISM. [postulated by Jean PIAGET]

moral relativism 1. the belief that the morality or immorality of an action is determined by social custom rather than by universal or fixed standards of right and wrong. Compare MORAL ABSOLUTISM; SITUATION ETHICS. **2.** in Jean PIAGET's theory, the ability of a child in the AUTONOMOUS STAGE of moral development to consider the intention behind an act along with possible extenuating circumstances when judging its rightness or wrongness. Compare MORAL REALISM.

morals *pl. n.* the ethical values or principles that people use to guide their behavior. See also MORAL; MORALITY.

moral therapy a form of psychotherapy from the 19th century based on the belief that a person considered insane could be helped by being treated in a kindly, moral manner that assumed rationality.

moral treatment the humane and ethical treatment of psychiatric patients. Such treatment originated in the family-care program established in the GHEEL COLONY, Belgium, during the 13th century, but came to fruition in the 19th century through the efforts of Philippe Pinel (see SALPÊTRIÈRE) and Jean Esquirol (1772–1840) in France, William Tuke (1732–1822) in England, and Benjamin Rush (1745–1813), Isaac Ray (1807–1881), and Thomas Kirkbride (1809–1883) in the United States. Mechanical restraint, physical punishments, bloodletting, and insanitary conditions were gradually replaced by a comparatively comfortable, healthy environment, occupational and social activities, and reassuring talks with physicians and attendants. The THERAPEUTIC COMMUNITY of today has its roots in this movement.

moratorium *n.* in Erik ERIKSON's theory of psychosexual development, the experimental period of adolescence in which, during the task of discovering who one is as an individual separate from family of origin and as part of the broader social context, young people try out alternative roles before making permanent commitments to an IDENTITY. Adolescents who are unsuccessful at negotiating this stage risk confusion over their role in life. See also ERIKSON'S EIGHT STAGES OF DEVELOPMENT; IDENTITY VERSUS ROLE CONFUSION.

morbid *adj.* **1.** unhealthy or diseased. **2.** in psychology, abnormal or deviating from the norm.

morbid dependency excessive reliance on or need for another person or situation such that the dependent person has difficulty functioning independently. See DEPENDENCY NEEDS.

morbidity *n.* a pathological (diseased) condition or state, either organic or functional.

morbidity rate the incidence of disease, expressed as a ratio denoting the number of people in a population who are ill or have a specific disease compared with the number who are well.

morbidity risk in EPIDEMIOLOGY, the statistical chance that an individual will develop a certain disease or disorder. The probability is often expressed in terms of risk factors, using 1.0 as a base: The larger the number, the greater the morbidity risk.

morbid jealousy see DELUSIONAL JEALOUSY.

morbid obesity OBESITY that causes disease. The excess body weight begins first to interfere with agility and then day-to-day movement. As the obesity increases, the massive weight of tissue on the chest interferes with breathing. Affected people gradually develop HYPOXEMIA (decreased blood oxygen) and SLEEP APNEA (periodic cessation of breathing while asleep), which may result in chronic fatigue and SOMNOLENCE and, eventually, high blood pressure, pulmonary hypertension, myocarditis, right-sided heart failure, and ultimately death. See also BODY MASS INDEX.

Morel's syndrome see STEWART–MOREL SYNDROME.

mores *pl. n.* social customs and usages that are accepted by members of a culture or population.

Morgan's canon see LLOYD MORGAN'S CANON.

moria *n.* an obsessive or morbid desire to joke, as in some cases of DEMENTIA, particularly when the humor is inappropriate. See also GALLOWS HUMOR.

Morita therapy a therapy for SHINKEISHITSU introduced in Japan in the early 20th century. Classical inpatient Morita therapy consists of four stages: (a) absolute isolated bed rest for 7 days; (b) light work; (c) intensive work; and (d) preparation for daily living, with the objective of teaching patients to accept their lives the way they are, a process called **arugamama**. [Shoma **Morita** (1874–1938), Japanese psychiatrist]

morning-after pill a popular name for postcoital, or emergency, oral contraception. It consists of two doses of a progestin, or a combined formulation of a progestin and an estrogen, taken at spaced intervals no later than 72 hours after intercourse.

morning erection an erection of the penis that occurs during the last period of REM SLEEP before awakening and is not necessarily related to sexual dreaming.

morning-glory seeds seeds of the plant *Rivea corymbosa*, which contain psychoactive agents and have been used as HALLUCINOGENS, notably in 16th-century Mexico.

morning sickness nausea and vomiting experienced by some (but not all) women during the first months of pregnancy or throughout the entire pregnancy. Although morning sickness usually occurs soon after arising in the morning, some women have the symptoms throughout the day. Also called **nausea gravidarum**.

moron *n.* an obsolete name for a person with MILD MENTAL RETARDATION. [first described by Henry GODDARD]

Moro reflex a reflex in which a newborn infant, when startled, throws out the arms, extends the fingers, and often quickly brings the arms back together as if clutching or embracing. In normal, healthy babies, the Moro reflex disappears during the 1st year. Also called **Moro response**. See also STARTLE RESPONSE. [Ernst **Moro** (1874–1951), German physician]

-morph *suffix* form or structure (e.g., ECTOMORPH).

morpheme *n.* in linguistic analysis, a unit of meaning that cannot be analyzed into smaller such units. For example, the word *books* is composed of two morphemes, *book* and the suffix *-s* signifying a plural noun. See BOUND MORPHEME; FREE MORPHEME. **—morphemic** *adj.*

morphine *n.* the primary active ingredient in OPIUM, first synthesized in 1806 and widely used as an analgesic and sedative, especially in terminally ill cancer patients (see OPIATES; OPIOID ANALGESIC). Prolonged administration or abuse can lead to dependence and to withdrawal symptoms on cessation. The substance is 10 times as potent as opium. See OPIOID ABUSE; OPIOID DEPENDENCE; OPIOID INTOXICATION; OPIOID WITHDRAWAL.

morpho- (**morph-**) *combining form* form or structure.

morphogenesis *n.* the development of the form and structure of an organism. **—morphogenetic** or **morphogenic** *adj.*

morphological index the index or relationship based on body proportions that describes a particular body build.

morphology *n.* **1.** the branch of biology concerned with the forms and structures of organisms. **2.** the branch of linguistics that investigates the form and structure of words. It is particularly concerned with the regular patterns of INFLECTION and word formation in a language. With SYNTAX, morphology is one of the two traditional subdivisions of GRAMMAR. **—morphological** *adj.*

morphophilia *n.* interest in sexual partners whose body characteristics (e.g., height, weight, or skin and hair color) are very different from one's own.

morphophoneme *n.* an abstract phonological unit used to represent the set of PHONEMES that constitute the ALLOMORPHS of a single MORPHEME.

morphophonemics *n.* a branch of linguistics that analyzes the interaction between MORPHOLOGY and PHONOLOGY, especially regarding the use of different ALLOMORPHS of the same morpheme in different phonological contexts. **—morphophonemic** *adj.*

Morris water maze a device used to test animal spatial learning, consisting of a water-filled tank with a platform hidden underwater. An animal is placed in the water and can escape only by finding and climbing on the hidden platform. Typically a variety of external cues are provided for spatial reference. The Morris water maze is often used to evaluate the effects of brain lesions or drug manipulations on spatial learning and memory. [devised in 1981 by Richard G. M. **Morris**, British neuroscientist]

morsicatio buccarum habitual biting of the inside of the cheeks (buccal mucosa), sometimes causing lesions or the formation of white excess tissue.

morsicatio labiorum see LIP BITING.

mortality *n.* **1.** the death rate in a population. **2.** see ATTRITION.

mortality salience the cognitive accessibility of thoughts about the inevitability of one's death. Such thoughts are believed by some theorists to be a motivating force behind a diverse set of actions designed to defend oneself or one's social group.

mort douce primarily in literary contexts, a peaceful death (French, literally "sweet death") in which all tensions are released in a manner reminiscent of the fulfillment of sexual intercourse. **Petit mort** (little or quiet death) makes use of the same analogy, but with a less dramatic conclusion. By contrast, **le grand mort** (the great death) of Elizabethan poets visualizes death as the ultimate tumultuous orgasm.

mortido *n.* in psychoanalytic theory, the energy of the DEATH INSTINCT and counterpart to the LIBIDO. See also DESTRUDO. [defined in 1936 by Austrian psychoanalyst Paul Federn (1872–1950)]

morula *n.* an early stage of embryological development, extending from the first CLEAVAGE of the zygote until the BLASTULA is formed by further divisions of daughter cells.

mosaicism *n.* a condition of genetic abnormality in which an individual is made up of two or more different cell lines derived from a single zygote. In a typical case, a mosaic individual may have one normal cell line and another with an extra chromosome, such as 45,X/46,XX. The cell lines may differ within tissues and organs of the same person. Mosaicism is associated with DOWN SYNDROME and TURNER'S SYNDROME.

mosaic test a PROJECTIVE TECHNIQUE in which the subject, usually a child, is asked to "make anything you like" out of about 400 pieces of different colors and shapes. Mosaic materials are also used in some intelligence tests.

mossy fiber any of certain nerve fibers that extend from the DENTATE GYRUS to the HIPPOCAMPUS, where they synapse in area CA3.

most comfortable loudness (**MCL**) the sound level at which speech is most comfortable for an individual.

mother archetype in Carl JUNG'S ANALYTIC PSYCHOLOGY, the primordial image of the generative and sustaining mother figure that has occurred repeatedly in various cultural concepts and myths since ancient times and is located within the COLLECTIVE UNCONSCIOUS. See also ARCHETYPE; MAGNA MATER.

motherese *n.* the distinctive form of speech used by parents and other caregivers when speaking to infants and young children. It is characterized by grammatically simple and phonologically clear utterances, often delivered in a high-pitched sing-song intonation.

mother figure 1. a person who occupies the mothering role in relation to a child. **2.** in psychoanalytic theory, a person onto whom the patient transfers feelings and attitudes that he or she had toward the real mother. Also called **mother substitute**.

mothering *n.* the process of nurturing, caring for, and protecting a child by a mother or maternal figure.

mother love the protective and possessive affection that a mother displays toward her child. Although it may be instinctive, it is also reinforced by pressures of the social group, which expects the mother to show tender feelings toward her offspring.

Mothers Against Drunk Driving (**MADD**) an organization whose mission is to stop drunk driving and to support its victims. It was known as **Mothers Against Drunk Drivers** until 1984. See SELF-HELP GROUP.

mother–son incest sexual activity between mother and son, which is rarer than FATHER–DAUGHTER INCEST. See also PHAEDRA COMPLEX.

mother substitute 1. see MOTHER FIGURE. **2.** see MOTHER SURROGATE.

mother surrogate a substitute for an individual's natural mother (e.g., a sister, father, friend, teacher, or foster mother) who assumes the basic functions of the biological mother. Harry HARLOW's classic research with young monkeys demonstrated that monkeys preferred a mother surrogate covered in cloth to one that was simply a wire frame, even though the latter was the source of food. Also called **mother substitute**; **surrogate mother**.

motility *n.* **1.** the capacity to move either voluntarily or involuntarily (as in sleepwalking). **2.** the style and speed of movement. See also MOBILITY. **—motile** *adj.*

motility disorder any abnormality of motion or movement, particularly with respect to the digestive tract (e.g., **esophageal motility disorder** or **gastrointestinal motility disorder**).

motility psychosis an obsolescent name for a BIPOLAR DISORDER that has as a prominent feature extreme PSYCHOMOTOR AGITATION or PSYCHOMOTOR RETARDATION.

motion aftereffect (**MAE**) the perception that a stationary object or scene moves following prolonged fixation of a moving stimulus. The aftereffect of illusory movement is in the opposite direction to the movement of the stimulus that induced the effect. Also called **kinetic aftereffect**.

motion agnosia the inability to perceive motion in a visual stimulus, as a result of brain damage to EXTRASTRIATE VISUAL AREAS. Patients with motion agnosia will report that the level of water in a cup does not rise, even though they are aware that water is being poured into the cup and they eventually notice that the cup overflows.

motion and time study see TIME AND MOTION STUDY.

motion detection the ability to detect movement. Many cells in the visual system act as motion detectors, and some are also sensitive to the direction of movement.

motion economy a set of principles for the efficient performance of industrial operations. Motion economy was developed largely by U.S. engineer Frank Gilbreth (1868–1924) and his wife, U.S. engineer and psychologist Lillian Moller Gilbreth (1878–1972). Its recommendations include: simultaneous use of both hands moving in opposite directions; use of continuous, curved movements rather than straight line motions; use of the fewest movements possible; use of such items as jigs and fixtures to relieve hands of unnecessary work as "holding devices"; arrangement of work to permit an easy, natural rhythm; and arrangement of work to avoid long reaches.

motion in limine a formal proposal to a court, usually made before a trial begins (Latin *in limine*, "preliminary"), requesting that certain statements, questions, or evidence not be introduced into the proceedings.

motion parallax the interrelated movements of elements in a scene that can occur when the observer moves relative to the scene. Motion parallax is a DEPTH CUE.

motion sickness a type of discomfort marked by nausea, dizziness, headache, pallor, cold sweats, and in some cases vomiting and prostration. The cause is irregular or abnormal motion that disturbs the normal sense of balance maintained by the semicircular canals of the inner ear. The condition may be aggravated or initiated by an emotional disturbance, such as anxiety or grief. Also called **kinesia**.

motivated forgetting a memory lapse motivated by a desire to avoid a disagreeable recollection. It is one of the cognitive mechanisms that has been suggested as a cause of delayed memories of childhood trauma.

motivation *n.* **1.** the impetus that gives purpose or direction to human or animal behavior and operates at a conscious or unconscious level (see UNCONSCIOUS MOTIVATION). Motives are frequently divided into (a) physiological, primary, or organic motives, such as hunger, thirst, and need for sleep, and (b) personal, social, or secondary motives, such as affiliation, competition, and individual interests and goals. An important distinction must also be drawn between internal motivating forces and external factors, such as rewards or punishments, that can encourage or discourage certain behaviors. See EXTRINSIC MOTIVATION; INTRINSIC MOTIVATION. **2.** in CONDITIONING, the variables, collectively, that alter the effectiveness of REINFORCERS. Compare ESTABLISHING OPERATION. **3.** a person's willingness to exert physical or mental effort in pursuit of a goal or outcome. See WORK MOTIVATION. **4.** the act or process of encouraging others to exert themselves in pursuit of a group or organizational goal. The ability to motivate followers is an important function of LEADERSHIP. **—motivate** *vb.* **—motivated** *adj.* **—motivational** *adj.*

motivational enhancement therapy a transtheoretical treatment, based on the STAGES OF CHANGE, that matches clients to interventions on the basis of individual differences in readiness to change. This treatment was initially applied to substance abuse but has now generalized to other problem behaviors.

motivational factor any physiological or psychological factor that stimulates, maintains, and directs behavior. Examples are BASIC PHYSIOLOGICAL NEEDS, interests, and EXTRINSIC REWARDS.

motivational hierarchy see MASLOW'S MOTIVATIONAL HIERARCHY.

motivational selectivity an explanation for the different ways that an event or object may be perceived by different people based on the influence of individual motives on cognitive processes. See SELECTIVE PERCEPTION.

motivational styles a way of classifying people with regard to their learning and performance, in which categories are based on individual differences in motivation, including but not limited to intrinsic–extrinsic motivation, mastery orientation, and competitiveness. The notion of motivational styles is particularly used in education, business, and sport to help people recognize both strengths and weaknesses and develop strategies to improve learning and performance.

motivation research in consumer psychology, research that uses clinical, intensive, and qualitative approaches to reveal the true motives behind the decisions of individuals to purchase a product. Motivation research also is employed to determine why consumers may refuse to buy a certain product.

motivators *pl. n.* in the two-factor theory of WORK MOTIVATION proposed by U.S. clinical psychologist Frederick Herzberg (1923–2000), those aspects of the working situation that can increase satisfaction and motivation. Motivators involve the work itself rather than the work context and are increased by means of JOB ENRICHMENT and vertical loading (see JOB ENLARGEMENT). Compare HYGIENE FACTORS.

motive *n.* **1.** a specific physiological or psychological state of arousal that directs an organism's energies toward a goal. See MOTIVATION. **2.** a reason offered as an explanation for or cause of an individual's behavior.

motoneuron *n.* see MOTOR NEURON.

motor *adj.* involving, producing, or referring to muscular movements.

motor agraphia a writing disorder resulting from impairment of muscular coordination in the hand.

motor amimia see AMIMIA.

motor amusia a form of AMUSIA in which a person loses the ability to reproduce melodies as a result of a cortical lesion. An individual may be able to recognize melodies but can no longer sing or play them, even though he or she may have studied music extensively.

motor aphasia a form of APHASIA in which, as a result of brain damage, a person is unable to perform specific muscular movements involved in speaking.

motor aprosodia an inability to produce the emotional inflections of language, that is, to express the normal rhythm, pitch, and "melody" of speech. This is most often due to damage in the right frontal lobe of the brain. Compare SENSORY APROSODIA.

motor area an area of the MOTOR CORTEX that, when stimulated, produces movements of skeletal muscles in various parts of the body. It has SOMATOTOPIC ORGANIZATION, with individual neurons controlling a specific movement direction of an associated body part that might involve coordinated action of several muscles. Also called **Brodmann's area 4**; **primary motor cortex**.

motor behavior 1. aspects of human movement that include MOTOR CONTROL, MOTOR DEVELOPMENT, and MOTOR LEARNING. **2.** see MOTOR FUNCTION.

motor control the influence of neurophysiological factors on human movement.

motor conversion symptoms one of two types of symptoms of CONVERSION DISORDER, the other being SENSORY CONVERSION SYMPTOMS. Examples of motor conversion symptoms include impaired coordination and balance, paralysis or weakness confined to a specific area of the body, difficulty in swallowing, aphonia (loss of voice), and urinary retention.

motor coordination the cooperative action of reflexive (or involuntary) and voluntary movements to carry out complex activities.

motor cortex the region of the frontal lobe of the brain responsible for the control of voluntary movement. It is divided into two parts. The **primary motor cortex**, or MOTOR AREA, is the main source of neurons in the CORTICOSPINAL TRACT. The **secondary** (or **nonprimary**) **motor cortex**, made up of the PREMOTOR AREA and the SUPPLEMENTARY MOTOR AREA, is specialized for planning upcoming movements and learning new movements. Lesions in the primary motor cortex due to stroke or traumatic injury usually cause initial paralysis that may improve to a condition involving weakness and poor muscle tone. Lesions in the secondary motor cortex usually cause complex disruptions in MOTOR PLANNING for complex movements (see APRAXIA). Also called **motor strip**.

motor development the changes in motor skills that occur over an entire life span, which reflect the development of muscular coordination and control and are also affected by personal characteristics, the environment, and interactions of these two factors.

motor disorder loss of the ability to perform simple or complex acts or skills because of temporary or permanent damage to tissues in the premotor or MOTOR AREAS of the central nervous system. The cause of the damage may be a congenital or inherited defect, injury, surgical excision, or a psychochemical factor.

motor disturbance any disturbance of motor behavior, such as hyperactivity, retarded activity, automatism, repetitive movements, rigid posture, grimacing, or tics.

motor dominance the controlling influence of one cerebral hemisphere shown in motor activity, such as writing or throwing a ball.

motor end plate the terminus of the axon of a motor neuron, opposite the cell membrane of the muscle fiber it innervates. See NEUROMUSCULAR JUNCTION.

motor equivalence the ability to use different movements, produced by either the same or different parts of the body, to perform a task under different conditions. For example, the task of writing one's name may be performed (a) on paper, with a pen held in the hand, by moving the fingers and wrist; (b) on a blackboard, with chalk held in the hand, by moving the arm; or (c) in the sand, using a toe, by moving the leg.

motor evoked potential a type of EVOKED POTENTIAL associated with motor neurons and motor cortex. For example, activity in spinal motor neurons may be studied by directly stimulating motor areas in the brain (see TRANSCRANIAL MAGNETIC STIMULATION) and observing the evoked potential in the spinal cord. Compare SENSORY EVOKED POTENTIAL.

motor function any activity that results from stimulation of MOTOR NEURONS, including glandular activity as well as reflexes and voluntary and involuntary muscle contractions. Also called **motor behavior**.

motor-function homunculus the SOMATOTOPIC ORGANIZATION of the MOTOR CORTEX as originally mapped by Canadian neurosurgeon Wilder Penfield (1891–1976). Within this mapping, the size of the brain region associated with a body part reflects the complexity of the activities carried out with that part of the body rather than its size.

motor habit a habit described in terms of movements.

motor imitation the ability, particularly striking in infants and children, to imitate movements, facial expressions, and so forth after viewing them and without practice.

motor impersistence an effect observed in some individuals with neurological damage in which the individual is able to initiate an activity (e.g., tongue protrusion) or assume a posture but, presumably because of a motor dysfunction, cannot maintain persistent control of the act or posture.

motor learning the process of acquiring and perfecting motor skills and movements, either simple acts or complex sequences of movements, which comes about through varying types of practice, experience, or other learning situations. See MOTOR BEHAVIOR; MOTOR CONTROL; MOTOR DEVELOPMENT.

motor manipulation see CURIOSITY.

motor memory the capacity to remember previously executed movements, such as the steps of a dance or the body movements of an exercise. See also MULTISTORE MODEL OF MEMORY; VERBAL MEMORY; VISUAL MEMORY.

motor milestones the significant achievements in MOTOR DEVELOPMENT that occur during an infant's first 2 years. Although individual children vary, on average infants will (a) support their head while prone at 3 months; (b) support their head in other positions at 4 months; (c) sit with props at 5 months; (d) sit supported by their hands and reach with one hand at 6 months; (e) pick up small items, using thumb opposition, and stand if holding onto a railing at 8 months; (f) creep, pull to a standing position, and take side steps while holding onto a support at 10 months; (g) walk alone, throw a ball, and walk backwards, sideways, upstairs, and downstairs with assistance at 16 months; and (h) run and walk up and down steps easily or with minimal assistance at 24 months. See also DEVELOPMENTAL SEQUENCE.

motor neglect underutilization of or failure to use motor functions on one side of the body despite the presence of normal strength and motor control. See NEGLECT.

motor nerve an efferent nerve that terminates in a muscle or gland.

motor neuron a neuron whose axon connects directly to muscle fibers. Because motor neurons are the final stage of output from the nervous system and are the only means of stimulating muscle fibers, they are known as the **final common path**. Also called **motoneuron**.

motor neuron disease any one of a group of degenerative disorders of the LOWER MOTOR NEURONS or both the lower and UPPER MOTOR NEURONS, marked by progressive weakness and wasting of skeletal muscles and paralysis. This group of disorders includes several forms, but—especially in the United States—the term often is applied specifically to AMYOTROPHIC LATERAL SCLEROSIS.

motor neuron lesion any damage to a MOTOR NEURON, particularly if it involves the cell body.

motor neuron pool a collection of MOTOR NEURONS whose axons all connect to the same muscle, although the motor neurons may be scattered through a few levels of the spinal cord.

motor overflow a condition in which intentional motor behavior in one muscle group is accompanied by unintentional movement in another muscle group as a result of a brain injury or disorder. For instance, while performing a fine motor task with the right hand, the left hand may move as well. Also called **synkinesia**; **synkinesis**.

motor pathway a NEURAL PATHWAY that originates in the brain or brainstem and descends down the spinal cord to control the motor neurons. The motor pathways can control posture, reflexes, and muscle tone, as well as the conscious voluntary movements associated with the MOTOR SYSTEM.

motor planning the ability of the brain to conceive, organize, and carry out a sequence of unfamiliar actions.

motor primacy theory the concept that body mechanisms associated with motor nerve functions develop before sensory nerve mechanisms.

motor process theory of imagery a theory to explain how IMAGERY can improve performance. It states that, during imagery, the brain sends impulses to the muscles. These impulses are identical to those that cause muscle contraction with movement but are of lower intensity; the neural pathways are thereby strengthened. Also called **ideomotor principle**; **psychoneuromuscular theory**.

motor program a stored representation, resulting from MOTOR PLANNING and refined through practice, that is used to produce a coordinated movement. Motor programs store the accumulated experience underlying SKILL at a task. See also GENERALIZED MOTOR PROGRAM.

motor root see VENTRAL ROOT.

Motor scale see BAYLEY SCALES OF INFANT AND TODDLER DEVELOPMENT.

motor set preparatory adjustments or readiness to make a certain response or begin an activity, for example, as prompted by "Ready, Set, Go!" at the start of a foot race.

motor speech disorder any of several communication disorders arising from inaccurate production of speech sounds because of lack of strength or coordination of the muscles involved in speaking, as occurs in CEREBELLAR ATAXIA or PARKINSON'S DISEASE.

motor strip see MOTOR CORTEX.

motor system the complex of skeletal muscles, neural connections with muscle tissues, and structures of the central nervous system associated with motor functions. Also called **neuromuscular system**.

motor tension a state of muscle tension in which the individual is restless and tires easily. This symptom is associated with GENERALIZED ANXIETY DISORDER.

motor test any test designed to measure motor skills, ranging from GROSS MOTOR to FINE MOTOR manipulation.

motor theory of speech perception the view that speech perception relies on the processes that are used in speech production, such that listeners interpret a spoken message by unconsciously computing what motor operations would be required to produce that sequence of sounds. The theory was advanced as an explanation of CATEGORICAL PERCEPTION in the processing of speech sounds.

motor theory of thought a concept popularized by behaviorists in the 1920s that motor-system responses are controlled by conditioned-reflex links between the MOTOR CORTEX and SENSORY AREA. The theory was subsequently challenged by investigators who noted a lack of physiological and anatomical evidence to support it. Also called **motor theory of consciousness**.

motor tract the nerve fibers that convey signals from the higher centers of the brain to the spinal cord.

motor unit a group of muscle fibers that respond collectively and simultaneously because they are connected by nerve endings to a single motor neuron.

mouches volantes see MUSCAE VOLITANTES.

mountain-climber's syndrome (**mountain sickness**) see ALTITUDE SICKNESS; ACUTE MOUNTAIN SICKNESS.

mourning *n.* the process of feeling or expressing grief following the death of a loved one, or the period during which this occurs. It typically involves feelings of apathy and dejection, loss of interest in the outside world, and diminution in activity and initiative. These reactions are similar to depression, but are less persistent and are not considered pathological. See also BEREAVEMENT.

mouse-movement adapter an adaptive device for a computer mouse that is used to control the movement of the pointer on the screen. The device is designed for use by individuals with motor disabilities who are not able to manipulate a standard computer mouse manually.

mouthstick *n.* a type of PHYSICAL EXTENSION DEVICE consisting of a piece fitting into the mouth of the user that is attached to an extension with a tip that may press against, grasp, pull, or point to an object.

movement *n.* a brief, unitary activity of a muscle or body part. A movement is less complex than an ACT.

movement chaining the generation of complex movement sequences when the occurrence of, or feedback from, each movement in the sequence acts as the stimulus to initiate the next. [originally described by British neurophysiologist Sir Charles Sherrington (1857–1952) in relation to sequences of reflexes]

movement conformity aligning one's values, judgments, or behaviors with those of a social or cultural movement. See CONFORMITY.

movement disorder any abnormality in motor processes, relating primarily to posture, coordination, or locomotion.

movement education a technique designed to help individuals develop or improve motor skills, creative expression, and self-awareness through physical movement. See also MOVEMENT THERAPY.

movement illusion an illusion that an object is in motion when it is not.

movement learning see MOTOR LEARNING; RESPONSE LEARNING.

movement perspective a visual ILLUSION produced by the relative distance of moving objects. For example, a nearby bird flying at 50 kmh (c. 30 mph) may appear to be traveling faster than a jet airliner in the distant sky moving at 960 kmh (nearly 600 mph).

movement sense see KINESTHESIS.

movement-sensitive retinal cells cells, most commonly found in the retinas of lower animals, that respond to various specific movements across the visual field. Examples include the bug-detector cells of amphibians, which respond best to small, dark, moving spots, and cells that adapt quickly to objects moving in a particular direction.

movement therapy a therapeutic technique in which individuals use rhythmic exercises and bodily movements to achieve greater body awareness and social interaction and enhance their psychological and physical functioning. See also DANCE THERAPY.

moving-edge detector any of the cells in the visual system that respond best to a dark-light border moved through the receptive field. A particular speed and direction of movement may be required to elicit the optimum response from a moving-edge detector. See also FEATURE DETECTOR.

moving-window technique in studies of reading, an experimental technique in which the words on a page are covered up except for a limited number that can be viewed through a "window," which moves forward through the text at a set rate.

Mowat sensor an aid to AMBULATION for individuals with visual impairment. It is a lightweight, hand-held device, similar to a flashlight, that detects objects by sending out brief pulses of high-frequency sound (ultrasound). The device vibrates when it detects an object, and users can tell how close they are to the object by the rate of vibration. The device ignores everything but the closest object within the beam.

Mowrer, O. Hobart (1907–1982) U.S. psychologist. Mowrer earned his doctorate from Johns Hopkins University in 1932, studying under Knight Dunlap (1873–1949). After several years at Yale University's Institute of Human Relations and at Harvard University, in 1948 he joined the faculty at the University of Illinois, where he remained until his retirement. Mowrer is best known for his contributions to theories of learning and language accuisition. His TWO-FACTOR THEORY of learning combined principles of PAVLOVIAN CONDITIONING with those of OPERANT CONDITIONING, both being necessary to explain such phenomena as avoidance of a feared object. Mowrer was the first psychologist to explain language acquisition via elementary principles of conditioning, which he did in a 1954 *American Psychologist* paper, "The Psychologist Looks at Language." Mowrer was also important in the field of applied psychology, inventing an early BIOFEEDBACK device to stop bed-wetting in children and writing on topics in psychopathology and psychotherapy. Among his most important publications were *Frustration and Aggression* (1939), *Learning Theory and the Symbolic Processes* (1960), *Learning Theory and Behavior* (1960), and *The New Group Therapy* (1964). Mowrer was president of the American Psychological Association in 1954.

Mowrer's theory see TWO-FACTOR THEORY.

MPI abbreviation for Maudsley Personality Inventory. See EYSENCK PERSONALITY INVENTORY.

mPOA abbreviation for MEDIAL PREOPTIC AREA.

MPS 1. abbreviation for MUCOPOLYSACCHARIDOSIS. **2.** abbreviation for myofascial pain syndrome (see CHRONIC MYOFASCIAL PAIN).

MPTP *n.* 1-*m*ethyl-4-*p*henyl-1,2,3,6-*t*etrahydro*p*yridine: a by-product of heroin synthesis that is used experimentally to induce symptoms of Parkinson's disease in laboratory animals. It was discovered accidentally in 1976 when it was synthesized and injected by a recreational drug user who was attempting to produce an analog of meperidine (Demerol). This individual developed acute symptoms of Parkinson's disease, as did other users of the drug. Autopsy revealed massive degeneration of dopamine-containing neurons in the NIGROSTRIATAL TRACT. MPTP is not in itself neurotoxic (damaging to nerve tissue), but it is converted to the methylphenylpyridinium ion (MPP^+), a potent neurotoxin at dopaminergic neurons, by the enzyme MONOAMINE OXIDASE B.

MR abbreviation for MENTAL RETARDATION.

MRH abbreviation for Müllerian regression hormone (see MÜLLERIAN-INHIBITING HORMONE).

MRI abbreviation for MAGNETIC RESONANCE IMAGING.

mRNA abbreviation for MESSENGER RNA.

MRT abbreviation for MODIFIED RHYME TEST.

MS abbreviation for MULTIPLE SCLEROSIS.

MSE abbreviation for MENTAL STATUS EXAMINATION.

MSH abbreviation for MELANOCYTE-STIMULATING HORMONE.

MSH2 a germ-line mutation located on the short arm of chromosome 2 and associated with hereditary nonpolyposis colon cancer (HNPCC) and Lynch syndrome.

MSIS abbreviation for MULTISTATE INFORMATION SYSTEM.

MSLT abbreviation for MULTIPLE SLEEP LATENCY TEST.

MSP abbreviation for MUNCHAUSEN SYNDROME BY PROXY.

MSQ abbreviation for MINNESOTA SATISFACTION QUESTIONNAIRE.

MST abbreviation for MCCARTHY SCREENING TEST.

MSUD abbreviation for MAPLE-SUGAR URINE DISEASE.

mucocutaneous skin the hairless skin of the lips. This type of skin is also found at other junctions between the inside and outside of the body (e.g., the nasal and anal orifices).

mucopolysaccharidosis (**MPS**) *n.* (*pl.* **mucopolysaccharidoses**) any of various metabolic disorders, classified into six groups (I–VI), that are marked by excess mucopolysaccharide—glycosaminoglycan (GAG), a complex carbohydrate—in the tissues. Certain forms of the disease are associated with mental retardation. See BETA-GLUCURONIDASE DEFICIENCY; HUNTER'S SYNDROME; HURLER'S SYNDROME; MAROTEAUX–LAMY SYNDROME; SANFILIPPO'S SYNDROME.

mucous colitis see IRRITABLE BOWEL SYNDROME.

mucous ophthalmia see OPHTHALMIA.

muina *n.* see BILIS.

muliebrity *n.* the state or condition of being a woman (from Latin *mulier*, "woman") or the qualities considered to be characteristic of women.

Müller fibers elongated glial cells that traverse and support all the layers of the retina. Also called **Müller cells**. [Heinrich **Müller** (1820–1864), German anatomist]

Müllerian ducts paired ducts that occur in a mammalian embryo and develop into female reproductive structures (fallopian tubes, uterus, and upper vagina) if testes are not present in the embryo. Compare WOLFFIAN DUCT. [Johannes **Müller** (1801–1858), German anatomist]

Müllerian-inhibiting hormone (**MIH**) a hormone produced by the testes early in prenatal development that inhibits feminization of the fetus by preventing the Müllerian ducts from differentiating into the female sex organs. Also called **anti-Müllerian hormone (AMH)**; **Müllerian-inhibiting substance (MIS)**; **Müllerian regression hormone (MRH)**.

Müllerian mimicry a form of MIMICRY in which two or more species, each of which is toxic or potentially harmful, have similar body shape or coloration. For predators, a single experience with a member of one of these species can lead to learned avoidance of all similar-looking animals, conferring protection on all the mimetic species. [Johann Friedrich Theodor **Müller** (1822–1897), German zoologist]

Müller-Lyer illusion a GEOMETRIC ILLUSION in which a difference is perceived in the length of a line depending upon whether arrowheads at either end are pointing toward each other or away from each other. Also called **arrowhead illusion**. [first described in 1889 by Franz **Müller-Lyer** (1857–1916), German psychiatrist]

Müller–Urban method a psychophysical procedure for estimating the DIFFERENCE THRESHOLD for data obtained using the METHOD OF CONSTANT STIMULI. It is based on the assumption that the best measure of the threshold is the median of the best fitting ogive (S-shaped function) for the distribution. [Georg Elias **Müller** (1850–1934), German experimental psychologist and philosopher; Frank M. **Urban**, 20th-century U.S. psychologist]

Müller–Urban weights a psychophysical procedure for determining the best value of *h* (the measure of PRECISION OF PROCESS) by fitting observations to the normal curve. Also called **Müller–Urban weighting**; **Urban's weights**. [Georg **Müller** and Frank M. **Urban**]

multa loca tenens principle a rule stating that if a drug can substitute for or mimic one action of a natural physiological agent, it may be able to simulate other natural functions as well. Because of such multiple effects, the administered drug may compete for receptors, enzymes, and other physiological targets.

multiattribute-utility analysis a method of using the ratings of judges to quantify the social utility or value of a given program. Dimensions relevant to program outcomes are ranked and then weighted in terms of their comparative social importance; each program is scored on all social-value dimensions. This form of analysis enables comparisons of different social programs to be made.

multiaxial classification a system of classifying mental disorders according to several categories of factors, for example, social and cultural influences, as well as clinical symptoms. DSM–IV–TR uses multiaxial classification, which takes account of the many factors involved in the etiology of these disorders and enables a more comprehensive clinical assessment to be made. See AXIS.

multicollinearity *n.* in MULTIPLE REGRESSION, a state that occurs when the INDEPENDENT (PREDICTOR) VARIABLES are extremely highly interrelated, making it difficult to determine separate effects on the DEPENDENT VARIABLE.

multicultural counseling 1. psychotherapies that take into account not only the increasing racial and ethnic diversity of clients in many countries but also diversity in spirituality, sexual orientation, ability and disability, and social class and economics; the potential cultural bias (e.g., racism, sexism) of the practitioner; the history of oppressed and marginalized groups; diversity within diversity; acculturation and issues involving living in two worlds; and the politics of power as they affect clients. Also called **cross-cultural counseling**; **multicultural therapy**. Compare TRANSCULTURAL PSYCHOTHERAPY. **2.** any form of therapy that assesses, understands, and evaluates a client's behavior in the multiplicity of cultural contexts (e.g., ethnic, national, demographic, social, and economic) in which that behavior was learned and is displayed.

multicultural education a progressive approach to education that emphasizes social justice, equality in education, and understanding and awareness of the traditions and language of other cultures and nationalities. Multicultural programs involve two or more ethnic or cultural groups and are designed to help participants define their own ethnic or cultural identity and to appreciate that of others. The purpose is to promote inclusiveness and cultural pluralism in society.

multiculturalism *n.* **1.** the quality or condition of a society in which different ethnic and cultural groups have equal status but each maintains its own identity, characteristics, and mores. **2.** the promotion or celebration of cultural diversity within a society. Also called **cultural pluralism**. Compare CULTURAL MONISM. **—multicultural** *adj.*

multicultural therapy see MULTICULTURAL COUNSELING.

multidetermination *n.* the interaction of several different factors in the etiology of a disorder (e.g., biological, psychological, environmental). **—multidetermined** *adj.*

multidetermined behavior the concept that human behavior is influenced by the interaction of multiple factors, past and present. In general, the major influences are genetic, environmental, physiological, and psychological.

multidimensional *adj.* **1.** describing any form of analysis in which factors or variables are represented on more than one dimension. **2.** of scales or measures, having a number of different dimensions. **3.** having many aspects that may engender many points of view. **4.** complex. Compare UNIDIMENSIONAL.

Multidimensional Scale for Rating Psychiatric Patients see INPATIENT MULTIDIMENSIONAL PSYCHIATRIC SCALE.

multidimensional scaling (**MDS**) a scaling method that represents perceived similarities among stimuli by arranging similar stimuli in spatial proximity to one another, while disparate stimuli are represented far apart from one another. Multidimensional scaling is an alternative to FACTOR ANALYSIS for dealing with large multidimensional matrices of data or stimuli.

multidisciplinary approach see INTERDISCIPLINARY APPROACH.

multidisciplinary team a group of individuals, each with expertise in a different field of study, who are brought together to examine a subject area or to assist people.

multifactorial inheritance inheritance of a trait, such as height or predisposition to a certain disease, that is determined not by a single gene but by many different genes acting cumulatively. Such traits show continuous, rather than discrete, variation among the members of a given population and are often significantly influenced by environmental factors, such as nutritional status. Also called **polygenic inheritance**.

multifactorial model a model of inheritance positing that the genetic and environmental causes of a trait constitute a single continuous variable, the **liability**, and if that liability is exceeded, the trait will manifest itself.

multigenerational transmission process the passing on of psychological problems, primarily anxiety, over several generations through family relationships. A central concept in FAMILY SYSTEMS THEORY, the principal process involves the unconscious passing on of a higher level of anxiety, which overrides adaptive thinking and behavior, to members in each succeeding generation. Interventions to change this transmission involve charting family relationships and coaching individuals on how to interact with targeted relatives, usually those who are lowest in anxiety and who function at the most adaptive level. [developed by U.S. psychiatrist Murray Bowen (1913–1990)]

multigravida *n.* a woman who has had two or more pregnancies. Compare PRIMIGRAVIDA.

multi-infarct dementia in *DSM–III*, DEMENTIA resulting from cerebrovascular disease. In *DSM–IV–TR*, this is referred to as VASCULAR DEMENTIA.

Multilevel Academic Survey Tests (**MAST**) a method of assessing academic performance in reading and mathematics that is used to identify specific content weaknesses and determine appropriate areas of enhanced instruction or remediation. The MAST is divided into three grade-level tests (Primary Form for kindergarten through grade 2, Short Form for grades 3 through 12, and Extended Form for grades 3 through 12) and a variety of criterion-referenced curriculum level tests. The former may be administered alone or in conjunction with any number and combination of the latter. [originally developed in 1985 by U.S. educators Kenneth W. Howell and Stanley H. Zucker, and Mada K. Morehead]

Multilingual Aphasia Examination (**MAE**) a neuropsychological test battery used to determine the presence, type, and severity of APHASIA. The 11 subtests, assessing various aspects of expressive and receptive language function, include Visual Naming, Sentence Repetition, CONTROLLED ORAL WORD ASSOCIATION, Oral Spelling, Written Spelling, Block Spelling, a TOKEN TEST, Aural Comprehension of Words and Phrases, Reading Comprehension of Words and Phrases, Rating of Articulation, and Rating of Praxic Features of Writing. The MAE was originally developed in 1978 and is now in its third edition (published in 2001). Despite the implications of its name, the MAE currently is available only in English and Spanish versions. [developed by U.S. psychologists Arthur Lester Benton (1909–), Kerry deS. Hamsher (1946–), and Abigail B. Sivan (1943–)]

multilingualism *n.* the sociolinguistic situation in which several languages are used within the same community, usually resulting from geographical, economic, or militaristic interactions. Typically, the various languages serve different social functions and have different status. See DIGLOSSIA.

multimodal theory of intelligence a theory that intelligence is a composite of many abilities.

multimodal therapy (**MMT**) a form of psychotherapy in which the therapist assesses the client's significant *B*ehaviors, *A*ffective responses, *S*ensations, *I*magery, *C*ognitions, *I*nterpersonal relationships, and the need for *D*rugs and other biological interventions. The first letters yield the acronym **BASIC ID**, which summarizes the seven basic interactive modalities of the approach. MMT posits that these modalities exist in a state of reciprocal transaction and flux, connected by complex chains of behavior and other psychophysiological processes. The therapist, usually in concert with the client, determines which specific problems across the BASIC ID are most salient. MMT uses an eclectic approach drawing mainly from a broad-based social and cognitive learning theory. Also called **multimodal behavior therapy**. [developed by South African-born U.S. clinical psychologist Arnold Allan Lazarus (1932–)]

multimodal treatment approach a manner of treating a disease, disorder, or syndrome by simultaneously applying several different methods, often from different disciplines or traditions.

multinomial distribution a theoretical probability distribution that describes the distribution of n objects sampled at random from a population of k kinds of things with regard to the number of each of the kinds that appears in the sample.

multiparous *adj.* **1.** describing a mother (a **multipara**) who has had two or more pregnancies resulting in live births. The pregnancies may be either successive or concurrent (as in the case of twins). **2.** giving birth to more than one offspring at a time. —**multiparity** *n.*

multipayer system see ALL-PAYER SYSTEM.

multiphilia *n.* interest in multiple, short-term sexual relationships only, with no desire for any long-term relationship or commitment.

multiple-aptitude test a battery of separate tests designed to measure a wide range of relatively independent functions and to yield a profile of the subject's abilities in different areas, as contrasted with a single global IQ. Different batteries measure different patterns of abilities. An example is the battery comprising the DIFFERENTIAL APTITUDE TESTS, primarily for use in educational and vocational counseling.

multiple baseline design an experimental design in which several items of behavior are assessed repeatedly before and after an experimental manipulation in order to determine which items systematically vary as a function of the manipulation.

multiple causation the view that events, including behaviors, seldom result from single causes, but instead that there are generally multiple causes, working in complex combinations to produce any event. Multiple causation contrasts with SIMPLE CAUSATION and (often) with LINEAR CAUSATION.

multiple-choice experiment an experiment in which a participant decides which of several possible choices is correct, usually on the basis of a specific cue that must be learned.

multiple-choice question see CLOSED-ENDED QUESTION.

multiple-choice test any test in which, for each item, the examinee chooses one of several given alternatives as being correct. See CLOSED-ENDED QUESTION.

multiple classification the ability to classify items in terms of more than one dimension simultaneously, such as shape and color. According to Jean PIAGET's theory of cognitive development, this ability is not achieved until the CONCRETE OPERATIONAL STAGE.

multiple comparisons a set of comparisons (differences) among the means of samples from *k* populations that are generally tested in a post hoc manner in order to keep the TYPE I ERROR rate controlled at a prespecified level. Also called **multiple contrasts**.

multiple correlation (symbol: *R*) a numerical index of the degree of relationship between a particular variable (e.g., a dependent variable) and two or more other variables (e.g., independent variables).

multiple correlation squared see COEFFICIENT OF MULTIPLE CORRELATION.

multiple cutoff model of selection in PERSONNEL SELECTION, a model in which an applicant for a job must meet a minimum score on each of several selection instruments (i.e., tests and inventories) in order to be hired. Unlike the MULTIPLE HURDLE MODEL OF SELECTION, the multiple cutoff procedure does not require applicants to take and pass the selection instruments in any particular order.

multiple delusions concurrent DELUSIONS, not necessarily interconnected.

multiple drafts hypothesis the theory that conscious perception occurs not in a specific location in the brain, but rather through many copies (drafts) of sensory input that are widely distributed over the sensory cortex. [proposed by U.S. philosopher Daniel Clement Dennett (1942–) and British physician Marcel Kinsbourne (1931–)]

multiple family therapy a form of GROUP PSYCHOTHERAPY in which a group of two or more family members meets with two or more therapists at once. See also FAMILY THERAPY; COTHERAPY.

multiple hurdle model of selection in PERSONNEL SELECTION, a model in which applicants for a job are required to pass each of a series of selection instruments (i.e., tests and inventories) before they are evaluated on the next instrument. The number of applicants is therefore reduced at each "hurdle." See also BANDING.

multiple-impact therapy a treatment method in which a group of mental health professionals works with a client family during an intensive, limited period.

multiple-intelligences theory the idea that intelligence is made up of eight distinct categories: linguistic, musical, bodily-kinesthetic, logical-mathematical, spatial, naturalist, intrapersonal, and interpersonal. [proposed in 1983 by U.S. psychologist Howard Gardner (1943–)]

multiple marital therapy a form of therapy in which each marital partner is treated independently by individual therapists. The two therapists may meet privately to discuss their clients, and sessions involving all four parties or a combination of the parties may be held. See also CONJOINT THERAPY.

multiple mating a strategy used by females to prevent CERTAINTY OF PATERNITY in males and as a MATE-SELECTION mechanism. A female mammal might mate with most males in its group, thus giving each male a potential stake in helping to protect the female and its young. Multiple mating is a form of CRYPTIC FEMALE CHOICE if the female can control which male mates with it at the time when conception is most likely.

multiple monitored electroconvulsive treatment (**MMECT**) a form of ELECTROCONVULSIVE THERAPY in which an attempt is made to shorten the overall period of treatment by inducing several seizures in a single session. Also called **multimonitored electroconvulsive treatment**.

multiple orgasm in women, the occurrence of more than one orgasm, without a resolution phase (see SEXUAL-RESPONSE CYCLE) separating the orgasms. Studies have found that as many as 30% of women experience this. Male multiple orgasm does not occur, because further arousal and response are not possible during the REFRACTORY PHASE following male orgasm. However, some men do carefully monitor and control their arousal and may experience the first elements of an orgasm, without ejaculation, more than once before having a complete orgasm, with ejaculation.

multiple personality disorder see DISSOCIATIVE IDENTITY DISORDER.

multiple regression a statistical technique for examining the linear relationship between a continuous DEPENDENT VARIABLE and a set of two or more INDEPENDENT VARIABLES. It is often used to predict the score of individuals on a criterion variable from multiple predictor variables.

multiple regression model of selection a model of PERSONNEL SELECTION in which the applicant is measured on each of several predictors and these scores are weighted to reflect the GOODNESS OF FIT between the predictor and performance on a given JOB CRITERION. The goodness of fit is measured using MULTIPLE REGRESSION techniques. The model assumes that the predictors are linearly related to the job criteria and that they are additive and can compensate for one another.

multiple reinforcement schedule a COMPOUND SCHEDULE OF REINFORCEMENT in which two or more schedules alternate and each schedule is associated with a different EXTEROCEPTIVE STIMULUS. For example, under a multiple fixed-interval extinction schedule, a tone could be present while the fixed-interval schedule is in effect and absent when extinction is in effect.

multiple relationship in a therapeutic context, a situation in which a psychologist has more than one type of relationship with a client. A multiple relationship occurs when a psychologist is in a professional role with a person and (a) concurrently is in another role with the same person, (b) concurrently is in a relationship with a person closely associated with or related to the client, or (c) promises to enter into another relationship in the future with the client or a person closely associated with or related to the client. Psychologists are ethically expected to refrain from entering into a multiple relationship because it might impair their objectivity, competence, or effectiveness in performing their functions as a psychologist or exploit or harm the client with whom the professional relationship exists. Also called **dual relationship**.

multiple-resource model a model of attention that views attention as comprising many pools of resources, each pool being specific to one stimulus modality or type of response. Different tasks place varying demands on different resources, and performance suffers less if two tasks draw on different resource pools than if they draw on the same pool. For example, talking while riding a bicycle presents fewer problems than trying to have two conversations at once. See MULTIPLE-TASK PERFORMANCE. Compare UNITARY-RESOURCE MODEL.

multiple-response test a MULTIPLE-CHOICE TEST in which more than one alternative is chosen for each test item.

multiple-role playing a MANAGEMENT DEVELOPMENT technique involving group ROLE PLAY. A large group is broken up into smaller groups, each of which comprises three people sitting in one row and the three people sitting directly behind them. Each six-person group is then given the same problem, with each member assigned one of six roles in the decision-making process. The solutions arrived at by each group are then reported to the entire body. See also BUSINESS GAME; CASE METHOD; CONFERENCE METHOD; SCENARIO ANALYSIS.

multiple roles in persuasion a postulate in the ELABORATION-LIKELIHOOD MODEL holding that variables can influence persuasion in one or more of four possible roles. When ELABORATION is likely to be low, a variable can influence persuasion by possibly serving as a PERIPHERAL CUE. When situational and dispositional factors do not cause elaboration to be extremely high or low, a variable can influence persuasion by determining the amount of elaboration. When elaboration is likely to be high, a variable can serve as an ARGUMENT if it is directly relevant to evaluating the ATTITUDE OBJECT or as a BIASING FACTOR in elaboration.

multiple sclerosis (**MS**) a DEMYELINATING DISEASE of the central nervous system (brain and spinal cord) characterized by inflammation and multifocal scarring of the protective MYELIN SHEATH of nerves, which damages and destroys the sheath and the underlying nerve, disrupting neural transmission. The initial symptom of MS is often a visual disturbance, such as blurred or double vision, red–green color distortion, or blindness in one eye. Later symptoms include fatigue, weakness in the hands and feet, numbness, stiffness or muscular spasms, muscle and back pain, difficulties with coordination and balance, loss of bladder or bowel control, and depression. Some individuals also experience cognitive impairments, such as difficulties with concentration, attention, memory, and judgment. The onset is usually between the ages of 20 and 40, and, with periods of remission, the disease may continue for 25 years or more. Rapid progression to death is rare. The cause of MS, which occurs twice as frequently in females as in males, is unknown. However, the destruction of myelin may be due to an autoimmune response (see AUTOIMMUNITY).

Multiple Sleep Latency Test (**MSLT**) an inpatient test performed in a SLEEP LABORATORY in which the individual is monitored during a series of five 20-minute nap periods scheduled 2 hours apart. The object is to assess daytime sleep tendency by measuring the number of minutes it takes the individual to fall asleep. The individual is monitored by means of electrodes that measure brain waves, eye movements, heartbeat, and muscle tone. The test is used in the diagnosis of PRIMARY HYPERSOMNIA and NARCOLEPSY.

multiple-spike recording the recording and analyzing of potentials from rapidly firing neurons using MICROELECTRODES connected to computer equipment.

multiple suicides see CLUSTER SUICIDES; MASS SUICIDE.

multiple-task performance a scenario in which a person must perform two or more tasks either simultaneously or contemporaneously. Success will depend on the degree to which the person can divide his or her attentional resources between tasks. See MULTIPLE-RESOURCE MODEL; UNITARY-RESOURCE MODEL. See also PERFORMANCE-OPERATING CHARACTERISTIC.

multiple trace hypothesis the hypothesis that when a stimulus is presented on multiple occasions, each occasion creates an entirely new record in memory rather than strengthening or otherwise updating an already existing record.

multiplex *n.* a method of coding information enabling two or more messages or data streams to be transmitted simultaneously over the same communication channel.

Multiplex Controller Aptitude Test a primary selection test completed by Air Traffic Control Specialist trainees to assess their aptitude for learning the principles and procedures of air traffic control.

multiplicity-versus-unity dimension a method of evaluating a work of art by its effects on the viewer. Arousal is heightened by complexity (multiplicity) factors and lowered by elements of harmony (unity). Multiplicity in art is sometimes held to be associated with historical periods of political or economic insecurity, when tensions are reflected in deformation of art styles. There is, however, little evidence for this contention.

multipolar neuron a NEURON that has many dendrites and a single axon extending from the CELL BODY. Compare BIPOLAR NEURON; UNIPOLAR NEURON.

multisensory learning learning in which the material to be learned is presented through several sensory modalities (e.g., seeing, hearing, and touching) rather than through only one modality.

multisensory method an approach to teaching reading and spelling that incorporates the visual, auditory, kinesthetic, and tactile modalities, often referred to as **VAKT**. See FERNALD METHOD.

multiskilled (**multiskill**) *adj.* **1.** displaying a level of proficiency in more than one area of expertise. **2.** having the ability to perform more than one task at the same time.

multistage sampling a sampling technique in which samples are drawn first from higher order groupings (e.g., states) and in later stages of the process from successively lower level groupings (e.g., counties within states, towns within counties) in order to avoid the necessity of having a SAMPLING FRAME for the entire population.

multistage theory any theory concerning a process that posits a series of steps or stages operating serially to accomplish that particular process.

multistate information system (**MSIS**) an automated record-keeping system designed to provide comparative statistics for evaluation of programs and treatment procedures in U.S. mental hospitals and community mental health facilities.

multistore model of memory any theory hypothesizing that information can move through and be retained in any of several memory storage systems, usually of a short-term and a long-term variety. Also called **stor-**

age-and-transfer model of memory. See DUAL-STORE MODEL OF MEMORY; MODAL MODEL OF MEMORY.

multisynaptic arc see POLYSYNAPTIC ARC.

multitrait–multimethod matrix an integrative multivariable framework for systematically gathering information about CONVERGENT VALIDITY and DISCRIMINANT VALIDITY in a single study. With this approach, one assesses two or more constructs (or traits) using two or more measurement techniques (or methods) and then intercorrelates these various measurements.

multivariate *adj.* consisting of many variables, especially in experimental design or correlational analysis.

multivariate analysis a statistical analysis that simultaneously models multiple DEPENDENT VARIABLES.

multivariate analysis of variance (**MANOVA**) an extension of the ANALYSIS OF VARIANCE (ANOVA) model that identifies the simultaneous effects of the independent variables upon a set of dependent variables.

mum effect see UPWARD COMMUNICATION.

Munchausen syndrome a severe and chronic form of FACTITIOUS DISORDER characterized by repeated and elaborate fabrication of clinically convincing physical symptoms and a false medical and social history (see PSEUDOLOGIA FANTASTICA). Other features are recurrent hospitalization and PEREGRINATION, and there may be multiple scars from previous (unnecessary) investigative surgery. The patient's motivation is a psychological need to assume the SICK ROLE. See also PATHOMIMICRY. [Baron Karl Friedrich Hieronymus von **Münchhausen** (1720–1797), German soldier-adventurer famous for his tall tales]

Munchausen syndrome by proxy (**MSP**) a psychological disorder in which caregivers fabricate or intentionally cause symptoms in those they are caring for in order to seek and obtain medical investigation or treatment. Typically, the caregiver is the mother, who behaves as if distressed about her child's illness and denies knowing what caused it: She is believed to be motivated by the hope that she will be seen as an exceptionally attentive parent, and her behavior may be an attempt to arouse sympathy. In *DSM–IV–TR* this condition is called **factitious disorder by proxy** (see FACTITIOUS DISORDER NOT OTHERWISE SPECIFIED).

mundane realism the extent to which an experimental situation resembles a real-life situation or event. This is related to EXPERIMENTAL REALISM, in which experiments are designed to elicit valid emotional responses even if the events of the experiment do not resemble ordinary occurrences.

Munsell color system a method of color notation devised for use mainly in science, industry, and technology. The system uses numerical designations for hue, saturation, and brightness of color for accurate identification and specification. See COLOR SYSTEM; COLOR VALUE. [Albert H. **Munsell** (1858–1918), U.S. artist]

Münsterberg, Hugo (1863–1916) German-born U.S. psychologist. Münsterberg received his doctorate from the University of Leipzig in 1885, studying with Wilhelm WUNDT, and earned a medical degree in 1887 from the University of Heidelberg. Münsterberg taught at the University of Freiburg until he was invited by William JAMES to direct the psychology laboratory at Harvard University in the early 1890s. He returned to Freiburg in 1895 for 2 years, but otherwise remained at Harvard for the rest of his career. Münsterberg's early research was on the psychology of the will, but once he came to the United States his interests rapidly shifted toward applied psychology, making him a pioneer in that field. He addressed such topics as EYEWITNESS TESTIMONY and lie detection, educational psychology, abnormal psychology, and the psychology of motion pictures. His popular writings on the role of psychology in business and industry made him a recognized founder of the field of INDUSTRIAL AND ORGANIZATIONAL PSYCHOLOGY. Münsterberg published a series of pathbreaking books, including *On the Witness Stand* (1908), *Psychotherapy* (1909), *Psychology and Industrial Efficiency* (1913), and *The Photoplay* (1916). He was also a self-appointed ambassador of cultural relations between Germany and the United States, writing a popular book about Americans for a German audience, *Die Amerikaner* (1903). Because of his prominence in German–American relations, Münsterberg became a target of anti-German sentiment during World War I. See also FORENSIC PSYCHOLOGY.

murder *n.* the unlawful killing of one person by another, particularly when the act involves premeditation. See also HOMICIDE.

murder–suicide the intentional killing of another person followed by the suicide of the killer. See also EXTENDED SUICIDE.

mu receptor see OPIOID RECEPTOR.

muscae volitantes particles or specks seen as floating before the eyes. Also called **mouches volantes**. [Latin, literally: flying flies]

muscarine *n.* a toxic alkaloid, isolated from FLY AGARIC (*Amanita muscaria*) and some other fungi, that stimulates certain types of acetylcholine receptors (the MUSCARINIC RECEPTORS) in smooth muscle, cardiac muscle, endocrine glands, and the central nervous system. See also NICOTINE.

muscarinic receptor a type of ACETYLCHOLINE RECEPTOR that responds to MUSCARINE as well as to acetylcholine. Muscarinic receptors mediate chiefly the inhibitory activities of acetylcholine. Compare NICOTINIC RECEPTOR.

muscimol *n.* see FLY AGARIC; GABA AGONISTS; IBOTENIC ACID.

muscle *n.* contractile tissue that generates force and moves parts of the body. The main types of muscle are SMOOTH MUSCLE, SKELETAL MUSCLE, and CARDIAC MUSCLE.

muscle action potential a wave of electric potential that sweeps across a muscle when it is stimulated. See ACTION POTENTIAL.

muscle contraction a shortening of the MUSCLE FIBERS in response to electrical stimulation from a MOTOR NEURON by which a muscle exerts force on the tissues to which it is attached. This stimulation initiates an electrochemical sequence in which myosin filaments, powered by ATP (adenosine triphosphate), detach from a nearby actin filament, swing forward to reattach further along the actin filament, and then swing back causing the actin and myosin filaments to slide in opposite directions. When this process is repeated in many muscle fibers, the overall muscle becomes shorter but thicker. See ISOMETRIC CONTRACTION; ISOTONIC CONTRACTION.

muscle-contraction headache a headache arising from increased muscle tension, frequently in the neck. Also called **muscle-tension headache**.

muscle dysmorphia a form of BODY DYSMORPHIA characterized by chronic dissatisfaction with one's muscularity and the perception that one's body is inadequate and undesirable, although objective observers would disagree with such an assessment. This condition often leads to excessive exercising, steroid abuse, and eating disorders. It is typically found in males, especially bodybuilders. Also called **bigorexia**. See also REVERSE ANOREXIA.

muscle fiber a microscopic strand of muscle tissue that functions as a molecular machine converting chemical energy into force. Thousands of muscle fibers are linked by connective tissue into a muscle. Each fiber is, in turn, composed of millions of longitudinally aligned protein filaments. It is the interaction of ACTIN and MYOSIN protein molecules (sometimes together referred to as **actomyosin**) in these filaments that creates MUSCLE CONTRACTION.

muscle relaxants drugs used in the management of spasms of skeletal muscle, generally resulting from mechanical injury, stroke, cerebral palsy, or multiple sclerosis. Most act on the central nervous system or its associated structures to reduce muscle tone and spontaneous activity. Although the precise mode of action varies with the drug, muscle relaxants generally act by depressing spinal reflexes without loss of consciousness. Common muscle relaxants include BENZODIAZEPINES, BACLOFEN, DANTROLENE, and botulinum toxin. Others used for localized muscle spasms include CARISOPRODOL, CYCLOBENZAPRINE, METHOCARBAMOL, and ORPHENADRINE.

muscle relaxation the release of tension from muscle, that is, the alteration of the state of the muscle on a continuum from full contraction to flaccidity.

muscle sensation a kinesthetic awareness of movements and tensions in muscles, tendons, and joints. See KINESTHETIC FEEDBACK.

muscle spindle a receptor that lies within a muscle, parallel to the main contractile MUSCLE FIBERS, and sends impulses to the central nervous system when the muscle is stretched.

muscle-tension gradient the rate of change of muscle tension during performance of a task. It is measured by ELECTROMYOGRAPHY.

muscle tonus see TONUS.

muscle twitch a small, sudden, and brief involuntary contraction of a muscle, as opposed to sustained contraction.

muscular dystrophy (**MD**) any of a group of inherited disorders marked by degeneration of the muscles, which gradually weaken and waste away due to abnormalities in the muscle structural protein dystrophin and in a series of glycoproteins that are critical to maintaining the structural integrity of muscle fibers. There are various kinds of muscular dystrophy, each differentiated by pattern of inheritance, age of onset, rate of progression, and distribution of weakness. One of the most common and severe types is **Duchenne muscular dystrophy** (pseudohypertrophic muscular dystrophy). This is inherited as a SEX-LINKED recessive trait and is therefore restricted to boys. It typically begins before the age of 6 with delayed walking and loss of muscle strength, first in the pelvic girdle followed by weakness in the shoulder girdle. Individuals with this disorder have difficulty in rising to a standing position and often fall. They usually are unable to walk by the age of 12 and frequently die from complications before the age of 20.

muscular rigidity stiffness in muscles that is resistant to changes in position. Individuals may misinterpret this symptom as weakness, but the condition usually occurs in the presence of normal strength. See COGWHEEL RIGIDITY; LEAD-PIPE RIGIDITY.

muscular type a constitutional type characterized by dominance of the muscular and locomotor systems over other body systems (see ROSTAN TYPES). It corresponds to the ATHLETIC TYPE in KRETSCHMER TYPOLOGY.

musculocutaneous nerve a nerve that innervates the muscles of the upper arm and cutaneous receptors of the lateral forearm.

musculoskeletal disorder any disease, injury, or significant impairment to tendons, muscles, bones, joints, and supporting connective (soft) tissues.

musculoskeletal system the system of SKELETAL MUSCLES and bones that generally function together to move parts of the body and maintain its general form.

musical ability the ability used to write, recall, play, and understand music. It is clear that musical ability involves multiple subabilities that may be relatively distinct from one another.

musical aphasia see TONAPHASIA.

musical intelligence in the MULTIPLE-INTELLIGENCES THEORY, the intelligence that involves the skills used in writing, playing, remembering, and understanding music.

musical interval the pitch or frequency spacing between two sounds. Two sounds that are an OCTAVE apart (i.e., with an interval of an octave) have a 2:1 ratio of their fundamental FREQUENCIES. See also CENT.

musical therapy see MUSIC THERAPY.

musician's cramp a type of OCCUPATIONAL CRAMP experienced by musicians, usually in the arm or hand, that prevents them from performing. The condition may be due to electrolyte imbalance. See also REPETITIVE STRAIN INJURY.

musicogenic epilepsy a type of REFLEX EPILEPSY in which seizures are precipitated by music.

music therapy the use of music as an adjunct to the treatment or rehabilitation of individuals to enhance their psychological, physical, cognitive, or social functioning. Also called **musical therapy**.

mussitation *n.* unintelligible muttering, or moving the lips without producing speech.

musturbation *n.* the behavior of individuals who believe that they must absolutely meet often perfectionist goals in order to achieve success, approval, or comfort. Cognitive and behavioral therapies may be useful in bringing awareness and perspective to such maladaptive cognitions. See also RATIONAL EMOTIVE BEHAVIOR THERAPY. [defined by U.S. psychotherapist Albert Ellis (1913–)]

musty *adj.* denoting one of the seven classes of odorants in the STEREOCHEMICAL SMELL THEORY.

mutagen *n.* see MUTATION. **—mutagenic** *adj.*

mutation *n.* a permanent change in the genetic material of an organism. It may consist of an alteration to the number or arrangement of chromosomes (a **chromosomal mutation**) or a change in the composition of DNA, generally affecting only one or a few bases in a particular gene (a **point mutation**). Mutations can occur spontaneously, but many are due to exposure to agents (**mutagens**) that significantly increase the rate of mutation; these include X-rays and other forms of radiation and certain chemicals. A mutation occurring in a body cell (i.e., a **somatic mutation**) cannot be inherited, whereas a mutation in a reproductive cell producing ova or spermatozoa (i.e., a **germ-line mutation**) can be transmitted to that individual's offspring. Most mutations either have no discernible effect or have a deleterious effect; however, a tiny majority are beneficial and thus give that individual and his or her descendants a selective advantage. Mutations responsible for SINGLE-GENE DISORDERS are sought in genetic testing of high-risk families or groups.

mutilation *n.* **1.** the destruction or removal of a limb or an essential part of the body. **2.** a destructive act causing a disfiguring injury to the body. See also SELF-MUTILATION.

mutism *n.* lack or absence of speaking due to physical or PSYCHOGENIC factors. The condition may result from neurological damage or disorder, a structural defect in the organs necessary for speech, congenital or early deafness in which an individual's failure to hear spoken words inhibits the development of speech, psychological disorders (e.g., CONVERSION DISORDER, CATATONIC SCHIZOPHRENIA), or severe emotional disturbance (e.g., extreme anger). The condition may also be voluntary, as in monastic vows of silence or the decision to speak only to selected individuals. See also AKINETIC MUTISM; ALALIA; SELECTIVE MUTISM; STUPOR.

muttering delirium a type of DELIRIUM in which an individual's speech is marked by low utterances, slurring, iteration, DYSARTHRIA, PERSEVERATION, or any combination of these. Typically, the individual's movements are dominated by restlessness and trembling.

mutual accommodation the situation in which two or more participants in a relationship adjust to each other's attitudes, desires, personal needs, and behavioral patterns so that they interact harmoniously. See SOCIAL ADAPTATION.

mutual gaze see EYE CONTACT.

mutual help a form of SELF-HELP that is not professionally guided and that involves joining with others similar to oneself to explore ways to cope with life situations and problems. Mutual help can occur in person, by telephone, or through the Internet.

mutualism *n.* an INTERSPECIES INTERACTION in which two species live together in close association, to the mutual benefit of both species. See also SYMBIOSIS. Compare COMMENSALISM; PARASITISM.

mutually exclusive events 1. two or more events that have no common elements, that is, disjoint events (see DISJOINT SETS). **2.** in probability theory, two or more events that cannot co-occur; the occurrence of one precludes the simultaneous or subsequent occurrence of the other(s). For example, the alternatives "heads" and "tails" in a single toss of a coin are mutually exclusive events.

mutual masturbation 1. sexual activity in which two individuals stimulate each other's genitals at the same time for the purpose of sexual gratification. This is more properly considered a type of PETTING BEHAVIOR, as masturbation is defined as self-stimulation. **2.** sexual activity in which two or more individuals stimulate their own genitals while jointly viewing erotic materials. Such activity, especially when involving adolescent males, is popularly known as "a circle jerk."

mutual pretense an interaction pattern in which all participants try to act as if they are unaware of the most crucial facts in a situation (e.g., a situation in which one of the participants is terminally ill). This pattern is often regarded by therapists and researchers as an anxiety-driven strategy that inhibits communication, increases tension, and leads to missed opportunities for meaningful mutual support.

mutual support groups groups composed of individuals who meet on a regular basis to help one another cope with a shared life problem. This term is sometimes used by self-help group researchers and practitioners instead of the traditional term SELF-HELP GROUPS, as it emphasizes the mutual, interdependent nature of SELF-HELP GROUP PROCESSES.

my- *combining form* see MYO-.

myasthenia *n.* muscular weakness or lack of muscular endurance.

myasthenia gravis an autoimmune disorder (see AUTOIMMUNITY) due to faulty transmission of nerve impulses at neuromuscular junctions resulting from a loss of ACETYLCHOLINE RECEPTORS. Affected muscles are easily fatigued and may become paralyzed. Muscles involved in eating may fail to function normally toward the end of a meal, or speech may become slurred and the voice weak after a period of talking. Drooping eyelids, double vision, and swallowing difficulties may also be present. The disease is progressive, eventually affecting muscles throughout the body.

mydriasis *n.* excessive dilation (widening) of the pupil of the eye caused by anticholinergic drugs (e.g., atropine and scopolamine) acting on MUSCARINIC RECEPTORS. **—mydriatic** *adj., n.*

myel- *combining form* see MYELO-.

myelencephalon *n.* see MEDULLA OBLONGATA.

myelin *n.* the substance that forms the insulating MYELIN SHEATH around the axons of many neurons. It consists mainly of phospholipids, with additional **myelin proteins**, and accounts for the whitish color of WHITE MATTER.

myelinated fiber a nerve fiber that is covered by a MYELIN SHEATH. The insulating properties of the myelin sheath enable myelinated fibers to conduct nerve impulses much faster than nonmyelinated fibers (see SALTATORY CONDUCTION).

myelination *n.* the formation and development of a MYELIN SHEATH around the AXON of a neuron, which is effected by neuroglia, such as SCHWANN CELLS. Researchers look to anomalies in this process to explain some forms of severe mental illness (e.g., schizophrenia). Also called **axonal myelination**; **medullation**; **myelinization**.

myelin sheath the insulating layer around many axons (see MYELINATED FIBER) that increases the speed of conduction of nerve impulses. It consists of MYELIN and is laid down by NEUROGLIA, which wrap themselves around adjacent axons. The myelin sheath is interrupted by small gaps, called NODES OF RANVIER, which are spaced about every millimeter along the axon. Also called **medullary sheath**.

myelitis *n.* inflammation of the spinal cord.

myelo- (**myel-**) *combining form* spinal cord or bone marrow.

myeloarchitecture *n.* the development and distribution of the fiber processes of the nerve cells of the brain, particularly the myelinated fibers. See also CORTICAL LAYERS.

myelocele *n.* protrusion of the spinal cord, found in SPINA BIFIDA. See MENINGOMYELOCELE; MYELOMENINGOCELE.

myelomeningocele *n.* a sac containing the spinal cord and its covering meninges that protrudes from the spine in individuals with SPINA BIFIDA. The sac usually is closed before birth but postnatally fills with cerebrospinal fluid to protrude from the lumbar, low thoracic, or sacral region of the spine. See also MENINGOMYELOCELE.

myenteric plexus a network of nerve fibers and neuron cell bodies located between the inner and outer muscle layers of the digestive tract, including the esophagus, stomach, and intestines. Together with other enteric plexuses, it controls the responses of the digestive tract.

Myers–Briggs Type Indicator (**MBTI**) a personality

test designed to classify individuals according to their expressed choices between contrasting alternatives in certain categories of traits. The categories, based on JUNGIAN TYPOLOGY, are (a) Extraversion–Introversion, (b) Sensing–Intuition, (c) Thinking–Feeling, and (d) Judging–Perceiving. The participant is assigned a type (e.g., INTJ or ESFP) according to the pattern of choices made. The test has little credibility among research psychologists but is widely used in educational counseling and human resource management to help improve work and personal relationships, increase productivity, and identify interpersonal communication preferences and skills. [Isabel Briggs **Myers** (1897–1980), U.S. personologist, and her mother Katharine Cook **Briggs** (1875–1968)]

myesthesia *n.* the muscle sense; that is, the sensation felt in muscle contractions and the awareness of movement in muscles and joints. Also called **myoesthesia**; **myoesthesis**. See also KINESTHESIS.

myo- (**my-**) *combining form* muscle.

myocardial infarction see INFARCTION.

myoclonic *adj.* of, relating to, or characterized by MYOCLONUS.

myoclonic epilepsy EPILEPSY characterized by MYOCLONIC SEIZURES or MYOCLONUS in conjunction with other types of seizure. Also called **myoclonus epilepsy**.

myoclonic movements movements characterized by rapid, involuntary muscle jerks (see MYOCLONUS).

myoclonic seizure a rare type of GENERALIZED SEIZURE characterized by rapid, involuntary muscle jerks.

myoclonus *n.* rapid, involuntary muscle jerks. This may occur normally, as when a limb or other part of the body suddenly jerks while falling asleep (see NOCTURNAL MYOCLONUS), or abnormally, as in CREUTZFELDT–JAKOB DISEASE, MYOCLONIC SEIZURES, and other neurological disorders. The condition may be limited to a single group of muscles or it may occur simultaneously or consecutively in unrelated muscle groups.

myoclonus epilepsy see MYOCLONIC EPILEPSY.

myoelectric prothesis an artificial limb (see PROSTHESIS), such as a **myoelectric arm**, that can be manipulated by nerve impulses generated by voluntary muscle movements. The nerve impulses are received by an electronic transducer that amplifies and converts them into appropriate movements of the prosthesis through tiny electric motors.

myoesthesia (**myoesthesis**) *n.* see MYESTHESIA.

myofascial pain syndrome (**MPS**) see CHRONIC MYOFASCIAL PAIN.

myography *n.* a technique that utilizes apparatus to record aspects of muscle activity. Some devices record the small electric potential that accompanies contraction of the muscle fibers. A **myograph** is an instrument that records the extent, force, or duration of ISOTONIC CONTRACTIONS or the tension and duration of ISOMETRIC CONTRACTIONS. A **myogram** is a graphic record of the velocity and intensity of muscle contractions. **—myographic** *adj.*

myoneural junction see NEUROMUSCULAR JUNCTION.

myopathy *n.* any muscular disorder, hereditary or acquired, involving defective functioning of muscle fibers. An example is MYASTHENIA GRAVIS, which involves a defect at NEUROMUSCULAR JUNCTIONS. The term is usually qualified by an adjective that specifies the type of myopathy or its cause. For example, ACUTE ALCOHOLIC MYOPATHY and **hereditary myopathy** suggest a cause, whereas **ocular myopathy** defines the affected area as the muscles that control eye movements.

myopia *n.* nearsightedness, or closesightedness, an ERROR OF REFRACTION due to an abnormally long eye: The retinal image is blurred because the focal point of one or both eyes lies in front of, rather than on, the retina. Specific types include **chromic myopia**, marked by defective color perception of distant objects; **progressive myopia**, a gradual loss of accommodation for distant vision associated with aging; and **prodromal myopia**, in which accommodation changes permit a return of normal sightedness after a period of myopia.

myosin *n.* a contractile protein that, together with ACTIN, occurs in MUSCLE FIBERS and mediates MUSCLE CONTRACTION.

myosis *n.* see MIOSIS.

myositis *n.* inflammation of a muscle.

myotatic reflex see STRETCH REFLEX.

myotonia *n.* increased tone and contractility of a muscle, with slow or delayed relaxation. **—myotonic** *adj.*

myotonic disorder any disease, generally inherited, in which voluntary muscles show increased tone and contractility but relax slowly and with great difficulty. The condition often affects the muscles of the hands or is manifested by general muscle stiffness.

myotonic muscular dystrophy a type of MUSCULAR DYSTROPHY marked by increased muscle tone and contractility (myotonia) and muscle wasting, most noticeably in the face and hands, and often accompanied by cataracts and cardiac abnormalities. It is an AUTOSOMAL DOMINANT disorder that is usually first noted in adolescence or early adulthood, although age of onset can vary. Also called **dystrophia myotonica**; **Steinert's disease**.

myriachit *n.* a CULTURE-BOUND SYNDROME found in Siberian populations. Similar to LATAH, it is characterized by indiscriminate, apparently uncontrolled imitations of the actions of other people encountered by the individual. Also called **ikota**; **irkunii**; **menkeiti**; **olan**. See also IMU; JUMPING FRENCHMEN OF MAINE SYNDROME.

Mysoline *n.* a trade name for PRIMIDONE.

mysophilia *n.* a pathological interest in dirt or filth, often with a desire to be unclean or in contact with dirty objects. Mysophilia may be expressed as a PARAPHILIA in which the person is sexually aroused by a dirty partner.

mystical participation a mode of engagement or type of mental activity in which the boundaries between the natural and the spiritual, and between oneself and one's environment, are either overcome or not established in the first place. The term was introduced by French philosopher and ethnologist Lucien Levy-Bruhl (1857–1939), who held that mystical participation is a characteristic of so-called primitive cultures. See LAW OF PARTICIPATION.

mysticism *n.* **1.** the view that there are real sources of knowledge and truth other than sensory experience and rational deduction. It is held that such knowledge comes through inspiration, revelation, or other experiences that are not strictly sensory, although there may be a sensory component. A common implication is that such knowledge cannot readily be shared with or conveyed to others but must be individually achieved. Mysticism thus carries a connotation of subjectivism. **2.** the belief that an immediate knowledge of, or union with, the divine can be achieved through personal religious experience. Accounts of mystical experiences in the writings of various spiritual traditions typically describe a state of intense, trancelike contemplation in which a sense of profound insight is accompanied by feelings of ecstatic self-surrender. **3.** any irrational or unscientific belief, especially one characterized by self-delusion or deliberate OBSCURANTISM. **—mystic** *n., adj.* **—mystical** *adj.*

mystic union the feeling of spiritual identification with God, nature, or the universe as a whole. See BUDDHISM; COSMIC IDENTIFICATION; OCEANIC FEELING; TRANSCENDENTAL MEDITATION; YOGA; ZEN THERAPY.

Mytelase *n.* a trade name for AMBENOMIUM.

mythology *n.* **1.** a body of traditional stories (myths) associated with the early history of a particular culture. Such stories generally involve supernatural beings and events and often seek to explain particular natural or cultural phenomena (e.g., the cycle of the seasons or a specific custom) in terms of their supposed origins. Myths are often distinguished from LEGENDS as having little or no basis in historical events. **2.** the study of myths. Sigmund FREUD compared myths to DREAMS, which contain hidden meanings, and believed they throw unique light on the cultures from which they stem, and in some instances, as in the myth of Oedipus, on human nature in general. **3.** in Carl JUNG'S ANALYTIC PSYCHOLOGY, primordial images, or ARCHETYPES, that are stored in the COLLECTIVE UNCONSCIOUS. **—mythological** *adj.*

mythomania *n.* **1.** a tendency to elaborate, exaggerate, and tell lies, including reports of imagined experiences, often involving SELF-DECEPTION. See also FACTITIOUS DISORDER; PATHOLOGICAL LYING. **2.** an abnormal interest in myths, in which the individual may believe fantasy to be reality, and a tendency to fabricate incredible stories. Also called **pseudologia fantastica**. See also FABULATION.

myxedema *n.* a metabolic disorder that develops in adulthood due to a deficiency of thyroid hormone (see HYPOTHYROIDISM). The condition is characterized by subnormal heart rate, circulation, and body temperature and a decrease in most other metabolic activities. Affected individuals tend to be fatigued, listless, and overweight, but usually respond to administration of thyroxine. **—myxedemic** *adj.*

Nn

n symbol for the number of scores or observations obtained from a particular experimental condition or subgroup.

N 1. symbol for the total number of cases (participants) in an experiment or study. **2.** abbreviation for NUMERICAL ABILITY.

NA abbreviation for NARCOTICS ANONYMOUS.

nabilone *n.* a synthetic cannabinoid, closely related to TETRAHYDROCANNABINOL, that is used clinically to manage nausea and vomiting in patients recovering from surgical anesthesia or undergoing chemotherapy. It is available in Canada but not in the United States. Canadian trade name: **Cesamet**.

n-Ach abbreviation for NEED FOR ACHIEVEMENT.

nadle *n.* see TWO-SPIRIT.

Nafe pattern theory a theory claiming that the pattern of firing of neurons is responsible for the quality of cutaneous sensations. [John Paul **Nafe** (1886–1970), U.S. psychologist]

n-Aff abbreviation for NEED FOR AFFILIATION.

Naglieri Nonverbal Ability Test (**NNAT**) a test of nonverbal reasoning and problem-solving ability for students in kindergarten through grade 12, regardless of language and educational or cultural background. It consists of 38 abstract matrix designs measuring pattern completion, reasoning by analogy, serial reasoning, and spatial visualization. The test can be used to screen for learning disabilities or as an assessment tool for students who lack verbal skills, have English only as a second language, or possess limited English abilities. An extension and modification of the 1985 **Matrix Analogies Test**, the NNAT was originally developed in 1997. [Jack A. **Naglieri** (1950–), U.S. psychologist]

naikan *n.* a Japanese therapy that emphasizes character building through rigorous self-reflection upon (a) what the client has received from others, (b) what the client has returned to others, and (c) how the client's actions may have hurt others. Through this process of self-reflection, guided by the therapist, the client acquires a sense of responsibility for his or her actions and an appreciation of the positive influences in his or her life. [introduced by Japanese Buddhist of the Jodo Shinshu sect Yoshimoto Ishin (1916–1988)]

nail biting the compulsive habit of chewing on one's fingernails, usually thought to be a means of releasing tension. Also called **onychophagia**; **onychophagy**.

naive analysis of action in ATTRIBUTION THEORY, a set of rules by which laypersons determine whether another person (an "actor") caused a certain action. Also called **lay psychology**; **naive psychology**. See CORRESPONDENT INFERENCE THEORY. [postulated in 1958 by Austrian-born U.S. psychologist Fritz Heider (1896–1988)]

naive hedonism in KOHLBERG'S THEORY OF MORAL DEVELOPMENT, the second of two stages in the PRECONVENTIONAL LEVEL, in which children make moral decisions based on what serves their own needs and what is negotiated with others according to precise interpretation of rules. Also called **instrumental-relativist orientation**; **naive instrumental hedonism**. Compare PUNISHMENT AND OBEDIENCE ORIENTATION.

naive observer 1. an observer who has little or no prior information about the events that he or she is observing or the people involved in them. In psychology experiments, the reactions of a naive observer may be highly revealing when contrasted with those of other observers who have been given selected pieces of information (or misinformation) about the observed situation or the actors in it (e.g., that a particular individual has a criminal conviction). **2.** in philosophy, an observer who adopts a position of NAIVE REALISM.

naive participant a participant who has not previously participated in a particular research study and has not been made aware of the experimenter's hypothesis. Compare CONFEDERATE.

naive personality theories a set of ideas that laypeople tend to hold about how specific personality traits cluster together within a person. Such theories, which are often held implicitly rather than explicitly, are a major concern of ATTRIBUTION THEORY. Also called **layperson theories**. See NAIVE ANALYSIS OF ACTION.

naive psychology see NAIVE ANALYSIS OF ACTION.

naive realism 1. the belief or assumption that one's sense perceptions provide direct knowledge of external reality, unconditioned by one's perceptual apparatus or individual perspective. Since the advent of CARTESIANISM, most philosophy has assumed that such a position is untenable. The cognitive development theory of Jean PIAGET stresses the child's progress away from naive realism and toward conceptualization and logical reasoning. As conceptualization and reasoning develop, naive realism is presumed to diminish. Also called **direct realism**; **phenomenal absolutism**. **2.** in social psychology, the tendency to assume that one's perspective of events is a natural, unbiased reflection of objective reality and to infer bias on the part of anyone who disagrees with one's views. See FALSE CONSENSUS; FALSE-CONSENSUS EFFECT.

Nalline test a test to determine abstinence from opiates, in which the subject is given an injection of the OPIOID ANTAGONIST nalorphine (Nalline). This precipitates withdrawal symptoms if opiates have been used recently.

nalmefene *n.* see OPIOID ANTAGONIST.

nalorphine *n.* see OPIOID ANTAGONIST.

naloxone *n.* a morphine-derived OPIOID ANTAGONIST that prevents the binding of opioids to OPIOID RECEPTORS, having primary activity at the mu receptor. Like other opioid antagonists, it can quickly reverse the effects of opioid overdose and is useful in emergency settings to reverse respiratory depression. U.S. trade name: **Narcan**.

naltrexone *n.* an OPIOID ANTAGONIST that, like the shorter acting NALOXONE, prevents the binding of opioid agonists to opioid receptors. Accordingly, both drugs may precipitate a rapid withdrawal syndrome. If naltrexone is taken prior to use of opiate drugs, it will prevent their reinforcing effects, and can therefore be used for the management of opioid dependence in individuals desiring abstinence. Naltrexone is also appropriate as an adjunctive treatment in the management of alcoholism. U.S. trade name: **ReVia**.

name-of-the-father *adj.* in the theory of French psychoanalyst Jacques Lacan (1901–1981), denoting the stage at which the infant first enters the realm of the SYMBOLIC. The child's ability to "name the father" as a symbol for the absence of the mother represents his or her first use of symbolization and the first recognition that the father is a rival at the beginning of the OEDIPUS COMPLEX. See also MIRROR PHASE.

NAMI abbreviation for NATIONAL ALLIANCE FOR THE MENTALLY ILL.

naming *n.* an association disturbance observed in schizophrenia, in which the individual relates to the external world solely by naming objects and actions (e.g., naming furniture or other objects in an examining room).

naming task a task in which an individual is required to name an object from its picture or its description or simply to produce names from a certain category (e.g., birds). Naming tasks are used to assess language impairments and difficulties recalling general knowledge from SEMANTIC MEMORY.

nanometer (symbol: nm) *n.* 10^{-9} m (i.e., one billionth of a meter). The wavelengths in the visible range of the electromagnetic spectrum extend from approximately 400 to 700 nm.

nanosomia body type see PYGMYISM.

Narcan *n.* a trade name for NALOXONE.

narcissism *n.* **1.** excessive self-love or egocentrism. See NARCISSISTIC PERSONALITY DISORDER. **2.** in psychoanalytic theory, the taking of one's own EGO or body as a sexual object or focus of the LIBIDO or the seeking or choice of another for relational purposes on the basis of his or her similarity to the self. See BODY NARCISSISM; PRIMARY NARCISSISM. **—narcissist** *n.* **—narcissistic** *adj.*

narcissistic character see NARCISSISTIC PERSONALITY.

narcissistic object choice in psychoanalytic theory, selection of a mate or other LOVE OBJECT similar to oneself. Compare ANACLITIC OBJECT CHOICE.

narcissistic personality a pattern of traits and behaviors characterized by excessive self-concern and overvaluation of the self. Also called **narcissistic character**.

narcissistic personality disorder in *DSM–IV–TR*, a personality disorder with the following characteristics: (a) a long-standing pattern of grandiose self-importance and exaggerated sense of talent and achievements; (b) fantasies of unlimited sex, power, brilliance, or beauty; (c) an exhibitionistic need for attention and admiration; (d) either cool indifference or feelings of rage, humiliation, or emptiness as a response to criticism, indifference, or defeat; and (e) various interpersonal disturbances, such as feeling entitled to special favors, taking advantage of others, and inability to empathize with the feelings of others. [originally formulated by U.S. psychiatrists Wilhelm Reich (1897–1957), Otto Kernberg, and Heinz Kohut (1913–1981), and U.S. psychologist Theodore Millon (1929–)]

narcissistic type see LIBIDINAL TYPES.

narcoanalysis *n.* a form of psychoanalysis in which injections of drugs (often opioids) are used to induce a semihypnotic state in order to facilitate exploration and ventilation of feelings, uncover repressed traumatic memories, and, through the analyst's review and interpretation with the patient afterward, promote the patient's insight into the unconscious forces that underlie his or her symptoms. The technique was developed initially to treat COMBAT STRESS REACTIONS in the 1940s and is rarely if ever used now.

narcolepsy *n.* a disorder consisting of excessive daytime sleepiness accompanied by brief "attacks" of sleep during waking hours. These sleep attacks may occur at any time or during any activity, including in potentially dangerous situations, such as driving an automobile. The attacks are often associated with HYPNAGOGIC HALLUCINATIONS, SLEEP PARALYSIS, and CATAPLEXY and are marked by immediate entry into REM sleep without going through the usual initial stages of sleep. Also called **paroxysmal sleep**. **—narcoleptic** *adj.*

narcolepsy–cataplexy syndrome a symptom pattern consisting of sudden, repeated loss of muscle tone (see CATAPLEXY) and recurrent sleep attacks (see NARCOLEPSY).

narcomania *n.* **1.** a pathological desire for narcotic drugs to relieve pain or discomfort. **2.** an obsolete name for psychosis resulting from long-term abuse of narcotic drugs.

narcosynthesis *n.* a treatment technique that involves the administration of narcotic drugs to stimulate recall of emotional traumas, followed by "synthesis" of these experiences with the patient's emotional life through therapeutic discussions in the waking state. [developed during World War II by U.S. psychiatrists Roy Richard Grinker and John P. Spiegel]

narcotherapy *n.* psychotherapy conducted while the patient is in a semiconscious state induced by injection of narcotic drugs, such as amobarbital (Amytal) or thiopental. Narcotherapy was used, for example, with individuals experiencing COMBAT STRESS REACTIONS during and after World War II. See also NARCOANALYSIS; NARCOSYNTHESIS.

narcotic 1. *n.* originally, any drug that induces a state of stupor or insensibility (narcosis). More recently, the term referred to strong OPIOIDS used clinically for pain relief but this usage is now considered imprecise and pejorative; the term is still sometimes used in legal contexts to refer to a wide variety of abused substances. **2.** *adj.* of or relating to narcotics or narcosis.

narcotic addiction see OPIOID DEPENDENCE.

narcotic agonist see OPIOID AGONIST.

narcotic analgesic see OPIOID ANALGESIC.

narcotic antagonist see OPIOID ANTAGONIST.

narcotic dependence see OPIOID DEPENDENCE.

Narcotics Anonymous (**NA**) a self-help organization for those who seek help with a drug addiction, based on a TWELVE-STEP PROGRAM and modeled after ALCOHOLICS ANONYMOUS. The only requirement for membership is the desire to stop using drugs.

narcotic stupor a state of lethargy or limited mobility and decreased responsiveness to stimulation due to the effects of an opioid drug. This state may border on loss of consciousness and be followed by coma.

NARHC abbreviation for NATIONAL ASSOCIATION OF RURAL HEALTH CLINICS.

narrative method 1. a method of questioning eyewitnesses to an event that reconstructs the event using both the known facts and personal accounts of the experience. **2.** a method of presenting either opening or closing arguments to the jury in a way that tells a story, with events placed in chronological order and including vivid details. See also STORY MODEL.

narrative psychotherapy treatment for individuals, couples, or families that helps clients reinterpret and rewrite their life events into true but more life-enhancing narratives or stories. Narrative therapy posits that individuals are primarily meaning-making beings who are the linguistic authors of their lives and who can reauthor these stories by learning to deconstruct them, by seeing patterns in their ways of interpreting life events or problems, and by reconstruing problems or events in a more helpful light. See also CONSTRUCTIVISM; CONSTRUCTIVIST PSYCHOTHERAPY.

narrative theory any theory of consciousness stating that beliefs arise as part of an explanatory narrative about oneself and society.

narrotophilia *n.* sexual interest and arousal obtained from speaking or hearing sexually explicit words during sexual activity. It most commonly occurs in telephone sex or online computer sex, in which partners talk while masturbating. There are commercial services that employ people to engage in narratophilia with clients for a fee. In some cases of narratophilia, however, people prefer to make obscene phone calls to strangers or randomly selected numbers, as the involvement of a noncooperating person adds to their pleasure. **—narratophile** *n.*

NAS abbreviation for NATIONAL ACADEMY OF SCIENCES.

nasal 1. *adj.* of or relating to the nose. **2.** *adj.* denoting a speech sound produced by letting all or most of the airstream pass through the nasal (rather than the oral) cavity, for example, [ng] in *sing*, or the sound of *-on* in the French word *bon*. **3.** *n.* a nasal speech sound.

nasal cavity the space within the nose, divided into two halves by the **nasal septum**, that communicates with the exterior via the two nostrils and leads to the NASOPHARYNX. Separated from the oral cavity by the hard palate, it is lined with mucous membrane containing OLFACTORY EPITHELIUM and also forms part of the VOCAL TRACT.

NASA Task Load Index (**NASA TLX**) a subjective rating procedure that enables raters to assess the total workload of operatives in a variety of HUMAN–MACHINE SYSTEMS. An overall workload score is derived from a weighted average of ratings on six subscales: mental demands, physical demands, temporal demands, own performance, effort, and frustration.

nasopharynx *n.* the portion of the PHARYNX that lies above the level of the SOFT PALATE. The nasopharynx is closed off from other parts of the pharynx during swallowing and speaking by reflex raising of the soft palate.

NASPSPA abbreviation for NORTH AMERICAN SOCIETY FOR THE PSYCHOLOGY OF SPORT AND PHYSICAL ACTIVITY.

natality *n.* see BIRTH RATE.

National Academy of Sciences (**NAS**) a private, nonprofit society of distinguished scholars engaged in scientific and engineering research, dedicated to the furtherance of science and technology and to their use for general welfare. Its headquarters are in Washington, DC. The NAS was founded by the U.S. Congress in 1863 and expanded to include the National Research Council in 1916, the National Academy of Engineering in 1964, and the Institute of Medicine in 1970. Collectively, the four organizations are known as the **National Academies**.

National Alliance for the Mentally Ill (**NAMI**) a network of SELF-HELP GROUPS that provides emotional and educational support for relatives and individuals affected by mental illness.

National Association of Rural Health Clinics (**NARHC**) an organization that seeks to promote, expand, improve, and protect the delivery of quality, cost-effective health care services in underserved rural areas. NARHC actively engages in the legislative and regulatory process with the U.S. Congress, federal agencies, and rural health organizations.

national character the general personality characteristics attributed to the people of a nation. Although culture has a recognized effect on character formation, the idea of a national character is not generally considered a useful construct, as it invariably consists of an unexamined STEREOTYPE. See also CULTURAL DETERMINISM.

National Committee for Quality Assurance (**NCQA**) a national organization, founded in 1979, that reviews and accredits MANAGED CARE plans and measures the quality of care offered by them.

National Health Interview Survey (**NHIS**) a questionnaire that provides the principal source of information on the health of the civilian noninstitutionalized population of the United States and is one of the major data-collection programs of the National Center for Health Statistics (NCHS). The survey includes core questions and sometimes questions relating to specific initiatives (e.g., aging, healthy people, AIDS).

National Institute of Mental Health (**NIMH**) an agency of the federal government established in 1949 to understand the mind, the brain, and behavior and thereby reduce the burden of mental illness through research. It is committed to scientific programs to educate and train future mental health researchers, including scientists trained in molecular science, cognitive and affective neuroscience, and other disciplines required for the study of mental illness and the brain.

nationalism *n.* **1.** strong, often excessive, feelings of pride in and allegiance to one's nation and its culture or belief in its superiority. **2.** a goal or policy of national independence, especially in relation to a dominant colonial or occupying power. **—nationalist** *n., adj.* **—nationalistic** *adj.*

National Labor Relations Act legislation passed by the U.S. Congress in 1935 that legalized the rights of employees to form and operate unions, engage in COLLECTIVE BARGAINING, and strike. It also identified and prohibited certain UNFAIR LABOR PRACTICES of employers and created the National Labor Relations Board to administer and enforce the provisions of the act. Sponsored by German-born U.S. politician Robert F. Wagner (1877–1953), it is also known as the **Wagner Act**. See also LABOR MANAGEMENT RELATIONS ACT.

National Mental Health Association (**NMHA**) the largest nonprofit organization in the United States, which addresses all aspects of mental health and illness. Established in 1909, it is dedicated to promoting mental health, preventing mental disorders, and achieving victory over mental illness through advocacy, education, research, and service.

National Parent Teachers Association see PARENT TEACHERS ASSOCIATION.

National Practitioner Data Bank a computerized database, established through Title IV of Public Law 99-660 (the Health Care Quality Improvement Act of 1986) and maintained and operated by the U.S. Department of Health and Human Services, that contains information on physicians and other health care professionals against whom MALPRACTICE claims have been paid or certain disciplinary actions taken. The database is primarily an alert or flagging system intended to facilitate a comprehensive review of health care practitioners' professional credentials.

National Register of Health Service Providers in Psychology a national, nonprofit CREDENTIALING organization for professional psychologists, founded in 1974 to advance psychology as a profession and improve the delivery of health services to the public.

National Research Council in the United States, the research arm of the NATIONAL ACADEMY OF SCIENCES, which undertakes scientific studies assigned to it by the U.S. Congress.

National Science Foundation (**NSF**) an independent agency of the U.S. government, established by the National Science Foundation Act of 1950. Its mission is to promote the progress of science; to advance national health, prosperity, and welfare; and to secure the defense of the nation. Activities that fall within its purview include the initiation and support of scientific and engineering research; exchange of information among scientists; technological development; distribution of federal monies to universities and other research organizations; and political advocacy for national policies and research in science and engineering.

native *adj.* see INNATE.

Native American a member of any of various indigenous peoples of the western hemisphere who populated that territory prior to European colonization. When referring to the indigenous peoples of North America, the term **American Indian** is also used.

native speaker a person who speaks a particular language as a mother tongue, rather than as a second or foreign language.

nativism *n.* **1.** the doctrine that the mind has certain innate structures and that experience plays a limited role in the creation of knowledge. See also INNATE IDEAS; NATIVISTIC THEORY. Compare CONSTRUCTIVISM; EMPIRICISM. **2.** the doctrine that mental and behavioral traits are largely determined by hereditary, rather than environmental, factors. See NATURE–NURTURE CONTROVERSY. **3.** the theory that individuals are born with all perceptual capabilities intact, although some capabilities may depend on the biological maturation of perceptual systems to reach adult levels. **—nativist** *adj., n.* **—nativistic** *adj.*

nativistic theory in linguistics, the theory that human beings are born with an innate knowledge of language that enables them to structure and interpret the data they encounter as language learners. Although certain theories about the origins of human language in prehistory have been termed nativistic (see LANGUAGE-ORIGIN THEORY), the term is now mainly associated with Noam CHOMSKY's theory of language acquisition in young children. See LANGUAGE ACQUISITION DEVICE; LANGUAGE UNIVERSAL.

N1 attention effect the first negative component of an EVENT-RELATED POTENTIAL. The N1 component is usually larger for attended stimuli than for unattended stimuli. The source of the N1 component is thought to be areas of the visual cortex. See also PI ATTENTION EFFECT.

natural aptitude see APTITUDE.

natural category 1. a category of like objects or events found in the real world, such as "songs" or "rabbits," as opposed to an AD HOC CATEGORY or an **artificial category** created in a laboratory setting to study categorization processes. **2.** see BASIC-LEVEL CATEGORY.

natural child 1. one of the child ego states in TRANSACTIONAL ANALYSIS, characterized as carefree, fun-loving, creative, impulsive, and impatient. Compare ADAPTED CHILD. **2.** a biological offspring of a parent, in contrast to an adopted child.

natural childbirth a method of labor and child delivery that does not include (or is designed to eliminate) the need for medical interventions, such as anesthetics. The mother receives preparatory education in such areas as breathing and relaxation coordination, exercise of the muscles involved in labor and delivery, and postural positions that make labor more comfortable and allow for conscious participation in delivery. See also LAMAZE METHOD.

natural consequences a form of discipline in which parents do not intervene in children's actions but let the consequences of the action serve as a punishment or lesson. For example, a lesson is learned by children when a toy they have failed to bring indoors during a rainstorm is ruined.

natural experiment a natural event, often a natural disaster (e.g., a flood, tornado, or volcanic eruption), that is treated as an experimental condition to be compared to some control condition. Since natural events cannot be manipulated or prearranged, natural experiments are "quasi experiments" rather than true experiments. Also called **experiment of nature**. See QUASI-EXPERIMENTAL RESEARCH.

natural family planning controlling the number of children in a family by the use of natural techniques of birth control, such as the RHYTHM METHOD, as opposed to the use of oral contraceptives, intrauterine devices, diaphragms, and similar methods.

natural fertility in physiology, the reproductive capacity of animals when unaffected by contraception or induced abortion.

natural group 1. any group formed through natural social processes, particularly when compared to ad hoc laboratory groups created by researchers in their studies of group processes. Examples include an audience, board of directors, clique, club, committee, crowd, dance troupe, family, gang, jury, orchestra, sorority, and support group. **2.** a group whose members are united through common descent or custom, such as a family or tribe.

natural high a state of well-being and happiness that is often associated with physical or mental exertion, in contrast to similar mood states induced by drugs. A natural high is produced by activities that are part of everyday life as opposed to methods that have a direct effect on brain chemistry.

naturalism *n.* **1.** in philosophy, the doctrine that reality consists solely of natural objects and that therefore the methods of natural science offer the only reliable means to knowledge and understanding of reality. Naturalism is closely related to PHYSICALISM and MATERIALISM and explicitly opposes any form of supernaturalism or MYSTICISM positing the existence of realities beyond the natural and material world. **2.** in literature and the other arts, a movement that developed in the late 19th century, often seen as arising out of REALISM, the literary movement and style that generally preceded it. Naturalistic writers aimed to depict life without idealistic illusions or literary artifice and often chose challenging or taboo subjects, such as divorce or prostitution. The plays and novels often show a strong leaning toward psychological DETERMINISM, with the behavior of the characters being explained in terms of their heredity or environments. Leading exponents of naturalism included French writers Émile Zola (1840–1902), Alphonse Daudet (1840–1897), and Guy de Maupassant (1850–1893), Norwegian dramatist Henrik Ibsen (1828–1906), and German dramatist Gerhart Hauptmann (1862–1946). See also POSITIVISM. **—naturalistic** *adj.*

naturalistic environment a type of laboratory environment that attempts to include many of the features found in natural environments. Examples are underground burrows for fossorial animals, flight cages for birds, and trees or other climbing structures for arboreal animals. Naturalistic environments allow the study of more species-typical behavior in captive animals while maintaining control over many other variables.

naturalistic fallacy **1.** a putative logical error that occurs when an attempt is made to define values in terms of natural properties. Values such as goodness and truth are held to be human perceptions and to have no ontological status, or independent existence, as properties of things. **2.** more specifically, the fallacy of basing a moral conclusion (i.e., a conclusion about what ought to be) on ontological premises (i.e., premises about what is or is not the case). An example would be arguing that war is morally acceptable because wars have occurred throughout history. Not all philosophers would agree that all such arguments are necessarily fallacious. [identified by British philosopher George Edward Moore (1873–1958)]

naturalistic observation data collection in a field setting, usually without laboratory controls or manipulation of variables. These procedures are usually carried out by a trained observer, who watches and records the everyday behavior of participants in their natural environments. Examples of naturalistic observation include an ethologist's study of the behavior of chimpanzees and an anthropologist's observation of playing children. See OBSERVATIONAL METHOD.

naturalist intelligence in the MULTIPLE-INTELLIGENCES THEORY, the intelligence involved in detecting patterns and regularities in natural phenomena, used, for example, in identifying varieties of plants or birds.

natural killer cell (**NK cell**) a type of LYMPHOCYTE that destroys infected or cancerous cells. Unlike the B lymphocytes and T lymphocytes, natural killer cells do not require the target cells to display on their surface foreign ANTIGENS combined with host histocompatibility proteins.

natural language a language that has evolved naturally for use among humans, as opposed to an ARTIFICIAL LANGUAGE, such as that used in computer programming.

natural language category a class of things, people, or the like that is defined as a category distinct from other categories by the semantic structure of a particular NATURAL LANGUAGE, rather than by an extralinguistic (scientific or logical) system of classification. Systems of categorization can vary widely from one language to another (see LINGUISTIC DETERMINISM; LINGUISTIC RELATIVITY). Some researchers believe that each natural language category is defined by a cognitive prototype and that membership in the category is determined by an entity's degree of resemblance to this prototype. For example, the category "birds" is defined by a prototype consisting of a set of features (has a beak, has feathers, can fly, etc.) representing the ideal or typical bird: An entity that has all or most of these features will be accepted as belonging to this category.

natural law **1.** in science and natural philosophy, a fundamental truth about the observed regularities of the natural world, such as the law of gravity. See LAW. See also CAUSAL LAW. **2.** in ethics and political philosophy, an ethical principle reflecting a natural or divine truth that is not derived from human reason or experience and that is universal in its application. A natural law is thus seen to provide a norm that should be reflected in human ethical and legal systems.

natural law theory in ethics and political philosophy, the position that there are certain ethical principles that are true and universal, originating in the very nature of reality itself or in the decrees of a divine law giver. In the dominant strain of natural law theory, it is assumed that these principles can be discerned by reason and apply only to beings capable of rational thought. Natural law theory can be traced back to the ancient Greek Stoic philosophers; it strongly influenced Roman law and was subsequently developed by Christian philosophers of the Middle Ages and later periods. Compare RELATIVISM.

natural monism the position that there is a single reality underlying both mental and physical phenomena and that this reality is material. Such a position implies that all sciences, including psychology, are ultimately reducible to physics and chemistry (and that even chemistry obeys the laws of physics). Compare IDEALISTIC MONISM; NEUTRAL MONISM. See also MIND–BODY PROBLEM.

natural reinforcer a stimulus or circumstance, such as food or water, that is inherently reinforcing and does not depend on learning to become desirable. Natural reinforcers are more precisely known as **unconditioned primary reinforcers** (see PRIMARY REINFORCEMENT).

natural selection the process by which such forces as competition, disease, and climate tend to eliminate individuals who are less well adapted to a particular environment and favor the survival and reproduction of better adapted individuals. Hence, over successive generations, the nature of the population changes. This is the fundamental mechanism driving the evolution of living organisms and the emergence of new species, as originally proposed independently by British naturalists Charles Darwin (1809–1882) and Alfred Russel Wallace (1823–1913). See DARWINISM; EVOLUTIONARY THEORY; SELECTION; SURVIVAL OF THE FITTEST. Compare ARTIFICIAL SELECTION.

natural work module a unit of work in which an employee or team of employees produces a whole item or otherwise completes a meaningful sequence of tasks from start to finish. Such an approach has been found to yield greater TASK IDENTITY and therefore greater motivation than one in which employees perform their tasks with little or no sense of context.

natural work team a group of employees who perform related or complementary tasks working together as a cooperative unit. It has been found that creating such teams has a positive effect on WORK MOTIVATION.

nature *n.* **1.** the entirety of physical reality. **2.** the phenomena of the natural world, including plants, animals, and physical features, as opposed to human beings and their creations. **3.** the fundamental or inherent qualities of something. See ESSENCE. **4.** the innate, presumably genetically determined, characteristics and behaviors of an individual. In psychology, those characteristics most often and traditionally associated with nature are temperament, body type, and personality. Compare NURTURE. **—natural** *adj.*

nature–nurture controversy the dispute over the relative contributions of hereditary and constitutional factors (NATURE) and environmental factors (NURTURE) to the development of the individual. Nativists emphasize the role of heredity, whereas environmentalists emphasize sociocultural and ecological factors, including family attitudes, child-rearing practices, and economic status. Most scientists now accept that there is a close interaction between hereditary and environmental factors in the ontogeny of behavior (see EPIGENESIS). Also called **heredity–environment controversy**; **nature–nurture issue**; **nature–nurture problem**.

naturopathy *n.* an alternative health care system that aims to prevent disease and promote physical and mental health by using natural therapies (e.g., dietary measures, acupuncture, and massage) to address underlying disease processes. Also called **naturopathic medicine**. See also COMPLEMENTARY AND ALTERNATIVE MEDICINE.

Naturwissenschaftliche Psychologie one of two approaches to the study of psychological problems and issues identified by German psychologists in the late 19th century. This approach (translated literally as "natural science psychology") adopted the experimental method and laboratory techniques as appropriate and useful for certain classes of phenomena, such as perceptual phenomena. These techniques were regarded as inappropriate for studying higher mental processes, language, and social phenomena, for which a different approach (see GEISTESWISSENSCHAFTLICHE PSYCHOLOGIE) was required.

nausea gravidarum see MORNING SICKNESS.

nauseous *adj.* in the ZWAARDEMAKER SMELL SYSTEM, denoting an odor quality that is smelled in feces and carrion flowers.

nautilus eye the eye of the nautilus mollusk, which is of particular value in studies of vision. It consists mainly of a spherical cavity lined with photosensitive cells that respond to light entering through a small hole at the top. This eye is thus virtually a pinhole camera made of living tissue.

navigation *n.* the mechanisms used by an organism to find its way through the environment, for example, to a migration site or to its home site. A variety of cues have been documented in nonhuman animals, including using the sun or stars as a compass (see SUN COMPASS), magnetic lines, olfactory cues, visual cues (e.g., rivers or coastlines), and wind-sheer effects from air masses crossing mountain ranges. See also HOMING; MIGRATION BEHAVIOR.

nay-saying *n.* a type of RESPONSE BIAS in which questions tend to be answered negatively regardless of their content. Compare RESPONSE ACQUIESCENCE (yea-saying).

NBAS abbreviation for Neonatal Behavioral Assessment Scale (see BRAZELTON NEONATAL BEHAVIORAL ASSESSMENT SCALE).

NCQA abbreviation for NATIONAL COMMITTEE FOR QUALITY ASSURANCE.

near-death experience (**NDE**) an image, perception, event, interaction, or feeling (or a combination of any of these) reported by some people after a life-threatening episode. Typical features include a sense of separation from the body, often accompanied by the ability to look down on the situation; a peaceful and pleasant state of mind; and an entering into the light, sometimes following an interaction with a spiritual being. There is continuing controversy regarding the cause and nature of NDEs. Spiritual, biomedical, and contextual lines of explanation are still in play, and there is no solid evidence to support the proposition that NDEs prove survival of death. See also DEATHBED ESCORTS AND VISIONS. [term coined in 1975 by U.S. parapsychologist Raymond A. Moody (1944–) in his book *Life After Life*]

near miss in hearing studies, a small deviation from WEBER'S LAW in which the WEBER FRACTION for intensity discrimination decreases over a wide range of intensities of the standard. The near miss is observed for sounds with a restricted bandwidth and is thought to result from nonlinear growth of excitation in the COCHLEA.

near point the shortest distance at which an object is in focus for a single eye. Also called **near point of accommodation**. Compare FAR POINT.

near point of convergence the shortest distance at which an object is in focus when viewed with both eyes, without appearing as a double image.

nearsightedness *n.* see MYOPIA.

necessary condition see CONDITION.

Necker cube a line drawing of a cube in which all angles and sides can be seen, as if it were transparent. It is an AMBIGUOUS FIGURE whose three-dimensionality fluctuates when viewed for a prolonged period of time. See also RUBIN'S FIGURE. [Louis Albert **Necker** (1730–1804), Swiss crystallographer]

neck–eye reflex a reflex involving compensatory movements of the eyes to maintain fixation on a target while the direction of the head is changed. It is important for maintaining image stability.

necro- (**necr-**) *combining form* death or dissolution.

necromancy *n.* **1.** a form of DIVINATION in which a person supposedly conjures up the spirits of the dead in order to gain knowledge of future events. **2.** more generally, black magic or sorcery. **—necromancer** *n.* **—necromantic** *adj.*

necromania *n.* a morbid preoccupation with corpses, usually including sexual desire for dead bodies, and a morbid interest in funerals, morgues, autopsies, and cemeteries. See NECROPHILIA.

necromimesis *n.* a delusion in which individuals act as if they were dead because they believe they are dead.

necrophilia *n.* sexual interest in or sexual contact with dead bodies. It is a PARAPHILIA that appears to be confined almost exclusively to men. In some cases they kill the victim themselves, but most frequently they gain access to female (or male) corpses from funeral parlors, mortuaries, morgues, or graves. See KATASEXUALITY. **—necrophile** *n.* **—necrophilic** *adj.*

necrophilic fantasies male (and, occasionally, female) fantasies about viewing or having heterosexual or same-sex intercourse with a corpse as a means of achieving sexual excitement. Such fantasies are sometimes acted out with the aid of prostitutes who satisfy necrophilic clients by simulating a lifeless appearance.

necrophobia *n.* a persistent and irrational fear of corpses. See also THANATOPHOBIA.

necrosis *n.* the death of cells (e.g., neurons, muscle cells) from any of a variety of causes, including obstruction of blood supply to the affected part, disease, injury, or toxins. **—necrotic** *adj.*

need *n.* **1.** a condition of tension in an organism resulting from deprivation of something required for survival, well-being, or personal fulfillment. **2.** a substance, state, or any other thing (e.g., food, water, security) whose absence generates this condition. See MASLOW'S MOTIVATIONAL HIERARCHY.

need arousal a motivational technique, used primarily by propagandists, advertisers, and politicians, in which an appeal is made to the desire of individuals for such attainments as status, health, money saving, beauty, or security.

need distribution of rewards the allocation of resources to members of a group based on need, such that individuals with greater needs receive more, irrespective of their overall contribution to the group.

need–fear dilemma **1.** a simultaneous need for and fear of close relationships with others. **2.** a conflicting set of conditions facing those who need structured control but have an aversion to external control or influence. In marked form, it is a characteristic condition in schizophrenia, particularly in terms of both greatly needing and greatly fearing other people.

need for achievement (**n-Ach**) a strong desire to accomplish goals and attain a high standard of performance and personal fulfillment. People with a high need for achievement often undertake tasks in which there is a reasonable probability of success and avoid tasks that are either too easy (because of lack of challenge) or too difficult (because of fear of failure). The need for achievement was proposed by U.S. psychologist Henry Alexander Murray (1893–1988) and investigated extensively by David MCCLELLAND.

need for affection the degree to which a person wants to be close or distant in a relationship with another. In intimate relationships, need for affection is often expressed concretely as a desire to be touched or held or to be commended verbally. An exaggerated need for affection and approval is one of the ten neurotic trends identified by German-born U.S. psychoanalyst Karen D. Horney (1885–1952). This exaggerated need is often seen as resulting from early deprivation, especially of physical affection.

need for affiliation (**n-Aff**) a strong desire to socialize and be part of a group. People with a high need for affiliation often seek the approval and acceptance of others. See AFFILIATIVE DRIVE. [proposed by David MCCLELLAND]

need for closure 1. the motivation to achieve finality and absoluteness in decisions, judgments, and choices. A person with a high need for closure will often have a low tolerance of ambiguity and uncertainty and may be attracted to dogmatic political or religious views. **2.** the need to achieve a sense of finality at the close of a painful or difficult episode in one's life. Some estranged couples, for example, feel a need to obtain a formal divorce for emotional as well as practical reasons. See CLOSURE.

need for cognition a personality trait reflecting a person's tendency to enjoy engaging in extensive cognitive activity. This trait primarily reflects a person's motivation to engage in cognitive activity rather than his or her actual ability to do so. Individuals high in need for cognition tend to develop attitudes or take action based on thoughtful evaluation of information. [originally investigated in 1994 by U.S. psychologists John T. Cacioppo (1951–) and Richard E. Petty (1951–)]

need for power the dispositional tendency to seek control over other people and over one's environment. See POWER.

need-hierarchy theory see MASLOW'S MOTIVATIONAL HIERARCHY.

need–press method in the THEMATIC APPERCEPTION TEST, a system of analyzing and scoring each sentence of the stories told by a participant as a means of evaluating his or her needs and the PRESS of environmental factors to which he or she is exposed.

need–press theory in the PERSONOLOGY of U.S. psychologist Henry Alexander Murray (1893–1988), an explanation of behavior in terms of the influence, or PRESS, of both the present environment and past experiences upon the expression and activation of a need.

need reduction the decrease of a need, often achieved through consummatory behavior (see CONSUMMATORY RESPONSE). Also called **need gratification**. See DRIVE-REDUCTION THEORY.

needs assessment 1. the identification of currently unmet service needs in a community or other group, done prior to implementing a new service program or modifying an existing service program. The perceived needs are generally assessed from multiple perspectives, including those of community or group leaders and those of each individual in the community or group. **2.** the identification of those areas that should be the focus of a PERSONNEL TRAINING program. Needs assessment involves analyses in three key areas: (a) the KNOWLEDGE, SKILLS, ABILITIES, AND OTHER CHARACTERISTICS of employees; (b) the requirements of the tasks performed by employees; and (c) the requirements of the organization. See also PERSON–NEEDS ANALYSIS.

need to belong the motivation to be a part of relationships, belong to groups, and to be viewed positively by others. See AFFILIATIVE DRIVE.

need to evaluate a personality trait reflecting a person's tendency to engage in extensive evaluative thinking when encountering people, issues, or objects. People who are high in need to evaluate tend to form attitudes and categorize objects spontaneously along a positive–negative scale. People who are low in need to evaluate tend to think of objects in evaluative terms only when the context encourages such categorization. [originally investigated in 1996 by U.S. psychologists William Blair Gage Jarvis and Richard E. Petty (1951–)]

nefazodone *n.* a MIXED-FUNCTION ANTIDEPRESSANT chemically related to TRAZODONE but with some important pharmacological distinctions. It is an antagonist at 5-HT_2 SEROTONIN RECEPTORS and an inhibitor of both serotonin and norepinephrine reuptake. This combination of actions is thought to be related to the lack of SSRI-like side effects associated with its antidepressant properties. Its sedative effects may be useful in the treatment of depression-related anxiety and insomnia.

negation *n.* **1.** in Jean PIAGET's theory of cognitive development, a mental process—a form of REVERSIBILITY—in which one realizes that any operation can always be negated, or inverted. Also called **inversion**. See IDENTITY, NEGATION, RECIPROCAL, AND CORRELATIVE OPERATIONS. **2.** see DENIAL. **—negate** *vb.*

negative *n.* in linguistics, the form of a sentence used to make a negative assertion about something rather than an AFFIRMATIVE statement or a question (see INTERROGATIVE). In modern English, negatives are nearly always formed using *not* or *no* and an auxiliary verb (usually *be, have,* or *do*). The structural relationship between positive and negative forms of a statement (e.g., between *I went* and *I did not go*) is of major interest in GENERATIVE GRAMMAR and PSYCHOLINGUISTICS.

negative acceleration a situation in which changes in the rate of development in a given activity or function decrease as a result of practice. For example, successive practice trials may produce smaller and smaller gains in learning or performance. See LEARNING CURVE. Compare POSITIVE ACCELERATION.

negative adaptation a gradual loss of sensitivity or weakening of response due to prolonged stimulation.

negative affect the internal feeling state (AFFECT) that occurs when one has failed to achieve a goal or to avoid a threat or when one is not satisfied with the current state of affairs. The tendency to experience such states is known as **negative affectivity**.

negative afterimage see AFTERIMAGE.

negative afterpotential the small additional negative membrane potential (HYPERPOLARIZATION) shown by nerve and muscle cells during recovery from an ACTION POTENTIAL. The nerve or muscle is less excitable during the negative afterpotential.

negative attitude in psychotherapy and counseling, the client's feeling of rejection or disapproval of the therapist or counselor or of the therapeutic or counseling process, another person, an object, or of him- or herself. Compare POSITIVE ATTITUDE.

negative binomial distribution a discrete theoretical probability distribution that describes the distribution of the number of trials that will occur before the *r*th success will occur in a sequence of *n* BERNOULLI TRIALS. Also called **Pascal distribution**.

negative conditioned stimulus in PAVLOVIAN CONDITIONING, a stimulus that, when presented in the context of CONDITIONED STIMULUS–UNCONDITIONED STIMULUS pairings, is not followed by an unconditioned stimulus.

negative contingency see CONTINGENCY.

negative discriminative stimulus (symbol: S^{Δ} or S–) in OPERANT CONDITIONING, a stimulus signifying that a given response will not be reinforced, implying that there is at least one other stimulus circumstance in which the response will be reinforced. Compare DISCRIMINATIVE STIMULUS.

negative emotion an unpleasant, often disruptive, emotional reaction designed to express a NEGATIVE AFFECT. Negative emotion is not conducive to progress toward obtaining one's goals. Examples are anger, envy, sadness, and fear. Compare POSITIVE EMOTION.

negative eugenics see EUGENICS.

negative exercise addiction an inordinate attraction to habitual participation in physical exercise activities that has a negative effect on physical, psychological, or social well-being. Also called **exercise compulsion**; **exercise obsession**. Compare POSITIVE EXERCISE ADDICTION.

negative feedback 1. an arrangement whereby some of the output of a system, whether mechanical or biological, is fed back to reduce the effect of input signals. Such systems, which measure the deviation from a desired state and apply a correction, are important in achieving HOMEOSTASIS, whereas systems employing POSITIVE FEEDBACK tend to amplify small deviations and become highly unstable. See FEEDBACK SYSTEM. **2.** in social psychology, nonconstructive criticism, disapproval, and other negative information received by a person in response to his or her performance.

negative hallucination a false perceptual experience characterized by failure to see a person or object while looking directly at it, as in failing to perceive a certain person in a group in response to hypnotic suggestion. Compare POSITIVE HALLUCINATION.

negative imagery mental images that incorporate sensations of performance errors, unwanted outcomes, DEMOTIVATION, or SELF-DEGRADING.

negative incentive an object or condition that constitutes an AVERSIVE STIMULUS and therefore facilitates avoidance behavior. Compare POSITIVE INCENTIVE.

negative induction a reduction in the response to one stimulus, in circumstances in which conditions remain fixed, as a result of a reduction of response brought about in another experiment in which stimuli were alternated. See also BEHAVIORAL CONTRAST.

negative Oedipus complex in psychoanalytic theory, the opposite or reverse aspect of the OEDIPUS COMPLEX, in which the son desires the father and regards the mother as rival, or the daughter is attached to the mother and regards the father as rival. The more familiar attachment is the heterosexual form (the positive Oedipus complex). Sigmund FREUD held that both aspects are part of the normal Oedipus complex in boys and girls. Also called **inverted Oedipus complex**.

negative priming the ability of a preceding stimulus to inhibit the response to a subsequent stimulus. This is measured by the detectability of the second stimulus or the time taken to make a response to the second stimulus. The most striking examples occur when the participant is instructed to ignore a feature of the first stimulus (e.g., its color) and then to attend to that same feature in the second stimulus. PRIMING effects are usually facilitative.

negative punishment punishment that results because some stimulus or circumstance is removed as a consequence of a response. For example, if a response results in a subtraction of money from an accumulating account, and the response becomes less likely as a result of this experience, then negative punishment has occurred. Compare POSITIVE PUNISHMENT.

negative recency in recalling a list of items, the tendency to recall fewer of the final items of the list than the middle and early items. Negative recency contrasts with the enhanced recall of final items seen in the RECENCY EFFECT. Also called **negative recency effect**.

negative reference group a group with which a person does not want to be identified and whose norms and standards he or she does not wish to match.

negative reinforcement the removal, prevention, or postponement of an AVERSIVE STIMULUS as a consequence of a response, which, in turn, increases the probability of that response. Compare POSITIVE REINFORCEMENT.

negative response a response that results in avoidance of or withdrawal from a stimulus.

negative schizophrenia a form of schizophrenia characterized by a predomination of NEGATIVE SYMPTOMS, suggesting deficiency or absence of behavior normally present in a person's repertoire, as shown in apathy, blunted affect, emotional withdrawal, poor rapport, and lack of spontaneity. Compare POSITIVE SCHIZOPHRENIA. [defined in 1982 by U.S. psychiatrist Nancy C. Andreasen and Scott A. Olsen]

negative self-talk the covert expression of ideas (see SELF-TALK) that are counter to the creation of an IDEAL PERFORMANCE STATE and are demotivating or self-degrading.

negative self-verification theory the theory that a depressed mood is exacerbated or maintained because depressed individuals solicit or inspire feedback or treatment from others that confirms or reinforces their negative beliefs about themselves.

negative-state-relief model the hypothesis that HELPING BEHAVIOR is used by some people in stress situations and periods of boredom and inactivity to avoid or escape negative moods.

negative stereotype a STEREOTYPE that purports to describe the undesirable, objectionable, or unacceptable qualities and characteristics of the members of a particular group or social category. Compare POSITIVE STEREOTYPE.

negative suggestion a statement intended to deter or suppress a feeling, thought, or action on the part of another person.

negative symptom a deficit in the ability to perform the normal functions of living—logical thinking, self-care, social interaction, planning, initiating, and carrying through constructive actions, and so forth—as shown in apathy, blunted affect, emotional withdrawal, poor rapport, and lack of spontaneity. In schizophrenia, a predominance of negative symptoms is often associated with a poor prognosis. Compare POSITIVE SYMPTOM. See NEGATIVE SCHIZOPHRENIA.

negative transfer 1. a process in which previous learning obstructs or interferes with present learning. For instance, tennis players who learn racquetball must often unlearn their tendency to take huge, muscular swings with the shoulder and upper arm. See also TRANSFER OF TRAINING. Compare POSITIVE TRANSFER. **2.** see LANGUAGE TRANSFER.

negative transference in psychoanalysis, transfer of anger or hostility felt toward the parents, or other individuals significant during childhood, onto the therapist. Compare POSITIVE TRANSFERENCE.

negative triad see COGNITIVE TRIAD.

negative tropism the orientation of an organism away from a particular source of stimulation. See TROPISM.

negativism *n.* **1.** an attitude characterized by persistent resistance to the suggestions of others (**passive negativism**) or the tendency to act in ways that are contrary to the expectations, requests, or commands of others (**active negativism**), typically without any identifiable reason for opposition. In young children and adolescents, such reactions may be considered a healthy expression of self-assertion. Negativism may also be associated with a number of disorders (extreme negativism is a feature of CATATONIC SCHIZOPHRENIA) and it can be an expression of opposition, withdrawal, or anger or a method of gaining attention. Also called **negativistic response**. See also OPPOSITIONAL DEFIANT DISORDER; PASSIVE-AGGRESSIVE PERSONALITY DISORDER. **2.** any philosophy or doctrine based on negation, such as nihilism or skepticism. **—negativistic** *adj.*

negativistic personality disorder see PASSIVE-AGGRESSIVE PERSONALITY DISORDER.

negativistic response see NEGATIVISM.

negativity bias see TRAIT-NEGATIVITY BIAS.

neglect *n.* **1.** failure to provide for the basic needs of a person in one's care. The neglect may be emotional (e.g., rejection or apathy), material (e.g., withholding food or clothing), or service-oriented (e.g., depriving of education or medical attention). See CHILD NEGLECT; ELDER NEGLECT. See also MALTREATMENT. **2.** a syndrome characterized by lack of awareness of a specific area or side of the body caused by a brain injury. It may involve failure to recognize the area as belonging to oneself or ignoring the existence of one side of the body or one side of the visual field (see UNILATERAL NEGLECT; VISUAL NEGLECT). This is most often associated with an injury to the right cerebral hemisphere with corresponding left-sided neglect. Neglect has also been found in auditory, tactile, and proprioceptive tasks. Also called **perceptual neglect**. See also MOTOR NEGLECT; SENSORY NEGLECT; SPATIAL NEGLECT.

neglect dyslexia a form of acquired dyslexia (see ALEXIA) associated with VISUAL NEGLECT, a condition in which a person is unaware of half of the visual field as a result of neurological damage. Either the initial parts of words are misread (left neglect) or the terminal parts of words are misread (right neglect), and the errors are not simple deletions but typically guesses of real though incorrect words with approximately the right number of letters.

neglected child 1. see CHILD NEGLECT. **2.** see ISOLATE.

negligence *n.* failure to fulfill a duty or to provide some response, action, or level of care that it is appropriate or reasonable to expect. In ergonomics, for example, negligence involves failure to take reasonable care to protect human safety or equipment in the design, development, or evaluation of a system. A variety of different types of negligence exist in law. See also MALPRACTICE. **—negligent** *adj.*

negligent hiring a basis for a civil lawsuit against an employer in which a person claims that he or she suffered injury, loss, or harm as a result of actions by an incompetent employee who would not have been hired had the organization followed responsible hiring practices.

negotiation *n.* a reciprocal communication process in which two or more parties to a dispute examine specific issues, explain their positions, and exchange offers and counteroffers in an attempt to identify a solution or outcome that is acceptable to all parties. Compare BARGAINING. **—negotiate** *vb.*

Neil v. Biggers a case resulting in an influential 1972 U.S. Supreme Court decision in which the court identified factors that should be considered when assessing the validity of eyewitness identification. These factors are: (a) certainty as to the identification, (b) delay between the witnessed event and identification, (c) ability to clearly view the witnessed event, (d) level of attention paid to the witnessed event, and (e) the accuracy of the witness's initial description of the individual involved in the event.

Nelson–Denny Reading Test a multiple-choice test of vocabulary, reading rate, and reading comprehension for high school and college students as well as adults. The vocabulary section consists of 80 one-sentence statements requiring participants to choose from among four choices the proper meaning of a specific word used in that sentence. The reading rate and reading comprehension sections are combined; the former requires participants to read as much of a given narrative passage as possible within one minute while the latter requires participants to answer questions about that same passage and six others. Originally developed in 1929, the Nelson–Denny Reading Test is now in its 5th edition (published in 1993). [M. J. **Nelson** (1894–1970) and E. C. **Denny** (1887–1984), U.S. educators]

Nembutal *n.* a trade name for PENTOBARBITAL.

neoassociationism *n.* theories of association formation developed subsequently to traditional philosophical ASSOCIATIONISM. Neoassociationism typically encompasses learning and conditioning theories, such as that of Clark L. HULL.

neoassociationist theory in general, any modern theory that accounts for behavior as a conditioned or unconditioned response to an antecedent event. Specifically, the term was applied by U.S. psychologist Leonard Berkowitz (1926–) to his theory explaining aggression as a response to triggering conditions that activate an associative network of responses. See also FRUSTRATION–AGGRESSION HYPOTHESIS; WEAPONS EFFECT.

neobehaviorism *n.* an approach to psychology, influenced by LOGICAL POSITIVISM, that emphasized the development of comprehensive theories and frameworks of behavior, such as those of Clark Leonard HULL and Edward C. TOLMAN, through empirical observation of behavior and the use of consciousness and mental events as explanatory devices. It thus contrasts with classical BEHAVIORISM, which was concerned with freeing psychology of mentalistic concepts and explanations. According to U.S. psychologist and philosopher Sigmund Koch (1917–1996), neobehaviorism replaced classical behaviorism as the dominant 20th-century program for experimental psychology in about 1930; its influence began to wane in the 1950s. See also RADICAL BEHAVIORISM. **—neobehaviorist** *adj., n.*

neocerebellum *n.* the dorsal and most recently evolved part of the CEREBELLUM, which appears only in mammals. It contains fibers that communicate with nuclei of the PONS. Compare PALEOCEREBELLUM.

neocortex *n.* the part of the CEREBRAL CORTEX that is the most recently evolved and contains six layers of cells. All the cortex seen at the surface of the human brain is neocortex, including the primary sensory and motor cortex and association cortex. Also called **isocortex**. See also CORTICAL LAYERS; CYTOARCHITECTURE. Compare ALLOCORTEX; ARCHICORTEX; PALEOCORTEX. **—neocortical** *adj.*

neodissociative theory a theory that explains the paradoxical phenomena of hypnosis as a result of DIVIDED CONSCIOUSNESS. For example, hypnotic analgesia can produce subjectively reported relief from pain while physiological measures indicate that pain is still being registered.

neo-Freudian 1. *adj.* denoting an approach that derives from the CLASSICAL PSYCHOANALYSIS of Sigmund FREUD, but with modifications and revisions that typically emphasize social and interpersonal elements over biological instincts. The term is not usually applied to the approaches of Freud's contemporaries, such as Alfred ADLER and Carl JUNG, who broke away from his school quite early. Erik ERIKSON, Erich FROMM, German-born U.S. psychoanalyst Karen Horney (1885–1952), and U.S. psychiatrist Harry Stack Sullivan (1892–1949) are considered to be among the most influential neo-Freudian theorists and practitioners. **2.** *n.* an analyst or theoretician who adopts such an approach.

neolalia *n.* the abnormal tendency to use NEOLOGISMS when speaking. Also called **neolallism**.

neolocal *adj.* denoting a living arrangement in which a newly married couple begins a new household separate from their kin, or a culture in which this is the norm. Compare MATRILOCAL; PATRILOCAL.

neologism *n.* a word made up by an individual. Neologisms, whose origins and meanings are usually nonsensical and unrecognizable (e.g., "klipno" for watch), are typically associated with APHASIA or SCHIZOPHRENIA. See also PORTMANTEAU NEOLOGISM. **—neologistic** *adj.*

neologistic jargon unintelligible speech containing a mixture of inappropriately combined words and bizarre expressions coined by the speaker. Also called **neologistic paraphasia**. See WORD SALAD.

neo-Malthusian *adj.* denoting the contemporary doctrine or movement that supports population control, especially by the use of family planning and contraception, in order to ensure adequate resources and protect the environment. See MALTHUSIAN THEORY.

neonatal *adj.* referring to a newborn child or to the period shortly after childbirth.

Neonatal Behavioral Assessment Scale (NBAS) see BRAZELTON NEONATAL BEHAVIORAL ASSESSMENT SCALE.

neonatal drug dependency syndrome a syndrome in which a baby is born with drug dependence due to the mother's drug abuse (most often opioid abuse) during the latter part of pregnancy. Such babies are often of low birth weight. Other severe problems that accompany drug abuse by pregnant women include increased risk of intrauterine death, premature delivery, and increased neonatal mortality.

neonatal imitation the ability of newborn babies to reproduce some behavior, such as a facial expression, that they see in others. See also ACTIVE INTERMODAL MAPPING.

neonatal period in human development, the period from birth to approximately 1 month of age for infants born after a full-term pregnancy (for infants born prematurely, the period is longer). Among nonhuman species, the neonatal period varies depending on the species. For example, in dogs the period extends from birth to approximately 12 to 14 days of age; for some rats it lasts approximately 21 days from birth. See also DEVELOPMENTAL LEVELS.

neonate *n.* a newborn human or nonhuman animal. Human infants born after the normal gestational period of 36 weeks are known as **full-term neonates**; infants born prematurely before the end of this period are known as **preterm neonates** (or, colloquially, as "preemies").

neonaticide *n.* the killing of an infant who is less than 24 hours old. See also FILICIDE; INFANTICIDE.

neonativism *n.* the belief that much cognitive knowledge, such as OBJECT PERMANENCE and certain aspects of language, is innate, requiring little in the way of specific experiences to be expressed. Neonativists hold that cognitive development is influenced by biological constraints and that individuals are predisposed to process certain types of information. Also called **structural constraint theory**. **—neonativist** *adj., n.*

NEO Personality Inventory (NEO-PI) a personality questionnaire designed to assess the factors of the FIVE-FACTOR PERSONALITY MODEL. First published in 1985 and revised in 1992 (**NEO-PI-R**), the inventory takes its name from three factors of the model: *n*euroticism, *e*xtraversion, and *o*penness to experience. It is available in two versions (Form S for self-reports and Form R for observer ratings), each comprising 240 statements to which participants respond using a 5-point LIKERT SCALE format, ranging from "strongly disagree" to "strongly agree." [developed by U.S. psychologists Paul T. Costa, Jr. (1942–) and Robert R. McCrae (1949–)]

neophasia *n.* a complex language system created by and idiosyncratic to a person, with its own vocabulary and rules of grammar.

neophenomenology *n.* an approach to psychology that emphasizes the role of the individual's phenomenological (immediate and conscious) experience in the determination of action. See PERSONALISTIC PSYCHOLOGY; PHENOMENOLOGY. [attributed to U.S. psychologists Donald Snygg (1904–1967) and Arthur W. Combs (1912–1999)]

neophilia *n.* a strong desire for anything new or different, such as new foods.

neophobia *n.* **1.** a persistent and irrational fear of change or of anything new, unfamiliar, or strange. **2.** the avoidance of new stimuli, especially foods. **—neophobic** *adj.*

neoplasm *n.* a new, abnormal growth, that is, a benign or malignant tumor. The term is generally used to specify a malignant tumor (see CANCER). A neoplasm usually grows rapidly by cellular proliferation but generally lacks structural organization. A malignant neoplasm is usually invasive, destroying or damaging neighboring normal tissues, and can spread to distant sites by the process of metastasis; benign neoplasms are usually encapsulated and do not spread, but may damage neighboring tissues by compression. **—neoplastic** *adj.*

Neoplatonism *n.* a school of philosophy based on a particular understanding of the teachings of Greek philosopher Plato (c. 427–c. 347 BCE), especially as interpreted by Alexandrian philosopher Plotinus (204–270). Neoplatonism retains Plato's view that there is another perfect and eternal world that accounts for the things of the physical world (see PLATONIC IDEALISM). In the strain developed by Plotinus, however, there is greater emphasis on an ultimate unity of the universe, and a new sense that MYSTICISM, as opposed to reason, is the way through which the other world is experienced. Neoplatonism was influential in the reconciliation of Christianity with classical philosophy in the Middle Ages and the Renaissance. **—Neoplatonist** *n., adj.*

neostigmine *n.* an anticholinesterase (see CHOLINERGIC DRUGS) used in the diagnosis and treatment of myasthenia gravis and glaucoma. U.S. trade name: **Prostigmin**.

neostriatum *n.* a portion of the BASAL GANGLIA that has evolved relatively recently. It includes the PUTAMEN and the CAUDATE NUCLEUS. It is contrasted with the phylogenetically older **paleostriatum**, which is represented by the GLOBUS PALLIDUS. **—neostriatal** *adj.*

neoteny *n.* **1.** in zoology, sexual maturation in the larval state. **2.** in evolution, the retention into adulthood of juvenile characteristics of an ancestral species, for example, the large ratio of brain size to body size in humans. **—neotenous** *adj.*

nephrogenic diabetes insipidus a form of diabetes in which the kidney is unable to produce a normal concentration of urine because the kidney tubules do not respond to VASOPRESSIN produced by the pituitary gland. The patient drinks enormous amounts of water and excretes large volumes of dilute urine. The disorder can be critical for infants, who cannot communicate their thirst and therefore suffer water depletion, which may lead to brain damage and mental retardation before the cause can be diagnosed.

nepiophilia *n.* sexual interest in and arousal by infants: a type of PEDOPHILIA. The person generally does not find adults, or sometimes even older children, sexually arousing. Nepiophilia is rarely seen in females.

Nernst equation an equation used to calculate the EQUILIBRIUM POTENTIAL at a membrane. [Walther Hermann **Nernst** (1864–1941), German chemist]

nerve *n.* a bundle of nerve fibers (see AXON) outside the central nervous system (CNS), enclosed in a sheath of connective tissue to form a cordlike structure. Nerves serve to connect the CNS with the tissues and organs of the body. They may be motor, sensory, or mixed (containing axons of both motor and sensory neurons). See CRANIAL NERVE; SPINAL NERVE. Compare TRACT.

nerve block the blocking of nerve impulses by drugs (e.g., anesthetics) or by mechanical means.

nerve cell see NEURON.

nerve deafness see SENSORINEURAL HEARING LOSS.

nerve ending the terminus of an AXON. There are various types of nerve ending, including ANNULOSPIRAL ENDINGS and FLOWER-SPRAY ENDINGS in muscle spindles, BASKET ENDINGS, KRAUSE END BULBS, MEISSNER'S CORPUSCLES, and FREE NERVE ENDINGS.

nerve fiber 1. the AXON of a neuron, extending from the cell body. **2.** loosely, the neuron itself.

nerve growth factor (**NGF**) an endogenous polypeptide that stimulates the growth and development of neurons in SPINAL GANGLIA and in the ganglia of the SYMPATHETIC NERVOUS SYSTEM.

nerve impulse a wave of DEPOLARIZATION, in the form of an ACTION POTENTIAL, that is propagated along a neuron or chain of neurons as the means of transmitting signals in the nervous system. Also called **nervous impulse**; **neural impulse**. See also SYNAPSE.

nerve–muscle preparation a muscle and its motor nerve, both at least partially dissected from the body, used for physiological experiments.

nerve of Wrisberg see GREATER SUPERFICIAL PETROSAL NERVE. [Heinrich A. **Wrisberg** (1739–1808), German anatomist]

nerve root the part of a nerve that connects directly to the brain or spinal cord. Spinal nerves arise from the spinal cord via a DORSAL ROOT and a VENTRAL ROOT, which then combine to form the spinal nerve. Certain CRANIAL NERVES also are formed by the combination of two nerve roots.

nerve tissue the cell bodies and fibrous processes of neurons that make up the functional components of the nervous system. Supporting tissues, such as NEUROGLIA, are sometimes also included. Also called **nervous tissue**.

nerve tract see TRACT.

nerve trunk the main body of a nerve, in which all the axons run together. The trunk of a typical spinal nerve is formed by the combination of the two SPINAL ROOTS and distributes to peripheral organs and tissues via its branches.

nervios *n.* a wide range of symptoms affecting Latino groups in the United States and Latin America (the word literally means "nerves") and attributed to stressful and difficult life experiences and circumstances. Symptoms include headache, dizziness, concentration difficulties, sleep disturbance, stomach upsets, and tingling sensations; mental disorder may or may not be present. See also ATAQUE DE NERVIOS.

nervous *adj.* **1.** in a transient emotional state of anxious apprehension. **2.** of an excitable, highly strung, or easily agitated disposition. **3.** referring to the structures or functions of the nervous system. See also NEURAL.

nervous breakdown a lay term for an emotional illness or other mental disorder that has a sudden onset, produces acute distress, and significantly interferes with one's functioning. Also called **nervous prostration**.

nervous exhaustion a lay term for a state of severe fatigue due to emotional strain. See also NEURASTHENIA.

nervous habit stereotyped behavior, such as nail biting or tics, presumed to be based on anxiety and performed to reduce tension.

nervous impulse see NERVE IMPULSE.

nervousness *n.* a state of restless tension and emotionality in which people tend to tremble, feel apprehensive, or show other signs of anxiety or fear.

nervous prostration see NERVOUS BREAKDOWN.

nervous system the system of NEURONS, NERVES, TRACTS, and associated tissues that, together with the ENDOCRINE SYSTEM, coordinates activities of the organism in response to signals received from the internal and external environments. The nervous system of higher vertebrates is often considered in terms of its divisions, principally the CENTRAL NERVOUS SYSTEM, the PERIPHERAL NERVOUS SYSTEM, and the AUTONOMIC NERVOUS SYSTEM. See also CONCEPTUAL NERVOUS SYSTEM.

nervous tissue see NERVE TISSUE.

nervus terminalis a collection of nerve fibers that originates near the OLFACTORY EPITHELIUM. Its origin suggests that it is part of the VOMERONASAL SYSTEM and is involved in the perception of PHEROMONES, although its true function is the subject of debate.

NES 1. abbreviation for NEUROLOGICAL EVALUATION SCALE. **2.** abbreviation for NONEPILEPTIC SEIZURE.

nest building a form of parental behavior, observed mainly in fish, birds, and mammals, that involves finding and preparing a site for laying eggs or giving birth to young. The forms of nest building vary widely, but generally all are associated with hormonal activity induced in the female by changes in day length, temperature, courtship with a male, or the presence of offspring. In species with biparental care, such as many monogamous birds and rodents, nest building may be done by both sexes. In some fish males are the exclusive nest builders. Nest building in nonpregnant female mammals can be induced by exposure to young animals (see CONCAVEATION).

nesting *n.* in an experimental design, the appearance of the levels of one factor (the **nested factor**) only within a single level of another factor. For example, classrooms are nested within a school because each specific classroom is found only within a single school; similarly, schools are nested within school districts. See HIERARCHICALLY NESTED DESIGN.

network *n.* **1.** the system of interpersonal interactions and relationships in an individual's environment that play an important part in the production of mental health or psychological disorder. The specific impact that these interactions and relationships have on the development of psychopathology is called the **network effect**. [defined by German-born psychoanalyst Sigmund Heinrich Foulkes (1868–1976)] **2.** in SOCIOMETRY, a complex chain of interrelations that shape social tradition and public opinion, either spontaneously or through propaganda. See PSYCHOLOGICAL NETWORK; SOCIAL NETWORK. [defined by Austrian psychiatrist and philosopher Jacob L. Moreno (1889–1974)] See also COMMUNICATION NETWORK; FRIENDSHIP NETWORK; GROUP NETWORK; KINSHIP NETWORK; SEMANTIC NETWORK.

network analysis the study of the relations among sampling units (e.g., individuals) within a specific NETWORK (e.g., a friendship network) and the implications of these networks for the system in which they occur. In industrial and organizational psychology, it involves the identification of patterns of communication, influence, liking, and other interpersonal behaviors and attitudes among a collection of people. Properties of systems are assumed to be emergent, that is, not immediately predictable from a knowledge of networks among individuals. See also SOCIOMETRY.

network-analysis evaluation a method of studying networks of services from the vantage point of either agencies within a system or the flow of service recipients through the system.

network effect see NETWORK.

networking *n.* **1.** establishing contacts and relationships inside and outside one's place of work with the intent of advancing one's career. **2.** forming networks of computing resources by connecting computers via communication systems. See COMPUTER NETWORK.

network-memory model the concept that LONG-TERM MEMORY is made up of a series of knowledge representations that are connected or linked together. The strength of the connections is determined by experience factors, such as repetition and associations. See also CONNECTIONIST MODELS OF MEMORY; SPREADING ACTIVATION.

network therapy individual PSYCHOTHERAPY or FAMILY THERAPY in which an attempt is made to involve not only family members but other relatives, friends, and neighbors as sources of emotional support and possible vocational opportunity. See also SOCIAL-NETWORK THERAPY.

neur- *combining form* see NEURO-.

neural *adj.* pertaining to the nervous system, its parts, and its functions.

neural arc the pathway followed by nerve impulses from a RECEPTOR to an EFFECTOR. In a REFLEX ARC a sensory neuron (or bundle of neurons) is connected either directly or via one or more INTERNEURONS to one or more MOTOR NEURONS; in more complex behaviors the pathways are longer and the connections are more complicated.

neural axis 1. the CENTRAL NERVOUS SYSTEM as a whole. **2.** the structures of the central nervous system that lie along the midline, including the spinal cord and brainstem but excluding the cerebral hemispheres and the cerebellar hemispheres. Also called **neuraxis**.

neural chain a simple type of NEURAL CIRCUIT in which neurons are attached end to end.

neural circuit an arrangement of NEURONS and their interconnections. Neural circuits often perform particular limited functions, such as NEGATIVE FEEDBACK circuits, POSITIVE FEEDBACK circuits, or OSCILLATOR CIRCUITS. In a **local circuit** the neurons are all contained within a level of brain organization of a particular region.

neural conduction the passage of a NERVE IMPULSE along a nerve fiber. See CONDUCTION. Compare NEUROTRANSMISSION.

neural constructivism the theory that brain development, and thus cognitive development, proceeds as a dynamic interaction between the development of the NEURAL SUBSTRATE and the environment.

neural crest an embryonic structure consisting of a ridgelike area of ectodermal tissue on either side of the NEURAL TUBE that develops into the spinal ganglia and various structures within the sympathetic and peripheral nervous systems.

neural Darwinism a biological theory of mind that attempts to explain specific cognitive functions, such as learning or memory, in terms of the selection of particular groups of neuronal structures inside individual brains. This selection of the best adapted structures is placed within the general framework of the Darwinian theory of NATURAL SELECTION. Critics of the theory argue that natural selection cannot apply without reproduction. Also called **neuronal group selection**; **selectionist brain theory**. [proposed by U.S. neuroscientist Gerald M. Edelman (1929–) in 1987]

neural facilitation see FACILITATION.

neural fibril see NEUROFIBRIL.

neural folds in the developing embryo, ridges of ectoderm on the NEURAL PLATE that form around a groove—the **neural groove**—and fuse to form the NEURAL TUBE.

neuralgia *n.* pain, typically recurrent, sharp, and spasmodic, that occurs along the course of a nerve or a group of nerves. See TRIGEMINAL NEURALGIA. —**neuralgic** *adj.*

neural groove see NEURAL FOLDS.

neural impulse see NERVE IMPULSE.

neural induction the influence of a neuron or group of neurons on the development of other cells, particularly other neurons.

neural integration the ALGEBRAIC SUMMATION of excitatory and inhibitory POSTSYNAPTIC POTENTIALS, which governs the excitability and firing of the postsynaptic neuron.

neural irritability a property of NERVE TISSUE that makes it sensitive to stimulation and capable of responding by transmitting ACTION POTENTIALS. It is dependent on rapid, transient movement of ions through ion channels in the plasma membrane, causing a reversible DEPOLARIZATION of the membrane.

neural network 1. a technique for modeling the neural changes in the brain that underlie cognition and perception in which a large number of simple hypothetical neural units are connected to one another. **2.** a form of

ARTIFICIAL INTELLIGENCE system used for learning and classifying data. Neural networks are usually abstract structures modeled on a computer and consist of a number of interconnected processing elements (**nodes**), each with a finite number of inputs and outputs. The elements in the network can have a "weight" determining how they process data, which can be adjusted according to experience. In this way, the network can be "trained" to recognize patterns in input data by optimizing the output of the network. The analogy is with the supposed action of neurons in the brain. Neural networks are used in research in such areas as pattern recognition, speech recognition, and machine translation of languages. They also have applications in such fields as financial prediction.

Neural networks are often structured into layers, including an **input layer** (in which properties of input parameters are encoded), possibly multiple **hidden layers** (in which generalizations of the input parameters are reflected), and an **output layer** (in which the response of the neural network system is reported to the environment). The connectivity of these layers often differs, usually reflecting the algorithms the neural network uses for learning. There are multiple families of algorithms used for learning patterns in data, including Hebbian learning and back-propagation learning. See also PERCEPTRON.

neural parenchyma the essential functioning tissue of the nervous system, as distinguished from the structural or supporting elements.

neural pathway any route followed by a nerve impulse through central or peripheral nerve fibers of the nervous system. A neural pathway may consist of a simple REFLEX ARC or a complex but specific routing, such as that followed by impulses transmitting a specific wavelength of sound from the COCHLEA to the auditory cortex. Also called **nerve pathway**. See also AFFERENT PATHWAY; DOPAMINERGIC PATHWAY; EFFERENT PATHWAY; MOTOR PATHWAY.

neural plasticity 1. the ability of the nervous system to change in response to experience or environmental stimulation. **2.** the change in reactivity of the nervous system and its components as a result of constant, successive activations. Also called **neuroplasticity**.

neural plate a specific region of the outer primary cell layer (ectoderm) on the dorsal surface of an embryo that develops ultimately into the central nervous system. As development proceeds, the neural plate folds into the NEURAL TUBE. See also NEURULATION.

neural quantum theory a theory to explain linear psychophysical functions, which are sometimes obtained instead of the ogival (S-shaped) form, whereby changes in sensation are assumed to occur in discrete steps and not along a continuum, based on the all-or-none law of neural activity. In this context, quantum refers to a functionally distinct unit in the neural mechanisms that mediate sensory experience—that is, to a perceptual rather than to a physical unit. Also called **quantal hypothesis**; **quantal theory**.

neural regeneration regrowth of injured neurons, which occurs at a very slow rate. Complete replacement of injured neurons is rare in mammals but common in some fish and amphibians. Even in mammals, severed axons in the peripheral nervous system regrow readily. Sprouts of the growing axons are guided by CELL ADHESION MOLECULES. Also called **neuronal regeneration**; **regeneration of nerves**.

neural reinforcement the strengthening of a neuron's response by the simultaneous or contingent activity of a second neuronal response.

neural retina see RETINA.

neural satiation a period of lessened reactivity or the inhibition of a neuronal response following strong stimulation of an area or adjacent regions.

neural set a disposition, often temporary, of a NEURAL PATHWAY to respond in a certain way.

neural substrate the part of the nervous system that mediates a particular behavior.

neural transmission see NEUROTRANSMISSION.

neural tube a structure formed during early development of an embryo, when folds of the NEURAL PLATE curl over and fuse. Cells of the neural tube differentiate along its length on the anterior–posterior axis to form swellings that correspond to the future FOREBRAIN, MIDBRAIN, and HINDBRAIN; the posterior part of the tube develops into the spinal cord. The cavity of the tube ultimately becomes the interconnected cerebral VENTRICLES and the central canal of the spinal cord. Many congenital defects of the nervous system originate at this stage of development (see NEURAL TUBE DEFECT). See also NEURULATION.

neural tube defect any of a group of congenital defects caused by faulty development of the NEURAL TUBE from the NEURAL PLATE. As a result, portions of the brain or spinal cord or their covering membranes (the meninges) protrude through a gap in the skull or spinal column, giving rise to neurological disorders, mental retardation, or physical disability of varying severity. ANENCEPHALY and SPINA BIFIDA are examples of such defects.

neurasthenia *n.* a condition marked by fatigue, weakness, insomnia, aches, and pains. The name (from Greek *neurastheneia*, "nerve weakness") originated in the 19th century, when the symptoms were believed to be due to exhaustion, primarily from overwork, and is rarely used today. The condition is now attributed primarily to emotional conflicts, tensions, frustrations, and other psychological factors, and in *DSM–IV–TR* it is classified as UNDIFFERENTIATED SOMATOFORM DISORDER. [coined in 1869 by U.S. neurologist George Miller Beard (1839–1883)] **—neurasthenic** *adj.*

neuraxis *n.* see NEURAL AXIS.

neuritic plaques see SENILE PLAQUES.

neuritis *n.* inflammation of a nerve, especially resulting from infection or autoimmune factors. See also NEUROPATHY.

neuro- (**neur-**) *combining form* nerves or the nervous system.

neuroanatomy *n.* the study of the structures and relationships among the various parts of the nervous system. **—neuroanatomist** *n.*

neurobiofeedback *n.* see NEUROFEEDBACK.

neurobiology *n.* a branch of biology that studies the structures and processes of the nervous system. **—neurobiological** *adj.*

neurobiotaxis *n.* the growth of a nerve fiber toward the tissue it will innervate, which occurs during embryological development. Those factors that influence neurobiotaxis are currently the subject of research on nerve growth in adult organisms, suggesting the possibility of nerve regeneration or replacement after injury or disease.

neuroblast *n.* an undifferentiated cell that is capable of developing into a neuron.

neuroblastoma *n.* a type of tumor that develops from nerve cells that resemble the primitive neural cells of the embryo. The cells of a neuroblastoma are very small with very large nuclei, often arranged in sheets, clumps, or cords. Most such tumors develop in the adrenal medulla or autonomic nervous system.

neurochemistry *n.* the branch of NEUROSCIENCE that deals with the roles of atoms, molecules, and ions in the functioning of nervous systems. Because chemical substances in a physiological system obey the laws of nature that apply in other environments, the activities of neurotransmitters, drugs, and other molecules in the nervous system can be explained in terms of basic chemical concepts.

neurocontrol *n.* **1.** the control of electronic devices by energy transformed from neural output. Such devices have been developed for the use of people with paralysis or other severe impairments of bodily function. See BIOENGINEERING. **2.** more generally, any method of controlling an automated system or device that is modeled on the neuronal architecture in human beings. Such methods have been developed in advanced robotics and in such high-tech applications as spacecraft navigation.

neurocrine *adj.* referring to neurons that secrete agonists, especially NEUROTRANSMITTERS, at synapses, or to those agonists themselves.

neurodermatitis *n.* an eczematous skin lesion that may be associated with psychological stress and is exacerbated by rubbing or scratching the skin.

neuroeffector junction the functional connection between a neuron and a muscle or a gland. See also NEUROMUSCULAR JUNCTION.

neuroeffector transmission the transmission of nerve impulses from neurons through NEUROEFFECTOR JUNCTIONS to the two general types of effectors, muscles and glands.

neuroendocrinology *n.* the study of the relationships between the nervous system, especially the brain, and the endocrine system. Some cells within the nervous system release hormones into the local or systemic circulation; these are called **neuroendocrine** (or **neurosecretory**) **cells**. The HYPOTHALAMUS, for example, produces RELEASING HORMONES that regulate secretion of pituitary hormones. Certain substances, such as NOREPINEPHRINE, act both as hormones and as neurotransmitters. **—neuroendocrinological** *adj.* **—neuroendocrinologist** *n.*

neuroethology *n.* a branch of biology that studies animal behavior in relation to neural processes and structures. See ETHOLOGY.

neurofeedback *n.* a learning strategy that enables people to alter their own brain waves using information about their brain-wave characteristics that is made available through electroencephalograph recordings that may be presented to them as a video display or an auditory signal. Also called **neurobiofeedback**. See BIOFEEDBACK.

neurofibril *n.* a fine fiber found in the cytoplasm of a neuron. It is composed of microscopic protein filaments and MICROTUBULES. Abnormal formation of neurofibrils leads to the development of NEUROFIBRILLARY TANGLES, which are characteristic of Alzheimer's disease. Also called **neural fibril**.

neurofibrillary tangles twisted strands of abnormal filaments within neurons that are associated with Alzheimer's disease. The filaments form microscopically visible knots or tangles consisting of tau protein, which normally is associated with MICROTUBULES. If the structure of tau is rendered abnormal, the microtubule structure collapses, and the tau protein collects in neurofibrillary tangles.

neurofibroma *n.* a tumor of peripheral nerves caused by abnormal proliferation of SCHWANN CELLS. A neurofibroma is very similar to a SCHWANNOMA but is distinguished by its lack of a capsule and resulting incorporation of nerve fibers into its mass. See VON RECKLINGHAUSEN'S DISEASE.

neurofibromatosis *n.* see VON RECKLINGHAUSEN'S DISEASE.

neurofilament *n.* a small, rodlike structure found in the axons of neurons. Neurofilaments are involved in the transport of materials along the axon. See AXONAL TRANSPORT.

neurogenesis *n.* the division of nonneuronal cells to produce neurons.

neurogenic *adj.* pertaining to a condition or event caused or produced by a component of the nervous system.

neurogenic communication disorder any speech or language problem due to nervous system impairment that causes some level of difficulty or inability in exchanging information with others.

neuroglia *n.* a tissue within the nervous system consisting of nonneuronal cells that provide structural, nutritional, and other kinds of support to neurons. Certain types of neuroglia form the MYELIN SHEATH around axons; these are OLIGODENDROCYTES in the central nervous system and SCHWANN CELLS in the peripheral nervous system. Other types of neuroglia are ASTROCYTES, MICROGLIA, and ependymal cells (see EPENDYMA). Also called **glial cells**. **—neuroglial** *adj.*

neuroglioma *n.* see GLIOMA.

neurogram *n.* **1.** see ENGRAM. **2.** a wavelike tracing, either printed or displayed on a monitor, that represents the electrical impulses of neurons. **3.** a three-dimensional image of nerves in the brain provided by a specialized MAGNETIC RESONANCE IMAGING technique.

neurohormone *n.* a hormone produced by neural tissue and released into the general circulation. See NEUROENDOCRINOLOGY.

neurohumor *n.* a NEUROTRANSMITTER or a local NEUROHORMONE.

neurohypophysis *n.* see PITUITARY GLAND.

neurokinin *n.* a neurotransmitter family comprising three related neuropeptides: SUBSTANCE P, **neurokinin A**, and **neurokinin B**. They appear to play roles in emotion and in pain perception.

neuroleptic malignant syndrome a rare complication of therapy with conventional (typical or first-generation) ANTIPSYCHOTICS, characterized by fever, inability to regulate blood pressure, difficulty in breathing, and changes in consciousness (including coma); mortality rates approaching 25% have been observed. It occurs primarily at the start of treatment or with a sudden increase in dose. The incidence of the syndrome, never high, has declined further with the abandonment of MEGADOSE PHARMACOTHERAPY with conventional antipsychotics and the advent of second-generation ATYPICAL ANTIPSYCHOTICS.

neuroleptics *pl. n.* see ANTIPSYCHOTICS.

neuroleptic syndrome the series of effects observed in individuals who have taken ANTIPSYCHOTICS. It is characterized by reduced motor activity and emotionality, an indifference to external stimuli, and a decreased ability to perform tasks that require good motor coordination. With high doses, patients may become cataleptic.

neurolinguistic programming (**NLP**) a set of techniques and strategies designed to improve interpersonal communications and relations by modifying the "mental programs," or MENTAL MODELS of the world, that individuals develop and use to respond to and interact with the environment and other people. This approach uses principles derived from NEUROLINGUISTICS and presumes that these programs, as well as the behaviors they influence, result from the interaction among the brain, language, and the body. In order to achieve desired change, one must first understand subjective experience and the structures of thought (i.e., mental programs) underlying that experience, and then learn to modify these programs as needed, for example, to enhance adaptive behavior across a variety of situations or to attain excellence in personal performance. Although originally applied to psychotherapy and counseling, neurolinguistic programming has developed applications in other fields, such as business management, artificial intelligence, and education. [developed in the United States in 1976 by U.S. mathematician and therapist Richard Bandler (1950–) and U.S. linguist John Grinder (1940–)]

neurolinguistics *n.* the branch of linguistics that investigates how language organization and language processing are encoded in the brain.

neurological amnesia a loss or impairment of memory due to disease or injury that affects the nervous system.

neurological evaluation analysis of the data gathered by an examining physician of an individual's mental status and sensory and motor functioning. The examination typically includes assessment of cognition, speech and behavior, orientation and level of alertness, muscular strength and tone, muscle coordination and movement, TENDON REFLEXES, cranial nerves, pain and temperature sensitivity, and discriminative senses.

Neurological Evaluation Scale (**NES**) an assessment instrument originally developed in 1989 to provide a standardized tool for the evaluation of neurological abnormalities and impairments associated with schizophrenia. Currently, it is often used in researching other severe mental illnesses, such as bipolar disorders, as well. [developed by U.S. psychiatrists Robert W. Buchanan and Douglas W. Heinrichs]

neurological examination see NEUROLOGICAL EVALUATION.

neurological impairment any condition marked by disruption of the nervous system as a result of disease, injury, or the effects of a drug or other chemical.

neurology *n.* a branch of medicine that deals with the nervous system in both healthy and diseased states. The diagnosis and treatment of diseases of the nervous system is called **clinical neurology**; **neurologists** diagnose and treat patients with stroke, dementia, headaches, and back pain, among other disorders. **—neurological** *adj.*

neuromodulator *n.* a substance that modulates the effectiveness of neurotransmitters by influencing the release of the transmitters or the RECEPTOR response to the transmitter.

neuromuscular disorder any pathological condition that involves the nerves and muscles. Common symptoms include weakness, cramps, and paralysis. Examples of such disorders include MUSCULAR DYSTROPHY, MYASTHENIA GRAVIS, and the MYOPATHIES.

neuromuscular junction the junction between a motor neuron and the muscle fiber it innervates. In skeletal muscle, the muscle-cell plasma membrane (sarcolemma) is greatly folded in the region opposite the terminus of a motor axon, forming a **motor end plate**. When impulses arrive at the axon terminus, neurotransmitter diffuses across the gap separating the axon and motor end plate. The neurotransmitter binds to receptors in the sarcolemma and causes an END-PLATE POTENTIAL, which can trigger muscle contraction. Also called **myoneural junction**.

neuromuscular system see MOTOR SYSTEM.

neuron (**neurone**) *n.* the basic cellular unit of the nervous system. Each neuron is composed of a CELL BODY; fine, branching extensions (DENDRITES) that receive incoming nerve signals; and a single, long extension (AXON) that conducts nerve impulses to its branching terminal. The axon terminal transmits impulses to other neurons, or to effector organs (e.g., muscles and glands), via junctions called SYNAPSES or NEUROMUSCULAR JUNCTIONS. Neurons can be classified according to their function as MOTOR NEURONS, SENSORY NEURONS, or INTERNEURONS. There are various structural types, including UNIPOLAR NEURONS, BIPOLAR NEURONS, and MULTIPOLAR NEURONS. The axons of vertebrate neurons are often surrounded by a MYELIN SHEATH. Also called **nerve cell**. [term coined by German physician Heinrich Wilhelm von Waldeyer-Hartz (1836–1921)] **—neuronal** *adj.*

neuronal cell death the selective, genetically programmed death of nerve cells that occurs during development of the nervous system. See also PROGRAMMED CELL DEATH.

neuronal group selection see NEURAL DARWINISM.

neuronal regeneration see NEURAL REGENERATION.

neuronal transmission see NEUROTRANSMISSION.

neuron doctrine the principle that the nervous system is composed of individual cells (NEURONS) that make contact with each other but do not interpenetrate. Before this doctrine was accepted, many assumed that the nervous system consisted of continuous tubelike networks. Also called **neuron theory**. [enunciated in 1891 by German physician Heinrich Wilhelm von Waldeyer-Hartz (1836–1921)]

neurone *n.* see NEURON.

Neurontin *n.* a trade name for GABAPENTIN.

neuroparalytic ophthalmia see OPHTHALMIA.

neuropathic pain pain caused by damage to peripheral nerves. It is often difficult to treat.

neuropathology *n.* the study of diseases of the nervous system. **—neuropathological** *adj.* **—neuropathologist** *n.*

neuropathy *n.* disease of the nervous system, particularly the peripheral nerves. See PERIPHERAL NEUROPATHY. **—neuropathic** *adj.*

neuropeptide *n.* any of several peptides that are released by neurons as NEUROTRANSMITTERS or NEUROHORMONES. They include the ENDOGENOUS OPIOIDS (e.g., enkephalin and endorphin); peptides found in both the brain and the peripheral nervous system (e.g., SUBSTANCE P and NEUROTENSIN); hypothalamic RELEASING HORMONES (e.g., thyrotropin-releasing hormone); pituitary hormones (e.g., GROWTH HORMONE and PROLACTIN); and other circulating peptides (e.g., atrial natriuretic peptide and bradykinin).

neuropeptide Y a NEUROPEPTIDE transmitter, found in the brain, heart, and adrenal glands, that stimulates vasoconstriction and regulates feeding behavior. Some research has shown that it may be involved in Alzheimer's disease.

neuropharmacology *n.* the scientific study of the effects of drugs on the nervous system. **—neuropharmacological** *adj.* **—neuropharmacologist** *n.*

neurophysiology *n.* a branch of NEUROSCIENCE that is concerned with the normal and abnormal functioning of the nervous system, including the chemical and electrical activities of individual neurons. **—neurophysiological** *adj.* **—neurophysiologist** *n.*

neuropil *n.* a weblike network of AXON and DENDRITE filaments that forms the bulk of the GRAY MATTER of the central nervous system. The CELL BODIES of the neurons are embedded in the net of fibers.

neuroplasticity *n.* see NEURAL PLASTICITY.

neuroprotective *adj.* denoting agents, such as drugs and hormones, that are believed to prevent damage to the brain or spinal cord.

neuropsychological assessment an evaluation of the presence, nature, and extent of brain damage or dysfunction derived from the results of various NEUROPSYCHOLOGICAL TESTS.

neuropsychological rehabilitation the use of psychological techniques to treat and manage cognitive, emotional, and behavioral problems that arise from brain damage or dysfunction.

neuropsychological test any of various clinical instruments for assessing cognitive impairment, including those measuring memory, language, learning, attention, and visuospatial and visuoconstructive functioning. Examples of batteries of such tests are the HALSTEAD–REITAN NEUROPSYCHOLOGICAL BATTERY and the LURIA–NEBRASKA NEUROPSYCHOLOGICAL BATTERY.

neuropsychology *n.* the branch of science that combines neuroscience and psychology. See also CLINICAL NEUROPSYCHOLOGY. **—neuropsychological** *adj.* **—neuropsychologist** *n.*

neuroreceptor *n.* a RECEPTOR molecule located in a neuron cell membrane that binds molecules of a particular neurotransmitter, hormone, drug, or the like and initiates a particular response within the neuron. Also called **neurotransmitter receptor**.

neuroscience *n.* the scientific study of the nervous system, including NEUROANATOMY, NEUROCHEMISTRY, NEUROLOGY, NEUROPHYSIOLOGY, and NEUROPHARMACOLOGY, and its applications in psychology and psychiatry. See also BEHAVIORAL NEUROSCIENCE; COGNITIVE NEUROSCIENCE.

neurosecretion *n.* **1.** the secretion of substances, such as hormones or neurotransmitters, by neural tissue. **2.** a substance secreted in this way.

neurosecretory cell see NEUROENDOCRINOLOGY.

neurosis *n.* any one of a variety of mental disorders characterized by significant anxiety or other distressing emotional symptoms, such as persistent and irrational fears, obsessive thoughts, compulsive acts, dissociative states, and somatic and depressive reactions. The symptoms do not involve gross personality disorganization, total lack of insight, or loss of contact with reality (compare PSYCHOSIS). In psychoanalysis, neuroses are generally viewed as exaggerated, unconscious methods of coping with internal conflicts and the anxiety they produce. In *DSM–IV–TR*, most of what used to be called neuroses are now classified as ANXIETY DISORDERS. Also called **psychoneurosis**. **—neurotic** *adj., n.*

neurosurgery *n.* surgical procedures performed on the brain, spinal cord, or peripheral nerves for the purpose of restoring functioning or preventing further impairment. See also PSYCHOSURGERY. **—neurosurgeon** *n.* **—neurosurgical** *adj.*

neurosyphilis *n.* a late manifestation of untreated or inadequately treated syphilis, usually occurring years after the initial infection, in which the causative bacterium, *Treponema pallidum*, damages and destroys the brain and spinal cord. This results in blindness and severe neurological deficits, including memory impairment, inability to concentrate, and behavioral deterioration. See ASYMPTOMATIC NEUROSYPHILIS; GENERAL PARESIS; LOCOMOTOR ATAXIA.

neurotensin (**NT**) *n.* a NEUROPEPTIDE released from the hypothalamus into the circulation and widely distributed throughout the central nervous system.

neurotic anxiety in psychoanalytic theory, anxiety that originates in unconscious conflict and is maladaptive in nature: It has a disturbing effect on emotion and behavior and also intensifies resistance to treatment. Neurotic anxiety contrasts with REALISTIC ANXIETY, about an external danger or threat, and with moral anxiety, which is guilt posited to originate in the superego.

neurotic character see CHARACTER NEUROSIS.

neurotic conflict **1.** in psychoanalytic theory, an INTRAPSYCHIC CONFLICT that leads to persistent maladjustment and emotional disturbance. **2.** in the approach of German-born U.S. psychoanalyst Karen D. Horney (1885–1952), the clash that occurs between opposing NEUROTIC NEEDS, such as an excessive need for power and independence and the need for love and dependence. See also NEUROTIC TREND.

neurotic depression **1.** see REACTIVE DEPRESSION. **2.** any MAJOR DEPRESSIVE EPISODE that does not include psychotic features.

neurotic disorder any mental disorder characterized by distressing symptoms that are recognized by the individual as being unacceptable and alien. REALITY TESTING is largely intact, and behavior does not actively violate social norms (although functioning may be markedly impaired). The disturbance is relatively enduring or recurrent without treatment, is not limited to a transitory reaction to stressors, and has no demonstrable organic cause. In *DSM–IV–TR*, neurotic disorders are not recognized as a valid diagnostic entity, and the individual disorders that were included under that heading in earlier editions of the *DSM* have been subsumed under various other categories.

neurotic inventory a questionnaire designed to reveal a person's tendency toward NEUROTICISM. Statements are taken from case histories and related material, and the participant indicates agreement or disagreement with each statement. Theoretically, the more statements with which participants agree, the greater their tendency toward neuroticism.

neuroticism *n.* **1.** the state of being neurotic or a proneness to NEUROSIS. **2.** a mild condition of neurosis. **3.** one of the dimensions of the FIVE-FACTOR PERSONALITY MODEL and the BIG FIVE PERSONALITY MODEL, characterized by a chronic level of emotional instability and proneness to psychological distress. **4.** in EYSENCK'S TYPOLOGY, one of three major dimensions whose polar opposite is emotional stability, the others being introversion versus EXTRAVERSION and PSYCHOTICISM versus impulse control. See also FACTOR THEORY OF PERSONALITY.

neurotic needs in psychoanalytic theory, excessive drives and demands that may arise out of the strategies individuals use to defend themselves against BASIC ANXIETY. German-born U.S. psychoanalyst Karen D. Horney (1885–1952) enumerated ten neurotic needs: for affection and approval, for a partner to take over one's life, for restriction of one's life, for power, for exploitation of others, for prestige, for admiration, for achievement, for self-sufficiency and independence, and for perfection.

When an individual's personality is dominated by a few neurotic needs he or she may exhibit a NEUROTIC TREND.

neurotic resignation the avoidance of any aspect of reality that may bring inner conflicts into one's awareness, involving withdrawal that may take the form of total inactivity or overactivity in other areas. Neurotic resignation is distinguished from **dynamic resignation**, which is viewed as a temporary decision to postpone action until more favorable circumstances emerge. See also ESCAPE FROM REALITY; FLIGHT FROM REALITY; FLIGHT INTO REALITY. [first described by German-born U.S. psychoanalyst Karen D. Horney (1885–1952)]

neurotic solution a method of resolving a NEUROTIC CONFLICT by removing it from awareness.

neurotic trend in the theory of German-born U.S. psychoanalyst Karen D. Horney (1885–1952), one of three basic tendencies stemming from an individual's choice of strategies to counteract BASIC ANXIETY. These strategies generate insatiable NEUROTIC NEEDS, which group themselves into three trends: (a) moving toward people, or clinging to others (see COMPLIANT CHARACTER); (b) moving away from people, or insisting on independence and self-dependence (see DETACHED CHARACTER); and (c) moving against people, or seeking power, prestige, and possessions (see AGGRESSIVE CHARACTER).

neurotoxicology *n.* the study of the effects of toxins and poisons on the nervous system. **—neurotoxicological** *adj.*

neurotoxin *n.* any substance that is destructive to the central or peripheral nervous system, causing temporary or permanent damage.

neurotransmission *n.* the process by which a signal or other activity in a neuron is transferred to an adjacent neuron or other cell. Synaptic transmission, which occurs between two neurons via a SYNAPSE, is largely chemical, by the release and binding of NEUROTRANSMITTER, but it may also be electrical (see ELECTRICAL SYNAPSE). Neurotransmission also occurs between a neuron and an effector organ or gland and between a neuron and a skeletal muscle cell (see NEUROMUSCULAR JUNCTION). Also called **neural transmission**; **neuronal transmission**.

neurotransmitter *n.* any of a large number of chemicals that can be released by neurons to mediate transmission or inhibition of nerve signals across the junctions (SYNAPSES) between neurons. When triggered by a nerve impulse, the neurotransmitter is released from the TERMINAL BUTTON, travels across the SYNAPTIC CLEFT, and binds to and reacts with RECEPTOR molecules in the postsynaptic membrane. Neurotransmitters include amines, such as ACETYLCHOLINE, NOREPINEPHRINE, DOPAMINE, and SEROTONIN; and amino acids, such as GAMMA-AMINOBUTYRIC ACID, GLUTAMATE, and GLYCINE. Also called **chemical transmitter**; **synaptic transmitter**.

neurotransmitter receptor see NEURORECEPTOR.

neurotrophic factor a polypeptide that is synthesized by and released from neurons and helps certain neurons to grow and survive. See also BRAIN-DERIVED NEUROTROPHIC FACTOR.

neurulation *n.* the process of development of the rudimentary nervous system in early embryonic life, including formation of the NEURAL TUBE from the NEURAL PLATE.

neutral color a color that lacks hue and saturation (e.g., gray, white, or black).

neutrality *n.* a role or a manner of behavior adopted by the therapist, who not only remains passive and permissive but also does not express judgments of right and wrong or suggest what is proper behavior on the part of the client.

neutralization *n.* in psychoanalytic theory, the use of sexual or aggressive energy in the service of the EGO rather than for gratification of the INSTINCTS, that is, in functions such as problem solving, creative imagination, scientific inquiry, and decision making. SUBLIMATION uses neutralized energy. Also called **taming of the instinct**. See also DESEXUALIZATION. **—neutralize** *vb.*

neutralizer *n.* a member of a therapy group who plays a role of modifying and controlling impulsive, aggressive, or destructive behaviors of other members of the group. [first described by 20th-century Russian-born U.S. psychotherapist Samuel Richard Slavson]

neutral monism a position holding that there is a single substance to reality, but that this is neither physical (body) nor mental (mind). It seeks to avoid both IDEALISM and MATERIALISM and the philosophical problems that attend them. William JAMES advocated such a position (see RADICAL EMPIRICISM), as did British philosopher Bertrand Russell (1872–1970). However, it has been difficult to convey satisfactorily what the nature of such a substance might be. Compare IDEALISTIC MONISM; NATURAL MONISM. See also MIND–BODY PROBLEM.

neutral point the single wavelength of visible light that appears uncolored (white or gray) to a person with DICHROMATISM, that is, someone with only two cone photopigments, rather than three. The specific wavelength of the neutral point varies according to which photopigment is missing. Those with normal color vision (TRICHROMATISM), and three cone photopigments, have no neutral point.

neutral stimulus in PAVLOVIAN CONDITIONING, a stimulus that does not elicit a response of the sort to be measured as an index of conditioning. For example, the sound of a bell has no effect on salivation, therefore it is a neutral stimulus with respect to salivation and a good candidate for conditioning of that response.

Nevo syndrome see SOTOS SYNDROME.

new-age therapy any of a number of popular treatments that lack a sound scientific basis and are generally not accepted by mental health professionals as valid, effective therapeutic practice. Support for such therapies does not come from independent scientific studies, but rather is derived primarily from the "insights" and observations of their founders or the analysis and evaluation of participant feedback. An example of a new-age therapy is REBIRTHING.

new-look theory of cognitive dissonance a version of COGNITIVE DISSONANCE THEORY postulating that COGNITIVE DISSONANCE is a result of behavior that causes unpleasant consequences. If a person assumes responsibility for these consequences (i.e., if the person freely chose to perform the behavior and the consequences were foreseeable), this results in physiological arousal. In order for cognitive dissonance to occur, people must then perceive this arousal state as negative and due to the consequences. [originally proposed by U.S. psychologists Joel Cooper (1943–) and Russell H. Fazio (1952–)]

Newman–Keuls test a MULTIPLE COMPARISON testing procedure used for making post hoc pairwise comparisons among a set of means.

Newtonian view see MAXWELLIAN VIEW. [Isaac **Newton** (1642–1727), British physicist and mathematician]

Newton's law of color mixture the principle that color mixtures appearing identical to one another will also produce the same perceived color when they are mixed with one another. [Isaac **Newton**]

nexus *n.* **1.** a bond or connection, especially between members of a group or series. **2.** a connection of mutual dependence or causality between variables.

NGF abbreviation for NERVE GROWTH FACTOR.

NGRI abbreviation for NOT GUILTY BY REASON OF INSANITY.

NGT abbreviation for NOMINAL GROUP TECHNIQUE.

NGU abbreviation for NONGONOCOCCAL URETHRITIS.

NHIS abbreviation for NATIONAL HEALTH INTERVIEW SURVEY.

NHST abbreviation for NULL HYPOTHESIS SIGNIFICANCE TESTING.

niacin *n.* see NICOTINIC ACID.

niche picking the active seeking and selection by an individual of a comfortable, suitable, or advantageous place or position within a group or organization.

nicotine *n.* an alkaloid obtained primarily from the TOBACCO plant (*Nicotiana tabacum*). Today nicotine is one of the most widely used psychoactive drugs; it is the primary active ingredient in tobacco and accounts for both the acute pharmacological effects of smoking or chewing tobacco (e.g., a discharge of EPINEPHRINE, a sudden release of glucose, an increase in blood pressure, respiration, heart rate, and cutaneous vasoconstriction) and the dependence that develops (see NICOTINE DEPENDENCE; NICOTINE WITHDRAWAL). The behavioral effects of the drug include enhanced alertness and feelings of calm. Nicotine produces multiple pharmacological effects on the central nervous system by activating NICOTINIC RECEPTORS, facilitating the release of several neurotransmitters, particularly dopamine (a reaction similar to that seen with such drugs as cocaine and heroin), along with other actions in the periphery. In large doses it is highly poisonous, producing such symptoms as dizziness, diarrhea, vomiting, tremors, spasms, unconsciousness, heart attack, and potentially death via paralysis of the muscles of respiration. Nicotine was isolated from the tobacco plant in 1828 and was named for the French diplomat Jean Nicot, who introduced tobacco into France in 1560. **—nicotinic** *adj.*

nicotine dependence in *DSM–IV–TR*, a cluster of cognitive, behavioral, and physiological symptoms indicating continued use of nicotine despite significant nicotine-related problems. There is a pattern of repeated nicotine ingestion resulting in tolerance, characteristic withdrawal symptoms if use is suspended (see NICOTINE WITHDRAWAL), and an uncontrollable drive to continue use. There is no *DSM–IV–TR* diagnosis of nicotine abuse. See also SUBSTANCE DEPENDENCE.

nicotine withdrawal a characteristic withdrawal syndrome that develops after cessation of (or reduction in) prolonged, heavy nicotine consumption. Two or more of the following are required for a *DSM–IV–TR* diagnosis of nicotine withdrawal: DYSPHORIA or depressed mood; insomnia; irritability, frustration, or anger; anxiety; difficulty in concentrating; restlessness; decreased heart rate; and increased appetite or weight gain.

nicotinic acid a vitamin of the B complex that serves as an essential precursor of the coenzyme NAD (nicotinamide adenine dinucleotide) and related coenzymes, which are vital for energy metabolism. U.S. biochemist Conrad Arnold Elvehjem (1901–1962) discovered in 1937 that nicotinic acid can prevent or cure PELLAGRA. Also called **niacin**.

nicotinic acid deficiency see PELLAGRA.

nicotinic receptor a type of ACETYLCHOLINE RECEPTOR that responds to NICOTINE as well as to acetylcholine. Nicotinic receptors mediate chiefly the excitatory activities of acetylcholine, including those at NEUROMUSCULAR JUNCTIONS. Compare MUSCARINIC RECEPTOR.

nictitating membrane a fold of transparent or semitransparent membrane, present in many vertebrates, that can be drawn laterally over the eye like a third eyelid, independently of the other eyelids. This "blink" (the nictitating-membrane response) can be conditioned in a nonhuman animal (e.g., a rabbit) by pairing a puff of air (the UNCONDITIONED STIMULUS) with a light or tone (the CONDITIONED STIMULUS).

Niemann–Pick disease an inherited lipid-storage disorder generally marked by a deficiency of the enzyme sphingomyelinase and accumulation of lipids in brain tissue and visceral organs. Massive liver and spleen enlargement (hepatomegaly and splenomegaly) may occur. Mental retardation, blindness, and death before adulthood are common. About 95% of individuals with this disorder have a defective *NPC1* gene (chromosomal locus 18q11–12). Also called **sphingomyelin lipidosis**. See also LIPID-METABOLISM DISORDERS. [Albert **Niemann** (1880–1921) and Ludwig **Pick** (1868–1944), German physicians]

night blindness a visual impairment marked by partial or complete inability to see objects in a dimly lighted environment. Night blindness can be inherited or due to defective DARK ADAPTATION or dietary deficiency of vitamin A. Also called **nyctalopia**.

night-eating syndrome an eating disorder characterized by INSOMNIA, nocturnal HYPERPHAGIA, and morning ANOREXIA that persist for at least 3 months. Recent research suggests night-eating syndrome is related to hormonal irregularities and a disturbed CIRCADIAN RHYTHM of food intake, although chronic stress may also be a contributing factor. This type of eating disorder is estimated to affect 1.5% of the global population and is thought to occur in 10–25% of obese individuals. [first described in 1955 by U.S. psychiatrist Albert J. Stunkard]

night hospital a unit within a hospital in which patients receive psychiatric care at night, having spent the day in the community. See also PARTIAL HOSPITALIZATION.

nightmare *n.* a frightening or otherwise disturbing dream, in which fear, sadness, despair, disgust, or some combination of these forms the emotional content. Nightmares contain visual imagery and some degree of narrative structure and typically occur during REM SLEEP. The dreamer tends to waken suddenly from a nightmare and is immediately alert and aware of his or her surroundings. In *DSM–IV–TR*, the occurrence of frequent nightmares is classified as NIGHTMARE DISORDER. Nightmares are also a symptom of POSTTRAUMATIC STRESS DISORDER. **—nightmarish** *adj.*

nightmare-death syndrome the unexpected and mysterious nocturnal death of a healthy individual that occurs among southeast Asian refugees, especially Hmong, arriving in the United States. It is attributed by Hmong informants to a nocturnal spirit encounter and is similar to the Filipino concept of BANGUNGUT. Also called **sudden unexpected nocturnal-death syndrome**.

nightmare disorder in *DSM–IV–TR*, a SLEEP DISORDER characterized by the repeated occurrence of frightening dreams that lead to awakenings from sleep. It was formerly known as **dream anxiety disorder**. See PARASOMNIA.

night terror see SLEEP TERROR DISORDER.

nigrostriatal tract the neural pathway that extends from the SUBSTANTIA NIGRA to the STRIATUM of the basal ganglia. It contains DOPAMINERGIC NEURONS and is associated with the production of voluntary movement.

nihil ex nihilo fit nothing arises from nothing (Latin): a succinct expression of a doctrine introduced by Greek philosopher Parmenides (c. 480 BCE) that nothing comes into being that does not already exist in some form. The doctrine runs counter to the orthodox religious dogma that God created the world *ex nihilo* (from nothing), although it might be argued that it does not apply to supernatural events.

nihilism *n.* **1.** the delusion of nonexistence: a fixed belief that the mind, body, or the world at large—or parts thereof—no longer exists. Also called **delusion of negation**; **nihilistic delusion**. **2.** the belief that existence is without meaning. **—nihilistic** *adj.*

nilutamide *n.* see ANTIANDROGEN.

NIMH abbreviation for NATIONAL INSTITUTE OF MENTAL HEALTH.

ninth cranial nerve see GLOSSOPHARYNGEAL NERVE.

nirvana *n.* **1.** in HINDUISM, a state of liberation or illumination, characterized by the extinction of individual consciousness as it merges into *brahman,* the eternal Absolute. Nirvana frees one from suffering, death and rebirth, and all other worldly bonds. **2.** in BUDDHISM, the state of perfect blessedness that is the goal of all spiritual practice. **3.** in general use, any place or condition of great peace or bliss. [Sanskrit, literally: "extinction"]

nirvana principle in psychoanalytic theory, the tendency of all INSTINCTS and life processes to remove tension and seek the stability and equilibrium of the inorganic state, that is, death. This is the trend of the DEATH INSTINCT, which Sigmund FREUD believed to be universal. See also PRINCIPLE OF INERTIA.

Nissl bodies microscopic particles, consisting of granular endoplasmic reticulum and ribosomes, found in large numbers in the cell bodies of neurons. Nissl bodies can be stained by toluidine blue (**Nissl stain**), which allows measurement of cell-body size and the density of neurons in different regions of the nervous system. Also called **Nissl granules**; **Nissl substance**; **tigroid bodies**. [Franz **Nissl** (1860–1919), German neuropathologist]

Nissl method any of certain techniques used to stain neurons for microscopic examination, especially the use of Nissl stain to reveal NISSL BODIES. [Franz **Nissl**]

nisus *n.* in the system of German philosopher Gottfried Wilhelm Leibniz (1646–1716), the inherent tendency in all MONADS to strive toward the perfect realization of their innate and appropriate ends. See also ENTELECHY. [Latin, literally: "effort"]

Nitoman *n.* a trade name for TETRABENAZINE.

nitrazepam *n.* a long-acting BENZODIAZEPINE with a HALF-LIFE of more than 24 hours, used as a hypnotic. Though nitrazepam has no active metabolic products, its lengthy half-life may cause unwanted accumulation with daily dosing. It is not currently marketed in the United States. Canadian trade name: **Mogadon**.

nitric oxide a compound present in numerous body tissues, where it has a variety of functions. In the body it is synthesized by the enzyme nitric oxide synthase from arginine, NADPH, and oxygen. Nitric oxide functions as a neurotransmitter, or an agent that influences neurotransmitters, in the brain and other parts of the central nervous system. In peripheral tissues it is involved in the relaxation of smooth muscle, and thus acts as a vasodilator, a bronchodilator, and as a relaxant of smooth muscle in the penis and clitoris, being involved in erection and other components of the sexual response.

nitrogen narcosis see RAPTURE-OF-THE-DEEP SYNDROME.

nitrous oxide an analgesic gas that is commonly used in outpatient dental procedures and as an adjunct in surgical anesthesia. It is also used as a propellant in aerosolized foods (e.g., whipping cream). In low doses nitrous oxide produces sensations of giddiness, elation, and euphoria. This property was apparent when it was initially synthesized in 1772 by British chemist Joseph Priestley (1733–1804), and nitrous oxide has long been known colloquially as **laughing gas**. Its euphoriant effects make nitrous oxide a popular inhalant in social settings. Also called **dinitrogen monoxide**.

Nizoral *n.* a trade name for KETOCONAZOLE.

NLD abbreviation for NONVERBAL LEARNING DISORDER.

NLP abbreviation for NEUROLINGUISTIC PROGRAMMING.

nm symbol for NANOMETER.

NMDA *N*-methyl-D-aspartate: an AGONIST that binds to a class of GLUTAMATE RECEPTORS that are both ligand-gated and voltage-sensitive (see NMDA RECEPTOR).

NMDA hypothesis of consciousness a speculative hypothesis proposing that because the NMDA RECEPTOR complex is centrally involved in working memory, and working memory is intimately involved in consciousness, NMDA may be a component in the neural underpinnings of consciousness.

NMDA receptor a type of GLUTAMATE RECEPTOR that binds NMDA as well as GLUTAMATE. NMDA receptors are coupled to LIGAND-GATED ION CHANNELS and are also voltage-sensitive, which enables them to participate in a variety of information-processing operations at synapses where glutamate is the neurotransmitter. The drugs of abuse KETAMINE and PCP are antagonists at NMDA receptors, preventing the influx of calcium ions at CALCIUM CHANNELS, which may cause the hallucinogenic effects of these drugs. Excessive flow of calcium ions into the presynaptic neuron via the NMDA receptor is thought to contribute to glutamate toxicity. A recently emerging hypothesis on the etiology of schizophrenia involves dysfunction of the NMDA glutamate receptor (see GLUTAMATE HYPOTHESIS). Compare AMPA RECEPTOR.

N-methyl-D-aspartate *n.* see NMDA.

NMHA abbreviation for NATIONAL MENTAL HEALTH ASSOCIATION.

NMR abbreviation for NUCLEAR MAGNETIC RESONANCE.

NNAT abbreviation for NAGLIERI NONVERBAL ABILITY TEST.

noble savage in ROMANTICISM, a conceit that posited people from nonindustrial or nontechnological societies as the most noble of human beings, because untouched by civilization, which was viewed as a degrading influence on human thought and behavior. [proposed by French philosopher and author Jean-Jacques Rousseau (1712–1778)]

nocebo *n.* an adverse or otherwise unwanted physical or emotional symptom caused by the administration of a PLACEBO.

nociception *n.* see PAIN PERCEPTION. **—nociceptive** *adj.*

nociceptive reflex a defensive reflex evoked by a painful stimulus or one that threatens damage to the organism.

nociceptor *n.* a sensory RECEPTOR that responds to stimuli that are generally painful or detrimental to the organism. Also called **pain receptor**.

noctambulation *n.* see SLEEPWALKING DISORDER.

nocti- (**noct-**) *combining form* night.

noctiphilia (**noctophilia**) *n.* see NYCTOPHILIA.

nocturia *n.* the need to urinate during the night. The condition may simply be the result of excessive fluid intake before going to sleep, but can be a sign of a disease of the heart, liver, or urinary system. Renal disease in which the kidneys lose their ability to concentrate urine may be a cause of nocturia.

nocturnal *adj.* active or occurring during the dark period of the daily cycle. Compare DIURNAL.

nocturnal emission an involuntary ejaculation that occurs during a nocturnal dream, known popularly as a **wet dream**. Studies show that the majority of males experience a nocturnal emission before the age of 21. A small percentage of total sexual release in a young adult male is through nocturnal emissions. Orgasm as part of nocturnal dreams is rare among adolescent females but increases among mature females.

nocturnal enuresis see ENURESIS.

nocturnal myoclonus involuntary jerking of the limbs (MYOCLONUS) that occurs when a person is falling asleep. The involuntary spasms may occur repeatedly and with sufficient activity to awaken the person. Nocturnal myoclonus is not necessarily a sign of a neurological disorder.

nodal behavior in group psychotherapy, a period of increased activity, which may be interpersonally challenging, aggressive, or disorderly, followed by a relatively quiet period of **antinodal behavior**.

nodal point the point in the optical axis of the eye that connects locations in the visual field with their projections on the retina.

node *n.* **1.** a point in a graph, tree diagram, or the like at which lines intersect or branch. **2.** a single point or unit in an associative model of memory. Nodes typically represent a single concept or feature, are connected to other nodes (usually representing semantically related concepts and features) by links in an associative network, and may be activated or inhibited to varying degrees, depending on the conditions. **3.** in communications, a point in a network at which two or more pathways are interconnected. **4.** in artificial intelligence, see NEURAL NETWORK. **—nodal** *adj.*

node of Ranvier any of successive regularly spaced gaps in the MYELIN SHEATH surrounding an axon. The gaps permit the exchange of ions across the plasma membrane at those points, allowing the nerve impulse to leap from one node to the next in so-called SALTATORY CONDUCTION along the axon. [Louis A. **Ranvier** (1835–1922), French pathologist]

noëgenesis *n.* the production of new knowledge from sensory or cognitive experience. There are three laws of noëgenesis: (a) the apprehension of experience (by which new stimuli are encoded), (b) the EDUCTION of relations (by which the nature of relations between stimuli is inferred), and (c) the eduction of correlates (by which a relation previously inferred is applied in a new context). [proposed in 1923 by Charles Spearman (1863–1945), British psychologist] **—noëgenetic** *adj.*

noesis *n.* **1.** in philosophy, the exercise of the higher reason or NOUS, especially in its role of apprehending truths that cannot be derived from experience. Compare DIANOIA. **2.** in psychology, the functioning of the intellectual or cognitive processes.

noetic *adj.* describing a level of knowledge or memory in which there is awareness of the known or remembered thing but not of one's personal experience in relation to that thing (see NOETIC MEMORY). **Noetic consciousness** is a state of consciousness in which one is aware of facts, concepts, words, and meanings but not of any connection to one's own experience. Compare ANOETIC; AUTONOETIC. [defined by Estonian-born Canadian psychologist Endel Tulving (1927–)]

noetic memory awareness of the general knowledge that one possesses. Synonymous with SEMANTIC MEMORY, it is the middle level of memory in the monohierarchic theory of memory proposed by Estonian-born Canadian psychologist Endel Tulving (1927–), being subordinate to AUTONOETIC MEMORY and superordinate to ANOETIC MEMORY. Also called **noetic awareness**.

no excuse in REALITY THERAPY, the concept that there are no acceptable reasons to condone irresponsible behavior or attribute it to another source. According to this concept, all behavior stems directly from the client and the client is therefore completely and solely responsible for his or her behavior. [devised by U.S. psychiatrist William Glasser (1925–)]

N-of-1 experimental design see SINGLE-CASE EXPERIMENTAL DESIGN.

noise *n.* **1.** any unwanted sound or, more generally, any unwanted disturbance (e.g., electrical noise). **2.** a random or aperiodic waveform whose properties are described statistically. There are many types of noise, which are distinguished by their spectral or statistical properties. **White noise** (or **background noise**) has equal energy at all frequencies; **broadband noise** has energy over a relatively wide frequency range (e.g., 50 Hz to 10 kHz for audition); **pink noise** has energy that is inversely proportional to frequency; **Gaussian noise** has instantaneous values that are determined according to a normal probability density function. **3.** anything that interferes with, obscures, reduces, or otherwise adversely affects the clarity or precision of an ongoing process, such as the communication of a message or signal.

noise abatement the application of legislation or technology to reduce the level of noise pollution. Noise abatement may require the redesign of automobile or aircraft engines, ordinances that prohibit use of airports at night, or routing of traffic away from residential areas. See also NOISE EFFECTS.

noise conditions the effects of traffic sounds, subway noise, jet booms, and other sources of noise pollution on the public.

noise dose a percentage indicating the amount of noise to which a person is exposed in his or her working environment relative to permissible levels of noise exposure. It is used to determine points at which the employer must apply ENGINEERING CONTROLS or ADMINISTRATIVE CONTROLS.

noise effects physiological stress responses to noise, especially if it is prolonged or occurs during demanding cognitive or physical tasks. Noise interferes with the performance of complex tasks and can produce LEARNED HELPLESSNESS, prevent or disturb sleep, and—with provocation—heighten aggression. See also ENVIRONMENTAL STRESS.

noise-induced hearing loss hearing loss that develops over time due to continuous exposure to noise. See EXPOSURE DEAFNESS.

noise pollution any environmental noise (e.g., traffic sounds) that is unwanted or detrimental to one's health or welfare.

nomadism *n.* **1.** a pathological tendency to wander from place to place and repeatedly change one's residence and occupation, often giving rise to instability and social MALADJUSTMENT. In milder form this tendency may be an attempt to escape from a distressing situation or from responsibility, but in extreme form it may be associated with brain damage, epilepsy, mental retardation, or psychosis. See also DROMOMANIA; PORIOMANIA. **2.** the lifestyle of a group of people with no fixed residence, characterized by frequent movement from place to place, often in search of resources or in accordance with seasonal changes.

nomenclature *n.* a systematic classification of technical terms used in an art or science.

nomifensine *n.* an antidepressant that is structurally different from any in current use. It blocks the synaptic reuptake of norepinephine and dopamine but not of serotonin. Due to severe, sometimes fatal, drug reactions, including acute hemolytic anemia, it was withdrawn worldwide in 1986. Former U.S. trade name: **Merital**.

nominal aphasia see AMNESTIC APHASIA.

nominal classification see CONCEPTUAL CLASSIFICATION.

nominal data see CATEGORICAL DATA.

nominal fallacy the false belief that a phenomenon is understood if it is merely named or labeled.

nominal group technique (**NGT**) a structured technique of group problem solving that aims to improve the quality of group decisions by reducing the pressures on group members to conform. Individuals first state their ideas privately and anonymously, and these ideas are posted for discussion and clarification. The group votes anonymously on the ideas and then goes through another round of discussion and clarification, followed by another round of voting. The intent is to reach a consensus on the relative merits of the ideas generated by the group.

nominalism *n.* in medieval philosophy, the position that only concrete particulars have real substantial existence, UNIVERSALS (i.e., general qualities, such as "redness" or "beauty") being mere names with, at most, a mental existence. Compare PLATONIC IDEALISM; REALISM. **—nominalist** *n., adj.*

nominal leader an individual who is named to direct and guide a group but does not perform the activities associated with that role. Compare FUNCTIONAL LEADER.

nominal realism a young child's conviction that the name of an object is not just a symbol but an intrinsic part of the object. The tendency toward this conviction also occurs in adults, as shown, for example, in one study in which adult participants refused food that was identified as toxic with a label they knew to be false. Also called **word realism**. See also MAGICAL THINKING. [first described by Jean PIAGET]

nominal scale a scale of measurement in which data are simply classified into mutually exclusive categories, without indicating order, magnitude, a true zero point, or the like. Also called **categorical scale**. See also INTERVAL SCALE; ORDINAL SCALE; RATIO SCALE.

nominal stimulus in stimulus–response experiments, the stimulus as defined and presented by the experimenter. This may be different from the EFFECTIVE STIMULUS (functional stimulus) experienced by the organism.

nominative *n.* the CASE of a noun, pronoun, or noun phrase that forms the SUBJECT of a clause or sentence. Compare ACCUSATIVE; DATIVE; GENITIVE.

nominative self the self as knower of the self, rather than the self so known. In the psychology of William JAMES the nominative self, or "I," is contrasted with the EMPIRICAL SELF, or "me."

nomological net a conceptual network, often comprising inferences about a variable. The CONSTRUCT VALIDITY of a test is ascertained through a nomological network reflecting research and other experience with the test.

nomology *n.* **1.** the science or study of law and lawfulness. **2.** the branch of science concerned with the formulation of NATURAL LAWS, especially CAUSAL LAWS. A nomological approach is one that strives for causal explanations of phenomena, rather than merely classifying them. See DEDUCTIVE-NOMOLOGICAL MODEL. **—nomological** *adj.*

nomothetic *adj.* relating to the formulation of general laws as opposed to the study of the individual case. A **nomothetic approach** involves the study of groups of people or cases for the purpose of discovering those general and universally valid laws or principles that characterize the average person or case. Compare IDIOGRAPHIC.

nomothetic score a score on a dimension that is common to all people tested (e.g., general intelligence), which implicitly or explicitly compares the individual receiving the score with other individuals receiving a score.

nonaccidental properties visual characteristics of objects that are unaffected by the viewpoint of the observer and therefore provide useful cues for object recognition.

nonactional verb see ACTIONAL VERB.

nonadaptive trait a trait that has no specific value with respect to NATURAL SELECTION, being neither useful nor harmful for REPRODUCTIVE SUCCESS. In human beings eye color, earlobe size, and being able to curl one's tongue are nonadaptive traits.

nonadditive *adj.* describing values or measurements that cannot be meaningfully summarized through addition because the resulting overall value does not correctly reflect the underlying properties of and associations between the component values.

nonadherence *n.* failure of a patient to adhere to a prescribed therapeutic regimen. Nonadherence may involve taking medications in incorrect doses, at incorrect times, or in inappropriate combination with prescribed or over-the-counter medications, alcohol, or foodstuffs. Nonadherence may also involve failure to follow through with recommendations made during psychotherapy. Nonadherence has traditionally been ascribed to oppositional behavior on the part of the patient; however, it probably is more commonly due either to inadequate communication between practitioner and patient, to physical or cognitive limitations that prevent the patient from following therapeutic recommendations (e.g., language differences between patient and practitioner, physical disabilities that prevent prescribed follow-through), or to adverse effects that are not being adequately addressed. A primary aspect of HEALTH PSYCHOLOGY involves methods of reducing nonadherence and increasing adherence. Also called **noncompliance**.

nonaffective hallucination a hallucination whose content is not thematically related to depressed or manic affect. See MOOD-INCONGRUENT PSYCHOTIC FEATURES.

nonaggressive erotica sexually explicit literature, pictures, or other artistic material that does not contain any violence, coercion, or exploitation, but instead presents a caring, consensual, mutually gratifying view of sexuality.

nonaggressive society a culture or subculture whose

goal is one of peaceful isolation from or coexistence with its neighbors. Socialization in such societies is marked by de-emphasis of achievement or power needs, disapproval of aggression, and affirmation of basic pleasures.

nonattitude *n.* an extremely weak attitude that has little persistence over time and minimal resistance to persuasion. Such attitudes have little impact on information processing and behavior. In extreme cases, nonattitudes may be reports of attitudes that reflect no meaningful evaluation of the ATTITUDE OBJECT. See also STRENGTH OF AN ATTITUDE. [originally proposed by Philip E. Converse (1928–)]

noncardiac chest pain recurrent chest pain that cannot be attributed to heart disease. It is commonly caused by problems with the esophagus (gullet), such as gastroesophageal reflux disease or esophageal spasm, or by musculoskeletal disorders, especially fibromyositis (muscle inflammation). Anxiety and panic attacks can also produce pain that resembles cardiac chest pain. See also PSEUDOANGINA.

noncentral chi-square distribution a CHI-SQUARE DISTRIBUTION in which the NONCENTRALITY PARAMETER is not equal to zero.

noncentral F distribution an F DISTRIBUTION in which the noncentrality parameter is not equal to zero.

noncentrality parameter a parameter in many probability distributions used in hypothesis testing that has a value different from zero when a sample is obtained from a population whose parameters have values different from those specified by the NULL HYPOTHESIS under test. This parameter is important in determining the POWER of a statistical procedure.

noncentral t distribution a T DISTRIBUTION in which the noncentrality parameter is not equal to zero.

noncommunicating hydrocephalus HYDROCEPHALUS associated with blockage of the ventricular system, which interferes with normal flow and reabsorption of cerebrospinal fluid. It is typically caused by a tumor. Also called **obstructive hydrocephalus**. Compare COMMUNICATING HYDROCEPHALUS.

noncompetitive *adj.* in pharmacology, referring to a drug that affects a neurotransmitter RECEPTOR while binding at a site other than that bound by the endogenous LIGAND.

noncompliance *n.* see NONADHERENCE.

non compos mentis in law, mentally deficient or legally insane and therefore not responsible for one's conduct. See INCOMPETENCE; INSANITY. Compare COMPOS MENTIS.

nonconformity *n.* expressing opinions, making judgments, or performing actions that are inconsistent with the opinions, judgments, or actions of other people or the normative standards of a social group or situation. Nonconformity can reflect individuals' ignorance of the group's standards, an inability to reach those standards, independence (as when individuals retain their own personally preferred position despite group pressure to change it), and the ANTICONFORMITY of individuals who deliberately disagree with others or act in atypical ways. Compare CONFORMITY.

nonconscious *adj.* describing anything that is not available to conscious report. See UNCONSCIOUS.

nonconscious processes processes that do not themselves reach consciousness, although their eventual outcomes or consequences may have conscious impact.

nonconscious self-regulation the process of moving toward a desired goal or away from an undesired goal without being aware of doing so. See SELF-REGULATION.

noncontingent reinforcement the process or circumstances in which a stimulus known to be effective as a REINFORCER is presented independently of any particular behavior. Because contingencies may arise by accident (see ACCIDENTAL REINFORCEMENT), behavior-independent presentation of stimuli cannot guarantee that no contingency exists between a response and the stimuli. See REINFORCEMENT.

nondeclarative memory a collection of various forms of memory that operate automatically and accumulate information that is not accessible to conscious recollection. For instance, one can do something faster if one has done it before, even if one cannot recall the earlier performance. Nondeclarative memory includes PROCEDURAL LEARNING and PRIMING. Nondeclarative memory does not depend on the MEDIAL TEMPORAL LOBES and is preserved in individuals with AMNESTIC DISORDER. Compare DECLARATIVE MEMORY.

nondecremental conduction the propagation of a nerve impulse along an axon in which the amplitude of the impulse is maintained as it progresses. Compare CONDUCTION WITH DECREMENT. See also ALL-OR-NONE LAW.

nondemand pleasuring caressing of a partner's body for the sensual pleasure involved, with no expectation of sexual arousal. In sex therapy this practice, which excludes any touching of breasts or genitals, is often prescribed to eliminate performance anxiety: It allows a couple with a sexual dysfunction to begin to enjoy physical relations with each other without the risk of experiencing another failure. Also called **nondemanding pleasuring**.

nondirected discussion method a discussion between two or more people about a specific topic without format of any type or the intervention of the leader, whose only role is to assign the topic. The goal is to generate participant-directed discussion.

nondirectional test see TWO-TAILED TEST.

nondirective approach an approach to psychotherapy and counseling in which the client leads the way by expressing his or her own feelings, defining his or her own problems, and interpreting his or her own behavior, while the therapist or counselor establishes an encouraging atmosphere and clarifies the client's ideas rather than directing the process. This approach is a cornerstone of CLIENT-CENTERED THERAPY. [originally advocated by Carl ROGERS]

nondirective counseling see CLIENT-CENTERED THERAPY.

nondirective play therapy a form of PLAY THERAPY based on the principle that a child has the capacity to revise his or her own attitudes and behavior. The therapist provides a variety of play materials and either assumes a friendly, interested role without giving direct suggestions or interpretations or engages the child in conversation that focuses on the child's present feelings and present life situations. The therapist's accepting attitude encourages the child to try new and more appropriate ways of dealing with problems.

nondirective teaching model a person-oriented teaching model, associated with Carl ROGERS's approach, that is primarily concerned with developing the capacity for self-instruction while emphasizing self-discovery, self-understanding, and the realization of one's innate potential.

nondirective therapy see CLIENT-CENTERED THERAPY.

nondisjunction *n.* the failure of pairs of chromosomes to separate during cell division with the result that both chromosomes move to the nucleus of one daughter cell, while the other daughter cell fails to receive its normal complement.

nonepileptic seizure (NES) an episode that resembles an epileptic seizure but is not produced by an abnormal electrical discharge in the brain. According to the Epilepsy Foundation, such seizures may be classified as **physiologic nonepileptic seizures**, which are associated with metabolic disturbances (e.g., changes in heart rhythm or sudden drops in blood pressure) and include SYNCOPE and TRANSIENT ISCHEMIC ATTACKS, or as PSYCHOGENIC NONEPILEPTIC SEIZURES. Nonepileptic seizures are also called **nonepileptic events** (or **attacks**), **pseudoseizures**, or **pseudoepilepsy**, although use of the latter two terms is now discouraged.

nonequivalent-groups design a nonrandomized research design (see NONRANDOMIZED DESIGN) in which the responses of a treatment group and a control group are compared on measures collected at the beginning and end of the research.

nonexperimental research see QUASI-EXPERIMENTAL RESEARCH.

nonfalsifiable explanation an explanation that is fundmentally incapable of being shown to be wrong by any empirical procedures. Such explanations are usually viewed as falling outside the realm of science.

nonfluency *n.* a type of speech that involves such disturbances as dysprosody (altered speech rhythms or intonation), dysarthria (impaired articulation), and agrammatism (deviation from grammatical rules).

nonfluent aphasia a form of APHASIA in which the individual understands language, but has difficulty expressing himself or herself through language. BROCA'S APHASIA is a classic example. Compare FLUENT APHASIA.

nongenetic inheritance the transmission of behavioral or physiological functions between generations without any direct genetic basis. For example, because dominant female macaques intervene more frequently and successfully on behalf of their offspring than do subordinate females, the offspring inherit the status of their female parents. The type of maternal care a young rodent or monkey receives can lead to permanent physiological and neurological changes that affect its subsequent adult parental behavior.

nongonococcal urethritis (NGU) an infection of the genital tract, usually sexually transmitted, caused by an agent other than the gonococcus (responsible for gonorrhea). The infectious organism is often a strain of chlamydia. The symptoms usually include inflammation of the urethra and sometimes a puslike discharge (see URETHRITIS). Also called **nonspecific urethritis (NSU)**.

nongraded school **1.** a school that groups students by academic achievement, mental and physical ability, or emotional development, rather than by age or grade level. **2.** a place of learning that does not use letter or number grades to reflect the quality of a student's work.

nonintentional learning see INCIDENTAL LEARNING.

noninvasive *adj.* **1.** denoting procedures or tests that do not require puncture or incision of the skin or insertion of an instrument or device into the body for diagnosis or treatment. **2.** of a tumor, not capable of spreading from one tissue to another (see NEOPLASM). Compare INVASIVE.

nonjudgmental approach in psychotherapy, the presentation or display of a neutral, noncritical attitude on the part of the therapist in order to encourage the client to give free expression to ideas and feelings. See also NEUTRALITY.

nonlanguage test a test in which the questions or problems as well as the answers or solutions are not conveyed in words. Mazes and PERFORMANCE TESTS are examples. Also called **nonverbal test**.

nonlinear *adj.* describing any relationship between two variables (X and Y) that cannot be expressed in the form $Y = a + bX$, where a and b are numerical constants. The relationship therefore does not appear to be a straight line when depicted graphically.

nonlinear dynamics theories a family of theories, including CHAOS THEORY, concerning the behavior of neurons and neural assemblies in stochastic processes. Nonlinear theories may be able to account for behavior of complex systems that would appear random in deterministic models.

nonlinear regression model any regression model that is not linear in its parameters. Such models cannot be solved by the methods of ordinary least squares regression techniques. Also called **curvilinear regression model**.

nonliterate *adj.* see PRELITERATE.

nonmanipulated variable a variable observed in research but not experimentally manipulated.

nonmembership reference group see REFERENCE GROUP.

nonmonotonic logic a mathematical reasoning system in which information previously considered correct can be revised and removed in the light of new information. This means that any other information believed to be correct, based on the removed information, must also be reconsidered. The system is said to be "nonmonotonic" because information considered correct does not remain the same or grow larger with further reasoning. These nonmonotonic systems are often controlled by "belief revision" or "truth maintenance" algorithms.

nonnormative influences influences on lifespan development that are irregular, in that they happen to just one or a few individuals and do not follow a predictable timetable.

nonnutritive sucking the sucking by infants of objects that do not provide milk (e.g., a thumb or a pacifier), in order, for example, to induce calm or aid sleep. The SUCKING REFLEX thus plays a part in the development of emotional control and self-regulation. Nonnutritive sucking has been used in research studies as a way of inferring infant preferences, by observing differences in sucking rate as infants are presented with different stimuli.

nonorganic hearing loss hearing loss that cannot be accounted for by a known biological cause.

nonorthogonal design a FACTORIAL DESIGN in which the number of subjects or observations in each CELL differs or in which the cell sizes do not have a certain constant of PROPORTIONALITY. Compare ORTHOGONAL DESIGN.

nonovert appeals in marketing and advertising, techniques in which the advertising message is presented by apparently ordinary people who make no deliberate attempt to persuade. In nonovert appeals, consumers may be given the impression that they are "overhearing" an independent endorsement of a product. Nonovert appeals are commonly used in television **slice-of-life commercials**.

nonparametric statistics statistical tests that do not make assumptions about the distribution of the attribute (or attributes) in the population being tested, such as normality and homogeneity of variance. Compare PARAMETRIC STATISTICS.

nonperson *n.* see PERSONALITY DETERIORATION.

nonprescription drugs see OVER-THE-COUNTER DRUGS.

nonprimary motor cortex see MOTOR CORTEX.

nonprimary sensory area see SECONDARY SENSORY AREA.

nonprobability sampling sampling without random selection of sampling units. See also CONVENIENCE SAMPLING; HAPHAZARD SAMPLING; OPPORTUNISTIC SAMPLING.

nonrandomized design any of a large number of research designs in which sampling units are not assigned to experimental conditions at random.

nonrapid-eye-movement sleep see NREM SLEEP.

nonrational *adj.* **1.** incapable of being validated by reason, as, for example, in the opinion of most modern philosophers, the proposition that God exists. A nonrational belief is not necessarily irrational. **2.** describing actions or behaviors that cannot easily be explained in terms of the rational self-interest of the actor.

nonreactive observation any observation that does not affect what is being observed.

nonregulatory drive a DRIVE that serves functions that are unrelated to preserving physiological HOMEOSTASIS and thus not necessary for the physical survival of the individual organism, for example, sex or achievement. Also called **general drive**. Compare REGULATORY DRIVE.

non-REM sleep see NREM SLEEP.

nonresponder bias the extent to which nonresponders (e.g., to a survey) differ from responders. See VOLUNTEER BIAS.

nonreversal shift in DISCRIMINATIONS involving two alternatives, a change in contingencies such that stimuli that were irrelevant in the initial phase of training become the relevant stimuli in a later phase. For example, in initial training involving the presentation of different shapes, white shapes might be designated correct and black ones incorrect. In a following condition, squares (which were one of the shapes in the original task) might be designated correct and circles (also present in the earlier phase) incorrect. Compare REVERSAL SHIFT.

nonsedating antihistamines see HISTAMINE ANTAGONISTS.

nonsense figure a figure that appears to have no meaning since it does not correspond to any common or familiar object and is not a recognizable geometric form, such as a circle or triangle.

nonsense syllable any three-letter nonword used in learning and memory studies to study learning of items that do not already have meaning or associations with other information in memory. See also CONSONANT TRIGRAM. [introduced in 1885 by Hermann EBBINGHAUS]

non sequitur 1. in logic, an inference that does not follow from the premises of an argument, especially when there is no appearance of logical argument at all. **2.** in general usage, any statement that appears puzzlingly unrelated to previous statements in a conversation, discussion, or the like. [Latin, literally: "it does not follow"]

nonshared environment in behavior genetic analyses, those aspects of an environment that individuals living together (e.g., in a family household) do not share and that therefore cause them to become dissimilar to each other. Examples of nonshared environmental factors include the different friends or teachers that siblings in the same household might have outside of the home. Also called **unshared environment**. Compare SHARED ENVIRONMENT.

nonspecific effect a result or consequence whose specific cause or precipitating factors are unknown, for example, the effect on a patient of the belief that he or she has received medication or some other intervention when no true treatment has been given. See also PLACEBO EFFECT.

nonspecificity theory see PATTERN THEORY.

nonspecific urethritis (NSU) see NONGONOCOCCAL URETHRITIS.

nonspectral hue see EXTRASPECTRAL HUE.

nonstate theories of hypnosis explanations of the hypnotic state simply as variations of the psychological, physiological, and behavioral aspects of waking consciousness, rather than as a unique altered state of consciousness. Compare STATE THEORIES OF HYPNOSIS.

nonsteroidal anti-inflammatory drugs see NSAIDS.

nonstriate visual cortex the many regions of cortex that surround the STRIATE CORTEX and participate in the processing of visual stimuli beyond the simple analysis of features that occurs in striate cortex. The nonstriate visual cortex includes parietal regions associated with visuospatial functions, temporal regions important for object recognition, and cortical areas that contribute to eye movements. It is thus somewhat more extensive than PRESTRIATE CORTEX.

nonsyphilitic interstitial keratitis see COGAN'S SYNDROME.

nontraditional education 1. an educational plan that does not conform to the accepted or customary ideas of an ordinary educational system and that may include innovative approaches to teaching, curriculum, grading, or degree requirements. **2.** an educational plan that allows an individual to gain credentials without going through the usual channels.

nontraditional marriage a marriage that deviates from the traditional patterns of marriage in a society. In the United States and western Europe, such marriages may include marriages without the intent of having children or that permit the partners to have sexual relations with other people. Compare TRADITIONAL MARRIAGE.

nonulcer dyspepsia see DYSPEPSIA.

nonverbal ability the ability to understand and manipulate nonverbal stimuli, such as colors, patterns, and shapes.

nonverbal auditory perception test a test that evaluates nonverbal auditory skills, such as the analysis of rhythm and tone and the recognition of nonverbal sounds (e.g., a bell, train, mooing cow).

nonverbal behavior actions that can indicate an individual's attitudes or feelings without the need for speech. Nonverbal behavior can be apparent in FACIAL EXPRESSION, gaze direction, INTERPERSONAL DISTANCE, posture and postural changes, and gestures. It serves a number of functions, including providing information to other people (if they can detect and understand the signals), regulating interactions among people, and revealing the degree of intimacy between those present. Nonverbal behavior is often used synonymously with NONVERBAL COMMUNICATION, despite the fact that nonverbal actions are not always intended for, or understood by, other people.

nonverbal communication (NVC) the act of conveying information without the use of words. Nonverbal communication occurs through facial expressions, gestures, body language, tone of voice, and other physical indications of mood, attitude, approbation, and so forth, some of which may require knowledge of the culture or subculture to understand. In psychotherapy, clients' nonverbal communication can be as important to note as their verbal communication. See also NONVERBAL BEHAVIOR.

nonverbal intelligence an expression of intelligence that does not require language. Nonverbal intelligence can be measured with PERFORMANCE TESTS. See NONLANGUAGE TEST.

nonverbal language see NONVERBAL BEHAVIOR; NONVERBAL COMMUNICATION.

nonverbal leakage see VERBAL LEAKAGE.

nonverbal learning the process of learning about nonverbal materials, such as pictures or drawings, odors, or nonlanguage sounds. Compare VERBAL LEARNING.

nonverbal learning disorder (**NLD**) a LEARNING DISABILITY that is characterized by limited skills in critical thinking and deficits in processing nonverbal information. This affects a child's academic progress as well as other areas of functioning, which may include social competencies, visual-spatial abilities, motor coordination, and emotional functioning. Also called **nonverbal learning disability**.

nonverbal reinforcement any form of NONVERBAL COMMUNICATION, such as a gesture, facial expression, or body movement, that increases the frequency of the behavior that immediately precedes it. For example, a parent's smile following a desired response from a child, such as saying "thank you," reinforces the child's behavior. See also REINFORCEMENT; SOCIAL REINFORCEMENT.

nonverbal test see NONLANGUAGE TEST.

nonverbal vocabulary test a test of vocabulary that does not require a verbal response, such as one in which the participant is required to point to a picture associated with a printed word. An example of such a test is the PEABODY PICTURE VOCABULARY TEST.

non-Western therapies alternatives or complements to traditional Western forms of and approaches to psychotherapy and counseling that emphasize the body (e.g., ACUPUNCTURE, YOGA) and the interdependency of all beings and de-emphasize individualism and rigid autonomy. These therapies have typically developed outside of Europe and North America. See also COMPLEMENTARY AND ALTERNATIVE MEDICINE.

nonzero-sum game in GAME THEORY, a situation in which the rewards and costs experienced by all players do not balance (i.e., they add up to less than or more than zero). In such a situation, unlike a ZERO-SUM GAME, one player's gain is not necessarily another player's loss.

noology *n.* the science of the human mind (from Greek *nous*, "mind, reason"). See NOUS. [coined by Austrian-born U.S. psychiatrist Viktor Frankl (1905–1997)]

Noonan's syndrome a genetic disorder that involves the skin, heart, gonads, and skeleton and is transmitted as an autosomal dominant trait. Affected individuals often have short stature, cardiovascular defects, and deafness. Intellectual development varies: Some have above average intelligence, most have mild to moderate mental retardation, and a few have profound retardation. Male patients are seldom fertile. Also called **familial Turner syndrome**; **Ullrich–Noonan syndrome**. [reported in 1963 by Jacqueline **Noonan** (1921–), U.S. pediatrician]

nootropic drugs drugs that are used to enhance cognitive function, usually in the treatment of progressive dementias, such as Alzheimer's disease, but also of cognitive dysfunction due to traumatic brain injury. They do not reverse the course of the dementia, but are reported to slow its progress in mild to moderate forms of the disease. Many of these drugs work by inhibiting the activity of acetylcholinesterase in the central nervous system, thereby counteracting the disruption of cholinergic neurotransmission observed in patients with Alzheimer's disease. Other drugs use different mechanisms for improving cognitive performance in patients with Alzheimer's disease, including NMDA RECEPTOR antagonism and potentially the prevention of BETA-AMYLOID plaque formation in the brain. Current nootropics include TACRINE, DONEPEZIL, RIVASTIGMINE, and GALANTAMINE. Also called **cognitive enhancers**; **memory-enhancing drugs**.

norepinephrine (**NE**) *n.* a catecholamine NEUROTRANSMITTER and hormone produced mainly by brainstem nuclei and in the ADRENAL MEDULLA. Also called **noradrenaline**.

norepinephrine receptor any of certain receptors in the central nervous system and sympathetic nervous system that bind and respond to NOREPINEPHRINE or substances that mimic its action. See ALPHA ADRENORECEPTOR; BETA ADRENORECEPTOR.

Norflex *n.* a trade name for ORPHENADRINE.

norm *n.* **1.** a standard or range of values that represents the typical performance of a group or of an individual (of a certain age, for example) against which comparisons can be made. **2.** a conversion of a raw score into a scaled score that is more easily interpretable, such as percentiles or IQ scores. **—normative** *adj.*

normal distribution a theoretical continuous PROBABILITY DISTRIBUTION that is a function of two parameters: the EXPECTED VALUE, μ, and the VARIANCE, σ^2. It is given by

$$P(x) = [\exp(-(x - \mu)^2/2\sigma^2)]/\sigma\sqrt{(2\pi)}$$

The normal distribution is the type of distribution expected when the same measurement is taken several times and the variation about the mean value is random. It has certain convenient properties in statistics, and unknown distributions are often assumed to be normal distributions. Also called **Gaussian distribution**.

normality *n.* a broad concept that is roughly the equivalent of MENTAL HEALTH. Although there are no absolutes and there is considerable cultural variation, some flexible psychological and behavioral criteria can be suggested: (a) freedom from incapacitating internal conflicts; (b) the capacity to think and act in an organized and reasonably effective manner; (c) the ability to cope with the ordinary demands and problems of life; (d) freedom from extreme emotional distress, such as anxiety, despondency, and persistent upset; and (e) the absence of clear-cut symptoms of mental disorder, such as obsessions, phobias, confusion, and disorientation.

normalization principle the concept that people with mental or physical disability should not be denied social and sexual relationships and participation in community life merely because of their disability. Social and sexual relationships can include a wide range of emotional and physical contacts, from simple friendship to sexual stimulation and satisfaction. Participation in community life includes engaging in typical life activities, such as work and recreation. See also SOCIAL ROLE VALORIZATION. [introduced in 1969 by Swedish psychologist Bengt Nirje]

normalize *vb.* to apply a TRANSFORMATION to a batch of data that produces a new set of scores that approximately follow the NORMAL DISTRIBUTION.

normal-pressure hydrocephalus (**NPH**) HYDRO-

CEPHALUS associated with ventricular enlargement but normal intracranial pressure. Most common in older adults, the condition frequently benefits from shunting procedures, though complications may occur. Also called **low-pressure hydrocephalus**.

normal probability curve see NORMAL DISTRIBUTION.

normal saline see PHYSIOLOGICAL SALINE.

normal science a science at the stage of development when it is characterized by a PARADIGM consisting of universal agreement about the nature of the science, its practices, assumptions, and methods, and satisfaction with its empirical progress. Compare IMMATURE SCIENCE; PREPARADIGMATIC SCIENCE. See PARADIGM SHIFT; SCIENTIFIC REVOLUTION. [proposed by U.S. philosopher of science Thomas Kuhn (1922–1996)]

normative compliance adjustments in an individual's behavior resulting from NORMATIVE INFLUENCE. See also COMPLIANCE. [defined in 1961 by German-born educator and sociologist Amitai Werner Etzioni (1929–)]

normative crisis see MATURATIONAL CRISIS.

normative ethics see ETHICS.

normative influence the personal and interpersonal processes that cause individuals to feel, think, and act in ways that are consistent with SOCIAL NORMS, standards, and conventions. Normative influence is partly personal, because individuals who have internalized their group's norms will strive to act in ways that are consistent with those norms. It is also interpersonal, because groups place direct and indirect pressure on members to comply with their norms. Those who consistently violate the group's norms are often subjected to negative interpersonal consequences (ostracism, ridicule, punishment), whereas those who conform are typically rewarded. Also called **normative social influence**. Compare INFORMATIONAL INFLUENCE; INTERPERSONAL INFLUENCE.

normative-reeducative strategy in social psychology, the idea that societal change should be based on active reeducation of people within the framework of their cultural milieu. Normative-reeducative strategy holds that a program for social change based only on rational appeal is inadequate because behavioral patterns are largely determined by traditional attitudes and cultural norms. See also EMPIRICAL-RATIONAL STRATEGY; POWER-COERCIVE STRATEGY.

normative research research conducted for the purpose of ascertaining NORMS.

normative science a scientific approach concerned with establishing NORMS or typical or desirable values for behavior, education, health, or other cultural or societal aspects. In contrast to **descriptive science**, which attempts to characterize behavior and other phenomena as they actually exist, normative science attempts to determine what they should be in order to satisfy various criteria.

normative social influence see NORMATIVE INFLUENCE.

norm group a group whose performance serves as the basis for establishing NORMS.

normosplanchnic type a constitutional body type that corresponds roughly to the ATHLETIC TYPE in KRETSCHMER TYPOLOGY. [described by Italian physician Giacinto Viola (1870–1943)]

normotensive *adj.* describing individuals whose blood pressure is within the normal range for their age and other factors considered.

normotype *n.* a constitutional body type that is morphologically average (EUMORPHIC).

norm-referenced testing an approach to testing based on a comparison of one person's performance with that of a NORM GROUP on the same test. Norm-referenced testing differentiates among individuals and ranks them on the basis of their performance. For example, a nationally standardized norm-referenced test will indicate how a given person performs compared to the performance of a national sample. See CRITERION-REFERENCED TESTING.

Norpramin *n.* a trade name for DESIPRAMINE.

Norrie's disease a type of congenital blindness that is transmitted as an X-linked genetic defect affecting only males. Progressive loss of hearing often accompanies the blindness. About two thirds of affected individuals show mental retardation, and some experience hallucinations or other psychological difficulties. [reported in 1927 by Gordon **Norrie** (1855–1941), Danish ophthalmologist]

North American Society for the Psychology of Sport and Physical Activity (NASPSPA) a multidisciplinary association of scholars from the behavioral sciences and related professions. The purpose of the association is to promote the scientific study of human behavior in sport and physical activity, to facilitate dissemination of scientific knowledge, and to advance the improvement of research and teaching in SPORT PSYCHOLOGY, MOTOR LEARNING, MOTOR CONTROL, and MOTOR DEVELOPMENT.

Northern blot a method of detecting a particular RNA fragment in a mixture, such as one derived from a tissue extract. It involves separating the various RNA molecules using GEL ELECTROPHORESIS, blotting the separated RNAs onto nitrocellulose, then using a NUCLEOTIDE probe to hybridize with, and highlight, the RNA fragment of interest. [named by analogy with SOUTHERN BLOT]

nortriptyline *n.* a TRICYCLIC ANTIDEPRESSANT, a so-called secondary tricyclic, that is the principal metabolic product of AMITRIPTYLINE. Although its clinical efficacy is the same as other tricyclics, nortriptyline and the other secondary tricyclic agent, DESIPRAMINE, were often preferred because they were less sedating and had fewer ANTICHOLINERGIC EFFECTS. A THERAPEUTIC WINDOW is thought to exist for nortriptyline: Although plasma levels do not always correlate with clinical effectiveness, optimum responses are thought to occur when serum levels of the drug are between 50 and 150 ng/ml. Plasma levels over 500 ng/ml are toxic. The availability of newer antidepressants that do not require therapeutic monitoring has led to a decline in its use. U.S. trade names: **Aventyl**; **Pamelor**.

NOS abbreviation for NOT OTHERWISE SPECIFIED.

nose *n.* the organ that contains the sensory tissue (about 600 mm^2) that underlies olfactory sensitivity (see OLFACTORY EPITHELIUM). The major functions of the nose are to modulate the temperature and adjust the humidity of inspired air and to direct that air toward the sensory tissue in the nasal cavity.

noso- (**nos-**) *combining form* disease.

nosocomial *adj.* denoting or relating to a hospital-acquired infection that is unrelated to the patient's primary illness.

nosogenesis *n.* see PATHOGENESIS.

nosological approach an approach that focuses on the naming and classifying of disorders together with the identification of PATHOGNOMONIC signs and symptoms and their grouping into syndromes for diagnostic purposes. The nosological approach contrasts with the PSYCHODYNAMIC APPROACH, which emphasizes causal factors.

nosology *n.* the scientific study and classification of diseases and disorders, both mental and physical. See also PSYCHIATRIC CLASSIFICATION. **—nosological** *adj.*

nosomania *n.* a rarely used term for an unfounded, abnormal belief that one is suffering from a particular disease. See HYPOCHONDRIASIS.

nostalgia *n.* **1.** a longing to return to an earlier period or condition of life recalled as being better than the present in some way. **2.** a longing to return to a place to which one feels emotionally bound (e.g., home or a native land). See also HOMESICKNESS. **—nostalgic** *adj.*

no-suicide contract a specific agreement, used when the potential for suicide is at issue, made between the client and the therapist that the client will not take his or her own life. It is often used as an intermediary measure for an agreed-upon period of time (e.g., until the next therapy session). See also CONTRACT.

not guilty by reason of insanity (NGRI) a final judgment made in a court of law if the defendant has been found to lack the mental capacity to be held criminally responsible for his or her actions. See CRIMINAL RESPONSIBILITY; INSANITY.

nothingness *n.* in EXISTENTIALISM, the belief that nothing is seen to structure existence. The nothingness or meaninglessness of human existence is thought to be the primary cause of anxiety or anguish.

Nothnagel's acroparesthesia see ACROPARESTHESIA. [Carl Wilhelm Hermann **Nothnagel** (1841–1905), German neurologist]

not me in the SELF-SYSTEM theory of U.S. psychoanalyst Harry Stack Sullivan (1892–1949), the part of the personified self that is based on interpersonal experiences that have evoked overwhelming anxiety, dread, and horror, and which may lead to nightmares, emotional crises, and schizophrenic reactions. Compare BAD ME; GOOD ME.

not otherwise specified (NOS) in *DSM–IV–TR*, denoting a broad-based diagnostic category, for example, DEPRESSIVE DISORDER NOT OTHERWISE SPECIFIED. The NOS diagnosis is chosen when the patient's problems seem to fall into a particular family of disorders (e.g., depressive disorders, anxiety disorders), but the syndrome is not typical or there is not enough information available at the time of diagnosis to specify more accurately the type of disorder that is present.

noumenon *n.* (*pl.* **noumena**) in the thought of German philosopher Immanuel Kant (1724–1804), a thing in itself as contrasted with a thing known through the senses and the understanding (see PHENOMENON). Although the noumena are the causes of one's experience, they can never themselves be experienced, as they lie outside time and space; nor can they be apprehended by speculative reason, because the general concepts of quantity, quality, relation, and so forth apply only to phenomena. The ideas of God, freedom, and immortality belong to the noumenal realm but are accessible to human beings through their experience as moral agents. **—noumenal** *adj.*

nous *n.* in classical Greek philosophy, reason or intellect. For Plato (c. 427–c. 347 BCE) nous is the highest form of reason, permitting the apprehension of the fundamental and unchanging principles of reality. Aristotle (384–322 BCE) likewise distinguished between nous, which enables understanding of the essential and nonaccidental, and the knowledge gained from experience, which enables understanding of the temporary and contingent. In later Platonic and Neoplatonic thought, nous was sometimes identified with the rational principle governing the universe itself (see NEOPLATONISM).

novel antipsychotics see ATYPICAL ANTIPSYCHOTICS.

novelty *n.* the quality of being new and unusual. It is one of the major determining factors directing attention. The attraction to novelty has been shown to begin as early as 1 year of age; for example, when infants are shown pictures of visual patterns, they will stare longer at a new pattern than at a pattern they have already seen. In consumer behavior, the attraction to novelty is manifested as a desire for a change, even in the absence of dissatisfaction with the present situation. For example, despite satisfaction with a particular product, many consumers will switch to a different brand simply because they want a change or, in some cases, just because it is new.

novelty fear see NEOPHOBIA.

novelty hypothesis the claim that the contents of CONSCIOUSNESS can be predicted by their novelty, based on the observation that novel or unexpected events frequently intrude in ongoing conscious functioning.

novelty preference task a task in which an infant is shown a new object simultaneously with a familiar one. It is used in studies of infant cognition, based on the fact that infants will visually inspect a new object in preference to looking at a familiar object. The duration of the infant's visual gaze is used to quantify attention, surprise, and novelty versus familiarity.

noxious stimulus an aversive stimulus that can serve as a negative reinforcer of behavior, in severe cases because it causes pain or damage to the experiencing organism and in lesser cases because it is unpleasant.

NPH abbreviation for NORMAL-PRESSURE HYDROCEPHALUS.

NPTA abbreviation for National Parent Teachers Association. See PARENT TEACHERS ASSOCIATION.

NREM sleep *non*rapid-*e*ye-*m*ovement sleep: periods of sleep in which dreaming, as indicated by RAPID EYE MOVEMENTS (REM), usually does not occur. During these periods, which occur most frequently in the first hours of sleep, the electroencephalogram shows only minimal activity, and there is little or no change in pulse, respiration, and blood pressure. Also called **non-REM sleep**. Compare REM SLEEP.

n=1 research see SINGLE-CASE EXPERIMENTAL DESIGN.

NSAIDs *n*on*s*teroidal *a*nti-*i*nflammatory *d*rugs: a large class of analgesic and anti-inflammatory agents that includes ASPIRIN, ibuprofen, naproxen, and many others. They achieve their effects by blocking the synthesis of PROSTAGLANDINS involved in inflammation and the pain response. Concurrent administration of NSAIDs and LITHIUM may cause increased serum levels of lithium.

NSF abbreviation for NATIONAL SCIENCE FOUNDATION.

NST abbreviation for nucleus of the solitary tract (see SOLITARY NUCLEUS).

NSU abbreviation for nonspecific urethritis (see NONGONOCOCCAL URETHRITIS).

nubile *adj.* **1.** describing a girl or young woman who is of marriageable age, ready for marriage, or going through puberty. **2.** describing a sexually attractive young woman. **—nubility** *n.*

nuchal rigidity rigidity along the back of the neck, which can be associated with injury or brain disease.

nuclear complex a central conflict or problem that is rooted in infancy, for example, feelings of inferiority (according to Alfred ADLER) or the OEDIPUS COMPLEX (according to Sigmund FREUD).

nuclear family a family unit consisting of two parents and their dependent children (whether biological or adopted). With various modifications, the nuclear family has been and remains the norm in developed Western societies. Compare EXTENDED FAMILY; PERMEABLE FAMILY.

nuclear imaging imaging that involves scanning for emissions from radioactive isotopes injected into the body. Techniques include POSITRON EMISSION TOMOGRAPHY (PET) and SINGLE PHOTON EMISSION COMPUTED TOMOGRAPHY (SPECT). These forms of scanning yield information not only about the anatomy of an organ but also about its functions; they are therefore valuable for medical diagnosis and research. See also BRAIN IMAGING.

nuclear magnetic resonance (**NMR**) the response of atomic nuclei to changes in a strong magnetic field. The atoms give off weak electric signals, which can be recorded by detectors placed around the body and used for imaging parts of the body, including the brain. See BRAIN IMAGING; MAGNETIC RESONANCE IMAGING.

nuclear schizophrenia a type of schizophrenia whose defining features, which include social inadequacy and withdrawal, blunted affect, and feelings of DEPERSONALIZATION and DEREALIZATION, are highly similar to those described by German psychiatrist Emil Kraepelin (1856–1926) for DEMENTIA PRAECOX. It is of early, insidious onset and is associated with a degenerative, irreversible course and poor prognosis. This term is often used interchangeably with PROCESS SCHIZOPHRENIA. Also called **authentic schizophrenia**; **true schizophrenia**; **typical schizophrenia**. Compare SCHIZOPHRENIFORM PSYCHOSIS. [proposed in the late 1930s by Norwegian psychiatrist Gabriel Langfeldt (1895–1983)]

Nuclear Surety Personnel Reliability Program a special assessment program to achieve safety consistent with operational readiness and to minimize the effects of accidents, incidents, and deficiencies in handling nuclear weapons. At least two authorized persons must be present whenever a task is performed with a nuclear weapon. Individuals qualified under the program are trained to perform these duties and to make the appropriate judgments.

nuclear warfare the use of nuclear weapons in combat, which causes enormous destruction with potentially both physical and psychological effects on the survivors.

nuclei *pl. n.* see NUCLEUS.

nucleic acid a large molecule that consists of a chain of NUCLEOTIDES. Nucleic acids are of two types, DNA and RNA, and are important constituents of living cells.

nucleolus *n.* (*pl.* **nucleoli**) a structure within a cell's NUCLEUS that is the site of assembly of RIBOSOMES. **—nucleolar** *adj.*

nucleoplasm *n.* the material contained within the NUCLEUS of a cell. It is bound by the **nuclear envelope**, which separates it from the CYTOPLASM.

nucleotide *n.* a compound consisting of a nitrogenous base, a sugar, and one or more phosphate groups. Nucleotides such as ATP are important in metabolism. The nucleic acids (DNA and RNA) comprise long chains of nucleotides (i.e., polynucleotides).

nucleus *n.* (*pl.* **nuclei**) **1.** a large membrane-bound compartment, found in the cells of nonbacterial organisms, that contains the bulk of the cell's genetic material in the form of chromosomes. **2.** in the central nervous system, a mass of CELL BODIES belonging to neurons with the same or related functions. Examples are the amygdaloid nuclei (see AMYGDALA), the basal nuclei (see BASAL GANGLIA), the thalamic nuclei (see THALAMUS), and the NUCLEUS ACCUMBENS. Compare GANGLION.

nucleus accumbens one of the largest of the septal nuclei (see SEPTAL AREA), which receives dopaminergic innervation from the VENTRAL TEGMENTAL AREA. Dopamine release in this region may mediate the reinforcing qualities of many activities, including drug abuse.

nucleus basalis magnocellularis see MAGNOCELLULAR NUCLEUS OF THE BASAL FOREBRAIN.

nucleus cuneatus the NUCLEUS in the medulla oblongata that is the termination of the CUNEATE FASCICULUS in the dorsal columns of the spinal cord. Also called **cuneate nucleus**.

nucleus gracilis the NUCLEUS in the medulla oblongata that is the termination of the GRACILE FASCICULUS in the dorsal columns of the spinal cord. Also called **gracile nucleus**.

nucleus of the raphe see RAPHE NUCLEUS.

nucleus of the solitary tract see SOLITARY NUCLEUS.

nuisance parameter a parameter of secondary interest that must be estimated in order to obtain an estimate of or test a hypothesis about a parameter of primary interest.

nuisance variable a variable that has no intrinsic significance to the experiment but may contribute to an increase in experimental error.

null finding the result of an experiment indicating that there is no relationship, or no significant relationship, between variables. Also called **null result**.

null hypothesis (symbol: H_0) the statement that an experiment will find no difference between the experimental and control conditions, that is, no relationship between variables. Statistical tests are applied to experimental results in an attempt to disprove or reject the null hypothesis at a predetermined SIGNIFICANCE LEVEL. See also ALTERNATIVE HYPOTHESIS.

null hypothesis significance testing (**NHST**) computation of a test of significance to evaluate the tenability of the NULL HYPOTHESIS. See SIGNIFICANCE TESTING.

null result see NULL FINDING.

null set see EMPTY SET.

number *n.* in linguistics, a grammatical classification of nouns, pronouns, and any words in AGREEMENT with them according to whether they are singular or plural (or in some languages, dual). In English, number is most commonly expressed by the plural noun ending *-s* (e.g., *boy* but *boys*) and in the inflection of the verb to agree with the number of the subject (e.g., *The boy runs* but *The boys run*).

number-completion test an intelligence test, or a component of one, in which the subject is required to supply a missing item in a series of numbers or to continue the series. A component of such a test might be: 6, 9, 13, 18, — (the next number is 24).

number factor an intelligence factor that is measured by tests of ability to handle numerical problems. See FACTOR THEORY OF INTELLIGENCE; PRIMARY ABILITIES.

numerical ability (**N**) one of THURSTONE's seven PRIMARY ABILITIES. Thurstone measured this ability with arithmetic computation problems and relatively simple word problems.

numerical competence the ability of some animals to identify the cardinal numbers associated with differing quantities of objects and to arrange these numbers in correct order. Some parrots and chimpanzees can count the number of items presented to them, and some can rank numbers, as in the ascending sequence 1, 5, 8.

numerical scale any scale or measurement instrument that yields a quantitative (numerical) representation of an attribute.

numerology *n.* the study of the occult significance of

numbers. For example, the date of someone's birth or a figure derived from the letters of his or her name may be interpreted in terms of its supposed influence on that person's character and future. See also GEMATRIA. **—numerological** *adj.* **—numerologist** *n.*

numerosity perception the perception of number (i.e., of constituent elements or of separate objects) by means of visual, auditory, or other sensory systems.

nurse *n.* a graduate of an approved school of nursing who meets prescribed standards of education and clinical practice and who is licensed by the state to provide nursing services. See also LICENSED PRACTICAL NURSE; REGISTERED NURSE.

nurse practitioner a REGISTERED NURSE who has undergone extensive postgraduate training (often in a specialty area, such as internal medicine or pediatrics) and is licensed to perform some of the activities of a physician, including the prescription of medicine. Nurse practitioners generally function under the supervision of physicians, but not in their presence.

nursery school see SCHOOL READINESS.

nurse's aide a person who works in a hospital or nursing home, has completed at least a brief course of health care training, and assists nursing staff in providing care for patients. Also called **nurse's assistant**.

nursing behavior the provision by a female of nourishment for her young offspring until they are capable of obtaining their own food. In mammals it involves primarily the secretion of milk from the mammary glands and assisting the offspring to find the nipple in order to suckle the milk. PROLACTIN stimulates mammary gland development, and OXYTOCIN stimulates the milk letdown reflex. Some male birds, such as the ringdove, produce a crop milk (a milklike substance in the part of their digestive tract known as the crop) that is regurgitated to feed young chicks.

nursing home a LONG-TERM CARE FACILITY that provides 24-hour nursing care in addition to supportive services for people with chronic disability or illness, particularly older people who have mobility, eating, and other self-care problems.

nurturance *n.* **1.** the provision of affectionate attention, protection, and encouragement to others. **2.** the need or tendency to provide such nurturance.

nurture *n.* the totality of environmental factors that influence the development and behavior of a person. Psychologists have shown particular interest in sociocultural and ecological factors, such as family attributes, child-rearing practices, and economic status. Compare NATURE. See also NATURE–NURTURE CONTROVERSY.

nutmeg *n.* the seed of the trees *Myristica acuminata* and *M. fragrans*, which are indigenous to the Moluccas (Indonesia) and cultivated in South America, the Philippines, and the West Indies. It has a history of folk use as a remedy for stomach and gastrointestinal complaints. Nutmeg has volatile oils containing elemecin, myristicin, and other active ingredients that in sufficient doses produce intoxicating effects, some of which have been compared to those produced by CANNABIS. In larger doses, however, nutmeg is poisonous; signs of toxicity include abnormally dilated or contracted pupils, hallucinations, severe nausea and vomiting, and rapid heartbeat. See also MACE.

nutrient *n.* any substance required as part of the diet for growth, maintenance, and repair of the body's tissues or as a source of energy. Nutrients include CARBOHYDRATES, fats (see FATTY ACID), PROTEINS (see also AMINO ACID), VITAMINS, and some minerals (e.g., calcium, sodium, potassium).

nutritional disorder any medical or psychological condition that results from MALNUTRITION. Such disorders include obesity and vitamin deficiency disorders. See also EATING DISORDER.

nutritional effects on intelligence the effects of essential vitamins and minerals on people's levels of intelligence. Research suggests that mild nutritional deficiencies have little, if any, effect on intelligence, but that moderate and (especially) severe deficiencies can result in intellectual deficits. There is no credible evidence that vitamin and mineral supplements beyond the levels achieved in a normal balanced diet contribute to further intellectual enhancement.

nux vomica the seed of a plant, *Strychnos nux vomica*, that grows in tropical Asia and has been used as an emetic (the name means literally "a nut that causes vomiting"). Nux vomica contains two substances, STRYCHNINE and BRUCINE, which are CNS STIMULANTS and highly poisonous, causing powerful, painful convulsions and eventually death from paralysis of respiratory muscles. In low doses, nux vomica increases glandular secretion in the gastrointestinal tract and has been used as a homeopathic remedy to stimulate digestion and treat a variety of gastrointestinal conditions.

NVC abbreviation for NONVERBAL COMMUNICATION.

NVD abbreviation for *n*ausea, *v*omiting, and *d*iarrhea.

nyakwana *n.* see EPENA.

nyctalopia *n.* see NIGHT BLINDNESS.

nyctophilia *n.* a strong preference for darkness or night. Also called **noctiphilia**; **noctophilia**; **scotophilia**.

nyctophonia *n.* a variation of SELECTIVE MUTISM in which the child speaks at night but is mute during daylight hours.

nympholepsy *n.* **1.** a type of PEDOPHILIA in which the individual has a strong preference or obsessive desire for young girls who are sexually precocious (nymphets: a word coined by Vladimir Nabokov in his 1955 novel *Lolita*). Also called **Lolita complex**. **2.** a mania or frenzy, especially of an erotic nature, characterized by a desire for some unattainable ideal. The name is derived from myths in which an individual glimpses a nymph and becomes possessed by a demonic frenzy in pursuit of her.

nymphomania *n.* excessive or uncontrollable desire for sexual stimulation and gratification in a woman. The word is often used loosely to denote a high degree of sexuality in a woman, reflecting negative cultural attitudes toward female sexuality and male fears of being unable to meet the sexual needs of women. **—nymphomaniac** *n., adj.*

nystagmus *n.* involuntary, rapid movement of the eyeballs. The eyeball motion may be rotatory, horizontal, vertical, or a mixture. See also PHYSIOLOGICAL NYSTAGMUS; VESTIBULAR NYSTAGMUS.

Oo

OA abbreviation for OVEREATERS ANONYMOUS.

OAEs abbreviation for OTOACOUSTIC EMISSIONS.

O&M abbreviation for orientation and mobility. See ORIENTATION AND MOBILITY TRAINING.

obedience *n.* behavior in compliance with a direct command. **—obedient** *adj.*

obesity *n.* the condition of having excess body fat resulting in overweight, variously defined in terms of absolute weight, weight–height ratio (see BODY MASS INDEX), distribution of subcutaneous fat, and societal and aesthetic norms. The basic causes are genetic, environmental, behavioral, or some interaction of these. Overeating may have a psychological cause (see BINGE-EATING DISORDER; FOOD ADDICTION; NIGHT-EATING SYNDROME) but in some cases it may be due to an organic disorder (see HYPERPHAGIA). The consequences of obesity are a matter for concern: It predisposes to heart disease, diabetes, and other serious medical conditions (see MORBID OBESITY), and obese individuals may develop emotional and psychological problems relating to BODY IMAGE. **—obese** *adj.*

obesity treatments therapeutic efforts used to produce substantial weight reduction in an individual. Treatments include long-term diets, crash diets, group support, HYPNOTHERAPY, exercise programs, nutritional education, drug therapy, BEHAVIOR MODIFICATION of eating patterns, hormonal treatment when indicated, and DYNAMIC PSYCHOTHERAPY focused on insight into the unconscious purposes served by the individual's excessive food intake.

object *n.* **1.** the "other," that is, any person or symbolic representation of a person that is not the self and toward whom behavior, cognitions, or affects are directed. The term is sometimes used to refer to nonpersonal phenomena (e.g., an interest might be considered to be an "object") but the other-person connotation is far more typical and central. **2.** in psychoanalytic theory, the person, thing, or part of the body through which an INSTINCT can achieve its AIM of gratification. See OBJECT CATHEXIS; OBJECT RELATIONS. **3.** the person who is loved by an individual's EGO: his or her LOVE OBJECT. **4.** in linguistics, a noun, pronoun, or complex noun that is governed by an active transitive verb or a preposition, such as *dinner* in *I ate dinner* or *I came after dinner*. Objects of verbs can be divided into **direct objects** (e.g., *cake* in *Mary ate the cake*) and **indirect objects** (e.g., *Mary* in *John gave Mary the cake*).

object and location memory a form of spatial cognition that involves locating and remembering objects in spatial arrays. It should not to be confused with the more common OBJECT-LOCATION MEMORY.

object-assembly test a test in which the task is to reassemble an object puzzle that has been broken up or dismantled.

object-based attention attention viewed as operating primarily on objects rather than on spatial locations. Compare SPACE-BASED ATTENTION.

object blindness see VISUAL AGNOSIA.

object cathexis in psychoanalytic theory, the investment of LIBIDO or PSYCHIC ENERGY in objects outside the self, such as a person, goal, idea, or activity. Also called **object libido**. Compare EGO CATHEXIS. See CATHEXIS.

object choice in psychoanalytic theory, the selection of a person toward whom LIBIDO or PSYCHIC ENERGY is directed. See ANACLITIC OBJECT CHOICE; NARCISSISTIC OBJECT CHOICE.

object color color attributed to a solid object, as opposed to a FILM COLOR, which has no object associated with it.

object concept see OBJECT PERMANENCE.

object constancy the tendency for an object to be perceived more or less unchanged despite variations in the conditions of observation.

object display a single display that uses a meaningful shape to present different types of information simultaneously. Object displays usually take the form of polygons, changes in the shape of which provide an indication of the status of the system (see EMERGENT FEATURES). Also called **configural display**.

object fetish sexual interest and arousal focused on a particular item. Common targets of such interest are feet, shoes, and undergarments, but almost anything can be the focus of an object fetish. See also RETIFISM.

objectifying attitude a tendency to react to an object, person, or event while disregarding personal feelings about it.

objective 1. *adj.* having actual existence in reality, based on observable phenomena. **2.** *adj.* impartial or uninfluenced by personal feelings, interpretations, or prejudices. Compare SUBJECTIVE. **3.** *n.* something that is to be obtained or worked toward. See AIM; GOAL. **4.** *n.* in linguistics, see ACCUSATIVE. **5.** *n.* the lens or lens system in an optical instrument, such as a microscope. Also called **object glass**; **objective lens**; **object lens**.

objective anxiety see REALISTIC ANXIETY.

objective competitive situation a situation in which one or more people evaluate the performance of an individual or team by comparing it either with the performance of another individual or team or with some standard of excellence. See also COMPETITION.

objective elaboration the tendency to generate particular evaluative responses based on the strength of the ARGUMENTS contained in a message rather than on factors external to the arguments. See also BIASED ELABORATION; BIASING FACTOR; ELABORATION.

objective examination an examination in which subjective judgments do not play a role in scoring. An example is a multiple-choice test in which scoring standards have been formulated to allow no difference of opinion among different scorers as to the correctness of a response. In contrast, an essay test is a SUBJECTIVE TEST.

objective indicator a marker or other measure of an entity, condition, emotion, or behavior that is free of subjective bias, that is, it is not an opinion or rating but an independent measure of the condition. An objective indicator is generally viewed as more reliable than a subjective assessment.

objective psychology an approach to psychology that focuses on measurement of behavioral processes or other observable phenomena. Compare SUBJECTIVE PSYCHOLOGY.

objective psychotherapy a treatment procedure developed primarily for use with institutionalized patients and patients with mild-to-moderate emotional disturbances. To reduce the subjectivity resulting from a personal relationship with the therapist, all therapeutic communication is carried out in writing. The patient answers written autobiographical questions, relates and comments on dreams, and reacts to assigned readings. In return, the therapist gives interpretations and points out underlying motivations in written memoranda, including a **memorandum as a whole**, which summarizes all the insights reached in the process. [developed by U.S. psychoanalyist Benjamin Karpman (1886–1962)]

objective reality the EXTERNAL WORLD of physical objects, events, and forces that can be observed, measured, and tested. See REALITY.

objective reference 1. the activity or condition by which one term or concept is related to another or to objects in the world. **2.** the actual object or sensation that is perceived by the senses.

objective responsibility in the moral judgment typical of children under the age of 10, the idea that the rightness or wrongness of an act is based almost exclusively on its objective, usually physical, consequences. For example, to a young child, the number of cups he or she has broken is more important than the reason for breaking them (see MORAL REALISM). This idea reflects a kind of literalism manifested by young children before they learn to take an individual's motives into account. Compare SUBJECTIVE RESPONSIBILITY. [proposed by Jean PIAGET]

objective scoring scoring a test by means of a key or formula, so that different scorers will arrive at the same score. It is contrasted with **subjective scoring**, in which the score depends on the scorer's opinion or interpretation.

objective self-awareness a reflective state of awareness in which a person regards himself or herself objectively, acknowledging personal limitations and the existing disparity between the IDEAL SELF and the ACTUAL SELF. Objective self-awareness is often a necessary part of SELF-REGULATION.

objective set a GESTALT PSYCHOLOGY factor in which the original grouping seen in a display based on objective factors, such as spatial location, will be maintained as the display changes and will continue to be seen when the grouping is objectively ambiguous. See PERCEPTUAL SET.

objective sociogram see SOCIOGRAM.

objective test a test designed to elicit a specific answer, correct or incorrect. A "true or false" test is an example of an objective test. Compare SUBJECTIVE TEST.

objectivism *n.* **1.** the position that judgments about the external world can be established as true or false independent of personal feelings, beliefs, and experiences. **2.** in ethics, the position that the ideals, such as "the good," to which ethical propositions refer are real. Objectivism holds that ethical prescriptions do not reduce to mere statements of personal or cultural preference. Compare SUBJECTIVISM. —**objectivist** *n., adj.*

objectivity *n.* **1.** the tendency to base judgments and interpretations on external data rather than on subjective factors, such as personal feelings, beliefs, and experiences. **2.** a quality of a research study such that its hypotheses, choices of variables studied, measurements, techniques of control, and observations are as free from bias as possible. Compare SUBJECTIVITY.

object language a type of computer programming language that emphasizes data rather than processes. Unlike imperative languages, with programs that consist primarily of commands to perform specified actions, object languages support programs that consist primarily of commands to data objects generally to modify themselves (e.g., change their values).

object libido see OBJECT CATHEXIS.

object-location memory the ability to remember the location of objects in the environment (e.g., where one put one's car keys).

object loss in psychoanalytic theory, the actual loss of a person who has served as a GOOD OBJECT, which precedes INTROJECTION and is involved in SEPARATION ANXIETY. Anxiety about the possible loss of a good object begins with the infant's panic when separated from its mother. Adult GRIEF and MOURNING are related to object loss and separation anxiety in infancy and childhood, which often intensifies and complicates the grief reaction.

object love in psychoanalytic theory, love of a person other than the self. It is a function of the EGO and not the instincts as in OBJECT CATHEXIS. See LOVE OBJECT.

object of consciousness in conscious perception, the perceived object as distinct from the perceiver. In BUDDHISM and VEDANTA Hinduism, there is a related notion that the real self is "overshadowed" by the object of perception. The separation of observer and observed is criticized as artificial in phenomenological philosophies (see PHENOMENOLOGY). Compare SUBJECT OF CONSCIOUSNESS.

object of instinct in psychoanalytic theory, that which is sought (the **external aim**, e.g., a person, object, or behavior) in order to achieve satisfaction (the **internal aim**). See AIM OF THE INSTINCT.

object-oriented play the manipulation of objects, such as banging or throwing them, in the context of play.

object permanence knowledge of the continued existence of objects even when they are not directly perceived. According to Jean PIAGET, object permanence develops gradually in infants over the SENSORIMOTOR STAGE of cognitive development. Milestones that indicate the acquisition of object permanence include reaching for and retrieving a covered object (about 8 months), retrieving an object at location B even though it was previously hidden several times at location A (the **A-not-B task**, about 12 months), and removing a series of covers to retrieve an object, even though the infant only witnessed the object being hidden under the outermost cover (**invisible displacement**, about 18 months). Recent research using nonreaching tasks suggests that infants display some knowledge of object permanence at an earlier age than that suggested by Piaget.

object relations 1. an individual's relationship to his or her entire external world. **2.** in psychoanalysis, an individual's relationships to his or her OBJECTS (real and imagined), that is, the persons, activities, or things that function as sources of libidinal or aggressive gratification.

object relations theory any psychoanalytically based theory that views the need to relate to OBJECTS as more central to personality organization and motivation than the vicissitudes of the INSTINCTS. These theories developed from and in reaction to classic Freudian theories of psychodynamics. Some theories view the personality as organized in terms of a complex world of internal object representations and their relationships with each other, for example, FAIRBAIRNIAN THEORY and the approach of Melanie KLEIN.

object-superiority effect in visual perception tasks, the finding that judgments about a briefly presented line are made more efficiently when the line is part of a drawing of a three-dimensional object than when it is part of a two-dimensional figure. See CONFIGURAL SUPERIORITY EFFECT.

obligate carrier an individual whose parent and child or whose monozygotic twin carries a particular genetic mutation, implying that the individual must also carry the mutation, even though he or she has not been tested for the mutation.

obligatory exercise exercise that an individual feels obliged to undertake. See EXERCISE ADDICTION.

oblique *adj.* **1.** correlated, not independent: used to describe the relationship between correlated factors in FACTOR ANALYSIS. **2.** not at right angles. Compare ORTHOGONAL.

oblique rotation a rotational system used in FACTOR ANALYSIS when two or more factors are correlated.

obnubilation *n.* CLOUDING OF CONSCIOUSNESS or STUPOR.

obscenity *n.* verbal expressions, drawings, gestures, and written material that grossly violate the norms of good taste and decency in a given society. See PORNOGRAPHY. **—obscene** *adj.*

obscurantism *n.* **1.** opposition to scientific inquiry, rational argument, and the progress of knowledge generally, especially when these appear to contradict a given set of political, social, or religious convictions. **2.** a deliberate or strategic failure to be clear and lucid in the expression of knowledge or opinion. **—obscurantist** *adj.*

observation *n.* **1.** the intentional examination of an object or process for the purpose of obtaining facts about it or reporting one's conclusions based on what has been observed. See CONTROLLED OBSERVATION; NATURALISTIC OBSERVATION; PARTICIPANT OBSERVATION. **2.** a piece of information (see DATA). **—observational** *adj.*

observational error the deviation of an observed value from the true value.

observational learning 1. the acquisition of information, skills, or behavior through watching the performance of others, either directly or via such media as films and videotapes. Also called **vicarious learning**. **2.** the conditioning of an animal to perform an act observed in a member of the same or a different species. For example, the mockingbird can learn to imitate the song patterns of other kinds of birds. Also called **vicarious conditioning**. See also MODELING THEORY.

observational method the scientific method in which observers are trained to watch and record behavior, events, or processes as precisely and completely as possible without personal bias or interpretation. Tape recorders, cameras, stopwatches, and other devices may be used to increase accuracy.

observational study a study based on direct observation of cases (participants) in which the experimenter passively observes the behavior of the participants without any attempt at intervention or manipulation of the behaviors being observed. Such studies typically involve observation of cases under naturalistic conditions rather than the random assignment of cases to experimental conditions. See OBSERVATIONAL METHOD.

observation commitment the confinement of a person in a hospital by a court order for a limited period of observation, usually to determine COMPETENCY TO STAND TRIAL or overall legal COMPETENCE.

observation delusion see DELUSION OF OBSERVATION.

observer *n.* **1.** one who makes or records an OBSERVATION. **2.** in TELEPATHY experiments, a participant who is neither the designated SENDER nor the designated RECEIVER. His or her function is often to guard against EXPERIMENTER BIAS or other methodological errors.

observer bias an experimental bias consisting of errors by an observer in one direction. Such a bias is often associated with the observer's expectations, beliefs, or personal preferences. See EXPERIMENTER BIAS; EXPERIMENTER EFFECT; EXPERIMENTER EXPECTANCY EFFECT.

observer drift gradual systematic changes over a period of time in the observations and recording of observations made by a particular observer. See EXPERIMENTER DRIFT.

observer's sociogram see SOCIOGRAM.

observing response behavior that results in the presentation or clarification (e.g., enhanced view) of DISCRIMINATIVE STIMULI.

obsession *n.* a persistent thought, idea, image, or impulse that is experienced as intrusive and inappropriate and results in marked anxiety, distress, or discomfort. Obsessions are often described as EGO-DYSTONIC in that they are experienced as alien or inconsistent with one's self and outside one's control. Common obsessions include repeated thoughts about contamination, a need to have things in a particular order or sequence, repeated doubts, aggressive or horrific impulses, and sexual imagery. Obsessions can be distinguished from excessive worrries about everyday occurrences in that they are not concerned with real-life problems. The response to an obsession is often an effort to ignore or suppress the thought or impulse or to neutralize it by a COMPULSION. See OBSESSIVE-COMPULSIVE DISORDER. **—obsessional** *adj.* **—obsessive** *adj.*

obsessional type see LIBIDINAL TYPES.

obsessive behavior behavior characteristic of obsessive-compulsive personality disorder or obsessive-compulsive disorder, such as persistent brooding, doubting, ruminating, worrying over trifles, cleaning up and keeping things in perfect order, or performing rituals.

obsessive-compulsive disorder (OCD) an ANXIETY DISORDER characterized by recurrent obsessions, compulsions, or both that are time consuming (more than one hour per day), cause significant distress, or interfere with the individual's functioning. The obsessions and compulsions are recognized as excessive or unreasonable.

obsessive-compulsive personality disorder in *DSM–IV–TR*, a personality disorder characterized by an extreme need for perfection, an excessive orderliness, an inability to compromise, and an exaggerated sense of responsibility. See COMPULSIVE PERSONALITY DISORDER.

obsessive personality an obsolete *DSM–I* personality trait disturbance characterized by excessive orderliness, perfectionism, indecisiveness, constant worry over trivia, and the imposition of rigid standards on others. See COMPULSIVE CHARACTER.

obstinate progression see SYNDROME OF OBSTINATE PROGRESSION.

obstruction method a technique for determining the relative strength of drives. An experimental animal is presented with one or more goals of various drives, for example, food (hunger) versus water (thirst), and is required to overcome an obstacle (e.g., an electrified grid) in order to reach the goal. The delay before attempting to overcome the obstacle, as well as the animal's choice of which goal to pursue, may be used to represent drive strength and drive dominance.

obstructive dysmenorrhea see DYSMENORRHEA.

obstructive hydrocephalus see NONCOMMUNICATING HYDROCEPHALUS.

obstruent *adj., n.* see PLOSIVE.

obtrusive idea an obsessive, unwanted, and alien idea that intrudes on a person's normal flow of thought. See also OBSESSION.

obtrusive measure a method of obtaining measurements or observations in which the participants are aware that a measurement is being made. Compare UNOBTRUSIVE MEASURE.

obturator *n.* **1.** any item that blocks an opening. **2.** a PROSTHESIS worn inside the mouth to close an opening in the palate. It is often used to improve the speech production of an individual with a CLEFT PALATE.

OCB abbreviation for ORGANIZATIONAL CITIZENSHIP BEHAVIOR.

Occam's razor (**Ockham's razor**) the maxim that, given a choice between two hypotheses, the one involving the fewer assumptions should be preferred. See also ELEGANT SOLUTION; LAW OF PARSIMONY. [William of **Occam** or **Ockham** (c. 1285–1347), English Franciscan monk and Scholastic philosopher]

occasional cause in the doctrine of OCCASIONALISM, a change in a material or mental condition that appears to cause a correlated change in some other condition but that, in reality, is merely an occasion for God to produce the observed change in the latter.

occasional inversion a form of same-gender sexual behavior that may occur when a person is deprived of the presence of individuals of the opposite sex, for example, in prison or in military service. See also SITUATIONAL HOMOSEXUALITY.

occasionalism *n.* the philosophical doctrine that events are not directly caused by the antecedent events that appear to produce them, and particularly that material things cannot cause mental phenomena or mental phenomena influence material things. Rather, all things material and mental are caused by God's volitional acts. A change in a mental or material condition provides God with the occasion to produce a change in some other mental or material condition. Thus, the material or mental phenomena that might appear to be real and direct causes are merely OCCASIONAL CAUSES. Extreme forms of occasionalism reject causal influence of any mental or material phenomena on any others. Occasionalism was first formulated by French philosopher Nicolas Malebranche (1638–1715), largely as a response to the MIND–BODY PROBLEM arising from CARTESIAN DUALISM. **—occasionalist** *adj.*

occasion setter in PAVLOVIAN CONDITIONING, a stimulus that is differentially paired with a stimulus–stimulus contingency. For example, after presentation of a light, a tone might be followed by the delivery of food. In the absence of the light, the tone is not followed by food. If the tone is effective in eliciting salivation only after the light is presented, the light is designated as an occasion setter. Compare CONDITIONAL DISCRIMINATION.

occipital cortex the CEREBRAL CORTEX of the occipital lobe of the brain. See VISUAL CORTEX.

occipital lobe the most posterior lobe of each cerebral hemisphere, associated with the visual sense. See CEREBRUM.

occlusion *n.* **1.** an obstruction or closure. Occlusion of a cerebral artery may cause a thrombotic or embolic STROKE. **2.** the simultaneous firing of two branches of the same neuron, which may result in a total output that is less than the sum of the separate responses. **—occlusive** *adj.*

occult *adj.* mysterious, incomprehensible, or secret. The term is mainly applied to certain esoteric traditions of magical belief and practice (see MAGIC) but is sometimes used of other alleged phenomena that cannot be explained in either everyday or scientific terms, such as PREMONITORY DREAMS, CLAIRVOYANCE, and telepathic communications (see TELEPATHY). See PARAPSYCHOLOGY. **—occultism** *n.* **—occultist** *n.*

occupation *n.* **1.** a family of jobs that involve the performance of similar tasks and have similar requirements in terms of skills, training, and personal attributes. For example, bookkeeping jobs in different organizations will differ to some extent in the tasks performed and level of skill required, but there is enough commonality to place them in the same occupation of bookkeeper. Occupations may also be defined in part by a common OCCUPATIONAL CULTURE. See also PROFESSION. **2.** in rehabilitation, see OCCUPATIONAL THERAPY. **3.** more generally, any activity or pastime. **—occupational** *adj.*

occupational ability the ability to perform vocational or professional tasks, generally measured by a series of OCCUPATIONAL TESTS.

occupational adjustment the degree to which an individual's abilities, interests, and personality are compatible with a particular OCCUPATION. The term differs from VOCATIONAL ADJUSTMENT in its emphasis on the interaction between an individual's personal characteristics and the objective requirements, conditions, and opportunities associated with the job.

occupational analysis the systematic collection, processing, and interpretation of information concerning specific OCCUPATIONS.

occupational biomechanics see BIOMECHANICS.

occupational classification the assignment of jobs to OCCUPATIONS using systems such as O–ET (the Occupational Information Network).

occupational counseling an early 20th-century approach to vocational guidance. Three steps were identified in the process: (a) relevant knowledge of self, (b) realistic knowledge of occupations, and (c) true reasoning in making sensible choices. [proposed by U.S. educator Frank Parsons (1854–1908)]

occupational cramp painful spasm of the muscles, usually in the hand or arm, that prevents the individual from engaging in his or her occupation, such as writing, driving, sewing, playing a musical instrument, or firing a gun. It is a form of DYSTONIA. See MUSICIAN'S CRAMP; WRITER'S CRAMP. See also REPETITIVE STRAIN INJURY.

occupational culture a distinctive pattern of thought and behavior shared by members of the same OCCUPATION and reflected in their language, values, attitudes, beliefs, and customs. For example, police officers can be regarded as having a distinct CULTURE of this kind. See also ORGANIZATIONAL CULTURE.

occupational disease any disease arising from factors involved with the patient's job or profession.

occupational ergonomics a specialty area of ERGONOMICS that attempts to make work systems and processes within particular occupations more responsive to the physical, cognitive, and psychosocial characteristics of workers.

occupational health psychology theory and research devoted to understanding workplace sources of health, illness, and injury and the application of this knowledge to improve the physical and mental well-being of employees. See also INDUSTRIAL AND ORGANIZATIONAL PSYCHOLOGY.

occupational interest measure see INTEREST TEST.

occupational neurosis a PSYCHOGENIC inhibition associated with employment in which the individual experiences distress and increasing aversion to work, which may be expressed as poor work performance or reactive symptoms of illness (e.g., fatigue, vertigo) that increase in severity as the individual continues to work. In some cases, there is a specific inhibition that interferes with the ability to work, often affecting an essential function necessary for that work, such as WRITER'S CRAMP, SEAMSTRESS'S CRAMP, or CARPAL TUNNEL SYNDROME. These inhibitions were originally believed to be CONVERSION symptoms reflecting inner conflicts but have increasingly been found to have a medical explanation. Also called **occupational inhibition**.

occupational norm the average or typical score obtained from tests of a particular ability, trait, or interest among members of a particular OCCUPATION.

occupational psychology see INDUSTRIAL AND ORGANIZATIONAL PSYCHOLOGY.

occupational rehabilitation see VOCATIONAL REHABILITATION.

Occupational Safety and Health Administration (OSHA) a federal agency of the U.S. Department of Labor created to enforce the Occupational Safety and Health Act of 1970 and to establish occupational safety and health standards for all places of employment involved in interstate commerce.

occupational segregation the extent to which people of the same gender or ethnicity are employed in some occupations to the exclusion of others. For example, the fact that a high proportion of nurses are women could suggest that this may be a sex-segregated occupation.

occupational status the degree of esteem accorded to members of an OCCUPATION by society. Occupations that are viewed positively are high-status occupations, whereas occupations that are viewed negatively are low-status occupations.

occupational stress tension and strain experienced by workers on the job, arising out of such factors as demanding schedules, difficult decisions, relationships with coworkers and supervisors, disagreeable working conditions, fatigue, occupational hazards, excessive competition, or anxiety over possible unemployment. See EXECUTIVE STRESS; STRESS.

occupational test a test designed to measure potential ability or actual proficiency in a given OCCUPATION. See EMPLOYMENT TEST; WORK-SAMPLE TEST.

occupational therapy (OT) a therapeutic, rehabilitative process that uses purposeful tasks and activities to improve health; prevent injury or disability; enhance quality of life; and develop, sustain, or restore the highest possible level of independence of individuals who have been injured or who have an illness, impairment, or other mental or physical disability or disorder. It typically includes assessment of an individual's FUNCTIONAL STATUS, the development and implementation of a customized treatment program, and recommendations for adaptive modifications in home and work environments as well as training in the use of appropriate ASSISTIVE TECHNOLOGY devices. The term **occupation** is used by practitioners of the therapy to denote three broad categories of human activity: (a) ACTIVITIES OF DAILY LIVING, (b) work and productive activities, and (c) play or leisure activities.

occurrence rate the frequency with which particular events are observed to occur.

OCD abbreviation for OBSESSIVE-COMPULSIVE DISORDER.

oceanic feeling an expansion of consciousness beyond one's body (limitless extension) and a sense of unlimited power associated with identification with the universe as a whole (see COSMIC IDENTIFICATION). According to psychoanalytic theory, this feeling originates in the earliest period of life, before the infant is aware of the outside world or the distinction between the ego and nonego. Oceanic feelings may be revived later in life as a delusion or as part of a religious or spiritual experience.

oceanic state a condition of perceived boundlessness of the self, sometimes involving the perception of omnipotence. It may be an ecstatic state, a state of altered awareness, a state of interpersonal connection or union or of spiritual union, or a dissociative experience. See also ALTERED STATE OF CONSCIOUSNESS; COSMIC CONSCIOUSNESS.

O'Connor v. Donaldson a 1975 lawsuit in the U.S. Supreme Court in which it was determined that people cannot be involuntarily committed to a facility on the basis of mental illness alone if they are not dangerous to themselves or others and are able to survive safely outside the facility. A lower court ruling in this case assisted the court in its final ruling in *Wyatt v. Stickney* (1972) regarding right to treatment with involuntary commitment (see FORCED TREATMENT; WYATT V. STICKNEY DECISION).

octave *n.* the interval between two sounds that have a frequency ratio of 2:1. The interval or frequency ratio in octaves between two sounds with frequencies f_2 and f_1 is given by $f_2/f_1 = 2^n$, where n is the number of octaves. A filter with a bandwidth of ⅓ octave, for example, has an upper frequency cutoff that is $2^{1/3} = 1.26$ times that of the lower frequency cutoff. See CENT; MUSICAL INTERVAL.

octave effect in conditioning, the phenomenon in which an experimental animal, after experiencing REINFORCEMENT at one sound frequency, will react to a new frequency an octave away from the original frequency because it is more similar to the original than it is to a frequency within that octave.

ocul- *combining form* see OCULO-.

ocular 1. *adj.* relating to the eye. **2.** *n.* the eyepiece of a microscope.

ocular accommodation see ACCOMMODATION.

ocular apraxia see OCULOMOTOR APRAXIA.

ocular dominance a response characteristic of neurons in the STRIATE CORTEX. Many neurons respond more vigorously to stimulation through one eye than they do to stimulation through the other eye. See also OCULAR DOMINANCE COLUMN.

ocular dominance column a vertical slab of STRIATE CORTEX in which the neurons are preferentially responsive to stimulation through one of the two eyes. It is important for binocular vision. Ocular dominance columns for each eye alternate in a regular pattern, so that an electrode inserted tangentially to the cortical surface encounters neurons that are responsive to stimulation through first the IPSILATERAL EYE, then the CONTRALATERAL EYE, then back to the ipsilateral eye; vertical electrode penetration of one column encounters neurons in all layers in which the response is dominated by stimulation through the same eye. See also MONOCULAR REARING. Compare ORIENTATION COLUMN.

ocular dominance histogram a graph that portrays the strength of response of a neuron to stimuli presented to either the left eye or the right eye. It is used to determine the effects of manipulating visual experience.

ocular dysmetria inability to direct saccadic eye movements (see SACCADE) to targets. Eye movements may either fall short of the target (undershooting: **ocular hypometria**) or go beyond it (overshooting: **ocular hypermetria**). Ocular dysmetria may be due to an oculomotor deficit (e.g., paralysis of eye muscles), defective visual localization, or impaired visuomotor coordination. Also called **saccadic dysmetria**.

ocular fixation see FIXATION.

ocular flutter a rapid horizontal oscillation occurring in both eyes when gazing straight ahead. Flutter may also appear following a SACCADE (**flutter dysmetria**). Ocular flutter is typically caused by injury to the cerebellum.

ocular hypertelorism see HYPERTELORISM.

ocular myopathy see MYOPATHY.

ocular palsy see OCULOMOTOR PALSY.

ocular pursuit see VISUAL PURSUIT.

oculo- (**ocul-**) *combining form* eye.

oculocerebral-hypopigmentation syndrome a hereditary disorder marked by eye anomalies, absence of hair and skin pigmentation, mental retardation, and spasticity. The cases studied have involved children of Old Order Amish families. The syndrome is believed to be due to an autosomal recessive trait that becomes manifested through consanguinity (relationship by blood).

oculocerebrorenal syndrome an X-linked recessive genetic disorder affecting male children and marked by renal-tubule dysfunction, mental retardation, and eye disorders, including congenital glaucoma, cataracts, and distension of the eyeball because of fluid accumulation. The renal disorders include acidosis, hypophosphatemia, and excess amino acids in the urine. Neurological deficits vary from absence-of-brain abnormalities to hydrocephalus and cerebral atrophy. Also called **Lowe's disease**; **Lowe's syndrome**; **oculocerebrorenal syndrome of Lowe**.

oculogravic illusion an illusory displacement of an object that may occur when the direction of gravity changes (e.g., a line may appear to tilt in an aircraft during a roll).

oculogyral illusion the APPARENT MOVEMENT of a stationary faint light in a dark room due to VESTIBULAR NYSTAGMUS of the eyes when the body is moved.

oculogyric crisis prolonged fixation of the eyeballs in a single position for minutes to hours. It may result from ENCEPHALITIS or be produced by certain antipsychotic drugs. Also called **oculogyric spasm**.

oculomotor apraxia a condition in which willed (i.e., purposeful) eye movements are impaired. Affected individuals appear to have lost the ability to move their eyes. SMOOTH-PURSUIT MOVEMENTS and SACCADES are impaired or even absent when elicited by a target stimulus and when the individual is asked to follow a target. A particular form of oculomotor apraxia is **lid apraxia**, the inability to close the eyes. Also called **ocular apraxia**. See also CONGENITAL OCULOMOTOR APRAXIA.

oculomotor changes a broad category of effects induced by alteration of the visual environment, such as the adaptation in movement trajectory that occurs with prolonged viewing of the world through prism goggles that invert or displace the visual image.

oculomotor nerve the third CRANIAL NERVE, which contains both motor and sensory fibers and innervates most of the muscles associated with movement and accommodation of the eye and constriction of the pupil (i.e., all the muscles of the eye except the external rectus and superior oblique muscles). Also called **cranial nerve III**.

oculomotor nucleus a nucleus in the brainstem that is associated with either of the OCULOMOTOR NERVES.

oculomotor palsy paralysis of any of the extrinsic EYE MUSCLES. This may be due to damage to the muscle itself (myogenic), the motor end plate (neuromuscular), or the third, fourth, or sixth cranial nerves (neurogenic). The most common causes are diabetes, hypertension, and multiple sclerosis. Also called **ocular palsy**.

oculosympathetic paralysis see HORNER'S SYNDROME.

oculovestibular response eye movements that occur when the head is moved. They are used to test integrity of the RETICULAR ACTIVATING SYSTEM after brain injury.

Od see REICHENBACH PHENOMENON.

OD 1. *n.* a colloquial name (an abbreviation) for an OVERDOSE, most often of an opioid or a sedative. **2.** *vb.* to take an overdose. **3.** abbreviation for ORGANIZATIONAL DEVELOPMENT.

O data information about an individual's personality based on judgments by *o*bservers, that is, evaluations provided by peers or others who have observed his or her daily functioning. See also L DATA; Q DATA; T DATA.

odd–even reliability a method of assessing the reliability of a test by correlating scores on the odd-numbered items with scores on the even-numbered items. It is a special case of SPLIT-HALF RELIABILITY.

oddity from sample a procedure similar to MATCHING TO SAMPLE except that reinforcement is arranged for responding to a stimulus that does not match the sample stimulus. Also called **oddity learning**.

oddity problem a learning task in which an animal is required to choose an object that is in some way different from other possible choices. The purpose is to test the animal's ability to perceive relationships and differences among a number of similar objects.

odds *n.* the ratio of the probability of an event occurring to the probability of the event not occurring, usually expressed as the ratio of integers (e.g., 3:2).

odds ratio the ratio of two ODDS. For example, in a study on a drug, the odds ratio is calculated as the odds of an effect in a treated group divided by the odds of the same effect in a control group.

odor *n.* the property of an ODORANT that is perceptible as a sensory experience produced by stimulation of the olfactory nerve. See SMELL; SMELL MECHANISM.

odorant *n.* an airborne volatile substance that produces an ODOR sensation. Odorants may differ in both intensity and quality.

odorant-binding protein any one of a small family of proteins that bind to odorants and are carriers of the odorant molecules to the mucus-covered neurons in the OLFACTORY EPITHELIUM.

odoriferous *adj.* producing an odor.

odorimetry *n.* see OLFACTOMETRY.

odor prism see HENNING'S ODOR PRISM.

odorvector *n.* the vapor of an ODORANT, which produces sensations of smell. The odorvector may be sensed via the nose (see ORTHONASAL OLFACTION) or via the nasopharynx (see RETRONASAL OLFACTION). Also called **odorivector**.

Odyle *n.* see REICHENBACH PHENOMENON.

oedipal conflict see OEDIPUS COMPLEX.

oedipal phase in psychoanalytic theory, the later portion of the PHALLIC STAGE of psychosexual development, usually between ages 3 and 5, during which the OEDIPUS COMPLEX manifests itself. Also called **oedipal stage**.

Oedipus complex in psychoanalytic theory, the erotic feelings of the son toward the mother, accompanied by rivalry and hostility toward the father, during the PHALLIC STAGE of development. The corresponding relationship between the daughter and father is referred to as the **female Oedipus complex**. The complete Oedipus complex includes both this heterosexual form, called the **positive Oedipus complex**, and its homosexual counterpart, the NEGATIVE OEDIPUS COMPLEX. Sigmund FREUD derived the name from the Greek myth in which Oedipus unknowingly killed his father and married his mother. Although Freud held the complex to be universal, most anthropologists question this universality because there are many cultures in which it does not appear. Freud saw the Oedipus complex as the basis for NEUROSIS when it is not adequately resolved by the boy's fear of castration and gradual IDENTIFICATION with the father. The female Oedipus complex is posited be resolved by the threat of losing the mother's love and by finding fulfillment in the feminine role. Contemporary psychoanalytic thought has decentralized the importance of the Oedipus complex and has largely modified the classical theory by emphasizing the earlier, primal relationship between child and mother. Also called **oedipal conflict**; **oedipal situation**. See also CASTRATION COMPLEX; NUCLEAR COMPLEX.

OEP abbreviation for olfactory-evoked potential. See CHEMOSENSORY EVENT-RELATED POTENTIAL.

off cells (**OFF cells**) neurons in the visual system, particularly the retina, that depolarize when the retina is stimulated by light offset. See OFF RESPONSE. Compare ON CELLS.

off-center bipolar cell a RETINAL BIPOLAR CELL that is inhibited by light in the center of its RECEPTIVE FIELD but is excited by light in the surround. See also OFF RESPONSE. Compare ON-CENTER BIPOLAR CELL.

off-center ganglion cell a RETINAL GANGLION CELL that is inhibited by light in the center of its RECEPTIVE FIELD but is excited by light in the surround. See also OFF RESPONSE. Compare ON-CENTER GANGLION CELL.

off-center/on-surround referring to a concentric RECEPTIVE FIELD in which stimulation of the center inhibits the neuron of interest, whereas stimulation of the surround excites it. See CENTER–SURROUND ANTAGONISM. Compare ON-CENTER/OFF-SURROUND.

officer selection procedures see MILITARY OFFICER SELECTION.

officer training military courses used to educate officers on leadership skills.

off-label *adj.* denoting or relating to the clinical use of a drug for a purpose that has not been approved by the U.S. Food and Drug Administration. Manufacturers generally do not promote drugs for off-label uses, although medical literature may support such uses.

offline *adj., adv.* see ONLINE.

off response (**OFF response**) the depolarization of a neuron in the visual system that occurs in response to light decrement. Neurons with off responses in the center of their receptive fields are often called OFF CELLS. See also CENTER–SURROUND ANTAGONISM. Compare ON RESPONSE.

offspring *n.* any of the immediate descendants of a human, animal, or plant.

off-the-job training interventions to increase the knowledge, skills, and abilities of employees that occur away from the workstation or workplace, often in classroom settings. Compare ON-THE-JOB TRAINING. See also VESTIBULE TRAINING.

off-time life events LIFE EVENTS that occur at a nontypical or unexpected point in the life span for members of a given population. Examples are cancer in a child and marriage for a 90-year-old. Compare ON-TIME LIFE EVENTS.

'ohana *n.* the family unit in the Hawaiian culture, characterized by a value system that emphasizes multigenerational kinship, including the prescription of age-appropriate roles, connection to one's ancestors, respect for the wisdom of elders, promotion of the welfare of children, and the overall sustenance of the family system. Similar ways of conceptualizing family are found in other Polynesian cultures.

6-OHDA abbreviation for 6-HYDROXYDOPAMINE.

Ohm's law the principle that the ear can analyze COMPLEX TONES into a series of individually perceptible PURE TONES. [Georg Simon **Ohm** (1787–1854), German physicist]

-oid *suffix* likeness or similarity (e.g., ANTHROPOID).

oikofugic *adj.* having or relating to an urge to travel or wander from home. See DROMOMANIA; NOMADISM.

oikomania *n.* see ECOMANIA.

oikotropic *adj.* affected with homesickness or nostalgia for home.

OKR abbreviation for OPTOKINETIC REFLEX.

olan *n.* see MYRIACHIT.

olanzapine *n.* an ATYPICAL ANTIPSYCHOTIC used for the treatment of acute mania, schizophrenia, and other psychotic disorders in adults. It is closely related to CLOZAPINE, but lacks the latter drug's association with agranulocytosis. Common side effects are sedation, lethargy, weight gain, and ORTHOSTATIC HYPOTENSION. Rarely, like all antipsychotics, it may be associated with TARDIVE DYSKINESIA or NEUROLEPTIC MALIGNANT SYNDROME. U.S. trade names: **Zydis**; **Zyprexa**.

Older Adult Resources and Services a questionnaire used as a community assessment tool to determine the level of functioning of older adults in five areas: mental health, physical health, social resources, economic resources, and ACTIVITIES OF DAILY LIVING. It must be administered by a trained individual and can be administered in separate segments if assessment of only one area is desired. The responses to the questionnaire can be used to determine choices of supportive services for the geriatric population.

oldest old adults older than 85 years of age. This group is the fastest growing segment of the population in many developed countries.

old-fashioned racism see MODERN RACISM.

old-old *adj.* describing adults aged over 75. See also OLDEST OLD. Compare YOUNG-OLD.

olfactie *n.* a unit for measuring odor intensity, used to calibrate early OLFACTOMETERS. It is equal to the intensity of an ODORANT that just exceeds the ABSOLUTE THRESHOLD.

olfaction *n.* the sense of smell, which is activated by ODORANT stimulation of receptor cells in the OLFACTORY

EPITHELIUM located in the nasal passages. **—olfactory** *adj.*

olfactometer *n.* an instrument used to regulate the presentation of ODORANTS. An olfactometer may have tubes that are inserted into the nostrils, or the odorant may be emitted more diffusely into the air surrounding the nose. See BLAST OLFACTOMETER; STREAM OLFACTOMETER.

olfactometry *n.* the measurement of odor sensations. Also called **odorimetry**.

olfactophilia *n.* sexual interest in and arousal by body odors, especially those from the genital areas.

olfactorium *n.* a test chamber devised for precise measurement of olfactory function, especially odor sensitivity. The highly controlled odor environment presents pure air or odorant-bearing air. The testee typically bathes and then puts on a protective suit prior to entering the chamber.

olfactory adaptation a decrease in olfactory sensitivity subsequent to stimulation of the sense of smell. This temporary phenomenon is measured by increases in odor thresholds and reported declines in odor intensities.

olfactory area a brain structure associated with the sense of smell. Experimental evidence of the exact functions of this area has been compiled by excision or ablation of a number of tissues in and around the RHINENCEPHALON, with varied and often conflicting results. Only lesions of the OLFACTORY BULB seem consistently to produce a disruption of olfactory functions. See PERIAMYGDALOID CORTEX; PYRIFORM AREA.

olfactory brain see PYRIFORM AREA; RHINENCEPHALON.

olfactory bulb a bulblike ending on the olfactory nerve in the anterior region of each cerebral hemisphere. This first synapse in the olfactory system picks up excitation from the nose, specifically from the cilia in the OLFACTORY EPITHELIUM. See also TUFTED CELL.

olfactory cell see OLFACTORY RECEPTOR.

olfactory cilium a hairlike structure arising from an OLFACTORY RECEPTOR.

olfactory cortex see PYRIFORM AREA.

olfactory cross-adaptation a reduction in sensitivity to an odor following adaptation to another odor. Unlike other senses, there are usually no changes in the perceived quality of single ODORANTS following adaptation to other single odorants. Cross-adaptation is observed, however, in an odorant mixture that contains the single odorant adapting stimulus.

olfactory dysfunction any alteration in the perception of odor quality or odor sensitivity. See ANOSMIA; DYSOSMIA; HYPOSMIA; MICROSMIA; PAROSMIA; PHANTOSMIA; TROPOSMIA.

olfactory epithelium an area of OLFACTORY RECEPTORS or nerve endings in the lining of the nose. The epithelium is separated from the OLFACTORY BULB by the CRIBRIFORM PLATE, through which the receptor cells synapse with cells in the olfactory bulb. See also SMELL MECHANISM.

olfactory eroticism pleasurable sensations, particularly of an erotic nature, associated with the sense of smell.

olfactory-evoked potential (**OEP**) see CHEMOSENSORY EVENT-RELATED POTENTIAL.

olfactory hallucination a false perception of odors, which are usually unpleasant or repulsive, such as poison gas or decaying flesh.

olfactory mucosa the superior portion of the nasal cavity containing mucus-secreting cells and subsuming the OLFACTORY EPITHELIUM, the OLFACTORY NERVE, and supporting cells.

olfactory nerve the first CRANIAL NERVE, which carries sensory fibers concerned with the sense of smell. It originates in the olfactory lobe and is distributed to the nasal mucous membrane (see OLFACTORY RECEPTOR). Also called **cranial nerve I**.

olfactory prism see HENNING'S ODOR PRISM.

olfactory receptor a spindle-shaped receptor cell in the OLFACTORY EPITHELIUM of the nasal cavity that is sensitive to ODORANTS. Cilia at the base of the olfactory receptors contain receptor sites for odorants. The receptors themselves collectively form the OLFACTORY NERVE, which synapses with cells in the OLFACTORY BULB. Also called **olfactory sense organ**. See OLFACTORY STIMULATION.

olfactory sense organ see OLFACTORY RECEPTOR.

olfactory stimulation the excitation of the cilia of OLFACTORY RECEPTORS in the nasal cavity by inhaled ODORANTS, which are absorbed into nasal mucus. There is little agreement on the precise mechanism involved in this excitation.

olfactory sulcus a groove on the surface of each cerebral hemisphere, on the inferior (lower) side of the frontal lobe.

olfactory system the primary structures and processes involved in an organism's detection of and responses to ODORANTS. The olfactory system includes several million OLFACTORY RECEPTORS in the nasal cavity, the OLFACTORY EPITHELIUM and VOMERONASAL SYSTEM, OLFACTORY TRANSDUCTION, neural impulses and pathways (see OLFACTORY NERVE), and associated brain areas and their functions.

olfactory tract a band of nerve fibers that originates in the OLFACTORY BULB and extends backward along the bottom side of the frontal lobe of the brain to a point called the **olfactory trigone**, at which point the tract divides into three strands leading to the medial and lateral olfactory gyri and the olfactory tubercle. See also LATERAL OLFACTORY TRACT.

olfactory transduction the sequence of events involved in converting chemical molecules into olfactory signals. As in other sense systems, the conjoint activation of many receptors and the modulating effects of SECOND MESSENGERS play important roles in olfactory transduction.

olfactory tubercle a small oval elevation near the base of the OLFACTORY TRACT that contains auxiliary olfactory nerve fibers and cells. The olfactory tubercle is rarely found in humans but is a common structure in animals that depend on a sense of smell to survive.

oligarchy *n.* **1.** rule by a small elite group. **2.** those who constitute such a group. **—oligarchic** *adj.*

oligo- (**olig-**) *combining form* few or deficient.

oligocephaly *n.* see OLIGOENCEPHALY.

oligodendrocyte *n.* a type of glial cell (see NEUROGLIA) that is associated with neurons in the central nervous system. Some oligodendrocytes (known collectively as **oligodendroglia**) form MYELIN SHEATHS around axons.

oligoencephaly *n.* a form of mental retardation associated with asymmetrical physical development and often marked by an abnormally small brain, nervous-system irregularities, and low resistance to disease. Also called **oligocephaly**.

oligohydramnios *n.* a deficiency of amniotic fluid, which can result in mechanical interference with fetal movements leading to possible congenital defects, such as clubfoot, torticollis, muscular dystrophy, or brain damage.

oligospermia *n.* an abnormally low content of spermatozoa in a sample of semen. Oligospermia is one of several factors responsible for male INFERTILITY. The usually accepted minimum level of sperm needed to insure fertility is 20 million per milliliter.

olisbos *n.* see DILDO.

olivary nucleus an olive-shaped mass of gray matter in the medulla oblongata, containing the cell bodies of neurons that connect the cerebral cortex with other parts of the brain.

olivocochlear bundle a tract of centrifugal or efferent fibers extending from the SUPERIOR OLIVARY COMPLEX through the descending neural pathways to the cochlear HAIR CELLS.

olivopontocerebellar atrophy a slowly progressive neurological disorder characterized by degeneration of neurons in the pons, cerebellum, and OLIVARY NUCLEUS. Symptoms are highly variable across individuals but typically include ATAXIA, difficulties with balance and walking, tremors, and DYSARTHRIA. In many cases onset is in middle adulthood and death occurs within 10–20 years.

-ology *suffix* see -LOGY.

ololiuqui *n.* the seed of a Latin American vine, *Rivea corymbosa*, which contains substances chemically related to LSD but less potent. Ololiuqui was first described in the reports of the 16th-century Spanish physician Francisco Hernández while studying the indigenous peoples of Mexico, who used it for both medicinal and religious purposes.

OLSAT acronym for OTIS–LENNON SCHOOL ABILITY TEST.

ombudsman *n.* a person or program responsible for investigating consumer complaints and grievances and acting as a consumer advocate in resolving problems. The concept and term originated in Scandinavia.

omega squared (symbol: ω^2) a measure of the STRENGTH OF ASSOCIATION based on the proportion of variance of one measure predictable from variance in other measures.

omen *n.* an event that is regarded, whether rationally or not, as a portent of future good or ill fortune. The study of supernatural omens was known as AUGURY.

omission training see DIFFERENTIAL REINFORCEMENT OF OTHER BEHAVIOR.

omnibus test a statistical test of significance in which more than two conditions are compared simultaneously or in which there are two or more INDEPENDENT VARIABLES.

omnipotence *n.* in psychology, the delusion that one can personally direct, or control, reality outside of the self by thought or wish alone. In psychoanalytic theory, the main emphasis is on the infant's feeling that he or she is all-powerful, which is thought to arise (a) out of the fact that the child's slightest gesture leads to satisfaction of the need for food; (b) out of increasing abilities; and (c) as a REACTION FORMATION to feelings of helplessness and anxiety. Psychology generally considers feelings of omnipotence to fall anywhere between neurosis, in its milder forms, and psychosis, when the delusion is expressed as alienation from or outright denial of reality. See also MEGALOMANIA. **—omnipotent** *adj.*

omnipotent therapist see PRESTIGE SUGGESTION.

onanism *n.* COITUS INTERRUPTUS or MASTURBATION. Onanism is named for the biblical character Onan, who "went to his brother's wife and spilled it [his seed] on the ground" (Genesis 38:9).

on cells (**ON cells**) neurons in the visual system, particularly the retina, that depolarize when the retina is stimulated by light onset. See ON RESPONSE. Compare OFF CELLS.

on-center bipolar cell a RETINAL BIPOLAR CELL that is excited by light in the center of its RECEPTIVE FIELD but is inhibited by light in the surround. See also ON RESPONSE. Compare OFF-CENTER BIPOLAR CELL.

on-center ganglion cell a RETINAL GANGLION CELL that is excited by light in the center of its RECEPTIVE FIELD but is inhibited by light in the surround. See also ON RESPONSE. Compare OFF-CENTER GANGLION CELL.

on-center/off-surround referring to a concentric RECEPTIVE FIELD in which stimulation of the center excites the neuron of interest, whereas stimulation of the surround inhibits it. See CENTER–SURROUND ANTAGONISM. Compare OFF-CENTER/ON-SURROUND.

oncology *n.* the study and treatment of benign and malignant tumors (see NEOPLASM). This branch of medicine and of behavioral or population sciences deals with CANCER and is subdivided into medical oncology, radiation oncology, surgical oncology, behavioral oncology, and oncology epidemiology. **—oncologist** *n.*

ondansetron *n.* a SEROTONIN ANTAGONIST at the 5-HT_3 SEROTONIN RECEPTOR that is used for the prevention and treatment of nausea resulting from chemotherapy or anesthesia. Recent studies have also demonstrated that, when combined with appropriate behavior therapy, it may be an effective adjunctive agent in managing certain types of alcoholism, although it is not officially approved by the U.S. Food and Drug Administration for such treatment. U.S. trade name: **Zofran**.

one-group pre–post design a PREEXPERIMENTAL DESIGN in which the reactions of only one group of participants are measured before and after exposure to the TREATMENT. See also BEFORE–AFTER DESIGN.

oneirism *n.* a dreamlike state in a condition of wakefulness. **—oneiric** *adj.*

oneiro- (**oneir-**) *combining form* dreams.

oneirodynia *n.* a form of dreaming characterized by NIGHTMARES or unpleasant dreams.

oneiromancy *n.* the art or practice of divining the future from DREAMS. See DIVINATION. See also CLAIRVOYANT DREAM; PREMONITORY DREAM.

oneirophrenia *n.* a dreamlike, hallucinatory state resembling schizophrenia in certain symptoms, such as disturbances of emotion and associations, but distinguished from schizophrenia by disturbances of the senses and clouding of consciousness. It is associated with prolonged sleep deprivation, sensory deprivation, or drug use, but currently is not widely considered a distinct clinical entity. [first described in the 1950s by Hungarian-born U.S. psychiatrist Ladislas von Meduna (1896–1964)]

one-juror verdict theory an approach sometimes used during the jury selection process that involves identifying among prospective jurors a potential leader sympathetic to one's case and then removing all other potential leaders through PEREMPTORY CHALLENGES, in the hope that during the deliberation process this person will be able to persuade the rest of the jury to agree with his or her views.

one-shot case study a research design in which a single group is observed only once after some event was presumed to have caused change. The degree of control in this design is so low that most research methodologists regard the design as unscientific.

one-sided message a message containing arguments that solely advocate one side of an issue. It is contrasted with a **two-sided message**, which predominantly advocates one side but also acknowledges—and sometimes refutes—the other side of an issue. One-sided messages tend to be most effective when recipients are unlikely to generate arguments on the other side of the issue. Two-sided messages are most successful when recipients are likely to generate opposing arguments.

one-tailed test a statistical test of an experimental hypothesis in which the expected direction of an effect or relationship is specified. Also called **directional test**. Compare TWO-TAILED TEST.

one-trial learning the mastery of a skill or an increment of learning on the first TRIAL.

one-way analysis of variance a statistical test of the probability that the means of three or more samples have been drawn from the same population; that is, an ANALYSIS OF VARIANCE with a single independent variable.

one-way design an experimental design in which the groups being compared vary along a single dimension. Also called **single-factor design**.

one-way mirror a mirror or screen that can be seen through from one side. One-way mirrors are used, for example, for the unobtrusive observation of participants in research studies, such as studies of the behavior of children. Also called **one-way screen**.

one-word stage the developmental period, between approximately 10 and 18 months, when children use one word at a time when speaking. Complex ideas are sometimes expressed with a single word, accompanied by gestures and emphasis. For example, depending on the context and how the word is spoken, *milk* may mean *That is milk, I want more milk*, or *I spilled the milk*. Also called **holophrastic stage**. See HOLOPHRASE.

oniomania *n.* compulsive shopping, or an uncontrollable impulse to spend money and to buy without regard to need or use.

online *adj., adv.* in computing contexts, connected to a computer resource (e.g., the WORLD WIDE WEB) through a COMPUTER NETWORK (e.g., the Internet). **Offline** means using only the resources available from a single computer.

online self-help group a self-help group composed of individuals who communicate via personal computer over the Internet on a regular basis to help one another cope with a shared life problem. Online groups overcome some of the traditional barriers to self-help participation, including lack of local group availability, rarity of problem, and time or transportation constraints. They are a relatively recent form of self-help group.

online therapy see E-THERAPY.

on–off cells neurons in the visual system, particularly the retina, that depolarize when the retina is stimulated with either light onset or light offset.

onomatopoeia *n.* the formation of a word whose sound replicates to a recognizable degree the sound of the thing or action that it represents, for example, *hiss, smack, cuckoo*. See also ICONIC SYMBOL. **—onomatopoeic** *adj.*

on response (**ON response**) the depolarization of a neuron in the visual system that occurs in response to light increment. Neurons with on responses in the center of their receptive fields are often called ON CELLS. See also CENTER–SURROUND ANTAGONISM. Compare OFF RESPONSE.

onset insomnia see SLEEP-ONSET INSOMNIA.

onset of action the point at which the activity of a drug is apparent, generally measured in terms of the time elapsed between administration and the appearance of its pharmacological effects.

on-the-job training training provided in the workplace during regular working hours for the purpose of developing or enhancing the knowledge, skills, and abilities of employees. Compare OFF-THE-JOB TRAINING. See also VESTIBULE TRAINING.

on-time life events LIFE EVENTS that occur at the typical or expected point in the life span for members of a given population. Examples are marriage in young adulthood and retirement in early old age. Compare OFF-TIME LIFE EVENTS.

ontoanalysis *n.* a form of EXISTENTIAL ANALYSIS that probes the ultimate nature of being.

ontogenetic fallacy the false assumption that anything that looks like a common pattern of change with age is a basic, normative process of aging. An example is the assumption that because disability is often seen in the elderly it is a natural, universally experienced outcome of the aging process. [proposed by 21st-century U.S. sociologist Dale Dannefer]

ontogenetic psychology the study of the psychological aspects of the biological development of the individual (see ONTOGENY) as opposed to that of the species (see PHYLOGENY). Also called **ontogenic psychology**.

ontogeny *n.* the biological origin and development of an individual organism from fertilization of the egg cell until death. Also called **ontogenesis**. Compare PHYLOGENY. See also RECAPITULATION THEORY. **—ontogenetic** *adj.*

ontogeny of conscious experience the developmental origins of conscious sensory experience in an organism. In humans, conscious experience can be demonstrated from the 5th or 6th month of gestation.

ontological confrontation the keen and immediate awareness of personal mortality that can occur when an individual's usual defenses against death awareness are pierced by circumstances or evoked memories. See also DEATH ANXIETY; TERROR MANAGEMENT THEORY.

ontology *n.* the branch of philosophy that deals with the question of existence itself. From some philosophical perspectives, ontology is synonymous with METAPHYSICS, in that both ask fundamental questions about what reality is. However, from the perspective of contemporary EXISTENTIALISM and HERMENEUTICS, ontology implies a concern with the meaning of existence that is largely lacking in traditional metaphysics. Whereas metaphysics asks "What is there?" or "What is fundamental?," the question of ontology is often posed as "What does it mean to 'be' at all?" For example, to say that Smith is a professor is to rely on a very different sense of the verb *be* than is present in a statement that Smith is hungry. Likewise, Smith is not a professor in the same way that a painting is beautiful. Contemporary approaches to ontology often take their analytical point of departure from the work of German philosopher Martin Heidegger (1889–1976). In this tradition, psychology is the pursuit of an adequate understanding of the ontology of human beings. It asks, or ought to ask, "What does it mean to be a human being?" See BEING-IN-THE-WORLD; DASEIN; EXISTENTIAL PHENOMENOLOGY. **—ontological** *adj.*

oocyte *n.* a cell in the ovary from which an ovum (egg cell) develops in the process of OOGENESIS.

oogenesis *n.* the process by which germ cells divide and differentiate to produce female gametes (ova). In human females, **primary oocytes** are formed in the ovary during embryonic development by the proliferation and differentiation of precursor cells called **oogonia** (*sing.* **oogonium**). The primary oocytes enter into the first division of MEIOSIS but then remain suspended at this stage of cell division until puberty. Thereafter, roughly once a month until the menopause, one primary oocyte resumes meiosis and completes the first meiotic division to produce two unequally sized daughter cells: The larger one is the **secondary oocyte**, while the smaller is a **polar body**. Following OVULATION, the secondary oocyte undergoes the second meiotic division to produce an ovum and another polar body. The first polar body might also divide to produce two tiny cells, resulting in three polar bodies, which are normally nonfunctional and degenerate.

oophorectomy *n.* see OVARIECTOMY.

opaque *adj.* unable to transmit light: neither transparent nor translucent.

OPD syndrome *o*to*p*alato*d*igital syndrome: a congenital disorder affecting males or females, believed to be X-linked, and marked by short stature, MILD MENTAL RETARDATION, bone anomalies, and a variety of other possible defects, including hearing impairment, cleft palate, and abnormalities of the digits.

open adoption a form of ADOPTION that allows varying degrees of pre- and postplacement contact between a child's birth family and adoptive family and makes possible a relationship between all three parties. Compare CLOSED ADOPTION.

open-book exam an examination within a particular subject area in which the instructor allows students to make use of reference books, textbooks, or lecture notes in order to answer the exam's questions. Also called **open-book test**.

open call system a system of VOCAL COMMUNICATION in which new vocalizations can be added throughout life. Whereas many songbirds rarely show change in song structure after the end of a CRITICAL PERIOD, other birds, including parrots, starlings, mynahs, and mockingbirds, can acquire new calls and songs throughout their lives. Few mammals have an open call system, but some dolphins and whales show evidence of acquiring new calls throughout life. Compare CLOSED CALL SYSTEM.

open-classroom design a design of classroom that provides a study environment based on results of BEHAVIOR-MAPPING techniques, as opposed to the traditional classroom design in which rows of desks are arranged in parallel lines. The open physical construction of the classroom, occasionally without walls, creates an environment suitable for less formal learning styles. For example, since the open-classroom design does not require that desks be arranged in parallel lines, an instructor may opt to arrange the desks in a circular formation to facilitate discussion or in groupings of four or six for small group work.

open-classroom method a system of education in which teaching is informally structured, often with an emphasis on personalized instruction or use of the OPEN-CLASSROOM DESIGN.

open class society a society that permits or encourages SOCIAL MOBILITY. Compare FIXED CLASS SOCIETY.

open-class words in a language, a category of words that readily admits new members, such as those arising through borrowing, word formation, or technological innovation. In practice, this category is virtually identical with the category of CONTENT WORDS because it usually excludes grammatical FUNCTION WORDS. Compare CLOSED-CLASS WORDS.

open design see OPEN-CLASSROOM DESIGN; OPEN-OFFICE DESIGN.

open-door hospital see OPEN HOSPITAL.

open-door policy the policy of maintaining an OPEN HOSPITAL or OPEN WARD (without locked doors or physical restraints). Such a policy is associated with the concept of a THERAPEUTIC COMMUNITY.

open economy an experimental design used in operant-conditioning experiments in which an organism's intake of food or water includes not only that provided during experimental sessions but also supplemental amounts provided independently of behavior in the home cage. This ensures that a particular level of body weight, or some other measure of deprivation, is maintained. Compare CLOSED ECONOMY.

open-ended question a question that respondents answer in their own words (e.g., an essay question). Compare CLOSED-ENDED QUESTION.

open-field chamber an enclosed space in which animals can move freely while their ambulatory and defecatory behavior is observed and measured. See also ANIMAL OPEN-FIELD BEHAVIOR.

open group a psychotherapy or counseling group to which new members may be admitted during the course of therapy. Also called **continuous group**. Compare CLOSED GROUP.

open head injury a HEAD INJURY, such as a gunshot wound, in which the skull is penetrated or broken open. See also PENETRATING HEAD INJURY. Compare CLOSED HEAD INJURY.

open hospital a psychiatric hospital without locked doors or physical restraints. Also called **open-door hospital**.

opening moves see OPENING TECHNIQUE.

opening technique the means by which a therapist establishes initial rapport and trust at the beginning of a professional relationship with a client in therapy or at the beginning of each session in individual or family therapy. Also called **opening moves**.

open-loop system **1.** a system that requires constant external inputs, as opposed to one that continually recycles the initial input. **2.** a system that will continue to follow a particular set of commands, irrespective of adverse results or altered conditions, because it has no capacity to monitor or regulate itself through FEEDBACK. An example would be a garden sprinkler system that is set to come on at specific times, even if it is raining. Compare CLOSED-LOOP SYSTEM.

open marriage **1.** a MARRIAGE in which both partners allow and encourage each other to grow and change over the years. Compare CLOSED MARRIAGE. **2.** a marital arrangement (formal or common-law) in which the partners permit each other to have sexual relations with other people. See also NONTRADITIONAL MARRIAGE.

open mind see OPENMINDEDNESS.

openmindedness *n.* a personality trait reflecting a relative lack of DOGMATISM. **—openminded** *adj.*

openness to experience a dimension of the BIG FIVE PERSONALITY MODEL and the FIVE-FACTOR PERSONALITY MODEL that refers to individual differences in the tendency to be open to new aesthetic, cultural, or intellectual experiences.

open-office design a type of office design consisting of a large area with very few separators or partitions between work spaces. A premium is placed on flexibility and visual accessibility, which are believed to support innovation and communication. Evidence indicates mixed results, with positive responses for team activities but problems with distraction and lack of privacy. There also appear to be individual differences in tolerance for open-plan spaces. See also LANDSCAPED OFFICE; OPEN-CLASSROOM DESIGN.

open shop a work arrangement in which union membership is voluntary and is not required as a condition of employment. Compare CLOSED SHOP; UNION SHOP. See also AGENCY SHOP.

open skills motor skills that are performed under varying conditions on each occasion, as in making a jump shot in a game of basketball. Compare CLOSED SKILLS.

open society a form of social organization characterized by respect for human rights, freedom to voice dissenting opinions, elective government, and the rule of law. Essential to this concept is an awareness of the imperfect nature of government and the need for constant critical evaluation of social policy so that it evolves with changing circumstances or new insights. A **closed society**, by contrast, is one characterized by inflexible social structures and a fixed ideology that cannot accept criticism or tolerate difference. See also DEMOCRACY. [described by French philosopher Henri Bergson (1859–1941) and later developed by Austrian-born British philosopher Karl Popper (1902–1994)]

open study a study in which new participants can be added after the study has begun.

open system 1. a system with permeable boundaries that permit exchange of information or materials with the environment. **2.** a biological system in which growth can occur without conforming to laws of thermodynamics or a demonstrated constancy of energy relations. Compare CLOSED SYSTEM.

open system theory a theoretical perspective that views the organization as open to influence from the environment. The organization is viewed as transforming human and physical resources from the environment into goods and services, which are then returned to the environment. The organization must import more resources than it outputs if it is to maintain itself.

open ward a hospital ward or unit in which the doors are not locked.

open word see PIVOT GRAMMAR.

operandum *n.* in OPERANT CONDITIONING, a device that an experimental animal operates or manipulates to produce automatic recording of a response. For example, in a simple conditioning experiment for a rat, a lever that the rat can press would be the operandum. See also MANIPULANDUM.

operant *n.* a class of responses that produces a common effect on the environment. An operant is defined by its effect rather than by the particular type of behavior producing that effect. A distinction may be made between the behavior required to achieve the effect and what alternative forms of behavior constitute the class and may also occur. In the former, the class might include all forms of behavior that result in a lever being moved 4 mm downward (see DESCRIPTIVE OPERANT). In the latter case, the class includes all forms of behavior that become more probable; for example, a rat's two-handed lever presses might increase in probability, but one-handed presses might not (see FUNCTIONAL OPERANT). Compare RESPONDENT.

operant aggression see AGGRESSION.

operant behavior behavior that produces an effect on the environment and whose likelihood of recurrence is influenced by consequences (see OPERANT). Operant behavior is nearly synonymous with VOLUNTARY BEHAVIOR.

operant chamber an apparatus for the laboratory study of OPERANT BEHAVIOR. It typically consists of a small enclosure and is equipped so that all stimuli are presented, and all responses are detected and recorded, automatically. See OPERANT CONDITIONING CHAMBER.

operant conditioning the process in which behavioral change (i.e., learning) occurs as a function of the consequences of behavior. Examples are teaching a dog to do tricks and rewarding behavioral change in a misbehaving child (see BEHAVIOR THERAPY). The term is essentially equivalent to INSTRUMENTAL CONDITIONING. Also called **operant learning**. See BEHAVIOR MODIFICATION; SHAPING. [first described by B. F. SKINNER]

operant conditioning chamber an apparatus used to study FREE-OPERANT behavior. Generally, it provides a relatively small and austere environment that blocks out extraneous stimuli. Included in the environment are devices that can present stimuli (e.g., reinforcers) and measure free-operant responses. For example, the apparatus for a rat might consist of a 25-cm^3 space containing a food tray, which can be filled by an automatic feeder located outside the space, and a small lever that the rat may press to release food from the feeder. Measurement of behavior and presentation of stimuli in the apparatus are usually automatic. The apparatus was initially developed in the 1930s by B. F. SKINNER. It later became known colloquially as the **Skinner box**, although Skinner himself disliked this term.

operant conditioning therapy a therapeutic approach that relies on the use of antecedents, behaviors, and consequences. For example, REINFORCEMENT through rewards may be used to improve behaviors in everyday situations.

operant learning see OPERANT CONDITIONING.

operant level a baseline probability or frequency of behavior that occurs naturally, before REINFORCEMENT is arranged, for example, the amount of lever pressing by a rat before any food reward or other reinforcer is introduced.

operant paradigm 1. the experimental arrangement of a CONTINGENCY between an operant response and a consequence, such as reinforcement. **2.** more generally, the assumption that much human behavior is controlled by its consequences.

operant response a single instance from an OPERANT class. For example, if lever pressing has been conditioned, each single lever press is an operant response.

operating space the space in WORKING MEMORY that can be allocated to the execution of intellectual operations. [defined by Canadian developmental psychologist Robbie Case (1944–2000)]

operation *n.* **1.** a type of cognitive SCHEME that is mental (that is, requires symbols), derives from action, exists in an organized system in which it is integrated with all other operations (**structures of the whole**), and follows a set of logical rules, most importantly that of REVERSIBILITY. See CONCRETE OPERATION; FORMAL OPERATIONS. [postulated by Jean PIAGET] **2.** a surgical procedure.

operational analysis analysis of the decision-making processes involved in the accomplishment of complex tasks. Generally the tasks involve the tracing of inputs through a process and the tracking of outputs. The analysis usually involves mathematical modeling and statistical techniques and aims at maximizing the effectiveness of the process.

operational definition a definition of something in terms of the operations by which it could be observed and measured. For example, the operational definition of anxiety could be in terms of a test score, behavioral withdrawal, or activation of the sympathetic nervous system. See OPERATIONISM.

operational evaluation see PROCESS EVALUATION.

operationalism *n.* see OPERATIONISM.

operational sex ratio the relative number of males and females available at the time when reproduction is possible. In mammals with internal gestation and lactation, there are often fewer females receptive to copulation than available males, creating an operational sex-ratio bias toward males, even though adults of both sexes may be present in equal numbers. In polygynous species (see POLYGYNY), there might be more receptive females than available males, creating an operational sex-ratio bias toward females.

operational thought in Jean PIAGET's theory, thought characteristic of the CONCRETE OPERATION and FORMAL OPERATIONS that occur in the last two stages of a child's cognitive development.

operationism *n.* the position that the meaning of a scientific concept depends upon the procedures used to establish it, so that each concept can be defined by a single observable and measurable operation. In concrete terms, operationism might define an emotional disorder as a particular score on a diagnostic test. This approach was mainly associated with radical BEHAVIORISM. Also called **operationalism**.

operationist view of consciousness the notion that conscious experiences may be reduced to publicly observable events, such as discriminative responses. [championed by U.S. psychophysicist Stanley S. Stevens (1906–1973) and E. G. BORING]

operations research the application of scientific methods to the study of complex organizations and to the solution of complex problems involving conflicting goals, concepts, and decisions.

operative knowledge knowledge acquired in the process of performing OPERATIONS, thought to be more basic and more predictive of later intellectual functioning than FIGURATIVE KNOWLEDGE (e.g., factual knowledge). [postulated by Jean PIAGET]

operators *pl. n.* the mental processes involved in comprehending the effect of different manipulations on quantity, as in knowing that adding an orange to a bowl of oranges changes the number, whereas rearranging the oranges does not. Compare ESTIMATORS. [first used in this sense by U.S. statistician Andrew Gelman]

ophidiophilia *n.* an abnormal fascination with snakes.

ophthalmia *n.* severe inflammation of the eye that may affect either the conjunctiva or deeper structures. **Mucous** (or **catarrhal**) **ophthalmia** is a form of conjunctivitis with a purulent secretion; **electric ophthalmia** is produced by exposure to the light of an electric welding torch; **neuroparalytic ophthalmia** is a corneal inflammation with possible ulceration associated with lesions of the trigeminal nerve. See also TRACHOMA.

ophthalmic nerve a division of the TRIGEMINAL NERVE that mediates sensation of the orbit of the eye, the anterior part of the nasal cavity, and the skin of the nose and forehead.

ophthalmology *n.* the medical specialty concerned with the study of the eye and the diagnosis and treatment of eye disease. A physician who specializes in ophthalmology is called an **ophthalmologist**. Compare OPTOMETRY.

ophthalmometer *n.* see KERATOMETER.

ophthalmoplegia *n.* paralysis of one or more of the internal or external muscles of the eye (see OCULOMOTOR PALSY). See also PROGRESSIVE SUPRANUCLEAR PALSY.

ophthalmoplegia externa see BALLET'S DISEASE.

ophthalmoscope *n.* a hand-held device used to examine the structures of the eye, especially the fundus (back). This examination may be direct, with the eye at close range so as to observe an erect image, or indirect, by use of a lens that produces an inverted image of the fundus. Compare RETINOSCOPE.

ophthalmoscopy *n.* the study of the fundus (back) of the eye with an OPHTHALMOSCOPE. Ophthalmoscopy is also used to measure refractive errors of the eye, in which case it is termed **metric ophthalmoscopy**.

-opia *suffix* defect of vision or the eyes (e.g., ANOPIA; MYOPIA).

opiates *pl. n.* natural and semisynthetic compounds derived from OPIUM. They include the alkaloids MORPHINE and CODEINE, first isolated from opium in the 19th century for medicinal use, and their derivatives (e.g., HEROIN [diacetylmorphine]). Opiates, together with synthetic compounds having the pharmacological properties of opiates, are known as OPIOIDS; the properties and uses of all these drugs are discussed in that entry.

opinion *n.* an ATTITUDE, BELIEF, or judgment.

opinionaire *n.* a questionnaire that measures opinions.

opinion giver the TASK ROLE adopted by a group member who regularly expresses his or her ideas, knowledge, attitudes, and beliefs during group discussions. Also called **information giver**. Compare OPINION SEEKER. [identified in 1948 by U.S. educational theorist Kenneth D. Benne (1908–1992) and 20th-century U.S. social psychologist Paul Sheats following studies of discussion groups conducted at the National Training Laboratories]

opinion leader an individual to whom others turn for advice before purchasing products or on whom others model their behavior. To be effective, the opinion leader needs to have social ties with other members of the group.

opinion poll a set of measures assessing attitudes toward a variety of different ATTITUDE OBJECTS. Such measures are administered in telephone interviews, questionnaires, or face-to-face interviews.

opinion seeker the TASK ROLE adopted by a group member who regularly seeks out other members' ideas, knowledge, attitudes, and beliefs during group discussions. Also called **information seeker**. Compare OPINION GIVER. [identified in 1948 by U.S. educational theorist Kenneth D. Benne (1908–1992) and 20th-century U.S. social psychologist Paul Sheats following studies of discussion groups conducted at the National Training Laboratories]

opinion testimony evidence that includes inferences or conclusions rather than actual facts observed or experienced. Opinion testimony is usually only allowed by EXPERT WITNESSES, because they have specialized knowledge that will aid the judge or jury in reaching a decision. See ULTIMATE OPINION TESTIMONY. See also LEARNED TREATISE EXCEPTION.

opioid abuse in *DSM–IV–TR*, a pattern of opioid use manifested by recurrent significant adverse consequences related to the repeated ingestion of an opioid. This diagnosis is preempted by the diagnosis of OPIOID

DEPENDENCE: If the criteria for opioid abuse and opioid dependence are both met, only the latter diagnosis is given. See also SUBSTANCE ABUSE; SUBSTANCE DEPENDENCE.

opioid agonist any drug with enhancing effects at OPIOID RECEPTORS in the central nervous system. Opioid agonists may be complete (pure) or partial agonists. MORPHINE is a pure opioid agonist; other examples include CODEINE, HEROIN, METHADONE, MEPERIDINE, and LAAM. Partial opioid agonists (e.g., BUPRENORPHINE, tramadol) have lower levels of activity than complete opioid agonists at the same receptors and consequently have less analgesic activity. Also called **narcotic agonist**.

opioid analgesic any OPIOID used clinically to reduce both the sensation of pain and the emotional response to pain. This analgesia results from agonist activity at the mu OPIOID RECEPTOR. CODEINE, **dihydrocodeine**, PROPOXYPHENE, and HYDROCODONE are among opioids used for the relief of mild to moderate pain; severe pain is managed with more potent agents, such as MORPHINE, MEPERIDINE, **oxycodone** (U.S. trade name: OxyContin), and LEVORPHANOL. METHADONE, FENTANYL, and BUPRENORPHINE are potent analgesics that have additional uses. Side effects associated with opioid analgesics include nausea and vomiting, constipation, sedation, and respiratory depression; many also have the potential for abuse and physical dependence. Also called **narcotic analgesic**. See also OPIOID ANTAGONIST.

opioid analgesic addiction psychological and physical dependence on an opioid drug, such as morphine, that is administered to relieve pain. A sign is the need to increase the dosage in order to obtain the same degree of relief. See OPIOID DEPENDENCE; OPIOID WITHDRAWAL.

opioid antagonist an agent that acts as an antagonist at OPIOID RECEPTORS. Generally, opioid antagonists are synthetic derivatives of morphine that, as a result of structural changes in the molecule, bind to opioid receptors but do not produce the effects of euphoria, respiratory depression, or analgesia that are observed with opioid agonists. Opioid antagonists may be complete (pure) or mixed. Complete antagonists, such as NALOXONE, NALTREXONE, **nalmefene** (U.S. trade name: Revex), and **nalorphine**, are generally used to reverse the effects of opiate overdose (notably respiratory depression). Mixed AGONIST–ANTAGONIST opioids, such as BUTORPHANOL and **pentazocine** (U.S. trade name: Talwin), were developed in attempts to produce opioid analgesics that did not possess the abuse potential of opioid agonists. Also called **narcotic antagonist**.

opioid blockade the inhibition of the euphoric effects of such opioids as heroin by administration of a blocking agent, especially METHADONE, as maintenance treatment for drug abuse. See METHADONE MAINTENANCE THERAPY; OPIOID ANTAGONIST.

opioid dependence in *DSM–IV–TR*, a cluster of cognitive, behavioral, and physiological symptoms indicating continued use of opioids despite significant opioid-related problems. There is a pattern of repeated opioid ingestion resulting in tolerance, characteristic withdrawal symptoms if use is suspended (see OPIOID WITHDRAWAL), and an uncontrollable drive to continue use. Also called **narcotic dependence**. See also OPIOID ABUSE.

opioid intoxication a reversible syndrome due to the recent ingestion of an opioid. It includes clinically significant behavioral or psychological changes (e.g., initial euphoria followed by apathy, DYSPHORIA, PSYCHOMOTOR AGITATION OR RETARDATION, impaired judgment, and impaired social or occupational func-tioning), as well as one or more signs of physiological involvement (e.g., pupillary constriction, drowsiness or coma, slurred speech, impairment in attention or memory).

opioid neurotransmitter see ENDOGENOUS OPIOID.

opioid receptor a RECEPTOR that binds OPIOIDS (including ENDOGENOUS OPIOIDS) and mediates their effects via G PROTEINS. It is generally agreed that there are at least three classes: delta (δ), kappa (κ), and mu (μ) receptors. Opioid receptors are widely distributed in the brain, spinal cord, and periphery and each type of receptor is differentially distributed. **Mu receptors** are largely responsible for the analgesic and euphoric effects associated with opioid use. Most exogenously administered opioids bind to mu receptors, which also mediate the respiratory depression, sedation, and reduced gastrointestinal motility associated with opioids. **Kappa receptors** are localized primarily in the DORSAL ROOT ganglia of the spinal cord. Stimulation of these receptors produces more modest analgesia and dysphoric responses, and may also be responsible for some of the perceptual and cognitive effects of opioids. **Delta receptors** may potentiate activity of opioids at the mu receptor site and have a less direct involvement in the production of analgesia. The more recently discovered **N/OFQ receptor** has not been completely characterized.

opioids *pl. n.* a group of compounds that include the naturally occurring OPIATES (e.g., morphine, codeine) and their semisynthetic derivatives (e.g., heroin); synthetic compounds with morphinelike effects (OPIOID AGONISTS, e.g., meperidine, methadone); OPIOID ANTAGONISTS (e.g., naloxone, naltrexone) and mixed agonist–antagonists (e.g., BUPRENORPHINE); and ENDOGENOUS OPIOIDS. The effects of opioids include analgesia, drowsiness, euphoria or other mood changes, RESPIRATORY DEPRESSION, and reduced gastrointestinal motility. Many natural opioids are subject to abuse and dependence (see OPIOID ABUSE; OPIOID DEPENDENCE; OPIOID INTOXICATION; OPIOID WITHDRAWAL).

Opioids are used clinically as pain relievers (see OPIOID ANALGESIC), anesthetics (e.g., FENTANYL), cough suppressants (e.g., DEXTROMETHORPHAN), and antidiarrheal drugs (e.g., LOPERAMIDE). Opioid agonists are used for (among other things) the management of opioid addiction.

opioid withdrawal a characteristic withdrawal syndrome that develops after cessation of (or reduction in) prolonged, heavy opioid consumption. Three or more of the following are required for a *DSM–IV–TR* diagnosis of opioid withdrawal: (a) dysphoric mood; (b) nausea or vomiting; (c) muscle aches; (d) lacrimation or rhinorrhea (runny nose); (e) dilation of the pupils, piloerection (goose flesh), or sweating; (f) diarrhea; (g) yawning; (h) fever; (i) insomnia. See SUBSTANCE WITHDRAWAL.

Opitz–Frias syndrome see TELECANTHUS-HYPOSPADIAS SYNDROME. [reported in 1969 by John M. **Opitz** (1935–) and Jaime L. **Frias**, U.S. geneticists]

opium *n.* the dried resin of the unripe seed pods of the opium poppy, *Papaver somniferum*. Opium contains more than 20 alkaloids (see OPIUM ALKALOIDS), the principal one being MORPHINE, which accounts for most of its pharmacological (including addictive) properties. Natural and synthetic derivatives (see OPIATES; OPIOIDS) are eaten, smoked, injected, sniffed, and drunk. Their action, due mainly to their morphine content, is to induce analgesia and euphoria and produce a deep, dreamless sleep from which the user can be easily aroused.

opium alkaloids alkaloids derived from opium, of which there are more than 20. The principal alkaloid is

MORPHINE; others include codeine, THEBAINE, and PAPAVERINE. See also OPIATES.

opponent cells neurons in the visual system that depolarize when a particular stimulus (e.g., red light) comes on in the center of the neuron's receptive field and when the "opposite" stimulus (e.g., green light) is extinguished in the surrounding zone of the receptive field. **Double-opponent cells** depolarize when the red light comes on or the green light is extinguished in the center of the receptive field, while the same stimuli produce the opposite effects in the receptive field surround.

opponent process theory of acquired motivation a theory that a stimulus or event simultaneously arouses a primary affective state, which may be pleasurable or aversive, and an opponent (opposite) affective state, which serves to reduce the intensity of the primary state: These two states together constitute emotional experience. According to this theory, the opponent state has a long latency, a sluggish course of increase, and a sluggish course of decay after the initiating stimulus is removed, all of which lead to its domination for a period following removal of the stimulus. In contrast to the primary state, it is also strengthened through use and weakened through disuse. This theory sought to account for such diverse acquired motives as drug addiction, love, affection and social attachment, and cravings for sensory and aesthetic experiences. Also called **opponent process theory of emotion; opponent process theory of motivation**. [originated by U.S. psychologist Richard Lester Solomon (1918–1995)]

opponents theory of color vision any one of a class of theories describing color vision on the basis of the activity of mechanisms, which may correspond to cells, that respond to red–green, blue–yellow, or black–white. The HERING THEORY OF COLOR VISION, the most highly developed opponents theory, contrasted with the YOUNG–HELMHOLTZ THEORY OF COLOR VISION, which relied on receptors sensitive to specific regions of the spectrum. Although both theories explained many phenomena, both had deficiencies. In the 1950s U.S. psychologists Leo Hurvich (1910–) and Dorothea Jameson (1921–1998) suggested that both theories were correct, the Young–Helmholtz model describing a first stage of processing in the visual system, while the outputs of that system were fed into an opponents process. This combined theory is known as the **dual process theory of color vision**. All three theories were proposed long before physiological studies of retinal neurons had been carried out, yet were successful in predicting the responses of cells under most conditions.

opportune family individuals considered to be family to someone, even though they may not be legally related to that person. These individuals are involved in decision making regarding the person's household, responsibilities, and significant relationships.

opportunism *n.* the ability to exploit resources not available to others. Species introduced to new habitats to control pests often have few or no predators and spread without any checks and balances. Some species are able to utilize new food resources rapidly: Kelp gulls introduced in Argentina rapidly expanded in numbers by feeding on refuse from fish factories and subsequently learned to attack and eat flesh from whales calving and nursing young in nearby waters. Other species show no opportunism and cannot exploit novel habitats or food resources.

opportunistic sampling the selection of participants or other sampling units for an experiment or survey simply because they are readily available.

opportunity class 1. an educational system that provides special-needs students with high-quality academic teaching in a stable, supportive environment with all the elements of a specialized curriculum. **2.** an instructional setting that provides guidance and counseling to promote each individual student's intellectual, social, emotional, and physical growth. **3.** a class in the PULL-OUT PROGRAM for students who do not fit the norm, such as gifted, emotionally challenged, or at-risk students.

opportunity structure a matrix that relates personal characteristics (e.g., age, disability, race, gender, education, financial status) to the cultural and social opportunities and options that are available to an individual throughout his or her life. According to some psychologists, barred or restricted access to legitimate opportunities for success, due to economic or social disadvantage, leads some individuals to seek success by illegitimate means (**illegitimate opportunity structure**), such as delinquency or other criminal activity. Also called **opportunity matrix**.

opposites test see ANTONYM TEST.

oppositional defiant disorder in *DSM–IV–TR*, a behavior disorder of childhood characterized by recurrent disobedient, negativistic, or hostile behavior toward authority figures that is more pronounced than usually seen in children of similar age and lasts for at least 6 months. It is manifest as temper tantrums, active defiance of rules, dawdling, argumentativeness, stubbornness, or being easily annoyed. The defiant behaviors typically do not involve aggression, destruction, theft, or deceit, which distinguishes this disorder from CONDUCT DISORDER. Oppositional defiant disorder should be distinguished from ATTENTION-DEFICIT/HYPERACTIVITY DISORDER, with which it often co-occurs.

opsin *n.* the protein component of visual PHOTOPIGMENTS. The other component is a vitamin A derivative known as **retinal**. There is one opsin for all rods (rod opsin, or scotopsin), which together with retinal forms the rod photopigment RHODOPSIN. There are three different cone opsins (photopsins), which convey different peak wavelength sensitivities to each of the three different cone photopigments (see IODOPSIN).

opt- *combining form* see OPTO-.

optical axis a theoretical line that passes through the center of an optical system. In the case of the eye it passes through both the cornea and the lens.

optical defect any condition of the eye that prevents light rays from focusing properly on the retina. See ERROR OF REFRACTION.

optical flow pattern the total field of apparent velocities of visual stimuli that impinge upon a physical or theoretical visual system when objects move relative to the visual system or the visual system moves relative to the objects.

optical illusion a false visual image produced by either physical or psychological factors. See ILLUSION.

optical projection 1. the formation of a visual image by means of a slide projector or similar device. **2.** the localization of objects in space that correspond to the image on the retina.

optical scanner 1. a device for examining small or isolated areas by means of reflected or projected light. It is used in various chemical and physiological studies, for example, to determine the density of red blood cells in a blood sample and to identify molecules of a sugar or amino acid. **2.** a device for converting photographs, print, and other visual material into DIGITAL representations that can be stored in a computer and treated as data (for transmission, modification, or printing out).

optic aphasia inability to name visually presented objects.

optic apraxia an impairment in the ability to associate tools and other objects with the corresponding action. Individuals with optic apraxia are disabled in everyday life because they use objects improperly, misselect the objects needed for an intended activity, perform a complex activity (e.g., preparing a cup of tea, dressing) in the wrong order, or do not complete the task at all. In most cases the temporoparietal or frontal association areas (or both) of the brain's left hemisphere are affected.

optic ataxia inability to direct limb movements (e.g., grasping objects) in the absence of paralysis, visual or visuospatial impairment, and visual neglect. Optic ataxia is typically caused by bilateral or unilateral (typically right-sided) damage to the parieto-occipital region of the brain; it is a feature of BÁLINT'S SYNDROME. Also called **visuomotor ataxia**.

optic atrophy degeneration of fibers of the optic nerve, as occurs in LOCOMOTOR ATAXIA, lead or methyl alcohol poisoning, or multiple sclerosis.

optic chiasm the location at the base of the brain at which the optic nerves from the two eyes meet. In humans, the nerve fibers from the nasal half of each retina cross, so that each hemisphere of the brain receives input from both eyes. This partial crossing is called a **partial decussation**.

optic disk the area of the retina at which the axons of the RETINAL GANGLION CELLS gather before leaving the retina to form the optic nerve. Because this region contains no photoreceptors, it creates a BLIND SPOT in the visual field.

optician *n.* see OPTOMETRY.

optic nerve the second CRANIAL NERVE, which carries the axons of RETINAL GANGLION CELLS and extends from the retina to the OPTIC CHIASM. Also called **cranial nerve II**.

optic neuritis inflammation of the optic nerve, which may lead to sudden, painful loss of vision in one eye.

optic radiations nerve fibers that project from the LATERAL GENICULATE NUCLEUS to the VISUAL CORTEX in the occipital lobe and to the pretectum, a structure in the midbrain important for the reflexive contraction of the pupils in the presence of light. As the optic radiations sweep around the lateral ventricles they are called **Meyer's loop**.

optics *n.* the study of the physics of light, including its relations to the mechanisms of vision.

optic tectum the portion of the TECTUM in the midbrain that serves the visual system. See SUPERIOR COLLICULUS.

optic tract the bundle of optic nerve fibers after the partial decussation of the optic nerves at the OPTIC CHIASM. The major targets of the optic tract are the LATERAL GENICULATE NUCLEUS in the thalamus and the SUPERIOR COLLICULUS in the midbrain.

optimal adjustment the ideal degree and quality of coping with life or with a specific stressful event.

optimal apparent motion the perception of movement that occurs when the conditions used to produce APPARENT MOVEMENT are ideal. For example, in the production of BETA MOVEMENT, the timing and spacing of individual stationary stimuli can be manipulated to produce optimal apparent motion.

optimal design a type of experimental design in which all the participants are assigned to the several CELLS of the design in order to optimize a feature of the design, for example, to obtain equally precise estimates of a parameter from each population.

optimal foraging theory a theory of FORAGING behavior arguing that NATURAL SELECTION has created optimal strategies for food selection (based on nutritional value and costs of locating, capturing, and processing food) and for deciding when to depart a particular patch to seek resources elsewhere. Many aspects of optimal foraging theory have been studied empirically using OPERANT CONDITIONING with different SCHEDULES OF REINFORCEMENT and REWARD quality. See also MARGINAL VALUE THEOREM.

optimal functioning the highest possible level of functioning, especially in the areas of meaningful relationships, work life, education, and subjective well-being.

optimal intensity a state in which the level of AROUSAL, commitment, effort, and assertiveness and the appropriateness of ATTENTIONAL FOCUS are consistent with the IDEAL PERFORMANCE STATE.

optimal interpersonal distance the physical distance between two or more people that they judge to be comfortable while interacting. Comfortable distance varies with the type of relationship, interaction, and setting as well as with differences in nationality, personality, and social class. See DISTANCE ZONE; INTERPERSONAL DISTANCE; fPROXEMICS.

optimality theory any of various concepts developed to determine the structures or behaviors that best cope with particular problems faced by organisms.

optimal level the maximum (highest) level of complexity of a skill that an individual can control, which can be attained only in the most supportive environment. It has been suggested that when acquiring a skill an individual moves from the optimal level, at which the skill can be performed with assistance from others, to the **functional level**, at which a skill can be performed independently but possibly at a lower than optimal level. See SKILL THEORY. [proposed by 21st-century U.S. psychologist Kurt W. Fischer]

optimal level theory any theory that emphasizes organisms' attempts to achieve optimal levels of some factor, such as stimulation or excitement (optimal level of arousal), tension, foraging, or movement.

optimal outbreeding see INBREEDING AVOIDANCE.

optimal stimulation principle see PRINCIPLE OF OPTIMAL STIMULATION.

optimal stopping rule a rule that specifies when one should cease data collection in a study. It is based on a model in which additional data is predicted to be of no further use: The magnitude of the effect is so large or so small that the collection of additional data could not reasonably be expected to change the conclusion that would be drawn on the basis of the data already collected.

optimism *n.* the attitude that things happen for the best and that people's wishes or aims will ultimately be fulfilled. **Optimists** are people who expect good things to happen to them and to others; they anticipate positive outcomes, whether serendipitously or through perseverance and effort. Optimism can be defined in terms of EXPECTANCY: confidence of attaining desired goals (compare PESSIMISM). Most individuals lie somewhere on the spectrum between the two polar opposites of pure optimism and pure pessimism but tend to demonstrate sometimes strong, relatively stable or situational tendencies in one direction or the other. See also EXPECTANCY-VALUE MODEL. **—optimistic** *adj.*

optimize *vb.* to create conditions that produce the best possible (**optimum**) outcome of something in the face of existing constraints. **—optimization** *n.*

opto- (**opt-**) *combining form* vision or the eyes.

optogram *n.* the physical image produced on the retina by the bleaching of RHODOPSIN by a visual stimulus (see PIGMENT BLEACHING). In the 19th century optograms were obtained by rapidly removing the retina of experimental animals after they had viewed a bright stationary stimulus and, in several instances, by examining the retinas of human prisoners immediately after execution.

optokinetic effect 1. any of a broad class of perceptual and motor responses to movement of the eyes. **2.** the movements of the eyes themselves in response to various moving stimuli. See OPTOKINETIC REFLEX.

optokinetic reflex (**OKR**) the compensatory eye movements that allow the eyes to maintain fixation on a visual target during relatively large, slow head movements. The optokinetic reflex is driven by visual signals. Compare VESTIBULO-OCULAR REFLEX.

optometry *n.* the clinical field concerned primarily with the optics of the eye and the devices and procedures that can correct optical defects. **Optometrists** can prescribe corrective lenses and exercises but are generally prohibited from prescribing drugs or performing eye surgery. Optometrists are more clinically oriented than **opticians**, who make spectacle lenses, but have fewer clinical privileges than ophthalmologists (see OPHTHALMOLOGY).

or- *combining form* see ORO-.

oracle *n.* **1.** in the ancient world, a shrine at which people sought advice or information about future events from a god, generally through the medium of a priest or priestess. The advice or prophesy given was usually enigmatic. **2.** in general usage, any person or thing considered to give infallible advice or information. **—oracular** *adj.*

oral administration see ADMINISTRATION.

oral-aggressive personality in psychoanalytic theory, a personality type resulting from fixation at the ORAL-BITING PHASE of the ORAL STAGE and marked by aggressiveness, envy, and exploitation. Compare ORAL-RECEPTIVE PERSONALITY. See ORAL PERSONALITY.

oral apraxia difficulty performing skilled movements with the face, lips, tongue, and cheeks on command. For example, individuals with oral apraxia make incorrect movements when asked to pretend to blow out a match or suck on a straw. Also called **buccofacial apraxia**.

oral behavior activities involving the mouth, such as thumb sucking, smoking, eating, kissing, nail biting, talking, and oral sex.

oral-biting phase in psychoanalytic theory, the second phase of the ORAL STAGE of PSYCHOSEXUAL DEVELOPMENT, from about the 8th to the 18th month of life. During this phase the child begins to feel that he or she is an independent person, develops ambivalent attitudes toward the mother, and expresses hostility by biting her breast or the nipple of the bottle. In later life the urge to bite may take the form of nail-biting, spitting, sticking out the tongue, or chewing on a pencil or gum. Also called **oral-sadistic phase**. Compare ORAL-SUCKING PHASE. See ORAL-AGGRESSIVE PERSONALITY; ORAL SADISM. [identified by German psychoanalyst Karl Abraham (1877–1925)]

oral character see ORAL PERSONALITY.

oral coitus see FELLATIO.

oral contraceptives tablets ("pills") taken regularly by women to prevent pregnancy. Most are combined formulations of a synthetic estrogen and a progestin; some are progestin-only formulations. The synthetic hormones in these pills alter the normal menstrual activities so that ovulation and related functions are prevented. Introduced in 1960, this type of contraceptive became known popularly as simply "the Pill."

oral eroticism in psychoanalytic theory, the pleasure derived from oral activities such as smoking, chewing, biting, talking, kissing, and oral-genital contact. Also called **oral erotism**; **oral gratification**. See also ORALITY; ORAL-SUCKING PHASE.

oral-eroticism phase see ORAL-SUCKING PHASE.

Oralet *n.* a trade name for FENTANYL.

oral–genital contact see OROGENITAL ACTIVITY.

oral gratification see ORAL EROTICISM.

oral impregnation fertilization that is rumored to occur by oral rather than genital contact. This myth is circulated in many variations, primarily as a warning that a girl can become pregnant by allowing a boy to kiss her.

oralism *n.* a method of improving the communication skills of individuals with hearing loss that focuses on the use of residual hearing, LIPREADING, and speech and deemphasizes or prohibits the use of sign language and other manual forms of communication. Also called **oral method**.

orality *n.* in psychoanalytic theory, the oral factor in EROTICISM or neurosis, ranging from pleasure in biting, sucking, smoking, or oral sex to such habits as speechmaking, overeating, alcoholism, and excessive generosity. See ORAL PERSONALITY.

oral–lingual dyskinesia see BUCCOLINGUAL MASTICATORY SYNDROME.

oral method see ORALISM.

oral-passive type see ORAL-RECEPTIVE PERSONALITY.

oral personality in psychoanalytic theory, a pattern of personality traits derived from fixation at the ORAL STAGE of PSYCHOSEXUAL DEVELOPMENT. If the individual has experienced sufficient sucking satisfaction and adequate attention from the mother during the oral-sucking phase, he or she is posited to develop an oral-receptive personality marked by friendliness, OPTIMISM, generosity, and dependence on others. If the individual does not get enough satisfaction during the sucking and biting phases, he or she is posited to develop an ORAL-AGGRESSIVE PERSONALITY marked by tendencies to be hostile, critical, envious, exploitative, and overcompetitive. Also called **oral character**.

oral phase see ORAL STAGE.

oral reading reading aloud.

oral-receptive personality in psychoanalytic theory, a personality pattern characterized by dependence, OPTIMISM, and expectation of nourishment and care from external sources (just as the mother provided these satisfactions in infancy), which is believed to be caused by fixation at the oral-sucking phase. Also called **oral-passive type**. Compare ORAL-AGGRESSIVE PERSONALITY. See also ORAL PERSONALITY; RECEPTIVE CHARACTER.

oral sadism in psychoanalytic theory, the primitive urge to use the mouth, lips, and teeth as instruments of aggression, mastery, or sadistic sexual gratification. This impulse is believed to originate in the ORAL-BITING PHASE of infancy. See also ORAL-AGGRESSIVE PERSONALITY.

oral-sadistic phase see ORAL-BITING PHASE.

oral sex stimulation of the external genitals by the partner's mouth (see OROGENITAL ACTIVITY). Oral sex may be carried to the point of orgasm or done as part of FOREPLAY. Research has shown that some adolescents who wish to remain virgins will have oral sex to orgasm, as this is not considered to constitute a loss of virginity.

oral sound a speech sound produced by airflow through the cavity of the mouth with little or no nasal quality in its production.

oral stage in psychoanalytic theory, the first stage of PSYCHOSEXUAL DEVELOPMENT, occupying the first year of life, in which the LIBIDO is concentrated on the mouth, which is the principal erotic zone. The stage is divided into the early oral-sucking phase, during which gratification is achieved by sucking the nipple during feeding, and the later ORAL-BITING PHASE, when gratification is also achieved by biting. FIXATION during the oral stage is posited to cause an oral personality. Also called **oral phase**. See also ORAL-AGGRESSIVE PERSONALITY; ORAL EROTICISM.

oral-sucking phase in psychoanalytic theory, the earliest part of the ORAL STAGE of PSYCHOSEXUAL DEVELOPMENT, in which the infant is posited to feel that he or she is ingesting the mother's being along with the milk swallowed (see INCORPORATION). This phase is believed to lay the foundation for feelings of closeness and dependence, as well as for possessiveness, greed, and voraciousness. Compare ORAL-BITING PHASE. See ORAL-RECEPTIVE PERSONALITY. [identified by German psychoanalyst Karl Abraham (1877–1925)]

oral test any test in which the questions are posed and answered orally.

Orap *n.* a trade name for PIMOZIDE.

ora serrata the most anterior portion of the retina, located adjacent to the ciliary body. The normal retinal layers are attenuated in the ora serrata. Also called **ora terminalis**.

Orbison illusion any one of a group of GEOMETRIC ILLUSIONS in which a figure or a line with straight edges, or a circle, appears distorted by a background pattern of repeated lines. [William Dillard **Orbison** (1911–1952), U.S. psychologist]

orbitofrontal cortex the CEREBRAL CORTEX of the ventral part of each FRONTAL LOBE, having strong connections to the HYPOTHALAMUS. Lesions of the orbitofrontal cortex can result in loss of inhibitions, forgetfulness, and apathy broken by bouts of euphoria, as in the well-known case of PHINEAS GAGE.

orchidectomy *n.* the surgical removal of one or both testes. An orchidectomy may be performed when a testis is injured or diseased, as when the male reproductive system has been affected by cancer. It does not necessarily cause impotence but may reduce the desire for coitus. Orchidectomy performed before puberty can affect the development of secondary male sex characteristics. Also called **orchiectomy**. See also CASTRATION.

order *n.* in BIOLOGICAL TAXONOMY, a main subdivision of a CLASS, containing a group of similar, related FAMILIES.

ordered metric scale an ordered scale of measurement in which differences between scaling units can be ranked from smallest to largest.

ordered scale a scale of measurement in which the scaling units can be ranked from smallest to largest.

order effect in REPEATED MEASURES DESIGNS, the effect of the order in which treatments are administered, that is, the effect of being the first administered treatment (rather than the second, third, and so forth). This is often confused with the SEQUENCE EFFECT.

orderliness *n.* the tendency to be neat and tidy and to keep everything in place. Excessive orderliness may be a symptom of OBSESSIVE-COMPULSIVE DISORDER or OBSESSIVE-COMPULSIVE PERSONALITY DISORDER.

order of magnitude the approximate magnitude of a number or value within a range, usually to the nearest power of 10. For example, 2,500 (2.5×10^3) and 4,300 (4.3×10^3) are of the same order of magnitude, but both are one order of magnitude greater than 240 (2.4×10^2).

order-of-merit ranking see MERIT RANKING.

order statistic a statistic based only on the position of an observation within a set of observations (e.g., the largest observation).

ordinality *n.* a basic understanding of "more than" and "less than" relationships.

ordinal position a place or rank, such as a child's position or birth order in a family, indicated by an ordinal number (e.g., first, second, etc.).

ordinal scale a measurement system developed in such a manner as to reflect the rank ordering of participants on the attribute being measured. See also INTERVAL SCALE; NOMINAL SCALE; RATIO SCALE.

ordinary creativity the ability to think divergently or to come up with unique and original ideas (e.g., generating as many uses as possible for a familiar object). Compare EXCEPTIONAL CREATIVITY.

ordinate *n.* the vertical coordinate in a graph or data plot; that is, the *y*-axis. See also ABSCISSA.

Orestes complex in classical Freudian psychoanalysis, a son's repressed impulse to kill his mother, which may result in the actual act of matricide. The name is derived from the ancient Greek story of Orestes, who killed his mother, Clytemnestra, and her lover, Agamemnon.

orexin *n.* any of a group of proteins, expressed in the LATERAL HYPOTHALAMUS, that trigger feeding and have also been implicated in NARCOLEPSY.

orexis *n.* the affective, appetitive character of an activity or behavior, as opposed to the cognitive aspects. Also called **orexia**. **—orectic** *adj.*

organelle *n.* a specialized, membrane-bound structure within a cell, such as a MITOCHONDRION or the GOLGI APPARATUS.

organ eroticism sexual arousal or sexual attachment associated with a particular organ of the body.

organic *adj.* **1.** denoting a condition or disorder that is basically somatic or physical, as contrasted with FUNCTIONAL or PSYCHOGENIC. **2.** relating to the fundamental, or essential, make-up of a thing, situation, or phenomenon and to the interworking of its components.

organic-affective syndrome in *DSM–III–R*, any disturbance of mood with symptoms that meet the criteria for a mood disorder but that result from a specific identifiable organic disorder. This diagnostic category has been removed from *DSM–IV–TR*. Also called **organic mood syndrome**.

organic amnesia see AMNESTIC DISORDER.

organic approach the theory that all disorders, mental and physical, have a physiological basis. Adherents of this view hold that all psychotic disorders (including schizophrenia and bipolar disorders), and possibly also the more severe nonpsychotic disorders, result from structural brain changes or biochemical disturbances of the nervous or glandular systems. Also called **organicism**.

organic brain syndromes in *DSM–III*, a group of disorders, including delirium, dementia, AMNESTIC DISORDER, ORGANIC DELUSIONAL SYNDROME, and ORGANIC PERSONALITY SYNDROME, each characterized by a pattern of psychological and behavioral symptoms (e.g., memory loss, impaired intellectual functioning, disorientation, poor judgment) associated with transient or permanent brain dysfunction, but without reference to cause. This diagnostic category has been removed from *DSM–IV–TR*. Also called **organic mental syndromes**. See also ORGANIC MENTAL DISORDERS.

organic defect a congenital disorder that is not the result of a genetic anomaly. For example, a mental or physical disability in an individual can result from maternal disorders or other conditions in pregnancy, including preeclampsia, viral infections (e.g., rubella), sexually transmitted infections, protozoan infections (e.g., toxoplasmosis), dietary deficiencies, or drug abuse (e.g., alcoholism).

organic delusional syndrome in *DSM–III*, a condition characterized by the occurrence of prominent delusions, usually persecutory in nature, that are produced most often by such substances as amphetamines, cannabis (marijuana), and hallucinogens but may also be associated with brain damage or dysfunction. This diagnostic category has been removed from *DSM–IV–TR*.

organic dementia in *DSM–III*, DEMENTIA due to any condition that causes injury to the brain.

organic disorder any illness resulting from a demonstrable abnormality in the structure or biochemistry of body tissues or organs. Also called **organic disease**. Compare PSYCHOGENIC DISORDER.

organic hallucinations hallucinations associated with a specific brain-based factor. Stimulation or irritation of part of the brain or a sensory pathway may be a factor, and precipitating causes include aneurysm, tumor, epilepsy, drug use (including some prescribed drugs), and abuse of alcohol, cocaine, amphetamines, or similar substances.

organic hallucinosis in *DSM–III*, a condition characterized by persistent or recurrent hallucinations produced by hallucinogens (which usually cause visual hallucinations), alcohol (which usually causes auditory hallucinations), brain damage or dysfunction, or, in some cases, sensory deprivation (blindness, deafness). This diagnostic category has been removed from *DSM–IV–TR*.

organicism *n.* see ORGANIC APPROACH.

organicity *n.* a former term for brain damage or dysfunction.

organicity test an obsolete name for a cognitive or behavioral test that has been shown to be differentially sensitive to the effects of brain damage or dysfunction. See NEUROPSYCHOLOGICAL TEST.

organic mental disorders in *DSM–III*, a heterogeneous group of mental disturbances resulting from transient or permanent brain dysfunction due to specific organic factors. Specification of cause is what distinguished these disturbances from ORGANIC BRAIN SYNDROMES. This diagnostic category has been removed from *DSM–IV–TR*.

organic mental syndromes see ORGANIC BRAIN SYNDROMES.

organic mood syndrome see ORGANIC-AFFECTIVE SYNDROME.

organic paralysis loss of function of voluntary muscles due to structural lesions of the nervous or muscular system. See PARALYSIS. Compare CONVERSION PARALYSIS.

organic personality syndrome in *DSM–III*, a disorder characterized by a marked change in personality or behavior due to a factor that damages the brain, for example, a tumor, head injury, or vascular disease. The personality change involves at least one of the following: emotional lability (temper outbursts, unprovoked crying), impulse dyscontrol (shoplifting, sexual indiscretions), marked apathy and lack of interest, and suspiciousness or paranoid ideation. This diagnostic category has been removed from *DSM–IV–TR*.

organic repression a retroactive form of amnesia in which the patient may be unable to recall events prior to the injury although examiners are unable to find a personal motive for the amnesia, such as the kind of repression observed in dissociative amnesia.

organic retardation failure of an organ or organ system to develop normally because of a genetic defect, dietary deficiency, or hormonal disorder. A failure of one or more parts of the skeletal system to grow normally could be caused by pituitary, hereditary, or dietary factors, or a combination of these.

organic selection see BALDWIN EFFECT.

organic sensation a sensation that arises from deep within the body (e.g., a rumbling stomach). Also called **visceral sensation**.

organic speech impairment see SPEECH IMPAIRMENT.

organic therapies somatic treatments for serious or recalcitrant mental disorder and disease, among which are ELECTROCONVULSIVE THERAPY, PSYCHOPHARMACOLOGY, and PSYCHOSURGERY.

organic variable a process or state within an organism that combines with a stimulus to produce a particular response. For example, a headache may be an organic variable, and the response may be an irritable reaction to a stimulus (e.g., noise in the neighborhood). Also called **O variable**.

organ inferiority the sense of being deficient or somehow less than others as a result of negative feelings about a physical trait. Any type of structural defect or developmental deformity, real or fancied, may produce such feelings of inferiority and efforts at compensation. [defined by Alfred ADLER]

organism *n.* an individual living entity, such as an animal, plant, or bacterium, that is capable of reproduction, growth, and maintenance.

organismic *adj.* having components (**organs**) serving various functions that interact to produce the integrated, coordinated total functioning that characterizes an organism.

organismic model the theory that development is directed by constraints inherent in the relationship among elements within the organism as they act upon themselves and each other. Not only are biological processes (e.g., maturation) seen as critical in directing development, but so also are the behaviors of the organism. See DEVELOPMENTAL SYSTEMS APPROACH.

organismic personality theory an approach to personality theory in which personal functioning is understood in terms of the action of the whole, coherent, integrated organism, rather than in terms of psychological variables representing one versus another isolated aspect of body or mind. [developed by German-born U.S. physician and psychiatrist Kurt Goldstein (1878–1965) and Hungarian psychologist Andras Angyal (1902–1960)]

organismic psychology an approach to psychology that emphasizes the total organism, rejecting distinctions between mind and body. It embraces a MOLAR APPROACH that takes account of the interaction between the organism and its environment. See HOLISM; HOLISTIC PSYCHOLOGY.

organismic valuing process in client-centered theory, the presumed healthy and innate internal guidance system that a person can use to "stay on the track" toward self-actualization. One goal of treatment within the client-centered framework is to help the client listen to this inner guide. See CLIENT-CENTERED THERAPY.

organismic variable one of the four factors considered in behavioral assessment using the SORC system, referring to the physiological and psychological features of the organism that influence behavior.

organization *n.* **1.** a structured entity consisting of various components that interact to perform one or more functions. Business, industrial, and service entities are constituted in this way. **2.** in GESTALT PSYCHOLOGY, an integrated perception composed of various components that appear together as a single whole, for example, a face. See GESTALT PRINCIPLES OF ORGANIZATION. **3.** in memory research, the structure discovered in or imposed upon a set of items in order to guide memory performance. **4.** in Jean PIAGET's theory, the coordinated biological activities of the organism as determined by genetic factors, interactions with the environment, and level of maturation. Inherent in this theory is the concept that every intellectual operation is related to all other acts of intelligence. Mental processes also become increasingly organized, developing through such stages as reflex behavior and responses to immediate stimulation and gradually becoming self-sustaining, self-generating, and capable of reflecting the child's own thoughts. See FUNCTIONAL INVARIANT. **—organizational** *adj.*

organizational approach in the study of emotion, a conceptual framework, based on GENERAL SYSTEMS THEORY, emphasizing the role of emotions as regulators and determinants of both intrapersonal and interpersonal behaviors, as well as stressing the adaptive role of emotions. The organizational approach also emphasizes how perception, motivation, cognition, and action come together to produce important emotional changes.

organizational assessment activities involved in evaluating the structure, process, climate, and environmental factors that influence the effectiveness of an organization and the morale and productivity of employees. General or specific evaluations (e.g., readiness to change, job satisfaction, turnover) may be performed by practitioners from a variety of disciplines, including CONSULTING PSYCHOLOGY and INDUSTRIAL AND ORGANIZATIONAL PSYCHOLOGY.

organizational behavior modification the application of the principles of learning theory to effect changes within an organization.

organizational career see PROTEAN CAREER.

organizational citizenship behavior (**OCB**) an action taken by an employee to benefit the organization that is not formally required by the job or that exceeds the formal requirements (e.g., voluntarily helping a coworker with a computer problem).

organizational climate the general character of the total organizational environment as perceived by those who work within it. It is an expression of the ORGANIZATIONAL CULTURE.

organizational commitment an employee's dedication to an organization and wish to remain part of it. Organizational commitment is often described as having both an emotional or moral element (AFFECTIVE COMMITMENT) and a more prudential element (CONTINUANCE COMMITMENT).

organizational culture a distinctive pattern of thought and behavior shared by members of the same organization and reflected in their language, values, attitudes, beliefs, and customs. The culture of an organization is in many ways analogous to the personality of an individual. See also ATTRACTION–SELECTION–ATTRITION MODEL; OCCUPATIONAL CULTURE.

organizational culture analysis a comprehensive organizational development intervention in which groups of managers and employees meet to describe the organizational culture and identify those aspects of the culture that are helpful to achieving the goals of the organization and those that are hindrances. [developed by U.S. organizational psychologist Edgar H. Schein (1928–)]

organizational development (**OD**) the application of principles and practices drawn from psychology, sociology, and related fields to the planned improvement of ORGANIZATIONAL EFFECTIVENESS. More specifically, OD emerged from the concerns with GROUP DYNAMICS and SELF-ACTUALIZATION that came to the fore in the 1950s and 1960s. Although many different types of interventions are included under the OD umbrella, the role of the OD consultant is typically described as helping organizational participants to (a) identify and diagnose their own problems and (b) generate solutions to these problems. The OD consultant facilitates the creation of an environment in which participants engage in self-renewal and continuous improvement.

organizational dynamics those forces and processes that stimulate growth, development, and change within an organization. See GROUP DYNAMICS; SOCIAL DYNAMICS.

organizational effect a long-term effect of hormonal action typically occurring in fetal development or the early postnatal period that leads to permanent changes in behavior and neural functioning. The presence of testosterone in young male rats leads to long-term male-typical behavior, and female rats can be masculinized by neonatal exposure to testosterone. Compare ACTIVATIONAL EFFECT.

organizational effectiveness a multidimensional construct defining the degree of success achieved by an organization. According to a GOAL-ATTAINMENT MODEL, effectiveness is the extent to which the organization is able to achieve its goals in an efficient manner. According to a SYSTEMS MODEL OF EVALUATION, effectiveness is the organization's ability to achieve long-term survival, which involves acquiring resources, adapting to changes in the environment, and maintaining the internal health of the system. From an ecological perspective, effectiveness is the ability of the organization to minimally satisfy the expectations of its strategic constituencies. All of these factors and more could be included in an assessment of an organization's effectiveness.

organizational efficiency see EFFICIENCY.

organizational hierarchy the chain of command in an organization, defining levels of authority and responsibility. Individuals occupying higher positions in the hierarchy have greater power than those lower in the hierarchy.

organizational humanism an approach to improving ORGANIZATIONAL EFFECTIVENESS based on the assumption that effectiveness is enhanced if organizational participants can achieve their full potential through SELF-ACTUALIZATION. See HUMANISTIC PSYCHOLOGY.

organizational hypothesis the hypothesis that steroids produced by the newly formed testis during development masculinize the developing brain to alter behavior permanently.

organizational identification a form of GROUP IDENTIFICATION in which an individual (e.g., an employee) defines himself or herself in terms of involvement or membership in a particular organization or group.

organizational justice employee perceptions of how fair an organization is. It consists of perceptions of the fairness of outcomes that employees receive (**distributive justice**) and the fairness of the procedures used in distributing these outcomes (**procedural justice**). See also EQUITY THEORY.

organizational politics behavior by individuals in an organization that is intended to further their own interests, or the interests of a particular unit or department, over the interests of other individuals or units.

organizational psychology see INDUSTRIAL AND ORGANIZATIONAL PSYCHOLOGY.

organizational structure the arrangement and interrelationship of the various parts or elements of an organization. Organizational structures can be described on several dimensions, including simple versus complex, centralized versus decentralized, and hierarchical versus nonhierarchical. A distinction can also be made between the FORMAL ORGANIZATIONAL STRUCTURE and the informal structures of an organization.

organized offender the type of offender who carefully plans his or her crimes and who is typically more intelligent and less socially isolated than DISORGANIZED OFFENDERS. This dichotomy is useful when profiling violent offenders (see CRIMINAL PROFILING).

organized play play that is structured, governed by rules, and controlled or directed by another individual, such as a teacher, group leader, or therapist. Compare FREE PLAY.

organ language in the context of classical psychoanalytic explanations of PSYCHOSOMATIC illness, the bodily expression of emotional conflict or disturbance. Some believe that knowledge of the significance to the patient of the organ affected by the illness is essential for accurate diagnosis and treatment. For example, chronic lumbago (lower backache) with no identifiable organic cause may mean that the patient is feeling put upon, is being a martyr, or is aiming too low in life. Also called **organ speech**.

organ of Corti a specialized structure that sits on the BASILAR MEMBRANE within the cochlea in the inner ear. It contains the HAIR CELLS (the sensory receptors for hearing), their nerve endings, and supporting cells. See also DEITERS CELLS; TECTORIAL MEMBRANE. [Alfonso **Corti** (1822–1876), Italian anatomist]

organogenesis *n.* **1.** the formation of organs during development. **2.** see SOMATOGENESIS. **—organogenic** or **organogenetic** *adj.*

organ speech see ORGAN LANGUAGE.

organum vasculosum of the lamina terminalis (OVLT) one of the CIRCUMVENTRICULAR ORGANS where the BLOOD–BRAIN BARRIER is weak, enabling neurons there to monitor substances in the blood.

orgasm *n.* the climax of sexual stimulation or activity, when the peak of pleasure is achieved, marked by the emission of semen (EJACULATION) in the male and vaginal contractions in the female. The peak period of sexual excitement lasts less than 1 min in most males and females. In addition to involuntary muscle contractions, it is characterized by increased blood pressure and heart rate and a mild clouding of consciousness. Also called **climax**. See also MULTIPLE ORGASM; SEXUAL-RESPONSE CYCLE; VAGINAL ORGASM; VULVAL ORGASM. **—orgasmic** or **orgastic** *adj.*

orgasmic dysfunction see FEMALE ORGASMIC DISORDER; MALE ORGASMIC DISORDER.

orgasmic phase see SEXUAL-RESPONSE CYCLE.

orgasmic platform the vascular tissue at the outer portion of the vagina and the labia minora that becomes engorged during sexual arousal or coitus.

orgastic impotence inability of a male to achieve orgasm in spite of normal erection and ejaculation. See MALE ORGASMIC DISORDER.

orgastic potency the ability of a man or woman to achieve full orgasm during the sex act. See POTENCY.

orgiastic *adj.* relating to a situation characterized by indulgence, revelry, frenzy, and indiscriminate sexual behavior.

orgone *n.* the "life energy" and creative force in nature that was believed by Austrian psychoanalyst Wilhelm Reich (1897–1957) to pervade the universe. According to Reich, orgone was emitted by energy vesicles called BIONS, which he claimed to find in organic material. He also posited that it related to cosmic radiation and speculated that it might be responsible for the origin of life from earth and water (biogenesis), as well as the formation of weather patterns and the sexual potency of human beings. See also ORGONE THERAPY.

orgone accumulator in the ORGONE THERAPY of Austrian psychoanalyst Wilhelm Reich (1897–1957), an enclosure in which the patient sat for the purpose of capturing vital ORGONE energy, which Reich supposed to have the effect of improving the flow of life energy and releasing energy blocks. Also called **orgone box**.

orgone therapy the therapeutic approach of Austrian psychoanalyst Wilhelm Reich (1897–1957), based on the concept that the achievement of "full orgastic potency" is the key to psychological well-being. Reich believed the orgasm to be the emotional-energy regulator of the body, the purpose of which is to dissipate sexual tensions that would otherwise be transformed into neuroses. He further held that the orgasm derives its power from a hypothetical cosmic force, ORGONE energy, which accounts not only for sexual capacity but also for all functions of life and for the prevention of disease. Also called **vegetotherapy**.

orgy *n.* a type of social gathering at which a number of people engage in unrestrained sexual activity, often with other forms of revelry, including singing, dancing, and drinking.

oriental nightmare-death syndrome see BANGUNGUT.

orientation *n.* **1.** awareness of the self and of outer reality, that is, the ability to identify one's self and to know the time, the place, and the person one is talking to. See also REALITY ORIENTATION. **2.** the act of directing the body or of moving toward an external stimulus, such as light, gravity, or some other aspect of the environment. **3.** in vision, the degree of tilt of the long axis of a visual stimulus. For example, a vertical bar is oriented at 0°; a horizontal bar is oriented at 90°. Many neurons in the visual system respond most vigorously to a stimulus of a certain orientation: They are said to be **orientation selective**. See also ORIENTATION COLUMN. **4.** relative position or alignment, for example, of a body part or an atom in a chemical compound. **5.** the process of familiarizing oneself with a new setting (e.g., a new home, neighborhood, or city) so that movement and use do not depend upon memory cues, such as maps, and eventually become habitual. **6.** an individual's general approach, ideology, or viewpoint. **7.** the process of introducing a newcomer to a job, company, educational institution, or other environment. **—orient** *vb.*

orientation and mobility training (**O&M training**) guided instruction in the cognitive and motor skills necessary for people with visual impairment to orient themselves in space and to move safely in the environment (sidewalk, street corner, crosswalk, stairwell, kitchen, bathroom, classroom, office building, and so on). O&M training includes instruction in the use of the long cane or the handling of a service animal (e.g., guide dog), as well as in the use of available senses, including any residual vision, to enable the individual to navigate safely. O&M training is a key component of VISION REHABILITATION and is usually provided by professional O&M specialists (formerly called **peripatologists**).

orientation column a vertical slab of STRIATE CORTEX in which all the neurons are maximally responsive to stimuli of the same ORIENTATION. Adjacent columns have slightly different orientation preferences, so that electrode penetration tangential to the cortical surface that passes through many columns would encounter neurons with orientation preferences that shift smoothly around a reference axis. Compare OCULAR DOMINANCE COLUMN.

orientation illusion see ILLUSION OF ORIENTATION.

orienting response 1. a behavioral response to an altered, novel, or sudden stimulus, for example, turning one's head toward an unexpected noise. Various physiological components of the orienting response have subsequently been identified as well, including dilation of pupils and blood vessels and changes in heart rate and electrical resistance of the skin. [described in 1927 by Ivan PAVLOV] **2.** any response of an organism in relation to the direction of a specific stimulus. See TAXIS; TROPISM. Also called **orienting reflex**.

original cause the first or primary cause of a phenomenon; that is, the first in a sequence of causes producing a particular effect. See CAUSAL CHAIN; REMOTE CAUSE.

originality *n.* see CREATIVITY.

original sin in the Judeo-Christian tradition, a state of sin held to be innate in all humankind as a result of the first sin committed by Adam and Eve, which led to their being expelled from the Garden of Eden. Although modern theologians tend to interpret this story symbolically rather than historically, the idea that there is a fundamental flaw in human nature remains important in Christian thought. The doctrine of original sin has sometimes been reinterpreted in psychological, existential, or socioeconomic terms.

origin-of-language theories see LANGUAGE-ORIGIN THEORY.

Orne effect the tendency for typical participants to try to discern the wishes or intent of an experimenter and to try to respond in accordance with these wishes or intent. See DEMAND CHARACTERISTICS. [Martin T. **Orne** (1927–2000), Austrian-born U.S. psychiatrist]

ornithinemia *n.* excessive ornithine in the blood, possibly due to an inborn error of amino acid metabolism or to liver disease. The condition sometimes occurs in siblings, who manifest mental retardation and severe speech disturbance.

oro- (**or-**) *combining form* mouth.

orofacial dyskinesia behavior characterized by abnormal chewing, mouthing, and tongue movements that resemble symptoms of TARDIVE DYSKINESIA.

orogenital activity the application of the mouth to the genitalia. The activity may be performed by couples of opposite sexes or the same sex, either as a precoital form of stimulation or carried to orgasm. Application of the mouth to the male genitalia is called FELLATIO; application of the mouth to the female genitalia is known as CUNNILINGUS. Also called **buccal intercourse**; **oral–genital contact**. See also ORAL SEX.

oropharynx *n.* the portion of the PHARYNX at the back of the mouth, extending from the level of the hyoid bone (at the base of the tongue) to the SOFT PALATE. It contains the functional crossing of the alimentary and respiratory canals. **—oropharyngeal** *adj.*

orphenadrine *n.* an ANTICHOLINERGIC DRUG used in the treatment of drug-induced parkinsonian symptoms, such as those produced by conventional antipsychotics. It is also used for the relief of localized muscle spasms (see MUSCLE RELAXANTS). Orphenadrine is also sold in combination with ANALGESICS (e.g., with aspirin and caffeine as **Norgesic** in the United States). U.S. trade name: **Norflex**.

Ortgeist *n.* the spirit of a place (German, "place spirit"). The term is mainly used to mean the influence of the physical or cultural environment on the development of social, economic, and artistic life in a particular place. Compare ZEITGEIST.

orthergasia *n.* see EUERGASIA.

ortho- (**orth-**) *combining form* **1.** straight or perpendicular (e.g., ORTHOGENESIS). **2.** correct or normal (e.g., ORTHOPSYCHIATRY).

orthodox psychoanalysis see CLASSICAL PSYCHOANALYSIS.

orthodox sleep a less common name for NREM SLEEP.

orthogenesis *n.* **1.** the theory that the evolution of a species follows a direction determined by factors inherent to the organisms and that successive generations follow the same plan irrespective of NATURAL SELECTION. **2.** the theory that all cultures pass through the same sequential stages. **—orthogenetic** *adj.*

orthogenetic principle the hypothesis that development of all aspects of functioning (including cognition, perception, etc.) progresses from lack of differentiation to increasing differentiation, articulation, and hierarchic integration. [proposed in 1957 by Austrian-born U.S. psychologist Heinz Werner (1890–1964)]

orthogonal *adj.* **1.** independent or unrelated. **2.** at right angles. Compare OBLIQUE.

orthogonal contrasts a set of comparisons (contrasts) among the CELL means of a factor that, as a set, are nonoverlapping and uncorrelated and completely partition the SUM OF SQUARES of that factor.

orthogonal design a FACTORIAL DESIGN in which all CELLS contain the same number of subjects or observations or in which there is a certain constant of proportionality in cell sizes. Compare NONORTHOGONAL DESIGN.

orthogonal polynomial contrasts a set of orthogonal contrast coefficients that code the linear, quadratic, and higher order trends in the data.

orthogonal rotation a class of transformations of multidimensional spaces in which the axis system remains at right angles. Also called **rigid rotation**.

orthography *n.* **1.** the formal writing system of a language. **2.** the study of the conventions of spelling in such a system. **—orthographic** *adj.*

orthokinesis *n.* an increase (positive orthokinesis) or decrease (negative orthokinesis) in the speed or frequency of movement, particularly in relation to increases or decreases in stimulation.**—orthokinetic** *adj.*

orthonasal olfaction sensations of smell arising via the introduction of an ODORANT through the nares (nostrils). This is the common route for olfactory sensation. Compare RETRONASAL OLFACTION.

orthonasia *n.* a program in which children are taught about death as a part of life, to enable them to incorporate healthy attitudes toward death in their coping repertoire. [introduced by Austrian-born U.S. psychologist Kurt R. Eissler (1908–1999)]

orthopsychiatry *n.* an interdisciplinary approach to mental health in which psychiatrists, psychologists, social workers, pediatricians, sociologists, nurses, and educators collaborate on the study and treatment of emotional and behavioral problems before they become severe and disabling. The approach is basically preventive, and the major emphasis is on child development, family life, and maintenance of mental health. **—orthopsychiatric** *adj.* **—orthopsychiatrist** *n.*

orthoptics *n.* **1.** the study and treatment of faulty binocular vision. **2.** the use of eye exercises to coordinate the vision in the left and right eyes of individuals with extrinsic EYE MUSCLE imbalance. **—orthoptic** *adj.* **—orthoptist** *n.*

orthoptoscope *n.* see AMBLYOSCOPE.

Ortho-Rater *n.* a portable visual testing device used for the rapid assessment of VISUAL ACUITY, COLOR VISION, and DEPTH PERCEPTION. A common use in the United States is for visual screening during application for a driver's license.

orthostatic hypotension a drop in blood pressure when moving from a lying or sitting position to a standing position. Blood pressure is normally maintained in the face of changes in position by activation of BARORECEPTORS in the walls of the heart and the major arteries. Activation of these receptors in turn activates ALPHA ADRENORECEPTORS in peripheral blood vessels, leading to arterial constriction and maintenance of blood pressure. Numerous psychotropic drugs (e.g., antidepressants, antipsychotics) block the activity of peripheral alpha adrenoreceptors, leading to orthostatic hypotension and an increased risk of falls, particularly in older adults. Orthostatic hypotension can also be caused by such disorders as diabetes mellitus, amyloidosis, and Parkinson's disease. Also called **postural hypotension**.

orthotist *n.* a health professional who specializes in designing, constructing, and fitting braces and other orthopedic (supportive or corrective) appliances. Compare PROSTHETIST.

oscillator circuit a circuit that produces a repeating pattern of output. Unlike an ENDOGENOUS OSCILLATOR, it is not necessarily biological. For example, oscillator circuits can be found in computers, and the term itself is often associated with artificial NEURAL NETWORKS.

oscillograph *n.* an instrument, often used in studies of body functions, that makes graphic recordings of wave forms of electrical energy.

oscillometer *n.* an instrument for measuring oscillations (variations or fluctuations), especially those associated with bodily functions, such as variations in arterial pulsation.

oscillopsia *n.* the sensation of perceiving oscillating movement of the environment. This illusory movement can be caused by (bilateral) vestibular cerebellar injury, paralysis of extrinsic eye muscles, or nystagmus, but may also be due to cerebral disorders (e.g., seizures, occipital lobe infarction).

oscilloscope *n.* an electronic device that records and displays visually an electrical or sound wave on a fluorescent screen of a cathode ray tube.

Osgood, Charles Egerton (1916–1991) U.S. psychologist. Osgood received his PhD in psychology at Yale University in 1946. He joined the faculty at the University of Illinois in 1950, remaining there throughout his career. His most important general contribution is the text *Method and Theory in Experimental Psychology* (1953). Osgood's research has been particularly relevant to the fields of PSYCHOLINGUISTICS and CROSS-CULTURAL PSYCHOLOGY. Influenced by Clark HULL'S NEOBEHAVIORISM, Osgood developed a theory that explicitly named mental representations as INTERVENING VARIABLES between stimulus and response in the behaviorist's model. Along with colleagues, he developed the SEMANTIC DIFFERENTIAL method of determining the meaning of words. Although this method was criticized by other linguists, such as Noam CHOMSKY and Roger BROWN, it was nonetheless very influential, inspiring a great deal of research. Osgood's views are summarized in *The Measurement of Meaning* (1957), coauthored with George J. Suci and Percy H. Tannenbaum. His later research focused on cross-cultural studies of meaning as well as language pathology. Among other honors, Osgood received the American Psychological Association's Distinguished Contributions Award and was elected to fellowships of the American Academy of Arts and Sciences and the National Academy of Sciences.

OSHA abbreviation for OCCUPATIONAL SAFETY AND HEALTH ADMINISTRATION.

-osis *suffix* **1.** diseased condition (e.g., NEUROSIS). **2.** process or state (e.g., METAMORPHOSIS). **3.** formation or development (e.g., GLIOSIS).

osmolagnia *n.* sexual interest in and pleasure derived from smells emanating from the body, especially from the genitals.

osmolarity *n.* the concentration of an osmotic solution, measured in osmoles per liter of solution.

osmometer *n.* **1.** an instrument for measuring OSMOTIC PRESSURE or the amount of osmotic action (passage across a membrane of solutes from higher to lower concentrations) in different liquids. **2.** an early type of OLFACTOMETER involving a sealed chamber containing an ODORANT. The participant opened the chamber, inhaled, and reported the odor detected.

osmometric thirst thirst resulting from a loss of cellular fluids and a relative increase in OSMOTIC PRESSURE. Also called **intracellular thirst**; **osmotic thirst**. See also OSMOREGULATION. Compare HYPOVOLEMIC THIRST.

osmoreceptor *n.* a hypothetical receptor in the HYPOTHALAMUS that responds to changes in the concentrations of various substances in the body's extracellular fluid and to cellular dehydration. It also regulates the secretion of VASOPRESSIN and contributes to thirst. See OSMOMETRIC THIRST; OSMOREGULATION.

osmoregulation *n.* a complex mechanism for maintaining the optimum content of water and electrolytes in the body cells and extracellular fluid of an organism. Also called **water regulation**. See OSMOMETRIC THIRST; OSMORECEPTOR.

osmosis *n.* the passive movement of solvent molecules through a differentially permeable membrane separating two solutions of different concentrations. The solvent tends to flow from the weaker solution to the stronger solution. **—osmotic** *adj.*

osmotic pressure the pressure required to prevent the passage of water (or other solvent) through a semipermeable membrane from an area of low concentration of solute to an area of higher concentration. It results from the spontaneous movement of molecules occurring when different concentrations are separated by a semipermeable membrane.

osphresiolagnia *n.* sexual arousal or erotic experience produced by odors.

osphresiophilia *n.* an abnormal attraction to odors.

ossicles *pl. n.* any small bones, but particularly the auditory ossicles: the chain of three tiny bones in the middle ear that transmit sound vibrations from the tympanic membrane (eardrum) to the OVAL WINDOW of the inner ear. They are the **malleus** (or hammer), which is attached to the tympanic membrane; the **incus** (or anvil); and the **stapes** (or stirrup), whose footplate nearly fills the oval window. The ossicles allow efficient transmission of sound from air to the fluid-filled cochlea.

osteoarthritis *n.* see ARTHRITIS.

osteomalacia *n.* see CALCIUM-DEFICIENCY DISORDERS.

osteopathy *n.* a health care system based on the belief that many disorders are caused by structural defects in the musculoskeletal system. It focuses on primary care, prevention, a holistic approach to patient health, and—especially—manipulation of the affected joints and muscles (particularly of the spine) in conjunction with traditional medical, surgical, and pharmacological treatment to address underlying disease processes. Also called **osteopathic medicine**. See also COMPLEMENTARY AND ALTERNATIVE MEDICINE. **—osteopath** *n.* **—osteopathic** *adj.*

osteopetrosis *n.* a rare genetic disorder characterized by increased bone density, which may lead to abnormalities in bone shape or size, due to abnormal resorption (breakdown, removal, and replacement) of bone. Although the bones are highly dense, they are brittle and liable to fracture.

osteoporosis *n.* see CALCIUM-DEFICIENCY DISORDERS.

-ostomy *suffix* see -STOMY.

Ostwald color system a method of organizing chromatic and achromatic samples. The system consists of 24 hues arranged around the outside of a circle, with the complementary colors for each hue located along the circle's diameters. By combining adjacent colors, any color on the **Ostwald scale** can be produced. [Wilhelm **Ostwald** (1853–1932), German chemist and physicist]

OT abbreviation for OCCUPATIONAL THERAPY.

ot- *combining form* see OTO-.

OTC drugs abbreviation for OVER-THE-COUNTER DRUGS.

Othello syndrome see DELUSIONAL JEALOUSY. [derived from the name of the protagonist of William Shakespeare's tragedy *Othello*]

other conditions that may be a focus of clinical attention in *DSM–IV–TR*, a category that includes various conditions or problems that warrant psychiatric attention or treatment even though they do not meet the criteria of MENTAL DISORDER.

other-conscious emotions see SELF-CONSCIOUS EMOTION.

other-directed *adj.* describing or relating to people whose values, goals, and behavior stem primarily from identification with group or collective standards rather than with individually defined standards. Also called **outer-directed**. Compare INNER-DIRECTED; TRADITION-DIRECTED. [introduced by U.S. sociologist David Riesman (1909–2002)]

other psychosexual disorders the *DSM–III* designation for what *DSM–IV–TR* terms SEXUAL DISORDER NOT OTHERWISE SPECIFIED.

other–total ratio (**OTR**) a formula for predicting the level of SELF-AWARENESS experienced by individuals in social settings. The formula states that self-awareness increases in direct proportion to the number of people in the group relative to the number of people in the individual's subgroup, that is, self-awareness = the number of people in the group/the number of people in the subgroup. [described in 1983 by U.S. social psychologist Brian Mullen (1955–)]

otic *adj.* pertaining to the ear.

Otis–Lennon School Ability Test (**OLSAT**) a multiple-choice assessment of verbal and nonverbal reasoning abilities that are predictors of success in school. Available in different levels for students in kindergarten through grade 12, it currently consists of various tasks (e.g., defining words, detecting likenesses and differences, following directions, and recalling words and numbers) designed to measure verbal comprehension, verbal reasoning, pictorial reasoning, figural reasoning, and quantitative reasoning. The OLSAT was originally published in 1979 as a modification and replacement of the earlier **Otis–Lennon Mental Ability Test**, which itself was a revision of the **Otis Quick Scoring Mental Ability Tests** (originally published in the mid-1930s). Now in its eighth edition (published in 2003), the OLSAT is usually administered in groups. [Arthur S. **Otis** (1886–1963) and Roger T. **Lennon** (1916–), U.S. psychologists]

otitis media an inflammation or infection of the middle ear commonly associated with sinusitis, upper respiratory infections, or allergies and resulting in a conductive hearing loss (see CONDUCTION DEAFNESS). **Acute otitis media** is common in young children, resulting from viral or bacterial infection. In **serous otitis media**, a thick fluid fills the middle ear. In **adhesive otitis media**, permanent adhesions develop in the middle ear due to the continued presence of fluid after the infection itself has been controlled. These adhesions cause damage to the OSSICLES.

oto- (**ot-**) *combining form* ear.

otoacoustic emissions (**OAEs**) weak sounds produced by the COCHLEA that are recorded using a microphone placed in the EXTERNAL AUDITORY MEATUS. **Spontaneous otoacoustic emissions** (SOAEs) are recorded in the absence of externally presented sound. **Evoked otoacoustic emissions** (EOAEs) are responses to sounds, typically transients (clicks), sustained PURE TONES, or pairs of tones. EOAEs are not the result of reflections, and thus the alternative term **cochlear echo** is not technically correct. All OAEs appear to require normal cochlear function and provide strong evidence for an active mechanical process occurring within the cochlea, probably mediated by movement of the outer HAIR CELLS. Measurement of EOAEs is becoming widespread in audiological assessment. Also called **cochlear emissions**.

otoconium *n.* (*pl.* **otoconia**) see OTOLITH.

otohemineurasthenia *n.* a unilateral deafness for which no organic cause can be found.

otolaryngologist *n.* a specialist physician or surgeon who assesses and treats diseases of the ears, nose, and throat and of the head and neck.

otolith *n.* any of numerous tiny calcium particles embedded in the gelatinous matrix of the VESTIBULAR SACS of the inner ear. See MACULA. Also called **otoconium**; **statoconium**.

otology *n.* the medical discipline concerned with the study, diagnosis, and treatment of disorders of the ear. **—otological** *adj.* **—otologist** *n.*

-otomy *suffix* see -TOMY. See also -ECTOMY.

otoneurology *n.* the study of neurology as related to audition. **—otoneurological** *adj.* **—otoneurologist** *n.*

otopalatodigital syndrome see OPD SYNDROME.

otosclerosis *n.* a formation of spongy bone that develops in the middle ear and immobilizes the STAPES at the point of attachment to the oval window facing the inner ear. Otosclerosis is marked by progressive deafness as the OSSICLES fail to transmit vibrations from the tympanic membrane to the inner ear. It is considered hereditary. **—otosclerotic** *adj.*

ototoxic *adj.* toxic to the ears, especially the middle ear or inner ear. **—ototoxicity** *n.*

OTR abbreviation for OTHER–TOTAL RATIO.

ought self in analyses of self-concept, a mental representation of a set of attributes that one is obligated to possess according to social norms or one's personal responsibilities.

Ouija board tradename for a board marked with numbers and letters on which a movable pointer, held by the participants, spells out messages under the supposed guidance of spirits. The process can be seen as a form of AUTOMATIC WRITING. [from a blend of the French and German words for "yes," *oui* and *ja*]

outbreeding *n.* **1.** the mating of humans who are unrelated or who originate from different groups. It is thus the converse of INBREEDING. **2.** the mating of an animal with an unrelated or distantly related member of the same species. This may produce HYBRID VIGOR. Also called **crossbreeding**.

outcome *n.* **1.** the result of an experiment, treatment, interaction, or any other event, for example, a client's condition after psychotherapy. **2.** in GAME THEORY, the factor determining a particular set of payments, one set being paid to each participant.

outcome dependence a social situation in which one person's outcomes, including the rewards or punishments experienced, are determined in whole or in part by the actions of another person. Compare OUTCOME INTERDEPENDENCE. [based on the social exchange theory of U.S. social psychologists John Thibaut (1917–1986) and Harold H. Kelley (1921–) as described in their book *The Social Psychology of Groups* (1959)]

outcome evaluation a process used to decide whether a program has achieved its stated goals and had the desired impact on the participants. Also called **payoff evaluation**. See also IMPACT ANALYSIS; SUMMATIVE EVALUATION.

outcome expectancies cognitive, emotional, and behavioral outcomes that individuals believe are associated with future, or intended, behaviors (e.g., alcohol consumption, exercise) and that are believed to either promote or inhibit these behaviors.

outcome goal a goal dependent on a social evaluation of performance (e.g., the result of a competitive event).

outcome interdependence a social situation in which two or more people have mutual influence over one another's outcomes. Compare OUTCOME DEPENDENCE. [based on the social exchange theory of U.S. social psychologists John Thibaut (1917–1986) and Harold H. Kelley (1921–), as described in their book *The Social Psychology of Groups* (1959)]

outcome measures assessments of the effectiveness of an intervention on the basis of measurements taken before, during, and after the intervention.

outcome research a systematic investigation of the effectiveness of a single type or technique of psychotherapy, or of the comparative effectiveness of different types or techniques, when applied to one or more disorders. See also PSYCHOTHERAPY RESEARCH.

outdoor training program a method of leadership development and team building in which employees are taken to an outdoor location, such as a wilderness area, and presented with a series of physical challenges that they must overcome as a group or as individuals. Afterward participants discuss what they learned about themselves, others, and working together, and how they can apply what they have learned back at work. Although outdoor training programs are popular, there is insufficient research to draw conclusions about their effectiveness.

outercourse *n.* noncoital sexual activity, which may include achieving orgasm by manual stimulation of the genitals or by ORAL SEX.

outer-directed *adj.* see OTHER-DIRECTED.

outer ear see EXTERNAL EAR.

outer hair cells see HAIR CELLS.

outer nuclear layer the layer of cell bodies of the rods and cones in the retina. Also called **outer granular layer**.

outer plexiform layer the synaptic layer in the retina in which contacts are made between PHOTORECEPTORS, RETINAL BIPOLAR CELLS, and RETINAL HORIZONTAL CELLS.

outer psychophysics an attempt to establish the direct relationship between the physical intensity of sensory stimuli and the intensity of the related mental experience. Compare INNER PSYCHOPHYSICS. See PSYCHOPHYSICAL LAW. [introduced by Gustav FECHNER]

outgroup *n.* **1.** in general, any group to which one does not belong or with which one does not identify, but particularly a group that is judged to be different from, and inferior to, one's own group (the INGROUP). **2.** a specific rival group that ingroup members ridicule, derogate, and sometimes express aggression against. Also called **theygroup**. [defined by U.S. sociologist William G. Sumner (1840–1910)]

outgroup extremity effect the tendency to describe and evaluate OUTGROUP members, their actions, and their products in extremely positive or extremely negative ways. Compare INGROUP EXTREMITY EFFECT. See also INGROUP BIAS; LINGUISTIC INTERGROUP BIAS.

outgroup homogeneity bias the perceptual tendency to assume that the members of other groups are very similar to each other, particularly in contrast to the assumed diversity of the membership of one's own groups. See also GROUP ATTRIBUTION ERROR; GROUP FALLACY; INGROUP BIAS; INGROUP EXTREMITY EFFECT; LINGUISTIC INTERGROUP BIAS.

outing *n.* revealing one's own or another person's same-sex sexual orientation to others. The term refers to COMING OUT of the closet (see CLOSET HOMOSEXUAL). **—out** *vb.*

outlier *n.* an extreme observation, measurement, or score, that is, one that significantly differs from all others obtained. Outliers may be the result of error, in which case they may distort research findings. Such scores can have a high degree of influence on summary statistics and estimates of parametric values and their precision.

out-of-body experience a dissociative experience in which the individual imagines that his or her mind, soul, or spirit has left the body and is acting or perceiving independently. Such experiences are often reported by those who have recovered from the point of death (see NEAR-DEATH EXPERIENCE); they have also been reported by those using hallucinogens or under hypnosis. Certain occult or spiritualistic practices may also attempt to induce such experiences. See ASTRAL PROJECTION.

outpatient *n.* a registered ambulatory patient who can be treated without overnight admission to a hospital, clinic, or other facility, for instance, in a physician's or group practice's office, a clinic, or a day-surgery center. See also AMBULATORY CARE. Compare INPATIENT.

outpatient commitment a form of court-ordered psychiatric or psychological treatment in which individuals are allowed to remain in the community so long as they are closely monitored and continue to receive treatment. Compare INVOLUNTARY CIVIL COMMITMENT.

outpatient services health care services performed for registered ambulatory patients in hospital units, clinics, doctors' offices, and mental health centers.

outplacement counseling practical and psychological assistance given to employees whose employment with an organization has been terminated. It can include VOCATIONAL GUIDANCE and coaching in job-hunting skills as well as psychological help in dealing with the transition. The program is usually conducted by specialty firms outside the organization. See also VOCATIONAL COUNSELING.

output *n.* in computing contexts, the information a computer produces. Compare INPUT.

output interference interference that occurs during the recall of memories because the act (or process) of retrieving an item interferes with the ability to later recall other items. For example, during an IMMEDIATE RECALL TEST, some items from a list (e.g., those not yet recalled) may be forgotten once other items have been recalled.

outsider *n.* **1.** a person who does not belong to one's group, particularly one who is viewed with suspicion. **2.** in group discussions, a group member who is not able to participate fully because he or she is not familiar with the issues under discussion.

ova *pl. n.* see OVUM.

oval window a membranous window in the bony wall of the cochlea in the ear (see SCALA VESTIBULI). Vibration of the stapes (see OSSICLES) is transmitted to the oval window and into the cochlear fluids.

O variable see ORGANIC VARIABLE.

ovarian follicle see GRAAFIAN FOLLICLE.

ovariectomy *n.* the surgical removal of one or both ovaries. This procedure may be performed when the ovaries are diseased or injured. Under some circumstances, as when a woman is at very high risk for ovarian cancer, it may be carried out for prevention or prophylaxis (see PROPHYLACTIC SURGERY). Removal of ovaries in premenopausal women will induce menopause. Also called **oophorectomy**.

ovary *n.* the female reproductive organ, which produces OVA (egg cells) and sex hormones (estrogens and progesterone). In humans the two ovaries are almond-shaped organs, normally located in the lower abdomen on either side of the upper end of the uterus, to which they are linked by the FALLOPIAN TUBES. The ovaries of the prepubertal human female contain about 350,000 immature oocytes, of which fewer than 400 will develop into mature ova to be released at a rate of about one per month between menarche (first menstruation) and menopause (see OOGENESIS). See also GRAAFIAN FOLLICLE; MENSTRUAL CYCLE. **—ovarian** *adj.*

overachiever *n.* a person, such as a student, who achieves above his or her capacity as calculated and predicted by aptitude and general-intelligence tests. Since it is impossible to achieve at a level above that at which one can perform, it is preferable to refer to **overachievement** as **achievement above predicted expectations**. Compare UNDERACHIEVER.

overactivity *n.* excessive, restless activity that may be related to anxiety or mania. Overactivity is usually somewhat less extreme than HYPERACTIVITY.

overage *adj.* describing a person who is beyond the average or usual age associated with a given behavior or trait. The term is sometimes applied to a child or student who is chronologically older than the others in his or her grade. **Underage** describes a student who is younger than his or her classmates.

overanxious disorder of childhood generalized and persistent anxiety or worry that occurs in childhood. In *DSM–IV–TR*, overanxious disorder of childhood is now classified as GENERALIZED ANXIETY DISORDER. Also called **overanxious reaction**.

overattribution bias see FUNDAMENTAL ATTRIBUTION ERROR.

overbreathing *n.* see HYPERVENTILATION.

overclassification *n.* a phenomenon in which, at levels ranging from local schools to national patterns of education, children who are members of ethnic minority groups are at heightened risk of being classified as SPECIAL EDUCATION students.

overcompensation *n.* see COMPENSATION. **—overcompensate** *vb.*

overconfidence *n.* **1.** a state of overestimating one's ability to perform or underestimating the ability of a competitor to perform. **2.** an unsupported belief or unrealistically positive expectation that a desired outcome will occur. **—overconfident** *adj.*

overcontrolled *adj.* denoting behavior that is inhibited and often driven by shyness or fear of rejection. The word is typically used to describe the behavior of children thought to be at risk for depression, but may also refer to similar behavior in adults.

overcorrection *n.* in therapy, a technique used when a client exhibits inappropriate behavior, in which the therapist asks the client to repeat the behavior in an appropriate but exaggerated way.

overcrowding *n.* a higher concentration of organisms per unit of space than is customary for a given species. Experimental overcrowding significantly increases abnormal behavior and aggression in rats, even when sufficient resources preclude the need for competition. In human societies, overcrowding is associated with stress patterns, such as stimulus overload but does not inevitably lead to increased aggression. See also DENSITY; OVERPOPULATION.

overdetermination *n.* in psychoanalytic theory, the

concept that several unconscious factors may combine to produce one symptom, dream, disorder, or aspect of behavior. Because drives and defenses operate simultaneously and derive from different layers of the personality, a dream may express more than one meaning, and a single symptom may serve more than one purpose or fulfill more than one unconscious wish. **—overdetermined** *adj.*

overdispersion *n.* in CATEGORICAL DATA ANALYSIS, a situation in which the observations display more variation than is predicted by the sampling model.

overdose 1. *n.* the ingestion of an excessive amount of a drug, with resulting adverse effects. The precise toxic effects differ according to many factors, including the properties and dosage of the drug, the body weight and health of the individual, and the individual's tolerance for the drug. **2.** *vb.* to take an excessive amount of a drug.

Overeaters Anonymous (**OA**) a voluntary organization of men and women who seek to help each other understand and overcome compulsive eating disorders through a TWELVE-STEP PROGRAM. See also SELF-HELP GROUP.

overexpectation *n.* in PAVLOVIAN CONDITIONING, a decrease in responding to two (or presumably more) conditioned stimuli when they are joined into a compound stimulus and then paired with the unconditioned stimulus previously used to establish each part of the compound as an independent conditioned stimulus.

overextension *n.* the tendency of very young children to extend the use of a word beyond the scope of its specific meaning, for example, by referring to all animals as "doggie."

overgeneralization *n.* **1.** a cognitive distortion in which an individual views a single event as an invariable rule, so that, for example, failure at accomplishing one task will predict an endless pattern of defeat in all tasks. **2.** the tendency of young children to generalize standard grammatical rules to apply to irregular words, for example, pluralizing *foot* to *foots*. See OVEREXTENSION; OVERREGULARIZATION.

overheating *n.* excessive ambient temperature. See HEAT EFFECTS; HEAT-INDUCED ASTHENIA; HEAT EXHAUSTION; HEATSTROKE.

overidentification *n.* in the GENERAL LINEAR MODEL, the presence of more parameters than are needed to specify the model correctly.

overinclusion *n.* failure of an individual to eliminate ineffective or inappropriate responses associated with a particular stimulus.

overintensity *n.* a state in which one or all of the following are above the optimal level for an individual's performance: arousal, commitment, effort, assertiveness, and attentional focus. See INTENSITY.

overjustification effect a paradoxical effect in which rewarding (or offering to reward) a person for his or her performance can lead to lower, rather than higher, effort and attainment. It occurs when the introduction of an EXTRINSIC REWARD weakens the strong INTRINSIC MOTIVATION that was the key to the person's original high performance.

overlapping factor in FACTOR ANALYSIS, a factor common to two or more tests.

overlapping psychological tasks in psychological testing, two tasks that overlap in time. A common finding is that performance of the second task is slowed when the stimulus for it is presented shortly after the stimulus for the first task. See PSYCHOLOGICAL REFRACTORY PERIOD.

overlearning *n.* practice that is continued beyond the point at which the individual knows or performs well. The benefits of overlearning may be seen in increased persistence of the learning over time. **—overlearned** *adj.*

overload *n.* a psychological condition in which situations and experiences are so cognitively, perceptually, and emotionally stimulating that they tax or even exceed the individual's capacity to process incoming information. See COGNITIVE OVERLOAD; INFORMATION OVERLOAD; SENSORY OVERLOAD; STIMULUS OVERLOAD.

overload principle a concept stating that to increase the size or functional ability of MUSCLE FIBERS, they must be pushed close to the limit of their current ability to respond.

overmedication *n.* see MEDICATION.

overpayment inequity an employee's perception that he or she is being paid at a rate that exceeds what is fair, especially in comparison with coworkers. This can lead to dissatisfaction, tension with coworkers, and efforts to restore equity. Compare UNDERPAYMENT INEQUITY. See EQUITY THEORY.

overpopulation *n.* a POPULATION DENSITY that is higher than desirable and may result in OVERCROWDING and stress. Evidence from animal behavior supports the view that overcrowding increases aberrant behavior and aggression. However, some human societies with very high population density have correspondingly low rates of violence and social pathology, suggesting that the negative effects of overpopulation may have social as well as biological origins. See also CROWDING.

overproduction *n.* **1.** the condition in which a species produces too many offspring for the available food, space, or other vital resources. **2.** production of goods beyond what is needed.

overproductive ideas racing thoughts or FLIGHT OF IDEAS often present in a MANIC EPISODE.

overprotection *n.* the process of coddling, sheltering, and indulging a child to such an extent that he or she fails to become independent, cannot endure frustration or competition, and may develop a passive–dependent personality.

overreaction *n.* a reaction, particularly an emotional response, that exceeds an appropriate level.

overregularization *n.* a transient error in linguistic development in which the child attempts to make language more regular than it actually is, for example, by saying *breaked* instead of *broken*. See also OVEREXTENSION; OVERGENERALIZATION.

overshadowing *n.* in PAVLOVIAN CONDITIONING, a decrease in conditioning with one conditioned stimulus because of the presence of another conditioned stimulus. Usually a stronger stimulus will overshadow a weaker stimulus. **—overshadow** *vb.*

overshoot *n.* the portion of an ACTION POTENTIAL that represents the stage when the membrane potential is transiently depolarized relative to the resting potential. Compare UNDERSHOOT.

overshooting *n.* in vision, the tendency for the eyes to move to a position beyond that needed to fixate a target.

oversimplification *n.* an explanation or characterization of something that omits recognized essential elements, making it appear less complicated than it really is. **—oversimplify** *vb.*

overstaffing *n.* a situation in which management

judges that more people than necessary are being employed by an organization or one of its subunits. Compare UNDERSTAFFING. **—overstaffed** *adj.*

overt *adj.* **1.** denoting anything that is directly observable, open to view, or publicly known. **2.** not hidden. Compare COVERT. **3.** deliberate or attracting attention.

overt behavior behavior that is explicit, that is, observable without instruments or expertise.

over-the-counter drugs (**OTC drugs**) drugs that can be purchased without a doctor's prescription, such as acetaminophen and aspirin. Also called **nonprescription drugs**.

overt homosexuality gay or lesbian tendencies that are consciously recognized and expressed in sexual contact, in contrast to LATENT HOMOSEXUALITY.

overt integrity test see INTEGRITY TESTING.

overtone *n.* see HARMONIC.

overtraining syndrome the unwanted physical and mental effects, collectively, of training beyond the individual's capacities. Characteristic symptoms include decreased performance, easily tiring, loss of motivation, emotional instability, inability to concentrate, and increased susceptibility to injury and infection. See BURNOUT.

overt response any observable or external reaction (e.g., a response that can be seen or heard). Compare COVERT RESPONSE.

overvalued idea a false or exaggerated belief that is maintained by an individual, but less rigidly and persistently than a delusion (e.g., the idea that one is indispensable in an organization). The presence of an overvalued idea implies an unconscious motivation that, if made conscious, would reduce its importance and corresponding dysfunctions.

oviduct *n.* the tube in female animals through which egg cells from the ovary are conveyed to other parts of the reproductive system. In mammals it is called the FALLOPIAN TUBE.

oviparity *n.* reproduction in which fertilized eggs are laid and hatch outside the mother's body. Compare VIVIPARITY. **—oviparous** *adj.*

OVLT abbreviation for ORGANUM VASCULOSUM OF THE LAMINA TERMINALIS.

ovulation *n.* the production of a mature secondary oocyte (see OOGENESIS) and its release from a GRAAFIAN FOLLICLE at the surface of the ovary. Rupture of the follicle causes the oocyte to be discharged into a fallopian tube. In humans, the oocyte matures into an OVUM in the strict sense only if it is penetrated by a sperm during its passage along the fallopian tube.

ovulatory cycle the cyclical changes in the ovary associated with the development of a GRAAFIAN FOLLICLE. See MENSTRUAL CYCLE.

ovum *n.* (*pl.* **ova**) a single female GAMETE that develops from a secondary oocyte following its release from the ovary at OVULATION. Also called **egg cell**. See also OOGENESIS.

own control a REPEATED MEASURES DESIGN in which multiple measurements are taken on the same group or individual. Such a design may not need an independent control group because the participants serve as their own control.

oxazepam *n.* a short-acting BENZODIAZEPINE that is the final active product of the metabolism of DIAZEPAM. Oxazepam possesses the advantage of having no metabolic products; it therefore has a predictable HALF-LIFE and elimination time and requires minimal processing in the liver. Because of this, some consider it to be the preferred agent in the management of alcohol withdrawal. However, the need for close monitoring of dosing schedules leads others to prefer longer acting agents for this condition. U.S. trade name: **Serax**.

oxidation *n.* a chemical reaction in which a substance combines with oxygen or in which electrons are lost. In DRUG METABOLISM, oxidation is a common mechanism of Phase I metabolism, in which drugs are made more polar (i.e., more water soluble) by the addition of an oxygen atom, often via the action of CYTOCHROME P450 enzymes.

oxycephaly *n.* a high, pointed condition of the skull. Also called **acrocephaly**. **—oxycephalic** *adj.*

oxycodone *n.* see OPIOID ANALGESIC.

oxytocics *pl. n.* drugs that are capable of stimulating contractions of the uterine muscles and are used clinically to induce labor and elective or therapeutic abortion and to control postpartum bleeding. They include ERGOT DERIVATIVES (e.g., ergonovine) and some PROSTAGLANDINS. See also OXYTOCIN.

oxytocin *n.* a hormone produced in the hypothalamus and secreted by the posterior lobe (neurohypophysis) of the PITUITARY GLAND in response to direct neural stimulation. It stimulates smooth muscle, particularly in the mammary glands during lactation and in the wall of the uterus during labor. In lactating women it is released by the tactile stimuli provided by a nursing infant and facilitates expression of milk—the so-called **milk letdown reflex**. Synthetic oxytocin can be administered at term to help induce uterine contractions.

Pp

p symbol for PROBABILITY.

P see PRIMARY ABILITIES.

p53 a tumor-suppressor gene that normally regulates the cell cycle and protects the cell's DNA from damage. Mutations in *p53* cause cells to become malignant. Germline mutations in *p53* are responsible for at least most cases of Li–Fraumeni syndrome. Carriers of *p53* mutations in Li–Fraumeni syndrome families have a 90% LIFETIME RISK of developing one or more kinds of cancer.

P300 see P3 COMPONENT.

PA abbreviation for PHYSICIAN ASSISTANT.

pacemaker *n.* a natural or artificial device that helps establish and maintain certain biological rhythms. Unqualified, the term usually refers to a CARDIAC PACEMAKER. Natural pacemakers include the sinoatrial node, which regulates heart rhythm, and the THALAMIC PACEMAKER.

pachygyria *n.* a brain malformation in which the convolutions (gyri) of the cerebral cortex are abnormally thick. It is usually accompanied by a reduction in the fissures between the gyri. Also called **macrogyria**.

pacing *n.* see EDUCATIONAL PACING.

Pacinian corpuscle a type of cutaneous receptor organ that is sensitive to contact and vibration. It consists of a nerve-fiber ending surrounded by concentric layers of connective tissue. Pacinian corpuscles are found in the fingers, the hairy skin, the tendons, and the abdominal membrane. Also called **Pacinian body**; **Pacini's corpuscle**; **Vater's corpuscle**. [Filippo **Pacini** (1812–1883), Italian anatomist]

package testing a form of product testing that emphasizes the effects of the package design on consumer purchasing decisions. One package-testing study found that 30% of female purchasers of cosmetics changed brands when a better package with a similar product was offered, and 50% said they would be willing to pay a higher price for the same product in a more convenient or efficient package.

packet switching a method of transmitting messages from point to point over a COMPUTER NETWORK that makes efficient use of the network's capacity and ensures transmission even if part of the network is down. The method involves dividing a digitized message into short segments called **packets**, each of which contains, in addition to its message segment, a header that identifies its destination, the position of the segment within the message, and so forth. Each packet finds its way to its destination, selecting its node-to-node route on the basis of the distribution of traffic load at any particular moment. At the destination the packets of a given message, which may have traveled by different routes, are assembled in the correct order to reconstruct the original message.

padded cell a room in a psychiatric hospital or ward that is lined with mattresses or other heavy padding on the floor and walls to protect a violent or self-destructive patient from self-injury or from injuring others. In most institutions padded cells have been replaced by some combination of physical restraints, psychological interventions, and tranquilizing medications.

paedo- *combining form* see PEDO-.

PAG abbreviation for PERIAQUEDUCTAL GRAY.

pain *n.* an unpleasant sensation due to damage to nerve tissue, stimulation of free nerve endings, or excessive stimulation (e.g., extremely loud sounds). Physical pain is elicited by stimulation of pain receptors, which occur in groups of myelinated or unmyelinated fibers throughout the body, but particularly in surface tissues. Pain that is initiated in surface receptors generally is perceived as sharp, sudden, and localized; pain experienced in internal organs tends to be dull, longer lasting, and less localized. Because of psychological factors, as well as previous experience and training in pain response, individual reactions vary widely. Although pain is generally considered a physical phenomenon, it involves various cognitive, affective, and behavioral factors: It is an unpleasant emotional as well as sensory experience. Pain may also be a feeling of severe distress and suffering resulting from acute anxiety, loss of a loved one, or other psychological factors (see PSYCHIC PAIN). Psychologists have made important contributions to understanding pain by demonstrating the psychosocial and behavioral factors in the etiology, severity, exacerbation, maintenance, and treatment of both physical and mental pain. See also GATE-CONTROL THEORY OF PAIN.

pain disorder in *DSM–IV–TR*, a SOMATOFORM DISORDER characterized by severe, prolonged pain that significantly interferes with a person's ability to function. The pain cannot be accounted for solely by a medical condition, and there is evidence of psychological involvement in its onset, severity, exacerbation, or maintenance. Although not feigned or produced intentionally (compare FACTITIOUS DISORDER; MALINGERING), the pain may serve such psychological ends as avoidance of distasteful activity or gaining extra attention or support from others. Pain disorder was formerly referred to as **psychogenic pain disorder** or **somatoform pain disorder**.

pain drawing a diagnostic tool for identifying the amount, severity, and type of pain. A front and back view of the human body is provided, and the individual is given instructions to identify the location and type of pain using specified symbols.

pain endurance the amount of time that pain of a certain intensity can be tolerated.

painful bruising syndrome see GARDNER–DIAMOND SYNDROME.

painful sexual intercourse discomfort occurring during coitus, which may range from irritation, if the vagina is inflamed because of a bacterial infection, to severe pain by deep penetration, particularly when the uterus is retroverted. A rigid hymen, urinary tract disease, vaginal tears, vaginal atrophy during menopause, and vaginal muscle disorders are other possible causes. Males seldom experience painful intercourse. See also DYSPAREUNIA.

pain management the prevention, reduction, or elimination of physical or mental suffering or discomfort, which may be achieved by pharmacotherapy (e.g., administration of opioids or other analgesics), behavioral therapies, neurological and anesthesiologic methods (e.g., nerve blocks, self-administered pumps), complementary or alternative methods (e.g., ACUPUNCTURE or ACUPRESSURE), or a combination of these. A wide range of psychological interventions have been used successfully in treatment to help people deal with or control their pain. For example, BIOFEEDBACK and RELAXATION have been used alone and in conjunction with other cognitive techniques to treat chronic headaches and facial pain. HYPNOTHERAPY has also been used successfully to treat acute pain and pain associated with burns and metastatic disease. Cognitive and behavioral COPING-SKILLS TRAINING, along with external ATTENTIONAL FOCUS, neutral or positive IMAGERY, problem solving, communication skills, and psychotherapeutic approaches, have been combined with physical modalities in the treatment of CHRONIC PAIN syndromes.

pain mechanisms neural mechanisms that mediate pain. These extend from peripheral nerve endings to the cerebral cortex, especially the CINGULATE GYRUS. Some investigators propose that sharp pain sensations are transmitted by rapidly conducting A FIBERS and dull pain sensations are transmitted by slowly conducting C FIBERS. See also GATE-CONTROL THEORY OF PAIN.

pain pathway any neural pathway that mediates sensations of pain. Afferent pain pathways include rapidly conducting myelinated A FIBERS and slowly conducting unmyelinated C FIBERS, ascending tracts in the ANTEROLATERAL SYSTEM, the CENTRAL GRAY matter, the RETICULAR FORMATION, and many thalamic and cerebral cortical areas, especially the CINGULATE GYRUS. There are also efferent pathways that inhibit pain signals at various levels down to spinal synapses, including release of ENDOGENOUS OPIOIDS that inhibit pain.

pain perception the perception of physiological pain, usually evoked by stimuli that cause or threaten to cause tissue damage. In some cases, such as PHANTOM LIMB pain and CAUSALGIA, the persistence of pain cannot be explained by stimulation of neural pathways. Pain perception can be measured in terms of its intensity and can be classified according to several categories: These include sharp or dull; focal or general; and chronic or intermittent or transitory. Also called **nociception**.

pain receptor see NOCICEPTOR.

pain scale a standardized rating scale for judging the experience of pain. It may take the form of verbal self-description, numerical rating, or graphical depictions of faces.

pain sense a sense, involving free nerve endings on the body surface and in some internal organs, that yields a specific effect identified as pain, especially when tissue injury occurs. See PAIN MECHANISMS; PAIN PATHWAY; PAIN PERCEPTION.

pain threshold the intensity at which a stimulus begins producing pain.

pain tolerance the greatest intensity of pain that can be endured voluntarily.

paint sniffing a type of substance abuse involving the inhalation of the fumes of paint thinners and other volatile solvents. See INHALANT ABUSE.

pair bond a relationship between two individuals characterized by close affiliative behavior between partners, emotional reaction to separation or loss, and increased social responsiveness on reunion. Pair bonds are important in species with biparental care, providing the female with increased likelihood of male cooperation in the care of the young and the male with increased CERTAINTY OF PATERNITY.

paired-associates learning a technique used in studying learning in which participants learn syllables, words, or other items in pairs and are later presented with one half of each pair to which they must respond with the matching half. Also called **paired-associates method**; **paired associations**. [introduced by Mary W. CALKINS]

paired comparison **1.** a systematic procedure for comparing a set of stimuli or other items. A pair of stimuli is presented to the participant, who is asked to compare them on a particular dimension, such as size, loudness, or brightness; the process is continued until every item in the set has been compared with every other item. The method is mainly associated with research into psychophysical judgments but has also been used to study preferences between works of art or different personality characteristics. **2.** in industrial and occupational settings, a method of employee evaluation in which each worker in a selected group is compared with every other worker on a series of performance measures. Employees are then rated on the basis of the number of favorable comparisons they receive.

pairing *n.* in behavioral studies, the juxtaposing of two events in time. For example, if a tone is presented immediately before a puff of air to the eye, the tone and the puff have been paired.

pairing hypothesis the hypothesis that the crucial feature of PAVLOVIAN CONDITIONING is the temporal conjunction (i.e., PAIRING) between a conditioned stimulus and an unconditioned stimulus.

pairmate *n.* either of the individuals involved in a PAIR BOND.

pairwise contrast a contrast that involves only two group means.

palatal lisp see LISP.

palate *n.* the roof of the mouth, consisting of an anterior bony portion (see HARD PALATE) and a posterior fibromuscular portion (see SOFT PALATE). See also CLEFT PALATE.

palatum durum see HARD PALATE.

paleo- (**palaeo-**) *combining form* ancient.

paleocerebellum *n.* a phylogenetically old part of the CEREBELLUM, including most of the vermis (central area) and the cerebellar pyramids. It is involved in control of the muscles of the trunk and girdle. Also called **spinocerebellum**. Compare NEOCEREBELLUM. **—paleocerebellar** *adj.*

paleocortex *n.* CEREBRAL CORTEX that has between three and five CORTICAL LAYERS and is phylogenetically older than NEOCORTEX. It is concerned mainly with olfactory functions and includes ENTORHINAL CORTEX and PERIAMYGDALOID CORTEX. See also ALLOCORTEX.

paleologic thinking PRELOGICAL THINKING characterized by concrete, dreamlike thought processes, as occurs in children. Mental activity is limited to feeling and perception and excludes logic and reasoning. [defined by Italian-born U.S. psychiatrist Silvano Arieti (1914–1982)]

paleopallium *n.* see RHINENCEPHALON.

paleopsychology (**palaeopsychology**) *n.* **1.** the study of certain psychological processes in contemporary humans that are believed to have originated in earlier stages of human and, perhaps, nonhuman animal evolution. These include unconscious processes, such as the COLLECTIVE UNCONSCIOUS. The term was introduced in this sense by Carl JUNG. **2.** the present-day reconstruction of the psychological reactions of prehistoric human beings. **—paleopsychological** *adj.*

paleostriatum *n.* see NEOSTRIATUM.

palilalia *n.* a speech disorder in which words and phrases are needlessly repeated with increasing speed.

palin- (**pali-**) *combining form* **1.** repetition (e.g., PALINPHRASIA). **2.** reversal of direction (e.g., PALINLEXIA).

palingraphia *n.* see MIRROR WRITING.

palinlexia *n.* reading letters or words in reverse order, for example, *deb* for *bed*, or *Car my is this* for *This is my car.*

palinopsia *n.* the persistence or reappearance of a visual image after the stimulus has been removed. Palinopsia is associated with posterior brain injury, drug effects, and seizures. Also called **palinopia**; **paliopsy**; **visual perseveration**. See also AFTERIMAGE; VISUAL ILLUSION.

palinphrasia *n.* involuntary repetition of words or phrases in speaking. Also called **paliphrasia**. See also PALILALIA.

paliopsy *n.* see PALINOPSIA.

paliphrasia *n.* see PALINPHRASIA.

palliative care terminal care that focuses on symptom control and comfort instead of aggressive, cure-oriented intervention. This is the basis of the HOSPICE approach. Emphasis is on careful assessment of the patient's condition throughout the end phase of life in order to provide the most effective medications and other procedures to relieve pain.

pallid data see VIVID DATA.

pallidotomy *n.* a neurosurgical technique in which electrodes are used to selectively lesion the GLOBUS PALLIDUS. Pallidotomy is used for the management of disorders involving damage to the EXTRAPYRAMIDAL TRACT, such as Parkinson's disease.

palmar *adj.* **1.** in humans, referring to the palms of the hands. **2.** in nonhuman primates, referring to the palm of any limb.

palmar conductance the electrical conductivity of the skin of the palm of the hand. See SKIN CONDUCTANCE.

palmar reflex a reflex in which the fingers are flexed when the palm is scratched. See GRASP REFLEX.

palmistry *n.* the practice of interpreting lines and other features of the palm of the hand as signs of personality traits or predictions of the individual's future. It has no scientific basis. Also called **chiromancy**; **chirosophy**. **—palmist** *n.*

palpebral fissure the hypothetical line between the upper and lower eyelids. When the eyelids are open, the palpebral fissure forms an elliptical space. Also called **rima palpebrarum**.

palpitation *n.* a rapid heartbeat associated with an anxiety attack, excessive tension, or physical exertion.

palsy *n.* an obsolete name for paralysis, still used in such compound names as CEREBRAL PALSY, BELL'S PALSY, and PROGRESSIVE SUPRANUCLEAR PALSY.

Pamelor *n.* a trade name for NORTRIPTYLINE.

PAN abbreviation for POSITIONAL ALCOHOL NYSTAGMUS.

pan- *combining form* all or every.

panacea *n.* a solution or remedy for everything that is wrong or that universally applies to a set of related problems.

panarteritis *n.* a diffuse inflammation of the walls of the small and medium arteries. Arteries of the skeletal muscles, kidneys, heart, and gastrointestinal tract may be involved.

pancreas *n.* a gland, located near the posterior wall of the abdominal cavity, that is stimulated by SECRETIN to secrete pancreatic juice, which contains various digestive enzymes. In addition, small clusters of cells within the pancreas (see ISLETS OF LANGERHANS) function as an ENDOCRINE GLAND, secreting the hormones INSULIN and GLUCAGON. **—pancreatic** *adj.*

pancreatitis *n.* an inflammation of the pancreas, marked by severe abdominal pain and caused by biliary tract disorders (e.g., gallstones), alcoholism, viral infection, or reactions to certain drugs (e.g., some antipsychotic agents).

pandemic 1. *adj.* occurring universally or over a large area (e.g., several countries) and therefore more widespread than EPIDEMIC. **2.** *n.* a pandemic disease. Compare ENDEMIC.

panel study a longitudinal study (see LONGITUDINAL DESIGN) in which one or more groups (panels) are followed over time.

panentheism *n.* see PANTHEISM.

panic *n.* a sudden, uncontrollable fear reaction that may involve terror, confusion, and irrational behavior, precipitated by a perceived threat (e.g., earthquake, fire, or being stuck in an elevator).

panic attack a sudden onset of intense apprehension and fearfulness, in the absence of actual danger, accompanied by the presence of such physical symptoms as palpitations, difficulty in breathing, chest pain or discomfort, choking or smothering sensations, excessive perspiration, and dizziness. The attack occurs in a discrete period of time and often involves fears of going crazy, losing control, or dying. In *DSM–IV–TR* the diagnosis of a panic attack requires the presence of at least 4 of 13 somatic or cognitive symptoms. Attacks may occur in the context of any of the ANXIETY DISORDERS as well as in other mental disorders (e.g., mood disorders, substance-related disorders) and in some general medical conditions (e.g., hyperthyroidism). See also CUED PANIC ATTACK; SITUATIONALLY PREDISPOSED PANIC ATTACK; UNCUED PANIC ATTACK.

panic control treatment a COGNITIVE BEHAVIOR THERAPY for panic disorder focusing on education about panic, training in slow breathing, and graded IN VIVO exposures to cues associated with panic. [developed by U.S. clinical psychologists Michelle G. Craske and David H. Barlow (1942–)]

panic disorder in *DSM–IV–TR*, an ANXIETY DISORDER characterized by recurrent, unexpected PANIC ATTACKS that are associated with (a) persistent concern about having another attack, (b) worry about the possible consequences of the attacks, (c) significant change in behavior related to the attacks (e.g., avoiding situations, engaging in SAFETY BEHAVIOR, not going out alone), or (d) a combination of any or all of these. Panic disorder associated with significant avoidance is classified as **panic disorder with agoraphobia** (see AGORAPHOBIA).

panpsychism *n.* the view that all elements of the natural world possess some quality of soul (psyche) or some form of sentience. Some equate this view with HYLOZOISM, which holds that all natural objects possess the quality of life, whereas others distinguish between life and soul or sentience. Also called **psychism**. See also ANIMISM; MIND STUFF.

pansexualism *n.* the view that all human behavior is motivated by the sexual drive. Sigmund FREUD has been popularly associated with such a view; however, although he emphasized the power of the sexual instinct, Freud also recognized nonsexual interests, such as the self-preservative drives (e.g., hunger and thirst) and the aggressive drive associated with the DEATH INSTINCT. **—pansexual** *adj.*

pantheism *n.* the doctrine that all of reality constitutes a unity and that this unity is divine. Thus, everything is part of God. Modern pantheism was first systematically propounded by Dutch Jewish philosopher Baruch Spinoza (1632–1677), who proposed that God and nature are coequivalent. Such a position is incompatible with traditional THEISM because it entails a God who is no more than the sum total of his creation. Some thinkers make a distinction between pantheism and **panentheism**, which maintains that God is everywhere in his creation but not coequivalent with it. **—pantheist** *adj., n.*

pantomime *n.* **1.** an expression of feelings and attitudes through gestures rather than words. **2.** a nonverbal therapeutic technique sometimes employed when verbal expression is blocked.

pantry-check technique an inspection of the kitchen shelves or cabinets of households to determine whether the subjects of advertising research actually use the products they claim to prefer. Interviews alone often prove inadequate: Some market-research control studies have shown that as many as 15% of individuals interviewed may claim to use, prefer, or at least be acquainted with a particular product that has never been marketed or advertised. See also RECOGNITION TECHNIQUE.

Panum phenomenon a visual illusion produced by binocular fusion of separate images presented to the left and right eyes, the fused image appearing closer to the eyes than the stimuli. [Peter Ludwig **Panum** (1820–1885), Danish physiologist]

Panum's fusional area the region in space surrounding a HOROPTER in which images that appear at different points on the two retinas are nonetheless fused by the visual system and so appear as single images. If visual targets appear outside this area (either in front of or behind it) they will appear as double images, and the observer will experience double vision. [Peter **Panum**]

papaverine *n.* an OPIUM ALKALOID first isolated in the 1840s. It has no psychopharmacological activity but is a potent vasodilator, being occasionally used in the treatment of angina pectoris, to increase blood flow in the cerebral arteries, or—when injected into the corpora cavernosa (see CORPUS CAVERNOSUM) of the penis—to produce erection in the management of impotence. U.S. trade name: **Para-Time S.R.**

paper-and-pencil test a test in which the questions or problems are written, printed, or drawn and the answers are written down.

paperless office a workplace in which computers, rather than papers, letters, and books, are used for communication, records, and so forth. The prediction that the advent of computers would result in the paperless office has proved false.

Papez circuit a circular network of nerve centers and fibers in the brain that is associated with emotion and memory. It includes the hippocampus, FORNIX, MAMMILLARY BODY, anterior thalamus, CINGULATE GYRUS, and PARAHIPPOCAMPAL GYRUS. Damage to any component of this system leads to amnesia. Also called **Papez circle**. See also PAPEZ'S THEORY OF EMOTION. [first described in 1937 by James W. **Papez** (1883–1958), U.S. neuroanatomist]

Papez–MacLean theory of emotion see MACLEAN'S THEORY OF EMOTION.

Papez's theory of emotion a modification of the CANNON–BARD THEORY proposing that the PAPEZ CIRCUIT is the site of integration and control of emotional experience in the higher brain centers. See also MACLEAN'S THEORY OF EMOTION. [James **Papez**]

papilla *n.* (*pl.* **papillae**) any of the four types of swellings on the tongue. In humans, some 200 FUNGIFORM PAPILLAE are toward the front of the tongue; 10–14 FOLIATE PAPILLAE are on the sides; 7–11 CIRCUMVALLATE PAPILLAE are on the back; and FILIFORM PAPILLAE, with no taste function, cover most of the tongue's surface. Also called **lingual papilla**.

papilledema *n.* a swelling of the OPTIC DISK due to an increase in intracranial pressure. The condition may occur because the meningeal membranes of the brain are continuous with the sheaths of the optic nerve, so that pressure can be transmitted to the eyeball. Also called **choked disk**.

PAQ abbreviation for POSITION ANALYSIS QUESTIONNAIRE.

para- (**par-**) *prefix* **1.** beside, near, or resembling (e.g., PARAPROFESSIONAL). **2.** abnormal or beyond (e.g., PARAPSYCHOLOGY).

parabiosis *n.* the artificial or natural joining of two individuals so their circulatory systems interconnect, as in the case of some CONJOINED TWINS.

parabiotic preparation two genetically similar animals that have been surgically joined at some anatomical structure, resulting in a shared circulation of blood. Parabiotic preparations are used for a variety of research purposes.

paracentral scotoma a small island of blindness in the central visual field surrounding, but not including, the fovea. **Monocular paracentral scotoma** (affecting one eye) results from impairment of the peripheral visual system, due, for example, to glaucoma or optic nerve atrophy; **homonymous paracentral scotoma** (affecting both eyes) is due to injury to the central visual system posterior to the LATERAL GENICULATE NUCLEUS. Patients with homonymous paracentral scotoma typically have difficulties with reading (**hemianopic dyslexia**). See also SCOTOMA.

paracentral vision a form of vision that utilizes the retinal area immediately surrounding, but not including, the FOVEA CENTRALIS. Compare CENTRAL VISION; PERIPHERAL VISION.

paracetamol *n.* see ACETAMINOPHEN.

parachlorophenylalanine *n.* a substance that blocks the synthesis of SEROTONIN from tryptophan, resulting in depletion of serotonin from brain cells.

parachromatopsia *n.* partial color blindness. Also called **parachromopsia**. See also DYSCHROMATOPSIA.

paracontrast *n.* a form of forward MASKING in which the perception of a visible stimulus (the target) is altered by the prior presentation of another visual stimulus (the mask) in a different spatial location. The target is often a small dot, while the mask is a ring that surrounds it. Each stimulus is presented very briefly (10–100 ms), at intervals that are varied systematically, and the quality of the target's percept is measured. Compare METACONTRAST.

paracrine *adj.* describing or relating to a type of cellular signaling in which a chemical messenger is released from a cell and diffuses to a nearby target cell, on which it exerts its effect, through the intervening extracellular space. Compare AUTOCRINE; ENDOCRINE.

paracusia *n.* **1.** partial deafness, especially to deeper tones. **2.** any abnormality of hearing other than simple deafness, such as **paracusia localis**, impairment in determining the direction from which a sound comes.

paracyesis *n.* see ECTOPIC PREGNANCY.

paradigm *n.* **1.** a model, pattern, or representative example, as of the functions and interrelationships of a process, a behavior under study, or the like. **2.** an experimental design or plan of the various steps of an experiment. **3.** a grammatical category or a collection of all inflectional forms of a word. **4.** a set of assumptions, attitudes, concepts, values, procedures, and techniques that constitutes a generally accepted theoretical framework within, or a general perspective of, a discipline.

paradigm clash in science or philosophy, the conflict that occurs when a new set of fundamental assumptions about reality or human knowledge proves incompatible with an established set of such assumptions. For example, the doctrine of organic evolution challenged established thinking about the origin and nature of the living world and ultimately replaced previous theories.

paradigm shift in the influential 1962 analysis of SCIENTIFIC REVOLUTIONS by U.S. historian and philosopher Thomas S. Kuhn (1922–1996), a very substantial and fairly rapid change in the whole pattern of ideas and assumptions defining the nature of a science and determining the methods and procedures employed.

paradox *n.* a surprising or self-contradictory statement that may nevertheless be true. In philosophy, paradoxes are traditionally classified as logical or semantic. A **logical paradox** occurs when apparently valid arguments lead to a conclusion that seems contradictory or absurd. For example: *God is omnipotent: Omnipotent beings can do anything: Therefore God can make a stone so big he cannot move it: Therefore he is not omnipotent.* A **semantic paradox** arises from the words in a proposition. For example: *This sentence is not true.* The language of paradox is particularly common in poetry and religion, where it may be used to disrupt conventional ways of thinking and perceiving. See also VICIOUS CIRCULARITY. **—paradoxical** *adj.*

paradoxical cold an effect produced in thermal nerve endings that are sensitive to both cold and heat. The nerve fibers have double peaks, including one for heat that is above the threshold of pain. Touching a hot object that fires a hot and cold receptor can produce an illusion of cold.

paradoxical directive an instruction by a therapist to the client to do precisely the opposite of what common sense would dictate in order to show the absurdity or self-defeating nature of the client's original intention. See also PARADOXICAL TECHNIQUE.

paradoxical intention a psychotherapeutic technique in which the client is asked to magnify a distressing, unwanted symptom. For example, an individual who is afraid of shaking in a social situation would be instructed to imagine the feared situation and purposely exaggerate the shakiness. The aim is to help clients distance themselves from their symptoms, often by appreciating the humorous aspects of their exaggerated responses. In this way clients can learn that the predicted catastrophic consequences attributed to their symptoms are very unlikely to occur. Paradoxical intention may be used to treat anxiety disorders but is not appropriate for suicidal behavior or schizophrenia. [originally developed by Austrian psychiatrist Viktor E. Frankl (1905–1997) for the treatment of phobias]

paradoxical motion the global perception of motion in a MOTION AFTEREFFECT even though the individual elements in the image do not appear to move.

paradoxical reaction in pharmacology, a drug reaction that is contrary to the expected effect, for example, worsening of anxiety after the administration of an anxiolytic agent.

paradoxical sleep see REM SLEEP.

paradoxical technique a therapeutic technique in which a client is directed by the therapist to continue undesired symptomatic behavior, and even increase it, to show that the client has voluntary control over the symptoms. Also called **paradoxical intervention**. See also PARADOXICAL DIRECTIVE.

paradoxical thinking cognition marked by contradiction of typical logical processes. Although this type of thinking can be associated with distorted thought processes, such as those present in SCHIZOID PERSONALITY DISORDER or some forms of schizophrenia, it can also be used as a way of reframing problems or negative beliefs in a positive manner. This approach is often embraced to promote creativity and used as a vehicle for personal, familial, and organizational change.

paradoxical warmth a sensation of warmth produced when a cold object of approximately 30 °C (86 °F) stimulates a cold receptor.

paradox of freedom a fundamental paradox that arises under assumptions of DETERMINISM in human behavior: namely, that although specific behaviors can be attributed to specific antecedent causes, humans almost universally experience a sense of being free to perform or refrain from performing any given behavior at the point of action. HARD DETERMINISM resolves this paradox by insisting that the sense of free choice is illusory, whereas SOFT DETERMINISM argues that such a sense is not in fact incompatible with causal explanations.

parafovea *n.* the region of the retina immediately surrounding the FOVEA CENTRALIS.

paragenital *adj.* relating to sexual intercourse in which conception is prevented. See BIRTH CONTROL.

parageusia *n.* **1.** a distorted sense of taste. **2.** a GUSTATORY HALLUCINATION. See also DYSGEUSIA.

paragigantocellular nucleus (**PGN**) a region of the brainstem RETICULAR FORMATION that is implicated in sleep.

paragrammatism *n.* a form of APHASIA consisting of substitutions, reversals, or omissions of sounds or syllables within words or reversals of words within sentences. Paragrammatic speech may be unintelligible if the disturbance is severe. **—paragrammatic** *adj.*

paragraphia *n.* a condition in which writing is distorted by transposition or omission of letters and words or insertion of incorrect and irrelevant words.

paragraph-meaning test an intelligence test, or a component of one, in which the participant is asked to explain the basic point, gist, or meaning of a paragraph.

parahippocampal gyrus a ridge (gyrus) on the medial (inner) surface of the TEMPORAL LOBE of cerebral cortex, lying over the HIPPOCAMPUS. It is a component of the LIMBIC SYSTEM thought to be involved in spatial or topographic memory. Also called **parahippocampal cortex**.

para I abbreviation for primipara. See PRIMIPAROUS.

parakinesia (**paracinesia**) *n.* awkwardness or clumsiness of movement.

parakinesis *n.* **1.** in parapsychology, see PSYCHOKINESIS. **2.** in medicine, an occasional synonym for PARAKINESIA.

paralalia *n.* **1.** a speech disorder or disturbance that involves the substitution of one speech sound for another (e.g., saying "wabbit" for *rabbit* or "lellow" for *yellow*). See also LALLING. **2.** a rarely used term for speech disorders generally.

paralanguage *n.* the vocal but nonverbal elements of

communication by speech. Paralanguage includes not only SUPRASEGMENTAL features of speech, such as tone and stress, but also such factors as volume and speed of delivery, voice quality, hesitations, and nonlinguistic sounds, such as sighs, whistles, or groans. These **paralinguistic cues** (or **paralinguistic features**) can be enormously important in shaping the total meaning of an utterance; they can, for example, convey the fact that a speaker is angry or sarcastic when this would not be apparent from the same words written down. In some uses, the term paralanguage is extended to include gestures, facial expressions, and other aspects of BODY LANGUAGE.

paraldehyde *n.* a sedative and hypnotic drug formerly used in the treatment of agitation or delirium tremens. It was relatively toxic, with a noted side effect of producing a characteristic breath odor, and has been abandoned in favor of safer alternatives. U.S. trade name: **Paral**.

paralexia *n.* the substitution or transposition of letters, syllables, or words during reading. See also VISUAL DYSLEXIA.

paralinguistic cues (**paralinguistic features**) see PARALANGUAGE.

parallax *n.* an illusion of movement of objects in the visual field when the head is moved from side to side. Objects beyond a point of visual fixation appear to move in the same direction as the head movement; those closer seem to move in the opposite direction. Parallax provides a monocular cue for DEPTH PERCEPTION.

parallel distributed circuit an interactive network that encompasses several different circuits at the same time to process the same stimuli. It is a relatively recent development in computers, but an ancient property of nervous systems.

parallel distributed processing (**PDP**) any model of cognition based on the idea that the representation of information is distributed as patterns of activation over a richly connected set of hypothetical neural units that function interactively and in parallel with one another. See DISTRIBUTED PROCESSING; PARALLEL PROCESSING. See also GRACEFUL DEGRADATION.

parallel fiber any of the axons of the GRANULE CELLS that form the outermost layer of the CEREBELLAR CORTEX.

parallel form see ALTERNATE FORM.

parallelism *n.* **1.** in general, the quality or condition of being parallel, structurally similar, or having corresponding features. **2.** in philosophy, the proposition that, although mind and body constitute separate realities, they function in parallel such that responses seem holistic and the two realms seem to assert causal control over each other. See MIND–BODY PROBLEM. See also OCCASIONALISM; PREESTABLISHED HARMONY. **3.** in anthropology, see CULTURAL PARALLELISM.

parallel play SOCIAL PLAY in which children play next to but not with each other. Compare ASSOCIATIVE PLAY; COOPERATIVE PLAY; SOLITARY PLAY.

parallel processing INFORMATION PROCESSING in which two or more sequences of operations are carried out simultaneously by independent processors. A capacity for parallel processing in the human mind would account for people's apparent ability to carry on different cognitive functions at the same time, as, for example, when driving a car while also listening to music and having a conversation. However, those who believe that there is no truly parallel processing in the brain explain this ability in terms of very rapid shifts between functions and information sources. The term parallel processing is usually reserved for processing at a higher, symbolic level, as opposed to the level of individual neural units described in models of PARALLEL DISTRIBUTED PROCESSING. Also called **simultaneous processing**. Compare SERIAL PROCESSING.

parallel search in a search task, the process of searching for many items at the same time, with no decrease in efficiency. Compare SERIAL SEARCH.

paralogia *n.* insistently illogical or delusional thinking and verbal expression, sometimes observed in schizophrenia. Swiss psychiatrist Eugen Bleuler (1857–1939) cited the example of a patient who justified his insistence that he was Switzerland by saying "Switzerland loves freedom. I love freedom. I am Switzerland." Also called **paralogical thinking**; **perverted logic**; **perverted thinking**. See also EVASION.

paralogism *n.* a fallacy or invalid argument, especially one that is unintentional and difficult to detect.

paralysis *n.* loss of function of voluntary muscles. A common cause is a lesion of the nervous or muscular system due to injury, disease, or congenital factors. The lesion may involve the central nervous system, as in a stroke, or the peripheral nervous system, as in GUILLAIN–BARRÉ SYNDROME. See also FLACCID PARALYSIS; SPASTIC PARALYSIS. **—paralytic** *adj.*

paralysis agitans an archaic name for PARKINSON'S DISEASE.

paralytic dementia see GENERAL PARESIS.

paramedic *n.* a health care professional who is specially trained and certified to assist medical professionals and, especially, to provide a wide range of emergency services prior to and during transportation to a hospital.

parameter *n.* **1.** a numerical constant that characterizes a population with respect to some attribute, for example, the location of its central point. **2.** an ARGUMENT of a function. **—parametric** *adj.*

parametric statistics statistical procedures that are based on assumptions about the distribution of the attribute (or attributes) in the population being tested. Compare NONPARAMETRIC STATISTICS.

paramimia *n.* the use of gestures inappropriate to or not congruent with one's underlying feelings.

paramimism *n.* a gesture or other movement that has a meaning to the patient although others may not understand its significance.

paramnesia *n.* see FALSE MEMORY.

paranoia *n.* **1.** a PARANOID STATE. **2.** in *DSM–III*, a relatively rare disorder, distinct from paranoid schizophrenia, in which the person reasons rightly from a wrong premise and develops a persistent, well-systematized, and logically constructed set of persecutory delusions, such as being conspired against or poisoned or maligned. The equivalent *DSM–IV–TR* diagnostic category is persecutory-type DELUSIONAL DISORDER. **3.** historically, any psychiatric disorder characterized by persistent delusions. See also CLASSICAL PARANOIA. **4.** in ancient times, any mental disorder or DELIRIUM. **—paranoiac** *n., adj.*

paranoiac character a personality type whose primary characteristic is a tendency to blame the environment for his or her difficulties.

paranoia querulans see LITIGIOUS PARANOIA.

paranoid *adj.* **1.** relating to or exhibiting extreme distrust or suspiciousness. See also PARANOID PERSONALITY DISORDER; PARANOID TENDENCY. **2.** relating to or characterized by DELUSIONS. See also DELUSIONAL DISORDER; PARANOID SCHIZOPHRENIA.

paranoid condition see PARANOID STATE.

paranoid delusion loosely, any of a variety of false personal beliefs tenaciously sustained even in the face of incontrovertible evidence to the contrary: DELUSIONS OF GRANDEUR, DELUSIONAL JEALOUSY, or, most frequently, DELUSIONS OF PERSECUTION.

paranoid disorder see DELUSIONAL DISORDER.

paranoid hostility anger and desire to harm others arising out of the delusion that they are persecuting or plotting against one.

paranoid ideation thought processes involving persistent suspiciousness and nondelusional beliefs of being persecuted, harassed, or treated unfairly by others.

paranoid litigious state see LITIGIOUS PARANOIA.

paranoid personality disorder in *DSM–IV–TR*, a personality disorder characterized by (a) pervasive, unwarranted suspiciousness and mistrust (such as expectation of trickery or harm, guardedness and secretiveness, avoidance of accepting blame, overconcern with hidden motives and meanings, and pathological jealousy); (b) hypersensitivity (such as being easily slighted and quick to take offense, making mountains out of molehills, and readiness to counterattack); and (c) restricted affectivity (such as emotional coldness, no true sense of humor, or absence of soft tender feelings).

paranoid pseudocommunity see PSEUDOCOMMUNITY.

paranoid psychosis a psychotic condition characterized by persecutory delusions without personality disorganization or deterioration. See DELUSIONAL DISORDER; PARANOID STATE.

paranoid-schizoid position in the OBJECT RELATIONS THEORY of Melanie KLEIN, the period from birth up to the 6th month of life during which infants perceive the world in terms of PART-OBJECTS and develop a fear of annihilation and persecutory anxiety due to the power of their DEATH INSTINCT. Infants use various primitive DEFENSE MECHANISMS to defend against these fears, including (a) PROJECTION of aggression onto an external object; (b) directing their own aggression against the imagined persecutory object; and (c) INTROJECTION and SPLITTING of the breast into a good object and a bad object (see BAD BREAST; GOOD BREAST). Compare DEPRESSIVE POSITION.

paranoid schizophrenia in *DSM–IV–TR*, a subtype of SCHIZOPHRENIA, often with a later onset than other types, characterized by prominent delusions or auditory hallucinations. Delusions are typically persecutory, grandiose, or both; hallucinations are typically related to the content of the delusional theme. Cognitive functioning and mood are affected to a much lesser degree than in other types of schizophrenia. The *DSM–III* designation was **paranoid type schizophrenic disorder**.

paranoid state a condition characterized by delusions of persecution or grandiosity that are not as systematized and elaborate as in a DELUSIONAL DISORDER or as disorganized and bizarre as in paranoid schizophrenia. Paranoid states are described in the *International Classification of Diseases* (9th edition) but not in *DSM–IV–TR*. Also called **paranoid condition**.

paranoid system of beliefs delusional beliefs of persecution, reference to the self, grandiosity, and the like. See also CIRCUMSCRIBED BELIEF.

paranoid tendency a propensity toward feelings of mistrust, persecutory beliefs, and negative perceptions of oneself and others. See also PARANOID PERSONALITY DISORDER; PARANOID STATE.

paranormal *adj.* denoting any phenomenon involving the transfer of information or energy that cannot be explained by existing scientific knowledge. The term is particularly applied to those forms of alleged EXTRASENSORY PERCEPTION that are the province of parapsychological investigation (see PARAPSYCHOLOGY). See also OCCULT; PRETERNATURAL; SUPERNATURAL.

paranormal cognition see EXTRASENSORY PERCEPTION.

paranosic gains see PRIMARY GAINS.

paraphasia *n.* a speech disturbance characterized by the use of incorrect, distorted, or inappropriate words, which in some cases resemble the correct word in sound or meaning and in other cases are irrelevant or nonsensical. For example, a wheelchair may be called a "spinning wheel," and a hypodermic needle might be called a "tie pin." The disorder occurs in a variety of forms (e.g., LITERAL PARAPHASIA, SEMANTIC PARAPHASIA) and is seen most commonly in organic brain disorders and PICK'S DISEASE. **—paraphasic** *adj.*

paraphemia *n.* a speech disorder marked by the habitual introduction of inappropriate words or by the meaningless combination of words.

paraphilia *n.* in *DSM–IV–TR*, a sexual disorder in which unusual or bizarre fantasies or behavior are necessary for sexual excitement. The fantasies or acts persist over a period of at least 6 months and may take several forms: preference for a nonhuman object, such as animals or clothes of the opposite sex; repetitive sexual activity involving real or simulated suffering or humiliation, as in whipping or bondage; or repetitive sexual activity with nonconsenting partners. Paraphilias include such specific types as FETISHISM, FROTTEURISM, PEDOPHILIA, EXHIBITIONISM, VOYEURISM, SEXUAL MASOCHISM, and SEXUAL SADISM. **—paraphiliac** *adj.*

paraphilia not otherwise specified in *DSM–IV–TR*, a residual category comprising PARAPHILIAS, such as COPROPHILIA, NECROPHILIA, and UROPHILIA, that do not meet the diagnostic criteria for any specific type.

paraphonia *n.* an abnormal change in voice quality.

paraphrase *vb.* to express the meaning of a text or utterance in different words, often for the sake of clarity or brevity. See also INTERPRET.

paraphrasia *n.* see WORD SALAD. **—paraphrasic** *adj.*

paraphrasic error an error that results in incoherent speech, most often from combining existing words, eliminating syllables from words, or creating new words. See WORD SALAD.

paraphrenia *n.* **1.** a late-onset psychotic condition that is marked by delusions and hallucinations but is distinct from schizophrenia by virtue of the absence of generalized intellectual impairment and distinct from degenerative dementias by virtue of the absence of a progressively deteriorating course. Although paraphrenia is not listed in *DSM–IV–TR* or *ICD–10*, it is still used as a diagnostic entity in some parts of the world. See also LATE PARAPHRENIA. [first described by German psychiatrist Emil Kraepelin (1856–1926)] **2.** any of various mental disorders that are associated with transitional periods of life (i.e., adolescence or old age). [defined in 1863 by German physician Karl Ludwig Kahlbaum (1828–1899)] **3.** loosely, any of a variety of conditions, such as LATE-ONSET SCHIZOPHRENIA, PARANOID SCHIZOPHRENIA, or certain PARANOID STATES.

paraplegia *n.* paralysis of the legs and lower part of the trunk. See also SPASTIC PARAPLEGIA. **—paraplegic** *adj.*

parapraxis *n.* an error that is believed to express unconscious wishes, attitudes, or impulses. Examples of such errors include slips of the pen, SLIPS OF THE TONGUE and other forms of VERBAL LEAKAGE, forgetting significant events, mislaying objects with unpleasant associations, unintentional puns, and motivated accidents. Also called **parapraxia**. See also FREUDIAN SLIP; SYMPTOMATIC ACT.

paraprofessional *n.* a trained but not professionally credentialed worker who assists in the treatment of patients in both hospital and community settings.

parapsychology *n.* the systematic study of alleged psychological phenomena involving the transfer of information or energy that cannot be explained in terms of presently known scientific data or laws. Such study has focused largely on the various forms of EXTRASENSORY PERCEPTION, such as TELEPATHY and CLAIRVOYANCE, but also encompasses such phenomena as alleged POLTERGEIST activity and the claims of MEDIUMS. Although parapsychology is committed to scientific methods and procedures, it is still regarded with suspicion by most scientists, including most psychologists. There are perhaps three main reasons for this: (a) the fact that admitting even one instance of paranormal causation would overthrow virtually all the established laws and principles of science; (b) the fact that even the best-documented positive findings in this area have proved impossible to replicate; and (c) the notorious fact that some researchers have been duped by charlatans. See also ZENER CARDS. **—parapsychological** *adj.* **—parapsychologist** *n.*

parareaction *n.* an abnormal or exaggerated reaction to a relatively minor incident (e.g., tripping), which may become the basis for a delusion.

parasexuality *n.* any form of sexual behavior not involving normal sexual acts performed with a consenting adult partner or normal masturbation. See PARAPHILIA.

parasite *n.* a species that depends on another for survival but generally does not kill it (see PARASITISM). There are many intestinal parasites that are of value in the digestion of food for their hosts. Some parasites induce illness or debilitation but do not weaken the host so severely that it (and therefore the parasite) will die. Others will survive if they can find an alternative host before the death of their current host. Some parasites can alter the behavior of their hosts to make transfer to another host more likely. **—parasitic** *adj.*

parasitism *n.* **1.** in biology, an INTERSPECIES INTERACTION in which one organism, the PARASITE, lives on or in an organism of another species, the host. The arrangement is beneficial to the parasite but usually harmful to the host. **2.** by analogy, a social relationship in which one individual habitually benefits from the generosity of others without making any useful return.

parasomnia *n.* a SLEEP DISORDER characterized by abnormal behavior or physiological events occurring during sleep or the transitional state between sleep and waking. In *DSM–IV–TR* parasomnias comprise NIGHTMARE DISORDER, SLEEP TERROR DISORDER, SLEEPWALKING DISORDER, and PARASOMNIA NOT OTHERWISE SPECIFIED and form one of two broad groups of primary sleep disorders, the other being DYSSOMNIAS. See also DYSFUNCTIONS ASSOCIATED WITH SLEEP, SLEEP STAGES, OR PARTIAL AROUSALS.

parasomnia not otherwise specified in *DSM–IV–TR,* a diagnostic category reserved for sleep disturbances that are characterized by abnormal behavior or physiological events during sleep but do not meet criteria for a more specific PARASOMNIA. Examples include REM BEHAVIOR DISORDER and SLEEP PARALYSIS.

parasuicide *n.* a range of behaviors involving deliberate self-harm that falls short of suicide and may or may not be intended to result in death. It includes ATTEMPTED SUICIDE and PASSIVE SUICIDE.

parasympathetic drugs see CHOLINERGIC DRUGS.

parasympathetic nervous system one of two branches of the AUTONOMIC NERVOUS SYSTEM (ANS, which controls smooth muscle and gland functions), the other being the SYMPATHETIC NERVOUS SYSTEM. Anatomically it comprises the portion of the ANS whose preganglionic fibers leave the central nervous system from the brainstem via the OCULOMOTOR, FACIAL, GLOSSOPHARYNGEAL, and VAGUS NERVES and the spinal cord via three sacral nerves (see SPINAL NERVE). It is defined functionally as the system controlling rest, repair, enjoyment, eating, sleeping, sexual activity, and social dominance, among other functions. The parasympathetic nervous system stimulates salivary secretions and digestive secretions in the stomach and produces pupillary constriction, decreases in heart rate, and increased blood flow to the genitalia during sexual excitement. Also called **parasympathetic division**.

parasympatholytic drugs see ANTICHOLINERGIC DRUGS.

parasympathomimetic drugs see CHOLINERGIC DRUGS.

parataxic distortion in psychoanalytic theory, a distorted perception or judgment of others on the basis of past experiences or of the unconscious. Also called **transference distortion**. [introduced by U.S. psychoanalyst Harry Stack Sullivan (1892–1949)]

parataxis *n.* **1.** broadly, a lack of integration among components of personality, cognitive style, or emotions. The term is now infrequently used. **2.** in language, joining syntactic units (e.g., words, phrases) without the use of conjunctions, as in *I came; I saw; I conquered.*

parateresiomania *n.* an abnormal desire to observe others undressing or engaging in sexual activities. In *DSM–IV–TR* this is called VOYEURISM.

parathyroid gland a small, paired endocrine gland found in the area of the thyroid gland. It secretes PARATHYROID HORMONE, which takes part in the control of calcium and phosphate metabolism.

parathyroid hormone a hormone secreted by the PARATHYROID GLANDS when blood-calcium levels are low. It promotes dissolution of bone tissue and absorption of calcium by the intestine, thereby increasing the concentration of calcium (and phosphate) in the blood. Thus, together with CALCITONIN, it participates in calcium regulation. Also called **parathyrin**.

Para-Time S.R. a trade name for PAPAVERINE.

paratype *n.* the totality of environmental influences that act on an organism to produce individual expression of a genetic trait or character.

paratypic *adj.* referring to the acquired properties (as opposed to genetic endowments) of an organism that result from exposure to environmental forces.

paraventricular nucleus (**PVN**) a nucleus of the HYPOTHALAMUS. Neurons in this nucleus synthesize the hormones oxytocin and vasopressin.

paraverbal therapy a method of psychotherapy, introduced in the 1970s, for children who have difficulty communicating verbally and are also affected by such conditions and disorders as hyperactivity, autism, withdrawal, or language disturbances. Assuming that these children would feel more intrigued and less threatened by a nonverbal approach, the therapy uses various expressive media, including the components of music (tempo and pitch), mime, movement, and art in unorthodox ways to help the children express themselves. The therapist participates on the children's level, and eventually the children feel safe enough to verbalize their real feelings, enabling them to participate in more conventional therapy. [developed by Evelyn P. Heimlich]

paraworld *n.* a hypothetical world of ideal conditions that serves as a basis for formulating a model of some system or process believed to be true in the actual world. Such model building can be an important strategy in science.

paregoric *n.* a medication containing a tincture of opium that is administered to control severe cases of diarrhea. It relieves pain and discomfort and reduces intestinal motility. It is also used to treat opioid withdrawal in neonates and may be used as well with children and adults. Besides opium, paregoric contains camphor, benzoic acid, glycerin, anise oil, and alcohol. It was developed in the early 18th century. Also called **camphorated tincture of opium**.

parenchyma *n.* the functioning tissues of an organ or gland, as distinguished from supporting or connecting tissues. **—parenchymatous** *adj.*

parens patriae a doctrine promoting the power and interest of the government (Latin, "parent of the country") in caring for and protecting minors and individuals who are unable to care for themselves or to provide for their own basic needs, even if this necessitates restricting their rights. In the United States, this power and interest is vested with the individual states.

parental behavior the process of preparing for the birth of offspring (often through nest building) and the actions of one or both parents that contribute to the survival or well-being of their young. The latter include (a) provisioning the young through NURSING BEHAVIOR (in mammals) or with food (in birds and weaned mammals), (b) RETRIEVING BEHAVIOR or carrying young in species that do not build permanent nests, and (c) weaning the offspring so that they can become independent. Many hormonal controls of parental behavior have been identified in females (as well as in males of those species in which males participate in care of young). Among human beings and other primates, parental behavior is less dependent on hormonal changes and more dependent on cultural and experiential factors than among other animals, although such hormonal changes still occur.

parental imperative a hypothesis stating that while raising children both men and women adopt distinct, stereotypical gender roles as a means of successfully fulfilling the demands of parenthood. Once this parental imperative lessens, however, these gender role orientations change in favor of more androgynous identities; for example, women become more assertive and competitive, while men become more contemplative and expressive. [proposed by U.S. psychologist David L. Gutmann (1925–)]

parental investment the amount of energy a parent expends in parental care. Because ova are much larger than sperm, and female mammals go through gestation and subsequent lactation, it is often assumed that female mammals have greater parental investment than males. However, there is considerable male parental investment in COOPERATIVE-BREEDING species, such as marmoset and tamarin monkeys, in which males can lose up to 10% of body weight during the period when offspring must be carried constantly. Male parental investment may also be high in species in which males defend the young from predators or attacks from other members of the same species.

parental investment theory the proposition that many sex differences in sexually reproducing species (including humans) can be understood in terms of the amount of time, energy, and risk to their own survival that males and females put into parenting versus mating (including the seeking, attaining, and maintaining of a mate). Differences in parenting and mating investment between males and females vary among species and as a function of environmental conditions. [proposed in 1972 by U.S. sociobiologist Robert L. Trivers (1943–)]

parental perplexity a parent–child relationship marked by a lack of parental spontaneity, extreme indecisiveness, and an inability to sense and satisfy the child's needs. Such primary relationships may result in psychological problems (e.g., overdependency) during childhood and have further consequences throughout development.

parental rejection persistent denial of approval, affection, or care by one or both parents, sometimes concealed beneath a cover of overindulgence or overprotection. The frequent result is corrosion of the child's self-esteem and self-confidence, a poor self-image, inability to form attachments to others, tantrums, generalized hostility, and development of psychophysical and emotional disturbances. See CHILD NEGLECT.

parent counseling professional guidance of parents on problems related to raising their children, including their own roles in this process.

parent effectiveness training (PET) a set of principles providing guidance for prosocial interactions between children and parents related to discipline, communication, and responsible relationships. Guidelines are also provided for client-centered discussions of principles, practices, and problems of child rearing conducted by a mental health professional on a group basis. A balance is maintained between the child's feelings and needs and those of the parents. One of the most notable concepts is to determine who is responsible for (i.e., owns) the problem and who owns the solution for resolving a conflict. [introduced in 1962 by U.S. psychologist Thomas Gordon (1918–2002)]

parenteral drug administration any route of administration of a drug other than via the digestive tract (parenteral literally means not enteric, or not through the gut). Such routes include subcutaneous, intramuscular, and intravenous injection; rectal and vaginal suppositories; inhalation; and absorption through the skin or mucous membranes.

parent image a representation of the parent that exists in the mind of the individual but not necessarily as an accurate image: for example, it may be an idealized version of the real parent.

parenting *n.* all actions related to the raising of offspring. Researchers have described different human **parenting styles**—ways in which parents interact with their children—with most classifications varying on the dimensions of emotional warmth (warm versus cold) and control (high in control versus low in control).

Parenting Stress Index (PSI) an instrument used to assess stress in parent–child interactions and to identify potentially dysfunctional parenting behaviors or potential behavior problems in the child. It currently consists of 120 questionnaire items to which parents respond using a 5-point LIKERT SCALE format, ranging from "strongly agree" to "strongly disagree." Originally published in 1983, the PSI is now in its third edition (published in 1995). [developed by U.S. educational psychologist Richard R. Abidin (1938–)]

parenting style see PARENTING.

parenting training any program that instructs parents and other caregivers in techniques for effectively dealing with problem behavior in their children. Also called **parent training**.

parent management training a treatment approach based on the principles of OPERANT CONDITIONING. Parents use antecedents, behaviors, and consequences to change child and adolescent behavior at home, at school, and in other settings. The goals are to help children develop prosocial behaviors and decrease oppositional, aggressive, and antisocial behaviors.

parent–offspring conflict a conflict that arises when parents cease providing care for current offspring and invest in producing the next set of offspring. The parents will benefit in terms of REPRODUCTIVE SUCCESS by breeding again as soon as the current offspring have a high probability of surviving independently. The offspring, however, will gain more by continued investment from their parents, creating the conflict. Parent–offspring conflict is manifested through regressive behavior, including tantrums, by the older offspring and through SIBLING RIVALRY.

Parents Anonymous a peer-led, professionally facilitated group for parents who would like to learn more effective methods of childrearing, thus strengthening families and providing a means of preventing child abuse.

Parents Without Partners an international organization providing mutual social support, educational programs, and activities for single parents and their children.

parent teachers association (**PTA**) an organization consisting of instructors and the parents of students. Its aims are to assist parents with parenting skills, to support and create a forum for students in the community and government, and to encourage public and parental involvement in public schools. The **National Parent Teachers Association** (**NPTA**) is a not-for-profit organization whose goal is to improve the welfare of children and young people. Its primary activities include public education, strengthening schools in large cities, and preventing substance abuse among students. It has also worked in many areas of child health and safety through various educational projects.

parergasia *n.* **1.** a symptom of SCHIZOPHRENIA in which the individual performs an action that is not intended, such as opening the mouth when asked to close the eyes. [defined by German psychiatrist Emil Kraepelin (1856–1926)] **2.** a former name for schizophrenia, introduced by Swiss-born U.S. psychiatrist Adolf Meyer (1866–1950) to replace DEMENTIA PRAECOX, since he believed this disorder is best described in terms of disorganized behavior and distorted thought processes.

paresis *n.* partial or incomplete paralysis.

paresthesia *n.* an abnormal skin sensation, such as tingling, tickling, burning, itching, or pricking, in the absence of external stimulation. Paresthesia may be temporary, as in the "pins and needles" feeling that many people experience (e.g., after having sat with legs crossed too long), or chronic and due to such factors as neurological disorder or drug side effects. **—paresthetic** *adj.*

paretic *adj.* relating to or experiencing PARESIS.

paretic psychosis see GENERAL PARESIS.

Pareto principle **1.** in economics, the principle that 80% of the wealth in any society will be owned by 20% of the population. **2.** more generally, the principle that 80% of any given output is produced by 20% of input. For example, in any retail organization 80% of the sales will be accounted for by 20% of the customers. Also called **80:20 rule**. [Vilfredo **Pareto** (1848–1923), Italian economist and sociologist]

parica *n.* see EPENA.

parietal cortex the cerebral cortex of the PARIETAL LOBE.

parietal drift see POSTURAL ARM DRIFT.

parietal lobe one of the four main lobes of each cerebral hemisphere (see CEREBRUM). It occupies the upper central area of each hemisphere, behind the FRONTAL LOBE, ahead of the OCCIPITAL LOBE, and above the TEMPORAL LOBE. Parts of the parietal lobe participate in somatosensory activities, such as discrimination of size, shape, and texture of objects; visual activities, such as visually guided actions; and auditory activities, such as speech perception.

parietal neglect see UNILATERAL NEGLECT.

parieto-occipital sulcus a groove (sulcus) that runs upward along the medial (inner) side of each cerebral hemisphere, extending from a junction with the CALCARINE FISSURE at a point posterior to the SPLENIUM, and forming the border between the CUNEUS and PRECUNEUS regions.

Paris Medical School a group of doctors and students at the Salpêtrière hospital in Paris who advanced the hypotheses and research of French neurologist Jean-Martin Charcot (1825–1893), particularly with regard to his neurological studies of a posited relation between hysteria and hypnotism. Sigmund FREUD, who studied through a fellowship under Charcot, was greatly influenced by the Paris Medical School in his early studies and in the direction of his future work.

Parkes–Weber syndrome see STURGE–WEBER SYNDROME.

parkinsonian *adj.* of or relating to Parkinson's disease or parkinsonism.

parkinsonian tremor see RESTING TREMOR.

parkinsonism *n.* any disorder whose symptoms resemble those of PARKINSON'S DISEASE without the actual presence of the disease entity. Antipsychotic agents with strong dopamine-blocking activity, particularly the HIGH-POTENCY ANTIPSYCHOTICS (e.g., haloperidol), may cause the reversible syndrome known as **drug-induced parkinsonism** (**pseudoparkinsonism**).

Parkinson's disease a progressive neurodegenerative disease caused by the death of dopamine-producing neurons in the SUBSTANTIA NIGRA of the brain, which controls balance and coordinates muscle movement. Symptoms typically begin late in life with mild tremors (see RESTING TREMOR), increasing rigidity of the limbs, and slowness of voluntary movements. Later symptoms include postural instability, impaired balance, and difficulty walking (see FESTINATING GAIT). DEMENTIA occurs in some 20–60% of patients, usually in older patients in whom the disease is far advanced. [first described in 1817 by James **Parkinson** (1755–1824), British physician]

Parlodel *n.* a trade name for BROMOCRIPTINE.

parole *n.* **1.** in psychology and psychiatry, a method of maintaining supervision of a patient whose treatment is mandated by the court and who has not been discharged, but who is away from the confines of a restrictive setting, such as a mental institution or halfway house. A patient on parole may be returned to the hospital at any time without formal action by a court. **2.** supervised release from confinement in a correctional facility.

parorexia *n.* a pathological compulsion to consume unusual foods or nonnutritive substances. See also CISSA; PICA.

parosmia *n.* a disorder of the sense of smell in which a person is unable to distinguish odors correctly. For example, when presented with an odor of beer the person might say it smells of bleach. Also called **parosphresia**. See also DYSOSMIA; TROPOSMIA.

paroxetine *n.* an antidepressant of the SSRI class. It is currently one of the most commonly prescribed antidepressants. Like other SSRIs, it is used to treat depression and anxiety disorders, such as panic disorder, social phobia, and obsessive-compulsive disorder. It differs from other SSRIs in that most patients find it to be sedating rather than activating; paroxetine should therefore be taken in the evening rather than on rising. It should not be taken by patients who are already taking MONOAMINE OXIDASE INHIBITORS. Paroxetine is available in immediate- and controlled-release preparations. U.S. trade name: **Paxil**.

paroxysm *n.* **1.** the sudden intensification or recurrence of a disease or an emotional state. **2.** a convulsion, spasm, or seizure. **—paroxysmal** *adj.*

paroxysmal sleep see NARCOLEPSY.

Parry's disease see GRAVES' DISEASE. [Caleb Hillier **Parry** (1755–1822), British physician]

parse *vb.* **1.** in vision, to deconstruct a complex stimulus into its component features and attributes. **2.** in linguistics, to analyze a sentence into its constituent parts, such as subject, verb, object, and the like, in order to map its syntactic structure.

parsimony *n.* see LAW OF PARSIMONY.

part correlation the correlation between two variables with the influence of a third variable removed from one (but only one) of the two variables. Also called **semipartial correlation**. Compare PARTIAL CORRELATION.

parthenogenesis *n.* literally, virgin birth: the production of offspring without fertilization of the egg cells by sperm. It is the usual means of reproduction in some species. **—parthenogenetic** *adj.*

partial *n.* any frequency component in a COMPLEX TONE. A partial is not necessarily a HARMONIC.

partial agonist a substance that binds to a receptor but fails to produce the same degree of response as a full AGONIST at the same receptor site or exerts only part of the action exerted by the endogenous neurotransmitter that it mimics. Partial agonists may exhibit the same affinity for the receptor site as do full agonists and may act as competitive inhibitors of full agonists. Minor variations in the chemical structure of either the receptor or the binding substance may dictate whether the substance acts as a full or partial agonist at any particular receptor site.

partial agraphia an older, less common name for DYSGRAPHIA.

partial concealment the concealment by a researcher only of who or what is being observed.

partial correlation the correlation between two variables with the influence of one or more other variables on their intercorrelation statistically removed or held constant. Compare PART CORRELATION.

partial decussation see OPTIC CHIASM.

partial hospitalization hospital treatment of patients on a part-time basis (i.e., less than 24 hours per day). See DAY HOSPITAL; NIGHT HOSPITAL; WEEKEND HOSPITALIZATION.

partial insanity a borderline condition in which mental impairment is present but is not sufficiently severe to render the individual completely irresponsible for his or her criminal acts. In legal proceedings, a conclusion of partial insanity may arise when there is evidence that a mental disorder was probably a contributing cause to a defendant's actions, or that the disorder rendered the individual incapable of deliberation, premeditation, malice, or another mental state usually requisite for first-degree offenses; in such circumstances it may lead to conviction for a lesser offense. See also DIMINISHED RESPONSIBILITY; INSANITY; MCNAUGHTEN RULE.

partial instinct see COMPONENT INSTINCT.

partialism *n.* a type of PARAPHILIA in which a person obtains sexual satisfaction from contact with a body part of the sexual partner other than the usual erotic areas such as lips, breasts, and genitals (e.g., a leg). Partialism is distinguished from FETISHISM in which an object, such as a shoe, replaces the sexual partner.

partial least squares a variant on MULTIPLE REGRESSION analysis designed for the construction of predictive models when there are many highly interrelated predictor variables.

partial lipodystrophy a LIPID-METABOLISM DISORDER that is usually acquired during infancy. There is a symmetric absence of adipose tissue in the face, but fat may or may not be absent from the regions above the legs. See LIPODYSTROPHY. See also TOTAL LIPODYSTROPHY.

partially ordered scale a scale of measurement that falls partway between a NOMINAL SCALE and an ORDINAL SCALE, such that the scaling units can, on average (but not always), be ordered or ranked from smallest to largest.

partial reinforcement see INTERMITTENT REINFORCEMENT.

partial reinforcement effect (**PRE**) increased RESISTANCE TO EXTINCTION after intermittent reinforcement rather than after continuous reinforcement. Also called **partial reinforcement extinction effect** (**PREE**).

partial report a method of testing memory in which only some of the total information presented is to be recalled. For example, if several rows of letters are shown to the participant, a cue given afterward may prompt recall of only one particular row. Partial report methods are used to minimize OUTPUT INTERFERENCE in studies of ICONIC MEMORY. Compare WHOLE REPORT.

partial schedule of reinforcement see INTERMITTENT REINFORCEMENT.

partial seizure a seizure that begins in a localized area of the brain, although it may subsequently progress to a GENERALIZED SEIZURE. **Simple partial seizures** produce no alteration of consciousness despite clinical manifestations, which may include sensory, motor, or autonomic activity. COMPLEX PARTIAL SEIZURES may produce similar sensory, motor, or autonomic symptoms but are also characterized by some impairment or alteration of consciousness during the event. Partial seizures of both types are most commonly focused in the temporal lobe. Also called **focal seizure**.

partial sight see LOW VISION.

participant *n.* a person who takes part in an investigation, study, or experiment, for example by performing tasks set by the experimenter or by answering questions set by a researcher. The participant may be further identified as an **experimental participant** (see EXPERIMENTAL GROUP) or a **control participant** (see CONTROL GROUP). Participants are also called SUBJECTS, although the former term is now often preferred when referring to humans.

participant modeling a procedure for changing behavior in which effective styles of behavior are modeled (e.g., by a therapist) for an individual and then various aids are introduced to help the individual master the tasks. [developed by Albert BANDURA]

participant observation a type of observational method in which a trained observer enters the group under study as a member, while avoiding a conspicuous role that would alter the group processes and bias the data. Cultural anthropologists become PARTICIPANT OBSERVERS when they enter the life of a given culture to study its structure and processes.

participant observer an individual who enters a group under study as a member while, at the same time, functioning as a scientific observer of the processes and structure of the group.

participation *n.* **1.** taking part in an activity, usually one that involves others in a joint endeavor. **2.** the interaction of two or more systems that mutually influence each other. **3.** in Jean PIAGET's theory of cognitive development, the tendency of children to confuse their wishes, fantasies, or dreams with reality. **—participate** *vb.*

participative decision-making (PDM) the management practice of allowing employees to participate in the decision-making process. The extent of participation can vary from a relatively low level, in which employees provide input or consult with decision-makers, to the highest level, in which employees are fully involved and actually make the decisions. See INDUSTRIAL DEMOCRACY; QUALITY CIRCLE; SCANLON PLAN.

participative leadership a LEADERSHIP STYLE in which followers are allowed to become involved in decision-making and are given autonomy in performing their tasks.

participative management a style of management that involves PARTICIPATIVE DECISION-MAKING and PARTICIPATIVE LEADERSHIP.

participatory design in ergonomics, design practice that supports direct input from end users during the DEVELOPMENT CYCLE.

participatory ergonomics a process in which employees at all levels within an organization are directly and actively involved in developing or enhancing ergonomic practices to improve worker health and safety.

participatory evaluation a type of PROGRAM EVALUATION in which the individuals who provided a service also have a role in the evaluation of the service or program. The official evaluator facilitates the evaluation and acts primarily as a resource person, rather than actually conducting the evaluation. Also called **collaborative evaluation**; **empowerment evaluation**.

particularism *n.* **1.** in philosophy, a solution to the so-called **criterion problem**, which states that one cannot know whether one has knowledge because to recognize particular bits of knowledge one would need to know the criteria by which they are judged to be knowledge, and in order to know the criteria, one would already have to be able to recognize bits of knowledge. Particularism resolves this problem by stating that no general criteria are necessary to determine particular bits of knowledge. **2.** in ethics, the doctrine that there are no general moral principles and that judgments of moral behavior cannot be made on the basis of such principles. Moral judgments must take account of many particular factors in a person's background and current situation. This position tends toward moral RELATIVISM. See also MORAL NIHILISM; SUBJECTIVISM. **—particularist** *adj.*

part-list cuing inhibition in a RECALL test, impairment of the capacity to recall individual items if some of the other items in the list studied are provided as retrieval CUES. Also called **part-set cuing effect**.

part method of learning a learning technique in which the material is divided into sections, each to be mastered separately in a successive order. Compare WHOLE METHOD OF LEARNING.

partner abuse see DOMESTIC VIOLENCE.

partner swapping see WIFE SWAPPING.

part-object *n.* **1.** in psychoanalytic theory, an OBJECT toward which a COMPONENT INSTINCT is directed. Such an object is usually a part of the body rather than a whole person. **2.** in the OBJECT RELATIONS THEORY of Melanie KLEIN, an early object representation that derives from SPLITTING the object into parts containing negative and positive qualities. It is held that such objects constitute the infant's first experience of the world, being perceived as a GOOD OBJECT or a BAD OBJECT according to whether they are gratifying or frustrating. INTERNALIZATION of part-objects is further posited to represent the beginning of the inner world of objects whose relationships create the infant's personality. See also DEPRESSIVE POSITION; PARANOID-SCHIZOID POSITION.

part-set cuing effect see PART-LIST CUING INHIBITION.

parturition *n.* the act or process of giving birth to a child (or children, in the case of a multiple birth).

part–whole problem 1. the controversy over whether to approach an issue, particularly a psychological one, from an atomistic or a holistic perspective, that is, whether to view some phenomenon as a structured set of components or as an integrated functioning totality. **2.** the problem of whether to learn something by memorizing its constituent parts or by attempting to commit the totality to memory.

parvocellular system the part of the visual system that projects to or originates from small neurons in the four dorsal layers (the **parvocellular layers**) of the LATERAL GENICULATE NUCLEUS. It allows the perception of fine details, colors, and large changes in brightness. The parvocellular system is expanded in primates compared to other animals; it conducts information relatively slowly because of its small cells and slender axons. Compare MAGNOCELLULAR SYSTEM.

PAS abbreviation for PRECATEGORICAL ACOUSTIC STORAGE.

pascal *n.* see SOUND PRESSURE.

Pascal distribution see NEGATIVE BINOMIAL DISTRIBUTION. [Blaise **Pascal** (1623–1662), French mathematician]

pasmo *n.* see SUSTO.

passband *n.* see FILTER.

passion *n.* **1.** an intense, driving, or overwhelming feeling or conviction. Passion is often contrasted with emotion, in that passion affects a person unwillingly. **2.** intense sexual desire. **3.** a strong liking or enthusiasm for or devotion to an activity, object, concept, or the like. **—passionate** *adj.*

passionate love a type of love in which sexual passion and a high level of emotional arousal are prominent features; along with COMPANIONATE LOVE, it is one of the two main types of love identified by social psychologists. Passionate lovers typically are greatly preoccupied with the loved person, want their feelings to be reciprocated, and are usually greatly distressed when the relationship seems awry. See also LIMERENCE; ROMANTIC LOVE; TRIANGULAR THEORY OF LOVE.

passionflower *n.* a climbing herb, *Passiflora incarnata*, indigenous to the southeastern United States and other subtropical areas but also cultivated as an ornamental plant. Parts of the plant have been used both externally and internally for a variety of medicinal purposes, ranging from treatment of burns and hemorrhoids to the alleviation of neuralgia and spasms or seizures. **Passionflower tea** has long been a folk remedy for the relief of nervous tension. Although some studies suggest passionflower has sedative properties and it has been approved by Commission E, a committee of 24 interdisciplinary health care professionals formed in 1978 by the German Federal Institute for Drugs and Medical Devices, for treatment of insomnia and anxiety, definitive clinical evidence of this effect has not been established. Adverse reactions are rare, but may include nausea, vomiting, and rapid heart rate.

passive *adj.* **1.** acted upon rather than acting. **2.** describing a personality pattern that is submissive, compliant, easily influenced by external forces, and dependent on others. See also DEPENDENT PERSONALITY DISORDER. **3.** in grammar, denoting the PASSIVE VOICE of a verb.

passive-aggressive *adj.* characteristic of behavior that is seemingly innocuous, accidental, or neutral but that indirectly displays an unconscious aggressive motive. For example, a child who appears to be compliant but is routinely late for school, misses the bus, or forgets his or her homework may be expressing unconscious resentment at having to attend school.

passive-aggressive personality disorder a personality disorder of long standing in which AMBIVALENCE toward the self and others is expressed by such means as procrastination, dawdling, stubbornness, intentional inefficiency, "forgetting" appointments, or misplacing important materials. These maneuvers are interpreted as passive expressions of underlying ambivalence and NEGATIVISM. The pattern persists even where more adaptive behavior is clearly possible; it frequently interferes with occupational, domestic, and academic success. This disorder is classified in the appendix of *DSM–IV–TR* and given an alternative name, **negativistic personality disorder**, in accordance with the theoretical proposals of U.S. psychologist Theodore Millon (1929–).

passive algolagnia interest and pleasure derived from experiencing pain during sexual activity, that is, from being the masochist in a relationship involving SADOMASOCHISM.

passive avoidance a type of OPERANT CONDITIONING in which the individual must refrain from an explicit act or response that will produce an aversive stimulus. Compare ACTIVE AVOIDANCE.

passive-avoidance learning a commonly used misnomer for PUNISHMENT. It is usually used in situations in which the behavior that is punished occurs without specific training. For example, a mouse on a platform might step down onto an electrified grid; subsequently, the mouse no longer steps down.

passive coping see EMOTION-FOCUSED COPING.

passive deception the withholding of certain information from research participants, such as not informing them of the full details of the study. Also called **deception by omission**.

passive-dependent personality see DEPENDENT PERSONALITY DISORDER.

passive euthanasia the intentional withholding of treatment that might prolong the life of a person who is approaching death. It is distinguished from ACTIVE EUTHANASIA, in which direct action (e.g., a lethal injection) is taken to end the life. Courts have ruled that physicians do not have to try every possible intervention to prolong life, but opinions differ on where the line should be drawn. There is also controversy regarding the significance of the passive–active distinction, since both approaches result in shortening the life. See also EUTHANASIA.

passive learning 1. learning that may occur without the intention to learn, through exposure to information or behavior. See INCIDENTAL LEARNING. **2.** learning that occurs without active mnemonic involvement (see MNEMONIC STRATEGY), as in DRILL and ROTE LEARNING.

passive listening in psychotherapy and counseling, attentive listening by the therapist or counselor without intruding upon or interrupting the client in any way. See also ACTIVE LISTENING.

passive management by exception a style of management in which the manager only intervenes and takes charge if subordinates fail to meet work standards.

passive negativism see NEGATIVISM.

passive noise protection see ACTIVE NOISE PROTECTION.

passive recreation a form of RECREATIONAL THERAPY in which the emphasis is on an individual's amusement or entertainment, for example, attending a musical concert. Compare ACTIVE RECREATION.

passive rehearsal a strategy for retaining information in short-term memory in which a person includes few (usually one) unique items per REHEARSAL set. Compare CUMULATIVE REHEARSAL.

passive resistance resistance to a government, policy, or law through nonviolent means, such as fasting, demonstrating, or CIVIL DISOBEDIENCE.

passive scopophilia sexual interest in and arousal by having others view one's genitals. Passive scopophilia differs from EXHIBITIONISM in that it usually involves the participation of a consenting partner rather than a stranger.

passive suicide ambiguous behavior that tends to be self-destructive, but not actively so, and is sometimes thought to reflect suicidal intentions. Examples of this behavior include failing to feed oneself or to engage in rudimentary self-care.

passive touch a form of touch characterized by sensory experiences that occur when the observer does not move. In passive touch, stimulation is imposed on the skin of the individual. Compare ACTIVE TOUCH.

passive transport the movement of substances across a cell membrane without expenditure of energy by the cell. It includes simple diffusion of ions through ion channels and facilitated diffusion of larger molecules assisted by transport proteins. Compare ACTIVE TRANSPORT.

passive vocabulary see RECEPTIVE VOCABULARY.

passive voice in linguistics, the category of a verb used when the PATIENT of the action appears as the grammatical SUBJECT of the clause or sentence and the AGENT appears as the grammatical OBJECT. The passive voice, which is much less common than the standard ACTIVE VOICE, is illustrated by the sentence *The purse was stolen by the thief*, as opposed to *The thief stole the purse*.

passivism *n.* an attitude of submissiveness, especially in sexual relations (e.g., male passivism).

passivity *n.* a form of adaptation, or maladaptation, in which the individual adopts a pattern of submissiveness, dependence, and retreat into inaction.

passivity phenomena phenomena in which individuals feel that some aspect of themselves is under the control of others. These aspects can include acts, impulses, movements, emotions, or thoughts; patients typically report feeling that they are being made to do or think things by someone else or that they are experiencing the behaviors or emotions of someone else.

PASS model a model of intelligence based on the theory of Alexander LURIA, according to which intelligence comprises separate abilities for simultaneous and successive processing. The four elements of the model are *p*lanning, *a*ttention, *s*imultaneous processing, and *s*uccessive processing. [proposed in 1990 by U.S. psychologists J. P. Das (1931–) and Jack A. Naglieri (1950–)]

pastoral counseling a form of counseling or psychotherapy in which insights and principles derived from the disciplines of theology and the behavioral sciences are used in working with individuals, couples, families, groups, and social systems to achieve healing and growth. Pastoral counseling is centered in theory and research concerning the interaction of religion and science, spirituality and health, and spiritual direction and psychotherapy. A **pastoral counselor** receives advanced training in one or several of the behavioral sciences (often psychology specifically) in addition to religious training, theological training, or both. Also called **pastoral psychotherapy**.

past-pointing *n.* see POINTING.

PAT abbreviation for PROGRESSIVE ACHIEVEMENT TESTS.

Patau's syndrome see CHROMOSOME-13 TRISOMY. [Klaus **Patau**, 20th-century U.S. geneticist]

patch-clamp technique the use of very fine-bore pipette MICROELECTRODES, clamped by suction onto tiny patches of the plasma membrane of a neuron, to record the electrical activity of a single square micrometer of the membrane, including single ION CHANNELS. [devised in the 1980s by German neuroscientists Erwin Neher (1944–) and Bert Sakmann (1942–)]

patellar reflex see KNEE-JERK REFLEX.

paternal behavior actions by males directed toward care and protection of their young. **Direct paternal behavior** consists of such actions as feeding, carrying, or otherwise nurturing the offspring; **indirect paternal behavior** consists of acquiring resources or defending the group from harm, which indirectly leads to increased survival of the young. Males of species with biparental care undergo some hormonal changes similar to those in females: increased secretion of PROLACTIN and ESTROGENS. Early experience with young offspring is important for competent paternal behavior in many species. See ANIMAL PATERNAL BEHAVIOR.

paternalism *n.* a policy or attitude in which those having authority over others extend this authority into areas usually left to individual choice or conscience (e.g., smoking or sexual behavior), usually on the grounds that this is necessary for the welfare or protection of the individuals concerned. **—paternalist** *n.* **—paternalistic** *adj.*

path *n.* **1.** a connection or link, as between items or points. **2.** see PATHWAY.

path analysis a set of quantitative procedures used to verify the existence of causal relationships among several variables, displayed in graph form showing the various hypothesized routes of causal influence. The causal relationships are theoretically determined, and the path analysis determines both the accuracy and the strength of the hypothesized relationships.

path coefficient in PATH ANALYSIS, any of the set of regression-like coefficients (partial REGRESSION COEFFICIENTS) that reflect the strength of relationships among the variables in the system.

path–goal theory of leadership a LEADERSHIP THEORY stating that leaders will be effective in so far as they make it clear to followers how they can achieve goals and obtain rewards. By doing so, leaders enhance their followers' expectancy that hard work will lead to task success and that task success will lead to valued rewards. The four basic LEADERSHIP STYLES proposed in this theory are instrumental (directive), supportive, participative, and ACHIEVEMENT-ORIENTED LEADERSHIP. Each of these styles can be effective or ineffective, depending on the nature of the work environment and the characteristics of subordinates. Also called **path–goal theory**. See also VALENCE–INSTRUMENTALITY–EXPECTANCY THEORY.

patho- (**path-**) *combining form* suffering or disease.

pathoclisis *n.* **1.** sensitivity to particular toxins. **2.** the tendency of particular toxins to target certain organs or systems of organs.

pathogenesis *n.* the origination and development of a mental or physical disease or disorder. Also called **nosogenesis**; **pathogeny**. **—pathogenetic** *adj.*

pathogenic *adj.* contributing to disease or leading to PATHOLOGY. A pathogenic agent (e.g., a bacterium or virus) is known as a **pathogen**. **—pathogenicity** *n.*

pathogenic family pattern negative or harmful family attitudes, standards, and behavior that lay the groundwork for mental and behavioral disorder. Examples are parental rejection; TRIANGULATION of the child into the marital relationship between the parents; and excessively harsh, excessively lenient, or inconsistent discipline.

pathogeny *n.* see PATHOGENESIS.

pathognomonic *adj.* **1.** describing a sign, symptom, or a group of signs or symptoms that is indicative of a specific physical or mental disorder and not associated with other disorders. **2.** in the RORSCHACH INKBLOT TEST, denoting signs that point toward maladjustment.

pathognomy *n.* the recognition of feelings, emotions, and character traits, particularly when they are signs or symptoms of disease.

pathological aging changes that occur because of age-related disease, as distinct from changes associated with normal healthy aging.

pathological doubt **1.** abnormal concern about having failed to perform a particular action, such as locking the door upon leaving the house. Pathological doubt is a common feature of OBSESSIVE-COMPULSIVE DISORDER. **2.** a negative belief about one's ability or future that often results in the inhibition of behavior and is commonly associated with a MAJOR DEPRESSIVE EPISODE.

pathological fallacy an error of overgeneralization in which pathological characteristics observed in one individual or in a limited group of individuals are extrapolated and attributed to the general population. For example, most non-Freudians contend that Sigmund FREUD's theories are tenuous because they are based on a handful of clinical cases.

pathological gambling an impulse-control disorder characterized by chronic, maladaptive wagering, leading to significant interpersonal, professional, or financial difficulties. In *DSM–IV–TR* it is included in the category

IMPULSE-CONTROL DISORDERS NOT ELSEWHERE CLASSIFIED.

pathological grief see COMPLICATED GRIEF.

pathological inertia 1. the inability to switch SETS or show flexibility due to a brain injury or psychological condition. **2.** severely impaired initiative, drive, or motivation sometimes associated with brain damage, particularly to the frontal lobes. See ABULIA.

pathological intoxication see IDIOSYNCRATIC INTOXICATION.

pathological jealousy see DELUSIONAL JEALOUSY.

pathological lying a persistent, compulsive tendency to tell lies out of proportion to any apparent advantage that can be achieved. This often occurs among people with alcohol dependence or brain damage, but it is most common among individuals with ANTISOCIAL PERSONALITY DISORDER, who in some cases do not seem to understand the nature of a falsehood. See also PSEUDOLOGIA FANTASTICA.

pathology *n.* **1.** functional changes in an individual or an organ related to or resulting from diseases or disorders. **2.** the scientific study of functional and structural changes involved in physical and mental disorders and diseases. **—pathological** *adj.* **—pathologist** *n.*

pathomimicry *n.* conscious or unconscious mimicking, production, or feigning of symptoms of disease or disorder. Also called **pathomimesis**. See FACTITIOUS DISORDER; LASTHENIE DE FERJOL SYNDROME; MALINGERING.

pathomiosis *n.* a patient's minimization or denial of his or her illness.

pathomorphism *n.* any abnormal or extreme body build. **—pathomorphic** *adj.*

pathophysiology *n.* the functional alterations that appear in an individual or organ as a result of disease or disorder, as distinguished from structural alterations. **—pathophysiological** *adj.*

pathway *n.* a route or circuit along which something moves. Also called **path**. See NEURAL PATHWAY.

-pathy *suffix* **1.** disease or disorder (e.g., PSYCHOPATHY). **2.** therapy or treatment (e.g., HOMEOPATHY). **3.** perception or feeling (e.g., EMPATHY).

patient *n.* **1.** a person receiving health care from a licensed health professional (including the services of most psychologists and psychiatrists). See INPATIENT; OUTPATIENT. See also PATIENT–CLIENT ISSUE. **2.** in linguistics, the entity that is affected by or undergoes the main action described in a clause or sentence, such as *door* in *James opened the door* or *James knocked on the door.* The patient is usually the grammatical OBJECT and is easiest to identify when this is the case; however, *door* is both subject and patient in such constructions as *The door was opened by James* (see PASSIVE VOICE), *The door swung open,* and (in some analyses) *The door is open.* In CASE GRAMMAR the term EXPERIENCER is sometimes used for a patient who is a sentient being, such as *Angus* in *Angus felt threatened* or *Angus saw it all.* Compare AGENT; INSTRUMENTAL.

patient–client issue the dilemma of how to identify the recipient of psychological services or intervention (i.e., the nomenclature used for the recipient). Psychiatrists, many clinical psychologists, and some other mental health providers tend to follow the traditional language of the medical model and refer to the people seeking their services as **patients**. Counseling psychologists, some clinical psychologists, social workers, and counselors tend to avoid the word "patient," which is associated with illness and dysfunction, using instead the word **client** to refer to the person seeking their services.

patients' rights see RIGHTS OF PATIENTS.

patriarchy *n.* **1.** a society in which descent and inheritance is **patrilineal**, that is, traced through the male only. See UNILATERAL DESCENT. See also DESCENT GROUP. **2.** more loosely, a family, group, or society directed and governed by men. Compare MATRIARCHY. **—patriarchal** *adj.*

patricide *n.* **1.** the murder of one's own father. **2.** a person who murders his or her own father. See also MATRICIDE. **—patricidal** *adj.*

patrilineal *adj.* see PATRIARCHY.

patrilocal *adj.* denoting a living arrangement in which a married couple resides with or in close proximity to the husband's father or relatives, or a culture in which this is the norm. Compare MATRILOCAL; NEOLOCAL.

P1 attention effect the first positive component of an EVENT-RELATED POTENTIAL. The P1 component is usually larger for attended stimuli than for unattended stimuli. The source of the P1 component is thought to be areas of the visual cortex. See also NI ATTENTION EFFECT.

pattern *n.* a spatial or temporal arrangement of separate elements to make a complex whole.

pattern coding the coding of information in sensory systems based on the temporal pattern of action potentials.

pattern discrimination the ability of humans and other animals to distinguish differences in patterns of visual, auditory, or other types of stimuli. See also PATTERN RECOGNITION.

patterned interview a type of interview, often used in PERSONNEL SELECTION, that is designed to cover certain specific areas (e.g., work history, education, home situation, etc.), but at the same time to give the interviewer the chance to steer the dialogue into side channels and ask questions on points that need to be clarified. Also called **semistructured interview**. Compare STRUCTURED INTERVIEW; UNSTRUCTURED INTERVIEW.

patterning *n.* **1.** establishing a system or pattern of responses to stimuli. **2.** a pattern of stimuli that will evoke a new or different set of responses.

patterning theory of taste coding a theory postulating that each GUSTATORY STIMULUS evokes a unique pattern of neural activity from the TASTE-CELL population and that this pattern serves as the neural representation of the evoking stimulus. Taste quality is coded in the shape of the evoked pattern, while intensity is represented by the total discharge rate. Compare LABELED-LINE THEORY OF TASTE CODING.

pattern matrix in FACTOR ANALYSIS, the matrix of regression-like weights that express the values of the MANIFEST VARIABLES in terms of the theoretical factors.

pattern recognition 1. the ability to recognize and identify a complex whole composed of, or embedded in, many separate elements. Pattern recognition is not only a visual ability; in audition, it refers to (a) the recognition of temporal patterns of sounds or (b) the recognition of patterns of excitation of the BASILAR MEMBRANE, such as that which occurs during the perception of vowels in speech. **2.** the identification and classification of meaningful patterns of data input by computers, based on the extraction and comparison of the characteristic properties or features of the data.

pattern theory a theory maintaining that the nerve impulse pattern for pain is produced by intense stimulation of nonspecific receptors, since there are no specific fibers or endings exclusively for the experience of pain. According to this theory, the nerves involved in detecting and reporting pain are shared with other senses, such as touch, and the most important feature of pain is the amount of stimulation involved. Also called **nonspecificity theory**. Compare GATE-CONTROL THEORY OF PAIN; SPECIFICITY THEORY.

pattern vision the ability to discriminate between shapes, sizes, and other features of objects in the environment by visual patterns. Pattern vision is lost following a lesion or excision of the STRIATE CORTEX, where many of the elements of patterns are processed.

pause *n.* in linguistics, a rest or delay in speech. Short (often barely distinguishable) pauses are used to mark the JUNCTURE between linguistic units, such as syllables, words, and sentences, whereas longer pauses may be used for deliberate effect or may indicate psychological activity in the speaker. The analysis of the location of pauses in speech is an active area of research. **—pausal** *adj.*

Pavlov, Ivan Petrovich (1849–1936) Russian physiologist. Pavlov earned a medical degree in 1883 at the Military-Medical Academy of Saint Petersburg and subsequently worked in the laboratories of the German physiologists Rudolph Heidenhain (1834–1897) and Carl Ludwig (1816–1895). He then returned to the Military-Medical Academy, where he remained for the rest of his career. Pavlov's major interest was in the physiology of digestion and the manner in which it is controlled by the nervous system. Although he was awarded the 1904 Nobel Prize in physiology or medicine for his research on the digestive processes, it is for his subsequent research on the conditioned response that he is best known in psychology (see PAVLOVIAN CONDITIONING). His observations led to further experiments that yielded the concepts of the UNCONDITIONED RESPONSE (or reflex), the CONDITIONED STIMULUS, DISCRIMINATION of stimuli, EXTINCTION of response, and the production and elimination of EXPERIMENTAL NEUROSES in animals. He later focused on human neuroses, developing the theory that they are due to an imbalance between the excitatory and inhibitory functions of the cortex; for this condition he advocated treatment by prolonged sleep, sedatives, and verbal and environmental therapy. **—Pavlovian** *adj.*

Pavlovian conditioning a type of learning in which an initially neutral stimulus—the CONDITIONED STIMULUS (CS)—when paired with a stimulus that elicits a reflex response—the UNCONDITIONED STIMULUS (US)—results in a learned, or conditioned, response (CR) when the CS is presented. For example, the sound of a tone may be used as a CS, and food in a dog's mouth as a US. After repeated pairings, namely, the tone followed immediately by food, the tone, which initially had no effect on salivation (i.e., was neutral with respect to it), will elicit salivation even if the food is not presented. Also called **classical conditioning**; **respondent conditioning**; **Type I conditioning**; **Type S conditioning**. See CONDITIONING. [discovered in the early 20th century by Ivan PAVLOV]

pavor *n.* a frightening dream characterized by its realism and residual feelings of terror on waking. **Pavor nocturnus** occurs during the night (see SLEEP TERROR DISORDER); **pavor diurnus** may occur in young children during a daytime nap. See also NIGHTMARE.

Paxil *n.* a trade name for PAROXETINE.

pay equity see COMPARABLE WORTH.

Payne v. Tennessee a case resulting in a 1991 U.S. Supreme Court decision establishing that the admissibility in court of VICTIM IMPACT STATEMENTS must be considered on a case-by-case basis and that such statements are not per se excluded from all sentencing proceedings.

payoff evaluation see OUTCOME EVALUATION.

payoff matrix a schedule or table that lists the costs and benefits arising from every possible course of action that could be chosen by an individual—for example, by a player in a game or a participant in a signal detection experiment. An ideal participant will show shifts in response or decision criteria that maximize the payoff.

Payton, Carolyn R. (1925–2001) U.S. psychologist. Payton is best known as director of the Peace Corps from 1977 to 1979 and as a major advocate for the mental health needs of African Americans. She earned a master's degree in psychology from the University of Wisconsin in 1948 and was awarded a doctorate in counseling and student administration from Columbia University in 1962. In the interim, she served on the faculty at a number of institutions before joining the psychology department at Howard University in 1959. From 1964 to 1970 she served as an officer for the Peace Corps, using her background in psychology to assess Peace Corps trainees and to debrief returning volunteers. She returned to Howard University in 1970 as director of Counseling Services (HUCS) and remained there until her retirement, apart from a brief period (1977–1979) serving as director of the Peace Corps under President Jimmy Carter. At Howard she built the HUCS into a major force in the area, offering mental health services not only to students at Howard but also to the local African American community. She also established the HUCS as an accredited training program for therapists and counselors, one of the few such programs existing at an African American institution. Payton's honors included the American Psychological Association's Award for Distinguished Professional Contributions to Public Service and its Award for Outstanding Lifetime Contribution to Psychology.

P3 component the third positive component of an EVENT-RELATED POTENTIAL, which is associated with postperceptual cognitive processes, such as attention. It is sometimes called the **P300** because it appears approximately 300 ms after stimulus onset.

PCP 1. *n.* 1-(1-*p*henyl*c*yclohexyl)*p*iperidine (phencyclidine): a hallucinogenic drug sometimes referred to as a "psychedelic anesthetic" because it was originally developed as an amnestic analgesic for use in surgical anesthesia and was later found to produce a psychedelic or dissociative reaction. Its medical use was discontinued because of adverse reactions, including agitation, delirium, disorientation, and hallucinations. PCP has a complex mechanism of action. It binds as an ANTAGONIST to the NMDA RECEPTOR; it also acts as a DOPAMINE-RECEPTOR AGONIST and blocks the reuptake of dopamine, norepinephrine, and serotonin, among other actions. Because intoxication with PCP can produce symptoms resembling both the positive and negative symptoms of schizophrenia, some consider it to be a useful drug model of schizophrenia. High doses of PCP may induce stupor or coma. PCP became common as an illicit drug in the 1970s. It can be smoked (often in combination with marijuana or tobacco), insufflated (inhaled nasally), or taken orally or intravenously (see ANGEL DUST). Despite speculation about its potential neurotoxicity (ability to damage nerve tissue), it remains a popular illicit drug. PCP is still used in veterinary medicine, primarily as an immobilizing anesthetic during surgical procedures. See also HALLUCINOGEN. **2.** abbreviation for PRIMARY CARE PROVIDER.

PCP intoxication a reversible syndrome due to the recent ingestion of PCP. It includes clinically significant behavioral or psychological changes (e.g., belligerence, assaultiveness, impulsiveness, unpredictability, PSYCHOMOTOR AGITATION, impaired judgment, and impaired social or occupational functioning), as well as one or more signs of physiological involvement (e.g., vertical or horizontal NYSTAGMUS, hypertension or tachycardia, numbness or diminished responsiveness to pain, unsteady gait, unclear speech, muscle rigidity, seizures, and coma). See also SUBSTANCE INTOXICATION.

PCP intoxication delirium a reversible syndrome that develops over a short period of time (usually hours to days) following heavy PCP consumption. It includes disturbance of consciousness (e.g., reduced ability to focus, sustain, or shift attention), accompanied by changes in cognition (e.g., memory deficit, disorientation, or language disturbance) in excess of those usually associated with PCP INTOXICATION. See also SUBSTANCE INTOXICATION DELIRIUM.

PCR abbreviation for POLYMERASE CHAIN REACTION.

Pcs abbreviation for PRECONSCIOUS.

PD abbreviation for personal DISPOSITION.

PDAT abbreviation for PRESENILE DEMENTIA OF THE ALZHEIMER'S TYPE.

PDDNOS abbreviation for PERVASIVE DEVELOPMENTAL DISORDER NOT OTHERWISE SPECIFIED.

PDM abbreviation for PARTICIPATIVE DECISION-MAKING.

PDP abbreviation for PARALLEL DISTRIBUTED PROCESSING.

Peabody Picture Vocabulary Test (**PPVT**) a test in which sets of four black-and-white drawings are presented to the participant, who selects the one that corresponds to a word uttered by the examiner. There are 204 total sets of stimuli, arranged in 17 groups of 12. The test, now in its third edition (**PPVT–III**, 1997), may be used with individuals aged 2½ to over 90 years to assess receptive vocabulary and verbal ability. [originally developed in 1959 by psychologists Lloyd M. Dunn (1917–) and Leota M. Dunn (1917–2001) at Peabody College of Vanderbilt University, Nashville]

peak clipping the elimination of high-amplitude portions of speech waves by electronic means, causing some loss of quality but little, if any, loss of intelligibility. Peak clipping makes it possible to reduce high-intensity noise and enable a hearing aid or public address system to make the best use of its available power.

peak experience in the humanistic theory of Abraham MASLOW, a moment of awe, ecstasy, or transcendence that may at times be experienced by self-actualizers (see SELF-ACTUALIZATION). Peak experiences represent sudden insights into life as a powerful unity transcending space, time, and the self. See also BEING COGNITION; TIMELESS MOMENT; TRANSPERSONAL PSYCHOLOGY.

peak performance a performance at the optimum level of an individual's physical and mental capabilities.

peak procedure a procedure, used in behavioral studies, in which repetitions of a FIXED-INTERVAL SCHEDULE of reinforcement are interspersed with periods, usually two or three times as long as the fixed interval, in which reinforcement is omitted.

peak shift 1. a phenomenon, seen in STIMULUS GENERALIZATION, that occurs after DISCRIMINATION TRAINING involving two stimuli along a common dimension (e.g., brightness). The peak of the response gradient (i.e., the point at which the organism shows maximum response) is shifted in a direction away from the less favorable stimulus (e.g., a dim light) to a point beyond the value of the stimulus associated with reinforcement (e.g., beyond the value of a bright light to that of a very bright light). **2.** in aesthetics, the phenomenon that an extreme form of a preferred stimulus (a SUPERNORMAL STIMULUS) is preferred over the normal form of that stimulus.

Pearson product–moment correlation see PRODUCT–MOMENT CORRELATION.

pecking order a usually linear sequence (HIERARCHY) of authority, status, and privilege that prevails in some organizations and social groups. The expression derives from observations of regular patterns of dominance (pecking, threatening, chasing, fighting, avoiding, crouching, and vocalizing) in chickens and other animals. See also DOMINANCE HIERARCHY; STATUS RELATIONS.

pectus carinatum a malformation of the chest wall in which the sternum (breastbone) protrudes prominently. The condition may be a symptom of such disorders as rickets and MARFAN'S SYNDROME. Also called **pigeon breast**.

ped- *combining form* see PEDO-.

pedagogy *n.* the activity or profession of imparting knowledge or instruction. —**pedagogical** *adj.*

pederasty *n.* anal sexual intercourse, especially between an adult male (**pederast**) and a boy or young man (see CATAMITE). Also called **pedicatio**; **pedication**.

pedestrian movement the generally regular and predictable flow of pedestrian traffic in a public area, such as a shopping mall, plaza, or street intersection. Despite apparently random patterns of foot traffic, pedestrians usually follow the most direct route to a destination, which may or may not conform to the pathways planned and constructed for pedestrian movement.

pediatric psychology an interdisciplinary field of research and practice that addresses the interaction of physical, behavioral, and emotional development with health and illness issues affecting children, adolescents, and families. Related to the larger field of HEALTH PSYCHOLOGY, pediatric psychology differs not only in the focus on children and adolescents, but also in its emphasis on the child in the contexts of the family, school, and health care settings. The field tends to take a normative developmental view of adaptation based on physical conditions, medical treatment, and psychosocial interactions with family and peers, rather than a psychopathological view of adjustment to disease and disorders.

pediatric psychopharmacology the branch of pharmacology that is involved in the understanding and administration of drugs used in the treatment of mental and behavioral disorders of childhood and adolescence. It helps determine the choice of drug according to the age of the child, the diagnosis, the duration of the disorder, the severity of the illness, and the availability of the patient for behavioral and laboratory monitoring of the drug effects.

pedicatio *n.* see PEDERASTY.

pedication *n.* see PEDERASTY.

pedigree *n.* **1.** in medical genetics, a pictoral representation of the history of an illness in a family. It depicts the relationship of family members and—for each member—current status (alive or not), the date of diagnosis, kind of relevant illness, and age at diagnosis. Geneticists can often estimate a family member's likelihood of developing the disease from reviewing such a pedigree. **2.** family lineage or ancestry, especially when this is regarded as distinguished or notable. **3.** the line of descent of a pure-bred animal, or a record of such descent.

pedigree method the study of family history and genealogy as a means of tracing traits that might be inherited. The method was applied by British scientist Francis Galton (1822–1911) in his studies of genius and by Henry Herbert GODDARD in his studies of mental retardation.

pedo- (**ped-**; **paedo-**; **paed-**) *combining form* children.

pedology *n.* an early 20th-century educational movement in Europe whose stated purpose was the scientific study of the physical and mental development of children. Interest in pedology manifested itself especially within the emerging Soviet psychology of the 1920s, and Lev VYGOTSKY was among its supporters. Because of its emphasis on ability testing and examination of individual differences, however, it was banned by the Soviets as a "false science" in 1936.

pedomorphism *n.* the attribution of childish behavior characteristics to adults. Compare ADULTOMORPHISM. —**pedomorphic** *adj.*

pedomorphosis *n.* the retention of juvenile characteristics in adult organisms.

pedophilia *n.* a PARAPHILIA in which sexual acts or fantasies with prepubertal children are the persistently preferred or exclusive method of achieving sexual excitement. The children are usually many years younger than the **pedophile** (or **pedophiliac**). Sexual activity may consist of looking and touching, but sometimes includes intercourse, even with very young children. Pedophilia is rarely seen in women. —**pedophilic** *adj.*

peduncle *n.* a stalklike bundle of nerve fibers, for example, the CEREBELLAR PEDUNCLE or the CEREBRAL PEDUNCLE. —**peduncular** *adj.*

peduncular hallucinosis recurrent visual hallucinations caused by pathological processes in the upper brainstem, which indirectly affect the central visual system. The hallucinations, which may be long-lasting, vivid, and scenic, are often accompanied by agitation and sleep disturbances. The hallucinations are usually recognized as such by the patient, who may see a panorama of people and events from his or her past life. Peduncular hallucinosis may be mixed with nonhallucinatory perceptions.

peeping Tom slang for a voyeur (see VOYEURISM), derived from the name of a tailor who, according to the 11th-century legend, peeked at Lady Godiva as she was riding naked through the streets of Coventry, England.

peer *n.* an individual who shares a feature or function (e.g., age, sex, occupation, social group membership) with one or more other individuals. In developmental psychology, a peer is typically an age mate with whom a child or adolescent interacts.

peer counseling counseling by an individual who has a status equal to that of the client, such as a college student trained to counsel other students or an employee trained to counsel his or her coworkers.

peer group a group of individuals who share one or more characteristics, such as age, social status, economic status, occupation, or education. Members of a peer group typically interact with each other on a level of equality and exert influence on each other's attitudes, emotions, and behavior (see PEER PRESSURE). Although children begin to interact before the age of 2, genuine peer groups based on shared age typically do not develop until the age of 5 years or later.

peer pressure the influence exerted by a PEER GROUP on its individual members to fit in with or adapt to group expectations by thinking, feeling, and (most importantly) behaving in a similar or acceptable manner (see CONFORMITY). Peer pressure may have positive SOCIALIZATION value but may also have negative consequences for mental or physical health. Also called **peer-group pressure**.

peer rating the evaluation of an individual's behavior by his or her associates (e.g., a physician peer review). In child development research, peer ratings are sometimes obtained from members of a child's peer group (e.g., school class members).

peer review the evaluation of scientific or academic work, such as research or articles submitted to journals for publication, by other qualified professionals practicing in the same field.

peer tutoring the teaching of one student by another, who has displayed sufficient competency in a subject to help a fellow student learn a skill or concept. Peer tutors often receive minimal training or guidance by the teacher.

pegboard test a test of manual dexterity and fine motor speed in which the participant—first with his or her dominant hand, then with the nondominant hand, and finally with both hands—inserts pegs in a series of holes as rapidly as possible. One of the best known examples is the **Purdue Pegboard Test** (developed at Purdue University, West Lafayette, Indiana).

peg-word mnemonic system a MNEMONIC STRATEGY used to remember lists, in which each item is associated in imagination with a number–word pair (the **peg**). For example, if the pegs are the rhyming pairs "one is a bun, two is a shoe," and so on, the first item to be remembered would be associated with a bun, the second with a shoe, and so on.

pejorism *n.* severe PESSIMISM.

Pelizaeus–Merzbacher disease a rare, progressive degenerative disorder of the central nervous system marked by involuntary, rapid eye movements (see NYSTAGMUS), muscular incoordination (see ATAXIA), and spasticity. It is caused by a mutation in the gene that controls the production of a specific MYELIN protein. Severity and onset vary widely, depending on the type of mutation, and extend from the mild, adult-onset, spastic paraplegia form to the severe form with onset at infancy and death in early childhood. [Friedrich **Pelizaeus** (1850–1917), German neurologist; Ludwig **Merzbacher** (1875–1942), German physician]

pellagra *n.* deficiency of the B vitamin NICOTINIC ACID (niacin), marked by weakness, gastrointestinal disturbances, skin disorders, and neurological symptoms, for example, apathy, confusion, disorientation, and neuritis. Also called **nicotinic acid deficiency**.

pellet *n.* a small piece of food used in studies with rats and other animals. Pellets are available in standard weights and sizes with standard contents.

pemoline *n.* a nonamphetamine CNS STIMULANT used for the management of attention-deficit/hyperactivity disorder (ADHD). Its effects resemble those of the AMPHETAMINES and METHYLPHENIDATE, and its mechanism of action includes blockade of dopamine reuptake. Pemoline has been associated with rare but occasionally fatal liver failure and with the development of TOURETTE'S DISORDER. Safety concerns led to its withdrawal from the Canadian market in 1999. Pemoline is no longer considered a FIRST-LINE MEDICATION in the management of ADHD. Baseline liver-function tests and complete patient education, including specific INFORMED CONSENT, are required before initiating therapy with pemoline. U.S. trade name (among others): **Cylert**.

PEN acronym for psychoticism, extraversion, neuroticism (see EYSENCK'S TYPOLOGY).

pendular knee jerk an abnormal KNEE-JERK REFLEX observed in patients with a lesion of the cerebellum, in which the leg continues to move several times after the initial reflex.

pendulum problem a PIAGETIAN TASK used to assess cognitive development. The participant is asked to work out what governs the speed of an object swinging on a piece of string. The ability to systematically examine the variables (length, weight, force of drop, height of drop) generally appears in early adolescence and is evidence of HYPOTHETICO-DEDUCTIVE REASONING, which marks the FORMAL OPERATIONS stage of development.

penetrance *n.* in genetics, the extent to which the effects of an ALLELE are manifest in the individuals possessing it, expressed as the fraction or percentage of individuals carrying that allele who manifest the trait associated with it. If all persons who possess a particular dominant allele develop the associated trait, the allele is said to show **complete penetrance** (100%). In contrast, **incomplete penetrance** occurs when some individuals with a particular allele do not develop the associated trait.

penetrating head injury a head injury in which an object, such as a bullet, penetrates the brain. See OPEN HEAD INJURY.

penetration *n.* the entry of the penis into the vagina. In the United States, legal definitions in cases of rape or illicit intercourse vary from state to state, but penetration is generally considered to have occurred if the glans penis passes beyond the labia majora. In some states, if penetration has not occurred during sexual assault, there cannot be a charge of rape. In such cases, the crime is some variety of felonious sexual assault, which usually has lower penalties than rape.

penetration response a response in a projective test that can be interpreted to contain a suggestion of weakness or penetrability (e.g., "a hole in the wall"). Such interpretation ultimately derives from an imprecise use of the psychoanalytic concept of PROJECTION and is of limited validity.

penile plethysmograph see PLETHYSMOGRAPH.

penile prosthesis an implanted device that is used to restore male sexual potency. Such devices are typically either made of malleable material or are inflatable, and their insertion requires surgery.

penilingus *n.* see FELLATIO.

penis *n.* the male organ for urination and intromission, which enters the female's vagina to deliver semen. The urethra runs through the penis, which is composed largely of erectile tissue (see CORPUS CAVERNOSUM; CORPUS SPONGIOSUM) and has a mushroom-shaped cap (GLANS PENIS). —**penile** *adj.*

penis envy in the classic psychoanalytic theory of Sigmund FREUD, the hypothesized desire of girls and women to possess a male genital organ. Freud held it to originate in the PHALLIC STAGE, between ages 3 and 6, when the girl discovers that she lacks this organ, and further posited that the girl feels "handicapped and ill-treated," blames her mother for the loss, and wants to have her penis back. German-born U.S. psychoanalyst Karen D. Horney (1885–1952), among others, later argued that penis envy is not an envy of the biological organ itself but represents women's envy of men's superior social status. In any sense, the concept has been actively disputed from the beginning and is rarely considered seriously in current psychology. See also CASTRATION COMPLEX.

Pennhurst Consent Decree a judicial decree ordering the closure of the Pennhurst State School and Hospital in Philadelphia, Pennsylvania, and the movement of its residents with mental retardation to least restrictive environments within the community. The decree further ordered team planning for individual movement to the community, provision of case management, and establishment of individual habilitation plans. The decree was based on the court's determination that conditions at the facility were dangerous to the well-being of residents and violated the due process and equal protection clauses of the U.S. Constitution and other federal and state legislation. The Pennhurst facility closed in 1980. See also YOUNGBERG V. ROMEO.

penology *n.* **1.** the scientific study of the management of correctional facilities and the rehabilitation of criminals. **2.** in older writings, the branch of CRIMINOLOGY concerned with the theory and practice of the punishment of crime.

Penrose triangle a three-dimensional IMPOSSIBLE FIGURE composed of three bars, each at 90° to the adjacent bar, that appear to make a twisted triangle. The figure is more accurately called a **tribar**, since true triangles have three angles that add up to 180° rather than the 270° of the Penrose triangle. [Roger **Penrose** (1931–), British physicist]

pentazocine *n.* see OPIOID ANTAGONIST.

pentobarbital *n.* a short- to intermediate-acting BARBITURATE formerly in common use as a sedative and hypnotic drug. Like all barbiturates, it has been supplanted by safer agents, such as the benzodiazepines. It is still used in the induction of anesthesia and very rarely in the treatment of a specific epileptic condition; otherwise it has no mental health applications. It was formerly used in psychotherapy to make clients less inhibited and therefore able to express themselves more effectively, but this use has been discredited. U.S. trade name: **Nembutal**.

Pentothal *n.* a trade name for THIOPENTAL.

people-first language language that places a person before his or her disability by describing what a person has rather than equating the person with the disability. Examples of the use of such language include "a child with a learning disability" (rather than "a learning-disabled child"), "a child with Down syndrome" (rather than "a Down child"), and "a person who uses a wheelchair" (rather than "a wheelchair-bound person").

pepsinogen *n.* the precursor of **pepsin**, a proteolytic enzyme necessary for the breakdown of proteins. It is secreted by the gastric glands of the stomach and is converted to pepsin in the presence of gastric acid, also secreted by glands of the stomach.

peptic ulcer see ULCER.

peptide *n.* a short chain of AMINO ACIDS linked by **peptide bonds**. Peptides are usually identified by the number of amino acids in the chain, for example, dipeptides have two, tripeptides three, tetrapeptides four, and so on. See also POLYPEPTIDE; PROTEIN.

peptide hormone any hormone that is classed chemically as a PEPTIDE. Peptide hormones include ADRENOCORTICOTROPIC HORMONE, CORTICOTROPIN-RELEASING HORMONE, OXYTOCIN, VASOPRESSIN, and CHOLECYSTOKININ.

perceive *vb.* **1.** to be conscious of or recognize through the senses. See PERCEPTION. **2.** to understand or grasp the meaning of something.

perceived behavioral control the extent to which a person believes a behavior is under his or her active control. See THEORY OF PLANNED BEHAVIOR.

perceived competence an individual's belief in his or her ability to learn and execute skills.

perceived reality a person's subjective experience of reality, in contrast to objective, external reality. Client-centered, humanistic-existential, and related phenomenological theories propose that individuals behave in accordance with perceived, rather than objective, reality.

perceived risk the extent to which individuals feel they are subject to a health threat. Risk is a joint function of the probability of occurrence of a negative event and the magnitude of its consequence.

perceived self the subjective appraisal of personal qualities that one ascribes to oneself.

perceived self-efficacy an individual's subjective perception of his or her capability for performance in a given setting or ability to attain desired results, proposed by Albert BANDURA as a primary determinant of emotional and motivational states and behavioral change.

perceived simultaneity the integration of stimuli into a single, conscious percept despite small discrepancies in their actual time of arrival, so that they are perceived as occurring simultaneously.

perceived susceptibility a subjective estimate of the likelihood of personally contracting a disease, without any consideration of severity. Also called **perceived vulnerability**.

percentage reinforcement in operant conditioning, a procedure in which a fixed percentage of scheduled reinforcers is omitted.

percentile *n.* the location of a score in a distribution coded to reflect the percentage of cases in the batch that have scores equal to or below the score in question. Thus, if a score is said to be at the 90th percentile, the implication is that 90% of the scores in the batch are equal to or lower than that score.

percentile reinforcement in operant conditioning, a procedure in which the likelihood that a response will be reinforced depends on the response exceeding (or being less than) a value based on a distribution from previous responses. Usually, the distribution is based on some set of the most recent responses and it is updated with each response. For example, the current response might be eligible for reinforcement if its peak force falls above the 90th PERCENTILE of the distribution of forces from the previous 50 responses. The most recent force then replaces the earliest one in the distribution so that the distribution remains based on 50 entries.

percept *n.* the product of PERCEPTION: the stimulus object or event as experienced by the individual.

perception *n.* the process or result of becoming aware of objects, relationships, and events by means of the senses, which includes such activities as recognizing, observing, and discriminating. These activities enable organisms to organize and interpret the stimuli received into meaningful knowledge.

perception deafness inability to analyze or perceive sounds normally, due to some impairment of the inner ear or auditory nerve pathways leading to the brain.

perception of spatial relations an awareness of the relative position of objects in space.

perceptive *adj.* describing an individual who is sensitive and discriminating, especially in the judgment of people, works of art, and so forth. **—perceptiveness** or **perceptivity** *n.*

perceptive impairment and nerve loss see SENSORINEURAL HEARING LOSS.

perceptron *n.* a connected network of input nodes and output nodes that acts as a useful model of associative NEURAL NETWORKS. A simple (single-layer) perceptron might stand for two connected neurons, while more complicated perceptrons have additional hidden layers between input and output. The connections between the inputs and outputs can be weighted to model the desired output. The goal is to develop a theoretical understanding of the way neural connections process signals and form associations (memories). **Back-propagation (backprop) algorithms** describe the most common process by which the weightings between input and output are adjusted. The output is compared to a desired endpoint and changes needed in the strengths of the connections are transmitted back through the perceptron.

perceptual *adj.* relating to the awareness of sensory stimuli.

perceptual aftereffect see AFTEREFFECT.

perceptual anchoring 1. the process in which the qualities of a stimulus are perceived relative to another, anchoring, stimulus. **2.** see SYMBOL GROUNDING.

perceptual classification in classification tasks, the grouping together of items on the basis of perceptual characteristics. Compare COMPLEMENTARY CLASSIFICATION; CONCEPTUAL CLASSIFICATION; IDIOSYNCRATIC CLASSIFICATION.

perceptual closure the process by which an incomplete stimulus (e.g., a line drawing of a circle with a segment missing) is perceived to be complete (e.g., an entire circle). See CLOSURE.

perceptual constancy the ability to maintain a perception of the properties of an object, (e.g., size, shape, color) regardless of changes in the actual stimulus conditions, such as the level of illumination, image size on the retina, or confounding contextual cues. See also SHAPE CONSTANCY; SIZE CONSTANCY; BRIGHTNESS CONSTANCY; WHITENESS CONSTANCY.

perceptual cues 1. features of a stimulus that are perceived and used by an organism in a particular situation or setting to identify and make judgments about that stimulus and its properties. **2.** features of a situation that indicate the expected behavior. See DEMAND CHARACTERISTICS.

perceptual cycle hypothesis the theory that cognition affects perceptual exploration but is in turn modified by real-world experience, creating a cycle of cognition, attention, perception, and the real world in which each influences the others. Thus, sensory experience is neither totally internal nor totally external. [proposed in 1976 by U.S. cognitive psychologist Ulric Neisser (1928–)]

perceptual decentration see DECENTRATION.

perceptual defect see PERCEPTUAL DEFICIT.

perceptual defense in psychoanalytic theory, a misperception that occurs when anxiety-arousing stimuli are unconsciously distorted. If taboo words are rapidly presented, they may be misinterpreted; for example, if the stimulus word *anal* is presented, participants may report seeing the innocuous *canal*.

perceptual deficit an impaired ability to organize and interpret sensory experience, causing difficulty in observing, recognizing, and understanding people, situations, words, numbers, concepts, or images. Also called **perceptual defect**.

perceptual development the acquisition of sensory

skills (i.e., those that enable a person to organize sensory stimuli into meaningful entities) in the course of physical and psychological development.

perceptual disorder see PERCEPTUAL DISTURBANCE.

perceptual distortion an inaccurate interpretation of perceptual experience. Examples include the distorted images produced by dreams or hallucinogenic drugs, geometric illusions (e.g., the MÜLLER-LYER ILLUSION), visions occurring in states of sensory deprivation or dehydration, and distortions produced by modifying auditory stimuli. Perceptual distortion may also occur as a consequence of acquired brain injury. See also METAMORPHOPSIA.

perceptual disturbance a disorder of perception, such as (a) recognizing letters but not words, (b) inability to judge size or direction, (c) confusing background with foreground, (d) inability to filter out irrelevant sounds or sights, (e) a body-image distortion, or (f) difficulty with spatial relationships (e.g., perceiving the difference between a straight line and a curved line). Also called **perceptual disorder**.

perceptual expansion 1. the development of the ability to recognize, interpret, and organize intellectual, emotional, and sensory data in a meaningful way. **2.** the enriched understanding of experience that takes place in psychotherapy when greater INSIGHT is achieved through the therapeutic process and dynamic.

perceptual extinction an effect of lesions in the parieto-occipital region on one side of the brain in which a stimulus, usually tactual or visual, is not detected. If a single stimulus is presented on either side of the midline, it is detected; however, when two similar stimuli are presented at the same time, one on each side of the midline, the stimulus on the side of the body opposite the location of the lesion is not detected. This phenomenon is utilized in neuropsychological research on attention mechanisms. Also called **sensory extinction**; **sensory inattention**.

perceptual field in GESTALT PSYCHOLOGY, the totality of the environment that an individual perceives at a particular time; that is, all of the aspects of the environment of which the person is aware at a given time.

perceptual filtering the process of focusing attention on a selected subset of the large number of sensory stimuli that are present at any one time. Perceptual filtering is necessary because the cognitive and physical capacity of an individual to process and respond to multiple sources of information is limited. See also BOTTLENECK MODEL.

perceptual fluency the ease with which a visual target is processed. The **perceptual fluency theory** of VISUAL ATTENTION holds that the repeated presentations of a given target between presentations of distractors in successive trials increases the perceptual fluency for that target, thus making it easier to distinguish from the distractors.

perceptualization *n.* **1.** see PERCEPTUAL ORGANIZATION. **2.** in schizophrenia, the transformation of abstract concepts into specific perceptions. For example, an individual who thinks poorly of him- or herself may later experience hallucinations that bad odors are emanating from his or her body; the rotten personality becomes the rotten body that smells. Perceptualization is the most advanced level of ACTIVE CONCRETIZATION. [defined by Italian-born U.S. psychiatrist Silvano Arieti (1914–1982)]

perceptual learning learning to perceive the relationships between stimuli and objects in the environment or the differences among stimuli.

perceptual localization the ability to determine the physical location of a stimulus (e.g., a sound). See AUDITORY LOCALIZATION.

perceptual maintenance in environmental design, the construction of an environment to facilitate sensory functions (e.g., seeing, hearing) and to provide an appropriate level of perceptual stimulation for the activity carried out (e.g., the lighting and soundproofing of a recording studio).

perceptual masking see MASKING.

perceptual–motor coordination the use of perceptually derived information (e.g., vision, touch) in the control of ongoing movements.

perceptual–motor learning the learning of a skill that requires linking the perceptual discrimination of important stimuli with appropriate motor responses (e.g., hitting a ball or driving an automobile).

perceptual–motor match the ability to correlate perceptual data with a previously learned set of motor responses. An individual with brain damage may have to touch everything he or she sees because of an inability to make the perceptual–motor match automatically.

perceptual neglect see NEGLECT.

perceptual network see GROUP NETWORK.

perceptual organization the process enabling such properties as structure, pattern, and form to be imposed on the senses to provide conceptual organization. Each of the senses establishes (or learns) such organizational schemata. According to traditional GESTALT PSYCHOLOGY, the parts of a group are organized to form whole figures that constitute more than the parts separately (see GESTALT PRINCIPLES OF ORGANIZATION). Recent research has more precisely defined the properties that enable such organized tasks. Artists have traditionally used the principles of perceptual organization to create desired moods or feelings and to challenge viewers' expectations. Also called **perceptualization**.

perceptual representation system (**PRS**) a MEMORY SYSTEM whose function is to identify objects and words, allowing quick recognition of previously encountered stimuli. Perceptions are specifically recognized in the form previously experienced, that is, a word as seen versus a word as heard. The PRS does not recognize the meaning of stimuli, which is handled by SEMANTIC MEMORY.

perceptual restructuring the process of modifying a perception to accommodate new information.

perceptual rivalry the incompatibility of different perceptions of the same object. When an AMBIGUOUS FIGURE that allows two different perceptual interpretations is viewed, only one perceptual diagnosis can be made at any one time, so that perception alternates between the two rival interpretations. This switching between percepts is primarily involuntary.

perceptual schema a mental model that provides a FRAME OF REFERENCE for interpreting information entering the mind through the senses or for activating an expectation of how a particular perceptual scene may look. See SCHEMA.

perceptual segregation the separation of one part of a PERCEPTUAL FIELD from the whole by physical boundaries or attention-diverting methods. See FIGURE–GROUND.

perceptual sensitization the lowering of an individual's sensory thresholds for events that are emotionally sensitive or threatening.

perceptual set 1. a temporary readiness to perceive certain objects or events rather than others. For example, a person driving a car has a perceptual set to identify anything that might impact his or her safety. See SELECTIVE PERCEPTION; SET. **2.** a SCHEMA or FRAME OF REFERENCE that influences the way in which a person perceives objects, events, or people. For example, an on-duty police officer and a painter might regard a crowded street scene with very different perceptual sets.

perceptual sociogram see SOCIOGRAM.

perceptual speed see PRIMARY ABILITIES.

perceptual style the characteristic way in which an individual attends to, selects, alters, and interprets sensory stimuli. Some believe perceptual functions are distorted among individuals manifesting various forms of psychological dysfunction.

perceptual synthesis 1. the integration of experience from all the senses to establish knowledge of the external world and one's interactions with it. This includes the elimination of unessential information with respect to similarities and differences. **2.** in auditory perception, a phenomenon in which people perceive missing sounds or faint sounds when the gap created by them is filled with white noise.

perceptual training a method of enhancing an individual's ability to interpret perceived objects or events in concrete terms. For example, the ability of a child to recognize letters of the alphabet may be enhanced by tracing the outlines of the letters.

perceptual transformation 1. any modification in a PERCEPT produced by (a) an addition to, deletion from, or alteration in a physical stimulus or (b) a novel interpretation of the stimulus, a change in a SET or attitude, or a sudden insight concerning the material. **2.** change in the way a problem, event, or person is perceived by the inclusion of new information or a different perspective.

perceptual user interface an interface that would enable a computer system to "perceive," interpret, and respond appropriately to the facial expressions, speech, gestures or movements, and other perceptually based patterns of communication typical of users. The intent is to provide realistic, interactive encounters similar to those experienced among people in the real world. Compare GRAPHICAL USER INTERFACE; TANGIBLE USER INTERFACE.

percipient 1. *adj.* capable of perception. **2.** *n.* in parapsychology, the alleged recipient of telepathic communications or other extrasensory impressions. Compare AGENT. See also RECEIVER.

perdida del alma see SUSTO.

peregrination *n.* widespread or excessive traveling from place to place. Peregrination is one of the essential features of MUNCHAUSEN SYNDROME: The patient feels impelled to travel from town to town or from hospital to hospital in order to find a new audience every time the false nature of the illness is discovered. Also called **itinerancy**.

peremptory challenge a request made to the judge during VOIR DIRE that a prospective juror be replaced without indicating a specific reason. In criminal trials, each side is allowed a particular number of peremptory challenges. Compare CHALLENGE FOR CAUSE.

perfectionism *n.* the tendency to demand of others or of oneself a higher level of performance than is required by the situation, thought by some to be a risk factor for depression. **—perfectionist** *adj., n.* **—perfectionistic** *adj.*

perfect pitch see ABSOLUTE PITCH.

perforant path the route of axons that perforate the SUBICULUM to provide the main inputs to the HIPPOCAMPUS.

performance *n.* **1.** any activity or collection of responses that leads to a result or has an effect upon the environment. **2.** the behavior of an organism (the **performer**) when faced with a specific task. **3.** in linguistics, see COMPETENCE.

performance anxiety anxiety associated with the apprehension and fear of the consequences of being unable to perform a task or of performing the task at a level that will lead to expectations of higher levels of performance achievement. TEST ANXIETY is a common example of performance anxiety. Other examples include fear of public speaking, participating in classes or meetings, playing a musical instrument in public, or even eating in public. If the fear associated with performance anxiety is focused on negative evaluation by others, embarrassment, or humiliation, the anxiety may be classified as a SOCIAL PHOBIA.

performance appraisal see PERFORMANCE REVIEW.

performance assessment 1. see PERFORMANCE REVIEW. **2.** an appraisal of growth or deterioration in learning, memory, or both through performance on ability and achievement tests.

performance contract a formal agreement between an employer and an employee regarding the work outcomes expected of the employee and the compensation and other rewards provided for these outcomes.

performance enhancement the act or process of taking performance to a higher level of achievement.

performance evaluation 1. see PERFORMANCE REVIEW. **2.** generally, any process of comparing the expected, planned, or ideal level of accomplishment or outcome for a particular activity or goal with the actual level of accomplishment or outcome.

performance goal 1. in the motivational theory of U.S. personality psychologist Carol Dweck (1946–), the goal of demonstrating to others who may be evaluating one's performance that one possesses a particular ability or other attribute. This is in contrast to a LEARNING GOAL, in which one aims to develop an ability or attribute. **2.** a goal that is set in terms of a specific level of achievement, such as running a mile in 5 min 30 s. See also GOAL SETTING; OUTCOME GOAL; PROCESS GOAL.

performance imagery 1. the use of IMAGERY to cognitively re-create all the sensations of a performance. See MENTAL REHEARSAL. **2.** the use of imagery during a performance as a cue to tell the body what to do, for example, imaging an explosion under the foot at the moment of takeoff for a high jump.

performance intensity see INTENSITY.

performance IQ see IQ.

performance-operating characteristic (**POC**) the measure of performance on one task plotted against the measure of performance on a second task that is performed simultaneously. The POC shows how improvements in performance on one of the tasks might trade with performance decrements in the other task.

performance review a formal appraisal of an employee's job performance, typically performed by his or her supervisor at least once a year. The review may be in the form of a quantitative rating or a more subjective appraisal and usually involves feedback to the employee. Also called **performance appraisal**; **performance assessment**; **performance evaluation**. See also EMPLOYEE EVALUATION; EVALUATION INTERVIEW; JOB CRITERION.

performance routine a predetermined set of physical and mental behaviors followed during a performance that allow an individual (e.g., an athlete) to maintain focus, energy levels, confidence, and control.

performance test any test of ability requiring primarily motor, rather than verbal, responses, such as a test requiring manipulation of a variety of different kinds of objects.

performative *adj.* denoting an utterance whose very delivery accomplishes the stated intention of the speaker, as in *I apologize, I promise,* and *I declare this mall open.* The nature of performative SPEECH ACTS received much attention in 20th-century linguistic philosophy. See also ILLOCUTIONARY ACT.

peri- *prefix* **1.** around or enclosing. **2.** near.

periamygdaloid cortex an ill-defined region surrounding the AMYGDALA of the brain that is associated with the sense of smell. The proportion of the brain that it occupies in a particular species seems to depend on the importance of the sense of smell for survival: the greater the importance, the larger the proportion. Dogs, for example, have a larger proportion of olfactory nerve tissue than do human beings. See also PYRIFORM AREA.

periaqueductal gray (**PAG**) a region of the brainstem, rich in nerve cell bodies (i.e., gray matter), that surrounds the CEREBRAL AQUEDUCT. A component of the LIMBIC SYSTEM, it plays an important role in organizing defensive behaviors (e.g., freezing).

perikaryon *n.* see CELL BODY.

perilymph *n.* the fluid that fills the space between the membranous LABYRINTH and the walls of the bony labyrinth in the inner ear. —**perilymphatic** *adj.*

perimeter *n.* a hemispherical instrument used to plot the limits of the visual field. An individual is seated within the hemisphere and is asked to fixate a central spot of light. The visual field is then probed with small flashes of light, which the participant is asked to detect. The size and brightness of the flashes can be varied to assess visual sensitivity at many points within the field.

perimetry *n.* the measurement of the extent of the visual field. See PERIMETER.

perinatal herpes-virus infection a complication of infection with herpes simplex Type 2 in which the virus in a pregnant woman may be transmitted to the fetus. The fetal infection may develop into a severe blood disorder and can also result in a fatal form of encephalitis. The complication is most likely to develop in late pregnancy. See HERPES INFECTION.

period *n.* **1.** the interval of time between the same point in successive cycles, such as sunset to sunset. **2.** see MENSTRUATION.

periodicity *n.* the state of recurring more or less regularly, that is, at intervals.

periodicity pitch see VIRTUAL PITCH.

periodicity theory the theory that pitch is encoded in the temporal structure of the neural responses to sounds, specifically in the timing of neural discharges ("spikes"). For periodic sounds, those that elicit strong pitch, the discharges of auditory nerve fibers tend to occur at integer multiples of the period of the sound. See PHASE LOCKING. Compare PLACE THEORY.

periodic reinforcement see FIXED-INTERVAL SCHEDULE.

period prevalence see PREVALENCE.

peripatologist *n.* the former name for an O&M specialist (see ORIENTATION AND MOBILITY TRAINING).

peripheral *adj.* **1.** in the nervous system, located or taking place outside the brain and spinal cord. Compare CENTRAL. **2.** in vision, toward the margins of the visual field, rather than close to the center. The onset of a peripheral stimulus tends to draw attention to that location. **3.** situated on the surface of a body. **4.** situated away from a center and toward the outside edge. **5.** incidental or superficial.

peripheral anticholinergic syndrome a syndrome observed in patients receiving combinations of agents with psychopharmacological effects and due to the additive ANTICHOLINERGIC EFFECTS on the peripheral nervous system of, among others, tricyclic antidepressants, the weaker phenothiazines, and antiparkinsonian drugs. The symptoms include dry mucous membranes, dry mouth, and hot, flushed skin and face. See also ANTICHOLINERGIC SYNDROME; CENTRAL ANTICHOLINERGIC SYNDROME.

peripheral auditory system see AUDITORY SYSTEM.

peripheral cue a factor external to the merits of an argument that can be used to provide a relatively low-effort basis for determining whether an ATTITUDE OBJECT should be positively or negatively evaluated. See also ELABORATION-LIKELIHOOD MODEL; PERIPHERAL ROUTE TO PERSUASION.

peripheral dysarthria see DYSARTHRIA.

peripheral dyslexia a form of acquired dyslexia (see ALEXIA) that is characterized by difficulties in processing the visual aspects of words (e.g., difficulties identifying letter forms) and—unlike CENTRAL DYSLEXIA—results from damage to the visual analysis system.

peripheral dysostosis with nasal hypoplasia a congenital abnormality characterized by short, wide hands and feet and a short, flat nose with nostrils bent forward. Most affected individuals show some degree of mental retardation. Because of foot anomalies, learning to walk may be slow.

peripheralism *n.* the view of some behaviorists that emphasizes events at the periphery of an organism, such as the skeletal and laryngeal muscles and sex organs, rather than the functions of the central nervous system. For example, John B. WATSON believed (falsely) that thinking was not a function taking place in the brain but involved minute movements of the vocal apparatus (SUBVOCAL SPEECH) and thus was an objective behavior. Also called **peripheralistic psychology**. Compare CENTRALISM.

peripheral nerve fiber classification the classification of peripheral nerve fibers (axons) according to their diameters, speeds of conduction, and locations. They fall into three main classes, which can be further divided into subclasses. A FIBERS vary from 6 to 20 μm in diameter; they are MYELINATED FIBERS and conduct rapidly. B FIBERS occur in the preganglionic AUTONOMIC NERVOUS SYSTEM; they are myelinated but of relatively small diameter, and conduct more slowly than A fibers. C FIBERS vary from 0.2 to 1.5 μm in diameter; they are unmyelinated and conduct slowly. See also VELOCITY OF CONDUCTION.

peripheral nervous system (**PNS**) the portion of the nervous system that lies outside the skull and spinal column, that is, all parts outside the CENTRAL NERVOUS SYSTEM. Afferent fibers of the PNS bring messages from the sense organs to the central nervous system; efferent fibers transmit messages from the central nervous system to the muscles and glands. It includes the CRANIAL NERVES, SPINAL NERVES, and parts of the AUTONOMIC NERVOUS SYSTEM.

peripheral neuropathy a neuromuscular disorder of the extremities caused by damage to the peripheral nervous system and usually characterized by weakness, numbness, clumsiness, and sensory loss. Causes are numerous and include diabetes, nutritional deficiencies, injury or trauma, and exposure to toxic substances. It is seen in 5–15% of chronic alcoholics (see ALCOHOLIC NEUROPATHY).

peripheral route to persuasion the process by which attitudes are formed or changed as a result of using PERIPHERAL CUES rather than carefully scrutinizing and thinking about the central merits of attitude-relevant information. See also ELABORATION; ELABORATION-LIKELIHOOD MODEL. Compare CENTRAL ROUTE TO PERSUASION.

peripheral vision vision provided by retinal stimulation considerably outside the FOVEA CENTRALIS. Compare CENTRAL VISION; PARACENTRAL VISION.

periphery *n.* in vision, the part of the visual field that is analyzed by the portions of the retina outside the FOVEA CENTRALIS.

perirhinal cortex a structure in the MEDIAL TEMPORAL LOBE adjacent to the hippocampus that plays an important role as an interface between visual perception and memory.

peritraumatic dissociation a transient dissociative experience (see DISSOCIATION) that occurs at or around the time of a traumatic event. Affected individuals may feel as if they are watching the trauma occur to someone else, as if in a movie, or they may feel "spaced out" and disoriented after the trauma. The occurrence of peritraumatic dissociation is a predictor for the later development of POSTTRAUMATIC STRESS DISORDER.

periventricular white matter tissue consisting largely of myelinated nerve fibers (i.e., WHITE MATTER) that surrounds the lateral cerebral VENTRICLES.

Perky effect the tendency for an imagined stimulus to interfere with seeing an actual target stimulus when the imagined form is close to that of the target. For example, a participant is positioned in front of a blank screen and asked to imagine a leaf, while simultaneously, without the participant's knowledge, a blurry picture of a leaf is projected onto the screen, gradually becoming brighter; the intensity of the picture is well above the threshold for detection before the participant reports seeing it. [described in 1910 by Cheves West **Perky** (1874–1940), U.S. psychologist]

perlocutionary act see ILLOCUTIONARY ACT.

permanence concept see OBJECT PERMANENCE.

permastore *n.* very long-term or permanent memory that develops after extensive learning, training, or experience. Details of foreign languages or algebra learned years ago in school, and even the names of classmates, are said to be stored in permastore. [first described by U.S. cognitive psychologist Harry P. Bahrick (1924–)]

permeability *n.* the state of being permeable to gases, liquids, or dissolved substances, for example by having fine pores through which substances can pass. A perfect membrane has no permeability, but most biological membranes are **selectively** (or **partially**) **permeable** (or **semipermeable**), permitting the selective passage of certain substances, such as the flow of nutrients through a cell membrane. See also OSMOTIC PRESSURE. **—permeable** *adj.*

permeable family a more fluid and flexible version of the NUCLEAR FAMILY that some sociologists regard as an emerging norm in contemporary Western society. The permeable family differs from the stereotypical nuclear family in five main areas: (a) the greater variety of family structures produced by divorce, remarriage, and the acceptance of COHABITATION and single-parent families; (b) a looser sense of family boundaries, so that the offspring of former relationships may be regarded as part of the family unit for some purposes but not for others (see BOUNDARY AMBIGUITY); (c) the erosion of traditional sex roles within the family produced by FEMINISM and the greater role played by women in the workforce; (d) the erosion of a sense of hierarchy and deference within the family, so that children and teenagers expect greater freedom and respect for their views and preferences; and (e) the tendency for all members of the family to expect greater autonomy, so that individual activities sometimes take precedence over shared pursuits and rituals (e.g., family meals). See also BLENDED FAMILY.

permissible exposure level the point at which an employer must use ENGINEERING CONTROLS or ADMINISTRATIVE CONTROLS to reduce employees' exposure to certain hazards, such as noise. See NOISE DOSE.

permissiveness *n.* **1.** an interpersonal style or approach that involves giving a wide range of freedom and autonomy to those with whom one has dealings or over whom one has authority. **2.** an approach to child rearing in which the child is given wide latitude in expressing his or her feelings and opinions, even in ACTING OUT, and in which artificial restrictions and punishment are avoided as much as possible. **—permissive** *adj.*

permissiveness with affection a societal standard that condones premarital sex for both men and women, provided the couples have a stable, affectionate relationship.

permissive parenting **1.** a relaxed parenting style in which the parent or caregiver behaves toward the child in a nonpunishing, accepting, and affirmative manner. A permissive parent tends to make few demands, avoids exercising control, and encourages children to govern their own behavior. Rules are explained, and the children participate in decision making. Compare AUTHORITARIAN PARENTING; AUTHORITATIVE PARENTING; REJECTING–NEGLECTING PARENTING. [first described by U.S. developmental psychologist Diana Baumrind (1927–)] **2.** see LAISSEZ-FAIRE PARENTING.

permutation *n.* an ordered sequence of elements from a set.

permutation test a technique of testing hypotheses based on all possible permutations (ordered sequences) of cases to groups.

peroneal muscular atrophy see CHARCOT–MARIE–TOOTH DISEASE.

perphenazine *n.* a conventional (typical or first-generation) ANTIPSYCHOTIC agent of the piperazine PHENOTHIAZINE class. It is used for the treatment of schizophrenia, and its efficacy and side effects are similar to those of other phenothiazines. As with all phenothiazines, long-term use may be associated with the production of TARDIVE DYSKINESIA or other neuromuscular deficits. U.S. trade name: **Trilafon**.

persecution delusional disorder a type of DELUSIONAL DISORDER in which the central delusion is persecutory (e.g., that one is being plotted against).

persecutory delusion see DELUSION OF PERSECUTION.

per se exclusion rule see STATE V. MACK.

perseverance *n.* see PERSISTENCE.

perseveration *n.* **1.** in general, persistence in doing something to an exceptional level or beyond an appropriate point. **2.** in neuropsychology, the inappropriate repetition of behavior that is often associated with damage to the FRONTAL LOBE of the brain. **3.** an inability to interrupt a task or to shift from one strategy or procedure to another. Perseveration may be observed, for example, in workers under extreme task demands or environmental conditions (mainly HEAT STRESS). **4.** according to the PERSEVERATION–CONSOLIDATION HYPOTHESIS, the repetition, after a learning experience, of neural processes that are responsible for memory formation, which is necessary for the consolidation of LONG-TERM MEMORY. **5.** in speech and language, the persistence of abnormal or inappropriate repetition of a sound, word, or phrase, as occurs in stuttering. **6.** the persistence or prolongation of a speech mode beyond the particular developmental stage at which it is typical or accepted, such as baby talk continuing into later childhood or adulthood. **—perseverate** *vb.*

perseveration–consolidation hypothesis the hypothesis that information passes through two stages in memory formation. During the first stage the memory is held by perseveration (repetition) of neural activity and is easily disrupted. During the second stage the memory becomes fixed, or consolidated, and is no longer easily disrupted. The perseveration–consolidation hypothesis guides much contemporary research on the biological basis of long-term learning and memory. Also called **consolidation hypothesis**; **consolidation–perseveration hypothesis**. See also DUAL TRACE HYPOTHESIS. [originally proposed in 1900 by German psychologists Georg Elias Müller (1850–1934) and Alfons Pilzecker (1865–1920)]

perseveration set a tendency or predisposition that is acquired in a previous situation and is transferred to another situation where it may facilitate or interfere with the task at hand.

perseverative error the continuing recurrence of an error, for example, continuing to call a square a circle even after feedback that the name is wrong, or repeating the same answer to a series of different questions.

persistence *n.* **1.** continuance or repetition of a particular behavior, process, or activity despite cessation of the initiating stimulus. **2.** the quality or state of maintaining a course of action or keeping at a task and finishing it despite the obstacles (such as opposition or discouragement) or the effort involved. Also called **industriousness**; **perseverance**. **3.** continuance of existence, especially for longer than is usual or expected. **—persistent** *adj.*

persistence of an attitude the extent to which an attitude is stable over time and remains constant in the absence of a direct challenge. See also STRENGTH OF AN ATTITUDE.

persistence of vision a sensation of visual stimulation that continues briefly after the actual stimulus is extinguished, perhaps caused by integration lag of visual signals. The light trail of a glowing stick moved rapidly in the dark is an example of the persistence of vision.

persistent puberism a condition in which secondary sexual characteristics become arrested in development and individuals remain in effect pubescent for the rest of their lives.

persistent vegetative state (**PVS**) a prolonged biomedical condition in which rudimentary brain function and, usually, spontaneous respiration continue but there is no awareness of self or environment, no communication, and no voluntary response to stimuli. The condition should be distinguished from BRAIN DEATH. Young trauma victims have sometimes recovered from PVS, but adults rarely recover after 3 months in this state. The term **permanent vegetative state** is sometimes used for people who have been in PVS for an extended period.

persona *n.* in the ANALYTIC PSYCHOLOGY of Carl JUNG, the public face an individual presents to the outside world, in contrast to more deeply rooted and authentic personality characteristics. The term is taken from the mask worn by actors in Roman antiquity.

personal adjustment 1. adaptation by an individual to living and working conditions in his or her family and community, especially in respect of social interactions with those with whom regular personal contacts are necessary. **2.** the degree to which a person is able to cope with the demands of life.

personal arousal scale a technique for self-assessment of the level of ACTIVATION using the same specific criteria for each assessment.

personal attribution see DISPOSITIONAL ATTRIBUTION.

personal audit an oral or written interview or questionnaire designed to encourage individuals to assess their own personal strengths and weaknesses.

personal-care attendant a person hired by an individual with a disability to provide assistance with ACTIVITIES OF DAILY LIVING (dressing, eating, etc.).

personal commitment an individual's adherence to a cause, attitude, or belief. Personal commitment does not necessarily reflect cultural values, attitudes, or beliefs. See also POSTCONVENTIONAL LEVEL.

personal construct one of the concepts by which an individual perceives, understands, predicts, and attempts to control the world. Understanding a client's personal constructs is a central way of beginning to help that person change rigid or negative beliefs. See REPERTORY GRID. [formulated by U.S. psychologist George A. Kelly (1905–1967)]

personal construct therapy a therapy based on the concept of the PERSONAL CONSTRUCT. The essence of the approach is to help individuals test the usefulness and validity of their constructs and to revise and elaborate them as necessary to enhance their understanding and positive interpretations of and interactions with the world. [developed in the 1950s by U.S. psychologist George A. Kelly (1905–1967)]

personal data sheet a questionnaire designed to obtain biographical facts about a person, including age, sex, education, occupation, interests, and health history.

personal disjunction an individual's feeling or perception of dissimilarity or discrepancy between what is or might be and the objective reality or likelihood.

personal disposition (**PD**) see DISPOSITION.

personal distance zone in social psychology, the DISTANCE ZONE adopted by those interacting with friends and personal acquaintances. The personal distance zone is defined as the area from 0.5 to 1.5 m (1½ to 4 ft). Compare INTIMATE ZONE; PUBLIC DISTANCE ZONE; SOCIAL ZONE. See also PROXEMICS.

personal documents writings (diaries, letters, essays, etc.), recordings, and similar material produced by a person that, when examined in **personal-document analysis**, may provide insights into that person's personality, values, attitudes, beliefs, fears, and so forth.

personal equation 1. the difference in performance attributed to INDIVIDUAL DIFFERENCES. **2.** historically, a difference in reaction time between two observers.

personal fable a belief in one's uniqueness and invulnerability, which is an expression of ADOLESCENT EGOCENTRISM and may extend further into the lifespan.

personal-growth group a small group of individuals that uses "encounter" methods, such as games, confrontation, and reenactment, for self-discovery and the development of the members' potential. See also ENCOUNTER GROUP; HUMAN-POTENTIAL MOVEMENT.

personal-growth laboratory a sensitivity-training course or group (see SENSITIVITY TRAINING) that seeks to develop the participants' capabilities for constructive relationships, creative effort, leadership, and understanding of others. This is achieved by various methods, such as art activities, intellectual discussions, sensory stimulation, and emotional interactions.

personal-history questionnaire a questionnaire that records information about a person's special abilities, interests, extracurricular activities, family life, and any medical, emotional, or other problems relating to performance of activities or social adjustment.

personal identity see IDENTITY.

personal involvement see EGO INVOLVEMENT.

personalism *n.* **1.** the view that personality should be the central subject matter of psychology. See PERSONALISTIC PSYCHOLOGY. **2.** a tendency to believe that another person's actions are directed at oneself rather than being an expression of that individual's characteristics.

personalistic approach a view of history holding that important events and accomplishments result mainly from the actions of key individuals. It contrasts with explanations of historical events and accomplishments that invoke a ZEITGEIST, or "spirit of the times." Also called **great man hypothesis**.

personalistic psychology a school of psychology in which the primary emphasis is on personality as the core of psychology (see PERSONALISM), the uniqueness of every human being, and the study of an individual's traits (and organization of traits) as the key to personality and adjustment to the environment. Personalistic psychology originated with German psychologist Edward Spranger (1882–1963), William STERN, and other Europeans and was developed in the United States by Gordon ALLPORT.

personality *n.* the configuration of characteristics and behavior that comprises an individual's unique adjustment to life, including major traits, interests, drives, values, self-concept, abilities, and emotional patterns. Personality is generally viewed as a complex, dynamic integration or totality, shaped by many forces, including: hereditary and constitutional tendencies; physical maturation; early training; identification with significant individuals and groups; culturally conditioned values and roles; and critical experiences and relationships. Various theories explain the structure and development of personality in different ways but all agree that personality helps determine behavior. See also PERSONALITY DEVELOPMENT; PERSONALITY PSYCHOLOGY; PERSONALITY STRUCTURE.

personality assessment the evaluation of such factors as intelligence, skills, interests, aptitudes, creative abilities, attitudes, and facets of psychological development by a variety of techniques. These include (a) observational methods that use behavior sampling, interviews, and rating scales; (b) personality inventories, such as the MINNESOTA MULTIPHASIC PERSONALITY INVENTORY; and (c) projective techniques, such as the RORSCHACH INKBLOT TEST and THEMATIC APPERCEPTION TEST. The uses of personality assessment are manifold, for example, in clinical evaluation of children and adults; in educational and vocational counseling; in industry and other organizational settings; and in rehabilitation.

personality-based integrity test see INTEGRITY TESTING.

personality breakdown a disintegration of personality structure and defenses that results in maladaptive and regressive behavior.

personality change a modification of psychological functioning in relation to personality that could be manifested in many ways. For example, there may be a change in the degree to which one is shy versus socially open or a shift in how internally controlled versus externally determined one views events and behavior.

personality correlates 1. personality traits that are associated with a particular illness or disorder. For example, personality correlates of stress sensitivity may include introversion, obsession, and dependency. **2.** variables that correlate with measures of personality. Correlations between personality traits and observed behaviors, for example, provide evidence for the validity of measures of such traits.

personality cult see CULT OF PERSONALITY.

personality deterioration a progressive decline in an individual's sense of personal identity, self-worth, motivational forces, and emotional life to the point at which he or she appears to be a "changed person" or even a "nonperson." See DETERIORATION.

personality development the gradual development of personality in terms of characteristic emotional responses or temperament, a recognizable style of life, personal roles and role behaviors, a set of values and goals, typical patterns of adjustment, characteristic interpersonal relations and sexual relationships, characteristic traits, and a relatively fixed self-image. See also PERSONALITY PSYCHOLOGY; PERSONALITY STRUCTURE.

personality disintegration a rapid breakdown in personality, cohesion, and functioning, usually owing to particularly stressful life circumstances.

personality disorders a group of disorders involving pervasive patterns of perceiving, relating to, and thinking about the environment and the self that interfere with long-term functioning of the individual and are not limited to isolated episodes. *DSM–IV–TR* recognizes 10 specific personality disorders—paranoid, schizoid, schizotypal, histrionic, narcissistic, antisocial, borderline, avoidant, dependent, and obsessive-compulsive—each of which has its own entry in the dictionary.

personality inventory a personality assessment device that usually consists of a series of statements covering various characteristics and behavioral patterns to which the participant responds by fixed answers, such as True, False, Always, Often, Seldom, or Never, as applied to himself or herself. The scoring of such tests is objective, and the results are interpreted according to standardized norms. An example is the MINNESOTA MULTIPHASIC PERSONALITY INVENTORY.

personality processes the dynamics of personality functioning, that is, personality systems that change over time and across situations as the individual interacts with different people and events in the environment. Personality processes are usually contrasted with PERSONALITY STRUCTURE, that is, the stable, enduring elements of an individual's personality.

personality psychology the systematic study of the human personality, including (a) the nature and definition of personality; (b) its maturation and development; (c) the structure of the self; (d) key theories (e.g., trait theories, psychoanalytic theories, role theories, learning theories, type theories); (e) personality disorders; (f) individual differences; and (g) personality tests and measurements. Personality psychologists tend to study more-or-less enduring and stable individual differences in adults and have traditionally assigned a central role to human motivation and the internal dynamics of human behavior, including both conscious and unconscious motivational forces, factors, and conflicts. Personality theories aim to synthesize cognitive, emotional, motivational, developmental, and social aspects of human individuality into integrative frameworks for making sense of the individual human life. The major families of personality theories include the psychodynamic, behavioral, and humanistic families.

personality structure the organization of the personality in terms of its basic components and their relationship to each other. Structural theories vary widely according to their key concepts, for example, clusters of PERSONALITY TRAITS in Gordon ALLPORT's approach; the surface traits and source traits in CATTELL'S FACTORIAL THEORY OF PERSONALITY; the ID, EGO, and SUPEREGO of Sigmund FREUD; the individual style of life of Alfred ADLER's approach; and needs and motivations in MASLOW'S MOTIVATIONAL HIERARCHY.

personality test any instrument used to help evaluate personality or measure personality traits. Personality tests may collect self-report data, in which participants answer questions about their personality or select items that describe themselves, or they may take the form of projective tests (see PROJECTIVE TECHNIQUE), which claim to measure unconscious aspects of a participant's personality.

personality trait a relatively stable, consistent, and enduring internal characteristic that is inferred from a pattern of behaviors, attitudes, feelings, and habits in the individual. Personality traits can be useful in summarizing, predicting, and explaining an individual's conduct, and a variety of **personality trait theories** exist, among them ALLPORT'S PERSONALITY TRAIT THEORY and CATTELL'S FACTORIAL THEORY OF PERSONALITY. However, because they do not explain the proximal causes of behavior nor provide a developmental account, they must be supplemented by dynamic and processing concepts, such as motives, schemas, plans, projects, and life stories.

personality type any of the specific categories into which human beings may be classified on the basis of personality traits, attitudes, behavior patterns, physique (see CONSTITUTIONAL TYPE), or other outstanding characteristics. Examples are the INTROVERSION–EXTRAVERSION distinction and FUNCTIONAL TYPES of Carl JUNG and Erich FROMM's character types, such as the EXPLOITATIVE ORIENTATION and MARKETING ORIENTATION.

personalization *n.* the alteration or adaptation of something to make it specific to or more meaningful or appropriate for a particular person, as in changing the content of material on a web page or in a magazine to address a particular individual.

personalized instruction 1. teaching focused on the exact level of students' needs in a subject, regardless of curriculum or grade designations. **2.** a process of imparting knowledge that emphasizes a one-on-one relationship between student and instructor. This process enables a student to ask in-depth questions and to gain a clear understanding of concepts introduced by the instructor.

Personal Orientation Inventory (**POI**) an inventory intended to measure SELF-ACTUALIZATION. Originally developed in 1966, it consists of 150 items that each contain two statements descriptive of values or behavior. For each item, the participant selects the statement most descriptive of him- or herself. The POI is scored for 2 major scales (time ratio, support ratio) plus 10 subscales: self-actualizing value, existentiality, feeling reactivity, spontaneity, self-regard, self-acceptance, nature of man, synergy, acceptance of aggression, and capacity for intimate contact. [developed by U.S. psychologist Everett L. Shostrom (1921–)]

personal plan 1. a conception of one's future that includes goals to be achieved. **2.** in psychotherapy, a written plan of intervention and action developed for a client with the participation of all parties concerned. Usually compiled with reference to diagnostic and other data relevant to the client's situation, it identifies a continuum of development outlining progressive steps to be achieved by the client.

personal projects the aims of an individual that involve an organized set of activities of personal relevance over an extended period. [analyzed by Canadian personality psychologist Brian R. Little]

personal protective equipment protective gear, such as gloves, face masks, or hearing protection, that acts as a barrier to reduce or eliminate an individual's exposure to a hazard (e.g., dangerous chemicals or high levels of noise). See also ADMINISTRATIVE CONTROLS; ENGINEERING CONTROLS.

personal space an area of defended space around an individual. Patterns of personal-space use may vary among species as well as among human cultures. Personal space differs from other types of defended space (e.g., territory) by being a surrounding "bubble" that moves with the individual (see BUBBLE CONCEPT OF PERSONAL SPACE). It may have been used by various species throughout evolutionary history to protect the individual organism against intraspecies aggression and threats to personal autonomy. Because human use of personal space varies among cultures, at least part of it must represent a learned behavior. See PROXEMICS.

personal-space invasion the intrusion by one person into the personal space of another. The intruder inappropriately and uncomfortably crowds the other person, without apparent motive. See PROXEMICS.

personal strivings personal goal systems that involve multiple interrelated aims, some of which may support one another while others may be in conflict. [analyzed by U.S. personality psychologist Robert A. Emmons (1958–)]

personal therapy see INDIVIDUAL THERAPY.

personal unconscious in the ANALYTIC PSYCHOLOGY of Carl JUNG, the portion of each individual's unconscious that contains the elements of his or her own experience as opposed to the COLLECTIVE UNCONSCIOUS, which contains the ARCHETYPES universal to humankind. The personal unconscious consists of everything subliminal, forgotten, and repressed in an individual's life. Some of these contents may be recalled to consciousness, as in Sigmund FREUD's notion of the PRECONSCIOUS, but others cannot and are truly unconscious. The personal unconscious also contains COMPLEXES based on the individual's personal experience. In Jung's view the personal unconscious must be integrated into the conscious EGO for INDIVIDUATION to occur.

personal web page a home page (the introductory page on a website) in which one's own preferences for news, stock and sport information, and the like might be displayed. Such a page also provides advertisers with the opportunity to display advertisements for products that are most likely to be of interest to the viewer.

person-centered planning an individual planning process that focuses on people's gifts, strengths, preferences, and achievements. In the case of a person with a developmental disability, emphasis is placed on the person, his or her family members, and the supports needed to enable the person to make choices, participate in the community, and achieve dignity. The process requires an extended commitment from participants and the development of an action-oriented plan. Methods of person-centered planning include Essential Lifestyles Planning, Making Action Plans (MAPS), Personal Future Planning, Planning Alternative Tomorrows with Hope (PATH), and Whole Life Planning. See also PERSON-CENTERED TEAM.

person-centered psychotherapy see CLIENT-CENTERED THERAPY.

person-centered team a group of people who meet periodically in order to develop plans for supports and services to enhance the lifestyle and self-determination of someone with mental retardation or a related condition. The team uses methods based on principles of PERSON-CENTERED PLANNING. Team participants are invited by the person with mental retardation or his or her advocate, rather than by a service organization or agency, and they need not be trained professionals in human services.

person–environment interaction the relationship between a person's psychological and physical capacities and the demands placed on those capacities by the person's social and physical environment (ENVIRONMENTAL PRESS). Quality of life is strongly influenced by **person–environment congruence**: Too little or too much environmental press can lead to poor quality of life.

personification *n.* **1.** in the approach of U.S. psychoanalyst Harry Stack Sullivan (1892–1949), the pattern of feelings and attitudes toward another person arising out of interpersonal relations with him or her. **2.** a figure of speech in which personal or human characteristics are attributed to an object or abstraction, as in saying *Fortune smiled on her.* **3.** a person viewed as representing or embodying some quality, thing, or idea. **—personify** *vb.*

person in the patient in the psychosomatic approach to therapy, the role of the patient's personality, character, and emotional factors as causative agents.

person–machine system see HUMAN–MACHINE SYSTEM.

person–needs analysis in industrial and organizational settings, a component of NEEDS ASSESSMENT in which data are collected to determine whether employees need training, which employees need training, and whether they are ready for training.

personnel *n.* see HUMAN RESOURCES.

personnel data 1. information on newly hired employees derived from application forms, interviews, EMPLOYMENT TESTS, physical examinations, and letters of reference, to be used in matching individuals and jobs. See also BIOGRAPHICAL DATA. **2.** information on employees held by a personnel or human resources department. This will usually include personal details, posts held within the organization, salary and other benefits, and evaluations of job performance.

personnel placement see PLACEMENT.

personnel psychology the branch of INDUSTRIAL AND ORGANIZATIONAL PSYCHOLOGY that deals with the selection, placement, training, promotion, evaluation, and counseling of employees.

personnel selection the process of selecting employees best suited for particular jobs using such procedures as the assembly and analysis of BIOGRAPHICAL DATA, EMPLOYMENT INTERVIEWS, and EMPLOYMENT TESTS.

personnel specification a list of certain precisely defined attributes that will be required in the successful candidate for a particular job, including educational or other qualifications, training, work experience, physical characteristics (e.g., strength and fitness), and specific work-related abilities. More general criteria, such as interests and personality traits, may also be included in the specification. Because these attributes are considered to be predictors of successful job performance, they will be emphasized in publicity and may be tested in the personnel selection process. Also called **job specification**. See JOB DIMENSIONS; JOB REQUIREMENTS; KNOWLEDGE, SKILLS, ABILITIES, AND OTHER CHARACTERISTICS. See also BONA FIDE OCCUPATIONAL QUALIFICATION.

personnel test any test used in PERSONNEL SELECTION, placement of newly hired or existing employees, or employee evaluation. Such tests include (a) aptitude tests, which measure basic abilities and skills; (b) achievement tests, which measure job-specific abilities such as typing skill; and (c) personality and interest inventories, which are used as predictors of job performance. See EMPLOYMENT TEST; OCCUPATIONAL TEST.

personnel training in industrial and organizational settings, a program designed to achieve such goals as orientation of new employees, development of knowledge and skills, or modification of supervisor or employee attitudes. The learning procedures used in personnel training may include classes or lectures (see LECTURE METHOD), use of audiovisual aids or simulator devices (see SIMULATION TRAINING), role play, laboratory training, case discussions (see CASE METHOD), behavioral modeling, business games, or PROGRAMMED INSTRUCTION. The training may be provided outside or inside the usual work setting (see OFF-THE-JOB TRAINING; ON-THE-JOB TRAINING; VESTIBULE TRAINING). Also called **employee training**. See also EXECUTIVE COACHING; MANAGEMENT DEVELOPMENT.

personology *n.* **1.** the study of personality from the holistic point of view, based on the theory that an individual's actions and reactions, thoughts and feelings, and personal and social functioning can be understood only in terms of the whole person. **2.** the theory of personality as a set of enduring tendencies that enable individuals to adapt to life, proposed by U.S. psychologist Henry Alexander Murray (1893–1988). According to Murray, personality is also a mediator between the individual's fundamental needs, both viscerogenic (see VISCEROGENIC NEED) and psychogenic (see PSYCHOGENIC NEED), and the demands of the environment.

person perception the processes by which people think about, appraise, and evaluate other people. An important aspect of person perception is the attribution of motives for action (see ATTRIBUTION THEORY).

person-to-person rating scale a rating scale (formerly called **man-to-man rating scale**) that compares traits of the ratee with the traits of a selected group of individuals who illustrate varying degrees of the traits in question. The rater selects the person in the comparison group with whom the ratee is most closely matched on the trait in question and assigns the ratee the same rating.

perspective *n.* **1.** the ability to view objects, events, and ideas in realistic proportions and relationships. **2.** the ability to interpret relative position, size, and distance of objects in a plane surface as if they were three-dimensional. **3.** the capacity of an individual to take into account and potentially understand the perceptions, attitudes, or behaviors of him- or herself and of other individuals.

perspective taking looking at a situation from a viewpoint that is different from one's usual viewpoint. This may involve adopting the perspective of another person or that associated with a particular social role, as in role play exercises.

perspective theory a theory postulating that self-reports of attitudes on rating scales depend on the content and perspective of a person's attitude. **Content** refers to the evaluative responses that a person actually associates with an ATTITUDE OBJECT. **Perspective** refers to the range of possible evaluative responses that a person considers when rating an attitude object. A self-report of an attitude can change as a result of a change in content or perspective, that is, an actual change in the attitude or a change in what a person defines as an extremely positive or negative attitude. [originally proposed by Harry S. Upshaw (1926–) and Thomas M. Ostrom (1936–)]

perspectivism *n.* a philosophical position applied to psychotherapy in which it is assumed that there is no objective, context-independent truth. [derived from the work of German philosopher Friedrich Nietzsche (1844–1900)]

perspiration *n.* see SWEATING.

persuasion *n.* an active attempt by one person to change another person's attitudes, beliefs, or emotions associated with some issue, person, concept, or object. See also DUAL PROCESS MODELS OF PERSUASION. **—persuasive** *adj.*

persuasion therapy a type of SUPPORTIVE PSYCHOTHERAPY in which the therapist attempts to induce the client to modify faulty attitudes and behavior patterns by appealing to the client's powers of reasoning, will, and self-criticism. The technique was advocated by Alfred ADLER and others, notably Swiss-born French physicians Paul-Charles Dubois (1848–1918) and Joseph Jules Déjerine (1849–1917), as a briefer alternative to reconstructive methods (see RECONSTRUCTIVE PSYCHOTHERAPY) in some therapies.

persuasive arguments theory an analysis of GROUP POLARIZATION that assumes that the opinions of group members discussing an issue or choice will tend to become more extreme when a majority of the members favor a basic position, because the group will generate more arguments favoring the majority position. See also CHOICE SHIFT; CHOICE-SHIFT EFFECT.

persuasive communication information that is intended to change or bolster a person's attitude or course of action and is presented in written, audio, visual, or audiovisual form.

pertinence model **1.** a model of attention in which various stimuli or sources of information are weighted in terms of their relevance. **2.** a model of perception according to which a stimulus that is highly relevant can attract attention even if it is weak.

perturbation *n.* **1.** an anxious or distressed mental state. In the context of a completed or attempted suicide, it is a measure of the extent to which a person is (or was) upset or disturbed. **2.** an influence or activity that causes an interruption or interference in a mental or physical phenomenon or system.

pertussis *n.* see WHOOPING COUGH.

pervasive developmental disorder not otherwise specified (**PDDNOS**) in *DSM–IV–TR*, a residual category comprising PERVASIVE DEVELOPMENTAL DISORDERS characterized by impaired development of social interaction skills associated with communication difficulties or stereotyped behavior that do not conform to the diagnostic criteria of other pervasive developmental disorders, such as AUTISTIC DISORDER, ASPERGER'S DISORDER, RETT SYNDROME, or CHILDHOOD DISINTEGRATIVE DISORDER. This category includes **atypical autism**, a disorder in which children have notable difficulties in play, nonverbal communication, social interaction, and speech but are more social than peers diagnosed with autistic disorder. Also, unlike this disorder, which must occur by the age of 3 years, onset of atypical autism may not be noted until the age of 5 to 6 years. Recent research has suggested that about half of the children with atypical autism also manifest varying degrees of mental retardation. See also AUTISTIC SPECTRUM DISORDER.

pervasive developmental disorders in *DSM–IV–TR*, a class of disorders characterized by severe and pervasive impairment in social interaction and verbal or nonverbal communication or the presence of stereotyped behavior, interests, and activities. These disorders are frequently apparent from an early age; they include ASPERGER'S DISORDER, AUTISTIC DISORDER, CHILDHOOD DISINTEGRATIVE DISORDER, RETT SYNDROME, and PERVASIVE DEVELOPMENTAL DISORDER NOT OTHERWISE SPECIFIED.

perversion *n.* a culturally unacceptable or prohibited form of behavior, particularly sexual behavior. See SEXUAL PERVERSION.

perverted logic (**perverted thinking**) see PARALOGIA.

pessimism *n.* the attitude that things will go wrong and that people's wishes or aims are unlikely to be fulfilled. **Pessimists** are people who expect unpleasant or bad things to happen to them and to others or who are otherwise doubtful or hesitant about positive outcomes of behavior. Pessimism can be defined in terms of expectancy: lack of confidence of attaining desired goals (compare OPTIMISM). Most individuals lie somewhere on the spectrum between the two polar opposites of pure optimism and pure pessimism but tend to demonstrate sometimes strong, relatively stable or situational tendencies in one direction or the other. See also EXPECTANCY-VALUE MODEL. **—pessimistic** *adj.*

PET **1.** abbreviation for PARENT EFFECTIVENESS TRAINING. **2.** acronym for POSITRON EMISSION TOMOGRAPHY.

pet-assisted therapy see ANIMAL-ASSISTED THERAPY.

petechial hemorrhage a minute HEMORRHAGE, often of pinpoint size.

Peter principle the theory that people in an organization will rise to their level of incompetence; that is, employees will continue to receive promotions and additional responsibilities until they can no longer successfully perform their work. It has not been substantiated in empirical work. [proposed in 1969 in a book of the same title by Lawrence J. **Peter** (1919–1990), Canadian-born U.S. educationalist]

pethidine *n.* see MEPERIDINE.

petitio principii see BEGGING THE QUESTION.

petit mal see ABSENCE SEIZURE.

petrification *n.* see FOSSIL.

pet therapy see ANIMAL-ASSISTED THERAPY.

petting behavior sexual activity that may not continue to orgasm or may be foreplay engaged in prior to orgasm. Petting behavior may include kissing, caressing the breasts and genitals, oral sex, and placing the genitals in apposition.

peyote *n.* a small, spineless cactus, *Lophophora williamsii*, that grows wild in Mexico and southern Texas. The name is derived from the Aztec word *peyotl*, which describes the plant as resembling a caterpillar's cocoon. The principal active ingredient is the hallucinogen MESCALINE, found in discoid protuberances on the crown of the plant that are called **mescal buttons**. These buttons are cut from the roots and dried, and then generally chewed or soaked in water to produce an intoxicating liquid. From earliest recorded time, peyote has been used by indigenous peoples of northern Mexico and the southwestern United States as a part of their religious ceremonies; it is still incorporated into the rituals of the Native American Church. Both peyote and mescaline are classified by the U.S. Drug Enforcement Administration as Schedule I controlled substances (see SCHEDULED DRUGS).

P factor analysis FACTOR ANALYSIS that involves statistically analyzing multiple responses provided by a single individual across multiple occasions, rather than studying multiple responses of a large number of individuals, each of whom is studied on only one occasion.

Pfaundler–Hurler syndrome see HURLER'S SYNDROME.

Pfeiffer's syndrome an inherited disorder marked by premature fusion of the cranial bones, causing a skull deformity (see CRANIOSYNOSTOSIS SYNDROME). The patients also have facial deformities with protruding, widely spaced eyes (which often show signs of strabismus), large thumbs, and large great toes. Some affected individuals have below average intelligence. The syndrome is inherited as a dominant trait (see ACROCEPHALOSYNDACTYLY). Also called **acrocephalosyndactyly Type V**. [Emil **Pfeiffer** (1846–1921), German physician]

PG abbreviation for PROSTAGLANDIN.

PGN abbreviation for PARAGIGANTOCELLULAR NUCLEUS.

PGO spikes pontine–geniculo–occipital spikes: peaks, recorded on an electroencephalogram, that occur during sleep and indicate neural activity in the pons, lateral geniculate nucleus, and occipital cortex. They are associated with dreaming. See DREAM STATE.

PGR abbreviation for psychogalvanic reflex. See GALVANIC SKIN RESPONSE.

pH see HYDROGEN-ION CONCENTRATION.

phacomatosis *n.* see PHAKOMATOSIS.

Phaedra complex the incestuous love of a mother for her son. The name derives from the Greek myth of Phaedra, wife of Theseus. When her stepson, Hippolytus, rejected her love, Phaedra accused him of violating her and hanged herself. See also MOTHER–SON INCEST.

phago- (**phag-**) *combining form* eating.

phagocytosis *n.* the process by which solid particles, including foreign substances, food particles, and other cells, are engulfed by cells called **phagocytes**. The substances are surrounded by membrane, forming a vacuole within the phagocyte that fuses with a **lysosome**, an organelle containing enzymes that digest the engulfed contents. Certain white blood cells act as phagocytes as part of the IMMUNE RESPONSE.

phagomania *n.* an insatiable hunger or morbid desire to consume food.

phakomatosis (**phacomatosis**) *n.* a hereditary disorder characterized by the growth of benign nodulelike tumors of the brain, eye, and skin. Types of phakomatosis include VON RECKLINGHAUSEN'S DISEASE, cerebroretinal angiomatosis, tuberous sclerosis, and encephalotrigeminal angiomatosis.

phakoscope (**phacoscope**) *n.* an instrument that enables the shape of the lens of the eye to be observed, as well as the changes in its shape that occur during ACCOMMODATION.

phallic *adj.* of, relating to, or resembling the penis.

phallic character see PHALLIC PERSONALITY.

phallicism *n.* reverence for the male genitalia, especially when regarded as symbolizing the creative forces of nature. See also PHALLOCENTRIC. Also called **phallism**; **phallus worship**.

phallic mother in psychoanalytic theory, the fantasy that the mother has a penis.

phallic personality in psychoanalytic theory, a pattern of narcissistic behavior exemplified by boastfulness, excessive self-assurance, vanity, compulsive sexual behavior, and in some cases aggressive or exhibitionistic behavior. Also called **phallic character**; **phallic-narcissistic character**; **phallic-narcissistic personality**.

phallic phase see PHALLIC STAGE.

phallic pride in psychoanalytic theory, the sense of superiority and feelings of power experienced by boys when they discover that they have a penis and girls do not. These feelings are believed to help master intense CASTRATION ANXIETY. See also PHALLIC STAGE.

phallic sadism in psychoanalytic theory, aggression that is associated with the child's PHALLIC STAGE of PSYCHOSEXUAL DEVELOPMENT. The child interprets sexual intercourse as a violent, aggressive activity on the part of the man, and particularly on the part of the penis. See also PRIMAL SCENE; SADISM.

phallic stage in the classic psychoanalytic theory of Sigmund FREUD, the stage of PSYCHOSEXUAL DEVELOPMENT occurring at about age 3, when the LIBIDO is focused on the genital area (penis or clitoris) and discovery and manipulation of the body become a major source of pleasure. During this period boys are posited to experience CASTRATION ANXIETY, girls to experience PENIS ENVY, and both to experience the OEDIPUS COMPLEX. Also called **phallic phase**.

phallic symbol any object that resembles or might be taken as a representation of the penis, such as a cigar, pencil, tree, skyscraper, snake, or hammer.

phallism *n.* see PHALLICISM.

phallocentric *adj.* **1.** denoting a culture or belief system in which the phallus (penis) is regarded as a sacred giver of life, source of power, or symbol of fertility. See PHALLICISM; PRIAPISM. See also ANDROCENTRIC. **2.** more generally, focused or fixated on the penis as a symbol of male potency. **—phallocentrism** *n.*

phallus *n.* (*pl.* **phalli**) the PENIS or an object that resembles the form of the penis. As a symbolic object, it often represents fertility or potency.

phallus worship see PHALLICISM.

phanerothyme *adj.* a term coined by British writer Aldous Huxley (1894–1964) to describe the effect of mind-altering drugs, such as LSD (from Greek *phanein*, "to reveal," and *thymos*, "mind, soul"). He first used the term in a letter (1956) to his friend Humphry Osmond, who counterproposed the term *psychedelic*, which has the same etymological sense of "mind-revealing." See PSYCHEDELIC DRUGS.

phantasm *n.* an illusion or apparition, often of an absent person appearing in the form of a spirit or ghost. The observer may recognize it as being imaginary or illusory, unlike a true hallucination, which is associated with lack of insight on the part of the observer.

phantasmagoria *n.* **1.** a shifting series of confused or deceptive images, as in a dream or hallucination. **2.** an apparition of ghosts or spirits. [from the name of a 19th-century theatrical show, in which magic lantern effects were used to create images of ghosts and specters] **—phantasmagoric** *adj.*

phantasticum *n.* (*pl.* **phantastica**) a category of drugs identified in the 1920s as capable of producing hallucinatory experiences. These drugs are now known as HALLUCINOGENS. [named by German toxicologist Louis Lewin (1850–1929)]

phantasy *n.* in the OBJECT RELATIONS THEORY of Melanie KLEIN, one of the unconscious constructions, wishes, or impulses that are presumed to underlie all thought and feeling. The *ph* spelling is used to distinguish this from the everyday form of FANTASY, which can include conscious daydreaming.

phantom *n.* **1.** an illusion without material substance. **2.** the feeling that an amputated body part (e.g., a limb or breast) is still present. See BREAST-PHANTOM PHENOMENON; PHANTOM LIMB; PSEUDOESTHESIA.

phantom breast see BREAST-PHANTOM PHENOMENON.

phantom color a color perceived during stimulation with a black and white pattern, such as a BENHAM'S TOP.

phantom limb the feeling that an amputated limb is still present, often manifested as a tingling or, occasionally, painful sensation in the area of the missing limb (**phantom limb pain**). In some cases the individual may even deny that the limb has been removed. It is thought that the brain's representation of the limb remains intact and, in the absence of normal SOMESTHETIC STIMULATION, becomes active spontaneously or as a result of stimulation from other brain tissue. See also BREAST-PHANTOM PHENOMENON.

phantom-lover syndrome a type of EROTIC DELUSION elaborated around a person who in fact does not exist. [defined in 1978 by Canadian psychiatrist Mary V. Seeman]

phantosmia *n.* perception of an odor when no smell stimulus is present (i.e., an olfactory hallucination). See also DYSOSMIA.

pharmacodynamics *n.* the study of the interactions of drugs with the RECEPTORS that are responsible for their actions on the body. It involves studying the effects of drugs on the body and their mechanism of action. Basic studies involve the activity of drugs at the receptor sites to which the drugs attach as well as the changes in cell function and behavior that result. **—pharmacodynamic** *adj.*

pharmacodynamic tolerance a form of drug TOLERANCE in which the chemistry of the brain becomes adjusted to the presence of the drug, which in turn then loses its capacity for modifying brain activity. Neurons adapt to continued drug presence by reducing the number or sensitivity of receptors available to the drug (i.e., down-regulation). This cellular-adaptive tolerance is associated with the use of many drugs, including sedative hypnotics and psychostimulants, and may be followed by withdrawal symptoms when regular doses of the drug are interrupted. This may be contrasted with **metabolic tolerance,** in which the body reacts to continued presence of the drug by metabolizing it at an increased rate. Both forms of tolerance lead to higher doses of the drug being needed to produce the same effects.

pharmacogenetics *n.* the study of genetic factors that influence the response of individuals to different drugs and to different dosages of drugs. Inherited variations in enzymes or other metabolic components can affect the efficacy of a drug or cause adverse reactions to normal doses. For example, some 40–70% of Caucasians have an enzyme variant that causes them to metabolize the antituberculosis drug, isoniazid, very slowly. They require only a fraction of the standard dose.

pharmacogenomics *n.* the study of the ways in which genetic knowledge can be utilized for the accurate and effective administration of medications and other drugs.

pharmacokinetics *n.* the study of how pharmacological agents are processed within a biological system, in vivo or in vitro, including factors that influence the absorption, distribution, metabolism, and elimination of the substance or its metabolic products.

pharmacological antagonism a form of antagonism between two drugs in which one acts as an AGONIST at a specified receptor site and the other acts as an ANTAGONIST at the same receptor site. It occurs, for example, between morphine and naloxone: Although both drugs occupy the mu OPIOID RECEPTOR, morphine (the agonist) produces physiological and psychological changes characteristic of opioid drugs, whereas naloxone (the antagonist) competitively binds to the same receptor site and reverses the effects of morphine. Compare PHYSIOLOGICAL ANTAGONISM.

pharmacology *n.* the branch of science that involves the study of substances that interact with living organisms to alter some biological process affecting the HOMEOSTASIS of the organism. **Therapeutic** (or **medical**) **pharmacology** deals with the administration of substances to correct a state of disease or to enhance well-being. **—pharmacological** or **pharmacologic** *adj.*

pharmacopeia (**pharmacopoeia**) *n.* a book, usually issued by a recognized authority, that lists drugs and their chemical properties, preparation, recommended dosages, method of administration, side effects, dangers, and other information.

pharmacotherapeutic regimen a plan for the treatment of a condition through the use of medication, outlining, for example, the type of drug or drugs to be used, dosage requirements, schedule of administration, and expected duration of use.

pharmacotherapy *n.* the treatment of a disorder by the administration of drugs, as opposed to such means as surgery, psychotherapy, or complementary and alternative methods. Also called **drug therapy**. See PSYCHOPHARMACOTHERAPY.

pharynx *n.* the muscular and membranous tube running from the mouth and nostrils to the entrance to the esophagus (gullet) that acts as the passage for food and respiratory gases. It consists of three major sections: the lower LARYNGOPHARYNX, the middle OROPHARYNX, and the upper NASOPHARYNX. **—pharyngeal** *adj.*

phase *n.* **1.** a stage in the development of life, such as puberty or adulthood. **2.** a recurrent state of any cyclical process.

phase cue see BINAURAL CUES.

phase locking the tendency for a neural ACTION POTENTIAL to occur at a certain phase of a PURE-TONE stimulus. In general, an action potential will not occur on every cycle, but when it is generated it tends to occur at the same point or phase in the stimulus. More generally, phase locking refers to the ability of a neuron to synchronize or follow the temporal structure of a sound. In the auditory nerve, fibers can phase-lock to frequencies below 4–5 kHz. Phase locking underlies the ability to localize sounds based on interaural phase differences or interaural time differences (see BINAURAL CUES). Its role in monaural hearing is uncertain, but it has been proposed as a mechanism for the coding of pitch.

phase modulation see MODULATION.

phase shift 1. a disruption of the normal sleep–wake cycle, with the result that the individual is alert during a usual sleeping period and sleepy when he or she should be alert. See CIRCADIAN RHYTHM SLEEP DISORDER; DISORDERS OF THE SLEEP–WAKE CYCLE SCHEDULE. **2.** a change in the diurnal or CIRCADIAN RHYTHM brought about by such things as changes in daylight exposure or changing time zones.

phase spectrum see SOUND SPECTRUM.

phasic activation a pattern of brain activation, associated with attention mechanisms, that is related to the DIFFUSE THALAMIC PROJECTION SYSTEM and is transitory rather than tonic or persistent in nature.

phasic receptor a RECEPTOR cell that shows a rapid fall in the frequency of discharge of nerve impulses as stimulation is maintained. Compare TONIC RECEPTOR.

phatic communication spoken or written communication that is intended primarily to establish or maintain social relationships rather than to convey information.

phencyclidine *n.* see PCP.

phenelzine *n.* a MONOAMINE OXIDASE INHIBITOR that exerts its antidepressant effects by irreversibly binding to monoamine oxidase, thus preventing the breakdown of monoamine neurotransmitters. As with other drugs in its class, phenelzine has been supplanted by safer drugs without the associated toxicities, dietary restrictions, and potentially fatal drug interactions. U.S. trade name: **Nardil**.

Phenergan *n.* a trade name for PROMETHAZINE.

phenobarbital *n.* an anticonvulsant BARBITURATE used for treatment of generalized tonic–clonic or partial seizures. Formerly widely used as a sedative and hypnotic, it has been largely supplanted for these purposes by safer medications lacking the toxicity and adverse effects associated with barbiturates. Phenobarbital is also sometimes used in the management of SEDATIVE, HYPNOTIC, OR ANXIOLYTIC WITHDRAWAL. U.S. trade name: **Luminal**.

phenocopy *n.* an imitation of a PHENOTYPE resulting from the interaction of an environmental factor and a GENOTYPE. An example is the effect of sunlight on skin or hair, resulting in variations that mimic the natural coloring or texture of other phenotypes.

phenomena *pl. n.* see PHENOMENON.

phenomenal absolutism see NAIVE REALISM.

phenomenal field see PHENOMENAL SPACE.

phenomenalism *n.* the doctrine that access to, and thus knowledge of, the external world is always through sensory experience of phenomena. Propositions about physical objects are therefore to be analysed in terms of actual or possible sensory experiences. The position is compatible with certain forms of IDEALISM, in that physical entities are defined in terms of mental experience, but also with EMPIRICISM and POSITIVISM. **—phenomenalist** *adj.*

phenomenal motion motion that may not be real but is perceived or experienced as being real. See APPARENT MOVEMENT. See also PHENOMENAL SPACE.

phenomenal self the SELF as experienced by the individual at a given time. Only a small portion of self-knowledge is active in working memory or consciousness at any time, with the remainder lying dormant or inactive. The same person might have a very different phenomenal self at different times, without any change in actual self-knowledge, simply because different views are brought into awareness by events. Also called **working self-concept**.

phenomenal space the environment as experienced by a given individual at a given time. The term refers not to objective reality but to personal and subjective reality, including everything within one's field of awareness. In the phenomenological personality theory of Carl ROGERS, it is also known as the **phenomenological field**. Also called **phenomenal field**.

phenomenistic causality in the theory of Jean PIAGET, an inference of causality between events, drawn only on the basis of spatial or temporal contiguity. Such inferences are typical of much thinking in prescientific cultures and of the thought processes of a child. For example: "It is dark outside because I am sleepy."

phenomenological analysis an approach to psychology in which mental experiences are described and studied without theoretical presuppositions or speculation as to their causes or consequences. In general, such an approach will favor observation and description over analysis and interpretation; it will also attempt to understand a person's experience from the point of view of that person, rather than from some more abstract theoretical perspective. See also PHENOMENOLOGY.

phenomenological death the subjective sense that one has become inert, insensitive, and unresponsive. Phenomenological death occurs in some psychotic conditions. Patients may speak of themselves as dead and behave (although inconsistently) in accord with that belief. Phenomenological death is conceived as the extreme point on a continuum of self-assessment; it is not necessarily a condition that is permanent.

phenomenological field see PHENOMENAL SPACE.

phenomenological theory an approach to personality theory that places questions of individuals' current experiences of themselves and their world at the center of analyses of personality functioning and change. See also PERSONAL CONSTRUCT. [proposed by U.S. psychologist George A. Kelly (1905–1967)]

phenomenological therapy any form of therapy, perhaps best exemplified by CLIENT-CENTERED THERAPY, in which the emphasis is on the client's process of self-discovery as opposed to an interpretive focus, such as that found in psychoanalysis.

phenomenology *n.* a movement in modern European philosophy initiated by German philosopher Edmund Husserl (1859–1938). In his writings of the 1910s and 1920s, Husserl argued for a new approach to human knowledge in which both the traditional concerns of philosophy (such as metaphysics and epistemology) and the modern concern with scientific causation would be set aside in favor of a careful attention to the nature of immediate conscious experience. Mental events should be studied and described in their own terms, rather than in terms of their relationship to events in the body or in the external world. However, phenomenology should be distinguished from introspection as it is concerned with the relationship between acts of consciousness and the objects of such acts (see INTENTIONALITY). Husserl's approach proved widely influential in psychology (especially GESTALT PSYCHOLOGY) and the social sciences; it also inspired the work of German philosopher Martin Heidegger (1889–1976), whose EXISTENTIAL PHENOMENOLOGY provided the basis for EXISTENTIALISM and EXISTENTIAL PSYCHOLOGY. **—phenomenological** *adj.* **—phenomenologist** *n.*

phenomenon *n.* (*pl.* **phenomena**) **1.** an observable event or physical occurrence. **2.** in philosophy, something perceived by the senses. In Greek philosophy, most notably that of Plato (c. 427–c. 347 BCE), phenomena are the sensible things that constitute the world of experience, as contrasted with the transcendent realities that are known only through reason. German philosopher Immanuel Kant (1724–1804) used the term *phenomena* to refer to things as they appear to the senses and are interpreted by the categories of the human understanding. For Kant, knowledge of phenomena is the kind of knowledge available to human beings, as knowledge of NOUMENA, or things in themselves, remains beyond human experience or reason. **3.** an occurrence or entity that defies explanation. **—phenomenal** *adj.*

phenothiazines *pl. n.* a group of chemically related compounds most of which are used as ANTIPSYCHOTIC drugs, originally developed as such in the 1950s. The drugs in this class of traditional (or first-generation) antipsychotics were formerly the most widely used agents for the treatment of schizophrenia. The phenothiazines were the first effective antipsychotic medications and largely responsible for the deinstitutionalization of tens of thousands of people with schizophrenia. It is commonly assumed that their therapeutic effects are produced by blockade of dopamine D2 receptors (see DOPAMINE-RECEPTOR ANTAGONISTS); they also block acetylcholine, histamine, and norepinephrine receptors, actions that are associated with many of their adverse effects. Phenothiazines are used for the treatment of acute mania, psychotic agitation, and schizophrenia as well as nausea and vomiting and for preanesthesia sedation. They can be divided into three subgroups: aliphatic, piperazine, and piperidine. A variety of adverse side effects is associated with their use, including EXTRAPYRAMIDAL EFFECTS, TARDIVE DYSKINESIA, sedation, and ANTICHOLINERGIC EFFECTS.

phenotype *n.* the observable characteristics of an individual, such as morphological or biochemical features and the presence or absence of a particular disease or condition. Phenotype is determined by the expression of the individual's GENOTYPE (i.e., genes) coupled with the effects of environmental factors (e.g., nutritional status or climate). **—phenotypic** *adj.*

phensuximide *n.* see SUCCINIMIDES.

phentermine *n.* an APPETITE SUPPRESSANT with a mechanism of action similar to the AMPHETAMINES. Like other appetite suppressants, it is effective only for short-term weight loss: Long-term results require concurrent adherence to effective behavioral weight-loss strategies. Phentermine was previously marketed in combination with fenfluramine or dexfenfluramine—a combination known as "phen-fen"—which was taken off the market after cases of pulmonary hypertension and heart-valve disease were reported in users. These serious side effects cannot be ruled out with the use of phentermine alone. Phentermine should not be given in combination with monoamine oxidase inhibitors, and should be used with caution in individuals taking SSRI antidepressants. U.S. trade names: **Adipex**; **Ionamin**.

phentolamine *n.* an alpha-ADRENORECEPTOR BLOCKING AGENT with direct action on heart and smooth muscle. It is a potent vasodilator used in management of severe hypertension associated with catecholamine excess, as in patients with PHEOCHROMOCYTOMAS. It is in infrequent clinical use. U.S. trade name: **Regitine**.

phenylalkylamines *pl. n.* a group of natural and synthetic drugs that can produce hallucinogenic effects. They include the PHENYLETHYLAMINES, such as MESCALINE, and the phenylisopropylamines (substituted phenylethylamines), such as MDMA.

phenylcyclohexyl derivatives a category of drugs introduced in 1960 as potential general anesthetics but discontinued because they caused serious psychological disturbances in patients. The prototype drug, PCP, produces sensory deprivation effects similar to those observed in some cases of schizophrenia. Drugs of this series are considered to be HALLUCINOGENS but may be used as anesthetics and analgesics in veterinary medicine.

phenylethylamines *pl. n.* a group of drugs with hallucinogenic effects and a common basic chemical structure. The prototype is MESCALINE, an alkaloid first isolated from the PEYOTE cactus in 1896. Mescaline is one of the least potent of the hallucinogens, but potency is increased by adding methyl groups to the basic molecule, thereby creating **substituted phenylethylamines**. The latter include the amphetamine derivatives DOM, MDA, and MDMA. See also PHENYLALKYLAMINES.

phenylketonuria (PKU) *n.* an inherited metabolic disease transmitted as an autosomal recessive trait and marked by a deficiency of an enzyme (phenylalanine hydroxylase) needed to utilize the amino acid phenylalanine. Unless it is diagnosed in early infancy and treated by a restricted dietary intake of phenylalanine, phenylketonuria leads to severe mental retardation and other nervous-system disorders. Most untreated patients have IQs below 20. Women who have been treated for the disease must adopt a restricted diet during pregnancy to prevent neurological damage to their children (see MATERNAL PKU).

phenylpyruvic acid an intermediate product of the metabolism of phenylalanine. In patients with PHENYLKETONURIA, phenylalanine is not converted to the normal end-product, tyrosine, but only to phenylpyruvic acid, which is excreted in their urine.

phenylpyruvic oligophrenia a severe form of mental retardation that is associated with or due to an inborn error of metabolism of phenylalanine, as in cases of PHENYLKETONURIA. Early dietary restriction of phenylalanine may bring intelligence up to average or near-average range.

phenytoin *n.* an ANTICONVULSANT drug: the prototype of the HYDANTOINS. Phenytoin is prescribed mainly for the management of partial and tonic–clonic seizures but is also used in the treatment of some cases of migraine and neuralgia. It is occasionally used to manage behavioral disturbances in children. U.S. trade name (among others): **Dilantin**.

pheochromocytoma *n.* a small tumor that usually develops in the adrenal medulla but may occur in tissues of the sympathetic paraganglia. Because it is composed of adrenal tissue, it can secrete epinephrine and norepinephrine, producing excessive levels of these catecholamines, hypertension with headaches, tachycardia, visual blurring, and other symptoms. It is believed to be an inherited disorder.

pheromone *n.* an EXTERNAL CHEMICAL MESSENGER that influences the behavior of other members of the same species. For example, it may serve to attract animals of the opposite sex or to act as an alarm. In nonhuman animals, sensitivity to pheromones occurs via the VOMERONASAL SYSTEM. The existence of true pheromones in humans is controversial, although scents (e.g., perfumes, body odors) may play a role in sexual attraction and arousal. Pheromones have also been suggested as a cause of MENSTRUAL SYNCHRONY. Also called **ectohormone**. Compare ALLOMONE.

phi coefficient (symbol: ϕ) a measure of association for two dichotomous RANDOM VARIABLES. The phi coefficient is the PRODUCT–MOMENT CORRELATION when both variables are coded (0,1).

phi–gamma function (symbol: $\phi(\gamma)$) for the METHOD

OF CONSTANT STIMULI, a plot of response probability based on stimulus magnitude that takes the ogival (S-shaped) form of the cumulative normal distribution.

-philia *suffix* abnormal craving or attraction (e.g., NECROPHILIA).

Phillips Rating Scale of Premorbid Adjustment in Schizophrenia a method of analyzing the PREMORBID ADJUSTMENT of patients with schizophrenia as part of a determination of their prognosis. It is based on questions derived by a researcher from case-history information. Also called **Phillips scale**; **Phillips scale of premorbid adjustment**. [developed in 1953 by psychopharmacologist Leslie **Phillips**]

philo- (**phil-**) *combining form* love of or interest in.

philology *n.* the study of the history of languages and of their relationships with one another, usually with a focus on the analysis of textual records. See also COMPARATIVE LINGUISTICS; DIACHRONIC LINGUISTICS; GENETIC LINGUISTICS. **—philological** *adj.*

philopatry *n.* attachment to the place where an individual was born or hatched. In species with sex-biased DISPERSAL, the nondispersing species is said to show philopatry. If males typically leave the natal group to join other groups, the species shows female philopatry.

philosophical psychology the branch of psychology that studies the philosophical issues relevant to the discipline and the philosophical assumptions that underlie its theories and methods. It approaches psychology from a wide perspective informed by a knowledge of metaphysics, epistemology, ethics, the history of ideas, the philosophy of science, and the tools of formal philosophical analysis. Philosophical psychologists tend to concentrate on the larger issues arising from the field rather than on model building and data gathering. See also RATIONAL PSYCHOLOGY.

philosophical psychotherapy psychotherapy based on philosophical principles of belief and attitude generally, as they relate to cognition, emotion, and behavior, or based on the principles of some particular philosophical perspective (e.g., EXISTENTIAL PSYCHOTHERAPY). Training in philosophy without appropriate training in the mental health field, however, is deemed inadequate for offering psychotherapy or counseling services.

philosophy *n.* the intellectual discipline that uses careful reasoned argument to elucidate fundamental questions, notably those concerning the nature of reality (METAPHYSICS), the nature of knowledge (EPISTEMOLOGY), and the nature of moral judgments (ETHICS). As such, it provides an intellectual foundation for many other disciplines, including psychology. Psychology as a scientific discipline has its roots in the epistemological preoccupations of 18th- and 19th-century philosophy and continues to be influenced by philosophical ideas. See PHILOSOPHICAL PSYCHOLOGY. **—philosopher** *n.* **—philosophical** *adj.*

philosophy of mind the branch of philosophy concerned with questions about the nature and functioning of mind and consciousness and the relationship of mind and mental activity to brain and body and to the external world (see MIND–BODY PROBLEM). It is deeply concerned with the relationships among language, thought, and action.

philosophy of science the branch of philosophy devoted to the study and understanding of science and its development. It is concerned with such matters as the methods of science, the nature of scientific knowledge and scientific explanation, and the meaning of the scientific enterprise.

phimosis *n.* a condition, congenital or acquired, in which the foreskin of the penis cannot be retracted over the glans. The acquired form of phimosis is usually due to an infection or edema. Phimosis may be corrected by circumcision. The condition is a frequent complication of sexually transmitted diseases.

Phineas Gage an individual, often featured in introductory psychology textbooks, who was made famous when a railroad tie passed through and damaged anterior parts of the frontal lobes of his brain without apparent cognitive deficits but who later showed marked changes in behavior and personality.

phi phenomenon 1. an illusion of APPARENT MOVEMENT seen when two lights flash on and off about 150 m apart. The light appears to move from one location to the other. The phi phenomenon is a form of BETA MOVEMENT. **2.** a sensation of pure movement independent of any other attributes of the stimulus, such as its form.

phlebotomy *n.* removal of blood from the body for diagnostic or therapeutic purposes. This is ordinarily achieved by inserting a needle or catheter into a vein and then applying negative pressure. Through the early and mid-19th century, this practice was known as **bloodletting** and involved the removal of considerable quantities of blood as a means of curing or preventing disease. Also called **venesection**.

phlegmatic type one of the original constitutional body types based on the four humors associated with Hippocrates (c. 460–c. 377 BCE) and described by Galen (129–199 CE), who attributed the apathetic character of the phlegmatic type to the dominance of phlegma, or mucus, over other body fluids, or humors. See CARUS TYPOLOGY; HUMORAL THEORY.

PHO abbreviation for PHYSICIAN–HOSPITAL ORGANIZATION.

phobia *n.* a persistent and irrational fear of a specific situation, object, or activity (e.g., heights, dogs, water, blood, driving, flying), which is consequently either strenuously avoided or endured with marked distress. In *DSM–IV–TR* the many types of individual phobia are classified under the heading SPECIFIC PHOBIA. See also SOCIAL PHOBIA. **—phobic** *adj.*

-phobia *suffix* irrational fear or dislike (e.g., CLAUSTROPHOBIA).

phobic anxiety anxiety that focuses on or is directed toward objects or situations (e.g., insects, telephone booths, open areas) that represent the real fear but pose little if any actual danger themselves.

phobic attitude a behavior pattern apparently characterized by disruptions in the awareness of and attention to experience in the present. An example is engaging in a fantasy of the future to escape a painful present reality. [defined by German-born U.S. psychotherapist Frederick (Fritz) S. Perls (1893–1970)]

phobic avoidance the active evasion of feared objects or situations by individuals with phobias.

phobic character in psychoanalytic theory, an individual who tends to deal with anxiety by extreme or fearful avoidance. [first used in 1945 by Austrian psychoanalyst Otto Fenichel (1897–1946)]

phobic disorders in *DSM–III*, a group of disorders in which the essential feature is a persistent, irrational fear and consequent avoidance of specific objects, activities, or situations (see PHOBIA). The fear is recognized as unreasonable, but is nevertheless so intense that it interferes with everyday functioning and is often a significant source of distress. Phobic disorders included SPECIFIC PHOBIAS, SOCIAL PHOBIA, and AGORAPHOBIA.

phocomelia *n.* congenital absence of the proximal portion of a limb or limbs, the hands or feet being attached to the trunk by a small, irregularly shaped bone.

Phoenix House an organization devoted to the treatment and prevention of substance abuse in adolescents and adults. Phoenix House offers both residential and outpatient programs, as well as other services related to or in support of the treatment process. See also THERAPEUTIC COMMUNITY.

phon *n.* see LOUDNESS.

phon- *combining form* see PHONO-.

phonasthenia *n.* **1.** voice fatigue, which may be attributable to overuse, general debilitation, or old age. **2.** see BREATHY VOICE.

phonation *n.* the production of VOICED sounds by means of vibrations of the VOCAL CORDS.

phone *n.* a single speech sound.

phoneme *n.* in linguistics, a speech sound that plays a meaningful role in a language and cannot be analyzed into smaller meaningful sounds, conventionally indicated by slash symbols: /b/. A speech sound is held to be meaningful in a given language if its contrast with other sounds is used to mark distinctions of meaning: In English, for example, /p/ and /b/ are phonemes because they distinguish between [pan] and [ban] and other such pairs (see MINIMAL PAIR). **—phonemic** *adj.*

phoneme–grapheme correspondence the relationship between PHONEMES and their graphic representation (see GRAPHEME) in a particular language. A high level of regularity in this correspondence is thought to facilitate early reading.

phonemic awareness the knowledge that words consist of separable sounds.

phonemic disorder a disturbance involving PHONEMES, the speech sounds that distinguish words from one another.

phonemic restoration effect a psycholinguistic phenomenon in which a person listening to speech recordings in which PHONEMES have been replaced by white noise or have otherwise been made inaudible does not notice the interruption. It is assumed that the listener's perceptual mechanism must have restored the missing phonemes. This is considered strong evidence for an active process of speech perception.

phonemics *n.* the branch of linguistics concerned with the classification and analysis of the PHONEMES in a language. While PHONETICS tries to characterize all possible sounds represented in human language, phonemics identifies which of the phonetic distinctions are considered meaningful by a given language. See EMIC–ETIC DISTINCTION.

phonetics *n.* the branch of linguistics that studies the physical properties of speech sounds and the physiological means by which these are produced and perceived. See ACOUSTIC PHONETICS; ARTICULATORY PHONETICS.

phonetic symbolism the hypothesis that there is a correspondence of some kind between the sounds of words and their REFERENTS, as opposed to an arbitrary relationship. Most schools of modern linguistics are based on the premise that words are essentially ARBITRARY SYMBOLS, the only exceptions being a small number of onomatopoeic coinages (see ONOMATOPOEIA). However, it is an observable fact that most languages contain clusters of words (mainly monosyllables) in which a similarity of sound seems to reflect a similarity of reference; an example in English would be the large cluster *track, trail, train, traipse, tramp, travel, trawl, tread, trek, trip, trot, truck, trudge,* and so on. Believers in phonetic symbolism would argue that for English speakers (at least) the sound [tr] and the physical actions involved in articulating it must have a deep psychological correspondence with the ideas of travel and laborious movement. Others would dismiss such speculations entirely, arguing that these word clusters can be explained by shared etymology, simple association of ideas, and coincidence. Also called **sound symbolism**.

phonics *n.* **1.** a method of teaching reading, popularly known as **sounding out**, that is based on the sounds of the letters in a word rather than on the word as a unit, that is, trying to match GRAPHEMES and PHONEMES. Also called **phonic method**. Compare WHOLE-WORD METHOD. **2.** a former name for ACOUSTICS.

phonism *n.* a form of SYNESTHESIA in which a sensation of hearing is effected through another sense, that is, by something that is seen, smelled, tasted, or felt.

phono- (phon-) *combining form* voice, speech, or sound.

phonogram *n.* a graphic or symbolic representation of a phoneme, syllable, or word.

phonological disorder in *DSM–IV–TR*, a communication disorder characterized by failure to develop and consistently use speech sounds that are appropriate for the child's age. It most commonly involves misarticulation of the later acquired speech sounds, such as [l], [r], [s], [z], [ch], [sh], or [th] (see LALLING; LISP), but may also include substitution of sounds (e.g., [t] for [k]) or omission of sounds (e.g., final consonants). These problems are not due to, or are in excess of those normally associated with, hearing loss, structural deficits in the mechanism of speech production (e.g., cleft palate), or a neurological disorder. In *DSM–III* this disorder was categorized as **developmental articulation disorder**.

phonological dysgraphia an impaired ability or an inability to sound out words or write them phonetically.

phonological dyslexia a form of acquired dyslexia (see ALEXIA) characterized primarily by difficulties in reading pronounceable nonwords. Semantic errors are not seen in this type of dyslexia, a feature that distinguishes it from DEEP DYSLEXIA. Phonological dyslexia manifested as a form of DEVELOPMENTAL DYSLEXIA has also been described. See also SURFACE DYSLEXIA. [first described in 1979 by Marie-France Beauvois and Jacqueline Derouesné]

phonological loop a component of SHORT-TERM MEMORY or WORKING MEMORY that retains verbal information by REHEARSAL over short intervals of time. See also CENTRAL EXECUTIVE. [proposed by British cognitive psychologist Alan D. Baddeley (1934–)]

phonological recoding the use of reading skills to translate written symbols into sounds and words.

phonology *n.* the branch of linguistics that studies the system of speech sounds in a language or in language generally. The term is less specific than either PHONEMICS or PHONETICS. **—phonological** *adj.*

phonopathy *n.* an obsolescent name for any voice disorder.

phonopsia *n.* see CHROMATIC AUDITION.

phonosurgery *n.* surgical intervention to maintain or improve the voice or the ease with which phonation occurs, such as the removal of polyps from the vocal cords or THYROPLASTY.

phoria *n.* the position of the two eyes when a target is viewed binocularly and appears as a single image. The term is most commonly used as part of compound words to describe changes in eye position that occur when images from the two eyes cannot be fused, such as ESOPHORIA and EXOPHORIA.

phosphene *n.* a sensation of a light flash in the absence of actual light stimulation to the eye. It may occur with the eyes closed and can be caused by mechanical stimulation of the retina, by rubbing the eyes, or by direct electrical stimulation of the visual cortex. Also called **visual phosphene**. See also PHOTOPSIA.

phosphoinositide *n.* any of a class of SECOND MESSENGERS that are common in postsynaptic cells. See INOSITOL PHOSPHATES.

phosphorylation *n.* the addition of one or more phosphate groups (PO_4) to a molecule (e.g., a protein). See also KINASE.

photic driving the effect in which the electrical activity of cortical neurons, as measured via ELECTROENCEPHALOGRAPHY, is altered by rhythmically presented light stimuli, such that the frequency of the activity becomes synchronized with the flashing or pulsing of the photic stimulation.

photism *n.* **1.** a false perception or hallucination of light. See PHOTOPSIA. **2.** a form of SYNESTHESIA in which light or color sensations occur in response to stimulation of other senses (e.g., hearing).

photo- (**phot-**) *combining form* **1.** light (e.g., PHOTOTAXIS). **2.** photography (e.g., PHOTOCOUNSELING).

photoaging *n.* the cumulative effect during a person's life of exposure of the skin to sunlight, which can be manifest as wrinkling or skin damage caused by ultraviolet radiation.

photobiology *n.* the study of the effects of light on organisms, including the more specific study of the effects of color on mood, cognition, physiology, and behavior and the use of color in treating a variety of disorders (**chromotherapy**). **—photobiological** *adj.* **—photobiologist** *n.*

photocoagulation *n.* the use of radiant energy, usually in the form of a laser or xenon-arc beam, to condense protein material in a tissue. Photocoagulation is used in the treatment of detached retina after surgery, benign skin tumors, and degeneration of peripheral tissues.

photocounseling *n.* the use of photographs or videotapes depicting aspects of a client's life to obtain insight into his or her behavior and needs and also to increase the rapport between the client and the therapist.

photogenic epilepsy a form of REFLEX EPILEPSY in which seizures are precipitated by a particular kind of visual aberration, such as a flickering light.

photographic memory see EIDETIC IMAGE.

photoma *n.* a visual hallucination in which sparks or light flashes are seen in the absence of external stimuli. See also PHOSPHENE; PHOTOPSIA.

photomania *n.* **1.** an abnormal craving for light, particularly sunlight. See also SEASONAL AFFECTIVE DISORDER. **2.** the practice of sun worship.

photometer *n.* a device that measures the intensity of light, taking into account the sensitivity of the human visual system to light of different wavelengths. This measurement is different from that of the amount of energy produced by a light source.

photometry *n.* the measurement of the intensity of light.

photon *n.* **1.** an individual quantum of electromagnetic radiation. **2.** a former name for TROLAND.

photoperiodism *n.* the behavioral and physiological reactions of animals and plants to changes in the length of days or in the intensity of light in the environment. Photoperiodism in animals is involved in the timing of seasonal migration behavior, reproductive cycles, changes in plumage or pelage, and hibernation. The shedding of leaves in autumn and winter dormancy are signs of photoperiodism in plants. Behavior affected by photoperiodism is usually in response to the direction of change in day length (i.e., increasing or decreasing) rather than absolute day length.

photophobia *n.* an extreme and often painful sensitivity to light. It may be associated with migraine headaches or with certain types of brain trauma. **—photophobic** *adj.*

photopic *adj.* relating to vision in conditions of bright illumination, especially daylight.

photopic luminosity the relative effectiveness of various wavelengths of light for visual acuity under light-adapted conditions.

photopic-sensitivity curve a graph of visual threshold as a function of wavelength under light-adapted conditions. The peak of the human photopic-sensitivity curve falls at approximately 555 nm; this means that less energy is needed for stimulus detection at this wavelength than at any other wavelength under daylight conditions. See PHOTOPIC VISION.

photopic stimulation visual stimulation under daylight conditions.

photopic vision the type of vision associated with light levels during daylight. Photopic vision is mediated by RETINAL CONES, while vision at twilight and at night is mediated by RETINAL RODS. Also called **daylight vision**. Compare SCOTOPIC VISION.

photopigment *n.* a substance in a RETINAL ROD or RETINAL CONE that interacts with light to initiate a chemical cascade resulting in the conversion of light energy into an electrical signal. All rods contain the photopigment RHODOPSIN, while cones have one of three different photopigments (IODOPSINS), each with a different wavelength sensitivity (see LONG-WAVELENGTH PIGMENT; MEDIUM-WAVELENGTH PIGMENT; SHORT-WAVELENGTH PIGMENT). Photopigment is located in disks of membrane in the outer segment of a rod or cone. Also called **visual pigment**.

photopsia *n.* visual sensations in the absence of external visual stimuli, which can be unstructured (see PHOSPHENE) or structured. Structured photopsia consists of regular achromatic or chromatic visual patterns (e.g., circles, squares, diamonds) and is caused by pathological activation of prestriate cortical neurons. See also VISUAL HALLUCINATION. Also called **photopsy**.

photopsin *n.* any one of three different proteins found, combined with 11-*cis* retinal, in RETINAL CONES. See IODOPSIN.

photoreceptor *n.* a visual receptor, especially a RETINAL ROD or a RETINAL CONE.

photosensitivity *n.* sensitivity to light, especially sunlight, as occurs in ALBINISM and PHOTOGENIC EPILEPSY. Conditions marked by increased sensitivity to the effects of sunlight on the skin include systemic LUPUS ERYTHEMATOSUS and XERODERMA PIGMENTOSUM. Photosensitivity may occur as an adverse reaction to certain drugs, such as the phenothiazines (e.g., chlorpromazine), carbamazepine, St. John's wort, thiazides, sulfonamides, and tetracyclines. In such cases it often takes the form of a rash or other skin reaction. Photosensitivity may also represent an immune reaction in some individuals who manifest allergy symptoms after exposure to intense light. **—photosensitive** *adj.*

phototaxis *n.* movement toward or away from a light source. Positive phototaxis is movement toward light; negative phototaxis is movement away from light. Some insects display a relationship between muscular activity and light orientation. When the left eye of a fly or bee is shaded or blinded, the legs on the side of the body with reduced vision work to keep the body turned toward the light that can be seen only with the right eye. See also TAXIS.

phototherapy *n.* therapy involving exposure to ultraviolet or infrared light, which is used for treating not only certain skin conditions or disorders (e.g., jaundice, psoriasis) but also depression, particularly for patients with SEASONAL AFFECTIVE DISORDER (SAD). Typically, in phototherapy for SAD, a specially designed lamp that delivers 5,000 to 10,000 lx of light is shone on the retina, and a signal is transmitted via the optic nerve to the pineal gland, which secretes MELATONIN in response to darkness. Inhibition of melatonin release by bright light relieves the symptoms of SAD. Also called **bright light therapy**.

phototropism *n.* an orienting response (see TROPISM), especially of a plant, either toward (positive phototropism) or away from (negative phototropism) light. It is distinct from PHOTOTAXIS, which is active movement of an organism in response to light.—**phototropic** *adj.*

PHR abbreviation for POINT–HOUR RATIO.

phrase *n.* a constituent of a sentence that is larger than a word but smaller than a CLAUSE. Phrases can be classified as noun phrases, verb phrases, prepositional phrases, and so on, according to their function within the clause. —**phrasal** *adj.*

phrase marker see BRANCHING.

phrase-structure grammar (**PSG**) a type of GENERATIVE GRAMMAR in which a system of **phrase-structure rules** (or **rewrite rules**) is used to describe a sentence in terms of the grammatical structures that generate its form and define it as grammatical. In practice, such a description will also be a CONSTITUENT analysis of the sentence in question. The phrase-structure rules used in this form of analysis are usually set out in the form X → Y + Z, in which the arrow is an instruction to reformulate ("rewrite") X in terms of its immediate constituents (Y + Z). So, for example, the sentence *The dogs chase the cats* can be described by the following set of rules:

sentence (S) → noun phrase (NP) + verb phrase (VP)
NP → determiner (det) + noun (N)
VP → verb (V) + NP
det → *the*
N → *cats, dogs*
V → *chase*

The same set of rules could also be shown in diagrammatic form as a tree diagram or phrase marker (see BRANCHING).

In the late 1950s formal phrase-structure analysis of this kind was developed by Noam CHOMSKY, who also, however, pointed out its limitations as a description of how language works. Chomsky's TRANSFORMATIONAL GENERATIVE GRAMMAR added an important new dimension by proposing that sentences have a DEEP STRUCTURE as well as the linear SURFACE STRUCTURE described in phrase-structure grammar, and that the relationship between the two levels can be described through a system of transformational rules.

phratry *n.* a social unit with common kinship bonds, typically composed of multiple CLANS claiming UNILATERAL DESCENT. See DESCENT GROUP.

phrenic nerve a nerve that originates in the CERVICAL PLEXUS of the neck and sends sensory and motor branches to the heart, diaphragm, and other parts of the chest and abdomen.

phreno- (**phren-**) *combining form* mind or brain.

phrenology *n.* a theory of personality formulated in the 18th and 19th centuries by German physician Franz Josef Gall (1757–1828) and Austrian philosopher and anatomist Johann Kaspar Spurzheim (1776–1832). It stated that specific abilities or personality traits are represented by specific areas of the brain: The size of these brain areas determines the degree of the corresponding skill or trait. Proponents of the theory argued that the size of such locations could be indicated by bumps and hollows on the skull surface, based on the observation that the contours of the brain follow the skull contours. Although wrong in most respects, the theory suggested the idea of LOCALIZATION OF FUNCTION. See also PHYSIOGNOMY. —**phrenological** *adj.* —**phrenologist** *n.*

phthinoid *adj.* denoting a variety of the asthenic constitutional body type in KRETSCHMER TYPOLOGY in which the physique is underdeveloped and usually characterized by a flat, narrow chest.

phthisic type a body type characterized as slender and flat-chested, as from a wasting disease such as tuberculosis (which was formerly called phthisis). See CARUS TYPOLOGY.

phylogenetic principle the theory that ONTOGENY recapitulates PHYLOGENY in the development of an organism: In humans, this supposes that human life, across development from embryo to adult, repeats the stages of organic and social evolution.

phylogeny *n.* **1.** the evolutionary origin and development of a particular group of organisms. Also called **phylogenesis**. Compare ONTOGENY. **2.** a diagram that shows genetic linkages between ancestors and descendants. Also called **phylogenetic tree**. —**phylogenetic** *adj.*

phylum *n.* (*pl.* **phyla**) in BIOLOGICAL TAXONOMY, a main subdivision of a KINGDOM, containing a group of similar, related CLASSES.

physiatrics (**physiatry**) *n.* see PHYSICAL MEDICINE.

physical abilities in industrial and organizational settings, personal characteristics such as strength, speed, and agility that are required to perform certain job-related tasks. If these are BONA FIDE OCCUPATIONAL QUALIFICATIONS they may be included in the PERSONNEL SPECIFICATION for a position.

physical activity any bodily movement produced by the contraction of skeletal muscle that increases energy expenditure above the basal level.

physical age see ANATOMICAL AGE.

physical anthropology see ANTHROPOLOGY.

physical dependence the state of an individual who has repeatedly taken a drug and will experience unpleasant physiological symptoms (see SUBSTANCE WITHDRAWAL) if he or she stops taking the drug. In *DSM–IV–TR*, SUBSTANCE DEPENDENCE with physical (or physiological) dependence is diagnosed if there is evidence of withdrawal or TOLERANCE. Compare PSYCHOLOGICAL DEPENDENCE.

physical determinism the type of DETERMINISM presumed to operate among physical objects in the natural world. In psychology, physical determinism is the assumption that psychological events and behaviors have physical causes and can be described in terms of models and theories borrowed from the physical sciences. See HARD DETERMINISM; PSYCHOLOGICAL DETERMINISM.

physical disorder see GENERAL MEDICAL CONDITION.

physical examination an assessment of the body and its specific functions, generally by a physician or other health care professional, using inspection, palpation, percussion, and auscultation. It also frequently includes laboratory tests and other forms of screening for various physiological abnormalities, malfunctions, and diseases.

physical extension device a piece of equipment or mechanism that extends the reach of an individual with a disability. See HEADSTICK; MOUTHSTICK.

physicalism *n.* **1.** the doctrine that reality is composed of matter and that mind is therefore reducible to matter. See IDENTITY THEORY; MATERIALISM; MIND–BODY PROBLEM. **2.** the view that all meaningful propositions can be stated in the language of the physical sciences and in operational definitions. See LOGICAL POSITIVISM; POSITIVISM. **—physicalist** *adj.*

physically correct doll see ANATOMICALLY DETAILED DOLL.

physical map a type of chromosome map that depicts the actual physical location of genes and genetic markers on the chromosome, with distances measured in base pairs, kilobases, or similar units. Various techniques are used in constructing physical maps, including positional cloning and DNA sequencing. The HUMAN GENOME PROJECT has provided a complete physical map of all human chromosomes. See also MAPPING OF GENES.

physical medicine the branch of medicine that specializes in the diagnosis and treatment of illness and disorders through physical means (e.g., exercise and massage) and mechanical devices. Physical medicine is also concerned with the REHABILITATION of patients with physical disabilities. Also called **physiatrics**; **physiatry**.

physical modality a therapeutic intervention that involves the use of a physical agent, such as heat or ice.

physical symbol system hypothesis a hypothesis concerning the necessity and sufficiency of capturing intelligence in computational systems. The hypothesis states that a necessary and sufficient condition for a physical system to exhibit general intelligent action is that it be a physical symbol system. "Necessary" means that any physical system that exhibits general intelligence will be an instance of a physical symbol system. "Sufficient" means that any physical symbol system can be organized further to exhibit general intelligent action. This hypothesis has been a driving factor for much research in ARTIFICIAL INTELLIGENCE and COGNITIVE SCIENCE. [proposed in 1976 by U.S. cognitive and computer scientist Allen Newell (1927–1992) and Herbert A. SIMON]

physical therapy (**PT**) **1.** the treatment of pain, injury, or disease using physical or mechanical methods, such as exercise, heat, water, massage, or electric current (diathermy). The treatment is administered by a trained **physical therapist**. Also called **physiotherapy**. **2.** a branch of medicine and health care that identifies, corrects, alleviates, and prevents temporary, prolonged, or permanent movement dysfunction or physical disability.

physician assistant (**PA**) a licensed health care professional who provides services under the direction of a supervising physician.

physician-assisted suicide see ASSISTED DEATH.

physician–hospital organization (**PHO**) an organization formed, owned, and governed by one or more hospitals and physician groups to obtain payer contracts and to further mutual interests.

physiodrama *n.* see PSYCHODRAMA.

physiogenic *adj.* pertaining to a disorder that is organic in origin.

physiognomic perception the tendency to see expressive properties in objects, such that, for example, dark objects may be perceived as gloomy, or bright ones may be perceived as happy. Initially described by Austrian-born U.S. psychologist Heinz Werner (1890–1964) in children, this perceptual tendency has since been investigated by others in adults.

physiognomy *n.* **1.** the form of a person's physical features, especially the face. **2.** the attempt to read personality from the facial features and expression, assuming, for example, that a person with a receding chin is weak or one with a high forehead is bright. The idea dates back to Greek philosopher Aristotle (383–322 BCE) and was later developed into a pseudoscientific system by Swiss pastor Johann Lavater (1741–1801) and Italian psychiatrist Cesare Lombroso (1835–1909). Also called **physiognomics**. See also CHARACTEROLOGY; PHRENOLOGY.

physiological age a measurement of the level of development or deterioration of an individual in terms of functional norms for various body systems.

physiological antagonism a form of antagonism (see ANTAGONIST) in which two substances have opposing physiological actions. For example, a stimulant (e.g., caffeine) would show physiological antagonism in combination with an anxiolytic drug (e.g., a benzodiazepine). Compare PHARMACOLOGICAL ANTAGONISM.

physiological arousal aspects of AROUSAL shown by physiological responses, such as increases in blood pressure and rate of respiration and decreased activity of the gastrointestinal system. Such primary arousal responses are largely governed by the SYMPATHETIC NERVOUS SYSTEM, but responses of the PARASYMPATHETIC NERVOUS SYSTEM may compensate or even overcompensate for the sympathetic activity. See also AUTONOMIC NERVOUS SYSTEM.

physiological assessment evaluation of the functioning state of the body, a tissue, or an organ, including physical and chemical factors and processes.

physiological correlate an association between a physiological measure and a behavioral measure. The existence of a physiological correlate may suggest a causal relation, but it does not establish a cause.

physiological cycle a series of regularly recurring changes in body activities, such as the SLEEP–WAKE CYCLE. See also BIOLOGICAL RHYTHM.

physiological factors factors pertaining to the functions of a living organism and its parts as well as to the chemical and physical processes involved in this functioning.

physiological motive a motive resulting from a BASIC PHYSIOLOGICAL NEED, such as the need for food. See DEFICIENCY MOTIVE; MOTIVATION.

physiological needs the lowest level of MASLOW'S MOTIVATIONAL HIERARCHY of needs, comprising food, water, air, sleep, and other survival needs. See also PRIMARY NEED; VISCEROGENIC NEED.

physiological nystagmus the normal small, rapid movement of the eyes that permits sustained viewing of a scene. Compare VESTIBULAR NYSTAGMUS. See also NYSTAGMUS.

physiological paradigm the concept that mental disorders are caused by abnormalities in neurological structures and processes. This perspective, which underlies the field and practice of psychiatry, holds that mental disorders can be treated with drugs, surgery, or other techniques ordinarily used to correct malfunctioning of the body.

physiological psychology 1. a former name for BIOLOGICAL PSYCHOLOGY. **2.** a term originally used by Wilhelm WUNDT to designate what is now known as SCIENTIFIC PSYCHOLOGY.

physiological response specificity the principle that an individual's physiological responses to a range of different stimuli will be of the same type. For example, one individual may tend to respond to many different stimuli with increases in heart rate, while another individual may respond to the same stimuli with breathing changes. [proposed by U.S. psychophysiologist John I. Lacey (1915–)]

physiological saline a mixture of water and salt (sodium chloride) in which the concentration of salt is 0.9% w/v, approximately equal in OSMOLARITY to mammalian extracellular fluid. Also called **normal saline**.

physiological zero the temperature at which an object in contact with the skin feels neither warm nor cold, that is, about 32 °C (90 °F) for an object in contact with the hands or feet.

physiologic nonepileptic seizure see NONEPILEPTIC SEIZURE.

physiology *n.* the science of the functions of living organisms, including the chemical and physical processes involved and the activities of the cells, tissues, and organs, as opposed to static anatomical or structural factors. **—physiological** *adj.* **—physiologist** *n.*

physiopathology *n.* the study of PATHOPHYSIOLOGY.

physiotherapy *n.* see PHYSICAL THERAPY. **—physiotherapist** *n.*

physique type the basic physical structure, build, and body type of an individual, particularly as related to his or her CONSTITUTIONAL TYPE.

physostigmine *n.* a CHOLINERGIC DRUG—an alkaloid derived from the dried seed of an African vine—used in the treatment of glaucoma and to cause the pupil of the eye to contract. It is also employed as a cholinesterase inhibitor to reverse the toxic effects on the central nervous system of overdoses of ANTICHOLINERGIC DRUGS. U.S. trade names: **Antilirium; Isopto Eserine**.

phytoestrogens *pl. n.* see ESTROGEN.

PI abbreviation for PROACTIVE INTERFERENCE.

pia-arachnoid *n.* the inner two coverings of the brain and spinal cord—the PIA MATER and ARACHNOID MATER—considered as a single structure. See MENINGES.

Piaget, Jean (1896–1980) Swiss child psychologist and epistemologist. Piaget earned his doctorate from the University of Neuchâtel in 1918, with a dissertation on the classification of mollusks. He then studied psychology and philosophy at the universities of Zürich and Paris before taking a position at the Jean-Jacques Rousseau Institute of Geneva, a center for research on child development. Piaget is best known for his research and theoretical work on cognitive development. He proposed that all children develop through a prescribed series of cognitive stages: sensorimotor, preoperational, concrete operational, and formal operational. He held that although the age of onset for each stage might vary due to cultural and historical factors, the order of the stages is the same for all cultures. In the SENSORIMOTOR STAGE, the child's ability to recognize OBJECT PERMANENCE develops; the older infant becomes aware that an object exists even when it is out of sight. During the PREOPERATIONAL STAGE, the child is egocentric, showing little awareness of the perspective of others; language develops, as well as a rudimentary number system. The CONCRETE OPERATIONAL STAGE is characterized by the development of conceptually based thinking rather than the earlier perceptually based thinking. Children in this stage become capable of such mental operations as REVERSIBILITY, CATEGORIZATION, and CONSERVATION. Finally, in the formal operational stage (see FORMAL OPERATIONS), abstract thinking, HYPOTHETICO-DEDUCTIVE REASONING, and moral reasoning develop. Among Piaget's most influential works are *The Origins of Intelligence* (1936), *The Construction of Reality* (1937), and (with Barbel Inhelder) *The Growth of Logical Thinking from Childhood to Adolescence* (1953) and *The Early Growth of Logic in the Child* (1959). In 1969 Piaget was awarded the Distinguished Scientific Contribution Award of the American Psychological Association. See also CONSTRUCTIVISM. **—Piagetian** *adj.*

Piagetian task any one of a variety of tasks developed by Jean PIAGET to assess the cognitive abilities of infants, children, or adolescents. Examples of such tasks include, in infancy: OBJECT PERMANENCE tasks and DEFERRED IMITATION; in childhood: CONSERVATION, tests of perceptual perspective taking (e.g., the THREE-MOUNTAINS TEST), and CLASS INCLUSION; in adolescence: the PENDULUM PROBLEM.

Piagetian theory of intelligence the theory of COGNITIVE DEVELOPMENT proposed by Jean PIAGET, according to which intelligence develops through four major stages: (a) the sensorimotor stage (roughly 0–2 years), (b) the preoperational stage (roughly 2–7 years), (c) the concrete operational stage (roughly 7–12 years), and (d) the formal operational stage (roughly 12 years and beyond). According to this theory, each stage builds upon the preceding one. The order is therefore fixed as are the relative ages at which different stages are achieved; Piaget did not believe it was feasible to hurry children through the unfolding of these stages. Passage through the stages is facilitated by a balance of two processes: ASSIMILATION, in which new information is incorporated into already existing cognitive structures; and ACCOMMODATION, in which new information that does not fit into already existing cognitive structures is used to create new cognitive structures.

pia mater a delicate membrane that covers the surface of the brain and spinal cord; it is the innermost layer of the three MENINGES. The cranial portion of the pia mater is richly supplied with blood vessels and closely follows the contours of the cerebral cortex, extending into the fissures and sulci.

p.i. basis abbreviation for per-inquiry basis. See COUPON-RETURN TECHNIQUE.

piblokto *n.* a CULTURE-BOUND SYNDROME observed primarily in female Inuit and other arctic populations. Individuals experience a sudden dissociative period of extreme excitement in which they often tear off clothes, run naked through the snow, scream, throw things, and perform other wild behaviors. This typically ends with convulsive seizures, followed by an acute coma and amnesia for the event. Also called **arctic hysteria**; **pibloktoq**.

pica *n.* a rare eating disorder found primarily in young children and marked by a persistent craving for unnatural, nonnutritive substances, such as plaster, paint, hair, starch, or dirt. In *DSM–IV–TR* it is classified with the FEEDING AND EATING DISORDERS OF INFANCY OR EARLY CHILDHOOD. **Lead pica** is often found in children living in older housing with lead paint and can lead to irreversible mental impairment. Studies on rats and monkeys demonstrated that lead pica can be induced by calcium deficiency. Animals with normal nutrition learn that lead ingestion is aversive, but calcium-deficient animals do not learn aversions to lead.

Pick's disease a form of DEMENTIA characterized by progressive degeneration of the frontal and temporal areas of the brain with the presence of particles called **Pick bodies** in the cytoplasm of the neurons. The disease is characterized by personality changes and deterioration of social skills and complex thinking; symptoms include problems with new situations and abstractions, difficulty in thinking or concentrating, loss of memory, lack of spontaneity, gradual emotional dullness, loss of moral judgment, and disturbances of speech. [described in 1892 by Arnold **Pick** (1851–1924), Czech psychiatrist and neuroanatomist]

Pickwickian syndrome a syndrome characterized by grotesque obesity associated with hypersomnolence, cyanosis, congestive heart failure, and muscle twitching. These symptoms are usually believed to result from respiratory disability induced by extreme obesity. The name of the syndrome is derived from the character in Dickens's *Pickwick Papers* (1836–1837).

picrotoxin *n.* a CNS STIMULANT derived from the berries of a southeast Asian shrub, *Anamirta cocculus*. Originally used as a fish poison, picrotoxin was introduced in the 1930s as therapy for barbiturate overdose. It is a convulsant agent and acts as a GABA ANTAGONIST by binding to a specific site on the $GABA_A$ receptor complex, blocking the effects of GABA agonists (e.g., the benzodiazepines). Picrotoxin has no modern clinical applications but may be used to induce seizures in nonhuman animals for research purposes.

pictophilia *n.* sexual interest in and arousal by viewing erotic pictures or films, alone or with a partner.

pictorial imagery see VISUAL IMAGERY.

pictorial realism a design principle holding that images on a visual display should match the MENTAL MODEL of the user. For example, a fluid-level indicator that communicates changing levels by moving a fluid-level image up and down has pictorial realism. In contrast, a fluid-level indicator that moves left to right is not designed on this basis and is likely to be less effective.

picture-anomalies test a type of nonverbal test of social intelligence that depends on the ability of the participant to detect absurdities in cartoon pictures.

picture-arrangement test a subtest of the Wechsler intelligence scales, in which the participant is required to arrange in proper order a series of sketches that tell a brief story. See also WECHSLER ADULT INTELLIGENCE SCALE.

picture-completion test a type of test consisting of drawings of familiar objects with features missing. The task is to recognize and specify the missing parts. See also INCOMPLETE-PICTURES TEST.

picture-interpretation test a test in which the participant is asked to interpret a visual image (e.g., a drawing, photograph, or painting). This type of test may aid in the assessment of intelligence or personality traits.

picture superiority effect the tendency for a picture or drawing to be remembered better than the name of the pictured object. For example, people are more likely to remember "dog" if they see a drawing of a dog than if they see the word *dog*.

picture-world test a PROJECTIVE TECHNIQUE for children in which the participant composes a story about realistic scenes, adding objects or figures as he or she wishes. The child is instructed to picture either a world that actually exists or one that he or she would like to exist.

pidgin *n.* an improvised CONTACT LANGUAGE incorporating elements of two or more languages, often devised for purposes of trading. Pidgins are characterized by simple rules and limited vocabulary. Compare CREOLE.

piecewise regression a variant on ordinary least squares regression in which a REGRESSION LINE consisting of several different lines is fitted to the data. The several pieces are, in general, of different slopes and meet at nodal points in order to form a continuous line.

piecework *n.* work for which employees are paid per unit of productivity. In a differential piece-rate system, the rate of compensation for each unit produced increases once the employee has surpassed the level of productivity that work studies determine to be the standard. See SCIENTIFIC MANAGEMENT.

pie chart a graphic display in which a circle is cut into pielike wedges, the area of the wedge being proportional to the percentage of cases in the category represented by that wedge.

Pierre Robin's syndrome a congenital disorder with anomalies that include micrognathia (abnormally small jaw) and cleft palate. Serious eye disorders occur in most affected individuals, along with a small, receding chin and a tongue that falls backward into the pharynx (glossoptosis), interfering with breathing and feeding. The incidence of mental retardation ranges from 5 to 50%. [initially reported in 1923 by **Pierre Robin** (1867–1950), French pediatrician]

Pigem's question a question designed to elicit projective responses by a patient undergoing a MENTAL STATUS EXAMINATION. The question is usually a variation of "What would you like most to change in your life?"

pigeon breast see PECTUS CARINATUM.

pigment bleaching the change in the photopigment RHODOPSIN that occurs when it absorbs photons. The color of the pigment changes from purple (visual purple) to a transparent light yellow (VISUAL YELLOW). See also VISUAL CYCLE.

pigment epithelium the single cuboidal layer of pigmented cells that abuts the tips of the photoreceptors in the RETINA. The pigment in the cells reduces light scatter by absorbing photons that elude the PHOTOPIGMENTS in the photoreceptors. The pigment epithelium is also critical for the health of the photoreceptors because it phagocytoses (engulfs) disks of membrane that are continually shed by the photoreceptors. Also called **retinal pigment epithelium** (**RPE**).

pigment regeneration the reconstitution of functional rhodopsin following PIGMENT BLEACHING. See also VISUAL CYCLE.

PIL abbreviation for PURPOSE IN LIFE.

Pillai's trace a multivariate test statistic used in MULTIVARIATE ANALYSIS OF VARIANCE, which is converted to an F RATIO to obtain a SIGNIFICANCE LEVEL. [Sreedharan **Pillai** (1920–1985), Indian statistician]

pilocarpine *n.* an alkaloid derived from several tropical American plants but mainly from *Pilocarpus jaborandi*. Pilocarpine is a powerful parasympathomimetic agent, affecting postganglionic cholinergic receptors (see CHOLINERGIC DRUGS). It is used in the treatment of glaucoma and to contract the pupil of the eye. U.S. trade names (among others): **Isopto Carpine**; **Pilocar**; **Pilostat**.

piloerection *n.* a temporary roughness of the skin caused by contraction of the piloerector muscles, which raise the hairs, and elicited by cold, fear, or sexual or other excitation. Also called **goose bumps**; **goose flesh**; **goose pimples**; **goose skin**.

pilomotor effect contraction of the piloerector muscles, which causes the hairs on the skin to stand erect. Also called **pilomotor response**.

pilot selection the assessment of a candidate in order to determine whether he or she possesses the aptitudes, dexterity, and psychomotor skills needed to become an aircraft pilot.

pilot study a preliminary research project designed to evaluate and (if required) modify procedures in preparation for a subsequent and more detailed research project. Pilot studies are designed to reveal information about the viability and, to a lesser extent, the potential outcomes of a proposed experiment.

pilot testing the evaluation of some aspect of the research materials or procedures used in a PILOT STUDY.

Piltz's reflex an automatic and involuntary increase in the size of the pupil when attending to an object or event. [Jan **Piltz** (1870–1931), Polish neurologist]

pimozide *n.* a first-generation (typical or conventional) ANTIPSYCHOTIC of the diphenylbutylpiperidine class. Like other conventional antipsychotics, it is a blocker of postsynaptic dopamine D2 receptors. In the United States it is officially approved by the Food and Drug Administration only for the management of vocal and motor tics associated with Tourette's disorder, although it is widely used as an antipsychotic drug in Europe and South America. Pimozide has been associated with potentially lethal disturbances of heart rhythm, and it should not be used in patients with histories of arrhythmias or in doses exceeding 10 mg/day. Because pimozide has no apparent special advantages over similar antipsychotics that are less damaging to the heart (e.g., haloperidol), it should be used in Tourette's disorder only if other medications have failed to produce the desired response. U.S. trade name: **Orap**.

pincer grip the manner of grasping an object between the thumb and forefinger. See also POWER GRIP; PRECISION GRIP.

pineal gland a small, cone-shaped gland attached by a stalk to the posterior wall of the THIRD VENTRICLE of the brain. In amphibians and reptiles, the gland appears to function as a part of the visual system. In mammals it secretes the hormone MELATONIN. Because it is an unpaired organ located in the middle of the brain, French philosopher René Descartes (1596–1650) believed it was the seat of the RATIONAL SOUL and the connection between mind and body. Also called **epiphysis cerebri**; **pineal body**.

Pinel's system a classification of mental disorders and symptoms outlined in the 18th century. The four major categories were melancholias, manias with delirium, manias without delirium, and dementia or mental deterioration. [Philippe **Pinel** (1745–1826), French psychiatrist]

pink noise see NOISE.

pinna *n.* (*pl.* **pinnae**) the part of the external ear that projects beyond the head. Also called **auricle**.

piperidinediones *pl. n.* a class of chemically related drugs formerly used for daytime sedation or the management of insomnia but no longer in common clinical use. Their mechanism of action and toxicity are similar to the BARBITURATES. The prototype of the class is GLUTETHIMIDE.

Piper's law the principle that for a uniformly stimulated retinal area peripheral to the fovea, the threshold for LUMINANCE is inversely proportional to the square root of the area stimulated. Compare RICCO'S LAW. [Hans Edmund **Piper** (1877–1915), German physiologist]

piriform area see PYRIFORM AREA.

pitch *n.* the subjective attribute that permits sounds to be ordered on a musical scale. The pitch of a PURE TONE is determined primarily by its frequency, the pitch of a complex periodic sound by its fundamental frequency. However, other physical parameters, such as intensity and duration, can affect pitch. The unit of pitch is the MEL.

pitch discrimination the ability to detect changes in sound based upon pitch. It is more appropriately called FREQUENCY DISCRIMINATION because of uncertainty that the discrimination is based on the subjective attribute of pitch. For example, under certain circumstances a change in frequency produces a change in loudness. In this case, frequency discrimination could be based on a loudness change rather than a pitch change.

pithiatism *n.* a former name (from Greek *pithanotes*, "persuasiveness") for SOMATIZATION DISORDER, proposed in 1918 by French neurologist Joseph Babinski (1857–1932) as a substitute for HYSTERIA. It was based on the theory that some hysterical symptoms are produced by suggestion and can therefore be eliminated by suggestion and would therefore distinguish hysterical disorders from those on which persuasion has no effect.

Pitres' rule a generalization stating that when a multilingual person recovers from APHASIA caused by a stroke or cerebral injury, the language recovered first is usually the one most used by the person prior to the onset of the aphasia. Other languages are reestablished in a slower and often less complete manner. Also called **Pitres' law**. Compare RIBOT'S LAW. [proposed in 1895 by Jean Albert **Pitres** (1848–1927), French neurologist]

pituitarism *n.* disordered functioning of the pituitary gland, which may be overactive (hyperpituitarism) or underactive (hypopituitarism).

pituitary adenoma see ADENOMA.

pituitary cachexia see HYPOPHYSEAL CACHEXIA.

pituitary gland a gland, pea-sized in humans, that lies at the base of the brain, connected by a stalk (the infundibulum) to the HYPOTHALAMUS. The pituitary gland is divided into an anterior and a posterior lobe, which differ in function. The anterior lobe (**adenohypophysis**) produces and secretes seven hormones—thyroid-stimulating hormone, follicle-stimulating hormone, adrenocorticotropic hormone, growth hormone, luteinizing hormone, prolactin, and melanocyte-stimulating hormone—in response to RELEASING HORMONES from the hypothalamus. The posterior lobe (**neurohypophysis**) secretes two hormones, vasopressin and oxytocin, which are synthesized in the hypothalamus and transported down axons in the infundibulum to the neurohypophysis in response to direct neural stimulation. The pituitary's role of secreting TROPIC HORMONES, which regulate the production of other hormones, has resulted in its designation as the "master gland of the endocrine system." Also called **hypophysis**; **hypophysis cerebri**.

pituitectomy *n.* see HYPOPHYSECTOMY.

pituri *n.* an Australian shrub, *Duboisia hopwoodii*, whose leaves have traditionally been used for their stimulant, analgesic, and hallucinogenic effects by members of Aboriginal tribes. The leaves were cured, powdered, and then rolled into a quid to be chewed or smoked. The primary active ingredient is NICOTINE. Although some indigenous peoples still use pituri, it was most popular during the 19th and early 20th centuries.

pity *n.* a feeling of sorrow and compassion for people who are unhappy, suffering, or otherwise unfortunate or in distress.

pivot grammar a type of simple grammar displayed in the early stages of language development (especially the TWO-WORD STAGE). Pivot grammar is characterized by two-word utterances in which one word (the **pivot word**) is typically a FUNCTION WORD, such as a determiner or preposition, and the other (the **open word**) is a CONTENT WORD, such as a noun or verb. A small child has relatively few pivot words in his or her vocabulary but uses them often and always in the same position relative to the open word. Open words are used less frequently, but the child learns more of them and can use them anywhere in a phrase. *More juice, light off,* and *all gone* are typical examples of pivot grammar: *More, off,* and *all* are pivot words; *juice, light,* and *gone* are open words.

PK abbreviation for PSYCHOKINESIS.

PKU abbreviation for PHENYLKETONURIA.

place attachment feelings of connection or affiliation with a geographic location that provides security and comfort and contributes to identity. Individually and collectively, people become attached to certain places, such as their homes or their neighborhoods. See also TERRITORIALITY.

placebo *n.* (*pl.* **placebos**) **1.** a pharmacologically inert substance, such as a sugar pill, that is often administered as a control in testing new drugs. Placebos used in DOUBLE-BLIND trials may be DUMMIES or ACTIVE PLACEBOS. Formerly, placebos were occasionally used as diagnostic or psychotherapeutic agents, for example, in relieving pain or inducing sleep by suggestion, but the ethical implications of deceiving patients in such fashion makes this practice problematic. **2.** any medical or psychological intervention or treatment that is believed to be "inert," thus making it valuable as a control condition against which to compare the intervention or treatment of interest. See PLACEBO EFFECT.

placebo control group a CONTROL GROUP that receives a PLACEBO.

placebo effect a clinically significant response to a therapeutically inert substance or nonspecific treatment. It is now recognized that placebo effects accompany the administration of any drug (active or inert) and contribute to the therapeutic effectiveness of a specific treatment. See PLACEBO.

place cells neurons in the HIPPOCAMPUS that fire selectively when an animal is in a particular spatial location or moving toward that location.

place conditioning see CONDITIONED PLACE PREFERENCE.

place learning 1. the learning of locations or physical positions of goals (e.g., where food can be found). Compare RESPONSE LEARNING. [defined by Edward C. TOLMAN] **2.** in conditioning, learning an association between a place and an unconditioned stimulus, such as food or poison. See CONDITIONED PLACE PREFERENCE.

placement *n.* **1.** in education, the assignment of students to a suitable course or curriculum on the basis of demonstrated ability or achievement. **2.** in organizations, the assignment of existing or newly hired employees to the particular jobs for which they are best qualified. Also called **job placement**; **personnel placement**; **selective placement**.

placement counseling 1. services designed to advise and assist individuals to find suitable or optimal employment. Placement counseling may include coaching or training for job interviews, procedures for filling out applications, and assistance with other activities relevant to obtaining a job. **2.** in education, a service that provides guidance to students in deciding upon an appropriate educational program, class, or level of instruction. **3.** in foster care, services provided to help children and their adoptive parents adjust to adoptive placement. **4.** in VOCATIONAL REHABILITATION, a service that advises and prepares people with disabilities for appropriate job opportunities.

placement test a test used by educational institutions to place students in classes appropriate to their abilities, achievements, and interests.

placenta *n.* the specialized organ produced by the mammalian embryo that attaches to the wall of the uterus to permit removal of waste products and to provide nutrients, energy, and gas exchange for the fetus via the maternal circulation. **—placental** *adj.*

placental mammal a mammal that produces a highly specialized PLACENTA to nourish the developing embryo or embryos in the uterus. All mammals except MARSUPIALS and monotremes are placental mammals.

place theory the theory that (a) different frequencies stimulate different places along the BASILAR MEMBRANE and (b) pitch is coded by the place of maximal stimulation. The first proposition is strongly supported by experimental evidence and stems from the fact that the mammalian auditory system shows TONOTOPIC ORGANIZATION. The second hypothesis remains controversial. See HELMHOLTZ THEORY. Compare PERIODICITY THEORY.

Placidyl *n.* a trade name for ETHCHLORVYNOL.

placing *n.* a reflex movement in which a baby lifts his or her foot onto a surface, which occurs during the first 3 months of life.

plain English law 1. in some states in the United States, a law requiring attorneys to use less arcane, more comprehensible language in drafting documents. **2.** a law written in a way that strives for simplicity of expression. Plain English laws reduce reliance on legal jargon, enabling them to be more easily understood by the general public.

plan *n.* in cognitive psychology, a MENTAL REPRESENTATION of an intended action, such as an utterance or a complex movement, that is presumed to guide the individual in carrying it out. See PREPARATION. See also COGNITIVE PLAN.

PLAN acronym for PROGRAM FOR LEARNING IN ACCORDANCE WITH NEEDS.

Planck's principle the notion that new scientific theories do not gain acceptance by a systematic process of validation that convinces opponents of their truth. Instead, as opponents of a new theory grow old and die, they are replaced by a new generation of scientists, who were exposed to the theory early in their careers and have come to accept it. This notion is a direct challenge to both VERIFICATION and FALSIFICATIONISM. [Max **Planck** (1858–1947), German physicist]

plane symmetry see SYMMETRY.

planned behavior behavior that is under the organism's direct control, as opposed to more reactive behavior or REFLEXIVE BEHAVIOR. In social psychology, the THEORY OF PLANNED BEHAVIOR suggests that the intent to engage in a specific behavior is determined by attitudes, norms, and perceived control surrounding the behavior in question.

planned comparison a comparison among two or more means in ANALYSIS OF VARIANCE or REGRESSION ANALYSIS that has been specified prior to the observation of the data. Also called **planned contrast**. Compare POST HOC COMPARISON.

planned parenthood the state of couples or individuals who plan the occurrence and timing of the births of their children, often in concert with career and other family decisions.

Planned Parenthood Federation of America (**PPFA**) an organization that promotes comprehensive reproductive and complementary health care services; advocates public policy that guarantees access to such services and the privacy and rights of individuals using such services; and supports research and technology in reproductive health care, as well as education on human sexuality. Formerly known as the AMERICAN BIRTH CONTROL LEAGUE, the organization adopted its current name in 1942.

plantar reflex the reflex flexing of the toes when the sole of the foot is stroked.

planum temporale a region of the superior temporal cortex of the brain, adjacent to the primary AUDITORY CORTEX, that includes part of WERNICKE'S AREA. In most people it is larger in the left cerebral hemisphere than in the right hemisphere.

plaque *n.* a small patch or area of abnormal tissue that usually has a different appearance from the surrounding normal tissue. Kinds of plaque include atherosclerotic (or atheromatous) plaques, consisting of lipid deposits on the lining of arterial walls (see ATHEROSCLEROSIS); DEMYELINATION plaques, which develop on the protective nerve sheaths of patients with multiple sclerosis; and SENILE PLAQUES, which occur in Alzheimer's disease.

-plasia *suffix* development or growth (e.g., HYPERPLASIA).

plasticity *n.* flexibility and adaptability. Plasticity of the nervous or hormonal systems makes it possible to learn and register new experiences. Early experiences can also modify and shape gene expression to induce long-lasting changes in neurons or endocrine organs. See also FUNCTIONAL PLASTICITY; NEURAL PLASTICITY. Compare RIGIDITY.

plastic surgery a branch of surgery that specializes in the restoration, reconstruction, and repair of damaged or diseased tissue to improve the form or function of a body structure or area. Plastic surgery is commonly used in reconstruction of the female breast (e.g., after surgical removal for cancer), facial features (e.g., the nose or a cleft lip or palate), and genital features (e.g., the vagina or penis in sex-reversal surgery). See also COSMETIC SURGERY; POSTRECONSTRUCTIVE SURGERY; RECONSTRUCTIVE SURGERY.

plastic tonus a state of voluntary muscles such that a limb can be passively moved into positions that are retained, sometimes for hours. It is characteristic of CATATONIA.

plateau *n.* a period in learning when the LEARNING CURVE flattens because the rate of increase has stopped temporarily, often because of fatigue, boredom, loss of motivation, or a change in the level of skill required.

plateau phase see SEXUAL-RESPONSE CYCLE.

Plateau's spiral a stimulus used to create a vivid MOTION AFTEREFFECT that consists of a black and white spiral rotated around its central point. Depending on the direction of rotation, the spiral will appear to expand or contract when steadily viewed while it is rotating. However, when the spiral is stopped it will appear to move in the opposite direction, producing a perception of expansion or contraction. Moreover, the illusory expansion or contraction will apply to any other stationary object viewed immediately after stopping the spiral. [Joseph Antoine Ferdinand **Plateau** (1801–1883), Belgian physicist]

Platonic idealism a general philosophical position deriving both directly and indirectly from the writings of Greek philosopher Plato (c. 427–c. 347 BCE), which holds that the phenomena of our world are to be truly known by contemplating them in their ideal forms or abstract essences. Such knowledge is to be achieved by the rational intellect or NOUS, rather than the senses or the understanding. In *The Republic,* Plato developed a philosophical system around the central notion that the things of this world are shadows or reflections of their ideal forms existing in a transcendent realm outside time and space (see ANALOGY OF THE CAVE). This realm is the "real" world because the forms that comprise it are perfect and eternal, not being subject to change, decay, or limitation like the things of our world. "Platonic idealism" is essentially a misnomer, as Plato's doctrine of ideas is actually a form of REALISM and not of IDEALISM.

Plato's THEORY OF FORMS is partly an attempt to solve the logical and other problems involved in relating particulars to UNIVERSALS (e.g., relating blue things to the term "blue" or good things to the concept "goodness"); however, it also had a metaphysical or religious dimension, which was later emphasized and extended by NEOPLATONISM.

Platonic love a type of love in which there is no overt sexual behavior or desire. The term derives from a misunderstanding of the teachings of Greek philosopher Plato (c. 427–c. 347 BCE).

platycephaly *n.* a condition in which the crown of the head is abnormally flat. —**platycephalic** *adj.*

platykurtic *adj.* describing a distribution of scores flatter than a normal distribution, that is, having more scores at the extremes and fewer in the center than in a normal distribution. See also MESOKURTIC; LEPTOKURTIC.

plausible rival hypothesis a proposition that provides a reasonable alternative to the research HYPOTHESIS being investigated.

play *n.* activities that appear to be freely sought and pursued solely for the sake of individual or group enjoyment. Although play is typically regarded as serving no immediate purpose beyond enjoyment, studies indicate that the motivation to play is as natural as the urge to eat or sleep and that it contributes significantly to development. In the research in this area, various types of play have been described, ranging from LOCOMOTOR PLAY to OBJECT-ORIENTED PLAY to SOCIAL PLAY to COGNITIVE PLAY, and numerous theories about play have been proposed. Jean PIAGET, for example, regarded it as advancing children's cognitive development through MASTERY PLAY, playing games with defined rules (such as hide-and-seek), and SYMBOLIC PLAY. Advocates of the **practice theory of play** propose that play prepares children for activities or roles they will encounter as adults, whereas others suggest that it serves a more immediate function, such as exercise, establishing social relations among peers, or—according to the SURPLUS ENERGY THEORY—using up excess energy. Although the preponderance of research on play focuses on the activities of children, the play behavior of nonhuman animals is also actively studied (see ANIMAL PLAY). Also called **ludic activity**.

playacting *n.* dramatic play in which children, adolescents, or adults (including group-therapy participants) take different roles. In the process, the participants test out relationships; rehearse different ways of dealing with situations; identify with significant figures; and play out any of a broad range of affective states and behaviors within the safe realm of make-believe. See also PSYCHODRAMA.

playfulness *n.* the tendency to see the light or bright side of life, to joke with others, and not to take matters too seriously. Playfulness is considered to be a foundation of humor. **—playful** *adj.*

playground design the design of recreational areas for children, which can influence their play behavior. For example, more complex levels of play are seen in adventure playgrounds than in traditional or contemporary playgrounds.

play-group psychotherapy a technique used in group therapy for preschool and early elementary school children. Materials of many kinds (e.g., clay, toys, blocks, and figurines) are used to foster the expression of conflicts and fantasies and to give the therapist an opportunity to ask questions and help the children in the group understand their feelings, behavior, and relationships within the context of the group. See also GROUP PSYCHOTHERAPY. [introduced in the early 1940s by 20th-century Russian-born U.S. psychotherapist Samuel Richard Slavson]

play therapy the use of play activities and materials (e.g., clay, water, blocks, dolls, puppets, drawing, and finger paint) in CHILD PSYCHOTHERAPY. Play-therapy techniques are based on the theory that such activities mirror the child's emotional life and fantasies, enabling the child to "play out" his or her feelings and problems and to test out new approaches and understand relationships in action rather than words. This form of psychotherapy, which focuses on a child's internal world and unconscious conflicts in addition to his or her daily life and current relationships, may be nondirective, but may alternatively be conducted on a more directive or a more analytic, interpretive level (see DIRECTIVE PLAY THERAPY; NONDIRECTIVE PLAY THERAPY). See also PROJECTIVE PLAY.

pleasantness *n.* a conscious, hedonic state, typically deemed highly desirable, that is experienced when an event is congruent with one's goals or is associated with pleasure. See also DIMENSIONAL THEORY OF EMOTION. **—pleasant** *adj.*

pleasure *n.* the emotion or sensation induced by the enjoyment or anticipation of what is felt or viewed as good or desirable.

pleasure center any of various areas of the brain (including areas of the hypothalamus and limbic system) that, upon INTRACRANIAL SELF-STIMULATION, have been implicated in producing pleasure. The existence of pure pleasure centers has not been definitively established, particularly because the self-stimulation response rate varies according to such factors as the duration and strength of the electrical stimulation. Also called **reward center**. [proposed by U.S. psychologist James Olds (1922–1976)]

pleasure principle the view that human beings are governed by the desire for instinctual gratification, or pleasure, and for the discharge of tension that builds up as pain or "unpleasure" when gratification is lacking. According to psychoanalytic theory, the pleasure principle is the psychic force that motivates people to seek immediate gratification of instinctual, or libidinal, impulses, such as sex, hunger, thirst, and elimination. It dominates the ID and operates most strongly during childhood. Later, in adulthood, it is opposed by the REALITY PRINCIPLE of the EGO. Also called **pleasure–pain principle**.

-plegia *suffix* paralysis (e.g., QUADRIPLEGIA).

pleniloquence *n.* a compulsion to talk incessantly. **—pleniloquent** *adj.*

pleonasm *n.* a form of verbal redundancy in which an excess of words is used to express an idea, as in *a great big giant*.

pleonexia *n.* **1.** an abnormal greediness or desire for the acquisition of objects. **2.** an abnormal intake of oxygen.

plethysmograph *n.* a device for measuring and recording volume or volume changes in organs or body tissues, such as the blood supply flowing through an organ. Examples include the **penile plethysmograph**, which records changes in the size of the penis and thus measures blood flow and erection; and the **vaginal plethysmograph**, which records changes in the amount of blood in the walls of the vagina and thus measures sexual arousal.

plexiform layer one of the two synaptic layers in the retina. See INNER PLEXIFORM LAYER; OUTER PLEXIFORM LAYER.

plexiform molecular layer see CORTICAL LAYERS.

plexus *n.* a network of similar structures (e.g., nerves, blood vessels) that are functionally or anatomically interconnected, for example, the BRACHIAL PLEXUS, CERVICAL PLEXUS, or CELIAC PLEXUS.

PLISSIT *n.* acronym for a model, developed in the 1970s, that is used in counseling clients about sexual problems. The model offers successive levels of communication or intervention: (a) *P*ermission, in which the client is told it is acceptable to do things he or she might think are not allowed; (b) *L*imited *I*nformation, in which the client is given information limited to that directly relevant to his or her concerns; (c) *S*pecific *S*uggestion, in which actions are specified; and (d) *I*ntensive *T*herapy, which may be required if the client has a complex problem (usually involving another therapist). The approach enables the counselor or therapist to determine at which point the problem is beyond his or her level of comfort and competence and it is appropriate to refer the client elsewhere.

plosive 1. *adj.* denoting a speech sound in which the airstream is partially or totally obstructed and suddenly released. A plosive sound may be VOICED (e.g., [b], [d], [g]) or UNVOICED (e.g., [p], [t], [k]). **2.** *n.* a plosive speech sound. Also called **obstruent**; **stop**.

Plummer's disease see THYROTOXICOSIS. [Henry Stanley **Plummer** (1874–1936), U.S. surgeon]

pluralism *n.* **1.** the idea that any entity has many aspects and that it may have a variety of causes and meanings. **2.** in philosophy, the doctrine that ultimate reality is composed of more than one substance or fundamental kind of entity. Compare DUALISM; MONISM. **3.** in sociology, the existence in a society of people having different religions, ethnic origins, and cultural backgrounds. **—pluralist** *adj.*

pluralistic ignorance the state of affairs in which virtually every member of a group privately rejects what are held to be the prevailing attitudes and beliefs of the group. Each member falsely believes that these standards are accepted by everyone else in the group. It has been suggested that apparently sudden changes in social mores (e.g., with regard to sexual behavior) can be explained by the gradual recognition by many individuals that others in the group think the same as themselves. [proposed in the 1920s by U.S. social psychologist Floyd Henry Allport (1890–1978)]

plural marriage POLYGAMY, especially in the form associated with the Mormon community. See also GROUP MARRIAGE.

plutomania *n.* an inordinate striving for money and possessions.

PM abbreviation for PRIMARY MEMORY.

PMS abbreviation for PREMENSTRUAL SYNDROME.

PNC abbreviation for PREFERRED NOISE CRITERION.

PNES abbreviation for PSYCHOGENIC NONEPILEPTIC SEIZURE.

pneumo- *combining form* **1.** air or gas (e.g., PNEUMOENCEPHALOGRAPHY). **2.** the lungs (e.g., PNEUMOGRAPH).

pneumoencephalography *n.* a diagnostic technique used from 1918 until the mid-1980s to examine the cerebral ventricles and subarachnoid space of the brain by injecting air into the cerebrospinal fluid. Because of the difference in opacity between the air and brain tissues, the air appears as a dark shadow on the resulting radiographic image (X-ray), which is known as a **pneumoencephalogram**. The development of COMPUTED TOMOGRAPHY and MAGNETIC RESONANCE IMAGING has eliminated the need for this test.

pneumograph *n.* an instrument that records the movements or volume change of the lungs. The record is produced either by electric monitoring of the rate and extent of respiratory movements or by X-ray imaging of the lungs after they have been injected with a gas to improve the visual contrast between tissue areas. Also called **pneumatograph**; **stethograph**.

PNS abbreviation for PERIPHERAL NERVOUS SYSTEM.

POC abbreviation for PERFORMANCE-OPERATING CHARACTERISTIC.

POE abbreviation for POSTOCCUPANCY EVALUATION.

poetry therapy a form of BIBLIOTHERAPY that employs the reading or writing of poetry to facilitate emotional expression in an individual and foster healing and personal growth. Also called **psychopoetry**.

Poetzl phenomenon see PÖTZL PHENOMENON.

Poggendorf illusion a visual illusion in which the two ends of a straight diagonal line seem to be offset from one another when the line appears to pass behind a figure with parallel vertical borders, such as a bar. [Johann Christian **Poggendorf** (1796–1877), German physicist]

POI abbreviation for PERSONAL ORIENTATION INVENTORY

poikilotherm *n.* see ECTOTHERM. **—poikilothermic** *adj.* **—poikilothermy** *n.*

point biserial correlation the correlation (association) between two random variables, one continuous and one dichotomous.

point estimate a single estimated numerical value of the population parameter. Compare INTERVAL ESTIMATE.

point–hour ratio (**PHR**) the average numerical grade earned by a student, determined by dividing earned GRADE POINTS by the total number of class hours attended in a semester or quarter. Also called **grade-point average**.

pointing *n.* a test in which the participant, first with the eyes open and then with the eyes closed, extends a forefinger and touches the forefingers of the examiner as they stand facing each other. Knowing the location of the examiner's fingers, participants should be able to touch them with their eyes closed. Failure to do so is called **past-pointing**.

point localization the ability to locate a point on the skin that is stimulated. The **point-localization test** is a somatosensory test in which a skin area, usually on the hand, is touched twice with an intervening period of 1 s. The participant is required to determine whether the points touched were in the same place. Also called **tactual localization**.

point method a method of evaluating jobs for the purpose of setting wage or salary levels in which a number of COMPENSABLE JOB FACTORS are identified, each factor is divided into degrees or levels, and points are assigned to each level; jobs can then be rated according to their total point score. The technique, which is essentially a development of the FACTOR-COMPARISON METHOD, is now the most widely used form of job evaluation. Also called **point factor method**. Compare CLASSIFICATION METHOD; HAY METHOD; JOB-COMPONENT METHOD; RANKING METHOD.

point mutation a deletion, change, or insertion of a single base pair, causing a change in the DNA sequence. See MUTATION.

point of subjective equality (**PSE**) the value of a comparison stimulus that, for a given observer, is equally likely to be judged as higher or lower than that of a standard stimulus.

point prevalence see PREVALENCE.

Poisson distribution a theoretical statistical distribution that generates the probability of occurrence of rare events that are randomly distributed in time or space. [Siméon D. **Poisson** (1781–1840), French mathematician]

Poisson regression model a NONLINEAR REGRESSION MODEL used to describe the occurrence of rare events as a function of one or more predictor variables. [Siméon **Poisson**]

polar body any of one or more tiny cells that are produced by division of oocytes during the formation of female gametes (see OOGENESIS).

polar continuum a series whose end points are opposites, such as hot–cold.

polarization *n.* **1.** a difference in electric potential between two surfaces or two sides of one surface because of chemical activity. Polarization occurs normally in living cells, such as neurons and muscle cells, which maintain a positive charge on one side of the plasma membrane and a negative charge on the other. See POLARIZED MEMBRANE. **2.** a condition in which light waves travel in parallel paths along one plane.

polarized membrane a membrane with a positive electrical charge on one surface and a negative charge on the other surface. All living cells maintain a potential difference across their plasma membrane—the membrane potential. In the resting condition, the outside of the membrane is positive in relation to the inside. See RESTING POTENTIAL.

polarized thinking see DICHOTOMOUS THINKING.

polar opposites end points of a polar continuum, in which a parameter moves from one pole (e.g., hot) to its opposite (e.g., cold).

police psychologist a psychologist whose chief role is to assist law enforcement. Typical duties may involve the screening and selection of recruits, FITNESS FOR DUTY EVALUATIONS, and counseling.

policy analysis a collection of techniques of synthesizing information (a) to specify alternative policy and program choices in cost–benefit terms, (b) to assess organizational goals in terms of input and outcome, and (c) to provide a guide for future decisions concerning research activities.

policy research empirical research conducted to guide the formulation of corporate or public policies.

polio *n.* see POLIOMYELITIS.

polioencephalitis *n.* inflammation of the gray matter of the brain, due to an infectious disease.

poliomyelitis *n.* an inflammatory process due to viral infection. In minor cases it is characterized by fever, headache, sore throat, and vomiting that typically disappear within 72 hours. In major cases, the inflammation affects the gray matter of the spinal cord and may lead to muscular weakness and paralysis, which can affect the muscles controlled by autonomic nerves, as well as skeletal muscles, so that breathing, swallowing, or similar functions are disrupted. Cognitive problems may arise as a secondary result of breathing difficulties. Also called **infantile paralysis**; **polio**.

political correctness advocacy of or conformity to the belief that anything, particularly language, that may be offensive to or discriminate against anyone on the basis of race, ethnicity, gender, sexuality, disability, or physical appearance should be avoided. The term is usually used disparagingly to connote dogmatism, excessive sensitivity, and the like.

political genetics any of various attempts to derive political theories or practices from the science of genetics. Most such programs have been repugnant, ranging from the policies of selective breeding and population control advocated by SOCIAL DARWINISM to Nazi conceptions of a master race. See also BEYONDISM.

political psychology **1.** the study of political issues and processes from the perspective of psychological principles. **2.** the application of psychological principles and knowledge to the formation of public policy, particularly as related to mental health and associated issues. See also PUBLIC SERVICE PSYCHOLOGY.

political socialization the transmission of political norms through social agents, such as schools, parents, peers, or the mass media. See SOCIAL TRANSMISSION.

political sociology an interdisciplinary field that examines the social basis of and social influences on political institutions, political movements, political power, and public policy.

poll *n.* see OPINION POLL.

Pollitt syndrome see TRICHORRHEXIS NODOSA WITH MENTAL RETARDATION. [reported in 1968 by Rodney J. **Pollitt**, British physician]

pollution *n.* the presence of toxins or contaminants in the environment. See AIR-POLLUTION ADAPTATION; AIR-POLLUTION BEHAVIORAL EFFECTS.

poltergeist *n.* an alleged paranormal phenomenon in which an unseen "presence" disturbs a household by noisy and destructive pranks, such as slamming doors, rapping on walls, upsetting furniture, and breaking crockery. Parapsychologists often approach such manifestations with the idea that they may be caused by conscious or unconscious PSYCHOKINESIS, rather than being INDEPENDENT PHENOMENA.

poly- *combining form* **1.** many or much (e.g., POLYGYNY). **2.** excessive (e.g., POLYDIPSIA).

polyandry *n.* **1.** in animals, a MATING SYSTEM in which a female mates with more than one male but a male mates with only one female. The female mates with and forms a social relationship with multiple males during one reproductive cycle. COOPERATIVE-BREEDING tamarins are thought to exhibit **facultative polyandry**, in which a female mates with multiple males who share in care of young when a new social group is formed, but once the group is established and has many helpers, the same female will become monogamous with one of the males. **2.** marriage of a woman to more than one husband at the same time, which is an accepted custom in certain cultures. Compare MONOGAMY; POLYGAMY; POLYGYNANDRY; POLYGYNY. **—polyandrous** *adj.*

polychoric correlation the correlation between two variables both of which are scored as ordered categories.

polydipsia *n.* excessive or abnormal thirst, typically for prolonged periods. It may result from organic causes, such as diabetes mellitus, or—in the case of **psychogenic polydipsia**—may be related to psychological factors. It may also be induced by conditioning procedures (see ADJUNCTIVE BEHAVIOR).

polydrug abuse SUBSTANCE ABUSE involving more than one drug.

polydrug dependence dependence (physical, psychological, or both) on more than one drug of abuse. Also called **polysubstance dependence**. See SUBSTANCE DEPENDENCE.

polydystrophic oligophrenia see SANFILIPPO'S SYNDROME.

polyestrous *adj.* see ESTRUS.

polyethism *n.* the division of labor that occurs especially among colonies of SOCIAL INSECTS, in which each individual has a specific job, such as care of larvae, foraging for food, defense of the colony, or nest construction. In some species there is an age-biased polyethism such that individuals progress through several tasks as they become older.

polygamy *n.* marriage to more than one spouse at the same time, which is an accepted custom in certain cultures. See also BIGAMY; GROUP MARRIAGE; PLURAL MARRIAGE; POLYANDRY; POLYGYNY. Compare MONOGAMY. **—polygamous** *adj.* **—polygamist** *n.*

polygenic trait a trait that is determined by numerous genes rather than only one. An example is average intelligence. Also called **polygenetic trait**. See MULTIFACTORIAL INHERITANCE.

polyglot *n.* see LINGUIST.

polyglot reaction recovery from APHASIA in which a multilingual person first uses a language other than his or her native language. See also PITRES' RULE; RIBOT'S LAW.

polygraph *n.* a device that measures and records several physiological indicators of anxiety or emotion, such as heart rate, blood pressure, and SKIN CONDUCTANCE or GALVANIC SKIN RESPONSE. The instrument has been widely used in the interrogation of criminal suspects and in employee screening to measure marked physiological reactions to questions about such issues as theft, sexual deviation, or untruthfulness. It has been colloquially referred to as a **lie detector**, although no one has ever documented a close relation between physiological patterns and deceptive behavior. The accuracy of polygraph examinations is controversial, and the results are not accepted as evidence in many U.S. courts of law. The polygraph was invented in 1917 by U.S. experimental psychologist William Marston (1893–1947); an improved version, the **Keeler polygraph**, was designed by U.S. criminologist Leonard Keeler (1903–1949).

polygynandry *n.* a MATING SYSTEM in which females mate with multiple males and males mate with multiple females. Compare MONOGAMY; POLYANDRY; POLYGYNY.

polygyny *n.* **1.** in animals, a MATING SYSTEM in which a male mates with more than one female but a female mates with only one male. See also HAREM; RESOURCE DEFENSE POLYGYNY. **2.** marriage of a man to more than one wife at the same time, which is an accepted custom in certain cultures. Compare MONOGAMY; POLYANDRY; POLYGAMY; POLYGYNANDRY. **—polygynous** *adj.*

polyiterophilia *n.* sexual interest and arousal focused on repeating the same sexual actions and behaviors many times, and with many different partners.

polymerase chain reaction (**PCR**) a method for reproducing a particular RNA or DNA sequence manyfold, allowing amplification for sequencing or manipulating the sequence.

polymodal *adj.* involving several sensory modalities.

polymorphic fusiform layer see CORTICAL LAYERS.

polymorphism *n.* **1.** in biology, the condition of having multiple behavioral or physical types within a species or population. In some fish species there are two distinct sizes of males: Larger males defend territory and attract females to mate with them; much smaller males, often with the physical appearance of females, stay close to the large male and inseminate some of the eggs. Peppered moths in England exist as black morphs (forms) in polluted areas and white morphs in nonpolluted areas. **2.** in genetics, the presence in a population of two or more variants of a gene (i.e., ALLELES) at a given genetic locus. For example, the variety of human blood groups is due to polymorphism of particular genes governing the characteristics of red blood cells. See also SINGLE-NUCLEOTIDE POLYMORPHISM. **—polymorphic** *adj.*

polymorphous perversity in the classic psychoanalytic theory of Sigmund FREUD, the response of the human infant to many kinds of normal, daily activities posited to provide sexual excitation, such as touching, smelling, sucking, viewing, exhibiting, rocking, defecating, urinating, hurting, and being hurt.

polyneuritis *n.* inflammation of several nerves at the same time, usually involving peripheral nerves as a result of infection. Symptoms include intense pain, muscle atrophy, and paralysis.

polyneuropathy *n.* any disease that affects many or all of the peripheral nerves. See PERIPHERAL NEUROPATHY.

polynomial regression a class of linear regression models (see LINEAR MODEL) in which one or more of the terms is raised to a power greater than 1 (e.g., $Y_i = \beta_0 + \beta_1 X_i + \beta_2 X_i^2 + \beta_3 X_i^3 + \ldots$).

polyopia *n.* the formation of multiple images of one object on the retina due to a refractive error of the eye, brain injury (see PALINOPSIA), fatigue, or PSYCHOGENIC DISORDER. See VISUAL ILLUSION.

polyorchidism *n.* the condition of having one or more supernumerary testes. **—polyorchid** *adj., n.*

polypeptide *n.* a molecule consisting of numerous (usually more than 10–20) AMINO ACIDS linked by peptide bonds (see PEPTIDE). The synthesis of polypeptides in living cells takes place at RIBOSOMES according to the genetic instructions encoded in the cell's DNA. Polypeptides are assembled by the cell into PROTEINS.

polyphagia *n.* an abnormal compulsion to eat excessive quantities of food.

polypharmacy *n.* the simultaneous use of a variety of drugs of the same or different classes with the intent of producing a more robust therapeutic response. Polypharmacy for mental disorders may, for example, involve the administration of two or more antidepressants in the hope that agents with different mechanisms of action will result in greater clinical improvement than that seen with any one drug alone. Polypharmacy is often criticized because of the lack of well-controlled studies supporting its use and the greater likelihood of drug interactions when two or more drugs are used simultaneously. However, for those individuals unsuccessfully treated with several trials of monotherapy, or for whom monotherapy achieves suboptimal results, polypharmacy may be therapeutically indicated and appropriately managed.

polyphasic activity see TYPE A BEHAVIOR.

polyphasic sleep a sleep pattern in which sleep occurs in relatively short naps throughout a 24-hour period. A human infant may begin life with a polyphasic sleep rhythm that consists of half a dozen sleep periods. The rhythm becomes monophasic, with one long, daily sleep period, by about school age. **Biphasic sleep** patterns, which include one daytime nap period in addition to the long, typically nocturnal, period of sleep, are seen in a variety of cultures (e.g., as the siesta) and in older adults. See also SLEEP–WAKE CYCLE. Compare MONOPHASIC SLEEP.

polysemy *n.* the condition in which a word has more than one meaning, as in *dear* meaning "loved" or "expensive." Psycholinguistic experiments to probe the structure of the MENTAL LEXICON frequently make use of polysemy. See also AMBIGUITY; HOMONYM; PUN. **—polysemic** *adj.*

polysensory unit a neuron in the central nervous system or a sensory receptor that normally responds to more than one type of stimulus, such as cutaneous sensory receptors that mediate prick-pain impulses and also produce sensations of itching.

polysomnography *n.* the recording of various physiological processes (e.g., eye movements, brain waves, heart rate, penile tumescence) throughout the night, for the diagnosis of sleep-related disorders. **—polysomnograph** *n.*

polysubstance dependence see POLYDRUG DEPENDENCE.

polysurgical addiction a condition characterized by a compulsive drive to undergo one surgical procedure after another even when organic pathology cannot be found. The condition may be a manifestation of FACTITIOUS DISORDER with predominantly physical signs and symptoms, HYPOCHONDRIASIS, or SOMATIZATION DISORDER.

polysynaptic arc a NEURAL ARC involving several SYNAPSES, for example, when one or more sensory neurons are connected to one or more motor neurons via one or several interneurons. Also called **multisynaptic arc**. Compare MONOSYNAPTIC ARC.

polysynaptic reflex any reflex whose pathway involves more than a single SYNAPSE.

POMC abbreviation for PROOPIOMELANOCORTIN.

POMR abbreviation for problem-oriented medical record. See PROBLEM-ORIENTED RECORD.

POMS acronym for PROFILE OF MOOD STATES.

pons *n.* a part of the brainstem lying between the MIDBRAIN and the MEDULLA OBLONGATA, appearing as a swelling on the ventral surface of the brainstem. It consists of bundles of transverse, ascending, and descending nerve fibers and nuclei, including FACIAL NERVE nuclei. It serves primarily as a bridge, or transmission structure, between different areas of the nervous system. It also works with the CEREBELLUM in controlling equilibrium, and with the CEREBRAL CORTEX in smoothing and coordinating voluntary movements. With the cerebellum it forms the region called the metencephalon. **—pontine** *adj.*

pontine–geniculo–occipital spikes see PGO SPIKES.

pontine nucleus any of several nuclei in the basal PONS. They receive fibers from the cerebral cortex and send fibers to the cerebellum via the middle CEREBELLAR PEDUNCLES.

pontine sleep dreaming sleep; sleep characterized by the presence of PGO SPIKES. See DREAM STATE.

pontocerebellar pathway a neural pathway in the brain consisting of nerve fibers that run from the PONTINE NUCLEI to the CEREBELLUM. The latter uses this information to coordinate and refine muscular activity initiated by the cerebral cortex.

Ponzo illusion a visual illusion in which the upper of two parallel horizontal lines of equal length appears to be longer than the bottom of the two lines when the horizontal lines are flanked by oblique lines that are closer together at the top than they are at the bottom. Also called **railway lines illusion**. [Mario **Ponzo** (1882–1960), Italian psychologist]

pooled interdependence a task condition in which the task is split among a number of individuals, units, or groups, each of which performs independently with no flow of work between them and little if any contact or coordination required. The output of each individual, unit, or group is eventually pooled and contributes to the overall goals of the organization as a whole. For example, each member of a particular organization's sales department works independently throughout the day to sell a particular organizational product, and at the end of the day the number of sales across all members is combined to yield a sales figure for the organization. Pooled interdependence means that the results achieved by each individual or group will depend very little on the accomplishments of the other individuals or groups.

pooled variance the estimate of a single common variance achieved by combining several independent estimates of that variance. Also called **pooled within-cell variance**; **within-cell variance**.

pooling *n.* a procedure for combining several independent estimates of a parameter into a single estimate. This may be done by calculating the average of the independent estimates, with or without WEIGHTING. However, note that a pooled estimate is not obtained by simply combining all data into a single data set and calculating the estimate of the parameter on the massed data points.

poor premorbid schizophrenia see PROCESS SCHIZOPHRENIA.

pop-out *n.* in visual search tasks, a target that is different from the DISTRACTORS. One or more basic features will mark the pop-out as distinct from the other stimuli, hence allowing the target to be easily detected and identified regardless of the number of distractors.

popular psychology 1. psychological knowledge as understood by members of the general public, which may be oversimplified, misinterpreted, and out of date. See also COMMONSENSE PSYCHOLOGY; FOLK PSYCHOLOGY. **2.** psychological knowledge intended specifically for use by the general public, such as self-help books and television and radio advice programs.

population *n.* **1.** the total number of individuals (humans or other organisms) in a given geographical area. **2.** in statistics, a theoretically defined, complete group of objects (people, animals, institutions) from which a sample is drawn in order to obtain empirical observations and to which results can be generalized. Also called **universe**.

population density the number of people or other organisms per unit of space.

population research the study of the numbers, and changes in the numbers, of people and other organisms, focusing on the reasons for growth and decline, the migration patterns and spatial distribution of the organisms, and related issues. Also called **demographic research**. See also DEMOGRAPHIC PATTERN; DEMOGRAPHY.

population stereotype in ergonomics, generalizations about the perceptual, cognitive, or physical characteristics of a group of users, such as an ethnic or cultural group, that are relevant to the design of systems or products for that group. For example, in the United States, users have a right bias (i.e., a tendency to move right, select doors on the right, etc.) and the color red carries connotations of "stop," "danger," or "turn off." See CULTURAL ERGONOMICS.

population vector the mechanism used in the MOTOR CORTEX to encode the direction of an intended movement. The activity in each neuron increases when the intended movement is close to its preferred direction. The direction of the intended movement is derived from the activity across the population of neurons.

POR abbreviation for PROBLEM-ORIENTED RECORD.

porencephaly *n.* see CEREBRAL DYSPLASIA.

poriomania *n.* an irresistible impulse to run away or wander off, either consciously or in a state of amnesia. The condition may occur in some types of epilepsy and dementia. Also called **poriomanic fugue**. See also FUGUE; NOMADISM.

pornographomania *n.* **1.** a morbid impulse to write obscene letters. **2.** sexual arousal associated with writing obscenities.

pornography *n.* writings or images (e.g., illustrations, films) with sexual content that are likely to cause sexual arousal in some individuals. Legal interpretations vary, but all focus on the violation of community standards and the lack of any redeeming artistic value. See also EROTICA. **—pornographic** *adj.*

pornolagnia *n.* an obscure term for attraction to prostitutes as sexual partners, in preference to partners who choose to have sex out of mutual interest.

porphyria *n.* a metabolic disorder involving the excretion of excessive or abnormal **porphyrins** (breakdown products of hemoglobin) in the urine. The acute intermittent form is characterized by abdominal pain, nausea, weakness or paralysis of the extremities, and psychiatric symptoms, such as irritability, depression, agitation, and delirium.

porropsia *n.* see TELEOPSIA.

PORT abbreviation for SCHIZOPHRENIA PATIENT OUTCOMES RESEARCH TEAM.

portal-systemic encephalopathy see HEPATIC ENCEPHALOPATHY.

Porter–Lawler model of motivation a model of work motivation that integrates the VALENCE–INSTRUMENTALITY–EXPECTANCY THEORY with other theoretical perspectives, including EXISTENCE, RELATEDNESS, AND GROWTH THEORY, EQUITY THEORY, and theories of INTRINSIC MOTIVATION. [Lyman W. **Porter** (1930–) and Edward E. **Lawler** III (1938–), U.S. management theorists]

Porter's law the principle that the CRITICAL FLICKER FREQUENCY increases with the logarithm of the brightness of the stimulus, independent of the stimulus wavelength. Also called **Ferry–Porter law**. [Thomas Cunningham **Porter** (1860–1933), British scientist; Edwin Sidney **Ferry** (1868–1956), U.S. physicist]

Porteus Maze Test one of the original paper-and-pencil intelligence tests, devised in 1913 and designed to assess ability to plan ahead and apply reasoning to the solution of a problem. In its various forms, the Porteus Maze Test consists of a complex set of straight pathways that turn abruptly at right angles and run into numerous blind alleys. Only one pathway leads directly through the maze. [Stanley D. **Porteus** (1883–1972), Australian-born U.S. psychologist]

Portman Clinic a major British clinic set up in 1933 in Portman Square, London, England, by three psychoanalysts to work with criminals and psychopaths. This led to the study and treatment of all mental and behavioral abnormalities and disorders. The clinic joined the TAVISTOCK CLINIC in the Tavistock and Portman National Health Service Trust in 1994. Apart from clinical and mental health services, this trust now provides training in forensic psychotherapy to qualified psychiatrists.

portmanteau neologism a new word formed by combining parts of several existing words, for example, *stagflation*, from *stagnation* and *inflation*. See BLENDING; NEOLOGISM.

port-wine stain a permanent birthmark consisting of a bluish red discoloration. A diffuse port-wine stain on the face may be a symptom of the STURGE–WEBER SYNDROME.

position *n.* **1.** the location in space of an object in relation to a reference point or other objects. **2.** in the social psychology of groups, an individual's situation relative to others in the group, particularly with regard to social standing or rank or to his or her stand on an issue.

positional alcohol nystagmus (**PAN**) a form of horizontal NYSTAGMUS that persists following a horizontal change in head position (e.g., with the individual supine, head turned right or left) and is produced by alcohol intoxication.

positional cloning a technique to locate a gene that causes a disease, utilized when little is known about the biochemical basis of the disease.

Position Analysis Questionnaire (**PAQ**) a standardized, structured JOB ANALYSIS questionnaire that analyzes the type and level of work behaviors required by a job, rather than the tasks or technologies involved. It consists of 194 items organized in six sections: information input; mental processes involved; relationships with others; job context (physical and social); work output; and other characteristics. A statistical analysis of data from the PAQ can be used in job evaluation for the purpose of setting pay rates (see JOB-COMPONENT METHOD) or in estimating the predictive validity of PERSONNEL TESTS (see JOB-COMPONENT VALIDITY). [developed in the 1970s by U.S. industrial and organizational psychologist Ernest J. McCormick (1911–1990), U.S. industrial and organizational psychologist Paul R. Jeanneret (1940–), and Robert C. Mecham]

position effect in parapsychology experiments using ZENER CARDS or similar targets, an effect in which the position of the target in a temporal series or a spatial array appears to influence the accuracy of the participant's "calls" or guesses. See also DECLINE EFFECT; DIFFERENTIAL EFFECT; FOCUSING EFFECT; PREFERENTIAL EFFECT; SHEEP–GOAT EFFECT.

positioning *n.* in psychotherapy, deviation of the therapist from his or her typical method of operation or of conducting a session. For example, the therapist may give information or direction contrary to that anticipated by the client on the basis of the therapist's usual approach.

position power a capacity to influence others based on the acceptance by these others that the influencer occupies a formal position in the organization or group that gives him or her the right to make decisions and to demand compliance. In other words, the power is associated with the position itself and is not dependent on the person in that position. See LEGITIMATE POWER; POWER.

positive acceleration a situation in which the successive gains as a result of learning or practice increase across trials. See LEARNING CURVE. Compare NEGATIVE ACCELERATION.

positive addiction a concept based on the assumption that some life activities in which a person feels a need or urge to participate, such as meditation or exercising, are positive even though they may possibly attain a level or a form of addiction. Positive addictions are considered healthy therapeutic alternatives relative to negative addictions, such as drug abuse, alcohol dependence, or cigarette smoking. [developed by U.S. psychiatrist William Glasser (1925–)]

positive affect the internal feeling state (AFFECT) that occurs when a goal has been attained, a source of threat has been avoided, or the individual is satisfied with the present state of affairs. The tendency to experience such states is called **positive affectivity**.

positive afterimage see AFTERIMAGE.

positive afterpotential a small, positive membrane potential (hypopolarization) shown by a neuron or muscle cell during recovery from an ACTION POTENTIAL. The nerve or muscle is more excitable during the positive afterpotential. See also AFTERPOTENTIAL.

positive attitude in psychotherapy and counseling, the client's feelings of self-approval and acceptance and approval of the therapist or counselor, the therapeutic or counseling process, another person, or an object. Compare NEGATIVE ATTITUDE.

positive contingency see CONTINGENCY.

positive definite a class of square symmetric matrices whose EIGENVALUES are all positive (i.e., >0).

positive discrimination preferential treatment, especially in employment or education, of groups that may be at a disadvantage, for example, on the basis of race or gender. See AFFIRMATIVE ACTION; EQUAL OPPORTUNITY. See also DISCRIMINATION.

positive discriminative stimulus (symbol: S+) a stimulus associated with a contingency of POSITIVE REINFORCEMENT.

positive emotion an emotional reaction designed to express a POSITIVE AFFECT, such as happiness when one attains a goal, relief when a danger has been avoided, or contentment when one is satisfied with the present state of affairs. Compare NEGATIVE EMOTION.

positive eugenics see EUGENICS.

positive exercise addiction an inordinate attraction to habitual participation in physical exercise activities that brings about a positive sense of physical and psychological well-being. Compare NEGATIVE EXERCISE ADDICTION.

positive family history a family history that shows the characteristics sufficient for the family to be considered to have a genetic syndrome or inherited disease. The AMSTERDAM CRITERIA, for example, are the criteria by which a family history of colon cancer is evaluated to determine whether the family has hereditary nonpolyposis colorectal cancer (HNPCC) or familial adenomatous polyposis (FAP).

positive feedback 1. an arrangement whereby some of the output of a system, whether mechanical or biological, is fed back to increase the effect of input signals. Positive feedback is rare in biological systems. See FEEDBACK SYSTEM. **2.** in social psychology, acceptance, approval, affirmation, or praise received by a person in response to his or her performance. Compare NEGATIVE FEEDBACK.

positive findings bias the tendency for researchers to hope for, perceive, and report results supporting research hypotheses rather than the NULL HYPOTHESIS. See EXPERIMENTER EFFECT.

positive hallucination a false perceptual experience characterized by perceiving that something is there when it is not there. In general, positive hallucination is an exaggeration of normal perception. Although positive hallucinations are a hallmark of psychotic disturbances, such as schizophrenia, these perceptual experiences can also be generated by hypnosis. See HALLUCINATION. Compare NEGATIVE HALLUCINATION.

positive hit rate 1. the number of instances in which the choice of a particular alternative proved correct divided by the total number of instances in which that alternative was chosen. **2.** in PERSONNEL SELECTION, the proportion of people hired who actually succeed on the job.

positive illusion a belief about oneself that is pleasant or positive and that is held regardless of its truth. The most common positive illusions involve exaggerating one's good traits (see BENEFFECTANCE), overestimating one's degree of control over personally important events (see ILLUSION OF CONTROL), and sustaining unrealistic optimism (see REPRESSIVE COPING STYLE).

positive incentive an object or condition that constitutes a desired goal and may result in GOAL-DIRECTED BEHAVIOR. Compare NEGATIVE INCENTIVE.

positive interdependence a relationship in which the success of one party increases the likelihood of another party's success and one party's failure increases the likelihood that others will fail. This type of interdependence tends to elicit cooperative, conflict-free interactions. Also called **promotive interdependence**. Compare CONTRIENT INTERDEPENDENCE.

positive motivation the impulse to engage in behaviors that result in desired outcomes, for example, wanting to work hard in order to obtain praise or promotion from an employer.

positive Oedipus complex see OEDIPUS COMPLEX.

positive psychology a field of psychological theory and research that focuses on the psychological states (e.g., contentment, joy), individual traits or CHARACTER STRENGTHS (e.g., intimacy, integrity, altruism, wisdom), and social institutions that make life most worth living. A manual, *Character Strengths and Virtues: A Handbook and Classification*, serves this perspective in a manner parallel to the *DSM–IV–TR* for the categorization of mental illness. [term coined by Abraham MASLOW and adapted by U.S. psychologist Martin P. Seligman]

positive punishment punishment that results because some stimulus or circumstance is presented as a consequence of a response. For example, if a response results in presentation of a loud noise and the response becomes less likely as a result of this experience, then positive punishment has occurred. Compare NEGATIVE PUNISHMENT.

positive regard 1. a parent's warm, caring, accepting feelings for a child. Positive regard is considered necessary for the child to develop a consistent sense of self-worth. **2.** the therapist's feelings for the client as a unique individual whom he or she cares for and values. See also CONDITIONAL POSITIVE REGARD; UNCONDITIONAL POSITIVE REGARD. [defined by Carl ROGERS]

positive reinforcement 1. an increase in the probability of occurrence of some activity because that activity results in the presentation of a stimulus or of some circumstance. **2.** the procedure of presenting a positive reinforcer after a response. See REINFORCEMENT. Compare NEGATIVE REINFORCEMENT.

positive schizophrenia a form of schizophrenia in which POSITIVE SYMPTOMS predominate, as evidenced in the person's bizarre behavior, illogical speech or writing, or expression of hallucinations and delusions. Although more dramatically evident than NEGATIVE SCHIZOPHRENIA, the positive aspect is usually less challenging to treat. [defined in 1982 by U.S. psychiatrist Nancy C. Andreasen and Scott A. Olsen]

positive self-regard an attitude of self-esteem or self-worth. Positive self-regard is often sought as a goal in treatment and is fostered by the therapist's regard for the client.

positive self-talk the covert expression of ideas (see SELF-TALK) that facilitate the creation of an IDEAL PERFORMANCE STATE and are motivating or self-enhancing.

positive stereotype a stereotype that purports to describe the admirable, desirable, or beneficial qualities and characteristics of the members of a particular group or social category. Although stereotypes about other groups are often negative, generalizations about one's own groups tend to be positive. Compare NEGATIVE STEREOTYPE.

positive symptom a symptom of schizophrenia that represents an excess or distortion of normal function, as distinct from a deficiency in or lack of normal function (compare NEGATIVE SYMPTOM). Positive symptoms include delusions or hallucinations, disorganized behavior, and manifest conceptual disorganization. Positive symptoms are more dramatic than negative symptoms and are less distinctive of schizophrenia: Swiss psychiatrist Eugen Bleuler (1857–1939) regarded them as SECONDARY SYMPTOMS. See POSITIVE SCHIZOPHRENIA.

positive transfer 1. the improvement or enhancement of present learning by previous learning. For instance, learning to program a videocassette recorder could facilitate learning to program a digital telephone. See also TRANSFER OF TRAINING. Compare NEGATIVE TRANSFER. **2.** see LANGUAGE TRANSFER.

positive transference in psychoanalytic theory, DISPLACEMENT onto the therapist of feelings of attachment, love, idealization, or other positive emotions that were originally experienced toward the parents or other significant individuals. Compare NEGATIVE TRANSFERENCE. See TRANSFERENCE.

positive tropism the orientation of an organism toward a source of stimulation. An example is the turning of a flower to face the sun. See TROPISM.

positivism *n.* a family of philosophical positions holding that all meaningful propositions must be reducible to sensory experience and observation, and thus that all genuine knowledge is to be built on strict adherence to empirical methods of verification. Positivism first became an explicit position in the work of French thinkers Auguste Comte (1798–1857) and Claude Henri de Rouvroy, Comte de Saint-Simon (1760–1825), although it is implicit to varying degrees in most earlier forms of EMPIRICISM. Its effect is to establish science as the model for all forms of valid inquiry and to dismiss the truth claims of religion, metaphysics, and speculative philosophy. Positivism, particularly LOGICAL POSITIVISM, was extremely influential in the early development of psychology and helped to form its commitment to empirical methods. It continues to be a major force in contemporary psychology. See also MACHIAN POSITIVISM. —**positivist** *adj.*

positivist criminology an approach that seeks to explain criminal behavior not as an exercise of free will or choice (as is the case in classical CRIMINOLOGY) but rather as a consequence of various internal factors (e.g., biological, psychological) and external factors (e.g., cultural and social) that affect human behavior. See also CRIMINAL ANTHROPOLOGY.

positron emission tomography (**PET**) a technique used to evaluate cerebral metabolism using radiolabeled tracers, such as 2-deoxyglucose labeled with fluorine-18, which emit positrons as they are metabolized. This technique enables documentation of functional changes that occur during the performance of mental activities.

possession *n.* see DEMONIC POSSESSION.

possession trance see DISSOCIATIVE TRANCE DISORDER.

possessiveness *n.* **1.** in general, excessive striving to claim possession or ownership. **2.** an abnormal tendency to control or dominate others, generally involving the restriction of their social relationships. In its most extreme form, this pattern of behavior is often associated with abusive relationships. See also JEALOUSY.

postcaptivity health problems health problems that develop after a period of captivity, especially in PRISONERS OF WAR, which may include injuries, posttraumatic stress reactions, affective reactions, or a combination of these. Many former captives, but not all, may show POSTTRAUMATIC STRESS DISORDER in the years following release, sometimes with a delayed onset.

postcentral area a sensory region of the PARIETAL LOBE of the brain, posterior to the CENTRAL SULCUS, that has neurons involved in the perception of touch, proprioception, kinesthesis, and taste.

postcentral gyrus a ridge in the PARIETAL LOBE of the brain, just behind the CENTRAL SULCUS, that is the site of the PRIMARY SOMATOSENSORY AREA.

postchiasmatic visual deficit a visual impairment caused by damage to visual processing areas posterior to (i.e., beyond) the OPTIC CHIASM, such as the OPTIC RADIATIONS or STRIATE CORTEX. Postchiasmatic injury or disease affects vision in both eyes (see HOMONYMOUS HEMIANOPIA). Also called **retrochiasmatic visual deficit**.

postcognition *n.* in parapsychology, the experiencing of a past event as if it were occurring in the present. In a test of postcognition, the participant would be asked to guess the outcome of an earlier set of trials involving ZENER CARDS or similar stimulus materials. See also BACKWARD DISPLACEMENT. Compare PRECOGNITION. —**postcognitive** *adj.*

postcompetition anxiety the apprehension or fear created after a competition as a result of not meeting goals during the competition, the perceived reaction of others to the performance or outcome, or the perceived expectations of others and oneself because of the performance or outcome.

postconcussion syndrome persistent, pervasive changes in cognitive abilities and emotional functioning that occur as a result of diffuse trauma to the brain during concussion. An individual with this syndrome may appear to be within normal limits neurologically but suffers from persistent depression, fatigue, impulse-control problems, and difficulties with concentration and memory. Postconcussion syndrome is frequently seen in individuals who have been repeatedly beaten on the head and face, such as battered children or women (see BATTERED-CHILD SYNDROME; BATTERED-WOMAN SYNDROME).

postconventional level in KOHLBERG'S THEORY OF MORAL DEVELOPMENT, the third and highest level of moral reasoning, characterized by an individual's commitment to moral principles sustained independently of any identification with family, group, or country. The earlier stage of the postconventional level (Stage 5 of the model as a whole; see SOCIAL CONTRACT ORIENTATION) is marked by concerns with individual rights in relation to the needs of society. The later stage (Stage 6; see PRINCIPLED STAGE) is concerned with the application of self-determined, rational principles that have universal validity. Compare CONVENTIONAL LEVEL; PRECONVENTIONAL LEVEL.

postcopulatory behavior activity that immediately follows COPULATORY BEHAVIOR. Male rats, for example, are inactive but produce an ultrasonic vocalization after ejaculation. In many species males remain alert and guard their mate to prevent other males from attempting to copulate with her. In some species females can eject or remove sperm or keep it, engaging in postcopulatory MATE SELECTION.

postcreolization continuum see DECREOLIZATION.

postemployment services 1. in VOCATIONAL REHABILITATION, follow-up assistance or programs designed to help recently employed individuals with disabilities adjust to their new job situation. Examples include counseling, financial support, and continuing medical treatment and care. **2.** training and services provided to help individuals who are economically disadvantaged (e.g., those receiving public assistance in the form of welfare) obtain employment, develop various work-related skills essential to sustained long-term employment, and enhance their potential for wage increases and career advancement. Such services may include access to and assistance with child care and transportation; flexible work hours; on-the-job training; continuing education classes; and mentoring programs designed to help newly hired individuals adjust to the workplace.

postencephalitic amnesia a memory disorder that occurs in some patients who have recovered from an attack of viral ENCEPHALITIS. The symptoms include a gross defect of recent memory and partial amnesia for events preceding the attack; intelligence, however, is unimpaired.

postencephalitis syndrome a pathological condition that occurs following or as a result of ENCEPHALITIS. An example is postencephalitic PARKINSONISM, which developed in patients who recovered from the 1915–1926 epidemic of ENCEPHALITIS LETHARGICA. The onset of symptoms in some cases was not observed until 10 years after recovery from the disease.

posterior *adj.* toward the back or tail of an animal. Compare ANTERIOR.

posterior cerebral artery an artery of the brain that arises from the terminal bifurcation of the BASILAR ARTERY and passes above the OCULOMOTOR NERVE to curve around the midbrain above the level of the TENTORIUM CEREBELLI. Its branches supply blood to the region of the THIRD VENTRICLE, including the thalamus and choroid plexus, the posterior surface of the occipital lobe, and the lingual, fusiform, and inferior temporal gyri.

posterior chamber see EYE.

posterior commissure a large bundle of nerve fibers in the brain that crosses the midline of the EPITHALAMUS just dorsal to the point where the CEREBRAL AQUEDUCT opens into the fourth VENTRICLE. It is composed mainly of myelinated fibers connecting oculomotor and related cells of the midbrain. See also COMMISSURE.

posterior communicating artery an artery that arises from the INTERNAL CAROTID ARTERY and passes just ventral to the optic tract to merge with the POSTERIOR CEREBRAL ARTERY, thus completing the ARTERIAL CIRCLE at the base of the brain. Branches of the posterior communicating artery supply the optic tract and part of the optic chiasm, the genu of the corpus callosum, the posterior hypothalamus, parts of the internal capsule, the third ventricle, and anterior and ventral nuclei of the thalamus.

posterior cortex in neuroanatomy, the OCCIPITAL CORTEX of mammals, including the STRIATE CORTEX (Brodmann area 17) and PRESTRIATE CORTEX (area 18).

posterior distribution in Bayesian analysis, the estimated distribution of the parameters of interest obtained by combining empirical data with one's prior expectation of the probable values of the parameters in question.

posterior fossa see FOSSA.

posterior horn see DORSAL HORN.

posterior nucleus see LATERAL POSTERIOR NUCLEUS.

posterior pituitary the posterior lobe of the PITUITARY GLAND. Also called **neurohypophysis**.

posterior rhizotomy see RHIZOTOMY.

posterior root see DORSAL ROOT.

postexperimental inquiry a procedure designed to reveal DEMAND CHARACTERISTICS in which participants are asked about the responses they gave in an experiment. Compare PREINQUIRY.

postfigurative culture a society or culture in which the young learn chiefly from their parents, grandparents, and other adults. Compare COFIGURATIVE CULTURE; PREFIGURATIVE CULTURE. [coined by U.S. anthropologist Margaret Mead (1901–1978)]

postformal thought the complex ways in which adults structure their thinking based on the complicated nature of adult life. It is an extension of Jean PIAGET's concept of FORMAL OPERATIONS, which are developed in adolescence, to adult cognition and includes an understanding of the relative, nonabsolute nature of knowledge; an acceptance of contradiction as a basic aspect of reality; the ability to synthesize contradictory thoughts, feelings, and experiences into more coherent, all-encompassing wholes; and the ability to resolve both ill- and well-defined problems.

postganglionic autonomic neuron any neuron of the SYMPATHETIC NERVOUS SYSTEM whose cell body lies in a ganglion of the SYMPATHETIC CHAIN. Such neurons innervate certain target organs, such as the kidneys, ovaries, and salivary glands. Compare PREGANGLIONIC AUTONOMIC NEURON.

postherpetic neuralgia see HERPETIC NEURALGIA.

post hoc comparison a comparison among two or more means in ANALYSIS OF VARIANCE or MULTIPLE REGRESSION analysis that is formulated after the data have been examined. Also called **post hoc contrast**. Compare PLANNED COMPARISON.

post hoc ergo propter hoc after this, therefore because of this (Latin). See FALSE CAUSE.

post hoc fallacy in statistics and experimental design, the erroneous inference that because B followed A (in a temporal sense), then A caused B. This is comparable to the concept of FALSE CAUSE in philosophy.

posthypnotic amnesia an individual's incapacity to remember what transpired during a hypnotic trance. Typically, the participant is instructed to forget the hypnotic experience until receiving a prearranged cue from the hypnotist; at that point, memory of the experience returns. However, highly susceptible individuals may show spontaneous posthypnotic amnesia.

posthypnotic suggestion a suggestion made to a person under hypnosis and acted upon after awakening from the hypnotic trance. Usually, the act is carried out in response to a prearranged cue from the hypnotist, and the participant does not know why he or she is performing the act.

postictal *adj.* following a sudden attack, especially a seizure or a stroke. During the **postictal period** following a seizure, the individual may be confused, disoriented, and unable to form new memories. The length of the postictal period may vary from less than a second to many hours and depends on the type of seizure.

postlingually deafened becoming deaf after the acquisition of language.

postmodernism *n.* **1.** a number of related philosophical tendencies that developed in reaction to classical MODERNISM during the late 20th century. Most postmodern positions reject traditional metaphysics for its pursuit of a reality independent of the world of lived experience, traditional epistemology for its pursuit of certain knowledge and objectivity, and traditional ethical theories because of their reliance on metaphysics and epistemology. More specifically, they see the ideal of objective truth that has been a guiding principle in the sciences and most other disciplines since the 17th century as basically flawed: There can be no such truth, only a plurality of "narratives" and "perspectives." Postmodernism emphasizes the construction of knowledge and truth through discourse and lived experience, the similar construction of the self, and RELATIVISM in all questions of value. It is therefore a form of radical skepticism. See also POSTSTRUCTURALISM. **2.** in the arts, a general movement away from the tenets and practices of MODERNISM that became apparent in the late 20th century. Postmodern culture is often held to be characterized by a free merging of genres and styles, a spirit of irony and pastiche, and a recognition of the importance of pop culture and the mass media. **—postmodern** *adj.*

postmortem examination see AUTOPSY.

postnatal period see POSTPARTUM PERIOD.

postnatal sensorineural lesions disorders of the inner ear or of auditory nerve pathways that are acquired sometime in life and result in loss of hearing. Causes include injury, drug toxicity, viral infections, such diseases as mumps, measles, or scarlet fever, and simply old age.

postoccupancy evaluation (**POE**) the measurement of user responses to a building or facility following its construction. POEs are a valuable source of information for designers, providing feedback on the validity of assumptions about how the built environment fulfills users' needs and affects their behaviors. POEs can also inform ARCHITECTURAL PROGRAMMING. In the United States, POEs are required when federal money is used for construction.

postpartum blues see BABY BLUES.

postpartum depression a MAJOR DEPRESSIVE EPISODE or, less commonly, MINOR DEPRESSIVE DISORDER that affects women within 4 weeks after childbirth. Compare BABY BLUES.

postpartum emotional disturbance **1.** any MOOD DISORDER that affects women following childbirth. **2.** fluctuations in mood following childbirth that do not meet the criteria for any mood disorder.

postpartum period the period of about 6 weeks following childbirth during which the mother's reproductive system gradually returns to its prepregnant state. Some women experience depression during this period (see BABY BLUES; POSTPARTUM DEPRESSION). Also called **postnatal period**; **puerperium**.

postpartum psychosis psychotic symptoms (e.g., delusions or hallucinations) that occur in women shortly after childbirth, often associated with POSTPARTUM DEPRESSION.

postpositivism *n.* **1.** the general position of U.S. psychology since the mid-20th century, when it ceased to be dominated by LOGICAL POSITIVISM, HYPOTHETICO-DEDUCTIVE METHODS, and OPERATIONISM. Postpositivistic psychology is a broader and more human endeavor, influenced by such philosophers of science as Thomas Kuhn (1922–1996) and by such developments as SOCIAL CONSTRUCTIONISM and the Continental tradition of PHENOMENOLOGY and EXISTENTIALISM. **2.** more generally, any approach to science and the PHILOSOPHY OF SCIENCE that has moved away from a position of strict POSITIVISM. See also POSTMODERNISM. **—postpositivist** *adj., n.* **—postpositivistic** *adj.*

postreconstructive surgery surgery performed after the original reconstructive procedure (see RECONSTRUCTIVE SURGERY). Such surgery, which is often required to achieve optimum functioning, may involve the transfer of muscle or tendon fibers between body areas or the redirection of nerve fibers. See also COSMETIC SURGERY; PLASTIC SURGERY.

postreinforcement pause in operant conditioning, the period of time that elapses from the end of REINFORCEMENT until the next response from the class that is being reinforced.

postrotational nystagmus the involuntary, rapid eye movements (see NYSTAGMUS) that occur when rapid rotation of the body ceases.

postschizophrenic depression a depressive episode that may follow an ACUTE SCHIZOPHRENIC EPISODE. Postschizophrenic depression is viewed variously as a routine event in recovery from schizophrenic decompensation, as a mood disturbance that existed previously and was masked by the schizophrenic episode, or as a side effect to drug treatment for schizophrenia.

poststructuralism *n.* a broad intellectual movement that developed from French STRUCTURALISM in the late 1960s and 1970s. It is represented by the work of Jacques Derrida (1930–2004) in philosophy and criticism, Jacques Lacan (1901–1981) in philosophy and psychoanalysis, Michel Foucault (1926–1984) in the history of ideas, and Hélène Cixous (1937–) and Julia Kristeva (1941–) in feminist theory, among others. Although these thinkers are very diverse, they share a starting point in the structuralist account of language given by Swiss linguist Ferdinand de Saussure (see STRUCTURALISM), which holds that linguistic SIGNS acquire meaning only through structural relationships with other signs in the same language system. Poststructuralism endorses the arbitrariness of the sign, but from this basis proceeds to question the whole idea of fixed and determinate meaning. In the DECONSTRUCTION of Derrida, structures and systems of meaning are found to be unstable, contradictory, and endlessly self-subverting. This skepticism extends to the idea of personal identity itself; according to Derrida, the self is merely another "text" to be deconstructed.

In psychology, poststructuralism is mainly significant because of its influence on the radical psychoanalytical theories of the 1960s and 1970s. Lacan, who trained and practiced as a psychiatrist, rejected the idea of a stable autonomous EGO and reinterpreted the Freudian UNCONSCIOUS in terms of Saussure's structural linguistics. His unconventional ideas and methods led to his exclusion from the International Society of Psychoanalysts in 1963. Both Kristeva (another practicing psychoanalyst) and Cixous were deeply influenced by Lacan's ideas of sexuality, consciousness, and language, which are given a radical feminist twist in their writings. The best-known work of Foucault, who worked in a psychiatric hospital as a young man, is his *Folie et déraison: Histoire de la folie à l'âge classique* (1961; translated as *Madness and Civilization: A History of Insanity in the Age of Reason*, 1965), which gives a tendentious history of Western attitudes to insanity, arguing that the categories of "madness" and "reason" are themselves oppressive. **—poststructuralist** *adj.*

postsynaptic *adj.* **1.** of or relating to the region of a neuron within a SYNAPSE that receives and responds to a neurotransmitter. **2.** of or relating to a neuron that receives a signal via a synapse. Compare PRESYNAPTIC.

postsynaptic potential (**PSP**) the electric potential at a dendrite or other surface of a neuron after an impulse has reached it across a SYNAPSE. Postsynaptic potentials may be either EXCITATORY POSTSYNAPTIC POTENTIALS or INHIBITORY POSTSYNAPTIC POTENTIALS.

postsynaptic receptor any receptor that is located on the cell membrane or in the interior of a postsynaptic neuron. Interaction with an effector substance (e.g., a neurotransmitter), released either by the presynaptic neuron or from another site, initiates a chain of biochemical events contributing, for example, to excitation or inhibition of the postsynaptic neuron.

posttest 1. *n.* a test administered after completion of the principal test or instruction program. It may be given in conjunction with a PRETEST to assess comprehension of the content and nature of the main test as well as its effectiveness as an assessment instrument. **2.** *n.* a test administered after the application of an intervention or control condition. **3.** *vb.* to administer a posttest.

posttest counseling a type of GENETIC COUNSELING that occurs during and after disclosure of genetic test results. Posttest counseling focuses on the individual's understanding of the meaning of the test result and of the options for SCREENING. Considerable attention is given to the psychological status of the individual and to assessing whether the individual needs further genetic or psychological services.

posttest-only control-group design an experimental design involving only a POSTTEST and comprising an EXPERIMENTAL GROUP and a CONTROL GROUP.

posttetanic potentiation (**PTP**) the increase in POSTSYNAPTIC POTENTIAL elicited in target neurons by a single action potential subsequent to the induction of a tetanus (a rapid series of action potentials) in the presynaptic neuron. It is a well-known example of NEURAL PLASTICITY.

posttraumatic amnesia (**PTA**) **1.** a period of amnesia following a psychological trauma. The traumatic event may be forgotten (retrograde amnesia), or events following the trauma may be forgotten (anterograde amnesia). The period of forgetting may be continuous, or the person may experience vague, incomplete recollections of the traumatic event. **2.** a disturbance of memory for events that immediately follow a head injury.

posttraumatic disorders emotional or other disturbances whose symptoms appear after a patient has endured a traumatic experience. Common posttraumatic disorders include POSTTRAUMATIC STRESS DISORDER, ACUTE STRESS DISORDER, the DISSOCIATIVE DISORDERS, and some types of PHOBIAS and ANXIETY DISORDERS.

posttraumatic epilepsy epileptic seizures that occur as a complication of traumatic brain injury. The seizures may occur either soon after the injury or, in some cases, months or years later.

posttraumatic personality disorder a personality disorder occasionally observed after a severe head injury. Some patients become indifferent and withdrawn, but most are irritable, impulsive, petulant, extremely selfish, and irresponsible. Older patients and those suffering from frontal-lobe damage may show impaired memory with CONFABULATION. See also POSTCONCUSSION SYNDROME.

posttraumatic stress disorder (**PTSD**) in *DSM–IV–TR*, a disorder that results when an individual lives through or witnesses an event in which he or she believes that there is a threat to life or physical integrity and safety and experiences fear, terror, or helplessness. The symptoms are characterized by (a) reexperiencing the trauma in painful recollections, flashbacks, or recurrent dreams or nightmares; (b) diminished responsiveness (emotional anesthesia or numbing), with disinterest in significant activities and with feelings of detachment and estrangement from others; and (c) chronic physiological arousal, leading to such symptoms as exaggerated startle response, disturbed sleep, difficulty in concentrating or remembering, guilt about surviving when others did not (see SURVIVOR GUILT), and avoidance of activities that call the traumatic event to mind. Subtypes are CHRONIC POSTTRAUMATIC STRESS DISORDER and DELAYED POSTTRAUMATIC STRESS DISORDER. See also ACUTE STRESS DISORDER.

posttreatment follow-up a periodic check on the progress of people who have received some form of psychotherapeutic or medical treatment. In research studies, posttreatment follow-up is used to see if the effects of treatment are maintained or if relapse occurs. If the effects of treatment are maintained, it is inferred that the treatment has lasting rather than temporary effects.

postulate *n.* see AXIOM.

postural aftereffect a change in posture that arises as an aftereffect of prior stimulation. For example, when viewing a moving scene, a person typically leans in the direction of the motion. When viewing ends, body posture returns to a vertical position and then, briefly, leans in the opposite direction.

postural arm drift the drift of the arms from their original position when an individual is required to hold them outstretched and in a static position, with the eyes closed. The drift, if it occurs, is usually toward the midline and may be an indication of a parietal lesion. Also called **parietal drift**.

postural control the ability to control the position of one's body. The first landmark in the development of postural control occurs at about 3 weeks of age, when a prone infant is first able to lift the head and raise the chin. Within a few weeks, further steps in postural control are achieved, such as holding the head erect and turning it, and sitting with and then without support.

postural hypotension see ORTHOSTATIC HYPOTENSION.

postural reflex any of a variety of automatic movements that serve to maintain body POSTURE. See also STANCE REFLEX.

postural set a body position, characterized by increased muscle tone, that is adopted in preparation for a response, for example, a baseball batter's stance before a pitch.

posture *n.* **1.** the position or bearing of the body. Types of posture include **erect** (upright), **recumbent** (reclining), **prone** (lying face down), or **supine** (lying face up). Movements typically involve coordinated changes in posture (e.g., to maintain balance or distribute forces). **2.** a rationalized mental position or attitude. **—postural** *adj.*

posturing *n.* the assumption of a bizarre or inappropriate body position or attitude for an extended period of time. It is commonly observed in CATATONIA.

postvention *n.* the emotional release needed by helpers and others who work with those who have survived a traumatic event or who have directly experienced personal trauma or natural catastrophe. It is similar to debriefing following experience in working with victims of disasters (see CRITICAL-INCIDENT STRESS DEBRIEFING). [defined by 20th-century U.S. psychologist Edwin S. Schneidman]

postventral nucleus see VENTROPOSTERIOR NUCLEUS.

pot *n.* slang for marijuana. See CANNABIS.

potassium channel see ION CHANNEL.

potency *n.* **1.** the ability of a male to perform sexual intercourse, that is, to maintain an erection and achieve ejaculation. Compare IMPOTENCE. **2.** in pharmacology, see DOSE–RESPONSE RELATIONSHIP. **—potent** *adj.*

potential *n.* **1.** the capacity to develop or come into existence. **2.** electric potential, measured in volts: a property of an electric field equal to the energy needed to bring unit electric charge from infinity to a given point. The potential difference between two points is the driving force that causes a current to flow. Because messages in the nervous system are conveyed by electrochemical potentials, many kinds of potential are of importance in neuroscience and biological psychology, including the ACTION POTENTIAL, AFTERPOTENTIAL, GRADED POTENTIAL, LOCAL POTENTIAL, MEMBRANE POTENTIAL, POSTSYNAPTIC POTENTIAL, and RESTING POTENTIAL. **3.** in philosophy, see ACTUAL.

potential-stress score see LIFE-CHANGE UNIT.

potentiation *n.* a form of DRUG INTERACTION in which the addition of a second drug intensifies certain properties of the first drug administered. It often refers to the ability of a nontoxic drug to render the effects of a toxic drug more severe than when the toxic agent is administered singly.

potlatch *n.* a ceremony among some Native American peoples of the northwestern United States that involves a ceremonial feast and the distribution of impressive gifts, typically to establish prestige or to affirm social status.

Pötzl phenomenon (**Poetzl phenomenon**) the phenomenon whereby words or pictures that are presented subliminally may appear in imagery or dreams a short time later. It is taken as an example of SUBLIMINAL PERCEPTION. [Otto **Pötzl** (1877–1962), Austrian neurologist and psychiatrist]

Pötzl's syndrome a form of PURE ALEXIA associated with visual field defects and disturbances of the color sense. The syndrome is believed to be the result of a lesion in the medullary layer of the LINGUAL GYRUS of the dominant hemisphere of the brain, with damage to the CORPUS CALLOSUM. [Otto **Pötzl**]

poverty of content of speech speech that is adequate in quantity but too vague, repetitious, and lacking in content to be qualitatively adequate. It is frequently observed in schizophrenia and is distinct from POVERTY

OF SPEECH, in which the quantity of speech is diminished.

poverty of ideas a thought disturbance, often associated with schizophrenia, dementia, and severe depression, in which there is reduced spontaneity and productivity of thought as evidenced by speech that is vague or full of simple or meaningless repetitions or stereotyped phrases. The term is sometimes used interchangeably with INTELLECTUAL IMPOVERISHMENT. See also POVERTY OF SPEECH.

poverty of speech excessively brief speech with few elaborations that occurs in schizophrenia or occasionally in the context of a major depressive episode. It is distinct from POVERTY OF CONTENT OF SPEECH, in which the quality of speech is diminished. Also called **laconic speech**.

POW abbreviation for PRISONER OF WAR.

power *n.* **1.** the capacity to influence others, even when they try to resist this influence. Social power derives from a number of sources: control over rewards (REWARD POWER) and punishments (COERCIVE POWER); a right to require and demand obedience (LEGITIMATE POWER); others' identification with, attraction to, or respect for the powerholder (REFERENT POWER); others' belief that the powerholder possesses superior skills and abilities (EXPERT POWER); and the powerholder's access to and use of informational resources (**informational power**). **2.** in hypothesis testing, the probability that the NULL HYPOTHESIS will be rejected when the ALTERNATIVE HYPOTHESIS is true. In this case, it is likely that the experiment will be able to yield the results that the researcher expects because the alternative hypothesis typically expresses the belief of the researcher. **3.** in mathematics, a notation that indicates the number of times a quantity is multiplied by itself.

power base the interpersonal origin of one individual's capacity to influence other individuals. For example, REWARD POWER is based on the influencer's control over valued resources, and LEGITIMATE POWER is based on a licit right to require and demand compliance.

power-coercive strategy in social psychology, a strategy based on the uses of economic, social, and political power to effect societal change, usually through nonviolent measures (e.g., organized boycotts, strikes, sit-ins, demonstrations, registration drives, and lobbying). See also EMPIRICAL-RATIONAL STRATEGY; NORMATIVE-REEDUCATIVE STRATEGY.

power distance the degree to which a culture accepts an unequal distribution of power in organizations, institutions, or society at large. Individuals in high power distance cultures are more accepting of large power differentials than those in low power distance cultures. [introduced by Dutch cultural psychologist Geert Hofstede (1928–)]

power elite the concept of a small number of powerful individuals, especially corporate, political, religious, or military leaders, who hold the highest positions of authority in their respective institutions and share a common outlook and values. This elite not only controls vast economic resources but is thought to shape the agendas of government, business, education, and the media through its actions and attitudes. Most sociologists now reject the idea of a single power elite, arguing that developed societies have a complex of overlapping elites, which often have competing values and interests. [coined by U.S. sociologist C. Wright Mills (1916–1962)]

power function 1. a relationship in which the values for one variable vary as a function of another variable raised to a power. In mathematics, it is expressed by the equation $Y = aX^b$, where X and Y are the variables and a and b are numerical constants. When plotted on LOG-LOG COORDINATE PAPER, a power function is linear. Power functions have been used to characterize the scales relating perceived and physical intensity, as well as to characterize the relationship between response speed and practice. **2.** in HYPOTHESIS TESTING, a functional relationship between the power of a statistical test and one of the variables that affect power, such as sample size.

power grip the manner of grasping an object between the pads of the fingers and the palm (e.g., when using a hammer). See also PINCER GRIP; PRECISION GRIP.

power law 1. the law stating that sensory magnitude grows as a POWER FUNCTION of stimulus magnitude. **2.** a generalization demonstrated by a LEARNING CURVE in which each increment in the performance variable (e.g., learning or memory) corresponds with a logarithmic increase in the practice variable. For instance, if the successive units of practice are 1 trial, 10 trials, 100 trials, the resulting learning curve is a straight line.

powerlessness *n.* a state of mind in which individuals feel they lack control or influence over factors or events that affect their health (mental or physical), personal lives, or the society in which they live.

power play an aggressive technique or strategy used to achieve an end, often through the coercion of others.

power spectral density see SPECTRUM LEVEL.

power spectrum see SOUND SPECTRUM.

power test a type of test intended to calculate the participant's level of mastery of a particular topic under conditions of little or no time pressure. The test is designed so that items become progressively more difficult. Compare SPEED TEST.

P-O-X triads see BALANCE THEORY.

PPA abbreviation for PREFERRED PROVIDER ARRANGEMENT.

PPFA abbreviation for PLANNED PARENTHOOD FEDERATION OF AMERICA.

PPO preferred provider organization: a formally organized entity created by contractual arrangements among hospitals, physicians, employers, insurance companies, or third-party administrators to provide health care services to subscribers at a negotiated, often discounted, price.

PPVT abbreviation for PEABODY PICTURE VOCABULARY TEST.

PQ4R one of a variety of study methods developed on the basis of research in cognitive psychology. The formula represents six steps required for acquiring information: *p*review, *q*uestion, *r*ead, *r*eflect, *r*ecite, and *r*eview.

practical intelligence the ability to apply one's intelligence in practical, everyday situations. In the TRIARCHIC THEORY OF INTELLIGENCE it is the aspect of intelligence that requires adaptation to, shaping of, and selection of new environments.

practical intelligence task a task requiring the display of PRACTICAL INTELLIGENCE, for example, consulting a map to find a location or using mathematics to compute the prices of tickets to an athletic event. Such tasks also may measure tacit knowledge that typically is not explicitly taught and that often is not even verbalized, that is, knowledge about adapting to, shaping, or selecting an environment. Compare ACADEMIC INTELLIGENCE TASKS.

practice *n.* repetition of an act, behavior, or series of activities, often to improve performance or acquire a skill.

For example, members of sports teams may engage in a preplanned series of activities organized for such purposes as learning a pattern of play or increasing physical fitness. See also DISTRIBUTED PRACTICE; MASSED PRACTICE.

practice effect in learning, any change or improvement that results from practice or repetition of task items or activities.

practice goal a GOAL established as a target for performance during PRACTICE.

practice guidelines criteria and strategies designed to assist mental health clinicians and practitioners and physicians in the recognition and treatment of specific disorders and diseases, as well as for ethical practice. Such guidelines are often based on the latest and best available scientific research or the considered judgment of expert panel committees representing specific professions or subdisciplines. See also CLINICAL PRACTICE GUIDELINES.

practice material introductory, unscored items or examples, presented before an experiment or test, that illustrate test procedure and acquaint the participant with the nature of the items.

practice theory of play see PLAY.

practice trial the first of a series of opportunities to respond to a test, which is given to participants to acquaint them with the procedure of the test and is therefore not scored.

practicum supervision a diversified and comprehensive training experience for students planning to become professional practitioners in a given field. Management of the on-site experience is provided by an instructor or other experienced practitioner.

Prader–Willi syndrome (PWS) a congenital disorder marked by mental retardation, short stature, hypotonia (flaccid muscles), hypogonadism (underdeveloped sex organs), obesity, insensitivity to pain, and short hands and feet. Caused by an abnormality of chromosome 15 (lack of the paternal segment 15q11.2–12), it is observed most frequently in males, perhaps because the gonadal abnormality is more easily detected in males. Affected individuals have an excessive appetite and are constantly foraging for food. When diabetes mellitus is associated with the condition, it is called **Royer's syndrome**. Also called **Prader–Labhart–Willi syndrome**; **Prader–Labhart–Willi–Fanconi syndrome**. [reported in 1956 by Andrea **Prader** (1919–) and Heinrich **Willi** (1900–1971), with Alexis **Labhart** (1916–), Swiss pediatricians]

pragmatic language the ability to use language appropriately in a specific context or situation.

pragmatics *n.* in linguistics, the analysis of language in terms of its functional communicative properties (rather than its formal and structural properties, as in PHONOLOGY, SEMANTICS, and GRAMMAR) and in terms of the intentions and perspectives of its users. See also FORM–FUNCTION DISTINCTION; FUNCTIONAL GRAMMAR.

pragmatism *n.* a philosophical position holding that the truth value of a proposition or a theory is to be found in its practical consequences: If, for example, the hypothesis of God makes people virtuous and happy, then it may be considered true. Although some forms of pragmatism emphasize only the material consequences of an idea, more sophisticated positions, including that of William JAMES, recognize conceptual and moral consequences. Arguably, all forms of pragmatism tend toward RELATIVISM, because they can provide no absolute grounds—only empirical grounds—for determining truth, and no basis for judging whether the consequences in question are to be considered good or bad. See also INSTRUMENTALISM. [coined by U.S. physicist and philosopher Charles Sanders Peirce (1839–1914)] **—pragmatist** *adj., n.*

Prägnanz *n.* see PRINCIPLE OF PRÄGNANZ.

prana *n.* see CHI.

prandial drinking intake of fluids that is stimulated by eating.

praxiology *n.* **1.** the study of human conduct, or the science of efficient action (from Greek *praxis,* "to do"). **2.** psychology as the study of human actions and overt behavior, to the exclusion of consciousness and metaphysical concepts. [employed by U.S. psychologist Knight Dunlap (1875–1949)]

praxis *n.* **1.** a medical name for MOTOR PLANNING. Inadequate praxis is APRAXIA. **2.** practice, as opposed to theory. Greek philosopher Aristotle (384–322 BCE) contrasted praxis, or practical activity, with theoretical or rational activity. The term is sometimes used to denote knowledge derived from and expressed chiefly in practical or productive activity, as opposed to theoretical or conceptual knowledge.

PRE abbreviation for PARTIAL REINFORCEMENT EFFECT.

preadolescence *n.* the period of CHILDHOOD preceding adolescence, comprising approximately the 2 years preceding the onset of puberty. Also called **prepubertal stage**; **prepuberty**; **prepubescence**. **—preadolescent** *adj., n.*

preattentive process see UNCONSCIOUS PROCESS.

preattentive processing unconscious mental processing of a stimulus that occurs before attention has focused on this particular stimulus from among the array of those present in a given environment. An example of this is the disambiguation of the meaning of a particular word from among an array of words present in a given visual stimulus before conscious perception of the word. Preattentive processing is thought to identify basic stimulus features in parallel, with no limit on capacity. Also called **preattentive analysis**; **preperceptual processing**; **unconscious processing**. See also PARALLEL PROCESSING.

preaversive stimulus in conditioning, a stimulus that precedes the presentation of an AVERSIVE STIMULUS. See CONDITIONED SUPPRESSION; ESTES–SKINNER PROCEDURE.

precategorical acoustic storage (PAS) a SENSORY MEMORY that momentarily retains auditory information before it is interpreted and comprehended: a theoretical explanation of the phenomenon of ECHOIC MEMORY. PAS is regarded as a parallel store to the visual system's ICONIC MEMORY. [proposed in 1969 by U.S. psychologist Robert George Crowder (1939–2000)]

precausal thinking the tendency of a young child (below the age of 8) to perceive natural events, such as rain, wind, and clouds, in terms of intentions and willful acts, that is, in anthropomorphic rather than mechanical terms. Compare ANIMISTIC THINKING. [first described by Jean PIAGET]

precedence effect **1.** the effect of the brain in locating the source of a sound without being aware of reflected sounds from different locations. For example, if a sound is produced by a particular source and is then reflected off the walls, the listener only perceives the first source, provided that the sound from the second source arrives within a short period of time (less than 70 ms). **2.** the tendency for global features of a stimulus to dominate local features in performance tasks.

precentral gyrus a ridge in the FRONTAL LOBE of the brain, just in front of the CENTRAL SULCUS, that is crucial for motor control, being the site of the MOTOR AREA.

prechiasmatic visual deficit a visual impairment caused by damage to the part of the visual system anterior to (i.e., earlier in visual processing than) the OPTIC CHIASM. This can affect one eye (e.g., in cases of disease or injury to the eye or optic nerve) or both eyes (e.g., in cases with involvement of the optic chiasm itself). See also HETERONYMOUS HEMIANOPIA; CHIASMAL SYNDROME.

precipitating cause the particular factor, sometimes a traumatic or stressful experience, that is the immediate cause of a mental or physical disorder. A single precipitating event may turn a latent condition into the manifest form of the disorder. Compare PREDISPOSING CAUSE.

precision *n.* a measure of accuracy. In statistics, an estimate with a small STANDARD ERROR is regarded as having a high degree of precision. **—precise** *adj.*

precision grip the manner of grasping an object between the opposed tactile pads of the thumb and fingertips (e.g., when using a pen). See also PINCER GRIP; POWER GRIP.

precision of process (symbol: h) an index of proximity of a series of measures to the mean. It is the reciprocal of the VARIANCE, that is, $h = 1/\sigma^2$.

preclinical psychopharmacology the area of psychopharmacology that precedes the actual clinical application of a new drug on an individual patient or patient population. It usually includes laboratory studies of the pharmacological mechanisms of the drug, extrapolation of research data into human-use terms, and evaluation of possible interactions with current drugs or in patients with various medical conditions.

precocial *adj.* describing animals that show a high degree of behavior development at birth or hatching. For example, young geese can follow their mother and forage for food a day after hatching, whereas other birds must be provisioned for several weeks before they leave the nest. In mammals, ungulates (e.g., cattle and sheep) are much more behaviorally advanced at birth than primates. Compare ALTRICIAL.

precocious puberty abnormally early development of sexual maturity, usually before the age of 8 in a female and 10 in a male. True precocious puberty is marked by mature gonads capable of ovulation or spermatogenesis, adult levels of female or male sex hormones, and secondary sexual characteristics. **Pseudoprecocious puberty** is a condition usually caused by an endocrine tumor that results only in premature development of secondary sex characteristics. Also called **pubertas praecox**.

precocity *n.* very early, often premature, development in a child of physical or mental functions and characteristics. **—precocious** *adj.*

precognition *n.* in parapsychology, the purported ability to see or experience future events through some form of EXTRASENSORY PERCEPTION. In a test of precognition, the participant would be asked to predict the outcome of a future set of trials involving ZENER CARDS or similar stimulus materials. Compare POSTCOGNITION. See also FORWARD DISPLACEMENT. **—precognitive** *adj.*

precompetition anxiety increased cognitive and physiological AROUSAL in the week before a competition. Precompetition anxiety may facilitate or inhibit performance, depending on the performer's perception of the activation level (i.e., as an indication of readiness or apprehension). See DEBILITATIVE ANXIETY; FACILITATIVE ANXIETY.

precompetition imagery the use of IMAGERY before a competition for the MENTAL REHEARSAL of performance segments or to assist in achieving an IDEAL PERFORMANCE STATE.

preconception *n.* a belief or expectation related to some ATTITUDE OBJECT that is held before substantial information about the object is gained.

preconscious (Pcs) 1. *n.* in the classical psychoanalytic theory of Sigmund FREUD, the level of the psyche that contains thoughts, feelings, and impulses not presently in awareness, but which can be more or less readily called into consciousness. Examples are the face of a friend, a verbal cliché, or the memory of a recent event. Compare CONSCIOUS; UNCONSCIOUS. **2.** *adj.* denoting or relating to thoughts, feelings, and impulses at this level of the psyche. Also called **foreconscious**.

preconscious thinking 1. the pictorial, magical, fantasy thinking of children that precedes the development of logical thinking. [introduced in 1938 by Austrian psychoanalyst Otto Fenichel (1897–1946)] **2.** in psychoanalytic theory, thinking that takes place at the level of the PRECONSCIOUS. Preconscious thinking has sometimes been cited to explain apparently unconscious, intuitive thought processes, as well as certain kinds of creative leaps and insights.

preconventional level in KOHLBERG'S THEORY OF MORAL DEVELOPMENT, the first level of moral reasoning characteristic of children and marked by obedience, unquestioning acceptance of parents' moral definitions, and evaluation of an act's material consequences only. The earlier stage of this level (Stage 1 of the model as a whole; see PUNISHMENT AND OBEDIENCE ORIENTATION) is characterized by concern with punishment and reward. In the later stage (Stage 2; see NAIVE HEDONISM), an act is still appraised for its potential for self-gratification, but awareness of others' needs has begun to emerge. Compare CONVENTIONAL LEVEL; POSTCONVENTIONAL LEVEL.

precue *n.* a piece of advance information available from the environment (in experimental situations, manipulated by the experimenter) giving partial details that can be used to constrain planning for an upcoming movement. Studies of how precues reduce the time necessary for MOTOR PLANNING once the full movement specification is made available have been an important tool in discerning the structure of motor plans.

precuneus *n.* an area on the medial (inner) surface of the PARIETAL LOBE of each cerebral hemisphere in the brain. Located between the PARIETO-OCCIPITAL SULCUS and the CINGULATE SULCUS, it is involved in a variety of cognitive functions. Immediately behind the precuneus is the wedge-shaped CUNEUS. **—precuneate** *adj.*

precursor *n.* in biochemistry, a compound from which another is formed by a chemical reaction. For example, TYROSINE is a precursor of the catecholamine neurotransmitters (e.g., norepinephrine, dopamine).

predation *n.* the act or practice of stalking, capturing, and killing other animals for food. **Prey choice** can be broad or highly specific, and some species store captured prey for future use. Captured prey may be shared with young or other group members and may not be consumed exclusively by the successful predator. See PREDATORY AGGRESSION; PREDATORY BEHAVIOR.

predator *n.* **1.** an animal that naturally preys on others to obtain its food. See PREDATION. **2.** a person or organization whose behavior is rapacious or exploitative. **—predatory** *adj.*

predator defense see ANTIPREDATOR DEFENSE.

predator pressure the effect of predators upon their prey, affecting both current numbers of prey and their survival for reproduction.

predatory aggression aggression directed toward the capture of prey. Predatory aggression is more properly a form of FORAGING than aggression. See ANIMAL AGGRESSION.

predatory behavior behavior in which one animal stalks, attacks, and kills another. Predatory behavior has been described in terms of FORAGING and eating, but some animals will hunt and kill others without eating the prey. A cat, for example, may hunt and kill a mouse but refrain from eating it. See also HUNTING BEHAVIOR; PREDATION.

predatory paraphilia sexual interest and arousal focused on an activity that involves an unwilling participant rather than a consenting partner (see PARAPHILIA). Examples include EXHIBITIONISM and FROTTEURISM.

predestination *n.* in Christian theology, the belief or doctrine that God has foreordained salvation for certain chosen individuals, not for any merit of their own but purely according to his grace. This doctrine was taught systematically by early Church father Augustine of Hippo (354–430) and revived by 16th-century reformers Martin Luther (1483–1546) and John Calvin (1509–1564). Calvin's system is sometimes described as one of **double predestination**, as it maintains that God also foreordained a portion of humankind to damnation, an idea that raises particular moral difficulties. Predestination is a form of theological DETERMINISM, as it effectively denies human FREE WILL and moral responsibility. The concept has always been the subject of intense debate and is now rejected by most mainstream Christian thinkers. See CALVINISM.

predicate *n.* **1.** in linguistics, the part of a sentence or clause that is not the SUBJECT but asserts a property, action, or condition of the subject. The predicate of a sentence may range from a single intransitive VERB (as in *She smiled*) to a long and complex construction. See also COMPLEMENT. **2.** in logic, a property or characteristic that is attributed to the subject of a proposition. In Aristotelian and Scholastic logic (see SCHOLASTICISM), a predicate is a second term that is stated to have a particular relation to the subject of a proposition, as, for example, *man* in *Edward is a man* or *mortal* in *Man is mortal.* —**predicative** *adj.*

predicate analysis the system of SYMBOLIC LOGIC that is concerned with the relationships between the elements within individual propositions, as well as with the relationships between propositions as wholes. Also called **predicate calculus**. Compare PROPOSITIONAL ANALYSIS.

predicate thinking a thought process in which objects are considered similar or even identical because they share a particular attribute. Jean PIAGET considered such thinking to be typical of the PREOPERATIONAL STAGE of early cognitive development. Likewise, psychoanalysis associates it with the PRIMARY PROCESS thinking typical of the ID, which manifests itself in dreams and fantasies.

prediction *n.* **1.** an attempt to foretell what will happen in a particular case, generally on the basis of past instances or accepted principles. A **theoretical prediction** gives the expected results of an experiment or controlled observation in accordance with the logic of a particular theory. In science, the use of prediction and observation to test hypotheses is a cornerstone of the empirical method (see FALSIFIABILITY; FALSIFICATIONISM; RISKY PREDICTION). However, by their very nature, the theories, constructs, and explanatory models current in psychology are not always open to direct validation or falsification in this way. In psychological assessment, personality tests and other psychometric instruments can often predict participants' behaviors or other characteristics with an impressive level of accuracy. In psychiatry, it may be possible to predict the general behavior or prognosis of patients whose personality pattern is known but not their specific behavior, since so many factors are involved. See also PROBABILISM; PSEUDOSCIENCE. **2.** in parapsychology and the occult arts, see DIVINATION; PRECOGNITION. —**predict** *vb.* —**predictable** *adj.* —**predictive** *adj.*

prediction interval a range of values within which one would predict a person to score on variable *b*, given his or her scores on the predictor variable *a*.

predictive efficiency the number or proportion of correct predictions that can be made from a particular test.

predictive testing see PREDISPOSITION.

predictive validity an index of how well a test correlates with a variable that is measured in the future, at some point after the test has been administered. For example, the predictive validity of a test designed to predict the onset of a disease would be calculated by the extent to which it was successful at identifying those individuals who did, in fact, later develop that disease.

predictive value the VALIDITY of a test as a predictor of a phenomenon of interest.

predictor *n.* a variable or other information used to estimate or predict future performance, health, or other status. In PERSONNEL SELECTION, for example, obvious predictors used to estimate an applicant's future job performance include qualifications, relevant work experience, and job-specific skills such as the ability to type or speak a particular language. Other predictors may include a candidate's interests, attitudes, and personality traits (see INTEREST FACTORS). See also FRAMINGHAM HEART STUDY; PERSONNEL SPECIFICATION.

predictor display in ergonomics, a display that includes preview information advising the operator of system status at some point in the future, should current controls and conditions remain unchanged.

predictor variable in REGRESSION ANALYSIS, a variable that may be used to predict the value of another variable; that is, an INDEPENDENT VARIABLE.

predisposing cause a factor that increases the probability that a mental or physical disorder or hereditary characteristic will develop but is not the immediate cause of it. Compare PRECIPITATING CAUSE.

predisposition *n.* **1.** a susceptibility to developing a disorder or disease, the actual development of which is initiated by the interaction of certain biological, psychological, or environmental factors. **2.** in genetics, any hereditary factor that, given the necessary conditions, will lead to the development of a certain trait or disease. **Predisposition testing** is genetic testing for mutations that are less than 100% penetrant (see PENETRANCE). Thus, a positive test result indicates that the individual has an increased predisposition to develop the disease, but might not necessarily do so. If a mutation is fully penetrant, the testing is referred to as **predictive testing**, since all those who carry the mutated gene will develop the disease.

PREE abbreviation for partial reinforcement extinction effect (see PARTIAL REINFORCEMENT EFFECT).

preeclampsia *n.* an increase in blood pressure (see HYPERTENSION), associated with edema or proteinuria (the presence of protein in the urine), or both, occurring in a pregnant woman. There may also be signs of headaches, dizziness, and nervous irritability. Preeclampsia may progress to the serious condition of ECLAMPSIA.

preening *n.* a form of ANIMAL GROOMING BEHAVIOR in which birds pick through their own feathers or those of another group member. **—preen** *vb.*

preestablished harmony a principle invoked by German philosopher Gottfried Wilhelm Leibniz (1646–1716) to explain how MONADS behave in a coordinated and orderly fashion, even though each is independent and follows its own preestablished end. The same principle is held to explain the coordinated interaction between the physical and nonphysical realms (see MIND–BODY PROBLEM). According to Leibniz, God is the origin of the preestablished harmony.

preexperimental design a research design in which there is no CONTROL GROUP and no random assignment of cases (participants) to experimental conditions (treatments). Such a design therefore is of minimal value in establishing causality.

preference *n.* **1.** in conditioning, the probability of occurrence of one of two or more concurrently available responses, usually expressed as either a RELATIVE FREQUENCY (compared to the frequency of all the measured responses) or a ratio. **2.** more generally, the act of choosing one alternative over others. **—preferential** *adj.*

preference for consistency a personality trait reflecting the extent to which a person desires to maintain consistency among elements in his or her cognitive system. See also COGNITIVE DISSONANCE; COGNITIVE DISSONANCE THEORY. [originally proposed by U.S. psychologists Robert B. Cialdini (1945–), Melanie R. Trost, and Jason T. Newsom (1965–)]

preference method a research technique in which an organism chooses one of several possible stimuli. Examples of such methods are those in which an animal chooses a certain food or a human chooses one of several paintings, activities, or vocations.

preference test a study in which consumers are asked to state a preference between competing products, such as two or more soft drinks.

preferential effect in parapsychology experiments, the finding that a participant's "calls" or guesses are more accurate for one set of TARGETS in an experiment (e.g., die faces with high values or ZENER CARDS with stars) than another (e.g., die faces with low values or Zener cards with crosses). See also DECLINE EFFECT; DIFFERENTIAL EFFECT; FOCUSING EFFECT; POSITION EFFECT; SHEEP–GOAT EFFECT.

preferential looking technique a method for assessing the perceptual capabilities of nonverbal human infants and animals. Infants will preferentially fixate a "more interesting" stimulus when it is presented at the same time as a "less interesting" stimulus, but only if the stimuli can be distinguished from one another. To minimize bias, on each trial the investigator is positioned so that he or she can observe the infant and make a judgment about which stimulus the infant fixates, but the stimuli themselves are visible only to the infant. To assess visual acuity, for example, on the first trial a coarse ACUITY GRATING is paired with a homogeneous gray stimulus of the same mean luminance. The infant preferentially looks at the grating. On successive trials the SPATIAL FREQUENCY of the grating is increased (the bars are made narrower) and the position of the grating versus the homogeneous field is randomized. When the grating can no longer be discriminated by the infant, the likelihood that the grating will be chosen for fixation will drop to chance.

preferential matching in an ESP FREE-RESPONSE TEST, the use of a judge to evaluate a participant's "calls" or guesses in terms of their similarity to possible TARGETS.

preferred noise criterion (**PNC**) a noise level set for steady ambient noise in enclosed spaces and used to determine or test for allowable background noise levels.

preferred provider arrangement (**PPA**) a contractual arrangement between a health care insurer and a health care provider or group of providers who agrees to provide services at reduced or prenegotiated rates.

preferred provider organization see PPO.

prefigurative culture a society or culture in which people typically learn from those younger than themselves. Because of the extremely rapid rate of social and technological change in the modern world, it has been proposed that contemporary Western society may be moving toward a prefigurative culture in which the young possess a keener intuition of the present than their elders. Compare COFIGURATIVE CULTURE; POSTFIGURATIVE CULTURE. [coined by U.S. anthropologist Margaret Mead (1901–1978)]

prefix *n.* in linguistics, a MORPHEME that is added to the beginning of a word to create a derived form, such as *un-* in *unlikely* or *ex-* in *ex-wife*. See AFFIXATION; INFIX; SUFFIX.

preformism *n.* the biological theory, now discredited, that development consists of the emerging into mature form of traits and capacities that exist in prototypical form in the germ cell. An early example of preformism was the 16th- and 17th-century notion of the HOMUNCULUS, a minute but completely formed human body believed to exist in the spermatozoon. Preformism contrasts with the epigenetic principle of successive differentiation in complex and cumulative stages of development (see EPIGENESIS).

prefrontal cortex the most anterior (forward) part of the FRONTAL LOBE of each cerebral hemisphere in the brain. It functions in attention, planning, and memory and is divided into a dorsolateral region and an orbitofrontal region (see ORBITOFRONTAL CORTEX). Damage to the prefrontal cortex in humans leads to emotional, motor, and cognitive impairments. Also called **frontal association area**.

prefrontal lobotomy see LEUKOTOMY.

preganglionic autonomic neuron any neuron of the SYMPATHETIC NERVOUS SYSTEM whose cell body is located in the central nervous system and that sends its axon to a ganglion in the SYMPATHETIC CHAIN. Here it may connect to a POSTGANGLIONIC AUTONOMIC NEURON, which can innervate such organs as the bladder and heart.

pregenital organization in psychoanalytic theory, organization of LIBIDO functions in the early stages of PSYCHOSEXUAL DEVELOPMENT preceding the GENITAL STAGE.

pregenital phase in psychoanalytic theory, the early stages of PSYCHOSEXUAL DEVELOPMENT that precede the organization of the LIBIDO around the genital zone (i.e., the ORAL STAGE and the ANAL STAGE). Some theorists also include the PHALLIC STAGE in the pregenital phase, whereas others use the term synonymously with the PREOEDIPAL phase.

pregnancy *n.* the state of a woman who is carrying a developing embryo, which normally lasts 266 days from conception until the birth of the baby (see PRENATAL PE-

RIOD). Embryonic development normally occurs within the uterus, but occasionally it may be extrauterine (see ECTOPIC PREGNANCY). Also called **fetation; gravidity**. See also ADOLESCENT PREGNANCY; FALSE PREGNANCY.

prehension *n.* the act of grasping, clasping, or seizing an object or supporting the body, usually with an appendage adapted for that purpose. For example, the hands of human beings and primates and the tails of certain New World monkeys are **prehensile.**

preinquiry *n.* a procedure designed to reveal the DEMAND CHARACTERISTICS of a particular study by asking participants to report on their perceptions at various points during the research before the study has been completed. Compare POSTEXPERIMENTAL INQUIRY.

prejudice *n.* **1.** a negative attitude toward another person or group formed in advance of any experience with that person or group. Prejudices include an affective component (emotions that range from mild nervousness to hatred), a cognitive component (assumptions and beliefs about groups, including STEREOTYPES), and a behavioral component (negative behaviors, including DISCRIMINATION and violence). They tend to be resistant to change because they distort the prejudiced individual's perception of information pertaining to the group. Prejudice based on racial grouping is RACISM; prejudice based on sex is SEXISM. **2.** any preconceived attitude or view, whether favorable or unfavorable.

prekindergarten *n.* see SCHOOL READINESS.

prelingually deafened being congenitally deaf or becoming deaf prior to the acquisition of language.

prelinguistic *adj.* denoting or relating to the period of an infant's life before it has acquired the power of speech. The **prelinguistic period** includes the earliest infant vocalizations as well as the babbling stage typical of the second half of the first year. HOLOPHRASES usually emerge around the time of the child's first birthday.

preliterate *adj.* **1.** denoting a child who has not yet acquired the ability to read and write. **2.** denoting a culture or social group that has not developed a written language. Also called **nonliterate**.

preloading *n.* an experimental procedure in which food, water, or some other nutritive substance is introduced into the stomach or another part of an animal's digestive system prior to giving the animal access to food or water. The effect of preloading on the animal's eating or drinking behavior is then measured.

prelogical thinking in psychoanalytic theory, primitive thought processes that are characteristic of early childhood, when thought is under the control of the PLEASURE PRINCIPLE rather than the REALITY PRINCIPLE. Such thinking may also occur later in life, as in daydreaming, in which WISH-FULFILLMENT is dominant. See also PRIMARY PROCESS.

Premack's principle the view that the opportunity to engage in behavior with a relatively high BASELINE probability will reinforce behavior of lower baseline probability. For example, a hungry rat may have a high probability of eating but a lower probability of pressing a lever. Making the opportunity to eat depend on pressing the lever will result in reinforcement of lever pressing. Also called **Premack's rule**. [David **Premack** (1925–), U.S. psychologist]

premarital counseling educational and supportive guidance provided to individuals planning marriage by a member of the clergy trained in counseling, a therapist, or some other appropriately qualified person. Premarital counseling may take the form of advice and answers to questions covering a wide range of matters, such as the timing of marriage, rights and responsibilities of spouses in marriage, birth-control methods, and sexual intimacy. Assessment instruments to identify potential conflicts in the marriage can help the premarital counselor to focus sessions appropriately.

premarital sex sexual relations before marriage. See also FORNICATION.

premature ejaculation a sexual dysfunction in which EJACULATION occurs with minimal sexual stimulation, before, on, or shortly after PENETRATION or simply earlier than desired. The diagnosis takes into account such factors as age, novelty of the sexual partner, and the frequency and duration of intercourse. The diagnosis does not apply if the disturbance is due to the direct effect of a substance (e.g., withdrawal from opioids). See also SQUEEZE TECHNIQUE.

premature termination see TERMINATION.

prematurity *n.* a state of underdevelopment, as in the birth of an offspring before it has completed the normal fetal processes of development. Premature (preterm) babies have low birth weight and are at risk for such complications as RESPIRATORY DISTRESS SYNDROME and JAUNDICE. See also PRENATAL STRESS.

premeditation *n.* a deliberate resolve to commit a crime, especially a violent crime, as revealed by evidence of planning or other forethought. A premeditated crime is often considered more serious than the same offense committed intentionally but without prior resolve. See MALICE AFORETHOUGHT. **—premeditated** *adj.*

premenstrual dysphoric disorder a MOOD DISORDER in women that begins in the week prior to the onset of menstruation and subsides within the first few days of menstruation. Women experience emotional mood swings, including markedly depressed mood, anxiety, feelings of helplessness, and decreased interest in activities. In contrast to PREMENSTRUAL SYNDROME, the symptoms must be severe enough to impair functioning in social activities, work, and relationships. The symptoms of premenstrual dysphoric disorder are of comparable severity to those experienced in MINOR DEPRESSIVE DISORDER. Also called **late luteal phase dysphoric disorder; premenstrual stress syndrome**. See also DEPRESSIVE DISORDER NOT OTHERWISE SPECIFIED.

premenstrual syndrome (PMS) a collection of psychological and physical symptoms experienced by women during the week prior to the onset of menstruation and subsiding within the first few days of menstruation. Symptoms can include mood swings, irritability, fatigue, headache, bloating, abdominal discomfort, and breast tenderness. In contrast to the more severe PREMENSTRUAL DYSPHORIC DISORDER, premenstrual syndrome has a less distinctive pattern of symptoms and does not involve major impairment in social and occupational functioning. Also called **premenstrual stress syndrome; premenstrual tension**.

premise *n.* a proposition forming part of a larger argument: a statement from which a further statement is to be deduced, especially as one of a series of such steps leading to a CONCLUSION.

premonitory dream a dream that appears to give advance notice or warning of some future event. See also CLAIRVOYANT DREAM.

premoral stage 1. in Jean PIAGET's theory of moral development, the stage at which young children (under the age of 5) are unaware of rules as cooperative agreements, that is, they are unable to distinguish right from wrong. Compare AUTONOMOUS STAGE; HETERONOMOUS STAGE. **2.** the stage that precedes the PRECONVENTIONAL LEVEL in KOHLBERG'S THEORY OF MORAL DEVELOPMENT and corresponds to infancy (birth to roughly 18 months).

premorbid *adj.* characterizing an individual's condition before the onset of a disease or disorder. **—premorbidity** *n.*

premorbid abilities an estimate of an individual's psychological abilities prior to a neurological trauma or disease that is used to determine the degree of loss caused by the damage. This estimate is based on testing and assessments conducted after the damage has occurred; it may include consideration of such factors as educational level, occupational history, and client and family reports.

premorbid adjustment a measure of the level of a person's functioning before the onset of an acute psychological disorder. The measure, as used in the PHILLIPS RATING SCALE OF PREMORBID ADJUSTMENT IN SCHIZOPHRENIA, has been found to be of value in predicting the course of schizophrenia.

premorbid personality 1. personality traits that existed before a physical injury or other traumatic event or before the development of a disease or disorder. **2.** personality strengths and weaknesses that predispose the individual toward mental health and well-being or to a particular mental disorder (e.g., depression or schizophrenia) or that affect the speed or likelihood of recovery from a disorder. Also called **primary personality**.

premorbid schizophrenia the quality of physical, psychological, and emotional functioning in an individual prior to the emergence of schizophrenia.

premortem clarity a state of mental alertness, after a period of clouded or confused cognition, that sometimes returns prior to death. Premortem clarity sometimes has consequential associations, such as the utterance of last words and the affirmation or modification of wills and testaments.

premotor area an area of the MOTOR CORTEX concerned with MOTOR PLANNING. In contrast to the SUPPLEMENTARY MOTOR AREA, input to the premotor area is primarily visual, and its activity is usually triggered by external events. Also called **Brodmann's area 6**; **intermediate precentral area**; **premotor cortex**.

premotor theory of attention a theory proposing that attention is a consequence of the mechanisms that generate actions or motor responses. It is based on neurophysiological evidence that space is coded in several cortical circuits that have specific motor purposes. Those circuits that represent space for programming eye movements are considered to play the primary role in spatial attention. Preparing to move the eyes to a specific location increases the readiness to act in that region of space and facilitates the processing of stimuli located in that region.

prenatal care medical, health, and educational services provided to or obtained by a woman during pregnancy. Such services are intended to prevent complications and decrease the risk of maternal or prenatal mortality.

prenatal counseling counseling given to couples or to single women who are expecting a baby or planning a pregnancy. It sometimes also covers advice on terminating the pregnancy (see ABORTION COUNSELING). For those who are considering adoption, prenatal counseling includes advice on the child's arrival and future, dealing with friends and relatives, and coping with any impact on the biological mother and father.

prenatal developmental anomaly a congenital abnormality that originates in the course of development before birth. Examples include cleft palate, spina bifida, and PHOCOMELIA.

prenatal diagnosis determination of a pathological condition or the presence of disease or genetic abnormalities in a fetus. See ALPHA-FETOPROTEIN TEST; AMNIOCENTESIS; CHORIONIC VILLUS SAMPLING; ULTRASOUND.

prenatal influence any influence on the developing organism between conception and birth. Prenatal influences include radiation effects, maternal diseases (e.g., rubella, toxoplasmosis), alcohol or drug abuse, excessive smoking, blood incompatibility, nutritional deficiency, and emotional stress.

prenatal masculinization the masculinizing effects of ANDROGENS on fetal sexual anatomy and on neural pathways in the brain prior to birth.

prenatal period the developmental period between conception and birth, in humans commonly divided into the GERMINAL STAGE (approximately the first two weeks), the EMBRYONIC STAGE (the following six weeks), and the FETAL STAGE (from two months to birth).

prenatal stress stress in a pregnant woman, which is marked by elevation of stress hormones and other biological changes, with an increased likelihood of intrauterine infection. Preterm births and low birth weight are among the most widely recognized effects of maternal stress during pregnancy. Women who experience high levels of psychological stress are significantly more likely to deliver preterm. Preterm babies are susceptible to a range of complications, including chronic lung disease. Some recent studies suggest that stress in the womb can also affect a baby's temperament and neurobehavioral development: Infants whose mothers experienced high levels of stress while pregnant, particularly in the first trimester, show signs of increased depression and irritability.

preoccupation *n.* a state of being self-absorbed and "lost in thought," which ranges from transient absentmindedness to a symptom of schizophrenia in which the individual withdraws from external reality and turns inward upon the self. Also called **preoccupation with thought**.

preoccupied attachment an adult attachment style that combines a negative INTERNAL WORKING MODEL OF ATTACHMENT of oneself, characterized by doubt in one's own competence and efficacy, and a positive internal working model of attachment of others, characterized by one's trust in the ability and dependability of others. Individuals with preoccupied attachment are presumed to seek others' help when distressed. Compare DISMISSIVE ATTACHMENT; FEARFUL ATTACHMENT; SECURE ATTACHMENT.

preoedipal *adj.* **1.** in psychoanalytic theory, pertaining to the first stages of PSYCHOSEXUAL DEVELOPMENT, before the development of the OEDIPUS COMPLEX during the PHALLIC STAGE. During this phase the mother is the exclusive love object of both sexes and the father is not yet considered either a rival or a love object. **2.** more generally, denoting organization or functions before the onset of the Oedipus complex. See also PREPHALLIC.

preoperational stage in Jean PIAGET's theory, the second major period of cognitive development, approximately between the ages of 2 and 7, when the child becomes able to record experience in a symbolic fashion and to represent an object, event, or feeling in speech, movement, drawing, and the like. During the later 2 years of the preoperational stage, egocentrism diminishes noticeably with the emerging ability to adopt the point of view of others. Also called **symbolic stage**. See also CONCRETE OPERATIONAL STAGE; FORMAL OPERATIONS; SENSORIMOTOR STAGE.

preoperational thought the symbolic, intuitive, and prelogical thinking characteristic of children during the second major stage of cognitive development (approximately between ages 2 and 7). See PREOPERATIONAL STAGE. [first described by Jean PIAGET]

preoptic area a region of the HYPOTHALAMUS lying above and slightly anterior to the OPTIC CHIASM. Nuclei here are involved in temperature regulation and in the release of HYPOTHALAMIC HORMONES. See also MEDIAL PREOPTIC AREA.

preorgasmic *adj.* **1.** relating to the state immediately before ORGASM. It is characterized by increased breathing, heart rate, and blood pressure; semispastic muscle contractions; and maximum increase in the size of the glans penis, testes, and upper vaginal walls. **2.** denoting the status of a person who has never experienced orgasm. See PRIMARY ORGASMIC DYSFUNCTION.

preparadigmatic science a science at a primitive stage of development, before it has achieved a PARADIGM and when there is no consensus about the true nature of the subject matter and how to approach it. Psychology has been considered a preparadigmatic science by many theorists, in contrast to physics and chemistry (regarded as NORMAL SCIENCES). See also IMMATURE SCIENCE; PARADIGM SHIFT; SCIENTIFIC REVOLUTION. [proposed by U.S. philosopher of science Thomas Kuhn (1922–1996)]

preparation *n.* in cognitive psychology, the process of increasing readiness for an activity, for example, by planning or imagining a movement before it is executed. See PLAN. **—prepare** *vb.*

preparatory adjustment the changes made by the brain and body that follow a warning signal and result in performance improvement. A period of about 500 ms is typically needed for optimal preparation.

preparatory interval the period between a warning signal or cue and the actual presentation of the stimulus.

preparatory response any response (except the final one) in a series of behaviors that leads to a goal or reinforcement. Preparatory responses themselves are not immediately goal-directed.

preparatory set a special alertness or preparedness to respond in a particular manner to an expected stimulus, action, or event. A preparatory set may be manifested physically, as with a tennis player preparing to receive a serve, or experienced mentally, as with a chess player anticipating an opponent's next move. See MENTAL SET; MOTOR TEST; PERCEPTUAL SET; SET.

prepared learning a species-specific and innate tendency to quickly learn a certain type of knowledge. Some associations between stimuli, responses, and reinforcers may be more easily formed than CONTRAPREPARED associations, due to biological PREPAREDNESS. For example, animals may be prepared to associate new foods with illness, and it has been suggested that humans learn certain phobias more readily due to preparedness. See also PRINCIPLE OF BELONGINGNESS; RESTRICTED LEARNING.

preparedness *n.* a genetically influenced predisposition for certain stimuli to be more effective than others in eliciting particular responses. For example, flavors may be more effective as stimuli in establishing a CONDITIONED TASTE AVERSION than are colors of lights.

preperceptual processing see PREATTENTIVE PROCESSING.

prephallic *adj.* in psychoanalytic theory, referring to the stages of PSYCHOSEXUAL DEVELOPMENT preceding the PHALLIC STAGE (i.e., the ORAL STAGE and the ANAL STAGE). See also PREGENITAL PHASE; PREOEDIPAL.

pre–post design see BEFORE–AFTER DESIGN.

prepotency *n.* **1.** the quality or state of possessing greater power, influence, or force. **2.** the capacity for one of two parents to transmit more of his or her genetic characteristics to an offspring than the other. **—prepotent** *adj.*

prepotent response a response that takes priority over other potential responses (e.g., a pain response).

prepotent stimulus any stimulus that is dominant over any other competing stimulus in that it is more likely to gain attention or elicit a response.

prepsychotic panic a stage in the development of schizophrenia in which self-image is disordered: Individuals feel guilty, unlovable, humiliated, or otherwise different, but have not yet acquired symptoms of delusions and hallucinations. [defined by Italian-born U.S. psychiatrist Silvano Arieti (1914–1982)]

prepsychotic personality characteristics and behavior of a person, such as eccentricities, withdrawal, litigiousness, apathy, or hypersensitivity, that may be indicative of later development of a psychotic disorder.

prepubertal stage see PREADOLESCENCE.

prepuberty *n.* see PREADOLESCENCE.

prepubescence *n.* see PREADOLESCENCE.

prepuce *n.* a covering fold of skin, especially the skin covering the glans penis (see FORESKIN) in males and the clitoris (see CLITORAL HOOD) in females. Also called **preputium**. **—preputial** *adj.*

prepulse inhibition diminution of a reflex response by presenting a weak stimulus just before the strong stimulus that elicits the response. For example, a loud noise can elicit a startle reaction, but presentation of a tone before the noise will diminish the startle reaction.

preputium *n.* see PREPUCE.

prepyriform area the olfactory PROJECTION AREA at the base of the temporal lobe of the brain.

prerelease anxiety state anxiety experienced by an individual about to leave an institutional setting and reenter the everyday world. For example, prison inmates may fear having to compete in the real world again.

presbycusis *n.* the gradual diminution of hearing acuity associated with aging. See also VASCULAR SCLEROSIS.

presbyopia *n.* a normal, age-related change in vision due to decreased lens elasticity and accommodative ability, resulting in reduced ability to focus vision on near tasks (e.g., reading). Usually beginning in middle age, presbyopia is correctable with reading glasses or glasses with bifocal or trifocal lenses.

preschool program an educational curriculum for children who are below the required minimum age for participation in regular classroom work. Preschool programs for intellectually or emotionally challenged children are designed to develop social skills and provide stimulation at levels appropriate for each child.

prescribing *n.* **1.** in psychotherapy and medicine, advising or telling a patient what to do in specific situations. **2.** ordering the use of a MEDICATION.

prescription privilege the legal right to prescribe drugs and other medications necessary for the treatment of medical or mental health disorders.

prescriptive eclectic psychotherapy see ECLECTIC PSYCHOTHERAPY.

prescriptive grammar an approach to grammar in which a series of rules is used to distinguish proper from improper usage and a standard version of the language is identified and promoted (see STANDARD LANGUAGE). It is often contrasted with **descriptive grammar**, in which the goal is to provide an accurate account of language use without specification as to correctness. Prescriptive grammarians seek to correct nonstandard forms, such as *I can't get no satisfaction*, whereas descriptive grammarians seek to characterize the rule system that produces such utterances.

prescriptive norms see INJUNCTIVE NORMS.

prescriptivism *n.* in linguistics, the practice of using PRESCRIPTIVE GRAMMAR to inculcate certain forms and varieties of language and to stigmatize others.

preselection *n.* a family's subjective assignment of the role of mutation carrier to one or more family members prior to knowledge of their actual genetic status. Family members often treat the preselected person in a special way, assuming that he or she is a mutation carrier.

presenile dementia DEMENTIA with an onset before the age of 65.

presenile dementia of the Alzheimer's type (**PDAT**) an older name for DEMENTIA of the Alzheimer's type with onset before age 65. See also ALZHEIMER'S DISEASE.

presenilin *n.* any member of a family of transmembrane proteins, mutations in which are associated with early-onset familial ALZHEIMER'S DISEASE.

presenility *n.* **1.** DEMENTIA that occurs prior to old age (typically, prior to age 65). **2.** the period of life immediately preceding dementia in old age.

presentation *n.* **1.** the way in which materials are set before an individual, often for the purpose of learning or understanding. **2.** the act of exposing a human participant or an animal subject to stimuli or learning materials during an experiment. **3.** in psychoanalytic theory, the means or vehicle through which an INSTINCT is expressed. **4.** in interpersonal relations and social interaction, the way in which an individual behaves or expresses himself or herself. Also called **instinct representation**. **5.** in animal behavior, see PRESENTING. **—present** *vb.*

presenting *n.* behavior in which a female animal turns its back toward a male and raises its posterior, which allows the male to mate. Presenting is also seen in subordinate animals directed toward dominant animals outside a mating context. LORDOSIS is a specific form of presenting seen in many rodents.

presenting symptom a symptom or problem that is offered by a client or a patient as the reason for seeking treatment. In psychotherapy, a client may present with depression, anxiety, panic, anger, chronic pain, or family or marital problems; such symptoms may become the focus of treatment or may represent a different, underlying problem that is not recognized or regarded by the client as requiring help. Also called **presenting problem**.

presentist 1. *adj.* denoting a perspective that attributes the influence of past events on present behavior to a representation of them that exists in the present. See AHISTORICAL. **2.** *n.* a person holding such a position. **—presentism** *n.*

Present State Examination (**PSE**) a structured interview comprising about 400 items, including a wide range of symptoms likely to be manifested during an acute episode of one of the functional psychoses. The PSE was developed for the WHO-sponsored INTERNATIONAL PILOT STUDY OF SCHIZOPHRENIA.

presolution variability the variability observed in behavior prior to arriving at a successful solution to a difficult problem.

prespeech development development of the earliest forms of perceptual experience, learning, and communication, which precedes actual speech and is necessary for its development. For example, babies attend to sound at birth and can differentiate the human voice from other sounds within the 1st month. Cross-cultural studies reveal that mothers routinely use techniques that help their infants acquire language; for example, they shorten their expressions, stress important words, simplify syntax, and speak in a higher register and with exaggerated distinctness. See BABBLING; INFANT-DIRECTED SPEECH; INFANTILE SPEECH.

press *n.* in the PERSONOLOGY of U.S. psychologist Henry Alexander Murray (1893–1988), an environmental stimulus, such as a person or situation, that arouses a need. Examples are the birth of a sibling, parental discord, feelings of social inferiority, or the sight of food when hungry. See NEED–PRESS THEORY.

pressor effect the effect of VASOCONSTRICTORS, such as VASOPRESSIN.

pressure *n.* in psychology, excessive or stressful demands, imagined or real, made on an individual by another individual or group to think, feel, or act in particular ways. The experience of pressure is often the source of cognitive and affective discomfort or disorder, as well as of maladaptive coping strategies, the correction of which may be a mediate or end goal in psychotherapy.

pressured speech accelerated and sometimes uncontrolled speech that often occurs in the context of a HYPOMANIC EPISODE or a MANIC EPISODE. Also called **pressure of speech**.

pressure gradient a gradual reduction in pressure extending in all directions when a stimulus is applied to the skin.

pressure of activity compulsive and occasionally uncontrolled activity and PSYCHOMOTOR AGITATION, usually occurring in the context of a MANIC EPISODE.

pressure of ideas a characteristic symptom of MANIA in which there is increased spontaneity and productivity of thought: Numerous, widely varied ideas arise quickly and pass through the mind rapidly. It is usually manifested as PRESSURED SPEECH or PRESSURE OF ACTIVITY. Also called **thought pressure**.

pressure of speech see PRESSURED SPEECH.

pressure sense the sensation of stress or strain, compression, expansion, pull, or shear, usually caused by a force in the environment. Pressure receptors may interlock or overlap with pain receptors so that one sensation is accompanied by the other. The pressure sense is similar to the sensation of contact.

pressure-sensitive spot see PRESSURE SPOT.

pressure sore see PRESSURE ULCER.

pressure spot any of the points on the body surface that are particularly sensitive to pressure stimuli. Also called **pressure-sensitive spot**.

pressure-threshold test a sensory test in which pressure sensitivity is measured with a series of hairs of graded stiffness.

pressure ulcer a localized area of cellular death (necrosis) affecting individuals with limited mobility. Pressure ulcers derive from increased pressure on small areas of tissue due to prolonged sitting or lying in one position. Also called **bedsore**; **decubitus ulcer**; **pressure sore**.

prestige *n.* the degree of respect, regard, and admiration afforded an individual by his or her peers or the whole community. Prestige derives from various sources, including success, achievement, rank, reputation, authority, illustriousness, or position within a social structure. **—prestigious** *adj.*

prestige suggestion a method of supportive, SYMPTOMATIC TREATMENT that relies on the prestige of the therapist in the eyes of the patient. The so-called **omnipotent therapist** may be able to abolish undesirable symptoms, at least temporarily, by suggestion.

prestriate cortex visually responsive regions in the cerebral cortex outside the STRIATE CORTEX. The prestriate cortex includes BRODMANN'S AREAS 18 and 19, as determined by CYTOARCHITECTURE, and additional areas in the temporal and parietal lobes. On the basis of function and connectivity, the prestriate cortex has been divided into multiple VISUAL AREAS, including V2, V4, and V5. Also called **extrastriate cortex**; **prestriate area**.

presupposition *n.* in linguistics, a PROPOSITION that underlies an utterance but is not stated explicitly within it. For example, the question *Has Simone finally given up smoking?* presupposes that Simone is, or used to be, a smoker. Compare IMPLICATURE.

presynaptic *adj.* **1.** referring to the region of a neuron within a SYNAPSE that releases neurotransmitter. **2.** referring to a neuron that is transmitting a signal to one or more other neurons via its synapses. Compare POSTSYNAPTIC.

preterm infants see PREMATURITY; PRENATAL STRESS.

preterm viability the ability of a fetus to survive outside the uterus. A fetus may be viable from around 20 weeks after conception.

preternatural *adj.* describing phenomena that appear to be inexplicable in terms of the known laws of the physical universe. Compare SUPERNATURAL.

pretest 1. *n.* a preliminary test or trial run to familiarize the person or group tested with the content and nature of a particular test. It may be given in conjunction with a POSTTEST. **2.** *n.* a trial run administered before the application of an intervention or control condition. **3.** *vb.* to administer a pretest.

pretest counseling a type of GENETIC COUNSELING undertaken before deciding whether to undergo genetic testing. Pretest counseling includes educating individuals about the contribution of genetics to the etiology of disease, taking a family history and creating a PEDIGREE, estimating risk, and discussing the risks, benefits, and limitations of genetic testing.

pretest–posttest design an experimental design in which participants are randomly assigned to either treatment or control conditions and are measured both before and after experiencing the treatment or control condition.

pretest sensitization the extent to which the administration of a PRETEST affects the subsequent responses of the participant to experimental treatments.

pretrial publicity media coverage of a case that occurs prior to the trial and can lead prospective jurors to form opinions about the case before hearing evidence in court. See CHANGE OF VENUE.

prevalence *n.* the total number of cases (e.g., of a disease or disorder) existing in a given population at a given time (**point prevalence**) or during a specified period (**period prevalence**). See also INCIDENCE.

prevention *n.* behavioral, biological, or social interventions intended to reduce the risk of disorders, diseases, or social problems for both individuals and entire populations. See PRIMARY PREVENTION; SECONDARY PREVENTION; TERTIARY PREVENTION.

prevention design in ergonomics, the design of tools or systems so as to reduce the possibility of HUMAN ERROR. See ENGINEERING CONTROLS. See also EXCLUSION DESIGN; FAIL-SAFE.

prevention research research directed toward finding interventions to reduce the likelihood of future pathology. Such research is often concentrated on individuals or populations considered to be particularly at risk of developing a condition, disease, or disorder.

preventive care care that aims to prevent disease or its consequences, emphasizing early detection and early treatment of conditions and generally including routine physical examination, immunizations, and well-person care. See also PREVENTION; PRIMARY PREVENTION.

preventive counseling counseling that aims to prevent anticipated problems or conflicts. It is most useful when individuals may be exposed to increased stress (e.g., during adolescence or prior to an important exam or commitment) or are at risk from high levels of stress.

preventive stress management an intervention involving a session or series of sessions prior to the occurrence of anticipated stressful situations during which information on stressors, coping strategies, and opportunities to practice these strategies are provided. See also PRIMARY PREVENTION; STRESS MANAGEMENT.

preverbal *adj.* before the acquisition of language. Preverbal children communicate using nonword sounds and gestures.

preverbal construct a concept that may have been formulated before one acquired language but that, even without a verbal symbol, may still be used to construe one's experiences in later life. [proposed by U.S. psychologist George A. Kelly (1905–1967)]

previous battle experience see BATTLE INOCULATION.

prevocational training programs designed to help individuals prepare to enter a competitive work situation and workplace environment. Training is not career- or position-specific but rather focuses on helping individuals develop good work habits and gain the basic skills and abilities essential for employment in any field, such as following directions and being punctual. Prevocational training may be provided to any individual who has not had actual work experience in a competitive job market, such as a college student nearing graduation or an adult entering the workforce late in life, but is typically offered to adolescents and adults with disabilities.

priapism *n.* **1.** persistent penile erection that occurs independently of sexual arousal or that continues long after orgasm has occurred and sexual activity ceased. The condition is associated with leukemia and sickle-cell anemia and is usually painful. Immediate causes may be thrombosis, cancer, hemorrhage, inflammation, lesions involving nerve tracts between the brain and the urethra, or overdose of drugs injected into the penis to treat ERECTILE DYSFUNCTION. **2.** another name for SATYRIASIS. Priapism is named for Priapus, the Greco-Roman god of procreation and of the generative force in nature, who was the basis of a cult that worshiped the phallus. See also PHALLOCENTRIC.

price–quality relationship the real or perceived relationship between the price and the quality of an item or experience. In general, consumers think that higher prices mean higher quality.

Price Waterhouse v. Hopkins a case resulting in a 1989 U.S. Supreme Court ruling that any employment decision made (even in part) on the basis of sex is discriminatory. In this case, the plaintiff was a woman who was denied partnership in an accounting firm because her conduct at work was judged to be excessively masculine.

prick experience the sensation produced when a pin, needle, or small electrical stimulus is applied to a receptor area of the skin. A prick experience may resemble other somatic sensations, such as itch, tickle, pain, or pressure, depending on how the stimulus is applied.

pride *n.* a SELF-CONSCIOUS EMOTION that occurs when a goal has been attained and one's achievement has been recognized and approved by others. It differs from JOY and HAPPINESS in that these emotions do not require the approval of others for their existence. Pride also has expressive reactions that differ from joy, such as puffing up of the chest and directing attention to others or an audience. Pride can become antisocial if the sense of accomplishment is not deserved or the reaction is excessive. See also HUBRIS. **—proud** *adj.*

primacy effect the tendency for facts, impressions, or items that are presented first to be better learned or remembered than material presented later in the sequence. This can occur in both formal learning situations and social contexts. For example, it can result in a **first-impression bias**, in which the first information gained about a person has an inordinate influence on later impressions and evaluations of that person. Also called **law of primacy**; **principle of primacy**. Compare RECENCY EFFECT.

prima facie at first sight; on the face of things (Latin, literally: "first face"). Prima facie evidence is evidence that, while not conclusive, is considered sufficiently strong to support an inference of fact in the absence of evidence to the contrary.

primal anxiety in psychoanalytic theory, the most basic form of anxiety, first experienced when the infant is separated from the mother at birth and suddenly has to cope with the flood of new stimuli. See also BIRTH TRAUMA; PRIMAL TRAUMA.

primal depression an obsolescent name for depression that occurs in early childhood and is theoretically attributed to absent or distant parents.

primal fantasy in psychoanalytic theory, any of a range of fantasies employed by children to fill gaps in their knowledge of sexual experience, especially one about conception and birth (see CLOACAL THEORY), parental intercourse, or castration.

primal father the head of a hypothetical primitive tribe who is slain and devoured by his sons (or other younger men) and later revered as a god, as described by Sigmund FREUD in 1913 in *Totem and Taboo*. The crime has a tragic effect on the son or sons who kill the dominant male and becomes enshrined in the culture of the tribe as a TOTEM. See also PRIMAL-HORDE THEORY.

primal-horde theory Sigmund FREUD's speculative reconstruction in *Totem and Taboo* (1913) of the original human family, which comprised a dominant male (the PRIMAL FATHER) holding sway over a subordinate group of females and younger men or sons. Freud used the theory to account for the origin of EXOGAMY, the INCEST TABOO, guilt, and totemism (see TOTEM).

primal repression see PRIMARY REPRESSION.

primal sadism in psychoanalytic theory, an aspect of the DEATH INSTINCT that is identical with MASOCHISM and remains within the person, partly as a component of the LIBIDO and partly with the self as an OBJECT.

primal scene in psychoanalytic theory, the child's first observation, in reality or fantasy, of parental intercourse or seduction, which is interpreted by the child as an act of violence (see PHALLIC SADISM). See also PRIMAL FANTASY.

primal therapy a therapeutic technique used to release deep-seated feelings and emotional frustration by crying, screaming, and hitting objects. The client is encouraged to reexperience traumatic early childhood (even peri- and prenatal) experiences and react vocally and physically to release the psychic pain associated with them. The technique, sometimes popularly and erroneously known as **primal scream therapy**, has received little scientific validation and is not advocated by most psychotherapists or counselors. [developed in the 1960s and 1970s by U.S. psychologist Arthur Janov (1924–)]

primal trauma in psychoanalytic theory, a painful situation to which an individual was subjected in early life that is presumed to be the basis of a neurosis in later life. The primal trauma is considered by some in psychoanalysis to be the BIRTH TRAUMA. See also PRIMAL ANXIETY.

primary abilities the unitary factors revealed by factor analysis to be essential components of intelligence. There are seven primary abilities: VERBAL ABILITY (V), WORD FLUENCY (WF), NUMERICAL ABILITY (N), SPATIAL INTELLIGENCE (S), MEMORY (M), perceptual speed (P), and reasoning (R). These factors are measured by the **Primary Mental Abilities Test**. Also called **primary mental abilities**. [proposed in about 1936 by Louis L. THURSTONE]

primary aging changes associated with normal AGING that are inevitable and caused by intrinsic biological or genetic factors. Examples include the appearance of gray hair and skin wrinkles. However, some age-related diseases have genetic influences, making the distinction between primary aging and SECONDARY AGING imprecise. See SENESCENCE.

primary amenorrhea see AMENORRHEA.

primary anxiety in psychoanalytic theory, anxiety experienced as a spontaneous response to trauma or in response to dissolution of the EGO. Also called **automatic anxiety**. Compare SIGNAL ANXIETY.

primary appraisal in the COGNITIVE APPRAISAL THEORY of emotions, evaluation of the relevance of an event to one's goals, one's moral norms, and one's personal preferences. It is followed by SECONDARY APPRAISAL. See also CORE RELATIONAL THEMES. [proposed by U.S. psychologist Richard S. Lazarus (1922–2002)]

primary attention attention that does not require conscious effort, such as attention to an intense, powerful, or arresting stimulus. Compare SECONDARY ATTENTION.

primary behavior disorder any of various behavior problems in children and adolescents, including habit disturbances (e.g., nail biting, temper tantrums), bedwetting, conduct disorders (e.g., vandalism, fire setting, alcohol or drug use, sex offenses, stealing), and school-centered difficulties (e.g., truancy, school phobia, disruptive behavior).

primary care the basic or general health care a patient receives when he or she first seeks assistance from a health care system. General practitioners, family practitioners, internists, obstetricians, and pediatricians are known as PRIMARY CARE PROVIDERS (PCPs). Also called **primary health care**. Compare SECONDARY CARE; TERTIARY CARE.

primary care provider (**PCP**) a physician who provides PRIMARY CARE services and may act as the GATEKEEPER controlling patients' access to the rest of the health care system through referrals. PCPs are usually generalist physicians (e.g., internists, pediatricians, family physicians, and general practitioners) and occasionally obstetricians and gynecologists. Also called **primary physician**.

primary care psychology a specialty discipline within health, clinical, and counseling psychology that involves providing psychological preventive and treatment services under the auspices of medical professionals in such settings as clinics, hospitals, and private practices, either on site or on a consultation basis.

primary caretaker standard a standard of evaluation used in CHILD CUSTODY disputes that awards custody of the child to the parent who has previously assumed the most responsibility for and spent the most time with the child. See also TENDER YEARS DOCTRINE.

primary cause a condition or event that predisposes an individual to a particular disorder, which probably would not have occurred in the absence of that condition or event. Sexual contact, for example, is a common primary cause of a sexually transmitted disease.

primary circular reaction in Jean PIAGET's theory of cognitive development, a type of repetitive action that represents the earliest nonreflexive infantile behavior. For example, in the first months of life, a hungry baby may repeatedly attempt to put a hand in the mouth. This does not result in effective goal-oriented behavior, but it does indicate a primitive link between goal (easing hunger) and action (attempting to suck on the hand). Primary circular reactions develop in the SENSORIMOTOR STAGE, following the activation of such reflexes as sucking, swallowing, crying, and moving the arms and legs. See also COORDINATION OF SECONDARY CIRCULAR REACTIONS; SECONDARY CIRCULAR REACTION; TERTIARY CIRCULAR REACTION.

primary colors the basic colors from which all the various hues can be produced by mixing different combinations. Some investigators believe human color perception involves combinations of the three primary colors, that is, blue, green, and red; others contend that yellow, violet, or both should be included because of visual color sensitivity peaks found at those wavelengths.

primary consciousness sensory experience. The descriptor implies that sensory experience is an early stage in the EVOLUTION OF CONSCIOUSNESS.

primary control behavior that is aimed at producing a sense of control through an individual's direct alteration of the environment. Compare SECONDARY CONTROL. See LOCUS OF CONTROL.

primary coping a type of COPING STRATEGY that enhances one's sense of control over environmental circumstances and oneself. Primary coping includes actions directed toward changing stressors (i.e., objective events or environmental conditions). Also called **primary control coping**. Compare SECONDARY COPING.

primary cortex any of the regions of the CEREBRAL CORTEX that receive the main input from sensory receptors or send the main output to muscles. Examples are primary motor cortex (see MOTOR AREA), primary visual cortex (see STRIATE CORTEX), PRIMARY TASTE CORTEX, and the PRIMARY SOMATOSENSORY AREA. The primary motor cortex has a lower threshold for elicitation of motor responses than do adjacent motor cortical regions. Most neurons in primary sensory regions have more direct sensory input than do neurons in adjacent sensory cortical regions.

primary data the original experimental or observational data before statistical treatment and analysis.

primary degenerative dementia in *DSM–III*, dementia of subtle onset with a gradually progressive course but no specific cause, usually starting after the age of 65 (senile onset) but in some cases before this age (presenile onset). Subtypes with delirium, delusions, or depression were also specified. This diagnostic category has been removed from *DSM–IV–TR*, since the current definition of dementia is based on symptom pattern and does not carry the historical implication of progressively worsening or irreversible course.

primary deviance in theories of deviance and identity, an initial rule-breaking act (such as NONCONFORMITY or disobedience) performed by an otherwise socially compliant individual. In most cases individuals amend their behaviors in response to social pressure, but if they continue to violate social norms (**secondary deviance**), other people may label them as deviant. See also LABELING THEORY.

primary drive an innate DRIVE, which may be universal or species-specific, that is created by deprivation of a needed substance (e.g., food) or the need to engage in a specific activity (e.g., nest building in birds). Compare SECONDARY DRIVE.

primary dysmenorrhea see DYSMENORRHEA.

primary emotion any one of a limited set of emotions that typically are manifested and recognized universally across cultures. They include FEAR, ANGER, JOY, SADNESS, DISGUST, CONTEMPT, and SURPRISE; some theorists also include SHAME, SHYNESS, and GUILT. Also called **basic emotion**. Compare SECONDARY EMOTION.

primary empathy an approach to CLIENT-CENTERED THERAPY in which the therapist actively tries to experience the client's situation as the client has and then tries to restate the client's thoughts, feelings, and experiences from the client's point of view.

primary environment an environment that is central in a person's life and in which personal or family interactions can be sustained, for example, a workplace or home. See also PRIMARY TERRITORY. Compare SECONDARY ENVIRONMENT.

primary erectile dysfunction a male sexual dysfunction in which the man has never been able to achieve penile erection sufficient for sexual intercourse. See ERECTILE DYSFUNCTION; IMPOTENCE; MALE ERECTILE DISORDER. Compare SECONDARY ERECTILE DYSFUNCTION.

primary familial xanthomatosis see WOLMAN'S DISEASE.

primary gains in psychoanalytic theory, the basic psychological benefits derived from possessing neurotic symptoms, essentially relief from anxiety generated by conflicting impulses or threatening experiences. Also called **paranosic gains**. Compare SECONDARY GAINS.

primary group any of the small, long-term groups characterized by face-to-face interaction and high levels of COHESION, solidarity, and GROUP IDENTIFICATION. These groups are primary in the sense that they are the initial socializers of the individual members, providing them with the foundation for attitudes, values, and a social orientation. Families, partnerships, and long-term psychotherapy groups are examples of such groups. Compare SECONDARY GROUP.

primary health care see PRIMARY CARE.

primary homosexuality same-sex sexual orientation in which the individual has never experienced sexual arousal or activity with a person of the opposite sex.

primary hue a less common name for PRIMARY COLOR.

primary hypersomnia in *DSM–IV–TR*, a sleep disorder characterized by excessive sleepiness (evidenced by prolonged episodes of sleep, daytime episodes of sleep on an almost daily basis, or both), the severity and persistence of which cause clinically significant distress or impairment in functioning. The disorder is not caused by a general medical condition and is not an aspect of another sleep disorder or mental disorder. See DYSSOMNIA. See also DISORDERS OF EXCESSIVE SOMNOLENCE. Compare PRIMARY INSOMNIA.

primary identification in psychoanalytic theory, the first and most basic form of IDENTIFICATION, which occurs during the ORAL STAGE of development when the infant experiences the mother as part of himself or herself. After weaning, the infant begins to differentiate between the self and external reality and then becomes capable of SECONDARY IDENTIFICATION. Primary identification is closely tied to oral INCORPORATION. Also called **primary narcissistic identification**.

primary impotence see PRIMARY ERECTILE DYSFUNCTION.

primary insomnia in *DSM–IV–TR*, a sleep disorder characterized by difficulty in initiating or maintaining a restorative sleep to a degree in which the severity and persistence of the sleep disturbance causes clinically significant distress, impairment in a significant area of functioning, or both. The disorder is not caused by a general medical condition or the effects of a substance and is not exclusively an aspect of another sleep disorder or mental disorder. See DYSSOMNIA. See also INSOMNIA. Compare PRIMARY HYPERSOMNIA.

primary line of sight a line connecting a target of fixation with the center of the pupil of the eye. Compare VISUAL AXIS.

primary masochism in psychoanalytic theory, the portion of the DEATH INSTINCT or AGGRESSIVE INSTINCT that is directed toward the self after the LIBIDO has absorbed it emotionally and directed a large portion of it toward the external world. Also called **erotogenic masochism**.

primary maternal preoccupation in the OBJECT RELATIONS THEORY of British psychoanalyst Donald Winnicott (1896–1971), a state immediately following childbirth in which a mother becomes preoccupied with her infant to the exclusion of everything else, which permits a heightened sensitivity to the child's needs.

primary memory (**PM**) memory that retains a few items for only several seconds, in contrast to SECONDARY MEMORY. The term was used in DUAL-STORE MODELS OF MEMORY before being replaced by SHORT-TERM MEMORY. [introduced by William JAMES]

primary mental abilities see PRIMARY ABILITIES.

Primary Mental Abilities Test see PRIMARY ABILITIES.

primary mental deficiency below average intelligence due to genetic factors.

primary microcephaly a congenital disorder in which MICROCEPHALY is the primary, and usually the only, evidence of anomalous fetal development. The most common characteristic is a normal-size face combined with a small cranium. The forehead is low and narrow but recedes sharply. The back of the head is flat, and the vertex often is pointed. Mental retardation and spasticity of limbs occur as neurological deficits. Compare PURE MICROCEPHALY.

primary mood disorder a MOOD DISORDER that does not occur in the context of another disorder.

primary motivation MOTIVATION created by the presence of a PRIMARY NEED. Compare SECONDARY MOTIVATION.

primary motor cortex see MOTOR AREA; MOTOR CORTEX.

primary narcissism in psychoanalytic theory, the earliest type of NARCISSISM, in which the infant's LIBIDO is directed toward his or her own body and its satisfaction rather than toward the environment or OBJECTS. At this stage the child forms a narcissistic EGO-IDEAL stemming from his or her sense of OMNIPOTENCE. See also BODY NARCISSISM.

primary narcissistic identification see PRIMARY IDENTIFICATION.

primary need an innate need that arises out of biological processes and leads to physical satisfaction, for example, the need for water and sleep. See also PHYSIOLOGICAL NEEDS; VISCEROGENIC NEED.

primary odor in various theories of odor perception, any of a number of posited odor qualities that somehow combine to produce the perception of an odor. See CROCKER–HENDERSON ODOR SYSTEM; HENNING'S ODOR PRISM; ZWAARDEMAKER SMELL SYSTEM.

primary oocyte see OOGENESIS.

primary orgasmic dysfunction a female sexual dysfunction in which the woman has never been able to achieve an orgasm with any type of stimulation, with or without a partner. Studies have found that 10–15% of sexually active women in the United States fall into this category. Rates in other cultures are related to how positive or negative the culture is toward female sexuality.

primary personality 1. the original personality, as opposed to a SECONDARY PERSONALITY or secondary personalities, of an individual with DISSOCIATIVE IDENTITY DISORDER. **2.** see PREMORBID PERSONALITY.

primary physician see PRIMARY CARE PROVIDER.

primary position in vision, the position for binocular fixation that is looking straight ahead when the body and head are upright.

primary prevention research and programs, designed for and directed to nonclinical populations or populations at risk, that seek to promote and lay a firm foundation for mental, behavioral, or physical health so that psychological disorders, illness, or disease will not develop. Compare SECONDARY PREVENTION; TERTIARY PREVENTION.

primary process in psychoanalytic theory, unconscious mental activity in which there is free, uninhibited flow of PSYCHIC ENERGY from one idea to another. Such thinking operates without regard for logic or reality, is dominated by the PLEASURE PRINCIPLE, and provides hallucinatory fulfillment of wishes. Examples are the dreams, fantasies, and magical thinking of young children. These processes are posited to predominate in the ID. Also called **primary-process thinking**. See also PRELOGICAL THINKING.

primary quality in the philosophy of English empiricist philosopher John Locke (1632–1704), a sensible quality of an object that is a physical property, or the result of a physical property, of the object itself, such as weight, size, or motion. Locke contrasted such properties with so-called SECONDARY QUALITIES, such as color, taste, and smell.

primary reinforcement 1. in OPERANT CONDITIONING, the process in which presentation of a stimulus or circumstance following a response increases the future probability of that response, without the need for special experience with the stimulus or circumstance. That is, the stimulus or circumstance, known as an **unconditioned primary reinforcer**, functions as effective REINFORCEMENT without any special experience or training. **2.** the contingent occurrence of such a stimulus or circumstance after a response. Also called **unconditioned reinforcement**. See also CONDITIONED REINFORCER.

primary relationship a person's closest relationship, in terms of the time, energy, and priority given to it. A primary relationship will typically include high degrees of intimacy, attraction, and commitment.

primary repression in psychoanalytic theory, the first phase of REPRESSION, in which ideas associated with instinctual wishes are screened out and prevented from becoming conscious. Primary repression contrasts with REPRESSION PROPER, in which the repressed material has already been in the realm of consciousness. Also called **primal repression**.

primary reward any stimulus that is innately reinforcing, for example, water to a thirsty person. See PRIMARY REINFORCEMENT; REWARD.

primary sensory area any area within the NEOCORTEX of the brain that acts to receive sensory input—for most senses, from the thalamus. The primary sensory area for hearing is in the temporal lobe, for vision in the occipital lobe (see STRIATE CORTEX), and for touch and taste in the parietal lobe (see PRIMARY SOMATOSENSORY AREA; PRIMARY TASTE CORTEX). Compare SECONDARY SENSORY AREA.

primary sensory ending see ANNULOSPIRAL ENDING.

primary sex characteristics see SEX CHARACTERISTICS.

primary sexual dysfunction any failure in sexual functioning that has always been present in the person and happens in all sexual situations. See SEXUAL DYSFUNCTION. Compare SECONDARY SEXUAL DYSFUNCTION.

primary skin senses the sensations of heat, cold, touch (i.e., contact), and pain. Other sensations from the skin, such as wetness, are considered sensory blends (see TOUCH BLENDS).

primary sleep disorder see SLEEP DISORDER.

primary social unit see SOCIUS.

primary somatosensory area (S1) an area of the cerebral cortex, located in a ridge of the anterior PARIETAL LOBE just posterior to the CENTRAL SULCUS, where the first stage of cortical processing of tactile information takes place (see SOMATOSENSORY AREA). It receives input from the ventroposterior nuclear complex of the thalamus (see VENTROPOSTERIOR NUCLEUS) and projects to other areas of the parietal cortex. See also SECONDARY SOMATOSENSORY AREA.

primary stuttering dysfluency in the speech of young children without accompanying signs of awareness, stress, or emotion. This simple, nonanxiety-producing stage is not accepted as true stuttering by some speech and language pathologists. Compare SECONDARY STUTTERING.

primary symptoms 1. see FUNDAMENTAL SYMPTOMS. **2.** symptoms that are a direct result of a disorder and essential for its diagnosis. **3.** symptoms that appear in the initial stage of a disorder. Compare SECONDARY SYMPTOMS.

primary task in ergonomics, the priority task in a situation requiring MULTIPLE-TASK PERFORMANCE. The operator is expected to allocate sufficient mental resources to the primary task to maintain an acceptable level of performance: He or she will then allocate remaining resources to other tasks. Compare SECONDARY TASK.

primary taste any of certain qualities posited as being basic to the entire sense of TASTE, in that all taste sensations are composed of them. The number of proposed primary tastes has ranged historically from 2 to 11, but SWEET, SALTY, SOUR, and BITTER, now joined by UMAMI, are the most widely accepted. However, the evidence that primary tastes exist is not definitive.

primary taste cortex the area of cerebral cortex that is the first cortical relay for taste. Located along the sharp bend that includes the frontal operculum laterally and the anterior INSULA medially, it receives taste, touch, visceral, and other sensory inputs from the thalamus and permits an integrated evaluation of a chemical. Its output goes to regions that control oral and visceral reflexes in response to foods. See SECONDARY TASTE CORTEX.

primary territory 1. in social psychology, a space controlled by and identified with the person or group who uses it exclusively and to whom it is essential, for example, an apartment or house. Primary territory is similar to PRIMARY ENVIRONMENT. Compare PUBLIC TERRITORY; SECONDARY TERRITORY. See also PROXEMICS. **2.** in animal behavior, a defended space. See TERRITORIALITY.

primary thought disorder a disturbance of cognition, observed primarily in schizophrenia, characterized by incoherent and irrelevant intellectual functions and peculiar language patterns (including bizarre syntax, NEOLOGISMS, and WORD SALAD). See SCHIZOPHRENIC THINKING.

primary visual cortex see STRIATE CORTEX.

primary visual system the major visual pathway in primates, in which processing of visual information is done by the FOVEA CENTRALIS, enabling careful analysis of stimulus properties. Signals pass from the retina to the OPTIC NERVE, OPTIC TRACT, LATERAL GENICULATE NUCLEUS, and OPTIC RADIATIONS, terminating in the STRIATE CORTEX. It is the phylogenetically more recent visual system and functions poorly in newborns. Compare SECONDARY VISUAL SYSTEM.

primary warfare situations operations involving personnel in combat, in containment, and frequently in inactivity. Such situations can involve combat systems, engineering, supply, and communications for operations at sea, in the air, on land, or below the surface.

primate *n.* a member of the Primates, an order of mammals that includes the lemurs, monkeys, apes, and humans. Characteristics of the order include an opposable thumb (i.e., a thumb capable of touching other digits), a relatively large brain, and binocular vision. The young are usually born singly and mature over an extended period.

primidone *n.* a barbiturate ANTICONVULSANT drug whose primary metabolic product is PHENOBARBITAL. It is appropriate for the treatment of partial and tonic–clonic seizures but has been largely supplanted by newer, safer agents. U.S. trade name: **Mysoline**.

primigravida *n.* a woman who is pregnant for the first time. Also called **gravida I**. Compare PRIMIPAROUS.

priming *n.* **1.** in cognitive psychology, the effect in which recent experience of a stimulus facilitates or inhibits later processing of the same or a similar stimulus. In REPETITION PRIMING, presentation of a particular sensory stimulus increases the likelihood that participants will identify the same or a similar stimulus later in the test. In SEMANTIC PRIMING, presentation of a word or sign influences the way in which participants interpret a subsequent word or sign. **2.** in animal behavior, the ability of a PHEROMONE to gradually alter the behavior of another member of the same species. —**prime** *vb.*

priming-the-pump technique see DOUBLE TECHNIQUE.

primiparous *adj.* describing a woman who has had only one pregnancy resulting in offspring, regardless of whether it was a single or multiple birth. Such a woman is called a **primipara**, or **para I**. Also called **uniparous**. Compare PRIMIGRAVIDA.

primitive *adj.* **1.** belonging to the earliest stages of the development of something, such as a language, a species, or a technology. **2.** describing a society or culture that is PRELITERATE, economically and technologically undeveloped, and appears to be characterized by relatively simple forms of social organization. The term is now generally avoided by social scientists, as it implies acceptance of the discredited view that all societies pass through the same stages of development and that certain cultural practices belong to an "earlier" stage of human evolution (see CULTURAL EPOCH THEORY; SOCIAL DARWINISM). Note also that technologically undeveloped societies may be highly developed in other respects, having complex religious and kinship systems. See also MODERNIZATION; TRADITIONALISM.

primitive defense mechanism in psychoanalytic theory, any DEFENSE MECHANISM that protects against anxiety associated with the DEATH INSTINCT. Primitive defense mechanisms include DENIAL, SPLITTING, PROJECTION, and IDEALIZATION.

primitive superego in OBJECT RELATIONS THEORY, an early SUPEREGO that is formed in the PREGENITAL PHASE by the INTROJECTION of especially harsh and terrifying BAD OBJECTS. [first used in 1934 by British psychoanalyst James Strachey (1887–1967)]

primitivization *n.* in psychoanalytic theory, the REGRESSION of higher EGO functions, such as objective thinking, reality testing, and purposeful behavior, with a return to primitive stages of development characterized by magical thinking (e.g., wish-fulfilling fantasies and hallucinations), helplessness, and emotional dependence. Primitivization occurs primarily in traumatic neuroses, in which higher functions are blocked by the overwhelming task of meeting the emergency, and in advanced schizophrenia, in which the ego breaks down and PSYCHIC ENERGY is withdrawn from external reality and concentrated on a narcissistic fantasy life. [first used in 1950 by Austrian psychoanalyst Ernst Kris (1900–1957)]

primordial image see ARCHETYPE.

primordial panic a reaction, observed in some children with schizophrenia, of fright and anger combined with unfocused, disorganized motor responses similar to the startle responses of infants. Also called **elementary anxiety**.

principal-axis factor analysis a factor extraction method in FACTOR ANALYSIS in which the COEFFICIENT OF MULTIPLE CORRELATION of a variable with all other variables in the system is used as the initial COMMUNALITY estimate for that variable.

principal component analysis a statistical technique in which the interrelationship among many correlated variables can be completely reproduced by a smaller number of new variables (called principal components) that are mutually orthogonal and ordered in terms of the percentage of the total system variance for which they account. Often, most of the total variance can be captured in the first few principal components. This technique is similar in its aims to FACTOR ANALYSIS but has different technical features.

principal-component factor analysis a factor extraction method in FACTOR ANALYSIS in which the initial COMMUNALITY estimate is set to 1 for each variable in the system.

principle *n.* **1.** a fundamental rule, standard, or precept, especially in matters of morality or personal conduct. **2.** a proposition deemed to be so fundamental and obvious as to need no defense or support. See AXIOM. **3.** in the empirical sciences, a statement of an established regularity, similar to a LAW.

principled negotiation a negotiation procedure to resolve the conflict between people or groups. The procedure has four main components: (a) separating the problems of the interpersonal relationships from the substantive issues and dealing with each individually, (b) focusing on the parties' real interests rather than on what they initially say they want, (c) developing possible solutions that benefit all parties, and (d) insisting on objective criteria for the decisions. [recommended by Roger Fisher (1922–) and William L. Ury, U.S. experts on negotiation]

principled stage in KOHLBERG'S THEORY OF MORAL DEVELOPMENT, the second of two stages in the POSTCONVENTIONAL LEVEL, in which people are guided by individual principles, conscience, and consistent, universal, ethical standards. Compare SOCIAL CONTRACT ORIENTATION.

principle of belongingness 1. the learning principle that connections between items are more readily formed if the items are closely related in some way, so that one may elicit the other (e.g., "Coney" and "Island"). [proposed by Edward L. THORNDIKE] **2.** the idea that associations between some stimuli and responses are readily acquired because of evolutionary predispositions. See PREPARED LEARNING.

principle of closure see CLOSURE.

principle of common fate see COMMON FATE.

principle of constancy in psychoanalytic theory, the idea that all mental processes tend toward a state of equilibrium and the stability of the inorganic state. Also called **constancy law**; **law of constancy**. See also DEATH INSTINCT; NIRVANA PRINCIPLE; PRINCIPLE OF INERTIA.

principle of continuity see LAW OF CONTINUITY.

principle of contradiction see CONTRADICTION PRINCIPLE.

principle of contrast see LAW OF CONTRAST.

principle of distributed repetitions the concept that better learning occurs when repetitions of the material are spread out or distributed in time rather than being massed together. See DISTRIBUTED PRACTICE.

principle of economy see LAW OF PARSIMONY. See also ELEGANT SOLUTION; OCCAM'S RAZOR.

principle of equipotentiality see LAW OF EQUIPOTENTIALITY.

principle of good shape see GOOD SHAPE.

principle of independent assortment see MENDELIAN INHERITANCE.

principle of inertia in psychoanalytic theory, the tendency of the organism to expend minimum energy by preferring unconscious automatic actions to conscious ones. This principle is posited to be the mechanism that underlies the REPETITION COMPULSION and is one type of ID RESISTANCE. Also called **inertia principle**. See also DEATH INSTINCT; NIRVANA PRINCIPLE.

principle of mass action see LAW OF MASS ACTION.

principle of noncontradiction see CONTRADICTION PRINCIPLE.

principle of optimal stimulation the theory that organisms tend to learn those responses that lead to an optimal or preferred level of stimulation or excitation. Also called **optimal stimulation principle**.

principle of Prägnanz in GESTALT PSYCHOLOGY, the principle that individuals tend to perceive forms as the simplest and most meaningful, stable, and complete structures that conditions permit (German *Prägnanz*, "terseness"). Also called **law of Prägnanz**. See also CLOSURE; GESTALT PRINCIPLES OF ORGANIZATION.

principle of primacy see PRIMACY EFFECT.

principle of proportionality the fundamental judicial principle that the severity of a punishment should be directly related to the seriousness of the crime. Excessively harsh punishments for repeat offenders who commit minor offenses may be considered to violate this principle.

principle of proximity see LAW OF PROXIMITY.

principle of recency see RECENCY EFFECT.

principle of segregation see MENDELIAN INHERITANCE.

principle of similarity see LAW OF SIMILARITY.

principle of symmetry see LAW OF SYMMETRY.

principle of the excluded middle see EXCLUDED MIDDLE PRINCIPLE.

print enlargement system a system for individuals with LOW VISION that enlarges and displays printed text or graphics on a computer or other monitor or screen. The system may be designed for use with a video camera and television or with a personal computer and scanner, or it may be a stand-alone device incorporating all necessary components into a single unit. See also CLOSED-CIRCUIT TELEVISION SYSTEM.

prion *n.* an aberrant counterpart of a normal cellular protein that acts as the infectious agent in certain brain diseases (see PRION DISEASE), notably CREUTZFELDT–JAKOB DISEASE.

prion disease any of a group of fatal neurodegenerative diseases caused by self-replicating abnormal PRION proteins in the brain. Symptoms include gait disturbance, lack of coordination, muscle tremors and jerks, and difficulty in swallowing. Human varieties include CREUTZFELDT–JAKOB DISEASE, FATAL FAMILIAL INSOMNIA, Gerstmann–Straussler–Scheinker syndrome, and KURU. Prion diseases are also known as **spongiform encephalopathies** because of the postmortem appearance of the brain.

prior entry see LAW OF PRIOR ENTRY.

prisoner of war (**POW**) a person held captive by an enemy during a war. Personality disturbances can occur in individuals subjected to the physical and psychological strains of a POW experience. The reactions vary greatly from individual to individual but can include (a) depression due to loss of freedom and identity; (b) personality changes, such as sullen withdrawal and suspiciousness; (c) inertia and loss of interest due to confinement and debilitating conditions; (d) the effects of coercive persuasion, particularly if BRAINWASHING is involved; (e) loss of ego strength; and (f) occasionally, death. These reactions, known as **prisoner-of-war syndrome**, have been compared to the ANACLITIC DEPRESSION observed in hospitalized and deprived children. See also POSTCAPTIVITY HEALTH PROBLEMS.

prisoner's dilemma a MIXED-MOTIVE GAME used in GAME THEORY investigations of competition and cooperation. Each participant in the game must choose between a self-beneficial course of action that could be costly for the other players and an action that would bring a smaller individual payoff but would lead to some benefits for all the players. The name derives from a police tactic, used when incriminating evidence is lacking, in which two suspects are separated and told that the one who confesses will go free or receive a light sentence. Each prisoner may choose silence (the cooperative strategy), hoping that the other does the same but risking a long sentence if the other confesses. Alternatively, either prisoner may confess (the competitive strategy), hoping to improve his or her own situation even though this will be at the expense of the other prisoner. Each prisoner has an incentive to confess regardless of what the other does. The prisoner's dilemma has implications for SOCIAL EXCHANGE THEORY and the study of SOCIAL DILEMMAS.

prison psychologist a psychologist specializing in CORRECTIONAL PSYCHOLOGY.

prison psychosis a severe emotional disturbance precipitated by actual or anticipated incarceration. The types of disturbance vary; in many cases they result from long-standing tendencies toward schizophrenia or are paranoid reactions released by the stress of imprisonment. Symptoms include delusions of innocence, pardon, ill treatment, or persecution; periods of excitement; or rage and destructiveness. See GANSER SYNDROME.

privacy *n.* **1.** the state in which an individual's or a group's desired level of social interaction is not exceeded. **2.** the right to control (psychologically and physically) others' access to one's personal world, for example by regulating others' input through use of physical or other barriers (e.g., doors, partitions) and by regulating one's own output in the form of communication with others. **3.** the right of patients and others (e.g., consumers) to control the amount and disposition of the information they divulge about themselves. See PRIVILEGED COMMUNICATION. **—private** *adj.*

private acceptance see CONVERSION.

private adoption see ADOPTION.

private event an activity or stimulus that is apparent only to the person engaged in or experiencing it. It usually denotes private behavior (e.g., imagining) or private stimuli (e.g., a headache). See also COVERT BEHAVIOR.

private mental hospital a hospital for patients with mental disorders that is organized and run by a group of health care professionals (e.g., psychiatrists, psychologists). A private mental hospital is typically considerably smaller than a PUBLIC MENTAL HOSPITAL, usually has a higher doctor–patient ratio, and generally offers specialized, intensive treatment rather than chronic care.

private practice 1. the practice of a medical or mental health care professional who operates as a self-employed individual. **2.** in the United Kingdom, any medical practice outside the National Health Service.

private self the part of the SELF that is known mainly to oneself, such as one's inner feelings and SELF-CONCEPT. The private self is distinguished from the PUBLIC SELF and the COLLECTIVE SELF.

private self-consciousness see SELF-CONSCIOUSNESS.

private speech see EGOCENTRIC SPEECH.

privation *n.* absence of the necessities of life or of the means required to satisfy needs.

privilege *n.* the legal right of an individual to confidentiality of personal information obtained by a professional in the course of their relationship, as between a patient and a health care professional during the course of treatment or diagnosis. See PRIVILEGED COMMUNICATION.

privileged access the relationship that an individual has with his or her private, subjective, conscious experience, which is accessible to and observable by only that person.

privileged communication confidential information, especially as provided by an individual to a professional in the course of their relationship, that may not be divulged to a third party without the knowledge and consent of that individual. This protection applies to communications not only between patients and physicians, clinical psychologists, psychiatrists, or other health care professionals, but also between clients and attorneys, confessors and priests, and spouses.

proactive aggression see ASSERTION.

proactive interference (**PI**) INTERFERENCE in new learning due to previous learning of similar or related material. For example, study of French in high school may proactively interfere with college learning of Spanish. Also called **proactive inhibition**. See also RELEASE FROM PROACTIVE INTERFERENCE. Compare RETROACTIVE INTERFERENCE.

proattitudinal behavior behavior that is consistent with an attitude. Having a positive attitude toward a political candidate and agreeing to donate money to that candidate's political campaign is an example of proattitudinal behavior. See also ATTITUDE–BEHAVIOR CONSISTENCY. Compare COUNTERATTITUDINAL BEHAVIOR.

probabilism *n.* **1.** in psychology and other empirical sciences, the concept that events or sequences of events can be predicted with a high, though not perfect, degree of probability and validity on the basis of rational and empirical data. In statistical hypothesis testing associated with empirical research, probabilism is fundamental to the practice of attaching a probability to the truth or falsity of the NULL HYPOTHESIS. See also STOCHASTIC. **2.** in ethical theory, the notion that when solutions to ethical questions are unclear, one should follow the course with the greatest estimated probability of being ethically correct. Evidence of a high probability of being correct can be found in agreement among persons of respected moral judgment. **—probabilist** *adj.* **—probabilistic** *adj.*

probabilistic functionalism 1. a theory of perception proposing that environmental cues are at best approximate indices of the objects they refer to, that organisms select the cues that are most useful for responding, and that the veracity of perceptions should therefore be considered probabilistic rather than certain. [proposed by Hungarian-born U.S. psychologist Egon Brunswick (1903–1955)] **2.** the view that behavior is best understood in terms of its probable success in attaining goals.

probabilistic hypothesis a hypothesis that focuses on the likelihood of an event happening rather than predicting a discrete outcome.

probability (symbol: p) *n.* the degree to which an event is likely to occur. **—probabilistic** *adj.*

probability curve a graphic representation of the expected frequency of occurrence of a variable.

probability density function a mathematical representation of the shape of a PROBABILITY DISTRIBUTION.

probability distribution a curve that specifies, by the areas below it, the probability that a random variable occurs at a particular point. The best known example is the bell-shaped NORMAL DISTRIBUTION; others include CHI-SQUARE DISTRIBUTION, Student's T DISTRIBUTION, and F DISTRIBUTION.

probability learning a principle of CHOICE BEHAVIOR in which the probability of a response tends to approach the probability of the REINFORCEMENT.

probability mass function a mathematical FUNCTION that relates a value with the probability that a discrete RANDOM VARIABLE will take on that value.

probability sample a sample chosen from a population in such a way that the likelihood of each unit in the population being selected is known in advance of the sampling. See RANDOM SAMPLING.

probability theory a branch of mathematics concerned with the study of probabilistic phenomena.

probabilogical model a theory of attitude and belief structure postulating that BELIEFS can be viewed as interlinked networks of syllogisms. These networks of syllogisms have vertical structure in that a syllogism containing two beliefs (i.e., the premises) can logically imply a third belief (i.e., the conclusion). They have horizontal structure in that the conclusion for one syllogism can serve as the conclusion for other syllogisms. [originally proposed by U.S. psychologist William J. McGuire (1925–)]

proband *n.* the family member whose possible genetic disease or disorder forms the center of the investigation into the extent of the illness in the family. He or she is the person around whom a PEDIGREE is drawn and from whom the information about other family members is obtained. Also called **index case**.

probation *n.* a criminal sentence in which an offender is not committed to a correctional facility but instead remains in the community under the supervision of a probation officer. Probation is typically accompanied by various conditions intended to control the offender's conduct (e.g., no use of alcohol or drugs, no association with known criminals). See also SHOCK PROBATION.

probe 1. *n.* a follow-up question in an interview or survey. **2.** *vb.* to investigate or explore in depth.

probe technique a memory test in which the participant is asked to recall whether a particular item was among a series of presented items. For example, if the participant hears 1, 3, 5, 7, the probe might be "Was 6 in the list?"

probing *n.* in psychotherapy, the use of direct questions intended to stimulate additional discussion, in the hope of uncovering relevant information or helping the client come to a particular realization or achieve a particular insight.

probit analysis a form of REGRESSION ANALYSIS for a dichotomous dependent variable. In this model an observable independent variable is thought to affect a latent continuous variable that determines the probability that a dichotomous event will occur.

problematic *adj.* describing a situation, event, thing, or idea that is difficult to deal with.

problem behavior any conduct that is maladaptive, destructive, or antisocial.

problem box a problem-solving test consisting of a box with latches, strings, or other fastenings that the participant must learn to manipulate in such a way as to get in or, in some cases, get out.

problem checklist a type of self-report scale listing various personal, social, educational, or vocational problems. The participant indicates the items that apply to his or her situation.

problem drinking see ALCOHOL ABUSE; ALPHA ALCOHOLISM.

problem finding the skills involved in locating problems worth solving (compare PROBLEM SOLVING). Research by psychologists Jacob W. Getzels (1912–2001) and Mihaly Csikszentmihalyi (1934–) has suggested that expert artists tend to be better problem finders than are less expert artists; research by sociologist Harriett Zuckerman (1937–) indicated that the same distinction applies to scientists. Educational psychologist Patricia Arlin has proposed a neo-Piagetian theory of cognitive development according to which problem finding represents a cognitive stage beyond the Piagetian stage of formal operations (see PIAGETIAN THEORY OF INTELLIGENCE).

problem-focused coping a type of COPING STRATEGY that is directed toward decreasing or eliminating stressors, for example, by generating possible solutions to a problem. The coping actions may be directed at the self, the environment, or both. Also called **active coping**. See also PRIMARY COPING. Compare EMOTION-FOCUSED COPING.

problem isomorphs problems that have the same underlying structure, so that they require essentially the same operations to achieve a solution. Such problems may vary enormously in their surface structure and in the degree of difficulty experienced by solvers. See ISOMORPHISM.

problem-oriented record (**POR**) a form of patient-care record that has four components: (a) a database (standardized information on history, physical examination, mental status, etc.); (b) a problem list, based on the database; (c) a treatment plan for each problem; and (d) progress notes as related to the problems and to the patient's response to each treatment. Also called **problem-oriented medical record** (**POMR**).

problem representation a scheme, often a drawing, that represents the relations among elements of a problem. For example, a table might be used to express the relations among two sets of items or a flow chart might be used to express the series of steps to be followed in solving a problem.

problems in living concrete problems with which patients with chronic mental illness (e.g., schizophrenia) frequently struggle (e.g., inability to keep a job or a place of residence), which are believed to be the most useful next focus of treatment after symptoms stabilize with medication. Problems in living are often addressed in day treatment or in aftercare following hospitalization. [proposed by Hungarian-born U.S. psychiatrist Thomas S. Szasz (1920–)]

problem solving the process by which individuals attempt to overcome difficulties, achieve plans that move them from a starting situation to a desired goal, or reach conclusions through the use of higher mental functions, such as reasoning and CREATIVE THINKING. Problem solving is seen in animals in laboratory studies involving mazes and other tests as well as in natural settings to obtain hidden foods. Many animals display problem-solving strategies, such as the WIN–STAY, LOSE–SHIFT STRATEGY, which allows an animal to solve a new problem quickly, based on whether the first response was successful or unsuccessful. In terms of CONDITIONING, problem solving involves engaging in behavior that results in the production of DISCRIMINATIVE STIMULI in situations involving new CONTINGENCIES.

problem-solving interview **1.** in PERSONNEL SELECTION, an employment interview in which the interviewee is presented with a problem that must be solved. The idea is that such an approach will reveal the applicant's analytical, creative, and problem-solving abilities under pressure. See also PATTERNED INTERVIEW; STRUCTURED INTERVIEW; UNSTRUCTURED INTERVIEW. **2.** an interview that is focused on specific job-related problems, with the aim of working with the interviewee on reaching constructive and mutually acceptable solutions to deficits in performance. This technique is used both with supervisors and with other employees.

problem space the set of all possible paths to the solution of a given problem.

procaine *n.* a local anesthetic used primarily in medical and dental procedures. Procaine was introduced in 1905 as the first synthetic substitute for cocaine.

procedural justice **1.** see ORGANIZATIONAL JUSTICE. **2.** in legal proceedings, the use of methods and procedures that are fair and impartial, as distinct from the making of just decisions. The various rules governing how witnesses are questioned and what evidence is admitted into court are examples of the application of procedural justice within the legal system.

procedural knowledge see PROCEDURAL MEMORY.

procedural learning the process of acquiring skill at a task, particularly a task that eventually can be performed automatically (i.e., without attention), as opposed to acquiring FACTUAL KNOWLEDGE about it.

procedural memory long-term memory for the skills involved in particular tasks. Procedural memory is demonstrated by skilled performance and is often separate from the ability to verbalize this knowledge (see DECLARATIVE MEMORY). Knowing how to type or skate, for example, requires procedural memory. Also called **procedural knowledge**.

procedural rationality the rationality of the processes used in arriving at a decision, as opposed to the rationality of the decision itself. Compare SUBSTANTIVE RATIONALITY.

procedure *n.* **1.** a sequence of steps or actions. **2.** the way in which a study is to be conducted or has been conducted.

proceptivity *n.* the period during MATING BEHAVIOR when females actively solicit males for copulation. Proceptivity is distinguished from the more passive RECEPTIVITY to indicate the female's active role in mating.

process analysis **1.** in psychotherapy, the examination of the interaction between the therapist and the client and of their evolving relationship, as opposed to the content of their discussions. **2.** in evaluation research, an analytic procedure that focuses on each element of a program in order to identify ways of improving program operations. See also IMPLEMENTATION EVALUATION.

process consultation an ORGANIZATIONAL DEVELOPMENT intervention in which work groups are observed by a consultant, who provides feedback on how to improve the effectiveness with which members work together.

process-dissociation method a method for objectively separating memory elements that are conscious from those that are not. Also called **method of opposition**. [developed by U.S. psychologist Larry L. Jacoby (1944–)]

process evaluation in evaluation research, an in-house function in which the evaluator quickly moves into the situation to be evaluated, conducts the evaluation, feeds back findings to the program administrator for immediate program modification (if necessary), then repeats the process. See also FORMATIVE EVALUATION.

process experiential psychotherapy an approach

to psychotherapy that focuses on the client's moment-to-moment experience and guides the client's cognitive and affective processing in the direction of client-defined goals. The THERAPEUTIC ALLIANCE, internal patterns of viewing the self and others, and an emphasis on therapeutic process over content are core elements of this therapy. See also CLIENT-CENTERED THERAPY; GESTALT THERAPY; HUMANISTIC THERAPY. [proposed by South African-born Canadian psychologist Leslie Greenberg (1945–)]

process goal a goal focused on the action necessary for optimal execution of a skill (e.g., in sport, to have high knee lift while running).

processing-efficiency theory a theory that attempts to explain the relationship between anxiety and performance (see AROUSAL–PERFORMANCE RELATIONSHIP). It suggests that anxiety serves two functions: (a) It increases worry and takes part of the attentional resources, and (b) the worry created serves a monitoring function by identifying the task as important, so that the individual increases the effort, which overcomes the depleted attentional capacity (see CAPACITY MODEL).

Processing Speed Index an index from the WECHSLER ADULT INTELLIGENCE SCALE and other Wechsler tests that measures the speed of nonverbal processing.

process loss in the social psychology of groups, any action, operation, or dynamic that prevents the group from reaching its full potential, such as reduced effort (SOCIAL LOAFING), inadequate coordination of effort (COORDINATION LOSS), poor communication, or ineffective leadership. See also COLLECTIVE EFFORT MODEL; RINGELMANN EFFECT; SOCIAL INTERFERENCE; SUCKER EFFECT.

process observer 1. in groups, the member who observes and comments on the group's functioning. This role may be formally designated or taken on informally by one or more group members. **2.** a consultant who helps groups to improve their performance by observing the unit as it works and discussing these observations with the unit.

processor *n.* **1.** in INFORMATION THEORY, any device or system that can perform specific operations on data that have been presented to it in proper format. **2.** in computer science, a computer or its principal operating part. See CENTRAL PROCESSOR.

process–reactive *adj.* relating to a disease model of schizophrenia based on the distinction between gradual and acute onset of symptoms. PROCESS SCHIZOPHRENIA is marked by a long-term gradual deterioration before the disease is manifest, whereas REACTIVE SCHIZOPHRENIA is associated with a rapid onset of symptoms after a relatively normal premorbid period.

process research the study of various psychological mechanisms or processes of psychotherapy as they influence the outcome of treatment or the reactions that the therapist or client may have. A basic goal of such research is to identify therapeutic methods and processes that are most effective in bringing about positive change, as well as inadequacies and other limitations. See also PSYCHOTHERAPY RESEARCH.

process schizophrenia a form of schizophrenia that begins early in life, develops gradually, is believed to be due to endogenous (biological or physiological) rather than environmental factors, and has a poor prognosis. Psychosocial development before the onset of the disorder is poor; individuals are withdrawn, socially inadequate, and indulge in excessive fantasies. This term is often used interchangeably with NUCLEAR SCHIZOPHRENIA. Also called **poor premorbid schizophrenia**. Compare REACTIVE SCHIZOPHRENIA. [proposed in 1959 by U.S. psychologists Norman Garmezy (1918–) and Eliot H. Rodnick (1911–1999)]

process study any investigation undertaken to assess the mechanisms and variables that contribute to and influence the outcome of a particular activity. For example, a process study of GROUP PSYCHOTHERAPY sessions may seek to determine characteristics of the therapeutic interaction that are associated with positive, neutral, or negative changes individually and across the group. See also PROCESS RESEARCH.

process variable 1. an interpersonal, affective, cognitive, or behavioral factor that is operative during the course of psychotherapy or counseling and influences the progress or the course of behavior. **2.** any set of PSYCHOLOGICAL FACTORS that has an effect on the development or modification of a process over time.

prochlorperazine *n.* a low-potency PHENOTHIAZINE used for the treatment of nausea and vomiting and, occasionally, for the control of anxiety. It was formerly used as an antipsychotic agent. U.S. trade name (among others): **Compazine**.

pro-choice *adj.* supporting a woman's right to make free, informed decisions regarding her reproductive options, including the right to safe, legal ABORTION. Compare PRO-LIFE.

procreative sex sexual activity that can result in pregnancy. In some cultures and religions this is regarded as the basis for what is considered to be normal sex, as opposed to deviant or sinful sexual activity.

Procrustes rotation a LINEAR TRANSFORMATION of the points represented in a MATRIX X to best conform, in a least-squares sense, to the points in a target matrix, Y. Usually the points in the target matrix represent some theoretical factor structure or the results of a FACTOR ANALYSIS on a different population. The name derives from the robber in Greek mythology who forced his victims to fit his bed by stretching them or cutting off their limbs.

procyclidine *n.* an ANTICHOLINERGIC DRUG that is used in the treatment of Parkinson's disease and drug-induced EXTRAPYRAMIDAL EFFECTS. U.S. trade name: **Kemadrin**.

prodigy *n.* an individual, typically a child, who displays unusual or exceptional talent or intelligence, quite often in a discrete area of expertise, such as mathematics, music, or chess. Even if naturally endowed with such exceptional abilities, prodigies still require the opportunity and dedication to train and develop their gifts. Prodigies do not always develop into accomplished adults: There appears to be an important transition between the two, and only a proportion of prodigies successfully negotiate this transition. See also GIFTEDNESS.

prodromal myopia see MYOPIA.

prodromal syndrome a set of traits, symptoms, or neurological deficits that may predispose an individual to developing a psychological or neurological disorder.

prodrome *n.* an early symptom or symptoms of a mental or physical disorder. A prodrome frequently serves as a warning or premonitory sign that may, in some cases, enable preventive measures to be taken. Examples are the AURAS that often precede epileptic seizures or migraine headaches and the headache, fatigue, dizziness, and insidious impairment of ability that often precede a stroke. Also called **prodromic phase**. **—prodromic** *adj.* **—prodromal** *adj.*

prodrug *n.* a drug that is either biologically inert or of limited activity until metabolized to a more active derivative.

product appeals advertising appeals directed toward a specific type of consumer personality. For example, a product appeal for a "conservative family car" might be directed toward married businesspeople with young children, while an appeal for a "sexy sports car" might be directed toward younger or older men and women with fewer family responsibilities.

product champion an individual who supports an innovation (e.g., a new technology) and provides information regarding its benefits so that the target user groups will adopt the innovation. Such individuals are held to play a key role in INNOVATION DIFFUSION and CHANGE MANAGEMENT.

product image the unique identity of a product, or special brand of product, established usually by careful psychological studies to create a receptive feeling for the product in the mind of the consumer. For example, some brands of coffee are identified as mountain-grown in Latin America, hand-picked by experts with Hispanic names, and carefully roasted to yield a rich, dark beverage, although the brand may actually contain coffees from Africa or Indonesia.

production deficiency 1. in problem solving, failure to find the right or best strategy for completing a task, as opposed to failure in implementing it. **2.** the inability of children to make spontaneous use of a strategy that they are capable of using when instructed. Compare MEDIATIONAL DEFICIENCY; UTILIZATION DEFICIENCY.

production method see MAGNITUDE PRODUCTION.

production rules the "if–then" statements describing the conditions under which a rule relating to a cognitive skill is to be applied (if…) and the action to be implemented (then…). See PRODUCTION SYSTEM.

production system a rule-based computer program that makes decisions or solves problems (see RULE-BASED SYSTEM). It operates according to a set of "if" (state)–"then" (action) rules, such that when a certain state occurs, an associated action is executed, thus altering the state, which produces a new action, and so on. A production system consists of three components: (a) the set of "production memory," represented as sets of "if–then" rules; (b) the "working memory," which contains information related to the present state of the problem solving, represented as patterns to be submitted to the production memory; and (c) a control regime that takes the patterns (representing the current state of the problem solving) from working memory to the set of production rules. When a production rule matches this pattern, it "fires" and produces a new pattern (reflecting the new state of the problem solving), which is then placed in working memory. This cycle continues until no patterns in working memory match the production rules. The production system approach is used as a COGNITIVE ARCHITECTURE by many researchers in cognitive science. See also ADAPTIVE PRODUCTION SYSTEM; SOAR.

productive language see EXPRESSIVE LANGUAGE.

productive love in psychoanalytic theory, the capacity of healthy individuals to establish close, interdependent relationships without abridging their individuality. Respect, care, responsibility, and knowledge of the other are essential components. According to Erich FROMM, productive love is accomplished through active effort and is an aspect of the productive orientation.

productive orientation in psychoanalytic theory, a personality pattern in which the individual is able to develop and apply his or her potentialities without being unduly dependent on outside control. Such an individual is highly active in feeling, thinking, and relating to others, and at the same time retains the separateness and integrity of his or her own self. [introduced by Erich FROMM]

productive thinking in the theory of Erich FROMM, thinking in which a given question or issue is considered with objectivity as well as respect and concern for the problem as a whole. It is a feature of the PRODUCTIVE ORIENTATION.

productive vocabulary an individual's vocabulary as defined by the words that he or she regularly uses, as opposed to those that he or she can understand when used by others. Also called **active vocabulary**; **working vocabulary**. Compare RECEPTIVE VOCABULARY.

productivity *n.* **1.** the relationship between the quantity or quality of output (goods created or services provided) and the input (time, materials, etc.) required to create it. **2.** the capacity to produce goods and services having exchange value. VOCATIONAL REHABILITATION programs often use the productivity of people with disabilities as a major measure of the effectiveness of the programs. **3.** one of the three formal properties of language, consisting of the ability to combine individual words to produce an unlimited number of sentences. See SEMANTICITY. [defined by Roger BROWN]

product–moment correlation (symbol: *r*) a statistic that indexes the degree of linear relationship between two variables. Invented by British statistician Karl Pearson (1857–1936), it is often known as the **Pearson product–moment correlation**.

product rule see DURHAM RULE.

product testing the testing of consumer response to a new product before or after it has been offered for sale. In the United States, such tests are usually conducted on a limited scale in certain markets, such as in Omaha, Nebraska, or Rochester, New York, which have been studied intensively and have populations with known consumer characteristics. Large-scale advertising campaigns are based on results of the localized product testing, which also may influence changes in product or package design.

proecological behavior behavior that promotes the quality of the natural environment. Examples include recycling, efficient use of energy, use of mass transportation, and birth control. Among topics examined in the analysis of these behaviors are ENVIRONMENTAL ATTITUDES, economic and political impediments, and sociodemographic factors. See also SOCIAL TRAP.

proestrus *n.* the period in the ESTROUS CYCLE that immediately precedes ESTRUS.

profession *n.* an OCCUPATION requiring specialized knowledge in which guidelines and rules of conduct have been established governing such matters as minimal qualifications for entrance into the profession, training, performance criteria, fees and general business practices, and ethical relations between members of the profession and their colleagues and clients. See PROFESSIONAL ETHICS; PROFESSIONAL LICENSING; PROFESSIONAL STANDARDS. See also VOCATION. **—professional** *adj., n.* **—professionalize** *vb.*

professional-aptitude test any test used for selecting candidates for professional training. Typical aptitudes tested include the mental capacity, ability to acquire information and skills, and cognitive style needed for general higher education and proficiency in specific professions, such as psychology, law, science, nursing, engineering, dentistry, medicine, accounting, theology, and teaching.

professional–client sexual relations a boundary

violation (see BOUNDARY ISSUES) in which a health care professional engages in sexual relations with a patient under his or her care. See also PROFESSIONAL ETHICS.

professional development the continuing education or training that is often expected or required of people employed in a PROFESSION. Professional organizations often assist the professional development of their members by providing courses, conferences, literature, and other services. See also CAREER DEVELOPMENT; MANAGEMENT DEVELOPMENT.

professional ethics rules of acceptable conduct that members of a given profession are expected to follow. See BOUNDARY ISSUES; CODE OF ETHICS; ETHICS; PROFESSIONAL STANDARDS; STANDARDS OF PRACTICE.

professional licensing the imposition of state-regulated minimal standards for legal employment as a member of a given profession. Professional licensing usually consists of three parts: provisional certification, full certification, and recertification. See LICENSE.

professional manager a person occupying a managerial position in an organization who has been extensively prepared and trained for that position and thus possesses specialized knowledge of important principles, practices, and procedures.

professional standards the levels of performance and conduct required or expected in a particular profession. See also CODE OF ETHICS; PROFESSIONAL ETHICS; STANDARDS OF PRACTICE.

profile *n.* **1.** a graphical representation of the scores of an individual (or the means of groups of individuals) on multiple measures. The *x*-axis of the graph usually represents the various measures, while the *y*-axis is the score of the individual on the corresponding measure. Usually the points are connected by short line segments. **2.** a group of characteristics indicating that a particular type of person is likely to engage in a certain behavior. See CRIMINAL PROFILING.

profile analysis a MULTIVARIATE statistical technique that compares groups of individuals with regard both to the shape of their score PROFILES on several variables and to the values of their scores on those variables.

profile matching system a method of PERSONNEL SELECTION in which decisions to hire or reject for employment are based on the GOODNESS OF FIT between an applicant's characteristics and a profile of the ideal or typical employee in the position. See also INTERVIEWER STEREOTYPE.

profile of a disorder a drawn or mechanically generated outline, often a graph, representing the symptoms and characteristics of a disorder.

Profile of Mood States (**POMS**) a brief self-report instrument measuring six dimensions of transient and fluctuating mood states over time: tension or anxiety, depression or dejection, anger or hostility, vigor or activity, fatigue or inertia, and confusion or bewilderment. Participants indicate on a 5-point scale ranging from "not at all" to "extremely" whether each of the 65 adjectives (e.g., confused, spiteful, energetic, good-natured) listed is descriptive of themselves within the specified time frame. A mentally healthy profile on the POMS is known as the ICEBERG PROFILE. [originally developed in 1971 by U.S. psychologist Douglas M. McNair (1927–), U.S. psychometrician Maurice Lorr (1910–), and U.S. psychologist Leo F. Droppleman (1936–)]

profiling *n.* **1.** see CRIMINAL PROFILING. **2.** in sport, an exercise in which athletes first identify the most important physical and mental components necessary for optimal performance and then assess the degree to which they possess each of these components at that time.

profound mental retardation a diagnostic category for those with IQs below 20, comprising about 1% of people with MENTAL RETARDATION. It is due to sensorimotor abnormalities as well as intellectual factors; typical developmental attainments include rudimentary speech and limited self-care, and affected individuals require lifelong, highly structured environments with constant aid and supervision.

progeria adultorum see WERNER'S DISEASE.

progesterone *n.* a hormone, secreted mainly by the CORPUS LUTEUM in the ovary, that stimulates proliferation of the ENDOMETRIUM (lining) of the uterus required for implantation of an embryo. If implantation occurs, progesterone continues to be secreted—first by the corpus luteum and then by the placenta—maintaining the pregnant uterus and preventing further release of egg cells from the ovary. It also stimulates development of milk-secreting cells in the breasts.

progestin *n.* see PROGESTOGENS.

progestogens *pl. n.* steroids that include the natural hormone PROGESTERONE and synthetic steroids (known as **progestins**) with physiological effects similar to those of progesterone. Progestins may be derived from progesterone or testosterone. While progesterone has an antiestrogenic action, progestins may have different effects, such as proestrogenic activity. They are used in oral contraceptives, HORMONE REPLACEMENT THERAPY, and medications for menstrual disorders.

prognosis *n.* **1.** in general medicine and mental health science, a prediction of the future course, duration, severity, and outcome of a condition, disease, or disorder. Prognosis may be given whether or not treatment is undertaken, in order to give the client an opportunity to weigh the benefits of different treatment options. **2.** more generally, any prediction or forecast. —**prognostic** *adj.*

program effectiveness conclusions drawn about PROGRAM OUTCOMES from testing an intervention as it is actually executed in the context of a routine everyday service delivery. This method contains several threats to INTERNAL VALIDITY because it must rely on procedures that are not scientifically controlled. Compare PROGRAM EFFICACY. See also PROGRAM EVALUATION.

program efficacy conclusions drawn about PROGRAM OUTCOMES from testing an intervention under closely controlled scientific conditions, which may narrowly define the type of patients treated, nature of services offered, and so forth. Because this method involves the provision of services under conditions that are very different from everyday real-world service delivery, there are dangers that it may not achieve a high degree of EXTERNAL VALIDITY. Compare PROGRAM EFFECTIVENESS.

program evaluation a process of applying social research tools that contributes to decisions on installing, continuing, expanding, certifying, or modifying programs, depending on their effectiveness. Program evaluation is also used to obtain evidence to rally support for or opposition to a program and to contribute to basic knowledge in the social and behavioral sciences about social interventions and social experimentation.

Program for Learning in Accordance with Needs (**PLAN**) an individualized instructional system covering language arts, mathematics, science, and social studies in grades 1 through 12. It is based on learning objectives developed by the teacher and the student together. This system illustrated how programmed learning and, ultimately, computers could play an important and integral role in individualizing education. [developed in the 1960s by U.S. psychologist John C. Flanagan (1906–1996)]

program impact the effects of a program designed to produce some type of good or service, measured in terms of success or failure in achieving these goals or objectives.

program integrity the extent to which an intended program is actually delivered. Also called **treatment integrity**; **treatment validity**.

programmed cell death the orderly death and disposal of surplus tissue cells, which occurs as part of tissue remodeling during development, or of worn-out and infected cells, which occurs throughout life. Also called **apoptosis**.

programmed instruction a learning technique, used for self-instruction and in academic and some applied settings, in which the material is presented in a series of sequential, graduated steps, or **frames**. The learner is required to make a response at each step: If the response is correct, it leads to the next step; if it is incorrect, it leads to further review. Also called **programmed learning**. See TEACHING MACHINE.

programming *n.* **1.** the planning of a sequential set of operations in such areas as social organization or experimental research. **2.** see COMPUTER PROGRAMMING.

programming language see COMPUTER PROGRAMMING LANGUAGE.

program monitoring the use of key indicators to measure program performance. The purposes and regularity of this activity vary widely and include PROCESS EVALUATION, information provided from management information systems, and performance measurement that assesses program outcomes. Typically, these methods do not assess the impact of the program. See also PROGRAM EFFECTIVENESS; PROGRAM IMPACT.

program outcome any or all of the effects that arise from the implementation of a program. Also called **program output**.

progression–regression hypothesis the hypothesis that learning leads to the use of more complex control strategies (progression) and that stress or forgetting leads to the use of simpler control strategies (regression).

Progressive Achievement Tests 1. (**PAT**) assessment tests that provide information on the reading vocabulary, reading comprehension, and mathematics achievement of students in comparison with national norms. Progressive Achievement Tests are generally used for diagnostic purposes at the beginning of a school year and are available for grades 4 through 10. They were developed by the New Zealand Council for Educational Research (NZCER). **2.** see CALIFORNIA ACHIEVEMENT TESTS.

progressive bulbar palsy see BULBAR PARALYSIS.

progressive education a broad educational approach originally associated with John DEWEY's philosophy. It emphasizes experimentalism as opposed to dogmatism in teaching, learning by doing, recognition of individual rates of learning, latitude in selecting areas of study according to interest, and a close relationship between academic learning and experience in the world outside the classroom.

progressive-interval schedule a SCHEDULE OF REINFORCEMENT in which the presentation of each reinforcer is dependent on the first response that occurs after a fixed interval of time has passed, with this interval increasing after each reinforcement. The amount by which the interval increases can be based on any of various functions. For example, a progressive-interval schedule might begin with an interval of 30 s, which is then increased by 30 s after each subsequent reinforcement. Compare FIXED-INTERVAL SCHEDULE.

progressive lipodystrophy see LIPODYSTROPHY.

progressively distributed process a technique used in memory studies in which the interval of time between repetitions is gradually increased so that they become progressively more distributed.

Progressive Matrices see COLORED PROGRESSIVE MATRICES.

progressive muscular atrophy see SPINAL MUSCULAR ATROPHY.

progressive myopia see MYOPIA.

progressive-ratio schedule a SCHEDULE OF REINFORCEMENT in which each reinforcer is presented on the completion of a particular number of responses and the number of responses required increases after each reinforcement. The amount by which the number increases can be determined by any of various functions, although most commonly the number increases by a fixed amount from reinforcement to reinforcement. Progressive-ratio schedules are often used to measure the effectiveness of reinforcers. Compare FIXED-RATIO SCHEDULE.

progressive relaxation a technique in which the individual is trained to relax the entire body by becoming aware of tensions in various muscle groups and then relaxing one muscle group at a time. In some cases, the individual consciously tenses specific muscles or muscle groups and then releases tension to achieve relaxation throughout the body. Also called **Jacobson relaxation method**. See also RELAXATION. [developed by U.S. physician Edmund Jacobson (1888–1983)]

progressive semantic dementia a progressively worsening DEMENTIA characterized by loss of the ability to understand abstract or higher level verbal constructs, particularly those that deal with values, ethics, and the like.

progressive spinal muscular atrophy see SPINAL MUSCULAR ATROPHY.

progressive supranuclear palsy a progressive neurological disorder usually starting in the 6th decade of life and characterized by OCULOMOTOR PALSY, with downward gaze particularly affected. The condition may be accompanied by PARKINSONISM, postural instability, speech and swallowing difficulties, DYSTONIA, personality changes, and typically mild cognitive impairment. Pathology often shows loss of neurons and GLIOSIS in various regions of the brainstem, basal ganglia, and midbrain. Also called **Steele–Richardson–Olszewski syndrome**; **supranuclear palsy**.

progressive teleologic regression the purposive return of a person with schizophrenia to the PRIMARY PROCESS level, in an attempt to avoid tension, stress and anxiety, and a self-image that has become bizarre, threatening, and frightening. The regression is progressive because it fails to accomplish its purpose and becomes more extreme. [first described by Italian-born U.S. psychiatrist Silvano Arieti (1914–1982)]

projected jealousy a type of behavior in which individuals who are unfaithful, or who repress impulses to be unfaithful, accuse their partners of being unfaithful, thereby projecting their own impulses. See PROJECTION.

Project Head Start a U.S. government-funded program designed to enhance early childhood education, with special emphasis on high-risk, inner-city, and minority children up to 5 years of age and their families.

Project Intelligence a project developed in 1979 to improve cognitive skills, formulated originally for use by children of early to middle adolescence in Venezuela. The project was evaluated and found to be effective in improving cognitive skills.

projection *n.* in psychoanalytic and psychodynamic theories, the process by which one attributes one's own individual positive or negative characteristics, affects, and impulses to another person or group. This is often a DEFENSE MECHANISM in which unpleasant or unacceptable impulses, stressors, ideas, affects, or responsibilities are attributed to others. For example, the defense mechanism of projection enables a person conflicted over expressing anger to change "I hate him" to "He hates me." Such defensive patterns are often used to justify prejudice or evade responsibility; in more severe cases, they may develop into paranoid delusions in which, for example, an individual who blames others for his or her problems may come to believe that those others are plotting against him or her. In classical psychoanalytic theory, projection permits the individual to avoid seeing his or her own faults, but modern usage has largely abandoned the requirement that the projected trait remain unknown in the self. **—project** *vb.*

projection area an area of the CEREBRAL CORTEX that receives inputs from a particular sense organ. Each sense sends messages to two or more projection areas.

projection fiber a nerve fiber that carries impulses from the cerebral cortex to subcortical structures (e.g., the thalamus, hypothalamus, or basal ganglia).

projection neuron a neuron with a long axon extending some distance from the cell body. Also called **Golgi Type I neuron**. Compare LOCAL CIRCUIT NEURON.

projective device in consumer psychology, a word-association technique employed in MOTIVATION RESEARCH. Key words are mixed with neutral background words and subjects are asked to make associations without being aware of which terms are the key words. Such projective devices enable advertisers to learn which words are likely to be most attractive to consumers when used in advertising copy. Some techniques also include cartoon characters or scenes in which individuals are asked to provide a dialogue.

projective doll play see DOLL PLAY.

projective identification 1. in psychoanalysis, a DEFENSE MECHANISM in which the individual projects qualities that are unacceptable to the self onto another individual and that person—through unconscious or conscious interpersonal pressure—internalizes the projected qualities and believes himself or herself to be characterized by them appropriately and justifiably. See PROJECTION. **2.** in the object relations theory of Melanie KLEIN, a defense mechanism in which a person fantasizes that part of his or her EGO is split off and projected into the OBJECT in order to control or harm it, thus allowing the individual to maintain a belief in his or her omnipotent control. Projective identification is a key feature of Klein's PARANOID-SCHIZOID POSITION.

projective method see PROJECTIVE TECHNIQUE.

projective play a variation of PLAY THERAPY in which dolls and other toys are used by children to express their feelings, which can be helpful in diagnosing mental disturbances.

projective psychotherapy a treatment procedure in psychotherapy in which selected responses on various projective tests are fed back to the client, who associates with them in much the same way that analytic patients make free associations to dreams. [developed by U.S. psychologist Molly Harrower (1906–1999)]

projective technique any personality assessment procedure that consists of a fixed series of relatively ambiguous stimuli designed to elicit unique, sometimes highly idiosyncratic, responses. Examples of this type of procedure are the RORSCHACH INKBLOT TEST, the THEMATIC APPERCEPTION TEST, and various sentence completion and word association tests. Projective techniques are quite controversial, with opinions ranging from the belief that personality assessment is incomplete without data from at least one or more of these procedures to the view that such techniques lack reliability and validity and that interpretations of personality organization and functioning derived from them are completely hypothetical and unscientific. Also called **projective method**.

project method a teaching structure in which students work alone or together to initiate, develop, and carry through learning projects with a minimal amount of direct guidance from the teacher.

prolactin *n.* a hormone, secreted by the anterior PITUITARY GLAND, that stimulates milk secretion by the mammary glands. Also called **lactogenic hormone**; **luteotropic hormone**.

prolapsed intervertebral disk see SLIPPED DISK.

pro-life *adj.* denoting a position or social movement that opposes or aims to limit the right to legal abortion, often on religious grounds. Compare PRO-CHOICE.

Prolixin *n.* a trade name for FLUPHENAZINE.

PROLOG *n.* PRO(gramming) LOG(ic): a high-level computer language, which is important for research in ARTIFICIAL INTELLIGENCE. Inference in PROLOG is a form of deduction but is not mathematically sound due to several pragmatic compromises, including the use of "cut" to control backtracking and "negation" as the failure to find correct results. A strength of the language is a powerful pattern matcher based on unification, for use in PRODUCTION SYSTEM applications.

promethazine *n.* a PHENOTHIAZINE used for the treatment of nausea, motion sickness, and allergies and as a sedative. Its mechanism of action includes blockade of H_1 HISTAMINE receptors and of dopamine receptors in the MESOLIMBIC SYSTEM. U.S. trade name: **Phenergan**.

promiscuity *n.* transient, casual sexual relations with a variety of partners. In humans, this type of behavior is generally regarded unfavorably; however, it has been argued that there can be healthy promiscuity in the simple enjoyment of casual, consensual, nonexploitative relationships. In bonobos (pygmy chimpanzees) sexual activity occurs frequently both between and within sexes in exchange for resources (e.g., food) or to calm tensions. In many species females appear to display promiscuity to prevent CERTAINTY OF PATERNITY but often mate with the most dominant or successful male at the time when conception is most likely. **—promiscuous** *adj.*

promotive interdependence see POSITIVE INTERDEPENDENCE.

prompt *n.* see CUE.

prompting *n.* in psychotherapy, suggesting or hinting at topics by the therapist to encourage the client to discuss certain issues. Prompting may include reminding the client of previously discussed material, tying previously discussed topics together, or finishing a sentence or thought for the client to aid in his or her understanding of an issue.

prompting method see ANTICIPATION LEARNING METHOD; CUED RECALL.

pronation *n.* **1.** the act of turning the arm and hand so that the palm faces downward and the two long bones of the forearm are crossed, or the condition resulting from this action. **2.** the act of turning the foot so that the sole faces outward and the lateral (outer) margin is raised (as in walking on the inside of one's feet), or the condition resulting from this action. **3.** the state or condition of being prone (see POSTURE). Compare SUPINATION. **—pronate** *vb.*

prone *adj.* see POSTURE.

pronoun *n.* in linguistics, a word that substitutes for a noun, noun phrase, or larger nominal unit, usually to avoid repetition. English pronouns include the personal pronouns (*I, you, she,* etc.), the demonstrative pronouns (*this, that,* etc.), and the relative pronouns (*that, which,* etc.). See ANAPHORA; ANTECEDENT. **—pronominal** *adj.*

pronoun reversal a speech phenomenon observed in children with AUTISTIC DISORDER, in which the child refers to him- or herself in the second or third person (e.g., *you, him, she*) while identifying others by first-person pronouns (e.g., *me*). Also called **pronominal reversal**.

proof *n.* **1.** the establishment of a proposition or theory as true, or the method by which it is so established. There is much debate as to whether propositions or theories can ever be truly proven. In logic and philosophy, even a valid argument can be untrue if its first premise is false. For example, it is a valid argument to say that *All trees are pines: I have a tree in my garden: Therefore my tree is a pine.* In empirical sciences such as psychology, both logical and methodological problems make it impossible to prove a theory or hypothesis true. Disciplines that rely on empirical science must settle for some type of PROBABILISM based on empirical support of its theories and hypotheses. See also FALSIFIABILITY. **2.** in mathematics and logic, a sequence of steps formally establishing the truth of a theorem or the validity of a proposition. **3.** in law, evidence that establishes and supports the truth of claims made by either party in a dispute. Only evidence presented at trial can constitute proof; the TRIER OF FACT must then decide whether such evidence constitutes adequate proof. In criminal cases the standard of proof required to obtain a conviction is proof BEYOND REASONABLE DOUBT.

proofreader's illusion a visual error in which a misspelling, omission, extra letter, transposition, or the like is overlooked, owing to TOP-DOWN PROCESSING in which the context and other cues outweigh the impact of the word or phrase as literally spelled or misspelled.

proopiomelanocortin (POMC) *n.* a protein, synthesized in the pituitary gland, that is the precursor of several hormones. It can be cleaved by enzymes at different positions to yield biologically active compounds, including BETA-ENDORPHIN, ALPHA-MELANOCYTE STIMULATING HORMONE, and ADRENOCORTICOTROPIC HORMONE.

propaedeutic *n.* **1.** introductory instruction provided by a teacher to a student before formal instruction of a full concept or idea begins. **2.** an introduction to any art or science.

propaganda *n.* a method of social control that attempts to strengthen or change the beliefs, attitudes, and actions of others by presenting highly biased information or sometimes DISINFORMATION. It usually involves an appeal to emotion that is designed to win support for an idea or course of action or to belittle or disparage the ideas or programs of others. See also CARD-STACKING; FEAR APPEAL; GLITTERING GENERALITIES; SUBLIMINAL PROPAGANDA.

propaganda analysis a study of the techniques, appeals, content, and effectiveness of propaganda.

propaganda inoculation see INOCULATION EFFECT; INOCULATION THEORY.

propanediols *pl. n.* a group of chemically related compounds derived from propyl alcohol and originally developed as antianxiety drugs. Their pharmacological actions include muscle relaxation, depression of the central nervous system, and a calming effect through interference with autonomic reactions. The prototype of the group is MEPROBAMATE. Due to their toxicity in overdose, propanediols have largely been supplanted as anxiolytics by benzodiazepines and other sedative hypnotics; CARISOPRODOL, a precursor of meprobamate, is currently used as a muscle relaxant.

propensity *n.* a strong tendency toward a behavior or action.

propensity analysis a statistical approach to the adjustment of group means to account for preexisting group differences on a set of variables. Propensity analysis is an alternative to matching or ANALYSIS OF COVARIANCE.

prophase *n.* the first stage of cell division, during which chromosomes shorten and thicken, dividing along their length into chromatids, and the nuclear envelope dissolves. In MEIOSIS, homologous pairs of chromosomes associate to form bivalents (pairs).

prophecy formula see SPEARMAN–BROWN PROPHECY FORMULA.

prophylactic maintenance see MAINTENANCE THERAPY.

prophylactic surgery the removal of an organ prior to the expected onset of cancer in that organ, usually because the individual has a POSITIVE FAMILY HISTORY of the disease or is a CARRIER of a predisposing mutation. Women who carry mutations in genes *BRCA1* or *BRCA2* (see BRCA1 AND BRCA2) or P53 are at greatly increased risk of breast and ovarian cancer and may consider prophylactic surgery. **Prophylactic mastectomy** is the surgical removal of one or both breasts prior to a diagnosis of breast cancer. **Prophylactic ovariectomy** is the surgical removal of the ovaries prior to a diagnosis of ovarian cancer. **Prophylactic thyroidectomy** is the surgical removal of the thyroid gland prior to the onset of medullary thyroid cancer in individuals at increased risk for MEN2 (multiple endocrine neoplasia, type 2), a hereditary cancer syndrome. The emotional impact of prophylactic surgery in such patients is under study.

prophylaxis *n.* the use of methods or procedures designed to avoid or prevent mental or physical disease or disorder. **—prophylactic** *adj., n.*

propinquity *n.* the geographic nearness of two or more people to each other, an element in the formation of close relationships. See also PROXEMICS.

proportionality *n.* in statistics, a relationship between two variables in which one changes in constant ratio to another. Two variables are directly proportional (written $x \propto y$) if $x = ay$, where a is a constant. They are inversely proportional ($x \propto 1/y$) if $x = a/y$. The constant a is called the **constant of proportionality**.

proposita *n.* a female PROBAND. Compare PROPOSITUS.

proposition *n.* **1.** in philosophy, anything that can be asserted or denied and that is capable of being either true or false, that is, the content of a typical declarative sentence, such as *Grass is green* or *Lenin was a great man.* **2.** in linguistics, a formal statement representing the underlying meaning of a sentence or sentence component, irrespective of its form. For example, the sentences *I scored the goal* and *The goal was scored by me* represent the same proposition, as would a translation of either sentence into a different language. See PROPOSITIONAL CONTENT. **—propositional** *adj.*

propositional analysis the system of SYMBOLIC LOGIC that is concerned only with the logical relationships between PROPOSITIONS as wholes, and not with relationships between the elements within individual propositions. Also called **propositional calculus**. Compare PREDICATE ANALYSIS.

propositional content the complete set of PROPOSITIONS expressed by a sentence, paragraph, or longer unit.

propositional knowledge the abstract representation of knowledge, words, or images. PROPOSITIONS are the smallest units of meaningful thought, and knowledge is represented as a series of propositional statements or as a network of interconnected propositions.

propositional network a diagram in which the terms of a PROPOSITION and the relations between them are represented as nodes linked together to form a network.

propositus *n.* a male PROBAND. Compare PROPOSITA.

propoxyphene *n.* a synthetic OPIOID ANALGESIC that has approximately half the pain-control efficacy of codeine. It is generally marketed in combination with a nonsteroidal anti-inflammatory agent, such as aspirin, for the management of moderate pain. U.S. trade names: **Darvon**; **Darvocet** (in combination with ACETAMINOPHEN).

propranolol *n.* a BETA BLOCKER used primarily to treat hypertension. In low doses it is used as an adjunctive agent in the treatment of certain forms of social phobia, such as fear of public speaking or performance, predominantly due to its ability to control certain peripheral symptoms of anxiety, such as tremor and vocal quavering. Because it produces a nonspecific blockade of BETA ADRENORECEPTORS, it should not be taken by individuals with asthma or reactive airway disease, due to its ability to constrict bronchial smooth musculature and thereby induce breathing difficulties. U.S. trade name: **Inderal**.

propriate striving the final stage in the development of the PROPRIUM. According to Gordon W. ALLPORT, who originated the concept, propriate striving emerges in adolescence with the search for identity and includes the experimentation common to adolescents before making long-range commitments. Because Allport believed in the independence of adult motivation, in contrast to childhood motivation, adolescence is considered especially significant as the time when conscious intentions and future-oriented planning begin to motivate the personality. See FUNCTIONAL AUTONOMY.

proprietary drug any chemical used for medicinal purposes that is formulated or manufactured under a name that is protected from competition by TRADEMARK or patent. The ingredients, however, may be components of generic drugs that have the same or similar effects.

propriety standards the legal and ethical requirements of an evaluation research study. These standards include having formal or written agreements between parties in the study, protecting the rights of participants, avoiding conflicts of interest by both program evaluators and participants, conducting complete and fair program assessments, fully reporting all findings, and maintaining fiscal soundness.. See also ACCURACY STANDARDS; FEASIBILITY STANDARDS; UTILITY STANDARDS.

proprioception *n.* the sense of body movement and position, resulting from stimulation of PROPRIOCEPTORS located in the muscles, tendons, and joints and of VESTIBULAR RECEPTORS in the labyrinth of the inner ear. Proprioception enables the body to determine its spatial orientation without visual clues and to maintain postural stability. Also called **proprioceptive sense**. **—proprioceptive** *adj.*

proprioceptive stimulus a stimulus that arises from within an organism based on stimulation from PROPRIOCEPTORS, the receptors that detect current body positions. Compare EXTEROCEPTIVE STIMULUS; INTEROCEPTIVE STIMULUS.

proprioceptor *n.* a receptor that is sensitive to body movement and position, including motion of the limbs. Examples are MUSCLE SPINDLES and GOLGI TENDON ORGANS. See PROPRIOCEPTION.

proprium *n.* a concept of the self, or that which is consistent, unique, and central in the individual, that was developed by Gordon W. ALLPORT. According to Allport, the proprium incorporates body sense, self-identity, self-esteem, self-extension, rational thinking, self-image, PROPRIATE STRIVING, and knowing.

propulsive gait see FESTINATING GAIT.

prosencephalon *n.* see FOREBRAIN.

prosocial *adj.* denoting or exhibiting behavior that benefits one or more other people. Compare ANTISOCIAL.

prosocial aggression any act of AGGRESSION that has socially constructive and desirable consequences, such as intervening to prevent a hold-up or rape or demonstrating against an unjust regime. Compare ANTISOCIAL AGGRESSION.

prosocial behavior any act that is socially constructive or in some way beneficial to another person or group. A broad range of behavior can be described as prosocial, including simple everyday acts, such as providing assistance to an elderly person crossing the street. Compare ANTISOCIAL BEHAVIOR. See ALTRUISTIC BEHAVIOR; HELPING BEHAVIOR.

prosodic *adj.* see SUPRASEGMENTAL.

prosody *n.* a phonological feature of speech, such as stress, intonation, intensity, or duration, that pertains to a sequence of PHONEMES rather than to an individual SEGMENT. See PARALANGUAGE; SUPRASEGMENTAL.

ProSom *n.* a trade name for ESTAZOLAM.

prosopagnosia *n.* a form of AGNOSIA characterized by an inability to recognize faces. In some cases it is a congenital condition, whereas in others it is a result of brain injury or disease.

prospective memory remembering to do something in the future, such as taking one's medicine later. Prospective memory contrasts with **retrospective memory**, or remembering past events.

prospective research research that is planned before the data have been collected; that is, research that starts with the present and follows subjects forward in time, as in randomized experiments and in longitudinal research. Compare RETROSPECTIVE RESEARCH.

prospective sampling a SAMPLING method that selects cases on the basis of their exposure to a risk factor. Participants are then followed in order to see if the condition of interest develops. A study design using this method is referred to as a **prospective study**. See RETROSPECTIVE SAMPLING.

prospect theory a theory of decision making that attempts to explain how people's decisions are influenced by their attitudes toward risk, uncertainty, loss, and gain. In general, it finds that people are motivated more strongly by the fear of loss than the prospect of making the equivalent gain. See ANTICIPATORY REGRET. [formulated by Israeli-born U.S. psychologists Daniel Kahneman (1934–) and Amos Tversky (1937–1996)]

prostaglandin (**PG**) *n.* any of a group of chemically related substances that act as local hormones in animal tissue and cause a variety of physiological effects. There are several basic types, designated by capital letters with subscript numbers indicating the degree of saturation of fatty acid side chains (e.g., PGE_2, PGH_2). Among their many activities, they influence blood pressure, cause stimulation of smooth muscle, and promote inflammation.

prostate gland a gland in male mammals, walnut-sized in humans, that surrounds the urethra immediately beneath the urinary bladder. It secretes a thin, alkaline fluid that increases in volume during sexual stimulation and becomes part of SEMEN during ejaculation. Tumors of the prostate gland occur frequently, especially in older men.

prosthesis *n.* (*pl.* **prostheses**) an artificial replacement for a missing or dysfunctional body part that is attached to or implanted in the body. Prostheses include artificial limbs, artificial joints, and plastic heart valves. Also called **prosthetic device**. **—prosthetic** *adj.*

prosthetist *n.* a health professional who specializes in designing, constructing, and fitting artificial body parts for individuals. Compare ORTHOTIST.

Prostigmin *n.* a trade name for NEOSTIGMINE.

prostitution *n.* a sex service that is based on the payment of money or the exchange of other property or valuables. Prostitution may involve heterosexual or same-sex services provided by male or female **prostitutes**. The sex service may be simple coitus, other common sexual acts (e.g., fellatio, cunnilingus, masturbation), or acts leading to gratification of PARAPHILIAS.

prot- see PROTO-.

protagonist *n.* in PSYCHODRAMA, the person selected as the central character in the drama or ROLE PLAY.

protanomaly *n.* a type of red color blindness in which the red-sensitive retinal cones do not function normally, although there is evidence that some red sensitivity is present. Compare PROTANOPIA.

protanopia *n.* a type of COLOR BLINDNESS in which the loss of color perception is in the red area of the spectrum. Red and green are confused with one another, and red stimuli appear very dim. The cause may be a deficiency of red-sensitive photopigment in the retinal cones or the absence of a receptor process required for normal perception of red. Compare PROTANOMALY.

protasis *n.* see ANTECEDENT.

protean career a career pattern that is characterized by a high degree of mobility between organizations, functions, and settings and that is shaped primarily by the needs, goals, and choices of the individual rather than any external structure. The protean career, which has become increasingly the norm in many areas of employment, is often contrasted with the traditional **organizational career**, in which an individual makes a long-term commitment to an organization in return for an implied promise of job security and steady advancement. The attributes required for success in this new kind of career include self-awareness, adaptability, and a capacity for self-direction and continuous learning. The measure of success is personal fulfillment rather than such external measures as salary, job title, or position.

protected relationships professional provider–client contacts that are subject to ethical standards regarding confidentiality of records and other information provided by the client, information about sessions, and the existence of the professional relationship itself.

protective reflex the reflex withdrawal of the body or a body part away from painful or annoying stimulation. Also called **protective response**.

protein *n.* a molecule that consists of a long-chain polymer of AMINO ACIDS. Proteins are involved in virtually every function performed by a cell; they are the principal building blocks of living organisms and, in the form of ENZYMES, the basic tools for construction, repair, and maintenance. Proteins play an essential role in human nutrition, including the provision of all of the essential amino acids that humans cannot produce themselves. PROTEIN DEFICIENCY leads to a variety of symptoms and conditions. Excess protein can cause overreaction of the immune system and liver dysfunction and is implicated in obesity. See also PEPTIDE.

protein deficiency lack of a normal quantity of proteins, particularly complete proteins, in the diet or body tissues. Complete proteins contain the essential AMINO ACIDS, which must be acquired from the external environment in meals since they cannot be synthesized by the body's own chemistry. In addition to being required for basic structural and functional processes, several amino acids, including glutamic acid, lysine, and cystine, are needed for learning and other mental activities. Protein deficiency may lead to fatigue, retarded growth, loss of muscle mass, hair loss, insulin resistance, and hormonal irregularities. It may occur as a result of a lack of carbohydrates or fats in the diet, a condition that causes the body to consume its own proteins as a source of energy. If this self-digestion process is not controlled, irreversible damage to vital organs results. See also KWASHIORKOR; MARASMUS.

protein hormone any of a class of hormones that are PROTEINS. Examples are PARATHYROID HORMONE, PROLACTIN, GROWTH HORMONE, and INSULIN.

protein kinase any of a class of enzymes that add one or more phosphate groups (PO_4) to protein molecules.

protein metabolism all the biochemical reactions involved in the manufacture and breakdown of proteins. The body makes a large variety of complex proteins from AMINO ACIDS, including enzymes, antibodies, certain hormones (e.g., insulin), and structural proteins, such as keratin, collagen, and the actin and myosin molecules of muscle. Proteins are broken down into their constituent amino acids during the basic turnover of cell proteins as well as for the elimination of toxic peptides and abnormal proteins. In case of severe energy starvation, with depletion of the body's fat reserves, protein can be broken down to provide carbon to make glucose, but this impairs normal body functions.

protensity *n.* the temporal attribute (i.e., duration spread) of a mental process or of consciousness.

Protestant work ethic see WORK ETHIC.

prothetic *adj.* describing a sensory dimension along which stimuli vary in degrees of magnitude or quantity, but not in quality. Compare METATHETIC.

proto- (**prot-**) *combining form* **1.** ancestral or original (e.g., PROTOLANGUAGE). **2.** first (e.g., PROTANOPIA).

protocol *n.* **1.** the original notes of a case, study, or experiment recorded during or immediately after a particular session or trial. **2.** a case history and WORK-UP. **3.** any account or transcript of a participant's thoughts, feelings, or ideas as verbally reported. **4.** a treatment plan.

protocol analysis a methodology in which people are encouraged to think out loud as they perform some task. Transcripts of these sessions (THINK-ALOUD PROTOCOLS) are then analyzed to investigate the cognitive processes underlying performance of the task. Also called **verbal protocol analysis**.

protolanguage *n.* in GENETIC LINGUISTICS, a posited common ancestor of the members of a language family. The most celebrated protolanguage is Proto-Indo-European, the unrecorded prehistoric language that is presumed to be the ancestor of all Indo-European languages. See SOUND CHANGE.

protopathic *adj.* denoting or relating to primary, primitive sensitivity, especially cutaneous sensitivity. See PROTOPATHIC SYSTEM.

protopathic sensation any of the most basic or primitive skin sensations, such as pain or intense warmth or coldness.

protopathic system one of the two divisions of the SOMATOSENSORY SYSTEM, the other being the EPICRITIC SYSTEM. The protopathic system carries fibers from receptors for extremes of cold, heat, pain, and crude applications of touch.

protoplasm *n.* all the living contents of a CELL, consisting of the CYTOPLASM and NUCLEOPLASM. **—protoplasmic** *adj.*

prototypal approach to classification the process of classifying abnormal behavior on the assumption that there are combinations of characteristics (prototypes of behavior disorders) that tend to occur together regularly. The prototypal approach recognizes that the ideal combination of traits does not exist in reality and that prototypes with similar characteristics can blend into one another.

prototype *n.* **1.** in CONCEPT FORMATION, the best or average exemplar of a category. For example, the prototypical bird is some kind of mental average of all the different kinds of birds of which a person has knowledge or with which a person has had experience. Also called **cognitive prototype**. **2.** more generally, an object, event, or person that is held to be typical of a category and comes to represent or stand for that category. See PROTOTYPE MODEL. **3.** an early model of something that represents or demonstrates its final form. **—prototypal**, **prototypical**, or **prototypic** *adj.*

prototype model a theory of CATEGORIZATION proposing that people form an average of the members of a category and then use the average as a PROTOTYPE for making judgments about category membership.

prototypicality *n.* the degree to which something is typical or exemplary of the category to which it belongs.

protriptyline *n.* see TRICYCLIC ANTIDEPRESSANTS.

Proust phenomenon the sudden evocation of a memory, including a range of related sensory and emotional expressions. The term is named for French writer Marcel Proust (1871–1922), who described, in the first section of his multivolume novel *À la recherche du temps perdu* (*In Search of Lost Time*), how the experience of eating a madeleine (a small, shell-shaped sponge cake) transported him in memory back to childhood. See RECOLLECTION; REDINTEGRATION.

proverb test a verbal test in which the participant attempts to explain the meaning of proverbs. The test is used most often to measure intelligence but has also been used to measure WISDOM.

provider *n.* a health care professional or facility, such as a psychologist, psychiatrist, physician, hospital, or skilled nursing or intensive care facility, that provides health care services to patients. See PRIMARY CARE PROVIDER. See also PPO; PREFERRED PROVIDER ARRANGEMENT.

Provigil *n.* a trade name for MODAFINIL.

provocative testing any type of testing in which symptoms of a condition are intentionally caused or reproduced in a patient or other person presenting for evaluation. This can be done in order to test the effectiveness of treatments for the condition, to rule in or rule out the possibility of a similar diagnosis, or, in the case of PSYCHOGENIC DISORDERS, to test the veracity of the condition. For example, provocative testing has been used somewhat controversially in distinguishing NONEPILEPTIC SEIZURES from neurologically based epileptic seizures.

proxemics *n.* in social psychology, the study of interpersonal spatial behavior. Proxemics is concerned with TERRITORIALITY, INTERPERSONAL DISTANCE, spatial arrangements, CROWDING, and other aspects of the physical environment that affect behavior.

proximal *adj.* **1.** situated near or directed toward the trunk or center of an organism. **2.** near, or mostly closely related, to the point of reference or origin. Compare DISTAL. **—proximally** *adv.*

proximal receptor a receptor that detects stimuli in direct or near-direct contact with the body (e.g., the receptors for taste and touch).

proximal response a response that occurs within an organism (e.g., a glandular or muscular response). Compare DISTAL RESPONSE.

proximal stimulus the physical energy from a stimulus as it directly stimulates a sense organ or receptor, in contrast to the DISTAL STIMULUS in the actual environment. In reading, for example, the distal stimulus is the print on the page of a book, whereas the proximal stimulus is the light energy reflected by the print that stimulates the photoreceptors of the retina. Also called **proximal variable**.

proximate cause the most direct or immediate cause of an event. In a CAUSAL CHAIN, it is the one that directly produces the effect. For example the proximate cause of Smith's aggression may be an insult, but the REMOTE CAUSE may be Smith's early childhood experiences. In law, proximate cause is important in liability cases where it must be determined whether the actions of the defendant are sufficiently related to the outcome to be considered causal, or if the action set in motion a chain of events that led to an outcome that could have been reasonably foreseen.

proximate explanation an explanation for behavior in terms of physiological mechanisms or developmental experiences, rather than in terms of the adaptive value of the behavior (see ULTIMATE EXPLANATION).

proximity compatibility in ergonomics, a design principle stating that a control should be placed next to or close to the area of the display that is activated by the control. See also DISPLAY–CONTROL COMPATIBILITY.

proximodistal development the progression of physical and motor development from the center of an organism toward the periphery. For example, children learn to control shoulder movements before they learn to control arm and finger movements. See also CEPHALOCAUDAL DEVELOPMENT.

proxy variable a variable, *B*, used in place of another, *A*, when *B* and *A* are substantially correlated but scores only on variable *B* are available, often because of the difficulty or costs involved in collecting data for variable *A*.

Prozac *n.* a trade name for FLUOXETINE.

PRP abbreviation for PSYCHOLOGICAL REFRACTORY PERIOD.

PRS abbreviation for PERCEPTUAL REPRESENTATION SYSTEM.

prudence *n.* farsighted and deliberate concern for the consequences of one's actions and decisions. It is a form of practical reasoning and self-management that resists the impulse to satisfy short-term pleasures at the expense of long-term goals. **—prudent** *adj.*

prudery *n.* the quality of being excessively modest or priggish, particularly in having a negative view of sexual matters. **—prude** *n.* **—prudish** *adj.*

pruning *n.* in neural development, the loss of neurons and neural connections that are not used or are unnecessary, especially in children. Children are born with considerably more neural connections than necessary for adult functioning, which enables the fast rate of cognitive development in children.

prurient interest in obscenity law, a morbid, degrading, or excessive interest in sexual matters. Material is only judged to be obscene if it is held to appeal predominantly to a prurient rather than a nonprurient interest in sex.

pruritus *n.* itching that may result from physiological or psychological conditions. See also PSYCHOGENIC PRURITUS. **—pruritic** *adj.*

PSE 1. abbreviation for POINT OF SUBJECTIVE EQUALITY. **2.** abbreviation for PRESENT STATE EXAMINATION.

pseudephedrine *n.* see EPHEDRA.

pseudesthesia *n.* see PSEUDOESTHESIA.

pseudo- (**pseud-**) *combining form* false or spurious.

pseudoachondroplasia *n.* a form of short-limb AUTOSOMAL DOMINANT dwarfism that is usually diagnosed at 2 to 3 years of age. Individuals have normal head size and facial features, short hands and feet, and leg deformities including bowlegs (genu varum) or knock-knee (genu valgum). Also called **pseudoachondroplastic spondyloepiphysial dysplasia**.

pseudoangina *n.* **1.** chest pain that resembles the pain (angina pectoris) of a HEART ATTACK but for which there is no clinical evidence of heart disease. **2.** chest pain that resembles angina pectoris but originates from damage to the SPINAL ROOTS in the neck (cervical) region. Compression of the root of the seventh cervical nerve by a prolapsed intervertebral disk (see SLIPPED DISK) is commonly identified as the cause. Also called **cervical angina**. See NONCARDIAC CHEST PAIN.

pseudoasthma *n.* a physical condition with symptoms and findings that suggest asthma, although no organic basis can be found. Differences between pseudoasthma and true asthma are detected during physical examination. For example, the patient generally has difficulty breathing in rather than breathing out, the respiratory attack is resolved quickly rather than gradually, and the severity of the attack decreases in the presence of distraction rather than remaining constant. Also called **nonorganic acute upper airway obstruction**; **vocal cord dysfunction**.

pseudochromesthesia *n.* see CHROMESTHESIA.

pseudocommunication *n.* distorted attempts at communication or vestiges of communication in the form of fragments of words, apparently meaningless sounds, and unfathomable gestures. The condition is sometimes observed in individuals with different types of schizophrenia.

pseudocommunity *n.* a group of real or imagined persons believed, in a persecutory delusion, to be organized for the purpose of conspiring against, threatening, harassing, or otherwise negatively focusing upon one. Also called **paranoid pseudocommunity**. [first described by 20th-century U.S. psychiatrist and clinical psychologist Norman A. Cameron]

pseudoconditioning *n.* in circumstances of PAVLOVIAN CONDITIONING, elicitation of a response by a previously neutral stimulus when it is presented following a series of occurrences of a conditioned stimulus. For example, after flinching in response to each of several presentations of electric shock, a person is likely to flinch if a loud tone is then presented.

pseudoconversation *n.* see COLLECTIVE MONOLOGUE.

pseudoconvulsion *n.* an older name for a type of NONEPILEPTIC SEIZURE in which the person collapses and experiences muscular contractions, although other signs (e.g., pupillary signs, loss of consciousness, and amnesia) are not observed.

pseudocopulation *n.* **1.** bodily contact between a man and a woman with EJACULATION but without actual PENETRATION. **2.** sexual activity in which a couple rub their genitals together, without penetration and sometimes while clothed, with or without orgasm occurring.

pseudocyesis *n.* see FALSE PREGNANCY.

pseudodementia *n.* **1.** deterioration or impairment of cognitive functions in the absence of neurological disorder or disease (compare DEMENTIA). The condition may occur, reversibly, in a MAJOR DEPRESSIVE EPISODE—particularly among older adults, in which case the preferred term is **dementia syndrome of depression**—or as a psychological symptom of FACTITIOUS DISORDER. **2.** see GANSER SYNDROME.

pseudoepilepsy *n.* see NONEPILEPTIC SEIZURE.

pseudoesthesia *n.* an illusory sensation, such as a feeling of irritation in a limb that has been amputated. Also called **pseudesthesia**. See PHANTOM LIMB.

pseudogiftedness *n.* an apparent talent in a child that develops not from any inborn ability or motivation but rather from an ability to imitate others. Thus, the giftedness is apparent rather than real.

pseudogroup *n.* **1.** a false, pretend, or artificial GROUP. **2.** a group of participants in a research procedure who are led to believe that they are working on tasks as a group, whereas in fact they are working individually. This procedure is used to study the psychological impact of group membership.

pseudohallucination *n.* a vivid hallucination, usually visual, that the individual recognizes as hallucinatory.

pseudohermaphroditism *n.* a congenital abnormality in which the gonads (ovaries or testicles) are of one sex, but one or more contradictions exist in the morphological criteria of sex. In female pseudohermaphroditism, the individual is a genetic and gonadal female with partial masculinization, such as an enlarged clitoris resembling a penis and labia majora resembling a scrotum. In male pseudohermaphroditism, the individual is a genetic and gonadal male with incomplete masculinization, including a small penis, perineal HYPOSPADIAS, and a scrotum that lacks testes. **—pseudohermaphrodite** *n.*

pseudohydrocephalus *n.* see SILVER–RUSSELL SYNDROME.

pseudohypertrophic muscular dystrophy see MUSCULAR DYSTROPHY.

pseudohypoparathyroidism *n.* a condition that resembles hypoparathyroidism (deficiency of PARATHYROID HORMONE) but fails to respond to parathyroid hormone treatment. Patients have a round face and thick-set figure and seem to have impaired senses of smell and taste. In most cases they have mild to moderate mental retardation. The disease is believed to be due to a genetic defect that blocks normal response to parathyroid hormone by receptor tissues. See also ALBRIGHT'S HEREDITARY OSTEODYSTROPHY.

pseudoidentification *n.* a DEFENSE MECHANISM in which individuals adopt or identify with the opinions, values, or orientations of others in order to protect themselves against attack or criticism.

pseudoinsomnia *n.* INSOMNIA reported by an individual who actually sleeps an adequate number of hours. The reason for reporting the complaint is often obscure and may involve a subtle misperception of sleep, dreaming of a sleepless night, or the use of the complaint as a symptom when the individual is anxious or depressed.

pseudoisochromatic charts a set of color plates used for testing color vision. See HARDY–RAND–RITTLER PSEUDOISOCHROMATIC PLATES; ISHIHARA TEST FOR COLOR BLINDNESS.

pseudologia fantastica a clinical syndrome characterized by elaborate fabrications, which are usually concocted to impress others, to get out of an awkward situation, or to give the individual an ego boost. Unlike the fictions of CONFABULATION, these fantasies are believed only momentarily and are dropped as soon as they are contradicted by evidence. Typical examples are the "tall tales" told by people with antisocial personality disorder, although the syndrome is also found among malingerers and individuals with factitious disorders, neuroses, and psychoses. See also PATHOLOGICAL LYING.

pseudomemory *n.* a fake memory, such as a spurious recollection of events that never took place, as opposed to a memory that is merely inaccurate (see FALSE MEMORY). Pseudomemory is a cause of particular concern when using hypnosis to help eyewitnesses retrieve memories (see HYPERMNESIA). It was formerly called **pseudomnesia**. See also CONFABULATION; RECOVERED MEMORY.

pseudomotivation *n.* a reason created by a person, particularly one with schizophrenia, to justify earlier behavior. The individual may or may not be aware of the inconsistencies in the excuse or may be indifferent to them. [first described by Swiss psychiatrist Eugen Bleuler (1857–1939)]

pseudomutuality *n.* a family relationship that has a superficial appearance of mutuality, openness, and understanding although in fact the relationship is rigid and depersonalizing. Family theories of schizophrenia and other forms of major psychopathology have identified pseudomutuality as a critical etiological factor.

pseudoneurological *adj.* suggesting a neurological condition. The term is generally used in reference to SOMATIZATION DISORDER: According to *DSM–IV–TR*, at least one pseudoneurological symptom must be present in order to diagnose this disorder.

pseudoneurotic schizophrenia a disorder characterized by all-pervasive anxiety and a wide variety of neurotic symptoms (persistent and irrational fears, obsessive thoughts, compulsive acts, dissociative states), with underlying psychotic tendencies (delusions, hallucinations, disorganized speech, thought, or behavior) that at times emerge very briefly, typically in response to stress (see MICROPSYCHOSIS). Pseudoneurotic schizophrenia is primarily considered to be a personality disorder rather than a type of schizophrenia; in *DSM–IV–TR*, such individuals are diagnosed with SCHIZOTYPAL PERSONALITY DISORDER or BORDERLINE PERSONALITY DISORDER. [described in 1949 by German-born U.S. psychiatrist Paul H. Hoch (1902–1964) and psychiatrist Phillip Polatin (1905–1980) and used in clinical practice and research for the next 25 years]

pseudonomania *n.* an abnormal urge to lie or to falsify information.

pseudoparalysis *n.* loss of limb movement or limb power due to pain, with no identifiable structural or functional etiology within the nervous system.

pseudoparkinsonism *n.* see PARKINSONISM.

pseudopersonality *n.* a fictitious characterization contrived by an individual in an effort to conceal facts about his or her true self from others.

pseudophone *n.* an instrument used in studying the localization of sound. It diverts to the left ear those sounds that would normally enter the right ear, and vice versa.

pseudoprecocious puberty see PRECOCIOUS PUBERTY.

pseudopregnancy *n.* see FALSE PREGNANCY.

pseudoprodigy *n.* an individual who develops an exceptionally high degree of skill or knowledge, usually at an early age and primarily as a result of overtraining by overzealous parents or teachers. Pseudoprodigies typically burn out at an early age.

pseudopsychology *n.* an approach to psychology that utilizes unscientific or fraudulent methods. Examples include PALMISTRY, PHRENOLOGY, and PHYSIOGNOMY. See PSEUDOSCIENCE. See also PARAPSYCHOLOGY. **—pseudopsychological** *adj.*

pseudopsychopathic schizophrenia a disorder in which psychotic tendencies characteristic of SCHIZOPHRENIA are masked or overlaid by antisocial tendencies, such as pathological lying, sexual deviations, and violent or other uninhibited behavior. Pseudopsychopathic schizophrenia is primarily considered to be a personality disorder rather than a type of schizophrenia; in *DSM–IV–TR*, such individuals are diagnosed with SCHIZOTYPAL PERSONALITY DISORDER or BORDERLINE PERSONALITY DISORDER.

pseudoretardation *n.* retarded intellectual development, usually consistent with MILD MENTAL RETARDATION due to adverse cultural or psychological conditions rather than congenital factors. Among these conditions are maternal deprivation, intellectual impoverishment, severe emotional disturbance, and perceptual deficits. The term may be a misnomer as it can be applied to individuals whose performance is consistent with mental retardation that may not be alleviated by educational intervention. Also called **psychosocial mental retardation**; **psychosocial mental developmental delay**. See also SIX-HOUR RETARDED CHILD.

pseudoscience *n.* a system of theories and methods that has some resemblance to a genuine science but that cannot be considered such. Examples range from ASTROLOGY, NUMEROLOGY, and esoteric MAGIC to such modern phenomena as SCIENTOLOGY. Various criteria for distinguishing pseudosciences from true sciences have been proposed, one of the most influential being that of FALSIFIABILITY. On this basis, certain approaches to psychology and psychoanalysis have sometimes been criticized as pseudoscientific, as they involve theories or other constructs that cannot be directly or definitively tested by observation (see PREDICTION; RISKY PREDICTION). See also PARAPSYCHOLOGY. **—pseudoscientific** *adj.*

pseudoscope *n.* an optical instrument designed to create visual illusions by transposing images between the left and right eyes and inverting distance relations so that solid objects appear hollow and hollow objects solid.

pseudoseizure *n.* see NONEPILEPTIC SEIZURE.

pseudosenility *n.* an acute, reversible confusional state or severe cognitive impairment in an older adult resulting from such factors as drug effects, malnutrition, depression, diminished cardiac output, fever, alcoholism, intracranial tumor, a fall, or a metabolic disturbance. This state is often confused with the irreversible state of DEMENTIA.

pseudotrisomy 18 a congenital disorder, believed to be due to an autosomal recessive trait, marked by the same general anomalies found in patients with chromosome-18 trisomy (e.g., a short neck with webbing, congenital heart disease). However, studies have failed to show signs of chromosome-18 trisomy, chromosomal translocation, or other abnormalities. All affected individuals observed have evidenced mental retardation.

PSG abbreviation for PHRASE-STRUCTURE GRAMMAR.

psi *n.* **1.** the Greek letter ψ, often used to symbolize psychology. **2.** unspecified mental functions held to be involved in TELEPATHY and other parapsychological processes that currently defy scientific explanation. **3.** the phenomena or alleged phenomena studied by PARAPSYCHOLOGY, including EXTRASENSORY PERCEPTION, PRECOGNITION, and PSYCHOKINESIS. The term is thought to be derived from PSYCHIC.

PSI abbreviation for PARENTING STRESS INDEX.

Psi Beta the national honor society in psychology for U.S. community and junior colleges, founded in 1981 and affiliated with the AMERICAN PSYCHOLOGICAL ASSOCIATION in 1988. It is the sister honor society to PSI CHI.

Psi Chi the national honor society in psychology for U.S. senior colleges and universities, founded in 1929 to encourage, stimulate, and maintain excellence in scholarship and to advance the science of psychology. It consists of a federation of over 1,000 chapters and is affiliated with the AMERICAN PSYCHOLOGICAL ASSOCIATION and the AMERICAN PSYCHOLOGICAL SOCIETY. It is the sister honor society to PSI BETA.

psi-hitting *n.* in parapsychology experiments, performance on a test that is significantly above chance expectations. Compare PSI-MISSING.

psilocin *n.* an indolealkylamine HALLUCINOGEN that is the principal psychoactive compound in "magic mushrooms" of the genus *Psilocybe,* which were used by the Aztecs for religious and ceremonial purposes. **Psilocybin,** first isolated in 1958, differs from psilocin only in having an additional phosphate group; it is rapidly metabolized in the body and converted to psilocin. Like other indolealkylamine hallucinogens (e.g., LSD, DMT), psilocin is active at various SEROTONIN RECEPTORS: Agonism at 5-HT_{1A} and 5-HT_{2A} receptors in the cerebral cortex of the brain appears to be responsible for the psychoactive effects of these drugs.

psilocybin *n.* see PSILOCIN.

psi-missing *n.* in parapsychology experiments, performance on a test that is significantly below chance expectations. Compare PSI-HITTING. See also CONSISTENT MISSING.

psittacism *n.* the mechanical repetition of words, phrases, or ideas with no understanding of their meaning. [from Latin *psittacus,* "parrot"]

PSP abbreviation for POSTSYNAPTIC POTENTIAL.

PST abbreviation for PSYCHOLOGICAL SKILLS TRAINING.

psychache *n.* intense psychological pain that is sometimes thought to be a risk factor for suicide.

psychagogy *n.* a method of reeducation that emphasizes the relationship of the client to the environment, particularly the social environment.

psychasthenia *n.* an archaic name for any of the ANXIETY DISORDERS. It is primarily still in use as an axis on the MINNESOTA MULTIPHASIC PERSONALITY INVENTORY.

psyche *n.* in psychology, the mind in its totality, as distinguished from the physical organism. The term also refers to the soul or the very essence of life and derives from Greek mythology, in which Psyche is a personification of the soul in the form of a beautiful girl who, having lost her divine lover, Eros, is eventually reunited with him and made immortal.

psychedelic drugs a name for HALLUCINOGENS (from Greek, literally: "mind-manifesting"), proposed in 1956 by Humphry Osmond (1917–2004), friend of British writer Aldous Huxley, in response to Huxley's proposal, PHANEROTHYME. Also called **psychedelics.**

psychedelic experience see HALLUCINOGEN; HALLUCINOGEN INTOXICATION.

psychedelic therapy the now-discredited use of HALLUCINOGENS (or psychedelics; so-called mind-expanding or mind-enhancing drugs) in the treatment of some types of mental or physical illness. LSD was used in the 1950s and 1960s in combination with psychotherapy to assist patients in enhancing their awareness of cognitive and psychological processes; it was also used in the management of a number of significant conditions, such as schizophrenia and alcoholism. MDMA was similarly used in the 1980s. However, various studies have revealed no lasting benefit; indeed, some patients claim to have been harmed by such treatments. These findings, coupled with reclassification of these drugs as illegal, ended the use of such agents in psychotherapy.

psychiatric classification the grouping of mental disorders and other psychological problems into diagnostic categories, as in the *Diagnostic and Statistical Manual of Mental Disorders* (see DSM–IV–TR). Classification serves the purpose of organizing symptomatic states and abnormal functioning to enhance the treatment of disorders and research aimed at understanding causes. Also called **psychiatric nosology.**

psychiatric diagnosis the diagnosis of mental disorders as currently based on the DSM–IV–TR. See CLINICAL DIAGNOSIS.

psychiatric disability chronic loss or impairment of function due to a mental disorder, resulting in severe difficulties in meeting the demands of life.

psychiatric disorder see MENTAL DISORDER.

psychiatric hospital a public or private institution providing a wide range of diagnostic techniques and treatment to individuals with mental disorders on an inpatient basis. Also called **mental hospital.** See also PRIVATE MENTAL HOSPITAL; PSYCHIATRIC UNIT; PUBLIC MENTAL HOSPITAL.

psychiatric illness see MENTAL DISORDER.

psychiatric nosology see PSYCHIATRIC CLASSIFICATION.

psychiatric unit a unit of a general hospital organized for treatment of acutely disturbed psychiatric patients on an inpatient basis. Such units usually include provision for emergency coverage and admission; treatment with psychotropic drugs or electroconvulsive therapy; group therapy; psychological examinations; and adjunctive modalities, such as social work services, occupational therapy, art therapy, movement therapy, music therapy, and discussion groups.

psychiatrist *n.* a physician who specializes in the diagnosis, treatment, prevention, and study of mental and emotional disorders. In the United States, education for this profession consists of 4 years of premedical training in college; a 4-year course in medical school, the final 2 years of which are spent in clerkships studying with physicians in at least five specialty areas; and a 4-year residency in a hospital or agency approved by the American Medical Association. One year of the residency is spent as a hospital intern, and the final 3 in psychiatric residency, learning diagnosis and treatment as well as the use of psychiatric medicines and other treatment modes. After completing residency, most psychiatrists take a voluntary examination for certification by the American Board of Psychiatry and Neurology.

psychiatry *n.* the medical specialty concerned with the study, diagnosis, treatment, and prevention of personality, behavioral, and mental disorders. As a medical specialty, psychiatry is based on the premise that biological causes are at the root of mental and emotional problems, although some psychiatrists do not adhere exclusively to the biological model and additionally treat problems as social and behavioral ills. Training for psychiatry includes the study of psychopathology, biochemistry, psychopharmacology, neurology, neuropathology, psychology, psychoanalysis, genetics, social science, and community mental health, as well as the many theories and approaches advanced in the field itself. **—psychiatric** *adj.*

psychic 1. *adj.* denoting phenomena associated with the mind. Ivan PAVLOV referred to conditioned responses as "psychic reflexes," because the idea of the physical stimulus evoked the reflexive response. **2.** *adj.* denoting a class of phenomena, such as TELEPATHY and CLAIRVOYANCE, that appear to defy scientific explanation. The term is also applied to any putative powers, forces, or faculties associated with such phenomena. See PSI. **3.** *n.* a MEDIUM, SENSITIVE, or other person with alleged paranormal abilities.

psychic apparatus in psychoanalytic theory, mental structures and mechanisms. Sigmund FREUD initially (1900) divided these into unconscious, preconscious, and conscious areas or systems and later (1923) into the ID, EGO, and SUPEREGO: The id is described as unconscious, and the ego and superego as partly conscious, partly preconscious, and partly unconscious. Also called **mental apparatus**. See also STRUCTURAL MODEL; TOPOGRAPHIC MODEL.

psychic blindness see FUNCTIONAL BLINDNESS.

psychic conflict see INTRAPSYCHIC CONFLICT.

psychic determinism the position, associated particularly with Sigmund FREUD, that mental (psychic) events do not occur by chance but always have an underlying cause that can be uncovered by analysis. See DETERMINISM. See also FREUDIAN SLIP.

psychic energizer a drug that has an antidepressant effect. The name, now rarely used, was introduced in the late 1950s by U.S. psychiatrist Nathan S. Kline (1916–1983) to identify MONOAMINE OXIDASE INHIBITORS derived from iproniazid, which had been developed for control of tuberculosis. Iproniazid was discontinued as a tuberculosis drug because of its powerful effects on the central nervous system.

psychic energy in psychoanalytic theory, the dynamic force behind all mental processes. According to Sigmund FREUD, the basic sources of this energy are the INSTINCTS or drives that are located in the ID and seek immediate gratification according to the PLEASURE PRINCIPLE. Carl JUNG also believed that there is a reservoir of psychic energy, but objected to Freud's emphasis on the pleasurable gratification of biological instincts and emphasized the means by which this energy is channeled into the development of the personality and the expression of cultural and spiritual values. Also called **mental energy**. See also LIBIDO.

psychic healing the treatment of physical or mental illness by parapsychological or spiritualistic means. See also CRYSTAL HEALING; FAITH HEALING.

psychic link in parapsychology and spiritualism, a direct connection between one mind and another, not mediated by any sensory channel. See TELEPATHY.

psychic numbing a posttraumatic symptom pattern in which the individual feels incapable of emotional expression, love, or closeness to others. See ALEXITHYMIA.

psychic pain intolerable pain caused by intense psychological suffering (rather than organic dysfunction). At its extreme, prolonged psychic pain can lead to suicide attempts. See also ALGOPSYCHALIA.

psychic paralysis of visual ideation a cluster of visual deficits comprising difficulty in spatial localization, difficulty in executing SACCADES or tracking a moving object, and a tendency for visual perception to be dominated at any one time by an object. This symptom is associated with BÁLINT'S SYNDROME, but there is evidence to suggest it can occur in isolation.

psychic reality the internal reality of fantasies, wishes, fears, dreams, memories, and anticipations, as distinguished from the external reality of actual events and experiences.

psychic research see PARAPSYCHOLOGY.

psychic resilience see RESILIENCE.

psychic seizure a type of COMPLEX PARTIAL SEIZURE marked by psychological disturbances, such as illusions, hallucinations, affective experiences, or cognitive alterations (e.g., déjà vu).

psychic suicide a purported form of self-destruction in which the individual decides to die and actually does so without resorting to a physical agency. See also VOODOO DEATH.

psychic tension a sense of emotional strain experienced in emergencies or other situations that generate inner conflict or anxiety. See STRESS; TENSION.

psychic trauma an experience that inflicts damage on the psyche, often of a lasting nature. Examples are sexual assault and child abuse. See TRAUMA.

psychic vaginismus a painful vaginal spasm that makes intercourse painful and in some cases impossible. The corresponding *DSM–IV–TR* designation is FUNCTIONAL VAGINISMUS.

psyching out techniques used to create fear, apprehension, and doubt in an opponent. The term probably originated in sport but has become generalized to numerous competitive situations.

psyching up undertaking a series of activities for the purpose of getting into an IDEAL PERFORMANCE STATE for an event, such as a competition.

psychism *n.* see PANPSYCHISM. See also SPIRITUALISM.

psycho- *combining form* mind.

psychoacoustics *n.* an interdisciplinary study of hearing that involves psychology, physiology, physics, audiology, music, engineering, and otolaryngology. It is a branch of PSYCHOPHYSICS.

psychoactive drugs a group of drugs that have significant effects on psychological processes, such as thinking, perception, and emotion. Psychoactive drugs include those deliberately taken to produce an altered state of consciousness (e.g., HALLUCINOGENS, OPIOIDS, INHALANTS, CANNABIS) and therapeutic agents designed to ameliorate a mental condition; these include ANTIDEPRESSANTS, MOOD STABILIZERS, SEDATIVES, HYPNOTICS, and ANXIOLYTICS (which are CNS depressants), and ANTIPSYCHOTICS. Psychoactive drugs are often referred to as **psychotropic drugs** (or **psychotropics**) in clinical contexts.

psychoanalysis *n.* an approach to the mind, psychological disorders, and psychological treatment originally developed by Sigmund FREUD at the beginning of the 20th century. The hallmark of psychoanalysis is the assumption that much of mental activity is unconscious and, consequently, that understanding people requires interpreting the unconscious meaning underlying their overt, or manifest, behavior. Psychoanalysis (often shortened to **analysis**) focuses primarily, then, on the influence of such unconscious forces as repressed impulses, internal conflicts, and childhood traumas on the mental life and adjustment of the individual. The foundations on which classic psychoanalysis rests are: (a) the concept of INFANTILE SEXUALITY; (b) the OEDIPUS COMPLEX; (c) the theory of INSTINCTS; (d) the PLEASURE PRINCIPLE and the REALITY PRINCIPLE; (e) the threefold division of the psyche into ID, EGO, and SUPEREGO; and (f) the central importance of anxiety and DEFENSE MECHANISMS in neurotic reactions. Psychoanalysis as a form of therapy is directed primarily to psychoneuroses, which it seeks to eliminate by bringing about basic modifications in the personality. This is done by establishing a constructive therapeutic relationship, or TRANSFERENCE, with the analyst, which enables him or her to elicit and interpret the unconscious conflicts that have produced the neurosis. The specific methods used to achieve this goal are FREE ASSOCIATION, DREAM ANALYSIS, analysis of RESISTANCES and defenses, and WORKING THROUGH the feelings revealed in the transference process. Also called **Freudian approach**; **Freudianism**. **—psychoanalytic** *adj.*

psychoanalyst *n.* a therapist who has undergone special training in psychoanalytic theory and practice and who applies the techniques developed by Sigmund FREUD to the treatment of mental disorders. In the United States, psychoanalysts are usually trained first as psychiatrists or clinical psychologists and then undergo extensive training at a psychoanalytic institute; European institutes permit so-called LAY ANALYSIS and accept other interested and qualified professionals for psychoanalytic training. All recognized training centers, however, require a thorough study of the works of Freud and others in the field, supervised clinical training, a TRAINING ANALYSIS, and a personal program of psychoanalysis. See also ANALYST.

psychoanalytic group psychotherapy GROUP PSYCHOTHERAPY in which basic psychoanalytic concepts and methods, such as FREE ASSOCIATION, analysis of RESISTANCES and defenses, and DREAM ANALYSIS, are used in modified form. The most prominent exponent of such therapy was British psychoanalyst Wilfred Bion (1897–1979).

psychoanalytic play technique a method of CHILD ANALYSIS developed by Melanie KLEIN during the 1920s, in which play activity is interpreted as symbolic of underlying fantasies and conflicts and substitutes for FREE ASSOCIATION. The therapist provides toys for the child and encourages free, imaginative play in order to reveal the child's unconscious wishes and conflicts.

psychoanalytic psychotherapy therapy conducted in the form of classical PSYCHOANALYSIS or in one of the generally shorter forms of treatment that evolved from the classical form, such as PSYCHODYNAMIC PSYCHOTHERAPY or DYNAMIC PSYCHOTHERAPY. Generally, it involves a systematic one-on-one interaction between a therapist and a client that emphasizes the importance of unconscious motives and conflicts as determinants of human behavior while helping the client overcome abnormal behavior or adjust to the problems of life. The use of FREE ASSOCIATION and therapist interpretation, as well as the development of a THERAPEUTIC ALLIANCE, are common techniques.

psychobiography *n.* a form of biographical literature that offers a psychological profile or analysis of an individual's personality in addition to the usual account of his or her life and experiences. **—psychobiographical** *adj.*

psychobiological factors the multiple determinants of personality and behavior—biological, psychological, and sociological—that are cited in the holistic, multidisciplinary approach of PSYCHOBIOLOGY.

psychobiology *n.* **1.** a school of thought in the mental health professions in which the individual is viewed as a holistic unit and both normal and abnormal behavior are explained in terms of the interaction of biological, sociological, and psychological determinants. Also called **ergasiology**. [developed by Swiss-born U.S. psychiatrist Adolf Meyer (1866–1950)] **2.** a rare synonym for BIOLOGICAL PSYCHOLOGY. **—psychobiological** *adj.*

psychochemistry *n.* the study of the relationships between chemicals, behavior (including the genetic or metabolic aspects of behavior), and psychological processes.

psychocultural stress psychological tension or anxiety and, in many cases, mental illness generated by cultural and SOCIOCULTURAL FACTORS (e.g., racial discrimination, rapid technological advance).

psychocutaneous disorder any skin (dermatological) disorder in which psychological factors are believed to play an important role (see PSYCHOSOMATIC DISORDER). In some cases (e.g., HIVES, PSYCHOGENIC PRURITUS) the disorder appears to be caused or exacerbated by psychological factors; in others (e.g., acne, psoriasis, eczema, dermatitis) there is a predisposition to the condition, which is precipitated by stress factors (see DIATHESIS–STRESS MODEL).

psychodance *n.* see PSYCHODRAMA.

psychodiagnosis *n.* **1.** any procedure designed to discover the underlying factors that account for behavior, especially disordered behavior. **2.** diagnosis of mental disorders through psychological methods and tests.

psychodrama *n.* a technique of psychotherapy in which clients achieve new insight and alter undesired patterns of behavior through acting out roles or incidents. The process involves: (a) a PROTAGONIST, or client, who presents and acts out his or her emotional problems and interpersonal relationships; (b) trained AUXILIARY EGOS, who play supportive roles representing significant individuals in the dramatized situations; and (c) a DIRECTOR, or therapist, who guides this process and leads an interpretive session when it is completed. Various special techniques are used to advance the therapy, among them exchanging roles, soliloquy, enactment of dreams, and hypnotic dramatizations. The various types of psychodrama include: (a) SOCIODRAMA, which deals with the active structuring of social worlds and collective ideologies; (b) **physiodrama**, which blends physical conditioning with psychodrama; (c) **axiodrama**, which deals with ethics and the eternal verities, such as truth, justice, and beauty; (d) HYPNODRAMA, which combines psychodrama with hypnosis; (e) **psychomusic**, in which spontaneous music is a part of psychodrama; and (f) **psychodance**, which uses spontaneous dance in psychodrama. See also THEATER OF SPONTANEITY. [developed in the 1920s by Austrian-born U.S. psychiatrist Jacob Levi Moreno (1889–1974)]

psychodynamic approach the psychological and psychiatric approach that views human behavior from the standpoint of unconscious motives that mold the personality, influence attitudes, and produce emotional disorder. The psychodynamic approach is interested in affect rather than cognition and rejects introspective methods in favor of clinical material as a basis for inference. The emphasis is on tracing behavior to its origins, as contrasted with the systematic approach (see TOPOGRAPHIC MODEL) and the NOSOLOGICAL APPROACH, which concentrate on overt events, personality characteristics, and symptoms. See DYNAMIC PSYCHOLOGY; DYNAMIC PSYCHOTHERAPY.

psychodynamic group psychotherapy PSYCHODYNAMIC PSYCHOTHERAPY conducted in a group that focuses on insight, with group members providing support and modeling for gaining awareness of previously disregarded aspects of their personality and behavior.

psychodynamic psychotherapy those forms of psychotherapy, falling within or deriving from the psychoanalytic tradition, that view individuals as reacting to unconscious forces (e.g., motivation, drive), that focus on processes of change and development, and that place a premium on self-understanding and making meaning of what is unconscious. Most psychodynamic approaches share common features, such as emphasis on dealing with the unconscious in treatment, emphasis on the role of analyzing TRANSFERENCE, and the use of dream analysis and INTERPRETATION.

psychodynamics *n.* **1.** any system or perspective emphasizing the development, changes, and interaction of mental and emotional processes, motivation, and drives. **2.** the pattern of motivational forces, conscious or unconscious, that gives rise to a particular psychological event or state, such as an attitude, action, symptom, or mental disorder. These forces include drives, wishes, emotions, and defense mechanisms, as well as biological needs (e.g., hunger and sex). See also DYNAMIC PSYCHOLOGY. —**psychodynamic** *adj.*

psychodynamic theory a constellation of theories of human functioning that are based on the interplay of drives and other forces within the person, especially (and originating in) the psychoanalytic theories developed by Sigmund FREUD and his colleagues and successors, such as Anna FREUD, Carl JUNG, and Melanie KLEIN. Later psychodynamic theories, while retaining concepts of the interworking of drives and motives to varying degrees, moved toward the contemporary approach, which emphasizes the process of change and incorporates interpersonal and transactional perspectives of personality development. See PSYCHODYNAMIC APPROACH; PSYCHODYNAMICS.

psychoeducational diagnostician a specialist trained in the diagnosis and assessment of children with learning disabilities.

psychoeducational problems problems in the education process substantial enough that some youth and adults experience significant emotional or psychological distress. See SCHOOL PSYCHOLOGY.

psychoendocrinology *n.* the study of the hormonal system in order to discover sites and processes that underlie and influence biological, behavioral, and psychological processes. It is often concerned with identifying biochemical abnormalities that may play a significant role in the production of mental disorders.

psychogalvanic reflex (**PGR**) see GALVANIC SKIN RESPONSE.

psychogender *n.* a less common name for GENDER IDENTITY or gender self-identity, used to distinguish between psychological sex identification and biological sex in the treatment of INTERSEXUALITY and GENDER IDENTITY DISORDER.

psychogenesis *n.* **1.** the origin and development of personality, behavior, and mental and psychic processes. **2.** the origin of a particular psychic event in an individual. See PSYCHOGENIC. —**psychogenetic** *adj.*

psychogenetics *n.* the study of the inheritance of psychological attributes. —**psychogenetic** *adj.*

psychogenic *adj.* resulting from psychological, mental, or emotional factors, as contrasted with ORGANIC or somatic factors. See FUNCTIONAL.

psychogenic amnesia see DISSOCIATIVE AMNESIA.

psychogenic cardiovascular disorder any disorder of the heart or circulation that cannot be accounted for by any identifiable organic dysfunction or a general medical condition and is thought to be related to psychological factors. It can include chest pain, racing heart, and tightness in the chest.

psychogenic disorder any disorder that cannot be accounted for by any identifiable organic dysfunction and is believed to be due to psychological factors, such as emotional conflict or stress. Psychogenic disorders include anxiety disorders, somatoform disorders, personality disorders, and functional psychoses. In psychology and psychiatry, psychogenic disorders are improperly considered equivalent to FUNCTIONAL DISORDERS.

psychogenic fugue see DISSOCIATIVE FUGUE.

psychogenic hallucination a HALLUCINATION arising from psychological factors, such as a need to enhance self-esteem or relief from a sense of guilt, as opposed to hallucinations produced primarily by physiological conditions, such as intoxication.

psychogenic hypersomnia episodes of sleep or sleep of excessive duration precipitated by psychological factors, such as a wish to escape from a threatening or other anxiety-provoking situation. Also called **somnolent detachment**. See also HYPERSOMNIA.

psychogenic mutism loss of speech due to psychological rather than physical factors. See also MUTISM.

psychogenic need in the PERSONOLOGY of U.S. psychologist Henry Alexander Murray (1893–1988), a need that is concerned with emotional satisfaction as opposed to biological satisfaction. The psychogenic needs defined by Murray include the AFFILIATIVE NEED, the DOMINANCE NEED, and the seclusion need. Compare VISCEROGENIC NEED.

psychogenic nocturnal polydipsia excessive nighttime thirst with a psychological rather than organic or physical basis. It is most often seen in patients with schizophrenia and is recognized as a dangerous and potentially life-threatening disorder, because chronic overconsumption of substantial amounts of water can fatally damage the body's fluid balance.

psychogenic nonepileptic seizure (**PNES**) a behavioral or emotional manifestation of psychological distress, conflict, or trauma that resembles an epileptic SEIZURE but is not produced by abnormal electrical activity in the brain. Most PNESs are CONVERSION NONEPILEPTIC SEIZURES, but they may also be associated with FACTITIOUS DISORDER or MALINGERING. Also called **psychogenic seizure**.

psychogenic pain disorder see PAIN DISORDER.

psychogenic polydipsia see POLYDIPSIA.

psychogenic pruritus a psychosomatic skin disorder characterized by a functional itching that resists treatment. Psychogenic pruritus often occurs in individuals with anxiety, depression, or obsessive-compulsive disorder.

psychogenic purpura see GARDNER–DIAMOND SYNDROME.

psychogenic seizure see PSYCHOGENIC NONEPILEPTIC SEIZURE.

psychogenic torticollis see TORTICOLLIS.

psychogenic vertigo an unpleasant, illusory sensation of movement of oneself or the environment that cannot be accounted for fully by any identifiable neurological or other organic dysfunction and is thought to be related to psychological factors. Psychogenic vertigo is common in a number of psychological disorders, including panic disorder, agoraphobia, schizophrenia, and somatoform disorder.

psychogram *n.* see TRAIT PROFILE.

psychographics *n.* in marketing or advertising, an extended form of demographics that surveys the values, activities, interests, and opinions of populations or population segments (**psychographic segmentation**) in order to predict consumer preferences and behavior. Psychographic profiling is generally carried out with proprietary techniques developed by private research firms. The information is then used in the development of advertising messages, as well as in products designed to appeal to individuals with specific profiles. Such analysis was formerly referred to as **activities, interests, opinions** (**AIO**). **—psychographic** *adj.*

psychography *n.* **1.** the natural history and description of mental phenomena, as in psychoanalysis. **2.** the art of literary characterization of an individual—real or fictional—making free use of psychological categories and theories. **3.** a psychological biography or character description. See also PSYCHOBIOGRAPHY; PSYCHOHISTORY.

psychohistory *n.* the application of psychoanalytic theory to the study of historical figures, events, and movements. Also called **historical psychoanalysis**.

psychokinesis (**PK**) *n.* in parapsychology, the alleged ability to control external events and move or change the shape of objects through the power of thought. Examples include the supposed ability of certain psychics to influence the roll of dice or to bend a piece of metal by exerting "mind over matter" (see CHANGE EFFECT). Also called **parakinesis**; **telekinesis**. **—psychokinetic** *adj.*

psycholepsy *n.* the sudden onset of a MAJOR DEPRESSIVE EPISODE, often occurring in the context of a BIPOLAR DISORDER.

psycholinguistics *n.* a branch of psychology that employs formal linguistic models to investigate language use and the cognitive processes that accompany it. In particular, the models of GENERATIVE GRAMMAR proposed by Noam CHOMSKY and others have been used to explain and predict LANGUAGE ACQUISITION in children and the production and comprehension of speech by adults. To this extent psycholinguistics is a specific discipline that can be distinguished from the more general area of psychology of language, which encompasses many other fields and approaches. **—psycholinguistic** *adj.*

psychological abuse see EMOTIONAL ABUSE.

psychological acculturation see ACCULTURATION.

psychological aesthetics a branch of psychology that deals with the psychological effects of different art forms, patterns, colors, composition, and other aspects of stimuli contained in paintings, music, sculpture, photographs, architecture, natural landscapes, etc. Certain colors or patterns, for example, may excite viewers, while others may have a calming effect. Psychological aesthetics may also be applied to the study of political, social, economic, or other influences on the work of artists.

psychological anaphylaxis a psychological hypersensitivity resulting from a previous disturbing or traumatic event. Exposure to circumstances or events that are similar to the one that produced the original sensitivity may result in a reappearance of the earlier psychological symptoms.

psychological assessment the gathering and integration of data in order to make a psychological evaluation, decision, or recommendation. Psychologists assess diverse psychiatric problems (e.g., anxiety, substance abuse) and nonpsychiatric concerns (e.g., intelligence, career interests), and assessment can be conducted with individuals, dyads, families, groups, and organizations. Assessment data may be gathered through various methods, such as CLINICAL INTERVIEWS, BEHAVIOR OBSERVATION methods, PSYCHOLOGICAL TESTS, physiological or psychophysiological measurement devices, or other specialized test apparatuses.

psychological atomism the view that the contents of mind consist ultimately of discrete and independent units of thought that cannot be further subdivided. These psychological atoms can be arrived at by breaking complex ideas down into simpler ones, until further division and discrimination is impossible. Some interpretations of structural psychology (see STRUCTURALISM) suggest that it is based on a type of psychological atomism.

psychological autopsy an analysis that is conducted following a person's death in order to determine his or her mental state prior to death. Psychological autopsies are often performed when a death occurs in a complex or ambiguous manner and are frequently used to determine if a death was the result of natural causes, accident, homicide, or suicide. Attention is given to the total course of the individual's life in order to reconstruct the facts, motivations, and meanings associated with the death. [pioneered in the 1970s by psychologists Edwin S. Shneidman and Norman L. Farberow and medical examiner Theodore J. Murphy at the Los Angeles Suicide Prevention Center]

psychological counseling interaction with a client for the purpose of exploring and, particularly, offering direct advice about affective, cognitive, or behavioral problems and reaching solutions. See also COUNSELING PSYCHOLOGY.

psychological deficit cognitive, behavioral, or emotional performance of any individual at a level that is significantly below, or less adept than, that of a typical person.

psychological dependence dependence on a psychoactive substance for the reinforcement it provides. It is signaled by a high rate of drug use, drug craving, and the tendency to relapse after cessation of use. Many believe reinforcement is the driving force behind drug addiction, and that TOLERANCE and PHYSICAL DEPENDENCE are related phenomena that sometimes occur but are probably not central to the development of dependency-inducing patterns of drug use. Compare PHYSICAL DEPENDENCE.

psychological determinism the general position that psychological phenomena, including behaviors, are determined, especially by physical and other factors outside the control of the person. See DETERMINISM; IDENTITY THEORY; PHYSICAL DETERMINISM.

psychological disorder see MENTAL DISORDER; PSYCHOPATHOLOGY.

psychological distance the degree of a person's detachment or DISENGAGEMENT from emotional involvement with one or more other people.

psychological distress a set of psychological and physical symptoms of both anxiety and depression that occur in individuals who do not meet the criteria for any particular psychological disorder. It is thought to be what is assessed by many putative self-report measures of depression. Psychological distress likely reflects normal fluctuations of mood in most people, but may indicate the beginning of a MAJOR DEPRESSIVE EPISODE in individuals with a history of MAJOR DEPRESSIVE DISORDER.

psychological dysfunction impaired or abnormal mental functioning and patterns of behavior.

psychological examination examination of a patient by means of interviews, observations of behavior, and administration of psychological tests in order to evaluate personality, adjustment, abilities, interests, and functioning in important areas of life. The purpose of the examination may be to assess the patient's needs, difficulties, and problems and contribute to the diagnosis of mental disorder and determination of the type of treatment required.

psychological factors functional factors—as opposed to organic (constitutional, hereditary) factors—that contribute to the development of personality, the maintenance of health and well-being, and the etiology of mental and behavioral disorder. A few examples of psychological factors are the nature of significant childhood and adult relationships, the experience of ease or stress in social environments (e.g., school, work), and the experience of trauma.

psychological factors affecting medical condition in *DSM–IV–TR*, a clinical category, classified under "Other Conditions," comprising psychological and behavioral factors that adversely affect the course, treatment, or outcome of a GENERAL MEDICAL CONDITION (e.g., by exacerbating symptoms or delaying recovery). The factors include mental disorders and psychological symptoms (e.g., major depressive disorder, anxiety), personality traits (e.g., hostile, denying), physiological response to stress, and behavior patterns detrimental to health (e.g., overeating, excessive alcohol consumption). A wide range of medical conditions can be affected by psychological factors: cardiovascular, gastrointestinal, neurological, and rheumatological disorders, cancers, and many others.

psychological field in the social psychology of Kurt LEWIN, the individual's LIFE SPACE or environment as he or she perceives it at any given moment. See also FIELD THEORY.

psychological intervention see INTERVENTION.

psychological kidnapping depriving a person of the free functioning of his or her personality. The term is commonly used to describe the psychological mind control attributed to cults. Compare BRAINWASHING.

psychological kinesiology the study of the behavior associated with human movement from a psychological perspective. See KINESIOLOGY.

psychological masquerade a medical condition that can present as a psychological disorder. Examples include epilepsy, multiple sclerosis, Alzheimer's disease, and brain tumors.

psychological me see EMPIRICAL SELF; ME.

psychological model 1. a theory, usually including a mechanism for predicting psychological outcomes, intended to explain specific psychological processes. See also CONSTRUCT; INTERVENING VARIABLE. **2.** a representation of human cognitive and response characteristics used to approximate and evaluate the performance of an actual individual in a complex situation, such as a novel aircraft cockpit.

psychological moment 1. the best possible moment for producing a particular effect on another person or other people, as in *He put in his counteroffer at the psychological moment.* **2.** the lived present as it is experienced. See SPECIOUS PRESENT; TIMELESS MOMENT.

psychological need 1. any need that is essential to mental health or that is otherwise not a biological necessity. It may be generated entirely internally, as in the need for pleasure, or it may be generated by interactions between the individual and the environment, as in the need for social approval, justice, or job satisfaction. See also SOCIAL MOTIVE. Compare BASIC PHYSIOLOGICAL NEED. **2.** any need from the four higher levels of MASLOW'S MOTIVATIONAL HIERARCHY. Compare PHYSIOLOGICAL NEEDS.

psychological network the set of individuals, families, and social groups with whom people interact in personally meaningful ways, whose opinions are of some concern to them, and who provide emotional support for them.

psychological rapport Carl JUNG's term for TRANSFERENCE, which he defined as an intensified tie to the analyst that acts as a compensation for the patient's defective relationship to his or her present reality. Jung saw this as an inevitable feature of every analysis.

psychological reactance see REACTANCE THEORY.

psychological refractory period (**PRP**) the period after response to a stimulus during which response to a second stimulus, presented shortly after the first, is delayed. Reaction time for the second task is increased when the stimulus for it occurs immediately (i.e., within one fourth of a second) after the stimulus for the first task. This **PRP effect** has been attributed to a response-selection bottleneck.

psychological rehabilitation the development or restoration of an effective, adaptive identity in an individual with a congenital or acquired physical impairment (e.g., through accident, injury, or surgery) through such psychological approaches as individual or group therapy, counseling, ability assessment, and psychopharmacology. The object is to help the individual to improve or regain his or her self-image, ability to cope with emotional problems, competence, and autonomy.

psychological resilience see RESILIENCE.

psychological scale 1. a scale of measurement for a psychological variable or function, such as intelligence. **2.** any instrument that can be used to make such a measurement.

psychological skills training (**PST**) a program of instruction and practice of psychological skills relevant to athletic performance, including RELAXATION, CONCENTRATION, IMAGERY, GOAL SETTING, and ENERGIZING.

psychological social psychology see SOCIAL PSYCHOLOGY.

psychological statistics statistical methods that are used in the psychological or behavioral sciences.

psychological test a standardized instrument (i.e., a test, inventory, or scale) used in measuring intelligence, specific mental abilities (reasoning, comprehension, abstract thinking, etc.), specific aptitudes (mechanical aptitude, manual coordination, dexterity, etc.), achievement (reading, spelling, arithmetic, etc.), attitudes, values, interests, personality or personality disorders, or other attributes of interest to psychologists.

psychological testing see PSYCHOMETRICS.

psychological time the subjective estimation or experience of time. This is mainly dependent upon the processing and interpretation by the brain of time-related internal or external stimuli (see TIME SENSE) but can be influenced by other factors. In general, time is experienced as passing more slowly when one is bored or inactive and more rapidly when one is engaged in an absorbing activity. Certain PEAK EXPERIENCES can produce a sense of time dissolving or being suspended (see TIMELESS MOMENT). Drugs and hypnosis can also be used to alter the perception of time. See also TACHYPSYCHIA.

psychological treatment various forms of treatment and psychoeducation—including psychotherapy, clinical intervention, and behavior modification, among others—aimed at increasing the client's adaptive and independent functioning. Psychological treatment is the specific purview of trained mental health professionals and incorporates a wide array of diverse theories and techniques for producing healthy and adaptive change in a client's actions, thoughts, and feelings. The term is sometimes used in contrast to treatment through the use of medication, although medication is sometimes used as an adjunct to various forms of psychological treatment (see ADJUNCTIVE THERAPY).

psychological tremor see TREMOR.

psychological universal a psychological feature that occurs and is recognized across diverse cultures, albeit sometimes in different forms. In 1980 U.S. psychologist Walter J. Lonner (1934–) proposed a seven-level structure to categorize ideas and concepts that may qualify as psychological universals: (a) **simple universals** (e.g., the absolute facticity of human aggression); (b) **variform universals** (e.g., aggression takes on various forms in different cultures, but it always occurs); (c) **functional universals** (societal variations that have the same social consequences, but equilibrated for local relevance); (d) **diachronic universals** (universals of behavior that are temporally invariant, but interpreted differently); (e) **ethologically oriented universals** (those with phylogenetic, Darwinian links); (f) **systematic behavioral universals** (various subcategories in psychology); and (g) **cocktail-party universals** (those things that all people feel but can only discuss as phenomena that defy measurement).

psychological warfare a broad class of activities designed to influence the attitudes, beliefs, and behavior of soldiers and civilians with regard to military operations. Such activities include attempts to bolster the attitudes and morale of one's own people as well as to change or undermine the attitudes and morale of an opposing army or civilian population.

psychologism *n.* any position or theoretical perspective that holds one or more of the following: (a) that the rules of logic are reflective of the way the mind works, so that logic is persuasive only because it "fits" the working of the mind; (b) that truth is established by verifying the correspondence of external facts to ideas in the mind; (c) that epistemological questions can be answered by an understanding of the laws by which the mind works; and (d) that the meanings of words are established by the ideas corresponding to them. The term is generally employed as a criticism of particular approaches or theories on the grounds that such positions make psychological processes that are accidental and contingent the foundation of knowledge: Because it takes the contingent to be fundamental, psychologism will be led toward epistemological relativism. This critical use of the term was introduced by German philosopher Gottlob Frege (1848–1925), whose work in mathematical logic can be seen as a rigorous attempt to eliminate psychologism. It was later taken up by the logical positivists (see LOGICAL POSITIVISM) and, from a different perspective, by German phenomenologist Edmund Husserl (1859–1938), who used it to criticize the British traditions of EMPIRICISM and ASSOCIATIONISM. The term was later turned against Husserl's own work by German philosopher Martin Heidegger (1889–1976): see EXISTENTIAL PHENOMENOLOGY.

psychologist *n.* an individual who is professionally trained in the research, practice, or teaching (or all three) of one or more branches or subfields of PSYCHOLOGY. Training is obtained at a university or a school of professional psychology, leading to a doctoral degree in philosophy (PhD), psychology (PsyD), or education (EdD). Psychologists work in a variety of settings, including laboratories, schools, colleges, universities, social agencies, hospitals, clinics, the military, industry and business, prisons, the government, and private practice. The professional activities of psychologists are also varied but can include psychological counseling, health care services, educational testing and assessment, research, teaching, and business and organizational consulting. Formal CERTIFICATION or PROFESSIONAL LICENSING is required in order to practice independently in many of these settings and activities.

psychologistic *adj.* **1.** superficially resembling psychology. **2.** characterized by an overuse of psychological explanation and jargon in dealing with some issue. **3.** having the qualities or characteristics of PSYCHOLOGISM.

psychology *n.* **1.** the study of the mind and behavior. Historically, psychology was an area of philosophy (see EPISTEMOLOGY). It is now a diverse scientific discipline comprising several major branches of research (e.g., experimental psychology, biological psychology, cognitive psychology, developmental psychology, personality, and social psychology), as well as several subareas of research and applied psychology (e.g., clinical psychology, industrial/organizational psychology, school and educational psychology, human factors, health psychology, neuropsychology, cross-cultural psychology). Research in psychology involves observation, experimentation, testing, and analysis to explore the biological, cognitive, emotional, personal, and social processes or stimuli underlying human and animal behavior. The practice of psychology involves the use of psychological knowledge for any of several purposes: to understand and treat mental, emotional, physical, and social dysfunction; to understand and enhance behavior in various settings of human activity (e.g., school, workplace, courtroom, sports arena, battlefield, etc.); and to improve machine and building design for human use. **2.** the supposed collection of behaviors, traits, attitudes, and so forth that characterize an individual or a group (e.g., the psychology of women). **—psychological** *adj.*

psychology of religion the empirical or academic study of spiritual experience or organized religion from a psychological perspective. This has involved the description and analysis of certain specialized types of experience, such as those associated with MYSTICISM, as well as an investigation of the more ordinary ways in which RELIGIOUS FAITH affects the behaviors and cognitive processes of believers. Pioneers in this field of study included Wilhelm WUNDT and William JAMES.

psychometric *adj.* **1.** of or relating to PSYCHOMETRICS or PSYCHOMETRY. **2.** of or relating to PSYCHOPHYSICS.

psychometric examination a series of psychological tests administered to determine intelligence, manual skills, personality characteristics, interests, or other mental factors.

psychometric function see PSYCHOPHYSICAL FUNCTION.

psychometrician *n.* an individual who is trained to administer psychological tests and interpret their results, working under the supervision of a licensed psychologist. Also called **psychometrist**.

psychometrics *n.* **1.** the psychological theory and technique (e.g., the science and process) of mental measurement. **2.** the branch of psychology dealing with measurable factors. Also called **psychometric psychology**; **psychometry**.

Psychometric Society a nonprofit professional organization founded in 1935 to promote the advancement of quantitative measurement practices in psychology, education, and the social sciences. It publishes the journal *Psychometrika*.

psychometric theories of intelligence theories of intelligence based on or tested by scores on conventional tests of intelligence, such as number-series completions and verbal analogies. These theories are often, but not always, based on FACTOR ANALYSIS, that is, they specify a set of factors alleged to underlie human intelligence. Among the most famous of such theories are Charles Spearman's TWO-FACTOR THEORY and THURSTONE's theory of PRIMARY ABILITIES. See also RADEX THEORY OF INTELLIGENCE; THREE-STRATUM MODEL OF INTELLIGENCE.

psychometry *n.* **1.** see PSYCHOMETRICS. **2.** in parapsychology, the reputed ability of some people to hold an object in their hands and become aware of facts about its history or about people who have been associated with it. There is, however, no verified evidence of such an ability.

psychomimetic *adj., n.* see PSYCHOTOMIMETIC.

psychomimic syndrome a condition in which an individual who lacks organic evidence of an illness develops symptoms of an illness suffered by another person, who may have died of the disorder. The symptoms usually occur around the anniversary of the death of the other person. See also ANNIVERSARY EVENT; ANNIVERSARY REACTION.

psychomotility *n.* a motor action or habit that is influenced or controlled by a mental process (e.g., a tic, handwriting, gait, stammering, or dysarthria), which may be an indicator of psychomotor disturbance.

psychomotor *adj.* relating to movements or motor effects that result from mental activity.

psychomotor agitation restless physical and mental activity that is inappropriate for its context. It includes pacing, hand wringing, and pulling or rubbing clothing and other objects and is a common symptom of both MAJOR DEPRESSIVE EPISODES and MANIC EPISODES. Also called **psychomotor excitement**.

psychomotor disorder 1. a disturbance in the psychological control of movement. **2.** a motor disorder precipitated by psychological factors. Examples include epileptic seizures brought on by stress, PSYCHOMOTOR RETARDATION associated with depression, and hyperactivity exhibited during a MANIC EPISODE.

psychomotor epilepsy an old name for **complex partial epilepsy**, a form of epilepsy characterized by COMPLEX PARTIAL SEIZURES.

psychomotor excitement see PSYCHOMOTOR AGITATION.

psychomotor hallucination the sensation that parts of the body are being moved to different areas of the body.

psychomotor retardation a slowing down or inhibition of mental and physical activity, manifested as slow speech with long pauses before answers, slowness in thinking, and slow body movements. Psychomotor retardation is a common symptom of depression (see MAJOR DEPRESSIVE EPISODE). It was formerly known as **hypokinesis**. Also called **hypoactivity**; **hypomotility**.

psychomotor seizure see COMPLEX PARTIAL SEIZURE.

psychomotor skill any ability (e.g., handwriting, drawing, or driving a car) whose performance draws on a combined and coordinated set of cognitive and motor processes.

psychomotor test a test requiring a coordination of cognitive and motor activities, as in the TRAIL MAKING TEST.

psychomusic *n.* see PSYCHODRAMA.

psychoneural parallelism see PARALLELISM.

psychoneuroendocrinology *n.* the study of the relations among psychological factors, the nervous system, and the endocrine system in determining behavior and health. It includes the effects of psychological stress on neuroendocrine systems (see NEUROENDOCRINOLOGY) and how changes in these systems affect behavior in normal and psychopathological states.

psychoneuroimmunology *n.* the study of how the brain and behavior affect immune responses. [originated by U.S. psychologist Robert Ader (1932–)] **—psychoneuroimmunological** *adj.*

psychoneuromuscular theory see MOTOR PROCESS THEORY OF IMAGERY.

psychoneurosis *n.* see NEUROSIS.

psychonomic *adj.* denoting an approach to psychology that emphasizes quantitative measurement, experimental control, and OPERATIONAL DEFINITIONS, especially in the area of experimental, laboratory psychology. The word was coined to provide a name for the PSYCHONOMIC SOCIETY, which was created in 1959 by a number of experimental psychologists who were opposed to what they regarded as a swing in the AMERICAN PSYCHOLOGICAL ASSOCIATION toward an emphasis on the mental health concerns of psychology. See EXPERIMENTAL PSYCHOLOGY.

psychonomics *n.* **1.** the science of the laws governing the mind. **2.** the science of the environmental factors that influence development. See NOMOLOGY.

Psychonomic Society a professional organization founded in 1959 to promote the communication of scientific research in psychology and allied sciences. It publishes six scholarly journals in psychology, mainly concerned with learning, behavior, and cognition.

psychonosology *n.* the systematic classification of mental disorders. See PSYCHIATRIC CLASSIFICATION.

psychooncology *n.* the study of psychological, behavioral, and psychosocial factors involved in the risk, detection, course, treatment, and outcome (in terms of survival) of cancer. The field examines responses to cancer on the part of patients, families, and caregivers at all stages of the disease. **—psychooncological** *adj.* **—psychooncologist** *n.*

psychopath *n.* a former name for an individual with ANTISOCIAL PERSONALITY DISORDER. **—psychopathic** *adj.*

psychopathia sexualis the name for SEXUAL DEVIANCY coined by German psychiatrist Richard von Krafft-Ebing (1840–1902) and used as the title of his classic work on the subject, first published in 1886.

psychopathic personality a former name for ANTISOCIAL PERSONALITY DISORDER.

psychopathology *n.* **1.** the scientific study of mental disorders, including theory, research, diagnosis, and treatment. This broad field of study may involve psychology, biochemistry, pharmacology, psychiatry, neurology, endocrinology, and other related subjects. A **psychopathologist** is a medical or psychological professional who studies the causes of mental disorders. **2.** patterns of behavior or thought processes that are abnormal or maladaptive. The term in this sense is sometimes considered to be synonymous with MENTAL ILLNESS or MENTAL DISORDER. **—psychopathological** *adj.*

psychopathy *n.* **1.** a former term for a personality trait marked by egocentricity, impulsivity, and lack of such emotions as guilt and remorse, which is particularly prevalent among repeat offenders diagnosed with ANTISOCIAL PERSONALITY DISORDER. **2.** formerly, any psychological disorder or mental disease. **—psychopathic** *adj.*

psychopharmacological drugs any medications used in the treatment of mental or behavioral disorders.

psychopharmacology *n.* the study of the influence of drugs on mental, emotional, and behavioral processes. Psychopharmacology is concerned primarily with the mode of action of various substances that affect different areas of the brain and nervous system, including drugs of abuse. See also CLINICAL PSYCHOPHARMACOLOGY; GERIATRIC PSYCHOPHARMACOLOGY; PEDIATRIC PSYCHOPHARMACOLOGY; PRECLINICAL PSYCHOPHARMACOLOGY. **—psychopharmacological** *adj.* **—psychopharmacologist** *n.*

psychopharmacotherapy *n.* the use of pharmacological agents in the treatment of mental disorders. For example, acute or chronic schizophrenia is treated by administration of antipsychotic drugs or other agents. Although such drugs do not cure mental disorders, they may—when used appropriately—produce significant relief from symptoms.

psychophysical *adj.* of or relating to the relationship between physical stimuli and mental events.

psychophysical dualism see DUALISM; MIND–BODY PROBLEM. See also CARTESIAN DUALISM.

psychophysical function a psychometric relationship between a stimulus and judgments about the stimulus, as expressed in a mathematical formula. In the METHOD OF CONSTANT STIMULI, it is the proportion of "yes" responses (i.e., that the stimulus was perceived) as a function of physical magnitude of the stimuli. Also called **psychometric function**.

psychophysical law a mathematical relationship between the strength of a physical stimulus and the intensity of the sensation experienced. Psychophysical laws were first developed from the empirical research conducted by German psychophysiologists Ernst H. Weber (1795–1878) and Gustav FECHNER, chiefly at the University of Leipzig. This work, aimed at direct scientific investigation of the MIND–BODY PROBLEM, established the foundation of psychology as an experimental science. Also called **psychophysical relationship**. See also INNER PSYCHOPHYSICS; OUTER PSYCHOPHYSICS.

psychophysical methods the standard techniques used in investigating psychophysical problems, such as the METHOD OF ADJUSTMENT, the METHOD OF EQUAL-APPEARING INTERVALS, and the METHOD OF LIMITS.

psychophysical parallelism see PARALLELISM. See also MIND–BODY PROBLEM.

psychophysical properties in Daniel Berlyne's theory of aesthetic preference (see AROUSAL POTENTIAL), factors (e.g., intensity, pitch, saturation) that are intrinsic to a stimulus.

psychophysical relationship see PSYCHOPHYSICAL LAW.

psychophysical scaling method any of the techniques used to construct scales relating physical stimulus properties to perceived magnitude. Methods are often classified as direct or indirect, based on whether the observer directly judges magnitude. See DIRECT SCALING.

psychophysical tuning curve see TUNING CURVE.

psychophysics *n.* a branch of psychology that deals with relationships between stimulus magnitudes, stimulus differences, and corresponding sensory processes.

psychophysiological assessment the use of physiological measures via electroencephalography, electrocardiography, electromyography, and electrooculography to infer psychological processes and emotion. Also called **psychophysiological monitoring**.

psychophysiological monitoring see PSYCHOPHYSIOLOGICAL ASSESSMENT.

psychophysiology *n.* the study of the relation between psychological and physiological functioning as they pertain to processes and behavior. See also PHYSIOLOGICAL PSYCHOLOGY; PSYCHOSOMATIC MEDICINE. **—psychophysiological** *adj.* **—psychophysiologist** *n.*

psychopoetry *n.* see POETRY THERAPY.

psychopolitics *n.* **1.** the study of the psychological aspects of political behavior and political structures, such as the effects of different types of system (democratic, fascist, socialist, etc.) on a society and its members. **2.** the use of psychological tactics or strategies to achieve a political objective. **—psychopolitical** *adj.*

psychorrhea *n.* a symptom of DISORGANIZED SCHIZOPHRENIA consisting of a stream of vague, bizarre, and usually incoherent theories of philosophy.

psychoscience *n.* any science that deals with the mind and mental behavior, with mental diseases and disorders, and with their treatment and cure. In particular, it refers to PSYCHOLOGY, PSYCHIATRY, and COGNITIVE SCIENCE.

psychosexual *adj.* relating to or denoting any aspects of human sexuality that are based on or influenced by psychological factors, as opposed to genetic, chemical, and other biologically based (organic) aspects.

psychosexual development in the classic psychoanalytic theory of Sigmund FREUD, the step-by-step growth of sexual life as it affects personality development. Freud posited that the impetus for psychosexual development stems from a single energy source, the LIBIDO, which is concentrated in different organs throughout infancy and produces the various **psychosexual stages**: the ORAL STAGE, ANAL STAGE, PHALLIC STAGE, LATENCY STAGE, and GENITAL STAGE. Each stage gives rise to its own characteristic erotic activities (e.g., sucking and biting in the oral stage) and the early expressions may lead to "perverse" activities later in life, such as SADISM, MASOCHISM, VOYEURISM, and EXHIBITIONISM. Moreover, the different stages leave their mark on the individual's character and personality, especially if sexual development is arrested in a FIXATION at one particular stage. Also called **libidinal development**.

psychosexual disorders in *DSM–III*, a group of disorders of sexuality stemming from psychological rather than organic factors. In *DSM–IV–TR* the category of SEXUAL AND GENDER IDENTITY DISORDERS is used for these problems.

psychosexual disorders not elsewhere classified in *DSM–III*, a residual category comprising psychological sexual disturbances not covered by the specific diagnostic categories. In *DSM–IV–TR* this category is termed SEXUAL DISORDERS NOT OTHERWISE SPECIFIED.

psychosexual dysfunction in *DSM–III*, a category of sexual disorders that in *DSM–IV–TR* is termed SEXUAL DYSFUNCTION.

psychosexual stages see PSYCHOSEXUAL DEVELOPMENT.

psychosexual trauma a frightening, degrading, or otherwise traumatic sexual experience in earlier life that is related to current emotional problems. Examples include incest or other forms of child SEXUAL ABUSE, SEXUAL ASSAULT, and DATE RAPE.

psychosis *n.* **1.** an abnormal mental state characterized by serious impairments or disruptions in the most fundamental higher brain functions—perception, cognition and cognitive processing, and emotions or affect—as manifested in behavioral phenomena, such as delusions, hallucinations, and significantly disorganized speech. See PSYCHOTIC DISORDER. **2.** historically, any severe mental disorder that significantly interferes with functioning and ability to perform activities essential to daily living. **3.** as initially used in 1845 by Austrian psychiatrist Ernst von Feuchtersleben (1806–1849), any mental abnormality, disturbance, or disorder.

psychosis with mental retardation episodes of excitement, depression, hallucinations, or paranoia that occur occasionally in people with mental retardation. Such episodes are usually mild and may recur, either regularly or unpredictably. They must be distinguished from emotional or behavioral characteristics consistent with the intellectual, social, and developmental status of the person.

psychosocial approach psychological theory, research, and practice that emphasizes social and cultural influences on mental health, personality development, and behavior.

psychosocial deprivation lack of adequate opportunity for social and intellectual stimulation. It may be a significant factor in emotional disturbance and delayed mental development or mental retardation in children. Also called **sociocultural deprivation**. See PSEUDORETARDATION.

psychosocial development **1.** according to Erik ERIKSON's theory, personality development as a process influenced by social and cultural factors throughout the life span. See ERIKSON'S EIGHT STAGES OF DEVELOPMENT. **2.** the development of normal social behavior, both PROSOCIAL BEHAVIOR (e.g., cooperation) and negative (e.g., aggressive) behavior. Psychosocial development involves changes not only in children's overt behavior but also in their SOCIAL COGNITION. For example, they become able to take the perspective of others and to understand that other people's behavior is based on their knowledge and desires.

psychosocial factors social, cultural, and environmental phenomena and influences that affect the mental health and behavior of the individual and of groups. Such influences include social situations, relationships, and pressures, such as competition for and access to education, health care, and other social resources; rapid technological change; work deadlines; and changes in the roles and status of women and minority groups.

psychosocial mental retardation (**psychosocial mental developmental delay**) see PSEUDORETARDATION.

psychosocial rehabilitation the process of restoring normal psychological, behavioral, and social skills to individuals after mental illness, often with assistance from specialized professionals using focused programs and techniques. It aims to help individuals who have been residing in mental institutions or other facilities (e.g., prisons) to reenter the community.

psychosocial stressor a life situation that creates an unusual or intense level of stress that may contribute to the development or aggravation of mental disorder, illness, or maladaptive behavior. Examples of psychosocial stressors include divorce, the death of a child, prolonged illness, unwanted change of residence, a natural catastrophe, or a highly competitive work situation.

psychosocial therapy psychological treatment with a strong emphasis on interpersonal aspects of problem situations, which is designed to help an individual with emotional or behavioral disturbances adjust to situations that require social interaction with other members of the family, work group, community, or any other social unit.

psychosomatic *adj.* characterizing an approach based on the belief that the mind (psyche) plays a role in all the diseases affecting the various bodily systems (soma).

psychosomatic disorder a type of disorder in which psychological factors are believed to play an important role in the origin or course (or both) of the disease. See also PSYCHOLOGICAL FACTORS AFFECTING MEDICAL CONDITION.

psychosomatic medicine a field of study that emphasizes the role of psychological factors in causing and treating disease.

psychostimulants *pl. n.* see CNS STIMULANTS.

psychosurgery *n.* the treatment of a mental or neurological disorder by surgical intervention on parts of the brain, for example, destruction of selective brain areas. Examples include TEMPORAL LOBECTOMY for severe temporal lobe epilepsy and, historically, prefrontal lobotomy (see LEUKOTOMY) for severe psychiatric disorders, particularly schizophrenia. Psychosurgery was most popular from 1935 to 1960 and is among the most controversial of all psychiatric treatments ever introduced. Contemporary psychosurgery approaches are far more precisely targeted and confined in extent than the early techniques, employing high-tech imaging and a variety of highly controllable methods of producing minute lesions.

psychosynthesis *n.* in psychoanalysis, an attempt to unify the various components of the UNCONSCIOUS, such as dreams, fantasies, and instinctual strivings, with the rest of the personality. This "constructive approach" was advocated by Carl JUNG, who contrasted it with what he saw as Sigmund FREUD's "reductive approach." **—psychosynthetic** *adj.*

psychotechnics *n.* **1.** the practical application of psychological principles, as in economics, sociology, and business. **2.** the application of psychological principles to alter or control behavior of an individual.

psychotechnology *n.* **1.** the body of psychological facts and principles involved in the practical applications of psychology. **2.** the application of such knowledge.

psychotherapeutic process whatever occurs between and within the client and psychotherapist during the course of psychotherapy. This includes the experiences, attitudes, emotions, and behavior of both client and therapist, as well as the dynamic, or interaction, between them. See also PROCESS RESEARCH.

psychotherapy *n.* any psychological service provided by a trained professional that primarily uses forms of communication and interaction to assess, diagnose, and treat dysfunctional emotional reactions, ways of thinking, and behavior patterns of an individual, family (see FAMILY THERAPY), or group (see GROUP PSYCHOTHERAPY). There are many types of psychotherapy, but generally they fall into four major categories: psychodynamic (e.g., PSYCHOANALYSIS; CLIENT-CENTERED THERAPY), cognitive-behavioral (see BEHAVIOR THERAPY; COGNITIVE BEHAVIOR THERAPY; COGNITIVE THERAPY), humanistic (e.g., EXISTENTIAL PSYCHOTHERAPY), and INTEGRATIVE PSYCHOTHERAPY. The **psychotherapist** is an individual who has been professionally trained and licensed (in the United States by a state board) to treat mental, emotional, and behavioral disorders by psychological means. He or she may be a clinical psychologist (see CLINICAL PSYCHOLOGY), PSYCHIATRIST, counselor (see COUNSELING PSYCHOLOGY), SOCIAL WORKER, or psychiatric nurse. Also called **therapy**; **talk therapy**. **—psychotherapeutic** *adj.*

psychotherapy by reciprocal inhibition a type of BEHAVIOR THERAPY in which emphasis is placed on the weakening of the bond between anxiety responses and anxiety-provoking stimuli by conditioning the anxiety-provoking response to an incompatible response, such as muscle relaxation. See RECIPROCAL INHIBITION; SYSTEMATIC DESENSITIZATION.

psychotherapy integration see INTEGRATIVE PSYCHOTHERAPY.

psychotherapy matching see MATCHING PATIENTS.

psychotherapy research the use of scientific methods to describe, explain, and evaluate psychotherapy techniques, processes, and effectiveness.

psychotic *adj.* of, relating to, or affected by PSYCHOSIS or a PSYCHOTIC DISORDER.

psychotic disorder any one of a number of severe mental disorders, regardless of etiology, characterized by gross impairment in REALITY TESTING. The accuracy of perceptions and thoughts is incorrectly evaluated, and incorrect inferences are made about external reality, even in the face of contrary evidence. Specific symptoms indicative of psychotic disorders are delusions, hallucinations, and markedly disorganized speech, thought, or behavior; individuals may have little or no insight into their symptoms. In *DSM–IV–TR*, the psychotic disorders include SCHIZOPHRENIA, SCHIZOPHRENIFORM DISORDER, SCHIZOAFFECTIVE DISORDER, DELUSIONAL DISORDER, BRIEF PSYCHOTIC DISORDER, SHARED PSYCHOTIC DISORDER, **psychotic disorder due to a general medical condition**, SUBSTANCE-INDUCED PSYCHOTIC DISORDER, and PSYCHOTIC DISORDER NOT OTHERWISE SPECIFIED.

psychotic disorder not otherwise specified in *DSM–IV–TR*, a category that includes disorders with psychotic symptoms (e.g., delusions, hallucinations, disorganized speech or behavior) that do not meet the criteria for any specific psychotic disorder. An example is POSTPARTUM PSYCHOSIS.

psychotic episode a period during which an individual exhibits psychotic symptoms, such as hallucinations, delusions, and disorganized speech. See also ACUTE PSYCHOTIC EPISODE.

psychotic features in mood disorders, delusions or hallucinations that occur during a MAJOR DEPRESSIVE EPISODE, MANIC EPISODE, or MIXED EPISODE. See MOOD-CONGRUENT PSYCHOTIC FEATURES; MOOD-INCONGRUENT PSYCHOTIC FEATURES.

psychoticism *n.* a dimension of personality in EYSENCK'S TYPOLOGY characterized by aggression, impulsivity, aloofness, and antisocial behavior, indicating a susceptibility to psychosis and psychopathic disorders (see ANTISOCIAL PERSONALITY DISORDER). It was originally developed as a factor for distinguishing between normal individuals and those with schizophrenia or bipolar disorders, using tests of judgment of spatial distance, reading speed, level of proficiency in mirror drawing, and adding rows of numbers.

psychotic mannerism a frequently repeated complex movement that appears to be related to or affected by psychosis (e.g., hand wringing, stroking one's hair).

psychotogenic 1. *adj.* describing a drug-induced state resembling PSYCHOSIS, marked, for example, by sensory illusions or distortions, hallucinations, delusions, and behavioral and emotional disturbances. **2.** *n.* an agent, such as a hallucinogen, that induces such a state. Also called **psychotogen**.

psychotomimetic 1. *adj.* tending to induce hallucinations, delusions, or other symptoms of psychosis. **2.** *n.* one of a group of drugs originally used in laboratory experiments to determine if they could induce psychoses, or states mimicking psychoses, on the basis of their effects. The group includes LSD and AMPHETAMINES. Also called **psychomimetic**.

psychotoxic *adj.* denoting or relating to agents that cause brain damage, such as excess alcohol, certain drugs and heavy metals, volatile solvents, and pesticides.

psychotropic drugs see PSYCHOACTIVE DRUGS.

PT abbreviation for PHYSICAL THERAPY.

PTA 1. abbreviation for PARENT TEACHERS ASSOCIATION. **2.** abbreviation for POSTTRAUMATIC AMNESIA.

PTC abbreviation for psychophysical TUNING CURVE.

P-technique factor analysis the FACTOR ANALYSIS of the time period × time period CORRELATION MATRIX, in which variables are correlated not over individuals but over occasions. Compare Q-TECHNIQUE FACTOR ANALYSIS; R-TECHNIQUE FACTOR ANALYSIS.

Ptolemaic theory see GEOCENTRIC THEORY.

ptosis *n.* (*pl.* **ptoses**) the sinking or dropping of an organ or part of the body, especially drooping of the eyelid. This may be caused by injury to the third cranial (oculomotor) nerve or the eye muscles. It is also a characteristic sign of MYASTHENIA GRAVIS and HORNER'S SYNDROME. **—ptotic** *adj.*

PTP abbreviation for POSTTETANIC POTENTIATION.

PTSD abbreviation for POSTTRAUMATIC STRESS DISORDER.

ptyalism *n.* **1.** the excessive production of saliva. Normal production of the parotid, submaxillary, and sublingual salivary glands is between 1,000 and 1,500 ml per day for an adult human. Ptyalism may be associated with epilepsy, encephalitis, certain medications, high blood pressure, deep emotion, or high anxiety. **2.** a condition in which saliva production is normal but the patient is unable to swallow the saliva as fast as it is secreted, as in cases of parkinsonism, bulbar or pseudo- bulbar paralysis, or bilateral facial-nerve palsy.

pubertas praecox see PRECOCIOUS PUBERTY.

puberty *n.* the stage of development when the genital organs reach maturity and secondary SEX CHARACTERISTICS begin to appear, signaling the start of ADOLESCENCE. It is marked by ejaculation of sperm in the male, onset of menstruation and development of breasts in the female, and, in both males and females, growth of pubic hair and increasing sexual interest. See also PRECOCIOUS PUBERTY; PERSISTENT PUBERISM. **—pubertal** *adj.*

puberty rite the initiation into adult life of a pubescent member of a community through ceremonies, cultural-lore indoctrination, and similar customs. For young males in traditional societies this may often involve a physical and psychological ordeal in which they are forced to experience pain, hardship, and fear. See RITE OF PASSAGE.

pubescence *n.* the period or process of reaching puberty. **—pubescent** *adj.*

pubescent growth spurt the rapid development of bone and muscle in response to increased secretion of growth hormone at PUBERTY. There is a dramatic increase in height and weight, accompanied by development of the reproductive organs and secondary SEX CHARACTERISTICS. Also called **adolescent growth spurt**.

public adoption see ADOPTION.

publication bias the extent to which the results of studies that are published differ from the results of studies that are not published.

publication ethics the principles and standards associated with the process of publishing the results of scientific research or scholarly work in general. These include such matters as giving the appropriate credit and authorship status to those who have earned it and not submitting for republication results that have already been published elsewhere without indicating that fact.

public distance zone in social psychology, the DISTANCE ZONE adopted by people in formal, official, or ceremonial interactions. The public distance zone is defined as an area of 3.5–7.5 m (11½–24½ ft). Compare INTIMATE ZONE; PERSONAL DISTANCE ZONE; SOCIAL ZONE. See also PROXEMICS.

public health approach a community-based approach to mental and physical health in which agencies and organizations focus on enhancing and maintaining the well-being of individuals by ensuring the existence of the conditions necessary for them to lead healthy lives. The approach involves such activities as monitoring community health status; identifying and investigating health problems and threats to community health; ensuring the competency of health care providers and personnel; disseminating accurate information and educating individuals about health issues; developing, modifying, and enforcing policies and other regulatory measures that support community health and safety; and ensuring the accessibility of quality health services. The approach involves various levels of disease and disorder prevention (primary, secondary, tertiary), the expansion and appropriate use of the scientific knowledge base, and the development and utilization of partnerships within and among communities.

public health nurse a REGISTERED NURSE or NURSE PRACTITIONER who has received additional training in social and public health sciences and services. Public health nurses are usually employed by government health departments and engaged in educational, informational, and preventive activities.

public health services 1. services intended to protect and improve community health. **2.** in some countries, health services provided by the state and financed mainly by general taxation.

public mental hospital a hospital for patients with mental disorders that is organized and run by the state, the county, or the U.S. Department of Veterans Affairs. Compare PRIVATE MENTAL HOSPITAL.

public opinion poll see OPINION POLL.

public relations a business practice associated with planned and sustained efforts to establish and maintain goodwill and understanding between an organization and its public.

public residential facility any residential setting directly operated by state or local government. Although generally referring to large institutions, such as developmental centers (formerly called TRAINING SCHOOLS or state schools), the number of smaller residential settings, such as COMMUNITY RESIDENCES, that are publicly operated now greatly exceeds the number of remaining public institutions.

public self information about the self, or an integrated view of the self, that is conveyed to others in actions, self-descriptions, appearance, and social interactions. An individual's public self will vary with the people who constitute the target or audience of such impressions. The public self is often contrasted with the PRIVATE SELF. See also COLLECTIVE SELF; SOCIAL SELF.

public self-consciousness see SELF-CONSCIOUSNESS.

public service psychology an area of psychology defined by the activities of psychologists employed by public sector agencies (e.g., in community mental health centers, state hospitals, correctional facilities, police and public safety agencies) and the psychological condition of people served by these agencies. Particular interests include advocacy, access to services, education and training, public policy formulation, research and program evaluation, and prevention efforts.

public-speaking anxiety fear of giving a speech or presentation in public in the expectation of being negatively evaluated or humiliated by others. This is a common fear, associated with SOCIAL PHOBIA.

public territory in social psychology, a public space temporarily used by a person or group (e.g., a park bench or bus seat). Compare PRIMARY TERRITORY; SECONDARY TERRITORY. See PROXEMICS.

pudendal nerve a combined sensory and motor nerve that carries fibers to the muscles and skin of the perineal region from branches of the second, third, and fourth SACRAL NERVES. It terminates as the dorsal nerve of the penis or clitoris.

pudendum *n.* (*pl.* **pudenda**) see VULVA. **—pudendal** *adj.*

puer aeternus the ARCHETYPE of eternal youth. [Latin, "eternal boy"; introduced by Carl JUNG]

puerilism *n.* immature, childish behavior.

puerperal disorder a medical or psychological disorder occurring in a woman during the puerperium, which extends from the termination of labor to the return of the uterus to its normal condition. Puerperal disorders include psychotic and depressive reactions and, occasionally, manic episodes or delirious states precipitated by biological, psychosocial, or environmental factors. See POSTPARTUM DEPRESSION; POSTPARTUM EMOTIONAL DISTURBANCE; POSTPARTUM PSYCHOSIS.

puerperium *n.* (*pl.* **puerperia**) see POSTPARTUM PERIOD. —**puerperal** *adj.*

Puerto Rican syndrome see MAL DE PELEA.

Pulfrich effect an illusion of depth that occurs when a pendulum swinging in one plane is viewed by one eye normally, but through a dimming filter by the other eye. The difference in the timing of the visual signals created by this situation is interpreted by the brain as RETINAL DISPARITY, and the pendulum appears to be traveling in an ellipse rather than back and forth. Also called **Pulfrich phenomenon**. Compare MACH–DVORAK STEREOILLUSION. [Carl **Pulfrich** (1858–1927), German scientist]

pull model a psychological theory emphasizing how positive experience draws a person to establish meaning or to set goals. Compare PUSH MODEL.

pull-out program an educational plan in which students who spend most of the day in traditional classrooms are, for a portion of the day, taken to a separate class for specialized work, either above or below the standard of instruction in their regular classrooms. See also OPPORTUNITY CLASS.

pulmonary embolism the lodgment of a blood clot or other obstructing material (see EMBOLISM) in a pulmonary artery with consequent obstruction of blood supply to the lung tissue. The clot most commonly derives from DEEP VEIN THROMBOSIS.

pulse *n.* **1.** the pressure waves caused by rhythmic contraction and relaxation of the walls of arteries as blood is pumped from the heart. The pulse, which can be detected manually at superficial arteries, provides a measure of the heart rate. The strength of the pulse at various points in the body (e.g., the ankle) gives an indication of the adequacy of circulation. **2.** an increase followed by a decrease in magnitude of a signal.

pulvinar *n.* a large NUCLEUS in the brain that forms the dorsal posterior region of the THALAMUS. It has afferent and efferent connections with the CINGULATE GYRUS.

pun *n.* an expression that makes deliberate use of verbal AMBIGUITY, generally for humorous effect. Most puns exploit the phenomenon of homophony, in which words sounding the same (or nearly the same) have different meanings. See also POLYSEMY.

punch-drunk *adj.* see BOXER'S DEMENTIA.

punctate *adj.* relating to or marked by small points or spots. **Punctate stimuli** are applied to points on the skin.

punctate sensitivity the variable distribution of sense receptors in the skin with the result that some points are more sensitive to certain types of stimuli than others. On most parts of the skin, pain spots are more densely distributed than touch, cold, and warm spots, in that order.

punctuated equilibrium a theory of EVOLUTION proposing that periods of rapid change, resulting in the development of new species, are separated by longer periods of little or no change.

pungent *adj.* denoting one of the seven classes of odorants in the STEREOCHEMICAL SMELL THEORY.

punishment *n.* **1.** in OPERANT CONDITIONING, the process in which the relationship, or CONTINGENCY, between a response and some stimulus or circumstance results in the response becoming less probable. For example, a pigeon's pecks on a key may at first occasionally be followed by presentation of food; this will establish some probability of pecking. Next, each peck produces a brief electric shock (while the other conditions remain as before). If pecking declines as a result, then punishment is said to have occurred, and the shock is called a **punisher**. **2.** the procedure of eliciting punishment using a punisher. **3.** a painful, unwanted, or undesirable event or circumstance imposed as a penalty on a wrongdoer. —**punish** *vb.*

punishment and obedience orientation in KOHLBERG'S THEORY OF MORAL DEVELOPMENT, the first of two stages in the PRECONVENTIONAL LEVEL, in which children make moral decisions based on obeying the rules of an authority figure and avoiding punishment. Compare NAIVE HEDONISM.

punitive damages a sum of money a defendant is ordered to pay to the plaintiff in a civil lawsuit when the goal of the court is to punish the defendant for malicious or evil acts and to deter others from engaging in similar conduct. Compare COMPENSATORY DAMAGES.

pupil *n.* the aperture through which light passes on entering the eye. It is located immediately in front of the LENS. The size of the opening is controlled by a circle of muscle (the IRIS) innervated by fibers of the autonomic nervous system.

pupillary reflex the automatic change in size of the pupil in response to light changes or a change of fixation point. The pupil constricts in response to bright light and dilates in dim light. Also called **light reflex**. See also ACCOMMODATION.

pupillary-skin reflex see CUTANEOUS-PUPILLARY REFLEX.

pupillometer *n.* an instrument for measuring the diameter of the pupil of the eye. Also called **coreometer**.

pupillometrics (**pupilometrics**) *n.* **1.** the scientific measurement of the pupil of the eye. Also called **pupillometry**. **2.** a research method in which pupillary responses to stimuli (usually visual images) are measured in order to determine the participant's interest in the stimuli. [devised by U.S. psychologist Ekhard Hess (1916–1986)]

puppetry therapy the use of puppets as a projective form of PLAY THERAPY. See also PROJECTIVE PLAY.

puppy love a type of ROMANTIC LOVE that flourishes during adolescence but is unstable and transient. Puppy love is regarded as marking a step toward emotional maturation. Also called **calf love**.

Purdue Pegboard Test see PEGBOARD TEST.

pure alexia a form of acquired dyslexia (see ALEXIA) in which reading is impaired while auditory recognition of letters and words and writing ability are intact. People with pure alexia are able to read a word only by naming each constituent letter aloud slowly. They are able to write spontaneously and take dictation but are unable to copy printed material or read sentences, even those they themselves have written. The condition is often associated with AGENESIS or lesions of the corpus callosum fibers in the OCCIPITAL LOBE of the brain. Also called **agnosic alexia**; **alexia without agraphia**; **letter-by-letter reading**. See also ALEXIA WITH AGRAPHIA.

pure color a sensation of color induced by monochromatic light, that is, light that contains a single wavelength,

pure consciousness awareness without content. It is a central concept in VEDANTA.

pure microcephaly a condition marked by an abnormally small cranium (see MICROCEPHALY) in the absence of other congenital anomalies. Affected individuals usually have a face of normal size and show mental retardation. They may be smaller than average in height and in many cases are affected by spasticity of the limbs. Compare PRIMARY MICROCEPHALY.

pure research research designed to answer a theoretical or academic question or to develop a theory, rather than to answer a practical question. Compare APPLIED RESEARCH; BASIC RESEARCH.

pure-stimulus act a behavioral response that does not move an organism toward its goal but whose sole function is to serve as a stimulus for other responses. It operates by activating proprioceptive stimuli that in turn initiate the appropriate goal-directed response. Also called **pure-stimulus response**. [first defined in 1930 by Clark L. HULL]

pure tone a sound whose instantaneous SOUND PRESSURE is a sinusoidal function of time. A pure tone has only one frequency component. Also called **simple tone**; **sinusoid**. Compare COMPLEX TONE.

pure-tone audiometry see AUDIOGRAM; AUDIOMETER; RANGE OF AUDIBILITY.

pure word deafness a condition in which an individual is unable to understand spoken language but can comprehend nonverbal sounds and read, write, and speak in a relatively normal manner. The syndrome is considered "pure" in the sense that it is relatively free of the language difficulties encountered in the APHASIAS.

purging *n.* the activity of expelling food that has just been ingested, usually by VOMITING or the use of laxatives. Purging often occurs in conjunction with an eating binge in ANOREXIA NERVOSA or BULIMIA NERVOSA; its purpose is to eliminate or reduce real or imagined weight gain.

Purkinje afterimage see BIDWELL'S GHOST. [Johannes Evangelista **Purkinje** (1787–1869), Czech physiologist and physician]

Purkinje cell a type of large, highly branched cell in the CEREBELLAR CORTEX of the brain that receives incoming signals about the position of the body and transmits signals to spinal nerves for coordinated muscle actions. [Johannes **Purkinje**]

Purkinje figures the observation of one's own network of retinal blood vessels, best seen by shining a bright light through the sclera at the margin of the eye. [Johannes **Purkinje**]

Purkinje–Sanson images three reflected images of a fixated object produced by the surface of the cornea and the front and back of the lens. [Johannes **Purkinje**; Louis Joseph **Sanson** (1790–1841), French surgeon]

Purkinje shift a visual phenomenon in which colors appear to change with the level of illumination. A rose, for example, may appear bright red and its leaves bright green at the beginning of twilight, then gradually change to a black flower with light gray leaves as the level of daylight declines. The Purkinje shift affects the brilliance of the red end of the spectrum before the blue end. [Johannes **Purkinje**]

purple *n.* a color that results from mixing short and long wavelengths of light. See EXTRASPECTRAL HUE.

purpose *n.* **1.** the reason for which something is done or for which something exists. **2.** a mental goal or aim that directs a person's actions or behavior. **3.** persistence or resolution in pursuing such a goal.

purposeful behavior behavior with a specific goal, as opposed to aimless or random behavior. See GOAL-DIRECTED BEHAVIOR.

purpose in life (**PIL**) the internal, mental sense of a goal or aim in the process of living or in existence itself. This concept is of special significance in EXISTENTIAL PSYCHOTHERAPY, in which it is considered to be central to the development and treatment of anxiety, depression, and related emotional states. Having a clear purpose in life reduces negative states.

purposeless hyperactivity a symptom of certain brain or mental disorders characterized by prolonged periods of excessive activity that has no purpose.

purposive accident an apparent accident that in fact was caused deliberately. It may have been motivated by psychological factors, such as unacknowledged wishes or needs. Also called **intentional accident**. See PARAPRAXIS.

purposive behaviorism a cognitive theory of learning postulating that behavioral acts have a goal or purpose that selects and guides the behavioral sequence until the goal or purpose is attained. Purposive behaviorism incorporates the gestalt concepts of Kurt LEWIN'S FIELD THEORY and contrasts with behavioral learning theories, which reduce behavior to smaller units of learned stimuli and responses. See also S–S LEARNING MODEL. [proposed by Edward C. TOLMAN]

purposive psychology an approach to psychology that makes the primary assumption that organisms usually have conscious goals that motivate and organize their behavior. See also HORMIC PSYCHOLOGY; PURPOSIVE BEHAVIORISM; TELEOLOGY.

purposive sampling SAMPLING from a subpopulation that is already known to have the same characteristics as the total population.

purposivism *n.* any approach that emphasizes goals or purposes to explain actions or behavior. See PURPOSIVE BEHAVIORISM.

pursuitmeter *n.* **1.** any instrument that measures the ability of a test participant to follow a moving target. **2.** an older term for a PURSUIT ROTOR.

pursuit movement see SMOOTH-PURSUIT MOVEMENT.

pursuit rotor a device to test VISUAL–MOTOR COORDINATION that consists of a small target embedded in a disk. The participant attempts to keep a stylus above the target, which moves as the disk rotates at varying speeds.

push-down stack a model of memory that compares its storage procedures to stacks of cafeteria trays in spring-loaded compartments. New items in memory are like trays added to the top of the stack, with other items being pushed down to accommodate them. Access to memory items is only from the "top." The model originated in computing but is now often applied to SHORT-TERM MEMORY in humans.

push model a psychological theory emphasizing how negative experience impels a person to establish meaning or to set goals. Compare PULL MODEL.

push switch a single- or multiple-button switch that can be activated by direct pressure from almost any body part and is therefore operable by users with disabilities.

putamen *n.* a part of the LENTICULAR NUCLEUS in the BASAL GANGLIA of the brain. It receives input from the motor cortex and is involved in control of movements.

putrid *adj.* denoting one of the seven classes of odorants in the STEREOCHEMICAL SMELL THEORY.

puzzle box in experimental research, a box in which an animal must manipulate some type of device, such as a latch, in order to escape from the box or to get a reward. It was originally used in 1898 in the form of the **Thorndike Puzzle Box** (a wooden box with slatted sides and a door that could be opened by the animal inside) by Edward L. THORNDIKE in studying animal learning and intelligence.

p-value *n.* see SIGNIFICANCE LEVEL.

PVS abbreviation for PERSISTENT VEGETATIVE STATE.

PWS abbreviation for PRADER–WILLI SYNDROME.

pycnodysostosis (**pyknodysostosis**) *n.* an autosomal recessive syndrome characterized by dense but defective bones, open skull sutures, and short stature. Affected individuals rarely reach an adult height of 5 ft (1.5 m), and about 20% are likely to show mental retardation.

Pygmalion effect an effect in which the expectations of a leader or superior lead to behavior on the part of followers or subordinates that is consistent with these expectations: a form of SELF-FULFILLING PROPHECY or EXPECTANCY EFFECT. For example, raising manager expectations regarding the performance of subordinate employees has been found to enhance the performance of those employees. Compare UPWARD PYGMALION EFFECT.

pygmalionism *n.* the act of falling in love with one's own creation. The term is derived from Greek mythology, in which Pygmalion fell in love with a statue of Aphrodite that he had sculpted.

pygmyism *n.* a constitutional hereditary anomaly consisting of a dwarfed but well-proportioned body, roughly equivalent to the primordial **nanosomia body type**. This body build is typical for certain groups of people, particularly in central Africa. Communities of similar small people have been described in myths and the ancient literatures of Europe.

pyknic type a body type characterized by a short, thickset, stocky physique. According to KRETSCHMER TYPOLOGY, such individuals tend to be jovial, extraversive, and subject to mood swings (in extreme cases, manic-depressive). See also CONSTITUTIONAL TYPE.

pyknodysostosis *n.* see PYCNODYSOSTOSIS.

pyknolepsy *n.* see CHILDHOOD ABSENCE EPILEPSY.

pyloric stenosis see STENOSIS.

pyr- *combining form* see PYRO-.

pyramid *n.* a bulge on the front of the MEDULLA OBLONGATA where fibers of motor neurons from higher centers cross from one side of the brain to the opposite side of the spinal cord. See also PYRAMIDAL TRACT.

pyramidal cell a type of large neuron that has a roughly pyramid-shaped CELL BODY and is found in the cerebral cortex. See CORTICAL LAYERS.

pyramidal tract the primary pathway followed by motor neurons that originate in the motor area of the cortex, the premotor area, somatosensory area, and the frontal and parietal lobes of the brain. Fibers of the pyramidal tract communicate with fibers supplying the peripheral muscles. Because of the contralateral relationship between left and right brain hemispheres and motor activity on the opposite sides of the body, pyramidal-tract fibers cross in the PYRAMIDS of the medulla. The pyramidal tract includes the CORTICOSPINAL TRACT, and the two terms are occasionally used synonymously. Also called **pyramidal motor system**; **pyramidal system**. See also EXTRAPYRAMIDAL TRACT.

pyramidotomy *n.* the surgical process of cutting the pyramidal (motor) tract in the brain.

pyridostigmine *n.* an anticholinesterase (see ANTICHOLINERGIC DRUGS) used in the treatment of myasthenia gravis. U.S. trade name (among others): **Mestinon**.

pyriform area (**piriform area**) a pear-shaped region of the RHINENCEPHALON, at the base of the medial temporal lobe of the brain, that contains clumps of STELLATE CELLS and PYRAMIDAL CELLS. It receives OLFACTORY TRACTS of the second order and input from the inferior temporal lobe, and relays impulses to the HIPPOCAMPAL FORMATION. Also called **olfactory cortex**; **pyriform cortex**; **pyriform lobe**.

pyro- (**pyr-**) *combining form* **1.** fire or burning (e.g., PYROMANIA). **2.** fever (e.g., PYROGEN).

pyrogen *n.* any agent that causes an increase in body temperature.—**pyrogenic** *adj.*

pyrolagnia *n.* the arousal of sexual excitement by large fires or conflagrations. Also called **erotic pyromania**.

pyromania *n.* an impulse-control disorder characterized by (a) repeated failure to resist impulses to set fires and watch them burn, without monetary, social, political, or other motivations; (b) an extreme interest in fire and things associated with fire; and (c) a sense of increased tension before starting the fire and intense pleasure, gratification, or release while committing the act. In *DSM–IV–TR* pyromania is included in the category IMPULSE-CONTROL DISORDERS NOT ELSEWHERE CLASSIFIED. An older name is **incendiarism**.

Qq

QALYs acronym for QUALITY ADJUSTED LIFE YEARS.

qat *n.* see KHAT.

Q data information about an individual's personality gleaned from responses to *q*uestionnaires, sometimes referred to as **S data** when the questionnaires are *s*elf-reports. See also L DATA; O DATA; T DATA.

qEEG abbreviation for QUANTITATIVE ELECTROENCEPHALOGRAPH.

qi *n.* see CHI.

qigong *n.* a Chinese health maintenance and self-healing practice that consists of coordination of specific breathing patterns with a variety of postures and body movements. Various forms are often taught as an auxiliary to Chinese martial arts.

QLT abbreviation for QUANTITATIVE TRAIT LOCI.

Q sort a technique used in personality measurement in which cards representing personal traits are sorted, by the participant or a rater observing the participant, into piles (of predetermined size) ranging from "most characteristic" to "least characteristic" of the participant.

QT abbreviation for QUICK TEST.

Q-technique factor analysis the FACTOR ANALYSIS of the subject × subject CORRELATION MATRIX, in which people are correlated with each other on particular variables. Also called **inverse factor analysis**. Compare P-TECHNIQUE FACTOR ANALYSIS; R-TECHNIQUE FACTOR ANALYSIS.

Q test see COCHRAN Q TEST.

Quaalude *n.* see METHAQUALONE.

quack 1. *n.* an unqualified person who makes false claims about, or misrepresents his or her ability or credentials in, medical diagnosis and treatment. **2.** *adj.* describing a treatment for which false or exaggerated claims are made. **—quackery** *n.*

quadrangular therapy marital therapy involving the married couple and each spouse's individual therapist working together (see COUPLES THERAPY). Each spouse may meet with his or her therapist separately and then come together as a group.

quadranopia *n.* a VISUAL FIELD DEFECT in which one fourth, or one quadrant, of the normal field is lost. **Homonymous quadranopia** is the loss of vision in both (upper or lower) quadrants of the same half (right or left) of the visual field of each eye (e.g., left upper quadranopia); it is caused by postchiasmatic brain injury (see POSTCHIASMATIC VISUAL DEFICIT). Also called **quadrantanopsia**; **quadrantic hemianopia**.

quadratic form a mathematical form that is central to MULTIVARIATE ANALYSIS. If $\boldsymbol{x}$ is a vector and A a square matrix, then the quadratic form is given by $\boldsymbol{x}'A\boldsymbol{x}$.

quadriparesis *n.* muscle weakness or partial paralysis in all four limbs due to loss of motor nerve function. This may be developmental, the result of a brain injury, or due to a disorder of the peripheral nervous system. Also called **tetraparesis**.

quadriplegia *n.* paralysis of all four limbs. It is usually associated with severe cerebral palsy, a spinal injury, or an acquired brain injury that results in paralysis from the neck down. Also called **tetraplegia**. Compare PARAPLEGIA. **—quadriplegic** *adj.*

quale *n.* (*pl.* **qualia**) **1.** the characteristic or quality that determines the nature of a mental experience (sensation or perception) and makes it distinguishable from other such experiences, so that (for example) the experiencer differentiates between the sensations of heat and cold. Qualia bear some conceptual relationship to the empiricist notion of PRIMARY QUALITIES and SECONDARY QUALITIES; in some systems, however, they take on the quality of basic or fundamental units of experience. Other thinkers, primarily those in the materialist tradition, reject the notion of qualia as an unnecessary construct with little explanatory value. **2.** the phenomenal, conscious state or feeling specific to each emotion. The ineffable phenomenal states of anger, happiness, fear, sadness, and so on are qualia of AFFECT.

qualitative data data that are not expressed numerically, such as descriptions of behavior and experience. If desired, qualitative data can often be expressed quantitatively. Compare QUANTITATIVE DATA.

qualitative evaluation an evaluation method that yields narratives gathered primarily from unstructured methods of data collection, naturalistic observation, and existing records. As an initial or divergent phase of PROGRAM EVALUATION, it seeks to allow maximum opportunity to frame EVALUATION OBJECTIVES. This approach is usually associated with a GOAL-FREE EVALUATION rather than a GOAL-BASED EVALUATION. Compare QUANTITATIVE EVALUATION.

qualitative research an approach to science that does not employ the quantification (expression in numerical form) of the observations made.

qualitative versus quantitative differences the debate concerning the degree to which a process, such as development, reflects changes (e.g., in cognition) in type or kind (qualitative) as opposed to amount or rate (quantitative).

quality *n.* a characteristic of a sensation or other entity that makes it unique. Quality denotes a difference in kind rather than in quantity, as between various sounds of the same note played on different instruments, which produces a different distribution of overtones, as opposed to the quantity or volume of the sound. Also called **sense quality**. See PRIMARY QUALITY; SECONDARY QUALITY. See also QUALE.

quality adjusted life years (**QALYs**) a measure that combines the quantity of life, expressed in terms of survival or life expectancy, with the quality of life. The value of a year of perfect health is taken as 1; a year of ill health is worth less than 1. The measure provides a method to assess the benefits to be gained from medical procedures and interventions.

quality assurance in health administration, a systematic process used to improve the quality of health care services; it involves evaluating them in terms of effectiveness, appropriateness, acceptability, adequacy of diagnostic evaluation, length of stay, and outcome.

quality circle a form of PARTICIPATIVE MANAGEMENT in which a small group of employees are given the task of improving the quality and reducing the costs of the goods or services produced in their jobs and resolving any other production and productivity problems. Employees in a quality circle are typically given autonomy in how they approach this task and may be trained in STATISTICAL PROCESS CONTROL. See also SCANLON PLAN.

quality control processes associated with manufacturing or packaging that are designed to reduce the number of defective products.

quality of care the extent to which health services are consistent with professional standards and increase the likelihood of desired outcomes.

quality of life the extent to which a person obtains satisfaction from life. The following are important for a good quality of life: emotional, material, and physical well-being; engagement in interpersonal relations; opportunities for personal (e.g., skill) development; exercising rights and making self-determining lifestyle choices; and participation in society. Enhancing quality of life is a particular concern for those with chronic disease or developmental and other disabilities and for those undergoing medical or psychological treatment.

quality of worklife (**QWL**) an area of theory, research, and application associated with industrial and organizational psychology and specifically concerned with enhancing employees' WORK MOTIVATION, JOB SATISFACTION, and ORGANIZATIONAL COMMITMENT by implementing policies of PARTICIPATIVE MANAGEMENT and JOB ENRICHMENT.

quality weighting the WEIGHTING of each of the studies in a META-ANALYSIS by the quality of its design, execution, and analysis.

quantal hypothesis (**quantal theory**) see NEURAL QUANTUM THEORY.

quantifier *n.* in linguistics, a DETERMINER used to express the notion of quantity, such as *many, most, some,* or *all.*

quantitative approach Sigmund FREUD's theory that mental processes, such as tensions, obsessions, pleasure, and unpleasure, differ in the quantity as well as quality of PSYCHIC ENERGY associated with them. Even though the amounts cannot be measured as exactly as in the physical sciences, they nevertheless are posited to exist: For example, the amount of tension existing in the psyche at one time can be compared with the amount at another time. See also ECONOMIC MODEL.

quantitative data data expressed numerically, such as test scores or measurements of length or width. Compare QUALITATIVE DATA.

quantitative electroencephalograph (**qEEG**) a version of the electroencephalograph that generates numerical results that can be statistically analyzed. See ELECTROENCEPHALOGRAPHY.

quantitative evaluation an evaluation method that yields numerical indices gathered primarily from formal (objective) methods of data collection, systematic and controlled observation, and a prescribed research design. As a final or convergent phase of PROGRAM EVALUATION, it seeks to provide precise answers to already defined EVALUATION OBJECTIVES. This approach is usually associated with a GOAL-BASED EVALUATION rather than a GOAL-FREE EVALUATION. Compare QUALITATIVE EVALUATION.

quantitative genetics the field of genetics that studies traits that differ in degree rather than in kind.

quantitative research an approach to science that employs the quantification (expression in numerical form) of the observations made.

quantitative score a number that represents the quantity or number of correctly fulfilled requirements for a given test or class.

quantitative semantics see CONTENT ANALYSIS.

quantitative trait loci (**QTL**) locations in the GENOME containing a number of genes that contribute to genetic variation in a given trait.

quantum *n.* (*pl.* **quanta**) **1.** in physics, a unit of radiant energy. **2.** in neuroscience, the minimal amount of neurotransmitter released by a neuron at a given time.

quantum hypothesis of consciousness an extension of NEURAL QUANTUM THEORY that quantum-level neuronal events are a crucial aspect of consciousness.

quantum theory see NEURAL QUANTUM THEORY.

quartile *n.* one fourth of a DISTRIBUTION of scores. For example, the first quartile of a distribution would be the lowest 25% of scores, the second quartile would range from 26% to 50%, and so on.

quartile deviation a measure of DISPERSION defined as half the distance between the first and third QUARTILES (i.e., half the interquartile range).

quartimax rotation in FACTOR ANALYSIS, an ORTHOGONAL ROTATION that maximizes the variance across the rows of the factor matrix.

quasi-control subjects research participants who are asked to reflect on the context in which an experiment is conducted and to speculate on the ways in which the context may influence their own and other participants' behaviors.

quasi-experimental design an experimental design in which assignment of participants to experimental or control groups cannot be made at random. A study using this design is called a **quasi experiment**.

quasi-experimental research research in which the investigator cannot control or manipulate the INDEPENDENT VARIABLE but can determine how the DEPENDENT VARIABLE is measured. Examples of quasi-experimental research are studies that deal with the responses of large groups to such variables as natural disasters or widespread changes in social policy. Also called **nonexperimental research**.

quasi-F ratio in the ANALYSIS OF VARIANCE, an F RATIO that must be formed by construction of the ERROR TERM as the weighted sum of several components of variance.

quasi group a collective with some, but not all, of the defining features of a true GROUP.

quasi need in the social psychology of Kurt LEWIN, a tension state that initiates goal-directed activity with an origin in intent or purpose rather than a biological deficit.

quaternity *n.* Carl JUNG's fourfold concept of personality, in which there are four functions of the ego: feeling, thinking, intuiting, and sensing (see FUNCTIONAL TYPES). For Jung, the quaternity is an ARCHETYPE exemplified in myriad ways, such as the four points of the compass and the four points of the cross.

quazepam *n.* a BENZODIAZEPINE used as a HYPNOTIC agent. It is of medium potency and is highly lipid soluble, enabling rapid penetration of the BLOOD–BRAIN BARRIER resulting in rapid onset of effects. Because its metabolic products are eliminated slowly, quazepam may accumulate in the body, leading to unwanted daytime sedation. U.S. trade name: **Doral**.

queer *adj., n.* controversial slang, in the main pejorative, referring (in both the adjectival and noun senses) to gays and lesbians or relating to same-sex sexual orientation. The original and still common use of the word, to describe anything that is unusual in an odd or strange way, was extended to refer to gays in the late 19th and throughout much of the 20th century, when it acquired a predominantly negative, derogatory connotation. During the late 1960s and onward (see SEXUAL REVOLUTION), it was appropriated by some members within the gay community as a term of identification that carried no negative connotation and, indeed, took on the role of a label of pride and self-respect. This usage is not embraced, however, by all members of the gay community.

querulent *adj.* quarrelsome, complaining, irritable, and suspicious. These qualities are frequently associated with a paranoid state and a tendency toward litigiousness. See also LITIGIOUS PARANOIA.

question begging see BEGGING THE QUESTION. See also CIRCULAR REASONING; THEORY BEGGING.

questionnaire *n.* a list of questions asked to obtain information about a topic of interest, such as an individual's lifestyle, attitudes, and other behaviors or characteristics.

quetiapine *n.* an ATYPICAL ANTIPSYCHOTIC used for the management of psychosis and schizophrenia. Like the conventional antipsychotics, its therapeutic effects are in part related to its ability to block D2 dopamine receptors (see DOPAMINE-RECEPTOR ANTAGONISTS); however, it differs from the older agents in its ability to also block 5-HT_2 SEROTONIN RECEPTORS. Sedation is a common adverse effect; thyroid dysfunction, weight gain, and ELECTROCARDIOGRAPHIC EFFECTS are more rarely observed. U.S. trade name: **Seroquel**.

queue *n.* a file of people who are waiting for some service, commodity, or opportunity. Although the members of the queue are often strangers who will likely not meet again, they nonetheless comply with social norms that determine the order in which members will receive service.

Quick Test (**QT**) a 50-item intelligence test used for screening purposes and for individuals with severe disabilities, who may respond to test items by pointing or nodding without using words. Participants are presented with a set of four black-and-white drawings and must indicate which one best represents a target word. The words vary from "easy" to "hard" and each has an assigned approximate difficulty level. [developed in 1962 by U.S. psychologists Robert Bruce Ammons (1920–1999) and Carol H. Ammons (1927–)]

quick trajectory see TRAJECTORIES OF DYING.

quid pro quo an advantage given in return for something done or promised (from Latin, literally: "one thing for another"). The phrase has come to be associated with a form of SEXUAL HARASSMENT in which sexual demands are made with the explicit or implicit suggestion that compliance will have positive employment consequences (e.g., promotion), while failure to comply could have the opposite effect (e.g., termination of employment).

Quincke's disease see ANGIONEUROTIC EDEMA. [Heinrich Irenaeus **Quincke** (1842–1922), German physician]

quintile *n.* one fifth of a distribution of scores. For example, the first quintile would be the lowest 20% of scores.

quota sampling a method of selecting participants for a study in which a prespecified number of individuals with specific background characteristics, such as a particular age, race, sex, or education, is selected in order to obtain a sample with the same proportional representation of these characteristics as the target population. Also called **quota control**.

quotient hypothesis an adaptation of WEBER'S LAW suggesting that the quotients or ratios of two successive DIFFERENCE THRESHOLDS in a given sensory series are equal.

QWL abbreviation for QUALITY OF WORKLIFE.

Rr

r symbol for PRODUCT-MOMENT CORRELATION.

$\mathbf{r}^2$ symbol for COEFFICIENT OF DETERMINATION.

$\mathbf{r}_{\mathbf{alerting}}$ symbol for ALERTING CORRELATION.

$\mathbf{r}_{\mathbf{contrast}}$ symbol for CONTRAST CORRELATION.

$\mathbf{r}_{\mathbf{effect\ size}}$ symbol for EFFECT-SIZE CORRELATION.

R 1. abbreviation for RESPONSE. **2.** symbol for MULTIPLE CORRELATION. **3.** see PRIMARY ABILITIES.

rabbit–duck figure an ambiguous figure that produces the appearance of the head of a duck or the head of a rabbit, but never both simultaneously.

rabies *n.* an infectious viral disease that can be transmitted from animals to humans. It is usually transmitted through the bite of an infected animal, although the virus may enter through any break in the skin. The virus travels along nerve fibers until it reaches the brain, causing pain, fever, excessive salivation, agitation, confusion, hallucinations, and paralysis or contractions of muscles, particularly those of the respiratory tract. Aversion to water is a major symptom, especially in later stages of the disease. This is due to painful spasms associated with the swallowing reflex. Unless antirabies vaccine is given before the virus reaches the brain and symptoms appear, the infection causes death within 2–10 days. Rabies was previously called **hydrophobia**.

rabies encephalitis a viral inflammation of the brain transmitted by the bite of a rabid animal (see RABIES).

race *n.* a socially defined concept sometimes used to designate a portion, or "subdivision," of the human population with common physical characteristics, ancestry, or language. The term is also loosely applied to geographic, cultural, religious, or national groups. The significance often accorded to racial categories might suggest that such groups are objectively defined and homogeneous; however, there is much heterogeneity within categories, and the categories themselves differ across cultures. Moreover, self-reported race frequently varies owing to changing social contexts and an individual's identification with more than one race. See also ETHNIC GROUP; ETHNIC IDENTITY; RACISM. **—racial** *adj.*

race norming in personnel selection, a type of AFFIRMATIVE ACTION in which different cutoff scores are determined for applicants from different ethnic groups. Race norming has been declared illegal in U.S. federal civil-rights legislation. See also BANDING.

race psychology an obsolete area of comparative psychology, which attempted the empirical study of RACIAL AND ETHNIC DIFFERENCES.

rachischisis *n.* a congenital fissure of the spinal column, as in SPINA BIFIDA.

racial and ethnic differences variation between two or more racial or ethnic groups on a variable of interest. Empirical studies have failed to show any innate differences between ethnic groups in terms of intelligence, character traits, or sensory acuity; a review of literature by U.S. psychologist Richard Nisbett (1941–) suggests that the preponderance of evidence supports an environmental interpretation of any racial or ethnic differences. See also RACE PSYCHOLOGY.

racial discrimination the differential treatment of individuals because of their membership in a racial group. Discrimination is in most cases the behavioral manifestation of PREJUDICE and therefore involves less favorable, negative, hostile, or injurious treatment of the members of rejected groups. See also RACISM.

racial identity an individual's sense of being a person whose identity is defined, in part, by membership of a particular RACE. The strength of this sense will depend on the extent to which an individual has processed and internalized the psychological, sociopolitical, cultural, and other contextual factors related to membership of the group. See also ETHNIC IDENTITY.

racial memory thought patterns, feelings, and traces of experiences held to be transmitted from generation to generation and to have a basic influence on individual minds and behavior. Carl JUNG and Sigmund FREUD both embraced the concept of a phylogenetic heritage (see PHYLOGENY), but focused on different examples. Freud cited religious rituals designed to relieve feelings of anxiety and guilt, which he explained in terms of the OEDIPUS COMPLEX and his PRIMAL-HORDE THEORY. Jung cited images, symbols, and personifications that spontaneously appear in different cultures, which he explained in terms of the ARCHETYPES of the COLLECTIVE UNCONSCIOUS. Also called **racial unconscious**.

racial prejudice see PREJUDICE.

racial unconscious see RACIAL MEMORY.

racism *n.* a form of PREJUDICE that assumes that the members of racial categories have distinctive characteristics and that these differences result in some racial groups being inferior to others. Racism generally includes negative emotional reactions to members of the group, acceptance of NEGATIVE STEREOTYPES, and RACIAL DISCRIMINATION against individuals; in some cases it leads to violence. See AVERSIVE RACISM; EVERYDAY RACISM; INSTITUTIONALIZED RACISM; MODERN RACISM. See also ETHNOCENTRISM. **—racist** *adj., n.*

radex theory of intelligence a PSYCHOMETRIC THEORY OF INTELLIGENCE postulating that the organization of mental abilities forms a radial order of complexity (or **radex**). The radex comprises two parts: (a) a simplex, which is the relative distance from the center of a circle, with abilities that are closer to the center of the circle therefore being closer to the construct of general intelligence, which is at dead center; and (b) a circumplex, which is the relative distance around the circle, with abilities that are more highly correlated therefore being located closer to each other. Thus the system identifies abilities through a set of polar coordinates (rather than the Cartesian coordinates used by other systems). [proposed by U.S. psychologist Louis Guttman (1916–1997)]

radial glial cells cells of the NEUROGLIA that form early in development, spanning the width of the emerging cerebral hemispheres to guide migrating neurons.

radial maze a type of maze that has a central starting point with several arms (typically six to eight) extending from the center. A nonhuman animal might be required to learn to find food in only certain of the arms or to search systematically through each arm without entering the same arm twice. Radial mazes have been used extensively to study SPATIAL MEMORY and learning.

radial nerve the combined sensory and motor nerve that innervates the medial (inner) side of the forearm and hand, including the thumb. Its fibers are derived from the fifth through eighth cervical SPINAL NERVES and the first thoracic spinal nerve and they pass through the BRACHIAL PLEXUS.

radiation *n.* **1.** energy transmitted in the form of waves, such as electromagnetic radiation (e.g., heat, light, microwaves, short radio waves, ultraviolet rays, or X-rays), or in the form of a stream of nuclear particles (e.g., alpha particles, beta particles, gamma rays, electrons, neutrons, or protons). Such waves or particles are used for diagnostic, therapeutic, or experimental purposes (see RADIATION THERAPY). **2.** in neuroscience, the spread of excitation to adjacent neurons. **3.** more generally, the outward spread of something from a central point.

radiation necrosis tissue death due to exposure to harmful radiation.

radiation therapy the use of RADIATION (e.g., X-rays) in the treatment of diseases. Radiotherapy is used mainly in the destruction of cancer cells by implanting RADIOACTIVE ISOTOPES in the body of the patient or delivering a known dose of radiation to a specific tissue area. Side effects may include fatigue, soreness and redness of the irradiated area, nausea and vomiting, loss of appetite, and a decreased white blood cell count. Also called **radiotherapy**.

radical behaviorism the view that behavior, rather than consciousness and its contents, should be the proper topic for study in psychological science. This term is often used to distinguish classical BEHAVIORISM, as originally formulated in 1913 by John B. WATSON, from more moderate forms of NEOBEHAVIORISM. However, it has evolved to denote as well the form of behaviorism later proposed by B. F. SKINNER, which emphasized the importance of reinforcement and its relationship to behavior (i.e., the environmental determinants of behavior). Skinner conceded the existence of private events, such as thinking, feeling, and imagining, but believed them to be irrelevant, viewing them not as causes of behavior but as more behavior in need of explanation or as private stimuli that function according to the same laws as public stimuli. See BEHAVIOR ANALYSIS; DESCRIPTIVE BEHAVIORISM.

radical empiricism **1.** a metaphysical position propounded by William JAMES in 1904: It holds that reality consists not of subject and object (mind and matter) but of pure experience. The position is therefore one of NEUTRAL MONISM. **2.** the associated position, also propounded by William James, that the whole of human experience is the legitimate domain for psychological investigation. This was in contrast to the tendency of certain schools of psychology, such as STRUCTURALISM, to define the subject much more narrowly. The methodological implication of radical empiricism is that psychology should not be restricted to a single method, but that it should employ methods appropriate to the study of any phenomenon that forms part of human experience. **3.** the general position that (a) empirical methods provide the only reliable sources of knowledge and (b) that only propositions that can be tested by such methods have real meaning. See EMPIRICISM; LOGICAL POSITIVISM; POSITIVISM.

radical feminism a branch of feminist thought, very influential in the late 20th century, that holds as its main tenets that: (a) the oppression of women is pandemic, the most fundamental of all historical instances of oppression, and thus a paradigm case of oppression; (b) since the oppression of women is systemic and ubiquitous, sweeping social change is the only remedy radical enough to overcome it; (c) traditional gender roles are constraining to both sexes and ought to be overcome; (d) biology should not determine the destiny or shape the lives of women; and (e) consciousness raising, in which women come to see their personal problems as symptomatic, is the beginning of liberation. These tenets have been adopted in one form or another by many subsequent strains of FEMINISM.

radical hysterectomy see HYSTERECTOMY.

radicalism *n.* **1.** any position that goes to the heart of an idea or issue. A radical criticism is one that strikes at the most fundamental aspect of its target; a radical theory is one that challenges the fundamental assumptions and implications of rival theories. **2.** a political or social position that calls for extreme or fundamental change to remedy a perceived problem. Compare REFORMISM. —**radical** *adj.*

radical psychiatry a variant of RADICAL THERAPY proposing that the psychological problems of individuals are the result of their victimization by the social, economic, and political system in which they live. As such, it is the system, not the individual, that should be the target of intervention and change. This view was most seriously considered during the 1970s and 1980s.

radical therapy any clinical intervention that focuses on the harmful psychological effects of social problems on individuals and that encourages individuals to help themselves by changing society. This approach was actively advanced by some psychologists in the 1970s and 1980s.

radiculitis *n.* inflammation of a SPINAL ROOT, particularly the portion between the spinal cord and the intervertebral canal. Symptoms commonly include pain or weakness or loss of sensation in the part of the body served by the affected spinal nerve.

radiculopathy *n.* any disorder of a SPINAL ROOT. Radiculopathies are often due to vertebrae compressing the nerve roots, as in the condition popularly known as SLIPPED DISK.

radioactive isotope an isotope of a chemical element that emits radiation during its decay to a stable form. All the isotopes of an element have the same number of nuclear protons, but different isotopes of an element have different numbers of neutrons. The radiation emitted by a radioactive isotope consists of alpha or beta particles or gamma rays, which are produced as the isotopes decay into simpler atoms and lose energy while gaining stability. Radioactive isotopes are widely used in diagnostic, research, and therapeutic techniques as they affect photographic film, produce an electric charge in the surrounding air, produce fluorescence with certain other substances, and have the ability to destroy or alter cells or microorganisms. Also called **radioisotope**.

radioactive tracer a chemical compound labeled with a RADIOACTIVE ISOTOPE, such as calcium (^{45}Ca) or carbon (^{14}C), so that its metabolic pathway can be traced through body tissues. Radioactive tracers may be used for diagnostic, therapeutic, or research purposes. For example, in tobacco research, nicotine molecules can be tagged with radioactive tracers, and the path of the alkaloid traced through the lungs and bloodstream of cigarette smokers.

radiograph *n.* a negative image produced on a sensitive surface (e.g., photographic film) by radiation, usually by

X-rays or gamma rays. The technique of producing such images is called **radiography**; it is widely used as a diagnostic aid. Also called **radiogram**. See also RADIOLOGY. **—radiographer** *n.* **—radiographic** *adj.*

radioimmunoassay (**RIA**) *n.* an immunological technique to measure the concentration of a substance of interest (e.g., a hormone) in a sample of blood or a tissue. A mixture of the substance to be assayed and a form of the substance tagged with a RADIOACTIVE ISOTOPE is allowed to react with an antibody specific to that substance. The amount of radioactivity that is bound by the antibody reflects the amount of substance in the sample: The greater the concentration of the substance in the sample, the less radioactivity will be bound.

radioisotope *n.* see RADIOACTIVE ISOTOPE.

radiological factors see EARLY TRANSIENT INCAPACITATION.

radiology *n.* the medical discipline or specialty in which radiographic imaging techniques (see RADIOGRAPH) are used to diagnose disease (**diagnostic radiology**) and radioactive substances and other forms of radiation are used to treat disease (**therapeutic radiology**). The latter is more commonly referred to as RADIATION THERAPY. **—radiological** *adj.* **—radiologist** *n.*

radiotherapy *n.* see RADIATION THERAPY.

RAE abbreviation for ROTATIONAL AFTEREFFECT.

rage *n.* intense, typically uncontrolled anger. It is usually differentiated from HOSTILITY in that it is not necessarily accompanied by destructive actions but rather by excessive expressions. In animals, rage appears to be a late stage of AGGRESSION when normal deterrents to physical attack, such as SUBMISSIVE SIGNALS, are no longer effective. It generally includes rapid respiration, thrusting and jerking of limbs, and clawing, biting, and snarling.

rage disorder any disturbance characterized by one or more episodes of rage, such as incidents of ROAD RAGE, or any clinical disorder in which episodes of rage are a primary symptom, such as INTERMITTENT EXPLOSIVE DISORDER.

railway lines illusion see PONZO ILLUSION.

railway spine see ERICHSEN'S DISEASE.

rami communicantes the nerve fibers that connect the ganglia of the SYMPATHETIC CHAIN to spinal nerves. They include both the gray rami communicantes (see GRAY RAMUS) and the WHITE RAMI COMMUNICANTES.

ramp movement a slow, sustained movement that is thought to be generated in the BASAL GANGLIA. Also called **smooth movement**.

ramus *n.* (*pl.* **rami**) **1.** a branch of a blood vessel or a nerve. **2.** any of the large branches of a SPINAL NERVE after it emerges from the spinal column, notably the anteriorly directed **ventral ramus** and the posteriorly directed **dorsal ramus**. These distribute motor and sensory nerve fibers to other, smaller nerves. **3.** any of the short nerve branches that arise from the ventral ramus and communicate with sympathetic ganglia (see RAMI COMMUNICANTES).

Rana pipiens a species of frog used in studies of neurophysiology and neuroanatomy.

random *adj.* without order or predictability.

random activity behavior that has no apparent goal or specific eliciting stimulus, but may have an intrinsic purpose.

random assignment see RANDOMIZE.

random classification see IDIOSYNCRATIC CLASSIFICATION.

random control a control condition for PAVLOVIAN CONDITIONING in which the conditioned stimulus and the unconditioned stimulus are presented with equal probability but independently of each other. Such an arrangement results in a zero CONTINGENCY.

random-digit dialing a method of telephone SAMPLING in which the researcher selects the first three digits of telephone numbers and then uses a computer program to select the last digits at random.

random-dot stereogram a type of STEREOGRAM consisting of two images, each composed of black and white dots (or squares). Many of the dots are identical in both images, but a subset of dots in one image is offset horizontally compared to the other image. The images themselves simply appear to contain random dots, but when the separate images are presented to the separate eyes they are fused by the visual system. The horizontal disparity of the subset of dots is interpreted as stereoscopic depth. [first devised in 1959 by Hungarian-born U.S. engineer Bela Julesz (1928–)]

random-effects model a statistical model in which the statistical parameters that index the effectiveness of treatments or experimental conditions are treated as having been randomly sampled from a population of such levels. Although random-effects designs tend to be less powerful than FIXED-EFFECTS MODELS, they enable generalization to be made to levels of the independent variable not actually employed in the study.

random error an error due to chance alone and randomly distributed around a true score. Also called **variable error**. Compare ABSOLUTE ERROR; CONSTANT ERROR.

random factor a factor in an experimental design whose levels are selected by a random process within some allowable range of values.

random-interval schedule (**RI schedule**) a SCHEDULE OF REINFORCEMENT in which the first response after an interval has elapsed is reinforced, the duration of the interval varies randomly from reinforcement to reinforcement, and a fixed probability of reinforcement over time is used to reinforce a response. For example, if every second the probability that reinforcement would be arranged for the next response was .1, then the random-interval schedule value would be 10 s (i.e., RI 10 s).

randomization test an approach to HYPOTHESIS TESTING in which all possible combinations of participants and conditions are tested.

randomize *vb.* to assign participants or other sampling units to the conditions of an experiment at random, that is, in such a way that each participant or sampling unit has an equal chance of being assigned to any particular condition. **—randomization** *n.*

randomized block design a research design in which participants are first classified into groups (blocks), on the basis of a variable for which the experimenter wishes to control. Individuals within each block are then randomly assigned to one of several treatment groups. Designs of this type allow the experimenter to take the BETWEEN-GROUPS VARIANCE into separate account. See also BLOCK DESIGN.

randomized clinical trial an experimental design in which patients are randomly assigned to either a group that will receive an experimental treatment or one that will receive a comparison treatment or PLACEBO. There may be multiple experimental and comparison groups, but each patient is assigned to only a single group.

randomized-group design an experimental design in which the participants are assigned at random to either experimental or control groups without matching on one or more background variables. Compare MATCHED-GROUP DESIGN.

randomized-response technique a procedure for reducing SOCIAL DESIRABILITY bias when measuring attitudes or other constructs at an aggregate group level. Participants are presented with a pair of questions that have dichotomous response options (e.g., agree or disagree, yes or no), one question being the target question and the other an innocuous filler question. They are instructed to roll a die (or use a similar randomization procedure) to determine which question they should answer and to conceal the result of this roll from the interviewer; they then provide the answer to that question but do not tell the interviewer which one it is. The ambiguity regarding which question has been answered is assumed to reduce participants' concerns about the social desirability of their answers. Despite the fact that the interviewer does not know which question each person has answered, PROBABILITY THEORY can be used to estimate the distribution of responses to the target question in the population.

random mating MATING BEHAVIOR without mate selection. Many early BEHAVIORAL ECOLOGY theories were based on the idea of random mating, but it is now recognized that most animals select specific mates and often show ASSORTATIVE MATING.

random model see COMPONENTS-OF-VARIANCE MODEL.

random noise see NOISE.

random number generator (**RNG**) a device or system used to produce random output, whether this be a "pseudorandom" output deriving from algorithms or other mathematical functions or a "true random" output based on unpredictable physical processes, such as electronic or thermal noise currents. In parapsychology experiments, true random number generators are used to test the supposed ability of certain psychics to influence random systems by mental intention (see PSYCHOKINESIS). RNGs are also used in cryptography, statistics, and financial and economic simulations. Also called **random event generator** (**REG**).

random numbers a set of numbers generated by chance alone, without a predictable pattern or order.

random observation any observation that is made spontaneously or by chance, is uncontrolled, or is not part of a schedule or pattern of organized observation.

random-ratio schedule (**RR schedule**) a SCHEDULE OF REINFORCEMENT in which the number of responses required for each reinforcement varies randomly from reinforcement to reinforcement. It is usually arranged by having the same probability of reinforcement for each response regardless of the history of reinforcement for prior responses. For example, a random-ratio 100 schedule would result from a reinforcement probability of .01 for any given response.

random sampling a process for selecting individuals for a study from a larger potential group of individuals in such a way that each is selected with a fixed probability of inclusion. This selected group of individuals is called a **random sample**.

random selection the procedure used for random sampling.

random variable a variable whose value depends upon the outcome of chance. Also called **stochastic variable**.

random walk model a model of reaction time and accuracy in which the evidence mounts in discrete steps, causing one to incline toward or away from alternative response criteria. A response is made when the evidence, or "walk," reaches one of the criteria.

R & T play abbreviation for ROUGH-AND-TUMBLE PLAY.

range *n.* in statistics, a measure of DISPERSION, obtained by subtracting the lowest score from the highest score in a distribution.

range effect in VISUAL PURSUIT, a tendency to make movements too large when the target motion is small and too small when the target motion is large.

range fractionation a hypothesis of perception of stimulus intensity, stating that a wide range of intensity values can be encoded by a group of cells, each of which is a specialist for a particular range of stimulus intensities.

range of attention the span or spread of attention.

range of audibility the sound frequencies that elicit the sensation of hearing. For humans with normal hearing the range of audibility is usually specified as 20 Hz to 20 kHz. However, humans are much less sensitive to frequencies at the extremes of this somewhat arbitrary range. The frequency range of speech is approximately 100 Hz to 4 kHz. In audiometry, PURE-TONE thresholds are typically measured at frequencies from 250 Hz to 8 kHz. Also called **audibility range**; **audible range**.

range of minus judgments the range of perceptual judgments given in a psychophysical experiment. It is obtained by subtracting the lowest judgment from the highest one.

range of motion (**ROM**) the degree of movement of a joint that can be achieved without tissue damage, such as how far a person can turn his or her neck. It is determined by the contour of the joint, the restraining bones, and the ligaments of the capsule surrounding the joint.

range restriction see RESTRICTION OF RANGE.

rank 1. *n.* a particular position along an ordered continuum. See RANK ORDER. **2.** *vb.* to arrange items in a graded order, for example, from highest to lowest value.

Rankian therapy see WILL THERAPY.

ranking method 1. in industrial and organizational settings, a method of evaluating jobs for the purpose of setting wages or salaries in which jobs are ranked according to their overall relative value to the company. The advantages of the method are that it is fast and simple; the disadvantage is that such whole-job comparisons tend to be subjective and become more difficult as the number of jobs in the organization increases. Compare CLASSIFICATION METHOD; FACTOR-COMPARISON METHOD; JOB-COMPONENT METHOD; POINT METHOD. **2.** an EMPLOYEE COMPARISON TECHNIQUE in which the employees in a selected group are ranked from the highest to the lowest on one or more CRITERION DIMENSIONS.

rank order the arrangement of a series of items (e.g., scores or individuals) in order of magnitude.

rank order correlation a measure of the degree of relationship between two variables that have each been placed in ranks. Also called **Spearman rank order correlation**.

rank transformation any of a class of TRANSFORMATIONS in which the actual numerical score of a participant is replaced by the rank position of the score within the entire batch of scores (i.e., without regard to the particular CELL of the design in which the participant resides). Rank transformations serve as the basis for a wide variety of nonparametric tests.

rape *n.* forced sexual penetration, against the will and without the consent of the individual; it also includes sexual penetration of an individual unable to give consent due to mental impairment or intoxication (see DATE RAPE). Local U.S. laws define specific variations, such as the absence or presence of genital penetration, the sex of perpetrator and victim, the marital status of the parties, or the interpretation of the term "valid consent." See also STATUTORY RAPE.

rape counseling provision of guidance and support for victims of rape and sexual assault. **Rape crisis centers** offer expert counseling for the psychological trauma that individuals typically experience following a sexual attack; both the affected individuals and their families are counseled. Community education and prevention outreach programs are increasingly part of the purview of this area of counseling.

rape-trauma syndrome the symptoms of POST-TRAUMATIC STRESS DISORDER (PTSD) experienced by an individual who has been sexually assaulted (the term was coined prior to the wide acceptance and use of the more inclusive concept of PTSD). The symptoms, which may include fear of being alone, phobic attitudes toward sex, VAGINISMUS, male impotence, or repeated washing of the body, may persist for a year or more after the rape. They may be aggravated by an attitude of others that the victim "invited" rape by dressing in a certain way or other behavior.

raphe nucleus a group of SEROTOGENIC NEURONS in the midline of the brainstem that project widely to the spinal cord, thalamus, basal ganglia, and cerebral cortex. Also called **nucleus of the raphe**; **raphe**.

rapid alternating movements changing hand positions rapidly in a sequenced pattern as a measure of motor control and coordination (i.e., cerebellar functioning). Failure to perform this task is called DYSDIADOCHOKINESIS.

rapid cycling mood disturbance that fluctuates over a short period, most commonly between manic and depressive symptoms. A rapid-cycling BIPOLAR DISORDER is characterized by four or more mood episodes over a 12-month period; the episodes must be separated by symptom-free periods of at least 2 months or must be delimited by switching to an episode of opposite polarity (e.g., a major depressive episode switches to a manic, mixed, or hypomanic episode).

rapid eye movement (**REM**) the rapid, jerky, but coordinated movement of the eyes behind closed lids, frequently observed during dreaming sleep. See DREAM STATE; REM SLEEP.

rapid neuroleptization see MEGADOSE PHARMACOTHERAPY.

rapid sequential visual presentation (**RSVP**) in psychophysical testing, a methodology in which a series of visual stimuli, such as shapes or words, are presented in a very short time span, often just a few milliseconds per item.

rapport *n.* a warm, relaxed relationship of mutual understanding, acceptance, and sympathetic compatibility between or among individuals. The establishment of rapport with the client in psychotherapy is frequently a significant mediate goal for the therapist in order to facilitate and deepen the therapeutic experience and promote optimal progress and improvement in the client.

rapprochement *n.* **1.** generally, a state of cordial relations between individuals or groups. **2.** in the theory of SEPARATION–INDIVIDUATION of Austrian child psychoanalyst Margaret Mahler (1897–1985), the phase, after about 18 months of age, in which the child makes active approaches to the mother. This contrasts with the preceding stage in which the child was relatively oblivious to the mother.

rapture-of-the-deep syndrome an acute, transient psychosis experienced by scuba and deep-sea divers, attributed to an excessively high blood-nitrogen level (**nitrogen narcosis**).

RAS abbreviation for RETICULAR ACTIVATING SYSTEM.

Rasch model the simplest model for ITEM RESPONSE THEORY, in which only a single parameter, item difficulty, is specified. [proposed in 1960 by Georg **Rasch** (1901–1980), Danish statistician]

rate 1. *n.* relative frequency (e.g., RESPONSE RATE). **2.** *vb.* to assign a score on some variable (e.g., friendliness) using a RATING SCALE.

rate dependence effect see LAW OF INITIAL VALUES.

rate dependency in behavioral pharmacology, the phenomenon in which the magnitude or direction (or both) of a drug's effect on response rate depends on the response rate observed when the drug is not present. Typically, low response rates are increased by a drug, and high rates are increased less or decreased.

ratee *n.* an individual who is assigned a RATING.

rate law the principle that the strength of a stimulus is indicated by the rate of firing of the nerve impulses it elicits.

rate of change the amount of change in a variable per unit time divided by the value of the variable before the change. If a score rises from 20 to 30 in unit time, the rate of change is $(30 - 20)/20 = 10/20 = 0.5$.

rate of occurrence see INCIDENCE.

rater *n.* one who assesses a person, object, or other unit, particularly for experimental purposes.

rating *n.* a score assigned to a person or object on some numerical scale. See RATING SCALE.

rating error an incorrectly assigned RATING.

rating scale an instrument used to assign scores to persons or objects on some numerical dimension.

rating scale judgment task a signal detection task in which participants assign confidence ratings to their "yes" or "no" responses. Each rating category defines a different response criterion relative to which the evidence is judged, allowing a RECEIVER-OPERATING CHARACTERISTIC CURVE to be constructed efficiently.

ratio *n.* the quotient of two numbers, that is, one number divided by the other number.

ratio IQ IQ as determined by the ratio of mental age to chronological age, multiplied by 100. Compare DEVIATION IQ.

rational *adj.* **1.** pertaining to REASONING or, more broadly, to higher thought processes. **2.** based on, in accordance with, or justifiable by accepted principles of reasoning or logic. Compare IRRATIONAL; NONRATIONAL. **3.** capable of or exhibiting reason. **4.** influenced by reasoning rather than by emotion. **—rationally** *adv.*

rational authority see AUTHORITY.

rational-economic man a construct introduced in the work of Scottish economist Adam Smith (1723–1790): The rational-economic man makes decisions based on the rational analysis of potential and desired outcomes and acts in his (or her) own rational self-interest. Such an assumption about the nature of human beings and their motivation lies behind the classical economic theories of capitalism and the classical political philosophies of liberalism. It can also be seen to be influential in psychology, most theories and models of which assume a human being capable of reason and highly motivated to act out of self-interest. See EUDEMONISM; HEDONISM. See also BOUNDED RATIONALITY.

rational emotive behavior therapy (**REBT**) a form of COGNITIVE BEHAVIOR THERAPY based on the concept that an individual's irrational or self-defeating beliefs and feelings influence and cause his or her undesirable behaviors and damaging self-concept. Originally called **rational emotive therapy** (**RET**), it became known as rational emotive behavior therapy during the 1990s. The therapy teaches the individual, through a variety of cognitive, emotive, and behavioral techniques, to modify and replace self-defeating thoughts to achieve new and more effective ways of feeling and behaving. In the process of the therapy, the irrational beliefs and feelings are first unmasked then altered by (a) showing how the beliefs and feelings produce the individual's problems and (b) indicating how they can be changed through behavior therapy. Also called **rational psychotherapy**. See also ABCDE TECHNIQUE; ABC THEORY. [developed in 1955 by U.S. psychotherapist Albert Ellis (1913–)]

rationalism *n.* **1.** any philosophical position holding that (a) it is possible to obtain knowledge of reality by reason alone, unsupported by experience, and (b) all human knowledge can be brought within a single deductive system. This confidence in reason is central to classical Greek philosophy, notably in its mistrust of sensory experience as a source of truth and the preeminent role it gives to reason in epistemology. However, the term "rationalist" is chiefly applied to thinkers in the Continental philosophical tradition initiated by French philosopher René Descartes (1596–1650), most notably Dutch Jewish philosopher Baruch Spinoza (1632–1677) and German philosopher Gottfried Wilhelm Leibniz (1646–1716). Rationalism is usually contrasted with EMPIRICISM, which holds that knowledge comes from or must be validated by sensory experience. In psychology, psychoanalytical approaches, humanistic psychology, and some strains of cognitive theory are heavily influenced by rationalism. **2.** in religion, a perspective that rejects the possibility or the viability of divine revelation as a source of knowledge. **3.** in general language, any position that relies on reason and evidence rather than on faith, intuition, custom, prejudice, or other sources of conviction. **—rationalist** *adj., n.*

rationality *n.* **1.** the quality of being reasonable or RATIONAL or of being acceptable to reason. **2.** a rational action, belief, or desire.

rationality of emotions the proposition that emotions show an implacable logic, in that they follow from APPRAISALS made by the individual as inevitably as logical conclusions follow from axioms and premises. This view, which counters the traditional idea that emotions and reason are in opposition to one another, is linked to the work of U.S. psychologist Richard S. Lazarus (1922–2002) and Swiss-born Canadian–British psychologist Ronald B. De Sousa (1940–).

rationalization *n.* in psychotherapy, an explanation, or presentation, in which apparently logical reasons are given to justify unacceptable behavior that is motivated by unconscious instinctual impulses. In psychoanalytic theory, such behavior is considered to be a DEFENSE MECHANISM. Examples are: "Doesn't everybody cheat" or "You have to spank children to toughen them up." Rationalizations are used to defend against feelings of guilt, to maintain self-respect, and to protect from criticism. In psychotherapy, rationalization is considered counterproductive to deep exploration and confrontation of the client's thoughts and feelings and of how they affect behavior. **—rationalize** *vb.*

rational knowledge knowledge gained through reason or arrived at by logical argument.

rational learning MEANINGFUL LEARNING that involves a clear understanding of the learned material and the relationships between its components.

rationally based persuasion see COGNITIVELY BASED PERSUASION.

rationally suicidal having SUICIDAL IDEATION or intent that could be considered an understandable response to an untenable situation.

rational problem solving problem solving based on reasoning that is generally agreed to be correct, optimal, or logical.

rational psychology an approach to the study and explanation of psychological phenomena that emphasizes philosophy, logic, and deductive reason as sources of insight into the principles that underlie the mind and that make experience possible. This approach is in sharp contrast to that of EMPIRICAL PSYCHOLOGY. See also PHILOSOPHICAL PSYCHOLOGY. [proposed by U.S. philosopher, theologian, and psychologist Laurens Perseus Hickok (1798–1888)]

rational psychotherapy see RATIONAL EMOTIVE BEHAVIOR THERAPY.

rational soul in the thought of Greek philosopher Aristotle (384–322 BCE), the type of soul possessed by human beings. Unlike the VEGETATIVE SOUL and the SENSITIVE SOUL, the rational soul has the capacity for rational thought. See also NOUS.

rational thinking thinking according to logical rules, which is a central part of intelligence according to many theories, in particular that of U.S. psychologist Jonathan Baron (1944–).

rational type in the ANALYTIC PSYCHOLOGY of Carl JUNG, one of the two major categories of FUNCTIONAL TYPE: It comprises the THINKING TYPE and the FEELING TYPE. Compare IRRATIONAL TYPE.

ratio reinforcement in OPERANT CONDITIONING, reinforcement presented after a prearranged number of responses, in contrast to reinforcement delivered on the basis of a time schedule only. In such schedules (e.g., FIXED-RATIO SCHEDULE, PROGRESSIVE-RATIO SCHEDULE), the rate of reinforcement is a direct function of the rate of responding. Also called **ratio schedule of reinforcement**. Compare INTERVAL REINFORCEMENT.

ratio scale a measurement scale having a true zero (i.e., zero on the scale indicates an absence of the measured attribute) and a constant ratio of values. Thus, on a ratio scale an increase from 3 to 4 (for example) is the same as an increase from 7 to 8.

ratio strain in operant-conditioning experiments, the occurrence of long periods of inactivity in the animal when FIXED-RATIO SCHEDULES are very large.

Rat Man a landmark case of Sigmund FREUD's, which he described in "Notes upon a Case of Obsessional Neurosis" (1909). The name was applied to a patient of Freud's, a 30-year-old lawyer whose obsessional fear of rats was traced to repressed death wishes toward his father generated by oedipal conflicts. One example of the patient's obsession was his belief that a rat that appeared to come out of his father's grave had eaten the corpse; another was a fantasy that a rat had been placed in his father's anus and had eaten through his intestines. Freud's analysis of these reactions laid the groundwork for the psychoanalytic interpretation of obsessional neurosis. See also OEDIPUS COMPLEX.

rauwolfia derivatives alkaloids obtained from plants

of the genus *Rauwolfia*, primarily *R. serpentina*, the ancient Hindu snakeroot. They have sedative and antihypertensive actions, and have been used in neuropsychopharmacology since about 1000 BCE by Hindu healers. The genus was named for 16th-century German botanist Leonhard Rauwolf, who reported its tranquilizing effect in 1575 while traveling in India. The prototype drug of the group is **reserpine**, which acts by depleting stores of catecholamine neurotransmitters in both central and peripheral nervous systems. Rauwolfia derivatives were initially used in the management of psychosis, but were erroneously thought to induce depression and therefore abandoned for this use in the 1950s.

Raven's Colored Progressive Matrices see COLORED PROGRESSIVE MATRICES.

Raven's Progressive Matrices a nonverbal test of mental ability consisting of abstract designs, each of which is missing one part. The participant chooses the missing component from several alternatives in order to complete the design. The test comprises 60 designs arranged in five groups of 12; the items within each group become progressively more difficult. Scales of different levels of difficulty are available (for children and adults), but all require some degree of logic and analytic ability. The test, introduced in 1938, is often viewed as the prototypical measure of GENERAL INTELLIGENCE. [John C. **Raven** (1902–1970), British psychologist]

RAVLT abbreviation for REY AUDITORY VERBAL LEARNING TEST.

raw score an original test score before it is converted to other units or another form.

Rayleigh equation a statement of the proportion of red and green stimuli needed for a normal human eye to perceive yellow. Observers who are red-weak or green-weak require different proportions from normal observers. [John William Strutt, Baron **Rayleigh** (1842–1919), British physicist]

Rayleigh scattering the scattering of sunlight by molecules in the atmosphere. The amount of scattering is dependent on the wavelength of the light, with short wavelengths producing stronger scattering than long wavelengths. The blue color of the sky is caused by the relatively large amount of Rayleigh scattering of short-wavelength light by the Earth's atmosphere. [Lord **Rayleigh**]

Raynaud's disease a disorder characterized by episodes of painful vasoconstriction of the blood vessels in the extremities, especially the fingers and toes. The attacks, usually lasting up to 15 min, are precipitated by cold exposure or, in one third of cases, by emotional stress. **Raynaud's phenomenon** refers to similar symptoms caused by another disease—for example, rheumatic arthritis (see ARTHRITIS)—or by toxic agents, such as vinyl chloride. Drug therapy and behavioral treatment (with thermal biofeedback) have proven effective in relieving the attacks. [identified in 1854 by Maurice **Raynaud** (1834–1881), French physician]

RBC theory abbreviation for RECOGNITION BY COMPONENTS THEORY.

RBD abbreviation for REM BEHAVIOR DISORDER.

rCBF (**RCBF**) abbreviation for REGIONAL CEREBRAL BLOOD FLOW.

RCFT abbreviation for Rey COMPLEX FIGURE TEST.

RdA abbreviation for READING AGE.

RDC abbreviation for RESEARCH DIAGNOSTIC CRITERIA.

reach envelope in ergonomics, the area that an operator can reach from a seated or standing position. It is used in WORKSPACE DESIGN to determine the placement of displays and tools to be used by the operator.

reactance theory a model stating that in response to a perceived threat to or loss of a behavioral freedom a person will experience **psychological reactance** (or, more simply, **reactance**), a motivational state characterized by distress, anxiety, resistance, and the desire to restore that freedom. According to this model, when people feel coerced or forced into a certain behavior, they will react against the coercion, often by demonstrating an increased preference for the behavior that is restrained, and may perform the opposite behavior to that desired. [proposed in 1966 by U.S. psychologist Jack W. Brehm (1928–)]

reaction *n.* a response to a stimulus.

reactional biography 1. in employment interviews, an applicant's account of his or her employment history or other experience that sheds significant light on how he or she reacted to these events. A skillful interviewer will attempt to elicit such information in addition to the factual data; similarly, a skillful interviewee will know how to present his or her experiences in terms of positive lessons learned or challenges overcome. **2.** in the INTERBEHAVIORAL PSYCHOLOGY of U.S. psychologist Jacob Robert Kantor (1888–1984), an organism's history of interactions with and responses to environmental stimuli, which influences that organism's subsequent psychological development and behavior.

reaction formation in psychoanalytic theory, a DEFENSE MECHANISM in which unacceptable or threatening unconscious impulses are denied and are replaced in consciousness with their opposite. For example, to conceal an unconscious prejudice an individual may preach tolerance; to deny feelings of rejection, a mother may be overindulgent toward her child. Through the symbolic relationship between the unconscious wish and its opposite, the outward behavior provides a disguised outlet for the tendencies it seems to oppose.

reaction potential in HULL'S MATHEMATICO-DEDUCTIVE THEORY OF LEARNING, the probability that a stimulus will facilitate a particular response. It is a multiplicative function of an organism's HABIT STRENGTH and DRIVE STRENGTH.

reaction time (**RT**) the time that elapses between onset or presentation of a stimulus and occurrence of a response to that stimulus. There are several specific types, including SIMPLE REACTION TIME and COMPOUND REACTION TIME. Also called **cognitive reaction time**; **response time**.

reaction-time apparatus any instrument used to measure REACTION TIME.

reaction type 1. any of the categories into which a psychiatric syndrome can be classified in terms of its predominant symptoms. For example, Swiss-born U.S. psychiatrist Adolf Meyer (1866–1950) distinguished affective, delirious, deteriorated, disguised-conflict, organic, and paranoid reaction types. **2.** in reaction-time experiments, a particular type of SET, or readiness of the participant or participants: motor (prepared to respond), sensory (prepared to receive a stimulus), or mixed.

reactivation of memory the RETRIEVAL of a memory, which may be triggered by stimuli or environmental conditions that were present when the memory was originally formed. See also PRIMING.

reactive *adj.* **1.** in general, responsive to a given stimulus or situation. **2.** describing or relating to an episode, such as a depressive or psychotic episode, that is secondary to a traumatic event, stress, or emotional upheaval in the life of the individual. A reactive episode generally has a more favorable prognosis than a similar episode that is ENDOGENOUS in origin and unrelated to a specific happening.

reactive aggression a physical act, usually in retaliation, committed with little forethought and with the intention of causing injury or harm to another person.

reactive attachment disorder in *DSM–IV–TR*, a disorder of infancy and early childhood characterized by disturbed and developmentally inappropriate patterns of social relating not resulting from mental retardation or pervasive developmental disorder. It is evidenced either by persistent failure to initiate or respond appropriately in social interactions (inhibited type) or by indiscriminate sociability without appropriate selective attachments (disinhibited type). There must also be evidence of inadequate care (e.g., ignoring the child's basic physical or emotional needs, frequent changes of primary caregiver), which is assumed to be responsible for the disturbed social relating. Also called **attachment disorder**.

reactive depression a MAJOR DEPRESSIVE EPISODE that is apparently precipitated by a distressing event or situation, such as a career or relationship setback. Also called **depressive reaction**; **exogenous depression**; **neurotic depression**; **neurotic-depressive reaction**. Compare ENDOGENOUS DEPRESSION.

reactive disorder an older name for a mental disorder that is apparently precipitated by severe environmental pressure or a traumatic event.

reactive inhibition in HULL'S MATHEMATICO-DEDUCTIVE THEORY OF LEARNING, a tendency for response magnitude to decrease with increasing practice or fatigue.

reactive mania a HYPOMANIC EPISODE or MANIC EPISODE that is precipitated by an external event.

reactive measure a measure that alters the response under investigation. For example, if participants are aware of being observed, their reactions may be influenced more by the observer and the fact of being observed than by the stimulus object or situation to which they are ostensibly responding. See also UNOBTRUSIVE MEASURE.

reactive psychosis see SITUATIONAL PSYCHOSIS.

reactive schizophrenia an acute form of schizophrenia that clearly develops in response to predisposing or precipitating environmental factors, such as extreme stress. The prognosis is generally more favorable than for PROCESS SCHIZOPHRENIA. [proposed in 1959 by U.S. psychologists Norman Garmezy (1918–) and Eliot H. Rodnick (1911–1999)]

reactivity *n.* the condition in which an object being observed is changed by the fact that it is the object of observation. See REACTIVE MEASURE.

readability level 1. the level at which a child is able to read successfully. It is a relative measure of skill, identified in terms of grade level. **2.** the degree of readability of a passage based on such factors as legibility of the printed page, vocabulary, sentence length and structure, human interest, and general intelligibility.

readership-survey technique a research method used in advertising to determine how thoroughly a consumer has read the copy in a print advertisement. The consumer is shown a list of products, brand names, or company names. If the consumer claims to have seen an advertisement for any of them in a particular magazine or newspaper, he or she is asked to recall information about the content of the advertising copy. See also RECOGNITION TECHNIQUE.

readiness *n.* **1.** a state of preparedness to act or to respond to a stimulus. **2.** the degree of preparation for a specific task or subject that is necessary to result in MEANINGFUL LEARNING.

readiness test a test designed to predict how well an individual is prepared to profit from instruction in a particular field, especially reading, mathematics (arithmetic, algebra, geometry), and foreign languages.

reading age (**RdA**) the reading abilities of a student as reflected in a scale stating the age of the peer group to which the student's reading abilities are equivalent. A child who reads well may have a reading age significantly above his or her chronological age.

reading delay inability to read at the ability level typical for a given age.

reading disability a reading ability that is below that expected for a child of a given age and stage of development. It is associated with neurological damage or impairment, perceptual deficit, faulty habit patterns (mouthing words, backtracking), poor comprehension, emotional problems, or environmental deprivation. See also DYSLEXIA.

reading disorder in *DSM–IV–TR*, a LEARNING DISORDER that is characterized by a level of reading ability substantially below that expected for a child of a given age, intellectual ability, and educational experience. The reading difficulty, which involves faulty oral reading, slow oral and silent reading, and often reduced comprehension, interferes with achievement or everyday life and is not attributable to neurological impairment, sensory impairment, mental retardation, or environmental deprivation. See also DYSLEXIA.

reading epilepsy a type of REFLEX EPILEPSY in which reading precipitates a seizure.

reading ladder 1. a means of advancing a student's reading abilities to a higher level, beginning with easy reading and progressing in a prescribed order through increasingly difficult reading. This process was developed to encourage students to expand their reading skills. **2.** a list of titles on a similar theme arranged in order of difficulty, with the easiest at the bottom and the most difficult at the top.

reading machine a device for individuals with visual impairment that uses an optical scanner and character-recognition software (**print scanning and reading technology**) and a SPEECH SYNTHESIZER to convert printed text into speech. Reading machines can either be standalone units or can be created by adding the appropriate components to a personal computer.

reading quotient a child's reading ability as determined by dividing reading-age test scores (see READING AGE) by chronological age.

reading readiness the development of the prerequisite skills and abilities for reading, such as auditory and visual discrimination, cognitive abilities, and fine motor coordination.

reading retardation the state of having a reading achievement level 2 or more years below the individual's MENTAL AGE.

reading span 1. the amount of written or printed material that a person can apprehend during a single FIXATION of the eye during reading. The greater the reading span, the fewer times the eye needs to stop along a line of text. A span of 7–10 characters is considered typical. Also called **eye span**; **recognition span**. See also EYE–VOICE SPAN. **2.** in memory tests, the number of words a person can remember on being asked to recall the last word of each sentence in a passage that he or she has just read.

readmission *n.* the admission to a hospital, clinic, mental hospital, or other institution of a patient who has been admitted previously. Also called **rehospitalization**. See also REVOLVING-DOOR PHENOMENON. **—readmit** *vb.*

reafference *n.* sensory signals that occur as a result of the movement of the sensory organ. For example, when the eye moves, the image of a stationary stimulus moves across the retina. This reafferent signal of motion is compared to that which would be expected as a result of the intended movement, and adjustments are made as necessary. See BRAIN COMPARATOR; COROLLARY DISCHARGE. **—reafferent** *adj.*

reafference principle a concept developed to explain the regulation and interaction of internal signals and sensory signals in directing and coordinating bodily movements. It requires storage of a copy of each spontaneous activation of a motor unit by the processing unit (see COROLLARY DISCHARGE). This copy fixes the reference value of the parameters required to execute the movement, which guides the response until the REAFFERENCE from a sensory unit to the processing unit indicates an accordance with the reference value or set point. The reafference principle has also been used to explain some perceptual phenomena. For example, a corollary discharge signal from neural units controlling how the eye moves has been hypothesized to be used in combination with reafferent motion signals from the retina to determine the motion of objects in the world.

Real *n.* the realm of nature or reality: one of three aspects of the psychoanalytic field defined by French psychoanalyst Jacques Lacan (1901–1981). The Real is posited to be unknown and unknowable—in effect, unreal—because all individuals ultimately possess are images and symbols. The other realms are the IMAGINARY and the SYMBOLIC.

real–ideal self congruence the degree to which the characteristics of a person's ideal self match his or her actual characteristics. The discrepancy between the two, when large enough, creates psychological pain; it is theorized to be a motivating force for entering treatment and is the focus of treatment in CLIENT-CENTERED THERAPY. In research studies it is measured by having participants sort cards describing themselves as they would like to be and as they are (see SELF-IDEAL Q SORT).

realism *n.* **1.** the philosophical doctrine that objects have an existence independent of the observer. Compare IDEALISM. See also NAIVE REALISM. **2.** the older philosophical doctrine that UNIVERSALS, such as general terms and abstract ideas, have a greater genuine reality than the physical particulars to which they refer, as in so-called PLATONIC IDEALISM. Compare NOMINALISM. **3.** in literature and the visual and performing arts, any mode of representation that seeks to present human experience and society in a way that appears to be true to life. The quest for verisimilitude usually involves both a sensitive and complex delineation of the psychology of characters and a detailed description of social contexts. The term "realism" is more particularly applied to a broad movement of this kind in 19th-century fiction, as represented by the work of French novelists Honoré de Balzac (1799–1850) and Gustave Flaubert (1821–1880); Russian novelists Ivan Turgenev (1818–1883), Fyodor Dostoevsky (1821–1881), and Leo Tolstoy (1828–1910); and American novelist William Dean Howells (1837–1920). Literary NATURALISM is usually considered an offshoot of literary realism. **—realist** *adj., n.*

realism factor in psychological aesthetics, the effect of independent and objective influences on art judgments, in contrast to judgments dominated by subjective or idealistic factors.

realistic anxiety anxiety in response to an identifiable threat or danger. This type of anxiety is considered a normal response to danger in the real world and serves to mobilize resources in order to protect the individual from harm. Also called **objective anxiety**.

realistic group-conflict theory a conceptual framework predicated on the assumption that intergroup tensions, including rivalries, prejudice, and warfare, will occur whenever groups must compete for scarce resources, including food, territory, jobs, wealth, power, natural resources, and energy. Also called **realistic conflict theory**. See CONFLICT THEORY.

realistic job preview see JOB PREVIEW.

realistic thinking thinking that is based or focused on the objective qualities and requirements that pertain in different situations. Realistic thinking permits adjustment of thoughts and behavior to the demands of a situation; it depends on the ability to interpret external situations in a fairly consistent, accurate manner. This, in turn, involves the capacity to distinguish fantasy and subjective experience from external reality. See also REALITY TESTING.

reality *n.* in philosophy, that which genuinely exists, usually in contrast to that which only appears or seems to exist. See ABSOLUTE REALITY; OBJECTIVE REALITY. See also ACTUAL. **—real** *adj.*

reality awareness the perception of external objects as different from the self and from each other. Also called **reality contact**.

reality confrontation an activity in which the therapist raises the possibility that the patient has misconstrued events or the intentions of others. The confrontation is thought to be helpful in reducing maladaptive behaviors that result from distorted thinking.

reality monitoring see SOURCE MONITORING.

reality orientation in psychotherapy, a form of REMOTIVATION that aims to reduce a client's confusion about time, place, or person. The therapist continually reminds the client who he or she is, what day it is, where he or she is, and what is happening or is about to take place.

reality principle in psychoanalytic theory, the regulatory mechanism that represents the demands of the external world and requires the individual to forgo or modify instinctual gratification or to postpone it to a more appropriate time. In contrast to the PLEASURE PRINCIPLE, which is posited to dominate the life of the infant and child and govern the ID, or instinctual impulses, the reality principle is posited to govern the EGO, which controls impulses and enables people to deal rationally and effectively with the situations of life.

reality testing **1.** in general, any means by which an individual determines and assesses his or her limitations in the face of biological, physiological, social, or environmental actualities or exigencies. **2.** the objective evaluation of sense impressions, which enables the individual to distinguish between the internal and external worlds, and between fantasy and reality. Defective reality testing is the major criterion of PSYCHOSIS.

reality therapy treatment that focuses on present ineffective or maladaptive behavior and the development of the client's ability to cope with the stresses of reality and take greater responsibility for the fulfillment of his or her needs (i.e., discover what he or she really wants and the optimal way of achieving it). To these ends, the therapist plays an active role in examining the client's daily activities, suggesting healthier, more adaptive ways for the client to behave. Reality therapy tends to be of shorter duration than many other traditional psychotherapies (see SHORT-TERM THERAPY). [developed by U.S. psychiatrist William Glasser (1925–)]

real-life test a period during which people seeking sex-reversal surgery (see TRANSSEXUALISM) are required to live as the sex they wish to become, for usually one or two years, before any surgical procedures are performed. As well as a name change, it involves changing clothing, hair, and other aspects of physical appearance to those of the opposite sex. The real-life test is used to give the individual (and the professionals involved) an indication of whether or not he or she will be able to cope with, and benefit from, a sex-reversal operation.

real self the individual's true wishes and feelings and his or her potential for further growth and development. See SELF. See also ACTUAL SELF; TRUE SELF. [defined by German-born U.S. psychoanalyst Karen D. Horney (1885–1952)]

real–simulator model an experimental design in which some participants are instructed to simulate hypnosis, or some other psychological state, while other participants are genuinely experiencing it. The experimenter is usually unaware which participants are experiencing the state and which are simulators. Also called **simulator–real model**. [originated by Austrian-born U.S. psychiatrist Martin Theodore Orne (1927–2000)]

real time the actual time in which a process occurs, particularly in computer applications.

real-time amplification a technique of AUDITORY FEEDBACK to improve voice quality and diction, in which individuals speak into a microphone attached by headphones to an amplifier that feeds back voice and speech patterns without time lapse. The amplifier filters out background noises outside of the bandwidth (typically set to 100–80000 Hz), allowing the speaker to experience optimal auditory feedback as he or she is talking in real time.

reason 1. *n.* consecutive thought, as in deduction or induction. Although at one time reason was considered a mental faculty, this is typically not intended in current usage. See DEDUCTIVE REASONING; INDUCTIVE REASONING. **2.** *n.* in philosophy, the intellect (or NOUS) regarded as the source of true knowledge. See RATIONALISM. **3.** *n.* soundness of mind. **4.** *n.* a statement offered to justify an action or decision or to explain the occurrence of an event. **5.** *vb.* see REASONING.

reasonable accommodations adjustments made within a work or school setting that allow an individual with a physical, cognitive, or psychiatric disability to perform required tasks and essential functions. Provisions for reasonable accommodations must be made by employers and educators according to the 1990 AMERICANS WITH DISABILITIES ACT and the 1973 Rehabilitation Act.

reasonable doubt see BEYOND REASONABLE DOUBT.

reasonable person standard a standard used to judge whether or not a particular form of conduct in the workplace constitutes SEXUAL HARASSMENT. This standard focuses on what a "reasonable person" would conclude, rather than being based on the views of either the victim or the perpetrator.

reasonable resistance standard in rape cases, the degree of resistance by the victim that is required to demonstrate that the sexual act was not consensual.

reasoned action model see THEORY OF REASONED ACTION.

reasoning *n.* **1.** thinking in which logical processes of an inductive or deductive character are used to draw conclusions from facts or premises. See DEDUCTIVE REASONING; INDUCTIVE REASONING. **2.** the sequence of arguments or proofs used to establish a conclusion in this way. **—reason** *vb.*

reasoning mania a MANIC EPISODE in which judgment is not impaired and there are no PSYCHOTIC FEATURES.

reasoning test a test of skills in inductive thinking, deductive thinking, or both. Examples include number series and classification of words (induction) as well as various kinds of syllogisms (deduction). See INDUCTIVE REASONING; DEDUCTIVE REASONING.

reassociation *n.* in HYPNOANALYSIS, a process of renewing or reviewing a forgotten or inhibited traumatic event so that the experience will be integrated with the individual's personality and consciousness.

reassurance *n.* in psychotherapy and counseling, a supportive approach that encourages clients to believe in themselves and in the possibilities of improvement. The technique is common and has widespread use across many forms of psychotherapy. It is used frequently in SUPPORTIVE PSYCHOTHERAPY and occasionally in RECONSTRUCTIVE PSYCHOTHERAPY to encourage a client in the process of exploring new relationships and feelings. Reassurance is also used to diminish anxiety, for example, by explaining to a client that a period of heightened depression or tension is temporary and not unexpected. Also called **assurance**.

rebelliousness *n.* resistance to authority, especially parental authority or its equivalent. **—rebellious** *adj.*

rebirthing *n.* **1.** the therapeutic use of continuous, focused breathing and reflection, initially under the guidance of a rebirthing practitioner (a **rebirther**), to release tension, stress, and intense emotions and attain a state of deep peace and total relaxation that leads to personal growth and positive changes in health, consciousness, and self-esteem (i.e., a personal and spiritual "rebirth"). This type of therapy is increasingly being termed **breathwork** or **rebirthing breathwork**. [developed in the 1970s by California-based New Age guru Leonard Orr] **2.** a highly controversial form of therapy, now largely discredited (both scientifically and ethically), in which an individual attempts to reexperience being born (e.g., through hypnotic age regression) in order to resolve supposed pre- and perinatal conflicts and emotions and to develop new and different outlooks on life.

rebound effect an increase in behavior or the strength of a process following a period of suppression.

rebound insomnia a phenomenon associated with the use of hypnotic agents, particularly short-acting BENZODIAZEPINES, and characterized by a temporary worsening of insomnia following abrupt discontinuation of the drug or an inability to return to sleep after the initial effects of the drug have worn off. Rebound insomnia of the latter type often makes administration of a second dose of the agent ineffective.

rebound phenomenon a test that demonstrates loss of the ability of the cerebellum to control coordinated movement: If the individual extends the forearm against resistance and the resistance is suddenly removed, the hand or fist will snap back toward the chest. Also called **Holmes's phenomenon**.

reboxetine *n.* a drug that inhibits the reuptake of norepinephrine but has little or no effect on neurotransmission of serotonin, dopamine, acetylcholine, or histamine. It was the first selective norepinephrine reuptake inhibitor developed for clinical use as an antidepressant. U.S. trade name (among others): **Vestra**.

REBT abbreviation for RATIONAL EMOTIVE BEHAVIOR THERAPY.

rebus writing the use of symbols to represent the sounds of language. If each phonetic sound is assigned its own unique symbol, the number of symbols needed within a writing system is substantially reduced.

recall 1. *vb.* to transfer prior learning or past experience to current consciousness: that is, to remember data or an experience. **2.** *n.* the process by which this occurs. See also FREE RECALL; RECALL METHOD.

recall memory see RECALL METHOD.

recall method a technique of evaluating memory in terms of the amount of learned material that can be correctly reproduced, as in an essay exam or in reproducing a list of words. Recall can be tested immediately after learning (see IMMEDIATE RECALL TEST) or after various delay intervals. Also called **recall test**. Compare RECOGNITION METHOD.

recall score method a technique in which the capacity to remember is given a numerical value according to the number of items, or the proportion of items, that can be recalled. Some memory tests, such as the CALIFORNIA VERBAL LEARNING TEST, produce recall scores that can be compared to normative values.

recall test see RECALL METHOD.

recapitulation theory 1. the hypothesis that the stages of embryological development of an organism mirror the morphological stages of evolutionary development characteristic of the species, that is, ONTOGENY recapitulates PHYLOGENY. The theory was abandoned early in the 20th century when embryology showed no consistent correspondence between ontogeny and phylogeny. Also called **biogenetic law**. [proposed by German biologist Ernst H. Haeckel (1834–1919)] **2.** the extension of the principle of recapitulation to a child's mental and behavioral development. [proposed by U.S. psychologist Granville Stanley HALL]

receiver *n.* **1.** in COMMUNICATION THEORY, a device or process, such as the sensory apparatus of vision or hearing or a radio receiver, that translates a signal into an intelligible message. In psychological applications of INFORMATION THEORY, the human being has sometimes been treated as a receiver; this analogy has motivated various aspects of research (e.g., the ability to cope with noise). **2.** in TELEPATHY experiments, the participant who attempts to receive information transmitted by the SENDER. See also PERCIPIENT.

receiver-operating characteristic curve (**ROC curve**) in a detection, discrimination, or recognition task, the relationship between the HIT RATE (the proportion of correct "yes" responses) and the FALSE-ALARM rate (the proportion of incorrect "yes" responses). This is plotted as a curve to determine what effect the observer's response criterion is having on the results. Also called **isosensitivity function**; **response-operating characteristic curve**. See also D PRIME.

receiving hospital a health facility that is specially equipped and staffed to handle new patients requiring diagnosis and preliminary treatment, for example, people with suspected mental disorder.

recency effect a memory phenomenon in which the most recently presented facts, impressions, or items are learned or remembered better than material presented earlier. This can occur in both formal learning situations and social contexts. For example, it can result in inaccurate ratings or impressions of a person's abilities or other characteristics due to the inordinate influence of the most recent information received about that person. Also called **law of recency**; **principle of recency**; **recency error**. Compare NEGATIVE RECENCY; PRIMACY EFFECT.

receptive amimia see AMIMIA.

receptive aphasia a type of APHASIA in which the ability to understand words, signs, or gestures is impaired. For example, a person may hear words but not understand them or may see words but be unable to read them. Such individuals were once identified as word-deaf or word-blind. Also called **impressive aphasia**; **logagnosia**; **logamnesia**; **receptive dysphasia**; **sensory aphasia**. Compare EXPRESSIVE APHASIA.

receptive character in the psychoanalytic theory of Erich FROMM, a passive, dependent, and compliant, or conforming, personality type: roughly equivalent to the ORAL-RECEPTIVE PERSONALITY or the passive-dependent personality (see DEPENDENT PERSONALITY DISORDER) described by others. Such an individual is said to be of a **receptive orientation.**

receptive dysphasia see RECEPTIVE APHASIA.

receptive field the spatially discrete region and the features associated with it that can be stimulated to cause the maximal response of a sensory cell. In vision, for example, the receptive field of a retinal ganglion cell is the area on the retina (containing a particular number of photoreceptors) that evokes a neural response. An auditory neuron has a receptive field that can be described either by the range of tones to which it responds or by the receptors that cause this response. Also called **receptor field**.

receptive language the language perceived and mentally processed by a person, as opposed to that which he or she originates. A person's receptive language skills may differ markedly from his or her EXPRESSIVE LANGUAGE skills.

receptive vocabulary an individual's vocabulary as defined by the words that he or she can understand, rather than the words that he or she normally uses. Also called **passive vocabulary**; **recognition vocabulary**. Compare PRODUCTIVE VOCABULARY.

receptivity *n.* the period of time when a female is responsive to sexual overtures from a male, typically (but not exclusively) around the time of ovulation. Receptivity has a connotation of passive female acceptance or tolerance of male sexual overtures. In contrast, PROCEPTIVITY conveys active solicitation of males by females. **—receptive** *adj.*

receptor *n.* **1.** the cell in a sensory system that is responsible for stimulus TRANSDUCTION. Receptor cells are specialized to detect and respond to specific stimuli in the external or internal environment. Examples include the RETINAL RODS and RETINAL CONES in the eye and the HAIR CELLS in the cochlea of the ear. Also called **receptor cell**. **2.** a SENSE ORGAN, such as the eye or the ear. **3.** a molecule in a cell membrane that specifically binds a particular molecular messenger (e.g., a neurotransmitter, hormone, or drug) and elicits a response in the cell. Also called **receptor molecule**. See also NEURORECEPTOR.

receptor adaptation the tendency of a receptor to stop responding to a constant stimulus.

receptor cell see RECEPTOR.

receptor field see RECEPTIVE FIELD.

receptor molecule see RECEPTOR.

receptor potential the electric potential produced by

stimulation of a receptor cell, which is roughly proportional to the intensity of the sensory stimulus and may be sufficient to trigger an ACTION POTENTIAL in a neuron that is postsynaptic to the receptor. Also called **generator potential**.

receptor site a region of specialized membrane on the surface of a cell (e.g., a neuron) that contains RECEPTOR molecules, which receive and react with particular messenger molecules (e.g., neurotransmitters).

recessive allele a version of a gene ALLELE whose effects are manifest only if it is carried on both members of a HOMOLOGOUS pair of chromosomes or on an unmatched sex chromosome (i.e., on the single X chromosome in normal males). See AUTOSOMAL RECESSIVE; RECESSIVE TRAIT. Compare DOMINANT ALLELE.

recessive trait in genetics, a trait that is expressed only if its determining ALLELE is carried on both members of a HOMOLOGOUS pair of chromosomes or on an unmatched sex chromosome. See RECESSIVE ALLELE. Compare DOMINANT TRAIT.

recidivism *n.* **1.** repetition of delinquent or criminal behavior, especially in the case of a habitual criminal, or **repeat offender**, who has been convicted several times. **2.** multiple relapses in patients with mental illness. **—recidivist** *n., adj.* **—recidivistic** *adj.*

recidivism rate the frequency with which delinquent or criminal behavior recurs or patients relapse. It is sometimes used as a marker of the effects of interventions; for example, the percentage of patients who are rearrested for rape following treatment intended to reduce the likelihood of committing this crime would indicate the effectiveness of the treatment.

recipient factors characteristics of the person receiving a persuasive message that influence the extent to which he or she is persuaded. Recipient factors include such characteristics as intelligence, self-esteem, and NEED FOR COGNITION.

reciprocal altruism a form of HELPING BEHAVIOR that is sustained when one individual (A) helps another (B) and at some future time B helps A or A's offspring. The requirements of reciprocal altruism are (a) that the participants are able to identify each other individually, (b) that they are able to remember past actions and who helped whom, (c) that the cost to the helper is less than the gain to the recipient, and (d) that there is a mechanism to protect against CHEATING. GAME THEORY provides a theoretical system for understanding reciprocal altruism. See also ALTRUISM.

reciprocal determinism a concept that opposes the radical or exclusive emphasis on environmental determination of responses and asserts that a reciprocal relation exists among environment, behavior, and the individual. That is, instead of conceptualizing the environment as a one-way determinant of behavior, reciprocal determinism maintains that the environment influences behavior, behavior influences the environment, and both influence the individual, who also influences them. This concept is associated with SOCIAL LEARNING THEORY.

reciprocal inhibition **1.** a technique in BEHAVIOR THERAPY that aims to replace an undesired response with a desired one by COUNTERCONDITIONING. It relies on the gradual substitution of a response that is incompatible with the original one and is potent enough to neutralize the anxiety-evoking power of the stimulus. See also SYSTEMATIC DESENSITIZATION. [devised by South African-born U.S. psychologist Joseph Wolpe (1915–1997)] **2.** in neuroscience, the inhibition of one SPINAL REFLEX when another is elicited. [proposed by British neurophysiologist Charles Scott Sherrington (1857–1952)] **3.** a neural mechanism that prevents opposing muscles from contracting at the same time. **4.** the inability to recall two associated ideas or items because of their interference with each other.

reciprocal innervation the principle of MOTOR NEURON activity stating that when one set of muscles receives a signal for a reflex action, the antagonistic set of muscles receives a simultaneous signal that inhibits reaction. See RECIPROCAL INHIBITION.

reciprocal liking the attraction and cordial attitudes that people have to others who are attracted to them.

reciprocal punishment a punishment that fits the crime. For example, a child who consistently neglects to feed his or her pet might be punished by forgoing a meal. In this way, the child gains insight into the consequences of the act. Compare EXPIATORY PUNISHMENT.

reciprocal regulation recurring or mutual adaptation of behavior of a person or people to changed conditions.

reciprocal roles the characteristic behavior patterns displayed by occupants of a particular position in a group or society in response to the behavior patterns of occupants of other positions.

reciprocal-teaching procedure an instructional process designed to improve student understanding of previously taught material and to provide efficient strategies for maintaining learned material.

reciprocity *n.* **1.** in Jean PIAGET's theory of cognitive development, see COMPENSATION. **2.** the quality of an act, process, or relation in which one person receives benefits from another and, in return, provides the giver with an equivalent benefit. **—reciprocal** *adj.*

reciprocity law a general principle that the magnitude of sensation is the product of the duration of the stimulus multiplied by its intensity. BLOCH'S LAW is an example of this principle for vision. Also called **reciprocity principle**.

reciprocity norm the SOCIAL NORM that people who help others will receive equivalent benefits from these others in return. Compare SOCIAL JUSTICE NORM; SOCIAL RESPONSIBILITY NORM.

recoding *n.* the translation of material held in memory from one form into another. For example, a series of random digits (e.g., 239812389712) could be recoded as a series of four-digit prices ($23.98, $12.38, $97.12), thereby making the series much easier to recall. See CHUNKING; ELABORATION. **—recode** *vb.*

recognition *n.* **1.** a sense of awareness and familiarity experienced when one encounters people, events, or objects that have been encountered before or when one comes upon material that has been learned in the past. See also RECOGNITION METHOD. **2.** the acknowledgment of an achievement by bestowing awards or words of praise.

recognition by components theory (**RBC theory**) the theory that perception of objects entails their decomposition into a set of simple three-dimensional elements called GEONS, together with the skeletal structure connecting them. [proposed by U.S. psychologist Irving Biederman (1939–)]

Recognition Memory Test (**RMT**) a verbal and nonverbal memory test that is used to detect neuropsychological deficits. In the Recognition Memory for Words subtest of the RMT, participants are presented with 50 stimulus words, one every 3 s, and must respond whether they consider each pleasant or unpleasant. Following the presentation of all 50 stimuli, each word is presented again concurrently with a distractor item, and participants must choose which of the two words had been presented previously. The procedure is the same for the Recognition Memory for Faces subtest, in which the stimuli used are photographs of unfamiliar faces. Also called **Warrington Recognition Memory Test**. [originally developed in 1984 by British neuropsychologist Elizabeth Kerr Warrington]

recognition method a technique of measuring the amount of material learned or remembered by testing a person's capacity to later identify the content as having been experienced before. During **recognition testing**, previously studied items are presented along with new items, or LURES, and the participant attempts to identify those items that were studied before and those items that were not. Also called **recognition test**. Compare RECALL METHOD.

recognition span see READING SPAN.

recognition technique a type of READERSHIP-SURVEY TECHNIQUE employed in consumer psychology. Consumers are asked to recall information about a product they claim to recognize from previous exposure to its advertisements. Consumers also may be asked questions about advertisements that have never appeared in order to determine their suggestibility or false-recognition level. See also PANTRY-CHECK TECHNIQUE.

recognition test see RECOGNITION METHOD.

recognition vocabulary see RECEPTIVE VOCABULARY.

recognitory assimilation a type of SENSORIMOTOR INTELLIGENCE characterized by the selective use of a SCHEME. For example, an infant applies a sucking scheme to a nipple for nursing and to various nonnutritive objects (e.g., a thumb) for comfort, to aid sleep, or for some other purpose.

recollection *n.* **1.** the act of recalling past events and experiences, a process that occurs spontaneously in ordinary life and during FREE ASSOCIATION but can also be stimulated by hypnotic suggestion, pictures, or visits. **2.** vivid and detailed memory for past events or information pertaining to a specific time or place. See EPISODIC MEMORY.

recombinant DNA a DNA molecule containing a fragment that has been inserted by genetic RECOMBINATION or some similar process, for example, using the techniques of GENETIC ENGINEERING. Recombinant DNA laboratory techniques involve the creation of novel or modified pieces of genetic material, which can then be inserted in the chromosomes of another species. These techniques allow for the study of the expression of a particular gene or the development of strains of bacteria that can produce natural substances of therapeutic value.

recombination *n.* the exchange of genetic material between paired chromosomes during the formation of sperm and egg cells. It involves the breaking and rejoining of CHROMATIDS of homologous chromosomes in a process called **crossing over**. It results in offspring having combinations of genes that are different from those of either parent.

recompensation *n.* an increase in the ability of an individual to adapt to the environment and alleviate stressful situations. Compare COMPENSATION; DECOMPENSATION.

reconditioning therapy a form of BEHAVIOR THERAPY in which the client is conditioned to replace undesirable responses with desirable responses. See also AVERSION THERAPY.

reconstituted family see BLENDED FAMILY.

reconstitution *n.* **1.** revision of one's attitudes or goals. **2.** an outcome of the grieving process experienced by some patients with catastrophic illnesses resulting in disability.

reconstruction *n.* **1.** in psychoanalysis, the revival and analytic interpretation of past experiences that have been instrumental in producing present emotional disturbance. **2.** the logical recreation of an experience or event that has been only partially stored in memory. **—reconstruct** *vb.*

reconstructive memory a form of remembering marked by the logical recreation of an experience or event that has been only partially stored in memory. It draws on general knowledge and SCHEMAS or on memory for what typically happens in order to reconstruct the experience or event.

reconstructive psychotherapy psychotherapy directed toward basic and extensive modification of an individual's character structure, by enhancing his or her insight into personality development, unconscious conflicts, and adaptive responses. Examples are Freudian PSYCHOANALYSIS, Adlerian INDIVIDUAL PSYCHOLOGY, Jungian ANALYTIC PSYCHOLOGY, and the approaches of German-born U.S. psychoanalyst Karen D. Horney (1885–1952) and U.S. psychiatrist Harry Stack Sullivan (1892–1949).

reconstructive surgery the surgical specialty or procedure concerned with the restoration or rebuilding of or improvement in shape and appearance of body structures that are missing, defective or diseased, damaged, or not considered aesthetically pleasing. See also COSMETIC SURGERY; PLASTIC SURGERY; POSTRECONSTRUCTIVE SURGERY.

recorder *n.* in the psychology of groups, see TASK ROLE.

record keeping an essential aspect of therapy, in which clinical notes are preserved for future reference, training purposes, or both. Clinical notes may be subpoenaed by the courts. The extent of detail in record keeping varies with the situation, but some degree of record keeping is deemed standard procedure for clinicians.

recovered memory the subjective experience of recalling details of a prior traumatic event, such as sexual or physical abuse, that has previously been unavailable to conscious recollection. Before recovering the memory, the person may be unaware that the traumatic event has occurred. The phenomenon is controversial: Because such recoveries often occur while the person is undergoing therapy, there is debate about their veracity vis-à-vis the role that the therapist may have played in suggesting or otherwise arousing them. Also called **repressed memory**. See also DISSOCIATIVE BARRIERS; POSTTRAUMATIC AMNESIA; PSEUDOMEMORY.

recovery *n.* the period during which an individual exhibits consistent progress in terms of measurable return of abilities, skills, and functions following illness or injury.

Recovery, Inc. a SELF-HELP GROUP for individuals with serious mental health problems that focuses on will-training techniques for controlling temperamental behavior and changing members' attitudes toward their problems. Founded in 1937 by U.S. neuropsychiatrist Abraham A. Low (1891–1954), it is one of the oldest self-help organizations in the world.

recovery of function recovery of function impaired as a result of damage to the central or peripheral nervous system.

recovery ratio see DISCHARGE RATE.

recovery time **1.** the time required for a neural unit (e.g., a neuron or muscle cell) to recover from a response before it is capable of responding to a stimulus again. See REFRACTORY PERIOD. **2.** the time required for a physiological process to return to a normal state after it has been altered by the response to a stimulus. An example is the REFRACTORY PHASE of the sexual-response cycle.

recreation *n.* rejuvenating and pleasurable pastimes or sports. **—recreational** *adj.*

recreational drug a drug of abuse.

recreational therapy the use of individualized recreational activities as an integral part of the rehabilitation or therapeutic process. Also called **therapeutic recreation**.

recruitment *n.* **1.** in neurophysiology, an increase in the number of neurons that respond as a stimulus is maintained or increased in strength. **2.** in auditory perception, a rapid increase in loudness after a stimulus exceeds the auditory threshold. It is characteristic of SENSORINEURAL HEARING LOSS.

rectal administration the administration of a drug by rectal insertion, usually in the form of a SUPPOSITORY, for absorption via the rectal mucosa.

rectal reflex see DEFECATION REFLEX.

rectangular array any two-dimensional arrangement of data.

rectangular distribution see UNIFORM DISTRIBUTION.

recumbent *adj.* see POSTURE.

recuperative theory a theory that the function of sleep is to allow the body to recuperate from the rigors of waking, to regather resources, and to reestablish internal HOMEOSTASIS.

recurrent *adj.* occurring repeatedly or reappearing after an interval of time or a period of remission: often applied to disorders marked by chronicity, relapse, or repeated episodes (e.g., depressive symptoms).

recurrent circuit a network of neurons and synapses in which a nerve impulse can make a complete path back to its starting point. This occurs in both POSITIVE FEEDBACK circuits and NEGATIVE FEEDBACK circuits. See also SELF-EXCITING CIRCUIT.

recurrent collateral inhibition a negative-feedback system that prevents rapid, repeated firing of the same MOTOR NEURON. To accomplish this, one branch of an axon loops back toward the cell body of the neuron and communicates with an inhibitory RENSHAW CELL. The Renshaw cell in turn inhibits the neuron.

recurrent depression MAJOR DEPRESSIVE DISORDER in which there have been two or more MAJOR DEPRESSIVE EPISODES.

recurrent dream a dream that occurs repeatedly. Sigmund FREUD saw recurrent dreams as punishment, rather than WISH-FULFILLMENT, dreams and linked them to a masochistic need for self-criticism arising from fantasies of excessive ambition. Carl JUNG regarded recurrent dreams as more revealing of the UNCONSCIOUS than single dreams, and found that in a dream series the later dreams often throw light on the earlier ones (see SERIAL INTERPRETATION). Other psychologists see them as an attempt to come to terms with disturbing experiences.

recurring-figures test a test of memory in which a person is shown a series of cards featuring generally nonsensical figures or geometric forms. Some figures appear on more than one card, and the participant must try to remember whether a figure has appeared on a previous card.

recurring-phase theories the view that certain specific issues continually dominate group interactions.

recursion *n.* in GENERATIVE GRAMMAR, a process in which certain grammatical rules can be repeatedly applied, with the output of each application being input to the next, in principle indefinitely. An example is the rule S → S *and* S, where S denotes sentence; the rule is recursive because it can be used to generate a potentially infinite string of sentences conjoined by *and*. A well-known example of recursion in action is the nursery rhyme "The House that Jack Built" (*This is the dog that worried the cat that killed the rat that ate the malt...*). **—recursive** *adj.*

red–green blindness a form of color blindness in which certain shades of red and green are confused. See also DEUTERANOPIA.

red–green responses a concept of color vision in which responses of certain retinal receptors are excitatory while others are inhibitory to the same wavelength. Since red and green are at opposite ends of the spectrum, it is assumed that a red excitatory response is accompanied by a green inhibitory response, each representing a different receptor process.

redintegration *n.* **1.** the process of reorganizing, or reintegrating, mental processes after they have been disorganized by psychological disorder, particularly in psychoses. **2.** more generally, restoration to health or to normal condition and functioning. **3.** the process of recovering or recollecting memories from partial cues or reminders, as in recalling an entire song when a few notes are played. **4.** the elicitation of a response by a part of the stimulus complex that was involved in the initial learning. Also called **reintegration**. **—redintegrative** *adj.*

redintegrative memory a less common name for REDINTEGRATION.

redirected behavior actions that do not appear relevant to the context in which they are performed. See DISPLACEMENT BEHAVIOR.

red nucleus a NUCLEUS in the brainstem that receives input from the cerebellum and gives rise to the RUBROSPINAL TRACT.

redout *n.* a condition resulting from blood being pushed into the head by negative g-forces. Capillaries in the eyes engorge and may burst, causing the visual field to appear red. Redout is experienced, for example, by fighter pilots. Compare BLACKOUT.

red reflex the red color reflected through a person's pupil when light is directed toward the retina along the LINE OF REGARD of the observer's eye. It occurs because the light is reflected by the vascular retina; the absence of a red reflex is a sign that may indicate lens opacities (cataract) or retinal abnormalities.

red sage a brushy shrub, *Salvia miltiorrhiza*, whose roots are known to Chinese herbalists as dan shen and have traditionally been used (powdered or whole) to treat cardiac and vascular disorders, including heart attacks, stroke, and atherosclerosis. Indeed, red sage has been shown in some studies to decrease the clotting capability of blood; it should not be taken in combination with prescribed blood thinners, as bleeding problems may result. Other studies suggest red sage may interfere with the development of scarlike fibers in the liver (associated primarily with chronic hepatitis and consumption of large quantities of alcohol) and may be effective in preventing the growth of cancer cells and the replication of the HIV virus, but these potential uses have not been confirmed and require further investigation. Side effects of red sage are mild and may include itching, stomach upset, and decreased appetite. The active compounds are miltirone and other diterpene quinones, which act as PARTIAL AGONISTS at the benzodiazepine–GABA receptor complex (see $GABA_A$ RECEPTOR). Because red sage is a partial agonist, it may interact with and enhance the sedative effects of drugs that are full BENZODIAZEPINE AGONISTS—commonly used in the treatment of generalized anxiety and insomnia—leading to extreme drowsiness.

reduced model in the GENERAL LINEAR MODEL, a model with fewer parameters than the most highly parameterized model in a set of models to be compared. In general, a reduced model is a proper subset of the most highly parameterized model.

reductio ad absurdum 1. a form of valid logical argument in which either (a) a premise is disproved by showing that it leads to a contradiction and is thus absurd or (b) a premise is indirectly proved by showing that its negation leads to a contradiction and is thus absurd. **2.** in general language, a persuasive technique in which an opposing position is presented in its most extreme or absurd form in order to discredit it. Such a move generally belongs to SOPHISTRY rather than to logic. [Latin, literally: "reduction to the absurd"]

reductionism *n.* the strategy of explaining or accounting for some phenomenon or construct A by claiming that, when properly understood, it can be shown to be some other phenomenon or construct B, where B is seen to be simpler, more basic, or more fundamental. The term is mainly applied to those positions that attempt to understand human culture, society, or psychology in terms of animal behavior or physical laws. In psychology, a common form of reductionism is that in which psychological phenomena are reduced to biological phenomena, so that mental life is shown to be merely a function of biological processes. Compare EMERGENTISM. See also EPIPHENOMENON; IDENTITY THEORY; MATERIALISM.

reduction to essence rule in FUZZY TRACE THEORY, the assumption that people of all ages are biased to extract the gist from a message.

redundancy *n.* **1.** the property of having more structure than is minimally necessary. Biological systems or structures often have redundancy so that impairment or failure of a unit will not prevent adequate functioning. See also DISTRIBUTIONAL REDUNDANCY. **2.** in linguistics and information theory, the condition of those parts of a communication that could be deleted without loss of essential content. In this sense, redundancy includes not only obvious padding, such as repetitions, tautologies, and polite formulas, but also the multiple markings of a given meaning that are required by many conventions of grammar and syntax. For example, in the sentence *All three men were running*, the plurality of the subject is signaled four times: by *all*, *three*, and the plural forms *men* and *were*. It is largely owing to redundancies of this kind that one can so often guess the correct content of messages that have been only partially heard or misprinted. It is calculated that redundancy constitutes roughly 50% of most written and spoken English. **—redundant** *adj.*

redundancy analysis a statistical technique for examining the degree to which the original manifest can be recovered from a set of summative canonical variates.

redundant coding in ergonomics, coding a display or control on two or more physical dimensions, for example, by both shape and color. Redundant coding enhances CONTROL DISCRIMINABILITY.

redundant prepuce an excessive growth of prepuce (foreskin). The condition may be pathological if the excess foreskin prevents the prepuce from being drawn back over the glans, which may be necessary to prevent inflammation from trapped smegma or urine.

reduplicated babbling babbling in which the same syllable is repeated (e.g., *ba-ba-ba-ba-ba*). It is characteristic of infants between about 8 and 10 months.

reduplicative paramnesia a disturbance of memory or CONFABULATION characterized by the subjective certainty that a familiar person or place has been duplicated, such as the belief that the hospital where one is treated is duplicated and relocated to another site. It can be caused by a variety of neurological disorders, but brain lesions commonly involve the frontal lobes, the right hemisphere, or both. See also CAPGRAS SYNDROME.

reeducation *n.* **1.** learning or training that focuses on replacing maladaptive cognitions, affects, or behaviors with healthier more adaptive ones or on learning forgotten or otherwise lost skills anew. **2.** a form of psychological treatment in which the client learns effective ways of handling and coping with problems and relationships through a form of nonreconstructive therapy, such as RELATIONSHIP THERAPY, BEHAVIOR THERAPY, hypnotic suggestion (see HYPNOSUGGESTION), COUNSELING, PERSUASION THERAPY, nonanalytic group therapy, or REALITY THERAPY. Also called **reeducative therapy**.

reenactment *n.* the process of reliving traumatic events and past experiences and relationships while reviving the original emotions associated with them. This technique is used in PSYCHODRAMA and PRIMAL THERAPY, among others. See also ABREACTION.

reentrant neural activity the mutual exchange of signals between neural areas along massively parallel connections, enabling the association of activity in different regions of the brain.

reentry *n.* **1.** the return of a patient or client to society after experiencing life in an institution (e.g., a psychiatric hospital) or being part of the relatively open and honest environment of an ENCOUNTER GROUP. **2.** the return of a mental health professional from a disaster experience in which he or she dealt with many victims suffering from trauma and other forms of psychological stress. See also POSTVENTION.

reevaluation counseling a therapeutic approach involving COCOUNSELING between individuals. In the process, two people take turns in counseling and being counseled. The process starts with one individual (acting as counselor) asking the other (acting as client) a provocative question and continues with other steps, such as asking the individual acting as client to cite two or three minor upsets that have recently occurred. The client is encouraged to react emotionally in his or her responses, to work through his or her emotions, and then to reverse roles and act as the counselor for the other person. Also called **reevaluation cocounseling**. [developed in the 1950s by U.S. personal counselor Harvey Jackins (1916–1999)]

reference database a source of bibliographic information, which is of value for, among other things, developing a comprehensive review of the literature in a particular field of study.

referenced cognitive test a test of cognitive function that has been standardized and normed so that performances can be compared across individuals.

reference group a group or social aggregate that individuals use as a standard or frame of reference when selecting and appraising their own abilities, attitudes, or beliefs. Reference groups include formal and informal groups that the individual identifies with and admires, statistical aggregations of noninteracting individuals, imaginary groups, and even groups that deny the individual membership (**nonmembership reference groups**).

See also SOCIAL COMPARISON THEORY. Compare ASPIRATIONAL GROUP; MEMBERSHIP GROUP.

reference-group theory a general conceptual framework that assumes that individuals' attitudes, values, and self-appraisals are shaped, in part, by their identification with, and comparison to, REFERENCE GROUPS. A reference-group theory of SELF-CONCEPT, for example, assumes that individuals compare their economic, intellectual, social, and cultural achievements to those attained by members of their reference group. Similarly, a reference-group theory of values suggests that individuals adopt, as their own, the values expressed by the majority of the members of their reference group.

referent *n.* in linguistics, the thing (or process or situation) in the external physical world to which a word or phrase refers. In the structuralist account of language (see STRUCTURALISM), verbal SIGNS (words) are held to consist of a SIGNIFIER (physical form) and signified (concept indicated by the signifier), with no need for any external referent.

referential attitude an expectancy attitude sometimes observed in certain individuals with schizophrenia or other forms of psychopathology who are seeking justification, via environmental aspects, for their IDEAS OF REFERENCE or DELUSIONS OF REFERENCE.

referential signal a communication signal given by an animal that appears to provide information about specific objects or events in the environment. Vervet monkeys have different types of calls specific to eagles, leopards, and snakes, three major predators. Many species of birds and monkeys have calls that are specific to the presence of food. Some have argued that referential signals are a form of symbolic communication and might be the primitive basis of words in language.

referent power a capacity to influence others that is based on these others' identification with, attraction to, or respect for the influencer. See POWER.

referral *n.* **1.** the act of directing a patient to a therapist, physician, agency, or institution for evaluation, consultation, or treatment. **2.** the individual who is so referred. **—refer** *vb.*

referred pain pain that is felt in a part of the body other than the site of the pain stimulus.

referred sensation a sensation that is localized (i.e., experienced) at a point different from the area stimulated. For example, when struck on the elbow, the mechanical stimulation of the nerve may cause one to feel tingling of the fingers. Also called **eccentric perception**.

reflectance *n.* the ratio of the intensity of light reflected from a surface (reflected flux) to the intensity of light shining on a surface (incident flux). The **reflectance spectrum** of a surface describes the percentage of reflected photons at each wavelength in the visible spectrum.

reflected appraisals the evaluative feedback that a person receives from others. Some theories of self have treated reflected appraisals as the most important basis for the SELF-CONCEPT, claiming that people learn about themselves chiefly from others. See LOOKING-GLASS SELF; SYMBOLIC INTERACTIONISM.

reflected glare see DIRECT GLARE.

reflection *n.* **1.** see MEDITATION. **2.** in FACTOR ANALYSIS, the change of sign or direction of scoring of a factor. **3.** in the thought of English philosopher John Locke (1632–1704), the process of introspective thought by which SIMPLE IDEAS derived from sensations are converted into more abstract COMPLEX IDEAS. For Locke, all knowledge has its source in either sensation or reflection (i.e., there are no INNATE IDEAS). **4.** a rebounding or throwing back, as of light rays from an impenetrable surface. **5.** an image produced by the reflection of light rays, as in a mirror. **—reflect** *vb.*

reflection–impulsivity *n.* see REFLECTIVITY–IMPULSIVITY.

reflection of feeling a statement made by a therapist or counselor that is intended to highlight the feelings or attitudes implicitly expressed in a client's communication. According to Carl ROGERS, the statement reflects and communicates the essence of the client's experience from the client's point of view so that hidden or obscured feelings can be exposed for clarification. Also called **reflection response**.

reflection response 1. in a RORSCHACH INKBLOT TEST, a response that the inkblot represents a bilateral reflection of one half of the card. That is, the image is perceived not as a single entity across both halves of the card but as two entities in the two halves, one entity being a mirror image of the other. **2.** see REFLECTION OF FEELING.

reflective *adj.* describing the type of individual who makes decisions about complex problems slowly and deliberately. Compare IMPULSIVE. See REFLECTIVITY–IMPULSIVITY. **—reflectivity** *n.*

reflective abstraction the ability to arrive at new knowledge by reflecting upon knowledge one already possesses, without the need for additional information from the external environment. [postulated by Jean PIAGET]

reflective consciousness aspects of consciousness that allow it to refer to its own activities. Also called **self-consciousness**; **self-reflection**.

reflectivity–impulsivity *n.* a dimension of COGNITIVE STYLE based on the observation that some people approach tasks impulsively, preferring to act immediately on their first thoughts or impressions, whereas others are more reflective, preferring to make a careful consideration of a range of alternatives before acting. This aspect of cognitive style—CONCEPTUAL TEMPO—can be assessed by means of the MATCHING FAMILIAR FIGURES TEST. Also called **reflection–impulsivity**. [first described in 1963 by U.S. developmental psychologist Jerome Kagan (1929–)]

reflex *n.* any of a number of automatic, unlearned, relatively fixed responses to stimuli that do not require conscious effort and that often involve a faster response than might be possible if a conscious evaluation of the input was required. Reflexes are innate in that they do not arise as a result of any special experience. An example is the PUPILLARY REFLEX. The concept of a reflex was first proposed by French philosopher René Descartes (1596–1650), who supposed, before the distinction between sensory and motor nerves had been made, that the sensory impulses flowed to the spinal cord, where they were reflected back down to the muscles.

reflex arc a NEURAL CIRCUIT that is involved in a REFLEX. In its simplest form it consists of an afferent, or sensory, neuron that conducts nerve impulses from a receptor to the spinal cord, where it connects directly or via an INTERNEURON to an efferent motor neuron that carries the impulses to an effector, that is, a muscle or gland. See also DISYNAPTIC ARC; MONOSYNAPTIC ARC; POLYSYNAPTIC ARC.

reflex epilepsy a type of epilepsy marked by seizures that are triggered by sensory input, such as sound, touch, or light (e.g., MUSICOGENIC EPILEPSY; PHOTOGENIC EPILEPSY).

reflex inhibition the reduction or prevention of a reflex because an incompatible reflex is occurring or has just occurred.

reflex integration the combining of two reflexes into a single, more complex response.

reflexive affect see AFFECT.

reflexive behavior responses to stimuli that are involuntary or free from conscious control (e.g., the salivation that occurs with the presentation of food) and therefore serve as the basis for PAVLOVIAN CONDITIONING. Compare PLANNED BEHAVIOR; VOLUNTARY BEHAVIOR.

reflexivity *n.* see STIMULUS EQUIVALENCE.

reflex latency the time that elapses between application of a stimulus and the start of a reflex response. See also CENTRAL REFLEX TIME.

reflexogenous zone an area of the body that when stimulated by particular stimuli elicits a particular reflex. For example, the sole of the foot is the reflexogenous zone for the BABINSKI REFLEX.

reflexology *n.* **1.** a school of psychology based on research dealing solely with the outwardly observed and fixed manifestations and reactions of the human being. It is credited to Russian physiologist Vladimir M. Bekhterev (1857–1927), who taught that all behavior could be constructed from the simple reflex as the elementary unit or building block. **2.** the physiological study of involuntary automatic responses to stimuli, particularly as they affect the behavior of humans and other animals. **3.** a type of therapy based on the principle that there are reflex points or zones in the feet and hands that correspond to every part of the body and that manipulating and pressing on these points has beneficial health effects. See also COMPLEMENTARY AND ALTERNATIVE MEDICINE. **—reflexologist** *n.*

reflex strength the potential strength of a response to a reflex stimulus (e.g., the potential for a STARTLE RESPONSE if an organism is touched), often measured by REFLEX LATENCY.

reflex sympathetic dystrophy overactivity of the SYMPATHETIC NERVOUS SYSTEM, which may occur following local injury, usually to an upper or lower limb, associated with damage to nerves and blood vessels, resulting in pain; limb disuse; shiny, thin skin; loss of hair; and bone demineralization.

reformatory paranoia a type of MEGALOMANIA expressed as a personality trait in individuals who concoct plans to reform the world and try to convince others to follow their ideas.

reformism *n.* any position that advocates change in an institution, law, practice, or theory without challenging its fundamental characteristics or tenets. Reformists accept the need for modernization and the correction of abuses but tend to decry violent or extreme change; their methods usually include publicity, education, and lobbying. Compare RADICALISM. **—reformist** *n., adj.*

refraction *n.* **1.** the bending of light rays as they pass from one medium to another, such as from air into water. **2.** the bending of light as it passes through the cornea and lens of the eye so that it is focused on the retina. **3.** the clinical description of the efficacy of this process for an individual eye.

refractive error (**refractive disorder**) see ERROR OF REFRACTION.

refractive index (symbol: n) a measure of the extent to which a ray of light is bent (refracted) in passing from one transparent medium to another. The refractive index of a transparent medium is equal to the ratio of the speed of light in a vacuum to the speed of light in that medium. The value of n can vary with the wavelength of the light. Also called **index of refraction**.

refractory *adj.* **1.** resistant to control, as in a case of a disease or disorder that fails to respond to previously effective therapy. **2.** in neurophysiology, describing a neuron or muscle cell that is unable to respond to a stimulus. See REFRACTORY PERIOD. **3.** stubborn, uncooperative, or unmanageable. **—refractoriness** *n.*

refractory mental illness a mental illness that is difficult to cure.

refractory period a period of inactivity after a neuron or muscle cell has undergone excitation. As the cell is being repolarized, it will not respond to any stimulus during the early part of the refractory period, called the **absolute refractory period**. In the subsequent **relative refractory period**, it responds only to a stronger than normal stimulus.

refractory phase the period following orgasm during which further sexual arousal or orgasm is not possible. It occurs only in the male SEXUAL-RESPONSE CYCLE; females can have immediate further arousal and multiple orgasm. The length of the refractory phase increases with advancing age: Older men may not be capable of sexual activity more than once per day.

reframing *n.* **1.** a process of reconceptualizing an idea for the purpose of changing an attitude by seeing it from a different perspective. In psychotherapy, the manner in which a client frames behavior may be part of the problem. Part of the therapist's response might be to reframe thoughts or feelings so as to provide alternative ways to evaluate the situation or respond to others. Compare RESTATEMENT. **2.** changing the conceptual context, emotional context, or both of a problem or situation and placing it in a different frame that fits the given facts of the problem or situation equally well, but changes its entire meaning. For example, perceptions of weakness or difficulty in handling a situation may be changed to strength and opportunity.

refutability *n.* see FALSIFIABILITY.

refutation *n.* in logic and philosophy, the act or process of showing that a statement, theory, or claim is false or invalid. In this sense, denying an argument or claim is not the same as refuting it. **—refute** *vb.*

REG abbreviation for random event generator (see RANDOM NUMBER GENERATOR).

regeneration of nerves see NEURAL REGENERATION.

regenerative medicine a branch of research and applied medicine that studies the body's capacities for and processes of self-healing, as well as the ability to create new tissues for transplant. See also STEM CELL.

regimen *n.* a particular course of action designed to achieve a specific goal. In medicine, it often refers to a detailed treatment program for the regulation of diet, exercise, rest, medication, and other therapeutic measures. Various forms of psychotherapy, such as COGNITIVE BEHAVIOR THERAPY, may also make use of regimens during the course of treatment. Such programs typically include a schedule and specify the components, methods, and duration of the program.

regional cerebral blood flow (**rCBF**; **RCBF**) the rate of flow of blood through a particular area of the brain, measured by BRAIN IMAGING techniques such as positron emission tomography and single photon emission computed tomography.

regional localization theory the theory, now universally accepted, that the brain has specialized areas that control specific functions.

region of acceptance see ACCEPTANCE REGION.

region of rejection see CRITICAL REGION.

register *n.* a form of a language associated with specific social functions and situations or with particular subject matter. Examples include the different types of language considered appropriate for a scientific meeting, a kindergarten class, or a barroom story. Register differs from DIALECT in that it varies with social context rather than with the sociological characteristics of the user. See ELABORATED CODE.

registered nurse (**RN**) a professional nurse who has completed an accredited educational program and passed a required state licensing examination. Registered nurses provide such services as observing and recording patient symptoms and reactions, developing a treatment plan in consultation with the attending physician, administering medication, and educating the patient or family on self-care methods.

Regitine *n.* a trade name for PHENTOLAMINE.

regression *n.* **1.** generally, a turning or going backward. In psychology, this typically indicates a return to a prior, lower state of cognitive, emotional, or behavioral functioning. **2.** in psychoanalytic theory, a DEFENSE MECHANISM in which the individual reverts to immature behavior or to an earlier stage of PSYCHOSEXUAL DEVELOPMENT when threatened with anxiety caused by overwhelming external problems or internal conflicts. **—regress** *vb.* **—regressive** *adj.*

regression analysis any of several statistical techniques that are designed to allow the prediction of the score on one variable, the DEPENDENT VARIABLE, from the scores on one or more other variables, the INDEPENDENT VARIABLES. Regression analysis is a subset of the GENERAL LINEAR MODEL.

regression coefficient the WEIGHT associated with an independent (predictor) variable in a REGRESSION ANALYSIS.

regression diagnostics a set of techniques used to uncover problems that arise from violations of assumptions in the application of regression methods to particular data sets.

regression effect the tendency for individuals scoring high or low on a test to score closer to the MEAN on a retest.

regression equation the mathematical expression of the relationship between the dependent variable and one or more independent variables that results from conducting a REGRESSION ANALYSIS.

regression in the service of the ego the adaptive circumvention of normal ego functioning in order to access primitive material (see PRIMARY PROCESS), often associated with the creative process. [first described by Swiss-born U.S. psychoanalyst Ernst Kris (1900–1957)]

regression line a straight or curved line fitting a set of data points, usually obtained by a least squares method. It is a geometric representation of the REGRESSION EQUATION for the variables.

regression of y on x the prediction of the dependent variable *y* from the independent variable *x*. Compare INVERSE PREDICTION.

regression therapy see REPARENTING.

regression toward the mean an example of BIAS due to the unreliability of measurement instruments, such that earlier measurements that were extremely deviant from a sample mean will tend, on retesting, to result in a value closer to the sample mean than the original value.

regressive electroshock therapy an obsolete form of ELECTROCONVULSIVE THERAPY that was administered several times a day to patients with schizophrenia when other treatment methods failed and the prognosis was poor. The patients typically regressed to a point where they were incontinent, out of contact, and had to be spoonfed. Recovery from treatment took from a week to a month.

regressive reconstructive approach a technique in psychotherapy in which the client is encouraged to reexperience with emotional intensity traumatic situations from an earlier stage of life. Through such concurrent or subsequent mechanisms as TRANSFERENCE and INTERPRETATION, the approach is posited to help bring about personality change and development of greater emotional adaptation and maturity in the client.

regret *n.* an emotional response to remembrance of a past state, condition, or experience that one wishes had been different.

regular *adj.* in linguistics, denoting a word or a form of a word that conforms to the usual patterns of INFLECTION in a language. Compare IRREGULAR.

regulation of consciousness any activity aimed at managing or changing the state and content of CONSCIOUSNESS, including pain avoidance, pleasure seeking, and variety seeking. Self-destructive activities, such as self-mutilation and chemical intoxication, may also be efforts to regulate states of consciousness.

regulatory behavior the actions of an organism that are geared to maintaining physiological balance by meeting PRIMARY NEEDS.

regulatory drive any drive that helps preserve physiological HOMEOSTASIS and thus is necessary for the survival of the individual organism. Compare NONREGULATORY DRIVE.

regulatory system a group of interacting mechanisms that acts to maintain HOMEOSTASIS or any other stable state in an organ or organism.

rehabilitation *n.* **1.** the process of restoring to the fullest possible degree the independence, well-being, and level of functioning of an individual who has been injured, experienced a trauma, or developed a physical or mental disability, disorder, or impairment. It involves providing appropriate resources, such as treatment or training, to enable such a person (e.g., one who has had a stroke) to redevelop skills and abilities he or she had acquired previously or to compensate for their loss. See also REHABILITATION PROGRAM. Compare HABILITATION. **2.** treatment designed to bring an individual to a condition of health or useful and constructive activity, as in criminal rehabilitation or alcohol rehabilitation (see ALCOHOLISM TREATMENT).

rehabilitation center a facility devoted to restoring individuals with mental or physical disorders or impairments, including those with multiple problems, to an adequate level of functioning. Rehabilitation centers use such techniques as vocational training, work in a sheltered situation, occupational therapy, physical therapy, educational therapy, social therapy, recreational therapy, and psychological therapy and counseling.

rehabilitation counselor a professional worker trained and equipped to evaluate and guide individuals who have a physical, mental, or emotional impairment in all major phases of the rehabilitation process: vocational, educational, personal, psychological, social, and recreational. The rehabilitation counselor typically helps to coordinate the various services offered by the rehabilitation team and to focus them on each individual's needs.

rehabilitation engineering a discipline that integrates multiple areas of research within various fields to develop products, processes, and environments to improve the quality of life for people with disabilities. See also BIOENGINEERING.

rehabilitation medicine the branch of medicine that specializes in the development of individuals to the fullest physical, psychological, cognitive, social, vocational, or educational potential that is consistent with their physiological or anatomical impairment and environmental limitations.

rehabilitation program the overall system of REHABILITATION services provided in support of an individual with an illness, injury, or physical or mental disability, disorder, or impairment. The program is typically customized to meet the specific needs of each individual and may include physical therapy, recreational therapy, and occupational therapy; psychological, social service, educational, and vocational programs; and appropriate specialty services, such as SPEECH THERAPY, AUDIOLOGY, and ORIENTATION AND MOBILITY TRAINING.

rehabilitation psychology a specialty branch of psychology devoted to the application of psychological knowledge and understanding to the study, prevention, and treatment of disabling and chronic health conditions. **Rehabilitation psychologists** consider the entire network of factors (biological, psychological, social, environmental, and political) that affect functioning to help individuals attain optimal physical, psychological, and interpersonal functioning.

rehabilitation team a group of health care specialists who coordinate their efforts in the rehabilitation of patients on an individual basis. A rehabilitation team may include plastic surgeons, orthopedic surgeons, neurologists, psychologists, psychiatrists, physical therapists, occupational therapists, and others, depending upon the needs of the patient.

rehearsal *n.* **1.** preparation for a forthcoming event or confrontation that is anticipated to induce some level of discomfort or anxiety. By practicing what is to be said or done in a future encounter, the event itself may be less stressful. Rehearsal may be carried out in psychotherapy with the therapist coaching or role-playing to help the client practice the coming event. See also BEHAVIOR REHEARSAL; MENTAL REHEARSAL; ROLE PLAY. **2.** the repetition of information in an attempt to maintain it longer in memory. According to the DUAL-STORE MODEL OF MEMORY, rehearsal occurs in SHORT-TERM MEMORY and may allow a stronger trace to be then stored in LONG-TERM MEMORY. Although rehearsal implies a verbal process, it is hypothesized to occur also in other modalities. See also DEPTH-OF-PROCESSING HYPOTHESIS.

rehospitalization *n.* see READMISSION.

Reichenbach phenomenon an "energy field" allegedly emanating from crystals and certain other natural objects. Adherents claim that it can be made visible by KIRLIAN PHOTOGRAPHY but is otherwise discernible only by certain "sensitive" individuals. The phenomenon was first described by the Austrian chemist and metallurgist Baron Karl von Reichenbach (1788–1869), who held it to be a manifestation of an all-pervading physical force that he named **Od** or **Odyle** after the Norse god Odin. Reichenbach considered this force to be distinct from electricity and magnetism but similar to the ANIMAL MAGNETISM of the Austrian physician Franz A. Mesmer (1734–1815). These ideas later influenced the Austrian-born psychologist Wilhelm Reich (1897–1957) and his theory of ORGONE energy. The Reichenbach phenomenon is now mainly cited by advocates of CRYSTAL HEALING. See also AURA; EFFLUVIUM.

Reicher–Wheeler effect see WORD-SUPERIORITY EFFECT. [Gerald M. **Reicher** (1939–) and Daniel D. **Wheeler** (1942–), U.S. psychologists]

Reichian analysis a highly controversial and largely scientifically discredited system of psychotherapy, developed by Austrian-born U.S. psychoanalyst Wilhelm Reich (1897–1957), in which ORGASTIC POTENCY is emphasized as the criterion of mental health. Notwithstanding the widespread judgment of the approach as alternative (see ALTERNATIVE PSYCHOTHERAPY) and unsupported by research, Reich made early contributions to psychology in his theories concerning emotional catharsis and authoritarianism.

reification *n.* **1.** treating an abstraction, concept, or formulation as though it were a real object or static structure. **2.** a type of thinking frequently observed in schizophrenia in which the abstract is confused with the real.

reiki *n.* a complementary therapy that aims to promote physical, emotional, and spiritual healing through the use of energy and the laying on of hands, which is believed to improve the flow of life energy in the patient. See also COMPLEMENTARY AND ALTERNATIVE MEDICINE. [Japanese, "universal life energy"]

reincarnation *n.* the doctrine found in some early Greek philosophy, in BUDDHISM and HINDUISM, and in some spiritualist traditions that the human psyche survives death and is reborn in other bodies (in most forms of the doctrine, in other human bodies). See FUTURE LIVES; METEMPSYCHOSIS.

reinforce *vb.* to enhance or increase the probability of a response by arranging a dependent relationship, or contingency, between the response and a REINFORCER.

reinforcement *n.* **1.** in OPERANT CONDITIONING, a process in which the frequency or probability of a response is increased by a dependent relationship, or contingency, with a stimulus or circumstance (the REINFORCER). See REINFORCEMENT CONTINGENCY. **2.** the procedure that results in the frequency or probability of a response being increased in such a way. **3.** in PAVLOVIAN CONDITIONING, the presentation of an unconditioned stimulus after a conditioned stimulus. See also NEGATIVE REINFORCEMENT; POSITIVE REINFORCEMENT; SCHEDULE OF REINFORCEMENT.

reinforcement analysis the system of evaluating negative versus positive reinforcement factors. In environmental psychology, POSITIVE REINFORCEMENT leads to rewards, such as development of community land for recreational purposes, good schools, and consumer markets, whereas NEGATIVE REINFORCEMENT has detrimental effects, such as deterioration of areas into ghettos or slums. See also SOCIAL TRAP.

reinforcement contingency the contingency (relationship) between a response and a REINFORCER. The contingency may be positive (if the occurrence of the reinforcer is more probable after the response) or negative (if it is less probable given the response). Reinforcement contingencies can be arranged by establishing dependencies between a particular type of response and a reinforcer (as when an experimenter arranges that a rat's lever presses are followed by presentation of food), or they can occur as natural consequences of a response (as when a door opens when pushed), or they can occur by accident (see ACCIDENTAL REINFORCEMENT). Also called **response–reinforcement contingency**.

reinforcement counseling a behavioral approach to counseling based on the idea that behavior is learned and can be predictably modified by various reinforcement techniques that strengthen or weaken specific types of behavior through schedules of positive or negative reinforcement. See also REINFORCEMENT THERAPY.

reinforcement delay the time between a response and the occurrence of a REINFORCER.

reinforcement of alternative behavior see REWARDED ALTERNATIVE METHOD.

reinforcement schedule see SCHEDULE OF REINFORCEMENT.

reinforcement survey schedule an assessment form that elicits information about activities, stimuli, or situations that a person finds rewarding or pleasurable. This information is used by behavior therapists to help patients organize contingencies that increase positive behaviors or decrease negative behaviors.

reinforcement theory any theory that is designed to account for the process of REINFORCEMENT.

reinforcement therapy a therapeutic process based on OPERANT CONDITIONING and the use of positive reinforcement to initiate and maintain behavioral change. See also REINFORCEMENT COUNSELING.

reinforcer *n.* a stimulus or circumstance that acts effectively to produce REINFORCEMENT when it occurs in a dependent relationship, or contingency, with a response. Also called **reinforcing stimulus**. See CONDITIONED REINFORCER; NATURAL REINFORCER.

reinforcing cause a condition that tends to maintain a healthy or maladaptive behavior or behavioral pattern in an individual. An example of the healthy–maladaptive range can be seen when special attention is given to a person who is ill, which can contribute either to a speedy or to a delayed recovery. It is typical, however, to use the term in relation to negative or maladaptive consequences.

reinforcing stimulus see REINFORCER.

reintegration *n.* see REDINTEGRATION.

Reissner's membrane a membrane of the AUDITORY LABYRINTH that separates the SCALA VESTIBULI from the SCALA MEDIA inside the cochlea. Also called **vestibular membrane**. [Ernst **Reissner** (1824–1878), German anatomist]

Reitan Indiana Aphasia Screening Test a 32-item test developed to evaluate language, CONSTRUCTIONAL PRAXIS, calculation, and right–left orientation. It is part of the HALSTEAD–REITAN NEUROPSYCHOLOGICAL BATTERY. [Ralph M. **Reitan** (1922–), U.S. psychologist]

Reitan–Klove Sensory Perceptual Examination a sensory examination, developed as part of the HALSTEAD–REITAN NEUROPSYCHOLOGICAL BATTERY, that includes measures of tactile, visual, and auditory sensory function on both sides of the body. Also called **Sensory Perceptual Examination**. [Ralph **Reitan**; Hallgrim **Klove** (1927–), Norwegian neuropsychologist]

Reix limen (**RL**) the German name for ABSOLUTE THRESHOLD.

rejected child in sociometric measures of peer acceptance, a child who is frequently mentioned in negative terms and is actively disliked by his or her peers. Compare ISOLATE.

rejecting–neglecting parenting an uninvolved parenting style in which the parent discourages emotional dependency and fails to enrich the child's environment. Compare AUTHORITARIAN PARENTING; AUTHORITATIVE PARENTING; PERMISSIVE PARENTING. [first described by U.S. developmental psychologist Diana Baumrind (1927–)]

rejection *n.* **1.** denial of love, attention, interest, or approval. **2.** an antagonistic or discriminatory attitude toward a group of people.

relapse *n.* the recurrence of symptoms of a disorder or disease after a period of improvement or apparent cure.

relapse prevention procedures that are used after successful treatment of a condition, disease, or disorder in order to reduce relapse rates. These often include a combination of cognitive and behavioral skills that are taught to clients before therapy is terminated. Such procedures are often used with disorders (e.g., addictions and depression) that have unusually high relapse rates. See also TERTIARY PREVENTION.

relapse-prevention model a cognitive-behavioral model to predict lapse and relapse of behavior from a healthy to an unhealthy form during a period of behavior change (e.g., stopping exercising when on a program to improve physical fitness).

relapse rate the incidence of clients or patients who have recovered or improved but who later experience a recurrence of their disorder or disease.

relatedness *n.* a reciprocal relationship of empathy, trust, and oneness between two or more people. **—related** *adj.*

relatedness needs see EXISTENCE, RELATEDNESS, AND GROWTH THEORY.

relation *n.* **1.** any kind of meaningful connection between two or more events or entities. The specific nature of this connection varies with the context and discipline. In science, for example, a relation is primarily a causal relation. See CAUSALITY; RELATIONSHIP. **2.** a pairing or mapping between the elements of two sets such that each element of the first (or leading) set is paired with only one corresponding element of the second (or trailing) set. **3.** an individual connected to another by blood, marriage, or adoptive ties. See also KINSHIP.

relational discrimination in conditioning, a DISCRIMINATION based on the relationship between or among stimuli rather than on absolute features of the stimuli. For example, an animal can be trained to respond to the larger of two stimuli, regardless of the absolute size of the two stimuli.

relational frame a hypothesized unit that permits one to describe the relationships between new entities based on previous experience. Entities can stand in several relationships to one another; for example, they may exhibit the relationship of sameness or the relationship of larger than. Through experience with many such relationships, frames are learned into which new entities can be placed. For example, after many experiences with conditions in which one thing is larger than another, and having learned in those situations to say, for example, "The cow is bigger than the dog," one is then in position to say "My cat is bigger than yours" when comparing the two cats for the first time.

relational learning learning to differentiate among stimuli on the basis of relational properties (e.g., the larger of two stimuli) rather than absolute properties (e.g., the stimulus that has a given size).

relational mapping the ability to apply what one knows about one set of elements to a different set of elements. For example, knowing the relation of A to B, one can deduce that C is related to D in the same way that A is related to B.

relational primacy hypothesis the hypothesis that

ANALOGICAL THINKING is available early in infancy, that is, young infants are able to comprehend or solve a problem in one event by comparing it with another. See also RELATIONAL SHIFT.

relational research research investigating the strength of the relationships between two or more variables.

relational shift the developmental change in ANALOGICAL THINKING that occurs when the child moves from focusing on perceptual similarity to focusing on relational similarity when solving problems.

relational word see FUNCTION WORD.

relationship *n.* **1.** a connection between objects, events, variables, or other phenomena. Research often involves the study of the relationship between variables. **2.** a continuing and usually binding association between two or more people, as in a family, friendship, marriage, partnership, or other interpersonal link in which the participants have some degree of influence on each other's thoughts, feelings, and even actions. In psychotherapy, the THERAPIST–PATIENT RELATIONSHIP is thought to be an essential aspect of patient improvement. As with other relationships in life, therapeutic relationships characterized by trust, warmth, respect, and understanding are more likely to result in positive outcomes for the patient.

relationship leader see SOCIAL-EMOTIONAL LEADER.

relationship-motivated *adj.* denoting a LEADERSHIP STYLE in which the leader concentrates on building and maintaining good relationships within the group, minimizing friction, and providing support and encouragement so that group and individual morale remain high. It is assessed using the LEAST PREFERRED COWORKER SCALE. Also called **relationship-oriented**. Compare TASK-MOTIVATED.

relationship role one of several identifiable roles adopted by members of a group who perform particular behaviors to maintain or enhance interpersonal relationships within the group. Although studies have listed and labeled these roles in various different ways, some commonly cited relationship roles are the **gatekeeper**, who controls the CHANNELS OF COMMUNICATION in such a way that everyone has a chance to contribute; the HARMONIZER; the COMPROMISER; the **encourager**, who offers praise and support; and the **comedian**, who relieves tension and raises morale through humor. Also called **maintenance role**; **socioemotional role**. Compare TASK ROLE. See also GROUP ROLES.

relationship system the system of interpersonal bonds recognized in a particular culture, society, or group. The term is broader than KINSHIP NETWORK or kinship system as it includes relationships that are not based on blood or AFFINITY.

relationship therapy 1. any form of psychotherapy, from direct guidance to psychoanalysis, in which the relationship between client and therapist is a key factor. Relationship therapy provides emotional support, creating an accepting atmosphere that fosters personality growth and elicits attitudes and past experiences for examination and analysis during sessions. **2.** the use of a warm, friendly relationship between the therapist and troubled children as a means of accelerating the capacity of the children to change. [first described by U.S. social worker Jessie Taft (1882–1960) and child psychiatrist Frederick H. Allen (1890–1964)]

relative accommodation the amount of ACCOMMODATION of the eyes that is possible when CONVERGENCE is kept constant.

relative deprivation the perception by an individual that the amount of a desired resource (e.g., money, social status) he or she has is less than some comparison standard. This standard can be the amount that was expected or the amount possessed by others with whom the person compares him- or herself. The concept was introduced as a result of studies of morale in the U.S. Army during World War II, which indicated that soldiers were dissatisfied if they believed they were not obtaining as many military rewards and benefits as their peers. In 1966 British sociologist Walter Garrison Runciman (1934–) distinguished between **egoistic relative deprivation**, the perceived discrepancy between an individual's own current position and the comparison standard; and **fraternalistic relative deprivation**, the perceived discrepancy between the position that the person's ingroup actually has and the position the person thinks it ought to have. According to some research, social unrest tends to be greatest in areas with high levels of relative deprivation. See also SOCIAL COMPARISON THEORY.

relative efficiency for two tests (A and B) of the same hypothesis operating at the same SIGNIFICANCE LEVEL, the ratio of the number of cases needed by test A to the number of cases needed by test B in order for the two tests to have the same POWER.

relative frequency the frequency of some type or category of event as a proportion of the total frequency of all types or categories. For example, the relative frequency of "yes" responses could be calculated as the number of "yes" responses divided by the total number of "yes," "no," and "I don't know" responses.

relative judgment see COMPARATIVE JUDGMENT.

relative pitch the ability to identify the pitch of a sound accurately by using an internal reference pitch. Compare ABSOLUTE PITCH.

relative position see INTERPOSITION.

relative refractory period see REFRACTORY PERIOD.

relative risk the ratio of the incidence of a certain disorder or condition in groups exposed to (or possessed of) a specific risk factor and groups not exposed to (or possessed of) that factor.

relative scotoma see SCOTOMA.

relative sensitivity the sensitivity to discriminate differences in stimuli (e.g., in terms of intensity or quality) when one stimulus is judged relative to another. When only one stimulus is presented at a time, sensitivity to stimulus differences is reduced.

relativism *n.* any position that challenges the reality of absolute standards of truth or value. In epistemology, relativism is the assertion that there exist no absolute grounds for truth or knowledge claims. Thus, what is considered true will depend on individual judgments and local conditions of culture, reflecting individual and collective experience. Such relativism challenges the validity of science except as a catalog of experience and a basis for ad hoc empirical prediction. In ethics, relativism is the claim that no moral absolutes exist. Thus, judgments of right and wrong are based on local culture and tradition, on personal preferences, or on artificial principles. Standards of conduct vary enormously across individuals, cultures, and historical periods, and it is impossible to arbitrate among them or to produce universal ethical principles because there can be no means of knowing that these are true. In this way, relativism in epistemology and relativism in ethics are related. See also MORAL NIHILISM; PARTICULARISM; POSTMODERNISM. **—relativist** *adj.*

relativity law see WEBER'S LAW.

relaxation *n.* **1.** abatement of intensity, vigor, energy, or tension, resulting in calmness of mind, body, or both. **2.** the return of a muscle to its resting condition after a period of contraction. **—relax** *vb.*

relaxation technique any therapeutic technique to induce relaxation and reduce stress.

relaxation therapy the use of muscle-relaxation techniques as an aid in the treatment of emotional tension. Also called **therapeutic relaxation**. See also DIFFERENTIAL RELAXATION; PROGRESSIVE RELAXATION.

relaxation training see PROGRESSIVE RELAXATION.

relay nucleus a NUCLEUS that relays nerve impulses from one tract to another within the central nervous system. For example, the LATERAL GENICULATE NUCLEI receive fibers from the optic tract and send fibers to the visual cortex. Relay nuclei are especially prominent in the THALAMUS.

relearning method the learning again of material that was once known but is now forgotten, a technique for measuring knowledge that may be present even if unrecallable. Savings in time or trials over the original learning indicate the amount of retention (see SAVINGS SCORE). Also called **savings method**.

release *n.* the letting go of physical, mental, or emotional tension or pent-up energy, which tends toward relaxation or arousal reduction. See also RELEASER.

release from proactive interference restoration of the capacity to readily remember items of one type after switching categories of materials to be recalled. For instance, successively trying to memorize dates leads to the buildup of PROACTIVE INTERFERENCE, causing a decline in immediate recall of dates; switching to remembering names releases proactive interference, and retention improves (i.e., names are remembered more easily than dates were).

release inhibitor a substance that prevents or interferes with the release of hormones or other agents from glands or tissue cells. For example, SOMATOSTATIN is a release-inhibiting hormone (or factor) that inhibits the normal rate of release of growth hormone from the pituitary gland.

release phenomenon unrestricted activity of a lower brain center when a higher center with inhibitory control is incapacitated, damaged, or excised.

releaser *n.* a stimulus that, when presented under the proper conditions, initiates a FIXED-ACTION PATTERN (see also MODAL ACTION PATTERN). In animal behavior, the stimulus is an environmental cue that routinely evokes a particular response or pattern of responses specific to a particular species. For example, the sight or presence of a hen elicits FOLLOWING BEHAVIOR in its chicks, and a red belly on a male stickleback fish elicits aggressive behavior from other male sticklebacks but is attractive to gravid female sticklebacks. Also called **releasing stimulus**; **sign stimulus**. See also IMPRINTING; INNATE RELEASING MECHANISM.

release theory of humor the theory that people laugh out of a need to release pent-up psychic energy. In Sigmund FREUD's version of this theory, humor permits the expression of normally taboo impulses and the energy it releases is that normally used in keeping such impulses out of consciousness. Compare INCONGRUITY THEORY OF HUMOR.

release therapy 1. any therapy whose ultimate value is in the release of deep-seated, forgotten, or inhibited emotional and psychic pain through open expression and direct experience of anger, sorrow, or hostility in the therapy context. The technique is used, for example, in PLAY THERAPY and in PSYCHODRAMA. **2.** a form of therapy in which young children reenact anxieties, frightening experiences, and traumatic events with such materials as figurines, toy animals, and water guns. [developed in the 1930s by U.S. psychiatrist David M. Levy (1892–1977)]

release zone the region of a PRESYNAPTIC axon terminal where synaptic vesicles discharge neurotransmitter molecules into the synaptic cleft. See SYNAPSE.

releasing hormone any of a class of HYPOTHALAMIC HORMONES that travel via the HYPOTHALAMIC–PITUITARY PORTAL SYSTEM to control the release of hormones by the anterior pituitary gland. Examples are CORTICOTROPIN-RELEASING HORMONE and GONADOTROPIN-RELEASING HORMONE.

releasing stimulus see RELEASER.

relevant–irrelevant test a question format used in POLYGRAPH testing in which physiological responses accompanying questions relevant to a crime (e.g., "Did you steal from the office?") are compared with responses accompanying questions irrelevant to the crime (e.g., "Are you 24 years old?"). In criminal investigations it has been increasingly replaced by the CONTROL QUESTION TEST. See also GUILTY KNOWLEDGE TEST.

reliability *n.* the ability of a measurement instrument (e.g., a test) to measure an attribute consistently, which is important in assessing the validity of data acquired using that instrument. The basic index of reliability is the CORRELATION COEFFICIENT. INTERNAL CONSISTENCY reliability is indexed by the correlations among items or subtests; RETEST RELIABILITY is indexed by the correlation among two or more occasions of measurement. See also INTERRATER RELIABILITY. **—reliable** *adj.*

reliability of components the average reliability of the items or subtests comprising a test. See ITEM-TO-ITEM RELIABILITY.

reliability of composites the overall reliability of a test made up of components (e.g., items or subtests). See COMPOSITE RELIABILITY.

relief *n.* a POSITIVE EMOTION that occurs as a response to a threat that has abated, disappeared, or failed to materialize.

relief–discomfort quotient (**relief–distress quotient**) see DISTRESS–RELIEF QUOTIENT.

religion *n.* a system of spiritual beliefs, practices, or both, typically organized around the worship of an all-powerful deity (or deities) and involving such behaviors as prayer, meditation, and participation in public rituals. Other common features of organized religions are the belief that certain moral teachings have divine authority and the recognition of certain people, places, texts, or objects as being holy or sacred. See also PSYCHOLOGY OF RELIGION. **—religious** *adj.*

religiosity *n.* pious, exaggerated religious zeal.

religious delusions DELUSIONS associated with religious beliefs and grandiose ideas with religious content. Delusional ideation frequently includes beliefs that the individual is the embodiment of a notable religious figure, such as a messiah or prophet, and that he or she possesses special powers, such as being able to cure all illness. Such beliefs may be a feature of grandiose-type DELUSIONAL DISORDER.

religious faith belief and trust in a deity or other spiritual force that sets standards of conduct, responds to prayer, and (typically) assures the ultimate triumph of good over evil. Religious faith may be intensely private in some of its aspects but usually involves the believer in adherence to a particular religious body and an organized system of ceremonials and doctrines. Most theologians in the monotheistic traditions insist that faith involves an orientation of the entire personality toward God, rather than the merely intellectual acceptance of certain teachings. See MYSTICISM; RELIGION; SPIRITUALITY. See also PSYCHOLOGY OF RELIGION.

religious healing see FAITH HEALING.

religious instinct hypothesis the hypothesis that human beings are naturally drawn to believe in and to worship a higher power. It is used by some believers as the basis of an argument for the existence of God and the validity of religion, and by some skeptics as an illustration of how human beings create myths in order to make themselves feel more comfortable or to find meaning in life. More recently it has been argued that the religious instinct may have a biological origin and serve an evolutionary purpose.

religious mania a state of acute hyperactivity, agitation, and restlessness accompanied by hallucinations of a religious nature.

religiousness *n.* a tendency to adhere to religious beliefs and to engage in religious practices.

religious therapy therapeutic intervention through such approaches as PASTORAL COUNSELING, scriptural study, and church-sponsored community activities. Such interventions are sometimes led by a mental health professional but often not. See also SUPPORTIVE PSYCHOTHERAPY.

REM abbreviation for RAPID EYE MOVEMENT.

remand *vb.* **1.** to send back a case from an appellate court to the lower court from which the appeal came, together with instructions on how to proceed. **2.** to send an accused person back into custody or admit him or her to bail, pending further legal proceedings.

REM behavior disorder (**RBD**) a SLEEP DISORDER involving motor activity during REM SLEEP, which typically includes an actual physical enactment of dream sequences. Because the dreams that are acted out are generally unpleasant or combative, this behavior is usually disruptive and can result in violence. In *DSM–IV–TR* this disorder is classified as a PARASOMNIA NOT OTHERWISE SPECIFIED.

remedial education a learning process that occurs after the initial, primary instruction of a subject or skill has been given. Remedial education is intended to improve skills that appear deficient or lacking in a particular subject or area.

remedial reading specialized instruction for individuals whose READING QUOTIENT is significantly below average or who have developed faulty reading patterns.

remedial therapy intervention aimed at assisting a person to achieve a normal or increased level of functioning when functioning is below expectation in a particular area (e.g., reading). Also called **remedial training**.

remembering *n.* the process of consciously reviving or bringing to awareness previous events, experiences, or information. Remembering also involves the process of retaining such material, which is essential to learning, since without it one would not profit from training, practice, or past experience. According to Estonian-born Canadian psychologist Endel Tulving (1927–), remembering is distinct from knowing (see REMEMBER–KNOW PROCEDURE). Methods of assessing remembering include the RECALL METHOD, RECOGNITION METHOD, and RELEARNING METHOD.

remember–know procedure a procedure used to measure two different ways of accessing events from one's past and as an assessment of EPISODIC MEMORY and SEMANTIC MEMORY, respectively. Remembering is the conscious and vivid recollection of a prior event such that a person can mentally travel to the specific time and place of the original event and retrieve the details; he or she is able to bring back to mind a particular association, image, or something more personal from the time of the event. Knowing refers to the experience in which a person is certain that an event has occurred but fails to recollect anything about its actual occurrence or what was experienced at the time of its occurrence; the retrieval of the event is not accompanied by any specific recollection about the time, place, or details. [introduced in 1985 by Estonian-born Canadian psychologist Endel Tulving (1927–)]

remembrance *n.* **1.** the act of remembering or the state of being remembered. **2.** in GROUP SOCIALIZATION, a late stage in the socialization process during which ex-members review their experiences in the group and continuing members discuss the contributions and activities of former members.

Remeron *n.* a trade name for MIRTAZAPINE.

remifentanil *n.* see FENTANYL.

reminder *n.* a cue that helps to refresh or reinvigorate some behavior, memory, habit, or goal.

reminiscence *n.* **1.** the recalling of previous experiences, especially those of a pleasant nature. Events that occurred in adolescence and early adulthood (often called the **reminiscence bump**) are most often remembered. Unlike RECOLLECTION, reminiscence does not necessarily involve vivid and detailed memory. See also AUTOBIOGRAPHICAL MEMORY; EPISODIC MEMORY; LIFE REVIEW. **2.** an increase in the amount remembered, or in performance, that occurs after a delay interval following the initial exposure to the information, instead of the more usual forgetting after a delay.

reminiscence theory of knowledge the theory of Greek philosopher Plato (c. 429–347 BCE) that knowledge originates in a hypothetical existence prior to birth in which humans are exposed to the true forms or essences of things. After birth this knowledge is retrieved through the mental process of recollection, or reminiscence. According to Plato, this is the only possible explanation for human knowledge of certain ideal concepts, such as perfect equality, that cannot be derived from experience. See PLATONIC IDEALISM; THEORY OF FORMS.

reminiscence therapy the use of LIFE HISTORIES—written, oral, or both—to improve psychological well-being. The therapy is often used with older people.

Reminyl *n.* a trade name for GALANTAMINE.

remission *n.* a reduction or significant abatement in symptoms of a disease or disorder, or the period during which this occurs. Remission of symptoms does not necessarily indicate that a disease or disorder is fully cured. See also SPONTANEOUS REMISSION.

REM latency the time between onset of sleep and the first occurrence of RAPID EYE MOVEMENT (REM).

remorse *n.* anguish caused by a sense of guilt, which may have a real or imagined basis. Various methods may be used to relieve feelings of guilt, including bestowing gifts and doing penance.

remote association an association between one item in a list or series and another item that does not adjoin it. Hermann EBBINGHAUS first reported that associations are formed not only between adjacent items but also between items further apart in the list or series.

remote-association test a creativity test in which the participant is asked to suggest a fourth word that links three apparently unrelated words, such as rat–blue–cottage (answer: cheese).

remote cause a cause that is removed from its effect in time or space but is nevertheless the ultimate or overriding cause. In a CAUSAL CHAIN, it may be considered to be the precipitating event without which the chain would not have begun (the original cause). For example, the PROXIMATE CAUSE of Smith's aggression may be a trivial snub, but the remote cause may be Smith's early childhood experiences. See also CAUSAL LATENCY; DELAYED EFFECT.

remote grandparent the type of grandparent who interacts with his or her grandchildren infrequently, due to physical distance or emotional detachment. Compare COMPANIONATE GRANDPARENT; INVOLVED GRANDPARENT.

remote masking the masking of a signal by a masker that is much higher in frequency than the signal. See AUDITORY MASKING.

remote memory recall or recognition of experiences or information dating from the distant past. See LONG-TERM MEMORY.

remote perception 1. in parapsychology, the perception of a scene, event, or the like at which one is not physically present. In the usual research protocol, one person is physically present at and studying a target location, while the remote perceiver is situated at some distance from the scene, with no prior knowledge of it, and attempts to perceive aspects of its ambience and detail. Both participants record their impressions on identical checklists, and the observations are later correlated for level of agreement. **2.** the perception of an object using means other than the senses normally used to perceive it. For example, rocks on Mars may be perceived using a video camera mounted on a robot. See TELEPRESENCE.

remote viewing see CLAIRVOYANCE.

remotivation *n.* intervention aimed at increasing the likelihood that a person will cooperate with and benefit from treatments. It includes efforts directed toward stimulating withdrawn patients with chronic disorders in mental hospitals, for example, by involving them in poetry-reading groups or conversation groups in which a **bridge to reality** is established by discussing current topics.

REM rebound the recurrence of REM SLEEP, the stage of sleep in which dreaming is associated with mild involuntary eye movements.

REM sleep *r*apid-*e*ye-*m*ovement sleep: the stage of sleep, formerly called **desynchronized sleep**, in which dreaming occurs and the electroencephalogram shows activity characteristic of wakefulness (hence it is also known as **paradoxical sleep**) except for inhibition of motor expression other than coordinated movements of the eyes. It accounts for one quarter to one fifth of total sleep time. Also called **activated sleep**. See DREAM STATE. Compare NREM SLEEP.

REM storm an intense burst of RAPID EYE MOVEMENT (REM) during sleep.

renal *adj.* referring to the kidney or kidneys.

renal system the kidneys and related structures, including the ureters, bladder, urethra, renal blood supply, and renal nerve supply, which are involved with the excretion of waste materials from the body.

Renard Diagnostic Interview a structured interview developed in 1977 at the Renard Hospital, Washington University (St. Louis), to elicit enough information to establish criteria for the diagnosis of 15 major psychiatric disorders. See RESEARCH DIAGNOSTIC CRITERIA.

renifleur *n.* a person with a morbid interest in body odors, especially as a means of sexual excitement. See OSPHRESIOLAGNIA.

renin *n.* an enzyme that is released by the kidneys when blood pressure falls. It specifically cleaves the plasma globulin protein angiotensinogen to form ANGIOTENSIN.

renin–angiotensin system a system of the liver and kidneys that regulates the production of ALDOSTERONE from the adrenal cortex and is therefore involved in the control of blood pressure. See ANGIOTENSIN; RENIN.

Renpenning's syndrome a condition that is inherited as an X-linked (see SEX-LINKED) trait, marked by eye defects, MICROCEPHALY, psychomotor retardation, short stature, small testes, and mental retardation. [Hans **Renpenning** (1929–), Canadian physician]

Renshaw cell a neuron that inhibits motor neurons near the spinal cord. Renshaw cells are a part of the NEGATIVE FEEDBACK system that prevents rapid, repeated firing of motor neurons. See also RECURRENT COLLATERAL INHIBITION. [Birdsay **Renshaw** (1911–1948), U.S. neurophysiologist]

renunciation *n.* **1.** in general, the act of giving something up or denying oneself. **2.** in psychoanalytic theory, a refusal of the EGO to follow impulses of the ID. **—renounce** *vb.*

reorganization principle in GESTALT PSYCHOLOGY, the principle that new learning or perception disrupts old cognitive structures, requiring a reorganized structure. This is in opposition to the associationist principle that new learning is essentially added on to existing structures (see ASSOCIATIONISM). See also DISCONTINUITY HYPOTHESIS.

repair *n.* in language, a correction made spontaneously in conversation to repair miscommunication. Also called **conversational repair**.

reparameterization *n.* the process of recasting the parameters of a model in different terms, usually for the purpose of removing technical difficulties in the solution of the GENERAL LINEAR MODEL from the original parameterization.

reparation *n.* **1.** amelioration of or expiation for harm previously done. See also RESTITUTION. **2.** in the OBJECT RELATIONS THEORY of Melanie KLEIN, acts that are performed during the DEPRESSIVE POSITION to repair the relationship with the GOOD OBJECT. Klein viewed all creative and positive acts in adulthood as examples of reparation.

reparative therapy therapy given to people who have experienced a sexual assault, including childhood sexual abuse and adult rape. Procedures generally involve working through the emotional trauma that was experienced and cognitive therapy on such issues as self-blame. The aim of reparative therapy is to turn a victim into a survivor, who is able to return to normal functioning emotionally, interpersonally, and sexually.

reparenting *n.* **1.** a controversial therapeutic procedure used to provide a client with missed childhood experiences. The client, who typically has severe problems, is treated as a child or infant; for example, he or she may be fed with a spoon or bottle, hugged, sung to, and provided with what the client or therapist feels the client missed in childhood. Reparenting has been unethically used to justify recreation of the birth process by wrapping a client in a blanket and having him or her struggle to get out. **2.** in self-help and some forms of counseling, a therapeutic technique in which individuals are urged to provide for themselves the kind of parenting attitudes or actions that their own parents were unable to provide.

repeatability *n.* the degree to which specific research studies obtain similar results when they are conducted again and again.

repeated acquisition a procedure in which sequences of responses are learned but the sequence changes from observation period to observation period. For example, a person might be asked to press a sequence of keys in the presence of seven different stimuli presented in sequence. Having learned to do so, the person would be required to learn a different sequence of key presses in response to the same seven stimuli in the next test period.

repeated measures design a research design in which the same individuals are measured on the same DEPENDENT VARIABLE (or variables) on multiple occasions.

repeat offender see RECIDIVISM.

repertoire *n.* the sum total of potential behavior or responses that a person or nonhuman animal is capable of performing. It usually refers to behavior that has been learned and is generally quantified through the study of past behavior. Also called **behavioral repertoire**.

repertory grid a technique used to analyze an individual's PERSONAL CONSTRUCTS. A number of significant concepts are selected, each of which is rated by the participant on a number of dimensions using a numerical scale. The findings are displayed in matrix form and can be subjected to statistical analysis to reveal correlations. The repertory grid was developed principally as a means of analyzing personal relationships but has also been used to determine the complexity of a person's thinking (COGNITIVE COMPLEXITY) and in various other applications. [introduced by U.S. psychologist George A. Kelly (1905–1967)]

repetition *n.* repeated presentation of material to be learned or remembered. Repetition forms the basis of DRILL and ROTE LEARNING methods. See also REPETITION EFFECT.

repetition compulsion in psychoanalytic theory, an unconscious need to reenact early traumas in the attempt to overcome or master them. In repetition compulsion the early painful experience is repeated in a new situation symbolic of the repressed prototype. Repetition compulsion acts as a RESISTANCE to therapeutic change, since the goal of therapy is not to repeat but to remember the trauma and to see its relation to present behavior. Also called **compulsion to repeat**.

repetition effect the fact that repeated presentation of information or items typically leads to better memory for the material. The repetition effect is a general principle of learning, although there are exceptions and modifiers. For instance, **spaced repetitions** are usually more effective than **massed repetitions**. See DISTRIBUTED PRACTICE; LAW OF FREQUENCY; MASSED PRACTICE.

repetition law see LAW OF FREQUENCY.

repetition priming a change in the processing of a stimulus (e.g., speed of response, number of errors) due to previous exposure to the same or a related stimulus.

repetitive strain injury (**RSI**) a MUSCULOSKELETAL DISORDER involving chronic inflammation of the muscles, tendons, or nerves and caused by overuse or misuse of a specific body part. RSI most commonly affects the hands, wrists, elbows, arms, shoulders, back, or neck and results in pain and fatigue of the affected areas. Examples include CARPAL TUNNEL SYNDROME and **tendinitis** (inflammation, irritation, and swelling of a tendon). Repetitive strain injuries are often associated with occupational situations, and their prevention is an important issue in ERGONOMICS and HUMAN FACTORS. Also called **cumulative trauma disorder** (**CTD**); **repetitive motion disorder** or **injury** (**RMD**; **RMI**); **repetitive stress injury**.

repetitive transcranial magnetic stimulation (**rTMS**) see TRANSCRANIAL MAGNETIC STIMULATION.

replacement memory see SCREEN MEMORY.

replacement sampling see SAMPLING WITH REPLACEMENT.

replacement therapy 1. treatment in which a natural or synthetic substance is substituted for one that is deficient or lacking in an individual. See HORMONE REPLACEMENT THERAPY. **2.** the process of replacing abnormal thoughts or behavior with healthier ones through the use of therapy focused on constructive activities and interests.

replication *n.* the repetition of an original experiment, or of a trial within an experiment, to gain information about its INTERNAL VALIDITY, its REPEATABILITY, or its application in other settings. In **exact replication**, procedures are identical to the original experiment or duplicated as closely as possible. In **modified replication**, alternative procedures and additional conditions may be incorporated. In **conceptual replication**, different techniques and manipulations are introduced to gain theoretical information. See also BALANCED REPLICATION.

replication plane a plane generated by crossing the EFFECT SIZE of a study with that of its attempted REPLICATION.

reportability *n.* the quality of psychological events that enables them to be reported by the experiencing individual. It is the standard behavioral index of conscious experience (see CONSCIOUSNESS). Also called **verbal report**.

representation *n.* **1.** a mental structure of encoded information that corresponds to some object or concept. See also REPRESENTATIONALISM. **2.** in psychoanalytic theory, the use of a SYMBOL to stand for a threatening object or a repressed impulse. **3.** more generally, the use of any object, figure, or image to stand for or signify something. See SYMBOLISM. **—represent** *vb.* **—representational** *adj.* **—representative** *adj.*

representational change a young child's false memory for an initial belief as demonstrated by performance in a FALSE-BELIEF TASK. For example, children shown a box marked as containing pencils and asked what it contains are likely to reply that it contains pencils; the box is then opened to reveal that it actually contains pennies. When later asked what they originally thought was in the box, most children of 3 years and younger say pennies, whereas older children remember their original belief.

representational constraints the ways in which representations are hard-wired into the brain so that some types of knowledge are innate. Several theorists have proposed that infants are born with, or develop very early in life, some basic ideas about the nature of objects (e.g., their solidity), mathematics (e.g., simple concepts of addition and subtraction), or grammar. Also called **representational innateness**. Compare ARCHITECTURAL CONSTRAINTS; CHRONOTOPIC CONSTRAINTS.

representational insight the knowledge that an entity (e.g., a word, photograph) can stand for something other than itself.

representationalism *n.* the view that in perception the mind is not directly aware of the perceived object but of a mental representation of it. See PHENOMENALISM. **—representationalist** *adj.*

representational redescription the mental processes by which a child produces a new description of his or her existing representations. This recoding of information enables the child to think more flexibly and use knowledge in a more sophisticated way. [proposed by British psychologist Annette Karmiloff-Smith]

representational skills cognitive skills involved in understanding the world of people, objects, and events in terms of mental representation, including the use of images and words.

representational stage in Jean PIAGET's theory, the period of cognitive development that begins with the PREOPERATIONAL STAGE and ends with the CONCRETE OPERATIONAL STAGE.

representational thought cognition based on use of symbols, including, but not limited to, language and images.

representative democracy see DEMOCRACY.

representative design an experimental design in which background variables are intentionally not controlled so that research results will apply more realistically to the real world. See ECOLOGICAL VALIDITY; MUNDANE REALISM.

representative factors in some studies of the higher primates, hypothetical mental functions that permit an animal to continue or renew a response after the original stimulus is discontinued. Such functions are presumed to involve some form of MENTAL REPRESENTATION of stimuli.

representativeness *n.* the correspondence between a sample and the population from which it is drawn such that the sample accurately symbolizes its population. A representative sample reproduces the essential characteristics and constitution of a population in correct proportions.

representativeness heuristic a method of generalization about a given person or target based on partial information or on how closely the exemplar matches the typical or average member of the category. For example, given a choice of the two categories "poet" and "accountant," judges are likely to assign a person in unconventional clothes reading a poetry book to the former category; however, the much greater frequency of accountants in the population means that such a person is more likely to be an accountant. The representativeness heuristic is thus a form of the BASE-RATE FALLACY. Compare AVAILABILITY HEURISTIC.

representative sampling the selection of a sample that accurately reflects the total population. See also RANDOM SAMPLING.

repressed memory see RECOVERED MEMORY.

repression *n.* **1.** in classic psychoanalytic theory and other forms of DEPTH PSYCHOLOGY, the basic DEFENSE MECHANISM that consists of excluding painful experiences and unacceptable impulses from consciousness. Repression operates on an unconscious level as a protection against anxiety produced by objectionable sexual wishes, feelings of hostility, and ego-threatening experiences of all kinds. It also comes into play in most other forms of defense, as in denial, in which individuals avoid unpleasant realities by first repressing them and then negating them. See PRIMARY REPRESSION; REPRESSION PROPER. **2.** the suppression or exclusion of individuals or groups within the social context, through limitations on personal rights and liberties. **3.** more generally, the process of restricting, restraining, or subduing something or someone. Compare SUPPRESSION. **—repress** *vb.*

repression proper in psychoanalytic theory, a form of REPRESSION that acts upon experiences and wishes that have been conscious to make them unconscious. This is in contrast to PRIMARY REPRESSION, which operates on material that has never been conscious. Sigmund FREUD also called this form of repression **afterexpulsion** because material is expelled from consciousness after it has become conscious. Also called **secondary repression**.

repression-resistance *n.* in psychoanalysis, the RESISTANCE deployed by the patient in order to maintain REPRESSION of unacceptable impulses. This may manifest itself in the patient's forgetting of events, an impeded flow of FREE ASSOCIATIONS, or in the patient's application of interpretations offered by the analyst to others but not to himself or herself. Also called **ego resistance**. Compare ID RESISTANCE.

repression–sensitization defense mechanisms involving approach and avoidance responses to threatening stimuli. The sensitizing process involves intellectualization in approaching or controlling the stimulus, whereas repression involves unconscious denial in avoiding the stimulus.

repressive coping style a pattern of dealing with life characterized by downplaying problems or misfortunes and maintaining an artificially positive view. Repressive coping is diagnosed by a combination of high scores on SOCIAL DESIRABILITY bias and low scores on reported anxiety. See also POSITIVE ILLUSION.

reproduction *n.* in biology, the production of new individuals from parent organisms, which perpetuates the species. Sexual reproduction involves the fusion of male and female GAMETES in the process of FERTILIZATION; ASEXUAL reproduction does not.

reproduction theory *n.* a theory suggesting that educational systems reproduce the social and economic structures and divisions of the societies in which they exist. [originated by French sociologist of education Pierre-Félix Bourdieu (1930–2002)]

reproductive behavior activity that leads to propagation of individuals. The mechanisms range from simple cell division in a unicellular organism or budding of new offspring in simple multicellular organisms to a merger of chromosomes contributed by the male and female parents in sexual reproduction, often followed by supervision of the offspring until they can survive independently. Courtship behavior, mate selection, copulatory behavior, and parental behavior are components of reproductive behavior.

reproductive failure failure to conceive or to bear offspring that will grow to maturity.

reproductive function the total process of creating a new organism, or a specific act of the process, such as sexual intercourse.

reproductive image in Jean PIAGET's theory of cognitive development, a mental image that is limited to evoking previously experienced sights and involves relatively static representations of objects. Compare ANTICIPATORY IMAGE.

reproductive imagination imagination used to reproduce images or objects with which one has become familiar in the past.

reproductive memory accurate recall of information. This type of memory is subject to errors of CONSTRUCTIVE MEMORY or RECONSTRUCTIVE MEMORY, especially when material consists of stories or prose passages. See BARTLETT TECHNIQUE.

reproductive success the degree to which an individual is successful in producing progeny that in turn are able to produce progeny of their own. Individuals vary in their success in finding mates and reproducing successfully. NATURAL SELECTION is based on this differential reproductive success. The genetic and behavioral traits that lead to greatest reproductive success survive in a population over generations, while traits producing low reproductive success eventually become extinct within a population. See also INCLUSIVE FITNESS.

reproductive suppression the inability of one or several individuals within a group to reproduce, despite having reached reproductive maturity. In many COOPERATIVE-BREEDING species, dominant, breeding individuals suppress reproduction in subordinates. Both behavioral and physiological cues can be involved. Reproductive suppression can be temporary, as in wolves, marmosets, or meerkats, in which an individual can quickly become a breeder in the absence of cues from the dominant animal, or it can be permanent, as in SOCIAL INSECTS.

reproductive type a CONSTITUTIONAL TYPE characterized by a dominance of the reproductive system over other body systems (see ROSTAN TYPES). It is roughly comparable to the HYPERGENITAL TYPE.

res cogitans the Latin term (literally: "thinking thing") used by French philosopher René Descartes (1596–1650) to refer to the mental realm as distinct from the realm of physical matter (RES EXTENSA). See CARTESIAN DUALISM.

Rescorla–Wagner theory an influential theory of PAVLOVIAN CONDITIONING that posits that conditioning proceeds from pairing to pairing as a fixed proportion of the maximum amount of conditioning that can be achieved with the UNCONDITIONED STIMULUS (US). For example, if food (the US) produces 100 ml of salivation (the unconditioned response [UR]), and after one pairing of a tone with food, the tone elicits a CONDITIONED RESPONSE (CR) of 40 ml of salivation (i.e., 0.4 of the maximum amount achievable), a second trial will increase the magnitude of the CR by 24 ml (i.e., 0.4 × [100–40]), so that the response will be 64 ml. After a third trial, the magnitude will be 78.4 ml—that is, 40 + 24 + (0.4 × [100–64]—and so on until the CR is 100 ml (the maximum achievable). Also called **Rescorla–Wagner model**. [proposed in 1972 by Robert **Rescorla** (1940–) and Alan **Wagner** (1934–), U.S. experimental psychologists]

research *n.* the systematic effort to discover or confirm facts or to investigate a problem or topic, most often by scientific methods of observation and experiment.

research design see EXPERIMENTAL DESIGN.

Research Diagnostic Criteria (**RDC**) a modification of criteria developed from the RENARD DIAGNOSTIC INTERVIEW for diagnosis of psychiatric disorders, expanding the number of disorders from the original 15 to 25. It focuses on present or past episodes of illness and gives inclusion and exclusion criteria for diagnosis of the different disorders.

research ethics the values, principles, and standards by which are judged the conduct of individual researchers and the moral status of the research procedures they employ. Also called **experimental ethics**.

research method see SCIENTIFIC METHOD.

research question a HYPOTHESIS under investigation.

research register a database of research studies, in progress or completed, about a specific topic, or funded by the same organization, or sharing a common design.

research sport psychologist an individual who is educated and trained in the nonclinical psychology of human movement as it relates to sport and whose primary focus is on the development of theory and the study of the efficacy of application strategies. See SPORT PSYCHOLOGY.

resentment *n.* a feeling of bitterness, animosity, or hostility elicited by something perceived as insulting or injurious.

reserpine *n.* see RAUWOLFIA DERIVATIVES.

reserve capacity the difference between performance on a psychological task and the individual's maximum capability to perform that task. Training, intervention, and practice can be used to minimize reserve capacity on a given task.

reserved *adj.* emotionally restrained, particularly in social interactions.

res extensa the Latin term (literally: "extended thing") used by French philosopher René Descartes (1596–1650) to refer to the physical realm of matter. By "extended" Descartes meant that material objects have the property of occupying space, in contrast to the mind, which has no spatial dimensions. Compare RES COGITANS. See CARTESIAN DUALISM.

residence rate the ratio of the number of people residing in institutions of a given type on a given date to the total population of the city, county, state, or other area.

residential care long-term care for older adults, patients with chronic illness, or individuals undergoing rehabilitation that provides housing and meals and may also provide medical, nursing, and social services. See also DOMICILIARY CARE.

residential habilitation a HOME AND COMMUNITY-BASED SERVICE provided for a person with mental retardation or a related condition. This service is similar to DAY HABILITATION but is delivered in a supervised or supportive residential setting or in a family home.

residential schools special educational facilities that provide residential services for children with mental retardation. Although historically significant, the use of such facilities greatly diminished during the latter part of the 20th century, and children with mental retardation now receive public education in their home communities.

residential treatment treatment that takes place in a hospital, special center, or other facility that offers a treatment program and residential accommodation. Some programs require residence for a specific time (e.g., a one-month treatment for addictions), and some may include provision for the client to learn or work in the community during the day.

residual 1. *n.* in statistics, the difference between the value of an empirical observation and the value of that observation predicted by a model. **2.** *n.* in general, any part of something that remains after most of the condition, entity, or process has been used up or removed. **3.** *adj.* denoting a condition in which acute symptoms have subsided but chronic or less severe symptoms remain. **4.** *adj.* denoting remaining ability (e.g., residual hearing) or a remaining disability (e.g., residual loss of vision) after a trauma or surgery.

residual analysis any of a series of analyses performed on a RESIDUAL to diagnose problems in the application of a model to a particular batch of data. See REGRESSION DIAGNOSTICS.

residual attention-deficit disorder in *DSM–III*, the condition (designated **attention-deficit disorder, residual type**) of a child previously diagnosed as having attention-deficit disorder with hyperactivity in whom the hyperactivity component has ceased. In *DSM–IV–TR* the equivalent diagnosis is ATTENTION-DEFICIT/HYPERACTIVITY DISORDER NOT OTHERWISE SPECIFIED or ATTENTION-DEFICIT/HYPERACTIVITY DISORDER, predominantly inattentive type.

residual schizophrenia in *DSM–IV–TR*, a subtype of SCHIZOPHRENIA diagnosed when there has been at least one schizophrenic episode but positive symptoms (e.g., delusions, hallucinations, disorganized speech or behavior) are no longer prominent. The person does, however, continue to display negative symptoms (e.g., flat affect, poverty of speech, or avolition) or mild behavioral and cognitive disturbances (e.g., eccentric behavior, mildly disorganized speech, or odd beliefs). The *DSM–III* designation was **residual type schizophrenic disorder**.

residual term see ERROR TERM.

residual vision relatively nonconscious visual processing that is spared when damage to the STRIATE CORTEX (primary visual cortex) produces loss of conscious vision. See BLINDSIGHT.

residue method see METHOD OF RESIDUES.

residue pitch see VIRTUAL PITCH.

resignation *n.* an attitude of apathetic surrender to one's situation or symptoms.

resilience *n.* the process and outcome of successfully adapting to difficult or challenging life experiences, especially through mental, emotional, and behavioral flexibility and adjustment to external and internal demands. A number of factors contribute to how well people adapt to adversities, predominant among them (a) the ways in which individuals view and engage with the world, (b) the availability and quality of social resources, and (c) specific COPING STRATEGIES. Psychological research demonstrates that resources and skills in each of these domains associated with more positive adaptation (i.e., greater resilience) can be cultivated and practiced. Also called **psychic resilience**; **psychological resilience**. See also COPING BEHAVIOR; COPING-SKILLS TRAINING. **—resilient** *adj.*

resinous *adj.* denoting one of the primary odor qualities in HENNING'S ODOR PRISM.

resistance *n.* **1.** generally, any action in opposition to, defying, or withstanding something or someone. **2.** in psychotherapy and analysis, unconscious obstruction, through the client's words or behavior, of the therapist's or analyst's methods of eliciting or interpreting psychic material brought forth in therapy. Psychoanalytic theory classically interprets resistance as a form of DEFENSE and distinguishes three types: CONSCIOUS RESISTANCE, ID RESISTANCE, and REPRESSION-RESISTANCE. **3.** the degree to which an organism can defend itself against disease-causing microorganisms. See IMMUNITY. **4.** the degree to which disease-causing microorganisms withstand the action of drugs. **—resist** *vb.* **—resistant** *adj.*

resistance of an attitude the extent to which an attitude remains unchanged in the face of attack or challenge.

resistance stage see GENERAL ADAPTATION SYNDROME.

resistance to change the measure of BEHAVIORAL MOMENTUM. Ongoing behavior is challenged by operations intended to disrupt it. The greater the degree that the behavior persists unperturbed, the greater is its resistance to change and, by inference, the greater its behavioral momentum.

resistance to extinction the endurance or persistence of a conditioned response during EXTINCTION.

resistance to interference the ability to ignore irrelevant information so that it does not impede task performance. Inability to ignore such information is called **interference sensitivity**.

resistant attachment see AMBIVALENT ATTACHMENT.

resistant estimator an estimator of a parameter that is less likely to be influenced by OUTLIERS (extreme scores). Also called **robust estimator**.

resocialization *n.* the process of enabling individuals with mental disorders to resume appropriate interpersonal activities and behaviors and, generally, to participate in community life through more adaptive attitudes and skills.

resolution *n.* a measure of the ability of the eye or an optical device or system to detect two distinct objects when these are close together. A system with high resolution can distinguish targets very close to one another as individual entities; a system with low resolution can only distinguish targets that are farther apart. Also called **resolving power**.

resolution phase see SEXUAL-RESPONSE CYCLE.

resolving power see RESOLUTION.

resonance *n.* see ACOUSTIC RESONANCE.

resource allocation the distribution of a program's effort across different parts of the program or service.

resource awareness knowledge by a therapist or counselor of community services and agencies that could assist clients in meeting their needs or in bolstering positive strategies, directions, or gains achieved in psychotherapy or counseling.

resource competition in consciousness, the process in which concurrent attentional or conscious processes compete for limited brain resources. See DUAL-TASK COMPETITION.

resource defense polygyny a form of POLYGYNY that can occur when males defend areas containing differing amounts of resources and some of the areas have sufficient resources to allow multiple females to breed successfully. The male defending the resources is able to benefit from polygyny not by being more attractive or having better genes but because the resources he controls are sufficient for multiple females and their offspring.

resource teacher a specialist who teaches children with SPECIAL NEEDS, gifted children, and other exceptional children and who is available to act as a consultant to other teachers.

resource theory a theory of interpersonal relationships holding that the amount of resources (e.g., information, love, status, money, goods, services) possessed by each of the participants greatly affects the nature of their relationship. Those having more resources than they require for themselves can distribute their excess to the other party and thus have power over the other to the extent that the other needs these resources. It is proposed that withholding needed resources from the other can heighten conflict, whereas the relationship is harmonious when each party is equally powerful and cooperative in the exchange of resources. [proposed in 1974 by U.S. psychologists Edna B. Foa (1937–) and Uriel G. Foa (1916–1990)]

respiration *n.* **1.** the series of chemical reactions that enables organisms to convert the chemical energy stored in food into energy that can be used by cells. Also called **cellular respiration**; **internal respiration**. **2.** the process by which an animal takes up oxygen from its environment and discharges carbon dioxide into it. Also called **external respiration**.

respiratory depression slow and shallow breathing that can be induced by opioids and other sedatives. These drugs raise the threshold level of respiratory centers in the medulla oblongata of the brain that normally would react to increased carbon dioxide in the tissues by increasing the rate and depth of breathing. Respiratory depression is a primary hazard of the use of morphine and other OPIOID ANALGESICS, but is also observed with CNS DEPRESSANTS, such as barbiturates. Respiratory depression is less common with BENZODIAZEPINES unless they are taken together with another CNS depressant, such as alcohol.

respiratory disorder any disorder involving one or more components of the respiratory system, such as the diaphragm, lungs, trachea, larynx, or nasal cavities. See also ASTHMA; HYPERVENTILATION; PSEUDOASTHMA.

respiratory distress syndrome a disorder of some newborn babies in which the lungs fail to expand due to deficiency of a natural surfactant that prevents the alveoli (air sacs) from collapsing. The alveoli are lined with a membrane of hyaline material. The condition, which is most common in premature infants, may worsen progressively before the lungs begin producing surfactant. Also called **hyaline membrane disease**.

respiratory sinus arrhythmia (**RSA**) the normal tendency for the heart rate to increase and decrease in synchrony but slightly out of phase with inhalation and exhalation. When observed, respiratory sinus arrhythmia can be taken as a sign of vagal function (see VAGAL TONE). It is sometimes used as a physiological index of temperamental disposition: According to U.S. psychologist Jerome Kagan (1929–), lack of RSA is associated with inhibited temperamental disposition.

respiratory type a CONSTITUTIONAL TYPE characterized by a dominance of the circulatory and respiratory systems over other body systems. See ROSTAN TYPES.

respite services assistance, supervision, and recreational or social activities provided for a person who is unable to care for him- or herself (e.g., because of a disability or chronic illness) for a limited period in order to temporarily relieve family members from caregiving responsibilities or enable them to conduct necessary personal or household affairs. These services may be provided for a child or adult on a scheduled or unscheduled basis, either regularly or occasionally, after school hours, at weekends, or overnight, and either in the home or at another location. Also called **respite care**; **in-home respite**.

respondent *n.* **1.** the organism that responds to a stimulus. **2.** a person who is interviewed or who replies to a survey or questionnaire. **3.** in conditioning, any REFLEX that can be conditioned by PAVLOVIAN CONDITIONING procedures. Compare OPERANT.

respondent behavior behavior that is evoked by a specific stimulus and will consistently and predictably occur if the stimulus is presented. Also called **elicited behavior**. See also REFLEX. Compare EMITTED BEHAVIOR.

respondent conditioning see PAVLOVIAN CONDITIONING.

respondent topography the physical characteristics of a RESPONDENT.

responder *n.* see ALLOCATOR.

response *n.* any glandular, muscular, neural, or other reaction to a stimulus. A response is a clearly defined, measurable unit of behavior discussed in terms of its result (e.g., pressing a lever) or its physical characteristics (e.g., raising an arm; see RESPONSE TOPOGRAPHY).

response acquiescence the tendency of a research participant, interviewee, or respondent to reply affirmatively to a question regardless of its content. Also called **yea-saying**. See ACQUIESCENT RESPONSE SET. Compare NAY-SAYING.

response amplitude the magnitude of a response, especially in conditioning.

response bias a tendency to give one response more than others, regardless of the stimulus condition. In SIGNAL DETECTION THEORY, response bias is the overall willingness to say "yes" (signal present) or "no" (signal not present), regardless of the actual presence or absence of the signal.

response-by-analogy principle the generalization that an organism in an unfamiliar situation will react in a manner similar to its reaction in a similar but familiar situation.

response circuit the neural pathway from a RECEPTOR to an EFFECTOR.

response class a category of behaviors that have the same or similar external outcomes.

response competition in choice reaction tasks, the interference of an irrelevant stimulus or stimulus feature in producing a response such that CHOICE REACTION TIME to produce the correct response is slowed. For example, in the STROOP COLOR–WORD INTERFERENCE TEST, in which participants are asked to name the color of letters that themselves spell the name of another color, reaction time is slowed because response activation from the irrelevant information (what the letters spell) competes with that from the relevant information (the color of the letters).

response cost a procedure in OPERANT CONDITIONING in which certain responses result in loss of a valued commodity. The intent of such procedures is to produce punishment. See NEGATIVE PUNISHMENT.

response deprivation in operant conditioning, an approach to identifying reinforcers before their effectiveness has been demonstrated. It holds that if the opportunity to engage in some activity is restricted below its normal level, then opportunity to engage in that activity can serve as reinforcement for some other behavior.

response differentiation see DIFFERENTIATION.

response frequency see RESPONSE RATE.

response generalization see INDUCTION.

response hierarchy the ordering of a group of responses or response sequences in the order in which they are likely to be evoked by a specific stimulus (RESPONDENT BEHAVIOR) or to occur in a particular stimulus situation (OPERANT BEHAVIOR). Also called **hierarchy of response**.

response integration the process of combining reflexes and simple movements into more complex responses.

response latency see LATENCY OF RESPONSE.

response learning learning to perform specific movements or responses. Edward C. TOLMAN contrasted response learning in mazes, in which the participant learns a sequence of left–right responses, with PLACE LEARNING, in which the participant learns a cognitive map of the maze. Also called **movement learning**.

response magnitude the amplitude, duration, or intensity of a response.

response maintenance the extent to which changes are maintained for a period of time after an intervention has been completed.

response-operating characteristic curve see RECEIVER-OPERATING CHARACTERISTIC CURVE.

response-oriented system a system of psychology that emphasizes responses as the target of primary study.

An example is OPERANT CONDITIONING. See ACT PSYCHOLOGY; S–R PSYCHOLOGY.

response prevention a type of behavior therapy used to treat OBSESSIVE-COMPULSIVE DISORDER, involving exposure to situations or cues that trigger OBSESSIONS or provoke COMPULSIONS, followed by the prevention of the compulsive behavior. Also called **exposure and response prevention**.

response probability the likelihood that a response will occur in a particular circumstance. It is often inferred from the RELATIVE FREQUENCY or the RESPONSE RATE.

response proposition the content of an imagined response to an imagined situation stimulus. Response propositions are part of the BIOINFORMATIONAL THEORY of how and why imagery works in performance enhancement. See also STIMULUS PROPOSITION.

response rate the number of responses that occur within a specified time interval. Also called **response frequency**.

response–reinforcement contingency see REINFORCEMENT CONTINGENCY.

response scenario any of a series of alternative behavior patterns that could occur when an individual is confronted with a specific stimulus. In sport, for example, a response scenario might consist of alternative offensive plays that could be run against a specific defensive formation.

response selection an intermediate stage of human information processing in which a response to an identified stimulus is chosen. Response selection is typically studied by varying relationships between the stimuli and their assigned responses.

response set 1. a tendency to answer questions in a systematic manner that is unrelated to their content. Examples include the ACQUIESCENT RESPONSE SET and SOCIAL DESIRABILITY RESPONSE SET. See also RESPONSE STYLE. [first extensively discussed and studied by Lee J. CRONBACH] **2.** in sport, the tendency for an athlete to exhibit the same pattern of play in specific situations (e.g., always faking to the right before driving for the basket).

response–shock interval (**R–S interval**) in a SIDMAN AVOIDANCE SCHEDULE, the time by which each response postpones the aversive stimulus (which is usually a shock). For example, with a response–shock interval of 20 s, each response restarts a 20-s timer that controls the time to the next shock. Therefore, if 20 s elapse without a response, a shock occurs.

response strength a hypothetical entity that summarizes the likelihood of occurrence, magnitude, and resistance to disruption of a class of responses, often measured by RESPONSE RATE or LATENCY OF RESPONSE.

response style a RESPONSE SET, specifically one arising from dispositional rather than situational factors.

response suppression a decrease in the rate or probability of a response due to some experimental operation. For example, PUNISHMENT results in response suppression.

response threshold see THRESHOLD.

response time see REACTION TIME.

response topography the physical characteristics of a response, including its duration, force, extent, and location. Also called **topography of response**.

response variable the DEPENDENT VARIABLE in a study.

restatement *n.* in psychotherapy and counseling, the verbatim repetition or rephrasing by the therapist or counselor of a client's statement. The purpose is not only to confirm that the client's remarks have been understood, but also to provide a "mirror" in which the client can see his or her feelings and ideas more clearly (see MIRRORING). Compare CLARIFICATION; INTERPRETATION; REFRAMING.

rest-cure technique a treatment approach, developed in the 19th century, for individuals with nervous disorders attributed to the hectic pace of life in the "railroad age." The regimen consisted not only of extended rest, but also physical therapy, massage, environmental change, mild exercise, and a nutritious diet. Although the technique itself is no longer used, the concept it embodies is still applied in such activities as taking time off work for a "mental health day" or spending time at a health spa. [developed by U.S. physician Silas Weir Mitchell (1829–1914)]

rest home a facility for convalescent care or for older adults who do not need continuous medical or nursing care. See ADULT HOME; ASSISTED LIVING FACILITIES.

resting potential the electric potential across the plasma membrane of an excitable cell, such as a neuron, when it is in the nonexcited, or resting, state. It is usually in the range –50 to –100 mV for vertebrate neurons, representing an excess of negatively charged ions on the inside of the membrane. See also ACTION POTENTIAL.

resting tremor a tremor that occurs when the individual's affected body part is at rest. It is a characteristic symptom of PARKINSON'S DISEASE, in which case it is referred to as a **parkinsonian tremor**.

restitution *n.* the act of restoring or compensating for something lost through prior damaging actions or events. Acts of restitution exist on a behavioral spectrum: They may be a healthy, even necessary, part of acknowledging and dealing with harm committed intentionally or unintentionally, but they may also, more pathologically, take such forms as a compulsive drive to "do for others" or a persistent pattern of martyrdom.

restitution of psychological function the return of psychological or cognitive functions to previous levels after decline as a result of a brain injury. See also RECOVERY OF FUNCTION.

restless-legs syndrome see EKBOM'S SYNDROME.

restlessness *n.* a form of activity that appears purposeless and limited in time or intensity. A human being may constantly move, become distractible, or pace the floor; an animal may move about its environment, changing positions frequently, or look around. See also LOCOMOTOR ACTIVITY. **—restless** *adj.*

restoration effect a phenomenon in which the mind unconsciously restores information missing from a stimulus. The best known example is the so-called PHONEMIC RESTORATION EFFECT, in which the perceiver fails to notice that certain PHONEMES have been masked out in speech recordings. The restoration effect is considered evidence of TOP-DOWN PROCESSING. See also CLOSURE.

restoration therapy 1. treatment that is directed toward the reestablishment of structure and function in a body part or system that has suffered a damaging loss or deficiency because of disease or injury. The therapy may be employed, for example, in restoring the structure of the larynx and the function of speech after a throat-cancer operation or restoring the use of affected limbs after a paralyzing stroke. **2.** the reestablishment of a prior level of functioning in an individual with a mental or emotional disorder. **3.** a form of COMPLEMENTARY AND ALTERNATIVE MEDICINE that uses techniques and concepts from massage, chiropractic, osteopathy, shiatsu, acupressure, and herbal formulas to treat specific ailments and enhance overall health by balancing the body's life-force energy (see CHI) and breaking down soft tissues, which then rebuild themselves. [created by Japanese professor Henry S. Okazaki (1890–1951)]

restorative environment an environment, often a natural setting, that rejuvenates and assists in recovery from stress or fatigue. Characteristic features of restorative environments include LEGIBILITY and elements that give rise to contemplation and provide a break from one's normal routine. There is growing interest in the incorporation of restorative elements into health care settings because of evidence that they speed recovery.

restorative justice an approach to criminal justice in which emphasis is placed on rehabilitation of offenders and repairing the harm done to victims rather than on punishing offenders.

Restorff phenomenon see VON RESTORFF EFFECT.

Restoril *n.* a trade name for TEMAZEPAM.

rest period a brief pause in work or any other taxing activity taken on either a regular or a discretionary basis for the purpose of rest, recreation, refreshment, entertainment, or avoidance of overfatigue or boredom. It is often viewed as a reward for effort.

restraint *n.* **1.** the ability to control or prevent actions or behaviors that are harmful or otherwise undesirable. See SELF-CONTROL. **2.** the use of control measures to prevent violent patients from injuring themselves or others.

restricted affect emotional expression that is reduced in range and intensity. It is common in depression, inhibited personalities, and schizophrenia. See FLAT AFFECT.

restricted code see ELABORATED CODE.

restricted environmental stimulation reduction in the level of ambient information (i.e., external stimuli) to which an organism or individual is exposed: used, for example, in experimental techniques.

restricted learning a process in which species-specific restrictions on an organism's reactions to certain stimuli lead to ready adaptation of that organism's behavior to ensure survival. For instance, there may be innate responses to food, mates, or predators. See also PREPARED LEARNING; PRINCIPLE OF BELONGINGNESS.

restriction of range the limitation by a researcher—via sampling, measurement procedures, or other aspects of experimental design—of the full range of total possible scores that may be obtained to only a narrow, limited portion of that total. For example, in a study of the grade-point averages of university students, restriction of range would occur if only students from the dean's list were included. Range restriction on a particular variable may lead to a failure to observe, or the improper characterization of, a relationship between the variables of interest.

resurgence *n.* in conditioning, the reappearance of previously reinforced and then extinguished responses during a period of EXTINCTION for a subsequently learned response. For example, a rat might be presented with two levers. First, presses on lever A are reinforced; next, presses on lever A are subjected to extinction and presses on lever B are reinforced. Pressing lever A will cease, and pressing lever B will occur. Finally, extinction is arranged for presses on lever B, so that no reinforcement is available in the situation. As responding on lever B declines, pressing on lever A will increase temporarily.

RET abbreviation for rational emotive therapy. See RATIONAL EMOTIVE BEHAVIOR THERAPY.

retardation *n.* **1.** the slowing down of any mental or physical activity. See also PSYCHOMOTOR RETARDATION. **2.** slow or delayed intellectual development, as in MENTAL RETARDATION. **3.** in conditioning, a delay in the appearance of a conditioned (learned or acquired) response due to prior experience. For example, presentation of a stimulus to be used later as a conditioned stimulus slows the development of conditioning.

retarded depression an obsolescent name for a MAJOR DEPRESSIVE EPISODE that includes PSYCHOMOTOR RETARDATION and appetite loss.

retarded ejaculation see MALE ORGASMIC DISORDER.

rete mirabile a network of blood vessels that is derived from a nearby artery or vein, for example, the web of small arterial vessels in the kidney glomeruli or of small veins in the liver. A cranial rete mirabile is found in the brains of certain domestic animals but does not occur normally in humans.

retention *n.* **1.** persistence of learned behavior or experience during a period when it is not being performed or practiced, as indicated by the ability to recall, recognize, reproduce, or relearn it. **2.** the storage and maintenance of a memory. Retention is the second stage of memory, after ENCODING and before RETRIEVAL. **3.** the inability or refusal of an individual to defecate or urinate. **—retentive** *adj.*

retention curve a graphic representation of a person's remembrance of material over a period of time. Also called **memory curve**. See EBBINGHAUS'S CURVE OF RETENTION.

retest **1.** *n.* the readministration of a measuring instrument or test. **2.** *vb.* to readminister a test.

retest reliability an estimate of the reliability of a measurement instrument (e.g., a test) obtained as the correlation between scores on two administrations of the test to the same individual. Also called **test–retest reliability**.

reticular activating system (**RAS**) a part of the RETICULAR FORMATION thought to be particularly involved in the regulation of arousal, alertness, and sleep–wake cycles.

reticular formation an extensive network of nerve cell bodies and fibers within the brainstem, extending from the medulla oblongata to the upper part of the midbrain, that is widely connected to the spinal cord, cerebellum, thalamus, and cerebral cortex. It is most prominently involved in arousal, alertness, and sleep–wake cycles, but also functions to control some aspects of action and posture. Also called **brainstem reticular formation**. See also RETICULAR ACTIVATING SYSTEM.

reticular membrane a stiff membrane in the ORGAN OF CORTI that forms a division between ENDOLYMPH and PERILYMPH, which differ in their ionic composition. The stereocilia of the HAIR CELLS protrude through this membrane. Also called **reticular lamina**.

reticulospinal tract a TRACT of axons arising from the brainstem RETICULAR FORMATION and descending to the spinal cord to modulate movement.

retifism *n.* a form of FETISHISM in which sexual excitement is achieved through contact or masturbation with a shoe or foot. Shoes or feet are among the most common varieties of OBJECT FETISH, but there is little understanding of why this occurs. The condition is named for French writer Nicolas-Edme Rétif (1734–1806), also known as Rétif de la Bretonne, who is said to have had a sexual interest in women's footwear.

retina *n.* the innermost, light-sensitive layer of the eye. A layer of neurons lines the inner surface of the back of the eye and provides the sensory signals required for vision. The retina contains the photoreceptors, that is, the RETINAL RODS and RETINAL CONES, as well as additional neurons that process the signals of the photoreceptors and convey an output signal to the brain by way of the OPTIC NERVE. This inner layer of the retina is sometimes called the **neural retina**, to distinguish it from the retinal PIGMENT EPITHELIUM, which abuts the tips of the photoreceptors. See also AMACRINE CELLS; RETINAL BIPOLAR CELLS; RETINAL HORIZONTAL CELLS; RETINAL GANGLION CELLS.

retinal 1. *adj.* of or relating to the retina. **2.** *n.* an aldehyde of vitamin A that is a component of the retinal photopigments. See OPSIN; RHODOPSIN. Also called **retinene**.

retinal bipolar cells neurons in the INNER NUCLEAR LAYER of the retina that receive input from the photoreceptors (RETINAL RODS and RETINAL CONES) and transmit signals to RETINAL GANGLION CELLS and AMACRINE CELLS. Rods and cones are served by different populations of retinal bipolar cells, called **rod bipolars** and **cone bipolars**, respectively.

retinal cones photoreceptors in the retina that require moderate to bright light for activation, as opposed to RETINAL RODS, which require very little light for activation. In primates retinal cones are concentrated in the FOVEA CENTRALIS of the retina, where their high spatial density and the pattern of connections within the cone pathway are critical for high-acuity vision. The cone pathways also provide information about the color of stimuli. This is achieved by the presence of three different populations of cones, each having their maximum sensitivity to light in the short, middle, or long wavelengths of the spectrum, respectively. Other animals may have additional populations of cones; for example, some fish have cones that are sensitive to ultraviolet wavelengths. See also PHOTOPIC VISION; PHOTOPIGMENT.

retinal densitometry a method of measuring the absorptance characteristics of retinal PHOTOPIGMENTS. A light is shone into the eye, travels through the retina, is reflected back out of the eye by tissues behind the retina, and is measured. The light that emerges is compared to the light that entered the eye to determine how much was absorbed.

retinal detachment see DETACHED RETINA.

retinal disparity the slight difference between the right and left retinal images. When both eyes focus on an object, the different position of the eyes produces a disparity of visual angle, and a slightly different image is received by each retina. The two images are automatically compared and fused; this unconscious comparison provides an important cue to DEPTH PERCEPTION. Also called **binocular disparity**. See also UNCROSSED DISPARITY.

retinal field an array of photoreceptors stimulated by a visual target. This is different from the retinal receptive field (see VISUAL RECEPTIVE FIELD).

retinal ganglion cells the only neurons in the retina that send signals to the brain resulting from visual stimulation. Retinal ganglion cells receive input from RETINAL BIPOLAR CELLS and AMACRINE CELLS, the axons of retinal ganglion cells forming the OPTIC NERVE.

retinal horizontal cells neurons in the retina that make lateral connections between photoreceptors, RETINAL BIPOLAR CELLS, and one another. Their cell bodies are located in the INNER NUCLEAR LAYER of the retina.

retinal image the image formed on the retina of an eye focused on an external object. The resolution of the image varies with the diameter of the pupil, the focus becoming sharper as illumination of the object increases and the aperture of the pupil decreases.

retinal light a sensation of light experienced in the absence of any type of stimulation, which is thought to result from intrinsic activity within the visual system. Also called **dark light**.

retinal oscillations the alternating sensations or a series of sensations that persist after a brief visual stimulation. Examples include CHARPENTIER'S BANDS and FLIGHT OF COLORS.

retinal pigment epithelium see PIGMENT EPITHELIUM.

retinal receptive field see VISUAL RECEPTIVE FIELD.

retinal rivalry see BINOCULAR RIVALRY.

retinal rods photoreceptors in the retina that respond to low light levels, as opposed to RETINAL CONES, which require moderate to bright light for activation. In primates, which have both rods and cones, the rods are excluded from the center of the retina, the FOVEA CENTRALIS. All rods contain the same photopigment, RHODOPSIN; therefore the rod pathways do not provide color information to the visual system. The connections of the rod pathway enhance retinal sensitivity to light, while acuity is relatively poor. See also RETINAL BIPOLAR CELLS; SCOTOPIC VISION.

retinal size the dimensions of the retinal image. Retinal size diminishes in proportion to a reflected object's distance from the eye. The perception of size is achieved as a compromise between retinal size and an object's actual size.

retinene *n.* see RETINAL.

retinex *n.* one of the three components required for the LAND THEORY OF COLOR VISION. Each retinex component represents the brightness value of a visual image as viewed through a filter that allows short (blue), middle (green), or long (red) wavelengths to pass.

retinitis *n.* inflammation of the retina.

retinitis pigmentosa a disorder of the retina marked by progressive atrophy of the photoreceptors (affecting rods more than cones) and disturbances in the retinal PIGMENT EPITHELIUM. Retinitis pigmentosa causes NIGHT BLINDNESS and visual field loss (see TUNNEL VISION). Although most commonly a hereditary condition, it has been associated with the use of PHENOTHIAZINE antipsychotics, such as chlorpromazine and, especially, thioridazine.

retinodiencephalic degeneration see LAURENCE–MOON–BIEDL SYNDROME.

retinol *n.* see VITAMIN A.

retinopathy of prematurity (**ROP**) a disease of the retina that affects infants born prematurely. In its severest form it leads to complete retinal detachment (see DETACHED RETINA) and total blindness. The greatest risk factor appears to be low birth weight (<1000 g); additional risk factors include below normal gestational age at birth, prolonged parenteral nutrition, apnea, sepsis, blood transfusions, and oxygen therapy.

retinoscope *n.* a device used to assess the refractive state of the eye. It projects a slit of light into the eye; by determining the direction in which the slit moves when the retinoscope is moved, the clinician can detect MYOPIA, HYPEROPIA, or ASTIGMATISM. Lenses of various power can be placed between the retinoscope and the eye to determine the correction that provides the best refraction for the patient. Compare OPHTHALMOSCOPE.

retinotopic map the point-by-point representation of the retinal surface in another structure in the visual system, such as the STRIATE CORTEX. **Visuotopic map** is sometimes used synonymously for retinotopic map but more properly refers to the representation of the visual field in any neural structure.

retirement counseling individual or group counseling of employees to help them prepare for retirement. Discussions usually include such topics as norms for this transition, mental and physical health, recreational activities, part-time or consultant work, finances, insurance, government programs, and issues related to change of residence.

retreat from reality see FLIGHT FROM REALITY.

retrieval *n.* **1.** the process of recovering or locating information stored in memory. Retrieval is the final stage of memory, after ENCODING and RETENTION. **2.** in information science, the recovery of information from a computer or other storage device.

retrieval block a brief RETRIEVAL FAILURE in which the inability to recall a specific piece of information is accompanied by the feeling that there is an impediment or block to its recollection, as in the well-known TIP-OF-THE-TONGUE PHENOMENON.

retrieval cue a prompt or stimulus used to guide memory recall. See CUE-DEPENDENT FORGETTING; ECPHORIA; ENCODING SPECIFICITY PRINCIPLE.

retrieval failure the inability to recollect information that is known to be available in memory.

retrieving behavior a component of animal parental behavior characterized by picking up and carrying to the nest young offspring that have wandered away or, in some cases, have been born outside the nest.

retroactive interference INTERFERENCE that occurs when new learning or exposure to new information impairs the ability to remember material or carry out activities previously learned, especially if the two sets of material are similar. For instance, studying French in college may retroactively interfere with what is remembered of Spanish learned in high school. Retroactive interference is one of the processes that account for forgetting. Also called **retroactive inhibition**. Compare PROACTIVE INTERFERENCE.

retrobulbar *adj.* behind the eyeball.

retrochiasmatic visual deficit see POSTCHIASMATIC VISUAL DEFICIT.

retrocochlear hearing loss an auditory disorder related to the neural pathways of the eighth cranial nerve (see AUDITORY NERVE) and the higher centers of the central nervous system (that is, beyond the cochlea). It results in difficulty understanding speech.

retrocognition *n.* see POSTCOGNITION.

retrograde amnesia loss of memory for events and experiences that occurred before the onset of the AMNESIA. For example, a soldier may forget events preceding the bursting of a shell that threw him or her to the ground. See also TEMPORAL GRADIENT. Compare ANTEROGRADE AMNESIA.

retrograde degeneration destruction of the CELL BODY of a neuron following injury to its AXON. Compare ANTEROGRADE DEGENERATION.

retrograde ejaculation the ejaculation of semen in a reverse direction, that is, into the urinary bladder, from which it is excreted later. This may be a result of surgery of the prostate gland, and it also occurs when the penis is squeezed just before ejaculation—a misguided attempt at preventing impregnation. Retrograde ejaculation is occasionally associated with the use of antidepressants, including the TRICYCLIC ANTIDEPRESSANTS and SSRIS, as well as conventional antipsychotic agents (particularly thioridazine). There are also reports of retrograde ejaculation with ATYPICAL ANTIPSYCHOTICS (e.g., risperidone).

retrograde transport the movement of substances along the axon of a neuron toward the cell body. See AXONAL TRANSPORT.

retrography *n.* see MIRROR WRITING.

retrogression *n.* the return to a previous inappropriate behavior or to a behavior appropriate to an earlier stage of maturation when more adult techniques fail to solve a conflict. It is approximately equivalent to REGRESSION, but without the full psychoanalytic connotations.

retrogressive formation see BACK-FORMATION.

retrolental fibroplasia a disorder of the tissues behind the lens of the eye, marked by the presence of an opaque substance that causes detachment of the retina and blindness. It occurs mainly in preterm infants and is associated with excessive administration of oxygen that leads to exudation of blood and serum through the walls of retinal blood vessels.

retronasal olfaction sensations of smell arising via the nasopharynx, from an odorant in the mouth (compare ORTHONASAL OLFACTION). Retronasal olfaction is easily confused with gustatory (taste) sensations.

retropulsion *n.* walking or running backward with short steps, observed in some patients with parkinsonism. **—retropulsive** *adj.*

retrospection *n.* an observation or review of an experience from the past, typically not the distant past. Compare INTROSPECTION.

retrospective audit in health administration, a method of determining medical necessity or appropriate billing practice for services that have already been rendered.

retrospective falsification **1.** the alteration of a story each time it is told in order to emphasize its favorable points or make it more interesting. It may be deliberate or unconscious and unintentional. [defined by Donovan Hilton Rawcliffe] **2.** the addition of false details to memories of past experiences, particularly as done by a person with PARANOID SCHIZOPHRENIA to support a persecutory delusional system.

retrospective information information that is gained by asking people to recall feelings, events, and behaviors from their distant past. This type of information is usually regarded as less accurate and reliable than information gained by recording events and experiences while they are occurring.

retrospective medical audit see MEDICAL AUDIT.

retrospective memory see PROSPECTIVE MEMORY.

retrospective research observational, nonexperimental research that tries to explain the present in terms of past events; that is, research that starts with the present and follows subjects backward in time. For example, a **retrospective study** may be undertaken in which individuals are selected on the basis of whether they exhibit a particular problematic symptom and are then studied to determine if they had been exposed to a risk factor of interest. Compare PROSPECTIVE RESEARCH.

retrospective sampling a SAMPLING technique that selects cases on the basis of their previous exposure to a risk factor or the completion of some particular process. Participants are then examined in the present to see if a particular condition or state exists, often in comparison to others who were not exposed to the risk or did not complete the particular process. See also PROSPECTIVE SAMPLING.

Rett syndrome a degenerative condition that occurs in

children (typically girls) who develop normally early in life but then, between 6 and 18 months, undergo rapid regression in motor, cognitive, and social skills; these skills subsequently stabilize at a level that leaves the child with mental retardation. Affected children exhibit autistic features and stereotyped hand movements (e.g., hand wringing); in some, seizures and scoliosis (sideways spinal curvature) occur, and deceleration of head growth is pronounced. In *DSM–IV–TR*, the condition is termed **Rett's disorder** and classified as a PERVASIVE DEVELOPMENTAL DISORDER. [Andreas **Rett** (1924–1997), Austrian pediatrician]

reuptake *n.* the process by which neurotransmitter molecules that have been released at a SYNAPSE are taken up by the presynaptic neuron that released them. Reuptake is performed by TRANSPORTER proteins in the presynaptic membrane.

revealed-differences technique a method of studying the behavior of members of a family in a laboratory setting by posing a question and observing how the members reach agreement on an answer.

reverberatory circuit a neural circuit that is more or less continuously active, recirculating nerve impulses that were initially activated in response to stimuli so that retrieval of information on demand is possible. A theory of reverberatory circuits has been proposed to explain learning and memory processes. Although reverberatory circuits have been demonstrated only in the autonomic nervous system, they are also believed to exist in the central nervous system. Also called **reverberating circuit**.

reverie *n.* a pleasant state of abstracted daydreaming or musing.

reversal design an experimental design that attempts to counteract the confounding effects (see CONFOUNDS) of sequence, order, and treatment in LATIN SQUARES by alternating baseline conditions (A) with treatment conditions (B), for example by employing two sets of three observations (A then B then A; B then A then B) to yield counterbalanced estimates of A versus B.

reversal error a mistake in which a letter or word is read or written backward (e.g. *tip* for *pit* or *b* as *d*). When reversal errors are marked and developmentally inappropriate, they are indicative of DYSLEXIA. See also STREPHOSYMBOLIA.

reversal learning in DISCRIMINATIONS involving two alternatives, the effects of reversing the contingencies associated with the two alternatives. For example, a monkey could be trained under conditions in which lever presses when a red light is present result in food presentation and lever presses when a green light is on are without effect. The contingencies are then reversed, so that presses when the red light is on are ineffective and presses when the green light is on result in food presentation. If the monkey's behavior adapts to the new contingencies (i.e., it presses the lever only when the green light is present), reversal learning has occurred.

reversal of affect in psychoanalytic theory, a change in the AIM OF THE INSTINCT into its opposite, as when a masochistic impulse to hurt the self is transformed into a sadistic impulse to hurt others, or vice versa. Also called **affect inversion**; **inversion of affect**.

reversal shift in DISCRIMINATIONS involving two alternatives, a reversal of contingencies as compared with an immediately preceding set of conditions. For example, in initial training a white stimulus might be designated as correct and black as incorrect. A reversal shift would mean that, in a later phase of the training, black becomes correct and white incorrect. Compare NONREVERSAL SHIFT.

reversal theory a theory of motivation, emotion, and personality that attempts to explain the relationship between AROUSAL and performance. It suggests that the way an individual interprets the arousal, rather than the amount of arousal, affects performance and that he or she can reverse the positive–negative interpretation from moment to moment.

reverse anorexia a condition characterized by an individual's desire to increase body size, particularly muscularity. As with ANOREXIA NERVOSA, in which the desire is to lose weight or reduce body size, the drive to alter body size is not diminished by achieving extensive body modification. The individual's unhappiness with self-image, despite excessive gains in muscle mass and definition, is still present. See also MUSCLE DYSMORPHIA.

reverse causality in seeking to understand causal relationships, the common error of mistaking cause for effect and vice versa. Asking if an event or condition commonly considered to be the cause of a phenomenon might in reality be its effect is always a useful check against preconceptions and can generate fresh, challenging ideas. For example, the poverty of Mr. X is usually thought to be an effect of his financial irresponsibility, but what if this acknowledged irresponsibility is in fact an effect of his poverty? Considering a reversed causality is also a useful strategy for dealing with questions of causality based on correlational data. See also FALSE CAUSE; HISTORICAL FALLACY.

reversed dependency trap a situation in which the personal SELF-WORTH of a parent or parents becomes dependent on the child's performance in school, sport, or some other context.

reverse tolerance an effect of certain drugs, usually psychoactive substances (particularly CNS stimulants), in which repeated use alters the body's sensitivity so that repeated administration of a drug will enhance the effects of that drug. Also called **sensitization**. Compare TOLERANCE.

reversibility *n.* in Jean PIAGET's theory of cognitive development, a mental operation that reverses a sequence of events or restores a changed state of affairs to the original condition. It is exemplified by the ability to realize that a glass of milk poured into a bottle will remain the same in amount when poured back into the glass. Reversibility can be expressed in terms of NEGATION or COMPENSATION. See also CONSERVATION.

reversible figure an AMBIGUOUS FIGURE in which the perspective is easily reversed. Examples include the NECKER CUBE and RUBIN'S FIGURE.

reversible figure-ground the changing perception of which elements constitute the figure and which elements constitute the background in such AMBIGUOUS FIGURES as RUBIN'S FIGURE.

reversible inhibitors of monoamine oxidase (RIMAs) see MONOAMINE OXIDASE INHIBITORS.

reversing lenses and prisms lenses and prisms used in the experimental investigation of visuomotor adaptation.

reversion *n.* in genetics, the expression of a hereditary trait that was not manifested in a parent. The offspring may resemble a remote ancestor more closely than a member of the immediate family.

Reversol *n.* a trade name for EDROPHONIUM.

ReVia *n.* a trade name for NALTREXONE.

revivification *n.* a hypnotic technique in which suggestion is used to induce an individual to revive and relive forgotten or inhibited memories.

revolutionary coalition a subgroup (COALITION) formed within a larger group or organization that seeks a radical and pervasive change in the functioning and structure of the group or organization.

revolving-door phenomenon the repeated readmission of patients to hospitals or other institutions, often because they were discharged before they had adequately recovered.

reward *n.* a lay word that is nearly synonymous with REINFORCEMENT. Sometimes it is used to describe the intent of someone providing consequences for behavior, rather than the effectiveness of a consequence (as is required in the definition of reinforcement) in influencing the frequency or probability of occurrence of a particular behavior.

reward center see PLEASURE CENTER.

rewarded alternative method a procedure that involves eliminating reward for an undesired behavior and replacing it with reward for a desired behavior. Also called **reinforcement of alternative behavior**.

reward expectancy the hypothesized state of an organism that has been exposed to a situation in which REINFORCEMENT occurs. [first described by Edward C. TOLMAN]

reward power a capacity to influence others that is based on the ability or the promise to deliver desired rewards. The strength of reward power increases with (a) the value of the rewards and (b) the extent to which the target of influence is dependent on the influencer for the rewards.

reward system a set of interrelated factors that link a particular stimulus with some form of satisfaction or pleasure.

rewrite rule see PHRASE-STRUCTURE GRAMMAR.

Rey Auditory Verbal Learning Test (**RAVLT**) a test for evaluating verbal learning and memory, including proactive inhibition, retroactive inhibition, retention, encoding versus retrieval, and organization. Originally developed in the 1940s, the RAVLT now has several variations. The standard format starts with a list of 15 words, and the participant is required to repeat all the words he or she can remember, in any order. This procedure is carried out a total of five times. Next, the examiner presents a second list of 15 words, allowing the participant only one attempt at recall. Immediately following this, the participant is asked to remember as many words as possible from the first list. A delayed recall trial as well as a recognition trial may also be administered. [André **Rey** (1906–1965), Swiss psychologist]

Rey Complex Figure Test (**RCFT**) see COMPLEX FIGURE TEST. [André **Rey**]

Rey–Osterrieth Complex Figure Test see COMPLEX FIGURE TEST. [André **Rey**; Paul Alex **Osterrieth**]

RFT abbreviation for ROD-AND-FRAME TEST.

rhabdomancy *n.* the art of DIVINATION by rod or wand, as in the practice of DOWSING for water, minerals, buried treasure, or the like using a forked stick. **—rhabdomancer** *n.*

Rh blood-group incompatibility an antigen-antibody reaction that occurs when blood from an Rh-positive individual is mixed with blood from an Rh-negative individual (see RH FACTOR) during transfusion or pregnancy. In pregnancy, this arises if an Rh-negative mother bears a child that has inherited Rh-positive blood: The fetal Rh antigens pass through the placental membrane, and maternal antibodies react through the placenta to destroy the fetal red blood cells. The damaged blood cells yield bilirubin, which the fetus cannot detoxify, and KERNICTERUS may result. Also called **rhesus incompatibility**. See also RH REACTION.

RHC abbreviation for RURAL HEALTH CLINIC.

rheoencephalography *n.* the measurement of blood flow of the brain, typically using a device known as a **rheoencephalograph** that records the impedance (resistance) of cerebral vessels to the passage of an electrical current. **—rheoencephalographic** *adj.*

rhesus factor see RH FACTOR.

rhesus monkey a small primate, native to India, Nepal, and Afghanistan, that is often used in psychological, biological, and medical research because of its high degree of similarity to humans.

rhetorical-question message a persuasive message that includes rhetorical questions as a means of encouraging more careful scrutiny of the message. See also MESSAGE FACTORS.

rheumatoid arthritis see ARTHRITIS.

Rh factor (**rhesus factor**) any of at least eight different antigens, each determined genetically, that may be attached to the surface of an individual's red blood cells (the name derives from the rhesus monkey, used in early studies of the factor). A person whose blood cells carry an Rh factor is said to be **Rh-positive**. One whose blood cells lack an Rh factor is **Rh-negative**. Some 99% of African Americans, Native Americans, and Asian Americans and 85% of Caucasians are Rh-positive. See also RH REACTION.

rhinal fissure a fissure on the anterior medial surface of each TEMPORAL LOBE in the brain. Also called **rhinal sulcus**.

Rhine cards see ZENER CARDS. [Joseph B. **Rhine** (1895–1980), U.S. psychologist]

rhinencephalon *n.* the portion of the brain that includes the limbic system; olfactory nerves, bulbs, and tracts; and related structures. The term literally means "smell brain," because early anatomists assumed it was an olfactory organ itself. Also called **paleopallium**.

rhino- (**rhin-**) *combining form* nose or sense of smell.

rhinolalia *n.* a speech quality characterized by unusual nasal resonance, sometimes due to abnormalities or obstruction within the nasal cavity.

rhizomelic *adj.* relating to or affecting the hip, shoulder, or both. Rhizomelic abnormalities are associated with certain congenital defects that may be accompanied by mental retardation. An affected individual may, for example, have one leg shorter than the other or contractures of the hip and shoulder joints.

rhizotomy *n.* a surgical procedure in which a spinal nerve root is severed within the spinal canal. A rhizotomy may be performed for the relief of pain or other discomfort or to control a disorder, such as hypertension. The different types of rhizotomy include **anterior rhizotomy**, in which an anterior spinal nerve is cut; **posterior rhizotomy**, in which a posterior spinal nerve is cut; and **trigeminal rhizotomy**, in which the sensory root fibers of the trigeminal nerve are transected.

rhodopsin *n.* a visual pigment associated mainly with function of the RETINAL ROD cells. Rhodopsin consists of the vitamin A aldehyde **11-cis retinal** bound to the protein OPSIN. When activated by photons, 11-*cis* retinal is transformed into all-*trans* retinal, which detaches from the opsin. This initiates a cascade of events that results in

VISUAL TRANSDUCTION. Also called **visual purple**. See SCOTOPSIN; VISUAL CYCLE.

rhombencephalon *n.* see HINDBRAIN.

Rh reaction an adverse effect that can occur in blood transfusions and pregnancies when an Rh-negative person's blood is mixed with Rh-positive blood from another individual (see RH FACTOR). This reaction is similar to the immune reaction that occurs in response to an invasion of the body tissues by a foreign agent. In pregnancy, an Rh-negative mother may carry an Rh-positive fetus, her body forming anti-Rh antibodies that destroy the red blood cells of the fetus. See also RH BLOOD-GROUP INCOMPATIBILITY.

rhyming delirium compulsive speaking or responding in rhymes, occasionally associated with a MANIC EPISODE.

rhythm *n.* **1.** a regular pattern of changes, fluctuations, or occurrences, for example, a BIOLOGICAL RHYTHM. **2.** the frequency of BRAIN WAVES, identified as alpha waves, beta waves, gamma waves, delta waves, and theta waves. **3.** the cadence or long-term temporal structure of similar sounds. **—rhythmic** or **rhythmical** *adj.*

rhythmic stereotypy a gross motor movement, such as body rocking or foot kicking, that has no apparent function. It is a form of LOCOMOTOR PLAY that occurs in the 1st year of life.

rhythmic stimulation an automatic effect of a flickering light characterized by synchronization of the electroencephalogram pattern to the frequency of the flicker. The effect of light flicker on brain waves may vary with different species of animals. Flickering lights may precipitate seizures in predisposed individuals.

rhythm method a technique of contraception in which the woman abstains from coitus during the days of her menstrual cycle in which she is most likely to become pregnant, that is, from just before until just after ovulation. The rhythm method is not very effective because of the difficulty in making advance predictions of the precise time of ovulation. The predictions are made by charting rectal or vaginal temperature changes daily or by testing changes in the sugar content of the cervical mucus. See also CALENDAR METHOD OF BIRTH CONTROL.

RI abbreviation for random interval. See RANDOM-INTERVAL SCHEDULE.

RIA abbreviation for RADIOIMMUNOASSAY.

ribonucleic acid see RNA.

ribosomal RNA see RNA.

ribosome *n.* an organelle, consisting of RNA and proteins, found in large numbers in all cells and responsible for the translation of genetic information (in the form of messenger RNA) and the assembly of proteins. Ribosomes can occur free in the cytoplasm or be attached to the ENDOPLASMIC RETICULUM. **—ribosomal** *adj.*

Ribot's law 1. the principle that the most recently acquired memories are the most vulnerable to disruption from brain damage. As a result, a TEMPORAL GRADIENT is observed in RETROGRADE AMNESIA. **2.** a generalization stating that when a multilingual person recovers from APHASIA caused by a stroke or cerebral injury, the language recovered first will be the person's native language. Compare PITRES' RULE. [Théodule **Ribot** (1839–1916), French psychologist]

Ricco's law the principle that VISUAL THRESHOLD is a function of the intensity of a visual image and its area on the fovea. Compare PIPER'S LAW. [Annibale **Ricco** (1844–1919), Italian astrophysicist]

rich interpretation an approach to analyzing the language of young children that goes beyond the literal sense of the word or words used and takes into account the surrounding verbal and nonverbal contexts to infer the full meaning of the utterance and draw conclusions about the child's linguistic COMPETENCE. See HOLOPHRASE.

rich medium see MEDIA RICHNESS.

rickets *n.* see CALCIUM-DEFICIENCY DISORDERS.

Riddoch's phenomenon the ability of patients with injury to the visual system beyond the optic chiasm to see moving, but not stationary, light stimuli (**statokinetic dissociation**). Riddoch's phenomenon can also be associated with damage to the optic nerve. See also CEREBRAL AMBLYOPIA. [first described in 1917 by George **Riddoch** (1888–1947), British neurologist]

ridge regression a variant on ordinary least squares regression designed to remedy problems that arise from MULTICOLLINEARITY.

Ridit analysis a scoring system for use in categorical analysis in which the score for the category is the mean rank score on the outcome variable of interest for all members of that category. [invented by U.S. biostatistician Irwin D. J. Bross (1921–2004)]

Rieger's syndrome an autosomal dominant disorder marked by dental and eye abnormalities. The dental anomalies may include missing teeth and hypoplasia (underdevelopment) of the enamel. Visual disorders usually involve anomalies of the iris and cornea. Mental retardation is sometimes present. Also called **hypodontia**. [initially reported in 1935 by Herwigh **Rieger** (1898–1986), German ophthalmologist]

right-and-wrong-cases method see METHOD OF CONSTANT STIMULI.

right-and-wrong test see MCNAUGHTEN RULE.

right brain the right cerebral hemisphere. The term is sometimes used to designate functions or COGNITIVE STYLE supposedly mediated by the right (rather than by the left) hemisphere, such as spatial perception. See also HEMISPHERIC LATERALIZATION.

right-handedness *n.* the preferential use of the right hand for major activities, such as eating, writing, and throwing. It is a component of DEXTRALITY and applies to about 90% of the population. See also LATERALITY. Compare LEFT-HANDEDNESS.

right hemisphere the right half of the CEREBRUM or CEREBELLUM in the brain. The two CEREBRAL HEMISPHERES differ somewhat in function; for example, in most people the right hemisphere has greater responsibility for spatial attention. See HEMISPHERIC LATERALIZATION. Compare LEFT HEMISPHERE.

right-hemisphere consciousness a hypothesis that the right cerebral hemisphere of the brain is conscious, like the left hemisphere, even though it has no control of spoken communication (compare LEFT-HEMISPHERE CONSCIOUSNESS). The right hemisphere is postulated to function in a holistic, nonlinear manner, specialized for spatial and SUPRASEGMENTAL (prosodic) perception. [attributed to Roger SPERRY]

righting reflex the automatic tendency of an organism to return to an upright position when it has been thrown off balance or placed in a supine position. Also called **righting reaction**.

right–left disorientation a disorder characterized by general difficulty in distinguishing between the right and left sides or right and left directions. It has been linked to APHASIA and other disorders of comprehension but also occurs in the absence of such disorders. Although thought to be related to disorders of the left parietal lobe of the cerebral cortex, it also occurs to a mild degree in otherwise healthy adults.

right–left orientation test any test that measures the ability to discriminate between right and left directions.

right-or-wrong test see MCNAUGHTEN RULE.

rights of patients in the United States, the rights of patients who are involuntarily hospitalized (i.e., legally committed). These rights are: (a) to communicate with people outside the facility, (b) to keep clothing and personal effects, (c) to vote, (d) to follow their religion, (e) to be employed if possible, (f) to execute wills or other legal instruments, (g) to enter into contractual relationships, (h) to make purchases, (i) to be educated, (j) to marry, (k) to retain licenses and permits, (l) to sue or be sued, and (m) not to be subjected to unnecessary restraint.

rights of people with mental retardation rights enshrined in the United Nations Standard Rules on the Equalization of Opportunities for Persons with Disabilities (1993). People with mental retardation have the same rights as other human beings. These include (a) the right to receive proper medical care, physical therapy, education, training, rehabilitation, assistive technology, and guidance; (b) the right to economic security and to work; (c) the right to live with their families or with foster parents or, if this is not feasible, to live in a residential setting under circumstances as close as possible to family life; and (d) the right to protection from abuse and exploitation.

Rightstart program a program to improve the mathematical abilities of young elementary-school children. It consists of 40 half-hour sessions. [devised in the late 1980s by Robbie Case (1944–2001), Canadian developmental psychologist]

right to die the right to physician-assisted suicide that some consider should be available for terminally ill patients (see ASSISTED DEATH). This is distinguished from the RIGHT TO REFUSE TREATMENT in cases in which the patient is on life support.

right to effective treatment the policy position or ethical stance that people with a disability or a disorder have the legal, civil, or moral right to receive services to alleviate or cure their condition. With respect to specific therapies, this entails the use of methods that have been empirically and scientifically validated for efficacy and effectiveness.

right to refuse treatment 1. the right of patients with mental illness to refuse treatment that may be potentially hazardous or intrusive (e.g., ELECTROSHOCK THERAPY or PSYCHOACTIVE DRUGS), particularly when such treatment does not appear to be in the best interests of the patient. In the United States, various state laws and court rulings support the rights of patients to receive or reject certain treatments, but there is a lack of uniformity in such regulations. See also FORCED TREATMENT. **2.** the right of terminally ill patients (e.g., those on life-support systems) to refuse treatment intended to prolong their lives. See also RIGHT TO DIE.

right to treatment 1. a statutory right, established at varying governmental levels, stipulating that people with disabilities or disorders, usually persistent or chronic in nature, have the right to receive care and treatment suited to their needs. Such statutory rights may apply nationally or to certain state or provincial areas, or they may be limited to certain conditions and disabilities. **2.** the principle that a facility that has assumed the responsibility of offering treatment for a patient is legally obligated to provide treatment that is adequate and appropriate.

rigid family a family structure in which rules are never questioned and there are no exceptions to rules. Such a structure can be a cause of emotional and behavioral problems for the children of the family.

rigidity *n.* **1.** stiffness or inflexibility, particularly MUSCULAR RIGIDITY. **2.** a personality trait characterized by strong resistance to changing one's behavior, opinions, or attitudes or inability to do this. **3.** the tendency, after brain injury, to be inflexible and complete a task in only one manner, despite more effective available alternatives. See also DECEREBRATE RIGIDITY. **—rigid** *adj.*

rigid rotation see ORTHOGONAL ROTATION.

Riley–Day syndrome see FAMILIAL DYSAUTONOMIA. [Conrad Milton **Riley** (1913–2005) and Richard Lawrence **Day** (1905–1989), U.S. pediatricians]

RIMAs abbreviation for reversible inhibitors of monoamine oxidase. See MONOAMINE OXIDASE INHIBITORS.

ring chromosome 18 a congenital chromosomal disorder characterized by MICROCEPHALY, ear and eye abnormalities, and severe mental retardation. The condition is not hereditary but due to breakage of the arms of chromosome 18, which fuse to form one or more rings of varying sizes.

Ringelmann effect the tendency for groups to become less productive in terms of output per member as they increase in size. The effect is named for Max Ringelmann (1861–1931), a French agricultural engineer who studied the productivity of horses, oxen, men, and machines in various agricultural applications. He found that groups often outperform individuals, but that the addition of each new member to the group yields less of a gain in productivity. Subsequent studies suggest that this loss of productivity is caused by the reduction of motivation experienced in groups (SOCIAL LOAFING) and the inefficiency of larger groups.

ring-finger dermatitis a skin disease involving an area of a finger where a ring usually is worn. The condition may be marked by itching, dryness, redness, or eruption of small blisters. In the absence of evidence that the condition is caused by irritation from or an allergic reaction to chemicals in the ring or in detergents trapped beneath the ring (the most common cause), ring-finger dermatitis may be a PSYCHOSOMATIC DISORDER.

Rinne test a tuning-fork test used to aid in differentiating between conductive and sensorineural hearing loss. The sensation produced by the tuning fork when presented via air conduction is compared to that produced by placing the tuning fork against the MASTOID process of the temporal bone. [Friedrich Heinrich A. **Rinne** (1819–1868), German otologist]

rise *n.* the distance along the *y*-axis between two points. Compare RUN.

risk *n.* **1.** the probability or likelihood that an event will occur, such as the risk that a disease or disorder will develop. **2.** the probability of experiencing loss or harm that is associated with an action. See also AT RISK; MORBIDITY RISK; RISK FACTOR. **—risky** *adj.*

risk-as-feelings theory a model stating that decision making in situations involving a degree of risk is often driven by emotional reactions, such as worry, fear, or anxiety, rather than by a rational assessment of (a) the desirability and (b) the likelihood of the various possible outcomes (see SUBJECTIVE-EXPECTED UTILITY).

risk assessment the process of determining the threat of dangerousness an individual would be likely to pose if released from the confinement in which he or she is held as a result of mental illness or criminal acts. See ACTUARIAL RISK ASSESSMENT; CLINICAL RISK ASSESSMENT.

risk-assessment matrix a method in which a table is used to prioritize hazards on the basis of risk, which is defined by the intersection between the probability of the hazards and the severity of their consequences. Also called **hazard-assessment matrix**.

risk aversion the tendency, when choosing between alternatives, to avoid options that entail a risk of loss, even if that risk is relatively small.

risk factor a clearly defined behavior or constitutional (e.g., genetic), environmental, or other characteristic that is associated with an increased possibility or likelihood that a disease or disorder will subsequently develop in an individual.

risk level the level or amount of risk of making a TYPE I ERROR that one is willing to accept in null hypothesis SIGNIFICANCE TESTING.

risk metrics numbers, formulas, graphs, or other means of presenting or describing the probability or likelihood of developing a disease or disorder.

risk perception an individual's subjective assessment of the level of risk associated with a particular hazard. Risk perceptions will vary according to such factors as past experiences, age, gender, and culture. For example, women tend to overestimate their risk of developing breast cancer. These exaggerated perceptions of risk often motivate people to seek genetic services, genetic testing, or prophylactic surgery.

risk-recreation model see ADVENTURE-RECREATION MODEL.

risk–rescue rating a formula comparing the inherent risk of a method of attempted suicide with the likelihood of discovery and rescue.

risk sensitivity the ability of an organism to choose an environment where the variance in stability of resources over time is low. Individuals that do not show risk sensitivity choose environments with high variance in stability of resources. If resources are good, these individuals and their offspring thrive; if resources are poor, they fare less well than risk-sensitive individuals.

risk taking 1. a pattern of unnecessarily engaging in activities or behaviors that are highly risky or dangerous. This pattern of behavior is often associated with substance abuse, gambling, and high-risk sexual behaviors. **2.** accepting a challenging task that simultaneously involves potential for failure as well as for accomplishment or personal benefit. It is often associated with creativity and taking calculated risks in the workplace or in educational settings.

risk tolerance 1. the level of risk to which an individual is willing to be exposed while performing an action or pursuing a goal. Tolerance of risk is usually based upon an assumption (justified or not) that the risk is slight, the consequences are minor, and that both are outweighed by immediate benefits. **2.** the degree of economic loss that a person, company, or other organization is willing to risk in pursuit of a possible gain.

risky prediction a prediction made on the basis of a scientific hypothesis that has a real possibility of proving that hypothesis wrong. According to Austrian-born British philosopher of science Karl Popper (1902–1994), certain ostensibly scientific theories and hypotheses, including many in psychology, have a capacity to be stretched in order to explain a range of possible experimental results. To the extent that this can occur, the theory or hypothesis is not genuinely falsifiable and thus not genuinely scientific. Popper held that scientific theories must be tested by means of risky predictions. See FALSIFIABILITY; FALSIFICATIONISM.

risky shift a tendency for the decisions of individuals to be more risky following group discussion. Research has revealed that group discussion does not make decisions more risky per se, but simply serves to polarize group members in the direction of their initial views.

risperidone *n.* an ATYPICAL ANTIPSYCHOTIC of the benzisoxazole class. It was the second atypical antipsychotic introduced into the U.S. market (CLOZAPINE was the first). It has a less frequent incidence of extrapyramidal symptoms than conventional antipsychotics when used at a lower dose range and it acts as a potent inhibitor of both D2 dopamine and 5-HT_2 serotonin receptors. U.S. trade name: **Risperdal**.

Ritalin *n.* a trade name for METHYLPHENIDATE.

rite *n.* a culture-bound ceremony or ritual, often religious in nature.

rite of passage a ritual that marks a specific life transition, such as birth, marriage, or death, or a developmental milestone, such as a bar mitzvah, graduation, or admission to a new profession or association. In many prescientific societies such rites are considered essential if the individual is to make a successful transition from one status to another. However, the persistence of rites of passage in modern secular societies where there is no such belief suggests that they can fulfill an important psychological function for both the individual and his or her social group. See BIRTH RITE; DEATH RITE; PUBERTY RITE.

ritual *n.* **1.** a form of COMPULSION involving a rigid or stereotyped act that is carried out repeatedly and is based on idiosyncratic rules that do not have a rational basis (e.g., having to perform a task in a certain way). Rituals may be performed in order to reduce distress and anxiety caused by an OBSESSION. **2.** a ceremonial act or rite, usually involving a fixed order of actions or gestures and the saying of certain prescribed words. Anthropologists distinguish between several major categories of ritual, although these can often overlap in practice: magic rituals, which involve an attempt to manipulate natural forces through symbolic, often imitative, actions (e.g., pouring water on the ground to make rain); calendrical rituals, which mark the changing of the seasons and the passing of time; liturgical rituals, which involve the reenactment of a sacred story or myth, as in the Christian eucharist and many other religious rituals; RITES OF PASSAGE; and formal procedures that have the effect of emphasizing both the importance and the impersonal quality of certain social behaviors, as in a court of law. **3.** more generally, any habit or custom that is performed routinely and with little or no thought. **—ritualism** *n.* **—ritualistic** *adj.*

ritual abuse organized, repetitive, and highly sadistic abuse of a physical, sexual, or emotional nature, perpetrated principally on children. The abuse is reported as using rituals and symbols from religion (e.g., upside-down crosses), the occult, or secret societies. It may also include the creation of pornography or the selling of sexual access to children. Victims may be forced to engage in heinous acts, such as the killing of animals, as a means of coercing their participation and silence.

ritualization *n.* the process by which a normal behavioral or physiological action becomes a communication signal representing the behavior or its physiological consequence. Among animals, THREAT DISPLAYS may result from the conflict between attack and escape and incorporate aspects of both actions. Courtship feeding of mates is similar to feeding of young and may signal the moment when both mates are ready to breed. In human beings the flushed face associated with anger and the pale face associated with fear initially derive from actions of the sympathetic nervous system related to vasodilation and vasoconstriction, respectively.

rivalry *n.* competition between individuals or groups for a specific goal or for status and prestige within a particular field. See SIBLING RIVALRY.

rivastigmine *n.* a CARBAMATE that is a reversible ACETYLCHOLINESTERASE INHIBITOR, used for the treatment of mild to moderate dementia associated with Alzheimer's disease (see NOOTROPIC DRUGS). Because it can cause nausea and loss of appetite, low starting doses with a slow upward TITRATION are recommended. U.S. trade name: **Exelon**.

RJP abbreviation for realistic job preview. See JOB PREVIEW.

RL abbreviation for REIX LIMEN.

RMD abbreviation for repetitive motion disorder (see REPETITIVE STRAIN INJURY).

RMI abbreviation for repetitive motion injury (see REPETITIVE STRAIN INJURY).

RMS abbreviation for ROOT-MEAN-SQUARE.

RMT abbreviation for RECOGNITION MEMORY TEST.

RN abbreviation for REGISTERED NURSE.

RNA *r*ibo*n*ucleic *a*cid: a nucleic acid that directs the synthesis of protein molecules in living cells. There are three main types of RNA. MESSENGER RNA carries the GENETIC CODE from the cell nucleus to the cytoplasm. **Ribosomal RNA** is found in ribosomes, small particles where proteins are assembled from amino acids. **Transfer RNA** carries specific amino acids for protein synthesis. Each of the 20 amino acids has a corresponding transfer RNA molecule to place the amino acid in the proper sequence in protein assembly. RNA is similar to DNA in structure except that it consists of a single strand of nucleotides (compared with the double strands of DNA), the base uracil (U) occurs instead of thymine (T), and the sugar unit is ribose, rather than deoxyribose.

RNG abbreviation for RANDOM NUMBER GENERATOR.

road rage aggressive or confrontational behavior while driving, typically triggered by an actual or imagined transgression by another driver. Often associated with traffic congestion, road rage varies in severity and can involve hostile verbal expression, hazardous driving, and interpersonal violence.

Robaxin *n.* a trade name for METHOCARBAMOL.

Robbers' Cave experiment a field study of the causes and consequences of conflict between groups. In the experiment two groups of 11-year-old boys from similar backgrounds, none of whom previously knew one another, were sent camping in the same area of wilderness. During the first stage, the two groups were allowed to develop their own rules, structures, and collective identities in complete independence of one another. During the second stage, they were made aware of each other's presence and encouraged to develop a sense of rivalry through a series of competitive exercises; the result was deepening hostility leading to open violence. In the third stage, staff deliberately created various urgent problems, such as a fault in the water supply, that could only be solved by the two groups working together; the result was a complete reconciliation. See also SUPERORDINATE GOAL. [performed in the early 1950s by Turkish-born U.S. social psychologist Muzafer Sherif (1906–1988) and colleagues; the study derives its name from the state park in Oklahoma that served as the site for the research]

Roberts syndrome an autosomal recessive disorder in which the child is born with abnormally short arms and legs as well as a cleft lip and palate. Other features include MICROCEPHALY and genital hypertrophy (enlargement). Few affected individuals survive early infancy; of those who do, 50% are likely to have mental retardation. Also called **Appelt–Gerken–Lenz syndrome**. [described in 1919 by John Bingham **Roberts** (1852–1924), U.S. physician, and in 1966 by Hans **Appelt** (1919–1988), H. **Gerken**, and Widukind **Lenz** (1919–1995), German physicians]

Robitussin *n.* a trade name for DEXTROMETHORPHAN.

robot *n.* **1.** a machine that performs functions similar to those of a human (e.g., a spot-welding robot). **2.** a human being whose rigid, insensitive, or detached behavior resembles that of a machine. **—robotic** *adj.*

robotics *n.* the science of designing and constructing machines (AUTOMATONS) capable of performing not only automated, repetitive, high-precision, or dangerous tasks but also functions similar to those of humans. For example, personal assistance robots are under development for individuals with disabilities. See CYBERNETICS.

robust estimator see RESISTANT ESTIMATOR.

robustness *n.* the ability of a hypothesis-testing or estimation procedure to produce valid results in spite of violations of the assumptions upon which the methodology is based.

ROC curve abbreviation for RECEIVER-OPERATING CHARACTERISTIC CURVE.

rocking *n.* a stereotyped motor behavior in which the body rocks to and fro, often observed in children or adults with severe or profound mental retardation, AUTISTIC DISORDER, or STEREOTYPIC MOVEMENT DISORDER. Also called **body rocking**.

Rock v. Arkansas a case resulting in a 1987 ruling by the U.S. Supreme Court stating that it is a violation of DUE PROCESS rights to prohibit a defendant from presenting evidence discovered after undergoing hypnosis.

Rod-and-Frame Test (**RFT**) a test used to study the role of visual and gravitational cues in judging the visual vertical. It is the most widely used measure of FIELD DEPENDENCE and FIELD INDEPENDENCE. The test consists of a movable rod inside a frame; the participant must adjust the rod to a true vertical position as the position of the frame is changed. Degree of error (i.e., the number of degrees away from 90°) is the measure used to score the test. The higher the score, the more field dependent the participant is; the lower the score, the more field independent he or she is. [developed in 1948 by U.S. psychologists Herman A. Witkin (1916–1979) and Solomon ASCH]

rod–cone break the shift in visual sensitivity that occurs during DARK ADAPTATION when the sensitivity of the RETINAL RODS first exceeds that of the RETINAL CONES. When visual sensitivity is measured in the dark following a very bright flash of light, the cones reach maximum sensitivity after about 7 minutes. However, overall visual sensitivity continues to improve for about 20 more minutes as RHODOPSIN regenerates and the rods reach their maximum sensitivity.

rods *pl. n.* see RETINAL RODS.

rods of Corti the two rows of stiff pillarlike structures that form an arch (the **arch of Corti**) in the ORGAN OF CORTI.

rod vision vision that depends solely upon the RETINAL

RODS, which are active in dim light. See also SCOTOPIC VISION.

Roelofs effect a distortion of space perception in which the subjective location of "straight ahead" is shifted by the presence of a large rectangle or frame whose center is located to one side of the true straight-ahead position. The subjective location of straight ahead moves in the same direction as the frame or rectangle. [C. Otto **Roelofs**, 20th-century Dutch physician]

roentgenogram *n.* a photographic record produced by X-RAY exposure. See RADIOGRAPH. [Wilhelm Konrad **Roentgen** (1845–1923), German physicist]

roentgen ray see X-RAY. [Wilhelm **Roentgen**]

Rogerian therapy see CLIENT-CENTERED THERAPY.

Rogers, Carl (1902–1987) U.S. psychologist. Rogers received his doctorate from Columbia University's Teachers College in 1931. He held a number of faculty positions in his career, but it was while teaching at the University of Chicago (1944–1957) that he most fully developed and described his distinctive approach to psychotherapy. Rogers originated CLIENT-CENTERED THERAPY and the NONDIRECTIVE APPROACH, which he conceived as providing the client with a warm, accepting climate that would foster personality growth and the realization of inner potential. Fitting within the loosely associated group of theories and techniques of HUMANISTIC PSYCHOLOGY, client-centered therapy offered an important alternative to the Freudian and behaviorist psychotherapies then dominant. Rogers viewed psychological dysfunction as typically resulting from CONDITIONAL POSITIVE REGARD, namely, the conditions put on love and affection by early authority figures, such as parents and teachers. He believed that individuals who suppressed their own needs in order to receive positive regard from others would develop low self-esteem and be unable to achieve self-actualization. Client-centered therapy was designed as a corrective, with the therapist providing a therapeutic atmosphere of UNCONDITIONAL POSITIVE REGARD, warmth, and UNCRITICALNESS that would theoretically enable the client to thrive and become what Rogers would call a fully functioning person. See also CONDITIONS OF WORTH; GROWTH PRINCIPLE. **—Rogerian** *adj.*

Rokeach Dogmatism Scale a 66-item scale developed in 1960 to measure individual differences in openness or closedness of belief systems (i.e., DOGMATISM) across several continua, such as "isolation and differentiation between belief and nonbelief systems" and "interrelations among primitive, intermediate, and peripheral beliefs." Some studies have found the scale more useful in assessing "general authoritarianism" and "general intolerance." [Milton **Rokeach** (1918–1988), U.S. psychologist]

Rokeach Value Survey (**RVS**) an instrument that assesses participants' values to help them determine what is most important in their lives and make good personal choices (often used as a career development instrument). "Value" is defined as "an enduring belief that a specific mode of conduct or end-state of existence is personally or socially preferable to an opposite or converse mode of conduct or end-state of existence." Two kinds of values are distinguished in the survey: instrumental, that is, modes of conduct and behavioral characteristics that are seen as socially desirable; and terminal, that is, end-states of existence or ultimate modes of living that have been idealized. [Milton **Rokeach**]

rok-joo *n.* see KORO.

Rolandic cortex a region of the CEREBRAL CORTEX that lies in and adjacent to the CENTRAL SULCUS (Rolandic fissure), which marks the boundary between the frontal and parietal lobes. [Luigi **Rolando** (1773–1831), Italian anatomist]

Rolandic fissure see CENTRAL SULCUS. [Luigi **Rolando**]

role *n.* a coherent set of behaviors expected of an individual in a specific position within a group or social setting. Since the term is derived from the dramaturgical concept of role (the dialogue and actions assigned to each performer in a play), there is a suggestion that individuals' actions are regulated by the part they play in the social setting rather than by their personal predilections or inclinations. See also GROUP ROLES; RELATIONSHIP ROLE; SOCIAL ROLE; TASK ROLE.

role ambiguity indefinite expectations about the behaviors to be performed by individuals who occupy particular positions within a group. Role ambiguity is often caused by lack of clarity in the role itself, lack of consensus within the group regarding the behaviors associated with the role, or the individual role taker's uncertainty with regard to the types of behaviors expected.

role categories see SOCIAL ROLE.

role conflict **1.** a state of tension or distress caused by inconsistent or discordant expectations associated with one's social or group ROLE, as when a role's demands are inconsistent with each other (INTRAROLE CONFLICT) or individuals occupy more than one role and the behaviors required by these roles are incompatible with one another (INTERROLE CONFLICT). **2.** in sport, the state of tension that arises when the athlete's perception of role requirements differs from that of the coach.

role confusion **1.** a state of uncertainty about a given social or group role. **2.** GENDER ROLE behavior in a male or female that is traditionally associated with the opposite sex. See also GENDER IDENTITY DISORDER; TRANSGENDER. **3.** see IDENTITY VERSUS ROLE CONFUSION.

role deprivation the denial of culturally and psychologically significant statuses and roles to certain individuals or groups. Individuals can be unfairly deprived of social roles, as when they are required to retire at a specific age, or unfairly denied group roles, as when they are excluded from leadership positions for no valid reason.

role differentiation in groups and other social systems, the gradual increase in the number of roles and decrease in the scope of these roles that tends to occur over time as each role becomes more narrowly defined and specialized. For example, in many cases the all-inclusive LEADERSHIP ROLE divides, over time, into two: the task leader role and the relationship leader role. See COLEADERSHIP.

role diffusion a state of confusion about one's social role that typically occurs during adolescence. See IDENTITY VERSUS ROLE CONFUSION. [described by Erik ERIKSON]

role-divided psychotherapy a form of GROUP PSYCHOTHERAPY in which members meet for part of the session without the therapist and part with the therapist. Also called **role-divided therapy**. See also COTHERAPY. [developed by Latvian-born U.S. therapist George R. Bach (1914–1986)]

role-enactment theory a social psychological explanation of hypnosis according to which the person under hypnosis takes on a role assigned by the hypnotist and behaves in accordance with this role while in the hypnotic condition. See also ASSUMED ROLE.

role expectations expectations regarding the traits, attitudes, and behaviors appropriate to a particular ROLE. These expectations may be communicated to the occupant of a role by other people in the occupant's ROLE SET or by the occupant himself or herself. See also PYGMALION EFFECT; SOCIAL ROLE; UPWARD PYGMALION EFFECT.

role model a person or group serving as an exemplar for the goals, attitudes, or behavior of an individual. The individual identifies with and seeks to imitate the role model.

role overload a situation in which one is asked to do more than one is capable of doing in a specific period of time (**quantitative overload**) or in which one is taxed beyond one's knowledge, skills, and abilities (**qualitative overload**).

role play a technique used in HUMAN RELATIONS TRAINING and PSYCHOTHERAPY in which participants act out various social roles in dramatic situations. Originally developed in PSYCHODRAMA, role play is now widely used in industrial, educational, and clinical settings for such purposes as training employees to handle sales problems, testing out different attitudes and relationships in group and family psychotherapy, and rehearsing different ways of coping with stresses and conflicts.

role-playing research research in which participants assume a role and attempt to behave as if the role were really theirs. Critics argue that it cannot be assumed that individuals really in a role would behave in the same way as those only playing that role.

role reversal a technique used for therapeutic and educational purposes in which an individual exchanges roles with another individual in order to experience alternative cognitive styles (e.g., in problem solving), feelings, and behavioral approaches. In PSYCHODRAMA, the PROTAGONIST exchanges roles with an AUXILIARY in acting out a significant interpersonal situation. Role reversal is also used in management development programs, for example, an exchange of roles between a supervisor and an employee.

role set the group of people (and their associated ROLES) who are related to and interact meaningfully with the occupant of a particular role, communicating the attitudes and behaviors appropriate to that role. See ROLE EXPECTATIONS. [defined in 1957 by U.S. sociologist Robert King Merton (1910–2003)]

role shift in any two-person relationship, the adoption by one partner of the characteristic behavior of the other. See also ROLE REVERSAL.

role taking adoption of the role or viewpoint of another person.

role therapy in psychotherapy, a system that uses real-life PSYCHODRAMA. The client selects a role model, works out the aspects of the model with the therapist, and then role-plays the model both in the therapeutic session and in real life. [developed by U.S. psychologist George A. Kelly (1905–1967)]

rolfing *n.* a deep-massage technique developed in the 1930s. It aims to relieve muscular tension, improve posture and balance, and enhance personal functioning through realignment of body structure. The technique is based on a theory that muscle massage will relieve both physical and psychological pain. Also called **structural integration**. [devised by Ida P. **Rolf** (1896–1979), U.S. physical therapist]

ROM abbreviation for RANGE OF MOTION.

Romanticism *n.* an artistic and intellectual movement in Europe and America in the late 18th and early 19th centuries that stressed the values of imagination, spontaneity, wonder, and emotional self-expression over the classical standards of balance, order, restraint, proportion, and objectivity. Its name derives from **romance**, the literary form in which desires and dreams prevail over everyday realities. As a reaction in part against the scientific and technological advances of the time, Romanticism can be viewed as a precursor to humanistic movements in psychology (see HUMANISM; HUMANISTIC PSYCHOLOGY).

romanticism factor see CLASSICISM FACTOR.

romantic love a type of love in which intimacy and passion are prominent features (see TRIANGULAR THEORY OF LOVE). Although the loved party is typically well liked and often idealized, research indicates that the lover's sexual arousal is an especially important component. In some taxonomies of love, romantic love is identified with PASSIONATE LOVE and distinguished from COMPANIONATE LOVE; in others, it is seen as involving elements of both. See also LIMERENCE; LOVE SCALE.

Romazicon *n.* a trade name for FLUMAZENIL.

Romberg's sign a diagnostic sign of certain neurological disorders, including LOCOMOTOR ATAXIA, that consists of a swaying motion and unsteadiness when the individual stands with the eyes closed, feet together, and arms outstretched. [Moritz **Romberg** (1795–1873), German physician]

rooming-in *n.* a practice in some hospitals in which the mother and her newborn child share the same room so that the mother can feed, care for, and establish a close relationship with the baby as soon after birth as is feasible.

root cause analysis a method that identifies the underlying cause or causes of a recurring problem (e.g., in the workplace) by using progressively more specific strategies to uncover the source.

rootedness *n.* in the psychoanalytic theory of Erich FROMM, the need to establish bonds or ties with others that provide emotional security and serve to reduce the isolation and insignificance that Fromm believed to lie at the heart of human existence. It is manifested positively in BROTHERLINESS and negatively in INCESTUOUS TIES.

rooting reflex a reflex in which the healthy newborn infant turns the head toward a gentle stimulus (e.g., the touch of a finger or nipple) applied to the corner of the mouth or to the cheek.

root-mean-square (**RMS**) the square root of the sum of the squares of a set of values divided by the number of values. For a set of values x_1, x_2, ... x_n the root-mean-square value is

$$\sqrt{[(x_1^2 + x_2^2 + \ldots x_n^2)/n]}$$

In the physical sciences the term is used as a synonym for STANDARD DEVIATION under certain circumstances.

rootwork *n.* a cultural or folk health belief system, common in the southern United States and the Caribbean, that attributes illness to witchcraft, hexing, voodoo, or spells (i.e., "roots"). The individual displays intense fear, symptoms of anxiety, and related somatic complaints and typically remains in this state until a traditional healer, called a **root doctor**, removes the root. Also called **brujeria**; **mal puesto**.

ROP abbreviation for RETINOPATHY OF PREMATURITY.

Rorschach, Hermann (1884–1922) Swiss psychiatrist. Rorschach earned his doctorate of medicine at the University of Zürich in 1912. He was the originator of the widely used RORSCHACH INKBLOT TEST of personality. For this, he standardized a set of inkblots, developed criteria for scoring them quantitatively, compared patients of varying diagnoses, and conceived the notion of different experience types that could be differentiated using the inkblot test. He was working on a general theory of personality when he died suddenly of peritonitis. The Rorschach test, developed between 1918 and 1922, did not come into widespread use until the 1950s, when it became, for a time, the test of choice in psychodiagnosis.

Rorschach Inkblot Test a PROJECTIVE test in which the participant is presented with ten unstructured inkblots (mostly in black and gray but sometimes in color) and is asked "What might this be?" or "What do you see in this?" The examiner classifies the responses according to such structural and thematic (content) factors as color (C), movement (M), detail (D), whole (W), popular or common (P), animal (A), form (F), and human (H). Various scoring systems, either qualitative or quantitative, are used. The object is to interpret the participant's personality structure in terms of such factors as emotionality, cognitive style, creativity, impulse control, and various defensive patterns. Perhaps the best known, and certainly one of the most controversial, assessment instruments in all of psychology—it is almost considered "representative" by the general public—the Rorschach is widely used and has been extensively researched, with results ranging from those that claim strong support for its clinical utility (e.g., for selecting treatment modalities or monitoring patient change or improvement over time) to those that demonstrate little evidence of robust or consistent validity and that criticize the instrument as invalid and useless. [developed in the early 1920s by Hermann RORSCHACH]

Rosenthal effect an effect in which the expectancy an experimenter has about the outcome of an experiment unwittingly affects the outcome of the experiment in the direction of the expectancy. The term is often used synonymously with EXPERIMENTER EXPECTANCY EFFECT. [Robert **Rosenthal** (1933–), U.S. psychologist]

Rostan types a system of body types classified on the basis of aspects of the inner structure of the body. See CEREBRAL TYPE; DIGESTIVE TYPE; MUSCULAR TYPE; REPRODUCTIVE TYPE; RESPIRATORY TYPE.

rostral *adj.* **1.** pertaining to a ROSTRUM. **2.** situated or occurring toward the nose, or beak, of an organism, or toward the front or anterior portion of an organ. Compare CAUDAL. **—rostrally** *adv.*

rostrum *n.* (*pl.* **rostra**) a beak-shaped or prowlike structure, such as the rostrum of the CORPUS CALLOSUM at its anterior bend where it curves backward under the frontal lobe.

rotarod *n.* a horizontally oriented rotating cylinder, about 3 cm in diameter, that is used to measure motor coordination and balance in rodents. A rat or mouse is placed on top of the rotarod, and the time taken for the rodent to fall off is measured.

rotary pursuit test any test that requires the participant to follow a revolving or irregularly moving target with a pointer or other indicator.

rotation *n.* in statistics, movement around the origin in a multidimensional space. See OBLIQUE ROTATION; ORTHOGONAL ROTATION; PROCRUSTES ROTATION; QUARTIMAX ROTATION; VARIMAX ROTATION. **—rotational** *adj.*

rotational aftereffect (**RAE**) a MOTION AFTEREFFECT produced by fixation of a rotating stimulus. When the motion of the stimulus is stopped, the stimulus appears to move in the opposite direction. See also PLATEAU'S SPIRAL.

rotational error a drawing or construction error that involves rotating the figure from the position of the copied stimulus.

rotational nystagmus see VESTIBULAR NYSTAGMUS.

rotation system a technique of GROUP PSYCHOTHERAPY in which the therapist works with each individual in sequence in the presence of other group members.

rotation treatment see GYRATOR TREATMENT.

rote learning the type of learning in which acquisition occurs through DRILL and REPETITION, sometimes in the absence of comprehension. Rote learning may lead to the production of correct answers, but without awareness of the reasoning behind or the logical implications of the response.

rote recall precise recollection of information that has been stored in its entirety (e.g., an address, chemical formula, color pattern, or piece of music). See also VERBATIM RECALL.

rote rehearsal repeating information over and over to oneself as a means of committing it to memory, as with a phone number, key facts for a test, the lines of a play, or the like. The recitation may be overt or covert. See REHEARSAL. See also ARTICULATORY LOOP.

Rotter Internal–External Locus of Control Scale (**RIELC**) a scale that is used to provide information regarding a client's feelings for causality of events. Clients who measure high on internal LOCUS OF CONTROL (see INTERNALIZERS) assume causality is primarily under their control; clients who measure high on external locus of control (see EXTERNALIZERS) assume causality is primarily outside their control. Those with high internal measures tend to take more responsibility for and control of their learning, resulting in better performance (e.g., on academic tasks). In contrast, those with high external measures have been shown to take less responsibility, resulting in poorer performance on tasks. [Julian Bernard **Rotter** (1916–), U.S. psychologist]

rough-and-tumble play (**R & T play**) a vigorous form of LOCOMOTOR PLAY, involving chasing, wrestling, and rough-housing, that is typical of childhood and observed more frequently in boys than in girls. R & T play is necessarily social as it involves another person, usually a peer. It is also observed in animals.

roughness *n.* **1.** the tactile quality of an object that is coarse, as in sandpaper. See also TOUCH BLENDS. **2.** a subjective quality used as part of a continuum to describe the percepts produced by amplitude-modulated sounds (see MODULATION). Slow, regular amplitude fluctuations that can be perceived as loudness changes are described as BEATS. Higher fluctuation rates, above approximately 15 Hz, are described as **flutter**, whereas those above approximately 40 Hz are described as being **rough**.

roughness discrimination test a test of somesthetic sensitivity in which participants are asked to determine by touch which of a choice of surfaces (e.g., grades of sandpaper) has a greater roughness. The ability is sometimes impaired following a lesion in a brain area related to the sense of touch.

round dance see BEE COMMUNICATION.

round-table technique a GROUP-PSYCHOTHERAPY technique used in a hospital setting. Three connecting rooms are required. In one, the therapist and others use a one-way window to watch the therapy session in progress. In the second room, selected patients also use a one-way window to watch the same session. The patients in the third room—the therapy room—sit around a table with a microphone in the center. Their task is to recommend a member of their group to go to a staff meeting for possible discharge and, if the member is discharged, to pick a member from the patient group in the adjoining room to join their group. A majority vote prevails. See also MILIEU THERAPY. [pioneered by U.S. psychologist Willis H. McCann (1907–1998)]

round window a membrane-covered opening in the cochlea where it borders the middle ear (see SCALA TYMPANI). Pressure changes in the cochlea produced by vibration of the OVAL WINDOW are ultimately transmitted to the round window. This permits displacement of the BASILAR MEMBRANE and stimulation of the sensory receptors.

Rouse v. Cameron see LEAST RESTRICTIVE ALTERNATIVE.

route learning learning to navigate within a spatial environment through the acquisition of specific directions, distances, and landmarks. **Route knowledge** is represented as a series of directions to follow to get from one place to another (compare SURVEY KNOWLEDGE). Also called **way finding**.

routes of administration see ADMINISTRATION.

routinized behavior a behavior that has been so well learned and frequently repeated that it no longer takes conscious control to execute (e.g., walking). ELITE ATHLETES, for example, routinize the behavior of executing the basic skills so that they have greater capacity to attend to other aspects of their sport. Also called **automatic performance**.

routinized thoughts see AUTOMATIC THOUGHTS.

Royer's syndrome see PRADER–WILLI SYNDROME.

RPE abbreviation for retinal pigment epithelium (see PIGMENT EPITHELIUM).

RPE scale see BORG SCALE.

RR abbreviation for random ratio. See RANDOM-RATIO SCHEDULE.

-rrhagia *suffix* excessive flow or discharge (e.g., MENORRHAGIA).

-rrhea *suffix* flow or discharge (e.g., LOGORRHEA).

RSA abbreviation for RESPIRATORY SINUS ARRHYTHMIA.

RSH syndrome see SMITH–LEMLI–OPITZ SYNDROME.

RSI abbreviation for REPETITIVE STRAIN INJURY.

R–S interval abbreviation for RESPONSE–SHOCK INTERVAL.

R→S relationship the relationship between *r*esponse and *s*timulus, as in TRIALS where a given response by an organism produces a particular change in the stimulus environment, such as reinforcement or escape from aversive stimuli.

r-strategy *n.* a reproductive strategy that involves a high rate of reproduction (r value, or ***r***) with low PARENTAL INVESTMENT. It implies that maximizing the rate of reproduction and producing a relatively large number of offspring are more likely to lead to REPRODUCTIVE SUCCESS than producing a few offspring that require high levels of parental investment (see K-STRATEGY).

RSTS abbreviation for RUBINSTEIN–TAYBI SYNDROME.

RSVP in cognitive psychology, abbreviation for RAPID SEQUENTIAL VISUAL PRESENTATION.

RT abbreviation for REACTION TIME.

R-technique factor analysis the FACTOR ANALYSIS of a CORRELATION MATRIX in which variable measurements are correlated, that is, relationships between the variables themselves are examined. Compare P-TECHNIQUE FACTOR ANALYSIS; Q-TECHNIQUE FACTOR ANALYSIS.

rTMS abbreviation for repetitive TRANSCRANIAL MAGNETIC STIMULATION.

rubber *n.* **1.** slang for a CONDOM. **2.** see FROTTEURISM.

rubella *n.* see GERMAN MEASLES.

Rubin's figure an ambiguous figure that may be perceived either as one goblet or as two facing profiles. Also called **goblet figure**. See also NECKER CUBE. [Edgar **Rubin** (1886–1951), Danish philosopher]

Rubinstein–Taybi syndrome (**RSTS**; **RTS**) a familial disorder marked by facial abnormalities, including MICROCEPHALY and HYPERTELORISM, broad thumbs and toes, and mental retardation, caused by several different genetic factors. Hypotonia (flaccid muscles) and a stiff gait are common. One study found more than 80% of affected individuals had IQs of less than 50. Also called **Rubinstein syndrome**. [Jack H. **Rubinstein** (1925–) and Hooshang **Taybi** (1919–), U.S. pediatricians]

rubrospinal tract a MOTOR PATHWAY that arises from the RED NUCLEUS in the brainstem and descends laterally in the spinal cord, where it stimulates flexor motor neurons and inhibits extensor motor neurons.

Ruffini's corpuscle a type of sensory-nerve ending in the subcutaneous tissues of human fingers. Ruffini's corpuscles are believed to mediate sensations of skin stretch, motion detection, and hand and finger position. Also called **Ruffini's endings**. [Angelo **Ruffini** (1864–1929), Italian anatomist]

rule *n.* **1.** a guideline or standard that is used to guide responses or behavior or that communicates situational NORMS. **2.** in linguistics, a formal mechanism used to account for the patterns of relationship between grammatical elements in a language. Formal linguistics draws distinctions between rules that are obligatory, optional, categorical, and variable.

rule-assessment approach a theory that explains cognitive development in terms of the rules and the increasingly powerful strategies children use to solve problems. See also ADAPTIVE STRATEGY CHOICE MODEL. [proposed by U.S. developmental psychologist Robert S. Siegler (1949–)]

rule-based system a computer program in which human knowledge is stored and used as a sequence of "if–then" relationships. See EXPERT SYSTEM; PRODUCTION SYSTEM.

rule-governed behavior any behavior that is influenced by verbal antecedents, such as following instructions (as when a child cleans his or her room because told to do so) or reacting to one's own private thinking (as when an adult begins an exercise program after thinking "I need to lose weight"). The term does not refer to behavior that can be described by a rule. For example, rats' behavior that adopts a WIN–STAY, LOSE–SHIFT STRATEGY cannot be described as rule-governed. Also called **verbally governed behavior**. Compare CONTINGENCY-GOVERNED BEHAVIOR.

rule learning in psychology experiments, the process in which a participant gradually acquires knowledge about a fixed but unstated standard that defines, for example, the acceptability of a response or membership of a category.

rule modeling an imitative technique in which people learn to control their behavior by following the same rules that have been followed by a model, even when there are slight situational variations.

rule of abstinence in psychoanalysis, the rule that the patient should abstain from all gratifications that might distract him or her from the analytic process or drain off instinctual energy, anxiety, and frustration that could be used as a driving force in the therapy. Examples of such gratifications are smoking, engaging in idle conversation, or ACTING OUT during the sessions, and unlimited sexual activity, absorbing interests, and other pleasures pursued outside the sessions. Also called **abstinence rule**.

rule of thumb a generally useful but by no means infallible strategy for approaching a problem or decision. See HEURISTIC.

rules of inference rules for the construction of logical arguments stating what kinds of inference are valid from what kinds of premise. See DEDUCTION; DEDUCTIVE REASONING.

rules of the game in developmental psychology, rules, laws, or social conventions toward which, according to Jean PIAGET, children's attitudes change as they get older. When children first learn the meaning of rules, they view them as utterly binding. Even when they break rules, they tend not to challenge their validity. However, as they approach adolescence (beginning around age 10), children tend to shift their attitudes and view rules as social conventions or laws that can be questioned and modified under conditions of mutual consent.

rumination *n.* **1.** obsessional thinking involving excessive, repetitive thoughts or themes that interfere with other forms of mental activity. It is a common feature of OBSESSIVE-COMPULSIVE DISORDER. **2.** the voluntary regurgitation of food from the stomach to the mouth, where it is masticated and tasted a second time. It frequently occurs among people with severe or profound mental retardation, and it is possible that delays in development may be due partly to the disorder. Also called **merycism**. **—ruminate** *vb.*

rumination disorder in *DSM–IV–TR*, a disorder characterized by the repeated voluntary regurgitation of ingested food involving ejection or reswallowing, but without nausea. Individuals may develop potentially fatal weight loss and malnutrition. It lasts for a period of at least 1 month and generally occurs during infancy (age 3 to 12 months), following a period of normal feeding; however, it may also be observed in individuals with severe mental retardation.

rumor *n.* a story or piece of information of unknown reliability that is passed from person to person. See also GOSSIP.

rumor-intensity formula a model that attempts to explain why some rumors persist and intensify whereas others peter out. In short, the strength of a rumor is the arithmetical product of the significance of the subject matter and the level of uncertainty about available information. [proposed by Gordon ALLPORT and Russian-born U.S. experimental psychologist Leo Postman (1918–2004)]

run *n.* **1.** a single presentation of a series of stimuli or tasks as part of an experiment. **2.** the distance along the *x*-axis between two points. Compare RISE.

runaway selection a theory of female MATE SELECTION proposing that certain traits in males are sexually attractive to females, which choose mates with these traits and thereby ensure that any male offspring will also be attractive to females, independent of genetic quality. Compare GOOD GENES HYPOTHESIS.

runner's high a euphoric sensation achieved while running, characterized by an elevated sense of awareness, a suppression of pain and discomfort, perfect rhythm, and ease of effort. See also ENDORPHINS.

running wheel see ACTIVITY WHEEL.

runway *n.* in animal experimentation, the pathway that leads from a starting box to a goal box or to the main part of a maze.

rural environment an environment usually characterized by open land, sparse settlement, some distance from cities and towns, and an economy that is usually agriculturally based but may alternatively be based on other types of economic activity, such as logging, mining, oil and gas exploration, or tourism. In environmental psychology, the rural environment is often used as a basis for comparison with the urban (city) environment with respect to air-pollution levels, crowding, crime, and other physical and social stressors. See also URBAN BEHAVIOR.

rural health clinic (**RHC**) a clinic, physician practice, or country health department that—in compliance with the Rural Clinic Services Act—is located in a medically underserved area and uses a physician, PHYSICIAN ASSISTANT, NURSE PRACTITIONER, or some combination of these to deliver primary outpatient health care. See also NATIONAL ASSOCIATION OF RURAL HEALTH CLINICS.

rush *n.* the effect reported when someone receives an intravenous injection of amphetamine, cocaine, or methamphetamine. The sensation is sometimes described as a dramatic awakening accompanied by a high and sudden degree of euphoria.

RVS abbreviation for ROKEACH VALUE SURVEY.

Ss

s symbol for SPECIAL FACTOR.

S see PRIMARY ABILITIES; SPATIAL INTELLIGENCE.

S– symbol for NEGATIVE DISCRIMINATIVE STIMULUS.

S+ symbol for POSITIVE DISCRIMINATIVE STIMULUS.

S^D symbol for DISCRIMINATIVE STIMULUS.

S^Δ symbol for NEGATIVE DISCRIMINATIVE STIMULUS.

SA abbreviation for SOCIAL AGE.

SAB abbreviation for STANDARD APPLICATION BLANK.

saccade *n.* a ballistic movement of the eyes that allows visual fixation to jump from one location to another in the visual field. Once initiated, a saccade cannot change course. See also MICROSACCADES. Compare SMOOTH-PURSUIT MOVEMENT. **—saccadic** *adj.*

saccadic dysmetria see OCULAR DYSMETRIA.

saccadic speed the speed of the rapid, ballistic eye movement known as a SACCADE. Human saccades reach speeds of 700° of VISUAL ANGLE per second.

saccadic time the duration of a SACCADE. Saccades last 15–100 ms, and approximately 150 ms elapses before the next saccade can be initiated.

saccule *n.* the smaller of the two VESTIBULAR SACS of the inner ear, the other being the UTRICLE. Like the utricle, it contains a sensory structure called a MACULA. Movements of the head relative to gravity exert a momentum pressure on hair cells within the macula, which then fire impulses indicating a change in body position in space. **—saccular** *adj.*

sacral division the nerves of the PARASYMPATHETIC NERVOUS SYSTEM that arise from the spinal cord in the sacral (lower back) region. Compare CRANIAL DIVISION.

sacral nerve see SPINAL NERVE.

sacred disease a name for epilepsy used by the ancient Greeks, based on the belief that seizures were evidence of divine visitation. Hippocrates, however, rejected this view, saying "Surely it, too, has its nature and causes whence it originates, just like other diseases, and is curable by means comparable to their cure."

sacrificial paraphilia sexual interest and arousal involving staged or actual death, with ritualistic sacrifice features. This may involve, as the sacrificial objects, animals or people. See also PARAPHILIA.

SAD abbreviation for SEASONAL AFFECTIVE DISORDER.

S-adenosylmethionine (SAM) *n.* a commonly used supplement thought by some to have efficacy in the treatment of depression. Randomized controlled trials have suggested it is of some benefit in relieving the condition. Its mechanism of action is unknown, but it is apparently involved in the metabolism of certain neurotransmitters and may increase levels of serotonin in the brain.

sadism *n.* **1.** the practice of obtaining gratification by inflicting pain or humiliation on a sexual partner (see SEXUAL SADISM). Sadism may be extended beyond the sexual partner to include animals. Although some activities or speech that might be considered sadistic by Western cultural standards do occur as an accepted part of foreplay in some non-Western cultures, true sadists prefer and need the infliction of pain for sexual enjoyment and functioning. **2.** any form of pleasure derived from cruelty. In psychoanalytic theory, sadism is attributed to the working of the DEATH INSTINCT and is manifested in innate aggressive tendencies expressed from the earliest stages of development. For example, during the ORAL-BITING PHASE the infant expresses sadism by taking pleasure in biting. See also ANAL SADISM; ORAL SADISM. Compare MASOCHISM. [Donatien Alphonse François, Comte (Marquis) de **Sade** (1740–1814), French soldier and writer] **—sadist** *n.* **—sadistic** *adj.*

sadistic personality disorder in *DSM–III–R* (but not in *DSM–IV–TR*), a personality disorder characterized by an abusive and intimidating manner, inclined to gain satisfaction in coercing and humiliating others. Such people are often reckless and undaunted by danger or punishment.

sadness *n.* an emotional state of unhappiness, ranging in intensity from mild to extreme and usually aroused by the loss of something that is highly valued, for example, by the rupture or loss of a relationship. Persistent sadness is one of the two defining symptoms of a MAJOR DEPRESSIVE EPISODE, the other being ANHEDONIA. **—sad** *adj.*

sadomasochism *n.* **1.** sexual activity between consenting partners in which one partner enjoys inflicting pain (see SEXUAL SADISM) and the other enjoys experiencing pain (see SEXUAL MASOCHISM). **2.** a PARAPHILIA in which a person is both sadistic and masochistic, deriving sexual arousal from both giving and receiving pain. **—sadomasochist** *n.* **—sadomasochistic** *adj.*

sadomasochistic personality formerly, in psychoanalysis, the characterization of people who enjoy both exhibiting and receiving aggressive behavior.

SADS abbreviation for SCHEDULE FOR AFFECTIVE DISORDERS AND SCHIZOPHRENIA.

Saethre–Chotzen syndrome see CHOTZEN'S SYNDROME.

safe compartment in a two-compartment CONDITIONING APPARATUS, the compartment that is not associated with an AVERSIVE STIMULUS.

safe sex sexual activity in which the exchange of bodily fluids is inhibited as much as possible to help reduce the risk of unwanted pregnancy or contracting sexually transmitted diseases. Precautions may include avoidance of high-risk behaviors, careful selection of one's partners, and the use of preventive barriers (e.g., condoms, dental dams).

safety and health education instruction regarding health-related matters, including the causes and prevention of malnutrition, alcoholism, drug addiction, and sexually transmitted disease, as well as safety on the roads, in the workshop, at home, and on the playing field. See also ACCIDENT PREVENTION.

safety behavior a behavior performed by an anxious individual in an attempt to minimize or prevent a feared catastrophe. For example, a person with PANIC DISORDER might only go out when accompanied, and a person with SOCIAL PHOBIA might wear sunglasses indoors to avoid eye contact. Safety behaviors may also include internal mental processes: A person with social phobia might memorize what he or she plans to say at a social gathering. Safety behavior contributes to the maintenance of anxiety disorders when people believe that the behavior, rather than the lack of actual danger, is what prevents the feared catastrophe. Also called **safety cues**; **safety-seeking behaviour**; **safety signals**. [first defined in 1991 by British psychologist Paul M. Salkovskis]

safety device in the therapeutic approach of German-born U.S. psychoanalyst Karen D. Horney (1885–1952), any psychic means used by an individual to protect himself or herself from threats, particularly the hostile elements of the environment. As such, the concept is similar to the classical psychoanalytic concept of the DEFENSE MECHANISM. See also BASIC ANXIETY.

safety engineering a discipline that applies multiple approaches to the design and evaluation of work systems and processes with the aim of eliminating or reducing hazard. See also HAZARD CONTROL.

safety needs the second level in MASLOW'S MOTIVATIONAL HIERARCHY of needs after basic PHYSIOLOGICAL NEEDS: It consists of the needs for freedom from illness or danger and the need for a secure, familiar, predictable environment.

safety psychology the study of the human and environmental factors involved in accidents and ACCIDENT PREVENTION. Human factors include safe and unsafe attitudes and behavior, relevant personality and physiological considerations, and stress conditions. Environmental factors include, for example, safe highway construction, safe working conditions, reduction of overcrowding, redesign of signs, noise abatement, use of seat belts, and improved design of kitchens and bathrooms. See also ACCIDENT PRONENESS.

sagittal *adj.* describing or relating to a plane that divides the body or an organ into left and right portions. A **midsagittal** (or **medial sagittal**) **plane** divides the body centrally into halves, whereas a **parasagittal plane** lies parallel but to one side of the center. **—sagittally** *adv.*

sagittal fissure see LONGITUDINAL FISSURE.

Saint Dymphna's disease an early name for mental illness, deriving from the name of the patron saint of those with nervous disorders or mental illness. According to legend, Dymphna, a medieval Irish princess, fled to Belgium to escape the incestuous advances of her mad father, who later put her to death near Gheel. See GHEEL COLONY.

St. John's wort a perennial flowering plant, *Hypericum perforatum*, that has an extensive history of folk use, particularly as a sedative, a treatment for nerve pain and malaria, and a balm for wounds, burns, and insect bites. It is currently a highly popular product used in the treatment of mild to moderate depression, anxiety, and insomnia. There is some research supporting its effectiveness for these purposes, but studies have not demonstrated the superiority of St. John's wort over placebo in the management of major depression. There is also some research suggesting the herb possesses anti-inflammatory and antioxidant properties as well. The active agents are presumed to be HYPERICIN and related compounds. Hypericin is known to exert some effects common to other ANTIDEPRESSANTS, such as inhibition of the reuptake of norepinephrine, dopamine, and serotonin. It may also exert some effects by modulating the neurotransmitters GAMMA-AMINOBUTYRIC ACID (GABA) and GLUTAMATE. The agent should be used with caution, as it may interact adversely with or limit the effectiveness of a number of other drugs, particularly those used to treat HIV/AIDS and cancer and to prevent transplant rejection. Although rare, side effects may include dry mouth, dizziness, diarrhea, nausea, increased sensitivity to sunlight, and fatigue.

Saint Vitus's dance an archaic name for Sydenham's CHOREA.

sales-survey technique a method of testing the effectiveness of advertising appeals by analyzing sales of a product after it has been advertised in one or more communities and comparing the results with sales of the same product in areas in which it has not been advertised. The method requires that various extraneous factors, such as weather conditions, that may have affected shopper behavior during the period studied are taken into account.

salicylates *pl. n.* a group of drugs that are based on **salicin**, a compound obtained from the bark of willow trees (*Salix*), and includes salicylic acid and its derivatives. The latter are used as analgesics, antipyretics, and anti-inflammatory agents. They act on both the peripheral and central nervous systems, particularly the thalamus, but also mimic some aspects of the adrenal hormones. The best known member is ASPIRIN (acetylsalicylic acid), introduced in 1899. Other salicylates include **salicylamide** and compounds used in topical formulations for the relief of muscle and joint pain.

salicylism *n.* poisoning with salicylates, the most common form of which is due to overdosage of ASPIRIN. Symptoms of mild salicylism include tinnitus, mental confusion, headache, nausea, and vomiting. More severe forms of salicylism are characterized by severe acidosis, hemorrhage, and changes in mental status that may lead to convulsions, coma, and death.

salience *n.* a parameter of a stimulus that indexes its effectiveness.

salience hypothesis a general theory of perception according to which highly salient stimuli (objects, people, meanings, etc.) will be perceived more readily than those of low salience. It has applications in social perception, advertising, and linguistics.

salient *adj.* distinctive or prominent. A salient stimulus in a multielement array will tend to be easily detected and identified. See POP-OUT.

saline *adj.* consisting of salt or having a SALTY taste.

saliromania *n.* sexual interest and arousal associated with objects that are filthy, disgusting, or deformed.

salivary gland any of several glands located in the wall of the mouth that secrete a fluid (saliva) containing the enzyme α-amylase (ptyalin). The major salivary glands are the paired parotid, submaxillary, and sublingual glands; smaller glands are scattered over the cheeks and tongue. See also SALIVATION.

salivary reflex a change in the secretion of the salivary glands caused by unconditioned or conditioned stimulation of their effector nerves. See CONDITIONED RESPONSE; UNCONDITIONED RESPONSE.

salivation *n.* the secretion of saliva by the SALIVARY GLANDS, typically as a reflex response to stimuli associated with food.

Salpêtrière *n.* an institution for women founded in Paris in 1656 as an asylum for the infirm, aged, and insane. At one time it contained nearly 10,000 people, and treatment was proverbially brutal. The Salpêtrière was transformed during the regime of Philippe Pinel (1745–1826), who became its director in 1794 and introduced many pioneering reforms in the treatment of people with mental illnesses. From the 1860s the hospital became the center for the psychopathological investigations of Jean-Martin Charcot (1825–1893), which involved the use of hypnosis; in 1885 one of Charcot's students was the young Sigmund FREUD.

salpingectomy *n.* the surgical removal of one or both fallopian tubes. A salpingectomy may be performed as a STERILIZATION measure or because of an infection or malignant growth in the reproductive tract. Also called **tubectomy**. See also TUBAL LIGATION.

saltation *n.* **1.** a dancing or leaping motion (from Latin, *saltatio*, "dance"), specifically one seen as a result of CHOREA. **2.** the mode of conduction of nerve impulses along myelinated nerve fibers. See SALTATORY CONDUCTION. **3.** the phenomenon in which a sensation is felt at a site other than that where it was evoked. **4.** a sudden variation or modification of a species. **5.** an abrupt transition or sudden change or development in the course of an illness.

saltatory conduction a type of conduction of nerve impulses that occurs in MYELINATED FIBERS, in which the impulses skip from one NODE OF RANVIER to the next. This permits much faster conduction velocities compared with unmyelinated fibers.

salty *adj.* denoting the TASTE elicited by sodium chloride or lithium chloride, by other sodium and lithium salts, and by the amino acid arginine. Sodium is the primary ion for generating osmotic forces in an organism and is an essential carrier of electrical potentials; it cannot be produced in the body, therefore it is essential to consume it. **—saltiness** *n.*

SAM 1. abbreviation for S-ADENOSYLMETHIONINE. **2.** abbreviation for SEARCH OF ASSOCIATIVE MEMORY.

same-sex marriage a long-term, intimate, stable, and in some jurisdictions legally recognized relationship between two people of the same sex. It is less frequently called **homosexual marriage**. See DOMESTIC PARTNERSHIP.

SAMHSA abbreviation for SUBSTANCE ABUSE AND MENTAL HEALTH SERVICES ADMINISTRATION.

sample *n.* **1.** a subset of a POPULATION of interest. **2.** the cases actually studied in an experiment.

sample distribution the distribution of scores in a particular SAMPLE (e.g., normal, skewed, bimodal).

sample overlap an incidence in which values are found in two or more SAMPLES from the same population.

sample space 1. the collection of all possible samples of a given size of ELEMENTARY EVENTS in a given population. **2.** a geometric representation of a sample in which the dimensions of the space represent the criteria defining the sample.

sampling *n.* the process of selecting a limited number of subjects or cases for participation in experiments, surveys, or other research. It is important to ensure that a sample is representative of the population as a whole. See QUOTA SAMPLING; RANDOM SAMPLING; SAMPLING POPULATION; STRATIFIED RANDOM SAMPLING.

sampling bias any flaw in SAMPLING processes that makes the resulting sample unrepresentative of the population, hence possibly distorting research results.

sampling distribution the distribution of a statistic over infinite repeated samples drawn from a population; that is, the theoretical distribution of a statistic.

sampling error 1. the extent to which a SAMPLE is not representative of the POPULATION from which it was drawn. **2.** the variation in the estimate of a parameter that occurs from sample to sample. **3.** the predictable margin of error that occurs in studies employing sampling.

sampling fraction the proportion of a population that is included in a sample: the ratio of the sample size to the population size for finite populations.

sampling frame a complete listing of all of the elements in a POPULATION from which a sample is to be drawn.

sampling methods the various means by which participants are chosen for research. See SAMPLING.

sampling plan a design or procedure that specifies how research participants are to be chosen, particularly in a survey study.

sampling population the POPULATION from which a SAMPLE is selected in experimental studies.

sampling theory the principles of drawing samples that accurately represent the population from which they are taken. See SAMPLING.

sampling unit any of the elements that make up a SAMPLE. Sampling units may, for example, be people, schools, or cities. For instance, if classrooms are selected at random, then it is the classroom that is the sampling unit and not the students in the class.

sampling variability the extent to which the value of a statistic differs across a series of samples from the mean value for all possible samples (i.e., the POPULATION). See SAMPLING ERROR.

sampling with replacement a SAMPLING technique in which a selected unit is returned to the pool and may subsequently be redrawn in another sample. In **sampling without replacement** the sampling unit is not returned to the pool.

samsara *n.* see METEMPSYCHOSIS.

sanatorium *n.* formerly, an institution for the treatment and convalescence of individuals with chronic diseases, such as rheumatism, tuberculosis, neurological disorders, or mental disorders. Also called **sanitarium**.

sanction *n.* a punishment or other coercive measure, usually administered by a recognized authority, that is used to penalize and deter inappropriate or unauthorized actions. See also SOCIAL SANCTION.

Sandimmune *n.* a trade name for CYCLOSPORINE.

S and M abbreviation for sadism and masochism. See SADOMASOCHISM.

sane society see Erich FROMM.

Sanfilippo's syndrome a disorder causing severe mental retardation associated with bone and joint defects and a tendency toward dwarfism. Affected children may also show signs of corneal opacities. The disease is transmitted as an autosomal recessive trait that causes a systemic form of MUCOPOLYSACCHARIDOSIS. After normal early mental development, the child shows mental regression. The ability to speak deteriorates and eventually is lost, as is motor control. Lifespan may be 10 to 20 years. Also called **heparitinuria**; **mucopolysaccharidosis Type III**; **polydystrophic oligophrenia**; **Sanfilippo (A, B, C, D)**. [described in 1963 by Sylvester **Sanfilippo**, U.S. pediatrician]

sangue dormido a CULTURE-BOUND SYNDROME found among inhabitants (indigenous and immigrant) of Cape Verde. Symptoms include pain, numbness, tremor, paralysis, convulsions, stroke, blindness, heart attack, infection, and miscarriage. [Portuguese, literally: "sleeping blood"]

sanguine type one of the four constitutional and temperamental types established by Roman physician Galen

(129–215), who believed that the ruddy complexion and cheerful outlook displayed by such individuals was due to the predominance of the blood over other body fluids. See HUMORAL THEORY.

sanitarium *n.* see SANATORIUM.

sanity *n.* **1.** in law, the state of being not legally insane (see INSANITY), and therefore not suffering from a mental disease or defect that impairs one's ability to understand or appreciate one's acts or to conform to the requirements of the law. **2.** more generally, soundness of mind or judgment. **—sane** *adj.*

Sansert *n.* a trade name for METHYSERGIDE.

sapid stimulus see GUSTATORY STIMULUS.

Sapir–Whorf hypothesis see LINGUISTIC DETERMINISM. [Edward **Sapir** (1884–1939) and Benjamin Lee **Whorf** (1897–1941), U.S. linguists]

sapphism *n.* see LESBIANISM.

Sarafem *n.* a trade name for FLUOXETINE.

sarcoma *n.* see CANCER.

SAR workshop abbreviation for SEXUAL ATTITUDE REASSESSMENT WORKSHOP.

SAT acronym for SCHOLASTIC ASSESSMENT TEST.

Satanic ritual abuse (**SRA**) see SATANISM. See also RITUAL ABUSE.

Satanism *n.* a religion based on the worship of Satan, the supreme personification of evil in Christian tradition, whether as a deity or a concept. Satanist cults vary from neopagan groups that revere Satan as a benevolent force of energy in nature to those that involve some kind of allegiance to Satan as an evil principle. In the latter case, worship takes the form of magical rituals that may involve an element of deliberate transgression (e.g., by parodies of Christian ceremonies or taboo sexual practices). **Satanic ritual abuse** (**SRA**) is the alleged psychological, sexual, or physical abuse of humans or animals committed as part of a religious ritual involving worship of Satan. See RITUAL ABUSE. See also DEMONOLOGY. **—Satanic** *adj.* **—Satanist** *n.*

satellite clinic a freestanding outpatient facility that is physically separate from but administratively attached to a parent medical facility. Staff interaction and sharing of services occur between the clinic and parent facility.

satellite male in animal behavior, a male peripheral to a territorial male, or present in a group of displaying males, that does not call or display. A satellite male will rapidly replace a territorial male that disappears and will often intercept females attracted to nearby displaying males to engage in SNEAK MATING.

satiation *n.* **1.** the satisfaction of a desire or need, such as hunger or thirst. See SATIETY. **2.** the temporary loss of effectiveness of a REINFORCER due to its repeated presentation. **—satiate** *vb.*

satiety *n.* the state of being fully satisfied to or beyond capacity, as, for example, when hunger or thirst have been fully assuaged, which inhibits any desire to eat or drink more.

satiety center see VENTROMEDIAL NUCLEUS.

satiety mechanism any of the bodily processes or systems that regulate food and fluid intake. See also APPETITIVE BEHAVIOR.

satisfaction of instincts in psychoanalytic theory, the gratification of basic needs, such as hunger, thirst, sex, and aggression, which discharges tension, eliminates UNPLEASURE, and restores the organism to a balanced state. Satisfaction may occur on a conscious, preconscious, or unconscious level. Also called **gratification of instincts**. See also LIBIDO.

satisfice *vb.* to choose an option that meets the requirements of a particular situation but that may not be the optimal choice when considered in the abstract. In economics, the hypothesis of **satisficing behavior** is the assumption that, given the constraints of BOUNDED RATIONALITY, economic agents seek a level of profit or utility that they find satisfactory rather than the optimal such level. [defined by U.S. social scientist Herbert Simon (1916–2001)]

satori *n.* in ZEN BUDDHISM, the state or moment of spiritual awakening (Japanese, "awakening") or enlightenment in which reality is perceived.

saturated model a model with as many parameters as there are CELLS (or possible effects) in the design that the model represents.

saturated test in FACTOR ANALYSIS, a test that is shown to have a high degree of correlation with a given factor.

saturation *n.* in color theory, the quality of a stimulus that describes the purity of a color and the degree to which it departs from white. Highly saturated colors have little if any gray, whereas colors of low saturation are more akin to gray.

saturation scale an index of the purity of a color, ranging from gray to the pure color. It is used in psychophysics to relate the perceived purity of a color to the percentage of light of a given wavelength that is present.

satyriasis *n.* excessive or insatiable desire in a male for sexual gratification. Sexual activity with one person is found not to be enough, and many other sexual partners are sought. See also DON JUAN; EROTOMANIA.

sauce béarnaise effect a lay term referring to a CONDITIONED TASTE AVERSION. If a person happens to become ill after tasting a new food, such as sauce béarnaise, he or she may subsequently dislike and avoid that food: Regardless of the actual cause of the illness, the sauce will be identified with it. See PREPARED LEARNING.

savant *n.* **1.** a learned individual, or an individual who demonstrates exceptional or remarkable and unusual intellectual prowess or skills. **2.** a person with mental retardation or an AUTISTIC SPECTRUM DISORDER who demonstrates exceptional, usually isolated, cognitive abilities. See IDIOT SAVANT.

savings method see RELEARNING METHOD.

savings score the amount of savings in relearning material that was once known but is now forgotten. Savings may be quantified by the amount of time or the number of study periods required for relearning relative to initial learning. See RELEARNING METHOD.

sawtooth waves bursts of small, sharp waves recorded on an electroencephalogram during REM SLEEP.

saxitoxin (**STX**) *n.* an animal toxin that blocks the passage of sodium ions across a cell's plasma membrane when applied to the outer surface of the cell.

SB abbreviation for STANFORD–BINET INTELLIGENCE SCALE.

sc abbreviation for *s*ub*c*utaneous.

scaffolding *n.* **1.** an epistemological approach to EMBODIED COGNITION, in which the world that an AGENT operates within is seen as a sine qua non of its intelligence. A simple example is the use of paper and pencil to perform complex arithmetic procedures. **2.** in education, a teaching style that supports and facilitates the student as he or she learns a new skill or concept, with the ultimate goal of the student becoming self-reliant. Derived from Lev VYGOTSKY's theories, in practice it involves teaching material just beyond the level at which the student could learn alone. Technology (e.g., computer software) that may be used to assist in this process is known as **scaffolded tools**.

scalability *n.* the characteristic of an item (e.g., in a test) that allows it to fit into a progression of scores or values.

scala media one of the three canals that run the length of the COCHLEA in the inner ear. Located between the scala vestibuli and scala tympani, it is filled with fluid (ENDOLYMPH) and is delimited by REISSNER'S MEMBRANE, the highly vascular **stria vascularis**, and the BASILAR MEMBRANE, which supports the ORGAN OF CORTI. Also called **cochlear duct**. See also AUDITORY LABYRINTH.

scala tympani one of the three canals within the COCHLEA in the inner ear. It is located below the scala media, from which it is separated by the BASILAR MEMBRANE, and contains PERILYMPH. At its basal end is the ROUND WINDOW.

scala vestibuli one of the three canals within the COCHLEA in the inner ear. It is located above the scala media, from which it is separated by REISSNER'S MEMBRANE, and contains PERILYMPH. At its basal end is the OVAL WINDOW.

scale *n.* a system for arranging items in a progressive series, for example, according to their magnitude or value.

scale development the process of constructing, standardizing, and validating a measuring instrument.

scaled test **1.** a test in which the items are arranged in order of increasing difficulty. **2.** a test in which the items are assigned a value or score.

Scale of Prodromal Symptoms (**SOPS**) a psychological assessment instrument designed to identify and assess the PRODROMAL SYNDROME of schizophrenia and other psychotic disorders. It includes behaviorally defined diagnosis criteria and provides a six-point scale to quantitatively rate the severity of five ATTENUATED POSITIVE SYMPTOMS, four disorganization symptoms, and four general symptoms. [originally developed in 2001 by U.S. psychiatrist Thomas H. McGlashan (1941–) and colleagues]

scale reproducibility the degree to which people's overall scores on a CUMULATIVE SCALE imply that they have endorsed all items in the scale that are less extreme than their overall scores and rejected all items in the scale that are more extreme than their overall scores.

scale value the number that represents the value of an observation or attribute on a scale.

scaling *n.* the process of constructing a SCALE to measure or assess some quantity or characteristic (e.g., height, weight, happiness, empathy).

scalogram *n.* see CUMULATIVE SCALE.

Scanlon plan a type of GAINSHARING program in which employees are motivated to improve productivity by monetary bonuses and participation in solving production problems. A production committee made up of supervisors and employees is formed within each unit in an organization; this committee screens suggestions from employees for reducing costs and improving productivity. Gains, such as cost savings or the value of improved production, are shared with the whole group, not just the individuals making the suggestions. See also INDUSTRIAL DEMOCRACY; PARTICIPATIVE DECISION-MAKING; QUALITY CIRCLE. [Joseph **Scanlon** (1899–1956), U.S. union leader]

scanning *n.* in medicine, the process of using radiological, magnetic, or other means of visualizing a portion of the body, for example, using a BRAIN SCAN in diagnosing a disorder.

scanning hypothesis the hypothesis that RAPID EYE MOVEMENTS observed during dreaming sleep correspond to subjective gaze shifts of the dreamer looking around in the dream with fixations in specific locations.

scanning speech speech that is slow with variable intonations and involuntary interruptions between syllables. It is a characteristic of ATAXIC DYSARTHRIA.

scapegoating *n.* a process in which anger and aggression are displaced (see DISPLACEMENT) onto other, usually less powerful, groups or individuals when the true source of the aggressor's frustration lies in someone or something that cannot be directly confronted. See also PROJECTION. **—scapegoat** *n., vb.*

scapegoat theory **1.** an analysis of violence and aggression that assumes that individuals undergoing negative experiences (such as failure or abuse by others) may blame an innocent individual or group for causing the experience. Subsequent mistreatment of this scapegoat then serves as an outlet for individuals' frustrations and hostilities (see DISPLACED AGGRESSION). It has also been suggested that when scapegoats have been targets for aggression over the years they may thus acquire the quality of a stimulus for aggression. **2.** an analysis of PREJUDICE that assumes that intergroup conflict is caused, in part, by the tendency of individuals to blame their negative experiences on other groups. The theory is supported by studies suggesting that racial prejudice increases during periods of economic downturn and high unemployment. See REALISTIC GROUP-CONFLICT THEORY. See also FRUSTRATION–AGGRESSION HYPOTHESIS.

scapular reflex a REFLEX involving contraction of the scapular muscle when the skin over the scapula (shoulder blade) is irritated.

SCAT acronym for SCHOOL AND COLLEGE ABILITY TEST.

scato- (**scat-**) *combining form* feces or filth.

scatologia *n.* preoccupation with obscenities, lewdness, and filth, mainly of an excremental nature. The term is derived from the Greek word for dung. In psychoanalytic theory, scatalogia is usually associated with ANAL EROTICISM. Also called **scatology**. **—scatological** *adj.*

scatophilia *n.* sexual interest and arousal derived from talking about sexual or excremental matters and using obscene language.

scatter *n.* the tendency of data points to diverge from each other. An example is the variation in scores across a series of tests on the same individual.

scatter diagram see SCATTERPLOT.

scattering *n.* a type of thinking characterized by tangential or irrelevant associations that may be expressed in incomprehensible speech. It is observed in individuals with schizophrenia.

scatterplot *n.* a graphical representation of the location of data points in a two-dimensional space whose axes are defined by the variables under consideration. Also called **scatter diagram**.

scavenging behavior feeding on dead organic matter, such as carrion or scraps left by other animals. Scavenging behavior is found in many species, including vultures, hyenas, jackals, and chimpanzees.

scenario analysis a process in which managers conceptualize a range of plausible, logically consistent situations (scenarios) that may arise in the future and attempt to identify the implications of these for their organization and its activities. The purpose is not so much to predict the future—some of the scenarios considered may be highly unlikely—as to promote better decision making and subject existing systems and processes to critical scrutiny, especially in terms of their ability to respond flexibly to unexpected events. Scenario analysis has important applications in such fields as politics, military strategy, business, ergonomics, and accident prevention.

scenario-based design in ergonomics, design practice in which a variety of different potential uses for a product or system are envisioned and then analyzed in order to help designers identify and correct potential problems or flaws.

scent marking the act by an animal of depositing ODORANTS on a substrate, often from specialized **scent glands** that produce them. Scent glands are commonly found in the anogenital region, in the axilla, in the suprapubic region, and around the mouth. Scent marking provides cues about species, sex, reproductive status, and dominance status that can remain on or diffuse slowly from a substrate after the marking individual has left.

Schachenmann's syndrome see CAT'S-EYE SYNDROME.

Schachter, Stanley (1922–1997) U.S. psychologist. Schachter received his doctorate at the University of Michigan in 1949, studying under Leon FESTINGER. He taught at the University of Minnesota from 1949 until 1961, when he joined the faculty at Columbia University, where he remained for the remainder of his career. Schachter's research has been very influential in the fields of social and health psychology. Importantly, he found ways to conduct rigorous laboratory experiments on complex topics in social psychology and then to validate them in real-world situations. His research focused on such issues as social pressure within groups, social communication, ATTRIBUTION THEORY, and such addictive behaviors as overeating and smoking. One of his most famous and controversial articles was "Cognitive, Social, and Physiological Determinants of Emotional State" (*Psychological Review*, 1962, coauthored with Jerome E. Singer). Scientists had long held that particular physiological factors led to particular emotional states. Schachter and Singer's work provided compelling evidence that the same state of physiological arousal (e.g., induced by a measured injection of Adrenalin) could be interpreted as fear, anger, or excitement depending on the social context in which an individual was placed. That is, physiological, cognitive, and emotional states were interdependent. Notable books coauthored by Schachter include *Social Pressures in Informal Groups* (1950), *Theory and Experiment in Social Communication* (1950), *When Prophecy Fails* (1956), and *The Psychology of Affiliation* (1959). Among Schachter's honors were the American Psychological Association's Award for Distinguished Scientific Contributions and membership in the National Academy of Sciences.

Schachter–Singer theory the theory that experiencing and identifying emotional states are functions of both physiological AROUSAL and cognitive interpretations of the physical state. Also called **attribution of emotion**; **cognitive arousal theory of emotion**; **Schachter theory**; **two-factor theory of emotion**. See also JAMES–LANGE THEORY. [Stanley SCHACHTER and Jerome E. **Singer** (1924–), U.S. psychologists]

schadenfreude *n.* the gaining of pleasure or satisfaction from the misfortune of others. [from German *Schaden*, "harm," and *Freude*, "joy"]

Schaffer collateral an axon branch from a neuron in area CA3 of the HIPPOCAMPUS that projects to area CA1.

scheduled awakening a form of behavior therapy for elimination of persistent nightmares (see NIGHTMARE DISORDER; SLEEP TERROR DISORDER). The procedure includes the regular wakening of the sleeper at intervals related to REM SLEEP.

scheduled drugs drugs whose prescription or use has been restricted by the U.S. Drug Enforcement Administration. Schedule I drugs are those for which all nonresearch use is illegal (e.g., LSD, heroin). Schedule II drugs include most opiates, stimulants (e.g., cocaine, amphetamines, and methylphenidate), barbiturates, and prescribed forms of tetrahydrocannabinol (dronabinol). For Schedule II drugs, no refills or telephone prescriptions are permitted. Schedule III drugs include some opioids, barbiturates, and stimulants subject to abuse; prescriptions must be rewritten after 6 months, with a maximum of five refills. Schedule IV drugs include certain opioids, some stimulants, and most of the benzodiazepines. Refills are limited to five, and prescriptions must be rewritten after 6 months. Schedule V drugs include several opiates with low abuse potential (low doses of codeine and others). The Schedule of Controlled Substances, originally designed to restrict the prescription of commonly abused drugs, is periodically updated as the popularity of new agents—generally drugs of abuse—reaches the attention of authorities.

Schedule for Affective Disorders and Schizophrenia (SADS) a STRUCTURED INTERVIEW to identify and describe in detail a range of psychopathological symptoms, used to make standardized and reliable diagnoses in adults. The SADS includes a progression of questions and criteria and provides for the rating of symptom severity, both for lifetime occurrence and most recent or current occurrence, using a 0–4, 0–6, or 0–7 scale. A version of the SADS for use with children and adolescents, the **Kiddie Schedule for Affective Disorders and Schizophrenia (KSADS)**, is also available. [originally developed in 1978 by U.S. psychiatrist Robert L. Spitzer and U.S. clinical psychologist Jean Endicott (1936–)]

schedule-induced polydipsia see ADJUNCTIVE BEHAVIOR.

schedule of reinforcement in conditioning, a rule that determines which instances of a response will be reinforced. There are numerous types of schedules of reinforcement, entries for which are provided elsewhere in the dictionary. Also called **reinforcement schedule**. See REINFORCEMENT.

Scheffé test a post hoc statistical test that allows for the testing of all possible contrasts (weighted comparisons of any number of means) while controlling the probability of a TYPE I ERROR for the set of contrasts at a prespecified level. [Henry **Scheffé** (1907–1977), U.S. mathematician]

schema *n.* (*pl.* **schemata**) **1.** a collection of basic knowledge about a concept or entity that serves as a guide to perception, interpretation, imagination, or problem solving. For example, the schema "dorm room" suggests that a bed and a desk are probably part of the scene, that a microwave oven might or might not be, and that expensive Persian rugs probably will not be. Also called **cognitive schema**. See also FRAME OF REFERENCE; PERCEPTUAL SCHEMA. **2.** an outlook or assumption that an individual has of the self, others, or the world that endures despite objective reality. For example, "I am a damaged person" and "Anyone I trust will eventually hurt me" are negative schemas that may result from actual or imagined abandonment in early childhood. A goal of treatment, particularly stressed in COGNITIVE THERAPY, is to help the client to develop more realistic, present-oriented schemas to replace those developed during childhood or through traumatic experiences. See also

SELF-IMAGE. **3.** in social psychology, a cognitive structure representing a person's knowledge about some entity or situation, including its qualities and the relationships between these. Schemas are usually ABSTRACTIONS and therefore simplify a person's world. In 1932 British psychologist Frederic C. Bartlett (1886–1969) showed that past experiences are stored in memory as schemas; impressions of other people are also thought to be organized in this way. **—schematic** *adj.*

schema change methods techniques to alter cognitive, emotional, and physical patterns of meaning that individuals have derived about the self, other individuals, social groups, and situations from early experiences and that now interfere with adaptive living. See also SCHEMA.

schematic classification see COMPLEMENTARY CLASSIFICATION.

schematic image a mental picture or representation of an object composed of that object's most conspicuous features. Once formed, the schematic image is the model against which similar perceptual configurations are judged.

schematic representation the representation of individuals, objects, events, or processes in terms of their real or potential interactions with each other.

scheme *n.* a cognitive structure that may develop at any stage of life, beginning from when infants and young children learn to adapt their behavior to environmental conditions. There are schemes for everything, ranging from the simple sucking scheme of infancy (applied first to a nipple or teat and later to a thumb, soft toy, etc.) to the complex scheme involved in driving a car; with age, the focus shifts from behavioral schemes toward cognitive schemes. [first described by Jean PIAGET]

schizencephalic *adj.* denoting or relating to abnormal clefts or divisions in the brain tissues. The deformities may result from maldevelopment during fetal life or early infancy or be produced by destructive lesions of the brain. **—schizencephaly** *n.*

schizo- (**schiz-**) *combining form* split or fissure.

schizoaffective disorder in *DSM–IV–TR*, an uninterrupted illness featuring at some time a MAJOR DEPRESSIVE EPISODE, MANIC EPISODE, or MIXED EPISODE concurrently with characteristic symptoms of SCHIZOPHRENIA (e.g., delusions, hallucinations, disorganized speech, catatonic behavior) and, in the same period, delusions or hallucinations for at least 2 weeks in the absence of prominent mood symptoms. Also called **schizoaffective psychosis**; **schizoaffective schizophrenia**.

schizoid *adj.* characterized by lack of affect, social passivity, and minimal introspection.

schizoid disorder of childhood or adolescence in *DSM–IV–TR*, a disorder characterized by absence of close friends other than relatives or isolated children, no apparent interest in making friends, no pleasure from peer interactions, general avoidance of social contacts, lack of interest in team sports and other activities that involve other children, and a duration of at least three months.

schizoidism *n.* a complex of behavioral traits that include seclusiveness, quietness, and general introversion, indicating a separation by the person from his or her surroundings, the confining of psychic interests to the self, and in many cases a tendency toward schizophrenia. Also called **schizoidia**. [defined by Swiss physician Eugen Bleuler (1857–1939)]

schizoid–manic state a psychotic state combining features of both manic and schizophrenic excitement. Also called **schizomania**. [identified by Swiss-born U.S. psychiatrist Adolf Meyer (1866–1950), Austrian-born U.S. psychiatrist Abraham Brill (1874–1948), and Swiss psychiatrist Eugen Bleuler (1857–1939)]

schizoid personality disorder in *DSM–IV–TR*, a personality disorder characterized by long-term emotional coldness, absence of tender feelings for others, indifference to praise or criticism and to the feelings of others, and inability to form close friendships with more than two people. The eccentricities of speech, behavior, or thought that are characteristic of SCHIZOTYPAL PERSONALITY DISORDER are absent in those with schizoid personality disorder.

schizomania *n.* see SCHIZOID–MANIC STATE.

schizophrenia *n.* a psychotic disorder characterized by disturbances in thinking (cognition), emotional responsiveness, and behavior. Schizophrenia was first formally described in the late 19th century by German psychiatrist Emil Kraepelin (1856–1926), who named it DEMENTIA PRAECOX; in 1911 Swiss psychiatrist Eugen Bleuler (1857–1939) renamed the disorder "schizophrenia" and described what he regarded as its FUNDAMENTAL SYMPTOMS. According to *DSM–IV–TR*, which provides the criteria for diagnosis that are now most widely used, the characteristic disturbances must last for at least 6 months and include at least 1 month of active-phase symptoms comprising two or more of the following: delusions, hallucinations, disorganized speech, grossly disorganized or catatonic behavior, or NEGATIVE SYMPTOMS (e.g., lack of emotional responsiveness, extreme apathy). These signs and symptoms are associated with marked social or occupational dysfunction. Disorganized thinking (see FORMAL THOUGHT DISORDER; LOOSENING OF ASSOCIATIONS; SCHIZOPHRENIC THINKING) has been argued by some (beginning with Bleuler) to be the single most important feature of schizophrenia. But, lacking an objective definition of THOUGHT DISORDER and limited to evaluation of an individual's speech, *DSM–IV–TR* and its predecessors have not emphasized this feature. The age of onset is typically between the late teens and mid-30s, occasionally later. Five distinct subtypes of schizophrenia are described in *DSM–IV–TR* (see CATATONIC SCHIZOPHRENIA; DISORGANIZED SCHIZOPHRENIA; PARANOID SCHIZOPHRENIA; RESIDUAL SCHIZOPHRENIA; UNDIFFERENTIATED SCHIZOPHRENIA). In *DSM–III*, schizophrenia was viewed as comprising a group of SCHIZOPHRENIC DISORDERS. **—schizophrenic** *adj.*

schizophrenia in remission a diagnosis for cases in which individuals have experienced at least one schizophrenic episode and are currently free of schizophrenic symptoms.

Schizophrenia Patient Outcomes Research Team (**PORT**) a team of researchers established in 1992 by the Agency for Health Care Policy and Research and the National Institute of Mental Health. The team conducted a 5-year study to assess the treatment and management of schizophrenia (including pharmacotherapies, psychological and family interventions, vocational rehabilitation, and assertive community treatment) and subsequently developed 15 recommendations for improving patient outcomes. The researchers reviewed the literature on schizophrenia treatment outcomes and also surveyed a random sample of 719 individuals diagnosed with schizophrenia in two U.S. states to determine how the scientific evidence compared with actual clinical practice in outpatient and inpatient settings in both urban and rural areas. It was found that the overall rates at which patients' treatment conformed to the study recommendations were generally below 50%, indicating the need for greater efforts to ensure that treatment research results are translated into practice, and that the key to improving patient outcomes is adoption of a comprehensive and individualized strategy that includes not only proper doses of appropriate medications but also patient and family education and support.

schizophrenic disorders in *DSM–III*, a group of disorders that in *DSM–IV–TR* are regarded as subtypes of SCHIZOPHRENIA, namely: **catatonic type** (see CATATONIC SCHIZOPHRENIA), **disorganized type** (see DISORGANIZED SCHIZOPHRENIA), **paranoid type** (see PARANOID SCHIZOPHRENIA, **residual type** (see RESIDUAL SCHIZOPHRENIA), and **undifferentiated type** (see UNDIFFERENTIATED SCHIZOPHRENIA).

schizophrenic episode a period during which an individual exhibits promiment symptoms of schizophrenia, such as hallucinations, delusions, disordered thinking, and disturbances in emotional responsiveness and behavior. See also ACUTE SCHIZOPHRENIC EPISODE.

schizophrenic personality either SCHIZOID PERSONALITY DISORDER or SCHIZOTYPAL PERSONALITY DISORDER.

schizophrenic reaction a former diagnosis for the symptoms of schizophrenia that has its origin in the theories of Swiss-born U.S. psychiatrist Adolf Meyer (1866–1950). See also REACTION TYPE.

schizophrenic thinking pervasive, marked impairment of thinking in terms of LOOSENING OF ASSOCIATIONS and slowness of associations, representing POSITIVE SYMPTOMS and NEGATIVE SYMPTOMS, respectively, of schizophrenia. Because thinking must be inferred rather than merely observed, and because no single definition or test or technique of inference has been universally accepted, evaluation is usually limited to examining samples of speech or writing that the individual is inclined to express. On certain psychological tests (e.g., Rorschach, MMPI), schizophrenic thinking is identified in terms of **deviant verbalizations**, which are unusual, exaggerated, or otherwise abnormal responses to items presented during the test, for example, inventing a word (see NEOLOGISM) to describe a Rorschach inkblot. On the Whitaker Index of Schizophrenic Thinking (WIST; 1980), which actively tests for both positive and negative schizophrenic thinking, schizophrenic impairment of thinking is defined as simultaneously illogical, impaired, and without apparent awareness, all to a marked degree.

schizophreniform disorder in *DSM–IV–TR*, a disorder whose essential features are identical to those of SCHIZOPHRENIA except that the total duration is between 1 and 6 months (i.e., intermediate between BRIEF PSYCHOTIC DISORDER and schizophrenia) and social or occupational functioning need not be impaired. The diagnosis applies without qualification to an episode of between 1 and 6 months' duration from which the individual has already recovered. The diagnosis is provisional when there is no certainty of recovery within the 6-month period. If the disturbance persists beyond 6 months, the diagnosis would be changed to schizophrenia.

schizophreniform psychosis a type of nonschizophrenic psychosis in which symptoms typical of NUCLEAR SCHIZOPHRENIA are present but there is good PREMORBID ADJUSTMENT, sudden onset in response to a clear precipitating event, and a good prognosis and high probability of return to normal levels of functioning. Characteristics of schizophreniform psychosis can be seen in the *DSM–IV–TR* diagnostic category of SCHIZOPHRENIFORM DISORDER. Also called **schizophreniform state**. [proposed in the late 1930s by Norwegian psychiatrist Gabriel Langfeldt (1895–1983)]

schizophrenogenic *adj.* denoting a factor or influence viewed as causing or contributing to the onset or development of schizophrenia.

schizophrenogenic mother the stereotypic mother of an individual with schizophrenia. She is held to be emotionally disturbed, cold, rejecting, dominating, perfectionistic, and insensitive. At the same time, however, she is overprotective, fosters dependence, and is both seductive and rigidly moralistic. Historically, this type of mother was considered to play a causal role in the development of schizophrenia, but this view is now no longer widely held. See also SCHIZOPHRENOGENIC PARENTS. [first defined in 1948 by German-born U.S. psychiatrist Frieda Fromm-Reichmann (1889–1957)]

schizophrenogenic parents parents whose harmful influences are presumed to cause schizophrenia in their offspring. This concept—the subject of much debate in the 1940s especially—is now considered an oversimplification. See also SCHIZOPHRENOGENIC MOTHER.

schizotaxia *n.* a genetic predisposition to schizophrenia, held to be necessary for the disorder to become manifest and to be activated by severe environmental stresses. [presented as a concept in 1962 by Paul Everett MEEHL]

schizotypal personality disorder in *DSM–IV–TR*, a severe personality disorder characterized by various oddities of thought, perception, speech, and behavior that are not severe enough, however, to warrant a diagnosis of schizophrenia. Affected individuals have several of the following symptoms: (a) MAGICAL THINKING, (b) IDEAS OF REFERENCE, (c) social isolation, (d) recurrent illusions (e.g., feeling that a dead relative is present) or DEPERSONALIZATION, (e) vague or metaphorical speech without incoherence, (f) inadequate rapport with others due to aloofness or lack of feeling, (g) suspicious or paranoid thoughts, and (h) undue sensitivity to real or imagined criticism.

schizotypy *n.* in research contexts, a type of personality organization defined by milder forms of POSITIVE SYMPTOMS of schizophrenia, such as COGNITIVE SLIPPAGE, and NEGATIVE SYMPTOMS, such as inability to experience pleasure (see ANHEDONIA). Schizotypy is studied in individuals and family members as a predictor of or liability for the later occurrence of schizophrenia.

Schmid-Fraccaro syndrome see CAT'S-EYE SYNDROME.

Schnauzkrampf *n.* see LIP PURSING.

scholastic acceleration see EDUCATIONAL ACCELERATION.

scholastic achievement test any test that measures a student's knowledge and ability in a specific area of academic study, such as chemistry, history, mathematics, Spanish, or literature.

Scholastic Assessment Test (**SAT**) a test used in selecting candidates for college admission, formerly called **Scholastic Aptitude Test**. It measures critical reading abilities, mathematical reasoning abilities, and writing abilities developed over time through work done in school and alone. The critical reading section (formerly called the verbal section) tests ability to understand and analyze what is read and to recognize relationships between parts of a sentence. The mathematics section tests ability to solve problems involving arithmetic, algebra, and geometry. The writing section tests ability to organize thoughts, develop and express ideas, use language, and adhere to grammatical rules. The SAT is accepted by most public and private colleges in the United States as a standardized evaluation test for the purpose of competitive admission discrimination.

Scholasticism *n.* the system of logic, philosophy, and theology taught by university scholars in medieval Europe. It was based on ARISTOTELIAN logic, the writings of the early Christian fathers, and the authority of tradition and dogma. Major preoccupations included the attempt to reconcile faith with reason and the dispute between NOMINALISM and REALISM. Prominent Scholastics included Italian churchman and philosopher Thomas Aquinas (1225–1274), French philosopher Jean Burridan (c. 1295–1358), Scottish theologian John Duns Scotus (c. 1226–1308), and English churchman and philosopher William of Occam (c. 1285–1347). **—Scholastic** *n., adj.*

school *n.* **1.** a place or institution where people receive instruction. **2.** a major division of a university consisting of specialized, related subdivisions devoted to teaching, research, and scholarship. **3.** the adherents, collectively, of an approach to some field of subject matter having a developed theoretical framework and an associated literature. Examples of schools of psychology are BEHAVIORISM, FUNCTIONALISM, GESTALT PSYCHOLOGY, STRUCTURALISM, and PSYCHOANALYSIS.

school-ability test an assessment designed to evaluate a student's educational achievements in order to obtain information that will enhance his or her learning. The assessment can include a variety of widely accepted tests and measurement techniques as the bases for judgment. Under the direction of trained and competent staff, the assessment will meet appropriate federal and state laws, Board of Education policy, and the criteria for ethical and professional teaching.

school-activity record **1.** a record of an individual's participation in the sports, clubs, and interscholastic and intramural activities of a school or institution. **2.** a listing of all the sports, clubs, and interscholastic and intramural activities that are offered by a school or institution.

School and College Ability Test (**SCAT**) an academic aptitude test in three levels, administered from grade 3 through grade 12. The test yields a verbal score, based on a verbal-analogies segment; a quantitative score, based on comparisons involving fundamental number operations; and a total score.

school avoidance see SCHOOL REFUSAL.

school counseling guidance, offered at or outside the school to students, parents, and other caregivers, that focuses on students' academic, personal, social, and career adjustment, development, and achievement. Counseling is offered by certified and licensed professionals at all educational levels, from elementary through college and professional school.

school grade **1.** a letter or number representing the quality of academic work. **2.** a group of students who are taught together at the same level, usually grouped by age, or the children who belong to such a grouping.

schooling *n.* **1.** in animal behavior, the gathering together of large AGGREGATIONS of fish. Schooling is thought to minimize predation through CONFUSION EFFECTS and DILUTION EFFECTS or to improve hydrodynamic properties so that individual fish can move more efficiently through water. **2.** the process of educating in a formal setting or the provision of education.

school integration **1.** the process of bringing all parts of a classroom or community environment together into a whole, using such means as computers, communication with local-government officials, and applied workplace learning. **2.** the reduction or elimination of racial separation or segregation in public schools. This has been attempted by artificially reconfiguring the racial balance within all school-district schools to reflect the proportionate racial balance in the community as a whole.

school phobia see SCHOOL REFUSAL.

school psychology a field of psychology concerned with the PSYCHOEDUCATIONAL PROBLEMS and other issues arising in primary and secondary schools. The responsibilities of the **school psychologist** include inolvement in overall curriculum planning, individualized curriculum assessment and planning, administration of psychoeducational tests, interviews with parents concerning their child's progress and problems, pupil behavior problems, counseling of teachers and students, and research on systematic educational questions and issues.

school readiness **1.** any of a variety of programs designed to prepare children of below kindergarten age for attending formal school. These programs are often referred to as **prekindergarten** or **nursery school**. **2.** efforts to help communities provide the best environments for children, especially in the areas of health, early education, and school entry. The emphasis is on reducing factors that could detract from children's readiness to attend school.

school refusal persistent reluctance to go to school, which usually occurs during the primary school years and is often a symptom of an educational, social, or emotional problem. School refusal may be a feature of SEPARATION ANXIETY DISORDER. It may be triggered by a stressor (e.g., loss of a pet or loved one, a change of school, loss of a friend due to a move) or it may occur after a summer vacation when the child has spent more time with the primary caregiver. School refusal is often associated with physical symptoms (e.g., upset stomach, nausea, dizziness, headache) and anxiety at the start of the day along with complaints that the child is too sick to go to school. Also called **school avoidance**; **school phobia**.

school truancy see TRUANCY.

Schröder staircase an AMBIGUOUS FIGURE of a staircase, which can be perceived as seen either from above, or from underneath, the stairs, depending on the perspective of the observer. Also called **staircase illusion**. [Heinrich **Schröder** (1810–1885), German bacteriologist and educator]

Schultze's acroparesthesia see ACROPARESTHESIA. [Friedrich **Schultze** (1848–1934), German neurologist]

schwa *n.* a nondistinct neutral vowel represented in the INTERNATIONAL PHONETIC ALPHABET by the symbol ə. In English it is very common in unstressed syllables, such as the first syllable of *alone*.

Schwann cell a type of glial cell (see NEUROGLIA) that forms the MYELIN SHEATH around axons in peripheral nerves. Extensions of a single Schwann cell wind tightly and many times around several neighboring axons, so that the myelin sheath consists of multiple layers of the Schwann-cell plasma membrane. [Theodor **Schwann** (1810–1882), German histologist]

schwannoma *n.* a type of solitary, encapsulated tumor of the tissue covering peripheral nerves. These tumors, which develop from SCHWANN CELLS, are typically benign but tend to displace and compress surrounding nerves as they grow. A schwannoma is very similar to a NEUROFIBROMA but is distinguished by its capsule, which prevents the incorporation of nerve fibers into its mass.

sciatic nerve a large peripheral nerve that connects the receptor and effector cells in the leg to the spinal cord. Pain in the leg, which may extend over the entire length of this nerve, from the buttocks to the foot, is called **sciatica**. The cause is most commonly a SLIPPED DISK pressing on the nerve root emerging from the spinal cord.

SCID-I acronym for STRUCTURED CLINICAL INTERVIEW FOR DSM–IV AXIS I DISORDERS.

SCID-II acronym for STRUCTURED CLINICAL INTERVIEW FOR DSM–IV AXIS II PERSONALITY DISORDERS.

scientific attitude an attitude characterized by an objective and impartial approach and the use of empirical methods in the search for knowledge.

scientific explanation an account of an occurrence couched in terms of an established set of scientific principles, facts, and assumptions. Typical forms of explanation may be reductionistic, analyzing phenomena into components and describing how they combine to produce the phenomenon; ontogenic, relating the phenomenon to a universal set of developmental stages; empiricistic, describing a phenomenon in terms of the conditions that have been observed to produce it; or metaphoric or categorical, identifying a phenomenon as similar in some important respects to other phenomena already understood. Such an explanation stated systematically is generally known as a THEORY.

scientific jury selection the use of the methods of social science to identify prospective jurors who may be favorably predisposed to one's side in a legal dispute.

scientific management generally, the application of scientific methods to achieve improved worker efficiency and work conditions. More specifically, the term refers to the school of management thought introduced by U.S. engineer Frederick W. Taylor (1856–1915) in the late 19th century and publicized in a 1911 book. This approach, also known as **Taylorism** or the **Taylor system of scientific management**, involved (a) studying the work to determine the most efficient way of performing tasks (see TIME AND MOTION STUDY) and (b) paying workers piece-rate incentives to adopt these methods (see PIECEWORK).

scientific method a group of procedures, guidelines, assumptions, and attitudes required for the organized and systematic collection, interpretation, and verification of data and the discovery of reproducible evidence, enabling laws and principles to be stated or modified.

scientific notation a compact way of reporting very large or very small numbers in which the reported number is represented by a value multiplied by 10 raised to a positive or negative number. For example, $p = .0025$ would be expressed as 2.5×10^{-3}.

scientific psychology the body of psychological facts, theories, and techniques that have been developed and validated through the use of the SCIENTIFIC METHOD. They thus depend on objective measurement and the replication of results under controlled or known conditions. See EXPERIMENTAL PSYCHOLOGY.

scientific rationality the qualities of reason and logic that characterize, or ought to characterize, scientific inquiry. For many, science is the epitome of rationality because of its adherence to the rules of logic and evidence, its rejection of supernatural explanations, its devotion to objectivity, and its careful public testing of hypotheses. A commitment to standards and procedures of this kind is usually taken to be the criterion by which a discipline, such as psychology, may be judged to be a science. More narrowly, scientific rationality is sometimes equated with POSITIVISM.

scientific reasoning a type of reasoning that involves the generation of hypotheses and the systematic testing of those hypotheses.

scientific revolution a major change in the theoretical framework of a field of science, as identified by U.S. philosopher of science Thomas Kuhn (1922–1996). Research carried out within the framework of a NORMAL SCIENCE, that is, one with an active PARADIGM that defines the subject matter and methods of the science, will over time yield ANOMALIES that are inconsistent with predicted results. When a sufficient number of anomalies occur, a CRISIS stage may emerge, which motivates scientists and theorists to rethink the fundamental assumptions and methods of the science, and a complete reformulation may take place. This drastically changes both the activities and perspective of the scientists involved and the nature and subject matter of the science, at which time a new normal science may emerge. See also PARADIGM CLASH; PARADIGM SHIFT.

scientism *n.* an uncritical commitment to a particular view of science and scientific methods that leads its adherents to dismiss all other approaches as intellectually invalid. The term is mainly used by those who criticize the assumptions of Western science as arrogant or flawed, who maintain that scientific methods are inappropriate in certain fields or incapable of apprehending certain kinds of truth, or who reject the implication that all philosophical questions will one day reduce to scientific questions. **—scientistic** *adj.*

scientist-practitioner model a concept for the university training of doctoral clinical (or other applied) psychologists in the United States that is intended to prepare individuals both to provide services and to conduct research on mental health problems, essentially integrating these two functions in their professional work by making a laboratory of their applied settings and studying their phenomena and the results of their administrations scientifically. The purpose of the model is to ensure that practitioners contribute to the scientific development of their field. The training emphasizes research techniques applicable to applied (therapeutic) settings. The model emerged from a conference held in Boulder, Colorado, in 1949, which was sponsored by the U.S. Veterans Administration and the National Institute of Mental Health. Also called **Boulder model**.

Scientology *n.* a movement and belief system that emphasizes the harmful effects of ENGRAMS (essentially memory traces) of past traumatic experiences. Adherents practice a technique known as DIANETICS, in which interactions with an "auditor" and the use of a device called an "E-meter" (essentially a gauge of the ELECTRODERMAL RESPONSE) can lead eventually to a posited liberated state known as "being clear." Scientology also has its own elaborate cosmology, in which humans are believed to be reincarnated "thetans": immaterial, divine beings who have become trapped in the material world. [founded by U.S. science-fiction writer L. Ron Hubbard (1911–1986)] **—Scientologist** *n.*

scieropia *n.* a visual anomaly in which objects appear to be in a shadow. Scieropia can have emotional or psychological causes, in which case the condition is identified as **scierneuropsia**.

SCII abbreviation for Strong–Campbell Interest Inventory. See STRONG INTEREST INVENTORY.

scintillating scotoma see SCOTOMA.

sciosophy *n.* any system of thought claiming knowledge of natural or supernatural phenomena that is not supported by scientific methods, such as astrology or PHRENOLOGY. See PSEUDOSCIENCE. [coined by U.S. biologist and icthyologist David Starr Jordan (1851–1931)]

scissors gait a type of gait observed, for example, in some patients with cerebral palsy who cross their legs in scissors fashion when walking.

sclera *n.* the tough, white outer coat of the eyeball, which is continuous with the cornea at the front and the sheath of the optic nerve at the back of the eyeball. Also called **sclerotic coat**.

sclero- (**scler-**) *combining form* hardness.

sclerosis *n.* hardening of tissues, usually as a consequence of disease or aging. It particularly affects the nervous system (see AMYOTROPHIC LATERAL SCLEROSIS; MULTIPLE SCLEROSIS) and the circulatory system (see ARTERIOSCLEROSIS; ATHEROSCLEROSIS). **—sclerotic** *adj.*

SCL-90-R abbreviation for SYMPTOM CHECKLIST-90-R.

SCN abbreviation for SUPRACHIASMATIC NUCLEUS.

scoliosis *n.* lateral curvature of the spine.

-scope *suffix* instrument for observing (e.g., OSCILLOSCOPE).

scopo- (**scop-**) *combining form* observation or watching.

scopolamine *n.* an ANTICHOLINERGIC DRUG found as an alkaloid in HENBANE and related plants. Its most common therapeutic use is for the prevention of motion sickness; in the past it was sometimes used in labor to produce twilight sleep (a conscious but drowsy state with lack of sensitivity to pain) and amnesia for the event. Small doses can have a sedative effect, but large doses may cause restlessness, agitation, or delirium. Also called **hyoscine**. U.S. trade names: **Scopace**; **Transderm-Scop**.

scopophilia *n.* sexual pleasure derived from watching others in a state of nudity, undressing, or engaging in sexual activity. If scopophilia is persistent, the condition is essentially VOYEURISM. Also called **scoptophilia**; **scotophilia**. See also ACTIVE SCOPOPHILIA; PASSIVE SCOPOPHILIA.

score 1. *n.* a quantitative value assigned to test results or other measurable responses. **2.** *vb.* to assign scores to responses.

score band see BANDING.

score equating the process of equilibrating test scores in such a way that the score distribution remains equivalent over versions or administrations of the test.

scoterythrous vision a type of color blindness in which reds appear darkened because of a deficiency in perceiving the red end of the spectrum.

scoto- (**scot-**) *combining form* **1.** darkness (e.g., SCOTOPIC). **2.** blindness (e.g., SCOTOMA).

scotoma *n.* an area of partial or complete loss of vision in the visual field. Vision may be depressed (**relative scotoma**), altered (**scintillating scotoma**), or completely lost (**absolute scotoma**). Scotomas can occur either in the central visual field (see CENTRAL SCOTOMA) or in the periphery (see PARACENTRAL SCOTOMA). See also VISUAL FIELD DEFECT.

scotomization *n.* in psychoanalytic theory, the tendency to ignore or be blind to impulses or memories that would threaten the individual's EGO. Scotomization is a defensive process and may also be a form of RESISTANCE. Also called **scotomatization**. See also BLIND SPOT.

scotophilia *n.* see SCOPOPHILIA.

scotopic *adj.* pertaining to low light levels.

scotopic stimulation visual stimulation with dim targets, usually under conditions that specifically activate the RETINAL ROD system. Compare PHOTOPIC STIMULATION.

scotopic vision vision that occurs in dim light by means of the RETINAL ROD system. As scotopic vision does not permit color discrimination, the visual scene appears in shades of gray. However, the closer the illumination of a target is to 510 nm in wavelength, the brighter it will appear relative to other targets with the same energy, since this is the peak wavelength sensitivity for the rod system. Also called **twilight vision**. Compare PHOTOPIC VISION.

scotopsin *n.* the specific form of OPSIN found in RETINAL RODS. Scotopsin combines with 11-*cis* retinal to form RHODOPSIN, which is the functional photopigment with sensitivity to photons in the rod.

Scott, Walter Dill (1869–1955) U.S. psychologist. Scott received his doctorate from the University of Leipzig in 1900, studying under Wilhelm WUNDT. He joined the faculty of Northwestern University and remained there for the bulk of his career, ultimately becoming president of the university in 1920. Scott is recognized as a key figure in the field of applied psychology, with significant contributions to ADVERTISING PSYCHOLOGY and to personnel selection and management in industry. During World War I he headed the Army's Committee on the Classification of Personnel, devising a highly successful test for the selection of army officers. The United States awarded him its Distinguished Service Medal for this work. Scott's most important published works include *The Theory of Advertising* (1903), *The Psychology of Advertising* (1908), *Increasing Human Efficiency in Business* (1911), and *Personnel Management* (1923).

scramble competition in animal behavior, the mating rivalry that ensues when females are broadly dispersed or synchronous in their breeding, so that males do not benefit from holding territories or defending resources. Instead, males range widely and mate with any female they encounter, with little or no courtship behavior or MATE SELECTION. The males that are able to mate first with a female generally have the most REPRODUCTIVE SUCCESS.

screen defense in psychoanalytic theory, a DEFENSE in which a memory, fantasy, or dream image is unconsciously employed to conceal the real but disturbing object of one's feelings.

screened touch matching in parapsychology experiments using ZENER CARDS, a technique in which the participant indicates his or her guess concerning the symbol on the top card in an inverted deck by pointing to one of five positions corresponding to each of the possible symbols. The card is then placed in this position, still face down, for later checking. Because the person handling the cards never sees them face up, the technique is used in tests of CLAIRVOYANCE as opposed to TELEPATHY. See also BASIC TECHNIQUE.

screening *n.* **1.** the initial evaluation of a patient to determine his or her suitability for medical or psychological treatment generally, a specific treatment approach, or referral to a treatment facility. This evaluation is made on the basis of medical or psychological history, MENTAL STATUS EXAMINATION, diagnostic formulation, or some combination of these. **2.** a procedure or program to detect early signs of a disease in an individual or population. Individuals at increased hereditary risk of developing a disease are advised to follow regular screening plans. See also SCREENING TEST. **3.** the process of selecting items for a psychological test. **4.** the process of determining, through a preliminary test, whether an individual is suitable for some purpose or task. See also SELECTION TEST.

screening audiometry rapid group measurement of audibility using a tone or tones of fixed level.

screening test any testing procedure designed to separate people or objects according to a fixed characteristic or property. Screening tests are typically used to distinguish people who have a disease, disorder, or predisease condition from those who do not; they may be used, for example, in primary health care settings to identify people who are depressed. Screening tests are designed to be highly sensitive, and subsequent highly specific or focused testing is often required to confirm the results of the initial screening test.

screening tests for young children checklists or assessment protocols that have been developed to detect DEVELOPMENTAL DELAYS, criterion behaviors, or other risk factors associated with certain conditions or disorders during infancy and early childhood through the primary school years. Such tests do not provide diagnostic information, but instead are used with large numbers of children in order to identify those who may require assessment for emotional disturbance, mental retardation, neurological conditions, or other disorders.

screen magnifier an adaptation for individuals with visual impairment that enlarges both text and graphical information displayed on a personal computer screen. Screen magnifiers may be built into the operating system provided by the computer manufacturer or purchased as separate products.

screen memory in psychoanalytic theory, a memory of a childhood experience, usually trivial in nature, that unconsciously serves the purpose of concealing or screening out an associated experience of a more significant and perhaps traumatic nature. Also called **cover memory**; **replacement memory**.

screen reader a software program for individuals with visual impairment that converts both text and graphical information on a personal computer screen to a form that can be spoken through a SPEECH SYNTHESIZER or displayed on a refreshable BRAILLE display.

scree plot in FACTOR ANALYSIS, a plot of the EIGENVALUES of the COMMUNALITY-adjusted correlation matrix in descending order. Break points in this distribution are used to help determine the number of factors to be retained.

script *n.* **1.** a cognitive schematic structure—a mental road map—containing the basic actions (and their temporal and causal relations) that comprise a complex action. For example, the script for cooking pasta might be: Open pan cupboard, choose pan, fill pan with water, put pan on stove, get out pasta, weigh correct amount of pasta, add pasta to boiling water, decide when cooked, remove from heat, strain, place in bowl. Also called **script schema**. **2.** a structured representation consisting of a sequence of CONCEPTUAL DEPENDENCIES grouped together to capture the semantic relationships implicit in everyday human situations. It was designed for the purpose of computer-based story understanding. [created in 1966 by U.S. cognitive and computer scientist Roger C. Schank and U.S. psychologist Robert P. Abelson (1928–)]

script analysis in TRANSACTIONAL ANALYSIS, the analysis of the client's unconscious life plan, or SCRIPT. The script is based on fantasies, attitudes, and games or ploys derived from the individual's early experiences. [developed by Canadian-born U.S. psychiatrist Eric Berne (1910–1970)]

script schema see SCRIPT.

script theory 1. in TRANSACTIONAL ANALYSIS, the theory that an individual's approach to social situations follows a sequence that was learned and established early in life. **2.** the proposition that discrete affects, such as joy and fear, are prime motivators of behavior and that personality structure and function can be understood in terms of self-defining affective scenes and scripts. [proposed by U.S. personality psychologist Silvan S. Tomkins (1911–1991)]

scrivener's palsy an archaic name for WRITER'S CRAMP.

scrying *n.* see CRYSTAL GAZING.

SCU abbreviation for SPECIAL CARE UNIT.

sculpting *n.* see FAMILY SCULPTING.

SDAT abbreviation for SENILE DEMENTIA OF THE ALZHEIMER'S TYPE.

S data see Q DATA.

SDT abbreviation for SIGNAL DETECTION THEORY.

seamstress's cramp a type of OCCUPATIONAL CRAMP affecting the hands and manifested by inability to perform such manual operations as threading a needle and using scissors in cutting cloth. See also REPETITIVE STRAIN INJURY.

search *n.* **1.** a mental process in which a set of memories or other MENTAL REPRESENTATIONS is checked for the presence or absence of a particular target item. For example, one might search one's memory for the name of a former teacher. **2.** a task in which a person is asked to search through an array of presented stimuli, or a previously memorized list of stimuli, to determine whether any of a set of target stimuli is in the array or list. See VISUAL SEARCH. See also CONSISTENT MAPPING; VARIED MAPPING. **3.** in problem solving, the process by which the solver attempts to find the correct answer or best solution from among a range of alternatives. See BACKWARD SEARCH; BEST-FIRST SEARCH; EXHAUSTIVE SEARCH; HEURISTIC SEARCH; SELF-TERMINATING SEARCH. **4.** in artificial intelligence, the systematic investigation of states of a problem or game as part of finding a solution. There are multiple approaches to search, including BACKTRACK SEARCH, DEPTH-FIRST SEARCH, BREADTH-FIRST SEARCH, and A* SEARCH. There are many techniques available for investigating the applicability of these approaches on different applications.

search asymmetry in studies of VISUAL SEARCH, the situation in which search for the presence of a feature produces one pattern of results but search for the absence of that feature produces another. For example, searching for a *Q* in a field of *O*s (i.e., searching for the "tail" segment in the *Q*) is relatively easy, but searching for an *O* in a field of *Q*s (i.e., searching for the absence of this segment) is difficult.

search image a mechanism to explain the persistence of predators in seeking one or a few types of prey even in the presence of other suitable prey and when the numbers of the preferred prey decline in an area. It is hypothesized that predators are more successful when they focus attention and perception on finding a limited number of prey types (i.e., they have a search image for such prey). They are essentially short-term specialists and switch to new prey types only when previous types become very scarce or disappear altogether.

search of associative memory (**SAM**) a GLOBAL MEMORY MODEL used to explain recall and recognition memory in laboratory studies. Information may reside in SHORT-TERM MEMORY, from which it may be stored in LONG-TERM MEMORY or used to search long-term memory. Associations can be formed among items in memory and between items and the context in which they occur. See also DUAL-STORE MODEL OF MEMORY. [described in 1981 by U.S. psychologist Richard M. Shiffrin (1942–) and Dutch psychologist Jeroen G. W. Raaijmakers]

Seashore audiometer an instrument used to measure threshold sound intensity. [Carl Emil **Seashore** (1866–1949), Swedish-born U.S. psychologist]

Seashore Measures of Musical Talents a series of recorded tests of the components of musical aptitude, including tonal memory, time awareness, rhythm awareness, pitch discrimination, timbre awareness, and loudness discrimination. In these six subtests, various pairs of tones, tonal sequences, or rhythmic patterns are presented, and the participant must distinguish each along the particular dimension of interest. For example, in the time awareness subtest the participant must indicate for each of 50 tone pairs whether the second tone is longer or shorter than the first. Also called **Seashore Measures of Musical Ability**. [originally developed in 1919 and subsequently revised in 1939 by Carl **Seashore**]

Seashore Rhythm Test a neuropsychological test in which the participant listens to a recording of pairs of rhythmic patterns and indicates whether they are the same or different. The test is used by neuropsychologists to measure generalized cerebral function, although it was developed as a subtest of the SEASHORE MEASURES OF MUSICAL TALENT to predict musical talent and knowledge. [Carl **Seashore**]

seasickness *n.* MOTION SICKNESS occasioned by sea travel.

seasonal affective disorder (**SAD**) a MOOD DISORDER in which there is a predictable occurrence of MAJOR DEPRESSIVE EPISODES, MANIC EPISODES, or both at particular times of the year. The typical pattern is the occurrence of major depressive episodes during the fall or winter months. Also called **seasonal mood disorder**.

seasonality effect the proposal that individuals with schizophrenia are most likely to have been born during the period January to April. The hypothesized significance of the season of birth is uncertain. See also VIRAL HYPOTHESIS OF SCHIZOPHRENIA. [advanced by U.S. psychiatrist E. Fuller Torrey (1938–)]

seasonal mood disorder see SEASONAL AFFECTIVE DISORDER.

seasonal variation behavioral, psychological, or physiological changes that vary over seasons or that are in response to seasonal changes. In animals and plants, seasonal variation is often controlled by PHOTOPERIODISM. Examples include the increased rate of food intake and body weight gain in hibernating animals in late summer, seasonal migrations, and seasonal changes in gonad size and hormone production in temperate-zone species leading to reproduction at optimal times.

seat of mind the proposed place or organ in the body that serves as the physical location of the mind (or, in CARTESIAN DUALISM, the location in the body where mind and body interact; see CONARIUM). In current thinking, the brain is the seat of the mind; historically, other organs have been proposed, such as the heart. Some theories suggest that the mind (or the spirit) is diffused throughout the body.

Seattle Longitudinal Study a comprehensive ongoing study of adult intelligence and cognitive functioning based on the Primary Mental Abilities Test (see PRIMARY ABILITIES) and using a sequential design (a combination of cross-sectional and longitudinal data-collection methods). The study began in 1956, with testing done in 7-year intervals up to the present. [conducted by U.S. psychologist K. Warner Schaie (1928–)]

Seckel's bird-headed dwarfism a familial disorder, now linked to a defect on chromosome 3 (locus 3q22.1–24), marked by MICROCEPHALY, a beaklike nose, prominent eyes, narrow face, and short stature. Typically, affected individuals show intellectual skills consistent with mild to profound mental retardation. Also called **Seckel nanism**; **Virchow–Seckel syndrome**. [reported in 1960 by Helmut P. G. **Seckel** (1900–1960), German physician; the term "bird-headed dwarf" was introduced by Rudolf **Virchow** (1821–1902), German pathologist]

seclusiveness *n.* the tendency to isolate oneself from social contacts or human relationships. See also PRIVACY. —**seclusive** *adj.*

secondary aging changes due to biological AGING, but accelerated by disabilities resulting from disease or produced by extrinsic factors, such as stress, trauma, lifestyle, and environment. Secondary aging is often distinguished from PRIMARY AGING, which is governed by inborn and age-related processes, but the distinction is not a precise one.

secondary amenorrhea see AMENORRHEA.

secondary appraisal in the COGNITIVE APPRAISAL THEORY of emotion, assessment of one's ability to cope with the consequences of an interaction with the environment, which follows a PRIMARY APPRAISAL. See also COPING POTENTIAL; CORE RELATIONAL THEMES. [proposed by U.S. psychologist Richard S. Lazarus (1922–2002)]

secondary attention active attention that requires conscious effort, such as the attention needed to analyze a painting or sculpture. Compare PRIMARY ATTENTION.

secondary autoeroticism a type of AUTOEROTICISM not involving direct masturbation but produced instead by indirect association with the erogenous zones (e.g., sexual arousal from contact with urine).

secondary care health care services provided by medical specialists (e.g., cardiologists, urologists, dermatologists), to whom, typically, patients are referred by the PRIMARY CARE PROVIDER. Compare PRIMARY CARE; TERTIARY CARE.

secondary cause a contributing factor to the onset of symptoms of a disorder that in itself would not be sufficient to cause the disorder.

secondary circular reaction in Jean PIAGET's theory of cognitive development, a repetitive action emerging at around 4 to 5 months that signifies the infant's aim of making things happen. The infant repeats actions, such as rattling the crib, that have yielded results in the past but is not able to coordinate them so as to meet the requirements of a new situation. This forward step occurs during the SENSORIMOTOR STAGE. See COORDINATION OF SECONDARY CIRCULAR REACTIONS; PRIMARY CIRCULAR REACTION; TERTIARY CIRCULAR REACTION.

secondary control behavior that, while not directly controlling, is aimed at producing a sense of control by altering oneself (e.g., one's values, priorities, behavior) so as to bring oneself in line with the environment. Compare PRIMARY CONTROL. See LOCUS OF CONTROL.

secondary coping a type of COPING STRATEGY that enhances one's ability to adapt to events and environmental conditions as they are, such as rethinking about the stressor or problem in such a way as to facilitate acceptance. Also called **secondary control coping**. Compare PRIMARY COPING.

secondary defense symptoms a set of defensive measures employed by obsessive individuals when their primary defenses against repressed memories no longer offer protection. The secondary defenses usually include obsessional thinking, DOUBTING MANIA, and speculations, which may be expressed as phobias, ceremonials, superstitions, or pedantry.

secondary deviance see PRIMARY DEVIANCE.

secondary drive a learned drive; that is, a drive that is developed through association with or generalization from a PRIMARY DRIVE. For example, in an AVOIDANCE CONDITIONING experiment in which a rat must go from one compartment into another to escape from an electric shock, the secondary drive is fear of the shock and the primary drive with which it is associated is avoidance of pain. Also called **acquired drive**.

secondary elaboration in psychoanalysis, the process of altering the memory and description of a dream to make it more coherent and less fragmentary or distorted. See also DREAM-WORK.

secondary emotion an emotion that is not recognized or manifested universally across cultures or that requires social experience for its construction. For some theorists, PRIDE represents a secondary emotion, stemming from the conjunction of a PRIMARY EMOTION (JOY) and a favorable public reaction. Other secondary emotions include ENVY, LOVE, and JEALOUSY.

secondary environment an environment that is incidental or marginally important in a person's life and in which interactions with others are comparatively brief and impersonal. An example is a bank or a shop. Compare PRIMARY ENVIRONMENT.

secondary erectile dysfunction **1.** a condition in which a man is no longer capable of producing or maintaining a penile erection sufficient for sexual intercourse, although he was previously capable of performing intercourse successfully. **2.** a condition in which a man can have an erection in some situations (e.g., during masturbation) or with some partners, but not during sexual activity with his current primary partner. See also ERECTILE DYSFUNCTION; IMPOTENCE; MALE ERECTILE DISORDER. Compare PRIMARY ERECTILE DYSFUNCTION.

secondary gains in psychoanalytic theory, advantages derived from a NEUROSIS in addition to the PRIMARY GAINS of relief from anxiety or internal conflict. Examples are extra attention, sympathy, avoidance of work, and domination of others. Such gains are secondary in that they are derived from others' reactions to the illness instead of causal factors. They often prolong the neurosis and create resistance to therapy. Also called **advantage by illness**.

secondary group one of the larger, less intimate, more goal-focused groups typical of more complex societies. These social groups influence members' attitudes, beliefs, and actions, but as a supplement to the influence of small, more interpersonally intensive PRIMARY GROUPS. Whereas primary groups, such as families and children's play groups, are the initial socializing agents, adolescents and adults are increasingly influenced by such secondary groups as work groups, clubs, congregations, associations, and so on.

secondary identification in psychoanalytic theory, identification with admired figures other than the parents.

secondary memory (**SM**) memory that retains a large number of items relatively permanently, in contrast to PRIMARY MEMORY. The term was used in DUAL-STORE MODELS OF MEMORY before being replaced by LONG-TERM MEMORY. [introduced by William JAMES]

secondary mental deficiency below average intelligence due to disease or brain injury rather than congenital factors.

secondary mood disorder a MOOD DISORDER that occurs in the context of another disorder and whose symptoms may be caused by the other disorder.

secondary motivation motivation that is created by personal or social incentives (e.g., the urge to learn classical music or become a movie star) rather than by primary, physiological needs (e.g., for food).

secondary motor cortex see MOTOR CORTEX.

secondary oocyte see OOGENESIS.

secondary personality a second discrete identity that repeatedly controls behavior in individuals with DISSOCIATIVE IDENTITY DISORDER. This personality state is in sharp contrast to the original, PRIMARY PERSONALITY and generally has a different name as well as dramatically different attitudes, behavior, manner of speaking, and style of dress.

secondary position any location of binocular fixation other than the PRIMARY POSITION.

secondary prevention intervention for individuals or groups that demonstrate early psychological or physical symptoms, difficulties, or conditions (i.e., subclinical-level problems), which is intended to prevent the development of more serious dysfunction or illness. Compare PRIMARY PREVENTION; TERTIARY PREVENTION.

secondary process in psychoanalytic theory, conscious, rational mental activities under the control of the EGO and the REALITY PRINCIPLE. These thought processes, which include problem-solving, judgment, and systematic thinking, enable individuals to meet both the external demands of the environment and the internal demands of their instincts in rational, effective ways. Also called **secondary process thinking**. Compare PRIMARY PROCESS.

secondary quality in the philosophy of English empiricist philosopher John Locke (1632–1704), a sensible quality of an object that does not exist in the object itself but rather in the experience of the perceiver. Color, for example, is a secondary quality, since the sensation of a particular color can only be produced by an object under certain conditions of light. Compare PRIMARY QUALITY.

secondary reinforcer see CONDITIONED REINFORCER.

secondary repression see REPRESSION PROPER.

secondary reward a reward with a learned value that facilitates the retrieval of a PRIMARY REWARD.

secondary sensation see SYNESTHESIA.

secondary sensory area any of the regions of the cerebral cortex that receive direct projections from the PRIMARY SENSORY AREA for any given sense modality. An example is the SECONDARY SOMATOSENSORY AREA. Also called **nonprimary sensory area**.

secondary sensory ending see FLOWER-SPRAY ENDING.

secondary sex characteristics see SEX CHARACTERISTICS.

secondary sexual dysfunction any disturbance in sexual functioning (see SEXUAL DYSFUNCTION) that is not lifelong or that occurs only with some partners or in some situations. Compare PRIMARY SEXUAL DYSFUNCTION.

secondary somatosensory area (**S2**) an area of the cerebral cortex, located in the PARIETAL LOBE on the upper bank of the LATERAL SULCUS, that receives direct projections from the PRIMARY SOMATOSENSORY AREA and other regions of the anterior parietal cortex and has outputs to other parts of the lateral parietal cortex and to motor and premotor areas. See also SOMATOSENSORY AREA.

secondary stuttering dysfluency in speech characterized by uncomfortable awareness and attempts to modify the dysfluency. Effort, fear, and anxiety are typically conveyed through abnormal or unusual movements of the face, head, or body (e.g., tics, blinking, lip tremor, head jerks, fist clenching). Compare PRIMARY STUTTERING.

secondary symptoms **1.** according to Swiss psychiatrist Eugen Bleuler (1857–1939), those symptoms of SCHIZOPHRENIA, such as delusions and hallucinations, that are shared with other disorders and therefore not specifically diagnostic of schizophrenia. Bleuler theorized that these symptoms do not stem directly from the disease but rather begin to operate when the person reacts to some internal or external process. Also called **accessory symptoms**. Compare FUNDAMENTAL SYMPTOMS. **2.** symptoms that are not a direct result of a disorder but are associated with or incidental to those that are (e.g., social avoidance accompanying obsessive-compulsive disorder). **3.** symptoms that appear in the second stage of a disorder or that are derived from an earlier traumatic event, disease process, or disordered condition.

secondary task in ergonomics, a task that is secondary or peripheral to a central or PRIMARY TASK in a situation requiring MULTIPLE-TASK PERFORMANCE. The operator is expected to allocate sufficient cognitive resources to processing the primary task before allocating remaining resources to processing the secondary task.

secondary task methodology an experimental design used in the study of attention in which participants perform a primary task as well as possible and a secondary task to the extent possible while maintaining performance on the primary task. Performance on the secondary task provides a profile of the attention required by the primary task at various phases.

secondary taste cortex the area of cerebral cortex, located in the ORBITOFRONTAL CORTEX, that is the second cortical relay for taste (see also PRIMARY TASTE CORTEX). It identifies GUSTATORY STIMULI as either pleasant and rewarding or unpleasant and undesirable. This information from the secondary taste cortex interacts with analyses from visual, touch, and olfactory cells to permit an integrated appreciation of flavor.

secondary territory **1.** in social psychology, a space routinely used by a person or group who does not control or use it exclusively (e.g., the local tennis court). Habitués may harbor feelings of possession but they will acknowledge others' claims. Compare PRIMARY TERRITORY; PUBLIC TERRITORY. See also PROXEMICS. **2.** in animal behavior, see HOME RANGE.

secondary visual system the visual pathway that lies outside the PRIMARY VISUAL SYSTEM and is phylogenetically older than it. Retinal input travels directly to the SUPERIOR COLLICULUS, then to visual nuclei in the thalamus other than the lateral geniculate nucleus (i.e., the PULVINAR and LATERAL POSTERIOR NUCLEUS) before terminating in the PRESTRIATE CORTEX. The vision supported by the secondary visual system is relatively poor for the detection of form, but allows localization and detection of movement. It functions relatively well in the newborn. See also BLINDSIGHT.

second childhood **1.** a lay term, sometimes used as a synonym for DOTAGE, for the hypothetical tendency of older adults to regress to a childish state of mind. **2.** childlike playfulness in an adult.

second cranial nerve see OPTIC NERVE.

second-degree relative a grandparent, aunt, uncle, or cousin. The closeness of a relative with a particular hereditary disease has implications in assessing the risk for a particular person. Compare FIRST-DEGREE RELATIVE.

second-generation antipsychotics see ATYPICAL ANTIPSYCHOTICS.

second messenger an ion or molecule inside a cell whose concentration increases or decreases in response to stimulation of a cell RECEPTOR by an agonist (e.g., a neurotransmitter, hormone, or drug). The second messenger acts to relay and amplify the signal from the receptor (the "first messenger") by triggering a range of cellular activities. For example, receptors for catecholamine neurotransmitters (epinephrine and norepinephrine) are coupled to G PROTEINS, whose activation in postsynaptic neurons affects levels of second messengers that act to open or close certain ION CHANNELS. Second messegers include CYCLIC AMP, IP_3 (see INOSITOL PHOSPHATES), and calcium ions.

second-order conditioning in PAVLOVIAN CONDITIONING, the establishment of a conditioned response as a result of pairing a neutral stimulus with a conditioned stimulus that gained its effectiveness by being paired with an unconditioned stimulus. See HIGHER ORDER CONDITIONING.

second-order factor a factor that results from the factoring of OBLIQUE factors by correlating the derived factors among themselves. Compare FIRST-ORDER FACTOR.

second-order language see METALANGUAGE.

second-order neuron the second neuron in any neural pathway. In the somatosensory system, for example, a second-order neuron receives input from a FIRST-ORDER NEURON in the spinal cord and transmits it to the thalamus.

second-order schedule a SCHEDULE OF REINFORCEMENT in which the units counted are not single responses but completions of a particular reinforcement schedule (the **unit schedule**). For example, in a second-order fixed-ratio 5 of fixed-interval 30-s schedule [FR 5 (FI 30 s)], reinforcement is delivered only after five successive FI 30-s schedules have been completed. Often, a brief stimulus of some sort is presented on completion of each unit schedule.

second-person perspective the point of view of one person addressing another and aware of the other's consciousness, characterized by "I–you" communication. Compare FIRST-PERSON PERSPECTIVE; THIRD-PERSON PERSPECTIVE.

second sight an alleged paranormal faculty that enables some individuals to see events that are remote in time or space. See CLAIRVOYANCE; PRECOGNITION.

secretin *n.* a hormone produced by the upper small intestine in response to the arrival of hydrochloric acid from the stomach. Secretin stimulates secretion of pancreatic juice by the pancreas and of bile by the liver. Its function was discovered in 1902 by British physiologists William Maddock Bayliss (1860–1924) and Ernest Starling (1866–1927), and it was the first substance demonstrated to be a hormone.

secretion *n.* **1.** the synthesis and discharge of specific substances from cells (which may be organized in glands) into other parts of the body. The substance produced may be released directly into the blood (ENDOCRINE secretion) or through a duct (see EXOCRINE GLAND). **2.** the substance discharged by this process. **—secretory** *adj.*

SECs abbreviation for STIMULUS EVALUATION CHECKS.

sect *n.* a group whose members adhere to a distinctive set of doctrines, beliefs, and rituals. The term is often applied to a dissenting faction that breaks away from a larger religious, political, or other social organization. **—sectarian** *adj.*

section *n.* **1.** a thin slice of tissue (e.g., brain tissue) that can be examined microscopically. See CROSS SECTION. **2.** an image of a body part in any plane obtained by such techniques as COMPUTED TOMOGRAPHY or MAGNETIC RESONANCE IMAGING.

sectioning *n.* the educational strategy of offering the same course, typically taught by the same teacher, several times during the day. This enables many students to take the same course but keeps the teacher-pupil ratio low.

sector therapy a therapeutic procedure in which patterns of association that have produced emotional problems in the client are replaced by more realistic and constructive patterns. Unlike DEPTH THERAPY, this process, described as **goal-limited adjustment therapy**, focuses on specific areas (sectors) revealed by the client's own autobiographical account. The procedure enables the client to understand his or her faulty associations and gradually establish new ones with the aid of the therapist. [developed by Felix Deutsch (1884–1964)]

secular *adj.* civil, temporal, and free from religious influence or affiliation. A secular society, for example, is one in which various religions may exist, but in which the laws and governing institutions have no basis in religious doctrine. **—secularism** *n.* **—secularist** *n.* **—secularize** *vb.*

secular humanism a broad perspective, increasingly influential in Western countries since the mid-20th century, that can be characterized by some or all of the following: (a) a belief in seeking solutions to human problems through science and rational thought, rather than religion or traditional forms of morality; (b) a focus on this world rather than a putative afterlife; (c) an emphasis on an intrinsic human potential for growth, rather than on human limitation or sinfulness; (d) a search for new truth, and a belief in free thought, free speech, and free inquiry as the means to find it; (e) an acceptance of cultural and human diversity, including sexual diversity; and (f) an acceptance of some degree of RELATIVISM in ethics, usually accompanied by some type of UTILITARIANISM in practice. See also HUMANISM.

secular trend the main trend or direction of a TIME SERIES, as distinguished from temporary or seasonal variations.

secure attachment 1. in the STRANGE SITUATION, the positive parent–child relationship, in which the child displays confidence when the parent is present, shows mild distress when the parent leaves, and quickly reestablishes contact when the parent returns. **2.** an adult attachment style that combines a positive INTERNAL WORKING MODEL OF ATTACHMENT of oneself, characterized by a view of oneself as worthy of love, and a positive internal working model of attachment of others, characterized by the view that others are generally accepting and responsive. Compare DISMISSIVE ATTACHMENT; FEARFUL ATTACHMENT; PREOCCUPIED ATTACHMENT.

secure base phenomenon the observation that infants use a place of safety, represented by an attachment figure (e.g., a parent), as a base from which to explore a novel environment. The infant often returns or looks back to the parent before continuing to explore.

secure treatment setting a locked residential setting providing safety and treatment services for adolescent or adult offenders, usually felons, with mental retardation or developmental disabilities.

security *n.* a sense of safety, confidence, and freedom from apprehension. In psychology, security is believed to be engendered by such factors as warm, accepting parents and friends; development of age-appropriate skills and abilities; and experiences that build EGO STRENGTH. The development of security in the psychotherapeutic context (most often referred to as **trust**) is seen as a mediating goal that encourages open exploration of emotional and behavioral issues and is viewed to be part of a strong and healthy THERAPIST–PATIENT RELATIONSHIP.

security blanket see TRANSITIONAL OBJECT.

security operations in the approach of U.S. psychoanalyst Harry Stack Sullivan (1892–1949), a variety of interpersonal defensive measures, such as arrogance, boredom, or anger, that are used as a protection against anxiety or loss of self-esteem.

sedative 1. *n.* a drug that has a calming effect, and therefore relieves anxiety, agitation, or behavioral excitement, by depressing the central nervous system. The degree of sedation depends on the agent, the size of the dose, the method of administration, and the condition of the patient. A drug that sedates in small doses may induce sleep in larger doses and may be used as a HYPNOTIC; such drugs are commonly known as **sedative–hypnotics**. BENZODIAZEPINES are commonly used as sedatives. **2.** *adj.* producing sedation.

sedative amnestic disorder see SEDATIVE-, HYPNOTIC-, OR ANXIOLYTIC-INDUCED PERSISTING AMNESTIC DISORDER.

sedative, hypnotic, and anxiolytic drugs CNS DEPRESSANTS that have been developed for therapeutic use because of their calming effect (i.e., sedatives) and ability to induce sleep (i.e., hypnotics) and reduce anxiety (i.e., anxiolytics). They include the BARBITURATES, MEPROBAMATE, and the BENZODIAZEPINES. At low doses these drugs are prescribed for daytime use to reduce anxiety; at higher doses many of the same drugs are prescribed as sleeping pills. Although efficacious when used sparingly, over the long term all induce marked tolerance, and cessation of use can precipitate potentially life-threatening withdrawal phenomena. Acute abuse can yield dangerous intoxication effects, and chronic abuse can cause a range of other serious, irreversible conditions.

sedative, hypnotic, or anxiolytic abuse in *DSM–IV–TR*, a pattern of use of sedative, hypnotic, or anxiolytic drugs manifested by recurrent significant adverse consequences related to the repeated ingestion of these substances. This diagnosis is preempted by the diagnosis of SEDATIVE, HYPNOTIC, OR ANXIOLYTIC DEPENDENCE: If the criteria for sedative, hypnotic, or anxiolytic abuse and sedative, hypnotic, or anxiolytic dependence are both met, only the latter diagnosis is given.

sedative, hypnotic, or anxiolytic dependence in *DSM–IV–TR*, a cluster of cognitive, behavioral, and physiological symptoms indicating continued use of sedative, hypnotic, or anxiolytic drugs despite significant problems related to these substances. There is a pattern of repeated ingestion resulting in tolerance, characteristic withdrawal symptoms on cessation of use (see SEDATIVE, HYPNOTIC, OR ANXIOLYTIC WITHDRAWAL), and an uncontrollable drive to continue use. See also SEDATIVE, HYPNOTIC, OR ANXIOLYTIC ABUSE.

sedative-, hypnotic-, or anxiolytic-induced persisting amnestic disorder a disturbance in memory due to the persisting effects of sedative, hypnotic, or anxiolytic drugs. The ability to learn new information or to recall previously learned information is impaired severely enough to interfere markedly with social or occupational functioning and to represent a significant decline from a previous level of functioning. Unlike those diagnosed with ALCOHOL-INDUCED PERSISTING

AMNESTIC DISORDER, people diagnosed with this disorder can recover memory functioning.

sedative, hypnotic, or anxiolytic intoxication a reversible syndrome specific to the recent ingestion of sedative, hypnotic, or anxiolytic drugs. It includes clinically significant behavioral or psychological changes (e.g., inappropriate sexual or aggressive behavior, mood lability, impaired judgment, and impaired social or occupational functioning), as well as one or more signs of physiological involvement (e.g., slurred speech, an unsteady gait, involuntary eye movements, memory or attentional problems, incoordination, and stupor or coma).

sedative, hypnotic, or anxiolytic withdrawal in *DSM–IV–TR*, a characteristic withdrawal syndrome, potentially life-threatening, that develops after cessation of (or reduction in) prolonged, heavy consumption of sedative, hypnotic, or anxiolytic drugs. Symptoms may include autonomic hyperactivity; increased hand tremor; insomnia; nausea or vomiting; transient visual, tactile, or auditory hallucinations or illusions; psychomotor agitation; anxiety; either a transient worsening (rebound) of the anxiety condition that prompted treatment or a recurrence of that condition; and tonic–clonic seizures. Risks of physiological dependence and withdrawal are present with long-term use of all benzodiazepines and similarly acting anxiolytics. Short-acting benzodiazepines pose particular withdrawal risks, and patients taking high doses of short-acting agents must be carefully withdrawn over an extended period to avoid adverse outcomes.

sedative, hypnotic, or anxiolytic withdrawal delirium a reversible syndrome that develops over a short period of time (usually hours to days) following cessation of prolonged, heavy consumption of sedative, hypnotic, or anxiolytic drugs. It involves disturbance of consciousness (e.g., reduced ability to focus, sustain, or shift attention), accompanied by changes in cognition (e.g., memory deficit, disorientation, or language disturbance) in excess of those usually associated with withdrawal from these substances. See also SEDATIVE, HYPNOTIC, OR ANXIOLYTIC WITHDRAWAL.

sedative–hypnotics *pl. n.* see SEDATIVE.

sedative occupation an activity or task, such as knitting or weaving, that has a soothing or sedating effect because of its repetitious nature. Compare STIMULATING OCCUPATION.

seduction *n.* **1.** the inducement of a person to participate in sexual intercourse, without the use of force. Local laws vary in their interpretation of seduction, and common law does not recognize it as a crime. However, some laws define seduction as a crime if it involves a promise by a man to marry a woman in the near future if she will submit to intercourse now. **2.** more generally, the act or process of attracting or alluring. **—seduce** *vb.*

segment *n.* in linguistics, a consonantal or vowel PHONEME occurring as part of a consecutive sequence of these. See SUPRASEGMENTAL. **—segmental** *adj.*

segmental reflex see SPINAL REFLEX.

segmentation *n.* **1.** a technique of BEHAVIOR MODIFICATION in which a complex sequence of behaviors is divided into parts so that the client can more easily learn and master one or two at a time. **2.** the division of an animal's body into a number of similar compartments (segments or metameres). Metameric segmentation is most apparent in annelid worms, in which the arrangement of muscles, blood vessels, nerves, and so on recurs in each segment. **3.** see CLEAVAGE.

segregated model in evaluation research, an administrative relationship, used in FORMATIVE EVALUATION, between the program director, the production unit, and the evaluation unit as three distinct entities. In this model the production unit and the evaluation unit share equal importance and improved access to the program director. Compare INTEGRATED MODEL.

segregation *n.* **1.** the separation or isolation of people (e.g., ethnic groups) or other entities (e.g., mental processes) so that there is a minimum of interaction between them. **2.** in genetics, the separation of the paired ALLELES of any particular gene during the cell division (see MEIOSIS), leading to sex-cell formation. **3.** in genetics, separation of the sister CHROMATIDS of each chromosome during normal cell division (mitosis).

segregation analysis a statistical method to determine if particular traits show MENDELIAN INHERITANCE.

seismic communication the use of the ground or other substrate by animals to transmit signals between individuals. Some frogs and kangaroo rats thump on the ground with their feet in distinctive patterns that provide cues for individual recognition and that may serve to attract mates or repel intruders. Elephants may also use seismic communication for long-distance communication.

seizure *n.* a discrete episode of uncontrolled, excessive electrical discharge of neurons in the brain. The resulting clinical symptoms vary based on the type and location of the seizure. See EPILEPSY; FEBRILE SEIZURE; GENERALIZED SEIZURE; PARTIAL SEIZURE.

seizure disorder see EPILEPSY.

selected group a SAMPLE explicitly selected with respect to specific criteria related to the purpose of the research. For example, a sample of citizens age 65 and over might be selected for a study of patterns in the attitudes of older adults.

selection *n.* **1.** in ANIMAL BEHAVIOR, the differential survival of some individuals and their offspring compared with others, causing certain physical or behavioral traits to be favored in subsequent generations. The general process is known as NATURAL SELECTION, with components of INDIVIDUAL SELECTION and KIN SELECTION. **2.** the process of choosing an item (e.g., an individual or object) for a purpose, such as study, testing, classifying, or working (employee selection).

selection bias BIAS in selecting participants or other units for research. This can occur, for example, when selecting specially motivated participants or when assigning participants to control or experimental groups. Selection bias is associated with nonrandom sampling and with nonrandom assignment to conditions.

selectionist brain theory see NEURAL DARWINISM.

selection pressure a measure of the intensity with which NATURAL SELECTION favors the survival of some genotypes over others and thus alters the genetic composition of a population over successive generations.

selection ratio the proportion of those eligible to be selected for a purpose (e.g., inclusion in research) that actually are selected. In personnel selection, for example, it is the number of applicants who are hired to perform a job in an organization divided by the total number of applicants. The lower the selection ratio, the more competitive the hiring situation will be and the more useful (all other factors being held constant) any given PREDICTOR will be in making selection decisions. See TAYLOR–RUSSELL TABLES.

selection research the use of empirical investigation to determine the reliability, validity, utility, and fairness of procedures used in PERSONNEL SELECTION and to maximize the effectiveness of these procedures.

selection test any physical or mental test that assesses an individual's appropriateness for a task. Such tests are usually used to screen and select people for occupational and educational placement. See also EMPLOYMENT TEST.

selective action an action whereby a reinforcer may have a greater effect on some responses than others, that is, its effects are selective.

selective adaptation 1. a psychophysical procedure in which repeated exposure to a stimulus produces sensory adaptation that influences perception of a subsequent stimulus. **2.** the observation that perceptual adaptation can occur in response to certain stimulus qualities while being unaffected by others. For example, color adaptation can take place independently of motion adaptation.

selective agent a factor in the environment that exerts SELECTION PRESSURE and brings about NATURAL SELECTION.

selective amnesia the forgetting of particular issues, people, or events that is too extensive to be explained by normal forgetfulness and that is posited to be organized according to emotional, rather than temporal, parameters. The selectivity appears to be of benefit to or convenient for the person who cannot remember. See also DISSOCIATIVE AMNESIA.

selective attention attention concentrated on certain stimuli in the environment and not others, enabling important stimuli to be distinguished from peripheral or incidental ones. Selective attention is typically measured by instructing participants to attend to some sources of information while ignoring others and then determining their effectiveness in doing this. Also called **controlled attention**; **directed attention**.

selective breeding breeding of animals with known genetic characteristics in order to achieve a particular kind of animal or to produce uniform animals with identical genetic characteristics for research purposes.

selective cell death an early developmental process in which neurons that are not activated by sensory and motor experience die.

selective dropout the nonrandom loss of participants from a study.

selective estrogen receptor modulators (SERMs) see ANTIESTROGEN.

selective inattention 1. unmindful absence or failure of attention to particular physical or emotional stimuli. **2.** a perceptual defense in which anxiety-provoking or threatening experiences are ignored or forgotten. [defined by U.S. psychiatrist Harry Stack Sullivan (1892–1949)]

selective information processing the processing of attitude-relevant information in a biased manner. Although a number of potential biases are possible, it has traditionally been assumed that when this type of processing occurs, the bias will be toward confirming the attitude. Bias can occur at one or more of the following stages of processing: exposure, attention, encoding, perception, and retrieval. See also BIASED ELABORATION; BIASING FACTOR; DEFENSIVE PROCESSING.

selective learning learning to make only one of several possible responses or learning about one stimulus when several stimuli are available. A particular response or stimulus could have a selective advantage due to biological PREPAREDNESS, previous experience, or salience in a given situation. See also BLOCKING; OVERSHADOWING; PREPARED LEARNING.

selective listening attending to only one stream of auditory stimuli when two or more streams are presented.

selective mutism in *DSM–IV–TR*, a rare disorder, most commonly but not exclusively found in young children, characterized by a persistent failure to speak in certain social situations (e.g., at school) despite the ability to speak and to understand spoken language. Age of onset is usually before 5 years, and the failure to speak lasts at least 1 month (not counting the first month at school, when many children are shy about talking). Generally, these individuals function normally in other ways, although some may have additional disabilities. Most learn age-appropriate skills and academic subjects. Currently, selective mutism is thought to be related to severe anxiety and SOCIAL PHOBIA, but the exact cause is unknown. It was formerly (in *DSM–III* and earlier editions) called **elective mutism**.

selective optimization with compensation a process used in SUCCESSFUL AGING to adapt to biological and psychological deficits associated with aging. The process involves emphasizing and enhancing those capacities affected only minimally by aging (optimization) and developing new means of maintaining functioning in those areas that are significantly affected (compensation). [described by German psychologists Paul Baltes (1939–) and Margret Baltes (1939–1999)]

selective perception the process in which people choose from the myriad array of stimuli presented to the senses at any one time that one or those few stimuli that will be attended. See ATTENTION. See also MOTIVATIONAL SELECTIVITY; PERCEPTUAL SET.

selective permeability the property of a membrane that allows some substances to pass through but not others. See also PERMEABILITY.

selective placement see PLACEMENT.

selective potentiation the enhancement of the sensitivity or activity of certain NEURAL CIRCUITS.

selective rearing an experimental paradigm in which an animal is raised from birth or from the time of eye opening under conditions that restrict its visual experience. This induces long-term changes in the structure and function of its visual system. For example, MONOCULAR REARING reduces the number of neurons in the STRIATE CORTEX that are sensitive to binocular stimulation and alters the structure of the OCULAR DOMINANCE COLUMNS; rearing with prism goggles that restrict the orientations that are visible can alter the orientation selectivity of neurons and the ORIENTATION COLUMNS in the striate cortex.

selective reminding test any memory test in which the participant is given the answer when it cannot be remembered so that he or she is more likely to answer correctly on subsequent trials. For instance, if the word "pencil" is presented on a list-learning task and the participant is unable to recall it, the word would then be presented along with other words not recalled.

selective response a response that has been differentiated from a group of possible alternative responses.

selective retention variation between individuals in the capacity to remember with respect to the vividness, accuracy, quantity, and specific contents of memory. This selectivity is usually determined by such factors as interest, experience, motivation, and emotional arousal.

selective serotonin reuptake inhibitors see SSRIS.

selective silence in psychotherapy, a prolonged silence imposed by the therapist to generate tension that may encourage the client to speak, thus beginning or resuming communication in a session.

selective value the relative importance of any factor in determining the evolution of organs, traits, or species through NATURAL SELECTION. See also SELECTIVE AGENT.

selegiline *n.* a drug used as an adjunct in the treatment of Parkinson's disease. At low doses it selectively inhibits the enzyme MONOAMINE OXIDASE B (MAO-B)—which degrades the neurotransmitter dopamine—and thereby increases levels of dopamine in the brain. Because selegiline is an irreversible MONOAMINE OXIDASE INHIBITOR (MAOI), and at higher doses it inhibits both MAO-A and MAO-B, great care must be taken not to exceed the therapeutic dosage in order to avoid the severe adverse effects of nonselective, irreversible MAOIs. Adverse drug interactions have been observed with commonly prescribed antidepressants, and concurrent administration of selegiline and these should be avoided. Also called **deprenyl**. U.S. trade name: **Eldepryl**.

self *n.* the totality of the individual, consisting of all characteristic attributes, conscious and unconscious, mental and physical. Apart from its basic reference to personal identity, being, and experience, the term's use in psychology is extremely wide-ranging and lacks uniformity. According to William JAMES, self can refer either to the person as the target of appraisal (i.e., one introspectively evaluates how one is doing) or to the person as the source of AGENCY (i.e., one attributes the source of regulation of perception, thought, and behavior to one's body or mind). Carl JUNG maintained that the self gradually develops by a process of INDIVIDUATION, which is not complete until late maturity is reached. Alfred ADLER identified the self with the individual's LIFESTYLE, the manner in which he or she seeks fulfillment. German-born U.S. psychoanalyst Karen D. Horney (1885–1952) held that one's REAL SELF, as opposed to one's idealized self-image, consists of one's unique capacities for growth and development. Gordon ALLPORT substituted the word PROPRIUM for self, and conceived of it as the essence of the individual, consisting of a gradually developing body sense, IDENTITY, self-estimate, and set of personal values, attitudes, and intentions. See also FALSE SELF; PHENOMENAL SELF; SENSE OF SELF; TRUE SELF.

self-abasement *n.* **1.** the act of degrading or demeaning oneself. **2.** extreme submission to the will of another person. Also called **self-debasement**.

self-abuse *n.* a euphemism for MASTURBATION. The term apparently evolved from an attempt by certain 18th-century religious and medical writers to identify masturbation as "the sin of Onan" (see ONANISM) and to substantiate unscientific claims that a number of disorders (e.g., blindness and mental retardation) were produced by masturbation.

self-acceptance *n.* a relatively objective sense or recognition of one's abilities and achievements, together with acknowledgment and acceptance of one's limitations. Lack of self-acceptance is often viewed as a major characteristic of emotional disturbance.

self-accusation *n.* the act of blaming oneself unjustifiably for negative occurrences. It is often associated with a MAJOR DEPRESSIVE EPISODE.

self-activity *n.* the performance of actions that have been decided upon by oneself, without dependence on outside activators.

self-actualization *n.* the realization of that of which one is capable. According to Abraham MASLOW, it is the "full use and exploitation of talent, capacities, potentialities" such that the individual develops to maximum self-realization, ideally integrating physical, social, intellectual, and emotional needs. The process of striving toward full potential is fundamental according to Maslow; however, he posited that self-actualization can only be fully realized if the basic needs of physical survival, safety, love and belongingness, and esteem are fulfilled. Also called **self-realization**. See also HUMANISTIC PSYCHOLOGY; MASLOW'S MOTIVATIONAL HIERARCHY.

self-administered test a type of test in which the instructions are sufficiently self-evident not to require further clarification by the tester. Also called **self-administering test**.

self-administration *n.* in animal research, a procedure used to study the rewarding effects of drugs. Animals (usually primates or rodents) are required to perform an OPERANT RESPONSE (e.g., lever pressing) in order to receive a drug infusion, which is delivered via an intravenous catheter or through a CANNULA implanted in the brain.

self-advocacy *n.* the process by which people make their own choices and exercise their rights in a self-determined manner. For people with developmental and other disabilities, for example, self-advocacy might entail promoting increased control of resources related to services and making informed decisions about what services to accept, reject, or insist be altered. See also CONSUMER EMPOWERMENT.

self-affirmation *n.* **1.** any behavior by which a person expresses a positive attitude toward his or her self, often by a positive assertion of his or her values, attributes, or group memberships. SELF-AFFIRMATION THEORY assumes that the desire for self-affirmation is basic and pervasive and that many different behaviors reflect this motive. **2.** in psychotherapy, a positive statement or set of such statements about the self that a person is required to repeat on a regular basis, often as part of a treatment for depression, negative thinking, or low self-esteem. **3.** see COMPENSATORY SELF-ENHANCEMENT. **4.** in performance or competitive situations, any thought about oneself that is believable and vivid and that reinforces positive characteristics, abilities, or skills.

self-affirmation theory a theory postulating that people are motivated to maintain views of themselves as well adapted, moral, competent, stable, and able to control important outcomes. When some aspect of this self-view is challenged, people experience psychological discomfort. They may attempt to reduce this discomfort by directly resolving the inconsistency between the new information and the self, by affirming some other aspect of the self, or both. Self-affirmation theory has been used to provide an alternative explanation to COGNITIVE DISSONANCE THEORY for some phenomena. See also DISSONANCE REDUCTION; SELF-CONSISTENCY PERSPECTIVE OF COGNITIVE DISSONANCE THEORY. [originally proposed by U.S. psychologist Claude M. Steele (1946–)]

self-alienation *n.* a state in which the individual feels a stranger to himself or herself, typically accompanied by significant emotional distancing. The self-alienated individual is frequently unaware of or largely unable to describe his or her own intrapsychic processes.

self-alien syndrome any of various conditions in which an aspect of oneself is perceived as outside one's normal experience and control. This perception is common in neurological and psychological disorders but also occurs in such everyday situations as failures of impulse control.

self-analysis *n.* **1.** generally, the investigation or exploration of the SELF for the purpose of better understanding of personal thoughts, emotions, and behavior. Self-analysis occurs consciously and unconsciously in many contexts of daily life. To some degree or other, and with the assistance and sometimes interpretation of the therapist, it is a particularly crucial process within most forms of psychotherapy. **2.** an attempt to apply the principles of PSYCHOANALYSIS to a study of one's own drives, feelings, and behavior. It was proposed by Sigmund FREUD early in his career as part of the preparation of an analyst but later dropped in favor of a TRAINING ANALYSIS. Much of Freud's early theory of psychoanalysis was based on his own self-analysis as described in *The Interpretation of Dreams* (1900). **—self-analytic** *adj.*

self-appraisal *n.* see SELF-CONCEPT.

self as agent the aspect of the self that has goals, plans, and some degree of control over actions. It contrasts with the self as object and is synonymous with the "I" of William JAMES (see NOMINATIVE SELF).

self as known the aspect of the self that is known through reflection (see EMPIRICAL SELF). It is sometimes contrasted with the self as knower (see NOMINATIVE SELF).

self as observer the aspect of the self that interprets sensory and linguistic information for executive control, that is, the self as knower (see NOMINATIVE SELF).

self-assertion *n.* the act of putting forward one's own opinions or taking actions that express one's needs, rights, or wishes. Self-assertion is often seen as a goal of treatment and in some cases is specifically targeted by structured group treatments. **—self-assertive** *adj.*

self-assessment *n.* see SELF-CONCEPT.

self-as-target effect the tendency to assume wrongly that, or to overestimate the degree to which, external events refer to the self. For example, a person may think quite wrongly that other people's conversations and actions, or even music lyrics, are directed at him or her. In its milder forms the self-as-target effect is common and normal, but extreme forms are associated with PARANOIA.

self-awareness *n.* **1.** see SELF-UNDERSTANDING. **2.** in animal behavior, see AWARENESS.

self-blaming depression a MAJOR DEPRESSIVE EPISODE in which unreasonable guilt is a prominent feature.

self-care *n.* activities required for personal care, such as eating, dressing, or grooming, that can be managed by an individual without the assistance of others. See ACTIVITIES OF DAILY LIVING.

self-care children see LATCHKEY CHILDREN.

self-censure *n.* an individual's conscious self-blame, condemnation, or guilt in judging his or her own behavior to be inconsistent with personal values or standards of moral conduct.

self-completion theory the theory that many behaviors are performed to claim desired identities, so that by behaving in a certain way one is symbolically "proving" oneself to be a certain kind of person. Insecurity about being the sort of person one wants to be is often the reason for engaging in such self-completing acts. For example, a person who takes pride in being very fit and active may respond to the first signs of illness or exhaustion by increasing, rather than reducing, his or her activities.

self-complexity *n.* the degree to which different aspects of the SELF-CONCEPT are disconnected from one another. Low self-complexity entails considerable integration; high self-complexity results from COMPARTMENTALIZATION, so that what affects one part of the self may not affect other parts.

self-concept *n.* one's conception and evaluation of oneself, including psychological and physical characteristics, qualities, and skills. Self-concepts contribute to the individual's sense of identity over time. The conscious representation of self-concept is dependent in part on unconscious schematization of the self (see SCHEMA). Although self-concepts are usually available to some degree to the consciousness, they may be inhibited from representation yet still influence judgment, mood, and behavioral patterns. Also called **self-appraisal**; **self-assessment**; **self-evaluation**; **self-rating**. See SELF-IMAGE; SELF-PERCEPTION.

self-concept test a personality test designed to determine how participants view their own attitudes, values, goals, body concept, personal worth, and abilities. Three types of techniques are most frequently used: ADJECTIVE CHECKLISTS, interpretation of PERSONALITY INVENTORY responses on personality tests, and the Q SORT technique.

self-confidence *n.* **1.** self-assurance, or trust in one's own abilities, capacities, and judgment. Because it is most typically viewed as a positive personality trait, the encouragement or bolstering of self-confidence is often a mediate or end goal in psychotherapeutic treatment. **2.** a belief that one is capable of successfully meeting the demands of a task. **—self-confident** *adj.*

self-confrontation *n.* examining one's own attitudes, behaviors, and shortcomings to provide an impetus to change and to gain insight into how one is perceived by others.

self-conscious emotion an emotion that celebrates or condemns the self and its actions, generated when the self is known to be the object of another person's evaluation. Self-conscious emotions include SHAME, PRIDE, GUILT, and EMBARRASSMENT. Recently, the term **other-conscious emotions** has been suggested as a better name for these emotions, to emphasize the importance of the appraisal of other human beings in generating them.

self-consciousness *n.* **1.** a personality trait associated with the tendency to reflect on or think about oneself. Psychological use of the term refers only to individual differences in self-reflection, not to embarrassment or awkwardness (see sense **3.** below). Some researchers have distinguished between two varieties of self-consciousness: (a) **private self-consciousness**, or the degree to which people think about private, internal aspects of themselves (e.g., their own thoughts, motives, and feelings) that are not directly open to observation by others; and (b) **public self-consciousness**, or the degree to which people think about public, external aspects of themselves (e.g., their physical appearance, mannerisms, and overt behavior) that can be observed by others. **2.** see REFLECTIVE CONSCIOUSNESS. **3.** extreme sensitivity about one's own behavior, appearance, or other attributes and excessive concern about the impression one makes on others, which leads to embarrassment or awkwardness in the presence of others. **—self-conscious** *adj.*

self-consistency *n.* **1.** behavior or personality that has a high degree of internal harmony and stability. **2.** the compatibility of all aspects of a theory or system.

self-consistency perspective of cognitive dissonance theory a variation of COGNITIVE DISSONANCE THEORY postulating that COGNITIVE DISSONANCE is particularly likely to occur when an inconsistency involves some aspect of the self. This perspective differs from SELF-AFFIRMATION THEORY in that it assumes that dissonance can only be reduced by resolving the specific inconsistency that gave rise to the discomfort; it does not allow for the possibility that dissonance can be reduced by affirming some other aspect of the self. [originally proposed by U.S. psychologist Elliot Aronson (1932–)]

self-consistency theory see CONSISTENCY THEORY.

self-construal *n.* any specific belief about the SELF. The term is used particularly in connection with the distinction between INDEPENDENT SELF-CONSTRUALS and INTERDEPENDENT SELF-CONSTRUALS. A self-construal is much more specific than a SELF-CONCEPT.

self-contradiction *n.* **1.** in logic, a fundamental inconsistency between two or more premises of a single argument, such that they cannot both be true. **2.** more generally, a deep inconsistency between two or more beliefs, intentions, desires, or behaviors of an individual or of a group. Such inconsistency often produces tension. **—self-contradictory** *adj.*

self-control *n.* the ability to be in command of one's behavior (overt, covert, emotional, or physical) and to restrain or inhibit one's impulses. In circumstances in which short-term gain is pitted against long-term loss or long-term greater gain, it is the ability to opt for the long-term outcome. Choice of the short-term outcome is called **impulsiveness** (see IMPULSIVE). See also SELF-DISCIPLINE; SELF-REGULATION. **—self-controlled** *adj.*

self-control technique a technique in BEHAVIOR THERAPY in which clients are trained to evaluate their own behavior and reinforce desired behavior with appropriate material or social rewards.

self-control therapy a form of BEHAVIOR THERAPY that involves self-monitoring (e.g., diaries of behavior), self-evaluation, goal setting, behavioral contracts, teaching, self-reinforcement, and relapse prevention. Also called **self-management therapy**. [developed by Austrian-born U.S. clinical psychologist Frederick H. Kanfer (1925–2002)]

self-correction *n.* any situation in which an individual makes an error but fixes it spontaneously, with no external instructions or cues.

self-criticism *n.* the examination and evaluation of one's behavior, with recognition of one's weaknesses, errors, and shortcomings. Self-criticism can have both positive and negative effects; for example, a tendency toward harsh self-criticism is thought by some to be a risk factor for depression. **—self-critical** *adj.*

self-debasement *n.* see SELF-ABASEMENT.

self-deception *n.* **1.** failure to recognize one's own limitations. **2.** the development of a false or unrealistic self-concept.

self-defeating behavior behavior that blocks an individual's own goals and wishes. Examples of such behavior include the tendency to compete so aggressively that one cannot hold a job and the tendency of antisocial individuals to take such great risks that they are almost bound to get caught.

self-defeating personality disorder in *DSM–III–R* (but not *DSM–IV–TR*), a personality disorder characterized by a reluctance to seek pleasurable activities, encouraging others to exploit or take advantage of oneself, focusing on one's very worst personal features, and a tendency to sabotage one's good fortunes. See also MASOCHISTIC PERSONALITY DISORDER.

self-definition *n.* personal independence. See AUTONOMY.

self-degrading *n.* NEGATIVE IMAGERY or NEGATIVE SELF-TALK that causes one to think less of oneself and one's ability.

self-demand schedule in animal or child-rearing studies, a feeding schedule regulated by the individual's needs and desires, in contrast to a fixed or rigid schedule. Also called **demand feeding**.

self-denial *n.* the act of suppressing desires and forgoing satisfactions.

self-derogation *n.* the tendency to disparage oneself, often unrealistically. It is often associated with a MAJOR DEPRESSIVE EPISODE.

self-desensitization *n.* a procedure used in BEHAVIOR THERAPY in which the individual, when confronted with objects or situations that arouse fear or anxiety, engages in coping strategies designed to reduce anxiety, for example, repeating positive self-statements, mentally rehearsing a potential confrontation, or employing muscle relaxation. See also DESENSITIZATION; SYSTEMATIC DESENSITIZATION.

self-destructiveness *n.* actions by an individual that are damaging and not in his or her best interests. The behavior may be repetitive and resistant to treatment, sometimes leading to suicide attempts. The individual may not be aware of the damaging influence of the actions or may on some level wish for the resulting damage. See also DEATH INSTINCT. **—self-destructive** *adj.*

self-determination *n.* the control of one's behavior by internal convictions and decisions rather than by external demands. Also called **self-direction**.

self-determination theory a theory that emphasizes the importance of AUTONOMY and INTRINSIC MOTIVATION for producing healthy adjustment. According to this theory, negative outcomes ensue when people are driven mainly by external forces and extrinsic rewards.

self-development *n.* the growth or improvement of one's own qualities and abilities.

self-differentiation *n.* the tendency to seek recognition for one's individuality and uniqueness, particularly in contrast to the other members of one's social group.

self-direction *n.* see SELF-DETERMINATION.

self-discipline *n.* the control of one's own impulses and desires, forgoing immediate satisfaction in favor of long-term goals or of improvement generally. See also SELF-CONTROL; SELF-REGULATION. **—self-disciplined** *adj.*

self-disclosure *n.* the act of revealing information about one's self, especially one's PRIVATE SELF, to other people. In psychotherapy, the revelation and expression by the client of personal, innermost feelings, fantasies, experiences, and aspirations is believed by many to be a requisite for therapeutic change and personal growth. In addition, pertinent revelation by the therapist of his or her personal details to the client can—if used with discretion—be a valuable tool to increase rapport and earn the trust of the client.

self-discovery *n.* the process of searching for and finding one's unique SELF or IDENTITY.

self-discrepancy *n.* an incongruence between different aspects of one's self-concept, particularly between one's ACTUAL SELF and either the IDEAL SELF or the OUGHT SELF. [derived from the theory of U.S. psychologist E. Tory Higgins (1946–)]

self-dynamism *n.* the pattern of motivations or drives that comprise one's SELF-SYSTEM, including especially the pursuit of biological satisfaction, security, and freedom from anxiety. [proposed by U.S. psychiatrist Harry Stack Sullivan (1892–1949)]

self-effacement *n.* **1.** acting in such a way as not to draw attention to oneself or make oneself noticeable. **2.** in the approach of German-born U.S. psychoanalyst Karen D. Horney (1885–1952), a neurotic idealization of compliancy, dependency, and selfless love as a reaction to identification with the hated self. See also COMPLIANT CHARACTER; NEUROTIC TREND. **—self-effacing** *adj.*

self-efficacy *n.* an individual's capacity to act effectively to bring about desired results, especially as perceived by the individual (see PERCEIVED SELF-EFFICACY).

self-enhancement *n.* any strategic behavior designed to increase esteem, either SELF-ESTEEM or the esteem of others. Self-enhancement can take the form of pursuing success or merely distorting events to make them seem to reflect better on the self. Compare SELF-PROTECTION. See also COMPENSATORY SELF-ENHANCEMENT.

self-enhancement motive the desire to think well of oneself and to be well regarded by others. This motive causes people to prefer favorable, flattering feedback rather than accurate but possibly unfavorable information. Compare APPRAISAL MOTIVE; CONSISTENCY MOTIVE.

self-enucleation *n.* see AUTOENUCLEATION.

self-esteem *n.* the degree to which the qualities and characteristics contained in one's SELF-CONCEPT are perceived to be positive. It reflects a person's physical self-image, view of his or her accomplishments and capabilities, and values and perceived success in living up to them, as well as the ways in which others view and respond to that person. The more positive the cumulative perception of these qualities and characteristics, the higher one's self-esteem. A high or reasonable degree of self-esteem is considered an important ingredient of mental health, whereas low self-esteem and feelings of worthlessness are common depressive symptoms.

self-evaluation *n.* see SELF-CONCEPT.

self-evaluation maintenance model a conceptual analysis of group affiliations that assumes that an individual maintains and enhances self-esteem by (a) associating with high-achieving individuals who excel in areas with low relevance to his or her sense of self-worth and (b) avoiding association with high-achieving individuals who excel in areas that are personally important to him or her. [developed by U.S. social psychologists Abraham Tesser (1941–), Jennifer D. Campbell (1944–), and their colleagues]

self-evident *adj.* perceived immediately by the mind to be true without need of supporting argument or empirical evidence. In DEDUCTIVE REASONING it is usual to begin an argument from a proposition that is considered to be self-evident (an AXIOM). Philosophers have also held various types of INNATE IDEA to be self-evident.

self-exciting circuit a NEURAL CIRCUIT or NEURAL PATHWAY in which part of the output is fed back to the original cell, thus maintaining activity. See POSITIVE FEEDBACK; RECURRENT CIRCUIT.

self-expression *n.* free expression of one's feelings, thoughts, talents, attitudes, or impulses through such means as verbal communication; the visual, decorative, literary, and performing arts; and other commonplace activities (e.g., gardening and sports).

self-extension *n.* according to Gordon ALLPORT, an early stage in the development of the PROPRIUM or self, beginning roughly at age 4 and marked by the child's emerging ability to incorporate people, objects, and abstractions into the self-concept. Self-extension is the investment of ego in those objects outside the self with which the individual feels affinity or identification.

self-extinction *n.* in psychoanalytic theory, a form of neurotic behavior in which the patient lacks experience of himself or herself as an entity and identifies vicariously with the experiences and lives of others. [introduced by German-born U.S. psychoanalyst Karen D. Horney (1885–1952)]

self-feeding *n.* the act of feeding oneself without the direct assistance of others. Some individuals with disabilities may not be capable of self-feeding, whereas others may be able to feed themselves with the help of certain ASSISTIVE TECHNOLOGY devices.

self-focus *n.* **1.** the ability of human beings to direct conscious attention on themselves and their own thoughts, needs, desires, and emotions. **Trait self-focus** refers to a chronic habit or pattern of self-attention, whereas **state self-focus** refers to any temporary occurrence of the state. **2.** the capacity of an individual to analyze and evaluate his or her mental and emotive states. **3.** excessive concern for the self and its needs: selfishness. **—self-focused** *adj.*

self-fulfilling prophecy a belief or expectation that helps to bring about its own fulfillment, as, for example, when a person expects nervousness to impair his or her performance in a job interview or when a teacher's preconceptions about a student's ability influence the child's achievement for better or worse. See PYGMALION EFFECT; UPWARD PYGMALION EFFECT. See also DEMAND CHARACTERISTICS; EXPECTANCY EFFECT.

self-gratification *n.* the satisfaction of the needs of the self.

self-guide *n.* a specific image or goal of the SELF that can be used to direct SELF-REGULATION. In particular, self-guides include mental representations of valued or preferred attributes, that is, ideals and notions of how one ought to be; these may be chosen by the self or may come from others.

self-handicapping *n.* a psychological ploy in which individuals deliberately lessen their chances of performing well at a task they expect to fail or do poorly, for example, by neglecting to rehearse before an audition. The purpose is to create an acceptable excuse for an anticipated poor showing so that shortcomings can be attributed to circumstance and not to lack of ability. **—self-handicap** *vb.*

self-hate *n.* extreme SELF-DEROGATION.

self-help *n.* a focus on self-guided, in contrast to professionally guided, efforts to cope with life problems. This can involve self-reliance, drawing upon publicly available information and materials, or joining together with others similar to oneself, as is the case in SELF-HELP GROUPS.

self-help clearinghouse an organization that serves as an information and referral source about self-help groups in a given locality or region, providing up-to-date directories of all groups in that jurisdiction, as well as national self-help group resources. It serves as an important resource for citizens, groups, and professionals. Some clearinghouses also provide consultation to groups and group leaders and attempt to educate the public and professionals about the nature, value, and availability of groups. *The Self-Help Sourcebook* of a well-known clearinghouse in the United States, the American Self-Help Clearinghouse, provides an international listing of self-help clearinghouses.

self-help group a group composed of individuals who meet on a regular basis to help one another cope with a common life problem. Unlike therapy groups, self-help groups are not led by professionals, do not charge a fee for service, and do not place a limit on the number of members. They provide many benefits that professionals cannot provide, including friendship, emotional support, experiential knowledge, identity, meaningful roles, and a sense of belonging (see also SELF-HELP GROUP PROCESSES). Psychologists have become increasingly active in researching and supporting the development of self-help groups. Examples of self-help groups are ALCOHOLICS ANONYMOUS, COMPASSIONATE FRIENDS, and RECOV-

ERY, INC. See also MUTUAL SUPPORT GROUPS. Compare SUPPORT GROUP.

self-help group ideology the set of beliefs about the cause and best means to address the problem that brings members of SELF-HELP GROUPS together. Each self-help group develops an ideology that is distinctive and that serves as an aid or "antidote" to its particular type of problem. For instance, in the case of ALCOHOLICS ANONYMOUS the group ideology includes the belief that alcoholism is a life-long problem and that the first step in addressing the problem is for group members to admit that they do not have control over it.

self-help group processes the means or mechanisms by which SELF-HELP GROUPS are thought to exert influence on their members. These include providing a sense of belonging, adaptive beliefs, emotional support, role models, specific coping approaches, practical information, and opportunities to contribute meaningfully to others and to expand or rebuild personal social networks.

self-help group typology classification of self-help groups according to type. Many typologies include addiction/compulsion groups (e.g., ALCOHOLICS ANONYMOUS), life stress/transition groups (e.g., COMPASSIONATE FRIENDS), mental illness/mental health problem groups (e.g., GROW, INC.), and physical illness/health/disability groups (e.g., the National Multiple Sclerosis Society).

self-hypnorelaxation *n.* a form of SELF-HYPNOSIS in which clients are trained to respond to their own relaxation suggestions.

self-hypnosis *n.* the process of putting oneself into a trance or trancelike state through AUTOSUGGESTION. See also AUTOHYPNOSIS.

self-ideal Q sort a technique designed to measure the discrepancy between an individual's SELF-CONCEPT and his or her **self-ideal** (see EGO-IDEAL). The technique requires participants to sort cards with descriptions of characteristics twice, once with regard to how they see themselves and then in terms of how they would like to be. See Q SORT.

self-identification *n.* the act of construing one's identity in particular terms, usually as a member of a particular group or category (e.g., "I am Hispanic," "I am a lesbian," "I am a father") or as a person with particular traits or attributes (e.g., "I am intelligent," "I am unlucky," "I am fat").

self-identity *n.* see IDENTITY.

self-image *n.* one's own view or concept of oneself. Self-image is a crucial aspect of an individual's personality that can determine the success of relationships and a sense of general well-being. A negative self-image is often a cause of dysfunctions and of self-abusive, self-defeating, or destructive behavior. See also SCHEMA.

self-image bias the tendency of people to judge others according to criteria on which they themselves score highly. The more favorably a person rates himself or herself on some trait, the more central and important that trait is likely to be in how the person perceives others. The self-image bias is one subtle way in which the SELF-CONCEPT biases how the person perceives others.

self-inflicted wound a physical injury that results from self-injurious behavior or ATTEMPTED SUICIDE.

self-injurious behavior apparently intentional actions that inflict damage upon one's own body.

self-insight *n.* understanding oneself in some depth (see INSIGHT). It is a mediate goal or the desired outcome of many types of psychotherapy. See also DERIVATIVE INSIGHT.

self-instructional imagery imagery that is used in the learning or perfection of a skill. It may be the image of a past performance used to detect errors for correction, or it may be the image of an unperformed alteration of a skill. See MENTAL PRACTICE.

self-instructional training a form of COGNITIVE BEHAVIOR THERAPY that aims to modify maladaptive beliefs and cognitions and develop new skills in an individual. In therapy, the therapist identifies the client's maladaptive thoughts (e.g., "Everybody hates me") and models appropriate behavior while giving spoken constructive **self-instructions** (or **self-statements**). The client then copies the behavior while repeating these instructions aloud. See also SELF-STATEMENT TRAINING. [developed by U.S. psychologist Donald Meichenbaum (1940–)]

self-interest *n.* one's personal advantage or benefit. Self-interested behavior includes both the pursuit of rewards and benefits and the avoidance of costs, dangers, and harm.

self-inventory *n.* a questionnaire or series of statements on which participants check characteristics or traits that they perceive to apply to themselves.

selfish gene hypothesis the postulate that the sole purpose of genes is to replicate themselves and that genes are the overriding units of selection (i.e., the entities upon which NATURAL SELECTION operates). Hence any mutation enhancing gene replication (and transmission) would be selected for. Many contemporary evolutionary biologists hold this view to oversimplify the relationship between genes and organisms and to be extreme in its notion that genes consistently override selection on the organism or population level, although they accept the principal notion of gene replication as consistent with a number of processes in evolution. [proposed by British biologist Richard Dawkins (1941–) in his book *The Selfish Gene* (1976)]

selfish herd in animal behavior, a gathering of highly selfish individuals each jostling to keep other individuals between them and a source of danger. Individuals end up clustered together in groups not for mutual defense or cooperation, but simply because each individual is looking after its own interests by using the others as a shield.

selfishness *n.* the tendency to act excessively or solely in a manner that benefits oneself, even if others are disadvantaged. **—selfish** *adj.*

self-love *n.* **1.** regard for and interest in one's own being or contentment. **2.** excessive self-regard, or a narcissistic attitude toward one's own body, abilities, or personality. See EGOTISM; NARCISSISM.

self-managed reinforcement see SELF-REINFORCEMENT.

self-management *n.* **1.** an individual's control of his or her own behavior. Self-management is usually considered a desirable aspect for the individual personally and within the social setting, but some forms of self-management may be detrimental to mental and physical health (see also COPING MECHANISM). Psychotherapy and counseling often seek to provide methods of identifying the latter and modifying them into the former. **2.** a BEHAVIOR-THERAPY program in which clients are trained to apply techniques that will help them modify an undesirable behavior, such as smoking, excessive eating, or aggressive outbursts. Clients learn to pinpoint the problem, set realistic goals for changing it, use various contingencies to establish and maintain the desired behavior, and monitor progress.

self-management therapy see SELF-CONTROL THERAPY.

self-marking test a type of test that automatically scores an examinee's responses as correct or incorrect.

self-medication *n.* see MEDICATION.

self-monitoring *n.* **1.** a method used in behavioral management in which individuals keep a record of their behavior (e.g., time spent, place of occurrence, form of the behavior, feelings during performance), especially in connection with efforts to change or regulate the self (see SELF-REGULATION). **2.** a personality trait reflecting an ability to modify one's behavior in response to situational pressures, opportunities, and norms. High self-monitors are typically more in tune with the demands of the situation, whereas low self-monitors tend to be more in tune with their internal feelings. **3.** a therapeutic technique in which the therapist assigns homework to encourage the client to record behavior, because behavior sometimes changes when it is closely self-monitored. **4.** a motivational technique used in exercise programs. See also TRAINING LOG.

self-mutilation *n.* the act of disfiguring oneself. The most common type of self-mutilation is cutting.

self-objectification *n.* the achievement of objective knowledge about the self or self-understanding. It is one of Gordon ALLPORT's set of seven adaptive characteristics for psychological maturity.

self-organizing system any system in which elements combine to create a higher level structure solely as a result of their intrinsic properties.

self-perception *n.* a person's view of his or her self or of any of the mental or physical attributes that constitute the self. Such a view may involve genuine self-knowledge or varying degrees of distortion. Also called **self-percept**. See also PERCEIVED SELF; SELF-CONCEPT.

self-perception theory a theory postulating that people often have only limited access to their attitudes, beliefs, traits, or psychological states. In such cases, people must attempt to infer the nature of these internal cues in a manner similar to the inference processes they use when making judgments about other people. For example, a person may infer what his or her attitude is by considering past behaviors related to the ATTITUDE OBJECT: Approach behaviors imply a positive attitude; avoidance behaviors imply a negative attitude. Self-perception theory has been offered as an alternative explanation for some phenomena traditionally interpreted in terms of COGNITIVE DISSONANCE THEORY. The theory has also been used to explain the success of the FOOT-IN-THE-DOOR TECHNIQUE. [originally proposed by U.S. psychologist Daryl J. Bem (1938–)]

self-presentation *n.* any behaviors designed to convey a particular image of, or particular information about, the self to other people. Self-presentational motives explain why an individual's behavior often changes as soon as anyone else is thought to be present or watching. Some common strategies of self-presentation include EXEMPLIFICATION, SELF-PROMOTION, and SUPPLICATION. See also IMPRESSION MANAGEMENT. **—self-presentational** *adj.*

self-preservation instinct the fundamental tendency of humans and nonhuman animals to behave so as to avoid injury and maximize chances of survival (e.g., by fleeing from dangerous situations or predators). In his early formulations of classic psychoanalytic theory, Sigmund FREUD proposed that the instinct of self-preservation was one of two instincts that motivated human behavior, the other being the SEXUAL INSTINCT. In his later formulations he combined both instincts into the concept of EROS, or the LIFE INSTINCT, and opposed them to THANATOS, the DEATH INSTINCT. Also called **self-preservative instinct**; **survival instinct**.

self-promotion *n.* in SELF-PRESENTATION theory, a strategy of making oneself look good to others by highlighting or exaggerating one's competence and abilities.

self-protection *n.* any strategic behavior that is designed to avoid losing esteem, either SELF-ESTEEM or the esteem of others. Self-protection fosters a risk-avoidant orientation and is often contrasted with SELF-ENHANCEMENT.

self psychology **1.** any system of psychology focused on the SELF. **2.** a school of psychoanalytical theory that stresses the importance of an individual's relationships with others to healthy self-development and locates the source of many psychological problems in caregivers' lack of responsiveness to the child's emotional needs. In self-psychological therapy the therapist attempts to build an empathetic relationship with the client, rather than keeping an emotional distance as in classic psychoanalytical practice. [pioneered by Austrian-born U.S. psychoanalyst Heinz Kohut (1913–1981)]

self-punishment *n.* the act of inflicting physical or psychological harm on oneself for one's perceived misdeeds. Self-punishment ranges from SELF-ACCUSATION to SELF-MUTILATION or ATTEMPTED SUICIDE and commonly occurs in severe cases of MAJOR DEPRESSIVE DISORDER.

self-rating *n.* **1.** see SELF-CONCEPT. **2.** in psychological measurement, the act of reporting on or describing characteristics of oneself.

self-rating scale any questionnaire, inventory, or other instrument used by participants to assess their own characteristics (e.g., attitudes, interests, abilities, or performance).

self-realization *n.* see SELF-ACTUALIZATION.

self-reference *n.* a persistent tendency to direct a discussion or the attention of others back to oneself, that is, to one's personal concerns and perceptions. **—self-refer** *vb.* **—self-referential** *adj.*

self-reference effect the widespread tendency for individuals to have a superior or enhanced memory for stimuli that relate to the SELF or SELF-CONCEPT.

self-referencing *n.* in advertising and marketing, prompting individuals to think about how products might relate to their own past experiences in order to make them appreciate the value of a current product offering.

self-referral *n.* the act of consulting a clinical service provider or health care practitioner without a referral from a medically qualified professional or similar person or without being forced to seek such help by an employer, a spouse, or the courts. Self-referred individuals are often viewed as more motivated for treatment and more likely to admit to problems.

self-reflection *n.* **1.** examination, contemplation, and analysis of one's thoughts and actions. The condition of or capacity for this is called **self-reflexivity**. **2.** see REFLECTIVE CONSCIOUSNESS.

self-regulation *n.* the control of one's own behavior through self-monitoring of the conditions that evoke desired and undesired behavior, structuring the personal environment to facilitate desired behavior and circumvent situations that tend to elicit undesired behavior, self-evaluation and self-administration of punishments and rewards, or some combination of these. Self-regulatory processes are stressed in BEHAVIOR THERAPY. See also SELF-CONTROL; SELF-MANAGEMENT.

self-regulation model a five-stage model of the process of self-management of directed behavior without the presence of external constraints. The stages are problem identification, commitment, execution, environment management, and generalization.

self-regulatory resources theory a model stating that SELF-REGULATION depends on a global, but finite, pool of resources that can be temporarily depleted by situational demands. See EGO DEPLETION; VOLITION.

self-reinforcement *n.* the rewarding of oneself for appropriate behavior or the achievement of a desired goal. The self-reward may be, for example, buying a treat after studying for an exam. Also called **self-managed reinforcement**.

self-relevance *n.* see EGO INVOLVEMENT.

self-report *n.* a statement or series of answers to questions provided by an individual as to his or her state, feelings, beliefs, and so forth. Self-report methods rely on the honesty and self-awareness of the participant (see SELF-REPORT BIAS) and are used especially to measure behaviors or traits that cannot easily be directly observed.

self-report bias a methodological problem that arises when researchers rely on asking people to describe their thoughts, feelings, or behaviors rather than measuring these directly and objectively. People may not give answers that are fully correct, either because they do not know the full answer or because they seek to make a good impression (see SOCIAL DESIRABILITY). The self-report bias is often cited as a reason to use direct observation rather than SELF-REPORTS whenever practicable.

self-report inventory a type of questionnaire on which participants indicate the degree to which the descriptors listed apply to them.

self-repudiation *n.* denial of one's own pleasure or rights, usually out of a sense of guilt or low self-esteem.

self-respect *n.* a feeling of self-worth and SELF-ESTEEM, especially a proper regard for one's values, character, and dignity.

self-schema *n.* a cognitive framework comprising organized information about the self in terms of roles and actions, often in relation to a specific realm of experience (e.g., a clear conception of oneself as parent or worker).

self-selected groups design an experimental design in which the participants have chosen their group or the condition to which they will be exposed. As the assignment of participants is nonrandom, causal inference from data gleaned in such experiments is questionable.

self-selection of diet the concept that animals, including human infants and children, tend to choose foods that maintain good health when available from among those offered. See also CAFETERIA FEEDING; SPECIFIC HUNGER. [proposed in 1928 by pediatrician Clara M. Davis]

self-serving bias the tendency to interpret events in a way that assigns credit to the self for any success but denies the self's responsibility for any failure, which is blamed on external factors. The self-serving bias is regarded as a form of self-deception designed to maintain high SELF-ESTEEM. Compare GROUP-SERVING BIAS.

self-statement *n.* see SELF-INSTRUCTIONAL TRAINING; SELF-STATEMENT TRAINING.

self-statement modification a technique designed to change maladaptive ideas about the self that are uncovered in COGNITIVE BEHAVIOR THERAPY. See also SELF-INSTRUCTIONAL TRAINING.

self-statement training (**SST**) a type of COGNITIVE REHEARSAL that involves periodically thinking or saying something positive, such as "I am a capable individual who is worthy of respect." It is used in SELF-INSTRUCTIONAL TRAINING. See also AFFIRMATION; INNER DIALOGUE.

self-stereotyping *n.* see AUTOSTEREOTYPING.

self-stimulation *n.* **1.** the act or process of inducing or increasing the level of arousal in oneself. It can be observed in various situations; for example, infants who are understimulated may explore their surroundings or babble to themselves. **2.** see INTRACRANIAL SELF-STIMULATION; PLEASURE CENTER. See also MASTURBATION; SELF-REINFORCEMENT.

self-suggestion *n.* see AUTOSUGGESTION.

self-synchrony *n.* see SYNCHRONY.

self-system *n.* the relatively fixed personality of the individual resulting from relationships with his or her parents and other significant adults, in which approved attitudes and behavior patterns tend to be retained and disapproved actions and attitudes tend to be blocked out. [first described by U.S. psychiatrist Harry Stack Sullivan (1892–1949)]

self-talk *n.* an internal dialogue in which an individual utters phrases or sentences to him- or herself. The self-talk often confirms and reinforces negative beliefs and attitudes, such as fears and false aspirations, which have a correspondingly negative effect on the individual's feelings and reactions. In certain types of psychotherapy, one of the tasks of the therapist is to encourage the client to replace self-defeating, negative self-talk with more constructive, positive self-talk. In sport, athletes are trained to use positive self-talk to cue the body to act in particular ways, to cue ATTENTIONAL FOCUS, to motivate, to reinforce SELF-EFFICACY, and to change mood. See also INTERNALIZED SPEECH; RATIONAL EMOTIVE BEHAVIOR THERAPY. [described by U.S. psychotherapist Albert Ellis (1913–)]

self-terminating search any SEARCH process in which the search is ended as soon as a given target is detected. This may be a search for target items in memory, a VISUAL SEARCH, or any problem-solving exercise that involves finding the correct solution among a number of alternatives. Compare EXHAUSTIVE SEARCH.

self-test *n.* a test that can be administered without the help of a trained professional.

self-transcendence *n.* the state in which an individual transcends preoccupation with the self and is able to devote him- or herself fully to another person, work, cause, or activity. Humanistic psychologists maintain that deep commitment or absorption in something beyond the self is a central feature of the healthy individual. [first described by Austrian psychiatrist Viktor Emil Frankl (1905–1998)]

self-understanding *n.* the attainment of insight into one's attitudes, motives, reactions, defenses, strengths, and weaknesses. The achievement of self-understanding is one of the major goals of psychotherapy. Also called **self-awareness**.

self-verbalization *n.* **1.** self-directed private speech or thinking aloud. Self-verbalization can be a cognitive strategy that fosters internal self-regulation by verbally controlling behavior. Often used as a learning tool, it can be used to teach new skills, enhance problem-solving abilities, or alter previously held beliefs. Varying perspectives on this type of speech include the work of Lev

VYGOTSKY, Jean PIAGET, and Alexander LURIA. **2.** see SELF-TALK.

self-verification hypothesis the hypothesis that people seek information about themselves that confirms their existing SELF-CONCEPT, regardless of whether this is good or bad. According to this theory, the CONSISTENCY MOTIVE, which seeks self-verification, is often stronger than the SELF-ENHANCEMENT MOTIVE, which seeks favorable information about the self, or than the APPRAISAL MOTIVE, which seeks accurate information about the self (DIAGNOSTICITY). People seek self-verification (a) by engaging in situations that confirm their self-concept, (b) by seeking out and choosing to believe self-verifying feedback, and (c) by trying to persuade others of the validity of their own views of themselves.

self-worth *n.* an individual's evaluation of him- or herself as a worthwhile human being. Positive feelings of self-worth tend to be associated with a high degree of SELF-ACCEPTANCE and SELF-ESTEEM.

SEM abbreviation for STRUCTURAL EQUATION MODELING.

sem- *combining form* signs or meaning.

semantic aphasia a form of APHASIA in which individuals are unable to comprehend the meaning of words even though they may be able to utter them. See also LOGICOGRAMMATICAL DISORDER.

semantic code the means by which the conceptual or abstract components of an object, idea, or impression are stored in memory. For example, the item "typewriter" could be remembered in terms of its functional meaning or properties. Compare IMAGERY CODE.

semantic counseling a type of COUNSELING in which emphasis is placed on interpretations of meanings, particularly those related to adjustment and maladjustment.

semantic dementia a selective, progressive impairment in SEMANTIC MEMORY, leading to difficulties in naming, comprehension of words, and appreciation and use of objects. Nonsemantic aspects of language, as well as perceptual and spatial skills, are preserved. The syndrome results from focal degeneration of the polar and inferolateral regions of the temporal lobes.

semantic differential a technique used to explore the connotative meaning that certain words or concepts have for the individuals being questioned. Participants are asked to rate the word or concept on a seven-point scale with reference to pairs of opposites, such as *good–bad, beautiful–ugly, hot–cold, big–small,* and so on. Responses are then averaged or summed to arrive at a final index of attitudes. This procedure is one of the most widely used methods of assessing attitudes and may be used in psychometric testing or (in advertising, politics, etc.) to gauge public reactions to a product, issue, or personality. See also ATTITUDE OBJECT; DIRECT ATTITUDE MEASURE. [developed in the 1950s by U.S. psychologists Charles E. OSGOOD, George J. Suci, and Percy H. Tannenbaum (1927–)]

semantic dissociation a distortion between words and their culturally accepted meanings that is characteristic of the THOUGHT DISORDER of individuals with schizophrenia. It includes **semantic dissolution**, marked by a complete loss of meaning and communication; **semantic dispersion**, in which meaning and syntax are lost or reduced; **semantic distortion**, in which meaning may be transferred to neologisms; or **semantic halo**, marked by coherent but vague and ambiguous language.

semantic encoding cognitive ENCODING of new information that focuses on the meaningful aspects of the material as opposed to its perceptual characteristics. This will usually involve some form of ELABORATION. See also CONCEPTUALLY DRIVEN PROCESS; DEEP PROCESSING; TOP-DOWN PROCESSING.

semantic fluency the ability to generate words in different categories (e.g., types of dogs). Also called **category fluency**.

semantic generalization a result of PAVLOVIAN CONDITIONING in which a word, phrase, or sentence functions as a conditioned stimulus because it shares the same (or highly similar) meaning with a word, phrase, or sentence that has been established, via direct pairing with an unconditioned stimulus, as a conditioned stimulus. For example, the word *delicious*, when paired with actual food, will eventually elicit the response of salivation. After *delicious* is established as a conditioned stimulus, related words or phrases (e.g., *tasty*) may elicit the same or similar responses. See STIMULUS EQUIVALENCE.

semanticity *n.* **1.** the property of language that allows it to represent events, ideas, actions, and objects symbolically, thereby endowing it with the capacity to communicate meaning. According to Roger BROWN, it is one of the three formal properties of language. See PRODUCTIVITY. **2.** in animal communication, the meaning conveyed through vocalizations (e.g., alarm calls).

semantic jargon a form of RECEPTIVE APHASIA associated with a lesion of the posterior-middle and superior-temporal GYRUS, either bilateral or unilateral. Individuals utter real words and sentences, but in combinations that have little meaning. For example, an individual asked about his poor vision replied "My wires don't hire right."

semantic knowledge general knowledge or information that one has acquired; that is, knowledge that is not tied to any specific object, event, domain, or application. It includes word knowledge (as in a dictionary) and general factual information about the world (as in an encyclopedia) and oneself. Also called **generic knowledge**.

semantic memory 1. memory for general knowledge or information, such as dictionary and encyclopedic knowledge (see SEMANTIC KNOWLEDGE). According to some theories, semantic memory is a form of DECLARATIVE MEMORY, that is, information that can be consciously recalled and related. See also NOETIC MEMORY. **2.** memory for knowledge of word meanings. Certain brain injuries or degenerative brain diseases may render words meaningless, leaving other information and memories intact.

semantic network a GRAPH used to capture semantic relationships. Created by the artificial intelligence research community, it was originally used in programs attempting to understand natural (human) language. Nodes in the network represented entities and their properties in a domain. The arc link reflected the semantic nature of the property. This system has been used in an attempt to model human information storage (particularly the means by which words are connected to meanings and associations in long-term memory), with latencies in retrieval times supposedly reflecting the length of the path of the network searched for the required response.

semantic paradox see PARADOX.

semantic paraphasia a form of PARAPHASIA in which conversational speech is fairly fluent but objects are misnamed, although some associative connection may exist. For example, a pipe may be called a "smoker" and glasses a "telescope."

semantic priming an effect in which the processing of a stimulus is found to be more efficient after the earlier processing of a meaningfully related stimulus, as opposed to an unrelated or perceptually related stimulus. For example, responses to the word *nurse* would be faster following *doctor* than following *purse*. See PRIMING.

semantic primitive in SEMANTICS, one of the fundamental building blocks thought to be involved in the construction of meaning. Many refer to a basic physical property or simple sensation; for example, the concept *car* could be reduced to the semantic primitives *moves, fast, noisy, shiny,* and so on. Semantic primitives are thought to play an important role in language development in young children.

semantic psychosis the tendency of antisocial individuals to distort the meaning of words. They might say, for example, *I shouldn't have done that* when they merely mean *I'll say that because that's what he wants to hear, and then he'll let me go.* [defined by U.S. psychiatrist H. M. Cleckley (1905–1984)]

semantics *n.* **1.** in linguistics, the study of meaning in language, as opposed to the study of formal relationships (GRAMMAR) or sound systems (PHONOLOGY). **2.** aspects of language that have to do with meaning, as distinguished from SYNTACTICS. **3.** in logic and philosophy, the study of the relationships between words or phrases and the things or concepts to which they refer. Compare SEMIOTICS.

semantic satiation the effect in which a word seems to lose its meaning after it has been repeated many times in rapid succession. The reasons for this effect remain little understood.

semantic therapy a form of psychotherapy in which the clients are trained to examine undesired word habits and distorted ideas so that they can think more clearly and critically about their aims, values, and relationships. This approach is based on an active search for the meaning of the key words the client uses and on practicing the formation of clear abstractions, as well as on uncovering hidden assumptions and increased awareness of the emotional tone behind the words the client has been using. Polish-born U.S. scientist Alfred Korzybski (1879–1950) and U.S. psychologist Wendell A. L. Johnson (1906–1965) were major early exponents of this approach. See also GENERAL SEMANTICS.

semantogenic disorder a mental disorder originating in a misinterpretation of the meanings of emotion-colored words.

semasiology *n.* the study of development and change in the meanings of words. Also called **historical semantics**. See also SEMANTICS.

semeiosis *n.* see SEMIOSIS.

semen *n.* the fluid released during EJACULATION. It contains sperm and secretions of the PROSTATE GLAND, BULBOURETHRAL GLANDS, and SEMINAL VESICLES. Also called **seminal fluid**.

semicircular canals a set of three looped tubular channels in the inner ear that detect movements of the head and provide the sense of dynamic equilibrium that is essential for maintaining balance. They form part of the VESTIBULAR APPARATUS. The channels are filled with fluid (endolymph) and are oriented roughly at right angles to each other. Hence they can monitor movements in each of three different planes. Each canal has an enlarged portion, the **ampulla**, inside which is a sensory structure called a **crista**. This consists of HAIR CELLS whose processes are embedded in a gelatinous cap (the **cupula**). When the head moves in a certain plane, endolymph flows through the corresponding canal, displacing the cupula and causing the hairs to bend. This triggers the hair cells to fire nerve impulses, thus sending messages to the brain about the direction and rate of movement.

semiconscious *adj.* describing states of partial wakefulness, or alertness, such as drowsiness, stupor, or intermittent coma.

semi-interquartile range the INTERQUARTILE RANGE divided by 2.

seminal *adj.* **1.** of or relating to SEMEN. **2.** formative, that is, strongly influencing development (e.g., ideas, events, conditions).

seminal analysis see SPERM ANALYSIS.

seminal discharge the discharge of semen, which normally occurs during coital ejaculation, nocturnal emission, or masturbation.

seminal duct see VAS DEFERENS.

seminal fluid see SEMEN.

seminal vesicle either of two membranous pouches, approximately 8 cm (3 in) long in human males, located between the bladder and the rectum. The seminal vesicles secrete and store a fluid that mixes with secretions of the prostate gland to form the bulk of the SEMEN.

seminiferous tubule any of numerous minute, convoluted tubules in the lobules of the TESTIS. The seminiferous tubules are lined with germ cells that give rise to spermatozoa (see SPERMATOGENESIS). They also contain SERTOLI CELLS. Each lobule of a testis may contain one to several seminiferous tubules, and a single testis may contain as many as 400 lobules.

semiology *n.* **1.** see SEMIOTICS. **2.** see SYMPTOMATOLOGY.

semiosis (**semeiosis**) *n.* the process by which objects, words, gestures, and other entities become associated with particular meanings and function as SIGNS within a particular sign system. See SEMIOTICS.

semiotic movement a trend toward formalization of systems of visual communication by the use of signs or symbols that are not a part of the standard alphabet. The semiotic movement, which has been particularly popular in the United States, promotes the acceptance of "rules of grammar" for symbolic logic, mathematical formulas, or other symbolic systems that may be analogous to language.

semiotics *n.* the study of verbal and nonverbal SIGNS and of the ways in which they communicate meaning within particular sign systems. Unlike SEMANTICS, which restricts itself to the meanings expressed in language, semiotics is concerned with human symbolic activity generally. As an academic discipline, semiotics developed within the general framework of 20th-century STRUCTURALISM, taking as its premise the view that signs can only generate meanings within a pattern of relationships to other signs. Also called **semiology**. [introduced by U.S. philosopher C. S. Peirce (1839–1914)]

semipartial correlation see PART CORRELATION.

semipermeable membrane a membrane that allows some but not all molecules to pass through. See also PERMEABILITY.

semistructured interview see PATTERNED INTERVIEW.

semitone *n.* a half-step on the musical scale. More precisely, it is the logarithm of a frequency ratio.

semivowel *n.* **1.** a vowel-like speech sound that functions as a consonant in that it forms a syllable when combined with a true VOWEL. Examples are [w] as in *well* and [y] as in *yellow*. See also SONANT. **2.** a LIQUID speech sound.

sender *n.* in TELEPATHY experiments, the participant who attempts to transmit information to the RECEIVER. See also AGENT.

senescence *n.* **1.** the biological process of growing old, or the period during which this process occurs. **2.** the state or condition of being old. **—senescent** *adj.*

senile *adj.* **1.** relating to DEMENTIA associated with advanced age. **2.** a lay term used to describe an older adult with dementia.

senile dementia DEMENTIA with an onset after the age of 65.

senile dementia of the Alzheimer's type (SDAT) an older name for dementia of the Alzheimer's type with onset after age 65. See ALZHEIMER'S DISEASE.

senile miosis a reduction in the size of the pupil in old age caused by atrophy of the muscles controlling dilation of the pupil, which restricts the amount of light that enters the eye.

senile plaques clumps of BETA-AMYLOID protein surrounded by degenerated dendrites that are particularly associated with symptoms of Alzheimer's disease. Their increased concentration in the cerebral cortex of the brain is correlated with the severity of dementia. Also called **neuritic plaques**.

senile psychosis an obsolete name for SENILE DEMENTIA.

senilism *n.* an obsolete name for the appearance of symptoms of SENILITY in old age or before.

senility *n.* a lay term for DEMENTIA associated with advanced age. See also PSEUDOSENILITY.

senior citizen a popular name for an older adult, especially one who is retired or has reached the age of retirement (generally 55 years or older).

senium *n.* an older, less commonly used term for the period of old age.

sensate focus therapy an approach to problems of sexual dysfunction in which people are trained to focus attention on their own natural, biological sensual cues and gradually achieve the freedom to enjoy sensory stimuli. Therapy is conducted by teams of male and female professionals in joint interviews with the partners. The procedures involve prescribed body-massage exercises designed to give and receive pleasure, first not involving breasts and genitals, and then moving to these areas. This eliminates performance anxiety about arousal and allows the clients to relax and enjoy the sensual experience of body caressing without the need to achieve erection or orgasm. Sensate focus therapy is one component of the program developed by U.S. gynecologist William H. Masters (1915–2001) and U.S. psychologist Virginia E. Johnson (1925–).

sensation *n.* **1.** the process or experience of perceiving through the senses. See SENSORY SYSTEM. **2.** an irreducible unit of experience produced by stimulation of a sensory RECEPTOR and the resultant activation of a specific brain center, producing basic awareness of a sound, odor, color, shape, or taste or of temperature, pressure, pain, muscular tension, position of the body, or change in the internal organs associated with such processes as hunger, thirst, nausea, and sexual excitement. Also called **sense datum**; **sense impression**; **sensum**. **3.** in the STRUCTURALISM of E. B. TITCHENER, one of the three structural elements of mental experience, the other two being images and feelings. **4.** in general usage, a thrilling or exciting experience. See SENSATION SEEKING. **—sensational** *adj.*

sensationalism *n.* in philosophy, the position that all knowledge originates in sensations and that even complex abstract ideas can be traced to elementary sense impressions. See ASSOCIATIONISM; EMPIRICISM. **—sensationalist** *adj.*

sensation increment in psychophysics, a just noticeable increase in the intensity of a sensory experience.

sensation level the perceived intensity of a particular sensation, for example, the intensity of an auditory stimulus as experienced by a given listener (**auditory sensation level**).

sensation seeking the tendency to search out and engage in thrilling activities as a method of increasing stimulation and arousal. Limited to human populations, it typically takes the form of engaging in highly stimulating activities accompanied by a perception of danger, such as skydiving or race-car driving.

sensation threshold see ABSOLUTE THRESHOLD.

sensation type in the ANALYTIC PSYCHOLOGY of Carl JUNG, a FUNCTIONAL TYPE dominated by sense perception, as opposed to thinking, feeling, or intuition. This type of individual lives a life of sense experience and enjoyment. The sensation type is one of Jung's two IRRATIONAL TYPES, the other being the INTUITIVE TYPE. See also FEELING TYPE; THINKING TYPE.

sensation unit **1.** a discriminable sensory experience. **2.** see DIFFERENCE THRESHOLD.

sense **1.** *n.* any of the media through which one perceives information about the external environment or about the state of one's body in relation to this. They include the five primary senses—vision, hearing, taste, touch, and smell—as well as the senses of pressure, pain, temperature, kinesthesis, and equilibrium. Each sense has its own receptors, responds to characteristic stimuli, and has its own pathways to a specific part of the brain. Also called **sense modality**; **sensory modality**. **2.** *n.* a particular awareness of a physical dimension or property (e.g., time, space) or of an abstract quality, usually one that is desirable (e.g., humor, justice). **3.** *n.* good judgment or intelligence manifested by, or absent from, a person. **4.** *n.* the gist or general meaning of something, such as an argument, play, or event. **5.** *vb.* to perceive something using the senses. **6.** *vb.* to make an emotional or cognitive judgment about something, such as another person's mood.

sense datum see SENSATION.

sense distance an interval between two distinct sensations along a given dimension, for example, the distance between C and G on the musical scale.

sense experience awareness produced by stimulation of a sensory RECEPTOR.

sense impression see SENSATION.

sense modality see SENSE.

sense of coherence **1.** a perception of having clarity or intelligibility, that is, of being capable of thinking and expressing oneself in a clear and consistent manner. **2.** the ability to present a narrative of oneself in a way that is understandable and easy to follow.

sense of equilibrium the sense that enables the maintenance of balance while sitting, standing, walking, or otherwise maneuvering the body. A subset of PROPRIOCEPTION, it is in part controlled by the VESTIBULAR SYSTEM in the INNER EAR, which contains receptors (see VESTIBULAR RECEPTORS) that detect motions of the head.

Also called **equilibratory sense**; **labyrinthine sense**; **static sense**; **vestibular sense**.

sense of free will the sense that one is not forced to act as one does, which is an aspect of normal voluntary control and should not be confused with metaphysical FREE WILL. It contrasts with the sense that one's actions are unwanted, coerced, or perceived to be controlled by external influences (see SELF-ALIEN SYNDROME).

sense of identity awareness of being a separate and distinct person. The first signs of a sense of identity are believed to appear when infants experience separation from their caregivers and begin to be aware of their ability to move and perceive the environment. As infants grow and mature, they gradually perceive themselves as unique individuals with their own feelings, impulses, aims, and personality characteristics. See IDENTITY; SELF; SEPARATION–INDIVIDUATION.

sense of presence **1.** the sense of being in a particular place or time. **2.** an awareness and understanding of one's current existence. **3.** in parapsychology, an awareness or consciousness of unusual phenomena, such as the existence or appearance of spirits.

sense of self an individual's feeling of IDENTITY, uniqueness, and self-direction. See also SELF-CONCEPT; SELF-IMAGE; SENSE OF IDENTITY.

sense organ an organ, such as the eye or ear, that contains or comprises RECEPTOR cells, which are sensitive to particular stimuli, together with associated structures specialized to receive this sensory input. Also called **sensory organ**; **sensory receptor organ**.

sense quality see QUALITY.

sense-ratios method a system of scaling sensory magnitudes by selecting stimuli that are perceived to be at equal intervals along the scale.

sensibilia *pl. n.* things that are capable of being sensed.

sensibility *n.* **1.** a capacity to respond to an emotional situation with refined or intense feeling. **2.** the capacity to receive sensory input.

sensible *adj.* **1.** showing reason and sound judgment. **2.** capable of receiving sensory input (e.g., feeling pain). **3.** receptive to external influences. **4.** felt or perceived as real or material.

sensitive **1.** *adj.* having well-developed or intense mental and affective SENSIBILITY. **2.** *n.* in spiritualism and parapsychology, a person who is supposedly capable of receiving knowledge by paranormal means, as in CLAIRVOYANCE and TELEPATHY, or of perceiving AURAS and similar alleged phenomena beyond the range of normal perception. See also MEDIUM; PSYCHIC.

sensitive dependence the tendency for complex, dynamic systems to be highly sensitive to initial conditions, so that two such systems with starting points that are almost identical may become extremely divergent over time. In other words, the future states of complex systems are very dependent on small differences in their initial states. The best-known example of sensitive dependence is the so-called BUTTERFLY EFFECT. One possible explanation for this phenomenon is that measurements in chaotic systems are imprecise, so that prediction becomes extremely difficult. See CHAOS THEORY.

sensitive period a stage in development when an organism can most advantageously form specific attachments or acquire necessary skills. For example, in humans the 1st year of life is considered sensitive or critical for the development of a secure attachment bond or basic trust. The notion that the consequences of a missed opportunity during the sensitive period are irreversible is still subject to debate. See also CRITICAL PERIOD; IMPRINTING.

sensitive soul in the thought of Greek philosopher Aristotle (384–322 BCE), the type of soul possessed by nonhuman animals. The sensitive soul has the capacity to receive and react to sense impressions but does not have a capacity for rational thought. Compare RATIONAL SOUL; VEGETATIVE SOUL.

sensitive zone any point on the body that is highly responsive to a particular type of stimulus, such as touch or pain.

sensitivity *n.* **1.** the capacity to detect and discriminate. In SIGNAL DETECTION THEORY, sensitivity is measured by D PRIME (d′). **2.** the probability that a test gives a positive diagnosis given that the individual actually has the condition for which he or she is being tested. Compare SPECIFICITY. **3.** in physiology, the ability of a cell, tissue, or organism to respond to changes in its external or internal environment: a fundamental property of all living organisms. Also called **irritability**. **4.** emotional and aesthetic awareness. **5.** responsiveness to the feelings of others.

sensitivity training a group process focused on the development of self-awareness, productive interpersonal relations, and sensitivity to the feelings, attitudes, and needs of others. The primary method used in sensitivity training is free, unstructured discussion with a leader functioning as an observer and facilitator, although other techniques, such as ROLE PLAY, may be used. Sensitivity training is employed in HUMAN RELATIONS TRAINING in industry and general life, with various types of groups (e.g., workers, executives, married couples) meeting, for example, once a week or over a weekend. See also ACTION RESEARCH; PERSONAL-GROWTH LABORATORY; T-GROUP. [originated by Kurt LEWIN and Carl ROGERS]

sensitization *n.* **1.** a form of nonassociative learning in which an organism becomes more responsive to most stimuli after being exposed to unusually strong or painful stimulation. Compare HABITUATION. **2.** the increased effectiveness of an eliciting stimulus as a function of its repeated presentation. Water torture, in which water is dripped incessantly onto a person's forehead, is a good example. **3.** see REVERSE TOLERANCE.

sensor *n.* **1.** a RECEPTOR cell or organ. **2.** a device that responds to the presence of something (e.g., a smoke detector).

sensorimotor *adj.* **1.** describing activity, behavior, or brain processes that combine sensory (afferent) and motor (efferent) function. **2.** describing a mixed nerve that contains both afferent and efferent fibers.

sensorimotor aphasia a combination of sensory or RECEPTIVE APHASIA and motor or EXPRESSIVE APHASIA, in which there is impairment or loss of ability to perceive and understand language as well as to use it. See also GLOBAL APHASIA.

sensorimotor arc a REFLEX ARC consisting of an afferent sensory branch and an efferent motor branch.

sensorimotor cortex areas of the cerebral cortex that are concerned with somatosensory and motor functions. The primary motor cortex (see MOTOR AREA) lies just anterior to the central sulcus, while the PRIMARY SOMATOSENSORY AREA is just posterior to it.

sensorimotor intelligence in Jean PIAGET's theory of cognitive development, knowledge that is obtained from sensory perception and motor actions involving objects in the environment. This form of cognition characterizes children in the SENSORIMOTOR STAGE.

sensorimotor memory a memory, commonly of a

traumatic experience, that is encoded in SENSORIMOTOR, rather than verbal, forms. Frequently these are memories of events that occurred during the period of INFANTILE AMNESIA, which commonly lasts up to the age of 3 years. See also BODY MEMORY.

sensorimotor rhythm (**SMR**) a rhythmical electrical impulse of 12–14 Hz recorded over the ROLANDIC CORTEX in the brain. It is used in BIOFEEDBACK studies and procedures. See BRAIN WAVES.

sensorimotor stage in Jean PIAGET's theory, the first major stage of cognitive development, extending from birth through the first 2 years of life. The sensorimotor stage is characterized by the development of sensory and motor processes and by the infant's first knowledge of the world acquired by interacting with the environment. Some rudimentary awareness of the reality of time, space, and cause and effect is present. See also CONCRETE OPERATIONAL STAGE; FORMAL OPERATIONS; PREOPERATIONAL STAGE.

sensorineural hearing loss the loss or absence of hearing function due to pathology in the inner ear or along the nerve pathway from the inner ear to the brainstem. Also called **nerve deafness**; **perceptive impairment and nerve loss**; **sensorineural deafness** (or **impairment**). See also ADULT SENSORINEURAL LESIONS; CHILDHOOD SENSORINEURAL LESIONS; PRESBYCUSIS.

sensorium *n.* **1.** the human sensory apparatus and related mental faculties considered as a whole. The state of the sensorium is tested through the traditional MENTAL STATUS EXAMINATION; the sensorium may be **clear** (i.e., functioning normally) or **clouded** (lacking ability to concentrate and think clearly). **2.** see SENSORIUM COMMUNE.

sensorium commune a hypothetical location in the brain formerly held to be the seat of sensation in humans and animals and the site for the operations of the SENSUS COMMUNIS. Also called **sensorium**.

sensory *adj.* relating to the SENSES, to SENSATION, or to a part or all of the neural apparatus and its supporting structures that are involved in any of these. See SENSORY SYSTEM.

sensory acuity the extent to which one is able to perceive stimuli of minimal size, intensity, or duration and to discriminate minimal differences between stimuli.

sensory adaptation reduced responsiveness in a sensory receptor or sensory system caused by prolonged stimulation. The adaptation may be specific, for example, to the wavelength of a visual stimulus or to the orientation of the stimulus.

sensory amimia see AMIMIA.

sensory amusia a form of AMUSIA marked by impairment or loss of the ability to perceive and comprehend musical tones and sequences.

sensory aphasia see RECEPTIVE APHASIA.

sensory aprosodia an inability to understand the emotional inflections of language, that is, the rhythm, pitch, and "melody" of speech. Compare MOTOR APROSODIA.

sensory area any area of the cerebral cortex that receives input from sensory neurons, usually via the thalamus. There are specific sensory areas for the different senses, and they are functionally differentiated into PRIMARY SENSORY AREAS and SECONDARY SENSORY AREAS. Also called **sensory cortex**; **sensory projection area**.

sensory ataxia lack of muscular coordination (see ATAXIA) due to the loss of the sense of limb movements (see PROPRIOCEPTION).

sensory awareness training 1. the methods used in SENSATE FOCUS THERAPY and similar therapies to help an individual become more acutely aware of his or her own feelings and sensations and to accept new ways of experiencing them. **2.** in sport, training an athlete to become aware of the kinesthetic sensations experienced while performing and of the sensations related to AROUSAL level.

sensory bias the display of sensory preferences that may or may not relate to species-typical signals. Female tungara frogs prefer a low-pitched chuck note that males add to courtship calls, and females of a closely related species also prefer low-pitched chuck notes, even though males of their species do not produce these notes. The preference for low-pitched chuck notes is a sensory bias that can be exploited by any males that can add such a note to their mating calls. See SENSORY EXPLOITATION.

sensory circle an area of the skin that gives rise to nervous activity when stimulated, analogous to a RECEPTIVE FIELD. It was thought that skin areas with greater spatial acuity would have smaller sensory circles. [first described by German physiologist Ernst Heinrich Weber (1795–1878)]

sensory conditioning see SENSORY PRECONDITIONING.

sensory consciousness consciousness of sensory stimuli, having visual, tactile, olfactory, auditory, and taste qualities. Compare HIGHER ORDER CONSCIOUSNESS.

sensory conversion symptoms one of two types of symptoms of CONVERSION DISORDER, the other being MOTOR CONVERSION SYMPTOMS. Examples of sensory conversion symptoms include loss of touch or pain sensation, double vision, blindness, deafness, tinnitus, and hallucinations.

sensory cortex see SENSORY AREA.

sensory cue a visual, tactual, olfactory, gustatory, or auditory stimulus that evokes a response or a behavior pattern.

sensory deficit a loss, absence, or marked impairment of a normal sensory function, such as vision, hearing, taste, touch, or smell.

sensory deprivation the reduction of sensory stimulation to a minimum in the absence of normal contact with the environment. Sensory deprivation may be experimentally induced (e.g., via the use of a **sensory deprivation chamber**) for research purposes or it may occur in a real-life situation (e.g., in deep-sea diving). Although short periods of sensory deprivation can be beneficial, extended sensory deprivation has detrimental effects, causing (among other things) hallucinations, delusions, hypersuggestibility, or panic.

sensory discrimination the perceptual differentiation of stimuli, particularly closely related sensory stimuli (e.g., very similar shades of blue).

sensory disorder 1. an anatomical or physiological abnormality that interferes with optimum transmission of information from a sense organ to its appropriate reception point in the brain or spinal cord. An auditory disorder, for example, may be due to an accumulation of earwax, an infection that involves the ear ossicles, damage from injury or disease to the cochlear structures, or injury to the brain. **2.** a disorder of sensory function that has no apparent anatomical cause and is thought to be related primarily to psychological factors. For example, certain cases of paresthesia may be of psychological origin. Also called **sensory disturbance**.

sensory drive see SENSORY EXPLOITATION.

sensory engineering see KANSEI ENGINEERING.

sensory epilepsy a type of epilepsy marked by seizures involving abnormal skin sensations (see PARESTHESIA), such as tingling, numbness, or burning. Such seizures may occur without loss of consciousness.

sensory evoked potential a type of EVOKED POTENTIAL recorded from electrodes placed on the scalp, overlying the cerebral cortex, in response to sensory stimulation. The stimuli may be visual, auditory, somatosensory, or olfactory, and the mapping of sensory evoked potentials in the cortex helps to locate the different SENSORY AREAS. See also AUDITORY EVOKED POTENTIAL; VISUAL EVOKED POTENTIAL. Compare MOTOR EVOKED POTENTIAL.

sensory exploitation the use of a preexisting SENSORY BIAS to gain increased REPRODUCTIVE SUCCESS by changing some feature of ornamentation or calling behavior to be more attractive to mates. If low-frequency call notes are attractive to mates, then the first individuals to use these notes in courtship calling will achieve the greatest reproductive success. Also called **sensory drive**.

sensory exploration see CURIOSITY.

sensory extinction see PERCEPTUAL EXTINCTION.

sensory feedback see BIOFEEDBACK.

sensory field the totality of the stimuli that impinge on a receptor or an individual at a given time.

sensory gating see GATING.

sensory homunculus a figurative representation, in distorted human form, of the relative sizes of the sensory areas in the brain that correspond to particular sensory parts of the body. The homunculus is arranged upside down with the largest proportional areas representing the face and hands. See HOMUNCULUS. Compare MOTOR-FUNCTION HOMUNCULUS.

sensory inattention see PERCEPTUAL EXTINCTION.

sensory-information store (SIS) see SENSORY MEMORY.

sensory input the stimulation of a sense organ, causing an impulse to travel to its appropriate destination in the brain or spinal cord.

sensory integration the neural processes involved in perceiving, organizing, and evaluating sensory information across modalities, such as vision and hearing, and producing an adaptive response via impulses transmitted through the motor nerves. Development or enhancement of **sensory-integrative functioning** is an important goal of OCCUPATIONAL THERAPY.

sensory integration dysfunction a condition characterized by difficulties in organizing, processing, and analyzing sensory input (touch, movement, body awareness, sight, sound, smell, and taste).

sensory intensity the perceived intensity of a physical stimulus, predictably related to its actual intensity by psychophysical laws. See STIMULUS-INTENSITY DYNAMISM.

sensory interaction the integration of sensory processes in performing a task, as in maintaining balance using sensory input from both vision and PROPRIOCEPTION. See also CROSS-MODAL ASSOCIATION; INTERSENSORY PERCEPTION; PERCEPTUAL SYNTHESIS.

sensory leakage in ESP experiments, the conveying of information about the TARGET to the SUBJECT through ordinary sensory channels, often by inadvertent cues given by the tester. See also DEMAND CHARACTERISTICS; EXPERIMENTER BIAS.

sensory memory brief storage of sensory information in each of the senses, which temporarily holds material (e.g., a perceptual experience) for recoding into another memory (such as SHORT-TERM MEMORY) or for comprehension. For instance, ICONIC MEMORY holds a visual image for less than a second, whereas AUDITORY MEMORY may retain sounds for a little longer. Also called **sensory-information store (SIS)**; **sensory register**.

sensory modality see SENSE.

sensory modulation dysfunction a type of SENSORY INTEGRATION DYSFUNCTION characterized by difficulties in responding appropriately to sensory input (touch, movement, body awareness, sight, sound, smell, and taste). A person may be overresponsive or underresponsive to sensations or alternate rapidly between both response patterns.

sensory neglect inability to attend to sensory information, usually from one side of the body, as a result of brain injury. See NEGLECT.

sensory nerve a NERVE that conveys impulses from a sense organ to the central nervous system.

sensory neuron a NEURON that receives information from the environment, via specialized RECEPTOR cells, and transmits this—in the form of nerve impulses—through SYNAPSES with other neurons to the central nervous system.

sensory organ see SENSE ORGAN.

sensory organization the neural process of organizing impulses from sensory receptors into meaningful perception.

sensory overload a state in which the senses are overwhelmed with stimuli, to the point that the person is unable to process or respond to all of them. See also COMMUNICATION OVERLOAD; INFORMATION OVERLOAD; STIMULUS OVERLOAD.

sensory paralysis a condition in which sensory function is impaired but movement is not necessarily lost.

sensory pathway any of the routes followed by nerve impulses traveling from sense organs toward sensory areas of the brain. See AFFERENT PATHWAY; NEURAL PATHWAY.

Sensory Perceptual Examination see REITAN–KLOVE SENSORY PERCEPTUAL EXAMINATION.

sensory preconditioning a form of PAVLOVIAN CONDITIONING established by initially pairing two neutral stimuli (A and B) and subsequently pairing A with an unconditioned stimulus. If B comes to elicit a response, then sensory preconditioning has occurred. Also called **sensory conditioning**.

sensory projection area see SENSORY AREA.

sensory psychophysiology the study of the relation between psychological and physiological functioning as it pertains to the senses and perception.

sensory receptor organ see SENSE ORGAN.

sensory register see SENSORY MEMORY.

sensory root see DORSAL ROOT.

sensory spot a skin spot or location of high sensitivity to tactile, thermal, or pain stimuli.

sensory stimulation the elicitation of a response in a sensory receptor by a stimulus.

sensory substitution the perception of a stimulus normally analyzed by one sense through the activity of another sense. Tactile sensations can substitute for visual input, for example, when the visual world is transcribed into tactile sensations for a blind individual. Sensory substitution requires an active translation of stimulation between sensory systems, in contrast to SYNESTHESIA, which is an involuntary association of one sense with another or one sensory attribute with another.

sensory summation the combining and integrating of

sensory inputs at different levels of the nervous system. For example, sensory input will increase when multiple stimuli are summated over time (see TEMPORAL SUMMATION) or across space (see SPATIAL SUMMATION).

sensory suppression the phenomenon occurring in any sensory modality when an individual is given two sensory inputs simultaneously (such as touching the hand and face) but perceives only one of the stimuli.

sensory system the total structure involved in SENSATION, including the sense organs and their RECEPTORS, afferent sensory neurons, and SENSORY AREAS in the cerebral cortex at which these tracts terminate. There are separate systems for each of the senses. See AUDITORY SYSTEM; GUSTATORY SYSTEM; OLFACTORY SYSTEM; SOMATOSENSORY SYSTEM; VISUAL SYSTEM; VESTIBULAR SYSTEM.

sensory test a test designed to measure any of various sensory abilities, such as visual acuity, depth perception, color discrimination, or auditory acuity.

sensory transduction see TRANSDUCTION.

sensual *adj.* **1.** referring to the senses, particularly gratification of or appeal to the senses. **2.** referring to physical or erotic sensation.

sensum *n.* (*pl.* **sensa**) see SENSATION.

sensuous *adj.* describing the sensory aspect of an experience or something that is capable of arousing the senses.

sensus communis in the thought of Greek philosopher Aristotle (384–322 BCE), the mental faculty that takes data provided by the five senses and integrates them into unified perceptions. The operations of the sensus communis (Latin, "common sense") were thought to occur in the SENSORIUM COMMUNE.

sentence-completion test a test in which the participant must complete an unfinished sentence by filling in the missing word or phrase. A specific word or phrase is required if the test is used as an ability test. However, the test is used more often to evaluate personality than to measure intelligence. In this case, the participant is presented with an introductory phrase to which he or she may respond in any way. An example might be "Today I am in a _ _ mood." As a projective test, the sentence-completion test is an extension of the WORD-ASSOCIATION TEST in that responses are free and believed to contain psychologically meaningful material. Also called **incomplete-sentence test**.

sentence-repetition test a test in which the participant must repeat sentences of increasing difficulty and complexity directly after the examiner reads them. The test measures primarily memory skills.

sentience *n.* **1.** the simplest or most primitive form of cognition, consisting of a conscious awareness of stimuli without association or interpretation. **2.** the state of being SENTIENT.

sentience need in the PERSONOLOGY of U.S. psychologist Henry Alexander Murray (1893–1988), a need to enjoy sights, sounds, and other sensuous experiences.

sentient *adj.* capable of sensing and recognizing stimuli.

sentimentality *n.* the quality or condition of being excessively or affectedly swayed by emotional situations, especially those of a romantic or maudlin nature. See also EMOTIONALITY. **—sentimental** *adj.*

sentinel behavior a form of animal behavior in which one member of a group watches for potential predators while others in the group forage, rest, or engage in social interactions. Sentinel behavior is often seen in COOPERATIVE-BREEDING species, with different individuals taking turns as sentinels with those carrying young or feeding.

sentinel event in health administration, an unexpected occurrence or variation to service delivery involving death or serious physical or psychological injury. The event is called "sentinel" because it sends a signal or sounds a warning that requires immediate attention.

separated display in ergonomics, a machine display that separates critical information from more secondary information. The design is based upon the need to highlight important pieces of information so they stand out separately from other information on the display. Compare INTEGRATED DISPLAY.

separation anxiety the normal alarm or fear experienced by a young child separated (or facing the prospect of separation) from the person or people to whom he or she is attached (particularly parents). Separation anxiety is most active between 6 and 10 months. Separation from loved ones in later years may elicit similar anxiety.

separation anxiety disorder in *DSM–IV–TR*, an anxiety disorder occurring in childhood or adolescence that is characterized by developmentally inappropriate, persistent, and excessive anxiety about separation from the home or from major attachment figures. Other features may include marked ANTICIPATORY ANXIETY over upcoming separation and persistent and excessive worry about harm coming to attachment figures or about major events that might lead to separation from them (e.g., getting lost). There may also be SCHOOL REFUSAL, fear of being alone or going to sleep without major attachment figures present, separation-related nightmares, and repeated complaints of physical symptoms (e.g., vomiting, nausea, headaches, stomachaches) associated with anticipated separation. These symptoms cause clinically significant distress or impairment in functioning.

separation distress discomfort and anxiety felt by an individual upon losing contact with an attachment figure, for example, by a child upon losing contact with a caregiver or by an adult in reaction to the traumatic loss of a spouse or partner. See SEPARATION ANXIETY.

separation–individuation *n.* the developmental phase in which the infant gradually differentiates himself or herself from the mother, develops awareness of his or her separate identity, and attains relatively autonomous status. [defined by Austrian child psychoanalyst Margaret Mahler (1897–1985)]

sepsis *n.* the condition of tissues contaminated by the presence of pus-forming bacteria or other microorganisms or the toxic substances produced by such microorganisms. When spread throughout the bloodstream, the condition is called septicemia (see BLOOD POISONING). **—septic** *adj.*

sept *n.* a subdivision of a CLAN or other large social unit, especially one based on (supposed) common ancestry. In Scotland and Ireland a clan is often composed of several septs, which may be affiliated through a common loyalty or interest rather than a common ancestor. See also DESCENT GROUP.

septal area a region of the forebrain that contains the **septal nuclei** and the SEPTUM PELLUCIDUM, which separates the lateral ventricles. The septal nuclei, which include the NUCLEUS ACCUMBENS, form an integral part of the LIMBIC SYSTEM; they contribute fibers to the MEDIAL FOREBRAIN BUNDLE and have interconnections with the amygdala, hippocampus, and regions of the hypothalamus. Functionality of this area includes pleasure and anger suppression.

septicemia *n.* see BLOOD POISONING.

septum *n.* (*pl.* **septa**) a thin partition or dividing wall, such as the nasal septum (see NASAL CAVITY) or the SEPTUM PELLUCIDUM. —**septal** *adj.*

septum pellucidum a triangular, two-layered translucent membrane separating the anterior horns of the two LATERAL VENTRICLES of the brain. It touches the CORPUS CALLOSUM and the body of the FORNIX and is part of the SEPTAL AREA.

sequela *n.* (*pl.* **sequelae**) a residual effect of an illness or injury, often (but not necessarily) in the form of persistent or permanent impairment. Examples include paralysis, which may be the sequela of POLIOMYELITIS, and flashbacks, which may be the sequelae of traumatic stress.

sequence completion see NUMBER-COMPLETION TEST.

sequence effect in REPEATED MEASURES DESIGNS, the effect of the treatments being administered in a particular sequence (e.g., the sequence ABC versus ACB, versus BCA, and so forth). This is often confused with the ORDER EFFECT.

sequential analysis a class of statistical procedures in which a decision as to whether to continue collecting data is made as the experiment progresses. This approach is contrasted with studies in which the sample size is determined in advance and data is not analyzed until the entire sample is collected.

sequential effect in choice-reaction tasks, the influence of an immediately preceding trial (or trials) on performance in the current trial. Like PRIMING effects, sequential effects have both automatic and strategic components.

sequential marriage see SERIAL POLYGAMY.

sequential processing see SERIAL PROCESSING.

sequestration *n.* the process of separating the unacceptable or pathological aspects of one's personality from the normal part. For example, patients who cannot control their impulses and desires may isolate them from the rest of the self and become totally unaware of them.

Serax *n.* a trade name for OXAZEPAM.

serendipitous finding the accidental discovery of facts, artifacts, or relationships of scientific value.

serendipity *n.* the knack of making fortunate discoveries by accident. Serendipity is often considered a characteristic of the creative scientist. The word was coined in 1754 by British writer Horace Walpole (1717–1797) from the title of his story "The Three Princes of Serendip" (Serendip was an old Arabic name for Sri Lanka, whose princes were said to have had this ability).

Serentil *n.* a trade name for MESORIDAZINE.

serial anticipation method see ANTICIPATION LEARNING METHOD.

serial behavior an integrated sequence of responses that elicit each other in fixed order (e.g., playing music). The individual responses that comprise, and occupy specific positions within, the sequence are referred to as **serial responses**.

serial exhaustive search a hypothesized process of searching for a particular target item in SHORT-TERM MEMORY that involves inspecting each item in turn for a match.

serial-exploration method see METHOD OF JUST NOTICEABLE DIFFERENCES.

serial interpretation a psychoanalytic technique in which the analyst studies a series of consecutive DREAMS that, when taken as a group, provide clues that would be overlooked in interpretation of a single, isolated dream. See also RECURRENT DREAM.

serial killer an individual who repeatedly commits HOMICIDE, typically with a distinct pattern in terms of the selection of victims, location, and method.

serial learning the learning of a sequence of items or responses in the precise order of their presentation. For example, actors must learn their lines in sequence. Also called **serial-order learning**.

serial memory remembering a list of items in sequence. See SERIAL POSITION EFFECT; SERIAL RECALL.

serial-memory search a RETRIEVAL process in which each item in SHORT-TERM MEMORY is examined in the order in which it was entered into memory.

serial method an experimental method in which stimuli or cues are presented in a specific sequence.

serial monogamy see MONOGAMY.

serial polygamy a pattern of repeated marriage and divorce. Also called **sequential marriage**.

serial position curve a graphic representation of the number of items that can be remembered as a function of the order in which they were presented. Items at the beginning and end of the list are usually remembered best, thus producing a U-shaped memory curve.

serial position effect the effect of an item's position in a list of items to be learned on how well it is remembered. The classic serial position effect shows best recall of the first items from a list (see PRIMACY EFFECT) and good recall of the last items (see RECENCY EFFECT), while the middle items are less well recalled.

serial processing INFORMATION PROCESSING in which only one sequence of processing operations is carried on at a time. Those who hold that the human information-processing system operates in this way argue that the mind's apparent ability to carry on different cognitive functions simultaneously is explained by rapid shifts between different information sources. Also called **intermittent processing**; **sequential processing**. Compare PARALLEL PROCESSING. See also SINGLE-CHANNEL MODEL.

serial recall recalling items in the order in which they were presented. For instance, to remember a telephone number, the digits must be correctly sequenced. See also SERIAL MEMORY.

serial response see SERIAL BEHAVIOR.

serial search in a search task, the process of searching for one target at a time. Compare PARALLEL SEARCH.

series *n.* a collection of items (e.g., in a test or experiment) arranged in order with each item leading to the next.

SERMs abbreviation for selective estrogen receptor modulators. See ANTIESTROGEN.

Sernyl *n.* trade name for a brand of phencyclidine hydrochloride, an animal anesthetic with hallucinogenic properties sometimes taken as a drug of abuse (see PCP).

Seroquel *n.* a trade name for QUETIAPINE.

serotonergic neuron a neuron that releases or is activated by the neurotransmitter SEROTONIN. In the brain most serotogenic pathways originate in the RAPHE NUCLEUS and project diffusely to other sites in the brain and to the spinal cord.

serotonin *n.* a common monoamine neurotransmitter in the brain and other parts of the central nervous system, also found in the gastrointestinal tract, in smooth muscles of the cardiovascular and bronchial systems, and in blood platelets. It is synthesized from the dietary amino acid L-tryptophan (see TRYPTOPHAN HYDROXYLASE), and in the pineal gland it is converted to MELATONIN. Significant amounts of serotonin are found in the upper brainstem, particularly the RAPHE NUCLEUS. Serotonin is primarily degraded by MONOAMINE OXIDASE, which yields its principal metabolic product, 5-HYDROXYINDOLEACETIC ACID (5-HIAA). Serotonin has roles in numerous bioregulatory processes, including emotional processing, mood, appetite, and sleep as well as pain processing, hallucinations, and reflex regulation. For example, levels of serotonin correlate negatively with aggression, and release of serotonin may promote sleep. It is implicated in many psychological conditions, including depressive disorders, anxiety disorders, sleep disorders, aggression, and psychosis; many common psychotropic drugs affect NEUROTRANSMISSION mediated by serotonin. Also called **5-hydroxytryptamine** (**5-HT**).

serotonin and norepinephrine reuptake inhibitors see SNRIS.

serotonin antagonists agents that oppose the action of SEROTONIN. They include CYPROHEPTADINE and METHYSERGIDE, which are used for the prevention of migraine attacks, and the antiemetic ONDANSETRON. Also called **serotonin inhibitors**.

serotonin receptor any of various receptors that bind and respond to SEROTONIN (5-hydroxytryptamine; 5-HT). They occur in the brain and in peripheral areas and have different sensitivities that can be measured by susceptibility to ligands or blockers. At least 15 classes of serotonin receptors, affecting a variety of physiological and psychological processes, have been identified. They are designated by subscript numbers and letters (e.g., 5-HT_{1A}, 5-HT_{1B}, 5-HT_{1D}, 5-HT_{2A}, etc.).

serotonin-receptor agonists agents that increase the affinity for, or availability of, SEROTONIN at various SEROTONIN RECEPTORS in the brain or peripheral tissues. Commonly used INDIRECT AGONISTS are the SSRIS (e.g., fluoxetine, citalopram), which work by blocking the presynaptic reuptake of serotonin, thereby increasing the availability of serotonin at postsynaptic receptor sites. Other serotonin agonists exert their effects directly at the receptor site; for example, the TRIPTANS are direct agonists at receptor subtypes 5-HT_{1B} and 5-HT_{1D}. The anxiolytic agent BUSPIRONE is a PARTIAL AGONIST at the postsynaptic 5-HT_{1A} receptor, whereas the serotonin-like HALLUCINOGENS (e.g., LSD) act as partial agonists at 5-HT_{2A} receptors.

serotonin reuptake inhibitors (**SRIs**) see SSRIS.

serotonin syndrome a collection of symptoms, including agitation, confusion, delirium, and increased heart rate, due to excess activity of the neurotransmitter serotonin. It may result from drug interactions that increase amounts of available serotonin to toxic levels.

serous otitis media see OTITIS MEDIA.

Sertoli cell any of the elongated cells lining the SEMINIFEROUS TUBULES that protect and nourish developing sperm. As the sperm approach maturity, they become oriented in the seminiferous tubules so that they are partly embedded in the Sertoli cells. [Enrico **Sertoli** (1842–1910), Italian histologist]

sertraline *n.* an SSRI that is used for the treatment of depressive and anxiety disorders, including major depression, panic disorder, posttraumatic stress disorder, and obsessive-compulsive disorder. It has also been indicated for the treatment of premenstrual dysphoric disorder. U.S. trade name: **Zoloft**.

service delivery system see HUMAN SERVICE DELIVERY SYSTEM.

servomechanism *n.* a device that automatically activates changes or corrections in the performance of certain functions according to a predetermined SET POINT. For example, the cruise control of an automobile automatically adjusts engine output to maintain a constant speed. Also called **servo**. See also COMPARATOR.

SES abbreviation for SOCIOECONOMIC STATUS.

sessile *adj.* **1.** describing an organism that is permanently attached to the substrate, such as a sea anemone. **2.** attached broadly by a base, rather than by a stalklike structure, as in a sessile lesion.

set *n.* **1.** in behavioral psychology, a temporary readiness to respond in a certain way to a specific situation or stimulus. For example, a motorist gets set to move ahead when the light changes (a MOTOR SET); a sleeping mother is set to awaken when her baby stirs (a PERCEPTUAL SET); a bridge player is set to obey the rules of the game (a MENTAL SET). See PREPARATORY SET. See also AUFGABE; DETERMINING TENDENCY; EINSTELLUNG. **2.** in mathematics and logic, a collection of entities that is itself regarded as an entity. A set that is defined by a condition, such that its members must possess a particular attribute or attributes, is known as a CLASS.

SET acronym for STUDENTS' EVALUATION OF TEACHING.

set-level compatibility effect see STIMULUS–RESPONSE COMPATIBILITY.

set point the desired value in a SERVOMECHANISM, such as the level at which a thermostat is set to maintain a reasonably constant temperature. By extension to physiological and behavioral systems, set point refers to the preferred level of functioning of an organism or of a system within an organism. When a set point is exceeded (i.e., when physiological responses become higher than the set point), compensatory events take place to reduce functioning; when a set point is not reached, compensatory processes take place to help the organism or system reach the set point. In ATTACHMENT THEORY, the set point of attachment is physical proximity to a primary caregiver in conditions of threat, that is, threat leads the threatened individual to seek physical closeness to an attachment figure.

set theory *n.* the branch of mathematics and logic that is concerned with the properties of SETS (i.e., collections of entities that are themselves treated as entities). See also CLASS THEORY.

set-up *n.* the arrangement of equipment, data collectors, and participants required for a study.

set zone the range of a variable that a FEEDBACK SYSTEM tries to maintain. See also CRITICAL RANGE.

SEU see SUBJECTIVE–EXPECTED UTILITY.

seven plus or minus two the number of items that can be held in short-term memory at any given time and therefore accurately perceived and recalled after a brief exposure (see CHUNKING). The phrase originated in the title of an article (1956) by U.S. cognitive psychologist George Armitage Miller (1920–   ), "The magical number seven, plus or minus two: Some limitations on our capacity for processing information."

seventh cranial nerve see FACIAL NERVE.

severe mental retardation a diagnostic category applying to those with IQs of 20 to 30, comprising about 7% of people with MENTAL RETARDATION. These individuals typically do not acquire academic skills and frequently have sensory and motor problems. However, they are able to talk and can learn to dress, feed, and take care of themselves and to perform simple work under close supervision.

severity error a type of rating error in which the ratings are consistently overly negative, particularly with regard to the performance or ability of the participants. It is caused by the rater's tendency to be too strict or negative and thus to give undeservedly low scores. Compare LENIENCY ERROR.

sex *n.* **1.** the traits that distinguish between males and females. Sex refers especially to physical and biological traits, whereas GENDER refers especially to social or cultural traits, although the distinction between the two terms is not regularly observed. **2.** the physiological and psychological processes related to procreation and erotic pleasure.

sex change see SEX REVERSAL.

sex characteristics the traits associated with sex identity. **Primary sex characteristics** (e.g., testes in males, ovaries in females) are directly involved in reproduction of the species. **Secondary sex characteristics** are features not directly concerned with reproduction, such as voice quality and the presence or absence of facial hair and breasts. Also called **sexual characteristics**.

sex chromatin a condensed mass of CHROMATIN that is observed in the nucleus of nondividing SOMATIC cells of females. It is not observed in the somatic cells of normal males. The substance represents X-chromosome material that is not involved in somatic-cell metabolism. The presence of sex chromatin in somatic cells is generally regarded as proof of the sexual identity of females. Also called **Barr body**. See also CHROMATIN NEGATIVE; CHROMATIN POSITIVE.

sex-chromosomal aberration any disorder of structure, function, or both that is associated with the complete or partial absence of a sex chromosome or with the presence of extra sex chromosomes. Examples of such disorders are KLINEFELTER'S SYNDROME, XYY SYNDROME, and TURNER'S SYNDROME.

sex chromosome a chromosome that determines the sex of an individual. Humans and other mammals have two sex chromosomes: the X CHROMOSOME, which carries genes for certain sexual traits and occurs in both females and males; and the smaller Y CHROMOSOME, which is normally found only in males. An individual usually is considered to be a female if the body cells contain the XX combination of chromosomes and male if the cells contain the XY combination, regardless of physical traits or signs of hermaphroditism. Disease genes that are carried only on a sex chromosome (usually the X chromosome) are responsible for SEX-LINKED inherited conditions.

sex counseling see SEXUAL COUNSELING.

sex determination the genetic mechanism that determines the sex of the offspring. In humans a fertilized egg with two X CHROMOSOMES becomes a female, and a fertilized egg with one X and one Y CHROMOSOME becomes a male. See SEX DIFFERENTIATION.

sex differences **1.** the differences in physical features between males and females. These include differences in brain structures as well as differences in primary and secondary SEX CHARACTERISTICS. **2.** the differences between males and females in the way they behave and think. Sex differences are often viewed as driven by actual biological gender disparity (nature), rather than by differing environmental factors (nurture), and affect both cognition and behavior. See also GENDER DIFFERENCES. Compare SEX ROLE.

sex differentiation the process of acquiring distinctive sexual features during the course of development. Human sexual differentiation is determined genetically at the time of fertilization, primarily by the presence or absence of a Y CHROMOSOME. Fertilized eggs containing a Y chromosome develop as male embryos, whereas ones lacking a Y chromosome develop as females. This is due to the presence on the Y chromosome of a particular gene, called *SRY* (*sex reversal on Y*). It encodes a testis-determining factor that, via a cascade of signals, triggers the development of testes and other male reproductive organs. In the absence of this gene, the embryo develops along the default, female pathway, with ovaries and other female organs.

sex discrimination differential treatment of individuals on the basis of their gender. Although such treatment may favor women relative to men, in contemporary society most sex discrimination favors men over women; its usual manifestations include unfair hiring and promotion practices, lower wages paid to women doing the same type of work as men, and a tendency to undervalue characteristics and interests associated with women rather than men. Changing attitudes toward marriage, improved availability of day-care facilities, increased educational opportunities, role changes in the home, and workforce shortages in certain industries have led to a heightened awareness of the erroneous nature of GENDER STEREOTYPES and altered conceptions of what men and women can do. In addition, in many societies, legislation prohibits sex discrimination. Nevertheless, sex discrimination persists and contributes to a number of social problems, including inadequate support for working women, lower standards of health care for women, and violence against women. Also called **gender discrimination**; **sexual discrimination**. See also GLASS CEILING; PREJUDICE; SEXISM.

sex distribution see SEX RATIO.

sex drive the drive for sexual gratification and, ultimately, for sexual reproduction. Although it is not necessary for an individual's survival, it is considered a PRIMARY DRIVE as it is essential for species survival. In many animals, sexual activity is cyclical (e.g., seasonal or dependent on cyclical hormone release), although a variety of factors (e.g., external stimulation) may arouse the drive. Also called **sexual drive**. See LIBIDO.

sex education a formal course of instruction in reproductive processes that is presented in a classroom setting. Sex education ideally provides young adolescents with authoritative and objective information about both the psychological and physical aspects of sexual behavior.

sex feeling the pleasurable feeling associated with coitus or other sexual contact. Also called **sexual feeling**.

sex hormone any of the hormones that stimulate various reproductive functions. Primary sources of sex hormones are the male and female gonads (i.e., testis and ovary), which are stimulated to produce sex hormones by the pituitary hormones FOLLICLE-STIMULATING HORMONE and LUTEINIZING HORMONE. The principal male sex hormones (ANDROGENS) include testosterone; female sex hormones include the ESTROGENS, PROGESTERONE, and PROLACTIN.

sex hygiene the health-maintenance procedures related to sexual activity, for example, the prevention or control of sexually transmitted infections. Also called **sexual hygiene**.

sex identification see SEXUAL IDENTIFICATION.

sex identity **1.** the purely biologically determined sexual condition or status of an individual. **2.** learned, or socialized, identity relating to an individual's sex. See also GENDER IDENTITY.

sex-influenced character an inherited trait that is dominant in one sex but recessive in the other. For example, male-pattern baldness is controlled by an allele that seems to be dominant in men but recessive in women. Hence its full effects usually appear only in men.

sex instinct see SEXUAL INSTINCT.

sex interest a readiness to engage or participate in discussions, viewing, or other activities related to or leading to sexual contact. Also called **sexual interest**.

sexism *n.* discriminatory and prejudicial beliefs and practices directed against one of the two sexes, usually women. A sexist culture assigns predetermined economic, social, familial, and emotional roles to men and women on the basis of SEX-ROLE STEREOTYPES, reinforced by economic and social organization and justified by reference to women's reproductive role as childbearer. See also SEX DISCRIMINATION; PREJUDICE. **—sexist** *adj.*

sex-limited *adj.* describing a trait or anomaly that is expressed only in one sex, despite being determined by genes carried on the AUTOSOMES rather than the sex chromosomes. For example, the genes governing the development of ovaries and breasts are expressed only in females, whereas genes determining sperm production are expressed only in males.

sex-linked *adj.* describing a gene that is located on one of the SEX CHROMOSOMES, usually the X CHROMOSOME (**X-linked**), or a trait determined by such a gene. Sex-linked diseases, such as hemophilia, generally affect only males, because the defective gene is usually a RECESSIVE ALLELE. In females, who have two X chromosomes, it would be masked by the normal, dominant allele on the other X chromosome. In males, with just a single X chromosome, any sex-linked defective allele is expressed.

sex-negativity *n.* a negative attitude or stance toward any sexual behavior other than procreative marital coitus. Compare SEX-POSITIVITY.

sex object see SEXUAL OBJECT.

sex offense a sex act that is prohibited by law. An individual who has committed such an offense is called a **sex offender**. Some crimes are acts of violence involving sex, and others are violations of social taboos; there is much variation, by culture and jurisdiction, concerning which behaviors are considered crimes and how they may be punished. Some jurisdictions consider certain consensual sex acts to be illegal. Examples of sex offenses include forcible and statutory rape, incest, prostitution and pimping, bestiality, sodomy, sex murder, and forcible sexual assault without coitus. Also called **sexual offense**. See also MOLESTATION.

sexological examination the study of an individual's sexual behavior in terms of physiological, psychological, sociological, and specific genetic and environmental influences.

sexology *n.* the study of sexuality, particularly among human beings, including the anatomy, physiology, and psychology of sexual activity and reproduction. **—sexological** *adj.* **—sexologist** *n.*

sex perversion see SEXUAL PERVERSION.

sex-positivity *n.* a positive attitude or stance toward sexual activity between consenting individuals where this is seen as promoting healthy relationships and forms of self-expression. Sex is seen as neither good nor bad, per se, and the purpose of sexual relations is not deemed to be confined exclusively to procreation through marital coitus. Compare SEX-NEGATIVITY.

sex preselection predetermination of the sex of offspring through sex-control technology.

sex ratio the proportion of males to females in a given population at a given specified life stage, primarily conception (see CONCEPTION RATIO) or birth (see BIRTH RATIO) but also at any stage between birth and death. Also called **sex distribution**.

sex reversal the alteration of an individual's sex characteristics, by means of surgery and hormone treatment, in order to make that person physically resemble, as closely as possible, a person of the opposite sex. The procedure is also used to establish the physical features of one particular sex in HERMAPHRODITES or pseudohermaphrodites (see PSEUDOHERMAPHRODITISM). Also called **sex change**. See also GENDER REASSIGNMENT; TRANSSEXUALISM.

sex reversal on Y (**SRY**) a region of the Y CHROMOSOME that determines the sex of the individual. See SEX DIFFERENTIATION.

sex role the behavior and attitudinal patterns characteristically associated with masculinity or femininity as defined in a given society. Sex roles reflect the interaction between biological heritage and the pressures of socialization. The term refers to overt behavior and must be distinguished from GENDER IDENTITY, although the two usually match. The extent to which an individual manifests typical sex-role behavior varies greatly according to familial and cultural influences. Also called **sexual role**.

sex-role inversion a former name for TRANSSEXUALISM.

sex-role reversal a form of animal behavior in which each sex behaves in a manner typical of the other sex. For example, in some insects and fish males take full responsibility for care of the offspring, and in some polyandrous birds females are aggressive and defend territories.

sex-role stereotype a fixed, overly simplified concept of the social roles that are believed to be appropriate to each sex. See also GENDER STEREOTYPES.

sex selection see SEXUAL SELECTION.

sex sensations the effects of stimulation of the genitalia and other erogenous zones. Also called **sexual sensations**.

sex service see PROSTITUTION.

sex steroid any of the steroid hormones secreted by the gonads. See SEX HORMONE.

sex therapy the treatment of sexual disorders using techniques that are specific to the problem and its severity. Sex therapy generally involves psychological or psychiatric treatment but may also include medical interventions with specific medications or procedures. The usual treatment involves cognitive-behavioral therapy plus systemic therapy for relationship-based problems. Additional elements include correcting misinformation and teaching the basic facts about sex anatomy, physiology, and techniques, often using educational books or videos.

sex typing any form of behavior or any attitude that results from the process of socialization regarding what a particular culture deems to be an appropriate activity or expression of maleness and femaleness.

sexual abuse violation or exploitation by sexual means. Sexual abuse of children includes all sexual contact between adults and children. Sexual abuse can also occur in other relationships of trust.

sexual addiction a problematic sexual behavior, such as a PARAPHILIA or HYPERSEXUALITY, regarded as a form of addiction similar to drug addiction. The defining features of a sexual addiction include sexual behavior that has become out of control, has severely negative consequences, and that the addict is unable to stop, despite a wish to do so. Other features include persistence in high-risk, self-destructive behavior; spending large amounts of time in sexual activity or fantasy; neglect of social, occupational, or other activities; and mood changes associated with sexual activity.

sexual adjustment the process of establishing a satisfactory relationship with one or more sexual partners. Sexual adjustment may depend on psychological as well as physical factors.

sexual aggression aggression directed by one sex toward the other, often in the context of MATING BEHAVIOR. In species where males are much larger than females, it is thought that a male uses sexual aggression to achieve copulation with females whether or not the females want to mate with that male. See ANIMAL AGGRESSION.

sexual and gender identity disorders in *DSM–IV–TR*, a category of disorders of sexuality stemming from psychological rather than organic factors. It includes SEXUAL DYSFUNCTIONS, PARAPHILIAS, and GENDER IDENTITY DISORDERS.

sexual anesthesia an absence of normal sensation during sexual activity, including coitus. Sexual anesthesia is usually psychogenic. However, although some patients report they obtain sexual pleasure in masturbation but not in sexual activity with a partner, many derive no pleasure from any form of sexual behavior. See also ERECTILE DYSFUNCTION; FEMALE SEXUAL AROUSAL DISORDER.

sexual anomaly a congenital or developmental abnormality of the reproductive system, for example, the presence of both male and female gonads in an infant.

sexual apathy lack of interest in sexual activity. See HYPOACTIVE SEXUAL DESIRE DISORDER.

sexual arousal a state of PHYSIOLOGICAL AROUSAL elicited by sexual contact or by other erotic stimulation (e.g., fantasies, dreams, odors, or objects), resulting in impulses being transmitted through the central nervous system to the sacral region of the spinal cord. The impulses also trigger the release of sex hormones, dilation of the arteries supplying the genital areas, and inhibition of vasoconstrictor centers of the lumbar nerves. The effects of sexual arousal are mediated through the hypothalamus. See SEXUAL-RESPONSE CYCLE.

sexual arousal disorders see MALE ERECTILE DISORDER; FEMALE SEXUAL AROUSAL DISORDER.

sexual assault violent sexual penetration of an individual. It includes forced vaginal, oral, and anal penetration. See also RAPE.

sexual attitude reassessment workshop (SAR workshop) a group educational experience in which participants view films on such issues as same-sex sexual orientation, sex in aging, sexual values, and education about sex. The workshop also involves group discussion and personal reflection on these issues.

sexual attitudes values and beliefs about sexuality. Manifested in a person's individual sexual behavior, these attitudes are based on family and cultural views about sexuality, sex education (both formal and informal), and prior sexual experiences.

sexual attraction the first step in the MATING BEHAVIOR of many animals, in which animals emit stimuli that attract members of the opposite sex.

sexual aversion disorder in *DSM–IV–TR*, negative emotional reactions (e.g., anxiety, fear, or disgust) to sexual activity, leading to active avoidance of it and causing distress in the individual or his or her partner. This can be lifelong or acquired, and although it usually applies to all sexual activity (**generalized type**), it may be specific to only some activities or some partners (**situational type**). This aversion is not caused by a medical condition, a medication, or a drug side effect.

sexual behavior actions related to reproduction or to stimulation of the sex organs for pleasurable satisfaction without conception. Sexual behavior may include orientation of the partners in some form of COURTSHIP BEHAVIOR, postural accommodations for intercourse, and genital reflexes. In some species, sexual behavior may occur only at certain seasons or at specific stages of the ESTROUS CYCLE. Nonconceptive sexual behavior occurs in many species, including human beings, and may function to maintain social relationships or PAIR BONDS or to confuse mates about CERTAINTY OF PATERNITY.

sexual burnout loss of sexual function or interest due to a period of excessively frequent or demanding sexual activity. Sexual burnout also sometimes refers to the effects of advancing age on sexual activity, although age itself does not lead to loss of sexual interest or functioning.

sexual characteristics see SEX CHARACTERISTICS.

sexual conditioning the learning of cues that predict opportunities for mating so that these learned cues subsequently control sexual behavior. In both fish and birds, sexual conditioning that predicts when a mate will be present increases the REPRODUCTIVE SUCCESS of the conditioned males. See also SEXUAL IMPRINTING.

sexual contact any person-to-person contact that involves touching or connection of genital or erogenous skin or membrane surfaces, as in fondling, kissing, biting, or coitus.

sexual counseling guidance provided by therapists to sex partners in such matters as birth control, infertility, and general feelings of inadequate sexual performance. Working on specific SEXUAL DYSFUNCTION problems is usually considered to be SEX THERAPY rather than sexual counseling. Also called **sex counseling**.

sexual curiosity curiosity and interest in learning about sex and sexuality. In some cases this alone may be sufficient to produce sexual gratification or orgasm.

sexual desire disorders see HYPOACTIVE SEXUAL DESIRE DISORDER; SEXUAL AVERSION DISORDER.

sexual development the progression toward sexual maturity, in attitudes and behavior as well as in physical characteristics, from infancy through puberty. See also PSYCHOSEXUAL DEVELOPMENT.

sexual deviancy any sexual behavior that is regarded as significantly different from the standards established by a culture or subculture. The corresponding term in *DSM–IV–TR* is PARAPHILIA. Deviant forms of sexual behavior may include voyeurism, fetishism, bestiality, necrophilia, transvestism, sadism, and exhibitionism. Same-sex sexual behavior is considered deviant in some cultures, but not by most mental health professionals. Also called **sexual deviation**. See also SEXUAL PERVERSION.

sexual differentiation see SEX DIFFERENTIATION.

sexual dimorphism the existence within a species of males and females that differ distinctly from each other in form. See SEX CHARACTERISTICS; SEX DIFFERENCES.

sexual discrimination see SEX DISCRIMINATION.

sexual disorder any impairment of sexual function or behavior. Sexual disorders include SEXUAL DYSFUNCTION and PARAPHILIAS. See also SEXUAL AND GENDER IDENTITY DISORDERS.

sexual disorder not otherwise specified in *DSM–IV–TR*, a sexual problem that does not meet diagnostic criteria for SEXUAL DYSFUNCTION or PARAPHILIA. Examples include feelings of inadequacy about sexual performance, persistent and marked distress about sexual orientation (see EGO-DYSTONIC HOMOSEXUALITY), and distress about a pattern of repeated unsatisfactory or exploitative sexual relationships.

sexual drive see SEX DRIVE.

sexual dysfunction in *DSM–IV–TR*, a category of sexual disorders characterized by problems in one or more phases of the SEXUAL-RESPONSE CYCLE. Sexual dysfunctions include HYPOACTIVE SEXUAL DESIRE DISORDER, SEXUAL AVERSION DISORDER, FEMALE SEXUAL AROUSAL DISORDER, PRIMARY ERECTILE DYSFUNCTION, SECONDARY ERECTILE DYSFUNCTION, PREMATURE EJACULATION, MALE ORGASMIC DISORDER, FEMALE ORGASMIC DISORDER, DYSPAREUNIA, and VAGINISMUS.

sexual dysfunction not otherwise specified in *DSM–IV–TR*, a category that includes sexual dysfunctions outside the standard specific categories, such as absence of erotic sensations despite physiologically normal sexual excitement and orgasm or a dysfunction that may be due to a medical condition or substance abuse.

sexual erethism abnormal irritability or unpleasant sensitivity to stimulation of the sexual organs. It may be seen in individuals with SEXUAL AVERSION DISORDER.

sexual fantasy pleasant mental images or stories of sexual activity, not constrained by such real-world issues as partner availability or setting and situation.

sexual feeling see SEX FEELING.

sexual functioning the performance of sexual intercourse or the capability of performing sexual intercourse.

sexual harassment conduct of a sexual nature that is unwelcome or considered offensive, particularly in the workplace. In the United States, under Title VII of the 1964 Civil Rights Act, an employee is entitled to sue employers for sexual harassment. According to the U.S. EQUAL EMPLOYMENT OPPORTUNITY COMMISSION (EEOC), there are two forms of sexual harassment: QUID PRO QUO and behavior that makes for a HOSTILE WORK ENVIRONMENT. See also HARRIS V. FORKLIFT SYSTEMS INC.; MERITOR SAVINGS BANK V. VINSON; REASONABLE PERSON STANDARD.

sexual hygiene see SEX HYGIENE.

sexual identification the gradual adoption of the attitudes and behavior patterns associated with being male or female. A clear concept of sexual identity gradually develops out of a perception of physical sex differences, starting during the first 3 or 4 years of life, and, somewhat later, awareness of psychological differences determined by the particular culture and particular family. Also called **sex identification**. See SEX ROLE.

sexual identity 1. the individual's internal identification with heterosexual, homosexual, or bisexual preference, that is, with his or her SEXUAL ORIENTATION. **2.** an occasional synonym for SEX IDENTITY or GENDER IDENTITY.

sexual imprinting the development of a preference for a sexual partner during a sensitive or CRITICAL PERIOD. For example, if zebra finches are cross-fostered to Bengalese finch parents for the first 40 days of life, they will prefer to mate with Bengalese finches as adults. Birds prefer to socialize with other birds that resemble those they were exposed to in the first month of life.

sexual infantilism the tendency of a mature person to engage in sexual behavior characteristic of a small child. Sexual infantilism may be manifested in certain sexual disorders, such as VOYEURISM, FETISHISM, or in lovemaking that is limited to acts of foreplay (e.g., kissing, biting, or stroking the skin).

sexual inhibition suppression of the sexual impulse or the inability to feel sexual desire, to perform sexually, or to experience sexual gratification. See HYPOACTIVE SEXUAL DESIRE DISORDER; FEMALE ORGASMIC DISORDER; MALE ORGASMIC DISORDER.

sexual instinct 1. the basic drive or urge to preserve the species through mating and the activities that precede it, or, by extension, simply to express the self and the self's physiological and psychological needs through sexual activity. **2.** in psychoanalytic theory, the instinct comprising all the erotic drives and sublimations of such drives. It includes not only genital sex, but also anal and oral manifestations and the channeling of erotic energy into artistic, scientific, and other pursuits. In his later formulations, Sigmund FREUD saw the sexual instinct as part of a wider LIFE INSTINCT that also included the self-preservative impulses of hunger, thirst, and elimination. Also called **sex instinct**. See also EROS; LIBIDO; SELF-PRESERVATION INSTINCT.

sexual intercourse see COITUS.

sexual interest see SEX INTEREST.

sexual inversion see INVERSION.

sexual involution sexual behavior that features deviant, unusual, involved, complicated, or ritualistic elements. PARAPHILIAS are considered to be an example of sexual involution.

sexuality *n.* **1.** the capacity to derive pleasure from all forms of sexual activity and behavior, particularly from sexual intercourse. **2.** all aspects of sexual behavior, including gender identity, orientation, attitudes, and activity. **3.** in psychoanalytic theory, the "organ pleasure" derived from all EROGENOUS ZONES and processes of the body, including the mouth, anus, urethra, breasts, skin, muscles, and genital organs, as well as such functions as sucking, biting, eating, defecating, urinating, masturbation, and intercourse.

Sexuality Information and Education Council of the United States (**SIECUS**) a nonprofit organization founded in 1964 that develops, collects, and disseminates information about sexuality, promotes sex education, and advocates the right of individuals to make sexual choices.

sexualization *n.* see EROTIZATION.

sexual latency in psychoanalytic theory, the period from about 6 years of age until puberty, when the child has little, if any, interest in sex.

sexual liberation 1. the state of being free from sexual mores or inhibitions that are considered restrictive. See FREE LOVE. **2.** any social trend or process toward increased sexual freedoms.

sexual lifestyle an individual pattern of sexual behavior in terms of orientation, number of partners, and types of sexual activity engaged in. Sexual lifestyle reflects such influences as early childhood observations of the family of origin, experiences with male and female contacts in childhood and adolescence, and cultural or religious values.

sexually dimorphic nucleus a NUCLEUS of the central nervous system that differs in size between males and females. In humans, for example, a nucleus in the MEDIAL PREOPTIC AREA of the hypothalamus that synthesizes GONADOTROPIN-RELEASING HORMONE tends to be larger and more active in males than in females because gonadotropin release is continuous (it is cyclical in females). In songbirds where males sing more than females, several brain nuclei associated with both song learning and song production are larger in males than in females.

sexually transmitted disease (**STD**) an infection transmitted by sexual activity. More than 20 STDs have been identified, including those caused by viruses (e.g., hepatitis B, herpes, and HIV) and those caused by bacteria (e.g., chlamydia, gonorrhea, and syphilis). STDs are also known as **venereal diseases**, the term used traditionally for syphilis and gonorrhea.

sexual masochism in *DSM–IV–TR*, a PARAPHILIA in which sexual interest and arousal is repeatedly or exclusively achieved through being humiliated, bound, beaten, or otherwise made to suffer physical harm or threat to life. For the diagnosis, these activities must occur in real life, not fantasy, and must actually cause pain, not merely simulate painful experiences.

sexual maturation the stage of development of the reproductive system at which coitus and reproduction can be achieved.

sexual metamorphosis a rare delusion in which the individual believes that his or her biological sex has been changed into the opposite sex.

sexual negativism a lack of interest in sex that can be attributed to a deficit of sexual hormones. [described by German sexologist Magnus Hirschfeld (1868–1935)]

sexual object 1. in general language, a person regarded only in terms of his or her sexual attractiveness. **2.** in psychoanalytic theory, a person, animal, or inanimate object external to the individual's own body or psyche toward whom or which the sexual energy of an individual is directed. Also called **sex object**.

sexual offense see SEX OFFENSE.

sexual orientation one's enduring sexual attraction to male partners, female partners, or both. Sexual orientation may be heterosexual, same-sex (gay or lesbian), or bisexual. Also called **gender orientation**; **object choice**.

sexual orientation grid a method of classifying SEXUAL ORIENTATION on the basis of seven factors: sexual fantasy, sexual attraction, sexual behavior, emotional attraction, social attraction, social behavior, and self-identity. Each of these factors is evaluated in three time periods: past, present, and ideal future. Thus, a person's sexual orientation is described in terms of positions in a 3 × 7 grid. [developed by U.S. psychiatrist Fritz Klein (1932–), who considered Alfred KINSEY's single-scale of sexual orientation to be too simplistic]

sexual pain disorders see DYSPAREUNIA; VAGINISMUS.

sexual perversion any sexual practice that is regarded by a community or culture as an abnormal means of achieving orgasm or sexual arousal. In some cultures, sexual perversion is applied to any practice other than penile–vaginal intercourse between a woman and her husband. In Western societies it refers to those practices that deviate most widely from the norm, such as sadism, masochism, necrophilia, exhibitionism, pedophilia, fetishism, voyeurism, and zoophilia. The *DSM–IV–TR* designation for sexual perversion is PARAPHILIA. Also called **sex perversion**.

sexual preference 1. loosely, SEXUAL ORIENTATION. **2.** any particular sexual interest and arousal pattern, which may range from the relatively common (e.g., particular patterns of foreplay, particular positions) to those associated with a PARAPHILIA.

sexual reassignment see GENDER REASSIGNMENT.

sexual receptivity see RECEPTIVITY.

sexual reflex 1. penile erection produced by stimulation of the male genitalia. **2.** vaginal secretion and lubrication and swelling of the clitoris produced by stimulation of the female genitalia. **3.** the reflex activity involved in ORGASM. **4.** components of sexual behavior, such as the CREMASTERIC REFLEX, that are not under direct control of the higher brain levels and may be stimulated through spinal or bulbar neural connections.

sexual response a reaction to sexual stimulation. The most noticeable sexual response in the male is erection of the penis. See SEXUAL AROUSAL.

sexual-response cycle a four-stage cycle of sexual response that is exhibited by both men and women, differing only in aspects determined by male or female anatomy. The stages include the **arousal** (or **excitement**) **phase**, which lasts several minutes to hours (see SEXUAL AROUSAL); the **plateau phase**, lasting 30 s to 3 min, marked by penile erection in men and vaginal lubrication in women; the **orgasmic phase**, lasting 15 s and marked by EJACULATION in men and ORGASM in women; and the **resolution phase**, lasting 15 min to 1 day (see REFRACTORY PHASE).

sexual revolution either of two periods in U.S. (and, to some extent, European) history marked by a significant change in sexual values and behavior. The first sexual revolution occurred in the early part of the 20th century, after the end of the Victorian era, and involved efforts to increase sexual knowledge, legitimize women's enjoyment of sex, and eliminate prostitution. The second sexual revolution, during the 1960s, was stimulated by such events as the development of oral contraception and the publication of the KINSEY reports on the sexual behavior of men and women. This led to more openness of sexual expression in literature and the media, an increase in sexual activity, more tolerance of what were previously considered "deviant" activities, and more acceptance of female sexuality.

sexual role see SEX ROLE.

sexual sadism a PARAPHILIA in which sexual excitement is achieved by intentional infliction of physical or psychological suffering on another person. The harm may be inflicted on a consenting partner, typically involving mildly injurious bodily suffering combined with humiliation. When practiced with nonconsenting partners, sexual sadism may involve inflicting extensive, permanent, or possibly fatal bodily injury. This activity is likely to be repeated, with the severity of the sadistic acts increasing over time. See also SADISM; SADOMASOCHISM.

sexual selection a theoretical mechanism for the evolution of anatomical and behavioral differences between males and females, based on the selection of mates (see MATE SELECTION). [proposed in 1871 by British naturalist Charles Darwin (1809–1882)]

sexual sensations see SEX SENSATIONS.

sexual stimulation see GENITAL STIMULATION.

sexual synergism sexual arousal that results from a combination of stimuli experienced at the same time. The stimuli may appear to be somewhat contradictory, such as love and hate, fear, pain, or fright.

sexual tension a condition of anxiety and restlessness associated with the sex drive and a normal desire for release of sexual energy. Sexual tension may be complicated by fear of inadequate performance, fear of an unwanted pregnancy, fear of discovery, or other concerns.

sexual trauma any disturbing experience associated with sexual activity. Rape, incest, and other sexual offenses may be causes of sexual trauma in older children and adults. It is one of the most common causes of POSTTRAUMATIC DISORDERS and DISSOCIATIVE DISORDERS.

sexual-value system 1. the system of sexual stimulation and response that an individual feels is necessary for a satisfactory sexual relationship. **2.** a person's beliefs about what is normal, moral, and acceptable sexual behavior and activity.

s factor abbreviation for a designated SPECIFIC FACTOR or SPECIAL FACTOR identified through the factor analysis of ability tests. The s factor for a particular test represents the SPECIFIC ABILITY required for successful performance in the tested area.

shade *n.* any colored or uncolored stimulus defined by the amount of black it contains.

shading *n.* gradations of darkness on the surface of a real object or a depiction of an object, providing a DEPTH CUE.

shadow *n.* in the ANALYTIC PSYCHOLOGY of Carl JUNG, an ARCHETYPE that represents the "darker side" of the human psyche, mainly the sexual and aggressive instincts that tend to be unacceptable to the conscious ego and that are more comfortably projected onto others.

shadowing *n.* in cognitive testing, a task in which a participant repeats aloud a message word for word at the same time that the message is being presented, often with other stimuli being presented in the background. It is mainly used in studies of ATTENTION.

shadow jury a group of people hired by a TRIAL CONSULTANT to watch trials and report their impressions of the evidence presented. Attorneys use this feedback in the development of their trial strategies.

shaken baby the neurological consequences of a form of child abuse in which a small child or infant is repeatedly shaken. The shaking causes diffuse, widespread damage to the brain; in severe cases it may cause death.

shaking palsy an archaic name for PARKINSON'S DISEASE.

Shakow, David (1901–1981) U.S. psychologist. Shakow earned a doctorate in psychology from Harvard University in 1942, having worked concurrently at the Worcester State Hospital in Massachusetts since 1928. He subsequently held positions at the College of Medicine at the University of Illinois, the University of Chicago, and the National Institute of Mental Health, where he was chief of the laboratory in psychology from 1956 to 1966. His main areas of research were in psychoanalysis and in the motor performance of patients with schizophrenia. However, he is perhaps best known for his work in helping the American Psychological Association to professionalize the field of CLINICAL PSYCHOLOGY in the mid- to late 1940s. Shakow was instrumental in developing a model and drafting criteria for the training of the clinical psychologist as therapist, researcher, and diagnostician—the SCIENTIST-PRACTITIONER MODEL. This training model dominated clinical psychology for several decades and is still prominent.

shallow affect impaired ability to react emotionally, even in situations that usually arouse intense feeling. Also called **shallowness of affect**. See also FLAT AFFECT.

shallow processing cognitive processing of a stimulus that focuses on its superficial, perceptual characteristics rather than its meaning. It is considered that processing at this shallow level produces weaker, shorter-lasting memories than DEEP PROCESSING. See LEVELS-OF-PROCESSING MODEL OF MEMORY. See also BOTTOM-UP PROCESSING; DATA-DRIVEN PROCESS. [proposed in 1972 by Canadian psychologists Fergus I. M. Craik (1935–) and Robert S. Lockhart]

shaman *n.* in various indigenous cultures, especially those that include nature and ancestor worship, a spiritual leader, male or female, who uses allegedly supernatural or magical powers for divination (particularly diagnosis) and to heal mental or physical illness. The status of shamans is not conferred by recognized organizations but is held to arise from a significant personal physical or mental crisis or to be hereditary. **Shamanism** includes a wide spectrum of traditional beliefs and practices, many of which involve communication with the spirit and animal worlds in pursuit of physical or mental healing. **—shamanic** *adj.* **—shamanistic** *adj.*

shamanic trance an ALTERED STATE OF CONSCIOUSNESS induced by hallucinogens, rhythmic actions and music, suggestion, experiences of possession, or by similar means. See SHAMAN.

sham disorder a colloquial name for FACTITIOUS DISORDER.

shame *n.* a highly unpleasant SELF-CONSCIOUS EMOTION arising from the sense of there being something dishonorable, ridiculous, immodest, or indecorous in one's conduct or circumstances. It is typically characterized by withdrawal from social intercourse, for example by hiding or distracting the attention of another from one's shameful action, which can have a profound effect on psychological adjustment and interpersonal relationships. Shame may motivate not only avoidant behavior, but also defensive, retaliative anger. Psychological research consistently reports a relationship between proneness to shame and a whole host of psychological symptoms, including depression, anxiety, eating disorders, subclinical sociopathy, and low self-esteem. Shame is also theorized to play a more positive adaptive function by regulating experiences of excessive and inappropriate interest and excitement and by diffusing potentially threatening social behavior. **—shameful** *adj.*

shame culture a society, or a trend or organizing principle within a society, characterized by a strong desire to preserve honor and avoid shame. Compare GUILT CULTURE.

shamelessness *n.* behavior marked by an apparent absence of feelings of shame. This may arise as the result of psychological problems or reflect a loss of judgment after brain injury. **—shameless** *adj.*

sham feeding in animal research, a procedure in which the subject chews and swallows food, but the food is extracted through a tube surgically implanted in the esophagus so that it does not reach the stomach.

sham surgery in experiments using surgical interventions, surgery that functions as a CONTROL because it mimics the features of the experimental surgery but does not result in the alteration or removal of any bodily structures, that is, it does not have the systemic effects of the experimental procedure. Also called **sham operation**.

shape *n.* the spatial form of an object as it stands out from its background.

shape coding in ergonomics, coding a control or display by shape so that it can be readily distinguished from other controls or displays. See CONTROL DISCRIMINABILITY.

shape constancy a type of PERCEPTUAL CONSTANCY in which an object is perceived as having the same shape when viewed at different angles. For example, a plate viewed at an angle still appears circular rather than elliptical.

shaping *n.* the production of new forms of OPERANT BEHAVIOR by reinforcement of successive approximations to the behavior (see METHOD OF SUCCESSIVE APPROXIMA-

TIONS). Also called **approximation conditioning**; **behavior shaping**.

Shapiro–Wilks test a statistical test for testing the hypothesis that a sample was drawn from a population with a NORMAL DISTRIBUTION. [Samuel S. **Shapiro** (1930–) and Samuel Stanley **Wilks** (1906–1964), U.S. statisticians]

shared attention see JOINT ATTENTION.

shared environment in behavior genetic analyses, those aspects of an environment that individuals living together (e.g., biologically related individuals in a family household) share and that therefore cause them to become more similar to each other than would be expected on the basis of genetic influences alone. Examples of shared environmental factors include parental child-rearing style, divorce, or family income and related variables. Compare NONSHARED ENVIRONMENT.

shared mental model see TEAM MENTAL MODEL.

shared paranoid disorder in *DSM–III*, a disorder characterized by a persecutory DELUSIONAL SYSTEM that develops as a result of a close relationship with another person or (rarely) persons who already have such delusional beliefs. This disorder has been subsumed under the *DSM–IV–TR* category of SHARED PSYCHOTIC DISORDER.

shared psychotic disorder in *DSM–IV–TR*, a disorder in which the essential feature is an identical or similar delusion that develops in an individual who is involved with another individual (sometimes called the **inducer** or the **primary case**) who already has a psychotic disorder with prominent delusions. Shared psychotic disorder can involve many people (e.g., an entire family), but is most commonly seen in relationships of only two, in which case it is known as FOLIE À DEUX. In *DSM–III–R*, shared psychotic disorder was referred to as **induced psychotic disorder**.

sharpening *n.* a phenomenon in which some details of a memory become more sharply defined and accentuated, and possibly exaggerated, over time in comparison to the original experience.

Sheehan's syndrome see HYPOPHYSEAL CACHEXIA. [Harold Leeming **Sheehan**, 20th-century British pathologist]

sheep–goat effect in parapsychology experiments using ZENER CARDS or similar targets, a supposed difference in outcomes found between trials involving participants who believe that they may succeed in the given task (sheep) and trials involving those who assume that this is impossible (goats). See also DECLINE EFFECT; DIFFERENTIAL EFFECT; FOCUSING EFFECT; POSITION EFFECT; PREFERENTIAL EFFECT. [coined by U.S. parapsychologist Gertrude Schmeidler]

Sheldon's constitutional theory of personality the theory that every person possesses some degree of three primary temperamental components that relate to three basic body builds (SOMATOTYPES), measured on a seven-point scale. The three body types ECTOMORPH, ENDOMORPH, and MESOMORPH are correlated with the three components of temperament CEREBROTONIA, VISCEROTONIA, and SOMATOTONIA. Constitution provides a substructure, but nutrition and early experiences also influence the physique and temperament, respectively. [William H. **Sheldon** (1899–1970), U.S. psychologist]

shell shock the name used during World War I for COMBAT STRESS REACTIONS. At the time the disorder was attributed solely to minor brain hemorrhages or brain concussion due to exploding shells and bombs, without involving psychological factors.

shelter care the provision of a facility without physical restrictions for the temporary care of children who have been taken into custody pending investigation and placement. Shelter care is a form of FOSTER CARE.

sheltered workshop a work-oriented rehabilitation facility for individuals with disabilities that provides a controlled, noncompetitive, supportive working environment and individually designed work settings, using work experience and related services to assist individuals with disabilities to achieve specific vocational goals. Sheltered workshops differ from SUPPORTED EMPLOYMENT in that the latter occurs in a competitive, noncontrolled working environment.

shenjing shuairuo see SHINKEISHITSU.

shen-k'uei (**shenkui**) *n.* a CULTURE-BOUND SYNDROME occurring in males of Chinese or Taiwanese cultures and characterized by symptoms of anxiety, panic, and SOMATIZATION, such as sexual dysfunction, insomnia, and dizziness. Symptoms cannot be linked to a physical cause and are typically ascribed to excessive loss of semen due to unrestrained sexual activity. See also DHAT; JIRYAN; SUKRA PRAMEHA.

shift work work scheduled during the swing shift (usually 4 p.m. to 12 a.m.) or night shift (12 a.m. to 8 a.m.). Studies show wide variations in the attitudes of employees toward shift work and their ability to adjust their CIRCADIAN RHYTHMS and adapt to changes in sleep, eating, and social patterns. See also CIRCADIAN RHYTHM SLEEP DISORDER.

shin-byung *n.* a CULTURE-BOUND SYNDROME found in Korea, characterized by anxiety and such physical complaints as general weakness, dizziness, loss of appetite, insomnia, and gastrointestinal problems, followed by dissociation and alleged possession by ancestral spirits (see DISSOCIATIVE TRANCE DISORDER). It is considered by those affected to be a "divine illness," in which the individual experiences hallucinations of becoming a shaman, and a cure occurs when this conversion takes place.

shinkeishitsu *n.* a CULTURE-BOUND SYNDROME prevalent in Japan, with symptoms that include obsessions, perfectionism, ambivalence, social withdrawal, physical and mental fatigue, hypersensitivity, and hypochondriasis. Japanese psychiatrist Shoma Morita (1874–1938), a pioneer in the study of shinkeishitsu, postulated that there is a shinkeishitsu-prone innate temperament, which he called "hypochondriacal temperament." According to Morita, people who are born with this temperament are overly sensitive, self-reflective, and notice even minimal changes in their mental and physical states. This disorder is also prevalent in China, where it is known as **shenjing shuairuo**. See also MORITA THERAPY.

Shipley Institute of Living Scale (**SILS**) a short assessment of general cognitive functioning consisting of two subtests: vocabulary, in which participants must choose which of a group of words is most similar in meaning to a target word; and abstraction, in which participants must provide the final element in a sequence of numbers, letters, or words. The scale was originally developed in 1940 for use in psychiatric settings to identify and evaluate the intellectual decline associated with certain mental disorders. Also called **Shipley–Hartford Institute of Living Scale**. [Walter C. **Shipley** (1903–1966), U.S. psychologist]

shock *n.* **1.** the application of electric current. See ELECTROSHOCK THERAPY. **2.** a condition of lowered excitability of neural centers following cutting of their connections with other neural centers. For example, SPINAL SHOCK occurs when connections between the spinal cord and the brain are severed. **3.** acute reduction of blood flow in the body due to failure of circulatory control or loss of blood or other bodily fluids, marked by hypotension, coldness of skin, usually TACHYCARDIA, and sometimes anxiety. **4.** a sudden disturbance of equilibrium.

shock phase see GENERAL ADAPTATION SYNDROME.

shock probation a criminal sentence in which an offender is incarcerated for a brief period and then released into the community under the supervision of a parole or probation officer. This approach is typically used for juveniles or for first-time offenders who have committed less serious offenses, the theory being that such offenders may be capable of successful rehabilitation into society after they have experienced the initial shock of incarceration. Also called **shock sentencing**.

shock–shock interval (**SS interval**) in a SIDMAN AVOIDANCE SCHEDULE, the time between successive presentations of the aversive stimulus (often an electric shock) in the absence of the specified response.

shock therapy the treatment of severe mental disorders by administering drugs or an electric current to produce shock to the central nervous system in order to induce loss of consciousness or convulsions. Also called **shock treatment**. See COMA THERAPY; ELECTROCONVULSIVE THERAPY.

shoe anesthesia see STOCKING ANESTHESIA.

shoe fetishism see RETIFISM.

shook yong see KORO.

short-answer test an objective test using such techniques as multiple choice, fill-in, true–false, and matching alternatives, as opposed to a test requiring lengthy or complex answers.

shortcut key in ergonomics, a key or combination of keys on a control panel that can be used to activate frequently used functions in a single step, thus reducing reliance on more complex selection methods. A familiar example is the function keys on a computer keyboard, which enable the user to select a function without going through a series of menus.

Short Portable Mental Status Questionnaire (**SPMSQ**) a brief questionnaire that is typically used to screen older adults for DEMENTIA and other neurologically based cognitive deficits and to determine the severity of impairment. It consists of 10 simple questions relating to orientation (e.g., "What is the date today?", "What is the name of this place?"), knowledge of current events, short- and long-term memory, and calculation. [developed in 1975 by U.S. geriatric psychiatrist Eric A. Pfeiffer]

short-term dynamic psychotherapy see BRIEF PSYCHODYNAMIC PSYCHOTHERAPY.

short-term memory (**STM**) the reproduction, recognition, or recall of a limited amount of material after a period of about 10–30 s. STM is often theorized to be separate from LONG-TERM MEMORY, and the two are the components of the DUAL-STORE MODEL OF MEMORY. STM is frequently tested in intelligence or neuropsychological examinations. See also IMMEDIATE MEMORY; MODAL MODEL OF MEMORY; MULTISTORE MODEL OF MEMORY; PRIMARY MEMORY.

short-term therapy psychotherapy aimed at treating intrapsychic conflict, maladaptive interpersonal patterns, or negative feelings about the self during a short period (generally 10–20 sessions). To be effective, short-term therapy relies on active techniques of inquiry, focus, and goal setting. Short-term approaches may be applied on a deeper level, as in DYNAMIC PSYCHOTHERAPY; on a level of emotional REEDUCATION; or on a more symptomatic level, as in reconditioning and other forms of BEHAVIOR THERAPY. Also called **brief psychotherapy**. See also DIRECTIVE COUNSELING; REALITY THERAPY; SECTOR THERAPY.

short-wavelength pigment the PHOTOPIGMENT, present in one of the three populations of RETINAL CONES, that has maximum sensitivity to a wavelength of 419 nm. The absence of the gene for the short-wavelength pigment causes TRITANOPIA, a form of color blindness in which blue and green are confused with one another. See also LONG-WAVELENGTH PIGMENT; MEDIUM-WAVELENGTH PIGMENT.

showup *n.* a witness identification procedure similar to a LINEUP, except that only one suspect is presented.

shrink *n.* slang for a psychologist, psychiatrist, or other mental health professional who conducts psychotherapy. It is short for **headshrinker**, an allusion to the practice of HEADSHRINKING.

SHRM abbreviation for STRATEGIC HUMAN-RESOURCE MANAGEMENT.

shuk yang see KORO.

shunning *n.* systematic ostracism of an individual by a group, usually taking the form of minimal physical or social contact with the outcast. **—shun** *vb.*

shunting *n.* the diversion of blood or cerebrospinal fluid from one part of an organ or body to another. The process may occur as a result of a congenital defect or it may be the result of a surgical procedure, as in the artificial shunting of cerebrospinal fluid from the brain to the external jugular vein to relieve symptoms of hydrocephalus. See also VENTRICULOATRIAL SHUNT.

shuttle box a two-compartment box used for avoidance-conditioning research with animals. An electric shock to the feet is scheduled to be delivered if the animal remains in the same compartment for more than a specified period of time (e.g., 30 s). The subject can avoid electric shocks by regularly moving from one compartment to the other (i.e., shuttling between them). There is sometimes a small barrier that the animal must jump over or push to get from one compartment to the other.

shy–bold continuum the tendency of some individuals within a group to be fearful or cautious of new stimuli and of others to explore novel stimuli. The more fearful individuals are less likely to be preyed on but also less able to use new resources. A shy–bold continuum has been demonstrated in many species, from fish through human beings, and may be a universal dimension of behavioral variation.

shyness *n.* anxiety and inhibition in social situations, typically involving three components: (a) global feelings of emotional arousal and specific physiological experiences (e.g., upset stomach, pounding heart, sweating, and blushing); (b) acute public self-consciousness, self-deprecation, and worries about being evaluated negatively by others; and (c) observable behavior such as cautiousness, quietness, gaze aversion, and social withdrawal. Extremely shy individuals are at an increased risk of developing anxiety disorders such as SOCIAL PHOBIA. Also called **timidity**. See also SOCIAL ANXIETY. **—shy** *adj.*

shyness disorder see AVOIDANT DISORDER OF CHILDHOOD OR ADOLESCENCE.

sialorrhea *n.* excessive production of saliva. It occurs in amyotrophic lateral sclerosis and Parkinson's disease and is a common side effect of the antipsychotic CLOZAPINE.

Siamese twins see CONJOINED TWINS.

sib *n.* **1.** short for SIBLING. **2.** in anthropology, a person's kindred collectively. See KINSHIP; KINSHIP NETWORK.

sibilant 1. *adj.* denoting a FRICATIVE produced by forcing the air through an opening between the tongue and the roof of the mouth and creating a hissing sound, for example, [s], [z], or [sh]. **2.** *n.* a sibilant speech sound.

siblicide *n.* the killing of one's siblings. In ASYNCHRONOUS BROODS the first-hatched bird often attacks and kills later hatched ones. This is an extreme form of SIBLING RIVALRY.

sibling *n.* one of two or more children born of the same two parents (i.e., a sister or brother). Also called **sib**.

sibling rivalry competition among siblings for the attention, approval, or affection of one or both parents or for other recognition or rewards, for example, in sports or school grades. See also PARENT–OFFSPRING CONFLICT.

sib-pair method a technique used in genetics, particularly in attempting to discover the extent of inherited psychiatric factors, in which the incidence of a disorder among blood relatives is compared with the distribution of the disorder in the general population. Sib-pair method studies have found a higher incidence of schizophrenia in twins and close family members than in the general population.

sibutramine *n.* an APPETITE SUPPRESSANT used for the management of obesity. Sibutramine acts on the central nervous system to inhibit the reuptake of the neurotransmitter epinephrine and, to a lesser extent, serotonin and dopamine. Sibutramine may cause raised blood pressure and, because of its ability to release monoamines, it should not be used in conjunction with MONOAMINE OXIDASE INHIBITORS. Like other appetite suppressants, it is effective only in conjunction with dietary restriction. U.S. trade name: **Meridia**.

sick headache see MIGRAINE.

sick role the behavior expected of a person who is physically ill, mentally ill, or injured. Such expectations can be the individual's own or those of the family, the community, or society in general. They influence both how the person behaves and how others will react to him or her. In his pioneering discussion of the subject, U.S. sociologist Talcott Parsons (1902–1979) noted in 1951 that people with a sick role were expected to cooperate with caregivers and to want to get well, but were also provided with an exemption from normal obligations. See also FACTITIOUS DISORDER.

side effects reactions other than the intended therapeutic effect that may occur following administration of a drug. Often these are undesirable, and occasionally unexpected (see ADVERSE DRUG REACTION). Side effects can occur as a result of an interaction between two simultaneously administered drugs (see DRUG INTERACTIONS); as a HYPERSENSITIVITY REACTION of the patient; or, in some cases, as an emotional effect.

Sidman avoidance schedule a procedure in which brief, inescapable aversive stimuli are presented at fixed intervals (SHOCK–SHOCK INTERVALS) in the absence of a specified response. If the response is made, the aversive stimulus is postponed by a fixed amount of time (the RESPONSE–SHOCK INTERVAL) from that response. Also called **avoidance without warning signal**; **continuous avoidance**; **free-operant avoidance**. [Murray **Sidman** (1923–), U.S. psychologist]

SIDS acronym for SUDDEN INFANT DEATH SYNDROME.

SIECUS abbreviation for SEXUALITY INFORMATION AND EDUCATION COUNCIL OF THE UNITED STATES.

sighting line a visual axis that extends along a line from a point of fixation to the point of clearest vision on the retina.

sight method see WHOLE-WORD METHOD.

sight words in reading, words that are recognized instantly without additional analysis. Also called **sight vocabulary**.

sigmatism *n.* **1.** a kind of LISP specifically involving incorrect production of the [s] and [z] sounds. **2.** an obsolescent name for lisping.

sign 1. *n.* an objective, observable indication of a disorder or disease. See also SOFT SIGN. **2.** *n.* in linguistics and SEMIOTICS, anything that conveys meaning; a sign may be either verbal (e.g., a spoken or written word) or nonverbal (e.g., a hairstyle). The term is now mainly associated with approaches deriving from the theory of Swiss linguist Ferdinand de Saussure (1857–1913), who emphasized the arbitrary nature of linguistic signs (i.e., the lack of any necessary relationship between the material SIGNIFIER and the idea signified). The application of this idea to nonlinguistic sign systems provided the basic method of STRUCTURALISM in the social sciences. **3.** *vb.* to communicate using SIGN LANGUAGE.

signal *n.* **1.** a presentation of information, usually one that evokes some action or response. **2.** a stimulus. See SIGNAL DETECTION THEORY. **3.** an intelligible sign communicated from one individual or electromagnetic device to another.

signal anxiety in psychoanalytic theory, anxiety that arises in response to internal conflict or an emerging impulse, and functions as a sign to the EGO of impending threat, resulting in the use of a DEFENSE MECHANISM. Compare PRIMARY ANXIETY.

signal detection task a task in which the observer is required to discriminate between trials in which a target stimulus (the signal) is present and trials in which it is not (the noise). Signal detection tasks provide objective measures of perceptual sensitivity. Also called **detection task**.

signal detection theory (**SDT**) a body of concepts and techniques from communication theory, electrical engineering, and decision theory that were applied during World War II to the detection of radar signals in noise. These concepts were applied to auditory and visual psychophysics in the late 1950s and are now widely used in many areas of psychology. An important methodological contribution of SDT has been the refinement of psychophysical techniques to permit the separation of sensitivity from criterial, decision-making factors. SDT has also provided a valuable theoretical framework for describing perceptual and other aspects of cognition and for quantitatively relating psychophysical phenomena to findings from sensory physiology. A key notion of SDT is that human performance in many tasks is limited by variability in the internal representation of stimuli due to internal or external NOISE. Many of the theoretical notions of SDT were anticipated by Louis THURSTONE. Also called **detection theory**. See D PRIME; RECEIVER-OPERATING CHARACTERISTIC CURVE.

signal-to-noise ratio (**S/N**) the ratio of signal power (intensity) to noise power, usually expressed in DECIBELS. When the signal is speech, it is called the **speech-to-noise ratio**.

signal word in ergonomics, a word used in risk communications (e.g., on a warning sign) to indicate the level of risk associated with a hazardous situation. Examples of signal words include DANGER, WARNING, CAUTION, and NOTICE.

signal word panel in ergonomics and risk communication, a warning sign that contains a specific SIGNAL WORD (e.g., DANGER). The size, color, and font of the lettering, as well as the design of the panel itself, will be selected for maximum clarity and impact. The signal word panel may also contain an alerting symbol, such as a skull and crossbones.

signature *n.* an identifiable unique object, message, or symbol left by a criminal at the scene of a crime. It plays no part in the criminal act but represents a coded clue to the offender's identity, which can be of use in CRIMINAL PROFILING. Usually a criminal leaves the same signature at the scene of all his or her crimes. Also called **calling card**.

significance *n.* the degree or extent to which a result is meaningful or of consequence. See also STATISTICAL SIGNIFICANCE.

significance level in null hypothesis SIGNIFICANCE TESTING, the probability of rejecting the null hypothesis when it is in fact true (i.e., of making a Type I error). It is set at some criterion, α, usually .01 or .05, and the actual value for a particular test is denoted *p*. Thus when the *p*-value is less than α, the null hypothesis is rejected. Also called **alpha level**.

significance testing a set of procedures that are used to differentiate between two models. In the most common form of significance testing, one model (the NULL HYPOTHESIS) specifies a condition in which the treatment being studied has no effect and the other model (the ALTERNATIVE HYPOTHESIS) specifies that the treatment has some effect. Significance testing may also be used to differentiate beween two models (as in MULTIPLE REGRESSION analysis) where the two models differ in terms of the number of parameters specified in them.

significant difference the situation in which a SIGNIFICANCE TESTING procedure indicates that the two models being compared are different.

significant other 1. a spouse or other person with whom one has a committed sexual relationship. **2.** any individual who has a profound influence on a person's emotional security and well-being.

signifier *n.* **1.** in linguistics and SEMIOTICS, the material form of a SIGN as opposed to the idea or concept indicated (the **signified**). In language, therefore, the signifier is the spoken or written word or component of a word. The distinction between signifier and signified is of central importance in STRUCTURALISM and POSTSTRUCTURALISM. See also REFERENT. [introduced by Swiss linguist Ferdinand de Saussure (1857–1913)] **2.** in the theory of French psychoanalyst Jacques Lacan (1901–1981), a symbol, such as a word or symptom, that stands for some aspect of the patient's unconscious. Lacan's use of the term reflects his central belief that the unconscious is structured as a language.

sign language a system of communication in which signs formed by hands, face, and body positions and gestures are used instead of spoken language, mainly for communication with and by people who have severe hearing impairment. Sign language has its own syntax and methods of conveying nuances of feeling and emotion and is now accepted by most linguists as exhibiting the full set of defining characteristics of human oral–aural language. Forms of sign language are sometimes used also to communicate with children with certain neurological disorders and with nonhuman primates, but these systems are far less sophisticated than those used by people with hearing impairment. Also called **signing**. See AMERICAN SIGN LANGUAGE; FINGER SPELLING.

sign stimulus see RELEASER.

sign system an epithet for PSYCHOTHERAPY, which highlights the discipline's dependence on language as the major tool for exploring and understanding the hidden causes of cognitive, affective, and behavioral problems and disorders. [introduced by Austrian-born U.S. psychologist Paul Schilder (1886–1940)]

sign test a nonparametric test of a hypothesis concerning the median of a distribution. It is commonly used to test the hypothesis that the median difference in matched pairs is zero.

sign tracking in conditioning, elicited behavior directed toward a stimulus that is reliably paired with a primary reinforcer.

SII abbreviation for STRONG INTEREST INVENTORY.

silent monitor in certain 19th-century factories, a simple device consisting of a wooden cube colored differently on each side that was hung next to the machine of each worker and used to indicate the quality of his or her conduct on a daily basis. The grade given to each employee was recorded daily in a "Book of Character." The monitor was the idea of British social and educational reformer Robert Owen (1771–1858): It is considered an early example of influencing behavior through feedback and reinforcement in an applied setting.

silok *n.* a CULTURE-BOUND SYNDROME found in the Philippines, with symptoms similar to those of LATAH.

SILS abbreviation for SHIPLEY INSTITUTE OF LIVING SCALE.

silver-cord syndrome a parental relationship in which the father is absent or passive and the mother is domineering. Historically, this family pattern was believed to increase susceptibility of the offspring to development of schizophrenia, but this view is no longer widely held. See SCHIZOPHRENOGENIC MOTHER; SCHIZOPHRENOGENIC PARENTS.

Silver–Russell syndrome a congenital disorder characterized by short stature, hypertrophy of one side of the body, and elevated urinary gonadotropin hormones without precocious sexual maturity. Motor development is often delayed because of muscle weakness. Physical features include **pseudohydrocephalus**, a condition of normal head circumference but a small face, giving the appearance of an enlarged head. Various studies have found a higher than average incidence of mental retardation among the patients. Also called **Silver's syndrome**. [Henry K. **Silver** (1918–), U.S. pediatrician; Alexander **Russell** (1914–), British pathologist]

Simenon's syndrome a delusional condition characterized by the false perception or belief that one is loved by or has had a sexual affair with a public figure or other individual. See EROTIC DELUSION; EROTIC PARANOIA. See also CLÉRAMBAULT'S SYNDROME. [named for Georges Joseph Christian **Simenon** (1903–1989), Belgian-born French novelist, possibly because the condition featured in one of his stories]

similarities test a test in which the participant must either state the likenesses between items or arrange items in categories according to their similarities.

similarity classification see CONCEPTUAL CLASSIFICATION.

simile *n.* see METAPHOR.

Simmonds' disease a disorder of the pituitary gland caused by necrosis and failure of the anterior lobe (adenohypophysis) of the gland, which may be partial or complete. This results in secondary failure of the gonads, adrenal cortex, and thyroid gland, which depend upon the hormonal stimulation of the pituitary. Anorexia, atrophy of sexual features, absence of libido, hypotension, bradycardia, and hypoglycemia are symptoms of the disorder. [Morris **Simmonds** (1855–1925), German physician]

Simon, Herbert Alexander (1916–2001) U.S. economist, political scientist, and psychologist. Simon earned a doctorate in political science from the University of Chicago in 1942. After joining a faculty at the Illinois Institute of Technology, he moved in 1949 to the Carnegie Mellon University, where he remained for the rest of his career. Simon is generally regarded as a founder of the fields of ARTIFICIAL INTELLIGENCE and COGNITIVE SCIENCE. He was among the first to use computers to model human decision making and problem solving. This work became the basis of the information-processing model of human cognition that Simon and Allen Newell (1927–1992) discussed in their influential book, *Human Problem Solving* (1972). Other important writings include *Models of Man* (1957), *The Sciences of the Artificial* (1996), and *Models of Thought* (2 volumes, 1979–1989). Simon's many honors include the Nobel Prize for economic sciences (1978), the National Medal of Science (1986), election to the National Academy of Sciences and the American Academy of Arts and Sciences, and the American Psychological Association's Award for Outstanding Lifetime Contributions to Psychology (1993).

Simon effect in a two-choice task, the finding that the response to a stimulus is facilitated if the location of the stimulus corresponds to the location of the response, even though stimulus location is irrelevant to the task. For example, if a left (rather than a right) keypress is the required response to a blue stimulus, reaction time will be quicker if this stimulus is presented on the left-hand side than if it is presented on the right (and vice versa). The Simon effect has been attributed to automatic activation of the corresponding response. [discovered in 1969 by U.S. psychologist J. Richard **Simon** (1929–)]

simple causation an instance of causation in which a single event is caused by a single identifiable antecedent, without multiple causes or other intervening processes. Compare MULTIPLE CAUSATION.

simple cell a neuron, most commonly found in the STRIATE CORTEX, that has a receptive field consisting of an elongated center region and two elongated flanking regions. The response of a simple cell to stimulation in the center of the receptive field is the opposite of its response to stimulation in the flanking zones. This means that a simple cell responds best to an edge or a bar of a particular width and with a particular direction and location in the visual field. Also called **simple cortical cell**. Compare COMPLEX CELL.

simple depression a less common name for MILD DEPRESSION.

simple deteriorative disorder in *DSM–IV–TR*, a disorder in which the essential feature is the development over the course of at least 1 year of prominent NEGATIVE SYMPTOMS, which represent a clear change from a preestablished baseline and are severe enough to result in a significant deterioration in occupational or academic functioning. The individual gradually loses emotional responsivity, ambition, and interest in self-care and becomes socially withdrawn or isolated. POSITIVE SYMPTOMS, if they appear, are not prominent. Historically, and in other classifications, this disorder is known as SIMPLE SCHIZOPHRENIA.

simple effects in a FACTORIAL DESIGN, the comparison of group means of one factor at specific levels of the other factor or factors.

simple eye the type of eye found in most vertebrates and some invertebrates. It consists of a single focusing element, which may be a thickening of the exoskeleton (in an arthropod), a pinhole in the surface of the eye (in a mollusk), or a crystalline lens (in a vertebrate), plus one or more photosensitive cells. Compare COMPOUND EYE.

simple factorial design an experimental design in which the two or more levels of each INDEPENDENT VARIABLE or factor are observed in combination with the two or more levels of every other factor. See also FACTORIAL DESIGN.

simple ideas in ASSOCIATIONISM, the simple, unorganized sensations, derived from the various senses, that form the basis of all knowledge. Through the rational process of REFLECTION, simple ideas can be transformed into more abstract COMPLEX IDEAS. [defined by English philosopher John Locke (1632–1704)]

simple phobia see SPECIFIC PHOBIA.

simple random sampling a sampling plan in which the participants are selected individually on the basis of a randomized procedure, such as by the use of a table of random digits.

simple reaction time (**SRT**) the REACTION TIME of a participant in a task that requires him or her to make an elementary response (e.g., pressing a key) whenever a stimulus (such as a light or tone) is presented. The individual makes just a single response whenever the only possible stimulus is presented. Compare CHOICE REACTION TIME; COMPLEX REACTION TIME. See also COMPOUND REACTION TIME; DISCRIMINATION REACTION TIME.

simple schizophrenia one of the four major types of schizophrenia described by German psychiatrist Emil Kraepelin (1856–1926) and Swiss psychiatrist Eugen Bleuler (1857–1939), characterized primarily by gradual withdrawal from social contact, lack of initiative, and emotional apathy. The equivalent *DSM–IV–TR* diagnostic category is SIMPLE DETERIORATIVE DISORDER.

simple sentence see COMPLEX SENTENCE.

simple stepfamily a STEPFAMILY in which only one of the parents brings a child or children from a previous union to the new family unit. Compare BLENDED FAMILY.

simple structure a set of criteria for adequacy of a rotated factor-analytic solution. These criteria require each factor to show a pattern of high loadings on some variables and near-zero loadings on others.

simple tone see PURE TONE.

simple universal see PSYCHOLOGICAL UNIVERSAL.

Simpson's paradox a phenomenon that can occur when the raw data of two or more studies are merged, giving results that differ from those of either study individually. For example, two studies, each showing a correlation of .00 between two variables, *X* and *Y*, may show a strong positive correlation between variables *X* and *Y* when the data are merged in an inappropriate manner. [Edward H. **Simpson**, 20th-century U.S. statistician]

simulated environment see SIMULATION.

simulated family a technique used in training and therapy in which hypothetical family situations are enacted. In training, the enactment is by clinicians or other professionals. In FAMILY THERAPY, one or more members of the family may participate with others, who play the roles of other family members. See also ROLE PLAY.

simulation *n.* **1.** an experimental method used to investigate the behavior and psychological processes and functioning of individuals in social and other environments, often those to which investigators cannot easily gain access, by simulating those environments in a realistic way. **2.** the artificial creation of experiment-like data through the use of a mathematical or computer model of behavior or data.

simulation training an OFF-THE-JOB TRAINING technique in which trainees learn a complex or hazardous task by practicing on a replica of the task. This may involve the use of computer simulations, mechanical training aids, or plausible but fictitious work scenarios (see BUSINESS GAME; CASE METHOD; SCENARIO ANALYSIS).

simulator *n.* a training device that simulates the conditions or environment of the actual operating situation or that resembles the actual equipment to be used, such as a flight simulator for pilots.

simulator–real model see REAL–SIMULATOR MODEL.

simulator sickness see SOPITE SYNDROME.

simultanagnosia *n.* a form of AGNOSIA characterized by an impairment in the ability to integrate multiple elements of complex visual stimuli, possibly caused by a lesion in the anterior portion of the left OCCIPITAL LOBE of the brain. For example, an individual may be able to name the objects represented in a picture but not to identify the action that is depicted.

simultaneous conditioning a PAVLOVIAN CONDITIONING technique in which the conditioned stimulus and the unconditioned stimulus are presented at the same time. Compare DELAY CONDITIONING.

simultaneous confidence intervals joint CONFIDENCE INTERVALS that are formed for estimating multiple parameters simultaneously from the same set of data.

simultaneous contrast the enhanced perception of the difference between two stimuli when these are presented in close proximity to one another in space. See also COLOR CONTRAST; CONTRAST ILLUSION; MACH BANDS. Compare SUCCESSIVE CONTRAST.

simultaneous discrimination in conditioning, DISCRIMINATION between two simultaneously available stimuli.

simultaneous lightness contrast see BRIGHTNESS CONTRAST.

simultaneous masking see MASKING.

simultaneous processing see PARALLEL PROCESSING.

Sinemet *n.* a U.S. trade name for a drug combination of LEVODOPA and **carbidopa**, used in the treatment of Parkinson's disease, the symptoms of which are due to lack of striatal dopamine. Carbidopa inhibits the action of the enzyme DOPA DECARBOXYLASE in peripheral tissues, thereby enabling levodopa to be administered in lower doses to achieve an effective concentration in the brain, where it is converted by striatal enzymes into dopamine.

Sinequan *n.* a trade name for DOXEPIN.

sine qua non an indispensable element (Latin, literally: "without which not"). In law, for example, a guilty mind (see MENS REA) is the sine qua non of CRIMINAL RESPONSIBILITY.

sine wave a mathematical expression involving the trigonometric functions sine or cosine. In much of physics a sine wave is a function of time. For example, in acoustics a PURE TONE is a variation in sound pressure that is a sinusoidal function of time. The parameters of a sine wave are its frequency, amplitude, and phase. A sine wave, unlike a complex wave, has only one frequency component.

single blind denoting an experimental procedure in which the participants, but not the experimenter, are unaware of the experimental treatment, manipulation, or drug administered. See BLIND. Compare DOUBLE BLIND; TRIPLE BLIND.

single-capacity model see UNITARY-RESOURCE MODEL.

single-case experimental design a REPEATED MEASURES DESIGN in which a single participant, group, or other sampling unit is observed over time. Individuals serve as their own controls, and typically a number of observations are obtained at different times over the course of treatment. Also called **intrasubject replication design**; **N-of-1 experimental design**; **n=1 research**; **single-subject design**.

single-case methods and evaluation a type of PSYCHOTHERAPY RESEARCH based on systematic study of one client before, during, and after intervention.

single-cell recording see MICROELECTRODE.

single-channel model a model of human INFORMATION PROCESSING in which only SERIAL PROCESSING is possible. Cognition is held to consist of a series of discrete sequenced steps involving one information source and one processing channel at a time. Compare DISTRIBUTED PROCESSING; PARALLEL PROCESSING.

single-episode depression a MAJOR DEPRESSIVE EPISODE in an individual who does not have a history of major depressive episodes. It is thought that the effects of treatment in people having single episodes may be different from those in individuals who have a history of depression.

single-factor design see ONE-WAY DESIGN.

single-gene disorder a disease or condition that is due to the presence of a single mutated gene. Single-gene disorders are relatively rare; many diseases exhibit MULTIFACTORIAL INHERITANCE and are also influenced by environmental factors. Huntington's disease and sickle-cell disease are examples of single-gene disorders. Generally, the single mutation causes a failure to synthesize a normally functioning enzyme that is required for a specific step in building body tissue or for a vital stage in the metabolism of a food component.

single-nucleotide polymorphism (**SNP**) a common, tiny variation in human DNA, occurring roughly every 1000 bases along the molecule and affecting single nucleotides. Such variations can be used as GENETIC MARKERS to track the inheritance of particular defective genes in families.

single parent a person who rears a child without the assistance of a partner.

single photon emission computed tomography (**SPECT**) a functional imaging technique that uses gamma radiation from a radioactive dye to create a picture of blood flow in the body. In the brain it can be used to measure cerebral blood flow, which is a direct measure of cerebral metabolism and activity.

single-session therapy (**SST**) therapy that ends after one session, usually by choice of the client but also as indicated by the type of treatment (e.g., ERICKSONIAN PSYCHOTHERAPY, SOLUTION-FOCUSED BRIEF THERAPY). Some clients claim enough success with one hour of therapy to stop treatment, although some therapists believe that this claim represents a FLIGHT INTO HEALTH or temporary relief from symptoms. Preparation for the session (e.g., by telephone) increases the likelihood of the single-therapy session being successful.

singles test in parapsychology experiments on PSYCHOKINESIS, a technique in which the participant attempts to influence the throw of a single die.

single-subject design see SINGLE-CASE EXPERIMENTAL DESIGN.

singleton *n.* **1.** a fetus that develops alone or an offspring born singly. **2.** sometimes, in popular usage, the only child of two parents.

singular matrix a square matrix whose inverse does not exist. A singular matrix has a zero determinant.

sinistral *adj.* left-handed.

sinistrality *n.* a tendency or preference to be left-handed or to use the left side of the body in motor activities. See also LEFT-HANDEDNESS. Compare DEXTRALITY.

sinistration *n.* leftward direction. MIRROR WRITING, for example, shows sinistration.

sinistro- (**sinistr-**) *combining form* on or toward the left.

sinusoid *n.* see PURE TONE.

SIQ abbreviation for SPORT IMAGERY QUESTIONNAIRE.

SIS abbreviation for sensory-information store (see SENSORY MEMORY).

sissy behavior slang for effeminate behavior in boys, which is often a source of ridicule by others. See ROLE CONFUSION; TOMBOYISM.

SIT 1. abbreviation for SLOSSON INTELLIGENCE TEST. **2.** abbreviation for SMELL IDENTIFICATION TEST. **3.** abbreviation for STRESS-INOCULATION TRAINING.

situated cognition cognition seen as inextricable from the context in which it is applied. From this it follows that intelligence also cannot be separated from its context of application (**situated intelligence**). See also STREET INTELLIGENCE.

situated identities theory the theory that individuals take on different roles in different social and cultural settings, so that a person's behavior pattern may shift radically according to the situation and the others with whom he or she is interacting.

situated intelligence see SITUATED COGNITION.

situated knowledge knowledge that is embedded in, and thus affected by, the concrete historical, cultural, linguistic, and value context of the knowing person. The term is used most frequently in perspectives arising from SOCIAL CONSTRUCTIONISM, RADICAL FEMINISM, and POSTMODERNISM to emphasize their view that absolute, universal knowledge is impossible. It sometimes carries the further implication that social, cultural, and historical factors will constrain the process of knowledge construction itself. To the extent that knowledge is situated, it is difficult to avoid some kind of epistemological RELATIVISM.

situated learning learning that occurs in specific physical and social contexts (e.g., in a classroom). Knowledge learning may be facilitated when people interact within the setting or if they interact with the physical setting (e.g., when map learning occurs in the actual physical space being studied). However, situated learning may be less meaningful than other types of learning if it does not transcend the particular situation in which it was acquired (see CONTEXT-SPECIFIC LEARNING).

situational analysis a method of studying behavior or other phenomena in a natural setting, as opposed to in a laboratory. See also NATURALISTIC OBSERVATION.

situational approach see CONTINGENCY MODEL.

situational attribution 1. in ATTRIBUTION THEORY, the ascription of one's own or another's behavior to external or circumstantial causes, such as pressure from other people. **2.** the ascription of an event or outcome to causes outside the person concerned, such as luck, other people, or the circumstances. Also called **environmental attribution**; **external attribution**. Compare DISPOSITIONAL ATTRIBUTION.

situational conditions in educational psychology, all the relevant external variables within a classroom setting that influence student learning and achievement. Situational conditions include the physical environment, teaching methods, time factors, goals, organization of material, methods of testing, consequences of performance, type of reinforcement, and social relationships.

situational determinants the environmental conditions that exist before and after an organism's response and influence the elicitation of this behavior: one of the four variables considered in behavioral analysis. See SORC.

situational effect the effect of different environmental situations on the behavior of participants or experimenters.

situational homosexuality same-sex sexual behavior that develops in a situation or environment in which the opportunity for heterosexual activity is missing and where close contact with individuals of the same sex occurs. Situational homosexuality may occur in a prison, school, or military setting where individuals are living together, segregated according to their sex. Once away from this setting, a previously heterosexual person typically returns to being exclusively heterosexual. See also OCCASIONAL INVERSION.

situational interview an EMPLOYMENT INTERVIEW in which applicants for a job are presented with scenarios and asked what they would do in those situations. Their potential to perform the job is then evaluated using BEHAVIORALLY ANCHORED RATING SCALES.

situationalism *n.* the view that an organism's interaction with the environment and situational factors, rather than personal characteristics and other internal factors, are the primary determinants of behavior. Also called **situationism**. [proposed by Kurt LEWIN]

situational leadership theory a CONTINGENCY THEORY OF LEADERSHIP that recommends leaders use varying amounts of directive (TASK-MOTIVATED) and supportive (RELATIONSHIP-MOTIVATED) leadership, depending on the maturity of followers. Maturity in this context refers to both job maturity (e.g., experience, ability, knowledge) and psychological maturity (e.g., level of motivation, willingness to accept responsibility). When maturity is low, leaders should be directive, concentrating on structure and task orientation (see DIRECTIVE LEADER). With increasing follower maturity, leaders need to increase supportive actions. At the highest levels of maturity, followers may need neither directive nor supportive leadership and a laissez-faire style can be effective (see LAISSEZ-FAIRE LEADER; SUBSTITUTES FOR LEADERSHIP THEORY). Also called **situational theory of leadership**. [proposed by U.S. management theorists Paul Hersey and Kenneth H. Blanchard]

situationally predisposed panic attack a PANIC ATTACK that occurs in response to a specific situational trigger but is not invariably induced by it. Compare CUED PANIC ATTACK; UNCUED PANIC ATTACK.

situational orgasmic dysfunction the inability of a woman to experience orgasm with a particular sex partner or in a particular situation. See FEMALE ORGASMIC DISORDER.

situational psychosis a severe but temporary reaction to a traumatic event or situation (such as imprisonment) involving such symptoms as delusions and hallucinations. Also called **reactive psychosis**; **traumatic psychosis**.

situational restraint the use of environmental arrangements (e.g., screens on windows, immovable furniture), as opposed to physical restraint of the individual, to minimize the risk of dangerous or destructive acts by patients with mental or emotional problems.

situational sampling the observation of individuals in several real-life situations, as opposed to experimental situations, as part of the study of their behavior.

situational semantics a branch of SEMANTICS holding that the meaning of utterances, particularly their truth value, must be understood by considering not only the correspondence of the utterance to what is the case in the world, but also the situation in which the utterance is made. A major implication of this notion is that truth is situational, and that language expresses primarily situations rather than transituational facts. This view is related to SOCIAL CONSTRUCTIONISM, POSTMODERNISM, and some species of FEMINISM.

situational-stress test a SITUATION TEST with stress as an integral component.

situational test see SITUATION TEST.

situational theory of leadership see SITUATIONAL LEADERSHIP THEORY.

situational therapy see ENVIRONMENTAL THERAPY.

situation awareness conscious knowledge of the immediate environment and the events that are occurring in it. Situation awareness involves perception of the elements in the environment, comprehension of what they mean and how they relate to one another, and projection of their future states. In ergonomics, for example, it refers to the operator's awareness of the current status and the projected future status of a system. Situation awareness is influenced by a number of factors, including stress; it may be impaired by COGNITIVE TUNNELING or SOCIAL TUNNELING.

situation ethics the view that the morality or immorality of an action must be evaluated within the context of a given situation as interpreted according to some ethical norms. Compare MORAL ABSOLUTISM; MORAL RELATIVISM.

situationism *n.* see SITUATIONALISM.

situation test a test that places an individual in a natural setting, or in an experimental setting that approximates a natural one, to assess either the individual's ability to solve a problem that requires adaptive behavior under stressful conditions or the individual's reactions to what is believed to be a stressful experience. For example, a course of DESENSITIZATION therapy aimed at reducing phobic reactions might begin with a situation test in which the individual encounters the phobic object. The individual's reactions are then assessed and considered in relation to individual needs or a specific therapy program. Also called **situational test**. See also SITUATIONAL-STRESS TEST.

six-hour retarded child a child mistakenly judged to be a slow learner in school (i.e., for about 6 hours a day) while functioning relatively well in the complex social world outside. This mistake, which can lead to a lifelong pattern of failure, has been made in the past by administrators, teachers, and school psychologists for a number of reasons, including acculturation issues, test bias, language proficiency of the child, undiagnosed learning problems, and behavioral considerations.

Sixteen Personality Factor Questionnaire (16PF) the fifth edition (1995) of a comprehensive self-report PERSONALITY INVENTORY. The instrument assesses personality on 16 key scales: warmth, vigilance, reasoning, abstractedness, emotional stability, privateness, dominance, apprehension, liveliness, openness to change, rule-consciousness, self-reliance, social boldness, perfectionism, sensitivity, and tension. The 16 factors are grouped into 5 "global factors": extraversion, independence, tough-mindedness, anxiety, and self-control. [developed by British psychologist Raymond B. Cattell (1905–1998) and his associates]

sixth cranial nerve see ABDUCENS NERVE.

sixth sense 1. in general language, an INTUITION or INSTINCT that enables a person to make a correct judgment or decision without conscious use of the five senses or normal cognitive processes. **2.** in parapsychology, the ostensible sensory modality responsible for mediating the phenomena of EXTRASENSORY PERCEPTION. See PSI. **3.** in Aristotelian philosophy, the SENSUS COMMUNIS ("common sense") in which information from the five special senses is integrated.

size constancy the awareness that objects do not change size when the retinal image changes as they move closer or farther away. See also PERCEPTUAL CONSTANCY.

size cue any of a variety of means used by the visual system to interpret the APPARENT SIZE of a stimulus. These include the size of the image that falls on the retina, the relationship of the object to others within the field, DEPTH CUES, and SIZE CONSTANCY.

size discrimination the ability to distinguish differences in the sizes of objects. In the absence of vision, this depends on tactile sensation.

size–distance paradox an illusion that an object is bigger or smaller than is actually the case caused by a false perception of its distance from the viewer. For example, in the so-called **moon illusion** the moon appears to be larger on the horizon, where DEPTH CUES make it appear to be farther away, than at its zenith, where there are no depth cues. Also called **distance paradox**.

size-invariant neurons see LOCATION-INVARIANT NEURONS.

size principle the principle that the order of RECRUITMENT of motor neurons serving a particular muscle is related to their size: To produce muscle responses of increasing strength, small, low-threshold neurons are recruited first, and large, high-threshold neurons are recruited last.

size–weight illusion the tendency to judge density when trying to judge weight, that is, to be influenced by the size of an object and thus perceive a large object as weighing less than an equally heavy but smaller, denser object.

Sjögren–Larsson syndrome an autosomal recessive condition characterized by scaly skin, spasticity, and mental retardation, caused by several different genetic factors. Sweat glands are sparse or deficient. The scaliness varies in specific cases among populations from different regions of the world. [reported in 1957 by Torsten **Sjögren** (1896–1974), Swedish physician, and Tage Konrad Leopold **Larsson** (1905–), Swedish scientist]

Sjögren's syndrome see XEROPHTHALMIA. [Henrik S. C. **Sjögren** (1899–1986), Swedish ophthalmologist]

skeletal age a measure of the degree to which the skeleton has matured. Skeletal age can be the same as, more than, or less than CHRONOLOGICAL AGE.

skeletal muscle a muscle that provides the force to move a part of the skeleton. Skeletal muscles are attached to the bones by tendons and usually span a joint, so that one end of the muscle is attached via a tendon to one bone and the other end is attached to another bone. Skeletal muscles work in reciprocal pairs (see ANTAGONISTIC MUSCLES) so that a bone can be moved in opposite directions. Skeletal muscle is composed of numerous slender, tapering MUSCLE FIBERS, each of which is bounded by a membrane (sarcolemma) and contains cytoplasm (sarcoplasm). Within the sarcoplasm are the longitudinal contractile fibrils (myofibrils), organized into arrays (sarcomeres) that give a striped appearance when viewed microscopically. Contraction of skeletal muscle is typically under voluntary control of the central nervous system. Each muscle fiber is stimulated to contract by nerve impulses conducted along a MOTOR NEURON and transmitted to the fiber via a NEUROMUSCULAR JUNCTION. A single neuron may activate from several up to hundreds of muscle fibers. Also called **striated muscle**; **voluntary muscle**. Compare CARDIAC MUSCLE; SMOOTH MUSCLE.

skelic index the ratio between length of the legs and length of the trunk. This index is used in ANTHROPOMETRY.

skeptical argument the element of the SPORT PERSONALITY DEBATE arguing that personality is not predictive of athletic success. See also CREDULOUS ARGUMENT.

skeptical postmodernism a perspective within POSTMODERNISM that is particularly reluctant to grant any foundations for meaning or morality. From such a perspective it is difficult to see why any political system or ideology should be thought preferable to any other, or how the idea of social progress can have any meaning. Skeptical postmodernism is often contrasted with AFFIRMATIVE POSTMODERNISM.

skepticism *n.* **1.** an attitude of disbelief or doubt. **2.** in philosophy, the position that certain knowledge can never be found. British philosopher David Hume (1711–1776) made skepticism a cornerstone of his system and provoked much later discussion when he taught that sensory experience provides no sure basis for knowledge of the external world and that nothing can be proved by observation. CAUSATION, for example, is only an inference that relates two observed events, and one has no knowledge that this relationship will apply in similar cases: It is a generalization that could be proved wrong by a different result. In modern philosophy, POSTMODERNISM, POSTSTRUCTURALISM, and DECONSTRUCTION are essentially systems of skepticism. **—skeptic** *n.* **—skeptical** *adj.*

skewness *n.* a measure of the degree or extent to which a batch of scores lack symmetry around their measure of CENTRAL TENDENCY.

skill *n.* an ability or proficiency acquired through training and practice. Motor skills are characterized by the ability to perform a complex movement or SERIAL BEHAVIOR quickly, smoothly, and precisely. Skills in other learned tasks include BASIC SKILLS, COMMUNICATION SKILLS, and SOCIAL SKILLS.

skilled nursing facility (**SNF**) a licensed or approved facility, whether freestanding or affiliated with a hospital, that provides continuous rehabilitation and medical care of a lesser intensity than that provided in an acute-care hospital setting. See also CONTINUING CARE UNIT; CONVALESCENT CENTER.

skill learning learning to perform a task with proficiency, as defined by ease, speed, and accuracy of performance, acquired through a high degree of practice. Skills may be motor, perceptual, cognitive, or a combination of these (as in reading and playing music).

skill theory the proposition that cognitive development is the result of a dynamic interaction between the individual and the environment. According to this theory, a **skill** (or **dynamic skill**) is the capacity to act in an organized way in a specific context, and in order for a skill to be developed to its OPTIMAL LEVEL, it must be exercised in the most supportive of environments. Also called **dynamic skill theory**. [proposed by 21st-century U.S. psychologist Kurt W. Fischer]

skimming *n.* a rapid, somewhat superficial, reading of material to get the general idea of the content. See also SCANNING. **—skim** *vb.*

skin *n.* the external covering of the body, consisting of an outer layer (epidermis) and a deeper layer (dermis) resting on a layer of fatty subcutaneous tissue. The skin is well supplied with nerves and blood vessels and forms an effective yet sensitive barrier. It prevents injury to underlying tissues, reduces water loss from the body, and forms part of the body's temperature-regulation mechanism through the evaporation of sweat secreted from sweat glands. Human skin typically has only a sparse covering of hair, except on the head and genital regions, and the hair has minimal value as insulation, although it is often highly significant in social terms. In humans, insulation is provided mainly by the subcutaneous ADIPOSE TISSUE. The root of each hair arises from a HAIR FOLLICLE, into which the ducts of sebaceous glands discharge sebum, an oily secretion that lubricates and waterproofs the skin surface. Various types of sensory nerve ending provide touch and pressure sensitivity, as well as sensations of pain and temperature (see CUTANEOUS RECEPTOR). The skin also prevents the entry of foreign substances and pathogens.

skin conductance a measure of the change in conductance of the skin to the passage of a small electric current between two electrodes, typically used to measure a person's level of AROUSAL or energy mobilization. In contrast to other autonomically mediated indices, skin conductance rarely shows relations with specific emotional states, such as fear or anger, responding instead to level of arousal. The mechanism of skin conductance is not fully known: It seems to be related to the electrical activity of sweat glands but not to sweating itself. See also GALVANIC SKIN RESPONSE.

skin graft a piece of skin, either of full thickness or split (i.e., partial) thickness, surgically applied to wounds to facilitate healing. Skin grafts can conform to irregular wounds and concavities.

Skinner, Burrhus Frederic (1904–1990) U.S. psychologist. Skinner earned his doctorate from Harvard University in 1931 and subsequently taught at the University of Minnesota and Indiana University before returning to Harvard in 1948. He spent the rest of his career there. Arguably the most famous experimental psychologist of the 20th century, Skinner was best known as the originator of OPERANT CONDITIONING, a distinctive form of BEHAVIORISM that he called RADICAL BEHAVIORISM. Operant conditioning, which he contrasted with PAVLOVIAN CONDITIONING, was based on the view that an organism's environment shapes its behavior; actions that are reinforced by the environment will increase in frequency, while those that are punished will decrease in frequency. Skinner invented a laboratory method utilizing the Skinner box (see OPERANT CONDITIONING CHAMBER) to make detailed studies of the SCHEDULES OF REINFORCEMENT that shape behavior in rats and pigeons. Not content to confine himself to laboratory research, Skinner initiated the field of APPLIED BEHAVIOR ANALYSIS by applying his ideas to educational methods (see PROGRAMMED INSTRUCTION; TEACHING MACHINE), child rearing, language acquisition, psychotherapy, and cultural analysis. His most famous writings include his *Behavior of Organisms* (1938) and *Verbal Behavior* (1957) as well as more popular works, such as *Walden Two* (1948),

Beyond Freedom and Dignity (1971), and *About Behaviorism* (1974). Among Skinner's many honors were his election to the National Academy of Sciences and the Society of Experimental Psychologists and his receipt of both the Distinguished Scientific Contribution Award and the Lifetime Scientific Contribution Award from the American Psychological Association. See also DESCRIPTIVE BEHAVIORISM.

Skinner box the colloquial name for an OPERANT CONDITIONING CHAMBER. [initially developed by B. F. SKINNER]

skin popping slang for the injection of a substance containing an opioid—usually HEROIN—under the skin, as opposed to mainlining (i.e., injecting into a vein).

skin receptor any of the nerve endings in the skin that respond to pain, pressure, temperature, or other stimuli.

skin sense see CUTANEOUS SENSE.

skin-sensory spot an area of the skin that contains nerve endings for stimuli, such as heat, cold, pain, and touch. Some parts of the body have a greater concentration of skin-sensory spots than others. For example, the fingertips have more skin-sensory spots per square centimeter than the skin of the back.

skin stimulation a cutaneous sensation experienced as pain, pressure, coldness, warmth, tickle, or itch through nerve receptors in the skin.

skull trephining see TREPHINATION.

sl abbreviation for *sub*lingual.

SLD abbreviation for SPECIFIC LEARNING DISABILITY.

SLE abbreviation for systemic lupus erythematosus (see LUPUS ERYTHEMATOSUS).

sleep *n.* a state of the brain characterized by partial or total suspension of consciousness, muscular relaxation and inactivity, reduced metabolism, and relative insensitivity to stimulation. Other mental and physical characteristics that distinguish sleep from wakefulness include amnesia for events occurring during the loss of consciousness and unique sleep-related electroencephalogram and brain-imaging patterns (see SLEEP STAGES). These characteristics also help distinguish normal sleep from a loss of consciousness due to injury, disease, or drugs. See also DREAM STATE; NREM SLEEP; REM SLEEP.

sleep apnea the temporary cessation of breathing while asleep, which occurs when the upper airway becomes completely or partially blocked by mucus or excessive tissue, interrupting regular breathing for short periods of time. It usually terminates in a loud snore, body jerk, arm flailing, or standing without awakening. Sleep apnea can cause severe daytime sleepiness, and evidence is building that untreated severe sleep apnea may be associated with high blood pressure and risk for stroke and heart attack. See also APNEA.

sleep attack see NARCOLEPSY.

sleep center an obsolete name for an area in the hypothalamus formerly thought to control sleep. It has now been shown that no single area of the brain governs the SLEEP–WAKE CYCLE; rather, multiple areas, including the hypothalamus and RETICULAR ACTIVATING SYSTEM, have been implicated in its regulation. See also WAKING CENTER.

sleep cycle a cyclical pattern of SLEEP STAGES in which a period of SLOW-WAVE SLEEP is followed by a period of REM SLEEP. In humans, a sleep cycle lasts approximately 90 min.

sleep deprivation deliberate prevention of sleep, sometimes for experimental purposes, but also used as a form of punishment or a means of exacting a "confession" from a prisoner. Studies show that the loss of one night's sleep does not have a substantial effect on physical or mental functioning; participants kept awake for 30 to 60 hours show little impairment in performing novel or challenging tasks, but cannot tolerate boring tasks, such as keeping watch. After this, speech begins to be slurred and performance on psychological tests becomes increasingly poor. Many of the symptoms of psychosis, such as disorientation, detachment from reality, perceptual distortion, and paranoid reactions, appear after 6 or 7 days without sleep.

sleep disorder a persistent disturbance of typical sleep patterns, including the amount, quality, and timing of sleep, or the chronic occurrence of abnormal events or behavior during sleep. In *DSM–IV–TR* sleep disorders are broadly classified according to apparent cause, which may be endogenous or conditioning factors (**primary sleep disorders**), another mental disorder, a medical condition, or substance use. Primary sleep disorders are subdivided into DYSSOMNIAS and PARASOMNIAS. A classification system introduced in 1979 by the Association of Sleep Disorders Centers groups sleep disorders according to individuals' presenting symptoms: DISORDERS OF INITIATING AND MAINTAINING SLEEP, DISORDERS OF EXCESSIVE SOMNOLENCE, DISORDERS OF THE SLEEP–WAKE CYCLE SCHEDULE, and DYSFUNCTIONS ASSOCIATED WITH SLEEP, SLEEP STAGES, OR PARTIAL AROUSALS.

sleep disorientation a state of being half-awake and half-asleep, with absence of normal orientation while the mind is under the influence of nightmarish thoughts. Some individuals become dangerously violent during this state and may inflict injury on people nearby. The condition was formerly called **somnolentia**.

sleep drive the basic physiological urge to sleep, particularly when in need of rest. It appears to be governed in part by the hypothalamus and the RETICULAR ACTIVATING SYSTEM.

sleep efficiency the ratio of total time asleep to total time in bed. Sleep efficiency can be reduced in various psychological conditions (e.g., depression, anxiety) as well as by the use of some pharmacological agents (e.g., certain antidepressants).

sleep enuresis see BED-WETTING.

sleep epilepsy 1. a type of epilepsy in which seizures occur exclusively or predominantly during sleep. **2.** a former name for NARCOLEPSY.

sleeper effect the finding that the impact of a persuasive message increases over time. This effect is most likely to occur when a person carefully scrutinizes a message with relatively strong arguments and then subsequently receives a discounting cue (i.e., some piece of information suggesting that the message should be disregarded). The discounting cue weakens the initial impact of the message, but if the cue and the arguments in the message are not well integrated in memory, the cue may gradually be forgotten. If this occurs, the impact of the arguments will be greater at a later point in time than they were at the time of their initial presentation.

sleep hygiene techniques for the behavioral treatment of insomnia that involve instruction given to the client to follow certain routines aimed at improving sleep patterns. Typical recommendations to the client include using the bed only for sleeping and sex (e.g., the client is instructed not to read in bed), not napping during the day, decreasing caffeine intake or eliminating it after a certain point in the day, going to bed regularly at a set time, and keeping a sleep diary.

sleepiness *n.* see SOMNOLENCE.

sleeping sickness an infection, found only in tropical Africa, caused by parasitic protozoans of the genus *Trypanosoma* (*T. gambiense* and *T. rhodesiense*), which are transmitted by the bite of infected tsetse flies. Initial symptoms include fever, headaches, sweating, and swollen lymph nodes, progressing—upon inflammation of the brain and its protective membranes (see MENINGES)—to lethargy, excessive sleepiness (see HYPERSOMNIA), and confusion. If untreated, sleeping sickness can result in coma and eventually death. In *DSM–IV–TR*, the condition is categorized as SLEEP DISORDER due to a general medical condition: hypersomnia type. Also called **African trypanosomiasis**.

sleeping state see S-STATE.

sleep inversion a tendency to sleep or be somnolent by day and to remain awake at night.

sleep laboratory a research facility designed to monitor patterns of activity during sleep, such as eye movement, breathing abnormalities, heartbeat, brain waves, and muscle tone. Sleep laboratories are typically found in neurology departments in hospitals and universities or in sleep disorder clinics.

sleep latency the amount of time it takes for an individual to fall asleep once the attempt to do so is made. Sleep latency is measured in the diagnosis of SLEEP DISORDERS. Sleeping pills (e.g., benzodiazepines) are designed to decrease sleep latency so that the individual can fall asleep more quickly.

sleep learning the learning of material presented while one is asleep. The possibility of true sleep learning is still a controversial issue. Simple learning, such as PAVLOVIAN CONDITIONING, may occur during sleep; more complex learning, such as the acquisition of a foreign language, has not been reliably demonstrated.

sleeplessness *n.* see INSOMNIA.

sleep-onset insomnia a DYSSOMNIA characterized by persistent difficulty initiating sleep. Also called **onset insomnia**. See also INSOMNIA; PRIMARY INSOMNIA.

sleep paralysis brief inability to move or speak just before falling asleep or on awakening, often accompanied by hallucinations. It may occur in any individual but is seen especially in individuals with NARCOLEPSY and may be due to a temporary dysfunction of the RETICULAR ACTIVATING SYSTEM.

sleep pattern a habitual, individual pattern of sleep, such as two 4-hour periods, daytime napping, various forms of insomnia (e.g., initial or intermittent insomnia), or excessive sleep. See also SLEEP–WAKE CYCLE.

Sleep Questionnaire and Assessment of Wakefulness (**SQAW**) an extensive questionnaire developed in 1979 by U.S. physician Laughton E. Miles at the Stanford University Sleep Disorders Clinic and Research Center to assess sleep behaviors and sleep disorders.

sleep recovery sleeping more than usual after a period of sleep deprivation, as though in compensation.

sleep rhythm see SLEEP–WAKE CYCLE.

sleep spindles characteristic spindle-shaped patterns recorded on an electroencephalogram (EEG) during STAGE 2 SLEEP. They are short bursts of waves with a frequency of about 15 Hz that progressively increase then decrease in amplitude and they indicate a state of light sleep. Sleep spindles are often accompanied by K COMPLEXES.

sleep stages the four-cycle progression in electrical activity of the brain during a normal night's sleep, as recorded on an electroencephalogram (EEG). The regular pattern of ALPHA WAVES characteristic of the relaxed state of the individual just before sleep becomes intermittent and attenuated in STAGE 1 SLEEP, which is marked by drowsiness with rolling eyeball movements. This progresses to STAGE 2 SLEEP (light sleep), which is characterized by SLEEP SPINDLES and K COMPLEXES. In STAGE 3 and STAGE 4 SLEEP (deep sleep), DELTA WAVES predominate (see SLOW-WAVE SLEEP). These stages comprise NREM SLEEP and are interspersed with periods of dreaming associated with REM SLEEP. After a period of deep sleep, the sleeper may return to either light sleep or REM sleep or to both, and the cycles can recur multiple times over the course of the sleep period.

sleep talking verbalization during sleep, either in the form of mumbling or an approximation of waking speech. It usually but not always occurs during NREM SLEEP, and the sleeper is sometimes responsive to questions or commands. It is generally not considered pathological, and occurs at one time or another in most people.

sleep terror disorder a SLEEP DISORDER characterized by repeated episodes of abrupt awakening from NREM SLEEP accompanied by signs of disorientation, extreme panic, and intense anxiety. More intense than NIGHTMARES and occurring during the first few hours of sleep, these episodes typically last between 1 and 10 min and involve screaming and symptoms of autonomic arousal, such as profuse perspiration, dilated pupils, rapid breathing, and a rapidly beating heart. The individual is difficult to wake or comfort and does not have detailed recall of the dream upon waking; complete loss of memory for the episode is common. The disorder occurs most often in children and generally resolves itself during adolescence. In adults, it is often associated with psychopathology and a more chronic course. See also PARASOMNIA. Compare NIGHTMARE DISORDER.

sleep–wake cycle the natural, brain-controlled bodily rhythm that results in alternate periods of sleep and wakefulness. The sleep–wake cycle may be disrupted by a number of factors, such as flight across time zones, shift work, drug use, or stress (see CIRCADIAN RHYTHM SLEEP DISORDER; DISORDERS OF THE SLEEP–WAKE CYCLE SCHEDULE). Also called **sleep rhythm**; **sleep–wakefulness cycle**. See also MONOPHASIC SLEEP; POLYPHASIC SLEEP.

sleep–wake schedule disorder see CIRCADIAN RHYTHM SLEEP DISORDER.

sleepwalking disorder a SLEEP DISORDER characterized by persistent incidents of complex motor activity during slow-wave NREM SLEEP. These episodes typically occur during the first hours of sleep and involve getting out of bed and walking, although the individual may also perform more complicated tasks, such as eating, talking, or operating machinery. While in this state, the individual stares blankly, is essentially unresponsive, and can be awakened only with great difficulty; he or she does not remember the episode upon waking. Also called **noctambulation**; **somnambulism**. See also PARASOMNIA.

slice-of-life commercials see NONOVERT APPEALS.

slip *n.* an error, such as a SLIP OF THE TONGUE, that is committed unintentionally, even while knowing that it is an error. It implies a momentary loss of conscious control.

slip of the pen see FREUDIAN SLIP; PARAPRAXIS.

slip of the tongue a minor error in speech, such as a SPOONERISM, that is episodic and not related to speech disorder or a stage of second-language acquisition. Psychoanalysts have long been interested in the significance of such slips, believing them to reveal unconscious associations, motivations, or wishes. Also called **lapsus linguae**; **speech error**. See also FREUDIAN SLIP; PARAPRAXIS; VERBAL LEAKAGE.

slippage *n.* see COGNITIVE SLIPPAGE.

slipped disk a condition in which the gelatinous interior of an intervertebral disk is pushed through a weakened portion of its fibrous coating, pressing on adjacent nerve roots and associated structures. This causes pain in the back, leg, or arm, depending on the position of the disk and the nerve involved, and sometimes nerve damage (resulting in numbness, weakness, etc.). The SCIATIC NERVE is most commonly affected. The medical name for this condition is **prolapsed intervertebral disk**.

slogan *n.* a phrase developed as an attention-seeking advertising device associated with a product image. Slogans may also help the consumer recall the name of a product brand, as in "good to the last drop" for Maxwell House Coffee, or "99 and 44/100 percent pure" for Ivory Soap. Slogans may be revised periodically as a result of continuing studies of consumer psychology.

slope *n.* in mathematics and statistics, the RISE divided by the RUN; that is, the change in vertical distance on a graph divided by the horizontal distance. It is represented by the slant of a line. See also ACCELERATION.

Slosson Intelligence Test (**SIT**) a brief individual test of verbal intelligence designed for use with individuals aged 4 and over. It consists of 187 oral questions assessing six cognitive domains: vocabulary, general information, similarities and differences, comprehension, quantitative ability, and auditory memory. Originally developed in 1963, the SIT was revised in 1991 (**SIT–R**) and in 2002 (**SIT–R3**). [Richard Lawrence **Slosson**, Jr. (1910–)]

slowdown *n.* a tactic used by employees to persuade management to make concessions. It involves intentionally slowing production to levels that are costly to management but not in violation of contractual agreements. Also called **go-slow**.

slow learner a child of lower-than-average intelligence. Such children are so designated despite the fact that a somewhat lower-than-average IQ does not necessarily imply slow learning. Slow learners are estimated at 15–17% of the average school population. They do not show marked variations from physical, social, and emotional norms and are usually placed in regular classes. The term "slow learner" is often imprecisely applied to children with MILD MENTAL RETARDATION as well as to children of normal capacity whose intellectual progress is slow.

slow muscle fiber a type of muscle fiber found in SKELETAL MUSCLE that contracts slowly but does not fatigue readily. Compare FAST MUSCLE FIBER.

slow-release preparation a drug preparation that is formulated in such a way that the active ingredient is released over an extended period. For example, drugs may be administered in the form of transdermal patches, which are applied to skin, through which they slowly release their contents; or as extended-release capsules, which contain quantities of the active drug surrounded by separate coatings that dissolve at different rates in stomach and intestines. Injectable slow-release forms (depot preparations) are often oil based; these are taken up into fat stores in the body and released over extended periods of days to weeks. Also called **extended-release preparation**; **sustained-release preparation**.

slow wave see DELTA WAVE.

slow-wave sleep a stage of DEEP SLEEP that is characterized by DELTA WAVES on the electroencephalogram. It is controlled by SEROTONIN-rich cells in the brainstem: Increased levels of serotonin stimulate slow-wave sleep, whereas abnormally low levels of serotonin result in insomnia. Slow-wave sleep has a restorative function that helps eliminate feelings of fatigue. See also SLEEP STAGES.

Sly syndrome see BETA-GLUCURONIDASE DEFICIENCY.

SM abbreviation for SECONDARY MEMORY.

smallest space analysis (**SSA**) a multivariate technique for analyzing MULTITRAIT–MULTIMETHOD MATRIX data.

small for dates the condition of a baby that is underweight for its GESTATIONAL AGE.

small group a small collection of research participants, typically 10 or fewer, whose responses to the experimental conditions are to be compared to those of one or more other groups.

small-N experimental design an experimental design for a small number of SAMPLING UNITS.

Smalltalk *n.* one of the first object-oriented computer languages, designed at Xerox in the 1970s. The name was chosen because the language was designed to be a communication medium for children. Window systems and mouse-driven control eventually emerged from this early research project.

Smart House a home that contains numerous devices that can be programmed to perform tasks automatically or be integrated into a single system that is controlled by a user through a single unit. For example, a door can be programmed to unlock automatically whenever a smoke detector sounds in the home, or a light can be turned on and off using a remote control rather than a light switch. Smart House technology can also incorporate elaborate systems and sensors that monitor household equipment, such as appliances and heating and cooling systems, as well as the activities of occupants, often providing alerts to individuals or external agencies as necessary. Such homes are especially important to older adults and individuals with disabilities because they enable increased independence and enhance quality of life.

smell 1. *n.* an ODOR, or the sense that enables an organism to detect the odors of volatile substances. Molecules of odorant chemicals carried by air currents are absorbed into nasal mucus and stimulate the OLFACTORY RECEPTORS, where they are converted to neural messages. See OLFACTION; OLFACTORY TRANSDUCTION; SMELL MECHANISM. **2.** *vb.* to detect an odor or odors by means of the olfactory system.

smell brain see RHINENCEPHALON.

smell compensation the perception of a combination of ODORANTS as less intense than the component odorants.

Smell Identification Test (**SIT**) a 40-item test of odor-identification ability for individuals aged 5 years and older. It is used to assess olfactory sensitivity and diagnose or evaluate olfactory impairment, which has been recognized as an important clinical indicator of neurological and psychiatric disorders (e.g., Alzheimer's disease, Parkinson's disease). Test participants scratch and sniff a scent-impregnated patch and then identify the odor from a list of four answer choices, repeating the procedure for all 40 test stimuli. A brief version of the test (**B–SIT**) using 12 odorant stimuli determines gross dysfunction of olfactory sensitivity. The SIT, initially developed in 1981, is now in its third edition. Also called **University of Pennsylvania Smell Identification Test (UPSIT)**. [developed by U.S. psychologist Richard L. Doty (1944–)]

smell mechanism the process and structures involved in the perception of odors. OLFACTORY RECEPTORS extend numerous cilia into the OLFACTORY MUCOSA in the roof of the nasal cavity; these cilia, together with villi of supporting tissue cells, form a layer of hairlike projections. Molecules of ODORANTS are absorbed into nasal mucus and carried to the OLFACTORY EPITHELIUM, where they stimulate the receptor sites of the cilia. The olfactory receptors carry impulses in axonal bundles through tiny holes in the CRIBRIFORM PLATE, the bony layer separating the base of the skull from the nasal cavity. On the top surface of the cribriform plate rests the OLFACTORY BULB, which receives the impulses and sends them on to the PERIAMYGDALOID CORTEX. See also INFRARED THEORY OF SMELL; STEREOCHEMICAL SMELL THEORY.

smell prism see HENNING'S ODOR PRISM.

SMIC abbreviation for SPORTS MEDICINE INJURY CHECKLIST.

smile *n.* a bilateral upturning of the lips, typically taking place when greeting another or sharing certain states of pleasure with another. See also DUCHENNE SMILE; ENDOGENOUS SMILE.

Smith–Lemli–Opitz syndrome an autosomal recessive disorder marked by MICROCEPHALY, a broad, short nose, syndactyly (fused digits) or polydactyly (extra digits), and mental retardation. Nearly all affected males have urethral or other genital anomalies, whereas females have no obvious abnormalities of the external genitalia, a factor that led early investigators to believe erroneously that the syndrome affected only males. This disorder may be caused by mutations in the sterol delta-7-reductase gene (*DHCR7*), on chromosome 11 (locus 11q12–13). Also called **RSH syndrome** (from the names of the three affected families originally reported); **Smith syndrome**. [reported in 1964 by David W. **Smith** (1926–1981), U.S. pediatrician, Luc **Lemli** (1935–), Belgian pediatrician, and John M. **Opitz** (1935–), U.S. geneticist]

smoking *n.* the act of drawing the smoke of burning TOBACCO or other substances, such as marijuana, into the mouth or lungs. See CANNABIS; NICOTINE; TOBACCO.

smoking cessation treatment interventions to help people quit smoking that typically involve behavioral techniques (e.g., reinforcement), social support, environmental change, and healthy activity substitution (e.g., exercise), which may be used in conjunction with nicotine replacement therapy or other drugs. Group treatment is often offered in community settings.

smoothed curve a curve that has been adjusted to eliminate erratic or sudden changes in slope, so that its fundamental shape and direction will be evident.

smoothing *n.* a collection of techniques used to reduce the irregularities in a batch of data or in a plot (curve) of that data, particularly in TIME SERIES analyses. The use of a "moving average" is one example of smoothing such data.

smooth movement see RAMP MOVEMENT.

smooth muscle any muscle that is not striated and is under the control of the AUTONOMIC NERVOUS SYSTEM (i.e., it is not under voluntary control). Smooth muscles are able to remain in a contracted state for long periods of time or maintain a pattern of rhythmic contractions indefinitely without fatigue. Smooth muscle is found, for example, in the digestive organs, blood vessels, and the muscles of the eyes. Also called **involuntary muscle**. Compare CARDIAC MUSCLE; SKELETAL MUSCLE.

smooth-pursuit movement an EYE MOVEMENT that enables continuous fixation on an object as it moves. Compare SACCADE.

SMR abbreviation for SENSORIMOTOR RHYTHM.

S/N abbreviation for SIGNAL-TO-NOISE RATIO.

snake phobia a persistent and irrational fear of snakes, formerly called **ophidiophobia**. This type of fear is classified as a SPECIFIC PHOBIA, animal type. See also ANIMAL PHOBIA.

sneak mating a practice in which male animals that do not form or defend territories or nest sites or that do not vocalize or give displays to attract mates intercept females and mate with them before the females reach the larger, more dominant territorial or displaying males. Sneak mating has a low success rate, but it is frequently the only reproductive strategy available to smaller, subordinate males.

Snellen chart a device for testing VISUAL ACUITY, consisting of printed letters ranging in size from very small to very large. The observer reads the letters at a given distance. Also called **Snellen test**. [Herman **Snellen** (1834–1908), Dutch ophthalmologist]

SNF abbreviation for SKILLED NURSING FACILITY.

snow *n.* slang for COCAINE or, sometimes, HEROIN or AMPHETAMINE.

snowball sampling a method of recruiting new participants for a study by asking existing participants to recommend additional potential participants.

snow blindness a visual distortion caused by exposure to extreme intensities of white light. It is marked by PHOTOPHOBIA, an illusion that all objects are red (see CHROMATOPSIA), or temporary loss of vision.

SNP abbreviation for SINGLE-NUCLEOTIDE POLYMORPHISM.

SNRIs serotonin and norepinephrine reuptake inhibitors: a class of antidepressants that apparently exert their therapeutic effects by inhibiting the reuptake of both serotonin and norepinephrine. They include VENLAFAXINE and duloxetine. Also called **mixed serotonin and norepinephrine reuptake inhibitors**.

SOA abbreviation for STIMULUS ONSET ASYNCHRONY.

Soar *n.* a COGNITIVE ARCHITECTURE, or a complete computational representation, intended to reflect a comprehensive view of human or machine processing, from input/output devices, the use of appropriate knowledge- and search-based processing, and including components that learn. Soar is based on the PRODUCTION SYSTEM model of human problem solving. See also ADAPTIVE PRODUCTION SYSTEM. [acronym for State, Operator, and Result; created in 1990 by U.S. cognitive and computer scientist Allen Newell (1927–1992)]

sociability *n.* the need or tendency to seek out companions, friends, and social relationships. See AFFILIATIVE DRIVE; GREGARIOUSNESS. **—sociable** *adj.*

sociability rating an evaluation of an individual's degree of sociability based on the amount of time devoted to social activities.

social *adj.* **1.** relating to human society. **2.** relating to the behavior and interactions of people as members of a group, a community, or society in general.

social acceptance 1. the formal or informal admission of an individual into a group. **2.** the absence of SOCIAL DISAPPROVAL.

social action 1. individual or group activities directed to achieving social benefits for the community or a segment of the population. See also ACTIVISM; COMMUNITY ACTION GROUP; SOCIAL MOVEMENT. **2.** in sociology, any human activity seen in terms of its social context. Thus defined, such activity is the characteristic subject matter of the discipline of sociology.

social action program a planned and organized effort to change some aspect of society, such as enactment of animal rights legislation or initiating improvements in psychiatric hospitals. See also SOCIAL MOVEMENT.

social activity an event or pursuit that brings individuals together and facilitates their interaction, for example, dancing, singing, games, or parties. Social activities are frequently a part of the rehabilitation process for individuals with mental or physical disabilities.

social adaptation adjustment to the demands, restrictions, and mores of society, including the ability to live and work with others harmoniously and to engage in satisfying social interactions and relationships. Also called **social adjustment**.

social-adjustive function of an attitude the role an attitude can play in facilitating social interaction and enhancing cohesion among members of a social group. For example, a teenager may adopt positive attitudes toward certain styles of dress and types of music as a means of gaining acceptance by a peer group. See also EGO-DEFENSIVE FUNCTION OF AN ATTITUDE; FUNCTIONAL APPROACH TO ATTITUDES; KNOWLEDGE FUNCTION OF AN ATTITUDE; UTILITARIAN FUNCTION OF AN ATTITUDE; VALUE-EXPRESSIVE FUNCTION OF AN ATTITUDE.

social adjustment see SOCIAL ADAPTATION.

social age (**SA**) an estimate of a person's social capacities in relation to normative standards, which can be made in a number of ways. In clinical situations with young children, social age often is assigned by interviewing parents and other adults to produce scores on the VINELAND ADAPTIVE BEHAVIOR SCALES.

social agency a private or governmental organization that supervises or provides personal services, especially in the fields of health, welfare, and rehabilitation. The general objective of a social agency is to improve the quality of life of its clients.

social anchoring basing one's attitudes, values, actions, and so forth on the positions taken by others, often to an extreme degree. Whereas social comparison (see SOCIAL COMPARISON THEORY) involves comparing one's position to that held by others, anchoring implies an inability to make an independent judgment.

social animal the concept that some animals are inherently social creatures with interpersonal needs and wants. When referring to humans, the term **social man** is sometimes used. Also called **social being**; **zoon politikon**. See also SOCIAL INSTINCT.

social anorexia loss of appetite associated with starvation or malnutrition, as in individuals who are undernourished.

social anthropology see ANTHROPOLOGY.

social anxiety fear of social situations (e.g., making conversation, meeting strangers, or dating) in which embarrassment may occur or there is a risk of being negatively evaluated by others (e.g., seen as stupid, weak, or anxious). Social anxiety involves apprehensiveness about one's social status, role, and behavior. When the anxiety causes an individual significant distress or impairment in functioning, a diagnosis of SOCIAL PHOBIA may be warranted.

social anxiety disorder see SOCIAL PHOBIA.

social approval positive appraisal and acceptance of someone or something (a behavior, trait, attribute, or the like) by a social group. Its manifestations may include compliments, praise, statements of approbation, and so on. Compare SOCIAL DISAPPROVAL.

social ascendancy see UPWARD MOBILITY.

social assimilation 1. the process by which two or more cultures or cultural groups are gradually merged, although one is likely to remain dominant. **2.** the process by which individuals are absorbed into the culture or mores of the dominant group. See ACCULTURATION.

social atom see SOCIUS.

social attitude 1. a person's general outlook on social issues and approach to his or her social responsibilities. **2.** a person's general disposition or manner toward other people, for example, friendly or hostile. **3.** an opinion or evaluation shared by a social group.

social behavior 1. any action performed by interdependent conspecifics (members of the same species). **2.** in humans, an action that is influenced, directly or indirectly, by others, who may be actually present, imagined, expected, or only implied. **3.** any one of a set of behaviors exhibited by gregarious, communal social species, including COOPERATION, AFFILIATION, ALTRUISM, and so on.

social bond an affective relation between individuals, such as the connection between two friends or the emotional link between family members.

social breakdown syndrome a symptom pattern observed primarily in institutionalized individuals with chronic mental illness but also in such populations as long-term prisoners and older people. Symptoms include withdrawal, apathy, submissiveness, and progressive social and vocational incompetence. Previously considered to be symptomatic of mental illness, this decline is now attributed to internalized negative stereotypes, such as identification with the SICK ROLE and the impact of labeling (see LABELING THEORY), the absence of social support, and such institutional factors as a lack of stimulation, overcrowding, unchanging routine, and disinterest on the part of the staff. Also called **chronicity**; **institutionalism**; **institutional neurosis**; **social disability syndrome**.

social casework see CASEWORK.

social category a group of people defined by SOCIAL CLASS or other common attributes of a social nature, such as homelessness, unemployment, or retirement.

social change any process in which the general structure or character of a society is altered, as in the Industrial Revolution of the 19th century or the introduction of freer sexual expression in the 20th century. Social change may be the result of impersonal economic and technological forces or determined action by individuals or groups. See also CULTURE CHANGE; SOCIAL EVOLUTION; SOCIAL MOVEMENT.

social class a major group or division of society that shares a common level of status, income, power, and prestige as well as many common values and, in some cases, similar religious and social patterns. See also SOCIOECONOMIC STATUS.

social climate the general character of the social milieu in which individuals and groups live, that is, the totality of the prevailing customs, mores, and attitudes that influence their behavior and adjustment.

social climbing an attempt to improve one's social standing by associating with people of a higher social class. It often involves efforts to impress such people, cater to their needs, or both.

social clock in a given culture, the set of norms governing the ages at which particular life events, such as beginning school, leaving home, getting married, having children, and retiring, are expected to occur.

social code the social rules and standards, including laws, adhered to by a specific community or by society in general.

social cognition 1. cognition in which people perceive, think about, interpret, categorize, and judge their own social behaviors and those of others. The study of social cognition involves aspects of both cognitive psychology and social psychology. Major areas of interest include ATTRIBUTION THEORY, PERSON PERCEPTION, SOCIAL INFLUENCE, and the cognitive processes involved in moral judgments. **2.** in animal behavior, the knowledge that an individual has about other members of its social group and the ability to reason about the actions of others based on this knowledge. In vervet monkeys, for example, after an individual in matriline (matrilineal line of descent) A attacks an individual in matriline B, other members of B are more likely to attack other animals from A.

social-cognitive theory a theoretical framework in which the functioning of personality is explained in terms of cognitive contents and processes acquired through interaction with the sociocultural environment. [advanced by Albert BANDURA and U.S. personality psychologist Walter Mischel (1930–)]

social cohesion see COHESION.

social comparison theory the proposition that people evaluate their abilities and attitudes in relation to those of others (i.e., through a process of comparison) when objective standards for the assessment of these abilities and attitudes are lacking. The way people compare themselves with others (their **comparison group** or REFERENCE GROUP) was most fully described by Leon FESTINGER in 1954. He also held that those chosen as the comparison group are generally those whose abilities or attitudes are relatively similar to the person's own abilities or views.

social competence skill in interpersonal relations, especially the ability to handle a variety of social situations effectively.

social constructionism the position, mainly associated with POSTMODERNISM, that any supposed knowledge of reality (as, for example, that claimed by science) is in fact a construct of language, culture, and society having no objective or universal validity. See also SITUATED KNOWLEDGE.

social constructivism the school of thought that an individual's motivations and emotions are shaped predominantly by cultural training in modes of acting, feeling, and thinking, rather than being largely determined by biological influences. See NATURE–NURTURE CONTROVERSY.

social contagion see CONTAGION.

social context the specific circumstance or general environment that serves as a social framework for individual or interpersonal behavior. This context frequently influences, at least to some degree, the actions and feelings that occur within it.

social contract in political theory, the idea that society is based upon an unwritten agreement whereby individuals freely surrender some of their natural freedoms in order to benefit from the greater security and other benefits that follow from government and the rule of law. The classic formulations of social contract theory are those of English philosopher Thomas Hobbes (1588–1679), English philosopher John Locke (1632–1704), and Swiss-born French philosopher Jean-Jacques Rousseau (1712–1778), each of whom developed it in a very different way: For Hobbes, the social contract justified autocracy as the only bulwark against anarchy; for Locke, it permitted the removal of unjust or arbitrary rulers; for Rousseau, it required the voluntary subjection of the individual to the "general will" of society.

social contract orientation in KOHLBERG'S THEORY OF MORAL DEVELOPMENT, the first of two stages in the POSTCONVENTIONAL LEVEL, in which people make moral decisions based on an understanding of social mutuality and an interest in the welfare of others. Compare PRINCIPLED STAGE.

social control 1. the power of the institutions, organizations, and laws of society to influence or regulate the behavior of individuals and groups. The human tendency to conform increases the power of social institutions to shape behavior. See also BEHAVIOR CONTROL. **2.** the impact of education, the media, religion, the economic system, and other social forces on individual or group behavior.

social conventions established rules, methods, procedures, and practices that have been accepted as guides for social conduct over a relatively long period. Often unwritten, arbitrary, and self-perpetuating, social conventions usually pertain to relatively mundane aspects of society, such as etiquette, social ceremonies, and decorum. See also SOCIAL NORMS.

social Darwinism the now discredited theory that social relations develop according to the principles of NATURAL SELECTION advanced by British naturalist Charles Darwin (1809–1882). As articulated by British philosopher Herbert Spencer (1820–1903) and others, the theory proposed that societies evolve through SURVIVAL OF THE FITTEST, the "fittest" being defined as those with wealth, power, and "natural" superiority in the struggle for existence. With its legitimizing of social, economic, and racial inequality, social Darwinism became a major ideological vehicle for justifying laissez-faire economics, imperialism, and EUGENICS in the late 19th and early 20th centuries.

social death a pattern of group behavior that ignores the presence or existence of another person. Social death occurs in situations in which verbal and nonverbal communication would be expected to include all participants but in which one or more individuals are excluded. See also PHENOMENOLOGICAL DEATH.

social-decision scheme a strategy or rule used in a group to select a single alternative from among the various alternatives proposed and discussed during the group's deliberations. These schemes or rules are sometimes explicitly acknowledged by the group, as when a formal tally of those favoring the alternative is taken and the proposal is accepted only when a certain proportion of those present favor it, but are sometimes implicit and informal, as when a group accepts the alternative that its most powerful members seem to favor.

social deficit inability, unwillingness, or poor judgment in the performance of social activities commensurate with chronological age, intelligence, or physical condition. Such a deficit is presumed to reduce a person's ability to obtain social support and is therefore a target of treatment, especially in behavior therapy and with severely disturbed individuals.

social degeneracy a condition in which social structures and norms of individual behavior no longer function constructively.

social density 1. density that can be changed by altering the number of individuals per given unit of space. Social density is a major determinant of CROWDING, and there is evidence that it has a more powerful effect on human response than SPATIAL DENSITY. **2.** the number of interpersonal interactions that are likely to occur in a given space. See also PROXEMICS.

social deprivation **1.** lack of adequate opportunity for social experience. **2.** limited access to society's resources due to poverty, discrimination, or other disadvantage. See CULTURAL DEPRIVATION.

social desirability **1.** the extent to which someone or something (a trait, attribute, or the like) is admired or considered valuable within a social group. **2.** a bias that prompts individuals to present themselves in ways that are likely to be seen as positive by the majority of other people. Social desirability bias often reduces the validity of interviews, questionnaires, and other self-reports, because respondents tend to provide answers based on perceived social desirability rather than accuracy. See IMPRESSION MANAGEMENT; RESPONSE SET.

social desirability response set the tendency of a respondent or participant to give answers that elicit a favorable evaluation rather than answers that genuinely represent their views. See RESPONSE SET; SOCIAL DESIRABILITY.

social determinism the theory or doctrine that historical events or individual behaviors are determined by social phenomena, such as economic forces. See also CULTURAL DETERMINISM; DETERMINISM.

social development the gradual acquisition of certain skills (e.g., language, social skills), attitudes, relationships, and behavior that enable the individual to interact with others and to function as a member of society.

social differentiation the process by which a hierarchy in social status develops within any society or social group. For example, in a care facility for older people, social differentiation might be based on age, level of mobility, or physical impairment.

social dilemma an interpersonal situation that tempts individuals to seek personal, selfish gain by putting at risk the interests of the larger collective to which they belong. Such mixed-motive situations have reward structures that favor individuals who act selfishly rather than in ways that benefit the larger social collective; however, if a substantial number of individuals seek maximum personal gain, their outcomes will be lower than if they had sought collective outcomes. Social dilemmas are simulated in MIXED-MOTIVE GAMES, such as the PRISONER'S DILEMMA. See also SOCIAL TRAP.

social disability syndrome see SOCIAL BREAKDOWN SYNDROME.

social disapproval condemnation and rejection of someone or something (a behavior, trait, attribute, or the like) by a social group. Its manifestations may include insults, criticism, disparagement, SHUNNING, and so on. Compare SOCIAL APPROVAL.

social discrimination the differential treatment of individuals based on their cultural background, social class, educational attainment, or other sociocultural distinction. See DISCRIMINATION.

social distance the degree to which, psychologically speaking, a person or group wants to remain separate from members of different social groups. This reflects the extent to which individuals or groups accept others of a different ethnic, racial, national, or other social background.

social distance scale a measure of intergroup attitudes that asks respondents to indicate their willingness to accept members of other ethnic, national, or social groups in situations that range from relatively distant ("would allow to live in my country") to relatively close ("would admit to close kinship by marriage"). See also BOGARDUS SOCIAL DISTANCE SCALE.

social drift see DRIFT HYPOTHESIS.

social drinker an imprecise categorization generally agreed to signify an individual who tends to drink alcohol only in a social setting and usually in moderation.

social drive the drive to establish social relationships and to be gregarious. See AFFILIATIVE DRIVE; GREGARIOUSNESS.

social dyad two people or groups who interact in a social context. Examples of such relationships are rivalry between two siblings or two sports teams, symbiosis between mother and infant, and harmony or hostility between business partners. See also DYAD; DYADIC RELATIONSHIP.

social dynamics **1.** an approach to sociology that focuses on the empirical study of specific societies and social systems in the process of historical change. Compare SOCIAL STATICS. [conceptualized by French philosopher Auguste Comte (1798–1857)] **2.** the forces or processes of change at work in any social group. See GROUP DYNAMICS.

social ecology the study of human or nonhuman organisms in relation to their social environment. See also ECOLOGICAL STUDIES; ECOLOGY; HUMAN ECOLOGY; URBAN ECOLOGY.

social-emotional leader an individual who guides others in their pursuits by performing supportive, interpersonally accommodative behaviors. Also called **relationship leader**.

Social–Emotional scale see BAYLEY SCALES OF INFANT AND TODDLER DEVELOPMENT.

social engineer **1.** a person engaged in planning social policy and in organizing community action programs to remedy such problems as crime, drug abuse, and urban decay. **2.** a pejorative term for a person who attempts to enforce social change by imposing certain abstract or theoretical ideas on society.

social evolution the process of gradual change in a society over time, especially as contrasted with the sudden and dramatic changes caused by political upheavals, natural disasters, or the like. See also CULTURAL DRIFT; SOCIAL CHANGE.

social exchange theory a theory envisioning social interactions as an exchange in which the participants seek to maximize their benefits within the limits of what is regarded as fair or just. Intrinsic to this hypothesis is the RECIPROCITY NORM: People are expected to reciprocate for the benefits they have received. Social exchange theory is similar to EQUITY THEORY, which also maintains that people seek fairness in social relationships and that fairness exists when each party in the relationship has the same ratio of outcomes (benefits) to inputs (resources brought to the relationship). [proposed by Austrian sociologists George C. Homans (1910–1989) and Peter Blau (1918–)]

social facilitation the improvement in an individual's performance of a task that often occurs when others are present. This effect tends to occur with tasks that are uncomplicated or have been previously mastered through practice. There is some disagreement as to whether the improvement is due to a heightened state of arousal, a greater self-awareness, or a reduced attention to unimportant and distracting peripheral stimuli. By contrast, the presence of other people is frequently an impediment to effective performance when the task is complicated, particularly if it is not well learned. See also AUDIENCE EFFECT.

social factors factors (e.g., attitudes) that affect thought or behavior in social contexts or that affect SELF-CONCEPT vis-à-vis other individuals or groups.

social feedback a direct report of the effect of one's behavior or speech on other people. An example of social feedback is laughter at one's jokes.

social fission the splitting of a social group into smaller groups, usually because of unresolvable internal conflict between factions.

social fixity see SOCIAL IMMOBILITY.

social flexibility see SOCIAL MOBILITY.

social force any global, systemic, and relatively powerful process that influences individuals in interpersonal settings, such as GROUP PRESSURE, NORMATIVE INFLUENCE, and CONTAGION. See also SOCIAL INFLUENCE; SOCIAL PRESSURE.

social gerontology the study of the social process of aging and the interaction of older adults with their environments, including such issues as the contributions of older adults to the community, services provided in the community for older adults, and the utilization of group residences and communities for older adults.

social group see GROUP.

social growth the development of the individual's knowledge and ability with regard to dealings with other individuals and groups. Social growth is not limited to conformity; much social growth can lie outside the range of cultural expectations.

social habit a common form of social behavior that is deeply ingrained and often appears to have an automatic quality (e.g., saying "Thank you").

social heritage culturally learned social behaviors that are constant across generations. Examples include giving gifts on particular occasions, greeting others when one enters a room, and shaking hands. See CULTURAL HERITAGE; SOCIAL TRANSMISSION.

social hunger a desire to be accepted by others.

social identity 1. the personal qualities that one claims and displays to others so consistently that they are considered to be part of one's essential, stable self. This public persona may be an accurate indicator of the private, personal self, but it may also be a deliberately contrived image (see SOCIAL IMAGE). **2.** see COLLECTIVE SELF.

social identity theory 1. a general social-psychological conceptualization of the personal and interpersonal factors that influence the publicly claimed and presented self. **2.** a conceptual perspective on group processes and intergroup relations that assumes that groups influence their members' self-concepts and self-esteem, particularly when individuals categorize themselves as group members and identify strongly with the group. According to this theory, people tend to favor their INGROUP over an OUTGROUP because the former is part of their self-identity. With its emphasis on the importance of group membership for the self, social identity theory contrasts with individualistic analyses of behavior that discount the importance of group belongingness.

social image an individual's public persona, that is, the identity presented to others in public contexts. See SOCIAL IDENTITY.

social immobility a feature of a society with fixed social norms or a rigid class system such that movement from one social class to another is virtually impossible and occurs only in very rare and prescribed instances. The traditional Hindu CASTE system is an example of such a FIXED CLASS SOCIETY. Also called **social fixity**. Compare SOCIAL MOBILITY.

social impact assessment the evaluation of the social effect of a proposed construction project while it is in the planning stage. It is based on studies of potential effects on land values, traffic flow, displacement of jobs and homes, ecological balance, air pollution, and related factors, as well as predicted benefits to the environment and to people who would make use of the new facility.

social impact theory a theory of social influence postulating that the amount of influence exerted by a source on a target depends on (a) the strength of the source compared to that of the target (e.g., the social status of the source versus that of the target); (b) the immediacy of the source to the target (e.g., the physical or psychological distance between them); and (c) the number of sources and targets (e.g., several sources influencing a single target). The impact of the source on the target increases as the source's strength, immediacy, and number increase relative to the target. See also DYNAMIC SOCIAL IMPACT THEORY. [originally proposed by U.S. psychologist Bibb Latané]

social imperception disorder a condition characterized by a lack of awareness of common social interaction and interpersonal behaviors, difficulty in recognizing and understanding other people's feelings and emotions, and a very limited awareness of typical social interpersonal issues.

social incentive an inducement to behave in particular approved ways involving the offer of such interpersonal rewards as acceptance, approval, inclusion, or status.

social indicator any variable by which the quality of life of a society can be assessed. Many social indicators have been suggested by different authorities—among them, per capita income, poverty, unemployment, labor conditions, education, mental health, general health, pollution, the cost of housing, opportunities for leisure and recreation, crime rates, nutrition, life expectancy, and the status of the elderly.

social influence 1. any change in an individual's thoughts, feelings, or behaviors caused by other people, who may be actually present, imagined, expected, or only implied. **2.** those interpersonal processes that can cause individuals to change their thoughts, feelings, or behaviors. See INFORMATIONAL INFLUENCE; INTERPERSONAL INFLUENCE; NORMATIVE INFLUENCE. See also SOCIAL FORCE; SOCIAL PRESSURE.

social information processing a type of human INFORMATION PROCESSING in which social information is encoded, compared with other pertinent information, and retrieved to influence one's interactions with others. [proposed by U.S. psychologist Kenneth A. Dodge (1954–)]

social inhibition the restraint placed on an individual's expression of her or his feelings, attitudes, motives, and so forth by the belief that others could learn of this behavior and disapprove of it. See also AUDIENCE EFFECT.

social-inquiry model a teaching model that emphasizes the role of social interaction. The social-inquiry model utilizes methods of resolving social issues through a process of logical reasoning coupled with academic inquiry.

social insects insects that live together in groups, exhibiting reproductive division of labor, cooperation in care of the young, and multiple generations working together. In colonies of some bees, ants, wasps, and termites, reproduction is limited to one or a few queens, and large numbers of workers (sterile females) build nests, forage for food, tend the larvae, and defend the nest. Social insects are haplodiploid (see HAPLODIP-

LOIDY), with males developing from unfertilized eggs. This means that workers share 75% of their genes (whereas queen and worker share only 50%), so they have greater INCLUSIVE FITNESS by tending their siblings than they would by breeding on their own. See also EUSOCIALITY.

social instinct **1.** the desire for social contact and a feeling of belonging, as manifested by the tendency to congregate, affiliate, and engage in group behaviors. **2.** in the INDIVIDUAL PSYCHOLOGY of Alfred ADLER, an innate drive for cooperation that leads normal individuals to incorporate social interest and the common good into their efforts to achieve self-realization. See also GREGARIOUSNESS; HERD INSTINCT.

social integration **1.** the process by which separate groups are combined into a unified society, especially when this is pursued as a deliberate policy. Whereas **desegregation** refers to the formal termination of practices that create a segregated society, integration implies a coming together based on individual acceptance of the members of other groups. **2.** the process by which an individual is assimilated into a group.

social intelligence the degree of ease and effectiveness displayed by a person in social relationships.

social interaction any process that involves reciprocal stimulation or response between two or more individuals. These can range from the first encounters between parent and offspring to the complex interactions with multiple individuals in adult life. Social interaction includes the development of cooperation and competition, the influence of status and social roles, and the dynamics of group behavior, leadership, and conformity. Persistent social interaction between specific individuals leads to the formation of SOCIAL RELATIONSHIPS. It is only through close observation of social interaction that SOCIAL ORGANIZATION and SOCIAL STRUCTURE can be inferred.

social interest in the INDIVIDUAL PSYCHOLOGY of Alfred ADLER, communal feeling based on a recognition that people live in a social context; are an integral part of their family, community, humanity, and the cosmos itself; and have a natural aptitude for acquiring the skills and understanding necessary to solve social problems and to take socially affirmative action. Adler believed, however, that social interest is only partially inherent in adaptive development and needs to be actively cultivated in any individual.

social interference **1.** any actions that conflict with, obstruct, hamper, or undermine the activities and experiences of others. **2.** the reduction of productivity that occurs when individuals work in the presence of others. Compare SOCIAL FACILITATION. See also SOCIAL LOAFING.

social intervention social action programs designed to increase some type of social goods or services.

social introversion a behavioral trait manifested by shy, inhibited, and withdrawn attitudes.

social isolation **1.** voluntary or involuntary absence of contact with others. See also ISOLATE; LONELINESS. **2.** in experimental research, the separation of an animal from other members of its species. Social isolation often produces abnormal behavioral and physiological changes in animals.

social isolation syndrome in animal experiments, a syndrome produced in animals by raising them in total isolation from other members of their species. It consists of severely abnormal behavior, such as rocking, huddling, self-clasping, and retreating into a corner, as well as impaired sexual behavior.

sociality *n.* the tendency to live as part of a group with clear organization of social interactions and the ability to cooperate with and adapt to the demands of the group. Benefits of sociality for nonhuman animals include better predator detection and avoidance, increased foraging success through sharing information, and protection of young. Costs include increased risk of parasites, increased competition between group members, and increased visibility to predators.

sociality corollary a concept proposing that an individual's ability to communicate or otherwise interact with another individual is based on an understanding of the other's PERSONAL CONSTRUCT. [proposed by U.S. psychologist George A. Kelly (1905–1967)]

socialization *n.* **1.** the process by which individuals acquire social skills, beliefs, values, and behaviors necessary to function effectively in society or in a particular group. **2.** the process by which employees adjust to the ORGANIZATIONAL CULTURE and learn the knowledge, skills, attitudes, and values expected of them by superiors, peers, subordinates, customers, and others. **3.** the process whereby individuals become aware of alternative lifestyles and behaviors. It enables individuals to learn the social or group value-system behavior pattern and what is considered normal or desirable for the social environment in which they will be members. **—socialize** *vb.*

socialized delinquency violations of the law by individuals under age 18 that result from their adherence to the attitudes and values of a SUBCULTURE, such as a gang, that glorifies criminal or antisocial conduct. Also called **subcultural delinquency**.

socialized drive any PRIMARY DRIVE that has been modified through SOCIAL LEARNING so that drive satisfaction is achieved through socially acceptable behaviors, for example, sexual gratification achieved through mutually consensual adult sex. Compare SOCIAL DRIVE.

social judgment theory a theory of ATTITUDE CHANGE postulating that the magnitude of PERSUASION produced by a particular message depends on how much the position advocated in the message differs from a person's attitude. Persuasion is likely to be greatest when a message advocates a position that a person finds neither clearly acceptable nor clearly objectionable. See also LATITUDE OF ACCEPTANCE; LATITUDE OF NONCOMMITMENT; LATITUDE OF REJECTION.

social justice norm the SOCIAL NORM stating that people should be helped by others only if they deserve to be helped. Compare RECIPROCITY NORM; SOCIAL RESPONSIBILITY NORM.

social learning learning that is facilitated through social interactions with other individuals. Several forms of social learning have been identified, including LOCAL ENHANCEMENT, SOCIAL FACILITATION, EMULATION, and IMITATION.

social learning theory the general view that learning is largely or wholly due to social interactions with others. Behavior is assumed to be developed and regulated (a) by external stimulus events, such as the influence of other individuals; (b) by external reinforcement, such as praise, blame, and reward; and (c) by the effects of cognitive processes, such as thinking and judgment, on the individual's behavior and on the environment that influences him or her. [developed by Albert BANDURA]

social limitation restriction attributed to social policy or barriers (structural or attitudinal) that limit individuals' fulfillment of roles or deny individuals access to the services and opportunities associated with full participation in society.

social loafing the reduction of individual effort that occurs when people work in groups compared to when they work alone. Compare SOCIAL FACILITATION. See also SOCIAL INTERFERENCE.

socially sensitive research research on topics likely to evoke emotional responses from participants or controversy among community members.

social maladjustment **1.** inability to develop relationships that satisfy affiliative needs. **2.** lack of social finesse or tact. **3.** a breakdown in the process of maintaining constructive social relationships.

social marketing the use of marketing techniques to prompt socially desirable behaviors, such as eating health foods, driving safely, undergoing regular medical examinations, and the like.

social maturity a level of behavior in accordance with the social standards that are the norm for individuals of a particular age.

social maturity scale a scale that measures the degree to which an individual performs age-appropriate behaviors. These behaviors are primarily concerned with functioning in the family and community and are sometimes considered in conjunction with measures of intellectual impairment to establish the presence of retardation.

social mobility the extent to which a society permits or encourages change in social class, social status, or social roles. Societies differ in the degree to which they permit or facilitate movement or change in their social hierarchy (see FIXED CLASS SOCIETY; OPEN CLASS SOCIETY). Also called **social flexibility**. Compare SOCIAL IMMOBILITY. See DOWNWARD MOBILITY; HORIZONTAL MOBILITY; UPWARD MOBILITY; VERTICAL MOBILITY.

social monogamy see MONOGAMY.

social mores customs and codes of behavior established by a social group that are not necessarily supported by legal sanctions, but which may be as binding as laws. See also SOCIAL CONVENTIONS; SOCIAL NORMS.

social motive any motive acquired as a result of interaction with others. It may be universal (e.g., NEED FOR AFFILIATION) or culture-specific (e.g., NEED FOR ACHIEVEMENT). See also PSYCHOLOGICAL NEED.

social movement a deliberate, relatively organized effort of individuals and groups seeking to achieve or resist social change. Social movements emerge and operate mainly outside accepted political institutions; they can be narrow in scope, targeting particular social issues (e.g., teenage pregnancy), or they can address fundamental issues in society, such as the WOMEN'S LIBERATION MOVEMENT or the Civil Rights movement of the 1950s and 1960s. Reformist movements seek the improvement of existing social institutions and practices, revolutionary movements seek large-scale revisions of the social order, reactionary movements oppose change, and communitarian movements strive to create harmonious living conditions in modern society. See also COMMUNITY ACTION GROUP; SOCIAL ACTION PROGRAM.

social needs see MASLOW'S MOTIVATIONAL HIERARCHY.

social network the structure of the relationships that an individual or group has with others. Sociologists and social psychologists have developed quantitative analytic methods for measuring social networks (**social-network analysis**).

social-network therapy a form of psychotherapy in which various people who maintain significant relationships with the patient or client in different aspects of life (e.g., relatives, friends, coworkers) are assembled with the client present in small or larger group sessions. See also NETWORK THERAPY.

social neuroscience an emerging discipline that aims to integrate the social and biological approaches to human behavior that have often been seen as mutually exclusive. Social neuroscientists use a range of methodologies to elucidate the reciprocal interactions of the brain's biological mechanisms (especially the nervous, immune, and endocrine systems) with the social and cultural contexts in which human beings operate.

social norms socially determined consensual standards that indicate (a) what behaviors are considered typical in a given context (DESCRIPTIVE NORMS) and (b) what behaviors are considered proper in the context (INJUNCTIVE NORMS). Whether implicitly or explicitly, these norms not only prescribe the socially appropriate way to respond in the situation (the "normal" course of action) but also proscribe actions that should be avoided if at all possible. Unlike statistical norms, social norms of both types include an evaluative quality such that those who do not comply and cannot provide an acceptable explanation for their violation are evaluated negatively. Social norms apply across groups and social settings, whereas **group norms** are specific to a particular group. See also SOCIAL CONVENTIONS.

social order **1.** the structures, institutions, and organizing principles that maintain a society in its customary or characteristic form. See SOCIAL ORGANIZATION. **2.** a stable or peaceful condition of society.

social-order-maintaining morality see LAW-AND-ORDER ORIENTATION.

social organism a social group or society regarded as an entity having dynamic, living qualities, such as intention and self-preservation.

social organization the complete set of SOCIAL RELATIONSHIPS among members of a society or other group, which determines the structure of the group and the place of individuals within it. These relationships can be based on several variables: kinship, age, sex, area of residence, and—in human beings—religion, matrimony, or common interests as well. The social organization is usually implemented by rules of behavior produced by social interactions involving DOMINANCE, TERRITORIALITY, the MATING SYSTEM, and COOPERATION.

social ossification ingrained social behavior that is difficult to change, for example, when a person moves to a new environment with different social rules and standards.

social penetration theory a model stating that close relationships grow closer with increasingly intimate SELF-DISCLOSURES.

social perception an individual's awareness of social phenomena, especially his or her ability to infer motives, attitudes, or values from the social behavior of other individuals or of groups. Also called **interpersonal perception**.

social phenomenon any process, event, or accomplishment that results from the interaction of two or more individuals.

social phobia an anxiety disorder that is characterized by extreme and persistent SOCIAL ANXIETY or PERFORMANCE ANXIETY that causes significant distress or prevents participation in everyday activities. The feared situation is most often avoided altogether or else it is endured with marked discomfort. Also called **social anxiety disorder**.

social physique anxiety worry, apprehension, and fear related to concerns about how others will perceive one's physical appearance.

social planning the development of strategies and plans in such areas as education, public health, and social services provision, with the goal of enhancing the quality of life for all members of the community.

social play 1. play that involves interacting with others for fun or sport. Examples include ROUGH-AND-TUMBLE PLAY and sometimes SOCIODRAMATIC PLAY. **2.** patterns of play identified by the 1932 classification system of U.S. child-development researcher Mildred Parten and used to characterize the level of social development and participation of preschool children. According to this system, the lowest level of social play is SOLITARY PLAY, and the highest is COOPERATIVE PLAY. See also ASSOCIATIVE PLAY; PARALLEL PLAY.

social power see POWER.

social pressure the exertion of influence on a person or group by another person or group. Like GROUP PRESSURE, social pressure includes rational argument and persuasion (INFORMATIONAL INFLUENCE), calls for conformity (NORMATIVE INFLUENCE), and direct forms of influence, such as demands, threats, or personal attacks on the one hand and promises of rewards or social approval on the other (INTERPERSONAL INFLUENCE). See also SOCIAL FORCE; SOCIAL INFLUENCE.

social psychology the study of how an individual's thoughts, feelings, and actions are affected by the actual, imagined, or symbolically represented presence of other people. **Psychological social psychology** differs from **sociological social psychology** in that the former tends to give greater emphasis to internal psychological processes, whereas the latter focuses on factors that affect social life, such as status, role, and class.

social psychology of the experiment the study of the ways in which the participant-related and experimenter-related ARTIFACTS operate.

social punishment a negative interpersonal stimulus, such as SHUNNING, emotional withdrawal, or some other sign of disapproval, that decreases the frequency of the behavior that immediately precedes it. Compare SOCIAL REINFORCEMENT.

social pyramid a hierarchic distribution of POWER in social structures, as represented in a pyramidlike shape. Ultimate power is concentrated in the hands of a few people at the apex of the pyramid, with each descending tier representing a larger number of people with a diminished level of power. The base of the pyramid represents the greatest number of people with the least power.

social quotient the ratio between SOCIAL AGE and CHRONOLOGICAL AGE. A social quotient is a parallel concept to an IQ, where a score of 100 indicates average performance for age and scores less than 100 indicate below-average functioning. See VINELAND SOCIAL MATURITY SCALE.

social reality the consensus of attitudes, opinions, and beliefs held by members of a group or society.

social recovery restoration of an adaptive, highly functional mental state through SOCIAL THERAPY and improvement in social skills. [first described by U.S. psychiatrist Harry Stack Sullivan (1892–1949)]

social reform program an intervention program developed and implemented to counter deleterious aspects of a social system, the primary objective being to reduce the effects of malfunctions in the system. Also called **countermeasure-intervention program**.

social rehabilitation 1. the achievement of a higher level of social functioning in individuals with mental disorders or disabilities through group activities and participation in clubs and other community organizations. **2.** the achievement of a higher level of independent functioning in individuals with physical impairments or disabilities through provision of assistance with ACTIVITIES OF DAILY LIVING as well as other more social aspects of living, such as employment and the need for transportation and appropriate housing, that often present barriers to participation for those with disabilities. **3.** services and assistance provided to help criminal offenders establish new, noncriminal ways of life and become productive members of the community.

social reinforcement a positive interpersonal stimulus, such as verbal praise, a smile, touch, or other sign of approval, that increases the frequency of the behavior that immediately precedes it. Compare SOCIAL PUNISHMENT. See REINFORCEMENT.

social relationship the sum of the SOCIAL INTERACTIONS between individuals over a period of time. Momentary social interactions can be described in terms of parental care, dominant–subordinate or aggressive–fearful interactions, and so on, but a social relationship is the emergent quality from repeated interactions. A DYAD (interacting pair) may have a generally positive or generally negative social relationship that is reciprocal or complementary. Dyads with long-term social relationships will adjust behavior with each other according to feedback received.

social repression the act or process of controlling, subduing, or suppressing individuals, groups, or larger social aggregations through interpersonal means. Techniques of social repression include information control, the elimination of grassroots reform movements, manipulation of local leaders, and so on.

social resistance 1. group opposition to the political, economic, or social actions and policies of a government or society. **2.** subgroup opposition to the values and strictures of a dominant culture.

social responsibility norm the social standard or NORM that, when possible, one should assist those in need. Compare RECIPROCITY NORM; SOCIAL JUSTICE NORM.

social role the functional role played by an individual who holds a formal position in a social group, such as the role of squadron leader, teacher, or vice president of an organization. Positions of this kind are termed **role categories**, and the attitudes and behavior associated with each category are termed ROLE EXPECTATIONS.

social role theory a model contending that all psychological differences between men and women can be attributed to cultural standards and expectations about GENDER, rather than to biological factors.

social role valorization a principle, developed in succession to the NORMALIZATION PRINCIPLE, that stresses the importance of creating or supporting socially valued roles for people with disabilities. According to this principle, fulfillment of valued social roles increases the likelihood that a person will be socially accepted by others and will more readily achieve a satisfactory quality of life. [formulated in 1983 by German-born Canadian sociologist and special educator Wolf Wolfensberger (1934–)]

social sanction a punishment or other coercive measure imposed on a group member for violation of group rules. See also SOCIAL PUNISHMENT.

social scale any system of assigning individuals to social classes or categories based on such factors as occupation, wealth, education, or lifestyle.

social science 1. any of a number of disciplines concerned with the social interactions of individuals, studied from a scientific and research perspective. These disciplines traditionally have included anthropology, economics, geography, history, linguistics, political science, psychiatry, psychology, and sociology, as well as associated areas of mathematics and biology. Additional fields include related psychological studies in business administration, journalism, law, medicine, public health, and social work. The focus of analysis ranges from the individual to institutions and entire social systems. The general goal is to understand social interactions and to propose solutions to social problems. **2.** these disciplines collectively.

Social Security a comprehensive social program providing basic retirement income and insurance, as well as disability, survivor, and MEDICARE benefits. Established in 1935, the program is operated by the U.S. Social Security Administration.

social self 1. the aspects of the SELF that are important to or influenced by social relations. See also COLLECTIVE SELF; PUBLIC SELF; SOCIAL IDENTITY. **2.** a person's characteristic behavior in social situations. **3.** the facade that an individual may exhibit when in contact with other people, as contrasted with his or her real self. See SOCIAL IMAGE.

social services 1. services provided by government and nongovernment agencies and organizations to improve social welfare for those in need, including people with low income, illness, or disability, older adults, and children. Services might include health care, insurance, subsidized housing, food subsidies, and the like. **2.** government services to improve standards of living for all citizens, including such services as roads and public transportation, clean water, electricity, telecommunications, and public health institutions.

social situation the configuration of social factors affecting the behavior of an individual at a particular time.

social skills a set of learned abilities that enable an individual to interact competently and appropriately in a given social context. The most commonly identified social skills include assertiveness, coping, communication and friendship-making skills, interpersonal problem-solving, and the ability to regulate one's cognitions, feelings, and behavior. See also SOCIAL COMPETENCE.

social skills training (**SST**) **1.** techniques for teaching effective social interaction in specific situations (e.g., job interviews, dating). **2.** a form of individual or group therapy for those who need to overcome social inhibition or ineffectiveness. It uses many techniques, including BEHAVIOR REHEARSAL, COGNITIVE REHEARSAL, and ASSERTIVENESS TRAINING.

social speech speech used with the intent to communicate. Also called **socialized speech**. See also EGOCENTRIC SPEECH.

social statics 1. an approach to sociology that focuses on the distinctive nature of human societies and social systems considered in the abstract, rather than on the empirical study of any particular society. Compare SOCIAL DYNAMICS. [conceptualized by French philosopher Auguste Comte (1798–1857)] **2.** an approach to sociology that examines human societies and sociopolitical systems as they exist at a particular time or moment in history, that is, relative to their current level of development.

social statistics the application of statistical methods to the understanding of social issues and problems. See also DEMOGRAPHY. [formulated by Belgian social statistician Adolphe Quetelet (1796–1874)]

social status the relative prestige, authority, and privilege of an individual or group. Social status can be determined by any number of factors—including occupation, level of education, ethnicity, religion, age, rank, achievements, wealth, reputation, authority, and ancestry—with different groups and societies stressing some qualities more than others when allocating status to members.

social stimulus 1. a STIMULUS with social significance that elicits a RESPONSE relevant to interpersonal relationships. **2.** an individual or group that elicits such a response.

social stratification the existence or emergence of separate socioeconomic levels in a society. See SOCIAL CLASS; SOCIOECONOMIC STATUS.

social structure the complex of processes, forms, and systems that organize and regulate interpersonal phenomena in a group or society. The social structure of a group includes the status, attraction, and communication relations that link one member to another as well as a system of norms and roles (see GROUP STRUCTURE). The social structure of a society includes the complex of relations among its constituent individuals, groups, institutions, customs, mores, and so on.

social studies a course of study that covers many aspects of the social environment, including such disciplines as geography, history, judicial systems, governments both past and present, anthropology, national customs, and sociology.

social subordination the relegation of an individual or group to a position of low status or prestige in society. [concept articulated by German philosopher and sociologist Georg Simmel (1858–1918)]

social support the provision of assistance or comfort to others, typically in order to help them cope with a variety of biological, psychological, and social stressors. Support may arise from any interpersonal relationship in an individual's social network, involving family members, friends, neighbors, religious institutions, colleagues, caregivers, or support groups. It may take the form of practical help with chores or money, informational assistance (e.g., advice or guidance), and, at the most basic level, emotional support that allows the individual to feel valued, accepted, and understood. Social support has generally been shown to have positive physical and psychological effects, particularly in protecting against the deleterious effects of stress. See also COPING; SOCIAL INTEGRATION.

social technology 1. use of the principles and methods of SOCIAL SCIENCE to develop practical strategies for confronting and resolving conflicts and problems of society. **2.** the techniques so developed.

social therapy therapeutic and rehabilitative approaches that use social structures and experiences to improve the interpersonal functioning of individuals, for example, MILIEU THERAPY and the THERAPEUTIC COMMUNITY.

social transmission the transfer from one generation to the next of customs, language, or other aspects of the CULTURAL HERITAGE of a group. See ENCULTURATION; HERITAGE; SOCIAL HERITAGE.

social trap a SOCIAL DILEMMA in which individuals can maximize their resources by seeking personal goals rather than collective goals, but if too many individuals act selfishly, all members of the collective will experience substantial long-term losses. Many social traps involve a dilemma over a public good. The TRAGEDY OF THE COMMONS is an example: A grazing area will be destroyed if too many of the farmers who share it increase the size of their herds. More broadly, a social trap is a situation in which human behavior is shaped by reinforcements that conflict with the consequences of that behavior (see REINFORCEMENT ANALYSIS). Immediate positive reinforcements can lead to behaviors that in the long run are bad for the individual (e.g., addiction) or for society (e.g., the tragedy of the commons). Immediate negative reinforcements can prevent behaviors that in the long run would be good for the individual (e.g., studying) or for society (e.g., using mass transportation). See also MIXED-MOTIVE GAME.

social tunneling a psychological state, usually associated with a demanding task or stressful environment, characterized by a tendency to ignore social cues that may be relevant to the task, such as spoken commands or alert signals from other people. Compare COGNITIVE TUNNELING.

social withdrawal retreat from society and interpersonal relationships, usually accompanied by an attitude of indifference, detachment, and aloofness. Social withdrawal is often associated with such disorders as schizophrenia, autism, and depression. See also WITHDRAWAL REACTION.

social worker a person trained in an accredited college or graduate school of social work to help individuals and families deal with personal and practical problems, including problems related to mental or physical disorder, poverty, living arrangements, social life, marital relationships, child care, occupational stress, and unemployment. Social workers, who in the United States must qualify by obtaining a master's degree in social work, are important members of treatment and rehabilitation teams in clinics, social agencies, mental health centers, mental hospitals, and general hospitals. See COMMUNITY SOCIAL WORKER; MEDICAL SOCIAL WORKER.

social zone in social psychology, the DISTANCE ZONE adopted between people engaged in relationships of a relatively formal nature, for example, that of attorney and client. The social zone is defined as the area of 1.25–3.5 m (4–11½ ft). See PROXEMICS. Compare INTIMATE ZONE; PERSONAL DISTANCE ZONE; PUBLIC DISTANCE ZONE.

societal-reaction theory see LABELING THEORY.

society *n.* **1.** an enduring social group living in a particular place whose members are mutually interdependent and share political and other institutions, laws and mores, and a common culture. **2.** any well-established group of individuals (human or animal) that typically obtains new members at least in part through sexual reproduction and has relatively self-sufficient systems of action. **3.** an organization formed for a particular purpose or to further a common interest or activity. **4.** the companionship of other people. **5.** popularly and loosely, an elite social level, typically comprising those of high SOCIOECONOMIC STATUS who possess money, power, and prestige and are considered in some way fashionable. **—societal** *adj.*

Society for Neuroscience a nonprofit organization of basic scientists and physicians who study the brain and nervous system. Formed in 1970, it publishes *The Journal of Neuroscience.*

Society for Psychical Research a British scholarly society founded in 1882 to promote the scientific investigation of parapsychological and paranormal phenomena. It publishes the *Journal of the Society for Psychical Research* (established 1884).

Society for Psychotherapy Research an international, interdisciplinary organization dedicated to the scientific study of psychotherapy in all of its various forms. It publishes the journal *Psychotherapy Research.*

Society for Research in Child Development (SRCD) a multidisciplinary, nonprofit, professional association founded in 1933 to promote research in the field of human development, to foster the exchange of information among scientists and other professionals of various disciplines, and to improve the application of research findings. It publishes the journal *Child Development.*

Society of Experimental Psychologists an organization whose object is to advance psychology by arranging conferences on experimental psychology. Founded in 1904 by Edward Bradford TITCHENER as the Society of Experimentalists, it was reorganized under its current name in 1927.

Society of Experimental Social Psychology a scientific organization dedicated to the advancement of social psychology. It publishes the *Journal of Experimental Social Psychology.*

sociobiology *n.* the systematic study of the biological basis for social behavior. **Sociobiologists** believe that populations tend to maintain an optimal level of density (neither overpopulation nor underpopulation) by such controls as aggression, stress, fertility, emigration, predation, and disease. Such controls are held to operate through the Darwinian principle of NATURAL SELECTION. [pioneered by U.S. biologist Edward Osborne Wilson (1929–)] **—sociobiological** *adj.*

sociocenter *n.* in SOCIOMETRY, the individual at the psychological center of the group, that is, the most popular member or most prominent STAR.

sociocentric bias see GROUP-SERVING BIAS.

sociocentrism *n.* **1.** the tendency to put the needs, concerns, and perspective of the social unit or group before one's individual, egocentric concerns. See also ALLOCENTRIC. **2.** the practice of perceiving and interpreting situations from the point of view of the social group rather than from one's own personal perspective. **3.** the tendency to judge one's own group as superior to other groups across a variety of domains. Whereas ETHNOCENTRISM refers to the selective favoring of one's ethnic, religious, racial, or national groups, sociocentrism usually means the favoring of smaller groups characterized by face-to-face interaction among members. Compare EGOCENTRISM. **—sociocentric** *adj.*

sociocognitive bias a subtle bias in judgment to which evaluators may be susceptible. Unlike values, sociocognitive biases are inaccurate judgments that result from shortcomings in cognitive processing; they appear to be universals that intrude regardless of values or ethics.

sociocultural deprivation see PSYCHOSOCIAL DEPRIVATION.

sociocultural factors environmental conditions that play a part in healthy and adaptive behavior and well-being or in maladaptive behavior and the etiology of mental disorder and social pathology. Examples of sociocultural factors of a positive nature are a strong sense of family and community support and mentorship, good education and health care, availability of recreational facilities, and exposure to the arts. Examples of a negative nature are slum conditions, poverty, extreme or restrictive occupational pressures, lack of good medical care, and inadequate educational opportunities.

sociocultural mental retardation see CULTURAL-FAMILIAL MENTAL RETARDATION.

sociocultural perspective 1. any viewpoint or approach to health, mental health, history, politics, economics, or any other area of human experience that emphasizes the environmental factors of society, culture, and social interaction. **2.** in developmental psychology, the view that cognitive development is guided by adults interacting with children, with the cultural context determining to a large extent how, where, and when these interactions take place. A major pioneer of this perspective was Lev VYGOTSKY, whose **sociocultural theory** posited that the developmental process was one of gradual mastery by children of their own "natural" cognitive functions through interaction with and guidance from more skilled individuals or mentors (e.g., parents, teachers) in their surrounding culture. See also GUIDED PARTICIPATION; ZONE OF PROXIMAL DEVELOPMENT.

sociocusis *n.* the loss of hearing acuity due to all the hazards of living in a modern society, including disease, noise exposure, and aging.

sociodrama *n.* a technique for enhancing human relations and social skills that uses dramatization and ROLE PLAY. See also PSYCHODRAMA.

sociodramatic play a form of SYMBOLIC PLAY in which children take on social roles, such as mother, father, police officer, doctor, and so on. The activity can either be solitary or involve other children.

socioeconomic status (**SES**) the position of an individual or group on the socioeconomic scale, which is determined by a combination or interaction of social and economic factors, such as income, amount and kind of education, type and prestige of occupation, place of residence, and (in some societies or parts of society) ethnic origin or religious background. See SOCIAL CLASS.

socioemotional role see RELATIONSHIP ROLE.

sociofugal *adj.* describing environmental conditions, such as rows of seats facing the same way (e.g., church pews) or ambient noise that interferes with communication, that discourage or prevent interaction among group members. A physical environment having these characteristics is termed a **sociofugal space**. Compare SOCIOPETAL.

sociogenetics *n.* the study of the origin and development of societies. **—sociogenetic** *adj.*

sociogenic *adj.* characterizing an idea, attitude, or other mental process that is based on sociocultural influences.

sociogenic hypothesis the idea that social conditions, such as living in impoverished circumstances, are major contributors to and causal agents of mental or behavioral disorders (e.g., schizophrenia or criminality).

sociogram *n.* a graphic representation of the relations among members of a social unit or group. In most cases each member of the group is depicted by a symbol, such as a lettered circle or square, and the types of relations among members (e.g., communication links, friendship pairings) are depicted by arrows. SOCIOMETRY, as originally developed by Austrian psychiatrist and philosopher Jacob L. Moreno (1889–1974), uses objective data collected by observers or the self-reports provided by members of the group to generate sociograms. Moreno himself used four types of sociograms to represent any given situation: (a) an intuitive sociogram, based on relationships noted by the therapist in the first session; (b) an observer's sociogram, consisting of the cotherapist's impressions; (c) an objective sociogram, based on a SOCIOMETRIC TEST; and (d) a perceptual sociogram, in which each member indicates which other members appear to accept or reject him or her. In practice, sociograms are used mainly to emphasize the patterns of liking and disliking (ATTRACTION RELATIONS) in a group.

sociohistorical development the series of changes in values, norms, and technologies that occur over time in one's society and that, according to Lev VYGOTSKY, shape the development of one's cognitive skills and pattern of thinking.

sociolect *n.* a DIALECT spoken by a particular social group.

sociolinguistics *n.* the study of the relationship between language and society and of the social circumstances of language usage, especially as related to such characteristics as gender, social class, and ethnicity. Using techniques and findings from linguistics and the social sciences, sociolinguistics is concerned with the individual's language use in the context of his or her social community or culture. One aspect of this field is the study of linguistic codes, that is, the culturally determined rules and conventions that govern language usage. Social factors are also important in analyzing how languages change over time.

sociological factors social conditions that affect human behavior. Examples of such factors are socioeconomic and educational level, environmental factors (e.g., crowding), and the customs and mores of an individual's social group.

sociological measure 1. a formal measure of aspects of society that may affect the development or maintenance of normal behaviors or mental health problems. Sociological measures may assess the interrelationships between people or the structural components of a society, for example, and include both quantitative and qualitative methods. See also SOCIOMETRY. **2.** see PRIMARY PREVENTION.

sociological social psychology see SOCIAL PSYCHOLOGY.

sociology *n.* the scientific study of the origin, development, organization, forms, and functioning of human society, including the analysis of the relationships between individuals and groups, institutions, and society itself. **—sociological** *adj.* **—sociologist** *n.*

sociometer theory a theory holding that SELF-ESTEEM is important to individuals mainly because it serves as a sociometer (measure of social appeal). Specifically, high self-esteem signifies that the self has traits, such as competence, likability, moral virtue, and physical attractiveness, that will promote acceptance by other people.

sociometric analysis an investigation of the structural properties of a group, with a particular focus on patterns of liking and disliking. See SOCIOMETRY.

sociometric differentiation the gradual development of stronger and more positive interpersonal ties between some members of a group, accompanied by decreases in the quality of relations between other members of the group. See also ATTRACTION RELATIONS; SOCIOMETRY.

sociometric distance the degree of closeness or acceptance between individuals or groups as measured on a social distance scale. See also BOGARDUS SOCIAL DISTANCE SCALE; PROXEMICS; SOCIAL DISTANCE.

sociometric structure see ATTRACTION RELATIONS.

sociometric test a self-report measure of intermember relations in a group, as used in SOCIOMETRY to analyze and develop a graphic representation of the group's structure (see SOCIOGRAM).

sociometry *n.* a field of research in which various techniques are used to analyze the patterns of intermember relations within groups and to summarize these findings in mathematical and graphic form. In most cases researchers ask the group members one or more questions about their fellow members, such as "Whom do you most like in this group?", "Whom in the group would you like to work with the most?", or "Whom do you like the least?". These choices can then be summarized in a SOCIOGRAM, in which each member is represented by a numbered or lettered symbol and the various choices are identified by lines between them with arrows indicating the direction of relationships. In most cases the diagram is organized into a meaningful pattern by placing those individuals who are most frequently chosen (STARS) in the center of the diagram and the ISOLATES about the periphery. The method also yields various indices of group structure and group cohesion, including choice status (the number of times a person is chosen by the other group members), rejection status (the number of times a person is rejected by others), the relative number of mutual pairs in a group, and so on. [developed by Austrian psychiatrist and philosopher Jacob L. Moreno (1889–1974)] —**sociometric** *adj.*

socionomics *n.* the study of nonsocial influences on social groups, that is, the ways in which the physical environment modifies society. This includes the effects of different terrains and climatic conditions on economic and social organization.

sociopath *n.* a former name for an individual with an ANTISOCIAL PERSONALITY DISORDER.

sociopathic behavior see DYSSOCIAL BEHAVIOR.

sociopathic disorder see ANTISOCIAL PERSONALITY DISORDER.

sociopathic personality see ANTISOCIAL PERSONALITY DISORDER.

sociopathy *n.* see ANTISOCIAL PERSONALITY DISORDER.

sociopetal *adj.* describing environmental conditions, such as circular seating arrangements and a comfortable ambient room temperature, that promote interaction among group members. A physical environment having these characteristics is termed a **sociopetal space**. Compare SOCIOFUGAL.

sociosexual assessment an assessment of an individual to identify or measure his or her awareness of cultural standards regarding social relationships and sexual activity, knowledge of facts about sexuality and the nature and consequences of sexual interaction, and engagement (type and nature) in sexual activities. It may also include an assessment of risks that the individual may engage in culturally sanctioned sexual activities.

sociotechnical systems approach an approach to the design and evaluation of WORK SYSTEMS that developed in Britain after World War II. It is based on the theory that tasks and roles, technology, and the social system constitute a single interrelated system, such that changes in one part require adjustments in the other parts. The introduction of new technologies, for example, may automate some job tasks and lead to decreased job satisfaction and group resistance to the changes. The goal of this approach is to optimize organizational or technological design by considering the ways in which people interact with technology in a variety of environments.

sociotherapy *n.* a supportive therapeutic approach based on modification of an individual's environment with the aim of improving the individual's interpersonal adjustment. The approach may be used in a variety of contexts, including working with parents and prospective foster parents, family counseling, vocational retraining, and assistance in readjusting to community life following hospitalization for severe mental illness.

sociotropy *n.* the tendency to place an inordinate value on relationships over personal independence, thought to leave one vulnerable to depression in response to the loss of relationships or to conflict.

socius *n.* the individual considered as the basic unit of society. Also called **primary social unit**; **social atom**.

Socratic dialogue a process of structured inquiry and discussion between two or more people to explore the concepts and values that underlie their everyday activities and judgments. In some psychotherapies, it is a technique in which the therapist poses strategic questions designed to clarify the client's core beliefs and feelings and, in the case of COGNITIVE THERAPY, to enable the client to discover the distortions in his or her habitual interpretation of a given situation. In psychotherapy, it is also known as the **Socratic-therapeutic method**.

Socratic effect the finding that mere expression of beliefs tends to produce greater logical consistency among belief structures. [originally documented by U.S. psychologist William J. McGuire (1925–)]

Socratic-therapeutic method see SOCRATIC DIALOGUE.

sodium Amytal interview see AMOBARBITAL.

sodium channel see ION CHANNEL.

sodium pump a membrane protein that uses energy to actively transport sodium ions out of a cell against their concentration gradient. The main sodium pump responsible for maintaining the RESTING POTENTIAL of animal cells, and hence the excitability of neurons and muscle cells, is called an **Na^+/K^+ ATPase**. In each cycle, this moves three sodium ions out of the cell, across the plasma membrane, in exchange for two potassium ions entering the cell, using energy derived from ATP.

sodium regulation maintenance of the concentration of sodium ions in blood plasma within normal limits. Sodium ions are the principal CATIONS of plasma and extracellular fluid and play a crucial role in fluid and electrolyte balance. Falling levels of plasma sodium trigger release of ALDOSTERONE from the adrenal cortex. This hormone stimulates reabsorption of sodium ions by the kidney tubules, thereby restoring plasma sodium levels. Severe sodium deficiency can be fatal, whereas excessive plasma sodium levels can result in hypertension.

sodomy *n.* **1.** ANAL INTERCOURSE between human beings or sexual intercourse of any kind between a human being and an animal (see ZOOERASTY). This word is derived from the name of the corrupt town of Sodom described in Genesis 18–19. **2.** in legal contexts, any sexual assault that does not involve penile–vaginal penetration.

soft data subjective data or data considered to be flawed in some way, for example because of lack of experimental randomization, lack of formal random sampling in survey research, or being based only on anecdote.

soft determinism the position that all events, including human actions and choices, have causes, but that free will and responsibility are compatible with such DETERMINISM. Compare HARD DETERMINISM.

soft key in ergonomics, a control key that activates multiple functions depending upon the state of the system. Soft keys are usually mapped to a specific area on the display.

soft neurological sign see SOFT SIGN.

soft palate the portion of the roof of the mouth that extends rearward from the HARD PALATE and terminates at a fleshy appendage, the **uvula**. Consisting of fibromuscular tissue covered by mucous membrane, it separates the oral cavity from the NASOPHARYNX and, when raised, closes off the nasopharynx to produce normal speech sounds. Also called **velum palatinum**.

soft psychology a usually pejorative name for those areas of psychology that do not always make rigorous use of scientific methods in developing, evaluating, and applying the principles and techniques of academic psychology. For example, experimental researchers may refer to clinical psychology as "soft psychology." Compare HARD PSYCHOLOGY.

soft sell see HARD SELL.

soft sign a clinical, behavioral, or neurological sign that may reflect the presence of neurological impairment. Soft signs are subtle, nonspecific, and ambiguous (because they are also seen in individuals without neurological impairment). Examples include slight abnormalities of speech, gait, posture, or behavior; sleep disturbances; slow physical maturation; sensory or perceptual deficits; and short attention span. Also called **equivocal sign**; **soft neurological sign**.

soft spot see FONTANEL.

Sohval–Soffer syndrome a rare, presumably hereditary, disease characterized by mental retardation and testicular deficiency, as well as skeletal anomalies and diabetes mellitus. A small number of affected individuals studied had psychotic disorder and low intelligence. The penis and testes are small, and facial and pubic hair is sparse. [reported in 1953 by Arthur R. **Sohval** (1904–) and Louis J. **Soffer** (1904–), U.S. physicians]

SOI abbreviation for STRUCTURE OF INTELLECT MODEL.

soldiers' disease dependence on MORPHINE during the U.S. Civil War.

solicitation behavior the actions shown by one animal seeking to mate with another, typically the behavior of females as they seek to interest a mate in copulation. In some primates, such as capuchin and patas monkeys, males rarely initiate sexual interactions without extensive female solicitation behavior. In many other species attempts by males to copulate are unsuccessful in the absence of female solicitation behavior.

solipsism *n.* the philosophical position that one can be sure of the existence of nothing outside the self, as other people and things may be mere figments of one's own consciousness. Although psychologically unacceptable, such a position is notoriously difficult to refute, either logically or empirically. The question posed by solipsism has been put in various ways, but all arise from the fact that one's experience of one's own consciousness and identity is direct and unique, such that one is cut off from the same kind of experience of other minds and the things of the world. See CARTESIAN SELF; EGOCENTRIC PREDICAMENT. **—solipsist** *n.* **—solipsistic** *adj.*

solitary nucleus a nucleus in the medulla oblongata of the brainstem that relays information from the intermediate nerve (see GREATER SUPERFICIAL PETROSAL NERVE), glossopharyngeal nerve, and vagus nerve. Gustatory (taste) neurons project to the anterior division of the nucleus, with touch and temperature afferents immediately lateral and visceral afferents medial and caudal. Gustatory neurons project from the solitary nucleus to control reflexes of acceptance or rejection, to anticipate digestive processes, and to activate higher levels of the taste system (see THALAMIC TASTE AREA). Also called **nucleus of the solitary tract** (**NST**).

solitary play playful activity in which a child engages by him- or herself, apparently unaware of others playing nearby. Compare ASSOCIATIVE PLAY; COOPERATIVE PLAY; PARALLEL PLAY. See also SOCIAL PLAY.

Solomon four-group design an experimental design that assesses the effect of having been pretested on the magnitude of the treatment effect. If the application of a pretest does affect the experimental outcome, this would be detected. [Richard L. **Solomon** (1919–1992), U.S. psychologist]

solute *n.* the substance that is dissolved in a SOLVENT to form a solution.

solution-focused brief therapy SHORT-TERM THERAPY that focuses on problems in the HERE AND NOW, with specific goals that the client views as important to achieve in a limited time.

solvent *n.* the liquid in which a substance (the SOLUTE) is dissolved in forming a solution.

solvent abuse see INHALANT ABUSE.

soma *n.* **1.** the physical body (Greek, "body"), as distinguished from the mind or spirit (see SOUL). See MIND–BODY PROBLEM. **2.** in neuroscience, the CELL BODY of a neuron. **3.** a plant regarded as sacred (and personified as the plant god Soma) by ancient Aryan peoples, which some experts have hypothesized to be FLY AGARIC (*Amanita muscaria*).

Soma *n.* a trade name for CARISOPRODOL.

somaesthesia *n.* see SOMESTHESIA.

somat- *combining form* see SOMATO-.

somatic *adj.* **1.** describing, relating to, or arising in the body as distinguished from the mind. **2.** describing, relating to, or arising in cells of the body other than the sex cells or their precursors (i.e., germ-line cells). Hence, a **somatic mutation** cannot be transmitted to the offspring of the affected individual.

somatic anxiety the level of reaction of the SYMPATHETIC NERVOUS SYSTEM that one experiences in any given situation.

somatic area see SOMATOSENSORY AREA.

somatic cell see BODY CELL.

somatic concern worries about one's bodily health, including concern over physical symptoms (e.g., chest pain, nausea, diarrhea, headaches, pain, shortness of breath) and distressing beliefs about bodily illness or dysfunction. See HYPOCHONDRIASIS.

somatic delusion the false belief that one or more bodily organs are functioning improperly or are diseased, injured, or otherwise altered. Although standard tests do not confirm this belief, the individual nonetheless continues to maintain this conviction. Also called **somatopsychic delusion**.

somatic depression a MAJOR DEPRESSIVE EPISODE in which physical symptoms are prominent.

somatic disorder an organic physical disorder, as distinguished from a FUNCTIONAL DISORDER or a PSYCHOGENIC DISORDER.

somatic function any function of sensation and muscular contraction that involves the SOMATIC NERVOUS SYSTEM.

somatic hallucination the false perception of a physical occurrence within the body, such as feeling electric currents.

somatic nervous system the part of the nervous system comprising the sensory and motor neurons that innervate the sense organs and the skeletal muscles, as opposed to the AUTONOMIC NERVOUS SYSTEM.

somatic obsession preoccupation with one's body or any part of it. This concern may be associated with compulsive checking of the body part (e.g., in a mirror or by touch), comparison with others, and seeking reassurance. Somatic obsession is the central feature of BODY DYSMORPHIC DISORDER but may also be a feature of OBSESSIVE-COMPULSIVE DISORDER if other obsessive-compulsive symptoms are present.

somatic receptor any of the sensory organs located in the skin, including the deeper kinesthetic sense organs (see KINESTHESIS). Types of somatic receptors include free nerve endings, MERKEL'S TACTILE DISKS, MEISSNER'S CORPUSCLES, KRAUSE END BULBS, GOLGI TENDON ORGANS, and BASKET ENDINGS.

somatic sense see SOMATOSENSE.

somatic sensory area see SOMATOSENSORY AREA.

somatic sensory system see SOMATOSENSORY SYSTEM.

somatic therapy the treatment of mental disorders by organic methods, such as the prescription of a psychotropic drug or the use of electroconvulsive therapy or megavitamin therapy. Also called **somatotherapy**.

somatic weakness the hypothesized vulnerability, due to congenital susceptibility, of an organ or organ system to the effects of psychological stress. The organ is thus predisposed to becoming the focus of a PSYCHOSOMATIC DISORDER.

somatist *n.* a person who considers mental disorders to be manifestations of organic disease.

somatization *n.* the organic expression of psychological disturbance. The first use of the word has controversially been attributed to Austrian psychoanalyst Wilhelm Stekel (1868–1940) to describe what is now called CONVERSION. Some investigators use the word in reference not only to the physical symptoms that occur in almost every type of anxiety disorder but also to the expression of symptoms in such PSYCHOSOMATIC DISORDERS as psychogenic asthma and peptic ulcers.

somatization disorder in *DSM–IV–TR,* a SOMATOFORM DISORDER involving a history of multiple physical symptoms (at least eight, one of which must be a PSEUDONEUROLOGICAL symptom) of several years' duration, for which medical attention has been sought but which are apparently not due to any physical disorder or injury. The complaints are often described in vague yet colorful or exaggerated terms by the patient, who often appears anxious or depressed. Among the complaints are feelings of sickliness, difficulty in swallowing or walking, blurred vision, abdominal pain, nausea, diarrhea, painful or irregular menstruation, sexual indifference, painful intercourse, pain in the back or joints, shortness of breath, palpitations, and chest pain.

somato- (**somat-**) *combining form* body.

somatoform disorder in *DSM–IV–TR,* any of a group of disorders marked by physical symptoms suggesting a specific medical condition for which there is no demonstrable organic evidence and for which there is positive evidence or a strong probability that they are linked to psychological factors. The symptoms must cause marked distress or significantly impair normal social or occupational functioning. See SOMATIZATION DISORDER; UNDIFFERENTIATED SOMATOFORM DISORDER; CONVERSION DISORDER; PAIN DISORDER; HYPOCHONDRIASIS; BODY DYSMORPHIC DISORDER.

somatoform disorder not otherwise specified in *DSM–IV–TR,* a diagnostic category reserved for disorders with unexplained physical symptoms that do not meet the criteria for a more specific SOMATOFORM DISORDER. It should not be confused with UNDIFFERENTIATED SOMATOFORM DISORDER.

somatoform pain disorder see PAIN DISORDER.

somatogenesis *n.* **1.** the process by which germ-cell material develops into body cells. **2.** the development of behavioral or personality traits or disorders as a result of anatomical, physiological, or biochemical changes in the body. Also called **organogenesis**. **—somatogenic** or **somatogenetic** *adj.*

somatognosia *n.* awareness of one's own body or body parts. Denial of one's body parts is called ASOMATOGNOSIA and is commonly seen in individuals with NEGLECT.

somatography *n.* a variety of body visualization techniques used in ENGINEERING ANTHROPOMETRY and EQUIPMENT DESIGN. **—somatographic** *adj.*

somatomedin *n.* any of a class of polypeptides, produced by the liver in response to stimulation by GROWTH HORMONE, that stimulate protein synthesis and promote growth.

somatometry *n.* the classification of individuals based on body form and relation of types of physique to psychological characteristics. **—somatometric** *adj.*

somatophrenia *n.* a tendency to imagine or exaggerate bodily ills. See also HYPOCHONDRIASIS.

somatoplasm *n.* the tissue cells of the body, collectively, as distinguished from the germ cells. Compare GERM PLASM.

somatopsychic delusion see SOMATIC DELUSION.

somatopsychology *n.* the study of the psychological impact of physiological disease or disability: The term is little used, and the subject matter of the study is now largely included under the rubric of HEALTH PSYCHOLOGY.

somatopsychosis *n.* **1.** a psychosis marked by delusions that involve the person's body or body parts. **2.** a psychosis that is due to a bodily (physical) disease. [defined by U.S. psychiatrist Elmer Ernest Southard (1876–1920)]

somatosense *n.* any of the senses related to touch and HAPTICS, including KINESTHESIS, the VISCERAL SENSE, the articular senses (see ARTICULAR SENSATION), and the CUTANEOUS SENSES. Also called **somatic sense**; **somesthetic sense**.

somatosensory area either of two main areas of the CEREBRAL CORTEX that can be mapped with EVOKED POTENTIALS to reveal points that respond to stimulation of the various SOMATOSENSES. The somatosensory areas vary somewhat among different species: In humans the PRIMARY SOMATOSENSORY AREA is located in the POSTCENTRAL GYRUS of the anterior parietal lobe, and the SECONDARY SOMATOSENSORY AREA is on the lateral surface of the parietal lobe just dorsal to the LATERAL SULCUS. Also called **somatic sensory area**; **somatic area**; **somatosensory cortex**.

somatosensory system the parts of the nervous system that serve perception of touch, vibration, pain, temperature, and position (see SOMATOSENSE). Nerve fibers from receptors for these senses enter the dorsal roots of the spinal cord and ascend mainly through tracts in the DORSAL COLUMNS to the VENTROPOSTERIOR NUCLEI of the thalamus, from which they are relayed (directly or indirectly) to the SOMATOSENSORY AREAS of the parietal cortex. Also called **somatic sensory system**.

somatostatin *n.* a hormone that is secreted by the hypothalamus and inhibits the release of the GROWTH HORMONE (somatotropin) by the anterior pituitary gland. It is also secreted by cells in the ISLETS OF LANGERHANS in the pancreas, where it inhibits the secretion of insulin and glucagon. Analogues of somatostatin are used therapeutically in the control of ACROMEGALY. Also called **somatotropin-release inhibiting factor (SRIF)**.

somatotherapy *n.* **1.** treatment of bodily or physical disorders. **2.** see SOMATIC THERAPY.

somatotonia *n.* the personality type that, according to SHELDON'S CONSTITUTIONAL THEORY OF PERSONALITY, is associated with a mesomorphic physique (see MESOMORPH). Somatotonia is characterized by a tendency toward energetic activity, physical courage, and love of power. **—somatotonic** *adj.*

somatotopagnosia *n.* see AUTOTOPAGNOSIA.

somatotopic organization the topographic distribution of areas of the MOTOR CORTEX relating to specific activities of skeletal muscles. The brain can be mapped to locate areas of somatotopic organization by electrically stimulating a point in the cortex and observing associated movement of a skeletal muscle in the face, the trunk, or a limb. See SOMATOSENSORY AREA. See also MOTOR-FUNCTION HOMUNCULUS.

somatotropin *n.* see GROWTH HORMONE.

somatotropin-release inhibiting factor (SRIF) see SOMATOSTATIN.

somatotype *n.* the body build or physique of a person as it relates to his or her temperament or behavioral characteristics. Numerous categories of somatotypes have been proposed by various investigators since ancient times. The classification of individuals in this way is called **somatotypology**. See CONSTITUTIONAL TYPE.

somber–bright dimension in psychological aesthetics, a method of classifying artistic styles on the basis of their emotional effects. Experimental evidence shows that intense brightness, high saturation, and hues that correspond to long wavelengths of light tend to excite a viewer.

Somers d an asymmetric measure of association between two ordinal variables. [Robert H. **Somers**]

somesthesia (**somaesthesia**) *n.* sensitivity to cutaneous, kinesthetic, and visceral stimulation. Also called **somesthesis**. **—somesthetic** *adj.*

somesthetic disorder any dysfunction involving the SOMATOSENSES, such as difficulty in maintaining postural or positional awareness or lack of sensitivity to pain, touch, or temperature. Somesthetic disorders are usually related to PARIETAL LOBE damage.

somesthetic sense see SOMATOSENSE.

somesthetic stimulation stimulation of kinesthetic, cutaneous, or visceral receptors.

somnambulism *n.* see SLEEPWALKING DISORDER.

somnambulistic state a state of mind in which walking, talking, or other complex acts occur during sleep (see SLEEPWALKING DISORDER). Historically, it refers to a hypnotic phase in which the individual in a deep TRANCE may appear to be awake and in control of his or her actions but is actually under the influence of the hypnotist.

somniloquy *n.* literally, SLEEP TALKING. Also called **somniloquence**; **somniloquism**. **—somniloquent** *adj.* **—somniloquist** *n.*

somnolence *n.* excessive sleepiness or drowsiness, which is sometimes pathological. The condition may be due, for example, to medication, a sleep disorder, or a medical condition (e.g., HYPOTHYROIDISM). **—somnolent** *adj.*

somnolentia *n.* **1.** unnatural drowsiness. **2.** see SLEEP DISORIENTATION.

somnology *n.* the study of sleep and sleep disorders. **—somnologist** *n.*

somnophilia *n.* an obsolete term for sexual interest and arousal derived from intruding on a sleeping person. It may involve fondling the person or masturbating while watching the person sleep.

SOMPA acronym for SYSTEM OF MULTICULTURAL PLURALISTIC ASSESSMENT.

sonant 1. *n.* a vowel or VOICED consonant that is capable of forming a syllable or the nucleus of a syllable. **2.** *n.* a NASAL or LIQUID consonant that functions as a vowel in a particular syllable. Also called **sonorant**. Compare SEMIVOWEL. **3.** *adj.* related to, having, or producing speech sounds.

Sonata *n.* a trade name for ZALEPLON.

sone *n.* the unit of LOUDNESS.

song *n.* in animal behavior, a complex, relatively long sequence of vocalizations that is often stereotyped in overall structure or sequence of calls. It is used to defend territories against members of the same sex and species as well as to attract mates. Song is thought to occur primarily in birds, but the term also has been used to describe long acoustic sequences produced by crickets and certain primates (e.g., gibbons). In the northern temperate zone, song is usually seasonal and under the control of gonadal steroids, but in the tropics there is little evidence of hormonal control.

sonic boom a high-pressure acoustic shock wave, often caused by an aircraft or projectile traveling at supersonic speeds.

Sonic Pathfinder a trademark for a mobility assistance device, worn on the head, that emits ultrasound and provides feedback through earphones for individuals with visual impairment. Feedback consists of the notes of a musical scale, which make a familiar tonal progression as the user approaches an object. The signal received is restricted to the nearest object to the user or, in certain cases, to the object directly ahead of the user.

sonography *n.* see ULTRASOUND.

sonorant *n.* see SONANT.

soothability *n.* the ability of infants and children to calm down and recover from distress.

sophistry *n.* a style of argumentation designed not to arrive at truth but to persuade others that one's position is correct. This is generally accomplished by careful strategic use of language and the skillful use of fallacious arguments (see FALLACY). For example, one common type of sophistry is to represent the other's point of view as more extreme and less plausible than it really is and then attack the extreme version of the position and show that it is wrong. A particular instance of sophistry is called a **sophism**. The term comes from the Sophists, a group of itinerant teachers in Greece in the 5th century BCE, who taught and practiced rhetoric.

sophrosyne *n.* an ideal of character recommended by Greek philosopher Plato (c. 427–c. 347 BCE). The word has no direct English equivalent but is often translated as "temperance" or "moderation" and carries the sense of being well balanced, prudent, self-disciplined, and sound in judgment.

Sopite syndrome a syndrome that may develop after prolonged exposure to VIRTUAL REALITY, as in driving or flight simulators. Symptoms include dizziness, nausea, chronic fatigue, lack of initiative, drowsiness, lethargy, apathy, and irritability. These characteristics can persist for prolonged periods even after exposure to a virtual environment is over. Also called **simulator sickness**; **space motion sickness**.

soporifics *pl. n.* agents that are capable of producing sleep, particularly a deep sleep. Also called **sopoforics**.

SOPS abbreviation for SCALE OF PRODROMAL SYMPTOMS.

S–O–R *s*timulus–*o*rganism–*r*esponse: a modification of the stimulus–response (S–R) relationship that emphasizes the role of the organism, including its drives and characteristics. The model has been most notably applied to theories of learning and perception. See S–O–R PSYCHOLOGY. See also DYNAMIC PSYCHOLOGY. Compare S–R LEARNING MODEL; S–R PSYCHOLOGY.

SORC *n.* an acronym for the four variables employed in behavioral analysis: stimuli (see SITUATIONAL DETERMINANTS), ORGANISMIC VARIABLES, responses, and consequences (reinforcement contingencies). A functional analysis of behavior may seek to determine how the presentation of certain stimuli leads to specific responses (perhaps influenced by individual, or organismic, variables), which are followed by consequences that may then reinforce the elicited responses.

sorcery drugs a group of plant alkaloids that includes belladonna, the opium alkaloids, mandrake, aconite, and hemlock. The substances have been chewed, smoked, or brewed into potions since ancient times for purposes of healing or intoxication. Medicinal herbs were usually grown and administered by shamans or native healers; some, such as the opiates and anticholinergics, are used in modern medical pharmacology.

Sorge *n.* care (German). The term has gained currency in psychology and philosophy chiefly through its use by German philosopher Martin Heidegger (1889–1976) to denote the uniquely human activity of caring or worrying about things.

S–O–R psychology *s*timulus–*o*rganism–*r*esponse psychology: an extension of the S–R PSYCHOLOGY of behaviorists incorporating the notion of R. S. WOODWORTH that factors within the organism help determine what stimuli the organism is sensitive to and which responses may occur. The O factors could be biological or psychological. S–O–R psychology has been extended beyond PAVLOVIAN CONDITIONING and INSTRUMENTAL CONDITIONING to encompass such disciplines as marketing and consumer behavior. For example, an individual's emotional state when shopping may influence how many products he or she purchases and the particular types or brands.

sorting test a technique for assessing the ability to conceptualize. The participant, usually a child, is asked to arrange an assortment of common objects by category. The method used in this task reflects the level of cognitive development; for example, a very young child may group random objects together for entirely subjective reasons, whereas an older child will categorize objects on the basis of functional relationships. See also CLASS INCLUSION.

sort-recall task a task used in memory research in which participants, usually children, have the opportunity to sort items into groups before having to recall the items at a later time.

Sotos syndrome an inherited condition characterized by MACROCEPHALY, distinctive facial features (including wide-set eyes), nonprogressive cerebral disorder, mental retardation, increased birth weight, and excessive growth during early childhood. Mild dilation of the cerebral ventricles, nonspecific EEG (electroencephalogram) changes, and seizures have been observed in affected individuals. Handicaps may be fewer than previously believed and tend to improve with age. Also called **cerebral gigantism**; **Nevo syndrome**. [reported in 1964 by J. F. **Sotos** (1927–), U.S. pediatrician]

soul *n.* the nonphysical aspect of a human being, considered responsible for the functions of mind and individual personality and often thought to live on after the death of the physical body. The English word corresponds to the Greek *psyche*, often also translated as "mind," and the Latin *anima*, usually translated as "spirit." The concept of the soul was present in early Greek thinking, and has been an important feature of many philosophical systems and most religions. Some traditional areas of debate have included whether the soul is material or immaterial, whether animals, plants, or seemingly inert natural objects have souls (see PANPSYCHISM), and whether the soul is individual, allowing the personality to persist after death, or whether it is a reflection of a universal "cosmic" soul. Because the existence of the soul has resisted empirical verification, science has generally ignored the concept, while those who adhere to MATERIALISM, POSITIVISM, or REDUCTIONISM reject it absolutely. Despite this, the term survives in the general language to mean the deepest center of a person's identity and the seat of his or her most important moral, emotional, and aesthetic experiences. See also RATIONAL SOUL; SENSITIVE SOUL; VEGETATIVE SOUL.

soul image in the ANALYTIC PSYCHOLOGY of Carl JUNG, the deeply unconscious portion of the psyche that is composed of the ANIMUS (or male archetype) and ANIMA (or female archetype).

soul kiss see FRENCH KISS.

sound *n.* variations in pressure that occur over time in an elastic medium, such as air or water. Sound does not necessarily elicit an auditory sensation—infrasound and ultrasound are respectively below and above the audible range of humans—but in psychology sound usually denotes a stimulus capable of being heard by an organism. See RANGE OF AUDIBILITY.

sound-attenuating chamber see ANECHOIC CHAMBER.

sound cage a device for measuring sound localization. See AUDITORY LOCALIZATION.

sound change in linguistics, a change over the course of time in the phonological patterns of a language. Modern languages have developed from their ancestor languages and become differentiated from other languages in the same family through a series of such changes occurring naturally over many centuries. See GENETIC LINGUISTICS; PROTOLANGUAGE.

sound frequency see FREQUENCY.

sounding out see PHONICS.

sound intensity the rate of flow of sound energy through a given area, measured in watts per square meter. In practice, sound intensity is seldom directly measured; it is indirectly determined using pressure measurements and often is expressed in DECIBELS. Sound intensity is proportional to the square of sound pressure.

sound-level meter a device used to measure sound pressure. The sound pressure is transduced by a microphone, processed, and typically expressed in decibels sound-pressure level (see DECIBEL). Some sound-level meters have frequency-weighting scales to approximate the characteristics of human hearing. The **dBC** scale gives approximately equal weight across most of the RANGE OF AUDIBILITY. The **dBA** scale is thought to better approximate the loudness or noisiness of environmental sounds.

sound localization see AUDITORY LOCALIZATION.

sound pressure the force per unit area exerted by a sound wave. The pressure is expressed as changes in the ambient or static pressure (e.g., atmospheric pressure), usually as root-mean-square (rms) pressure changes. The unit of measurement of sound pressure is the **pascal** (Pa). Also called **acoustic pressure**. See also DECIBEL.

sound-pressure level (**SPL**) see DECIBEL.

soundproof room a room that cannot be penetrated by audible sound.

sound shadow an area in which sound is blocked by a nontransmitting object, such as the head.

sound spectrograph an electronic instrument that analyzes a sound source (typically human speech) in terms of its variations in frequency and intensity over time. The visual record so produced is a **sound spectrogram**, a quasi-three-dimensional representation of sound, often shortened to **spectrogram**. The SOUND SPECTRUM, measured over a relatively brief interval, is plotted by the sound spectrograph as a function of time on the *x*-axis, while frequency is plotted on the *y*-axis, and intensity is depicted by shading or color. A spectrogram provides an imperfect representation of the perceptually relevant aspects of sound.

sound spectrum the representation of sound in terms of its frequency composition. Any physically realizable sound and, more generally, any waveform can be represented as a function of time or of frequency. These representations are uniquely related by the Fourier transform or Fourier series (see FOURIER ANALYSIS). The spectrum is the frequency-domain representation and consists of the **amplitude spectrum** (or **power spectrum**) and the **phase spectrum**. Both are necessary to describe the sound completely. For example, a sound played backward has the same amplitude spectrum but an altered phase spectrum, and usually the sounds are perceptually very different. Periodic sounds have a **line spectrum** with a nonzero amplitude only at discrete frequencies. Other sounds have a **continuous spectrum**: The spectrum is then described in terms of **spectral density**, which involves units of amplitude or power per hertz. Sound spectra are useful partly because the mammalian auditory system performs an imperfect Fourier analysis. Also called **acoustic spectrum**; **auditory spectrum**; **tonal spectrum**. See TONOTOPIC ORGANIZATION.

sound symbolism see PHONETIC SYMBOLISM.

sour *adj.* denoting the TASTE elicited by acids. Increasing sourness generally occurs with declining pH. Acids are involved in many physiological processes and also characterize unripe or spoiled foods; thus their detection is essential for an organism's ion HOMEOSTASIS and food selection. **—sourness** *n.*

source amnesia impaired memory for how, when, or where information was learned despite good memory for the information itself. Source amnesia is often linked to frontal lobe pathology.

source attractiveness the extent to which the source of a persuasive message is seen as physically attractive. Source attractiveness is a SOURCE FACTOR.

source confusion misattribution of the origins of a memory. This may distort eyewitness accounts of the events surrounding a crime. For example, an eyewitness hearing from a police officer that the perpetrator carried a gun may later believe that he or she saw the gun at the crime scene. See also UNCONSCIOUS TRANSFER.

source credibility the extent to which the source of a persuasive message is seen as likely to provide accurate information, which is determined by SOURCE EXPERTISE and SOURCE TRUSTWORTHINESS. Source credibility is a SOURCE FACTOR.

source expertise the extent to which the source of a persuasive message is seen as knowledgeable about the topic of the message. Source expertise is a SOURCE FACTOR. See also SOURCE CREDIBILITY.

source factors characteristics of the source of a persuasive message that are likely to influence the effectiveness of the message. SOURCE ATTRACTIVENESS, SOURCE CREDIBILITY, SOURCE EXPERTISE, SOURCE MAJORITY OR MINORITY STATUS, and SOURCE TRUSTWORTHINESS are all source factors.

source language 1. the language (usually a person's native tongue) used as a starting point when attempting to learn or use another language. **2.** the language from which a TRANSLATION has been or is being made. Compare TARGET LANGUAGE.

source majority or minority status a SOURCE FACTOR indicating (a) that the source of a message holds a position that is shared by a numerical majority or minority of the population or (b) that the source of a message is a member of a social group that is a numerical majority or minority.

source memory remembering the origin of a memory or of knowledge, that is, memory of where or how one came to know what one now remembers. Compare FACT MEMORY.

source monitoring determining the origins of one's memories, knowledge, or beliefs, for example, whether an event was personally experienced, witnessed on television, or overheard. Also called **reality monitoring**.

source traits in CATTELL'S FACTORIAL THEORY OF PERSONALITY, a group of 12 personality traits, determined by FACTOR ANALYSIS, that underlie and determine SURFACE TRAITS. Examples are cyclothymia (emotionally expressive and changeable) and schizothymia (reserved, anxious, laconic). See also ABILITY TRAIT; DYNAMIC TRAIT; TEMPERAMENT TRAIT.

source trustworthiness the extent to which the source of a persuasive message is seen as honest. Source trustworthiness is a SOURCE FACTOR. See also SOURCE CREDIBILITY.

Southern blot a method of detecting a particular DNA sequence in a mixture of DNA molecules. It involves separating the DNAs with GEL ELECTROPHORESIS, blotting the separated DNAs onto nitrocellulose, then using a labeled DNA or RNA probe to hybridize with, and highlight, the DNA sequence of interest. Compare NORTHERN BLOT; WESTERN BLOT. [developed in the 1970s by Edward **Southern** (1938–), British biochemist]

SOV abbreviation for ALLPORT–VERNON–LINDZEY STUDY OF VALUES.

space adaptation syndrome a type of motion sickness probably caused by an astronaut's inability to distinguish up from down while in orbit. This confusion results in dizziness and nausea.

space-based attention attention viewed as operating primarily on a representation of visual space, that is, attention is directed toward spatial locations rather than objects. Compare OBJECT-BASED ATTENTION.

spaced practice see DISTRIBUTED PRACTICE.

spaced repetition see REPETITION EFFECT.

space factor a hypothesized ability, proposed by Louis Leon THURSTONE in 1938, that accounts for some individual differences in the capacity to perceive and reason about spatial relations. This factor may be related to individual differences in mathematical abilities.

space motion sickness see SOPITE SYNDROME.

space orientation see SPATIAL ORIENTATION.

space perception an awareness, derived from sensory input, of the spatial properties of objects in the environment, including their shape, dimension, and distance.

space psychology the application of psychological procedures to the problems of humans functioning in outer space.

spam *n.* unwanted e-mail messages, typically sent to addressees on extensive mailing lists. They usually advertise or promote products or services but may also be used for disseminating political or other propaganda. See WORM.

spandrel *n.* see EXAPTATION.

span of apprehension see APPREHENSION SPAN.

spasm *n.* a sudden, involuntary muscle contraction, which may vary in severity from a twitch to a convulsion. A **tonic spasm** is continuous or sustained; a **clonic spasm** alternates between contraction and relaxation, as in **hiccups**. A spasm may be restricted to a particular body part: for example, a **vasospasm** involves a blood vessel, and a **bronchial spasm** involves the bronchi. **—spasmodic** *adj.*

spasmodic dysphonia a rare VOICE DISORDER whose symptoms include momentary periods of uncontrolled vocal spasms, stuttering, tightness in the throat, and recurrent hoarseness. The cause is unknown, but the condition may be attributed to a neurological or physiological disturbance or to psychological factors. Spasmodic dysphonia (formerly known as **spastic dysphonia**) particularly affects public speakers.

spasmodic fixation a condition in which an individual is unable to change gaze until the target of fixation is removed. Also called **spasm of fixation**.

spastic *adj.* **1.** relating to SPASM. **2.** relating to increased muscle tension (see SPASTICITY).

spastic colitis see IRRITABLE BOWEL SYNDROME.

spastic dysarthria see DYSARTHRIA.

spastic dysphonia see SPASMODIC DYSPHONIA.

spastic hemiparesis partial paralysis on one side of the body complicated by spasticity of the limbs on the affected side, which may be quite painful.

spasticity *n.* a state of increased tension of resting muscles resulting in resistance to passive stretching. It is caused by damage to UPPER MOTOR NEURONS and is marked by RIGIDITY and exaggerated TENDON REFLEXES.

spastic paralysis a type of paralysis marked by increased muscle tension (see SPASTICITY). It is caused by damage to UPPER MOTOR NEURONS and frequently occurs in CEREBRAL PALSY. Compare FLACCID PARALYSIS.

spastic paraplegia a form of PARAPLEGIA characterized by spasticity of the leg muscles. Also called **tetanoid paraplegia**.

spatial ability the ability to orient or perceive one's body in space or to detect or reason about SPATIAL RELATIONSHIPS. A deficit in spatial ability may be observed in people with brain injuries, who are unable to perform effectively in map-reading tests and jigsaw puzzles or who have difficulties in recognizing shapes tactually.

spatial apractagnosia see APRACTAGNOSIA.

spatial attention the manner in which an individual distributes attention over the visual scene. Spatial attention is usually directed at the part of the scene on which a person fixates (see FIXATION).

spatial coherence see COHERENCE.

spatial contrast sensitivity see CONTRAST SENSITIVITY.

spatial density density that can be changed by altering the amount of space while keeping the number of individuals constant. There is some evidence that the impact of spatial density on CROWDING is less than that of SOCIAL DENSITY.

spatial discrimination the ability to detect differences in spatial location.

spatial disorder a disorder of space perception, usually associated with a lesion of the PARIETAL LOBE of the brain. It includes impaired memory for locations, CONSTRUCTIONAL APRAXIA, route-finding difficulties, and poor judgment of the localization of stimuli. Individuals may underestimate the distance of far objects, overestimate the distance of near objects, or be unable to align objects according to instructions.

spatial frequency the number of repeating elements in a pattern per unit distance. In a simple pattern of alternating black and white vertical bars (an example of a square-wave grating), the spatial frequency is the number of pairs of black and white bars per degree of visual angle, usually expressed as cycles per degree (cpd). See also CONTRAST SENSITIVITY).

spatial intelligence the ability to mentally manipulate objects in space and to imagine them in different locations and positions. It is one of the distinct intelligences in Gardner's MULTIPLE-INTELLIGENCES THEORY and also a primary mental ability (S) in Thurstone's theory of PRIMARY ABILITIES.

spatial memory the capacity to remember the position and location of objects or places, which may include orientation, direction, and distance. Spatial memory is essential for ROUTE LEARNING and navigation.

spatial neglect a disorder in which individuals have difficulty recognizing and using space, usually on the left side. For example, if approached on the left side, an individual with spatial neglect may not notice the approaching person. However, this individual would respond normally when approached on the right side. Spatial neglect can affect imagined space, as well as physical, personal, or extrapersonal space. See also NEGLECT.

spatial orientation the ability to perceive and adjust one's location in space in relation to objects in the external environment. See SPATIAL ABILITY.

spatial relationships the three-dimensional relationships of objects in space, such as their distance apart and their position relative to each other. Also called **spatial relations**. See also DEPTH PERCEPTION; SPATIAL ABILITY; SPATIAL INTELLIGENCE.

spatial summation a neural mechanism in which an impulse is propagated by two or more POSTSYNAPTIC POTENTIALS occurring simultaneously at different synapses on the same neuron, when the discharge of a single synapse would not be sufficient to activate the neuron. Compare TEMPORAL SUMMATION.

spatial threshold see TWO-POINT THRESHOLD.

spatial vision the perception of patterns and details in images. Spatial vision is distinguished from visual acuity, movement vision, or other categories of visual perception and discrimination.

spaying *n.* the surgical removal of the ovaries of a female mammal as a sterilization procedure.

SPC abbreviation for STATISTICAL PROCESS CONTROL.

speaking in tongues see GLOSSOLALIA.

Spearman–Brown prophecy formula the mathematical formulation of a basic theory of CLASSICAL TEST

THEORY concerning the length (number of items) of a test and its reliability, whereby increasing the number of items results in increased reliability for the test. [Charles Edward **Spearman** (1863–1945), British psychologist and psychometrician; W. **Brown**, 20th-century British psychologist]

Spearman rank order correlation see RANK ORDER CORRELATION. [Charles **Spearman**]

Spearman's G in the TWO-FACTOR THEORY of intelligence, GENERAL ABILITY, represented by the factor *g*. [proposed in 1904 by Charles **Spearman**]

Spearman's S in the TWO-FACTOR THEORY of intelligence, a SPECIFIC ABILITY, represented by the factor *s*. [proposed in 1904 by Charles **Spearman**]

special-ability test a focused examination given in order to determine if a student possesses any extraordinary or unusual skills, talents, or abilities.

special aptitude see SPECIFIC ABILITY.

special care unit (**SCU**) a unit in a health care institution designed to provide specialized care for people with severe problems, such as dementia, head injuries, or spinal cord injuries.

special child a child with SPECIAL NEEDS who requires SPECIAL EDUCATION and training. Such children may have learning disabilities, mental retardation, physical disabilities, or emotional difficulties. See also EXCEPTIONAL CHILD.

special education specially designed programs, services, and instruction provided to children with learning, behavioral, or physical disabilities (e.g., visual impairment, hearing loss, or neurological disorders) or to children with intellectual ability far above or below the norm whose characteristics and educational needs differ from those who can be taught through standard methods and materials.

special factor (symbol *s*) a mathematical representation of a specialized ability that is postulated to come into play in particular kinds of cognitive tasks (see SPECIFIC ABILITY). Special factors, such as mathematical ability, are contrasted with the GENERAL FACTOR (*g*), which underlies every cognitive performance. [proposed in 1904 by British psychologist and psychometrician Charles Edward Spearman (1863–1945)]

special needs the requirements of individuals with physical, mental, or emotional disabilities or financial, community-related, or resource disadvantages. Special needs may include SPECIAL EDUCATION, training, or therapy.

special psychiatric rapid intervention team (**SPRINT**) a multidisciplinary U.S. Navy team, consisting of psychologists, psychiatrists, social workers, and chaplains, that provides short-term mental health and emotional support immediately after a crisis. The team may also provide educational and consultative services to local supporting agencies.

special school a facility that provides focused and individualized education for children with disabilities or other disadvantages who are not prepared to cope with the intellectual and social skills demanded in regular school settings.

special senses those SENSES whose receptors are located only in the head: hearing, vision, taste, and smell.

speciation *n.* the formation of new SPECIES. The process involves one population splitting into two or more populations that are reproductively isolated from each other. Over time, the accrued genetic differences between these populations become so great as to prevent successful interbreeding.

species *n.* in BIOLOGICAL TAXONOMY, the basic unit of classification, consisting of a group of organisms that can interbreed to produce fertile offspring. It is the main subdivision of a GENUS.

species recognition the ability of an animal to determine whether another animal is from the same or a different species. Species recognition is important in MATE SELECTION to avoid breeding with another species. Cues used for species recognition include species-specific coloration, vocalizations, and odors and species-specific behavior.

species-specific behavior behavior that is common to most members of a particular species, appears to be unlearned (though expression may be modified by experience), and is manifested by all species members in essentially the same way. Also called **species-typical behavior**. See also INSTINCT.

species-specific defense reaction (**SSDR**) the characteristic responses of members of a species to aversive stimuli in the absence of previous experience with the stimuli. This bias determines the rate of learning an organism may demonstrate for ESCAPE BEHAVIOR in response to aversive stimuli.

species specificity of language the theory that language is an innate characteristic unique to the species *Homo sapiens*. See LANGUAGE-ORIGIN THEORY; TASK SPECIFICITY OF LANGUAGE.

species-typical behavior see SPECIES-SPECIFIC BEHAVIOR.

specific ability an ability used only for a particular intellectual task or a single test in a battery of tests. It does not correlate with other abilities, as opposed to GENERAL ABILITY, which correlates at least moderately with other abilities. Also called **special aptitude**. See also SPECIAL FACTOR.

specific aptitude see APTITUDE.

specific-attitudes theory the viewpoint that certain psychosomatic disorders are associated with particular attitudes. An example is an association between the feeling of being mistreated and the occurrence of hives. See also SPECIFIC-REACTION THEORY.

specific developmental disorders in *DSM–III*, disorders in which some distinctive and circumscribed ability or area of functioning fails to develop properly from an early age, but difficulties are not attributable to mental retardation, autism, or any other condition. In *DSM–IV–TR*, such disorders are categorized as LEARNING DISORDERS or COMMUNICATION DISORDERS.

specific-energy doctrine the concept that the quality of a sensory experience is determined by the type of sensory receptor and its nerve channels; thus, the sense of pain originates with stimulation of pain receptors, hearing with receptors in the inner ear, and so on. Originally it was supposed that the different sensory channels had different forms of neural energy, but it was later realized that the specificity lies in the connections from sensory receptors to sensory areas in the cerebral cortex. Also called **specific energy of nerves**; **specific energy of the senses**; **specific nerve energies**. [proposed in the 1830s by German physiologist Johannes Peter Müller (1801–1858)]

specific exploration see INSPECTIVE EXPLORATION.

specific factor a factor in a FACTOR ANALYSIS that is significant only in a single test; that is, the factor that represents ability in one particular type of cognitive (or other) task.

specific hunger hunger for foods that satisfy a biological need for a specific nutrient found in those foods. For instance, a protein-deprived animal will seek protein-rich foods even though more palatable but protein-deficient foods are available. See also SELF-SELECTION OF DIET.

specificity *n.* **1.** the quality of being unique, of a particular kind, or limited to a single phenomenon. For example, a stimulus that elicits a particular response or a symptom localized in a particular organ (e.g., the stomach) is said to have specificity. **2.** the probability that a test yields a negative diagnosis given that the individual does not have the condition for which he or she is being tested. Compare SENSITIVITY.

specificity doctrine of traits the proposition that personality traits are expressed with respect to specific classes of social contexts, rather than being expressed globally in all situations.

specificity of behavior **1.** the fact that certain behavior is elicited only by particular stimuli and therefore does not generalize beyond specific situations. **2.** a fixed pattern of expected behavior in a situation.

specificity theory a theory holding that the mechanism of pain is—like vision and hearing—a specific modality with its own central and peripheral apparatus. According to this theory, pain is produced by nerve impulses that are generated by an injury and are transmitted directly to a pain center in the brain. Compare GATE-CONTROL THEORY OF PAIN; PATTERN THEORY.

specific learning disability (**SLD**) a substantial deficit in scholastic or academic skills that does not pervade all areas of learning but rather is limited to a particular aspect, for example, reading or arithmetic difficulty. In U.S. federal legislation, this term is used interchangeably with LEARNING DISABILITY.

specific nerve energies see SPECIFIC-ENERGY DOCTRINE.

specific phobia an ANXIETY DISORDER, formerly called **simple phobia**, characterized by a marked and persistent fear of a specific object, activity, or situation (e.g., dogs, blood, flying, heights). The fear is excessive or unreasonable and is invariably triggered by the presence or anticipation of the feared object or situation; consequently, this is either avoided or endured with marked anxiety or distress. In *DSM–IV–TR*, specific phobias are classified into five subtypes: (a) **animal type**, which includes fears of animals or insects (e.g., cats, dogs, birds, mice, insects, or snakes); (b) **natural environment type**, which includes fears of objects in the natural surroundings (e.g., heights, storms, water, or lightning); (c) **blood-injection-injury type**, which includes fears of seeing blood or an injury and of receiving an injection or other invasive medical procedure; (d) **situational type**, which includes fear of public transportation, elevators, bridges, driving, flying, enclosed places (see CLAUSTROPHOBIA), and so forth; and (e) **other type**, which includes fears that cannot be classified under any of the other subtypes (e.g., fears of choking, vomiting, or contracting an illness and children's fears of clowns or loud noises).

specific-reaction theory a concept that an innate tendency of the autonomic nervous system to react in a particular way to a stressful situation accounts for psychosomatic symptoms. See also SPECIFIC-ATTITUDES THEORY.

specific-status characteristics behavioral and personal characteristics relevant to the setting that people intentionally and unintentionally take into account when making judgments of their own and others' competency, ability, and social value. Compare DIFFUSE-STATUS CHARACTERISTICS. See EXPECTATION-STATES THEORY.

specific thalamic projection system the direct sensory pathways via the THALAMUS for visual, auditory, and somesthetic impulses; that is, neurons that project to the thalamus from specific receptors and then from the thalamus to each of the specific sensory cortices.

specific transfer transfer of skills and knowledge acquired in one task to a similar task in which they are directly relevant. Compare GENERAL TRANSFER.

specious present the lived present, experienced as a distinct "moment" characterized by certain sense impressions and mental events. This sense of inhabiting a particular moment called "the present" is psychologically strong but actually specious, because (a) time is continuous and ongoing and (b) the present instant is so infinitely short that it cannot be experienced. See also PSYCHOLOGICAL MOMENT; TIMELESS MOMENT.

SPECT acronym for SINGLE PHOTON EMISSION COMPUTED TOMOGRAPHY.

spectator effect the effect on performance when a task is carried out in the presence of others. When an individual is confident of being able to perform the task, that is, has high task confidence, spectators improve performance; when task confidence is low, they worsen it.

spectator role a behavior pattern in which one's natural sexual responses are blocked by performance anxiety. It involves observing oneself closely and worrying about how well or poorly one is performing sexually, rather than participating fully in the sexual activity; this prevents sexual arousal from occurring. [first described by U.S. gynecologist William H. Masters (1915–2001) and U.S. psychologist Virginia E. Johnson (1925–)]

spectator therapy the beneficial effect upon members of a therapy group of observing the therapy of fellow members with similar or related problems.

spectral absorption the ability of chemicals to absorb light of specific wavelengths. This is determined by passing lights of nearly pure wavelengths through solutions of the chemicals and measuring the amount of light absorbed. In visual spectral absorption the principle is applied by measuring the degree to which different wavelengths of light alter retinal photopigment molecules.

spectral color any one of the colors of the visible spectrum, produced when white light is refracted by a prism. The visible spectrum can be divided into some 130 distinguishable spectral colors by human observers. Also called **spectral hue**. Compare EXTRASPECTRAL HUE.

spectral density see SOUND SPECTRUM.

spectral envelope see ENVELOPE.

spectral hue see SPECTRAL COLOR.

spectrally opponent cell a visual receptor cell (see RETINAL CONES) that is excited by light in certain regions of the visible SPECTRUM and inhibited by light in other regions.

spectral scale a scale that depicts the colors of the spectrum for light of different wavelengths or frequencies by just noticeable differences (see DIFFERENCE THRESHOLD).

spectral sensitivity the relative degree to which light of different wavelengths is absorbed by the photopigments of the retina. Each type of photoreceptor has its own characteristic spectral sensitivity.

spectrogram *n.* see SOUND SPECTROGRAPH.

spectroscopy *n.* the study of the SPECTRUM of electromagnetic radiation, especially the visible spectrum, as it interacts with matter. The interpretation of the spectra so produced is used in chemical analysis, examining molecular structure, and for many other purposes. Spectroscopy is performed using **spectroscopes, spectrometers,** or **spectrophotometers.**

spectrum *n.* (*pl.* **spectra**) **1.** a distribution of electromagnetic energy displayed by decreasing wavelength. In the case of the **visible spectrum**, it is the series of visible colors (with wavelengths in the range 400–700 nm) produced when white light is refracted through a prism. **2.** a wide range of associated elements, qualities, actions, or occurrences. **—spectral** *adj.*

spectrum level the spectral density of a sound, usually expressed in DECIBELS sound-pressure level (dB SPL). For a waveform with a continuous spectrum, the **power spectral density** is the power in a band Δf Hz wide centered at frequency f as Δf approaches zero. The spectrum level at frequency f is the power spectral density expressed in decibels sound-pressure level.

spectrum of consciousness 1. in TRANSPERSONAL PSYCHOLOGY, the full range of human psychological and spiritual experiences concomitant with states of being. **2.** in neuroscience, the full range of awareness. See CONSCIOUSNESS.

speculation *n.* **1.** conjectural thinking that is not necessarily supported by scientifically determined evidence. **2.** a loosely supported theory or explanation. **—speculative** *adj.*

speculative psychology a view of a psychological subject or issue that is based on SPECULATION rather than experiment or research. See ARMCHAIR PSYCHOLOGY; RATIONAL PSYCHOLOGY.

speech *n.* communication through conventional vocal and oral symbols.

speech, language, and hearing center a professionally staffed clinic or center that provides diagnostic and treatment services to people with communication impairments. Staff typically consists of experts in audiology, speech and language pathology, and speech and hearing sciences. Also called **community speech and hearing center**.

speech act an instance of the use of speech considered as an action, especially with regard to the speaker's intentions and the effect on a listener. A single utterance usually involves several simultaneous speech acts (see ILLOCUTIONARY ACT). The study of speech acts is part of the general field of PRAGMATICS.

speech-activated control in ergonomics, the use of voice commands to activate functions or enter information (e.g., in voice-activated dialing). Also called **voice-activated control**.

speech amplification system a system consisting of a microphone attached to a headset and a small amplifier designed to increase the volume of the voice of an individual who is unable to speak loudly because of a voice disorder or respiratory problem.

speech and language acquisition disorders a wide range of disorders resulting in failure, or reduced ability, to acquire and use the conventional symbolic system of speaking and understanding language.

speech and language pathology 1. inadequate or maladaptive communication behavior and disorders of speech, language, and hearing. **2.** the clinical field that studies, evaluates, and treats speech, voice, and language disorders.

speech and language therapist a specialist with a degree or other appropriate certification in SPEECH AND LANGUAGE PATHOLOGY. Also called **speech and language clinician**.

speech anxiety see PUBLIC-SPEAKING ANXIETY.

speech aphasia see EXPRESSIVE APHASIA.

speech area any of the areas of the cerebral cortex that are associated with verbal (oral, rather than written) communication. The speech areas are located in the left hemisphere in most individuals; they include BROCA'S AREA in the third convolution of the frontal lobe and WERNICKE'S AREA in the temporal lobe. Maps of the speech areas have been quite well plotted, originally by studying cortical lesions in patients with specific speech defects and more recently by brain imaging of normal speakers.

speech audiometry the measurement of hearing in terms of the reception of spoken words presented at controlled levels of intensity.

speech community a community consisting of the speakers of a particular language or variety of a language (e.g., a dialect).

speech derailment see DERAILMENT.

speech development see LANGUAGE DEVELOPMENT.

speech discrimination test a phonetically balanced word list used to measure an individual's ability to understand speech.

speech disorder any disorder that affects the production of speech. Among such problems are the following: poor audibility or intelligibility; unpleasant tonal quality; unusual, distorted, or abnormally effortful sound production; lack of conventional rhythm and stress; inappropriateness in terms of age or physical or mental development. See also COMMUNICATION DISORDER; LANGUAGE DISORDER; MOTOR SPEECH DISORDER; VOICE DISORDER.

speech error see SLIP OF THE TONGUE.

speech functions the various purposes for which spoken language is used: primarily, to communicate ideas or information, to maintain social relationships, and to express feeling or emotion. See also SPEECH ACT.

speech impairment any problem that affects the production of speech: an occasional synonym for SPEECH DISORDER.

speech impediment in general usage, any speech impairment or disorder. The term is no longer used in formal research or therapeutic practice.

speech intelligibility the degree to which speech sounds (whether conversational or communication-system output) can be correctly identified and understood by listeners in a particular environment. Background or other system noise is one of the most important factors influencing speech intelligibility. See also ARTICULATION INDEX.

speech lateralization the hemispheric asymmetry in the control of verbal communication. For most individuals, speech centers are located in the left cerebral hemisphere, which is relatively specialized for the speech function. See also LANGUAGE LOCALIZATION; SPEECH AREA; WADA TEST.

speech origin see LANGUAGE-ORIGIN THEORY.

speech perception the psychological process in which a listener processes an incoming stream of speech into a phonological representation.

speech processor a device that converts microphone or other input into patterns of electrical stimulation, such as the element of a COCHLEAR IMPLANT that converts sounds into electrical impulses to stimulate the auditory nerve, thus enabling comprehension of sound and speech.

speech production the process by which a person uses his or her neural, articulatory, and respiratory capacities to produce spoken language.

speech reading see LIPREADING.

speech-reception threshold (**SRT**) the sound level in DECIBELS sound-pressure level (dB SPL) at which speech is just intelligible.

speech recognition system a computer software program capable of recognizing and responding to human speech. Such programs enable individuals to control computers and create and manipulate documents by dictation, which is especially important for individuals with disabilities who are unable to provide commands and data input using other methods, such as a keyboard or mouse.

speech register see REGISTER.

speech rehabilitation training to restore a lost or impaired speech function. Also called **speech reeducation**.

Speech-Sounds Perception Test a test in the HALSTEAD–REITAN NEUROPSYCHOLOGICAL BATTERY that measures the ability to match a spoken nonsense word containing a double *e* (such as *teeg*) with its written counterpart.

speech synthesizer a computer or other system capable of producing artificial speech. Synthesizers may produce speech in response to input (e.g., from a keyboard) or they may convert written text into speech. See also AUDIOTACTILE DEVICE.

speech therapy the application of remedies, treatment, and counseling for the improvement of speech and language.

speech-tolerance level the level in DECIBELS sound-pressure level (dB SPL) at which continuous speech is judged to be uncomfortably loud.

speech-to-noise ratio see SIGNAL-TO-NOISE RATIO.

speed *n.* slang for an amphetamine, especially METHAMPHETAMINE.

speed–accuracy tradeoff the tendency, when performing a task, for either speed or accuracy to be sacrificed in order to prioritize the other. In experiments, by varying the speed–accuracy criterion through instructions, payoffs, and deadlines, a person can respond quickly with many errors, slowly with few errors, or anywhere in between. In the area of motor control, FITTS LAW is a specific example of a speed–accuracy tradeoff.

speedball *n.* a colloquial name for a mixture of HEROIN and a powerful stimulant (e.g., COCAINE or an AMPHETAMINE).

speed test **1.** a type of test intended to calculate the number of problems or tasks the participant can solve or perform in a predesignated block of time. The participant is often, but not always, made aware of the time limit. **2.** any test in which a person must operate within specified time restraints. **3.** a test in which the participant's speed contributes to the final score. Also called **timed test**. Compare POWER TEST.

spell *n.* **1.** a hypnotic influence or suggestion. **2.** a lay term for an episode of a physical or mental disorder.

spelling dyslexia see WORD-FORM DYSLEXIA.

Spence, Kenneth Wartinbee (1907–1967) U.S. psychologist. Spence received his PhD in 1933 from Yale University, where he studied with Robert M. YERKES. He spent the bulk of his career at the University of Iowa, heading its psychology department for 22 years. Spence was an experimental psychologist whose research involved a skillfully designed series of experiments on DISCRIMINATION LEARNING in animals and Pavlovian eyeblink conditioning in humans. Together with Clark L. HULL, he developed a version of NEOBEHAVIORISM that was very influential in the 1940s and 1950s. The Hull–Spence model offered a theoretical system that explained animal learning and motivation based on principles of PAVLOVIAN CONDITIONING, in contrast to Skinnerian (OPERANT CONDITIONING) principles. Spence was awarded many honors, including election to the National Academy of Sciences and the Society of Experimental Psychologists and receipt of the Distinguished Scientific Contribution Award from the American Psychological Association in 1956. See also ASSOCIATIONISM; CONTIGUITY LEARNING THEORY; MAZE LEARNING.

sperm *n.* see SPERMATOZOON.

sperm analysis the evaluation of male fertility based on the sperm count per milliliter of ejaculate and on sperm morphology (i.e., form and structure) and motility. Also called **seminal analysis**.

spermatid *n.* an immature spermatozoon. See SPERMATOGENESIS.

spermatocyte *n.* an intermediate stage in the development of spermatozoa in the male testis.

spermatogenesis *n.* the process of production of spermatozoa in the seminiferous tubules of the TESTIS. Male germ cells (**spermatogonia**) lining the seminiferous tubules mature into **primary spermatocytes**, which undergo MEIOSIS eventually resulting in mature spermatozoa (four per spermatocyte). In the first meiotic division, each primary spermatocyte gives rise to two HAPLOID **secondary spermatocytes**, each of which then undergoes a further division to form two **spermatids**. The latter, attached to SERTOLI CELLS, mature into spermatozoa. The process is controlled by pituitary GONADOTROPINS, which (among other functions) promote the release of testosterone from the interstitial cells of the testis, which stimulates sperm production. Spermatogenesis is continuous in humans after the onset of puberty and seasonal in some other animal species. —**spermatogenetic** *adj.*

spermatogonium *n.* (*pl.* **spermatogonia**) a male germ cell. See SPERMATOGENESIS.

spermatorrhea *n.* the involuntary discharge of semen in the absence of orgasm.

spermatozoon *n.* (*pl.* **spermatozoa**) the GAMETE produced by males, which fuses with a female gamete (see OVUM) in the process of fertilization. Also called **sperm**.

sperm competition competition between the sperm of different males to fertilize the eggs of females that mate with multiple males. Males have several strategies for dealing with sperm competition, including MATE GUARDING, leaving an ejaculatory plug in the female genitalia to prevent other males from mating, or removing sperm from previous males prior to mating. Females have tactics to counter these strategies (see CRYPTIC FEMALE CHOICE). In the muriqui monkey of Brazil, males produce sperm plugs that block the vagina, but both females and other males can remove these plugs before mating again.

Sperry, Roger Wolcott (1913–1994) U.S. psychologist. Sperry earned his master's degree in psychology from Oberlin College in 1937 and his doctorate in zoology from the University of Chicago in 1941, studying under the neuroembryologist Paul Weiss (1898–1989). He spent four postdoctoral years working with Karl LASHLEY at the Yerkes Laboratories of Primate Biology in Florida and then several years on the faculty of the University of Chicago. In 1954 he accepted a newly created chair of psychobiology at the California Institute of Technology, where he spent the remainder of his career. Sperry is best known for his nerve-regeneration theory and his research into the functions of the two hemispheres of the brain using the split-brain technique (see COMMISSUROTOMY). Throughout his career, Sperry sought answers to fundamental questions regarding the nature of consciousness and its interaction with the body. Representative works include "Neurology and the Mind–Brain Problem" (*American Scientist*, 1952), "Hemispheric Disconnection and Unity in Conscious Awareness" (*American Psychologist*, 1968), and his book *Science and Moral Priority* (1983). Sperry's many honors included membership in the American Academy of Arts and Sciences and receipt of the American Psychological Association's Lifetime Achievement Award. In 1981 he received the Nobel Prize for Physiology or Medicine.

spherical aberration the failure of light rays to converge at the same focal point because of the curvature of a lens. See ABERRATION; ASTIGMATISM.

spherical lens a lens in which either or both of the surfaces are portions of a sphere.

sphericity *n.* an assumption encountered in the analysis of data obtained when individuals are measured on two or more occasions that requires the correlation among the time points to be constant for all time points. See REPEATED MEASURES DESIGN.

sphincter *n.* a ring-shaped muscle that partly or wholly closes a body orifice, such as the anal sphincters or the IRIS of the eye.

sphincter control the ability to control the muscles that open and close the openings of the body, particularly the anal and urinary sphincters. This ability is an important stage in physical development. See DEFECATION REFLEX; TOILET TRAINING.

sphincter morality in psychoanalytic theory, personality characteristics and behaviors such as obstinacy, extreme orderliness, and parsimony, which are associated with an anal-retentive personality. See also ANAL PERSONALITY; ANAL STAGE.

sphingomyelin *n.* a phospholipid that occurs abundantly in animal cell membranes. It makes up about one tenth of the lipids of the brain.

sphingomyelin lipidosis see NIEMANN–PICK DISEASE.

sphygmograph *n.* an instrument for measuring the strength, rapidity, and other characteristics of the pulse.

sphygmomanometer *n.* an instrument for measuring blood pressure, especially in the arteries.

spicy *adj.* **1.** denoting the taste of highly flavored foods. Spiciness is carried mainly through the trigeminal nerve (see TRIGEMINAL CHEMORECEPTION) rather than the GUSTATORY SYSTEM. **2.** denoting one of the primary odor qualities in HENNING'S ODOR PRISM. **—spiciness** *n.*

spider phobia a persistent and irrational fear of spiders. In *DSM–IV–TR*, spider phobia is classified as a SPECIFIC PHOBIA, animal type. Also called **arachneophobia**; **arachnophobia**. See also ANIMAL PHOBIA.

spike-and-wave discharges a pattern of BRAIN WAVES on an electroencephalogram (see ELECTROENCEPHALOGRAPHY) that is characteristic of ABSENCE SEIZURES. It consists of a sharp spike followed by a low-amplitude DELTA WAVE and occurs at a frequency of three per second.

spike potential see ACTION POTENTIAL.

spike-wave activity the pattern produced by an ACTION POTENTIAL of a neuron when amplified and projected onto the screen of an OSCILLOSCOPE or a computer monitor. The waveform appears as a sharp, high peak, followed by a short dip below the baseline (the AFTERPOTENTIAL), then a return to the predischarge level. The amplitude of the wave spike indicates the intensity of the discharge.

spina bifida a developmental defect resulting from a failure of the vertebral canal to close normally around the spinal cord (see NEURAL TUBE DEFECT). This results in part of the spinal cord protruding from the body surface (see MYELOMENINGOCELE). Individuals with spina bifida have difficulty with sensation, ambulation, and bowel and bladder control; they may also experience weakness or paralysis of the muscles of the legs or feet, susceptibility to infection, and, in 90% of cases, HYDROCEPHALUS. MENINGOMYELOCELE is the most common form of spina bifida. See also MENINGOCELE.

spinal animal an animal whose spinal cord has been surgically severed and therefore separated from communication with its brain, so that peripheral processes of the body are controlled only by the spinal cord and nerves.

spinal canal the canal that runs through the SPINAL COLUMN and contains the spinal cord.

spinal column the backbone, consisting of a series of bones (vertebrae) connected together by disks of cartilage (intervertebral disks) and held together by muscles and tendons. It extends from the cranium to the coccyx, encloses the spinal cord, and forms the main axis of the body. Also called **spine**; **vertebral column**.

spinal cord the part of the CENTRAL NERVOUS SYSTEM that extends from the lower end of the MEDULLA OBLONGATA, at the base of the brain, through a canal in the center of the spine as far as the lumbar region. In transverse section, the cord consists of an H-shaped core of gray matter (see CENTRAL GRAY; ANTERIOR HORN; DORSAL HORN) surrounded by white matter consisting of tracts of long ascending and descending nerve fibers on either side of the cord that are linked by the WHITE COMMISSURE. The spinal cord is enveloped by the MENINGES and is the origin of the 31 pairs of SPINAL NERVES. See also SPINAL ROOT.

spinal cord disease any pathological condition caused by infection, injury, or a congenital defect of the spinal cord. Examples include Brown-Séquard syndrome, Horner's syndrome, spinal meningitis, amyotrophic lateral sclerosis, multiple sclerosis, and syringomyelia.

spinal cord injury any damage to the spinal cord caused by sudden or progressive external forces. Kinds of spinal cord injury include contusion (bruising), hemorrhage, laceration, transection, spinal shock, and compression. See also INCOMPLETE SPINAL CORD INJURY; RADICULOPATHY; SLIPPED DISK.

spinal ganglion a GANGLION found in the DORSAL ROOT of each SPINAL NERVE and containing the cell bodies of sensory neurons.

spinal gate in the GATE-CONTROL THEORY OF PAIN, a mechanism in cells of the SUBSTANTIA GELATINOSA of the spinal cord that transmits the net effect of both excitatory and inhibitory signals to the brain. The mechanism can modify the pain signals in accordance with messages from higher centers that reflect previous experience and the influence of emotional and other factors on PAIN PERCEPTION. Also called **gating mechanism**.

spinal muscular atrophy (**SMA**) a hereditary (autosomal) MOTOR NEURON DISEASE characterized by wasting (atrophy) of skeletal muscles associated with degeneration of nerve cells in the ANTERIOR HORN of the spinal cord. There are three common types, based on age of onset and symptom severity. Type I (also called **infantile spinal muscular atrophy** or **Werdnig–Hoffmann disease**) is evident at birth or within the first few months of life and is the most severe, resulting in death usually prior to age 2. Type II (also called **intermediate spinal muscular atrophy**) has an onset of symptoms between 6 months and 2 years and results in delayed motor development, progressive loss of strength, and variable loss of ambulation. Type III (also called **juvenile spinal muscular atrophy** or **Kugelberg–Welander disease**) is identified between ages 1 and 15 and is the least severe, associated with slower progression and lower incidence. There is also a Type IV (also called **adult-onset spinal muscular atrophy** or **Aran–Duchenne disease**), with an onset typically after age 30 and symptoms ranging from mild to severe. Also called **progressive muscular atrophy**; **progressive spinal muscular atrophy**.

spinal nerve any of the 31 pairs of nerves that originate in the gray matter of the SPINAL CORD and emerge through openings between the vertebrae of the spine to extend into the body's dermatomes (skin areas) and skeletal muscles. The spinal nerves comprise 8 cervical nerves, 12 thoracic nerves, 5 lumbar nerves, 5 sacral nerves, and 1 coccygeal nerve. Each attaches to the spinal cord via two short branches, a DORSAL ROOT and a VENTRAL ROOT. See also SPINAL ROOT.

spinal puncture see LUMBAR PUNCTURE.

spinal reflex a REFLEX that involves neural circuits in the spinal cord, often controlling posture or locomotion. They are sometimes classed as **segmental reflexes**, if the circuit involves only one segment of the spinal cord, or as **intersegmental reflexes**, if the impulses must travel through more than one spinal segment. Reflexes that require brain activity are **suprasegmental reflexes**.

spinal root the junction of a SPINAL NERVE and the SPINAL CORD. Near the cord, each spinal nerve divides into a DORSAL ROOT, carrying sensory fibers, and a VENTRAL ROOT, carrying motor fibers, as stated by the BELL–MAGENDIE LAW.

spinal shock a temporary loss of reflex functions below the site of an injury to the spinal cord.

spinal stenosis see STENOSIS.

spinal tap see LUMBAR PUNCTURE.

spindle *n.* see MUSCLE SPINDLE; SPINDLE WAVES.

spindle cell a type of small neuron whose CELL BODY is spindle-shaped, that is, wider in the middle and tapering at the two ends. It should not be confused with a MUSCLE SPINDLE.

spindle waves electroencephalogram patterns associated with light sleep. See SLEEP SPINDLES.

spine *n.* see SPINAL COLUMN.

spinocerebellar tract a major nerve tract that carries impulses from the muscles and other proprioceptors through the spinal cord to the CEREBELLUM.

spinothalamic tracts two ascending pathways for somatosensory impulses that travel through the spinal cord to the thalamus. They form subdivisions of the ANTEROLATERAL SYSTEM. The **anterior spinothalamic tract** serves touch and pressure sensations; the **lateral spinothalamic tract** carries principally pain and temperature information.

spiral ganglion the mass of cell bodies of the auditory nerve. It is located in the inner wall of the COCHLEA near the organ of Corti.

spiral omnibus test an assessment in which the focused themes being tested are distributed throughout the test, instead of being grouped together, and become increasingly difficult as the test progresses. Each subsequent spiral of difficulty covers a different domain of intelligence. Also called **spiral test**.

spirit *n.* **1.** the nonphysical part of a person: the mental, moral, and emotional characteristics that make up the core of someone's identity (e.g., *a noble spirit; it broke her spirit*). **2.** a vital force seen as animating the bodies of living creatures, sometimes identified with the SOUL and seen as surviving death. **3.** an immaterial being, possessed of some permanence, to which are ascribed many or most of the activities of a living person. **4.** a supernatural being, such as a ghost or a deity. **5.** in idealist philosophies, a universal mind or idea seen as a fundamental reality and a moving force of events in the world. See ABSOLUTE IDEALISM. **6.** the mood, temper, or disposition that temporarily or permanently characterizes a person. **7.** loyalty or morale.

spiritism *n.* see SPIRITUALISM.

spirit photography the attempt, popular in the late 19th century, to render the spirits of deceased individuals visible by photography. In particular, it was claimed that spirits often left faint imprints on photographs of their loved ones. The first alleged spirit photograph was produced in 1862 by the U.S. engraver William H. Mumler, who was subsequently tried (inconclusively) for fraud. Most of the supposed spirit images produced at this time seem to have been created using a simple process of double exposure or specially prepared plates.

spiritual factor any moral, religious, or mystical belief that plays a role in influencing behavior, emotions, or thoughts.

spiritual healing see FAITH HEALING.

spiritualism *n.* **1.** in metaphysics, the position that the fundamental reality of the universe is nonmaterial. **2.** the belief that the spirits of the dead survive in another world or dimension, and that it is possible for the living to receive communications from them through MEDIUMS. With MAGIC and the OCCULT arts, spiritualism may be considered the philosophical and religious counterpart to PARAPSYCHOLOGY. Also called **spiritism**. **3.** the belief that all humans, animals, plants, and natural objects possess souls and are part of a larger, universal spirit. See PANPSYCHISM. **—spiritualist** *adj., n.* **—spiritualistic** *adj.*

spirituality *n.* **1.** a concern for or sensitivity to the things of the SPIRIT or SOUL, especially as opposed to material things. **2.** more specifically, a concern for God and religion and a sensitivity to religious experience. **3.** the fact or state of being incorporeal.

spiritual self see EMPIRICAL SELF.

spirograph *n.* an instrument for measuring and recording the rate and amount of breathing.

spirometer *n.* an instrument used for measuring the air capacity in the lungs. In speech and language therapy, it may be used to record breathing functions associated with speech production.

SPL abbreviation for sound-pressure level. See DECIBEL.

splanchnic *adj.* denoting the abdominal organs, or viscera. In combination with a qualifying prefix, this word is used in the names of various body types to indicate the abdomen (e.g., NORMOSPLANCHNIC TYPE, MICROSPLANCHNIC TYPE, MACROSPLANCHNIC TYPE).

splanchnic nerve any of certain nerves that serve the abdominal VISCERA. They originate in the ganglia of the SYMPATHETIC CHAIN.

spleen *n.* **1.** an organ that produces lymphocytes, filters and stores blood, and destroys old red blood cells. Although it is not necessary to maintain life, the absence of a spleen may predispose an individual to certain infections. **2.** bad temper or ill will. **3.** an old term for melancholy or depression.

splenium *n.* (*pl.* **splenia**) a blunt enlargement at the posterior end of the CORPUS CALLOSUM.

split brain a brain in which the cerebral hemispheres have been separated by severence of the corpus callosum (see COMMISSUROTOMY). Surgical transection of the corpus callosum is used to create split-brain laboratory animals for experimental purposes and is also occasionally performed on humans to alleviate some forms of severe epilepsy. Split brain can also occur without surgical intervention as a result of injury or disease of the corpus callosum. Study of individuals or animals with split brain helps to define the roles of the two hemispheres. Also called **divided brain**.

split-brain technique see COMMISSUROTOMY.

split-half reliability a measure of the internal consistency of a test, obtained by correlating responses on one half of the test with responses on the other half. Also called **split-half correlation**.

split-litter method in animal research, the assignment of litter mates to different groups in an experiment (e.g., the experimental group and the control group). This is an attempt to minimize genetic differences between the members of the different groups. Also called **split-litter technique**.

split personality a lay term for an individual with DISSOCIATIVE IDENTITY DISORDER. It is sometimes confused with SCHIZOPHRENIA, which means literally "splitting of the mind" but does not involve the formation of a second personality.

split run a method of testing the effectiveness of advertising and other promotions by showing an advertisement to one half of a product's potential customers and showing no advertisement (or a different advertisement) to the other half. Sales figures can be assessed from data provided by stores in which coupons are used, or the consumer provides other identifying information (for example, an identification card or membership card for a particular store).

split-span test a test in which brief auditory messages in the form of two different lists of digits or words are presented rapidly and simultaneously, one list to each ear. Participants are required to report as many digits or words as possible in any order. Typically, participants report first the stimuli presented to one ear, then those presented to the other.

splitting *n.* **1.** in KLEINIAN ANALYSIS, the most primitive of all DEFENSE MECHANISMS, in which OBJECTS that evoke ambivalence and therefore anxiety are dealt with by compartmentalizing positive and negative emotions (see PART-OBJECT), leading to images of the self and others that are not integrated. In general, it results in polarized viewpoints that are projected onto different people. This mechanism is found not only in infants and young children, who are as yet incapable of combining these polarized viewpoints, but also in adults with dysfunctional patterns of dealing with ambivalence; it is often associated with BORDERLINE PERSONALITY DISORDER. Splitting plays a central role in FAIRBAIRNIAN THEORY. Also called **splitting of the object**. **2.** in COTHERAPY, an appeal by a client to one of the therapists when he or she feels that that therapist would be more sympathetic than the other. Also called **splitting situation**.

SPMSQ abbreviation for SHORT PORTABLE MENTAL STATUS QUESTIONNAIRE.

spongiform encephalopathy see PRION DISEASE.

spongioblast *n.* a type of ectodermal cell (see ECTODERM) that can develop into cells of the NEUROGLIA.

spontaneity test a type of SOCIOMETRIC TEST in which an individual in a therapy group is encouraged to improvise freely in reenactments of typical life situations with other members of the group who have been judged to be emotionally related, positively or negatively, to that individual. The object is to gain insight into interpersonal relationships not revealed by the standard sociometric test, which deals only with attraction and repulsion. [devised by Austrian-born U.S. psychiatrist Jacob Levi Moreno (1889–1974)]

spontaneity training a personality-training program in which a client learns to act naturally and spontaneously in real-life situations by practicing such behavior in graduated sessions. Also called **spontaneity therapy**. [introduced by Austrian-born U.S. psychiatrist Jacob Levi Moreno (1889–1974)]

spontaneous abortion an interruption of pregnancy with loss of the fetus as a result of natural causes. A common cause of spontaneous abortion is an imbalance of hormones required to support the pregnancy. Emotional disturbances may also be causative factors. More than 10% of all human pregnancies terminate by spontaneous abortion. See also MISCARRIAGE.

spontaneous alternation the instinctive, successive alternation of responses between alternatives in a situation involving discrete choices or exploration. For example, in a learning and memory experiment, a rat in a T MAZE tends to choose the left arm on one trial, the right arm on the next, the left arm again, and so on.

spontaneous discharge the firing of nerve impulses without direct influence of an external stimulus.

spontaneous human combustion the claim that the human body can spontaneously burst into flame, without the aid of any external ignition, and burn completely to ashes. Despite a number of alleged cases, this is generally considered an URBAN LEGEND.

spontaneous imagery the unintended or nonwilled emergence of mental IMAGES. See also IMAGERY.

spontaneous memorialization voluntary public response to unexpected and violent death. Examples include the placement of messages, flowers, and other objects at sites associated with terrorist attacks or personal tragedies (e.g., when a shopkeeper has been murdered or a child struck down by a hit-and-run driver). The hallmark of spontaneous memorialization is an immediate emotional response on the part of individuals and small groups of people, as distinguished from institutionalized patterns of response. See also TRAUMATIC GRIEF.

spontaneous movement movement that results from impulse, occurring without premeditation or planning. Spontaneous movement decreases in some disorders, such as Parkinson's disease.

spontaneous neural activity the apparently automatic firing of neurons, or firing in the absence of observable stimuli. See SPONTANEOUS DISCHARGE.

spontaneous recovery the reappearance of a conditioned response, after either operant or Pavlovian conditioning, after it has been experimentally extinguished (see EXTINCTION).

spontaneous regression a phenomenon in which a person suddenly relives an event from an earlier age (e.g., childhood) and may exhibit appropriate behavior for that age.

spontaneous remission a reduction or disappearance of symptoms without any therapeutic intervention, which may be temporary or permanent. It most commonly refers to medical, rather than psychological, conditions. See also WAITING-LIST PHENOMENON.

spontaneous speech speech that is not in response to a specific question or direction.

spontaneous trait inference a judgment about an individual's personality traits that is made automatically, without any conscious intent to make such a judgment.

spoonerism *n.* a SLIP OF THE TONGUE in which two sound elements (usually initial consonants) are unintentionally transposed, resulting in an utterance with a different and often amusing sense, for example, *sons of toil* for *tons of soil*. [W. A. **Spooner** (1844–1930), British academic noted for slips of this kind]

sport *n.* **1.** a physical contest between individuals or teams conducted under codified rules, controlled by nonparticipants, and in which there is only one winner. **2.** in genetics, an organism that has undergone mutation and is distinctly different from its parents.

sport and exercise psychology the application and development of psychological theory for the understanding of human behavior in the sport and physical exercise environment. This discipline evolved from SPORT PSYCHOLOGY and is progressively becoming two separate disciplines as EXERCISE PSYCHOLOGY merges with HEALTH PSYCHOLOGY.

Sport Imagery Questionnaire (**SIQ**) **1.** an instrument used to measure the degree to which an athlete uses each of five different functions of IMAGERY: (a) motivational general, arousal (images related to physiological and emotional AROUSAL); (b) motivational general, mastery (images of being a master of self-control); (c) motivational specific (images of winning, achieving a goal, etc.); (d) cognitive general (images of strategies to be used in a game); and (e) cognitive specific (images of proper execution or improvement of a skill). The SIQ currently consists of 30 statements (e.g., "I imagine the excitement associated with competing") to which participants respond using a 7-point LIKERT SCALE, ranging from "rarely" to "often." [developed in 1998 by Craig R. Hall, Diane E. Mack, experimental psychologist Allan U. Paivio (1925–), and health psychologist Heather A. Hausenblas (1970–)] **2.** an instrument used to measure the imaging abilities of athletes. A participant is asked to imagine four different situations in his or her sport (practicing alone, practicing in front of others, watching a teammate, competing) and then to rate five different characteristics of the resulting imagery on a 5-point LIKERT SCALE, ranging from "no image present" to "extremely clear and realistic image." [originally developed in 1982 by sport psychologist Rainer Martens (1942–)]

sport injury a physical injury that occurs as a result of participation in sport or exercise.

sport personality debate a debate about the role that personality characteristics have in decisions to participate in sport and in the ability to perform in sport. Research evidence supports the position that personality is not a relevant factor. See CREDULOUS ARGUMENT; SKEPTICAL ARGUMENT.

sport psychologist an individual who uses psychological theory to study the circumstances and consequences of participation in sport and who applies this theory to enhance sport performance and make it consistent. See CLINICAL SPORT PSYCHOLOGIST; EDUCATIONAL SPORT PSYCHOLOGIST; RESEARCH SPORT PSYCHOLOGIST.

sport psychology the application and development of psychological theory for the understanding and enhancement of human behavior in the sport environment. Sport psychologists are identified as CLINICAL SPORT PSYCHOLOGISTS, EDUCATIONAL SPORT PSYCHOLOGISTS, or RESEARCH SPORT PSYCHOLOGISTS, depending on their education, training, and work in the field.

sport-related life skills psychological skills learned for sport-related purposes that can be applied to behavior in other environments and situations.

sport science the application of biophysical and social-scientific methods to study sport behavior. Sport science includes biological, mechanical, psychological, sociological, and managerial disciplines.

sport self-talk log see TRAINING LOG.

sports hypnosis hypnosis used to assist participants in sport to eliminate mind-sets that interfere with athletic performance or to develop those that enhance it.

sports imagery imagery used by participants in sport for learning and perfecting new skills, for MENTAL REHEARSAL, and for controlling emotions. See KINESTHETIC IMAGERY; MENTAL PRACTICE; SPORT IMAGERY QUESTIONNAIRE.

sportsmanship *n.* a situation-specific set of behaviors involving concern for and respect of rules, opponents, and officials and a positive approach to participation. The nature of sportsmanship depends on such factors as the type of sport, the level of play, and the age of the participant.

Sports Medicine Injury Checklist (**SMIC**) a guide for assessing athletic (sport) injury. The guide lists a series of factors that have particular relevance to sport injuries, including aspects related to the acute phase, the chronic phase, and the participant's history.

sport socialization the process of using sport as a medium for teaching and learning the skills and characteristics necessary to function effectively in a society. It includes learning respect for authority (e.g., a referee), fulfilling commitments (going to practice, not quitting the team), and so on.

sport sociology the application and development of sociological theory related to sport. Its primary focus is the role sport plays in societies, the organizations of sport, and the impact of culture on sport and of sport on culture.

spotlight model of attention a model of attention that likens the focus of attention to a spotlight. Information outside the spotlight is presumed not to receive processing that requires attention.

Spranger's typology a system of classification that sorts humans by six basic cultural values: theoretical, economic, aesthetic, social, political, and religious. [proposed by German philosopher and psychologist Eduard **Spranger** (1882–1963)]

spread *n.* see DISPERSION.

spreading activation 1. in neuroscience, a hypothetical process in which the activation of one neuron is presumed to spread to connected neurons, making it more likely that they will fire. **2.** in cognitive psychology, an analogous model for the association of ideas, memories, and the like, based on the notion that activation of one item stored in memory travels through associated links to activate another item. As each item is activated, further activation may spread through the network, making it more likely that associated items will be recalled. Spreading activation is a feature of some NETWORK-MEMORY MODELS of SEMANTIC MEMORY.

spreading depression a propagating wave of silence in neuronal activity accompanied by a relatively large negative electric potential. Spreading depression occurs in regions of gray matter, including the cerebral cortex and hippocampus. It may occur spontaneously or be evoked by intense local electrical, chemical, or mechanical stimuli. Cortical spreading depression is related to migraine headaches.

spread of effect see GENERALIZATION; STIMULUS GENERALIZATION.

spree murder the act of killing people at two or more locations within a short period of time. See also MASS MURDER.

SPRINT acronym for SPECIAL PSYCHIATRIC RAPID INTERVENTION TEAM.

spurious correlation a situation in which variables are correlated through their common relationship with one or more other variables but not through a causal mechanism. See THIRD-VARIABLE PROBLEM.

spurt *n.* a sudden, sharp increase in the rate of a process, such as a growth spurt around the time of puberty. See also END SPURT; INITIAL SPURT.

SQAW acronym for SLEEP QUESTIONNAIRE AND ASSESSMENT OF WAKEFULNESS.

SQ3R one of a variety of study methods developed on the basis of research in cognitive psychology. The formula represents a method for enhanced learning of reading material. It consists of five steps: *s*urvey, *q*uestion, *r*ead, *r*ecite, and *r*eview.

squared multiple correlation see COEFFICIENT OF MULTIPLE CORRELATION.

squeeze technique a technique for overcoming PREMATURE EJACULATION. The penis is stimulated until the man is well aroused, then the partner squeezes the penis briefly where the head of the penis joins the shaft. When the squeeze is released, a pause in stimulation is taken for 30 s to 1 min. The squeeze and pause lowers arousal, and stimulation is then resumed. After several stimulate–squeeze–pause–stimulate cycles, the man is stimulated to ejaculation. This procedure conditions the man to maintain an erection longer before ejaculation. [devised by U.S. gynecologist William H. Masters (1915–2001) and U.S. psychologist Virginia E. Johnson (1925–)]

SQUID acronym for SUPERCONDUCTING QUANTUM INTERFERENCE DEVICE.

squint *n.* see CROSS-EYE; STRABISMUS.

S–R abbreviation for stimulus–response.

SRA abbreviation for Satanic ritual abuse. See SATANISM. See also RITUAL ABUSE.

SRCD abbreviation for SOCIETY FOR RESEARCH IN CHILD DEVELOPMENT.

SRIF abbreviation for somatotropin-release inhibiting factor (see SOMATOSTATIN).

SRIs abbreviation for serotonin reuptake inhibitors. See SSRIS.

S–R learning model the hypothesis that learning leads to the formation of *s*timulus–*r*esponse connections. In PAVLOVIAN CONDITIONING, this connection is between the conditioned stimulus and the unconditioned response (e.g., between the tone and salivation in PAVLOV's procedure); in INSTRUMENTAL CONDITIONING, the connection is between the discriminative stimulus and the response (e.g., between a tone and bar pressing).

S–R–O learning model *s*timulus–*r*esponse–*o*utcome learning model: in INSTRUMENTAL CONDITIONING, the hypothesis that associations are acquired between a discriminative stimulus, the instrumental response, and the outcome of reinforcement or punishment.

S–R psychology an approach to psychology that conceptualizes behavior in terms of *s*timulus and *r*esponse. The fundamental goal is therefore describing functional relationships between stimulus and response, that is, manipulating a stimulus and observing the response. S–R psychology developed from E. L. THORNDIKE's connectionism and J. B. WATSON's behaviorism. **S–R theories** tend to be behavioral rather than cognitive. Examples include C. L. HULL's reinforcement theory (see HULL'S MATHEMATICO-DEDUCTIVE THEORY OF LEARNING) and E. R. GUTHRIE'S CONTIGUITY LEARNING THEORY. S–R theories are sometimes contrasted with cognitive theories of learning (see S–S LEARNING MODEL), such as PURPOSIVE BEHAVIORISM or Gestalt psychology.

SRT 1. abbreviation for SIMPLE REACTION TIME. **2.** abbreviation for SPEECH-RECEPTION THRESHOLD.

S–R theory see S–R PSYCHOLOGY.

SRY abbreviation for SEX REVERSAL ON Y. See SEX DIFFERENTIATION.

SSA abbreviation for SMALLEST SPACE ANALYSIS.

SSDR abbreviation for SPECIES-SPECIFIC DEFENSE REACTION.

SSE abbreviation for subacute spongiform encephalopathy (see CREUTZFELDT–JAKOB DISEASE).

SS interval abbreviation for SHOCK–SHOCK INTERVAL.

S–S learning model *s*timulus–*s*timulus learning model: any learning theory that is cognitive and emphasizes the formation of associations between stimuli, in contrast to theories based on stimulus–response connections (see S–R PSYCHOLOGY). Examples include TOLMAN'S PURPOSIVE BEHAVIORISM and Gestalt learning theory. In PAVLOVIAN CONDITIONING, the S–S learning model postulates associations between conditioned and unconditioned stimuli; in INSTRUMENTAL CONDITIONING, the association is between the discriminative stimulus and the reinforcing stimulus.

S sleep abbreviation for SLOW-WAVE SLEEP or SYNCHRONIZED SLEEP, that is, NREM SLEEP. Compare D SLEEP.

SSRIs selective serotonin reuptake inhibitors: a class of antidepressants that are thought to act by blocking the reuptake of serotonin into serotonin-containing presynaptic neurons in the central nervous system (see also SEROTONIN-RECEPTOR AGONISTS). The SSRIs have demonstrated efficacy in the treatment of not only depression but also panic disorder and obsessive-compulsive disorder as well as eating disorders and premenstrual dysphoric disorder. However, the relationship of the reuptake mechanism to the therapeutic qualities of these agents has not been clearly elucidated. SSRIs also block the activity of certain subtypes of serotonin AUTORECEPTORS, and this may also be associated with their therapeutic effects. SSRIs have less adverse side effects than the TRICYCLIC ANTIDEPRESSANTS and the MONOAMINE OXIDASE INHIBITORS; common side effects include nausea, headache, anxiety, and tremor, and some patients may experience sexual dysfunction. SSRIs include FLUOXETINE, PAROXETINE, SERTRALINE, CITALOPRAM, and FLUVOXAMINE. Also called **SRIs** (serotonin reuptake inhibitors).

SST 1. abbreviation for SELF-STATEMENT TRAINING. **2.** abbreviation for SINGLE-SESSION THERAPY. **3.** abbreviation for SOCIAL SKILLS TRAINING. **4.** abbreviation for STIMULUS SAMPLING THEORY.

S-state *n.* the *s*leeping (or *s*leep) state, as opposed to the D-state (see DREAM STATE) and the W-state (waking state).

s-structure *n.* abbreviation for SURFACE STRUCTURE.

SSW abbreviation for STAGGERED SPONDAIC WORD TEST.

stabilimeter *n.* an instrument for measuring postural stability and body sway when a person is standing erect and blindfolded and is asked to remain immobile.

stability *n.* **1.** the absence of variation or motion, as applied to genetics (invariance in characteristics), personality (few emotional or mood changes), or body position (absence of body sway). **2.** in developmental psychology, the degree to which a person maintains over time the same rank order with respect to a particular characteristic (e.g., intelligence test performance) in comparison with peers.

stability–instability bipolar dimensions of the single trait of EMOTIONAL STABILITY.

stabilized image an image on the retina that does not move when the eye is moved. A stabilized image will fade rapidly since neurons in the visual system are sensitive to change rather than to maintained stimulation. Even during FIXATION images are normally not truly stabilized, because very small eye movements (MICROSACCADES) continually refresh the stimulation of the retina by moving the eyes relative to a target.

stabilizing selection the tendency of NATURAL SELECTION to maintain the existing mean of a population characteristic (e.g. mean height, mean neck length) over successive generations.

Stablon *n.* a trade name for TIANEPTINE.

Stadol *n.* a trade name for BUTORPHANOL.

staffing theory an analysis from an ECOLOGICAL PERSPECTIVE of the psychological and interpersonal consequences of interacting in situations that are overstaffed or understaffed. It was formerly known as **manning theory**.

staff of Asclepius see CADUCEUS.

staff turnover see TURNOVER.

stage *n.* a relatively discrete period of time in which functioning is qualitatively different from functioning at other periods.

stage fright an anxiety reaction associated with speaking or performing in public. The individual becomes tense and apprehensive and may stutter, forget lines, or escape the situation. The apprehension may develop into panic symptoms or even a PANIC ATTACK. See also PERFORMANCE ANXIETY.

stage 1 sleep the initial stage of sleep, which is characterized by low-amplitude BRAIN WAVES (4–6 Hz) of irregular frequency, slow heart rate, and reduced muscle tension. See SLEEP STAGES.

stage 2 sleep a stage of sleep that is defined by regular bursts of 14–18 Hz waves (called SLEEP SPINDLES) that progressively increase and then decrease in amplitude. See SLEEP STAGES.

stage 3 sleep a stage of SLOW-WAVE SLEEP that is defined by the SLEEP SPINDLES seen in STAGE 2 SLEEP interspersed with larger amplitude DELTA WAVES (slow waves of 1–4 Hz). See SLEEP STAGES.

stage 4 sleep a stage of SLOW-WAVE SLEEP that is defined by the presence of high-amplitude DELTA WAVES (slow waves of 1–4 Hz). See SLEEP STAGES.

stages of change the five steps involved in changing health behavior proposed in the TRANSTHEORETICAL MODEL: (a) precontemplation (not thinking about changing behavior), (b) contemplation (considering changing behavior), (c) preparation (occasionally changing behavior), (d) action (participating in the healthful behavior on a regular basis, resulting in major benefits), and (e) maintenance (continuing the behavior after 6 months of regular use). [developed by U.S. clinical psychologist James O. Prochaska (1942–)]

stages of dying a hypothetical sequence of events, moods, or coping strategies that occur during the DYING PROCESS. Buddhist tradition specifies eight stages, including physiological, psychological, and spiritual phenomena, some of which occur before and some after the point at which a death would be certified by a physician. More familiar in Western nations is the sequence of stages described in 1969 by Swiss-born U.S. psychiatrist Elisabeth Kübler-Ross (1926–2004). These begin with the DENIAL AND SHOCK STAGE, followed by the ANGER STAGE, BARGAINING STAGE, DEPRESSION STAGE, and ACCEPTANCE STAGE. Although the term implies a fixed sequence, the stages do not always occur in the same order and may overlap.

stage theory of strategy development see ADAPTIVE STRATEGY CHOICE MODEL.

Staggered Spondaic Word Test (**SSW**) a test of auditory-processing abilities using equally stressed, two-syllable words in which the first syllable of one word is presented to one ear and simultaneously the second syllable of another word is presented to the other ear. [originally published in 1962 by U.S. audiologist Jack Katz]

stagnation *n.* see GENERATIVITY VERSUS STAGNATION.

STAI abbreviation for STATE–TRAIT ANXIETY INVENTORY.

stain *n.* a chemical dye that is applied to sections of tissues to render them more easily visible during microscopic examination. The choice of stain is determined by the type of tissue and the study objective.

staircase illusion see SCHRÖDER STAIRCASE.

staircase method a variation of the METHOD OF LIMITS in which stimuli are presented in ascending and descending order. When the observer's response changes, the direction of the stimulus sequence is reversed. This method is efficient because it does not present stimuli that are well above or below threshold.

staircase phenomenon 1. any of various phenomena that display graduated or stepwise changes of response of physical or physiological systems to a series of stimuli. **2.** in cardiac muscle, the increase in the force of cardiac contractions as heart rate is increased. **3.** in skeletal muscle, the graduated sequence of increasingly stronger muscle contractions that occur when a sequence of identical stimuli is applied to a rested muscle. Also called **treppe**.

stakeholder *n.* in evaluation research, any of a program's sponsors, funders, decision makers, personnel, or service recipients who either have a stake in the functioning of the program or are potentially affected by information resulting from the evaluation of its processes and outcomes. Conflict can occur between any groups of stakeholders with different interests, especially in the specification or weighting of the EVALUATION OBJECTIVES.

staleness *n.* in sport, the physical and psychological result of overtraining, which persists over time (e.g., 2 weeks or more) and causes a deterioration in performance.

stalking *n.* **1.** a repeated pattern of following or observing a person in an obsessional, intrusive, or harassing manner. Often associated with a failed relationship with the one pursued, stalking may involve direct threats, the intent to cause distress or bodily harm, and interpersonal violence. It may alternatively be an aspect of EROTIC PARANOIA. See also DOMESTIC VIOLENCE. **2.** in animal behavior, see PREDATION; PREDATORY BEHAVIOR.

stalking law a law that makes it a crime to willfully, maliciously, and repeatedly follow, harass, or threaten another with the intent of causing that person reasonable fear for his or her safety (see STALKING). Stalking laws in the United States vary from state to state.

stammering *n.* see STUTTERING. **—stammer** *vb., n.*

stance reflex 1. the reflex response of skeletal muscle that maintains the stability of the standing posture. **2.** any reflex that maintains a special standing posture, such as the stance reflexes of a sow in estrus that maintain the animal with its back arched and its body rigid.

standard *n.* **1.** a criterion for evaluating the goodness or worth of a person, action, or event. **2.** any positive idea about how things might be, such as an ideal, norm, value, expectation, or previous performance, that is used to measure and judge the way things are. Evaluation of the self is often based on comparing the current reality (or perceptions of the current reality) against one or more standards.

standard application blank (**SAB**) in PERSONNEL SELECTION, a standardized application form used to obtain basic BIOGRAPHICAL DATA, such as age, sex, education, qualifications, employment history, leisure interests, and the like. Compare WEIGHTED APPLICATION BLANK.

standard deviation (symbol: *SD*) a measure of the dispersion of a set of scores, indicating how narrowly or broadly they are distributed around the MEAN. It is equal to the square root of the VARIANCE. If a population of n values has a mean μ, then the standard deviation is

$$\sqrt{[\Sigma(X_i - \mu)^2/n]}$$

For a sample of the population, with a mean value $\bar{X}$, the **sample standard deviation** is taken to be

$$\sqrt{[\Sigma(X_i - \bar{X})^2/(n-1)]},$$

that is, the divisor is $(n - 1)$ rather than n. See also ROOT-MEAN-SQUARE.

standard error the standard deviation of a sampling distribution.

standard error of estimate a measure of the degree to which a REGRESSION LINE fits a set of data. If y' is an estimated value from a regression line and y is the actual value, then the standard error of estimate is

$$\sqrt{[\Sigma(y - y')^2/n]},$$

where n is the number of points.

standard error of measurement (symbol: *SEM*) in measurement theory, the error in estimating true scores from observed scores.

standard error of the mean (symbol: σ_M) the standard deviation of the sampling distribution of the mean, equal to $\sigma/\sqrt{n}$, where σ is the standard deviation of the original distribution and n is the sample size.

standardization *n.* the process of establishing NORMS or uniform procedures for a test.

standardization group a sample used to establish reliable norms for the population that it represents. This is done by analysing the results of the test administered to the sample and ascertaining the average performance level and the relative frequency of each deviation from the mean. Also called **standardization sample**.

standardized instructions instructions for a standardized measuring instrument that are to be presented to all participants exactly as prepared as part of the standard experimental or assessment procedure.

standardized interview schedule a type of STRUCTURED INTERVIEW with fixed questions and procedures that is used in PERSONNEL SELECTION and other fields. These are designed to enhance the predictive value of the interview by (a) providing criteria for objective scoring and (b) eliminating interviewer bias and other sources of variability. Compare PATTERNED INTERVIEW; UNSTRUCTURED INTERVIEW.

standardized measuring device a test or instrument that has been administered to a large and representative sample of the population for which it is to provide reliable norms.

standardized test a test whose VALIDITY and RELIABILITY have been established by thorough empirical investigation and analysis and which has clearly defined norms.

standard language the generally accepted version of a language that is associated with formal and official contexts and with high-status users. Generally speaking, it will be the version used in the mainstream media and taught to schoolchildren and second-language learners. Most languages have a number of nonstandard varieties that differ from the standard language in pronunciation, vocabulary, and grammar.

standard network see GROUP NETWORK.

standard observer the hypothetical ideal observer.

standard score a score obtained from an original score by subtracting the mean value of all scores in the batch and dividing by the standard deviation of the batch. This conversion from raw scores to standard scores allows comparisons to be made between measurements on different scales. A standard score is often given the symbol z and is sometimes referred to as a **z score**.

standards of practice a set of guidelines that delineate the expected techniques and procedures, and the order in which to use them, for interventions with individuals experiencing a range of psychological, medical, or educational conditions. Standards of practice have been developed by the American Psychological Association and other professional associations to ensure that practitioners use the most researched and validated treatment plans.

standard stimulus a stimulus used as the basis of comparison for other stimuli in an experiment, for example, in comparing loud sounds to a sound of a given intensity.

Stanford Achievement Test an assessment tool utilizing multiple-choice and open-ended questions designed to measure progress in reading, mathematics, language, spelling, listening, science, and social science. There is also an emphasis on higher level thinking and writing skills. Currently in its tenth edition (2003), the test reflects contemporary education practice with each new edition.

Stanford–Binet Intelligence Scale (**SB**) a standardized assessment of intelligence and cognitive abilities for individuals aged 2 to 89 years. It currently includes five verbal subtests and five nonverbal subtests that yield Verbal, Nonverbal, and Full Scale IQs (with a mean of 100 and a standard deviation of 15) as well as Fluid Reasoning, Knowledge, Quantitative Reasoning, Visual-Spatial Processing, and Working Memory index scores. The Stanford–Binet test was so named because it was brought to the United States by Lewis M. TERMAN, a professor at Stanford University, in 1916, as a revision and extension of the original **Binet–Simon Scale** (the first modern intelligence test) developed in 1905 by Alfred BINET and French physician Théodore Simon (1873–1961) to assess the intellectual ability of French children. The present Stanford–Binet Intelligence Scale (**SB5**), developed by U.S. psychologist Gale H. Roid (1943–) and published in 2003, is the fourth revision of the test; the first and second revisions were made in 1937 and 1960, respectively, by Terman and U.S. psychologist Maud Merrill (1888–1978), and the third in 1986 by U.S. psychologists Robert L. Thorndike (1910–1990), Elizabeth P. Hagen (1915–), and Jerome M. Sattler (1931–).

Stanford Hypnotic Susceptibility Scale a standardized 12-item scale used to measure HYPNOTIC SUSCEPTIBILITY by means of the participant's response to such suggestions as falling forward, closing the eyes, or lowering an outstretched arm for mild hypnosis and hallucinating a fly or posthypnotic amnesia for deeper hypnosis. [developed at Stanford University by Ernest R. HILGARD]

Stanford v. Kentucky a case resulting in a 1989 U.S. Supreme Court ruling that it is permissible to sentence to death people as young as 16 years of age.

stanine *n.* a division of a range of scores into nine parts, the scores having a NORMAL DISTRIBUTION. The stanine scale has a mean of 5 (i.e., stanine 5 is the average) and a standard deviation of 2. In a given set of scores, the lowest 4% fall in stanine 1, the next 7% in 2, the next 12% in 3, 17% in 4, 20% in 5, 17% in 6, 12% in 7, 7% in 8, and 4% in 9 (the highest scoring range). The scale was developed in World War II by the U.S. Air Force. It is now used mainly in assessing educational performance.

stanolone *n.* a semisynthetic analog of DIHYDROTESTOSTERONE used in the treatment of some breast cancers because of its tumor-suppressing capabilities.

stapedius muscle a middle ear muscle that controls the movement of the stapes, one of the ear OSSICLES. Its activation (the **stapedius reflex**) is part of the ACOUSTIC REFLEX.

stapes *n.* (*pl.* **stapedes**) the stirrup-shaped ossicle that is the innermost of the three bones of the middle ear. Also called **stirrup**. See OSSICLES.

star *n.* **1.** in SOCIOMETRY, an individual who is frequently chosen when group members select the other members whom they like the most, prefer to work or associate with, admire, and so on. Such individuals are the most popular, best liked group members, and if only a single star emerges in a group he or she will be the group's SOCIOCENTER. Compare ISOLATE. **2.** see CHANNELS OF COMMUNICATION.

star compass see SUN COMPASS.

startle response an unlearned, rapid, reflexlike response to sudden, unexpected, intense stimuli (loud noises, flashing lights, etc.). This response includes behaviors that serve a protective function, such as closing the eyes, frowning by drawing the eyebrows together, compressing the lips, lowering the head, hunching the shoulders, and bending the trunk and knee. The reaction can be neutralized by context, inhibition, and habituation. Also called **startle reaction**.

starvation reactions physical and psychological effects of chronic undernourishment, which is experienced by perhaps well over one quarter of the world's population. Common physical effects include general weakness or asthenia, hunger pangs, sluggishness, and susceptibility to disease. Psychological effects include slowing down of thought processes, difficulty in concentration, apathy, irritability, reduced sexual desire, and loss of care in appearance. Psychotic reactions seldom occur except when starvation is accompanied by infection or extreme stress.

stasis *n.* a condition of stability, equilibrium, or inactivity, as opposed to a state of flux or change.

STAT abbreviation for STERNBERG TRIARCHIC ABILITIES TEST.

state *n.* the condition or status of an entity or system at a particular time that is characterized by relative stability of its basic components or elements. Although the components or elements are essentially qualitatively stable, it is possible for them also to be dynamic, as in a hyperactive state or a state of flux.

state anxiety anxiety in response to a specific situation that is perceived as threatening or dangerous. State anxiety varies in intensity and fluctuates over time. Compare TRAIT ANXIETY. [defined in 1972 and 1983 by U.S. psychologist Charles D. Spielberger (1927–)]

state-dependent behavior actions that are affected by one's emotional state, for example, saying something hurtful to another while in a state of anger.

state-dependent learning learning that occurs in a particular biological or psychological state and is better recalled when the individual is subsequently in the same state. Recall may be diminished when the individual is in a different state. For example, an animal trained to run a maze while under the influence of a psychoactive drug (e.g., pentobarbital) may not run it successfully without the drug. Also called **dissociated learning**. See also CONTEXT-SPECIFIC LEARNING.

state-dependent memory a condition in which memory for a past event is improved when the person is in the same biological or psychological state as when the memory was initially formed. Thus, alcohol may improve recall of events experienced when previously under the influence of alcohol (although this level of recall is lower than recall under conditions where both ENCODING and RETRIEVAL occur in sober states). A distinctive state may arise from a drug, a mood, or a particular place. See CONTEXT-SPECIFIC LEARNING; MOOD-DEPENDENT MEMORY; STATE-DEPENDENT LEARNING.

statement validity analysis techniques used to assess the truth of allegations made by children during interviews concerning sexual abuse. These provide various criteria enabling interviewers to distinguish between plausible and implausible accounts. See also CRITERION-BASED CONTENT ANALYSIS.

state of consciousness see CONSCIOUSNESS; ALTERED STATE OF CONSCIOUSNESS.

state orientation a style of responding to dilemmas or conflicts that is characterized by prolonged analysis and assessment of alternatives rather than by swift, decisive action. Compare ACTION ORIENTATION.

state self-focus see SELF-FOCUS.

state space a graphical representation used to characterize game playing and other search-based problem solving. A state space has four components: (a) a set of nodes or states, (b) a set of arcs linking subsets of the states or nodes, (c) a nonempty set of nodes indicated as the start nodes of the space, and (d) a nonempty set of goal nodes of the space. The goal nodes are identified by either a property of the state itself (e.g., a checkmate) or a property of the path leading to the goal state (e.g., a shortest path). An architecture such as a PRODUCTION SYSTEM or CLASSIFIER SYSTEM can generate a state space search. See also GRAPH; SEARCH; TREE.

state-specific science the concept of science as being dependent on a particular state of consciousness, so that a change in consciousness might yield a different kind or content of science. [proposed by U.S. psychologist Charles T. Tart (1937–)]

states versus transformations in Jean PIAGET's theory, the extent to which a child's attention is focused on states (e.g., the appearance of an object) rather than transformations (i.e., what is done to the object), and vice versa, at different stages of cognitive development. At the PREOPERATIONAL STAGE children center their attention on specific states and ignore the transformations between states, whereas the reverse is true for children at the CONCRETE OPERATIONAL STAGE.

state theories of hypnosis theories positing that HYPNOTIC INDUCTION evokes a unique altered state of consciousness in the participant. Compare NONSTATE THEORIES OF HYPNOSIS.

State–Trait Anxiety Inventory (**STAI**) a self-report assessment device that includes separate measures of STATE ANXIETY and TRAIT ANXIETY. The state anxiety items measure the intensity of anxiety experienced by participants in specific situations; the trait anxiety items assess the frequency with which respondents experience anxiety in the face of perceived threats in the environment. [devised in 1970 by U.S. psychologist Charles D. Spielberger (1927–) and colleagues]

State v. Mack a case resulting in an influential 1980 Minnesota Supreme Court ruling that testimony based on memories uncovered during hypnosis, or after an eyewitness has undergone a hypnotic induction, is not admissible in court because hypnosis is an unreliable method of retrieving memories. This has been referred to as the **per se exclusion rule**. However, this rule banning hypnotically retrieved evidence does not apply to defendants. See ROCK V. ARKANSAS.

static ataxia loss of the ability to maintain a fixed position, including excessive swaying and tottering when standing still with the eyes closed or inability to balance the body on one leg or to extend the arm steadily.

static marriage see CLOSED MARRIAGE.

static response a POSTURAL REFLEX that orients the body against a force, such as gravity. Also called **static reflex**.

static sense see SENSE OF EQUILIBRIUM.

statistic *n.* any function of the observations in a set of data. Statistics may be used to describe a batch of data, to estimate parameters in optimal ways, or to test hypotheses.

statistical analysis analysis of data through the use of probabilistic models.

statistical association see ASSOCIATION.

statistical control the use of statistical methods to reduce the effect of factors that could not be eliminated or controlled during an experiment.

statistical decision theory a branch of statistical science concerned with the use of data to arrive at decisions. Specific equations are used to calculate the amount of loss associated with each course of action in order to determine the most advantageous choice.

statistical error any error of sampling, measurement, or treatment that interferes with drawing a valid conclusion from experimental results.

statistical learning theory a theoretical approach that uses mathematical models to describe processes of learning. The term is often specifically applied to STIMULUS SAMPLING THEORY but can be more generally applied to other theories.

statistical process control (**SPC**) in organizational and industrial theory, a method of monitoring, evaluating, and continuously improving the performance of products, systems, or employees through the statistical analysis of performance data.

statistical psychology the branch of psychology that uses statistical models and methods to derive descriptions and explanations of phenomena.

statistical significance the degree to which a result cannot reasonably be attributed to the operation of chance or random factors alone.

statistical test a specific mathematical technique used to test the correctness of an empirical hypothesis. See HYPOTHESIS TESTING.

statistics *n.* the branch of mathematics that uses data descriptively or inferentially to find or support answers for scientific and other quantifiable questions. **—statistical** *adj.* **—statistician** *n.*

statoconium *n.* (*pl.* **statoconia**) see OTOLITH.

statokinetic dissociation see RIDDOCH'S PHENOMENON.

status *n.* **1.** the state or position of an individual or group, for example, an individual's standing in a social group. **2.** a persistent condition, as in STATUS EPILEPTICUS.

status comparison the comparison of one's own abilities and status with those of others.

status differentiation the gradual rise to positions of greater authority by some individuals within a group, accompanied by decreases in the authority exercised by other members.

status epilepticus a continuous series of SEIZURES, sometimes resulting in death. It requires immediate medical treatment, usually by intravenous medication.

status generalization the tendency for individuals who are known to have achieved or been ascribed authority, respect, and prestige in one context to enjoy relatively higher status in other, unrelated, contexts. Well-known athletes or wealthy individuals, for example, may rise rapidly to positions of authority in groups even when these DIFFUSE-STATUS CHARACTERISTICS (athleticism, wealth) are not relevant in the current group context. See also EXPECTATION-STATES THEORY.

status offense a nondelinquent, noncriminal act considered to be illegal because the perpetrator is not an adult. Truancy, curfew violations, and underage drinking are examples of status offenses.

status planning see LANGUAGE PLANNING.

status relations patterns of relative prestige and respect that determine deference and authority within a group or organization, that is, the "chain of command," DOMINANCE HIERARCHY, or PECKING ORDER. Also called **authority relations**.

status role 1. a prestigious, high-ranking, or otherwise influential position within a group. **2.** the special position in a group held by an individual who lends prestige to the group as a whole because of reputation, special abilities, or achievements.

status symbol any indicator of a person's prestige or high status in a group or society, such as expensive or rare possessions, an extravagant lifestyle, or membership in prestigious clubs. The term applies particularly to those indicators that individuals deliberately choose to communicate their status level to others.

statutory rape the criminal offense of having sexual intercourse with an individual who is not qualified to give lawful consent because she or he is below the statutory age of consent. In the United States, the age of consent ranges from 14 to 18, depending on each state's law.

STD abbreviation for SEXUALLY TRANSMITTED DISEASE.

steady state in behavioral studies, a state in which behavior is practically the same over repeated observations in a particular context. See BEHAVIORAL BASELINE.

stealing thunder a courtroom strategy in which admissions to the jury are made by one attorney before these same facts are brought up by the opposing attorney. It is designed to reduce the impact this information may have on the jury.

stealth juror a juror who conceals his or her biases from the judge or attorneys during VOIR DIRE.

steatopygia *n.* the presence of large quantities of fat in the buttocks. In some cultures steatopygia is considered an element of female beauty.

Steele–Richardson–Olszewski syndrome see PROGRESSIVE SUPRANUCLEAR PALSY. [John C. **Steele** and John Clifford **Richardson**, 20th-century Canadian neurologists; Jerzy **Olszewski** (1913–1964), Polish-born Canadian neuropathologist]

Steinert's disease see MYOTONIC MUSCULAR DYSTROPHY. [Hans Gustav Wilhelm **Steinert**, 20th-century German physician]

Steinzor effect in discussion groups, the tendency for individuals to speak immediately after those sitting opposite them speak. The effect is strongest in leaderless groups. Compare HEAD-OF-THE-TABLE EFFECT. [Bernard **Steinzor** (1920–) U.S. clinical psychologist]

Stelazine *n.* a trade name for TRIFLUOPERAZINE.

stellate cell any of a number of types of small nerve cells that have many branches. See also CORTICAL LAYERS.

stem-and-leaf plot a graphical method for the display of data that resembles a HISTOGRAM but carries more detailed information about the values of the data points.

stem cell a cell that is itself undifferentiated but can divide to produce one or more types of specialized tissue cells (e.g., blood cells, nerve cells). Because of this ability, stem cells act as a kind of continual repair system for the living organism by replenishing specialized cells. Stem cells are found in embryos (see EMBRYONIC STEM CELL) but also occur in adults as **tissue stem cells**. Adult and embryonic stem cell research have the potential for changing treatment of disease through use of the cells to repair specific tissues and, even, to grow organs (see REGENERATIVE MEDICINE). Although the ethics of the more recent embryonic stem cell research are the subject of debate, stem cell research and treatments using adult cells has occurred since the 1960s (e.g., the use of bone marrow stem cells in the treatment of leukemia and lymphoma). Current research shows the potential to develop treatments for some neurological and cardiovascular conditions (e.g., growing new blood vessels) and, even, for regenerative dentistry (i.e., to grow replacement teeth).

stem-completion task a task in which people are asked to provide complete words when given the first few letters. For example, given *ele—*, a participant might say *elevate* or *elephant*. See COMPLETION TEST.

steno- *combining form* narrow or contracted.

stenosis *n.* the abnormal narrowing of a body conduit or passage. **Carotid stenosis** is narrowing of a CAROTID ARTERY, for example by atherosclerosis, which limits blood flow to the brain; **aortic stenosis** is narrowing of the aortic valve leading from the left ventricle, thereby restricting blood flow from the heart to the general circulation; **pyloric stenosis** restricts the flow of stomach contents into the small intestine; **spinal stenosis** is a narrowing of the opening in the spinal column, thereby restricting the space needed for the spinal cord and resulting in numbness and pain in the lower back and legs. **—stenotic** *adj.*

stenosis of aqueduct of Sylvius a hereditary or familial disorder, transmitted as an X-linked recessive gene, marked by massive head enlargement at birth and hydrocephalus due to narrowing of the CEREBRAL AQUEDUCT (aqueduct of Silvius). In some cases, the disorder develops insidiously after adulthood rather than as a congenital condition.

step-down test a memory test used in studies of shock-avoidance learning in rats and mice. When the animal first steps down from an elevated platform in the test chamber, it is given an electric shock. On subsequent test trials, the time taken to step down is measured as an indication of memory for the shock experience.

stepfamily *n.* a family unit formed by the union of parents one or both of whom brings a child or children from a previous union (or unions) into the new household. See BLENDED FAMILY; SIMPLE STEPFAMILY.

step function a mathematical function that changes only in discrete jumps or steps, rather than continuously.

stepping reflex a REFLEX movement elicited during the first few weeks of human life by holding an infant upright with his or her feet touching a flat surface and moving the infant gently forward.

stepwise phenomenon any process that changes over time in accordance with a STEP FUNCTION.

stepwise regression a group of regression techniques that enter predictor (independent) variables into (or delete them from) the REGRESSION EQUATION one variable (or block of variables) at a time according to some predefined criterion. It is contrasted with ordinary **least squares regression**, which enters all variables simultaneously.

stereoacuity *n.* see STEREOSCOPIC ACUITY.

stereoblindness *n.* the inability to see depth using the cue of RETINAL DISPARITY, causing impaired depth perception. Stereoblindness is thought to affect 5–10% of the general population. It is associated with STRABISMUS during early childhood, but may also be caused by occipitotemporal brain injury.

stereochemical smell theory the concept that certain odors are perceived because they are produced by ODORANTS whose stereochemical properties have certain shapes. Seven classes of odorants are postulated: camphoraceous, ethereal, floral, minty, musty, pungent, and putrid. The odorant molecules are thought to fit receptors in a lock-and-key manner that causes the neural membrane to become depolarized or hyperpolarized, which in turn is the cue that produces an odor experience (see LOCK-AND-KEY THEORY). Since many odorants that share a similar molecular structure produce different odor experiences, it has been hypothesized that the lock-and-key principle may be modified by the orientation of the molecules at the receptor surfaces. Also called **steric theory of odor**. See also SMELL MECHANISM.

stereocilia *pl. n.* see HAIR CELLS.

stereognosis *n.* the ability to recognize an object by touch.

stereogram *n.* a picture perceived to have depth because it is produced by the binocular summation of two separate images of the same scene, each image slightly offset from the other in the horizontal plane. Although a STEREOSCOPE is commonly used to view the images, some observers can fuse the two images by simply crossing or uncrossing their eyes.

stereopsis *n.* DEPTH PERCEPTION provided by means of the RETINAL DISPARITY of the images in the two eyes. Also called **stereoscopic depth perception**; **stereoscopic vision**. See also ANAGLYPH.

stereoscope *n.* a device that presents two slightly disparate pictures of the same scene, one to each eye. The separate retinal images fuse to produce a binocular, three-dimensional image (see STEREOGRAM).

stereoscopic acuity visual acuity for the perception of depth. Also called **stereoacuity**.

stereoscopic depth perception see STEREOPSIS.

stereoscopic motion picture a motion picture in which the dimension of depth is provided by recording the scene through two cameras, each with the perspective of one eye. When each sequence of images is presented to the correct eye at the same time, stereoscopic depth is perceived (see DEPTH PERCEPTION; STEREOPSIS).

stereoscopic vision see STEREOPSIS.

stereotactic atlas a map of the brain featuring a coordinate system and consisting of images (obtained using various methods to depict structures, nerve fibers, etc.) and schematic representations of serial sections of the brain. Also called **stereotaxic atlas**.

stereotactic instrument a device designed to permit experimental work on the brains of animals without damaging neighboring tissues. The stereotactic instrument holds the animal's head in a position that, when coordinated with information from a STEREOTACTIC ATLAS, allows an ELECTRODE, CANNULA, or surgical device to be inserted into a precise area or structure of the brain.

stereotaxis *n.* active movement of an organism in response to touch or direct contact with a solid object or surface. Also called **thigmotaxis**. See TAXIS. —**stereotaxic** *adj.*

stereotaxy *n.* determination of the exact location of a specific area within the body (e.g., the exact location of a nerve center in the brain) by means of three-dimensional measurements. Stereotaxy is used for positioning MICROELECTRODES in the brain for diagnostic, experimental, or therapeutic purposes and for locating an area of the brain prior to surgery. Also called **stereotactic localization**; **stereotactic technique**. —**stereotactic** or **stereotaxic** *adj.*

stereotropism *n.* an orienting response of an organism to touch or contact with a solid object or surface. —**stereotropic** *adj.*

stereotype *n.* a set of cognitive generalizations (e.g., beliefs, expectations) about the qualities and characteristics of the members of a particular group or social category. Stereotypes, like SCHEMAS, simplify and expedite perceptions and judgments, but they are often exaggerated, negative rather than positive, and resistant to revision even when perceivers encounter individuals with qualities that are not congruent with the stereotype (see PREJUDICE). Unlike individually held expectations about others based on their category memberships, stereotypes are widely shared by group members. See NEGATIVE STEREOTYPE; POSITIVE STEREOTYPE. See also INSTANCE THEORY; GENDER STEREOTYPES; KERNEL-OF-TRUTH HYPOTHESIS. —**stereotypic** *adj.*

stereotype accuracy the ability to determine accurately in what way and to what extent a person's traits correspond to a STEREOTYPE associated with his or her age group, ethnic group, professional group, or other relevant group. Compare DIFFERENTIAL ACCURACY.

stereotyped behavior 1. inflexible behavior that follows a particular pattern and does not alter with changing conditions. **2.** see STEREOTYPY.

stereotyped movement a repeated movement or gesture, such as a tic, rocking, or head banging.

stereotype threat an individual's expectation that NEGATIVE STEREOTYPES about his or her member group will adversely influence others' judgments of his or her performance. This expectation may in turn undermine the individual's actual ability to perform well. In an academic setting, for example, it has been shown that African American students' performance in tests of intellectual ability can suffer because of anxiety induced by thinking that they are expected to perform poorly and will be judged according to negative stereotypes about Black intelligence. See also PREJUDICE. [identified in 1995 by U.S. psychologists Claude M. Steele (1946–) and Joshua Aronson (1961–)]

stereotypic movement disorder in *DSM–IV–TR*, a disorder characterized by repetitive, nonfunctional, and often self-injurious behaviors, such as head banging, biting or hitting parts of the body, rocking, or hand waving. It may be associated with mental retardation and can arise at any age. Stereotypic movement disorder is distinguished from other disorders marked by stereotyped movements, such as TIC DISORDERS and PERVASIVE DEVELOPMENTAL DISORDERS.

stereotypy *n.* **1.** persistent pathological repetition of the same words, phrases, sounds, or movements. It is a common symptom in children with autism and in individuals with obsessive-compulsive disorder or catatonic schizophrenia. Stereotypy is also seen in nonhuman animals under conditions of social isolation, early social deprivation, or neglect. Also called **stereotyped behavior**. See STEREOTYPIC MOVEMENT DISORDER. **2.** repetitive behavior or gestures that are within the normal spectrum.

steric theory of odor see STEREOCHEMICAL SMELL THEORY.

sterility *n.* **1.** the condition of being incapable of producing offspring, either because of INFERTILITY or surgical or medical intervention (see STERILIZATION). **2.** the condition of being incapable of supporting microbial life because of treatment with chemicals, radiation, or heat. —**sterile** *adj.*

sterilization *n.* the process of rendering an organism incapable of sexual reproduction. This may be accomplished surgically (see VASECTOMY; CASTRATION; HYSTERECTOMY; OVARIECTOMY; SALPINGECTOMY; TUBAL LIGATION) or it may result from injury or from exposure to radiation, heat, or chemicals.

Stern, Louis William (1871–1938) German psychologist. Stern earned his doctorate in 1893 at the University of Berlin under Hermann EBBINGHAUS. He was a member of the faculty at the University of Breslau from 1897 until 1916, when he moved to the University of Hamburg, where he became director of the psychological institute. Following the Nazi rise to power in Germany, Stern emigrated to the United States, working at Duke University for the last 5 years of his life. Stern was influential in a number of psychological fields. He was a pioneer of developmental psychology with three early books, including the popular *The Psychology of Early Childhood up to the Sixth Year of Age* (1914). He founded the German-language *Journal of Applied Psychology* and published numerous articles on various topics in that field. Stern is perhaps best known for developing the notion of the intelligence quotient (see IQ) to express the outcome of intelligence tests. His books *On the Psychology of Individual Differences* (1900) and *Methodological Foundations of Differential Psychology* (1911) are basic works in the field of DIFFERENTIAL PSYCHOLOGY. His philosophical system of critical personalism, which focused on the problem of human individuality, is less well known, although he considered that it underpinned his entire life's work.

Sternberg Triarchic Abilities Test (**STAT**) a GROUP INTELLIGENCE TEST, used for research purposes, that measures analytical, creative, and practical abilities using multiple-choice verbal, quantitative, and figural items, as well as essays. Revised versions of the test also include other types of items, such as writing stories, telling stories, designing things, and watching movies with practical problems for the examinees to solve. The test yields separate scores for the analytical, creative, and practical components. [developed in the 1980s by Robert J. **Sternberg** (1949–), U.S. psychologist]

steroid *n.* any organic molecule that is based on four interconnected hydrocarbon rings. The male and female SEX HORMONES are steroids, as are the CORTICOSTEROIDS and other natural substances, such as vitamin D and CHOLESTEROL.

steroid hormone any of a class of hormones whose molecular structure is based on the steroid nucleus of four interconnected rings of carbon atoms. Examples include the SEX HORMONES and CORTICOSTEROIDS.

steroid use the practice of taking steroids for the purpose of increasing muscle bulk. This practice is against the rules that govern the Olympic Games and most amateur sport.

stethograph *n.* see PNEUMOGRAPH.

Stevens–Johnson syndrome a condition marked by eruptions of fluid-filled blisters on the skin, mucous membranes, eyes, and genitals. It has a fatality rate of 1–5% and may be associated with an adverse reaction to ANTICONVULSANT and antibiotic agents. Also called **erythema multiforme bullosum**; **erythema multiforme exudativum**; **erythema multiforme major**. [Albert M. **Stevens** (1884–1945) and Frank C. **Johnson** (1894–1934), U.S. pediatricians]

Stevens law a psychophysical relationship stating that the psychological magnitude of a sensation is proportional to a power of the stimulus producing it. This can be expressed as $\psi = ks^n$, where ψ is the sensation, k is a constant of proportionality, s is the stimulus magnitude, and n is a function of the particular stimulus. See also FECHNER'S LAW; WEBER'S LAW. [Stanley Smith **Stevens** (1906–1973), U.S. psychophysicist]

Stevens power law a logarithmic relationship between the impulse frequency of a visual stimulus (S) and its intensity (I). It is expressed as $S = I^b$, where b is an empirical constant that is approximately 0.33 for the human eye.

Stewart–Morel syndrome a disorder characterized by hypertrophy of the frontal bone of the skull, obesity, headache, disturbances affecting the nervous system, and a tendency toward mental retardation. Also called **Morel's syndrome**. [Douglas Hunt **Stewart** (1860–1943), U.S. surgeon; Ferdinand **Morel** (1888–1957), Swiss psychiatrist]

sthenic type a constitutional type characterized by strength and vigor; it is roughly equivalent to the ATHLETIC TYPE in KRETSCHMER TYPOLOGY.

sthenometer *n.* an instrument for measuring muscle strength.

stick shaker in ergonomics, a device within a joystick or other stick control that uses vibration to provide feedback to the operator in certain situations (e.g., the stall of an aircraft engine, wind, turbulence).

stiffness *n.* **1.** inflexibility of the muscles and joints due to injury, DYSTONIA, or over- or underuse. **2.** a characteristic, due to the springlike properties of muscles, that determines how the force exerted by a muscle varies as a function of its length for a fixed level of activation.

stigma *n.* the negative social attitude attached to a characteristic of an individual that may be regarded as a mental, physical, or social deficiency. A stigma implies social disapproval and can lead unfairly to discrimination against and exclusion of the individual.

stigmatophilia *n.* sexual interest in and arousal by a partner who is tattooed or has scars, or by having oneself tattooed, particularly in the genital area.

Stiles–Crawford effect a difference in the perceived brightness or perceived color of a stimulus depending on whether light rays enter the pupil near the edge or through the center. [Sir Walter **Stiles** (1901–1985), British physicist; Brian H. **Crawford**, 20th-century British physiologist]

Stiller's sign a floating tenth rib, which is associated with a tendency to neurasthenia. Also called **costal stigma**; **Stiller's rib**. [Berthold **Stiller** (1837–1922), Hungarian physician]

Stilling Color Vision Test a test consisting of PSEUDOISOCHROMATIC CHARTS containing dots of various hues, saturations, and intensities developed for the detection of color weakness. Some of the dots form numbers that are visible to the normal eye but not to the color-blind or color-weak eye. Now obsolete, it is the predecessor to the commonly used ISHIHARA TEST FOR COLOR BLINDNESS. [developed in 1877 by Jakob **Stilling** (1842–1915), German ophthalmologist]

stilted speech formal, affected, or pompous speech. It may be characteristic of a particular individual, but is also observed as a speech disturbance in some individuals with particular disorders, such as schizophrenia or certain forms of APHASIA.

stim test a technique used by some POLYGRAPH examiners to convince examinees that the test is infallible. An examinee selects a card from a deck of playing cards, and the examiner ostensibly uses questions and the examinee's physiological readings to determine which card was selected. In reality, examiners rely on a marked deck to identify correctly the card chosen by the examinee.

stimulants *pl. n.* agents that excite functional activity in an organism or in a part of an organism. Stimulants are usually classified according to the body system or function excited (e.g., cardiac stimulants, respiratory stimulants). In psychology, the term usually refers to the CNS STIMULANTS (or psychostimulants).

stimulate *vb.* **1.** to animate, excite, or rouse to activity or heightened action. **2.** to apply a STIMULUS to a sensory receptor or to an excitable cell (e.g., neuron or muscle cell).

stimulating occupation an activity or task, such as dancing, that has an arousing and stimulating effect. Compare SEDATIVE OCCUPATION.

stimulation *n.* **1.** the act or process of increasing the level of activity of an organism. **2.** in perception, see SENSORY STIMULATION. **3.** in neuropsychology, see ELECTRICAL STIMULATION. See also STIMULUS.

stimulation effects the physiological changes produced when a stimulus alters the MEMBRANE POTENTIAL of a neuron or muscle cell, resulting in a nerve impulse or muscle contraction. Changes in electric potentials are frequently measured, as are resultant changes in localized blood flow and temperature.

stimulator *n.* a device used to apply electric current to excite or stimulate a RECEPTOR. An early type of stimulator was an induction coil wired to a vibrator that would convert direct-current electricity into pulsations. Modern stimulators incorporate a device for controlling the rate of change in the electric current, since a steady current flow has little stimulus effect.

stimulus *n.* (*pl.* **stimuli**) **1.** any agent, event, or situation—internal or external—that elicits a response from an organism. See CONDITIONED STIMULUS; UNCONDITIONED STIMULUS. **2.** any change in physical energy that activates a sensory RECEPTOR. See DISTAL STIMULUS; PROXIMAL STIMULUS.

stimulus-bound *adj.* **1.** relating to a perception that is largely dependent on the qualities of the stimulation and thus involves little or no interpretation. **2.** describing behavior that occurs in response to the presence of a specific stimulus (e.g., hungering for and eating a specific food after seeing it). **3.** characterizing an individual whose behavior tends to be inflexible and determined primarily by the nature of the stimulus. **4.** describing a person, usually a child, who has a poor attention span, is distracted by irrelevant stimuli, and therefore performs below his or her intellectual capacity.

stimulus continuum a series of stimuli related to each other along a specific dimension (e.g., a series of tones in the diatonic scale or an unbroken series of shades of blue).

stimulus control the extent to which behavior is influenced by different stimulus conditions. It can refer to different responses occurring in the presence of different stimuli or to differences in the rate, temporal organization, or topography (see RESPONSE TOPOGRAPHY) of a single response in the presence of different stimuli.

stimulus differentiation **1.** a process whereby an organism learns to discriminate between two stimuli by responding differently to them, for example, by responding in the presence of one stimulus but not the other. See also DISCRIMINATION LEARNING. **2.** in Gestalt psychology, the process of distinguishing different parts or patterns in a visual field.

stimulus discrimination **1.** the ability to distinguish among different stimuli (e.g., to distinguish a circle from an ellipse). **2.** differential responding in the presence of different stimuli. See DISCRIMINATION.

stimulus element any of the individual features of a complex stimulus, such as its shape or color.

stimulus equivalence the condition in which two or more related stimuli elicit the same response. Stimuli meet the mathematical definition of equivalence if they can be shown to exhibit **reflexivity**, **symmetry**, and **transitivity**. For example, in the context of an ARBITRARY MATCHING TO SAMPLE procedure, if a stimulus is chosen when it also appears as the sample, reflexivity has been shown. If stimulus A is chosen when B is the sample, and B is chosen when A is the sample, symmetry has been shown. If B is chosen when A is the sample, C is chosen when B is the sample, and C is chosen when A is the sample, transitivity has been shown.

stimulus error an error in response that consists of focusing on the meaning or semantic status of a stimulus (e.g., "chair"), rather than on its other properties (size, shape, etc.).

stimulus evaluation checks (**SECs**) assessments made on several dimensions when an individual evaluates the impact of an event and hence its emotional intensity and quality. Examples of SECs include checks for novelty, goal relevance, and congruity–incongruity of actions or events with social expectations. See also APPRAISAL DIMENSION. [proposed by Swiss psychologist Klaus Scherer (1943–) in his theory of appraisal]

stimulus filtering the specialization of the nervous system so that only critical stimuli reach the brain and irrelevant stimuli do not. Female bullfrogs have two auditory organs that respond only to the two dominant frequencies in male courtship calls. Moths have ears with only two neurons: The neurons respond only to sounds in the frequency range of bat ultrasound, and successive filters in the moth's central nervous system ensure that only bat-produced sounds reach the brain.

stimulus function **1.** the role of a stimulus in evoking a response. For example, in an INSTRUMENTAL CONDITIONING procedure, a stimulus is designed to function as a signal, cue, or prompt to evoke responding. **2.** the mathematical relationship between the magnitude of a stimulus and the size of the response.

stimulus generalization the spread of effects of conditioning (either operant or Pavlovian) to stimuli that differ in certain aspects from the stimulus present during original conditioning. If responding is indistinguishable from that seen in the presence of the original stimulus, GENERALIZATION is said to be complete (or no attention is commanded by the stimulus difference). If responding is different enough to be detected, DISCRIMINATION is evident as well as generalization. See also STIMULUS CONTROL.

stimulus gradient the variations in a stimulus along a given dimension (e.g., a change in loudness).

stimulus-intensity dynamism in HULL'S MATHEMATICO-DEDUCTIVE THEORY OF LEARNING, the concept that the greater the STIMULUS STRENGTH, the greater the organism's response strength.

stimulus object any object (i.e., a thing, person, or condition) that elicits a response from an organism.

stimulus onset asynchrony (**SOA**) the time between the onset of one stimulus and the onset of the following stimulus. The term is used mainly in experiments with MASKING. Compare INTERSTIMULUS INTERVAL.

stimulus overload the condition in which the environment presents too many stimuli to be comfortably processed, resulting in stress and behavior designed to restore equilibrium. See also COMMUNICATION OVERLOAD; INFORMATION OVERLOAD; SENSORY OVERLOAD.

stimulus proposition the content of a situation brought up as a mental image. Stimulus propositions are part of the BIOINFORMATIONAL THEORY of how and why imagery works to enhance performance. See also RESPONSE PROPOSITION.

stimulus–response (**S–R**) see S–R LEARNING MODEL; S–R PSYCHOLOGY.

stimulus–response compatibility the extent to which the relationship between stimulus and response facilitates response. Speed and accuracy are affected by this relationship; for example, a left keypress in response to a stimulus on the left will be quicker and more accurate than a right keypress for a stimulus on the left. This is an example of an **element-level compatibility effect**, which results from the mapping of individual stimuli to responses within a set. A verbal response to a verbal stimulus is quicker and more accurate than a spatial response to a verbal stimulus. This is an example of a **set-level compatibility effect**.

stimulus–response theory see S–R PSYCHOLOGY.

stimulus sampling a procedure for increasing the generalizability of research results by SAMPLING not only participants but also the stimulus or treatment conditions to which they were exposed.

stimulus sampling theory (**SST**) a MATHEMATICAL LEARNING THEORY stating that stimuli are composed of hypothetical elements and that on any given learning trial a sample of those elements becomes associated with the desired response. [developed by W. K. ESTES]

stimulus set in reaction-time experiments, the expectancy or readiness associated with concentration on the stimulus. Compare RESPONSE SET.

stimulus situation all the components of an occurrence or experience that, taken as a whole, comprise a stimulus to which an organism responds. The term is used to highlight the complexity of behavior-arousing events that are unitary patterns comprising many elements (e.g., a concert, an athletic competition). This approach differs from that of traditional behavior analysts, who tend to break down stimuli into smaller, separate elements.

stimulus–stimulus learning model see S–S LEARNING MODEL.

stimulus strength the actual intensity of a stimulus or its ability to elicit a desired response.

stimulus substitution a way of characterizing the outcome of PAVLOVIAN CONDITIONING, when the conditioned stimulus is said to have taken on the functions of the unconditioned stimulus. For example, in PAVLOV's early experiments, the sound of a tone paired with food eventually came to elicit salivation, just as the food does; that is, the tone substituted for the food. This characterization is no longer widely accepted.

stimulus value 1. the strength of a given stimulus, measured in standard units (e.g., a shock of 40 volts). **2.** a theoretical characteristic of a stimulus said to index its effectiveness as a REINFORCER.

stimulus word a word presented to a participant with the object of eliciting a response.

stirrup *n.* see STAPES.

STM abbreviation for SHORT-TERM MEMORY.

stochastic *adj.* describing a system or process that follows a random probability pattern, such that events may be analyzed according to their statistical probability but not accurately predicted. See PROBABILISM.

stochastic independence the condition in which two systems or processes are statistically unrelated, so that one is in no way contingent upon the other.

stochastic model in artificial intelligence, a model based on co-relational analysis, usually Bayesian, used for simulating situations as well as fault diagnosis. Although mathematically well founded, unless simplifying assumptions are made, such models are computationally intractable for complex situations. See BAYESIAN BELIEF NETWORK; GRAPH.

stochastic variable see RANDOM VARIABLE.

Stockholm syndrome a mental and emotional response in which a captive (e.g., a hostage) displays seeming loyalty to—even affection for—the captor. The captive may come to see law enforcement or rescuers as the enemy because they endanger the captor. The name derives from the case of a woman who in 1973 was held hostage at a bank in Stockholm, Sweden, and became so emotionally attached to one of the robbers that she broke her engagement to another man and remained faithful to her former captor during his prison term. [term coined by Swedish psychiatrist and criminologist Nils Bejerot (1921–1988)]

stocking anesthesia a SENSORY CONVERSION SYMPTOM in which there is a loss of sensitivity in the foot and in part of the calf (i.e., areas that would be covered by a stocking) that cannot be explained by a general medical condition or organic dysfunction. Also called **foot anesthesia**; **shoe anesthesia**. See also GLOVE ANESTHESIA.

stomach loading in animal experiments, the process of expanding a balloon in the subject's stomach or filling the stomach with water or an inert substance.

-stomy (**-ostomy**) *suffix* surgical opening (e.g., TRACHEOSTOMY).

stooge *n.* a colloquial name for a CONFEDERATE.

stop *n.* see PLOSIVE.

stop-signal task a procedure used in choice-reaction tasks in which a signal instructing the participant to withhold the response is presented on some trials at varying intervals after presentation of the stimulus. This is done to determine at what point in processing a response can no longer be inhibited.

storage *n.* the state of an item that is retained in memory, after ENCODING and before RETRIEVAL. See also RETENTION.

storage-and-transfer model of memory see MULTISTORE MODEL OF MEMORY.

storage capacity the amount of information that can be retained in memory. SENSORY MEMORY and SHORT-TERM MEMORY are believed to have limited capacities; LONG-TERM MEMORY may have an unlimited capacity.

storm-and-stress period a period of emotional turmoil. The phrase was used by G. Stanley HALL to characterize adolescence, which he believed to correspond to the turbulent transition from savagery to civilization. It is a translation of the German *Sturm und Drang,* which was the title of a 1776 drama by Friedrich Maximilian von Klinger and was subsequently applied to a German literary movement. Also called **Sturm und Drang period**.

story model a theory of juror decision making that proposes that jurors organize trial information into narratives or stories to aid comprehension and retention of evidence. See also NARRATIVE METHOD.

story-recall test a test that requires an individual to recall details of a story that is told or read to him or her.

storytelling *n.* **1.** the recounting by a client of the events, concerns, and problems that led him or her to seek treatment. Therapists can learn much about the motives and origins of conflicts by attending carefully (see ACTIVE LISTENING) to the stories that clients bring to the session. **2.** the use of symbolic talk and allegorical stories by the therapist to aid the client's understanding of issues. Also called **therapeutic storytelling**.

stotting *n.* a stiff-legged jumping display, given by many species of ungulates, in which all four legs are off the ground at the same time. Stotting appears to communicate to predators that the individual has detected the predator and has enough vigor to make capture difficult. Studies show that predators are more likely to fail or simply give up a hunt when an animal displays stotting.

STP see DOM.

strabismic amblyopia see DEVELOPMENTAL AMBLYOPIA.

strabismometer *n.* an instrument for measuring the amount of strabismus.

strabismus *n.* any chronic abnormal alignment of the

eyes, making normal binocular fixation and thus binocular vision impossible. Because strabismic eyes look in different directions, they give the brain conflicting messages, which may result in DOUBLE VISION. Alternatively, the brain may simply ignore, or suppress, one eye's view altogether. The most common form of strabismus occurs horizontally: One or both eyes deviate inward (**convergent strabismus**, see CROSS-EYE) or outward (**divergent strabismus**). However, the deviation may be upward (**hypertropia**), downward (**hypotropia**), or, in rare cases, twisted clockwise or counterclockwise (**cyclotropia**). Also called **heterotropia**; **squint**. **—strabismic** *adj.*

straight 1. *adj.* a colloquial term for heterosexual. **2.** *n.* slang for a heterosexual person.

strain 1. *n.* the state of a system on which excessive demands are made. Examples include muscular strain (excessive tension in a muscle usually due to an activity overload) and psychological strain, usually due to an emotional overload. **2.** *n.* a specific group within a species whose members possess a common distinguishing characteristic. **3.** *n.* excessive effort or exertion. **4.** *vb.* to distort, alter, or injure as a result of such excess or the application of external force. **5.** *vb.* to filter.

straitjacket *n.* an article of clothing that was formerly used to restrain patients in mental hospitals from injuring themselves or others and, in some cases, for punishment. It consisted of a canvas shirt with long sleeves that could be fastened behind the patient's back after folding his or her arms in front of the body. If a means of physical restraint for a mental patient is needed now, a system of belts that limit the patient's range of motion is used. Also called **camisole**.

strange-hand sign a TACTILE PERCEPTUAL DISORDER characterized by an inability to recognize one's own left hand. Individuals may be able to write with the left hand but do not believe the writing is their own or, when clasping the two hands, may be unable to acknowledge without visual clues the left hand as their own. The disorder is caused by a defect of the CORPUS CALLOSUM of the brain.

stranger anxiety the distress, fear, and unhappiness experienced by young children when they are around individuals who are unfamiliar to them. Stranger anxiety is a normal part of cognitive development: Babies differentiate caregivers from other people and display a strong preference for familiar faces. Stranger anxiety usually begins around 8 or 9 months of age (but can begin as early as 6 months) and typically lasts into the 2nd year. Also called **fear of strangers**; **stranger fear**. See also SEPARATION ANXIETY; XENOPHOBIA.

stranger distress see DISTRESS.

Strange Situation an experimental technique used to assess quality of ATTACHMENT in infants and young children (up to the age of 2). The procedure subjects the child to increasing amounts of stress induced by a strange setting, the entrance of an unfamiliar person, and two brief separations from the parent. The reaction of the child to each of these situations is used to evaluate the security or insecurity of his or her attachment to the parent. See AMBIVALENT ATTACHMENT; AVOIDANT ATTACHMENT; DISORGANIZED ATTACHMENT; INSECURE ATTACHMENT; SECURE ATTACHMENT. [devised in 1978 by Canadian-born U.S. psychologist Mary D. Salter Ainsworth (1913–1999)]

strangulated affect in psychoanalytic theory, an inhibition or retention of the normal discharge of emotion, leading to a substitute discharge in the form of physical symptoms. This theory was advanced in Sigmund FREUD's early formulations to explain the dynamics of CONVERSION HYSTERIA; it was later supplanted by the concept of REPRESSION. See also AFFECT.

strata *pl. n.* see STRATUM.

strategic family therapy a group of approaches to FAMILY THERAPY in which the focus is on identifying and applying novel interventions to produce behavioral change rather than on helping the family gain insight into the sources of their problems. Also called **strategic intervention therapy**.

strategic human-resource management (**SHRM**) planned and systematic efforts to help organizations improve their competitive performance and achieve their goals by effectively utilizing HUMAN RESOURCES.

strategic intervention therapy see STRATEGIC FAMILY THERAPY.

strategy *n.* **1.** a program of action designed to achieve a goal or accomplish a task. **2.** in artificial intelligence, a specific approach used for designing SEARCHES of a problem or game space. Strategies, which are used to determine which state in the search is to be considered next, are often called HEURISTICS. They do not always guarantee a minimal path search but can support good enough solutions. **3.** in biology, see K-STRATEGY; R-STRATEGY.

stratification *n.* in sociology, see SOCIAL STRATIFICATION. **—stratify** *vb.*

stratified random sampling RANDOM SAMPLING conducted within strata or subdivisions of a population, so that the sample obtained (called a **stratified sample**) includes individuals representing each stratum (e.g., young and old or men and women). The proportion of the sample to be collected from each stratum is determined before sampling begins.

stratum (*pl.* **strata**) **1.** a level or class within society (see SOCIAL STRATIFICATION). **2.** any of the subpopulations in survey SAMPLING. **3.** a layer (typically one of a number of parallel layers) in a structure.

streaming *n.* **1.** in audition, the perception of a sequence of sounds as a unitary object. Under certain conditions several streams may be perceived nearly simultaneously, as in musical counterpoint. See FISSION. **2.** in educational psychology, the continual flow of learning opportunities, with all successive learning linked to prior documented successive mastery.

streaming media displays that are seen or heard as they are delivered by media. Typically the term refers to computer presentations, but television and radio are also considered to be streaming media.

stream of action the continuous activities of an organism. Also called **action stream**.

stream of consciousness the concept of consciousness as a continuous, dynamic flow of ideas and images rather than a static series of discrete components. It emphasizes the subjective quality of conscious experience as a never-ending and never-repeating stream. Apart from its context in philosophy of mind and studies of perception, the concept also found highly influential expression in the MODERNISM of early 20th-century writers, such as James Joyce, Marcel Proust, and Virginia Woolf. Also called **stream of thought**. [introduced in 1890 by William JAMES]

stream olfactometer an OLFACTOMETER that has a constant flow or stream of air into which an odorant can be introduced. See also BLAST OLFACTOMETER.

street hustlers see MALE HOMOSEXUAL PROSTITUTION.

street intelligence the intelligence people apply in their everyday lives. The term evolved from research conducted in the 1990s by psychologists Terezhina Nunes,

David Carraher, and others, who found that street children in Brazil who successfully negotiated life on the street did very poorly in paper-and-pencil tests of the skills that they showed themselves well able to use in street contexts. The street intelligence of these children can be viewed as situated intelligence (see SITUATED COGNITION) that failed to transfer to a specific testing environment.

strength of an attitude the extent to which an attitude persists over time, resists change, influences information processing, and guides behavior. Strong attitudes possess all four of these defining features, whereas weak attitudes lack these features. A number of attitude properties have been shown to be predictors of an attitude's strength, including ACCESSIBILITY OF AN ATTITUDE, AMBIVALENCE OF AN ATTITUDE, CENTRALITY OF AN ATTITUDE, PERSISTENCE OF AN ATTITUDE, and several others.

strength of association in statistics, the degree of relationship between two or more variables. Common measures are OMEGA SQUARED and COEFFICIENT OF MULTIPLE CORRELATION.

strephosymbolia *n.* **1.** a perceptual disorder characterized by the mirrorlike reversal of objects. **2.** a reading difficulty characterized by a tendency to transpose or reverse letters while reading or writing (e.g., *tap* for *pat* or *p* for *q*). Also called **twisted symbols**. [defined in 1937 by U.S. psychiatrist Samuel Torrey Orton (1879–1948)]

stress *n.* **1.** a state of physiological or psychological response to internal or external stressors. Stress involves changes affecting nearly every system of the body, influencing how people feel and behave. For example, it may be manifested by palpitations, sweating, dry mouth, shortness of breath, fidgeting, faster speech, augmentation of negative emotions (if already being experienced), and longer duration of stress fatigue. Severe stress is manifested by the GENERAL ADAPTATION SYNDROME. By causing these mind–body changes, stress contributes directly to psychological and physiological disorder and disease and affects mental and physical health, reducing the quality of life. [first described in the context of psychology around 1940 by Canadian physician Hans Selye (1907–1982)] **2.** in linguistics, emphasis placed on a word or syllable in speech, generally by pronouncing it more loudly and deliberately than its neighboring units and slightly prolonging its duration. See also ACCENT.

stress casualty a member of the armed forces who is unable to perform his or her duties because of exposure to operational stresses or risk factors. Such stress may result in somatic and behavioral symptoms. The primary cause is an imminent external threat to life, leading to inability to cope with the threat and a consequent overwhelming feeling of helplessness.

stress-decompensation model a concept of the development of abnormal behavior as a result of high levels of stress that lead to the gradual but progressive deterioration of normal behavior to a level that is highly disorganized and dysfunctional.

stress immunity 1. a highly developed capacity to tolerate emotional strain. **2.** failure to react to stressful situations or events.

stress immunization the concept that mild stress early in life makes an individual better able to handle stress later in life.

stress incontinence 1. a type of URINARY INCONTINENCE that occurs during exertion or other physical activities, such as laughing or coughing, that apply increased pressure to the abdomen and bladder. **2.** any form of INCONTINENCE whose origin is a high level of stress.

stress-induced analgesia a reduced sensitivity to pain that an organism may experience when exposed to extreme physical trauma. For example, soldiers in combat may ignore injuries and instead respond to other threats to their lives, and injured animals fleeing predators may ignore their injuries in order to avoid capture. The precise mechanism is uncertain but may be related to the production of large quantities of ENDORPHINS.

stress-inoculation training (**SIT**) a four-phase training program for stress-management often used in COGNITIVE BEHAVIOR THERAPY. Phase 1 entails the identification of reactions to stress and their effects on functioning and psychological well-being; phase 2 involves learning relaxation and self-regulation techniques; phase 3 consists of learning coping self-statements (see SELF-STATEMENT TRAINING); phase 4 involves assisted progression through a series of increasingly stressful situations using imagery, video, role playing, and real-life situations until the individual is eventually able to cope with the original stress-inducing situation or event. [developed by U.S. psychologist Donald Meichenbaum (1940–)]

stress interview an interview in which the person being questioned is deliberately subjected to confrontational, hostile, emotionally unsettling, or otherwise stressful conditions, such as a combination of aggressive questioning and environmental influences (e.g., harsh lighting). Such techniques are mainly associated with police or military interrogations; in PERSONNEL SELECTION they have sometimes been used to test an individual's ability to manage pressure and handle stress but are generally considered of questionable validity.

stress management the use of specific techniques, strategies, or programs—such as relaxation training, anticipation of stress reactions, and breathing techniques—for dealing with stress-inducing situations and the state of being stressed. See also COPE MODEL; PREVENTIVE STRESS MANAGEMENT; TIME-OUT THEORY.

stressor *n.* any event, force, or condition that results in physical or emotional stress. Stressors may be internal or external forces that require adjustment or COPING STRATEGIES on the part of the affected individual.

stressor aftereffects the residual effects that follow exposure to environmental stressors. Immediately after exposure to acute or chronic stressors (e.g., noise, crowding, traffic congestion, social conflict), individuals may manifest negative effects, such as reduced motivation to persist with a task or a decrease in altruistic behavior.

stress reaction maladaptive or pathological behavior resulting from conditions of pressure or strain. Examples are extreme feelings of tension or panic, disorganized speech patterns, and accidents caused by the effects of alcohol, drugs, or emotional stress.

stress test 1. an examination or evaluation designed to ascertain an individual's capacity to perform a relatively complex task under purposefully stressful conditions. **2.** a medical evaluation designed to assess the effects of stress, typically induced by physical exercise, on cardiac function. The most common of such procedures is a test in which the patient walks or runs on a treadmill while cardiac, respiratory, or other physiological processes are monitored.

stress tolerance the capacity to withstand pressures and strains and the consequent ability to function effectively and with minimal anxiety under conditions of stress. See also STRESS IMMUNITY.

stress training activities designed to help individuals understand the causes of stress and learn strategies for managing and preventing it. Realistic training and simulation (e.g., water survival, escape training, firefighting) are seen as necessary instructional strategies to prepare personnel in certain types of work to operate in stressful environments.

stress–vulnerability model in schizophrenia and mood disorders, the theory that a genetic or biological predisposition to these illnesses exists and that psychological and social factors can increase the likelihood of symptomatic episodes. See also DIATHESIS–STRESS MODEL.

stretch receptor a RECEPTOR cell that responds primarily to stretching of muscles. Stretch receptors include the MUSCLE SPINDLES of skeletal muscle.

stretch reflex the contraction of a muscle in response to stretching of that muscle. Stretch reflexes support the body against the pull of gravity. Also called **myotatic reflex**. See also EXTENSOR THRUST.

stria atrophica purplish scarlike lesions, later becoming white, on the breast, thighs, abdomen, and buttocks. They are associated with pregnancy, rapid growth during puberty and adolescence, Cushing's syndrome, and topical or prolonged treatment with corticosteroids.

striate cortex the first region of the cerebral cortex that receives visual input from the thalamus, particularly from the LATERAL GENICULATE NUCLEUS. The striate cortex is located in the occipital lobe and contains a dense band of myelinated fibers in layer IVb that appears as a white stripe (stripe of Gennari). Neurons in the striate cortex project to visual areas in the PRESTRIATE CORTEX and to subcortical visual nuclei. Also called **Brodmann's area 17**; **primary visual cortex**. See also VI.

striated muscle see SKELETAL MUSCLE.

stria terminalis the smaller of the two efferent pathways from the AMYGDALA in the brain (see also VENTRAL AMYGDALOFUGAL PATHWAY). Its fibers carry impulses from the CORTICOMEDIAL GROUP of amygdaloid nuclei to the septal, hypothalamic, and thalamic areas.

striatum *n.* the input region of the BASAL GANGLIA, comprising mainly the CAUDATE NUCLEUS, PUTAMEN, and NUCLEUS ACCUMBENS.

stria vascularis see SCALA MEDIA.

strict scrutiny a test used to ascertain whether a law violates a fundamental right granted under the U.S. Constitution. The government must show that although such a law treats some people favorably and others unfavorably, it is nevertheless the least inequitable way of handling an important issue. The test is often invoked in the context of discrimination based on race, gender, or nationality.

stridor dentium see BRUXISM.

stridulation *n.* see VOCAL COMMUNICATION.

string *n.* in linguistics, a linear sequence of words or word elements that can be subjected to formal analysis.

striving for superiority in the INDIVIDUAL PSYCHOLOGY of Alfred ADLER, the idea that human beings are motivated by an innate, sovereign drive for realizing their full potential. This drive is defined as the urge for completion and perfection rather than for superiority in the sense of social status or domination over others.

stroboscope *n.* a device that allows very rapid presentation or illumination of a sequence of images. When sequential still images are presented by a stroboscope, the perception of movement is created, as in a motion picture.

stroboscopic illusion 1. the apparent motion of a series of separate stimuli occurring in close consecutive order, as in motion pictures. **2.** the apparent lack of motion or reverse motion of a moving object, such as a rotating fan, produced by illuminating it with a series of intermittent light flashes. Also called **stroboscopic effect**.

stroke *n.* disruption of blood flow to the brain, which deprives the tissue of oxygen and nutrients, causing tissue damage and loss of normal function and, potentially, tissue death. A stroke may result from a hemorrhage of a blood vessel in the brain (see HEMORRHAGIC STROKE) or an embolism or thrombus blocking an artery in the brain (see EMBOLIC STROKE; THROMBOTIC STROKE). This term is often used interchangeably with CEREBROVASCULAR ACCIDENT. See also CEREBRAL INFARCTION; CEREBRO VASCULAR DISEASE; LACUNAR STROKE; TRANSIENT ISCHEMIC ATTACK.

Strong, Edward Kellogg, Jr. (1884–1963) U.S. psychologist. Strong received his doctorate in psychology from Columbia University in 1911, writing a dissertation on the psychology of advertising. He taught briefly at George Peabody College for Teachers in Tennessee, served in the army during World War I as a member of the Committee on the Classification of Personnel, and then joined the faculty of the Carnegie Institute of Technology following the war. In 1923 he moved to Stanford University, where he remained until his retirement. Strong is considered to be one of the founders of APPLIED PSYCHOLOGY, especially in the areas of personnel classification and occupational analysis. He is best known for creating, with colleagues, a test that assesses a person's interests and relates them to possible career choices. Originally called the Strong Vocational Interest Blank, it is now known as the STRONG INTEREST INVENTORY and is still widely used in vocational guidance programs. His writings include *Psychology of Selling Life Insurance* (1922), *Job Analysis and the Curriculum* (1923), and *Vocational Interests of Men and Women* (1943). Strong was awarded the Butler Silver Medal Award from Columbia University in 1944.

strong ego see EGO STRENGTH.

Strong Interest Inventory (**SII**) an INTEREST TEST based on the concept that people who achieve success in one occupation are likely to have common interests and preferences that differentiate them from people who are successful in other occupations. The most recent version of the test, published in 2004, presents an inventory of 291 items, which the subject marks "strongly like," "like," "indifferent," "dislike," or "strongly dislike." The items pertain to occupations, subject areas, activities (including leisure activities), contact with various kinds of people, and self-descriptive characteristics. The test provides 6 general occupational themes and 244 occupational scales, 30 basic interest scales, and 5 personal style scales. The Strong Interest Inventory was formerly known as the **Strong–Campbell Interest Inventory** (**SCII**), which was itself a revision of the **Strong Vocational Interest Blank**. [Edward Kellogg STRONG, Jr.]

strong law of effect see LAW OF EFFECT.

strong methods 1. problem-solving techniques that are specific to a particular domain or application, for example, medical diagnosis. **2.** in artificial intelligence, programs that incorporate knowledge specific to a particular application or domain: for example, knowledge of the rules of chess in building a chess-playing program. Compare WEAK METHODS.

Stroop Color–Word Interference Test a three-part test in which (a) color names are read as fast as possible; (b) the colors of bars or other shapes are rapidly named;

and, most importantly, (c) color hues are named quickly when used to print the names of other colors (such as the word *green* printed in the color red). The degree to which the participants are subject to interference by the printed words is a measure of their cognitive flexibility and selective attention. Also called **Stroop test**. See also RESPONSE COMPETITION. [John Ridley **Stroop** (1897–1973), U.S. psychologist]

Stroop effect the finding that the time it takes a participant to name the color of ink in which a word is printed is longer for words that denote incongruent color names than for neutral words or for words that denote a congruent color. For example, if the word *blue* is written in red ink (incongruent), participants take longer to say "red" than if the word *glue* is written in red ink (neutral) or if the word *red* is written in red ink (congruent). See STROOP COLOR–WORD INTERFERENCE TEST. [John **Stroop**]

structural analysis 1. in psychology, any theory of the organization of mind or personality that attempts to differentiate between component parts and to define the relationship of part to part and part to whole. Such an analysis can be contrasted with one based on function, dynamics, or behavior. See PERSONALITY STRUCTURE; STRUCTURAL MODEL. **2.** in linguistics, an analysis of a word, phrase, sentence, or longer unit in terms of its formal CONSTITUENTS. See PHRASE-STRUCTURE GRAMMAR. **3.** any analysis based on the ideas or methods of STRUCTURALISM.

structural approach see STRUCTURAL MODEL.

structural constraint theory see NEONATIVISM.

structural disorder a disorder related to a defect in or damage to the structure of an organ or tissue, such as the nervous system.

structural equation modeling (**SEM**) a statistical modeling technique that includes LATENT VARIABLES as causal elements. SEM is an advanced statistical method for testing causal models involving constructs that cannot be directly measured but are, rather, approximated through several measures presumed to assess part of the given construct.

structural family therapy a type of FAMILY THERAPY that provides a method for the rational solution of problems, based on the theory that these problems are the result of poorly structured family relationships. For example, a father may behave more like a teenage son, whereas an elder daughter may behave more like a parent, a situation that eventually causes problems for one or both. To improve this structure, the entire family system and the part each person plays in that system must be modified. Also called **structural therapy**.

structural group a therapeutic group made up of individuals selected for those characteristics that would make them most likely to be successful in achieving the goals sought in the therapy. People of different types, temperaments, personalities, and educational levels are combined in a group, based on the concept that their interaction will maximize each other's benefits in the therapeutic process. Also called **structured group**. [devised by Austrian-born U.S. psychiatrist Jacob Levi Moreno (1889–1972)]

structural hypothesis see STRUCTURAL MODEL.

structural integration see ROLFING.

structuralism 1. a movement considered to be the first school of psychology as a science, independent of philosophy. Usually attributed to Wilhelm WUNDT, but probably more strongly and directly influenced by Edward Bradford TITCHENER, structuralism defined psychology as the study of mental experience and sought to investigate the structure of such experience through a systematic program of experiments based on trained INTROSPECTION. Also called **structural psychology**. **2.** a movement in various disciplines that study human behavior and culture that enjoyed particular currency in the 1960s and 1970s. The movement took its impetus from the radically new approach to linguistic analysis pioneered by Swiss linguist Ferdinand de Saussure (1857–1913). Against the prevailing historical and comparative approaches, Saussure maintained that a language is a closed system that must be approached through the detail of its internal structure; linguistic SIGNS (written or spoken words) acquire meaning not through their relationships to external REFERENTS but through their structural relationships to other signs in the same system (see ARBITRARY SYMBOL). The meaning of any particular use of language is therefore grounded in the total abstract system of that language, which is largely defined by a pattern of functional contrasts between elements (see BINARY FEATURE; MINIMAL PAIR). The structuralist model of language was extended to cover essentially all social and cultural phenomena, including human thought and action, in the work of French anthropologist Claude Lévi-Strauss (1908–). For structuralists in anthropology and the other social sciences, there is a connection between the events of the lived world and a deeper structure of abstract relationships and ideas that provides meaning to the events. Structuralist explanations play down individual autonomy and agency, positivistic science, and linear-time causation in favor of explanations in terms of structural and systemic influences operating in the present to produce rule-governed behavior, the true nature of which can be revealed as the underlying structures are revealed. In the 1960s structuralist ideas exerted a major influence on literary studies; they also provided a basic intellectual framework for the new field of SEMIOTICS, which studies the ways in which verbal and nonverbal signs acquire meaning within particular codes of signification. During subsequent decades structuralism increasingly gave way to POSTSTRUCTURALISM.

structuralist 1. *n.* a therapist who believes that changing the organizational structure of a group or system, such as a family, will change and improve its patterns of interaction. **2.** *n.* an adherent of structuralism. **3.** *adj.* of or relating to structuralism.

structural matrix see STRUCTURED INTERACTIONAL GROUP PSYCHOTHERAPY.

structural model in psychoanalytic theory, the view that the total personality comprises three divisions or functions: (a) the ID, which represents instinctual drives; (b) the EGO, which controls id drives and mediates between them and external reality; and (c) the SUPEREGO, which comprises moral precepts and ideals. Sigmund FREUD proposed this model in 1923 to replace his earlier TOPOGRAPHIC MODEL, in which the mind was divided into three regions: the UNCONSCIOUS, PRECONSCIOUS, and CONSCIOUS. Also called **structural approach**; **structural hypothesis**; **structural theory**. See also DYNAMIC MODEL; ECONOMIC MODEL.

structural psychology see STRUCTURALISM.

structural therapy 1. see STRUCTURAL FAMILY THERAPY. **2.** a system of treatment for children with AUTISTIC DISORDER, which provides a structured environment emphasizing physical and verbal stimulation in a gamelike setting. The purpose is to increase the amount and variety of stimuli received by the children, thereby helping them to relate to their environment in a more realistic manner.

structural zero a coefficient whose value is set to zero for theoretical reasons, as opposed to a coefficient that has an empirical value of zero.

structure *n.* **1.** a relatively stable arrangement of elements or components organized so as to form an integrated whole. Structure is often contrasted with FUNCTION to emphasize how something is organized or patterned rather than what it does. See also BIDIRECTIONALITY OF STRUCTURE AND FUNCTION. **2.** a complex entity consisting of organized components. **3.** in Jean PIAGET's theory, any of the entities that together comprise the enduring KNOWLEDGE BASE by which children interpret their world. A structure is equivalent to a SCHEME. **—structural** *adj.*

structured autobiography see AUTOBIOGRAPHY.

Structured Clinical Interview for DSM–IV Axis I Disorders (**SCID-I**) an instrument used by clinicians to make standardized and reliable diagnoses of the 37 most frequently seen *DSM–IV* Axis I clinical disorders and avoid the common problem of premature focus on one diagnostic possibility. Assessment involves a standard set of questions asked in an interview with the patient.

Structured Clinical Interview for DSM–IV Axis II Personality Disorders (**SCID-II**) an instrument used by researchers and clinicians to make standardized and reliable diagnoses of the 10 *DSM–IV* personality (Axis II) disorders, as well as DEPRESSIVE PERSONALITY DISORDER, PASSIVE-AGGRESSIVE PERSONALITY DISORDER, and personality disorder not otherwise specified. Assessment involves a set of questions asked in an interview with the patient.

structured group see STRUCTURAL GROUP.

structured interactional group psychotherapy a form of GROUP PSYCHOTHERAPY in which the therapist provides a **structural matrix** for the group's interactions. This is usually achieved by selecting a different member of the group to be the focus of the interaction—the TARGET PATIENT—in each session. [developed by U.S. psychiatrists Harold I. Kaplan (1928–1998) and Benjamin J. Sadock (1933–)]

structured interview an interview consisting of a predetermined set of questions or topics. Structured interviews are popular in marketing research because they produce data that can be easily tabulated; they may also be used in personnel selection and other fields. Compare PATTERNED INTERVIEW; UNSTRUCTURED INTERVIEW. See also STANDARDIZED INTERVIEW SCHEDULE.

structured item a response item with fixed options.

structured learning a complex system of psychotherapy based on the idea of psychological skills training, that is, teaching individuals the skills and behaviors associated with leading healthy and satisfying lives and then helping them gain the ability to consistently and reliably apply these skills outside of the therapeutic setting. This approach involves four essential components: MODELING, ROLE PLAY, performance feedback, and TRANSFER OF TRAINING. The individual is provided with examples of specific behavior to be imitated, is allowed to practice that behavior, is given feedback regarding the performance of the behavior, and completes HOMEWORK assignments that encourage the use of the behavior in real-world situations. [developed in the mid-1970s by U.S. psychologists Arnold P. Goldstein (1933–), Robert P. Sprafkin (1940–), and N. Jane Gershaw (1945–)]

structured learning group a type of INTERPERSONAL LEARNING GROUP that helps participants gain self-insight, develop improved interpersonal skills, and solve interpersonal problems through a series of relatively specific exercises, activities, and assignments.

structured observational measures methods for measuring overt behaviors and interpersonal processes that require that each observed unit of action be classified into an objectively defined category. Investigators who use such a CATEGORY-SYSTEM METHOD must (a) select which behaviors are of interest and which are not, (b) clearly define the characteristics of the behavior so that observers all agree on the classification of the action, and (c) note the occurrence and frequency of these targeted behaviors in the situation under analysis. INTERACTION-PROCESS ANALYSIS and SYMLOG are examples of such classification systems.

structured stimulus a well-defined, well-organized stimulus. Compare UNSTRUCTURED STIMULUS.

structure of an attitude the set of properties related to the content of mental representations associated with an attitude, the number of these representations, and the strength and the pattern of associations among these representations. See also TRIPARTITE THEORY OF ATTITUDES.

structure of intellect model (**SOI**) a model of intelligence that postulates five operations (cognition, memory, divergent production, convergent production, evaluation), six products (units, classes, relations, systems, transformations, implications), and five contents (symbolic, semantic, behavioral, auditory, visual), for a total of 150 separate factors of intelligence (120 in an earlier version of the theory). The evidence for the theory is fairly weak and in large part has been refuted by the work of U.S. psychologist John L. Horn (1928–). See also GUILFORD DIMENSIONS OF INTELLIGENCE. [initially proposed in the 1950s by Joy Paul GUILFORD]

structures of the whole see OPERATION.

structure word see FUNCTION WORD.

structuring *n.* **1.** the explanation by a counselor or therapist, usually during the first session of a course of treatment, of the specific procedures and conditions of the process. This includes the intended results of treatment, time restrictions, fees, and the function and responsibilities of both client and counselor or therapist. See also CONTRACT. **2.** in education, the use of behavioral instructions to a student to decrease disruptions in the classroom.

struggle for existence see COMPETITION FOR RESOURCES.

strychnine *n.* an alkaloid derived from NUX VOMICA. It is a stimulant of the central nervous system (see CNS STIMULANTS)—through its ability to antagonize the inhibitory neurotransmitter glycine—and a powerful convulsant, with death usually resulting from paralysis of muscles of respiration. Strychnine has long been used as a rodenticide, and this use continues to the present; there are, however, no clinical applications for strychnine. No marked tolerance develops for strychnine, and increased susceptibility to poisoning is likely from repeated exposure.

student counseling see EDUCATIONAL COUNSELING.

student's disease the condition of individuals who believe they have the symptoms of a disease or mental disorder that they have been studying or that they have read or heard about.

students' evaluation of teaching (**SET**) a controversial practice, begun in the 1960s in the United States, in which students evaluate a teacher's performance. Students are given the opportunity to fill out questionnaires or forms regarding the capabilities and performance of their instructor, commonly toward the end of a learning sequence, and instructors then use the information to modify their format or teaching style. It often includes informal, individualized evaluations, as well as more formal, standardized forms. There is currently a movement to create a national standard for student evaluation. Also called **student–teacher evaluation**.

Student's t distribution see T DISTRIBUTION. [**Student**, pseudonym of William S. Gosset (1876–1937), British statistician]

student–teacher evaluation see STUDENTS' EVALUATION OF TEACHING.

study 1. *n.* a research project, such as a survey or systematic observation, that is less rigorously controlled than a true EXPERIMENT. **2.** *n.* loosely, any research investigation. **3.** *n.* any attempt to acquire and remember information. **4.** *vb.* to engage in study.

Study of Values see ALLPORT–VERNON–LINDZEY STUDY OF VALUES.

study skill any method used to facilitate the process of learning material, such as outlining, taking notes, underlining, or silent recitation.

stupor *n.* **1.** a mental state in which an individual is totally or almost totally unresponsive and immobile and experiences DISORIENTATION. **2.** inability to speak (see MUTISM).

Sturge–Weber syndrome a congenital disorder marked by malformation of meningeal blood vessels (hemi- or leptomeningeal angioma), a facial PORT-WINE STAIN, glaucoma, and focal-motor seizures. Skin pigmentation may occur on one or both sides of the face or extend into the scalp area. About half of affected individuals have mental retardation, and others may have specific cognitive difficulties or disabilities detected by neuropsychological testing. Other characteristics may include contralateral hemiplegia, intracranial calcification, and emotional or behavioral disorders. Also called **encephalofacial angiomatosis**; **Kalischer syndrome**; **Parkes–Weber syndrome**; **Sturge–Weber–Dimitri syndrome**. [William A. **Sturge** (1850–1919) and Frederick Parkes **Weber** (1863–1962), British physicians; Vicente **Dimitri** (1885–1955), Austrian physician; S. **Kalischer**, German physician]

Sturm und Drang period see STORM-AND-STRESS PERIOD.

stuttering *n.* in *DSM–IV–TR*, a disturbance in the normal fluency and time patterning of speech. It is characterized by frequent repetition or prolongation of sounds, syllables, or words, with hesitations and pauses that disrupt speech. The disorder occurs in about 1% of all children. Mild cases usually recover spontaneously by the age of 16; chronic stuttering is exacerbated in situations where communication is important or stressful. Also called **stammering**. See also PRIMARY STUTTERING; SECONDARY STUTTERING. **—stutter** *vb., n.*

stuttering gait a gait characterized by hesitancy in taking steps: a walking pattern observed in certain patients with schizophrenia or conversion disorder. In some cases it is neurological in origin, as with PARKINSON'S DISEASE.

STX abbreviation for SAXITOXIN.

style theories of leadership see LEADERSHIP STYLE; LEADERSHIP THEORIES.

stylistic ratings a system of evaluating works of art in terms of their technical attributes, as opposed to the reactions or moods of those who view the art. Stylistic ratings may be based on such factors as importance of shapes, lines, composition, surface textures, and reproduction of objects or people portrayed. Stylistic dimensions include classicism, subjectivism, and expressionism.

stylus maze a maze that is "run" by moving a stylus through the various pathways. The task may be performed visually or tactually.

subacute spongiform encephalopathy (**SSE**) see CREUTZFELDT–JAKOB DISEASE.

subarachnoid hemorrhage bleeding into the subarachnoid space surrounding the brain. It may be the result of trauma or a ruptured ANEURYSM. Initial symptoms are caused by increasing INTRACRANIAL PRESSURE and can include headache and loss of consciousness as escaping blood distends the spaces beneath the arach- noid (see CISTERNA), causing compression or spasm of the blood vessels of the thalamus and upper brainstem.

subarachnoid space a space beneath the delicate ARACHNOID MATER, the middle of the three MENINGES that surround the brain and spinal cord. It is occupied by cerebrospinal fluid, which drains into the SUPERIOR SAGITTAL SINUS through ARACHNOID GRANULATIONS.

subcallosal gyrus a portion of the LIMBIC SYSTEM behind the CINGULATE GYRUS. Its functions are reciprocal to those of the cingulate gyrus: It inhibits motor neuron activity, whereas the cingulate gyrus enhances motor neuron functions.

subception *n.* a reaction to an emotion-provoking stimulus that is not clearly enough perceived to be reportable, although its effects may be observed indirectly by the electrodermal response or by a longer than expected reaction time.

subcommissural organ a group of secretory ependymal cells (see EPENDYMA) on the dorsal wall of the third ventricle of the brain, near the CEREBRAL AQUEDUCT. It is one of the CIRCUMVENTRICULAR ORGANS whose exact function is unknown.

subconscious 1. *adj.* denoting mental processes that occur outside consciousness. **2.** *n.* in Sigmund FREUD'S structural model, the concept of the mind beneath the level of consciousness, comprising the PRECONSCIOUS and the UNCONSCIOUS.

subcortical *adj.* relating to structures or processes of the nervous system that are located or take place below the level of the cerebral cortex. See also SUBCORTICAL CENTER.

subcortical aphasia aphasia resulting from damage to subcortical (deeper) areas of the brain (e.g., the basal ganglia) rather than cortical areas.

subcortical arteriosclerotic encephalopathy see BINSWANGER'S DISEASE.

subcortical center any region of the brain at a level below the CEREBRAL CORTEX that has a particular function or functions. Subcortical centers include the THALAMUS, HYPOTHALAMUS, and BASAL GANGLIA. Within each subcortical structure may be several special centers, such as nuclei of the hypothalamus that regulate sleep, water balance, protein metabolism, and sexual activity.

subcortical dementia dementia caused by damage to or dysfunction of the subcortical (deeper) structures of the brain that may be due, for example, to Parkinson's disease. It is marked by cognitive slowing, memory impairment, visuospatial abnormalities, and mood and affect disturbances. Compare CORTICAL DEMENTIA.

subcortical learning 1. learning that occurs in areas of the brain underneath the cortex. For example, some simple habits or associations may be learned subcortically. **2.** learning that occurs during cortical spreading depression, that is, during a temporary suppression of cortical activity induced by an injection of potassium chloride into the cortex.

subcultural delinquency see SOCIALIZED DELINQUENCY.

subculture *n.* a group that maintains a characteristic set of religious, social, ethnic, or other customs or beliefs that serve to distinguish it from the larger culture in which the members live. See also COUNTERCULTURE. —**subcultural** *adj.*

subculture of violence see CULTURE OF HONOR.

subcutaneous injection injection of a drug beneath the skin, often in the upper arm or thigh, where there is an adequate layer of subcutaneous tissue. Although the subcutaneous route is used mainly to inject fluids, medications may also be administered subcutaneously in the form of slowly absorbed pellets. Also called **hypodermic injection**. See also ADMINISTRATION.

subcutaneous sensibility the sensitivity of nerve receptors (e.g., PACINIAN CORPUSCLES) beneath the skin.

subdelirious state the precursor of full DELIRIUM, marked by restlessness, headache, irritability, hypersensitivity to sound and visual stimuli, and emotional instability. Also called **subdelirium**.

subdural *adj.* lying beneath the DURA MATER, the outermost of the coverings (meninges) of the brain and spinal cord.

subdural hematoma an accumulation of blood due to bleeding between the DURA MATER membrane and the brain surface. Because the hematoma enlarges and cannot escape through the skull, it causes pressure that distorts brain structures. The bleeding may occur over a period of days or weeks, producing symptoms of confusion, memory loss, or other neurological deficits that may be mistaken as signs of dementia in an older person.

subdural hemorrhage bleeding beneath the DURA MATER, the outermost of the meningeal membranes that surround the brain. It typically occurs as a result of head injury, and the specific symptoms may vary according to the brain area affected by the bleeding.

subfecundity *n.* see FECUNDITY.

subfornical organ a structure in the brain that is responsive to ANGIOTENSIN II and contributes to thirst and drinking behavior. One of the CIRCUMVENTRICULAR ORGANS, it is located below the FORNIX.

subgoal *n.* a goal that serves as an intermediary step to attaining an ultimate goal (i.e., the GOAL OBJECT). For example, completing an outline of an essay may be a subgoal of completing the essay itself—the ultimate goal.

subiculum *n.* (*pl.* **subicula**) a region of the forebrain adjacent to the HIPPOCAMPUS that has reciprocal connections with the hippocampus and the DENTATE GYRUS. It forms part of the HIPPOCAMPAL FORMATION. Also called **hippocampal gyrus**.

subitize *vb.* to perceive at a glance how many objects are presented, without counting (from Latin *subito*, "at once").

subject *n.* **1.** the individual human or nonhuman animal that takes part in an experiment or research study and whose responses or performance are reported or evaluated. PARTICIPANT is now often the preferred term for human subjects, because the word "subject" is depersonalizing and implies passivity and submissiveness on the part of the experimentee. **2.** in linguistics, the principal noun phrase in a clause or sentence about which something is stated (compare PREDICATE). The subject is usually (but not always) the AGENT of the main action and in English can usually be identified as the noun phrase whose number and person govern the form of the main verb. **3.** an area or branch of knowledge or a course of study.

subjection *n.* the state of being under the control of another individual or of a government or other organization, especially where this is felt to be oppressive. See also SOCIAL SUBORDINATION.

subjective *adj.* **1.** taking place or existing only within the mind. **2.** particular to a specific person and thus intrinsically inaccessible to the experience or observation of others. **3.** based on or influenced by personal feelings, interpretations, or prejudices. Compare OBJECTIVE.

subjective assessment of performance determination of the level of achievement of a task based on one's own observations or those of another individual and grounded in specific criteria.

subjective attribute a perceptual quality that is uniquely dependent on the individual who experiences it (e.g., a particular taste or color).

subjective colors see FECHNER'S COLORS.

subjective competitive situation an individual's perception, evaluation, and acceptance of a situation as meeting the criteria of an OBJECTIVE COMPETITIVE SITUATION.

subjective contour an edge or border perceived in an image as a result of the inference of the observer. A common form of a KANIZSA FIGURE contains a triangle with sides that consist of subjective contours. Also called **illusory contour**.

subjective-equality point see POINT OF SUBJECTIVE EQUALITY.

subjective examination see SUBJECTIVE TEST.

subjective–expected utility (**SEU**) a hypothetical value that people are presumed to compute (nearly always unconsciously) in making a rational choice between alternatives, especially in economic matters. When choosing from a fixed set of alternatives, each associated with (a) a given utility value and (b) a SUBJECTIVE PROBABILITY estimate of the desired outcome, people act so as to maximize the value of the sum (a) × (b).

subjective–expected value in analyses of decision making, the extent to which an outcome is (a) desired or valued and (b) thought to be probable by the decision maker. The choice of one alternative over others is to a considerable extent a function of the personal (or subjective) value placed by an individual on a specific act or outcome as well as the perceived probability (expectation) that the given alternative will lead to that outcome. Many analyses assume that the alternative selected is the one for which the product of the expectation and the subjective value is the highest.

subjective idealism in philosophy, the metaphysical position that what is normally considered the EXTERNAL WORLD is in fact constructed partly or wholly by individual perceiving minds. See IDEALISM; SOLIPSISM.

subjective norms perceptions that a person has regarding whether people important to that person believe that he or she should or should not perform a particular behavior. See also THEORY OF PLANNED BEHAVIOR; THEORY OF REASONED ACTION.

subjective organization the creation of one's own idiosyncratic set of associations or groupings among items to be learned in order to facilitate memory. [proposed by Estonian-born Canadian psychologist Endel Tulving (1927–)]

subjective probability a person-specific estimate, derived from subjective experience, of the likelihood of a given event or outcome. The subjective probability estimate is used in calculating the SUBJECTIVE–EXPECTED UTILITY.

subjective psychology a psychological approach that focuses on introspective or phenomenological data. Compare OBJECTIVE PSYCHOLOGY.

subjective responsibility in the moral reasoning typical of children over the age of 10, the idea that an individual's motives should be taken into account when judging an act. Compare OBJECTIVE RESPONSIBILITY. [proposed by Jean PIAGET]

subjective scoring see OBJECTIVE SCORING.

subjective test an assessment tool that is scored according to personal judgment or to standards that are less systematic than those used in OBJECTIVE TESTS, as in some essay examinations. Most subjective tests attempt to measure the degree to which a student can articulate the core or essential features of a concept. Also called **subjective examination**.

subjective tone the perception of a tonal-like sound that is not present in the acoustic input. This covers a broad range of percepts, including COMBINATION TONES, TINNITUS, and AUDITORY HALLUCINATIONS.

subjective visual field the VISUAL FIELD as assessed from the observer's point of view.

subjective well-being a judgment that people make about the overall quality of their lives by summing emotional ups and downs to determine how well their actual life circumstances match their wishes or expectations concerning how they should or might feel.

subjectivism *n.* **1.** in ethics, the proposition that the ideals, such as "the good," to which ethical propositions refer are reflections of personal judgment rather than independent realities. Subjectivism holds that ethical prescriptions reduce to mere statements of personal or cultural preference. **2.** in general, any position holding that judgments of fact or value reflect individual states of mind rather than states of affairs that can be said to be true or false independently of individuals. Compare OBJECTIVISM. **—subjectivist** *n., adj.*

subjectivity *n.* **1.** in general, the tendency to interpret data or make judgments in the light of personal feelings, beliefs, or experiences. **2.** in empirical research, the failure to attain proper standards of OBJECTIVITY.

subject of consciousness the observing ego, the "I," or an individual's subjectivity. See also SELF AS AGENT. Compare OBJECT OF CONSCIOUSNESS.

subject variable a variable of individual differences in a study (e.g., the participant's sex or occupation). A variable of this type is neither manipulated by the experimenter, as an INDEPENDENT VARIABLE might be, nor is it usually changed in the course of the experiment, as a DEPENDENT VARIABLE might be.

subjunctive *n.* in linguistics, the MOOD of a verb used to indicate that a situation is hypothetical or not yet realized, as in *If I were in your position* or *I insist that she go now*. Compare IMPERATIVE; INDICATIVE; INTERROGATIVE.

sublimation *n.* in psychoanalytic theory, a DEFENSE MECHANISM in which unacceptable sexual or aggressive drives are unconsciously channeled into socially acceptable modes of expression. Thus, the unacceptable drives and energies are redirected into new, learned behaviors, which indirectly provide some satisfaction for the original instincts. For example, an exhibitionistic impulse may gain a new outlet in choreography; a voyeuristic urge may lead to scientific research; and a dangerously aggressive drive may be expressed with impunity on the football field. As well as allowing for substitute satisfactions, such outlets are posited to protect individuals from the anxiety induced by the original drive. **—sublimate** *vb.*

Sublimaze *n.* a trade name for FENTANYL.

subliminal *adj.* denoting or relating to stimuli that are below the threshold of perception or awareness. **—subliminally** *adv.*

subliminal consciousness a level of consciousness in which a stimulus may affect behavior even though the person is not aware of it. See SUBLIMINAL PERCEPTION.

subliminal learning information, habits, or attitudes acquired from exposure to stimuli that were presented below the threshold for conscious awareness (i.e., subliminally).

subliminal perception the registration of stimuli below the level of awareness, particularly stimuli that are too weak (or too rapid) to affect the individual on a conscious level. It is questionable whether responses to subliminal stimuli actually occur and whether it is possible for subliminal commands or advertising messages to influence behavior. Evidence indicates that subliminal commands do not directly affect behavior but may influence responses via SUBLIMINAL PRIMING.

subliminal persuasion the presentation of information in a manner that changes people's attitudes without their being consciously aware of the content of the information to which they have been exposed. Subliminal persuasion usually involves extremely brief presentations of visual stimuli (e.g., words, pictures).

subliminal priming unconscious stimulation that increases the probability of the later occurrence of related cognitive tasks. See PRIMING.

subliminal process see UNCONSCIOUS PROCESS.

subliminal propaganda a form of propaganda in which images or words are displayed too quickly for the conscious mind to perceive. They may, however, influence a person unconsciously.

subliminal stimulation stimulation that is below the threshold intensity required to elicit a response (see SUBLIMINAL PERCEPTION). Also called **subliminal stimulus**.

submission *n.* compliance with or surrender to the requests, demands, or will of others. Compare DOMINANCE; ASSERTIVENESS.

submissiveness *n.* a tendency to comply with the wishes or obey the orders of others. See COMPLIANCE. **—submissive** *adj.*

submissive signal a signal given by a SUBORDINATE to a dominant animal indicating that it will not continue to compete with the other for resources. By using submissive signals low-ranking individuals avoid being attacked, and overall levels of physical aggression are reduced. See THREAT DISPLAY.

subnormal *adj.* denoting something that is below (often significantly below) the normal or expected level. The use of this term with reference to intelligence is now largely obsolete, and the term BELOW AVERAGE is generally used.

subnormal period of neuron a period of time, measured in milliseconds, when neuron excitability is below normal. It follows an absolute REFRACTORY PERIOD or a period of supernormal excitability.

suboccipital puncture an alternative procedure to LUMBAR PUNCTURE for obtaining access to the SUBARACHNOID SPACE for diagnostic or therapeutic purposes. It involves the insertion of a needle into the

CISTERNA MAGNA through an area near the base of the skull to collect cerebrospinal fluid. Also called **cisternal puncture**; **cistern puncture**.

subordinate *n.* **1.** one who is subject to the control or authority of another, as in the subordinate–supervisor relationship in the workplace. **2.** in animal social groups, an individual who in competition for resources is less likely to obtain the resource than another animal. In a stable social group, individuals readily learn which are dominant and which are subordinate so that resource distribution occurs with minimal fighting or direct aggression. See also ANIMAL DOMINANCE.

subordinate category a subdivision of a BASIC-LEVEL CATEGORY formed at a more specific level of categorization. So, for example, "Siamese cat" is a subordinate category of the basic-level category "cat," and "rocking-chair" is a subordinate category of "chair." A subordinate category is usually characterized by (a) high levels of resemblance among its members and (b) a relatively low level of difference between its members and those of neighboring categories (e.g., Siamese cats tend to look quite similar to each other but do not look very different from Orientals). The name of the subordinate category often incorporates the name of the basic-level category, as in the examples given above.

subordinate clause see CLAUSE; EMBEDDED SENTENCE.

subordination *n.* **1.** in linguistics, see COORDINATION. **2.** in general, the placing of something into a lower ranking category or group.

subspecies *n.* see BREED.

substance *n.* **1.** in psychopathology, a drug of abuse (e.g., alcohol, cannabis, cocaine, an inhalant), a medication (e.g., a sedative or anxiolytic), or a toxin that is capable of producing harmful effects when ingested or otherwise taken into the body. See SUBSTANCE-RELATED DISORDERS. **2.** in philosophy, that which has an independent, self-sufficient existence and remains unalterably itself even though its attributes or properties may change. Philosophers have differed over what qualifies as a substance and whether reality consists of a single substance (see MONISM) or more (see DUALISM; PLURALISM).

substance abuse in *DSM–IV–TR*, a pattern of substance use manifested by recurrent significant adverse consequences related to the repeated ingestion of a substance, which may be a drug of abuse or a medicinal drug. This diagnosis is preempted by the diagnosis of SUBSTANCE DEPENDENCE: If the criteria for substance abuse and substance dependence are both met, only the latter diagnosis is given.

Substance Abuse and Mental Health Services Administration (**SAMHSA**) an agency of the U.S. Department of Health and Human Services (HHS), established in 1992, charged with improving the quality and availability of prevention, treatment, and rehabilitative services in order to reduce illness, death, disability, and cost to society resulting from substance abuse and mental illness. SAMHSA has three program divisions: the Center for Mental Health Services, the Center for Substance Abuse Prevention, and the Center for Substance Abuse Treatment. See also ALCOHOL, DRUG ABUSE AND MENTAL HEALTH ADMINISTRATION.

substance abuse treatment inpatient and outpatient programs for individuals diagnosed with substance dependence (i.e., dependence on alcohol or any other drug) to achieve abstinence. These include but are not limited to short- and long-term residential programs (colloquially known as "rehab"), clinic- and hospital-based outpatient programs, METHADONE MAINTENANCE THERAPY, and TWELVE-STEP PROGRAMS. Also called **drug abuse treatment**. See also ALCOHOLISM TREATMENT.

substance dependence in *DSM–IV–TR*, a cluster of cognitive, behavioral, and physiological symptoms indicating continued use of a substance despite significant substance-related problems. There is a pattern of repeated substance ingestion resulting in tolerance, withdrawal symptoms if use is suspended, and an uncontrollable drive to continue use. See ALCOHOL DEPENDENCE; AMPHETAMINE DEPENDENCE; CANNABIS DEPENDENCE; COCAINE DEPENDENCE; HALLUCINOGEN DEPENDENCE; INHALANT DEPENDENCE; NICOTINE DEPENDENCE; OPIOID DEPENDENCE; SEDATIVE, HYPNOTIC, OR ANXIOLYTIC DEPENDENCE. See also SUBSTANCE ABUSE.

substance-induced anxiety disorder clinically significant anxiety (e.g., generalized anxiety, panic attacks, phobic symptoms, or obsessive-compulsive symptoms) caused by the direct physiological effects of exposure to a drug, toxin, or other substance. The anxiety symptoms may be associated with substance intoxication (e.g., alcohol, amphetamines, caffeine), substance withdrawal (e.g., alcohol, cocaine, sedatives), medication use (e.g., anesthetics, anticholinergics, thyroid medication), or exposure to heavy metals and toxins (e.g., gasoline, paint, carbon dioxide).

substance-induced mood disorder in *DSM–IV–TR*, significant and persistent mood disturbance (with depressive symptoms, manic symptoms, or both) believed to be caused directly by the physiological effects of a substance, which may be a drug of abuse, a medicinal drug, or a heavy metal or toxin (e.g., gasoline, paint, an organophosphate insecticide). When caused by a drug of abuse, the mood disturbance must occur during or within a month of intoxication or withdrawal and must be more severe than that normally experienced as part of a SUBSTANCE INTOXICATION or SUBSTANCE WITHDRAWAL syndrome. Medications that can cause mood disturbance include antihypertensives, steroids, psychotropic drugs, and many others.

substance-induced persisting amnestic disorder a disturbance in memory due to the persisting effects of a substance (see AMNESTIC DISORDER). The ability to learn new information or to recall previously learned information is impaired severely enough to interfere markedly with social or occupational functioning and to represent a significant decline from a previous level of functioning. See ALCOHOL-INDUCED PERSISTING AMNESTIC DISORDER; SEDATIVE-, HYPNOTIC-, OR ANXIOLYTIC-INDUCED PERSISTING AMNESTIC DISORDER.

substance-induced persisting dementia multiple COGNITIVE DEFICITS due to the persisting effects of substance abuse. The most notable feature is impaired memory, but there may also be aphasia (impaired expression or understanding of language), apraxia (inability to perform skilled or complex movements), agnosia (impaired ability to interpret sensations correctly), and EXECUTIVE DYSFUNCTION. See also ALCOHOL-INDUCED PERSISTING DEMENTIA.

substance-induced psychotic disorder prominent hallucinations or delusions due to the direct physiological effects of a substance. Also called **hallucinosis**. See ALCOHOL-INDUCED PSYCHOTIC DISORDER; AMPHETAMINE-INDUCED PSYCHOTIC DISORDER; CANNABIS-INDUCED PSYCHOTIC DISORDER; HALLUCINOGEN-INDUCED PSYCHOTIC DISORDER.

substance intoxication a reversible syndrome due to the recent ingestion of a specific substance, including clinically significant behavioral or psychological changes, as well as one or more signs of physiological involvement. See ALCOHOL INTOXI-CATION; AMPHETAMINE INTOXICATION; CANNABIS INTOXICATION; COCAINE INTOXICATION; HALLUCINOGEN INTOXICATION; INHALANT INTOXICATION; OPIOID INTOXICATION; SEDATIVE, HYPNOTIC, OR ANXIOLYTIC INTOXICATION.

substance intoxication delirium a reversible substance-specific syndrome that develops over a short period of time (usually hours to days) following heavy consumption of the substance. It includes disturbance of consciousness (e.g., reduced ability to focus, sustain, or shift attention), accompanied by changes in cognition (e.g., memory deficit, disorientation, or language disturbance) in excess of those usually associated with intoxication with that substance. See ALCOHOL INTOXICATION DELIRIUM; AMPHETAMINE INTOXICATION DELIRIUM; COCAINE INTOXICATION DELIRIUM; PCP INTOXICATION DELIRIUM.

substance P a NEUROPEPTIDE that functions as a neurotransmitter in both peripheral and central nervous systems. It belongs to the NEUROKININ family of transmitters. High concentrations of neurons containing substance P are localized in the DORSAL HORN of the spinal cord, where they play a role in the modulation of pain. In peripheral tissues, substance P acts as a vasodilator. It also has a role in sexual behavior and has been implicated in the regulation of mood.

substance-related disorders in *DSM–IV–TR*, a category of disorders caused by the effects of SUBSTANCES and encompassing the substance use disorders (substance abuse and substance dependence) and the substance-induced disorders (e.g., intoxication).

substance withdrawal a syndrome that develops after cessation of (or reduction in) prolonged, heavy consumption of a substance. Also called **detoxification effects**. See ALCOHOL WITHDRAWAL; AMPHETAMINE WITHDRAWAL; COCAINE WITHDRAWAL; NICOTINE WITHDRAWAL; OPIOID WITHDRAWAL; SEDATIVE, HYPNOTIC, OR ANXIOLYTIC WITHDRAWAL.

substantia gelatinosa a gelatinous-appearing mass of extensively interconnected small neurons at the tip of the DORSAL HORN of the spinal cord. Some cells in the substantia gelatinosa contain ENDORPHINS and are involved in regulation of pain. Neurons of the substantia gelatinosa extend into the MEDULLA OBLONGATA, where they form the spinal TRIGEMINAL NUCLEUS.

substantia nigra a region of gray matter in the midbrain, named for its dark pigmentation, that sends DOPAMINERGIC NEURONS to the BASAL GANGLIA. Depletion of dopaminergic neurons in this region has been implicated in PARKINSON'S DISEASE.

substantive rationality the rationality of a decision itself, as opposed to the rationality of the processes used to arrive at the decision. Compare PROCEDURAL RATIONALITY.

substantive universal see LANGUAGE UNIVERSAL.

substitute formation see SYMPTOM FORMATION.

substitutes for leadership theory a CONTINGENCY THEORY OF LEADERSHIP proposing that leadership is not important to effective group performance in some work situations. For instance, a highly structured task (see TASK STRUCTURE) may substitute for a structuring or directive leader and a highly cohesive work group may substitute for a considerate, supportive leader. See SITUATIONAL LEADERSHIP THEORY. [developed in 1978 by Steven Kerr and U.S. organizational behaviorist John Michael Jermier (1950–)]

substituting *n.* in GROUP PSYCHOTHERAPY, providing social support by such behavior as a smile, a pat, or a hug, rather than by words.

substitution *n.* the replacement of unacceptable emotions or unattainable goals with alternative satisfactions or feelings. Substitution may be viewed as a positive adaptation or solution (e.g., adoption when one cannot have a child of one's own) or as a negative, maladaptive response (e.g., emotional eating after a frustrating day at the office). See also DEFENSE MECHANISM.

substitution hypothesis see ALTERATION HYPOTHESIS.

substitution test any test in which the examinee substitutes one set of symbols for another. An example is a code test in which symbols or letters are substituted for numbers.

substrate *n.* **1.** a basis or foundation, such as the physical medium on which an animal or plant lives or grows. **2.** a chemical compound that is acted on by an enzyme. The substrate binds specifically to the enzyme's active site, thereby lowering the energy required for the reaction, which therefore can proceed much faster. When the process is over, the enzyme is unchanged but the substrate has been changed into different molecules called reaction products. The released enzyme then repeats the process with another substrate of the same composition.

subtest *n.* a separate division of a test or test battery, usually with an identifiable content (e.g., the multiplication subtest of a mathematics test).

subthalamic nucleus a part of the subthalamus that receives fibers from the GLOBUS PALLIDUS as a part of the descending pathway from the BASAL GANGLIA. It forms part of the EXTRAPYRAMIDAL TRACT.

subthalamus *n.* a part of the DIENCEPHALON of the brain, wedged between the THALAMUS and the HYPOTHALAMUS. It contains the subthalamic nucleus and functions in the regulation of movements controlled by skeletal muscles, together with the BASAL GANGLIA and the SUBSTANTIA NIGRA. **—subthalamic** *adj.*

subtherapeutic dose a dose of a drug that does not achieve a particular therapeutic effect. Although this is generally not desired, drugs intended for one purpose may be administered in subtherapeutic doses to achieve a different effect. For example, the TRICYCLIC ANTIDEPRESSANTS are rarely used in current practice in doses sufficient to alleviate depression; however, they are often used in low (subtherapeutic) doses to promote sleep or alleviate pain.

subthreshold potential a type of GRADED POTENTIAL resulting from a stimulus that is not of sufficient intensity to elicit an ACTION POTENTIAL and does not travel far beyond the immediate region of stimulation. See also CONDUCTION WITH DECREMENT; LOCAL POTENTIAL.

subtotal hysterectomy see HYSTERECTOMY.

subtraction method see DONDERS'S METHOD.

subtractive bilingualism see ADDITIVE BILINGUALISM.

subtractive mixture a form of COLOR MIXTURE in which pigments are combined, causing some wavelengths to be absorbed or subtracted from the mixture. Compare ADDITIVE COLOR MIXTURE. See also COLOR SUBTRACTION.

subtractive principle a rule of COLOR MIXTURE stating that the perceived color of a target that absorbs some wavelengths of light will be complementary to the absorbed wavelengths.

subvocal speech COVERT SPEECH associated with faint movements of the lips, tongue, and larynx that resemble speech movements but are inaudible. People often use subvocal speech, for example, when commenting to themselves on their own and others' actions, perceptions, and feelings.

successful aging 1. avoidance of disease and disability, maintenance of cognitive capacity, and continued active engagement in life. **2.** adaptation to the aging process through such strategies as SELECTIVE OPTIMIZATION WITH COMPENSATION.

successful intelligence in the TRIARCHIC THEORY OF INTELLIGENCE, the ability to succeed in life according to one's own definition of success, via adaptation to, shaping of, and selection of environments. Successful intelligence involves capitalizing on strengths and compensating for or correcting weaknesses. The three main abilities used to attain it are analytical, creative, and practical abilities, which in combination enable one to perform a wide variety of tasks.

successive-approximations method see METHOD OF SUCCESSIVE APPROXIMATIONS.

successive contrast the enhanced perception of the difference between two stimuli when these are presented in close temporal proximity to one another. See also COLOR CONTRAST. Compare SIMULTANEOUS CONTRAST.

successive discrimination in conditioning, a DISCRIMINATION between stimuli that are presented in succession.

successive induction the succession of movements of limbs or other body parts in a pattern of antagonistic reflex actions. In walking, for example, successive induction requires alternate flexion and extension of muscles in the lower limbs.

successive-intervals method see METHOD OF SUCCESSIVE INTERVALS.

successive reproduction a method used to study the way in which information in LONG-TERM MEMORY is altered by RECONSTRUCTION. Participants are asked to reproduce or recall the same material several times in succession, and the variations in their reproductions are recorded.

succinimides *pl. n.* a group of chemically related drugs that are effective in the treatment of absence seizures. Discovered in a search for an antidote for drug-induced convulsions, they produce a sedative effect and may cause behavioral changes. **Ethosuximide** is an example of a succinimide and is sold in the United States under the trade name **Zarontin**.

succinylcholine *n.* a drug that relaxes skeletal muscles, used intravenously in anesthesia and before electroconvulsive treatment. It is a neuromuscular blocking agent that does not relieve pain or produce sedation. U.S. trade name (among others): **Anectine**.

succorance need in the PERSONOLOGY of U.S. psychologist Henry Alexander Murray (1893–1988), the need for protection, aid, and support.

succubus *n.* a demon or evil spirit in female form believed to have sexual intercourse with sleeping men. Compare INCUBUS.

sucker effect an effect in which individuals reduce their personal investment in a group endeavor because of their expectation that others will think negatively of someone who works too hard or contributes too much (considering them to be a sucker). Compare COMPENSATION EFFECT. See also COLLECTIVE EFFORT MODEL.

sucking reflex a basic reflex in which the young of many mammals (including human infants) grasp the nipple with their lips and draw milk into their mouths by suction.

sudden infant death syndrome (**SIDS**) the sudden and unexpected death of a seemingly healthy infant during sleep for no apparent reason. Also called **crib death**; **cot death**.

sudden insight sudden knowledge or understanding of the truth or essential nature of something, for example, a problem or complex situation. See AHA EXPERIENCE; DISCONTINUITY HYPOTHESIS; EUREKA TASK; INSPIRATION.

sufentanil *n.* a short-acting OPIOID that binds to OPIOID RECEPTORS and is used as an analgesic supplement in the maintenance of balanced general anesthesia. See also FENTANYL. U.S. trade name: **Sufenta**.

suffering *n.* the experience of pain or acute distress, either psychological or physical. Suffering may be proportionate to the situation, as in the loss of a loved one or the experience of physical trauma, or it may be exaggerated to satisfy hidden drives or motives, such as a need for sympathy, attention, or control over others. It may also be self-induced, as in self-mutilation. See MASOCHISM; SADISM. See also UNPLEASURE.

sufficient condition see CONDITION.

sufficient statistic a statistic that uses all the information in a sample for estimating a parameter of interest.

suffix *n.* in linguistics, a MORPHEME that is added to the end of a word or word stem to create an inflected or derived form, for example, *-s* in *books*, *-ing* in *driving*, and *-ment* in *encouragement*. See AFFIXATION; INFIX; PREFIX.

suffix effect impaired memory of the last items of an auditorily presented list when the list is followed by an item that does not need to be recalled.

suggestibility *n.* **1.** a state in which the ideas, beliefs, attitudes, or actions of others are readily and uncritically adopted. **2.** an occasional synonym for HYPNOTIC SUSCEPTIBILITY.

suggestion *n.* **1.** the process of inducing acceptance of an idea or course of action in an individual through indirect means. Suggestion is usually expressed in words but may also be pictorial, as in advertisements, or subliminal. **2.** an idea or potential course of action presented to another for consideration. See also AUTOSUGGESTION; PRESTIGE SUGGESTION.

suggestion therapy a type of psychotherapy in which distressing symptoms are alleviated by direct suggestion and reassurance. The technique is sometimes used in HYPNOTHERAPY. A suggestion may be accompanied by an explanation of the meaning and the purpose of the symptoms, but no attempt is made to modify the client's basic personality.

suicidal crisis a situation in which suicide is threatened or attempted.

suicidal gesture an ATTEMPTED SUICIDE or similar self-destructive behavior, especially when the risk of death is quite low.

suicidal ideation suicidal thoughts or a preoccupation with suicide, often as a symptom of a MAJOR DEPRESSIVE EPISODE. Most instances of suicidal ideation do not progress to ATTEMPTED SUICIDE.

suicidality *n.* the risk of suicide, usually indicated by suicidal ideation or intent.

suicide *n.* the act of killing oneself. Frequently, suicide occurs in the context of a MAJOR DEPRESSIVE EPISODE, but it may also occur as a result of a substance-use disorder or schizophrenia. It sometimes occurs in the absence of any psychiatric disorder, especially in untenable situations, such as bereavement or declining health. See also ATTEMPTED SUICIDE; PASSIVE SUICIDE. **—suicidal** *adj.*

suicide attempt see ATTEMPTED SUICIDE.

suicide by cop the act, by a person who is suicidal, of purposely eliciting police gunfire.

suicide-prevention center a CRISIS-INTERVENTION facility dealing primarily with individuals who have suicidal thoughts or who have threatened or attempted suicide. Suicide-prevention centers are usually staffed by social workers or paraprofessionals with mental health preparation who are trained to deal with such emergencies in person or over a telephone hotline. Suicide-prevention centers additionally provide community education and outreach, and staff may provide bereavement support for the relatives and loved ones of an individual who has killed himself or herself.

suicidology *n.* a multiprofessional discipline devoted to the study of suicidal phenomena and their prevention. Major groups involved are (a) scientists (epidemiologists, sociologists, statisticians, demographers, and social psychologists), (b) clinicians (clinical psychologists, psychiatrists, social workers, trained volunteers, and members of the clergy), and (c) educators (public health educators and school and college personnel).

sui juris having the ability to make legal decisions and possessing full civil rights (Latin, literally: "of his own right"). A person who is *sui juris* must have reached the age of maturity (typically 18 years old), be fully mentally competent, and not be under the guidance or protection of another (e.g., a CONSERVATOR).

sukra prameha a CULTURE-BOUND SYNDROME found in Sri Lanka, with symptoms similar to those of SHEN-K'UEI.

suk-yeong *n.* see KORO.

sulcus *n.* (*pl.* **sulci**) a groove, especially one on the surface of the cerebral cortex. The term is often used synonymously with FISSURE. **—sulcal** *adj.*

sulcus centralis see CENTRAL SULCUS.

sulcus principalis in the brain of monkeys, a groove that marks the boundary between the dorsolateral FRONTAL CORTEX and the ventrolateral frontal cortex. Adjacent cortical tissue has been implicated in perception and in working memory.

Sullivan's interpersonal theory a theory that emphasizes social influences on development, focusing on key relationships and how they develop and change over time. It proposes that an individual's concept of selfhood is a reflection of others' attitudes toward that person (i.e., arising out of interpersonal relationships and situations) and posits that, although personal self-concept develops slowly, the need for personal security is present from the beginning of existence. Sullivan hypothesized that threats to self-respect are experienced as anxiety and that assaults on self-esteem emanate from sources outside the person, particularly those most intimately related to the individual across early and adolescent development. The theory proposes three phases of relationship development: (a) during preadolescence, intimacy with a same-sex friend; (b) in early adolescence, changes from same-sex cliques to mixed-sex cliques; (c) in late adolescence, full participation in intimate reciprocal relationships with a romantic partner. [Harry Stack **Sullivan** (1892–1949), U.S. psychiatrist]

sumatriptan *n.* see TRIPTANS.

summa libido see ACME.

summarizer *n.* in the psychology of groups, see TASK ROLE.

summated ratings method a method of constructing a scale to measure an attitude that uses ITEM ANALYSIS to select the best items.

summating potential a slowly changing electric potential that is recorded in the COCHLEA and is evoked by sound.

summation *n.* **1.** the process in which a neural impulse is propagated by the cumulative effects of two or more stimuli that alone would not be sufficient to activate the neuron. See SPATIAL SUMMATION; TEMPORAL SUMMATION. **2.** the increased intensity experienced in a sensation when two stimuli are presented to a receptor in rapid succession or to adjacent areas. **3.** (symbol: Σ) a mathematical operation involving the addition of numbers, quantities, or the like. For example, in a set of related values ($x_1, x_2, x_3, \ldots x_n$), a summation of all values of a general member of the set (x_i; the *i*th value), that is, the values of x_i from $i = 1$ to $i = n$, is indicated by:

$$\sum_{i=1}^{i=n} x_i, \sum_{1}^{n}, \text{ or } \sum_{i}$$

Often, the limits on the summation sign are omitted when what is intended is otherwise obvious.

summation effect a feature of BINOCULAR CELLS in the visual cortex in which the activity of the cell is greater when stimulation occurs through both eyes than when stimulation occurs through one eye. A similar phenomenon occurs in the auditory system; when both ears are stimulated there is a **binaural summation effect** of enhanced loudness.

summation time 1. the longest interval over which the perceived intensity of a stimulus is determined by the total amount of energy during the interval. **2.** the longest interval between two successive stimuli such that they are perceived as a single, continuous stimulus.

summative evaluation 1. in educational evaluation research, the appraisal of a student's achievement at the conclusion of an educational program. Also called **terminal assessment**. **2.** in evaluation research, an attempt to assess the overall effectiveness of a program after it is in operation (in contrast to FORMATIVE EVALUATION, which is used to help in the development of the program). Also called **ex post facto evaluation**. See also OUTCOME EVALUATION.

summer depression an atypical variant of SEASONAL AFFECTIVE DISORDER in which MAJOR DEPRESSIVE EPISODES tend to occur in the summer months.

Sumner, Francis Cecil (1895–1954) U.S. psychologist. Sumner received his PhD in psychology from Clark University in 1920. He was the first African American to receive a doctorate in psychology in the United States. Mentored by G. Stanley HALL, he wrote his dissertation on the psychoanalytic theories of Sigmund FREUD and Alfred ADLER. Sumner taught at a number of African American colleges and universities before joining the faculty of Howard University in Washington, DC, where he became head of the psychology department in 1928 and remained throughout his career. He is best known for his administrative and teaching roles, creating programs to train Black psychologists before the era of desegregation. Under Sumner's leadership, Howard University trained more Black psychologists than all other American colleges and universities combined. Sumner is also noted for establishing the first psychology of religion courses at African American institutions in the United States and for conducting research assessing attitudes of Black and White students toward justice in the American legal system. See also PSYCHOLOGY OF RELIGION.

sum of cross products a statistical value obtained for two sets of variables X_i and Y_i defined by the summation

$$\Sigma\,(X_i - \bar{X})\,(Y_i - \bar{Y}),$$

where $\bar{X}$ is the mean value of X_i and $\bar{Y}$ the mean value of Y_i. It is used in MULTIVARIATE ANALYSIS OF VARIANCE.

sum of squares the total obtained by adding together the squares of each deviation score in a sample (i.e., each score minus the sample mean squared, and then added together). Thus, for a set of variables X_i,

$\Sigma(X_i - \bar{X})^2$,

where $\bar{X}$ is the mean value of X_i. See ROOT-MEAN-SQUARE.

sum strategy a simple addition strategy used by young children that involves counting together the two addends of a problem. For example, for the problem 3 + 2 = ?, a child would say, "1, 2, 3...4, 5."

sun compass the use of the sun as a directional stimulus in orientation and navigation. Because the sun appears to move across the sky during the day and has different trajectories in different seasons, a sun compass must be coupled with some form of TIME ESTIMATION. To head south at 9 a.m. one needs to keep the sun on the left, but at 3 p.m. one needs to keep the sun on the right. Studies of several species, ranging from bees to fish and birds, have demonstrated a time-compensated sun compass. For nocturnal species, there is evidence of a **star compass**.

sundown syndrome the tendency, particularly among older adults with dementia or individuals in institutional care, to experience reduced levels of psychological functioning late in the day. Also called **sundowning**.

Sunset procedures U.S. federal legislation requiring (a) that all federal programs be reauthorized every 10 years in compliance with an established schedule, (b) that such reauthorization be preceded by standardized committee reviews, (c) that inventories of federal programs be established and maintained, and (d) that Congressional committees select a few programs for in-depth reexamination. **Sunset bills** are laws proposed to the legislature recommending standards and guidelines for formalized procedures to evaluate programs that are funded by federal or state governments. **Sunset acts** comprise legislation established by federal and state governments that requires assessment of federally or state-funded programs by evaluation researchers.

suo yang see KORO.

superconducting quantum interference device (**SQUID**) a device used in MAGNETOENCEPHALOGRAPHY for detecting magnetic waves in the brain. These highly sensitive devices must be used in rooms that are screened from all outside magnetic sources. They are useful in the study of in vivo human brain processes.

superconscious *n.* **1.** a New Age term for transpersonal awareness. **2.** in certain Eastern traditions, with variation (see BUDDHISM; HINDUISM; TAOISM), a state in which the individual attains highest knowledge, freedom from pain, and perfect spiritual insight because the mind is free from passion and desire. At their most profound level, the practices of MEDITATION and YOGA (among others) may be directed toward the ultimate achievement of the superconscious state.

superego *n.* in psychoanalytic theory, the moral component of the personality that represents society's standards and determines personal standards of right and wrong, or conscience, as well as aims and aspirations (see EGO-IDEAL). In the classic Freudian tripartite structure of the psyche, the EGO, which controls personal impulses and directs actions, operates by the rules and principles of the superego, which basically stem from parental demands and prohibitions. The formation of the superego occurs on an unconscious level, beginning in the first 5 years of life and continuing throughout childhood and adolescence and into adulthood, largely through identification with the parents and later with admired models of behavior. See also HETERONOMOUS SUPEREGO; PRIMITIVE SUPEREGO.

superego anxiety in psychoanalytic theory, anxiety caused by unconscious superego activity that produces feelings of guilt and demands for atonement. Compare EGO ANXIETY; ID ANXIETY.

superego resistance in psychoanalytic theory, a type of RESISTANCE to the psychoanalytic process created by the superego. It generates a sense of guilt and gives rise to the need for punishment in the form of persistent symptoms. Compare REPRESSION-RESISTANCE; ID RESISTANCE.

superego sadism in psychoanalytic theory, the aggressive, rigid, and punitive aspect of the superego, or conscience. Its energy is derived from the destructive forces of the ID, and its intensity and strength are dependent upon the violent and sadistic fantasies of the child's primordial strivings. See SADISM.

superficial *adj.* **1.** in anatomy, located close to or at the surface of the body or of an organ. **2.** having no deep significance or real substance.

superior *adj.* in anatomy, higher, above, or toward the head. Compare INFERIOR.

superior colliculus either of a pair of rounded prominences (colliculi) in the brain, one of which lies near each CEREBRAL PEDUNCLE, rostrally to the INFERIOR COLLICULUS and immediately beneath the PINEAL GLAND. The superior colliculus receives fibers from the OPTIC TRACT and projects fibers to several stations, including the LATERAL GENICULATE NUCLEUS and the RETICULAR FORMATION. The superior colliculus gives rise to the TECTOSPINAL TRACT and is involved in orienting movements of the head and eye toward external stimuli.

superior function in the ANALYTIC PSYCHOLOGY of Carl JUNG, the dominating function among the four basic functions—seeing, thinking, intuiting, and feeling—that rules the conscious ego and dominates the other three, which become INFERIOR FUNCTIONS in the unconscious. The superior function determines the FUNCTIONAL TYPE of the individual.

superior intelligence an arbitrary category of general intelligence attained by only 15% of the population. It includes individuals with an IQ of 120 or more on both the WECHSLER ADULT INTELLIGENCE SCALE and the STANFORD–BINET INTELLIGENCE SCALE.

superiority complex in the INDIVIDUAL PSYCHOLOGY of Alfred ADLER, an exaggerated opinion of one's abilities and accomplishments that derives from an overcompensation for feelings of inferiority (see COMPENSATION). Compare INFERIORITY COMPLEX.

superior longitudinal fasciculus a bundle of nerve fibers that connects ridges (gyri) in the cerebral cortex as distant as the FRONTAL LOBE and the OCCIPITAL LOBE. Most are shorter fibers that connect closer gyri. Near the middle of the fasciculus, some fibers coming from both directions turn abruptly upward into the motor and somatosensory areas of the cortex.

superior oblique the extrinsic EYE MUSCLE that rotates the eye upward when the eye is pointing toward the nose and contributes to upward motion (together with the SUPERIOR RECTUS) when it contracts with the eye pointing straight ahead.

superior olivary complex a collection of brain nuclei located in the PONS. The cells receive excitatory input from the contralateral COCHLEAR NUCLEI in the brainstem and inhibitory input from the ipsilateral cochlear nuclei. The contralateral input comes through the TRAPEZOID BODY, a concentration of transverse nerve fibers in the pons. Also called **superior olive**.

superior rectus the extrinsic EYE MUSCLE that rotates the eye upward when the eye is pointing away from the nose and that contributes to upward motion (together with the SUPERIOR OBLIQUE) when it contracts with the eye pointing straight ahead.

superior sagittal sinus a part of the system of veins that drain blood from the cerebral tissues. It runs across the top of the cerebral cortex, draining venous blood from an area above the eye to the transverse sinus, which empties into the internal jugular vein.

superior temporal gyrus a ridge (gyrus) that extends along the upper surface of the TEMPORAL LOBE of the brain, bounded above by the LATERAL SULCUS and laterally by the superior temporal sulcus.

superman *n.* the usual English translation of the German word *Ubermensch*, introduced by German philosopher Friedrich Wilhelm Nietzsche (1844–1900). For Nietzsche the superman is an ideal type of a human life, one who brings into reality the most creative and powerful attributes of humanity, who seizes life courageously in response to the Wille zur Macht (see WILL TO POWER), and avoids the "slave mentality" that Nietzsche took to be characteristic of the culture of his time. As Nietzsche considered few capable of such affirmative, authentic living, the ideal is essentially aristocratic and nondemocratic. Although the concept has no racial elements, the Nazis later used it to affirm the supposed superiority of the Aryan race and to justify aggression and oppressive racial policies.

supernatural *adj.* of or relating to phenomena that appear to depart from or transcend the laws of the physical universe, especially when these phenomena are taken to be the work of gods, demons, or spirits. Compare PRETERNATURAL. **—supernaturalism** *n.*

supernormal *adj.* **1.** exceeding or beyond the normal. **2.** in psychometrics, denoting a category of individuals or their attributes that are far above the normal range.

supernormal stimulus a stimulus that by virtue of being larger or more intense than those normally encountered has a greater behavioral effect than the natural stimulus. For example, a gull presented with its own egg and a much larger, artificial egg will attempt to incubate the larger egg. The exaggerated response to supernormal stimuli may be involved in the evolution of certain ornaments, such as peacock tails or the antlers of some ungulates. See PEAK SHIFT; SENSORY BIAS.

superordinate category a high-level category that subsumes a number of BASIC-LEVEL CATEGORIES and reflects a more abstract level of categorization. So, for example, "animal" is a superordinate category including the basic-level categories "cat," "fish," "elephant," and so on. A superordinate category is usually characterized by (a) low levels of resemblance between members and (b) fundamental differences between its members and those of other categories (e.g., an elephant is not much like a fish but both are very different from a tree).

superordinate goal **1.** a goal that takes precedence over one or more other, more conditional, goals. **2.** a goal that can be attained only if the members of two or more groups work together by pooling their skills, efforts, and resources. In the ROBBERS' CAVE EXPERIMENT studying intergroup conflict reduction, superordinate goals were introduced by creating emergencies and problems that could only be resolved through the joint efforts of both groups.

superposition *n.* see LINEAR SYSTEM.

supersensitivity *n.* heightened responsiveness to a particular neurotransmitter. For example, prolonged blockade of DOPAMINE RECEPTORS by some antipsychotic drugs leads to an increase in the number of dopamine receptors; discontinuation of the drug may then result in a marked increase of psychotic symptoms, a condition called **supersensitivity psychosis**.

superstition *n.* **1.** a belief or practice founded upon the operation of supernatural or magical forces, such as charms or omens. **2.** any unscientific belief accepted without question. **—superstitious** *adj.*

superstitious behavior the behavior that results from ACCIDENTAL REINFORCEMENT of an action so that the organism continues to repeat it. For example, a rat that turned in a circle before accidentally hitting a bar and obtaining food might continue turning in a circle before each bar press.

superstitious control the illusion that one can influence outcomes through various practices designed to protect oneself, alter the environment, or affect a situation. Such practices include following specific behavior patterns (see SUPERSTITIOUS RITUAL). Some people maintain that superstitious control serves a positive psychological function in averting the development of LEARNED HELPLESSNESS. See FAITH HEALING; MAGICAL THINKING.

superstitious ritual a specific pattern of behavior that is believed to control one's performance and its outcome. Failure to follow the ritual is believed to have negative effects on performance and outcome. In sport, for example, such rituals might include putting items of a uniform on in a specific order, listening to a specific piece of music before beginning to play, and entering the competition venue in a specific order. Also called **superstitious routine**.

supertaster *n.* a person with uncommonly low gustatory thresholds and strong responses to moderate concentrations of taste stimuli. Supertasters have unusually high numbers of TASTE BUDS.

supervalent thought an extreme preoccupation with a single topic. See OBSESSION; RUMINATION.

supervenience *n.* in philosophy, the condition of being dependant on a set of facts or properties in such a way that change only occurs subsequent to change in the original facts or properties themselves. Thus, for example, conscious experience depends on (supervenes) a level of reality that transcends the brain and mental processes. **—supervene** *vb.* **—supervenient** *adj.*

supervised analysis see CONTROL ANALYSIS.

supervision *n.* in psychotherapy and counseling, clinical guidance and direction (i.e., critical evaluation) that is provided by a qualified and experienced therapist or counselor—the **supervisor**—to a trainee. Supervision is required while the trainee learns therapeutic techniques; the trainee may also provide the supervisor with process notes, audiotapes, and videotapes of a therapeutic session. A prescribed number of hours of supervision is required by state licensing boards as part of the requirements for obtaining a license in a mental health field. Also called **therapy supervision**.

supervisory analysis see CONTROL ANALYSIS.

supervisory attentional system see EXECUTIVE.

supervisory control in ergonomics, the role allocated to the human operator in highly automated systems. The operator is responsible for system monitoring, interpretation, decision making, and manual correction or intervention. Reducing the operator's role to one of supervisory control may result in either optimal or degraded performance, depending chiefly on system design. See also CLUMSY AUTOMATION; FUNCTION ALLOCATION.

superwoman syndrome a set of characteristics found in a woman who performs or attempts to perform all the duties typically associated with several different full-time roles, such as wage earner, mother, homemaker, and wife.

supination *n.* **1.** the act of turning the forearm so that the palm faces upward, or the condition resulting from this action. **2.** the act of turning the foot so that the sole faces inward and the medial (inner) margin is raised (as in walking on the outside of one's feet), or the condition resulting from this action. **3.** the state or condition of being supine (see POSTURE). Compare PRONATION. **—supinate** *vb.*

supplementary motor area an area of the MOTOR CORTEX with SOMATOTOPIC ORGANIZATION involved in planning and learning new movements that have coordinated sequences. In contrast to the PREMOTOR AREA, neuronal input to the supplementary motor area is triggered more by internal representations than by external events.

supplication *n.* in SELF-PRESENTATION theory, a strategy that involves depicting oneself as weak, needy, or dependent, so as to motivate others to provide assistance or care. **—supplicate** *vb.*

supported employment a VOCATIONAL REHABILITATION program that places individuals with disabilities directly into the paid competitive working environment as quickly as possible. With an emphasis on matching an individual with an appropriate employer and work environment rather than adapting the person to the environment, it involves individualized, rapid placement and ongoing support, training, and assessment that integrates both vocational and personal needs. Supported employment differs from a SHELTERED WORKSHOP in that the latter occurs in a controlled, noncompetitive working environment. See also TRANSITIONAL EMPLOYMENT.

supported living a situation in which people with mental retardation live singly or in small groups in apartments or houses (usually rented but sometimes leased or purchased) where drop-in assistance in performing activities of daily living and learning independent living skills is available. Varying degrees of assistance are provided by staff, depending on the skills of the particular residents.

supported retirement a daily or regular program or schedule of activity for an aging or aged person with mental retardation that emphasizes socialization and recreational engagement, rather than the habilitation activities and vocational involvement typical of adult mental retardation day services.

support group a group similar in some ways to a SELF-HELP GROUP, in that members who share a problem come together to provide help, comfort, and guidance. A primary distinguishing feature of support groups is in their leadership: a professional or agency-based facilitator who often does not share the problem of members. In addition, support groups often last for only a limited predetermined number of sessions, and a fee for attendance is sometimes charged.

supportive ego a member of an ACTIVITY-THERAPY group who helps a fellow member work out difficulties within his or her psyche, mind, or personality. [first described by 20th-century Russian-born U.S. psychotherapist Samuel Richard Slavson]

supportive-expressive psychotherapy a form of brief DYNAMIC PSYCHOTHERAPY that focuses on the therapist–client relationship and on relationships outside of therapy to define a central relationship pattern that is the focus of treatment. [developed by U.S. clinical psychologists Lester Luborsky (1920–) and Paul Crits-Christoph]

supportiveness *n.* in psychotherapy and counseling, an attitude or response of acceptance, encouragement, or reassurance displayed by the therapist or counselor.

supportive psychotherapy a form of therapy that aims to relieve emotional distress and symptoms without probing into the sources of conflicts or attempting to alter basic personality structure. Specific methods used include reassurance, reeducation, advice, persuasion, environmental changes, pastoral counseling, bereavement therapy, bibliotherapy, remotivation, and encouragement of desirable behavior. Such measures are frequently applied to individuals with relatively minor or limited problems, as well as to fragile or hospitalized patients, as a means of maintaining morale and preventing deterioration.

supportive services 1. programs ancillary to the treatment or rehabilitation of people with illnesses or disabilities. **2.** social service programs (e.g., child care or transportation) that are necessary to enable an individual to participate in the workforce or function more independently.

suppository *n.* a bullet-shaped medicinal preparation for rectal administration. It dissolves in the rectum to release its active component, which is absorbed through the rectal mucosa. Vaginal suppositories are available for treating gynecological conditions.

suppression *n.* a conscious effort to put disturbing thoughts and experiences out of mind, or to control and inhibit the expression of unacceptable impulses and feelings. It is distinct from the unconscious DEFENSE MECHANISM of REPRESSION in psychoanalytic theory. **—suppress** *vb.*

suppressive therapy a form of psychotherapy directed toward the reinforcement of the client's defense mechanisms and the suppression (rather than expression) of distressing experiences and feelings. Compare EXPRESSIVE THERAPY.

suppressor variable a variable that reduces (suppresses) the apparent relationship between two other variables. See THIRD-VARIABLE PROBLEM.

suprachiasmatic nucleus (**SCN**) a small region of the HYPOTHALAMUS in the brain, above the OPTIC CHIASM, that is the location of the CIRCADIAN OSCILLATOR, which controls circadian rhythms. It receives direct input from the retina. See also BIOLOGICAL CLOCK.

supraliminal *adj.* describing stimulation that is above the DIFFERENCE THRESHOLD or ABSOLUTE THRESHOLD. **Supraliminal difference** is the difference between stimuli that are above the difference threshold.

supraliminal perception 1. the processing of sensory data that are above the threshold of perception (i.e., that are not subliminal). **2.** the processing of information that can be detected by the senses but that is not consciously interpreted by the perceiver. Examples include the hum of conversation in a crowded room or visual information displayed very briefly during experiments on perception. Compare SUBLIMINAL PERCEPTION.

supranuclear palsy see PROGRESSIVE SUPRANUCLEAR PALSY.

supraoptic nucleus a nucleus of the HYPOTHALAMUS that lies above the OPTIC CHIASM. Neurons in this nucleus secrete the hormones OXYTOCIN and VASOPRESSIN.

suprarenal gland see ADRENAL GLAND.

suprasegmental *adj.* in linguistics, denoting those phonological features of speech that extend over a series of SEGMENTS rather than forming individual PHONEMES. In English the principal suprasegmental features are TONE (pitch), STRESS, and JUNCTURE. Also called **prosodic**. See also PARALANGUAGE; PROSODY.

suprasegmental reflex see SPINAL REFLEX.

surd *n.* an UNVOICED consonant.

surface color a color perceived as localized on a surface, as opposed to a color that permeates an object (BULKY COLOR) or a FILM COLOR that is not localized to a surface or an object.

surface dyslexia a form of acquired dyslexia (see ALEXIA) in which a person is overly reliant on spelling-to-sound correspondence and therefore has difficulty reading irregularly spelled words. Surface dyslexia manifested as a form of DEVELOPMENTAL DYSLEXIA has also been described. See also DEEP DYSLEXIA. [first described in 1973 by British neuropsychologists John C. Marshall and Freda Newcombe (1925–2001)]

surface structure (**s-structure**) in the TRANSFORMATIONAL GENERATIVE GRAMMAR developed by Noam CHOMSKY, the structure of a grammatical sentence as it actually occurs in speech or writing, as opposed to its underlying DEEP STRUCTURE or abstract logical form. In Chomsky's theory, the surface structure of a sentence is generated from the deep structure by a series of transformational rules involving the addition, deletion, or reordering of sentence elements. Psycholinguists have investigated whether and to what extent this may serve as a model for the cognitive processes involved in forming and interpreting sentences.

surface therapy psychotherapy directed toward relieving the client's symptoms and emotional stress through such measures as reassurance, suggestion, and direct attempts to modify attitudes and behavior patterns, rather than through exploration and analysis of unconscious motivation and underlying dynamics. Compare DEPTH THERAPY.

surface traits in CATTELL'S FACTORIAL THEORY OF PERSONALITY, a group of 35 characteristics that can be directly inferred from an individual's observable behavior. Surface traits appear consistently and are thought to cluster and form SOURCE TRAITS, which are regarded as the underlying building blocks of personality.

surgency *n.* in trait psychology, a personality trait marked by cheerfulness, responsiveness, spontaneity, and sociability, but at a level below that of EXTRAVERSION or MANIA. [defined by British psychologist Raymond Cattell (1905–1998)] **—surgent** *adj.*

surplus energy theory the hypothesis that children and young animals engage in LOCOMOTOR PLAY because they have excess energy that needs to be expended. See also PLAY.

surplus meaning 1. any significance attributed to observed data that goes beyond what is strictly observable. In behaviorist schools of psychology, explanatory concepts that refer to vague or undetectable internal processes are often dismissed as surplus meaning. **2.** in literary analysis, the idea that every use of language involves a range of meanings beyond the surface or intended use. This is a basic principle of DECONSTRUCTION and POSTSTRUCTURALISM.

surprisal *n.* in INFORMATION THEORY, a measure of the predictability of a SIGNAL. A signal conveys information to the extent that it reduces the uncertainty that existed before it was received. In general, the less predictable a signal, the more information it conveys. A highly informative signal is highly unpredictable and therefore considerably reduces uncertainty; such a signal is sometimes said to have a high surprisal value.

surprise *n.* an emotion typically resulting from the violation of an expectation or the detection of novelty in the environment. According to various theories, it is considered to be one of the emotions that have a universal pattern of facial expression. The physiological response includes raising or arching the eyebrows, opening the eyes wide, opening the mouth wide in an oval shape, and gasping.

surprisingness *n.* in psychological aesthetics, a measure of the degree to which one's expectations are disconfirmed.

surrogate *n.* a person or object that substitutes for the role of an individual who has a significant position in a family or group. The surrogate may substitute for a parent, child, or mate who is absent from the scene. Young animals may use soft cloth material as a surrogate mother, and young humans may use stuffed toys as surrogate companions.

surrogate decision making a provision in law or a regulation permitting the appointment of a surrogate for a person, frequently a person with mental retardation, dementia, or a mental disorder, who is not competent to make specific decisions regarding consent to medical, surgical, or other health care procedures. The surrogate makes these determinations on behalf of the person.

surrogate father see FATHER SURROGATE.

surrogate mother see MOTHER SURROGATE.

sursumvergence *n.* the deviation or turning upward of one eye in relation to the other. See STRABISMUS.

survey 1. *n.* a study in which a group of participants is selected from a population and some selected data about or opinions of those participants are collected, measured, and analyzed. The results thus obtained may then be extrapolated to the whole population. See also SURVEY RESEARCH. **2.** *vb.* to carry out a survey.

survey error any biased or unbiased (i.e., random) error obtained in SURVEY RESEARCH.

survey feedback an ORGANIZATIONAL DEVELOPMENT technique in which employees are surveyed on their attitudes toward various workplace issues. The summarized results are then discussed by a series of small groups who suggest interpretations and solutions.

survey knowledge a mental representation of a spatial environment that resembles a map, as if one has a bird's-eye view of the environment, as contrasted with route knowledge (see ROUTE LEARNING).

survey research a research method in which the investigator attempts to determine the current state of a population with regard to one or more attributes. Survey research does not involve any intervention imposed by the investigator.

survival analysis a set of statistical procedures used to build models calculating the time until some event occurs (e.g., the death of a patient, the failure of a piece of equipment). Also called **event history analysis**.

survival instinct see SELF-PRESERVATION INSTINCT.

survival of the fittest the tendency of individuals that are better adapted to a particular environment to be more successful at surviving and producing offspring. This concept is inherent in the theory of evolution by NATURAL SELECTION, as proposed by British naturalists Charles Darwin (1809–1882) and Alfred Russel Wallace (1823–1913). See also COMPETITION FOR RESOURCES; DARWINIAN FITNESS.

survival value the degree to which a behavioral, physiological, or physical trait will contribute to REPRODUCTIVE SUCCESS. A trait that can be shown to increase the probability of reproductive success in a given environment has high survival value.

survivor guilt remorse or guilt for having survived a catastrophic situation when others did not or for not suffering the ills that others had to endure. It is a common reaction stemming in part from a feeling of having failed to do enough to prevent the tragedy or to save those who did not survive. Survivor guilt is also experienced by family members who are found not to carry deleterious genetic mutations that have led to disease and, often, death in other family members or simply by family or friends who feel that they did not do enough to succor their loved ones prior to death.

survivorship *n.* **1.** the state of having a typical life and life span after overcoming severe diseases (e.g., cancer), traumatic life events (e.g., child abuse), or environmental disaster (e.g., earthquake). **2.** the state of living into very old age.

susceptibility *n.* **1.** vulnerability to, or the increased likelihood of being affected by, a physical or mental disease or disorder. **2.** capacity for deep feeling or emotional arousal.

susceptibility rhythms cyclical variations in sensitivity to infections or allergic responses.

SUSOPS acronym for SUSTAINED OPERATIONS.

suspense *n.* a state of anxious expectancy.

suspensory ligament see ZONULES.

suspiciousness *n.* an attitude of mistrust toward the motives or sincerity of others. Although a degree of suspiciousness in certain situations can be natural and likely serves the purposes of self-preservation or survival, extreme, pervasive suspiciousness is a common characteristic of individuals with PARANOID PERSONALITY DISORDER.

sustained attention attentional focus on a task for an extended length of time.

sustained operations (**SUSOPS**) an extended work schedule under demanding conditions. A sustained workload can combine with fatigue and reduced or fragmented sleep to degrade performance, productivity, safety, and the effectiveness of an operation.

sustained-release preparation see SLOW-RELEASE PREPARATION.

susto *n.* a CULTURE-BOUND SYNDROME occurring among Latinos in the United States and populations in Mexico, Central America, and South America. After experiencing a frightening event, individuals fear that their soul has left their body. Symptoms include weight loss, fatigue, muscle pains, headache, diarrhea, unhappiness, troubled sleep, lack of motivation, and low self-esteem. Also called **chibih**; **espanto**; **pasmo**; **perdida del alma**; **tripa ida**.

swallowing *n.* the process by which ingested material (food, liquid, etc.) is transferred from the mouth cavity to the stomach, which involves a complex series of reflex muscle contractions and relaxations. The muscles of the cheeks, tongue, and roof of the mouth first contract to form a chute, after which the tongue presses upward and backward against the hard palate. As the substance to be swallowed passes toward the back of the mouth, the SOFT PALATE is raised to close the opening to the nasopharynx. At the same time, the epiglottis is lowered over the opening to the trachea (windpipe) to prevent food or fluid entering the respiratory system, and the larynx moves upward to form a seal against the lower side of the epiglottis. As the substance swallowed enters the esophagus, it is moved along by alternate contractions of two layers of muscles, composed of, respectively, longitudinal and circular muscle fibers. Hence, the food or fluid is advanced toward the stomach, regardless of body position. Also called **deglutition**.

sweating *n.* the discharge of a secretion (sweat) from the sweat glands in the skin. Sweating is important in control of body temperature and is a route of excretion of water, salts, and some urea. Also called **perspiration**.

sweet *adj.* denoting the pleasurable taste associated with sugars, an immediate source of energy. Sugars are detected by specialized proteins contained in a subset of taste receptor cells mainly toward the front of the tongue (see FUNGIFORM PAPILLAE). **—sweetness** *n.*

swinging *n.* slang for uninhibited sexual expression, for example, such activities as wife swapping, one-night stands, group sex, and experimentation with unusual sexual activities (e.g., bondage and discipline).

switch cost in studies of task switching, the loss of efficiency associated with redirecting attention from one task to another.

switch device the input mechanism that allows a person to activate an ENVIRONMENTAL CONTROL DEVICE. See also CONTROL DEVICE; FEEDBACK DEVICE; TARGET DEVICE.

switching *n.* **1.** in psychotherapy, changing the course of the discussion during a session. This may be done by the client, either purposefully or unconsciously, when the discussion is too close to sensitive issues. Switching may also be done by the therapist to change the discussion to more relevant therapeutic issues. **2.** in multiple personality disorders, the often rapid movement between one personality and another.

switch process the process by which a person with a BIPOLAR DISORDER experiences the transition from a MAJOR DEPRESSIVE EPISODE to a MANIC EPISODE or vice versa. These processes usually include brief periods of relatively unimpaired functioning.

Sydenham's chorea see CHOREA. [Thomas **Sydenham** (1624–1689), English physician]

syllabary *n.* a writing system that represents each SYLLABLE (rather than each PHONEME) with a separate symbol. Compare ALPHABET.

syllable *n.* in linguistics, a unit of articulation consisting of a stand-alone vowel or a vowel combined with one or more consonants. The syllable length of a speaker's sentences is often used as a standard of comparison in psycholinguistic research and in psychometric tests of language development and mental ability. **—syllabic** *adj.*

syllogism *n.* a form of DEDUCTIVE REASONING in which a categorial proposition (i.e., one taking the form *all X are Y*, *no X are Y*, *some X are Y*, or *some X are not Y*) is combined with a second such proposition having one of its terms in common with the first to yield a third such proposition (the conclusion). For example: *All men are mortal; some men are tall; therefore some mortals are tall.* Of the numerous possible combinations of terms, only 24 are formally valid. An example of an invalid syllogism would be: *Some women are tall; all mothers are women; therefore some mothers are tall.* Although the conclusion is doubtless empirically correct, it cannot be deduced from these premises. **—syllogistic** *adj.*

Sylvian fissure see LATERAL SULCUS.

sym- *prefix* see SYN-.

symbiosis *n.* **1.** in animal behavior, any relationship in which two species live together in close association, especially one in which both species benefit (see MUTUALISM). For example, in tropical Amazonia, a species of ant lives on a particular tree species that it uses for food and shelter, at the same time removing lichen and other parasites that might harm the tree. Also called **biological symbiosis**. **2.** in developmental psychology, the stage in infantile development when the infant's dependence is total and he or she is neither biologically nor psychologically separated from the mother. See also SEPARATION–INDIVIDUATION. [proposed by Hungarian-born U.S. psychoanalyst Margaret S. Mahler (1897–1985)] **3.** a mutually reinforcing relationship in which one individual is overdependent on another to satisfy needs. Such a relationship hampers the development or independence of both individuals and usually results in dysfunction when the dominant individual is unwilling to provide for the dependent individual. Also called **symbiotic relationship**. **—symbiotic** *adj.*

symbiotic infantile psychosis see SYMBIOTIC PSYCHOSIS.

symbiotic marriage a marriage or partnership of two individuals who are dependent upon each other for the gratification of certain psychological needs. Both partners may have neurotic or otherwise unusual needs that could not be satisfied easily outside of their relationship. Compare SYNERGIC MARRIAGE.

symbiotic psychosis an obsolete name for a condition, occurring in children between the ages of 2 and 5, that is characterized by complete emotional dependence on the mother, inability to tolerate separation from her, reactions of anger and panic if any separation is threatened, and developmental lag. Some of these features are characteristic of SEPARATION ANXIETY DISORDER. Also called **symbiotic infantile psychosis**; **symbiotic infantile psychotic syndrome**. [first described by Hungarian-born U.S. psychoanalyst Margaret Mahler (1897–1985)]

symbiotic relationship see SYMBIOSIS.

symbol *n.* **1.** any object, figure, or image that represents something else, such as a flag, a logo, a pictogram, or a religious symbol (e.g., a cross). A written or spoken word can be regarded as a particular kind of symbol (see ARBITRARY SYMBOL; SIGNIFIER). In literature and art, symbols are generally suggestive rather than explicit in their meaning: For example, a rose may suggest ideas of beauty, love, femininity, and transience without being limited to any of these meanings in particular. Carl JUNG maintained that the symbols of religion, mythology, and art throw special light on the racial unconscious. See also SIGN. **2.** in psychoanalytic theory, a disguised representation of a repressed idea, impulse, or wish. See also SYMBOLISM. **3.** in safety engineering, a pictorial device used in risk communications to warn workers or consumers of the hazards associated with tools or systems. See SIGNAL WORD PANEL. **—symbolic** *adj.*

symbol–digit test a task in which a person is given a list of symbols, each with a corresponding digit, and then a long list of symbols without the digits, each of which the participant has to fill in. The test measures the number of symbol–digit pairs completed in a fixed time or the time taken to complete a fixed number of pairs. See also CODE TEST.

symbol grounding the process of establishing and maintaining the correspondence between symbolic representations of objects and the actual physical objects in the real-world environment. For example, if a child is instructed to retrieve the green box from the shelf, he or she cannot do so properly unless able to associate the internal representation of the item conveyed by the concepts of "green" and "box" with the appropriate sensory experience actually associated with the physical object itself. Also called **perceptual anchoring**.

Symbolic *n.* the realm of symbols or SIGNIFIERS: one of three aspects of the psychoanalytic field defined by French psychoanalyst Jacques Lacan (1901–1981). The achievement of symbolization marks the beginning of ego differentiation and is associated with the infant's entrance into the world of language, culture, law, and morality. The other two realms are the IMAGINARY and the REAL. See also MIRROR PHASE; NAME-OF-THE-FATHER.

symbolic action see SYMPTOMATIC ACT.

symbolic attitude the evaluation of an ATTITUDE OBJECT based on the extent to which it is seen as consistent or inconsistent with a person's moral values. See also VALUE-EXPRESSIVE FUNCTION OF AN ATTITUDE.

symbolic consciousness awareness of events whose meaning goes beyond their sensory contents.

symbolic displacement the process of transferring a response, usually emotional, from its original stimulus to one that represents it. For example, a man who harbors homicidal impulses might develop a morbid fear of knives or guns.

symbolic function in Jean PIAGET's theory, the underlying symbolic nature of cognition, occurring toward the end of the SENSORIMOTOR STAGE and expressed through DEFERRED IMITATION, language, SYMBOLIC PLAY, and mental IMAGERY. Also called **semiotic function**.

symbolic interactionism a sociological theory that assumes that self-concept is created through interpretation of symbolic gestures, words, actions, and appearances exhibited by others during social interaction. In contrast to Freudian and other approaches that postulate extensive inner dispositions and regard social interaction as resulting from them, symbolic interactionists believe that inner structures result from social interactions. U.S. social thinkers George Herbert Mead (1863–1931) and Charles Horton Cooley (1864–1929) are recognized exponents of this view. See GENERALIZED OTHER; LOOKING-GLASS SELF; REFLECTED APPRAISALS.

symbolic learning theory a theory that attempts to explain how IMAGERY works in PERFORMANCE ENHANCEMENT. It suggests that imagery develops and enhances a coding system that creates a mental blueprint of what has to be done to complete an action.

symbolic logic the systematic use of symbols in logical analysis. In modern symbolic logic, the symbols used are those of mathematics, particularly those of SET THEORY. The language of mathematics is well suited to the investigation of the precise conditions of validity in arguments because it is an ARTIFICIAL LANGUAGE, lacking the connotations and subjective meanings present in a NATURAL LANGUAGE, and because relations between mathematical entities are simple and precisely defined. See LOGIC.

symbolic matching to sample see ARBITRARY MATCHING TO SAMPLE.

symbolic mode a stage of cognitive development in which SYMBOLIC REPRESENTATION enables the young child to depict and convey ideas through the use of words, sounds, and play. The child can, for example, imagine he or she is a fire engine and make siren noises while pushing a block that represents a speeding engine. Also called **symbolic stage**. Compare ENACTIVE MODE; ICONIC MODE. [proposed by U.S. developmental psychologist Jerome Seymour Bruner (1915–)]

symbolic play a form of play in which the child pretends to be another person, real or imaginary, and imitates activities involved in such situations as preparing a dinner or putting a baby to bed. Symbolic play may or may not be social and may or may not include objects. Also called **make-believe**. See also FANTASY PLAY; IMAGINARY COMPANION; SOCIODRAMATIC PLAY.

symbolic process **1.** in cognitive psychology, any cognitive activity in which ideas, images, or other MENTAL REPRESENTATIONS serve as mediators of thought. The term is often used to distinguish the HIGHER MENTAL PROCESSES from either (a) lower cognitive functions, such as perception, or (b) those neurophysiological processes that underlie processing at the symbolic level. See also SYMBOLIC THINKING; THINKING. **2.** in psychoanalysis, any operation in which a SYMBOL is substituted for a repressed thought or impulse. See also SYMBOLIZATION.

symbolic realization the fulfillment of a blocked desire or goal through a substitute that represents it. For example, a person who has not been able to rebel against an authoritarian father may rebel against all symbols of authority, such as the laws or customs of the society in which he or she lives.

symbolic representation the process of representing experiences in the mind symbolically, for example, through words and sounds: one of three modes of representing knowledge (compare ENACTIVE REPRESENTATION; ICONIC REPRESENTATION). See SYMBOLIC MODE. [proposed by U.S. developmental psychologist Jerome Seymour Bruner (1915–)]

symbolic reward something that has no intrinsic value but is nevertheless prized because it represents something of value. For example, being listed in a city's social register may be regarded as a symbolic reward for attainment of high social standing.

symbolic stage **1.** see PREOPERATIONAL STAGE. **2.** see SYMBOLIC MODE.

symbolic thinking the ability to think in terms of signs, symbols, concepts, and abstract relations, as evidenced by language, numeracy, and artistic or ritual expression. Archaeological finds suggest that symbolic thinking may have evolved in humans much earlier than previously thought, possibly toward the end of the Lower Paleolithic (i.e., over 70,000 years ago). See also SYMBOLIC PROCESS.

symbolism *n.* **1.** in psychoanalytic theory, the substitution of a SYMBOL for a repressed impulse or threatening object in order to avoid censorship by the superego (e.g., dreaming of a steeple or other PHALLIC SYMBOL instead of a penis). Also called **symbolization**. **2.** the use of symbols in literature and the visual arts or in human culture generally (see SEMIOTICS). A specific, early modernist movement, referred to as **Symbolism**, developed in France in the mid- to late 19th century as a reaction to REALISM and NATURALISM. The writing, primarily poetry and drama, was highly evocative and made extensive use of indirect symbolic language to represent character, situation, and action. Leading exponents were the French poets Charles Baudelaire (1821–1867), Arthur Rimbaud (1854–1891), and Stéphane Mallarmé (1842–1898), and the Belgian dramatist Maurice Maeterlinck (1862–1949). The writings of these authors had a profound influence on other important literary figures, such as the Irish poet William Butler Yeats (1865–1939), the Irish novelist James Joyce (1882–1941), and the U.S.-born British poet T. S. Eliot (1888–1965).

symbolization *n.* **1.** see SYMBOLISM. **2.** in Albert BANDURA'S SOCIAL-COGNITIVE THEORY, the ability to think about one's social behavior in terms of words and images. **—symbolize** *vb.*

symbol-substitution test see CODE TEST.

SYMLOG *n.* *Sy*stematic *M*ultiple *L*evel *O*bservation of *G*roups: a theory and observational system for studying group behavior. The model assumes that group activities and group members can be classified along three dimensions (dominance–submissiveness, friendliness–unfriendliness, and acceptance–nonacceptance of authority) and that groups whose behavioral profiles are characterized by dominance, friendliness, and acceptance of authority usually work together more effectively. See also STRUCTURED OBSERVATIONAL MEASURES. [developed by U.S. social psychologist Robert Freed Bales (1916–)]

Symmetrel *n.* a trade name for AMANTADINE.

symmetrical distribution a distribution in which the values above the MEAN are a mirror image of those below the mean.

symmetry *n.* **1.** see STIMULUS EQUIVALENCE. **2.** in mathematics and statistics, equality relative to some axis. **3.** in aesthetics, balance and harmony in the proportions of objects or works of art, an aesthetically pleasing quality. Distinct patterns of symmetry are widely produced. For example, almost all ornamental bands fall into one of seven types of **band symmetry**, and essentially all patterned wallpaper can be grouped into 17 types of **plane symmetry**. **4.** the mirrorlike correspondence of parts on opposite sides of a center. See also BILATERAL SYMMETRY. **—symmetrical** *adj.*

symmetry compulsion a compulsion to arrange objects in a certain way (e.g., in a room) or in a particular order (e.g., on a desk). Symmetry compulsion is associated with obsessions about neatness or perfection. It can be a symptom of OBSESSIVE-COMPULSIVE DISORDER or, sometimes, of OBSESSIVE-COMPULSIVE PERSONALITY DISORDER.

sympathectomy *n.* a surgical procedure in which portions of the SYMPATHETIC NERVOUS SYSTEM are excised, severed, or otherwise disrupted. In **chemical sympathectomy**, this is accomplished by the administration of specific drugs.

sympathetic chain either of two beadlike chains of GANGLIA of the SYMPATHETIC NERVOUS SYSTEM, one chain lying on each side of the spinal column.

sympathetic division see SYMPATHETIC NERVOUS SYSTEM.

sympathetic ganglion any of the ganglia that form part of either SYMPATHETIC CHAIN.

sympathetic induction the process in which one person's expressed emotion elicits a similar emotion in another person. See EMPATHY; SYMPATHY.

sympathetic nervous system one of the two divisions of the AUTONOMIC NERVOUS SYSTEM (ANS, which controls smooth muscle and gland functions), the other being the PARASYMPATHETIC NERVOUS SYSTEM. Anatomically it consists of PREGANGLIONIC AUTONOMIC NEURONS whose fibers run from the thoracic and lumbar regions of the spinal cord to the chains of sympathetic ganglia. From these arise the fibers of POSTGANGLIONIC AUTONOMIC NEURONS, which innervate organs ranging from the eye to the reproductive organs. It is defined functionally in terms of its ability to act as an integrated whole in affecting a large number of smooth muscle systems simultaneously, usually in the service of enhancing "fight or flight" (see FIGHT–FLIGHT REACTION). Typical sympathetic changes include dilation of the pupils to facilitate vision, constriction of the peripheral arteries to supply more blood to the muscles and the brain, secretion of epinephrine to raise the blood-sugar level and increase metabolism, and reduction of stomach and intestinal activities so that energy can be directed elsewhere. Thus, the sympathetic nervous system tends to antagonize the effects of the parasympathetic nervous system. Also called **sympathetic division**.

sympathetic vibration a state in which the thoughts and feelings of two or more people are in harmony.

sympathism *n.* see SYMPATHY SEEKING.

sympathomimetic drugs drugs that stimulate activity in the SYMPATHETIC NERVOUS SYSTEM because they potentiate the activity of norepinephrine or epinephrine or have effects similar to these neurotransmitters (hence they are also known as **adrenergic drugs**). Sympathomimetic drugs act as agonists at ADRENORECEPTORS; they include the amphetamines and ephedrine.

sympathy *n.* **1.** feelings of concern or compassion resulting from an awareness of the suffering or sorrow of another. **2.** more generally, a capacity to share in and respond to the concerns or feelings of others. See also EMPATHY. **3.** an affinity between individuals on the basis of similar feelings, inclinations, or temperament. **—sympathetic** *adj.* **—sympathize** *vb.*

sympathy seeking the tendency to seek emotional support or elicit the assistance of others by arousing sympathy. Also called **sympathism**.

sympatric species species that occupy the same habitat or overlapping habitats. Species that do not occur together or occupy the same habitat are described as **allopatric**.

symphorophilia *n.* sexual interest and arousal derived from stage-managing the occurrence of a disaster and then watching it. The person may masturbate either while the disaster occurs or afterward, with memories or pictures of the event. **—symphorophile** *n.*

symptom *n.* **1.** any deviation from normal functioning that is considered indicative of physical or mental disorder. A recognized pattern of symptoms is usually necessary in order for an individual to be judged as having a SYNDROME or psychological disorder. **2.** in general contexts, any event that is indicative of another event; for example, a series of strikes is a symptom of economic unrest. **—symptomatic** *adj.*

symptomatic act an action that appears to be intended for one purpose (or to have no particular purpose) but that betrays a hidden intention or meaning. In psychoanalytic theory, such acts are thought to represent repressed impulses. See also FREUDIAN SLIP; PARAPRAXIS; SYMPTOM FORMATION.

symptomatic epilepsy see EPILEPSY.

symptomatic treatment in mental health practice, treatment directed toward the relief of distressing symptoms, as opposed to treatment focused on underlying causes and conditions and the reconstruction of the patient's personality. Major techniques used in symptomatic treatment are hypnotherapy, suggestion therapy, drug therapy, and narcotherapy.

symptomatology *n.* **1.** the combined signs, markers, or indications of a disease or disorder. **2.** the scientific study of the markers and indications of a disease or disorder. Also called **semiology**.

symptom bearer see IDENTIFIED PATIENT.

Symptom Checklist-90-R (**SCL-90-R**) a 90-item self-report inventory that measures the psychological symptoms and distress of community, medical, and psychiatric respondents along nine primary symptom dimensions and three global indices. The SCL-90-R adds four dimensions to the five assessed in the HOPKINS SYMPTOM CHECKLIST, of which it is a direct outgrowth: hostility, phobic anxiety, paranoid ideation, and psychoticism.

symptom cluster a group of related symptoms that usually occur together, as in a SYNDROME.

symptom complex see SYNDROME.

symptom-context method a system of gathering data as symptoms arise in vivo in the psychotherapy session as an aid to psychotherapy research, case formulation, and treatment. It is similar to the CORE CONFLICTUAL RELATIONSHIP THEME method. [developed by U.S. clinical psychologist Lester Luborsky (1920–)]

symptom formation 1. in psychoanalytic theory, the development of a somatic or behavioral manifestation of an unconscious impulse or conflict that provokes anxiety. Also called **substitute formation**. **2.** the process by which the indications of physical or psychological illness or disease develop.

symptom removal in psychotherapy, elimination of symptoms through direct treatment without addressing underlying issues and unconscious motivation. See also SURFACE THERAPY.

symptom specificity a hypothesis stating that people with PSYCHOSOMATIC DISORDERS display abnormal responses to stress in particular physiological systems. According to this hypothesis, a person's complaints will center around a particular organ (e.g., the heart) and set of related symptoms (e.g., cardiovascular symptoms) rather than involving a variety of complaints about different organs or systems.

symptom substitution in the classic psychoanalytic theory of Sigmund FREUD, the development of a symptom to replace one that has cleared up as a result of treatment. It is said to occur if the unconscious impulses and conflicts responsible for the original symptom are not dealt with. Symptom substitution is often used as an argument against therapies aimed at symptom removal alone, as in behavior therapy, suggestion, and some forms of hypnotherapy; however, this hypothesis has not been validated.

syn- (**sym-**) *prefix* **1.** with or together (e.g., SYNCHRONIZATION). **2.** union or fusion (e.g., SYNCRETISM).

Synanon *n.* a residential drug treatment program that utilized confrontation and peer pressure to encourage its members to deal with their addiction. Founded in California in 1958 by Charles Dederich (1914–1997), himself a recovering alcoholic, Synanon was the first major drug treatment program in the United States, and its TOUGH LOVE approach to overcoming addiction was widely publicized as innovative and effective. It evolved into an experimental commune that Dederich proclaimed as a religion in the mid-1970s. Thereafter, amid accusations of authoritarian practices within the community and Dederich's no-contest plea to charges of attempted murder, Synanon declined in prominence and was eventually disbanded in 1991.

synapse *n.* the specialized junction through which neural signals are transmitted from one neuron (the presynaptic neuron) to another (the postsynaptic neuron). In most synapses the knoblike ending (TERMINAL BUTTON) of the axon of a presynaptic neuron faces the dendrite or cell body of the postsynaptic neuron across a narrow gap, the synaptic cleft. The arrival of a neural signal triggers the release of NEUROTRANSMITTER from SYNAPTIC VESICLES in the terminal button into the synaptic cleft. Here the molecules of neurotransmitter activate receptors in the postsynaptic membrane and cause the opening of ION CHANNELS in the postsynaptic cell. This may lead to excitation or inhibition of the postsynaptic cell, depending on which ion channels are affected. Also called **synaptic junction**. See also AXO-AXONAL SYNAPSE; ELECTRICAL SYNAPSE. **—synaptic** *adj.*

synapse rearrangement the loss of some synapses and the establishment of others that occurs as a refinement of synaptic connections often seen in development or that follows loss of or damage to some neurons.

synaptic bouton see TERMINAL BUTTON.

synaptic cleft the gap within a synapse between the TERMINAL BUTTON of one neuron and the dendrite or cell body of a neighboring neuron. The synaptic cleft is typically 20–30 nm wide. Also called **synaptic gap**.

synaptic depression the reduced ability of a SYNAPSE to transmit a neural signal. It is a form of NEURAL PLASTICITY.

synaptic junction see SYNAPSE.

synaptic knob see TERMINAL BUTTON.

synaptic pruning a neurodevelopmental process, ocurring both before birth and up to the second decade of life, in which the weakest synapses between neurons are eliminated. In schizophrenia research, it is hypothesized that premature or excessive pruning may account for some forms of the disease.

synaptic transmission see NEUROTRANSMISSION.

synaptic transmitter see NEUROTRANSMITTER.

synaptic vesicle any of numerous small spherical sacs in the cytoplasm of the TERMINAL BUTTON of a presynaptic neuron that contain molecules of NEUROTRANSMITTER. The transmitter is released into the SYNAPTIC CLEFT when a nerve impulse arrives at the terminal button.

synaptogenesis *n.* the formation of synapses between neurons as axons and dendrites grow. See also EXPERIENCE-DEPENDENT PROCESS; EXPERIENCE-EXPECTANT PROCESS.

synchronicity *n.* in the ANALYTIC PSYCHOLOGY of Carl JUNG, the simultaneous occurrence of events that appear to have a meaningful connection when there is no explicable causal relationship between these events, as in extraordinary coincidences or purported examples of telepathy. Jung suggested that some simultaneous occurrences possess significance through their very coincidence in time.

synchronic linguistics see DIACHRONIC LINGUISTICS.

synchronism *n.* the simultaneous occurrence or existence of phenomena. **—synchronic** *adj.* **—synchronous** *adj.*

synchronization *n.* a pattern of brain-wave activity that appears to be coordinated, so that one set of neurons may oscillate in phase with another set. Originally, synchronization referred to the delta rhythm of deep sleep. See DELTA WAVE.

synchronized sleep the type of sleep associated primarily with DEEP SLEEP, when electroencephalogram recordings show slow, synchronous waves. See also SLEEP STAGES.

synchronous brood see ASYNCHRONOUS BROOD.

synchronous correlation in LONGITUDINAL DESIGNS, a correlation that represents the degree of relationship between variables at a specific moment in time.

synchrony *n.* **1.** the simultaneous occurrence of things or events. **2.** the act of moving together in harmony, which tends to bring people closer together and is used particularly in DANCE THERAPY. In **self-synchrony**, an individual's movements are synchronized with his or her own speech. In **interactional synchrony**, the movements of a listener correspond with the speech and movements of the speaker. **—synchronous** *adj.*

syncope *n.* a transient loss of consciousness resulting from sudden reduction in the blood supply to the brain. Such attacks may be experienced by individuals with cerebrovascular disorders or they may be precipitated by psychological or other factors (e.g., extreme fear, severe pain). Also called **fainting**. **—syncopal** *adj.*

syncretic thought the first, or prelogical, stage of thinking in a child's life, characterized by egocentric and frequently animistic thought processes. For example, a simple block may be called a car, or a broomstick may be ridden as a horse. At this stage, connections are likely to be purely accidental: If the sun shines brightly on the child's birthday, the child may think that the birthday is the reason for the sun to shine. See ANIMISTIC THINKING; PRIMARY PROCESS. [proposed by Jean PIAGET]

syncretism *n.* the integration of elements from two or more systems, theories, or concepts into a new system, theory, or concept. The term is mainly applied to systems in which cultures, beliefs, or doctrines that may appear incompatible are nevertheless combined. **—syncretic** *adj.*

syndrome *n.* a set of symptoms and signs that are usually due to a single cause (or set of related causes) and together indicate a particular physical or mental disease or disorder. Also called **symptom complex**.

syndrome of obstinate progression a syndrome in which there is continuous forward progression by leg movements, caused by lesions of the interpeduncular nucleus in the brainstem (between the two CEREBRAL PEDUNCLES) and adjacent areas of the brain. Animals with these lesions persistently walk in a single direction, without regard for obstacles or restraint, until the obstacles give way or the animal falls and begins walking in another direction or finally becomes exhausted and dies. [discovered in 1942 by U.S. neurosurgeon and physiologist Percival Bailey (1892–1973) and Edward W. Davis]

synecdoche *n.* see METONYMY.

synectics model an educational approach that emphasizes creative problem solving and the development of teaching methods that enhance student creativity, such as encouraging metaphorical thinking.

synergic marriage a marriage or partnership that is enhanced by the contributions the partners can make in satisfying each other's psychological needs in a positive manner. Compare SYMBIOTIC MARRIAGE.

synergism *n.* the joint action of different elements (e.g., drugs, muscles) such that their combined effect is greater than the sum of their individual effects. See DRUG SYNERGISM. **—synergistic** *adj.*

synergistic muscles muscles that work together to produce a specific action, such as flexion or extension of a limb. See also AGONIST. Compare ANTAGONIST.

synergogy *n.* cooperative learning that focuses on problem solving, learning within group activities, and joint projects. Synergogy has been demonstrated to be effective at every level of education. In adult learning, for example, students can acquire and retain more information with this method than in lecture and standard discussion formats. Also called **circles of learning**.

synergy *n.* the coordination of forces or efforts to achieve a goal, as when a group of muscles work together in order to move a limb. Also called **coordinative structure**. **—synergic** *adj.*

synesthesia *n.* a condition in which stimulation of one sensory system arouses sensations in another. For example, sounds (and sometimes tastes and odors) may be experienced as colors while they are being heard, and specific sounds (e.g., different musical notes) may yield specific colors. Research suggests that about one in 2,000 people regularly experience synesthesia, and some experts suspect that as many as one in 300 people have some variation of the condition. Also called **concomitant sensation**; **secondary sensation**. See also CHROMESTHESIA.

synkinesis (**synkinesia**) *n.* see MOTOR OVERFLOW.

synonym *n.* a word that has exactly or almost exactly the same meaning as another word in the same language, so that the two are ordinarily interchangeable. Compare ANTONYM. **—synonymous** *adj.*

synopsia *n.* a form of SYNESTHESIA in which specific colors are associated with specific tones. Also called **synopsy**.

synoptic *adj.* in the form of a summary or synopsis.

syntactical aphasia a form of APHASIA characterized by errors in the combinations or sequences of words in sentences. Also called **cataphasia**. See also AGRAMMATISM.

syntactics *n.* the structural and grammatical aspects of language, as distinguished from SEMANTICS.

syntax *n.* the set of rules that describes how words and phrases in a language are arranged into grammatical sentences, or the branch of linguistics that studies such rules. With MORPHOLOGY, syntax is one of the two traditional subdivisions of grammar. **—syntactic** or **syntactical** *adj.*

syntaxic mode the highest stage in experiencing the world, characterized by CONSENSUAL VALIDATION, the development of syntaxic thinking, and the expression of ideas in a commonly accepted language. [defined by U.S. psychiatrist Harry Stack Sullivan (1892–1949)]

syntaxic thinking the highest level of cognition, which includes logical, goal-directed, reality-oriented thinking. [defined by U.S. psychiatrist Harry Stack Sullivan (1892–1949)]

syntaxis *n.* a way of thinking and communicating that is logical and based on reality. See SYNTAXIC MODE; SYNTAXIC THINKING. **—syntaxic** *adj.*

synthesis *n.* **1.** the bringing together of disparate parts or elements—whether they be physical or conceptual—into a whole; for example, the integration of personality factors, such as attitudes, impulses, and traits, into a totality. **2.** in GESTALT PSYCHOLOGY, the perception or recognition of phenomena as a whole. See PSYCHOSYNTHESIS. **3.** the process by which chemical or biochemical compounds are formed from their constituents. See BIOSYNTHESIS. **4.** in philosophy, the final stage of a dialectical process: a third proposition that resolves the opposition between THESIS and ANTITHESIS. The synthesis then serves as the thesis in the next phase of the ongoing dialectic. This use of the term is particularly associated with the thought of German philosopher Georg Wilhelm Friedrich Hegel (1770–1831). See also DIALECTICAL MATERIALISM. **—synthetic** *adj.*

synthetic approach the combining (synthesizing) of various processes, systems, skills, or other components into a more complex whole as a means of learning or better understanding the whole. For example, a synthetic approach to learning to read is one in which the child first learns to recognize written letters and understand their associated sounds before learning to combine letters into syllables and words. Compare ANALYTIC APPROACH.

synthetic language see FUSIONAL LANGUAGE.

synthetic opioids see OPIOIDS.

synthetic speech speech produced by a machine, usually a computer. Speech synthesis algorithms differ in complexity and in other ways, therefore the speech they produce varies in quality (intelligibility and naturalness). Compare COMPRESSED SPEECH; DIGITIZED SPEECH.

synthetic validity in industrial and organizational settings, a technique for inferring the validity of a selection test or other predictor of job performance from a JOB ANALYSIS. It involves systematically analyzing a job into its elements, estimating the validity of the test or predictor in predicting performance on each of these elements, and then combining the validities for each element to form an estimate of the validity of the test or predictor for the job as a whole. Synthetic validity can be useful in estimating the validity of selection procedures in small organizations where the larger samples required in CONCURRENT VALIDITY and PREDICTIVE VALIDITY are not available. See also JOB-COMPONENT VALIDITY.

syntonia *n.* a high degree of emotional responsiveness to the environment. **—syntonic** *adj.*

syphilis *n.* a contagious disease caused by infection with the spirochete bacterium *Treponema pallidum*. Syphilis is usually a SEXUALLY TRANSMITTED DISEASE, but it can be transmitted through a break or cut in the skin or mucous membrane; it can also be transmitted by an infected pregnant woman to an unborn child. Untreated, syphilis progressively destroys body tissues, particularly those of the heart and nervous system. See also CEREBRAL SYPHILIS; GENERAL PARESIS.

syringomyelia *n.* a disorder marked by the presence of a fluid-filled cavity in the spinal cord that expands and elongates over time, causing progressive damage to the spinal cord and resulting in weakness in the arms and legs and loss of temperature and pain sensation. Syringomyelia may occur as a complication of trauma, meningitis, hemorrhage, a tumor, or congenital defects.

syrinx *n.* (*pl.* **syringes**) see VOCAL COMMUNICATION.

system *n.* **1.** any collective entity consisting of a set of interrelated or interacting elements that have been organized together to perform a function. **2.** an orderly method of classification or procedure (e.g., the Library of Congress system). **3.** a structured set of facts, concepts, and hypotheses that provide a framework of thought or belief, as in a philosophical system. See CONCEPTUAL SYSTEM. **4.** a living organism or one of its major bodily structures (e.g., the respiratory system). **—systematic** *adj.*

systematic approach see TOPOGRAPHIC MODEL.

systematic behavioral universal see PSYCHOLOGICAL UNIVERSAL.

systematic desensitization a form of BEHAVIOR THERAPY in which COUNTERCONDITIONING is used to reduce anxiety associated with a particular stimulus. It involves the following stages: (a) The client is trained in deep-muscle relaxation; (b) various anxiety-provoking situations related to a particular problem, such as fear of death or a specific phobia, are listed in order from weakest to strongest; and (c) each of these situations is presented in imagination or in reality, beginning with the weakest, while the client practices muscle relaxation. Since the muscle relaxation is incompatible with the anxiety, the client gradually responds less to the anxiety-provoking situations. See also COVERT DESENSITIZATION; IN VIVO DESENSITIZATION; RECIPROCAL INHIBITION. [introduced by South African-born U.S. psychologist Joseph Wolpe (1915–1997)]

systematic error an error in data or in a conclusion

drawn from the data that is regular and repeatable as a result of improper collection methods or statistical treatment of the data.

Systematic Multiple Level Observation of Groups see SYMLOG.

systematic observation the gathering of data according to an objective, well-ordered method that will yield reliable information about some phenomenon or aspect of behavior.

systematic rational restructuring a system of psychotherapy in which the client is encouraged to imagine anxiety-provoking situations while talking about them in a realistic manner that reduces his or her anxieties. See also IMPLOSIVE THERAPY.

systematics *n.* see BIOLOGICAL TAXONOMY.

systematic sampling a type of SAMPLING in which all the members of a population are listed and then some systematic procedure is applied to select specific cases, for example, the population might be listed alphabetically and every seventh case selected.

systematized delusion a false, irrational belief that is highly developed and organized, with multiple elaborations that are coherent, consistent, and logically related. Compare FRAGMENTARY DELUSION.

system flow diagram in ergonomics, a flow chart used to illustrate the movement of materials or people within a WORK SYSTEM or to illustrate the direction of movement of information.

systemic 1. *adj.* concerning or having impact on an entire system. For example, a systemic disorder affects an entire organ system or the body as a whole. **2.** *n.* the interplay of reciprocal processes between interactional partners, as in a family.

systemic lupus erythematosus (**SLE**) see LUPUS ERYTHEMATOSUS.

systemic mucopolysaccharidosis see MAROTEAUX–LAMY SYNDROME.

systemic thinking a combination of analytical and synthetic thinking that takes account of the impact of a system (or organization) and all its components together. Analytical thinking is concerned with breaking down a concept into its component parts, whereas synthetic thinking is the process of combining components to make a complete whole.

system model of evaluation a method of assessing organizational effectiveness in terms of a working model of a social unit that is capable of achieving a goal. It is concerned with assessing the allocation of resources by the organization to reach an optimum level of operation, rather than with assessing the effectiveness of the organization in achieving public goals.

System of Multicultural Pluralistic Assessment (**SOMPA**) an assessment for children aged 5 through 11 that is designed to estimate intellectual potential in a culturally and ethnically equitable manner. A collection of nine instruments whose scores are interpreted according to a unique ideological perspective, the SOMPA purportedly circumvents cultural and linguistic differences and reveals all student capabilities and requisite skills that would make them eligible for special educational programs. [developed in 1978 by sociologists Jane R. Mercer and June F. Lewis]

systems engineering a discipline that adopts an integrated, multidisciplinary approach to the design and analysis of WORK SYSTEMS in order to account for the complex interdependencies of system components, people, and processes. Its goal is to enhance efficiency and safety. See ERGONOMICS; MACROERGONOMICS; SOCIOTECHNICAL SYSTEMS APPROACH. See also ENGINEERING PSYCHOLOGY; HUMAN FACTORS ENGINEERING.

systems of support a framework for identifying the nature and profile of services and supports required by a person with mental retardation. This is based on considerations of intellectual functioning and adaptive skills, psychological and emotional factors, physical health and etiological factors, and environmental or situational factors.

systems theory see GENERAL SYSTEMS THEORY.

systolic blood pressure the pressure of the blood against the arterial walls produced by the contraction of the heart muscles, as the blood is forced into the aorta and the pulmonary artery. See BLOOD PRESSURE. Compare DIASTOLIC BLOOD PRESSURE.

Tt

T in psychophysics, abbreviation for a transition point in judgments.

T_3 abbreviation for TRIIODOTHYRONINE.

T_4 abbreviation for THYROXINE.

TA abbreviation for TRANSACTIONAL ANALYSIS.

tabanka (**tabanca**) *n.* a CULTURE-BOUND SYNDROME found in Trinidad, with symptoms that include depression associated with a high rate of suicide. It is seen in men who have been abandoned by their wives.

tabes dorsalis see LOCOMOTOR ATAXIA.

table of random numbers a table of numbers that has been generated by a random process.

table-tilting *n.* in SPIRITUALISM, movements of a table during a séance, ostensibly reflecting the efforts of spirits to communicate with the participants. In parapsychology, the same movements might be attributed to PSYCHOKINESIS. Also called **table-tipping**; **table-turning**.

taboo (**tabu**) **1.** *n.* a religious, moral, or social convention prohibiting a particular behavior, object, or person. The word derives from *tabu,* the Polynesian term for "sacred," which was used specifically in reference to objects, rites, and individuals consecrated to sacred use or service and, therefore, seen as forbidden, unclean, or untouchable in secular contexts. **2.** *adj.* prohibited or strongly disapproved.

tabula rasa concept the idea that at birth the mind is like a "blank tablet" (from Latin) and that all knowledge is subsequently derived from sensory experience. The notion of INNATE IDEAS is thus dismissed as a fiction. The phrase is mainly associated with English empiricist philosopher John Locke (1632–1704), although he never in fact used it: Locke's actual phrase was "white paper." See EMPIRICISM.

tachisme *n.* see ACTION PAINTING.

tachistoscope *n.* an instrument that exposes visual material on a screen for very brief intervals. Words, numbers, pictures, and symbols can be rapidly presented in the right or left visual field. Also called **T-scope**.

tachy- *combining form* fast or accelerated.

tachycardia *n.* pathologically rapid heartbeat, often associated with drugs or anxiety. See ARRHYTHMIA.

tachyphagia *n.* a pathological form of rapid eating.

tachyphemia *n.* speech that is characterized by persistent volubility and rapidity. See LOGORRHEA. See also PRESSURED SPEECH.

tachyphrenia *n.* mental hyperactivity. **—tachyphrenic** *adj.*

tachyphylaxis *n.* a rapidly developing TOLERANCE to a drug, as indicated by progressively decreasing response to repeated administration. For example, the blood pressure of a patient might continue to rise despite repeated injections of a drug that normally would lower the blood pressure. **—tachyphylactic** *adj.*

tachypsychia *n.* an altered perception of time, in which time seems to speed up or slow down. See PSYCHOLOGICAL TIME. **—tachypsychic** *adj.*

tacit knowledge knowledge that is informally acquired rather than explicitly taught (e.g., knowledge of social rules) and allows a person to succeed in certain environments and pursuits. It is stored without self-reflective awareness and therefore not easily articulated. PRACTICAL INTELLIGENCE requires a facility for acquiring tacit knowledge. Also called **implicit knowledge**; **unconscious knowledge**. See TRIARCHIC THEORY OF INTELLIGENCE. [proposed by U.S. psychologist Robert J. Sternberg (1949–)]

tacrine *n.* an ACETYLCHOLINESTERASE INHIBITOR used for the treatment of mild to moderate dementia associated with Alzheimer's disease (see NOOTROPIC DRUGS). A common adverse reaction to tacrine is liver dysfunction, which limits its use. U.S. trade name: **Cognex**.

tact- *combining form* touch.

tactic *adj.* see TAXIS.

tactile agnosia see ASTEREOGNOSIS.

tactile aid see TACTILE SENSORY AID.

tactile amnesia see ASTEREOGNOSIS.

tactile circle an area of the skin where two tactile stimuli presented simultaneously are perceived as one. See also SENSORY CIRCLE.

tactile communication the use of touch as a means of communication. In dogs and wolves, the placing of one individual's head and neck on the back of another is a signal of dominance. In many primates, including human beings, ALLOGROOMING is important in maintaining social relationships and may release hormones that serve to provide a physiological calming or reward effect.

tactile extinction see DOUBLE-SIMULTANEOUS TACTILE SENSATION.

Tactile Finger Recognition see FINGER LOCALIZATION TEST.

Tactile Form Perception a test in which participants use one hand to feel a geometric figure made of sandpaper, which is hidden from view, and then identify it from among a set of 12 drawings. There is a total of 20 geometric figures; 10 are presented to one hand and 10 to the other. The test assesses nonverbal tactile information-processing ability and is scored for the number of correct identifications. [developed in 1983 by U.S. neuropsychologist Arthur Lester Benton (1909–) and colleagues]

tactile form recognition any test of the ability to recognize an object by touch alone. Such tests usually involve blindfolding the participants and asking them to name objects placed in their hands.

tactile hallucination a false perception involving the sense of touch. These sensations may include itching, feeling electric shocks, and feeling insects biting or crawling under the skin. Also called **haptic hallucination**; **tactual hallucination**.

tactile illusion an illusion involving the touch sense. Tactile illusions may occur when patterns are pressed on the skin rather than when patterns are experienced through voluntary movement to gain information about the object or surface. Compare HAPTIC ILLUSION.

tactile perception the ability to perceive objects or judge sensations through the sense of touch. The term often refers to judgments of spatial stimulation of the skin and patterns imposed on the skin. Tactile perception may also involve judging sensory events involving stimulation of the skin, for example, the thermal properties of a liquid. Some researchers restrict this term to PASSIVE TOUCH. Compare HAPTIC PERCEPTION.

tactile perceptual disorder a condition, due to brain damage, that is characterized by difficulty in discriminating sensations that involve touch receptors. Individuals may be unable to determine the shape, size, texture, or other physical aspects of an object merely by touching it.

tactile receptor any of the CUTANEOUS RECEPTORS or other receptors involved in the SOMATOSENSES.

tactile sense see TOUCH SENSE.

tactile sensory aid a device that makes use of touch to help individuals cope with perceptual impairment. An example of a tactile sensory aid is a vibrator that cues a person who has a hearing impairment that the doorbell is ringing. Other aids provide assistance with reading, and a number of electronic travel aids facilitate orientation and mobility for people with visual impairment. Although tactile sensory aids are also called **tactile aids**, the latter term is sometimes used more explicitly to refer only to devices that convert auditory information into patterns of skin stimulation—either vibratory (for a **vibrotactile aid**) or electrical (for an **electrotactile aid**)—for use in communicating with and teaching speech production to people with profound hearing loss. See also TACTUAL DISPLAY.

tactile stimulation activation of a sensory receptor by a touch stimulus. Also called **tactual stimulation**.

tactile test any test that involves the sense of touch.

tactual display a device for transmitting information that is to be read or otherwise processed through the use of touch. Tactual displays may provide BRAILLE output from a computer or information in letter shapes. They may use simple vibrators, raised pins, or electrocutaneous stimulation of the skin. Tactual displays are useful for people with visual impairment, and some are used for assisting people with hearing loss. See also TACTILE SENSORY AID.

tactual hallucination see TACTILE HALLUCINATION.

tactual localization see POINT LOCALIZATION.

Tactual Performance Test (**TPT**) a NEUROPSYCHOLOGICAL TEST—part of the HALSTEAD–REITAN NEUROPSYCHOLOGICAL BATTERY—that requires a blindfolded individual to place wooden shapes (e.g., stars) into a formboard placed at a 45° angle to the vertical. Performances for the dominant, nondominant, and both hands simultaneously are obtained, and then the blindfold is removed and the individual is asked to draw the shapes and their relative positions on the formboard. The test measures motor skills, tactile perception, nonverbal memory, problem solving, and other executive functions.

tactual shape discrimination the ability to determine shapes of objects by touch alone. A person may be required to differentiate between a cylinder and another object when unable to see the objects.

tactual size discrimination the ability to judge the comparative size of two invisible objects through the sense of touch. It is used as a test for the possible presence of a cortical lesion that would interfere with this ability.

tactual stimulation see TACTILE STIMULATION.

Tadoma method a technique of communicating with people having both hearing and visual impairment. People with these disabilities learn to place their fingers on the cheek and neck and their thumb on the mouth of the person speaking and translate the vibrations and muscle movements into words. [originated in the 1930s by U.S. teacher Sophia Alcorn (1883–1967); the name is derived from Tad and Oma, two of her students]

TAE abbreviation for TILT AFTEREFFECT.

Taft–Hartley Act see LABOR MANAGEMENT RELATIONS ACT.

TAG acronym for TALENTED AND GIFTED.

tagging *n.* the process of attaching a RADIOACTIVE ISOTOPE to a molecule to label it and create a RADIOACTIVE TRACER. The tagging enables observation of the route and distribution of a substance through the body and also its measurement.

tag question in linguistics, a short INTERROGATIVE clause attached to the end of a statement to invite the agreement of a listener, as in *The bird flew away, didn't it?* or *We've not been here before, have we?* In English, the form of the tag question is determined by the structure of the main statement and a combination of linguistic rules involving pronominalization, negation, interrogation, and truncation, as seen in the examples given above. The ability of young children to form appropriate tag questions is considered a prime illustration of their early mastery of linguistic rules.

taijin kyofusho a phobia, similar to SOCIAL PHOBIA and unique to Japan, that is characterized by an intense fear that one's body parts, bodily functions, or facial expressions are embarrassing or offensive to others (e.g., in appearance, odor, or movement).

tail flick a test used to measure pain sensitivity in nonhuman animals (usually rodents). An intense beam of light is focused on a specific spot on the animal's tail. After a period, the animal abruptly moves its tail to avoid the beam of light. The time that elapses before this tail flick is used as an index of pain sensitivity; analgesic drugs (e.g., morphine) increase the LATENCY OF RESPONSE.

TAIS abbreviation for TEST OF ATTENTIONAL AND INTERPERSONAL STYLE.

Takayasu's disease a circulatory disorder involving arteries that carry blood from the aortic arch above the heart toward the brain. Occlusion of the innominate, left subclavian, and left carotid arteries results in a loss of pulses in the arms and neck, cramplike pain in the arms, and fainting spells due to CEREBRAL ISCHEMIA. The disease seems to affect mainly young females. [Michishige **Takayasu** (1872–1938), Japanese physician]

talbot *n.* a unit of light energy equal to one LUMEN second, that is, the energy carried by one lumen in one second.

Talbot–Plateau law the principle that if a light flickers so rapidly that it is perceived as continuous, its brightness will be determined by the ratio of the duration of the on to the off periods. Thus the perceived brightness of the stimulus that appears continuous is actually an average of the brightness over time of the intermittent on and off periods. [William Henry Fox **Talbot** (1800–1877), British physicist; Joseph Antoine Ferdinand **Plateau** (1801–1883), Belgian physicist]

talent *n.* an innate skill or ability, or an aptitude to excel in one or more specific activities or subject areas. Talent cannot be accounted for by normal development patterns and is often not maximized, as it requires time, energy, sacrifice, dedication, and money on the part of parents, mentors, and the talented person. Ideal circumstances for the development of a talent include enjoyment of the talent for its own sake and a clear perception of how it can be exploited to fulfill the individual's long-term aspirations. **—talented** *adj.*

talented and gifted (**TAG**) describing children who display a level of intelligence significantly above average, special abilities, or both as measured by appropriate standard assessment procedures. **Talented and Gifted** is an organization that promotes education advocacy, research, and the sharing of ideas between educators and parents of such children.

talion *n.* retaliation, especially retaliation in kind, as in the biblical injunction "an eye for an eye, a tooth for a tooth." The **talion principle** or **law** plays an important part in psychoanalytic theory, because it includes the general idea of retribution for defying the SUPEREGO and the specific fear (**talion dread**) that all transgressions, accidental or intentional, will be punished in kind. For example, a person wishing consciously or unconsciously for the death of another person might suffer extreme anxiety caused by the fear that he himself or she herself is dying.

talipes *n.* see CLUBFOOT.

talking book a book recorded on audio cassette or CD for use by individuals with visual impairment or certain learning disabilities (e.g., dyslexia), which requires the use of specially designed playback equipment. Talking books do not include audiobooks intended for widespread use by the general public, for example, in situations in which they cannot or prefer not to read (e.g., while traveling).

talking cure a synonym for psychotherapy, sometimes, but not always, used dismissively. The term is apt in that the very essence of certain psychotherapeutic approaches is for the client to "talk out" his or her problems with the therapist. First used in the context of psychoanalysis, the term was coined by the landmark patient ANNA O.

talk therapy see PSYCHOTHERAPY.

tally sheet an instrument used to record the frequency of occurrence of various behaviors or other events.

taming of the instinct see NEUTRALIZATION.

tandem reinforcement a SCHEDULE OF REINFORCEMENT for a single response in which two or more schedule requirements must be completed in sequence before reinforcement occurs and no stimulus change accompanies completion of each requirement. For example, in a tandem, fixed-interval 1-min, fixed-ratio 10 schedule, the first response after 1 min (see FIXED-INTERVAL SCHEDULE) would initiate the FIXED-RATIO SCHEDULE, and the 10th response would result in reinforcement. Also called **tandem schedule of reinforcement**. Compare CHAINED SCHEDULE.

tandem therapy in marriage therapy (see COUPLES THERAPY), a practice in which the therapist meets individually with each partner.

tangentiality *n.* a thought disturbance that is marked by oblique speech in which the person constantly digresses to irrelevant topics and fails to arrive at the main point. In extreme form it is a manifestation of LOOSENING OF ASSOCIATIONS, a symptom most frequently found in schizophrenia. Compare CIRCUMSTANTIALITY.

tangential speech verbal communication that repeatedly diverges from the original subject. Often resulting from disorganized thought processes or a diminished ability to focus attention, these digressions may continue until the original subject is no longer the focus of the conversation. This type of conceptual disorganization is often associated with schizophrenia and delirium.

tangent screen a vertical screen on which is plotted the location of a VISUAL RECEPTIVE FIELD for a neuron by moving a spot or bar of light across the screen and noting the regions of maximum response.

tangible user interface (**TUI**) in computing, several experimental types of user interface that enable on-screen data to be manipulated by direct physical means. Rather than appearing in graphical form, devices such as windows, icons, and handles are embodied as graspable, physical objects that can be used to access and manipulate data. The general goal of TUI development is to find solutions that bridge the gap between the digital world and the physical environment. Areas currently under investigation include (a) the transformation of architectural surfaces such as walls, doors, and tables into active interfaces with the digital world; (b) the creation of direct links between tangible objects, such as books, pictures, or models, and related digital information; and (c) the use of ambient media, such as light and sound, to convey background information to an operator. Compare GRAPHICAL USER INTERFACE; PERCEPTUAL USER INTERFACE.

tantric sex an approach to sex based on the Chinese philosophical and religious system of TAOISM. The approach highly values sex, with the belief that long life and even immortality can be reached by sexual activity. Sexual techniques are aimed at mutual and equal sexual pleasure for each partner. Prolonged love-making sessions, with much general body stroking, and techniques to prolong intercourse are stressed in the tantric approach.

tantrum *n.* see TEMPER TANTRUM.

Taoism (**Daoism**) *n.* a classical Chinese philosophy formulated by Laozi (Lao Tzu) in the 5th century BCE. The *Tao,* meaning "way" or "path," is seen as the origin of all creation, unknowable in its essence but observable in its manifestations and the basis of a spiritual approach to living. **—Taoist** *adj., n.*

tapering *n.* in pharmacology, a gradual reduction in the dose of a drug in order to avoid undesirable effects that may occur with rapid cessation. Such effects may be extreme (e.g., convulsions) or relatively mild (e.g., head pain, mild gastrointestinal distress). Drugs that produce physiological dependence (e.g., opiates, benzodiazepines) must be tapered to prevent a withdrawal syndrome; seizures can result from sudden cessation of benzodiazepines (see SEDATIVE, HYPNOTIC, OR ANXIOLYTIC WITHDRAWAL).

tapetum *n.* a light-reflecting layer behind the retina of some animals, such as the domestic cat. The tapetum enhances visual sensitivity in nocturnal animals by reflecting back any photons that have passed through the retina, so that these have a second chance to interact with the photopigments in the photoreceptors.

taphophilia *n.* a morbid attraction to cemeteries.

tapping test see DOTTING TEST; FINGER TAPPING TEST.

Taractan *n.* a trade name for CHLORPROTHIXENE.

Tarasoff decision the 1976 California Supreme Court decision in *Tarasoff v. Regents of the University of California,* which placed limits on a client's right to confidentiality by ruling that mental health practitioners who know or reasonably believe that a client poses a threat to another person are obligated to protect the potential victim from danger. Depending on the circumstances, that protection may involve such things as warning the potential victim, notifying the police of the potential threat posed by the client, or both. The decision was based on a case in which an individual confided to his therapist that he intended to kill a friend and later did so. See also DUTY TO PROTECT; DUTY TO WARN.

Tarchanoff phenomenon see GALVANIC SKIN RESPONSE. [Ivan Romanovich **Tarchanoff** (1846–1908), Russian physiologist]

tardive *adj.* denoting delayed or late-arriving symptoms or disease characteristics, as in TARDIVE DYSKINESIA.

tardive dyskinesia a movement disorder associated with the use of ANTIPSYCHOTICS, particularly conventional antipsychotics that act primarily as DOPAMINE-RECEPTOR ANTAGONISTS. It is more common with prolonged use (months or years), and older patients, females, and patients with mood disorders are thought to be more susceptible. Symptoms include tremor, so-called choreoathetoid movements (see CHOREOATHETOSIS), and spasticity of muscle groups, particularly orofacial muscles and muscles in the extremities. Onset is insidious and may be masked by continued use of the antipsychotic, only appearing when the drug is discontinued or the dose lowered. Its incidence is estimated at up to 40% of long-term users of conventional antipsychotics; the incidence is lower with atypical antipsychotics. No effective treatment is known.

tardive dysmentia a behavioral disorder associated with long-term use of antipsychotic drugs and characterized by changes in affect, social behavior, and level of activity. Symptoms may include an inappropriately loud voice and loquaciousness, euphoria, intrusive behavior (including invasion of others' privacy), and thought disorder. In addition, the individual may exhibit episodes of social withdrawal interspersed with episodes of hyperactivity, as well as excessive emotional reactivity and explosive hostility. The condition is considered the behavioral equivalent of TARDIVE DYSKINESIA. Also called **iatrogenic schizophrenia**; **tardive psychosis**.

target *n.* **1.** an area or object that is the focus of a process, inquiry, or activity. **2.** the goal object in a task. For example, the target in a VISUAL SEARCH might be to find a letter *S* in a randomly arranged array of letters. In some CONCEPT-DISCOVERY TASKS, the target is the rule that classifies objects as belonging or not belonging to a category. Where a search has more than one item as its goal, these are known as the **target set**. **3.** a tissue, organ, or type of cell that is selectively affected by a particular hormone, neurochemical, drug, or microorganism. **4.** a NEURON that attracts the growth of the DENDRITES or AXONS of other neurons toward it. **5.** in parapsychology experiments, the object or event that the participant attempts to identify in tests of CLAIRVOYANCE, the message that he or she attempts to respond to in tests of TELEPATHY, or the object that he or she attempts to influence in tests of PSYCHOKINESIS.

target behavior the specific behavior or behavioral pattern selected for modification in BEHAVIOR THERAPY.

target device the appliance, furnishing, or equipment that responds to commands from a CONTROL DEVICE. See also ENVIRONMENTAL CONTROL DEVICE; FEEDBACK DEVICE; SWITCH DEVICE.

target language 1. the second or additional language that a nonnative speaker is attempting to use or learn. See also INTERLANGUAGE. **2.** the language into which a translation has been or is being made. Compare SOURCE LANGUAGE.

target patient in STRUCTURED INTERACTIONAL GROUP PSYCHOTHERAPY, the group member who becomes the focus of attention and discussion.

target population the population that a study is intended to research and to which generalizations from samples are to be made.

target response the response (or response class) chosen to be studied or for which consequences are to be arranged.

target stimulus a specific stimulus to which participants in a test or experimental procedure must attend or respond. For example, in tests of hearing the target stimulus may be a specific tone that must be identified; in studies of MASKING, it is the stimulus obscured or altered by the masker.

Tartini's tone a COMBINATION TONE, specifically a difference tone. [first noted by Giuseppe **Tartini** (1692–1770), Italian musician]

TAS abbreviation for TELLEGEN ABSORPTION SCALE.

task *n.* **1.** any goal-oriented activity undertaken by an individual or a group. **2.** a laboratory activity in which participants are set particular objectives and their attempts to achieve these are monitored. Such tasks are used in studies of problem solving, decision making, group interaction, and many other fields. **3.** in perception and cognition, a laboratory activity in which the presentation of stimuli and the possible responses to be made by the participant are controlled by the experimenter so that precise inferences may be made about how perception or cognition changes as a function of changes in task parameters. See also SEARCH.

task analysis 1. the breakdown of a complex task into component tasks to identify the different skills needed to correctly complete the task. In education, for example, it entails the breakdown of a subject or field of study to identify the specific skills the student must possess in order to master it; in industrial and organizational settings, a job is broken down into the skills, knowledge, and specific operations required. See also JOB ANALYSIS. **2.** in ergonomics, a method of evaluating a product or system in which researchers interview actual or target users in order to find out (a) what tasks are performed; (b) which of these are most frequently performed and which are most important; (c) how and in what sequence the tasks are performed; (d) what standards of performance apply; and (e) how different categories of user vary in their answers to the above. Although some scripted questions are asked, the interviews are otherwise unstructured, the better to reflect users' actual experience. Compare COGNITIVE WALKTHROUGH METHOD; CONVERSATION ANALYSIS; HEURISTIC.

task cohesion the degree to which members of a team or group are attracted to a task and work together through the integration of their skills to complete the task successfully.

task complexity the degree to which there is a need to integrate complicated interactions among different mental and physical aspects of a task.

task demands the impact of a task's characteristics, including its divisibility and difficulty, on the procedures that an individual or group can use to complete the task.

task-focused thinking thought that is related solely to the task being undertaken.

task force a small group of individuals given responsibility for a comparatively short-term assignment with specific objectives.

task identity a motivating characteristic of tasks specified in the JOB-CHARACTERISTICS MODEL of U.S. psychologist J. Richard Hackman (1940–) and U.S. organizational behaviorist Greg R. Oldham (1947–). A job is high in task identity if it entails responsibility for a complete and identifiable piece of work (see NATURAL WORK MODULE), as in writing a book or planning and executing an action program from start to finish. Compare TASK SIGNIFICANCE.

task inventory in industrial and organizational settings, a list of the specific tasks required by a job or position. Also called **job inventory**. See also JOB ANALYSIS; JOB DESCRIPTION; TASK ANALYSIS.

task-motivated *adj.* denoting a LEADERSHIP STYLE in which the leader concentrates on structuring the tasks the group must complete, providing task-related feedback, and setting goals. It is assessed using the LEAST PREFERRED COWORKER SCALE. Also called **task-oriented**. Compare RELATIONSHIP-MOTIVATED.

task orientation a motivational focus on mastering a task. Task orientation is a component of the ACHIEVEMENT GOAL THEORY.

task-oriented group a group primarily devoted to solving a problem, providing a service, creating a product, or other goal-directed behavior. See ACTION GROUP; WORK GROUP. See also INSTRUMENTAL ORIENTATION.

task role one of several identifiable ROLES adopted by group members who perform particular behaviors that promote completion of tasks and activities. Although studies have listed and labeled these roles in various different ways, some commonly cited task roles include the INITIATOR, who sets goals and suggests ways of attaining them; the OPINION GIVER (or information giver); the OPINION SEEKER (or information seeker); the **summarizer**, who clarifies what others have said and pulls ideas together; and the **recorder**, who writes down suggestions and decisions. Compare RELATIONSHIP ROLE. See also GROUP ROLES.

task significance a motivating characteristic of tasks specified in the JOB-CHARACTERISTICS MODEL developed by U.S. psychologist J. Richard Hackman (1940–) and U.S. organizational behaviorist Greg R. Oldham (1947–). Jobs high in task significance are those jobs that are perceived to be important to the organization or to have high impact on the lives of others. Compare TASK IDENTITY.

task specificity of language the theory, mainly associated with Noam CHOMSKY, that language use differs from other cognitive tasks in qualitative ways and makes use of components that are specific to this purpose. The theory accords with Chomsky's ideas of AUTONOMOUS SYNTAX and intuited GRAMMATICALITY but is incompatible with the approaches taken in FUNCTIONAL GRAMMAR, COGNITIVE GRAMMAR, or behaviorist accounts of language (see VERBAL BEHAVIOR). See also MODULARITY; SPECIES SPECIFICITY OF LANGUAGE.

task structure the extent to which there is a clear relationship of means to ends in the performance of a task. In a highly structured task the procedures required to perform the task successfully are known, whereas in an unstructured task there is uncertainty about how to proceed.

task switching a procedure in which the participant switches between two or more tasks, typically according to a regular schedule. The usual finding is that responses are slower when the task switches than when the same task is merely repeated.

tastant *n.* a substance that can be tasted.

taste *n.* the sense devoted to the detection of molecules dissolved in liquids (also called **gustation**), or the sensory experience resulting from perception of GUSTATORY QUALITIES. Dissolved molecules are delivered to the taste receptors—TASTE CELLS—on the tongue, soft palate, larynx, and pharynx. Of the proposed five PRIMARY TASTES, three are dedicated to detecting nutrients: SWEET (sugars), SALTY (sodium), and UMAMI (proteins), and two are for protection: SOUR (from unripe or spoiled foods) and BITTER (from toxins). Taste combines with smell, texture, and appearance to generate a sense of FLAVOR.

taste adaptation a decrease in sensitivity to a stimulus that has been presented continuously to the GUSTATORY SYSTEM. Adaptation can be complete, and the perception lost, after minutes of stimulation. Adaptation is used to determine whether two stimuli share the same receptor population by inducing adaptation to the first stimulus and then evaluating the degree to which the perception of the second stimulus is diminished.

taste aversion avoidance of a particular taste. See CONDITIONED TASTE AVERSION.

taste-aversion learning see CONDITIONED TASTE AVERSION.

taste blindness reduced sensitivity to the bitter taste of phenylthiocarbamide (PTC) or propylthiouracil (PROP). Originally thought to be a simple Mendelian RECESSIVE TRAIT, taste blindness is now known to extend to other bitter tastes, as well as to salty and sweet tastes, and is associated with having fewer TASTE BUDS.

taste bud a goblet-shaped structure, 30 × 50 μm, about 6,000 of which occur in the human mouth. Each bud is a collection of about 50 TASTE CELLS arranged like sections of an orange. At its apex is a TASTE PORE through which each taste cell sends a MICROVILLUS studded with receptor proteins to sample the environment.

taste cell a receptor cell for GUSTATORY STIMULI. Each has a hairlike extension (see MICROVILLUS) that protrudes from the opening in the TASTE BUD. Humans have about 300,000 taste cells, though the number can vary across individuals, and there are about 50 cells per taste bud. Taste cells can be divided into four anatomical types: TYPE I CELLS comprise 60% of the total, TYPE II CELLS 20%, TYPE III CELLS 15%, and TYPE IV CELLS 5%. All but Type IV cells may be involved in TASTE TRANSDUCTION. See also GUSTATORY NEURON TYPES.

taste pore a 6-μm opening at the top of each taste bud through which the MICROVILLI of its 50 taste cells project to sample the chemical environment.

taste stimulus see GUSTATORY STIMULUS.

taste system see GUSTATORY SYSTEM.

taste transduction the sequence of events involved in converting the detection of chemical molecules into taste signals. GUSTATORY STIMULI interact with the MICROVILLUS of a taste cell, which results in changes in activity in the ion channels within taste receptors. The subsequent DEPOLARIZATION within these receptors triggers the release of neurotransmitters that stimulate sensory neurons in the peripheral nervous system (see GREATER SUPERFICIAL PETROSAL NERVE). The mechanisms of transduction vary with the type of gustatory stimulus, although each taste cell is capable of transducing different stimuli. Also called **gustatory transduction**.

TAT abbreviation for THEMATIC APPERCEPTION TEST.

tau effect 1. the effect of the timing of stimuli on their perceived spatial location. For example, if three equidistant lights are flashed in succession, but the time interval between the first two is shorter than that between the second and third, then the first two lights are perceived to be closer together than the second and third. **2.** the invariant that the time to contact between an object and an observer moving at a constant speed toward each other is inversely proportional to the rate of expansion of the observer's retinal image of the object, regardless of the size of the object or the speed at which it travels. Research suggests that the tau effect is used in a variety of situations involving the control of movements, for example, by a ballplayer when preparing to catch a ball and by a diving gull in retracting its wings before hitting the surface of the water to catch a fish.

tautology *n.* **1.** in logic, a statement that is always and necessarily true by virtue of the meaning of its component terms and that therefore has no propositional content, as *Either he is alive or he is not alive*. See also CIRCULAR REASONING. **2.** in general use, needless repetition of an idea in a different word, phrase, or sentence, as in *necessary essential* or *individual person*. **—tautological** *adj.*

Tavistock Clinic a major British provider of clinical mental health services, set up in Tavistock Square, London, England, in 1919. It became a part of the National Health Service in 1947, when the separate **Tavistock Institute of Human Relations** was founded to relate the psychological and social sciences to the needs of society. In 1994 the Tavistock Clinic and the PORTMAN CLINIC became a trust of the National Health Service and its leading organization for providing postgraduate training in mental health.

taxis *n.* (*pl.* **taxes**) active movement of motile organisms in response to a stimulus. Taxis can be a negative response, marked by movement away from the stimulus, or positive, in which case the organism moves toward the stimulus. Taxis differs from TROPISM, which refers to a simple orientation to or from a natural force (e.g., light or gravity) without changing place, as in plants. Kinds of taxis include PHOTOTAXIS, in which movement is toward a light source; GEOTAXIS, marked by a movement toward the earth; and **chemotaxis**, in which the movement is in response to chemicals in the environment. **Tropotaxis** indicates a direct path toward a source, such as a food smell; **klinotaxis** is a movement interrupted by pauses to evaluate the sources of stimuli. Also called **taxic behavior**. Compare KINESIS. **—taxic** or **tactic** *adj.*

taxonomic classification see CONCEPTUAL CLASSIFICATION.

taxonomy *n.* the science of classification, for example, BIOLOGICAL TAXONOMY. **—taxonomic** *adj.* **—taxonomist** *n.*

taxonomy of educational objectives a hierarchy of levels of cognitive performance that include knowledge, comprehension, application, analysis, synthesis, and evaluation. Students must first successfully complete initial objectives, then build on these to reach higher level objectives of critical thinking and skill. The taxonomy accommodates a student who memorizes facts and uses them in simple problem solving and who can also understand component parts of information, put that information into a new whole, and then make judgments about the importance of that information. These categories have been widely accepted as forming the distinctions between lower level thinking and higher level or critical thinking. The taxonomy is ultimately a guideline for understanding the critical mental processing that is generally defined as rational, analytical, and evaluative thinking. [described in 1956 by U.S. educator Benjamin S. Bloom (1913–1999)]

Taylorism *n.* see SCIENTIFIC MANAGEMENT.

Taylor Manifest Anxiety Scale a 65-item self-report scale, derived from the MINNESOTA MULTIPHASIC PERSONALITY INVENTORY, that was first developed in 1951 and modified and shortened to 50 items in 1953. The scale, consisting of statements (e.g., "I cannot keep my mind on one thing") to which participants respond "true" or "false," formerly enjoyed frequent use in research as a general measure of anxiety symptoms. It correlates with other anxiety measures and with physiological indicators of anxiety. Also called **Manifest Anxiety Scale**. See ANXIETY SCALE. [devised by U.S. psychologist Janet **Taylor** Spence (1923–)]

Taylor–Russell tables in industrial and organizational theory, tables that allow those responsible for personnel selection to estimate the potential value of a test or other predictor on the basis of (a) the SELECTION RATIO, (b) the VALIDITY of the predictor, and (c) the BASE RATE of success of employees hired under current procedures. [Harold C. **Taylor** and James T. **Russell**, 20th-century U.S. personnel psychologists]

Tay–Sachs disease (**TSD**) an AUTOSOMAL RECESSIVE disorder primarily affecting Ashkenazi Jews of central and eastern European origin. The disease is due to a deficiency of the enzyme hexosaminidase A, resulting in the accumulation of G_{M2} gangliosides in all tissues (see GANGLIOSIDOSIS). This process gradually destroys the brain and nerve cells by altering the shape of neurons. Development is normal until the 6th month of infancy, after which there is a deterioration of motor, visual, and cognitive abilities. Death usually occurs between 3 and 5 years of age. Also called **G_{M2} gangliosidosis**. [Warren **Tay** (1843–1927), British physician; Bernard **Sachs** (1858–1944), U.S. neurologist]

TBI abbreviation for TRAUMATIC BRAIN INJURY.

TBR items abbreviation for TO-BE-REMEMBERED ITEMS.

TCAs abbreviation for TRICYCLIC ANTIDEPRESSANTS.

T cell see LYMPHOCYTE.

T data information about an individual's personality that has been obtained through *t*ests. See also L DATA; O DATA; Q DATA.

TDD abbreviation for TELECOMMUNICATION DEVICE.

t distribution a theoretical PROBABILITY DISTRIBUTION that plays a central role in testing hypotheses about population means among other parameters. It is the sampling distribution of the statistic $(M - \mu_0)/s$, where μ_0 is the population mean of the population from which the sample is drawn, M is the data estimate of the mean of the population, and s is the standard deviation of the batch of scores. Also called **Student's t distribution**.

teacher-effectiveness evaluation an assessment of specific criteria for instructors, including classroom management, curriculum, parental communication, and the effectiveness of the instructor as shown by student progress. See also STUDENTS' EVALUATION OF TEACHING.

teaching games classroom instruction in the form of games designed to engage students' active interest as they work on specific skills (e.g., vocabulary or mathematics). Teaching games can provide a unique opportunity to give students incentives, such as specific rewards or the pleasure of winning.

teaching machine a simple or elaborate instrument that (a) automatically presents programmed material to the learner, (b) provides an opportunity to check understanding at each step through problems or questions, and (c) provides feedback as to whether the response is right or wrong. One equivalent of the teaching machine is PROGRAMMED INSTRUCTION, which B. F. SKINNER advocated. The modern-day equivalent of teaching machines is the personal computer, which is widely accepted as a supplement for teaching complex tasks, concepts, or skills, in addition to specific content areas. See BRANCHING.

teaching model see DEVELOPMENTAL TEACHING MODEL.

teaching style the personal attributes that define a teacher's classroom methods and behavior. Qualities associated with teacher effectiveness include mastery of subject matter, pedagogical thinking, organizational ability, enthusiasm, warmth, calmness, and the establishment of a rapport with students.

team *n.* an organized task-focused group. Members of such groups combine their individual inputs in a deliberate way in the pursuit of a common goal and are typically cohesive and united.

team building a structured intervention designed to increase the extent to which a group functions as a team. Such interventions often involve assessing the current level of GROUP DEVELOPMENT, clarifying and prioritizing goals, and increasing group cohesiveness.

team goals **1.** goals set collectively by a team. **2.** goals set by coaches for team performance.

team mental model in ergonomics, a MENTAL MODEL of a work system that is held in common by the members of a team. Ideally, team members should have a shared mental picture of the system and its attributes, a shared knowledge of all relevant tasks, and a shared understanding of the team's progress toward its goal. Coordination, efficiency, and accuracy will increase as team members converge on a common mental model that is accurate and complete yet flexible. Also called **shared mental model**.

teamwork *n.* cooperative effort toward a common goal or on a common project.

tease *vb.* to bother, provoke, or torment another person through various types of irritating behavior, such as name-calling, insults, or repetitive annoyances. Teasing can be playful and affectionate or malicious and bullying.

technical *adj.* **1.** relating to specialized skills, abilities, or techniques. **2.** relating to skills or abilities that are mechanical, industrial, or technological. **3.** denoting scientific specialization or character.

technical eclecticism in INTEGRATIVE PSYCHOTHERAPY, the use of techniques from various theoretical frameworks to deal with the complex issues of a client. Technical eclecticism uses a systematic and carefully thought out approach that balances theoretical perspectives and treatment processes. [developed by South African-born U.S. psychologist Arnold Allan Lazarus (1932–)]

technical term a word or phrase used in a specialized field to refer to objects or concepts that are particular to that field and for which there are no adequate terms in ordinary language. See also JARGON.

technological gatekeeper an organizational or GROUP ROLE that involves channeling information about technological innovations into the organization from the outside. People occupying this role communicate with professionals inside and outside the organization, serving as the conduit for new technical information.

technological illiteracy lack of knowledge of technology, especially a lack of the technological knowledge that a well-educated layperson would generally be expected to have. Technological illiteracy, in this sense, can be a handicap in modern society. See COMPUTER ILLITERACY.

tectal nucleus any of certain NUCLEI located in the SUPERIOR COLLICULUS and INFERIOR COLLICULUS in the dorsal part of the midbrain. They perform relay functions for the visual and auditory systems and they integrate reflex functions. Some neurons in these nuclei are bimodal, responding to both visual and auditory stimuli.

tectorial membrane part of the ORGAN OF CORTI in the cochlea. It consists of a semigelatinous membrane in which the stereocilia of the outer HAIR CELLS are embedded.

tectospinal tract a tract of nerve fibers that starts at the SUPERIOR COLLICULUS, crosses the midline at the midbrain, and descends through the midbrain, pons, and medulla oblongata to terminate in the cervical (neck) region of the spinal cord. It functions in turning the head in response to visual, auditory, and somatosensory stimuli. See also VENTROMEDIAL PATHWAYS.

tectum *n.* (*pl.* **tecta**) the roof of the MIDBRAIN, dorsal to the CEREBRAL AQUEDUCT. The tectum contains the SUPERIOR COLLICULI, which act as relay and reflex centers for the visual system, and the INFERIOR COLLICULI, which are sensory centers for the auditory system. **—tectal** *adj.*

teenage pregnancy see ADOLESCENT PREGNANCY.

teeth grinding see BRUXISM.

teething *n.* the process in which the teeth erupt through the gums, typically occurring between 4 and 9 months of age. During this process, the infant may exhibit several accompanying symptoms, such as an increase in irritability, sleep disturbance, temporary rejection of breast or bottle feeding, gum inflammation, and excessive drooling.

tegmentum *n.* (*pl.* **tegmenta**) the central core of the MIDBRAIN and PONS. It contains sensory and motor tracts passing through the midbrain and also several nuclei, including the OCULOMOTOR NUCLEUS, RED NUCLEUS, and SUBTHALAMIC NUCLEUS. **—tegmental** *adj.*

Tegretol *n.* a trade name for CARBAMAZEPINE.

tele- (**tel-**) *combining form* **1.** distant or over a distance (e.g., TELEPATHY). **2.** television or telephone (e.g., TELECONFERENCING).

telecanthus-hypospadias syndrome a hereditary disorder marked by widely spaced eyes, a high nose bridge, and a urethral opening on the ventral side of the penis. Some affected individuals also show mental retardation, with IQs in the 40s and 50s. Recent research suggests that the condition is genetically heterogeneous, with both X-linked and autosomal forms. Also called **BBBG** (or **GBBB**) **syndrome** (from the names of the affected families originally reported); **Opitz–Frias syndrome**.

teleceptor *n.* a sensory nerve ending that can detect stimuli from a distance (e.g., a receptor in the eye, nose, or ear). Also called **distance receptor**.

telecommunication device (**TDD**) a device used by individuals with hearing loss or speech impairments to communicate via telephone lines. It typically consists of a keyboard, a letter display, and a cradle for the telephone receiver and may also include a printer. An individual types a message and sends it, and another individual with a telecommunication device receives the message, views it on the display, and then types and sends a response. Also called **text telephone** (**TTY**).

telecommuting *n.* working from home using a computer, telephone, and (possibly) a fax machine to communicate with people at the central workplace or at other locations. Also called **teleworking**. **—telecommute** *vb.* **—telecommuter** *n.*

teleconferencing *n.* the use of telecommunications links (e.g., telephone or video systems) to enable real-time group meetings of individuals who are physically distant from one another. **—teleconference** *n., vb.*

telegnosis *n.* in parapsychology, alleged knowledge of distant events without direct communication, as by CLAIRVOYANCE or TELEPATHY. See EXTRASENSORY PERCEPTION.

telegraphic speech **1.** condensed or abbreviated speech in which only the most central words, carrying the highest level of information, are spoken. Nouns and verbs are typically featured, while adjectives, adverbs, articles, and connective parts of speech are omitted. **2.** the speech of children roughly between the ages of 18 and 30 months, which is usually in the form of two-word expressions. Such speech is telegraphic in that it uses only the most germane and prominent features of language, bypassing articles, prepositions, and other ancillary words. **3.** the speech of children approximately 24 to 30 months of age that develops after the TWO-WORD STAGE and is characterized by short but multiword expressions (e.g., *dog eat bone*). Also called **telegraphic stage**.

telehealth *n.* the use of telecommunications and information technology to provide access to health assessment, diagnosis, intervention, and information across a distance, rather than face to face. Also called **telemedicine**.

telekinesis *n.* see PSYCHOKINESIS.

telemedicine *n.* see TELEHEALTH.

telemetry *n.* the process of measuring and transmitting quantitative information to a remote location, where it can be recorded and interpreted. For example, a small radio transmitter may be implanted inside an animal to measure general activity level as well as a variety of physiological variables, including body temperature, heart rate, and blood pressure. This transmitter sends signals to a receiver located outside the animal. **—telemetric** *adj.*

telencephalon *n.* see CEREBRUM.

teleologic regression see PROGRESSIVE TELEOLOGIC REGRESSION.

teleology *n.* **1.** the position that certain phenomena are best understood and explained in terms of their purposes rather than their causes. In psychology, its proponents hold that mental processes are purposive, that is, directed toward a goal. The view that behavior is to be explained in terms of ends and purposes is frequently contrasted with explanations in terms of causes, such as INSTINCTS and CONDITIONED RESPONSES. See also HORMIC PSYCHOLOGY; PURPOSIVE PSYCHOLOGY. **2.** the doctrine that the universe or human history or both have purpose and direction and are moving toward a particular goal. This position is usually, but not always, a religious one. **—teleologic** or **teleological** *adj.*

teleonomy *n.* **1.** the property of being goal-directed in terms of structures, functions, and behaviors that is a fundamental characteristic of living organisms. **2.** the apparently directional or "purposeful" character of evolutionary adaptation. The term is used in this context in order to avoid the metaphysical implications of TELEOLOGY. **3.** the scientific study of living organisms in terms of evolutionary adaptation. **—teleonomic** *adj.*

teleoperator *n.* a remote-controlled device or system that augments the operator's physical capabilities while remaining immediately responsive to his or her control (unlike fully automated robotics). Some teleoperators are designed to imitate the body movements of the operator. Teleoperators are used in space, underwater, on high buildings or other inaccessible structures, and in dangerous tasks, such as landmine clearance.

teleopsia *n.* a VISUAL ILLUSION in which an object appears to be more distant than it is in reality. Teleopsia is often associated with STEREOBLINDNESS but may occur independently of the perception of the actual size. Also called **porropsia**. See also METAMORPHOPSIA.

telepathic dream a dream that is allegedly stimulated or influenced by the dream of another person sleeping in the same room. [described by Wilhelm Stekel (1868–1940), Austrian physician]

telepathy *n.* the alleged direct communication of information from one mind to another, in the absence of any known means of transmission. It is a form of EXTRASENSORY PERCEPTION. See also MIND READING; THOUGHT TRANSFERENCE. **—telepath** *n.* **—telepathic** *adj.*

telephone counseling **1.** a method of treating and dealing with the problems of clients by telephone. The skills for telephone counseling include (a) careful selection of problems that lend themselves to the medium, (b) ACTIVE LISTENING for cues to issues and ramifications of the problems, (c) good verbal skills that guide the client appropriately, and (d) ability to respond quickly to avoid gaps and awkward silences. **2.** free HOTLINE telephone services that provide listening and referral services rather than formal counseling. Hotline volunteers are trained to provide emotional support in serious situations, especially those involving suicidal thoughts, but not to give formal advice. See also DISTANCE THERAPY.

telephone interview an interview that is conducted by telephone rather than face to face.

telephone scatologia a PARAPHILIA in which an individual obtains sexual pleasure by making obscene telephone calls. See SCATOPHILIA.

telephone theory see HEARING THEORIES.

teleplasm *n.* see ECTOPLASM. **—teleplasmic** *adj.*

telepresence *n.* the sense of being at a remote site when provided with sensory information (e.g., sights, sounds, or textures) from that distant place. See also REMOTE PERCEPTION.

telepsychotherapy *n.* see DISTANCE THERAPY.

telergy *n.* in parapsychology, the alleged ability of a SENSITIVE to confer paranormal abilities on another person via TELEPATHY.

telesis *n.* purposeful, planned efforts directed toward achieving a particular goal.

telesthesia (**telaesthesia**) *n.* see CRYPTESTHESIA. **—telesthetic** *adj.*

Telfaire instructions cautionary instructions read to juries in cases in which eyewitness identification may be the most critical evidence against the defendant. The instructions address issues that are suspected to lead to eyewitness misidentification and were originally proposed by the judge hearing the appeal in the case *United States v. Telfaire* (1972), in which the defendant had been convicted solely on the evidence of an identifying witness who was of a different race.

telic *adj.* purposeful or goal-directed in nature, as in **telic behavior**. See also TELEOLOGY.

telic continuum a typically J-shaped curve that describes purposeful behavior, plotting the degree of conformity to an established rule or principle. Also called **conformity curve**.

Tellegen Absorption Scale (**TAS**) a measure of a person's ability to become deeply involved in a task or other aspect of the environment. Consisting of 34 statements (e.g., "I like to watch cloud shapes change in the sky") to which participants respond "true" or "false," it is considered to be a reliable indication of the ease with which an individual can be hypnotized. See ABSORPTION. [devised in 1974 by U.S. psychologist Auke **Tellegen** (1930–)]

telodendron *n.* see END BRUSH.

temazepam *n.* an intermediate-acting BENZODIAZEPINE used for the short-term treatment of insomnia. Temazepam is readily processed in the liver to form an inactive metabolic product; it therefore has a relatively predictable HALF-LIFE and does not accumulate in the body with repeated doses. However, as with other benzodiazepine HYPNOTICS, TOLERANCE can occur with repeated use. U.S. trade name: **Restoril**.

temper *n.* **1.** a display of irritation or anger. See also TEMPER TANTRUM. **2.** a tendency to be quick to anger. **3.** a personality characteristic, disposition, or mood.

temperament *n.* the basic foundation of personality, usually assumed to be biologically determined and present early in life, including such characteristics as energy level, emotional responsiveness, response tempo, and willingness to explore. In animal behavior, temperament is defined as an individual's constitutional pattern of reactions, with a similar range of characteristics. Studies of animals ranging from fish to primates have documented differences in temperament, particularly along the SHY–BOLD CONTINUUM. Within each population there are individuals that show high levels of exploratory behavior toward novel features and others that appear to display NEOPHOBIA.

temperament theory the belief that behavioral tendencies are biologically based and present from birth, forming the DISPOSITION of the individual.

temperament trait 1. a biologically based, inherited personality characteristic. **2.** a personality trait that involves emotional qualities and affective styles of behavior. It is one of three classes of SOURCE TRAITS in CATTELL'S FACTORIAL THEORY OF PERSONALITY, the other two being ABILITY TRAITS and DYNAMIC TRAITS.

temperance *n.* any form of auspicious self-restraint, manifested as self-regulation in monitoring and managing one's emotions, motivation, and behavior and as self-control in the attainment of adaptive goals.

temperature illusion a misinterpretation of a temperature stimulus. PARADOXICAL COLD is an example: A very hot shower may cause goose bumps and a feeling of cold. Also called **thermal illusion**.

temperature sense a part of the SOMATOSENSORY SYSTEM concerned with the perception of hotness and coldness, with receptors at various depths in the skin and other body surfaces (e.g., the tongue) that may be exposed to the environment. Also called **thermoesthesia**; **thermesthesia**.

temperature spot an area of the skin that contains temperature-sensitive receptors.

temper tantrum a violent outburst of anger commonly occurring between the ages of 2 and 4 and involving such behavior as screaming, kicking, biting, hitting, and head banging. The episodes are usually out of proportion to immediate provocation and sometimes regarded as an expression of accumulated tensions and frustrations. Also called **tantrum**. See also OPPOSITIONAL DEFIANT DISORDER.

template-matching theory the hypothesis that PATTERN RECOGNITION proceeds by comparing an incoming sensory stimulation pattern to mental images or representations of patterns (templates) until a match is found. This theory is largely considered too simplistic, since the same stimulus can be viewed from multiple perspectives, thereby altering the input pattern, and since a particular stimulus can have many different variations (e.g., a letter of the alphabet can be printed in numerous styles, sizes, orientations, etc.); it is impossible to store a template for each specific perspective or variation.

temporal *adj.* **1.** of or pertaining to time or its role in some process, as in TEMPORAL CONDITIONING or TEMPORAL SUMMATION. **2.** relating or proximal to the temple, as in TEMPORAL LOBE. **—temporally** *adv.*

temporal appraisal theory a model stating that people's evaluations of themselves in the past tend to be more negative than their current evaluations of themselves.

temporal arteritis see ARTERITIS.

temporal aspects of consciousness properties of consciousness relating to time, including the FLEETING PRESENT, the length of time necessary for sensory stimulation to come to awareness, and the subjective perception of duration. See PROTENSITY.

temporal bone the bone, located in the side and base of the skull, that contains the MIDDLE EAR and the INNER EAR.

temporal coherence see COHERENCE.

temporal conditioning a procedure in PAVLOVIAN CONDITIONING in which the unconditioned stimulus is presented at regular intervals but in the absence of an accompanying conditioned stimulus. Compare TRACE CONDITIONING.

temporal construal theory a model stating that people rely on largely abstract representations (high-level construals) of future situations when making decisions for the distant future but on more concrete representations (low-level construals) when making decisions for the near future.

temporal discrimination in conditioning, a DISCRIMINATION in which the duration of a stimulus or circumstance is the controlling variable.

temporal-frequency discrimination the ability to distinguish different temporal patterns in visual, auditory, or other types of stimuli (e.g., different pulse rates by touch). See also PATTERN DISCRIMINATION.

temporal gradient a pattern of RETROGRADE AMNESIA characterized by greater loss of memory for events from the recent past (i.e., close to the onset of the amnesia) than for events from the remote past. See also RIBOT'S LAW.

temporal hallucinations see TEMPORAL LOBE ILLUSIONS.

temporal lobe one of the four main lobes of each CEREBRAL HEMISPHERE in the brain, lying immediately below the LATERAL SULCUS on the lower lateral surface of each hemisphere. It contains the auditory projection and auditory association areas and also areas for higher order visual processing. The MEDIAL TEMPORAL LOBE contains regions important for memory formation.

temporal lobe amnesia a memory disorder, secondary to injury of the temporal lobe (particularly medial structures, such as the hippocampus), that prevents the formation of new memories.

temporal lobectomy the surgical excision of a temporal lobe or a portion of the lobe. It may be performed in the treatment of temporal lobe epilepsy, the location and size of the lesion determining which tissues and related functions may be affected.

temporal lobe epilepsy a type of epilepsy characterized by recurrent COMPLEX PARTIAL SEIZURES of temporal lobe origin.

temporal lobe illusions distorted perceptions that may be associated with COMPLEX PARTIAL SEIZURES arising from abnormal discharge of neurons in the temporal lobe. They often include distortions of the sizes or shapes of objects, recurring dreamlike thoughts, or sensations of déjà vu. Hallucinations, such as the sound of threatening voices, may also be experienced. Also called **temporal hallucinations**; **temporal lobe hallucinations**.

temporal lobe syndrome a group of personality and behavioral disturbances associated with temporal lobe epilepsy in some individuals. These may include a profound sense of righteousness, preoccupation with details, compulsive writing or drawing, religiosity, and changes in sexual attitudes.

temporal modulation transfer function (**TMTF**) a function describing the ability to follow temporal changes in the magnitude of a stimulus. In PSYCHOACOUSTICS, a TMTF is usually obtained by measuring the amount of sinusoidal amplitude MODULATION that is necessary to detect the modulation (a **modulation threshold**) as a function of frequency of modulation. TMTFs are similarly measured in other modalities. The utility of the TMTF is grounded in linear systems theory, specifically the principle that the transfer function of a LINEAR SYSTEM provides a complete description of the system.

temporal perceptual disorder a condition, observed in some individuals with lesions in the left hemisphere of the brain, that is characterized by difficulty in temporal perception of visual and auditory stimuli. For example, individuals may be unable to identify the sequences of vowels repeated at measured time intervals.

temporal precedence the principle that what is labeled as the cause must be shown to have occurred before the effect.

temporal summation a neural mechanism in which an impulse is propagated by two successive POSTSYNAPTIC POTENTIALS (PSPs), neither of which alone is of sufficient intensity to cause a response. The partial DEPOLARIZATION caused by the first PSP continues for a few milliseconds and is able, with the additive effect of the second PSP, to produce an above-threshold depolarization sufficient to elicit an ACTION POTENTIAL. Compare SPATIAL SUMMATION.

temporary commitment emergency INVOLUNTARY HOSPITALIZATION of a patient with a mental disorder for a limited period of observation or treatment.

temporary lesion a nonpermanent disruption of the normal functioning of a specific brain area in an organism. This is produced by an injection of drugs into that brain area or by electromagnetic stimulation of the area.

temporary threshold shift (**TTS**) a temporary condition in which the normal level of hearing is altered or disrupted. For example, after relatively prolonged exposure to very loud noise, the absolute threshold may shift so that minimal sound intensities one could normally detect are temporarily inaudible. A similar shift can occur in vision.

temporomandibular joint syndrome see TMJ SYNDROME.

temptation *n.* a desire, or a stimulus that facilitates a desire, to behave in a certain way, especially in a way that is contrary to one's own or society's standards of behavior.

tendentious apperception the tendency to perceive what one wishes to perceive in an event or situation. See APPERCEPTION; APPERCEPTIVE MASS. See also PERCEPTUAL SET.

tender-mindedness *n.* a personality trait characterized by intellectualism, idealism, optimism, dogmatism, religiousness, and monism. Compare TOUGH-MINDEDNESS. [first described by William JAMES] **—tender-minded** *adj.*

tender years doctrine the assumption in CHILD CUSTODY cases that mothers should be awarded custody of their children during the formative years of development. See also PRIMARY CARETAKER STANDARD.

tendinitis *n.* see REPETITIVE STRAIN INJURY.

tendon *n.* a strong band of tissue that connects a muscle to a bone.

tendon reflex the reflex contraction of a muscle elicited by stretching a tendon. Such reflexes are mediated by tendon stretch detectors, called GOLGI TENDON ORGANS. An example of a tendon reflex is the KNEE-JERK REFLEX, elicited by tapping or stretching the patellar tendon just below the kneecap. Also called **deep reflex**.

tendon sensation the kinesthetic sensation produced by stimulation of receptors in a tendon, for example, by stretching it.

Tenex *n.* a trade name for GUANFACINE.

Tennessee Self-Concept Scale (**TSCS**) a self-report assessment currently consisting of descriptive statements to which participants respond using a 5-point scale, ranging from "always false" to "always true." It is available in two forms—Adult, containing 82 items for use with individuals aged 13 years and older, and Child, containing 76 items for use with individuals aged 7 to 14 years—and yields measurements on six substantive dimensions of SELF-CONCEPT (Physical, Moral, Personal, Family, Social, Academic/Work) within three domains (Identity, Satisfaction, Behavior). The TSCS was originally published in 1964; the most recent version is the **TSCS–2**, published in 1996. [originally developed by U.S. psychologist William H. Fitts (1918–)]

TENS *t*ranscutaneous *e*lectrical *n*erve *s*timulation: a procedure in which mild electrical pulses are delivered through small electrodes attached to the skin. TENS is most commonly used to relieve or reduce chronic pain: The pulses stimulate nerves that supply the region in which the pain is felt and thus inhibit transmission of pain signals.

tense 1. *adj.* in a state of nervous activity. **2.** *adj.* stretched tight or strained. **3.** *n.* in linguistics, one of a set of forms taken by a verb in order to mark the relation between the time of the reported action (or state or condition) and the time of the utterance. In addition to the simple present (*I run*) and simple past (*I ran*), English has a future tense formed using the AUXILIARY VERBS *shall* and *will*; additional **aspects** of the verb, expressing completed or continuous action, can be formed using the auxiliary verbs *be*, *have*, and *do* (*I did run*, *I am running*, etc.).

tension *n.* **1.** a feeling of physical and psychological strain accompanied by discomfort, uneasiness, and pressure to seek relief through talk or action. **2.** the force resulting from contraction or stretching of a muscle or tendon.

tension headache a persistent headache produced by acute or prolonged emotional tension and usually accompanied by insomnia, irritability, and painful contraction of the neck muscles.

tension law a concept that any deviation from an organism's optimal level of external conditions (e.g., temperature, atmospheric pressure) produces a state of tension. Compare HOMEOSTASIS. [Joseph Jean **Delboeuf** (1831-1896), Belgian psychologist]

tension reduction alleviation of feelings of tension.

A variety of techniques may be used for this purpose, for example, RELAXATION THERAPY, tranquilizing drugs, muscle relaxants, hypnotic suggestion, periods of MEDITATION, verbal CATHARSIS, or MOVEMENT THERAPY.

tensor tympani a middle ear muscle that controls the movement of the TYMPANIC MEMBRANE (eardrum). Its activation (the **tympanic reflex**) is part of the ACOUSTIC REFLEX.

tenth cranial nerve see VAGUS NERVE.

tenting *n.* lengthening and expansion of the vagina and elevation of the uterus during the excitement and plateau phases of the female SEXUAL-RESPONSE CYCLE. These changes facilitate entry of the penis and make intercourse more pleasurable.

tentorial herniation see TRANSTENTORIAL HERNIATION.

tentorium cerebelli a fold of DURA MATER that separates the upper (dorsal) surface of the cerebellum from the lower (basal) surfaces of the occipital and temporal lobes of the cerebrum. The tentorium cerebelli is attached at the midline to the falx cerebri, a vertical fold of dura mater that lines the inner (medial) surface of each cerebral hemisphere.

ten–twenty system a standardized system of imaginary lines on the head that allows for placement of electrodes during ELECTROENCEPHALOGRAPHY.

Tenuate *n.* a trade name for DIETHYLPROPION.

tenure *n.* see JOB TENURE.

teratogenic *adj.* inducing developmental abnormalities in a fetus. A **teratogen** is an agent or process that causes such abnormal developments, a process called **teratogenesis**; a **teratomorph** is a fetus or offspring with developmental abnormalities.

teratological defect a structural or functional abnormality in an individual caused by hereditary factors or an environmental influence, such as exposure to drugs or X-rays during the mother's pregnancy. Examples of such defects include Down syndrome, associated with abnormal genetic factors; and the THALIDOMIDE syndrome, marked by deformed arms and legs, caused by thalidomide taken during the mother's pregnancy.

teratology *n.* the study of developmental abnormalities and their causes (see TERATOLOGICAL DEFECT). **—teratological** *adj.*

term *n.* the time when a normal pregnancy is completed. Also called **full term**. See also GESTATION PERIOD; PRETERM VIABILITY.

Terman, Lewis Madison (1877–1956) U.S. psychologist. Terman earned his doctorate at Clark University in 1905, worked for 4 years at the Los Angeles Normal School, and then went to Stanford University, where he spent the remainder of his career. Terman's career was primarily devoted to the development and application of psychological tests. He was responsible for validation and revision of the Binet scales for use in the United States, resulting in the STANFORD–BINET INTELLIGENCE SCALE; construction of the ARMY TESTS administered during World War I; development of the Stanford Achievement Test; and creation of questionnaires designed to reveal *Psychological Factors in Marital Happiness* (1938). He is also noted for developing a series of studies of gifted children and eminent adults (see GENIUS; TERMAN'S GIFTEDNESS STUDY).

Terman–McNemar Test of Mental Ability an early GROUP INTELLIGENCE TEST designed for grades 7 through 12 and consisting of 162 four- or five-option multiple-choice items within seven types of verbal subtests: synonyms, classification, logical selection, information, analogies, opposites, and best answer. It was a modification and replacement of the 1920 **Terman Group Test of Mental Ability**, which was also a group-administered test but consisted of two-option multiple-choice items within 10 subtests (classification, logical selection, information, analogies, best answer, word meaning, sentence meaning, mixed sentences, arithmetic, and number series). [developed in 1942 by Lewis TERMAN and Quinn **McNemar** (1900–1986), U.S. psychologists]

Terman's giftedness study a longitudinal study that examined 1,528 gifted children in California over their lifetimes, beginning in the 1920s. The participants—aged 3 to 19 years—had IQs over 135. The study suggested that individuals who are gifted as children tend to exhibit greater success throughout the course of their lives, as measured by conventional societal standards, than those who are not. It also suggested that 2% of the population is gifted and that gifted children had better health and happier lives than their counterparts. [initiated in 1921 by Lewis TERMAN]

terminal 1. *adj.* referring to the end. **2.** *n.* the end of a structure, such as an AXON TERMINAL.

terminal assessment see SUMMATIVE EVALUATION.

terminal behavior 1. in FREE-OPERANT conditioning under INTERMITTENT REINFORCEMENT, behavior that is predominant in the period shortly before reinforcement occurs. Compare ADJUNCTIVE BEHAVIOR. **2.** a response that either falls outside an organism's current behavioral repertoire or is not occurring at a desired rate, strength, or magnitude. Increasing terminal behavior is the aim of specific behavioral interventions.

terminal button the terminal portion of an AXON from which a neural signal is transmitted, through discharge of a NEUROTRANSMITTER, across a SYNAPSE to a neighboring neuron's dendrites or cell body. Terminal buttons are about 1 μm in diameter, and there may be several on a single axon. As stated in the LAW OF FORWARD CONDUCTION, the normal direction of travel of a nerve impulse is from the dendritic zone toward the terminal buttons of the same neuron. Also called **bouton terminal**; **end button**; **synaptic bouton**; **synaptic knob**; **terminal bulb**.

terminal care services for people with terminal illness, now usually provided by HOSPICES, which may be either freestanding units or associated with a hospital, nursing home, or extended care facility. The emphasis is on palliative care, pain control, supportive psychological services, and involvement in family and social activities, with the goal of enabling patients to live out their lives in comfort, peace, and dignity.

terminal drop a rapid decline in cognitive abilities immediately before death. The cognitive abilities that appear to be most prone to terminal drop are those least affected by normal aging (see HOLD FUNCTIONS). Also called **terminal decline phenomenon**; **terminal drop-decline**.

terminal insomnia a form of INSOMNIA in which the individual habitually awakens very early, feels unrefreshed, and cannot go back to sleep. It is a common symptom of a MAJOR DEPRESSIVE EPISODE. Compare INITIAL INSOMNIA; MIDDLE INSOMNIA.

terminal link the schedule in a CHAINED SCHEDULE that ends in primary reinforcement. It is most often a feature of CONCURRENT-CHAINS PROCEDURES.

terminal threshold the maximum stimulus intensity that will produce a sensation.

termination *n.* in therapy, the conclusion of treatment.

Termination may be suggested by the client or therapist or may be by mutual agreement. Termination can be immediate or prolonged; in the latter case, a date for the final session is established and sessions are sometimes scheduled less frequently over a period. In **premature termination**, treatment is ended before either the therapist or client considers the therapy complete. This may result, for example, from difficulties in the relationship between the therapist and client, misunderstanding of the required length of treatment, a change in the client's financial circumstances, or departure of the client to another location.

territorial aggression the act of defending a defined space (territory) by fighting or threatening intruders of the same species. See also ANIMAL AGGRESSION; TERRITORIALITY.

territorial dominance 1. the ability of resident animals to protect a defined space (their territory) as well as to drive out intruders that may be larger and stronger. Residents typically have a competitive advantage over intruders that they would not have in a neutral environment. See TERRITORIALITY. **2.** the ability of people to dominate interpersonal interactions to a greater extent when in their own homes or offices.

territoriality *n.* **1.** the defense by an animal of a specific geographic area (its **territory**) against intrusion from other members of the same species. Territory (or PRIMARY TERRITORY) differs from HOME RANGE (see also SECONDARY TERRITORY) in being an area that is actively defended and from PERSONAL SPACE in being a geographic area. Territoriality is observed in a wide range of animals and is found most often where there are specific defensible resources, such as a concentration of food or shelter. Groups with DOMINANCE–SUBORDINATION RELATIONSHIPS are generally found when resources are spread out over a large area. Territoriality is maintained through singing in birds and through SCENT MARKING in many mammals (e.g., antelope and dogs), as well as by active patrolling of territory boundaries. A resident is more likely to attack an intruder than vice versa, but attack probability decreases rapidly when the territory holder leaves its own territory. **2.** in humans, behavior associated with the need or ability to control and regulate access to a space, which reflects feelings of identity derived from use of and attachment to a familiar place. See also PUBLIC TERRITORY.

territorial marking the use of SCENT MARKING to indicate territory boundaries.

territory *n.* see TERRITORIALITY.

terror *n.* intense and overwhelming fear.

terrorism *n.* systematic intimidation or coercion to attain political or religious objectives using unlawful and unpredictable force or violence against property, persons, or governments. **—terrorist** *adj., n.*

terror management theory a theory proposing that control of death-related anxiety is the primary function of society and the main motivation in human behavior. Individual SELF-ESTEEM and a sense of being integrated into a powerful human culture are regarded as the most effective ways for human beings to defend themselves against the frightening recognition of their own mortality (see DEATH ANXIETY). The need for such defense is heightened by ONTOLOGICAL CONFRONTATION and any weakening of social institutions (see also DEATH SYSTEM). [based on the work of U.S. cultural anthropologist Ernest Becker (1925–1974) and developed by U.S. psychologists Jeff Greenberg (1954–), Sheldon Solomon (1953–), and Tom Pyszczynski (1954–)]

tertiary care highly specialized care given to patients who are in danger of disability or death. Tertiary care often requires sophisticated technologies provided by highly specialized practitioners and facilities, for example, neurologists, neurosurgeons, thoracic surgeons, and intensive care units. Compare PRIMARY CARE; SECONDARY CARE.

tertiary circular reaction in Jean PIAGET's theory of cognitive development, an infant's action that creatively alters former SCHEMES to fit the requirements of new situations. Tertiary circular reactions emerge toward the end of the SENSORIMOTOR STAGE, at about the beginning of the 2nd year; they differ from earlier behaviors in that the child can, for the first time, develop new schemes to achieve a desired goal. Also called **discovery of new means through active experimentation**. See also PRIMARY CIRCULAR REACTION; SECONDARY CIRCULAR REACTION.

tertiary prevention intervention and treatment for individuals or groups with already established psychological or physical conditions, disorders, or diseases. Tertiary interventions include attempts to minimize negative effects, prevent further disease or disorder related to complications, prevent relapse, and restore the highest physical or psychological functioning possible. Compare PRIMARY PREVENTION; SECONDARY PREVENTION.

test 1. *n.* any procedure or method to examine or determine the presence of some factor or phenomenon. **2.** *n.* a standardized set of questions or other items designed to assess knowledge, skills, interests, or other characteristics of an examinee. See PSYCHOLOGICAL TEST. **3.** *n.* a set of operations, usually statistical in nature, designed to determine the VALIDITY of a hypothesis. **4.** *vb.* to administer a test.

testability *n.* the degree to which a hypothesis or theory is capable of being evaluated empirically.

test administration the giving of a test for the purpose of obtaining information.

test age see AGE EQUIVALENT.

testamentary capacity the legal ability or mental competence to make a will. It involves being able to understand and remember the nature and extent of one's property and knowing who or what will receive that property.

test anxiety tension and apprehensiveness associated with taking a test (see PERFORMANCE ANXIETY).

test battery a group or series of related tests administered at one time, with scores recorded separately or combined to yield a single score. Also called **battery of tests**.

test bias the tendency of a test to systematically over- or underestimate the true scores of individuals to whom that test is administered or those who are members of particular groups (e.g., ethnic minorities, sexes, etc.). See also BIAS.

test construction the creation of a test, usually with a clear intent to meet the usual criteria of VALIDITY, RELIABILITY, NORMS, and other elements of test standardization.

test cutoff 1. the prearranged ending point or limit for an assessment. The limit may be in terms of time, number of answers given incorrectly, or number of questions administered. **2.** a predetermined score performance standard for a given test. Those who perform at or above this score will be considered, for example, for certain programs or colleges; those who perform below this score will not.

testicle *n.* a TESTIS and its surrounding structures, including the system of ducts within the scrotum. **—testicular** *adj.*

testicular atrophy reduction of size or loss of function of a testis as a result of obstruction of its blood supply, injury, infection, or surgical repair of an inguinal hernia. Pressure testicular atrophy may result from failure of a testis to descend normally from the abdominal cavity during sexual development.

testicular feminization syndrome see ANDROGEN-INSENSITIVITY SYNDROME.

testimony *n.* evidence given in court by an individual who is under oath. See EXPERT TESTIMONY; EYEWITNESS TESTIMONY; OPINION TESTIMONY; ULTIMATE OPINION TESTIMONY.

testing the limits 1. a method used to study adult age differences in cognition in which research participants are required to perform a task to the best of their ability and are then tested after extensive practice on the task. See also RESERVE CAPACITY. [developed by German psychologist Paul Baltes (1939–) and his associates] **2.** in psychological testing, allowing a participant to proceed beyond time limits (or waiving other standardized requirements) to see if he or she can complete an item or do better under alternate conditions. **3.** in general psychology, attempts by an individual to see how far he or she can test rules before the rules are enforced. An example would be seeing how much talking one can get away with in a class before being reprimanded by the teacher.

test interpretation the clinical, educational, vocational, or other practical implications given to a particular test result. Such conclusions are typically drawn by an expert in testing or by suitable computer software.

testis *n.* (*pl.* **testes**) the principal reproductive organ in males, a pair of which is normally located in the scrotum. The testes produce sperm in the SEMINIFEROUS TUBULES (see SPERMATOGENESIS) and male sex hormones (ANDROGENS) in INTERSTITIAL CELLS. Also called **orchis**. See TESTICLE. See also ARRESTED TESTIS; HYPERMOBILE TESTES.

testis-determining factor see SEX DIFFERENTIATION.

test item a constituent part, or the smallest scoreable unit, of a test.

test marketing research undertaken to assess consumer reactions to new products, prices, or options. Companies often try to carry out this research discreetly so that competitors are unaware of any potential changes. Based on results of test marketing, products may be introduced, changed, or not introduced into the general market.

Test of Attentional and Interpersonal Style (**TAIS**) a self-report inventory that determines an individual's dominant attentional style (see ATTENTIONAL FOCUS) and profiles his or her style of interacting with others. Widely used in sports to predict and enhance athletic performance and in business to select and train individuals for particular jobs, the TAIS consists of 144 items (e.g., "All I need is a little information and I can come up with a large number of ideas") grouped into 17 subscales. [developed in 1976 by U.S. psychologist Robert M. Nideffer (1942–)]

test of significance any of a set of procedures used to assess the probability that a set of empirical results could have been obtained if the NULL HYPOTHESIS were true.

test of simple effects a statistical test of differences between levels of one factor (INDEPENDENT VARIABLE) in a FACTORIAL DESIGN at a single level of the other factors in the design.

test, operate, test, exit (**TOTE**) see FEEDBACK LOOP.

testosterone *n.* a male sex hormone and the most potent of the ANDROGENS produced by the testes. It stimulates the development of male reproductive organs, including the prostate gland, and secondary SEX CHARACTERISTICS, such as beard, bone, and muscle growth. Women normally secrete small amounts of testosterone from the adrenal cortex and ovary.

test profile a chart depicting an examinee's relative standing (performance) on a series of tests or subtests.

test–retest correlation a CORRELATION that represents the stability of a variable over time.

test–retest reliability see RETEST RELIABILITY.

test score a numerical value assigned as a measure of performance on a test.

test selection the process of choosing the most useful or appropriate test or set of assessment instruments in order to provide accurate diagnostic or other psychological information. Test selection is made on the basis of psychological history (often in conjunction with medical history), interviews, other pretest knowledge of the individual or group to be tested, or some combination of these.

test sophistication familiarity with a particular test or type of test, which might affect the score attained on subsequent tests. See TEST-WISE.

test–study–test method an approach to the teaching of spelling (and other similar, content-acquisition subjects) that uses a pretest to determine the words a child knows, followed by study of the words the child did not know, and then a retest.

test theory see CLASSICAL TEST THEORY.

test-tube baby a colloquial term for a baby born after IN VITRO FERTILIZATION.

test-wise *adj.* describing individuals who have taken a number of tests and are therefore more adept at taking them than those who are relatively new to the testing process. See TEST SOPHISTICATION.

tetanic contraction a sustained contraction of a muscle, usually induced by repeated, rapid stimuli.

tetanizing shock an electric shock that produces sustained muscular contractions.

tetanoid paraplegia see SPASTIC PARAPLEGIA.

tetany *n.* see CALCIUM-DEFICIENCY DISORDERS.

tetartanopia *n.* a rare form of color blindness marked by difficulty in discriminating between yellow and blue. Luminosity perception is normal, but the yellow and blue perception processes have confused or possibly merged connections.

tetra- (**tetr-**) *combining form* four.

tetrabenazine *n.* a drug used in the treatment of HUNTINGTON'S DISEASE and other hyperkinetic movement disorders. It acts by depleting brain stores of the monoamine neurotransmitters dopamine, norepinephrine, and serotonin and produces such side effects as PARKINSONISM, sedation, and depression. It is not currently available in the United States. Canadian trade name: **Nitoman**.

tetrachoric correlation the estimated correlation between two continuous variables both of which have been dichotomized and for which only the dichotomized values are available.

tetrachromatism *n.* the theory that normal color vision is based upon perception of the four colors red, green, blue, and yellow.

tetrahydrocannabinol (**THC**) *n.* one of a number of

CANNABINOIDS occurring in the CANNABIS plant that is the agent principally responsible for the psychoactive properties of cannabis. THC is available in a synthetic pharmaceutical preparation known as **dronabinol** (U.S. trade name: **Marinol**) for use in the treatment of chemotherapy-induced nausea and vomiting and as an appetite stimulant for the treatment of HIV-related anorexia. Research suggests it may also be effective in reducing intraocular pressure and as an analgesic.

tetraparesis *n.* see QUADRIPARESIS.

tetraplegia *n.* see QUADRIPLEGIA.

tetrodotoxin (**TTX**) *n.* a toxin from puffer fish ovaries that blocks the voltage-gated sodium channels in neuron plasma membranes (see VOLTAGE-GATED ION CHANNEL), thus preventing the conduction of action potentials.

textons *pl. n.* elemental features of visual stimuli that provide the basis for preattentive segmentation of a visual scene, prior to the direction of focused attention on any one object within the scene (see FEATURE-INTEGRATION THEORY). There are three categories of textons: elongated blobs (with their attendant color, orientation, and width); terminators, which convey the end of a line segment; and crossings of line segments. [proposed in the 1980s by Hungarian-born U.S. engineer Bela Julesz (1928–)]

text telephone (**TTY**) see TELECOMMUNICATION DEVICE.

texture gradient see GRADIENT OF TEXTURE.

texture perception perception of the surface characteristics of an object or substance, typically using the HAPTIC or visual senses (see VISUAL TEXTURE).

texture segregation task any detection task in which the figure to be detected is defined by textural elements so that it must be distinguished from some background pattern of a different texture.

tft strategy abbreviation for TIT-FOR-TAT STRATEGY.

TGA abbreviation for TRANSIENT GLOBAL AMNESIA.

T-group *n.* training group: a type of experiential group, usually of up to a dozen or so people, concerned with fostering the development of "basic skills," such as effective leadership and communication, and attitude change. **T-group training** was developed by the National Training Laboratory in Group Development in the late 1940s and grew out of Kurt LEWIN's work in the area of small-group dynamics. Although sometimes used synonymously with ENCOUNTER GROUP, the emphasis is less on personal growth and more on SENSITIVITY TRAINING and practical interpersonal skills, for example, as stressed in management training. One of the goals of T-groups is to foster greater understanding of group dynamics and of the individual members' roles within the group or organization.

thalamic lesion a loss of structure or function of a part of the THALAMUS resulting in such effects as avoidance-learning deficits. Animals that have experienced a thalamic lesion take much longer to learn to avoid an electric shock, although they learn eventually. Effects vary somewhat with the part of the thalamus affected.

thalamic nucleus any of the various nuclei of the THALAMUS.

thalamic pacemaker groups of nuclei in the THALAMUS that trigger waves of electrical activity in the cerebral cortex. Several thalamic nuclei have been found to initiate cortical discharges, including the intralaminar, midline, reticular, and ventralis anterior nuclei. Pacemaker neurons in the reticular nucleus excite cortical cells to fire synchronously in the pattern of SLOW-WAVE SLEEP.

thalamic taste area the area of the thalamus that relays taste information from the SOLITARY NUCLEUS to the PRIMARY TASTE CORTEX. About one third of its neurons respond to taste; others are activated by touch or temperature stimulation of the mouth or even the anticipation of an approaching taste stimulus.

thalamic theory of Cannon see CANNON–BARD THEORY.

thalamocortical system the THALAMUS and CEREBRAL CORTEX: parts of the brain that—especially in mammals—are so closely and reciprocally interconnected that they are often treated as a single system. Normal functioning of this system appears to be necessary for normal conscious experience and action.

thalamus *n.* (*pl.* **thalami**) a mass of gray matter, forming part of the DIENCEPHALON of the brain, whose two lobes form the walls of the THIRD VENTRICLE. It consists of a collection of sensory, motor, autonomic, and associational nuclei, serving as a relay for nerve impulses traveling between the spinal cord and brainstem and the cerebral cortex. Specific areas of the body surface and cerebral cortex are related to specific parts of the thalamus. Many structural and functional regions of the thalamus have been identified, including the DORSOMEDIAL NUCLEUS, the LATEROVENTRAL NUCLEUS, and the VENTROPOSTERIOR NUCLEUS. See also EPITHALAMUS; SUBTHALAMUS. **—thalamic** *adj.*

thalidomide *n.* a drug reintroduced into the United States in 1998 as an immunosuppressant for treatment of cutaneous manifestations of erythema nodosum leprosum (a severe, acute form of leprosy). A derivative of the sedative GLUTETHIMIDE, it was originally (in the late 1950s and early 1960s) used to treat anxiety and morning sickness in pregnancy until its association with severe, life-threatening birth defects became apparent. Numerous fetal abnormalities, including abnormal limb development (see PHOCOMELIA) and gastrointestinal, cardiac, and neurological deficits were common, and the drug was withdrawn. Prescription requires special training by prescribers and pharmacists, and thalidomide must not be taken by women who are pregnant; both women and men who are taking thalidomide must comply with various mandatory conditions and contraceptive measures. Its mechanism of action is unclear. U.S. trade name: **Thalomid**.

thanato- (**thanat-**) *combining form* death.

thanatology *n.* the study of death-related behaviors, thoughts, feelings, and phenomena. Death was mostly the province of theology until the 1960s, when existential thinkers and a broad spectrum of care providers, educators, and social and behavioral scientists became interested in death-related issues. **—thanatologist** *n.*

thanatomania *n.* see VOODOO DEATH.

thanatomimesis *n.* behavior that bears a strong resemblance to death and may be thought to serve as a strategy for preventing death. Examples from the human and animal kingdoms can be seen in various children's games and death-feigning spiders and opossums. **—thanatomimetic** *adj.*

thanatophobia *n.* a persistent and irrational fear of death or dying. This fear may focus on the death of oneself or of loved ones and is often associated with HYPOCHONDRIASIS. Sigmund FREUD suggested that expressed fears of death are disguised ways of communicating other sources of anxiety: The unconscious is incapable of believing in its own death, and thanatophobia therefore draws its terror from threats the individual has actually experienced. Also called **death phobia**. See also DEATH ANXIETY. **—thanatophobic** *adj.*

Thanatos *n.* the personification of death and the brother of Hypnos (sleep) in Greek mythology, whose name was chosen by Sigmund FREUD to designate a theoretical set of strivings oriented toward the reduction of tension and life activity (see DEATH INSTINCT). In Freud's DUAL INSTINCT THEORY, Thanatos is seen as involved in a dialectic process with EROS (love), the striving toward sexuality, continued development, and heightened experience (see LIFE INSTINCT). See also DESTRUDO; NIRVANA PRINCIPLE; PRINCIPLE OF INERTIA.

that's-not-all technique a two-step procedure for enhancing compliance that consists of presenting an initial, large request and then, before the person can respond, immediately reducing it to a more modest target request. The target request is sometimes made more attractive by offering some additional benefit. Compliance with the target request is greater following the initial request than would have been the case if the target request had been presented on its own. See also DOOR-IN-THE-FACE TECHNIQUE; FOOT-IN-THE-DOOR TECHNIQUE; LOW-BALL TECHNIQUE.

THC abbreviation for TETRAHYDROCANNABINOL.

theater of consciousness a metaphor for, or conceptualization of, consciousness in which conscious events are compared to a play on a stage, while unconscious psychological functions are represented by the audience and the backstage crew.

Theater of Spontaneity an experimental theater established in Vienna in 1921 by Austrian-born U.S. psychiatrist Jacob Levi Moreno (1889–1974). The process of playing unrehearsed, improvised parts in the theater proved to be not only effective training for actors but frequently had a beneficial effect on their interpersonal relationships. This technique evolved into PSYCHODRAMA, which Moreno brought to the United States in 1925.

thebaine *n.* an OPIUM ALKALOID that is chemically similar to morphine but has stimulatory effects. It comprises about 0.2% of natural opium. Although thebaine lacks the analgesic effect of morphine, it can be converted to several important opioid agonists and antagonists (e.g., buprenorphine, naloxone).

theism *n.* belief in God, especially a personal God considered to be the creator and sustainer of the universe, who cares for and intervenes in creation but is distinct from it. Theism is central to orthodox Judeo-Christian belief and may be distinguished from both DEISM and PANTHEISM. **—theist** *adj., n.*

thema *n.* in the PERSONOLOGY of U.S. psychologist Henry Alexander Murray (1893–1988), a unifying "theme," or unit of interplay, between an individual and the environment in which a need and a PRESS interact to yield satisfaction.

Thematic Apperception Test (**TAT**) a projective test, developed by U.S. psychologist Henry Alexander Murray (1893–1988) and his associates, in which participants are held to reveal their attitudes, feelings, conflicts, and personality characteristics in the oral or written stories they make up about a series of relatively ambiguous black-and-white pictures. Prior to administering the test, the examiner assures the participant that there are no right or wrong answers and indicates that the narratives should have a beginning, middle, and ending. At the end, the stories are discussed for diagnostic purposes. Systematic coding schemes, with demonstrated reliability and validity, have been developed to assess different aspects of personality functioning derived from TAT stories, including motivation for achievement, power, affiliation, and intimacy; gender identity; DEFENSE MECHANISMS; and mental processes influencing interpersonal relations. The TAT is one of the most frequently used and researched tests in psychology, particularly in clinical settings for diagnosis, personality description, and assessment of strengths and weakness in personality functioning.

thematic classification see COMPLEMENTARY CLASSIFICATION.

thematic paralogia a speech characteristic marked by the incessant, distorted dwelling of the mind on a single theme or subject.

thematic paraphasia incoherent speech that wanders from the theme or subject.

thematic test any examination in which a participant is required to tell a story from which interpretations are made about the individual's psychological functioning, especially his or her unconscious wishes and needs.

theobromine *n.* a METHYLXANTHINE alkaloid that occurs naturally in the seeds of *Theobroma cacao*, the COCOA plant. Theobromine is structurally similar to caffeine in coffee and theophylline in tea but has less pharmacological potency than these methylxanthines.

theomania *n.* a delusion in which the person believes himself or herself to be inspired by or possessed of divinity.

theophagy *n.* literally, the eating of God. In most uses the term refers to the symbolic consuming of the body or blood of a deity, as in the Christian eucharist, as a means of communing more fully with the divine. However, it can also refer to certain rites in which adherents attempt to absorb the attributes of a deity by consuming the body or blood of a slaughtered animal or human considered to be its representative.

theophylline *n.* see METHYLXANTHINES.

theorem *n.* in mathematics and logic, a formula or proposition that can be deduced in a series of logical steps.

theoretical integration the integration of theoretical concepts from different approaches to produce meaningful frames of reference that may help explain the dynamics or causes of problems or the functioning of an individual when any single traditional theoretical approach individually fails to explain the behavior adequately.

theory *n.* **1.** a principle or body of interrelated principles that purports to explain or predict a number of interrelated phenomena. See CONSTRUCT; MODEL. **2.** in the philosophy of science, a set of logically related explanatory hypotheses that are consistent with a body of empirical facts and that may suggest more empirical relationships. See SCIENTIFIC EXPLANATION. **3.** in general usage, abstract or speculative thought as opposed to practice or reality. **—theoretical** *adj.*

theory begging an informal FALLACY in which evidence for the truth of a theory is derived from a logical or empirical process that already assumes the truth, language, or perspective of that same theory. An example might be citing examples of "stimulus–response connections" established in empirical studies in order to verify that behavioristic accounts of learning are true, when the terminology "stimulus–response connection" was generated by a behavioristic account in the first place. Theory begging is thus a form of CIRCULAR REASONING or BEGGING THE QUESTION.

theory-laden *adj.* **1.** describing a term or expression that can only be understood in the context of a particular theory. For example, some specialized vocabulary used in accounts of behavioral phenomena can be understood only in the context of the theory that generated the vocabulary and in the context of other constructs that are part of the theory's explanatory accounts. **2.** describing a proposition or observation that reflects theoretical presuppositions on the part of the person who deploys it. Often these presuppositions, which may be a source of bias, are unconscious or unacknowledged. Some claim that all observations are theory-laden, and thus that OBJECTIVITY is impossible.

theory of aging any of several hypotheses about the biological, psychological, or social causes of the aging process.

theory of evolution see EVOLUTIONARY THEORY.

theory of forms the doctrine of Greek philosopher Plato (c. 429–347 BCE) that all things have a real permanent existence as ideas or forms independent of one's senses and of the impoverished examples that one can perceive. Also called **theory of ideas**. See ANALOGY OF THE CAVE; PLATONIC IDEALISM; REMINISCENCE THEORY OF KNOWLEDGE.

theory of mental self-government a model of COGNITIVE STYLES that proposes several dimensions to describe the preferred ways in which individuals think or express their cognitive abilities. The dimensions include (a) governmental—preferences in the legislative, executive, and judicial functions of cognition (i.e., in planning, implementing, and evaluating); (b) problem solving—styles labeled monarchic (a tendency to pursue one goal at a time), hierarchic (multiple goals with different priorities), oligarchic (multiple, equally important goals), and anarchic (unstructured, random problem solving); (c) global versus local thinking—preferring to think about large, abstract issues on the one hand or concrete details on the other; (d) internal versus external thinking—related to introversion–extraversion, social skills, and cooperativeness; and (e) conservative or progressive—rule-based leanings versus those that are creative and change-oriented. [proposed in 1988 by U.S. psychologist Robert J. Sternberg (1949–)]

theory of mind the ability to imagine or make deductions about the mental states of other individuals: What does the other individual know? What actions is that individual likely to take? Theory of mind is an essential component of attributing beliefs, intentions, and desires to others, specifically in order to predict their behavior. It begins to appear around 4 years of age in human beings; there has been considerable controversy about whether nonhuman animals have this ability. See also BELIEF–DESIRE REASONING; FALSE-BELIEF TASK; MINDBLINDNESS.

theory of misapplied constancy a theory of illusions proposing that the underlying cause is the inappropriate use of cues that normally allow accurate perception of such properties as size and shape. For example, depth might be misestimated if a display has converging lines that do not actually recede in depth: An object inside the lines would be seen as further away than it actually is, and thus its size would also be misperceived.

theory of personal investment a motivational theory stating that the degree to which an individual will invest personal resources of time and effort in an activity, in anticipation of benefits, is a function of personal incentives (mastery orientation, competitive orientation, affiliation, status), beliefs about oneself (sense of competence, self-reliance, goal directedness, identity), and perceived options (behavioral options perceived to be available in the specific situation).

theory of planned behavior a theory that resembles the THEORY OF REASONED ACTION but also incorporates the construct of PERCEIVED BEHAVIORAL CONTROL. Perceived behavioral control is added to attitude toward behavior and SUBJECTIVE NORMS as the antecedents influencing both the intention to perform a behavior and the performance of the behavior itself. [originally proposed by U.S. social psychologist Icek Ajzen (1942–)]

theory of reasoned action the theory that attitudes toward a behavior and SUBJECTIVE NORMS (perceived expectations) regarding a behavior determine a person's intention to perform that behavior. Intentions are in turn assumed to cause the actual behavior. Also called **reasoned action model**. See also THEORY OF PLANNED BEHAVIOR. [originally proposed by U.S. psychologists Martin Fishbein (1936–) and Icek Ajzen (1942–)]

theory theory any model of cognitive development that combines NEONATIVISM and CONSTRUCTIVISM, proposing that cognitive development progresses by children generating, testing, and changing theories about the physical and social world.

theory verification the process of developing and citing empirical evidence to increase or decrease the tenability of theories.

Theory X and Y two contrasting types of managerial philosophy: Theory X managers assume that workers are passive, lazy, and motivated only by money and security, whereas Theory Y managers assume that workers want to grow psychologically and are desirous of autonomy and responsibility. It is hypothesized that these assumptions are self-fulfilling: Workers who are subjected to Theory X management will act in a lazy and untrustworthy manner, whereas those who are subjected to Theory Y management and are provided with a workplace that encourages psychological growth will show creativity and initiative. A Theory X manager is authoritarian in leadership style, whereas a Theory Y manager is participative and democratic. [described by Douglas McGregor (1906–1964), U.S. management consultant and social psychologist]

Theory Z a managerial philosophy that attempts to incorporate aspects of JAPANESE MANAGEMENT practices into U.S. corporate culture. It emphasizes PARTICIPATIVE DECISION-MAKING by employees, the encouragement of team spirit, and measures to develop greater mutual respect between managers and employees. See also DEMING MANAGEMENT METHOD; TOTAL QUALITY MANAGEMENT. [identified by U.S. management theorist William G. Ouchi (1943–)]

therapeutic 1. *adj.* pertaining to **therapeutics**, the branch of medical science concerned with the treatment of diseases and disorders and the discovery and application of remedial agents or methods. **2.** *adj.* having beneficial or curative effects. **3.** *n.* a compound that is used to treat specific diseases or medical conditions.

therapeutic abortion an abortion that is performed for medical reasons, for example, to preserve the mother's health or life.

therapeutic agent any means of advancing the treatment process, such as a drug, occupational therapy, a therapist, or a THERAPEUTIC COMMUNITY. The therapeutic agent is presumed to be the causative agent in patient change.

therapeutic alliance a cooperative working relationship between client and therapist, considered by many to be an essential aspect of successful therapy. Derived from the concept of the psychoanalytic working alliance, the therapeutic alliance comprises bonds, goals, and tasks. BONDS are constituted by the core conditions of therapy, the client's attitude towards the therapist, and the therapist's style of relating to the client; goals are the mutually negotiated, understood, agreed upon, and regularly reviewed aims of the therapy; and tasks are the activities carried out by both client and therapist. See THERAPIST–PATIENT RELATIONSHIP. [concept developed by U.S. psychologist Edward S. Bordin (1913–1992)]

therapeutic atmosphere an environment of acceptance, empathic understanding, and UNCONDITIONAL POSITIVE REGARD in which clients feel most free to verbalize and consider their thoughts, behaviors, and emotions and make constructive changes in their attitudes and reactions.

therapeutic camp a camp that may provide part-time care, therapeutic treatment, rehabilitation, or a combination of these for individuals, often children and adolescents, with a variety of conditions, disorders, and illnesses. Examples include camps for children with learning disabilities, for children and adolescents living with HIV/AIDS, for SCHOOL REFUSAL adolescents, and for individuals with head injury.

therapeutic communication any comment or observation by the therapist that increases the client's awareness or self-understanding.

therapeutic community a setting for individuals requiring therapy for a range of psychosocial problems and disorders that is based on an interpersonal, socially interactive approach to treatment, both among residents and among residents and staff (i.e., "community as method or therapy"). The term covers a variety of short- and long-term residential programs as well as day treatment and ambulatory programs. The staff is typically multidisciplinary and may consist of human services professionals and clinicians providing mental health, medical, vocational, educational, fiscal, and legal services, among others. Originating as an alternative to conventional medical and psychiatric approaches, therapeutic communities have become a significant form of psychosocial treatment. See MILIEU THERAPY. [developed by 20th-century British psychiatrist Maxwell Shaw Jones]

therapeutic crisis a turning point in the treatment process, usually due to sudden insight or a significant revelation on the part of the client or patient. The crisis may have positive or negative implications and may lead to a change for the better or the worse, depending on how it is handled.

therapeutic factors curative factors that operate across models and techniques in GROUP PSYCHOTHERAPY. Factors identified include altruism, catharsis, cohesion, family reenactment, feedback, hope, identification, interpersonal learning, reality testing, role flexibility, universality, and vicarious learning. Therapeutic factors are often confused with COMMON FACTORS because both delineate effective change factors across theoretical models and techniques of therapy; however, common factors refer to individual psychotherapy, whereas therapeutic factors refer to group psychotherapy.

therapeutic group a group of individuals who meet under the leadership of a therapist for the express purpose of working together toward improvement in the mental and emotional health of the members.

therapeutic group analysis see GROUP-ANALYTIC PSYCHOTHERAPY.

therapeutic index any of several indices relating the clinical effectiveness of a drug to its safety factor, the most common being the THERAPEUTIC RATIO. Other therapeutic indices include the ratio of the minimum toxic dose to the minimum EFFECTIVE DOSE and the difference between the minimum effective dose and the minimum toxic dose.

therapeutic jurisprudence the study of law as a therapeutic agent. Therapeutic jurisprudence involves the examination of how laws, procedures, and people who play an active role within the legal system (e.g., judges, law enforcement agents) may either help or harm the various other individuals involved (e.g., defendants, victims).

therapeutic matrix in COUPLES THERAPY, the specific combination of therapist and clients that is used in the sessions, for example, a different therapist for each partner in COLLABORATIVE THERAPY or seeing the couple together in CONJOINT THERAPY.

therapeutic process see PSYCHOTHERAPEUTIC PROCESS.

therapeutic ratio an index relating the clinical effectiveness of a drug to its safety factor, calculated by dividing the median LETHAL DOSE (LD_{50}) by the median EFFECTIVE DOSE (ED_{50}). A drug is often considered safe only if its therapeutic ratio is at least 10. [introduced by German bacteriologist and immunologist Paul Ehrlich (1854–1915)]

therapeutic recreation see RECREATIONAL THERAPY.

therapeutic relaxation see RELAXATION THERAPY.

therapeutic role the functions of the therapist or other THERAPEUTIC AGENT in treating psychological disorders, alleviating painful responses or symptoms resulting from a distressing condition, or altering maladaptive thinking or behavior.

therapeutic soliloquy a procedure in which clients speak about themselves to a group without interruption. [developed by Austrian-born U.S. psychiatrist Jacob Levi Moreno (1889–1974)]

therapeutic storytelling see STORYTELLING.

therapeutic touch see TOUCH THERAPY.

therapeutic window the range of plasma levels of a drug within which optimal therapeutic effects occur. Suboptimal effects may occur both below and above the therapeutic window. Evidence for true therapeutic windows was never well established; perhaps the best evidence existed for the tricyclic antidepressant NORTRIPTYLINE. Few modern psychotropic drugs require therapeutic monitoring, although LITHIUM is a notable exception; it has a very narrow therapeutic range below which it has no therapeutic effect and above which adverse effects and toxicity dominate. Therapeutic windows are increasingly becoming less significant in modern clinical psychopharmacology.

therapeutist *n.* a former name for a THERAPIST.

therapist *n.* an individual who has been trained in and practices one or more types of therapy to treat mental or physical disorders or diseases: often used synonymously with psychotherapist (see PSYCHOTHERAPY).

therapist–patient relationship the relationship formed in therapy between a psychotherapist and the patient (client) receiving therapy. There has been much theory and research concerning this interaction: how it varies and changes over time and the significant implications that the dynamic has for the way in which treatment is offered and its outcomes. The relationship has ethical dimensions that are often specified in PRACTICE GUIDELINES. See also THERAPEUTIC ALLIANCE.

therapy *n.* **1.** remediation of physical, mental, or behavioral disorders or disease. **2.** see PSYCHOTHERAPY.

therapy group climate see GROUP CLIMATE.

therapy puppet a puppet used for ROLE PLAY in therapy with children. The use of a therapy puppet is sometimes more conducive to the child's revelation of thoughts and feelings than direct communication by the child with the therapist.

therapy supervision see SUPERVISION.

therblig *n.* a unit of movement sometimes used to describe and record industrial operations for the purposes of TIME AND MOTION STUDIES. It represents any one of the 18 fundamental, standardized activities involved in such operations: search, find, select, grasp, hold, position, assemble, use, disassemble, inspect, transport loaded, transport unloaded, pre-position for next operation, release load, unavoidable delay, avoidable delay, plan, and rest to overcome fatigue. [coined by U.S. engineer and efficiency expert Frank B. Gilbreth (1868–1924) and his wife, U.S. engineer and psychologist Lillian Moller Gilbreth (1878–1972), from a backward spelling of their surname]

there-and-then approach a historical approach to therapy, focusing on the roots of the client's difficulties in past experience, as opposed to the here-and-now approach (see HERE AND NOW).

thermal comfort subjective evaluation of feelings with respect to temperature. Major contributing factors include humidity, air velocity, clothing, and level of physical exertion. Contrary to widespread belief, the range of thermal comfort is remarkably stable cross-culturally.

thermal discrimination the ability to detect differences in temperature among stimuli. Some animals (e.g., snakes) are able to locate prey by differences of a fraction of a degree between the temperature of the environment and that produced by the body heat of potential prey. Humans, however, are much less sensitive to temperature change.

thermalgesia *n.* an abnormal reaction to heat in which a warm stimulus produces pain.

thermalgia *n.* a condition characterized by intense, burning pain.

thermal illusion see TEMPERATURE ILLUSION.

thermal sensitivity the ability to detect temperature, which is generally perceived relative to the body's temperature. See TEMPERATURE SENSE.

thermal stimulation stimulation of the skin with heat or cold.

thermic fever see HEATSTROKE.

thermistor *n.* a device used to measure temperatures according to their effects on the electrical resistance of semiconducting materials. Tiny thermistors can be implanted in NEURONS of animals to measure such data as the energy of metabolic activity during nervous-system functions.

thermo- (**therm-**) *combining form* heat.

thermoanesthesia *n.* **1.** loss or absence of the ability to distinguish between heat and cold by touch. **2.** insensitivity to heat. Also called **thermanesthesia**.

thermode *n.* a device made of copper through which water can be circulated at a controlled temperature. A thermode can be implanted in an organ of an animal in order to determine the effects of temperature changes on surrounding tissues. Much information about thermal receptors has been obtained in this manner.

thermoesthesia (**thermesthesia**) *n.* see TEMPERATURE SENSE.

thermography *n.* a diagnostic technique using thermally sensitive liquid crystals or infrared photography to detect temperature changes over the surface of the body. Thermography functions on the basis that diseased tissues, such as tumors, produce more heat than surrounding tissues and the heat can be measured in terms of infrared radiation.

thermoreceptor *n.* **1.** a receptor or sense organ that is activated by temperature stimuli (e.g., cold or warm stimuli). **2.** a part of the central nervous system that monitors and maintains the temperature of the body core and its vital organs. There is evidence for separate thermoregulatory regions in the spinal cord, brainstem, and hypothalamus.

thermoregulation *n.* the behavioral and physiological processes, collectively, that maintain normal body temperature. These processes include sweating and shivering. See also HOMEOSTASIS.

thesis *n.* (*pl.* **theses**) **1.** in logic, a proposition to be subjected to logical analysis in the interest of proof or disproof. **2.** more generally, any idea or proposition put forward in argument. **3.** in philosophy, the first stage of a dialectical process: a proposition that is opposed by an ANTITHESIS, thereby generating a new proposition referred to as a SYNTHESIS. The synthesis serves as thesis for the next phase of the ongoing process. This use of the term is particularly associated with the work of German philosopher Georg Wilhelm Friedrich Hegel (1770–1831). See also DIALECTICAL MATERIALISM. **4.** a dissertation based on original research, especially one required for an advanced academic degree.

theta feedback BIOFEEDBACK involving theta waves, of frequency 4–7 Hz.

theta wave in electroencephalography, a type of BRAIN WAVE with a frequency of 4–7 Hz. Theta waves are observed in the REM SLEEP of animals, STAGE 2 SLEEP in humans, and in the drowsiness state of newborn infants, adolescents, and young adults. Theta waves are also recorded in TRANCES, HYPNOSIS, and deep DAYDREAMS. Neurologically, the hippocampus is one well-known source of theta activity. Also called **theta rhythm**.

they-group *n.* see OUTGROUP.

thiamine (**thiamin**) *n.* a vitamin of the B complex present in various foods and also normally present in blood plasma and cerebrospinal fluid. Deficiency of thiamine results in neurological symptoms, as in BERIBERI, ALCOHOLIC NEUROPATHY, and KORSAKOFF'S SYNDROME. In severe cases, WERNICKE'S ENCEPHALOPATHY may result. Also called **vitamin B_1**.

thiazide diuretics a group of synthetic chemicals developed in the 1950s and widely used as DIURETICS in the treatment of hypertension. Thiazides cause the excretion of approximately equal amounts of sodium and chloride with an accompanying volume of water, thereby lowering blood pressure. Also called **benzothiadiazides**.

thick stripes broad bands of increased CYTOCHROME OXIDASE activity in the region of the prestriate cortex known as V2. The thick stripes receive input from layer IVb of the STRIATE CORTEX and analyze signals carried by the MAGNOCELLULAR SYSTEM.

thienobenzodiazepine *n.* any member of a class of chemically related compounds that include OLANZAPINE, an ATYPICAL ANTIPSYCHOTIC introduced into the U.S. market in 1996.

thigmesthesia *n.* sensitivity to pressure. See TOUCH SENSE.

think-aloud protocol a transcript of ongoing mental activity, as reported by a participant engaged in some task. The participant thinks aloud while performing the task, thus creating a record of his or her cognitive processing for later analysis. See PROTOCOL ANALYSIS.

thinking *n.* cognitive behavior in which ideas, images, MENTAL REPRESENTATIONS, or other hypothetical elements of thought are experienced or manipulated. In this sense thinking includes imagining, remembering, problem solving, daydreaming, FREE ASSOCIATION, concept formation, and many other processes. Thinking may be said to have two defining characteristics: (a) It is covert, that is, it is not directly observable but must be inferred from behavior or self-reports; and (b) it is symbolic, that is, it seems to involve operations on mental symbols or representations, the nature of which remains obscure and controversial (see SYMBOLIC PROCESS).

thinking aside a type of ASYNDETIC THINKING in which an individual's thoughts shift abruptly from one topic to another that is insignificantly or only tangentially related to it (i.e., to a "side topic"), and from this side topic to a second side topic, and so on, such that the individual is unable to develop a logical, coherent sequence of thoughts.

thinking style see COGNITIVE STYLE.

thinking through a typically multistage, multilayered thought process in which the individual attempts to understand and achieve insight into his or her own reactions, thought processes, or behavior, for example through consideration and analysis of cause and effect.

thinking type in the ANALYTIC PSYCHOLOGY of Carl JUNG, a FUNCTIONAL TYPE exemplified by the individual who evaluates information or ideas rationally and logically. The thinking type is one of Jung's two RATIONAL TYPES, the other being the FEELING TYPE. See also INTUITIVE TYPE; SENSATION TYPE.

thinning *n.* in CONDITIONING, a gradual increase in the intermittency of reinforcement.

thin stripes thin bands of increased CYTOCHROME OXIDASE activity in the region of the prestriate cortex known as V2. The thin stripes receive input from the CYTOCHROME OXIDASE BLOBS of the striate cortex and contain neurons that are sensitive to color.

thiopental *n.* an ultrashort-acting BARBITURATE used primarily as an anesthetic that can be administered intravenously to produce almost immediate loss of consciousness. It may also be used as an antidote to overdosage of stimulants or convulsants. Formerly it was occasionally used in psychotherapy to induce a state of relaxation and suggestibility. In nonmedical circles, it gained notoriety as a TRUTH SERUM. U.S. trade name: **Pentothal**.

thioridazine *n.* a low-potency antipsychotic of the piperidine PHENOTHIAZINE class that, like others of its class, causes sedation and significant anticholinergic effects. Adverse effects unique to thioridazine include the potential to cause retinal changes possibly leading to blindness (retinitis pigmentosum) at doses exceeding 800 mg/day. It can also cause severe disturbances in heart rhythm: Its ability to prolong the Q-T interval may cause fatal arrhythmias (see ELECTROCARDIOGRAPHIC EFFECT). It should not be taken by patients who have cardiac arrhythmias or who are taking other drugs that may prolong the Q-T interval. U.S. trade name: **Mellaril**.

thioxanthenes *pl. n.* a group of ANTIPSYCHOTIC drugs, generally of intermediate potency, that resemble the PHENOTHIAZINES in pharmacological activity and molecular structure. Thioxanthenes are used mainly in the treatment of psychotic disorders. Like the phenothiazines, they are associated with cardiovascular and anticholinergic side effects, as well as EXTRAPYRAMIDAL EFFECTS common to all dopamine-blocking agents. Their use has largely been supplanted by newer antipsychotics. Thioxanthenes include **thiothixene** (U.S. trade name: Navane), flupenthixol, and ZUCLOPENTHIXOL. Only thiothixene is currently available in the United States.

third cranial nerve see OCULOMOTOR NERVE.

third-party administrator (**TPA**) in health insurance, a fiscal intermediary organization that provides administrative services, including claims processing and underwriting, for other parties (e.g., insurance companies or employers) but does not carry any insurance risk.

third-party payer an organization, usually an insurance company, prepayment plan, or government agency, that pays for the health expenses incurred by the insured. The third party (to the agreement) is distinguished from the first party, the individual receiving the services, and the second party, the individual or institution providing the services.

third-person perspective a public, external, objective point of view on human behavior and experience. Compare FIRST-PERSON PERSPECTIVE; SECOND-PERSON PERSPECTIVE.

third-variable problem the fact that an observed correlation between two variables may be due to the common correlation between each of the variables and a third variable rather than because the two variables have any underlying relationship (in a causal sense) with each other.

third ventricle a cavity of the brain, filled with CEREBROSPINAL FLUID, that forms a cleft between the two lobes of the THALAMUS beneath the cerebral hemispheres (see VENTRICLE). It communicates with the LATERAL VENTRICLES and caudally with the fourth ventricle through the CEREBRAL AQUEDUCT.

thirst *n.* the sensation caused by a need for increased fluid intake in order to maintain an optimum balance of water and electrolytes in the body tissues. Water is lost from the body mainly in urine, sweat, and via the lungs. Dehydration causes reduced production of saliva and the feeling of a "dry mouth." In addition, a specialized area of the hypothalamus in the brain detects and responds to the changes in OSMOTIC PRESSURE that result from increased concentration of electrolytes in extracellular fluid subsequent to water loss (see OSMORECEPTOR). See also HYPOVOLEMIC THIRST; OSMOMETRIC THIRST.

Thomas S. class action a class action lawsuit in North Carolina that established a special class of people with mental retardation who lived in state psychiatric hospitals. Many class members had both mental retardation and severe and persistent or recurring mental illness (MR/MI). The court order specified required services and supports. Although the class was dissolved in 1998, the case resulted in the establishment of a division that administers MR/MI services within the state-led agency for mental retardation services.

Thomistic psychology the psychological principles found in the writings of Italian philosopher and theologian St. Thomas Aquinas (1225–1274) and revived in the early 20th century by a number of Roman Catholic thinkers. Aquinas emphasized ARISTOTELIAN logic, the compatibility of reason with faith, human free will, and the knowledge of God as ultimate happiness.

thoracic *adj.* pertaining to the **thorax**—the portion of the mammalian body cavity bounded by the ribs, shoulders, and diaphragm—or to a structure contained within this region, such as the thoracic vertebrae or the thoracic segments of the SPINAL CORD.

thoracic nerve see SPINAL NERVE.

thoracolumbar system a less common name for the SYMPATHETIC NERVOUS SYSTEM.

Thorazine *n.* a trade name for CHLORPROMAZINE.

Thorndike, Edward Lee (1874–1949) U.S. psychologist. After completing a master's degree at Harvard University under William JAMES, Thorndike earned his doctorate in 1898 at Columbia University under James McKeen CATTELL. Except for a year at Western Reserve University, Thorndike spent his career as a faculty member at Columbia University. His dissertation was published as the now classic *Animal Intelligence* (1898). Thorndike carried out the first laboratory studies of animal learning. He developed the concept of TRIAL-AND-ERROR LEARNING and the theory of CONNECTIONISM, which specified that associative bonds between situations and responses are the basis of learning new habits and behaviors. He further contributed to learning theory with the laws of readiness, exercise, and effect: Organisms (including humans) are more likely to repeat behaviors that are followed by satisfying consequences (satisfiers) and less likely to repeat those that are followed by unpleasant consequences. Thorndike also compiled a junior dictionary based on frequency of word use and published treatises on military and applied psychology. See also PRINCIPLE OF BELONGINGNESS; PUZZLE BOX; S–R PSYCHOLOGY.

Thorndike–Lorge list an early and influential list of word frequencies in the English language, compiled in 1944. There have been many subsequent updated lists, but this term is still sometimes used generically to mean an empirical list of word frequencies in a language. [Edward THORNDIKE and Irving D. **Lorge** (1905–1961), U.S. psychologists]

Thorndike Puzzle Box see PUZZLE BOX.

Thorndike's trial-and-error learning see TRIAL-AND-ERROR LEARNING. [Edward THORNDIKE]

thought *n.* **1.** the process of THINKING. **2.** an idea, image, opinion, or other product of thinking. **3.** attention or consideration given to something or someone.

thought avoidance the ability to evade or not consider unpleasant or dissonant mental events. It is a kind of psychological DEFENSE MECHANISM as well as a means of therapeutic change.

thought broadcasting the delusion that one's thoughts are being disseminated throughout the environment for all to hear.

thought deprivation see BLOCKING.

thought derailment disorganized, disconnected thought processes, as manifested by a tendency to shift from one topic to another that is indirectly related or completely unrelated to the first. Thought derailment is a symptom of schizophrenia; the term is essentially equivalent to COGNITIVE DERAILMENT. See DERAILMENT.

thought disorder a disturbance in the cognitive processes that affects communication, language, or thought content, including POVERTY OF IDEAS, NEOLOGISMS, PARALOGIA, WORD SALAD, and DELUSIONS. A thought disorder is considered by some to be the most important mark of schizophrenia (see also SCHIZOPHRENIC THINKING), but thought disorders are also associated with mood disorders, dementia, mania, and neurological diseases (among others). Also called **thought disturbance**. See CONTENT-THOUGHT DISORDER; FORMAL THOUGHT DISORDER.

thought echoing see ÉCHO DES PENSÉES.

thought experiment the process of imagining a theoretical research SET-UP and what the result might be of conducting the imagined experiment, in the hope that this process will lead to a better designed real experiment. In cases in which the experiment cannot actually be performed, the intent is to arrive at a well-reasoned conclusion. In physics, such experiments—called **Gedanken experiments**—are sometimes held in high regard.

thought insertion a delusion in which the individual believes that thoughts are irresistibly forced into his or her mind and ascribes these thoughts to outside sources.

thought intrusion interruption of the stream of consciousness by unwanted mental contents. See INTRUSIVE THOUGHTS.

thought monitoring the process of tracking and making note of one's own thoughts.

thought obstruction see BLOCKING.

thought pressure see PRESSURE OF IDEAS.

thought process any of the COGNITIVE PROCESSES involved in mental activities that are beyond perception, such as reasoning, remembering, imagining, problem solving, and making judgments. See THINKING. See also HIGHER MENTAL PROCESS; MEDIATION PROCESS; SYMBOLIC PROCESS.

thought-process disorder see FORMAL THOUGHT DISORDER.

thought sampling the process of noting the contents of the STREAM OF CONSCIOUSNESS, for therapeutic or empirical purposes. See THOUGHT MONITORING.

thought stopping the skill of using a physical or cognitive cue to stop negative thoughts and redirect them to a neutral or positive orientation. This skill is taught in some behavior therapies, when the therapist shouts "Stop!" to interrupt a trend toward undesirable thoughts and trains clients to apply this technique to themselves.

thought suppression the attempt to control the content of one's mental processes and specifically to rid oneself of undesired thoughts or images.

thought transference a supposed phenomenon in which the mental activities of one person are transmitted without physical means to the mind of another person. With MIND READING it is one of the two main forms of TELEPATHY.

thought withdrawal the delusion that one's thoughts are being removed from one's mind by other people or forces outside oneself.

threat *n.* **1.** a condition that is appraised as a danger to one's self or well-being or to a group. **2.** an indication of unpleasant consequences for failure to comply with a given request or demand, used as a means of coercion. **3.** any event, information, or feedback that is perceived as conveying negative information about the self. —**threaten** *vb.* —**threatening** *adj.*

threat appraisal the cognitive and emotional processes involved in assessing the potentiality and level of threat.

threat display any of various ritualized animal communication signals used to indicate that attack or aggression might follow. Examples are fluffed-out fur or feathers, certain facial expressions or body postures, and low-frequency vocalizations (e.g., growls). Animals that are responsive to a threat display can submit or flee before an attack begins. The use of ritualized threat displays can minimize direct physical aggression to the benefit of both individuals.

threat to self-esteem model a theory stating that help from another is sometimes perceived as a threat to the self, because it implies that the recipient is incapable or inferior. In these circumstances the recipient may respond negatively.

three-burst pattern see TRIPHASIC PATTERN.

three-day schizophrenia before 1970, the name for an ACUTE PSYCHOTIC EPISODE precipitated by terrifying external (real-life) events.

360° feedback system a procedure for evaluating JOB PERFORMANCE and providing feedback to employees. It involves asking supervisors, peers, and subordinates of an employee, as well as the employee himself or herself, to evaluate the employee's performance. A comparison of the employee's self-rating with the ratings of the others is then provided as feedback.

three-mountains test a PIAGETIAN TASK used to assess visual perspective taking in children. A doll is placed at various locations around a three-dimensional display of three mountains, and children must indicate how the doll sees the display. Children much below 8 years of age have difficulty performing this test correctly, although they are able to understand that others have a visual perspective that is different from their own when less complicated tasks are used.

three-stage theory the view that skill acquisition proceeds through three stages that progressively require less attention and become more automatic. According to U.S. psychologist Paul M. Fitts (1912–1965), the stages are cognitive, associative, and autonomous.

three-stratum model of intelligence a psychometric model of intelligence based on a factorial reanalysis of several hundred data sets available in the literature. It is considered by some researchers to be the most thoroughly supported of the various PSYCHOMETRIC THEORIES OF INTELLIGENCE. The three strata correspond to (a) minor group factors at the first (lowest) level, (b) major group factors at the second level (fluid intelligence, crystallized intelligence, general memory and learning, broad visual perception, broad auditory perception, broad retrieval ability, broad cognitive speediness, and processing speed), and (c) the general factor at the third (highest) level. [proposed in the 1990s by U.S. psychologist John B. Carroll (1916–)]

three-term contingency specification of the stimulus circumstances, the response, and the outcome in a REINFORCEMENT CONTINGENCY. It is formulated as $S^D{:}R \rightarrow S^R$ or denoted ABC (for *a*ntecedent, *b*ehavior, and *c*onsequence).

threshold *n.* **1.** in psychophysics, the magnitude of a stimulus that will lead to its detection 50% of the time. **2.** the minimum intensity of a stimulus that is necessary to evoke a response. For example, an AUDITORY THRESHOLD is the slightest perceptible sound; an excitatory threshold is the minimum stimulus that triggers an ACTION POTENTIAL in a neuron; a renal threshold is the concentration of a substance in the blood required before the excess is excreted. Also called **limen**; **response threshold**. See ABSOLUTE THRESHOLD; DIFFERENCE THRESHOLD.

threshold for bodily motion the minimum rate of rotation, acceleration, or deceleration necessary for the perception of bodily motion.

threshold of consciousness the psychological level at which stimuli enter awareness, characterized in terms of stimulus intensity, duration, and relevance. It applies to sensory stimuli (visual, auditory, olfactory, tactile, and gustatory) as well as memories and mood.

threshold shift a change in threshold as a result of a change in such variables as level of adaptation or context.

threshold theory a hypothesis in GROUP DYNAMICS positing that conflict is beneficial and useful provided it does not exceed the tolerance threshold of the group members for too long. [developed by U.S. communication theorist Ernest G. Bormann (1925–)]

threshold traits analysis (**TTA**) in personnel selection, a method of identifying the traits required for acceptable performance in a given position. Subject-matter experts (usually supervisors or current holders of a position) rate the importance, uniqueness, relevance, level, and practicality of 33 traits for a particular position. [proposed by industrial and organizational psychologist Felix Manuel Lopez (1917–)]

thrombosis *n.* the presence or formation of a blood clot (THROMBUS) in a blood vessel, including blood vessels in the heart (**coronary thrombosis**). Formation of a blood clot in a vein is called **venous thrombosis** (see DEEP VEIN THROMBOSIS). Thrombosis is likely to develop where blood flow is impeded by disease, injury, or a foreign substance. A thrombosis in the brain (**cerebral thrombosis**) can cause a THROMBOTIC STROKE or CEREBROVASCULAR ACCIDENT. See also AUDITORY THROMBOSIS. **—thrombotic** *adj.*

thrombotic stroke the most common type of STROKE, occurring when blood flow to the brain is blocked by a cerebral THROMBOSIS. A thrombotic stroke typically results from narrowing or occlusion of a large blood vessel in the brain, especially the carotid or middle cerebral artery, by ATHEROSCLEROSIS. Onset of symptoms can be gradual and is frequently preceded by TRANSIENT ISCHEMIC ATTACKS.

thrombus *n.* a blood clot that forms in a blood vessel (see THROMBOSIS). A thrombus that becomes detached from its point of origin and is carried in the blood to obstruct another site is called an embolus (see EMBOLISM).

thumb opposition the ability to coordinate the thumb and forefinger in PINCER GRIP movements. Thumb opposition begins to develop around the 3rd or 4th month of infancy, although it is not fully achieved until the second half of the 1st year, as eye–hand coordination grows more skillful.

thumb sucking a common though not universal habit among infants and young children, formerly classified as a habit disturbance when persisting beyond 3 or 4 years. It is commonly explained as a basic sucking impulse from which the child derives pleasure as well as comfort and relaxation.

Thurstone, Louis Leon (1887–1955) U.S. psychologist. After receiving a master's degree in engineering from Cornell University in 1912, Thurstone began studying psychology at the University of Chicago under James Rowland ANGELL and at the Carnegie Institute of Technology under Walter Van Dyke BINGHAM. He was awarded his doctorate in 1917 from the University of Chicago. Thurstone is best known as a pioneer in PSYCHOMETRICS, the field of psychological tests and measurements. He and his wife, Thelma Gwinn Thurstone (1897–1993), developed and maintained for more than 20 years the American Council of Education's Examination for High School Graduates and College Freshmen, which was the forerunner of the SCHOLASTIC ASSESSMENT TEST (SAT). His contributions to methodology include his development of the statistical technique of factor analysis to tease out PRIMARY ABILITIES. Thurstone founded the Psychometric Society in 1936 and launched the Society's journal *Psychometrika.* Among his many honors were his election to the National Academy of Sciences and the American Academy of Arts and Sciences.

Thurstone attitude scales a DIRECT ATTITUDE MEASURE that involves generating a large set of statements designed to reflect varying levels of negativity or positivity toward an ATTITUDE OBJECT. A group of judges are then asked to rate how positive or negative each statement is, usually on a 9- or 11-point scale. The central tendency and dispersion of the judges' ratings for each statement are computed, and a set of statements with low dispersions is selected. This set contains two statements reflecting each of the scale points on the rating scale (i.e., two statements having an average rating of 1, two statements having an average rating of 2, and so on) and makes up the final attitude scale. When the scale is administered, respondents are instructed to indicate which statements they endorse, and their attitude score is the median of the scale values for these statements. See also LIKERT SCALE; SEMANTIC DIFFERENTIAL. [Louis THURSTONE]

thymine (symbol: T) *n.* a pyrimidine compound that is one of the four bases found in DNA. In RNA, uracil replaces thymine. See also GENETIC CODE.

thymus *n.* an organ, located in the lower neck region, that is part of the IMMUNE SYSTEM. The thymus reaches maximum size at puberty, then shrinks. During infancy it is the site of formation of T LYMPHOCYTES.

thyro- *combining form* thyroid gland.

thyroid gland an endocrine gland forming a shieldlike structure on the front and sides of the throat, just below the thyroid cartilage. It produces the iodine-containing THYROID HORMONES (thyroxine and triiodothyronine) in response to THYROID-STIMULATING HORMONE from the anterior pituitary gland. C cells (parafollicular cells) in the thyroid produce the hormone CALCITONIN, which controls levels of calcium and phosphate in the blood. See also GOITER.

thyroid hormones any of the hormones synthesized and released by the THYROID GLAND. The primary thyroid hormone, THYROXINE (T_4), is metabolized to TRIIODOTHYRONINE (T_3) within target tissues. Plasma levels of T_4 are much higher than those of T_3, but T_3 has the more potent physiological activity. Both hormones play a central role in regulating basic metabolic processes and the early development and differentiation of the brain. Extremes in secretion of these hormones have major effects on metabolism and cognitive function (see CONGENITAL HYPOTHYROIDISM; MYXEDEMA; THYROTOXICOSIS). CALCITONIN, a hormone released by parafollicular cells of the thyroid gland, plays a crucial role in calcium and phosphate metabolism.

thyroid-stimulating hormone (**TSH**) a hormone produced by the anterior PITUITARY GLAND that stimulates production and release of thyroxine and triiodothyronine (see THYROID HORMONES) from the THYROID GLAND. Its secretion is controlled by THYROTROPIN-RELEASING HORMONE from the hypothalamus. It is used in the differential diagnosis of disorders of the thyroid gland. Also called **thyrotropin**; **thyrotropic hormone**.

thyroplasty *n.* any surgical procedure to the cartilages of the LARYNX to alter the length or position of the VOCAL CORDS in order to improve voice and sound production. Also called **laryngeal framework surgery**.

thyrotoxicosis *n.* a condition caused by an excess of THYROID HORMONES, which may be produced by an overactive thyroid gland or administered therapeutically. **Endogenous thyrotoxicosis** may be familial and can involve an autoimmune reaction in which the patient's antibodies stimulate rather than destroy the cells producing thyroid hormone. Thyrotoxicosis is characterized by nervousness, tremor, palpitation, weakness, heat sensitivity with sweating, and increased appetite with weight loss. There may be EXOPHTHALMOS associated with GOITER. Thyrotoxicosis is frequently associated with HYPERPLASIA (enlargement) of the thyroid gland, as in GRAVES' DISEASE, or the development of thyroid nodules (**Plummer's disease**), which occurs in older people. See also HYPERTHYROIDISM.

thyrotropin *n.* see THYROID-STIMULATING HORMONE.

thyrotropin-releasing hormone (**TRH**) a hormone produced by the HYPOTHALAMUS that regulates the release of THYROID-STIMULATING HORMONE. See RELEASING HORMONE.

thyroxine (**T_4**) *n.* an iodine-containing hormone produced by the thyroid gland: the principal THYROID HORMONE. It helps regulate metabolism by controlling oxidation rate in cells. See also TRIIODOTHYRONINE.

TIA abbreviation for TRANSIENT ISCHEMIC ATTACK.

tianeptine *n.* a novel antidepressant compound with a modified tricyclic structure that—unlike the majority of antidepressants—enhances, rather than blocks, the presynaptic reuptake of serotonin (see SSRIS) and thus decreases serotonin neurotransmission. Its efficacy compares favorably to currently used antidepressants, and it is being investigated for clinical use in the United States. French trade name: **Stablon**.

tic *n.* a sudden, involuntary contraction of a small group of muscles (motor tic) or vocalization (vocal tic) that is recurrent, nonrhythmic, and stereotyped. Tics may be simple (e.g., eye blinking, shoulder shrugging, grimacing, throat clearing, grunting, yelping), or complex (e.g., hand gestures, touching, jumping, ECHOLALIA, COPROLALIA). Tics may be psychogenic in origin; alternatively, they may occur as an adverse effect of a medication or other substance or result from a head injury, neurological disorder, or general medical condition.

tic disorder in *DSM–IV–TR*, any one of a group of disorders characterized by the occurrence many times a day of motor tics, vocal tics, or both that is not due to a general medical condition or the effects of a medication. The group includes TOURETTE'S DISORDER, CHRONIC MOTOR OR VOCAL TIC DISORDER, TRANSIENT TIC DISORDER, and TIC DISORDER NOT OTHERWISE SPECIFIED.

tic disorder not otherwise specified in *DSM–IV–TR*, a disorder characterized by the presence of tics that does not meet the diagnostic criteria for a specific TIC DISORDER. Examples are bouts of tics lasting less than 4 weeks and tics that appear after the age of 18.

tic douloureux see TRIGEMINAL NEURALGIA.

tickle experience a sensation produced by impulses from adjacent skin receptors that are stimulated lightly in rapid succession. It is assumed that the receptors involved are also responsible for the sensations of itch and pain and that the method of stimulation accounts for the different sensation.

tie-in *n.* an idea or product that is developed as part of or in relation to a project or initiative. In marketing and advertising, examples of tie-ins are the music, clothes, and other products that are developed in connection with a movie.

tight culture a homogeneous social group whose members share the same cultural attributes (e.g., language, social customs, religion) and tend toward a rigid adherence to the collective norms of their group. Compare LOOSE

CULTURE. [defined by U.S. psychologist Harry C. Triandis (1926–)]

tightrope test a test of the ability of rats to maintain their balance while climbing a sloping wire in order to obtain food.

tigroid bodies see NISSL BODIES.

tilt aftereffect (**TAE**) the distorted perception of the orientation of a vertical line or lines that occurs after prolonged viewing of lines tilted to the left or right from vertical. The visual system becomes adapted to the tilted lines, and the vertical lines then appear to be tilted in the opposite direction. The locus of the TAE is presumed to be in the STRIATE CORTEX or beyond, since adaptation through one eye can produce a TAE when the vertical lines are viewed through the other eye, a phenomenon known as INTEROCULAR TRANSFER.

timbre *n.* the perceptual attribute relating to the quality of a sound. Two perceptually different sounds with the same pitch and loudness differ in their timbre. Timbre is determined primarily by the SOUND SPECTRUM but also is affected by temporal and intensive characteristics. Also called **tone color**. **—timbral** *adj.*

time *n.* a concept by which events are ordered into past, present, and future and duration is measured. Time is used to mark the ubiquitous phenomenon of change. Through the observation of recurrent phenomena, such as the rotation of the earth, time is divided into periods and used to measure the duration of events and rates of change. Time appears to be so abstract, and at the same time so fundamental, that no universally satisfactory definition has been formulated. It is a matter of debate whether time is an abstract construct arising from humanity's marking of change, or whether it is some sort of medium through which change occurs. Although classical mechanics regarded time as absolute, the special theory of relativity maintains that time is relative to motion. Philosophers have also differed over whether time is absolute or relative to particular perspectives and conditions.

time agnosia an inability to perceive the passage of time, usually due to a disorder involving the temporal area of the brain. Awareness of the existence of time is retained. Causes may include a stroke, alcoholic coma, or a head injury; soldiers have experienced time agnosia after a combat trauma. Individuals are unable to estimate short time intervals and believe long periods of time to be much shorter than they actually are.

time and motion study an analysis of industrial operations or other complex tasks into their component steps, observing the time required for each. Common in the early years of scientific management, such studies may serve a number of different purposes, enabling an employer to set performance targets, increase productivity, rationalize pay rates and pricing policy, reduce employee fatigue, and prevent accidents. Also called **motion and time study**. See also THERBLIG.

time and rhythm disorders speech and language problems related to the timing of sounds and syllables, including repetitions, prolongations, and stuttering. The disorders are often functional and may be complicated by feelings of guilt. The condition may be treated with a combination of psychotherapy and speech therapy, using such techniques as cancellation (interrupted stuttering), voluntary stuttering, or rewarding or reinforcing fluent speech.

time-compressed speech words and phrases presented to the ear with small elements removed, which has the effect of increasing the rate of presentation. Time-compressed speech is used to measure auditory perceptual abilities. Also called **time-altered speech**. See also DISTORTED SPEECH TEST.

time discounting giving less weight or importance to future events than to present events, often in connection with the utility values associated with these events.

time disorientation loss of the ability to keep track of time or the passage of time. Inability to accurately state the correct year, month, day, or hour is a common symptom of mental disorder. See DISORIENTATION.

time distortion a type of perceptual distortion, sometimes experienced in altered states of consciousness, in which time appears to pass either with great rapidity or with extreme slowness. Perception of past and future may also be transformed.

timed test see SPEED TEST.

time error in psychophysics, a misjudgment due to the relative position of stimuli in time. For example, the first of two identical tones sounded consecutively tends to be judged as louder than the second.

time estimation the ability to monitor elapsed time. In operant-conditioning studies using FIXED-INTERVAL SCHEDULES, animals can estimate the time between one reward and the occurrence of the next reward. In nature, time estimation is important for finding prey that emerge at a fixed time of day or season and is essential for navigation when sun or star cues are used (see SUN COMPASS).

time-extended therapy a form of GROUP PSYCHOTHERAPY in which prolonged sessions replace or alternate with sessions of normal length. The experience is usually highly emotional and revealing since, due to fatigue and other reasons, the participants have insufficient energy for defensive games. See also ACCELERATED INTERACTION; MARATHON GROUP.

time-lag effect age differences seen in cross-sectional studies that are due to differences between COHORTS. This effect can be measured by testing people of the same age at different times and comparing the results (e.g., comparing 1998 results for people born in 1948 with 2003 results for people born in 1953).

time-lagged correlation the correlation of a measure at one point in time with the value of that same measure at a different point in time; for example, the correlation of IQ scores of individuals at 5 years of age with their IQ scores when they are 10 years of age.

timeless moment 1. the infinitely small dimension of the present instant as conceptualized by traditional linear time. See PSYCHOLOGICAL MOMENT; SPECIOUS PRESENT. **2.** an experience in which one's normal awareness of time dissolves and one feels a sense of holistic involvement with another person or thing or with the universe as a whole. Such PEAK EXPERIENCES are of particular interest in HUMANISTIC PSYCHOLOGY. See BEING COGNITION.

time-limited day treatment an outpatient all-day therapeutic community approach used with clients diagnosed with personality disorders that capitalizes on the positive attributes of the clients as a group. [developed by Canadian psychologist William E. Piper (1945–)]

time-limited psychotherapy (**TLP**) therapy that is limited to a predetermined and agreed-upon number of sessions over a specified period of time. Also called **limited-term psychotherapy**. See also SHORT-TERM THERAPY.

time management the use of techniques and strategies

to organize oneself in a way that makes the most efficient use of one's time.

time-of-measurement effect an effect that is due to the social and historical influences present at the time a measurement is made. These effects are difficult to separate from age effects in longitudinal designs.

time out (**TO**) **1.** a technique, originating in BEHAVIOR THERAPY, in which undesirable behavior is weakened and its occurrence decreased, typically by moving the individual away from the area that is reinforcing the behavior. For example, a child may be temporarily removed from an area when misbehaving. The technique is used in schools and by parents to decrease the undesirable behavior by isolating the misbehaver for a period. Also called **time out from reinforcement**. **2.** in OPERANT CONDITIONING, a time interval during which a behavior does not occur. A time-out procedure may be used to eliminate stimulus effects of earlier behaviors or as a marker in a series of events.

time-out theory a theory to explain the positive effect of exercise as a stress-management technique. It proposes that when exercising, the individual is taking a time-out from the real world and its stress inducers, thereby allowing the body to shut down the physical and mental manifestations of stress.

time perception the ability to perceive the passage of time. See PSYCHOLOGICAL TIME; TIME SENSE.

timer *n.* an instrument measuring the passage of time.

time sampling the process of obtaining observations over time. The process may involve fixed time periods (e.g., every 5 min) or random time intervals. Observations taken during these periods are known as **time samples**.

time score a score based on the amount of time used to complete a particular task, for example, the number of minutes a 3-year-old child requires to solve a simple puzzle.

time sense the ability to estimate time intervals or the time of day without information from clocks. Numerous external and internal cues and stimuli contribute to a sense of time, including the position of the sun in the sky, regular daily events (e.g., mealtimes, school or college classes), and internal body rhythms (see BIOLOGICAL CLOCK). However, one's estimation of the passage of time can be influenced and distorted by many factors (see PSYCHOLOGICAL TIME).

time series a set of measures on a single attribute measured repeatedly over time.

time-series design an experimental design that involves the observation of units (e.g., people or countries) over a defined time period.

time sharing the process of rapidly switching attention from one task to another when two or more tasks are performed together. An individual's time-sharing ability can be used to predict his or her performance in complex tasks.

timidity *n.* **1.** the tendency to take great caution in approaching a perceived risk or to avoid the risk altogether. **2.** see SHYNESS. **—timid** *adj.*

tinnitus *n.* noises in one or both ears, including ringing, buzzing, or clicking sounds due to acute ear problems, such as MÉNIÈRE'S DISEASE, disturbances in the receptor mechanism, side effects of drugs (especially tricyclic antidepressants), or epileptic aura. Occasionally tinnitus is due to psychogenic factors (see SENSORY CONVERSION SYMPTOMS).

tip-of-the-tongue phenomenon (**TOT phenomenon**) the experience of attempting to retrieve from memory a specific name or word but not being able to do so: The fact is ordinarily accessible and seems to hover tantalizingly on the rim of consciousness. See also RETRIEVAL BLOCK.

tissue *n.* a structure composed of identical or similar cells with the same or similar function, as in ADIPOSE TISSUE, erectile tissue (of the penis), or muscle tissue.

tissue damage injury to body tissue causing impairment of function, such as nerve damage in multiple sclerosis or damage caused by radiation. Tissue damage is a common cause of pain. Cuts, pinpricks, or other painful experiences are accompanied by the release of HISTAMINE or other substances known to excite pain receptors.

Titchener, Edward Bradford (1867–1927) British-born U.S. psychologist. One of the founding generation of American psychologists, Titchener studied under Wilhelm WUNDT, earning his doctorate from the University of Leipzig in 1892. After a brief period at Oxford University, in 1895 Titchener became a professor of psychology at Cornell University, where he spent the remainder of his career. Determined to make psychology a rigorously experimental science, Titchener became the chief exponent of STRUCTURALISM in America, emphasizing the use of systematic introspection in a laboratory setting to uncover the elements of experience (sensations, images, and feelings). He also developed experimental techniques, which were more fully accepted than his atomistic approach. To promote further his vision of psychology as an experimental science, Titchener founded a club called The Experimentalists, which eventually became the SOCIETY OF EXPERIMENTAL PSYCHOLOGISTS. His club was controversial among psychologists because of its exclusivity (membership was by invitation only and did not include experimentalist women). Titchener's multivolume textbook, *Experimental Psychology: A Manual of Laboratory Practice* (1901–1905), was widely influential. See also IMAGELESS THOUGHT.

tit-for-tat strategy (**tft strategy**) a bargaining strategy in which a party initially cooperates with another party but thereafter imitates the other party's behavior: Cooperation is met with cooperation, competition with competition.

Title IX a 1972 amendment to the United States Education Act that prohibited discrimination in offering educational programs based on sex. In sport this means that all educational institutions have to provide equal athletic opportunities for both sexes.

titration *n.* a technique used in determining the optimum dose of a drug needed to produce a desired effect in a particular individual. The dosage may be either gradually increased until a noticeable improvement is observed in the patient or adjusted downward from a level that is obviously excessive because of unwanted adverse effects or toxicity. To avoid unpleasant side effects when starting pharmacotherapy, some drugs must be slowly titrated upward to a therapeutic dose. Likewise, many drugs should be slowly titrated downward upon cessation of therapy both to avoid discontinuation side effects as well as to monitor for the recurrence of symptoms. See TAPERING.

TLP abbreviation for TIME-LIMITED PSYCHOTHERAPY.

T lymphocyte see LYMPHOCYTE.

TM abbreviation for TRANSCENDENTAL MEDITATION.

TMA 1. abbreviation for transcortical motor aphasia. See COMBINED TRANSCORTICAL APHASIA. **2.** abbreviation for TRIMETHOXYAMPHETAMINE.

T maze a maze shaped like the letter T and consisting of a start box and stem leading to a choice between left and right arms, one being incorrect while the other leads to the goal box. More complicated mazes can be formed by joining several T mazes in sequence.

TMJ syndrome a disorder of muscles operating the lower jaw at the *t*emporo*m*andibular *j*oint (TMJ) just in front of the ear. The condition, which may be due to tension or stress, arthritis, dislocation or other injury, or a tumor, is often marked by facial pain, limited jaw movement, and clicking of the jaw during movement.

TMS abbreviation for TRANSCRANIAL MAGNETIC STIMULATION.

TMTF abbreviation for TEMPORAL MODULATION TRANSFER FUNCTION.

TO abbreviation for TIME OUT.

tobacco *n.* the dried leaves of the plant *Nicotiana tabacum* and other *Nicotiana* species (native to tropical America but now cultivated worldwide), which are smoked, chewed, or sniffed for their stimulant effects. The main active ingredient is NICOTINE. The leaves also contain volatile oils, which give tobacco its characteristic odor and flavor. Tobacco was used by the native tribes of North and South America when the first European explorers arrived and was quickly transplanted to gardens and plantations throughout the world. Tobacco has no therapeutic value but is of great commercial and medical importance because of its widespread use and associated detrimental cardiovascular, pulmonary, and carcinogenic effects. Indeed, smoking tobacco cigarettes was identified by the U.S. Surgeon General more than 30 years ago as the major preventable cause of death and disability.

tobacco dependence see NICOTINE DEPENDENCE.

to-be-remembered items (**TBR items**) in experiments on memory, the specific items presented to the participant to remember, such as a list of letters, numerals, or words.

toe drop a loss of muscular control of the toes. It is a sign of the onset of CHARCOT–MARIE–TOOTH DISEASE, in which the peripheral nerves of the extremities gradually degenerate and cease transmitting impulses. Toe drop progresses to FOOT DROP.

Tofranil *n.* a trade name for IMIPRAMINE.

toilet training the process of teaching a child to control the emptying of the bowel and bladder by learned inhibition of natural reflexes and to excrete in the appropriate place and manner. Although defecation and urination involve functions of the autonomic nervous system, toilet training conditions the individual to override the reflex action with voluntary nerve control. See DEFECATION REFLEX; MICTURITION REFLEX. See also ENCOPRESIS; ENURESIS.

token economy in BEHAVIOR THERAPY, a program, sometimes conducted in an institutional setting (e.g., a hospital or classroom), in which desired behavior is reinforced by offering tokens that can be exchanged for special foods, television time, passes, or other rewards. See also BACKUP REINFORCER; BEHAVIOR MODIFICATION; OPERANT CONDITIONING THERAPY.

token identity theory see IDENTITY THEORY.

token reinforcer an object that has no inherent reinforcing value in itself but that can be exchanged for a REINFORCER. The best known example is money. Also called **token reward**. See CONDITIONED REINFORCER.

Token Test a test of auditory-language processing in which participants are asked to manipulate tokens of different shapes, sizes, and colors in response to increasingly complex instructions. The Token Test is used to identify and evaluate receptive language dysfunction associated with APHASIA. [originally developed in 1962 by Italian neuropsychologists Ennio De Renzi and Luigi A. Vignolo]

tolerance *n.* **1.** a condition, resulting from persistent use of a drug, characterized by a markedly diminished effect with regular use of the same dose of the drug or by a need to increase the dose markedly over time to achieve the same desired effect. Tolerance is one of the two prime indications of physical dependence on a drug, the other being a characteristic withdrawal syndrome. Development of drug tolerance involves several mechanisms, including pharmacological ones (i.e., metabolic tolerance and PHARMACODYNAMIC TOLERANCE) and a behavioral one (i.e., a behavioral conditioning process). Also called **drug tolerance**. See SUBSTANCE DEPENDENCE. **2.** acceptance of others whose actions, beliefs, physical capabilities, religion, customs, ethnicity, nationality, and so on differ from one's own. **3.** a fair and objective attitude toward points of view different from one's own. **4.** permissible or allowable deviation from a specified value or standard. **—tolerant** *adj.*

tolerance limit the allowable error in a measurement process.

tolerance of ambiguity the degree to which one is able to accept, and to function without distress or disorientation in, situations having conflicting or multiple interpretations or outcomes. Also called **ambiguity tolerance**.

Tolman, Edward Chace (1886–1959) U.S. psychologist. Tolman earned his doctorate from Harvard University in 1915, studying under Hugo MÜNSTERBERG. After teaching for 3 years at Northwestern University, he joined the faculty of the University of California, Berkeley, where he remained for the rest of his career. Tolman, along with Clark Leonard HULL and B. F. SKINNER, is known as a founder of NEOBEHAVIORISM who followed in the path set by John B. WATSON and his theory of behaviorism. Tolman differed from Hull, Skinner, and Watson, however, in the importance that he gave such mentalist concepts as purpose and COGNITIVE MAPS. In his theory of PURPOSIVE BEHAVIORISM, Tolman held that behavior, far from being randomly initiated, was persistently directed toward a goal until the goal was attained. Drawing on the FIELD THEORY of Gestalt psychologist Kurt LEWIN, Tolman also argued that behavior can be described in terms of goal-directed vectors and valences within a field. His selected papers are collected in two important books, *Purposive Behavior in Animals and Men* (1932) and *Behavior and Psychological Man* (1951). Among Tolman's many honors were election to the National Academy of Sciences (1937) and to the presidency of the American Psychological Association (1937). He also received the American Psychological Association's Distinguished Scientific Contribution Award (1957).

toloache *n.* a plant, *Datura innoxia*, belonging to the nightshade family and closely related to JIMSONWEED, that contains numerous alkaloids with powerful ANTICHOLINERGIC EFFECTS. The plant has been used by indigenous peoples of North and Central America in religious ceremonies and adolescent rituals.

toluene *n.* a volatile solvent that, when chronically inhaled, can cause kidney failure and death. See INHALANT.

Tolvon *n.* a trade name for MIANSERIN.

tomato effect the rejection of an effective treatment because it does not fit an established medical model or because it does not make sense in light of currently accepted medical theories. It has been applied to BIOFEED-

BACK TRAINING. The tomato effect is so named because in America the tomato—known to be a member of the nightshade family—was originally thought to be poisonous; for this reason, tomatoes were not consumed in America until 1820, even though Europeans had been eating them for generations without harm.

tomboyism *n.* the tendency of girls to adopt behavior traditionally associated with boys. See also ROLE CONFUSION; SISSY BEHAVIOR.

tomography *n.* a technique for revealing the detailed structure of a tissue or organ through a particular plane. Examples include COMPUTED TOMOGRAPHY and POSITRON EMISSION TOMOGRAPHY. **—tomographic** *adj.*

tomomania *n.* a compulsive urge to undergo surgery. See also MUNCHAUSEN SYNDROME.

-tomy (**-otomy**) *suffix* surgical cutting (e.g., LOBOTOMY). See also -ECTOMY.

ton- *combining form* see TONO-.

tonal attribute a perceptual characteristic of a sound. The primary tonal attributes are PITCH, LOUDNESS, and TIMBRE.

tonal chroma see TONALITY.

tonal fusion the blending of two or more tones into a single tonal experience.

tonal gap a range of pitches to which a person may be partially or totally insensitive (**island deafness**), although able to perceive tones on either side of the gap.

tonal island a region of normal pitch acuity surrounded by TONAL GAPS.

tonality *n.* the musical PITCH of a sound. Also called **tonal chroma**.

tonal language see TONE.

tonal scale the normal range of sound frequencies perceived by a young adult, usually given as from 20 to 20,000 Hz.

tonal sensation an auditory sensation that produces PITCH. The term is sometimes loosely used to describe any auditory sensation.

tonal spectrum see SOUND SPECTRUM.

tonal volume the extensity or space-filling quality of a sound.

tonaphasia *n.* inability or loss of the ability to recall musical tunes. Also called **musical aphasia**.

tone *n.* **1.** a PURE TONE. **2.** a sound that has PITCH. **3.** in linguistics, a phonetic variable along the dimension of pitch. In a **tonal language**, such as Mandarin or Thai, tone has a phonemic function (see PHONEME), in that differences in tone are sufficient to mark a distinction between words that are otherwise pronounced identically. In English, tone is an important SUPRASEGMENTAL feature of speech, with different patterns of **intonation** serving to distinguish between different types of utterance, such as statements and questions. **—tonal** *adj.*

tone color see TIMBRE.

tone deafness see ASONIA.

tongue kiss see FRENCH KISS.

tongue tie see ANKYLOGLOSSIA.

tonic *adj.* of or relating to muscle tone, especially a state of continuous muscle tension or contraction, which may be normal (see TONUS) or abnormal. For example, a tonic phase of facial muscles prevents the lower jaw from falling open, a normal function. Abnormally, in the tonic phase of a TONIC–CLONIC SEIZURE, the muscles controlling respiration may undergo tonic SPASM, resulting in a temporary suspension of breathing.

tonic activation a form of AROUSAL mediated by the RETICULAR FORMATION and identified as tonic because of its persistent effect. Compare PHASIC ACTIVATION.

tonic–clonic seizure a seizure characterized by both TONIC and CLONIC motor movements (it was formerly known as a **grand mal seizure**). In the tonic phase the muscles go into spasm and the individual falls to the ground unconscious; breathing may be suspended. This is followed by the clonic phase, marked by rapidly alternating contraction and relaxation of the muscles, resulting in jaw movements (the tongue may be bitten) and urinary incontinence. Also called **generalized tonic–clonic seizure**. See also EPILEPSY.

tonic conduction see ELECTROTONIC CONDUCTION.

tonic contraction the sustained contraction of different groups of muscle fibers within a muscle to maintain continual muscular tension (tonus).

tonic epilepsy a type of EPILEPSY in which TONIC, but not clonic (see CLONUS), muscle contractions occur.

tonic immobility see DEATH FEIGNING.

tonic labyrinth reflex a reflex occurring normally during infancy and pathologically thereafter that involves contraction of FLEXOR MUSCLES (those that bend limbs) if the head is tilted forward and contraction of EXTENSOR MUSCLES (those that straighten limbs) if the head is tilted backward.

tonic pupil of Adie a unilateral eye defect, caused by damage to the nerves supplying the intrinsic EYE MUSCLES, in which the pupil responds poorly to light and very slowly to convergence. [William John **Adie** (1886–1935), Australian-born British physician and neurologist]

tonic receptor a receptor in which the frequency of discharge of nerve impulses declines slowly or not at all as stimulation is maintained. Compare PHASIC RECEPTOR.

tonic reflex **1.** any reflex involving a significant delay between muscle contraction and relaxation. **2.** any reflex that enables a muscle or group of muscles to maintain a certain level of tension, or tonus. Signals from stretch receptors in muscles and tendons are integrated within the spinal cord, and the signals in the efferent motor neurons are adjusted accordingly. Such reflexes are crucial for maintaining posture and for movement.

tonic spasm see SPASM.

tono- (**ton-**) *combining form* **1.** sound or tone (e.g., TONOTOPIC ORGANIZATION). **2.** tension or pressure (e.g., TONOMETRY).

tonometer *n.* **1.** a device that can produce a tone of a given pitch or can measure the pitch of other tones. **2.** see TONOMETRY.

tonometry *n.* a method of measuring INTRAOCULAR PRESSURE in the diagnosis of GLAUCOMA and ocular hypertension. Tonometry is usually performed with a device (called a **tonometer**) that blows a puff of air against the eyeball and automatically measures the amount of indentation (resistance of the surface of the eye), which indicates the intraocular pressure.

tonotopic organization the fundamental principle that different frequencies stimulate different places within structures of the mammalian auditory system. This organization begins in the COCHLEA, where different frequencies tend to cause maximal vibration at different places along the BASILAR MEMBRANE and thus stimulate different HAIR CELLS. The hair cells are discretely innervated, and thus different auditory nerve fibers respond to a relatively limited range of frequencies, with the maximal response at the **best frequency** of the fiber. This frequency-to-place mapping is preserved in the AUDITORY CORTEX.

tonus *n.* a continuous, slight stretching, tension, or contraction in muscles when they are at rest. For example, the jaw muscles exhibit tonus when not used for eating or talking. Tonus serves to keep the muscles ready for action. See also TONIC.

tool design in HUMAN ENGINEERING, the design of instruments and tools with concern for such HUMAN FACTORS as the avoidance of muscle fatigue or injury. See also EQUIPMENT DESIGN; WORKSPACE DESIGN.

tool of intellectual adaptation a method of thinking, learning, or remembering or a problem-solving strategy that children internalize from their interactions with more competent members of society. [defined by Lev VYGOTSKY]

tool-using behavior the ability of animals to use objects as tools. Human beings are not the only tool-using and tool-making animals, as was previously thought: A finch may use a cactus spine to probe for insects; an antlion may hurl grains of sand at prey to make them fall into a pit; chimpanzees frequently use sticks to push into ant nests, use leaves as sponges for drinking or cleaning themselves, and use stones of different sizes as hammers and anvils to break open nuts. Distinctive patterns of tool use are found in different populations of chimpanzees across Africa, suggesting "cultural traditions" of tool-using behavior. Chimpanzees, orangutans, and capuchin monkeys in captivity also demonstrate the ability to use novel objects as tools to reach otherwise inaccessible food. Tool-using behavior requires a capacity to generalize relationships between the presence of an object in the environment and its usefulness in extending the animal's reach. See also ANIMAL TOOL USE.

topagnosis *n.* **1.** loss of the ability to localize touch. Individuals can feel tactile stimuli but cannot recognize the site of stimulation. **2.** loss of the ability to recognize familiar surroundings.

topalgia *n.* pain that is localized in one spot or small area without any lesion or trauma to account for it. Topalgia often is a symptom of a SOMATOFORM DISORDER, particularly in cases in which the pain seems to occur in unlikely segments of nerve or circulatory patterns.

Topamax *n.* a trade name for TOPIRAMATE.

topdog *n.* a set of internal moral standards or rules of conduct that produce anxiety and conflict in the individual when they are not fulfilled or carried out. The topdog is an ego state of superiority over the UNDERDOG. [defined by German-born U.S. psychiatrist Frederick (Fritz) R. Perls (1893–1970)]

top-down analysis 1. a deductive approach to problem solving that begins with a hypothesis or general principle and proceeds from this to an examination of empirical data or specific instances. Compare BOTTOM-UP ANALYSIS. Also called **above-down analysis**. **2.** in information processing, see TOP-DOWN PROCESSING.

top-down design a deductive approach to the design of a system or product, such that the design is driven by conceptual guidelines rather than empirical data (e.g., test results or user feedback). An example would be the design of menus or other displays of functions on a computer interface. These generally follow a hierarchical structure from general function categories to groupings or specific tasks via a series of submenus. Compare BOTTOM-UP DESIGN.

top-down processing INFORMATION PROCESSING that proceeds from a hypothesis about what a stimulus might be to a decision about whether the hypothesis is supported by an incoming stimulus. For example, in reading, knowledge about letter and word frequencies, syntax, and other regularities in language guides recognition of incoming information (see PROOFREADER'S ILLUSION). In this type of processing, a person's higher level knowledge, concepts, or expectations influence the processing of lower level information. Typically, perceptual or cognitive mechanisms use top-down processing when information is familiar and not especially complex. Also called **top-down analysis**. Compare BOTTOM-UP PROCESSING. See also CONCEPTUALLY DRIVEN PROCESS; DEEP PROCESSING; SEMANTIC ENCODING.

topectomy *n.* a former psychosurgical procedure in which selected areas of the frontal cortex were excised in cases of refractory mental illness (e.g., schizophrenia) that had not responded to electroconvulsive therapy or other types of treatment.

topical application the administration of a drug by applying it to the surface of the skin or other tissue surface, such as a mucous membrane. The drug is absorbed through the surface and produces its effects on underlying tissues. Some therapeutic drugs that are poorly absorbed through the skin are formulated with inert substances with better penetrating powers, which act as carriers.

topical flight see FLIGHT OF IDEAS.

topiramate *n.* an ANTICONVULSANT drug that is also used as a MOOD STABILIZER in the treatment of bipolar disorders. Topiramate works by slowing neurotransmission through blockade of sodium channels (see ION CHANNEL); it also apparently facilitates the activity of the neurotransmitter GAMMA-AMINOBUTYRIC ACID (GABA) and limits activity at GLUTAMATE RECEPTORS. Psychomotor slowing and somnolence are commonly reported adverse effects. U.S. trade name: **Topamax**.

topo- (**top-**) *combining form* place or position.

topoanesthesia *n.* loss of the ability to sense touch localization. Individuals with topoanesthesia cannot feel tactile stimuli at all.

topographagnosia *n.* a disturbance of topographical orientation resulting from damage to the PARIETAL LOBE in either hemisphere of the brain. Individuals have difficulty navigating through their environments and may get lost in the streets, be unable to find their way about their homes, or be unable to draw or locate significant features on a map. Topographagnosia is most commonly attributed to an AGNOSIA for landmarks.

topographic *adj.* pertaining to a detailed description of a structural entity, including its surface features and the spatial relations among its parts. Also called **topographical**. See also TOPOGRAPHIC ORGANIZATION. **—topographically** *adv.* **—topography** *n.*

topographical amnesia impairment in TOPOGRAPHICAL MEMORY, that is, memory for places and spatial layouts.

topographical disorientation a disorder of spatial visualization resulting from lesions in the cerebral cortex. It is exemplified by difficulty or inability to recall the arrangement of rooms in a house or the furniture in a room of a house in which the individual lives. Individuals with topographical disorientation also may be unable to recall or describe the location of landmarks or other objects in their neighborhoods.

topographical memory memory for the arrangement and relationships of objects in a spatial environment.

topographical psychology the process of mapping the mind, or locating the various mental processes in different regions or systems of the mind. Carl JUNG, for example, divided the mind into the conscious ego, the PERSONAL UNCONSCIOUS, and the COLLECTIVE UNCONSCIOUS; Sigmund FREUD divided the mind into three levels: CONSCIOUS, PRECONSCIOUS, and UNCONSCIOUS. Also called **mental topography**. See also TOPOGRAPHIC MODEL.

topographic hypothesis see TOPOGRAPHIC MODEL.

topographic mapping of the brain the orderly description and categorization of different parts of the brain in terms of their physical relations to each other.

topographic model the original division of the psyche into three regions or systems as proposed by Sigmund FREUD in 1913. The divisions are: (a) the system UNCONSCIOUS (Ucs), made up of unconscious impulses clustering around specific drives or instincts, such as hunger, thirst, and sex, as well as repressed childhood memories associated with them; (b) the system CONSCIOUS (Cs), which enables the individual to adapt to society, distinguish between inner and outer reality, delay gratification, and anticipate the future; and (c) the system PRECONSCIOUS (Pcs), which stands between the conscious and unconscious systems and is made up of logical, realistic ideas intermingled with irrational images and fantasies. Also called **descriptive approach**; **systematic approach**; **topographic hypothesis**. Compare DYNAMIC MODEL; ECONOMIC MODEL. See also STRUCTURAL MODEL.

topographic organization the arrangement of components in a structure, for example, the orderly spatial relationship between the distribution of neural receptors in an area of the body and a related distribution of neurons representing the same functions in cortical sensory regions of the brain. Thus, the motor cortex shows SOMATOTOPIC ORGANIZATION, the primary visual cortex shows a topographic mapping of the retina (see RETINOTOPIC MAP), and the auditory system shows TONOTOPIC ORGANIZATION.

topography of response see RESPONSE TOPOGRAPHY.

topological psychology a system of psychology in which phenomena are described and classified in terms of the formal relationships of attractions and repulsions (VALENCES) in an individual's LIFE SPACE. The result is a geometric map, or TOPOLOGY, of needs, purposes, and goals. [proposed by Kurt LEWIN]

topology *n.* the study of geometric forms and their transformations in space. Jean PIAGET found that most children of 3 or 4 years of age could identify common objects (e.g., key, comb, pencil) by HAPTIC PERCEPTION (exploring through touch alone), but only about one in five could identify simple geometric shapes without using sight. Kurt LEWIN used topological concepts in describing behavior in the LIFE SPACE. See also TOPOLOGICAL PSYCHOLOGY.

torpor *n.* a condition of total inactivity or lethargy. Only a very strong stimulus can elicit a response from an individual in such a condition.

Torrance Tests of Creative Thinking (**TTCT**) two batteries of pencil-and-paper test items—a verbal test (thinking creatively with words) and a figural test (thinking creatively with pictures)—that can be used at all stages from kindergarten to graduate school. Typical "activities," as they are called, involve listing possible consequences of the action in an intriguing picture, citing ways of improving a toy, and incorporating a curved line in drawing an unusual picture. The object is to test for four characteristics of creative thinking: fluency, flexibility, originality, and elaboration. See ARP TESTS; CREATIVITY TEST. [originally devised in 1966 by Ellis Paul **Torrance** (1915–2003), U.S. psychologist]

torsades de pointes see ELECTROCARDIOGRAPHIC EFFECT.

torsion *n.* in vision, the movement of the eyeball around an axis running horizontally from the pupil through the back of the eye.

tort *n.* a wrongful act, not including a breach of contract, that may be subject to recoverable damages in a civil lawsuit.

torticollis *n.* a continuous or spasmodic contraction of the neck muscles, resulting in rotation of the chin and twisting of the head to one side. This form of DYSTONIA may be neurological or congenital and may respond to drug treatment or BIOFEEDBACK TRAINING. However it may also be psychogenic. Torticollis is sometimes classed as a complex (dystonic) TIC. **—torticollar** *adj.*

torture *n.* the subjection of individuals to severe, painful physical abuse and violence, which often includes treatment that simulates death or near-death experiences. Torture may also involve mental or psychological abuse.

total aphasia see GLOBAL APHASIA.

total color blindness see ACHROMATISM.

total hysterectomy see HYSTERECTOMY.

total institution **1.** a highly organized and restrictive social INSTITUTION that maintains a high degree of control over the activities of those individuals who are members of, or confined to, it. Prisons, mental health facilities, and military bases are (in many cases) examples, because nearly all the activities of prisoners, patients, and personnel are regulated by the staff or officers. **2.** a traditional social institution that becomes so rigid that it takes on many of the qualities of a restrictive social institution. Marriage, for example, has been characterized as a total institution because it often creates a high degree of uniformity in the lifestyles and choices of adults.

total lipodystrophy a form of LIPODYSTROPHY, often congenital but occasionally acquired, characterized by absence of adipose tissue in the subcutaneous tissues, perirenal area, epicardium, and mesentery. See also PARTIAL LIPODYSTROPHY.

total-package arbitration a form of dispute resolution in which the parties in conflict submit their preferred terms for a settlement to a neutral party (the arbitrator), who must select the entire package of demands submitted by one of the parties rather than selectively accepting some demands from one party and some demands from the other. The knowledge that a dispute will be settled in this way often motivates parties in conflict to reach consensus prior to arbitration, since a compromise will yield a better outcome than the binding imposition of the other party's package.

total processing space the sum of storage and operating space (i.e., the total mental space) in WORKING MEMORY that is available to a person for the execution of a task. [first described by Canadian developmental psychologist Robbie Case (1944–2000)]

total quality management (**TQM**) in industrial and organizational theory, a comprehensive approach to management that involves a commitment to continuous improvements in quality and productivity. It usually entails improved training and communications in the workplace, greater participation of employees in making decisions, redesign of the work process, and the use of statistical techniques to monitor quality (see STATISTICAL PROCESS CONTROL). TQM programs are customer-focused: Employees identify internal and external customers, assess their needs, and commit themselves to meeting these needs in total at the first attempt.

total recall **1.** the ability to remember an event completely and accurately. **2.** in a recall task, the total number of items recalled across conditions or tests.

TOTE abbreviation for test, operate, test, exit. See FEEDBACK LOOP.

totem *n.* **1.** a revered animal, plant, natural force, or inanimate object that is conceived as the ancestor, symbol, protector, or tutelary spirit of a people, CLAN, or community. It is usually made the focus of certain ritual activities and TABOOS, typically against killing or eating it. **2.** as interpreted by Sigmund FREUD in *Totem and Taboo* (1912–1913), any symbol or representation of the primal father. **—totemic** *adj.* **—totemism** *n.*

TOTE model see FEEDBACK LOOP.

TOT phenomenon abbreviation for TIP-OF-THE-TONGUE PHENOMENON.

touch *n.* the sensation produced by contact of an object with the surface of the skin. Sensitivity to touch varies in different parts of the body; for example, the lips and fingers are far more sensitive than the trunk or back. See also TOUCH SENSE.

touch blends complex touch experiences derived from engaging in ACTIVE TOUCH to experience different qualities of an object, including hardness, softness, roughness, smoothness, wetness or dryness, stickiness, and other object qualities.

toucherism *n.* sexual interest and arousal obtained from touching a stranger on a erotic part of the body, particularly the breasts, buttocks, or genitals. This is often done as an apparent accident, in doorways or hallways. See also FROTTEURISM.

touch fiber a nerve fiber that is a receptor for a mechanical stimulus, such as stroking or light contact.

touching *n.* **1.** see TOUCH THERAPY. **2.** a DISTURBANCE OF ASSOCIATION, similar to NAMING, in which individuals with schizophrenia are unable to recognize an object unless they can touch it.

touch sense the ability to perceive a stimulus (e.g., an object, surface, material) that comes into contact with the surface of the skin (e.g., by pressure, stroking). Also called **tactile sense**. See HAPTIC PERCEPTION; TACTILE PERCEPTION. See also CUTANEOUS SENSE.

touch spot any of the small areas of the skin that are particularly sensitive to light contact.

touch therapy treatment that involves touching or manipulating parts of an individual's body to ease physical pain or to promote relaxation and a general sense of well-being. Touch therapy has been shown to have numerous benefits for children (among others), improving, for example, the physical and psychological development of preterm infants and bringing about a greater tolerance of touch by children with autism, which has resulted in improved bonding and communication with their parents. Also called **therapeutic touch**. See also COMPLEMENTARY AND ALTERNATIVE MEDICINE; MASSAGE.

tough love the fostering of individuals' well-being by requiring them to act responsibly and to seek professional assistance when they find it difficult to act in their own best interests. Often, strict oversight and restrictions of personal freedom and privileges must be willingly accepted by the target individual. Tough love is sometimes seen as a stance taken by a therapist or counselor or in interventions by family and friends of individuals with problem behaviors (e.g. substance abuse, violent behavior).

ToughLove International a voluntary organization for parents, children, or communities who seek help in dealing with the out-of-control behavior of a family member. Parent SUPPORT GROUPS aim to help parents take a firm stand in helping their children take responsibility for their behavior.

tough-mindedness *n.* **1.** a personality trait reflecting the extent to which people demonstrate low levels of compassion and high levels of aggression in social interactions. [proposed by Hans J. EYSENCK] **2.** a personality trait characterized by empiricism, materialism, skepticism, and fatalism. Compare TENDER-MINDEDNESS. [first described by William JAMES] **—tough-minded** *adj.*

Tourette's disorder a TIC DISORDER characterized by many motor tics and one or more vocal tics, such as grunts, yelps, barks, sniffs, and in a few cases an irresistible urge to utter obscenities (see COPROLALIA). The tics occur many times a day for more than a year, during which time any period free of tics is never longer than 3 months. The age of onset for the disorder is before 18 years; in most cases it starts during childhood or early adolescence. Also called **Gilles de la Tourette's syndrome**. [first described in 1885 by Georges Gilles de la Tourette (1857–1904), French physician]

Tower of Hanoi a puzzle often used in studies of problem solving and tests of EXECUTIVE FUNCTIONS. In the most basic version, the puzzle starts with three disks of successively decreasing diameter stacked on one of three vertical pegs. The solver's task is to move the stack from one peg to another by moving one disk at a time from one peg to another, never stacking a larger disk on a smaller one, in the fewest possible moves. [invented in 1883 by French mathematician Edouard Lucas (1842–1891)]

tox- (**toxic-**; **toxo-**; **toxico-**) *combining form* poison or poisoning.

toxemia of pregnancy a syndrome of edema, hypertension, and proteinuria that may develop in the last trimester of a pregnancy. It is now more commonly known as PREECLAMPSIA, which may progress to ECLAMPSIA.

toxic delirium DELIRIUM resulting from the action of a poison.

toxic disorder a brain disorder due to acute or chronic intoxication, including mercury, manganese, lead, bromide, alcohol, or barbiturate poisoning.

toxicity *n.* the capacity of a substance to produce toxic (poisonous) effects in an organism. The toxicity of a substance—whether a drug, an industrial or household chemical, or other agent—generally is related to the size of the dose per body weight of the individual, expressed in terms of milligrams of chemical per kilogram of body weight. Toxicity also may be expressed in terms of the median LETHAL DOSE (LD_{50}). See also BEHAVIORAL TOXICITY.

toxic-metabolic encephalopathy see METABOLIC ENCEPHALOPATHY.

toxicomania *n.* **1.** a morbid desire to consume poisons. **2.** a severe dependency on drugs.

toxicosis *n.* (*pl.* **toxicoses**) see CONDITIONED TASTE AVERSION.

toxic psychosis any PSYCHOSIS resulting from ingestion of poisons or drugs or caused by toxins produced within the body.

toxin *n.* a poisonous substance, especially one produced by a living organism.

toxo- *combining form* see TOX-.

toxoplasmosis *n.* a disease caused by infection with the protozoan parasite *Toxoplasma gondii*, which invades and multiplies within the tissues of mammals and birds. For example, the parasites reproduce in the intestinal cells of cats, and the disease may be transmitted to humans through accidental ingestion (via careless handling) of cat feces. Human infection may also result from eating raw or undercooked meat or, very rarely, from blood transfusion or organ transplantation. When acquired by a pregnant woman, the parasite can be transmitted to the fetus (**congenital toxoplasmosis**), causing hydrocephalus, blindness, mental retardation, and other congenital neurological disorders.

toy test any of a variety of projective tests for children that make use of dolls, puppets, or other toys. See PROJECTIVE TECHNIQUE.

TPA abbreviation for THIRD-PARTY ADMINISTRATOR.

TPD abbreviation for trance and possession disorder (see DISSOCIATIVE TRANCE DISORDER).

TPT abbreviation for TACTUAL PERFORMANCE TEST.

TQM abbreviation for TOTAL QUALITY MANAGEMENT.

trace *n.* see MEMORY TRACE.

trace conditioning a procedure in PAVLOVIAN CONDITIONING in which a conditioned stimulus and an unconditioned stimulus are separated by a constant interval, with the conditioned stimulus presented first. Compare TEMPORAL CONDITIONING.

trace-decay theory see DECAY THEORY.

tracer *n.* see RADIOACTIVE TRACER.

tracheostomy *n.* surgery to create an opening into the trachea (windpipe) through the neck to relieve impaired or obstructed breathing due, for example, to removal of the LARYNX or to swelling in the larynx or upper throat.

trachoma *n.* an infection of the eye, involving mainly the conjunctiva and cornea, caused by a strain of the bacterium *Chlamydia trachomatis*. Trachoma begins with pain, tearing, and photophobia; untreated, it progresses to blindness. It is common in Asia and Africa; in some parts of Africa, entire populations are infected. The causative bacterium is also responsible for a form of NONGONOCOCCAL URETHRITIS. See OPHTHALMIA.

tracing *n.* see RADIOACTIVE TRACER.

tracking *n.* **1.** the process of following a moving object with the eyes or using eye movements to follow a path of some kind. See VISUAL PURSUIT. **2.** a type of CONTINUOUS MOVEMENT TASK in which the goal is to make movements that follow a constantly moving target. See COMPENSATORY TRACKING. **3.** monitoring the progress of a student by means of recording test and homework scores, observing behavior within the classroom, eliciting a self-report, or a combination of these. **—track** *vb.*

tract *n.* **1.** a bundle or group of nerve fibers within the central nervous system. The name of a tract typically indicates its site of origin followed by its site of termination; for example, the RETICULOSPINAL TRACT runs from the reticular formation of the brainstem to the spinal cord. Compare NERVE. **2.** a series of organs that as a whole accomplishes a specific function (e.g., the digestive tract). **3.** a region, passage, or pathway.

tractotomy *n.* the surgical interruption of a nerve tract in the brainstem or spinal cord. One form of tractotomy is of benefit in bipolar disorder that is resistant to other forms of treatment.

trademark *n.* any word, phrase, name, symbol, device, or combination thereof used by manufacturers or merchants to identify their products (e.g., Oreo cookies, Lycra stretch fiber, Crayola crayons) and to distinguish them from the products of others. Typical trademarks include slogans and logos, while more unusual trademarks include sounds and specific packaging designs. While a trademark identifies products, a **trade name** identifies the company that makes or sells them. According to the International Trademark Association, the term trade name should therefore not be used to refer to a product but should be restricted to its manufacturer or purveyor. However, in certain circumstances, trade names may also function as trademarks (e.g., Polaroid Corporation and Polaroid One Instant Camera; American Express and American Express traveler's checks). In addition, in the area of pharmacology, the two terms are often used interchangeably to refer to PROPRIETARY DRUGS.

trade union see UNION.

tradition *n.* a set of social customs or other ethnic or family practices handed down from generation to generation. See also HERITAGE. **—traditional** *adj.*

traditional authority see AUTHORITY.

traditionalism *n.* **1.** a set of social practices and conditions considered typical of societies that are economically and technologically undeveloped, relatively static in their structures and customs, rural rather than urban, religious rather than secular, and which tend to emphasize family or collective responsibilities rather than individual rights and aspirations. The adequacy of this description, and of the dichotomy between traditional and modern societies that it implies, is by no means universally accepted. See MODERNIZATION. See also CULTURAL EPOCH THEORY; PRIMITIVE. **2.** more generally, adherence to any set of political, religious, or cultural traditions. **—traditionalist** *n.* **—traditionalistic** *adj.*

traditional marriage **1.** a marriage according to the traditional norms of a given society, usually for the primary purpose of establishing a family. Although prenuptial customs vary in different cultures, a traditional marriage generally follows a period of courtship, public announcement of wedding plans, and a wedding ceremony. Compare NONTRADITIONAL MARRIAGE. **2.** a marriage of husband and wife, wherein the former is the primary or sole breadwinner and the latter holds primary or sole responsibility for maintaining the home and managing child care.

tradition-directed *adj.* describing or relating to individuals whose values, goals, and behavior are largely determined by their traditional cultural heritage, that is, by the social norms transmitted by their parents. Compare INNER-DIRECTED; OTHER-DIRECTED. [introduced by U.S. sociologist David Riesman (1909–2002)]

tragedy of the commons a SOCIAL DILEMMA that occurs when a course of action benefiting individual members of a community in the short term is detrimental to the long-term welfare of the community. In the original example of this dilemma, if each herdsman in a village seeks to maximize his individual gain by keeping as many of his cattle as possible on common grazing land, this will eventually make the land unusable by all, since the grass of the pasture is a limited resource. The tragedy is that complete freedom in a society brings ruin to all. [introduced in 1968 by U.S. biologist Garrett Hardin (1915–)]

Trail Making Test (**TMT**) a connect-the-dot task that forms part of the HALSTEAD–REITAN NEUROPSYCHOLOGICAL BATTERY. **Trails A** requires the connection in sequence of 25 dots labeled by numbers. **Trails B** requires the connection in sequence of 25 dots labeled by alternating numbers and letters (1–A–2–B–3–C). The test, one of the most widely used for cognitive impairment, is purported to measure several functions, particularly cognitive flexibility, attention, sequencing, visual search, and motor speed. The TMT, originally developed in 1938 by U.S. psychologists John E. Partington and Russell G. Leiter, was initially known as the **Divided Attention Test** and subsequently as **Partington's Pathways Test**.

train 1. *vb.* to teach or condition an individual to perform certain responses, behaviors, tasks, or activities, particularly in a learning experiment. **2.** *n.* a succession of mild electrical impulses, such as is given in brain stimulation.

trainability *n.* the capacity of an individual to benefit from training and to gain proficiency in a particular skill. **—trainable** *adj.*

trainable mentally retarded formerly, describing people, usually children or young adults, with moderate mental retardation (IQ 35 to 49) who did not appear to profit from academic education in special classes but were able to achieve a degree of self-care, social adjustment at home, and vocational usefulness in such settings as sheltered workshops.

trainer *n.* **1.** in mental health, a professional leader or facilitator of a sensitivity-training group (see T-GROUP). **2.** a teacher or supervisor of individuals learning to practice psychotherapy.

training *n.* systematic instruction and practice by which an individual acquires competence in a specific discipline, talent, or vocational or recreational skill or activity.

training analysis PSYCHOANALYSIS of a trainee analyst. Its purpose is not only to provide training in the concepts and techniques of psychoanalysis, but also to increase insight into personal sensitivities or other emotional reactions that might interfere with the process of analyzing patients in the form of a COUNTERTRANSFERENCE. Also called **didactic analysis**.

training evaluation see EVALUATION OF TRAINING.

training group see T-GROUP.

training log a form of SELF-MONITORING, in which athletes record sleep patterns, food intake, mood, anxiety levels, and causal situations, as well as physical training activities. Also called **sport self-talk log**.

training school formerly, a rehabilitation facility for children or adults with mental retardation, utilizing interdisciplinary teams of therapists and allied health care practitioners to provide residential, health, training, vocational, and leisure services. Although such facilities attempted to provide homelike settings, this was seldom achieved in practice. Their use, once common, greatly diminished in the late 20th century. See also PUBLIC RESIDENTIAL FACILITY.

training study a study in which a participant's task performance is assessed after he or she has been instructed in the use of a strategy. In cognitive developmental research, training studies are used to assess MEDIATIONAL DEFICIENCY and PRODUCTION DEFICIENCY.

training systems design a specialty area in which principles drawn from COGNITIVE ERGONOMICS and general educational theory are applied to the design and evaluation of systems designed to facilitate learning and transfer of knowledge and skills.

training validity the success of a training program as judged by the performance of trainees on criteria that form part of the program. For example, the success of a program focusing on truck-driving skills might be evaluated on the basis of how well the trainees perform in driving a simulator used for instruction. This is to be distinguished from **transfer validity**, in which the program is evaluated on how well the trainees perform in the workplace after training (i.e., how well the trainee performs in driving real trucks on the job). See EVALUATION OF TRAINING.

trait *n.* **1.** an enduring personality characteristic that describes or determines an individual's behavior across a range of situations. **2.** in genetics, an attribute resulting from a hereditary predisposition (e.g., hair color or facial features).

trait anxiety proneness to experience anxiety. People with high trait anxiety tend to view the world as more dangerous or threatening than those with low trait anxiety and to respond with STATE ANXIETY to situations that would not elicit this response in people with low trait anxiety. [defined in 1972 and 1983 by U.S. psychologist Charles D. Spielberger (1927–)]

trait-negativity bias the tendency for negative personality traits to play a greater role than positive personality traits in determining overall impressions and to be more often cited in attributions of motive. Also called **negativity bias**. See BAD IS STRONGER THAN GOOD.

trait organization the way in which an individual's personal traits are related and comprise a unique, integrated whole.

trait profile a graphic display of test scores in which each score represents an individual trait. These scores or ratings are often arranged on a common scale to enable them to be interpreted quickly. Also called **psychogram**. See TEST PROFILE.

trait rating a technique in which a given behavioral feature or trait (e.g., a character trait or attribute) is observed, rated, and recorded.

trait self-focus see SELF-FOCUS.

trait theories of leadership approaches to leadership that consider cognitive and noncognitive abilities and personality characteristics as important determinants of success in a leadership role. Among the traits that have been shown to be positively related to successful leadership are general intelligence, extraversion, self-confidence, supervisory ability, decisiveness, and ACTION ORIENTATION. See LEADERSHIP THEORIES.

trait theory approaches that explain personality in terms of TRAITS, that is, internal characteristics that are presumed to determine behavior. Some examples are ALLPORT'S PERSONALITY TRAIT THEORY, CATTELL'S FACTORIAL THEORY OF PERSONALITY, and the FIVE-FACTOR PERSONALITY MODEL.

trajectories of dying the rate of movement and the length of the passage from a life-threatening condition to death. The **lingering trajectory** is often characteristic of long-term, terminally ill patients who seldom receive aggressive, all-out treatment. By contrast, the expected **quick trajectory** is an emergency situation in which life and death hang in the balance and any possible intervention might be attempted.

trajectory *n.* the sequence of positions through which a object travels over time during a movement.

trance *n.* **1.** a state characterized by markedly narrowed consciousness and responsiveness to stimuli. **2.** a state induced by HYPNOSIS or AUTOSUGGESTION and characterized by openness, or availability, to suggestion (see HYPNOTIC SUSCEPTIBILITY). The hypnotized person may experience a **light trance**, accepting such suggestions as inability to open the eyes or rigidity or lack of sensation in a limb, or a **medium trance**, in which there might be partial amnesia, POSTHYPNOTIC AMNESIA, and POSTHYPNOTIC SUGGESTION. A DEEP TRANCE might be characterized by such effects as an inability to open the eyes without affecting the trance, complete somnambulism, positive and negative posthypnotic hallucinations, and hyperesthesia (excessive sensibility). Also called **hypnotic trance**.

trance and possession disorder (**TPD**) see DISSOCIATIVE TRANCE DISORDER.

trance disorder see DISSOCIATIVE TRANCE DISORDER.

trance logic the presumed tendency of hypnotized individuals to engage simultaneously in logically contradictory or paradoxical trains of thought. It has been suggested that trance logic represents evidence of PARALLEL PROCESSING in that there appears to be simultaneous registration of information at different levels of awareness. See DIVIDED CONSCIOUSNESS; NEODISSOCIATIVE THEORY.

tranquilizer *n.* a drug that is used to reduce physiological and subjective symptoms of anxiety. In the past, distinctions were made between so-called **major tranquilizers** (ANTIPSYCHOTICS) and **minor tranquilizers** (ANXIOLYTICS, e.g., benzodiazepines).

tranquilizer chair a heavy wooden chair used in early psychiatry in which patients were strapped at the chest, abdomen, ankles, and knees, with their head inserted in a wooden box. This method of restraint was preferred to the STRAITJACKET because it reduced the flow of blood to the head and did not interfere with bloodletting, one of the standard treatments of the time. [devised by U.S. physician and psychiatrist Benjamin Rush (1745–1813)]

transaction *n.* **1.** any interaction between the individual and the social or physical environment, especially during encounters between two or more people. **2.** in some psychotherapies, the interplay between the therapist and the patient and ultimately between the patient and other individuals in his or her environment.

transactional analysis (**TA**) a theory of personality and a form of dynamic group or individual psychotherapy focusing on characteristic interactions that reveal internal EGO STATES and the games people play in social situations. Specifically, the approach involves: (a) a study of three primary ego states (parent, child, adult) and determination of which one is dominant in the transaction in question; (b) identification of the tricks and expedients, or games, habitually used in the client's transactions; and (c) analysis of the total script (see SCRIPT ANALYSIS), or unconscious plan, of the client's life, in order to uncover the sources of his or her emotional problems. [developed in the 1950s by Canadian-born U.S. psychologist Eric Berne (1910–1970)]

transactional contingent reward an interaction between two individuals in which one party offers rewards to the other contingent on specific actions or outcomes.

transactional evaluation an attempt to apply the principles of GENERAL SYSTEMS THEORY to the area of program innovation. It is designed to minimize the disruption of the reallocation process that occurs when changes are introduced in an organization and thereby to minimize any personal threat and defensiveness felt by participants in the system.

transactionalism *n.* **1.** an approach to ENVIRONMENTAL PSYCHOLOGY that emphasizes the continuing process of interaction between a person and his or her physical and social environment. This process is characterized as an ongoing series of "transactions" in which the person's behaviors are modified by environmental factors and vice versa. **2.** an approach to perception that emphasizes the interaction of people and their environment. Rather than being mere passive observers, people draw on past experiences in order to form perceptions of present situations and even of novel stimuli. **—transactionalist** *adj., n.*

transactional leadership a style of leadership in which the emphasis is on ensuring followers accomplish tasks. Transactional leaders influence others through exchange relationships in which benefits are promised in return for compliance. Compare TRANSFORMATIONAL LEADERSHIP. [introduced by U.S. political scientist James McGregor Burns (1918–)]

transactional model of development a framework that views development as the continuous and bidirectional interchange between an active organism with a unique biological constitution and its changing environment. See also DEVELOPMENTAL SYSTEMS APPROACH.

transactional psychotherapy psychotherapy that emphasizes the daily interactions between the client and others in his or her life. TRANSACTIONAL ANALYSIS is a specific type of therapy that is based on types of transactions that are considered dysfunctional.

transactive memory system a system in which information to be remembered is distributed among various members of a group, who can then each be relied on to provide that information when it is needed.

transcendence *n.* in METAPHYSICS and in the study of CONSCIOUSNESS, a state of existence or perception that exceeds—and is not definable in terms of—normal understanding or experience. The term implies states that go beyond the physical world and the nature of material existence. **—transcendent** *adj.*

transcendence need in the psychoanalysis of Erich FROMM, the human need to create so as to rise above passivity and attain a sense of meaning and purpose in an impermanent and seemingly random or accidental universe. Both creativity and destructiveness are considered by Fromm to be manifestations of the transcendence need.

transcendence therapy a form of therapy that is spiritually oriented and intended to help people achieve an inner sense of peace by first understanding their role in the larger picture of life and then using that understanding to overcome disappointments, difficulties, and other hardships. It is based on the concept of **formative spirituality**, which postulates that humans are not passive givers or receivers of information or experience but, rather, active interpreters of reality, engaging in an inner dialogue to recognize, relate to, and modify individual construals of existence. [developed by Dutch-born U.S. psychologist Adrian van Kaam (1920–)]

transcendentalism *n.* any philosophical position holding that ultimate reality lies beyond the level of sensory appearances or empirical investigation, such as the THEORY OF FORMS of Greek philosopher Plato (c. 429–347 BCE). The philosophies of German thinkers Immanuel Kant (1724–1804), Georg Wilhelm Friedrich Hegel (1770–1831), and Johann Gottlieb Fichte (1762–1814) are later examples of transcendentalism. The philosophical ideas of U.S. essayist and poet Ralph Waldo Emerson (1803–1882) and some of his New England contemporaries, which are based upon a search for reality through intuition, are also described as transcendentalist. See also IDEALISM; MYSTICISM. **—transcendental** *adj.* **—transcendentalist** *adj.*

transcendental meditation (**TM**) a technique of CONCENTRATIVE MEDITATION for achieving a TRANSCENDENTAL STATE of consciousness. Based on the *Bhagavad-gita* and other ancient Hindu writings, it was introduced in the United States in 1959 by Indian-born guru Maharishi Mahesh Yogi. The modern version of the original discipline consists of six steps that culminate in sitting with one's eyes closed, while repeating a MANTRA, for two 20-minute periods a day. Repetition of the mantra serves to block distracting thoughts and to induce a state of relaxation in which images and ideas can arise from deeper levels of the mind and from the cosmic source of all thought and being. The result is said to be not only a greater sense of well-being but also more harmonious interpersonal relations and the achievement of a state of ultimate self-awareness and restful alertness. See also MYSTIC UNION.

transcendental state a level of consciousness believed to reach beyond waking, sleeping, and hypnotic states. It is characterized physically by lowered metabolism and reduced adrenergic functions and psychologically by alleviation of tension, anxiety, and frustration and a high level of tranquillity. See also TRANSCENDENTAL MEDITATION.

transcendent counseling a form of counseling that is based on the notion that behavior is a product of an individual's lifestyle and that behavior change can only be achieved through lifestyle change. Various directive and action-oriented techniques and activities are employed, such as interpersonal counseling, the use of relaxation and meditation, and adoption of exercise and nutrition programs. [developed by U.S. psychologist Frederick D. Harper (1943–)]

transcortical *adj.* referring to the passage of activity from one part of the cerebral cortex to another.

transcortical aphasia a type of APHASIA caused by a lesion between BROCA'S AREA and WERNICKE'S AREA that results in these areas being isolated from the rest of the brain. As a result, the individual will be able to repeat spoken words but will have difficulty producing independent speech or understanding speech.

transcortical motor aphasia see COMBINED TRANSCORTICAL APHASIA.

transcortical sensory aphasia see COMBINED TRANSCORTICAL APHASIA.

transcranial magnetic stimulation (**TMS**) localized electrical stimulation of the brain through the skull caused by changes in the magnetic field in coils of wire placed around the head. Depending on the parameters, TMS may elicit a response or disrupt functioning in the region for a brief time. The technique was originally devised and is primarily used as an investigatory tool to assess the effects of electrical stimulation of the motor cortex. It is also being investigated as a possible therapy for some types of movement disorders and psychological conditions, such as depression, obsessive-compulsive disorder, and Tourette's disorder. **Repetitive transcranial magnetic stimulation** (**rTMS**) consists of a series of TMS pulses.

transcription *n.* in genetics, the process whereby the genetic information contained in DNA is transferred to a molecule of MESSENGER RNA (mRNA), which subsequently directs protein synthesis. The base sequence of the mRNA is complementary to that of the coding DNA strand and faithfully represents the instructions for assembling the component amino acids of the protein encoded by the gene (see GENETIC CODE).

transcultural psychotherapy forms of PSYCHODYNAMIC PSYCHOTHERAPY that emphasize cultural sensitivity and awareness, including culturally defined concepts of emotion, psychodynamics, and behavior. In the psychiatric community the term is used somewhat more often in a sense similar to MULTICULTURAL COUNSELING in clinical psychology.

transcutaneous electrical nerve stimulation see TENS.

transdermal patch an adhesive application that is designed to release a drug at a steady rate through absorption through the skin into the bloodstream. Transdermal patches are used, for example, to administer nicotine in progressively smaller doses to people who are trying to give up smoking.

Transderm-Scop *n.* a trade name for SCOPOLAMINE.

transducer *n.* a device or system that converts energy from one form to another. Sensory RECEPTOR cells are an example.

transduction *n.* the process by which one form of energy is converted into another, especially **sensory transduction**: the transformation of the energy of a stimulus into a change in the electric potential across the membrane of a RECEPTOR cell. See OLFACTORY TRANSDUCTION; TASTE TRANSDUCTION; VISUAL TRANSDUCTION.

transductive reasoning the tendency of a child in the PREOPERATIONAL STAGE of cognitive development to see a connection between unrelated instances, using neither deductive nor inductive means to do so. For example, the child might say, *I haven't had my nap, so it isn't afternoon.* [proposed by Jean PIAGET]

transection *n.* the severing or cutting of something transversely, such as a nerve tract or fiber or the spinal cord. **—transect** *vb.*

transfer 1. *vb.* to shift or change from one location to another, one form to another, or one situation or condition to another. **2.** *n.* the shift or change thus produced, as in TRANSFER OF TRAINING. **3.** *n.* in GESTALT PSYCHOLOGY, the use of the solution to one problem in solving a second problem that has elements in common with the first.

transfer-appropriate processing a concept of mental processing based on the idea that memory performance is better when a person processes material during study in the same way as the material will be processed during testing. For example, test performance should be relatively good if both study and test conditions emphasize either semantic processing on the one hand or perceptual processing on the other; but test performance will not be as good if study conditions emphasize one (e.g., semantic) and test conditions emphasize another (e.g., perceptual).

transferase *n.* any of a class of enzymes that catalyze the transfer of atoms or groups from one molecule to another; for example, the AMINOTRANSFERASES.

transfer by generalization see GENERAL TRANSFER.

transference *n.* in psychoanalysis, the DISPLACEMENT or PROJECTION onto the analyst of unconscious feelings and wishes originally directed toward important individuals, such as parents, in the patient's childhood. This process, which is at the core of the psychoanalytic method, brings repressed material to the surface where it can be reexperienced, studied, and worked through. In the course of this process, it is posited that the sources of neurotic difficulties are frequently discovered and their harmful effects alleviated. Although quite specific to psychoanalysis, the term's meaning has had an impact far beyond its narrow confines, and transference—as unconscious repetition of earlier behaviors and projection onto new subjects—is acknowledged as ubiquitous in human interactions. The role of transference in counseling and short-term dynamic psychotherapy is well recognized, and ongoing attempts to study its role in a range of therapeutic encounters promise to expand and elucidate its meanings. See also ANALYSIS OF THE TRANSFERENCE;

COUNTERTRANSFERENCE; NEGATIVE TRANSFERENCE; POSITIVE TRANSFERENCE; TRANSFERENCE RESISTANCE.

transference analysis see ANALYSIS OF THE TRANSFERENCE.

transference cure see FLIGHT INTO HEALTH.

transference neurosis in psychoanalysis, neurotic reactions released by the TRANSFERENCE process that result from the revival and reliving of the patient's early conflicts and traumas. These reactions are posited to replace the original neurosis and help the patient become aware that his or her attitudes and behavior are actually repetitions of infantile drives. It is believed that the transference neurosis must be resolved if the patient is to free himself or herself from the harmful effects of past experiences and adopt more appropriate attitudes and responses.

transference remission see FLIGHT INTO HEALTH.

transference resistance in psychoanalysis, a form of RESISTANCE to the disclosure of unconscious material, in which the patient maintains silence or attempts to act out feelings of love or hate transferred from past relationships to the analyst. See also ANALYSIS OF THE TRANSFERENCE.

transfer of principles see GENERAL TRANSFER.

transfer of training the influence of prior learning on new learning, either to enhance it (see POSITIVE TRANSFER) or to hamper it (see NEGATIVE TRANSFER). Solving a new problem is usually easier if previously learned principles or components can be applied, but in some cases these may confuse or mislead. The general principles of mathematics, for example, transfer to computer programming, but a knowledge of Spanish may have both positive and negative effects in learning Italian. See also GENERAL TRANSFER; SPECIFIC TRANSFER.

transfer RNA see RNA.

transfer validity see TRAINING VALIDITY.

transformation *n.* **1.** any change in appearance, form, function, or structure. See also METAMORPHOSIS. **2.** the conversion of data to a different form through a rule-based, usually mathematical process. **3.** in psychoanalytic theory, the process by which unconscious wishes or impulses are disguised in order that they can gain admittance to CONSCIOUSNESS. **—transform** *vb.* **—transformational** *adj.*

transformational generative grammar in linguistics, a type of GENERATIVE GRAMMAR based on the idea that sentences have an underlying DEEP STRUCTURE as well as the SURFACE STRUCTURE observable in speech or writing, and that the former gives rise to the latter through the operation of a small number of **transformational rules** involving the movement, addition, and deletion of constituents. This approach to syntactic structures was pioneered by Noam CHOMSKY in the late 1950s as a means of supplementing the more limited analysis made possible by PHRASE-STRUCTURE GRAMMAR. Also called **transformational grammar**. See also KERNEL SENTENCE.

transformational leadership a charismatic, inspiring style of leading others that usually involves heightening followers' motivation, confidence, and satisfaction, uniting them in the pursuit of shared, challenging goals, and changing their beliefs, values, and needs. Compare TRANSACTIONAL LEADERSHIP. [introduced by U.S. political scientist James McGregor Burns (1918–)]

transformational rules see TRANSFORMATIONAL GENERATIVE GRAMMAR.

transformation theory the theory that, over the course of time, one biological SPECIES can change into a different species. See DARWINISM; EVOLUTION.

transgender *adj.* having or relating to gender identities that differ from culturally determined gender roles and biological sex. Transgender states include transsexualism, some forms of transvestism, and intersexuality. These states should not be confused with same-sex sexual orientation. Also called **transgendered**. See also GENDER IDENTITY DISORDER. **—transgenderism** *n.*

transgenerational design see UNIVERSAL DESIGN.

transgenerational patterns patterns of behavior or personality characteristics that appear in successive generations, often referring to negative or maladaptive behaviors (e.g., drug abuse, adolescent pregnancy, child abuse).

transgenic *adj.* describing an organism in which a foreign or altered gene has been deliberately introduced into the GENOME.

transience *n.* impermanence that implies ending and may invoke anticipation of loss. In classical psychoanalytic theory, the idea that everything is transient may interfere with enjoyment and preclude the establishment of deep or lasting relationships. **—transient** *adj.*

transient global amnesia (**TGA**) a sudden GLOBAL AMNESIA—a form of transient AMNESTIC DISORDER—that typically resolves within 24 hours and occurs in the absence of any other neurological abnormalities. Individuals with TGA appear confused and disoriented and ask frequent repetitive questions to try and make sense of their experience. They are unable to acquire new memories (see ANTEROGRADE AMNESIA); they also exhibit RETROGRADE AMNESIA for recently experienced events. As the episode of TGA clears, new learning gradually returns to normal and retrograde amnesia shrinks; individuals are left with a dense memory gap for the period of TGA. TGA may be triggered by precipitating events, such as physical exertion. The mechanism responsible for its occurrence is poorly understood.

transient group a temporary, short-lived NATURAL GROUP or crowd.

transient ischemic attack (**TIA**) an episode during which an area of the brain is suddenly deprived of oxygen because its blood supply is temporarily interrupted, for example by thrombosis, embolism, or vascular spasm. Symptoms are the same as those of STROKE but disappear completely, typically within 24 hours.

transient monocular blindness see AMAUROSIS FUGAX.

transient situational disturbance a *DSM–II* category for disturbances that in *DSM–IV–TR* are classified as ADJUSTMENT DISORDERS. See also ADJUSTMENT REACTION.

transient situational personality disorder a *DSM–I* designation for POSTTRAUMATIC STRESS DISORDER, replacing the older term **traumatic neurosis**. This category also included what are classified in *DSM–IV–TR* as ADJUSTMENT DISORDERS. See also ADJUSTMENT REACTION.

transient tic disorder a TIC DISORDER involving the presence of single or multiple tics occurring many times a day for a period of between 4 weeks and 1 year. The tics may be simple (e.g., eye blinking, facial grimacing, throat clearing, or sniffing) or more complex (e.g., hand gestures, stomping, ECHOLALIA, or meaningless change in vocal pitch or volume).

transient tremor see TREMOR.

transitional employment a VOCATIONAL REHABILI-

TATION program that places individuals with disabilities or those who are economically, socially, or otherwise disadvantaged (e.g., those who are homeless or dependent on long-term welfare) in paid entry-level positions in a competitive working environment to gain the skills and experience needed to eventually obtain a permanent job in the community workforce. Positions are often provided by participating companies, and each placement typically lasts 6–9 months. Program participants may hold several transitional employment positions before obtaining permanent employment. See also SUPPORTED EMPLOYMENT.

transitional living a supervised living situation that allows psychiatric or neurological patients to make the transition from the dependence of a hospital setting to greater independence before returning to fully independent living.

transitional object **1.** a thing (e.g., a doll or a blanket) used by a child to ease the anxiety of separation from his or her first external OBJECT, the mother, until the child has established a secure internal object, or mental representation of her, that provides a sense of security and comfort. [first described by British psychoanalyst Donald W. Winnicott (1896–1971)] **2.** by extension, any person or thing that provides comfort, security, and emotional well-being.

transitional phenomenon an internal representation of the relationship between an individual's inner subjective representation of the world and the objective reality of that world. See also TRANSITIONAL OBJECT. [first described by British psychoanalyst Donald W. Winnicott (1896–1971)]

transitional probability the probability of moving from one state or condition to another state or condition.

transitive inference task a type of task used to assess children's ability to make transitive inferences, that is, to infer the relationship between two concepts or objects based on earlier acquired information. In one example a series of sticks is arranged in increasing length (e.g., A, B, C, D, E); if children know that D > C and C > B, they will make a correct transitive inference if they state that D > B, even though they have never seen these two sticks together.

transitivism *n.* the illusory assumption of one's symptoms or other characteristics by other people. For example, individuals with schizophrenia might believe that others are also experiencing their hallucinations (e.g., hearing voices) or delusions (e.g., of being persecuted).

transitivity *n.* **1.** the quality of a relationship among elements such that the relationship transfers across elements. For example, a transitive relationship would be: Given that a > b, and b > c, it must be the case that a > c. Compare INTRANSITIVITY. **2.** see STIMULUS EQUIVALENCE. **—transitive** *adj.*

transitory problem **1.** a passing or short-lived symptom, sequela, or other sign of an illness or disorder. **2.** a problem or cause of concern that is short-lived and of brief duration.

translation *n.* **1.** the act or process of rendering words, sentences, or texts into a different language, or the written or spoken rendering so produced. The degree to which a good translation reproduces the form as well as the content of the original will depend on a range of factors, notably the compatibility of the SOURCE LANGUAGE and the TARGET LANGUAGE, the nature of the original speech or text, and the purpose of the translation. See also INTERPRET. **2.** in genetics, the process whereby the genetic information contained in MESSENGER RNA, in the form of a sequence of CODONS, is "translated" into a sequence of amino acids in protein synthesis. See GENETIC CODE.

translation and back-translation a method of ensuring that the translation of an assessment instrument into another language is adequate, used primarily in cross-cultural research. A bilingual person translates items from the source language to the target language, and a different bilingual person then independently translates the items back into the source language. The researcher can then compare the original with the back-translated version to see if anything important was changed in the translation.

translocation *n.* the breakage of a large segment of DNA from one chromosome and its subsequent attachment to a different chromosome. It is a type of chromosomal MUTATION.

transmission *n.* **1.** the act or process of causing something (e.g., a disease) to pass from one place or person to another. See also HORIZONTAL TRANSMISSION. **2.** in neurology, see NEUROTRANSMISSION. **3.** the inheritance of traits through successive generations. **4.** the handing down of customs and mores from generation to generation. See SOCIAL TRANSMISSION. See also CULTURAL HERITAGE. **—transmissible** *adj.* **—transmit** *vb.*

transmitter *n.* **1.** an instrument or device that encodes and sends a message or impulse to a receiver or aids in its transmission. **2.** a NEUROTRANSMITTER.

transneural degeneration see TRANSSYNAPTIC DEGENERATION.

transneuronal degeneration see TRANSSYNAPTIC DEGENERATION.

transorbital lobotomy a former psychosurgical procedure in which a leukotome (a narrow rotating blade) was introduced through the socket above the eyes and carefully swung through a 30° angle to sever connections between the frontal lobe and the thalamus.

transparency *n.* **1.** genuineness in relating to other people, with minimal attempts to make a good impression. **2.** the state of being "invisible," that is, trying not to be noticed in certain social situations (e.g., when volunteers are sought for a task), for example, by avoiding eye contact, remaining still, or hiding behind another person.

transpersonal psychology an area in HUMANISTIC PSYCHOLOGY concerned with the exploration of the nature, varieties, causes, and effects of "higher" states of consciousness and transcendental experiences. "Transpersonal" refers to the concern with ends that transcend personal identity and individual, immediate desires. See also BEING COGNITION; PEAK EXPERIENCE.

transplacental transmission see HORIZONTAL TRANSMISSION.

transplantation *n.* **1.** the surgical implantation of a tissue or organ from one part of the body to another or from one person (the donor) to another (the recipient). Such procedures often induce pre- and postoperative anxieties, resistance, and other behavioral manifestations that may have ramifications for psychological health and intervention. **2.** the removal of a person from a permanent home to a temporary residence or nursing home, which may result in anxiety, depression, and other disturbances.

transporter *n.* a protein complex that spans a cell membrane and conveys ions, neurotransmitters, or other substances between the exterior and interior of the cell. For example, at SYNAPSES between neurons, transporters in the PRESYNAPTIC membrane recognize and bind to neurotransmitter molecules and return them to the presynaptic neuron for reuse (see REUPTAKE). Transporters may utilize passive transport, in which a substance is transported into or out of a cell according to its concentration gradient across the cell membrane; or active transport, which is an energy-dependent process often relying on the hydrolysis of ATP to provide energy to facilitate movement of a substance from one side of the cell membrane to the other.

transpose *n.* in matrix algebra, a matrix formed by interchanging the rows and columns of the original matrix.

transposition *n.* **1.** the process of learning a relationship between stimuli rather than learning the absolute characteristics of the stimuli. For example, if an organism is trained to select a 10-cm diameter disk over a 7-cm disk, and then in a transfer test chooses a 13-cm disk over a 10-cm disk (even though reinforcement has been obtained only for choosing a 10-cm disk), transposition has been observed. **2.** generally, an interchange of positions among two or more elements in a system. **—transpositional** *adj.*

transposition of affect the transfer of the affective component associated with a particular idea or object to an unrelated idea or object, as frequently occurs in OBSESSIVE-COMPULSIVE DISORDER. Also called **displacement**; **displacement of affect**.

transsexualism *n.* a GENDER IDENTITY DISORDER consisting of a persistent sense of discomfort and inappropriateness relating to one's anatomical sex, with a persistent wish to be rid of one's genitals and to live as a member of the other sex. In *DSM–IV–TR,* the diagnosis is applicable only if the condition is not due to another mental disorder, such as schizophrenia, and is not associated with INTERSEXUALITY or genetic abnormality. Many transsexuals feel that they belong to the opposite sex and are somehow trapped in the wrong body. They therefore seek to change their sex through surgical and hormonal means (see SEX REVERSAL). **—transsexual** *adj., n.*

transsynaptic degeneration the degeneration of a neuron that results from the death of a neighboring neuron with which it formed SYNAPSES. Also called **transneural degeneration**; **transneuronal degeneration**.

transtentorial herniation HERNIATION that occurs when increased INTRACRANIAL PRESSURE (resulting, for example, from a tumor or head injury) displaces the medial TEMPORAL LOBE or the deep hemisphere structures of the brain medially and downward through the tentorial notch (an opening in the fold of dura mater that separates the cerebellum from the cerebrum). This causes displacement of the midbrain laterally and downward, which in turn may cause death. Also called **tentorial herniation**; **uncal herniation**.

transtheoretical model (**TTM**) a five-stage theory to explain changes in people's health behavior (see STAGES OF CHANGE). It suggests that change takes time, that different interventions are effective at different stages, and that there are multiple outcomes occurring across the stages (e.g., belief structure, self-efficacy). [developed in the 1970s by U.S. clinical psychologist James O. Prochaska (1942–)]

transverse plane see HORIZONTAL PLANE.

transvestic fetishism in *DSM–IV–TR,* a PARAPHILIA consisting of the persistent wearing by a heterosexual male of female clothes with the purpose of achieving sexual excitement and arousal. It typically begins in childhood or adolescence and should not be confused with transvestism, the nonpathological CROSS-DRESSING by men or women of any sexual preference.

transvestism *n.* the process or habit wearing the clothes of the opposite sex. Transvestism, or CROSS-DRESSING, is distinct from TRANSVESTIC FETISHISM. Also called **transvestitism**. **—transvestic** *adj.* **—transvestite** *n.*

Tranxene *n.* a trade name for CLORAZEPATE.

tranylcypromine *n.* see MONOAMINE OXIDASE INHIBITORS.

trapezoid body a bundle of transverse nerve fibers in the PONS carrying afferent fibers from the COCHLEAR NUCLEI to the SUPERIOR OLIVARY COMPLEX and the nuclei of the LATERAL LEMNISCUS, and efferent fibers from the INFERIOR COLLICULI and lateral lemnisci to the cochlear nuclei.

trauma *n.* **1.** an event in which a person witnesses or experiences a threat to his or her own life or physical safety or that of others and experiences fear, terror, or helplessness. The event may also cause DISSOCIATION, confusion, and a loss of a sense of safety. Traumatic events challenge an individual's view of the world as a just, safe, and predictable place. Traumas that are caused by human behavior (e.g., rape, assault, toxic accidents) commonly have more psychological impact than those caused by nature (e.g., earthquakes). **2.** a physical injury. Such traumas include head injuries, such as blows to the head; brain injuries, such as hemorrhages and CEREBROVASCULAR ACCIDENTS; and injuries to other parts of the body, such as burns or amputations. **—traumatic** *adj.*

traumatic aphasia APHASIA resulting from brain injury.

traumatic brain injury damage to brain tissue caused by external mechanical forces, as evidenced by objective neurological findings, posttraumatic amnesia, skull fracture, or loss of consciousness because of brain trauma.

traumatic disorder any disorder that results from physical or psychological trauma.

traumatic encephalopathy an ENCEPHALOPATHY secondary to a brain trauma.

traumatic grief a severe form of separation distress that usually occurs following the sudden and unexpected death of a loved one. Numbness and shock are frequently accompanied by a sense of futility and purposelessness. A defining characteristic of traumatic grief is a sense of the meaninglessness of life, although the total syndrome includes many other painful and dysfunctional responses.

traumatic hemorrhage a type of CEREBRAL HEMORRHAGE that results from brain trauma.

traumatic neurosis see TRANSIENT SITUATIONAL PERSONALITY DISORDER.

traumatic psychosis see SITUATIONAL PSYCHOSIS.

traveling wave the wave of displacement along the BASILAR MEMBRANE that occurs when sound reaches the cochlea in the inner ear. In response to a PURE TONE the instantaneous displacement of the basilar membrane appears to move over time from the basal end toward the apical opening, or HELICOTREMA. At a point on the basilar membrane, however, the displacement will be approximately sinusoidal with a frequency equal to that of the pure tone.

traveling wave theory see HEARING THEORIES.

trazodone *n.* a chemically unique antidepressant that was introduced as a safer alternative to the tricyclic agents. However, it was of limited use as an antidepressant due to its pronounced sedative effects and its association with prolonged, painful, and unwanted erections (priapism) in a very small number of men who took the drug. Its mechanism of antidepressant action is unclear; it is not a potent inhibitor of either serotonin or norepinephrine reuptake and it is an antagonist at the 5-HT_2 serotonin receptor. Although of little use as an antidepressant, trazodone is commonly used in low doses for bedtime sedation or in controlling agitation and hostility in geriatric patients. A related agent, NEFAZODONE, which is less sedating and less associated with priapism, is now available. U.S. trade name: **Desyrel**.

Treacher Collins syndrome a principally autosomal dominant hereditary disorder characterized by facial anomalies, including a small retracted chin, small eyes with defects of the iris, and deformed external ears. It is caused by several genetic variations, including one that is autosomal recessive. Many affected individuals have conductive hearing loss, and some have mental retardation. Also called **Berry syndrome**; **Franceschetti–Zwahlen–Klein syndrome**; **mandibulofacial dysostosis**. [Edward **Treacher Collins** (1862–1919), British ophthalmologist]

treatment *n.* **1.** the administration of appropriate measures (e.g., drugs, surgery, therapy) that are designed to relieve a pathological condition. **2.** the level of an INDEPENDENT VARIABLE in an experiment, or the independent variable itself. See TREATMENT LEVEL.

treatment audit a procedure that measures quality assurance in health care. Audit activities include assessment of the structure, process, and outcome of the services provided. Audits occur in a cyclical process, thus enabling the results of the assessment to be fed back to improve or maintain the services assessed. See also PROGRAM INTEGRITY; PROGRAM MONITORING.

treatment bias 1. a tendency for the type of treatment given to a patient to be determined or influenced by the social class or cultural background of that patient. **2.** a practitioner's or researcher's unrealistically positive or negative bias toward a particular type of intervention stategy.

treatment combination 1. the particular combination of treatments administered to a participant in a study. **2.** the combination of levels of different FACTORS in a FACTORIAL DESIGN.

treatment effect the magnitude of the effect of a treatment (i.e., the INDEPENDENT VARIABLE) upon the response variable (i.e., the DEPENDENT VARIABLE) in a study. It is usually measured as the difference between the level of response under a control condition and the level of response under the treatment condition in standardized units.

treatment integrity see PROGRAM INTEGRITY.

treatment level the specific condition to which a group or participant is exposed in a study or experiment. For example, in a design employing four groups, each of which is exposed to a different dosage of a particular drug, each dosage amount represents a level of the treatment factor.

treatment plan the recommended steps for intervening that the therapist or counselor devises after an assessment of the client has been completed. Many MANAGED CARE plans require submission of formal, written treatment plans prior to approving mental health treatment. Compare TREATMENT PROTOCOL.

treatment protocol the formal procedures used in a system of psychotherapy. In some systems, such as EXPERIENTIAL PSYCHOTHERAPY, few explicit "rules" apply, whereas in others, such as BEHAVIOR THERAPY, strict adherence to a treatment protocol is often used to guide the work of the therapist. Compare TREATMENT PLAN.

treatment resistance 1. refusal or reluctance on the part of an individual to accept psychological or medical treatment or unwillingness to comply with the therapist's or physician's instructions or prescribed regimens. In psychotherapy it is the lack of a positive response by a client to the techniques being used or to what the client feels is a rupture in the THERAPEUTIC ALLIANCE, which requires the use of other strategies or efforts to repair the alliance by the therapist. Examples of treatment resistance are noncompliance with assignments, extended silences, talking about tangential issues, and seemingly pointless debates about the therapist's approach, suggestions, and interpretations. See also NONADHERENCE. **2.** failure of a disease or disorder to respond positively or significantly to a particular treatment method.

treatment-seeking behavior the active pursuit of treatment by a person who is mentally or physically ill, uneasy, or disturbed. See HELP-SEEKING BEHAVIOR.

treatment validity see PROGRAM INTEGRITY.

treatment withholding discontinuing medical treatment that has no benefit to the patient in terms of an eventual cure or short-term alleviation of symptoms.

tree *n.* in computer programming, a type of GRAPH in which there is a unique path between every pair of nodes, that is, a tree has no cycles. A **rooted tree** has all paths directed away from a root state, so that each node in the rooted tree has a unique parent. A rooted tree is often used to represent single- or multiple-person games.

tree diagram see BRANCHING.

tremor *n.* any involuntary trembling of the body or a part of the body (e.g., the hands) due to neurological or psychological causes. **Psychological** (or **psychogenic**) **tremor** may be mild, due to tension, or violent and uncontrolled in severe disturbances. Toxic effects of drugs or heavy metals may produce a **transient tremor**. A **coarse tremor** involves a large muscle group in slow movements, whereas a **fine tremor** is caused by a small bundle of muscle fibers that move rapidly. Some tremors occur only during voluntary movements (see ACTION TREMOR); others occur in the absence of voluntary movement (see RESTING TREMOR). A **senile tremor** is one that is associated with aging. See also ESSENTIAL TREMOR.

trend analysis any of several analytic techniques designed to uncover systematic changes (trends) in a set of variables, such as linear growth over time or quadratic increases in response with increased dosage levels.

trephination *n.* a surgical procedure in which a disk of bone is removed, usually from the skull, with a circular instrument (a **trephine**) having a sawlike edge. On the basis of evidence found in skulls of prehistoric humans, **skull trephining** is believed to be one of the oldest types of surgery. Among the numerous conjectural reasons given for the practice is the possibility that it was a treatment for headaches, infections, skull fractures, convulsions, mental disorders, or supposed demonic possession. Also called **trepanation**. **—trephine** *vb.*

treppe *n.* see STAIRCASE PHENOMENON.

TRH abbreviation for THYROTROPIN-RELEASING HORMONE.

triad *n.* a set of three people involved in a dynamic relationship, for example, a father, mother, and child or a therapist and a couple receiving marital therapy. The three people are presumed to form a triangle that has peculiar group characteristics and internal alliances.

triad training model an approach to training therapists and counselors that fosters greater understanding of clients of other cultures and develops greater multicultural counseling competencies. The didactic simulation matches a trainee therapist or counselor from a particular culture with a three-person team: (a) a "procounselor," representing the trainee therapist's or counselor's own culture; (b) a coached "client," who is hostile or resistant to the trainee, the therapy, or the trainee's culture; and (c) a catalyst "anticounselor," who represents the client's ethnic group, religion, or other affiliation. The catalyst serves as a bridge of communication and support for the client, and the dynamic among all parties reveals issues, content, and effective approaches to the trainee. See also MULTICULTURAL COUNSELING. [developed by U.S. psychologist Paul Bodholdt Pedersen (1936–)]

triage *n.* **1.** a method of enhancing the effects of treatment that involves the selection and sorting of patients in an orderly and systematic fashion. The patients are then routed to the most appropriate treatment services available. **2.** in evaluation research, a method of allocating scarce resources among social programs in which only programs that need and are most likely to benefit from the resources are considered.

trial *n.* **1.** in tests or experiments, one practice session or performance of a given task (e.g., one run through a maze). **2.** see CLINICAL TRIAL. **3.** in parapsychology research, any single attempt by a participant to identify a TARGET by CLAIRVOYANCE or TELEPATHY or to influence a target by PSYCHOKINESIS. In experiments using ZENER CARDS, each turn of a card is therefore a separate trial.

trial-and-error learning a type of learning in which the organism successively tries various responses in a situation, seemingly at random, until one is successful in producing the goal. In successive trials, the successful response appears earlier and earlier. MAZE LEARNING, with its eventual elimination of blind-alley entrances, is an example of trial-and-error learning. Trial and error derives from the S–R theory of Edward L. THORNDIKE, as an explanation of instrumental or reinforcement learning, although Thorndike initially preferred the more descriptive phrase **trial and accidental success**.

trial consultant a social scientist who assists attorneys with various aspects of a trial in which his or her expertise is relevant. **Trial consultation** typically includes helping to prepare individuals for testimony, developing surveys to help in jury selection and trial strategy development, and conducting CHANGE OF VENUE surveys. Also called **jury consultant**.

trial design an outline or plan of the conditions of a CLINICAL TRIAL that must be satisfied in order to optimally evaluate the efficacy of a new treatment.

trial lesson a diagnostic technique that provides information about a child's learning style and the individualized teaching approach that would be most effective for that child.

trial marriage an arrangement by which a couple attempt to determine their compatibility and suitability for formal marriage by living together for a period of time.

trial therapy a planned process of temporary treatment, either in the early sessions of therapy or as a set of sessions prior to the initiation of long-term therapy, to test whether the client is suitable or ready for a commitment to the therapeutic process. Trial therapy is also used to assess whether the therapist believes that his or her treatment approach is compatible with the client and is able to resolve the problem.

triangular theory of love the proposition that the various kinds of love can be characterized in terms of the degree to which they possess the three basic components of love relationships: passion, intimacy, and commitment. See COMPANIONATE LOVE; EROTIC LOVE; PASSIONATE LOVE; ROMANTIC LOVE. [advanced in 1988 by U.S. psychologist Robert J. Sternberg (1949–)]

triangulation *n.* **1.** the process of confirming a hypothesis by collecting evidence from multiple sources or experiments or using multiple procedures. The data from each source, experiment, or procedure supports the hypothesis from a somewhat different perspective. **2.** in FAMILY THERAPY, a situation in which two members of a family in conflict each attempt to draw another member onto their side. Triangulation can occur, for example, when two parents are in conflict and their child is caught in the middle. **—triangulate** *vb.*

triangulation *n.* **1.** the process of confirming a hypothesis by collecting evidence from multiple sources or experiments or using multiple procedures. The data from each source, experiment, or procedure supports the hypothesis from a somewhat different perspective. **2.** in FAMILY THERAPY, a situation in which two members of a family in conflict each attempt to draw another member onto their side. Triangulation can occur, for example, when two parents are in conflict and their child is caught in the middle. **—triangulate** *vb.*

triarchic theory of intelligence a theory of intelligence proposing three key abilities—analytical, creative, and practical—which are viewed as largely although not entirely distinct. According to the theory, intelligence comprises a number of information-processing components, which are applied to experience (especially novel experiences) in order to adapt to, shape, and select environments. The theory is triarchic because it contains three subtheories: one specifying the components of intelligence (see COMPONENTIAL SUBTHEORY), another specifying the kinds of experience to which the components are applied (see EXPERIENTIAL SUBTHEORY), and a third specifying how the components are applied to experience to be used in various kinds of environmental contexts (see CONTEXTUAL SUBTHEORY). [proposed in 1985 by Robert J. Sternberg (1949–), U.S. psychologist]

Triavil *n.* a trade name for a combination of the tricyclic antidepressant AMITRIPTYLINE and the antipsychotic PERPHENAZINE, used for the treatment of concurrent anxiety and depression.

triazolam *n.* a short-acting BENZODIAZEPINE used primarily as a HYPNOTIC and also to manage anxiety associated with dental procedures. Following reports of severe psychological disturbances associated with its use, including behavioral disinhibition, aggression, agitation, and short-term memory impairment (anterograde amnesia), its sale was prohibited in the United Kingdom in 1991. U.S. trade name: **Halcion**.

tribade *n.* a woman who achieves sexual pleasure by rubbing her genitals against those of another woman. This activity is known as **tribadism**, which is also occasionally used as a synonym for lesbianism. **—tribadic** *adj.*

tricho- (**trich-**) *combining form* hair or hairlike formation.

trichomegaly-retinal degeneration syndrome a rare disorder marked by abnormally short stature, long eyebrows and eyelashes, and poor vision due to retinal pigment degeneration. Some affected individuals exhibit slow psychomotor development and may have IQs of less than 70; in others, average-range intelligence has been reported.

trichophagy *n.* the act of persistently biting and eating one's hair.

trichorrhexis nodosa with mental retardation a congenital disorder marked by stubby, brittle hair, thin tooth enamel, defective nails, and severe mental retardation. Affected individuals who have been studied have shown MICROCEPHALY; X-rays have revealed a small cranial vault. Also called **Pollitt syndrome**.

trichotillomania *n.* an impulse-control disorder characterized by persistent hair pulling at any part of one's body on which hair grows, often with conspicuous hair loss. Feelings of increasing tension before the act and feelings of release or satisfaction on completion are common. In *DSM–IV–TR* trichotillomania is included in the category IMPULSE-CONTROL DISORDERS NOT ELSEWHERE CLASSIFIED.

trichromatic theory one of several concepts of the physiological basis of color vision based on evidence from experiments on color mixture in which all hues were able to be matched by a mixture of three primary colors. The YOUNG–HELMHOLTZ THEORY OF COLOR VISION is the best known trichromatic theory. Subsequent studies determined that there are three different retinal cone photopigments (see IODOPSIN) with peak sensitivities roughly corresponding to the three primary colors of trichromatic theory: blue, green, and red. Also called **three-component theory**. See also OPPONENTS THEORY OF COLOR VISION.

trichromatism *n.* normal color vision: the capacity to distinguish the three primary color systems of light–dark, red–green, and blue–yellow. Also called **trichromatopsia**.

tricomponent theory of attitudes see TRIPARTITE THEORY OF ATTITUDES.

tricyclic antidepressants (**TCAs**) a group of drugs, developed in the 1950s, that were the original FIRST-LINE MEDICATIONS for treatment of depression. They are presumed to act by blocking the reuptake of monoamine neurotransmitters (serotonin, dopamine, and norepinephrine) into the presynaptic neuron, thereby increasing the amount of neurotransmitter available for binding to postsynaptic receptors. Tricyclic antidepressants have a characteristic three-ring molecular core. They may be tertiary amines (e.g., IMIPRAMINE, AMITRIPTYLINE) or their metabolites, which are secondary amines (e.g., DESIPRAMINE, NORTRIPTYLINE). Other members of the group include CLOMIPRAMINE, **protriptyline** (U.S. trade name: **Vivactil**), DOXEPIN, and **trimipramine** (U.S. trade name: **Surmontil**). Side effects of TCAs include significant anticholinergic effects (e.g., dry mouth, blurred vision, constipation, urinary retention), drowsiness or insomnia, confusion, anxiety, nausea, weight gain, and impotence. They can also cause cardiovascular complications (particularly disturbances in heart rhythm). The tricyclics represented the mainstay of antidepressant treatment from the introduction of imipramine in 1957 until fluoxetine (Prozac)—the first SSRI—was introduced in 1987. Although they are effective as antidepressants, their adverse side effects and—more significantly—their lethality in overdose have led to a profound decline in their use. They remain, however, the standard against which other antidepressants are compared; no other class of antidepressants has demonstrated more clinical efficacy.

tridimensional theory of feeling see FEELING THEORY OF THREE DIMENSIONS.

trier of fact the person or party in a court of law who hears the evidence and decides the case. This may be either a judge or a jury. Also called **fact finder**.

trifluoperazine *n.* a HIGH-POTENCY ANTIPSYCHOTIC of the piperazine PHENOTHIAZINE class. Like other agents of this class, it acts primarily by blocking postsynaptic dopamine D2 receptors. Trifluoperazine is appropriate for the treatment of schizophrenia in both adults and children and severe, nonpsychotic anxiety in adults only. It may also be used to control behavioral symptoms associated with dementia. Because of its potentially severe side effects (e.g., TARDIVE DYSKINESIA, NEUROLEPTIC MALIGNANT SYNDROME)—and the availability of other, relatively nontoxic anxiolytics (e.g., the benzodiazepines)—it is not recommended for routine use in anxiety. U.S. trade name: **Stelazine**.

trigeminal chemoreception the stimulation of free nerve endings of the trigeminal nerve in the nasal cavity by odorous chemicals, leading to sensations of tickling, stinging, warming, or cooling. The trigeminal nerve is also sensitive to the airflow changes that occur during breathing.

trigeminal nerve the fifth and largest CRANIAL NERVE, which carries both sensory and motor fibers. The motor fibers are primarily involved with the muscles used in chewing, tongue movements, and swallowing. The sensory fibers innervate the same areas, including the teeth and most of the tongue in addition to the jaws. Some fibers of the trigeminal nerve innervate the cornea, face, scalp, and the dura mater membrane of the brain. Also called **cranial nerve V**.

trigeminal neuralgia a form of unilateral facial NEURALGIA involving the trigeminal nerve, characterized by paroxysms of excruciating pain. Also called **tic douloureux**.

trigeminal nucleus either of two nuclei associated with the three main roots of each trigeminal nerve. The **spinal trigeminal nucleus** extends downward in the medulla oblongata to the upper region of the spinal cord and receives fibers from pain and temperature receptors. The **principal sensory trigeminal nucleus** receives large myelinated fibers from pressure receptors in the skin and relays impulses upward to the thalamus.

trigeminal rhizotomy see RHIZOTOMY.

trigger 1. *n.* a stimulus that elicits a reaction. For example, an event could be a trigger for a memory of a past experience and an accompanying state of emotional arousal. **2.** *vb.* to act as a trigger.

trigger feature a specific feature, simple or complex, of a stimulus that may cause a response in a specific neuron. For example, some cells in the visual cortex respond to bars of light with specific orientations, while others respond to more complex visual patterns, such as faces. Also called **trigger mechanism**.

triggering cause a stimulus or phenomenon that initiates the immediate onset of a behavior problem. See also PRECIPITATING CAUSE. Compare PREDISPOSING CAUSE.

trigger zone a low-threshold region for eliciting a response. In a neuron the trigger zone for evoking an action potential is the AXON HILLOCK, where POSTSYNAPTIC POTENTIALS summate. In the brain, stimulation of the CHEMORECEPTOR TRIGGER ZONE in the medulla oblongata provokes vomiting.

trigram *n.* any three-letter combination. See NONSENSE SYLLABLE.

trigraph *n.* see DIGRAPH.

trihexyphenidyl *n.* an ANTICHOLINERGIC DRUG used in the treatment of drug-induced parkinsonian symptoms, such as those produced with use of conventional antipsychotics, and as an adjunctive treatment for PARKINSON'S DISEASE. It acts by exerting a direct inhibitory effect on the parasympathetic nervous system and a relaxing effect on smooth musculature. U.S. trade name: **Artane**.

triiodothyronine (**T_3**) *n.* an iodine-containing hormone that, together with THYROXINE, regulates metabolic activity. See THYROID HORMONES.

Trilafon *n.* a trade name for PERPHENAZINE.

tri-mean *n.* a measure of CENTRAL TENDENCY computed as the average of the MEDIAN, the upper HINGE, and the lower hinge of the distribution of cases.

trimester *n.* any of the three approximately 3-month periods into which a pregnancy is divided.

trimethoxyamphetamine (**TMA**) *n.* a synthetic AMPHETAMINE derivative that is a CNS STIMULANT with purported hallucinogenic properties similar to LSD and the naturally occurring hallucinogen MESCALINE. Side effects and toxicity of TMA and other "designer psychedelics" are similar to those of MDMA.

trimming *n.* the exclusion of a fixed percentage of cases at each end of a distribution before calculating a statistic on the batch of data in order to eliminate the influence of extreme scores on the estimate.

trinucleotide repeat a contiguous repetition of the same three NUCLEOTIDES within a nucleic acid (DNA or RNA). The occurrence of extra trinucleotide repeats in certain genes causes genetic dysfunction, as in HUNTINGTON'S DISEASE and FRAGILE X CHROMOSOME.

tripa ida see SUSTO.

tripartite theory of attitudes a theory of attitude structure proposing that an attitude is based on or consists of affective, cognitive, and behavioral components. Also called **tricomponent theory of attitudes**. See also BASES OF AN ATTITUDE; STRUCTURE OF AN ATTITUDE.

triphasic pattern a characteristic sequence of muscle activations—AGONIST, then ANTAGONIST, and finally agonist again—observed in rapid, unidirectional movements toward a target. Also called **three-burst pattern**.

triple blind denoting or relating to a research procedure in which the participants, the researcher, and the statistician analyzing the results are all unaware of the treatment group membership of the participants. See BLIND. Compare DOUBLE BLIND; SINGLE BLIND.

triple-code model of imagery a theory that attempts to explain why IMAGERY works in performance enhancement. It suggests three effects of imagery: (a) the image itself, an internal sensation that is representative of the outside world and its objects; (b) the somatic response, that is, the psychophysiological response to the image; and (c) the meaning of the image, which is unique to the individual.

triple-X condition see XXX SYNDROME.

triptans *pl. n.* a class of VASOCONSTRICTOR drugs used in the treatment of migraine headache, the prototype of which is **sumatriptan**. Triptans exert their therapeutic effect by acting as SEROTONIN-RECEPTOR AGONISTS at $5\text{-}HT_{1B}$ and $5\text{-}HT_{1D}$ receptors, causing the constriction of cerebral blood vessels. Triptans should not be administered concurrently with MONOAMINE OXIDASE INHIBITORS and should be used cautiously with SSRIS to avoid the risk of precipitating a SEROTONIN SYNDROME.

trisomy *n.* a condition in which a HOMOLOGOUS pair of chromosomes is joined by an extra matching chromosome in each cell nucleus. Trisomy is the cause of several disorders, including DOWN SYNDROME, in which there are three copies of chromosome 21. —**trisomic** *adj.*

trisomy 13–15 see CHROMOSOME-13 TRISOMY.

trisomy 17–18 a congenital disorder characterized by low birth weight with various facial anomalies, a prominent occiput, overlapping of the index finger over the third finger, and visual abnormalities. Severe mental retardation accompanies the defect, which is due to NONDISJUNCTION of one of the chromosomes in the 17–18 group. Also called **Edwards syndrome**; **E trisomy**.

trisomy 21 a condition associated with 85% of instances of DOWN SYNDROME, characterized by the presence of three number 21 chromosomes in the body cells rather than the normal pair. The extra chromosome may be contributed by either the father or the mother. Also called **21 trisomy**.

tritanopia *n.* a relatively rare form of color blindness in which there is some loss of luminosity in the blue portion of the visual spectrum as a result of a deficiency of SHORT-WAVELENGTH PIGMENT.

triune brain the view, now outmoded, that the brain consists of three layers reflecting its evolutionary development. The first and oldest is the archipallium, or R-complex (meaning reptilian complex and including the BRAINSTEM and CEREBELLUM); the second is the paleomammalian system, or LIMBIC SYSTEM; and the most recently evolved is the neopallium, or NEOCORTEX. [proposed by U.S. physician and neurophysiologist Paul D. MacLean (1913–)]

trochlear nerve the fourth CRANIAL NERVE, which contains motor fibers supplying the superior oblique muscle of the eyeball. Also called **cranial nerve IV**.

troilism *n.* sexual activity involving three people. A **troilist** is a person who, in such a relationship, enjoys engaging in heterosexual activities with a partner as well as observing the partner in sexual activities with a third person. The third person may be of the same sex as the partner or the troilist. If the third person is of the same sex as the troilist, only observation occurs. If the third person is of the same sex as the troilist's partner, the troilist may engage in sexual activity with both of them.

troland (symbol: td) *n.* the unit of illumination at the retina, defined as the illumination when a light source of 1 cd/m^2 is viewed through a standard pupil with an area of 1 mm^2.

trophic *adj.* **1.** describing or relating to activities associated with nourishment, or the ingestion of food and metabolism of nutrients. **2.** describing or relating to the nourishing and supportive functions of the CELL BODY of a neuron, as distinct from the activity of impulse reception and transmission. See also NEUROTROPHIC FACTOR.

trophic hormone see TROPIC HORMONE.

trophic nerve any nerve that regulates the nutrition of a tissue.

trophotropic *adj.* related to or concerning a capacity or propensity for renewal of energy, that is, for rest. Compare ERGOTROPIC.

tropia *n.* the relative deviation of the visual axes during binocular viewing of a single target, resulting in abnormal alignment of the eyes that convergence cannot correct (see STRABISMUS). The term is most commonly used in compound words, such as **exotropia** (outward deviation) and **esotropia** (inward deviation).

tropic hormone (**trophic hormone**) any of a class of ANTERIOR PITUITARY HORMONES that affect the secretion of other endocrine glands. The tropic hormones include THYROID-STIMULATING HORMONE, ADRENOCORTICOTROPIC HORMONE, FOLLICLE-STIMULATING HORMONE, and LUTEINIZING HORMONE.

tropism *n.* a form of orientation observed in both plants and animals toward or away from a stimulus, such as sunlight or gravity. The flower of a plant may turn gradually to face the sun as it moves across the sky (**heliotropism**), while its roots follow magnetic lines of force and the pull of gravity. Tropism contrasts with TAXIS, which is a directed movement toward or away from a stimulus. Compare KINESIS. **—tropic** *adj.*

troposmia *n.* a distorted odor perception in the presence of an odor. Typically, pleasant or neutral stimuli are perceived as unpleasant. See also DYSOSMIA; PAROSMIA.

tropotaxis *n.* see TAXIS.

truancy *n.* absence from school without permission. Persistent truancy before the age of 13 is an example of a serious violation of major rules, one of the symptoms of CONDUCT DISORDER. Also called **school truancy**. **—truant** *adj.*

true experiment a study in which participants are assigned at random to two or more experimentally manipulated treatment conditions.

true–false test a test in which statements must be categorized as being either true or false.

true schizophrenia see NUCLEAR SCHIZOPHRENIA.

true score in CLASSICAL TEST THEORY, that part of a measurement or score that reflects the actual amount of the attribute possessed by the individual being measured.

true self in psychoanalytic theory, the total of an individual's potentialities that could be developed under ideal social and cultural conditions. The term is used in the context of Erich FROMM's approach to neurosis as a reaction to cultural pressures and repressed potentialities. The concept is also used in the CLIENT-CENTERED THERAPY of Carl ROGERS. The realization of the true self is a major goal of therapy.

true variance naturally occurring variability within or among research participants. This variance is inherent in the nature of the participant and is not due to measurement error, imprecision of the model used to describe the variable of interest in the research (e.g., a particular behavior), or other extrinsic factors.

truncated distribution a distribution of cases that lacks one or both ends of the distribution of values.

trust 1. *n.* reliance on or confidence in the worth, truth, or value of someone or something. Trust is considered by most psychological researchers to be a primary component in mature relationships with others, whether intimate, social, or therapeutic. See BASIC TRUST; INTERPERSONAL TRUST; SECURITY; TRUST VERSUS MISTRUST. **2.** *vb.* to have trust in someone or something.

trust exercise a common procedure in GROUP PSYCHOTHERAPY and GROWTH GROUPS intended to help members of the group learn to trust other people. The trust exercise may involve putting a member in a vulnerable position so that he or she depends on the other group members for support. See also BLIND WALK.

trust versus mistrust the first of ERIKSON'S EIGHT STAGES OF DEVELOPMENT. It covers the first year of life and corresponds roughly to Sigmund FREUD'S ORAL STAGE. During this stage, the infant's attitudes of trust or mistrust toward other people and himself or herself is influenced by the kind of care received. See also BASIC MISTRUST; BASIC TRUST.

truth serum a colloquial name for drugs, especially the barbiturates AMOBARBITAL, PENTOBARBITAL, or THIOPENTAL, that are injected intravenously in mild doses to help elicit information by inducing a relaxed, semihypnotic state in which an individual is less inhibited and more communicative. The term is derived from the reported use of such drugs by police to extract confessions from suspects.

truth value in logic and philosophy, the truth or falsity of a proposition. See BIVALENCE; INFINITE-VALUED LOGIC.

tryptamine derivatives a group of drugs that are chemically related to SEROTONIN (5-hydroxytryptamine). They include a number of agents with hallucinogenic effects similar to those of LSD, including DMT (dimethyltryptamine), DET (diethyltryptamine), BUFOTENIN, and PSILOCIN. Tryptamine derivatives may also be classified as substituted indolealkylamines.

tryptophan *n.* one of the essential amino acids of the human diet. It is a precursor of the neurotransmitter SEROTONIN and plays a role in general physiological processes. In plants and many animals it is also a precursor of the B vitamin NICOTINIC ACID. Tryptophan depletion—loss of tryptophan in the brain—may be induced for research purposes.

tryptophan hydroxylase an enzyme that catalyzes the first step in the biosynthesis of SEROTONIN. It uses tetrahydrobiopterin as a coenzyme to transform the dietary amino acid L-tryptophan to 5-HYDROXYTRYPTOPHAN (5-HTP). This reaction is the rate-limiting step in serotonin synthesis, limited by levels of tryptophan in the brain as well as by levels of activity of neurons that use serotonin as a neurotransmitter.

TSA abbreviation for transcortical sensory aphasia. See COMBINED TRANSCORTICAL APHASIA.

T-scope *n.* see TACHISTOSCOPE.

T score any of a set of scores scaled so that they have a MEAN equal to 50 and STANDARD DEVIATION equal to 10.

TSCS abbreviation for TENNESSEE SELF-CONCEPT SCALE.

TSD abbreviation for TAY–SACHS DISEASE.

TSH abbreviation for THYROID-STIMULATING HORMONE.

TTCT abbreviation for TORRANCE TESTS OF CREATIVE THINKING.

t test any of a class of statistical tests based on the fact that the test statistic follows the T DISTRIBUTION when the null hypothesis is true. Most *t* tests deal with hypotheses about the mean of a population or about differences between means of different populations.

TTM abbreviation for TRANSTHEORETICAL MODEL.

TTR abbreviation for TYPE–TOKEN RATIO.

TTS abbreviation for TEMPORARY THRESHOLD SHIFT.

TTX abbreviation for TETRODOTOXIN.

TTY abbreviation for text telephone (see TELECOMMUNICATION DEVICE).

tubal ligation a surgical procedure for female STERILIZATION by cutting, cauterizing, tying, or blocking the FALLOPIAN TUBES. Tubal ligation does not affect sex drive, ability for coitus, or menstrual cycles. Although the effects of the procedure may sometimes be reversed and the ability to conceive restored, tubal ligation is usually considered permanent.

tubal pregnancy a pregnancy in which the fertilized ovum is implanted in the wall of a FALLOPIAN TUBE rather than in the lining of the uterus. It is the most common form of ECTOPIC PREGNANCY. Also called **fallopian-tube pregnancy**.

tubectomy *n.* see SALPINGECTOMY.

tuberculous meningitis a complication of tuberculosis resulting from spread of the tubercle bacilli from the lungs to the brain via the bloodstream. Tuberculous lesions in the SUBARACHNOID SPACE rupture to cause inflammation of the middle and innermost meninges (the arachnoid and pia). The symptoms are those of other forms of BACTERIAL MENINGITIS, and HYDROCEPHALUS may develop.

tuberoinfundibular tract one of three major neural pathways in the brain that use dopamine as their principal neurotransmitter (see DOPAMINERGIC NEURON). The cell bodies of this tract, which is a local circuit in the hypothalamus, project short axons to the pituitary gland. The tuberoinfundibular tract is associated with regulation of hypothalamic function and specific hormones (e.g., prolactin). Alterations in hormone function involving this tract are often seen in patients taking phenothiazine ANTIPSYCHOTICS.

tuberomammillary nucleus a nucleus in the HYPOTHALAMUS that contains neurons responsive to HISTAMINE and is involved in maintaining wakefulness and arousal.

tubular vision see TUNNEL VISION.

tufted cell one of the specialized types of cells involved in the sense of smell. The tufted cells are efferent neurons located in the OLFACTORY BULB. They synapse with receptor neurons in the glomerular layer (see GLOMERULUS) and exit the bulb in the LATERAL OLFACTORY TRACT.

TUI abbreviation for TANGIBLE USER INTERFACE.

TUITs acronym for task-unrelated images and thoughts (see INTRUSIVE THOUGHTS).

Tukey's Honestly Significant Difference Test (**Tukey's HSD Test**) a post hoc testing procedure that allows for the comparison of all pairs of groups while maintaining the overall SIGNIFICANCE LEVEL of the set of tests at a prescribed level. [John Wilder **Tukey** (1915–2000), U.S. statistician]

Tukey Test of Additivity a statistical test of the assumption that there are no interactions in experimental designs in which there is only one individual per CELL. It is used as a preliminary step to utilizing the interaction SUM OF SQUARES to estimate the within-cell error. [John **Tukey**]

tulipmania *n.* **1.** the extraordinary overvaluing of tulip bulbs that occurred in Holland in the 17th century. First introduced into Holland in the late 1500s, bulbs soon became highly prized and costly. Their value escalated over a period of 40 years until some of the rarer bulbs cost as much as a private home; such bulbs were no longer planted but instead displayed as an indication of the owner's wealth. Some individuals willingly traded all their possessions and savings to purchase bulbs, which they then hoped to resell for a much higher price as the market price escalated. The price of bulbs plummeted unexpectedly in 1637, causing financial ruin for many who had speculated in the bulb market. Also called **tulipomania**. **2.** any investment craze that is marked by a rapid increase in the price of a commodity with relatively little value.

tumescence *n.* a state of swelling or being swollen, as in swelling of the penis or clitoris as a result of sexual stimulation. Compare DETUMESCENCE. **—tumescent** *adj.*

tumor *n.* **1.** see NEOPLASM. **2.** swelling, one of the cardinal signs of inflammation.

tuning curve a graph of neuronal response (usually measured in action potentials or spikes per unit time) as a function of a continuous stimulus attribute, such as orientation, wavelength, or frequency. A neuron is said to be "tuned" for the stimulus that evokes the greatest response, and the width of the curve from the half-maximum response on either side of the peak indicates how broadly or narrowly tuned a neuron is for a particular stimulus attribute. In the auditory system it is a measure of FREQUENCY SELECTIVITY. For example, in recordings from an auditory nerve fiber, the threshold is usually defined as a fixed increase in firing rate in response to a pure tone. Typically, tuning curves are V-shaped with a **characteristic frequency** (**CF**) or **best frequency** (**BF**) at which the fiber requires the minimal sound level to reach the threshold response. A **psychophysical tuning curve** (**PTC**) is the relationship between the level and frequency of a pure-tone masker (see AUDITORY MASKING) that is necessary to just mask a PROBE signal of fixed level and frequency. PTCs bear a strong resemblance to those measured in auditory nerve fibers. See CRITICAL BAND; TONOTOPIC ORGANIZATION.

T-unit *n.* in linguistics, short for minimal terminable unit. T-units are the shortest grammatically complete units into which a string of written or spoken language can be divided (i.e., by insertion of periods and capital letters). The mean length of T-units is often used as a measure of the structural complexity of student writing. [first described in 1965 by U.S. educationalist Kellogg W. Hunt]

tunnel vision a VISUAL FIELD DEFECT producing the effect of perceiving the world through a long tunnel or tube. Peripheral vision may be entirely lost. Tunnel vision can occur in one or both eyes in uncontrolled GLAUCOMA and RETINITIS PIGMENTOSA and in both eyes after bilateral injury to visual processing areas beyond the optic chiasm. It may also be a conversion symptom. Also called **tubular vision**.

turbinate *n.* any of three bony shelves in the nasal cavity. The turbinates produce turbulence in the airflow passing from the nostrils to the OLFACTORY MUCOSA, and this turbulence distributes air across the OLFACTORY RECEPTORS in the mucosa.

Turing machine a machine designed in the 1930s to determine whether an algorithm could be described and used to prove any mathematical problem that was provable. The Turing machine consisted of four components: an alphabet of tokens, a finite-state machine, an infinite tape, and a read/write head that was used for reading and recording information produced by the finite-state machine from and onto the tape. The tape was infinite only in that it was expected that the read/write head would always be supplied with data as well as have space to write new data. There are multiple ways of describing the state of the Turing machine. One approach is with a set of five values, supplied by the alphabet of tokens: (a) the state of the finite-state machine, (b) the token read from the tape, (c) the token written to the tape, (d) the instruction for moving the read/write head, and (e) the next state of the finite-state machine. Sets of these patterns of five tokens make up the program for the machine. When the program is able to be located on the tape of the machine it is called a **universal Turing machine**. It was later demonstrated that the Turing machine was an example of a class of maximally powerful machines that could compute any function that was computable. See also GÖDEL'S PROOF. [Alan Mathison **Turing** (1912–1954), British mathematician]

Turing test a test proposed in 1950 (originally called the **imitation game**) to determine in what situations a computer program might be said to be intelligent. The test isolates in a room an individual who is connected to either a computer or another person. If the person in the room cannot tell, by asking questions, whether he or she is talking to the computer or to the other person, then the program on the machine must be seen as intelligent. [Alan **Turing**]

Turner's syndrome a chromosomal disorder marked by the absence of all or a part of one of the two X (female) chromosomes. The effects include sexual infantilism, webbing of the neck, short stature, and an IQ that is slightly below average. Nerve deafness and space-perception abnormalities also may be present. The KARYOTYPE in most cases is 45,XO (i.e., complete deletion of the X chromosome), resulting in infertility, but the syndrome may occur in females who are fertile, because only part of the chromosome is deleted. Also called **gonadal dysgenesis**; **XO syndrome**. See also NOONAN'S SYNDROME. [reported in 1938 by Henry H. **Turner** (1892–1970), U.S. endocrinologist]

turnover *n.* in industrial and organizational settings, the number of employees who leave their jobs during a given period. A distinction is generally made between **controllable turnover**, as by dismissal or voluntary resignation, and **uncontrollable turnover**, as by retirement or redundancy. The **turnover rate** is calculated by dividing controllable turnover by the average number of employees in the organization or unit during this period. This rate can be an indicator of the general level of job satisfaction among employees. Also called **labor turnover**; **staff turnover**. See INVOLUNTARY TURNOVER; VOLUNTARY TURNOVER.

turn taking in social interactions, alternating behavior between two or more individuals, such as the exchange of speaking turns between people in conversation, or the back-and-forth grooming behavior that occurs among some animals.

twelfth cranial nerve see HYPOGLOSSAL NERVE.

twelve-step program a distinctive approach to overcoming addictive, compulsive, or behavioral problems that was developed initially in ALCOHOLICS ANONYMOUS (AA) to guide recovery from alcoholism and is now used, often in an adapted form, by a number of other SELF-HELP GROUPS. In the context of alcoholism, for instance, the twelve-step program in AA asks each member to (a) admit that he or she cannot control his or her drinking; (b) recognize a supreme spiritual power, which can give the member strength; (c) examine past errors, a process that is carried out with another member who serves as sponsor; (d) make amends for these errors; (e) develop a new code and style of life; and (f) help other alcoholics who are in need of support. Variations of this model also exist for drug abuse and addiction, gambling addiction, and other problems.

21 trisomy see TRISOMY 21.

twenty-four-hour therapy a procedure in psychotherapy in which a patient is supervised 24 hours a day by the therapist, who has legal, medical, and financial control over the patient, or by the therapist's assistants, who maintain control over the patient under the direction of the therapist. Sometimes mobile telephones or other communication devices are used by the assistants to receive and obtain direction and information from the therapist. Often a parent or partner of the patient initiates this process when the situation is so desperate that no other method seems possible. [developed by U.S. psychologist Eugene E. Landy (1934–)]

twilight state a state of clouded consciousness in which the individual is temporarily unaware of his or her surroundings, experiences fleeting auditory or visual hallucinations, and responds to them by performing irrational acts, such as undressing in public, running away, or committing violence. The disturbance occurs primarily in temporal lobe epilepsy, dissociative reactions, and alcoholic intoxication. On regaining normal consciousness, individuals usually report that they felt they were dreaming and have little or no recollection of their behavior. See also DREAM STATE.

twilight vision see SCOTOPIC VISION.

twin control in twin studies, a method in which the target twin—that is, the one who has had certain experiences or training or has been exposed to the experimental conditions—is compared against the twin who has not had the experiences, training, or treatment and therefore serves as a CONTROL. Also called **cotwin control**.

twinning *n.* **1.** the simultaneous production of two or more embryos within a single uterus. **2.** the production of two symmetrical objects from a single object by division.

twins *pl. n.* see DIZYGOTIC TWINS; MONOZYGOTIC TWINS.

twin studies research utilizing twins. The purpose of such research is usually to assess the relative contributions of heredity and environment to some attribute. Specifically, twin studies often involve comparing the characteristics of identical and fraternal twins and comparing twins of both types who have been reared together or reared apart. For example, two types of study have been used to investigate intelligence in twins. (1) Identical twins reared apart. Here the genotypes (genetic makeups) are identical but as there is no shared environment disparity in intelligence must result from the different environments. (2) Comparisons between identical twins reared together and fraternal twins reared together. Here one can assume that each pair of twins shares the same environment, but while the identical twins have 100% of their genes in common, the fraternal twins share only 50% of their genes. The assumptions made in these studies are, however, never completely fulfilled. For example, the identical twins reared apart have had some common environment, if only their intrauterine experiences. Moreover, identical twins reared together usually have more similar environments than fraternal twins raised together. These differences can make the estimations of heritability of intelligence open to some doubts.

twisted symbols see STREPHOSYMBOLIA.

twitching *n.* a series of small muscular contractions.

two-by-two factorial design an experimental design in which there are two INDEPENDENT VARIABLES each having two levels. When this design is depicted as a matrix, two rows represent one of the independent variables and two columns represent the other independent variable. See FACTORIAL DESIGN.

two-chair technique see EMPTY-CHAIR TECHNIQUE.

two-dimensional leader behavior space see BLAKE–MOUTON MANAGERIAL GRID.

two-factor design a FACTORIAL DESIGN in which two INDEPENDENT VARIABLES are manipulated. Also called **two-way factorial design**.

two-factor theory 1. a theory of avoidance learning holding that avoidance behavior is the result of two kinds of conditioning. Initially, stimuli that precede the presentation of the stimulus to be avoided (e.g., an electric shock) are established by PAVLOVIAN CONDITIONING (Factor 1) as aversive. Next, the subject escapes (Factor 2) from the conditioned aversive stimulus (see ESCAPE LEARNING). [proposed by O. Hobart MOWRER] **2.** a theory that intelligence comprises two kinds of factors: a GENERAL FACTOR, whose influence pervades all tests of intelligence; and specific factors of intelligence, each of whose influence extends only to a single test in a test battery (see SPECIAL FACTOR). [proposed in 1904 by British psychologist Charles Spearman (1863–1945)]

two-factor theory of emotion see SCHACHTER–SINGER THEORY.

two-factor theory of work motivation see HYGIENE FACTORS; MOTIVATORS.

two-neuron arc see MONOSYNAPTIC ARC.

two-plus-two phenomenon a FALLACY of reasoning in which observed or accepted facts are considered to make a certain conclusion so "obvious" that the logical analysis necessary to justify the conclusion is omitted.

two-point discrimination the ability to sense the contact of a touch stimulus at two different points on the hand at the same time. The **two-point discrimination test** is used in studies of the effects of parietal lesions of the brain, particularly in patients with open head injuries.

two-point threshold the point of stimulus separation, that is, the smallest distance between two points of stimulation on the skin at which the two stimuli are perceived as two stimuli rather than as a single stimulus. Also called **spatial threshold**.

two-process model of recall the hypothesis that RECALL of a memory can involve two stages: a search that locates material in memory followed by a decision regarding whether this is the information sought. This model was proposed to explain the occurrence of higher rates of accurate memory in the RECOGNITION METHOD than in the RECALL METHOD. Also called **generate–recognize model**; **two-process model of retrieval**.

two-sided message see ONE-SIDED MESSAGE.

two-spirit *n.* in some Native American cultures, a person, typically male, who takes on the gender identity of the opposite sex with the approval of the society. The culture often views such individuals as having a special spiritual or guidance role in the community. In the Navajo culture such a person is termed a **nadle**, in the Lakota culture the term **winkte** is used, and in other cultures a literal translation of "man-woman" might be used. The traditional scholarly term **berdache** is now used less frequently because of its negative implications of male prostitution or of a "kept" status.

two-stage memory theory a concept that information acquired by learning is stored first in an IMMEDIATE MEMORY from which items are transferred into a permanent memory (see LONG-TERM MEMORY; PERMASTORE). For example, a new telephone number might be retained in immediate memory at first, but with REPETITION eventually transfers to permanent memory. This transfer is described sometimes in psychological terms, as due to REHEARSAL, and sometimes in biological terms, as in memory CONSOLIDATION. See DUAL-STORE MODEL OF MEMORY.

two-tailed test a statistical test of an experimental hypothesis that does not specify the expected direction of an effect or a relationship. Also called **nondirectional test**. Compare ONE-TAILED TEST.

two-way analysis of variance a statistical test analyzing the joint and separate influences of two INDEPENDENT VARIABLES on a DEPENDENT VARIABLE.

two-way factorial design see TWO-FACTOR DESIGN.

two-way table a table in which the joint FREQUENCY DISTRIBUTION of two INDEPENDENT VARIABLES is arrayed.

two-word stage the developmental period, between approximately 18 and 24 months of age, when children use two words at a time when speaking (e.g., *dog bone, mama cup*). See PIVOT GRAMMAR; TELEGRAPHIC SPEECH.

Tylenol *n.* a trade name for ACETAMINOPHEN.

tympanic cavity see MIDDLE EAR.

tympanic membrane a conically shaped membrane that separates the external ear from the middle ear and serves to transform the pressure waves of sounds into mechanical vibration of the OSSICLES. The first ossicle (malleus) is attached to the inner surface of the tympanic membrane. Also called **eardrum**.

tympanic reflex see TENSOR TYMPANI.

tympanometry *n.* the measurement of the mobility of the tympanic membrane. It is used in the diagnosis of CONDUCTION DEAFNESS. **—tympanometric** *adj.*

tympanoplasty *n.* surgery to repair the eardrum or the bones of the middle ear.

Type A behavior a behavior pattern that may be associated with increased risk of coronary heart disease. It is marked by competitiveness, achievement motivation, aggression and hostility, impatience and a distorted sense of time urgency, and **polyphasic activity** (e.g., shaving or eating while reading a newspaper). Compare TYPE B BEHAVIOR.

Type A personality a personality pattern characterized by chronic competitiveness, high levels of ACHIEVEMENT MOTIVATION, and hostility. The lifestyles of Type A individuals are said to predispose them to coronary heart disease. Compare TYPE B PERSONALITY. [outlined in the 1970s by U.S. physicians Meyer Friedman (1910–2001) and Ray H. Rosenman]

Type B behavior a behavior pattern that is free of aggression and hostility, marked by an absence of time urgency and lack of a need to display or discuss one's accomplishments and achievements. Compare TYPE A BEHAVIOR.

Type B personality a personality pattern characterized by low levels of competitiveness and frustration and a relaxed, easy-going approach. Type B individuals typically do not feel the need to prove their superiority or abilities. Compare TYPE A PERSONALITY. [outlined in the 1970s by U.S. physicians Meyer Friedman (1910–2001) and Ray H. Rosenman]

Type I cell a type of TASTE CELL that is electron-dense, that is, it appears dark when viewed by electron microscopy. Type I cells comprise about 60% of the cells in a TASTE BUD. Located peripherally in the bud, they may help hold its goblet shape. Each cell sends a spray of 30–40 MICROVILLI through the TASTE PORE to sample the chemical environment. Also called **dark cell**.

Type II cell a type of TASTE CELL that is electron-lucent, that is, it appears light when viewed by electron microscopy. Type II cells comprise 20% of the cells in a TASTE BUD. They are larger than TYPE I CELLS, though their volume comes from girth rather than length. They send short, blunt MICROVILLI through the TASTE PORE to sample the chemical environment. Also called **light cell**.

Type III cell a type of TASTE CELL that, when viewed by electron microscopy, is similar to a TYPE II CELL but has dense-cored vesicles in its basal region. Type III cells comprise 15% of the cells in a TASTE BUD; they contain acetylcholine and serotonin for activation of peripheral nerve fibers. Also called **intermediate cell**.

Type IV cell a type of cell assumed to be a STEM CELL for the creation of TASTE CELLS. Type IV cells comprise 5% of the cells in a TASTE BUD and are confined to its basal lamina. These cells have no receptor function, possessing neither access to the TASTE PORE nor synapses with peripheral nerve fibers. Also called **basal cell**.

type-changing plastic surgery plastic surgery that modifies one's features from one type to another (e.g., a "nose job"), as contrasted with restorative methods that return features to their previous condition (e.g., a face lift).

Type I conditioning see PAVLOVIAN CONDITIONING.

Type II conditioning see INSTRUMENTAL CONDITIONING.

Type I error the error of rejecting the NULL HYPOTHESIS when it is in fact true. Investigators make this error when they believe they have detected an effect or a relationship that does not actually exist. Also called **alpha error**.

Type II error the error of failing to reject the NULL HYPOTHESIS when it is in fact not true. Investigators make this error if they conclude that a particular effect or relationship does not exist when in fact it does. Also called **beta error**.

type identity theory see IDENTITY THEORY.

Type R conditioning see INSTRUMENTAL CONDITIONING.

Type S conditioning see PAVLOVIAN CONDITIONING.

type–token distinction in semantics and semiotics, the distinction between a general category of items having certain defining features (type) and a particular exemplar of that category (token). A token is taken to possess the essential properties of the type to which it belongs and will thus have a representative function. According to some theories, the type–token distinction plays an important role in semantic memory. [introduced by U.S. scientist and philosopher Charles S. Peirce (1839–1914)]

type–token ratio (**TTR**) a comparison, expressed as a ratio, of the number of types (distinct groups or categories of words) to the number of tokens (the total quantity of words) in a particular communication. The type–token ratio is used in linguistics analyses and studies to assess an individual's verbal diversification. The greater the number of types compared with the number of tokens, the higher the index and therefore the greater the diversification.

Type-T personality a predisposition of an individual to seek situations that cause or increase arousal, stimulation, thrills, and an adrenaline rush. See SENSATION SEEKING.

typhomania *n.* DELIRIUM occurring in individuals with typhoid fever and typhus.

typical antipsychotics see ANTIPSYCHOTICS.

typicality effect the finding that people are quicker to make category judgments about typical members of a category than they are to make such judgments about atypical members. For example, people are able to judge that a dog is a mammal faster than they are able to judge that a whale is a mammal.

typical schizophrenia see NUCLEAR SCHIZOPHRENIA.

typing *n.* **1.** identifying as a type, as in SEX TYPING and GENDER TYPING. **2.** representing something in terms of its common or typical characteristics. See CLASSIFICATION. **3.** typewriting: a much studied example of a SERIAL BEHAVIOR skill.

typology *n.* any analysis of a particular category of phenomena (e.g., individuals, things) into classes based on common characteristics, for example, a typology of personality. **—typological** *adj.*

tyramine *n.* a BIOGENIC AMINE found in high concentrations in a variety of sources, including ripe cheese, broad beans, ergot, mistletoe, some wines, and many foodstuffs that are aged or produced via enzymatic action. Tyramine is derived from the amino acid tyrosine and is sympathomimetic, causing an increase in blood pressure and heart action. Foods containing tyramine react with MONOAMINE OXIDASE INHIBITORS, preventing normal metabolism of the tyramine and resulting in a greatly aggravated effect on blood pressure. As a consequence, the patient may suffer a hypertensive crisis.

tyrosine *n.* a nonessential AMINO ACID present in most proteins. It is a precursor of the CATECHOLAMINE neurotransmitters DOPAMINE, norepinephrine, and epinephrine, which differ structurally only in the group at one position of the molecule. Tyrosine is derived from the essential amino acid phenylalanine.

tyrosine hydroxylase an enzyme that catalyzes the first, and rate-limiting, step in the biosynthesis of the catecholamine neurotransmitters DOPAMINE, norepinephrine, and epinephrine. It transforms dietary tyrosine, using the coenzyme tetrahydrobiopterin and molecular oxygen, to L-DOPA.

Uu

UCR abbreviation for UNCONDITIONED RESPONSE.

UCR fees abbreviation for usual, customary, and reasonable fees (see CUSTOMARY, PREVAILING, AND REASONABLE FEES).

Ucs abbreviation for UNCONSCIOUS.

UCS abbreviation for UNCONDITIONED STIMULUS.

U fiber a nerve fiber that loops through the white matter beneath the cerebral cortex to connect one cortical area to another. U fibers provide the fastest route for cortical transmission of impulses; the alternative intracortical pathway is composed of very fine fibers with slow transmission rates.

UG abbreviation for UNIVERSAL GRAMMAR.

ulcer *n.* an erosion of a tissue surface, such as the mucosal lining of the digestive tract. **Peptic ulcers**, which affect the stomach and duodenum, are associated with increased secretion of hydrochloric acid and pepsin, a digestive enzyme, or increased susceptibility of the lining of the stomach and duodenum to the effects of these substances (see GASTRODUODENAL ULCERATION). See also DYSPEPSIA.

Ullrich–Noonan syndrome see NOONAN'S SYNDROME. [Otto **Ullrich** (1894–1957), German pediatrician; Jacqueline **Noonan** (1921–), U.S. pediatrician]

ulnar nerve the sensory and motor nerve that innervates the lateral (outer) side of the forearm and hand. Its fibers are derived from the eighth cervical and first thoracic SPINAL ROOTS, and they pass through the medial section of the BRACHIAL PLEXUS.

ultimate attribution error see GROUP-SERVING BIAS.

ultimate explanation an account or explanation for a particular behavior in terms of its adaptive value. Compare PROXIMATE EXPLANATION.

ultimate opinion testimony OPINION TESTIMONY by an expert witness that directly informs the court about the issue in dispute. For example, an expert witness who testifies that the defendant is insane is giving ultimate opinion testimony.

Ultiva *n.* a trade name for remifentanil. See FENTANYL.

ultradian rhythm any periodic variation in physiological or psychological function (see BIOLOGICAL RHYTHM) recurring in a cycle of more than 24 hours, such as the human menstrual cycle. Compare CIRCADIAN RHYTHM; INFRADIAN RHYTHM.

ultrasonic communication the use of sound frequencies above the range of human hearing (i.e., above 20 kHz) for animal communication. Ultrasonic communication is commonly used by bats and dolphins, in which ECHOLOCATION is important for navigation or finding prey. High-frequency signals do not travel very far but, because of their short wavelength, they can provide excellent spatial resolution of prey and other objects in the environment. Compare INFRASONIC COMMUNICATION.

ultrasonic irradiation a form of psychosurgery in which sound waves of a frequency of 1000 kHz are directed through trephine openings in the skull for up to 14 min. It is an alternative to prefrontal lobotomy (see LEUKOTOMY) and is rarely used now.

ultrasound *n.* sound whose frequency exceeds the RANGE OF AUDIBILITY of humans, that is, above 20 kHz. In medicine, ultrasound is used to measure and record structures within the body in the imaging technique of **ultrasonography** (or **sonography**). By analyzing echoes of ultrasound waves reflected from tissue surfaces of varying densities, images of internal organs and structures can be recorded. The technique is used, for example, to examine the growing fetus during pregnancy and to produce images of organs, such as the heart, liver, kidneys, and gallbladder.

ultraviolet (UV) *n.* the portion of the electromagnetic spectrum between 0.5 nm and 400 nm. The upper range of the ultraviolet portion of the spectrum is just below the wavelengths perceived as blue. Ultraviolet stimuli can be seen by some insects and fish because they have photopigments in their retinas that are sensitive to these wavelengths.

ululation *n.* **1.** a shrill lament or wailing associated with emotional expression and ritual behavior in various cultures. **2.** a rare name for the incoherent wailing of some individuals with psychosis.

umami *adj.* denoting the taste of foods rich in protein (e.g., meats, fish, some vegetables, cheeses), represented by the taste of monosodium glutamate, which is used primarily to enhance other flavors. Umami is sometimes described as "savory" and is widely considered to be a PRIMARY TASTE quality, joining sweet, salty, sour, and bitter. [Japanese, "delicious"]

umbilical cord a cordlike structure containing two arteries and a vein in a cylindrical membrane that connects the fetus to the PLACENTA during pregnancy.

UMP test abbreviation for UNIFORMLY MOST POWERFUL TEST.

Umweg problem see DETOUR PROBLEM.

Umwelt *n.* in the thought of German philosopher Martin Heidegger (1889–1976), that aspect of DASEIN (human being-in-the-world) that is constituted by a person's engagement with the world immediately around him or her. The term was introduced into the vocabulary of psychology chiefly through the work of Swiss existential psychologist Ludwig Binswanger (1881–1966). Compare EIGENWELT; MITWELT. [German, literally: "around world"]

unaspirated sound see ASPIRATION.

unattended input any stimulus that is not a focus of attention. In DUAL-TASK PERFORMANCE tests, it is the flow of information that participants do not intend to monitor and are not aware of. See also DUAL-TASK COMPETITION.

unbalanced bilingual a person who speaks two languages but is more proficient in one than in the other. Compare BALANCED BILINGUAL.

unbiased *adj.* without BIAS or net error. In unbiased procedures, studies, and the like any errors that do occur are random and therefore self-cancelling in the long run.

unbiased estimator a statistic whose expected value is the value of the parameter being estimated. Thus if G is used to estimate the parameter Θ, G is said to be unbiased if and only if $E(G) = \Theta$.

unbiased estimator of variance a statistic whose expected value is σ^2, where σ is the VARIANCE.

unbiased sampling plan a survey design in which the values produced by the samples coincide in the long run with the true values in the population.

uncal herniation see TRANSTENTORIAL HERNIATION.

uncertainty *n.* **1.** the state or condition in which something (e.g., the probability of a particular outcome) is not accurately or precisely known. **2.** lack of confidence or clarity in one's ideas, decisions, or intentions. See also UNCERTAINTY PRINCIPLE. **—uncertain** *adj.*

uncertainty-arousal factor in psychological aesthetics, a response that reflects autonomic reactions by a viewer to a work of art, as opposed to cortical arousal. The factor contains simple–complex, clear–indefinite, and disorderly–orderly components, which are said to reflect subjective uncertainty.

uncertainty avoidance 1. a COGNITIVE STYLE characterized by a tendency to adhere to what is already known, thought, or believed. It contrasts with **uncertainty orientation**, which is the tendency to seek out new information and ideas and to enjoy exploring and mastering uncertainty. **2.** an intolerance of ambiguity or uncertainty and a psychological need for formal rules. See also NEED FOR CLOSURE. [defined by Dutch cultural psychologist Geert Hofstede (1928–)]

uncertainty factor in psychological aesthetics, a property of a work of art that is associated with high positive ratings on simple–complex and clear–indefinite scales and high negative ratings on a disorderly–orderly scale.

uncertainty orientation see UNCERTAINTY AVOIDANCE.

uncertainty principle the principle, introduced by German physicist Werner Heisenberg (1901–1976), that it is impossible to measure accurately both the position and the momentum of a particle at a specific moment in time. It arises from the fact that the act of measurement will itself interfere with the system being measured in unpredictable ways. The same principle applies to other paired variables, such as energy and time. The uncertainty principle has implications for philosophy, in that it appears to undermine the laws of cause and effect. Also called **Heisenberg principle**; **indeterminacy principle**.

uncertainty reduction theory (**URT**) a social theory of relationship development proposing that there is a need to gain information about other people through communication (reducing uncertainty) in order to be better able to predict and explain the behavior of those individuals. [developed in the early 1970s by U.S. communication theorist Charles R. Berger (1939–)]

uncinate fasciculus a bundle of nerve fibers that connects the anterior and inferior portions of the FRONTAL LOBE of each cerebral hemisphere in the brain. It forms a compact bundle as the fasciculus bends around the LATERAL SULCUS and spreads into a fan shape at either end.

unconditional love see UNCONDITIONAL POSITIVE REGARD.

unconditional positive regard 1. an attitude of caring, acceptance, and prizing on the part of the therapist, which is considered conducive to self-awareness and personality growth on the part of the client. This attitude is emphasized in CLIENT-CENTERED THERAPY. [proposed by Carl ROGERS] **2.** a parent or caregiver's spontaneous love and affection given without conditions, a universal need in infancy and a prerequisite for healthy development. It is internalized by the child and contributes to the development of an enduring sense of self-worth. Unconditional positive regard does not imply license; disapproval of specific types of behavior can be expressed without withdrawing love or inducing feelings of unworthiness. Compare CONDITIONAL POSITIVE REGARD.

unconditioned primary reinforcer see NATURAL REINFORCER; PRIMARY REINFORCEMENT.

unconditioned reflex a response to a stimulus that is innate, reflexive, and occurs without prior conditioning (learning). See UNCONDITIONED RESPONSE.

unconditioned reinforcement see PRIMARY REINFORCEMENT.

unconditioned response (**UCR**; **UR**) the unlearned response to a stimulus: any original response that occurs naturally and in the absence of conditioning (e.g., in Ivan PAVLOV's experiment, the dog's salivation in response to the presentation of food). The unconditioned response serves as the basis for establishment of the conditioned response; it is frequently reflexive in nature. See PAVLOVIAN CONDITIONING. Compare CONDITIONED RESPONSE.

unconditioned stimulus (**UCS**; **US**) a stimulus that elicits an UNCONDITIONED RESPONSE, as in withdrawal from a hot radiator, contraction of the pupil on exposure to light, or salivation when food is in the mouth. Also called **unconditional stimulus**. Compare CONDITIONED STIMULUS.

unconscious 1. (**Ucs**) *n.* in psychoanalytic theory, the region of the psyche that contains memories, emotional conflicts, wishes, and repressed impulses that are not directly accessible to awareness but that have dynamic effects on thought and behavior. Sigmund FREUD sometimes used the term **dynamic unconscious** to distinguish this concept from that which is merely descriptively unconscious but "static" and with little psychological significance. Compare CONSCIOUS; PRECONSCIOUS. See also COGNITIVE UNCONSCIOUS; COLLECTIVE UNCONSCIOUS; PERSONAL UNCONSCIOUS. **2.** *adj.* relating to or marked by absence of awareness or lack of consciousness.

unconscious cognition cognitive processes, such as thinking, memory processing, and linguistic processing, that occur in the absence of awareness. See COGNITIVE UNCONSCIOUS.

unconscious context those psychological processes and knowledge structures that shape awareness without themselves being conscious, for example, beliefs or memories.

unconscious homosexuality see LATENT HOMOSEXUALITY.

unconscious inference theory the hypothesis that perception is indirectly influenced by inferences about current sensory input that make use of the perceiver's knowledge of the world and prior experience with similar input. For example, consider two trees of the same height but different distances from the perceiver. The images of the trees that appear on the retina are of different sizes, but the knowledge that one tree is farther away than the other leads the perceiver to infer, without conscious effort, that in actuality the two trees are the same size. [proposed by German physiologist Hermann von Helmholtz (1821–1894)]

unconscious intentions goals or motivational structures that influence thought and behavior without themselves becoming conscious or being reportable. Compare CONSCIOUS INTENTIONS.

unconscious knowledge see TACIT KNOWLEDGE.

unconscious learning the acquisition of TACIT KNOWLEDGE. See IMPLICIT LEARNING.

unconscious motivation in psychoanalytic theory, wishes, impulses, aims, and drives of which the self is not aware. Examples of behavior produced by unconscious motivation are purposive accidents, slips of the tongue, and dreams that express unfulfilled wishes. See also PARAPRAXIS.

unconscious perception a phenomenon, the existence of which is controversial, in which a stimulus that is not consciously perceived nonetheless influences behavior. See PREATTENTIVE PROCESSING.

unconscious process **1.** in psychoanalytic theory, a psychical process that takes place in the UNCONSCIOUS, for example, REPRESSION. **2.** in cognitive psychology, a mental process that occurs without a person's awareness and subserves cognitive activity. Also called **preattentive process**; **subliminal process**. Compare CONSCIOUS PROCESS.

unconscious processing see PREATTENTIVE PROCESSING.

unconscious resistance in psychoanalytic theory, RESISTANCE proper, as opposed to CONSCIOUS RESISTANCE.

unconscious transfer a memory distortion that results from confusing the source of the information recalled (see SOURCE CONFUSION). In legal contexts, for example, a witness may mistakenly recognize an individual in the lineup as the perpetrator, when in fact the individual's face is familiar because it was earlier presented in a photograph. Also called **unconscious transference**.

uncontrollable turnover see TURNOVER.

uncontrolled *adj.* not regulated or measured, particularly by an investigator in the course of research.

uncontrolled variable a variable that is not regulated or measured by the investigator during an experiment or study.

unconventional therapy treatment that may be unique, controversial, or both, in that it is not traditionally accepted by the health care professions. See COMPLEMENTARY AND ALTERNATIVE MEDICINE.

uncovering *n.* in psychotherapy, the process of peeling away an individual's defenses and passing beyond a focus on symptoms to get to the underlying roots of a problem. **Uncovering techniques** may include psychoanalysis and other psychodynamic or depth therapies, deep exploration of issues, and the use of trust to encourage truthfulness on the part of the client.

uncriticalness *n.* a nonjudgmental attitude on the part of the therapist, which is considered essential in Carl ROGERS's nondirective approach (see CLIENT-CENTERED THERAPY) as well as in other forms of psychotherapy. Criticism is held to inhibit clients' efforts to recognize and revise their self-defeating patterns of thought and behavior.

uncrossed disparity the RETINAL DISPARITY produced by images that lie beyond the HOROPTER in visual space. Uncrossed disparity causes the images on both retinas to move nasally relative to the location of images of objects on the horopter, whereas **crossed disparity** does the opposite. Objects closer than the horopter will move temporally on both retinas, compared to objects on the horopter. See also DEPTH CUE.

uncued panic attack a PANIC ATTACK that occurs unexpectedly rather than being brought on by a specific situation or trigger. It is therefore perceived to have occurred spontaneously. Also called **unexpected panic attack**. Compare CUED PANIC ATTACK; SITUATIONALLY PREDISPOSED PANIC ATTACK.

uncus *n.* a hook-shaped part of the rhinal sulcus (cleft) of the hippocampal formation in the RHINENCEPHALON. The LATERAL OLFACTORY TRACT makes connections with the uncus.

underachiever *n.* a person, usually a student, who consistently achieves below his or her demonstrated capacity. **Underachievement** may be specific to an area of study or it may be general. It is more prevalent among boys than girls and is quite common in bright and even gifted children. It is also prevalent among average students and children with SPECIAL NEEDS. Compare OVERACHIEVER.

underage *adj.* see OVERAGE.

underclass *n.* **1.** a SOCIAL CLASS existing beneath the usual socioeconomic scale, often concentrated in the inner cities and usually characterized by poverty, inadequate educational or vocational opportunities, high unemployment or chronic underemployment, violent crime, substance abuse, poor social services, and few community-supporting institutions. **2.** more broadly, any group without equal or direct access to the economic, educational, legal, medical, or other provisions of a society. For example, the term **genetic underclass** has been used to identify those who are classified as susceptible to a particular disease following genetic testing and who may as a result encounter discrimination by insurance companies or employers.

underdog *n.* the rationalizations and self-justifications employed by an individual to allay the sense of guilt or shame arising from an inability to meet the demands of internal moral standards or other rules of conduct (the TOPDOG). [first described by German-born U.S. psychiatrist Frederick (Fritz) R. Perls (1893–1970)]

underextension *n.* the incorrect restriction of the use of a word, which is a mistake commonly made by young children acquiring language. For example, a child may believe that the label *dog* applies only to Fido, the family pet.

underintensity *n.* a state in which one or all of the following are below the optimal level: arousal, commitment, effort, assertiveness, and attentional focus.

underload *n.* the situation in which a low level of task demand creates distress in such forms as boredom and fatigue. Compare OVERLOAD.

underpayment inequity in industrial and organizational settings, an employee's perception that he or she is being paid less than is fair, especially in comparison to coworkers. This can lead to dissatisfaction and tension and, in some cases, to lowered productivity. Compare OVERPAYMENT INEQUITY. See EQUITY THEORY.

undershoot *n.* the portion of an ACTION POTENTIAL that represents the stage when the membrane potential is transiently hyperpolarized relative to the resting potential. Compare OVERSHOOT.

understaffing *n.* the condition in which the number of people available for a program or function falls below that required to maintain it. Compare OVERSTAFFING. —**understaffed** *adj.*

understanding *n.* **1.** the process of gaining insight about oneself or others or of comprehending the meaning or significance of something, such as a word, concept, argument, or event. See also APPREHENSION; COMPREHENSION. **2.** in counseling and psychotherapy, the process of discerning the network of relationships between a client's behavior and his or her environment, history, aptitudes, motivation, ideas, feelings, relationships, and modes of expression. **3.** in some philosophical writings, the faculty of organizing and interpreting the information acquired from the senses, as opposed to the NOUS or higher reason. See also DIANOIA. **—understand** *vb.*

undescended testicle see ARRESTED TESTIS.

undifferentiated schizophrenia in *DSM–IV–TR*, a subtype of SCHIZOPHRENIA in which the individual exhibits prominent psychotic features, such as delusions, hallucinations, disorganized thinking, or grossly disorganized behavior, but does not meet the criteria for any of the other subtypes of the disorder. The *DSM–III* designation was **undifferentiated type schizophrenic disorder**.

undifferentiated somatoform disorder in *DSM–IV–TR*, a SOMATOFORM DISORDER in which one or more physical complaints persist for 6 months or longer and cannot be explained by a known medical condition. Unlike FACTITIOUS DISORDER or MALINGERING, these symptoms are not intentionally feigned or produced. It should not be confused with SOMATOFORM DISORDER NOT OTHERWISE SPECIFIED.

undulatio reflexa reflexive action (Latin): the term used by French philosopher René Descartes (1596–1650) to explain bodily movements that are not under volitional control but instead occur as a response to the surrounding environment. The concept arose from Descartes's notion of the body as a machine that is wholly distinct from the mind (see CARTESIAN DUALISM). It served as a basis for later psychological theories that took the reflex arc as the basic unit, as well as the basic model, of behavior.

unfair labor practices practices by a labor union or employer that are defined as unfair under the LABOR MANAGEMENT RELATIONS ACT and subsequent amendments. These include the enforcement of CLOSED SHOPS and the use of secondary boycotts and secondary picketing to further a labor dispute.

unfalsifiable *adj.* denoting the quality of a proposition, hypothesis, or theory such that no empirical test can establish that it is false. For Austrian-born British philosopher of science Karl Popper (1902–1994), a theory or hypothesis that is unfalsifiable is to be judged nonscientific. See FALSIFIABILITY; FALSIFICATIONISM; RISKY PREDICTION.

unfinished business in therapy and counseling, the personal experiences that have been blocked or tasks that have been avoided because of feared emotional or interpersonal effects. Gestalt and many other therapists believe that people have an urge to complete unfinished business in order to achieve satisfaction and peace. Therapists and counselors working with the dying and their families believe that dealing with unfinished business is an important aspect of the dying and grieving processes.

unfinished story a PROJECTIVE TECHNIQUE in which participants are required to complete a story by role play, discussion, or writing. It is intended to reveal information about the participants' concerns.

unfitness *n.* **1.** the state or condition of lacking fitness or health. **2.** in biology, the inability of an organism to produce viable offspring in a given environment. Compare FITNESS.

unfolding *n.* a scaling procedure in which respondents' evaluations of a set of choices are used to form a continuum along which each respondent is placed in such a way as to reflect that respondent's relative evaluations of the set of choices.

unfreezing *n.* a therapeutic goal to rid an individual of rigid beliefs and stereotypes of self, others, and the world.

unidimensional *adj.* having a single dimension or composed of a single or a pure factor. Compare MULTIDIMENSIONAL.

unidimensional concept see BIPOLAR CONCEPT.

unified positivism an approach to the problem of the fragmentation of psychology that seeks to unify the field by emphasizing scientific work that integrates disparate findings and thus draws theories and models together. It derives its inspiration from one of the basic assumptions of LOGICAL POSITIVISM: that all science could be united, on the model of physics, through a strict empiricist approach. See also UNITY OF SCIENCE. [introduced by U.S. psychologist Arthur Staats (1923–)]

unified theory of cognition any theory that attempts to provide a single architecture for explaining all cognitive activity, whether in humans, animals, or artificial intelligence. An example is the SOAR model, proposed by U.S. cognitive psychologist and computer scientist Allen Newell (1927–1992).

Unified Tri-Service Cognitive Performance Assessment Battery (**UTCPAB**) a battery of assessment tests compiled in 1984 by a group of experimental research psychologists. It presents computerized, clinically relevant psychomotor and neuropsychological tests for the rapid assessment of the integrity of the nervous system.

uniform crime reports a nationwide database of reported crimes that contains information from all local and state law enforcement agencies within the United States. Its purpose is to set a consistent and reliable measure of criminal activity.

uniform-density factor see COMMON FATE.

uniform distribution a theoretical continuous distribution with a probability distribution of $f(x) = 1/(b - a)$, where a is the lower limit of the distribution and b is its upper limit. Also called **rectangular distribution**.

Uniform Guidelines for Employee Selection Procedures a formal set of guidelines developed by the EQUAL EMPLOYMENT OPPORTUNITY COMMISSION that provide employers with advice on how they can comply with civil-rights legislation in the hiring of employees. See FOUR-FIFTHS RULE.

uniformly most powerful test (**UMP test**) the test from among a set of competing tests, each with the same operational SIGNIFICANCE LEVEL, that has the highest POWER against all alternative hypotheses.

unilateral *adj.* denoting or relating to one side (e.g., of the body or an organ) or to one of two or more parties. **—unilaterally** *adv.*

unilateral couple counseling the counseling of one partner on his or her relationship to the other. Even when only one partner participates in counseling, the focus is on the partners' relationship. See also COUPLES COUNSELING.

unilateral descent in anthropology, a system of descent or inheritance in which descent is traced through the male line only (PATRIARCHY) or through the female line only (MATRIARCHY). Also called **unilineal descent**. Compare BILATERAL DESCENT. See also DESCENT GROUP.

unilateral lesion a lesion on one side or lobe of an organ or part. For example, a unilateral cerebral lesion involves one cerebral hemisphere, left or right, with effects that may vary according to the dominance of the hemisphere and the function affected. The motor and sensory effects of the lesion are generally on the contralateral side, that is, on the side opposite to that of the lesion.

unilateral neglect a disorder resulting from damage to the PARIETAL LOBE of the brain and characterized by a loss of conscious perception of objects in the half of the visual field (usually the left half) that is opposite the location of the lesion, ALIEN LIMB SYNDROME, and other striking neuropsychological features. Also called **hemineglect**.

unimodal distribution a set of scores that has one mode (represented by one peak in their geographical distribution), reflecting a tendency for scores to cluster around a specific value. Compare BIMODAL DISTRIBUTION.

uniocular *adj.* see MONOCULAR.

union *n.* an organization that represents employees in dealings with their employer. The union is responsible for negotiating contracts with employers that determine employees' compensation and conditions of employment and for seeing that the terms of these contractual agreements are fulfilled. Also called **labor union**; **trade union**. See COLLECTIVE BARGAINING.

union shop a work arrangement in which it is a condition of employment that new employees who are not union members join the union within a certain time after being hired. See also AGENCY SHOP; CLOSED SHOP; OPEN SHOP.

uniparous *adj.* see PRIMIPAROUS.

unipolar depression any DEPRESSIVE DISORDER, that is, any mood disorder marked by one or more MAJOR DEPRESSIVE EPISODES or a prolonged period of depressive symptoms with no history of manic or hypomanic symptoms or MIXED EPISODES.

unipolar mania a BIPOLAR DISORDER in which only MANIC EPISODES have occurred. Except in rare cases, manic episodes tend eventually to be followed by one or more MAJOR DEPRESSIVE EPISODES.

unipolar neuron a neuron that has only a single extension of the CELL BODY. This extension divides into two branches, oriented in opposite directions and representing the axon. One end is the receptive pole, and the other is the output zone. Unipolar neurons transmit touch information from the body surface to the spinal cord. Also called **monopolar neuron**. Compare BIPOLAR NEURON; MULTIPOLAR NEURON.

unipolar rating scale see BIPOLAR RATING SCALE.

unipolar stimulation electrical stimulation in which one electrode is placed on or in the tissue and the other is outside the tissue.

unique factor in FACTOR ANALYSIS, a factor that contributes only to a single variable.

unique hue see BINARY HUE.

uniqueness *n.* in FACTOR ANALYSIS, $1 - h_j^2$, where h_j^2 is the COMMUNALITY of the *j*th variable. The uniqueness is the part of the variance of a variable that it does not share with any other variable in the system.

unique trait see IDIOGRAPHIC TRAIT.

unitary-resource model a model of attention that views attention as a single pool of undifferentiated resources that can be devoted to a variety of processes. Tasks place demands on the general pool, rather than on particular resources. The extent to which the total resources are taxed by a primary task will determine the performance decrement on other tasks carried out at the same time; when the demand on resources exceeds the supply, allocation strategies become important. Also called **single-capacity model**. Compare MULTIPLE-RESOURCE MODEL.

United Nations Declaration on the Rights of Mentally Retarded Persons a 1971 declaration by the United Nations affirming the human rights of people with mental retardation. These issues were largely subsumed under the 1993 Standard Rules on the Equalization of Opportunities for Persons with Disabilities. See RIGHTS OF PEOPLE WITH MENTAL RETARDATION.

Unit Manning System a U.S. Army personnel program promoted in the 1980s to stabilize selected light-infantry division troops in cohort units. It was designed to build unit cohesion, reduce personnel turbulence, and enhance readiness and performance.

unit of analysis in experimental design and research, the group of people, things, or entities that are being investigated or studied. Also called **analysis unit**.

unit schedule see SECOND-ORDER SCHEDULE.

unity *n.* see FUSION.

unity in variety the concept that a stimulus with maximal unity and maximal variety is preferred.

unity of command a principle of management stating that each employee should have to report to one and only one immediate boss. See LINE MANAGEMENT; MATRIX ORGANIZATION. [proposed by French engineer Henri Fayol (1841–1925) and other classical management theorists]

unity of consciousness the concept of the contents of awareness being coherent, internally consistent, or shaped by a common goal. From this it follows that mutually inconsistent events cannot simultaneously appear in awareness.

unity of science the view that the principles of any and all sciences can be derived from or reduced to the laws of physics. See CONSILIENCE; UNIFIED POSITIVISM.

univariate *adj.* characterized by a single variable.

univariate research research that employs only one DEPENDENT VARIABLE.

universal *n.* **1.** in social psychology, see PSYCHOLOGICAL UNIVERSAL. See also UNIVERSALS. **2.** in linguistics, see LANGUAGE UNIVERSAL.

universal design a quality of a product or built environment so conceived as to make it optimally usable and comfortable for people of all ages and abilities. Universal design as a concept goes beyond mere accessibility and removal of barriers, in accordance with the mandates of such laws as the AMERICANS WITH DISABILITIES ACT (ADA), by emphasizing the inclusiveness of design to accommodate a wide range of physical and cognitive abilities. Also called **transgenerational design**. See also BARRIER-FREE ENVIRONMENT. Compare DESIGN FOR ADJUSTABLE RANGE; DESIGN FOR THE AVERAGE.

universal grammar (**UG**) in the linguistics of Noam CHOMSKY and his followers, a hypothetical metagrammar that is assumed to underlie the grammatical structures found in all natural languages (see LANGUAGE UNIVERSAL). The concept of a universal grammar is of considerable interest to psycholinguists, especially those working in the field of language acquisition.

universalism *n.* the position that certain aspects of the human mind, human behavior, and human morality are universal and essential and are therefore to be found in all cultures and historical periods. Universalism is a form of ESSENTIALISM and is opposed to RELATIVISM. **—universalist** *adj.*

universality *n.* **1.** the tendency to assume that one's personal qualities and characteristics, including attitudes and values, are common in the general social group or culture. See also FALSE CONSENSUS. **2.** in mob and crowd settings, the tendency for individuals to assume that atypical, unusual behaviors are allowable because many others in the situation are performing such actions ("everybody's doing it"). See COLLECTIVE BEHAVIOR; CONTAGION; EMERGENT-NORM THEORY. **3.** in self-help and psychotherapy groups, a curative factor fostered by the members' recognition that their problems and difficulties are not unique to them, but instead are experienced by many of the group members. Also called **impression of universality**. See also CURATIVE FACTORS MODEL.

universality of emotions the finding that certain emotional expressions, appraisals, and manifestations are the same or highly similar across cultures and societies. Compare CULTURAL SPECIFICITY OF EMOTIONS. See also PRIMARY EMOTION.

universalizability *n.* in ethics, the principle that particular moral judgments always carry an implied universal judgment. So, for example, to say *Daphne shouldn't have lied to him* implies the universal judgment that anybody in the identical situation to Daphne should not have lied. The principle of universalizability is related to that of the CATEGORICAL IMPERATIVE. **—universalizable** *adj.*

universals *pl. n.* in philosophy, general qualities, such as "blueness" or "courage," as opposed to the particulars that instantiate them. The status of universals and their relationship to particulars has been a matter of much debate in philosophy. See also ABSTRACT IDEA; PSYCHOLOGICAL UNIVERSAL.

universe *n.* in statistics, see POPULATION.

universe of discourse 1. the total system of ideas, concepts, terms, and expressions within which a given topic can be analyzed and understood. The universe of discourse defines both what can be said about a subject and how it can be said. Statements that are meaningful within a particular universe of discourse may well be nonsensical within another; to say *The sad skies are weeping,* for example, might be permissible in poetry but would hardly be so in meteorology. The idea of universes of discourse has also been explored by radical thinkers in the traditions of MARXISM, FEMINISM, and POSTSTRUCTURALISM; such critics argue that by controlling the universe of discourse in a particular society, the power elite controls what can and cannot be said or thought. **2.** in the field of artificial intelligence, any set of objects that can be represented within a given domain.

University of Pennsylvania Smell Identification Test (**UPSIT**) see SMELL IDENTIFICATION TEST.

unlearning *n.* see DECONDITIONING.

unmyelinated *adj.* describing a nerve fiber that lacks a MYELIN SHEATH, such as a C FIBER.

unobtrusive measure a measure obtained without disturbing the participant or alerting him or her that a measurement is being made. The behavior or responses of such participants are thus assumed to be unaffected by the investigative process or the surrounding environment. See also REACTIVE MEASURE. Compare OBTRUSIVE MEASURE.

unpleasantness *n.* an emotional state that is experienced when an event is incongruent with one's goals or is associated with pain. See also DIMENSIONAL THEORY OF EMOTION. **—unpleasant** *adj.*

unpleasure *n.* in psychoanalytic theory, the psychic pain, tension, and EGO suffering that is consciously felt when instinctual needs and wishes, such as hunger and sex, are blocked by the ego and denied gratification. [translation of German *Unlust,* "listlessness"]

unprepared learning see CONTRAPREPARED.

unresolved *adj.* **1.** in psychotherapy, denoting emotional or psychic conflicts not yet sufficiently dealt with and assimilated or understood. See also UNFINISHED BUSINESS. **2.** describing any stimulus whose characteristics cannot be determined by the perceiver.

unselected sample an informal name for a random sample. See RANDOM SAMPLING.

unshared environment see NONSHARED ENVIRONMENT.

unsociable *adj.* lacking SOCIABILITY because of a disinclination to interact and form relationships with others.

unspecified mental retardation the diagnosis made when an individual is presumed to have mental retardation but is too severely impaired or uncooperative to be evaluated by standard intelligence tests and adaptive behavior measures. The *DSM–IV–TR* designation is **mental retardation, severity unspecified**.

unstable personality disorder see BORDERLINE PERSONALITY DISORDER.

unstructured *adj.* denoting an object, situation, or set of ideas that does not have a definite pattern or organization.

unstructured autobiography see AUTOBIOGRAPHY.

unstructured interview an interview that imposes minimal structure by asking open-ended (rather than set) questions and allowing the interviewee to steer the discussion into areas of his or her choosing. In personnel selection, the idea is that such an approach will reveal more of the applicant's traits, interests, priorities, and interpersonal and verbal skills than a STRUCTURED INTERVIEW. The appropriateness of the technique will depend on the nature of the occupation or position; it will also require an experienced and confident interviewer. See also PATTERNED INTERVIEW.

unstructured stimulus a vague, poorly organized, and not clearly identifiable stimulus, such as an inkblot in the RORSCHACH INKBLOT TEST. Compare STRUCTURED STIMULUS.

Unusual Uses Test a test that measures DIVERGENT-THINKING ability. In this test participants are asked to think of unusual uses for common objects, such as a paper clip. The number and novelty of unusual responses contribute to the overall score. [devised by Joy Paul GUILFORD]

unvoiced *adj.* denoting speech sounds that are articulated through breath, without vibration of the vocal cords. The unvoiced (or voiceless) sounds comprise some consonants (e.g., [p], [t], and [f]). Compare VOICED. See BINARY FEATURE.

unweighted means analysis in the ANALYSIS OF VARIANCE, an analytic approach in which the size of the individual CELLS of the design is ignored.

unweighted test a statistical procedure in which each observation or score (or set of observations or scores) contributes equally to the results, that is, there is no differential WEIGHTING.

upper motor neuron any of the neurons of the primary motor cortex that contribute to the CORTICOSPINAL TRACT and influence and modulate the LOWER MOTOR NEURONS.

uppers *pl. n.* slang for various drugs that stimulate the central nervous system, such as amphetamine and methamphetamine. See CNS STIMULANTS.

upper threshold 1. for a DIFFERENCE THRESHOLD, the threshold at which the stimulus is judged to be greater than the standard. **2.** the maximum intensity of a stimulus that can be perceived without pain.

up-regulation *n.* the formation of additional RECEPTOR molecules by target cells in response to increased levels of hormones. Compare DOWN-REGULATION.

UPSIT abbreviation for University of Pennsylvania SMELL IDENTIFICATION TEST.

up through a technique for testing CLAIRVOYANCE in which the participant is asked to state the order of a stacked deck of ZENER CARDS from bottom to top. Compare DOWN THROUGH. See also BASIC TECHNIQUE.

upward appraisal in organizations, the evaluation of those in supervisory positions by their subordinates.

upward communication written and oral messages that originate with individuals lower in the hierarchy of an organization and that flow upward to those occupying positions higher in the hierarchy. Upward communication is subject to distortions such as the **mum effect**, in which subordinates are unwilling to convey bad news to their superiors. The more levels in the hierarchy through which a message must pass, the more subject it is to distortion as the result of filtering at each level. Compare DOWNWARD COMMUNICATION; HORIZONTAL COMMUNICATION.

upward grade homogenization see GRADE INFLATION.

upward mobility the movement of a person or group to a higher social class. Upward mobility tends to be a feature of relatively relaxed class systems operating within expanding economies. Also called **social ascendancy**. See also SOCIAL MOBILITY. Compare DOWNWARD MOBILITY.

upward Pygmalion effect an effect in which the expectations of followers or subordinates lead to behavior on the part of the leader or superior that is consistent with these expectations. The behavior of the leader does not reflect his or her true abilities or personality traits, but rather the perception of the leader by subordinates. Compare PYGMALION EFFECT. See ROLE EXPECTATIONS; SELF-FULFILLING PROPHECY.

UR 1. abbreviation for UNCONDITIONED RESPONSE. **2.** abbreviation for UTILIZATION REVIEW.

ur- *combining form* see URO-.

uracil (symbol: U) *n.* a pyrimidine compound that is one of the four bases found in RNA. In DNA, thymine occurs instead of uracil. See also GENETIC CODE.

uranoschisis *n.* see CLEFT PALATE.

urban behavior the behavior of people living in cities, who appear to be less attentive to the needs of strangers, walk faster, make less eye contact, and are exposed to more violence and aggressive behavior than their rural or suburban counterparts. The prevailing features of the urban environment—its size, density, and pace—led to the theory, proposed by Stanley MILGRAM, that urban behavior is characterized by adaptation to the INFORMATION OVERLOAD of city life, resulting in anonymity, powerlessness, aggression, indifference to others, and narrow self-interest among city dwellers.

urban ecology the study of the dynamics and organization of city life, particularly in relation to population density and the nature of the city environment. Urban ecology is based on principles derived from biology, sociology, psychology, and environmental science. See also URBANIZATION.

urbanism *n.* the way of life characteristic of cities. Urbanism has been a central area of research in sociology (most notably by the CHICAGO SCHOOL) and psychology since the early 20th century, with psychologists principally focused on the implications of urban life for mental health and social norms.

urbanization *n.* **1.** the trend toward living in cities, which are defined by the United States Bureau of the Census as having populations of 50,000 or more. **2.** the process of becoming a community with urban characteristics. Psychological research on urbanization initially focused, in the early 20th century, on the impact of urban life on mental health, purporting to find a link between inner-city residence and increased rates of mental illness; this position was later qualified (see DRIFT HYPOTHESIS). Inquiry has since expanded to investigate the psychological, physical, and behavioral consequences of the urban environment (e.g., population density, crowding, noise, and pollution) and the social, economic, and cultural dimensions of city life. See also URBAN ECOLOGY. **—urbanize** *vb.*

urban legend an incredible or lurid story, often involving a mixture of horror and humor, that is widely repeated as if true (often as the experience of a "friend of a friend") but can never be firmly documented. Urban legends differ from myths and folktales in that they nearly always have a contemporary setting and often involve modern technology (e.g., the many such tales about microwave ovens).

Urban's weights see MÜLLER–URBAN WEIGHTS.

Urecholine *n.* a trade name for BETHANECHOL.

urethra *n.* a membrane-lined duct that carries urine from the urinary bladder to the exterior. In males it passes through the CORPUS SPONGIOSUM of the penis and also serves as a channel for semen at ejaculation. In females the urethra is less than 4 cm long and runs almost directly to an opening anterior to the vaginal orifice. **—urethral** *adj.*

urethral eroticism in psychoanalytic theory, sexual pleasure derived from urination. Also called **urethral erotism**. See UROLAGNIA.

urethritis *n.* inflammation of the urethra, with symptoms of painful urination (DYSURIA) and urethral discharge. The infection may be transmitted by sexual contact, as in cases of GONORRHEA and NONGONOCOCCAL URETHRITIS.

urge incontinence a type of URINARY INCONTINENCE involving a sudden, strong desire to urinate followed by involuntary contractions of the bladder regardless of the amount of urine in the bladder. Because the bladder actually contracts, urine is released quickly, making it difficult for people with urge incontinence to predict or control the occurrence of the problem.

URI abbreviation for Uniform Resource Identifier. See URL.

urinary incontinence loss of conscious control of urination due to an organic condition, such as a neurological disorder or age-related changes in the bladder or kidneys. See STRESS INCONTINENCE; URGE INCONTINENCE. Compare ENURESIS.

urination *n.* the discharge of urine from the bladder, which is effected by voluntary relaxation of the SPHINCTER at the junction of the bladder and urethra and reflex contraction of the bladder wall (see MICTURITION REFLEX). Also called **micturition**.

URL Uniform Resource Locator: a string of letters and numbers that serves as a pointer to a resource (e.g., a document, service, file, or e-mailbox) on the WORLD WIDE WEB. Also called **URI** (Uniform Resource Identifier).

uro- (**ur-**) *combining form* urine or the urinary system.

urogenital *adj.* referring to organs concerned with both excretion and reproduction. Also called **urinogenital**.

urolagnia *n.* sexual interest focused on urine and urination. This may involve watching others urinate, being urinated on during sexual activity, urinating on the partner during sexual activity, or drinking one's own urine. See also URETHRAL EROTICISM.

urophilia *n.* a PARAPHILIA involving urine and urination as a major source of arousal during sexual activity.

URT abbreviation for UNCERTAINTY REDUCTION THEORY.

urticaria *n.* see HIVES.

US abbreviation for UNCONDITIONED STIMULUS.

usability engineering a specialty that applies knowledge of human capabilities and limitations to the design of systems (typically human–computer systems) with the goal of ensuring ease of use. This can be achieved by enhancing such attributes as design intuitiveness, learnability, and comprehensibility. See also ENGINEERING PSYCHOLOGY; USER-CENTERED DESIGN.

usable *adj.* in ergonomics, describing a product or system that is designed to be easy to use with a minimum of frustration, errors, and inconvenience. **—usability** *n.*

U.S. Department of Veterans Affairs (**VA**) an agency of the U.S. government established in 1930 to administer the laws providing benefits and other services to veterans, their dependents, and their beneficiaries. Its mission is to serve U.S. veterans and their families with compassion; to be their principal advocate in ensuring that they receive medical care, benefits, social support, and lasting memorials; and to promote the health, welfare, and dignity of all veterans in recognition of their service to the nation.

use-and-disuse theory see LAMARCKISM.

useful field of view denoting a brief computer-administered test of cognitive selective attention in the visual periphery that predicts accident risk while driving. Performance on the test typically declines with adult age but can be improved through training.

user-centered design in ergonomics, design practice with a central focus on understanding the characteristics of the target group in order to produce USABLE products or systems. See also ENGINEERING PSYCHOLOGY; USABILITY ENGINEERING.

user-friendly *adj.* describing a product or system that is easy to understand or use.

Usher syndrome a genetic disorder, inherited as an AUTOSOMAL RECESSIVE trait, causing SENSORINEURAL HEARING LOSS, deterioration of vision due to RETINITIS PIGMENTOSA, and, in some cases, loss of balance. [Charles Howard **Usher** (1865–1942), British ophthalmologist]

U statistic *n.* the statistic used in the MANN–WHITNEY U TEST.

usual, customary and reasonable fees (**UCR fees**) see CUSTOMARY, PREVAILING, AND REASONABLE FEES.

us-versus-them effect the tendency to view other groups and their members as competitors for scarce resources, including food, territory, wealth, power, natural resources, and energy.

UTCPAB abbreviation for UNIFIED TRI-SERVICE COGNITIVE PERFORMANCE ASSESSMENT BATTERY.

uterine orgasm see VULVAL ORGASM.

utero- (**uter-**) *combining form* womb (uterus).

uterus *n.* the hollow muscular organ in female mammals in which the embryo develops from the time of IMPLANTATION until birth. It is connected to the ovaries via the FALLOPIAN TUBES and to the exterior via the vagina, into which the cervix (neck) of the uterus projects. The ENDOMETRIUM (lining) of the uterus undergoes changes during the MENSTRUAL CYCLE. Also called **womb**. **—uterine** *adj.*

utilitarian function of an attitude the role an attitude can play in obtaining rewards, avoiding punishments, or both. For example, a person might adopt a positive attitude toward a particular product because it is effective and a negative attitude toward its chief competitor because it is ineffective. See also FUNCTIONAL APPROACH TO ATTITUDES.

utilitarianism *n.* an ethical theory based on the premise that the good is to be defined as that which brings the greatest amount or degree of happiness; thus, an act is considered moral if, compared to possible alternatives, it provides the greatest good for the greatest number of people. The doctrine is often reduced to the single maxim: The greatest good for the greatest number. The classical formulation of utilitarianism is that of British jurist and philosopher Jeremy Bentham (1748–1832), especially as popularized by British economist and philosopher John Stuart Mill (1806–1873). Utilitarianism is heavily influenced by HEDONISM and EUDEMONISM; it also shares with BEHAVIORISM the notion that the fundamental motive for action is pleasure or benefit. Because it rejects the idea that actions may be intrinsically good or bad, irrespective of their consequences, and can provide no objective means of calculating the amount of happiness that derives from particular actions, utilitarianism is in practice a species of ethical RELATIVISM. Compare NATURAL LAW THEORY. **—utilitarian** *adj.*

utility *n.* **1.** in decision making and economic theory, the subjective value of some outcome to the individual. **2.** in industrial and organizational psychology, the value of an intervention or program judged on the basis of its monetary worth to the organization. For example, there are methodologies for assessing the monetary gains achieved from using particular tests to select employees or particular training programs. **3.** in biology, the usefulness of a characteristic in preserving the life of an organism or continuing the species. Both ARTIFICIAL SELECTION and NATURAL SELECTION operate to increase utility. **4.** in UTILITARIANISM, the "goodness" of an act as determined by the amount or degree of happiness derived from it. **5.** in general, the capacity of a thing to accomplish its designed purpose, as in the explanatory utility of a psychological theory.

utility standards the information requirements of those for whom an evaluation research study is carried out. These standards include identifying all STAKEHOLDERS, selecting evaluation objectives appropriate to the intended recipients of the findings, providing clear and timely reporting of information, and following procedures that maximize the study's utilization. See also ACCURACY STANDARDS; FEASIBILITY STANDARDS; PROPRIETY STANDARDS.

utility theory in decision making, any normative theory of UTILITY that attempts to describe rational or optimal choice behavior.

utilization deficiency the inability of individuals to improve task performance by using strategies that they have already acquired and demonstrated the ability to use because they are not spurred to do so by memory. Although historically most frequently studied in children, current research suggests that such deficiencies are not developmental per se but may occur at any age as a by-product of diminished WORKING MEMORY capacity. Compare MEDIATIONAL DEFICIENCY; PRODUCTION DEFICIENCY.

utilization-focused evaluation attempts to maximize the usefulness of the results of an evaluation research study for its intended users or STAKEHOLDERS. All aspects of the design and the execution of the evaluation should be directed to this end. See also UTILITY STANDARDS; PARTICIPATORY EVALUATION.

utilization review (**UR**) a formal review of the necessity and quality of services provided in a hospital or clinic or by an individual provider. Conducted by a specially appointed committee, a utilization review often addresses whether the level of service provided is the most appropriate to the severity of the presenting problem. See also CONTINUED-STAY REVIEW; EXTENDED-STAY REVIEW.

utopia *n.* an idealized, perfect society. Coined by English statesman and author Sir Thomas More (1478–1535) in his speculative political fiction *Utopia* (1516), the term is of Greek derivation (literally, "no place"). By contrast, the term **dystopia**, coined in about 1950, refers to an imaginary society of nightmarish conditions. **—utopian** *adj.*

utopianism *n.* **1.** belief in the possibility of establishing an ideal social system (see UTOPIA) based on rational and moral principles. **2.** any idealistic approach to political or social questions that is thought to depend on an unrealistic view of human nature.

utricle *n.* the larger of the two VESTIBULAR SACS in the inner ear, the other being the SACCULE. Like the saccule, the utricle senses not only the position of the head with respect to gravity but also acceleration and deceleration. This is achieved by a special patch of epithelium—the MACULA—inside both the utricle and saccule. **—utricular** *adj.*

utterance *n.* a unit of spoken language, which may be of any length but can usually be identified by conversational turn taking or by clear breaks in the stream of speech. MEAN LENGTH OF UTTERANCE is considered an important index of language development in young children.

uveal tract see EYE.

uvula *n.* **1.** a fleshy appendage that hangs from the SOFT PALATE. It plays an important role as part of the apparatus for sound production of the human voice (see UVULAR). Also called **palatine uvula**. **2.** any similarly shaped structure, such as those located in the urinary bladder and the cerebellum.

uvular 1. *adj.* of or relating to the UVULA. **2.** *n.* a speech sound produced with the back of the tongue pressing against the uvula, such as the [r] sound in Parisian French.

uxoricide *n.* the murder of a wife by her husband.

uxorilocal *adj.* see MATRILOCAL.

Vv

V abbreviation for VERBAL ABILITY.

V1 VISUAL AREA 1, which in primates is coextensive with the STRIATE CORTEX (primary visual cortex). Neurons in V1 have relatively simple stimulus requirements for maximum activation, unlike the visual areas that V1 projects to, which include V2, V4, and V5. V1 is the preferred name of this cortex for discussions of the functional differences between cortical regions; striate cortex, primary visual cortex, and area 17 are the preferred names for discussions of cortical anatomy.

V2 VISUAL AREA 2, which in primates is a band of cerebral cortex located adjacent and anterior to V1. It is coextensive with Brodmann's area 18 (see PRESTRIATE CORTEX) and receives its major input from V1.

V4 VISUAL AREA 4, which in primates is located in the occipitotemporal cortex. Most neurons in V4 are sensitive to wavelength, and damage to a similar area in the human brain causes CEREBRAL ACHROMATOPSIA, a form of cortical color blindness.

V5 VISUAL AREA 5, which in primates is located in the temporal cortex. Most neurons in V5 are sensitive to the rate and direction of motion of a stimulus, and damage to a similar area in the human brain causes MOTION AGNOSIA.

VA abbreviation for U.S. DEPARTMENT OF VETERANS AFFAIRS.

VABS abbreviation for VINELAND ADAPTIVE BEHAVIOR SCALES.

vacuum activity the occurrence of a FIXED-ACTION PATTERN in the absence of the usual external stimulus (the RELEASER, or sign stimulus) that triggers the pattern. This is believed to be caused by a build-up of action-specific or motivational energy that overrides the INNATE RELEASING MECHANISM. Also called **vacuum response**. [proposed by Austrian ethologist Konrad Z. Lorenz (1903–1989)]

vagabond neurosis see DROMOMANIA.

vagal tone a measure of the variability of the heart rate associated with inhalation and exhalation (see RESPIRATORY SINUS ARRHYTHMIA), which is thought to reflect parasympathetic influence via the VAGUS NERVE.

vagina *n.* a tubelike structure in female mammals that leads from the cervix (neck) of the uterus to the exterior. The muscular walls of the vagina are lined with mucous membrane, and two pairs of VESTIBULAR GLANDS around the vaginal opening secrete a fluid that facilitates penetration by the penis during coitus. **—vaginal** *adj.*

vagina dentata in psychoanalytic theory, the unconscious fantasy that the vagina is a mouth with teeth that can castrate the male partner. In women, the fantasy is believed to stem from intense PENIS ENVY and a desire to castrate the partner as an act of revenge; in men, it is believed to stem from CASTRATION ANXIETY.

vaginal administration see ADMINISTRATION.

vaginal envy a psychological characteristic of men who desire the ability to become pregnant and bear children. See also FEMININITY COMPLEX; WOMB ENVY.

vaginal orgasm 1. female orgasm achieved through vaginal stimulation. **2.** in early psychoanalytic theory, the "mature, feminine" orgasm, as opposed to "immature, masculine" orgasms produced from clitoral stimulation. This view has long since been refuted. Indeed, researchers have demonstrated that the clitoris is the focus of female sexual response and that vaginal orgasms are primarily related to indirect stimulation of the clitoris and labia during intercourse. See COITAL ANORGASMIA.

vaginal plethysmograph see PLETHYSMOGRAPH.

vaginal sex sexual intercourse by means of vaginal penetration. See COITUS.

vaginismus *n.* a sexual dysfunction in which spasmic contractions of the muscles around the vagina occur during or immediately preceding sexual intercourse, causing the latter to be painful or impossible. Vaginismus is not diagnosed if the dysfunction is due solely to the effects of a medical condition, although medical conditions may be involved as a factor in the problem. See also FUNCTIONAL VAGINISMUS.

vagotomy *n.* surgical cutting or interruption of the VAGUS NERVE, which has motor, sensory, and physiological functions.

vagus nerve the tenth CRANIAL NERVE, a mixed nerve with both sensory and motor fibers that serves many functions. The sensory fibers innervate the external ear, vocal organs, and thoracic and abdominal VISCERA. The motor nerves innervate the tongue, vocal organs, and—through many ganglia of the PARASYMPATHETIC NERVOUS SYSTEM—the thoracic and abdominal viscera. Also called **cranial nerve X**; **pneumogastric nerve**.

VAKT abbreviation for visual, auditory, kinesthetic, and tactile (senses). See FERNALD METHOD.

valence *n.* **1.** in the FIELD THEORY of Kurt LEWIN, the subjective value of an event, object, person, or other entity in the LIFE SPACE of the individual. An entity that attracts the individual has **positive valence**, while one that repels has **negative valence**. **2.** in certain theories of motivation, the anticipated satisfaction of attaining a particular goal or outcome.

valence–instrumentality–expectancy theory a theory of WORK MOTIVATION holding that the level of effort exerted by employees will depend on a combination of three variables: (a) the EXPECTANCY of employees that effort will lead to success in the job, (b) the belief of employees that success will lead to particular outcomes (see INSTRUMENTALITY THEORY), and (c) the value of these outcomes (see VALENCE). A numerical value can be obtained for variable (a) using the SUBJECTIVE PROBABILITY estimates of employees, for variable (b) by measuring the correlation of performance to rewards, and for variable (c) by asking employees to rate the desirability of the rewards. The motivational force, or the amount of effort employees will exert, can then be calculated. See also PATH–GOAL THEORY OF LEADERSHIP; PORTER–LAWLER MODEL OF MOTIVATION. [proposed in 1964 by Canadian organizational psychologist Victor H. Vroom (1932–)]

validating marriage a long-lasting marriage in which the partners express mutual respect even when they disagree.

validation *n.* the process of determining the accuracy of an instrument in measuring what it is designed to measure.

validity *n.* **1.** the characteristic of being founded on truth, accuracy, fact, or law. **2.** the degree to which a test or measurement accurately measures or reflects what it purports to measure. There are various types of validity, including CONCURRENT VALIDITY, CONSTRUCT VALIDITY, and ECOLOGICAL VALIDITY. **—valid** *adj.*

validity criterion an external CRITERION that is used to define the attribute that an instrument is purported to measure and that is used to estimate the VALIDITY of the measurement instrument.

validity generalization a quantitative summary of all empirical research relevant to the VALIDITY of a particular measuring instrument.

validity generalization model of selection in personnel selection, an approach to assessing whether or not a test or predictor has validity in predicting performance on a particular JOB CRITERION. A study is conducted in which the average validity for the predictor is assessed on the basis of previous validation studies. A determination is then made of the extent to which variations in validities can be attributed to differences across studies in artifacts such as criterion measures, sample sizes, and the range of test scores. If small variations are found after correcting for these artifacts, it is concluded that the validity of the predictor generalizes across situations; in other words, the validity found in previous studies can be generalized or transported to a new situation. Based on this evidence, an employer may be justified in concluding that the predictor will be valid in selecting employees in a different employment setting.

Valium *n.* a trade name for DIAZEPAM.

valor *n.* see COURAGE.

valproic acid a carboxylic acid (also formulated as **valproate sodium**; U.S. trade name: **Depacon**) used as an ANTICONVULSANT and MOOD STABILIZER. Although exact mechanisms of action remain unclear, valproic acid may exert its effects by reducing membrane sodium-channel activity (see ION CHANNEL), thereby slowing neuronal activity. It may also stimulate the synthesis of the inhibitory neurotransmitter gamma-aminobutyric acid (GABA). Valproic acid and valproate sodium are officially approved by the U.S. Food and Drug Administration for the management of seizures and of manic episodes associated with bipolar disorders. Although in general less toxic than lithium, these drugs have been associated with fatalities due to liver failure, particularly in children under 2 years of age, as well as pancreatitis; serum monitoring of drug levels and liver function is therefore required, particularly on starting treatment. Valproic acid and valproate sodium should not be taken during pregnancy due to risks of NEURAL TUBE DEFECTS in the fetus. U.S. trade name: **Depakene**.

VALS abbreviation for VALUES LIFESTYLE GROUPS.

value *n.* **1.** the mathematical magnitude or quantity of a variable. **2.** a moral, social, or aesthetic principle accepted by an individual or society as a guide to what is good, desirable, or important. **3.** the worth, usefulness, or importance attached to something. **4.** in economics, the monetary worth of a good or service.

value analysis a type of CONTENT ANALYSIS of written material consisting of a table, or other systematic notation, documenting the frequency of appearance in the material of all expressions referring to specified values.

value-expressive function of an attitude the role an attitude can play in the expression of core values. For example, a person might adopt a positive attitude toward a religious symbol because that symbol is associated with important religious values. See also FUNCTIONAL APPROACH TO ATTITUDES.

value-free evaluation see GOAL-FREE EVALUATION.

value judgment an assessment of individuals, objects, or events in terms of the values held by the observer rather than in terms of their intrinsic characteristics objectively considered. The idea that social scientists should, wherever possible, avoid value judgments in their work was introduced by German sociologist Max Weber (1864–1920). In some other fields, such as aesthetics or morality, value judgments may be essential.

values clarification 1. any process intended to promote an individual's awareness and understanding of his or her moral principles and ethical priorities and their relationships to behavior. **2.** in psychotherapy, a series of exercises used to help an individual identify his or her personal values and evaluate their impact on or place in daily life.

values education 1. instruction that is focused on principles, moral standards, or ethical qualities that are considered desirable, in addition to academic instruction. **2.** education focused on socially acceptable or correct living.

Values Lifestyle Groups (VALS) groups of consumers segmented by their personal characteristics. Eight categories of consumers are identified, based on responses to proprietary questionnaires.

value system the moral, social, aesthetic, economic, and religious concepts accepted either explicitly or implicitly by an individual or a particular society.

vampirism *n.* a belief in the existence of vampires. In the portrayal of vampirism in literature, sexual pleasure is often associated with sucking blood from another person, a representation of the "love bite." Vampirism is variously interpreted by some psychoanalytic thinkers as oral sadism, oedipal strivings, fear of castration, or aggressive hostile feelings.

van Buchem's syndrome an AUTOSOMAL ABERRATION marked by thickening and osteosclerosis of bones of the face, skull, and trunk, resulting in facial paralysis and loss of hearing and vision. The symptoms usually begin around the age of puberty. [Francis Steven Peter **van Buchem** (1897–1979), Dutch physician]

vandalism *n.* willful defacement or destruction of property. A persistent pattern of vandalism is one symptom of CONDUCT DISORDER.

Vandenbergh effect the effects of CHEMICAL COMMUNICATION in influencing age of puberty in rodent populations. Adult males produce an odor that can accelerate puberty in young females, leading to earlier reproduction. However, adult females produce odors that inhibit puberty in females. As a result, in low-density populations with more males than females, young females mature earlier, but in dense populations with many adult females, young females mature more slowly, leading to a regulation of population density. See also WHITTEN EFFECT. [John G. **Vandenbergh** (1935–), U.S. biologist]

vanishing cues methodology a computer-assisted training technique designed to teach new, complex knowledge to individuals with memory impairment. The technique takes advantage of the patient's preserved ability to respond to partial cues. Initially, as much information is provided as is needed for the patient to make a correct response. Across learning trials, information is gradually withdrawn until the patient can respond correctly in the absence of any cues.

variability *n.* **1.** the quality of being subject to change or variation in behavior or emotion. **2.** in statistics and experimental design, the degree to which members of a group or population differ from each other.

variable *n.* a quantity in an experiment or test that varies, that is, takes on different values (such as test scores, ratings assigned by judges, and other personal, social, or physiological indicators) that can be quantified (measured). Also called **variate**.

variable error see RANDOM ERROR.

variable-interval reinforcement schedule (**VI schedule**) in free-operant conditioning, a type of INTERVAL REINFORCEMENT in which the reinforcement or reward is presented for the first response after a variable period has elapsed since the previous reinforcement. Reinforcement does not depend on the number of responses during the intervals. The value of the schedule is given by the average interval length; for example, "VI 3" indicates that the average length of the intervals between potential reinforcements is 3 min. This type of schedule generally produces a relatively constant rate of responding. It was formerly known as an **aperiodic reinforcement schedule**. Compare FIXED-INTERVAL SCHEDULE.

variable-ratio reinforcement schedule (**VR schedule**) in free-operant conditioning, a type of INTERMITTENT REINFORCEMENT in which a response is reinforced after a variable number of responses. The value of the schedule is given by the average number of responses per reinforcer; for example, "VR 10" indicates that the average number of responses before reinforcement is 10. Compare FIXED-RATIO SCHEDULE.

variable stimulus any one of a set of experimental stimuli that are to be systematically compared to a constant stimulus.

variable-time schedule (**VT schedule**) a schedule of stimulus presentation in which stimuli are presented, independently of any behavior, at variable time intervals. The value of the schedule is given as the mean of the intervals. See also NONCONTINGENT REINFORCEMENT.

variance (symbol: σ^2) *n.* a measure of the spread, or DISPERSION, of scores within a sample, whereby a small variance indicates highly similar scores, all close to the sample mean, and a large variance indicates more scores at a greater distance from the mean and possibly spread over a larger range. Also called **index of variability**.

variance–covariance matrix in MULTIVARIATE statistics, a MATRIX whose diagonal elements are the variances of variables and whose off-diagonal elements are the covariances among the variables.

variance stabilizing transformation any of a class of TRANSFORMATIONS whose purpose is to eliminate the relationship between the CELL mean and the variance of the observations within the cell over the cells in the design.

variant *n.* in a group of objects or events, one that differs from the others in some way while remaining essentially similar to them.

variate *n.* **1.** see VARIABLE. **2.** a specific value of a particular variable.

variation *n.* the existence of qualitative differences in form, structure, behavior, and physiology among the individuals of a population, whether due to heredity or to environment. Both ARTIFICIAL SELECTION and NATURAL SELECTION operate on variations among organisms, but only GENETIC VARIATION is transmitted to the offspring.

variations of aging individual differences in the effects of aging caused either by intrinsic factors (e.g., disease, genetics) or by extrinsic factors (e.g., lifestyle, environment, culture).

varicella *n.* see CHICKEN POX.

varicella-zoster *n.* see CHICKEN POX; HERPES INFECTION.

varied mapping in a SEARCH task, a condition in which target and distractor stimuli change roles randomly over the course of an experiment, so that a stimulus may be a target in one trial and a distractor in the next. Compare CONSISTENT MAPPING.

variety *n.* **1.** in BIOLOGICAL TAXONOMY, a subdivision of a species comprising those members of the species that are distinct with reference to particular minor characteristics that do not affect their ability to interbreed to produce fertile offspring. The various BREEDS of domestic animals are examples of varieties. **2.** in linguistics, a version of a language that is phonologically or grammatically distinct from the STANDARD LANGUAGE and may be associated with such categories as region, ethnicity, or social class. See also DIALECT; REGISTER.

variform universal see PSYCHOLOGICAL UNIVERSAL.

varimax rotation in FACTOR ANALYSIS, a method of ORTHOGONAL ROTATION that attempts to maximize the number of near-0 and near-1 loadings within each factor.

vas- *combining form* see VASO-.

vascular dementia severe loss of cognitive functioning as a result of cerebrovascular disease. It is often due to repeated strokes. See DEMENTIA.

vascular depression a MAJOR DEPRESSIVE EPISODE that occurs shortly after the onset or treatment of cardiovascular disease or that is assumed to be caused by cardiovascular disease. Often, this episode is characterized by ANHEDONIA rather than depressed mood. The concept of vascular depression is increasingly invoked to explain a first episode of depression occurring relatively late in life.

vascular insufficiency failure of the cardiovascular system to deliver an adequate supply of blood to the body tissues. This may involve large regions of the body or a particular organ or area of an organ. ATHEROSCLEROSIS, for example, can reduce the blood supply to the leg muscles, causing cramplike pains and limping; the heart, resulting in angina pectoris; or the brain, causing symptoms of stroke.

vascular sclerosis thickening of the walls of the blood vessels, possibly related to hypertension. In audition, the condition can lead to hearing loss, often seen as a function of aging (see PRESBYCUSIS).

vasculitis *n.* inflammation of a blood vessel.

vas deferens (*pl.* **vasa deferentia**) the duct of the testis that conveys spermatozoa from the EPIDIDYMIS to the ejaculatory duct, formed by union of the vas deferens and the duct of the SEMINAL VESICLE, and thence to the urethra. Also called **ductus deferens**; **seminal duct**; **spermatic duct**.

vasectomy *n.* a surgical procedure for male STERILIZATION in which the vas deferens, which carries sperm from the testes to the urethra, is removed, segmented, or cut and the resulting openings blocked.

vaso- (**vas-**) *combining form* **1.** blood vessel (e.g., VASODILATION). **2.** the vas deferens (e.g., VASECTOMY).

vasoconstriction *n.* narrowing of blood vessels, which is controlled by VASOMOTOR nerves of the sympathetic nervous system or by such agents as VASOPRESSIN or SYMPATHOMIMETIC DRUGS. It has the effect of increasing blood pressure. See also ERGOT DERIVATIVES.

vasoconstrictor *n.* any drug or other agent (e.g., the hormone vasopressin) that causes constriction of blood vessels so that the diameter of the vessels is reduced. The vasomotor nerves of the SYMPATHETIC NERVOUS SYSTEM also serve as vasoconstrictors. Vasoconstrictor drugs are used to increase blood pressure that has fallen to dangerously low levels. Also called **vasopressor**.

vasodilation *n.* widening of blood vessels, as by the action of a VASOMOTOR nerve or a drug, which has the effect of lowering blood pressure.

vasodilator *n.* any drug or other agent that serves to increase the diameter of blood vessels, generally by relaxing smooth muscle in arterial walls. Vasodilators are commonly used in the treatment of hypertension and angina pectoris.

vasomotor *adj.* describing or relating to nerve fibers, drugs, or other agents that can affect the diameter of blood vessels, especially small arteries, by causing contraction or relaxation of the smooth muscle of their walls. Fibers of the sympathetic and parasympathetic divisions of the AUTONOMIC NERVOUS SYSTEM have a vasomotor effect.

vasopressin *n.* a peptide hormone synthesized in the hypothalamus and released by nerve terminals in the posterior PITUITARY GLAND. It plays an important role in the retention of water in the body and in regulation of blood pressure (by constricting small blood vessels, which raises blood pressure). Vasopressin secretion may also activate the HYPOTHALAMIC–PITUITARY–ADRENOCORTICAL SYSTEM and may be associated with mechanisms of learning and memory. Also called **antidiuretic hormone** (**ADH**).

vasopressor 1. *adj.* causing constriction of blood vessels and thereby raising blood pressure. **2.** *n.* see VASOCONSTRICTOR.

vasospasm *n.* see SPASM.

Vater's corpuscle see PACINIAN CORPUSCLE. [Abraham **Vater** (1684–1751), German anatomist and botanist]

VCP abbreviation for VISUAL COMFORT PROBABILITY.

VD abbreviation for venereal disease. See SEXUALLY TRANSMITTED DISEASE.

vector *n.* **1.** in matrix algebra, a row or column of a matrix. **2.** in MULTIVARIATE ANALYSIS, a one-dimensional array in which the scores of *n* individuals on a particular measure are arrayed. **3.** a mathematical entity with magnitude and direction.

Vedanta *n.* a collection of metaphysical theories and mental disciplines that emerged in India around the 6th century BCE and derived from the sacred texts of HINDUISM, the *Upanishads.* The sophistication of certain of these philosophies has influenced modern science, including the development of QUANTUM THEORY. See OBJECT OF CONSCIOUSNESS; PURE CONSCIOUSNESS.

vegetative *adj.* **1.** pertaining to basic physiological functions, such as those involved in growth, respiration, sleep, digestion, excretion, and homeostasis, which are governed primarily by the AUTONOMIC NERVOUS SYSTEM. **2.** living without apparent cognitive neurological function or responsiveness, as in PERSISTENT VEGETATIVE STATE. **3.** denoting ASEXUAL reproduction, especially in plants.

vegetative soul in the thought of Greek philosopher Aristotle (384–322 BCE), the type of soul possessed by plants. The vegetative soul has the capacity for growth and reproduction but does not have the capacity to receive and react to sense impressions or the capacity for rational thought. Compare RATIONAL SOUL; SENSITIVE SOUL.

vegetative state a condition in which an individual is immobile and noncommunicative, unaware of self or the environment, and unresponsive to stimuli. The condition occurs primarily in individuals with serious brain injury and is characterized by a nonfunctioning cerebral cortex. See PERSISTENT VEGETATIVE STATE.

vegetotherapy *n.* see ORGONE THERAPY.

velar 1. *adj.* of or relating to the SOFT PALATE. **2.** *adj.* denoting a speech sound articulated by the soft palate, for example, the [hl] in Welsh *Llandovery* or the [kh] in Scottish *loch* or German *Bach.* **3.** *n.* a speech sound made in this way.

velleity *n.* **1.** a low level of VOLITION. **2.** a vague or weak inclination or tendency.

velocity of conduction the speed at which nerve impulses travel along the axon of a neuron. Measurements by various techniques show that axons vary considerably in velocity of conduction, from 80–120 m/s for large, myelinated A FIBERS to 0.5–2 m/s for small, unmyelinated C FIBERS. Conduction velocity was first measured by German physiologist Hermann von Helmholtz (1821–1894). See also PERIPHERAL NERVE FIBER CLASSIFICATION.

velum *n.* (*pl.* **vela**) **1.** an anatomical structure resembling a veil, such as the **velum medullare superior**, a thin layer of white matter that forms the roof of the superior part of the fourth VENTRICLE of the brain. **2.** the SOFT PALATE.

velum palatinum see SOFT PALATE.

venereal disease see SEXUALLY TRANSMITTED DISEASE.

venesection *n.* see PHLEBOTOMY.

venire *n.* a panel of prospective jurors drawn from the community. Typically, they are randomly selected from large lists, such as voter registration lists or lists of licensed drivers. Before individuals are included in the venire, they may be screened for such factors as age, citizenship, criminal history, and prior jury service.

venlafaxine *n.* an antidepressant that works by inhibiting the reuptake of both serotonin and norepinephrine; it belongs to a class called the SNRIs (serotonin and norepinephrine reuptake inhibitors). Its mechanism of action therefore differs from that of the SSRIS, which—some believe—makes it a more effective treatment for depression than SSRIs. It is also appropriate for treatment of generalized anxiety disorder and social anxiety disorder. Like other antidepressants, it should not be administered concurrently with MONOAMINE OXIDASE INHIBITORS. U.S. trade name: **Effexor**.

Venn diagram a visual representation of elements and relations in set algebra. It is a figure in which circles represent the elements of a set, and the union and intersection between or among the circles represent relationships between the sets (i.e., the degree to which they are mutually inclusive or exclusive). [John **Venn** (1834–1923), British logician]

ventilation *n.* in psychotherapy and counseling, a client's full and free expression of feelings or emotions, especially in session.

ventr- *combining form* see VENTRO-.

ventral *adj.* pertaining to the front (anterior side) of the body or the lower (inferior) surface of the brain. Compare DORSAL. **—ventrally** *adv.*

ventral amygdalofugal pathway the larger of the two efferent pathways from the AMYGDALA in the brain (see also STRIA TERMINALIS). It carries fibers from the basolateral group of nuclei and the central nucleus to the hypothalamus and various regions of the forebrain (including the CINGULATE GYRUS and ORBITOFRONTAL CORTEX) and brainstem (with which it has reciprocal connections).

ventral anterior nucleus a nucleus of the anterior THALAMUS that receives inputs from the BASAL GANGLIA and sends connections to the precentral cerebral cortex.

ventral horn see ANTERIOR HORN.

ventral lateral nucleus see LATEROVENTRAL NUCLEUS.

ventral root any of the SPINAL ROOTS that carry motor nerve fibers and arise from the spinal cord ventrally on each side. Also called **anterior root**; **motor root**. Compare DORSAL ROOT. See also BELL–MAGENDIE LAW.

ventral stream a series of specialized visual regions in the cerebral cortex of the brain that originate in the STRIATE CORTEX (primary visual cortex) of the occipital lobe and project forward and downward into the lower temporal lobe. It is known informally as the "what" pathway of perception. Compare DORSAL STREAM.

ventral tegmental area an area in the midbrain ventral to the PERIAQUEDUCTAL GRAY and dorsal to the SUBSTANTIA NIGRA. It forms part of the LIMBIC SYSTEM, sending DOPAMINERGIC NEURONS to the MESOCORTICAL SYSTEM and MESOLIMBIC SYSTEM.

ventral white commissure see WHITE COMMISSURE.

ventricle *n.* **1.** an anatomical cavity in the body, such as any of the ventricles of the heart. **2.** any of the four interconnected cavities inside the brain, which serve as reservoirs of CEREBROSPINAL FLUID. Each of the two LATERAL VENTRICLES communicates with the THIRD VENTRICLE via the INTERVENTRICULAR FORAMEN; the third and fourth ventricles communicate with each other, via the CEREBRAL AQUEDUCT, and with the central canal of the spinal cord and the SUBARACHNOID SPACE. Also called **cerebral ventricle**. **—ventricular** *adj.*

ventricular puncture a surgical procedure in which an opening from the outside is made to the lateral ventricle areas of the brain. The procedure may be performed in order to reduce INTRACRANIAL PRESSURE, to inject medications (e.g., antibiotics) directly into the brain, or to obtain cerebrospinal fluid. See also VENTRICULOATRIAL SHUNT.

ventricular system the network of VENTRICLES and passageways in the brain, spinal cord, and subarachnoid space through which the CEREBROSPINAL FLUID circulates as a source of nutrients for tissues of the central nervous system.

ventricular zone a region of actively dividing tissue cells lining the cerebral VENTRICLES that provides neurons mainly early in development and glial cells (see NEUROGLIA) throughout life.

ventriculoatrial shunt a surgically created passage for draining cerebrospinal fluid from the ventricles of the brain to the external jugular vein, as in the treatment of HYDROCEPHALUS. The shunt carries the fluid through a catheter to the venous system that empties into the right atrium of the heart.

ventriculomegaly *n.* abnormal enlargement of a ventricle.

ventriculostomy *n.* a treatment for HYDROCEPHALUS in which an opening is created between the floor of the third ventricle of the brain and the underlying cisterna to permit the free flow of cerebrospinal fluid.

ventriloquism effect see VISUAL CAPTURE.

ventro- (**ventr-**) *combining form* front.

ventrodorsal *adj.* oriented or directed from the front (anterior) to the back (posterior) of the body. Compare DORSOVENTRAL. **—ventrodorsally** *adv.*

ventromedial hypothalamic syndrome a set of symptoms caused by experimental lesions in the VENTROMEDIAL NUCLEUS of the hypothalamus in the brain. The syndrome consists of two stages. The first (or **dynamic**) stage is characterized by HYPERPHAGIA (overeating) and subsequent weight gain, resulting in obesity. The second (or **static**) stage includes stabilization of body weight, resistance to food-getting behavior, and finickiness, such that the animal is willing to eat only easily obtainable and palatable foods. Also called **hypothalamic hyperphagia**. Compare LATERAL HYPOTHALAMIC SYNDROME.

ventromedial nucleus an area of the hypothalamus in the brain that receives input from the AMYGDALA and is associated particularly with eating and sexual behavior. The ventromedial nucleus traditionally has been referred to as the **satiety center** because of its presumed dominance over the cessation of eating (indeed, structural or functional damage results in excessive eating), but it is now known that other neural areas are involved in this function as well. See also VENTROMEDIAL HYPOTHALAMIC SYNDROME.

ventromedial pathways some of the major descending pathways of the MOTOR SYSTEM, conveying information from diffuse areas of the cerebral cortex, midbrain, and cerebellum. These pathways include the anterior CORTICOSPINAL TRACT, which descends directly from motor cortex to the anterior horn of the spinal cord; the VESTIBULOSPINAL TRACT, which carries information from the VESTIBULAR NUCLEI for control of equilibratory responses; the TECTOSPINAL TRACT, for control of head and eye movements; and the RETICULOSPINAL TRACT, for maintaining posture.

ventroposterior nucleus a nucleus of the THALAMUS in the brain that relays messages from the spinal cord to the PRIMARY SOMATOSENSORY AREA in the anterior parietal cortex. It includes the medial and lateral ventroposterior subnuclei, representing the face and body respectively, and receives input from CUTANEOUS RECEPTORS. The ventroposterior nucleus is part of the **ventroposterior nuclear complex**; this also includes the ventroposterior superior nucleus, which receives input from muscle spindles, and the ventroposterior inferior nucleus, which receives spinothalamic terminations related to touch, pain, and temperature. Also called **posterior ventral lateral nucleus**; **postventral nucleus**; **ventral posterior lateral nucleus**.

VEP abbreviation for VISUAL EVOKED POTENTIAL.

verapamil *n.* see CALCIUM-CHANNEL BLOCKERS.

veratrine *n.* see HELLEBORE.

verb *n.* a word or phrase used to describe an action, occurrence, or state, forming the essential part of the PREDICATE of a sentence. The verb is also identifiable as the element of the sentence that marks temporality (TENSE), MOOD, voice (see ACTIVE VOICE; PASSIVE VOICE), and number AGREEMENT with the SUBJECT. See also ACTIONAL VERB; AUXILIARY VERB; CAUSATIVE VERB.

verbal ability (**V**) demonstrated skill to comprehend and communicate effectively with words. Sometimes a distinction is made between receptive abilities (comprehension) and productive abilities (fluency). Brain areas necessary for normal speech appear to be distributed over a broad region of the cerebral cortex and can be mapped by electrical stimulation. For right-handed individuals, language is primarily localized in the left hemisphere. See also PRIMARY ABILITIES.

verbal alexia a form of AGNOSIA in which an individual may recognize single letters but not whole words or combinations of letters.

verbal amnesia a loss of the ability to remember words

due to neurological disorder or disease. See NEUROLOGICAL AMNESIA.

verbal aphasia see EXPRESSIVE APHASIA.

verbal automatism see AUTOMATISM.

verbal behavior all behavior that involves words, including speaking, listening, writing, and reading. The term is used by those who favor a behavioristic account of language (see BEHAVIORISM) in which human verbal behavior is thought to be explained by general laws of learning and behavior observable in other species; that is, its reinforcement is socially mediated by the responses of others. This contrasts with the cognitive approach dominant in PSYCHOLINGUISTICS and specifically with the theory of the cognitive TASK SPECIFICITY OF LANGUAGE. [first described by B. F. SKINNER in 1957]

verbal behavior therapy a form of BEHAVIOR THERAPY, developed in the 1960s, that is based upon the principles of OBSERVATIONAL LEARNING and CONDITIONING and incorporates the notion of RECIPROCAL DETERMINISM. The process involves a thorough inventory of symptoms and behavioral problems, the identification of those problems that will be the focus of the therapy, a careful FUNCTIONAL ANALYSIS of these target problems, development of specific reasonable goals for behavior change for each target problem, and the selection of appropriate therapeutic techniques to achieve the specific goal for each target problem. [developed by Albert BANDURA]

verbal comprehension an individual's ability to understand the language used by others, as determined by his or her RECEPTIVE VOCABULARY and RECEPTIVE LANGUAGE skills.

Verbal Comprehension Index on the WECHSLER ADULT INTELLIGENCE SCALE and other Wechsler tests, a subset of verbal tests thought to measure verbal knowledge and comprehension more purely than all the tests included in the VERBAL IQ.

verbal conditioning the conditioning of a verbal response (such as the use of a specific word) through reinforcement, usually given in the form of attention or praise. For instance, the experimenter might respond "Okay" whenever the participant uses the pronoun "I" but does not respond to the use of other pronouns. [introduced in 1955 by U.S. behaviorist Joel Greenspoon (1921–)]

verbal factor a factor obtained by FACTOR ANALYSIS that represents the latent trait underlying verbal abilities.

verbal fluency test any of a group of tests in which participants are required, within a limited period, to generate words that fit a specific category or have specific characteristics (e.g., they may all start with the same letter). Compare DESIGN FLUENCY TEST.

verbal intelligence the ability to use words and combinations of words effectively in communication and problem solving.

verbal IQ a broad measure of verbal ability as obtained on standardized intelligence tests and affected by native verbal skills, experience, education, test tasking skills, and test motivation. See IQ.

verbalization *n.* **1.** the expression of thoughts, feelings, and fantasies in words. Verbalization is a common feature of most forms of psychotherapy, which has led to the use of the terms SIGN SYSTEM and TALKING CURE to refer to the discipline and practice. Apart from the general communication that occurs between therapist and client as part of the PSYCHOTHERAPEUTIC PROCESS, a particularly striking form of verbalization occurs in the use of FREE ASSOCIATION. **2.** in psychiatry, a symptom involving excessive or uncontrolled speech, as in CIRCUMSTANTIALITY or PRESSURED SPEECH. —**verbalize** *vb.*

verbal leakage SLIPS OF THE TONGUE, verbal ambiguities, or other aspects of speech thought to reveal information about an individual's motives and behavior that he or she has attempted to conceal. Body language that is similarly revealing is described by some psychologists as **nonverbal leakage**. See also FREUDIAN SLIP; PARAPRAXIS; SYMPTOMATIC ACT.

verbal learning the process of learning about verbal stimuli and responses, such as letters, digits, nonsense syllables, or words. The methods used include PAIRED-ASSOCIATES LEARNING and SERIAL LEARNING. Researchers in the **verbal learning tradition**, influenced by Hermann EBBINGHAUS and by ASSOCIATIONISM, sought to uncover basic laws of learning by studying simple materials under controlled conditions.

verbally governed behavior see RULE-GOVERNED BEHAVIOR.

verbal masochism a sexual disorder in which an individual enjoys hearing words that are humiliating and insulting and derives sexual excitement from the abuse. According to Austrian-born U.S. psychologist Theodore Reik (1888–1969), the sexual excitement may depend on the choice and emphasis of words or sentences used.

verbal memory the capacity to remember something written or spoken that was previously learned (e.g., a poem). Compare MOTOR MEMORY; VISUAL MEMORY.

verbal overshadowing the tendency for the verbal description of a stimulus to impair later accurate memory of the stimulus. For instance, verbally describing a face that has just been seen may reduce later recognition or identification of that face in a picture lineup.

verbal paraphasia a form of PARAPHASIA characterized by the inclusion of inappropriate words and phrases in a person's speech.

verbal protocol analysis see PROTOCOL ANALYSIS.

verbal report see REPORTABILITY.

verbal test 1. any test or scale in which performance depends upon one's ability to deal with words. **2.** any test that measures verbal ability.

verbal thought a reasoning process that requires language and thus represents the merging of language and thought. Children first use language to guide thought by speaking out loud; only later does speech go underground to become covert verbal thought. See EGOCENTRIC SPEECH; INNER LANGUAGE. [proposed by Lev VYGOTSKY]

verbatim recall recollection of the exact wording of verbal material (e.g., a conversation, poem, or quotation). See also ROTE RECALL.

verbatim trace a precise, literal memory representation. According to FUZZY TRACE THEORY, verbatim traces are less easily accessed, generally require more effort to use, and are more susceptible to interference and forgetting than FUZZY TRACES.

verbigeration *n.* apparently meaningless repetition of specific words or phrases. Also called **catalogia**; **cataphasia**.

verbomania *n.* see LOGORRHEA.

vergence *n.* a turning movement of the eyes. If they turn inward, the movement is CONVERGENCE; if outward, it is DIVERGENCE.

veridical *adj.* **1.** truthful. **2.** of mental phenomena, such as memories or beliefs, corresponding to external reality. **3.** of dreams or visions, apparently confirmed by later events or knowledge.

veridical hallucination in PARAPSYCHOLOGY, an apparently illusory or impossible event, such as the APPARITION of a ghost, that is nevertheless witnessed by more than one person. Because it consists of a perception in the absence of a stimulus, the experience is classified as a HALLUCINATION; however, because it is shared by two or more people, it is said to be veridical rather than illusory. See also GHOST IMAGE.

veridical perception accurate perception of what is real.

verification *n.* the process of establishing the truth or accuracy of something, especially the use of objective, empirical data to test or support the truth of a statement, conclusion, or hypothesis.

verification time in studies of cognition, a measure of the time taken by a participant to indicate whether a statement is true or not, or to verify that a particular stimulus meets some prespecified condition.

vermis *n.* (*pl.* **vermes**) the median lobe of the CEREBELLUM, which lies between the two cerebellar hemispheres. Also called **vermis cerebelli**. **—vermicular** *adj.*

vernacular *n.* the indigenous language or DIALECT spoken routinely by a SPEECH COMMUNITY. It usually coexists with an official formal language used in schools and government. See DIGLOSSIA.

Versed *n.* a trade name for MIDAZOLAM.

verstehende Psychologie understanding psychology (German): an approach to psychology advocated by German philosopher Wilhelm Dilthey (1833–1911). Dilthey argued that psychology belonged to the human sciences (*Geisteswissenschaften*) as opposed to the natural sciences (*Naturwissenschaften*), and that its goal was therefore understanding (*Verstehen*) rather than explanation in terms of natural laws. For psychology, the object of understanding is lived experience (*Erlebnis*), and the goal must be articulation of the meaning of the experience from the perspective of the person living it. This approach was influential in the development of PHENOMENOLOGY, modern HERMENEUTICS, and EXISTENTIAL PSYCHOLOGY. See GEISTESWISSENSCHAFTLICHE PSYCHOLOGIE; NATURWISSENSCHAFTLICHE PSYCHOLOGIE.

vertebral artery a paired artery that runs upward alongside the vertebrae of the neck. Each vertebral artery enters the skull through the FORAMEN MAGNUM near the top of the spinal column, where it joins the vertebral artery from the other side to form the BASILAR ARTERY.

vertebral column see SPINAL COLUMN.

vertex potential a brain potential recorded by electrodes placed at the vertex of the skull. The vertex potential seems to be evoked by a variety of stimuli but is closely associated with attention.

vertical décalage in Jean PIAGET's theory of cognitive development, the invariable sequence in which the different stages of development (sensorimotor, preoperational, concrete operational, formal operational) are attained. Compare HORIZONTAL DÉCALAGE.

vertical group a group composed of individuals who come from different social classes. Compare HORIZONTAL GROUP.

vertical–horizontal illusion see HORIZONTAL–VERTICAL ILLUSION.

vertical job enlargement see JOB ENLARGEMENT.

vertical loading see JOB ENLARGEMENT.

vertical mobility the movement or displacement of individuals or groups from one social class to another. This may take the form of UPWARD MOBILITY or DOWNWARD MOBILITY. Compare HORIZONTAL MOBILITY. See SOCIAL MOBILITY.

vertical transmission see HORIZONTAL TRANSMISSION.

vertigo *n.* an unpleasant, illusory sensation of movement or spinning of oneself or one's surroundings due to neurological disorders, psychological stress (e.g., anxiety), or activities that disturb the labyrinth (which contains the organs of balance) in the inner ear (as in a roller-coaster ride).

vesicle *n.* a fluid-filled saclike structure, such as any of the SYNAPTIC VESICLES in axon terminals that contain neurotransmitter molecules. **—vesicular** *adj.*

vested interest the extent to which an ATTITUDE OBJECT is seen as being related to a person's material self-interest. It is assumed to be a determinant of related constructs, such as the IMPORTANCE OF AN ATTITUDE and EGO INVOLVEMENT. It is also a determinant of the STRENGTH OF AN ATTITUDE.

vestibular adaptation an effect of repeated stimulation that can result in suppression of the vestibular (balance) function and may be observed in individuals whose daily activities require frequent or repeated turning of the head (e.g., ballet dancers and figure skaters).

vestibular apparatus the organ of balance and equilibrium, which is situated in the inner ear and contains receptors that detect the position and changes in the position of the head in space. It consists of the SEMICIRCULAR CANALS and VESTIBULAR SACS. See also VESTIBULAR SYSTEM.

vestibular glands two pairs of glands situated on either side of the vaginal orifice. Their secretions lubricate the vulva and vagina and assist penetration by the penis during coitus. The larger pair (the **greater vestibular glands**) are also called **Bartholin's glands**.

vestibular illusion a spatial disorientation due to inaccurate vestibular (balance) information, for example, following adaptation of a VESTIBULAR RECEPTOR.

vestibular membrane see REISSNER'S MEMBRANE.

vestibular nerve a division of the VESTIBULOCOCHLEAR NERVE that carries nerve fibers from the VESTIBULAR SYSTEM in the inner ear; it is associated with the sense of balance and orientation in space. Fibers of the vestibular nerve terminate in the VESTIBULAR NUCLEI of the brainstem.

vestibular nuclei NUCLEI in the dorsolateral part of the PONS and the MEDULLA OBLONGATA in the brain that receive fibers from the VESTIBULAR NERVE and serve the sense of balance and orientation in space. They send fibers to the cerebellum, reticular formation, thalamus, and the VESTIBULOSPINAL TRACT.

vestibular nystagmus involuntary eye movements consisting of slow drift in one direction followed by a rapid movement in the opposite direction, caused by stimulation of the vestibular apparatus during rotation of the head. Also called **rotational nystagmus**. Compare PHYSIOLOGICAL NYSTAGMUS.

vestibular receptors nerve cells associated with the sense of balance, located in the cristae of the SEMICIRCULAR CANALS and in the MACULAE of the UTRICLE and SACCULE. They occur in two similar forms: a HAIR CELL enclosed in a chalicelike nerve ending and a cylindrical hair cell that synapses at its base with a nerve ending.

vestibular sacs two sacs in the inner ear—the UTRICLE and SACCULE—that, together with the SEMICIRCULAR CANALS, comprise the VESTIBULAR APPARATUS (see also VESTIBULAR SYSTEM). The vestibular sacs respond to gravity and encode information about the head's orientation. Low-frequency stimulation of the vestibular sacs can produce dizziness and rhythmic eye movements called NYSTAGMUS.

vestibular sense see SENSE OF EQUILIBRIUM.

vestibular system a system in the body that is responsible for maintaining balance, posture, and the body's orientation in space and plays an important role in regulating locomotion and other movements. It consists of the VESTIBULAR APPARATUS in the inner ear, the VESTIBULAR NERVE, and the various cortical regions associated with the processing of vestibular (balance) information.

vestibule *n.* a chamber that leads to a body cavity or that connects one cavity to another. The **vestibule of the vagina** is the cavity in the VULVA, between the two LABIA minora, into which the vagina, urethra, and greater vestibular glands open. The **vestibule of the inner ear** is the cavity of the bony LABYRINTH that contains the utricle and saccule (the VESTIBULAR SACS) and is connected to the semicircular canals and cochlea. **—vestibular** *adj.*

vestibule training an approach to personnel training in which new employees, before starting their work duties, spend some time learning in a special section, or "vestibule," apart from the actual work environment that duplicates as precisely as possible the setting and conditions in which the employees will actually be working once their training is complete. See OFF-THE-JOB TRAINING; ON-THE-JOB TRAINING.

vestibulocochlear nerve the eighth cranial nerve: a sensory nerve containing tracts that innervate both the sense of hearing and the sense of balance. It has two divisions, the VESTIBULAR NERVE, originating in the vestibule and the semicircular canals, and the AUDITORY NERVE (acoustic or cochlear nerve), originating in the cochlea. The vestibulocochlear nerve transmits impulses from the inner ear to the medulla oblongata and pons and has fibers that continue into the cerebrum and cerebellum. Also called **cranial nerve VIII**.

vestibulo-ocular reflex (**VOR**) the involuntary compensatory movement of the eyes that occurs to maintain fixation on a visual target during small, brief head movements. It is triggered by vestibular signals. Compare OPTOKINETIC REFLEX.

vestibulospinal tract a TRACT that sends impulses from the VESTIBULAR NUCLEI to the spinal cord. It is divided into lateral and medial branches and serves to control balance and orientation in space.

vestigial body image the subjective or internal image of one's appearance that is not necessarily modified by changes to one's external features. For example, individuals who have lost large amounts of weight may continue to have a vestigial body image of an overweight individual.

Vestra *n.* a trade name for REBOXETINE.

vestured genital apposition sexual activity in which clothed participants place their genital regions together and thrust or rub against each other, simulating COITUS. The activity may or may not be carried to the point of orgasm for one or both partners.

VI abbreviation for variable interval. See VARIABLE-INTERVAL REINFORCEMENT SCHEDULE.

vibration *n.* a periodic motion of an object, such as a tuning fork, with a frequency that is usually measured in HERTZ.

vibration disease an occupational health hazard resulting from acoustic or mechanical vibration and shock to the hand and arm. The extent of the damage depends on the frequencies of vibrations and the duration of exposure.

vibration environment an environment in which the oscillations of an operational vehicle in motion are transmitted to humans by supporting seats, floors, walls, and handles. Such vibration can have mechanical effects on the human body that are similar to those caused by acceleration. The magnitude of the vibration effects depends on the frequency range of the vibration force and its relationship to the body's dynamic response.

vibration experience a sensation produced by contact with a pulsating or rapidly vibrating object that stimulates receptors in the skin. The vibration sense can be measured with a mechanical vibrator that can be adjusted for threshold frequencies of the effect.

vibration receptor a nerve ending that responds to various ranges of vibration frequencies. Vibration receptors have been identified through histological studies as PACINIAN CORPUSCLES. They have been located at depths ranging from the skin surface to the connective tissue covering the surface of a bone. Some vibration receptors seem most sensitive to vibrations between 100 and 500 Hz, whereas others are most sensitive to those below 100 Hz.

vibration sense see VIBRATION EXPERIENCE.

vibration white finger see HAND–ARM VIBRATION SYNDROME.

vibrator *n.* an appliance containing a small electric motor that produces a vibrating action, used to stimulate the genitals and other sensitive areas during masturbation or sexual activity with a partner. The device may be powered by batteries or by household electric current. Some vibrators strap on the hand, making the fingers vibrate during sexual stimulation. Another type has a vibrating mechanism on which a number of attachments of different size, shape, and texture can be placed, and these stimulate the body directly. Other vibrators are cylinders that can be used externally or inserted into the vagina or anus.

vibratory sensitivity responsiveness to contact with a vibrating stimulus.

vibrotactile aid see TACTILE SENSORY AID.

vibrotactile masking the interference of one vibrotactile stimulus pattern with another that may occur if the two patterns are presented in close temporal proximity. MASKING may be forward or backward.

vibrotactile threshold the minimum level of stimulation at which a vibration is perceived. Different types of MECHANORECEPTORS are sensitive to different specific frequencies of vibration.

Vicadin *n.* a trade name for a combination of HYDROCODONE and ACETAMINOPHEN.

vicarious *adj.* substitutive or second-hand: applied, for example, to the satisfaction obtained by viewing the experiences of others in television programs. It is widely believed that human conditioning of fear responses can occur through vicarious means, and that gratification of needs can be partially accomplished through watching the actions of others.

vicarious brain process see ALTERNATIVE BRAIN PROCESS THEORY; VICARIOUS FUNCTION.

vicarious conditioning see OBSERVATIONAL LEARNING.

vicarious enjoyment the pleasure one derives as a result of another's attainments or other positive experiences, often because of an identification with this other individual. Also called **vicarious pleasure**.

vicarious function a theory to explain the ability to recover from the effects of brain damage. It is based on evidence that many functions are not strictly localized in the brain, and that many brain areas can assume a function previously performed by a brain area that has been damaged. Also called **vicarious brain process**.

vicarious learning see OBSERVATIONAL LEARNING.

vicarious traumatization (**VT**) the impact on a therapist of repeated emotionally intimate contact with trauma survivors. More than COUNTERTRANSFERENCE, VT affects the therapist across clients and situations. It results in a change in the therapist's own worldview and sense of the justness and safety of the world. Therapist isolation and overinvolvement in trauma work can increase the risk of vicarious traumatization.

vicious circle a situation or behavioral pattern in which an individual's or group's problems become increasingly difficult because of a tendency to "address" or ignore them repetitively through unhealthy defensive reactions that, in fact, compound them.

vicious circularity 1. the logical problem that is presented by certain kinds of self-referring PARADOX, such as *This sentence is a lie*, and by certain related cruxes in SET THEORY, notably those arising from the idea that a set can be the member of itself. **2.** see CIRCULAR REASONING.

victim *n.* **1.** an individual who is the target of another person's violent, discriminatory, harassing, or assaultive behaviors. **2.** an individual who has experienced an accident or natural disaster. **—victimization** *n.*

victim blaming see BLAMING THE VICTIM.

victim impact statement a spoken or written statement, made during the sentencing phase of a trial by the victim of a crime, describing the harm and suffering experienced as a result of the defendant's acts.

videotape methods in clinical psychology and psychiatry, the use of videotape recordings of therapy sessions for therapeutic, research, or teaching purposes. Videotaped sessions are typically reviewed as a part of clinical supervision and are useful in providing trainees with feedback. Occasionally patients are invited to view the videotape with the therapist and recall their thoughts and emotions.

Vienna Circle a group of philosophers, logicians, and mathematicians who were based in Vienna in the 1920s and 1930s. The unifying theme of their work was an attempt to systematize the empirical and positivist tradition using the methods of modern SYMBOLIC LOGIC—an approach that became known as LOGICAL POSITIVISM. Prominent members of the group included German philosopher Rudolf Carnap (1891–1970) and Czech-born mathematical logician Kurt Gödel (1906–1978).

Vienna Psychoanalytic Society see WEDNESDAY EVENING SOCIETY.

Viennese School a group of early 20th-century practitioners of psychoanalysis, based in Vienna, who followed the theories of Sigmund FREUD. Also called **Vienna School**; **Wiener Schule**. See also WEDNESDAY EVENING SOCIETY.

Vierordt's law the principle that the TWO-POINT THRESHOLD for a stimulus is lower in mobile body parts than in those that are less mobile. [Karl von **Vierordt** (1817–1884), German physiologist]

Vieth–Müller circle a theoretical circle in space in front of an observer containing points that will fall on corresponding retinal locations in the two eyes when a point on the circle is fixated. A Vieth–Müller circle is an example of a HOROPTER. [G. U. **Vieth**; J. P. **Müller**]

vigilance *n.* a state of extreme awareness and watchfulness directed by one or more members of a group toward the environment, often toward potential threats (e.g., predators, intruders, enemy forces in combat). In animal behavior, vigilance increases in females after the birth of their young and in response to ALARM CALLS. In large groups there can be a division of labor, with individuals taking turns in vigilance. In a military context, vigilance tasks (e.g., sentry duty, ship and air traffic control, antiaircraft and missile defense tracking) demand maximum physiological and psychological attention and readiness to react, characterized by an ability to attend and respond to stimulus changes for uninterrupted periods of time. This level of vigilance can produce significant cognitive stress and occasional physiological stress reactions. **—vigilant** *adj.*

vigilance decrement in a vigilance task, a decrease in the number of targets detected that occurs after a short period on the task. In many situations the decrement is due to a shift in the response criterion, although in some cases it reflects a decrease in sensitivity for detecting the target.

vigor *n.* physical and mental robustness and energy. **—vigorous** *adj.*

Vigotsky, Lev Semenovich see VYGOTSKY, LEV SEMENOVICH.

Vineland Adaptive Behavior Scales (**VABS**) an assessment of an individual's personal and social functioning in four domains: communication, daily living skills, socialization, and motor skills. The VABS, which is a modification and replacement of the 1935 **Vineland Social Maturity Scale**, currently contains items covering the age range from birth to 90 years. Data are gathered through a rating form or semistructured interview with the person's parents or caregivers. The scales are used not only to diagnose and evaluate individuals with various disabilities—dementia, brain injuries, mental retardation, autism, or other developmental problems—but also to formulate educational and treatment (habilitative or rehabilitative) programs. The VABS was originally published in 1984; the most recent version is the **VABS–II**, published in 2005. [originally developed by psychologists Sara S. Sparrow (1933–), David A. Balla, and Domenic V. Cicchetti (1937–)]

violation-of-expectation method a technique, based on habituation and dishabituation procedures, in which increases in an infant's looking time are interpreted as evidence that the outcome expected by the infant has not occurred.

violence *n.* **1.** the expression of hostility and rage with the intent to injure or damage people or property through physical force. See also DOMESTIC VIOLENCE. **2.** passion or intensity of emotions or declarations. **—violent** *adj.*

viral hypothesis of schizophrenia the theory, first suggested in the early 20th century, that psychoses resembling schizophrenia are associated with influenza epidemics. It was later observed that several types of viral ENCEPHALITIS may include schizophrenia-like symptoms, and many studies have investigated the effect of exposure to viral agents, especially in utero, on subsequent development of schizophrenia. In particular, U.S. psychiatrist E. Fuller Torrey (1938–) has noted that the viral hypothesis accounts for the greater number of people with schizophrenia who are born from January to April (see SEASONALITY EFFECT), a period during which there is a high incidence of viral infections. More recently, however, it has been suggested that virus exposure is a risk factor for—rather than a key causative event in—the development of schizophrenia.

viral marketing a form of Internet marketing in which consumers tell other consumers about new products or services by sending e-mails either directing these consumers to a website or endorsing the product.

viral meningitis see MENINGITIS.

Virchow–Seckel syndrome see SECKEL'S BIRD-HEADED DWARFISM.

virgin 1. *n.* a person who has never had sexual intercourse. **2.** *adj.* referring to a pure or natural state, as in virgin forest. **—virginal** *adj.*

virginity *n.* the state of a person who has not participated in sexual intercourse. Traditionally, a woman was assumed to be a virgin if her HYMEN was not ruptured, but a ruptured hymen is no longer regarded as prima facie evidence of loss of virginity, as other events can cause this.

virilism *n.* the presence in a female of secondary sexual characteristics that are peculiar to men, such as muscle bulk and hirsutism. The condition is due to overactivity of the adrenal cortex, with excessive secretion of androgen, which can be corrected in some cases. Also called **masculinization**.

virility *n.* the state of possessing the qualities of an adult male, especially capacity for coitus. See also MALENESS; MASCULINITY. **—virile** *adj.*

virtual pitch the low pitch of a complex sound. For a complex periodic sound, the virtual pitch generally corresponds to that of the fundamental FREQUENCY even when the fundamental is not present in the sound (the phenomenon of the **missing fundamental**). The terms **periodicity pitch** and **residue pitch** are now used synonymously with virtual pitch, although they have different historical antecedents.

virtual reality a simulated three-dimensional environment created through the memory, graphics, and processes of a computer. It is often used to create simulated environments for such activities as flying a plane or exploring space, which are expensive or dangerous to experience directly. A number of supporting hardware and software tools, including gloves and head monitors with real-time feedback, are often used to immerse and train humans in this virtual reality.

virtual reality therapy a form of IN VIVO EXPOSURE THERAPY in which clients are active participants immersed in a three-dimensional computer-generated interactive environment that allows them a sense of actual presence in scenarios related to their presenting problems. This treatment is currently used primarily for anxiety-related disorders, such as fear of flying.

virtue *n.* **1.** a quality or characteristic that has positive connotations in a particular society and that is considered beneficial to psychological health. **2.** moral goodness. **—virtuous** *adj.*

virus *n.* **1.** a microscopic parasitic agent that consists of an RNA or DNA core surrounded by a protective protein coat. As viruses cannot replicate on their own but must invade a living host cell in an organism to do so, they are generally considered nonliving. Viral infection is responsible for many human illnesses and diseases, including influenza, poliomyelitis, mumps, several forms of cancer, and AIDS (see HIV). **2.** a computer program designed to disrupt the functioning of other programs or to scramble or destroy computer files. It gains access to programs or systems surreptitiously, often by means of an attachment to an innocent-looking e-mail. Viruses are typically designed to spread from computer to computer; for that reason, they can be extremely destructive.

Visatoner *n.* an electronic device that enables people with severe visual impairment to read printed material. Moving the Visatoner over a line of print results in a series of tones that can be translated by the user, who has received extensive training, into patterns of letters of the alphabet.

viscera *pl. n.* (*sing.* **viscus**) the organs in any major body cavity, especially the abdominal organs (stomach, intestines, kidneys, etc.). **—visceral** *adj.*

visceral brain in MACLEAN'S THEORY OF EMOTION, the area of the brain that is involved in the neurophysiological control of emotional behavior and experience (including motivated behavior). Its major structures are the AMYGDALA, HIPPOCAMPAL FORMATION, and SEPTAL AREA. These structures are considered to regulate responses organized, in principle, by the hypothalamus and basal ganglia and to provide them with much of the necessary information. It integrates cognitive aspects with commands for action.

visceral drive a drive that is derived from a physiological need. Also called **viscerogenic drive**. See PHYSIOLOGICAL MOTIVE.

visceral learning see LEARNED AUTONOMIC CONTROL.

visceral reaction a response of the visceral (internal or abdominal) organs, such as contractions of the stomach.

visceral sensation see ORGANIC SENSATION.

visceral sense the sense associated with functions of the viscera.

viscerogenic need in the PERSONOLOGY of U.S. psychologist Henry Alexander Murray (1893–1988), one of the primary, physiological needs that arise from organic processes and lead to physical gratification. They include the needs for air, water, food, sex, urination, and defecation. Compare PSYCHOGENIC NEED.

viscerotonia *n.* the personality type that, according to SHELDON'S CONSTITUTIONAL THEORY OF PERSONALITY, is associated with an endomorphic physique (see ENDOMORPH) and is characterized by a tendency toward love of comfort, love of food, relaxation, and sociability. **—viscerotonic** *adj.*

viscus *n.* see VISCERA.

visible spectrum see SPECTRUM.

vision *n.* **1.** the sense of sight, in which the eye is the receptor and the stimulus is radiant energy in the visible SPECTRUM. See also VISUAL SYSTEM. **2.** a visual hallucination often involving a religious or mystical experience. **3.** a mental image of something or someone produced by the imagination. **—visual** *adj.*

vision rehabilitation the REHABILITATION of individuals with visual impairment ranging from blindness to low vision. Services provided include functional assessments of a person's visual abilities, if any; ORIENTATION AND MOBILITY TRAINING; rehabilitation teaching (e.g., adaptive skills training in managing one's ACTIVITIES OF DAILY LIVING); instruction in the use of optical devices and ASSISTIVE TECHNOLOGY; career services and training; and psychological counseling.

visitation rights see CHILD VISITATION.

visiting nurse a REGISTERED NURSE who provides nursing services to patients in their homes. Visiting nurses are usually employed by a local visiting nurse association.

Vistaril *n.* a trade name for HYDROXYZINE.

visual acuity the degree of clarity, or sharpness, of visual perception. It may be measured in several ways, for example, by testing one's ability to detect very small gaps between two parts of a figure (the MINIMUM SEPARABLE method) or to discern a fine dark line on a light background or a fine light line on a dark background. See also ACUITY GRATING; LANDOLT CIRCLES; SNELLEN CHART.

visual adaptation the changes that occur in the visual system itself or in visual perception as a result of continuous stimulation. For example, the range of light intensities over which photoreceptors are responsive changes with prolonged exposure to dark, and many visual AFTEREFFECTS are caused by adaptation of neurons within the visual system. See also DARK ADAPTATION; LIGHT ADAPTATION.

visual agnosia an inability to recognize visual stimuli, such as objects. This may be due to a defect in visual perception (**apperceptive visual agnosia**) or to factors other than perceptual impairment (**associative visual agnosia**). The condition is observed in humans with brain lesions, although a similar effect has been noted in nonhuman animals, who need to touch objects in order to identify them. Also called **object blindness**. See also CONGENITAL VISUAL AGNOSIA; VISUAL FORM AGNOSIA.

visual agraphia an impaired ability to write resulting from a failure to recognize letters, numbers, or words. The condition is caused by lesions in the occipitoparietal area of the brain. See AGRAPHIA.

visual allachesthesia a symptom of a PARIETAL LOBE lesion manifested as a transposition of visual images to an opposite point in space (e.g., from one half of the visual field to the other).

visual allesthesia see VISUAL ILLUSION.

visual amnesia loss of the ability to recognize familiar objects, printed words, or handwriting by sight, due to neurological disease or injury.

visual angle the angle subtended by a visual target at the nodal point of the eye. The width of an adult thumb at arm's length subtends about 1° of visual angle, and there are 360° of visual angle around the entire head.

visual anomia failure to name visual stimuli correctly despite intact visual recognition.

visual anosognosia see ANTON'S SYNDROME.

visual aphasia see ALEXIA.

visual apperception test a PROJECTIVE TECHNIQUE in which participants (most often children and adolescents) are presented with a visually oriented task, for example, to draw a person, object, or situation; to finish an incomplete drawing; or to create a narrative from a single or multiple visual stimuli.

visual area any of many regions of the cerebral cortex in which the neurons are primarily sensitive to visual stimulation. Together, all the visual areas comprise the VISUAL CORTEX. Most visual areas can be distinguished from one another on the basis of their anatomical connections (i.e., their CYTOARCHITECTURE) and their specific visual sensitivities. Individual areas are designated by "V" and a number (which indicates roughly how distant the area is from STRIATE CORTEX). See V1; V2; V4; V5.

visual association cortex any of the VISUAL AREAS in the cerebral cortex that lie outside the striate cortex, including V2, V4, and V5. See also PRESTRIATE CORTEX.

visual attention the process by which one item, the target, is selected for analysis from among several competing items, the distractors. See also FEATURE-INTEGRATION THEORY.

visual attention disorder any disturbance of a person's ability to detect and attend to visual stimuli. Examples include BÁLINT'S SYNDROME and VISUAL NEGLECT. See also PERCEPTUAL EXTINCTION.

visual aura see AURA.

visual axis a straight line that extends from the external fixation point through the nodal point of the eye to the fovea. Compare PRIMARY LINE OF SIGHT.

visual blurring the sensation resulting from impairment of the ability to perceive form in the central field region, which is typically associated with poor visual acuity and reduced spatial CONTRAST SENSITIVITY. Visual blurring can occur as a result of retinal disease (e.g., MACULAR DEGENERATION, DIABETIC RETINOPATHY) or damage to the optic nerve (e.g., associated with multiple sclerosis) or visual cortex; it has also been reported as a side effect of anticholinergic drugs and as a consequence of ACCOMMODATIVE SPASM. Patients experience difficulties with reading and face perception (especially in black and white photographs).

visual capture the tendency for sounds to appear to emanate from plausible visual objects, regardless of the actual source of the sound. For example, the voices of actors in a movie are localized to the images on the screen, rather than to the speakers that produce the sound. Also called **ventriloquism effect**.

visual cliff an apparatus to investigate the development of DEPTH PERCEPTION in nonverbal human infants and animals, in particular, whether depth perception is an innate ability or learned through visuomotor experience. The apparatus consists of a table with a checkerboard pattern, dropping steeply down a "cliff" to a surface with the same pattern some distance below the tabletop. The apparatus is covered with a transparent surface, and the participant is positioned on this at the border between the tabletop and the cliff. Reluctance to crawl onto the surface covering the cliff is taken as an indication that the participant can discriminate the apparent difference in depth between the two sides of the apparatus. Most infants as young as 6 months of age will not cross over to the side over the cliff. [devised by Eleanor J. GIBSON]

visual closure the ability to identify a familiar object from an incomplete visual presentation.

visual comfort probability (**VCP**) a measure of the acceptability of discomfort glare (interference with vision caused by excessive illumination), calculated as the percentage of users who are likely to find the level of glare in a room or work area acceptable.

visual communication the use of distinctive colors, shapes, or movements that are detected by the visual system as a means of communication between individuals. For example, animals may have distinctive colors in the breeding season to indicate reproductive state, fluff out fur to appear larger in a threat context, or gesture with limbs or head in a variety of other contexts.

visual consciousness the contents of visual awareness. Operationally, it consists of those visual events that can be reported, distinguished from each other, and acted upon on request.

visual constructional impairment see VISUOCONSTRUCTIONAL IMPAIRMENT.

visual-construction test see VISUOCONSTRUCTIVE TEST.

visual cortex the cerebral cortex of the occipital lobe, specifically the STRIATE CORTEX (primary visual cortex). In humans this occupies a small region on the lateral surface of the occipital pole of the brain, but most is buried in the banks of the calcarine fissure on the medial surface of the brain. The visual cortex receives input directly from the LATERAL GENICULATE NUCLEUS via the OPTIC

TRACT and sends output to the multiple visual areas that make up the VISUAL ASSOCIATION CORTEX.

visual cycle the biophysical and biochemical sequence of events that includes the release of all-*trans* retinal from RHODOPSIN during light stimulation, followed by its conversion to 11-*cis* retinal in the retinal PIGMENT EPITHELIUM, and then the return of the 11-*cis* retinal to the photoreceptor for the reconstitution of rhodopsin.

visual discrimination the ability to distinguish shapes, patterns, hidden figures, or other images from similar objects that differ in subtle ways.

visual dominance 1. the phenomenon in which visual stimuli, when presented simultaneously with auditory or other stimuli, tend to dominate awareness. **2.** the phenomenon in which the view from one eye dominates the PERCEPT when viewing a scene with two eyes. See OCULAR DOMINANCE.

visual dyslexia a form of acquired dyslexia (see ALEXIA) characterized by multiple reading errors involving the substitution or transposition of letters within words (see PARALEXIA). The resulting misread words are often very similar to the actual words (e.g., reading *wife* as *life*, or *bug* as *dug*). [proposed in 1973 by British neuropsychologists John C. Marshall and Freda Newcombe (1925–2001)]

visual evoked potential (VEP) an electric potential recorded from the scalp overlying the visual cortex in response to visual stimulation.

visual extinction a form of VISUAL NEGLECT in which a previously visible stimulus in one half of the visual field disappears when a stimulus appears simultaneously in the other half of the visual field. Visual extinction occurs as a result of brain damage, usually to the parieto-occipital cortex contralateral to the visual field in which the extinction occurs.

visual fatigue the fading of visual images, particularly in bright light. Visual fatigue is often experienced by patients with optic neuritis; it can also occur after head injuries, especially after prolonged visual testing or when reading, as a result of reduced VISUAL ATTENTION.

visual field the extent of visual space over which vision is possible with the eyes held in a fixed position. The outer limit of vision for each eye extends approximately 60° nasally, 90° temporally, 50° superiorly, and 70° inferiorly. The extent varies with age: Very young children and older people have a smaller visual field. Objects nearest to the fixation point are seen with greatest clarity because visual acuity, spatial contrast sensitivity, and color vision are best in the foveal region.

visual field defect a reduction in the normal extent of the visual field, characterized by partial or total blindness. This is caused by an interruption in the flow of visual impulses between the retina and the visual cortex, which may be caused by a lesion before, after, or in the OPTIC CHIASM or in all or a part of the OPTIC RADIATIONS; it can involve tracts of one or both eyes. Each possible lesion produces a different defect.

visual field sparing the extent to which normal vision is preserved in a visually impaired or deprived half of a visual field, expressed in degrees of VISUAL ANGLE measured from the fovea. **Foveal sparing** means that the foveal region (1°) is spared; **macular sparing** refers to the preservation of the macular region (5°); **macular splitting** denotes sparing ranging from 1° to 5°.

visual fixation the orientation of the eyes so that images fall on the foveas, in the central part of the retinas. See FIXATION.

visual form agnosia a type of VISUAL AGNOSIA in which an individual is unable to recognize complex objects or pictures, even though basic visual functions, such as acuity and visual thresholds, are intact in the same part of the visual field. Linguistic and general intellectual functioning is also intact; thus when individuals touch the object, they can recognize it correctly. Visual form agnosia usually results from damage to VISUAL AREAS in the INFEROTEMPORAL CORTEX. In contrast, damage to earlier levels in the visual system, such as the LATERAL GENICULATE NUCLEUS or V1, produces a SCOTOMA. Also called **visual object agnosia**.

visual form discrimination the ability to discriminate visually between different shapes.

visual function the ability to process visual stimuli.

visual hallucination visual perception in the absence of any external stimulus. Visual hallucinations may be unformed (e.g., shapes, colors) or complex (e.g., figures, faces, scenes). In hallucination associated with psychoses (e.g., paranoid schizophrenia, alcohol- or hallucinogen-induced psychotic disorder), the individual is unaware of the unreality of the perception, whereas insight is retained in other conditions (e.g., pathological states of the visual system). Visual hallucinations may arise in association with lesions of the peripheral or central visual pathway or visual cortical areas; they are often present in temporal-lobe epilepsy and may appear during prolonged isolation. See also PEDUNCULAR HALLUCINOSIS.

visual hearing the substitution of vision for hearing. This may be accomplished, within limits, by LIPREADING and gesture interpretation.

visual illusion a misperception of external visual stimuli that occurs as a result of either a pathological condition or a misinterpretation of the stimuli (see ILLUSION). Typical pathological visual illusions are persistence or recurrence of a visual image after the external stimulus is no longer in view (see PALINOPSIA), seeing multiple images on viewing one object (see POLYOPIA), transposition of visual images from one position to another (**visual allesthesia**), and distortion in color perception (see CEREBRAL DYSCHROMATOPSIA). Compare VISUAL HALLUCINATION.

visual imagery mental imagery that involves the sense of having "pictures" in the mind. Such images may be memories of earlier visual experiences or syntheses produced by the imagination (as, for example, in visualizing a pink kangaroo). Visual imagery can be used for such purposes as dealing with traumatic events, establishing DESENSITIZATION hierarchies, or improving physical performance. See VISUALIZATION.

visual impairment partial or total inability to see, or to see normally, due to partial or complete loss or absence of vision or to visual dysfunction. Visual impairment encompasses the continuum from BLINDNESS to LOW VISION. It can result from disease or degenerative disorder (e.g., cataract, glaucoma, diabetic retinopathy, or macular degeneration), injury, or congenital defects (e.g., refractive errors, astigmatism). The degree of visual impairment is assessed in terms of disability in everyday life. Also called **vision impairment**. See also ADVENTITIOUS VISUAL IMPAIRMENT; CONGENITAL VISUAL IMPAIRMENT.

visual induction the influence that one visual stimulus or part of the VISUAL FIELD can have on the perception of an adjacent stimulus or the remainder of the visual field. COLOR CONTRAST effects are examples of visual induction.

visualization *n.* **1.** the process of creating a visual image in one's mind (see VISUAL IMAGERY) or mentally rehearsing a planned movement in order to learn skills or enhance performance. **2.** in psychotherapy, the intentional formation by a client of mental visual images of a scene or historical incident that may be inhibited or the source of anxiety. The purpose is to bring the visualized scene into the present therapeutic situation where it can be discussed and worked out to reduce its negative implications. See also GUIDED AFFECTIVE IMAGERY. **3.** a hypnotic method used to induce or increase relaxation in which the individual is asked to imagine, for example, sitting comfortably at home and then to use all senses in perceiving the scene (e.g., the curtains blowing in the windows, the texture of the armchair). The more fully the individual concentrates on these features, the more deeply relaxed he or she becomes. **4.** in consumer psychology, a motivation-research technique using imaginary or fictitious situations or conditions in order to induce consumers to reveal the true reasons for their choice of products. For example, instead of being asked why they like or dislike a product, consumers may be asked to characterize the type of individual they would expect to buy the product. **—visualize** *vb.*

visual learning training or CONDITIONING that depends upon visual cues. The brain center for visual learning is believed to be in the INFEROTEMPORAL CORTEX, where cortical cells have been demonstrated to be highly active in analyzing visual inputs.

visually guided reaching movements in which concurrent visual information is used to locate a target and avoid obstacles. Visually guided reaching is contrasted with movements to remembered, but unseen, targets and with movements guided by other senses (e.g., touch).

visual masking the ability of one visual stimulus to render another stimulus invisible. See MASKING.

visual memory the capacity to remember in the form of visual images what has previously been seen. Compare MOTOR MEMORY; VERBAL MEMORY.

visual memory span see MEMORY SPAN.

visual–motor coordination the ability to synchronize visual information with the movements of different parts of the body.

visual neglect a form of SENSORY NEGLECT in which the individual is unaware of half the visual field. This occurs most often in the left visual field following right parietal damage or dysfunction. See NEGLECT.

visual object agnosia see VISUAL FORM AGNOSIA.

visual organization in GESTALT principles of perception, a visual field that appears to be organized and meaningful.

visual organization test any test that involves the organization of visual, nonverbal stimuli.

visual perception the awareness of visual sensations that arises from the interplay between the physiology of the VISUAL SYSTEM and the internal and external environments of the observer.

visual perseveration see PALINOPSIA.

visual persistence see PERSISTENCE OF VISION.

visual phosphene see PHOSPHENE.

visual pigment see PHOTOPIGMENT.

visual-placing reflex the reflex act of animals in placing their legs to reach a surface they can see. Animals that have undergone surgical DECORTICATION may lose this normally automatic response and fail to stretch their legs toward a visible surface.

visual preference paradigm a research technique for studying visual discrimination in infants in which the amount of time spent looking at different visual stimuli is measured to determine which stimulus the infants prefer. It is assumed that the stimulus looked at more often is the one that is preferred and that such preferences indicate an ability to discriminate between stimuli.

visual processing the modification and analysis of visual signals at all levels of the VISUAL SYSTEM.

visual projection 1. the rendering of a three-dimensional object into two dimensions to produce a silhouette. **2.** any technique for the presentation of visual stimuli.

visual purple see PIGMENT BLEACHING; RHODOPSIN.

visual pursuit movements of the eyes in an attempt to maintain fixation on a moving target. Also called **ocular pursuit**; **visual tracking**.

visual receptive field that region of VISUAL SPACE in which stimulation will evoke a response from a neuron in the retina. Also called **retinal receptive field**.

visual receptor see PHOTORECEPTOR.

visual recognition the ability to recognize an object visually.

visual recognition test any test in which participants are asked to identify a series of familiar objects during single or multiple visual presentations of the objects.

visual reproduction the ability to draw or create an object presented visually.

visual-righting reflex any of the reflexes that automatically orient the head to the visual fixation point of the moment.

visual search the process of detecting a target visual stimulus among distractor stimuli. In experimental studies, the characteristics of the target and distractors are manipulated to explore the mental operations that underlie VISUAL ATTENTION. See also FEATURE-INTEGRATION THEORY.

visual-search perceptual disorder a disorder exemplified by difficulty in locating a specific number in a random array on a board as a result of a lesion in one cerebral hemisphere. Normally, participants perform better when the number sought is to the left of the midline. Participants with left-hemisphere damage also do better when the number is to the left of the midline, whereas those with right-hemisphere damage perform better when the number is to the right of the midline.

visual sensory store see ICONIC MEMORY.

visual space the three-dimensional perspective of the visual field.

visual–spatial ability the ability to comprehend and conceptualize visual representations and spatial relationships in learning and in the performance of such tasks as reading maps, navigating mazes, conceptualizing objects in space from different perspectives, and doing various geometric operations. Beginning in adolescence, males, on average, show a definite superiority in certain aspects of visual–spatial ability whereas females, on average, display superiority in certain aspects of VERBAL ABILITY.

visual stimulation stimulation by light that triggers a response in the receptor cells in the retina.

visual system the components of the nervous system and the nonneural apparatus of the eye that contribute to the perception of visual stimulation. The anterior structures of the eye, such as the CORNEA and LENS, focus light on the RETINA, which transduces photons into neural signals. These are transmitted via the OPTIC NERVE and OPTIC TRACT to nuclei in the thalamus and brainstem. These in turn transmit the signals either to the VISUAL AREAS of the cerebral cortex for conscious analysis or directly to motor centers in the brainstem and spinal cord to produce eye movements.

visual texture an attribute of a two-dimensional figure or a two-dimensional rendering of a three-dimensional object that describes its surface characteristics. Visual texture is related to, but not the same as, texture in the tactile sense. For example, the words "shiny" or "speckled" describe visual texture, while "smooth" or "wavy" describe tactile texture. Gradients of visual texture are often used to infer depth in a two-dimensional scene.

visual threshold 1. the minimum level of stimulation that can be detected visually. **2.** any of the thresholds for detecting various aspects of visual stimulation, including intensity, resolution, contrast sensitivity, movement acuities, position acuities, and so on.

visual tracking see VISUAL PURSUIT.

visual transduction the biochemical and biophysical process in which light energy is converted to a neural signal in a retinal PHOTORECEPTOR. See also ISOMERIZATION; VISUAL CYCLE.

visual yellow the bleached form of the photopigment RHODOPSIN. Also called **xanthopsin**. See PIGMENT BLEACHING.

visuoconstructional impairment an impairment characterized by difficulty in construction tasks, such as drawing or assembling the various parts of an object into a complete structure. See CONSTRUCTIONAL APRAXIA. Also called **visual constructional impairment**.

visuoconstructive test any of a wide range of tests that require a combination of visual and motor skills in the construction of an end product as an evaluation of these nonverbal skills. The most common examples of these tests are drawing tests, BLOCK-DESIGN TESTS, and jigsaw-puzzle tests. Also called **visual-construction test**.

visuomotor ataxia see OPTIC ATAXIA.

visuomotor behavior rehearsal a program of combining PROGRESSIVE RELAXATION and imagery for performance enhancement.

visuospatial agnosia a disorder of spatial orientation, which may be tested by asking the individual to point to objects or other stimuli located in different parts of his or her visual field. Individuals can report objects in their visual fields, but not the spatial relationships of the objects to one another.

visuospatial function the ability to recognize the spatial (relational) aspects of a figure or object in two and three dimensions.

visuospatial scratchpad a component or subsystem of WORKING MEMORY used for rehearsing or manipulating visual, imaginal, or spatial information. See also CENTRAL EXECUTIVE.

visuotopic map see RETINOTOPIC MAP.

vital capacity the capacity of the lungs to hold air, measured as the maximum volume of air that can be exhaled after maximum inspiration.

vital functions functions of the body (e.g., respiration, the circulation of the blood) that sustain life. Many vital functions are controlled by the brainstem.

vitalism *n.* **1.** the theory that the functions of living organisms are determined, at least in part, by a life force or principle. German biologist Hans Driesch (1867–1941) was the chief exponent of this view, holding that life processes are autonomous and purposive and that potentialities for growth and development are realized through the operation of an agent to which he applied the term ENTELECHY. French philosopher Henri Bergson (1859–1941) named this creative, vital force the ÉLAN VITAL. **2.** more generally, any theory that opposes NATURALISM and the reduction of psychological life to biological structures and processes. **—vitalist** *adj., n.*

vitality *n.* physical or intellectual vigor or energy: the state of being full of zest and enthusiastic about ongoing activities. See also FITNESS.

vital spirits see ANIMAL SPIRITS.

vital statistics data, usually compiled by a government agency, on specific life events (e.g., birth, death, disease, marriage, etc.) in a population.

vitamin *n.* an organic substance that in minute quantities is essential for normal growth and health. Many vitamins function as COENZYMES, aiding in the metabolism of carbohydrates, fats, and proteins. A few vitamins can be synthesized in the human body, but most must be supplied in the diet. The most important are vitamin A, the vitamin B complex (including THIAMINE, riboflavin, pyridoxine, cyanocobalamin [B_{12}], folic acid, NICOTINIC ACID, and pantothenic acid), vitamin C (ASCORBIC ACID), vitamin E, and vitamin K. Vitamins were so named in 1913 by Polish-born U.S. biochemist Casimir Funk (1884–1967), based on his belief that all vitamins were amines.

vitamin A a fat-soluble vitamin. Its aldehyde, retinal, is a component of the photopigments in the retina. Vitamin A deficiency results in night blindness and other visual disorders. Also called **retinol**. See also VISUAL CYCLE.

vitamin A toxicity a condition caused by excessive intake of vitamin A (retinol). A large overdose of vitamin A—500,000 IU or more—can cause headache, vomiting, bone pain, weakness, blurred vision, irritability, and flaking of the skin. Long-term intake of 100,000 IU or more per day can also lead to toxicity. Symptoms include hair loss, headache, bone thickening, an enlarged liver and spleen, anemia, menstrual problems, stiffness, joint pain, weakness, and dry skin. On the other hand, high doses of beta-carotene (which can be converted to vitamin A in the body) have no toxic effects.

vitamin C see ASCORBIC ACID.

vitamin deficiency lack of a vitamin needed for normal bodily functions. For example, deficiency of thiamine (vitamin B_1) is often associated with severe and chronic alcoholism (see WERNICKE'S ENCEPHALOPATHY; WERNICKE–KORSAKOFF SYNDROME).

vitamin D toxicity a condition caused by excessive intake of vitamin D. Long-term overdose of vitamin D can cause irreversible damage to the kidneys and cardiovascular system and can retard growth in children. Excessive amounts of the vitamin may lead to high blood pressure and premature hardening of the arteries. Nausea, abdominal pain, loss of appetite, weight loss, seizures, and an irregular heartbeat may be signs of overdose.

vitamin model of employee satisfaction a model proposing nine attributes of work that influence employee satisfaction. As with vitamins, employees will require some minimal amount or dosage of each attribute to be satisfied with their jobs. In the case of three attributes (money, physical security, and valued social position) employees can have an overabundance with no negative effects. However, as with some vitamins, too much of the remaining six attributes (externally generated goals, variety, clarity, control, skill use, and interpersonal contact) can lead to problems. [proposed by British organizational psychologist Peter B. Warr]

vitamin therapy the treatment of mental or physical conditions through a daily intake of diagnostic-specific vitamins in specific dosages.

vitex agnus castus see AGNUS CASTUS.

vitreous hemorrhage a complication of diabetes mellitus marked by bleeding within the eyeball due to the rupture of capillaries of the retina. See also DIABETIC RETINOPATHY.

vitreous humor the thick, transparent fluid filling the cavity (the **vitreous body**) behind the lens of the eye.

vivid data data that are salient or important to an individual (compared to so-called **pallid data**). Such data comprise observations (or, more generally, information), collected either by direct sensory experience or indirectly (e.g., by reading about something), that may then be used by the person to make deductions and generally reason about the world. A datum's vividness is a function of individual interests, the concreteness of the datum, its power, or its proximity. Vivid data are more likely to be recognized, attended to, and recalled, generating a greater cognitive influence.

vividness training training to improve the ability to produce very clear, crisp mental images in which the colors are distinct and the details of the imaged situation are present.

viviparity *n.* literally, live birth: reproduction in which the embryo develops within the female until a well-formed individual emerges. Compare OVIPARITY. **—viviparous** *adj.*

vivisection *n.* dissection performed on a living animal for research or experimental purposes. Many scientists and researchers oppose the practice, questioning its scientific validity and necessity, and numerous others criticize it as inhumane and unethical. See also ANIMAL CARE AND USE; ANIMAL RIGHTS.

VMI abbreviation for DEVELOPMENTAL TEST OF VISUAL–MOTOR INTEGRATION.

VNO abbreviation for vomeronasal organ (see VOMERONASAL SYSTEM).

vocabulary growth the development of vocabulary in children. In estimating vocabulary size, a distinction is commonly drawn between RECEPTIVE VOCABULARY and PRODUCTIVE VOCABULARY; more recent research has concentrated on the process of vocabulary acquisition and the organization of the child's MENTAL LEXICON.

vocabulary test a test designed to determine the number and level of words that an individual can use (**active vocabulary**) or understand (**passive vocabulary**).

vocal communication communication through auditory signals usually produced by a vibrating organ, such as the larynx in the throats of mammals or the two **syringes** located in the bronchial branches in birds. Vibrations produced by these organs are altered by changing configurations of the tongue, lips, and shape of the oral and nasal cavities. Other sound-producing mechanisms in animals include **stridulation**, the rubbing of body parts together, as in crickets. See also ANIMAL VOCALIZATION.

vocal cords a pair of tissue folds that project from the walls of the LARYNX. They vibrate, producing sounds, when expired air passes through the narrow space (**glottis**) between them. Also called **vocal folds**.

vocal-image voice audible speech patterns that have been electronically transformed into visual patterns that can be read by people with severe hearing loss.

vocalization *n.* the production of sounds by means of vibrations of the vocal cords, as in speaking, babbling, singing, screaming, and so forth. See also ANIMAL VOCALIZATION. **—vocalize** *vb.*

vocal reaction time in studies of cognition, the time that a participant takes to begin a spoken response to a stimulus. See REACTION TIME.

vocal register the tonal or pitch range of an individual's voice. See also CHEST VOICE; FALSETTO; HEAD VOICE.

vocal tract the structures, collectively, that are involved in vocalization, including the VOCAL CORDS and glottis of the larynx together with the pharynx, nasal cavity, mouth, and ARTICULATORS.

vocation *n.* an occupation or profession to which one is particularly suited, especially one involving a sense of mission or calling. **—vocational** *adj.*

vocational adjustment the degree to which an individual succeeds in choosing the kind of work or career best suited to his or her interests, traits, and talents. The term differs from OCCUPATIONAL ADJUSTMENT in emphasizing the match of career to personal goals and aptitudes, rather than the match of the individual to objective work conditions.

vocational appraisal the prediction by a vocational counselor of a client's potential for success and fulfillment in a particular occupation. A vocational appraisal is based on the counselor's understanding of occupational opportunities in relation to the client's personality, intelligence, abilities, and interests as revealed in interviews and tests. See VOCATIONAL COUNSELING.

vocational aptitude the personal abilities and traits required for successful performance of the tasks involved in a particular occupation.

vocational aptitude test any test designed to assess the abilities, interests, personality traits, and other factors deemed essential for success in a particular occupation. Such tests are often used to assess how well the participant's profile on these dimensions matches the profile of the typical or ideal person in the occupation.

vocational choice the choice of an occupation or career. A realistic process of this kind often begins in adolescence, with a conscious examination of individual interests, strengths, and limitations in relation to a given vocational context. A mature vocational choice requires sufficient self-understanding to match personal interests and resources to the requirements of and conditions in a specific vocation or profession. Also called **vocational selection**. See also VOCATIONAL ADJUSTMENT; VOCATIONAL MATURITY.

vocational counseling 1. a counseling service provided to employees who seek guidance on such matters as adjusting to new jobs or roles, developing their careers within organizations, or any personal or other problems affecting job satisfaction or job performance. See also OUTPLACEMENT COUNSELING. **2.** see VOCATIONAL GUIDANCE.

vocational education see VOCATIONAL TRAINING.

vocational guidance the process of helping an individual to choose an appropriate vocation through such means as (a) in-depth interviews; (b) administration of aptitude, interest, and personality tests; and (c) discussion of the nature and requirements of specific types of work in which the individual expresses an interest. Also called **vocational counseling**.

vocational maturity a developmentally advanced and competent orientation to issues of employment and occupational choice. A person with high vocational maturity is realistic about his or her options and takes a relatively rational approach to exploring the possibilities and making career decisions.

vocational rehabilitation the REHABILITATION of individuals with mental or physical disabilities or those who have been injured or ill in order to develop or restore PRODUCTIVITY. A vocational rehabilitation program includes assessment, VOCATIONAL GUIDANCE, and training and involves helping the individual to develop skills that have been lost or neglected and to find or return to employment in the competitive job market or another setting (see SHELTERED WORKSHOP; TRANSITIONAL EMPLOYMENT). Also called **occupational rehabilitation**. See also WORK REHABILITATION CENTER.

vocational selection 1. see VOCATIONAL CHOICE. **2.** a rare synonym of PERSONNEL SELECTION.

vocational services VOCATIONAL GUIDANCE, testing, and training, together with practical assistance in finding employment, as provided by a school, college, hospital, clinic, or rehabilitation center.

vocational training an organized program of instruction designed to equip individuals with the requisite skills and qualifications for placement in specific jobs or trades. Also called **vocational education**. See also VOCATIONAL REHABILITATION.

vodun *n.* see VOODOO.

voice *n.* **1.** the sound produced by the larynx and modified by other elements of the vocal tract (e.g., lips, tongue) before it issues from the mouth. **2.** in phonetics, the quality of a VOICED, as opposed to an UNVOICED, speech sound. **3.** in linguistics, see ACTIVE VOICE; PASSIVE VOICE. **4.** the distinctive tone or quality of a person's speaking or singing voice.

voice-activated control see SPEECH-ACTIVATED CONTROL.

voice-activated switch an interface between a device and the user that is activated by the user's voice and is often useful for individuals with disabilities. For example, an individual with a motor impairment can use a voice-activated switch to turn lights, appliances, and other household devices on and off.

voiced *adj.* denoting speech sounds that are articulated with accompanying vibration of the vocal cords. Voiced sounds include all the vowels and a number of consonants. The dichotomy voiced–UNVOICED is an important BINARY FEATURE in English and many other languages.

voice disorder any disorder that affects the pitch, loudness, tone, or resonance of the voice. See also COMMUNICATION DISORDER NOT OTHERWISE SPECIFIED.

voice key an apparatus, connected to a microphone, that starts or stops a timing device when a person speaks.

voiceless sound see UNVOICED.

voice-onset time (**VOT**) in phonetics, the brief instant that elapses between the initial movement of the speech organs as one begins to articulate a VOICED speech sound and the vibration of the vocal cord. Voice-onset time has been the subject of intense research in adult and infant speech perception because of evidence that this continuous acoustic dimension is perceived categorically (see CATEGORICAL PERCEPTION).

voice-output system a system that creates a voice for a computer to provide auditory feedback for individuals with visual impairment. For example, the system may create verbal output describing a file.

voiceprint *n.* a digital image of a voice, produced by electronic recording, that can be used for identification and authentication purposes. Voiceprints may also be used to analyze such vocal and speech characteristics as frequency, duration, and amplitude.

voice–stress analyzer an instrument that detects minute alterations in the voice, undetectable to the human ear, that presumably occur when a person is under stress. It is sometimes used as a lie detector, although its reliability and validity are controversial, and the results are not accepted as evidence in many U.S. courts of law.

voice therapist a specialist in the physiology and pathology of voice production who is involved with the diagnosis and remediation of voice disorders. See also SPEECH AND LANGUAGE THERAPIST.

voicing *n.* **1.** the use of vocal cord vibrations to produce speech sounds. See VOICED; UNVOICED. **2.** giving expression to ideas, observations, opinions, and the like through spoken communication.

voir dire the process of questioning prospective jurors to determine if they hold biases that may reasonably interfere with their ability to act impartially in a particular trial (from Norman French, literally: "to speak the truth"). The questions may be asked in private or in open court and may be posed by the attorneys, the judge, or both. Jurors may be asked to stand down by a CHALLENGE FOR CAUSE or a PEREMPTORY CHALLENGE.

volatile marriage a long-lasting marriage marked by both passionate arguments and expressions of affection, but with more positive than negative interactions.

volition *n.* **1.** the faculty by which an individual decides upon and commits to a particular course of action, especially when this occurs without direct external influence. The term encompasses a crucial set of activities involving the self, including choice and decision, self-control, intentional action, and an active rather than passive response to events. According to SELF-REGULATORY RESOURCES THEORY, volition depends on a limited resource that is expended whenever the self makes a decision or exerts control. **2.** the act of exercising this faculty. See also FREE WILL; WILL. **—volitional** *adj.*

volitional tremor see ACTION TREMOR.

volley *n.* a synchronous discharge, as when nerve impulses occur in phase along different fibers of a nerve.

volley theory the principle that individual fibers in an auditory nerve respond to one or another stimulus in a rapid succession of rhythmic sound stimuli, whereas other fibers in the nerve respond to the second, third, or *n*th stimulus. The result is that successive volleys of impulses are fired to match the inputs of stimuli, yet no single fiber is required to respond to every stimulus. Thus a nerve can reflect a more rapid frequency of stimulation (e.g., 1000 Hz) than any individual fiber could follow. Also called **volley principle**. See also HEARING THEORIES. [proposed in 1949 by U.S. psychologist Ernest Glen Wever (1902–1999)]

vol scale a scale of subjective loudness, measured in **vols**. One vol is the apparent volume of a 1000-Hz, 40-dB tone.

volt (symbol: V) *n.* the SI (International System) unit for measuring the difference of electric potential between two regions.

voltage-gated ion channel an ION CHANNEL that opens or closes in response to the voltage difference across the membrane, such as the voltage-gated sodium (Na^+) channel that mediates the ACTION POTENTIAL. Also called **voltage-activated gate**. Compare LIGAND-GATED ION CHANNEL.

volubility *n.* excessive, uncontrollable talkativeness: a common symptom of a MANIC EPISODE.

volume color see BULKY COLOR.

volume of distribution (symbol: V_d) the amount of a drug in the body in relation to its concentration in various body fluids (e.g., blood, plasma, extracellular fluid). It is expressed by the equation V_d = dose (amount of drug in body)/concentration in body fluid.

volumetric thirst see HYPOVOLEMIC THIRST.

voluntarism *n.* **1.** in psychology, the view that human behaviors are, at least in part, the result of the exercise of volition. See also FREE WILL. **2.** the general position that willing and choice are important factors in all human activities. For example, in ethics, voluntarism emphasizes that commitment to any moral principle is, in large part, a "will to believe," over which the person has some control. In epistemology, the same is held to be true of knowledge. In the field of historical studies, voluntarism holds that the exercise of will has been a major factor in the course of human events. It is therefore opposed to such approaches as MARXISM, which emphasize the role of impersonal economic forces. **3.** in metaphysics, the position that will, rather than mind, spirit, or some other substance, is the basis of reality. The best-known philosophy of this kind is that of German thinker Arthur Schopenhauer (1788–1866).

voluntary *adj.* describing activity, movement, behavior, or other processes produced by choice or intention and under cortical control, in contrast to automatic movements (e.g., reflexes) or action that is not intended (see IDEOMOTOR ACTIVITY).

voluntary admission admission of a patient to a mental hospital or other inpatient unit at his or her own request, without coercion. Such hospitalization can end whenever the patient sees fit, unlike INVOLUNTARY HOSPITALIZATION, the length of which is determined by a court or the hospital. Also called **voluntary commitment**; **voluntary hospitalization**.

voluntary agencies and organizations nonprofit groups supported in whole or in part by public contributions and devoted to the amelioration of public health or social welfare problems. The term "voluntary" distinguishes such groups from government agencies.

voluntary behavior behavior that is intentional in nature (e.g., walking, tapping at a key to receive food), as opposed to REFLEXIVE BEHAVIOR. See also OPERANT BEHAVIOR.

voluntary commitment see VOLUNTARY ADMISSION.

voluntary control the regulation of activities or behavior (e.g., movements, impulses, emotions) by conscious intention.

voluntary dehydration see DEHYDRATION.

voluntary hospitalization see VOLUNTARY ADMISSION.

voluntary movement movement by choice or intention, in contrast to automatic movements, such as reflexes.

voluntary muscle see SKELETAL MUSCLE.

voluntary process any process marked by intention and volition. Such activities are consciously desired, chosen, planned, regulated, and under CORTICAL CONTROL, in contrast to reflex actions or involuntary behavior.

voluntary response a deliberately chosen reaction to a stimulus that may require a complex coordination of excitatory and inhibitory impulses with feedback from visual and other systems.

voluntary turnover the number of employees who leave an organization or unit voluntarily during a given period, usually to take up a position in another organization. A high rate of voluntary turnover can be an indicator of low job satisfaction. Compare INVOLUNTARY TURNOVER. See TURNOVER.

volunteer *n.* an individual who contributes his or her services through personal choice and without compensation, for example, to a public or private health or social welfare agency or organization.

volunteer bias any systematic difference between participants who volunteer to be in a study versus those who do not.

volunteerism *n.* the act or practice of donating (i.e., without pay) one's time and energy to activities that contribute to the common good.

vomeronasal system a set of specialized receptor cells that in nonhuman mammals is sensitive to PHEROMONES and thus plays an important role in the sexual behavior and reproductive physiology of these animals. In humans this system responds physiologically to chemical stimulation and, in turn, excites brain centers, but its role in human olfaction is not known. Also called **Jacobson's organ**; **vomeronasal organ** (**VNO**).

vomiting *n.* ejecting the contents of the stomach through the mouth. Normally occurring as an autonomic physiological reaction to the ingestion of toxic substances, vomiting may also be self-induced, as in BULIMIA NERVOSA, as an inappropriate means of managing body weight (see PURGING).

vomiting center a nerve center in the medulla oblongata of the brain that is thought to partially govern vomiting. Another area, the CHEMORECEPTOR TRIGGER ZONE, also contributes to vomiting.

von Domarus principle an explanation of SCHIZOPHRENIC THINKING based on the concept that the individual perceives two things as identical merely because they have identical predicates or properties. [developed by Eilhard **von Domarus**, German psychiatrist]

von Economo's disease see ENCEPHALITIS LETHARGICA. [Constantin **von Economo** (1876–1931), Austrian neurologist]

von Frey hairs see FREY ESTHESIOMETER.

von Frey specificity theory a 19th-century theory, now disputed, that attempted to explain sensations of coldness, warmth, contact, and pain by linking them to different, specific receptors in the skin. The von Frey theory was premature, since not enough was known about anatomy at the time. [proposed in 1894 by Maximilian **von Frey** (1852–1932), German physiologist]

von Recklinghausen's disease an autosomal dominant hereditary disorder in which the common anomalies are pigmented (pale brown) patches on the skin and tumors of the peripheral nervous system (NEUROFIBROMAS); the latter may be firm subcutaneous nodules or soft cutaneous lumps that invaginate (form a pocket) when pressed. Visual, hearing, and other neurological anomalies may occur, and about a quarter of affected individuals show mental retardation. It is popularly called **Elephant Man's disease** (so named after a 19th-century patient, John Merrick, who was known as "the Elephant Man"). Also called **neurofibromatosis**. [described in 1882 by Friedrich D. **von Recklinghausen** (1833–1910), German pathologist]

von Restorff effect a memory-process theory stating that an item that is distinctive from others in a series will be remembered better than the nondistinctive items. For instance, if most of the words in a list are printed in blue ink, one word printed in red will be better remembered than the blue words. Also called **distinctiveness effect**; **isolation effect**; **Restorff phenomenon**. [proposed in 1933 by Hedwig **von Restorff** (1906–1962), German psychologist]

voodoo *n.* a synthetist religion, practiced chiefly in the Caribbean, in which west African traditions of magic and ancestor worship are combined with rites derived in part from Roman Catholicism. These typically involve the use of singing or chanting, drumbeating, and dancing to induce an ECSTATIC TRANCE, in which it is believed that spirits take possession of the worshippers, speaking and acting through them. Also called **vodun**; **voodooism**. **—voodooistic** *adj.*

voodoo death a CULTURE-BOUND SYNDROME observed in Haiti, Africa, Australia, and islands of the Pacific and the Caribbean. An individual who has disobeyed a ritual or taboo is hexed or cursed by a medicine man or sorcerer (often by pointing a bone at the culprit) and dies within a few days. U.S. physiologist Walter B. Cannon (1871–1945), one of the first researchers of voodoo death, suggested that the individual's strong belief in the curse caused physiological reactions in the body resulting in death. Also called **bone pointing**; **thanatomania**. See also PSYCHIC SUICIDE.

VOR abbreviation for VESTIBULO-OCULAR REFLEX.

VOT abbreviation for VOICE-ONSET TIME.

vowel *n.* **1.** a VOICED speech sound that is produced when the breath stream vibrating the vocal cords has unobstructed passage through the vocal tract. **2.** one of the letters of the alphabet used to represent these sounds in writing. Compare CONSONANT.

voyeurism *n.* a PARAPHILIA in which preferred or exclusive sexual interest and arousal is focused on observing unsuspecting people who are nude or in the act of undressing or engaging in sexual activity. Although the **voyeur** seeks no sexual activity with the person observed, orgasm is usually produced through masturbation during the act of "peeping" or later, while visualizing and remembering the event. Also called **inspectionalism**. See also PEEPING TOM. **—voyeuristic** *adj.*

VR abbreviation for variable ratio. See VARIABLE-RATIO REINFORCEMENT SCHEDULE.

Vroom–Yetton–Jago model of leadership a model that can be used by leaders in judging how much they should allow followers to participate in decision making in different situations. The model consists of a set of decision rules and a decision tree in which the leader assesses several key situational attributes, such as the nature of the task (e.g., whether high or low in TASK STRUCTURE), the degree of conflict expected among followers over preferred solutions, the degree of confidence that followers will accept decisions they do not agree with, and the extent to which such acceptance is important. On the basis of this assessment, the leader chooses from among several degrees of employee participation ranging from autocratic decision-making by the leader, through consultative approaches, to full participation and delegation. [Victor H. **Vroom** (1932–), Canadian organizational psychologist; Philip W. **Yetton**, 21st-century Australian management expert; Arthur G. **Jago** (1949–), U.S. organizational psychologist]

VT abbreviation for VICARIOUS TRAUMATIZATION.

VT schedule abbreviation for VARIABLE-TIME SCHEDULE.

vulnerability *n.* susceptibility to developing a condition, disorder, or disease when exposed to specific agents or conditions. **—vulnerable** *adj.*

vulnerability factor a variable that, if experienced or triggered, affects the probability that an individual will develop a condition, disorder, or disease.

vulva *n.* (*pl.* **vulvae**) the external female genitalia, including the CLITORIS, the LABIA, and the VESTIBULE of the vagina. Also called **pudendum**. **—vulval** *adj.*

vulval orgasm orgasm produced from stimulation of the VULVA (including the clitoris and labia). Some researchers have proposed that there are two types of orgasm, vulval and uterine, the latter involving deep vaginal penetration that results in contractions of the uterus during orgasm. Uterine contractions are said not to occur with vulval orgasms. This theory suggests that a more complete or satisfying orgasm results from intercourse than from stimulation of the vulva alone. However, many women have reported that whether or not uterine contractions accompany orgasm does not depend on the type of stimulation or sexual activity, but rather on how intense the orgasm is, and that the most intense orgasms occur in such activities as cunnilingus or during vibrator stimulation of the clitoris. See also VAGINAL ORGASM.

vulvectomy *n.* the surgical excision of all or part of the VULVA (external female genitalia). A vulvectomy is performed as a form of treatment for cancer of the vulva. It is also traditionally performed for cultural reasons (see FEMALE GENITAL MUTILATION).

Vygotskian theory of intelligence the theory that intelligence develops largely as a result of INTERNALIZATION, that is, by children absorbing what they observe in the environment and making it a part of themselves. Development occurs in part through a zone of proximal development, which distinguishes what children can do on their own from what they can do with the assistance of an adult mediator. [Lev VYGOTSKY]

Vygotsky, Lev Semenovich (or **Vigotsky**; 1896–1934) Russian psychologist. Vygotsky earned his doctorate in 1925 from the Psychological Institute in Moscow, where he remained on the research staff for the remainder of his career, although he also lectured and supervised research in Leningrad and Kharkov. Vygotsky is best known for his sociocultural theory of cognitive development, stressing the interaction of the child's natural capabilities with the symbolic mediators (e.g., written and oral language) available in his or her culture. In contrast to Jean PIAGET, who held that cognitive stages unfold naturally and inevitably and that education should follow these stages, Vygotsky held that the stages are in part driven by education and that therefore education should take place within a ZONE OF PROXIMAL DEVELOPMENT, aiming to stretch the child's capabilities beyond the current stage. Vygotsky's views were banned in the Soviet Union for political reasons from the 1930s to mid-1950s; they reached the West only after considerable delay, but are now quite influential. Among his most important writings are *Thought and Language* (1934) and the posthumously published *Mind in Society* (1978).

Ww

W symbol for COEFFICIENT OF CONCORDANCE.

Waardenburg's syndrome a hereditary disorder marked by a white or gray forelock, abnormal pigmentation of the iris, nerve deafness due to malfunction of the auditory nerves, and lateral displacement of the eyelids giving a false appearance that the eyes are widely separated. Mental retardation may occur, but deafness can be a factor in testing for intelligence. [Petrus Johannes **Waardenburg** (1886–1979), Dutch ophthalmologist]

WAB 1. abbreviation for WEIGHTED APPLICATION BLANK. **2.** abbreviation for WESTERN APHASIA BATTERY.

Wada test a presurgical and diagnostic technique for determining hemispheric functions, typically memory and language, by injecting a small dose of a barbiturate into an internal carotid artery. While each hemisphere is separately anesthetized, various cognitive tasks are administered; impairments on these tasks suggest that these functions are represented in the anesthetized hemisphere. The Wada test is typically used prior to TEMPORAL LOBECTOMY in severe epilepsy. Also called **intracarotid amobarbital procedure**; **intracarotid sodium amytal test** (**ISA**); **Wada dominance test**; **Wada technique**. [Juhn Atsushi **Wada** (1924–), Japanese-born Canadian neurosurgeon]

wage compression the tendency for the gap in salaries between established employees and those more recently hired to narrow as the rate of growth of the senior employees' salaries falls below that of junior employees' salaries. In extreme cases, an inversion may occur in which junior employees are paid more than senior employees.

waggle dance see BEE COMMUNICATION.

Wagner Act see NATIONAL LABOR RELATIONS ACT.

Wainwright v. Witt a case resulting in a 1985 U.S. Supreme Court decision that increased the prosecution's ability to exclude jurors from DEATH-QUALIFIED JURIES. According to this decision, excluded jurors need not be completely opposed to the death penalty: Any doubts they have over the morality of the death penalty may justify their exclusion. This decision therefore altered the criteria for acceptance from those earlier established in *Witherspoon v. Illinois* (see WITHERSPOON EXCLUDABLES).

WAIS abbreviation for WECHSLER ADULT INTELLIGENCE SCALE.

waist-to-hips ratio the circumference of the waist divided by the circumference of the hips. This ratio has been widely used in cross-cultural studies of attractiveness.

waiting-list control group a CONTROL GROUP, usually randomized, that will receive the same intervention given to the EXPERIMENTAL GROUPS but at a later time.

waiting-list phenomenon in psychotherapy and counseling, the unusual occurrence of a "cure" in a person who is on a waiting list for treatment. Such occurrences suggest that the anticipation of treatment in and of itself has profound psychological effects, which are similar to the PLACEBO EFFECT.

wakefulness *n.* a condition of awareness of one's surroundings generally coupled with an ability to communicate with others or to signal understanding of what is being communicated by others. It is characterized by low-amplitude, random, fast-wave electrical activity in the brain as recorded on an electroencephalogram.

waking center an obsolete name for an area of the posterior hypothalamus formerly thought to control waking from sleep. It has now been shown that the SLEEP–WAKE CYCLE is governed by a number of areas in the brain, including the hypothalamus and RETICULAR ACTIVATING SYSTEM. See also SLEEP CENTER.

waking dream 1. a metaphor for a vision. **2.** a dreamlike phenomenon occurring in the GANZFELD. **3.** a dream process in the psychoanalytic theory of British psychiatrist Wilfred Ruprecht Bion (1897–1979).

waking hypnosis a state of hypnosis induced without reference to sleep by requiring the participant to fix his or her attention on an object and to close the eyes tightly.

waking state see W-STATE.

Walden Two the title of a 1948 novel by B. F. SKINNER that describes an experimental community based on psychological principles. The name derives from *Walden, or Life in the Woods* (1854), a series of essays in which U.S. naturalist and writer Henry David Thoreau (1817–1862) describes his experiences of living as a recluse.

Wald–Wolfowitz test a nonparametric test of the NULL HYPOTHESIS that two samples have been taken from identical populations. [Abraham **Wald** (1902–1950), Hungarian-born psychologist; Jacob **Wolfowitz** (1910–1981), U.S. psychologist]

walk-in clinic a clinic in which diagnostic or therapeutic service is available without an appointment. See also DROP-IN CENTER.

walk–talk counseling session a therapy technique that uses walking or jogging during a counseling session.

walk-through performance testing (**WTPT**) a form of employee evaluation in which the employee is observed, interviewed, and rated as he or she performs the tasks required by the position.

Wallerian degeneration see ANTEROGRADE DEGENERATION. [Augustus **Waller** (1816–1870), British physiologist]

walleye *n.* see DIVERGENCE; EXOTROPIA.

Walter Reed Army Institute of Research a U.S. Army research institute that conducts a variety of applied-research programs.

wandering attention an attention disturbance in which the individual appears fully alert but is distracted by almost any external stimulus. The condition may result from disorders of the central nervous system, such as tumors occurring higher in the NEURAL AXIS than is the case in DRIFTING ATTENTION.

wandering behavior a disturbance of motor activity that involves directionless, disoriented movement. This behavior typically occurs in individuals with neurological impairment, dementia, alcohol dependence, or extreme stress.

wanderlust *n.* a tendency or compulsion to wander or roam. See also DROMOMANIA.

warehousing *n.* the practice of confining patients with mental disorders to large institutions for long-term, often lifetime, custodial care. This colloquial term implies lack of treatment beyond housing and feeding.

warm-blooded animal see ENDOTHERM.

warm spot any point on the surface of the skin that is particularly sensitive to stimuli producing the sensation of warmth.

warm stimulus a stimulus that is above skin temperature.

warmth *n.* the sensation experienced on the skin and some internal parts when the stimulus exceeds the normal skin temperature of about 33 °C (91 °F). However, a degree of adaptation may occur, which may cause variations in this temperature. For example, after putting a foot in a hot bath, a bowl of warm water will feel cool.

warm-up *n.* **1.** the use of a physical routine to prepare the body physiologically for physical exertion. **2.** the use of a physical routine to prepare the motor pathways for the performance of specific skills.

warm-up effect a phenomenon observed in learning and motor tasks in which individuals perform inexactly and slowly at the start of a session, even if familiar with the task, but then progress quickly to more proficient performance.

warning coloration the bright colors or patterns indicating that an organism is dangerous or unpalatable. Predators can learn quickly from a single encounter to avoid other organisms with similar markings. Examples include the black and white coloration of skunks, the yellow and black markings of many stinging insects, and the red, yellow, and black bands of a coral snake. Also called **aposematic coloration**. See BATESIAN MIMICRY.

warning overload in ergonomics and SAFETY ENGINEERING, the situation in which an operator receives visual, auditory, or other types of warnings that exceed his or her ability to process them and react appropriately. Warning overload may result from excessive visual awareness campaigns in the workplace, overreliance on auditory alerts, or excessive use of visual alerts.

war psychology the application of psychological principles and methods to military settings and operations during wartime. It covers human functioning in a variety of stressful environments, especially during times of crisis. See MILITARY PSYCHOLOGY.

Warrington Recognition Memory Test see RECOGNITION MEMORY TEST. [Elizabeth Kerr **Warrington**, British neuropsychologist]

Washburn, Margaret Floy (1871–1939) U.S. psychologist. Washburn earned her doctorate at Cornell University in 1894, studying under Edward B. TITCHENER. After several years of teaching at various institutions, in 1903 she joined the faculty of Vassar College, her undergraduate alma mater, and remained there throughout her career. She was active as an administrator, teacher, and researcher, publishing a wide variety of experimental studies in the areas of perception, memory, aesthetics, comparative psychology, and emotion. Washburn is best known as the author of *The Animal Mind* (1908), the first U.S. textbook of COMPARATIVE PSYCHOLOGY. Defying the odds for women of her generation, Washburn achieved both success and recognition among her predominantly male colleagues: She was elected president of the American Psychological Association in 1921, and in 1932 became only the second woman scientist to be elected to the National Academy of Sciences.

Washoe *n.* the name of the first chimpanzee to learn to communicate using the AMERICAN SIGN LANGUAGE.

Wason task see FOUR-CARD SELECTION PROBLEM. [Peter Cathcart **Wason** (1924–2003), British psychologist]

waterfall illusion the best known example of a MOTION AFTEREFFECT, produced by watching a waterfall for a period and then shifting one's gaze to stationary surrounding objects. These objects will appear to move upward, that is, in the opposite direction to the movement of the falling water—the adapting stimulus.

water-jug problems a set of problems in which participants are asked how they would measure out a specific amount of water using a number of jugs (often three) of specified capacity. For example, they might be asked to obtain exactly 39 ml of water using jugs that hold 207 ml, 165 ml, and 42 ml. Actual jugs are not usually provided. Also called **water-jar problems**. [devised by U.S. psychologist Abraham S. Luchins (1914–) and U.S. mathematician and psychologist Edith H. Luchins (1922–2002)]

water on the brain a colloquial name for CEREBRAL EDEMA.

water regulation see OSMOREGULATION.

watershed infarction necrosis (death) of neurons due to interruption of normal blood flow to an area lying at the periphery of a vascular bed, that is, in a WATERSHED ZONE.

watershed zone a zone that lies between the vascular distribution areas (vascular beds) of two arteries. Although the cerebral cortex is well supplied by arteries with collateral branches, there are areas at the junction of the parietal and occipital lobes and between the parietal and temporal lobes that are watershed zones. Such areas are particularly sensitive to anoxic injury (see WATERSHED INFARCTION).

Watson, John Broadus (1878–1958) U.S. psychologist. Watson earned his PhD in 1903 from the University of Chicago, where he studied biology and neurophysiology with Jacques Loeb (1859–1924) and Henry H. Donaldson (1857–1938), as well as philosophy and psychology with James Rowland ANGELL and John DEWEY. He then became an instructor and head of the university's psychological laboratory. From 1908 to 1920 he headed the program in experimental psychology at Johns Hopkins University, but was forced to resign because of a divorce scandal. Thereafter, he worked for the J. Walter Thompson advertising company in New York City while continuing to write popular psychological works. Watson, an important figure in the early history of COMPARATIVE PSYCHOLOGY, is best known as the founder of BEHAVIORISM, which eschewed the then-current emphasis on the study of consciousness through the method of INTROSPECTION and favored instead an objective study of observable, measurable behavior, molded on the methods of natural science. In applying this approach, major emphasis was placed on learned behavior, stimulus–response connections, and PAVLOVIAN CONDITIONING, which Watson introduced to American psychology. Watson served as president of the American Psychological Association in 1915, its youngest president. Among his most influential works were his 1913 *Psychological Review* article, "Psychology as the Behaviorist Views It," and *Psychology from the Standpoint of a Behaviorist* (1919). He also published the popular bestsellers *Behaviorism* (1924) and *The Psychological Care of Infant and Child* (1928).

Watson–Glaser critical thinking appraisal a measure of CRITICAL THINKING in which participants are asked to read and evaluate various statements, such as arguments, theses, problems, and interpretations. [Goodwin B. **Watson** (1899–1976) and Edward Maynard **Glaser** (1911–1993), U.S. psychologists]

wave-interference patterns in holographic photography, patterns created by light waves that converge from different angles: These can be recorded on film and projected into space to create a three-dimensional image. The principle has been invoked as an analogy for the ability of the mind to store spatial information and to reconstruct a three-dimensional image by recall processes.

wavelength *n.* the distance between successive peaks in a wave motion, such as a sound wave or a wave of electromagnetic radiation. The wavelength is equal to the speed of propagation of the wave motion divided by its frequency.

wavelength thresholds the minimum and maximum light or sound wavelengths that can be perceived. In the human visual system, wavelength thresholds vary somewhat with intensity but are generally around a minimum of 380 nm and maximum of 760 nm. Rod and cone functions also may be limiting factors, and species differences account for wavelength thresholds beyond human limits. In the human auditory system, wavelength thresholds are generally between 20 Hz and 20,000 Hz. Wavelength thresholds also vary in the auditory system for different species and intensities of sound.

wave of excitation in physiology, the propagation of electrical activity through tissue, as through nerve or muscle tissue.

waxy flexibility see CATALEPSY.

way finding see ROUTE LEARNING.

Ways of Coping Questionnaire (**WAYS**) a 66-item questionnaire administered to identify thoughts and behaviors that adults use to cope with stressful encounters in everyday life. It consists of statements (e.g., "I talked to someone to find out more") to which participants must respond using a 4-point LIKERT SCALE, ranging from "does not apply and/or not used" to "used a great deal." The WAYS measures coping processes, not coping styles. [developed by U.S. psychologists Susan Folkman (1938–) and Richard S. Lazarus (1922–2002)]

WBIS abbreviation for WECHSLER–BELLEVUE INTELLIGENCE SCALE.

WCST abbreviation for WISCONSIN CARD SORTING TEST.

weak ego see EGO WEAKNESS.

weak law of effect see LAW OF EFFECT.

weak methods 1. problem-solving techniques based on general principles rather than specific, domain-based knowledge. Such methods can be applied to a wide variety of problems but may be inefficient in many cases. **2.** in artificial intelligence, programs based on general principles that do not take into account knowledge specific to any particular application or domain. Compare STRONG METHODS.

weaning *n.* the process of acclimating a young child or animal to obtaining all nutriments from sources other than milk. It usually refers to the cessation of breast feeding.

weaning aggression animal aggression directed by mothers toward infants at the time of weaning to prevent them from suckling.

weapon-focus effect the tendency for eyewitnesses to focus their attention on any weapon present at the scene of a crime, thereby limiting their ability to remember other details of the crime scene, such as the perpetrator's face.

weapons effect increased hostility or a heightened inclination to aggression produced by the mere sight of a weapon. If provoked, individuals who have previously been exposed to the sight of a weapon will behave more aggressively than those who have not. Subsequent research has shown that this aggressive behavior is primed by the sight of weapons (see PRIMING) and that any other object associated with aggression can have the same effect. [identified in 1967 by U.S. psychologists Leonard Berkowitz (1926–) and Anthony LePage]

wear-and-tear theory of aging a theory of biological aging suggesting that aging results from an accumulation of damage to cells, tissues, and organs in the body caused by environmental agents. This leads to the weakening and eventual death of the cells, tissues, and organs.

Weber–Fechner law the law stating that to increase the intensity of a sensation in arithmetical progression, it is necessary to increase the intensity of the stimulus in geometric progression. The law is usually given in the form $s = k \log i$, where s is sensory magnitude, k is a constant, and i is the physical intensity of the stimulus. Also called **Bouguer–Weber law**. [Ernst Heinrich **Weber** (1795–1878), German physiologist and psychophysicist; Gustav Theodor FECHNER]

Weber fraction the ratio of the just noticeable difference (JND: see DIFFERENCE THRESHOLD) to the intensity of a stimulus. Increases in the intensity of a stimulus that are just noticeably different to the observer are a constant fraction of the stimulus intensity. The Weber fraction is calculated by dividing the JND by the intensity of the standard stimulus. The size of the Weber fraction varies as a function of stimulus condition and sense modalities. See WEBER'S LAW. [Ernst **Weber**]

Weber's experiment an experiment in which it was demonstrated that discrimination of weight was a constant fraction of 1/40 between two weights. [Ernst **Weber**]

Weber's law the law stating that the magnitude needed to detect change in a stimulus is proportional to the absolute magnitude of that stimulus. Thus the ratio of the magnitude of a stimulus to the amount that magnitude must be changed in order for the change to be perceived is a constant. This can be expressed as $\Delta I/I = k$, where I is the original stimulus magnitude and k is a constant. Thus the more intense the stimulus, the greater the change that must be made in it to be noticed. Also called **relativity law**. See also FECHNER'S LAW; STEVENS LAW. [proposed in 1834 by Ernst **Weber**]

website *n.* a site on the WORLD WIDE WEB that provides information, usually about a particular person or organization or about a commercial or professional service (e.g., sales or banking). The information at a given site is provided and maintained (i.e., kept current) by the owner of that site.

Wechsler, David (1896–1981) German-born U.S. psychologist. Wechsler earned his doctorate at Columbia University in 1925 under Robert S. WOODWORTH. During World War I he worked under Edwin G. BORING, scoring the Army's Alpha tests of intelligence and administering and scoring the Beta tests (see ARMY TESTS). After the war Wechsler studied with Charles Spearman (1863–1945) and Karl Pearson (1857–1936) in London, then went into private practice until becoming chief psychologist at Bellevue Psychiatric Hospital in New York City in 1932. It was there that Wechsler first developed the WECHSLER–BELLEVUE INTELLIGENCE SCALE, which provided subtest scores for different components of intelligence, such as verbal and quantitative ability, in contrast to the single-score tests of the STANFORD–BINET INTELLI-

GENCE SCALE. Wechsler's test was ultimately standardized as the WECHSLER ADULT INTELLIGENCE SCALE (WAIS). It and the WECHSLER INTELLIGENCE SCALE FOR CHILDREN (WISC) are still the dominant tests worldwide for measuring cognitive abilities. See also WECHSLER PRESCHOOL AND PRIMARY SCALE OF INTELLIGENCE.

Wechsler Adult Intelligence Scale (WAIS) an intelligence test for individuals aged 16 years to 89 years. A modification and replacement of the WECHSLER–BELLEVUE INTELLIGENCE SCALE, the WAIS currently includes seven verbal subtests (Information, Comprehension, Arithmetic, Similarities, Digit Span, Vocabulary, Letter–Number Sequencing) and seven performance subtests (Digit Symbol, Picture Completion, Block Design, Picture Arrangement, Object Assembly, Matrix Reasoning, Symbol Search). Depending on the specific combination of subtests administered, the test yields a Verbal Comprehension, a Perceptual Organization, a Processing Speed, and a Working Memory index score; a Verbal IQ, a Performance IQ, and a Full Scale IQ with a mean of 100 and a standard deviation of 15; or both index scores and IQs. The WAIS was originally published in 1955; the most recent version is the **WAIS-III**, published in 1997. [David WECHSLER]

Wechsler–Bellevue Intelligence Scale (WBIS) an individual intelligence scale for adults and older children consisting of six verbal and five performance subtests that yield separate verbal and performance IQs as well as an overall IQ. This test, published in 1939, has now been replaced by the WECHSLER ADULT INTELLIGENCE SCALE. [devised by David WECHSLER at Bellevue Psychiatric Hospital, New York City]

Wechsler Intelligence Scale for Children (WISC) an intelligence test developed initially in 1949 and standardized for children aged from 6 years to 16 years 11 months. It currently includes 10 core subtests (Similarities, Vocabulary, Comprehension, Block Design, Picture Concepts, Matrix Reasoning, Digit Span, Letter–Number Sequencing, Coding, Symbol Search) and 5 supplemental subtests (Word Reasoning, Information, Picture Completion, Arithmetic, Cancellation) that measure verbal comprehension, perceptual reasoning, processing speed, and working memory capabilities, yielding index scores for each as well as a Full Scale IQ with a mean of 100 and a standard deviation of 15. The most recent version of the test is the **WISC–IV**, published in 2003. [David WECHSLER]

Wechsler Memory Scale (WMS) a collection of memory tests, originally published in 1945, that assesses verbal (auditory) and nonverbal (visual) memory in older adolescents and adults by means of recall and recognition measures. The most recent version of the test (**WMS–III**, published in 1997) is a revised and elaborated version of the original scale and the **Wechsler Memory Scale–Revised** (**WMS–R**, published in 1987). The WMS–III contains 11 subtests, several of which measure memory both immediately and following a delay. Six of these subtests are considered primary because they are used to calculate summary index scores. The Immediate Memory Index, which is a combination of the Auditory Immediate Index and the Visual Immediate Index, provides a measure of overall immediate memory performance. The General Memory Index, which is a combination of the Auditory Delayed Index, the Visual Delayed Index, and the Auditory Recognition Delayed Index, provides a measure of overall delayed memory performance. Finally, the Working Memory Index provides a measure of an individual's capacity to manipulate information in short-term memory. [David WECHSLER]

Wechsler Preschool and Primary Scale of Intelligence (WPPSI) an intelligence test for children aged 2 years 6 months to 7 years 3 months that currently includes seven verbal subtests (Information, Vocabulary, Receptive Vocabulary, Word Reasoning, Similarities, Comprehension, Picture Naming) and seven performance subtests (Picture Completion, Picture Concepts, Block Design, Object Assembly, Matrix Reasoning, Symbol Search, Coding). These subtests yield Verbal, Performance, and Full Scale IQs with a mean of 100 and a standard deviation of 15 as well as General Language and Processing Speed index scores. The WPPSI was originally published in 1967; the most recent version is the **WPPSI–III**, published in 2002. [David WECHSLER]

Wednesday Evening Society an informal group of Sigmund FREUD's disciples who met with him for instruction in psychoanalysis, beginning in 1902. The Society evolved into the larger **Vienna Psychoanalytic Society** in 1910. See also VIENNESE SCHOOL.

weekend hospitalization a form of PARTIAL HOSPITALIZATION in which psychiatric patients function in the community during the week but spend the weekend in the hospital.

we-group *n.* see INGROUP.

weight *n.* **1.** heaviness: the extent of downward gravitational force exerted on an object or body. **2.** a coefficient or multiplier used in an equation or statistical investigation and applied to a particular variable to reflect the contribution to the data.

weight discrimination the ability to distinguish differences in weight among stimuli.

weighted application blank (WAB) in personnel selection, a scored application form used to obtain and evaluate BIOGRAPHICAL DATA. The applicant's response to each question on the form is scored according to both (a) the answer given and (b) the relative importance of the question as a means of differentiating between suitable and unsuitable candidates. Compare STANDARD APPLICATION BLANK.

weighted item an item on a test or scale that is multiplied by a WEIGHT other than 1.0 before scores on items are combined. See WEIGHTING.

weighted kappa a variant on the KAPPA statistic for interrater agreement in which the magnitude of differences between categories is included in the analysis. Thus if two raters differ by two categories, that difference is weighted more heavily than if they differ only by one category.

weighted least squares a variation on the ordinary least squares procedures utilized in the GENERAL LINEAR MODEL in which the variables are weighted by constants of PROPORTIONALITY. Weighted least squares is most often used when assumptions of HOMOGENEITY OF VARIANCE are violated.

weighted test a test in a test battery that has been multiplied by a WEIGHT other than 1.0 before scores on tests are combined. See WEIGHTING.

weight experiment a psychophysical experiment in which participants lift weights and their sensitivity to small differences in weight is judged.

weighting *n.* the process of multiplying test items, subtests, tests that are part of a test battery, or other measures that are components of a total score by a WEIGHT other than 1.0. If all components were to be weighted by 1.0, the result would be **equal weighting**, which is essentially no weighting.

weight regulation a process, governed by a complex

array of neural mechanisms and structures (including the hypothalamus), in which the brain seeks an optimum balance between food intake and energy expenditure by the organism after a certain body weight is achieved. A number of other factors, such as environmental stimuli, may influence the process.

Weight Watchers a widely available weight loss and control program that includes aspects of both SUPPORT GROUPS and SELF-HELP GROUPS.

Weismannism *n.* see GERM PLASM.

Welch–Aspin t test a variant on the T TEST that is used when the assumption of HOMOGENEITY OF VARIANCE is violated.

well-being *n.* a state of happiness, contentment, low levels of distress, overall good physical and mental health and outlook, or good quality of life.

Wellbutrin *n.* a trade name for BUPROPION.

well-defined problem a problem with clear initial conditions and goals and standard methods for proceeding from the former to the latter.

well-integrated personality see INTEGRATED PERSONALITY.

wellness concept the idea that health care programs should be actively involved in the promotion of **wellness**, seen as a dynamic state of physical, mental, and social well-being, rather than merely concerned with the treatment and prevention of illness. Wellness is viewed as the result of four key factors over which an individual has some control: human biology, environment, health care organization, and lifestyle.

wellness program a health care program emphasizing the WELLNESS CONCEPT.

Welsh Figure Preference Test (**WFPT**) a nonverbal personality assessment in which participants indicate "like" or "dislike" for each of 400 black-and-white figures varying in complexity from simple line drawings of geometric figures to detailed, multiline abstractions. Initially designed to diagnose psychiatric disorders, the WFPT currently includes several scales intended to measure a variety of constructs, both pathological (e.g., anxiety, repression) and nonpathological (e.g., creativity, originality). See also BARRON–WELSH ART SCALE. [originally developed in 1949 by George S. **Welsh** (1918–1990), U.S. psychologist]

Weltanschauung *n.* any fundamental understanding of the universe, and of humankind's place within it, held by a person, a culture, or a subculture (German, "worldview"). Such a worldview will be influential in the material development of a culture, as well as in those theories and philosophies that a culture may produce. It establishes the UNIVERSE OF DISCOURSE that prevails among its adherents, affecting their practical attitudes and behaviors as well as their theoretical commitments.

Werdnig–Hoffmann disease see SPINAL MUSCULAR ATROPHY. [Guido **Werdnig** (1862–1919), Austrian neurologist; Johann **Hoffmann** (1857–1919), German neurologist]

Werner's disease a rare hereditary disorder affecting both sexes and characterized by signs of premature aging that may appear before the age of 20. The patients are usually of short stature. The symptoms include graying and loss of hair, skin atrophy, underactivity of the endocrine glands, accumulation of calcium deposits in the tissues, and a form of arthritis. Also called **progeria adultorum**; **Werner's syndrome**. [Carl Otto **Werner** (1879–1936), German physician]

Wernicke–Korsakoff syndrome a syndrome resulting from chronic alcoholism or nutritional insufficiency, associated with deficiency of vitamin B_1 (thiamine). The syndrome is characterized by an acute confusional stage, ATAXIA, and oculomotor problems (see WERNICKE'S ENCEPHALOPATHY), followed by chronic changes in mental status and memory (see KORSAKOFF'S SYNDROME). Lesions are centered in the midbrain, cerebellum, and DIENCEPHALON. [Karl **Wernicke** (1848–1904), German neurologist; Sergei S. **Korsakoff** (1854–1900), Russian psychiatrist]

Wernicke's aphasia a loss of the ability to comprehend sounds or speech (auditory amnesia), and in particular to understand or repeat spoken language (see AUDITORY APHASIA) and to name objects or qualities (see ANOMIA). The condition is a result of brain damage and may be associated with other disorders of communication, including ALEXIA, ACALCULIA, or AGRAPHIA. Also called **Bastian's aphasia**; **cortical sensory aphasia**. See APHASIA. [Karl **Wernicke**]

Wernicke's area a region in the posterior temporal gyrus of the left hemisphere of the cerebrum in the brain, containing nerve tissue associated with the interpretation of sounds. Also called **Wernicke's speech area**. See also SPEECH AREA. [Karl **Wernicke**, who reported in 1874 a lack of comprehension of speech in patients who had suffered a brain lesion in that area]

Wernicke's encephalopathy a neurological disorder caused by a deficiency of vitamin B_1 (thiamine). The principal symptoms are confusion, oculomotor abnormalities (GAZE PALSY and NYSTAGMUS), and ataxia. The disorder is most frequently associated with chronic alcoholism but is also found in cases of pernicious anemia, gastric cancer, and malnutrition. These symptoms are likely to resolve with thiamine treatment, although most individuals then develop severe retrograde and anterograde amnesia as well as impairment in other areas of cognitive functioning, including executive functions (see KORSAKOFF'S SYNDROME). Also called **cerebral beriberi**; **Wernicke's disease**. [first described in 1881 by Karl **Wernicke**]

Wernicke's theory a theory that integrates the contributions of WERNICKE'S AREA and BROCA'S AREA in the production and understanding of speech. [proposed in 1874 by Karl **Wernicke**]

Wertheimer, Max (1880–1943) German-born U.S. psychologist. Wertheimer earned his doctorate at the University of Würzburg in 1904, studying with Karl Marbe (1869–1953) and Oswald Külpe (1862–1915). After a number of years lecturing at the University of Frankfurt, he moved to the University of Berlin, where he was appointed professor in 1922. He returned to Frankfurt as chair in 1929, but with the Nazi rise to power he emigrated to the United States in 1933 and taught at the New School for Social Research in New York City. Wertheimer is widely regarded as the founder of GESTALT PSYCHOLOGY, along with Wolfgang KÖHLER and Kurt KOFFKA. His most important contributions included his early experiments on the PHI PHENOMENON, which is the perception of APPARENT MOVEMENT when two separate stationary lines are presented in rapid succession. Unable to account for this phenomenon on the basis of existing theories of perception, Wertheimer suggested in a 1912 paper that certain perceptions, such as the phi phenomenon, were based not on the isolated elements contained in the thing perceived but in the PERCEPT taken as a whole (gestalt). Wertheimer is also famous for his work on the GESTALT PRINCIPLES OF ORGANIZATION and PRODUCTIVE THINKING. The latter research was published posthumously as the book *Productive Thinking* (1945), which has been influential in the field of cognitive psychology.

Werther syndrome CLUSTER SUICIDES induced by the suicide of a well-known or popular role model whose death is given extensive coverage by the media. The phenomenon is named for the first identified instance of media-triggered suicide, which occurred in 1774 following the publication of Goethe's novel *Die Leiden des jungen Werthers* (The Sorrows of Young Werther). The book triggered a fad, in that many young men of the time imitated the eccentric style of dress of the book's hero, Werther, by dressing in blue and yellow. Some young men also killed themselves in the same way Werther did in the novel, causing the book to be banned in some communities.

Westermarck effect the proposal that people who grow up in close proximity in the same household do not find one another sexually attractive later in life. It is based on the observation that people who had extensive contact with one another as children rarely ever married, despite being available as mates. [Edward **Westermarck** (1862–1939), Finnish anthropologist]

Western Aphasia Battery (**WAB**) a test battery that evaluates numerous aspects of language—spontaneous speech, comprehension, repetition, naming, etc.—and is used to determine the severity and type of a language disturbance as well as to assess such skills as writing, reading, and calculation. [developed by Canadian psychologist Andrew Kertesz (1935–)]

Western blot a method of detecting a particular protein molecule in a mixture (e.g., a sample from a tissue or organ). It involves separating the proteins with GEL ELECTROPHORESIS, blotting the separated proteins onto nitrocellulose, then using an isotopically labeled or enzyme-linked antibody to bind to and highlight the protein of interest. [named by analogy with SOUTHERN BLOT]

wet dream see NOCTURNAL EMISSION.

wet-globe bulb temperature a measure to account for effects of temperature and humidity and to monitor stress in order to prevent heat-related injuries or illnesses.

wet nurse a lactating woman who nurses an infant other than her own.

wet pack see HYDROTHERAPY.

Wever–Bray effect see COCHLEAR MICROPHONIC. [Ernest Glen **Wever** (1902–1991), U.S. psychologist; Charles **Bray** (1904–1982), U.S. otologist]

WF abbreviation for WORD FLUENCY.

WFPT abbreviation for WELSH FIGURE PREFERENCE TEST.

WGTA abbreviation for WISCONSIN GENERAL TEST APPARATUS.

what pathway see VENTRAL STREAM.

wheelchair *n.* a chair with wheels designed to increase the mobility of individuals unable to walk without assistance. One of the oldest ASSISTIVE TECHNOLOGY devices, wheelchairs may be manual (i.e., self-propelled by pushing on the wheels or propelled by an assisting individual from behind) or motorized (battery powered).

wheelchair sport a type of recreational or rehabilitative activity in which individuals with physical disabilities participate in competitive individual and team sports with the use of a wheelchair.

where pathway see DORSAL STREAM.

whiplash effect a painful injury to the soft tissues of the neck, which can persist for months, resulting from a sudden change of motion of the body. This most usually results from car accidents in which the car is struck from behind, causing the head to be snapped back suddenly. Also called **cervical sprain syndrome**.

whipping *n.* striking a person with a rod, lash, or similar instrument. See FLAGELLATION.

Whipple's disease see LIPODYSTROPHY. [George Hoyt **Whipple** (1878–1976), U.S. pathologist]

whipsawing *n.* **1.** increasing productivity by pairing two or more individuals or groups on a joint task, often with a competitive orientation. The term derives from the whipsaw, a type of saw with handles on both ends of the cutting blade used by paired workers to saw large timbers. **2.** undermining the unity of employees (and their unions) by pitting them against one another in competitive work settings.

whirl sensation the sensation of spinning, mediated by the VESTIBULAR SYSTEM. See DIZZINESS; VERTIGO.

whisker barrel a barrel-shaped column of neurons in the SOMATOSENSORY AREA of some animals that receives information from a particular whisker.

White, Robert W. (1904–2001) U.S. psychologist. White earned his doctorate in psychology at Harvard University in 1937, working with personality researcher Henry A. Murray (1893–1988). He joined the faculty at Harvard and remained there throughout his career, eventually chairing the Department of Social Relations. White is best known for the holistic study of the personality. He argued for INTRINSIC MOTIVATION at a time when dominant personality theories viewed humans as motivated solely by the need to reduce such basic drives as sex, hunger, and thirst. He also countered the increasing use of statistical methods in personality research, urging the importance of the CASE-STUDY method rather than the statistical method that emphasizes aggregating data from many individuals and analyzing that aggregate data. White's most important writings include *The Abnormal Personality* (1948), *Lives in Progress: A Study of the Natural Growth of Personality* (1952), and *The Enterprise of Living: A View of Personal Growth* (1972). He was awarded the Murray Award of the Society for Personality and Social Psychology.

white blood cell see LEUKOCYTE.

white-collar crime criminal activities committed by people of high respectability and social status in the course of their jobs. Examples include fraud and embezzlement.

white-collar worker an employee whose work involves very little or no physical labor, especially one in a salaried professional position. Such people have traditionally worked in an office environment. Compare BLUE-COLLAR WORKER.

white commissure a bundle of MYELINATED FIBERS, both sensory and motor, that crosses from one side of the spinal cord to the other, linking the ascending and descending columns of WHITE MATTER fibers on either side. It arches around the ventral median fissure of the spinal cord. Also called **anterior white commissure**; **ventral white commissure**.

white light 1. light that is a mixture of all of the visible wavelengths in the spectrum. White light can also be produced by a mixture of three single wavelengths of appropriate intensity, the PRIMARY COLORS. **2.** a brilliant white visual field reported to be experienced by some people when dying or undergoing NEAR-DEATH EXPERIENCES.

white matter parts of the nervous system composed of nerve fibers that are enclosed in a MYELIN SHEATH, which gives a white coloration to otherwise grayish neural structures. The sheaths cover only the fibers, so regions containing mainly CELL BODIES are gray. Compare GRAY MATTER.

whiteness constancy a perception of white surfaces as having the same brightness even when lighting changes are made. See also PERCEPTUAL CONSTANCY; BRIGHTNESS CONSTANCY.

white noise see NOISE.

whiteout syndrome a psychosis occurring in individuals (e.g., arctic explorers and mountaineers) who are exposed to the same white, impoverished environment for long periods of time.

white rami communicantes the MYELINATED FIBERS of the preganglionic branches running from SPINAL ROOTS to ganglia of the SYMPATHETIC CHAIN in the thoracic and upper two lumbar segments.

whitiko *n.* see WINDIGO.

Whitten effect the effect of CHEMICAL COMMUNICATION in inducing ovulation. In some rodent species, females ovulate when exposed to odors or scents from adult males. Other effects of chemical signals on reproduction include the BRUCE EFFECT and the LEE–BOOT EFFECT. See also VANDENBERGH EFFECT. [Wesley K. **Whitten** (1918–), Australian reproductive physiologist]

WHO abbreviation for WORLD HEALTH ORGANIZATION.

whole-channel *adj.* denoting or relating to an approach to teaching in which information is taught using methods that employ all the possible senses.

whole-language approach a top-down approach to teaching reading that emphasizes the reader's active construction of meaning and often excludes the use of phonics.

whole method of learning a learning technique in which the entire block of material is memorized, as opposed to learning the material in parts. Compare PART METHOD OF LEARNING.

whole report a method used in studies of ICONIC MEMORY in which the participant attempts to recall all of the presented information. Compare PARTIAL REPORT.

whole-word method a widely used method of language and reading instruction based on the idea that students should grasp the meaning of entire words at a time and use complete words when they talk, without focusing on the individual sounds that make up those words. This method is based on learning strategies originally used to teach deaf children to read, although current findings show that deaf children actually use phonetics for learning and practicing sign language. Also called **look-say**; **sight method**. Compare PHONICS. [developed by U.S. educator and cleric Thomas H. Gallaudet (1787–1851)]

whooping cough a highly contagious bacterial infection that affects the respiratory tract from the nasopharynx to the bronchioles. It is characterized by spasmodic coughing that commonly ends in a prolonged high-pitched whooping inspiration. Complications can include brain hemorrhage, convulsions, ANOXIA, and damage to vision and hearing. Also called **pertussis**.

Whorfian hypothesis see LINGUISTIC DETERMINISM. [Benjamin Lee **Whorf** (1897–1941), U.S. linguist]

WHO (10) Well-Being Index a 10-item questionnaire, commissioned by the World Health Organization, that includes negative and positive aspects of well-being in a single unidimensional scale. The index has been used to examine well-being in patients experiencing chronic diseases.

Wh- question a question that begins with *Who, What, Where, When,* or *How*.

wicca *n.* see WITCHCRAFT.

wideband procedures testing and measurement techniques that are relatively more subjective in nature, such as PROJECTIVE TECHNIQUES and interviews. Wideband procedures typically provide a broader range of information (i.e., have greater BANDWIDTH) but are less accurate (i.e., have reduced FIDELITY) than relatively more objective techniques.

Wide Range Achievement Test (**WRAT**) a standard assessment tool used to obtain a quick, accurate assessment of reading, spelling, and arithmetic skills. The most recent version, the **Wide Range Achievement Test–Third Edition (WRAT-3)**, was published in 1993 for use with children, adolescents, and adults in determining skill deficits as well as appropriate levels of instruction; it can be one component in identifying a learning disability. The **Wide Range Achievement Test–Expanded Edition** (**WRAT–Expanded**), published in 2001, is designed to measure academic achivement in children and adolescents. [originally developed in 1936 by U.S. psychologist Joseph F. Jastak]

wide-range test a test with relatively low floor and high ceiling, that is, a test with items that measure performance at very low and very high levels of scoring.

Widow-to-Widow Program a peer support program focusing on bereavement, grief, and mourning, thought to be the first of its kind and serving as a model for many subsequent organizations. U.S. social worker Phyllis R. Silverman started the Widow-to-Widow Program in 1964. The program draws on the experience and compassion of people who have suffered similar losses, providing support as an alternative or complementary approach to professional GRIEF COUNSELING and therapy and to medical management.

Wiener Schule see VIENNESE SCHOOL.

wife beating see BATTERED WOMEN.

wife swapping a form of GROUP SEX in which two or more married couples exchange spouses by mutual agreement for the purpose of sexual intercourse. The practice of wife swapping may also include watching the husband or wife participate in sexual intercourse with another person's spouse. Also called **mate swapping**; **partner swapping**. See also SWINGING.

wihtigo (**wihtiko**) *n.* see WINDIGO.

Wilcoxon test a nonparametric test of the difference in distribution for matched sets of research participants or for repeatedly observed participants. [Frank **Wilcoxon** (1892–1965), Irish mathematician and statistician]

wild boy of Aveyron a supposed feral child, unsocialized and nonliterate, found living in the woods near Aveyron around 1800 and studied by French physician Jean Itard (1775–1838). It has been suggested that the boy was actually autistic and abandoned in the woods by his parents. Itard's attempts to teach the boy inspired his pupil, French-born U.S. physician Edouard Séguin (1812–1880), to develop materials and methods for training those with learning difficulties. See also WOLF CHILDREN.

wilderness experience a group program in which demanding outdoor expeditions are undertaken for extended periods to foster enhanced self-efficacy, motivation, and social skills in the participants. The approach often benefits adolescents with behavioral problems.

Wilder's law of initial values see LAW OF INITIAL VALUES. [Joseph **Wilder** (1895–1976), U.S. psychiatrist]

Wildervanck's syndrome a hereditary disorder associated with KLIPPEL–FEIL SYNDROME and characterized by deafness and paralysis of the abducens nerve. Cranial asymmetry and mental retardation may also occur. [reported in 1952 by L. S. **Wildervanck**, Dutch geneticist]

Wilks's lambda (symbol: Λ) a statistic based on the difference in mean VECTORS among *k* samples used to test hypotheses about group mean vector differences in multivariate testing procedures, such as MULTIVARIATE ANALYSIS OF VARIANCE. [Samuel Stanley **Wilks** (1906–1964), U.S. mathematician]

will *n.* the capacity or faculty by which a human being is able to make choices and determine his or her own behaviors in spite of influences external to the person. See FREE WILL; VOLITION.

will disturbance a deficiency or lack of willpower identified by Swiss psychiatrist Eugen Bleuler (1857–1939) as a basic symptom of schizophrenia. The person may appear apathetic and lacking in objectives and motivation. Another form of will disturbance is characterized by a high degree of activity that is trivial, inappropriate, or purposeless.

will-do factors factors contributing to an employee's performance in a job that are attributable to his or her motivation rather than to his or her knowledge or ability.

Wille zur Macht see WILL TO POWER.

Williams syndrome (**Williams–Barratt syndrome**; **Williams–Beuren syndrome**) see HYPERCALCEMIA SYNDROME. [described in the 1960s by J. C. P. **Williams**, 20th-century New Zealand cardiologist; Brian Gerald **Barratt–Boyes** (1924–), British cardiologist; and Alois J. **Beuren** (1919–1984), German cardiologist]

Williams v. Florida an influential 1970 U.S. Supreme Court ruling that juries of less than 12 people are constitutionally permissible. The court indicated that although the size of a jury is an important factor in its effectiveness, juries having as few as 6 members could function as effectively as juries of 12 members.

Willie M. class action a class action lawsuit in North Carolina, settled out of court in 1979, that established a special class of children aged 18 years and younger. Class members have emotional, mental, or neurological disabilities, are violent or assaultive, have been placed in residential programs, and have not received appropriate treatment or educational services. Related service entitlements are specified in the agreement between the defendants and plaintiffs. The class persists to the present day.

Willowbrook Consent Judgment a landmark agreement in 1975 between agencies, parents, and friends of the court (the plaintiffs) and New York State (the defendant), detailing the rights of people with mental retardation who lived at the Willowbrook State School in Staten Island, NY, for several years. It set out standards for the residents' living environment, evaluation of services, personnel, education, recreation, food and nutrition services, dental services, psychological services, physical therapy services, speech and audiology services, medical and nursing services, safety procedures, treatment and medication, building maintenance, emergencies, records, and movement to community settings. Willowbrook State School was later renamed Staten Island Developmental Center; it closed during the 1980s. Also called **Willowbrook Consent Decree**.

willpower *n.* the ability to carry out one's intentions. See SELF-CONTROL.

will psychology see ACTION THEORY.

will therapy a form of psychotherapy based on the theory that neuroses can be avoided or overcome by asserting the will (or "counterwill") and by achieving independence. According to this theory, life is a long struggle to separate oneself from the mother psychologically, just as one separates oneself physically from the mother during birth. Also called **Rankian therapy**. See also BIRTH TRAUMA. [developed by Austrian psychologist Otto Rank (1884–1939)]

will to live see WILL TO SURVIVE.

will to meaning the need to find a suitable meaning and purpose for one's life. Will to meaning is the basis and fundamental motivation of LOGOTHERAPY, a technique for addressing problems related to the contemporary experience of MEANINGLESSNESS. See EXISTENTIAL VACUUM. [defined by Austrian psychiatrist Viktor Emil Frankl (1905–1998)]

will to power 1. in the individual psychology of Alfred ADLER, the determination to strive for superiority and domination, which he believed to be particularly strong in men who feel a need to escape the feelings of insecurity and inferiority that they associate with femininity. **2.** in the thought of German philosopher Friedrich Nietzsche (1844–1900), the determination to affirm oneself through courage, strength, and pride, which necessitates casting off the "slave morality" of Christianity, democracy, and false compassion. The will to power is the motive principle of the SUPERMAN. Also called **Wille zur Macht**.

will to survive the determination to live in spite of an adverse situation (e.g., a severe illness or disabling disorder) or extreme conditions (e.g., lack of food and water or imprisonment in a concentration camp). Also called **will to live**.

windigo *n.* a severe CULTURE-BOUND SYNDROME occurring among northern Algonquin Indians living in Canada and the northeastern United States. The syndrome is characterized by delusions of becoming possessed by a flesh-eating monster (the windigo) and is manifested in symptoms including depression, violence, a compulsive desire for human flesh, and sometimes actual cannibalism. Also called **whitiko**; **wihtigo**; **wihtiko**; **witigo**; **witiko**; **wittigo**.

windmill illusion an illusion of motion of rotating objects, such as windmills and automobile wheels, which appear to reverse direction intermittently.

wind tunnel a structure designed as a corridor through which air can be blown at controlled velocities and patterns of turbulence. Wind tunnels are mainly used to test the performance of aircraft or other objects or materials in a simulated outdoor environment. They may also be utilized in experiments to study the effects of wind or changing air pressures on the performance or behavior of humans or nonhuman animals. See also AIR-PRESSURE EFFECTS.

winkte *n.* see TWO-SPIRIT.

win–lose dynamic the conflict-promoting processes that occur in situations whose COMPETITIVE REWARD STRUCTURES cause participants to feel they can only succeed if others fail.

winner effect the increased likelihood that an individual will win aggressive encounters as a result of having won previous encounters. The winner effect may be associated with increased levels of testosterone. Compare LOSER EFFECT.

win–stay, lose–shift strategy in discrimination learning, a mental or behavioral strategy in which an organism continues to give the same response as long as it is being rewarded for doing so but changes the response once it is no longer being rewarded. The opposite **win–shift, lose–stay strategy** may also be seen: An organism changes responses when rewarded and maintains the response when not rewarded.

wireless *adj.* denoting or relating to communication (e.g., radio, broadcast television) without the use of wires to connect the communicating sites. Wireless communication is used both for very long-range transmission (as with communication satellites) and for very short-range transmission (to connect computers within the same building).

WISC abbreviation for WECHSLER INTELLIGENCE SCALE FOR CHILDREN.

Wisconsin Card Sorting Test (**WCST**) a test that requires participants to deduce from feedback (right vs. wrong) how to sort a series of cards depicting different geometric shapes in various colors and quantities. Once the participant has identified the underlying sorting principle (e.g., by color) and correctly sorts 10 consecutive cards, the principle is changed without notification. Although the task involves many aspects of brain function, it is primarily considered a test of EXECUTIVE FUNCTIONS. [originally developed in 1948 by U.S. psychologists David A. Grant (1916–) and Esta A. Berg]

Wisconsin General Test Apparatus (**WGTA**) an apparatus used to study primate learning that consists of a tray on which various objects can be placed and a movable partition over the tray separating the animal from the experimenter. A small piece of food is hidden beneath one of the objects, and the animal must displace that object to obtain the food reward. This basic design has been modified to create a number of learning tasks of varying complexity. [developed by Harry F. HARLOW]

wisdom *n.* the ability of an individual to make sound decisions, to find the right—or at least good—answers to difficult and important life questions, and to give advice about the complex problems of everyday life and interpersonal relationships. In his theory of wisdom, German psychologist Paul Baltes (1939–) emphasized the role of knowledge and life experience in achieving wisdom. In his **balance theory of wisdom**, U.S. psychologist Robert Sternberg (1949–) emphasized the importance of applying one's intelligence toward a common good through balancing of one's own, others', and institutional interests.

wish *n.* **1.** in psychoanalytic theory, the psychological manifestation of a biological INSTINCT that operates on a CONSCIOUS or UNCONSCIOUS level. **2.** in general language, any desire or longing.

wish-fulfillment *n.* in psychoanalytic theory, the gratification in fantasy or in a dream of a WISH associated with a biological INSTINCT.

wishful thinking a thought process in which one interprets a fact or reality according to what one wishes or desires it to be.

wit *n.* **1.** a mental function consisting of the ability to make amusing, incisive comments that throw light on a subject or person. **2.** in psychoanalysis, a verbal retort, jibe, or pun that suddenly and strikingly releases a repressed or hidden feeling or attitude. **—witty** *adj.*

witchcraft *n.* **1.** the supposed use of magical powers and practices to cause harm to other people or their property, including crops and livestock. In Christian countries, witches were believed to derive their powers from a compact with the devil, whom they worshipped in orgiastic rites known as witches' sabbaths. Such beliefs led to outbreaks of fanatical persecution in the 16th and 17th centuries (so-called **witch hysteria** or **witch mania**), in which the great majority of the victims were women (especially poor, old, and illiterate women). Belief in the power of witchcraft remains prevalent in many traditional societies (notably in Africa). **2.** a neopagan religion revolving around reverence for nature and goddess worship. Also called **wicca**.

witch doctor in many traditional societies, a person believed to possess magical powers who uses these chiefly to cure sickness and protect people from the WITCHCRAFT of others. See also SHAMAN.

withdrawal *n.* see SUBSTANCE WITHDRAWAL.

withdrawal-destructiveness *n.* in the psychoanalysis of Erich FROMM, a style of relating based on withdrawal and isolation from others, destructive behavior directed toward others, or a combination of the two. Fromm held that this style of relating was motivated by a need to establish emotional distance arising from a fear of dependency.

withdrawal dyskinesia distortion of voluntary movements (see DYSKINESIA) associated with withdrawal from drugs or other substances.

withdrawal reaction **1.** an extreme form of SOCIAL WITHDRAWAL that sometimes occurs in severe cases of MAJOR DEPRESSIVE EPISODE. **2.** a reemergence or exacerbation of symptoms as a result of cessation of treatment with medication, such as anxiolytics.

withdrawal reflex a reflex that may be elicited by any painful stimulus or unexpected threat to the well-being of the individual. It is characterized by sudden movement away from the potentially damaging stimulus, which requires rapid coordination of neuromuscular units.

withdrawing response in behavioral psychology, any behavior designed to sever contact with a noxious stimulus. See also ESCAPE BEHAVIOR.

Witherspoon excludables prospective jurors who so strongly oppose the death penalty that they are unwilling to consider it as a sentencing option and are therefore excludable from a DEATH-QUALIFIED JURY. The allusion is to the 1968 U.S. Supreme Court decision in *Witherspoon v. Illinois*. See also WAINWRIGHT V. WITT.

within-cell variance see POOLED VARIANCE.

within-dimension attitude consistency the extent to which pieces of ATTITUDE-RELEVANT KNOWLEDGE related to a single underlying dimension (i.e., a distinct category of information) are evaluatively consistent with one another. If the information within each underlying dimension of the attitude is evaluatively consistent (e.g., all positive or all negative), within-dimension attitude consistency is high. However, this type of consistency does not necessarily imply that CROSS-DIMENSION ATTITUDE CONSISTENCY is high. For example, the information related to one dimension could be extremely positive, and the information related to a second dimension could be extremely negative, resulting in high within-dimension consistency but low cross-dimension consistency. Likewise, high cross-dimension consistency does not necessarily imply high within-dimension consistency. See also AMBIVALENCE OF AN ATTITUDE; COMPLEXITY OF AN ATTITUDE.

within-group variance the variance among identically treated individuals within the same group or population. Also called **intraclass variance**.

within-subjects design an experimental design in which the effects of treatments are seen through the comparison of scores of the same participant observed under all the treatment conditions. Compare BETWEEN-SUBJECTS DESIGN.

witigo (**witiko**) *n.* see WINDIGO.

Witmer, Lightner (1867–1956) U.S. psychologist. Witmer earned his doctorate in 1892 at the University of Leipzig under Wilhelm WUNDT, after initial graduate study under James McKeen CATTELL at the University of Pennsylvania. He returned to the University of Pennsylvania as an instructor in psychology and remained there for the rest of his career. Witmer is best known as the founder of CLINICAL PSYCHOLOGY in the United States, establishing the first psychological clinic in 1896 and founding the first clinical psychology journal, *The Psychological Clinic,* in 1907. At a time when prominent experimentalists, such as Edward B. TITCHENER, were arguing that psychology should be a pure research science, Witmer was a powerful force arguing for and demonstrating the importance of the applied aspects of psychology. His students went on to become leaders in vocational guidance, speech therapy, and school psychology, as well as clinical psychology.

wittigo *n.* see WINDIGO.

Wittmaack–Ekbom syndrome see EKBOM'S SYNDROME. [Theodor **Wittmaack**, German physician; Karl-Axel **Ekbom** (1907–1977), Swedish physician]

Witzelsucht *n.* a type of joking mania (from German, literally, "compulsive wisecracking"), characterized by a morbid desire to tell poor jokes and meaningless stories, that can be a symptom of damage to the FRONTAL LOBE of the brain. See also MORIA.

WLM abbreviation for WOMEN'S LIBERATION MOVEMENT.

WMS abbreviation for WECHSLER MEMORY SCALE.

wobble switch an interface between a device and the user that is similar to a joystick. The switch is activated when the stick is pushed off-center in any direction and can therefore be activated by gross body movements of users with physical disabilities.

Wohlwill–Corino Andrade syndrome see ANDRADE'S SYNDROME.

wolf children two girls who were apparently raised by wolves in India and who adopted all the major lupine life patterns, such as bolting food, howling in the night, and running on all fours. When captured, they were approximately 18 months and 8 years old, respectively; the younger girl died within a year. The older girl lived until about age 17 and, though never fully civilized, learned to walk on two feet in a half-crouch, acquired a 50-word vocabulary, and learned to wear clothes and run errands. See also WILD BOY OF AVEYRON.

Wolffian duct a rudimentary duct system in the embryo that develops into structures of the male reproductive system (the epididymis, vas deferens, and seminal vesicles). In the female, the Wolffian duct does not develop. Compare MÜLLERIAN DUCTS. [Kaspar F. **Wolff** (1734–1794), German embryologist]

Wolf Man in the annals of psychoanalysis, a landmark case reported by Sigmund FREUD in 1918. It involved a conversion symptom (constipation), a phobia (for wolves and other animals), a religious obsession (piety alternating with blasphemous thoughts), and an appetite disturbance (anorexia), all of which proved to be reactions to early experiences. Freud saw this case as confirmation for his theory of infantile sexuality.

Wolman's disease a genetic metabolic disorder characterized by a deficiency of acid lipase, an enzyme needed to break down lipid molecules. The adrenal glands become enlarged and calcified. Psychomotor development in affected infants appears delayed, and mental retardation may be present but difficult to document due to overriding effects of vomiting, diarrhea, and other signs of acute illness. Also called **primary familial xanthomatosis**. [Moshe **Wolman** (1914–), Polish-born Israeli pathologist]

woman-centered psychology an approach to psychology that emphasizes the physical, psychological, and social experiences that are particularly characteristic of women. See ENGENDERING PSYCHOLOGY; FEMINIST PSYCHOLOGY.

womb envy 1. in psychoanalytic theory, the envy felt by some men for the reproductive capacity of women, regarded as an unconscious motive that leads them to denigrate women. See also VAGINAL ENVY. [proposed by German-born U.S. psychoanalyst Karen D. Horney (1885–1952)] **2.** the desire of a transsexual, or of a transvestite male whose gender identity is female, to wear female clothing or have sex-change surgery.

womb fantasy in psychoanalytic theory, the FANTASY of returning to the womb or existing in the womb, usually expressed in symbolic form, for example, living under water or being alone in a cavern.

women's liberation movement (**WLM**) **1.** a SOCIAL MOVEMENT, derived from earlier womens' social activism (e.g., the suffragist movement of the 19th and early 20th centuries), that came into existence in the late 1960s and campaigned for a wide range of feminist goals. These included the securing of (a) equal employment and educational opportunities through legislation and government policy; (b) freedom from male domination through social action against pornography and male violence toward women; and (c) the overthrow of capitalism, which was regarded as essential to achieving gender equality. The movement comprised numerous local women's groups and benefited from an influx of women from the student movement, the anti-Vietnam War movement, and the Civil Rights movement. **2.** more generally, a movement among some women to free themselves from the sexual DOUBLE STANDARD, from total responsibility for child-rearing and homemaking, and from the traditional stereotype of women as fragile, passive, dependent individuals who are governed by emotion rather than reason. See also FEMINISM; RADICAL FEMINISM.

Woodcock–Johnson Psychoeducational Battery an assessment, now in its third edition, that measures cognitive ability and academic achievement in children, young people, or adults. The tests of cognitive ability produce a full-scale intelligence score and determine strengths and weaknesses of information processing. The tests of academic achievement assess abilities in reading, written language, mathematics, and knowledge. They also assess basic skills in each of these areas and the level of application of those skills by the person being assessed. This battery is one of the main diagnostic tools used to evaluate a student for specific learning disabilities. Test results on the cognitive portion, when combined and compared with the results of the achievement portion, reveal the learning style of a student who may have a learning disability, documented by a statistically significant numerical difference between actual performance and cognitive potential. [Richard W. **Woodcock** (1928–), U.S. psychologist; M. Bonner **Johnson**]

Woodworth, Robert Sessions (1869–1962) U.S. psychologist. Woodworth received his doctorate in psychology from Columbia University in 1899, studying under James McKeen CATTELL. In 1903 he joined the faculty of Columbia, where he remained throughout his career. Woodworth is best known for his textbooks, which influenced generations of psychologists and shaped the field of EXPERIMENTAL PSYCHOLOGY for decades. His most important works include the introductory textbook *Psychology* (1921), *Contemporary Schools of Psychology* (1931), and *Experimental Psychology* (1938), which underwent two subsequent revisions. *Experimental Psychology* drew together in a single source the diverse methodologies and areas of research that constituted the growing field. It was so widely influential and provided such a high standard for the field that it was dubbed the "Columbia Bible." A leader in psychology in the United States, Woodworth was president of the American Psychological Association in 1914 and president of the Social Science Research Council in 1931–1932. His honors included the Gold Medal of the American Psychological Foundation (its first such award) and election to the American Academy of Arts and Sciences.

word approximation a speech disturbance in which conventional words are used in unconventional or inappropriate ways (as in METONYMY), or new but understandable words are constructed out of ordinary words (e.g., *easify* for *simplify*).

word-association test a projective test in which the participant responds to a stimulus word with the first word that comes to mind. The technique was invented by British scientist Sir Francis Galton (1822–1911) in 1879 for use in exploring individual differences, and German psychiatrist Emil Kraepelin (1856–1926) was the first to apply it to the study of abnormality.

word attack the method used to break down an unfamiliar word into its basic PHONEMES.

word blindness see ALEXIA.

word count a study of the rate of occurrence or the prevalence of specific words in a designated sample of spoken or written speech, for example, in 50 children's books for third- and fourth-graders or in a particular Presidential address.

word deafness see AUDITORY APHASIA.

word dumbness see EXPRESSIVE APHASIA.

word fluency (**WF**) the ability to list words rapidly in certain designated categories, such as words that begin with a particular letter of the alphabet. The ability is associated with a part of the brain anterior BROCA'S AREA in the dominant frontal lobe. Individuals with lesions in that part of the brain are likely to experience word-fluency deficits in verbal tests and tasks. See also PRIMARY ABILITIES.

word-form dyslexia a type of acquired dyslexia (see ALEXIA) characterized by the inability to recognize and read whole words, which can be read only by spelling them out letter by letter. Also called **spelling dyslexia**.

word-fragment completion task an indirect way of detecting memory for a word presented previously. A word fragment consists of some of the letters of the word with blank spaces for deleted letters; the participant's task is to fill in the blanks. Word fragments are frequently used in tests of IMPLICIT MEMORY.

word-frequency study a study in which the frequency of to-be-remembered words is manipulated to investigate the effect of this variable on later memory. Typically, in studies of FREE RECALL, higher frequency words are better remembered, but in studies of RECOGNITION memory, lower frequency words are better remembered. See also FREQUENCY JUDGMENT.

word hash see WORD SALAD.

word-length effect in a test of MEMORY SPAN, the fact that one can usually remember a greater number of shorter words than longer words. Short-term retention is affected by the length of time it takes to rehearse the words.

word of mouth the unofficial channel of communication in which facts, opinions, rumors, and gossip are transmitted orally from person to person.

word realism see NOMINAL REALISM.

word-recognition skills the cluster of strategies that are used to recognize words in reading, including the instant recognition of SIGHT WORDS, the interpretation of CONTEXT CLUES, and the use of phonics and structural analysis.

word-recognition threshold in tests involving word recognition, the minimum amount of time that a word must be exposed for a person to identify it correctly.

word salad an extreme form of thought disorder, manifest in severely disorganized and virtually incomprehensible speech or writing, marked by severe LOOSENING OF ASSOCIATIONS strongly suggestive of schizophrenia. The person's associations appear to have little or no logical connection. Also called **jargon aphasia**; **paraphrasia**; **word hash**. See also NEOLOGISTIC JARGON; SCHIZOPHRENIC THINKING.

word-span test a test of one's ability to remember in sequential order a list of words.

word spurt the rapid increase in word learning that occurs at about 18 months of age, when it is mostly nouns that are acquired.

word-superiority effect (**WSE**) the finding that, when presented briefly, individual letters are more easily identified in the context of a word than when presented alone. A similar but weaker effect is obtained when letters are presented as part of a pronounceable but meaningless vowel-consonant combination, such as *deet* or *pling*. Also called **Reicher–Wheeler effect**. See CONFIGURAL SUPERIORITY EFFECT; OBJECT-SUPERIORITY EFFECT.

work *n.* **1.** any physical, mental, or emotional activity directed toward accomplishing a task or transforming inputs in the form of physical materials, information, and other resources into goods or services. **2.** the tasks or duties involved in earning a livelihood. **3.** in physics, the product of a force and the distance through which its point of application moves, measured in joules. **—worker** *n.*

workaholic *n.* a colloquial name for an individual who has a compulsive need to work, works to an excessive degree, and has trouble refraining from work. This type of driven overinvolvement in work is often a source of significant stress, interpersonal difficulties, and health problems. See also ERGOMANIA (workaholism).

work decrement 1. a decline in the size or rate of output on a task. **2.** in an experiment, a decline in the magnitude of responses as a function of frequency of the response.

work ethic an emphasis (frequently an overemphasis) on the importance of work or other forms of effortful activity as a social, moral, and psychological good. Associated attitudes include individualism, competitiveness, high personal expectations, and an emphasis on self-discipline, self-improvement, and deferred gratification. The term was introduced by German sociologist Max Weber (1864–1920), who drew a celebrated correlation between the emergence of such an ethic in 16th-century Protestant thought and the origins of European capitalism. Also called **Protestant work ethic**. See also ACHIEVEMENT ETHIC.

work evaluation see EMPLOYEE EVALUATION.

work-flow integration the engineering of work tasks to provide a more efficient coordination of activities among employees involved in interdependent activities.

work-for-pay unit an inpatient or aftercare work facility constituting a component of a comprehensive rehabilitation program for patients with mental disorders. Such units offer prevocational screening and evaluation, vocational training, ego-strength assessment, and simple to complex work-related tasks, performed under supervision, for which patients receive payment. See SHELTERED WORKSHOP.

work function scale in FUNCTIONAL JOB ANALYSIS, any of the dimensions on which tasks are rated to determine the degree of complexity of dealing with data, people, and things.

work group any group of people whose primary objective is to perform a set of assigned tasks. The degree to which this collection becomes a cohesive unit with a distinct identity determines whether a work group becomes a TEAM. See also ACTION GROUP; TASK-ORIENTED GROUP.

working backward a problem-solving strategy in which the solver begins at the goal state and attempts to find a path back to the problem's starting conditions. Compare WORKING FORWARD. See also BACKWARD SEARCH.

working forward a problem-solving strategy in which the solver proceeds from the initial conditions to find a path to the desired goal state. Compare WORKING BACKWARD.

working hypothesis a provisional HYPOTHESIS readily subject to revision upon further experimentation.

working knowledge see ATTITUDE-RELEVANT KNOWLEDGE.

working memory a multicomponent model of SHORT-TERM MEMORY or ACTIVE MEMORY that has a PHONOLOGICAL LOOP to retain verbal information, a VISUOSPATIAL SCRATCHPAD to manipulate visual information, and a CENTRAL EXECUTIVE to deploy attention between them. [first described by British cognitive psychologist Alan D. Baddeley (1934–)]

Working Memory Index an index used in the WECHSLER MEMORY SCALE as well as the Wechsler intelligence tests that evaluates the ability to manipulate and process visual and auditory stimuli in short-term or working memory.

working mother a mother who works outside the home, especially one with small or school-aged children.

working self-concept see PHENOMENAL SELF.

working through 1. in psychotherapy, the process by which clients identify, explore, and deal with psychological issues, on both an intellectual and emotional level, through the presentation of such material to, and in discussion with, the therapist. **2.** in psychoanalysis, the process by which patients gradually overcome their RESISTANCE to the disclosure of unconscious material and are repeatedly brought face to face with the repressed feelings, threatening impulses, and internal conflicts at the root of their difficulties.

working vocabulary see PRODUCTIVE VOCABULARY.

work-limit test a test in which all examinees perform the same task with scores based on the time required for the performance.

work motivation the desire or willingness to make an effort in one's work. Motivating factors may include salary and other benefits, desire for status and recognition, a sense of achievement, relationships with colleagues, and a feeling that one's work is useful or important. A variety of theories of work motivation exist, including the EXISTENCE, RELATEDNESS, AND GROWTH THEORY, the JOB-CHARACTERISTICS MODEL, the PORTER–LAWLER MODEL OF MOTIVATION, the VALENCE–INSTRUMENTALITY–EXPECTANCY THEORY, and the two-factor theory of work motivation (see HYGIENE FACTORS; MOTIVATORS). See also MOTIVATION.

work psychology see INDUSTRIAL AND ORGANIZATIONAL PSYCHOLOGY.

work rehabilitation center a facility in which employees who have been injured recuperate and prepare for returning to employment. Rehabilitation efforts focus on an individual's specific therapeutic needs, include participation in simulated work activities, and incorporate workplace education designed to prevent future injury. See also VOCATIONAL REHABILITATION.

work–rest cycle any fixed or recurring sequence in which time spent performing tasks is interspersed with rest breaks. SCIENTIFIC MANAGEMENT has attempted to determine empirically the ideal work–rest cycle for the optimal performance of tasks.

work-sample test in personnel selection, a job-specific test that replicates the day-to-day tasks required in the job. The applicant may be required to use actual or simulated equipment in a controlled testing situation (e.g., driving a loaded forklift truck around a standard course) or to respond to typical problems or scenarios that occur at work, as in an IN-BASKET TEST. See also SITUATIONAL INTERVIEW.

work satisfaction see JOB SATISFACTION.

workspace *n.* the physical area in which an employee performs his or her main work tasks, together with any fixed equipment. Some typical workspaces include a desk with computer, a station on an assembly line, or the cab of a vehicle.

workspace design in HUMAN ENGINEERING, the design of fixed workstations for effective, comfortable, and safe performance of tasks. Aspects of good workspace design include the placement of materials, tools, machines, and controls within easy reach (see REACH ENVELOPE) and a comfortable, adjustable seat adapted to the particular task. See also EQUIPMENT DESIGN; TOOL DESIGN.

work-study program any of a variety of educational programs combining classroom study with job experience for the purpose of providing students with financial assistance or practical training.

work system 1. from a traditional time and motion perspective (see TIME AND MOTION STUDY), the structures, operations, and schedules required to meet the demands of a production or process system. **2.** from a more holistic, ergonomic perspective, the totality of the technological and environmental factors (physical and social) that are relevant to the human achievement of an organizational objective. See MACROERGONOMICS; SOCIOTECHNICAL SYSTEMS APPROACH; SYSTEMS ENGINEERING.

work team a group of employees working together as a cooperative unit.

work therapy the use of compensated or uncompensated work activities as a therapeutic agent for individuals with mental or physical disorders.

work-up *n.* in health care, a total patient evaluation, which may include laboratory assessments, radiologic series, medical history, and diagnostic procedures.

world design in EXISTENTIAL PSYCHOLOGY, a person's worldview or fundamental orientation toward life: his or her essential mode of BEING-IN-THE-WORLD. The term and concept come from the work of Swiss psychiatrist

Ludwig Binswanger (1881–1966). A person's world design includes the way in which that person integrates the totality of his or her personality with the world as he or she experiences it. Understanding a person's world design is essential in understanding the person.

World Federation for Mental Health an international, nongovernmental association of organizations and individuals formed in 1948 to advance the prevention of mental and emotional disorders, the proper treatment and care of those with such disorders, and the promotion of mental health worldwide. The federation organizes World Mental Health Day.

World Health Organization (**WHO**) a specialized agency of the United Nations that promotes technical medical cooperation among nations, carries out programs to control and eradicate disease, and strives to improve the quality of human life. Founded in 1948, the WHO has four main functions: (a) to give worldwide guidance in the field of health; (b) to set global standards for health; (c) to cooperate with governments in strengthening national health programs; and (d) to develop and transfer appropriate health technology, information, and standards. The WHO defines health as "a state of complete physical, mental and social well-being and not merely the absence of disease or infirmity." Its headquarters are in Geneva, Switzerland.

world regions in the thought of German philosopher Martin Heidegger (1889–1976), three different aspects of a person's lived experience characterized as three worlds simultaneously inhabited by DASEIN: the EIGENWELT, or private and subjective world; the MITWELT, or social world; and the UMWELT, or immediate physical environment.

worldview *n.* see WELTANSCHAUUNG.

World Wide Web (**WWW**) a worldwide system of repositories of information (WEBSITES) about people and organizations that can be accessed by computer users via the Internet. Also called **the Web**.

worm *n.* a computer program designed to replicate itself and to pass its self-replicating code from computer to computer. See also VIRUS.

worry *n.* a state of mental distress or agitation due to concern about an impending or anticipated event, threat, or danger.

worship *n.* **1.** reverence or adoration for a divine or supernatural being, a person, or a principle. **2.** the formal expression of RELIGIOUS FAITH in ritual, prayer, and other prescribed practices.

WPPSI abbreviation for WECHSLER PRESCHOOL AND PRIMARY SCALE OF INTELLIGENCE.

wraparound services a philosophy of care and related services that includes a planning process involving a focal person, concerned family members, and providers of services. It results in a highly individualized set of closely coordinated community services and natural supports for the person and his or her family, which achieves a variety of intervention outcomes. Wraparound services have been developed in several service sectors, including mental health, child welfare, and developmental disabilities, and have been proven effective as an alternative to residential services for multiproblem individuals and their families.

WRAT abbreviation for WIDE RANGE ACHIEVEMENT TEST.

writer's block inhibited ability to start or continue working on a piece of writing. Such difficulty is attributed primarily to psychological factors (e.g., fear of failure) but may also result from fatigue or BURNOUT. Suggested remedies often include writing spontaneously about an unrelated topic, doing more reading, and changing something about the physical environment.

writer's cramp a painful spasm of the muscles involved in writing or typing, which may be a form of OCCUPATIONAL CRAMP or a FUNCTIONAL DISORDER. See also REPETITIVE STRAIN INJURY.

writing angle a characteristic of an individual's handwriting defined by the angle between the horizontal baseline and an imaginary line connecting the top and bottom of individual letters.

writing disorder any motor, sensory, or language disorder that interferes with the ability to write.

writing test any test designed to sample and measure writing skills, which can include the motor act of writing, spelling, grammar, and content.

written aphasia see AGRAPHIA.

wrong number technique a method for assessing individuals' willingness to help members of specific social groups and categories. Researchers call participants on a telephone and emphasize their identity as members of a particular social or ethnic group, such as male or female, Black or White. They claim that they are experiencing a minor emergency (an automobile breakdown), that they have mistakenly dialed the wrong number from a payphone, and that they have now used the last of their coins. The researchers then ask the participants to place a call for them to an auto repair shop, for which they give a number. Willingness to help is indicated if the participant makes the call. [first used by U.S. psychologists Samuel L. Gaertner (1942–) and Leonard B. Bickman (1941–) and described in their 1971 research report]

WSE abbreviation for WORD-SUPERIORITY EFFECT.

W-state *n.* the *w*aking state (see WAKEFULNESS), as opposed to the D-state (see DREAM STATE) and the S-state (sleeping state).

WTPT abbreviation for WALK-THROUGH PERFORMANCE TESTING.

Wundt, Wilhelm Max (1832–1920) German psychologist and physiologist. Wundt received his medical degree in 1855 and his second doctorate in 1857, studying under Johannes Müller (1801–1858). He then served as an assistant to Hermann Von Helmholtz (1821–1894), who had a great influence on him. Wundt became the founder of EXPERIMENTAL PSYCHOLOGY when he established the first official psychological laboratory in Leipzig in 1879. There he and his students applied introspective and psychophysical methods to a wide range of subjects, including reaction time, word associations, attention, judgment, and emotions. A man of encyclopedic knowledge, Wundt published monumental works not only on the history and foundations of psychology, but also on logic, ethics, and the psychological interpretation of history and anthropology. Because his research laboratory became the premier locus of study for the new science of psychology in the late 19th century, Wundt's influence extended around the globe, with his students founding laboratories and university departments when they returned to their countries of origin. His most important works include his *Grundzüge der physiologischen Psychologie* (1873–1874), *Völkerpsychologie: Eine Untersuchung der Entwicklungsgesetze von Sprache, Mythus, und Sitte* (1900–1920), and his many papers published in the journal he founded in 1881, *Philosophische Studien.* See also FOLK PSYCHOLOGY; STRUCTURALISM.

Wundt curve an illusion in which straight lines that appear to be curved when viewed through a prism appear to curve in the opposite direction when the prism is removed. [described in 1898 by Wilhelm Max WUNDT]

Wundt gravity phonometer an apparatus for finding the DIFFERENCE THRESHOLDS for sound intensity. [Wilhelm Max WUNDT]

Wundt's tridimensional theory of emotion see FEELING THEORY OF THREE DIMENSIONS.

Würzburg school a school of psychology developed at the end of the 19th century by German psychologist Oswald Külpe (1862–1915) and his associates in Würzburg, Germany. It arose largely as a reaction to the structuralist approach of Edward B. TITCHENER, who insisted that conscious experience consisted of images that could be analyzed into basic elements (sensations, feelings). For the Würzburg school, the focus was on intangible mental activities, such as judgments, meanings, and DETERMINING TENDENCIES, which were conscious but had no image quality associated with them (see IMAGELESS THOUGHT). See also AUFGABE.

WWW abbreviation for WORLD WIDE WEB.

Wyatt v. Stickney decision a 1972 Alabama District Court decision stipulating that the state could not hold people involuntarily in hospital facilities without proper standards. These standards include a humane environment, adequate staff, and appropriate treatment.

Xanax *n.* a trade name for ALPRAZOLAM.

xanthines *pl. n.* see METHYLXANTHINES.

xantho- (**xanth-**) *combining form* yellow.

xanthocyanopsia *n.* a form of color blindness in which red and green are not perceived and therefore objects are seen in shades of yellow or blue.

xanthomatosis *n.* any of several disorders marked by an accumulation of excess lipids, such as cholesterol, in the body due to a metabolic disturbance. This leads to the formation of foam cells in skin lesions and other symptoms. These disorders include **bulbi xanthomatosis**, marked by fatty degeneration of the cornea; WOLMAN'S DISEASE; **hypercholesterolemic xanthomatosis**, or Type II hyperlipoproteinemia, associated with accelerated atherosclerosis and premature heart attacks; and normal cholesterolemic xanthomatosis (see HAND–CHRISTIAN–SCHÜLLER SYNDROME). A related form of xanthomatosis results in cutaneous lesions and other effects in some people with diabetes.

xanthopsia *n.* see CHROMATOPSIA.

xanthopsin *n.* see VISUAL YELLOW.

x-axis *n.* the horizontal axis on a graph. See ABSCISSA.

X chromosome the SEX CHROMOSOME that is responsible for determining femaleness in humans and other mammals. The body cells of normal females possess two X chromosomes (XX), whereas males have one X chromosome and one Y CHROMOSOME (XY). In humans the X chromosomes carries over 1,000 genes, including many responsible for hereditary diseases (see SEX-LINKED). Abnormal numbers of X chromosomes lead to genetic imbalance and a range of disorders and syndromes. See also FRAGILE X CHROMOSOME.

xeno- (**xen-**) *combining form* different, strange, or foreign. [from Greek *xenos*, "stranger"]

xenoglossophilia *n.* a tendency to use strange or foreign words, particularly in a pretentious manner.

xenoglossy *n.* in parapsychology, the ostensible ability of a person to speak or write in a language that is entirely unknown to him or her. See also LANGUAGE ESP.

xenophobia *n.* **1.** a pathological fear of strangers. **2.** hostile attitudes or aggressive behavior toward people of other nationalities, ethnic groups, or even different regions or neighborhoods. In animals xenophobia is manifested by territorial behavior (see TERRITORIALITY) and is also seen in social groups where intruders are typically attacked and repelled. **—xenophobic** *adj.*

xenorexia *n.* the pathological ingestion of inedible objects.

xeroderma pigmentosum a syndrome acquired as an AUTOSOMAL RECESSIVE trait and marked by extreme photosensitivity. It is caused by a defect in the ability of the body to repair damage to DNA resulting from exposure to ultraviolet light, which leads to cancerous changes in skin cells and increased mortality. MICROCEPHALY, mental retardation, and dwarfism may also be present.

xerophthalmia *n.* excessive dryness of the eyes, due to histological changes in the cornea and conjunctiva. Xerophthalmia is a characteristic symptom of **Sjögren's syndrome**, a systemic autoimmune disease with an onset between 40 and 65 years. Xerophthalmia is also one of the ocular effects of vitamin A deficiency.

X-linked *adj.* see SEX-LINKED.

XO syndrome see TURNER'S SYNDROME.

X-ray *n.* an electromagnetic emission of short wavelength (less than 100 nm) produced by bombarding a heavy metal target, such as tungsten, with high-energy electrons in a vacuum tube. X-rays are used for diagnostic purposes to visualize internal body structures: The radiation can penetrate most substances and produce images of objects on photographic film (see RADIOGRAPH) or can cause certain chemicals to fluoresce. X-rays are also used therapeutically to destroy malignant cells (see RADIATION THERAPY). Also called **roentgen ray**.

XX see SEX CHROMOSOME.

XXX syndrome a rare chromosomal disorder characterized by the presence of three X (female) chromosomes. The majority of affected females are physically and mentally normal. Delays in mental development, when present, are usually mild. This disorder is sometimes associated with PRADER–WILLI SYNDROME. Also called **triple-X condition**.

XXXX syndrome a chromosomal disorder in which a female has four X chromosomes instead of the normal pair. Affected females are likely to have minor physical anomalies and mental retardation; IQs of affected individuals have ranged from 30 to 80 in studies.

XXXXX syndrome a rare chromosomal disorder in which a female has five X chromosomes instead of the normal pair. All affected individuals studied had mental retardation, and some had ocular or other anomalies, such as patent ductus arteriosus (a heart defect), MICROCEPHALY, or limb abnormalities.

XXXXY syndrome a rare chromosomal disorder in which a male inherits three extra X chromosomes resulting in a variety of anomalies, including abnormally small genitalia, a short, broad neck, and hypotonia (flaccid muscles). Most affected individuals have mental retardation, with IQs of less than 60.

XXXY syndrome a relatively rare chromosomal disorder in which a child inherits the full complement of both male and female sex chromosomes. Affected individuals have a normal penis but small testes and prostate, and about half develop enlarged breasts. IQs of those tested have ranged from 20 to 76. Most cases have been found by screening projects in mental institutions and may not represent the spectrum of cases in the general population.

XXY syndrome see KLINEFELTER'S SYNDROME.

XXYY syndrome a chromosomal disorder in which a male is born with a double complement of the normal XY chromosome pair. Skeletal deformities, genital anomalies, and mental retardation are common effects. More than half the affected individuals tested had IQs below 70, and some exhibited bizarre behavior. Enlarged breasts and eunuchoid abdominal and hip fat are among the physical traits.

XY see SEX CHROMOSOME.

xylene *n.* a volatile solvent that, when chronically inhaled, can cause kidney failure and death. See INHALANT.

Xyrem *n.* a trade name for GHB.

XYY syndrome a chromosomal anomaly discovered in 1961 and associated with males who were aggressive or violent in institutions for criminals. It was originally assumed that the extra Y chromosome predisposes males to such behavior, but the theory was modified as XYY anomalies were later found among normal males. Also called **double-Y condition**.

XYZ grouping a program in which school administrators assign students to classes by virtue of their test scores and school records. Students with similar abilities are placed in the same class, with very little diversity. These classes are known as high, middle, and low classes; all of the groups follow the same basic curriculum. Students in the middle and lower classes in XYZ programs do not increase their achievement as compared to students in traditional classes, but students in the higher classes in XYZ programs increase their achievement by about one month on a GRADE-EQUIVALENT scale as compared to students in traditional classes. Self-esteem of lower ability students rises slightly, and self-esteem of higher ability students drops slightly, in XYZ classes. See also ABILITY GROUPING.

XYZ system a theoretical system for specifying colors in terms of three abstract primary colors, X, Y, and Z.

Yy

yagé *n.* see AYAHUASCA.

yakee *n.* see EPENA.

Yale model see MESSAGE-LEARNING APPROACH.

yantra *n.* a visual pattern on which attention is focused during CONCENTRATIVE MEDITATION. Compare MANTRA.

Yates correction a CORRECTION FOR CONTINUITY used in computing chi-square in order to improve the accuracy of the test. See CHI-SQUARE DISTRIBUTION. [Frank **Yates** (1902–1994), British statistician]

yaupon *n.* see CASSINA.

yawning *n.* the act of drawing in through the mouth a volume of air that is much larger than that inhaled in normal respiration, serving to improve oxygen supplies to the brain. Some research indicates that yawning is mediated by the same NEUROTRANSMITTERS in the brain that affect emotions, mood, appetite, and so forth (i.e., serotonin, dopamine, glutamic acid, and nitric oxide). The more of these compounds that are activated in the brain, the greater the frequency of yawns. Yawns can be a form of NONVERBAL COMMUNICATION in that they are contagious and can indicate boredom or disagreement as well as sleepiness.

y-axis *n.* the vertical axis on a graph. See ORDINATE.

Y chromosome the SEX CHROMOSOME that is responsible for determining maleness in humans and other mammals. The body cells of normal males possess one Y chromosome and one X CHROMOSOME (XY). The Y chromosome is much smaller than the X chromosome and is thought to carry just a handful of functioning genes. Hence, males are far more susceptible to SEX-LINKED diseases than females, because the Y chromosome cannot counteract any defective genes carried on the X chromosome.

yea-saying *n.* see RESPONSE ACQUIESCENCE.

yellow-sightedness *n.* see CHROMATOPSIA.

Yerkes, Robert Mearns (1876–1956) U.S. psychobiologist. Earning his doctorate at Harvard University in 1902 under the direction of Hugo MÜNSTERBERG, Yerkes remained there as an instructor until World War I. In 1917, as president of the American Psychological Association, he lobbied to involve psychologists in the war effort and was instrumental in developing the Army Alpha and Beta tests (see ARMY TESTS), which helped establish psychology as an important applied science. After the war he stayed in Washington for several years, working at the National Research Council of the National Academy of Sciences. In 1924, Yerkes moved to Yale University, where he took part in founding its Institute of Psychology. Apart from his role as an organizer and promoter of psychology, Yerkes is chiefly noted for his illuminating experiments in the field of COMPARATIVE PSYCHOLOGY at the Yale Laboratories of Primate Biology, later renamed the Yerkes Laboratories in his honor. There he broadened existing knowledge of animal behavior by showing, for example, that chimpanzees are capable of imitating humans and each other and can solve problems, stacking boxes to reach for food and transferring this learning to other problems. He also proved that lower animals can solve simple multiple-choice problems and that mouse killing in kittens is not instinctual, but learned. Experiments of this kind earned him recognition as the leading comparative psychologist in the United States. His works include, among others, *The Dancing Mouse* (1907), *Introduction to Psychology* (1911), *Chimpanzee Intelligence and its Vocal Expressions* (1925, with Blanche W. Learned), and *The Great Apes* (1929, with Ada W. Yerkes). He was a member of the National Academy of Sciences and a fellow of the American Academy of Arts and Letters.

Yerkes–Dodson law a law stating that the relation between motivation (AROUSAL) and performance can be represented by an inverted U-curve (see INVERTED-U HYPOTHESIS). [Robert M. YERKES and John Dillingham **Dodson** (1879–1955), U.S. psychologists]

Yerkish *n.* a language consisting of geometric forms that has been taught to nonhuman primates in studies of language acquisition and use. There has been some debate about whether animals trained with Yerkish demonstrate true language ability. [developed by U.S. psychologist Duane Rumbaugh (1929–) and named for Robert Mearns YERKES]

yes–no judgment task in psychophysics, a signal detection task in which participants undergo a series of trials in which they must judge the presence ("yes") or absence ("no") of a signal.

yin and yang in Chinese philosophy, the two opposite but complementary aspects of the fundamental principle governing the universe. Originally, the words referred to the shady and the sunny side of a hill. Yin and yang are the two forces or principles that can be seen at work in all phenomena. Sometimes one is dominant, sometimes the other, and all things ultimately revert to their opposites. In simple terms, yin is characterized as negative, passive, and feminine, among many other things, whereas yang is seen as positive, active, and masculine, among many other things. Understanding the principles of opposition, interaction, and harmony inherent in yin and yang is, however, as important as understanding the particular characteristics associated with each of them.

Y-linked inheritance a form of SEX-LINKED inheritance in which a recessive trait is inherited by way of a single gene on the Y CHROMOSOME.

yoga *n.* a school or tradition of Hindu philosophy and practical teaching that ultimately seeks to achieve MYSTIC UNION of the self with the Supreme Being, or of the human spirit with the universal spirit, through a prescribed mental discipline and physical exercises. Yoga exercises, including regulation of breathing and the adaptation of bodily postures (see ASANA), are used as a means of releasing tension and redirecting energy (i.e., prana; see CHI) and achieving a state of self-control, physical and mental relaxation, and finally deep contemplation. [Sanskrit, "union" or "yoke"]

yohimbine *n.* a stimulant alkaloid derived from the bark of the African tree *Pausinystalia yohimbe* and from *Rauwolfia serpentina* root. It acts as an antagonist at α_2-adrenoreceptors (see ALPHA ADRENORECEPTOR); at high doses, it is a MONOAMINE OXIDASE INHIBITOR and can cause serious adverse effects when taken concomitantly with antidepressants, tyramine-containing foods (e.g., liver, cheeses), or over-the-counter products containing phenylpropanolamine, such as nasal decongestants and diet aids. Yohimbine has achieved a reputation as a sexual enhancer in men, but there is little clinical evidence suggesting its efficacy is greater than placebo. It has also been studied as a potential treatment for erectile dysfunction, with contradictory results regarding its effectiveness. Chemically related to reserpine (see RAUWOLFIA DERIVATIVES), yohimbine is a SYMPATHOMIMETIC DRUG and may increase anxiety or produce panic attacks in susceptible individuals. Side effects may include nervousness, irritability, dizziness, skin flushing, or headache. More serious effects, including renal failure, seizures, and death, have also been reported, calling into question the safety of yohimbine-containing products. Yohimbine should not be taken by people with hypotension (low blood pressure), diabetes, or heart, liver, or kidney disease. It is available as an herbal remedy and also in prescription form (U.S. trade name: **Yocon**).

yoked control an experimental procedure designed to ensure that stimulus presentations occur in the same pattern with respect to time or behavior. For example, in one condition a nonhuman animal might behave so as to avoid electric shocks. In a yoked-control condition, the same temporal pattern of shocks received in the first case would be presented to the control animal independently of its behavior.

yoked-control group research subjects in a CONTROL GROUP who are specifically exposed to some of the same experiences (e.g., receipt of reinforcement or punishment in an OPERANT CONDITIONING study) as subjects in the EXPERIMENTAL GROUP, but not including the experimental treatments, manipulations, or conditions. This procedure is intended to make the control group as similar as possible to the experimental group in their experiences during research.

Youngberg v. Romeo the initial lawsuit that culminated in the PENNHURST CONSENT DECREE. In this action, the U.S. Supreme Court held that people with mental retardation who were involuntarily committed to state mental retardation institutions have a constitutional right to reasonably safe conditions, freedom from unreasonable restraints, and the services reasonably required to protect their liberty and interests.

Young–Helmholtz theory of color vision a theory to explain color vision in terms of components or processes sensitive to three different parts of the spectrum corresponding to the colors red, green, and blue. According to this theory, other colors are perceived by stimulation of two of the three processes, while light that stimulates all three processes equally is perceived as white. The components are now thought to be RETINAL CONES, although the original theory was not tied to a particular (or indeed to any) cell type. See TRICHROMATIC THEORY. Compare HERING THEORY OF COLOR VISION; OPPONENTS THEORY OF COLOR VISION. [Thomas **Young** (1773–1829), British physician and physicist; Hermann Ludwig Ferdinand von **Helmholtz** (1821–1894), German physiologist and physicist]

young-old *adj.* describing adults aged between 60 or 65 and 75. Compare OLD-OLD.

youpon *n.* see CASSINA.

you statement see I STATEMENT.

youth counseling counseling that provides advice, information, and support to young people, usually in adolescence or slightly younger. Youth counseling may focus on any issue that raises concerns or conflicts related to studying, family involvement, sexuality and gender identity, or peer relationships. It may be used to counter low self-image and feelings of inadequacy that are often experienced by young people.

youth culture **1.** a society that places a high premium on youth, physical health and beauty, and the values, tastes, and needs of young people. Such a society tends to derogate the values, experience, and needs of middle-aged and older people and may produce subtle psychological pressures for older adults to adapt to the culture of youth. **2.** the distinctive culture of teenagers and young adults, which often involves forms of dress, speech, music, and behavior that are deliberately at variance to those of the dominant culture. See also COUNTERCULTURE.

Yule's Q a measure of association for two DICHOTOMOUS VARIABLES. [George Udny **Yule** (1871–1951), British statistician]

Zz

Z a statistic used to transform CORRELATION COEFFICIENTS, often for the purpose of averaging them. See also FISHER'S R TO Z TRANSFORMATION.

zaar *n.* see ZAR.

zaleplon *n.* a HYPNOTIC drug that—unlike benzodiazepine and barbiturate hypnotics—does not relieve anxiety at lower doses. Like the related compounds ZOLPIDEM and ZOPICLONE, zaleplon does not relax skeletal muscles. It acts at a specific subunit on the $GABA_A$ RECEPTOR complex (the ω1 receptor) that results only in the production of sleep. U.S. trade name: **Sonata**.

zar (**zaar**) *n.* a CULTURE-BOUND SYNDROME, common in North African and Middle Eastern cultures, that is attributed to spirit possession. Occurring most frequently in women, zar often involves dissociative, somatic, and affective symptoms, such as shouting, laughing, apathy, and refusal to perform daily tasks.

Zarontin *n.* a trade name for ethosuximide. See SUCCINIMIDES.

Zeigarnik effect the tendency for interrupted, uncompleted tasks to be better remembered than completed tasks. [described in 1927 by Bluma **Zeigarnik** (1900–1988), Russian psychologist]

Zeitgeber *n.* a cue, such as day length, used to activate or time a BIOLOGICAL RHYTHM. See ENTRAINMENT. [German, "time giver": first defined scientifically in 1954 by German biologist Jürgen Aschoff (1913–1998)]

Zeitgeist *n.* the spirit of the times (German, "time spirit"). The term was used by German philosopher Georg Wilhelm Friedrich Hegel (1770–1831) to refer to a type of supraindividual mind at work in the world and manifest in the cultural worldview (see WELTANSCHAUUNG) that pervades the ideas, attitudes, and feelings of a particular society in a specific historical period. Used in this way, the term has a distinctly deterministic flavor. A Zeitgeist theory of history stresses the role of such situational factors as economics, technology, and social influences in contrast to the PERSONALISTIC APPROACH to history. The term was first used in English by British poet and literary critic Matthew Arnold (1822–1888) and introduced to psychology in 1929 by Edwin BORING, who used the concept as an organizing theme for his discussions of creativity, scientific change, and historiography. Compare ORTGEIST.

Zelmid *n.* a trade name for ZIMELDINE.

zelotypia *n.* extreme overzealousness in advocating a cause.

Zen Buddhism a Japanese school of BUDDHISM, dating from the 6th century CE, in which enlightenment is sought through direct, intuitive experience rather than through an intellectual approach to the scriptures. One method of preparing the way for such insight is to devote oneself to the solution of an insoluble paradox, such as "What is the sound of one hand clapping?" Another is prolonged, motionless meditation. In both cases the aim is to transcend rational, instrumental thought and the limitations of human language. Zen Buddhism has become increasingly popular in the West since the 1960s.

Zener cards a standardized set of stimulus materials, similar to a deck of playing cards, designed for use in experiments on EXTRASENSORY PERCEPTION and other parapsychological phenomena. The set consists of 25 cards, each of which bears one of 5 printed symbols (star, wavy lines, cross, circle, or square), with 5 cards in each category. In a typical test of TELEPATHY, the cards are shuffled (usually mechanically) and a designated SENDER turns the cards over one at a time to inspect the symbol, while a RECEIVER attempts to guess the symbol by reading the thoughts of the sender. In an experiment on CLAIRVOYANCE, the receiver might attempt to identify the order of the shuffled deck without any inspection of cards by the sender (see SCREENED TOUCH MATCHING). In an experiment on PSYCHOKINESIS, the participant would attempt to control the outcome of the shuffle directly. Also called **Rhine cards**. See also BASIC TECHNIQUE; ESP FORCED-CHOICE TEST; GENERAL EXTRASENSORY PERCEPTION. [named in honor of Karl E. **Zener** (1903–1964), U.S. perceptual psychologist who designed the symbols, by his colleague U.S. psychologist Joseph B. **Rhine** (1895–1980), who devised the deck]

Zeno's paradoxes several arguments proposed by Greek philosopher Zeno of Elea (early 5th century BCE) against the ideas of plurality and motion. Individuals making a trip must first go halfway to their destination, then cover half of the remaining distance, then half again, in an indefinite sequence of such steps that appears impossible to complete. Alternatively, if Achilles gives a tortoise a head start in a race and attempts to catch up, he must first run to where the tortoise was, then to where it has moved to, and so on for an infinite sequence of such moves, seemingly never catching up with the tortoise.

Zen therapy psychotherapy that is informed by and incorporates the philosophy and practices of ZEN BUDDHISM and that, like EXISTENTIALISM, is concerned with the unique meaning of the client's life within the universal context, rather than with simple adjustment to or removal of symptoms. Contemplation, through meditation and intuition, of human nature and human existence are believed to lead to a therapeutic alignment of the client with a sense of the oneness of the universe and to spiritual (and, thus, cognitive, affective, and behavioral) transformation. See also MYSTIC UNION.

zero-delay matching to sample see DELAYED MATCHING TO SAMPLE.

zero population growth the condition in which the number of births and deaths in a society is balanced, so that there is very little increase or decrease in population. This is now the norm in many developed societies.

zero-sum game in GAME THEORY, a type of game in which the players' gains and losses add up to zero. The total amount of resources available to the participants is fixed, and therefore one player's gain necessarily entails the others' loss. The term is used in analyses of bargaining and economic behavior.

zest *n.* see VITALITY.

ZIFT acronym for ZYGOTE INTRAFALLOPIAN TRANSFER.

zimeldine *n.* an antidepressant with SSRI properties that was removed from the worldwide market in 1983 due to its severe neurological side effects. Former European trade name: **Zelmid**.

zinc *n.* an element that is needed in minute amounts in the diet for normal functioning. The zinc ion is required for the activity of many enzymes.

ZIOF abbreviation for zone of individual optimal functioning (see ZONE OF OPTIMAL FUNCTIONING).

Zipf's law in linguistics, the observation that the length of words in any language is inversely related to their frequency of usage, so that high-frequency words are generally short, and uncommon words are generally long. Also called **Zipfian distribution**; **Zipf's distribution**. [George Kingsley **Zipf** (1902–1950), U.S. statistician and linguist]

ziprasidone *n.* an ATYPICAL ANTIPSYCHOTIC that is used for the treatment of schizophrenia and of acute manic or mixed episodes associated with bipolar disorders. It may prolong the Q-T interval of the cardiac cycle (see ELECTROCARDIOGRAPHIC EFFECT) and should therefore not be taken by patients with abnormal heart rhythms or by those who have had a recent heart attack or are taking antiarrhythmic drugs. Common side effects include ORTHOSTATIC HYPOTENSION and sedation. U.S. trade name: **Geodon**.

zoanthropy *n.* see LYCANTHROPY.

ZOF abbreviation for ZONE OF OPTIMAL FUNCTIONING.

Zofran *n.* a trade name for ONDANSETRON.

Zöllner illusion a visual illusion in which parallel lines appear to diverge when one of the lines is intersected by short diagonal lines slanting in one direction, and the other by lines slanting in the other direction. [Johann Karl Friedrich **Zöllner** (1834–1882), German astrophysicist]

Zoloft *n.* a trade name for SERTRALINE.

zolpidem *n.* a nonbenzodiazepine hypnotic introduced into the U.S. market in 1993 for short-term management of insomnia. Although structurally different from the benzodiazepines, it acts similarly by binding to a specific subtype of the $GABA_A$ RECEPTOR. It has primarily sedative rather than ANXIOLYTIC properties. U.S. trade name: **Ambien**.

Zomaril *n.* a trade name for ILOPERIDONE.

zombie argument a philosophical debate that focuses on the difficulty of distinguishing conscious beings (humans) from nonconscious beings (robots or zombies) that are capable of performing all the functions of conscious beings.

zone of comparison test a method of positioning questions in a CONTROL QUESTION TEST to facilitate objective analysis of physiological responses on POLYGRAPH charts and to minimize an examinee's potential to habituate to the question format.

zone of optimal functioning (**ZOF**) the range of physiological AROUSAL within which an individual can perform at the peak of physical, mental, and skillful ability. Also called **zone of individual optimal functioning** (**ZIOF**).

zone of potentiality the range of a student's capacity for growth, development, or achievement in a particular skill or subject area.

zone of proximal development in Lev VYGOTSKY'S sociocultural theory, the difference between a child's actual level of ability and the level of ability that he or she can achieve when working under the guidance of an instructor. See SOCIOCULTURAL PERSPECTIVE.

zonules *pl. n.* the delicate elastic fibers that connect the capsule of the LENS of the eye to the CILIARY PROCESSES. Also called **suspensory ligament**; **zonules of Zinn**. See also CILIARY MUSCLE.

zoo- *combining form* animals.

zooerasty *n.* sexual excitement or gratification obtained through anal or genital intercourse or other sexual contact with an animal. In *DSM–IV–TR* the corresponding term is ZOOPHILIA. Also called **zooerastia**; **bestiality**. See also SODOMY.

zoolagnia *n.* sexual attraction to animals. See ZOOERASTY; ZOOPHILIA.

zoomania *n.* an extremely intense or active form of ZOOERASTY or ZOOPHILIA.

zoomorphism *n.* **1.** the attribution of animal traits to human beings, deities, or inanimate objects. **2.** the use of animal psychology or physiology to explain human behavior. Compare ANTHROPOMORPHISM.

zoopharmacognosy *n.* the ability of nonhuman animals to select plants and plant parts (leaves, pith, etc.) for medicinal purposes to reduce fevers or eliminate parasites. In Tanzania, the plants used by chimpanzees to reduce fever or parasite load are the same as those used by human beings to treat the same ailments.

zoophilia *n.* a PARAPHILIA in which animals are repeatedly preferred or exclusively used to achieve sexual excitement and gratification. The animal, which is usually a household pet or farm animal, is either used as the object of intercourse or is trained to lick or rub the human partner, referred to as a **zoophile**. The most commonly used animals are pigs and sheep, in rural settings. Also called **zoophilism**. See also ZOOERASTY.

zoosadism *n.* a PARAPHILIA in which sexual arousal and satisfaction are obtained from torturing an animal. This may occur during direct sexual contact with the animal, or the person may masturbate later, using memories of the event as masturbatory fantasies.

zopiclone *n.* a nonbenzodiazepine HYPNOTIC that, like the related drug ZALEPLON, is relatively selective for a specific subunit on the $GABA_A$ RECEPTOR complex, which results only in profound sedation and sleep. It is used for the short-term treatment of insomnia in adults. Side effects include excessive sedation or confusion, dry mouth, and a bitter taste. U.S. trade name: **Lunesta**.

z score see STANDARD SCORE.

zuclopenthixol *n.* a conventional (typical or first-generation) ANTIPSYCHOTIC of the THIOXANTHENE class. Side effects include sedation, neuromuscular rigidity, and dystonia, and—like similar agents—it is associated with long-term risk of TARDIVE DYSKINESIA. Zuclopenthixol is not available in the United States. Canadian trade name: **Clopixol**.

Zugunruhe *n.* see MIGRATORY RESTLESSNESS.

Zung Self-Rating Depression Scale (**SDS**) a widely used adult self-report depression-screening instrument designed to measure the intensity of depressive or mood-related symptoms. It is also a tool for tracking a client's response to depression treatment over time. The SDS consists of 20 statements to which participants must respond using a 4-point LIKERT SCALE, ranging from "none or little of the time" to "most or all of the time." Half of the questions are worded positively (e.g., "I have trouble sleeping") and half are worded negatively (e.g., "I do not feel hopeful"). [originally developed in 1965 by William W. K. **Zung**, U.S. psychiatrist]

Zurich School a group of psychoanalysts who were early followers of Carl JUNG in Zurich, as opposed to the VIENNESE SCHOOL of Sigmund FREUD'S followers.

Zwaardemaker olfactometer an early OLFACTOM-

ETER consisting of a single glass tube open at both ends: One end was inserted into a nostril, and the other end was fitted into a tube filled with an ODORANT. Sniffing caused the odorant to reach the OLFACTORY EPITHELIUM. [Hendrik **Zwaardemaker** (1857–1930), Dutch physiologist]

Zwaardemaker smell system a system for classifying odor qualities based on a scheme originally developed by Swedish botanist Carolus Linnaeus (1707–1778). According to this system, there are nine PRIMARY ODOR qualities: ETHEREAL, AROMATIC, FRAGRANT, AMBROSIAC, ALLIACEOUS, EMPYREUMATIC, HIRCINE, FOUL, and NAUSEOUS. These qualities combine to produce the perceptions of smells. [Hendrik **Zwaardemaker**]

Zyban *n.* a trade name for BUPROPION.

Zydis *n.* a trade name for OLANZAPINE.

zygomaticus *n.* the set of muscles, innervated by the FACIAL NERVE, that activates the movement of the upper lip outward, upward, and backward. Its activity is recorded in studies of emotion.

zygote *n.* a fertilized egg, or ovum, with a DIPLOID set of chromosomes, half contributed by the mother and half by the father. The zygote divides to become an EMBRYO, which continues to divide as it develops and differentiates—in humans eventually forming a FETUS. **—zygotic** *adj.*

zygote intrafallopian transfer (**ZIFT**) a form of IN VITRO FERTILIZATION in which ova and sperm are mixed together in a laboratory container and the fertilized eggs (zygotes) are implanted into the fallopian tubes. Compare GAMETE INTRAFALLOPIAN TRANSFER.

Zyprexa *n.* a trade name for OLANZAPINE.

Appendixes

Biographical Entries

Adler, Alfred (1870–1937), Austrian psychiatrist
Allport, Gordon Willard (1897–1967), U.S. psychologist
Anastasi, Anne (1908–2001), U.S. psychologist
Angell, James Rowland (1869–1949), U.S. psychologist
Asch, Solomon E. (1907–1996), Polish-born U.S. psychologist
Baldwin, James Mark (1861–1934), U.S. psychologist
Bandura, Albert (1925–), Canadian-born U.S. psychologist
Bayley, Nancy (1899–1994), U.S. psychologist
Beers, Clifford (1876–1943), U.S. philanthropist
Binet, Alfred (1857–1911), French psychologist
Bingham, Walter Van Dyke (1880–1952), U.S. psychologist
Boring, Edwin Garrigues (1886–1968), U.S. psychologist
Bowlby, Edward John Mostyn (1907–1990), British psychiatrist
Broadbent, Donald E. (1926–1993), British psychologist
Brown, Roger (1925–1997), U.S. psychologist
Calkins, Mary Whiton (1863–1930), U.S. psychologist
Campbell, Donald Thomas (1916–1996), U.S. psychologist
Cattell, James McKeen (1860–1944), U.S. psychologist
Chomsky, Noam (1928–), U.S. linguist
Clark, Kenneth Bancroft (1914–2005), U.S. psychologist
Cronbach, Lee J. (1916–2001), U.S. psychologist
Dewey, John (1859–1952), U.S. philosopher, educator, and psychologist
Ebbinghaus, Hermann (1850–1909), German psychologist
Erikson, Erik H. (1902–1994), German-born U.S. psychologist
Estes, William Kaye (1919–), U.S. psychologist
Eysenck, Hans Jurgen (1916–1997), German-born British psychologist
Fechner, Gustav Theodor (1801–1887), German physician and philosopher
Festinger, Leon (1919–1989), U.S. psychologist
Freud, Anna (1895–1982), Austrian-born British psychoanalyst
Freud, Sigmund (1856–1939), Austrian neurologist and psychiatrist
Fromm, Erich (1900–1980), German-born U.S. psychoanalyst
Gibson, Eleanor Jack (1910–2002), U.S. psychologist
Gibson, James Jerome (1904–1979), U.S. psychologist
Goddard, Henry Herbert (1866–1957), U.S. psychologist
Guilford, Joy Paul (1897–1987), U.S. psychologist
Guthrie, Edwin Ray (1886–1959), U.S. psychologist
Hall, Granville Stanley (1844–1924), U.S. psychologist
Harlow, Harry Frederick (1905–1981), U.S. psychologist
Hebb, Donald Olding (1904–1985), Canadian psychobiologist
Hilgard, Ernest R. (1904–2001), U.S. psychologist
Hollingworth, Harry L. (1880–1956), U.S. psychologist
Hollingworth, Leta Stetter (1886–1939), U.S. psychologist
Hull, Clark Leonard (1884–1952), U.S. psychologist
James, William (1842–1910), U.S. psychologist and philosopher
Jung, Carl Gustav (1875–1961), Swiss psychiatrist and psychoanalyst
Kinsey, Alfred (1894–1956), U.S. zoologist and sex researcher
Klein, Melanie (1882–1960), Austrian-born British psychoanalyst
Koffka, Kurt (1886–1941), German experimental psychologist
Kohlberg, Lawrence (1927–1987), U.S. psychologist
Köhler, Wolfgang (1887–1967), German experimental psychologist
Ladd-Franklin, Christine (1847–1930), U.S. psychologist and mathematician
Lashley, Karl Spencer (1890–1958), U.S. psychologist
Lewin, Kurt (1890–1947), German-born U.S. psychologist
Luria, Alexander R. (1902–1977), Russian neuropsychologist
Maslow, Abraham Harold (1908–1970), U.S. psychologist
May, Rollo (1909–1994), U.S. psychologist, psychoanalyst, and existentialist
McClelland, David (1917–1998), U.S. psychologist
Meehl, Paul Everett (1920–2003), U.S. psychologist
Milgram, Stanley (1933–1984), U.S. social psychologist
Miller, Neal Elgar (1909–2002), U.S. psychologist
Mowrer, O. Hobart (1907–1982), U.S. psychologist
Münsterberg, Hugo (1863–1916), German-born U.S. psychologist
Osgood, Charles Egerton (1916–1991), U.S. psychologist
Pavlov, Ivan Petrovich (1849–1936), Russian physiologist
Payton, Carolyn R. (1925–2001), U.S. psychologist
Piaget, Jean (1896–1980), Swiss child psychologist and epistemologist
Rogers, Carl (1902–1987), U.S. psychologist
Rorschach, Hermann (1884–1922), Swiss psychiatrist
Schachter, Stanley (1922–1997), U.S. psychologist
Scott, Walter Dill (1869–1955), U.S. psychologist
Shakow, David (1901–1981), U.S. psychologist
Simon, Herbert Alexander (1916–2001), U.S. economist, political scientist, and psychologist

Skinner, Burrhus Frederic (1904–1990), U.S. psychologist

Spence, Kenneth Wartinbee (1907–1967), U.S. psychologist

Sperry, Roger Wolcott (1913–1994), U.S. psychologist

Stern, Louis William (1871–1938), German psychologist

Strong, Edward Kellogg, Jr. (1884–1963), U.S. psychologist

Sumner, Francis Cecil (1895–1954), U.S. psychologist

Terman, Lewis Madison (1877–1956), U.S. psychologist

Thorndike, Edward Lee (1874–1949), U.S. psychologist

Thurstone, Louis Leon (1887–1955), U.S. psychologist

Titchener, Edward Bradford (1867–1927), British-born U.S. psychologist

Tolman, Edward Chace (1886–1959), U.S. psychologist

Vygotsky, Lev Semenovich (or Vigotsky; 1896–1934), Russian psychologist

Washburn, Margaret Floy (1871–1939), U.S. psychologist

Watson, John Broadus (1878–1958), U.S. psychologist

Wechsler, David (1896–1981), Romanian-born U.S. psychologist

Wertheimer, Max (1880–1943), German-born U.S. psychologist

White, Robert W. (1904–2001), U.S. psychologist

Witmer, Lightner (1867–1956), U.S. psychologist

Woodworth, Robert Sessions (1869–1962), U.S. psychologist

Wundt, Wilhelm Max (1832–1920), German psychologist and physiologist

Yerkes, Robert Mearns (1876–1956), U.S. psychobiologist

Institutional and Organizational Entries

Academy of Certified Social Workers (ACSW)
Acoustical Society of America (ASA)
Adult Children of Alcoholics (ACOA)
Al-Anon
Alateen
Alcohol, Drug Abuse and Mental Health Administration (ADAMHA)
Alcoholics Anonymous (AA)
Alzheimer's Disease and Related Disorders Association, Inc.
American Academy of Clinical Sexologists (AACS)
American Alliance for Health, Physical Education, Recreation and Dance (AAHPERD)
American Association for Counseling and Development (AACD)—see American Counseling Association
American Association for the Advancement of Science (AAAS)
American Association of Applied and Preventive Psychology (AAAPP)
American Association of Applied Psychology (AAAP)
American Association of Clinical Psychologists (AACP)
American Association of Mental Retardation (AAMR)
American Association of Sex Educators, Counselors and Therapists (AASECT)
American Birth Control League (ABCL)
American Board of Medical Specialties (ABMS)
American Board of Professional Psychology (ABPP)
American College of Sports Medicine (ACSM)
American Counseling Association (ACA)
American Educational Research Association (AERA)
American Orthopsychiatric Association (AOA)
American Pain Society (APS)
American Parkinson Disease Association, Inc.
American Philosophical Society (APS)
American Psychiatric Association (APA)
American Psychoanalytic Association (APsaA)
American Psychological Association (APA)
American Psychological Association of Graduate Students (APAGS)
American Psychological Foundation (APF)
American Psychological Society (APS)
American Psychosomatic Society (APS)
American Society for Psychical Research
Army Research Institute (ARI)
Association for Research in Otolaryngology (ARO)
Association for the Advancement of Applied Sport Psychology (AAASP)
Association for the Advancement of Psychology (AAP)
Big Brothers Big Sisters of America
British Psychological Society (BPS)
Canadian Psychological Association (CPA)
Candlelighters Childhood Cancer Foundation
Centers for Disease Control and Prevention (CDC)
Centers for Medicare and Medicaid Services (CMS)
Cocaine Anonymous
Co-Dependents Anonymous
Compassionate Friends
Educational Testing Service (ETS)
Equal Employment Opportunity Commission (EEOC)
European Federation of Professional Psychologists' Associations (EFPPA)
European Federation of the Psychology of Sport and Physical Activity (FEPSAC)
Federation of Behavioral, Psychological, and Cognitive Sciences
Gamblers Anonymous (GA)
GROW, INC.
Health Care Financing Administration (HCFA)—see Centers for Medicare and Medicaid Services
Indian Health Service (IHS)
Interamerican Society of Psychology
International Association of Applied Psychology (IAAP)
International Council of Psychologists
International Military Testing Association
International Society for Sport Psychology (ISSP)
International Union of Psychological Science (IUPsyS)
Joint Commission on Accreditation of Healthcare Organizations (JCAHO)
Kinsey Institute for Research in Sex, Gender, and Reproduction
Military Testing Association—see International Military Testing Association
Mothers Against Drunk Driving (MADD)
Narcotics Anonymous (NA)
National Academy of Sciences (NAS)
National Alliance for the Mentally Ill (NAMI)
National Association of Rural Health Clinics (NARHC)
National Committee for Quality Assurance (NCQA)
National Institute of Mental Health (NIMH)
National Mental Health Association (NMHA)
National Parent Teachers Association (NPTA)—see parent teachers association
National Register of Health Service Providers in Psychology
National Research Council
National Science Foundation (NSF)
North American Society for the Psychology of Sport and Physical Activity (NASPSPA)
Occupational Safety and Health Administration (OSHA)
Overeaters Anonymous (OA)
Parents Anonymous
Parents Without Partners

Phoenix House
Planned Parenthood Federation of America (PPFA)
Portman Clinic
Psi Beta
Psi Chi
Psychometric Society
Psychonomic Society
Recovery, Inc.
Sexuality Information and Education Council of the United States (SIECUS)
Society for Neuroscience
Society for Psychical Research
Society for Psychotherapy Research
Society for Research in Child Development (SRCD)
Society of Experimental Psychologists
Society of Experimental Social Psychology
Substance Abuse and Mental Health Services Administration (SAMHSA)
Tavistock Clinic
ToughLove International
U.S. Department of Veterans Affairs (VA)
Walter Reed Army Institute of Research
World Federation for Mental Health
World Health Organization (WHO)

Psychological Test and Assessment Instrument Entries

ACT Assessment (American College Testing Assessment)
Allport–Vernon–Lindzey Study of Values (SOV)
Armed Forces Qualification Test (AFQT)
Armed Services Vocational Aptitude Battery (ASVAB)
Army tests
ARP tests (Aptitude Research Project tests)
Athletic Coping Skills Inventory (ACSI)
Athletic Motivation Inventory (AMI)
Auditory Consonant Trigram (ACT)
Auditory Continuous Performance Test (ACPT)
Autobiographical Memory Interview (AMI)
Barron–Welsh Art Scale (BWAS)
Barthel Index
Basic Achievement Skills Individual Screener (BASIS)
Basic Nordic Sleep Questionnaire (BNSQ)
Bayley Scales of Infant and Toddler Development
Beck Anxiety Inventory (BAI)
Beck Depression Inventory (BDI)
Beck Hopelessness Scale (BHS)
Beck Scale for Suicide Ideation (BSS)
Bem Sex Role Inventory (BSRI)
Bender Visual–Motor Gestalt Test (Bender–Gestalt)
Benton Visual Retention Test (BVRT)
Biographical Evaluation and Screening of Troops
Blessed Dementia Scale (BDS)
Body Image Assessment (BIA)
Bogardus Social Distance Scale
Borg scale
Boston Naming Test (BNT)
Brazelton Neonatal Behavioral Assessment Scale
Brief Psychiatric Rating Scale (BPRS)
Bruininks–Oseretsky Test of Motor Proficiency (BOT)
CAGE
California Achievement Tests (CAT)
California Psychological Inventory (CPI)
California Verbal Learning Test (CVLT)
Category Test
Cattell inventory
Center for Epidemiologic Studies Depression Scale (CES-D)
Child Behavior Checklist (CBCL)
Children's Depression Inventory (CDI)
Children's Embedded Figures Test (CEFT)
Children's Manifest Anxiety Scale (CMAS)
Children's Personality Questionnaire (CPQ)
Choice Dilemma Questionnaire (CDQ)
CIRCUS
Coaching Behavior Assessment System (CBAS)
Cognitive Abilities Test (CogAT)
Cognitive Assessment System (CAS)
Colored Progressive Matrices
Competitive State Anxiety Inventory (CSAI)
Complex Figure Test
Computerized Adaptive Screening Test (CAST)
Comrey Personality Scales (CPS)
Constructive Thinking Inventory (CTI)
Constructivist Learning Environment Survey (CLES)
Controlled Oral Word Association (COWA)
Coolidge Assessment Battery (CAB)
Cooper–Harper Handling Qualities Rating Scale
Cornell Medical Index (CMI)
Dementia Rating Scale (DRS)
Developmental Test of Visual–Motor Integration (VMI)
Diagnostic Interview Schedule (DIS)
Differential Ability Scales (DAS)
Differential Aptitude Tests (DAT)
Digit Span
Digit Symbol
Disability Rating Scale (DRS)
Doerfler–Stewart test
Dysexecutive Questionnaire (DEX)
Edwards Personal Preference Schedule (EPPS)
Embedded Figures Test (EFT)
Eriksen flankers task
Eysenck Personality Inventory (EPI)
Fear Survey Schedule (FSS)
Finger Localization Test
Finger Tapping Test
Functional Independence Measure (FIM)
Geriatric Depression Scale (GDS)
Glasgow Coma Scale (GCS)
Glasgow Outcome Scale (GOS)
Global Assessment of Functioning scale (GAF scale)
Global Deterioration Scale (GDS)
Gordon Diagnostic System (GDS)
Graduate Record Examinations (GRE)
Grip Strength Test
Guilford–Zimmerman Temperament Survey (GZTS)
Halstead–Reitan Neuropsychological Battery (HRNB)
Hamilton Rating Scale for Depression (HAM-D; HRSD)
Hollingshead scales
Holmgren Test for Color Blindness
Home Observation for Measurement of the Environment (HOME)
Hopkins Symptom Checklist (HSCL)
Hopkins Verbal Learning Test (HVLT)

Illinois Test of Psycholinguistic Abilities (ITPA)
Inpatient Multidimensional Psychiatric Scale (IMPS)
Iowa Tests of Basic Skills (ITBS)
Ishihara Test for Color Blindness
Jenkins Activity Survey (JAS)
Job Descriptive Index (JDI)
Job Diagnostic Survey (JDS)
Katz Index of Activities of Daily Living
Kaufman Adolescent and Adult Intelligence Test (KAIT)
Kaufman Assessment Battery for Children (K–ABC)
Kirton Adaption–Innovation Inventory (KAI)
Kohs Block Design Test
Krantz Health Opinion Survey (KHOS)
Kuder Preference Record
Learning Potential Assessment Device (LPAD)
Least Preferred Coworker Scale (LPC scale)
Letter–Number Sequencing
Luria–Nebraska Neuropsychological Battery (LNNB)
McCarthy Scales of Children's Abilities
McCarthy Screening Test (MST)
Machover Draw-a-Person Test (DAP test)
Mach scale
Marlowe–Crowne Social Desirability Scale (M–C SDS)
Maslach Burnout Inventory (MBI)
Matching Familiar Figures Test (MFF)
Metropolitan Achievement Tests (METROPOLITAN)
Michigan Alcoholism Screening Test (MAST)
Miller Analogies Test (MAT)
Mill Hill Vocabulary Scale (MHV)
Millon Clinical Multiaxial Inventory (MCMI)
Mini-Mental State Examination (MMSE)
Minnesota Multiphasic Personality Inventory (MMPI)
Minnesota Satisfaction Questionnaire (MSQ)
Modified Rhyme Test (MRT)
Multilevel Academic Survey Tests (MAST)
Multilingual Aphasia Examination (MAE)
Multiple Sleep Latency Test (MSLT)
Myers–Briggs Type Indicator (MBTI)
Naglieri Nonverbal Ability Test (NNAT)
NASA Task Load Index (NASA TLX)
Nelson–Denny Reading Test
NEO Personality Inventory (NEO-PI)
Neurological Evaluation Scale (NES)
Older Adult Resources and Services
Otis–Lennon School Ability Test (OLSAT)
Parenting Stress Index (PSI)
Peabody Picture Vocabulary Test (PPVT)
Personal Orientation Inventory (POI)
Phillips Rating Scale of Premorbid Adjustment in Schizophrenia
Porteus Maze Test
Position Analysis Questionnaire (PAQ)
Present State Examination (PSE)
Profile of Mood States (POMS)
Progressive Achievement Tests (PAT)
Quick Test (QT)
Raven's Progressive Matrices
Recognition Memory Test (RMT)
Reitan Indiana Aphasia Screening Test
Reitan–Klove Sensory Perceptual Examination
Renard Diagnostic Interview
Research Diagnostic Criteria (RDC)
Rey Auditory Verbal Learning Test (RAVLT)
Rod-and-Frame Test (RFT)
Rokeach Dogmatism Scale
Rokeach Value Survey (RVS)
Rorschach Inkblot Test
Rotter Internal–External Locus of Control Scale (RIELC)
Scale of Prodromal Symptoms (SOPS)
Schedule for Affective Disorders and Schizophrenia (SADS)
Scholastic Assessment Test (SAT)
School and College Ability Test (SCAT)
Seashore Measures of Musical Talents
Seashore Rhythm Test
Shipley Institute of Living Scale (SILS)
Short Portable Mental Status Questionnaire (SPMSQ)
Sixteen Personality Factor Questionnaire (16PF)
Sleep Questionnaire and Assessment of Wakefulness (SQAW)
Slosson Intelligence Test (SIT)
Smell Identification Test (SIT)
Speech-Sounds Perception Test
Sport Imagery Questionnaire (SIQ)
Staggered Spondaic Word Test (SSW)
Stanford Achievement Test
Stanford–Binet Intelligence Scale (SB)
Stanford Hypnotic Susceptibility Scale
State–Trait Anxiety Inventory (STAI)
Sternberg Triarchic Abilities Test (STAT)
Stilling Color Vision Test
Strong Interest Inventory (SII)
Stroop Color–Word Interference Test
Structured Clinical Interview for DSM–IV Axis I Disorders (SCID-I)
Structured Clinical Interview for DSM–IV Axis II Personality Disorders (SCID-II)
Symptom Checklist-90-R (SCL-90-R)
System of Multicultural Pluralistic Assessment (SOMPA)
Tactile Form Perception
Tactual Performance Test (TPT)
Taylor Manifest Anxiety Scale
Tellegen Absorption Scale (TAS)
Tennessee Self-Concept Scale (TSCS)
Terman–McNemar Test of Mental Ability
Test of Attentional and Interpersonal Style (TAIS)
Thematic Apperception Test (TAT)
Token Test
Torrance Tests of Creative Thinking (TTCT)
Tower of Hanoi
Trail Making Test (TMT)
Unified Tri-Service Cognitive Performance Assessment Battery (UTCPAB)
Unusual Uses Test

Vineland Adaptive Behavior Scales (VABS)
Ways of Coping Questionnaire (WAYS)
Wechsler Adult Intelligence Scale (WAIS)
Wechsler–Bellevue Intelligence Scale (WBIS)
Wechsler Intelligence Scale for Children (WISC)
Wechsler Memory Scale (WMS)
Wechsler Preschool and Primary Scale of Intelligence (WPPSI)
Welsh Figure Preference Test (WFPT)
Western Aphasia Battery (WAB)
WHO (10) Well-Being Index
Wide Range Achievement Test (WRAT)
Wisconsin Card Sorting Test (WCST)
Woodcock–Johnson Psychoeducational Battery
Zung Self-Rating Depression Scale (SDS)

Psychotherapy and Psychotherapeutic Approach Entries

acceptance and commitment therapy
action-oriented therapy
active analytic psychotherapy
active therapy
activity-group therapy
activity-interview group psychotherapy
adaptational approach
adjunctive therapy
adjuvant therapy
affirmative therapy
ahistoric therapy
analytical psychotherapy
analytic group psychotherapy
anamnestic analysis
anger control therapy
animal-assisted therapy
art therapy
assignment therapy
atropine-coma therapy (ACT)
attitude therapy
attribution therapy
aversion therapy
Beck therapy
behavioral couples therapy
behavioral family therapy
behavioral group therapy
behavioral relaxation training
behavioral sex therapy
behavioral weight control therapies
behavior modification
behavior therapy
bereavement therapy
bibliotherapy
biological therapy
brain-wave therapy
brief group therapy
brief intensive group cognitive behavior therapy
brief psychodynamic psychotherapy
brief stimulus therapy (BST)
carbon dioxide therapy
cerebral electrotherapy (CET)
child analysis
child psychotherapy
chronotherapy
client-centered therapy
cognitive-analytic therapy
cognitive behavioral couples therapy
cognitive behavioral group therapy
cognitive behavior therapy (CBT)
cognitive processing therapy (CPT)
cognitive therapy (CT)
collaborative therapy
coma therapy
combination therapy
combined therapy
computerized therapy
concurrent therapy
configurational analysis
conjoint therapy
constructivist psychotherapy
contact desensitization
convulsive therapy
coping-skills training
core conflictual relationship theme
correspondence training
cortical undercutting
cotherapy
couples therapy
covert desensitization
covert sensitization
creative arts therapy
dance therapy
Dauerschlaf
depth-oriented brief therapy
depth therapy
developmental therapy
dialectical behavior therapy
didactic group therapy
directive group psychotherapy
directive play therapy
distance therapy
drama therapy
dynamic psychotherapy
eclectic psychotherapy
ecosystemic approach
educational therapy
ego analysis
electroconvulsive therapy (ECT)
electronarcosis
electrosleep therapy
electrotherapy
emergency psychotherapy
emetic therapy
emotional reeducation
emotion-focused couples therapy
emotion-focused therapy

environmental therapy
Ericksonian psychotherapy
e-therapy
ethnotherapy
evocative therapy
exercise therapy
existential analysis
existential–humanistic therapy
existential psychotherapy
experiential psychotherapy
exposure therapy
expressive therapy
extended-family therapy
eye-movement desensitization therapy
family group psychotherapy
family therapy
feminist family therapy
feminist therapy
focal psychotherapy
frontal lobotomy
functional family therapy
geriatric psychotherapy
gestalt therapy
group-analytic psychotherapy
group psychotherapy
half-show
holistic education
horticultural therapy
humanistic therapy
hydrotherapy
hypnotherapy
imaginal flooding
imago therapy
implosive therapy
indirect method of therapy
individual therapy
insight therapy
instigation therapy
integrative behavioral couples therapy
integrative psychotherapy
integrity group
intensive psychotherapy
interpersonal group psychotherapy
interpersonal psychotherapy (IPT)
interpersonal reconstructive psychotherapy
interpretive therapy
in vivo exposure therapy
Kleinian analysis
leaderless group therapy
leukotomy
light therapy
logotherapy
long-term therapy
LSD psychotherapy
maintenance therapy
manual arts therapy
manualized therapy
marital therapy
medical family therapy
medical psychotherapy
megadose pharmacotherapy
megavitamin therapy
metaphor therapy
methadone maintenance therapy
Metrazol shock treatment
milieu therapy
Milligan annihilation method
monotherapy
moral therapy
Morita therapy
motivational enhancement therapy
movement therapy
multicultural therapy
multimodal therapy (MMT)
multiple family therapy
multiple-impact therapy
multiple marital therapy
multiple monitored electroconvulsive treatment (MMECT)
music therapy
naikan
narcotherapy
narrative psychotherapy
network therapy
nondirective play therapy
nondirective therapy
objective psychotherapy
operant conditioning therapy
organic therapies
panic control treatment
paraverbal therapy
parent effectiveness training (PET)
parent management training
pastoral counseling
personal construct therapy
persuasion therapy
phenomenological therapy
phototherapy
play-group psychotherapy
play therapy
poetry therapy
polypharmacy
process experiential psychotherapy
projective play
projective psychotherapy
psychedelic therapy
psychoanalysis
psychoanalytic group psychotherapy
psychoanalytic play technique
psychoanalytic psychotherapy
psychodynamic group psychotherapy
psychodynamic psychotherapy
psychopharmacotherapy
psychosocial therapy
psychosurgery
psychotherapy by reciprocal inhibition

puppetry therapy
quadrangular therapy
radical therapy
rational emotive behavior therapy (REBT)
reality therapy
reconditioning therapy
reconstructive psychotherapy
recreational therapy
reeducation
regressive electroshock therapy
reinforcement therapy
relationship therapy
release therapy
reminiscence therapy
reparative therapy
response prevention
restoration therapy
role-divided psychotherapy
role therapy
scheduled awakening
sector therapy
self-control therapy
self-instructional training
self-management
semantic therapy
sensate focus therapy
sex therapy
shock therapy
short-term therapy
single-session therapy (SST)
social-network therapy
social skills training (SST)
social therapy
sociotherapy
solution-focused brief therapy
somatic therapy
spontaneity training
strategic family therapy
stress-inoculation training (SIT)
structural family therapy
structural therapy
structured interactional group psychotherapy
structured learning
suggestion therapy
supportive-expressive psychotherapy
supportive psychotherapy
suppressive therapy
surface therapy
systematic desensitization
systematic rational restructuring
tandem therapy
time-extended therapy
time-limited day treatment
time-limited psychotherapy (TLP)
topectomy
tractotomy
transactional psychotherapy
transcendence therapy
transcultural psychotherapy
transorbital lobotomy
trial therapy
ultrasonic irradiation
verbal behavior therapy
virtual reality therapy
vitamin therapy
will therapy
work therapy
Zen therapy